# THE UNIVERSAL ALMANAC 1992

Edited by
## JOHN W. WRIGHT

**ANDREWS AND McMEEL**
A Universal Press Syndicate Company
**Kansas City · New York**

## Staff and Contributors

*General Editor,* John W. Wright
*Senior Editor,* Lincoln P. Paine

**Executive Editor for Science**
Bryan Bunch, Pace University; President, Scientific Publishing

**Consulting and Contributing Editors**
*Business and Economics:* Peter Cappelli, The Wharton School, University of Pennsylvania; Contributing Editor, Allison Paxton Paine
*History* (U.S.): Stanley Kutler, University of Wisconsin; Contributing Editor, Glen Gendzel
*The Media:* James Monaco, President, Baseline II (Electronic); Mary Quigley, New York University (Print); Contributing Editor, James Pallot, Baseline II
*Nations of the World:* John L. Connelly, Regis H.S. (Europe); John Major, Historian (Nations of Africa and Asia); James Malloy, University of Pittsburgh (Latin America); Patricia Szczerba (World Statistics)
*Sports:* David Klatell, Institute for Broadcast Sports, Boston University

**Data Entry**
Dorothy C. Green, Diane Cavanaugh (DMC Lexicon)

**Maps**
David Lindroth, West Milford, New Jersey

**Section Editors**
Curtis Church (The Fifty States); Edward J. Dwyer (U.S. Cities and Counties); Sherwood Harris (Education); Lawrence Lorimer (Religion); Sarah Myers (World Geography); Patricia Szczerba (The United Nations; International Organizations; Global Issues); Jenny Tesar (Health and Medicine)

**Senior Writers**
Glen Gendzel, Fredrica Harvey, Deborah Kaple, Jerold Kappes, Thomas LaRosa, Stephen Lichtman, John Major, Allison Paxton Paine, John Rosenthal, Marilyn Rosenthal

**Staff Writers**
Ellen Chodosh, Charles Epstein, Melody Kimmel, David Lippmann, Eugene McCaffrey, Frances N. McSherry, Barbara Mujica, William Mullaney, Charles Myers, Lisa Renaud, Eric Rosenthal, Peggy Rosenthal, Strom Thacker, Robert White

**Researchers**
Ben Fischler, William Hubbard, Ralph A. Lee, Josh Leifer, Paul Miller, David Myers, Candace Ovesey, Dee Shedd

**Fact Checkers and Proofreaders**
Gretchen Brown, Maureen Chiofalo, Richard Crowe, William Frucht, Jerold Kappes, David Lichtman, Robert L. Spring

*Editorial Director,* Donna Martin
*Designers,* Barrie Maguire, Cameron Poulter

**Production Manager**
Lisa Shadid

**Word Processors**
Kathy Holder, Patricia Rice

**Production Editor**
Jean Lowe

**Chief Copyeditor**
Matt Lombardi

**Editorial Coordinator/Word Processing**
Patty Donnelly

**Copyeditors, Proofreaders**
Leslee Anderson, Barbara Schalk Glessner, Libby Koch, Stephanie Stapp

The manuscript for this book was prepared in electronic form.
Typography by Connell-Zeko Type & Graphics, Kansas City, Missouri.

ISBN: 0-8362-7991-3 (hd)
ISBN: 0-8362-7990-5 (ppb)
ISSN: 1045-9820

# Contents

## 1992

### JANUARY

| S | M | T | W | T | F | S |
|---|---|---|---|---|---|---|
| | | | 1 | 2 | 3 | 4 |
| 5 | 6 | 7 | 8 | 9 | 10 | 11 |
| 12 | 13 | 14 | 15 | 16 | 17 | 18 |
| 19 | 20 | 21 | 22 | 23 | 24 | 25 |
| 26 | 27 | 28 | 29 | 30 | 31 | |

### FEBRUARY

| S | M | T | W | T | F | S |
|---|---|---|---|---|---|---|
| | | | | | | 1 |
| 2 | 3 | 4 | 5 | 6 | 7 | 8 |
| 9 | 10 | 11 | 12 | 13 | 14 | 15 |
| 16 | 17 | 18 | 19 | 20 | 21 | 22 |
| 23 | 24 | 25 | 26 | 27 | 28 | 29 |

### MARCH

| S | M | T | W | T | F | S |
|---|---|---|---|---|---|---|
| 1 | 2 | 3 | 4 | 5 | 6 | 7 |
| 8 | 9 | 10 | 11 | 12 | 13 | 14 |
| 15 | 16 | 17 | 18 | 19 | 20 | 21 |
| 22 | 23 | 24 | 25 | 26 | 27 | 28 |
| 29 | 30 | 31 | | | | |

### APRIL

| S | M | T | W | T | F | S |
|---|---|---|---|---|---|---|
| | | | 1 | 2 | 3 | 4 |
| 5 | 6 | 7 | 8 | 9 | 10 | 11 |
| 12 | 13 | 14 | 15 | 16 | 17 | 18 |
| 19 | 20 | 21 | 22 | 23 | 24 | 25 |
| 26 | 27 | 28 | 29 | 30 | | |

### MAY

| S | M | T | W | T | F | S |
|---|---|---|---|---|---|---|
| | | | | | 1 | 2 |
| 3 | 4 | 5 | 6 | 7 | 8 | 9 |
| 10 | 11 | 12 | 13 | 14 | 15 | 16 |
| 17 | 18 | 19 | 20 | 21 | 22 | 23 |
| 24 | 25 | 26 | 27 | 28 | 29 | 30 |
| 31 | | | | | | |

### JUNE

| S | M | T | W | T | F | S |
|---|---|---|---|---|---|---|
| | 1 | 2 | 3 | 4 | 5 | 6 |
| 7 | 8 | 9 | 10 | 11 | 12 | 13 |
| 14 | 15 | 16 | 17 | 18 | 19 | 20 |
| 21 | 22 | 23 | 24 | 25 | 26 | 27 |
| 28 | 29 | 30 | | | | |

### JULY

| S | M | T | W | T | F | S |
|---|---|---|---|---|---|---|
| | | | 1 | 2 | 3 | 4 |
| 5 | 6 | 7 | 8 | 9 | 10 | 11 |
| 12 | 13 | 14 | 15 | 16 | 17 | 18 |
| 19 | 20 | 21 | 22 | 23 | 24 | 25 |
| 26 | 27 | 28 | 29 | 30 | 31 | |

### AUGUST

| S | M | T | W | T | F | S |
|---|---|---|---|---|---|---|
| | | | | | | 1 |
| 2 | 3 | 4 | 5 | 6 | 7 | 8 |
| 9 | 10 | 11 | 12 | 13 | 14 | 15 |
| 16 | 17 | 18 | 19 | 20 | 21 | 22 |
| 23 | 24 | 25 | 26 | 27 | 28 | 29 |
| 30 | 31 | | | | | |

### SEPTEMBER

| S | M | T | W | T | F | S |
|---|---|---|---|---|---|---|
| | | 1 | 2 | 3 | 4 | 5 |
| 6 | 7 | 8 | 9 | 10 | 11 | 12 |
| 13 | 14 | 15 | 16 | 17 | 18 | 19 |
| 20 | 21 | 22 | 23 | 24 | 25 | 26 |
| 27 | 28 | 29 | 30 | | | |

### OCTOBER

| S | M | T | W | T | F | S |
|---|---|---|---|---|---|---|
| | | | | 1 | 2 | 3 |
| 4 | 5 | 6 | 7 | 8 | 9 | 10 |
| 11 | 12 | 13 | 14 | 15 | 16 | 17 |
| 18 | 19 | 20 | 21 | 22 | 23 | 24 |
| 25 | 26 | 27 | 28 | 29 | 30 | 31 |

### NOVEMBER

| S | M | T | W | T | F | S |
|---|---|---|---|---|---|---|
| 1 | 2 | 3 | 4 | 5 | 6 | 7 |
| 8 | 9 | 10 | 11 | 12 | 13 | 14 |
| 15 | 16 | 17 | 18 | 19 | 20 | 21 |
| 22 | 23 | 24 | 25 | 26 | 27 | 28 |
| 29 | 30 | | | | | |

### DECEMBER

| S | M | T | W | T | F | S |
|---|---|---|---|---|---|---|
| | | 1 | 2 | 3 | 4 | 5 |
| 6 | 7 | 8 | 9 | 10 | 11 | 12 |
| 13 | 14 | 15 | 16 | 17 | 18 | 19 |
| 20 | 21 | 22 | 23 | 24 | 25 | 26 |
| 27 | 28 | 29 | 30 | 31 | | |

## 1993

### JANUARY

| S | M | T | W | T | F | S |
|---|---|---|---|---|---|---|
| | | | | | 1 | 2 |
| 3 | 4 | 5 | 6 | 7 | 8 | 9 |
| 10 | 11 | 12 | 13 | 14 | 15 | 16 |
| 17 | 18 | 19 | 20 | 21 | 22 | 23 |
| 24 | 25 | 26 | 27 | 28 | 29 | 30 |
| 31 | | | | | | |

### FEBRUARY

| S | M | T | W | T | F | S |
|---|---|---|---|---|---|---|
| | 1 | 2 | 3 | 4 | 5 | 6 |
| 7 | 8 | 9 | 10 | 11 | 12 | 13 |
| 14 | 15 | 16 | 17 | 18 | 19 | 20 |
| 21 | 22 | 23 | 24 | 25 | 26 | 27 |
| 28 | | | | | | |

### MARCH

| S | M | T | W | T | F | S |
|---|---|---|---|---|---|---|
| | 1 | 2 | 3 | 4 | 5 | 6 |
| 7 | 8 | 9 | 10 | 11 | 12 | 13 |
| 14 | 15 | 16 | 17 | 18 | 19 | 20 |
| 21 | 22 | 23 | 24 | 25 | 26 | 27 |
| 28 | 29 | 30 | 31 | | | |

### APRIL

| S | M | T | W | T | F | S |
|---|---|---|---|---|---|---|
| | | | | 1 | 2 | 3 |
| 4 | 5 | 6 | 7 | 8 | 9 | 10 |
| 11 | 12 | 13 | 14 | 15 | 16 | 17 |
| 18 | 19 | 20 | 21 | 22 | 23 | 24 |
| 25 | 26 | 27 | 28 | 29 | 30 | |

### MAY

| S | M | T | W | T | F | S |
|---|---|---|---|---|---|---|
| | | | | | | 1 |
| 2 | 3 | 4 | 5 | 6 | 7 | 8 |
| 9 | 10 | 11 | 12 | 13 | 14 | 15 |
| 16 | 17 | 18 | 19 | 20 | 21 | 22 |
| 23 | 24 | 25 | 26 | 27 | 28 | 29 |
| 30 | 31 | | | | | |

### JUNE

| S | M | T | W | T | F | S |
|---|---|---|---|---|---|---|
| | | 1 | 2 | 3 | 4 | 5 |
| 6 | 7 | 8 | 9 | 10 | 11 | 12 |
| 13 | 14 | 15 | 16 | 17 | 18 | 19 |
| 20 | 21 | 22 | 23 | 24 | 25 | 26 |
| 27 | 28 | 29 | 30 | | | |

### JULY

| S | M | T | W | T | F | S |
|---|---|---|---|---|---|---|
| | | | | 1 | 2 | 3 |
| 4 | 5 | 6 | 7 | 8 | 9 | 10 |
| 11 | 12 | 13 | 14 | 15 | 16 | 17 |
| 18 | 19 | 20 | 21 | 22 | 23 | 24 |
| 25 | 26 | 27 | 28 | 29 | 30 | 31 |

### AUGUST

| S | M | T | W | T | F | S |
|---|---|---|---|---|---|---|
| 1 | 2 | 3 | 4 | 5 | 6 | 7 |
| 8 | 9 | 10 | 11 | 12 | 13 | 14 |
| 15 | 16 | 17 | 18 | 19 | 20 | 21 |
| 22 | 23 | 24 | 25 | 26 | 27 | 28 |
| 29 | 30 | 31 | | | | |

### SEPTEMBER

| S | M | T | W | T | F | S |
|---|---|---|---|---|---|---|
| | | | 1 | 2 | 3 | 4 |
| 5 | 6 | 7 | 8 | 9 | 10 | 11 |
| 12 | 13 | 14 | 15 | 16 | 17 | 18 |
| 19 | 20 | 21 | 22 | 23 | 24 | 25 |
| 26 | 27 | 28 | 29 | 30 | | |

### OCTOBER

| S | M | T | W | T | F | S |
|---|---|---|---|---|---|---|
| | | | | | 1 | 2 |
| 3 | 4 | 5 | 6 | 7 | 8 | 9 |
| 10 | 11 | 12 | 13 | 14 | 15 | 16 |
| 17 | 18 | 19 | 20 | 21 | 22 | 23 |
| 24 | 25 | 26 | 27 | 28 | 29 | 30 |
| 31 | | | | | | |

### NOVEMBER

| S | M | T | W | T | F | S |
|---|---|---|---|---|---|---|
| | 1 | 2 | 3 | 4 | 5 | 6 |
| 7 | 8 | 9 | 10 | 11 | 12 | 13 |
| 14 | 15 | 16 | 17 | 18 | 19 | 20 |
| 21 | 22 | 23 | 24 | 25 | 26 | 27 |
| 28 | 29 | 30 | | | | |

### DECEMBER

| S | M | T | W | T | F | S |
|---|---|---|---|---|---|---|
| | | | 1 | 2 | 3 | 4 |
| 5 | 6 | 7 | 8 | 9 | 10 | 11 |
| 12 | 13 | 14 | 15 | 16 | 17 | 18 |
| 19 | 20 | 21 | 22 | 23 | 24 | 25 |
| 26 | 27 | 28 | 29 | 30 | 31 | |

## 1994

### JANUARY

| S | M | T | W | T | F | S |
|---|---|---|---|---|---|---|
| | | | | | | 1 |
| 2 | 3 | 4 | 5 | 6 | 7 | 8 |
| 9 | 10 | 11 | 12 | 13 | 14 | 15 |
| 16 | 17 | 18 | 19 | 20 | 21 | 22 |
| 23 | 24 | 25 | 26 | 27 | 28 | 29 |
| 30 | 31 | | | | | |

### FEBRUARY

| S | M | T | W | T | F | S |
|---|---|---|---|---|---|---|
| | | 1 | 2 | 3 | 4 | 5 |
| 6 | 7 | 8 | 9 | 10 | 11 | 12 |
| 13 | 14 | 15 | 16 | 17 | 18 | 19 |
| 20 | 21 | 22 | 23 | 24 | 25 | 26 |
| 27 | 28 | | | | | |

### MARCH

| S | M | T | W | T | F | S |
|---|---|---|---|---|---|---|
| | | 1 | 2 | 3 | 4 | 5 |
| 6 | 7 | 8 | 9 | 10 | 11 | 12 |
| 13 | 14 | 15 | 16 | 17 | 18 | 19 |
| 20 | 21 | 22 | 23 | 24 | 25 | 26 |
| 27 | 28 | 29 | 30 | 31 | | |

### APRIL

| S | M | T | W | T | F | S |
|---|---|---|---|---|---|---|
| | | | | | 1 | 2 |
| 3 | 4 | 5 | 6 | 7 | 8 | 9 |
| 10 | 11 | 12 | 13 | 14 | 15 | 16 |
| 17 | 18 | 19 | 20 | 21 | 22 | 23 |
| 24 | 25 | 26 | 27 | 28 | 29 | 30 |

### MAY

| S | M | T | W | T | F | S |
|---|---|---|---|---|---|---|
| 1 | 2 | 3 | 4 | 5 | 6 | 7 |
| 8 | 9 | 10 | 11 | 12 | 13 | 14 |
| 15 | 16 | 17 | 18 | 19 | 20 | 21 |
| 22 | 23 | 24 | 25 | 26 | 27 | 28 |
| 29 | 30 | 31 | | | | |

### JUNE

| S | M | T | W | T | F | S |
|---|---|---|---|---|---|---|
| | | | 1 | 2 | 3 | 4 |
| 5 | 6 | 7 | 8 | 9 | 10 | 11 |
| 12 | 13 | 14 | 15 | 16 | 17 | 18 |
| 19 | 20 | 21 | 22 | 23 | 24 | 25 |
| 26 | 27 | 28 | 29 | 30 | | |

### JULY

| S | M | T | W | T | F | S |
|---|---|---|---|---|---|---|
| | | | | | 1 | 2 |
| 3 | 4 | 5 | 6 | 7 | 8 | 9 |
| 10 | 11 | 12 | 13 | 14 | 15 | 16 |
| 17 | 18 | 19 | 20 | 21 | 22 | 23 |
| 24 | 25 | 26 | 27 | 28 | 29 | 30 |
| 31 | | | | | | |

### AUGUST

| S | M | T | W | T | F | S |
|---|---|---|---|---|---|---|
| | 1 | 2 | 3 | 4 | 5 | 6 |
| 7 | 8 | 9 | 10 | 11 | 12 | 13 |
| 14 | 15 | 16 | 17 | 18 | 19 | 20 |
| 21 | 22 | 23 | 24 | 25 | 26 | 27 |
| 28 | 29 | 30 | 31 | | | |

### SEPTEMBER

| S | M | T | W | T | F | S |
|---|---|---|---|---|---|---|
| | | | | 1 | 2 | 3 |
| 4 | 5 | 6 | 7 | 8 | 9 | 10 |
| 11 | 12 | 13 | 14 | 15 | 16 | 17 |
| 18 | 19 | 20 | 21 | 22 | 23 | 24 |
| 25 | 26 | 27 | 28 | 29 | 30 | |

### OCTOBER

| S | M | T | W | T | F | S |
|---|---|---|---|---|---|---|
| | | | | | | 1 |
| 2 | 3 | 4 | 5 | 6 | 7 | 8 |
| 9 | 10 | 11 | 12 | 13 | 14 | 15 |
| 16 | 17 | 18 | 19 | 20 | 21 | 22 |
| 23 | 24 | 25 | 26 | 27 | 28 | 29 |
| 30 | 31 | | | | | |

### NOVEMBER

| S | M | T | W | T | F | S |
|---|---|---|---|---|---|---|
| | | 1 | 2 | 3 | 4 | 5 |
| 6 | 7 | 8 | 9 | 10 | 11 | 12 |
| 13 | 14 | 15 | 16 | 17 | 18 | 19 |
| 20 | 21 | 22 | 23 | 24 | 25 | 26 |
| 27 | 28 | 29 | 30 | | | |

### DECEMBER

| S | M | T | W | T | F | S |
|---|---|---|---|---|---|---|
| | | | | 1 | 2 | 3 |
| 4 | 5 | 6 | 7 | 8 | 9 | 10 |
| 11 | 12 | 13 | 14 | 15 | 16 | 17 |
| 18 | 19 | 20 | 21 | 22 | 23 | 24 |
| 25 | 26 | 27 | 28 | 29 | 30 | 31 |

## 1995

### JANUARY

| S | M | T | W | T | F | S |
|---|---|---|---|---|---|---|
| 1 | 2 | 3 | 4 | 5 | 6 | 7 |
| 8 | 9 | 10 | 11 | 12 | 13 | 14 |
| 15 | 16 | 17 | 18 | 19 | 20 | 21 |
| 22 | 23 | 24 | 25 | 26 | 27 | 28 |
| 29 | 30 | 31 | | | | |

### FEBRUARY

| S | M | T | W | T | F | S |
|---|---|---|---|---|---|---|
| | | | 1 | 2 | 3 | 4 |
| 5 | 6 | 7 | 8 | 9 | 10 | 11 |
| 12 | 13 | 14 | 15 | 16 | 17 | 18 |
| 19 | 20 | 21 | 22 | 23 | 24 | 25 |
| 26 | 27 | 28 | | | | |

### MARCH

| S | M | T | W | T | F | S |
|---|---|---|---|---|---|---|
| | | | 1 | 2 | 3 | 4 |
| 5 | 6 | 7 | 8 | 9 | 10 | 11 |
| 12 | 13 | 14 | 15 | 16 | 17 | 18 |
| 19 | 20 | 21 | 22 | 23 | 24 | 25 |
| 26 | 27 | 28 | 29 | 30 | 31 | |

### APRIL

| S | M | T | W | T | F | S |
|---|---|---|---|---|---|---|
| | | | | | | 1 |
| 2 | 3 | 4 | 5 | 6 | 7 | 8 |
| 9 | 10 | 11 | 12 | 13 | 14 | 15 |
| 16 | 17 | 18 | 19 | 20 | 21 | 22 |
| 23 | 24 | 25 | 26 | 27 | 28 | 29 |
| 30 | | | | | | |

### MAY

| S | M | T | W | T | F | S |
|---|---|---|---|---|---|---|
| | 1 | 2 | 3 | 4 | 5 | 6 |
| 7 | 8 | 9 | 10 | 11 | 12 | 13 |
| 14 | 15 | 16 | 17 | 18 | 19 | 20 |
| 21 | 22 | 23 | 24 | 25 | 26 | 27 |
| 28 | 29 | 30 | 31 | | | |

### JUNE

| S | M | T | W | T | F | S |
|---|---|---|---|---|---|---|
| | | | | 1 | 2 | 3 |
| 4 | 5 | 6 | 7 | 8 | 9 | 10 |
| 11 | 12 | 13 | 14 | 15 | 16 | 17 |
| 18 | 19 | 20 | 21 | 22 | 23 | 24 |
| 25 | 26 | 27 | 28 | 29 | 30 | |

### JULY

| S | M | T | W | T | F | S |
|---|---|---|---|---|---|---|
| | | | | | | 1 |
| 2 | 3 | 4 | 5 | 6 | 7 | 8 |
| 9 | 10 | 11 | 12 | 13 | 14 | 15 |
| 16 | 17 | 18 | 19 | 20 | 21 | 22 |
| 23 | 24 | 25 | 26 | 27 | 28 | 29 |
| 30 | 31 | | | | | |

### AUGUST

| S | M | T | W | T | F | S |
|---|---|---|---|---|---|---|
| | | 1 | 2 | 3 | 4 | 5 |
| 6 | 7 | 8 | 9 | 10 | 11 | 12 |
| 13 | 14 | 15 | 16 | 17 | 18 | 19 |
| 20 | 21 | 22 | 23 | 24 | 25 | 26 |
| 27 | 28 | 29 | 30 | 31 | | |

### SEPTEMBER

| S | M | T | W | T | F | S |
|---|---|---|---|---|---|---|
| | | | | | 1 | 2 |
| 3 | 4 | 5 | 6 | 7 | 8 | 9 |
| 10 | 11 | 12 | 13 | 14 | 15 | 16 |
| 17 | 18 | 19 | 20 | 21 | 22 | 23 |
| 24 | 25 | 26 | 27 | 28 | 29 | 30 |

### OCTOBER

| S | M | T | W | T | F | S |
|---|---|---|---|---|---|---|
| 1 | 2 | 3 | 4 | 5 | 6 | 7 |
| 8 | 9 | 10 | 11 | 12 | 13 | 14 |
| 15 | 16 | 17 | 18 | 19 | 20 | 21 |
| 22 | 23 | 24 | 25 | 26 | 27 | 28 |
| 29 | 30 | 31 | | | | |

### NOVEMBER

| S | M | T | W | T | F | S |
|---|---|---|---|---|---|---|
| | | | 1 | 2 | 3 | 4 |
| 5 | 6 | 7 | 8 | 9 | 10 | 11 |
| 12 | 13 | 14 | 15 | 16 | 17 | 18 |
| 19 | 20 | 21 | 22 | 23 | 24 | 25 |
| 26 | 27 | 28 | 29 | 30 | | |

### DECEMBER

| S | M | T | W | T | F | S |
|---|---|---|---|---|---|---|
| | | | | | 1 | 2 |
| 3 | 4 | 5 | 6 | 7 | 8 | 9 |
| 10 | 11 | 12 | 13 | 14 | 15 | 16 |
| 17 | 18 | 19 | 20 | 21 | 22 | 23 |
| 24 | 25 | 26 | 27 | 28 | 29 | 30 |
| 31 | | | | | | |

## 1996

### JANUARY

| S | M | T | W | T | F | S |
|---|---|---|---|---|---|---|
| | 1 | 2 | 3 | 4 | 5 | 6 |
| 7 | 8 | 9 | 10 | 11 | 12 | 13 |
| 14 | 15 | 16 | 17 | 18 | 19 | 20 |
| 21 | 22 | 23 | 24 | 25 | 26 | 27 |
| 28 | 29 | 30 | 31 | | | |

### FEBRUARY

| S | M | T | W | T | F | S |
|---|---|---|---|---|---|---|
| | | | | 1 | 2 | 3 |
| 4 | 5 | 6 | 7 | 8 | 9 | 10 |
| 11 | 12 | 13 | 14 | 15 | 16 | 17 |
| 18 | 19 | 20 | 21 | 22 | 23 | 24 |
| 25 | 26 | 27 | 28 | 29 | | |

### MARCH

| S | M | T | W | T | F | S |
|---|---|---|---|---|---|---|
| | | | | | 1 | 2 |
| 3 | 4 | 5 | 6 | 7 | 8 | 9 |
| 10 | 11 | 12 | 13 | 14 | 15 | 16 |
| 17 | 18 | 19 | 20 | 21 | 22 | 23 |
| 24 | 25 | 26 | 27 | 28 | 29 | 30 |
| 31 | | | | | | |

### APRIL

| S | M | T | W | T | F | S |
|---|---|---|---|---|---|---|
| | 1 | 2 | 3 | 4 | 5 | 6 |
| 7 | 8 | 9 | 10 | 11 | 12 | 13 |
| 14 | 15 | 16 | 17 | 18 | 19 | 20 |
| 21 | 22 | 23 | 24 | 25 | 26 | 27 |
| 28 | 29 | 30 | | | | |

### MAY

| S | M | T | W | T | F | S |
|---|---|---|---|---|---|---|
| | | | 1 | 2 | 3 | 4 |
| 5 | 6 | 7 | 8 | 9 | 10 | 11 |
| 12 | 13 | 14 | 15 | 16 | 17 | 18 |
| 19 | 20 | 21 | 22 | 23 | 24 | 25 |
| 26 | 27 | 28 | 29 | 30 | 31 | |

### JUNE

| S | M | T | W | T | F | S |
|---|---|---|---|---|---|---|
| | | | | | | 1 |
| 2 | 3 | 4 | 5 | 6 | 7 | 8 |
| 9 | 10 | 11 | 12 | 13 | 14 | 15 |
| 16 | 17 | 18 | 19 | 20 | 21 | 22 |
| 23 | 24 | 25 | 26 | 27 | 28 | 29 |
| 30 | | | | | | |

### JULY

| S | M | T | W | T | F | S |
|---|---|---|---|---|---|---|
| | 1 | 2 | 3 | 4 | 5 | 6 |
| 7 | 8 | 9 | 10 | 11 | 12 | 13 |
| 14 | 15 | 16 | 17 | 18 | 19 | 20 |
| 21 | 22 | 23 | 24 | 25 | 26 | 27 |
| 28 | 29 | 30 | 31 | | | |

### AUGUST

| S | M | T | W | T | F | S |
|---|---|---|---|---|---|---|
| | | | | 1 | 2 | 3 |
| 4 | 5 | 6 | 7 | 8 | 9 | 10 |
| 11 | 12 | 13 | 14 | 15 | 16 | 17 |
| 18 | 19 | 20 | 21 | 22 | 23 | 24 |
| 25 | 26 | 27 | 28 | 29 | 30 | 31 |

### SEPTEMBER

| S | M | T | W | T | F | S |
|---|---|---|---|---|---|---|
| 1 | 2 | 3 | 4 | 5 | 6 | 7 |
| 8 | 9 | 10 | 11 | 12 | 13 | 14 |
| 15 | 16 | 17 | 18 | 19 | 20 | 21 |
| 22 | 23 | 24 | 25 | 26 | 27 | 28 |
| 29 | 30 | | | | | |

### OCTOBER

| S | M | T | W | T | F | S |
|---|---|---|---|---|---|---|
| | | 1 | 2 | 3 | 4 | 5 |
| 6 | 7 | 8 | 9 | 10 | 11 | 12 |
| 13 | 14 | 15 | 16 | 17 | 18 | 19 |
| 20 | 21 | 22 | 23 | 24 | 25 | 26 |
| 27 | 28 | 29 | 30 | 31 | | |

### NOVEMBER

| S | M | T | W | T | F | S |
|---|---|---|---|---|---|---|
| | | | | | 1 | 2 |
| 3 | 4 | 5 | 6 | 7 | 8 | 9 |
| 10 | 11 | 12 | 13 | 14 | 15 | 16 |
| 17 | 18 | 19 | 20 | 21 | 22 | 23 |
| 24 | 25 | 26 | 27 | 28 | 29 | 30 |

### DECEMBER

| S | M | T | W | T | F | S |
|---|---|---|---|---|---|---|
| 1 | 2 | 3 | 4 | 5 | 6 | 7 |
| 8 | 9 | 10 | 11 | 12 | 13 | 14 |
| 15 | 16 | 17 | 18 | 19 | 20 | 21 |
| 22 | 23 | 24 | 25 | 26 | 27 | 28 |
| 29 | 30 | 31 | | | | |

## 1997

### JANUARY

| S | M | T | W | T | F | S |
|---|---|---|---|---|---|---|
| | | | 1 | 2 | 3 | 4 |
| 5 | 6 | 7 | 8 | 9 | 10 | 11 |
| 12 | 13 | 14 | 15 | 16 | 17 | 18 |
| 19 | 20 | 21 | 22 | 23 | 24 | 25 |
| 26 | 27 | 28 | 29 | 30 | 31 | |

### FEBRUARY

| S | M | T | W | T | F | S |
|---|---|---|---|---|---|---|
| | | | | | | 1 |
| 2 | 3 | 4 | 5 | 6 | 7 | 8 |
| 9 | 10 | 11 | 12 | 13 | 14 | 15 |
| 16 | 17 | 18 | 19 | 20 | 21 | 22 |
| 23 | 24 | 25 | 26 | 27 | 28 | |

### MARCH

| S | M | T | W | T | F | S |
|---|---|---|---|---|---|---|
| | | | | | | 1 |
| 2 | 3 | 4 | 5 | 6 | 7 | 8 |
| 9 | 10 | 11 | 12 | 13 | 14 | 15 |
| 16 | 17 | 18 | 19 | 20 | 21 | 22 |
| 23 | 24 | 25 | 26 | 27 | 28 | 29 |
| 30 | 31 | | | | | |

### APRIL

| S | M | T | W | T | F | S |
|---|---|---|---|---|---|---|
| | | 1 | 2 | 3 | 4 | 5 |
| 6 | 7 | 8 | 9 | 10 | 11 | 12 |
| 13 | 14 | 15 | 16 | 17 | 18 | 19 |
| 20 | 21 | 22 | 23 | 24 | 25 | 26 |
| 27 | 28 | 29 | 30 | | | |

### MAY

| S | M | T | W | T | F | S |
|---|---|---|---|---|---|---|
| | | | | 1 | 2 | 3 |
| 4 | 5 | 6 | 7 | 8 | 9 | 10 |
| 11 | 12 | 13 | 14 | 15 | 16 | 17 |
| 18 | 19 | 20 | 21 | 22 | 23 | 24 |
| 25 | 26 | 27 | 28 | 29 | 30 | 31 |

### JUNE

| S | M | T | W | T | F | S |
|---|---|---|---|---|---|---|
| 1 | 2 | 3 | 4 | 5 | 6 | 7 |
| 8 | 9 | 10 | 11 | 12 | 13 | 14 |
| 15 | 16 | 17 | 18 | 19 | 20 | 21 |
| 22 | 23 | 24 | 25 | 26 | 27 | 28 |
| 29 | 30 | | | | | |

### JULY

| S | M | T | W | T | F | S |
|---|---|---|---|---|---|---|
| | | 1 | 2 | 3 | 4 | 5 |
| 6 | 7 | 8 | 9 | 10 | 11 | 12 |
| 13 | 14 | 15 | 16 | 17 | 18 | 19 |
| 20 | 21 | 22 | 23 | 24 | 25 | 26 |
| 27 | 28 | 29 | 30 | 31 | | |

### AUGUST

| S | M | T | W | T | F | S |
|---|---|---|---|---|---|---|
| | | | | | 1 | 2 |
| 3 | 4 | 5 | 6 | 7 | 8 | 9 |
| 10 | 11 | 12 | 13 | 14 | 15 | 16 |
| 17 | 18 | 19 | 20 | 21 | 22 | 23 |
| 24 | 25 | 26 | 27 | 28 | 29 | 30 |
| 31 | | | | | | |

### SEPTEMBER

| S | M | T | W | T | F | S |
|---|---|---|---|---|---|---|
| | 1 | 2 | 3 | 4 | 5 | 6 |
| 7 | 8 | 9 | 10 | 11 | 12 | 13 |
| 14 | 15 | 16 | 17 | 18 | 19 | 20 |
| 21 | 22 | 23 | 24 | 25 | 26 | 27 |
| 28 | 29 | 30 | | | | |

### OCTOBER

| S | M | T | W | T | F | S |
|---|---|---|---|---|---|---|
| | | | 1 | 2 | 3 | 4 |
| 5 | 6 | 7 | 8 | 9 | 10 | 11 |
| 12 | 13 | 14 | 15 | 16 | 17 | 18 |
| 19 | 20 | 21 | 22 | 23 | 24 | 25 |
| 26 | 27 | 28 | 29 | 30 | 31 | |

### NOVEMBER

| S | M | T | W | T | F | S |
|---|---|---|---|---|---|---|
| | | | | | | 1 |
| 2 | 3 | 4 | 5 | 6 | 7 | 8 |
| 9 | 10 | 11 | 12 | 13 | 14 | 15 |
| 16 | 17 | 18 | 19 | 20 | 21 | 22 |
| 23 | 24 | 25 | 26 | 27 | 28 | 29 |
| 30 | | | | | | |

### DECEMBER

| S | M | T | W | T | F | S |
|---|---|---|---|---|---|---|
| | 1 | 2 | 3 | 4 | 5 | 6 |
| 7 | 8 | 9 | 10 | 11 | 12 | 13 |
| 14 | 15 | 16 | 17 | 18 | 19 | 20 |
| 21 | 22 | 23 | 24 | 25 | 26 | 27 |
| 28 | 29 | 30 | 31 | | | |

## 1998

### JANUARY

| S | M | T | W | T | F | S |
|---|---|---|---|---|---|---|
| | | | | 1 | 2 | 3 |
| 4 | 5 | 6 | 7 | 8 | 9 | 10 |
| 11 | 12 | 13 | 14 | 15 | 16 | 17 |
| 18 | 19 | 20 | 21 | 22 | 23 | 24 |
| 25 | 26 | 27 | 28 | 29 | 30 | 31 |

### FEBRUARY

| S | M | T | W | T | F | S |
|---|---|---|---|---|---|---|
| 1 | 2 | 3 | 4 | 5 | 6 | 7 |
| 8 | 9 | 10 | 11 | 12 | 13 | 14 |
| 15 | 16 | 17 | 18 | 19 | 20 | 21 |
| 22 | 23 | 24 | 25 | 26 | 27 | 28 |

### MARCH

| S | M | T | W | T | F | S |
|---|---|---|---|---|---|---|
| 1 | 2 | 3 | 4 | 5 | 6 | 7 |
| 8 | 9 | 10 | 11 | 12 | 13 | 14 |
| 15 | 16 | 17 | 18 | 19 | 20 | 21 |
| 22 | 23 | 24 | 25 | 26 | 27 | 28 |
| 29 | 30 | 31 | | | | |

### APRIL

| S | M | T | W | T | F | S |
|---|---|---|---|---|---|---|
| | | | 1 | 2 | 3 | 4 |
| 5 | 6 | 7 | 8 | 9 | 10 | 11 |
| 12 | 13 | 14 | 15 | 16 | 17 | 18 |
| 19 | 20 | 21 | 22 | 23 | 24 | 25 |
| 26 | 27 | 28 | 29 | 30 | | |

### MAY

| S | M | T | W | T | F | S |
|---|---|---|---|---|---|---|
| | | | | | 1 | 2 |
| 3 | 4 | 5 | 6 | 7 | 8 | 9 |
| 10 | 11 | 12 | 13 | 14 | 15 | 16 |
| 17 | 18 | 19 | 20 | 21 | 22 | 23 |
| 24 | 25 | 26 | 27 | 28 | 29 | 30 |
| 31 | | | | | | |

### JUNE

| S | M | T | W | T | F | S |
|---|---|---|---|---|---|---|
| | 1 | 2 | 3 | 4 | 5 | 6 |
| 7 | 8 | 9 | 10 | 11 | 12 | 13 |
| 14 | 15 | 16 | 17 | 18 | 19 | 20 |
| 21 | 22 | 23 | 24 | 25 | 26 | 27 |
| 28 | 29 | 30 | | | | |

### JULY

| S | M | T | W | T | F | S |
|---|---|---|---|---|---|---|
| | | | 1 | 2 | 3 | 4 |
| 5 | 6 | 7 | 8 | 9 | 10 | 11 |
| 12 | 13 | 14 | 15 | 16 | 17 | 18 |
| 19 | 20 | 21 | 22 | 23 | 24 | 25 |
| 26 | 27 | 28 | 29 | 30 | 31 | |

### AUGUST

| S | M | T | W | T | F | S |
|---|---|---|---|---|---|---|
| | | | | | | 1 |
| 2 | 3 | 4 | 5 | 6 | 7 | 8 |
| 9 | 10 | 11 | 12 | 13 | 14 | 15 |
| 16 | 17 | 18 | 19 | 20 | 21 | 22 |
| 23 | 24 | 25 | 26 | 27 | 28 | 29 |
| 30 | 31 | | | | | |

### SEPTEMBER

| S | M | T | W | T | F | S |
|---|---|---|---|---|---|---|
| | | 1 | 2 | 3 | 4 | 5 |
| 6 | 7 | 8 | 9 | 10 | 11 | 12 |
| 13 | 14 | 15 | 16 | 17 | 18 | 19 |
| 20 | 21 | 22 | 23 | 24 | 25 | 26 |
| 27 | 28 | 29 | 30 | | | |

### OCTOBER

| S | M | T | W | T | F | S |
|---|---|---|---|---|---|---|
| | | | | 1 | 2 | 3 |
| 4 | 5 | 6 | 7 | 8 | 9 | 10 |
| 11 | 12 | 13 | 14 | 15 | 16 | 17 |
| 18 | 19 | 20 | 21 | 22 | 23 | 24 |
| 25 | 26 | 27 | 28 | 29 | 30 | 31 |

### NOVEMBER

| S | M | T | W | T | F | S |
|---|---|---|---|---|---|---|
| 1 | 2 | 3 | 4 | 5 | 6 | 7 |
| 8 | 9 | 10 | 11 | 12 | 13 | 14 |
| 15 | 16 | 17 | 18 | 19 | 20 | 21 |
| 22 | 23 | 24 | 25 | 26 | 27 | 28 |
| 29 | 30 | | | | | |

### DECEMBER

| S | M | T | W | T | F | S |
|---|---|---|---|---|---|---|
| | | 1 | 2 | 3 | 4 | 5 |
| 6 | 7 | 8 | 9 | 10 | 11 | 12 |
| 13 | 14 | 15 | 16 | 17 | 18 | 19 |
| 20 | 21 | 22 | 23 | 24 | 25 | 26 |
| 27 | 28 | 29 | 30 | 31 | | |

## 1999

### JANUARY

| S | M | T | W | T | F | S |
|---|---|---|---|---|---|---|
| | | | | | 1 | 2 |
| 3 | 4 | 5 | 6 | 7 | 8 | 9 |
| 10 | 11 | 12 | 13 | 14 | 15 | 16 |
| 17 | 18 | 19 | 20 | 21 | 22 | 23 |
| 24 | 25 | 26 | 27 | 28 | 29 | 30 |
| 31 | | | | | | |

### FEBRUARY

| S | M | T | W | T | F | S |
|---|---|---|---|---|---|---|
| | 1 | 2 | 3 | 4 | 5 | 6 |
| 7 | 8 | 9 | 10 | 11 | 12 | 13 |
| 14 | 15 | 16 | 17 | 18 | 19 | 20 |
| 21 | 22 | 23 | 24 | 25 | 26 | 27 |
| 28 | | | | | | |

### MARCH

| S | M | T | W | T | F | S |
|---|---|---|---|---|---|---|
| | 1 | 2 | 3 | 4 | 5 | 6 |
| 7 | 8 | 9 | 10 | 11 | 12 | 13 |
| 14 | 15 | 16 | 17 | 18 | 19 | 20 |
| 21 | 22 | 23 | 24 | 25 | 26 | 27 |
| 28 | 29 | 30 | 31 | | | |

### APRIL

| S | M | T | W | T | F | S |
|---|---|---|---|---|---|---|
| | | | | 1 | 2 | 3 |
| 4 | 5 | 6 | 7 | 8 | 9 | 10 |
| 11 | 12 | 13 | 14 | 15 | 16 | 17 |
| 18 | 19 | 20 | 21 | 22 | 23 | 24 |
| 25 | 26 | 27 | 28 | 29 | 30 | |

### MAY

| S | M | T | W | T | F | S |
|---|---|---|---|---|---|---|
| | | | | | | 1 |
| 2 | 3 | 4 | 5 | 6 | 7 | 8 |
| 9 | 10 | 11 | 12 | 13 | 14 | 15 |
| 16 | 17 | 18 | 19 | 20 | 21 | 22 |
| 23 | 24 | 25 | 26 | 27 | 28 | 29 |
| 30 | 31 | | | | | |

### JUNE

| S | M | T | W | T | F | S |
|---|---|---|---|---|---|---|
| | | 1 | 2 | 3 | 4 | 5 |
| 6 | 7 | 8 | 9 | 10 | 11 | 12 |
| 13 | 14 | 15 | 16 | 17 | 18 | 19 |
| 20 | 21 | 22 | 23 | 24 | 25 | 26 |
| 27 | 28 | 29 | 30 | | | |

### JULY

| S | M | T | W | T | F | S |
|---|---|---|---|---|---|---|
| | | | | 1 | 2 | 3 |
| 4 | 5 | 6 | 7 | 8 | 9 | 10 |
| 11 | 12 | 13 | 14 | 15 | 16 | 17 |
| 18 | 19 | 20 | 21 | 22 | 23 | 24 |
| 25 | 26 | 27 | 28 | 29 | 30 | 31 |

### AUGUST

| S | M | T | W | T | F | S |
|---|---|---|---|---|---|---|
| 1 | 2 | 3 | 4 | 5 | 6 | 7 |
| 8 | 9 | 10 | 11 | 12 | 13 | 14 |
| 15 | 16 | 17 | 18 | 19 | 20 | 21 |
| 22 | 23 | 24 | 25 | 26 | 27 | 28 |
| 29 | 30 | 31 | | | | |

### SEPTEMBER

| S | M | T | W | T | F | S |
|---|---|---|---|---|---|---|
| | | | 1 | 2 | 3 | 4 |
| 5 | 6 | 7 | 8 | 9 | 10 | 11 |
| 12 | 13 | 14 | 15 | 16 | 17 | 18 |
| 19 | 20 | 21 | 22 | 23 | 24 | 25 |
| 26 | 27 | 28 | 29 | 30 | | |

### OCTOBER

| S | M | T | W | T | F | S |
|---|---|---|---|---|---|---|
| | | | | | 1 | 2 |
| 3 | 4 | 5 | 6 | 7 | 8 | 9 |
| 10 | 11 | 12 | 13 | 14 | 15 | 16 |
| 17 | 18 | 19 | 20 | 21 | 22 | 23 |
| 24 | 25 | 26 | 27 | 28 | 29 | 30 |
| 31 | | | | | | |

### NOVEMBER

| S | M | T | W | T | F | S |
|---|---|---|---|---|---|---|
| | 1 | 2 | 3 | 4 | 5 | 6 |
| 7 | 8 | 9 | 10 | 11 | 12 | 13 |
| 14 | 15 | 16 | 17 | 18 | 19 | 20 |
| 21 | 22 | 23 | 24 | 25 | 26 | 27 |
| 28 | 29 | 30 | | | | |

### DECEMBER

| S | M | T | W | T | F | S |
|---|---|---|---|---|---|---|
| | | | 1 | 2 | 3 | 4 |
| 5 | 6 | 7 | 8 | 9 | 10 | 11 |
| 12 | 13 | 14 | 15 | 16 | 17 | 18 |
| 19 | 20 | 21 | 22 | 23 | 24 | 25 |
| 26 | 27 | 28 | 29 | 30 | 31 | |

## 2000

### JANUARY

| S | M | T | W | T | F | S |
|---|---|---|---|---|---|---|
| | | | | | | 1 |
| 2 | 3 | 4 | 5 | 6 | 7 | 8 |
| 9 | 10 | 11 | 12 | 13 | 14 | 15 |
| 16 | 17 | 18 | 19 | 20 | 21 | 22 |
| 23 | 24 | 25 | 26 | 27 | 28 | 29 |
| 30 | 31 | | | | | |

### FEBRUARY

| S | M | T | W | T | F | S |
|---|---|---|---|---|---|---|
| | | 1 | 2 | 3 | 4 | 5 |
| 6 | 7 | 8 | 9 | 10 | 11 | 12 |
| 13 | 14 | 15 | 16 | 17 | 18 | 19 |
| 20 | 21 | 22 | 23 | 24 | 25 | 26 |
| 27 | 28 | 29 | | | | |

### MARCH

| S | M | T | W | T | F | S |
|---|---|---|---|---|---|---|
| | | | 1 | 2 | 3 | 4 |
| 5 | 6 | 7 | 8 | 9 | 10 | 11 |
| 12 | 13 | 14 | 15 | 16 | 17 | 18 |
| 19 | 20 | 21 | 22 | 23 | 24 | 25 |
| 26 | 27 | 28 | 29 | 30 | 31 | |

### APRIL

| S | M | T | W | T | F | S |
|---|---|---|---|---|---|---|
| | | | | | | 1 |
| 2 | 3 | 4 | 5 | 6 | 7 | 8 |
| 9 | 10 | 11 | 12 | 13 | 14 | 15 |
| 16 | 17 | 18 | 19 | 20 | 21 | 22 |
| 23 | 24 | 25 | 26 | 27 | 28 | 29 |
| 30 | | | | | | |

### MAY

| S | M | T | W | T | F | S |
|---|---|---|---|---|---|---|
| | 1 | 2 | 3 | 4 | 5 | 6 |
| 7 | 8 | 9 | 10 | 11 | 12 | 13 |
| 14 | 15 | 16 | 17 | 18 | 19 | 20 |
| 21 | 22 | 23 | 24 | 25 | 26 | 27 |
| 28 | 29 | 30 | 31 | | | |

### JUNE

| S | M | T | W | T | F | S |
|---|---|---|---|---|---|---|
| | | | | 1 | 2 | 3 |
| 4 | 5 | 6 | 7 | 8 | 9 | 10 |
| 11 | 12 | 13 | 14 | 15 | 16 | 17 |
| 18 | 19 | 20 | 21 | 22 | 23 | 24 |
| 25 | 26 | 27 | 28 | 29 | 30 | |

### JULY

| S | M | T | W | T | F | S |
|---|---|---|---|---|---|---|
| | | | | | | 1 |
| 2 | 3 | 4 | 5 | 6 | 7 | 8 |
| 9 | 10 | 11 | 12 | 13 | 14 | 15 |
| 16 | 17 | 18 | 19 | 20 | 21 | 22 |
| 23 | 24 | 25 | 26 | 27 | 28 | 29 |
| 30 | 31 | | | | | |

### AUGUST

| S | M | T | W | T | F | S |
|---|---|---|---|---|---|---|
| | | 1 | 2 | 3 | 4 | 5 |
| 6 | 7 | 8 | 9 | 10 | 11 | 12 |
| 13 | 14 | 15 | 16 | 17 | 18 | 19 |
| 20 | 21 | 22 | 23 | 24 | 25 | 26 |
| 27 | 28 | 29 | 30 | 31 | | |

### SEPTEMBER

| S | M | T | W | T | F | S |
|---|---|---|---|---|---|---|
| | | | | | 1 | 2 |
| 3 | 4 | 5 | 6 | 7 | 8 | 9 |
| 10 | 11 | 12 | 13 | 14 | 15 | 16 |
| 17 | 18 | 19 | 20 | 21 | 22 | 23 |
| 24 | 25 | 26 | 27 | 28 | 29 | 30 |

### OCTOBER

| S | M | T | W | T | F | S |
|---|---|---|---|---|---|---|
| 1 | 2 | 3 | 4 | 5 | 6 | 7 |
| 8 | 9 | 10 | 11 | 12 | 13 | 14 |
| 15 | 16 | 17 | 18 | 19 | 20 | 21 |
| 22 | 23 | 24 | 25 | 26 | 27 | 28 |
| 29 | 30 | 31 | | | | |

### NOVEMBER

| S | M | T | W | T | F | S |
|---|---|---|---|---|---|---|
| | | | 1 | 2 | 3 | 4 |
| 5 | 6 | 7 | 8 | 9 | 10 | 11 |
| 12 | 13 | 14 | 15 | 16 | 17 | 18 |
| 19 | 20 | 21 | 22 | 23 | 24 | 25 |
| 26 | 27 | 28 | 29 | 30 | | |

### DECEMBER

| S | M | T | W | T | F | S |
|---|---|---|---|---|---|---|
| | | | | | 1 | 2 |
| 3 | 4 | 5 | 6 | 7 | 8 | 9 |
| 10 | 11 | 12 | 13 | 14 | 15 | 16 |
| 17 | 18 | 19 | 20 | 21 | 22 | 23 |
| 24 | 25 | 26 | 27 | 28 | 29 | 30 |
| 31 | | | | | | |

# OBITUARIES

**Abdul Rahman, Tunku**, 87, Malay prince who served as prime minister of Malaya and Malaysia after independence from Britain, 1957–70. Of undisclosed causes, Kuala Lumpur, Dec. 6, 1990.

**Allen, George H.**, 72, U.S. football coach known chiefly for his winning records with Los Angeles Rams and Washington Redskins. Of natural causes, Palos Verdes, Calif., Dec. 31, 1990.

**Anderson, Sigurd**, 86, Republican governor of South Dakota, 1951–55, and member of Federal Trade Commission, 1955–64. Of natural causes, Webster, S.Dak., Dec. 21, 1990.

**Appling, Luke**, 83, Hall of Fame shortstop (Chicago White Sox, 1930–50), twice winner of AL batting title; finished career with .310 average. Of an abdominal aneurysm, Cumming, Ga., Jan. 3, 1991.

**Arden, Eve** (Eunice Quedens), 78, U.S. actress best known as title character of "Our Miss Brooks" on radio (1948–52) and on TV (1952–57), for which she won an Emmy Award. Of cancer, Beverly Hills, Calif., Nov. 12, 1990.

**Arrau, Claudio**, 88, Chilean pianist noted for luminous style he brought to 19th-century works, especially those of Liszt and Beethoven; after emergency surgery, Mürzzuschlag, Austria, June 9, 1991.

**Arrupe, Pedro, S.J.**, 83, Spanish Jesuit, superior general of Society of Jesus, 1965–83; led Jesuits through period of significant change following Second Vatican Council, and emphasized liberal, sometimes experimental policies in theology and social programs. Rome, Feb. 5, 1991.

**Arthur, Jean**, 90, U.S. actress whose distinctive vocal quaver brought comic flair to films such as *Mr. Deeds Goes to Town* and *Mr. Smith Goes to Washington*; her last film was *Shane*. Of heart disease, Carmel, Calif., June 19, 1991.

**Ashcroft, Dame Peggy**, 83, British actress who early shone as Juliet and other Shakespeare heroines, and later played Albee and Beckett women to great acclaim. Her films include *A Passage to India* (Academy Award) and TV's *The Jewel in the Crown*. After a stroke, London, June 14, 1991.

**Atwater, Lee**, 40, Reagan and Bush campaign strategist and chairman of Republican National Committee. Known for hard-edged tactics, after being diagnosed with brain tumor that caused his death he apologized to some of his Democratic opponents. Washington, D.C., Mar. 29, 1991.

**Barbie, Klaus**, 77, Nazi war criminal; the "Butcher of Lyons" was believed responsible for murder of over 10,000 people in France during World War II. With covert help of U.S. Army officials he fled to Bolivia in 1951. Discovered in 1972 and extradited in 1983, he was convicted after long, sensational trial, and sentenced to life in prison. Of cancer, Lyons, Sept. 25, 1991.

**Bardeen, John**, 82, U.S. scientist who twice shared Nobel Prize in Physics, for invention of the transistor (1956), and for development of a theory of superconductivity (1972). Awarded Presidential Medal of Freedom in 1976. Of natural causes, Boston, Jan. 30, 1991.

**Barnet, Charlie**, 77, U.S. band leader whose saxophone playing shone in arrangement of many swing-era hits including "Cherokee" and "I Hear a Rhapsody." Of Alzheimer's disease and pneumonia, San Diego, Calif., Sept. 4, 1991.

**Barrera, Laz**, 66, Racing Hall of Fame thoroughbred horse trainer who won Triple Crown in 1978 with Affirmed. Of cardiopulmonary failure, Downey, Calif., Apr. 25, 1991.

**Bell, James (Cool Papa)**, 87, baseball player in Negro leagues for 20 seasons, known for outstanding speed and hitting ability. Elected to Baseball Hall of Fame in 1974. Of a heart attack, St. Louis, Mar. 7, 1991.

**Bennett, Joan**, 80, U.S. actress whose dark beauty was outstanding in 1940s *films noirs* such as Fritz Lang's *Woman in the Window* and *Scarlet Street*. A wise and knowing mother to Elizabeth Taylor in *Father of the Bride*, she later starred in TV's *Dark Shadows*. Of a heart attack, Scarsdale, N.Y., Dec. 7, 1990.

**Bigart, Homer**, 83, U.S. journalist famed for his colorful and observant coverage of World War II, Korean War, and beginning of Vietnam conflict; winner of two Pulitzer Prizes. Of cancer, Portsmouth, N.H., Apr. 16, 1991.

**Bolling, Richard**, 74, congressman (D-Mo.) 1948–81, effective in leading efforts to liberalize House rules and in bringing about passage of Civil Rights Act of 1964. Of heart failure, Washington, D.C., Apr. 21, 1991.

**Brown, Paul**, 82, U.S. football coach and part-owner of Cleveland Browns and, later, Cincinnati Bengals; his methods and tactics transformed the game. Of pneumonia, Cincinnati, Ohio, Aug. 5, 1991.

**Busch, Niven**, 88, U.S. author of *Duel in the Sun*, source of the popular film, and many other novels and screenplays expressive of cowboy mythology of the American West. Of heart disease, San Francisco, Aug. 25, 1991.

**Capra, Frank**, 94, Italian-born U.S. film director whose belief in commonsense values and old-fashioned American democracy pervades his Hollywood classics *It Happened One Night*, *Mr. Deeds Goes to Town*, *Meet John Doe*, *Mr. Smith Goes to Washington*, the perennial Christmas favorite, *It's a Wonderful Life*, and many others. Winner of three Academy Awards. Of natural causes, La Quinta, Calif., Sept. 3, 1991.

**Castro, Bernard**, 87, Italian-born inventor of easily opened convertible sofa who turned his idea into a multimillion-dollar business; also a pioneer in the use of TV commercials. Of cardiac arrest, Ocala, Fla., Aug. 24, 1991.

**Caulfield, Joan**, 69, U.S. fashion model-turned-actress who appeared in such films as *Blue Skies* and *Dear Ruth* in 1940s, and later in comedies. Of cancer, Los Angeles, June 18, 1991.

**Chandler, A.B. (Happy)**, 92, former Kentucky governor (1935–39 and 1955–59) and senator (1939–44), he was also second commissioner of major league baseball (1944–51), bringing Jackie Robinson and other black players into the game. Of a heart attack, Versailles, Ky., June 15, 1991.

**Coleman, J.P.**, 77, Democratic governor of Mississippi (1956–60); a moderate on the race issue, he also served as chief judge of U.S. Circuit Court of Appeals. Of complications from a stroke, Ackerman, Miss., Sept. 28, 1991.

**Collins, LeRoy**, 82, Democratic governor of Florida 1955–61 who despite campaign endorsement of segregation promoted desegregation in schools and public establishments. Of cancer, Tallahassee, Fla., Mar. 12, 1991.

**Conte, Silvio O.**, 69, congressman (R-Mass.) known for his support of programs aiding the poor, education, and medical research. Was starting 17th term at time of death. From cancer, Bethesda, Md., Feb. 8, 1991.

**Convy, Bert**, 57, U.S. film and stage actor best known for *Cabaret* and *Fiddler on the Roof*; later hosted many TV game shows. Of a brain tumor, Los Angeles, July 15, 1991.

**Cooper, John Sherman**, 89, Senator (R-Ky.) 1946–73. A liberal who opposed Sen. Joseph McCarthy and military involvement in Cambodia during Vietnam conflict. Served as ambassador to India. Of heart failure, Washington, D.C., Feb. 21, 1991.

**Copland, Aaron**, 90, U.S. composer whose works range from popular successes *Appalachian Spring* and *Lincoln Portrait* to more austere 12-tone works such as *Piano Variations* and *Third Symphony*. An outstanding teacher, conductor, and author, he received a Pulitzer Prize, Academy Award, and Presidential Medal of Freedom. North Tarrytown, N.Y., Dec. 2, 1990.

**Cousins, Norman**, 75, editor of influential *Saturday Review* (1942–71 and 1973–78), author of very popular *Anatomy of an Illness*. Of a heart attack, Los Angeles, Nov. 30, 1990.

**Dahl, Roald**, 74, enormously popular Welsh-born author of children's novels (*James and the Giant Peach* and *Charlie and the Chocolate Factory*). Of unreported causes, Oxford, England, Nov. 23, 1990.

**Daly, John Charles Jr.**, 77, U.S. journalist and TV personality best known as long-time host of "What's My Line?" Later an ABC executive and director of Voice of America. Of cardiac arrest, Chevy Chase, Md., Feb. 25, 1991.

**Dante, Nicholas**, 49, U.S. dancer and coauthor of *A Chorus Line*, to which he contributed much of his own theatrical experience. Of AIDS, New York, May 21, 1991.

**Davis, Miles**, 65, U.S. jazz great whose distinctive trumpet solos were imitated around the world. His many albums include *Milestones*, *Bitches Brew*, and *Sketches of Spain*. Of pneumonia and a stroke, Santa Monica, Calif., Sept. 28, 1991.

**Delacorte, George T.**, 97, U.S. publisher and philanthropist who built Dell Publishing and Delacorte Press into major publishing houses. Of natural causes, New York, May 4, 1991.

**Dewhurst, Colleen**, 67, U.S. actress whose theatrical, earth-mother presence shone on stage, screen, and television. Her affinity with work of Eugene O'Neill illuminated revivals of *Mourning Becomes Electra* and *A Moon for the Misbegotten*. Winner of two Tony and four Emmy awards. Of cancer, South Salem, N.Y., Aug. 22, 1991.

**Dr. Seuss** (Theodore Seuss Geisel), 87, creator of the most popular children's books in history, including *The Cat in the Hat*, *Green Eggs and Ham*, *How the Grinch Stole Christmas*, and his own favorite, *The Lorax*. Winner of three Academy Awards, two for documentaries in 1940s and one for cartoon creation "Gerald McBoing Boing" (1951). He was childless. In his sleep, La Jolla, Calif., Sept. 26, 1991.

**Dunnock, Mildred**, 90, U.S. actress of uncommon emotional power, best known for her role as Linda Loman in *Death of a Salesman*. Of old age, Martha's Vineyard, Mass., July 5, 1991.

**Durocher, Leo,** 86, baseball player and manager who won three pennants (Brooklyn Dodgers and N.Y. Giants twice) and one World Series (Giants). Known as "The Lip" for his fiery encounters with umpires, he coined the phrase, "Nice guys finish last." Of natural causes, Palm Springs, Calif., Oct. 7, 1991.

**Durrell, Lawrence George,** 78, British expatriate novelist best known for his *Alexandria Quartet*. Of emphysema, Sommières, France, Nov. 7, 1990.

**Dürrenmatt, Friedrich,** 69, Swiss playwright, novelist, and essayist whose bleak view of humanity is exemplified in such powerful dramas as *The Visit* and *The Physicist*. From diabetes and heart disease, Neuchâtel, Switzerland, Dec. 14, 1990.

**Fairbank, John K.,** 84, U.S. authority on China, professor, and author of standard works on Asian history and culture; director of Harvard East Asian Research Center, 1955–73. Of a heart attack, Cambridge, Mass., Sept. 14, 1991.

**Fender, Clarence Leo,** 82, U.S. manufacturer and developer of mass-produced electric guitars such as the Fender Stratocaster, which transformed rock music as played by stars like Buddy Holly and Jimi Hendrix. Of Parkinson's disease, Fullerton, Calif., Mar. 21, 1991.

**Fish, Hamilton,** 102, congressman (R-N.Y.) 1920–44. Opposed Pres. Roosevelt's New Deal policies and, before Pearl Harbor, U.S. entrance into World War II. His grandfather, father, and son also served in government. Of old age, Cold Spring, N.Y., Jan. 18, 1991.

**Fodor, Eugene,** 85, Hungarian-born writer of travel guides, now worldwide best-sellers numbering more than 140 titles. Of a brain tumor, Torrington, Conn., Feb. 18, 1991.

**Fonteyn, Margot,** 71, British ballerina, the outstanding lyrical and classical dancer of the later 20th century, best known for her *Sleeping Beauty* and *Swan Lake* with the Royal Ballet in the 1940s and 1950s, and her partnership with Rudolf Nureyev. Of cancer, Panama City, Panama, Feb. 21, 1991.

**Franciscus, James,** 57, U.S. actor who achieved fame as TV's Mr. Novak, a high school English teacher; appeared in many other TV productions. Of emphysema, Los Angeles, July 8, 1991.

**Frye, Northrop,** 78, Canadian critic and teacher who sought a vision of the social ideal in literature through a study of Judeo-Christian myths and symbols. Important works are *Anatomy of Criticism* and several studies of literature and the Bible. Of a heart attack, Toronto, Jan. 23, 1991.

**Getz, Stan,** 64, U.S. jazz musician; a tenor saxophonist noted for his unique sound and melodic improvisations, his *Jazz Samba* album brought international fame in the 1960s; he won 11 Grammys. Of liver cancer, Malibu, Calif., June 6, 1991.

**Ghandi, Rajiv,** 46, the former prime minister of India, assassinated during his campaign for re-election. The grandson of Jawaharlal Nehru, independent India's first prime minister, and the son of Indira Ghandi, Rajiv succeeded his mother as prime minister after she was assassinated in 1984. His rule was marked by political instability and sectarian bloodshed and he lost power in 1989. Sriperumbudur, India, May 21, 1991.

**Gobel, George,** 71, comedian known for his low-

key, deadpan delivery and homey material who had his own TV show for several seasons and later appeared often on the "Hollywood Squares" TV game show. Of complications during bypass surgery, Encino, Calif., Feb. 24, 1991.

**Goody, Sam,** 87, U.S. record store owner who built LP sales after World War II into nationwide chain bearing his name. Of heart failure, Far Rockaway, N.Y., Aug. 8, 1991.

**Goren, Charles,** 90, U.S. contract bridge player, who popularized the now-standard point-counting system through many championship appearances in the 1940s and '50s, numerous popular books, and a TV show (1959–64). Of a heart attack, Encino, Calif., Apr. 3, 1991.

**Graham, Martha,** 96, American dancer, choreographer, and teacher, the last of the 20th-century modernists in the arts. Her distinctive technique of pelvic-centered contraction and release combined with powerful psychosexual images from sources as diverse as mythology and the American frontier defined modern dance. Creator of more than 180 works, including *Appalachian Spring*, *Seraphic Dialogue*, and *Clytemnestra*. Of cardiac arrest, New York, Apr. 1, 1991.

**Grange, Harold (Red),** 87, star football running back—the "Galloping Ghost"—for the Univ. of Illinois and Chicago Bears in the 1920s and '30s. Of pneumonia, Lake Wales, Fla., Jan. 28, 1991.

**Greene, Graham,** 86, British author and Catholic convert whose intense moral fiction (*The Power and the Glory*, *The Heart of the Matter*, *The Quiet American*) probes the torment of individual conscience in the modern world; also wrote thrillers, or "entertainments" (*The Third Man*, *Our Man in Havana*), plays, travel books, film criticism, and memoirs. Of a blood disease, Vevey, Switzerland, Apr. 3, 1991.

**Guard, Dave,** 56, U.S. folk singer; an original member of the Kingston Trio, whose hits ("Tom Dooley") dominated the folk music flowering of the 1950s and '60s. Of lymphoma, Rollinsford, N.H., Mar. 22, 1991.

**Guthrie, A.B.,** 90, U.S. writer of western historical fiction, including *The Big Sky* and *The Way West*, for which he received the Pulitzer Prize. Also known for the screenplay of *Shane*. Of lung failure, Choteau, Mont., Apr. 26, 1991.

**Hammer, Armand,** 92, chairman of Occidental Petroleum, known for his diversified interests in business, international peace, and philanthropy, and as a goodwill ambassador between the United States and Soviet leaders from Lenin to Gorbachev. From cerebral arteriosclerosis, Los Angeles, Dec. 10, 1990.

**Heidelberger, Michael,** 103, U.S. scientist. Discovered that antibodies are proteins and made many advances in modern immunology; awards include National Medal of Science and Louis Pasteur Gold Medal. Of a stroke, New York, June 25, 1991.

**Heinz, John,** 52, congressman and senator (R-Pa.) 1976–91, noted for contributions to trade and Social Security legislation. Heir to the H.J. Heinz food company fortune. Private plane crash, Philadelphia, Apr. 4, 1991.

**Hofstadter, Robert,** 75, U.S. physicist and Stanford professor; winner of 1961 Nobel Prize for studies of electron scattering in atomic nuclei and discoveries concerning the structure of nucleons. Of a heart attack, Stanford, Calif., Nov. 17, 1990.

**Honda, Soichiro,** 84, Japanese automaker whose independence and openness to change transformed his motorcycle manufacturing company into a worldwide automobile giant and a strong component of the postwar Japanese turnaround. Of liver failure, Tokyo, Aug. 5, 1991.

**Irwin, James B.,** 61, U.S. astronaut whose 1971 moon walk inspired his religious regeneration and the founding of an interdenominational evangelical organization. Of a heart attack, Glenwood Springs, Colo., Aug. 8, 1991.

**Jagger, Dean,** 87, long-time U.S. character actor whose many films include *Twelve O'Clock High*, (supporting-role Academy Award); also appeared frequently on television. Of heart disease, Santa Monica, Calif., Feb. 5, 1991.

**Jiang Quing,** 77, the widow of Mao Zedong, and Chinese political leader during the highly repressive era known as the Cultural Revolution (1966–76). Shortly after Mao's death in 1976 she and three associates ("The Gang of Four") were imprisoned after a famous "show" trial in which she was sentenced to death (later reduced to life imprisonment). Officially listed as a suicide, Quincheng Prison, China, May 14, 1991.

**Johnson, Clarence L. (Kelly),** 80, U.S. aircraft designer whose designs included World War II P-38 "Lightning," the first jet fighter, the U-2 spy plane, and SR-71 "Blackbird." Awarded Medal of Freedom. Of undisclosed causes, Burbank, Calif., Dec. 21, 1990.

**Kahane, Meir** (Martin David), 58, U.S. rabbi and Jewish activist who founded Jewish Defense League and after immigrating to Israel in 1971 led militant anti-Arab movement. A member of knesset 1984–88, until his Kach party was outlawed for antidemocratic, racist activities. Assassinated by Egyptian-American, New York, Nov. 5, 1990.

**Kosinski, Jerzy,** 57, Polish-born writer whose first novel, *The Painted Bird*, a harrowing account of his escape from the Holocaust, brought him great fame; his novel *Steps* won National Book Award in 1969. A suicide, New York, May 3, 1991.

**Land, Edwin H.,** 81, U.S. scientist and inventor of Polaroid Land instant camera in 1948, whose Polaroid Corp. is leader in field of instant photography. Received 533 patents and was awarded Medal of Freedom. Of cancer, Cambridge, Mass., Mar. 1, 1991.

**Landon, Michael,** 54, U.S. actor in films and highly popular television series, *Bonanza*, *Little House on the Prairie*, and *Highway to Heaven*, all featuring sentimental family values. Of cancer, Malibu, Calif., July 1, 1991.

**Le Gallienne, Eva,** 92, London-born actress who achieved Broadway stardom in *Liliom* and *The Swan*. In 1920s she founded Civic Repertory Theater in New York. Of heart failure, Weston, Conn., June 3, 1991.

**Lean, David,** 83, British film director known for exacting and tasteful craftsmanship in both small- and large-scale productions that won a total of 28 Academy Awards, including Best Picture for *Bridge on the River Kwai* and *Lawrence of Arabia*. His versions of *Great Expectations* and *Oliver Twist* were also highly praised. Of pneumonia, London, Apr. 16, 1991

**Lefebvre, Archbishop Marcel,** 85, French prelate excommunicated by Pope John Paul II in 1988 for defiance of Vatican authority; opposed Catholic reforms of Second Vatican Council. Of cancer,

Martigny, Switzerland, Mar. 26, 1991.

**Lewis, Sir W. Arthur,** 76, St. Lucia-born economist, long-time Princeton professor and cowinner of 1979 Nobel Prize in Economics. Of undisclosed causes, Barbados, June 15, 1991.

**Luria, Salvador E.,** Italian-born U.S. scientist who shared 1969 Nobel Prize in Physiology and Medicine for discoveries concerning the genetic structure of viruses. Of a heart attack, Lexington, Mass., Feb. 6, 1991.

**Maw, Herbert B.,** 97, Democratic governor of Utah 1940–48 who liberalized labor laws and welfare programs. Of undisclosed causes, Salt Lake City, Nov. 17, 1990.

**McCone, John A.,** 89, chairman of Atomic Energy Commission 1958–60, and CIA director 1961–65. Of cardiac arrest, Pebble Beach, Calif., Feb. 14, 1991.

**McKissick, Floyd,** 69, U.S. civil rights promoter, director of Congress of Racial Equality (CORE) 1966–67. He angered fellow blacks by supporting Nixon in 1972. Of lung cancer, Durham, N.C., Apr. 28, 1991.

**McMillan, Edwin M.,** 83, U.S. scientist, cowinner of 1951 Nobel Prize in Chemistry for discovery of plutonium and neptunium; awarded National Medal of Science. Of diabetes complications, El Cerrito, Calif., Sept. 7, 1991.

**Motherwell, Robert,** 76, U.S. artist, leading practitioner and spokesman of abstract expressionism for almost 50 years. His characteristic mode of oval shapes confined by vertical bars dominates such works as "Elegy to the Spanish Republic," a series of more than 100 canvases. After a stroke, on Cape Cod, Mass., July 16, 1991.

**Muggeridge, Malcolm Thomas,** 87, British journalist whose deft wit served him 60 years as a correspondent, editor of *Punch*, memoirist (*Chronicles of Wasted Time*), and essayist. After a stroke, Croydon, Surrey, England, Nov. 14, 1990.

**Murray, Arthur,** 95, U.S. teacher of ballroom dancing who built a worldwide mail-order and franchise dance studio empire from the 1920s to 1960s. "The Arthur Murray Party" was an early TV staple. Of natural causes, Honolulu, Mar. 3, 1991.

**Nemerov, Howard,** 71, U.S. poet whose formal rhyming verse ran gamut of subjects from everyday objects to history and cosmic black holes. Winner of Pulitzer Prize and National Book Award; U.S. poet laureate 1988–90. Of cancer, St. Louis, Mo., July 5, 1991.

**O'Faolain, Sean,** 91, Irish writer of novels, biographies, and plays, but best known for his masterful short stories often depicting realities of Irish life from an ironic but warm point of view. Of natural causes, Dublin, Apr. 20, 1991.

**Olav V,** 87, king of Norway since 1957; as crown prince, he was focal point of Norwegian resistance to Nazi occupation. Of a heart attack, Oslo, Jan. 17, 1991.

**Pandit, Vijaya Lakshmi,** 90, Indian diplomat who served as ambassador to U.S., USSR, and Spain, and first woman elected president of UN General Assembly, 1953; was sister of Prime Minister Jawaharlal Nehru. Of undisclosed causes, Dehra Dun, India, Dec. 1, 1990.

**Pasternak, Joe,** 89, Hungarian-born producer of more than 100 films, many of them bright musicals like *Anchors Aweigh*. Credited with

promoting careers of Judy Garland, Deanna Durban, and many others. Of Parkinson's disease, Beverly Hills, Calif., Sept. 13, 1991.

**Porter, Sylvia,** 77, U.S. financial writer whose many books and syndicated columns translated specialized economic and business information for millions of general readers. Of emphysema, Pound Ridge, N.Y., June 5, 1991.

**Rains, Albert McKinley,** 89, congressman (D-Ala.) 1944–65, noted for housing, agriculture, and Social Security legislation. Of pneumonia, Gadsden, Ala., Mar. 22, 1991.

**Ray, Aldo,** 64, U.S. movie actor known for portrayals of dim-witted, lovable brutes in such 1950s films as *Battle Cry* and *The Naked and the Dead*. Of throat cancer, Crockett, Calif., Mar. 27, 1991.

**Reasoner, Harry,** 68, U.S. journalist and anchor for network TV news, particularly *60 Minutes*. Of cardiopulmonary arrest after cancer treatment, Norwalk, Conn., Aug. 6, 1991.

**Remick, Lee,** 55, U.S. actress who worked on Broadway and in TV and film, most notably *A Face in the Crowd* and *Days of Wine and Roses*. Of cancer, Los Angeles, July 2, 1991.

**Revelle, Roger,** 82, U.S. scientist who as director of Scripps Institution of Oceanography at La Jolla led research on early theories of global warming and plate tectonics. Of cardiac arrest, San Diego, Calif., July 15, 1991.

**Revere, Anne,** 87, U.S. actress whose career playing supportive mothers (*National Velvet* (Academy Award), *A Place in the Sun*) was ended by 1950s blacklisting. She later won Tony Award for *Toys in the Attic*. Of pneumonia, Locust Valley, N.Y., Dec. 19, 1990.

**Ritt, Martin,** 76, U.S. film director who promoted social causes in such movies as *Edge of the City, Hud, Sounder,* and *Norma Rae*. Of a heart disease, Santa Monica, Calif., Dec. 8, 1990.

**Rizzo, Frank,** 70, former police commissioner and mayor of Philadelphia during 1960s and '70s whose "law and order" campaigns and policies won middle-class approval but brought minority criticism during turbulent times. Of a heart attack, Philadelphia, July 16, 1991.

**Robles, Alfonso García,** 80, Mexican diplomat, cowinner of 1982 Nobel Peace Prize for his promotion of nuclear disarmament. Of kidney failure, Mexico City, Sept. 2, 1991.

**Roosevelt, James,** 83, congressman (D-Calif.) and son of Pres. Franklin D. Roosevelt; he also served as a UN delegate and worked in private business. Of Parkinson's disease and a stroke, Newport Beach, Calif., Aug. 13, 1991.

**Salah Khalif** (Abu Iyad), cofounder of al-Fatah, predecessor and now a faction of PLO. Formed Black September group responsible for murder of 11 Israelis at Munich Olympics and assassination of U.S. ambassador and chief of mission in Sudan in 1972. Murdered in Tunis, Jan. 14, 1991.

**Schaefer, Jack,** 83, U.S. writer of westerns, most notably *Shane*. Of congestive heart failure, Santa Fe, N.Mex., Jan. 24, 1991.

**Schuyler, James,** 67, U.S. poet and winner of Pulitzer Prize for *The Morning of the Poem*. After a stroke, New York, Apr. 12, 1991.

**Serkin, Rudolf,** 88, Austrian-born pianist whose intense performances of classical and romantic music inspired awe and affection in his audiences. Of cancer, Marlboro, Vt., May 8, 1991.

**Siegel, Don,** 78, U.S. film director of *The Inva-*

*sion of the Body Snatchers* and action movies featuring strong, silent, antiheros sometimes operating outside the law, such as Dirty Harry. Of cancer, Nipomo, Calif., Apr. 20, 1991.

**Singer, Issac Bashevis,** 87, Polish-born writer who fled Nazis and lived in U.S. Winner of 1978 Nobel Prize for Literature, his many novels and short stories (*A Crown of Feathers and Other Stories, Enemies, a Love Story*) rooted in Jewish culture are deeply felt narratives of suffering, love, and betrayal. After several strokes, Surfside, Fla., July 24, 1991.

**Smith, Jabbo,** 82, U.S. musician whose personal style of trumpet playing was favorably compared to Louis Armstrong's in the 1920s and '30s. Of pneumonia, New York, Jan. 16, 1991.

**Snelling, Richard A.,** 64, Republican governor of Vermont (1977–85 and 1991), who promoted balanced budgets and environmental concerns. Of cardiac arrest, Shelburne, Vt., Aug. 13, 1991.

**Tamayo, Rufino,** 91, Mexican artist whose hundreds of paintings glow with color and light and feature subjects derived from Mexican folk art and pre-Columbian sculpture. Of pneumonia, Mexico City, June 24, 1991.

**Thomas, Danny,** 79, comedian and star of top-rated TV show "Make Room for Daddy." A gifted storyteller, he first made his mark in radio and later in nightclub appearances. His deep religious belief caused him to found St. Jude Children's Research Hospital. Of a heart attack, Los Angeles, Feb. 6, 1991.

**Tower, John G.,** 65, Senator (R-Tex.) 1961–85; chairman of Armed Services Committee and powerful voice on defense and national security matters. His nomination as Sec. of Defense in 1990 was rejected by Senate in a bitter confirmation hearing. In a commuter plane crash near Brunswick, Ga., Apr. 5, 1991.

**Tsedenbal, Yumzhagiin,** 74, Mongolian political leader who as premier and head of Communist party ruled from 1958 until his overthrow in 1984. A pawn of Soviet leader Brezhnev, he was exiled to Russia. Of an unspecified illness, Moscow, Apr. 20, 1991.

**Wagner, Robert F.,** 80, mayor of New York City 1954–65, known for opposition to machine politics and credited with honesty and integrity throughout a long political life that included essential support for development of Lincoln Center. Of heart failure, New York, Feb.12, 1991.

**West, Dottie,** 59, U.S. singer, first woman to win Grammy Award for country music; hits included "Country Sunshine" and "Here Comes My Baby." Of auto accident injuries, Nashville, Tenn., Sept. 4, 1991.

**Wilson, Sir Angus,** 77, British writer of 50 books, including fiction and biography. Novels like *Anglo-Saxon Attitudes* and *The Middle Age of Mrs. Eliot* are wry, satiric observations of postwar British middle class. After a stroke, Bury St. Edmunds, England, May 31, 1991.

**Zwicker, Ralph W.,** 88, retired Army general whose harassment in 1954 by Sen. Joseph McCarthy brought about hearings that led to McCarthy's censure by U.S. Senate. Of heart disease, Fort Belvoir, Va., Aug. 11, 1991.

# THE 1992 PRESIDENTIAL ELECTIONS

The presidential election campaign moved into high gear during September and October of 1991 as Pres. Bush declared that only serious illness would keep him from pursuing a second term and the field of Democratic candidates continued to expand rapidly. Familiar old names such as Eugene McCarthy and former California governor Jerry Brown joined with such rising stars as Nebraska senator Bob Kerrey, a Vietnam veteran and Congressional Medal of Honor winner, and Bill Clinton, the highly successful governor of Arkansas, to present a picture of Democratic viability that the polls seemed to dispute. Other declared candidates for the Democratic nomination were, as of October 20, 1991, former representative Paul Tsongas of Massachusetts; Gov. Doug Wilder of Virginia; Sen. Tom Harkin of Iowa; and Larry Agran, former mayor of Irvine, Calif.

Defeating an incumbent president is always difficult, but the apparent success of Bush's foreign policy and his ability to hold congressional Republicans together so that his many vetoes of Democratic legislation are never overridden make him an exceptionally solid favorite for reelection. Experts and pundits agree that only a continuing downturn in the economy, with a significant growth in unemployment, could make him seriously vulnerable. If the economy does not take off, other related issues such as the federal deficit, the savings and loan crisis, health insurance, and the lack of movement in either the war on drugs or a national education policy—both of which were cornerstones of Bush's 1988 campaign—could come to the fore.

If that happens, several other leading Democrats may yet declare, and they could emerge as obvious front-runners. These include Mario Cuomo, governor of New York, who is the clearcut choice of many Democrats; Lloyd Bentsen, senator from Texas and chairman of the Senate Finance Committee, who was a very effective candidate for vice president in 1988; and Jesse Jackson, who is the most well-known Democrat and clearly the party's most vibrant leader.

## Democratic Candidates, 1992

As of Oct. 20, 1991, nine Democrats had declared their candidacy for the 1992 presidential elections. The Democratic contenders are (in the order in which they declared their candidacy): former representative Paul Tsongas of Massachusetts; Gov. Doug Wilder of Virginia; Sen. Tom Harkin of Iowa; Gov. Bill Clinton of Arkansas; former governor Jerry Brown of California; Sen. Bob Kerrey of Nebraska; Larry Agran, former mayor of Irvine, Calif.; and former senator Eugene McCarthy of Minnesota.

**Larry Agran for President** P.O. Box 159, Irvine, Calif. 92650; (714) 250-8087. (FAX) (714) 250-7838.

**Jerry Brown for President** 8075 West 3rd St., Suite 402, Los Angeles, Calif. 90048; (213) 393-4110.

**Clinton for President Committee** P.O. Box 615, (917 West 7th St.), Little Rock, Ark. 72203; (501) 372-1992. (FAX) (501) 372-2292.

**Americans for Harkin** P.O. Box 2308, Washington, DC 20013; or 7910 Woodmontack Ave., Bethesda, Md. 20814; (301) 656-1992. (FAX) (301) 656-1323.

**Bob Kerrey for President** 1511 K St., NW, Suite 640, Washington, DC 20005; (202) 393-4110. (FAX) (202) 393-4388.

**McCarthy '92** P.O. Box 2008, Washington, DC 20013; (703) 448-0199. (FAX) (703) 893-4228.

**Paul Tsongas for President** 2 Oliver St., 5th floor, Boston, Mass. 02109; (617) 422-0100. (FAX) (617) 261-6575.

**Doug Wilder for President** 3050 Chain Bridge Rd., Suite 404, Fairfax, Va. 22030; (703) 218-5000. (FAX) (703) 385-3641.

## Republican Candidates, 1992

As of Oct. 20, 1991, no Republicans had declared their candidacy for the 1992 presidential elections, though Pres. George Bush is likely to receive the GOP nomination.

## THE PARTIES

The Democratic and Republican parties dominate American politics. While there are some independent and third-party officeholders sprinkled around the nation's statehouses, there is only one independent in all of Congress not affiliated with either party, Rep. Bernard Saunders of Vermont. The candidates whose names appear on the ballot in November are chosen at a nominating convention comprised of active party members—4,284 for the Democrats and 2,207 for the Republicans—selected on the basis of the outcome of party caucuses and primary elections held throughout the spring. These include "pledged" delegates who are obliged to vote for the candidate (at least on the first ballot at the convention) who wins the majority of votes in that state's primary or caucus, as well as "unpledged" delegates who include party leaders and officials, and elected federal officials such as governors, representatives, and senators.

For additional information about the nominating process and party platforms, as well as candidates who have declared their intentions to run for president contact:

**Democratic National Committee** Ron Brown, chairman, 430 South Capitol St., SE, Washington, DC 20003; (202) 863-8020.

**Republican National Committee** Clayton Yeutter, chairman, 310 First St., SE, Washington, DC 20003; (202) 863-8550.

## PRESIDENTIAL CAMPAIGN CALENDAR 1992

The following is a schedule of *caucuses* (in italics) and primary elections by which delegates to the Democratic and Republican conventions are selected in 1992. Numbers in parentheses indicate the number of delegates at stake.

| Date | Democratic | Republican |
|---|---|---|
| Feb. 17 | *Iowa caucus* (49) | *Iowa caucus* (23) |
| Feb. 18 | New Hampshire primary (18) | New Hampshire primary (23) |
| Feb. 23 | *Maine* (23) | *Maine* (22) |
| Feb. 25 | South Dakota (15) | South Dakota (19) |
| Mar. 3 | Colorado (47), Maryland (67) | Colorado (37), Maryland (42) |
| Mar. 7 | *Arizona* (41), South Carolina (43), *Wyoming* (13) | *Arizona* (37), South Carolina (36), *Wyoming* (20) |
| Mar. 8 | *Nevada* (17) | *Nevada* (21) |
| Mar. 10 Super Tuesday | *Delaware* (14), Florida (148), Georgia (76), *Hawaii* (20), Louisiana (60), Massachusetts (94), Mississippi (39), *Missouri* (77), Oklahoma (45), Rhode Island (22), Tennessee (68), Texas[1] (196) | *Delaware* (19), Florida (97), Georgia (52), *Hawaii* (14), Louisiana (38), Massachusetts (38), Mississippi (32), *Missouri* (47), Oklahoma (34), Rhode Island (15), Tennessee (45), Texas[1] (121) |
| Mar. 17 | Illinois (164), Michigan (131) | Illinois (85), Michigan (72) |
| Mar. 24 | Connecticut (53) | Connecticut (35) |
| Mar. 31 | *Vermont* (14) | *Vermont* (19) |

| Date | Democratic | Republican |
|---|---|---|
| Apr. 7 | Kansas (36), Minnesota (78), New York (244), Wisconsin (82) | Kansas (30), Minnesota (32), New York (100), Wisconsin (35) |
| Apr. 11 | *Virginia* (78) | *Virginia* (54) |
| Apr. 28 | Pennsylvania (169) | Pennsylvania (90) |
| May 3 | *Guam* (3) | *Guam* (NA) |
| May 5 | District of Columbia (17), Indiana (77), North Carolina (84), Ohio (151) | District of Columbia (14), Indiana (51), North Carolina (57), Ohio (83) |
| May 12 | Nebraska (25), West Virginia (31) | Nebraska (24), West Virginia (18) |
| May 19 | Oregon (47), Washington (71) | Oregon (23), Washington (35) |
| May 26 | Arkansas (36), Idaho (18), Kentucky (52) | Arkansas (27), Idaho (22), Kentucky (35) |
| June 2 | Alabama (55), *Alaska* (13), California (348), Montana (16), New Jersey (105), New Mexico (25) | Alabama (38), *Alaska* (19), California (201), Montana (20), New Jersey (60), New Mexico (25) |
| June 9 | North Dakota (14) | North Dakota (17) |
| July 13–16 | Democratic Convention, New York, N.Y. | |
| Aug. 17–20 | | Republican Convention, Houston, Tex. |
| **Nov. 3** | **ELECTION DAY** | |

**Note:** American Samoa, Puerto Rico, and the Virgin Islands had not decided on a date for their primaries as of Oct. 21, 1991. While most dates are final, some may be subject to change.
1. Delegates from Texas are selected by both caucus and primary.

# CALENDAR OF THE YEAR

## Understanding Calendars

**The day**  Earth turns at a fairly steady pace about the imaginary line that defines the North and South poles. This line through the poles is called Earth's axis. Each turn about the axis, called a rotation, takes slightly less than 24 hours. Since Earth is also traveling around the Sun, however, the time from noon to noon is longer than the time it takes for one rotation—about 3 minutes and 56 seconds longer, or almost exactly 24 hours. The time from noon to noon changes slightly during the year, depending on where Earth is in its path. If you average all the days in a year, the average time from noon to noon is exactly 24 hours.

**The year**  All the nine planets of the solar system travel in nearly circular paths, called orbits, around the Sun. Each trip around the Sun is called a revolution. The planets all revolve in the same direction, which can be observed from Earth by noting the position the Sun has among the background stars, which are traditionally grouped into constellations. (Since you can't see the Sun and stars at the same time, you can observe where the Sun rises or sets each day and then note the stars that appear in the same region.) Over the course of a year, the Sun appears to pass through the 12 constellations that make up the zodiac.

Earth's trip around the Sun, reflected in the Sun's trip through the zodiac, takes about 365.25 days. This varies slightly from time to time, so astronomers add or delete a second in some years to keep their records in tune with Earth's motion. (See also "Precession of the equinoxes" below.)

**Seasons**  Most of us have learned that the seasons change on the 21st of March, June, September, and December. However in some years the dates in these months may be as early as the 20th or as late as the 23d.

The seasons do *not*, strictly speaking, coincide with climate changes. In the northeastern United States, it still snows after Mar. 21, it gets quite hot before June 21, and there is not much "winter" until sometime in January. What the seasons mark is the change in the pattern of daylight over the course of the year.

The Earth is tilted with respect to its path around the Sun; different parts receive different amounts of sunlight during Earth's annual orbit, the time we know as a year. Between late

September (around the 21st) and late March, Earth's Northern Hemisphere is tilted away from the Sun. This period constitutes the fall and winter seasons for the Northern Hemisphere, during which there are less than 12 hours of daylight each day. For the rest of the year, spring and summer, the Northern Hemisphere is tilted toward the sun, and daylight hours constitute more than half of each day. In the Southern Hemisphere the situation is reversed: spring and summer last from late September to late March, while fall and winter make up the other half of the year.

At the points of transition from long days and short nights to short days and long nights, and vice versa, the *equinoxes* occur—the two days of the year when periods of daylight and darkness are equal. The *vernal equinox*, marking the first day of spring, takes place on or around Mar. 21 in the Northern Hemisphere, while the *autumnal equinox*, marking the beginning of fall, is on or around Sept. 21. Officially, summer begins on the day of the longest daytime during the year, about June 21 in the Northern Hemisphere, called the *summer solstice*. The *winter solstice*, about Dec. 21 in the Northern Hemisphere, has the shortest amount of daylight and the longest night of the year. The word *solstice* means "standing-still sun." These two days are so called because the apparent movement of where the Sun rises or sets reaches its extreme positions on the solstices and then reverses direction.

**Precession of the equinoxes**  Ancient Greek astronomers determined that the direction Earth's axis points is constantly, but very slowly, changing in a regular pattern. The kind of change is similar to the way a spinning top slowly leans first one way then another as its axis changes direction. This movement is called *precession*. The precession of both the Earth and the top is a result of neither being perfect spheres. Earth's diameter is about 27 miles greater from one side of the equator to the other than it is from one pole to the other. (Earth is oblate, or fat around the middle, as a result of its rotation.)

Picture Earth without considering its revo-

## SOLAR PHENOMENA: THE SEASONS, 1992

| Solar phenomenon | Month | Day | Hour | Min. |
|---|---|---|---|---|
| Perigee[1] | Jan. | 3 | 15 | — |
| Vernal equinox | Mar. | 20 | 03 | 02 |
| Summer solstice | June | 21 | 03 | 14 |
| Apogee[2] | July | 3 | 12 | — |
| Autumnal equinox | Sept. | 22 | 18 | 43 |
| Winter solstice | Dec. | 21 | 14 | 43 |

**Note:** Shown in universal time (UT). To convert to local time, see "Timing Planetary Phenomena." 1. Sun closest to the Earth, 91.4 million miles. 2. Sun farthest from the Earth, 94.5 million miles. **Source:** U.S. Naval Observatory, *Astronomical Phenomena for the Year 1992* (1989).

lution. Keep Earth's center in the same place mentally, and think about how the axis changes position during precession. Any point on Earth's axis (except the center of the planet) moves in a slow circle as a result of precession. This movement is so slow that it takes 26,000 years for a point to return to its original spot. In the meantime, the axis gradually changes its position in relation to the stars. While what we call the North Star (officially known as Polaris) is currently positioned directly above the North Pole, over time the axis will shift, so that in A.D. 14,980, for example, the star Vega will be directly above the North Pole. By A.D. 27,990, Polaris will have returned to its present position.

As the precession continues, one of its effects is to change the times of the year that seasons occur. Instead of the vernal equinox being around Mar. 21, 13,000 years from now it will occur around Sept. 21, the date at which the autumnal equinox is now. With this in mind, the precession of Earth is generally known as the precession of the equinoxes.

Although the precession of the equinoxes is slow, it can be easily observed. The year of about 365.25 days is the time it takes from one vernal equinox to the next. Because of the precession of the equinoxes, however, the time it takes the Sun to appear in the same position with respect to the stars is 20 minutes 24 seconds longer than the period from one equinox to the next. For this reason, accurate star maps have to specify both the date and year for which they are intended.

### Lunar Calendar

There is some evidence that very early humans (c. 25,000 B.C.) used marks on bone to indicate the passage of time, which they may have measured by the Moon's phases. A calendar for the year can be based upon the Moon's phases, which gives a year of 12 periods from new moon to new moon (hence the word *month*) lasting about 354 days. This is about 11 days shorter than the time it takes Earth to revolve around the Sun. The Chinese, who still use a version of this calendar, resolve the discrepancy by inserting extra months at fixed intervals to bring the lunar and solar years into alignment. The Chinese year is divided into months that are either 29 or 30 days long, since the time from new moon to new moon is approximately 29.5 days. (The Moon takes about 27.33 days to orbit Earth, but Earth is moving with respect to the Sun during that time, so the combined movement produces the period of about 29.5 days.) The New Year begins at the first new moon over China between Jan. 21 and Feb. 19, and is celebrated for a four-day period. Each year has both a number and a name. The year 1992—or 4629 in the Chinese era—is the Year of the Monkey.

### Solar Calendar

The ancient Egyptians were the first people known to have instituted a solar calendar. In actuality their calendar might be called a stellar calendar, since the year began with the rising of Sirius—the brightest star in the sky—at the same place the Sun rises, which generally happened at the same time the Nile flooded. The Egyptians determined that a year was 365 days, about 0.25 day short of the true solar year, so gradually the Egyptian calendar no longer coincided with the seasons. Historical records reveal when the Egyptian calendar and the rising of Sirius coincided, from which astronomers inferred that the Egyptian calendar must have been instituted in either 4241 B.C. or 2773 B.C. The Egyptian calendar had 12 30-day months and five days of festival, a system adopted by various early cultures, although some continued to use lunar calendars.

### Julian Calendar

In 46 B.C. Julius Caesar realized that various parts of the land controlled by Rome used different calendars, so he asked the astronomer Sosigenes to develop a uniform calendar. Sosigenes proposed that since the year was 365.25 days long (which is not exact), a 365-day calendar be kept with one day added (a "leap day") every fourth year. When Caesar introduced the new system, he also added days to the year 46 B.C., to bring the seasons in line with the calendar. With a total of 445 days, 46 B.C. is the longest calendar year on record. A year at that time began in what we call March, and the months were numbered. *September, October, November,* and *December* derive from this system, and mean "seventh," "eighth," "ninth," and "tenth" months, respectively.

There was a little further adjustment of the calendar, however, by Augustus Caesar, the first Roman emperor. The name of the fifth month (our July) was changed from Quintilis to honor Julius Caesar. Augustus named the sixth month after himself, August. So that August would not be shorter than 31-day July, Augustus borrowed a day from February.

Because of the Roman Empire's great sphere of influence, the Julian calendar became the ordinary calendar of Western nations.

### Gregorian Calendar

From at least A.D. 730, it was known that the solar year—measured from vernal equinox to vernal equinox—was somewhat short of 365.25 days. Each century the solar year gets about half a second shorter. In 1990 the solar year is calculated at 365 days 5 hours 48 minutes 45.5 seconds long, not 365 days 6 hours, which is what the Julian calendar assumes. Because the date of Easter (the Sunday following the first full Moon after the vernal equinox) was slipping, Pope Gregory XIII instituted calendrical reform in 1582. He proclaimed that the day following Oct. 4 would be Oct. 15, which dropped 10 days from the year. Furthermore, on the advice of astronomer Christoph Clavius, the new calendar would be kept in line by omitting the leap year in century years unless they were divisible by 400. Thus 1900 was not a leap year in the Gregorian calendar, as it came to be called, but 2000 would be.

Most Roman Catholic countries and some other Western countries adopted the new sys-

tem, but England did not. Finally, in 1752, England and its colonies adopted the Gregorian calendar, but they had to drop 11 days to fit common Western practice. It was at this time that New Year's Day in England was moved from Mar. 25 to Jan. 1, changing the number of the year for the almost three months affected. Thus, George Washington was born according to the Julian calendar on Feb. 11, 1731, but came to celebrate his birth as Feb. 22, 1732, on the Gregorian calendar.

Because the solar year is shortening, astronomers today keep the Gregorian calendar in line by making a one-second adjustment as needed, usually on Dec. 31 at midnight, whenever the error's accumulation nears one second.

### Julian Day Count

A year after the Gregorian calendar was first instituted, Joseph Justus Scaliger developed a system of counting days instead of years, which is still used by astronomers. Called the Julian Day Count (after his father, Julius Caesar Scaliger), it begins with 1 on Jan. 1, 4713 B.C. On this date the Julian calendar, the lunar calendar, and the Roman tax system (which had its own calendar) all coincided—something that won't happen again until A.D. 3267. Each day within such a 7,980-year period is numbered. Jan. 1, 1992, is Julian Day 2,448,621.

---

## HOLIDAYS AND HOLY DAYS
### Federal Holidays
### in the United States

Congress and the president have designated 10 days as federal holidays. Although these are so widely observed as to be considered "national" holidays, they technically apply only to federal employees and the District of Columbia. It is up to the individual states to designate their own holidays. When a federal holiday falls on a Saturday or a Sunday, it is observed on the preceding Friday or the following Monday.

**New Year's Day** (Jan. 1) The observance of the New Year dates back to pre-Christian times when rites were performed to ensure the return of spring. It was observed in England on March 25 until 1752, when it was changed to Jan. 1.

**Martin Luther King, Jr., Day** (Third Monday in January) Before his assassination in 1968, Martin Luther King, Jr., was the foremost civil rights leader of the 1950s and 1960s, and in 1964 he won the Nobel Peace Prize. In 1983

Congress set aside this day to celebrate his life and accomplishments.

**Presidents' Day** (Third Monday in February) Presidents' Day combines the observance of George Washington's birthday (Feb. 22), first observed in 1782, and Abraham Lincoln's birthday (Feb. 12), which became a federal holiday in 1892.

**Memorial Day** (Last Monday in May) Memorial Day (also known as Decoration Day) honors soldiers fallen in battle. Dating from the Civil War, it is traditionally marked with parades and memorial services.

**Independence Day** (Fourth of July) The most important U.S. holiday, Independence Day commemorates the signing of the Declaration of Independence on July 4, 1776, an event that marked America's birth as a free nation. The holiday was first observed in 1777 and is celebrated with fireworks, parades, and oratory.

**Labor Day** (First Monday in September) The idea of Peter J. McGuire, president of the United Brotherhood of Carpenters and Joiners of America, the official observance of a day celebrating the American worker was signed into law on June 28, 1894.

**Columbus Day** (Second Monday in October) On Oct. 12, 1492, Christopher Columbus and his crew landed in the Bahama Islands after sailing across the Atlantic. First celebrated in 1792, Columbus Day was not officially recognized until 1909. Its observance is of special national pride to Italian-Americans who claim the Genoese Columbus for their own.

**Veterans' Day** (Nov. 11) Armistice Day, which marked the end of World War I on Nov. 11, 1918, was made a legal holiday in 1938. The name was changed to Veterans' Day in 1954 to honor all of America's veterans.

**Thanksgiving Day** (Fourth Thursday in November) Thanksgiving Day was first observed in Plymouth Colony (Mass.) in 1621, the year in which the Pilgrims landed in the New World and gave thanks for their first harvest and for the new land they had colonized. President Lincoln proclaimed Thanksgiving a national holiday in 1863.

**Christmas Day** is celebrated on Dec. 25. (See also "Christian Holy Days.")

### U.S. Minor Holidays and Occasions

**April Fools' Day** (Apr. 1) A day for practical jokes; the origin of April Fools' Day is obscure, but it bears some resemblance to an ancient Roman festival honoring the goddess of nature.

**Arbor Day** (Last Friday in April) Dedicated to

### CHINESE YEARS, 1900–95

| Rat | Ox | Tiger | Hare (Rabbit) | Dragon | Snake | Horse | Sheep (Goat) | Monkey | Rooster | Dog | Pig |
|-----|-----|-------|---------------|--------|-------|-------|--------------|--------|---------|------|------|
| 1900 | 1901 | 1902 | 1903 | 1904 | 1905 | 1906 | 1907 | 1908 | 1909 | 1910 | 1911 |
| 1912 | 1913 | 1914 | 1915 | 1916 | 1917 | 1918 | 1919 | 1920 | 1921 | 1922 | 1923 |
| 1924 | 1925 | 1926 | 1927 | 1928 | 1929 | 1930 | 1931 | 1932 | 1933 | 1934 | 1935 |
| 1936 | 1937 | 1938 | 1939 | 1940 | 1941 | 1942 | 1943 | 1944 | 1945 | 1946 | 1947 |
| 1948 | 1949 | 1950 | 1951 | 1952 | 1953 | 1954 | 1955 | 1956 | 1957 | 1958 | 1959 |
| 1960 | 1961 | 1962 | 1963 | 1964 | 1965 | 1966 | 1967 | 1968 | 1969 | 1970 | 1971 |
| 1972 | 1973 | 1974 | 1975 | 1976 | 1977 | 1978 | 1979 | 1980 | 1981 | 1982 | 1983 |
| 1984 | 1985 | 1986 | 1987 | 1988 | 1989 | 1990 | 1991 | 1992 | 1993 | 1994 | 1995 |

## IMPORTANT DATES IN THE U.S. AND CANADA, 1990–95

| Event | 1990 | 1991 | 1992[1] | 1993 | 1994 | 1995 |
|---|---|---|---|---|---|---|
| New Year's Day[2] | Jan. 1 | Jan. 1 | Jan. 1 | Jan. 1 | Jan. 1 | Jan. 1 |
| Martin Luther King, Jr., Day[2] | Jan. 15 | Jan. 21 | Jan. 20 | Jan. 18 | Jan. 17 | Jan. 16 |
| Groundhog Day | Feb. 2 | Feb. 2 | Feb. 2 | Feb. 2 | Feb. 2 | Feb. 2 |
| St. Valentine's Day | Feb. 14 | Feb. 14 | Feb. 14 | Feb. 14 | Feb. 14 | Feb. 14 |
| Susan B. Anthony Day | Feb. 15 | Feb. 15 | Feb. 15 | Feb. 15 | Feb. 15 | Feb. 15 |
| Presidents' Day[2] | Feb. 19 | Feb. 18 | Feb. 17 | Feb. 15 | Feb. 21 | Feb. 20 |
| Mardi Gras | Feb. 27 | Feb. 12 | Mar. 3 | Feb. 23 | Feb. 15 | Feb. 28 |
| St. Patrick's Day | Mar. 17 | Mar. 17 | Mar. 17 | Mar. 17 | Mar. 17 | Mar. 17 |
| April Fools' Day | Apr. 1 | Apr. 1 | Apr. 1 | Apr. 1 | Apr. 1 | Apr. 1 |
| Daylight Saving begins | Apr. 1 | Apr. 7 | Apr. 5 | Apr. 4 | Apr. 3 | Apr. 2 |
| Arbor Day | Apr. 27 | Apr. 26 | Apr. 24 | Apr. 30 | Apr. 29 | Apr. 28 |
| National Teacher Day | May 8 | May 7 | May 5 | May 4 | May 3 | May 8 |
| Mother's Day | May 13 | May 12 | May 10 | May 9 | May 8 | May 14 |
| Armed Forces Day | May 19 | May 18 | May 16 | May 15 | May 21 | May 20 |
| Victoria Day[3] | May 21 | May 20 | May 18 | May 24 | May 23 | May 22 |
| National Maritime Day | May 22 | May 22 | May 22 | May 22 | May 22 | May 22 |
| Memorial Day[2] | May 28 | May 27 | May 25 | May 31 | May 30 | May 29 |
| Flag Day | June 14 | June 14 | June 14 | June 14 | June 14 | June 14 |
| Father's Day | June 17 | June 16 | June 21 | June 20 | June 19 | June 18 |
| Canada Day[3] | July 1 | July 1 | July 1 | July 1 | July 1 | July 1 |
| Independence Day[2] | July 4 | July 4 | July 4 | July 4 | July 4 | July 4 |
| Labor Day[2, 3] | Sept. 3 | Sept. 2 | Sept. 7 | Sept. 6 | Sept. 5 | Sept. 4 |
| Citizenship Day | Sept. 17 | Sept. 17 | Sept. 17 | Sept. 17 | Sept. 17 | Sept. 17 |
| Columbus Day[2] | Oct. 8 | Oct. 14 | Oct. 12 | Oct. 11 | Oct. 10 | Oct. 9 |
| Thanksgiving Day (Can.)[3] | Oct. 8 | Oct. 14 | Oct. 12 | Oct. 11 | Oct. 10 | Oct. 9 |
| United Nations Day | Oct. 24 | Oct. 24 | Oct. 24 | Oct. 24 | Oct. 24 | Oct. 24 |
| Daylight Saving ends | Oct. 28 | Oct 27 | Oct. 25 | Oct. 31 | Oct. 30 | Oct. 29 |
| Halloween | Oct. 31 | Oct. 31 | Oct. 31 | Oct. 31 | Oct. 31 | Oct. 31 |
| Election Day (U.S.) | Nov. 6 | Nov. 5 | Nov. 3 | Nov. 2 | Nov. 8 | Nov. 7 |
| Veterans' Day[2] | Nov. 11 | Nov. 11 | Nov. 11 | Nov. 11 | Nov. 11 | Nov. 11 |
| Remembrance Day[3] | Nov. 11 | Nov. 11 | Nov. 11 | Nov. 11 | Nov. 11 | Nov. 11 |
| Thanksgiving Day (U.S.)[2] | Nov. 22 | Nov. 28 | Nov. 26 | Nov. 25 | Nov. 24 | Nov. 23 |
| Christmas Day[2, 3] | Dec. 25 | Dec. 25 | Dec. 25 | Dec. 25 | Dec. 25 | Dec. 25 |
| Boxing Day[3] | Dec. 26 | Dec. 26 | Dec. 26 | Dec. 26 | Dec. 26 | Dec. 26 |
| New Year's Eve | Dec. 31 | Dec. 31 | Dec. 31 | Dec. 31 | Dec. 31 | Dec. 31 |

**Note:** For dates of Jewish, Christian, and Muslim holy days 1990–95, see below. 1. Leap year; February has 29 days. 2. Federal holiday in the United States. 3. Federal holiday in Canada.

trees and their preservation; its observance is meant to encourage preservation of the environment. Internationally, it is observed on Dec. 22.

**Armed Forces Day** (Third Saturday in May) A day to honor members of the U.S. Armed Forces.

**Citizenship Day** (Sept. 17) First observed by presidential proclamation in 1952, Citizenship Day falls on the same day as the old Constitution Day, which it replaces, though the old name is still commonly used.

**Daylight Saving Time** During this period, clocks are set one hour ahead of standard time; daylight saving time lasts from the first Sunday in April to the last Sunday in October, when clocks are turned back one hour—"Spring ahead, fall back."

**Election Day** (the Tuesday after the first Monday in November) In years evenly divisible by four, presidential elections are held; in years evenly divisible by two, elections for all members of the House of Representatives and for one-third of the members of the Senate are held.

**Father's Day** (Third Sunday in June) A uniquely American institution, Father's Day was first observed in West Virginia in 1908, but it was not until 1972 that the president signed a congressional resolution designating its official observance.

**Flag Day** (June 14) The first observance of Flag Day was in 1877, the centenary of the Flag Resolution, which adopted the design of the American flag flown today. Pres. Harry Truman signed the Flag Day Bill in 1949.

**Groundhog Day** (Feb. 2) On this day, as legend has it, the groundhog peeks out of his burrow to look for his shadow, and if he sees his shadow, six weeks of winter will follow; if he doesn't, spring is just around the corner.

**Halloween** (Oct. 31) All Hallow's Eve began as a pagan custom honoring the dead and as a celebration of autumn. The wearing of costumes can be traced back to medieval religious practice in which parishioners dressed as saints and angels and paraded through the churchyard. The modern practice of "trick or treating" is of recent American origin.

**Mother's Day** (Second Sunday in May) Conceived by Anne M. Jarvis of Philadelphia, Pa., where it was first observed, as a day for children to pay tribute to their mothers, this was declared a national holiday by presidential proclamation in 1914.

**National Maritime Day** (May 22) Designated by presidential proclamation in 1935, this commemorates the anniversary of the departure of the SS *Savannah* on the first successful transoceanic voyage of a steam-powered vessel, in 1819. It is also a day of remembrance of merchant mariners who died in defense of their country.

**National Teacher Day** (Tuesday of the first full week in May) The day when students and communities around the country honor their teachers and the teaching profession.

**St. Patrick's Day** (Mar. 17) A day in honor of Ireland's patron saint, St. Patrick's Day is a religious, political, and social event rolled into one. In Ireland St. Patrick is honored by church ceremonies and a three-day period of devotion. In the United States, Mar. 17 is celebrated with parades and the "wearing of the green."

**St. Valentine's Day** (Feb. 14) Originally, an occasion to honor two Christian saints martyred by the Roman Emperor Claudius (214–270). Since the Middle Ages, the day has been dedicated to lovers, probably because it is believed to be the day birds choose their mates.

**Susan B. Anthony Day** (Feb. 15) Anthony (1820–1906) was one of the first women's rights advocates, working especially for equal suffrage. She was a cofounder and later president of the National Woman Suffrage Association.

**United Nations Day** (Oct. 24) Commemorates the ratification of the UN Charter on this date in 1945 by the five permanent members of the Security Council and a majority of the other charter signatories.

### Christian Holy Days

**Christmas** is the celebration of Christ's birth. The exact date of his birth is unknown, but the date of Dec. 25 was probably chosen because it coincided with the ancient midwinter celebrations honoring pagan deities. The 12 days of Christmas fall between Christmas and Epiphany (Jan. 6), the day the Wise Men visited the Christ child.

**Easter** is the most important holy day in the Christian religion. It is the celebration of Christ's Resurrection from the dead, which gave Christians the hope of salvation and eternal life. Although Easter is only one day, the full observance of the holy day spans from Septuagesima Sunday (70 days before Easter Sunday), which may fall as early as January, to Pentecost, which can occur as late as June.

*Shrove Tuesday (Mardi Gras; Fat Tuesday)* Originally a day of penance, the last day before the beginning of Lent is now celebrated with feasting and merrymaking.

*Ash Wednesday* derives its name from the rite of burning the palms carried on the Palm Sunday of the year before and using the ashes to mark worshipers' foreheads with a cross.

*Lent,* a 40-day period of fasting and penitence beginning on Ash Wednesday and ending on Easter Sunday, is traditionally observed by fasting, performing acts of charity, and by giving up certain pleasures and amusements.

*Palm Sunday,* the Sunday before Easter, cel-

## CALENDAR OF CHRISTIAN HOLY DAYS

| Year A.D. | Ash Wednesday | Easter Sunday | Pentecost | Trinity Sunday | Advent |
|---|---|---|---|---|---|
| 1990 | Feb. 28 | Apr. 15 | June 3 | June 10 | Dec. 2 |
| 1991 | Feb. 13 | Mar. 31 | May 19 | May 26 | Dec. 1 |
| 1992 | Mar. 4 | Apr. 19 | June 7 | June 14 | Nov. 29 |
| 1993 | Feb. 24 | Apr. 11 | May 30 | June 6 | Nov. 28 |
| 1994 | Feb. 16 | Apr. 3 | May 22 | May 29 | Nov. 27 |
| 1995 | Mar. 1 | Apr. 16 | June 4 | June 11 | Dec. 3 |

ebrates Jesus' triumphant entry into Jerusalem, where palm branches were spread before him to honor his path.

*Holy (Maundy) Thursday* is the anniversary of the Last Supper. The traditional services mark three events that occurred during the week before Jesus was crucified: he washed the feet of his 12 disciples; he instituted the Eucharist (the sacrament of Holy Communion); and he was arrested and imprisoned.

*Good Friday* marks the day of Christ's Crucifixion. The holy day is observed with fasting, mourning, and penitence.

*Holy Saturday* is the day that anticipates the Resurrection. In the Catholic church, special vigils are held on Holy Saturday evening.

*Easter Sunday* marks the day of Christ's Resurrection. Many worshipers celebrate the holy day with sunrise services, a custom believed to be inspired by the example of Mary Magdalene, who went to Christ's tomb "early, while it was yet dark."

*Pentecost* (literally, 50th day) is the end of the full ecclesiastical observance of Easter. It takes place on the seventh Sunday after Easter Sunday and commemorates the descent of the Holy Spirit upon the Apostles.

**The Annunciation** This holy day marks the archangel Gabriel's announcement to Mary that she would conceive and give birth to Jesus. It is celebrated by Roman Catholics on Mar. 25; it is not observed by Protestant denominations.

**Trinity Sunday** The Sunday after Pentecost, this occasion honors the Father, Son, and Holy Ghost. It was declared a part of the church calendar in 1334 by Pope John XXII and is observed by Roman Catholics and by some Protestant denominations.

**Corpus Christi** This feast celebrates the presence of the body (corpus) of Christ in the Eucharist. At one time this was the principal feast of the church year, but today it is observed only by Catholic churches. Corpus Christi is celebrated on the Thursday following Trinity Sunday.

**All Saints' Day,** celebrated on Nov. 1, honors all of the Christian saints. In America many churches mark the Sunday nearest Nov. 1 as a day to pay tribute to those who have died during the year. All Saints' Day is observed primarily by Roman Catholics.

**Advent,** a religious season that begins on the Sunday closest to Nov. 30 and lasts until Christmas, both celebrates the birth of Jesus and anticipates his second coming. At one time Advent was a solemn season observed by fasting, but this is no longer the case.

**Holy Days of Obligation** are feast days in the Catholic calendar, observed by attendance at Mass and rest from unnecessary work. Six holy days of obligation are observed in the United States:

1. Solemnity of Mary, Jan. 1
2. Ascension Thursday (of Jesus to Heaven), 40 days after Easter
3. Assumption of the Blessed Virgin into Heaven, Aug. 15
4. All Saints' Day, Nov. 1
5. Mary's Immaculate Conception (honoring the Mother of God as the only person conceived without original sin), Dec. 8
6. Christmas, Dec. 25

### The Jewish Calendar

The months of the Jewish year are Tishri, Heshvan, Kislev, Tebet, Shebat, Adar, Nisan, Iyar, Sivan, Tammuz, Ab, and Elul. The Jewish era dates from the year of the creation (*anno mundi,* or A.M.), which is equal to 3761 B.C.E. (before the Christian era). Thus 5751 begins in 1990 and ends in 1991 of the Gregorian calendar. (Tishri, the first month of the Jewish year, falls in either September or October of the Gregorian calendar.)

Because the Jewish calendar is a blend of solar and lunar calendars, there are intercalated months to keep the lunar and solar years in alignment. (Intercalation is the insertion of an extra day, month, or other unit—Feb. 29 in a

leap year, for example—into a calendar. The intercalated month here is called Adar Sheni, or Veadar—"Second Adar." The year 5749 was a leap year).

### Jewish Holy Days

**Sabbath** is the first and most important Jewish holy day, occurring each week from sundown Friday to sundown Saturday. It is a day of rest and spiritual growth, given to men and women so they will remember the sweetness of freedom and keep it. Sabbath takes precedence over all other observances.

**Rosh Hashanah (New Year),** held to be the birthday of the world, is also called the Day of Judgment and Remembrance, and the day of the shofar—a ram's horn—which is blown to remind Jews of Abraham's willingness to sacrifice his son Isaac. The holiday takes place on the first and second days of Tishri (in September or October).

**Yom Kippur (Day of Atonement)** concludes the 10 days of repentance that Rosh Hashanah begins and takes place from sundown on the ninth day of Tishri until sundown on the 10th. The observance begins with the recitation of the most famous passage in the Jewish liturgy—the *Kol Nidre*—which nullifies unfulfilled vows made in the past year. The entire day is spent praying and fasting.

**Sukkoth (Tabernacles)** is a harvest festival celebrated from the 15th through the 22nd of Tishri. Sukkoth also commemorates the journey of the Jewish people through the wilderness to the land of Israel. Jewish families take their meals this week in a roughly constructed *sukkah* (booth)—a reminder of an agricultural society, of the Exodus, and of how precarious and fragile life can be. On the Simchath Torah, the 23rd of Tishri, a congregation finishes reading the last book of the Torah and immediately starts again with the first.

**Hanukkah (Feast of Dedication; Festival of Lights)** The importance of the eight-day feast, which begins on the 25th day day of Kislev, is its commemoration of the first war in human history fought in the cause of religious freedom. The Maccabees vanquished not just the military threat to Judaism but also the internal forces for assimilation into the Hellenistic culture of Israel's rulers. Jews light candles for eight nights to mark a miracle: a day's supply of oil, found in the recaptured Temple, that burned for eight days.

**Purim (Feast of Lots),** set on the 14th day of Adar, is another celebration of survival, noting the events described in the Book of Esther. At

## CALENDAR OF JEWISH HOLY DAYS

| Year A.M. | Rosh Hashanah | Yom Kippur | Sukkoth | Hanukkah | Purim | Pesach | Shavuoth |
|---|---|---|---|---|---|---|---|
| 5751 | Sept. 20, 1990 | Sept. 29, 1990 | Oct. 4, 1990 | Dec. 12, 1990 | Feb. 28, 1991 | Mar. 30, 1991 | May 19, 1991 |
| 5752 | Sept. 9, 1991 | Sept. 18, 1991 | Sept. 23, 1991 | Dec. 2, 1991 | Mar. 19, 1992 | Apr. 18, 1992 | June 7, 1992 |
| 5753 | Sept. 28, 1992 | Oct. 7, 1992 | Oct. 12, 1992 | Dec. 20, 1992 | Mar. 7, 1993 | Apr. 6, 1993 | May 26, 1993 |
| 5754 | Sept. 16, 1993 | Sept. 25, 1993 | Sept. 30, 1993 | Dec. 9, 1993 | Feb. 25, 1994 | Mar. 27, 1994 | May 16, 1994 |
| 5755 | Sept. 6, 1994 | Sept. 15, 1994 | Sept. 20, 1994 | Nov. 28, 1994 | Mar. 16, 1995 | Apr. 15, 1995 | June 4, 1995 |
| 5756 | Sept. 25, 1995 | Oct. 4, 1995 | Oct. 9, 1995 | Dec. 18, 1995 | Mar. 5, 1996 | Apr. 4, 1996 | May 24, 1996 |

**Source:** *Encyclopedia Judaica.*

**Purim** Jews rejoice at Queen Esther's and her cousin Mordecai's defeat of Haman, the Persian King Ahaseurus's adviser who plotted to slaughter all the Persian Jews. Ahaseurus ruled around 400 B.C.

**Pesach (Passover),** beginning on the 15th day of Nisan and lasting seven days, commemorates the exodus of the Hebrews from Egypt in about 1300 B.C. The name Passover also recalls God's sparing (passing over) the Jewish firstborn during the plagues upon the land brought by God through Moses. The holiday is marked by eating only unleavened foods and participating in a seder, or special meal.

**Shavuoth (Feast of Weeks)** is observed on the sixth or seventh day of Sivan. Originally an agricultural festival, Shavuoth is a celebration of the revelation of the Torah at Mt. Sinai, by which God established his covenant with the Jewish people.

## The Islamic Calendar

The 12 months of the Islamic year are: Muharram, Safar, Rabi I, Rabi II, Jumada I, Jumada II, Rajab, Sha'ban, Ramadan, Shawwal, Dhu'l-Qa'dah, Dhu'l-Hijja. The Islamic calendar is based on a lunar year of 12 months of 30 and 29 days (alternating every month), and the year is equal to 354 days. It runs in cycles of 30 years, of which the second, fifth, seventh, 10th, 13th, 16th, 18th, 21st, 24th, 26th, and 29th are leap years. Leap years have 355 days, the extra day being added to the last month, Dhu'l-Hijja. The year A.H. 1410 (*anno hegirae,* in the year of the hejira) is the 30th year in the cycle. There are no intercalated months or leap years, so the Islamic year does not keep a constant relationship to the solar year—which dictates the seasons—and months occur about 10 or 11 days earlier than in the year before.

The caliph Abu Bakr adopted A.D. 622—the year of the hejira (Muhammad's migration from Mecca to Medina)—as the first year of Islam. However, dating of the Muslim era varies throughout the Islamic world. In some countries the year of the Muslim era is obtained by subtracting 622 from the Gregorian year; A.D. 1990 equals A.H. 1368.

Other countries (Saudi Arabia, Yemen, and the principalities of the Persian Gulf) continue to use a purely lunar year. To approximate the Muslim era equivalent of the Gregorian year, subtract 622 (the year of hejira in the Gregorian calendar) from the current year and multiply the result by 1.031 (days in the year of the Gregorian calendar divided by days in the lunar year): A.D. 1990 = (1990 – 622) × 1.031 = A.H. 1410.

## Muslim Holy Days

**Ramadan,** the ninth month of the Islamic calendar, is the Islamic faith's holiest period. To honor the month in which the Koran was revealed, all adult Muslims of sound body and mind observe fasting—eschewing food, water, or even a kiss—between the hours of sunrise and sunset. Exempted from the fast are women in menstruation or childbirth bleeding, the chronically ill, or people on a journey, all of whom must make up the fast days at a later date.

**Id al-Fitr** This day of feasting is celebrated at the end of Ramadan. To mark the fast's break, worshipers also attend an early morning service, Salat-ul-'Id, at which they give alms in staple foodstuffs or their monetary value.

**Id al-Adha** The Feast of Sacrifice takes place on the 10th day of Dhu'l-Hijja, the last month of the year and the season of the *haj,* or pilgrimage. The day begins with a service in the mosques or other places of gathering, and for those who are not pilgrims continues with the ritual slaughter of a sheep in commemoration of God's ransom of Abraham's son from sacrifice. At least a third of the meat of the animal is to be set aside for charity.

**Fridays** At noontime Muslims attend mosque or comparable gathering places to say the congregational Friday prayer that ends the week. While Friday—Jumuah—is the holy day of the weekly Muslim calendar, it is not a Sabbath comparable to Christian Sundays or Jewish Saturdays, and there are no restrictions on work or other worldly enterprises.

## MONTHS OF THE YEAR

| Gregorian | Hebrew | Hindu | Muslim |
|---|---|---|---|
| *January* | Shebat | Magha | *Muharram* |
| February | Adar | Phalguna | Safar |
| March | Nisan | *Caitra* | Rabi I |
| April | Iyar | Vaisakha | Rabi II |
| May | Sivan | Jyaistha | Jumada I |
| June | Tammuz | Asadha | Jumada II |
| July | Ab | Sravana | Rajab |
| August | Elul | Bhadrapada | Sha'ban |
| September | *Tishri* | Asvina | Ramadan |
| October | Heshvan | Karttika | Shawwal |
| November | Kislev | Margasivsa | Dhu'l-Qa'dah |
| December | Tebet | Pansa | Dhu'l-Hijja |

**Note:** The months of the Gregorian, Hebrew, Hindu, and reformed Muslim calendars occur at roughly the same time of year, while those of the traditional (lunar) Muslim calendar occur at different times every year. Months in italics indicate the first month of the year in the respective calendars.

## The Hindu Year

The Hindu year consists of 12 months: Caitra, Vaisakha, Jyaistha, Asadha, Sravana, Bhadrapada, Asvina, Karttika, Margasivsa, Pansa, Magha, and Phalguna. Calendrically, holidays are of two types, lunar and solar. Solar holidays in the Hindu calendar include the following:

**Mesasamkranti** is the beginning of the new astrological year, when the sun enters the constellation Aries.

**Makaraj-Samkranti,** the winter solstice, occurs when the sun enters the constellation Capricorn.

**Mahavisuva Day** is New Year's Eve.

Principal holidays determined by the lunar year are these:

**Ramanavami** (Caitra 9) celebrates the birth of Rama, in Hindu folklore the epitome of chivalry, courage, and obedience to sacred law. Rama is considered an incarnation of Vishnu, and his name is synonymous with God.

**Rathayatra** (Asadha 2) is the pilgrimage of the chariot festival of Orissa.

**Janmastami** (Sravana 8) is the birthday of Krishna, an incarnation of the supreme deity, Vishnu, celebrated as a philosopher-king and hero.

**Dasahra** (Asvina 7–10) commemorates Rama's victory over the demon Ravana.

**Laksmipuja** (Asvina 15) honors Laksmi, goddess of good fortune.

**Dipavali** (Karttika 15) occasions the festival of lights and exchanging of presents.

**Mahasivaratri** (Magha 13) honors the god Shiva, one of the three supreme Hindu gods. Shiva, whose name means "Auspicious One," is a god of both reproduction and destruction.

## ASTRONOMICAL EVENTS, 1992

The main astronomical events included in this section are the phases of the Moon, the Moon's perigee (when it is closest to the Earth) and apogee (when it is farthest away), lunar and solar eclipses, and the visibility of the planets.

## Phases of the Moon

A lunation is the cycle from new moon to new moon and takes about 29.53 days. During this period, the relative position of the Earth, Moon, and Sun affect what, if any, part of the Moon we can see illuminated by the sun during our night. A *new moon* occurs when the Moon is in conjunction with the Sun, and the Moon is invisible from the Earth. When the Moon is at *first quarter* (90° from the Sun relative to the Earth), its sunlit part appears in the shape of a D (in the Southern Hemisphere, a backward D). A *full moon,* when the Moon shows an almost fully illuminated face, occurs when the Moon is 180° around the sky from the sun. The *last quarter* (or third quarter) is when the Moon is again moving toward a position between the Earth and the Sun, and it appears as a backward D (a normal D in the Southern Hemisphere). Intermediate phases are the *crescent moon*—between the new moon and first quarter

| CALENDAR OF MUSLIM HOLY DAYS | | | | |
|---|---|---|---|---|
| Year A.H. (A.D.) | New Year's Day, 1 Muharram | 1 Ramadan | Id al-Fitr, 1 Shawwal | Id al-Adha, 10 Dhu al-Hijja |
| 1410 (1989–90) | Aug. 30, 1989 | Mar. 28, 1990 | Apr. 27, 1990 | July 3, 1990 |
| 1411 (1990–91) | July 23, 1990 | Mar. 17, 1991 | Apr. 16, 1991 | June 23, 1991 |
| 1412 (1991–92) | July 13, 1991 | Mar. 5, 1992 | Apr. 4, 1992 | June 11, 1992 |
| 1413 (1992–93) | July 2, 1992 | Feb. 23, 1993 | Mar. 25, 1993 | June 1, 1993 |
| 1414 (1993–94) | June 20, 1993 | Feb. 12, 1994 | Mar. 14, 1994 | May 21, 1994 |
| 1415 (1994–95) | June 9, 1994 | Feb. 1, 1995 | Mar. 3, 1995 | May 10, 1995 |

(waxing), and between the last quarter and new moon (waning); and the *gibbous moon*, occurring before and after the full moon.

## VISIBILITY OF PLANETS IN MORNING AND EVENING TWILIGHT

| Planet | Morning | Evening |
|---|---|---|
| Venus | Jan. 1–May 7 | July 20–Dec. 31 |
| Mars | Jan. 1–Dec. 31 | — |
| Jupiter | Jan. 1–Feb. 29, and Oct. 1–Dec. 31 | Feb. 29–Sept. 4 |
| Saturn | Feb. 16–Aug. 7 | Jan. 1–13, and Aug. 7–Dec. 31 |

**Source:** U.S. Naval Observatory, *Astronomical Phenomena for the Year 1992* (1989).

## Visibility of the Planets

**Mercury** can only be seen low in the east before sunrise, or low in the west after sunset. It is visible in the mornings between the following approximate dates: Jan. 1–30; Apr. 3–May 24; Aug. 11–Sept. 6; and Nov. 28–Dec. 31. The planet is brighter at the end of each period. The best conditions for viewing occur in low northern latitudes for a few days in early January and during the third week in August, and in most northern latitudes for the first three weeks of December, and in southern latitudes from the second week in April until mid-May.

It is visible in the evenings between the following approximate dates: Feb. 23–Mar. 19; June 8–July 26; and Sept. 27–Nov. 16. The planet is brighter at the beginning of each period. The best conditions for viewing in northern latitudes occur during the first half of March, and in southern latitudes from the third week in June until the third week in July, and from the third week in October until just before mid-November.

**Venus** is a brilliant object in the evening sky from the beginning of the year until the second week in May, when it becomes too close to the Sun for observation. During the second half of July it reappears in the evening sky, where it stays until the end of the year. Venus is in conjunction with Mars on Feb. 19, with Saturn on Feb. 29 and Dec. 21, with Mercury on Apr. 5 and July 25, and with Jupiter on Aug. 23.

**Mars** can be seen at the very beginning of January in the morning sky in Ophiuchus. It then passes through Sagittarius, Capricornus, Aquarius, Pisces, briefly into Cetus, and back into Pisces, Aries, Taurus (passing 5° N. of Aldebaran on Aug. 1), Gemini (passing 5° S. of Pollux on Nov. 4, by which time it can be seen for more than half the night), Cancer, and back into Gemini in mid-December, where it remains for the rest of the year. (It passes 3° S. of Pollux on Dec. 22.) Mars is in conjunction with Mercury on Jan. 10, with Venus on Feb. 19, and with Saturn on Mar. 6.

## PHASES OF THE MOON, 1992

| | New moon | | | | First quarter | | | | Full moon | | | | Last quarter | | |
|---|---|---|---|---|---|---|---|---|---|---|---|---|---|---|---|
| Month | d | h | m | Month | d | h | m | Month | d | h | m | Month | d | h | m |
| Jan. | 4 | 23 | 10 | Jan. | 13 | 02 | 32 | Jan. | 19 | 21 | 28 | Jan. | 26 | 15 | 27 |
| Feb. | 3 | 19 | 00 | Feb. | 11 | 16 | 15 | Feb. | 18 | 08 | 04 | Feb. | 25 | 07 | 56 |
| Mar. | 4 | 13 | 22 | Mar. | 12 | 02 | 36 | Mar. | 18 | 18 | 18 | Mar. | 26 | 02 | 30 |
| Apr. | 3 | 05 | 01 | Apr. | 10 | 10 | 06 | Apr. | 17 | 04 | 42 | Apr. | 24 | 21 | 40 |
| May | 2 | 17 | 44 | May | 9 | 15 | 43 | May | 16 | 16 | 03 | May | 24 | 15 | 53 |
| June | 1 | 03 | 57 | June | 7 | 20 | 47 | June | 15 | 04 | 50 | June | 23 | 08 | 11 |
| June | 30 | 12 | 18 | July | 7 | 02 | 43 | July | 14 | 19 | 06 | July | 22 | 22 | 12 |
| July | 29 | 19 | 35 | Aug. | 5 | 10 | 58 | Aug. | 13 | 10 | 27 | Aug. | 21 | 10 | 01 |
| Aug. | 28 | 02 | 42 | Sept. | 3 | 22 | 39 | Sept. | 12 | 02 | 17 | Sept. | 19 | 19 | 53 |
| Sept. | 26 | 10 | 40 | Oct. | 3 | 14 | 12 | Oct. | 11 | 18 | 03 | Oct. | 19 | 04 | 12 |
| Oct. | 25 | 20 | 34 | Nov. | 2 | 09 | 11 | Nov. | 10 | 09 | 20 | Nov. | 17 | 11 | 39 |
| Nov. | 24 | 09 | 11 | Dec. | 2 | 06 | 17 | Dec. | 9 | 23 | 41 | Dec. | 16 | 19 | 13 |
| Dec. | 24 | 00 | 43 | | | | | | | | | | | | |

**Note:** Shown in universal time (UT). To convert to local time, see "Timing Planetary Phenomena." **Source:** U.S. Naval Observatory, *Astronomical Phenomena for the Year 1992* (1989).

**Jupiter** can be seen in January for more than half of the night in Leo, its westward elongation gradually increasing until it is at opposition on Feb. 29, when it can be seen throughout the night. Its eastward elongation then gradually decreases until by early June it can be seen only in the evening sky. In early September it becomes too close to the Sun for observation. In the beginning of October it reappears in the morning sky in Virgo, where it remains for the rest of the year. Jupiter is in conjunction with Venus on Aug. 23.

---

## TIMING PLANETARY PHENOMENA

The times for astronomical data shown here are expressed in universal time (UT), which is the standard time of the Greenwich meridian (0° of longitude), also known as Greenwich mean time (GMT). To convert to local time, determine your longitude and subtract one hour for every 15° of longitude west of 0°; or add one hour for every 15° of longitude east of 0.°

The first new moon of 1992 occurs Jan. 4 at 2310 hours in UT. The equivalent time in New York (74°W) is five hours earlier, or Jan. 4 at 1810 hours; in Chicago (87°W), it is six hours earlier, or Jan. 4 at 1710 hours; in Denver (105°W), it is seven hours earlier, or Jan. 4 at 1610 hours; and in San Francisco (122°W), it is eight hours earlier, or Jan. 4 at 1510. (To obtain the p.m. equivalent of UT times later than 1200, subtract 12: 1550 = 3:50 p.m.) Note that local clock times may differ from these standard times, especially in summer when clocks are often advanced by one hour.

---

**Saturn** can be seen in the evening sky in Capricornus until mid-January, when it becomes too close to the Sun for observation. It reappears in the morning sky in mid-February still in Capricornus, where it remains throughout the year. Its westward elongation gradually increases until it is at opposition on Aug. 7, when it is visible throughout the night. Its eastward elongation then gradually decreases until from early November it can only be seen in the evening sky. Saturn is in conjunction with Venus on Feb. 29 and Dec. 21, and with Mars on Mar. 6.

**Uranus** is too close to the Sun for observation until toward the end of January, when it appears in the morning sky in Sagittarius, where it remains throughout the year. It is at opposition on July 7, when it can be seen throughout the night, after which its eastward elongation gradually decreases. From early October it can only be seen in the evening sky until the second half of December, when it again becomes too close to the Sun for observation.

**Neptune** is too close to the Sun for observation until late January, when it can be seen in the morning sky shortly before sunrise in Sagittarius, where it remains throughout the year. It is at opposition on July 9, when it can be seen throughout the night. From mid-October until mid-December it can only be seen in the evening sky, after which it again becomes too close to the sun for observation.

### Do not confuse

1) Mercury with Mars during the first half of January; the reddish tint of Mars should assist in its identification.

2) Venus with Mars from mid-February to early March; with Saturn from late February to early March and mid-December to late December; with Mercury in early April and the third week of May; and with Jupiter in late August. On all occasions Venus is the brighter object.

3) Mars with Saturn for the first half of March, when Mars is the brighter object.

## TOTAL SOLAR ECLIPSES IN THE 1990s

A total eclipse is one of nature's most spectacular sights, and many people will travel halfway around the world to see one. A total eclipse occurs when the Moon is close enough to Earth to cover the entire Sun. As the Earth turns below, the shadow of the Moon races roughly from west to east in a long curving path. People not near the midline of that path see only a partial eclipse. Since the period of totality is only a few minutes, weather along the path is especially important. The viewing notes here are based on historical records of cloud cover at the time of the eclipse for places along the path.

| Date | Path | Remarks | Date | Path | Remarks |
|---|---|---|---|---|---|
| July 22, 1990 | Near Helsinki, Finland, along USSR's Arctic Coast, to Aleutian Islands | View at dawn in Finland, where weather is most likely to be best; cloud cover 99% of time in Aleutians | Oct. 24, 1995 | From Iran; across Afghanistan, Pakistan, India, Southeast Asia; and into western Pacific | Shortest eclipse of decade, lasting little over 2 minutes over China Sea; best viewing in Great Indian Desert near Calcutta, India |
| July 11, 1991 | Island of Hawaii, over the Pacific to Baja California, through Mexico and Central America, into South America to Brazil's rain forest | Best eclipse of decade because of 3 excellent viewing sites: Hawaii, Baja California, and Brazil; longest total-eclipse period until 2137 | Mar. 9, 1997 | From Mongolia, across Siberia, almost to North Pole | If you can stand the cold of March in Siberia, best viewing is between Magadan and Yakutsk on banks of frozen Lena |
| June 30, 1992 | From coast of South America to tip of South Africa, almost entirely in Atlantic Ocean | Over 5 min. long in mid-Atlantic; best seen from ship | Feb. 26, 1998 | From eastern Pacific; past Galapagos; across Panama, Columbia, and Venezuela; into Caribbean | North of Maracaibo, Venezuela, should provide good viewing, or vicinity of Leeward Islands in Caribbean |
| Nov. 3, 1994 | Starts in eastern Pacific but reaches land near Arequipa, Peru; crosses Chile, Bolivia, Paraguay, Brazil; and heads into Atlantic | Best viewing in inland Peru in terms of chance of clouds, but total-eclipse longest in Atlantic | Aug. 11, 1999 | From western Atlantic off Nova Scotia to Isles of Scilly and the southwest tip of Great Britain; through central Europe, Middle East, India, and Pakistan, to Bay of Bengal | First total eclipse for central Europe since 1961, but best viewing should be in Iran and Iraq; southeastern Europe and Turkey also should be good |

**Source:** Jay Anderson, "Eclipse Prospects for the 1990s," *Astronomy* (Feb. 1989).

## ECLIPSES OF THE MOON, 1992

A lunar eclipse occurs when the Sun, Earth, and Moon are in a straight line and the shadow of the Earth falls on the Moon. There are three kinds of lunar eclipses. A *total eclipse* is when the Moon passes completely into the Earth's umbra, or shadow, so the Sun cannot be seen from the Moon. A *partial eclipse* occurs when only part of the Earth's umbra falls across the Moon and the Sun is partially visible from some places on the Moon. A *penumbral eclipse* occurs when only the Earth's penumbra (partial shadow) shades the Moon, and from the Moon one's view of the Sun would be only partially blocked by the Earth. It is usually difficult to detect a penumbral eclipse from the Earth.

During 1992, there are two lunar eclipses, one partial and one total. Whether the eclipse can be viewed depends on one's location and the time of day. Since the Moon must be on the opposite side of the Earth from the Sun for a lunar eclipse to occur, eclipses occurring during daylight hours cannot be seen. (All times below shown in universal time (UT). To convert to local time, see "Timing Planetary Phenomena.")

**June 15, 1992—Partial eclipse** *Moon enters penumbra* June 15, 0209. *Middle of eclipse* June 15, 0457. *Moon leaves penumbra* June 15, 0744. The beginning of the umbral phase is visible in South America, Central America, the U.S. except the northwest, southeastern Canada, Antarctica, the eastern South Pacific Ocean, extreme western Europe, Africa except the northeast, and the Atlantic Ocean. The end is visible in New Zealand, Hawaii, South America, Central America, North America except Alaska and northern Canada, Antarctica, extreme western Africa, the South Pacific Ocean, the southeastern North Pacific Ocean, and most of the Atlantic Ocean except the northeast.

**Dec. 9–10, 1992—Total eclipse** *Moon enters penumbra* Dec. 9, 2055. *Moon enters totality* Dec. 9, 2306. *Middle of eclipse* Dec. 9, 2344. *Moon leaves totality* Dec. 10, 0021. *Moon leaves penumbra* Dec. 10, 0232. The beginning of the umbral phase is visible in northeastern South America, eastern and northern North America, Greenland, the Arctic regions, Africa, Europe, most of Asia, most of the Atlantic Ocean, and the Indian Ocean. The end is visible in South America, Central America, most of North America, Greenland, the Arctic regions, Africa, Europe, northern and western Asia, the eastern Pacific Ocean, the Atlantic Ocean, and the western Indian Ocean.

## SOLAR ECLIPSES

A solar eclipse occurs when the Moon passes between the Earth and the Sun; there are three types. A *total eclipse* occurs when the Moon completely covers the Sun and the sky turns dark. Total eclipses occur along a narrow path (typically 100–200 miles wide) called the track of totality and last only a few minutes at any point on the track. During the 1990s, no total eclipse will be visible from the continental United States, but on July 11, 1991, an excellent one was visible from Hawaii to Mexico City. A *partial eclipse* occurs when the Moon covers only a portion of the Sun. Whether an eclipse is total or partial depends on where one is standing; the July 11, 1991, eclipse that was total over a narrow strip of Mexico was partial over much of North and Central America. An *annular* (ring-shaped) *eclipse* occurs when the Moon is too far from the Earth to cover the Sun completely, so that at the height of the eclipse a ring of light surrounds the Moon. The most prominent annular eclipse in the United States during the 1990s will take place May 10, 1994, and will be visible from Texas to Maine.

# THE YEAR IN REVIEW

## Chronology of the Year's Key Events

### November 1990

**1** In an attempt to introduce its own currency, remedy inflation pressures and the scarcity of goods, and prevent outsiders from leaving with scarce consumer items, the Ukraine becomes first Soviet republic to issue rationing coupons, to be used with Soviet rubles when purchasing consumer goods such as food and gasoline.

In India, death toll rises to 210 people in a week of religious riots, mostly in Uttar Pradesh State where Hindu fundamentalists are waging a campaign to build a temple on the site of a Muslim mosque.

Soviet immigrants arriving in Israel in October reached 20,000 for the first time, despite inadequate housing, few job opportunities, and threat of war. Total for 1990 is 121,752, and Israel government expects 400,000 Soviet Jews to arrive in 1991.

National Transportation Safety Board finds United Airlines at fault for 1989 accident in which a DC-10's engine broke apart, severing its hydraulic lines and leaving it virtually uncontrollable; 112 people died during a crash landing at Sioux City, Iowa.

In London, 43 countries sign London Dumping Convention banning industrial waste dumping at sea; the ban is legally binding on all 64 nations that signed the Convention in 1970.

In Ayacucho, Peru, seven people, including leader of Pres. Alberto Fujimori's Change '90 political party, are killed by guerrillas suspected of being part of the Shining Path.

**2** While the October unemployment rate remained steady at 5.7%, the number of jobs fell by 68,000; construction and manufacturing industries led the decline. Nine of the 11 leading economic indicators fell, increasing the belief that expansion of the 1980s is over.

South African government agrees to a phased release of political prisoners and return of political exiles in accordance with the African National Congress's suspension of armed struggle. The two sides disagree on the timing of the release and the number of prisoners involved, the government claiming 250 to 600 prisoners affected by the agreement and the ANC counting 3,622 political prisoners.

In Moldavia, six are killed and 30 wounded when Moldavian nationalists travel to the town of Dubossary to crush separatist sentiment among Russian speakers and Ukrainians of Moldavia's Dniester River region.

**3** Oil production in Saudi Arabia surpasses 8.2 mil. barrels a day and is expected to rise to 8.5 mil. by next year, the highest level in a decade. Despite embargo on Kuwaiti and Iraqi oil, world oil supply is higher than before Persian Gulf crisis began in August.

In Budapest, Warsaw Pact members sign an agreement in one of their last joint efforts to redistribute weapons remaining in Eastern Europe after drastic reductions. Agreement provides Soviet Union with 13,150 of 20,000 tanks and 13,175 of 20,000 artillery systems to be distributed in the region.

Congress cuts all military and economic aid to Zaire because of human rights violations and suspicion that Pres. Mobutu's wealth is largely stolen. Some $40 mil. in economic aid is to be channeled through humanitarian agencies.

In Norway, Labor party leader Gro Harlem Brundtland becomes prime minister for third time, replacing Conservative Jan P. Syse.

**4** Defense Dept. calls up combat reserve units and extends combat reservists' 180-day call-up limit to 360 days.

**5** Rabbi Meir Kahane is assassinated at the Zionist Emergency Evacuation Rescue Operation conference in New York City by El Sayyid a Nosair, an Egyptian-born Muslim who is wounded by a police officer after wounding a bystander and fleeing the scene. (See "Obituaries.")

State Dept. dismisses career diplomat Felix Bloch, the first American diplomat disciplined on espionage-related charges since 1961; criminal charges have never been proved.

The Gulf Crisis Financial Coordination Group pledges $13 bil. in special aid to countries suffering from trade sanctions against Iraq. The group includes the U.S., the European Community, Japan, and Persian Gulf oil-producing states.

In Damascus, Syria, the two rival Lebanese Shiite Muslim militias sign a peace agreement ending three years of conflict over a strategic area in southern Lebanon that has claimed at least 2,500 lives.

**6** In an 8-to-0 decision, Supreme Court rules to disallow award of monetary damages for lost future earnings or loss of social ties to families of American seamen killed on the job.

Nawaz Sharif is sworn in as prime minister of Pakistan, after a 153 to 39 vote by the National Assembly in his favor. Sharif is the first prime minister in 30 years who is not a feudal landowner from Sind province.

In nationwide elections, U.S. voters unseat one senator and 15 representatives, and unseat the governing party in 14 states. Only one-third of eligible voters cast ballots. Final results: governors—28 Democrats, 19 Republicans, 2 independent; Senate—56 Democrats, 44 Republicans; House—267 Democrats, 165 Republicans, 1 Socialist, 2 undecided.

**7** After losing a parliamentary vote of confidence by a margin of 142 to 346, Prime Minister V.P. Singh of India resigns after 11 months in office. He lost popularity because he refused to allow the construction of a Hindu temple on the site of a 16th-century mosque in Ayodhya.

An earthquake measuring 7.0 on the Richter scale hits southern Iran, leaving 22 people dead, 100 injured, and 12,000 homeless.

**8** Increasing U.S. troop strength by 65%, Pres. Bush orders 150,000 American air, ground, and sea forces to the Persian Gulf region.

Former Japanese prime minister Yasuhiro Nakasone meets with Pres. Hussein and achieves the release of 74 of 305 Japanese citizens held in Iraq since August.

**9** The Pentagon announces that it will not rotate troops through Saudi Arabia and that forces now in place will remain for the duration of the crisis.

Despite a court order barring its broadcast and a threat of being held in contempt, Cable News Network airs a tape-recorded conversation between Gen. Manuel Antonio Noriega, former leader of Panama, and a member of his legal team. The conversation is about the arrests of two men in Panama who Noriega feared might testify against him.

Seven months after his absolute monarchy was overthrown by protestors, King Birendra of Nepal approves a new constitution that allows multiparty democracy and human rights, limits executive power of the king, guarantees a free and independent press, abolishes the death penalty, and allows for such civil liberties as habeas corpus.

**10** After 15 years of civil war, Lebanese army soldiers are allowed into parts of Beirut previously controlled by the militia. Members of rival Shiite Muslim factions, Amal and the Party of God, are pulling out of the capital as part of a plan to create a militia-free Beirut.

Following the collapse of V.P. Singh's 11-month-old government, Chandra Shekhar, a socialist politician who has never held a government post, is sworn in as India's eighth prime minister.

**11** In Colombia, about 1,000 guerrillas attack an army base and police station in Taraza and a municipal building and police station in Caceres, leaving 40 people dead. The attack is carried out by the Revolutionary Armed Forces of Colombia and the National Liberation Army just days after the guerrilla groups offered to take part in peace talks and release hostages.

**12** Japan installs Emperor Akihito as the 125th occupant of the Chrysanthemum Throne, before an audience of 2,500 dignitaries from around the world. In keeping with the postwar constitution, this coronation is first to acknowledge emperor only as a symbol and vests national sovereignty in the people.

In continuing student unrest in France, more than 100,000 demonstrators in Paris and 150,000 throughout France protest poor conditions in the nation's 4,700 senior high schools. The protest turns violent in Paris, where 200 people are wounded, 83 arrested, 100 cars burned, and 120 stores looted. Government announces emergency plan to increase the number of teaching, maintenance, and security positions at the schools.

**13** In an accord signed in Tokyo, Singapore agrees to serve as a base for increased American training missions, warships, and air force and navy personnel.

After a six-week interruption of the seven-year-old civil war, Sudanese government resumes bombing of civilian targets in rebel territory, killing 12 people and wounding more than 20 in Torit in southern Sudan.

**14** 1,500 armed policemen attempt to clear a large squatter settlement of thousands of people in Berlin with tear gas and water cannons; 450 are arrested and 260 people injured. Squatters are living in the estimated 27,000 apartments left vacant in eastern Berlin by East Germans who have moved west. As a result, the city's two-party coalition government collapses.

The Philippines are hit by a typhoon packing 150-mph winds, killing 112 people and destroying the sugarcane crop, area's principal product.

In Zurich, Switzerland, an Alitalia DC-9 crashes into a mountainside; all 40 passengers and 6 crew members are killed.

Poland and Germany sign treaty guaranteeing their mutual border, after months of doubt by the Polish government that a united Germany would honor their existing border.

**15** Because of its poor human rights record and its opposition to political pluralism, Kenya is denied U.S. military aid for 1991, and a share in the $200 mil. in increased U.S. economic development aid made available to African countries.

Iraq invites International Atomic Energy Agency to inspect its 27.6-pound stock of uranium, the size of an orange, in order to ascertain that it has not been made into a nuclear weapon.

Cable News Network claims that the FBI illegally took confidential material concerning the prosecution of Gen. Manuel Antonio Noriega of Panama and the U.S. government's mishandling of the case from an Atlanta hotel where a CNN reporter was staying.

Space shuttle *Atlantis* launched with a secret military cargo, thought to be a spy satellite for monitoring activities in the Persian Gulf.

Pres. Bush signs Clean Air Act of 1990. An overhaul of the antipollution law to impede acid rain, urban smog, and toxic chemicals, the act requires gas stations to sell cleaner-burning gas, calls for new pollutant-capturing equipment, and sets tighter emission controls for cars.

**16** Five U.S. senators, whose campaigns or causes collected $1.3 mil. from Charles H. Keating, Jr., an executive of the now insolvent Lincoln Savings & Loan Association, defend themselves to the Senate Ethics Committee concerning their conduct and relationship with Keating. "The Keating Five"—John Glenn (D-Ohio), John McCain (R-Ariz.), Donald W. Riegle, Jr. (D-Mich.), Dennis DeConcini (D-Ariz.), and Alan Cranston (D-Calif.)—all deny any wrongdoing.

Agudat Israel party, the Israeli religious party, signs coalition agreement with Prime Minister Yitzhak Shamir, to give Shamir's ruling Likud party an increased majority in parliament and strengthen his hold on power after narrowly surviving several recent no-confidence votes in parliament.

**17** On first U.S. presidential visit to Czechoslovakia, Pres. Bush rings replica of Liberty Bell in Prague before a crowd of 100,000 to mark first anniversary of Czechoslovakian revolution.

Soviet Pres. Mikhail Gorbachev announces adoption of new emergency power structure that centers power in Gorbachev and the Federation Council, made up of the leaders of the 15 repub-

lics, and abolishes post of prime minister. A new security council will oversee army, police, and KGB, in a concentration of power intended to facilitate transition to market economy.

FBI confirms reports of French intelligence spying on foreign offices of IBM and Texas Instruments Corp. between 1987 and 1989 in an effort to gain industry secrets for a French computer company.

**18** In India, 22 are killed by Sikh militants fighting for an independent Sikh nation in Punjab. Continued fighting brings death toll to 170 in 10 days, and more than 2,900 this year.

In Sofia, Bulgaria, 70,000 demonstrators gather to protest government rationing and shortages and to demand the resignation of Prime Minister Andrei Lukanov and his government because of shortages and rationing.

Pres. Saddam Hussein announces that all Western hostages held in Iraq will be released by late March 1991.

**19** Leaders of 34 NATO and Warsaw Pact countries meet in Paris for Conference on Security and Cooperation in Europe and sign an arms-control treaty authorizing destruction of thousands of weapons and declaring that the two groups are no longer enemies and will work to establish friendships.

Pres. Bush vetoes a bill imposing mandatory penalties on nations and companies that promote spread of chemical or biological weapons.

**20** To punish army for human rights abuses, Salvadoran rebels attack military installations, leaving 20 dead and 46 wounded.

**21** Michael R. Milken is sentenced to 10 years in prison for violating federal securities laws, the longest sentence ever received by an executive involved in securities fraud on Wall Street.

Thirty-seven people are reported killed when heavy rain causes their plane to crash on the island of Koh Samui, Thailand.

Ethiopian government asks for more than 800,000 tons of emergency food aid to prevent 4.3 million people from starving in 1991 due to drought conditions and civil war. Government and Eritrean rebels subsequently agree to open rebel-held port of Massawa to UN relief vessels.

**22** British Prime Minister Margaret Thatcher resigns after eleven-and-a-half years in power.

Black and white rebel army troops unsuccessfully attempt a coup in Transkei, South Africa, leaving 17 people dead.

**23** Despite protests by the opposition calling for its resignation, Bulgaria's Socialist government survives a vote of no confidence. Tens of thousands of workers walk off their jobs in protest, shutting down schools, factories, and offices.

**24** In an effort to end 15-year-old civil war and leave Beirut militia-free for first time since 1975, Christian militia begin withdrawing and are replaced by reunified national army.

**25** Lech Walesa, leader of anti-Communist Solidarity labor movement, wins Poland's presidential election, according to early returns.

In Israel, 10 die and at least 24 are wounded in three separate incidents of violence: an Egyptian border policeman kills four Israelis in passing vehicles; a teenage girl blows herself up in a security zone; and Israeli navy sinks a small boat carrying guerrillas from Lebanon toward the Israeli shore.

**26** Lee Kuan Yew, Singapore's only prime minister since independence and longest serving prime minister in the world, resigns after 31 years in power. His chosen successor is Goh Chok Tong.

Indian government imposes curfew in Punjab state after continued violence by Sikh separatists leaves 15 Hindus dead in Jullundur.

Ivory Coast's ruling Democratic party wins an overwhelming majority in parliamentary multiparty elections, ending 30 years of one-party rule.

Railway workers in eastern Germany strike for higher wages and guaranteed jobs. Tens of thousands of workers halt rail traffic around major ports and cause long delays.

MCA Inc. agrees to be acquired by the Matsushita Electric Industrial Co. of Japan for $6.13 bil. plus stock, the largest Japanese purchase of an American company.

**27** John Major, British chancellor of the Exchequer, is chosen to replace Margaret Thatcher as prime minister of Britain.

Soviet government authorizes military to use force to defend military installations, monuments, and servicemen against threats in rebellious republics.

**28** Pres. Collor of Brazil and Pres. Menem of Argentina sign an accord to renounce formally nuclear weapons manufacturing.

Two Liberian rebel factions, a West African peacekeeping force and army officials of the late Pres. Samuel K. Doe, agree to an immediate cease-fire in the yearlong civil war.

Syria and Britain reestablish diplomatic relations, four years after Britain accused Syria of fostering international terrorism and broke off diplomatic ties.

In Dhaka, Bangladesh, 50 people are killed and more than 1,000 wounded in clashes between police and demonstrators calling for resignation of Pres. H.M. Ershad and for lifting his declaration of a state of emergency.

**29** UN Security Council votes to authorize member states to use force to oust Iraqi troops from Kuwait if Iraq does not withdraw by Jan. 15.

Bulgaria's Prime Minister Andrei Lukanov resigns after four days of nationwide anti-Communist strikes and two weeks of street protests.

**30** Pres. Bush invites Iraqi Foreign Minister Tariq Aziz to Washington and stands ready send Secretary of State James A. Baker III to Baghdad for Persian Gulf peace talks.

Twelve white men are arrested in Louis Trichardt, South Africa, in connection with the assault by 30 white men on several hundred black children at Sunday school picnic in a newly desegregated park.

Saudi Arabia, the United Arab Emirates, and Kuwait grant $3 bil. in loans to the USSR to shore up the Soviet economy.

### December 1990

**1** In a flag-waving, champagne-toasting ceremony at 11:11 a.m., 130 ft. below the English Channel, Britain is joined to the European continent by the Chunnel. Begun in 1987, the 31-mile-long car and train tunnel between England and France will open in mid-1993.

Iraq accepts Pres. Bush's offer to send Sec. of State James Baker to Baghdad in an attempt to settle diplomatically the Persian Gulf crisis before the Jan. 15 deadline set by the UN.

Pres. Hissen Habré of Chad and his cabinet flee the country and seek refuge in Cameroon when guerrillas led by Idris Deby march into the capital and take control. The rebel offensive, which began Nov. 10, seeks to transform the political system into a multiparty democracy with general elections to be held within 45 days, as dictated by Chad's constitution. On Dec. 3, Idris Deby dissolves Chad's parliament and suspends the constitution.

One million dollars in gold ingots and cash are stolen by robbers who board a Brinks Inc.-chartered plane in Montreal and flee undetected.

In the latest such action over the last five months, armed government security men and members of Kenya's only political party bulldoze the Kibagare shanty village on the outskirts of Nairobi, leaving 30,000 homeless.

Two Israeli fighter jets launch their second attack in a week, and 20th air strike this year, on Palestinian guerrilla bases in Lebanon, leaving five wounded.

**2** In the first free all-German election since 1932, Chancellor Helmut Kohl of the Christian Democratic party and Foreign Minister Hans-Dietrich Genscher of the Free Democratic party are elected to head a unified Germany.

**3** A Northwest Airlines DC-9 collides with a Northwest 727 on the ground at the Detroit Metropolitan Airport in heavy fog, leaving eight people dead and 22 injured.

Dr. Jack Kevorkian, an advocate of voluntary euthanasia, is arrested in Clarkston, Mich., and charged with first-degree murder of a woman suffering from Alzheimer's disease. In June, Janet Adkins used a device Dr. Kevorkian invented to inject herself with lethal drugs and commit suicide as the doctor watched. Charges are later dropped.

Supreme Court rules that if a criminal suspect requests the assistance of a lawyer, police may not question the suspect further until the lawyer is present; ruling is intended to protect suspects from self-incrimination.

Loyalist troops in and around Buenos Aires, Argentina, retake army headquarters and four other installations, after 12 hours of fighting with approximately 300 army dissidents. Thirteen people are reported dead.

Violence between rival ethnic groups, mainly Zulu and Xhosa, leaves 71 dead in four black townships near Johannesburg, South Africa.

**4** Iraqi officials give permission for all 3,300 Soviet citizens in Iraq to return to the Soviet Union over the next few weeks, contingent on a guarantee by the USSR to compensate Iraq for broken Soviet worker contracts.

U.S. government lifts decade-long ban on blood donations by Haitians and requires that additional questions about a donor's sexual history be answered before donations are accepted.

In an effort to ease credit to businesses and consumers and slow a general economic downturn, the Federal Reserve lowers banks' reserve requirements, the portion of deposits held by banks as cash reserves or interest-free accounts. The move makes an additional $13 bil. available for lending.

Pres. H.M. Ershad of Bangladesh resigns

under pressure from opposition parties after a week of demonstrations and general strikes in which 70 are killed and 500 wounded; Chief Justice Shahabuddin Ahmed is chosen to head the interim government the next day.

Due to concern over the instability of Pres. Gorbachev's government, the American relief agency CARE begins distributing 50,000 packages, each containing a two-week supply of food for one person, in Moscow and Leningrad. Reversing its opposition to aiding the USSR, Japan sends $20 mil. medical aid package to victims of the 1986 Chernobyl nuclear power disaster through the World Health Organization.

In the northern province of Chalatenango, El Salvador, guerrilla troops shoot down a government military plane, marking the second rebel attack in two weeks. Rebels seek a better negotiating position in peace talks to end the 11-year-old civil war, which has claimed 170 lives since Nov. 20, bringing the death toll to 75,000 since 1979. On Dec. 7, the U.S. approves $48.1 mil. in military aid to be sent to the El Salvadoran government.

**5** One year after the U.S. invasion of Panama to oust Gen. Manuel Noriega, 500 American troops help put down a 12-hour rebellion led by a former chief of national police, Col. Eduardo Herrera Hassan, who escaped from prison and seized the police headquarters.

During a blackout in Pétionville, Haiti, seven miles outside Port-au-Prince, five are killed and 43 wounded in a grenade attack and drive-by shooting after a presidential campaign rally for leftist priest Jean-Bertrand Aristide.

**6** Pres. Saddam Hussein of Iraq announces he will free all foreigners held hostage in Iraq and Kuwait, including 2,000 westerners, 900 of whom are Americans.

In Casalecchio, Italy, outside Bologna, a burning military jet crashes into a high school, killing 12 students and injuring 70 others.

A boat carrying traders between fishing communities in Cross River state, Nigeria, capsizes and sinks drowning 60 passengers in the Atlantic Ocean.

**7** American unemployment rises to 5.9%, the highest level since October 1987, after the economy loses more than 250,000 jobs in November.

In Brussels, international negotiations on trading rules, which govern $4 trillion in annual world trade, break off when the U.S. and the European Community resist compromise on issues of European farm subsidies and U.S. trade in financial services.

One week after resignation of Prime Minister Andrei Lukanov, Bulgarian parliament elects political independent Dimitar Popov.

Montgomery, Ala., Federal District Court jury finds *Soldier of Fortune* magazine liable for $12.4 mil. in damages for publishing a "gun for hire" advertisement placed by Richard Savage that resulted in the 1985 death of Richard Braun.

**8** Thailand's Prime Minister Chatichai Choonhavan resigns amid charges of incompetence and corruption. The next day Chatichai is reappointed by King Bhumibol Adulyadej and returns as prime minister.

**9** Solidarity movement leader Lech Walesa is elected president of Poland in a landslide victory.

In continued violence over Hindus' plans to

build a temple on the site of a Muslim mosque in Ayodhya, Hindu-Muslim rioting results in 93 deaths and at least 350 arrests in India.

After a power outage at the 12,000-student Tirana Univ. in Albania, 500 to 1,000 students take part in the first known antigovernment student protest under communist rule.

Colombia's former guerrilla group M-19 wins largest bloc of 70 elected seats in the constitutional convention. In Casa Verde, army troops overrun the rebel Revolutionary Armed Forces command center; 71 are killed.

**10** Congo's governing party ends a seven-day congress, officially abandoning its Marxist ideology and adopting a social democrat platform, after more than two decades of one-party politics.

FDA approves a new birth control device for the first time in 25 years. Norplant consists of hormone-releasing skin implants effective for five years.

Snowstorms and heavy rain across Europe leave 12 dead and 9 missing, and thousands without electricity.

**11** All UN personnel are evacuated from Somalia, after one UN employee is shot in the head during civil war.

A chain-reaction accident involving 75 vehicles on a highway near Calhoun, Tenn., leaves 15 people dead and 50 injured in dense fog.

**12** Pres. Bush approves $1 bil. in federal loans to the USSR for the purchase of food and agricultural goods.

Sec. of Education Lauro F. Cavazos, first ever Hispanic cabinet member, resigns under pressure by the Bush administration.

One day after Albania's Communist party central committee endorses "the creation of independent political organizations" for the first time since 1946, opposition forces form the Democratic party, and two days of rioting follow. The Communist government formally recognizes the Democratic party one week later.

H.M. Ershad, former president of Bangladesh, and his wife are arrested on charges of gold smuggling, plundering money from the nation, and nepotism, and 13 former cabinet officials are sought in connection with similar crimes committed at Mr. Ershad's behest.

**13** In eastern Sicily, an earthquake measuring 5.1 on the Richter scale kills 18 people, injures 200, and causes $400 mil. in damage, leaving up to 2,500 people homeless.

Oliver Tambo, president of the African National Congress, returns to South Africa after 31 years in exile and is greeted by 5,000 supporters.

U.S. Ambassador to Kuwait W. Nathaniel Howell, 31 other Americans, and 96 passengers from Great Britain, Canada, Italy, and Japan fly to Frankfurt, Germany, aboard the last U.S.-sponsored evacuation flight from Iraq and Kuwait.

**14** U.S.-Iraqi peace talks between Sec. of State James Baker and Pres. Saddam Hussein are postponed indefinitely because of a dispute over setting the date.

In Rome, the 12 EC countries agree to give $2.4 bil. in emergency food, medical aid, and technical assistance to the USSR.

Industrial output of the U.S. declines by 1.7% in November, the largest monthly decline in eight years.

In Jaffa, Israel, the stabbing and killing of

three Israeli factory workers sets off widespread anti-Arab rioting.

In Carthage, Mo., a county probate judge issues the authorization for Nancy Beth Cruzan, 33 years old, to be disconnected from the feeding tube on which she has depended since a 1983 car accident left her in a coma. She dies Dec. 26, 1990.

Jim Bakker, head of the now-bankrupt PTL Ministry, is found liable for $130 mil. in damages in a lawsuit filed by 145,000 major contributors.

Lynn Martin, an Illinois congresswoman for 10 years, is named Sec. of Labor.

**15** In response to talks between the South African government and the African National Congress, the EC lifts its ban on new investments in South Africa. At the ANC's first legal conference in Johannesburg in 30 years, 1,600 delegates call for continued sanctions to keep pressure on the government to end apartheid.

**16** In Fez, Morocco, two days of rioting leave 33 people dead, more than 100 injured, and at least 200 arrested. Riots began during a general strike to protest economic hardship.

In Haiti's first democratic national elections, the Rev. Jean-Bertrand Aristide, 37-year-old Roman Catholic priest, is elected president.

*Pioneer 6*, the oldest working spacecraft, marks 25th anniversary since launching Dec. 16, 1965, from Cape Canaveral, Fla. The spacecraft has orbited the sun more than 24 times and traveled 15.4 billion miles.

Brazilian ranchers Darly Alves da Silva and his son are convicted in 1988 murder of environmentalist and union leader Chico Mendes and sentenced to 19 years in prison.

**17** Pres. Bush names Lamar Alexander, former governor of Tennessee, to replace Lauro Cavazos as Sec. of Education and orders department to reverse its ruling that scholarships designated solely for minority students are illegal.

Israeli police block thousands of Palestinians from entering Jerusalem in an attempt to head off violence caused by Arab-Israeli tensions over Israel's planned deportation of four Muslim leaders. In subsequent protests Israeli soldiers shoot and wound 18 Palestinians in the Gaza Strip.

Zambia's Pres. Kenneth Kaunda legalizes opposition parties, after 17 years of one-party rule.

**18** In a move designed to prompt consumers and businesses to borrow more money to spend, invest, and stimulate the sluggish economy, the Federal Reserve reduces the discount rate, the rate the central bank charges for loans to commercial banks, from 7% to 6.5%.

In Jalapa, Nicaragua, 60 former Contra guerrillas seize a police post, leaving 11 dead and 20 wounded. Army soldiers capture most of the guerrillas and regain control of the post.

Following the lead of the U.S., Germany, and the EC, Japan agrees to lend $100 mil. to the USSR to alleviate food shortages.

In light of new evidence and witnesses, Mississippian Byron de la Backwith is charged with the 1963 murder of civil rights leader Medgar Evers for the third time since 1964; two previous trials ended in deadlocked juries.

**19** The Burmese opposition, which won free elections in May but whose leader has been under house arrest since 1989 and prevented from governing, declares a rival government to Myanmar's ruling military regime, which has

been in power since it put down a democracy movement in 1988. The opposition party is subsequently outlawed.

**20** Soviet Foreign Minister Eduard A. Shevardnadze resigns, accusing hard-line reactionaries of leading the USSR toward dictatorship.

UN Security Council adopts a resolution criticizing the Israeli deportation order of four Palestinians and calling on the UN to monitor Palestinians' safety in occupied territories.

Parliamentary approval is given Bulgaria's first multiparty government since 1950. The eight-party government, formed in November, is to rule until elections in mid-1991.

**21** Outgoing Ohio Gov. Richard Celeste grants clemency to 25 women convicted of killing or assaulting husbands or companions who physically abused them.

Between 200,000 and 1.5 million Iraqis participate in a one-day evacuation drill in and around Baghdad and travel to assembly points outside the capital where they will stay in case of war.

In Bucharest, Romania, 20,000 demonstrators rally to honor Romanians killed one year ago during the revolution that ousted Nicolae Ceausescu, and to protest food shortages.

**22** Lech Walesa, founder of the Solidarity movement, is sworn in as Poland's president.

In the Mediterranean Sea, off the Israeli port of Haifa, 21 American sailors are drowned when a ferry carrying 102 crew members of the aircraft carrier *Saratoga* capsizes and sinks.

At the 11th annual summit of the Gulf Cooperation Council, representatives from Saudi Arabia, the UAE, Oman, Qatar, Bahrain, and Kuwait discuss strategies for more effective security and Kuwait's liberation. The GCC's statement calls for Iraq's unconditional withdrawal from Kuwait before Jan. 15, and declares Iraq responsible for compensating Kuwait for looting and plundering.

**23** In an effort to end 20 years of war in Cambodia, the country's four warring factions approve cease-fire and free election provisions of a UN peace plan to be ratified later.

In Slovenia, Yugoslavia, voters overwhelmingly favor independence from federal government in Belgrade, and endorse a six-month plan to take over military, foreign, and monetary policies.

**24** Iraq recalls more than 20 ambassadors from major European countries, the U.S., Japan, and the USSR, among others, for consultations with Pres. Hussein. Ambassadors return to their posts Dec. 27, reasserting that Hussein wants a Persian Gulf resolution linked to a settlement of the Palestinian issue.

Led by Cdr. Ivan Graanoogst, Suriname's army overthrows elected government of Pres. Ramsewak Shankar in a bloodless coup and promises to yield power to an elected government within 100 days.

**25** King Michael of Romania, forced into exile in Switzerland by Communist rulers in 1947, returns to Bucharest for the first time in 43 years with his wife and one daughter for a 24-to-36-hour visit. Authorities, who have denied King Michael's previous requests for entry, expel him after 12 hours.

Voters in Serbia, Yugoslavia's most populous republic, cast ballots in favor of the Socialists (ex-

Communists), electing them to 194 of 250 seats in parliament; it is Serbia's first free vote in 50 years.

Federal employees enjoy raises of between 4.1% and 29.5%; the president is the only federal employee whose salary remains frozen at its present level, $200,000, where it has been for 22 years.

**26** Census Bureau releases official 1990 census figures: U.S. population was 249,632,692 as of Apr. 1, 1990, a 10.2% increase over 1980.

**27** Communist party politburo member and former head of the official labor unions Gennadi I. Yanayev is elected to the newly created post of vice president of the USSR.

In continuing violence by rebel groups attempting to overthrow Pres. Mohammed Siad Barre, in power since 1969, 30 are killed when Somali government troops engage armed gangs after an attack on a fuel depot near Mogadishu.

**28** An electrical explosion in a Brooklyn, N.Y., subway tunnel kills two passengers, injures 149, and traps 1,000 for 40 minutes, as smoke fills a nine-car train during morning rush hour.

U.S. and UK announce they will vaccinate Persian Gulf–based troops against biological weapons, particularly anthrax.

**29** Israeli troops shoot and kill two Palestinians who refuse to stop and be searched in the Gaza Strip. The army later kills two demonstrators and wounds 125 more protesting news of the shooting.

In San Salvador, the guerrilla organization Farabundo Martí National Liberation Front (FNLM) suspends a five-week military campaign to present proposals to the government to end an 11-year civil war.

In Algiers, two army deserters hijack an Air Algeria Boeing 737, force it to land in Annaba, and stage a two-day standoff with authorities before freeing all 88 passengers and crew members and being taken into custody.

**30** In Moscow, police bulldoze a shantytown opposite the Kremlin, inhabited for five months by protestors of Gorbachev's reforms. Officials say it had begun to attract the mentally disturbed and petty criminals.

In Chita, Siberia, tens of thousands riot to protest lack of wine and vodka with which to celebrate the New Year.

**31** In Sidon, Lebanon, predawn Israeli air raid on a PLO headquarters kills 12 guerrillas; it is the 21st such raid on Lebanon this year, leaving 40 dead and 82 wounded.

Fighting between United Somali Congress and presidential guards and security forces moves to area of the presidential residence in Mogadishu, Somalia, while Pres. Mohammed Siad Barre reportedly takes refuge at the airport. Combat between the congress, predominantly members of the Hawiye tribe, and Pres. Barre's troops, mostly from the Marehan tribe, has led to 50,000 deaths over the last 18 months.

## January 1991

**1** Four Palestinians are killed in clashes between Israeli authorities and Palestinian demonstrators in the West Bank and the Gaza Strip on the 26th anniversary of the first military operation by Al Fatah, the main guerrilla group of the PLO.

Czechoslovakia implements new economic program to remove price controls on 85% of goods, close inefficient state enterprises, slow growth of the money supply, and make its currency (the crown) convertible.

Gov. Bruce Sundlun of Rhode Island declares bank emergency and closes 45 privately insured, state-chartered banks and credit unions until federal insurance for their 300,000 deposits worth $1.7 bil. can be arranged.

In Sri Lanka, a cease-fire takes effect after seven months of fighting between Tamil separatist guerrillas and the government.

Under pressure from the Kremlin, Moldavia agrees to modify law making Romanian official language and to consider measures to guarantee equal rights for all ethnic groups; two-thirds of Moldavia's residents speak Romanian.

California imposes ban on the sale of 56 types of semiautomatic weapons and puts into effect a 15-day waiting period for rifle and shotgun purchases; 12,000 people register their semiautomatic weapons before the midnight deadline. There are an estimated 300,000 semiautomatic weapons in private hands in California.

**2** Large U.S. banks cut their prime lending rate to 9.5% to stimulate demand for business and consumer loans.

Three thousand Albanians, mostly ethnic Greeks, cross Mt. Tsamanta into Greece over four days, fleeing Communist rule and economic hardship. Prime Minister Constantine Mitsotakis declares a state of emergency in the frontier region.

A U.S. military helicopter is shot down by Salvadoran leftist guerrillas of the Farabundo Martí National Liberation Front over Lolotique, El Salvador, killing three Americans on board. Members of the FMNL subsequently admit to shooting two of the three airmen; the third died from crash injuries.

FDA approves a new drug, erythropoietin, to treat anemia in people with AIDS; anemia is a common side effect of the AIDS drug AZT.

**3** Sec. of Health and Human Services Louis Sullivan lifts the ban on visitors infected with the AIDS virus, leaving only infectious tuberculosis on the list of diseases that can keep someone from entering the U.S.

Israel opens consulate in Moscow, 24 years after diplomatic relations were broken during the Six-Day War.

After public threats by Iraqis, Great Britain expels eight staff members of the Iraqi Embassy in London, and 67 Iraqi private citizens, mostly students, in the interest of national security.

**4** Iraq accepts U.S. offer for a high-level meeting in Geneva, in last ditch efforts to head off armed conflict.

Polish parliament approves 39-year-old Jan Krzysztof Bielecki, chosen by Pres. Lech Walesa, as youngest prime minister in postwar Polish history in a vote of 276 to 58. Bielecki vows to continue unpopular reforms necessary to achieve market economy.

Speaker pro tem of the South Carolina House Jack Rogers and highway commissioner Wade Crow are indicted on extortion charges, bringing to 13 the number of South Carolina state officials exposed by an FBI undercover operation.

**5** At close of first political trials in connection with 1989 Tienanmen Square demonstrations, seven protestors are sentenced to two-to-four years in jail for inciting "subversion against the People's Government and the overthrowing of the socialist system."

U.S. marines and Italian military personnel rescue nearly 300 foreigners, including 23 Americans, from Italian and American embassies in Mogadishu, Somalia, after they were trapped there for almost a week in the midst of factional fighting; about 250 foreigners remain.

**6** In response to withdrawals of more than $1 bil. in two days, U.S. government seizes Bank of New England and two affiliates, the Connecticut Bank and Trust Co. and the Maine National Bank, and promises to protect all depositors until banks can be sold. The move will cost taxpayers $2.3 bil., the costliest bailout in history.

High winds gusting up to 100 mph in Ireland and Britain leave 28 people dead or lost at sea in 12 separate incidents involving fallen trees and walls, wind-fanned fires, and capsized ships.

Backed by Guatemala's ex-dictator Rios Montt, Jorge Serrano is elected president of Guatemala in runoff elections, defeating publisher Jorge Carpio Nicolle.

**7** Moving to block the February inauguration of president-elect Jean-Bertrand Aristide, Roger Lafontant, a supporter of former Duvalier regime, attempts a coup and takes control of presidential palace in Port-au-Prince, Haiti, for 12 hours and holds outgoing Pres. Ertha Pascal-Trouillot hostage before being arrested by loyalist troops. Violence leaves 44 people dead.

Soviet Defense Ministry announces it will deploy thousands of paratroops to Baltic states of Estonia, Lithuania, and Latvia, and to Armenia, Georgia, Moldavia, and Ukraine to enforce military draft and find deserters. Draft-dodging is popular expression of anti-Soviet sentiment, with only 79% of the draft filled nationwide, 12% in Lithuania and 10% in Georgia.

**8** Pan Am, the third largest U.S. carrier, files for bankruptcy to protect it from creditors while it reorganizes.

In Lithuania, Prime Minister Kazimiera Prunskiene and her cabinet resign in a dispute with parliament and Pres. Vytautas Landsbergis over food-price increases and free-market policies. Concurrently, more than 100 Soviet military vehicles enter the capital, Vilnius, in a show of force for upcoming roundup of draftees.

In Tehran, during highest-level meeting between Iran and Iraq since before their eight-year war, the two countries agree to pull back forces on their mutual border to create a buffer zone about half a mile wide, a move that signals greater normalization of relations even though Iran condemns Iraq's invasion of Kuwait.

Republican party chooses Houston, Tex., as site of their 1992 national convention. Houston city officials expect convention to boost economy by $50 mil. to $100 mil.

**9** After six hours of talks in Geneva, Switzerland, U.S. Sec. of State James Baker and Iraqi Foreign Minister Tariq Aziz fail to agree on peaceful resolution of Persian Gulf crisis.

In Washington, Defense Dept. approves rules for reporters covering Persian Gulf crisis, widely disputed by newspaper and television executives as too strict. Among protested rules are a re-striction that reporters must operate as part of officially designated reporter pools under a military escort and that reports be subject to "security review."

Studies by climatologists in U.S. and Britain find that 1990 was warmest year since measurements of Earth's surface temperature began in 1880, supporting fears of global warming.

South Africa opens its school year with admittance of black students to 195 previously all-white public schools, one-tenth of South Africa's white public schools, as a result of a vote by parents of schools' white students.

**10** Ohio Gov. Richard F. Celeste commutes sentences of 11 prisoners, including eight convicted murderers on death row (commuted to life imprisonment), four days before leaving office. Incoming Ohio Attorney General Lee Fisher subsequently challenges action.

During a Belgrade meeting of Yugoslavian republic leaders, Slobodan Milosevic warns that if Yugoslavia becomes a confederation of independent states, Serbia will demand additional territory to unite the country's 8.5 million Serbs in a single state.

In Athens, four people are killed and more than 100 injured when Greek high school students and leftists clash with police in violent protests over educational changes introduced by the government to provide students with more work, less free time, and more discipline.

**11** In Vilnius, Lithuania, Soviet troops storm press center and civilian militia building with tanks and live ammunition, leaving seven people injured. Subsequent raids on police, telephone, and railroad installations are met with Lithuanian resistance in the form of truck barricades and human chains.

**12** In Brooklyn, N.Y., civil rights advocate Rev. Al Sharpton is stabbed in the chest at outset of march to protest light sentences for white defendants in the Yousef Hawkins murder trial of eight youths, only one of whom was convicted of murder. Sharpton's wound is not life threatening.

Congress votes to give Pres. Bush authority to use military force against Iraq pursuant to UN Security Council Resolution 678.

In Sebokeng, South Africa, gunmen suspected to be a local criminal gang or Inkatha members kill 35 people and wound 40 as they fire automatic weapons at mourners during a vigil for an African National Congress youth organizer slain a week ago.

**13** In Vilnius, Lithuania, Soviet Army seizes power for Communist party loyalist National Salvation Committee. Using tanks and machine guns, the committee captures state broadcast studios and transmitter, declares a curfew, bans public gatherings, tape recorders, and television cameras, and imposes personal searches and random document checks. Overnight violence between independence-minded Lithuanians and pro-Communists leaves 15 people dead and more than 100 wounded. Pres. Gorbachev blames leaders of separatist Lithuanian parliament for violence but disavows any prior knowledge of army attack.

In a last-minute effort to avoid conflict in Persian Gulf, UN Secretary General Javier Pérez de Cuéllar meets with Iraqi Pres. Hussein in

Baghdad, but no progress is made.

In Orkney, South Africa, a soccer game between two black teams from Soweto ends in violence, as fans clash over a referee's decision; 40 people are killed and 50 injured.

**14** In Baghdad, Iraqi parliament votes unanimously to follow Pres. Hussein into combat against coalition forces.

PLO leaders Saleh Khalef, second in command behind Yasir Arafat, and chief of security Hayel Abdel-Hamid are shot and killed in Tunis by a bodyguard, three days after slaying of another PLO leader, Khalil al-Wazir.

Jorge Serrano is sworn in as president of Guatemala, in first transfer of power from one elected civilian leader to another. Serrano is also first protestant elected president in Latin America.

**15** Deadline for withdrawal of Iraqi forces from Kuwait passes, as last-minute peace initiatives fail.

In Bogotá, Colombia, Jorge Luis Ochoa, second in command in the Medellín cocaine cartel, surrenders in exchange for government promise not to extradite him to U.S. to face drug charges.

**16** Operation Desert Storm begins at 6:30 p.m. (EST) as U.S. and allied forces attack Iraq and Kuwait by air. Oil prices immediately jump by $3 a barrel in cash trading at stock exchanges. Israel declares a state of emergency minutes after word of allied attack.

**17** Turkish parliament authorizes U.S. to launch strikes from its base in Incirlik, opening a second front for air attacks against Iraq.

Members of Spacewatch team at Univ. of Arizona observe an asteroid measuring 30 feet in diameter pass by Earth at a distance of 106,000 miles, less than half the distance to the Moon; it is the closest asteroid ever observed passing safely by Earth.

**18** In retaliation for allied air attacks on Iraq and Kuwait, seven Iraqi missiles hit Israel from Tel Aviv to Haifa, wounding seven people. Iraqi missile launched against Saudi Arabia is intercepted by a Patriot antimissile rocket before it strikes Dhahran. Allied air attacks cut electricity, telephone, and water services in Baghdad.

Eastern Airlines, eighth-largest airline in U.S., flies for last time, begins to sell off its planes and other assets, and immediately dismisses 5,000 of its 18,000 workers.

As part of upcoming trial of Panamanian Gen. Manuel Noriega, federal prosecutors disclose that CIA and U.S. Army paid Gen. Noriega $322,000 in cash and gifts over 31 years.

Peabody Coal, the largest U.S. coal company, pleads guilty to criminal charges of tampering with safety devices used to measure concentrations of dust that may cause black lung disease in mines in West Virginia, Kentucky, and Illinois, and agrees to pay $500,000 in fines. In 1982, the company pleaded guilty to similar charges and paid $130,000 in fines.

Albania's first legal Muslim service since 1967 is held at Tirana's Etem Bey mosque to a crowd of hundreds inside the mosque and 15,000 onlookers outside.

Lithuanian government resumes television broadcasting from inside parliament building where independence leaders are barricaded. Although range of a newly constructed antenna

is limited to downtown Vilnius, it is the only means by which the independence government can relay its version of recent insurgence by Soviet army, which demands resignation of the republic's government.

**19** Iraq attacks Tel Aviv for second time with conventional explosives, injuring only a few.

National Liberation Army ELN guerrillas attack workers building an oil pipeline for French consortium 200 miles northwest of Bogotá, Colombia, take 104 hostages, including four French nationals, and burn machinery, causing $2.5 mil. in property damage.

**20** In continuing violence over Latvian independence, 50 to 100 "black berets" of the Soviet Interior Ministry raid a Latvian Interior Ministry building in Riga, killing five people and wounding nine in a 90-minute gun battle.

Iraqi television broadcasts taped interviews with seven allied pilots shot down and taken prisoner. The pilots, from the U.S., Britain, Italy, and Kuwait, are heard stating their names, ages, and denouncing "aggression against peaceful Iraq." U.S. protests to Iraq's chargé d'affaires in Washington that Iraq's treatment of U.S. prisoners of war contravenes Geneva Convention.

In Zagreb, Yugoslavia, special police units take up positions across Croatia to defend independence-minded republic against possible attack by Yugoslav army.

In Moscow, 100,000 demonstrators protest Pres. Gorbachev's bloody crackdown in Latvia, calling for resignation of Gorbachev and his military and state security ministers. Protests are also reported in Leningrad, Kiev, Sverdlovsk, Donetsk, Kishinev, and Kaliningrad.

**21** Iraq announces that more than 20 POWs have been moved to civilian, educational, scientific, and economic targets as "human shields" to deter allied attack.

During emergency landing to refuel in Burgas, Bulgaria, police capture hijacker of a Soviet plane carrying 159 passengers and crew.

Three teenagers are trampled to death in surge of a crowd watching a heavy-metal group, AC/DC, perform in Salt Lake City.

**22** Iraqi troops set fire to two Kuwaiti oil refineries and an oil field near Kuwait/Saudi Arabia border. U.S. forces attack and sink two Iraqi ships, including a mine-laying vessel.

Iraqi Scud missile attack on Israel leaves three people dead, 70 wounded, and 20 apartment buildings damaged in Tel Aviv suburb.

In protest of Moscow crackdown on Baltic republics, European Parliament delays $1 bil. EC food-aid package and $550 mil. technical assistance agreement for USSR.

In an attempt to control the black market for commodities and to stabilize prices, Soviet government withdraws from circulation all 50- and 100-ruble notes, which account for more than one-third of money in circulation.

**23** In district capital of Ruhengeri, Rwanda, foreigners are evacuated as government forces and 400 to 600 rebels led by exiled members of Rwanda's minority Tutsi tribe battle for control of the city.

The Cuban- and Soviet-backed Marxist Angolan government accepts in principle a peace plan outlined by Portuguese, Soviet, and U.S. diplomats that will end the 15-year-old civil war

against the U.S.-backed guerrilla movement.

Germany pledges $165 mil. to Israel for humanitarian aid after Iraqi attacks, and additional funds to support the anti-Iraq alliance in the Persian Gulf.

Under investigation for overcharging U.S. government by millions of dollars for research over the last decade, Stanford Univ. announces it will refund about $500,000 of government research money used for maintenance of the university president's home.

**24** Iraq closes its border with Jordan, cutting off escape route for refugees and thousands of foreigners. A four-man CBS News crew is reported missing since Jan. 21 near Kuwait/Saudi border.

In Atlanta, the Federal Centers for Disease Control reports that 100,777 people in the U.S. have died from AIDS, a third of them in 1990, and projects that of the one million Americans now infected with the virus that causes AIDS, 165,000 to 215,000 will die by the end of 1993.

**25** Iraq releases millions of gallons of Kuwaiti crude oil into Persian Gulf.

For fifth time in eight days, Iraq attacks Israel at Haifa and Tel Aviv, killing one and wounding 42 when shrapnel from midair explosions falls to the ground. In Riyadh, Saudi Arabia, Iraqi Scud missiles destroy two office buildings and kill at least one person.

Gov. Norman Bangerter of Utah signs into law the strictest antiabortion measure in the U.S., allowing abortion only in cases of rape or incest, threatened damage to pregnant woman's health, or to prevent birth of a child with defects.

U.S. Dept. of Commerce reports that GNP dropped 2.1% for fourth quarter of 1990, the largest quarterly contraction in eight years.

In Guarne, Colombia, Diana Turbay, magazine publisher and daughter of former Pres. Julio César Turbay, is shot and killed by police officers in an attempt to rescue her from Medellín cartel kidnappers who held her captive for five months. The cartel releases television cameraman Richard Becerra but still holds three other journalists.

**26** In Somalia, United Somali Congress rebels claim control of Mogadishu, after forcing Pres. Mohammed Siad Barre to flee presidential palace minutes before rebels seized it; he had ruled for 21 years.

U.S. forces bomb two manifolds that regulate flow of oil entering pipelines in the Persian Gulf, in an effort to stem the flow of oil.

In Beijing, eight leading dissidents are sentenced to two-to-seven years in prison on charges of counterrevolutionary propaganda and incitement during the Tiananmen democracy movement in mid-1989; 66 others are released.

In Dhaka, Bangladesh, former Pres. H.M. Ershad—ousted from power in December 1990—is arrested and charged with possession of illegal arms, an offense punishable by up to 20 years.

**27** After 80 Iraqi warplanes fly to Iran to seek sanctuary and protect planes for future action, Iran announces it will hold planes until end of conflict.

**28** In Mogadishu, rebels in control of Somali capital announce formation of broad-based democratic government.

Iraq announces that allied bombing has killed at least 324 civilians and wounded 416, and holds UN Secretary General Pérez de Cuéllar personally responsible.

**29** South Africa's two largest black political movements, the African National Congress and Inkatha Freedom party, agree to end their rivalry, declare that both political organizations have the right to exist independently, and call for mutual tolerance by supporters. This marks first time in nearly three decades that Nelson Mandela and Chief Mangosuthu Gatsha Buthelezi, the rival parties' leaders, have met.

Pres. Bush delivers his second State of the Union Message, promising Americans that the country will overcome Saddam Hussein and domestic economic woes.

In Window Rock, Ariz., Peter MacDonald, chairman of the Navajo Nation for 16 years during the 1970s and 1980s, is convicted in tribal court of bribery, fraud, conspiracy, and ethics violations in connection with a plot to influence tribe to buy a ranch for an inflated price, for which he was to receive an $850,000 payoff.

**30** In first sustained ground combat of Persian Gulf war, Iraqi tank battalions attack allied positions near Kuwait border before being driven back by U.S. Marines and Arab infantry to coastal town of Khafji; 12 marines are killed and 2 wounded, the first allied ground troops to fall. After 36 hours of combat, Iraq surrenders Khafji and 400 prisoners are taken, leaving 200 Iraqis dead and wounded in the fighting.

In Bogotá, Colombia, members of Medellín drug cartel, the "Extraditables," suspend their all-out war against the government after Pres. Gaviria extends date for lenient court treatment of surrendering drug cartel leaders.

During first formal talks between Japan and North Korea to establish normal relations in Pyongyang, North Korea, Japan apologizes for its harsh colonial rule from 1910 to 1945, but refuses to compensate North Korea for economic hardships over the last 80 years.

For second consecutive day, Israeli troops and Palestinian guerrillas battle in southern Lebanon, as PLO fires dozens of rockets toward northern Israel for first time since Yasir Arafat announced he was giving up terrorism two years ago.

**31** Yugoslav authorities return 368 Albanian refugees who crossed into Yugoslavia to escape economic hardship under the Communist government, which reportedly imprisons escapees for up to three years. More than 1,000 people demonstrate in Tirana, Albania, calling for resignation of Foreign Minister Reis Malile.

State Dept. officials in Washington disclose that 11 acts of terrorism against U.S. and allied interests outside the U.S. were committed over the past 24 hours, bringing the total to 70 acts since the Persian Gulf war began.

### February 1991

**1** South African Pres. F.W. de Klerk announces that racial discrimination laws, particularly the Land Acts of 1913 and 1936, Group Areas Act of 1966, and Black Communities Act of 1984, will be repealed.

After unemployment rate rises to 6.2% in January, the highest since 1987, Federal Reserve sharply reduces interest rates; in response large banks reduce prime rate.

In Los Angeles, a collision between a landing USAir jet and a commuter plane waiting to take off leaves 29 dead and 30 injured; 67 USAir passengers survive. The collision occurs when an air traffic controller tells the two planes to use the same runway.

An earthquake measuring 6.8 on Richter scale hits Pakistan, killing 300, injuring 500, and destroying 100 houses along Afghanistan border.

Government-decreed joint patrols of police and army soldiers begin throughout USSR, a move met with resistance by governments of Lithuania, Armenia, Georgia, Moldavia, and Estonia. Within five days there are 5,000 arrests, mainly for hooliganism, and joint patrols expand to include 86 cities nationwide.

**2** American Persian Gulf command announces it has rendered useless the Iraqi Navy, comprised of 55 attack boats, 46 of which are destroyed or heavily damaged.

**3** An Iraqi Scud missile is destroyed near Riyadh, Saudi Arabia; falling debris injures 29 people. A U.S. B-52 crashes into the Indian Ocean; three crewmen are rescued.

In Rabat, Morocco, 300,000 people rally in support of Iraq and Saddam Hussein, burning U.S., British, French, and Israeli flags; 1,700 Moroccan troops are in Persian Gulf to fight against Iraq.

Prime Minister Chandra Shekhar and dismisses leader of southern Indian state of Tamil Nadu, and brings state under direct control of New Delhi. It is the fourth such action in three months, in an attempt by Rajiv Gandhi's Congress party to deprive opposition parties of their bases before the next election.

**4** Iran's Pres. Hashemi Rafsanjani offers to mediate peace talks between U.S. and Iraq; there is no reaction from Iraq, and U.S. says it will stop war only when Iraq complies with 12 UN resolutions.

Because of decreasing water levels, all water from California State Water Project is cut off to 15% of farmers in state's Central Valley.

Trial of Winnie Mandela and seven supporters charged with 1988 kidnapping and assault of four Soweto youths—one of whom was later found dead—opens in Johannesburg, South Africa.

**5** Attempting to convince Colombian government troops to withdraw from Revolutionary Armed Forces of Colombia headquarters it seized in December, guerrilla rebels launch attacks throughout Colombia; 40 rebels, civilians, and policemen are killed.

Israel attacks Palestinian guerrilla camps near Sidon, Lebanon, where an estimated 6,000 PLO fighters are entrenched, leaving 12 dead and 30 wounded. After subsequent attacks, 1,000 Lebanese army troops move in to defend area for first time in 13 years, and to urge Israel to abandon its occupation of its "security zone" in southern Lebanon.

**6** It is disclosed that information about terrorist activities in Syria supplied by U.S. to the Damascus government led to death of Israeli agents working among Syrian terrorist groups last fall.

Pres. Bush authorizes direct shipment of emergency medical supplies to Estonia, Latvia, Lithuania, and the Ukraine, in an attempt to court opposition leaders and send a message to Kremlin that the U.S. disagrees with Pres. Gorbachev's

treatment of independence-minded republics.

King Hussein of Jordan ends neutrality in the Persian Gulf war and publicly backs Iraq.

**7** IRA attacks British Prime Minister John Major's Downing Street offices, where cabinet is in session. Three are wounded after three mortar rounds are fired from a nearby van.

Father Jean-Bertrand Aristide, a Roman Catholic priest, is inaugurated as Haiti's first democratically elected president in 186 years of independence.

Soviet space station *Salyut 7* turns into huge fireball upon entering Earth's atmosphere, breaks apart, and falls to Earth in a trash dump in southern Argentina. Eyewitnesses say bulk of the craft fell into Atlantic Ocean.

Senate unanimously confirms former Rep. Lynn Martin (R-Ill.) as new sec. of labor.

**8** After an attack on an Israeli bus in which four soldiers are wounded, three Jordanian infiltrators are hunted down and killed.

**9** Defense Sec. Dick Cheney and Joint Chiefs Chairman Gen. Colin L. Powell meet with U.S. field commanders in Saudi Arabia to discuss timing for start of combined air-ground campaign.

Iraqi Scud missile hits a Tel Aviv neighborhood, wounding 26 people and damaging 150 homes after it is intercepted by a Patriot defense missile in midflight.

In a republic-wide plebiscite, Lithuanians vote 9-to-1 in favor of independence from the Kremlin.

In Durres, Albania, 10,000 people hoping to flee Albania and cross the Adriatic Sea by ferry to Italy, but lacking visas, tickets, and other travel documents, clash with police; two are killed.

In South Africa, 30,000 police make 11,361 arrests in a 10-hour period for crimes ranging from murder to cattle theft.

**10** African National Congress gunmen ambush Inkatha Freedom party motorcade outside Pietermaritzburg, South Africa, killing 17 and wounding 29, in worst violence in Natal Province since ANC and Inkatha reached a peace accord on Jan. 29.

**11** On opening day of Winnie Mandela's trial on charges of kidnapping and assault in 1988, a main witness against Mandela disappears and is presumed kidnapped.

After 46 years on display at a military college in Lexington, Va., a 15th-century bronze bell, a Japanese national symbol, is to be returned to Naha, Okinawa, where it was seized by marines in World War II.

**12** Soviet special envoy Yevgeny M. Primakov delivers plea from Pres. Gorbachev to Pres. Hussein of Iraq to withdraw from Kuwait and conform with UN resolutions. Hussein states he is willing to cooperate with USSR to end war, but makes no mention of a withdrawal.

In Beijing, two democracy advocates receive sentences of 13 years in prison, the longest sentences to date for protestors associated with 1989 Tienanmen Square demonstrations.

**13** American Stealth fighter-bombers hit a residential neighborhood in Baghdad and kill 400 civilians housed in a single building. Iraq claims building is a civilian air raid shelter, while U.S. officials identify it as a military communications center. Bombers hit two buses in Kuwait and Iraq, killing 60 civilians bound for Jordan.

In Mexico, 36 worshipers die and 25 are injured as they try to cram into an Ash Wednesday mass at Sanctuary of Our Lord of Chalma church, celebrated for a miracle-working icon it houses.

**14** Cuba and Yemen propose Persian Gulf peace plan at UN, calling for a halt to allied bombing and formation of a Security Council commission to explore means of ending conflict and report their findings to the council by Feb. 25.

In light of recent civilian casualties in Iraq, USSR becomes increasingly critical of anti-Iraq forces in Saudi Arabia, asserting that they may have gone beyond UN mandate.

In Miami, Amet Paredes, a codefendant of Gen. Manuel Noriega, pleads guilty to conspiracy to distribute and import 732 pounds of cocaine into U.S. in 1985 and 1986 and agrees to testify against Noriega.

**15** In southern Lebanon, battles between two rival camps within the PLO loyal to Yasir Arafat leave 17 dead and 40 wounded. A subsequent trial leads to the execution of 20 guerrillas who participated in a mutiny.

In Thailand, 100 people are killed, 86 injured, and 50 homes destroyed when a tractor-trailer carrying dynamite explodes after it overturns.

**16** In Bogotá, Colombia, Medellín cocaine ring drug trafficker Juan David Ochoa follows lead of his two brothers, and surrenders to authorities in exchange for lenient treatment, including no extradition to the U.S.

In Kabul, eight civilians are killed by missiles in fighting between guerrillas and Soviet-backed government of Afghanistan.

A car bomb explodes after a bullfight in Medellín, Colombia, killing 22 and injuring 176. Police blame hired assassins for drug traffickers.

**17** Iraqi Foreign Minister Tariq Aziz travels to Moscow for peace talks.

**18** IRA bombs two central London railroad stations, Victoria and Paddington, leaving one dead and 40 wounded in IRA's first civilian-targeted attack in seven years.

In effort to postpone an all-out ground offensive by anti-Iraqi forces, Soviet Pres. Gorbachev presents Iraq with another peace plan, including unconditional Iraqi withdrawal from Kuwait, a pledge of Soviet aid in preserving Iraq's sovereignty, and a call for Middle East peace conference.

On the Amherst, Mass., town common, a man carrying a cardboard peace sign sets himself on fire in protest of Persian Gulf war and dies.

**19** Pres. Bush states that Soviet peace plan falls short of what would be required for a ceasefire. Tariq Aziz returns to Baghdad.

Accusing him of amassing "absolute personal power" and "deceiving the people" with a failed plan for national renewal, Russia's Pres. Boris Yeltsin calls for Soviet Pres. Gorbachev's immediate resignation and demands Gorbachev turn power over to new Federation Council.

Maryland Gov. W.D. Schaefer commutes sentences of eight women convicted of killing men who abused them; the women claimed they acted in self-defense.

**20** USSR awaits Iraq's reply to Soviet ceasefire proposal, but U.S. and UK call proposal inadequate since it lacks a timetable for Iraqi withdrawal from Kuwait and Iraqi compliance with all UN Security Council resolutions.

Arguing that it shoulders an unfair burden of expenses for federal operations, the parliament of Yugoslavia's relatively affluent republic of Slovenia passes resolution to take over banking and defense functions from central government.

U.S. approves a $400 mil. loan guarantee to Israel earmarked for construction of housing for Soviet Jewish immigrants with stipulation that it not be used for housing in Gaza Strip, East Jerusalem, or West Bank.

**21** Prince al-Waleed bin Talal of Saudi Arabia agrees to invest $590 mil. in Citicorp, becoming largest single shareholder in largest U.S. banking company; he agrees not to try to take control of the company.

As thousands of Albanians demonstrate in the streets, destroying statues and symbols of former Stalinist dictator Enver Hoxha, Pres. Ramiz Alia takes personal control of Albanian government and promises to replace cabinet.

In Yugoslavia, Croatian parliament adopts measures giving the republic's government veto power over federal laws that threaten its sovereignty, and calls for federal authorities to rescind an order demanding that Croatian paramilitary units disband.

**22** In Moscow, Soviet officials announce that Pres. Hussein agrees to withdraw from Kuwait on second day after a cease-fire. Pres. Bush registers "serious concerns" about the peace plan, and gives Hussein 24 hours to withdraw from Kuwait or face a ground attack.

In effort to calm anti-Communist unrest that resulted in four deaths after a clash between security forces and civilians in Tirana, Albania's Pres. Ramiz Alia appoints caretaker government to serve until national elections Mar. 31.

**23** Army Day in Moscow is marked by a rally of 30,000 soldiers denouncing nation's democratic opposition and calling on them to stop interfering with Gorbachev.

Military forces in Thailand led by Gen. Sunthorn Kongsompong overthrow the elected government of Prime Minister Chatichai Choonhavan, accusing it of corruption and protecting enemies of monarchy. Gen. Sunthorn assumes position of prime minister, imposes martial law, and abolishes 1978 constitution.

**24** After Pres. Hussein fails to respond to Pres. Bush's deadline for withdrawal from Kuwait, thousands of allied tanks, troops, and helicopters enter Iraq and Kuwait from Saudi Arabia before dawn as ground war begins.

About 40,000 people march in Moscow to demand resignation of Soviet Pres. Gorbachev and show support for Russian republic Pres. Boris Yeltsin.

**25** Iraqi Scud missile destroys a U.S. barracks in Dhahran, Saudi Arabia, killing 28 and wounding 90, including the first three women to die in the war.

In Budapest, Warsaw Pact signs an agreement to dissolve itself by Mar. 31, after 36 years as a military alliance.

In one of the largest private "debt for nature" swaps to date, Mexico agrees to help preserve its Lacandona rain forest and other natural resources in exchange for reduction of its foreign debt by $4 mil.; it is helped by U.S. group Conservation International.

**26** Pres. Hussein announces Iraq is withdrawing from Kuwait and troops will be gone by day's end, but does not mention UN resolutions nor say they will lay down their arms. Allied forces press their attack and liberate Kuwait City after a two-day battle over Kuwait International Airport.

USSR and South Africa reestablish relations, agreeing to open "interest sections" in each other's capitals. USSR vows to reestablish full diplomatic relations with South Africa, severed in 1955, when apartheid is completely abolished.

In French Indian Ocean possession of Réunion, eight people are killed, cars overturned, and store windows broken when rioters protest closing of a pirate television station that broadcasts sex and karate films. About 440 paramilitary reinforcements and riot police officers are dispatched from France to help quell violence.

**27** Pres. Hussein agrees to give up all claims to Kuwait, release prisoners, and make war reparations in return for cease-fire and lifting of international sanctions. Pres. Bush later declares Kuwait liberated and Iraq defeated, and orders a halt to the 100-hour ground war.

At conclusion of a 14-month investigation of the "Keating five," Sen. Alan Cranston (D-Calif.) is singled out by the Senate Ethics Committee for disciplinary action by full Senate for his dealings with contributions from savings and loan executive Charles H. Keating, Jr.

In Bangladesh, Khaled Zia, widow of former Pres. Gen Ziaur Rahman, assassinated in 1981, and her Bangladesh Nationalist party win 140 of 330 parliamentary seats in national elections.

**28** In eastern Germany, about 20,000 workers strike for a second day to protest high unemployment and low wages. German government vows to raise taxes beginning in July to speed economic recovery.

### March 1991

**1** For the first time in their 10-year campaign against the government, Salvadoran guerrilla leaders from Farabundo Martí National Liberation Front (FMLN) order their forces not to interfere with upcoming national elections. In Chalatenango, 17 government soldiers and six guerrillas are killed when FMLN attacks country's main hydroelectric plant, leaving north and central El Salvador without power for several hours.

After 23 years of military insurgency in Colombia, 2,000 members of Popular Liberation Army lay down their arms in exchange for two political seats in 73-member national government assembly; it is the third guerrilla group to make such a deal with the government in order to take part in a revision of Colombia's 104-year-old constitution.

**2** Units of Yugoslavia's Federal Army are sent to Croatia to protect Serbian minority after violence erupts between Croatian security forces and Serbian villagers who seized police station.

In Colombo, Sri Lanka, a car bomb explodes and kills 19 people, including Deputy Defense Minister Ranjan Wijeratne, head of the government campaign against Tamil separatists.

CBS News correspondent Bob Simon and his three-man crew are freed after Soviet Pres. Mikhail Gorbachev appeals to Pres. Saddam Hussein for their release; the four were held in Baghdad for 41 days.

**3** During a two-hour meeting in Safwan, Iraq, between eight Iraqi military leaders and allied generals, Iraq agrees formally to end Persian Gulf war by promising to return all prisoners and Kuwaiti civilian detainees and comply with all UN resolutions. In southeastern Iraq, civil unrest erupts as anti-Hussein Shiite Muslim forces and deserting soldiers battle Republican Guard troops around Basra.

Sudafed, a cold remedy, is recalled nationwide after two people die and one becomes ill from taking cyanide-laced capsules in Washington state.

Latvians and Estonians vote overwhelmingly for independence from Moscow, with 77% favoring self-rule in both republics.

Pres. Elias Hrawi of Lebanon forbids Palestinian guerrillas to mount missile attacks on Israel from southern Lebanon, where 3,000 government soldiers have been deployed since mid-February to protect Lebanese citizens from Palestinian-Israeli violence.

In Colorado Springs, Colo., a United 737 jet crashes in high, gusty winds into a park four miles from the airport and kills all 25 people aboard.

In Los Angeles, a home videotape captures three police officers beating Rodney Glen King, a handcuffed and prone suspect, after the suspect is stopped for speeding, while other officers look on. The officers hit the suspect 53 to 56 times with nightsticks, and kicked him at least seven times. The three officers who beat King, who was not resisting arrest, face felony criminal charges of assault, and all 15 officers present face departmental charges of neglect of duty. The incident results in a grand jury investigation and sparks public complaints of racial discrimination against blacks and other minorities by police; public calls for resignation of Los Angeles Chief of Police Daryl Gates.

**4** In Baghdad, 10 allied prisoners, including six Americans, are released by Iraq, the first group released since end of Persian Gulf war.

**5** Baghdad voids annexation of Kuwait and agrees to return Kuwait assets of gold, currency, airliners, and art in keeping with allied conditions of permanent cease-fire; 35 prisoners are released in Baghdad. In southern Iraq, 36 journalists covering civil strife disappear.

U.S. and Israel agree on aid package to deliver $650 mil. in cash to help cover Israeli military and civil defense expenses.

Philadelphia family court judge grants city health officials right to immunize six children belonging to Faith Tabernacle Congregation against measles and requires member families to report incidence of disease and undergo monthly examinations by public health doctors. Since Jan. 1, 500 cases of measles have been reported in the city, and five children of Faith Tabernacle Congregation, which shuns medical treatment, have died of the disease.

**6** Following boycott of Indian parliament by Rajiv Gandhi's Congress party because of police surveillance of Gandhi's home, Prime Minister Chandra Shekhar and his minority government resign and call for general elections.

In Soviet Georgia, ethnic fighting between minority Ossetians and Georgian militants leaves 37 people dead and 150 wounded.

A Línea Aeropostal Venezolana DC-9 veers off course and crashes in Andes in western Venezuela, killing all 43 on board.

The Trinidadian tank barge *Vesta Bella* sinks off St. Kitts and spews 570,000 gallons of oil into the Caribbean for a month. Oil fouls beaches on St. Kitts, Nevis, St. Thomas, St. John and Tortola, St. Croix, Antigua, St. Barthélemy, St. Martin, and Saba.

**7** Approximately 1,000 of 7,000 Kuwaitis arrested or kidnapped and held in Iraq are released in an exchange of prisoners with Iraq.

Sec. of State James Baker begins Middle East peace initiative, with visits to Saudi Arabia, Egypt, Israel, Syria, Kuwait, Turkey, and the USSR.

Washington expands list of chemical or biological arms ingredients subject to export control from 11 to 50 and designates the entire Middle East and southwest Asia for special scrutiny.

More than 90 exiled African National Congress supporters, including leader of South African Communist party, Joe Slovo, return to South Africa from Zambia, in first wave of returns since Pres. F.W. de Klerk legalized opposition groups last year.

Military junta in Thailand appoints Anand Panyarachun as interim prime minister to lead country until new constitution can be drafted.

House of Representatives votes to appropriate additional $15 bil. for Persian Gulf war to pay for domestic costs, Israeli aid, veteran pensions, military health care, and nuclear-waste cleanup, among other programs, to augment the $4.3 bil. already appropriated by congress and $54.5 bil. in pledges from other countries.

**8** Labor Dept. announces that U.S. unemployment reached 6.5% in February, the highest rate in four years, and that 450,000 individuals lost their jobs in February.

In Soviet republics of Kazakhstan and Ukraine, coal miners strike to demand higher wages, better working conditions, and earlier retirement, and demand Pres. Gorbachev surrender power to independence-minded republics.

In light of civil unrest in Iraq, Iranian Pres. Ali-Akbar Rafsanjani denounces Iraqi Pres. Hussein and calls for his resignation.

Peru receives 35 tons of medicine from the U.S. to fight cholera epidemic responsible for 259 deaths. The epidemic, spread by consuming contaminated fish and unboiled water, has infected 55,000 people in Latin America.

**9** In Belgrade, Yugoslavia, army and police clash with 100,000 antigovernment demonstrators demanding resignation of Serbian Pres. Milosevic and his Socialist party

In the black township Alexandra near Johannesburg, South Africa, factional fighting breaks out between African National Congress and Inkatha Freedom party. Violence results in seven deaths and threatens truce agreed upon by ANC and Inkatha leaders in late January.

Israeli troops fire on Palestinian protesters on strike in Israeli-occupied Gaza Strip to mark 39 months of revolt against occupation, leaving 55 wounded.

**10** In Riyadh, Saudi Arabia, eight Arab countries agree to support Pres. Bush's Middle East peace plan, encompassing a larger American military presence, economic development programs, and arms control agreements; they disagree only about Arab-Israeli peace talks.

In Moscow, more than 100,000 supporters of Russian Republic Pres. Boris Yeltsin march to

demand Pres. Gorbachev's resignation and call for defeat of upcoming unity referendum.

Benin holds first free presidential election in 30 years; Marxist-Leninist Pres. Brig. Gen. Mathieu Kérékou could become first African president to be forced from power by popular vote since independence movements of 1960s. Close election returns necessitate a runoff election between Kérékou and Prime Minister Nicephore Soglo.

Four Israeli women are stabbed to death and one other wounded in West Jerusalem by a Palestinian claiming he wants to send a message to U.S. Sec. of State James Baker on eve of his visit to discuss Arab-Israeli peace talks.

El Salvador's governing right-wing Arena party wins legislative elections but loses majority in National Assembly, and leftist FMLN wins right to enter legislature for first time after 11 years of civil war.

**11** Six Arab guerrillas armed with automatic rifles, rocket-propelled grenade launchers, and dynamite enter Israel from Jordan and are shot and killed by Israeli troops during a two-hour gun battle near kibbutz Tirat Zvi.

Iraqi officials report that 500 Shiite fighters and civilians are killed in two days of battles with troops loyal to Pres. Hussein near holy city of Karbala, south of Baghdad. In Iraq's northern Kurdish region, 5,000 Kurds are used as human shields to deter attack on oil city of Kirkuk, after Kurdish rebels seize the oil town of Khanaqin.

Under pressure to disclose U.S. government-approved exports to Iraq of goods that may be used for weapons, the Commerce Dept. makes public a list of $500 mil. in advanced American manufactured goods, including computers and lasers, sold to Iraqi government agencies and private concerns since 1985.

**12** Exxon agrees to plead guilty to criminal charge and pay $100 mil. fine (largest ever paid for pollution), as part of $1.1 bil. settlement for *Exxon Valdez* oil spill; fine will be paid over 10 years and covers suits brought by U.S. and state of Alaska. At least 330 separate suits brought by fishermen and environmentalists are pending.

South African Pres. de Klerk introduces legislation to revise land tenure laws, end all racial discrimination in land ownership, and allow all South Africans to live where they choose. Currently, 87% of all land is reserved for 5 million whites, 13% of South Africa's population.

U.S. Sec. of State James Baker ends talks with Israeli and Palestinian leaders, as his proposals for peace negotiations are rejected by both sides. Israelis refuse to consider trading land for peace, and Palestinians insists on representation by PLO in talks with Israel.

After 52 years of nonrecognition, U.S. and Albanian officials announce the two countries will resume full diplomatic relations on Mar. 15, as a result of recent democratic developments in Albania, including planned multiparty elections. In Tirana, Albanian government pardons all political prisoners, estimated to number 200.

Former congressman Edward Madigan (R-Ill.) is sworn in as sec. of agriculture in Washington, vowing to break down trade barriers.

**13** As Iraqi civil unrest continues, protestors march in Baghdad, battles between loyalist troops and rebels rage in southern Basra and northern Kirkuk, and Kurdish rebels free 4,000 prisoners.

A week after Prime Minister Chandra Shekhar resigns, India's president dismisses parliament and calls for national elections in May.

Suffering from kidney and heart ailments, former East German Prime Minister Erich Honecker is transferred to a hospital in the USSR. Germany claims transfer is a violation of international law, since Honecker is to be brought up on criminal charges for ordering shooting of East Germans attempting to escape to West.

**14** Scientists from institutions around the world, including Johns Hopkins, Univ. of Utah, and Cancer Institute in Tokyo, report discovery of gene that triggers colon cancer.

Emir of Kuwait, Sheik Jaber al-Ahmed al-Sabah, returns to Kuwait City, seven and a half months after he departed for Saudi Arabia, and 16 days after Iraqi occupiers left.

The Court of Appeals in London rules that evidence in case against "Birmingham Six" from Northern Ireland, jailed since November 1974 for IRA bombings of two Birmingham pubs, has been discredited and releases them.

**15** The Paris Club, an informal group of western governments, agrees to forgive half of Poland's $33 bil. debt to facilitate the country's transition to market economy, the largest percentage of foreign debt ever forgiven a debtor nation by the group.

Borisav Jovic, leader of Yugoslavia's eight-member ruling council, resigns when his colleagues deny him power to mobilize the 250,000-man armed forces to quell civil unrest. The next day Serbian Pres. Slobodan Milosevic refuses to recognize authority of collective federal executive body, effectively declaring Serbia's secession from Yugoslav federation.

Four Los Angeles policemen are indicted in Mar. 3 beating of motorist Rodney King on charges of assault with a deadly weapon, misuse of authority, and falsifying police reports; the four officers plead not guilty on Mar. 26.

**17** Iran and Saudi Arabia resume diplomatic relations, broken in 1988, the year after 400 people, mostly Iranians, were killed in Mecca battling Saudi security forces.

Soviet voters support Pres. Gorbachev's referendum for national unity, favoring "preservation of the USSR as a renewed federation of equal sovereign republics." Six republics, accounting for 10 mil. voters, boycott the vote.

**18** Sudanese Pres. Bashir allows international famine relief of 1.1 million tons of food to enter northern and southern regions of the war-torn country, where eight million people are threatened by famine.

Throughout eastern Germany, 70,000 people demonstrate to protest economic hardships and low standards of living in contrast to west.

**19** Khaleda Zia becomes first woman named prime minister of Bangladesh.

In Miami, Brian Davidow and William Saldarriaga are convicted of conspiracy to import cocaine and distribution with intent to import in connection with a 1986 operation to trade M-16 automatic rifles for cocaine involving Gen. Manuel Noriega of Panama.

**20** Supreme Court rules that employers may not practice sex discrimination by excluding women from jobs in which exposure to toxic substances could harm a developing fetus. At least a dozen large U.S. manufacturing companies have such policies in place, allowing only women who can provide proof of sterility to be considered for such positions.

In Washington, National Institutes of Health finds that Dr. David Baltimore, a Nobel laureate and president of Rockefeller Univ., and coauthor Dr. Thereza Imanishi-Kari falsified crucial data in a 1986 study that finds that transplanted genes could stimulate production of antibodies.

April Glaspie, former U.S. ambassador to Iraq who was barred by State Dept. from speaking publicly, testifies before Senate Foreign Relations Committee that she warned Pres. Hussein in July 1990 against use of force in Kuwait border dispute. Iraq's account of meeting omits any such warning and portrays Glaspie as sympathetic to Iraq's position.

Five New York City police officials are charged with murder in death of a handcuffed car-theft suspect, Federico Pereira. Pereira died of asphyxiation after being punched, kicked, and strangled by the officers, who plead not guilty.

On Lech Walesa's first visit to Washington as president of Poland, Pres. Bush forgives $800 mil. in debt, to encourage U.S. investment.

In Antilias, Lebanon, a car bomb hits motorcade of Lebanese Defense Minister Michel al-Murr. He escapes relatively unharmed, but 10 others are killed and 25 wounded.

Under increasing criticism by Kuwaiti citizens, Prime Minister Sheik Saad al-Abdullah al-Sabah of Kuwait and his cabinet resign after failing to restore basic public services to Kuwait City, including food, water, and electricity.

**21** In Washington, L. William Seidman, chairman of the FDIC and Resolution Trust Corp., announces that the agency will need the authority to borrow $70 bil. from Federal Reserve System, an increase of $45 bil. over previous estimates, to reinforce the program that protects deposits from bank collapse.

A Saudi air force C-130 transport plane carrying 95 Senegalese soldiers crashes at a Saudi air base; six Saudi crew members and 92 soldiers are killed. Crash is blamed on reduced visibility due to black smoke from burning oil wells.

By a vote of 88 to 12, Senate confirms former Florida governor Bob Martinez as director of Office of National Drug Control Policy.

In response to Mar. 4 release of report on human rights abuses, including details on the death or disappearance of 2,025 Chileans under dictatorship of Gen. Pinochet, week-long violence results in bombing of three Santiago police stations, six bank robberies, and execution of chief investigator Héctor Hidalgo by leftist extremist group Rebel and Popular Forces of Lautaro.

**22** American F-15 fighter plane downs second Iraqi jet in three days over northern Iraq.

In Bamako, Mali, Pres. Gen. Moussa Traoré declares state of emergency as prodemocracy riots by demonstrators demanding end to one-party rule leave 100 dead and an estimated 1,000 wounded over three days.

UN Security Council lifts embargo on food to Iraq and restrictions on preapproved shipments of humanitarian goods, such as fuel, electrical generators, and sewage treatment equipment.

U.S. Congress revokes $55 mil. in aid to Jordan and bans military sales to allies who fail to contribute to Persian Gulf war costs.

In Exeter, N.H., high school teacher Pamela Smart is sentenced to life in prison without possibility of parole, in plotting with her 15-year-old student-lover, William Flynn, to murder her husband Gregory Smart. In January, Flynn and two student accomplices pleaded guilty to shooting Smart in May 1990.

**23** An estimated 20 tornadoes in Tennessee and Kentucky kill five people.

**24** After ordering the crowd to disperse, police fire on African National Congress supporters at rally in black township of Daveyton, South Africa, leaving 12 dead and 29 wounded. Factional violence over three days claims lives of at least 17 in neighboring Alexandra and Tembisa.

Pres. Aylwin of Chile wins congressional approval to free 195 leftist political prisoners jailed by former Pres. Pinochet from 1973 to 1990, marking first constitutional change since Aylwin took office in March 1990.

**25** In response to growing demonstrations supporting his chief rival, Russian republic Pres. Boris Yeltsin, Soviet Pres. Gorbachev bans all public rallies and demonstrations in Moscow for three weeks.

**26** Supreme Court rules 5 to 4 that a coerced or involuntary confession in a criminal trial does not automatically invalidate a conviction, and may be excused as "harmless error" if other evidence is adequate to sustain a guilty verdict.

After 23 years in power, Mali's dictator Gen. Traoré is overthrown in a violent overnight coup led by Lt. Col. Amadou Toumani Touré; 59 people are killed. The new National Reconciliation Council agrees to share power with civilians and organize elections by year's end.

In Singapore, all four Pakistani hijackers of a Singapore Airlines jet are killed by government commandos; passengers and crew members are safe. The hijackers demanded that Pakistani government release former Prime Minister Benazir Bhutto's imprisoned husband.

Supreme Court rules 6 to 3 that Americans employed overseas by U.S.-based companies do not enjoy protection under the Civil Rights Act of 1964, an antidiscrimination law, since federal laws apply only within U.S. borders.

Gen. H. Norman Schwarzkopf admits he wanted to continue allied offensive action to destroy Iraq's forces completely after Pres. Bush halted fighting; the White House rebukes Gen. Schwarzkopf's comments, claiming he was in on decision to call cease-fire, and general subsequently apologizes for statement and claims he was in agreement with Pres. Bush's decision to call for a cease-fire on Feb. 27.

**27** In continuing factional fighting in Alexandra, South Africa, Zulu gunmen raid a funeral vigil, kill 15 mourners, and wound 16 people associated with the African National Congress.

In first South Korean local elections in three decades, Pres. Roh Tae Woo's governing party wins more than 70% of local council seats with 55% of voters casting ballots.

**28** On 10th anniversary of an attempt on his life by John Hinckley, former U.S. Pres. Ronald Reagan, a lifelong member of the National Rifle Association, reverses his criticism of gun control and endorses a seven-day waiting period for handgun purchases as part of the "Brady bill."

The bill is named for White House press secretary James Brady, who was brain-damaged in the attack.

Up to 150,000 Iraqi troops launch an attack on northern city of Kirkuk, which has been under Kurdish control for a week.

In Moscow, 100,000 pro-Yeltsin demonstrators rally to defy Pres. Gorbachev's ban on public gatherings.

Because of a need for more new stamps than planned due to a recent increase in postal rates, the Bureau of Engraving and Printing in Washington commissions Canada to produce first U.S. stamp printed in a foreign country.

**29** In Brussels, Germany, France, Italy, Belgium, the Netherlands, and Luxembourg agree to allow Poles to travel visa-free, after Warsaw agrees to increase its controls on Eastern Europeans to avoid a vast migration to the west.

In Rome, six-time Prime Minister Giulio Andreotti resigns, paving the way for country's 50th government since World War II.

Two American sailors, Airman Apprentice Abdul H. Shaheed and Seaman Apprentice James L. Moss, are charged with attempting to sabotage aircraft carrier USS *Ranger* and kidnap skipper in the Persian Gulf and are ordered to face a court-martial. Sailors' actions were in direct response to Pres. Hussein's call for a worldwide Muslim holy war against the U.S.

Thunderstorms, tornadoes, and 70-mph winds claim lives of 23 people in parts of the South, including Georgia, Alabama, Texas, Louisiana, Arkansas, Mississippi, North Carolina, and Virginia, over two days.

**30** Nelson Mandela and Mangosuthu Gatsha Buthelezi meet in Durban, South Africa, in an attempt to put an end to factional violence between African National Congress and Inkatha Freedom party in black townships.

**31** U.S. Army announces it will withdraw about 20,000 troops—a quarter of American combat forces in Persian Gulf region—from southern Iraq within two weeks.

With 95% of eligible voters casting ballots, Albania's newly formed opposition Democratic party wins one-third of parliamentary seats in country's first multiparty legislative elections in 68 years. Ruling Communist party wins remaining two-thirds, but Pres. Ramiz Alia is defeated in his parliamentary election district. He will remain as president, since his party holds a majority of seats.

Police and Serbian rebels battle for control of a rebel-held national park in Krajina, an ethnic Serb enclave in Croatia, Yugoslavia, leaving one dead and 13 wounded. Police retake control of the park and arrest 29 rebels. Krajina declares it will secede from Croatia and join Serbia.

Iraqi loyalist forces retake three Kurdish towns in northern Iraq, including Dohuk, Erbil, and oil town of Kirkuk.

After 36 years of Soviet control, Warsaw Pact formally ends existence as a military force when Soviet commanders surrender powers over Eastern Europe in agreement between pact members, including USSR, Poland, Czechoslovakia, Hungary, Bulgaria, and Romania.

### April 1991

**1** In Moscow, food stores close to curb panic buying in anticipation of government price increases. Soviet prices increase by an average of 250% on Apr. 2.

Supreme Court rules that white defendants are entitled to new trials if convicted by juries from which blacks were excluded because of their race, a violation of the constitution.

**2** Iraq's army crushes month-long rebel insurgencies by northern Kurds and southern Shiite Muslims.

U.S. minimum wage increases 45 cents to $4.25 an hour, and below-minimum training wage for teenagers in their first job rises from $3.35 to $3.62 an hour. An estimated 3 million Americans earn the minimum wage.

In attempt to disperse 30,000 demonstrators from in front of Communist party headquarters in Shkodër, Albania, troops kill three people and wound 30; demonstrators are protesting election results giving victory to ruling Communist party.

Soumana Sacko, a civilian official with UN Development Program, is named interim prime minister of Mali by country's new military rulers under Gen. Lt. Col. Amadou Touré.

Roger Cooper, British businessman held by Iran since 1985 and charged with spying for British intelligence, is released in Teheran and returns to London.

A 30-year-old woman claims she was raped Mar. 30 on grounds of Kennedy family estate in Palm Beach, Fla.

Six pipe bombs shot from launchers near the Fresno, Calif., IRS center over a 24-hour period explode, shattering windows and rupturing a natural gas line, but causing no injuries. Investigating agents are looking for "someone possibly who doesn't like the IRS."

In response to growing criticism of Los Angeles Police Dept. since Mar. 3 beating of motorist by police officers, Mayor Tom Bradley calls for resignation of police chief Daryl F. Gates, who refuses to resign. Two days later he is temporarily relieved of command and is put on 60 days' administrative leave with pay by the mayor-appointed Police Commission. The order is rescinded and Gates returns to power within 24 hours.

**3** UN Security Council approves resolution to end war and lift sanctions against Iraq conditional upon Pres. Saddam Hussein's acceptance of financial and military terms. In Teheran, Iran announces it will accept Kurdish refugees and petitions UN High Commission for Refugees and Red Cross International for aid.

**4** In Minsk, capital of Soviet Byelorussia, tens of thousands of workers walk off the job and rally to demand wages increases to offset recent nationwide price increases and call for resignation of Pres. Mikhail Gorbachev.

EPA announces that ozone layer in latitude of the U.S. has been depleted at twice the rate previously expected, and that it has weakened 4.5% to 5% over last decade.

In Lower Merion Township, Pa., Sen. John Heinz (R-Pa.) and four others die when their chartered plane collides with a helicopter in mid-air over a school yard. Two school children are also killed.

Ertha Pascal Trouillot, former president of Haiti, is arrested and placed under house arrest by Pres. Jean-Bertrand Aristide in connection with an unsuccessful military coup in January.

**5** In Sacramento, Calif., four members of the Oriental Boys Asian youth gang hold 41 hostages at a Good Guys store for eight-and-a-half hours before police storm the building. After a gunman kills three hostages, all Good Guys employees, police kill three gunmen and critically wound the fourth; 10 other hostages are wounded.

Former Sen. John Tower (R-Tex.) and 22 others, including space shuttle astronaut Manley Lanier (Sonny) Carter, Jr., die when their commuter plane crashes in Brunswick, Ga.

Several earthquakes, measuring between 5.8 and 6.9 on the Richter scale, strike Peru within 24 hours, killing at least 38 people in northern region of San Martin.

An estimated 10 million people, half of Peru's population, lose electrical power in and around Lima after Maoist guerrilla attack on electrical distribution system. Armed with bombs, dynamite, and bazookas, guerrillas also bomb six banks, a gasoline depot, and Israeli and Colombian embassies.

**6** At the UN, Iraq accepts terms for formal cease-fire in Persian Gulf war.

In Cuba's worst rail crash, a passenger train derails and crashes near Manacas, 140 miles east of Havana, leaving 56 dead and 200 injured.

**7** At the Iraq-Turkey border, six U.S. planes airlift 36 tons of food, water, and medical gear to Kurdish refugees, and plan to continue airlift for two more weeks. Iran closes its borders after about 500,000 Kurds cross over.

**8** National Association of Insurance Commissioners chooses nine basic health insurance packages to supplement coverage provided to elderly by Medicare, to replace thousands of confusing private supplemental policies, known as "Medigap" insurance.

Germany, the Netherlands, Belgium, Luxembourg, and France begin allowing Polish citizens to enter without visas; as a result, lines of vehicles waiting to cross Polish-German border stretch as far as 25 miles.

In Yugoslavia, the trial of seven people, including Croatia's defense minister, charged with plotting a Croatian armed revolt against government, is postponed when thousands of Croatian nationalists throw stones, potatoes, and eggs at federal military courthouse in Zagreb.

On the eve of Sec. of State James Baker's visit to Israel, Israeli Defense Ministry announces it will free more than 1,000 of 14,000 Palestinian prisoners.

**9** While Soviet Pres. Gorbachev presents a crisis program in Moscow demanding a moratorium on strikes and demonstrations and stepped-up transition to a market economy to save federation from dissolution, Georgian republic declares independence in a unanimous parliamentary decision.

Washington suspends U.S. aid to non-Communist Cambodian factions because past aid is believed to have benefited Communist Khmer Rouge.

**10** In Minsk, the capital of Soviet Byelorussia, tens of thousands of workers rally in defiance of Pres. Gorbachev's proposal for a yearlong moratorium on strikes and protests as part of a package to avoid economic collapse.

*Moby Prince*, an Italian ferry en route to Sardinia, collides with an oil tanker near Leghorn, Italy, killing 151 passengers and crew; all 28 members of tanker crew survive.

**11** California insurance regulators seize control of Executive Life Insurance Co., in largest failure of an insurer. Executive Life, one of the industry's top 20 companies, invested two-thirds of its assets in high-risk junk bonds that are now declining in value.

In Italy, prime minister–designate Giulio Andreotti forms a coalition cabinet to serve as Italy's 50th postwar government, two weeks after Socialists caused Andreotti to resign.

**13** After U.S. forgives billions of dollars of Poland's and Egypt's official debt, Japan retracts promise to make loans to either country and announces it will refuse new loans to other countries seeking debt forgiveness.

**14** In shortest-lived art theft on record, 20 major paintings by Van Gogh are stolen by two gunmen from the Van Gogh National Museum, Amsterdam, and abandoned 35 minutes later.

In accordance with UN resolution to end Persian Gulf war, U.S. forces retreat to narrow buffer zone extending six miles into Iraq and three miles into Kuwait. In Erbil, Iraq, Pres. Hussein makes first public appearance since end of war.

**15** EC lifts remaining economic sanctions against South Africa, allowing import of South African gold coins, iron, and steel, despite pleas by African National Congress to maintain sanctions.

**16** Bush administration announces that five or six temporary encampments managed by American troops are to be built as deep as 60 miles inside Iraq for tens of thousands of Kurdish refugees.

Supreme Court rules 6-to-3 to limit number of appeals by death-row inmates and other state prisoners to challenge constitutionality of their convictions or sentences. Under the ruling, a prisoner's second habeas corpus petition or subsequent challenges must be dismissed except in unusual circumstances.

In defiance of U.S. request to stop settlement activity in West Bank and Gaza Strip in order to facilitate Arab-Israeli peace talks, first Jewish settlement under current Israeli government is opened in occupied territories.

In first visit of a Soviet leader to Japan, Pres. Gorbachev and Prime Minister Toshiki Kaifu open talks in Tokyo over enhanced political relations, Japanese aid and investment in USSR, and settlement of territorial dispute over Kurile Islands seized by USSR during World War II. Talks end after three days with signing of 15 agreements on trade fairs, cultural centers, air rights, and fishery accords, but without resolution of territorial disputes.

**17** For first time ever, Dow Jones industrial average closes above 3,000, at 3004.46, in anticipation of end to current recession.

Jordanian guerrillas shoot four farmers at Neveh Ur kibbutz, two miles from Jordanian border, killing one and wounding three, in second attack on area in one week. In 1991, armed Jordanian guerrillas have crossed border an average of once every 10 days.

One day after nationwide freight railroad strike begins, Congress passes bill stopping strike, which would affect 37% of all freight transportation, and creates three-member board to impose settlement within 65 days.

**18** Near Cape Canaveral, Fla., NASA officials

blow up by remote control a $100 mil. Atlas-Centaur rocket carrying a Japanese broadcasting satellite, after two of its engines failed to ignite, causing it to begin falling to Earth. Debris falls into ocean 240 miles offshore.

**19** In Patras, Greece, a parcel bomb explodes, killing seven people and wounding seven, at a building that houses United Parcel International, an American concern. Four days later, a Palestinian chemistry student surrenders.

UN releases Iraqi report claiming that chemical and ballistic weapons survived Persian Gulf war, including 10,000 nerve-gas warheads, 1,000 tons of nerve and mustard gas, 1,500 chemical weapons bombs and shells, and 52 Scud missiles armed with chemical and conventional warheads. Iraq denies possession of nuclear arms, nuclear-weapons-grade materials, or biological weapons.

**20** In Hanoi, Vietnam, U.S. special envoy Gen. John W. Vessey, Jr., announces U.S. will open temporary office to investigate unresolved cases of 2,278 American soldiers listed as missing in action or prisoners of war.

In Cheju, South Korea, Pres. Roh Tae Woo and Soviet Pres. Gorbachev agree to expand trade tenfold by 1996 and to negotiate mutual cooperation treaty.

Amid widespread criticism, Kuwaiti prime minister names new cabinet, including five members of ruling al-Sabah family but no opposition groups.

An Afghani guerrilla group, Hezb-i-Islami, or Party of Islam, reports that Kabul government fired two Scud missiles into bazaar in rebel-controlled Asadabad, killing 300 and wounding 500.

**21** Chancellor Helmut Kohl loses control of upper house in parliament as a result of local elections in Rhineland-Palatinate, his home state. Voters support Social Democrats over ruling Christian Democrats because of Kohl's reversal to allow tax increases to pay for German unity.

**22** An earthquake lasting 35 seconds and measuring 7.4 on the Richter scale strikes Costa Rica, killing at least 70 people and injuring 500 in Costa Rica and neighboring Panama, mostly on Caribbean coast near quake's epicenter.

**23** After case is aired on television's "America's Most Wanted," Virgilio Pablo Paz Romero is arrested in Boynton Beach, Fla., for 1976 car-bomb murder of Chilean Ambassador Orlando Letelier in Washington, D.C.

U.S. Air Force ends five-year weapons contract competition by selecting team comprised of Lockheed, General Dynamics, and Boeing to build 650 F-22 radar-evading fighter planes to replace F-15 Eagles, at a cost of $95 bil.

Supreme Court unanimously upholds National Labor Relations Board regulation to facilitate organization of community hospital workers. Fewer than 20% of hospital workers are now unionized.

During meeting between Pres. F.W. de Klerk and Prime Minister John Major in London, British government agrees to lift ban on trade and sports competition with South Africa.

In Slovakia, Prime Minister Vladimir Meciar and seven of his ministers are dismissed by parliamentary leaders in dispute over pace of economic change in the republic.

Massachusetts Institute of Tech. announces it will repay $731,000 in grant funds to U.S.

government, including $27,000 in lobbying expenses used to head off congressional investigation into charges of scientific fraud by MIT affiliate Dr. David Baltimore in 1986.

**24** In Baghdad, Kurdish leader Jalal Talabani and Iraqi Pres. Hussein reach an agreement in principle to allow safe return of Kurdish refugees living along borders with Turkey and Iran.

In Moscow, Pres Gorbachev and leaders of nine of nation's 15 republics make pact urging striking coal miners to return to work. Gorbachev promises revisions of unpopular price and tax programs and transfer of greater share of power to republics.

Federal district judge H. Russell Holland in Alaska rejects plea agreement between Exxon Corp. and the Justice Dept. for 1989 Valdez oil spill, declaring the agreed-upon criminal fine of $100 mil. too small to "achieve deterrence."

Sec. of State Baker's latest diplomatic mission fails to result in agreement between Israel and Syria over organization of Middle East peace conference. Israel rejects both of Syria's proposals to allow UN to play prominent role and to create permanent negotiating body that appeals to UN and superpower sponsors in case of deadlock. In Syria, Baker criticizes Israel for establishing new Jewish settlement on West Bank.

Angolan Pres. José Eduardo dos Santos accepts proposal to hold multiparty elections in 1992, the first such since independence in 1958, and accepts Portuguese proposal for cease-fire to end 16-year civil war.

In Budapest, Hungarian president votes to partially compensate owners of property seized by Communists, including spouses and descendants, who can receive up to $70,000 in coupons that can be sold or used to buy property.

Cpl. Greddie Stowers of South Carolina, a black World War I corporal, is posthumously awarded Medal of Honor; he is first black to receive highest medal for valor in combat.

**25** Pres. Gorbachev announces resignation as Communist party leader at Central Committee meeting; 24-member politburo unanimously refuses to consider his resignation and 349-member Central Committee votes 322 to 13, with 14 abstentions, to support the politburo.

Soviet Foreign Minister Aleksandr Bessmertnykh announces that USSR would cosponsor Middle East peace conference with U.S., adding that Arab clients of USSR must be satisfied with organization of conference before Soviets would commit themselves completely.

In Cape Town, South Africa, Justice Minister H.J. Coetsee extends deadline for release of all political prisoners whose crime did not result in death or injury, estimated by African National Congress to number 3,500.

Federal government cuts Stanford Univ.'s research funds by $20 mil. annually in response to charges that university overbilled government up to $200 mil.

State Dept. announces first financial assistance to Hanoi since the 1960s, in form of $1 mil. to produce artificial limbs in Vietnam for Vietnamese disabled during the war.

**26** Commerce Dept. reports that U.S. economy shrank for two consecutive quarters for first time since 1981–82 recession, as GNP contracted by 2.8% for Jan.–Mar. 1991, following a 1.6% decline in fourth quarter of 1990.

Procter and Gamble Co. agrees to drop "fresh" from name of Citrus Hill Fresh Choice brand orange juice because it is made from concentrate and FDA, which took company to court over name change, believes it is misleading.

A small fraction of the 500,000 Kurdish refugees move to safe zone administered by U.S. forces from mountains that border Turkey, and hundreds of Iraqi troops withdraw.

Six Japanese minesweepers carrying 500 crew members and Japanese fleet's flagship embark on their first overseas military mission since World War II, a 40-day journey to Persian Gulf. Japan announces it will contribute $100 mil. for emergency relief for Iraqi refugees.

**27** In mountains southeast of Beirut, Druse fighters of the Progressive Socialist party surrender 300 tons of ammunition to Syrian troops.

In St. Louis, Mo., Judge Barbara Ann Hoffa Crancer, daughter of former Teamsters union leader James R. Hoffa, sues Justice Dept. to open files on her father's presumed murder, unsolved since Hoffa's disappearance outside Detroit in 1975.

An estimated 70 tornadoes in Kansas, Texas, Oklahoma, Arkansas, Missouri, Nebraska, and Iowa claim lives of 23 people and leave thousands homeless as winds gust up to 200 mph.

After 12 days of deliberation, White Plains, N.Y., love-triangle murder trial of Carolyn Warmus ends with hung jury, leaving prosecutors to seek new trial. Warmus is accused of murdering her lover's wife, in what is known as the "Fatal Attraction" case.

In Mexico City, government of El Salvador and guerrilla opponents agree on constitutional amendments limiting powers of armed forces and imposing changes in judicial system and electoral process; no agreement is made on a cease-fire.

**28** In Seoul, South Korean Pres. Roh Tae Woo dismisses interior minister after antigovernment demonstrations at Yonsei Univ. break out following death of student protester beaten by police on Apr. 26. Protests continue for two days, as 20,000 students at campuses across South Korea demonstrate and one student sets herself on fire.

Suffering a major political setback, Winnie Mandela loses bid for presidency of ANC Women's League; the league reelects its current president, Gertrude Shope.

In Jerusalem, Israeli government disavows Foreign Minister David Levy and retracts his agreement made two days earlier with Sec. of State Baker on format for Arab-Israeli peace talks, stating that Israel had only agreed on a one-time meeting, not periodic talks Levy agreed to.

**29** In northern Iraq, Kurdish checkpoints are opened and refugees begin moving into allied-built tent city in a safe-haven zone.

In South Ossetia, in Soviet Georgia, an earthquake measuring 7.0 on the Richter scale kills over 100 people and destroys hospitals, schools, factories, and 17,000 homes.

In Damascus, Syria, Pres. Hafez al-Assad and Pres. Hashemi Rafsanjani of Iran agree to allow Iranian-backed forces to remain in Lebanon along Israeli border, contrary to 1989 accord disbanding all militias in Lebanon by May 1991.

**30** Former senator Paul E. Tsongas (D-Mass.) becomes first Democrat to announce his candidacy for president in 1992.

A cyclone with winds of up to 145 mph and waves 20 feet high kills 138,868 people and leaves up to 10 million homeless in 14 southeastern coastal districts of Bangladesh. Government appeals to world community for $1.4 bil. in relief and reconstruction aid.

In attempt to spur economic activity, Federal Reserve lowers discount rate (on its loans to banks) from 6% to 5½%, and lowers federal funds rate (rate banks charge each other on loans) from 6% to 5¾%.

As opposition abstains from participating in election, Albania's Communist leader Ramiz Alia is elected to presidency in first free elections in four decades with 68% of vote.

In Belfast, first political talks between Roman Catholic nationalists and Protestant unionists in 15 years begin with discussions about power of Catholic minority and relations between province of Northern Ireland and the Republic of Ireland.

Pres. Bush bars export to China of American components for a communications satellite, citing Chinese weapons exports to third-world countries, including sales of ballistic missiles to Pakistan and nuclear power reactor to Algeria.

In Taipei, Taiwanese Pres. Lee Teng-hui ends 43 years of emergency rule, authorizes presidential elections by year's end, and renounces use of force to reunify China.

## May 1991

**1** In Lisbon, Portuguese-backed Angolan leftist government of Pres. José Eduardo dos Santos and U.S.-backed UNITA rebels led by Jonas Savimbi sign accord calling for a cease-fire to take effect by month's end and the holding of free national elections by end of 1992. Civil war has claimed 300,000 lives over 16 years.

In Beirut, thousands of Lebanese army troops are deployed in a 1,000-square-mile area around the capital and secure 80 miles of coastal highway to rid the area of the Christian and Muslim militias that have controlled it for 16 years.

In Cambodia, a temporary cease-fire scheduled to last a month between Phnom Penh government and coalition partners, including Communist Khmer Rouge, followers of Prince Norodom Sihanouk, and Khmer People's National Liberation Front of Son Sann, lasts only a few hours before tank and artillery battles break out in Kompong Thom and Siem Reap provinces.

For third consecutive day, violent demonstrations and clashes between 4,000 police and 20,000 students break out in Seoul, South Korea, and two students set themselves on fire to protest the beating death of a student by police on Apr. 26.

In northern Sri Lanka, government forces battle Liberation Tigers of Tamil Eelam in continued fighting that has left 950 guerrillas and 180 troops dead since mid-March; rebels have suffered eroding public support and have resorted to suicidal attacks.

**2** In Croatian town of Borovo Selo, Yugoslavia, federal soldiers arrive after shooting begins between Serb rebels and Croatian police. Incident marks fourth time this year federal troops have been deployed to break up Serbo-Croatian violence, in which 12 officers and 20 civilians have been killed and 21 officers wounded.

Pope John Paul II delivers the "Centesimus

Annus" (the Hundredth Year) encyclical, praising free-market capitalism, but warns capitalist nations to correct injustices in their own countries and throughout the world.

Nuclear Regulatory Commission approves opening of Browns Ferry, Ala., nuclear reactor, nation's second largest atomic power plant, owned and operated by the TVA. The reactor has been closed due to safety problems for six years.

**3** Serb militants and police officers clash in secessionist Croatian villages of Borovo Selo and Polaca, Yugoslavia; 13 Croatian policemen and three civilians are killed.

A $1.1 bil. agreement to settle civil suits between Exxon and federal and state governments collapses when both Alaska's Gov. Walter J. Hickel and Exxon withdraw, paving way for years of court battles. Collapse results from criticism by Alaska House of Representatives, environmentalists, a federal judge, and Alaskan residents who claim that Exxon is not paying enough for its spill of 11 million gallons of oil into Prince William Sound.

Pres. Bush chooses Texas A & M Univ. as site for his presidential library, slated to open as early as 1996.

**4** Pres. Bush suffers shortage of breath while jogging and is admitted to Bethesda Naval Hospital for apparent heart irregularity. He is released two days later after his erratic heartbeat is brought under control by drugs. He is diagnosed to have Graves disease (from which his wife Barbara also suffers), an affliction in which immune system inexplicably attacks thyroid gland.

Number of protestors in South Korea swells to 70,000 students, older dissidents, and labor unionists, who call for resignation of Pres. Roh Tae Woo over beating death of a student by policemen.

**6** In Moscow, Soviet government transfers control of Siberian coal industry to Russian republic in response to demands of strikers.

**7** EPA directs nearly all water suppliers in U.S. to test drinking water in hundreds of thousands of homes to check lead content.

In Kuwait City, Sec. of Defense Dick Cheney announces that U.S. air patrols over southern Iraq have ceased and U.S. troops will withdraw from demilitarized zone on Iraq-Kuwait border; at invitation of Kuwaiti government, troops will remain in Kuwait.

In Baghdad, Kurdish rebels and Iraqi government begin talks on Kurdish autonomy.

In northern Iraq, Iraqis fire on a U.S. Navy plane just outside security zone for Kurdish refugees; it is reportedly the fifth such incident since cease-fire took effect.

**8** Along Armenia-Azerbaijan border, Soviet helicopters fire on Armenian village of Paravakar in retaliation for an ambush on government troops that left one soldier dead and eight injured. The two-week campaign to disarm Armenian border settlements by Soviet troops and Azerbaijani police has left 48 Armenians dead.

After four years in the job, William H. Webster resigns as director of CIA to return to practicing law.

In order to pressure government into negotiating a cease-fire to end 11-year-old civil war, Salvadoran leftist guerilla group FMLN sabotages power system, leaving El Salvador with about half its normal electricity supply.

**9** Under criticism for taxpayer subsidy of political travel, Pres. Bush orders chief of staff John H. Sununu and national security adviser Brent Scowcroft to seek advance approval from White House counsel for all flights, and bans use of military aircraft for most political and personal travel.

Baghdad rebuffs UN Secretary General Javier Pérez de Cuéllar's proposal for UN police force in northern Iraq, prompting continued coalition administration of Kurdish refugee camps.

Saudi Arabia, Kuwait, the UAE, Qatar, Oman, and Bahrain agree to allow U.S. to store weapons and matériel in the region and to perform joint exercises and training to facilitate a long-term U.S. military presence in Persian Gulf.

Albanian Prime Minister Fatos Nano, reappointed last week by Pres. Ramiz Alia, selects an all-Communist 25-member cabinet. In first multiparty voting since the 1920s, on Mar. 31, Communist party won two-thirds majority in parliament.

Manashit and Uzlu, two Armenian villages in Azerbaijan SSR, are attacked and occupied by Soviet army in attempt to disarm Armenians battling Azerbaijani gunmen for control of Nagorno-Karabakh, a predominantly Armenian enclave within Azerbaijan.

Federal government puts 250 universities on notice that they may be audited for overhead charges in connection with research grants; 21 other institutions have been named for inappropriately charging government for general expenses.

William K. Smith, nephew of Sen. Edward Kennedy, is charged in Palm Beach, Fla., with Mar. 30 rape and battery of woman who said she was assaulted on Kennedy estate.

**10** Saudi Arabia, Kuwait, Qatar, Bahrain, UAE, and Oman agree to send Gulf Cooperation Council representative to Israeli/Arab peace talks cosponsored by the U.S. and USSR. Sec. of State James Baker visits Middle East for fourth time in attempt to secure commitments of attendance.

New Hampshire House votes 243-to-105 to create paid state holiday honoring civil rights, without mention of Rev. Martin Luther King, Jr. New Hampshire is one of two states without a holiday honoring King, arguing that no single person should be honored for civil rights campaign.

**11** Mass repatriation of Kurdish refugees from Turkey to Iraq begins. Approximately 200,000 Kurds have already returned on their own; 260,00 remain in Turkey.

In Atlanta, 6,000 Southern Baptists create Cooperative Baptist Fellowship and begin to operate independent of conservative Southern Baptist Convention; fellowship members reject a literal reading of the Bible.

**12** Over 1,000 Zulus from Inkatha Freedom party raid squatter settlement of Kagiso, South Africa, killing 27, wounding 30, and burning down 82 houses; raid is thought to be in retaliation for kidnapping of an Inkatha supporter.

In Operation SEA ANGEL, first of 8,000 U.S. troops arrive in Bangladesh to distribute relief packages containing rice, molasses, water, clothing, and decontamination tablets for victims of cyclone in late April.

In The Simple Truth concert, 20 performers on three continents raise $17 mil. for International Committee of the Red Cross to support Kurdish relief efforts; audience is estimated at 300 million television viewers in 37 countries.

In first open elections in Nepal in 32 years, Communists win 70 of 205 seats in House of Representatives; ruling Nepali Congress party is officially declared winner with 106 seats and will form a new government. Nepali Congress party loses four of five seats in Kathmandu, and Prime Minister Krishna Prasad Bhattarai resigns; Nepal Congress party general secretary Girija Prasad Koirala is expected to be new prime minister.

**13** In Johannesburg, South Africa, Winnie Mandela is found guilty of being accessory after the fact and sentenced to six years in prison in assault of four youths who were kidnapped and taken to her home in late 1988. One youth was found dead nearby.

To accommodate overburdened criminal justice system, Supreme Court rules that people arrested without a warrant may be held for up to 48 hours while a judge decides if arrest is justified for probable cause, a standard already upheld by many states.

Russian Television, first television channel run by Russian republic, begins broadcasting alternative views, ending Soviet government monopoly on television.

**14** Queen Elizabeth II and Prince Philip visit White House at start of tour of U.S.; she is first British monarch to address Congress.

Pres. Bush nominates Robert M. Gates, deputy national security adviser, for director of CIA. Gates, a 25-year veteran of government bureaucracy, was denied the office four years ago due to Iran-Contra investigation.

In Seoul, 60,000 students and laborers march in funeral procession for student beaten to death in April and protest by setting streets on fire and calling for resignation of Pres. Roh Tae Woo.

In Birmingham, Ala., David Chandler is sentenced to death for murder of Marlin Shuler, a police informer. Chandler, who runs a marijuana operation in Alabama and Georgia, is first person sentenced to death for drug-trafficking violence.

**15** In Belgrade, Yugoslavia, republic of Serbia and two autonomous provinces block installation of Stipe Mesic, a Croat, as federal president.

In Paris, Edith Cresson, a Socialist and former trade minister, agricultural minister, and minister of European affairs, becomes first woman to serve as prime minister of France.

**16** In Moscow, 13 of 15 Soviet republics agree on an emergency economic plan to ban strikes while increasing wages and worker productivity, allow more freedom for open market trading, and cut budgets. Georgia and Estonia decline to take part.

In Moscow, headquarters of leading anti-Communist opposition group, the 1.3-million-member Democratic party, is bombed, and thousands of petitions supporting Boris Yeltsin in upcoming elections are destroyed.

**17** Commerce Dept. announces that trade deficit fell to $4.05 bil. in March, lowest in eight years; drop is due to strong exports in aircraft and computers and weak oil and auto imports as domestic demand remained low.

Iraq allows international commission under direction of the UN to locate, inspect, and destroy Iraqi chemical and biological weapons, ballistic missiles, and weapons-grade nuclear material.

Pres. Bush suspends all economic aid to Yugoslavia for violations of human rights in accordance with a law passed by congress last November. Aid is restored after 20 days.

For third day, thousands of strikers march through Tirana and throughout Albania demanding wage increases and investigation into killing of Democratic party members.

**18** In Johannesburg, African National Congress abandons negotiations with government until moves are made to stop factional fighting that ANC claims is permitted by police.

Rival drug gangs at Tamaulipas state prison in Matamoros, Mexico, battle for three hours using guns, knives, and firebombs; 18 are killed and five wounded. Oliveiro Chávez Araujo, a Mexican cocaine trafficker who was wounded and nearly blinded in the attack, controls prison for 12 days until guaranteed safety from federal police whom he claims hired an assassin to kill him. High-ranking prison and police officials are arrested immediately after his surrender.

In retaliation for Shiite raid in Israeli security zone that killed four a day earlier, two Israeli warplanes attack Shiite militia base in southern Lebanon, killing four and wounding 15.

Helen Sharmon, a chemist, becomes first Briton in space when she blasts off with two Soviet astronauts from Baikonur space center in Soviet central Asia aboard Soviet spacecraft.

**19** American Red Cross directors vote unanimously to reorganize its collection and handling of blood donations at its 53 blood centers and retrain all employees to avoid distributing contaminated blood. Half the nation's blood supply comes from Red Cross.

The first of hundreds of alleged Iraqi collaborators go on trial in Kuwait City, and five men are sentenced to prison terms, one for 15 years for wearing a T-shirt featuring Saddam Hussein's picture. Witnesses and evidence are disallowed in proceedings.

In Yugoslav republic of Croatia, 94% of voters support becoming independent nation linked only by a loose confederation with other Yugoslav republics.

**20** Soviet parliament votes 320-to-37, with 32 abstentions, to allow citizens to travel and emigrate freely by January 1993, paving way for USSR's qualification for most-favored-nation status in U.S. trading.

Threatening to veto any UN Security Council proposals to the contrary, Pres. Bush announces he will support lifting trade sanctions against Iraq only after Hussein is forced from power.

Indian national elections begin with political violence that leaves 40 dead and hundreds wounded, polling stations closed, and curfews imposed. Less than half the 500 million eligible voters actually turn out in seven-day election.

**21** Rajiv Gandhi, former prime minister of India, is assassinated when a bomb is placed near him while campaigning southwest of Madras. In aftermath, national elections are postponed. Congress party names Gandhi's widow, Sonia, to succeed him as party president, but she declines. Officials suspect a Sri Lankan Tamil woman carried out suicide bomb attack.

Ethiopian Pres. Mengistu Haile Mariam resigns, transfers power to Vice Pres. Lt. Gen. Tesfaye Gebre-Kidan, and flees country for Zimbabwe after 14 years at head of Marxist government. Rebels advance to within 50 miles of capital.

In Berlin, former East German Prime Minister Willi Stoph and three other senior officials are arrested for ordering border guards to shoot people attempting to cross to the west; more than 200 people were killed since order was issued in 1974.

South Korea's Prime Minister Ro Ja Bong resigns after four weeks of protests by students demanding resignation of president and his cabinet. Three days later, former cabinet minister Chung Won Shik is named prime minister and political prisoners are freed.

**22** In Damascus, Pres. Elias Hrawi of Lebanon and Syrian Pres. Hafez al-Assad sign Treaty of Brotherhood, Cooperation and Coordination to facilitate cooperation in defense, foreign policy, and their respective economies.

In Tunis, nearly 300 members of Muslim militant group Nahdha, including 100 soldiers, are arrested for conspiring to overthrow government and attempting to create an Islamic state.

Soviet Pres. Gorbachev asks Group of Seven industrialized democracies for $100 bil. in economic aid in loans and outright grants to bolster Soviet economy. It later turns out that $100 bil. was a figure of speech, meant to stress the importance of recovery. Gorbachev also asks for invitation to Group of Seven meeting in July.

**23** Supreme Court rules 5-to-4 to uphold federal regulations prohibiting 4,500 federally funded clinics that serve 4 million women from discussing abortion with patients, and directs them to advise women seeking abortion that clinics don't consider abortion an appropriate birth control method. Many clinics announce they will continue to advise patients on abortion even though they will lose federal funding as a result.

House of Representatives votes 231-to-192 to authorize Pres. Bush to negotiate free-trade agreements that lower trade barriers.

In Paris, the 17 members of the Coordinating Committee for Multilateral Export Controls (COCOM) agree to open trade with USSR and other Communist countries by allowing many high-technology items, most notably computer and aviation equipment, to be exported there without special licenses.

**24** Israel begins sudden mass evacuation of approximately 14,500 Ethiopian Jews from Ethiopia to Israel. Operation is completed in just under 36 hours. Israel admits to paying former Ethiopian government $35 mil. in order to facilitate airlift.

For third time in six months, UN Security Council votes 15-to-0 to urge Israel to stop deporting Palestinians from occupied territories.

Asmara, second largest city in Ethiopia, falls to Eritrean People's Liberation Front, separatist guerrillas who have fought for 31 years to control province of Eritrea. One day later, last government-controlled Red Sea port of Assab falls to rebels. Allied rebel group Ethiopian People's Revolutionary Democratic Front surrounds Addis Ababa.

Colombian businessman William Saldarriaga, a codefendant of Gen. Manuel Noriega, is sentenced to 20 years in prison for conspiring to trade rifles from Panama to Colombian drug dealers in exchange for cocaine.

**25** Due to 40,000 letters from conservative opposition, Dept. of Health and Human Services reverses January decision to allow people infected with AIDS virus to enter the U.S.

Last Cuban soldiers leave Angola after 16 years there in support of government against South African- and U.S.-backed rebels; Cuban troops once numbered 50,000 in Angola.

**26** A Lauda Air Boeing 767-300 carrying 223 passengers explodes over Thailand after take off outside Bangkok, killing all on board. The incident, the first crash of a Boeing 767, is caused by a computer malfunction that switched an engine into reverse.

U.S. forgives half of Egypt's $20.2 bil. debt for its support in Persian Gulf war and agrees to compensate Egypt for heavy financial losses.

In Soviet Georgia, separatist Zviad Gamsakhurdia is elected president in Georgia's first direct presidential election with 87% of the vote. In Moldavia, an Assembly of National Fronts is created, including Georgia, Moldavia, Armenia, Estonia, Latvia, and Lithuania, republics that have declared their intentions to secede. Aim of the assembly is to coordinate political and economic activities.

**27** Pres. Bush announces he will continue China's trading privileges as most-favored-nation for one more year, but restricts some exports, notably computers used for missile testing.

Ethiopia's acting president Lt. Gen. Tesfaye Gebre-Kidan surrenders Addis Ababa to rebel forces.

**28** In response to collapse of Warsaw Pact, NATO agrees to reorganize forces in Europe, including a 50% reduction in the 320,000 U.S. troops now in Europe.

Meles Zenawi, leader of Ethiopian People's Revolutionary Democratic Front, establishes temporary government in Addis Ababa.

**29** Scientists from Emory Univ. School of Medicine discover gene that causes fragile-X syndrome, an untreatable mental retardation that manifests itself in learning disabilities and, in severe cases, renders victims unable to talk or function.

P.V. Narasimha Rao, former Indian foreign minister and senior leader of the Indian Congress party, succeeds the late Rajiv Gandhi as party president, and will lead the party into national elections, interrupted by Gandhi's assassination.

In response to U.S. pressure, Argentina announces that a secret ballistic missile program, Condor II, will be halted, and the program's scientists, materials, and bases will be dedicated to developing space satellites in cooperation with Brazil.

In accordance with results of May 19 referendum, Croatia declares itself an independent state.

**30** In Addis Ababa, Ethiopia, thousands of demonstrators protest the new government and American political involvement, leaving 388 wounded and 10 dead.

In Glenanne, Northern Ireland, Irish Republican Army attacks Protestant Ulster Defense regiment base with truck filled with 2,000 pounds of explosives; blast kills three soldiers and wounds 10 soldiers and four civilians in nearby town.

**31** In Jerusalem, U.S. Sec. of Defense Dick Cheney announces that U.S. has begun storing unspecified military supplies in Israel for use in future conflicts in region, in accordance with an agreement made years ago.

In Lisbon, Soviet-backed Angolan government ends 16 years of civil war with U.S.-backed rebel group National Union for the Total Independence of Angola, or UNITA, by signing peace agreement providing for free elections in 1992, a market economy, and unified armed forces, and implementing immediate cease-fire.

In his first court appearance in West Palm Beach, William K. Smith pleads not guilty to rape charges.

## June 1991

**1** Allied commanders close last of seven Kurdish refugee camps along Turkey-Iraq border set up in an 11-nation effort. All refugees in Turkey have been repatriated to northern Iraq, but hundreds of thousands remain in Iran.

In Lisbon, U.S. Sec. of State James Baker and Soviet Foreign Minister Aleksandr Bessmertnykh resolve differences over conventional weapons reduction treaty signed last November. Treaty limits tanks, armored personnel carriers, artillery pieces, and combat aircraft and helicopters held by NATO and Warsaw Pact countries.

Approximately 55,000 students protest in Seoul and port city of Pusan to call for resignation of South Korean Pres. Roh Tae Woo and protest presence of 43,000 U.S. troops that students claim hinder unification procedures.

**2** In response to Jordanian King Hussein's proposal for "face-to-face" contacts, Israel's Foreign Minister David Levy invites Hussein to meet him in Israel and agrees to meet Hussein in Jordan.

Emir of Kuwait announces parliamentary elections to be held in October 1992.

Supreme Court rules 6-to-3 that jurors may not be excluded from civil cases on account of race.

**3** France signs 1968 Nuclear Nonproliferation Treaty, which prohibits signatories from helping other countries to acquire nuclear weapons, from making or acquiring nuclear weapons, and from exporting materials used in making bombs. France, which previously refused to sign on grounds of political independence but claimed to abide by treaty regulations, is 143rd party to the treaty; principal nonsignatories are Argentina, Brazil, China, India, Israel, Pakistan, and South Africa.

On Japanese island of Kyushu, Mt. Unzen volcano erupts; 37 people are killed, 20 injured, and nearly 10,000 evacuated from area. Dormant since 1792, when an estimated 15,000 people were killed, Mt. Unzen erupts again on June 8 and June 13.

**4** Attorney General Dick Thornburgh announces intent to resign from Bush cabinet on Aug. 16 to run for Senate from Pennsylvania.

Chinese government announces that Mao's widow, Jian Qing, committed suicide on May 14 in prison where she was serving life sentence for her role in 1966–76 Cultural Revolution.

In Sidon, Lebanon, the most intense Israeli air raids on Palestinian and Lebanese guerrilla bases in nine years leave seven people dead.

Albania's Communist cabinet resigns under pressure from a general strike and demonstrations by opposition groups, ending 46 years of Communist rule.

In Addis Ababa, Ethiopia, a grenade attack on a munitions depot results in 100 deaths and leaves 10,000 residents of neighboring shanty-town homeless; suspects include members of dissolved Ethiopian army.

**5** After two weeks of clashes between Algerian police and Muslim fundamentalists of the Islamic Salvation Front, who seek an Islamic state in Algeria, Algerian Pres. Chedli Bendjedid declares state of emergency and postpones upcoming parliamentary elections, first multiparty general elections since independence from France in 1962.

In Washington, D.C., an openly homosexual woman, Elizabeth L. Carl, is ordained to priesthood by Episcopal bishop of Washington, even though Episcopal Church resolved in 1979 not to ordain sexually active homosexuals.

In Johannesburg, South African legislators repeal Land Acts of 1913 and 1936, which reserved 87% of country's land for whites (14% of population), and Group Areas Act, which dictated where people could live according to race.

For third time in two days, Israeli planes attack Palestinian guerrilla bases around Sidon, which Israel claims are used to launch attacks on northern Israel, raising number of casualties to 22 killed and 82 wounded.

Space shuttle *Columbia* lifts off at 9:24 a.m., carrying a crew of seven astronauts, 29 rats, 2,478 jellyfish, and a medical laboratory where dizziness and nausea associated with weightlessness in space will be studied during a nine-day flight. Shuttle lands at Edwards Air Force Base, Calif., 10 days after liftoff.

**6** In Moscow, the KGB releases secret documents from 1941 that show Rudolf Hess, Hitler's deputy, was lured to duke of Hamilton's estate by British intelligence correspondence that promised a peace settlement.

**7** Islamic fundamentalists in Algeria stop protests and general strike in return for government promises to hold elections within six months; 40 to 50 people have been killed since demonstrations began May 25.

Prime Minister Yitzhak Shamir of Israel rejects U.S. calls for compromise to convene a Middle East peace conference; Israel refuses to reconvene a peace conference periodically, as Syria wants, and it will meet with the U.S., USSR, the EC, a Palestinian delegate from Jordan, and Arab countries only for the purpose of turning negotiations over to Israel and Arab countries for direct talks.

**8** In Washington, a two-mile, two-hour parade for Persian Gulf war veterans, including 8,000 troops, tanks, missiles, jets, helicopters, trucks, and other military equipment, draws 200,000 spectators. The parade cost $12 mil., $7 mil. of which was paid for by Defense Dept. and balance by 20 veterans' organizations.

North Korea agrees to international inspection of all nuclear installations by International Atomic Energy Agency, including installations U.S. claims are used to build nuclear weapons.

**9** Thirty-four years after political parties were banned in Jordan, King Hussein and Jordanian politicians sign National Charter, which sketches guidelines for government and parliament to draft democratic laws and expands freedoms for women and press.

**10** In the Philippines, Mt. Pinatubo erupts, spewing debris as far as 20 miles; over next 17

days, several moderate earthquakes and 100 smaller tremors send ash and smoke up to 80,000 feet into atmosphere, and blanket surrounding area. Located 55 miles northwest of Manila and 10 miles from Clark Air Force Base, the eruption causes evacuation of 20,000 Filipinos and 14,000 Americans from surrounding area. Mt. Pinatubo's last major eruption was in 1380.

In New York City's Canyon of Heroes, a privately funded ticker tape parade honors veterans of Persian Gulf war; parade includes 24,000 marchers and numerous marching bands, and is attended by 4.7 million spectators.

Iranian television reports that Iraqi forces attack thousands of Shiite Muslims in southern marshlands of Iraq and around cities of Amara and Nasiriya.

**11** In Washington, Pres. Bush approves agricultural loans totaling $1.5 bil. for Soviet farms to help buy feed grain and other farm goods; this follows on approval of similar loans totaling $1 bil. in December 1990.

House of Representatives votes to continue aid to Angolan rebels, in form of $20 mil. in nonmilitary aid, two weeks after Angolan government and rebels sign a peace accord to end 16 years of civil war. Aid is to feed and support UNITA fighters as they make their transition into civilian life.

The Red Sea port of Assab, Ethiopia, and the country's capital Addis Ababa, 400 miles away, are relinked by the opening of the only road between the two cities. The road opening makes possible the delivery of relief supplies to 7.3 million drought victims.

The General Assembly of the Presbyterian Church (U.S.A.) votes 491-to-26 to adopt its first policy on sexual misconduct by the clergy, prohibiting sexual contact between a clergy member and a parishioner or church employee, even if the parishioner or employee initiates it.

**12** Testifying before Congress, Gen. Norman Schwarzkopf complains about poor quality of U.S. intelligence reports on Iraqi military during Persian Gulf war.

PLO announces its refusal to give up bases in southern Lebanon, thus complicating Lebanese government's efforts to demobilize all armed factions in its 16-year-old civil war.

In Bangladesh, former president H.M. Ershad is sentenced to 10 years in prison for illegal weapons possession; deposed in December 1990, Ershad also faces corruption charges.

Albania's Communist party changes name to Socialist party, and parliament approves new cabinet headed by Prime Minister Ylli Bufi.

Russian republic, Soviet Union's largest, holds its first-ever direct presidential elections. Six-way race is won by Boris Yeltsin, an advocate of radical economic change and decentralization of power. His main opponent is former prime minister Nikolai Ryzhkov, an advocate of more gradual change. In Leningrad referendum held the same day, 55% of voters favor restoration of city's prerevolution name St. Petersburg.

**13** Revising discriminatory policy with roots in McCarthy era, Bush administration agrees to remove almost all 250,000 names on secret list maintained by government of ideologically unacceptable aliens. Among those barred from entering the U.S. were authors Graham Greene and

Gabriel García Márquez, and politicians such as PLO Chairman Yasir Arafat and Nicaragua's then president Daniel Ortega.

Reacting to land-mine death of three soldiers the day before, Sri Lankan army troops slaughter 150 Tamil villagers near Batticaloa. Defense ministry spokesmen claim that Tamil guerrillas used villagers as human shields during an attack on army troops.

Italy pledges $50 mil. in food, medical, and economic aid to Albania to aid that country's faltering economy and help stem tide of Albanian refugees to Italy.

Arguing that the bill did not provide adequate exceptions for victims of rape and incest, or cases in which the mother's life is in danger, Louisiana Gov. Buddy Roemer vetoes legislation that would have strictly limited abortions.

**14** The United States' NATO allies and five Eastern European countries approve compromise to end dispute over Soviet-U.S. treaty limiting conventional armies in Europe; treaty now goes to the U.S. Senate for approval.

Federal Centers for Disease Control report that 26% of babies born in U.S. in 1988 were born to single women, the highest proportion ever.

**15** In Punjab, India, gunmen kill 110 passengers on two trains, five hours after polling closes in national elections in all states except Punjab, where voting is scheduled to take place on June 22 under army protection. Although no group has taken responsibility for massacre, Punjab police suspect Sikh militants.

In Kuwait City, six journalists are sentenced to death in martial law court for collaborating with Iraq by working for *Al Nida*, an Iraqi newspaper published during the occupation.

An earthquake measuring 6.3 on Richter scale kills at least six people, injures 75, and destroys eight villages in mountainous Bakuriani region of Soviet Georgia. Scientists describe earthquake as an aftershock from Apr. 29 earthquake that killed 100 people and left 100,000 homeless. Three other major earthquakes are reported, two on Japanese islands and one in South Sandwich Islands near Antarctica.

**16** Defense Dept. orders 20,000 Americans to leave Philippines, where 140 people have been killed by molten rock and ash, 100 families left homeless, and hundreds reported missing after a week of volcanic eruptions from Mt. Pinatubo.

**17** In India, Congress party of assassinated Rajiv Gandhi wins 210 to 215 of 511 seats in parliament in country's 10th parliamentary elections. Party names P.V. Narasimha Rao, former foreign minister, as ninth prime minister.

In Johannesburg, South Africa, Pres. F.W. de Klerk repeals Population Registration Act, enacted in 1950, which classifies South Africans by race from birth. Act is fourth and final apartheid law to be repealed in less than a year, eliminating the legal foundation for apartheid.

Supreme Court rules 5-to-4 that hardships of prison life brought about by poor sanitation or overcrowding do not violate constitutional prohibition of cruel and unusual punishment unless authorities deliberately ignore basic human needs.

In Bonn, Germany, Polish Prime Minister Jan Krzysztof Bielecki and German Chancellor Helmut Kohl sign treaty of friendship and cooperation committing Germany to back Poland for EC membership and help resolve Poland's debt.

UN Security Council unanimously approves plan to prohibit export of military supplies to Iraq. Security Council also declares that Iraq must pay for destruction of its own weapons.

Zachary Taylor, 12th president of the U.S., is exhumed from his crypt after 141 years to investigate a theory of Clara Rising, a former humanities professor at Univ. of Florida, that he was assassinated in 1850 by arsenic poisoning. A week later it is determined that Taylor died of natural causes, as originally thought.

**18** The Palestinian Hebron Chamber of Commerce holds first election in occupied territories in 15 years. Six of 11 seats are won by Islamic fundamentalist movement Hamas, four by the PLO, and one by an independent.

Predominantly white Denver elects its first black mayor, Democrat Wellington Webb.

Both houses of Louisiana state legislature override Gov. Buddy Roemer's veto of abortion bill that allows abortion only in cases of rape, incest, or to save life of the mother. The law is to come into effect in early fall.

King Hussein of Jordan dismisses cabinet and chooses the Palestinian foreign minister Tahir Masri to become prime minister and form new government.

A mud slide caused by torrential rains in Antofagasta, Chile, kills 61 people, injures 750, leaves 1,000 people homeless.

In Karachi, Pakistan, Judge Nabi Sher Junejo is killed by four masked gunmen; Judge Junejo was trying the husband of former prime minister Benazir Bhutto on charges of conspiring to kill political opponents.

**19** Senate approves first overhaul of federal transportation system in 35 years and allocates $123 bil. to repair roads and bridges. For first time, states will be allowed to choose projects.

First popularly elected president of Russian republic, Boris N. Yeltsin, visits Washington, D.C., and is greeted by of members of Congress.

Dept. of Health and Human Services health economist Fred Hellinger announces that $5.8 bil. will be spent to treat AIDS in the U.S. in 1991; the amount is expected to rise to $40.4 bil. by 1994. The annual cost of treatment for one person infected with AIDS is $32,000.

**20** German parliament votes 337-to-320 in favor of moving its capital from Bonn to the historic capital of Berlin; move will take place slowly over 12 years.

In Washington, Pres. Bush meets Russia's newly elected president Boris Yeltsin, but vows to continue to deal with central government of Soviet Pres. Gorbachev.

Supreme Court rules 7-to-2 that fabricated quotations of public figures are libelous only if an alteration changes meaning of what person said.

In South Korea, local elections are won by governing Democratic Liberal party, which wins 564 of 866 council seats, despite widespread discontent and protests by student activists.

**21** Supreme Court votes 5-to-4 to allow states to ban nude dancing to protect order and morality.

In Tokyo, Nomura Securities Co., the world's largest brokerage house, admits it improperly compensated its biggest clients $120 mil. for stock market losses, and executive vice president

Yasuhiro Mizuuchi discloses that company provided $150 mil. in financing to Susumu Ishii, a member of a powerful Japanese crime family, for a share-manipulation scheme. Nikko Securities admits same indiscretions and improper compensation to clients totaling $122 mil.

In Washington, U.S. and European allies announce they will leave 5,000-member contingency force in Turkey to protect Kurds after forces withdraw in mid-July.

Terrorist suicide car bombing of Sri Lankan army command center in Colombo, used in anti-Tamil guerrilla campaign, kills 60 people, including 20 civilians, and wounds 50.

**22** In Tirana, Sec. of State Baker is greeted by 300,000 Albanians during first visit ever by a U.S. official. Baker urges Albanians to move toward democracy.

First Palestinian rival to PLO is formed by Kamel Tabanja in West Bank town of Ramallah; the Palestinian National party advocates only peaceful opposition.

The South African government, African National Congress, and Inkatha Freedom party meet for first time in Johannesburg to discuss ending factional violence.

Militant Mohawk Warrior Society in St. Regis Indian Reservation, N.Y., discloses it received $250,000 from Col. Muammar el-Qaddafi of Libya on June 11 in Tripoli.

**23** In London, Group of Seven industrialized democracies (Italy, Canada, U.S., Britain, Japan, Germany, and France) agree to offer the USSR associate membership in the IMF, entitling it to technical assistance for economic reform, but not financial aid.

After meeting in Thailand, Cambodian government and three opposition groups, Khmer Rouge, Khmer People's National Liberation Front, and a group headed by exiled Prince Norodom Sihanouk, agree to indefinite cease-fire to end 12 years of civil war, on eve of new round of peace talks.

**24** Supreme Court rules 5-to-4 that a news organization is not protected from lawsuits if it reveals name of a source after promising to keep it secret.

Supreme Court votes 6-to-3 to overturn 1963 decision guaranteeing state prison inmates right to challenge state convictions or sentences in federal court, known as "petitions for writs of habeas corpus." Such petitions are not allowed if inmate fails to meet state court requirements before turning to federal court.

In Hanoi, Vietnam, at seventh meeting of national congress since party formed in 1930, ruling Communist party announces it will not yield absolute power over the country, despite free-market reforms currently underway.

On eve of the 41st anniversary of start of Korean War, U.S. and North Korea reach agreement in principle to return remains of U.S. soldiers missing in Korean War, and North Korea delivers remains of 11 of 8,000 missing soldiers.

Northrop Corp. agrees to pay $8 mil. to settle lawsuit brought by two employees for falsifying tests on air force cruise missile parts.

**25** Parliaments of Slovenia and Croatia declare independence that will lead to secession from Yugoslavia if negotiations for loose confederation of republics collapse.

In Peru, Shining Path guerrilla movement

mounts major offensive against Pres. Alberto Fujimori's government, killing 60 people in one week, in commemoration of fifth anniversary of government's execution of 100 imprisoned guerrillas in Lima.

In Brazil, Pres. Fernando Collor de Mello abolishes tax subsidies for farmers and ranchers who cut down the Amazon rain forest and dismisses head of Indian protection agency for failing to give legal protection to 237 Indian homelands, a stalled project to be completed by 1993.

In Prague, Lt. Gen. Eduard Vorobyov, commander of Soviet forces, and Lt. Gen. Rudolf Duchacek of Czechoslovakian army sign protocol formally ending 23 years of Soviet military occupation, symbolically restoring Czechoslovakia's national sovereignty.

As state of siege imposed June 5 by Pres. Bendjedid continues, Algerian security forces battle with hundreds of Islamic fundamentalists in Algiers; seven people are dead and 34 wounded.

**26** Martial law ends in Kuwait and martial law court proceedings are transferred to civil court. Kuwait prime minister commutes sentences of all 29 collaborators sentenced to death to life in prison.

In London, 1976 convictions of seven people who served prison terms of 4 to 14 years for operating a bomb factory for the Irish Republican Army are overturned.

In Straits of Malacca, 150 miles southwest of Kuala Lumpur, 120 Indonesians, mostly illegal aliens deported from Malaysia, are lost after an Indonesian trawler and an unidentified ship collide; there are 13 survivors.

**27** South Africa announces it will sign Nuclear Nonproliferation Treaty and agrees not to develop nuclear weapons.

Supreme Court rules 5-to-4 that constitution permits mandatory life sentences without parole for nonviolent first offenses. By a vote of 6-to-3, court also overrules two earlier decisions preventing prosecutors in death penalty case from introducing evidence about murder victim's character and crime's effect on victim's family during sentencing.

Justice Thurgood Marshall, Supreme Court's only black justice and one of its few liberals, retires from the court after 24 years.

Party loyalist Do Muoi is elected general secretary of Vietnamese Communist party and immediately makes an international appeal for economic aid.

**28** Yugoslav army is deployed to Slovenia to take control of airports and border posts and prevent republic from putting into effect declared independence; skirmishes result in 150 people wounded or dead. One day later Croatia and Slovenia agree to suspend declarations of independence in response to federal officials' promise to recall federal troops from Slovenia and allow a Croatian to assume rotating presidency. A cease-fire is called immediately and collapses hours later with sporadic fighting in Slovenia.

At a military compound near Baghdad, Iraqi soldiers fire warning shots over heads of UN delegation attempting to inspect machinery used to make nuclear weapons; it is third such incident.

Senate approves "Brady bill" creating five-day waiting period for handgun purchases and providing penalties for states that fail to run background checks to identify felons. Bill receives enough votes to override a presidential veto.

In Paris, members of Comecon, Soviet-led trading bloc set up in 1949, agree to disband organization and liquidate jointly owned assets.

An earthquake measuring 6.0 on the Richter scale, centered 15 miles northeast of downtown Los Angeles and seven miles beneath San Gabriel Mountains, damages cities of Pasadena and Sierra Madre. One death is reported.

In Minnesota, Walter Leroy Moody, Jr., is convicted on 71 counts, including first degree murder, in death of a federal judge and a civil rights lawyer by delivering mail bombs in the southeast.

**29** An estimated 1,200 Kuwaiti refugees fearing punishment for collaboration with Iraqis during occupation flee to Iraq from a border camp.

The European Community lifts its sports boycott of South Africa, citing its progress in abolishing apartheid; the EC also announces $1.4 bil. in aid for the USSR.

**30** In biggest military reduction in 20 years, Federal Defense Base Closure and Realignment Commission recommends closure of Philadelphia naval shipyard, Long Beach, Calif., naval station, Fort Ord, Calif., army base, and 11 smaller installations.

## July 1991

**1** Former Soviet foreign minister Eduard Shevardnadze joins prominent Soviet citizens, including Gorbachev adviser Aleksandr Yakovlev and Russian republic Vice President Aleksandr Rutskoy, founding new political opposition movement to unite insurgents and Communist reformers.

Soviet parliament passes law allowing private ownership of industrial enterprises, breaking government's 70-year monopoly.

In Moscow, citizens of Russian republic register for unemployment benefits for first time.

After 50 years of silence, Romanian government admits that military and police killed 400,000 men, women, and children in Romanian pogroms in 1941; government previously claimed murders were carried out by Germans and Hungarians.

Unable to agree on tax increases and spending cuts, California, Connecticut, Illinois, Louisiana, Maine, Massachusetts, North Carolina, Ohio, and Pennsylvania miss June 30 deadline to balance their budgets; government shutdowns are planned for many states.

Pres. Bush nominates Judge Clarence Thomas to U.S. Supreme Court to fill seat vacated by Thurgood Marshall. A conservative, black appellate court judge for the District of Columbia circuit, Thomas is subsequently opposed by a number of organizations, including the National Organization for Women, National Association for the Advancement of Colored People, AFL-CIO, League of United Latin American Citizens, Congressional Black Caucus, and National Abortion Rights Action League.

In largest hashish bust on record, U.S. naval and law-enforcement officials seize 100 tons, worth $1.2 bil., aboard St. Vincent–registered freighter *Lucky Star* in Pacific Ocean 600 miles west of Midway; 15 people are arrested.

**2** Fighting breaks out between Yugoslav army and independent Slovenian forces in Ljubljana, Yugoslavia; 12 Yugoslav soldiers are killed. In Zagreb, Croatia, 1,000 demonstrators try to block an army convoy; three people are killed.

As Lebanese government continues effort to regain control of countryside from militias, its army battles Palestinians at guerrilla bases and arms depots in southern Lebanon; 80 Palestinian guerrillas are killed, 70 wounded, and 200 captured over four days. By July 9, government completes takeover of PLO bases in Lebanon.

At Univ. of Durban's Westville campus, African National Congress holds its first full conference of 2,244 delegates inside South Africa in 30 years; Nelson Mandela is elected to succeed ANC Pres. Oliver Tambo.

In first visit by South Korean head of state since 1966, Pres. Roh Tae Woo visits Washington to discuss his country's role as an economic power in Asia, and military and political conditions in North Korea.

**3** Soviet Pres. Mikhail Gorbachev denounces Communist party leaders for infighting that will likely bring on party collapse, and approves of progressive Democratic Reform Movement.

Industry rivals IBM and Apple Computer sign letter of intent to join forces to create new software and powerful computers to gain control over production of microprocessors and operating systems now manufactured by Intel Corp. and Microsoft Corp.

In Addis Ababa, Ethiopian political factions sign charter recognizing right of ethnic groups to secede and create their own countries. Eritrean People's Liberation Front expects to hold referendum on independence in two years, and agrees to give Ethiopia free access to Red Sea port of Assab in Eritrea.

**4** National Civil Rights Museum is dedicated on site of Lorraine Hotel in Memphis, where Rev. Martin Luther King, Jr., was assassinated in 1968.

**5** Colombia's new constitution, written by government officials, Indian leaders, former guerrillas, and clergymen, goes into effect. Among its sweeping changes are legalized civil divorce, institution of multiparty system, and popular elections for state governors.

Bank of Credit and Commerce International (BCCI), with $20 bil. in assets worldwide, is seized by regulators in the U.S., Cayman Islands, France, Great Britain, Luxembourg, Spain, and Switzerland, on charges of widespread fraud including concealed losses and false accounting methods.

As EC freezes arms sales and aid to Yugoslavia and threatens further measures if Yugoslav army continues to battle in Slovenia and Croatia, Yugoslavia's central government offers control of border posts to Slovenia on condition that Slovenia turn over customs revenues to federal government. Slovenia releases 2,500 Yugoslav soldiers. In Croatia, rebel Serbs continue to battle Croatian officials, resulting in the deaths of 25 policemen in one week.

**7** King Hussein of Jordan repeals martial law, in effect since 1967 Arab-Israeli war, legalizing large public meetings and lifting restrictions on freedom of speech and press.

**8** On island of Brioni, Yugoslav leaders sign accord calling for internationally observed ceasefire in Slovenia and Croatia, and recall of all federal troops and local militias to bases. In Croatia, Croats and minority Serbs battle for eight hours, leaving five combatants dead before Yugoslav army tanks put a stop to the fighting.

In Baghdad, Iraq admits to UN that it conducted three previously undisclosed projects to produce enriched uranium, which can be used in atomic bombs, and has produced about one pound of enriched uranium, not sufficient for nuclear weapons. U.S. intelligence denounces list of Iraqi nuclear sites as misleading and incomplete.

**9** Chinese newspaper *China Daily* reports that flooding from unusually heavy rain in eastern and central China has killed 1,729 people in two months and damaged crops and industrial centers; nine dams are blasted on Huangpu, Yangtze, and Yellow rivers to relieve rising water levels.

In response to South Africa's commitment to end racial discrimination in sports, International Olympic Committee lifts 21-year ban on country's athletes and allows them to participate in 1992 games in Barcelona.

In federal court in Washington, D.C., Alan D. Fiers, Jr., director of CIA Central American covert operations from 1984 to 1986, admits he told his superiors, including third-ranking CIA official, deputy director for operations Clair E. George (retired 1987), about Iran-Contra deals months before they were publicly disclosed, and was ordered by George not to disclose his knowledge to Congress.

**10** Pres. Bush lifts U.S. trade sanctions against South Africa, making it possible for U.S. to engage in trade with South Africa, make bank loans to South African government, engage in new investments, and coordinate air transportation. African National Congress disputes whether all five conditions set by Comprehensive Anti-Apartheid Act (1986), including releasing all political prisoners, have been met. Still in place are limits on lending by IMF and Export-Import Bank, a ban on exports to military and police, a UN arms embargo, and ban on intelligence cooperation.

In Moscow, Boris N. Yeltsin is inaugurated as first freely elected president of Russian republic.

Slovenian parliament ratifies EC-sponsored peace agreement and suspends republic's independence declaration for three months.

Peruvian national police, reportedly drunk, shoot down a commercial airplane in Amazon jungle 360 miles northeast of Lima shortly after takeoff, killing seventeen people on board.

L'Express commuter plane en route from Mobile, Ala., to Birmingham crashes, killing 13 people.

**11** A total eclipse of the Sun, seen most clearly in Hawaii at 7:30 a.m., local time, blackens skies across Pacific Ocean and Central America for five minutes.

Nationair DC-8 flying from Jeddah, Saudi Arabia, to Sokoto, Nigeria, crashes while making an emergency landing just after takeoff; all 247 passengers, mostly Muslim pilgrims returning to Nigeria, and 14 crew are killed.

Pan Am agrees to sell routes to Africa, Europe, and Asia and its shuttle operations connecting New York, Washington, and Boston to Delta Air Lines for $260 mil.

In attempt to improve Japanese-American relations during visit with Pres. Bush in Kennebunkport, Me., Japanese Prime Minister Toshiki Kaifu agrees to pay U.S. additional $500 mil. requested for military expenses in Persian Gulf.

House Democrats elect David Bonior (D-Mich.)

as majority whip.

**12** Senate Foreign Relations Committee chairman Claiborne Pell (D-R.I.) and Alan Cranston (D-Calif.) accuse former U.S. ambassador to Iraq April Glaspie of misleading Congress during her testimony about prewar meetings with Iraqi Pres. Hussein. Glaspie claims she warned Pres. Hussein not to invade Kuwait, but cables from Glaspie to Pres. Bush are conciliatory in tone and make no mention of such warnings.

In the second reported attack on someone connected with Salman Rushdie's *The Satanic Verses* of the month, Japanese translator of the book Hitoshi Igarashi is found dead at Tsukuba Univ. near Tokyo. Italian translator Ettore Capriolo was stabbed, not fatally, in Milan on July 3.

**13** Indian Central Bureau of Investigations discloses that a Sri Lankan Tamil militant is being sought for masterminding May 21 assassination of former prime minister Rajiv Gandhi.

**14** Syrian Pres. Hafez al-Assad accepts Pres. Bush's compromise proposal for Middle East peace conference. Israel subsequently refuses to accept compromise, stating it will only accept unreserved, direct negotiations with Syria.

In Meru, Kenya, boys at a boarding school riot over school's failure to pay fees for interscholastic athletics and take their anger out on girls who refuse to join protest at St. Kizito secondary school, breaking into girls' dormitory and raping 71 girls; 19 girls are suffocated or crushed to death when beds collapse on them. Thirty-nine boys are arrested and St. Kizito is closed.

Heads of state of Group of Seven largest industrialized nations and members of EC gather in London for 17th annual summit conference, focusing mainly on USSR's move to a market economy. After presummit meeting, Pres. Bush and Pres. François Mitterrand of France announce they will use military action against Iraq if it continues to develop nuclear weapons.

A 97-car Southern Pacific freight train derails and spills 19,000 gallons of metam sodium, a chemical used to kill insects and weeds, into Sacramento River 45 miles north of Lake Shasta; spill eventually enters lake, which supplies drinking water to entire state.

**15** New federal guidelines issued by Centers for Disease Control in Atlanta recommend that health care workers who perform surgery should voluntarily be tested for AIDS virus and hepatitis B, and if infected should inform their patients and stop performing surgery.

To stave off largest-ever failure of an insurer, officials in Newark, N.J., seize financially distressed Mutual Benefit Life Insurance Co., which is threatened by bad real estate investments.

An estimated 3,300 coalition troops complete withdrawal from northern Iraq, establishing rapid-deployment force stationed in Silopi, Turkey, comprised of 2,500 troops from the U.S., Belgium, Britain, France, Italy, the Netherlands, Spain, and Turkey as a safeguard against attack by Pres. Hussein on Kurds.

Weakened by bad real estate loans and loans to developing countries, Chemical Bank and Manufacturers Hanover announce plans for largest bank merger in U.S. history, with combined assets of $135.5 bil.

Claiming that revised figures are unreliable for small communities, Commerce Sec. Robert

Mosbacher announces that 1990 census will not be adjusted to add an estimated 5 million people missed during 1990 census.

U.S. announces it will abandon Clark Air Base, in the Philippines, because of extensive damage caused by recent volcanic eruptions from Mt. Pinatubo, but will retain nearby Subic Bay Naval Station.

KLM and Indonesian national airline join Lufthansa, Northwest, Federal Express, and Challenge Air Cargo in agreeing to halt shipments to U.S. and Europe of wild birds caught in South America, Africa, and Asia.

In Washington, a former POW releases photograph showing three U.S. servicemen missing in Southeast Asia since Vietnam War and holding sign dated May 25, 1990. Its authenticity is determined to be inconclusive, and Defense Dept. concludes that one of the men pictured is dead.

**16** In order to investigate extent of Robert Gates's knowledge of Iran-Contra affair in 1986, when he served as deputy CIA director, Senate Intelligence Committee delays confirmation hearings for Gates as director of CIA until September.

In Athens, leftist organization "November 17" bombs car carrying Turkey's ambassador to Greece, and detonates five other bombs in protest of Pres. Bush's upcoming visit. Group believes Bush sides with Turkish separatists in predominantly Greek Cyprus.

At London summit conference, Group of Seven agrees to support USSR economic reforms, and support USSR's admission to International Monetary Fund.

**17** Group of Seven agrees to provide technical expertise, but not financial assistance, to aid USSR in its move to a market economy. Pres. Gorbachev and Pres. Bush agree on strategic arms treaty to be signed later.

In Beijing, Cambodia's four competing factions agree to share a UN seat; delegation would include a representative of exiled Cambodian leader Prince Norodom Sihanouk, two representatives of Vietnamese-backed Communist government in Phnom Penh, and Khmer Rouge leader Khieu Samphan. Factions also unanimously elect Prince Sihanouk as president of Cambodian Supreme National Council to lead country until elections are held.

Senate votes to raise its own salaries by $23,000 to $124,900 per year, and to eliminate allowance to accept up to $23,068 in speaking fees annually.

**18** First Ibero-American Summit Conference opens in Guadalajara, Mexico, attended by leaders of 21 Spanish- and Portuguese-speaking countries. Conference provides forum for economic integration and cooperation.

In Jerusalem, Judge Ezra Kama announces findings of investigation into October 1990 shootings at Al-Aksa Mosque in Jerusalem's Old City that resulted in deaths of 17 Palestinians. Contrary to report of government-appointed commission, Judge Kama finds that Israeli police, not the Palestinians, instigated violence.

In Damascus, U.S. Sec. of State James Baker announces that Syria agrees to direct talks with Israel. Jordan, the Palestinians, and Israel must agree to same before invitations to Middle East peace conference are issued by cosponsors, the USSR and the U.S.

Yugoslav federal presidency begins withdrawing federal troops from Slovenia, an operation to be completed within three months.

**19** South African Law and Order Minister Adriaan Vlok admits government made payments of up to $100,000 to Inkatha Freedom party, archrival of African National Congress, to finance rallies and undermine popularity of ANC in 1989-90, when government claimed it was impartial. Vlok later admits to giving $600,000 to Inkatha and the Inkatha-sponsored United Workers Union of South Africa over six years.

At Elephant Pass camp in northern Sri Lanka, nine days of combat between Tamil rebels and Sri Lankan soldiers leave more than 600 rebels and 78 soldiers dead in fiercest fighting since separatist guerrilla warfare broke out in 1983; fighting ends after 25 days when government successfully destroys rebel bunkers.

**20** UN reports that Kurdish guerrillas control Sulaimaniya after three days' fighting with Iraqi army; battle resulted in up to 80 dead and 600 wounded.

In Moscow, Russian Pres. Boris Yeltsin bans Communist party organization from government workplaces, including offices, farms, and factories.

Peruvian congressional committee uncovers preliminary evidence that former president Alan García removed as much as $50 mil. of government funds for his private use to Panama branch of BCCI, where more than half of Peru's cash was kept during García's term from 1985 to 1990; García denies any wrongdoing.

**21** Jordan joins Syria, Lebanon, Egypt, and Saudi Arabia in agreeing to regional peace talks. Israeli Prime Minister Yitzhak Shamir declares he needs more time.

**22** Bank regulators in UK disclose that BCCI concealed losses of billions of dollars and may never have been profitable. BCCI hid this fact from banking officials through bribery, fabricated loans, unrecorded deposits, and rapid transfers of funds from one bank division to another.

In Croatian village of Mirkovci, fighting between Serbian and Croatian forces leaves at least 20 dead. At the same time, in Ohrid, Macedonia, leaders of six Yugoslavian republics call for disarmament of illegal paramilitary organizations, recall of mobilized military and police reserve units, and an end to violence in Yugoslavia for three months while leaders develop new organizational plan. The next day Croatian leaders declare their refusal to sign peace accord.

In Managua, Nicaragua, 600 delegates of Sandinista Front vote to become a democratic political party and elect former Nicaraguan president Daniel Ortega Saavedra as secretary general; party will continue to identify itself as socialist, revolutionary, and anti-imperialist, but will drop references to being Marxist-Leninist.

Two weeks after release of independent commission report stating that Los Angeles police department allowed racism and brutality and urging police chief Daryl F. Gates to step down, Gates announces his retirement by April 1992.

Off Cape Flattery, Wash., a Chinese freighter collides with and sinks Japanese fish-processing boat; one crew member is lost at sea and two injured. Sunken vessel carried 350,000 gallons of fuel, a third of which spills and washes ashore along 70 miles of Pacific Northwest, killing hundreds of sea birds and mammals.

After would-be victim calls police, Milwaukee police arrest Jeffrey Dahmer and remove three human heads, boxes holding body parts of up to 11 men, photographs of mutilated bodies, and a barrel of acid from his apartment. Dahmer confesses to drugging, strangling, dismembering, and photographing his victims and in some cases boiling their skulls to preserve them; he is charged with four counts of first-degree intentional homicide and habitual criminality, and held on $1 mil. bail. Believed to have killed at least 17 people over a 13-year period, Dahmer subsequently pleads innocent by reason of insanity.

**23** Two weeks after House votes 313–112 to pass a similar bill, Senate votes 55-to-44 to place restrictions on China's most-favored-nation status as of July 1992, but fails to secure enough votes to override likely presidential veto. Conditions to be attached include China's ending arms sales, releasing political prisoners, and stopping export of prisoner-made products to the U.S. Chinese government accuses Congress of interference in its internal affairs.

In one of first cases of acquaintance rape to come to trial, three white male students at St. John's Univ. are acquitted of all charges of sodomy, sexual abuse, and assault against a black female student who claims she was abused after being made drunk and becoming unconscious.

In Washington, Soviet government applies for full membership to IMF and World Bank, to the surprise of the Group of Seven leading industrialized nations who recommended a limited "special association" for USSR at summit talks in London. Full membership in organizations enables USSR to borrow funds, while associate status permits access to technical assistance.

**24** In anticipation of Communist party central committee meetings and upcoming visit to USSR by Pres. Bush, Soviet Pres. Gorbachev reaches agreement with nine of 15 Soviet republics on draft treaty to decentralize political and economic power.

In Madagascar, forces opposed to emergency decree imposed by Pres. Didier Ratsiraka take over two government ministries, bringing to six the number of offices taken in one week. Tens of thousands of people rally daily to call for Ratsiraka's resignation and free multiparty elections.

In Lebanon, for second time in a week, the Islamic group Holy Warriors for Freedom threatens action against German hostages unless it is apprised of condition of two Shiite Muslim terrorists held in Germany in connection with 1985 TWA hijacking and murder of an American.

At nuclear power plant in Sofia, Bulgaria, a radioactive leak between two reactors scheduled to be closed due to safety hazards results in radiation levels 100 times higher than normal.

**25** South African government admits it donated $35 mil. to support political parties opposing South-West Africa People's Organization in pre-independence Namibian elections. SWAPO was victorious in November 1989 elections, but fell short of two-thirds majority needed to institute socialist constitution.

Rearmed Contras attack northern Nicaraguan town of Auilalí, protesting abuses of power and police threats of violence by Sandinista security

forces left in place after Chamorro government took office. An estimated 1,000 former rebels have rearmed since laying down weapons.

Muslim rebels ambush Indian army convoy, killing 100 soldiers in Jammu and Kashmir. Three days later, Indian security forces kill 11 Muslims and arrest 47 in the same area.

**26** At Brooks Memorial Hospital in Dunkirk, N.Y., Dr. Neal Rzepkowski is asked to resign because he is HIV positive, in part due to newly issued Centers for Disease Control guidelines (see July 15). Authorities do not believe Dr. Rzepkowski infected any patients.

Following democratic reforms, including free elections in 1990, Sec. of State James Baker becomes first Western diplomat to address Mongolian parliament and promises U.S. aid of $6.4 mil. to offset losses incurred when USSR withdrew aid in 1990.

In Moscow, Communist party leaders approve new party charter proposed by Pres. Gorbachev, declaring it a "party of democratic reforms." Pres. Gorbachev vows to fight Russian Pres. Yeltsin's ban on Communist party from workplace to extent constitutionally possible.

**27** Death toll from battles between Serbs and Croats in Croatia rises to 80 and 100 wounded in one week, the most violent week in Croatian history since World War II. Government of Serbian republic supplies rebels with medicine, canteens, clothing, and food. The EC invites Yugoslavia's collective presidency to Brussels for urgent talks.

**28** In Santa Barbara, Calif., a 39-car Southern Pacific freight train derails and spills 440 gallons of military jet fuel component onto a highway, forcing evacuation of 350 residents.

**29** Pres. Bush visits USSR for fourth summit meeting with Pres. Gorbachev. Bush vows to ask Congress to grant USSR most-favored-nation status, but criticizes Moscow's treatment of Baltic republics and aid to Cuba. Bush also meets with Russian Pres. Yeltsin.

Stanford Univ. president Donald Kennedy resigns effective May 1992, in wake of scandal concerning overcharging government for millions of dollars in indirect research costs to pay for Kennedy's antiques, fresh flowers, etc.

Federal Reserve seeks $200 mil. penalty against BCCI for violating U.S. banking laws, largest fine in Federal Reserve's history, and seeks to bar permanently nine foreign businessmen from American banks. New York grand jury indicts BCCI and former executives Aga Hassan Abedi and Swaleh Naqvi on charges of fraud, theft, and money-laundering.

In Brussels, EC decides to send unarmed observer force of 100 to Croatia to seek ceasefire.

In Jerusalem, Israeli Prime Minister Yitzhak Shamir reconfirms refusal to attend Arab-Israeli peace talks if delegates from East Jerusalem or PLO are allowed to attend.

Islamic security forces in Isfahan, Iran, arrest 300 people trying to prevent arrest of women wearing improper dress. Improper dress, including showing one's hair and wearing stockings or makeup, is punishable by imprisonment and up to 70 lashes of the whip.

**30** After inspection of chemical weapons in Iraq, special UN commission announces it found 46,000 chemical shells and warheads and 3,000

tons of raw materials for weapons—quantities four times greater than Baghdad had admitted.

In Western India, rivers swollen from torrential rains during unusually harsh monsoon season burst through a dike, killing 500 people and destroying 2,000 houses in village of Mohad.

In Haiti, former head of Tontons Macoute terror squads during Duvalier regime, Roger Lafontant, is sentenced to life in prison for January 1991 attempt to keep Pres. Jean-Bertrand Aristide's government from taking office.

In second week of protests against an abortion clinic in Wichita, Kans., police arrest 177 people, bringing to 1,300 the number of people arrested for blocking the clinic entrance over two weeks. Subsequent arrests bring the total to 1,600, and Wichita's three abortion clinics are closed.

**31** Declaring arms race over, U.S. Pres. Bush and Soviet Pres. Gorbachev sign 700-page arms reduction treaty in Moscow, agreeing to cut stocks of long-range nuclear weapons. Meanwhile, six Lithuanian border guards are killed by unidentified gunmen.

Overturning 43-year-old law, Senate votes to allow women to fly military warplanes in combat.

Rear six cars of an 18-car train bound from Miami to New York jump the track at a freight siding near Camden, S.C., killing seven people and injuring 125.

Energy Dept. discloses that security personnel at nuclear weapons plants throughout U.S. illegally acquired and used surveillance equipment, for purposes including wiretapping and eavesdropping. Security officers at Hanford nuclear reservation in Richland, Wash., deny allegations that include wiretapping the phones of employees who publicly complained of safety, security, and environmental problems at the site.

### August 1991

**1** Israeli Prime Minister Yitzhak Shamir agrees to take part in Middle East peace talks so long as Palestinian delegation includes no members of PLO and no stateless or East Jerusalem Palestinians. Cabinet supports him.

Visiting Soviet Ukraine, Pres. Bush says U.S. will not take sides between Soviet government and republic governments.

An estimated 50,000 Croatians flee their homes to escape air and ground attacks by Yugoslav army and Serbian forces.

Two-year study of Bureau of Alcohol, Tobacco and Firearms concludes that domestic and imported wines sold in U.S. contain levels of lead up to three times legal amount for drinking water, due in part to lead foil caps that cover the cork.

**2** Senate Ethics Committee finds Sen. Alfonse D'Amato (R-N.Y.) innocent of nearly all accusations that he violated Senate rules and federal laws in his dealings with campaign contributors.

Senate votes 97-to-2 to use force to stop Iraq from producing atomic, biological, or chemical weapons, supporting Pres. Bush's threat to use military force to destroy Iraqi nuclear arsenal.

At Cape Canaveral, space shuttle *Atlantis* lifts off for its ninth flight (the 42nd overall for the shuttle program), carrying five crew and a T.D.R.S. communications satellite that completes network to make continuous communications possible between Earth and spacecraft, including Hubble telescope, spy satellites, and space shuttles.

**3** Because of the number of Cuban tourists overstaying their visas and illegally staying in U.S., Bush administration suspends processing of six-month tourist visas to Cubans, who are applying for tourist visas at triple 1990's rate.

Comoros Pres. Said Mohammed Djohar survives attempted coup staged by opposition party members and senior judge.

Japanese Finance Minister Ryutaro Hashimoto publicly apologizes, but refuses to resign, for involvement in loans worth $10 mil. made to three friends. Loans were arranged by Hashimoto's top aide and a Fuji Bank executive who forged deposit receipts used as loan collateral in largest bank fraud in Japanese history.

**4** During a weekend cruise from East London to Durban, South Africa, Greek liner *Oceanos* sinks in heavy seas two miles off coast. Helicopters and ships rescue all 571 passengers and crew.

In Tunis, Tunisia, Palestine Liberation Organization spokesman announces that PLO agrees to attend regional peace conference and offers to compromise with Israel on makeup of Palestinian delegation.

Responding to meager harvest and threat of famine in coming winter, Soviet Pres. Mikhail Gorbachev issues executive order to lower customs duties on imports of food and medicine and restricts import of luxury items.

In Yugoslavia, Serbia refuses to comply with EC-proposed cease-fire between Serbian rebels and authorities in Croatian republic, where 200 people have died since Croatia declared independence. Serbia agrees to cease-fire on Aug. 6.

**5** Iraq admits it secretly extracted three grams of plutonium from fuel at internationally monitored nuclear plant in Tuwaitha, Iraq, but denies it did so to make nuclear weapons. It also admits it misled UN inspectors about secret biological weapons.

House Speaker Thomas S. Foley and Senate majority leader George Mitchell order inquiries into allegations that Ronald Reagan's 1980 presidential campaign delayed release of 52 American hostages from Iran until after national elections.

For fifth time since 1949, South Korea applies for UN membership; North Korea applies for third time. On Aug. 8, UN Security Council unanimously approves Korean applications.

Arrested in Gulfport, Tex., for strangulation of a 10-year-old homeless girl, Donald Leroy Evans, a drifter, confesses to killing more than 60 people in 20 states since 1977.

**6** *Asian Wall Street Journal Weekly* discloses that Pol Pot, who the Khmer Rouge claimed resigned from official duties in 1989, secretly directed the group's negotiations in Cambodian peace talks in June. Pol Pot led the Khmer Rouge during late 1970s.

In Miami, David Rodrigo Ortiz Hermida becomes sixth of Gen. Manuel Noriega's codefendants to plead guilty to drug charges and agree to testify against him in exchange for federal protection for his family and light sentencing.

**7** Twelve people die as thousands of Albanians attempt to flee to Italy aboard freighter *Vlora*.

In New Orleans, federal judge Adrian G. Duplantier rules Louisiana's recently passed antiabortion law unconstitutional under *Roe* v. *Wade*.

In Wichita, federal district judge Patrick Kelly, who barred antiabortion protesters from blocking entrances to area abortion clinics, receives numerous death threats and is placed under protection of U.S. marshals.

**8** In Lebanon, British television journalist John McCarthy is released by the pro-Iranian militant group Islamic Holy War, after being held hostage since Apr. 17, 1986; he reports that three other hostages held by the same group, Americans Terry Anderson and Thomas Sutherland (held since 1985) and Briton Terry Waite (held since 1987) are alive and in good health. Jerome Leyraud, a French aid worker, is kidnapped in Beirut by Organization for the Defense of Prisoners' Rights; he is freed three days later.

In Bari, Italy, 10,000 Albanians seeking work, food, and shelter are taken to Victory soccer stadium to await their forced return to Albania. Clashes with police break out when émigrés attempt to escape.

Shahpur Bakhtiar, Iran's prime minister before being exiled to France by the Islamic revolution in February 1979, and his chief aide are stabbed to death outside Paris.

**9** Wall Street firm Salomon Bros. suspends two executives in charge of buying government securities and admits to violating government rules limiting buyers to purchase 35% of a single Treasury issue and preventing use of customers' names without authorization. Salomon Bros. made illegal bids in four auctions in 1990–91, and admits that John Gutfreund, chairman and chief executive, Thomas Strauss, president, and Deryk Maughan, vice chairman, knew about misconduct since April and attempted a cover-up; all three are forced to resign.

During speech by Pres. F.W. de Klerk in Ventersdorp, South Africa, two people are killed and 54 wounded as policemen clash with proapartheid Afrikaner Resistance Movement protesters attempting to keep de Klerk from speaking.

Vietnamese Prime Minister Do Muoi resigns after three years; he is succeeded by Vo Van Kiet, a former mayor of Saigon, who vows to transform Vietnam into a market economy.

Pentagon discloses that U.S. fire was responsible for 15% of U.S. forces killed or wounded in Persian Gulf war.

In Chicago, 10 members of the powerful 30-year-old street gang El Rukns ("The Foundation" in Arabic) are convicted on several charges, including racketeering, drug distribution, narcotics conspiracy, and conspiracy to commit murder. Three members are acquitted, and 65 additional members await upcoming trials. In 1987, members of El Rukns were convicted of conspiracy to conduct terrorist attacks in U.S. for Libya. On Sept. 2, businessman Noah Robinson, Rev. Jesse Jackson's half brother, and six El Rukn leaders are convicted of similar charges.

**10** At living quarters of Wat Promkunaram Thai Buddhist temple in Phoenix, Ariz., six monks, a nun, and two acolytes are shot to death by at least two gunmen who ransack temple.

Prime Minister Toshiki Kaifu of Japan visits Beijing. During meeting between Kaifu and Prime Minister Li Peng, China agrees in principle to sign Nuclear Nonproliferation Treaty.

**11** Revolutionary Justice Organization releases American book salesman Edward Austin Trace to Syrian officials in Beirut; Trace was a captive since Oct. 21, 1986. In an effort to free other hostages, Israel offers to discuss release of Arab prisoners in exchange for information about seven Israeli soldiers missing in Lebanon.

**12** BankAmerica Corp. announces it will acquire Security Pacific Corp., uniting the two largest banks in the western U.S. to create a bank approaching the size of the largest U.S. bank, Citicorp.

In Madagascar, antigovernment protests over three days leave 51 dead and several hundred wounded; 31 casualties result when Pres. Didier Ratsiraka's guard fire on 400,000 marchers outside the presidential palace, and 20 others die in political violence in northern city of Mahajanga. A general strike shuts down most businesses.

**13** In Washington, former presidential adviser Clark M. Clifford, chairman of First American Bankshares, Inc., Washington's largest bank holding company, resigns under pressure from federal regulators investigating BCCI, which secretly controlled the company.

UN announces up to $100,000 in compensation will be made available to anyone whose spouse, child, or parent was killed in Persian Gulf war, anyone who sustained serious personal injury, or anyone who left Iraq or Kuwait between Aug. 2, 1990, and Mar. 2, 1991, due to Iraq's invasion of Kuwait; funds will come from Iraq's future oil revenues.

In Plymouth, Mass., teenage vandals paint a black swastika on Plymouth Rock.

**14** In connection with suit filed by a General Electric employee under Federal False Claims Act, Justice Dept. accuses GE of fraud for billing Pentagon $30 mil. for sale of F-16 fighter engines and services to Israeli military that never took place.

In Soviet Azerbaijan, Armenians in Nagorno-Karabakh take 33 Soviet soldiers hostage and demand release of 16 Armenians detained by the military for carrying weapons. Armenian residents abduct eight more soldiers Aug. 15 and threaten to transfer them to Armenia if demands are not met.

**15** Congressional Budget Office discloses that federal budget deficit will rise to record $362 bil. for coming year, due to increasing Medicaid costs and cost of rescuing financial institutions.

During typhoon in South China Sea, 16 people die and 168 are rescued after oil worker barge capsizes and sinks 65 miles from Hong Kong.

UN Security Council adopts resolution to allow Iraq to sell up to $1.6 bil. in oil to buy food and medical supplies, but keeps all other sanctions against Iraq in place; 30% of the $1.6 bil. is earmarked for war compensation and to repay UN for its border surveying and monitoring.

The U.S. and USSR send joint letter to UN Secretary General Javier Pérez de Cuéllar urging him to facilitate stalled peace talks in El Salvador, where the U.S. and USSR previously supported opposing sides in 11-year civil war.

**16** UN high commissioner for refugees and South African government agree to establish a UN office inside the country for one year to help resettle as many as 40,000 political exiles living in other African nations.

An Indian Airlines Boeing 737-200 catches fire and crashes 27 miles from Imphal in eastern India, killing all 69 people aboard.

Aleksandr Yakovlev, an adviser to Gorbachev, warns that a reactionary coup is possible.

Organizers for International Conference on AIDS planned for Boston in May 1992 announce conference will be canceled because U.S. government restricts entry of people infected with AIDS virus; the U.S. is the only developed nation with such restrictions in place.

Exactly one year after their arrest by under cover FBI agents, four eastern Kentucky county sheriffs and one police chief are convicted of taking bribes totaling $92,500 to protect drug dealers; one sheriff is acquitted.

**17** Lebanese government grants amnesty to former Christian army commander Gen. Michel Aoun and allows him to leave French embassy in Beirut after 10 months in hiding to seek political asylum in France; he had been avoiding charges on embezzlement of $35 mil. in public funds.

**18** Treasury Dept. suspends Salomon Bros. from bidding in Treasury auctions until an investigation into the firm's admission of illegal bidding is undertaken. Hours later, Treasury Sec. Nicholas Brady softens punishment by allowing Salomon to bid in auctions for itself, but not on behalf of clients.

National midterm elections in Mexico result in victory for ruling Institutional Revolutionary party, PRI, the party of Pres. Carlos Salinas de Gortari.

With winds of 115 mph, Hurricane Bob hits barrier islands of North Carolina before moving northward. By nightfall on Aug. 19, Bob has sideswiped the mid-Atlantic and New England states, especially Long Island, Cape Cod, and Rhode Island, causing two deaths, knocking out electricity for millions of homes and businesses, and flooding areas from North Carolina to Maine.

**19** One day before Pres. Gorbachev is to sign new union treaty giving wide powers to the republics, he is detained in a coup by Soviet military and KGB while on vacation in the Crimea.

Cuban refugee Julio Gonzalez is convicted of 174 counts of murder, two for each victim, for setting fatal fire at Happy Land Social Club in the Bronx, N.Y., on Mar. 25, 1990. He is later given maximum sentence of 25 years to life.

As a 12-day-old cease-fire collapses in Yugoslavia, fighting resumes between Serbians and republic forces in Croatia.

Madagascar's Active Forces coalition announces it is taking power from Pres. Didier Ratsiraka, claiming he is no longer in control of the country. In response, Pres. Ratsiraka extends state of emergency for 15 days.

In Wichita, Kans., 95 antiabortion demonstrators from Operation Rescue are arrested for blocking entrance to two clinics, bringing to 2,300 the total arrests in a month. One day later, an additional 130 protesters are arrested for rushing toward an abortion clinic entrance. Three protest leaders are jailed indefinitely and a federal judge fines them each $5,000 to $10,000 per day until they comply with his conditions that they end protests and leave Wichita.

**20** In Moscow, three people die in midnight clashes with police as hundreds of thousands of demonstrators rally around Russian Pres. Yeltsin outside Russian parliament in defiance of a military curfew and in support of Yeltsin's call for the resignation and criminal trial of eight coup

plotters; Pres. Bush telephones Yeltsin to offer support and cuts off relations with coup leaders; EC cuts off humanitarian aid to the USSR.

Seven Sri Lankan Tamils suspected of planning the May 21 assassination of former prime minister Rajiv Gandhi commit suicide as Indian forces close in on them in Bangalore. The leader, Raja Arumainayagam, also known as Sivarasan and One-Eyed Jack, shoots himself in the head, and six of his followers consume cyanide.

At Cape Canaveral, Fla., an Aries Rocket carrying secret experiments for Star Wars program is destroyed by remote control after going out of control after liftoff.

**21** Coup to oust Soviet Pres. Gorbachev collapses, and he returns to Moscow and resumes full duties after three days under house arrest in the Crimea. One coup leader, KGB chairman Vladimir Kryuchkov, is arrested.

Mud slides set off by monsoon rains on the Philippines's Mt. Pinatubo kill 24 people and destroy hundreds of homes.

At a federal prison in Talladega, Ala., 121 Cuban inmates demanding cancellation of upcoming deportation of 34 Cubans seize 10 hostages. On Aug. 30, federal assault team storms prison, freeing hostages and taking custody of inmates without injury. One day later, 31 Cuban inmates are deported to Cuba.

South Carolina State Sen. Bud Long becomes 18th legislator and 28th person charged in an FBI undercover legislative vote-selling operation. Long is convicted of selling his vote to an undercover agent for $2,800.

**22** In wake of failed Soviet coup, Interior Minister Boris Pugo commits suicide, Prime Minister Valentin Pavlov is hospitalized with hypertension, Vasily Starodubtsev is sought for arrest, and five remaining coup plotters are arrested. Anatoly Lukyanov is accused of masterminding coup and submits resignation as speaker of Soviet parliament to Pres. Gorbachev.

Pres. Gorbachev refuses to join Boris Yeltsin in holding the Communist parliament responsible for the coup and remains party leader. Russian republic adopts tricolor flag of white, blue, and red, first used by Czar Peter the Great.

In Latvia and Lithuania, Communist party is outlawed by parliaments and Latvian Communist party leader Alfred Rubiks is sought for arrest for his support in the takeover.

Croatian president Franjo Tudjman sets Aug. 31 as deadline for Yugoslav federal presidency to withdraw Yugoslav troops from Croatia; if troops fail to withdraw, Tudjman says they will be treated as an occupying force and he will mobilize Croatian forces against them.

**23** Russian Pres. Yeltsin pressures Soviet Pres. Gorbachev into replacing his whole cabinet, in many cases with men loyal to Yeltsin. In Russian republic, Communist party members either defect or are locked out of their offices, and publication of party newspaper *Pravda* is halted. Latvian Communist parliament leader Alfred Rubiks is arrested in Riga.

In Madagascar, Pres. Ratsiraka gives Prime Minister Guy Willy Razanamasy full powers to form new government to include opposition forces.

Typhoon Gladys strikes the tip of Korea, bringing a record 16 inches of rain in one day to Pusan, South Korea's second-largest city; 55

people are killed and damage totals $11 mil.

**24** Pres. Gorbachev resigns as general secretary of Communist party's central committee, bans party from any official role in Soviet government, orders cabinet to resign, and names Ivan Silayev, a Yeltsin aide, to head committee to steer Soviet Union's national economy.

At least 100,000 people attend funeral of three men killed by Soviet troops in Moscow during anticoup demonstrations.

Russian Pres. Yeltsin formally recognizes independence of Estonia and Latvia, and has already recognized Lithuania as sovereign state after it declared independence in March. Ukrainian SSR declares independence, to be ratified by a Dec. 2 referendum.

Fighting between rebel Serbs and Croatian militia erupts immediately after German Foreign Minister Hans-Dietrich Genscher warns Yugoslavia's ambassador to Bonn, Boris Frlec, that if fighting in Croatia continues, Germany may recognize Croatia and Slovenia as separate states.

**25** Denmark, Norway, and Finland formally recognize secession of Estonia, Latvia, and Lithuania from Soviet Union. Republic of Byelorussia declares independence.

In Wichita, Kans., where antiabortion demonstrators organized by Operation Rescue have been blocking entrances to three area abortion clinics for a month, 25,000 abortion opponents attend rally at Wichita State Univ.

**26** College Board releases figures that show results of Scholastic Aptitude Test for college-bound high school seniors are at an all-time low for verbal scores (average 422—for men 426, and for women 418), and that math scores have fallen for first time since 1980 (average 474—for men 497, and for women 453).

Nikolai Kruchina, business manager of Soviet Communist party central committee responsible for budget, finance, and property worth $9 bil., commits suicide; Communist party anticipates financial collapse due to $500 mil. deficit.

**27** At Brussels meeting of the 12 European Community foreign ministers, EC recognizes Estonia, Latvia, and Lithuania as independent nations.

Soviet republic of Moldavia declares its independence from Soviet Union; republics of Russia, Kazakhstan, and Kirghizia agree to begin negotiating new union treaty.

American Bar Association evaluation committee rates Pres. Bush's nomination for Supreme Court justice, Judge Clarence Thomas, "qualified" for the job; two members give him an "unqualified" rating. None of the 15 committee members finds Thomas "well qualified."

In Pattaya, Thailand, Cambodian government and rebel factions agree to a disarmament pact, including disbanding 70% of military forces and putting 30% under UN supervision.

**28** In worst New York City subway disaster in 63 years, a subway derails at high speed and crashes, killing five people and injuring more than 200. Motorman Robert Ray is arrested five hours after he left the accident scene, and alcohol tests indicate he was legally drunk.

One day after cease-fire agreement is reached between Yugoslav army and Croatian leaders, Yugoslav army and rebel Serbs bombard Croatian republic near Vikovar.

After 24 years in power, Togo's military ruler,

Pres. Gnassingbé Eyadéma, hands over power to Prime Minister Kokou Koffigoh.

In Moscow, career bureaucrat and Soviet ambassador to Prague Boris Pankin is named new Soviet foreign minister.

**29** Soviet parliament votes to bar Communist party activities until its role in the coup is investigated. Party assets in republics are seized and offices closed.

In Kiev, republics of Russia and the Ukraine sign an agreement to remain in Soviet Union and negotiate loose federation. U.S. Pres. Bush and British Prime Minister John Major increase direct food aid to independent Soviet republics.

In Washington, the Occupational Safety and Health Admin. announces Citgo Petroleum Corp.'s agreement to pay $5.8 mil. in fines to settle charges of safety violations that led to Louisiana refinery fire in which six people died on Mar. 3, 1991; Citgo denies any fault or liability. Settlement is largest in OSHA's 20-year history.

**30** In the journal *Science*, neurobiologist Dr. Simon LeVay and his colleagues at Salk Institute in La Jolla, Calif., report findings that a segment of hypothalamus in the brains of homosexual men is different from that of heterosexual men, linking sexual behavior for the first time to biological traits.

NASA scientists make public first photographs of a landslide caused by a venusquake, a fracture of the planet Venus's crust.

Federal officials in Boston, Mass., disclose that they seized more than 6,000 pounds of hashish worth $100 mil. smuggled into the U.S. from Lebanon earlier this month.

**31** Yugoslav republic of Serbia accepts an EC peace proposal that includes international observers to oversee a cease-fire in Croatia and an arbitration commission to settle disputes.

In parliamentary elections in Singapore, ruling People's Action party of Prime Minister Goh Chok Tong claim an easy victory, taking 77 of 81 seats in parliament; but prime minister sees results as a vote of no confidence for his mandate for a more open government that promotes political debate and eases censorship because his party received only 62% of the overall vote, a smaller share than in the 1988 general election.

Soviet republics of Uzbekistan and Kirghizia declare independence, leaving only five republics agreeing to membership in union.

A crowd of 250,000 people, mostly union members and civil rights advocates, rally in Washington, D.C., to call for improved health care, education, and workers' rights.

### September 1991

**1** EC observers arrive in Belgrade, Yugoslavia, to oversee peace plan between Croatia and Serbia, as renewed fighting breaks out in Croatia.

Pres. Bush establishes diplomatic relations with Latvia, Lithuania, and Estonia.

British Prime Minister John Major becomes first Western European leader to visit China since Tienanmen Square massacre in 1989.

**3** Fire destroys Imperial Food Products chicken-processing plant in Hamlet, N.C.; 25 people are killed and 55 injured trying to escape through blocked or locked fire exits.

Iraqi government allows opposition political parties to exist, but not to serve in armed forces.

In Houston, Wanda Webb Holloway is convicted of solicitation of murder for hiring her former brother-in-law to kill the mother of her daughter's junior high school cheerleading rival. She is later sentenced to 15 years in prison and a fine of $10,000; plot was never carried out.

**4** South African Pres. F.W. de Klerk proposes new constitution that provides universal voting rights, creates two-chamber parliament open to all races, and replaces presidency with a three-to-five-member executive council.

Lithuania issues 1,000 certificates of rehabilitation, exonerating people convicted by Soviet courts on charges that they were Nazi war criminals; certificates entitle bearer to compensation for wrongful imprisonment.

A Grumman G-2 jet carrying 12 American employees of Conoco and DuPont crashes in Borneo en route from Tokyo to Jakarta, Malaysia.

Zambia's Pres. Kenneth Kaunda lifts 27-year state of emergency.

**5** Justice Dept. officials divulge they withheld tape recordings made by U.S. Attorney's office in Tampa for three years from bank examiners investigating illegal acquisition of U.S. banks by BCCI. Six BCCI officials and a Medellín drug cartel leader are charged with laundering cocaine profits through the bank from 1983 to 1989.

Soviet Congress of People's Deputies yields power to interim government controlled by Pres. Gorbachev and representatives from participating republics; they will write a new constitution.

Crimean parliament votes to become autonomous and independent republic within the Ukraine, which declared independence from Soviet Union.

**6** Soviet State Council recognizes independence of Estonia, Latvia, and Lithuania, after 51 years of Soviet occupation.

Former third-ranking CIA official, Clair E. George, is charged by federal grand jury with 10 felonies, including perjury and false statements in connection with Iran-Contra affair.

In Dolisie, Congo, more than 100 people are killed and 66 injured in collision of passenger and freight trains.

**7** An EC-sponsored Yugoslav peace conference opens in The Hague amid verbal sparring between Croatian and Serbian presidents.

**8** In township of Thokoza, South Africa, gunmen open fire on a crowd of nearly 300 Inkatha Freedom party members; in Soweto, a grenade is hurled at another group of Inkatha members; incidents leave 42 dead and 50 wounded.

Voters in republic of Macedonia, Yugoslavia, support independence from Yugoslavia by a margin of 3-to-1.

**9** South African government declares state of unrest in four townships after two days of violence between rival black factions results in nearly 100 deaths.

Iraq grounds foreign helicopters carrying UN weapons-plant inspectors. Iraq returns to Kuwait gold bullion worth about $700 mil. and 120,000 books and rare manuscripts from national library. UN reports renewed battles between Kurds and government forces in northern Iraq.

**10** Confirmation hearings begin for Clarence Thomas, Pres. Bush's nominee for Supreme Court justice.

**11** Soviet Pres. Mikhail Gorbachev announces he will begin negotiating to withdraw 11,000

Soviet military advisers from Cuba and eliminate a $2 bil. annual subsidy. Cuba demands that U.S. troops simultaneously withdraw from Guantánamo Bay Naval Station in eastern Cuba.

After confirming that an Israeli soldier missing in Lebanon is dead, Israel releases 51 Lebanese prisoners held by army in south Lebanon and turns over remains of nine guerrillas; more than 300 Arab prisoners remain in Israeli custody.

EPA issues national standards to prevent leakage of lead, plastics, and other chemicals into drinking water, and requires landfill operators to monitor leakage and buildup of methane gas.

**12** Pres. Bush asks Congress to delay considering Israel's request for $10 bil. in loan guarantees for settlement of Soviet Jews, fearing that Israeli construction in occupied territories could jeopardize Arab-Israeli peace talks. Prime Minister Yitzhak Shamir vows to continue settlements.

U.S. Senate votes 78-to-22 for a bill allowing abortion counseling in federally funded clinics and providing Medicaid payment for abortion in cases of rape and incest.

Space shuttle *Discovery* is launched carrying Upper Atmosphere Research Satellite, which will study effects of pollution on upper atmosphere during two-year orbit.

**13** The U.S. and USSR declare they will cease arms sales to Afghanistan by Jan. 1, 1992.

Virginia Gov. L. Douglas Wilder announces his bid for Democratic nomination for president.

North Korean defector discloses that North Korea will be able to make nuclear weapons within three years. North Korea has refused to allow inspection of its weapons plants.

Federal Reserve cuts discount rate to 5%, the lowest level since the 1970s, and cuts federal funds rate to 5.25%; banks cut prime lending rate in hopes that consumers and business will borrow and spend more and speed recovery.

**14** In South Africa, the government, ANC, Inkatha Freedom party, and 20 smaller anti-apartheid groups sign peace accord to end black factional violence.

Resolution Trust Corp. closes Columbia Savings and Loan Assoc. of Los Angeles, with $4.76 bil. in deposits; RTC estimates bailout will cost the public $1.2 bil.

**15** Sen. Tom Harkin (D-Iowa) announces his bid for Democratic nomination for president.

Swedish voters, angry over high taxes and sluggish economy, defeat ruling Social Democrats and give 53% of vote to five non-Socialist parties. Prime Minister Ingvar Carlsson announces resignation.

**16** Senate confirmation hearings for Pres. Bush's nominee for director of the CIA, Robert M. Gates, open. In Gates's second attempt to win post, he claims he should have done more to investigate wrongdoing by government in Iran-Contra affair, which kept him from being named director in 1987.

Yugoslav air force MIG fighters attack Croatia's capital, Zagreb; incident marks collapse of fourth EC-sponsored cease-fire since late June.

After independent prosecutor Lawrence Walsh announces he will abandon prosecution of former National Security Council aide Oliver North in Iran-Contra affair, Federal Judge Gerhard Gesell drops three felony charges on which North was convicted and dismisses case against him.

Philippine senate rejects U.S. lease on Subic Bay Naval Station, largest U.S. military installation in Southeast Asia; U.S. is later given three years to close down base.

Georgian government of Pres. Zviad Gamsakhurdia arrests leader of opposition National Democratic party and two aides; thousands of demonstrators call for president's resignation.

**17** Yugoslav army joins air force in its attack on Zagreb, Croatia.

The 46th UN General Assembly opens and admits North Korea, South Korea, the Marshall Islands, Micronesia, and Estonia, Latvia, and Lithuania to the UN, raising membership to 166 nations.

Soviet Union drops charges of treason against Aleksandr Solzhenitsyn after 17 years. The writer lives in exile in Vermont and plans to return to USSR shortly.

At a West African summit, Liberian rebel leader Charles Taylor agrees to surrender arms and confine his followers to camps under supervision of multinational peacekeeping force.

**18** The GAO discloses that members of Congress bounced 8,331 personal checks in year ended June 1990 at members-only House bank, subsidized by taxpayers. Bank covered all checks and charged no penalties. On Oct. 3, the bank is closed effective end of 1992, and members' records are sent to House ethics committee to determine repeated abuses. GAO reports that House members' unpaid bills at House restaurant total $300,000.

Pres. Bush authorizes U.S. military planes to protect UN inspectors in Iraq barred by Pres. Hussein from carrying out their mission.

Earthquake measuring 5.3 on Richter scale hits near Guatemala City, causing collapse of houses; seven people are killed and 60 injured.

**19** UN Security Council authorizes Iraq to sell $1.6 bil. in oil to buy food and essential supplies. One third of proceeds will compensate Persian Gulf war victims and their families.

Tropical storm Luke hits Japan, flooding 6,400 homes, resulting in five deaths, eight injuries, and many missing.

After USSR announces it would withdraw troops and end economic subsidies, Cuba excludes foreign delegations and journalists from Congress for first time in 32 years.

**20** Cambodian government and three rebel factions agree on form of future UN-supervised elections.

Yugoslav tanks and planes attack Croatia's coast despite pleas for truce by Croatian officials.

**21** Armenia is twelfth Soviet republic to declare independence.

Officials at Huntington Library in San Marino, Calif., allow unrestricted access to 3,000 photographic negatives of Dead Sea scrolls, 800 Hebrew and Aramaic manuscripts that date from 200 B.C. to the first century of the Christian era found in caves near the Dead Sea between 1947 and 1956; they include oldest known manuscript of Old Testament.

**22** Former British intelligence agent John Cairncross admits to being "fifth man" in British spy ring that collected information for Moscow from 1930s to 1950s; other agents were Kim Philby, Guy Burgess, Donald Maclean, and Anthony Blunt.

At Montana State Prison in Deer Lodge, five inmates are killed by fellow inmates when 68 prisoners seize facility for four-and-a-half hours.

**23** Iraq holds 40 UN nuclear inspectors captive for 12 hours after they attempt to remove nuclear weapons plans from a Baghdad building. Inspectors are allowed to leave without documents.

After government suspends party activities, Communist party members depose Tadzhikistan Pres. Kadreddin Aslonov and impose state of emergency; thousands protest.

Soviet republics of Armenia and Azerbaijan sign cease-fire agreement in conflict over Nagorno-Karabakh, an ethnic-Armenian area within Azerbaijan.

After several months without pay, 3,000 Zairean paratroopers loot stores and homes and close Kinshasa international airport; 30 are reported killed. The next day, France and Belgium deploy troops to evacuate foreign nationals.

**24** Kidnapped on Dec. 5, 1989, 77-year-old British hostage Jack Mann is fourth western hostage released by Lebanese-based terrorist group in four weeks.

Georgian Pres. Zviad Gamsakhurdia declares state of emergency.

**25** UN Security Council adopts resolution barring sale of military equipment to Yugoslavia.

At request of Pres. Bush, U.S. and Israel agree to postpone consideration of Israel's request for $10 bil. in loan guarantees for four months.

Remains of Bronze Age man who died around 4,000 years ago are found on Similaun Glacier in Tirolean Alps, along with an ax, backpack, leather pouch, bow, stone necklace, and stone knife.

**26** In Oracle, Ariz., eight researchers enter Biosphere 2, a 3.15-acre glass and steel enclosure containing 3,800 species of plants and animals, where they plan to live for two years. The $150 mil. ecological experiment will earn money through tourism and environment-related patents.

Romanian Prime Minister Petre Roman resigns amid protests by miners calling for higher pay, better working conditions, and Roman's ouster.

**27** In a move designed to convince Soviets to reduce their nuclear arsenal, Pres. Bush announces that U.S. will unilaterally remove and destroy all 2,400 land-based short-range nuclear weapons in Europe and Asia and withdraw short-range weapons from navy ships at sea; many long-range bombers and missiles are called off 24-hour alert status.

PLO legislature votes 314-to-18 to support U.S.- and Soviet-sponsored Middle East peace talks, but demands that Israel withdraw from occupied territories.

In Baghdad, 44 UN inspectors with Iraqi nuclear weapons documentation are freed after being held four days.

**28** Salvadoran army Col. Guillermo Alfredo Benavides Moreno is found guilty of murder and terrorism in connection with deaths of six Jesuit priests, their cook, and her daughter in 1989. Despite their confessions, actual gunmen are found innocent.

Typhoon Mireille causes damage in 41 of Japan's 47 prefectures; 45 people are killed and 700 injured.

**29** UNITA leader Jonas Savimbi returns to Angola after 16 years in exile to campaign for president in multiparty election expected in 1992.

Sharing power for first time in 26 years, Zaire's Pres. Mobuto Sese Seko names opposition leader Étienne Tshisekedi prime minister and forms an interim government; opposition will occupy 6 of 11 seats in new cabinet.

**30** Pres. Jean-Bertrand Aristide, Haiti's first popularly elected president, is overthrown in military coup; Aristide leaves country and later appeals to Organization of American States as the U.S., France, the EC, and Canada refuse to acknowledge ruling junta and suspend aid worth $570 mil.

Nebraska Sen. Bob Kerrey announces candidacy for Democratic presidential nomination.

## October 1991

**1** In Massachusetts, Yankee Rowe nuclear reactor, oldest nuclear power plant in U.S., voluntarily halts operations, a day before NRC reports findings of reduced safety and calls for its shutdown.

**2** Senate approves bill granting employees up to 12 weeks of unpaid leave to tend to family emergencies, including sickness or care of newborn; 65-to-32 vote is enough to sustain a presidential veto, but bill must be considered by House.

Organization of American States resolves to diplomatically isolate Haiti's military junta led by Brig. Gen. Raoul Cedras, and to send delegation to Port-au-Prince to discuss economic and diplomatic sanctions with junta leaders.

In major policy reversal, Hanoi government agrees to accept 100,000 Vietnamese refugees who fled Vietnam for economic reasons; they are to be returned by force from camps throughout Southeast Asia.

Philippine senators allows U.S. military three years to withdraw troops from Subic Bay Naval Station, and Pres. Aquino drops plans to hold national referendum on the issue.

**3** Yugoslav navy blocks ports in Croatia, in retaliation for continued Croatian blockade of army installations throughout the republic. In Belgrade, four pro-Serbian members of federal presidency take over parliamentary powers.

In Tel Aviv, opposition Labor party leader Shimon Peres calls for Israel to relinquish occupied Arab land and stop construction of housing in occupied territories.

Salvadoran military launches air and artillery bombardment of Guazapa volcano, a guerrilla stronghold, days after signing a partial peace accord at the UN.

Arkansas Gov. Bill Clinton announces candidacy for Democratic presidential nomination.

**4** In Madrid, 24 countries, including the U.S., sign protocol to 1959 Antarctic Treaty, banning mineral and oil exploration for 50 years, and providing wildlife protection and regulation of waste disposal and marine pollution. U.S. had withheld approval for months.

Voters in Memphis, where 55% of population is black, elect Willie Herenton as city's first black mayor.

**5** In response to U.S. arms reductions, Soviet Pres. Gorbachev announces similar reductions exceeding requirements of latest strategic arms treaty, including cut in strategic warheads to 5,000 by 1998, reduction of Soviet troops by 700,000, halt in nuclear testing for a year, and removal of missiles and bombers from battle-alert status.

In Jakarta, Indonesia, a C-130 Hercules transport plane carrying military personnel crashes into government building after take-off; all 132 aboard and a building guard are killed.

In Moscow, Pres. Gorbachev signs agreement with IMF granting Soviet Union special association status. Agreement provides for IMF technical assistance in statistics gathering, restructuring banking system, and establishing social programs for those suffering economic hardship in country's transition to a market economy.

**6** U.S. calls for ousted Haitian Pres. Jean-Bertrand Aristide of Haiti publicly to disavow mob violence and agree to share power with Haitian parliament, to gain support for his return to office.

Anita F. Hill, Univ. of Oklahoma law professor and former personal assistant to Supreme Court justice nominee Clarence Thomas, accuses Judge Thomas of sexual harassment over two years beginning in 1981, while Thomas was head of civil rights in the Dept. of Education and chairman of Equal Employment Opportunity Commission. Senate vote to confirm Thomas is delayed until Oct. 15 as hearings continue.

Videotape of American hostage Terry Anderson, former Middle East bureau chief for the Associated Press, is released by his captors, Islamic Holy War, in which Anderson states that his captors implied he, Thomas Sutherland, or Terry Waite would be freed soon.

In Jerusalem, Israeli peace campaigner Abi Nathan is sentenced to 18 months in prison for meeting PLO chairman Yasir Arafat in Tunis in July.

Under pressure by opposition forces, Communist Pres. Rakhmon Nabiyev of Soviet republic of Tadzhikistan resigns to make way for popular presidential elections. State of emergency has been repealed and ban on Communist party restored.

In Portugal, national elections result in victory for Prime Minister Aníbal Cavaco Silva (who will remain in office another four years) and his center-right Social Democratic party.

Prince Aleksandar Karadjordjevic, heir to defunct Yugoslav throne, holds monarchist rallies attended by 70,000 people in Belgrade and offers himself as peacemaker and alternative to government of Pres. Slobodan Milosevic of Serbia.

**7** UN inspectors discover intact Iraqi nuclear weapons research center, Al Atheer, which was believed destroyed by bombing, and a previously unidentified installation, Furat, used for enriching uranium to weapons grade.

Former assistant secretary of state Elliott

Abrams pleads guilty to charges of withholding information from Congress in 1986 concerning aid to Nicaraguan Contras and agrees to cooperate with Iran-Contra prosecutors.

Croatian presidential palace in Zagreb is attacked by Yugoslav air force, narrowly missing the federal Prime Minister Stipe Mesic, Croatian Pres. Franjo Tudjman, and Croatian Prime Minister Ante Markovic, who were in the building. Pres. Tudjman formally declares independence.

At midnight, Slovenia declares full independence and creates national currency, the tolar, to be exchanged one-to-one with Yugoslav dinar.

In northern Iraq, Kurdish rebels execute 60 Iraqi soldiers captured in recent combat in Sulaimaniya. Over 400 are wounded or killed over four days of fighting.

During OAS delegation visit to Port-au-Prince, Haitian legislature declares presidency vacant to make way for interim president and new elections. Supreme Court Justice Joseph Nerette is sworn in as provisional president one day later.

**8** A week of violence in Lomé, Togo, results in third unsuccessful coup attempt by mutinous troops who try to kidnap Prime Minister Joseph Koffigoh and kill four prodemocracy protesters.

In Anchorage, Alaska, Federal District Judge H. Russel Holland approves a $1 bil. settlement of criminal and civil charges against Exxon for *Exxon Valdez* oil spill, ending two years of court proceedings.

**9** Philippine Pres. Aquino allows return of former president Ferdinand Marcos's body for burial in his home province of Ilocos Norte, not in Manila as Mrs. Marcos insists.

Romanian diplomat Livia Radu, acting ambassador to India, is kidnapped by gunmen in New Delhi, in an attempt to gain freedom for two Sikhs held in Bucharest for attacking Indian ambassador to Romania, Julio Francis Ribeiro, two months ago.

Nimbus-7 satellite passing over Antarctica reports lowest stratospheric ozone level ever at 110 Dobson units, a measurement that is normally about 500 Dobson units.

**10** Syria refuses to participate in a phase of Middle East peace conference that includes regional issues such as water rights, economic development, and arms control, until Israel agrees to give up Golan Heights.

Czechoslovakia halts plans to export Soviet tanks to Syria until after Middle East peace conference takes place.

Pres. Bush increases to 142,000 number of

refugees that will be admitted to U.S. in fiscal year 1992.

**11** In Washington, Prof. Anita Hill and Judge Clarence Thomas testify before Senate Judiciary Committee concerning Hill's allegations of sexual harassment.

Ten of 12 Soviet republics reach agreement to form free-market economic community, to be formally signed in one week.

In Japan, ruling Liberal Democratic party endorses Kiichi Miyazawa, former finance minister, as next prime minister, essentially assuring his victory in upcoming elections.

**12** In Pakistan, Muslim guerrillas bomb Jalabad with surface-to-surface rockets, followed by government bombing of guerrilla bases around the city, after a week of clashes that began with a guerrilla assault on Gardez in which 100 guerrillas were killed.

Turkish government sends 3,000 troops, planes, and helicopters into Iraq to battle rebels belonging to Marxist Kurdish Workers party, a group that has been fighting for an autonomous state in southeastern Turkey since 1984.

For first time in U.S. a woman gives birth to her own grandchildren, a boy and a girl; Arlette Schweitzer was implanted with her own daughter's eggs that were fertilized with her son-in-law's sperm.

For second time in 11 years, Pope John Paul II visits Brazil, the country with most Roman Catholics, but where 600,000 Catholics leave the church each year.

**13** In Bangkok, Thailand, Group of Seven industrialized democracies agree to formulate Soviet economic reform program with the USSR.

**14** In Bulgarian parliamentary elections, opposition group Union of Democratic Forces claims victory over ruling Socialist (formerly Communist) government, amid rallies by 50,000 opposition supporters in Sofia.

In Kinshasa, Zaire, Pres. Mobutu Sese Seko accepts opposition-led cabinet for first time in Zaire's history.

**15** Senate confirms Judge Clarence Thomas as associate justice of the U.S. Supreme Court by a vote of 52-to-48, the most negative votes ever cast against a successful nominee.

Yugoslav republic of Bosnia-Herzegovina becomes fourth Yugoslav republic to declare independence. In Moscow, leaders of Croatia and Serbia agree to seventh cease-fire in four months at talks moderated by Soviet Pres. Mikhail Gorbachev.

## MAJOR NEWS STORIES OF THE YEAR
### Nov. 1, 1990 – Oct. 1, 1991

### The Gulf War

On Aug. 2, 1990, 120,000 Iraqi troops marched into Kuwait, overthrew the government, and took control of Kuwait City. About two weeks earlier, Iraqi Pres. Saddam Hussein threatened violence against Arab states whose

oil policies of overproduction resulted in low prices and lost revenues for Iraq. In addition to demanding that Kuwait abide by OPEC production quotas of 1.8 million barrels of oil a day, Iraq demanded that Kuwait return over $2.4 billion Pres. Hussein accused it of making on oil it illegally pumped out of the Rumaila oil field, exceeding its production quota set by OPEC. Hussein also wanted Kuwait to write off the $10-billion interest-free loan it extended to Iraq during the Iran-Iraq war, since overproduction by Kuwait cost Iraq $14 million in lost revenues when oil prices dropped.

The invasion met with almost universal disapproval. The U.S. and the European Community froze all Iraqi and Kuwaiti assets in their territo-

ries, banned nearly all Iraqi imports, and halted sales of arms and military equipment to Baghdad. The UN Security Council voted unanimously to condemn the invasion and demanded an Iraqi withdrawal, while the Soviet Union suspended delivery of arms and military hardware to Iraq.

On Aug. 6, the UN Security Council ordered a trade and financial boycott on occupied Kuwait and Iraq, prohibiting all UN members from buying oil from either country or having any other commercial or financial dealings with them. Iraq, which controlled one-fifth of the world's proven oil reserve, reduced daily exports of oil 40% and began to round up Westerners in Kuwait and Iraq and restrict their movement within and departure from either country. A day later, U.S. troops launched Operation Desert Shield and began moving tens of thousands of combat-ready troops into Saudi Arabia to defend it and its oil reserves against a possible invasion by Iraq. Pres. Hussein announced the annexation of Kuwait, an act immediately condemned by the UN Security Council, which voted unanimously to declare the annexation null and void in international law, making the decision legally binding on all UN members.

In response to a U.S. naval blockade of oil exports and all but food imports, Pres. Hussein removed Western citizens from Baghdad hotels to Iraqi military bases, oil production sites, and industrial installations to serve as human shields against attack, and severed their contact with the outside world. On Sept. 1, Pres. Hussein released 700 Western hostages, mostly women and children, but the last of the Western hostages were not released until Dec. 6. Millions of foreigners from third-world nations attempted to get out of the country as well, most via Jordan, where they arrived at the rate of 10,000 per day. Jordan's resources were stretched to the limit and it was forced to close its borders.

On Aug. 18, Saudi Arabia increased oil production to make up for at least half the amount lost to the world market as a result of the blockade of Iraqi exports. On Aug. 29, OPEC announced plans to make up for nearly all that had been lost. Before the invasion, Iraq had won support at the midyear OPEC meeting to boost oil prices to $21 per barrel. During the crisis oil prices fluctuated between $24 and $40 per barrel, but Iraq was unable to take advantage of the high prices because of the trade embargo.

In addition to its specific territorial and remunerative demands on Kuwait, Iraq demanded that military forces withdraw from Saudi Arabia before Western "guests" would be freed, that the U.S. promise not to attack, and that the UN lift the economic blockade. Multinational forces in turn demanded Iraq's complete withdrawal from Kuwait before UN sanctions would be dropped.

Iraq's only allies were King Hussein (no relation) of Jordan and Yasir Arafat, principal leader of the Palestine Liberation Organization, who both attempted to mediate between Pres. Hussein and the coalition opposing him. Pres. Hussein continued to keep international diplomats guessing with rumors of his willingness to negotiate on withdrawal from Kuwait, interlaced with statements that he was not willing to compromise his demands. The waters were muddied when the PLO called for linking a resolution of the Persian Gulf crisis to a resolution of the violence in Israeli-occupied territories, following the killing of 21 Arabs by Israeli security forces in Jerusalem on Oct. 8.

November was a decisive month both in the military buildup and in the diplomatic maneuvering to prevent war and to enable the Iraqis a face-saving withdrawal from Kuwait. The Bush administration believed the embargo and trade sanctions were having little effect in Iraq, and they were certainly not causing Pres. Hussein to negotiate seriously about withdrawing his forces from Kuwait.

On Nov. 8, Pres. Bush ordered another 200,000 U.S. troops into the region, half from the highly mechanized forces stationed in Germany. The next day the Pentagon announced that U.S. troops would not be rotated home at regular intervals but would remain in the region for the duration of the crisis, a clear signal that U.S. regarded war as a strong possibility. Ten days later Iraq declared that 250,000 more troops would be sent to the Kuwait region, bringing the total to an estimated 550,000. Bush responded with a dramatic Thanksgiving trip to the gulf. The president mingled with the troops and spoke constantly of the American people's support for their sacrifice; he also vowed that this would not be another Vietnam, that the U.S. would fight to win the war, and that no American serviceman would die in vain. This trip effectively personalized the struggle as a battle of wills between Bush and Hussein, and as a result, Bush's Gallup Poll ratings soared to the highest approval levels of any president in history.

With the military battle lines so clearly drawn, the diplomatic efforts of the Soviet Union, Germany's Chancellor Helmut Kohl, and UN General Secretary Javier Pérez de Cuéllar during these days came to naught. On Nov. 29, the UN Security Council approved Resolution 678 authorizing the use of all "necessary means" to expel Iraq from Kuwait and setting a Jan. 15, 1991, deadline for Hussein to withdraw peaceably.

Over the next six weeks, the coalition continued its intense military planning and Iraqi forces continued to dig in. Early in December, the U.S. had offered to hold high-level talks and Iraq immediately agreed; but neither side could agree on a date and the meeting was repeatedly postponed. Finally, on Jan. 4, Iraq and the U.S. agreed to meet in Geneva. However, it took

## COALITION FORCES

The coalition against Iraq included representatives of 37 countries from around the world who stationed army, navy, air force, or noncombatant forces in the Persian Gulf region for all or part of the crisis.

**Army** (695,000 ground troops): Afghanistan, Bahrain, Bangladesh, Egypt (40,000), France (15,000), Kuwait, Morocco, Nigeria, Oman, Pakistan, Qatar, Saudi Arabia (110,000), Senegal, Syria (15,000), United Arab Emirates, UK (25,000), United States (425,000).

**Navy** (175 warships): Argentina, Australia, Belgium, Denmark, France, Greece, Italy, Japan, Netherlands, Norway, Poland, Spain, UK, United States (65).

**Air force** (1,650 combat aircraft): Canada, France, Italy, Kuwait, New Zealand, Saudi Arabia, South Korea, UK, United States (1,200+).

**Medical:** Czechoslovakia, Hungary, Philippines, Romania, Sierra Leone, Singapore, Sweden.

**Financial contributions:** Saudi Arabia ($16.8 bil.), Kuwait ($16.0 bil.), Japan ($10.7 bil.), Germany ($6.6 bil.), UAE ($4.0 bil.), Korea ($0.4 bil.).

until Jan. 9—only six days before the UN deadline—for Secretary of State James Baker and Iraqi Foreign Minister Tariq Aziz to sit down together. After only six hours they decided an agreement was not possible. The Iraqi press reported that Hussein told his advisers he would now make the U.S. military "swim in their own blood."

A few days later Congress gave its approval of the use of force if Bush decided to attack; but the vote was much closer (52-to-47 in the Senate, 250-to-183 in the House) than the overwhelming public support for war might have indicated. Shortly thereafter the Iraqi parliament voted unanimously for war.

Jan. 15 passed in tense anticipation throughout much of the world. A little more than 18 hours past the midnight deadline, at 2:30 a.m., Jan. 18 in the gulf (6:30 p.m. Jan. 17 EST), coalition forces launched Operation Desert Storm with a ferocity not seen since the end of World War II. Over the first two days, coalition planes flew about 3,100 sorties (a sortie is one flight by one aircraft) aimed principally at destroying Iraqi command and control centers in Baghdad and rendering Hussein's air force useless. Coalition aircraft hit every strategically important site in the Iraqi capital, as well as many Iraqi airstrips. Although Iraq's air power was significant on paper (950 aircraft, including 665 combat planes), only 25 planes took to the air during the first two days of the war; eight were destroyed. On the third day 55 Iraqi aircraft were launched and six were destroyed, while the allies lost none in these initial engagements. Before the first week was over the allies lost 10 planes, but they had clear and complete control of he skies from Kuwait to Iraq—so complete in fact that more than 100 of Iraq's best aircraft were flown to Iran for safekeeping until the war was over.

To many observers, the U.S. and its allies actually assured their victory during the first 72 hours of the war. Despite all the official hype about the strength and toughness of Hussein's ground and tank forces, dug in and without air protection they were an easy, stationary target for allied aircraft. Over the next six weeks the allies flew more than 100,000 sorties, dropping 89,000 tons of explosives on entrenched Iraqi forces and on strategic targets in an assault unprecedented in the history of warfare, but intended to minimize the loss of life in the upcoming ground campaign. In addition to 360 carrier-based and 1,200 land-based fighter and attack aircraft, the U.S. deployed B-52s that introduced carpet bombing to desert warfare from their little known island base of Diego Garcia in the Indian Ocean. Other sophisticated weaponry included laser-guided "smart bombs," the most accurate bombing devices ever known; bombs that not only caused enormous craters but implanted explosive devices that made repair work extremely hazardous; and about 300 Tomahawk cruise missiles armed with conventional warheads launched from ships in the Red Sea and Persian Gulf. In addition, the battleship USS *Wisconsin* fired 1,900-pound projectiles from its 16-inch guns against Iraqi positions 23 miles inside Kuwait. So intense was the allied bombing that Jordan's King Hussein publicly accused the U.S. of trying to destroy Iraq.

With his air force rendered impotent and without a semblance of naval power, Hussein's strategy was to hold out for a prolonged and decisive ground war in which his battle-hardened veterans would inflict such heavy casualties on the inexperienced U.S. forces that American public opinion would turn against the war just as it had in Vietnam. From the outset, he also attempted to tear apart the delicate coalition of Arab and Western forces by trying to drag Israel into the conflict, an action that would have caused Arabs to rethink the purposes of the war.

Iraq's only effective weapon in this campaign was the Scud missile, a powerful but not very accurate weapon launched from highly mobile trucks. Over the course of the war, Iraq launched 86 Scuds, 40 at Israel, where they caused extensive damage, mostly in and around Tel Aviv, and wounded over 200 people but killed only one. Forty-six Scuds were also launched against Saudi Arabia, where the most extensive damage occurred at Dharan on Feb. 25, when 28 American soldiers were killed.

What made the Scuds so effective as a weapon of terror was the fear that Hussein would arm them with chemical or biological weapons. While allied bombings were thought to have destroyed the plants that made these weapons, Hussein was believed to have stockpiled and hidden 2,000 to 4,000 tons, and all Israelis and coalition troops were equipped with gas masks throughout the war. Such attacks never materialized.

On Jan. 28, two U.S. planes mistakenly bombed a civilian air raid shelter, killing 324 and wounding over 400. Capitalizing on the horror felt by the American people over this tragedy, Hussein seized the moment to propose a conditional withdrawal from Kuwait, which was quickly dismissed by Bush as a "cruel hoax." As the possibility of a ground war intensified, the Soviet Union attempted to convince Iraq to announce an unconditional withdrawal from Kuwait. Bush rejected the offer, but the Soviets kept pushing for an agreement and Bush finally made a counterdemand for an Iraqi withdrawal from Kuwait within 24 hours. Since this was not humanly possible, the world watched and waited for the start of the ground war.

Despite widespread predictions that the ground war would be a long and bloody affair—estimates of U.S. casualties ranged from 5,000 to 40,000—the allied victory came quickly and with a minimal loss of life. This was clearly the result of allied air supremacy: Hussein had no aerial reconnaissance capability and his command centers in Baghdad had been destroyed, while allied commanders could monitor Iraqi troop and tank movements continuously on the ground or from space-based spy satellites.

What allied commander Gen. Norman Schwarzkopf and his staff observed was that while Iraqi forces in Kuwait continued to build defensive fortifications, they never defended their right flank. On the night of Feb. 23–24, Schwarzkopf launched an envelopment attack that brought almost total victory in exactly 100 hours. With the bulk of the allied forces poised for both a frontal assault on Kuwait and an amphibious attack from the gulf, Schwarzkopf sent two mechanized divisions on a wide, sweeping movement into southern Iraq. While Hussein's commanders thought the only serious attack was coming into Kuwait, thousands of allied soldiers, as well as tanks, armored vehicles, and supplies for a 60-day war, drove through the desert without serious opposition. Within two days they had moved clear across the desert, taken about 25,000 prisoners (as ill-equipped Iraqi soldiers literally begged to be captured), and cut off the only escape route from Kuwait City. A tank battle with Iraq's elite Republican Guard contingent was hard fought but ended quickly in a decisive allied victory. In Kuwait the allies met strong initial resistance, but not enough to warrant an amphibious assault. Iraqi soldiers surrendered by the thousands, while many others fled toward Iraq in panic only to be massacred in allied air attacks. About 60,000 Iraqis were POWs by the end of the war.

In desperation, Hussein resorted to terrorist attacks, setting fire to over 600 Kuwaiti oil wells and deliberately spilling about a million barrels of oil into the Persian Gulf, creating an enormous oil slick that fouled wildlife and threatened the Saudi water supply. Ecological damage is still being assessed and crews will be working for two to three years to cap burning wells, which are causing widespread health and environmental problems.

At midnight on Feb. 17, Bush declared a cease-fire, although there is much evidence that Hussein had tried to surrender days earlier. Only 38 Americans died during the four-day ground war, and a total of 144 for the entire war. The number of Iraqi casualties will probably never be known, but estimates of 100,000 to 150,000 killed and 300,000 wounded are not officially disputed. Hussein lost more than 80% of his tanks and almost all his armored vehicles and artillery, and could no longer be considered a serious military threat in the region. But only a few days after signing the preliminary peace agreement (Mar. 3) declaring he would comply with all UN resolutions and compensate Kuwait, he turned his remaining military arsenal against two groups of rebellious forces in southern and northern Iraq.

With the outspoken encouragement of Bush and the Iranian government, Shiite Muslims took up arms in 12 southern Iraqi cities while Kurdish forces seized several important oil centers in the north. Neither group had the resources to prevent Hussein from suppressing the rebellions, which he did quickly and without interference. On Mar. 26, Bush, apparently under pressure from the UN, declared these uprisings to be an internal matter and not subject to action by the U.S. military, and the U.S. refused to keep Iraqi helicopters out of the sky, Hussein's one overwhelming advantage.

Fearing Hussein's brutality and the possibility he would use poison gas against them as he had in the 1980s, an estimated 1.5 million Kurds fled to Iran and Turkey, where large numbers of Kurds had lived for centuries. Americans were horrified to see that their stunning victory had left Hussein in control of a military force strong enough to keep him in power for the foreseeable future; the U.S. responded to the Kurdish plight by sending 10,000 soldiers to set up camps, provide humanitarian aid, and protect them from government soldiers. With the guarantee of U.S. protection, many Kurds returned to Iraq during the summer months.

Throughout the summer of 1991, the U.S. painstakingly attempted to lay the groundwork for a full-scale Middle East peace conference. Over 35,000 U.S. troops remained in the region, together with a substantial contingent of air and sea power. Under the terms of the peace agreement (accepted by Iraq on Apr. 6), the UN undertook inspections throughout Iraq to ensure that all chemical and biological weapons were destroyed and that no nuclear weapons existed or were planned. (See the August and September entries in the "Chronology of the Year's Key Events" for further developments.)

## A New Order in the USSR

Between the end of 1990 and the fall of 1991, the international political map was altered drastically as the world's largest Communist superpower, the USSR, fell into disarray. Massive power shifts from the central government to the people occurred in the USSR, as the Soviet people grew more vocal, and as Boris Yeltsin took center stage over Mikhail Gorbachev. The central government's loss of control over politics during the past year precipitated a struggle between Communist party hardliners, who were loathe to give up power, and the reformers, who advocated drastic changes. In August 1991, a coalition of party, military, and KGB leaders attempted to oust Gorbachev in a coup, which failed in three days, and as a result accelerated the demise of the Communist party and the drive for independence by the republics. Eastern Europe also ended its long forced association with the USSR, as both the Warsaw Pact and Comecon were dissolved in the spring of 1991. With everyone agreeing that communism was dead, the Soviet Union and its former satellites began their search for a new economic and political order.

A major force behind the changes was the rapidly deteriorating Soviet economy. In November, the Ukraine became the first republic to issue rationing coupons. Prompted by worries about the failing Gorbachev regime, the American relief agency CARE began to distribute food, Japan sent aid through the World Health Organization, and Germany, France, and the European Community agreed to lend money. U.S. Pres. George Bush also approved a billion-dollar loan to the Soviets for food. Meanwhile, the Soviet government could do little to quell international disquiet in the Middle East, as government shifts continued with the formation of a new Federation Council headed by Gorbachev, the resignation of Foreign Minister

Shevardnadze, and the appointment, in late December, of hardliner Gennadi Yanaev, the former head of the official Soviet labor unions, as vice president.

In a move meant to placate hardliners, Gorbachev sent Soviet troops in to suppress Lithuania's pro-independence movement at the beginning of 1991. In mid-January, Soviet black beret troops cracked down on Latvia's independence movement, prompting huge demonstrations in major Soviet cities to protest the repressive measures and to demand Gorbachev's resignation.

The world also viewed Soviet intervention in the Baltics unfavorably, and the European Community delayed promised aid in protest. In the meantime, the Gorbachev government, in a feeble attempt at regulating the black market, tried to remove all 50- and 100-ruble notes from circulation. Several republics defied the order, and ordinary citizens despaired.

Government repression of antigovernment resistance groups in the republics continued, as did the loud protests both within and outside the USSR. The American government, in a sign of displeasure over the crackdown, authorized shipments of medical supplies directly to the republics. In early February, Lithuania voted overwhelmingly for independence, and in the Russian republic (the RSFSR), Pres. Yeltsin called for Gorbachev's resignation. The political confusion continued, with more public rallies in major cities, one on Army Day (Feb. 23) in support of Gorbachev, and one the next day in support of Yeltsin and against Gorbachev.

The USSR's waning power in the world was brought home by the Feb. 25 agreement that signed the Warsaw Pact out of existence after 36 years. Internally, the diminished power of the central government was demonstrated by increased ethnic fighting in Georgia, striking coal miners in Kazakhstan and the Ukraine, and pro-independence votes in both Latvia and Estonia. Soviet citizens continued to gather in mass rallies, voicing their support of Yeltsin and their demand that Gorbachev surrender power to the republics. On Mar. 17, Soviet citizens voted in favor of Gorbachev's proposed union referendum, which would preserve the union of republics but give more power to the republics. Six republics refused to participate in the vote.

Gorbachev continued to demonstrate his unwillingness to loosen the grip of centralized control over the union republics, as he banned demonstrations (Mar. 25) and put Interior Ministry patrols in charge of law enforcement. Nevertheless, 100,000 people gathered in Moscow the next day to defy the ban. The trend toward freedom for the republics continued unabated, as Soviet Georgia voted to free itself from the Soviet government.

On the economic front, the Soviet government increased consumer prices on Apr. 1 by 250%, setting off a wave of panic buying and strikes around the country. Gorbachev responded by banning strikes, then made a deal with nine of the republics to rescind the price hikes and to decentralize government power. He later transferred control of the Siberian coal industry to the Russian republic, thus giving up central control

of an important industry and handing responsibility to the republic. In late April, Gorbachev offered to resign from the Communist party to stave off criticism, but his offer was rejected.

Two more blows to central power occurred in the spring, as the first non-government-controlled television station began broadcasting in the RSFSR, and the Soviet parliament voted to allow free travel abroad and emigration from the USSR. In the meantime, 13 republics agreed to emergency economic measures to ban strikes, even while they continued their struggle for political liberation. Zviad Gamsakhurdia became Georgia's first elected president on May 26; at the same time, Armenia and Moldavia declared their intentions to secede.

During the summer, the USSR and the U.S. continued talks about the weapons reduction treaty signed in November 1990. Bush approved agricultural loans of $1.5 billion to the Soviet Union, while the World Bank increased its involvement in the former Soviet satellites in Eastern Europe. On June 12, Yeltsin was elected president of the Russian republic in the RSFSR's first election. A week later, he was welcomed in Washington by Bush, in an attempt by the U.S. government to show support for the fledgling democratic movements. Popular opposition to communism continued in the USSR, as Leningraders in a dramatic vote decided to restore the city's prerevolutionary name of St. Petersburg.

The state of the failing Soviet economy remained in the forefront of the news. In June, American and Soviet economists unveiled a new proposal for reform that required nearly $100 billion dollars of outside investment. But Gorbachev was still not reconciled to radical reform, and he doomed the plan by suggesting that economists merge it with Prime Minister Pavlov's more conservative economic plan. On June 28, the Group of Seven (G-7) industrialized democracies agreed to offer the USSR associate membership in the International Monetary Fund (IMF). The G-7 stressed that it would hold out for genuine economic reform in the USSR before substantial amounts of money could be committed.

The summer witnessed the real decline of Communist party hegemony in Soviet politics, and the rise of Yeltsin. Former foreign minister Shevardnadze, Gorbachev adviser Yakovlev, and others formed a new political opposition party; two days later Shevardnadze resigned from the Communist party after 43 years. On July 20, Yeltsin banned Communist party activities at all workplaces; Gorbachev immediately vowed to fight the ban. Soon thereafter, the Russian republic recognized the independence of both Estonia and Latvia, as it had done earlier for Lithuania.

Bush arrived in Moscow for his fourth summit meeting with Gorbachev in late July, saying that while he remained committed to working with Gorbachev, he was opposed to the Soviet crackdowns in the Baltics and Soviet support of Cuba. On July 29, Bush and Gorbachev signed a lengthy nuclear arms reduction treaty.

On the domestic front, the Soviet economy continued its downward spiral. The Soviet parliament voted on July 1 to allow private

ownership of industrial enterprises for the first time in decades, but Gorbachev still appeared to be counting on outside help. The G-7 on July 17 reiterated its reservations about an economic bailout, and announced that it had agreed only to provide technical assistance to the USSR. In a surprise move, the Soviet government applied to the IMF and World Bank for full membership, which would permit it to borrow money, instead of just access to technical assistance that the offered associate status would bring. A historic first and highly symbolic act came in the summer when the Soviet government offered to sell at least 30% of the state-owned automobile company, the Volga Automotive Plant Association, which produces the Fiat-like Lada.

At the end of July, nine of the fifteen republics announced agreement with Gorbachev's draft union treaty, which would dramatically reduce central control and transfer power to the republics. In a prescient announcement in mid-August, Gorbachev adviser Aleksandr Yakovlev warned of an upcoming coup by hardliners who were dissatisfied with the union treaty.

On Aug. 19, while Gorbachev was on vacation, he was ousted in a coup by the Soviet military, the party, and the KGB. Gorbachev's own vice president, Gennadi Yanaev, backed by the newly formed State Committee for the State of Emergency, assumed the presidency. All of the eight coup plotters were Gorbachev appointees. The coup was badly planned and poorly executed, and failed after three dramatic days.

There was much popular resistance to the coup, most of which was led by Yeltsin. Despite the presence of tanks in Moscow and the threat of violence, Yeltsin defied the coup plotters and called for a general strike. Western nations threw their support behind Yeltsin and refused to recognize the legitimacy of the coup plotters. On Aug. 21, the coup collapsed and Gorbachev returned to Moscow from the Crimea, where he had been under house arrest.

After the coup, Gorbachev refused to join Yeltsin in censuring the Communist party for its role in the coup, but within a few days it was clear that Yeltsin had the upper hand. He berated Gorbachev in public for bad judgment in hiring the coup plotters, and he forced him to replace almost his entire cabinet with Yeltsin loyalists. On Aug. 24, Gorbachev resigned as general secretary of the Communist party's Central Committee, banned the party from any official role in the Soviet government, ordered the cabinet to resign, and named Yeltsin aide Ivan Silaev to head the new committee to reform the national economy. The Communist party newspaper *Pravda* also was forced to cease publication for its role in supporting the coup.

Failure of the coup caused the union of Soviet republics to disintegrate at an even faster rate. Just days after the failed coup, the Ukraine declared independence, followed by similar declarations from Byelorussia, Moldavia, Uzbekistan, and Kirghizia. This left only five republics in the original union. The move toward independence, however, has been fraught with both ethnic and political tensions; in one instance,

Kirghizia's Communists rose up and forced the republic's president to resign in September. In early fall, Yeltsin, as the newly anointed peacemaker, traveled to Nagorno-Karabakh to mediate the long-standing and violent struggle between the Armenians and Azerbaijanis.

The unstable political situation in various regions across the USSR has raised Western fears about who controls the country's vast arsenal of nuclear and tactical weapons. Soviet strategic weapons are located in the republics of Russia, the Ukraine, Belorussia, and Kazakhstan, but battlefield weapons are scattered throughout the country. This fear prompted Pres. Bush on Sept. 27, in a surprise announcement, to state that the U.S. is unilaterally reducing weapons, and to call on the Soviets to respond in kind. Although the Soviet reaction to Bush's proposal was positive, both the Ukraine and Kazakhstan have indicated that they may want to keep control of the weapons on their territories, instead of allowing the RSFSR to manage them as they earlier had proposed.

This troubled year has made clear that fighting for freedom was simple compared to the struggle that each ethnic group and former republic will encounter in the search for peace and prosperity. The political map of the territory that until recently defined the USSR, at this point, can only be imagined. (See also "Chronology of the Year's Key Events.")

## Secession and Civil War in Yugoslavia

The year 1991 witnessed the growing disintegration of Yugoslavia, as parliaments in three of the six republics—Slovenia and Croatia (on June 25) and Macedonia (on Sept. 9)—proclaimed their independence. A bitter and destructive civil war erupted between secessionist Croatia on one side and Serbian militias, abetted by the Yugoslav army, on the other.

So long as the Communist party dominated Yugoslavia after the 1980 death of Marshal Josip Tito, his scheme of a presidency that would rotate annually among the six republics worked smoothly. But matters changed dramatically with the 1989 collapse of communism in so much of Europe. Yugoslav elections in 1990 returned Communists (now named Socialists) to power only in Serbia and Montenegro. The other four republics established non- and even anticommunist governments.

In Serbia, rigid Marxist ideologue turned radical Serbian nationalist Slobodan Milosevic was elected president. His Socialists carried 194 of the 250 seats in the Serbian parliament. Milosevic's campaign for a greater Serbia had begun in 1987, when he became chairman of the Serbian Communist party. By stacking local parties and parliaments in the autonomous provinces of Kosovo and Vojvodina, he compelled these provinces to surrender their governing authority to Serbia.

Also in December 1990, Slovenia voted by referendum for independence from Yugoslavia. Milosevic warned the other presidents that if Yugoslavia were to become a loose confedera-

tion, all ethnic Serbs would have to be citizens of the Republic of Serbia. Over half a million Serbs live across the border from Serbia in Croatia, about 12% of that republic's population; most are descended from 17th-century Serbs who fled Ottoman oppression to serve in the army of Habsburg Hungary (which ruled Croatia) as soldiers in the "frontier military district" along the border of the two empires.

The deeply felt differences between Serbs and Croats, who share the same language, are rooted in the distant past; conflicts of East versus West, Ottoman versus Habsburg, Orthodox versus Catholic—even alphabets, Cyrillic versus Latin—all heighten ethnic differences. But more recent history adds virulence to the dispute. The Croats (like most non-Serbs) viewed the creation of Yugoslavia in 1918 as merely a disguise for Serbian domination. Disputes were so serious that in 1929 the king felt constrained to abolish parliament to preserve national unity.

When Germany invaded and destroyed Yugoslavia in 1941, the Germans allowed Croatia to emerge as an Italian client state that attempted to enforce mass conversions to the Catholic faith and embarked on a bloody series of massacres of perhaps 100,000 Serbs and Jews. In the three-way struggle between Germans and Croats, Serbian Chetniks, and Tito's Partisans, the royalist Chetniks and the Partisans repaid the debt with interest.

So at the core of the current struggle are deeply felt hatreds between Serbs and Croats. The absence of such enmity accounts for the lack of Serbian opposition to Slovenian independence. In late June and early July 1991, the Yugoslav army was handed a humiliating defeat and forced to withdraw from Slovenia by the Slovenian militia.

But in August, Serbian rebel militias in Croatia tried to seize ethnically Serbian territory before Croatia could gain its independence. They held about one-third of Croatia, principally in the provinces of Krajina and eastern Slovenia adjacent to Vojvodina. Essential to these successes was the support of Milosevic and the Yugoslav army, which entered Croatia under the guise of keeping Serbs and Croats apart but which actively aided the Serbian militia with tanks, artillery, air power, and the Adriatic fleet.

The secessions and Serbian intransigence have reduced Yugoslavia's central government to virtual nonexistence, and the army seems to be the only functioning organ of the federal government. Yet its officer corps is perhaps 70% Serbian and its war against Croatia has been patently more in the interest of Serbia than of Yugoslavia. With time, the Croat forces were better armed and more experienced and were able to isolate Yugoslav garrisons in Croatia. Slovenian and Croatian supply sources for the army were cut off, leaving it short of fuel and parts for tanks and planes. There were signs also of restiveness within the army itself as defections and draft resistance were on the rise (even in Serbia less than half of the draftees reported for duty), and the commander of the Yugoslav air force went over to the Croatian side.

Countless cease-fires negotiated under various auspices, including those of the EC, have lasted only days or even hours. The survival of Yugoslavia is in doubt and the shape of the successor states impossible to predict. As of Oct. 1, an estimated 1,000 people had been killed and 200,000 made homeless. (For further developments through September and October see the "Chronology of the Year's Key Events.")

## Africa in Change

The decades since independence in the 1960s have been hard ones for Africa. The autocratic and dictatorial regimes prevalent around much of the continent have often been no better, and in some cases markedly worse, than the colonial regimes they replaced. In 1989, the UN-affiliated Economic Commission for Africa (ECA) attributed Africa's economic ills to a "pervasive lack of democracy." In 1990, these ills included crushing external debt totaling $272 bil., which represents 90% of the region's GDP (112% of GDP in sub-Saharan Africa), GNP growth averaging 1% to 2% annually, and a decline in average per capita GDP of more than 2% per annum. In addition, the continent-wide literacy rate is only 54%, and in 1991 the UN estimated that 30 million people would require some type of emergency food relief.

As the 1990s opened, profound political, economic, and diplomatic changes swept the continent. By September 1991, strikes and violent protests for democracy had forced 17 of Africa's 49 sub-Saharan nations to legalize political opposition in 1990–91. Entrenched military leaders in Benin, Congo, Mali, and Niger were ousted, and Gabon's civilian president Omar Bongo was forced to hold multiparty elections that led to power-sharing with the opposition. While opposition grievances and tactics differ radically from one country to the next, some common threads have found expression in integrated regional efforts, especially under the aegis of the 51-member Organization of African Unity (OAU).

The cornerstone of the new approach is a commitment to multiparty democracy, which has been all but unknown throughout much of Africa. The coming of political pluralism is attributable to a number of factors, including the end of the Cold War and the social and economic failure of single-party authoritarian rule in general. In May 1991, the Conference on Security, Stability, Development and Cooperation in Africa, held in Kampala, Uganda, noted that it is the absence of "full democratic and human rights . . . as well as the precedence given to military expenditures, that is the root cause of insecurity and instability in Africa."

OAU member states endorsed the following principles outlined in the Kampala initiative: adherence to the rule of law legislated by freely elected representatives; respect for human rights and fundamental freedoms; popular participation in governance; the existence of pluralist political structures and freedom of expression; the establishment of the African Court of Justice on Human Rights; and procedures for monitoring member states' observance of these principles.

At the same time, the OAU is developing plans to achieve regional economic integration which will ultimately take the form of the African Economic Community (AEC). While total economic integration may be 30 years off, short-term initiatives include strengthening regional communities such as the Economic Community of West African States (ECOWAS) and Southern African Development Coordination Conference (SADCC), and stabilizing tariffs, customs duties, and other barriers to free trade.

Two regions in Africa are undergoing especially dramatic change: the Horn of Africa and South Africa.

**Horn of Africa** The Horn of Africa, which comprises the countries of Somalia, Ethiopia, Sudan, and the region's only peaceful enclave, tiny Djibouti, has long been wracked by civil wars punctuated by devastating drought. By the summer of 1991, the twin disasters had brought the threat of famine to 24 million people, and there were 3.7 million refugees and returnees, the majority of whom were at risk of malnutrition or starvation. The resolution of several long-standing conflicts could signal significant improvements throughout much of the region.

In Ethiopia, a collection of antigovernment forces, some of whom had been in the field for 30 years, succeeded in toppling the Marxist regime of Haile Mariam Mengistu. Of paramount significance, however, is the victorious coalition's recognition of the right of ethnic groups to secede and create their own countries. Eritrea shows every sign of doing so, in what could be the first recognized redrawing of African boundaries since the 1960s.

In Somalia, Mohamed Siad Barre was ousted in January 1991 after 23 years in power, but he remains in the southern part of the country, hoping to return to power. A meeting of six rival opposition movements produced a new government under the presidency of the United Somali Congress's Ali Mahdi Moammad. Absent from the meeting were Barre's group and the Somali National Movement, which on May 17, 1991, had declared an independent Republic of Somaliland in what was British Somaliland in northern Somalia. Although that action went all but unnoticed by the world community, the SNM remains the only effective government (Abd al-Rahman, president) in northern Somalia, and it must cope with the return of vast numbers of refugees who had fled Barre's violent campaign against the north between 1988 and 1991.

The situation is least hopeful in Sudan, geographically Africa's largest country. Eight years of sectarian violence between the ruling Muslim north and the animist and Christian south has helped to put an estimated 8 million Sudanese at risk of starvation, mostly in the south where there are an additional 1 million refugees from war-torn Ethiopia and elsewhere. The government has blocked relief efforts. Among the opposition there is also growing dissatisfaction with the leadership of the Sudan People's Liberation Movement;

some feel that the leadership has not pressed hard enough for a peace settlement and that it has done too little to promote civilian relief efforts. There is also evidence that factions in the south are considering secession.

**South Africa** Following the release of African National Congress leader Nelson Mandela in 1990, the government embarked on a number of sweeping institutional changes, including the release of political prisoners and tolerance of the return of political exiles, desegregation of previously all-white schools, and complete repeal of the legal foundation for apartheid—the Land Acts of 1913 and 1936, the Group Areas Act, and the Population Registration Act. Progress was marred by ethnic violence between Mandela's predominantly Xhosa ANC and Mangosuthu Buthelezi's Zulu Inkatha Freedom party, and by revelations in July that the government had given $700,000 to Inkatha over six years in an effort to undermine the popularity of the ANC.

In September 1991, de Klerk, Mandela, Buthelezi, and leaders of 20 smaller antiapartheid groups signed an accord to end factional violence that has claimed almost 6,000 lives in four years. The agreement sets standards of conduct for political parties and security forces and provides for special courts to settle political violence. At the same time, de Klerk proposed a new constitution that would provide for universal suffrage, create a two-chamber parliament open to all races, and replace the presidency with an executive council. Negotiations on the proposed constitution are to begin by early 1992.

The U.S., the EC, the Soviet Union, and other nations have responded favorably to these changes and have lifted trade and diplomatic sanctions against South Africa, and de Klerk has visited more than 10 African nations, as well as the U.S. and other Western countries, since coming to power in 1989.

## The Confirmation of Clarence Thomas

On July 1, 1991, Pres. Bush announced his intention to nominate Clarence Thomas, a prominent, controversial black conservative, to replace the retiring Thurgood Marshall as an associate justice of the Supreme Court. Although Thomas had been raised in poverty in rural Georgia, he worked his way through college and eventually received a degree from the Yale Law School. He served in the Reagan administration first as head of civil rights in the Dept. of Education, and then as chairman of the Equal Employment Opportunity Commission. In 1989, Pres. Bush appointed him to the Federal Court of Appeals in Washington, D.C.

Known for his outspoken views that minority organizations believed too strongly in welfare and that blacks needed to rely more on their own resources if they were to succeed, Thomas had crossed swords with the leading activist groups, including the NAACP, which immediately opposed his nomination. Within a short time, other major groups, including the AFL-CIO and the National Organization for

Women, also spoke out against Thomas, vowing to stop his appointment as they had Robert Bork's several years before. Many women's groups feared Thomas would provide the crucial vote to overturn *Roe* v. *Wade*, so they were prepared for a dramatic confrontation.

Confirmation hearings before the Senate Judiciary Committee opened on Sept. 10 and lasted less than two weeks. Unlike the Bork hearings, these lacked any moments of conflict or challenge. Liberal white senators who had hammered home their points relentlessly during Bork's proceedings seemed reluctant to confront this black man who was clearly not Bork's equal in learning and who insisted that his previous writings on the law, though meager, were no longer relevant to his current thinking. Thomas had been carefully coached by his White House "handlers" not to answer any questions regarding how he might vote, especially in regard to abortion. Thomas went even further and denied having ever discussed *Roe* v. *Wade* with anyone, an astonishing assertion that led some to believe he should not be on the bench for that reason alone.

The committee hearings ended on Sept. 20, with a vote scheduled for the following week. Most observers believed the committee vote would split along party lines, making the outcome so close as to be indecisive and passing the true test along to the full Senate. Intense lobbying began immediately as many black leaders and an array of powerful interest groups spoke out against the nomination. In addition to the NAACP and NOW, the Leadership Conference on Civil Rights, the National Abortion Rights League, the Alliance for Justice, People for the American Way, as well as five black congressmen and several leading black legal scholars, joined the fight against Thomas.

Despite such formidable opposition, the president and Senate Republicans remained confident, even after the Judiciary Committee vote (Sept. 27) deadlocked at 7–7, meaning there was no recommendation to the full Senate. The nomination still had a strong chance for success. The necessary votes would come from southern Democrats, who not only appreciated Thomas's conservatism, but who knew that a large number of their black constituents clearly supported the appointment. On the Friday before the scheduled vote of Tuesday, Oct. 8, all the news media predicted Thomas would win by seven to ten votes, perhaps more.

On Sunday, Oct. 6, however, this cut and dried issue was suddenly blown apart by a story in New York's *Newsday* that serious charges of sexual harassment against Thomas had been brought to the Senate committee's attention, but had never been made public. In an interview on National Public Radio late that day, Anita Hill, a tenured professor at the University of Oklahoma, claimed that as a young assistant to Clarence Thomas, both at the Department of Education and at EEOC, she had been sexually harassed by him. She also said that she had been approached by the committee staff in early September and had told them of her experiences on the condition that she remain anonymous. Toward the end of the hearings, when it was clear that nothing was being done concerning her charges, she was approached by committee staff members and she agreed to be interviewed by the FBI. While this meant that Clarence Thomas would have to be told and also be interviewed, she would still not have to go public with her story. What she never counted on, however, was that a committee or Senate staff member would leak her story to the press, a gross violation of every bipartisan rule established by Congress to guarantee confidentiality. In less than a day, the name of Anita Hill had become a permanent part of American political history.

On Monday, Oct. 7, while the White House and the Republican leaders in the Senate tried frantically to hold together the delicate coalition of support for Thomas, Professor Hill held a dramatic news conference at her law school in Norman, Oklahoma. Her reasonable and deliberate manner, combined with the serious nature of her allegations, stunned most of the 98 male senators and sowed serious doubts among all but Judge Thomas's staunchest supporters. Even more telling, perhaps, was the immediate and massive evidence that women all over the nation believed sexual harassment in the workplace to be a serious problem that the male power structure refused to address.

By late afternoon on Tuesday, it was clear to the Republican leadership that they no longer had enough support to secure the nomination, so the vote was postponed and Anita Hill asked to appear before the Judiciary Committee on Friday, Oct. 11. Over the following week, the entire country, already polarized by gender-related issues of abortion and equal pay for women, would learn about the meaning of sexual harassment, as well as about some matters many would have preferred not to hear. For the first time in U.S. history, sex had become a public issue in a Supreme Court nomination hearing.

On Friday, Oct. 11, the Judiciary Committee reconvened and heard testimony for over twelve and a half hours. Judge Thomas appeared first and after a searing attack on the Senate for dragging out "sleaze," "dirt," and "lies," he denied all of Hill's allegations and called the process "Kafkaesque." Anita Hill followed him immediately to the witness table, where she remained for over seven hours. She told a long and detailed story of how Clarence Thomas had harassed her when she was his assistant in the early 1980s by continually asking her for dates, discussing the contents of pornographic movies, asserting his own sexual prowess with women, and describing the size of his own penis. Under highly critical cross-examination by Republican senators, she answered almost every question in a concise, straightforward manner, while her deportment remained utterly calm throughout the proceeding. By all accounts, this was a remarkable and, for the judge, quite damning performance.

Thomas returned to the committee that night and again on Saturday and tried to recapture the ground he had so clearly lost. At first, he was very emotional, once or twice on the verge of tears, as he described the impact of this on him and his family. But, he also aggressively attacked the committee, implying that racism was an underlying cause in their willingness to let this happen. He called the proceedings a "high-tech lynching for uppity blacks" who dared to think for themselves. Later, on Saturday, the Republicans attacked Anita Hill and her testimony without restraint. They accused her of perjury, of being delusional, and of concocting her story from sources as diverse as *The Exorcist* and a Kansas sexual harassment case.

The nation, it seemed, was riveted by the senate hearings. Not only were television ratings significantly higher on both Friday and Saturday, the hearings trounced the major league baseball playoffs in the ratings race. Everywhere Americans were discussing this case and pondering or arguing, Was Hill telling the truth? Why would she lie? Why did she wait so long? And what exactly is sexual harassment? How can the accusations of one person against another person concerning events that took place in private without any witnesses be allowed to bring such enormous harm to someone's reputation?

On Sunday, the committee took testimony for over 12 hours, until 2:00 a.m. Monday morning. First came a panel of four witnesses, two men and two women, all former colleagues and friends of Anita Hill, who testified that she had told them about sexual harassment on the job around the time she alleged it happened. Not even the most strenuous questioning from Thomas's supporters on the committee could in any way move these witnesses from their positions, thus corroborating Hill's testimony.

Shortly after this panel was dismissed, Anita Hill's lawyers held an impromptu news conference to announce that Hill had taken a lie detector test that morning and had shown not one instance of deception. The lawyers asserted that while such a test would not be admissible in a court of law, it was administered by a former FBI expert and should help convince the American people that Hill was not deluded, not fantasizing, and not lying.

When the committee reconvened, the Republicans were, of course, infuriated by the timing of this and used every opportunity to attack the veracity of such tests. The panel of four women called to testify on behalf of Judge Thomas refused to be upstaged. In strong and measured statements, they each recounted their experiences as women working for Thomas in the Dept. of Education and EEOC. None of the four believed Anita Hill, they said and two of them characterized her as "arrogant," "aloof," and "ambitious" (one said Hill wanted to be "the Rosa Parks of sexual harassment"). One witness said she believed Hill felt "scorned" by Thomas at EEOC because he had many more assistants there and had less time for her.

At 10:30, Anita Hill requested that her second panel of witnesses be excused because of the lateness of the hour, but Judge Thomas's panel agreed to testify. These four were male friends and colleagues of the judge, and they each attested to his upstanding character. At 1:00 a.m., both sides agreed to end the hearings, even though two women who agreed to testify that Thomas had made inappropriate remarks to them had not been heard. The confirmation vote was set for Tuesday, Oct. 15, at 6:00 p.m., after an entire day of debate on the issue.

On Tuesday, the senate and the rest of America woke up to learn that all the opinion polls showed more people in the final analysis believed Judge Thomas than Anita Hill. It was less clear that a majority of Americans thought he should be confirmed, but many were convinced that he had been treated unfairly.

The Senate debate was long and long-winded, and produced little if any change in the record or in the opinions of the various cliques. The Democrats, faced with a major test of wills with the president that would set the tone for the 1992 election year, failed miserably in their attempt to stop Bush from having his way, despite their majority control of Congress. Clarence Thomas was confirmed on Tuesday, Oct. 15, by a vote of 52 to 48, the closest vote in this century.

---

### NOBEL PRIZES, 1991

**Chemistry** Richard R. Ernst (Switzerland), of the Eidgenössische Technische Hochschule in Zurich, for his work in refining nuclear magnetic resonance spectroscopy, which is used not only in medicine but in chemical analysis as well.

**Physics** Pierre-Gilles de Gennes (France), Collège de France, Paris, for his discoveries about the ordering of molecules in a variety of substances but especially liquid crystals, where his work has helped in understanding superconductivity.

**Physiology or Medicine** Erwin Neher (Germany) Max-Planck Institute for Biophysical Chemistry in Göttingen, and Bert Sakmann (Germany) Max-Planck Institute for Medical Research in Heidelberg, for establishing existence of ion channels by developing technique that allows detection of "incredibly small electrical currents that pass through a single ion channel."

**Literature** Nadine Gordimer (South Africa), for her "involvement on behalf of literature and free speech in a police state where censorship and persecution of books and people exist." Novels include *A Guest of Honour, Burger's Daughter,* and *My Son's Story.*

**Peace** Aung San Suu Kyi (Myanmar), leader of opposition National League for Democracy who has been under house arrest by Myanmar's military regime since 1989, "for her nonviolent struggle for democracy and human rights."

**Economic Sciences** Ronald H. Coase (UK) Univ. of Chicago Law School, for his work on the role of firms in the economy and on social cost of industry, notably his articles "The Theory of the Firm" (1937) and "The Problem of Social Cost" (1960).

# U.S. GEOGRAPHY

**Location** The United States of America shares the North American continent with Canada, Mexico, and the Central American nations. The 48 conterminous states lie in a broad landmass from approximately latitude 24° N to 49° N (south to north), and longitude 67° W to 124° W (east to west). It is bordered on the north by Canada, on the south by Mexico and the Gulf of Mexico, on the east by the Atlantic Ocean, and on the west by the Pacific Ocean. The state of Alaska is located to the northwest on the North American continent; Hawaii is in the Pacific Ocean Basin approximately 2,100 miles southwest of the state of California.

## Political-Geographic Divisions

The Bureau of the Census groups the states in a number of divisions and subdivisions.

**Northeast**
**New England** Maine, New Hampshire, Vermont, Massachusetts, Rhode Island, Connecticut.
**Middle Atlantic** New York, New Jersey, Pennsylvania.
**Midwest**
**East North-Central** Ohio, Indiana, Illinois, Michigan, Wisconsin.
**West North-Central** Minnesota, Iowa, Missouri, North Dakota, South Dakota, Nebraska, Kansas.
**South**
**South Atlantic** Delaware, Maryland, District of Columbia, Virginia, West Virginia, North Carolina, South Carolina, Georgia, Florida.
**East South-Central** Kentucky, Tennessee, Alabama, Mississippi.
**West South-Central** Arkansas, Louisiana, Oklahoma, Texas.
**Pacific**
**Mountain** Montana, Idaho, Wyoming, Colorado, New Mexico, Arizona, Utah, Nevada.
**Pacific** Washington, Oregon, California, Alaska, Hawaii.

## Physiographic Regions

The physiographic regions, that is the primary geological features and landforms, of the United States are:

**Atlantic and Gulf Coast Plains** Run from the islands of southern New England, Cape Cod, and Long Island, through New Jersey, Delaware, Maryland, Virginia, North Carolina, South Carolina, Georgia, Florida, Alabama, Mississippi, Louisiana, Texas; include lower Mississippi Valley in Arkansas, Missouri, Tennessee.
**Appalachian System** Divided into five parts:
**New England** White Mountains (New Hampshire), Green Mountains (Vermont), Champlain

Lowland and Hudson Valley (Vermont, New York), Catskill Mountains (New York).
**The Piedmont** Pennsylvania, Virginia, North Carolina, South Carolina, Georgia, Alabama.
**Great Smoky and Blue Ridge Mountains** Pennsylvania (Poconos), [discontinuous], Virginia, North Carolina, Georgia.
**Ridge and Valley** Pennsylvania, West Virginia, Virginia, Kentucky, Tennessee, Alabama.
**Appalachian Plateau** Pennsylvania, Ohio, West Virginia, Kentucky, Tennessee, Alabama.
**Canadian (or Laurentian) Shield** Covers much of eastern Canada and extends into the U.S. in two places:
**Adirondack Mountains** New York.
**Superior Upland** Upper Michigan, Wisconsin, Minnesota.
**Central Lowland** Includes most of the U.S. interior and is divided into four parts:
**Interior Lowlands** Ohio, Kentucky, Tennessee.
**Mississippi Great Lakes Basin** Ohio, Indiana, Illinois, Michigan, Wisconsin, Iowa, North Dakota, South Dakota.
**Interior Highlands** Ozark Mountains: Missouri, Arkansas, Oklahoma; Ouachita Mountains: Arkansas, Oklahoma.
**Great Plains** North Dakota, South Dakota, Nebraska, Kansas, Oklahoma, Texas, Montana, Wyoming, Colorado, New Mexico.

## Cordilleran Province
**Rocky Mountains** New Mexico, Colorado, Wyoming, Montana.
**Intermontane Range** Divided into four sections:
**Colorado Plateau** Colorado, Utah, New Mexico, Arizona (including Grand Canyon).
**Basin and Range Plateau** Nevada, Utah (including Wasatch Range).
**Desert Basin and Range** California (including Death Valley), Arizona.
**Snake and Columbia River Basins** Idaho, Washington, Oregon.
**Pacific Coastlands** Divided into four sections, three oriented north-south, the other east-west.
**Cascade Mountains and Sierra Nevada** Washington, Oregon, California.
**Puget Sound, Willamette Valley, and Central Valley** Washington, Oregon, California.
**Coast Ranges** Washington, Oregon, California.
**Los Angeles Extension** Tehachapi Mountains (east-west), San Gabriel Mountains, San Bernardino Mountains.

**Source:** J.H. Paterson, *North America*, 8th ed. (New York: Oxford University Press, 1989).

## NATIONAL PARK SYSTEM

The national park system of the United States began in March 1872 with the establishment of Yellowstone National Park in the Territories of Montana and Wyoming, "as a public park or pleasuring ground for the benefit and enjoyment of the people," placed "under exclusive control of the Secretary of the Interior."

The founding of Yellowstone began a worldwide national park movement, and today more than 100 countries contain some 1,200 national parks or equivalent preserves.

The U.S. national park system comprises 354 areas covering some 76 million acres (3% of total U.S. area) in the 50 states, the District of Columbia, Guam, Puerto Rico, Saipan, and the Virgin Islands. Additions to the national park system are generally made through acts of Congress, and national parks can be created only through such acts. But under the Antiquities Act of 1906, the president has authority to proclaim national monuments on lands already under federal jurisdiction.

The diversity of the parks managed by the National Park Service (NPS) is reflected in the variety of titles given to them. Although the system is best known for its scenic parks, more than half the areas of the national park system preserve places and commemorate persons, events, and activities important in the nation's history. Brief definitions of the most common titles follow, together with the number of areas and total federal acreage.

**National capital parks** include more than 346 sites (The Ellipse; Lafayette Park) throughout the Washington, D.C., area. (6,469 acres)
**National historic sites** include areas of prehistoric and modern historical interest (Tuskegee Institute, Miss.), archaeological sites, historic structures, and the like. (69; 18,274 acres)
**National historical parks** are commonly areas of greater physical extent and complexity than historic sites (Nez Perce, Idaho). (31; 140,436 acres)
**National lakeshores/seashores** (Cape Cod National Seashore, Mass.; Pictured Rocks National Lakeshore, Mich.) preserve shoreline areas and offshore islands while providing water-oriented recreation. (10 seashores, 596,663 acres; 4 lakeshores, 227,262 acres)
**National memorial** commonly designates an area or structure that is commemorative in nature (Ft. Clatsop, Oreg.). (26; 7,949 acres)
**National battlefield/battlefield park/battlefield site/military park** cover a variety of areas associated with U.S. military history (Antietam National Battlefield, Md.). (1 battle site, 1 acre; 9 military parks, 34,031 acres; 11 battlefields, 11,210 acres; 3 battlefield parks, 8,725 acres)
**National monuments** are intended to preserve at least one nationally significant resource—whether natural (Rainbow Bridge, Utah) or man-made (Mt. Rushmore, S.Dak.). They are usually smaller than national parks and lack the diversity of attractions. (78; 5,302,748 acres)
**National parks** contain a variety of resources and encompass large land and water areas (Grand Canyon, Ariz.) to help provide adequate protection of resources. (50; 56,376,732 acres)
**National parkways** are ribbons of land flanking roadways (Natchez Trace, Miss.-Tenn.-Ala.) that offer an opportunity for leisurely driving through areas of scenic interest. (4; 168,600 acres)
**National preserves** serve primarily to protect certain resources (Big Thicket, Tex.). Activities

such as hunting and fishing or mineral extraction may be permitted. (14; 9,899,724 acres)

**National recreation areas** were originally areas surrounding reservoirs (Lake Mead, Ariz.-Nev.), but now include other lands and waters set aside for recreational use. (18; 3,507,442 acres)

**National rivers/wild and scenic riverways** preserve ribbons of land bordering on free-flowing streams that have not been dammed, channelized, or otherwise altered (Delaware River, Pa.-N.J.). Activities such as hiking, boating, and hunting may be permitted. (14; 596,663 acres)

**National scenic trails** are usually long-distance footpaths winding through areas of natural beauty (Appalachian Trail, Maine-Ga.). (3; 92,863 acres)

**National wilderness areas** are designated under the Wilderness Act of 1964, which provides that "there shall be no commercial enterprise and no permanent road within any wilderness area . . . and (except for emergency uses) no temporary road, no use of motor vehicles, motorized equipment or motorboats, no landing of aircraft, no other form of mechanical transport,

and no structure or installation." Wilderness areas are usually part of other larger entities.

In addition to the national park system, there are three groups of areas that are closely linked in importance and purpose to areas managed by the NPS.

**Affiliated areas** (designated by Act of Congress, 1970) are areas in the United States and Canada that preserve significant areas outside the national park system but that rely on NPS assistance.

**Wild and scenic rivers system** (designated by Act of Congress, 1968) preserves undeveloped rivers as free-flowing streams accessible for public use. Wild rivers are free of dams and generally accessible only by trails; scenic rivers have relatively primitive shorelines and are largely undeveloped but may be accessible by road.

**National trails system** (designated by National Trails System Act of 1968) includes trails in both urban and rural settings for persons of all ages, interests, skills, and physical abilities.

**Source:** U.S. National Park Service, *The National Parks: Index 1987* (1987), and *National Park Service Statistical Abstract 1990* (1991).

## LARGEST NATIONAL PARKS IN THE CONTERMINOUS U.S.

| Rank/park | Acreage |
| --- | --- |
| 1. Yellowstone National Park, Idaho-Mont.-Wyo. | 2,219,785 |
| 2. Death Valley National Monument, Calif.-Nev. | 2,067,628 |
| 3. Lake Mead National Recreation Area, Ariz.-Nev. | 1,496,600 |
| 4. Everglades National Park, Fla. | 1,398,938 |
| 5. Grand Canyon National Park, Ariz. | 1,218,375 |
| 6. Glacier National Park, Mont. | 1,013,572 |
| 7. Olympic National Park, Wash. | 914,818 |
| 8. Yosemite National Park, Calif. | 761,170 |
| 9. Big Bend National Park, Tex. | 735,416 |
| 10. Isle Royale National Park, Mich. | 571,790 |
| 11. Big Cypress National Preserve, Fla. | 570,000 |
| 12. Joshua Tree National Monument, Calif. | 559,954 |

**Note:** Includes federal and nonfederal acreage. **Source:** U.S. National Park Service, *The National Parks: Index 1987* (1987).

## AREA CODES OF THE UNITED STATES AND CANADA, BY STATE AND PROVINCE, AND OF THE CARIBBEAN ISLANDS

| | | | | | | | |
| --- | --- | --- | --- | --- | --- | --- | --- |
| Alabama | 205 | Illinois (Schaumberg, Waukegan) | 708 | Nebraska (Grand Island, North Platte) | 308 | Pennsylvania (Allentown, Philadelphia) | 215 |
| Alaska | 907 | Illinois (Joliet, Rockford) | 815 | Nebraska (Lincoln, Omaha) | 402 | Pennsylvania (Pittsburgh) | 412 |
| Alberta, Canada | 403 | Indiana (Ft. Wayne, Gary) | 219 | Nevada | 702 | Pennsylvania (Harrisburg, Scranton) | 717 |
| Arizona | 602 | Indiana (Indianapolis, Muncie) | 317 | New Brunswick, Canada | 506 | Pennsylvania (Altoona, Erie) | 814 |
| Arkansas | 501 | Indiana (Evansville, Terre Haute) | 812 | New Hampshire | 603 | Prince Edward Island, Canada | 902 |
| Bermuda | 809 | Iowa (Cedar Rapids, Dubuque) | 319 | New Jersey (Jersey City, Newark) | 201 | Puerto Rico | 809 |
| British Columbia, Canada | 604 | Iowa (Ames, Des Moines) | 515 | New Jersey (Atlantic City, Trenton) | 609 | Quebec, Canada (Quebec City) | 418 |
| | | Iowa (Council Bluffs, Sioux City) | 712 | New Jersey (Elizabeth, New Brunswick) | 908 | Quebec, Canada (Montreal) | 514 |
| California (Fresno) | 209 | | | | | Quebec, Canada (Sherbrooke) | 819 |
| California (Los Angeles) | 213 | Kansas (Emporia, Wichita) | 316 | New Mexico | 505 | | |
| California (Long Beach, Santa Monica) | 310 | Kansas (Kansas City, Salina, Topeka) | 913 | New York City (Bronx, Manhattan) | 212 | Rhode Island | 401 |
| | | Kentucky (Bowling Green, Louisville) | 502 | New York (Syracuse, Utica) | 315 | Saskatchewan, Canada | 306 |
| California (San Jose) | 408 | Kentucky (Covington, Lexington) | 606 | New York (Hempstead, Long Island) | 516 | South Carolina | 803 |
| California (San Francisco) | 415 | | | New York (Albany, Schenectady) | 518 | South Dakota | 605 |
| California (Berkeley, Oakland) | 510 | Louisiana (Lafayette, Shreveport) | 318 | New York (Binghampton, Elmira) | 607 | Tennessee (Chattanooga, Knoxville, Nashville) | 615 |
| California (San Diego) | 619 | Louisiana (Baton Rouge, New Orleans) | 504 | New York (Buffalo, Rochester) | 716 | | |
| California (Santa Rosa, Eureka) | 707 | | | New York City (Brooklyn, Queens, Staten Island) | 718 | Tennessee (Jackson, Memphis) | 901 |
| California (Anaheim, Orange) | 714 | Maine | 207 | | | Texas (Dallas) | 214 |
| California (Bakersfield) | 805 | Manitoba, Canada | 204 | New York (White Plains, Yonkers) | 914 | Texas (Galveston) | 409 |
| California (Burbank) | 818 | Maryland | 301 | Newfoundland, Canada | 709 | Texas (Austin, San Antonio) | 512 |
| California (Sacramento) | 916 | Massachusetts (Amherst, Springfield) | 413 | North Carolina (Asheville, Charlotte) | 704 | Texas (Houston) | 713 |
| Caribbean islands[1] | 809 | | | North Carolina (Raleigh, Winston-Salem) | 919 | Texas (Amarillo) | 806 |
| Colorado (Aspen, Denver) | 303 | Massachusetts (Cape Cod, Lowell, Worcester) | 508 | | | Texas (Arlington, Ft. Worth) | 817 |
| Colorado (Colorado Springs, Pueblo) | 719 | Massachusetts (Boston) | 617 | North Dakota | 701 | Texas (Abilene, El Paso) | 915 |
| Connecticut | 203 | Michigan (Ann Arbor, Detroit, Flint) | 313 | Northwest Territories, Canada | 403 | Utah | 801 |
| | | Michigan (Lansing, Midland, Saginaw) | 517 | Nova Scotia, Canada | 902 | Vermont | 802 |
| Delaware | 302 | | | | | Virginia (Alexandria, Roanoke) | 703 |
| Florida (Ft. Lauderdale, Miami) | 305 | Michigan (Grand Rapids, Kalamazoo) | 616 | Ohio (Akron, Cleveland) | 216 | Virginia (Richmond, Virginia Beach) | 804 |
| Florida (Melbourne, Orlando) | 407 | | | Ohio (Sandusky, Toledo) | 419 | | |
| Florida (Ft. Myers, Tampa) | 813 | Michigan (Escanaba, Upper Peninsula) | 906 | Ohio (Cincinnati, Dayton) | 513 | Virgin Islands | 809 |
| Florida (Jacksonville, Tallahassee) | 904 | | | Ohio (Columbus, Steubenville) | 614 | Washington (Seattle, Vancouver) | 206 |
| Georgia (Atlanta, Columbus) | 404 | Minnesota (Duluth) | 218 | Oklahoma (Lawton, Oklahoma City) | 405 | Washington (Spokane, Yakima) | 509 |
| Georgia (Macon, Savannah) | 912 | Minnesota (Rochester, Winona) | 507 | Oklahoma (Muskogee, Tulsa) | 918 | Washington, D.C. | 202 |
| | | Minnesota (Minneapolis–St. Paul, Minnetonka) | 612 | Ontario, Canada (Toronto) | 416 | West Virginia | 304 |
| Hawaii | 808 | | | Ontario, Canada (London) | 519 | Wisconsin (Green Bay, Milwaukee) | 414 |
| Idaho | 208 | Mississippi | 601 | Ontario, Canada (Ottawa) | 613 | Wisconsin (La Crosse, Madison) | 608 |
| Illinois (Decatur, Springfield) | 217 | Missouri (Jefferson City, St. Louis) | 314 | Ontario, Canada (North Bay) | 705 | Wisconsin (Eau Claire, Wausau) | 715 |
| Illinois (Moline, Peoria) | 309 | Missouri (Joplin, Springfield) | 417 | Ontario, Canada (Ft. William, Thunder Bay) | 807 | Wyoming | 307 |
| Illinois (Chicago) | 312 | Missouri (Kansas City, St. Joseph) | 816 | | | Yukon, Canada | 403 |
| Illinois (Centralia, East St. Louis) | 618 | Montana | 406 | Oregon | 503 | | |

**Note:** When no cities are listed, the area code is for the entire state or province. 1. Includes Anguilla, Antigua, the Bahamas, Barbados, Bequia, Bermuda, British Virgin Islands, Cayman Islands, Dominica, Dominican Republic, Grenada, Jamaica, Montserrat, Mustique, Nevis, Puerto Rico, St. Kitts, St. Lucia, St. Vincent and the Grenadines, Trinidad and Tobago, Turks and Caicos Islands, Virgin Islands.

## SELECTED NATIONAL PARK SERVICE AREAS—ACREAGE, 1988, AND VISITS TO OVERNIGHT AREAS, 1988–90

| Area | Federal acres ('000s) 1988 | Visits (mil.) 1988 | Visits (mil.) 1990 | Overnight stays ('000s) 1988 | Overnight stays ('000s) 1990 |
|---|---|---|---|---|---|
| Acadia National Park, Maine | 41 | 4.5 | 5.4 | 221 | 220 |
| Big Bend National Park, Tex. | 708 | 0.2 | 0.3 | 212 | 215 |
| Blue Ridge Parkway, N.C.-Va. | 79 | 20.0 | 16.9 | 246 | 222 |
| Cape Cod National Seashore, Mass. | 27 | 5.2 | 5.4 | 19 | 23 |
| Death Valley National Monument, Calif.-Nev. | 2,049 | 0.7 | 0.7 | 346 | 293 |
| Gateway National Recreation Area, N.Y.-N.J. | 20 | 6.2 | 5.8 | 2 | 3 |
| George Washington Memorial Parkway, Va.-Md. | 7 | 9.5 | 5.3 | — | — |
| Glacier National Park, Mont. | 1,013 | 1.8 | 2.0 | 326 | 330 |
| Glen Canyon National Recreation Area, Ariz.-Utah | 1,194 | 3.5 | 3.1 | 1,929 | 2,376 |
| Grand Canyon National Park, Ariz. | 1,179 | 3.9 | 3.8 | 868 | 908 |
| Grand Teton National Park, Wyo. | 307 | 1.2 | 1.6 | 428 | 597 |
| Great Smoky Mountain National Park, N.C.-Tenn. | 520 | 8.8 | 8.2 | 494 | 463 |
| Gulf Island National Seashore, Miss.-Fla. | 99 | 5.2 | 4.9 | 186 | 174 |
| Independence National Historical Park, Pa. | (Z) | 5.4 | 3.3 | — | — |
| Kings Canyon National Park, Calif. | 462 | 1.0 | 1.1 | 287 | 302 |
| Lake Mead National Recreation Area, Ariz.-Nev. | 1,469 | 8.3 | 8.6 | 1,409 | 1,457 |
| Mesa Verde National Park, Colo. | 52 | 0.8 | 0.6 | 229 | 159 |
| Natchez Trace Parkway, Miss.-Tenn.-Ala. | 52 | 11.7 | 5.5 | 21 | 22 |
| National Capital Parks, D.C.-Md.-Va.[1] | 6 | 9.0 | 7.5 | — | — |
| Olympic National Park, Wash. | 911 | 3.0 | 2.8 | 424 | 404 |
| Ozark National Scenic Riverways, Mo. | 61 | 1.5 | 1.7 | 233 | 224 |
| Rocky Mountain National Park, Colo. | 265 | 2.5 | 2.6 | 215 | 209 |
| Sequoia National Park, Calif. | 402 | 1.0 | 1.1 | 359 | 345 |
| Shenandoah National Park, Va. | 195 | 1.9 | 1.8 | 358 | 323 |
| Valley Forge National Historical Park, Pa. | 3 | 4.2 | 1.7 | 2 | 1 |
| Virgin Island National Park, USVI | 13 | 0.8 | 0.7 | 222 | 173 |
| Yellowstone National Park, Idaho-Mont.-Wyo. | 2,220 | 2.2 | 2.8 | 1,109 | 1,345 |
| Yosemite National Park, Calif. | 759 | 3.2 | 3.1 | 2,286 | 2,220 |
| Zion National Park, Utah | 143 | 1.9 | 2.1 | 287 | 292 |
| **Total National Parks Sytstem** | **258,683** | — | **258.7** | — | **17,622** |

**Note:** Z = less than 500 acres. Area selection based on a minimum of 4 million visits or 200,000 overnight stays in 1988. 1. Includes 346 units in the District of Columbia, Maryland, and Virginia; not all report visits. **Source:** U.S. National Park Service, *National Park Statistical Abstract* (annual).

## STATE PARKS AND RECREATION AREAS BY STATE, 1989

| State | Acreage ('000s) | Visitors ('000s) Total | Visitors ('000s) Day | Revenue Total ('000s) | Revenue Percent of operating budget |
|---|---|---|---|---|---|
| Alabama | 49 | 5,775 | 4,770 | $21,656 | 87.5% |
| Alaska | 3,237 | 5,520 | 4,886 | 530 | 11.1 |
| Arizona | 39 | 2,017 | 1,696 | 1,846 | 28.9 |
| Arkansas | 48 | 6,660 | 6,007 | 10,023 | 57.9 |
| California | 1,287 | 77,307 | 70,920 | 42,112 | 26.0 |
| Colorado | 230 | 7,912 | 7,524 | 9,293 | 96.2 |
| Connecticut | 32 | 8,612 | 8,254 | 2,525 | 16.2 |
| Delaware | 12 | 1,742 | 1,548 | 3,447 | 69.9 |
| Florida | 419 | 15,147 | 14,113 | 15,381 | 42.7 |
| Georgia | 62 | 14,351 | 10,763 | 10,850 | 48.2 |
| Hawaii | 25 | 17,340 | 17,254 | 1,251 | 21.9 |
| Idaho | 47 | 2,130 | 1,901 | 1,337 | 44.0 |
| Illinois | 384 | 35,452 | 34,920 | 2,622 | 9.5 |
| Indiana | 57 | 9,397 | 7,787 | 8,324 | 69.4 |
| Iowa | 52 | 10,787 | 10,276 | 2,014 | 24.2 |
| Kansas | 30 | 5,109 | 3,337 | 2,458 | 45.5 |
| Kentucky | 42 | 28,192 | 25,189 | 34,158 | 63.6 |
| Louisiana | 38 | 1,028 | 732 | 1,525 | 26.9 |
| Maine | 70 | 2,217 | 2,000 | 1,399 | 36.8 |
| Maryland | 96 | 8,907 | 8,551 | 6,372 | 32.5 |
| Massachusetts | 60 | 14,133 | 13,235 | 7,324 | 37.0 |
| Michigan | 282 | 24,707 | 19,099 | 15,717 | 73.4 |
| Minnesota | 200 | 7,687 | 6,880 | 5,805 | 43.6 |
| Mississippi | 23 | 4,385 | 3,800 | 4,430 | 45.8 |
| Missouri | 109 | 14,375 | 13,350 | 2,631 | 16.4 |
| Montana | 51 | 4,195 | 3,636 | $ 300 | 12.1% |
| Nebraska | 149 | 8,739 | 7,443 | 14,414 | 218.8 |
| Nevada | 142 | 2,961 | 2,812 | 775 | 20.2 |
| New Hampshire | 33 | 4,439 | 4,241 | 6,910 | 89.1 |
| New Jersey | 92 | 10,620 | 10,164 | 4,754 | 19.9 |
| New Mexico | 119 | 4,826 | 2,179 | 2,860 | 37.6 |
| New York | 258 | 56,056 | 53,043 | 25,041 | 23.5 |
| North Carolina | 129 | 7,938 | 7,577 | 1,487 | 21.5 |
| North Dakota | 17 | 1,006 | 876 | 826 | 45.7 |
| Ohio | 208 | 83,218 | 65,571 | 11,439 | 27.8 |
| Oklahoma | 96 | 16,817 | 14,547 | 11,324 | 56.7 |
| Oregon | 90 | 39,030 | 36,926 | 7,564 | 39.0 |
| Pennsylvania | 276 | 36,324 | 34,754 | 21,000 | 52.9 |
| Rhode Island | 9 | 6,167 | 5,979 | 1,959 | 40.8 |
| South Carolina | 79 | 8,392 | 7,325 | 9,503 | 64.3 |
| South Dakota | 92 | 5,470 | 5,087 | 3,678 | 73.4 |
| Tennessee | 133 | 26,060 | 24,964 | 16,432 | 49.6 |
| Texas | 433 | 20,828 | 18,504 | 11,625 | 30.6 |
| Utah | 116 | 4,894 | 4,400 | 2,709 | 24.5 |
| Vermont | 47 | 982 | 603 | 3,671 | 93.2 |
| Virginia | 52 | 3,873 | 3,419 | 2,030 | 21.5 |
| Washington | 231 | 40,637 | 38,459 | 6,646 | 26.6 |
| West Virginia | 127 | 8,787 | 8,019 | 11,633 | 66.5 |
| Wisconsin | 71 | 11,563 | 10,220 | 6,812 | 60.2 |
| Wyoming | 119 | 1,796 | 1,349 | 136 | 3.9 |

**Note:** Figures are not strictly comparable with those of earlier years. **Source:** National Association of State Park Directors (Austin, Tex.) *1990 Annual Information Exchange* (1990).

## LAND COVER AND USE, BY STATE, 1982 (thousands of acres)

| State | Total surface area[1] | Federal surface area | Nonfederal land areas | | | | | |
|---|---|---|---|---|---|---|---|---|
| | | | Urban and built-up land[2] | Rural transportation[3] | Cropland | Pasture-land | Rangeland | Forest-land |
| United States[4] | 1,937,725 | 404,063 | 46,416 | 26,914 | 420,994 | 132,356 | 405,914 | 393,197 |
| Alabama | 33,091 | 904 | 906 | 639 | 4,510 | 3,817 | — | 20,633 |
| Arizona | 72,960 | 32,056 | 711 | 291 | 1,206 | 79 | 30,948 | 4,760 |
| Arkansas | 34,040 | 3,114 | 636 | 540 | 8,102 | 5,794 | 162 | 14,340 |
| California | 101,572 | 45,552 | 3,265 | 1,037 | 10,518 | 1,393 | 18,125 | 15,218 |
| Colorado | 66,618 | 23,611 | 672 | 609 | 10,603 | 1,260 | 24,233 | 4,030 |
| Connecticut | 3,212 | 9 | 603 | 55 | 245 | 114 | — | 1,828 |
| Delaware | 1,309 | 33 | 128 | 26 | 519 | 35 | — | 348 |
| Florida | 37,545 | 3,129 | 2,770 | 601 | 3,557 | 4,273 | 3,804 | 12,430 |
| Georgia | 37,702 | 2,068 | 1,632 | 504 | 6,568 | 2,977 | — | 21,884 |
| Hawaii | 4,141 | 342 | 126 | 23 | 333 | 974 | — | 1,474 |
| Idaho | 53,481 | 33,445 | 189 | 255 | 6,390 | 1,274 | 6,733 | 3,977 |
| Illinois | 36,061 | 493 | 1,846 | 870 | 24,727 | 3,157 | — | 3,429 |
| Indiana | 23,159 | 489 | 1,102 | 517 | 13,781 | 2,212 | — | 3,640 |
| Iowa | 36,016 | 172 | 623 | 1,061 | 26,441 | 4,536 | — | 1,756 |
| Kansas | 52,658 | 585 | 721 | 1,104 | 29,118 | 2,241 | 16,909 | 626 |
| Kentucky | 25,862 | 1,125 | 636 | 570 | 5,934 | 5,880 | — | 10,158 |
| Louisiana | 30,561 | 1,104 | 823 | 546 | 6,409 | 2,369 | 241 | 12,895 |
| Maine | 21,290 | 135 | 212 | 270 | 953 | 569 | — | 16,770 |
| Maryland | 6,695 | 158 | 763 | 114 | 1,794 | 534 | — | 2,425 |
| Massachusetts | 5,302 | 89 | 883 | 128 | 297 | 202 | — | 2,970 |
| Michigan | 37,457 | 3,087 | 1,966 | 873 | 9,443 | 2,911 | — | 15,360 |
| Minnesota | 54,017 | 3,373 | 904 | 1,154 | 23,024 | 3,590 | 199 | 13,956 |
| Mississippi | 30,521 | 1,618 | 582 | 539 | 7,415 | 3,975 | — | 15,243 |
| Missouri | 44,606 | 2,094 | 1,117 | 977 | 14,998 | 12,573 | 168 | 10,986 |
| Montana | 94,109 | 27,107 | 197 | 784 | 17,197 | 3,036 | 37,837 | 5,228 |
| Nebraska | 49,507 | 639 | 415 | 826 | 20,277 | 2,125 | 23,096 | 732 |
| Nevada | 70,759 | 60,189 | 199 | 152 | 860 | 304 | 7,908 | 357 |
| New Hampshire | 5,938 | 727 | 236 | 109 | 158 | 125 | — | 4,085 |
| New Jersey | 4,984 | 145 | 1,163 | 69 | 809 | 240 | — | 1,848 |
| New Mexico | 77,819 | 26,420 | 267 | 382 | 2,413 | 163 | 40,982 | 4,734 |
| New York | 31,429 | 237 | 1,811 | 594 | 5,912 | 3,872 | — | 16,517 |
| North Carolina | 33,708 | 2,116 | 1,622 | 727 | 6,695 | 1,980 | — | 16,729 |
| North Dakota | 45,250 | 1,879 | 198 | 1,036 | 27,039 | 1,272 | 10,948 | 438 |
| Ohio | 26,451 | 346 | 2,187 | 645 | 12,447 | 2,714 | — | 6,380 |
| Oklahoma | 44,772 | 1,192 | 851 | 789 | 11,568 | 7,138 | 15,060 | 6,539 |
| Oregon | 62,127 | 32,122 | 526 | 365 | 4,356 | 1,966 | 9,392 | 11,889 |
| Pennsylvania | 28,997 | 668 | 2,073 | 613 | 5,896 | 2,593 | — | 15,300 |
| Rhode Island | 776 | 4 | 140 | 14 | 27 | 36 | — | 406 |
| South Carolina | 19,912 | 1,150 | 839 | 475 | 3,579 | 1,208 | — | 11,026 |
| South Dakota | 49,354 | 2,824 | 231 | 833 | 16,947 | 2,703 | 22,784 | 562 |
| Tennessee | 26,972 | 1,343 | 1,000 | 588 | 51,592 | 5,356 | — | 11,529 |
| Texas | 170,756 | 2,998 | 4,388 | 2,234 | 33,320 | 17,043 | 95,353 | 9,324 |
| Utah | 54,336 | 35,819 | 274 | 152 | 2,039 | 490 | 8,489 | 3,235 |
| Vermont | 6,153 | 315 | 97 | 101 | 648 | 501 | — | 4,087 |
| Virginia | 26,091 | 2,347 | 1,219 | 329 | 3,397 | 3,392 | — | 13,625 |
| Washington | 43,609 | 12,474 | 990 | 492 | 7,793 | 1,345 | 5,637 | 12,690 |
| West Virginia | 15,508 | 1,104 | 312 | 205 | 1,093 | 1,869 | — | 10,423 |
| Wisconsin | 35,938 | 1,800 | 1,125 | 770 | 11,457 | 3,394 | — | 13,393 |
| Wyoming | 62,598 | 29,315 | 148 | 330 | 2,587 | 755 | 26,915 | 987 |

1. Includes 107.9 million acres of water area and minor land cover and uses that are not shown separately. 2. In urbanized areas and places of 2,500 or more population outside of urbanized areas. 3. Rural highway, road, and railroad rights-of-way, and airports. 4. Does not include Alaska. **Source:** U.S. Dept. of Agriculture, Soil Conservation Service, and Iowa State University, Statistical Laboratory, *Basic Statistics—1982, National Resources Inventory* (1987).

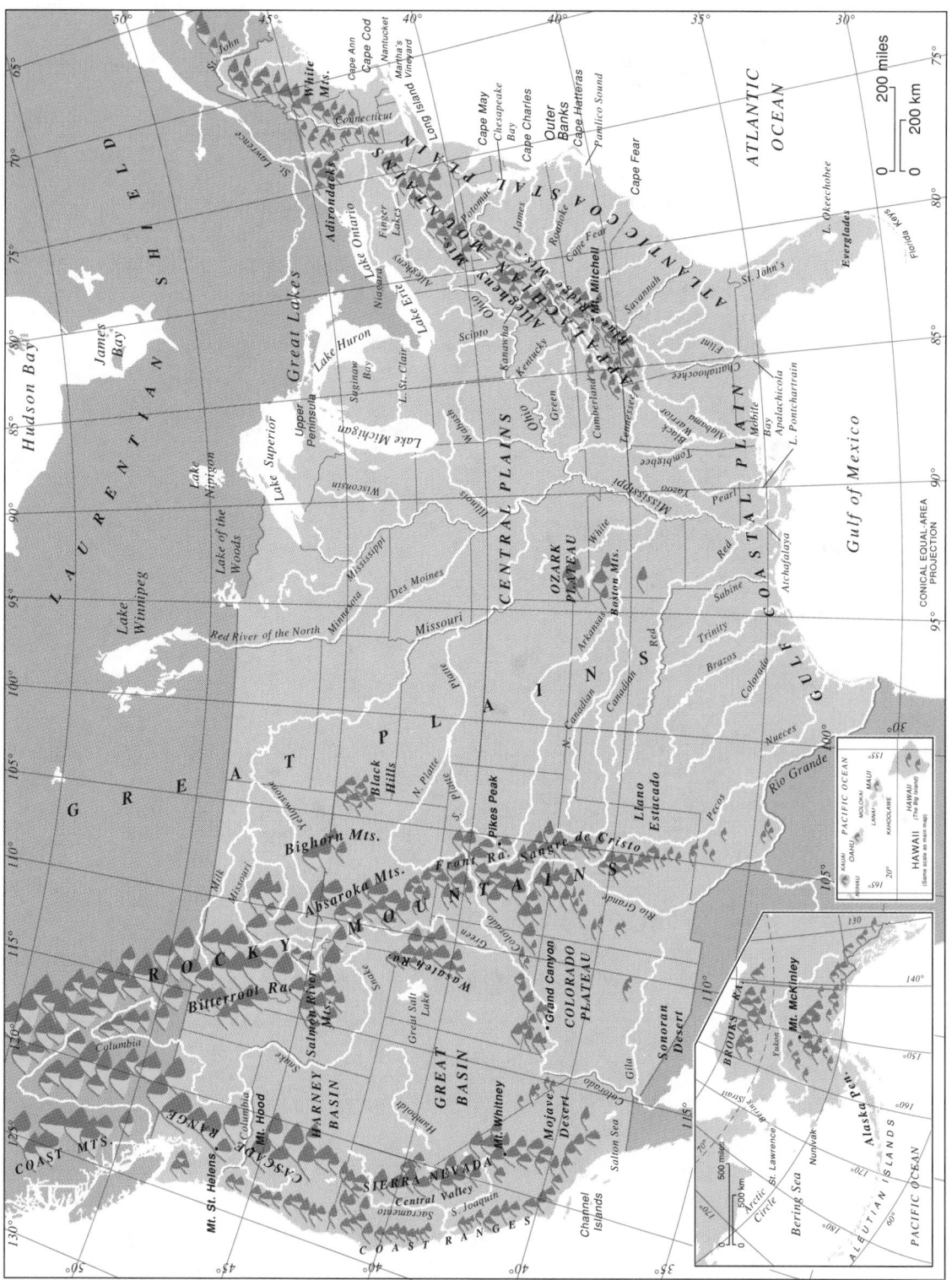

THE UNITED STATES PHYSICAL MAP 43

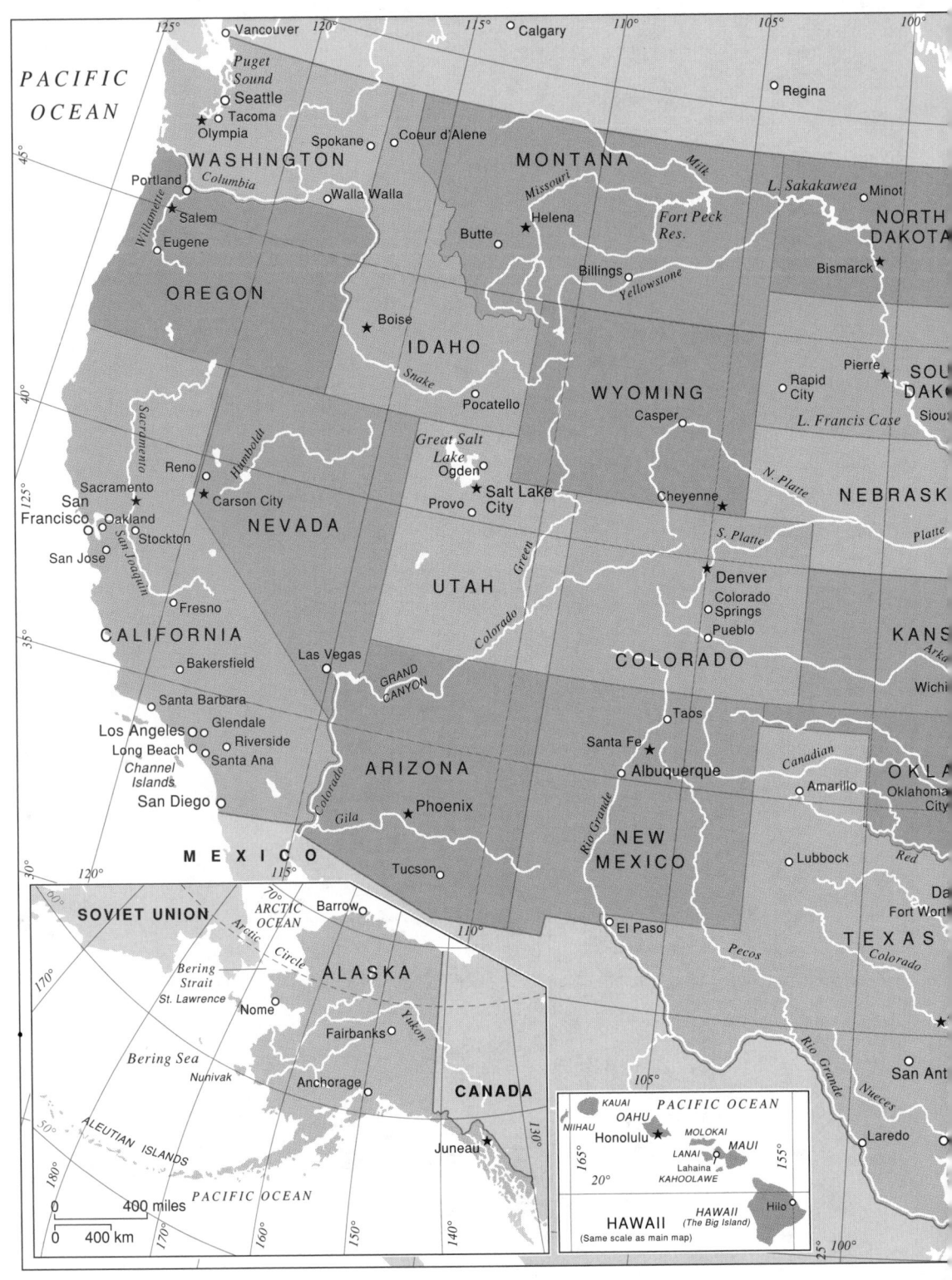

PACIFIC OCEAN

Vancouver
Calgary
Regina

Puget Sound
Seattle
Tacoma
Olympia
Spokane
Coeur d'Alene

WASHINGTON
Portland
Columbia
Walla Walla

MONTANA
Milk
Missouri
L. Sakakawea
Minot
NORTH DAKOTA

Salem
Eugene

Helena
Butte
Fort Peck Res.

Bismarck

OREGON

Billings
Yellowstone

Boise

IDAHO

Snake

WYOMING

Rapid City
Pierre
SOU DAK
Siou

Pocatello

Casper

L. Francis Case

Sacramento
Reno
Humboldt

Great Salt Lake
Ogden
Salt Lake City
Provo

N. Platte

Cheyenne

NEBRASK

Sacramento
San Francisco
Oakland
Stockton
San Jose
San Joaquin

Carson City

NEVADA

Green

S. Platte

Platte

Fresno

UTAH

Denver
Colorado Springs
Pueblo

KANS

CALIFORNIA

Colorado

COLORADO

Arka
Wichi

Bakersfield

Las Vegas

GRAND CANYON

Santa Barbara
Glendale
Los Angeles
Long Beach
Riverside
Santa Ana
Channel Islands
San Diego

Taos
Santa Fe
Albuquerque

Canadian

OKLA
Oklahoma City

ARIZONA

Colorado
Gila
Phoenix

NEW MEXICO

Amarillo

Lubbock

Red

MEXICO

Tucson

Rio Grande

El Paso

Pecos

TEXAS
Colorado

Da
Fort Wort

SOVIET UNION

ARCTIC OCEAN
Barrow
Arctic Circle

ALASKA

San Ant

Bering Strait
St. Lawrence
Nome

Fairbanks
Yukon

CANADA

Rio Grande
Nueces

Laredo

Bering Sea
Nunivak

Anchorage

ALEUTIAN ISLANDS

Juneau

KAUAI
OAHU
NIIHAU
Honolulu
MOLOKAI
MAUI
LANAI
Lahaina
KAHOOLAWE

PACIFIC OCEAN

PACIFIC OCEAN

0      400 miles
0      400 km

HAWAII
HAWAII
(The Big Island)
Hilo

HAWAII
(Same scale as main map)

CANADA

Lake of the Woods
L. Nipigon
Thunder Bay
L. Superior
Duluth
Sault Ste. Marie
MICHIGAN
Québec
MAINE
Montréal
Ottawa
St. Lawrence
Augusta
Burlington
Montpelier
NEW HAMPSHIRE
Portland
Concord
Portsmouth
Lake Champlain
VERMONT
MINNESOTA
St. Paul
minneapolis
Green Bay
WISCONSIN
L. Michigan
L. Huron
Toronto
L. Ontario
NEW YORK
Albany
MASSACHUSETTS
Boston
Worcester
Cape Cod
Milwaukee
Madison
Lansing
Grand Rapids
Warren
Detroit
L. Erie
ERIE CANAL
Rochester
Buffalo
Syracuse
Providence
Nantucket
RHODE ISLAND
Hartford
CONNECTICUT
IOWA
Cedar Rapids
Chicago
Toledo
Cleveland
OHIO
Scranton
PENNSYLVANIA
New Haven
Long Island
New York
Des Moines
Fort Wayne
Columbus
Pittsburgh
Harrisburg
Newark
NEW JERSEY
Trenton
Philadelphia
Wilmington
ILLINOIS
INDIANA
Dayton
Cincinnati
WEST VIRGINIA
Baltimore
Dover
DELAWARE
Springfield
Indianapolis
Ohio
WASHINGTON D.C.
Annapolis
MARYLAND
Chesapeake Bay
Kansas City
St. Louis
Louisville
Frankfort
Charleston
VIRGINIA
Richmond
Jefferson City
Lexington
Green
Roanoke
Norfolk
Virginia Beach
MISSOURI
KENTUCKY
James
Greensboro
Raleigh
Outer Banks
ARKANSAS
Nashville
Knoxville
NORTH CAROLINA
Charlotte
Asheville
TENNESSEE
Chattanooga
Greenville
Wilmington
Cape Fear
ATLANTIC OCEAN
Fort Smith
Little Rock
Memphis
Huntsville
Columbia
SOUTH CAROLINA
Cape Fear
Atlanta
Birmingham
Charleston
Shreveport
MISSISSIPPI
ALABAMA
Macon
Columbus
GEORGIA
Savannah
Jackson
Montgomery
Mobile
Pensacola
Tallahassee
Jacksonville
Baton Rouge
New Orleans
Apalachicola
FLORIDA
Cape Canaveral
LOUISIANA
Orlando
Tampa
St. Petersburg
Gulf of Mexico
L. Okeechobee
West Palm Beach
Fort Myers
Fort Lauderdale
Naples
Miami
Miami Beach
Hialeah
Key West
Florida Keys

0    200 miles
0    200 km

CONICAL EQUAL-AREA PROJECTION

## RIVERS AND LAKES

### Major Navigable Waterways of the United States

The U.S. inland and intracoastal waterway system handles over 500 million tons of traffic each year, carried by a fleet of more than 5,000 towboats and 31,000 barges on over 11,000 miles of primary channels. Ninety percent of these channels have depths of between 9 and 14 feet. Maintenance and improvement of the waterways—including channel dredging, bridge and levee maintenance, and the construction of canals and locks—are in large measure the responsibility of the U.S. Army Corps of Engineers. The 522-mile New York State Barge Canal System is the only major non-federal waterway in the country.

**Mississippi River System** The major inland river transportation network is the Mississippi River and its tributaries. This north-south-oriented system includes the Mississippi River, the Ohio River System, the Illinois Waterway, and the Arkansas and Missouri rivers, among others. In this system there are about 7,000 miles of heavily used, improved navigable channels, 85 percent of which have at least nine-foot navigable channel depths.

> *"The Missouri and the Mississippi have made a deeper impression on me than any other part of the world."*
>
> —T.S. Eliot (1888–1965)

**Intracoastal Waterways** At its mouth the Mississippi River is intersected by the Gulf Intracoastal Waterway (GIWW), which parallels the Gulf Coast for 1,180 miles from St. Marks River, Florida, to Brownsville, Texas, at the Mexican border. The GIWW is intersected by a number of river systems in addition to the Mississippi, including the Mobile River, the Apalachicola, and the Houston Ship Channel.

This network of major inland and coastal waterways connects some of the largest Gulf Coast ports—New Orleans, La.; Houston, Beaumont, and Corpus Christi, Tex.; and Mobile, Ala.—with some of the largest inland ports—St. Louis, Mo.; Pittsburgh, Pa.; Huntington, W. Va.; Cincinnati, Ohio; Memphis, Tenn.; and Chicago, Ill. The 40-foot controlling depth of the Mississippi River between the Gulf of Mexico and Baton Rouge allows ocean shipping to join the barge traffic, making this segment especially vital to both the domestic and foreign commerce of the United States.

The Atlantic Intracoastal Waterway provides 1,329 miles of protected channels for commercial and recreational navigation along the Atlantic Coast from Key West, Fla., to Norfolk, Va. Partially protected segments of the waterway continue north from Norfolk along the Delmarva Peninsula, the New Jersey coast, and Long Island. Among the major Atlantic Coast ports located along this waterway are Miami, Fla.; Savannah, Ga.; Baltimore, Md.; Philadelphia, Pa.; and the Port of New York and New Jersey.

**Pacific Coast** In comparison with the Mississippi River system and the intracoastal waterways of the Atlantic and Gulf coasts, the inland and coastal waterways of the Pacific are few. Shallow draft waterways include the Columbia-Snake Waterway and the Willamette River above Portland, Oreg.; the Sacramento River above Sacramento, Calif.; the San Joaquin River above Stockton, Calif.; and a few short navigable rivers stretching along the Washington and Oregon coasts.

The accompanying table shows the major navigable rivers in the United States, their total length, the distance commercially navigable, the body of water they flow into and the head of navigation—the upriver point beyond which commercial ships cannot pass—and the states through or by which the rivers pass, from source to mouth.

### The Great Lakes and St. Lawrence Seaway

The Great Lakes have been crucial to the development of the United States and Canada. They were the highways along which people and finished goods moved west, and along which raw materials such as lumber, minerals, and grains were transported to eastern markets. Later the cities of the Great Lakes, such as Chicago, Duluth, Detroit, and Buffalo, became important centers of finance, industry, and trade in their own right. So important was the maritime trade of the Great Lakes that in the 1890s, Chicago was the fourth-largest port in the world, despite being closed by ice for as many as five months a year.

An early obstacle to Great Lakes navigation was the fact that the lakes are not all at the same elevation: there is a difference of 354 feet between the level of the westernmost Lake Superior and easternmost Lake Ontario, and there is another 246 feet descent from Lake Ontario down the St. Lawrence River to where it empties into the Atlantic Ocean.

The first canal (1799) was built on the St.

## THE GREAT LAKES

| Lake | Area | | Depth | | Height above sea level | |
|---|---|---|---|---|---|---|
| | Sq. mi. | Sq km | Feet | Meters | Feet | Meters |
| Ontario | 7,540 | 19,529 | 802 | 244 | 246 | 75 |
| Erie | 9,940 | 25,745 | 210 | 64 | 571 | 174 |
| Michigan | 22,400 | 58,016 | 923 | 281 | 577 | 176 |
| Huron | 23,010 | 59,596 | 750 | 229 | 577 | 176 |
| Superior | 31,820 | 82,414 | 1,333 | 406 | 600 | 183 |

**Source:** U.S. Environmental Protection Agency and Environment Canada, *The Great Lakes: An Environmental Atlas and Resource Book* (1987).

Marys River between Lake Superior and Lake Huron. (Today there are two Sault Sainte Marie [or Soo] Canals—one U.S. and one Canadian—along the 70-mile river.) In 1825 the United States opened the way between the upper lakes (all but Lake Ontario) and the Atlantic via the 353-mile Erie Canal between Buffalo, on Lake Erie, and Albany, on the Hudson River north of New York City. Canada followed with the 27-mile Welland Canal (1833) connecting Welland on Lake Erie and St. Catherine's on Lake Ontario.

The most ambitious undertaking was the construction of the St. Lawrence Seaway, a joint Canadian-American effort to open the entire length of the St. Lawrence and the Great Lakes to oceangoing navigation. Started in 1955 and opened to navigation in 1959, the seaway's system of canals and locks allows ships of up to 730 feet in length and 27 feet draft to sail the entire 2,342 miles from the mouth of the St. Lawrence to Duluth, Minn., at the western end of Lake Superior. The seaway also provides hydroelectric power for Canada and the United States.

### The Panama Canal

One of the great engineering feats of the world, the 44-mile Panama Canal bisects the continents of North and South America, making it possible for ships to sail between the Atlantic and Pacific Oceans without rounding the treacherous Cape Horn at the tip of South America. The U.S. government began construction of the canal in 1904, and it was opened to commercial navigation Aug. 15, 1914. For interocean shippers the savings in distance and time afforded by the canal are enormous. A ship sailing from New York to San Francisco via the Panama Canal travels a distance of 5,263 miles, a savings of more than 7,800 miles—or about 20 days—over the 13,100-mile route around Cape Horn. The minimum depth of the canal is 41 feet, the minimum width 300 feet, and the highest elevation above sea level 85 feet.

The Canal Zone, a 10-mile-wide strip of land around the canal in the Republic of Panama, was acquired in 1903 by the United States, who governed it until 1979. The Panama Canal Treaty of 1977 abolished the Canal Zone as an independent political entity, but the canal's maintenance and operation remain the responsibility of the U.S. Panama Canal Commission until 1999, when the Republic of Panama assumes full responsibility.

## MAJOR NAVIGABLE RIVERS AND CANALS IN THE UNITED STATES

| Ultimate outflow/river | Length (miles) | Navigable length (mi.) | Mouth to head of navigation | States/provinces (from source to mouth) |
|---|---|---|---|---|
| **Atlantic Ocean** | | | | |
| St. Lawrence | 760 | 760 | Gulf of St. Lawrence to Lake Ontario | N.Y.; Ontario, Québec (Can.) |
| Cape Cod Canal | 17 | 17 | Sandwich to Buzzards Bay, Mass. | Mass. |
| Connecticut | 407 | 52 | Long Island Sound to Hartford, Conn. | N.H., Vt., Mass., Conn. |
| Hudson | 306 | 134 | New York Bay to Troy, N.Y.; New York State Barge Canal (522 mi.) links to Lake Erie (353 mi. Troy to Buffalo) and to Lakes Champlain, Ontario, Cayuga, Seneca | N.Y. |
| Delaware | 367 | 77 | Delaware Bay to Trenton, N.J. | N.Y., Pa., N.J., Del. |
| Chesapeake and Delaware Canal | 14 | 14 | Delaware Bay to Chesapeake Bay | Del., Md. |
| Potomac | 287 | 101 | Chesapeake Bay to Washington, D.C. | Va., Md., D.C. |
| James | 340 | 87 | Chesapeake Bay to Richmond, Va. | Va. |
| Roanoke | 410 | 112 | Atlantic Ocean to Altavista, N.C. | Va., N.C. |
| Cape Fear | 202 | 111 | Atlantic Ocean to Fayetteville, N.C. | N.C. |
| Savannah | 314 | 181 | Atlantic Ocean to Augusta, Ga. | S.C., Ga. |
| Saint Johns | 285 | 160 | Atlantic Ocean to Lake Harney, Fla. | Fla. |
| **Gulf of Mexico** | | | | |
| Chattahoochee | 436 | 194 | Apalachicola River to Columbus, Ga. | Ga., Ala. |
| Apalachicola | 90 | 90 | Gulf of Mexico to Chattahoochee, Fla. | Fla. |
| Mobile | 45 | 45 | Mobile Bay to confluence of Alabama and Tombigbee rivers | Ala. |
| Alabama | 318 | 305 | Mobile River to Montgomery, Ala. | Ala. |
| Tombigbee | 362 | 362 | Mobile River to Amory, Miss.; linked to Tennessee River by Tennessee-Tombigbee Waterway (253 mi.) | Miss., Ala. |
| Black Warrior | 217 | 217 | Tombigbee River to Birmingham, Ala. | Ala. |
| Houston Ship Channel | 57 | 57 | Galveston Bay to Houston, Tex. | Tex. |
| Rio Grande[1] | 1,885 | 13 | Gulf of Mexico to Brownsville, Tex. | Colo., N. Mex., Tex., Mexico |
| **Mississippi River System** | | | | |
| Mississippi | 2,348 | 1,807 | Gulf of Mexico to Minneapolis, Minn. | Minn., Wis., Iowa, Ill., Mo., Ky., Tenn., Ark., Miss., La. |
| EASTERN TRIBUTARIES | | | | |
| Illinois | 273 | 271 | Mississippi River to Joliet, Ill.; also linked to Mississippi by Illinois and Mississippi Canal, and to Lake Michigan (at Chicago, Calumet, East Chicago, Gary) by Illinois Waterway | Ill. |
| Ohio | 981 | 981 | Mississippi River to Pittsburgh, Pa. | Pa., Ohio, W.Va., Ind., Ky., Ill. |
| Monongahela | 129 | 129 | Ohio River to Fairmont, W.Va. | W.Va., Pa. |
| Allegheny | 325 | 72 | Ohio River to East Brady, Pa. | N.Y., Pa. |
| Kanawha | 97 | 91 | Ohio River to Charleston, W.Va. | W.Va. |
| Kentucky | 259 | 82 | Ohio River to Beattyville, Ky. | Ky. |
| Green | 360 | 103 | Ohio River to Bowling Green, Ky. | Ky. |
| Cumberland | 694 | 387 | Ohio River to Burnside, Ky. | Ky., Tenn. |
| Tennessee | 652 | 648 | Ohio River to Knoxville, Tenn. | Tenn., Ala., Miss., Ky. |
| Yazoo | 169 | 165 | Mississippi River to Greenwood, Miss. | Miss. |
| WESTERN TRIBUTARIES | | | | |
| Missouri | 2,315 | 753 | Mississippi River to Ponca, Nebr. | Mont., N.Dak., S.Dak., Nebr., Iowa, Kans., Mo. |
| Arkansas | 1,396 | 448 | McClellan-Kerr Arkansas River system from Mississippi River to Catoosa, Okla.; incorporates sections of White, Arkansas, Verdigris rivers | Colo., Kans., Okla., Ark. |
| Ouachita[2] | 605 | 351 | Mississippi River to Camden, Ark. | Ark., La. |
| Red | 1,018 | 106 | Mississippi River to Alexandria, La. | N.Mex., Tex., Okla., Ark., La. |
| Atchafalaya[3] | 220 | 220 | Atchafalaya Bay to Mississippi River | La. |
| **Pacific Ocean and Arctic Ocean** | | | | |
| San Joaquin | 340 | 103 | Sacramento River to Hills Ferry, Calif. | Calif. |
| Sacramento | 374 | 163 | San Francisco Bay to Chico Landing, Calif. | Calif. |
| Columbia | 1,210 | 285 | Pacific Ocean to Pasco, Wash. | British Columbia (Can.), Wash., Oreg. |
| Snake | 1,083 | 192 | Columbia River to Johnson Bar Landing, Idaho | Wyo., Idaho, Oreg., Wash. |
| Willamette | 294 | 133 | Columbia River to Harrisburg, Oreg. | Oreg. |
| Yukon | 1,979 | 1,699 | Bering Sea to Whitehorse, Yukon | Yukon (Can.), Alaska |

**Note:** All distances in nautical miles except for the Mississippi River system. One nautical mile = 1.151 statute miles. 1. In Mexico, known as the Río Bravo del Norte. 2. Lower 57 miles known as the Black River. 3. Flows from the Mississippi River to the Gulf of Mexico. **Source:** National Oceanic and Atmospheric Administration, *Distances between United States Ports, 1987* (1987).

## EXTREME AND MEAN ELEVATIONS, STATES AND OUTLYING AREAS

| State | Highest point Name | Elevation Feet | Elevation Meters | Lowest point Name | Elevation Feet | Elevation Meters | Approximate mean elevation Feet | Approximate mean elevation Meters |
|---|---|---|---|---|---|---|---|---|
| United States | Mount McKinley (Alaska) | 20,320 | 6,198 | Death Valley (Calif.) | −282 | −86 | 2,500 | 763 |
| Alabama | Cheaha Mountain | 2,405 | 733 | Gulf of Mexico | | Sea level | 500 | 153 |
| Alaska | Mount McKinley | 20,320 | 6,198 | Pacific Ocean | | Sea level | 1,900 | 580 |
| American Samoa | Lata Mountain | 3,160 | 964 | Pacific Ocean | | Sea level | 1,300 | 397 |
| Arizona | Humphreys Peak | 12,633 | 3,853 | Colorado River | 70 | 21 | 4,100 | 1,251 |
| Arkansas | Magazine Mountain | 2,753 | 840 | Ouachita River | 55 | 17 | 650 | 198 |
| California | Mount Whitney[1] | 14,494 | 4,421 | Death Valley | −282 | −86 | 2,900 | 885 |
| Colorado | Mount Elbert | 14,433 | 4,402 | Arkansas River | 3,350 | 1,022 | 6,800 | 2,074 |
| Connecticut | Mount Frissell, on south slope | 2,380 | 726 | Long Island Sound | | Sea level | 500 | 153 |
| Delaware | Elbright Rd., New Castle Co. | 442 | 135 | Atlantic Ocean | | Sea level | 60 | 18 |
| Dist. of Columbia | Tenleytown | 410 | 125 | Potomac River | 1 | (Z) | 150 | 46 |
| Florida | Sec. 30, T6N, R20W, Walton Co. | 345 | 105 | Atlantic Ocean | | Sea level | 100 | 31 |
| Georgia | Brasstown Bald | 4,784 | 1,459 | Atlantic Ocean | | Sea level | 600 | 183 |
| Guam | Mount Lamlam | 1,332 | 406 | Pacific Ocean | | Sea level | 330 | 101 |
| Hawaii | Puu Wekiu | 13,796 | 4,208 | Pacific Ocean | | Sea level | 3,030 | 924 |
| Idaho | Borah Peak | 12,662 | 3,862 | Snake River | 710 | 217 | 5,000 | 1,525 |
| Illinois | Charles Mound | 1,235 | 377 | Mississippi River | 279 | 85 | 600 | 183 |
| Indiana | Franklin Township, Wayne Co. | 1,257 | 383 | Ohio River | 320 | 98 | 700 | 214 |
| Iowa | Sec. 29, T100N, R41W, Osceola Co. | 1,670 | 509 | Mississippi River | 480 | 146 | 1,100 | 336 |
| Kansas | Mount Sunflower | 4,039 | 1,232 | Verdigris River | 679 | 207 | 2,000 | 610 |
| Kentucky | Black Mountain | 4,139 | 1,262 | Mississippi River | 257 | 78 | 750 | 229 |
| Louisiana | Driskill Mountain | 535 | 163 | New Orleans | −8 | −2 | 100 | 31 |
| Maine | Mount Katahdin | 5,267 | 1,606 | Atlantic Ocean | | Sea level | 600 | 183 |
| Maryland | Backbone Mountain | 3,360 | 1,025 | Atlantic Ocean | | Sea level | 350 | 107 |
| Massachusetts | Mount Greylock | 3,487 | 1,064 | Atlantic Ocean | | Sea level | 500 | 153 |
| Michigan | Mount Arvon | 1,979 | 604 | Lake Erie | 572 | 174 | 900 | 275 |
| Minnesota | Eagle Mountain, Cook Co. | 2,301 | 702 | Lake Superior | 602 | 184 | 1,200 | 366 |
| Mississippi | Woodall Mountain | 806 | 246 | Gulf of Mexico | | Sea level | 300 | 92 |
| Missouri | Taum Sauk Mountain | 1,772 | 540 | St. Francis River | 230 | 70 | 800 | 244 |
| Montana | Granite Peak | 12,799 | 3,904 | Kootenai River | 1,800 | 549 | 3,400 | 1,037 |
| Nebraska | Johnson Township, Kimball Co. | 5,426 | 1,655 | Southeast corner of state | 840 | 256 | 2,600 | 793 |
| Nevada | Boundary Peak | 13,140 | 4,007 | Colorado River | 470 | 143 | 5,500 | 1,678 |
| New Hampshire | Mount Washington | 6,288 | 1,918 | Atlantic Ocean | | Sea level | 1,000 | 305 |
| New Jersey | High Point | 1,803 | 550 | Atlantic Ocean | | Sea level | 250 | 76 |
| New Mexico | Wheeler Peak | 13,161 | 4,014 | Red Bluff Reservoir | 2,817 | 867 | 5,700 | 1,739 |
| New York | Mount Marcy | 5,344 | 1,630 | Atlantic Ocean | | Sea level | 1,000 | 305 |
| North Carolina | Mount Mitchell[2] | 6,684 | 2,039 | Atlantic Ocean | | Sea level | 700 | 214 |
| North Dakota | White Butte, Slope Co. | 3,506 | 1,069 | Red River | 750 | 229 | 1,900 | 580 |
| Ohio | Campbell Hill | 1,549 | 472 | Ohio River | 455 | 139 | 850 | 259 |
| Oklahoma | Black Mesa | 4,973 | 1,517 | Little River | 289 | 88 | 1,300 | 397 |
| Oregon | Mount Hood | 11,239 | 3,428 | Pacific Ocean | | Sea level | 3,300 | 1,007 |
| Pennsylvania | Mount Davis | 3,213 | 980 | Delaware River | | Sea level | 1,100 | 336 |
| Puerto Rico | Cerro de Punta | 4,390 | 1,339 | Atlantic Ocean | | Sea level | 1,800 | 549 |
| Rhode Island | Jerimoth Hill | 812 | 248 | Atlantic Ocean | | Sea level | 200 | 61 |
| South Carolina | Sassafras Mountain | 3,560 | 1,086 | Atlantic Ocean | | Sea level | 350 | 107 |
| South Dakota | Harney Peak | 7,242 | 2,209 | Big Stone Lake | 966 | 295 | 2,200 | 671 |
| Tennessee | Clingmans Dome | 6,643 | 2,026 | Mississippi River | 178 | 54 | 900 | 275 |
| Texas | Guadalupe Peak | 8,749 | 2,668 | Gulf of Mexico | | Sea level | 1,700 | 519 |
| Utah | Kings Peak | 13,528 | 4,126 | Beaverdam Creek | 2,000 | 610 | 6,100 | 1,861 |
| Vermont | Mount Mansfield | 4,393 | 1,340 | Lake Champlain | 95 | 29 | 1,000 | 305 |
| Virginia | Mount Rogers | 5,729 | 1,747 | Atlantic Ocean | | Sea level | 950 | 290 |
| Virgin Islands | Crown Mountain | 1,556 | 475 | Atlantic Ocean | | Sea level | 750 | 229 |
| Washington | Mount Rainier | 14,410 | 4,395 | Pacific Ocean | | Sea level | 1,700 | 519 |
| West Virginia | Spruce Knob | 4,861 | 1,483 | Potomac River | 240 | 73 | 1,500 | 458 |
| Wisconsin | Timms Hill | 1,951 | 595 | Lake Michigan | 581 | 177 | 1,050 | 320 |
| Wyoming | Gannett Peak | 13,804 | 4,210 | Belle Fourche River | 3,009 | 945 | 6,700 | 2,044 |

**Note:** Z = less than 0.5 meter. Sec. = section; T = township; R = range; N = north; W = west. 1. Highest point in 48 conterminous states. 2. Highest point east of Mississippi River. **Source:** U.S. Geological Survey. *Elevations and Distances in the United States* (1989).

# UNITED STATES HISTORY

## Documents of U.S. History

## THE DECLARATION OF INDEPENDENCE

After a year of war with Britain, American patriots were driven to make the final break in 1776. On June 7, before the Continental Congress in Philadelphia, Richard Henry Lee of Virginia proposed a declaration that the colonies "are, and of right ought to be, free and independent States." A committee of five, headed by Thomas Jefferson, was appointed to draw up the formal Declaration of Independence on June 10. The committee brought its version, mainly the work of Jefferson, back to Congress on June 28. Congress voted unanimously to declare independence on July 2, and after making several changes in the Jefferson committee's draft, they unanimously adopted the Declaration of Independence on July 4. Copies of the declaration were dispatched to the states for approval. The original document is on display today at the National Archives in Washington, D.C.

### In Congress, July 4, 1776,
### THE UNANIMOUS DECLARATION OF THE THIRTEEN UNITED STATES OF AMERICA,

When in the Course of human events, it becomes necessary for one people to dissolve the political bands which have connected them with another, and to assume among the Powers of the earth, the separate and equal station to which the Laws of Nature and of Nature's God entitle them, a decent respect to the opinions of mankind requires that they should declare the causes which impel them to the separation.

We hold these truths to be self-evident, that all men are created equal, that they are endowed by their Creator with certain unalienable Rights, that among these are Life, Liberty and the pursuit of Happiness. That to secure these rights, Governments are instituted among Men, deriving their just powers from the consent of the governed. That whenever any Form of Government becomes destructive of these ends, it is the Right of the People to alter or to abolish it, and to institute new Government, laying its foundation on such princi-

ples and organizing its powers in such form, as to them shall seem most likely to effect their Safety and Happiness. Prudence, indeed, will dictate that governments long established should not be changed for light and transient causes; and accordingly all experience hath shown, that mankind are more disposed to suffer, while evils are sufferable, than to right themselves by abolishing the forms to which they are accustomed. But when a long train of abuses and usurpations, pursuing invariably the same Object evinces a design to reduce them under absolute Despotism, it is their right, it is their duty, to throw off such Government, and to provide new Guards for their future security. Such has been the patient sufferance of these Colonies; and such is now the necessity which constrains them to alter their former Systems of Government. The history of the present King of Great Britain is a history of repeated injuries and usurpations, all having in direct object the establishment of an absolute Tyranny over these States. To prove this, let Facts be submitted to a candid world.

He has refused his Assent to Laws, the most wholesome and necessary for the public good.

He has forbidden his Governors to pass Laws of immediate and pressing importance, unless suspended in their operation till his Assent should be obtained; and when so suspended, he has utterly neglected to attend to them.

He has refused to pass other Laws for the accommodation of large districts of people, unless those people would relinquish the right of Representation in the Legislature, a right inestimable to them and formidable to tyrants only.

He has called together legislative bodies at places unusual, uncomfortable, and distant from the depository of their Public Records, for the sole purpose of fatiguing them into compliance with his measures.

He has dissolved Representative Houses repeatedly, for opposing with manly firmness his invasions on the rights of the people.

He has refused for a long time, after such dissolutions, to cause others to be elected; whereby the Legislative Powers, incapable of Annihilation, have returned to the People at large for their exercise; the State remaining in the mean time exposed to all the dangers of invasion from without, and convulsions within.

He has endeavoured to prevent the population of these States; for that purpose obstructing the Laws of Naturalization of Foreigners; refusing to pass others to encourage their migration hither, and raising the conditions of new Appropriations of Lands.

He has obstructed the Administration of Justice, by refusing his Assent to Laws for establishing Judiciary Powers.

He has made Judges dependent on his Will alone, for the tenure of their offices, and the amount and payment of their salaries.

He has erected a multitude of New Offices,

and sent hither swarms of Officers to harass our People, and eat out their substance.

He has kept among us, in times of peace, Standing Armies without the Consent of our legislature.

He has affected to render the Military independent of and superior to the Civil Power.

He has combined with others to subject us to a jurisdiction foreign to our constitution, and unacknowledged by our laws; giving his Assent to their acts of pretended legislation:

For quartering large bodies of armed troops among us:

For protecting them, by a mock Trial, from Punishment for any Murders which they should commit on the Inhabitants of these States:

For cutting off our Trade with all parts of the world:

For imposing taxes on us without our consent:

For depriving us in many cases, of the benefits of Trial by Jury:

For transporting us beyond Seas to be tried for pretended offences:

For abolishing the free System of English Laws in a neighbouring Province, establishing therein an Arbitrary government, and enlarging its Boundaries so as to render it at once an example and fit instrument for introducing the same absolute rule into these Colonies:

For taking away our Charters, abolishing our most valuable Laws, and altering fundamentally the forms of our Government:

For suspending our own legislature, and declaring themselves invested with Power to legislate for us in all cases whatsoever.

He has abdicated Government here, by declaring us out of his Protection and waging War against us.

He has plundered our seas, ravaged our Coasts, burnt our towns, and destroyed the lives of our people.

He is at this time transporting large armies of foreign mercenaries to compleat the works of death, desolation and tyranny, already begun with circumstances of Cruelty & perfidy scarcely paralleled in the most barbarous ages, and totally unworthy of the Head of a civilized nation.

He has constrained our fellow Citizens taken Captive on the high Seas to bear Arms against their Country, to become the executioners of their friends and Brethren, or to fall themselves by their Hands.

He has excited domestic insurrections amongst us, and has endeavoured to bring on the inhabitants of our frontiers, the merciless Indian Savages, whose known rule of warfare, is an undistinguished destruction of all ages, sexes and conditions.

In every stage of these Oppressions We have Petitioned for Redress in the most humble terms: Our repeated Petitions have been answered only by repeated injury. A prince, whose character is thus marked by every act which may define a Tyrant, is unfit to be the ruler of a free People.

Nor have We been wanting in attention to our British brethren. We have warned them from time to time of attempts by their legislature to extend an unwarrantable jurisdiction over us. We have reminded them of the circumstances of our emigration and settlement here. We have appealed to their native justice and magnanimity, and we have conjured them by the ties of our common kindred to disavow these usurpations, which would inevitably interrupt our connections and correspondence.

They too have been deaf to the voice of justice and of consanguinity. We must, therefore, acquiesce in the necessity, which denounces our Separation and hold them, as we hold the rest of mankind, Enemies in War, in Peace Friends.

We, therefore, the Representatives of the United States of America, in General Congress, Assembled, appealing to the Supreme Judge of the world for the rectitude of our intentions, do, in the Name, and by Authority of the good People of these Colonies, solemnly publish and declare, That these United Colonies are, and of Right ought to be Free and Independent States;

that they are Absolved from all Allegiance to the British Crown, and that all political connection between them and the State of Great Britain, is and ought to be totally dissolved; and that as Free and Independent States, they have full Power to levy War, conclude Peace, contract Alliances, establish Commerce, and to do all other Acts and Things which Independent States may of right do. And for the support of this Declaration, with a firm reliance on the Protection of Divine Providence, we mutually pledge to each other our Lives, our Fortunes and our sacred Honor.

## Signers of the Declaration of Independence

| Delegate | Colony | Born/Died | Delegate | Colony | Born/Died | Delegate | Colony | Born/Died |
|---|---|---|---|---|---|---|---|---|
| Adams, John | Massachusetts | 1735–1826 | Hooper, William | North Carolina | 1742–90 | Read, George | Delaware | 1733–98 |
| Adams, Samuel | Massachusetts | 1722–1803 | Hopkins, Stephen | Rhode Island | 1707–85 | Rodney, Caesar | Delaware | 1728–84 |
| Bartlett, Josiah | New Hampshire | 1729–95 | Hopkinson, Francis | New Jersey | 1737–91 | Ross, George | Pennsylvania | 1730–79 |
| Braxton, Carter | Virginia | 1736–97 | Huntington, Samuel | Connecticut | 1731–96 | Rush, Benjamin | Pennsylvania | 1745–1813 |
| Carroll, Charles | Maryland | 1737–1832 | Jefferson, Thomas | Virginia | 1743–1826 | Rutledge, Edward | South Carolina | 1749–1800 |
| Chase, Samuel | Maryland | 1741–1811 | Lee, Francis Lightfoot | Virginia | 1734–97 | Sherman, Roger | Connecticut | 1721–93 |
| Clark, Abraham | New Jersey | 1726–94 | Lee, Richard Henry | Virginia | 1732–94 | Smith, James | Pennsylvania | 1713–1806 |
| Clymer, George | Pennsylvania | 1739–1813 | Lewis, Francis | New York | 1713–1803 | Stockton, Richard | New Jersey | 1730–81 |
| Ellery, William | Rhode Island | 1727–1820 | Livingston, Philip | New York | 1716–78 | Stone, Thomas | Maryland | 1743–87 |
| Floyd, William | New York | 1734–1821 | Lynch, Thomas, Jr. | South Carolina | 1749–79 | Taylor, George | Pennsylvania | 1716–81 |
| Franklin, Benjamin | Pennsylvania | 1706–90 | McKean, Thomas | Delaware | 1734–1817 | Thornton, Matthew | New Hampshire | 1714–1803 |
| Gerry, Elbridge | Massachusetts | 1744–1814 | Middleton, Arthur | South Carolina | 1742–87 | Walton, George | Georgia | 1741–1804 |
| Gwinnett, Button | Georgia | 1732–77 | Morris, Lewis | New York | 1726–98 | Whipple, William | New Hampshire | 1730–85 |
| Hall, Lyman | Georgia | 1724–90 | Morris, Robert | Pennsylvania | 1734–1806 | Williams, William | Connecticut | 1731–1811 |
| Hancock, John | Massachusetts | 1737–93 | Morton, John | Pennsylvania | 1724–77 | Wilson, James | Pennsylvania | 1742–98 |
| Harrison, Benjamin | Virginia | 1726–91 | Nelson, Thomas, Jr. | Virginia | 1738–89 | Witherspoon, John | New Jersey | 1723–94 |
| Hart, John | New Jersey | ?–1779 | Paca, William | Maryland | 1740–99 | Wolcott, Oliver | Connecticut | 1726–97 |
| Hewes, Joseph | North Carolina | 1730–79 | Paine, Robert Treat | Massachusetts | 1731–1814 | Wythe, George | Virginia | 1726–1806 |
| Heyward, Thomas, Jr. | South Carolina | 1746–1809 | Penn, John | North Carolina | 1741–88 | | | |

## THE U.S. CONSTITUTION

During and after the Revolution, the United States was governed by the Continental Congress under the Articles of Confederation, which delegated very limited powers to the national government and reserved the rest to the states. Economic chaos, political confusion, and widespread dissatisfaction with the lack of central authority peaked with Shays's Rebellion in 1786. George Washington lent his prestige to the call for a convention to consider a new form of government. Congress endorsed the plan on

Feb. 21, 1787, "for the sole and express purpose of revising the Articles of Confederation." All states but Rhode Island sent delegates to the convention, which opened in Philadelphia on May 14. The delegates moved at once to discard the articles, draw up a new Constitution, and conduct their meetings in secrecy, while Washington presided and James Madison took notes. A long summer of debate and compromise finally produced the document that most of the delegates signed on Sept. 17. Congress ordered the

Constitution sent to the states for ratification on Sept. 28, requiring approval by at least nine of them to validate the new charter. Whether the Constitution would be adopted was in doubt until June 21, 1788, when New Hampshire became the ninth state to ratify it. The Constitution went into effect on Mar. 4, 1789. All of the original 13 states eventually ratified the Constitution, ending with Rhode Island on May 29, 1790. The U.S. Constitution remains the world's oldest written constitution.

## THE CONSTITUTION OF THE UNITED STATES OF AMERICA

### Preamble

WE, THE PEOPLE OF THE UNITED STATES, in order to form a more perfect union, establish justice, insure domestic tranquillity, provide for the common defense, promote the general welfare, and secure the blessing of liberty to ourselves and our posterity, do ordain and establish this Constitution for the United States of America.

### Article I

SECTION 1 All legislative powers herein granted shall be vested in a Congress of the United States, which shall consist of a Senate

and House of Representatives.

SECTION 2 [1] The House of Representatives shall be composed of members chosen every second year by the people of the several States, and the electors in each State shall have the qualifications requisite for electors of the most numerous branch of the State legislature.

[2] No person shall be a Representative who shall not have attained to the age of twenty-five years, and been seven years a citizen of the United States, and who shall not, when elected, be an inhabitant of that State in which he shall be chosen.

[3] Representatives and direct taxes shall be apportioned among the several States which may be included within this Union, according to their respective numbers, which shall be determined by adding to the whole number of free persons, including those bound to service for a term of years, and excluding Indians not taxed, three-fifths of all other persons. The actual enumeration shall be made within three years after the first meeting of the Congress of the United States, and within every subsequent term of ten years, in such manner as they shall by law direct. The number of Representatives shall not exceed one for every thirty thousand,

but each State shall have at least one Representative; and until such enumeration shall be made, the State of New Hampshire shall be entitled to choose three; Massachusetts, eight; Rhode Island and Providence Plantations, one; Connecticut, five; New York, six; New Jersey, four; Pennsylvania, eight; Delaware, one; Maryland, six; Virginia, ten; North Carolina, five; South Carolina, five; and Georgia, three.

[4] When vacancies happen in the representation from any State, the executive authority thereof shall issue writs of election to fill such vacancies.

[5] The House of Representatives shall choose their Speaker and other officers, and shall have the sole power of impeachment.

SECTION 3 [1] The Senate of the United States shall be composed of two Senators from each State, chosen by the legislature thereof for six years; and each Senator shall have one vote.

[2] Immediately after they shall be assembled in consequence of the first election, they shall be divided as equally as may be into three classes. The seats of the Senators of the first class shall be vacated at the expiration of the second year, of the second class at the expiration of the fourth year, and of the third class at the expiration of the sixth year, so that onethird may be chosen every second year; and if vacancies happen by resignation or otherwise during the recess of the legislature of any State, the executive thereof may make temporary appointments until the next meeting of the legislature, which shall then fill such vacancies.

[3] No person shall be a Senator who shall not have attained to the age of thirty years, and been nine years a citizen of the United States, and who shall not, when elected, be an inhabitant of that State for which he shall be chosen.

[4] The Vice-President of the United States shall be President of the Senate, but shall have no vote, unless they be equally divided.

[5] The Senate shall choose their other officers and also a President *pro tempore* in the absence of the Vice-President, or when he shall exercise the office of President of the United States.

[6] The Senate shall have the sole power to try all impeachments. When sitting for that purpose, they shall be on oath or affirmation. When the President of the United States is tried, the Chief Justice shall preside; and no person shall be convicted without the concurrence of two-thirds of the members present.

[7] Judgment in cases of impeachment shall not extend further than to removal from office, and disqualification to hold and enjoy any office of honor, trust, or profit under the United States; but the party convicted shall, nevertheless, be liable and subject to indictment, trial, judgment, and punishment, according to law.

SECTION 4 [1] The times, places, and manner of holding elections for Senators and Representatives shall be prescribed in each State by the legislature thereof; but the Congress may at any time by law make or alter such regulations, except as to the places of choosing Senators.

[2] The Congress shall assemble at least once in every year, and such meeting shall be on the first Monday in December, unless they shall by law appoint a different day.

SECTION 5 [1] Each House shall be the judge of the elections, returns, and qualification of its own members, and a majority of each shall constitute a quorum to do business; but a smaller number may adjourn from day to day, and may be authorized to compel the attendance of absent members, in such manner, and under such penalties, as each House may provide.

[2] Each House may determine the rules of its proceedings, punish its members for disorderly behavior, and with the concurrence of two-thirds, expel a member.

[3] Each House shall keep a journal of its proceedings, and from time to time publish the same, excepting such parts as may in their judgment require secrecy; and the yeas and nays of the members of either House on any question shall, at the desire of one-fifth of those present, be entered on the journal.

[4] Neither House, during the session of Congress, shall, without the consent of the other, adjourn for more than three days, nor to any other place than that in which the two Houses shall be sitting.

SECTION 6 [1] The Senators and Representatives shall receive a compensation for their services, to be ascertained by law and paid out of the Treasury of the United States. They shall, in all cases except treason, felony, and breach of the peace, be privileged from arrest during their attendance at the session of their respective Houses, and in going to and returning from the same; and for any speech or debate in either House they shall not be questioned in any other place.

[2] No Senator or Representative shall, during the time for which he was elected, be appointed to any civil office under the authority of the United States, which shall have been created, or the emoluments whereof shall have been increased during such time; and no person holding any office under the United States shall be a member of either House during his continuance in office.

SECTION 7 [1] All bills for raising revenue shall originate in the House of Representatives; but the Senate may propose or concur with amendments as on other bills.

[2] Every bill which shall have passed the House of Representatives and the Senate shall, before it becomes a law, be presented to the President of the United States; if he approves he shall sign it, but if not he shall return it, with his objections, to that House in which it shall have originated, who shall enter the objections at large on their journal and proceed to reconsider it. If after such reconsideration two-thirds of that House shall agree to pass the bill, it shall be sent, together with the objections, to the other House, by which it shall likewise be reconsidered, and if approved by two-thirds of that House it shall become a law. But in all such cases the vote of both Houses shall be determined by yeas and nays, and the names of the persons voting for and against the bill shall be entered on the journal of each House respectively. If any bill shall not be returned by the President within ten days (Sundays excepted) after it shall have been presented to him, the same shall be a law, in like manner as if he had signed it, unless the Congress by their adjournment prevent its return, in which case it shall not be a law.

[3] Every order, resolution or vote to which the concurrence of the Senate and House of Representatives may be necessary (except on a question of adjournment) shall be presented to the President of the United States; and before the same shall take effect shall be approved by him, or being disapproved by him, shall be repassed by two-thirds of the Senate and House of Representatives, according to the rules and limitations prescribed in the case of a bill.

SECTION 8 [1] The Congress shall have power to lay and collect taxes, duties, imposts and excises, to pay the debts and provide for the common defense and general welfare of the United States; but all duties, imposts and excises shall be uniform throughout the United States;

[2] To borrow money on the credit of the United States;

[3] To regulate commerce with foreign nations, and among the several States, and with the Indian tribes;

[4] To establish an uniform rule of naturalization, and uniform laws on the subject of bankruptcies throughout the United States;

[5] To coin money, regulate the value thereof, and of foreign coin, and fix the standard of weights and measures;

[6] To provide for the punishment of counterfeiting the securities and current coin of the United States;

[7] To establish post offices and post roads;

[8] To promote the progress of science and useful arts by securing for limited times to authors and inventors the exclusive right to their respective writings and discoveries;

[9] To constitute tribunals inferior to the Supreme Court;

[10] To define and punish piracies and felonies committed on the high seas and offenses against the law of nations.

[11] To declare war, grant letters of marque and reprisal, and make rules concerning captures on land and water;

[12] To raise and support armies, but no appropriation of money to that use shall be for a longer term than two years;

[13] To provide and maintain a navy;

[14] To make rules for the government and regulation of the land and naval forces;

[15] To provide for calling forth the militia to execute the laws of the Union, suppress insurrections, and repel invasions;

[16] To provide for organizing, arming and disciplining the militia, and for governing such part of them as may be employed in the service of the United States, reserving to the States respectively the appointment of the officers, and the authority of training the militia according to the discipline prescribed by Congress;

[17] To exercise exclusive legislation in all cases whatsoever over such district (not exceeding ten miles square) as may, by cession

of particular States and the acceptance of Congress, become the seat of the Government of the United States, and to exercise like authority over all places purchased by the consent of the legislature of the State in which the same shall be, for the erection of forts, magazines, arsenals, dockyards, and other needful buildings;

[18] To make all laws which shall be necessary and proper for carrying into execution the foregoing powers, and all other powers vested by this Constitution in the Government of the United States, or in any department or officer thereof.

SECTION 9 [1] The migration or importation of such persons as any of the States now existing shall think proper to admit shall not be prohibited by the Congress prior to the year one thousand eight hundred and eight, but a tax or duty may be imposed on such importation, not exceeding ten dollars for each person.

[2] The privilege of the writ of habeas corpus shall not be suspended, unless when in cases of rebellion or invasion the public safety may require it.

[3] No bill of attainder or ex post facto law shall be passed.

[4] No capitation or other direct tax shall be laid, unless in proportion to the census or enumeration hereinbefore directed to be taken.

[5] No tax or duty shall be laid on articles exported from any State.

[6] No preference shall be given by any regulation of commerce or revenue to the ports of one State over those of another; nor shall vessels bound to or from one State be obliged to enter, clear or pay duties in another.

[7] No money shall be drawn from the Treasury but in consequence of appropriations made by law; and a regular statement and account of the receipts and expenditures of all public money shall be published from time to time.

[8] No title of nobility shall be granted by the United States; and no person holding any office of profit or trust under them shall, without the consent of the Congress, accept of any present, emolument, office, or title of any kind whatever from any king, prince, or foreign state.

SECTION 10 [1] No State shall enter into any treaty, alliance, or confederation; grant letters of marque and reprisal; coin money, emit bills of credit, make anything but gold and silver coin a tender in payment of debts; pass any bill of attainder, ex post facto law or law impairing the obligation of contracts, or grant any title of nobility.

[2] No State shall, without the consent of the Congress, lay any imposts or duties on imports or exports, except what may be absolutely necessary for executing its inspection laws; and the net produce of all duties and imposts, laid by any State on imports or exports, shall be for the use of the Treasury of the United States; and all such laws shall be subject to the revision and control of the Congress.

[3] No State shall, without the consent of Congress, lay any duty of tonnage, keep troops and ships of war in time of peace, enter into any agreement or compact with another State or with a foreign power, or engage in war, unless actually invaded or in such imminent danger as will not admit of delay.

## Article II

SECTION 1 [1] The executive power shall be vested in a President of the United States of America. He shall hold his office during the term of four years, and together with the Vice-President, chosen for the same term, be elected as follows:

[2] Each State shall appoint, in such manner as the legislature thereof may direct, a number of Electors, equal to the whole number of Senators and Representatives to which the State may be entitled in the Congress; but no Senator or Representative, or person holding an office of trust or profit under the United States shall be appointed an Elector.

[3] The Electors shall meet in their respective States and vote by ballot for two persons, of whom one at least shall not be an inhabitant of the same State with themselves. And they shall make a list of all the persons voted for, and of the number of votes for each; which list they shall sign and certify, and transmit sealed to the seat of government of the United States, directed to the President of the Senate. The President of the Senate shall, in the presence of the Senate and House of Representatives, open all the certificates, and the votes shall then be counted. The person having the greatest number of votes shall be the President, if such number be a majority of the whole number of Electors appointed; and if there be more than one who have such majority, and have an equal number of votes, then the House of Representatives shall immediately choose by ballot one of them for President; and if no person have a majority, then from the five highest on the list the said House shall in like manner choose the President. But in choosing the President the votes shall be taken by States, the representation from each State having one vote; a quorum for this purpose shall consist of a member or members from two-thirds of the States, and a majority of all the States shall be necessary to a choice. In every case, after the choice of the President, the person having the greatest number of votes of the Electors shall be the Vice-President. But if there should remain two or more who have equal votes, the Senate shall choose from them by ballot the Vice-President.

[4] The Congress may determine the time of choosing the Electors and the day on which they shall give their votes, which day shall be the same throughout the United States.

[5] No person except a natural-born citizen, or citizen of the United States at the time of the adoption of this Constitution, shall be eligible to the office of President; neither shall any person be eligible to that office who shall not have attained to the age of thirty-five years, and been fourteen years a resident within the United States.

[6] In case of the removal of the President from office, or of his death, resignation, or inability to discharge the powers and duties of the said office, the same shall devolve on the Vice-President, and the Congress may by law provide for the case of removal, death, resignation, or inability, both of the President and Vice-President, declaring what officer shall then act as President, and such officer shall act accordingly until the disability be removed or a President shall be elected.

[7] The President shall, at stated times, receive for his services a compensation, which shall neither be increased nor diminished during the period for which he shall have been elected, and he shall not receive within that period any other emolument from the United States or any of them.

[8] Before he enter on the execution of his office he shall take the following oath or affirmation:

"I do solemnly swear (or affirm) that I will faithfully execute the office of President of the United States, and will to the best of my ability preserve, protect, and defend the Constitution of the United States."

SECTION 2 [1] The President shall be Commander-in-Chief of the Army and Navy of the United States, and of the militia of the several States when called into the actual service of the United States; he may require the opinion, in writing, of the principal officer in each of the executive departments, upon any subject relating to the duties of their respective offices, and he shall have power to grant reprieves and pardons for offenses against the United States, except in cases of impeachment.

[2] He shall have power, by and with the advice and consent of the Senate, to make treaties, provided two-thirds of the Senators present concur; and he shall nominate, and, by and with the advice and consent of the Senate, shall appoint ambassadors, other public ministers and consuls, judges of the Supreme Court, and all other officers of the United States whose appointments are not herein otherwise provided for, and which shall be established by law; but the Congress may by law vest the appointment of such inferior officers, as they think proper, in the President alone, in the courts of law, or in the heads of departments.

[3] The President shall have power to fill up all vacancies that may happen during the recess of the Senate, by granting commissions which shall expire at the end of their next session.

SECTION 3 He shall from time to time give to the Congress information of the state of the Union, and recommend to their consideration such measures as he shall judge necessary and expedient; he may, on extraordinary occasions, convene both Houses, or either of them, and in case of disagreement between them with respect to the time of adjournment, he may adjourn them to such time as he shall think proper; he shall receive ambassadors and other public ministers; he shall take care that the laws be faithfully executed, and shall commission all the officers of the United States.

SECTION 4 The President, Vice-President and all civil officers of the United States shall be removed from office on impeachment for and conviction of treason, bribery, or other high crimes and misdemeanors.

## Article III

SECTION 1 The judicial power of the United

States shall be vested in one Supreme Court, and in such inferior courts as the Congress may from time to time ordain and establish. The judges, both of the Supreme and inferior courts, shall hold their offices during good behavior, and shall, at stated times, receive for their services a compensation which shall not be diminished during their continuance in office.

SECTION 2 [1] The judicial power shall extend to all cases, in law and equity, arising under this Constitution, the laws of the United States, and treaties made, or which shall be made, under their authority; to all cases affecting ambassadors, other public ministers, and consuls; to all cases of admiralty and maritime jurisdiction; to controversies to which the United States shall be a party; to controversies between two or more States; between a State and citizens of another State; between citizens of different States; between citizens of the same State claiming lands under grants of different States, and between a State, or the citizens thereof, and foreign states, citizens, or subjects.

[2] In all cases affecting ambassadors, other public ministers and consuls, and those in which a State shall be party, the Supreme Court shall have original jurisdiction. In all the other cases before mentioned the Supreme Court shall have appellate jurisdiction, both as to law and fact, with such exceptions and under such regulations as the Congress shall make.

[3] The trial of all crimes, except in cases of impeachment, shall be by jury; and such trial shall be held in the State where the said crimes shall have been committed; but when not committed within any State, the trial shall be at such place or places as the Congress may by law have directed.

SECTION 3 [1] Treason against the United States shall consist only in levying war against them, or in adhering to their enemies, giving them aid and comfort. No person shall be convicted of treason unless on the testimony of two witnesses to the same overt act, or on confession in open court.

[2] The Congress shall have power to declare the punishment of treason, but no attainder of treason shall work corruption of blood or forfeiture except during the life of the person attained.

### Article IV

SECTION 1 Full faith and credit shall be given in each State to the public acts, records, and judicial proceedings of every other State. And the Congress may by general laws prescribe the manner in which such acts, records, and proceedings shall be proved, and the effect thereof.

SECTION 2 [1] The citizens of each State shall be entitled to all privileges and immunities of citizens in the several States.

[2] A person charged in any State with treason, felony, or other crime, who shall flee from justice, and be found in another State, shall, on demand of the executive authority of the State from which he fled, be delivered up, to be removed to the State having jurisdiction of the crime.

[3] No person held to service or labor in one State, under the laws thereof, escaping into another, shall, in consequence of any law or regulation therein, be discharged from such service or labor, but shall be delivered up on claim to the party to whom such service or labor may be due.

SECTION 3 [1] New States may be admitted by the Congress into this Union; but no new State shall be formed or erected within the jurisdiction of any other State; nor any State be formed by the junction of two or more States or parts of States, without the consent of the legislatures of the States concerned as well as of the Congress.

[2] The Congress shall have power to dispose of and make all needful rules and regulations respecting the territory or other property belonging to the United States; and nothing in this Constitution shall be so construed as to prejudice any claims of the United States or of any particular State.

SECTION 4 The United States shall guarantee to every State in this Union a republican form of government, and shall protect each of them against invasion, and on application of the legislature, or of the executive (when the legislature cannot be convened), against domestic violence.

### Article V

The Congress, whenever two-thirds of both Houses shall deem it necessary, shall propose amendments to this Constitution, or, on the application of the legislatures of two-thirds of the several States, shall call a convention for proposing amendments, which in either case shall be valid to all intents and purposes as part of this Constitution, when ratified by the legislatures of three-fourths of the several States, or by conventions in three-fourths thereof, as the one or the other mode of ratification may be proposed by the Congress; provided that no amendment which may be made prior to the year one thousand eight hundred and eight shall in any manner affect the first and fourth clauses in the Ninth Section of the First Article; and that no State, without its consent, shall be deprived of its equal suffrage in the State.

### Article VI

[1] All debts contracted and engagements entered into, before the adoption of this Constitution, shall be as valid against the United States under this Constitution as under the Confederation.

[2] This Constitution, and the laws of the United States which shall be made in pursuance thereof, and all treaties made, or which shall be made, under the authority of the United States, shall be the supreme law of the land; and the judges in every State shall be bound thereby, anything in the Constitution or laws of any State to the contrary notwithstanding.

[3] The Senators and Representatives before mentioned and the members of the several State legislatures, and all executive and judicial officers both of the United States and of the several States, shall be bound by oath or affir-

mation to support this Constitution; but no religious test shall ever be required as a qualification to any office or public trust under the United States.

### Article VII

The ratification of the conventions of nine States shall be sufficient for the establishment of this Constitution between the States so ratifying the same.

## Amendments to the Constitution

[The first 10 amendments, known collectively as The Bill of Rights, were adopted in 1791.]

### Amendment I

Congress shall make no law respecting an establishment of religion, or prohibiting the free exercise thereof; or abridging the freedom of speech or of the press; or the right of the people peaceably to assemble, and to petition the government for a redress of grievances.

### Amendment II

A well-regulated militia being necessary to the security of a free State, the right of the people to keep and bear arms shall not be infringed.

### Amendment III

No soldier shall, in time of peace, be quartered in any house without the consent of the owner, nor in time of war, but in a manner to be prescribed by law.

### Amendment IV

The right of the people to be secure in their persons, houses, papers, and effects, against unreasonable searches and seizures, shall not be violated, and no warrants shall issue but upon probable cause, supported by oath or affirmation, and particularly describing the place to be searched, and the persons or things to be seized.

### Amendment V

No person shall be held to answer for a capital, or otherwise infamous crime, unless on a presentment or indictment of a grand jury, except in cases arising in the land or naval forces, or in the militia, when in actual service in time of war or public danger; nor shall any person be subject for the same offense to be twice put in jeopardy of life or limb; nor shall be compelled in any criminal case to be a witness against himself, nor be deprived of life, liberty or property, without due process of law; nor shall private property be taken for public use without just compensation.

### Amendment VI

In all criminal prosecutions, the accused shall enjoy the right to a speedy and public trial, by an impartial jury of the State and district wherein the crime shall have been committed, which district shall have been previously ascertained by law, and to be informed of the nature and cause of the accusation; to be confronted with the witnesses against him; to have compulsory process for obtaining witnesses in his favor, and to have the assistance of counsel for his defense.

### Amendment VII

In suits at common law, where the value in controversy shall exceed twenty dollars, the right of trial by jury shall be preserved, and no fact tried by a jury shall be otherwise re-examined in any court of the United States, than according to the rules of the common law.

### Amendment VIII

Excessive bail shall not be required, nor excessive fines imposed, nor cruel and unusual punishments inflicted.

### Amendment IX

The enumeration in the Constitution of certain rights shall not be construed to deny or disparage others retained by the people.

### Amendment X

The powers not delegated to the United States by the Constitution, nor prohibited by it to the States, are reserved to the States respectively, or to the people.

### Amendment XI

[Adopted Jan. 8, 1798]

The judicial power of the United States shall not be construed to extend to any suit in law or equity, commenced or prosecuted against one of the United States by citizens of another State, or by citizens or subjects of any foreign state.

### Amendment XII

[Adopted Sept. 25, 1804]

[1] The Electors shall meet in their respective States and vote by ballot for President and Vice-President, one of whom, at least, shall not be an inhabitant of the same State with themselves; they shall name in their ballots the person voted for as President, and in distinct ballots the person voted for as Vice-President, and they shall make distinct lists of all persons voted for as President and of all persons voted for as Vice-President, and of the number of votes for each; which lists they shall sign and certify, and transmit sealed to the seat of the government of the United States, directed to the President of the Senate. The President of the Senate shall, in the presence of the Senate and House of Representatives, open all the certificates and the votes shall then be counted. The person having the greatest number of votes for President shall be the President, if such number be a majority of the whole number of Electors appointed; and if no person have such majority, then from the persons having the highest numbers not exceeding three on the list of those voted for as President, the House of Representatives shall choose immediately, by ballot, the President. But in choosing the President the votes shall be taken by States, the representation from each State having one vote; a quorum for this purpose shall consist of a member or members from two-thirds of the States, and a majority of all the States shall be necessary to a choice. And if the House of Representatives shall not choose a President whenever the right of choice shall devolve upon them, before the fourth day of March next following, then the Vice-President shall act as President, as in the case of the death or other constitutional disability of the President.

[2] The person having the greatest number of votes as Vice-President shall be the Vice-President, if such number be a majority of the whole number of Electors appointed; and if no person have a majority, then from the two highest numbers on the list the Senate shall choose the Vice-President; a quorum for the purpose shall consist of two-thirds of the whole number of Senators, and a majority of the whole number shall be necessary to a choice. But no person constitutionally ineligible to the office of President shall be eligible to that of Vice-President of the United States.

### Amendment XIII

[Adopted Dec. 18, 1865]

SECTION 1 Neither slavery nor involuntary servitude, except as a punishment for crime whereof the party shall have been duly convicted, shall exist within the United States, or any place subject to their jurisdiction.

SECTION 2 Congress shall have power to enforce this article by appropriate legislation.

### Amendment XIV

[Adopted July 28, 1868]

SECTION 1 All persons born or naturalized in the United States, and subject to the jurisdiction thereof, are citizens of the United States and of the State wherein they reside. No State shall make or enforce any law which shall abridge the privileges or immunities of citizens of the United States; nor shall any State deprive any person of life, liberty or property, without due process of law; nor deny to any person within its jurisdiction the equal protection of the laws.

SECTION 2 Representatives shall be apportioned among the several States according to their respective numbers, counting the whole number of persons in each State, excluding Indians not taxed. But when the right to vote at any election for the choice of Electors for President and Vice-President of the United States, Representatives in Congress, the executive and judicial officers of a State, or the members of the legislature thereof, is denied to any of the male inhabitants of such State, being twenty-one years of age, and citizens of the United States, or in any way abridged except for participation in rebellion or other crime, the basis of representation therein shall be reduced in the proportion which the number of such male citizens shall bear to the whole number of male citizens twenty-one years of age in such State.

SECTION 3 No person shall be a Senator or Representative in Congress, or elector of President and Vice-President, or hold any office, civil or military, under the United States or under any State, who, having previously taken an oath as a member of Congress, or as an officer of the United States, or as a member of any State legislature, or as an executive or judicial officer of any State, to support the Constitution of the United States, shall have engaged in insurrection or rebellion against the same, or given aid or comfort to the enemies thereof. But Congress may, by a vote of two-thirds of each House, remove such disability.

SECTION 4 The validity of the public debt of the United States, authorized by law, including debts incurred for payment of pensions and bounties for services in suppressing insurrection or rebellion, shall not be questioned. But neither the United States nor any State shall assume or pay any debt or obligation incurred in aid of insurrection or rebellion against the United States, or any claim for the loss or emancipation of any slave; but all such debts, obligations, and claims shall be held illegal and void.

SECTION 5 The Congress shall have power to enforce, by appropriate legislation, the provisions of this article.

### Amendment XV

[Adopted Mar. 30, 1870]

SECTION 1 The right of citizens of the United States to vote shall not be denied or abridged by the United States or by any State on account of race, color, or previous condition of servitude.

SECTION 2 The Congress shall have power to enforce this article by appropriate legislation.

### Amendment XVI

[Adopted Feb. 25, 1913]

The Congress shall have power to lay and collect taxes on incomes, from whatever source derived, without apportionment among the several States, and without regard to any census or enumeration.

### Amendment XVII

[Adopted May 31, 1913]

SECTION 1 The Senate of the United States shall be composed of two Senators from each State, elected by the people thereof, for six years; and each Senator shall have one vote. The electors in each State shall have the qualifications requisite for electors of the most numerous branch of the State legislatures.

SECTION 2 When vacancies happen in the representation of any State in the Senate, the executive authority of such State shall issue writs of election to fill such vacancies: Provided, that the legislature of any State may empower the executive thereof to make temporary appointments until the people fill the vacancies by election as the legislature may direct.

SECTION 3 This amendment shall not be so construed as to affect the election or term of any Senator chosen before it becomes valid as part of the Constitution.

### Amendment XVIII

[Adopted Jan. 29, 1919]

SECTION 1 After one year from the ratification of this article the manufacture, sale or transportation of intoxicating liquors within, the importation thereof into, or the exportation thereof from the United States and all territory subject to the jurisdiction thereof, for beverage purposes, is hereby prohibited.

SECTION 2 The Congress and the several States shall have concurrent power to enforce this article by appropriate legislation.

SECTION 3 This article shall be inoperative unless it shall have been ratified as an amendment to the Constitution by the legislatures of the several States, as provided in the Constitution, within seven years from the date of the submission hereof to the States by the Congress.

### Amendment XIX
[Adopted Aug. 26, 1920]

SECTION 1 The right of citizens of the United States to vote shall not be denied or abridged by the United States or by any State on account of sex.

SECTION 2 Congress shall have power to enforce this article by appropriate legislation.

### Amendment XX
[Adopted Feb. 6, 1933]

SECTION 1 The terms of the President and Vice-President shall end at noon on the 20th day of January, and the terms of Senators and Representatives at noon on the 3d day of January, of the years in which such terms would have ended if this article had not been ratified; and the terms of their successors shall then begin.

SECTION 2 The Congress shall assemble at least once in every year, and such meeting shall begin at noon on the 3d day of January, unless they shall by law appoint a different day.

SECTION 3 If, at the time fixed for the beginning of the term of the President, the President-elect shall have died, the Vice-President-elect shall become President. If a President shall not have been chosen before the time fixed for the beginning of his term or if the President-elect shall have failed to qualify, then the Vice-President-elect shall act as President until a President shall have qualified; and the Congress may by law provide for the case wherein neither a President-elect nor a Vice-President-elect shall have qualified, declaring who shall then act as President, or the manner in which one who is to act shall be selected, and such person shall act accordingly until a President or Vice-President shall have qualified.

SECTION 4 The Congress may by law provide for the case of the death of any of the persons from whom the House of Representatives may choose a President whenever the right of choice shall have devolved upon them, and for the case of death of any of the persons from whom the Senate may choose a Vice-President whenever the right of choice shall have devolved upon them.

SECTION 5 Sections 1 and 2 shall take effect on the 15th day of October following the ratification of this article.

SECTION 6 This article shall be inoperative unless it shall have been ratified as an amendment to the Constitution by the legislatures of three-fourths of the several States within seven years from the date of its submission.

### Amendment XXI
[Adopted Dec. 5, 1933]

SECTION 1 The eighteenth article of amendment to the Constitution of the United States is hereby repealed.

SECTION 2 The transportation or importation into any State, territory, or possession of the United States for delivery or use therein of intoxicating liquors, in violation of the laws thereof, is hereby prohibited.

SECTION 3 This article shall be inoperative unless it shall have been ratified as an amendment to the Constitution by conventions in the several States, as provided in the Constitution, within seven years from the date of the submission hereof to the States by the Congress.

### Amendment XXII
[Adopted Feb. 26, 1951]

SECTION 1 No person shall be elected to the office of President more than twice, and no person who has held the office of President, or acted as President, for more than two years of a term to which some other person was elected President shall be elected to the office of President more than once. But this Article shall not apply to any person holding the office of President when this Article was proposed by the Congress, and shall not prevent any person who may be holding the office of President, or acting as President, during the term within which this Article becomes operative from holding the office of President or acting as President during the remainder of such term.

SECTION 2 This article shall be inoperative unless it shall have been ratified as an amendment to the Constitution by the legislatures of three-fourths of the several States within seven years from the date of its submission to the States by the Congress.

### Amendment XXIII
[Adopted Apr. 3, 1961]

SECTION 1 The District constituting the seat of Government of the United States shall appoint in such manner as the Congress may direct:

A number of electors of President and Vice-President equal to the whole number of Senators and Representatives in Congress to which the District would be entitled if it were a State, but in no event more than the least populous State; they shall be in addition to those appointed by the States, but they shall be considered, for the purposes of the election of President and Vice-President, to be electors appointed by a State; and they shall meet in the District and perform such duties as provided by the twelfth article of amendment.

SECTION 2 The Congress shall have power to enforce this article by appropriate legislation.

### Amendment XXIV
[Adopted Jan. 23, 1964]

SECTION 1 The right of citizens of the United States to vote in any primary or other election for President or Vice-President, for electors for President or Vice-President, or for Senator or Representative in Congress, shall not be denied or abridged by the United States or any State by reason of failure to pay any poll tax or other tax.

SECTION 2 The Congress shall have power to enforce this article by appropriate legislation.

### Amendment XXV
[Adopted Feb. 10, 1967]

SECTION 1 In case of the removal of the President from office or of his death or resignation, the Vice-President shall become President.

SECTION 2 Whenever there is a vacancy in the office of the Vice-President, the President shall nominate a Vice-President who shall take office upon confirmation by a majority vote of both Houses of Congress.

SECTION 3 Whenever the President transmits to the President pro tempore of the Senate and the Speaker of the House of Representatives his written declaration that he is unable to discharge the powers and duties of his office, and until he transmits to them a written declaration to the contrary, such powers and duties shall be discharged by the Vice-President as Acting President.

SECTION 4 Whenever the Vice-President and a majority of either the principal officers of the executive departments or of such other body as Congress may by law provide, transmit to the President pro tempore of the Senate and the Speaker of the House of Representatives their written declaration that the President is unable to discharge the powers and duties of his office, the Vice-President shall immediately assume the powers and duties of the office as Acting President.

Thereafter, when the President transmits to the President pro tempore of the Senate and the Speaker of the House of Representatives his written declaration that no inability exists, he shall resume the powers and duties of his office unless the Vice-President and a majority of either the principal officers of the executive department or of such other body as Congress may by law provide, transmit within four days to the President pro tempore of the Senate and the Speaker of the House of Representatives their written declaration that the President is unable to discharge the powers and duties of his office. Thereupon Congress shall decide the issue, assembling within forty-eight hours for that purpose if not in session. If the Congress, within twenty-one days after receipt of the latter written declaration, or, if Congress is not in session, within twenty-one days after Congress is required to assemble, determines by two-thirds vote of both Houses that the President is unable to discharge the powers and duties of his office, the Vice-President shall continue to discharge the same as Acting President; otherwise the President shall resume the powers and duties of his office.

### Amendment XXVI
[Adopted June 30, 1971]

SECTION 1 The right of citizens of the United States, who are eighteen years of age or older, to vote shall not be denied or abridged by the United States or by any State on account of age.

SECTION 2 The Congress shall have power to enforce this article by appropriate legislation.

## THE EMANCIPATION PROCLAMATION

On July 22, 1862, Abraham Lincoln read to his cabinet a preliminary draft of an emancipation proclamation. Secretary of State William Seward suggested that the proclamation not be issued until a military victory had been won. The battle of Antietam gave Lincoln his desired opportunity, and on Sept. 22, he read to his cabinet a second draft of the proclamation. After some changes this was issued as a preliminary proclamation; the formal and definite proclamation came Jan. 1, 1863.

## THE PRESIDENT OF THE UNITED STATES OF AMERICA:

### *A Proclamation.*

Whereas on the 22nd day of September, A.D. 1862, a proclamation was issued by the President of the United States, containing among other things, the following, to wit:

"That on the 1st day of January, A.D. 1863, all persons held as slaves within any State or designated part of a State the people whereof shall then be in rebellion against the United States shall be then, thenceforward, and forever free; and the executive government of the United States, including the military and naval authority thereof, will recognize and maintain the freedom of such persons and will do no act or acts to repress such persons, or any of them, in any efforts they may make for their actual freedom.

"That the executive will on the 1st day of January aforesaid, by proclamation, designate the States and parts of States, if any, in which the people thereof, respectively, shall then be in rebellion against the United States; and the fact that any State or the people thereof shall on that day be in good faith represented in the Congress of the United States by members chosen thereto at elections wherein a majority of the qualified voters of such States shall have participated shall, in the absence of strong countervailing testimony, be deemed conclusive evidence that such State and the people thereof are not then in rebellion against the United States."

Now, therefore, I, Abraham Lincoln, President of the United States, by virtue of the power in me vested as Commander-in-Chief of the Army and Navy of the United States in time of actual armed rebellion against the authority and government of the United States, and as a fit and necessary war measure for suppressing said rebellion, do, on this 1st day of January, A.D. 1863, and in accordance with my purpose so to do, publicly proclaimed for the full period of one hundred days from the first day above mentioned, order and designate as the States and parts of States wherein the people thereof, respectively, are this day in rebellion against the United States the following, to wit:

Arkansas, Texas, Louisiana (except the parishes of St. Bernard, Plaquemines, Jefferson, St. John, St. Charles, St. James, Ascension, Assumption, Terrebonne, Lafourche, St. Mary, St. Martin, and Orleans, including the city of New Orleans), Mississippi, Alabama, Florida, Georgia, South Carolina, North Carolina, and Virginia (except the forty-eight counties designated as West Virginia, and also the counties of Berkeley, Accomac, Northhampton, Elizabeth City, York, Princess Anne, and Norfolk, including the cities of Norfolk and Portsmouth), and which excepted parts are for the present left precisely as if this proclamation were not issued.

And by virtue of the power and for the purpose aforesaid, I do order and declare that all persons held as slaves within said designated States and parts of States are, and henceforward shall be, free; and that the Executive Government of the United States, including the military and naval authorities thereof, will recognize and maintain the freedom of said persons.

And I hereby enjoin upon the people so declared to be free to abstain from all violence, unless in necessary self-defense; and I recommend to them that, in all cases when allowed, they labor faithfully for reasonable wages.

And I further declare and make known that such persons of suitable condition will be received into the armed service of the United States to garrison forts, positions, stations, and other places, and to man vessels of all sorts in said service.

And upon this act, sincerely believed to be an act of justice, warranted by the Constitution upon military necessity, I invoke the considerate judgment of mankind and the gracious favor of Almighty God.

## THE GETTYSBURG ADDRESS

Abraham Lincoln's most famous and most eloquent words were delivered on Nov. 19, 1863, at the dedication of the cemetery that held the remains of the 45,000 soldiers who fell at the Battle of Gettysburg, a significant Union victory. A powerful summation of Lincoln's war aims as well as a moving tribute to those who died for a just cause, the Gettysburg Address has become justly famous as a rhetorical masterpiece as well as a stirring example of Lincoln's statesmanship.

"Four score and seven years ago our fathers brought forth on this continent, a new nation, conceived in Liberty, and dedicated to the proposition that all men are created equal.

"Now we are engaged in a great civil war, testing whether that nation or any nation so conceived and so dedicated, can long endure. We are met on a great battle-field of that war. We have come to dedicate a portion of that field, as a final resting place for those who here gave their lives that that nation might live. It is altogether fitting and proper that we should do this.

"But, in a larger sense, we can not dedicate—we can not consecrate—we can not hallow—this ground. The brave men, living and dead, who struggled here, have consecrated it, far above our poor power to add or detract. The world will little note, nor long remember what we say here, but it can never forget what they did here. It is for us the living, rather, to be dedicated here to the unfinished work which they who fought here have thus far so nobly advanced. It is rather for us to be here dedicated to the great task remaining before us—that from these honored dead we take increased devotion to that cause for which they gave the last full measure of devotion—that we here highly resolve that these dead shall not have died in vain—that this nation, under God, shall have a new birth of freedom—and that government of the people, by the people, for the people, shall not perish from the earth."

## PLEDGE OF ALLEGIANCE

The original version of the Pledge of Allegiance appeared in the Sept. 8, 1892, issue of *Youth's Companion* magazine. Authorship was disputed until 1939, when the United States Flag Association declared Francis Bellamy the author. Congress mandated two changes by substituting "the flag of the United States of America" for "my flag" in 1923 and adding "under God" in 1954. Public schools throughout the United States made the daily Pledge of Allegiance obligatory, until the Supreme Court ruled in *West Virginia Board of Education* v. *Barnette* (1943) that the First Amendment protected the "right of silence" as well as freedom of speech.

"I pledge allegiance to the flag of the United States of America, and to the Republic for which it stands, one nation, under God, indivisible, with liberty and justice for all."

## "I HAVE A DREAM"

On Aug. 28, 1963, the Rev. Martin Luther King, Jr., addressed a crowd of more than 200,000 people at the Lincoln Memorial in Washington, D.C. Dr. King's speech, excerpted here, enunciated the very highest hopes of the civil rights movement in the United States.

"I say to you today, my friends, that in spite of the difficulties and frustrations of the moment I still have a dream. It is a dream deeply rooted in the American dream.

"I have a dream that one day this nation will rise up and live out the true meaning of its creed: 'We hold these truths to be self-evident, that all men are created equal.'

"I have a dream that one day on the red hills of Georgia the sons of former slaves and the sons of former slave owners will be able to sit down together at the table of brotherhood. . . .

"I have a dream that my four little children will one day live in a nation where they will not be judged by the color of their skin but by the content of their character.

"I have a dream today."

# Chronology of U.S History

**c. 1000** Viking explorer Leif Ericson explores North American coast and founds temporary colony called Vinland.

**1492** On first voyage to America, Christopher Columbus lands at San Salvador island in Bahamas.

**1493** Pope Alexander VI divides New World between Spain and Portugal.

**1497** John Cabot claims Newfoundland for King Henry VII of England.

**1499** Florentine merchant Amerigo Vespucci visits New World and begins writing popular accounts of his voyages.

**1506** Columbus dies poor and embittered, convinced he found new route to Asia and refusing to believe he discovered new continent.

**1507** German mapmaker Martin Waldseemüller, after reading Amerigo Vespucci's descriptions of New World, names it America after him.

**1513** Juan Ponce de León discovers Florida. Vasco Nuñez de Balboa crosses Panama and sights Pacific Ocean.

**1519** Hernán Cortés lands in Mexico.

**1520** Ferdinand Magellan, first to sail around world, discovers South American straits, named after him.

**1522** Cortés captures Mexico City and conquers Aztec empire.

**1524** Giovanni de Verrazano, commissioned by King Francis I of France, discovers New York harbor and Hudson River.

**1534** Jacques Cartier of France explores coast of Newfoundland and Gulf of St. Lawrence.

**1536** Traveling overland from Gulf of Mexico, Alvar Núñez Cabeza de Vaca reaches Gulf of California.

**1539** Fernando de Soto conquers Florida and begins three-year trek across Southeast.

**1540** Francisco Vásquez de Coronado explores Southwest, discovering Grand Canyon and introducing horses to North America.

**1541** Coronado discovers Mississippi River.

**1542** João Rodrígues Cabrilho (Cabrillo) explores coast of California, missing San Francisco Bay.

**1565** Don Pedro Menéndez de Aviles founds first permanent European settlement in North America, at St. Augustine, Florida.

**1572** Sir Francis Drake of England makes first voyage to America, landing in Panama.

**1576** English explorer Martin Frobisher searches for Northwest Passage.

**1577** Drake begins voyage of plunder around world.

**1579** Drake lands north of San Francisco Bay and claims region for Queen Elizabeth I.

**1584** Sir Walter Raleigh discovers Roanoke Island and names land Virginia, after Queen Elizabeth.

**1585** Raleigh establishes England's first American colony at Roanoke.

**1586** Drake evacuates surviving Roanoke settlers.

**1587** Raleigh resettles Roanoke with 150 new colonists. Virginia Dare first child of English parents born in America.

**1591** Relief expedition returns to Roanoke colony; all settlers have disappeared without trace.

**1602** Capt. Bartholomew Gosnold, first Englishman to set foot in New England, explores Cape Cod and Martha's Vineyard.

**1603** Samuel de Champlain of France explores St. Lawrence River; later founds Quebec.

**1607** First permanent English settlement in America established at Jamestown, Va. Only 32 of original 105 colonists survive first winter.

**1608** Capt. John Smith imprisoned by Indians and saved by Pocahontas, daughter of Chief Powhatan.

**1609** Henry Hudson sets out in search of Northwest Passage. Champlain sails into Great Lakes.

**1611** Hudson cast adrift by mutinous crewmen to die in bay later named for him.

**1612** First Dutch trading post appears on Manhattan Island.

**1616** Smallpox epidemic decimates Indian tribes from Maine to Rhode Island.

**1619** Dutch traders bring first African slaves to Virginia for sale. Americans hold first election when Virginia planters vote for House of Burgesses.

**1620** Pilgrims and others arrive in Plymouth, Mass., aboard *Mayflower*. They draw up Mayflower Compact.

**1622** Most of Virginia colony wiped out in Indian attack.

**1624** King James I revokes Virginia's charter and makes it royal colony.

**1626** Dutch colony of New Amsterdam founded on Manhattan Island, bought from Indian people for about $24.

**1630** John Winthrop sets sail for Massachusetts with 900 Puritans and others, beginning Great Migration to New England.

**1632** King Charles I of England grants Lord Baltimore charter to establish colony in Maryland.

**1634** Massachusetts adopts representative government. Jean Nicolet of France begins trading with Indians in Wisconsin.

**1635** Roger Williams, banished from Massachusetts, founds dissident colony of Rhode Island.

**1636** New Englanders massacre hundreds of Indians in Pequot War. Harvard College established.

**1638** First Swedish colony founded in Delaware.

**1639** "Oath of a Free Man" the first English document printed in America. First public school appears in Dorchester, first post office in Boston, and Connecticut writes first colonial constitution.

**1644** Indians make last, unsuccessful attempt to expel English settlers from Virginia. First American ship built in Boston.

**1647** Margaret Brent of Maryland first American woman to demand right to vote. Massachusetts passes first compulsory education law. First witchcraft execution takes place in Hartford, Conn.

**1648** Boston shoemakers and coopers establish first American labor unions.

**1651** British Parliament passes first Navigation Act regulating colonial trade.

**1652** Rhode Island first colony to outlaw slavery. First American coins minted in Boston.

**1654** Jacob Barsimon, first American Jew, arrives in New Amsterdam, followed by 23 more Jews from Brazil.

**1655** Dutch colonists capture Swedish colony in Delaware. Lady Deborah Moody of Long Island first American woman to vote.

**1656** First Quakers arrive in America; imprisoned in Boston, beaten, and deported.

**1659** Massachusetts hangs two Quakers on Boston Common.

**1660** British Parliament forbids Americans to export goods to countries other than England. Massachusetts outlaws celebration of Christmas.

**1661** Virginia first colony to recognize slavery as legal.

**1662** Connecticut granted royal charter. Massachusetts appoints official press censors and institutes "half-way" covenant.

**1663** British Parliament requires colonial imports from Europe to pass first through England. King Charles II grants charters to Carolina and Rhode Island.

**1664** New Amsterdam captured by Richard Nicolls, who renames it New York. New Jersey established.

**1670** Charles Town, later called Charleston, first permanent settlement in Carolina.

**1672** British Parliament tightens trade restrictions on colonies and appoints American customs collectors.

**1673** French explorers Jacques Marquette and Louis Jolliet paddle down Mississippi River to Arkansas. Regular mail service begins between Boston and New York. Dutch forces recapture New York.

**1674** Treaty of Westminster restores New York to England. King Louis XIV of France sends Sieur de La Salle to explore Mississippi River.

**1675** Thousands die in King Philip's War between New Englanders and five Indian tribes.

**1676** Bacon's Rebellion overthrows government of Virginia and burns down Jamestown.

**1680** New Hampshire separated from Massachusetts and made royal colony.

**1681** King Charles II names William Penn proprietor of Pennsylvania.

**1682** Penn founds Philadelphia. Sieur de La Salle claims North American interior for France, naming it Louisiana.

**1683** First German-Americans, a group of Mennonites, arrive in Philadelphia.

**1684** King Charles II revokes Massachusetts charter.

**1686** King James II appoints Sir Edmund Andros governor-general of Dominion of New England, dissolving colonial governments.

**1688** Quakers publish first antislavery tracts in Pennsylvania.

**1689** Andros surrenders to Boston mobs, and colonial self-government is reestablished. Jacob Leisler seizes power in New York uprising. King William's War begins in America.

**1690** Massachusetts issues first colonial paper money. American campaigns against French Canada fail. French and Indians burn Schenectady, N.Y.

**1691** Jacob Leisler surrenders and is hanged. Massachusetts rechartered with religious freedom.

**1692** Witchcraft hysteria breaks out in Salem, Mass., leading to 20 executions.

**1693** College of William and Mary chartered, the second college in America.

**1695** New York City organizes public relief for poor and homeless.

**1696** British Parliament places more commercial restrictions on colonies. American merchants join slave trade.

**1697** Treaty of Ryswick ends King William's War.

**1701** Antoine de la Mothe Cadillac establishes French outpost at Detroit, Mich. Yale College founded. Delaware separated from Pennsylvania.

**1702** Queen Anne's War breaks out.

**1704** *Boston News-Letter* first regularly published newspaper in America.

**1710** German Migration to America begins. British and American forces capture Port Royal, Nova Scotia.

**1711** Anglo-American attack on Quebec fails. Tuscarora Indian War breaks out in North Carolina.

**1712** Militia quell slave rebellion in New York City. Pennsylvania prohibits importing slaves.

**1713** Treaty of Utrecht ends Queen Anne's War.

**1714** Americans begin drinking tea. *Androborus*, a political satire, first play written in America.

**1716** First theater in America built in Williamsburg, Va. Slavery introduced to French Louisiana.

**1718** Jean Baptiste Le Moyne founds French city of New Orleans.

**1721** Sir Robert Walpole loosens colonial trade restrictions with policy of "salutary neglect."

**1722** France declares New Orleans capital of Louisiana.

**1723** America's first business corporation chartered in Connecticut.

**1724** France expels all Jews from Louisiana.

**1728** First American synagogue built in New York City.

**1729** North and South Carolina receive royal charters.

**1731** Benjamin Franklin founds first American library in Philadelphia.

**1732** King George II grants charter to Georgia. Only Catholic church in colonial America opens in Philadelphia. Benjamin Franklin begins publishing *Poor Richard's Almanack*. George Washington born in Virginia.

**1733** British Parliament passes Molasses Act, taxing imports from non-British sugar islands.

**1734** Beginning of Great Awakening, widespread religious revival.

**1735** French begin settling in Illinois.

**1737** Boston holds its first public celebration of St. Patrick's Day.

**1739** War of Jenkins' Ear begins. South Carolina slaves mount Stono Rebellion. French explorers Pierre and Paul Mallet discover Rocky Mountains.

**1741** Danish navigator Vitus Bering, hired by Peter the Great of Russia, explores coast of Alaska. *American Magazine*, the first in colonies, begins publishing in Philadelphia. Slave insurrection panic sweeps New York City.

**1742** First sugarcane planted in Louisiana.

**1744** King George's War breaks out.

**1745** British and Americans capture Ft. Louisbourg on Cape Breton Island. French and Indians raid Maine.

**1748** Ft. Louisbourg restored to France by Treaty of Aix-la-Chapelle, ending King George's War.

**1751** British Parliament forbids New England colonies to issue paper money.

**1752** Benjamin Franklin conducts famous kite experiment. Liberty bell is cracked in Philadelphia.

**1753** Governor Robert Dinwiddie of Virginia sends George Washington into Ohio country to demand withdrawal of French. First steam engine arrives in America.

**1754** Washington skirmishes with French patrol, touching off French and Indian War. Franklin presents Albany Plan of Union for colonies.

**1755** Quakers withdraw from Pennsylvania assembly rather than vote for military spending. Washington leads retreat from Battle of the Wilderness.

**1758** British and American forces lose Battle of Ticonderoga but capture Louisbourg and Ft. Duquesne. New Jersey sets aside first Indian reservation for Onami tribe.

**1759** General Wolfe defeats General Montcalm as British capture Quebec. Both generals fall in battle.

**1760** After fall of Montreal, all of New France surrenders to Britain. King George III crowned in England.

**1762** King Louis XV of France secretly cedes Louisiana to Spain.

**1763** Treaty of Paris ends French and Indian War. France cedes Canada to Britain. King George III prohibits Americans to settle in West. Conspiracy of Pontiac threatens frontier.

**1764** British Parliament passes Sugar Act and forbids all colonies to issue paper money. French settlers found St. Louis. "Paxton Boys" march on Philadelphia. In Boston James Otis protests, "No taxation without representation."

**1765** Parliament passes Stamp Act (tax on newspapers, legal documents, etc.) and Quartering Act (requiring housing of British soldiers in homes). Sons of Liberty organize resistance and nonimportation throughout colonies. Stamp Act Congress meets in New York.

**1766** Parliament repeals Stamp Act but passes Declaratory Act, affirming its right to pass laws binding on colonies. Chief Pontiac makes peace.

**1767** Parliament enacts Townshend Duties and suspends New York assembly for resisting Quartering Act.

**1768** "Regulators" rebel in North Carolina. Boston riots against Townshend Duties.

**1769** Daniel Boone explores Kentucky. Father Junipero Serra founds San Diego, the first Spanish mission in California. Gaspar de Portola sails into San Francisco Bay.

**1770** Five Americans perish in Boston Massacre (Mar. 5). British Parliament repeals Townshend Duties, except tax on tea.

**1771** North Carolina "Regulators" defeated by militia.

**1772** Rhode Island mob burns British revenue ship *Gaspee*. Boston appoints first Committee of Correspondence.

**1773** British Parliament passes Tea Act, leading to Boston Tea Party (Dec. 16).

**1774** Parliament passes "Intolerable Acts," punishing colonists for Tea Party. Boston is occupied by British forces under Gen. Thomas Gage. First Continental Congress meets in Philadelphia.

**1775** American Revolution begins with Battle of Lexington and Concord (Apr. 19). Second Continental Congress appoints George Washington as commander of Continental Army. British win Battle of Bunker Hill. First abolition society organized in Pennsylvania.

**1776** Tom Paine's *Common Sense* published. Declaration of Independence signed. Congress adopts name United States of America. British occupy New York City. George Washington crosses Delaware to win Battle of Trenton, N.J.

**1777** Americans win battles at Princeton and Saratoga. British occupy Philadelphia. Congress adopts Stars and Stripes flag and endorses Articles of Confederation. Washington's army spends winter at Valley Forge, Pa.

**1778** France makes alliance with U.S. and declares war on Britain. When French fleet arrives, British evacuate Philadelphia.

**1779** Congress offers to make peace in exchange for independence. British withdraw from New York City.

**1780** Pennsylvania first state to abolish slavery. British occupy Charleston, S.C. Washington quells Continental Army mutiny. Benedict Arnold defects to British.

**1781** French and American victory at Battle of Yorktown ends American Revolution. Articles of Confederation take effect. Los Angeles founded by Spanish missionaries.

**1782** British Parliament votes for peace with U.S. Negotiations in Paris lead to provisional Anglo-American peace treaty. Virginia permits owners to free their slaves. First English Bible printed in America.

**1783** Massachusetts, Connecticut, and Rhode Island abolish slavery. Treaty of Paris signed (Sept. 3), officially ending American Revolution. Washington retires to Mount Vernon, Va.

**1784** Congress ratifies Treaty of Paris. Spain closes Mississippi River to American trade. First bale of American cotton shipped to Britain.

**1785** First state university chartered in Georgia.

**1786** Virginia proclaims religious freedom. Shays's Rebellion put down in Massachusetts. Annapolis Convention calls for revising Articles of Confederation. New Jersey abolishes slavery.

**1787** Convention in Philadelphia writes Constitution. Congress passes Northwest Ordinance and submits Constitution for states' approval.

**1788** Constitution ratified and takes effect.

**1789** First presidential election results in victory for George Washington. Federal government begins meeting in New York City. Congress enacts first federal tariff.

**1790** First antislavery petitions are submitted to Congress. Temporary capital moved to Philadelphia. Pope Pius VI appoints John Carroll first Catholic bishop in U.S. First U.S. census lists population at 3,929,625.

**1791** Congress sets up First Bank of the United States and first internal revenue law, a tax on whiskey. Vermont enters Union as 14th state. Bill of Rights takes effect. Pres. Washington selects site of new U.S. capital on Potomac River.

**1792** New York stock traders begin meeting under a tree on Wall Street. Pres. Washington unanimously reelected. Construction begins on White House.

**1793** Eli Whitney invents cotton gin. Congress passes first Fugitive Slave Act. Pres. Washington holds first official cabinet meeting and lays cornerstone for Capitol. Britain begins confiscating American ships trading with France.

**1794** Pres. Washington defeats Whiskey Rebellion in Pennsylvania. U.S. and Britain sign Jay's Treaty. Ohio Indians defeated at Battle of Fallen Timbers.

**1795** Georgia stung by scandal of Yazoo land frauds. Senate ratifies Jay's Treaty with Britain.

**1796** Pres. Washington delivers "Farewell Address." France begins to confiscate ships trading with Britain.

**1797** France insults American diplomats in XYZ affair. Spanish begin building Mission San Juan Capistrano in California.

**1798** Georgia last state to abolish slave trade. Congress passes Alien and Sedition Acts. U.S. renounces alliance with France as unofficial naval war breaks out.

**1799** Russian-American trading company set up in Alaska. New York abolishes slavery. George Washington dies.

**1800** Library of Congress founded. Convention of 1800 signed, ending quasi-war between U.S. and France. Spain secretly cedes Louisiana to France. Congress begins meeting in Washington, D.C.

**1801** Election of Thomas Jefferson results in first transfer of executive power between rival parties. Congress takes jurisdiction over District of Columbia. Tripoli pirates declare war on U.S. for not paying tribute.

**1802** U.S. Military Academy established at West Point, N.Y.

**1803** Louisiana Purchase from France doubles size of U.S. Federal outpost founded at Ft. Dearborn, Ill., future site of Chicago.

**1804** Lewis and Clark expedition sets out from St. Louis. New Jersey begins gradual emancipation. Alexander Hamilton killed in duel with Aaron Burr.

**1805** Barbary War with Tripoli ends.

**1806** Congress authorizes construction of Cumberland Road. Noah Webster's first dictionary published. Aaron Burr conspires to create private frontier empire.

**1807** Britain and France enact blockades in Europe, confiscating American trading ships. British attack USS *Chesapeake*. Embargo Act forbids all American exports.

**1808** Congress declares end to African slave trade.

**1809** Embargo Act replaced with Non-Intercourse Act, outlawing exports to Britain and France. Henry Clay of Kentucky enters U.S. Senate. First steamboat sea voyage made from New York City to Philadelphia.

**1810** Pres. James Madison annexes West Florida.

**1811** Russians settle at Ft. Ross, Calif. First Bank of the United States fails to obtain recharter. Gen. William Henry Harrison defeats Indians at Battle of Tippecanoe. New Madrid earthquakes rock Ohio-Mississippi valleys.

**1812** War of 1812 begins by close vote in Congress. New England resists war. Daniel Webster of Massachusetts elected to Congress. British clamp blockade on U.S. ports, capture Detroit, and repel American attack on Canada at Queenstown.

**1813** Americans regain Detroit, attack Toronto and Ft. George in Canada, but surrender to British at Beaver Dams, Ontario. Capt. Oliver H. Perry wins control of Great Lakes. British and Indians burn Buffalo, N.Y.

**1814** British destroy Ft. Oswego, N.Y., and set fire to Washington, D.C. Francis Scott Key writes "The Star Spangled Banner." New Englanders opposed to war meet secretly at Hartford Convention. First textile mill established at Waltham, Mass. Treaty of Ghent ends War of 1812.

**1815** Gen. Andrew Jackson routs British at Battle of New Orleans, before news arrives that War of 1812 is over.

**1816** Congress charters Second Bank of the United States.

**1817** Rush-Bagot Treaty between Britain and U.S. demilitarizes Great Lakes. Harvard Law School founded. New York Stock and Exchange Board organized. Work begins on Erie Canal. Indian attack touches off first Seminole War in Florida.

**1818** Cumberland Road opened. Congress adopts present format for American flag. Canadian boundary dispute with Britain settled.

**1819** Panic of 1819 plunges South and West into depression. U.S. obtains Florida from Spain in Adams-Onís Treaty, settling border of Louisiana. *Savannah* makes first successful transatlantic crossing under steam power.

**1820** Missouri Compromise solves crisis over admission of Missouri as slave state. Abolitionists begin colonizing freed slaves in Africa.

**1821** First Catholic cathedral in U.S. built in Baltimore.

**1822** Denmark Vesey and 36 others executed for organizing rebel slave conspiracy in Charleston, S.C.

**1823** Monroe Doctrine, masterminded by Sec. of State John Quincy Adams, announced by Pres. James Monroe.

**1824** Russia and U.S. sign treaty settling territorial disputes in Pacific Northwest. First presidential nominating convention held in Utica, N.Y.

**1825** John Quincy Adams chosen president in infamous "Corrupt Bargain" with Henry Clay, who becomes secretary of state. Erie Canal opened. Mexico invites Americans to settle in Texas.

**1826** Anti-Mason party organized. John Adams and Thomas Jefferson die on 50th anniversary of Declaration of Independence. Jedediah Smith leads first overland expedition to California.

**1827** Joseph Smith has visions of Book of Mormon. U.S. and Britain agree to joint occupation of Pacific Northwest.

**1828** Congress passes protectionist "Tariff of Abominations" over southern protests.

**1829** Mexico refuses Pres. Andrew Jackson's offer to buy Texas.

**1830** Webster-Hayne Debate in U.S. Senate reveals sectional tension. Church of Latter-day Saints (the Mormons) founded by Joseph Smith in Fayette, N.Y. Mexico forbids further American immigration to Texas.

**1831** Nat Turner leads bloodiest of all slave rebellions, killing 57 whites in Virginia. Abolitionists petition Congress for end to slavery.

**1832** Black Hawk War fought in Illinois and Wisconsin. First nationwide Democratic party convention held in Baltimore. Pres. Jackson vetoes bill to recharter national bank. South Carolina nullifies "Tariff of Abominations."

**1833** Massachusetts last state to end tax support for churches. Congress lowers tariff and passes "Force Bill" to pressure South Carolina, which nullifies nullification. American Anti-Slavery Society organized. Oberlin College becomes first coeducational college.

**1834** Whig party organized by Senators Henry Clay and Daniel Webster in opposition to Pres. Jackson. Antiabolitionist riots break out in New York and Philadelphia.

**1835** Samuel Morse invents telegraph. National debt completely paid off. Pres. Jackson survives first attempt to assassinate a president. Second Seminole War begins in Florida.

**1836** Samuel Colt invents revolver. Texas declares independence from Mexico and requests U.S. annexation. Mexican army captures Alamo, but Texans are victorious at San Jacinto.

**1837** Panic of 1837 begins lengthy economic depression.

**1838** Joshua Giddings of Ohio is first abolitionist elected to Congress. Transatlantic steamship service established. Congress blocks abolitionist petitions with "Gag Rule."

**1839** Abner Doubleday of Cooperstown, N.Y., codifies rules of baseball. Congress outlaws dueling in Washington, D.C.

**1840** "Log Cabin Campaign" between William Henry Harrison and Martin Van Buren begins era of mass political participation. Liberty party founded by abolitionists in Albany, N.Y.

**1841** First emigrant train of 48 covered wagons arrives in California. Pres. William Henry Harrison dies after month in office. First Japanese immigrant arrives in New Bedford, Mass.

**1842** Webster-Ashburton Treaty settles Canada boundary disputes between U.S. and Britain. U.S. accidentally seizes California, then returns it with apology to Mexico.

**1843** End of Second Seminole War. B'Nai B'rith founded in New York. Mormons begin practicing polygamy.

**1844** Baptist is first church to split North and South over slavery. Samuel Morse sends first telegraph message. James K. Polk, first dark horse candidate, elected president.

**1845** Potato Famine begins massive Irish immigration. U.S. annexes Texas, over Mexican protests. U.S. Naval Academy opens at Annapolis, Md.

**1846** Mexican War begins when U.S. troops are attacked in disputed Texas territory. American settlers in California stage Bear Flag Revolt. Oregon Treaty gives U.S. sole possession of Pacific Northwest up to 49th parallel. First recorded baseball game played in Hoboken, N.J.

**1847** Wilmot Proviso, forbidding slavery expansion, passes House and sets off wave of panic in South. Gen. Winfield Scott conquers Mexico City. Brigham Young leads Mormons to Utah. Abraham Lincoln of Illinois arrives in Congress.

**1848** Treaty of Guadalupe-Hidalgo ends Mexican War, ceding Southwest to U.S. Revolution of 1848 begins wave of German immigration. New York-Chicago telegraph line completed. Chicago Board of Trade established. Free Soil party organized. Gold discovered in California. First Chinese immigrants arrive in San Francisco. Lucretia Mott and Elizabeth Cady Stanton hold first Women's Rights Convention in Seneca Falls, N.Y.

**1849** Gold Rush brings hundreds of thousands to California. Over 20 killed in New York City riot between fans of rival actors. Elizabeth Blackwell first American woman to receive medical degree.

**1850** Sen. Henry Clay's Compromise of 1850 solves crisis over slavery expansion. Clayton-Bulwer Treaty pledges Anglo-American cooperation in building any Central American canal. John C. Calhoun of South Carolina delivers last address to Senate.

**1851** Young Men's Christian Association (YMCA) established. Northern mobs resist Fugitive Slave Act. Maine is first state to pass prohibition laws. Hungarian patriot Louis Kossuth draws huge crowds touring country. *New York Times* founded. Herman Melville's *Moby Dick* published.

**1852** Harriet Beecher Stowe's *Uncle Tom's Cabin* published.

**1853** U.S. buys Gila River valley from Mexico in Gadsden Purchase. American, or "Know-Nothing," party founded. Commodore Matthew C. Perry opens trade with Japan.

**1854** Congress passes Kansas-Nebraska Act, setting off mass protests across North. Republican party founded. U.S. threatens to seize Cuba from Spain in Ostend Manifesto.

**1855** "Bleeding Kansas" fighting begins as proslavery and antislavery settlers hold rival state conventions. First railroad train crosses Mississippi River at Rock Island, Ill., into Davenport, Iowa.

**1856** Congressman Preston Brooks of South Carolina beats Sen. Charles Sumner of Massachusetts unconscious on Senate floor for insulting a southern senator. John Brown leads Pottawatomie massacre in Kansas. First Republican national convention nominates John C. Frémont for president in Pittsburgh, Pa.

**1857** New York-St. Louis railroad completed. Supreme Court hands down controversial *Dred Scott* decision protecting slavery. Panic of 1857 sends North into depression.

**1858** Lincoln-Douglas Debates dramatize issue of slavery expansion in Illinois race for Senate. First transatlantic telegraph cable laid.

**1859** John Brown's raid on Harper's Ferry arsenal to launch abolitionist war against slavery ends in his capture and execution. Slave insurrection panic sweeps South. Comstock Lode discovered in Nevada. First producing oil well in U.S. flows in Titusville, Pa.

**1860** Democratic party splits into northern and southern wings. South Carolina is first Southern state to secede from Union after victory of Abraham Lincoln. Crittenden Compromise fails to preserve Union. Pony Express begins mail delivery between California and Missouri.

**1861** Civil War begins with attack on Ft. Sumter in South Carolina (Apr. 12). Pres. Abraham Lincoln calls for 75,000 volunteers to put down rebellion. Jefferson Davis of Mississippi elected president of Confederate States of America. New York-San Francisco telegraph link completed. Yale awards first American Ph.D. Congress enacts first federal income tax.

**1862** Congress issues "greenbacks," subsidizes transcontinental railroad, abolishes slavery in District of Columbia, and passes Homestead Act. Pres. Lincoln issues Emancipation Proclamation after Battle of Antietam, bloodiest fight of Civil War.

**1863** Emancipation Proclamation takes effect (Jan. 1). Union victories at Vicksburg, Miss., and Gettysburg, Pa., signal turning point of Civil War. West Virginia secedes from Virginia and rejoins Union. Hundreds killed in New York City draft riot. Pres. Lincoln proclaims Thanksgiving national holiday.

**1864** Pres. Lincoln names Gen. Ulysses S. Grant as commander of Union armies. Gen. William T. Sherman destroys Atlanta and conducts "March to the Sea." Confederate army of Gen. Robert E. Lee crippled in Wilderness Campaign. Cheyenne and Arapaho slaughtered in Sand Creek Massacre in Colorado.

**1865** Gen. Lee surrenders to Gen. Grant at Appomattox Court House, Virginia (Apr. 9). Pres. Lincoln assassinated by John Wilkes Booth in Washington, D.C. (Apr. 14). Confederacy dissolved, ending Civil War. Pres. Andrew Johnson proclaims amnesty for most rebels. Slavery outlawed by adoption of 13th Amendment. Ku Klux Klan founded in Pulaski, Tenn.

**1866** In the struggle over Reconstruction policy, Congress overrides Pres. Johnson's vetoes of Civil Rights Act and New Freedmen's Bureau Bill. Whites riot in New Orleans to protest black suffrage. Grand Army of the Republic organized by Union veterans. Young Women's Christian Association (YWCA) founded in Boston.

**1867** Congress takes control of Reconstruction in South by passing First Reconstruction Act over Pres. Johnson's veto and Tenure of Office Act. U.S. purchases Alaska from Russia for $7.2 million (2¢ an acre). Farmers organize Patrons of Husbandry, beginning Granger movement. Cigarettes appear on American market. First elevated trains begin running in New York City.

**1868** For violating Tenure of Office Act of 1867, Pres. Johnson is impeached in the House (Feb. 24), but acquitted in the Senate by a single vote (May 16). U.S. and China sign Burlingame Treaty to allow immigration. Fourteenth Amendment grants equal citizenship and protection to freedmen (July 28). Half a million black votes help elect Gen. Ulysses S. Grant to presidency. Typewriter invented. University of California chartered.

**1869** "Hard Money" prevails when Congress passes Public Credit Act, promising repayment of government debts in gold. Transcontinental railroad completed when Union Pacific and Central Pacific lines meet at Promontory Point, Utah (May 10). Jay Gould and James Fisk cause financial panic by trying to corner gold market on "Black Friday" (Sept. 24). Knights of Labor national union organized. National Women's Suffrage Association formed in New York. Wyoming Territory grants first U.S. women's suffrage.

**1870** Fifteenth Amendment guarantees right to vote for all U.S. citizens, though only Wyoming and Utah territories allow women's suffrage (Mar. 30). Congress passes first Ku Klux Klan Act to enforce 15th Amendment. First black senator and black congressman elected. Yale and Harvard initiate first graduate studies programs in U.S. All states represented in Congress for first time since 1860.

**1871** Congress passes second Ku Klux Klan Act to enforce 14th Amendment in South. U.S. and Britain resolve Civil War disputes with Treaty of Washington. Tammany Hall ring overthrown in New York City when *New York Times* begins publishing exposé of William Marcy "Boss" Tweed. Most of Chicago destroyed in Great Fire (Oct. 8–11). Anti-Chinese race riots in Los Angeles. Illinois enacts first railroad regulations.

**1872** Liberal Republicans bolt from Pres. Grant and nominate newspaperman Horace Greeley for president. Crédit Mobilier scandal implicates Vice Pres. Schuyler Colfax and embarrasses Grant administration. Yellowstone National Park created. Susan B. Anthony arrested for leading suffragists to the polls. Jehovah's Witnesses, originally called Russellites, founded by Charles Taze Russell. Montgomery Ward opens for business in Chicago.

**1873** Silver withdrawn from money supply in "Crime of '73." Congressmen raise their own salaries 50%, retroactive for two years, and double president's pay in "Salary Grab" Act. Panic of 1873, triggered by failure of Jay Cooke's banking house, begins depression of 1870s. New York Stock Exchange forced to close for 10 days. Great Bonanza silver lode discovered in Nevada. San Francisco installs first cable cars.

**1874** Granger movement begins passing railroad regulations in midwestern states. Women's Christian Temperance Union founded in Cleveland, Ohio. Young Men's Hebrew Association organized in New York. Democrats recapture Congress for first time since Civil War. Greenback party formed in Indianapolis, Ind. Black rioters attack courthouse in Vicksburg, Miss. Chautauqua movement begins bringing educational speakers to rural communities across the country.

**1875** Congress passes Specie Resumption Act to reduce money supply by redeeming greenbacks for gold, and Civil Rights Act to guarantee equal rights for freedmen. Whiskey Ring scandal casts further pall on Grant administration. Archbishop John McCloskey of New York first American bishop. Aristides wins first Kentucky Derby at Churchill Downs, Ky.

**1876** U.S. awards patent to Alexander Graham Bell for telephone. Gen. George A. Custer and 265 men massacred by Sioux Indians at Little Big Horn, Mont. (June 25). Centennial of U.S. celebrated. Democrat Samuel Tilden outpolls Republican candidate Rutherford B. Hayes as presidential election is thrown into the House (Nov. 7). Professional baseball's National League established. Kappa Alpha opens first college fraternity house at Williams College. Central Park in New York completed.

**1877** Congress appoints Electoral Commission to solve impasse over disputed 1876 election (Jan. 29). House votes 185 to 184 to declare Rutherford B. Hayes president-elect, three days before his inauguration (Mar. 2). Reconstruction officially ends with withdrawal of federal troops from South (Apr. 24). Pres. Hayes sends in troops as Great Railroad Strike paralyzes much of nation (July 17). Anti-Chinese riots break out in San Francisco. Colorado silver rush begins.

**1878** Sen. A.A. Sargent introduces Women's Suffrage Amendment in Congress (Jan. 10). Greenback-Labor party formed in Toledo, Ohio. Coinage of silver resumes with Bland-Allison Act. Democrats win control of both houses of Congress for first time since 1858. American Bar Association organized in Saratoga, N.Y. Edison Electric begins operating in New York City. New Haven, Conn., sets up first commercial telephone network.

**1879** U.S. resumes specie payments for greenbacks. Pres. Hayes battles with Congress over use of federal troops in elections. F.W. Woolworth opens his first store in Utica, N.Y. First Church of Christ, Scientist, founded in Boston. Thomas Edison invents light bulb. California adopts state constitution forbidding employment of Chinese labor. Henry George's radical social critique, *Progress and Poverty*, becomes national best-seller.

**1880** Pres. Hayes declares U.S. must control any Isthmian canal. Ex-pres. Grant fails in attempt to regain Republican nomination. U.S. and China agree to Chinese Exclusion Treaty (Nov. 17). National Farmers' Alliance organized in Chicago. American branch of Salvation Army founded in Philadelphia, Pa. Census lists U.S. population over 50 million for first time (50,155,783).

**1881** Pres. James Garfield assassinated by Charles Guiteau in Washington, D.C. (July 2; dies Sept. 19). Chester A. Arthur becomes president (Sept. 20). Clara Barton creates American Red Cross. Booker T. Washington founds Tuskegee Institute for black education in Alabama. First summer camp for children opens in Squam Lake, N.H. Russian Jews begin immigrating to U.S. to escape pogroms.

**1882** John D. Rockefeller organizes Standard Oil trust, first such combination. Congress passes first Chinese Exclusion Act (May 10), which would be renewed for decades, and legislates first immigration restrictions: no paupers, convicts, or mental defectives (Aug. 3). Polygamists forbidden to vote or hold office. Knights of Columbus founded with permission from Roman Catholic church.

**1883** Congress passes Pendleton Act, requiring civil service competition for federal jobs. Brooklyn Bridge opened in New York. Supreme Court strikes down Civil Rights Act of 1875 (Oct. 15). New York–Chicago telephone service begins. Ohio River floods devastate Cincinnati. U.S. Navy builds its first steel ships. Railroads agree on standard time zones for North America.

**1884** "Mugwumps" bolt Republican party. Statue of Liberty cornerstone laid (Aug. 5). Belva A. Lockwood of Equal Rights party first woman candidate for president. Grover Cleveland of New York first Democrat elected president since Civil War. Home Insurance building of Chicago first skyscraper in world. Moses Fleetwood Walker first black professional baseball player.

**1885** Washington Monument completed after 36 years of construction. U.S. Post Office begins Special Delivery service. U.S. Marines land in Panama (Apr. 24). Senate refuses to ratify treaty for building canal across Nicaragua. Congress outlaws building fences on public lands in West. Stanford University founded in Palo Alto, Calif. Josiah Strong's best-seller *Our Country* argues for American imperialism.

**1886** Knights of Labor rail strike sets off national wave of strikes for eight-hour day. Haymarket Riot in Chicago leads to execution of seven anarchists. Pres. Cleveland has first White House wedding (June 2). Statue of Liberty in New York Harbor dedicated (Oct. 28). American Federation of Labor (AFL) founded in Columbus, Ohio. Indian wars end with capture of Geronimo. U.S. Treasury begins accumulating large revenue surplus.

**1887** Congress creates Interstate Commerce Commission, the first federal regulatory agency, but with weak enforcement powers. Pres. Cleveland orders Confederate battle flags returned to South, provoking outcry (June 7). Congress distributes reservation land to Indians; also bans opium imports. First electric trolley line built in Richmond, Va. U.S. Navy leases base at Pearl Harbor, Hawaii. First American golf club founded in Foxburg, Pa.

**1888** Snow falls for 36 hours in New York, killing 400 people in Great Blizzard of '88 (Mar. 12). First secret-ballot election held in Louisville, Ky. George Eastman brings first Kodak camera onto market. National Geographic Society founded in Washington, D.C. Edward Bellamy's utopian novel, *Looking Backward*, becomes sensational best-seller.

**1889** Four new states—N.Dak., S.Dak., Mont., Wash.—all admitted in one day (Feb. 22). Oklahoma Land Rush results when former Indian territory opened for settlement (Apr. 22). Johnstown Flood claims thousands of lives in Pennsylvania (May 31). Kansas passes first antitrust law. Jane Addams founds Hull House in Chicago. First all-American college football players chosen. Tower Building, the first New York skyscraper, completed.

**1890** Congress passes Sherman Antitrust Act (July 2) and Sherman Silver Purchase Act. Wyoming admitted as first state with women's suffrage (July 10). Sioux uprising ends at Battle of Wounded Knee (Dec. 29). Yosemite National Park created. Mormons renounce polygamy. Mississippi leads South in disfranchising black voters. Jacob Riis's *How the Other Half Lives* awakens Americans to problem of urban poverty. First Army-Navy football game played—Navy 24, Army 0.

**1891** Pres. Grover Cleveland denounces "dangerous and reckless experiment" of silver coinage. New Orleans mob lynches 11 Italian immigrants. People's, or Populist, party organized in Cincinnati. U.S. and Chile nearly go to war over death of two American sailors in Valparaiso (Oct. 16). Dr. James A. Naismith invents basketball in Springfield, Mass. Thomas Edison patents first American-made motion picture camera.

**1892** Immigrants begin landing at Ellis Island in New York (Jan. 1). Populist candidate James B. Weaver of Iowa receives over million votes for president. Violent strikes break out among steelworkers in Homestead, Pa., and among silver miners in Coeur d'Alene, Idaho. Chinese immigrants forced to register with federal government. George W.G. Ferris invents Ferris Wheel. First gasoline-powered American automobile built in Chicopee, Mass. Boll weevil first appears in Texas.

**1893** U.S. gold reserve falls below $100 million (Apr. 21). Panic of 1893, touched off by New York stock market crash (June 27), begins second-worst depression in U.S. history. Congress repeals Sherman Silver Purchase Act (Oct. 30). Hawaii requests U.S. annexation. Mormon Temple dedicated in Salt Lake City, Utah. Thousands perish in Louisiana cyclone. Frank Lloyd Wright completes first solo project, the Winslow home in Chicago.

**1894** Coxey's Army of unemployed march on Washington, D.C. (Apr. 30). U.S. Treasury issues two $50-million bond offerings to shore up dwindling gold reserves. Congress enacts first peacetime federal income tax, denounced as "socialism, communism, devilism" (Aug. 27). Pullman strike paralyzes railroads across nation. Senate refuses to annex Hawaii. Thomas Edison exhibits his kinetoscope.

**1895** Billionaire banker J.P. Morgan bails out U.S. Treasury, faced with gold drain. "Silver Democrats" appeal for unlimited silver coinage as way out of depression. Supreme Court rules income tax unconstitutional (May 20). Venezuelan boundary dispute brings U.S. and Britain close to war. Cuban insurrection against Spanish rule begins, winning American sympathy. National Association of Manufacturers formed in Cincinnati. First professional football game played in Latrobe, Pa.

**1896** Supreme Court approves segregation (*Plessy* v. *Ferguson*). William Jennings Bryan, "Silver Democrat" of Nebraska, wins nomination with "Cross of Gold" speech (July 7). Gold discovered in Klondike, Alaska, defusing money question (Aug. 16). American athletes sweep nine of 12 events at first International Olympics. Henry Ford builds his first automobile. First American motion pictures appear in theaters. "The Yellow Kid," first comic strip, begins running in New York *World*. First American hockey league organized in New York.

**1897** U.S. and Britain consent to arbitration of boundary disputes in Olney-Pauncefote Convention (Jan. 11). Venezuelan boundary dispute ends with Britain accepting arbitration. Klondike gold rush to Alaska moves into full swing. Senate again refuses to annex Hawaii. U.S. offers to mediate Cuban rebellion; lodges official complaint against Spanish brutality. "Yellow press" newspapers keep up constant assault on Spain. First American subway completed in Boston.

**1898** After mysterious explosion of battleship *Maine* in Havana harbor (Feb. 15), Spanish-American War breaks out (Apr. 21). Commodore George Dewey destroys Spanish fleet at Manila Bay (May 1), and U.S. takes Manila (Aug. 13). After Battle of San Juan Hill (July 1), Spanish garrison at Santiago, Cuba, surrenders (July 17). U.S. takes Cuba, Puerto Rico, Guam, Wake Island, and Philippines from Spain in Treaty of Paris (Dec. 10). Senate finally agrees to annex Hawaii.

**1899** Philippine Revolt against U.S. rule erupts. Sec. of State John Hay issues Open Door notes to European powers and Japan, requesting no spheres of influence in China (Sept. 6). U.S. and Germany agree to partition Samoan Islands (Dec. 2). Congress investigates incompetence in War Department, revealed during Spanish-American War. William McKinley first president to ride in an automobile.

**1900** "Hard Money" triumphs as U.S. returns to single gold standard (Mar. 14). Puerto Rico and Hawaii become U.S. territories by acts of Congress (Apr. 12 and 30). U.S. troops relieve foreign legations under siege in Peking, China, during Boxer Rebellion (Aug. 14). Olds Co. opens first Detroit, Mich., auto factory. Carrie Nation leads hatchet-wielding women into Kansas saloons to smash liquor barrels. Professional baseball's American League organized. Census lists U.S. population above 75 million for first time (75,994,575).

**1901** J.P. Morgan creates U.S. Steel, first billion-dollar corporation. U.S. retains control over Cuba with Platt Amendment. Pres. McKinley shot by anarchist Leon Czolgosz in Buffalo, N.Y. (Sept. 6; dies Sept. 14). Hay-Pauncefote Treaty secures British approval for U.S.-built canal in Panama (Nov. 18). First great Texas oil strike made near Beaumont, Tex. Army War College opens in Washington, D.C. Pres. Theodore Roosevelt promises to "speak softly and carry a big stick."

**1902** End of Philippine Insurrection. Reclamation Act initiates federal policy of conservation of natural resources (June 17). Congress declares Philippines an unorganized territory and its inhabitants non-U.S. citizens (July 1). Pres. Roosevelt escapes injury in trolley car accident near Pittsfield, Mass. First Tournament of Roses football game (later known as Rose Bowl) played—Michigan 49, Stanford 0. Pres. Roosevelt helps mediate Pennsylvania coal strike.

**1903** U.S. prevails over Canada in Alaskan boundary dispute. Pres. Roosevelt helps Panama gain independence from Colombia, then negotiates treaty to build Panama Canal (Nov. 2–18). Orville and Wilbur Wright conduct first powered flight near Kitty Hawk, N.C. (Dec. 17). *The Great Train Robbery*, first feature-length motion picture, appears in theaters. Wisconsin holds first primary elections. Ford Motor Co. formed. Boston defeats Pittsburgh in first baseball World Series.

**1904** Supreme Court upholds antitrust dissolution of Northern Securities company (Mar. 14). Pres. Roosevelt wins reelection and says he will not run again (Nov. 8). "Roosevelt Corollary" to Monroe Doctrine justifies U.S. intervention to keep other powers out of western hemisphere (Dec. 6). First New York City subway opened. New York State enacts first speed limit: 20 mph on open roads. Publication of Lincoln Steffens's *The Shame of the Cities*, well-known muckraking book. Deaf, dumb, and blind, Helen Keller graduates with honors from Radcliffe College.

**1905** Supreme Court disallows limits on length of working day. Industrial Workers of the World, a radical labor union, formed in Chicago. Pres. Roosevelt mediates Treaty of Portsmouth, ending Russo-Japanese War (Sept. 5). U.S. takes control of Santo Domingo trade. Black leaders hold Niagara Falls Conference, calling for equal rights. Winslow's Soothing Syrup for babies found to contain morphine and poison.

**1906** San Francisco destroyed by earthquake and fire (Apr. 18–19). Responding to consumer pressure, Congress passes Pure Food and Drug Act and Meat Inspection Act (June 30). Race riot breaks out in Atlanta (Sept. 22). Japan protests segregation of Asian students in California schools (Oct. 25). Pres. Roosevelt first American to win Nobel Peace Prize and first sitting president to leave U.S. on visit to Panama.

**1907** Panic of 1907 triggers crash on Wall Street (Mar. 13) and run on banks across nation. Pres. Roosevelt orders exclusion of Japanese laborers (Mar. 14). U.S. Navy's Great White Fleet embarks on tour around world (Dec. 16). Congress outlaws corporate contributions to political campaigns. Hundreds killed in coal mine explosions in Monongah, W.Va., and Jacobs Creek, Pa. All-time-record 1,285,349 immigrants arrive in one year.

**1908** U.S. and Japan conclude "Gentleman's Agreement" limiting immigration. Ford Model T appears on market (Oct. 1). Root-Takahira Agreement promises U.S. and Japan will respect each other's interests in Pacific. Pres. Roosevelt appoints National Conservation Commission. Federal Bureau of Investigation established. New York City outlaws women smoking in public. Lt. Thomas W. Selfridge, U.S. Army, first American air crash fatality. Gideons place their first Bible in hotel in Iron Mountain, Mont.

**1909** Robert E. Peary plants American flag at North Pole (Apr. 6). Pres. William Howard Taft opens 700,000 acres for settlement in West. W.E.B. DuBois founds National Association for the Advancement of Colored People (NAACP), advocating racial equality. U.S. Mint issues first Lincoln-head pennies. U.S. troops land in Nicaragua.

**1910** Theodore Roosevelt calls for "New Nationalism" in speech at Osawatomie, Kans. (Aug. 31). *Los Angeles Times* building destroyed by terrorist bomb (Oct. 1). Glacier National Park created. Mann Act cracks down on "white slave" trade. Milwaukee, Wis., elects socialist mayor and congressman. Boy Scouts of America chartered. Ballinger-Pinchot controversy reveals major differences over conservation policy in Taft administration. Barney Oldfield sets land speed record (133 mph) in Daytona Beach, Fla.

**1911** Sen. Robert M. LaFollette of Wisconsin founds National Progressive Republican League to promote reform (Jan. 21). Pres. Taft orders U.S. troops to border during Mexican Revolution. Supreme Court upholds antitrust break-ups of Standard Oil (May 15) and American Tobacco (May 29). Calbraith P. Rodgers makes first transcontinental airplane flight. U.S. bankers take control of Nicaragua's finances. Steel magnate Andrew Carnegie donates $125 million for philanthropic purposes.

**1912** *Titanic* sinks on maiden voyage from England (Apr. 15). Congress approves free-trade tariff reciprocity with Canada (July 22), rejected by Canadian Parliament (Sept. 21). Progressive, or "Bull Moose," party founded by Theodore Roosevelt, who survives assassination attempt by John Schrank in Milwaukee, Wis. (Oct. 14). Massachusetts adopts first minimum wage law. U.S. Marines land in Honduras, Cuba, Nicaragua, and Santo Domingo. Textile strike in Lawrence, Mass.

**1913** Sixteenth Amendment empowers federal government to collect income taxes (Feb. 25), and 17th Amendment allows for popular election of U.S. senators (May 31). Congress creates Federal Reserve system. Ford Motor Co. introduces assembly line. John D. Rockefeller donates $100 million to philanthropic Rockefeller Foundation. Civil War veterans hold 50th anniversary reunion at Gettysburg. Grand Central Station opens in New York City.

**1914** Pres. Woodrow Wilson nearly goes to war with Mexico over arrests of American sailors in Tampico (Apr. 14). U.S. Navy shells Vera Cruz and lands marines in retaliation (Apr. 21). U.S. declares neutrality in World War I (Aug. 4). Congress passes Clayton Act, toughening antitrust standards. Yale Bowl, the first full-size football stadium, opened in New Haven, Conn. Congress proclaims Mother's Day.

**1915** *Birth of a Nation* first movie blockbuster. Panama-Pacific International Exposition opens in miraculously rebuilt San Francisco. Pres. Wilson strongly protests German sinking of *Lusitania* with 128 Americans aboard (May 7). U.S. Marines land in Haiti (July 28). J.P. Morgan arranges $500-million war loan to France and Britain. Ku Klux Klan revived in Atlanta, Ga. Coast-to-coast long-distance telephone service begins.

**1916** House-Grey Memorandum warns Germany that refusal to negotiate may bring U.S. into World War I. Gen. John Pershing chases Pancho Villa into Mexico after border raid on Columbus, N.Mex. (Mar. 15). Britain blacklists U.S. firms doing business with Germany. U.S. acquires Virgin Islands from Denmark for $25 million (Aug. 4). Pres. Wilson wins reelection with slogan He Kept Us out of War (Nov. 7). Jeanette Rankin of Montana first woman elected to Congress. Louis D. Brandeis first Jewish member of Supreme Court. Margaret Sanger opens first birth-control clinic in Brooklyn, N.Y. National Park Service created.

**1917** Germany resumes unrestricted submarine warfare, leading U.S. to sever diplomatic relations (Feb. 3). Gen. John Pershing withdraws from Mexico. Zimmerman Telegram, intercepted by British intelligence and made public, reveals German overtures to Mexico in case of war (Feb. 24). U.S. merchant ships armed for self-defense against German submarines (Mar. 13). After Pres. Wilson proclaims "world must be made safe for democracy," Congress declares war on Germany (Apr. 6) and Austria-Hungary (Dec. 7), bringing U.S. into World War I. Prohibition begins as wartime conservation measure (Aug. 10). Race riot breaks out in East St. Louis, Mo. American soldiers begin fighting in Europe.

**1918** Pres. Wilson announces U.S. war aims in "Fourteen Points" speech (Jan. 8). U.S. troops join Allied intervention in Russian Revolution (Aug. 2). Congress passes Sedition Act. Over million U.S. troops participate in monthlong Meuse-Argonne campaign (Sept. 26–Nov. 11). Republicans win control of Congress, a rebuke to Pres. Wilson (Nov. 5). Armistice Day ends World War I (Nov. 11); mass celebrations break out across country. Pres. Wilson goes to Europe for peace conference (Dec. 4). Supreme Court approves draft laws and strikes down child labor laws. Influenza epidemic takes hundreds of thousands of American lives.

**1919** Eighteenth Amendment establishes Prohibition (Jan. 29). Strike wave sweeps country, triggering Red Scare. American Communist party organized in Chicago. Race riots in Washington, D.C., and Chicago (July 19 and 27). Pres. Wilson suffers incapacitating stroke during nationwide speaking tour (Sept. 26). Volstead Act implements national Prohibition enforcement. Versailles Treaty, including League of Nations, rejected by Senate (Nov. 19). Grand Canyon National Park created. New York–Chicago daily airmail service begins.

**1920** Atty. Gen. A. Mitchell Palmer stages "Palmer Raids," arresting and deporting thousands of radicals and immigrants. Sacco and Vanzetti arrested for murder in Braintree, Mass. (May 5). Supreme Court upholds Prohibition. Nineteenth Amendment establishes women's suffrage (Aug. 26). National League of Women Voters organized. Wall Street rocked by terrorist bomb, killing 30 bystanders (Sept. 16). First regular radio broadcasts begin in East Pittsburgh, Pa. Pres. Wilson receives Nobel Peace Prize. U.S. population, more urban than rural for first time, tops 100 million (105,710,620).

**1921** Pres. Warren G. Harding, promising "return to normalcy," takes office. U.S. agrees to compensate Colombia for supporting Panama revolution and seizing Panama Canal. Former Pres. William Howard Taft receives job he wants most, chief justice of U.S. (June 30). U.S. negotiates separate peace with Germany, Austria, and Hungary. Ku Klux Klan spreads terror in South. International disarmament conference meets in Washington, D.C. Jack Dempsey defeats Georges Carpentier in first million-dollar prize fight.

**1922** Washington Conference concludes with nine international treaties to limit naval arms race, relax tensions in Pacific, and protect China. Supreme Court upholds women's suffrage. Lincoln Memorial dedicated in Washington, D.C. (May 30). Pres. Harding vetoes "Bonus Bill" for World War I veterans. Congress passes joint resolution in favor of Jewish homeland in Palestine (Sept. 21). Narcotics Control Board established. First commercial radio show broadcast in New York.

**1923** Last U.S. occupation troops leave Germany (Jan. 10). Senate begins investigating corruption in Veterans Bureau and Teapot Dome oil leases (Oct. 25). Pres. Harding dies mysteriously of "apoplexy" in San Francisco (Aug. 2). Pres. Calvin Coolidge's address to Congress, calling for economy in government, first radio broadcast of a presidential speech (Dec. 6). Oklahoma declares martial law to crack down on Ku Klux Klan. Yankee Stadium opens in New York.

**1924** Congress provides bonuses for World War I veterans over Pres. Coolidge's veto. Congress passes Immigration Act, imposing strict national quota system. European powers accept Dawes Plan for repayment of war debts and reparations. U.S. Marines withdraw from Santo Domingo. Coast-to-coast airmail service begins. Ford Motor Co. turns out its 10-millionth automobile.

**1925** Tennessee outlaws teaching evolution in school, leading to Scopes Trial in Dayton, Tenn. (July 10–21). Ku Klux Klan marches on Washington, D.C. (Aug. 8). Nellie Tayloe Ross of Wyoming first woman governor. Florida land boom draws hordes of speculators. Col. Billy Mitchell suspended from U.S. Army for advocating stronger air force. Chicago gang wars break out as Al Capone consolidates bootlegging operations.

**1926** Sec. of Treasury Andrew Mellon's drastic tax cuts approved. Adm. Richard E. Byrd and Floyd Bennett first to fly over North Pole (May 9). Henry Ford institutes eight-hour day and five-day work week at Ford Motor Co. factories (Sept. 25). Hurricane sweeps Florida, killing 372 people. Book of the Month Club founded. California evangelist Aimee Semple MacPherson fakes her own kidnapping to draw publicity. U.S. Marines return to Nicaragua.

**1927** Charles Lindbergh completes nonstop solo flight from New York to Paris (May 20–21); returns home to huge welcoming crowds. Sacco and Vanzetti executed in Massachusetts, despite international protests (Aug. 23). *The Jazz Singer* with Al Jolson becomes first "talkie" motion picture (Oct. 6). Holland Tunnel in New York opened. Mississippi River floods, causes $300-million damage. Ford Model A unveiled. Mechanical cotton picker invented. New York–London commercial telephone service begins.

**1928** U.S. joins 14 countries in signing Kellogg-Briand Pact for "outlawry of war" (Aug. 27). Clark Memorandum disavows future U.S. interventions in Latin America. Pres. Coolidge refuses to aid American farmers mired in agricultural depression. Walt Disney creates "Steamboat Willie," first Mickey Mouse cartoon. George Eastman demonstrates color motion-picture technology. Republicans promise a "chicken in every pot, a car in every garage."

**1929** St. Valentine's Day Massacre claims six lives in Chicago gang wars. Young Plan replaces Dawes Plan for payment of war debts and reparations. Ramsay MacDonald first prime minister of Great Britain to address Congress (Oct. 7). Albert B. Fall, former secretary of interior, found guilty in Teapot Dome scandal (Oct.

25). Stock market crash on "Black Friday" (Oct. 29) ushers in Great Depression. Supreme Court upholds "pocket veto." Pres. Hoover insists business confidence is intact.

**1930** Wave of bank failures sweeps U.S., wiping out millions of savings accounts and leading to private hoarding of gold. Chicago bootlegging outfit worth $50 million broken up. U.S., Britain, and Japan sign London Naval Treaty limiting naval arms race (Apr. 22). Hawley-Smoot Tariff raises barriers to world trade, worsening depression (June 17). Congress creates Veteran's Administration (July 3). Hoover Dam begun near Las Vegas, Nev. The planet Pluto discovered.

**1931** World War I veterans offered "Bonus Loans" to combat Great Depression. "Star Spangled Banner" becomes national anthem. "Scottsboro Boys" arrested for rape in Alabama. Empire State Building, tallest building in world, opened in New York City. Pres. Herbert Hoover declares moratorium on international debt and reparations payments. George Washington Bridge over Hudson River completed.

**1932** Stimson Doctrine announces U.S. disapproval of Japanese invasion of China. Congress approves Reconstruction Finance Corporation to help recovery. Norris-LaGuardia Act restricts use of injunctions against labor strikes. Franklin D. Roosevelt, promising "New Deal" for Americans, elected president in Democratic landslide. Stock market drops to 10% of its 1929 value; national income cut in half. "Bonus Army" of poor veterans marches on Washington, D.C. Amelia Earhart first woman to fly solo across Atlantic.

**1933** Giuseppe Zangara kills Chicago Mayor Anton J. Cermak in Miami, Fla., motorcade, narrowly missing president-elect Franklin D. Roosevelt (Feb. 15). Banks closed for four days by presidential order (Mar. 5). During "Hundred Days" (Mar. 9-June 16), Pres. Roosevelt pushes New Deal through Congress, conducts first "fireside chat" on radio, and takes U.S. off gold standard. Beer and wine made legal again (Mar. 22). Congress passes National Industrial Recovery Act (June 16). U.S. recognizes Soviet Union (Nov. 16). U.S. Marines withdraw from Nicaragua. Frances Perkins, secretary of labor, becomes first woman cabinet member.

**1934** Dust storms inundate Southwest, driving "Okies" and "Arkies" to California. General strike paralyzes San Francisco (July 16). John Dillinger, public enemy number one, killed by FBI agents (July 22). Upton Sinclair mounts unsuccessful EPIC (End Poverty in California) campaign for governor. Sen. Gerald P. Nye of North Dakota begins investigating role of U.S. munitions manufacturers in World War I. U.S. releases Cuba from Platt Amendment. U.S. troops withdrawn from Haiti. Roman Catholic Legion of Decency begins censoring motion pictures.

**1935** Supreme Court invalidates National Industrial Recovery Act. Pres. Roosevelt pushes more "Second New Deal" legislation through Congress, notably Wagner Act protecting unions (July 5), Social Security Act (Aug. 14), and "soak-the-rich" Wealth Tax Act (Aug. 30). Sen. Huey

P. Long of Louisiana assassinated (Sept. 8). Congress of Industrial Organization (CIO) formed (Nov. 9). Congress passes first Neutrality Act. Alcoholics Anonymous founded.

**1936** Congress passes second Neutrality Act. France, Britain, and U.S. sign New London Naval Treaty (Mar. 25). U.S. declares neutrality in Spanish Civil War (Aug. 7). Congress of Industrial Organizations auto workers begin sit-down strikes in Flint, Mich. (Dec. 30). *Life* magazine begins publishing. William "Liberty Bell" Lemke, Republican of North Dakota, runs for president on Union party ticket endorsed by radio demagogue Father Charles E. Coughlin. Jesse Owens wins four gold medals at "Nazi Olympics" in Berlin.

**1937** Congress passes third Neutrality Act. Pres. Roosevelt proposes controversial "court-packing" plan. German dirigible *Hindenburg* explodes and burns in Lakehurst, N.J. (May 6). Pres. Roosevelt angers isolationists with "Quarantine Speech" (Oct. 5). Japanese planes sink U.S. Navy gunboat *Panay* in China (Dec. 12). Golden Gate Bridge completed in San Francisco. Slow recovery ends abruptly as economic depression worsens.

**1938** Republican gains in Congress signal end of New Deal. Pres. Roosevelt calls for military buildup (Jan. 28). Mexico seizes U.S.-owned oil wells (Mar. 18). Rep. Martin Dies of Texas begins House Un-American Activities Committee (HUAC) investigations of Communists and Fascists. Howard Hughes sets record for around-the-world flight in less than four days (July 14). "Invasion from Mars" radio broadcast by Orson Welles causes widespread panic (Oct. 30). Hurricane devastates Atlantic Coast, killing 700 people.

**1939** Supreme Court upholds Tennessee Valley Authority. First food stamp program begins in Rochester, N.Y. (May 16). Pan Am begins first regular transatlantic passenger service from New York to Lisbon, Portugal (June 28). U.S. declares neutrality in World War II (Sept. 5). Congress passes fourth Neutrality Act, approving Pres. Roosevelt's request for "cash-and-carry" arms sales to belligerents. Nylon stockings appear on market.

**1940** As World War II engulfs Europe, Pres. Roosevelt announces U.S. has moved from "neutrality" to "non-belligerency" (June 10). U.S. and Britain conclude Destroyers-for-Bases deal (Sept. 2). Congress enacts a peacetime draft (Sept. 16) and massive increases in military spending. Over 16 million men register for draft as Pres. Roosevelt's embargo on strategic exports takes effect. Roosevelt, reelected to unprecedented third term, calls for U.S. to become "arsenal of democracy" (Dec. 20). Both the Committee to Defend America by Aiding the Allies and the isolationist America First Committee organized.

**1941** Congress appropriates $7 billion in Lend-Lease aid to Britain. German submarine sinks merchant ship *Robin Moor*, first U.S. casualty of war (May 21). Roosevelt responds by declaring "unlimited national emergency" (May 27), freezing German and Italian assets in U.S. (June

14) and promising aid to USSR (June 24). Roosevelt freezes Japanese assets in retaliation for invasion of Indochina (July 25). Pres. Roosevelt and Prime Minister Winston Churchill issue Atlantic Charter (Aug. 12). U.S. Navy is ordered to "shoot on sight" at German warships (Sept. 11). "America has been attacked, the shooting has started," Pres. Roosevelt informs nation (Oct. 27). Japanese planes attack Pearl Harbor, Hawaii, killing 2,400 U.S. servicemen and civilians (Dec. 7). U.S. declares war on Japan (Dec. 10). Germany and Italy declare war on U.S. (Dec. 11). U.S. declares war on Germany and Italy (Dec. 11).

**1942** Roosevelt creates War Production Board, calls for mass mobilization, and puts New Deal on hold. U.S. troops land in North Ireland, first to arrive in Europe (Jan. 26). Pres. Roosevelt approves internment of Japanese-Americans for duration of war (Feb. 20). Japanese submarine shells an oil refinery in Santa Barbara, Calif. (Feb. 23). Maj. James H. Doolittle stages carrier-launched bombing raid on Tokyo (Apr. 18). U.S. forces surrender in Philippines (May 6) but win major naval victories over Japan in Coral Sea (May 4–8) and at Midway (June 3–6). U.S. offensive begins in Pacific with invasion of Guadalcanal Island (Aug. 7). First all-U.S. bombing attack launched against German forces at Rouen, France (Aug. 17). Congress approves "Victory Tax" on wartime incomes (Oct. 21). Allies land 400,000 men in North Africa (Nov. 7–8). Eight German saboteurs apprehended in New York; six executed. Cocoanut Grove nightclub fire in Boston claims lives of 492 patrons.

**1943** Congress appropriates $100 billion for war effort. Roosevelt and Prime Minister Winston Churchill demand "unconditional surrender" at Casablanca conference in Morocco (Jan. 24). U.S. Marines drive last Japanese from Guadalcanal (Feb. 9). U.S. troops defeated in first battle with Germans at Kasserine Pass, Tunisia (Feb. 20). Pres. Roosevelt declares wage-and-price freeze to stem inflation (Apr. 8). U.S. and Britain invade Sicily (July 10) and Italy proper (Sept. 3). Roosevelt and Churchill meet with Chiang Kai-shek of China in Cairo, Egypt (Nov. 22), and with Josef Stalin of Soviet Union in Tehran, Iran (Dec. 4–6). Gen. Dwight D. Eisenhower named Supreme Commander of Allied Forces in Europe. Congress approves federal income tax withholding. Race riots in Detroit and Harlem leave 40 dead. Chicago opens its first subway.

**1944** U.S. and British planes begin around-the-clock bombing of Berlin. Allied forces land at Anzio, Italy (Jan. 22). Congress approves $1.35 billion for UN Relief and Reconstruction Agency, first U.S. foreign aid (Mar. 29). Allied forces enter Rome (June 5) as reconquest of Europe begins with D-Day invasion of Normandy (June 6). Allied breakout from Normandy sends German forces reeling across France (July 25). Postwar financial arrangements made at international conference in Bretton Woods, N.H. (July 1–22). Plans for UN made at Dumbarton Oaks conference (Aug. 21–Oct. 7). Gen. Douglas MacArthur begins reconquest of Philippines with landings at Leyte Gulf (Oct. 20). Congress passes

Servicemen's Readjustment Act, known as "GI Bill of Rights." Roosevelt wins fourth term.

**1945** Roosevelt, Churchill, and Stalin meet for last time at Yalta in Soviet Crimea to begin postwar planning (Feb. 4–11). Allied forces cross Rhine River and drive into heart of Germany (Mar. 7). U.S. air raids destroy Tokyo (Mar. 10–11). Pres. Roosevelt dies suddenly of cerebral hemorrhage in Warm Springs, Ga. (Apr. 12). UN Conference begins meeting in San Francisco (Apr. 24). Germany surrenders, ending war in Europe (May 7). Fifty nations sign UN Charter (June 26). First atomic explosion occurs in test at Alamagordo, N. Mex. (July 16). Pres. Harry S Truman meets with Churchill and Stalin at Potsdam, Germany (July 17–Aug. 2). Atomic bombs dropped on Hiroshima (Aug. 6) and Nagasaki (Aug. 9); Japan surrenders (Aug. 14), ending World War II. Council of Allied Foreign Ministers meets in London, unable to agree on peace treaty (Dec. 16–27). Television channels are allotted for commercial use. Empire State Building hit by B-25 bomber in heavy fog.

**1946** Strike wave sweeps U.S., idling 4.6 million U.S. workers. Congress passes Employment Act, committing federal government to postwar economic management. Winston Churchill warns Americans about Communist expansion with "Iron Curtain" speech at Westminster College in Fulton, Mo. (Mar. 5). Pres. Truman seizes control of railroads and coal mines during strikes. Paris Peace Conference ends in failure (July 29–Oct. 15). U.S. presents Baruch Plan for international control of atomic energy, grants independence to Philippines (July 4), and agrees to loan Britain $3.5 billion for postwar reconstruction. Congress creates Atomic Energy Commission. UN General Assembly begins meeting in New York. John D. Rockefeller, Jr., donates $8.5 million for UN Headquarters. Most wartime wage and price controls lifted. Dr. Benjamin Spock publishes influential guidebook on baby care.

**1947** Council of Foreign Ministers meets in Moscow, again unable to agree on peace treaty (Mar. 10–Apr. 24). Pres. Truman announces Truman Doctrine, promising aid to countries threatened by subversion (May 12). Sec. of State George C. Marshall announces Marshall Plan for postwar reconstruction of Europe (June 5). Republican-dominated Congress restricts union organizing with Taft-Hartley Act. House Committee on Un-American Activities (HUAC) begins investigating communism in Hollywood (Oct. 20). Council of Foreign Ministers meets for last time in London (Nov. 25–Dec. 16). Texas City, Tex., wiped out when munitions ship explodes, killing over 500 people. Jackie Robinson of Brooklyn Dodgers breaks color line in baseball.

**1948** Postwar inflation keeps prices rising fast. Congress approves $5.3 billion for Marshall Plan aid to Europe with Foreign Assistance Act. U.S. recognizes new state of Israel (May 14) and admits 205,000 war refugees from Europe. Britain and U.S. begin airlifting supplies into West Berlin after Soviets cut off all traffic into city (June 26). Pres. Truman orders peacetime draft and desegregation of U.S. armed forces. HUAC charges Alger Hiss with spying for

Soviet Union. Pres. Truman wins upset reelection victory over Republican candidate Thomas E. Dewey of New York, despite Progressive and Dixiecrat walkouts from Democratic party. Idlewild International Airport, largest in world, opens in New York.

**1949** Pres. Truman calls for "Fair Deal" domestic programs and "Point Four" foreign aid programs. U.S., Canada, and 10 Western European nations sign treaty that will lead to North Atlantic Treaty Organization (NATO). Berlin Airlift ends when Soviets finally lift blockade (May 12). State Department issues "white paper" disclaiming responsibility for Communist takeover in China. Pres. Truman announces Soviet atomic bomb test (Sept. 23). Eleven U.S. Communist leaders convicted of conspiring to overthrow government. UN Headquarters on East River dedicated in New York City (Oct. 24). Steel strike idles half a million workers nationwide (Oct. 1–Nov. 11). *Lucky Lady II* of U.S. Air Force completes first nonstop around-the-world flight.

**1950** Sen. Joseph R. McCarthy of Wisconsin issues his first accusations of Communists in government at speech in Wheeling, W.Va. North Korea invades South Korea, beginning Korean War (June 25). Pres. Truman orders U.S. intervention (June 27), obtains UN support (July 7), asks Congress for a $10-billion rearmament program (July 20), and calls up reserves (Aug. 4). Inchon landing begins rout of North Korean invaders (Sept. 15). Congress passes Internal Security Act, requiring registration of Communist organizations, over Pres. Truman's veto (Sept. 23). UN troops recapture Seoul (Sept. 26) and invade North Korea (Oct. 7). Puerto Rican nationalists nearly assassinate Pres. Truman in Washington (Nov. 11). After China intervenes in Korean War, Pres. Truman proclaims national emergency (Dec. 16). U.S. population tops 150 million (150,697,361).

**1951** Gen. Dwight D. Eisenhower comes out of retirement to accept command of Allied forces in Europe (Apr. 4). Julius and Ethel Rosenberg sentenced to death for spying (atom bomb secrets) for Soviets (Apr. 5). Pres. Truman removes Gen. Douglas MacArthur from command in Korea for insubordination (Apr. 11). MacArthur returns to U.S., greeted by exultant crowds, to deliver address to Congress. Missouri River floods devastate Kansas City, causing over $1 billion in damages (July 11–25). U.S. concludes a mutual defense pact with Australia and New Zealand and signs a peace treaty with Japan (Sept. 8). Congress passes Mutual Security Act, providing $7 billion for foreign aid and military cooperation with pro-U.S. nations. Sen. Estes Kefauver of Tennessee investigates gambling and organized crime. CBS transmits first color television broadcast from New York.

**1952** Pres. Truman seizes steel mills paralyzed by strikes (Apr. 8). U.S., Britain, and France sign peace treaty with West Germany (May 26). GI Bill extended to Korean War veterans. Construction begins on USS *Nautilus*, first atomic submarine. Supreme Court upholds barring subversives from teaching in schools. Sen. Richard M. Nixon of California, Republican candidate for vice president, delivers "Checkers Speech" on national television to explain his "secret slush fund." Republicans win control of White House and both houses of Congress for first time since 1928. Supreme Court rejects appeal of Julius and Ethel Rosenberg. U.S. announces first successful hydrogen bomb test at Eniwetok Atoll in Marshall Islands (Nov. 16). Pres.-elect Dwight D. Eisenhower visits U.S. troops in Korea.

**1953** Sen. John W. Bricker of Ohio proposes sharp limits on presidential powers to make treaties. Thirteen more Communist leaders convicted of conspiring to overthrow government. Julius and Ethel Rosenberg executed in Ossining, N.Y. (June 19). Pres. Eisenhower lifts wage and price controls, increases U.S. support for French war effort in Indochina, negotiates armistice ending Korean War (June 27). Congress creates Department of Health, Education, and Welfare (Apr. 1). U.S. pledges aid to Spain in exchange for military bases (Sept. 26). First "atomic cannon" tested in Nevada. Maj. Chuck Yeager of U.S. Air Force sets new air speed record in rocket-powered X-1 jet plane. *The Robe* first motion picture in CinemaScope.

**1954** Sec. of State John Foster Dulles vows "massive retaliation" against Soviet aggression (Jan. 12). Foreign Ministers Conference in Berlin fails to achieve reunification of Germany (Jan. 25–Feb. 18). Puerto Rican nationalists shoot five Congressmen on floor of House of Representatives (Mar. 1). U.S. negotiates the Southeast Asia Treaty Organization (SEATO) security pact (Sept. 8). Army-McCarthy hearings discredit Sen. Joseph McCarthy and his methods. Supreme Court orders school desegregation in *Brown* decision (May 17). CIA helps overthrow Arbenz government in Guatemala (June 29). Congress passes Communist Control Act. Senate censures Sen. McCarthy. France announces that U.S. has paid for most of Indochina war. New York Stock Exchange prices finally reattain 1929 levels.

**1955** Pres. Eisenhower promises to use atomic weapons in case of war and conducts first televised press conference. U.S., Soviet Union, and Allies agree on Austrian peace treaty to end occupation. Summit conference of U.S., British, French, and Soviet leaders in Switzerland produces "spirit of Geneva." Supreme Court orders school desegregation to proceed "with all deliberate speed." Pres. Eisenhower hospitalized for three weeks following heart attack. Interstate Commerce Commission orders desegregation on interstate trains and buses. AFL and CIO labor federations merge to form AFL-CIO, with 15 million members (Dec. 5). Dr. Jonas Salk perfects polio vaccine. Civil rights leader Dr. Martin Luther King, Jr., leads bus boycott in Montgomery, Ala.

**1956** Pres. Eisenhower refuses to intervene against Soviet invasion of Hungary and exerts pressure on Allies to withdraw from Suez. Congressmen signing Southern Manifesto promise "massive resistance" to school desegregation. Atomic Energy Commission approves commercial nuclear power plants. Congress passes Highway Act, appropriating $32 billion for construction of vast nationwide road system. TWA and United airliners collide in midair and crash in

Grand Canyon, killing 128 people (June 30). *Peyton Place* blockbuster best-seller of year. First transatlantic telephone cable begins operating. Albert Woolson, last Union veteran of Civil War, dies at age 109. American actress Grace Kelly marries Prince Rainier III of Monaco.

**1957** Pres. Eisenhower announces Eisenhower Doctrine, promising aid to any Middle Eastern country threatened by communism. McClellan Committee begins investigating corruption and racketeering in International Brotherhood of Teamsters union. Sen. J. Strom Thurmond of South Carolina sets all- time filibuster record (24 hrs., 27 min.) with speech against civil rights (Aug. 30). Congress eventually approves first Civil Rights Act since Reconstruction (Sept. 9). Pres. Eisenhower sends troops to Little Rock, Ark., to enforce federal desegregation order (Sept. 24). First underground atomic test conducted in Nevada (Sept. 19). Sen. John F. Kennedy of Massachusetts wins Pulitzer Prize for *Profiles in Courage*.

**1958** In response to Soviet launch of Sputnik, U.S. launches Explorer I, first American satellite; Congress creates National Aeronautics and Space Administration (NASA) and passes National Defense Education Act. Vice Pres. Richard M. Nixon nearly killed by angry mob in Caracas, Venezuela. At request of weak government in Beirut, Pres. Eisenhower orders U.S. Marines to land in Lebanon (July 15). Nuclear submarine *Nautilus* performs first undersea crossing of North Pole (Aug. 5). Presidential assistant Sherman Adams forced to resign in scandal over accepting favors (Sept. 22). Dr. Linus Pauling predicts 5 million birth defects from radioactivity already released into atmosphere by atomic tests.

**1959** Fidel Castro's takeover of Cuba begins rapid deterioration of U.S.-Cuba relations (Jan. 1). Alaska becomes 49th state (Jan. 3), and Hawaii 50th (Aug. 21). Joint U.S.-Canada St. Lawrence Seaway project completed. Congress passes Landrum-Griffin Act to suppress racketeering in labor unions. Vice Pres. Nixon holds impromptu "kitchen debate" in Moscow with Soviet Premier Nikita Khrushchev, who later visits U.S. USS *George Washington,* the first U.S. Navy ballistic-missile submarine, launched. Charles Van Doren testifies that his victory on "$64,000 Question" TV game show was fixed. Walter Williams, last surviving Civil War veteran, dies at age 117.

**1960** U.S. and Japan conclude new security treaty (Jan. 19). Black students stage first sit-in at Woolworth's lunch counter in Greensboro, N.C. (Feb. 1). U-2 spy plane, with American pilot Francis Gary Powers, shot down over Soviet Union (May 1). Congress passes second Civil Rights Act since Reconstruction. Congress investigates "payola" in radio industry, leading to arrest of Alan Freed, "father of rock 'n' roll." After Cuba rejects American protests over confiscated property, Pres. Eisenhower imposes trade embargo. John F. Kennedy and Richard M. Nixon hold first televised presidential campaign debates. Kennedy wins by 0.3% of popular vote, closest presidential election since 1884 (Nov. 8).

**1961** Pres. Eisenhower breaks diplomatic relations with Cuba, warns Americans to beware of "military-industrial complex." CIA-backed Bay of Pigs invasion fails to overthrow Castro regime in Cuba (Apr. 17). Commander Alan B. Shephard, Jr., U.S. Navy, first American in space on Mercury rocket (May 5). Soviet construction of Berlin Wall creates temporary crisis (Aug. 13). Pres. Kennedy creates Peace Corps and Alliance for Progress. American families advised to build nuclear fallout shelters. "Freedom Rides" civil rights protests broken up by riots in Anniston and Birmingham, Ala. American Medical Association reports link between smoking and heart disease. National Council of Churches endorses birth control for families.

**1962** Lt. Col. John H. Glenn, Jr., first American to orbit Earth. Stock market has worst day since 1929 (May 28). Pres. Kennedy convinces steel companies to rescind price increases. U.S. conducts first successful test of sea-launched long-range ballistic missile with nuclear warhead. Pres. Kennedy sends U.S. marshals to protect James H. Meredith, a black student at University of Mississippi. U.S. extends $100-million emergency loan to the UN. Threat of nuclear war during Cuban Missile Crisis averted when Soviet Union agrees to withdraw missiles from Cuba (Oct. 22–28). Rachel Carson's *Silent Spring* draws attention to environmental crisis. U.S. Military Assistance Command set up in South Vietnam.

**1963** Pres. Kennedy proposes Medicare program. U.S., Great Britain, and Soviet Union conclude Nuclear Test–Ban Treaty outlawing atmospheric testing (July 25). "Hot line" between Washington and Moscow put in place. Civil rights movement reaches climax with mass demonstrations in Birmingham, Ala., and epic March on Washington, where Martin Luther King delivers his "I Have a Dream" speech (Aug. 28). Pres. Kennedy assassinated in Dallas, Tex., by Lee Harvey Oswald (Nov. 22), who is murdered by Jack Ruby (Nov. 24). Joseph Valachi testifies before Congress about extent of organized crime in U.S. Arnold Palmer first pro golfer to earn over $100,000 in one year.

**1964** Pres. Lyndon B. Johnson, taking up Pres. Kennedy's cause, calls for "War on Poverty." Supreme Court orders states to redraw Congressional boundaries to ensure fair representation. Alaska declared disaster area after major earthquake rocks Anchorage (Mar. 28). Mississippi "Freedom Summer" begins with murder of three civil rights workers (June 22). Pres. Johnson pushes landmark Civil Rights and Economic Opportunity acts through Congress. After alleged North Vietnamese attack on U.S. Navy destroyers, Congress passes Tonkin Gulf Resolution, giving Pres. Johnson free hand in Vietnam (Aug. 7). Warren Commission reports there was no conspiracy to assassinate Pres. Kennedy (Sept. 27). Martin Luther King wins Noble Peace Prize. Verrazano Narrows Bridge, the longest suspension bridge in world, opened in New York.

**1965** Pres. Johnson calls for "Great Society." Black nationalist Malcolm X assassinated in New York City (Feb. 21). Pres. Johnson orders U.S. Marines into South Vietnam (Mar. 8) and into Santo Domingo (Apr. 28). U.S. troops authorized to undertake offensive operations in South Vietnam (June 8). Martin Luther King leads civil rights marches from Selma to Montgomery, Ala., and in white neighborhoods of Chicago. Congress approves Medicare (July 30) and Voting Rights Act (Aug. 6). Watts Riot in Los Angeles leaves 34 dead and over $200 million in damage (Aug. 11–16), accelerating wave of ghetto riots. Tornadoes sweep Midwest, killing 271 and injuring 5,000. East Coast power blackout affects over 30 million Americans and Canadians (Nov. 9–10).

**1966** East Coast blizzard results in 165 deaths (Jan. 29–31). Pres. Johnson orders first B-52 strategic bombing raids on North Vietnam (Apr. 12). Supreme Court rules police must advise suspects of their rights (June 13). Cesar Chavez leads United Farm Workers strike and boycott against California grape growers. Stokeley Carmichael of Student Non-Violent Coordinating Committee demands "Black Power." Congress enacts safety standards for automobiles. Edward W. Brooke of Massachusetts is first black senator since Reconstruction. National Football League and American Football League agree to play Super Bowl championship game. Number of blacks voting in South nearly doubles in one year. U.S. troops in Vietnam increase from 215,000 to over 400,000.

**1967** The 500th U.S. plane shot down over North Vietnam (Apr. 4). Hundreds of thousands of antiwar protesters march on Washington (Apr. 15 and Oct. 21–22). Pres. Johnson announces U.S. troop level will reach 525,000 by end of 1968. Worst race riot in U.S. history erupts in Detroit, Mich. (July 23), leaving 43 dead, while riot in Newark, N.J. (July 12), kills another 26. Sen. Eugene McCarthy of Minnesota announces antiwar candidacy for president (Nov. 30). U.S. agrees to refrain from placing nuclear weapons in space and joins General Agreement on Tariffs and Trade (GATT). Albert DeSalvo, the "Boston Strangler," sentenced to life in prison. Stalin's daughter Svetlana Aliluyeva defects to U.S. Thurgood Marshall becomes first black justice on Supreme Court.

**1968** North Korea seizes USS *Pueblo*, holding 82 crewmen hostage (Jan. 23). North Vietnam and Viet Cong launch massive Tet Offensive (Jan. 30). Pres. Johnson makes surprise announcement that he will not seek reelection (Mar. 31). Martin Luther King murdered by James Earl Ray in Memphis, Tenn. (Apr. 4). Student protesters take over Columbia University (Apr. 23). Washington-Hanoi peace talks begin in Paris (May 10). After winning California primary, Sen. Robert F. Kennedy of New York murdered by Sirhan Sirhan in Los Angeles (June 5). U.S. signs Nuclear Non-Proliferation Treaty. Democratic Convention in Chicago marred by riots and police violence against antiwar demonstrators. Shirley Chisholm of New York is first black woman elected to Congress. Apollo VIII completes first moon orbit.

**1969** Oil spill off Santa Barbara, Calif., draws attention to need for environmental protection

(Feb. 5). Pres. Richard Nixon asks Congress to fund Anti-Ballistic Missile program (ABM) as "safeguard" for strategic defense. U.S. losses in Vietnam exceed losses in Korean War. U.S. troop withdrawals from Vietnam begin (July 8). Sen. Edward M. Kennedy of Massachusetts drives off bridge at Chappaquiddick, Mass., killing Mary Jo Kopechne (July 18). After $25 billion spent on U.S. space program, Neil Armstrong and Buzz Aldrin of Apollo XI are first men to walk on moon (July 20). Hurricane Camille claims over 300 victims in South. Trial of Chicago Eight (later Chicago Seven, after Bobby Seale tried separately) begins. Woodstock music festival near Bethel, N.Y., draws 400,000 young fans (Aug. 15–18). Vietnam Moratorium and "March against Death" antiwar demonstrations draw hundreds of thousands to Washington. U.S. and the USSR begin Strategic Arms Limitation Talks (SALT) in Helsinki, Finland.

**1970** Pres. Nixon calls for "Vietnamization" to decrease U.S. involvement in war. U.S. bombing of North Vietnam escalates dramatically; nationwide protests break out when U.S. invades Cambodia (Apr. 29). Four students killed and nine wounded by National Guard units at Kent State University in Ohio (May 4). SALT negotiations reopen in Vienna, Austria. Lt. William L. Calley court-martialed for massacre of 102 civilians in My Lai, South Vietnam (Nov. 12). Supreme Court upholds new 18-year-old voting age (Dec. 21). Congress passes Water Quality Improvement Act, Air Quality Control Act, and Occupational Safety and Health Act. U.S. troops in Vietnam down to 340,000 at year's end. U.S. population tops 200 million (203,235,000).

**1971** Pres. Nixon proposes federal revenue sharing with states. Charles Manson and three women followers convicted for Tate-LaBianca murders in Los Angeles (Jan. 25). Major earthquake rocks Southern California, killing 64 and injuring over 1,000 (Feb. 9). U.S. Ping-Pong team visits China, relaxing Cold War tensions. Supreme Court approves of busing to achieve school integration. Indian occupation of Alcatraz Island in San Francisco Bay comes to an end. Prison riot in Attica, N.Y., kills 43 inmates and guards. *New York Times* begins publishing "Pentagon Papers," top-secret history of Vietnam War (June 13). U.S. devalues dollar (Dec. 18). U.S. troops in Vietnam reach 139,000; U.S. air attacks are heaviest since 1968. Billie Jean King first woman athlete to earn over $100,000 in one year.

**1972** Nixon first president to visit China (Feb. 21–28) and Soviet Union (May 22–30). Airlines begin screening passengers to prevent hijackings. Congress passes Equal Rights Amendment and submits it to states for ratification. Gov. George Wallace of Alabama shot and seriously wounded by Arthur Bremer while campaigning for president in Laurel, Md. (May 15). Five men arrested for breaking into Democratic National Committee headquarters at Watergate complex in Washington, D.C. (June 17). Federal grand jury indicts five burglars and two former White House aides in Watergate trial (Sept. 15). Pres. Nixon angers farmers with "Great Grain Robbery," a secret deal to

sell wheat at discount to Soviet Union. National security adviser Henry Kissinger announces "peace is at hand" in Vietnam in time for Pres. Nixon to carry 49 states in election. U.S. troops in Vietnam fall to 69,000 as Nixon orders resumption of heavy bombing of North Vietnam (Dec. 18).

**1973** Supreme Court disallows state restrictions on abortions (*Roe* v. *Wade*). U.S. signs Paris peace accords ending Vietnam War (Jan. 27). North Vietnam releases U.S. prisoners of war. Trial of Watergate burglars reveals conspiracy to conceal White House involvement. Top presidential aides H.R. Haldeman, John Ehrlichman, John Dean, and Atty. Gen. Richard Kleindienst resign amid charges of White House cover-up (Apr. 30). Sen. Sam Ervin of North Carolina chairs Senate investigation of Watergate scandal on national television (May 17–Nov. 15). Vice Pres. Spiro Agnew resigns after threat of indictment for tax evasion (Oct. 10). Gasoline prices skyrocket after Arab nations embargo oil exports to U.S. in retaliation for U.S. aid to Israel in Yom Kippur War (Oct. 17). Pres. Nixon fires Watergate Special Prosecutor Archibald Cox and others in "Saturday Night Massacre" (Oct. 20). Pres. Nixon turns over first White House tapes, which include mysterious 18½-minute gap (Nov. 26). Gerald R. Ford of Michigan sworn in as first vice president chosen under 25th Amendment (Dec. 6). Indians defy federal authority in Wounded Knee, S.D.

**1974** Arab oil embargo of U.S. lifted (Mar. 18). Pres. Nixon admits owing nearly $500,000 in back taxes (Apr. 3). Supreme Court rules that Pres. Nixon must submit all White House tapes to Special Prosecutor Leon Jaworski (July 24). House Judiciary Committee votes three articles of impeachment (July 24–30). Pres. Nixon releases transcripts of tapes that show he ordered cover-up (Aug. 5). Citing "political" difficulties, Pres. Nixon announces resignation (Aug. 8), elevating Vice Pres. Ford to presidency (Aug. 9). Pres. Ford shocks nation by pardoning Nixon for all crimes he may have committed in office (Sept. 8). Democrats make major gains in midterm elections. Pres. Ford meets with Soviet Premier Leonid Brezhnev in Vladivostock to approve SALT treaty (Nov. 23–24). FBI and CIA efforts to disrupt civil rights and antiwar movements in 1960s revealed. Newspaper heiress Patty Hearst kidnapped in Berkeley, Calif., by radical Symbionese Liberation Army, which extorts $2-million food giveaway for needy.

**1975** Nixon aides convicted of obstructing justice in Watergate investigation (Jan. 1). Senate committee chaired by Frank Church begins investigation into illegal CIA and FBI activities. Last Americans evacuate Saigon as South Vietnam falls to North Vietnamese invasion (Apr. 30). Cambodia seizes USS *Mayaguez* (May 12), and Pres. Ford orders rescue operation (May 14). Apollo-Soyuz, joint Soviet-American space mission, achieves linkup in space (July 17). Lynette "Squeaky" Fromme and Sarah Jane Moore attempt to assassinate Pres. Ford in separate California incidents (Sept. 5 and 22). Congress votes to admit women to army, navy, and air force academies. President's Commission on Civil Rights reports southern schools more integrated than northern schools. Democrats in House of Representatives dismantle seniority system. Church Committee discovers CIA helped overthrow Salvador Allende of Chile and plotted to assassinate Fidel Castro of Cuba.

**1976** Congress repeatedly overrides Pres. Ford's vetoes of bills providing for jobs, health, education, and welfare programs. Senate investigators find Lockheed Corp. paid $22 million in bribes to foreign officials. Supreme Court upholds death penalty (July 3). Bicentennial of U.S. celebrated coast to coast. Congressman Wayne Hays of Ohio, chairman of House Ways and Means Committee, resigns over sex scandal. Sec. of Agriculture Earl Butz forced to resign for telling racist joke. Pres. Ford, in campaign debate with Democratic candidate James E. "Jimmy" Carter, insists there is "no Soviet domination of Eastern Europe" (Oct. 7). Justice Department begins probing South Korean bribery of congressmen and other officials. NASA's Viking I and Viking II space probes land on Mars and transmit scientific data, along with color photographs, back to Earth. "Legionnaire's Disease" breaks out at American Legion convention in Philadelphia, eventually claiming 29 victims. Patty Hearst convicted of armed robbery in California. Hundreds of West Point cadets found to have cheated on exams.

**1977** Cold winter and heavy snows hit eastern states. Pres. Carter pardons Vietnam War draft evaders, threatens to reduce foreign aid to countries violating human rights, calls for "moral equivalent of war" in energy conservation, and signs Panama Canal treaty (Sept. 7). U.S. declares 200-mi. sovereignty zone in Atlantic and Pacific oceans to exclude foreign fishing vessels. Power blackout sets off arson and looting spree in New York City (July 13–14). Oil begins flowing through Alaska pipeline. Pres. Carter accuses oil industry of "biggest rip-off in history" (Oct. 13). National Women's Conference held in Houston, Tex. Severe drought leads to water rationing on West Coast. ABC's weeklong TV series *Roots*, based on Alex Haley's best-seller about his slave ancestors, draws about 130 million viewers.

**1978** Pres. Carter postpones production of neutron bomb. California voters approve Proposition 13, reducing property taxes and setting off nationwide "taxpayers' revolt." Supreme Court gives limited approval to affirmative action programs but disallows quotas for college admissions (June 28). In private talks with Anwar Sadat and Menachem Begin, Pres. Carter mediates peace between Egypt and Israel with landmark Camp David Accords (Sept. 17). Nearly 1,000 American followers of the Rev. Jim Jones commit mass suicide in Jonestown, Guyana, after cult members murder Congressman Leo Ryan of California and others (Nov. 18). Federal loan guarantees rescue New York City from financial crisis.

**1979** U.S. resumes diplomatic relations with China (Jan 1). Pres. Carter commutes Patty Hearst's sentence, releasing her from jail. Farmers drive thousands of tractors into Washington to dramatize grievances. Worst nuclear accident in U.S. history takes place at Three Mile Island power plant near Harrisburg, Pa., releasing giant clouds of radioactive steam (Mar. 28) Pres. Carter and Premier Brezhnev sign SALT II treaty in Vienna (June 18). Shah of Iran and Anastasio Somoza of Nicaragua, both U.S.-supported dictators, flee revolutions in their countries. Iranian militants seize U.S. embassy in Tehran, taking 66 American hostages and demanding return of shah from U.S. (Nov. 4). Iranians release 13 American hostages, all blacks or women. Pres. Carter deports illegal Iranian students, freezes Iranian assets, and bars oil imports from Iran. Pope John Paul II visits U.S. Inflation reaches highest level in 33 years as Organization of Petroleum Exporting Countries (OPEC) doubles price of oil.

**1980** Canadian embassy officials help six Americans escape from Iran (Jan. 29). In response to Soviet invasion of Afghanistan, Pres. Carter embargoes grain and high-tech exports to Soviet Union, approves arms sales to China, and secures U.S. boycott of Olympics in Moscow. Congress grants Pres. Carter's request for Crude Oil Windfall Profits Tax and for resumption of Selective Service draft registration. Pres. Carter's secret rescue mission for American hostages in Iran fails when U.S. Navy helicopter crashes in desert, killing eight servicemen (Apr. 24). Race riot breaks out in Miami, protesting police brutality (May 17). Mt. St. Helens erupts in Washington State, killing 26 people and causing $2.7 billion in damage (May 18). Banking and trucking industries deregulated. FBI's "Abscam" operation implicates over 30 public officials, including a senator and seven congressmen, for accepting bribes. Republicans capture control of Senate for only second time in 50 years.

**1981** Minutes after Pres. Ronald Reagan is sworn in, Iran releases 52 American hostages after 444 days in captivity. Pres. Reagan shot by John Hinckley in Washington, D.C. (Mar. 30); undergoes surgery and makes full recovery. *Columbia* completes first successful space shuttle mission (Apr. 12–14). Federal air-traffic controllers go on strike and lose jobs when Pres. Reagan fires all 13,000 of them. Senate votes 99 to 0 to confirm Sandra Day O'Connor as first woman justice of Supreme Court. Pres. Reagan lifts grain embargo against Soviet Union but imposes new sanctions after Poland declares martial law. Congress accepts Pres. Reagan's plans for tax cuts, lower domestic spending, and major defense buildup. U.S. sends military advisers and aid to El Salvador. Professional baseball players stage two-month strike.

**1982** Ending 13-year antitrust suit, American Telephone and Telegraph agrees to surrender control of local Bell System phone companies in return for expansion into new business pursuits (Jan. 8). Pres. Reagan calls for "New Federalism," transferring programs to state and local control. Half a million Americans demonstrate in New York City in favor of nuclear freeze (June 12). Congress rejects nuclear freeze (Aug. 5). U.S. supports Great Britain in Falklands War with Argentina. Unemployment exceeds 10% for first time since Great Depression, and

federal budget deficit exceeds $100 billion a year for first time ever. After a decade, Equal Rights Amendment fails, falling three states short of ratification.

**1983** Inflation slows as oil prices decline sharply. Congress admits internment of Japanese-Americans during World War II was unjust and agrees to bail out Social Security system. National Commission on Excellence in Education reports U.S. is "nation at risk" because of inferior elementary and secondary schools. Sally Ride, aboard space shuttle *Challenger*, is first American woman astronaut. Klaus Barbie, Nazi war criminal, revealed to be living in U.S. with government protection. Pres. Reagan strongly condemns Soviet Union for shooting down Korean airliner with 269 people aboard (Sept. 1). U.S. Marines join multinational peacekeeping force in Beirut, Lebanon, where Muslim terrorists kill 240 of them in suicide bombing (Oct. 23). With several Caribbean nations, U.S. invades Grenada to overthrow Cuban-backed regime (Oct. 25). Pres. Reagan calls for large-scale funding of Strategic Defense Initiative, or "Star Wars."

**1984** Reagan recovery under way as unemployment falls, inflation rate declines, economic growth accelerates, and U.S. dollar soars on international markets. Pres. Reagan orders U.S. Marines out of Lebanon (Feb. 7). Congress censures Pres. Reagan for misusing funds to mine Nicaraguan harbors, later condemned by World Court. Pres. Reagan visits China (Apr. 26–May 1). Rep. Geraldine Ferraro, Democrat of New York, first woman to receive major party nomination for vice president. Soviet bloc countries boycott Olympics in Los Angeles. Jesse Jackson, Democrat of Illinois, mounts first major challenge by black candidate for major party nomination. Walter Mondale, Democratic candidate for president, carries only his home state of Minnesota.

**1985** Pres. Reagan calls for more tax and budget cuts to sustain economic growth (Feb. 4–6). Despite worldwide protests from Jewish organizations, Pres. Reagan visits West Germany to deliver address at Bitburg cemetery, where Nazi SS troops are buried (May 5). Muslim terrorists hijack TWA airliner (June 14), kill one American hostage, then release rest in Beirut (June 30). Palestinian terrorists kill an American hostage aboard hijacked Italian cruise ship *Achille Lauro* (Oct. 9). Pres. Reagan and Soviet Premier Mikhail Gorbachev hold their first summit meeting in Geneva (Nov. 19–21). Pres. Reagan signs Gramm-Rudman Act, requiring automatic spending cuts if Congress cannot reduce burgeoning federal deficit. Plane crash in Gander, Newfoundland, kills 248 U.S. troops coming home for Christmas (Dec. 12).

**1986** Pres. Reagan, blaming Libya for supporting terrorism, freezes Libyan assets in U.S. Space shuttle *Challenger* explodes in midair over Florida, killing six astronauts and civilian passenger (Jan. 28); investigations reveal NASA relaxed safety regulations to speed up launch date. U.S. Navy repels attack by Libyan forces during maneuvers in Gulf of Sidra (Mar. 24). Pres. Reagan blames Libya for death of two

Americans in terrorist bombing of West Berlin disco, then orders retaliatory air raids on Tripoli and Benghazi (Apr. 14). Jonathan Jay Pollard found guilty of spying for Israel (June 4). Congress overrides Pres. Reagan's veto of trade sanctions against South Africa (Oct. 2). Second Reagan-Gorbachev summit in Reykjavík, Iceland, reaches impasse over arms control and "Star Wars" (Oct. 12). Congress approves sweeping revision of U.S. tax structure. Democrats regain control of Senate. Pres. Reagan denies trading arms for hostages as Iran-Contra scandal breaks (Nov. 19). Wall Street financier Ivan Boesky fined $100 million for illegal insider-trading on stock market. Acquired immune deficiency syndrome (AIDS) has killed well over 10,000 Americans.

**1987** Pres. Reagan submits first trillion-dollar U.S. budget to Congress as national debt mounts steadily. Stock market closes above 2,000 for first time. Tower Commission inquiry into Iran-Contra affair criticizes White House staff and Pres. Reagan's "management style," prompting Chief of Staff Donald Regan to resign. TV evangelist Jim Bakker resigns after admitting his extramarital affair with Jessica Hahn. U.S.-Japan trade war erupts. After Pres. Reagan orders U.S. Navy into Persian Gulf to escort Kuwaiti oil tankers, an Iraqi warplane accidentally attacks USS *Stark*, killing 37 sailors (May 17). Congressional hearings on Iran-Contra affair bestow fame on former White House aide Lt. Col. Oliver North. Stock market crashes 508 points in one day, an all-time record, jolting markets around world (Oct. 16). Third Reagan-Gorbachev summit in Washington, D.C., produces agreement to dismantle medium-range missiles in Europe (Dec. 8).

**1988** Vice Pres. Bush denies involvement in Iran-Contra scandal. Congress rejects Pres. Reagan's request for aid to Contras. U.S. pressure on Gen. Manuel Noriega to step down plunges Panama into economic turmoil. After Iran lays mines in Persian Gulf, U.S. Navy warships and planes destroy two Iranian oil platforms and repel Iranian counterattacks (Apr. 18-19). USS *Vincennes* accidentally shoots down Iranian passenger plane, killing 290 people (July 3). Summer drought afflicts North America; fires burn 4 million acres of forest. Pres. Reagan vis-

its Moscow to meet with Premier Gorbachev. Atty. Gen. Edwin Meese resigns amid accusations of financial misdealings. *Discovery* completes first space shuttle mission since *Challenger* disaster. George Bush becomes first sitting vice president elected president since 1836. Terrorist bomb aboard Pan Am Flight 103 kills all 259 aboard, mostly Americans, and 11 on the ground in Lockerbie, Scotland (Dec. 21). Drexel Burnham Lambert agrees to pay record $650 million penalty for securities fraud (Dec. 21). Kohlberg Kravis Roberts acquires RJR Nabisco for $25 billion, largest leveraged buyout in history. Pentagon procurement scandal reveals influence peddling and other irregularities.

**1989** *Exxon Valdez* supertanker spills over 11 million gallons of oil off Alaska coast (Mar. 24). Abortion rights rally brings 500,000 marchers to Washington, D.C. (Apr. 9). HUD scandal reveals fraud, mismanagement, and influence peddling under Reagan administration. Top Democrats Jim Wright—Speaker of the House—and Tony Coelho—majority whip—resign from House over ethics violations. Pres. Bush visits Poland and Hungary, pledging aid to new democracies. Supreme Court upholds right to burn U.S. flag and approves state limits on abortion. Pres. Bush signs $300 billion savings and loan bailout (Aug. 9). Over 30 killed when Hurricane Hugo hits Charleston, S.C. (Sept. 22). U.S.-backed Panama coup fails (Oct. 3). Severe earthquake, second worst in U.S. history, inflicts $6 billion damage and leaves 62 dead in San Francisco Bay area (Oct. 17). L. Douglas Wilder of Virginia is first black elected governor; New York City and Seattle elect their first black mayors (Nov. 7). Pres. Bush and Premier Gorbachev hold shipboard summit off Malta (Dec. 2-3). After Panama declares "state of war" with U.S., Pres. Bush orders invasion by 24,000 U.S. troops to overthrow Noriega regime and install U.S.-backed popularly elected government (Dec. 20). Congress approves first minimum wage increase in eight years. FBI investigation of Chicago Board of Trade and Chicago Mercantile Exchange yields 46 indictments for fraud and racketeering. Annual inflation rate of 4.6% is highest since 1981.

**1990** After Iraq's invasion of Kuwait (Aug. 2), U.S. launches Operation Desert Shield:

more than 200,000 U.S. troops move into Saudi Arabia, and the navy blockades all oil exports from Iraq and all imports except food. Pres. Bush refuses any compromise with Iraq's dictator, Saddam Hussein, and works with UN Security Council to obtain condemnation of invasion and imposition of stringent economic sanctions. Bush and Gorbachev meet twice: U.S. agrees to provide some economic aid, grants USSR most-favored-nation trade status, and secures some arms reductions and agreement that Iraq must withdraw from Kuwait. John Poindexter, national security adviser to Pres. Reagan, convicted in Iran-Contra scandal and sentenced to six months in jail. Savings and loan scandal continues to unfold as five U.S. senators ("The Keating Five") are called before ethics committee to answer allegations they helped Charles Keating, head of Lincoln Savings; Neil Bush, the president's son, sued by FDIC for his role in a Colorado bank failure. Pres. Bush breaks campaign pledge of "no new taxes." Washington, D.C., Mayor Marion Barry convicted on drug-use charge. Nelson Mandela makes triumphant tour of U.S. and addresses joint session of Congress (June 26). A major flaw in the $1.5 billion Hubble Space Telescope is discovered shortly after its deployment. Longest and costliest criminal trial in U.S. history ends with the acquittal of Peggy Buckey and her son on 52 counts of child molestation at their Los Angeles school. Wall Street firm Drexel Burnham Lambert defaults on $100 million in loans, and Michael Milken, head of "junk bond" department, is fined $600 million and sentenced to jail. About 200,000 antiabortion protesters march in Washington, D.C. Worst floods in 80 years hit Texas, Louisiana, Arkansas, and Oklahoma. In the Bronx, N.Y., 87 people die in fire at Happy Land Social Club. Seventy-three die in Avianca crash when plane runs out of fuel over suburban Long Island. Imelda Marcos acquitted of fraud and racketeering charges. Three New York teenagers are convicted of raping and beating a Central Park jogger but acquitted of attempted murder. George Steinbrenner, owner of New York Yankees, banned from baseball; baseball great Pete Rose imprisoned for filing false income-tax returns.

# Biographies of U.S. Presidents

died only four years later, leaving his property to George, who went on to become one of Virginia's foremost landowners, ultimately acquiring more than 100,000 acres in Virginia and what is now West Virginia. In 1753 Washington joined the French and Indian War as an officer in the Virginia militia and fought bravely if poorly. The war provided Washington with the beginnings of his anti-British sentiments, exposing him to the arrogance of his British commanders. Upon returning to plantation life, and marrying Martha Custis, in 1759, Washington's resentment of the British was further fueled by their commercial restrictions. With the passage of the Stamp Act of 1765, Washington joined opposition to imperial rule in the Virginia House of Burgesses, becoming ever more active in resisting the

British. He went as a delegate to the Continental Congress, which chose him to command the Continental Army when war with Britain broke out in 1775. Washington proved an uncommonly resourceful general, keeping his ragtag army together through years of defeat, retreat, and hard winters to outlast the British and finally prevail at Yorktown in 1781. Here, as in all his life, Washington earned respect for his judgment, dignity, and bearing. Retiring to Mount Vernon after the war, the general quashed suggestions that he assume military dictatorship of the fledgling republic, not wanting to subvert the very principles for which the Americans had fought. But because of his belief in a strong central government, Washington felt compelled to return to public life to salvage his country from the chaotic Articles of Con-

## 1. George Washington
### (1789-1797)

Born in Westmoreland County, Virginia, on Feb. 22, 1732, the first president, with a love for the land, trained as a surveyor in his teens. At age 16 he went to live with his brother Lawrence, who built Mount Vernon. Lawrence

federation. In 1787 he presided over the Constitutional Convention in Philadelphia, which framed the presidency with him in mind, the only president ever elected unanimously in the electoral college (twice).

Washington's renowned judgment equaled the task of setting presidential precedent, for, as he wrote, "It is devoutly wished on my part, that these precedents may be fixed on true principles." His first act as president was to urge adoption of the Bill of Rights. Other notable achievements included national unity, quelling the Whiskey Rebellion, bolstering the treasury with a national bank, settling Jay's Treaty of commerce with Britain, and maintaining neutrality in the French Revolution. Washington successfully implemented executive power and quieted fears and suspicions of executive tyranny. But he regretted the rivalry between Thomas Jefferson and Alexander Hamilton, which led to the birth of political parties in his own cabinet; Washington feared that allegiance to "factions" would someday eclipse the guiding light of patriotism. After refusing a third term in 1796, Washington in his Farewell Address warned against party spirit, sectionalism, and "entangling alliances" with other nations. He died on Dec. 14, 1799, "first in war, first in peace, and first in the hearts of his countrymen," as his friend Henry Lee eulogized him.

## 2. John Adams
### (1797–1801)

A fifth-generation American directly descended from a Mayflower passenger, John Adams was born on Oct. 30, 1735, in Braintree, Massachusetts. At Harvard Adams considered the ministry but turned to law. He joined his cousin Sam Adams as an early opponent of the Stamp Act of 1765, organizing the Sons of Liberty and defending Americans accused of smuggling. Yet he also defended the British soldiers brought to trial for the Boston Massacre in 1770. In the Revolution, Adams persuaded the Continental Congress to commission George Washington as commander in chief, declare independence, and put stars and stripes on the flag. He wrote the Massachusetts state constitution in 1779 and negotiated peace with Britain in 1782. The first vice president, Adams called that position the "most insignificant office that ever the invention of man contrived or his imagination conceived."

Elected president as a Federalist in 1796, Adams retained Washington's cabinet, but Alexander Hamilton turned the party against him for refusing to make war on France. Adams built up the navy and kept the peace, but disaffecting the Federalists and signing the Alien and Sedition Acts (1798) politically weakened "His Rotundity." Adams lost the 1800 election to the increasingly popular Thomas Jefferson. The first president to reside in the White House, Adams lived to be 90, able to see his son John Quincy Adams become the sixth president in 1824. John Adams died on the same day that Thomas Jefferson did: July 4, 1826, the 50th anniversary of the Declaration of Independence they both signed.

## 3. Thomas Jefferson
### (1801–1809)

Thomas Jefferson was born on Apr. 13, 1743, in Albemarle County, Virginia, son of a self-made Virginian who died when Jefferson was 14. Jefferson graduated from William and Mary in 1762, began practicing law in 1767, and joined the Virginia House of Burgesses in 1769. With his pen Jefferson sharply criticized British rule, winning a place on Virginia's Committee of Correspondence to keep in touch with patriots in other colonies. His writings amassed great respect, earning him the right, as a delegate to the Continental Congress in 1776, to draft the Declaration of Independence. He then returned to Virginia as wartime governor, narrowly escaping capture when British troops destroyed his home. Congress sent Jefferson to Europe in 1784; he was minister to France during the Constitutional Convention and the early French Revolution, an event that affected him profoundly. As secretary of state under Washington, Jefferson's faith in democracy and states' rights clashed repeatedly with Alexander Hamilton's pursuit of central executive power. Jefferson resigned in 1793 and led opposition to the Federalists, whom Jefferson called "monarchists in principle." As vice president after 1796, Jefferson speeded the Federalists' downfall by secretly authoring the Kentucky Resolutions, critical of the Alien and Sedition Acts.

The House of Representatives chose Jefferson (ironically, with Hamilton's support) over Aaron Burr, whose electoral votes for president equaled his in 1800. "We are all Republicans—we are all Federalists," appealed Jefferson in his inaugural address, easing the transfer of power. In his first term, Jefferson slashed the budget, lowered taxes, reduced the national debt, and sent marines to fight Barbary pirates. Despite some concern over his constitutional authority to make the acquisition, Jefferson's greatest feat was the Louisiana Purchase from France in 1803, which doubled the size of the United States. "The less said about the constitutional difficulties, the better," wrote Jefferson, sending Lewis and Clark to explore the new lands. In his second term, Jefferson's unpopular Embargo Act (1807) was an attempt to avoid war with Britain or France, but it ruined American merchants. Retiring to Monticello in 1809, Jefferson busied himself with inventions and designing the University of Virginia. He died on the 50th anniversary of the Declaration of Independence, July 4, 1826. His amazingly broad interests spanned music, science, architecture, agronomy, and the classics, as well as politics and government.

## 4. James Madison
### (1809–1817)

James Madison was born to a wealthy family on Mar. 16, 1751, in Port Conway, Virginia. A Princeton graduate, Madison attended the first Virginia state convention in 1776, drafting a bill that guaranteed religious liberty. As the youngest member of the Continental Congress in 1780, he led the movement to revise the Articles of Confederation. At the Constitutional

Convention in Philadelphia in 1787, Madison's Virginia Plan became the pivot of discussion. Madison, dubbed the Father of the Constitution, tirelessly directed debate and applied his political wisdom. His voluminous notes provide the best record of the convention. Madison helped ratify the Constitution by coauthoring *The Federalist* (1787–88) with John Jay and Alexander Hamilton. A four-term congressman, Madison drafted the Bill of Rights and cofounded the Democratic-Republican party. In 1794 he married a young and ebullient widow, Dolley Payne Todd, an especially popular first lady. Madison led the opposition to the Federalists' Alien and Sedition Acts with the Virginia Resolutions, arguing the acts were unconstitutional attacks on liberty. Jefferson chose Madison as his secretary of state and later as his successor. Madison easily won the election of 1808. Britain and France preyed on American shipping throughout Madison's first term. Pushed by war hawks in Congress, Madison asked for a declaration of war to defend American rights against British outrages. Reelected despite numerous American defeats in the War of 1812, Madison barely escaped Washington as the British burned the White House. Yet he persisted in "Mr. Madison's War" until the Peace of Ghent (1814) and belated victory at New Orleans (1815) vindicated him. War expenses forced Madison to recharter the national bank and raise the tariff, contrary to his Jeffersonian principles. But by 1817 Madison could retire confident of secure independence, surging nationalism, and the total collapse of his Federalist opponents who had opposed the war. He died on June 28, 1836, having outlived all the founding fathers. Madison's presidency pales beside his greatest contributions—the Constitution and the Bill of Rights.

## 5. James Monroe
### (1817–1825)

The last Revolutionary hero and member of the "Virginia Dynasty" to become president, James Monroe was born on Apr. 28, 1758, in Westmoreland County, Virginia. He left the College of William and Mary to answer the call to arms in 1775. Wounded at Trenton, Monroe fought courageously and rose to lieutenant colonel under Gen. Washington. He learned law as an aide to Thomas Jefferson, who helped Monroe into Congress and the Senate. Much diplomatic experience followed Monroe's appointment as minister to France in 1794. Governor of Virginia from 1799 to 1802, Monroe returned to Europe to negotiate the Louisiana Purchase and later served in Britain and Spain. James Madison appointed him secretary of state in 1811 and secretary of war in 1814. Chosen to succeed Madison, Monroe won the 1816 election and presided over the Era of Good Feeling, a period marked by minimal sectional or partisan discord. Monroe bought Florida from Spain in 1819, and his popularity survived the Panic of 1819 as well as rancorous debates over the admission of Missouri as a slave state. Monroe toured the nation to jubilant crowds, winning reelection with all but one electoral vote in 1820. John Quincy Adams, his secretary of state, suggested Monroe proclaim American opposition to European encroachment in the Western Hemisphere, which he did in 1823; decades later this became known as the Monroe Doctrine. After retiring, Monroe became a regent of the University of Virginia (1826) and a member of the Virginia constitutional convention of 1829. Because of lack of attention over the years, his private affairs had suffered greatly, and Monroe discovered he was lapsing into bankruptcy. He sold his plantation and died all but penniless on Independence Day, July 4, 1831.

## 6. John Quincy Adams
### (1825–1829)

The only president's son to become president, John Quincy Adams was born on July 11, 1767, in Braintree, Massachusetts. A true child of the Revolution, Adams watched the Battle of Bunker Hill while holding his mother's hand, and he spent his teens in Europe with his father, John Adams, on diplomatic missions for the new nation. He entered Harvard in 1785, already an experienced diplomat fluent in seven languages. After a brief career as a Boston lawyer, Adams was minister to Holland in 1794 and to Prussia in 1797. As a Federalist, Adams was elected to the Senate in 1803, but after supporting Thomas Jefferson, he had to resign. James Madison made Adams minister to Russia in 1809, in time to witness Napoleon's invasion. Adams helped negotiate the Peace of Ghent (1814) before serving as ambassador to England, the second of three Adams generations to hold that post. James Monroe recalled Adams from Europe—where he had spent most of his life—to appoint him secretary of state in 1817, and in that post, Adams purchased Florida from Spain, patched relations with Britain, and conceived the Monroe Doctrine.

Running for president in 1824, Adams was beaten by Andrew Jackson in both popular and electoral votes; but with Henry Clay's support, the House of Representatives made Adams president. No one ever became president with less than Adams's 31 percent of the vote, yet he refused to conciliate his foes or even act like a politician. Adams posed above politics and made no effort to deal with Congress or use patronage. Consequently, elaborate plans for internal improvements and national academies came to naught. Adams, like his father, could not win a second term, as Jackson gained revenge at the polls in 1828. Massachusetts rescued Adams from despair by sending him to Congress in 1830, and "Old Man Eloquent" remained a powerful antislavery leader until he collapsed on the floor of the House at age 80; he died in the Speaker's Room on Feb. 23, 1848. John Quincy Adams, who considered himself a failure as president, worked for the first 11 presidents and numbers among the most important architects of early American foreign policy.

## 7. Andrew Jackson
### (1829–1837)

Born to Scotch-Irish immigrants in Waxhaw, South Carolina, on Mar. 15, 1767, Andrew Jackson was the first first-generation American to become president, as well as the first president from the western frontier and the first of seven to be born in a log cabin. Orphaned at 15, he was by then already a revolutionary veteran, a former prisoner of war, and scarred by the saber of a British officer whose boots he refused to clean. Jackson read law and made his way to the Tennessee frontier, marrying Rachel Donelson Robards in 1791. She neglected to divorce her first husband, but Jackson challenged to a duel anyone who questioned his marriage, once even killing a man on the field of honor. Jackson's frontier law practice prospered, and Tennessee elected him its first congressman in 1796. He served only briefly in the Senate; Washington so disgusted the rough-hewn Jackson that he resigned. Back in Tennessee, Jackson became a respected judge and honorary major general of the militia. In the War of 1812, Jackson led troops to victory at the Battle of New Orleans (1815), his men routing British invaders twice their number.

"Old Hickory" was now a national icon, reentering the Senate in 1823 and running for president as a hero above party. Jackson won more popular and electoral votes than anyone in 1824 but lost when the election was thrown into the House and Henry Clay supported John Quincy Adams. Vowing revenge against the politicians, Jackson swept to victory in 1828 as the "people's choice" reform candidate. Jackson's wife died on the eve of his inauguration. As president, Jackson aggrandized the power of his office on behalf of the common man by expanding suffrage, rotating officeholders (the "spoils system"), and economizing in government. Under Jackson the federal government completely paid off the national debt. Jackson vetoed federal road-building and banking—yet he asserted federal authority by ordering troops to South Carolina in the Nullification Crisis of 1832–33. The Whig party arose in opposition to "King Andrew I," especially to his high-handed veto of the national bank, but voters endorsed Jackson's war on privilege by reelecting him in 1832. In his second term, Jackson seized land from the Native Americans, ignoring the Supreme Court, and he recognized Texas in hopes of taking more land from Mexico. He became the first president to ride a train (1833) and to survive an assassination attempt (1835). After placing his friend Martin Van Buren in the White House, Jackson retired to the Hermitage, his plantation in Tennessee. He remained quite influential behind the scenes, persuading the Democrats to discard Van Buren and nominate James K. Polk in 1844. Andrew Jackson finally succumbed to dropsy and old wounds on June 8, 1845.

## 8. Martin Van Buren
### (1837–1841)

The first president to have played no part in the Revolution, Martin Van Buren was born to a Dutch family in Kinderhook, New York, on Dec. 5, 1782. Apprenticed to a lawyer at 14, Van Buren took to law and politics—so well, in fact, that he came to be called the Little Magician. By 1821 staunch party loyalty elevated him to the Senate, where Van Buren led northern supporters of Andrew Jackson and guided his victory in 1828. Brief service as New York governor ended when Jackson appointed him secretary of state in 1829. Van Buren helped build the Democratic party, and Jackson made him vice president in 1832. As Jackson's heir apparent, Van Buren won the 1836 election, but two months after he took office, the Panic of 1837 launched a severe depression that spoiled his presidency. "Martin Van Ruin" responded by creating the independent treasury system, but his lack of popularity was beyond repair. He made enemies in the North by protecting slavery and in the South by refusing to annex Texas. Though the self-made son of an innkeeper, Van Buren was cast by his opponents as an aristocrat; William Henry Harrison's "Hard Cider" campaign of 1840 (touting that Van Buren sipped champagne while Harrison preferred hard cider) washed him out of office. In 1844 Van Buren lost the Democratic nomination when Jackson abandoned him over the Texas issue. But in 1848 Van Buren guaranteed a Democratic defeat by founding the Free Soil party and running for president, which split the decisive New York vote. Van Buren died a Unionist on July 24, 1862, the only president whose life touched both the Revolution and the Civil War.

## 9. William Henry Harrison
### (1841)

Son of a signatory of the Declaration of Independence and grandfather of a president, William Henry Harrison was born in Charles City County, Virginia, on Feb. 9, 1773. Campaign legend held that his birthplace was a log cabin, but in fact it was a plantation mansion. Harrison left medical school to join the army and fight Native Americans in the Northwest in 1791. After an illustrious military career, he served in Congress (1816–19), the U.S. Senate (1825–28), and as ambassador to Colombia (1828–29) before falling victim to Andrew Jackson's spoils system. Harrison fit Whig designs of defeating Jacksonians with a war hero of their own and received the Whig nomination to face Martin Van Buren in 1840. Harrison's campaign sidestepped issues to cast him as a plain frontiersman who guzzled hard cider while Van Buren sipped champagne. In the first modern election full of hoopla and hype, "Tippecanoe and Tyler Too"—the Whig slogan—linked Harrison's most famous victory with his obscure running mate. A huge turnout gave Harrison the victory at age 67, the oldest president before Ronald Reagan. Harrison delivered a record 8,500-word inaugural address hatless and coatless on a drizzly winter day. He caught a cold that never left and succumbed to pneumonia on Apr. 4, 1841, the first president to die in the White House—where he lived for only 31 days. His grandson, Benjamin Harrison, was the 23d president.

## 10. John Tyler
### (1841–1845)

The first vice president to become president by succession, the first president to see impeachment proposed against him, and the only president to change parties in office, John Tyler was born on Mar. 29, 1790, in Charles City County, Virginia. He was a Virginia legislator, congressman, senator, and governor before the Whigs chose him as William Henry Harrison's running mate in 1840. Though a strict constructionist and states' rights advocate, Tyler earned the Whigs' favor by opposing Andrew Jackson. But as president after Harrison's death, "His Accidency" earned their ire by vetoing, in mid-1842, two tariff bills vital to the Whig party. Eventually, his cabinet resigned and his party expelled him. Outraged members of Congress called for his impeachment. On July 10, 1842, John Minor Botts, a Whig representative from Richmond, Virginia, proposed the appointment of a special committee to investigate Tyler's conduct in office with an eye toward impeachment. The proposal was defeated on Jan. 10, 1843, by a vote of 127 to 83. This was the first time presidential impeachment proceedings were introduced in Congress. Tyler concluded the Webster-Ashburton Treaty (1842), which adjusted the northeastern boundary of the United States, and the Texas annexation (1845), but without popular or partisan support, he was powerless and decided against running for reelection. A veto on his last day in office became the first ever to be overridden. Tyler died on Jan. 18, 1862, awaiting his seat in the Confederate Congress.

### 11. James Knox Polk
#### (1845–1849)

The first dark-horse president, James Knox Polk was born in Mecklenburg County, North Carolina, on Nov. 2, 1795. A star orator in Tennessee politics, Polk idolized Andrew Jackson. "Young Hickory" took Jackson's old seat in Congress in 1825 and was reelected seven times. Polk was speaker of the house from 1835 to 1839 and governor of Tennessee until 1841. He lost two bids for reelection, and his political career seemed over when the Democrats nominated him for president in 1844. Polk's name had not even appeared on the first seven ballots, but the deadlocked convention latched onto Polk as a proexpansion dark horse. In the election he defeated Henry Clay by 1.5 percent of the vote on a platform that ignored slavery. From his inaugural address onward, Polk pursued expansion in the West. In 1846, he bluffed the British into believing the United States would go to war over Oregon, extracting a treaty for it. When Mexico attacked U.S. troops in disputed Texas territory, Polk called it an invasion and got a declaration of war. The ensuing Mexican War (1846–48) won California and the Southwest for the United States in the Treaty of Guadalupe-Hidalgo. Polk declined a second term, having fulfilled the nation's "Manifest Destiny" to span the continent. The last strong president before Abraham Lincoln, Polk added a million square miles to the United States. But the issue of slavery in the new territories split the Democrats and soon the whole country. "The presidency is not a bed of roses," complained Polk, who left the White House totally ex-

hausted and died three months later, on June 15, 1849.

### 12. Zachary Taylor
#### (1849–1850)

Zachary Taylor, the first president to have no previous political experience, was born on Nov. 24, 1784, in Montebello, Virginia. His father was a colonel in the Revolutionary War, and Taylor—along with four brothers—served as a professional soldier for nearly 40 years. After distinguished service against the British and Native Americans, Gen. Taylor's finest hour came during the Mexican War, when he captured Monterrey and smashed Gen. Santa Ana's much larger army at the Battle of Buena Vista (1847). Though Taylor had never held office or even voted, the Whigs eagerly nominated "Old Rough and Ready" for president in 1848; Taylor, like William Henry Harrison, was an apolitical war hero above the slavery controversy. He won the election when the new Free Soil party siphoned off Democratic votes, but Taylor took office with Congress in chaos over the admission of California as a free state. Taylor opposed the Compromise of 1850 and probably would have vetoed it, but he died suddenly of acute indigestion on July 9, 1850. (A long, hot Fourth of July at Washington Monument ceremonies had no doubt contributed to his weakened state.) Backers of the compromise rejoiced that Taylor's death saved the Union. Taylor was both the last of eight slave owners and the last Whig to be elected president.

### 13. Millard Fillmore
#### (1850–1853)

Born in a log cabin on Jan. 7, 1800, Millard Fillmore was the son of a poor farmer in Locke Township, New York. Apprenticed to a cloth maker in his youth, Fillmore struggled for an education and got a job teaching even though he never attended college. Clerking for a judge taught Fillmore enough law to join the bar at age 23, and he became a prosperous New York attorney. Fillmore entered politics as an Anti-Mason and was a four-term congressman when the Whigs made him Zachary Taylor's vice president in 1848. Dignified good looks were Fillmore's main political asset; he was quite unprepared for the presidency when Taylor died suddenly in 1850. Fillmore delayed civil war another decade by signing the Compromise of 1850, but he lost the nomination in 1852 when the Whigs turned to Gen. Winfield Scott, yet another genial war hero and their last candidate. In 1856 Fillmore ran again for president as candidate of the American, or "Know-Nothing," party. Fillmore hoped to unite the country behind anti-Catholicism and nativism, submerging the slavery issue, but he carried only Maryland. Though a Unionist in the Civil War, Fillmore denounced Abraham Lincoln and remained sharply critical of Republicans until his death on Mar. 8, 1874.

### 14. Franklin Pierce
#### (1853–1857)

Son of a Revolutionary War hero, Franklin Pierce was born in Hillsboro, New Hampshire,

on Nov. 23, 1804—the first president born in the 19th century. A leader of Jacksonian Democrats in Congress in the 1830s, Pierce had been absent from national politics for a decade when the deadlocked Democratic convention nominated him for president on the 49th ballot in 1852. A dark horse candidate, Pierce won enough southern votes to defeat Gen. Winfield Scott, his Mexican War commander, becoming the youngest president as of that date. Pierce greatly hastened the coming of the Civil War by signing the Kansas-Nebraska Act (1854), which repealed the Missouri Compromise and reopened the dangerous issue of slavery expansion. He continually appeased the South by backing proslavery ruffians in "Bleeding Kansas," encouraging slavery expansionists who coveted Cuba, and buying the land known as the Gadsden Purchase from Mexico for a southern railroad. As a result Pierce's party lost elections to Republicans who charged that "slave power" controlled the White House. In 1856 Pierce became the only elected president to be denied his own party's renomination. During the Civil War, Pierce criticized the Emancipation Proclamation and was nearly lynched by angry New Englanders. He died a forgotten, depressed alcoholic, in Concord, New Hampshire, on Oct. 8, 1869, the only president from New Hampshire.

### 15. James Buchanan
#### (1857–1861)

Considered one of the worst presidents because of his lack of good judgment and moral courage, and also the only bachelor president, James Buchanan was born in Mercersburg, Pennsylvania, on Apr. 23, 1791. A lawyer and veteran of the War of 1812, Buchanan compiled more than 40 years of public service as legislator and diplomat. The Democrats nominated Buchanan in 1856 largely because he was in England during the Kansas-Nebraska debate and thus remained untainted by either side of the issue. Millard Fillmore's "Know-Nothing" candidacy helped Buchanan defeat John C. Frémont, the first Republican candidate for president. Buchanan favored "popular sovereignty" over slavery in the territories and was the last of the Doughfaces, or northern politicians submissive to the South. Few Americans shared Buchanan's faith that the Supreme Court's *Dred Scott* decision (1857) would end conflict over slavery expansion "speedily and finally." When it did not, Buchanan tried to close the issue himself by urging that Kansas be admitted as a slave state—an even worse miscalculation. Democrats deserted him, and Republicans won the House in 1858, but Buchanan's vetoes and southern votes in the Senate stalemated the government. He inadvertently helped Abraham Lincoln win in 1860 by refusing to conciliate his own party. The secession crisis paralyzed Buchanan, who denied both the southern right to secede and the federal government's right to do anything about it; he was relieved to hand Lincoln the reins. Buchanan died on June 1, 1868. On the day before, he predicted that "history will vindicate my memory," but historians continue mainly to denigrate him.

## 16. Abraham Lincoln
### (1861–1865)

A largely unpopular president until he was assassinated (the first assassinated president), Abraham Lincoln was born in a log cabin in Hodgenville, Kentucky, on Feb. 12, 1809. He accumulated barely a year's total education while growing up, though he did learn to write and developed a fondness for reading. Family moves took him to Indiana and then to Illinois by the time he was 21. At age 19 Lincoln had worked his way down the Mississippi and came away appalled at slavery. He served in the Black Hawk War (1832) before losing an election for the state legislature. A failed storekeeper, Lincoln worked odd jobs while he taught himself law, sometimes walking 20 miles to borrow books. He finally made the state legislature in 1834 as a Whig, and in 1842 married Mary Todd, having canceled their engagement once previously.

Elected to Congress in 1846, Lincoln denounced James K. Polk for precipitating the Mexican War. He returned to his Springfield, Illinois, law practice after only one term. But the repeal of the Missouri Compromise shocked Lincoln back into politics, and he helped organize the Illinois Republicans. An unsuccessful candidate for the Senate in 1858, Lincoln drew national attention in debates with Stephen A. Douglas, the nation's leading Democrat. Lincoln was rewarded with his party's nomination for president in 1860, the least objectionable candidate among several more prominent Republicans. He defeated three opponents in the election, though his name did not even appear on the ballot in the South. As Southern states left the Union, Lincoln preached conciliation and promised no harm to slavery—but he vowed to crush secession and forced the issue at Ft. Sumter. After early reverses in the Civil War, Lincoln decided slavery had to be abolished altogether to restore the Union, and he issued the Emancipation Proclamation (1862). Lincoln's management of the war was thwarted by incompetent generals, feuding politicians, and his own inexperience, which matched that of his troops. Yet, like them, Lincoln learned on the job, settling on Ulysses S. Grant as his top general by 1864. The powers of the presidency expanded dramatically under Lincoln, who stretched the Constitution on behalf of the war effort. Lincoln defeated Gen. George McClellan for reelection in 1864, vowing to "bind up the nation's wounds." Before he had the chance, Lincoln was shot on Good Friday, five days after the war's end, by John Wilkes Booth, an arch-Confederate. Lincoln died the next morning, on Apr. 15, 1865. His martyrdom spurred the vengefulness of Reconstruction, ironically against Lincoln's own wishes. Millions of Americans lined the 1,700-mile route of Lincoln's funeral train, their mournful cries resounding all the way back to Illinois. Lincoln's prestige has grown with time, until many have come to regard him as the greatest president.

## 17. Andrew Johnson
### (1865–1869)

The only president ever impeached, Andrew Johnson was born in Raleigh, North Carolina, on Dec. 29, 1808, the son of a poor laborer. No president could claim humbler origins: Johnson's father died when he was three, his mother worked as a washerwoman, and he never attended a day of school in his life. As a teenager he ran away to Tennessee, opened a successful tailor's shop, and got elected mayor of Greeneville by age 21. A fiery Democratic stump speaker, Johnson's attacks on Whigs and rich planters won him a seat in the state legislature in 1835 and in Congress in 1843, made him governor in 1853, and took him to the Senate in 1857. Alone among 22 southern senators, Johnson stayed loyal to the Union in 1861, though a mob of Virginians nearly lynched him for it. Lincoln appointed Johnson military governor of Tennessee, and he was nominated for vice president on the "National Union" ticket in 1864. Suddenly made president by Lincoln's assassination, Johnson vowed to carry on Lincoln's policy of leniency toward the South, but radical Republican opposition and his own coarse ineptitude led to serious clashes with Congress. Johnson vetoed 29 bills and was overridden 15 times, more than any other president to that time. A former slave owner, Johnson resisted Republican efforts to aid the freedmen. His only victory was the unpopular purchase of Alaska in 1867. Congress systematically stripped him of power until Johnson fought back by removing his disloyal secretary of war, Edwin M. Stanton. Impeached in the House for defying the Tenure of Office Act, Johnson was tried in the Senate and acquitted by a single vote on May 26, 1868. Few presidents were so stymied in office. Tennessee helped vindicate Johnson by making him the only former president elected to the Senate, but he died a few months later, on July 31, 1875.

## 18. Ulysses S. Grant
### (1869–1877)

A better general than president, Ulysses Simpson Grant was born in Point Pleasant, Ohio, on Apr. 27, 1822. Having barely passed West Point's height requirement for entrance, Grant attended the academy and graduated in the middle of his class in 1843. Fifty of Grant's classmates fought with or against him as Civil War generals. He served under Gen. Zachary Taylor in the Mexican War before marrying his sweetheart, Julia Dent, in 1848. Assigned to isolated posts after 1852, Grant grew bored away from his family and reportedly turned to heavy drinking. Finally resigning from the army in 1854, he went to Missouri, only to fail in farming and real estate. When the Civil War began, Grant was working in his younger brother's leather shop in Galena, Illinois. He received a commission and rose rapidly to brigadier general. U.S. Grant acquired the nickname Unconditional Surrender for his string of western victories, notably at Vicksburg and Chattanooga in 1863. Once Abraham Lincoln made him supreme commander in 1864, Grant

opened a relentless offensive that quickly ended the war. He personally accepted Gen. Robert E. Lee's surrender at Appomattox in 1865. After feuding with Andrew Johnson, Grant joined the Republicans and was elected president in 1868. Grant pressed radical Reconstruction in the South with mixed results. Corruption—notably the Jay Gould (1869), Crédit Mobilier (1872), and Whiskey Ring (1875) scandals—marred Grant's presidency; nevertheless, he easily won reelection in 1872. The Panic of 1873 triggered a deep economic depression that dissuaded Grant from a third term in 1876. Reconsidering in 1880, he sought the Republican nomination again and nearly succeeded. Afterward Grant retired and went bankrupt. To provide for his family, he began writing his memoirs. Developing cancer, Grant valiantly hung on to finish the project, which would earn him some literary fame and his family half a million dollars. He died on July 23, 1885, just four days after completing his autobiography.

## 19. Rutherford B. Hayes
### (1877–1881)

Rutherford Birchard Hayes was born a frail child on Oct. 4, 1822, in Delaware, Ohio, where he was raised by his mother. After attending Harvard Law School, he set up a successful Cincinnati law practice in 1849. Hayes defended fugitive slaves and helped found the Ohio Republicans. In 1852 he married Lucy Ware Webb, the first college graduate first lady. A decorated Civil War veteran, Hayes was wounded five times and promoted to general. From 1868 to 1876 he served as governor of Ohio. Republicans turned to Hayes as a scandal-free hero in 1876 and nominated him for president. He lost the election to Samuel Tilden of the Democrats, but Republicans in Congress disputed enough state vote totals to connive "Rutherfraud" into office with the support of southern Democrats. Hayes's first acts were to appoint an ex-Confederate to his cabinet and to withdraw federal troops from the South. He never overcame the resulting stigma of political bargain, and facing a Democratic Congress, Hayes seemed destined for a weak presidency. Yet he put the nation back on the gold standard, put down railroad strikes, reformed the civil service, and banished liquor from the White House before keeping his promise to serve only one term. Hayes viewed the return of prosperity and Republican majorities in Congress as personal triumphs. He worked quietly for charitable causes until his death on Jan. 17, 1893.

## 20. James A. Garfield
### (1881)

The last log cabin president, James Abram Garfield was born near Orange, Ohio, on Nov. 19, 1831, and like Rutherford B. Hayes, Garfield was raised by his mother. Garfield graduated from Williams College in 1856, became a classics professor, president of Hiram College, a lawyer, and at age 30 the youngest Union general in the Civil War. Garfield left the battlefield in 1864 to enter Congress, where he remained until the Republicans nominated him for president in 1880, a dark-horse compromise between Grant and James G. Blaine. Garfield defeated Gen. Winfield Scott Hancock and the Democrats by 0.1 percent of the vote in a campaign stressing tariffs. Republicans immediately swarmed to Garfield, demanding patronage for their rival "Stalwart" and "Half-Breed" factions. After only four months in office, Garfield was shot in a train station by Charles J. Guiteau, a disappointed Stalwart office-seeker. Garfield died 80 days later, on Sept. 19, 1881, the second presidential assassination ending the second-shortest presidency. When hordes of Republican hopefuls had besieged the White House begging for jobs, Garfield had exclaimed: "My God! What is there in this place that a man should ever want to get in it?"

### 21. Chester A. Arthur
### (1881–1885)

Chester Alan Arthur was born a preacher's son on Oct. 5, 1829, in Fairfield, Vermont. He grew up in Vermont and in New York to become an ardent abolitionist like his father. A true machine politician, Arthur worked for Republican candidates in New York and enjoyed several patronage jobs during the Civil War. Ulysses S. Grant appointed him collector of the port of New York in 1871, and Arthur prospered there until 1879, when Rutherford B. Hayes removed him in the name of reform. In 1880 "Half-Breed" Republicans nominated Arthur for vice president in a conciliatory gesture to his "Stalwart" faction. "The office of Vice President is a greater honor than I ever dreamed of attaining," he said. But Arthur acceded to the presidency on Sept. 19, 1881, when another Stalwart assassinated James A. Garfield. Perhaps shamed into supporting civil service reform, Arthur signed the Pendleton Act (1883) and rooted out post office graft. Democrats in Congress thwarted the rest of Arthur's initiatives; Republicans, whose calls for spoils Arthur ignored, denied him renomination in 1884. He lost a Senate race in New York and died two years later, on Nov. 18, 1886. Arthur was the last of three presidents in the single year 1881.

### 22, 24. Grover Cleveland
### (1885–1889; 1893–1897)

The only president to serve two nonconsecutive terms, Stephen Grover Cleveland was a minister's son, born in Caldwell, New Jersey, on Mar. 18, 1837. The family moved to New York, where Cleveland's uncle made him a lawyer. He showed scant interest in politics until Buffalo elected him mayor in 1881, and the next year Cleveland became governor. His war on corrupt Tammany Hall made Cleveland the perfect Democratic reform candidate for president in 1884. During the election campaign, backers of James G. Blaine, the Republican candidate, accused Cleveland of fathering an illegitimate child. He admitted it and won anyway—by 0.3 percent of the vote— but not before the Republicans came up with the immortal campaign chant "Ma! Ma! Where's my Pa?/Gone to the White House,/Ha! Ha! Ha!" The first Democratic president after

the Civil War, Cleveland pushed for civil-service reform and lower tariffs. In the first White House wedding, Cleveland married Frances Folsom in 1886. Cleveland cast over 300 vetoes—more than twice the combined total of all previous presidents. He cut Civil War pensions, seized 81 million acres of unused land from railroads, and signed the Interstate Commerce Act (1887). Defeated in the 1888 election, Cleveland claimed there was "no happier man in the United States"; yet four years later he won a rematch with Benjamin Harrison. Back in the White House, Cleveland underwent a secret operation to remove his cancerous upper jaw. His tight-money policies did nothing to help the depression after the Panic of 1893. Cleveland sent federal troops to break up the Pullman strike (1894) and supported William McKinley, a Republican, for president in 1896. "I have tried so hard to do right," Cleveland said on his deathbed on June 24, 1908.

### 23. Benjamin Harrison
### (1889–1893)

Benjamin Harrison was born on Aug. 20, 1833, at the North Bend, Ohio, farm of his grandfather William Henry Harrison, the ninth president. He took up the law in Indiana before joining the Union Army in 1862. Harrison finished the Civil War a brigadier general and returned to Indiana, where he was a prominent Republican, defeated for governor in 1876 but elected senator in 1881. A colorless compromise candidate for president, Harrison won the 1888 election despite receiving fewer popular votes than Grover Cleveland. Harrison bowed to the "Billion Dollar Congress" of free-spending Republicans who escalated Civil War pensions, transportation subsidies, naval construction, and spoils patronage. The McKinley Tariff, the Sherman Anti-Trust Act, the Sherman Silver Purchase Act (all 1890), and Secretary of State James G. Blaine's vigorous foreign policy were hallmarks of Harrison's administration, which oversaw the admission of six new states. Democrats won back Congress in 1890 and the White House in 1892, when Harrison lost to Cleveland in their rematch. A legal expert, Harrison taught at Stanford University and defended Venezuela in a boundary dispute with Britain before his death, on Mar. 13, 1901. Harrison referred to the White House as "my jail."

### 25. William McKinley
### (1897–1901)

The last Civil War veteran to become president, William McKinley was born in Niles, Ohio, on Jan. 29, 1843, son of an iron founder. A college dropout, McKinley was a post office clerk when the Civil War began. He volunteered as a private and mustered out as a 22-year-old major. McKinley studied law and was elected to Congress in 1876. A longtime Republican floor leader, he authored the record-high McKinley Tariff of 1890, before losing his seat that same year. Ohio millionaire Marcus Hanna, McKinley's political manager, engineered two governor's terms for him and funded McKinley's run for the presidency in 1896. William Jennings Bryan opposed him on

a free-silver platform, but McKinley's dignified front porch campaign stressed sound money, tariffs, and the "full dinner pail." He won the election with the first popular majority since Grant's reelection. Strongly probusiness, McKinley raised the tariff still higher and reluctantly led the country into the Spanish-American War (1898). By acquiring the Philippines and other islands, the country became a world power under McKinley, who went on to proclaim the open-door policy in China. McKinley defeated Bryan by an even larger margin in 1900 and was enjoying great popularity when anarchist Leon Czolgosz shot him in Buffalo, New York. McKinley died two weeks later, on Sept. 14, 1901.

### 26. Theodore Roosevelt
### (1901–1909)

Theodore Roosevelt was born in New York City on Oct. 27, 1858, the only president born there. A small, sickly child plagued by asthma, Roosevelt overcame a pampered youth to live the "strenuous life": he boxed, hiked, hunted, rode horses, and climbed the Matterhorn. After graduating Phi Beta Kappa from Harvard in 1880, he attended Columbia Law School and became the youngest member of New York's legislature. Rich men of his day did not consider politics a suitable avocation, but Roosevelt desperately wanted "to be of the governing class." His first wife, Alice Hathaway Lee, died on the same day his mother died in 1884. Roosevelt wrote books and ran a cattle ranch in North Dakota until he married Edith Kermit Carow in 1886 and they moved to Oyster Bay, New York. During the Spanish-American War, Roosevelt left a job at the Navy Department in 1898 to lead the Rough Riders volunteer regiment in Cuba, achieving glory in the Battle of San Juan Hill. Elected governor of New York immediately upon returning home, Roosevelt soon thereafter was named William McKinley's vice-presidential running mate, in 1900. Roosevelt learned of McKinley's death while on a mountain-climbing expedition.

The youngest president at 42, "T.R." promised a Square Deal to close the gap between capital and labor. He mounted well-publicized campaigns against big business and successfully arbitrated major strikes. "Teddy's" popularity soared when he humbled billionaire J. P. Morgan in the Northern Securities case, and a record plurality reelected him in 1904. Roosevelt signed progressive laws to regulate railroads, inspect food and drugs, and create more than 150 million acres of national parks and forests. No less vigorous in foreign policy, Roosevelt's corollary to the Monroe Doctrine asserted the country would intervene to prevent European involvement in Latin America. For helping to end the Russo-Japanese War, Roosevelt became the first American to win the Nobel Prize, but he considered the Panama Canal his greatest achievement. Roosevelt kept his pledge not to seek a third term in 1908—but in 1912 he ran against his chosen successor, William Howard Taft. Denied his party's nomination, Roosevelt survived an assassination attempt and won more than 4 million votes as the Progressive, or Bull Moose, candidate. During World War I, Roosevelt bitterly denounced the neutrality policy of Woodrow Wilson, who then denied Roosevelt's request to lead troops in France. Roosevelt's four sons fought there; Quentin, the youngest, was killed in action. While laying plans for another run at the White House, Roosevelt died suddenly of a cardiac embolism on Jan. 6, 1919. "No President has ever enjoyed himself as much as I have enjoyed myself," he said.

## 27. William Howard Taft
### (1909–1913)

By far the largest president at over 330 pounds, William Howard Taft was born in Cincinnati, Ohio, on Sept. 15, 1857. He graduated from Yale in 1878, then followed his father into law and Republican politics: "I always had my plate right side up when offices were falling," Taft wrote. William McKinley sent him to govern the Philippines in 1900, and Theodore Roosevelt appointed him secretary of war in 1904. Taft traveled around the world as Roosevelt's personal emissary, becoming T.R.'s chosen successor in 1908. As president, Taft tried to carry on Roosevelt's policies, but he wrecked the Republican party by alienating progressives from conservative "Stand-Patters" over tariff and conservation issues. Taft initiated the income tax and pursued antitrust suits against big business—but generally he sided with wealthy interests. An infuriated Roosevelt challenged Taft unsuccessfully for the Republican nomination in 1912, then outpolled him in the election, giving Woodrow Wilson the victory. With eight electoral votes, Taft suffered the worst-ever defeat for an incumbent president. But the better part of his career lay ahead: Taft, always more comfortable as a jurist, taught law at Yale until he was appointed chief justice of the United States in 1921. He served with distinction, alternating a liberal nationalism in economic affairs with political and social conservatism. Taft died on Mar. 8, 1930. Never nostalgic for the White House, Taft once said, "I don't remember that I ever was President."

## 28. Woodrow Wilson
### (1913–1921)

Born on Dec. 28, 1856, in Staunton, Virginia, the son of a Presbyterian minister, Thomas Woodrow Wilson grew up in Virginia, Georgia, South Carolina, and North Carolina—the first southern president since Andrew Jackson. Probably dyslexic, Wilson was slow to read; yet he became the most highly educated president. Graduated from Princeton in 1879, Wilson studied law before taking a Ph.D. in political science at Johns Hopkins in 1886. He taught at Bryn Mawr and Wesleyan University before Princeton appointed him professor in 1890. Wilson attracted the attention of Democratic bosses after he was elected Princeton's president in 1902, and they persuaded him to run for New Jersey governor in 1910. A strong progressive, Wilson won easily—and then turned on party bosses by sponsoring antimachine reforms. In 1912 the Democrats nominated Wilson for president on the 46th ballot, and he won, with Theodore Roosevelt and William

Howard Taft splitting the Republican vote.

Wilson's expert knowledge of government and strong party leadership pushed the Underwood Tariff, the Federal Reserve Act, the Federal Trade Commission, and the Clayton Antitrust Act through Congress by 1914. Restoring competition to the monopoly-plagued economy was the goal of Wilson's "New Freedom," until war in Europe made neutrality his top priority. German attacks on Allied ships carrying Americans strained Wilson's commitment, but he was narrowly reelected in 1916 on the slogan He Kept Us Out of War. After Germany spurned Wilson's mediation and resumed attacks on Allied shipping, Congress declared war at Wilson's behest in April 1917. World War I would "make the world safe for democracy," Wilson vowed, and he issued "Fourteen Points" for a just peace. After the armistice in November 1918, Wilson became the first president to visit Europe when he attended the Paris peace conference that produced the Versailles Treaty. Wilson's dream of "peace without vengeance" was frustrated at Versailles, where he compromised away his Fourteen Points to obtain the League of Nations for collective security. In July 1919, Wilson returned home to face hostile Republicans in the Senate, where his treaty languished. On a nationwide speaking tour, Wilson collapsed from exhaustion in Colorado and suffered a paralytic stroke in October 1919. Wilson, all but incapacitated, refused to compromise as the Senate rejected the Versailles Treaty. Wilson's second wife, Edith Bolling Galt, whom he married in 1915, shielded the disabled president from the press and politicians until the end of his term in 1921. Woodrow Wilson died in his sleep on Feb. 3, 1924, frustrated by his own country's refusal to join the League of Nations.

## 29. Warren G. Harding
### (1921–1923)

The first president born after the Civil War, Warren Gamaliel Harding was born in Blooming Grove, Ohio, which earlier had been named Corsica, on Nov. 2, 1865. He taught, studied law, and sold insurance before following his father into the newspaper business. Marriage to Florence DeWolfe, a wealthy widow, in 1891 helped finance Harding's paper, the *Marion Star*. A staunch Republican, Harding's pro-business editorials got him elected state senator and lieutenant governor. Although defeated for governor in 1910, Harding was elected senator four years later. Republicans turned to him in 1920 as a compromise candidate for president, the "best of the second-raters"; his good looks were expected to win over women first-time voters. Elected by an unprecedented 61 percent majority, Harding promised a return to "normalcy" for Americans tired of war and Woodrow Wilson. Harding's administration featured higher tariffs, lower taxes, and immigration restriction—but perhaps most notably, pervasive corruption and incompetence by Harding's crooked appointees. Harding was disturbed by the dishonesty of "my God-damn friends," two of whom committed suicide to avoid prosecution. While

visiting San Francisco, Harding died suddenly of an embolism on Aug. 2, 1923. Scandals involving secret love affairs, official graft, and the vast Teapot Dome swindle erupted soon thereafter. Mrs. Harding zealously tracked down Harding's letters and destroyed them, leaving him the most enigmatic president, and certainly one of the worst.

## 30. Calvin Coolidge
### (1923–1929)

The only president to share the nation's birthday, John Calvin Coolidge was born in Plymouth, Vermont, on July 4, 1872. Descended from a long line of New Englanders, he graduated from Amherst in 1895, practiced law in Massachusetts, and entered Republican politics in 1899. Coolidge rose slowly through a succession of state offices until he was elected governor of Massachusetts in 1918. Acclaimed for crushing the Boston police strike in 1919, Coolidge became the unexpected Republican vice-presidential nominee in 1920. After Warren G. Harding's death while still in office, Coolidge's own father swore him in as the new president. "Silent Cal" was the butt of jokes for his laconic utterances, but his minimalist approach to government fit the public mood, and he restored respectability to the White House, tainted by Harding's corrupt appointees and all-night poker parties. Instead of the whiskey that once flowed freely there, ice water in paper cups was served to visitors. Coolidge, untouched by leftover scandals, won the election in his own right in 1924. Pronouncing that the "business of America is business," he ushered in the heady years of Coolidge Prosperity, as the stock market soared higher and higher. Coolidge ignored foreign affairs and made frugality his trademark, slashing the budget at the expense of farmers and veterans, even driving out a White House cook who could not abide Coolidge's cost cutting. "It's a pretty good idea to get out when they still want you," Coolidge said, surprising the nation at the peak of his success by declining to run again in 1928. A popular president, Coolidge was safely out of politics when the Great Depression arrived. He died on Jan. 5, 1933, on the eve of the New Deal.

## 31. Herbert Hoover
### (1929–1933)

Born in West Branch, Iowa, on Aug. 10, 1874, Herbert Clark Hoover was the first president from west of the Mississippi. Orphaned at eight and raised by Quaker relatives in Iowa and Oregon, Hoover joined the first graduating class of Stanford University in 1895. He became a world-famous mining engineer and a multimillionaire by age 40. In World War I, Hoover helped rescue Americans stranded in Europe, distributed food supplies to occupied Belgium, and convinced the nation to save food ("Hooverize") for the war effort. Hoover was Woodrow Wilson's economic adviser at Versailles, and he organized relief for famine-struck Russia during the revolution. Joining the Republicans in 1919, Hoover earned prominence as the secretary of commerce in the 1920s and was elected president in 1928—the only electoral victory of his life. He promised a "chicken in every pot," but a few months later, the Wall Street crash brought on the Great Depression. Paralyzed by his conservative instincts, Hoover could not halt the spread of bank failures, bankruptcy, unemployment, and despair. Government should not get involved, he believed, and public relief would ruin American morals—so Hoover called for a balanced budget while promising the return of prosperity. He sent tanks to disperse veterans begging for pensions, and shanty towns across the country were dubbed Hoovervilles. Massively defeated by Franklin D. Roosevelt in 1932, Hoover called the New Deal "socialistic, collectivistic, fascistic and communistic." For decades Americans blamed Hoover for the depression and criticized his hard-hearted refusal to help the needy. Hoover lived another 31 years, the longest postpresidential lifespan, and he salvaged his reputation with more relief work after World War II. In retirement Hoover chaired two bipartisan commissions on government reorganization, issuing many important recommendations for federal reform. Boulder Dam on the Colorado River was renamed to honor Hoover before he died, at age 90, on Oct. 20, 1964.

### 32. Franklin D. Roosevelt (1933–1945)

The only president elected more than twice, Franklin Delano Roosevelt was born to a wealthy Hyde Park, New York, family on Jan. 30, 1882. He followed his cousin, Theodore Roosevelt, into Harvard and Columbia Law School—but not into the Republican party. F.D.R. was a Democratic state senator, assistant secretary of the navy, and nominee for vice president in 1920. Paralyzed by polio in 1921, Roosevelt learned to walk with braces and canes. As governor of New York after 1928, he pioneered unemployment relief in the Great Depression, earning him the Democratic nomination for president in 1932. Herbert Hoover, brooding and baffled by the depression, posed little challenge to the beaming, magnetic Roosevelt, who won the election by 23 million to 16 million votes. F.D.R. promised vague but bold experimentation ("above all, try something"), and as he took office in the worst inaugural crisis since Abraham Lincoln's, he assured Americans they had "nothing to fear but fear itself." F.D.R.'s first 100 days set a breakneck pace as compliant congressmen approved his New Deal for relief and recovery. Major landmarks were the National Industrial Recovery Act, the Agricultural Adjustment Act, the Tennessee Valley Authority, the Works Progress Administration, the National Labor Relations Act (Wagner Act), and the Social Security Act (1933–35). Though often contradictory and ineffective, the New Deal established the federal government's responsibility for protecting farmers, workers, and the unemployed while actively regulating the economy to prevent another crash. F.D.R.'s high-profile "fireside chats," public works projects, and Social Security programs overcame despair and restored public confidence in the economy and government.

Reelected by a huge margin in 1936, Roosevelt proved incapable of ending the depression, as he ran afoul of the "nine old men" on the Supreme Court. Almost as many Americans called Roosevelt a Communist as praised him for rescuing the common man. Despite alienating many voters with his court-packing plan and "soak the rich" taxes, F.D.R. won an unprecedented third term in 1940. As war loomed in Europe, F.D.R. used his mastery of public opinion to lead Americans away from isolation, helping Britain with the destroyers-for-bases deal (1940) and Lend-Lease Act (1941) even before Pearl Harbor. World War II then occupied F.D.R.'s full attention as he shelved the New Deal and orchestrated the mammoth war effort. Roosevelt crisscrossed the globe to meet with Allied leaders and kept close personal control of diplomacy and grand strategy. He rallied a powerful sense of national purpose in the war, winning his fourth election in 1944. Together with Winston Churchill and Josef Stalin, F.D.R. planned a postwar peace of UN cooperation. Just after the Yalta Conference, Roosevelt died suddenly of a cerebral hemorrhage on Apr. 12, 1945, days before the war's end. His wife of 40 years, Eleanor Roosevelt, easily the most influential first lady, led her husband's campaign on behalf of disadvantaged Americans and continued it long after his death.

### 33. Harry S Truman (1945–1953)

A plain midwestern farmer and World War I artilleryman, Harry S Truman (the S does not stand for a middle name) was born on May 8, 1884, in Lamar, Missouri. After his Kansas City haberdashery failed, Truman entered politics as a Democrat in the 1920s, and the local Pendergast machine arranged his election to the Senate as a New Dealer in 1934. National attention came to Truman when he headed a congressional committee investigating government waste during World War II. When Franklin D. Roosevelt needed a new vice president in 1944, he chose Truman. After only a few weeks in office, Truman had the presidency thrust upon him by Roosevelt's sudden death in April 1945. "Pray for me boys," he told his first press conference. Utterly unprepared, Truman did not even know about the atomic bomb project, but he vowed to carry on Roosevelt's policies. Truman proved a remarkably capable chief executive, educating himself in foreign affairs and dispatching crucial decisions rapidly. In his first four months, Truman approved the United Nations, accepted the German surrender, met with Allied leaders at Potsdam, and ordered atomic bombs dropped on Japan. As the Cold War commenced, Truman talked tough with the Soviets, accusing them of breaking agreements and intimidating helpless neighbors. In 1947 he proclaimed the Truman Doctrine, promising U.S. aid to threatened countries, and the Marshall Plan to aid European recovery and contain communism. The next year Truman ordered the Berlin airlift when the Soviets cut off West Berlin, and he promised to help Third World countries with the Point Four program. No less assertive at

home, Truman made progress on civil rights, subdued restive unions, and prevented the Republican-controlled Congress from dismantling the New Deal—a specter that he effectively raised to win surprise reelection in 1948. Truman committed the country to the NATO alliance in 1949 and sent troops to South Korea when Communist armies invaded in 1950. But as Congress rejected Truman's ambitious Fair Deal domestic program and the Korean War bogged down, Truman's last years were barren. He had more vetoes overridden than all presidents but Andrew Johnson, and his poll ratings were lower than all but Jimmy Carter's. Truman, who initially raised fears of subversion with his loyalty program, could not quell the Red Scare that swept his party from power in 1952, as Republicans hammered away on the theme that Democrats were "soft on communism." Truman was convinced that he saved the world from communism, prevented World War III, and could have won another term if he chose to run in 1952. "He did his damndest" was the only eulogy Harry Truman desired on his death, on Dec. 26, 1972. Out of favor when he left office, Truman has gained rising respect since his death.

### 34. Dwight D. Eisenhower (1953–1961)

The last war hero president, Dwight David Eisenhower was born in Denison, Texas, on Oct. 14, 1890, and grew up poor in Kansas. A military history buff, Eisenhower graduated with the 1915 class of West Point that produced 59 generals. He married Mamie Doud, his wife of 52 years, and spent World War I as a tank-training instructor. Eisenhower, only a major at age 40, rose rapidly during World War II, promoted past 350 senior officers to become commander of U.S. forces in Europe in 1942. By the end of 1944, he was the first U.S. five-star general and Supreme Allied Commander, taking the German surrender in May 1945. By that point a global celebrity, Eisenhower was army chief of staff until 1948, when he resigned to become president of Columbia University. Harry S Truman named him to command NATO forces in 1950, but two years later Eisenhower retired again to take the Republican nomination and run for president against Adlai E. Stevenson.

"Ike" became perhaps the most popular president in U.S. history, though many questioned his lax work habits, detached management style, and baffling speeches. Prominent millionaires in Eisenhower's cabinet and arch-conservatives such as Secretary of State John Foster Dulles seemed to have free rein, and Eisenhower acquiesced in Sen. Joe McCarthy's wild charges of subversion. His administration stockpiled atomic weapons and promised "massive retaliation" against Soviet aggression—yet did nothing when the Red Army rolled into Hungary in 1956. Eisenhower did end the Korean War, concluded several alliance agreements, and cut the defense budget. The "Eisenhower Doctrine" promised U.S. aid to Middle Eastern countries fighting communism. When Britain, France, and Israel invaded the Suez Canal in 1956, Eisenhower led UN condemnation and forced them to withdraw, though he sent U.S. marines into Lebanon two years later. He began heavy U.S. involvement in Vietnam by backing the French and then the puppet Diem regime. At home Eisenhower promised to scale back the government—yet he expanded Social Security; created the Department of Health, Education, and Welfare; and spent billions on public housing and freeways. He pointedly stressed religious devotion. The Supreme Court's *Brown* decision (1954), which Eisenhower deeply regretted, inaugurated the civil rights movement. Eisenhower defeated Stevenson again in 1956, but Soviet domination of space, revolution in Cuba, embarrassment over the Soviets' shooting down of a U.S. spy plane, and his own ill health marred his second term. Eisenhower reluctantly sent paratroopers to enforce desegregation in Little Rock, Arkansas, in 1957. Democrats controlled Congress for all but two years of Eisenhower's presidency, and they called for more active leadership when he ended his term as the oldest president before Ronald Reagan. In retirement Eisenhower approved of U.S. intervention in Vietnam and counseled presidents until his death, on Mar. 28, 1969.

### 35.  John F. Kennedy
### (1961–1963)

The youngest man elected president, the only Roman Catholic, and the first born in the 20th century, John Fitzgerald Kennedy was born in Brookline, Massachusetts, on May 29, 1917, to a family of Irish politicos. His father, Joseph P. Kennedy, was ambassador to England and one of the richest men in America. Kennedy attended Dexter and Choate academies, the London School of Economics, and Princeton before graduating from Harvard in 1940. A patrol boat commander in World War II, Kennedy was decorated for bravery in saving the lives of wounded crew members. Kennedy's father arranged his election to Congress, where he served three undistinguished terms before entering the Senate in 1952. After 1953, the year he married wealthy socialite Jacqueline Bouvier, Kennedy's health deteriorated from Addison's disease and agonizing back ailments. He won the Pulitzer Prize for *Profiles in Courage* (1957), a study of principled politicians supposedly written from his hospital bed. Kennedy positioned himself for a presidential run by lambasting Republicans for insufficient anticommunism and "vigor." In 1960, Kennedy prevailed over three prominent opponents for the Democratic nomination, then scraped past Richard M. Nixon in the election by 118,000 votes out of 69 million cast. The campaign featured the first televised presidential debates, capitalizing on Kennedy's exceptional poise and polish.

In accepting the Democratic nomination, Kennedy had pledged a New Frontier, but his social programs languished in Congress. Undaunted, Kennedy plunged into foreign affairs, his primary interest. Just after taking office, he approved the disastrous Bay of Pigs invasion, and a year later he terrified the world by confronting the Soviets over the presence of their missiles in Cuba. He visited the Berlin Wall and expressed solidarity with Germans under the Russian gun. Kennedy's bellicosity eventually subsided as he set up the Washington-Moscow hotline and signed the Nuclear Test Ban Treaty (1963). Thousands of U.S. troops went to Vietnam as Kennedy escalated the commitment to containing communism. Kennedy vastly increased spending for defense and space programs, vowing to put a man on the moon. He also engineered a $10-billion tax cut that eventually brought prosperity and increased revenues. As racial unrest spread, Kennedy cautiously supported the civil rights movement, introducing sweeping legislation that would not pass in his lifetime—nor would his plans for aid to education and medical care for the elderly reach fruition before his death. Gearing up for reelection, Kennedy embarked on a speaking tour across the South, where he was least popular. In a Dallas, Texas, motorcade on Nov. 22, 1963, he was fatally shot. Kennedy's alleged assassin, Lee Harvey Oswald, a left-wing ex-marine, was in turn murdered by Jack Ruby two days later. While doubts persisted that Oswald acted alone, Kennedy's martyrdom helped realize his legislative legacy, and subsequent revelation of his many peccadilloes have not tarnished the "Kennedy myth."

### 36.  Lyndon B. Johnson
### (1963–1969)

The eighth vice president to succeed by death of a president, Lyndon Baines Johnson was born on his father's Texas ranch near Stonewall on Aug. 27, 1908. He worked his way through Southwest Texas State Teachers College, taught briefly, then took a job in Washington—where he would live for all but two years until he left the White House. Government fascinated Johnson, and he reveled in making connections, marrying heiress Claudia Alta "Lady Bird" Taylor after a two-month courtship in 1934. An ardent New Dealer, Johnson won election to Congress as a Democrat in 1937. Reelected three times without opposition, Johnson became the first congressman to volunteer for combat in World War II, winning a Silver Star before returning to Washington. In 1948, on his second try, "Landslide Lyndon" was elected to the Senate by just 87 votes. Hard work and Texas oil money made Johnson the youngest Senate majority leader by 1955. A huge and hearty man, Johnson's powers of persuasion were legendary, but he failed in his bid for the Democratic nomination for president in 1960. Johnson accepted John F. Kennedy's offer of the vice presidency and campaigned hard in the South to aid their narrow victory. Made president a thousand days later by the tragedy in Dallas, Johnson vowed to continue Kennedy's programs, pushing them through Congress with surprising ease. Notable were the Civil Rights Act outlawing segregation and the Equal Opportunity Act, which declared "war on poverty." After less than a year in office, Johnson defeated Barry Goldwater by the biggest plurality in history.

Now president in his own right, Johnson unveiled plans for a Great Society free from poverty and discrimination and passed the Education Act, Medical Care Act, and the Voting Rights Act in 1965. But Johnson came to grief in Vietnam, where he broke his 1964 campaign promise not to send "American boys to fight Asian wars." Earlier administrations committed the U.S. to defending South Vietnam, but Johnson intervened massively to prove American credibility to allies and enemies alike. No doubt he also feared resurgent McCarthyism if another nation were "lost" to communism. Following the Tonkin Gulf incident (1964), Johnson steadily expended American power and lives in Vietnam, but victory, or a means to achieve it, never came within reach—despite the presence of over half-a-million U.S. troops by 1968. Johnson's presidency unraveled as American losses mounted, antiwar protests grew strident, race riots exploded in inner cities across the nation, and the government developed a credibility gap. Virtually a prisoner of the White House, Johnson faced a war he could neither win nor leave behind and a nation more deeply divided than at any time since the Civil War. In March 1968 Johnson effectively resigned by announcing he would not seek another term. He retired to his sprawling Texas ranch and stayed out of politics until his death, on Jan. 22, 1973. Johnson left a domestic reform legacy second only to the New Deal; but he squandered it in Vietnam by raising expectations he could not meet at home and abroad. The day after he died, diplomats signed the Paris peace agreement, formally ending the war.

### 37.  Richard M. Nixon
### (1969–1974)

The only president to resign from office, Richard Milhous Nixon was born in Yorba Linda, California, to a poor Quaker family on Jan. 9, 1913. A graduate of Whittier College and Duke University Law School, Nixon married Thelma "Pat" Ryan in 1940, saw noncombat service in World War II, and rode into Congress on the Republican wave of 1946. He gained fame in the anti-Communist trial of Alger Hiss before entering the Senate in 1950. Dwight D. Eisenhower made Nixon his running mate in 1952, but Nixon was nearly forced to resign for accepting questionable contributions. He appealed for national exoneration in the televised "Checkers" speech. A well-traveled vice president, Nixon almost lost his life to hostile Latin American mobs in 1958, and he waged an impromptu debate in Moscow with Soviet premier Nikita Khrushchev in 1959. Eisenhower's obvious successor in 1960, Nixon narrowly lost the election to John F. Kennedy, and when he lost a California gubernatorial race in 1962, Nixon's career seemed over. Yet he practiced law in New York until the Republicans nominated him again in 1968. To a nation riven by the Vietnam War, Nixon promised "law and order," appealing to calm and unity against a background of riots, assassinations, and protest. Nixon defeated Hubert H. Humphrey with the smallest victor's share of the vote since 1912.

Vowing to "bring us together," Nixon tried to thwart the bureaucracy and Democrats in

Congress by centralizing executive power. To control inflation, he ordered wage-price controls and devalued the dollar for the first time since the depression. Seeking "peace with honor" in Vietnam, Nixon built up the South Vietnamese army and withdrew U.S. troops—while massively escalating bombing of North Vietnam. Antiwar protests reached fever pitch when the United States invaded Cambodia in 1970. Nixon responded with appeals to the "silent majority," attacks on press freedom, and clandestine harassment of administration critics. High points of his first administration were the Apollo moon landing in 1969, Nixon's path-breaking visit to China in 1972, and the first Strategic Arms Limitation Treaty with the Soviet Union. Twelve days after announcing "peace is at hand" in Vietnam, Nixon was reelected by a landslide, carrying an unprecedented 49 states. During the campaign five burglars were arrested in the Democratic party headquarters, and by early 1973, they were linked to the White House. The ensuing "Watergate" scandal exposed the Nixon administration's rampant corruption, illegality, and deceit. Nixon himself downplayed the scandal as mere politics, but when his aides resigned in disgrace, Nixon's role in ordering an illegal cover-up came to light in the press, courts, and congressional investigations. Nixon evaded taxes, accepted illicit campaign contributions, ordered secret bombings, and harassed opponents with executive agencies, wiretaps, and break-ins. Vice President Spiro T. Agnew resigned in October 1973 for accepting bribes, but Nixon hung on to power, claiming, "I am not a crook," as the House began impeachment proceedings. Subpoenas and Supreme Court orders forced Nixon to release tapes of his White House conversations authorizing the Watergate cover-up. Ultimately, he resigned to avoid impeachment for obstruction of justice, abuse of power, and contempt of Congress. Claiming to have lost his "political base," Nixon announced his resignation on national television on Aug. 9, 1974. He never admitted wrongdoing, though he later conceded errors of judgment. Saved by a blanket pardon from Gerald R. Ford, his second vice president and successor as president, Nixon retired to his California mansion, later moving to New York and then New Jersey.

## 38. Gerald R. Ford
### (1974–1977)

The only vice president and president never elected to either office, Gerald Rudolph Ford was born in Omaha, Nebraska, on July 14, 1913. An Eagle Scout, he grew up in Michigan and attended the University of Michigan on a football scholarship, playing on the national championship teams of 1932 and 1933. After graduating in 1935, Ford coached football and boxing at Yale while attending law school; he received his degree in 1941. In the navy he earned 10 battle stars in the Pacific during World War II. Ford ran for Congress in 1948 as a Republican, marrying divorcée Betty Bloomer during the campaign, which he won. Thereafter he would be reelected 12 times, never by less than 60 percent of the vote. In

Congress Ford's solid conservative record elevated him to House Republican minority leader by 1965. For supporting Richard M. Nixon in Congress, Ford was rewarded with the vice presidency in December 1973, replacing Spiro T. Agnew under the 25th Amendment. "I do not think the public would stand for it," Ford said at his confirmation hearings, when asked if he would ever pardon Nixon. For eight months Ford stayed loyal to Nixon, until his resignation made Ford the new president on Aug. 9, 1974. Ford announced "our long national nightmare is over," but a month later he shocked the nation by giving Nixon a blanket pardon. Ford denied any deal had been made, but his public standing never recovered. He struggled with huge Democratic majorities in Congress to stem soaring inflation and unemployment, casting 66 vetoes in all. Ford asked for tax increases in 1974, tax rebates in 1975, and in 1976 his budget contained the largest peacetime deficit to that date. Congress refused Ford's request for aid to South Vietnam and intervention in the Angolan civil war. In the *Mayaguez* incident, Ford sent the marines to rescue 39 Americans captured by Cambodia, and 41 of the servicemen died in the effort.

Breaking a 1973 pledge, Ford decided to seek reelection, and while campaigning, he survived two assassination attempts by California women. Fending off Ronald Reagan's bid for the Republican nomination in 1976, Ford was far behind Jimmy Carter in the polls, but he carried four more states than Carter in the election—which Ford lost by 57 electoral votes. It was the first defeat of an incumbent president since Herbert Hoover's. Gerald Ford reminded Americans after Watergate that not all politicians were dishonest, and Congress passed a resolution commending his "openness and honesty that have done much to restore confidence in our government." Of himself, he said, "I'm a Ford, not a Lincoln."

## 39. Jimmy Carter
### (1977–1981)

James Earl Carter, the first deep-southerner elected president in 128 years, was born in Plains, Georgia, on Oct. 1, 1924. He grew up on a farm with no plumbing or electricity but realized his dream of attending the U.S. Naval Academy. Carter graduated in 1946 and married Rosalynn Smith, his sister's best friend. He joined the submarine fleet and studied nuclear physics, leaving the navy in 1953 to run the family peanut business. He was elected to the Georgia state senate in 1962. Defeated for governor in 1966, Carter campaigned constantly for the next four years, winning on his second try in 1970. Carter reorganized the government and hired more blacks, declaring that the "time for racial discrimination is over." A month before leaving office in 1974, Carter was the first Democrat to announce his candidacy for president in 1976, again campaigning constantly. "Jimmy Who?" burst into headlines by winning narrow pluralities over nine rivals in early primaries. Carter's grinning, homespun style and earnest vows of honesty ("I will never lie to you") struck a chord with voters after Watergate. Carter won

the nomination and defeated incumbent Gerald R. Ford by 2 percent of the vote. Lack of Washington connections helped his candidacy but not his presidency, for Carter never shook his image as the provincial amateur. Democratic majorities in Congress ignored Carter's pleas for tax reform and energy policy. Transportation deregulation, environmental protection, and new departments of energy and education were Carter's main domestic achievements.

But as federal spending mounted and oil prices doubled, most Americans blamed Carter for runaway inflation. His 20 percent approval rating in August 1979 was the lowest ever recorded in opinion polls. In foreign affairs Carter obtained a Panama Canal treaty, normalized relations with China, and mediated the Camp David peace accords between Israel and Egypt. He moved toward closer relations with the Soviet Union, signing the SALT II treaty in 1979, but the Soviet invasion of Afghanistan led Carter to embargo grain sales to the USSR and to order a boycott of the 1980 Moscow Olympics. The Carter Doctrine announced the United States would defend the Persian Gulf, where ironically, Carter soon met his downfall in the Iran hostage crisis. Early public support for Carter's restraint gradually withered under the glare of relentless media coverage that kept tensions high throughout 1980. Carter himself became a hostage of Iran, trapped in the White House as Edward Kennedy nearly deprived him of the Democratic nomination. In April 1980, Carter approved a military rescue mission, its tragic failure reinforcing his image of incompetence and weakness, which Republican candidate Ronald Reagan flayed. Carter's patience paid off with the safe return of all American hostages in January 1981—but by then he had lost the election in a Reagan landslide. Carter left the White House thoroughly discredited, his informal style ridiculed as inappropriate, his platitudes betraying lack of vision, his appeals for support seen as poor leadership. Yet Carter was a hard-working president wrecked by a hostile press, extortionate oil exporters, military miscues, Iranians, and other forces beyond his control. Carter, a born-again Christian, has resumed low-profile charity work and Sunday-school teaching.

## 40. Ronald Reagan
### (1981–89)

Ronald Wilson Reagan was born in Tampico, Illinois, on Feb. 6, 1911. He excelled at acting and campus politics in high school and at Eureka College. Reagan was a radio sports announcer when he made his first movie in 1937. Over 50 more films would follow in Reagan's prolific Hollywood career. In 1940 he married actress Jane Wyman, who divorced him in 1948. During World War II, Reagan made training films, and after the war he was president of the Screen Actors Guild. Then a Democrat, Reagan assailed Communists in Hollywood. He married Nancy Davis, another actress, in 1952. As his movie career waned, Reagan hosted television shows and espoused conservative causes, switching to the Republican party in 1960. Reagan made a dramatic speech at the end of the 1964 campaign, and despite his total lack of experience he was elected governor of California in 1966 by a million votes. As governor, Reagan broke all promises by raising taxes, increasing spending, and expanding the state government—yet he easily won reelection in 1970. He made a stab at the Republican presidential nomination in 1968, then bided his time until 1976, when he almost wrested the nomination from Gerald R. Ford. In 1980 he finally won the Republican nomination, and he swept past Jimmy Carter in the crushing "Reagan Revolution" of 1980, carrying 44 states and making huge Republican gains in Congress.

"Reaganomics" promised to cut taxes and social spending while vastly increasing the defense budget and somehow balancing the budget. Congress was unmoved until Mar. 20, 1981, when a crazed youth named John Hinckley shot Reagan twice in the chest. Reagan's good humor and rapid recovery charmed Americans—especially the press, which had questioned his age and health. Reagan then prevailed over Congress to pass mammoth tax cuts. The national debt began its meteoric rise under Reagan as defense spending outweighed cuts in social programs. By 1986 the U.S. had become a net borrower for the first time since World War I, but falling oil prices slowed inflation and rekindled economic growth, for which Reagan took credit. Calling the Soviet Union an "evil empire," Reagan built up the armed forces, deployed U.S. nuclear missiles in Europe, and began the Strategic Defense Initiative. He sent U.S. marines to Lebanon, where 240 of them died in a terrorist attack. To halt the spread of communism, Reagan ordered the invasion of Grenada and isolated the Sandinista government of Nicaragua. Reelected by another landslide in 1984, with the economy booming and his public esteem high, Reagan seemed headed for an even more successful second term. He ordered bombing raids on Libya and met with Soviet leader Mikhail Gorbachev, eventually producing historic arms control agreements. But in 1987 Reagan's invincible popularity finally succumbed to the Iran-Contra scandal: White House staff secretly sold arms to Iran in hopes of freeing American hostages held in Lebanon, using the profits illegally to fund Contra fighters in Nicaragua. Many top Reagan aides had to resign, but more damaging was the president's apparent loss of control over his own administration.

By 1988 Reagan was reduced to "lame duck" status, and bestowed his mantle on Vice President George Bush. He left office with the highest approval rating of any departing president since Franklin Roosevelt. In retirement Reagan was knighted by Queen Elizabeth and traveled around the globe, accepting $2 million from a Japanese media company for a pair of 20-minute speeches. As the Iran-Contra trials continued in 1990, Reagan was ordered to testify under oath on videotape. Questioned at length about his role in the scandal, Reagan responded 130 times with "I don't recall" or "I don't remember." In 1989 Simon & Schuster signed Reagan to a two-book deal worth an estimated $6 million. The first, a tepid autobiography, was a dismal failure, critically and commercially.

## 41. George Bush
### (1989–    )

The first sitting vice president elected president in over 150 years, George Herbert Walker Bush was born in Milton, Massachusetts, on June 12, 1924. His father was Prescott Sheldon Bush, Wall Street banker and U.S. senator from Connecticut from 1952 to 1963. Bush grew up in Greenwich, Connecticut, and he was elected senior class president at Phillips Academy, Andover, Massachusetts. One of the navy's youngest pilots in World War II, Bush was shot down over the Pacific and rescued at sea. For bravery in combat, Bush received the Distinguished Flying Cross and three Air Medals. He married Barbara Pierce, a Smith College student, on Jan. 6, 1945. After the war he went to Yale University, graduating Phi Beta Kappa in economics in 1948. Spurning an offer from his father's Wall Street firm, Bush chose to pursue a career in the Texas oil fields that eventually made him a millionaire in his own right. He cofounded Zapata Petroleum Corporation in 1953 and served as president of its offshore subsidiary before entering politics in the early 1960s.

Bush won the Republican nomination for Senate in 1964, mounting a conservative anti-Communist and anti–civil rights campaign in support of Barry Goldwater. For a Republican in Texas, Bush captured a record share of the vote but lost anyway. Two years later he was elected to Congress from a wealthy suburban Houston district which reelected him in 1968. Despite strong backing from President Richard Nixon and the oil industry, Bush lost another Senate race in 1970, this time to Lloyd Bentsen, Jr. Nixon compensated Bush by appointing him U.S. ambassador to the United Nations, though Bush had no diplomatic experience at the time. In 1973, as the Watergate scandal unfolded, Nixon appointed him chairman of the Republican National Committee, and Bush firmly supported the president to the end. His reward was an appointment as chief of the U.S. Liaison Office in China in 1974. Bush returned home when President Gerald R. Ford appointed him director of the CIA in 1976, but President Jimmy Carter removed him in 1977. Bush campaigned hard for the Republican presidential nomination in 1980, defeating heavily favored Ronald Reagan in some early primaries before he withdrew and accepted Reagan's offer to join him on the winning ticket.

As vice president, Bush traveled the globe, chaired various presidential task forces, and participated in national security policy decisions—though he denied any involvement in the Iran-Contra affair. Reagan formally designated Bush as acting president (under the 25th Amendment) when Reagan was incapacitated by surgery in 1985. Bush carefully maintained a low profile in office and avoided any appearance of disagreement with the president. By 1988 he was the obvious choice as Reagan's successor, besting Robert Dole in a brief contest for the Republican nomination in the primaries. With Reagan's endorsement, Bush handily defeated Michael S. Dukakis, renewing the Reagan pledge of "No New Taxes."

Bush vowed to uphold the Reagan legacy of less government, strong defense, and family values. He suffered early criticism for lack of leadership. For months, many key administration posts went unfilled, and the Senate rejected John Tower as Bush's nominee for defense secretary. But Bush struck back with major initiatives, including the savings and loan bailout, major arms control proposals, a stepped-up war on drugs, trips to Eastern Europe and Colombia, and two summit meetings with Soviet premier Mikhail Gorbachev. In December 1989, Bush ordered the invasion of Panama to protect U.S. citizens and overthrow the regime of Gen. Manuel Noriega.

By 1990 opinion polls showed Bush enjoying the highest public approval rating of any postwar president, even after he announced his willingness to consider new taxes. His ratings rose higher still after his tough stand opposing Iraq's seizure of Kuwait, and they reached record levels during the ensuing war (see Part I, "The Year in Review").

## THE PRESIDENTS

All 40 U.S. presidents (counting Grover Cleveland once) have been white, Christian males between the ages of 42 (Teddy Roosevelt's age when he took office) and 77 (Reagan's age when he left).

**Origins** The most common ancestries of presidents are English (18) and Scotch-Irish (7). Virginia is the leading birthplace of presidents (8), followed by Ohio (7), Massachusetts (4), and New York (4). New York, however, is the leading state of residence for successful presidential candidates (8), followed by Ohio (6), and Virginia (5).

**Religion** Although all 40 have been Christians, only one (Kennedy) was not a protestant; 11 presidents (including George Bush) were Episcopalians, 7 Presbyterians, and 4 Unitarians. Only three presidents (Jefferson, Lincoln, and A. Johnson) claimed no religious affiliation.

**Education** Andrew Johnson was the president with the least formal education (his wife taught him to read); Wilson the only one to earn a Ph.D. Only 12 presidents were not college graduates, but only one of these (Truman) held office in the 20th century. Harvard has graduated the most presidents (5).

**Marriage and family** Buchanan was the only president who never married, Reagan the only one ever divorced. Only six presidents had no children: Washington, Madison, Jackson, Polk, Buchanan, and Harding (although recent evidence indicates he fathered an illegitimate child while president); Grover Cleveland is the only president to publicly admit he had an illegitimate child. Tyler had 15 children.

# PRESIDENTIAL ELECTIONS, 1789–1988

## 1789 and 1792

George Washington of Virginia ran unopposed for president in 1789 and 1792. He received 69 and 132 electoral votes, respectively, in those years. John Adams of Massachusetts was elected vice president in both years, receiving 34 and 77 electoral votes, respectively.

## 1796

| Party | Candidate | Popular vote | Percent | Electoral vote |
|---|---|---|---|---|
| Federalist | John Adams (Mass.) | N.A. | N.A. | 71 |
| | and Thomas Pinckney (S.C.) | N.A. | N.A. | 59 |
| Democratic-Republican | Thomas Jefferson (Va.) | N.A. | N.A. | 68 |
| | and Aaron Burr (N.Y.) | N.A. | N.A. | 30 |

**Key Issues** Washington set a precedent by refusing to run for a third term. Though the Founders hoped to avoid parties, factions developed around Hamilton and Jefferson during Washington's first term. Hamilton's Federalists supported a strong central government that would play a major role in the national economy and represent the commercial interests of the North. Jefferson's Republicans advocated states' rights and the agrarian interests of the South. **Regional Influences** Though led by Hamilton, the Federalists nominated the more moderate Adams. Jefferson's strength in the South was balanced by Adams's power in the North. Eleven Federalist electors in New Hampshire failed to vote for Pinckney, their party's vice-presidential nominee, giving the position to Jefferson.

## 1800

| Party | Candidate | Popular vote | Percent | Electoral vote |
|---|---|---|---|---|
| Democratic-Republican | Thomas Jefferson (Va.) | N.A. | N.A. | 73 |
| | and Aaron Burr (N.Y.) | N.A. | N.A. | 73 |
| Federalist | John Adams (Mass.) | N.A. | N.A. | 65 |
| | and Charles C. Pinckney (S.C.) | N.A. | N.A. | 64 |
| Federalist | John Jay (N.Y.) | N.A. | N.A. | 1 |

**Key Issues** Adams divided the Federalists by keeping the United States out of war with France over seizures of American ships. In the meantime the Republicans under Jefferson organized nationally. They accused the Federalists of aristocratic and monarchial leanings, citing large taxes levied to maintain a standing army and navy, the Alien and Sedition Acts seeking to silence the administration's critics, and suppression of the Whiskey Rebellion. **Regional Influences** The Republicans again carried the South but also won New York through the efforts of vice-presidential nominee Burr. The election was thrown into the House when Jefferson and Burr received an equal number of electoral votes. With Hamilton's support, Jefferson won the election in the Federalist-dominated House.

## 1804

| Party | Candidate | Popular vote | Percent | Electoral vote |
|---|---|---|---|---|
| Democratic-Republican | Thomas Jefferson (Va.) | N.A. | N.A. | 162 |
| | and George Clinton (N.Y.) | N.A. | N.A. | 162 |
| Federalist | Charles C. Pinckney (S.C.) | N.A. | N.A. | 14 |
| | and Rufus King (N.Y.) | N.A. | N.A. | 14 |

**Key Issues** In 1804 Vice President Burr, a northern Republican, joined with a group of northeastern Federalists in a plot to unite New York and New England in a separate nation. The plot was exposed, discrediting the Federalists. Jefferson, already popular for his personal qualities as well as the Louisiana Purchase, swept to an easy victory. **Regional Influences** Jefferson lost only three states and even swept all of New England with the exception of Connecticut.

## 1808

| Party | Candidate | Popular vote | Percent | Electoral vote |
|---|---|---|---|---|
| Democratic-Republican | James Madison (Va.) | N.A. | N.A. | 122 |
| | and George Clinton (N.Y.) | N.A. | N.A. | 113 |
| Federalist | Charles C. Pinckney (S.C.) | N.A. | N.A. | 47 |
| | and Rufus King (N.Y.) | N.A. | N.A. | 47 |

**Note:** Clinton received six electoral votes for president. Madison and James Monroe of Virginia both received three electoral votes for vice president.

**Key Issues** Jefferson refused to run for a third term. Madison, his chosen successor, easily won the Republican nomination and the presidency. **Regional Influences** Pinckney and the Federalists regained most of the New England votes lost four years earlier and increased their strength in Congress as a result of commercial opposition to the embargo imposed by Jefferson on the export of American goods to warring European nations.

## 1812

| Party | Candidate | Popular vote | Percent | Electoral vote |
|---|---|---|---|---|
| Democratic-Republican | James Madison (Va.) | N.A. | N.A. | 128 |
| | and Elbridge Gerry (Mass.) | N.A. | N.A. | 131 |
| Federalist | DeWitt Clinton (N.Y.) | N.A. | N.A. | 89 |
| | and Jared Ingersoll (Pa.) | N.A. | N.A. | 86 |

**Key Issues** The election was a referendum on Madison's bid for a declaration of war against Great Britain in response to Britain's attempts to block the sale of southern raw materials in European markets. **Regional Influences** Commercial interests in the Northeast were opposed to war with Great Britain. The original 13 states split evenly, favoring Madison 90–89. New England, except Vermont, voted for Clinton, as did most Middle Atlantic states. The South and western states voted unanimously for Madison and thus for war.

## 1816

| Party | Candidate | Popular vote | Percent | Electoral vote |
|---|---|---|---|---|
| Democratic-Republican | James Monroe (Va.) | N.A. | N.A. | 183 |
| | and D.D. Tompkins (N.Y.) | N.A. | N.A. | 183 |
| Federalist | Rufus King (N.Y.) | N.A. | N.A. | 34 |
| | and John E. Howard (Md.) | N.A. | N.A. | 22 |

**Key Issues** The postwar period was a time of national and economic growth that saw widespread internal improvements despite opposition from Federalists. **Regional Influences** Monroe's landslide victory seemed to validate Madison's nationalist program, which called for a stronger standing army, a protective tariff, uniform currency, and a nationwide system of roads and canals, including the Cumberland Road. The Federalists won only three states, all in New England.

## 1820

| Party | Candidate | Popular vote | Percent | Electoral vote |
|---|---|---|---|---|
| Democratic-Republican | James Monroe (Va.) | N.A. | N.A. | 231 |
| | and D.D. Tompkins (N.Y.) | N.A. | N.A. | 218 |
| Democratic-Republican | John Q. Adams (Mass.) | N.A. | N.A. | 1 |

**Key Issues** The election was held at the height of the Era of Good Feelings, though sectional differences over slavery earlier in the year led to the Missouri Compromise. The Federalists ceased to exist as a party by the time of the election and failed to run a candidate against Monroe. **Regional Influences** Monroe ran unopposed for reelection. One elector from New Hampshire voted for Adams so that only Washington would hold the honor of being elected to the presidency by a unanimous vote.

## 1824

| Party | Candidate | Popular vote | Percent | Electoral vote |
|---|---|---|---|---|
| Democratic-Republican | John Q. Adams (Mass.) | 113,122 | 30.92 | 84 |
| Democratic-Republican | Andrew Jackson (Tenn.) | 151,271 | 41.34 | 99 |
| Democratic-Republican | William H. Crawford (Ga.) | 40,876 | 11.17 | 41 |
| Democratic-Republican | Henry Clay (Ky.) | 47,531 | 12.99 | 37 |
| Other | | 13,053 | 3.57 | — |
| | Total vote | 365,833 | | |
| | Jackson plurality | 38,149 | | |

**Key Issues** Personalities dominated an election in which all four candidates ran as Democratic-Republicans. John C. Calhoun of South Carolina ran unopposed for vice president. **Regional Influences** Each candidate represented his region: Adams the commercial Northeast, Crawford the cotton South, Clay and Jackson the agrarian West. Jackson won a clear plurality of the popular vote, and was the only candidate with support outside his home region. But no candidate won a majority of the electoral vote and the election was decided in the House, where Speaker Clay's support gave the victory to Adams.

## 1828

| Party | Candidate | Popular vote | Percent | Electoral vote |
|---|---|---|---|---|
| Democratic-Republican | Andrew Jackson (Tenn.) | 642,553 | 55.97 | 178 |
| | and John C. Calhoun (S.C.) | | | 171 |
| National-Republican | John Q. Adams (Mass.) | 500,987 | 43.63 | 83 |
| | and Richard Rush (Pa.) | | | 83 |
| Other | | 4,568 | 0.40 | — |
| | Total vote | 1,148,018 | | |
| | Jackson plurality | 141,656 | | |

**Key Issues** Personalities again overshadowed issues. The Jackson campaign catered to popular prejudices, portraying the contest as one between democracy and aristocracy. The Jackson coalition was a forerunner of the modern Democratic party and reestablished two-party politics in the country. **Regional Influences** Jackson won the South and West easily and appealed to discontented laborers in the North. Adams carried only New England, New Jersey, Maryland, and Delaware.

## 1832

| Party | Candidate | Popular vote | Percent | Electoral vote |
|---|---|---|---|---|
| Democrat | Andrew Jackson (Tenn.) | 701,780 | 54.23 | 219 |
| | and Martin Van Buren (N.Y.) | | | 189 |
| National-Republican | Henry Clay (Ky.) | 484,205 | 37.42 | 49 |
| | and John Sergeant (Pa.) | | | 49 |
| Anti-Masonic | William Wirt (Md.) | 100,715 | 7.78 | 7 |
| | and Amos Ellmaker (Pa.) | | | 7 |
| Independent | John Floyd (Va.) | N.A. | N.A. | 11 |
| | and Henry Lee (Mass.) | | | 11 |
| Other | | 7,273 | 0.56 | — |
| | Total vote | 1,293,973 | | |
| | Jackson plurality | 217,575 | | |

**Key Issues** The Anti-Masons, the first third-party in American politics, began in opposition to secret societies and privileged groups but were at heart an anti-Jackson party. All three parties held national conventions to select a presidential nominee. While Jackson's opposition to the Bank of the United States was made an issue by the two major parties, the election was more a referendum on Jackson himself. **Regional Influences** Anti-Masonic strength was concentrated in rural sections of New England and the Middle Atlantic states where National-Republicans and Anti-Masons supported the same ticket. With the forces against him divided, Jackson won easily. Clay won only half of the New England states, Wirt only Vermont. Jackson captured Maine and New Hampshire. In South Carolina, where electors still were chosen by the legislature, nullificationists cast their ballots for Floyd.

## 1836

| Party | Candidate | Popular vote | Percent | Electoral vote |
|---|---|---|---|---|
| Democrat | Martin Van Buren (N.Y.) | 764,716 | 50.83 | 170 |
| | and Richard M. Johnson (Ky.) | | | 147 |
| Whig | William Henry Harrison (Ohio) | 550,816 | 36.63 | 73 |
| Whig | Hugh L. White (Tenn.) | 146,107 | 9.72 | 26 |
| Whig | Daniel Webster (Mass.) | 41,201 | 2.74 | 14 |
| | Willie P. Mangum (N.C.) | N.A. | N.A. | 11 |
| Other | | 1,234 | 0.08 | — |
| | Total vote | 1,503,534 | | |
| | Van Buren plurality | 213,360 | | |

**Key Issues** Jackson's heavy-handed tactics, especially his battle against the national bank, led the National-Republicans to rename themselves Whigs, after the 18th-century British party that tried to lessen the power of the Crown. But lacking effective national leadership, the anti-Jackson forces could not agree on one candidate and ran three regional candidates. **Regional Influences** Whig strategy was to throw the election into the House, where they could unite around a single candidate. Webster was to win New England, Harrison the West, and White the South. But Van Buren, forced on the Democrats by Jackson, picked up enough states throughout the nation to win by a slim majority. Johnson fell one electoral vote short of a majority for vice president and was selected by the Senate.

## 1840

| Party | Candidate | Popular vote | Percent | Electoral vote |
|---|---|---|---|---|
| Whig | William Henry Harrison (Ohio) | 1,275,390 | 52.88 | 234 |
| | and John Tyler (Va.) | | | |
| Democrat | Martin Van Buren (N.Y.) | 1,128,854 | 46.81 | 60 |
| Liberty | James G. Birney (N.Y.) | 6,797 | 0.28 | — |
| Other | | 767 | 0.03 | — |
| | Total vote | 2,411,808 | | |
| | Harrison plurality | 146,536 | | |

**Key Issues** With the country still reeling from the Panic of 1837, the Democrats were on the defensive. The Whigs rallied around Harrison and turned the tables on Jackson's party. Harrison, despite his wealthy origins, was portrayed as the "log-cabin, hard-cider candidate" opposing the allegedly aristocratic Van Buren. The Democrats left the selection of a vice-presidential candidate to each state. **Regional Influences** Van Buren won only seven states, just one outside of the South or West. Harrison was long associated with the West, and Tyler was a conservative southerner and friend of Henry Clay. For the first time, active two-party politics was established across the nation.

## 1844

| Party | Candidate | Popular vote | Percent | Electoral vote |
|---|---|---|---|---|
| Democrat | James K. Polk (Tenn.) | 1,339,494 | 49.54 | 170 |
| | and George M. Dallas (Pa.) | | | |
| Whig | Henry Clay (Ky.) | 1,300,004 | 48.08 | 105 |
| | and Theodore Frelinghuysen (N.J.) | | | |
| Abolitionist | James G. Birney (N.Y.) | 62,103 | 2.30 | — |
| Other | | 2,058 | 0.08 | — |
| | Total vote | 2,703,659 | | |
| | Polk plurality | 39,490 | | |

**Key Issues** Manifest Destiny was the central issue because of the pending annexation of Texas. Opponents of slavery led the Senate to reject a treaty between Texas and the Tyler administration that would have preserved slavery in Texas and made the state a U.S. territory. Clay and Van Buren tried to ignore the Texas issue. But Polk snatched the Democratic nomination with his clear advocacy of annexation of Texas and general territorial expansion. **Regional Influences** Expansionism was immensely popular, especially in the South and West. Support for Manifest Destiny more than made up for antislavery sentiment elsewhere, and Polk won a narrow plurality but a clear victory.

## 1848

| Party | Candidate | Popular vote | Percent | Electoral vote |
|-------|-----------|-------------:|--------:|---------------:|
| Whig | Zachary Taylor (La.) and Millard Fillmore (N.Y.) | 1,361,393 | 47.28 | 163 |
| Democrat | Lewis Cass (Mich.) and William O. Butler (Ky.) | 1,223,460 | 42.49 | 127 |
| Free Soil | Martin Van Buren (N.Y.) and Charles Francis Adams (Mass.) | 291,501 | 10.12 | — |
| Other | | 2,830 | 0.10 | — |
| | Total vote | 2,879,184 | | |
| | Taylor plurality | 137,933 | | |

**Key Issues** The Wilmot Proviso forbidding the extension of slavery dominated the election. But both major parties evaded the issue. Slavery foes banded together to form the Free Soil party, which drew enough popular support away from the Democrats to throw the election to Old Rough and Ready, Zachary Taylor, a slaveholder. **Regional Influences** Both major parties balanced their tickets with a northerner and southerner. Free Soilers were mostly northern Democrats, antislavery Whigs and abolitionists. Free Soil strength in New York gave the state and the election to the Whigs.

## 1852

| Party | Candidate | Popular vote | Percent | Electoral vote |
|-------|-----------|-------------:|--------:|---------------:|
| Democrat | Franklin Pierce (N.H.) and William R.D. King (Ala.) | 1,607,510 | 50.84 | 254 |
| Whig | Winfield Scott (Va.) and William A. Graham (N.C.) | 1,386,942 | 43.87 | 42 |
| Free Soil | John P. Hale (N.H.) and George Washington Julian (Ind.) | 155,210 | 4.91 | — |
| Other | | 12,168 | 0.38 | — |
| | Total vote | 3,161,830 | | |
| | Pierce plurality | 220,568 | | |

**Key Issues** The election was a referendum on the Compromise of 1850, in which Congress voted to admit California as a free state, create the territories of New Mexico and Utah with no restriction on slavery, abolish the slave trade in the District of Columbia, purchase disputed land from Texas on behalf of New Mexico, and toughen the Fugitive Slave Act. The Democrats strongly endorsed the Compromise, but the bitterly divided Whigs only vaguely accepted it. **Regional Influences** The Democrats won a resounding electoral victory, capturing 27 states to the four taken by the Whigs: Massachusetts, Vermont, Kentucky, and Tennessee. Free Soilers returned to the Democrats and the Whigs never again were a political force in a nation that believed the slave question was behind it.

## 1856

| Party | Candidate | Popular vote | Percent | Electoral vote |
|-------|-----------|-------------:|--------:|---------------:|
| Democrat | James Buchanan (Pa.) and John C. Breckinridge (Ky.) | 1,836,072 | 45.28 | 174 |
| Republican | John C. Frémont (Calif.) and William L. Dayton (N.J.) | 1,342,345 | 33.11 | 114 |
| Whig | Millard Fillmore (N.Y.) and Andrew J. Donelson (Tenn.) | 873,053 | 21.53 | 8 |
| Other | | 3,177 | 0.08 | — |
| | Total vote | 4,054,647 | | |
| | Buchanan plurality | 493,727 | | |

**Key Issues** The Democrats firmly endorsed "popular sovereignty," even though it led to great turmoil in the territory of Kansas. But they chose as their nominee Buchanan, largely because he had been out of the country and was untainted by the "Bleeding Kansas" battle, which pitted supporters and foes of slavery trying to organize the territory into a slave or free state. The Republicans, a new party of northern Whigs and Democrats committed to the containment of slavery, ran Frémont, a popular

general and explorer. **Regional Influences** Frémont carried all but five of the free states. But Buchanan won all of the South in addition to the five northern states and was elected. Fillmore, supported by the "Know-Nothings" and Whig remnants, won only Maryland but strongly challenged the Democrats in the South.

## 1860

| Party | Candidate | Popular vote | Percent | Electoral vote |
|-------|-----------|-------------:|--------:|---------------:|
| Republican | Abraham Lincoln (Ill.) and Hannibal Hamlin (Maine) | 1,865,908 | 39.82 | 180 |
| Democrat | Stephen A. Douglas (Ill.) and Herschel V. Johnson (Ga.) | 1,380,202 | 29.46 | 12 |
| Democrat | John C. Breckinridge (Ky.) and Joseph Lane (Oreg.) | 848,019 | 18.09 | 72 |
| Constitutional Union | John Bell (Tenn.) and Edward Everett (Mass.) | 590,901 | 12.61 | 39 |
| Other | | 531 | 0.01 | — |
| | Total vote | 4,685,561 | | |
| | Lincoln plurality | 485,706 | | |

**Key Issues** Sectional differences over slavery came to a head in 1860. The Democrats could not agree on a candidate and split into northern and southern factions. The northern faction backed Douglas and popular sovereignty, the southern faction Breckinridge and federal protection of slavery in the territories. The Republicans, virtually all northerners, were a protariff, nationalist party that opposed the extension of slavery but did not seek to overturn it where it already existed. Bell, the candidate of Whigs and Know-Nothings who backed Fillmore in 1856, ran for the Constitutional Union, a compromise party expressing support for preservation of the Union. **Regional Influences** In effect there were two separate contests in 1860: Lincoln versus Douglas in the North, Breckinridge versus Bell in the South. Free states outnumbered slave states and cast half again as many electoral votes. Lincoln won every northern state except New Jersey and, though not even on the ballot in 10 southern states, was elected president. Breckinridge captured 11 of the 15 southern states. The four southern states won by Douglas and Bell were in the upper South.

## 1864

| Party | Candidate | Popular vote | Percent | Electoral vote |
|-------|-----------|-------------:|--------:|---------------:|
| Republican | Abraham Lincoln (Ill.) and Andrew Johnson (Tenn.) | 2,218,388 | 55.02 | 212 |
| Democrat | George B. McClellan (N.Y.) and George H. Pendleton (Ohio) | 1,812,807 | 44.96 | 21 |
| | Total vote | 4,031,887 | | |
| | Lincoln plurality | 405,581 | | |

**Key Issues** Lincoln's renomination was not assured. Radical Republicans thought he was not aggressive enough in his conduct of the war or plans for the eventual peace, but moderation ultimately prevailed. The Republicans ran as the Union party and nominated Johnson, a pro-Union Democrat, for vice president. The Democrats ran a peace campaign, calling the war a failure. But McClellan, a popular general, broke with his party's platform and denied the war was a failure, denouncing members of his party who seemed to advocate peace at any price. He opposed emancipation as a goal of the war. **Regional Influences** Military victories around election time helped the embattled incumbent. Lincoln won a convincing popular and electoral victory with the support of middle-class professionals, farmers, laborers, and the strongly pro-Union voters who voted for Bell four years earlier. McClellan was strongest in areas carried by Breckinridge four years before. Eleven Confederate states did not participate in the election.

## 1868

| Party | Candidate | Popular vote | Percent | Electoral vote |
|---|---|---|---|---|
| Republican | Ulysses S. Grant (Ohio) and Schuyler Colfax (Ind.) | 3,013,650 | 52.66 | 214 |
| Democrat | Horatio S. Seymour (N.Y.) and Francis P. Blair (Mo.) | 2,708,744 | 47.34 | 80 |
| Other | | 46 | — | — |
| | Total vote | 5,722,440 | | |
| | Grant plurality | 304,906 | | |

**Key Issues** The Republicans waved the "bloody shirt" of the war and ran on their program of Radical Reconstruction. While calling for Negro suffrage in the South, the Republicans asserted it was a matter for individual northern states to decide for themselves. Democrats ran against Reconstruction, declaring that the question of Negro suffrage should be decided by individual southern states as well. **Regional Influences** Despite Grant's popularity, the Republicans were just able to win the election. Seymour carried only eight states. Without black votes in the South, Grant would not have received a majority of the popular vote. The votes of the "unreconstructed" states of Mississippi, Texas, and Virginia were not counted.

## 1872

| Party | Candidate | Popular vote | Percent | Electoral vote |
|---|---|---|---|---|
| Republican | Ulysses S. Grant (Ohio) and Henry Wilson (Mass.) | 3,598,235 | 55.63 | 286 |
| Liberal Republican/Democrat | Horace Greeley (N.Y.) and Benjamin Gratz Brown (Mo.) | 2,834,761 | 43.83 | 66 |
| Straight Democrat | Charles O'Conor (N.Y.) | 18,602 | — | — |
| Other | | 16,081 | — | — |
| | Total vote | 6,467,679 | | |
| | Grant plurality | 763,474 | | |

**Key Issues** Liberal Republicans broke with Grant over corruption in his administration, high tariffs, and continued Radical Reconstruction. They nominated Greeley, editor of the *New York Tribune.* The Democrats endorsed Greeley and the Liberal platform. But the great scandals of the Grant administration were not yet revealed, and the Republicans again waved the bloody shirt to victory. **Regional Influences** Greeley carried only two states in the lower South and four border states. He died shortly after the election.

## 1876

| Party | Candidate | Popular vote | Percent | Electoral vote |
|---|---|---|---|---|
| Republican | Rutherford B. Hayes (Ohio) and William A. Wheeler (N.Y.) | 4,034,311 | 47.95 | 185 |
| Democrat | Samuel J. Tilden (N.Y.) and Thomas A. Hendricks (Ind.) | 4,288,546 | 50.97 | 184 |
| Greenback | Peter Cooper (N.Y.) | 75,973 | 0.90 | — |
| Other | | 14,271 | 0.17 | — |
| | Total vote | 8,413,101 | | |
| | Tilden plurality | 254,235 | | |

**Key Issues** The Republicans were in trouble as 1876 approached, due to rampant corruption in the Grant administration and the economic depression that followed the Panic of 1873. Hayes, a three-term Ohio governor known for his unassailable integrity, was nominated to run against Tilden, a New York reform governor whose reputation was made in opposition to the Tweed political machine. Both men espoused conservative economics. Cooper and the Greenbacks advocated currency expansion. **Regional Influences** As election day approached, Tilden could count on winning all of the South except for the three states still controlled by Republican carpetbaggers: South Carolina, Louisiana, and

Florida. He seemed assured of victory when those states appeared to vote for him, along with several northern states, including New York and New Jersey. But Republicans claimed South Carolina, Louisiana, and Florida for Hayes, arguing that thousands of blacks who would have voted for Hayes were barred from voting there. Election boards in those Republican-controlled states gave Hayes the needed majority, and thus the election. In the uproar that followed, Congress set up an Election Commission to validate the returns. The commission voted strictly along party lines, eight to seven, to give the election to Hayes. Despite charges that Republicans stole the election, Hayes was later inaugurated peaceably after he let it be known that as president he would end military reconstruction by withdrawing federal troops from the South and would restore "efficient local government" there.

## 1880

| Party | Candidate | Popular vote | Percent | Electoral vote |
|---|---|---|---|---|
| Republican | James A. Garfield (Ohio) and Chester A. Arthur (N.Y.) | 4,461,158 | 48.27 | 214 |
| Democrat | Winfield S. Hancock (Pa.) and William H. English (Ind.) | 4,444,260 | 48.25 | 155 |
| Greenback | James B. Weaver (Iowa) and Benjamin J. Chambers (Tex.) | 305,997 | 3.32 | — |
| Other | | 14,005 | 0.15 | — |
| | Total vote | 9,210,420 | | |
| | Garfield plurality | 16,898 | | |

**Key Issues** With the war and Reconstruction behind, no major issues arose over which the major parties disagreed. The Democrats, the party of secession 20 year earlier, nominated Gen. Hancock to help combat the stigma of treason. Garfield made a protectionist tariff central to his campaign. **Regional Influences** The balance between Republican strength in the Midwest and West and Democratic strength in the South resulted in a plurality of less than 17,000 for Garfield out of more than 9 million votes cast. Four months into his term, Garfield was shot by a disappointed office-seeker.

> *"Ma, Ma, where's my Pa?"*
> *"Gone to the White House, ha, ha, ha."*
>
> —Chant poking fun at Cleveland, who admitted siring an illegitimate child

## 1884

| Party | Candidate | Popular vote | Percent | Electoral vote |
|---|---|---|---|---|
| Democrat | Grover Cleveland (N.Y.) and Thomas A. Hendricks (Ind.) | 4,874,621 | 48.50 | 219 |
| Republican | James G. Blaine (Maine) and John A. Logan (Ill.) | 4,848,936 | 48.25 | 182 |
| Greenback | Benjamin F. Butler (Mass.) | 175,096 | 1.74 | — |
| Prohibitionist | John P. St. John (Kans.) | 147,482 | 1.47 | — |
| Other | | 3,619 | 0.04 | — |
| | Total votes | 10,049,754 | | |
| | Cleveland plurality | 25,685 | | |

**Key Issues** The private lives and morals of the candidates were the focus of a campaign notable for mudslinging. Blaine was accused of accepting bribes from a railroad company for whom he obtained a federal grant, and Republicans taunted Cleveland for fathering a son out of wedlock. Still, Cleveland, known for his independence and integrity in public life, attracted the votes of many liberal Republicans and reformers unable to stomach Blaine, a Radical Republican leader. **Regional Influences** Cleveland carried all of the southern states as well as the key swing states of Indiana, New Jersey, Connecticut, and New York, becoming the first Democrat elected president since the Civil War. Cleveland carried his home state of New York and its 36 electoral votes by less than 1,200 votes.

## 1888

| Party | Candidate | Popular vote | Percent | Electoral vote |
|---|---|---|---|---|
| Republican | Benjamin Harrison (Ind.) and Levi P. Morton (N.Y.) | 5,443,892 | 47.82 | 233 |
| Democrat | Grover Cleveland (N.Y.) and Allen G. Thurman (Ohio) | 5,534,488 | 48.62 | 168 |
| Prohibitionist | Clinton B. Fisk (N.J.) | 249,813 | 2.19 | — |
| Union Labor | Alson J. Streeter (Ill.) | 146,602 | 1.29 | — |
| Other | | 8,519 | 0.07 | — |
| | Total vote | 11,383,320 | | |
| | Cleveland plurality | 90,596 | | |

**Key Issues** Cleveland made tariff reform central to his administration, while the Republicans campaigned to maintain high wages by keeping a high tariff on imported goods. **Regional Influences** Despite the emphasis on the tariff, Cleveland still carried manufacturing states such as New Jersey and Connecticut as well as most of the South. But though Cleveland won the popular vote, Harrison carried the protariff swing states of Indiana and New York by slight margins to win the election in the electoral college in one of the most corrupt campaigns in history.

## 1892

| Party | Candidate | Popular vote | Percent | Electoral vote |
|---|---|---|---|---|
| Democrat | Grover Cleveland (N.Y.) and Adlai E. Stevenson (Ill.) | 5,551,883 | 46.05 | 277 |
| Republican | Benjamin Harrison (Ind.) and Whitelaw Reid (N.Y.) | 5,179,244 | 42.96 | 145 |
| Populist | James B. Weaver (Iowa) and James G. Field (Va.) | 1,024,280 | 8.50 | 22 |
| Prohibitionist | John Bidwell (Calif.) | 270,770 | 2.25 | — |
| Other | | 29,920 | 0.25 | — |
| | Total votes | 12,056,097 | | |
| | Cleveland plurality | 372,639 | | |

**Key Issues** Cleveland and Harrison again fought over the tariff, which the Republicans drastically raised in 1890. Both men were out of touch with the growing agrarian and populist discontent. Weaver, campaigning for free silver, became the first third-party candidate to gain electoral votes since the war. **Regional Influences** Cleveland improved on his 1884 and 1888 showings to win the most decisive presidential victory in 20 years. He carried the swing states of New York, New Jersey, Connecticut, and Indiana as well as traditionally Republican Illinois, California, and Wisconsin.

## 1896

| Party | Candidate | Popular vote | Percent | Electoral vote |
|---|---|---|---|---|
| Republican | William McKinley (Ohio) and Garret A. Hobart (N.J.) | 7,108,480 | 51.01 | 271 |
| Democrat/Populist | William J. Bryan (Nebr.) and Democrat Arthur Sewall (Maine) and Populist Thomas E. Watson (Ga.) | 6,511,495 | 46.73 | 176 149 |
| National Democrat | John M. Palmer (Ill.) | 133,435 | 0.96 | — |
| Prohibition | Joshua Levering (Md.) | 125,072 | 0.90 | — |
| Other | | 57,256 | 0.41 | — |
| | Total vote | 13,935,738 | | |
| | McKinley plurality | 596,985 | | |

**Key Issues** The Democrats abandoned the conservatism of Cleveland by nominating Bryan and adopted key elements of the Populist program, especially the call for free silver. The protariff and progold Republicans led by McKinley and Mark Hanna outspent the Democrats by almost 12 to 1, but Bryan amassed more votes than any victorious candidate before him. **Regional Influences** Bryan did not appeal to labor, and carried no state north of Virginia or east of Missouri. His hold on the agricultural South and West was broken by Republican victories in key states.

## 1900

| Party | Candidate | Popular vote | Percent | Electoral vote |
|---|---|---|---|---|
| Republican | William McKinley (Ohio) and Theodore Roosevelt (N.Y.) | 7,218,039 | 51.67 | 292 |
| Democrat | William J. Bryan (Nebr.) and Adlai E. Stevenson (Ill.) | 6,358,345 | 45.51 | 155 |
| Prohibition | John C. Woolley (Ill.) | 209,004 | 1.50 | — |
| Social Democrat | Eugene V. Debs (Ind.) | 86,935 | 0.62 | — |
| Other | | 98,147 | 0.70 | — |
| | Total vote | 13,970,470 | | |
| | McKinley plurality | 859,694 | | |

**Key Issues** Imperialism in the Philippines joined free silver and the tariff as the key issues in a replay of the 1896 election. Bryan tried to unite the silver interests in the West and South with supporters of the gold standard in a coalition against imperialism, which the Democratic platform called the "paramount issue" of the campaign. But voters did not desert McKinley in a time of prosperity. **Regional Influences** Bryan carried only the solid South and four silver states in the West and was defeated in the silver states of Kansas, South Dakota, Utah, and Wyoming as well as his home state of Nebraska. Both houses of Congress were led by significant Republican majorities.

## 1904

| Party | Candidate | Popular vote | Percent | Electoral vote |
|---|---|---|---|---|
| Republican | Theodore Roosevelt (N.Y.) and Charles W. Fairbanks (Ind.) | 7,626,593 | 56.41 | 336 |
| Democrat | Alton B. Parker (N.Y.) and Henry G. Davis (W. Va.) | 5,082,898 | 37.60 | 140 |
| Socialist | Eugene V. Debs (Ind.) | 402,489 | 2.98 | — |
| Prohibition | Silas C. Swallow (Pa.) | 258,596 | 1.91 | — |
| Other | | 148,388 | 1.10 | — |
| | Total votes | 13,518,964 | | |
| | Roosevelt plurality | 2,543,695 | | |

**Key Issues** Roosevelt stole the mantle of reform from the Democrats with his campaigns against the "malefactors of great wealth." The Democrats turned to the right by nominating the lackluster Parker, a judge with close ties to Wall Street. Parker turned his back on Bryan Democrats by renouncing free silver. **Regional Influences** Roosevelt won a landslide victory based largely on his own personality and popularity. The Democrats won only 13 states, none outside the South.

## 1908

| Party | Candidate | Popular vote | Percent | Electoral vote |
|---|---|---|---|---|
| Republican | William H. Taft (Ohio) and James S. Sherman (N.Y.) | 7,662,258 | 51.58 | 321 |
| Democrat | William J. Bryan (Nebr.) and John W. Kern (Ind.) | 6,406,801 | 43.05 | 162 |
| Socialist | Eugene V. Debs (Ind.) | 420,380 | 2.82 | — |
| Prohibition | Eugene W. Chafin (Ill.) | 252,821 | 1.70 | — |
| Other | | 126,474 | 0.85 | — |
| | Total vote | 14,882,734 | | |
| | Taft plurality | 1,269,457 | | |

**Key Issues** The immensely popular Roosevelt declined to run. Taft, his secretary of war and handpicked successor, debated Bryan over who was better qualified to complete TR's progressive program. Bryan abandoned silver and courted labor but ran a lackluster, losing campaign. **Regional Influences** Bryan again carried the South. But the appeal of Roosevelt's reform programs helped the Republicans do well in the West, and Taft's background as a Yale graduate and federal jurist enabled him to carry the East as well.

## 1912

| Party | Candidate | Popular vote | Percent | Electoral vote |
|---|---|---|---|---|
| Democrat | Woodrow Wilson (N.J.) and Thomas Marshall (Ind.) | 6,293,152 | 41.84 | 435 |
| Progressive | Theodore Roosevelt (N.Y.) and Hiram Johnson (Calif.) | 4,119,207 | 27.39 | 88 |
| Republican | William H. Taft (Ohio) and James S. Sherman (N.Y.) | 3,486,333 | 23.18 | 8 |
| Socialist | Eugene V. Debs (Ind.) | 900,369 | 5.99 | — |
| Other | | 241,902 | 1.61 | — |
| | Total vote | 15,040,963 | | |
| | Wilson plurality | 2,173,945 | | |

**Key Issues** Taft's conservatism and political ineptitude led Roosevelt to challenge him within the party from the left. Unable to wrest the nomination from Taft, Roosevelt ran a third-party campaign. The election boiled down to a contest between Roosevelt and Wilson and their respective conceptions of progressivism. Roosevelt's "New Nationalism" called for strong federal regulations to control the trusts and big businesses. Wilson's "New Freedom" sought instead to revive competition through vigorous application of antitrust laws. The Progressives advocated a broad array of social reforms to be implemented by the federal government, while the Democrats emphasized the primacy of the states in such matters. **Regional Influences** Though he amassed fewer votes than did Bryan in 1908, Wilson took advantage of the split in the Republican ranks to win a decisive plurality of the vote. He did best in traditional Democratic states but was able to win most traditionally Republican states as well. Roosevelt won only six states, including California, which he carried by fewer than 200 votes. Taft carried Utah and Vermont. The Democrats also won control of both houses of Congress, their best overall performance since the Civil War.

> *"He kept us out of the war."*
>
> —Wilson campaign slogan

## 1916

| Party | Candidate | Popular vote | Percent | Electoral vote |
|---|---|---|---|---|
| Democrat | Woodrow Wilson (N.J.) and Thomas Marshall (Ind.) | 9,126,300 | 49.24 | 277 |
| Republican | Charles Evans Hughes (N.Y.) and Charles W. Fairbanks (Ind.) | 8,546,789 | 46.11 | 254 |
| Socialist | Allen L. Benson (N.Y.) | 589,924 | 3.18 | — |
| Prohibitionist | James F. Hanly (Ind.) | 221,030 | 1.19 | — |
| Other | | 50,979 | 0.28 | — |
| | Total vote | 18,535,022 | | |
| | Wilson plurality | 579,511 | | |

**Key Issues** The campaign was a referendum on Wilson's first term: his program of domestic reform and his policy toward the war in Europe. He ran a peace campaign with the slogan He Kept Us Out of War and attracted the votes of many Bull Moosers. Voters who felt Wilson was either too harsh or too lenient toward Germany tended to vote Republican. Irish-American and German-American extremists, virulently opposed to aiding Great Britain, embarrassed Hughes with their vocal support. A coalition of labor, farmers, reformers, and intellectuals won the election for Wilson. **Regional Influences** Hughes, a former reform governor of New York who left the Supreme Court to challenge Wilson, carried all of the East except New Hampshire and all of the Old Northwest, except Ohio. But the South was again solid for the Democrats as was every state west of the Mississippi except Minnesota, Iowa, South Dakota, and Oregon, which Wilson lost by close margins. The electoral vote was the closest since 1876.

## 1920

| Party | Candidate | Popular vote | Percent | Electoral vote |
|---|---|---|---|---|
| Republican | Warren G. Harding (Ohio) and Calvin Coolidge (Mass.) | 16,133,314 | 60.30 | 404 |
| Democrat | James M. Cox (Ohio) and Franklin D. Roosevelt (N.Y.) | 9,140,884 | 34.17 | 127 |
| Socialist | Eugene V. Debs (Ind.) | 913,664 | 3.42 | — |
| Farmer-Labor | Parley P. Christensen (Utah) | 264,540 | 0.99 | — |
| Other | | 301,384 | 1.13 | — |
| | Total Vote | 26,753,786 | | |
| | Harding plurality | 6,992,430 | | |

**Key Issues** The voters turned against Wilsonian progressivism and internationalism by electing Harding, a vacuous party hack who promised a "return to normalcy" after the turbulent years of domestic reform and world war. The undistinguished Cox ran in support of the League of Nations and little else. **Regional Influences** Harding carried every state outside of the South, except Tennessee. The Republicans added to their majorities in both houses of Congress, regained in 1918.

## 1924

| Party | Candidate | Popular vote | Percent | Electoral vote |
|---|---|---|---|---|
| Republican | Calvin Coolidge (Mass.) and Charles G. Dawes (Ohio) | 15,717,553 | 54.00 | 382 |
| Democrat | John W. Davis (N.Y.) and Charles W. Bryan (Nebr.) | 8,386,169 | 28.84 | 136 |
| Progressive Socialist | Robert M. LaFollette (Wis.) and Burton K. Wheeler (Mont.) | 4,814,050 | 16.56 | 13 |
| Other | | 158,187 | 0.55 | — |
| | Total vote | 29,075,959 | | |
| | Coolidge plurality | 7,331,384 | | |

**Key Issues** The country "kept cool with Coolidge," since the Democrats could not overcome prosperity or themselves. Davis, a conservative Wall Street lawyer, was a compromise nominee selected by a bitterly divided party after 103 ballots. Reformers, laborers, and farmers flocked to the LaFollette candidacy. **Regional Influences** All 12 of the Democratic states were from the South. LaFollette's 13 electoral votes came from his home state of Wisconsin.

## 1928

| Party | Candidate | Popular vote | Percent | Electoral vote |
|---|---|---|---|---|
| Republican | Herbert C. Hoover (Calif.) and Charles E. Curtis (Kans.) | 21,411,911 | 58.20 | 444 |
| Democrat | Alfred E. Smith (N.Y.) and Joseph T. Robinson (Ark.) | 15,000,185 | 40.77 | 87 |
| Socialist | Norman Thomas (N.Y.) | 266,453 | 0.72 | — |
| Workers' | William Z. Foster (Ill.) | 48,170 | 0.13 | — |
| Other | | 63,565 | 0.17 | — |
| | Total vote | 36,790,364 | | |
| | Hoover plurality | 6,411,806 | | |

**Key Issues** Booze, bigotry, Tammany, and prosperity did in the Democrats. Rural America would not vote for an anti-Prohibition, big-city, Catholic machine-politician, despite Smith's success as governor of New York, especially while the Republicans could convincingly cite the success of their economic leadership. **Regional Influences** The solid South was shattered as Hoover Democrats gave Republicans the states of Virginia, North Carolina, Tennessee, Florida, and Texas for the first time since Reconstruction. Smith lost his own state and every western and border state. But Smith set the stage for the New Deal coalition: with the votes of urban ethnics, he carried the nation's 12 largest cities, all of which had been won by the Republicans four years earlier. The Democrats also won votes in the traditionally Republican West among farmers uncertain about prosperity.

## 1932

| Party | Candidate | Popular vote | Percent | Electoral vote |
|---|---|---|---|---|
| Democrat | Franklin D. Roosevelt (N.Y.) and John Nance Garner (Tex.) | 22,825,016 | 57.42 | 472 |
| Republican | Herbert C. Hoover (Calif.) and Charles E. Curtis (Kans.) | 15,758,397 | 39.64 | 59 |
| Socialist | Norman Thomas (N.Y.) | 883,990 | 2.22 | — |
| Communist | William Z. Foster (Ill.) | 102,221 | 0.26 | — |
| Other | | 179,758 | 0.45 | — |
| | Total vote | 39,749,382 | | |
| | Roosevelt plurality | 7,066,619 | | |

**Key Issues** The Democrats won by blaming the Republicans for the Great Depression. Roosevelt, the first presidential nominee of a major party to address his nominating convention, pledged to help the "forgotten man at the bottom of the economic pyramid." In a vague and contradictory platform, the Democrats promised to balance the federal budget by drastically reducing expenses and vowed to spend federal dollars to attack the nation's economic woes. **Regional Influences** Roosevelt lost only six states—Maine, New Hampshire, Vermont, Connecticut, Delaware, and Pennsylvania—carrying all of the agricultural West and South, improving on Smith's margins of victory in the nation's big cities.

## 1936

| Party | Candidate | Popular vote | Percent | Electoral vote |
|---|---|---|---|---|
| Democrat | Franklin D. Roosevelt (N.Y.) and John Nance Garner (Tex.) | 27,747,636 | 60.79 | 523 |
| Republican | Alfred M. Landon (Kans.) and Frank Knox (Ill.) | 16,679,543 | 36.54 | 8 |
| Union | William Lemke (N.Dak.) | 892,492 | 1.96 | — |
| Socialist | Norman Thomas (N.Y.) | 187,785 | 0.41 | — |
| Other | | 134,847 | 0.30 | — |
| | Total vote | 45,642,303 | | |
| | Roosevelt plurality | 11,068,093 | | |

**Key Issues** The great public appeal of the New Deal was confirmed in the most one-sided election since 1820 and sweeping victories for the Democrats in Congress. The populist forces of the late Huey Long coalesced around Lemke but failed to gather widespread support. **Regional Influences** Roosevelt carried every state except Maine and Vermont, and every large city. The middle class, farmers in the West and South, big-city ethnics, laborers, and reform intellectuals flocked to the Democrats. Northern blacks also began to vote heavily Democratic for the first time.

## 1940

| Party | Candidate | Popular vote | Percent | Electoral vote |
|---|---|---|---|---|
| Democrat | Franklin D. Roosevelt (N.Y.) and Henry A. Wallace (Iowa) | 27,263,448 | 54.70 | 449 |
| Republican | Wendell L. Willkie (Ind.) and Charles L. McNary (Ore.) | 22,336,260 | 44.82 | 82 |
| Socialist | Norman Thomas (N.Y.) | 116,827 | 0.23 | — |
| Prohibitionist | Roger W. Babson (Mass.) | 58,685 | 0.12 | — |
| Other | | 65,223 | 0.13 | — |
| | Total vote | 49,840,443 | | |
| | Roosevelt plurality | 4,927,188 | | |

**Key Issues** With war raging in Europe, the electorate turned its attention to foreign affairs. The Democrats broke with tradition and renominated FDR for a third term. The Republicans turned to businessman and political neophyte Willkie, a charismatic former Democrat. Willkie's internationalism and the pledge of both candidates to keep the country out of the war minimized the role of foreign policy in the campaign. **Regional Influences** Willkie carried only 10 states, mostly in the Midwest. But Roosevelt's percentage of the popular vote was markedly down from 1936.

## 1944

| Party | Candidate | Popular vote | Percent | Electoral vote |
|---|---|---|---|---|
| Democrat | Franklin D. Roosevelt (N.Y.) and Harry S Truman (Mo.) | 25,611,936 | 53.39 | 432 |
| Republican | Thomas E. Dewey (N.Y.) and John W. Bricker (Ohio) | 22,013,372 | 45.89 | 99 |
| Socialist | Norman Thomas (N.Y.) | 79,100 | 0.16 | — |
| Prohibitionist | Claude A. Watson (Calif.) | 74,733 | 0.16 | — |
| Other | | 195,778 | 0.41 | — |
| | Total vote | 47,974,819 | | |
| | Roosevelt plurality | 3,598,564 | | |

**Key Issues** Both candidates expressed support for New Deal social legislation and an international organization to maintain peace after the war. Big-city bosses and southern conservatives, with FDR's private support, ousted Henry Wallace from the ticket in favor of Truman. **Regional Influences** Roosevelt won 36 states, and the Democrats improved their control over Congress and the nation's statehouses. The Republicans won only a handful of western and New England states.

## 1948

| Party | Candidate | Popular vote | Percent | Electoral vote |
|---|---|---|---|---|
| Democrat | Harry S Truman (Mo.) and Alben W. Barkley (Ky.) | 24,105,587 | 49.51 | 303 |
| Republican | Thomas E. Dewey (N.Y.) and Earl Warren (Calif.) | 21,970,017 | 45.12 | 189 |
| States' Rights | Strom Thurmond (S.C.) and Fielding L. Wright (Miss.) | 1,169,134 | 2.40 | — |
| Progressive | Henry A. Wallace (Iowa) and Glen H. Taylor (Idaho) | 1,157,057 | 2.38 | — |
| Other | | 290,647 | 0.60 | — |
| | Total vote | 48,692,442 | | |
| | Truman plurality | 2,135,570 | | |

**Key Issues** The Republicans were sure of victory after 16 years of Democratic rule and the desertion of the Democrats by conservative Dixiecrats and the ultraliberal Wallace faction. But Dewey's dour personality and Truman's intense whistle-stop campaign against the "do-nothing, good-for-nothing" Republican 80th Congress resulted in one of the biggest upsets in presidential history. **Regional Influences** Dewey captured all of the Middle Atlantic and New England states, except Massachusetts and Connecticut, along with the Dakotas, Nebraska, Kansas, and Oregon. Thurmond won South Carolina, Mississippi, Alabama, and Louisiana.

## 1952

| Party | Candidate | Popular vote | Percent | Electoral vote |
|---|---|---|---|---|
| Republican | Dwight D. Eisenhower (Kans.) and Richard M. Nixon (Calif.) | 33,936,137 | 55.13 | 442 |
| Democrat | Adlai E. Stevenson (Ill.) and John J. Sparkman (Ala.) | 27,314,649 | 44.38 | 89 |
| Progressive | Vincent W. Hallinan (Calif.) | 140,416 | 0.23 | — |
| Prohibition | Stuart Hamblen (Calif.) | 73,413 | 0.12 | — |
| Other | | 86,503 | 0.14 | — |
| | Total vote | 61,551,118 | | |
| | Eisenhower plurality | 6,621,485 | | |

**Key Issues** Eisenhower swept to victory after uniting the internationalist and isolationist factions of the Republican party. He promised to kick out alleged crooks and Communists in Washington, wage a more aggressive fight against Communists worldwide, and "go to Korea," implying that he had a plan to end the war there. **Regional Influences** Stevenson appealed to northern liberals and southern states' rights Democrats, but carried only nine states in the South. The Republicans also won slight majorities in Congress and were in control of the national government for the first time in 20 years.

## 1956

| Party | Candidate | Popular vote | Percent | Electoral vote |
|---|---|---|---|---|
| Republican | Dwight D. Eisenhower (Kans.) and Richard M. Nixon (Calif.) | 35,585,247 | 57.37 | 457 |
| Democrat | Adlai E. Stevenson (Ill.) and Estes Kefauver (Tenn.) | 26,030,172 | 41.97 | 73 |
| Constitution/States' Rights | T. Coleman Andrews (Va.) | 108,055 | 0.17 | — |
| Socialist-Labor | Eric Hass (N.Y.) | 44,300 | 0.07 | — |
| Other | | 257,600 | 0.42 | 1 |
| | Total vote | 62,025,372 | | |
| | Eisenhower plurality | 9,555,073 | | |

**Key Issues** Eisenhower won an easy victory in a rematch of the 1952 election. His popularity did not translate into victories for his party elsewhere, as Democrats increased their control of Congress—regained in 1954—and their hold on the nation's governorships. **Regional Influences** Winning even more handsomely than he did in 1952, Eisenhower lost only seven southern states.

## 1960

| Party | Candidate | Popular vote | Percent | Electoral vote |
|---|---|---|---|---|
| Democrat | John F. Kennedy (Mass.) and Lyndon B. Johnson (Tex.) | 34,221,344 | 49.72 | 303 |
| Republican | Richard M. Nixon (Calif.) and Henry Cabot Lodge (Mass.) | 34,106,671 | 49.55 | 219 |
| Socialist-Labor | Eric Hass (N.Y.) | 47,522 | 0.07 | — |
| Other | | 337,175 | 0.48 | 15 |
| Unpledged | | 116,248 | 0.17 | — |
| | Total vote | 68,828,960 | | |
| | Kennedy plurality | 114,673 | | |

**Key Issues** Kennedy called for the government to play a larger role in stimulating the national economy in order to fund domestic social programs as well as to sustain a defense buildup and keep ahead militarily of the USSR. The election was the first in which there were nationally televised debates between the two candidates. Kennedy's slick television performance played a role in his narrow triumph. **Regional Influences** The Democrats won a thin victory by narrowly defeating the Republicans in the Middle Atlantic states, the Deep South, Illinois, and Texas. Nixon carried most of the Midwest, border, and western states. The conservative Democrat Senator Harry F. Byrd of Virginia received 15 electoral votes, including all eight of Mississippi's, six of Alabama's 11, and one of Oklahoma's eight.

## 1964

| Party | Candidate | Popular vote | Percent | Electoral vote |
|---|---|---|---|---|
| Democrat | Lyndon B. Johnson (Tex.) and Hubert H. Humphrey (Minn.) | 43,126,584 | 61.05 | 486 |
| Republican | Barry M. Goldwater (Ariz.) and William E. Miller (N.Y.) | 27,177,838 | 38.47 | 52 |
| Socialist-Labor | Eric Hass (N.Y.) | 45,187 | 0.06 | — |
| Socialist Workers | Clifton DeBerry (N.Y.) | 32,701 | 0.05 | — |
| Other | | 258,794 | 0.37 | — |
| | Total vote | 70,641,104 | | |
| | Johnson plurality | 15,948,746 | | |

**Key Issues** Johnson ran for election in his own right on the basis of his "Great Society" domestic programs. The reactionary Goldwater campaigned against the New Deal and for the bombing of North Vietnam. **Regional Influences** Johnson won all but six states—Goldwater's home state of Arizona and five states in the Deep South—in the biggest popular and electoral landslide since 1936. Forty new northern Democrats were elected to the House on LBJ's coattails.

## 1968

| Party | Candidate | Popular vote | Percent | Electoral vote |
|---|---|---|---|---|
| Republican | Richard M. Nixon (Calif.) and Spiro T. Agnew (Md.) | 31,785,148 | 43.42 | 301 |
| Democrat | Hubert H. Humphrey (Minn.) and Edmund S. Muskie (Maine) | 31,274,503 | 42.72 | 191 |
| American Independent | George C. Wallace (Ala.) and Curtis LeMay (Ohio) | 9,901,151 | 13.53 | 46 |
| Socialist-Labor | Henning A. Blomen (Mass.) | 52,591 | 0.07 | — |
| Other | | 189,977 | 0.20 | — |
| | Total vote | 73,203,370 | | |
| | Nixon plurality | 510,645 | | |

**Key Issues** With the country divided over Vietnam, Humphrey failed to emerge from the shadow of the unpopular Johnson, while the previously hawkish Nixon pledged to end the war. Wallace attacked desegregation, "pointy-headed" intellectuals, the administration's timidity in Vietnam, and federal encroachment on states' rights. **Regional Influences** Barely more than 500,000 votes separated Nixon and Humphrey, but the Republican edge in the Electoral College was comfortable, and the combined anti-Democratic vote was a repudiation of the Johnson-Humphrey administration. Humphrey's strength was in the eastern seaboard states. Wallace won five states in the Deep South.

## 1972

| Party | Candidate | Popular vote | Percent | Electoral vote |
|---|---|---|---|---|
| Republican | Richard M. Nixon (Calif.) and Spiro T. Agnew (Md.) | 47,170,179 | 60.69 | 520 |
| Democrat | George S. McGovern (S.Dak.) and R. Sargent Shriver (Md..) | 29,171,791 | 37.53 | 17 |
| American Independent | John G. Schmitz (Calif.) | 1,090,673 | 1.40 | — |
| People's | Benjamin Spock | 78,751 | 0.10 | — |
| Other | | 216,196 | 0.28 | — |
| | Total vote | 77,727,590 | | |
| | Nixon plurality | 17,998,388 | | |

**Key Issues** Seeking to convert Wallace Democrats, Nixon pursued a "Southern strategy" of denouncing busing, the welfare state, the media, and intellectuals. McGovern was unable to overcome Republican charges that he was the candidate of "acid, abortion, and amnesty." **Regional Influences** The GOP gained southern Democratic votes when an assassination attempt knocked Wallace out of the race. Nixon lost only Massachusetts and the District of Columbia, but Democrats added to their majority in the Senate and kept control of the House.

## 1976

| Party | Candidate | Popular vote | Percent | Electoral vote |
|---|---|---|---|---|
| Democrat | Jimmy Carter (Ga.) and Walter F. Mondale (Minn.) | 40,830,763 | 50.06 | 297 |
| Republican | Gerald R. Ford (Mich.) and Robert Dole (Kans.) | 39,147,793 | 48.00 | 241 |
| Independent | Eugene J. McCarthy (Minn.) | 756,691 | 0.93 | — |
| Libertarian | Roger MacBride (Va.) | 173,011 | 0.21 | — |
| Other | | 647,631 | 0.79 | — |
| | Total vote | 81,555,889 | | |
| | Carter plurality | 1,682,970 | | |

**Key Issues** In the wake of Watergate, Carter ran a moralistic campaign as a political outsider. He railed against the Washington bureaucracy and vowed to lead a "government that is as good and honest and decent . . . as filled with love as are the American people." **Regional Influences** Despite an unimpressive campaign filled with miscues, Ford nearly overcame a huge early deficit in the polls. But Carter's background as a southern moderate enabled him to eke out a victory through wins in a combination of northern, southern, and border states.

## 1980

| Party | Candidate | Popular vote | Percent | Electoral vote |
|---|---|---|---|---|
| Republican | Ronald Reagan (Calif.) and George Bush (Tex.) | 43,901,812 | 50.75 | 489 |
| Democrat | Jimmy Carter (Ga.) and Walter F. Mondale (Minn.) | 35,483,820 | 41.02 | 49 |
| Independent | John B. Anderson (Ill.) and Patrick J. Lucey (Wis.) | 5,719,722 | 6.61 | — |
| Libertarian | Edward E. Clark (Calif.) | 921,188 | 1.06 | — |
| Other | | 486,754 | 0.56 | — |
| | Total vote | 86,513,296 | | |
| | Reagan plurality | 8,417,992 | | |

**Key Issues** Inflation, an energy shortage, the taking of American hostages by Iran, and a strong primary challenge from Edward Kennedy of Massachusetts weakened Carter. Reagan, promising to get government "off the backs of the American people," pledged to cut taxes, increase defense spending, and balance the federal budget. Anderson, a Republican, ran as an independent to the left of both Carter and Reagan. **Regional Influences** Reagan swept to a landslide win in the Electoral College, with Carter carrying only six states and the District of Columbia.

## 1984

| Party | Candidate | Popular vote | Percent | Electoral vote |
|---|---|---|---|---|
| Republican | Ronald Reagan (Calif.) and George Bush (Tex.) | 54,450,603 | 58.78 | 525 |
| Democrat | Walter F. Mondale (Minn.) and Geraldine Ferraro (N.Y.) | 37,573,671 | 40.56 | 13 |
| Libertarian | David Bergland (Calif.) | 227,949 | 0.25 | — |
| Other | | 570,343 | 0.61 | — |
| | Total vote | 92,628,458 | | |
| | Reagan plurality | 16,876,932 | | |

**Key Issues** The economy was flying after emerging in late 1983 from the worst economic downturn since the Great Depression. Reagan, whose commercials proclaimed it was "morning in America," ridiculed Mondale as an old-fashioned "tax-and-spend, gloom-and-doom" Democrat. Controversy over her husband's finances blunted Ferraro's appeal as the first woman on a major party ticket. **Regional Influences** Mondale carried only his home state of Minnesota and the District of Columbia, while Reagan won the greatest electoral victory in American history and the fifth-highest share of the popular vote.

**Source:** Congressional Quarterly, Inc., *Presidential Elections since 1789* (1983).

## 1988

| Party | Candidate | Popular vote | Percent | Electoral vote |
|---|---|---|---|---|
| Republican | George Bush (Tex.) and Dan Quayle (Ind.) | 48,881,011 | 53.37 | 426 |
| Democrat | Michael S. Dukakis (Mass.) and Lloyd Bentsen (Tex.) | 41,828,350 | 45.67 | 112 |
| Libertarian | Ron Paul (Tex.) | 431,499 | 0.47 | — |
| New Alliance | Leonora Fulani (N.Y.) | 218,159 | 0.24 | — |
| Populist | David Duke | 48,267 | 0.05 | — |
| Consumer | Eugene J. McCarthy | 30,510 | 0.03 | — |
| American Independent | James Griffin | 27,818 | 0.03 | — |
| National Economic Recovery | Lyndon H. LaRouche, Jr. | 25,082 | 0.03 | — |
| Right-to-Life | William Mara | 20,497 | 0.02 | — |
| Worker's League | Ed Winn | 18,579 | 0.02 | — |
| Socialist Workers | James Warren | 13,338 | 0.01 | — |
| Peace Freedom | Herbert Lewin | 10,312 | 0.01 | — |
| Prohibition | Earl F. Dodge | 7,984 | 0.01 | — |
| Worker's World | Larry Holmes | 7,719 | 0.01 | — |
| Socialist | Willa Kenoyer | 3,800 | — | — |
| American | Delmar Dennis | 3,456 | — | — |
| Grassroots | Jack Herer | 1,949 | — | — |
| Independent | Louie Youngkite | 372 | — | — |
| Third World Assembly | John Martin | 235 | — | — |
| Other | | 6,934 | — | — |
| | Total vote | 91,585,871 | | |
| | Bush plurality | 7,052,661 | | |

*"Great men are not chosen president, firstly, because great men are rare in politics; secondly, because the method of choice does not bring them to the top; thirdly, because they are not, in quiet times, absolutely necessary."*

—English jurist, historian, and diplomat James Bryce, *The American Commonwealth* (1888)

## The 1988 Presidential Vote

Vice President George Bush defeated Massachusetts Gov. Michael S. Dukakis in every major section of the country and among most segments of the electorate in the 1988 presidential election. The result was a comfortable win for Bush in the popular vote, 48,881,278 to 41,805,374, and an easy victory in the Electoral College, 426 to 111. (One Democratic elector from West Virginia voted for the Democratic vice-presidential nominee, Texas Sen. Lloyd Bentsen, instead of Dukakis.)

Bush eked out a victory in the East, Dukakis's home region, won easily in the Midwest and West, and crushed Dukakis in the South, where he amassed 4.4 million of his national plurality of more than 7 million votes. The only significant gaps in the Republican victory, according to a *New York Times*/CBS News poll, were among minorities—especially blacks and Hispanics—Jewish voters, union households, low-income voters and, of course, voters identifying themselves as Democrats or liberals. In percentages the vote broke down as follows:

• Men voted 57–41 for Bush, while women went for the Republican 50–49.

• Dukakis swept the black vote (86–12) and won handily among Hispanics (69–30).

• Bush overwhelmed Dukakis in the South, 58–41. The Republican also won in the East (50–49), the Midwest (52–47) and the West (52–46).

• Bush won in all age categories surveyed: 18–29 years old, 30–44, 45–59, and 60+.

• Bush trounced Dukakis among white Protestants (66–33) and won the Catholic vote (52–47). White fundamentalists and evangelical Christians voted overwhelmingly for the GOP (81–18). Jews were the only religious group in the Democratic column (64–35).

• The only economic group to vote Democratic was the lowest-income voters. Those from families with an income under $12,500 voted for Dukakis 66–33, while voters with family incomes between $12,500 and $24,999 narrowly voted for the Massachusetts governor. A comfortable majority of voters from every other income category voted for Bush.

• Students, teachers, and the unemployed were the only groups classified by occupation to vote Democratic. The GOP won large victories among professionals, white-collar workers, and farmers.

• Blacks once again were by far the most reliable Democratic voters, despite widely reported tensions between the Dukakis campaign and supporters of the Rev. Jesse L. Jackson. But while nearly 90% of black voters voted Democratic, studies indicate that black voters showed up at the polls in smaller numbers than in other recent presidential elections.

• While white Democrats were four times as likely as black Democrats to desert the party and vote for Bush, Dukakis did surprisingly well in garnering the votes of so-called Reagan Democrats. Dukakis captured 51% of the votes of Democrats who voted for Reagan in

1984. Jimmy Carter received the votes of only 23% of these voters in 1980.

- Bush's top state was Utah, where he received nearly two-thirds of the vote. He collected at least 60% of the vote in eight states. Dukakis's strongest tally was in the District of Columbia, where he received 82.6% of the vote. In no other state did he even approach 60% of the vote.

**Key issues** Bush fought back from an early-summer 17-point Dukakis lead with a relentless attack on his opponent's "liberalism." Bush accused Dukakis of coddling up to criminals and made a household name out of Willie Horton, a Massachusetts prison inmate who raped a Maryland woman while out of jail on a furlough. He also attacked Dukakis for the pollution in Boston Harbor. Dukakis said early in the campaign that the election was about "competence, not ideology." Bush responded that the values of the Massachusetts governor were not those of the American people.

Dukakis failed to respond to the charges made by the Bush campaign and ran away from the "liberal" label until late in the campaign. He hammered unsuccessfully at Bush's links to the Iran-Contra scandal and Panama's drug-running leader, Gen. Mañuel Noriega, and mocked Bush's running mate, Sen. Dan Quayle. Ultimately, the voters decided to stay with the Republicans in a time of peace, prosperity, and continued popularity for the GOP incumbent, Ronald Reagan.

**Regional influences** Dukakis won only 10 states and the District of Columbia. Pockets of Democratic strength were found on the West Coast and in the northern Midwest: Dukakis won in Washington, Oregon, and Hawaii in the West and in Minnesota, Wisconsin, and Iowa in the Midwest. The Democrat also captured New York, West Virginia, Rhode Island, and his home state of Massachusetts. Bush swept the rest of the country easily and did especially well in the formerly Democratic "solid South."

## Nonvoter Study

Voter turnout hit a 64-year low in 1988, with 50.16% of the voting age population turning up at the presidential polls. The total number of voters also declined in absolute terms by more than a million, despite an increase of nearly 8 million people in the eligible voting pool. Turnout of registered voters also fell, from 72.6% in 1984 to 70.5% in 1988.

The decrease continues a trend that began in 1960, when 62.8% of eligible voters cast presidential ballots. The only increase in voter turnout during that period came in 1984, when 53.1% of the voting-age population voted, compared to 52.8% in 1980. The 3% decline from 1984 was the third largest since 1920. Only the Dewey-Truman race of 1948 and the Nixon-McGovern race of 1972 had bigger drop-offs from the previous election. Additionally, voter-turnout figures for the 1972 race were exaggerated by the enfranchisement of voters in the low-voting 18–20 age range.

Minnesota ranked highest in voter turnout,

### VOTER TURNOUT IN PRESIDENTIAL ELECTIONS, 1928–88

| Year | Total vote | Voting-age population (VAP) | % of VAP voting | Est. no. of registered voters | % of registered voters voting |
|------|-----------|---------------------------|----------------|------------------------------|------------------------------|
| 1928 | 36,879,414 | 71,185,000 | 51.8% | N.A. | N.A. |
| 1932 | 39,816,522 | 75,768,000 | 52.6 | N.A. | N.A. |
| 1936 | 45,646,817 | 80,354,000 | 56.8 | N.A. | N.A. |
| 1940 | 49,815,312 | 84,728,000 | 58.8 | N.A. | N.A. |
| 1944 | 48,025,684 | 95,573,000 | 56.1 | N.A. | N.A. |
| 1948 | 48,833,680 | 95,573,000 | 51.1 | N.A. | N.A. |
| 1952 | 61,551,919 | 99,929,000 | 61.6 | N.A. | N.A. |
| 1956 | 62,033,908 | 104,515,000 | 59.4 | N.A. | N.A. |
| 1960 | 68,838,000 | 109,672,000 | 62.8 | 82,500,000 | 75.4% |
| 1964 | 70,645,000 | 114,090,000 | 61.9 | 87,000,000 | 76.7 |
| 1968 | 73,212,000 | 120,285,000 | 60.9 | 90,000,000 | 74.8 |
| 1972 | 77,625,000 | 140,777,000 | 55.2 | 103,000,000 | 73.0 |
| 1976 | 81,603,000 | 152,308,000 | 53.5 | 106,500,000 | 70.0 |
| 1980 | 86,497,000 | 164,595,000 | 52.6 | 115,000,000 | 69.9 |
| 1984 | 92,653,000 | 174,467,000 | 53.1 | 127,500,000 | 73.1 |
| 1988 | 91,609,673 | 182,628,000 | 50.2 | 129,483,000 | 70.9 |

**Source:** Committee for the Study of the American Electorate, *Non-Voter Study* (1989).

with 66.33% of its voting population casting ballots. Georgia ranked lowest with only 38.79% of its eligible voters going to the polls. In 12 states (Maine, Minn., Miss., Mont., Nebr., Nev., N.C., N. Dak., Utah, Vt., Wash., and Wyo.), turnout for the presidential race was lower than for Senate and governor races.

## THE FEDERAL ELECTION CAMPAIGN ACT

In 1971 Congress passed the Federal Election Campaign Act to deal with various aspects of campaign financing. The law was amended and strengthened in 1974 and 1976, and the Federal Election Commission (FEC) was established to administer the law, which affects candidates for the U.S. House of Representatives, the U.S. Senate, and the presidency, as well as the political committees that support them. The act requires disclosure of sources and uses of funds for federal elections, provides public financing for presidential elections, and sets limits on campaign contributions. The specific requirements of each of these three parts of the act are detailed below.

**Public disclosure** Candidates for federal office and the political committees that support them must register and file periodic disclosures of their campaign finance activities with the clerk of the House, the secretary of the Senate, or the FEC. These reports are available to the public within 48 hours of their disclosure. A candidate is defined as one who has raised or spent more than $5,000 in any given year in campaigning for federal office. A political committee is defined as a club, committee, association, or organization that receives contributions or makes expenditures of more than $1,000 to a federal candidate in any calendar year. In recent years they have come to be called PACs, for Political Action Committee.

**Public financing** Public financing is provided for eligible presidential candidates in primary and general elections, and for national party committees for the nominating conventions. Financing is given in the form of matching payments to primary candidates, public grants to nominees in the general elections, and public grants to the national party committees for the conventions. The money for public financing is raised by the Presidential Election Campaign Fund, which collects one dollar from the tax payment of every taxpayer who checks off this box on his or her federal income-tax return.

**Contribution limits and prohibitions** In federal elections the act prohibits contributions from the treasuries of national banks, corporations, and labor organizations; contributions from government contractors; contributions from foreign nationals (green-card holders); cash contributions in excess of $100 per person; contributions supplied by one person in the name of another person.

Additionally, the act sets contribution limits as shown in the accompanying table.

### CAMPAIGN CONTRIBUTION LIMITS FOR INDIVIDUALS AND PACS

| Recipient | Contributor | | |
|-----------|-------------|---|---|
| | Individual contributor | Multi-candidate committee | Other political committee |
| Each candidate or candidate committee[1] | $ 1,000 | $ 5,000 | $ 1,000 |
| National party committee[1] | 20,000 | 15,000 | 20,000 |
| Other political committee[2] | 5,000 | 5,000 | 5,000 |
| **Total per calendar year** | **$25,000** | **no limit** | **no limit** |

1. Per election year. 2. Per calendar year. **Source:** Federal Election Commission.

### Campaign Finances, 1988

According to the FEC, primary and general election congressional candidates in 1987–88 raised $478 million and spent $459 million—an increase in spending of only 1.8% over the

## PACS: COMMITTEES AND CONTRIBUTIONS, 1979–88

| | Committees | | Contributions | |
|---|---|---|---|---|
| Year | Number | Percent change[1] | Amount | Percent change[1] |
| **Corporate** | | | | |
| 1987–88 | 2,008 | 5.4% | $56,155,259 | 13.3% |
| 1985–86 | 1,906 | 5.4 | 49,566,619 | 27.1 |
| 1983–84 | 1,809 | 16.2 | 39,008,465 | 32.8 |
| 1981–82 | 1,557 | 24.5 | 29,364,443 | 36.2 |
| 1979–80 | 1,251 | N.A. | 21,560,863 | N.A. |
| **Trade/Membership/Health** | | | | |
| 1987–88 | 848 | 7.5% | $41,213,596 | 19.3% |
| 1985–86 | 789 | 4.2 | 34,551,531 | 21.9 |
| 1983–84 | 757 | 13.2 | 28,346,541 | 23.4 |
| 1981–82 | 669 | 5.4 | 22,939,475 | 35.0 |
| 1979–80 | 635 | N.A. | 16,988,685 | N.A. |
| **Labor** | | | | |
| 1987–88 | 401 | –3.8% | $35,495,780 | 14.4% |
| 1985–86 | 417 | –4.8 | 31,038,885 | 18.6 |
| 1983–84 | 438 | 4.3 | 26,164,349 | 25.1 |
| 1981–82 | 420 | 26.9 | 20,916,367 | 47.2 |
| 1979–80 | 331 | N.A. | 14,213,099 | N.A. |
| **Total[2]** | | | | |
| 1987–88 | 4,832 | 5.1% | $159,243,241 | 13.9% |
| 1985–86 | 4,596 | 5.7 | 139,839,718 | 23.8 |
| 1983–84 | 4,347 | 16.8 | 112,970,044 | 29.0 |
| 1981–82 | 3,722 | 33.6 | 87,553,326 | 45.5 |
| 1979–80 | 2,785 | N.A. | 60,189,696 | N.A. |

1. Change over year before. 2. Includes other types of PACs not shown separately, classified as nonconnected, cooperative, and cooperative with shares. **Source:** Federal Election Commission, *FEC Reports on Financial Activity, 1987-88; U.S. Senate and House Campaigns, Final Report* (1989).

1986 election year. (By comparison, spending increased 20.6% from 1984 to 1986.) In the same period, spending for House seats increased 7.6%, to $257 million, while spending for Senate seats went down 4.8%, to $201.4 million. Winning campaigns showed spending increases of 18.5% for the Senate and 10.3% for the House over 1986 levels.

Contributions from PACs were also up by 11% over 1986. Although that was the smallest increase in the 1980s, contributions from PACs in 1988 made up 31% of net campaign receipts, compared with 28% in 1986 and only 17% in 1978. In 1988, contributions from individuals made up 64% of net receipts for the 210 Senate candidates and PAC contributions constituted 22.9%. Overall, the 1,582 candidates for the House raised $278 million: $130 million–46.7%–from individuals and $102 million–36.7%–from PACs. The balance of campaign funds came from candidates, loans, and political parties.

While PAC contributions more than doubled between 1979–80 and 1987–88, PAC contributions as a percentage of total campaign receipts grew from 26% to 37%. Over the same period, the number of candidates running for office fell in every election year, from 2,228 in 1979–80 to 1,792 in 1987–88—a drop of 28%.

PAC contributions to presidential candidates in the 1988 elections totaled $3.4 million: Republicans received $1.8 million of the total

and Democratic candidates $1.6 million. The leading PAC contributors to the Republican campaign were corporate PACs, 66%, and trade/membership/health PACs, 12.3%. Of Democratic presidential PAC contributions labor PACs accounted for 35.6% and corporate PACs for 35.3%.

# THE ELECTORAL COLLEGE

The Electoral College is the body of electors chosen by all of the states that ultimately is responsible for selecting the president of the United States. The Constitution's framers did not want the nation's chief executive chosen by either the national legislature or the people directly. Instead they set up what came to be known as the Electoral College—probably based on the Sacred College of Cardinals responsible for electing the pope—under Article II, section 1, of the Constitution to provide for indirect election of the president: "Each State shall appoint, in such manner as the legislature thereof may direct, a number of Electors, equal to the whole number of Senators and Representatives to which the State may be entitled in the Congress; but no Senator or Representative, or person holding an office of trust or profit under the United States, shall be appointed an Elector."

Electors were supposed to be distinguished, enlightened citizens who would cast a disinterested vote for president. From the start, though, electors have been instruments of partisan passions. At first most state legislatures were responsible for choosing electors. By 1828, however, all states except South Carolina allowed electors to be chosen by direct popular election. (In South Carolina the legislature continued to select electors until the Civil War.) When electors began being selected by popular vote, parties presented slates of candidates for presidential electors who were tacitly pledged to support the party's nominees for president and vice president. This is how the practice began of state's voting as a unit. Subsequently, many states passed laws requiring their electors to vote as a bloc. Where it is not required by law, it is customary for all of a state's electors to vote for the candidate receiving a plurality of the popular vote in that state. The names of the candidates for electors may or may not appear on the ballot alongside the names of the candidates to whom they are pledged. Voters really vote for presidential electors, though, even when they seem to be casting a ballot for a presidential candidate.

The presidential electors chosen by the voters in November meet in their state capitals on the first Monday after the second Wednesday in December to cast their vote for president and vice president. The results of this balloting are sent to the president of the U.S. Senate, the directors of the U.S. General Services Administration, the state's secretary of state, and to the judge of the federal district court of the district in which the electors gathered. Sealed state ballots are opened and counted at a joint session of Congress on Jan. 6 following the election year.

Originally, electors voted for two individuals

for president on a single ballot. The winner of a majority of the vote was elected president; the runner-up, vice president. The framers fully expected there to be many elections in which no candidate would gain a majority of the vote, and the president would have to be selected by the House of Representatives, where each state delegation would cast a single vote. But in 1789 and 1792, every elector voted for George Washington. In both years John Adams was the runner-up and thus vice president.

Problems inherent in this system became apparent once Washington no longer was a candidate. In 1796 Adams and Thomas Jefferson finished first and second in the balloting and were elected president and vice president, respectively, despite their being fierce foes. By 1800 two formal parties had evolved that nominated candidates specifically for president and vice president. A Federalist elector purposely failed to vote for the party's vice-presidential nominee, Thomas Pinckney, in order to assure a potential majority for John Adams. But overzealous Republican electors all voted for both Jefferson and the party's vice-presidential nominee, Aaron Burr. Both men received the same majority of the electoral vote, and the election had to be decided by the House, where Jefferson won. This led to adoption of the 12th Amendment to the Constitution, implemented in 1804, which required that electors cast separate ballots for president and vice president. If no candidate achieves a majority of the electoral vote for vice president, the position is determined by the Senate, with each senator casting a single ballot. This has happened only once, when the Senate selected Richard M. Johnson after he fell one electoral vote short of a majority for vice president in 1836.

Currently, 270 votes are needed to reach a majority in the Electoral College. There have been two elections in which no candidate received a majority of the electoral vote—in 1824 and in 1876, when disputed results in several states prevented either Rutherford B. Hayes or Samuel J. Tilden from achieving a majority. (John Quincy Adams and Hayes won those contests, respectively.) A candidate also can be elected president despite losing the popular vote. This occurred, again in 1824 and 1876, when the House selected Adams and Hayes, though they lost the popular vote to Andrew Jackson and Tilden, respectively, and in 1888, when Benjamin Harrison was elected over Grover Cleveland despite receiving a minority of the popular vote.

Critics of the Electoral College throughout the years have sought to diminish the power of the states in the selection of presidents. It is said to be unfair for all of a state's electoral votes to go to a candidate who merely achieved a plurality of the vote in that state. The many proposals offered to bypass the states and provide for the direct, popular election of the president have foundered, however, on the fear that while such a system might encourage third-and fourth-party candidates to run for office, it would make it even more likely for a candidate to be elected president with a minority of the total popular vote.

# Political Office Holders

## The Vice Presidency

The vice president is a member of the executive branch (to which he is elected with the president) and of the legislative branch, in which he serves as president of the Senate (see the Constitution Article I, section 3). Unlike the office of president, that of vice president has sometimes been left vacant after the death of the vice president or the latter's assumption of higher office on the death of the president. Until adoption of the 25th Amendment to the Constitution in 1967, there was no provision to fill a vacancy in the vice presidency. Under the amendment the president must name a vice president when the office is vacant, and the nominee must pass a majority vote of approval in both houses of Congress. Gerald Ford, Richard Nixon's choice to replace Spiro Agnew after the latter's resignation in 1973, was the first vice president to gain the office under the amendment. While the 25th Amendment does not supersede the presidential order of succession, it decreases the likelihood of the office's ever falling to the Speaker of the House or a sitting cabinet member.

## Presidential order of succession

Article II of the Constitution gives to Congress the power to determine the presidential order of succession should both the president and vice president die, become incapacitated, or be disqualified from office. The present law, passed in 1947, puts the Speaker of the House first in line to the presidency, followed by the president pro tempore of the Senate. The order of succession then goes through the members of the cabinet, in the order in which the executive departments were established: (1) Secretary of State, (2) Secretary of the Treasury, (3) Secretary of Defense, (4) Attorney General, (5) Secretary of the Interior, (6) Secretary of Agriculture, (7) Secretary of Commerce, (8) Secretary of Labor, (9) Secretary of Health and Human Services, (10) Secretary of Housing and Urban Development, (11) Secretary of Transportation, (12) Secretary of Energy, (13) Secretary of Education, (14) Secretary of Veterans Affairs.

Until the 1970 legislation removing the postmaster general from the cabinet and establishing an independent postal service, the postmaster general was fifth in line to the presidency. The heads of new departments are automatically added to the line of succession as the new departments are created.

A cabinet member must be a U.S. citizen and at least 35 years old in order to become acting president. If a cabinet member next in line to fill a presidential vacancy is not yet 35, the presidency passes to the next cabinet member in the order of succession.

## VICE PRESIDENTS OF THE UNITED STATES, 1789–1991

| Name | Party | Tenure | State, birth–death | Name | Party | Tenure | State, birth–death |
|------|-------|--------|--------------------|------|-------|--------|--------------------|
| 1. John Adams | Fed. | 1789–97 | Mass., 1735–1826 | 23. Adlai E. Stevenson | D | 1893–97 | Ill., 1835–1914 |
| 2. Thomas Jefferson | D-R | 1797–1801 | Va., 1743–1826 | 24. Garret A. Hobart | R | 1897–1901† | N.J., 1844–99 |
| 3. Aaron Burr | D-R | 1801–05 | N.Y., 1756–1836 | 25. Theodore Roosevelt | R | 1901[7] | N.Y., 1858–1919 |
| 4. George Clinton | D-R | 1805–13† | N.Y., 1739–1812 | 26. Charles W. Fairbanks | R | 1905–09 | Ind., 1852–1918 |
| 5. Elbridge Gerry | D-R | 1813–17† | Mass., 1744–1814 | 27. James S. Sherman | R | 1909–13† | N.Y., 1855–1912 |
| 6. Daniel D. Tompkins | D-R | 1817–25 | N.Y., 1774–1825 | 28. Thomas R. Marshall | D | 1913–21 | Ind., 1854–1925 |
| 7. John C. Calhoun | D-R | 1825–33[1] | S.C., 1782–1850 | 29. Calvin Coolidge | R | 1921–23[8] | Mass., 1872–1933 |
| 8. Martin Van Buren | D | 1833–37 | N.Y., 1782–1862 | 30. Charles G. Dawes | R | 1925–29 | Ill., 1865–1951 |
| 9. Richard M. Johnson | D | 1837–41[2] | Ky., 1780–1850 | 31. Charles Curtis | R | 1929–33 | Kans., 1860–1936 |
| 10. John Tyler | Whig | 1841[3] | Va., 1790–1862 | 32. John Nance Garner | D | 1933–41 | Tex., 1868–1967 |
| 11. George M. Dallas | D | 1845–49 | Pa., 1792–1864 | 33. Henry A. Wallace | D | 1941–45 | Iowa, 1888–1965 |
| 12. Millard Fillmore | Whig | 1849–50[4] | N.Y., 1800–74 | 34. Harry S Truman | D | 1945[9] | Mo., 1884–1972 |
| 13. William R. King | D | 1853–57† | Ala., 1786–1853 | 35. Alben W. Barkley | D | 1949–53 | Ky., 1877–1956 |
| 14. John C. Breckenridge | D | 1857–61 | Ky., 1821–75 | 36. Richard M. Nixon | R | 1953–61 | Calif., 1913– |
| 15. Hannibal Hamlin | R | 1861–65 | Maine, 1809–91 | 37. Lyndon B. Johnson | D | 1961–63[10] | Tex., 1908–73 |
| 16. Andrew Johnson | D | 1865[5] | Tenn., 1808–75 | 38. Hubert H. Humphrey | D | 1965–69 | Minn., 1911–78 |
| 17. Schuyler Colfax | R | 1869–73 | Ind., 1823–85 | 39. Spiro T. Agnew | R | 1969–73[11] | Md., 1918– |
| 18. Henry Wilson | R | 1873–77† | Mass., 1812–75 | 40. Gerald R. Ford | R | 1973–74[12] | Mich., 1913– |
| 19. William A. Wheeler | R | 1877–81 | N.Y., 1819–87 | 41. Nelson A. Rockefeller | R | 1974–77[13] | N.Y., 1908–79 |
| 20. Chester A. Arthur | R | 1881[6] | N.Y., 1829–86 | 42. Walter F. Mondale | D | 1977–81 | Minn., 1928– |
| 21. Thomas A. Hendricks | D | 1885† | Ind., 1819–85 | 43. George Bush | R | 1981–89 | Tex., 1924– |
| 22. Levi P. Morton | R | 1889–93 | N.Y., 1824–1920 | 44. J. Danforth Quayle | R | 1989– | Ind., 1947– |

**Notes:** Fed. = Federalist. D = Democrat. D–R = Democratic-Republican. R = Republican. † = Died in office. 1. Resigned to become senator from South Carolina (1832–43). 2. Voted in by Senate after no candidate for vice president gained a majority in the Electoral College. 3. Became president after William Henry Harrison's death. 4. Became president after Zachary Taylor's death. 5. Nominated by Republicans to run with Abraham Lincoln on the Union ticket; became president after Lincoln's assassination. 6. Became president after James Garfield's assassination. 7. Became president after William McKinley's assassination. 8. Became president after Warren Harding's death. 9. Became president after Franklin D. Roosevelt's death. 10. Became president after John F. Kennedy's assassination. 11. Resigned while under investigation for receiving kickbacks as governor of Maryland. 12. First vice president named under terms of the 25th Amendment; assumed presidency after Richard Nixon resigned. 13. Named vice president by Ford.

## SPEAKERS OF THE U.S. HOUSE OF REPRESENTATIVES, 1789–1991

| Name | Party | State | Tenure | Name | Party | State | Tenure |
|------|-------|-------|--------|------|-------|-------|--------|
| 1. Frederick A.C. Muhlenberg | D-R | Pa. | 1789–91 | 30. Schuyler Colfax | R | Ind. | 1863–69 |
| 2. Jonathan Trumbull | Fed. | Conn. | 1791–93 | 31. James G. Blaine | R | Maine | 1869–75 |
| 3. Frederick A.C. Muhlenberg | D-R | Pa. | 1793–95 | 32. Michael C. Kerr | D | Ind. | 1875–76 |
| 4. Jonathan Dayton | Fed. | N.J. | 1795–97 | 33. Samuel J. Randall | D | Pa. | 1876–81 |
| 5. George Dent | Fed. | Md. | 1797–99 | 34. J. Warren Keifer | R | Ohio | 1881–83 |
| 6. Theodore Sedgwick | Fed. | Mass. | 1799–1801 | 35. John G. Carlisle | D | Ky. | 1883–89 |
| 7. Nathaniel Macon | D-R | N.C. | 1801–07 | 36. Thomas B. Reed | R | Maine | 1889–91 |
| 8. Joseph B. Varnum | D-R | Mass. | 1807–11 | 37. Charles F. Crisp | D | Ga. | 1891–95 |
| 9. Henry Clay | D-R | Ky. | 1811–14 | 38. Thomas B. Reed | R | Maine | 1895–99 |
| 10. Langdon Cheves | D-R | S.C. | 1814–15 | 39. David B. Henderson | R | Iowa | 1899–1903 |
| 11. Henry Clay | D-R | Ky. | 1815–20 | 40. Joseph G. Cannon | R | Ill. | 1903–11 |
| 12. John W. Taylor | D-R | N.Y. | 1820–21 | 41. Champ Clark | D | Mo. | 1911–19 |
| 13. Philip Barbour | D-R | Va. | 1821–23 | 42. Frederick H. Gillett | R | Mass. | 1919–25 |
| 14. Henry Clay | D-R | Ky. | 1822–24 | 43. Nicholas Longworth | R | Ohio | 1925–31 |
| 15. John W. Taylor | D-R | N.Y. | 1825–27 | 44. John N. Garner | D | Tex. | 1931–33 |
| 16. Andrew Stevenson | D | Va. | 1827–34 | 45. Henry T. Rainey | D | Ill. | 1933–34 |
| 17. John Bell | D | Tenn. | 1834–35 | 46. Joseph W. Byrns | D | Tenn. | 1935–36 |
| 18. James K. Polk | D | Tenn. | 1835–39 | 47. William B. Bankhead | D | Ala. | 1936–39 |
| 19. Robert M.T. Hunter | Whig | Va. | 1839–41 | 48. Sam Rayburn | D | Tex. | 1940–46 |
| 20. John White | Whig | Ky. | 1841–43 | 49. Joseph W. Martin, Jr. | R | Mass. | 1947–49 |
| 21. John W. Jones | D | Va. | 1843–45 | 50. Sam Rayburn | D | Tex. | 1949–52 |
| 22. John W. Davis | D | Ind. | 1845–47 | 51. Joseph W. Martin, Jr. | R | Mass. | 1953–54 |
| 23. Robert C. Winthrop | Whig | Mass. | 1847–49 | 52. Sam Rayburn | D | Tex. | 1955–61 |
| 24. Howell Cobb | D | Ga. | 1849–51 | 53. John W. McCormack | D | Mass. | 1962–71 |
| 25. Linn Boyd | D | Ky. | 1851–55 | 54. Carl B. Albert | D | Okla. | 1971–76 |
| 26. Nathaniel Banks | R | Mass. | 1855–57 | 55. Thomas P. O'Neill, Jr. | D | Mass. | 1977–87 |
| 27. James L. Orr | D | S.C. | 1857–59 | 56. James C. Wright, Jr. | D | Tex. | 1987–89 |
| 28. William Pennington | Whig | N.J. | 1859–61 | 57. Thomas S. Foley | D | Wash. | 1989– |
| 29. Galusha A. Grow | R | Pa. | 1861–63 | | | | |

**Note:** D = Democrat, D-R = Democratic-Republican, Fed. = Federalist, R = Republican.

## CABINET MEMBERS, 1789–1991

### Washington Administration (1789–97)

| | | |
|---|---|---|
| Secretary of State | Thomas Jefferson | 1789–93 |
| | Edmund Randolph | 1794–95 |
| | Timothy Pickering | 1795–97 |
| Secretary of Treasury | Alexander Hamilton | 1789–95 |
| | Oliver Wolcott | 1795–97 |
| Secretary of War | Henry Knox | 1789–94 |
| | Timothy Pickering | 1795–96 |
| | James McHenry | 1796–97 |
| Attorney General | Edmund Randolph | 1789–93 |
| | William Bradford | 1794–95 |
| | Charles Lee | 1795–97 |
| Postmaster General | Samuel Osgood | 1789–91 |
| | Timothy Pickering | 1791–94 |
| | Joseph Habersham | 1795–97 |

### John Adams Administration (1797–1801)

| | | |
|---|---|---|
| Secretary of State | Timothy Pickering | 1797–1800 |
| | John Marshall | 1800–01 |
| Secretary of Treasury | Oliver Wolcott | 1797–1800 |
| | Samuel Dexter | 1800–01 |
| Secretary of War | James McHenry | 1797–1800 |
| | Samuel Dexter | 1800–01 |
| Attorney General | Charles Lee | 1797–1801 |
| Postmaster General | Joseph Habersham | 1797–1801 |
| Secretary of Navy | Benjamin Stoddert | 1798–1801 |

### Jefferson Administration (1801–09)

| | | |
|---|---|---|
| Secretary of State | James Madison | 1801–09 |
| Secretary of Treasury | Samuel Dexter | 1801 |
| | Albert Gallatin | 1801–09 |
| Secretary of War | Henry Dearborn | 1801–09 |
| Attorney General | Levi Lincoln | 1801–05 |
| | Robert Smith | 1805 |
| | John Breckinridge | 1805–06 |
| | Caesar Rodney | 1807–09 |
| Postmaster General | Joseph Habersham | 1801 |
| | Gideon Granger | 1801–09 |
| Secretary of Navy | Robert Smith | 1801–09 |

### Madison Administration (1809–17)

| | | |
|---|---|---|
| Secretary of State | Robert Smith | 1809–11 |
| | James Monroe | 1811–17 |
| Secretary of Treasury | Albert Gallatin | 1809–13 |
| | George Campbell | 1814 |
| | Alexander Dallas | 1814–16 |
| | William Crawford | 1816–17 |
| Secretary of War | William Eustis | 1809–12 |
| | John Armstrong | 1813–14 |
| | James Monroe | 1814–15 |
| | William Crawford | 1815–17 |
| Attorney General | Caesar Rodney | 1809–11 |
| | William Pinckney | 1811–14 |
| | Richard Rush | 1814–17 |
| Postmaster General | Gideon Granger | 1809–14 |
| | Return Meigs | 1814–17 |
| Secretary of Navy | Paul Hamilton | 1809–13 |
| | William Jones | 1813–14 |
| | Benjamin Crowninshield | 1814–17 |

### Monroe Administration (1817–25)

| | | |
|---|---|---|
| Secretary of State | John Quincy Adams | 1817–25 |
| Secretary of Treasury | William Crawford | 1817–25 |

### Monroe Administration (cont'd)

| | | |
|---|---|---|
| Secretary of War | George Graham | 1817 |
| | John C. Calhoun | 1817–25 |
| Attorney General | Richard Rush | 1817 |
| | William Wirt | 1817–25 |
| Postmaster General | Return Meigs | 1817–23 |
| | John McLean | 1823–25 |
| Secretary of Navy | Benjamin Crowninshield | 1817–18 |
| | Smith Thompson | 1818–23 |
| | Samuel Southard | 1823–25 |

### John Quincy Adams Administration (1825–29)

| | | |
|---|---|---|
| Secretary of State | Henry Clay | 1825–29 |
| Secretary of Treasury | Richard Rush | 1825–29 |
| Secretary of War | James Barbour | 1825–28 |
| | Peter Porter | 1828–29 |
| Attorney General | William Wirt | 1825–29 |
| Postmaster General | John McLean | 1825–29 |
| Secretary of Navy | Samuel Southard | 1825–29 |

### Jackson Administration (1829–37)

| | | |
|---|---|---|
| Secretary of State | Martin Van Buren | 1829–31 |
| | Edward Livingston | 1831–33 |
| | Louis McLane | 1833–34 |
| | John Forsyth | 1834–37 |
| Secretary of Treasury | Samuel Ingham | 1829–31 |
| | Louis McLane | 1831–33 |
| | William Duane | 1833 |
| | Roger B. Taney | 1833–34 |
| | Levi Woodbury | 1834–37 |
| Secretary of War | John H. Eaton | 1829–31 |
| | Lewis Cass | 1831–37 |
| | Benjamin Butler | 1837 |
| Attorney General | John M. Berrien | 1829–31 |
| | Roger B. Taney | 1831–33 |
| | Benjamin Butler | 1833–37 |
| Postmaster General | William Barry | 1829–35 |
| | Amos Kendall | 1835–37 |
| Secretary of Navy | John Branch | 1829–31 |
| | Levi Woodbury | 1831–34 |
| | Mahlon Dickerson | 1834–37 |

### Van Buren Administration (1837–41)

| | | |
|---|---|---|
| Secretary of State | John Forsyth | 1837–41 |
| Secretary of Treasury | Levi Woodbury | 1837–41 |
| Secretary of War | Joel Poinsett | 1837–41 |
| Attorney General | Benjamin Butler | 1837–38 |
| | Felix Grundy | 1838–40 |
| | Henry D. Gilpin | 1840–41 |
| Postmaster General | Amos Kendall | 1837–40 |
| | John M. Niles | 1840–41 |
| Secretary of Navy | Mahlon Dickerson | 1837–38 |
| | James Paulding | 1838–41 |

### William Harrison Administration (1841)

| | | |
|---|---|---|
| Secretary of State | Daniel Webster | 1841 |
| Secretary of Treasury | Thomas Ewing | 1841 |
| Secretary of War | John Bell | 1841 |
| Attorney General | John J. Crittenden | 1841 |
| Postmaster General | Francis Granger | 1841 |
| Secretary of Navy | George Badger | 1841 |

### Tyler Administration (1841–45)

| | | |
|---|---|---|
| Secretary of State | Daniel Webster | 1841–43 |
| | Hugh S. Legaré | 1843 |
| | Abel P. Upshur | 1843–44 |

### Tyler Administration (cont'd)

| | | |
|---|---|---|
| | John C. Calhoun | 1844–45 |
| Secretary of Treasury | Thomas Ewing | 1841 |
| | Walter Forward | 1841–43 |
| | John C. Spencer | 1843–44 |
| | George Bibb | 1844–45 |
| Secretary of War | John Bell | 1841 |
| | John C. Spencer | 1841–43 |
| | James M. Porter | 1843–44 |
| | William Wilkins | 1844–45 |
| Attorney General | John J. Crittenden | 1841 |
| | Hugh S. Legaré | 1841–43 |
| | John Nelson | 1843–45 |
| Postmaster General | Francis Granger | 1841 |
| | Charles Wickliffe | 1841 |
| Secretary of Navy | George Badger | 1841 |
| | Abel P. Upshur | 1841 |
| | David Henshaw | 1843–44 |
| | Thomas Gilmer | 1844 |
| | John Y. Mason | 1844–45 |

### Polk Administration (1845–49)

| | | |
|---|---|---|
| Secretary of State | James Buchanan | 1845–49 |
| Secretary of Treasury | Robert J. Walker | 1845–49 |
| Secretary of War | William L. Marcy | 1845–49 |
| Attorney General | John Y. Mason | 1845–46 |
| | Nathan Clifford | 1846–48 |
| | Isaac Toucey | 1848–49 |
| Postmaster General | Cave Johnson | 1845–49 |
| Secretary of Navy | George Bancroft | 1845–46 |
| | John Y. Mason | 1846–49 |

### Taylor Administration (1849–50)

| | | |
|---|---|---|
| Secretary of State | John M. Clayton | 1849–50 |
| Secretary of Treasury | William Meredith | 1849–50 |
| Secretary of War | George Crawford | 1849–50 |
| Attorney General | Reverdy Johnson | 1849–50 |
| Postmaster General | Jacob Collamer | 1849–50 |
| Secretary of Navy | William Preston | 1849–50 |
| Secretary of Interior | Thomas Ewing | 1849–50 |

### Fillmore Administration (1850–53)

| | | |
|---|---|---|
| Secretary of State | Daniel Webster | 1850–52 |
| | Edward Everett | 1852–53 |
| Secretary of Treasury | Thomas Corwin | 1850–53 |
| Secretary of War | Charles Conrad | 1850–53 |
| Attorney General | John J. Crittenden | 1850–53 |
| Postmaster General | Nathan Hall | 1850–52 |
| | Sam D. Hubbard | 1852–53 |
| Secretary of Navy | William A. Graham | 1850–52 |
| | John P. Kennedy | 1852–53 |
| Secretary of Interior | Thomas McKennan | 1850 |
| | Alexander Stuart | 1850–53 |

### Pierce Administration (1853–57)

| | | |
|---|---|---|
| Secretary of State | William L. Marcy | 1853–57 |
| Secretary of Treasury | James Guthrie | 1853–57 |
| Secretary of War | Jefferson Davis | 1853–57 |
| Attorney General | Caleb Cushing | 1853–57 |
| Postmaster General | James Campbell | 1853–57 |
| Secretary of Navy | James C. Dobbin | 1853–57 |
| Secretary of Interior | Robert McClelland | 1853–57 |

### Buchanan Administration (1857–61)

| | | |
|---|---|---|
| Secretary of State | Lewis Cass | 1857–60 |
| | Jeremiah S. Black | 1860–61 |
| Secretary of Treasury | Howell Cobb | 1857–60 |

## Buchanan Administration (cont'd)

| | | |
|---|---|---|
| | Philip Thomas | 1860–61 |
| | John A. Dix | 1861 |
| Secretary of War | John B. Floyd | 1857–61 |
| | Joseph Holt | 1861 |
| Attorney General | Jeremiah S. Black | 1857–60 |
| | Edwin M. Stanton | 1860–61 |
| Postmaster General | Aaron W. Brown | 1857–59 |
| | Joseph Holt | 1859–61 |
| | Horatio King | 1861 |
| Secretary of Navy | Isaac Toucey | 1857–61 |
| Secretary of Interior | Jacob Thompson | 1857–61 |

## Lincoln Administration (1861–65)

| | | |
|---|---|---|
| Secretary of State | William H. Seward | 1861–65 |
| Secretary of Treasury | Salmon P. Chase | 1861–64 |
| | William P. Fessenden | 1864–65 |
| | Hugh McCulloch | 1865 |
| Secretary of War | Simon Cameron | 1861–62 |
| | Edwin M. Stanton | 1862–65 |
| Attorney General | Edward Bates | 1861–64 |
| | James Speed | 1864–65 |
| Postmaster General | Horatio King | 1861 |
| | Montgomery Blair | 1861–64 |
| | William Dennison | 1864–65 |
| Secretary of Navy | Gideon Welles | 1861–65 |
| Secretary of Interior | Caleb B. Smith | 1861–63 |
| | John P. Usher | 1863–65 |

## Andrew Johnson Administration (1865–69)

| | | |
|---|---|---|
| Secretary of State | William H. Seward | 1865–69 |
| Secretary of Treasury | Hugh McCulloch | 1865–69 |
| Secretary of War | Edwin M. Stanton | 1865–67 |
| | Ulysses S. Grant | 1867–68 |
| | John M. Schofield | 1868–69 |
| Attorney General | James Speed | 1865–66 |
| | Henry Stanbery | 1866–68 |
| | William M. Evarts | 1868–69 |
| Postmaster General | William Dennison | 1865–66 |
| | Alexander Randall | 1866–69 |
| Secretary of Navy | Gideon Welles | 1865–69 |
| Secretary of Interior | John P. Usher | 1865 |
| | James Harlan | 1865–66 |
| | Orville H. Browning | 1866–69 |

## Grant Administration (1869–77)

| | | |
|---|---|---|
| Secretary of State | Elihu B. Washburne | 1869 |
| | Hamilton Fish | 1869–77 |
| Secretary of Treasury | George S. Boutwell | 1869–73 |
| | William Richardson | 1873–74 |
| | Benjamin Bristow | 1874–76 |
| | Lot M. Morrill | 1876–77 |
| Secretary of War | John A. Rawlins | 1869 |
| | William T. Sherman | 1869 |
| | William W. Belknap | 1869–76 |
| | Alphonso Taft | 1876 |
| | James D. Cameron | 1876–77 |
| Attorney General | Ebenezer Hoar | 1869–70 |
| | Amos T. Ackerman | 1870–71 |
| | G.H. Williams | 1871–75 |
| | Edwards Pierrepont | 1875–76 |
| | Alphonso Taft | 1876–77 |
| Postmaster General | John A. J. Creswell | 1869–74 |
| | James W. Marshall | 1874 |
| | Marshall Jewell | 1874–76 |
| | James N. Tyner | 1876–77 |
| Secretary of Navy | Adolph E. Borie | 1869 |
| | George M. Robeson | 1869–77 |

## Grant Administration (cont'd)

| | | |
|---|---|---|
| Secretary of Interior | Jacob D. Cox | 1869–70 |
| | Columbus Delano | 1870–75 |
| | Zachariah Chandler | 1875–77 |

## Hayes Administration (1877–81)

| | | |
|---|---|---|
| Secretary of State | William M. Evarts | 1877–81 |
| Secretary of Treasury | John Sherman | 1877–81 |
| Secretary of War | George W. McCrary | 1877–79 |
| | Alex Ramsey | 1879–81 |
| Attorney General | Charles Devens | 1877–81 |
| Postmaster General | David M. Key | 1877–80 |
| | Horace Maynard | 1880–81 |
| Secretary of Navy | Richard W. Thompson | 1877–80 |
| | Nathan Goff, Jr. | 1881 |
| Secretary of Interior | Carl Schurz | 1877–81 |

## Garfield Administration (1881)

| | | |
|---|---|---|
| Secretary of State | James G. Blaine | 1881 |
| Secretary of Treasury | William Windom | 1881 |
| Secretary of War | Robert T. Lincoln | 1881 |
| Attorney General | Wayne MacVeagh | 1881 |
| Postmaster General | Thomas L. James | 1881 |
| Secretary of Navy | William H. Hunt | 1881 |
| Secretary of Interior | Samuel J. Kirkwood | 1881 |

## Arthur Administration (1881–85)

| | | |
|---|---|---|
| Secretary of State | James G. Blaine | 1881 |
| | F.T. Frelinghuysen | 1881–85 |
| Secretary of Treasury | William Windom | 1881 |
| | Charles J. Folger | 1881–84 |
| | Walter Q. Gresham | 1884 |
| | Hugh McCulloch | 1884–85 |
| Secretary of War | Robert T. Lincoln | 1881–85 |
| Attorney General | Wayne MacVeagh | 1881 |
| | Benjamin H. Brewster | 1881–85 |
| | Thomas L. James | 1881 |
| Postmaster General | Timothy O. Howe | 1881–83 |
| | Walter Q. Gresham | 1883–84 |
| | Frank Hatton | 1884–85 |
| Secretary of Navy | William H. Hunt | 1881–82 |
| | William E. Chandler | 1882–85 |
| Secretary of Interior | Samuel J. Kirkwood | 1881–82 |
| | Henry M. Teller | 1882–85 |

## Cleveland Administration (1885–89)

| | | |
|---|---|---|
| Secretary of State | Thomas F. Bayard | 1885–89 |
| Secretary of Treasury | Daniel Manning | 1885–87 |
| | Charles S. Fairchild | 1887–89 |
| Secretary of War | William C. Endicott | 1885–89 |
| Attorney General | Augustus H. Garland | 1885–89 |
| Postmaster General | William F. Vilas | 1885–88 |
| | Don M. Dickinson | 1888–89 |
| Secretary of Navy | William C. Whitney | 1885–89 |
| Secretary of Interior | Lucius Q.C. Lamar | 1885–88 |
| | William F. Vilas | 1888–89 |
| Secretary of Agriculture | Norman J. Colman | 1889 |

## Benjamin Harrison Administration (1889–93)

| | | |
|---|---|---|
| Secretary of State | James G. Blaine | 1889–92 |
| | John W. Foster | 1892–93 |
| Secretary of Treasury | William Windom | 1889–91 |
| | Charles Foster | 1891–93 |
| Secretary of War | Redfield Proctor | 1889–91 |
| | Stephen B. Elkins | 1891–93 |

## Benjamin Harrison Administration (cont'd)

| | | |
|---|---|---|
| Attorney General | William H. H. Miller | 1889–93 |
| Postmaster General | John Wanamaker | 1889–93 |
| Secretary of Navy | Benjamin F. Tracy | 1889–93 |
| Secretary of Interior | John W. Noble | 1889–93 |
| Secretary of Agriculture | Jeremiah M. Rusk | 1889–93 |

## Cleveland Administration (1893–97)

| | | |
|---|---|---|
| Secretary of State | Walter Q. Gresham | 1893–95 |
| | Richard Olney | 1895–97 |
| Secretary of Treasury | John G. Carlisle | 1893–97 |
| Secretary of War | Daniel S. Lamont | 1893–97 |
| Attorney General | Richard Olney | 1893–95 |
| | James Harmon | 1895–97 |
| Postmaster General | Wilson S. Bissell | 1893–95 |
| | William L. Wilson | 1895–97 |
| Secretary of Navy | Hilary A. Herbert | 1893–97 |
| Secretary of Interior | Hoke Smith | 1893–96 |
| | David R. Francis | 1896–97 |
| Secretary of Agriculture | Julius S. Morton | 1893–97 |

## McKinley Administration (1897–1901)

| | | |
|---|---|---|
| Secretary of State | John Sherman | 1897–98 |
| | William R. Day | 1898 |
| | John Hay | 1898–1901 |
| Secretary of Treasury | Lyman J. Gage | 1897–1901 |
| Secretary of War | Russell A. Alger | 1897–99 |
| | Elihu Root | 1899–1901 |
| Attorney General | Joseph McKenna | 1897–98 |
| | John W. Griggs | 1898–1901 |
| | Philander C. Knox | 1901 |
| Postmaster General | James A. Gary | 1897–98 |
| | Charles E. Smith | 1898–1901 |
| Secretary of Navy | John D. Long | 1897–1901 |
| Secretary of Interior | Cornelius N. Bliss | 1897–99 |
| | Ethan A. Hitchcock | 1899–1901 |
| Secretary of Agriculture | James Wilson | 1897–1901 |

## Theodore Roosevelt Administration (1901–09)

| | | |
|---|---|---|
| Secretary of State | John Hay | 1901–05 |
| | Elihu Root | 1905–09 |
| | Robert Bacon | 1909 |
| Secretary of Treasury | Lyman J. Gage | 1901–02 |
| | Leslie M. Shaw | 1902–07 |
| | George B. Cortelyou | 1907–09 |
| Secretary of War | Elihu Root | 1901–04 |
| | William H. Taft | 1904–08 |
| | Luke E. Wright | 1908–09 |
| Attorney General | Philander C. Knox | 1901–04 |
| | William H. Moody | 1904–06 |
| | Charles J. Bonaparte | 1906–09 |
| Postmaster General | Charles E. Smith | 1901–02 |
| | Henry C. Payne | 1902–04 |
| | Robert J. Wynne | 1904–05 |
| | George B. Cortelyou | 1905–07 |
| | George von L. Meyer | 1907–09 |
| Secretary of Navy | John D. Long | 1901–02 |
| | William H. Moody | 1902–04 |
| | Paul Morton | 1904–05 |
| | Charles J. Bonaparte | 1905–06 |
| | Victor H. Metcalf | 1906–08 |
| | Truman H. Newberry | 1908–09 |
| Secretary of Interior | Ethan A. Hitchcock | 1901–07 |
| | James R. Garfield | 1907–09 |
| Secretary of Agriculture | James Wilson | 1901–09 |
| Secretary of Labor and Commerce | George B. Cortelyou | 1903–04 |
| | Victor H. Metcalf | 1904–06 |
| | Oscar S. Straus | 1906–09 |

## Taft Administration (1909–13)

| | | |
|---|---|---|
| Secretary of State | Philander C. Knox | 1909–13 |
| Secretary of Treasury | Franklin MacVeagh | 1909–13 |
| Secretary of War | Jacob M. Dickinson | 1909–11 |
| | Henry L. Stimson | 1911–13 |
| Attorney General | George W. Wickersham | 1909–13 |
| Postmaster General | Frank H. Hitchcock | 1909–13 |
| Secretary of Navy | George von L. Meyer | 1909–13 |
| Secretary of Interior | Richard A. Ballinger | 1909–11 |
| | Walter Fisher | 1911–13 |
| Secretary of Agriculture | James Wilson | 1909–13 |
| Secretary of Labor and Commerce | Charles Nagel | 1909–13 |

## Wilson Administration (1913–21)

| | | |
|---|---|---|
| Secretary of State | William J. Bryan | 1913–15 |
| | Robert Lansing | 1915–20 |
| | Bainbridge Colby | 1920–21 |
| Secretary of Treasury | William G. McAdoo | 1913–18 |
| | Carter Glass | 1918–20 |
| | David F. Houston | 1920–21 |
| Secretary of War | Lindley M. Garrison | 1913–16 |
| | Newton D. Baker | 1916–21 |
| Attorney General | James C. McReynolds | 1913–14 |
| | Thomas W. Gregory | 1914–19 |
| | A. Mitchell Palmer | 1919–21 |
| Postmaster General | Albert S. Burleson | 1913–21 |
| Secretary of Navy | Josephus Daniels | 1913–21 |
| Secretary of Interior | Franklin K. Lane | 1913–20 |
| | John B. Payne | 1920–21 |
| Secretary of Agriculture | David F. Houston | 1913–20 |
| | Edwin T. Meredith | 1920–21 |
| Secretary of Commerce | William C. Redfield | 1913–19 |
| | Joshua W. Alexander | 1919 |
| Secretary of Labor | William B. Wilson | 1913–21 |

## Harding Administration (1921–23)

| | | |
|---|---|---|
| Secretary of State | Charles E. Hughes | 1921–23 |
| Secretary of Treasury | Andrew Mellon | 1921–23 |
| Secretary of War | John W. Weeks | 1921–23 |
| Attorney General | Harry M. Daugherty | 1921–23 |
| Postmaster General | Will H. Hays | 1921–22 |
| | Hubert Work | 1922–23 |
| | Harry S. New | 1923 |
| Secretary of Navy | Edwin Denby | 1921–23 |
| Secretary of Interior | Albert B. Fall | 1921–23 |
| | Hubert Work | 1923 |
| Secretary of Agriculture | Henry C. Wallace | 1921–23 |
| Secretary of Commerce | Herbert C. Hoover | 1921–23 |
| Secretary of Labor | James J. Davis | 1921–23 |

## Coolidge Administration (1923–29)

| | | |
|---|---|---|
| Secretary of State | Charles E. Hughes | 1923–25 |
| | Frank B. Kellogg | 1925–29 |
| Secretary of Treasury | Andrew Mellon | 1923–29 |
| Secretary of War | John W. Weeks | 1923–25 |
| | Dwight F. Davis | 1925–29 |
| Attorney General | Harry M. Daugherty | 1923–24 |
| | Harlan F. Stone | 1924–25 |
| | John G. Sargent | 1925–29 |
| Postmaster General | Harry S. New | 1923–29 |
| Secretary of Navy | Edwin Denby | 1923–24 |
| | Curtis D. Wilbur | 1924–29 |
| Secretary of Interior | Hubert Work | 1923–28 |
| | Roy O. West | 1928–29 |
| Secretary of Agriculture | Henry C. Wallace | 1923–24 |
| | Howard M. Gore | 1924–25 |
| | William M. Jardine | 1925–29 |

## Coolidge Administration (cont'd)

| | | |
|---|---|---|
| Secretary of Commerce | Herbert C. Hoover | 1923–28 |
| | William F. Whiting | 1928–29 |
| Secretary of Labor | James J. Davis | 1923–29 |

## Hoover Administration (1929–33)

| | | |
|---|---|---|
| Secretary of State | Henry L. Stimson | 1929–33 |
| Secretary of Treasury | Andrew Mellon | 1929–32 |
| | Ogden L. Mills | 1932–33 |
| Secretary of War | James W. Good | 1929 |
| | Patrick J. Hurley | 1929–33 |
| Attorney General | William D. Mitchell | 1929–33 |
| Postmaster General | Walter F. Brown | 1929–33 |
| Secretary of Navy | Charles F. Adams | 1929–33 |
| Secretary of Interior | Ray L. Wilbur | 1929–33 |
| Secretary of Agriculture | Arthur M. Hyde | 1929–33 |
| Secretary of Commerce | Robert P. Lamont | 1929–32 |
| | Roy D. Chapin | 1932–33 |
| Secretary of Labor | James J. Davis | 1929–30 |
| | William N. Doak | 1930–33 |

## Franklin D. Roosevelt Administration (1933–45)

| | | |
|---|---|---|
| Secretary of State | Cordell Hull | 1933–44 |
| | Edward R. Stettinius, Jr. | 1944–45 |
| Secretary of Treasury | William H. Woodin | 1933–34 |
| | Henry Morgenthau, Jr. | 1934–45 |
| Secretary of War | George H. Dern | 1933–36 |
| | Henry A. Woodring | 1936–40 |
| | Henry L. Stimson | 1940–45 |
| Attorney General | Homer S. Cummings | 1933–39 |
| | Frank Murphy | 1939–40 |
| | Robert H. Jackson | 1940–41 |
| | Francis Biddle | 1941–45 |
| Postmaster General | James A. Farley | 1933–40 |
| | Frank C. Walker | 1940–45 |
| Secretary of Navy | Claude A. Swanson | 1933–40 |
| | Charles Edison | 1940 |
| | Frank Knox | 1940–44 |
| | James V. Forrestal | 1944–45 |
| Secretary of Interior | Harold L. Ickes | 1933–45 |
| Secretary of Agriculture | Henry A. Wallace | 1933–40 |
| | Claude R. Wickard | 1940–45 |
| Secretary of Commerce | Daniel C. Roper | 1933–39 |
| | Harry L. Hopkins | 1939–40 |
| | Jesse Jones | 1940–45 |
| | Henry A. Wallace | 1945 |
| Secretary of Labor | Frances Perkins | 1933–45 |

## Truman Administration (1945–53)

| | | |
|---|---|---|
| Secretary of State | Edward R. Stettinius, Jr. | 1945 |
| | James F. Byrnes | 1945–47 |
| | George C. Marshall | 1947–49 |
| | Dean G. Acheson | 1949–53 |
| Secretary of Treasury | Fred M. Vinson | 1945–46 |
| | John W. Snyder | 1946–53 |
| Secretary of War[1] | Robert P. Patterson | 1945–47 |
| | Kenneth C. Royall | 1947 |
| Attorney General | Tom C. Clark | 1945–49 |
| | J. Howard McGrath | 1949–52 |
| | James P. McGranery | 1952–53 |
| Postmaster General | Frank C. Walker | 1945 |
| | Robert E. Hannegan | 1945–47 |
| | Jesse M. Donaldson | 1947–53 |
| Secretary of Navy[1] | James V. Forrestal | 1945–47 |
| Secretary of Interior | Harold L. Ickes | 1945–46 |
| | Julius A. Krug | 1946–49 |
| | Oscar L. Chapman | 1949–53 |

## Truman Administration (cont'd)

| | | |
|---|---|---|
| Secretary of Agriculture | Clinton P. Anderson | 1945–48 |
| | Charles F. Brannan | 1948–53 |
| Secretary of Commerce | Henry A. Wallace | 1945–46 |
| | W. Averell Harriman | 1946–48 |
| | Charles W. Sawyer | 1948–53 |
| Secretary of Labor | Lewis B. Schwellenbach | 1945–48 |
| | Maurice J. Tobin | 1948–53 |
| Secretary of Defense[1] | James V. Forrestal | 1947–49 |
| | Louis A. Johnson | 1949–50 |
| | George C. Marshall | 1950–51 |
| | Robert A. Lovett | 1951–53 |

1. On July 26, 1947, the Dept. of War and the Dept. of the Navy were consolidated under the Dept. of Defense, which replaced the War Dept. in order of precedence.

## Eisenhower Administration (1953–61)

| | | |
|---|---|---|
| Secretary of State | John Foster Dulles | 1953–59 |
| | Christian A. Herter | 1959–61 |
| Secretary of Treasury | George M. Humphrey | 1953–57 |
| | Robert B. Anderson | 1957–61 |
| Secretary of Defense | Charles E. Wilson | 1953–57 |
| | Neil H. McElroy | 1957–59 |
| | Thomas S. Gates, Jr. | 1959–61 |
| Attorney General | Herbert Brownell, Jr. | 1953–58 |
| | William P. Rogers | 1958–61 |
| Postmaster General | Arthur E. Summerfield | 1953–61 |
| Secretary of Interior | Douglas McKay | 1953–56 |
| | Fred A. Seaton | 1956–61 |
| Secretary of Agriculture | Ezra T. Benson | 1953–61 |
| Secretary of Commerce | Sinclair Weeks | 1953–58 |
| | Lewis L. Strauss[1] | 1958–59 |
| | Frederick H. Mueller | 1959–61 |
| Secretary of Labor | Martin P. Durkin | 1953 |
| | James P. Mitchell | 1953–61 |
| Secretary of Health, Education, and Welfare | Oveta Culp Hobby | 1953–55 |
| | Marion B. Folsom | 1955–58 |
| | Arthur S. Flemming | 1958–61 |

1. Apppointed Oct. 1958 but not confirmed.

## Kennedy Administration (1961–63)

| | | |
|---|---|---|
| Secretary of State | Dean Rusk | 1961–63 |
| Secretary of Treasury | C. Douglas Dillon | 1961–63 |
| Secretary of Defense | Robert S. McNamara | 1961–63 |
| Attorney General | Robert F. Kennedy | 1961–63 |
| Postmaster General | J. Edward Day | 1961–63 |
| | John A. Gronouski | 1963 |
| Secretary of Interior | Stewart L. Udall | 1961–63 |
| Secretary of Agriculture | Orville L. Freeman | 1961–63 |
| Secretary of Commerce | Luther H. Hodges | 1961–63 |
| Secretary of Labor | Arthur J. Goldberg | 1961–62 |
| | W. Willard Wirtz | 1962–63 |
| Secretary of Health, Education, and Welfare | Abraham A. Ribicoff | 1961–62 |
| | Anthony J. Celebrezze | 1962–63 |

## Lyndon Johnson Administration (1963–69)

| | | |
|---|---|---|
| Secretary of State | Dean Rusk | 1963–69 |
| Secretary of Treasury | C. Douglas Dillon | 1963–65 |
| | Henry H. Fowler | 1965–69 |
| Secretary of Defense | Robert F. McNamara | 1963–68 |
| | Clark Clifford | 1968–69 |
| Attorney General | Robert F. Kennedy | 1963–64 |
| | Nicholas Katzenbach | 1965–66 |
| | Ramsey Clark | 1967–69 |
| Postmaster General | John A. Gronouski | 1963–65 |
| | Lawrence F. O'Brien | 1965–68 |
| | Marvin Watson | 1968–69 |
| Secretary of Interior | Stewart L. Udall | 1963–69 |

## Lyndon Johnson Administration (cont'd)

| | | |
|---|---|---|
| Secretary of Agriculture | Orville L. Freeman | 1963–69 |
| Secretary of Commerce | Luther H. Hodges | 1963–64 |
| | John T. Connor | 1964–67 |
| | Alexander B. Trowbridge | 1967–68 |
| | Cyrus R. Smith | 1968–69 |
| Secretary of Labor | W. Willard Wirtz | 1963–69 |
| Secretary of Health, Education, and Welfare | Anthony J. Celebrezze | 1963–65 |
| | John W. Gardner | 1965–68 |
| | Wilbur J. Cohen | 1968–69 |
| Secretary of Housing and Urban Development | Robert C. Weaver | 1966–69 |
| | Robert C. Wood | 1969 |
| Secretary of Transportation | Alan S. Boyd | 1967–69 |

## Nixon Administration (1969–74)

| | | |
|---|---|---|
| Secretary of State | William P. Rogers | 1969–73 |
| | Henry A. Kissinger | 1973–74 |
| Secretary of Treasury | David M. Kennedy | 1969–70 |
| | John B. Connally | 1971–72 |
| | George P. Shultz | 1972–74 |
| | William E. Simon | 1974 |
| Secretary of Defense | Melvin R. Laird | 1969–73 |
| | Elliot L. Richardson | 1973 |
| | James R. Schlesinger | 1973–74 |
| Attorney General | John N. Mitchell | 1969–72 |
| | Richard G. Kleindienst | 1972–73 |
| | Elliot L. Richardson | 1973 |
| | William B. Saxbe | 1973–74 |
| Postmaster General | Winton M. Blount | 1969–71 |
| Secretary of Interior | Walter J. Hickel | 1969–70 |
| | Rogers Morton | 1971–74 |
| Secretary of Agriculture | Clifford M. Hardin | 1969–71 |
| | Earl L. Butz | 1971–74 |
| Secretary of Commerce | Maurice H. Stans | 1969–72 |
| | Peter G. Peterson | 1972–73 |
| | Frederick B. Dent | 1973–74 |
| Secretary of Labor | George P. Shultz | 1969–70 |
| | James D. Hodgson | 1970–73 |
| | Peter J. Brennan | 1973–74 |
| Secretary of Health, Education, and Welfare | Robert H. Finch | 1969–70 |
| | Elliot L. Richardson | 1970–73 |
| | Caspar W. Weinberger | 1973–74 |
| Secretary of Housing and Urban Development | George Romney | 1969–73 |
| | James T. Lyon | 1973–74 |
| Secretary of Transportation | John A. Volpe | 1969–73 |
| | Claude S. Brinegar | 1973–74 |

## Ford Administration (1974–77)

| | | |
|---|---|---|
| Secretary of State | Henry A. Kissinger | 1974–77 |
| Secretary of Treasury | William E. Simon | 1974–77 |
| Secretary of Defense | James R. Schlesinger | 1974–75 |
| | Donald Rumsfeld | 1975–77 |
| Attorney General | William Saxbe | 1974–75 |
| | Edward Levi | 1975–77 |
| Secretary of Interior | Rogers Morton | 1974–75 |
| | Stanley K. Hathaway | 1975 |
| | Thomas Kleppe | 1975–77 |
| Secretary of Agriculture | Earl L. Butz | 1974–76 |
| | John A. Knebel | 1976–77 |
| Secretary of Commerce | Frederick B. Dent | 1974–75 |
| | Rogers Morton | 1975–76 |
| | Elliot L. Richardson | 1976–77 |
| Secretary of Labor | Peter J. Brennan | 1974–75 |
| | John T. Dunlop | 1975–76 |
| | W.J. Usery | 1976–77 |
| Secretary of Health, Education, and Welfare | Caspar Weinberger | 1974–75 |
| | Forrest D. Mathews | 1975–77 |
| Secretary of Housing and Urban Development | James T. Lynn | 1974–75 |
| | Carla A. Hills | 1975–77 |

## Ford Administration (cont'd)

| | | |
|---|---|---|
| Secretary of Transportation | Claude S. Brinegar | 1974–75 |
| | William T. Coleman | 1975–77 |

## Carter Administration (1977–81)

| | | |
|---|---|---|
| Secretary of State | Cyrus R. Vance | 1977–80 |
| | Edmund Muskie | 1980–81 |
| Secretary of Treasury | W. Michael Blumenthal | 1977–79 |
| | G. William Miller | 1979–81 |
| Secretary of Defense | Harold Brown | 1977–81 |
| Attorney General | Griffin Bell | 1977–79 |
| | Benjamin R. Civiletti | 1979–81 |
| Secretary of Interior | Cecil D. Andrus | 1977–81 |
| Secretary of Agriculture | Robert Bergland | 1977–81 |
| Secretary of Commerce | Juanita M. Kreps | 1977–79 |
| | Philip M. Klutznick | 1979–81 |
| Secretary of Labor | F. Ray Marshall | 1977–81 |
| Secretary of Health, Education, and Welfare[1] | Joseph A. Califano | 1977–79 |
| | Patricia R. Harris | 1979 |
| Secretary of Health and Human Services[1] | Patricia R. Harris | 1979–81 |
| Secretary of Housing and Urban Development | Patricia R. Harris | 1977–79 |
| | Moon Landrieu | 1979–81 |
| Secretary of Transportation | Brock Adams | 1977–79 |
| | Neil E. Goldschmidt | 1979–81 |
| Secretary of Energy | James R. Schlesinger | 1977–79 |
| | Charles W. Duncan | 1979–81 |
| Secretary of Education[1] | Shirley M. Hufstedler | 1979–81 |

1. The Dept. of Health, Education, and Welfare was redesignated the Dept. of Health and Human Services by the Department of Education Organization Act, effective May 4, 1980.

## Reagan Administration (1981–89)

| | | |
|---|---|---|
| Secretary of State | Alexander M. Haig | 1981–82 |
| | George P. Shultz | 1982–89 |
| Secretary of Treasury | Donald Regan | 1981–85 |
| | James A. Baker III | 1985–88 |
| | Nicholas F. Brady | 1988–89 |
| Secretary of Defense | Caspar Weinberger | 1981–87 |
| | Frank Carlucci | 1987–89 |
| Attorney General | William F. Smith | 1981–85 |
| | Edwin A. Meese III | 1985–88 |
| | Richard L. Thornburgh | 1988–89 |
| Secretary of Interior | James Watt | 1981–83 |
| | William P. Clark, Jr. | 1983–85 |
| | Donald P. Hodel | 1985–89 |
| Secretary of Agriculture | John Block | 1981–86 |
| | Richard E. Lyng | 1986–89 |
| Secretary of Commerce | Malcolm Baldrige | 1981–87 |
| | C. William Verity, Jr. | 1987–89 |
| Secretary of Labor | Raymond Donovan | 1981–85 |
| | William E. Brock | 1985–87 |
| | Ann McLaughlin | 1987–89 |
| Secretary of Health and Human Services | Richard Schweiker | 1981–83 |
| | Margaret Heckler | 1983–85 |
| | Otis R. Bowen | 1985–89 |
| Secretary of Housing and Urban Development | Samuel Pierce | 1981–89 |
| Secretary of Transportation | Drew Lewis | 1981–83 |
| | Elizabeth Hanford Dole | 1983–87 |
| | James H. Burnley | 1987–89 |
| Secretary of Energy | James Edwards | 1981–82 |
| | Donald P. Hodel | 1982–85 |
| | John S. Herrington | 1985–89 |
| Secretary of Education | Terrel H. Bell | 1981–85 |
| | William J. Bennett | 1985–88 |
| | Lauro D. Cavazos | 1988–89 |

## Bush Administration (1989–   )

| | | |
|---|---|---|
| Secretary of State | James A. Baker III | 1989– |
| Secretary of Treasury | Nicholas F. Brady | 1989– |
| Secretary of Defense | Richard B. Cheney | 1989– |
| Attorney General | Richard L. Thornburgh | 1989–91 |
| | William P. Barr[1] | 1991– |
| Secretary of Interior | Manuel Lujan, Jr. | 1989– |
| Secretary of Agriculture | Clayton K. Yeutter | 1989–91 |
| | Edward Madigan | 1991– |
| Secretary of Commerce | Robert A. Mosbacher | 1989– |
| Secretary of Labor | Elizabeth Hanford Dole | 1989–90 |
| | Lynn Martin | 1991– |
| Secretary of Health and Human Services | Louis W. Sullivan | 1989– |
| Secretary of Housing and Urban Development | Jack F. Kemp | 1989– |
| Secretary of Transportation | Samuel K. Skinner | 1989– |
| Secretary of Energy | James D. Watkins | 1989– |
| Secretary of Education | Lauro D. Cavazos | 1989–90 |
| | Lamar Alexander | 1991– |
| Secretary of Veterans Affairs | Edward J. Derwinski | 1989– |

1. Acting.

# Executive Office of the White House, 1991

A number of executive orders in 1939 transferred various government agencies to the Executive Office of the President and established the divisions of the Executive Office and defined their functions. Since then, presidents have used executive orders, reorganization plans, and legislative initiatives to reorganize the Executive Office to make its composition compatible with the goals of their administrations. The following list shows the key personnel in President Bush's Executive Office.

## The White House Office

| | |
|---|---|
| Chief of Staff to the President | John H. Sununu |
| Assistants to the President: | |
| Press Secretary | Max Marlin Fitzwater |
| National Security Affairs | Brent Scowcroft |
| Legislative Affairs | Frederick D. McClure |
| Economic and Domestic Policy | Roger B. Porter |
| Communications | David F. Demarest, Jr. |
| Dir. of Presidential Personnel | Charles G. Untermeyer |
| Public Events and Initiatives | Sigmund A. Rogich |
| Office of National Service | C. Gregg Petersmeyer |
| Counsel to the President | C. Boyden Gray |

## Executive Office of the President

| | |
|---|---|
| Office of Management and Budget | Richard G. Darman |
| Council of Economic Advisors | Michael J. Boskin |
| National Security Council | Brent Scowcroft |
| Office of Policy Development | William L. Roper |
| Office of the U.S. Trade Representative | Carla A. Hills |
| Council on Environmental Quality | Michael R. Deland |
| Office of Science and Technology Policy | D. Allen Bromley |
| Office of National Drug Control Policy | Bob Martinez |
| Office of Administration | Paul W. Bateman |
| Office of the Vice President | J. Danforth Quayle |

# The U.S. Supreme Court

## Important Supreme Court Decisions

**Marbury v. Madison (1803)** The Court struck down a law "repugnant to the constitution" for the first time and set the precedent for judicial review of acts of Congress. In a politically ingenious ruling on the Judiciary Act of 1789, Chief Justice John Marshall asserted the Supreme Court's power "to say what the law is," while avoiding a confrontation with Pres. Thomas Jefferson. Not until the *Dred Scott* case of 1857 would another federal law be ruled unconstitutional.

**Fletcher v. Peck (1810)** The Court ruled that Georgia could not deprive land speculators of their title, even though the previous owners had obtained the land from the state through fraud and bribery. Arising from the infamous Yazoo land frauds of 1795, this decision followed the Constitution's obligation of contracts clause and was the first time the Court invalidated a state law.

**Dartmouth College v. Woodward (1819)** The Court encouraged business investment with this decision by treating corporate charters as fully protected contracts. Not even the state legislatures that originally granted them could tamper with charters to private corporations, unless they retained the power to do so. Dartmouth College remained a private institution despite New Hampshire's attempt to take it over. This decision, which opened the way for abuse of corporate privileges, would later be modified in the *Charles River Bridge v. Warren Bridge* (1837) and *Munn v. Illinois* (1877) cases.

**McCulloch v. Maryland (1819)** "Broad," as opposed to "strict," construction of the Constitution received high-court approval in Chief Justice John Marshall's opinion upholding the constitutionality of the national bank against a Maryland challenge. This ruling enhanced federal governmental authority by liberally interpreting the power of Congress to make laws "necessary and proper" for its specified powers. At a time when states were trying to tax the Bank of the United States out of existence, this decision also forbade such state interference with the federal government. "The power to tax," Marshall wrote, "involves the power to destroy."

**Cohens v. Virginia (1821)** With this ruling, the Court reiterated its power to hear appeals from state courts, and affirmed the national supremacy of federal judicial power. Virginia's conviction of the Cohens for selling lottery tickets in violation of state law was

upheld, but so too was the Cohens' right to appeal to the Court, which Virginia had challenged. Critics of judicial "consolidationism" were reminded of the Court's comprehensive powers as the ultimate appellate court for all Americans.

**Gibbons v. Ogden (1824)** In a dispute arising from a New York ferry monopoly, the Court ruled that states could not restrain interstate commerce in any way, and that congressional power to regulate interstate commerce "does not stop at the jurisdictional lines of the several states." The decision helped prevent interstate trade wars, quite common under the Articles of Confederation, from breaking out under the Constitution. Chief Justice Marshall's opinion also confirmed the broad potential power of the Constitution's commerce clause.

**Charles River Bridge v. Warren Bridge (1837)** A key decision for economic development, this case arose when state-chartered proprietors of a Boston toll bridge objected that a new state-chartered bridge across the Charles River would put them out of business. Chief Justice Roger B. Taney, in his first constitutional ruling, held that state charters implied no vested rights and that ambiguities must be construed in favor of the public, who would benefit from the new toll-free bridge. This decision balanced private property rights against the public welfare.

**Dred Scott v. Sanford (1857)** Dred Scott, a Missouri slave, sued for his liberty after his owner took him into free territory. The Court ruled that Congress could not bar slavery in the territories. Scott remained a slave because the Missouri Compromise of 1820, prohibiting slavery from part of the Louisiana Purchase, violated the Fifth Amendment by depriving slave owners of their right to enjoy property without due process of law. Scott himself could not even sue, for he was held to be property, not a citizen. This decision sharpened sectional conflict by sweeping away legal barriers to the expansion of slavery.

**Ex Parte Milligan (1866)** Pres. Abraham Lincoln's suspension of some civil liberties during the Civil War was attacked in this decision, which upheld the right of habeas corpus. The Court ruled that the president could not hold military tribunals in areas remote from battle and where civil courts were open and functioning. Milligan's conviction by such a Civil War tribunal in Indianapolis, Indiana, was overturned. The Constitution, admonished the Court, applies "at all times, and under all circumstances."

**Slaughter-House Cases (1873)** In its first ruling on the Fourteenth Amendment, the Court held that Louisiana's grant of a butcher monopoly did not violate the privileges and immunities of competitors, nor deny them equal protection of the laws, nor deprive them of property without due process. Only a few rights deriving from "federal citizenship" were subject to federal protection, while states still protected most civil and property rights. Federal protection of civil rights, even for former slaves, was very narrowly interpreted in this ruling. But

## CHIEF JUSTICES OF THE UNITED STATES, 1789–1991

| Chief Justice | Tenure[1] | Appointed by |
|---|---|---|
| John Jay | 1789–95 | George Washington |
| John Rutledge[2,3] | 1795 | George Washington |
| Oliver Ellsworth | 1796–1800 | George Washington |
| John Marshall[4] | 1801–35 | John Adams |
| Roger B. Taney | 1836–64 | Andrew Jackson |
| Salmon P. Chase | 1864–73 | Abraham Lincoln |
| Morrison R. Waite | 1874–88 | Ulysses S. Grant |
| Melville W. Fuller | 1888–1910 | Grover Cleveland |
| Edward D. White | 1910–21 | William Howard Taft |
| William Howard Taft[5] | 1921–30 | Warren G. Harding |
| Charles Evans Hughes[2] | 1930–41 | Herbert Hoover |
| Harlan F. Stone[2] | 1941–46 | Franklin D. Roosevelt |
| Fred M. Vinson | 1946–53 | Harry S Truman |
| Earl Warren | 1953–69 | Dwight D. Eisenhower |
| Warren E. Burger | 1969–87 | Richard M. Nixon |
| William H. Rehnquist[2] | 1987– | Ronald Reagan |

1. Dates are for tenure as chief justice. For complete tenure on Supreme Court, see "Supreme Court Justices." 2. Served as associate justice prior to appointment as chief justice. 3. Served one term, but appointment not confirmed by Senate. 4. Longest tenure as chief justice. 5. Formerly served as 27th president of the United States.

this decision broadly upheld business regulation by states until *Santa Clara Co. v. Southern Pacific Railroad Co.* (1886) applied the Fourteenth Amendment to defense of corporate property rights.

**Munn v. Illinois (1877)** This decision, in one of the "Granger Cases," enabled states to regulate private property in the public interest when the public had an interest in that property. The Court held that Illinois laws setting maximum rates for grain storage did not violate the Fourteenth Amendment's ban on deprivation of property without due process of law and did not restrain interstate commerce. But for the next half-century, the Court imposed the burden of proof on the states for their regulatory laws.

**Civil Rights Cases (1883)** Racial equality was postponed 80 years by this decision, which struck down the Civil Rights Act of 1875 and allowed for private segregation. The Fourteenth Amendment's guarantee of equal protection, the Court ruled, applied against state action—but not against private individuals, whose discrimination unaided by the states was beyond federal control. Segregation of public facilities was approved soon afterward in *Plessy v. Ferguson* (1896).

**United States v. E.C. Knight Co. (1895)** The first ruling on the Sherman Antitrust Act of 1890, this decision curtailed federal regulation of monopolies by placing national manufacturers beyond the reach of the Constitution's commerce clause. Only the actual interstate commerce of monopolies, not their production activities, was subject to federal control. The Court's distinction between production and commerce impeded federal regulation of manufacturing until *National Labor Relations Board v. Jones & Laughlin Steel Corp.* (1937).

## JUSTICES OF THE U.S. SUPREME COURT, 1789–1991

| Name | Tenure | Appointed by | Name | Tenure | Appointed by | Name | Tenure | Appointed by |
|---|---|---|---|---|---|---|---|---|
| Baldwin, Henry | 1830–44 | Andrew Jackson | Gray, Horace | 1881–1902 | Chester A. Arthur | Pitney, Mahlon | 1912–22 | William Howard Taft |
| Barbour, Philip P. | 1836–41 | Andrew Jackson | Grier, Robert C. | 1846–70 | James K. Polk | Powell, Lewis F., Jr. | 1972–87 | Richard M. Nixon |
| Black, Hugo L. | 1937–71 | Franklin D. Roosevelt | Harlan, John Marshall | 1877–1911 | Rutherford B. Hayes | Reed, Stanley F. | 1938–57 | Franklin D. Roosevelt |
| Blackmun, Harry A. | 1970– | Richard M. Nixon | Harlan, John Marshall[3] | 1955–71 | Dwight D. Eisenhower | Rehnquist, William H.[1] | 1972– | Richard M. Nixon |
| Blair, John | 1789–96 | George Washington | Harrison, Robert H. | 1789–90 | George Washington | Roberts, Owen J. | 1930–45 | Herbert Hoover |
| Blatchford, Samuel | 1882–93 | Chester A. Arthur | Holmes, Oliver Wendell | 1902–32 | Theodore Roosevelt | Rutledge, John[1] | 1789–91 | George Washington |
| Bradley, Joseph P. | 1870–92 | Ulysses S. Grant | Hughes, Charles Evans[1,4] | 1910–16 | William Howard Taft | Rutledge, John[1] | 1795 | George Washington |
| Brandeis, Louis D. | 1916–39 | Woodrow Wilson | Hughes, Charles Evans[1,4] | 1930–41 | Herbert Hoover | Rutledge, Wiley B. | 1943–49 | Franklin D. Roosevelt |
| Brennan, William J., Jr. | 1956–90 | Dwight D. Eisenhower | Hunt, Ward | 1872–82 | Ulysses S. Grant | Sanford, Edward T. | 1923–30 | Warren G. Harding |
| Brewer, David J. | 1889–1910 | Benjamin Harrison | Iredell, James | 1790–99 | George Washington | Scalia, Antonin | 1986– | Ronald Reagan |
| Brown, Henry B. | 1890–1906 | Benjamin Harrison | Jackson, Howell E. | 1893–95 | Benjamin Harrison | Shiras, George | 1892–1903 | Benjamin Harrison |
| Burger, Warren E.[1] | 1969–87 | Richard M. Nixon | Jackson, Robert H. | 1941–54 | Franklin D. Roosevelt | Souter, David H. | 1990– | George Bush |
| Burton, Harold H. | 1945–58 | Harry S Truman | Jay, John[1] | 1789–95 | George Washington | Stevens, John Paul | 1975– | Gerald R. Ford |
| Butler, Pierce | 1922–39 | Warren G. Harding | Johnson, Thomas | 1791–93 | George Washington | Stewart, Potter | 1959–81 | Dwight D. Eisenhower |
| Byrnes, James F. | 1941–42 | Franklin D. Roosevelt | Johnson, William | 1804–34 | Thomas Jefferson | Stone, Harlan F.[1] | 1925–46 | Calvin Coolidge |
| Campbell, John A. | 1853–61 | Franklin Pierce | Kennedy, Anthony M. | 1987– | Ronald Reagan | Story, Joseph | 1811–45 | James Madison |
| Cardozo, Benjamin N. | 1932–38 | Herbert Hoover | Lamar, Joseph R. | 1911–16 | William Howard Taft | Strong, William | 1870–80 | Ulysses S. Grant |
| Catron, John | 1837–65 | Martin Van Buren | Lamar, Lucius Q. C. | 1888–93 | Grover Cleveland | Sutherland, George | 1922–38 | Warren G. Harding |
| Chase, Salmon P.[1] | 1864–73 | Abraham Lincoln | Livingston, H. Brockholst | 1806–23 | Thomas Jefferson | Swayne, Noah H. | 1862–81 | Abraham Lincoln |
| Chase, Samuel | 1796–1811 | George Washington | Lurton, Horace H. | 1910–14 | William Howard Taft | Taft, William Howard[1,5] | 1921–30 | Warren Harding |
| Clark, Tom C. | 1949–67 | Harry S Truman | Marshall, John[1] | 1801–35 | John Adams | Taney, Roger B.[1] | 1836–64 | Andrew Jackson |
| Clarke, John H. | 1916–22 | Woodrow Wilson | Marshall, Thurgood | 1967–91 | Lyndon B. Johnson | Thompson, Smith | 1823–43 | James Monroe |
| Clifford, Nathan | 1858–81 | James J. Buchanan | Matthews, Stanley | 1881–89 | James A. Garfield | Todd, Thomas | 1807–26 | Thomas Jefferson |
| Curtis, Benjamin R. | 1851–57 | Millard Fillmore | McKenna, Joseph | 1898–1925 | William McKinley | Trimble, Robert | 1826–28 | John Quincy Adams |
| Cushing, William | 1789–1810 | George Washington | McKinley, John | 1837–52 | Martin Van Buren | Van Devanter, Willis | 1910–37 | William Howard Taft |
| Daniel, Peter V. | 1841–60 | Martin Van Buren | McLean, John | 1829–61 | Andrew Jackson | Vinson, Fred M.[1] | 1946–53 | Harry S Truman |
| Davis, David | 1862–77 | Abraham Lincoln | McReynolds, James C. | 1914–41 | Woodrow Wilson | Waite, Morrison R.[1] | 1874–88 | Ulysses S. Grant |
| Day, William R. | 1903–22 | Theodore Roosevelt | Miller, Samuel F. | 1862–90 | Abraham Lincoln | Warren, Earl[1] | 1953–69 | Dwight D. Eisenhower |
| Douglas, William O.[2] | 1939–75 | Franklin D. Roosevelt | Minton, Sherman | 1949–56 | Harry S Truman | Washington, Bushrod | 1798–1829 | John Adams |
| Duval, Gabriel | 1811–36 | James Madison | Moody, William H. | 1906–10 | Theodore Roosevelt | Wayne, James M. | 1835–67 | Andrew Jackson |
| Ellsworth, Oliver[1] | 1796–1800 | George Washington | Moore, Alfred | 1799–1804 | John Adams | White, Byron R. | 1962– | John F. Kennedy |
| Field, Stephen J. | 1863–97 | Abraham Lincoln | Murphy, Frank | 1940–49 | Franklin D. Roosevelt | White, Edward D.[1] | 1894–1921 | Grover Cleveland |
| Fortas, Abe | 1965–69 | Lyndon B. Johnson | Nelson, Samuel | 1845–72 | John Tyler | Whittaker, Charles E. | 1957–62 | Dwight D. Eisenhower |
| Frankfurter, Felix | 1939–62 | Franklin D. Roosevelt | O'Connor, Sandra Day | 1981– | Ronald Reagan | Wilson, James | 1789–98 | George Washington |
| Fuller, Melville W.[1] | 1888–1910 | Grover Cleveland | Paterson, William | 1793–1806 | George Washington | Woodbury, Levi | 1845–51 | James K. Polk |
| Goldberg, Arthur J. | 1962–65 | John F. Kennedy | Peckham, Rufus W. | 1895–1910 | Grover Cleveland | Woods, William B. | 1880–87 | Rutherford B. Hayes |

**Note:** As of Aug. 31, 1991. Dates reflect complete tenure on the Supreme Court, including tenure as chief justice. 1. Served as chief justice. See "Chief Justices of the United States." 2. Longest-serving justice. 3. The two Harlans were grandfather and grandson. 4. Stepped down as associate justice to run for president in 1916; later appointed chief justice. 5. Formerly served as 27th president of the United States.

**Plessy v. Ferguson (1896)** The "separate but equal" doctrine supporting public segregation by law received the Court's approval in this ruling, which originated with segregated railroad cars in Louisiana. The Court held that as long as equal accommodations were provided, segregation was not discrimination and did not deprive blacks of equal protection of the laws under the Fourteenth Amendment. This decision was overturned in *Brown* v. *Board of Education* (1954).

**Lochner v. New York (1905)** This decision struck down a New York law placing limits on maximum working hours for bakers. The law violated the Fourteenth Amendment by restricting individual "freedom of contract" to buy and sell labor and was an excessive use of state police power, the Court held. The ruling was soon modified in *Muller* v. *Oregon* (1908), which approved state-regulated limits on women's labor after the Court utilized sociological and economic data to consider the health and morals of women workers.

**Standard Oil Co. of New Jersey v. United States (1911)** Federal efforts to break up monopolies under the Sherman Antitrust Act had to follow the "rule of reason," according to this ruling. Only those combinations in restraint of trade that were contrary to the public interest, and therefore unreasonable, were illegal. Although the Taft administration's prosecution of Standard Oil was upheld, breaking up one of the nation's leading monopolies, further antitrust suits were impaired by this decision, which facilitated the 1920s' merger movement.

**Schenk v. United States (1919)** The Court unanimously upheld that World War I limits on freedom of speech did not violate the First Amendment—if the speech in question represented a "clear and present danger." That famous doctrine of Justice Oliver Wendell Holmes, which approved the arrest of a draft resister for handing out pamphlets to soldiers in wartime, became an important standard for interpreting the First Amendment. But in subsequent cases of this period, the Court added that the mere "bad tendency" of speech to cause danger could be grounds for censorship.

**Schechter Poultry Corp. v. United States (1935)** At the height of its assault on the New Deal, the Court struck down the National Industrial Recovery Act in the famous "Sick Chicken Case." The NIRA was found to delegate excessive legislative regulatory powers to the executive without constitutional authority, and to regulate commerce within states in violation of the commerce clause. Schechter's kosher chicken supply house in New York did not have to abide by the NIRA's rigid industry codes, the Court ruled.

**National Labor Relations Board v. Jones & Laughlin Steel Corp. (1937)** Under pressure from public opinion and Pres. Franklin D. Roosevelt, the Court made an abrupt about-face and began approving New Deal legislation. In this case, laws protecting unions and barring "unfair labor practices" were upheld by the "stream of commerce" doctrine, holding that employers who sold their goods and obtained their raw materials through interstate commerce were subject to federal regulation. This ruling overturned *United States* v. *E.C. Knight Co.* (1895) and became the basis for the modern, expansive understanding of commerce power.

**West Virginia Board of Education v. Barnette (1943)** The Court reversed its earlier ruling in *Minersville School District* v. *Gobitis* (1940), which had required Jehovah's Witnesses to salute the flag in school. In this case, also brought against a Jehovah's Witness, the Court recognized that refusing to salute the flag did not violate anyone's rights, and that the First Amendment protected the "right of silence" as well as freedom of speech.

### Korematsu v. United States (1944)

Pres. Franklin D. Roosevelt's Executive Order No. 9066, which approved the West Coast evacuation and internment of 120,000 Japanese-Americans during World War II, was upheld on the grounds of "military necessity" in this ruling. The Court was reluctant to interfere with executive authority in time of national emergency. But in *Ex parte Endo* (1944), the Court held that persons of proven loyalty should not be interned. In August 1988 Congress made a formal apology to former internees and appropriated $1.25 billion in compensation for the 60,000 survivors.

### Dennis v. United States (1951)

At the height of the postwar "Red Scare," the Court upheld the conviction of 11 American Communist leaders under the Smith Act of 1940, which made it a crime to belong to organizations teaching or advocating the violent overthrow of the government. The "clear and present danger" doctrine could be disregarded, the Court held, if "the gravity of the 'evil,' discounted by its improbability, justifies such invasion of free speech as is necessary to avoid the evil." Over 100 Communists were indicted as a result, effectively destroying the Communist party as a political force.

### Youngstown Sheet and Tube Co. v. Sawyer (1952)

During the Korean War, when Pres. Harry S Truman seized steel plants to keep them operating despite a strike, the Court held that his action was an unconstitutional usurpation of legislative authority. Only an act of Congress, not the president's inherent executive powers or military powers as commander in chief, could justify such a sizable confiscation of property, despite the wartime emergency.

### Brown v. Board of Education of Topeka (1954)

Chief Justice Earl Warren led the Court unanimously to decide that segregated schools violated the equal protection clause of the Fourteenth Amendment. The "separate but equal" doctrine of *Plessy* v. *Ferguson* (1896) was overruled after a series of cases dating back to *Missouri ex. rel. Gaines* v. *Canada* (1938) had already limited it. "Separate educational facilities are inherently unequal," held the Court. Efforts to desegregate southern schools after the *Brown* decision met with massive resistance for many years.

### Baker v. Carr (1962)

Overrepresentation of rural districts in state legislatures, which effectively disfranchised millions of voters, led the Court to abandon its traditional noninterference in drawing legislative boundaries. Tennessee citizens deprived of full representation by "arbitrary and capricious" malapportionment were denied equal protection under the Fourteenth Amendment, ruled the Court. All states eventually reapportioned their legislatures in conformance with the "one man, one vote" doctrine of *Reynolds* v. *Sims* (1964).

### Gideon v. Wainwright (1963)

Reversing an earlier ruling in *Betts* v. *Brady* (1942), the Court held that the Sixth Amendment guaranteed access to qualified counsel, which was "fundamental to a fair trial." Gideon was entitled to a retrial because Florida failed to provide him with an attorney. After this decision, states were required to furnish public defenders for indigent defendants in felony cases. In *Argersinger* v. *Hamlin* (1972), the ruling was extended to all cases that might result in imprisonment.

### Heart of Atlanta Motel, Inc. v. United States (1964)

The Court upheld Title II of the Civil Rights Act of 1964, outlawing private discrimination in public accommodations, as a legitimate exertion of federal power over interstate commerce. Congress had "ample power" to forbid racial discrimination in facilities that affected commerce by serving interstate travelers. The Heart of Atlanta Motel was located on two interstate highways, so the Court could sidestep the *Civil Rights Cases* (1883) protection of private discrimination to overrule it.

### South Carolina v. Katzenbach (1966)

Federal intervention on behalf of voting rights was upheld in this decision. South Carolina sued the attorney general, contending that the 1965 Voting Rights Act encroached on the reserved powers of the states, treated the states unequally, and violated separation of powers. Chief Justice Warren ruled that the Fifteenth Amendment gave Congress broad powers to "use any rational means to effectuate the constitutional prohibition of racial discrimination in voting." After this decision blacks registered and voted in massive numbers in the South.

### Miranda v. Arizona (1966)

Expanding on *Gideon* v. *Wainright* (1963) and *Escobedo* v. *Illinois* (1964), the Court set forth stringent interrogation procedures for criminal suspects, to protect their Fifth Amendment freedom from self-incrimination. Miranda's confession to kidnapping and rape was obtained without counsel and without his having been advised of his right to silence, so it was ruled inadmissable as evidence. This decision obliged police to advise suspects of their rights upon taking them into custody.

### New York Times Co. v. United States (1971)

When the *New York Times* and the *Washington Post* published the top-secret "Pentagon Papers" in 1971, revealing government duplicity in the Vietnam War, the Nixon administration obtained an injunction against the *Times* on grounds of national security. But in a brief *per curiam* opinion, the Court observed that in this case the government had not met the "heavy burden of showing justification" for "prior restraint" on freedom of the press.

### Roe v. Wade (1973)

In a controversial ruling, the Court held that state laws restricting abortion were an unconstitutional invasion of a woman's right to privacy. Only in the last trimester of pregnancy, when the fetus achieved viability outside the womb, might states regulate abortion—except when the life or health of the mother was at stake. Feelings ran high on both sides in the aftermath of this decision. In *Planned Parenthood of Central Missouri* v. *Danforth* (1976), the Court added further that wives did not need their husbands' consent to obtain abortions.

### United States v. Nixon (1974)

In a unanimous ruling, the Court held that the secret White House recordings of Pres. Richard M. Nixon's conversations with aides were subject to subpoena in the Watergate cover-up trial. Nixon's claim to "executive privilege" was rejected as invalid because military and national security issues were not at stake, and Chief Justice Warren Burger cited *Marbury* v. *Madison* (1803) to assert the Court's primacy in constitutional issues. Once the tapes were released, documenting Nixon's obstruction of justice, the president resigned to avoid impeachment.

### University of California Regents v. Bakke (1978)

Twice refused admission to medical school, Bakke sued the University of California for giving "affirmative action" preference to less-qualified black applicants. In an ambiguous 5–4 ruling, the Court agreed that Bakke's right to equal protection was denied, that he should be admitted, and that affirmative action quotas should be discarded. But at the same time, the Court recognized race as a "factor" in admissions and hiring decisions. Affirmative action could continue as long as rigid quotas did not constitute, in effect, "reverse discrimination."

### Immigration and Naturalization Service v. Chadha (1983)

The legislative veto, contained in hundreds of federal statutes since 1932, was disallowed in this decision. Congress exceeded its constitutional powers when it blocked the attorney general's suspension of a deportation order for Jagdish Rai Chadha, a Kenyan student who overstayed his visa. The Court held that the Immigration and Nationality Act's legislative veto provision violated the constitutional separation of powers. Chief Justice Warren Burger recognized that Congress would prefer to delegate authority to the executive branch and reserve the right to veto administrative regulations, but "we have not found a better way to preserve freedom" than the separation of powers.

### Bowers v. Hardwick (1986)

In a controversial 5–4 decision applauded by fundamentalists but protested by gay activists, the Court ruled that the constitutional right to privacy does not protect homosexual relations, even between consenting adults in their own homes. Georgia's law against oral and anal sex, passed in 1816, could be applied to homosexuals—though the Court declined to rule on whether heterosexuals might also be prosecuted. The decision raised fears of bedroom patrols and sexual surveillance, despite the constitutional right to privacy in intimate personal matters established in cases dating back to the 1920s. Justice Byron White ruled that "none of the rights announced in those cases bears any resemblance to the claimed constitutional right of homosexuals to engage in acts of sodomy."

# THE FEDERAL GOVERNMENT

In their desire to create a government based on an elaborate system of "checks and balances," the Founding Fathers divided the sources of power into three separate and distinct branches of government—the legislative, the judicial, and the executive. The fundamental purpose, organization, and workings of these three branches are set down in the first three articles of the Constitution. Despite the passing of more than two centuries, the creation of dozens of departments, agencies, and commissions, the ongoing employment of over 2½ million civilian workers, and the creation of a standing peacetime military force of over 2 million, this structure remains essentially unchanged.

Below is a list of every major body within the federal government. Every entry mentions the date each entity was founded and summarizes its official function. (The primary source of this information is the National Archives and Record Administration, Office of the Federal Register, *United States Government Manual 1990-91*.)

## HOW A BILL BECOMES LAW

Usually bills are raised in any of the various committees of the Senate or House of Representatives. If the bill is supported by a majority of the committee, it is brought to the floor of the house in which it originated, and voted on. If it gains majority support in the full Senate or House, the other house of Congress votes on it. If the bill is passed in both the Senate and House, it is sent to the president, who may either sign it, veto it, or not act on it.

If the president signs it or refuses to act within 10 days and the Congress is still in session, the bill becomes law. If the president vetoes it, it is returned to the Senate and the House for another vote; a two-thirds majority in each house is then required to overturn the veto. However, if the president refuses to act on a bill and Congress adjourns before the end of the 10-day period, the legislation is dead. This is known as a pocket veto.

Occasionally bills are raised on the floor of the Senate or the House, in which case the first step of committee voting is avoided and the legislation process begins with the full Senate or House vote. All other processes remain the same.

## The Legislative Branch

**Architect of the Capitol** U.S. Capitol Building, Washington, DC 20515. (202) 225-1200. First Architect appointed in 1793 by president. Permanent authority for care of Capitol established by act of Aug. 15, 1876. Responsible for care and maintenance of Capitol building and grounds, Library of Congress buildings, and U.S. Supreme Court building. Operates Senate and House restaurants. Maintains, operates, and cares for House and Senate office buildings. Plans future construction, renovation, reconstruction, and alterations to existing buildings.

**Congressional Budget Office (CBO)** Second and D Sts. SW, Washington, DC 20515. (202) 226-2600. Created by Congressional Budget Act of 1974. Provides Congress with basic budget data. Analyzes and evaluates alternative fiscal and budgetary policy options and programs and makes recommendations to Congress. Publishes annual report on budget.

**Copyright Royalty Tribunal** Suite 450, 1111 20th St. NW, Washington, DC 20036. (202) 653-5175. Created by act of Oct. 19, 1976. Establishes and monitors copyright royalty rates for various recorded and published materials.

**General Accounting Office (GAO)** 441 G St. NW, Washington, DC 20548. (202) 275-2812. Created in 1921 by Budget and Accounting Act. Provides legal, accounting, auditing, and claims-settlement services for Congress. Facilitates more efficient and effective government operations.

**Government Printing Office (GPO)** North Capitol and H Sts. NW, Washington, DC 20401. (202) 783-3238. Created June 23, 1860, by Congressional Joint Resolution 25. Provides printing and binding services for Congress and departments and establishments of federal government. Furnishes blank paper, ink, and supplies to all agencies. Prepares and distributes catalogs and publications.

**Library of Congress** 101 Independence Ave. SE, Washington, DC 20540. (202) 707-2905. Created by law of Apr. 24, 1800. Librarian appointed by president. Buys books necessary for use by Congress and/or other governmental agencies. National library of U.S. Develops and maintains national book classification systems such as Library of Congress and Dewey Decimal systems. Maintains and publishes *The National Union Catalogs*.

**Office of Technology Assessment (OTA)** 600 Pennsylvania Ave. SE, Washington, DC 20510. (202) 224-8996. Created by Technology Assessment Act of 1972. Provides objective analyses and evaluations of scientific and technological public-policy issues.

**U.S. Botanic Garden** Director's Office: 245 First St. SW, Washington, DC 20024. (202) 225-8333. Conservatory: Maryland Ave.- First to Second Sts. SW, Washington, DC 20024. (202) 225-6646. Nursery: Poplar Point, 700 Howard Rd. SE, Anacostia, DC 20020. (202) 225-6420. Created in 1820. Collects, cultivates, and grows vegetable and plant matter of U.S. and other countries for exhibition and display. Provides study materials on vegetable and plant matter for students, botanists, horticulturists, floriculturists, and garden clubs.

**U.S. Tax Court** 400 Second St. NW, Washington, DC 20217. (202) 376-2751. Created by Article I of Constitution. Independent judicial body in legislative branch. Tries and adjudicates controversies involving deficiencies or overpayments of income, estate, and gift taxes.

## THE 102ND CONGRESS OF THE UNITED STATES

The House of Representatives is composed of 435 members. The number representing each state is determined by population every ten years; every state is entitled to at least one representative. Members are elected by popular vote for two-year terms, all terms running for the same period. In addition to state representatives, there are delegates from the District of Columbia, American Samoa, Guam, and the Virgin Islands (also elected for two years), and a resident commissioner from Puerto Rico (elected for four years). Delegates and the resident commissioner may take part in floor debates, but they have no vote.

The Senate is composed of 100 members, two from each state, elected to terms of six years. Senators are divided into three classes, and a new class is elected every two years.

The accompanying tables show each congressman's rating according to three prominent political groups of differing viewpoints. The Americans for Democratic Action (ADA), a liberal group founded in 1947, rates members of Congress on a wide variety of issues, but they stand basically for slowing defense spending, preventing violations of civil rights, and for government activity to end inequality. The American Conservative Union (ACU) rates members for their votes on budgetary, social, and foreign-policy issues from a conservative perspective. The American Security Council's rating, called the National Security Index (NSI), has been measuring congressional votes on defense since 1965; a high rating indicates support for developing large weapons systems and support of the peace-through-strength approach to foreign policy.

## THE 102ND CONGRESS OF THE UNITED STATES

| The Senate | Senate Offices | | The House of Representatives | House Offices | |
|---|---|---|---|---|---|
| The Capitol | President | J. Danforth Quayle (R) | The Capitol | Speaker | Thomas S. Foley (D) |
| Washington, DC 20510 | President pro tem | Robert C. Byrd (D) | Washington, DC 20515 | Majority leader | Richard A. Gephardt (D) |
| (202) 224-3121 | Majority leader | George J. Mitchell (D) | (202) 224-3121 | Majority whip | David E. Bonior (D) |
| | Majority whip | Wendell Ford (D) | | Minority leader | Robert H. Michel (R) |
| | Minority leader | Robert Dole (R) | | Minority whip | Newt Gingrich (R) |
| | Minority whip | Alan K. Simpson (R) | | | |

## THE 102ND CONGRESS: U.S. SENATE

| State | Senator | ADA[1] | ACU[2] | NSI[3] | State | Senator | ADA[1] | ACU[2] | NSI[3] |
|---|---|---|---|---|---|---|---|---|---|
| Alabama | Howell Heflin (D) | 28 | 55 | 100 | Montana | Max Baucus (D) | 56 | 41 | 10 |
| | Richard C. Shelby (D) | 33 | 48 | 100 | | Conrad Burns (R) | 6 | 91 | 100 |
| Alaska | Ted Stevens (R) | 33 | 65 | 100 | Nebraska | J. James Exon (D) | 33 | 61 | 90 |
| | Frank H. Murkowski (R) | 11 | 76 | 100 | | Bob Kerrey (D) | 83 | 13 | 30 |
| Arizona | Dennis DeConcini (D) | 61 | 20 | 30 | Nevada | Harry Reid (D) | 61 | 30 | 30 |
| | John McCain (R) | 11 | 87 | 100 | | Richard H. Bryan (D) | 56 | 30 | 90 |
| Arkansas | Dale Bumpers (D) | 72 | 23 | 10 | New Hampshire | Robert C. Smith (R) | N.A. | N.A. | N.A. |
| | David Pryor (D) | 67 | 18 | 0 | | Warren Rudman (R) | 17 | 77 | 90 |
| California | Alan Cranston (D) | 100 | 0 | 0 | New Jersey | Bill Bradley (D) | 94 | 13 | 11 |
| | John Seymour (R) | N.A. | N.A. | N.A. | | Frank R. Lautenberg (D) | 100 | 4 | 10 |
| Colorado | Hank Brown (R) | N.A. | N.A. | N.A. | New Mexico | Peter V. Domenici (R) | 22 | 50 | 100 |
| | Timothy E. Wirth (D) | 83 | 10 | 11 | | Jeff Bingaman (D) | 67 | 19 | 38 |
| Connecticut | Christopher J. Dodd (D) | 61 | 9 | 40 | New York | Daniel Patrick Moynihan (D) | 94 | 4 | 10 |
| | Joseph L. Lieberman (D) | 83 | 22 | 30 | | Alfonse M. D'Amato (R) | 28 | 70 | 80 |
| Delaware | William V. Roth, Jr. (R) | 22 | 87 | 100 | North Carolina | Jesse A. Helms (R) | 6 | 100 | 100 |
| | Joseph R. Biden, Jr. (D) | 83 | 17 | 10 | | Terry Sanford (D) | 67 | 17 | 40 |
| Florida | Robert Graham (D) | 67 | 30 | 100 | North Dakota | Quentin N. Burdick (D) | 89 | 9 | 20 |
| | Connie Mack III (R) | 0 | 96 | 100 | | Kent Conrad (D) | 67 | 30 | 20 |
| Georgia | Sam Nunn (D) | 50 | 32 | 100 | Ohio | John H. Glenn, Jr. (D) | 89 | 9 | 70 |
| | Wyche Fowler, Jr. (D) | 72 | 35 | 50 | | Howard M. Metzenbaum (D) | 78 | 10 | 10 |
| Hawaii | Daniel K. Inouye (D) | 72 | 13 | 50 | Oklahoma | David Lyle Boren (D) | 56 | 23 | 80 |
| | Daniel K. Akaka (D) | 100 | 11 | 10 | | Don Nickles (R) | 0 | 96 | 100 |
| Idaho | Larry E. Craig (R) | N.A. | N.A. | N.A. | Oregon | Mark O. Hatfield (R) | 78 | 35 | 10 |
| | Steven D. Symms (R) | 6 | 100 | 100 | | Robert W. Packwood (R) | 72 | 35 | 80 |
| Illinois | Alan J. Dixon (D) | 44 | 39 | 80 | Pennsylvania | Harris Wofford (D) | N.A. | N.A. | N.A. |
| | Paul Simon (D) | 94 | 13 | 0 | | Arlen Specter (R) | 39 | 48 | 80 |
| Indiana | Richard G. Lugar (R) | 6 | 83 | 100 | Rhode Island | Claiborne Pell (D) | 94 | 19 | 0 |
| | Daniel R. Coats (R) | 0 | 96 | 100 | | John H. Chafee (R) | 50 | 43 | 60 |
| Iowa | Charles E. Grassley (R) | 17 | 87 | 80 | South Carolina | Strom Thurmond (R) | 6 | 83 | 100 |
| | Tom Harkin (D) | 94 | 22 | 0 | | Ernest F. Hollings (D) | 50 | 48 | 100 |
| Kansas | Robert Dole (R) | 0 | 83 | 100 | South Dakota | Larry Pressler (R) | 22 | 83 | 70 |
| | Nancy L. Kassebaum (R) | 44 | 64 | 80 | | Thomas A. Daschle (D) | 83 | 9 | 10 |
| Kentucky | Wendell H. Ford (D) | 39 | 35 | 40 | Tennessee | James R. Sasser (D) | 72 | 9 | 10 |
| | Mitch McConnell (R) | 0 | 87 | 100 | | Albert Gore, Jr. (D) | 78 | 9 | 70 |
| Louisiana | J. Bennett Johnston, Jr. (D) | 39 | 38 | 60 | Texas | Lloyd Bentsen (D) | 44 | 32 | 80 |
| | John B. Breaux (D) | 33 | 39 | 60 | | Phil Gramm (R) | 0 | 91 | 100 |
| Maine | William S. Cohen (R) | 61 | 48 | 70 | Utah | Edwin Jacob Garn (R) | 6 | 95 | 100 |
| | George J. Mitchell (D) | 83 | 9 | 20 | | Orrin G. Hatch (R) | 11 | 87 | 100 |
| Maryland | Paul S. Sarbanes (D) | 83 | 4 | 10 | Vermont | Patrick J. Leahy (D) | 94 | 4 | 10 |
| | Barbara A. Mikulski (D) | 94 | 5 | 0 | | James M. Jeffords (R) | 72 | 26 | 30 |
| Massachusetts | Edward M. Kennedy (D) | 100 | 0 | 0 | Virginia | John William Warner (R) | 28 | 70 | 100 |
| | John F. Kerry (D) | 94 | 5 | 20 | | Charles S. Robb (D) | 61 | 22 | 100 |
| Michigan | Donald W. Riegle, Jr. (D) | 83 | 9 | 0 | Washington | Brock Adams (D) | 94 | 9 | 0 |
| | Carl Levin (D) | 78 | 22 | 10 | | Slade Gorton (R) | 17 | 78 | 90 |
| Minnesota | David Durenburger (IR) | 44 | 45 | 70 | West Virginia | Robert C. Byrd (D) | 56 | 26 | 80 |
| | Paul David Wellstone (DFL) | N.A. | N.A. | N.A. | | John D. Rockefeller IV (D) | 83 | 13 | 20 |
| Mississippi | Thad Cochran (R) | 0 | 87 | 100 | Wisconsin | Robert W. Kasten, Jr. (R) | 6 | 91 | 100 |
| | Trent Lott (R) | 0 | 91 | 100 | | Herbert H. Kohl (D) | 94 | 9 | 10 |
| Missouri | John C. Danforth (R) | 39 | 43 | 90 | Wyoming | Malcolm Wallop (R) | N.A. | 95 | 100 |
| | Christopher S. Bond (R) | 11 | 77 | 100 | | Alan K. Simpson (R) | 11 | 73 | 90 |

**Note:** D = Democrat; DFL = Democratic-Farmer-Labor (Minn.); IR = Independent Republican (Minn.); R = Republican. 1. Americans for Democratic Action: based on 18 Senate votes in 1990. 2. American Conservative Union: based on 21 Senate votes in 1990. 3. National Security Index of the American Security Council: based on 10 Senate votes in 1990. **Source:** Americans for Democratic Action; The American Conservative Union; American Security Council; Clerk of the U.S. House of Representatives.

# THE 102ND CONGRESS: U.S. HOUSE OF REPRESENTATIVES

| State/Dist. | City | Representative | ADA[1] | ACU[2] | NSI[3] |
|---|---|---|---|---|---|
| **Alabama** | | | | | |
| 1st | Mobile | H.L. (Sonny) Callahan (R) | 6 | 87 | 100 |
| 2d | Montgomery | William L. Dickinson (R) | 0 | 88 | 100 |
| 3d | Anniston | Glen Browder (D) | 33 | 58 | 100 |
| 4th | Jasper | Tom Bevill (D) | 22 | 58 | 100 |
| 5th | Huntsville | Robert E. Cramer, Jr. (D) | N.A. | N.A. | N.A. |
| 6th | Birmingham | Ben Erdreich (D) | 39 | 54 | 90 |
| 7th | Tuscaloosa | Claude Harris, Jr. (D) | 33 | 58 | 100 |
| **Alaska** | | | | | |
| 1st | At Large | Don Young (R) | 33 | 67 | 100 |
| **Arizona** | | | | | |
| 1st | Tempe | John J. Rhodes III (R) | 17 | 63 | 100 |
| 2d | Phoenix | Vacant | | | |
| 3d | Flagstaff | Bob Stump (R) | 6 | 100 | 100 |
| 4th | Scottsdale | Jon L. Kyl (R) | 6 | 92 | 100 |
| 5th | Tucson | Jim Kolbe (R) | 22 | 61 | 100 |
| **Arkansas** | | | | | |
| 1st | Jonesboro | Bill Alexander (D) | 50 | 17 | 50 |
| 2d | Little Rock | Ray Thornton (D) | N.A. | N.A. | N.A. |
| 3d | Fort Smith | John Paul Hammerschmidt (R) | 6 | 82 | 100 |
| 4th | Pine Bluff | Beryl F. Anthony, Jr. (D) | 67 | 17 | 40 |
| **California** | | | | | |
| 1st | Santa Rosa | Frank D. Riggs (R) | N.A. | N.A. | N.A. |
| 2d | Chico | Wally Herger (R) | 6 | 96 | 100 |
| 3d | Sacramento | Robert T. Matsui (D) | 94 | 0 | 20 |
| 4th | Sacramento | Vic Fazio (D) | 89 | 4 | 20 |
| 5th | San Francisco | Nancy Pelosi (D) | 100 | 4 | 0 |
| 6th | Marin County | Barbara Boxer (D) | 94 | 4 | 0 |
| 7th | Richmond | George Miller (D) | 100 | 4 | 0 |
| 8th | Oakland | Ronald V. Dellums (D) | 100 | 4 | 0 |
| 9th | Hayward | Fortney H. (Pete) Stark (D) | 100 | 4 | 0 |
| 10th | San José | Don Edwards (D) | 100 | 4 | 0 |
| 11th | San Mateo County | Tom Lantos (D) | 78 | 17 | 33 |
| 12th | Sunnyvale | Tom Campbell (R) | 44 | 46 | 50 |
| 13th | San José | Norman Y. Mineta (D) | 94 | 0 | 10 |
| 14th | Stockton | John T. Doolittle (R) | N.A. | N.A. | N.A. |
| 15th | Modesto | Gary Condit (D) | 56 | 29 | 25 |
| 16th | Monterey | Leon E. Panetta (D) | 83 | 8 | 10 |
| 17th | Fresno | Calvin M. Dooley (D) | N.A. | N.A. | N.A. |
| 18th | Fresno | Richard H. Lehman (D) | 94 | 4 | 10 |
| 19th | Santa Barbara | Robert J. Lagomarsino (R) | 11 | 92 | 100 |
| 20th | Bakersfield | William M. Thomas (R) | 17 | 74 | 100 |
| 21st | Thousand Oaks | Elton Gallegly (R) | 11 | 92 | 100 |
| 22d | Pasadena | Carlos J. Moorhead (R) | 6 | 96 | 100 |
| 23d | Beverly Hills | Anthony C. Beilenson (D) | 83 | 8 | 10 |
| 24th | Hollywood | Henry A. Waxman (D) | 100 | 4 | 22 |
| 25th | Los Angeles | Edward R. Roybal (D) | 100 | 4 | 0 |
| 26th | Van Nuys | Howard L. Berman (D) | 100 | 4 | 0 |
| 27th | Santa Monica | Mel Levine (D) | 100 | 4 | 20 |
| 28th | Culver City | Julian C. Dixon (D) | 100 | 4 | 13 |
| 29th | Los Angeles | Maxine Waters (D) | N.A. | N.A. | N.A. |
| 30th | El Monte | Matthew G. Martinez (D) | 78 | 9 | 30 |
| 31st | Compton | Mervyn M. Dymally (D) | 100 | 4 | 0 |
| 32d | Long Beach | Glenn M. Anderson (D) | 94 | 4 | 30 |
| 33d | Pomona | David Dreier (R) | 17 | 83 | 100 |
| 34th | West Covina | Esteban Edward Torres (D) | 89 | 0 | 10 |
| 35th | Redlands | Jerry Lewis (R) | 6 | 76 | 100 |
| 36th | Riverside | George E. Brown, Jr. (D) | 89 | 4 | 10 |
| 37th | Palm Springs | Alfred A. McCandless (R) | 6 | 92 | 100 |
| 38th | Santa Ana | Robert K. Dornan (R) | 6 | 91 | 100 |
| 39th | Anaheim | William E. Dannemeyer (R) | 6 | 100 | 100 |
| 40th | Newport Beach | C. Christopher Cox (R) | 11 | 88 | 100 |
| 41st | San Diego | William Lowery (R) | 11 | 70 | 100 |
| 42d | Long Beach | Dana Rohrabacher (R) | 6 | 96 | 100 |
| 43d | Carlsbad | Ronald C. Packard (R) | 11 | 88 | 100 |
| 44th | San Diego | Randy "Duke" Cunningham (R) | N.A. | N.A. | N.A. |
| 45th | Coronado | Duncan L. Hunter (R) | 6 | 96 | 100 |
| **Colorado** | | | | | |
| 1st | Denver | Patricia Schroeder (D) | 100 | 13 | 0 |
| 2d | Boulder | David E. Skaggs (D) | 89 | 8 | 20 |
| 3d | Pueblo | Ben Nighthorse Campbell (D) | 56 | 33 | 70 |
| 4th | Greeley | Wayne Allard (R) | N.A. | N.A. | N.A. |
| 5th | Colorado Springs | Joel Hefley (R) | 6 | 92 | 100 |
| 6th | Lakewood | Dan Schaefer (R) | 11 | 79 | 100 |
| **Connecticut** | | | | | |
| 1st | Hartford | Barbara B. Kennelly (D) | 83 | 8 | 20 |
| 2d | New London | Samuel Gejdenson (D) | 94 | 4 | 10 |
| 3d | New Haven | Rosa L. DeLauro (D) | N.A. | N.A. | N.A. |
| 4th | Stamford | Christopher Shays (R) | 72 | 25 | 30 |
| 5th | Waterbury | Gary A. Franks (R) | N.A. | N.A. | N.A |
| 6th | New Britain | Nancy L. Johnson (R) | 44 | 50 | 80 |
| **Delaware** | | | | | |
| 1st | At Large | Thomas R. Carper (D) | 78 | 17 | 20 |
| **Florida** | | | | | |
| 1st | Pensacola | Earl Dewitt Hutto (D) | 28 | 78 | 100 |
| 2d | Tallahassee | Pete Peterson (D) | N.A. | N.A. | N.A. |
| 3d | Jacksonville | Charles E. Bennett (D) | 39 | 42 | 50 |
| 4th | Daytona Beach | Craig T. James (R) | 17 | 71 | 100 |
| 5th | Orlando | Bill McCollum (R) | 17 | 88 | 100 |
| 6th | Ocala | Clifford B. Stearns (R) | 17 | 83 | 100 |
| 7th | Tampa | Sam M. Gibbons (D) | 61 | 27 | 40 |
| 8th | St. Petersburg | C.W. (Bill) Young (R) | 17 | 79 | 100 |
| 9th | Clearwater | Michael Bilirakis (R) | 17 | 80 | 100 |
| 10th | Winter Haven | Andy Ireland (R) | 11 | 82 | 100 |
| 11th | Melbourne | Jim Bacchus (D) | N.A. | N.A. | N.A. |
| 12th | N. Palm Beach | Tom Lewis (R) | 6 | 90 | 100 |
| 13th | Ft. Myers | Porter J. Goss (R) | 33 | 79 | 100 |
| 14th | W. Palm Beach | Harry A. Johnston (D) | 83 | 25 | 20 |
| 15th | Ft. Lauderdale | E. Clay Shaw, Jr. (R) | 6 | 83 | 100 |
| 16th | Hollywood | Lawrence J. Smith (D) | 94 | 9 | 20 |
| 17th | N. Miami Beach | William Lehman (D) | 89 | 0 | 0 |
| 18th | Miami | Ileana Ros-Lehtinen (R) | 33 | 65 | 100 |
| 19th | Coral Gables | Dante B. Fascell (D) | 83 | 8 | 22 |
| **Georgia** | | | | | |
| 1st | Savannah | Robert Lindsay Thomas (D) | 28 | 50 | 90 |
| 2d | Albany | Charles F. Hatcher (D) | 28 | 50 | 90 |
| 3d | Columbus | Richard B. Ray (D) | 22 | 50 | 80 |
| 4th | Dunwoody | Ben Jones (D) | 61 | 33 | 40 |
| 5th | Atlanta | John Lewis (D) | 100 | 4 | 0 |
| 6th | Carrollton | Newt Gingrich (R) | 17 | 86 | 100 |
| 7th | Marietta | George (Buddy) Darden (D) | 28 | 58 | 100 |
| 8th | Macon | J. Roy Rowland (D) | 33 | 42 | 90 |
| 9th | Dalton | Ed Jenkins (D) | 39 | 54 | 90 |
| 10th | Augusta | Doug Barnard, Jr. (D) | 22 | 81 | 100 |
| **Hawaii** | | | | | |
| 1st | Honolulu | Neil Abercrombie (D) | N.A. | N.A. | N.A. |
| 2d | Outer Islands | Patsy T. Mink (D) | N.A. | N.A. | N.A. |
| **Idaho** | | | | | |
| 1st | Boise | Larry LaRocco (D) | N.A. | N.A. | N.A. |
| 2d | Pocatello | Richard H. Stallings (D) | 39 | 46 | 50 |
| **Illinois** | | | | | |
| 1st | Chicago | Charles A. Hayes (D) | 100 | 4 | 0 |
| 2d | S. Chicago | Gus Savage (D) | 89 | 9 | 0 |
| 3d | Oak Lawn | Martin A. Russo (D) | 78 | 17 | 10 |

| State/Dist. | City | Representative | ADA[1] | ACU[2] | NSI[3] |
|---|---|---|---|---|---|
| 4th | Joliet | George E. Sangmeister (D) | 56 | 33 | 20 |
| 5th | Chicago | William O. Lipinski (D) | 44 | 54 | 75 |
| 6th | Wheaton | Henry J. Hyde (R) | 11 | 88 | 100 |
| 7th | Chicago | Cardiss Collins (D) | 94 | 5 | 0 |
| 8th | Chicago | Dan Rostenkowski (D) | 67 | 14 | 13 |
| 9th | Chicago | Sidney R. Yates (D) | 100 | 5 | 0 |
| 10th | Evanston | John Edward Porter (R) | 22 | 67 | 60 |
| 11th | Chicago | Frank Annunzio (D) | 56 | 38 | 40 |
| 12th | Palatine | Philip M. Crane (R) | 11 | 100 | 100 |
| 13th | Oak Brook | Harris W. Fawell (R) | 11 | 88 | 90 |
| 14th | Elgin | J. Dennis Hastert (R) | 6 | 79 | 100 |
| 15th | Bloomington | Vacant | | | |
| 16th | Rockford | John W. Cox, Jr. (D) | N.A | N.A. | N.A. |
| 17th | Moline | Lane Evans (D) | 100 | 4 | 0 |
| 18th | Peoria | Robert H. Michel (R) | 11 | 76 | 100 |
| 19th | Danville | Terry L. Bruce (D) | 83 | 8 | 20 |
| 20th | Springfield | Richard J. Durbin (D) | 83 | 4 | 0 |
| 21st | East St. Louis | Jerry F. Costello (D) | 67 | 29 | 30 |
| 22d | Carbondale | Glenn Poshard (D) | 78 | 29 | 0 |
| **Indiana** | | | | | |
| 1st | Gary | Peter J. Visclosky (D) | 72 | 13 | 30 |
| 2d | Muncie | Philip R. Sharp (D) | 67 | 22 | 38 |
| 3d | South Bend | Tim Roemer (D) | N.A. | N.A. | N.A. |
| 4th | Fort Wayne | Jill L. Long (D) | 50 | 38 | 30 |
| 5th | Kokomo | James Jontz (D) | 89 | 17 | 10 |
| 6th | Indianapolis | Dan Burton (R) | 11 | 96 | 100 |
| 7th | Terre Haute | John T. Myers (R) | 11 | 83 | 100 |
| 8th | Evansville | Francis X. McCloskey (D) | 83 | 8 | 10 |
| 9th | Bloomington | Lee H. Hamilton (D) | 67 | 13 | 20 |
| 10th | Indianapolis | Andrew Jacobs, Jr. (D) | 78 | 25 | 30 |
| **Iowa** | | | | | |
| 1st | Davenport | James A.S. Leach (R) | 61 | 21 | 30 |
| 2d | Cedar Rapids | Jim Nussle (R) | N.A. | N.A. | N.A. |
| 3d | Waterloo | David R. Nagle (D) | 83 | 8 | 20 |
| 4th | Des Moines | Neal Smith (D) | 83 | 8 | 30 |
| 5th | Council Bluffs | Jim Ross Lightfoot (R) | 6 | 92 | 90 |
| 6th | Sioux City | Fred Grandy (R) | 28 | 42 | 70 |
| **Kansas** | | | | | |
| 1st | Dodge City | Pat Roberts (R) | 6 | 75 | 80 |
| 2d | Topeka | James Slattery (D) | 61 | 22 | 30 |
| 3d | Kansas City | Jan Meyers (R) | 22 | 67 | 80 |
| 4th | Wichita | Dan Glickman (D) | 72 | 17 | 40 |
| 5th | Emporia | Dick Nichols (R) | N.A. | N.A. | N.A. |
| **Kentucky** | | | | | |
| 1st | Paducah | Carroll Hubbard, Jr. (D) | 39 | 52 | 60 |
| 2d | Owensboro | William H. Natcher (D) | 61 | 25 | 40 |
| 3d | Louisville | Romano L. Mazzoli (D) | 78 | 13 | 50 |
| 4th | Covington | Jim Bunning (R) | 6 | 87 | 100 |
| 5th | Somerset | Harold Rogers (R) | 6 | 83 | 100 |
| 6th | Lexington | Larry J. Hopkins (R) | 11 | 83 | 80 |
| 7th | Ashland | Carl C. Perkins (D) | 78 | 13 | 20 |
| **Louisiana** | | | | | |
| 1st | New Orleans | Robert L. Livingston, Jr. (R) | 6 | 83 | 100 |
| 2d | New Orleans | William J. Jefferson (D) | N.A. | N.A. | N.A. |
| 3d | New Iberia | W.J. (Billy) Tauzin (D) | 22 | 58 | 100 |
| 4th | Shreveport | Jim McCrery (R) | 17 | 88 | 100 |
| 5th | Monroe | Thomas J. Huckaby (D) | 22 | 71 | 100 |
| 6th | Baton Rouge | Richard H. Baker (R) | 0 | 86 | 100 |
| 7th | Lafayette | James A. Hayes (D) | 22 | 55 | 90 |
| 8th | Alexandria | Clyde C. Holloway (R) | 11 | 91 | 100 |
| **Maine** | | | | | |
| 1st | Portland | Thomas H. Andrews (D) | N.A. | N.A. | N.A. |
| 2d | Bangor | Olympia J. Snowe (R) | 28 | 54 | 40 |
| **Maryland** | | | | | |
| 1st | Eastern Shore | Wayne T. Gilchrest (R) | N.A. | N.A. | N.A. |
| 2d | Towson | Helen Delich Bentley (R) | 11 | 83 | 100 |
| 3d | Baltimore | Benjamin L. Cardin (D) | 83 | 4 | 0 |
| 4th | Annapolis | C. Thomas McMillen (D) | 56 | 17 | 50 |
| 5th | Landover | Steny H. Hoyer (D) | 89 | 0 | 20 |
| 6th | Hagerstown | Beverly B. Byron (D) | 33 | 48 | 100 |
| 7th | Baltimore | Kweisi Mfume (D) | 94 | 13 | 0 |
| 8th | Montgomery Co. | Constance A. Morella (R) | 67 | 17 | 20 |
| **Massachusetts** | | | | | |
| 1st | Pittsfield | John Oliver (D) | N.A. | N.A. | N.A. |
| 2d | Springfield | Richard E. Neal (D) | 83 | 18 | 11 |
| 3d | Worcester | Joseph D. Early (D) | 72 | 19 | 0 |
| 4th | Newton | Barney Frank (D) | 94 | 4 | 0 |
| 5th | Lowell | Chester G. Atkins (D) | 89 | 4 | 10 |
| 6th | Lynn | Nicholas Mavroules (D) | 94 | 8 | 10 |
| 7th | Malden | Edward J. Markey (D) | 94 | 4 | 0 |
| 8th | Cambridge | Joseph P. Kennedy II (D) | 89 | 4 | 0 |
| 9th | Boston | John Joseph Moakley (D) | 78 | 4 | 10 |
| 10th | Cape Cod | Gerry E. Studds (D) | 100 | 4 | 0 |
| 11th | Boston | Brian J. Donnelly (D) | 61 | 29 | 20 |
| **Michigan** | | | | | |
| 1st | Detroit | John Conyers, Jr. (D) | 78 | 0 | 0 |
| 2d | Ann Arbor | Carl D. Pursell (R) | 28 | 57 | 70 |
| 3d | Lansing | Howard E. Wolpe (D) | 100 | 13 | 10 |
| 4th | Benton Harbor | Frederick S. Upton (R) | 17 | 71 | 90 |
| 5th | Grand Rapids | Paul B. Henry (R) | 33 | 63 | 70 |
| 6th | Pontiac | Robert Carr (D) | 72 | 25 | 20 |
| 7th | Flint | Dale E. Kildee (D) | 94 | 4 | 0 |
| 8th | Bay City | Bob Traxler (D) | 56 | 9 | 30 |
| 9th | Traverse City | Guy Vander Jagt (R) | 6 | 83 | 100 |
| 10th | Midland | Dave Camp (R) | N.A. | N.A. | N.A. |
| 11th | Upper Peninsula | Robert W. Davis (R) | 56 | 43 | 100 |
| 12th | Port Huron | David E. Bonior (D) | 94 | 8 | 10 |
| 13th | Detroit | Barbara-Rose Collins (D) | N.A. | N.A. | N.A. |
| 14th | Warren | Dennis M. Hertel (D) | 94 | 17 | 10 |
| 15th | Wayne | William D. Ford (D) | 78 | 5 | 0 |
| 16th | Dearborn | John D. Dingell (D) | 67 | 4 | 11 |
| 17th | Southfield | Sander M. Levin (D) | 89 | 4 | 20 |
| 18th | Birmingham | William S. Broomfield (R) | 17 | 83 | 100 |
| **Minnesota** | | | | | |
| 1st | Rochester | Timothy J. Penny (DFL) | 67 | 25 | 40 |
| 2d | Willmar | Vin Weber (IR) | 22 | 83 | 100 |
| 3d | Bloomington | Jim Ramstad (IR) | N.A. | N.A. | N.A. |
| 4th | St. Paul | Bruce F. Vento (DFL) | 100 | 4 | 0 |
| 5th | Minneapolis | Martin Olav Sabo (DFL) | 94 | 0 | 10 |
| 6th | Stillwater | Gerry Sikorski (DFL) | 89 | 0 | 10 |
| 7th | St. Cloud | Colin C. Peterson (DFL) | N.A. | N.A. | N.A. |
| 8th | Duluth | James L. Oberstar (DFL) | 78 | 0 | 0 |
| **Mississippi** | | | | | |
| 1st | Oxford | Jamie L. Whitten (D) | 44 | 43 | 60 |
| 2d | Vicksburg | Mike Espy (D) | 67 | 17 | 25 |
| 3d | Meridian | G.V. (Sonny) Montgomery (R) | 22 | 63 | 100 |
| 4th | Jackson | Mike Parker (D) | 22 | 63 | 100 |
| 5th | Pascagoula | Gene Taylor (D) | 28 | 63 | 100 |
| **Missouri** | | | | | |
| 1st | St. Louis | William (Bill) Clay (D) | 94 | 4 | 11 |
| 2d | Kirkwood | Joan Kelly Horn (D) | N.A. | N.A. | N.A. |
| 3d | St. Louis | Richard A. Gephardt (D) | 83 | 4 | 20 |
| 4th | Jefferson City | Ike Skelton (D) | 33 | 50 | 80 |
| 5th | Kansas City | Alan Wheat (D) | 100 | 4 | 0 |

| State/Dist. | City | Representative | ADA[1] | ACU[2] | NSI[3] |
|---|---|---|---|---|---|
| 6th | St. Joseph | E. Thomas Coleman (R) | 28 | 65 | 90 |
| 7th | Springfield | Melton D. Hancock (R) | 11 | 100 | 100 |
| 8th | Cape Girardeau | Bill Emerson (R) | 11 | 78 | 100 |
| 9th | Hannibal | Harold L. Volkmer (D) | 39 | 38 | 50 |
| **Montana** | | | | | |
| 1st | Helena | Pat Williams (D) | 89 | 9 | 10 |
| 2d | Billings | Ron Marlenee (R) | 6 | 87 | 100 |
| **Nebraska** | | | | | |
| 1st | Lincoln | Douglas K. Bereuter (R) | 17 | 67 | 80 |
| 2d | Omaha | Peter Hoagland (D) | 72 | 29 | 30 |
| 3d | Grand Island | Bill Barrett (R) | N.A. | N.A. | N.A. |
| **Nevada** | | | | | |
| 1st | Las Vegas | James H. Bilbray (D) | 50 | 25 | 50 |
| 2d | Reno | Barbara F. Vucanovich (R) | 6 | 88 | 100 |
| **New Hampshire** | | | | | |
| 1st | Manchester | William H. Zeliff, Jr. (R) | N.A. | N.A. | N.A. |
| 2d | Concord | Dick Swett (D) | N.A. | N.A. | N.A. |
| **New Jersey** | | | | | |
| 1st | Pine Hill | Robert E. Andrews (D) | N.A. | N.A. | N.A. |
| 2d | Ocean City | William J. Hughes (D) | 78 | 13 | 30 |
| 3d | Toms River | Frank Pallone, Jr. (D) | 61 | 29 | 40 |
| 4th | Trenton | Christopher H. Smith (R) | 56 | 63 | 60 |
| 5th | Ridgewood | Margaret S. Roukema (R) | 28 | 59 | 50 |
| 6th | Edison | Bernard J. Dwyer (D) | 83 | 9 | 30 |
| 7th | Union | Matthew J. Rinaldo (R) | 50 | 46 | 100 |
| 8th | Paterson | Robert A. Roe (D) | 67 | 18 | 38 |
| 9th | Hackensack | Robert G. Torricelli (D) | 83 | 10 | 33 |
| 10th | Newark | Donald M. Payne (D) | 89 | 4 | 0 |
| 11th | Parsippany | Dean A. Gallo (R) | 17 | 65 | 100 |
| 12th | Hackettstown | Dick Zimmer (R) | N.A. | N.A. | N.A. |
| 13th | Bordentown | James A. Saxton (R) | 33 | 63 | 90 |
| 14th | Jersey City | Frank J. Guarini (D) | 78 | 13 | 44 |
| **New Mexico** | | | | | |
| 1st | Albuquerque | Steven Schiff (R) | 22 | 58 | 100 |
| 2d | Picacho | Joseph R. Skeen (R) | 6 | 71 | 100 |
| 3d | Santa Fe | Bill Richardson (D) | 61 | 26 | 70 |
| **New York** | | | | | |
| 1st | E. Long Island | George Hochbrueckner (D) | 89 | 13 | 20 |
| 2d | Babylon | Thomas J. Downey (D) | 100 | 8 | 10 |
| 3d | Huntington | Robert J. Mrazek (D) | 100 | 9 | 20 |
| 4th | E. Rockaway | Norman F. Lent (R) | 17 | 63 | 100 |
| 5th | Valley Stream | Raymond J. McGrath (R) | 50 | 52 | 90 |
| 6th | Jamaica | Floyd H. Flake (D) | 89 | 4 | 0 |
| 7th | Flushing | Gary L. Ackerman (D) | 94 | 0 | 0 |
| 8th | Queens | James H. Scheuer (D) | 89 | 0 | 10 |
| 9th | Astoria | Thomas J. Manton (D) | 67 | 9 | 20 |
| 10th | Flatbush | Charles E. Schumer (D) | 94 | 4 | 0 |
| 11th | Brooklyn | Edolphus Towns (D) | 94 | 4 | 0 |
| 12th | Brooklyn | Major R. Owens (D) | 94 | 4 | 0 |
| 13th | Brooklyn | Stephen J. Solarz (D) | 89 | 0 | 10 |
| 14th | Staten Island | Susan Molinari (R) | 31 | 57 | 100 |
| 15th | Manhattan | Bill Green (R) | 61 | 13 | 30 |
| 16th | Harlem | Charles B. Rangel (D) | 89 | 4 | 0 |
| 17th | Manhattan | Theodore S. Weiss (D) | 100 | 4 | 0 |
| 18th | Bronx | José E. Serrano (D) | 88 | 0 | 0 |
| 19th | Bronx | Eliot L. Engel (D) | 100 | 9 | 11 |
| 20th | Westchester | Nita M. Lowey (D) | 100 | 4 | 10 |
| 21st | Poughkeepsie | Hamilton Fish, Jr. (R) | 56 | 32 | 70 |
| 22d | Middletown | Benjamin A. Gilman (R) | 61 | 29 | 70 |
| 23d | Albany | Michael R. McNulty (D) | 78 | 21 | 70 |
| 24th | Saratoga Springs | Gerald B.H. Solomon (R) | 22 | 83 | 100 |
| 25th | Utica | Sherwood L. Boehlert (R) | 61 | 33 | 70 |
| 26th | Watertown | David O'B. Martin (R) | 28 | 63 | 100 |
| 27th | Syracuse | James T. Walsh (R) | 44 | 58 | 100 |
| 28th | Binghamton | Matthew F. McHugh (D) | 89 | 4 | 10 |
| 29th | Rochester | Frank J. Horton (R) | 61 | 25 | 50 |
| 30th | Rochester | Louise McIntosh Slaughter (D) | 94 | 19 | 10 |
| 31st | Buffalo | L. William Paxon (R) | 19 | 88 | 100 |
| 32d | Niagara Falls | John J. LaFalce (D) | 72 | 21 | 20 |
| 33d | Buffalo | Henry J. Nowak (D) | 89 | 4 | 10 |
| 34th | Corning | Amory Houghton, Jr. (R) | 33 | 43 | 90 |
| **North Carolina** | | | | | |
| 1st | Greenville | Walter B. Jones (D) | 50 | 39 | 33 |
| 2d | Durham | Tim Valentine (D) | 33 | 42 | 50 |
| 3d | Goldsboro | H. Martin Lancaster (D) | 39 | 50 | 70 |
| 4th | Raleigh | David E. Price (D) | 61 | 21 | 20 |
| 5th | Winston-Salem | Stephen L. Neal (D) | 50 | 32 | 20 |
| 6th | Greensboro | Howard Coble (R) | 6 | 83 | 70 |
| 7th | Wilmington | Charles G. Rose (D) | 61 | 21 | 22 |
| 8th | Salisbury | W.G. (Bill) Hefner (D) | 44 | 38 | 70 |
| 9th | Charlotte | J. Alex McMillan III (R) | 11 | 67 | 100 |
| 10th | Hickory | Cass Ballenger (R) | 6 | 83 | 100 |
| 11th | Asheville | Charles H. Taylor (R) | N.A. | N.A. | N.A. |
| **North Dakota** | | | | | |
| 1st | At Large | Byron L. Dorgan (D) | 72 | 21 | 20 |
| **Ohio** | | | | | |
| 1st | Cincinnati | Charles J. Luken (D) | N.A. | N.A. | N.A. |
| 2d | Cincinnati | Willis D. Gradison, Jr. (R) | 11 | 75 | 80 |
| 3d | Dayton | Tony P. Hall (D) | 72 | 8 | 10 |
| 4th | Findlay | Michael G. Oxley (R) | 0 | 79 | 100 |
| 5th | Bowling Green | Paul E. Gillmor (R) | 11 | 74 | 100 |
| 6th | Portsmouth | Bob McEwen (R) | 6 | 100 | 100 |
| 7th | Springfield | David L. Hobson (R) | N.A. | N.A. | N.A. |
| 8th | Hamilton | John A. Boehner (R) | N.A. | N.A. | N.A. |
| 9th | Toledo | Marcy Kaptur (D) | 72 | 8 | 10 |
| 10th | Lancaster | Clarence E. Miller (R) | 0 | 91 | 100 |
| 11th | Cleveland | Dennis E. Eckart (D) | 56 | 29 | 30 |
| 12th | Columbus | John R. Kasich (R) | 11 | 92 | 100 |
| 13th | Oberlin | Donald J. Pease (D) | 89 | 4 | 20 |
| 14th | Akron | Thomas C. Sawyer (D) | 89 | 0 | 10 |
| 15th | Columbus | Chalmers P. Wylie (R) | 11 | 74 | 100 |
| 16th | Canton | Ralph S. Regula (R) | 17 | 63 | 90 |
| 17th | Youngstown | James A. Traficant, Jr. (D) | 72 | 13 | 20 |
| 18th | Steubenville | Douglas Applegate (D) | 50 | 33 | 40 |
| 19th | Cleveland | Edward F. Feighan (D) | 94 | 9 | 22 |
| 20th | Cleveland | Mary Rose Oakar (D) | 83 | 4 | 10 |
| 21st | Cleveland | Louis Stokes (D) | 100 | 4 | 11 |
| **Oklahoma** | | | | | |
| 1st | Tulsa | James M. Inhofe (R) | 11 | 88 | 100 |
| 2d | Muskogee | Michael L. Synar (D) | 94 | 8 | 10 |
| 3d | Ada | Bill K. Brewster (D) | N.A. | N.A. | N.A. |
| 4th | Norman | Dave McCurdy (D) | 56 | 33 | 50 |
| 5th | Bartlesville | Mickey Edwards (R) | 6 | 92 | 100 |
| 6th | Oklahoma City | Glenn English (D) | 50 | 54 | 90 |
| **Oregon** | | | | | |
| 1st | Portland | Les AuCoin (D) | 78 | 0 | 11 |
| 2d | Medford | Robert F. (Bob) Smith (R) | 6 | 88 | 90 |
| 3d | Portland | Ron Wyden (D) | 89 | 4 | 10 |
| 4th | Eugene | Peter A. DeFazio (D) | 83 | 14 | 0 |
| 5th | Salem | Michael J. Kopetski (D) | N.A. | N.A. | N.A. |
| **Pennsylvania** | | | | | |
| 1st | Philadelphia | Thomas M. Foglietta (D) | 78 | 4 | 0 |
| 2d | Philadelphia | William H. Gray III (D) | 94 | 0 | 11 |
| 3d | Philadelphia | Robert A. Borski (D) | 83 | 8 | 20 |

| State/Dist. | City | Representative | ADA[1] | ACU[2] | NSI[3] |
|---|---|---|---|---|---|
| 4th | New Castle | Joseph P. Kolter (D) | 44 | 30 | 50 |
| 5th | Chester | Richard T. Schulze (R) | 17 | 71 | 70 |
| 6th | Reading | Gus Yatron (D) | 44 | 33 | 22 |
| 7th | Swarthmore | Curt Weldon (R) | 33 | 54 | 100 |
| 8th | Bucks County | Peter H. Kostmayer (D) | 89 | 0 | 0 |
| 9th | Altoona | E.G. (Bud) Shuster (R) | 11 | 96 | 100 |
| 10th | Scranton | Joseph M. McDade (R) | 33 | 57 | 100 |
| 11th | Wilkes Barre | Paul E. Kanjorski (D) | 67 | 21 | 20 |
| 12th | Johnstown | John P. Murtha (D) | 56 | 22 | 100 |
| 13th | Villanova | Lawrence Coughlin (R) | 33 | 35 | 70 |
| 14th | Pittsburgh | William J. Coyne (D) | 100 | 4 | 10 |
| 15th | Allentown | Donald L. Ritter (R) | 6 | 83 | 100 |
| 16th | Lancaster | Robert S. Walker (R) | 11 | 96 | 100 |
| 17th | Harrisburg | George W. Gekas (R) | 0 | 91 | 100 |
| 18th | Pittsburgh | Rick Santorum (R) | N.A. | N.A. | N.A. |
| 19th | York | William F. Goodling (R) | 22 | 68 | 70 |
| 20th | McKeesport | Joseph M. Gaydos (D) | 50 | 33 | 33 |
| 21st | Erie | Thomas J. Ridge (R) | 22 | 58 | 70 |
| 22d | Monangahela | Austin J. Murphy (D) | 50 | 33 | 20 |
| 23d | Warren | William F. Clinger, Jr. (R) | 28 | 55 | 90 |
| **Rhode Island** | | | | | |
| 1st | Providence | Ronald K. Machtley (R) | 61 | 25 | 80 |
| 2d | Warwick | John F. Reed (D) | N.A. | N.A. | N.A. |
| **South Carolina** | | | | | |
| 1st | Charleston | Arthur Ravenel, Jr. (R) | 28 | 63 | 100 |
| 2d | Columbia | Floyd D. Spence (R) | 17 | 79 | 100 |
| 3d | Aiken | Butler Derrick (D) | 44 | 33 | 40 |
| 4th | Spartanburg | Elizabeth J. Patterson (D) | 44 | 54 | 100 |
| 5th | Rock Hill | John M. Spratt, Jr. (D) | 56 | 33 | 40 |
| 6th | Florence | Robin M. Tallon, Jr. (D) | 50 | 42 | 70 |
| **South Dakota** | | | | | |
| 1st | At Large | Tim Johnson (D) | 67 | 25 | 20 |
| **Tennessee** | | | | | |
| 1st | Kingsport | James H. Quillen (R) | 6 | 83 | 100 |
| 2d | Knoxville | John J. Duncan, Jr. (R) | 11 | 88 | 80 |
| 3d | Chattanooga | Marilyn Lloyd (D) | 44 | 46 | 100 |
| 4th | Shelbyville | Jim Cooper (D) | 56 | 29 | 30 |
| 5th | Nashville | Bob Clement (D) | 44 | 29 | 40 |
| 6th | Murfreesboro | Bart Gordon (D) | 67 | 13 | 30 |
| 7th | Memphis | Don Sundquist (R) | 6 | 79 | 100 |
| 8th | Jackson | John S. Tanner (D) | 44 | 29 | 60 |
| 9th | Memphis | Harold E. Ford (D) | 89 | 5 | 0 |
| **Texas** | | | | | |
| 1st | Texarkana | Jim Chapman, Jr. (D) | 33 | 27 | 60 |
| 2d | Lufkin | Charles Wilson (D) | 44 | 40 | 100 |
| 3d | Dallas | Sam Johnson (R) | N.A. | N.A. | N.A. |
| 4th | Tyler | Ralph M. Hall (D) | 6 | 71 | 100 |
| 5th | Dallas | John Bryant (D) | 83 | 17 | 33 |
| 6th | Ennis | Joe L. Barton (R) | 6 | 87 | 100 |
| 7th | Houston | Bill Archer (R) | 0 | 88 | 100 |
| 8th | Humble | Jack Fields (R) | 6 | 88 | 100 |
| 9th | Beaumont | Jack Brooks (D) | 61 | 17 | 33 |
| 10th | Austin | J.J. (Jake) Pickle (D) | 61 | 25 | 67 |
| 11th | Waco | Chet Edwards (D) | N.A. | N.A. | N.A. |
| 12th | Fort Worth | Pete Geren (D) | 39 | 46 | 100 |
| 13th | Amarillo | Bill Sarpalius (D) | 28 | 74 | 80 |
| 14th | Victoria | Greg Laughlin (D) | 28 | 59 | 80 |
| 15th | McAllen | E. (Kika) de la Garza (D) | 61 | 23 | 50 |
| 16th | El Paso | Ronald D. Coleman (D) | 67 | 17 | 50 |
| 17th | Abilene | Charles W. Stenholm (D) | 22 | 67 | 90 |

| State/Dist. | City | Representative | ADA[1] | ACU[2] | NSI[3] |
|---|---|---|---|---|---|
| 18th | Houston | Craig A. Washington (D) | 94 | 5 | 0 |
| 19th | Lubbock | Larry Combest (R) | 0 | 96 | 100 |
| 20th | San Antonio | Henry B. Gonzalez (D) | 100 | 4 | 0 |
| 21st | Midland | Lamar S. Smith (R) | 11 | 83 | 100 |
| 22d | Houston | Thomas M. DeLay (R) | 6 | 92 | 100 |
| 23d | San Antonio | Albert G. Bustamante (D) | 50 | 17 | 40 |
| 24th | Dallas | Martin Frost (D) | 67 | 8 | 20 |
| 25th | Houston | Michael A. Andrews (D) | 56 | 25 | 70 |
| 26th | Arlington | Richard K. Armey (R) | 6 | 96 | 100 |
| 27th | Corpus Christi | Solomon P. Ortiz (D) | 56 | 21 | 40 |
| **Utah** | | | | | |
| 1st | Ogden | James V. Hansen (R) | 0 | 92 | 100 |
| 2d | Salt Lake City | Wayne Owens (D) | 72 | 13 | 10 |
| 3d | Provo | Bill Orton (D) | N.A. | N.A. | N.A. |
| **Vermont** | | | | | |
| 1st | At Large | Bernard Sanders (I) | N.A. | N.A. | N.A. |
| **Virginia** | | | | | |
| 1st | Newport News | Herbert H. Bateman (R) | 6 | 83 | 100 |
| 2d | Norfolk | Owen B. Pickett (D) | 50 | 42 | 80 |
| 3d | Richmond | Thomas J. Bliley, Jr. (R) | 17 | 83 | 100 |
| 4th | Portsmouth | Norman Sisisky (D) | 39 | 42 | 78 |
| 5th | Danville | Lewis F. Payne (D) | 33 | 33 | 70 |
| 6th | Roanoke | James R. Olin (D) | 50 | 38 | 20 |
| 7th | Charlottesville | D. French Slaughter, Jr. (R) | 6 | 92 | 100 |
| 8th | Alexandria | James P. Moran (D) | N.A. | N.A. | N.A. |
| 9th | Blacksburg | Rick Boucher (D) | 72 | 13 | 20 |
| 10th | Arlington | Frank R. Wolf (R) | 6 | 83 | 100 |
| **Washington** | | | | | |
| 1st | Seattle | John R. Miller (R) | 39 | 46 | 80 |
| 2d | Everett | Al Swift (D) | 89 | 4 | 20 |
| 3d | Olympia | Jolene Unsoeld (D) | 83 | 9 | 0 |
| 4th | Yakima | Sid Morrison (R) | 22 | 50 | 100 |
| 5th | Spokane | Thomas S. Foley (D)[4] | N.A. | N.A. | N.A. |
| 6th | Tacoma | Norman D. Dicks (D) | 83 | 4 | 30 |
| 7th | Seattle | James A. McDermott (D) | 94 | 0 | 10 |
| 8th | Seattle | Rodney Chandler (R) | 28 | 50 | 70 |
| **West Virginia** | | | | | |
| 1st | Wheeling | Alan B. Mollohan (D) | 61 | 21 | 90 |
| 2d | Morgantown | Harley O. Staggers, Jr. (D) | 72 | 13 | 20 |
| 3d | Charleston | Robert E. Wise, Jr. (D) | 72 | 13 | 33 |
| 4th | Huntington | Nick Joe Rahall II (D) | 78 | 13 | 11 |
| **Wisconsin** | | | | | |
| 1st | Kenosha | Les Aspin (D) | 61 | 8 | 38 |
| 2d | Madison | Scott L. Klug (R) | N.A. | N.A. | N.A. |
| 3d | Eau Claire | Steve Gunderson (R) | 33 | 63 | 100 |
| 4th | Milwaukee | Gerald D. Kleczka (D) | 89 | 17 | 10 |
| 5th | Wauwatosa | Jim Moody (D) | 94 | 14 | 20 |
| 6th | Oshkosh | Thomas E. Petri (R) | 22 | 75 | 50 |
| 7th | Wausau | David R. Obey (D) | 83 | 9 | 0 |
| 8th | Green Bay | Toby Roth (R) | 6 | 83 | 80 |
| 9th | Sheboygan | F. James Sensenbrenner, Jr. (R) | 6 | 83 | 60 |
| **Wyoming** | | | | | |
| 1st | At Large | Craig Thomas (R) | 11 | 79 | 100 |

**NON-VOTING REPRESENTATIVES**

| | |
|---|---|
| **American Samoa** | Delegate Eni F.H. Faleomavaega (D) |
| **Guam** | Delegate Ben Blaz (R) |
| **District of Columbia** | Delegate Eleanor Holmes Norton (D) |
| **Puerto Rico** | Resident Commissioner Jaime B. Fuster (D) |
| **Virgin Islands** | Delegate Ron de Lugo (D) |

**Note:** As of July 31. D = Democrat; DFL = Democratic-Farmer-Labor (Minn.); I = Independent; IR = Independent Republican (Minn.); R = Republican. 1. Americans for Democratic Action: based on 18 House votes in 1990. 2. American Conservative Union: based on 22 House votes in 1990. 3. National Security Index of the American Security Council: based on 10 House votes in 1990. 4. The Speaker of the House rarely votes. **Source:** Americans for Democratic Action; The American Conservative Union; American Security Council; Clerk of the U.S. House of Representatives.

# Judicial Branch

## SUPREME COURT OF THE UNITED STATES

United States Supreme Court Building; 1 First St. NE; Washington, DC 20543. (202) 479-3000. Created by Judiciary Act of Sept. 24, 1789, in accordance with Article III, Section 1 of Constitution. Composed of chief justice and a number of associate justices to be fixed by Congress. Justices (including the chief justice) are chosen by president with advice and consent of Senate and have lifetime tenure. Court terms begin first Monday of October and usu-ally last until end of June. The court deals with approximately 5,000 cases a year.

Jurisdiction of Supreme Court is outlined by Constitution in Article III, Section 2. In general, Supreme Court has original jurisdiction in cases in which a state or an ambassador is party; it has appellate jurisdiction in other federal cases involving the various states or in which U.S. is party.

### THE SUPREME COURT, 1991

| Name | Appointed by | Born | State | Law school |
|------|-------------|------|-------|-----------|
| William H. Rehnquist | Nixon, 1972 (justice) Reagan, 1986 (chief justice) | 1924 | Arizona | Stanford |
| Byron R. White | Kennedy, 1962 | 1917 | Colorado | Yale |
| Harry A. Blackmun | Nixon, 1970 | 1908 | Minnesota | Harvard |
| John Paul Stevens | Ford, 1975 | 1920 | Illinois | Northwestern |
| Sandra Day O'Connor | Reagan, 1981 | 1930 | Arizona | Stanford |
| Antonin Scalia | Reagan, 1986 | 1936 | Virginia | Harvard |
| Anthony M. Kennedy | Reagan, 1987 | 1936 | California | Harvard |
| David H. Souter | Bush, 1990 | 1939 | New Hampshire | Harvard |
| Clarence Thomas | Bush, 1991 | 1948 | Georgia | Yale |

## LOWER COURTS

**U.S. Courts of Appeals** These intermediate appellate courts were created by act of Mar. 3, 1981, to relieve Supreme Court of having to reconsider all trials originally decided by federal courts. Decisions of these courts are final except when law provides for direct review by the Supreme Court. Each of the 50 states is assigned to one of 12 judicial circuits that compose the court of appeals system.
**Circuit** District of Columbia
**Circuit Justice** William H. Rehnquist
**Circuit Judges** Abner J. Mikva (chief judge), Patricia M. Wald, Harry T. Edwards, Ruth B. Ginsburg, Laurence H. Silberman, James L. Buckley, Stephen F. Williams, Douglas Ginsburg, David Bryan Sentelle, Clarence Thomas, Karen L. Henderson, A. Raymond Randolph

**First Circuit** Districts of Maine, New Hampshire, Massachusetts, Rhode Island, and Puerto Rico
**Circuit Justice** David H. Souter
**Circuit Judges** Stephen G. Breyer (chief judge), Levin H. Campbell, Juan R. Torruella, Bruce M. Selya, Conrad K. Cyr (vacancy)

**Second Circuit** Districts of Vermont, Connecticut, northern New York, southern New York, eastern New York, and western New York
**Circuit Justice** Vacant
**Circuit Judges** James L. Oakes (chief judge), Thomas J. Meskill, Jon O. Newman, Amalya Lyle Kearse, Richard J. Cardamone, Ralph K. Winter, Jr., George C. Pratt, Roger J. Miner, Frank X. Altimari, J. Daniel Mahoney, John M. Walker, Jr., Joseph M. McLaughlin

**Third Circuit** Districts of New Jersey, eastern Pennsylvania, middle Pennsylvania, western Pennsylvania, Delaware, and the Virgin Islands
**Circuit Justice** David H. Souter
**Circuit Judges** Dolores Korman Sloviter (chief judge), Edward R. Becker, Walter K. Stapleton, Carol Los Mansmann, William D. Hutchinson, Robert E. Cowen, Morton I. Greenberg, Anthony J. Scirica, Richard Lowell Nygaard, Samuel A. Alito

**Fourth Circuit** Districts of Maryland, northern West Virginia, southern West Virginia, eastern Virginia, western Virginia, eastern North Carolina, middle North Carolina, western North Carolina, and South Carolina
**Circuit Justice** William H. Rehnquist
**Circuit Judges** Sam J. Ervin III (chief judge), Donald S. Russell, H. Emory Widener, Jr., Kenneth K. Hall, James Dickson Phillips, Jr., Francis D. Murnaghan, Jr., James M. Sprouse, Robert F. Chapman, James Harvie Wilkinson III, William W. Wilkins, Jr., Paul V. Nicmeyer

**Fifth Circuit** Districts of northern Mississippi, southern Mississippi, eastern Louisiana, middle Louisiana, western Louisiana, northern Texas, southern Texas, eastern Texas, and western Texas
**Circuit Justice** Antonin Scalia
**Circuit Judges** Charles Clark (chief judge), Thomas C. Gee, Henry A. Politz, Carolyn Dineen King, Samuel D. Johnson, Jr., William L. Garwood, E. Grady Jolly, Patrick E. Higginbotham, W. Eugene Davis, Edith H. Jones, Jerry Edwin Smith, John M. Duhe, Jr., Rhesa H. Barksdale, Jacques L. Wiener, Jr.

**Sixth Circuit** Districts of northern Ohio, southern Ohio, eastern Michigan, western Michigan, eastern Kentucky, western Kentucky, eastern Tennessee, middle Tennessee, and western Tennessee
**Circuit Justice** John Paul Stevens
**Circuit Judges** Gilbert S. Merritt (chief judge), Damon J. Keith, Cornelia G. Kennedy, Boyce F. Martin, Jr., Nathaniel R. Jones, Robert B. Krupansky, H. Ted Milburn, Ralph B. Guy, Jr., James L. Ryan, David A. Nelson, Danny J. Boggs, Alan E. Norris, Richard F. Suhrheinrich

**Seventh Circuit** Districts of northern Indiana, southern Indiana, northern Illinois, central Illinois, southern Illinois, eastern Wisconsin, and western Wisconsin
**Circuit Justice** John Paul Stevens
**Circuit Judges** William J. Bauer (chief judge), Walter J. Cummings, Harlington Wood, Jr., Richard D. Cudahy, Richard A. Posner, John L. Coffey, Joel M. Flaum, Kenneth F. Ripple, Frank H. Easterbrook, Daniel A. Manion, Michael S. Kanne

### HOW A CASE GETS TO THE SUPREME COURT

In both civil and criminal law, the United States Supreme Court is the ultimate court of appeal. All other remedies must be exhausted before petitioning the Court for appeal or review of a lower court decision. Cases originating in state courts can be appealed to the Court directly from state supreme courts; cases originating in federal court must go through the United States District Court and the United States Court of Appeals first. The Constitution limits the Court to original jurisdiction only in cases involving the United States or citizens of different states or foreign ambassadors or a state against a state. The Court itself decides whether to hear a case or let a decision stand. When the Court accepts a case, it grants a *writ of appeal*—or more often, a *writ of certiorari*—which announces the Court's intention to review a decision. Very rarely, the Court grants a *writ of certification* in response to a lower court's direct request for the Court's opinion. But in all cases, the Court will decline to review decisions lacking a "substantial federal question" at issue, which is what happens to the vast majority of cases brought before it. Yet the mounting backlog of cases awaiting the Court's attention periodically raises calls for easing the Court's work load by changing its review and appeal procedures, or even by adding another layer of appellate courts.

**Eighth Circuit** Districts of Minnesota, northern Iowa, southern Iowa, eastern Missouri, western Missouri, eastern Arkansas, western Arkansas, Nebraska, North Dakota, and South Dakota

**Circuit Justice** Harry A. Blackmun

**Circuit Judges** Donald P. Lay (chief judge), Theodore McMillian, Richard S. Arnold, John R. Gibson, George G. Fagg, Pasco M. Bowman II, Roger L. Wollman, Frank J. Magill, Clarence Arlen Beam, James B. Loken

**Ninth Circuit** Districts of northern California, eastern California, central California, southern California, Oregon, Nevada, Montana, eastern Washington, western Washington, Idaho, Arizona, Alaska, Hawaii, Territory of Guam, and District Court for the Northern Mariana Islands

**Circuit Justice** Sandra Day O'Connor

**Circuit Judges** J. Clifford Wallace (chief judge), James R. Browning, Proctor Hug, Jr., Thomas Tang, Mary M. Schroeder, Betty B. Fletcher, Jerome Farris, Harry Pregerson, Arthur L. Alarcon, Cecil F. Poole, Dorothy W. Nelson, William C. Canby, Jr., William A. Norris, Stephen A. Reinhardt, Robert B. Beezer, Cynthia Holcomb Hall, Charles E. Wiggins, Melvin Brunetti, Alex Kozinski, David R. Thompson, John T. Noonan, Jr., Diarmuid F. O'Scannlain, Edward Leavy, Stephen S. Trott, Ferdinand F. Fernandez, Pamela A. Rymer

**Tenth Circuit** Districts of Colorado, Wyoming, Utah, Kansas, eastern Oklahoma, western Oklahoma, northern Oklahoma, and New Mexico

**Circuit Justice** Byron R. White

**Circuit Judges** William J. Holloway, Jr. (chief judge), Monroe G. McKay, James K. Logan, Stephanie K. Seymour, John P. Moore, Stephen H. Anderson, Deanell Reece Tacha, Bobby R. Baldock, Wade Brorby, David M. Ebel

**Eleventh Circuit** Districts of northern Georgia, middle Georgia, southern Georgia, northern Florida, middle Florida, southern Florida, northern Alabama, middle Alabama, and southern Alabama

**Circuit Justice** Anthony M. Kennedy

**Circuit Judges** Gerald B. Tjoflat (chief judge), Peter T. Fay, Phyllis A. Kravitch, Frank M. Johnson, Jr., Joseph Woodrow Hatchett, R. Lanier Anderson III, Thomas A. Clark, J.L. Edmondson, Emmett Ripley Cox, Stanley F. Birch, Jr.

**U.S. Court of Appeals for the Federal Circuit** Established under Article III of Constitution pursuant to Federal Courts Improvement Act of 1982 to replace U.S. Court of Customs and Patent Appeals and Court of Claims. Has nationwide jurisdiction over patent, trademark, and copyright cases. Hears appeals from district and territorial courts in contract, internal revenue, and other cases in which U.S. is a defendant.

**Circuit Justice** William H. Rehnquist

**Circuit Judges** Helen W. Nies (chief judge), Howard T. Markey, Giles S. Rich, Glenn L. Archer, Jr., Pauline Newman, Haldane Robert Mayer, Paul R. Michel, S. Jay Plager, Alan D. Lourie, Raymond C. Clevenger III

**U.S. District Courts** These are trial courts of general federal jurisdiction. There are

## CASES BEFORE U.S. SUPREME COURT, U.S. COURTS OF APPEALS, AND U.S. DISTRICT COURTS, 1970–89

| Status | 1970 | 1975 | 1980 | 1985 | 1988 | 1989 |
|---|---|---|---|---|---|---|
| **U.S. Supreme Court[1]** | | | | | | |
| Total cases on docket | 4,212 | 4,761 | 5,144 | 5,158 | 5,657 | 4,980 |
| Cases argued | 151 | 179 | 154 | 171 | 170 | 144 |
| Number of signed opinions | 109 | 138 | 123 | 146 | 133 | 68 |
| **U.S. Courts of Appeals[2]** | | | | | | |
| Cases commenced | 11,662 | 16,658 | 23,200 | 33,360 | 37,524 | 38,734 |
| Cases terminated | 10,699 | 16,000 | 20,887 | 31,387 | 35,888 | 37,372 |
| Cases disposed of[3] | 6,139 | 9,077 | 10,607 | 16,369 | 19,178 | 19,322 |
| Median months to final disposition[4] | 8.2 | 7.4 | 8.9 | 10.3 | 10.1 | 10.3 |
| **U.S. District Courts[2]** | | | | | | |
| Civil cases commenced | 87,300[5] | 117,300[5] | 168,800[5] | 273,700[5] | 239,600[5] | 233,500[5] |
| Civil trials[6] | 9,449 | 11,603 | 13,191 | 14,254 | 12,536 | 12,085 |
| Jury trials | 3,371 | 3,700 | 3,937 | 5,437 | 5,448 | 5,207 |
| Criminal cases commenced[7] | 38,100 | 41,000 | 28,000 | 38,500 | 43,500 | 44,900 |
| Criminal trials[6] | 6,583 | 7,633 | 6,634 | 6,475 | 7,365 | 8,017 |
| Jury trials | 4,226 | 4,907 | 3,418 | 3,697 | 4,150 | 4,484 |

1. Statutory term of court begins first Monday in October. 2. For year ending June 30. 3. Terminated on the merits after hearing or submission. Beginning 1975, data not comparable with earlier years due to changes in criteria. 4. Prior to 1985, the figure is from filing of complete record to final disposition; beginning 1985, figure is from filing notice of appeal to final disposition. 5. Figures rounded in source. 6. A trial is defined as a contested proceeding (other than a hearing on a motion) before either court or jury in which evidence is introduced and final judgment sought. 7. Excludes transfers. **Sources**: Office of the Clerk, Supreme Court of the United States, unpublished data; Administrative Office of the U.S. Courts, *Annual Report of the Director*.

89 courts, including at least one in each state and the District of Columbia. Each has from 2 to 27 federal district judgeships. Overall, there are 541 permanent district judges in the 50 states, 15 in the District of Columbia, and 7 in Puerto Rico. Usually one judge is required to decide a case, but in some cases it is required that three judges be called together to compose the court.

**Territorial Courts** Estab. pursuant to Article IV, Section 3 of the Constitution. In Guam and the Virgin Islands these have jurisdiction not only over the subjects described in the judicial article of the Constitution but also over many local matters that, within the states, are decided by state courts.

**Judicial Panel on Multidistrict Legislation** Created Apr. 29, 1968, this body of seven judges is authorized to temporarily transfer civil actions pending in different districts and involving common questions of fact to a single district for coordinated or consolidated pretrial proceedings.

## Special Courts

The power to create special courts is vested in Congress in part by Article III of the Constitution and in part by Supreme Court decree. Appeals from these special courts may be taken to the U.S. Court of Appeals for the Federal Circuit.

**Temporary Emergency Court of Appeals** Estab. by Economic Stabilization Act Amendments of 1971. Has exclusive jurisdiction over all appeals from district courts arising from economic stabilization and energy conservation laws.

**U.S. Claims Court** Estab. Oct. 1, 1982, to replace the Court of Claims. Composed of 16 judges appointed for 15-year terms by president with advice and consent of Senate. President designates chief judge; has jurisdiction over monetary claims against the United States based on the Constitution or acts of Congress.

**U.S. Court of International Trade** Estab. June 10, 1890 as Board of United States General Appraisers. Has jurisdiction over civil actions against the U.S. involving federal laws governing imports.

**U.S. Court of Military Appeals** Estab. May 5, 1950. Serves as final court of appeal to review court-martial convictions for all the armed services. Subject only to certiorari review by the Supreme Court in a limited number of cases.

**U.S. Court of Veterans Appeals** Estab. Nov. 18, 1988. Exclusive jurisdiction to review decisions of the Board of Veterans Appeal.

**Administrative Office of the U.S. Courts** Washington, DC 20544. Created by act of Aug. 7, 1939. Its areas of primary concern are administering courts, supervising probation offices, and overseeing administration of bankruptcy courts, magistrate offices, and public defender's offices.

**Federal Judicial Center** Dolley Madison House, 1520 H St. NW, Washington, DC 20005. (202) 633-6011. Created by act of Dec. 20, 1967. Conducts research, develops improvement of personnel and data systems, and recommends improvements in administration and management.

# Executive Branch

## EXECUTIVE OFFICE OF THE PRESIDENT

**White House Office** 1600 Pennsylvania Ave. NW, Washington, DC 20500. (202) 456-1414. Serves president in performance of duties incident to his office. Maintains communication with Congress, individual members of Congress, heads of executive agencies, media, and public.

**Council of Economic Advisers** Old Executive Office Building, Washington, DC 20500. (202) 395-5084. Created by Employment Act of 1946. Council's three members—appointed by president—analyze the various segments of the economy, appraise and assess existing economic programs, recommend new economic programs, and assist in preparation of president's economic reports to Congress.

**Council on Environmental Quality** 722 Jackson Place NW, Washington, DC 20503. (202) 395-5750. Created by National Environmental Policy Act of 1969. Recommends national policies to improve quality of environment. Analyzes environmental changes and trends. Assesses and evaluates existing environmental programs. Assists president in compiling annual environmental quality report to Congress.

**National Critical Materials Council** 725 17th St. NW, Washington, DC 20506. (202) 395-7200. Estab. by National Critical Materials Act of 1984. Advises president on policies related to maintaining sufficient supplies of strategic minerals and materials for national security, economic well-being, and industrial productivity.

**National Security Council (NSC)** Old Executive Office Building, Washington, DC 20506. (202) 395-4974. Created by National Security Act of 1947. Chaired by president. Members include vice president and secretaries of state and defense. Chairman of Joint Chiefs of Staff is statutory military adviser; CIA director is intelligence adviser. Advises president on integration of domestic, foreign, and military policies relating to national security.

**Office of Administration** 725 17th St., Washington, DC 20503. (202) 395-6963. Created Dec. 12, 1977, by Reorganization Plan No. 1. Provides administrative services to all units within executive office except those in direct support of president.

**Office of Management and Budget (OMB)** Executive Office Building, Washington, DC 20503. (202) 395-3080. Created July 1, 1970, by Reorganization Plan No. 2 of 1970. Assists president in reviewing and assessing efficiency of structure and management of executive branch. Expands interagency cooperation. Assists president in preparing government's budget and fiscal program. Supervises, controls, and administers budget. Coordinates departmental advice and makes recommendations to president based on this advice. Plans, conducts, and promotes evaluation efforts to help president assess program objectives, performance, and efficiency. Keeps president informed of work planned and performed by the various government agencies.

**Office of National Drug Control Policy** Executive Office of the President, Washington, DC 20500. (202) 673-2520. Estab. by National Narcotics Leadership Act of 1988, effective Jan. 29, 1989. Coordinates federal, state, and local efforts to control illegal drug abuse and devises national strategies to ensure that national antidrug activities are carried out effectively.

**Office of Policy Development (OPD)** 1600 Pennsylvania Ave. NW, Washington, DC 20500. (202) 456-1414. Created in 1981 to replace Domestic Policy Staff (estab. Mar. 26, 1978). Advises and assists president in formulating, evaluating, and coordinating long-range economic and domestic public policy.

**Office of Science and Technology Policy** New Executive Office Building, Washington, DC 20506. (202) 395-7347. Created May 11, 1976, by National Science and Technology Policy, Organization, and Priorities Act of 1976. Serves as source of scientific, engineering, and technological analysis and expertise for president with respect to public policy in areas of economy, national security, health, foreign relations, and environment. Appraises sale, quality, and effectiveness of U.S. efforts in science and technology.

**Office of the U.S. Trade Representative** 600 17th St. NW, Washington, DC 20506. (202) 395-3230. Created as Office of the Special Representative for Trade Negotiations by Executive Order 11075 of Jan. 15, 1963. Congress made it agency of executive office under Trade Act of 1974. Administers trade agreements program of Tariff Act of 1930, Trade Expansion Act of 1962, and Trade Act of 1974. Sets and administers overall trade policy. Representative is chief representative of U.S. for all activities of General Agreement on Tariffs and Trade (GATT) and at discussions, meetings, and negotiations in most conferences in which trade and commodity are issues.

**Office of the Vice President of the United States** Old Executive Office Building, Washington, DC 20501. (202) 456-2326. Vice president participates in cabinet meetings and is, by statute, a member of National Security Council and board of regents of the Smithsonian Institution; serves as president of Senate; empowered to succeed to presidency pursuant to Article II and the 20th and 25th amendments to the Constitution.

## The Cabinet

The president is the administrative head of the executive branch of the federal government. A creation of custom and tradition dating back to George Washington's administration, the cabinet functions at the pleasure of the president. Its purpose is to advise the president on any subject on which he requests information. The cabinet is composed of the heads of the 14 executive departments and certain other executive officials to whom the president accords cabinet rank. The Office of Management and Budget and the Office of the U.S. Trade Representative have cabinet rank in the Bush administration. The vice president also participates regularly in cabinet meetings.

| Department | Cabinet officer |
|---|---|
| State | James Addison Baker III |
| Treasury | Nicholas F. Brady |
| Defense | Richard B. Cheney |
| Justice | William P. Bell (acting) |
| Interior | Manuel Lujan, Jr. |
| Agriculture | Edward Madigan |
| Commerce | Robert Adam Mosbacher |
| Labor | Lynn Martin |
| Health and Human Services | Louis W. Sullivan |
| Housing and Urban Development | Jack Kemp |
| Transportation | Samuel Knox Skinner |
| Energy | James D. Watkins |
| Education | Lamar Alexander |
| Veterans Affairs | Edward J. Derwinski |
| Office of Management and Budget | Richard G. Darman, director |
| U.S. Trade Representative | Carla Anderson Hills |

## EXECUTIVE DEPARTMENTS

**Department of Agriculture (USDA)** 14th St. and Independence Ave. SW, Washington, DC 20250. (202) 447-2791. Created by act of May 15, 1862. Works to improve farms and farm income, expand foreign markets for U.S. agriculture, and curb poverty, hunger, and malnutrition. Helps maintain natural resources such as soil, water, and forests. Maintains food quality standards through inspection and grading. Among the most important of its services are the following:

**Agricultural Marketing Service** Estab. Apr. 2, 1972. Administers standardization, grading, and classing of more than 600 agricultural commodities. Provides inspection, market news, and research, promotion, and regulatory programs.

**Agricultural Stabilization and Conservation Service** Estab. June 5, 1961. Administers commodity and related land-use programs designed for voluntary production adjustment, resource protection, and price, market, and farm income stabilization.

**Commodity Credit Corporation** Estab. July 1, 1948 (first organized 1933). Stabilizes, supports, and protects farm income and prices; assists in maintaining balanced and adequate supplies of agricultural commodities and their products, and facilitates orderly distribution of commodities.

**Extension Service** Created 1914. As part of Cooperative Extension System—with land-grant universities, Tuskegee University, and 3,150 local county offices—links research, science, and technology to farmers' needs. Assists in science and technology transfer; mitigation of natural disasters and catastrophes.

**Farmers Home Administration (FHA)** Estab. by Consolidated Farm and Rural Development Act of 1921. Provides loans for farm and home ownership, natural resource conservation, farm improvement, and other needs for those unable to get credit from other sources at reasonable rates and terms.

**Forest Service** Created Feb. 1, 1905. Provides sustained flow of renewable resources to meet current and future needs. Manages 156 national forests, 19 national grasslands, 15 land utilization projects on 191 million acres in 44 states, the Virgin Islands, and Puerto Rico. Some 32 million acres are set aside as wilderness, and 175,000 acres as primitive areas where timber will not be harvested.

**Rural Electrification Administration** Estab. May 11, 1935, by executive order. Credit agency that helps obtain financing through loans, loan guarantees, or other assistance for construction, expansion, or improvement; has provided 1,000 rural electric and 1,000 rural telephone utilities in 47 states and in U.S. territories.

**Soil Conservation Service** Estab. 1935. Develops and implements soil and water conservation programs. Assists in agricultural pollution control, environmental improvement, and rural community development.

## Department of Commerce

14th St. between Constitution Ave. and E St. NW, Washington, DC 20230. (202) 377-2000. Created Feb. 14, 1903, as part of Department of Commerce and Labor. Redesignated Department of Commerce by act of Mar. 4, 1913. Promotes international trade, economic growth, and technological advancement through encouragement of competitive free-enterprise system, prevention of unfair trade, granting of patents, economic promotion of domestic development, research in telecommunications, promotion of tourism, and assistance in growth of minority businesses. Department is divided into 12 operating units.

**National Technical Information Service (NTIS)** Clearinghouse for sale of government-sponsored research, development, and engineering reports. Its library exceeds 1.5 million titles.

**Bureau of the Census** Estab. Mar. 6, 1902, by act of Congress. Collects, tabulates, and publishes census statistics about America, its people, and its economy. Statistics are used by Congress, president, and public to aid development and evaluation of public policy. Population and housing censuses are performed every 10 years. Censuses of agriculture, state and local governments, manufacturers, mineral industries, distributive trades, and construction and transportation industries are performed every five years. Special censuses are performed on demand from state and local governments.

**Bureau of Economic Analysis (BEA)** Estab. Dec. 1, 1953, by secretary of commerce. Prepares diagnoses of health of economy through compilation and assessment of economic indicators.

**Bureau of Export Administration (BXA)** Estab. Oct. 1, 1987, by secretary of commerce. Licenses exporters, advises on matters of economic export regulations, and enforces U.S. export control laws.

**Economic Development Administration (EDA)** Estab. by Public Works and Economic Development Act of 1965. Promotes new jobs, protects existing jobs, and stimulates job growth in areas where unemployment is high or incomes are low. Programs are carried out through sponsorship of industrial parks, water and sewer lines, and airport developments; loan guarantees to industrial and commercial firms; planning grants to states, cities, districts, and Indian reservations; technical assistance for existing firms; planning grants; and emergency aid to communities to avoid long-term economic deterioration.

**International Trade Administration (ITA)** Estab. Jan. 2, 1980. Promotes world trade and strengthens U.S. position in relation to world trade and investment.

**Minority Business Development Agency (MBDA)** Estab. Nov. 1, 1979. Promotes minority business. Ensures effective, equitable, and competitive participation by minority business in free enterprise system.

**National Institute of Standards and Technology** Estab. by act of Mar. 3, 1901, as National Bureau of Standards; redesignated by Omnibus Trade and Competitiveness Act of 1988. Nonregulatory agency. Performs scientific research for specific purpose of aiding U.S. industry and science. Its four areas of primary research are engineering, physical and chemical measurements, materials science, and computer sciences. Through this research, the Institute increases U.S. productivity and innovation in world scientific market.

**National Oceanic and Atmospheric Administration (NOAA)** Estab. Oct. 3, 1970. Investigates and maps oceans of world. Discovers, utilizes, and conserves living resources of oceans. Monitors and predicts conditions of atmosphere, sun, and oceans; warns against deterioration of these conditions arising from natural and man-made events and circumstances. Provides weather reports and forecasts. Forecasts floods, hurricanes, and other weather-related natural disasters.

**National Telecommunications and Information Administration (NTIA)** Estab. Mar. 27, 1978. Fosters development and use of telecommunication and information services.

**Patent and Trademark Office (PTO)** Estab. by Congress in Article I, Section 8 of Constitution. Promotes incentives to invent and make inventions public through granting of exclusive patents. Issues more than 75,000 patents and 55,000 trademarks every year. Patents are of three kinds: design, plant, and utility.

**United States Travel and Tourism Administration (USTTA)** Estab. 1981 by National Tourism Policy Act of 1981. Ensures fullest utilization of U.S. tourism resources. Expands tourism where possible. Stimulates demand abroad for tourism in U.S.

## Department of Defense (DOD)

The Pentagon, Washington, DC 20301-1155. (703) 545-6700. Created by National Security Act Amendments of 1949. Provides necessary military forces to deter war and protect security of the country. Advises president on matters of war and military security. Includes 14 defense agencies, various field organizations, 5 colleges, 4 institutes, and 2 universities, as well as other offices in addition to those listed below. (See also "The National Defense.")

**Organization of the Joint Chiefs of Staff** Consists of chairman of Joint Chiefs of Staff; chief of staff of U.S. Army; chief of naval operations; chief of staff of U.S. Air Force; and commandant of Marine Corps. Advises and assists president and secretary of defense on most military issues. Assists president and secretary of defense in planning, direction, and allocation of strategic resources. Compares strengths and capabilities of American forces with those of potential adversaries.

**Department of the Air Force** Estab. Sept. 18, 1947, by National Security Act of 1947. Works in conjunction with other armed forces to protect peace and security of the U.S. Focuses on air missions and protecting American interests from invasion by air.

**Department of the Army** U.S. Army estab. June 14, 1775, by Continental Congress. Dept. of the Army estab. 1947 by National Security Act of 1947. Organizes, trains, and equips active and reserve forces to protect peace, security, welfare, and defense of U.S. Works in conjunction with other armed forces. Its mission focuses on land operations and maneuvers.

**Department of the Navy** U.S. Navy estab. Oct. 13, 1775, by Continental Congress. Dept. of the Navy estab. by act of April 30, 1798. Protects U.S. from attack by sea. Encompasses Marine Corps. Maintains freedom of the seas. Seizes or defends naval bases. Supports and works together with other armed forces.

## Department of Education

400 Maryland Ave. SW, Washington, DC 20202. (202) 708-5366. Created Oct. 17, 1979, by Department of Education Organization Act. Establishes policy for, administers, and coordinates almost all federal assistance to education. Department's budget includes funding for four corporations:

**American Printing House for the Blind** Distributes Braille books, books on tape, and educational aids for the blind.

**Gallaudet University** Provides college education for deaf who need special facilities. Encourages further education and study by its students.

**Howard University** Has special responsibility for admission and education of black students.

**National Technical Institute for the Deaf (NTID)** (Rochester Institute of Technology) Educates large numbers of deaf students within university designed for hearing students. Helps deaf students adapt to and join mainstream American hearing society.

## Department of Energy (DOE)

1000 Independence Ave. SW, Washington, DC 20585. (202) 586-5000. Created Aug. 4, 1977, by Department of Energy Organization Act. Coordinates and administrates energy functions of federal government, including research and development of energy technology, marketing federal power, energy conservation, nuclear weapons, and energy regulation. Three administrations are included under its aegis.

**Energy Information Administration (EIA)** Collects, processes, and publishes statistics and information regarding energy resources, energy production, consumption, demand, distribution, and technology. Performs analyses of these data to help users understand energy trends and their impact.

**Economic Regulatory Administration (ERA)** Administers all regulatory programs not administered by Federal Energy Regulatory Commission.

**Federal Energy Regulatory Commission** Sets rates for sale and transport of oil, natural gas, and electricity. Sets rates for and licenses hydroelectric power plants.

## Department of Health and Human Services (HHS) 200 Independence Ave.

SW, Washington, DC 20201. (202) 619-0257. Created Apr. 11, 1953, as Department of Health, Education, and Welfare. Redesignated Department of Health and Human Services Oct. 17, 1979, by Department of Education Organization Act. Advises president in formulation of public policy regarding health, welfare, and income and security programs. Department is divided into five operating administrations.

**Office of Human Development Services (HDS)** Advises secretary of HHS on human-development services and human-service programs. Provides leadership in planning and developing HDS programs. Supervises use of research funds. Controls equal employment opportunity and civil rights policies and programs.

**Public Health Service (PHS)** Estab. by Public Health Service Act of July 1, 1944. Promotes national physical and mental health. Coordinates national health policy between and among the states. Conducts medical research. Sponsors research for improved health care, disease prevention and control, and alcohol and drug abuse prevention. Enforces laws to assure safety and efficiency of foods, drugs, cosmetics, and medical devices. Encompasses *National Institute of Mental Health, Centers for Disease Control, Food and Drug Administration,* and *National Institutes of Health,* among others.

**Health Care Financing Administration (HCFA)** Estab. Mar. 8, 1977. Oversees Medicare and Medicaid health insurance and grant programs. (See also "Key Government Functions.")

**Social Security Administration (SSA)** Estab. July 16, 1946, by Federal Security Agency Reorganization Plan II of 1946. Administers national social insurance program known as Social Security. (See also "Key Government Functions.")

**Family Support Administration (FSA)** Advises secretary of HHS on programs to aid children and low-income families. Coordinates Work Incentive Program (WIN) with Department of Labor and directs Office of Child Support Enforcement.

## Department of Housing and Urban Development (HUD) 451 Seventh St.

SW, Washington, DC 20410. (202) 708-1422. Created Nov. 9, 1965, by Department of Housing and Urban Development Act. Administers mortgage programs to help families become home owners. Fosters construction of new housing and renovation of existing rental housing. Provides aid for low-income families who cannot afford their rent. Enacts programs to prevent housing discrimination. Encourages strong private-sector housing industry. Department's program areas are considered neither bureaus nor administrations. They include Community Planning and Development, Fair Housing and Equal Opportunity Housing, Public and Indian Housing, Government National Mortgage Association, and Policy Development and Research. The field operations of HUD are carried out through a series of regional and field offices. Regional offices are located in Boston, New York, Philadelphia, Atlanta, Chicago, Fort Worth, Kansas City, Denver, San Francisco, and Seattle.

## Department of the Interior 1849 C St.

NW, Washington, DC 20240. (202) 208-3171. Created by act of Mar. 3, 1849. Principal U.S. conservation agency. Directs use and conservation of public lands and natural resources; administers over 500 million acres of federal land and has trust responsibilities for approximately 50 million acres, mostly Indian reservations. Prescribes use of land and water resources, fish and wildlife, national parks and historic places, and mineral resources; aids in preservation of American Indian reservation communities. There are nine service bureaus.

**United States Fish and Wildlife Service** Conserves and protects fish and wildlife and their habitats. Assesses environmental impact of pesticides, thermal pollution, hydroelectric dams, and nuclear power sites.

**National Park Service** Estab. by act of Aug. 25, 1916. Administers, protects, and maintains diverse system of national parks, monuments, historic areas, and recreation areas and encourages understanding of the historic value of these sites through lectures, tours, exhibits, and films. Operates campgrounds, concessions, and transportation services.

**Bureau of Mines** Estab. July 1, 1910, by Organic Act of May 16, 1910. Ensures that U.S. has enough nonfuel minerals for security. Attempts to replace imported minerals with domestic ones. Seeks to suppress pollution, increase mine safety, and encourage recycling.

**Office of Surface Mining Reclamation and Enforcement (OSMRE)** Estab. by Surface Mining Control and Reclamation Act of 1977. Protects society from adverse effects of coal mining. Ensures continuing surface coal mining without permanent damage to land and water resources.

**Geological Survey** Estab. by act of Mar. 3, 1879. Identifies and classifies land, water, energy, and mineral resources. Investigates potential hazards such as earthquakes and volcanoes. Conducts topographic mapping.

**Bureau of Indian Affairs** Estab. 1824 as part of Department of War. Transferred to Department of Interior in 1849. Trains American Indian and Alaska native peoples to manage their own affairs under trust relationship to

federal government. Facilitates public and private aid to advancement of these peoples.

**Minerals Management Service (MMS)** Estab. Jan. 19, 1982, by Secretarial Order No. 3071. Assesses nature, extent, value, and recoverability of leasable minerals on outer continental shelf. Collects royalties on use of these minerals.

**Bureau of Land Management (BLM)** Estab. July 16, 1946, by consolidation of the General Land Office and the Grazing Service. Manages 270 million acres of public lands primarily in Far West and in Alaska. Resources in these lands include timber, oil, gas, hard minerals, and wildlife habitats.

**Bureau of Reclamation** Estab. 1902 as Reclamation Service, within U.S. Geological Survey, by Reclamation Act of 1902. Renamed Bureau of Reclamation in 1923. Provides year-round water and irrigation supply for towns, farms, and industries in western states. Generates hydroelectric power, regulates rivers and flood control, and enhances fish and wildlife habitats.

## Department of Justice Constitution

Avenue and 10th St. NW, Washington, DC 20530. (202) 514-2007. Created by act of June 22, 1870. Enforces the law in the public interest. Ensures fair competition in free enterprise system; enforces drug, immigration, and naturalization laws; aids in law enforcement, crime prevention, crime detection, and prosecution and rehabilitation of criminals. Conducts all Supreme Court suits in which U.S. is party or is concerned. Advises president on legal matters. Encompassed in department's authority are seven bureaus.

**Federal Bureau of Investigation (FBI)** Estab. 1908. Principal investigative bureau of Justice Department. Investigates violations of federal law. Areas of primary concern are organized crime (including drug-trafficking), terrorism, white-collar crime, and foreign counterintelligence. Gathers and reports facts, locates witnesses, and compiles evidence in federal cases.

**Bureau of Prisons** Imprisons and rehabilitates criminals convicted of federal crimes and sentenced to serve time in federal prison.

**United States Marshals Service** Provides security and support to federal court system. Apprehends federal fugitives. Ensures safety of federal witnesses. Executes court orders and arrest warrants. Maintains custody, manages, and sells property seized from criminals.

**International Criminal Police Organization (INTERPOL)** Estab. in 1923. Promotes international cooperation in prevention and suppression of international crime.

**Immigration and Naturalization Service (INS)** Estab. by act of Mar. 3, 1891. Controls immigration into U.S. by facilitating entry to qualified persons and denying admission to unqualified aliens. Deports illegal aliens already in U.S. Encourages and facilitates naturalization and citizenship.

**Drug Enforcement Administration (DEA)** Estab. July 1973. Investigates interstate drug-trafficking. Enforces government regulations regarding manufacture, distribution, sale, and dispensing of controlled substances; manages national narcotics intelligence system; performs research, training, and information exchange to foster drug traffic prevention and control.

**Office of Justice Programs (OJP)** Estab. by Justice Assistance Act of 1984. Fosters cooperation and coordination among the various arms of criminal justice system to create more effective justice.

## Department of Labor
200 Constitution Ave. NW, Washington, DC 20210. (202) 523–8165. Created by act of Mar. 4, 1913. Improves welfare and working conditions of wage earners. Guarantees minimum wages and overtime pay as well as unemployment insurance and workers' compensation. Prevents employment discrimination. Protects pension rights. Provides for job training programs. Strengthens collective bargaining. Helps workers find jobs. Pays special attention to labor-related needs of minority workers, old and young, women, and disabled people. Department has nine administrations and bureaus.

**Employment and Training Administration (ETA)** Provides employment security through unemployment insurance, worker dislocation programs, and federal-state employment service system. Trains or retrains and finds employment for disadvantaged workers through Job Training Partnership Act (JTPA).

**Office of Labor-Management Standards (OLMS)** Estab. May 3, 1984. Regulates union procedures. Protects rights of members in 48,000 unions. Areas of concern include handling of union funds, reporting of unions' financial transactions and administrative practices, and election of union officers.

**Pension and Welfare Benefits Administration (PWBA)** Estab. Sept. 2, 1974, by Employment Retirement Income Security Act of 1974. Requires private pension and welfare plan administrators to give participants summaries of pension and welfare plans. Keeps summaries on file. Regulates financial operations of pension and welfare plans.

**Bureau of Labor-Management Relations and Cooperative Programs (BLMRCP)** Provides information and technical assistance to employers, unions, and other organizations for purpose of improving labor relations. This goal is achieved through sponsoring conferences, publishing special reports, preparing training materials, and reviewing economic efficiency of and adherence to collective-bargaining relationships.

**Employment Standards Administration** Administers and directs programs dealing with minimum wage and overtime requirements, wages for government-sponsored work, affirmative action, and workers' compensation.

**Occupational Safety and Health Administration (OSHA)** Estab. 1970 by Occupational Safety and Health Act. Promotes safety and health standards in work place. Issues regulations, conducts investigations, issues citations, and proposes penalties for violations of health standards and regulations.

**Mine Safety and Health Administration (MSHA)** Estab. 1977 by Federal Mine Safety and Health Amendments Act of 1977. Responsible for all mine safety and health regulations.

Issues regulations, investigates violations, assesses penalties for noncompliance, and in coordination with Department of Health and Human Services, improves mine safety and health research.

**Bureau of Labor Statistics (BLS)** Data-gathering agency. Collects, processes, interprets, and distributes data involving employment, unemployment, wages, family income and expenditures, workers' compensation, industrial relations, productivity, and technological change.

**Veterans' Employment and Training Service (VETS)** Maximizes training and employment opportunities for veterans and disabled. Ensures that legislation involving veterans is carried out by local public employment services and by private enterprise.

## Department of State
2201 C St. NW, Washington, DC 20520. (202) 647–4000. Created by act of July 27, 1789, as Department of Foreign Affairs. Renamed Department of State by act of Sept. 15, 1789. Advises president on foreign policy. Formulates and executes policy to protect and defend American interests overseas. Negotiates treaties and agreements with foreign countries.

**United States Mission to the United Nations** Represents U.S. at UN. Carries out U.S. foreign policy as it relates to UN.

**Foreign Service** Maintains relations with more than 140 nations around world. Reports to State Department on developments relating to safety and welfare of U.S., its citizens, and their interests. Ambassadors to each country are personal representatives of the president and have full responsibility for carrying out U.S. foreign policy within the country. Ambassadors negotiate agreements between host country and U.S., explain and administer U.S. foreign policy, and maintain relations with government and public of host country.

## Department of Transportation (DOT)
400 Seventh St. SW, Washington, DC 20590. (202) 366-4000. Created by act of Oct. 15, 1966. Establishes nation's comprehensive transportation policy. Its nine umbrella administrations are responsible for highway planning, development, and construction; urban mass transit; railroads; aviation; and the safety of waterways, ports, highways, and oil and gas pipelines. Decisions made in conjunction with state and local authorities have strong bearing on land planning, energy conservation, and resource utilization policies.

**United States Coast Guard** Estab. by act of Jan. 28, 1915. Included in Dept. of Transportation Apr. 1, 1967. Coast Guard is at all times a branch of armed forces and a service with Dept. of Transportation except when operating as part of navy during war. Primary maritime law enforcement agency for U.S. Suppresses drug smuggling and trafficking. Licenses marine vessels. Administers and inspects violations of safety standards for design, construction, equipment, and maintenance of commercial marine vessels and offshore structures in U.S. waters. Provides search and rescue functions for saving lives and property in U.S. waters. Provides flood relief and removes hazards to navigation. Enforces rules ensuring safe and

orderly navigation through ports, waterways, and bridges. Operates ice-breaking vessels to facilitate marine transportation. Provides military and reserve training.

**Federal Aviation Administration (FAA)** Estab. 1958 by Federal Aviation Act. Included in Dept. of Transportation in 1967 by Dept. of Transportation Act. Regulates air commerce in effort to promote safety and secure national defense interests. Directs use of navigable U.S. airspace. Promotes and encourages civil aeronautics. Installs and operates air-navigation facilities. Develops and operates system of air traffic control for both civil and military aircraft. Regulates aircraft noise and other environmental effects of civil aviation.

**Federal Highway Administration (FHWA)** Included in Dept. of Transportation in 1967 by Dept. of Transportation Act. Promotes highway safety. Provides aid for construction and maintenance of state and federal highway systems. Facilitates and provides aid for safety improvements to state and federal highway systems. Helps states formulate agreed-upon size and weight regulations for trucks and commercial traffic. Administers highway planning and beautification programs.

**Federal Railroad Administration (FRA)** Estab. 1966 by section 3(e)(1) of Dept. of Transportation Act of 1966. Administers and enforces railroad safety regulations such as track maintenance, inspection and equipment standards, and operating practices. Maintains research and development programs and Transportation Test Center to foster further safety and efficiency of rail travel.

**National Highway Traffic Safety Administration** Estab. 1970 by Highway Safety Act of 1970. Promotes highway safety through various programs. These include enforcing a uniform and nationwide speed limit, administering laws to prevent odometer tampering, issuing theft prevention standards, setting average fuel-economy and air-pollution standards for motor vehicles, and enforcing inspection standards. Research and development programs are aimed at reducing number of highway collisions, reducing severity of injuries and economic loss involved in highway accidents, and reducing fatalities resulting from highway crashes.

**Urban Mass Transportation Administration (UMTA)** Estab. July 1, 1968, by Reorganization Plan No. 2 of 1968, Section 3. Improves equipment and methods used in urban mass transit. Encourages planning of cost-effective mass transit systems. Provides economic and technical assistance for mass transit programs. Encourages private sector involvement in local mass-transit systems.

**Maritime Administration (MARAD)** Estab. May 24, 1950, by Reorganization Plan No. 21 of 1950. Included in Dept. of Transportation Aug. 6, 1981, by Maritime Act of 1981. Constructs or supervises construction of U.S.-flag merchant ships for federal government. Generates business for U.S. ships. Develops ports and facilities for maritime transport. Promotes domestic shipping. Provides economic and technical aid to private shipbuilding. Regulates sales of ships.

**Saint Lawrence Seaway Development Corporation** Estab. by act of May 13, 1954. Owns, develops, maintains, and operates St. Lawrence Seaway between Montreal and Lake Erie within territorial limits of U.S. Provides safe and efficient waterway for maritime commerce. Charges user tolls and encourages traffic. Operates in coordination with Canadian owners, St. Lawrence Seaway Authority of Canada.

**Research and Special Programs Administration (RSPA)** Estab. Sept. 23, 1977; reorganized 1985. Its six umbrella organizations regulate transportation of hazardous materials; enforce safety standards for pipeline transportation of liquid and gaseous materials involved in or affecting interstate commerce; maintain information and research offices devoted to transportation, safety, and economics of aviation; and prepare emergency transportation programs.

**Department of the Treasury** 1500 Pennsylvania Ave. NW, Washington, DC 20220. (202) 566–2000. Created by act of Sept. 2, 1789. Formulates and recommends economic, financial, tax, and fiscal policies. Acts as financial agent for U.S. government. Enforces the law. Manufactures coins and currency. Department is divided into 12 bureaus, offices, and administrations.

**Bureau of Alcohol, Tobacco and Firearms** Estab. July 1, 1972, by Treasury Dept. Order No. 221. Enforces and administers laws regulating production, use, distribution, and sale of alcohol and tobacco products, firearms, and explosives. Bureau's objectives are to eliminate illegal trafficking, possession, and use of firearms and explosives, to suppress illegal alcohol and tobacco trafficking, and to ensure safety of storage facilities for explosives.

**Office of the Comptroller of the Currency** Estab. by act of Feb. 25, 1863. Issues and executes laws regulating national banks. Inspects, examines, and issues official approvals of national banks, their operations, and their financial soundness.

**United States Customs Service** Estab. Mar. 3, 1927, as Bureau of Customs. Redesignated Customs Service Apr. 4, 1973, by Treasury Dept. Order 165–23. Collects revenue from imports. Enforces customs treaties. Assesses and collects customs duties, excise taxes, fees, and penalties on imported merchandise. Seizes contraband including narcotics and illegal drugs. Processes people, mail, carriers, and cargo in and out of U.S. Apprehends violators of U.S. customs regulations and related laws including copyright, patent, and trademark, and import quotas. Intercepts high-technology exports to Soviet-bloc countries. Suppresses traffic of illegal narcotics, pornography, counterfeit monetary instruments, and quarantined animals, plants, and foods.

**Bureau of Engraving and Printing** Estab. by act of July 11, 1862. Designs, prints, and finishes Federal Reserve notes, U.S. postage stamps, identification cards, and Treasury securities. Inhibits counterfeiting of these documents.

**Federal Law Enforcement Training Center** Estab. Mar. 2, 1970, by Treasury Dept. Order 217. Teaches basic law-enforcement skills to police and investigators. Also teaches courses in white-collar crime, computer crime, law-enforcement photography, contract fraud, and marine law enforcement.

**Financial Management Service** Manages money of federal government. Improves cash management, credit management, and debt collection and payment programs. Invests social security and other trust funds. Serves as government's central accounting system. Publishes daily, monthly, and quarterly reports of government's financial operations and status.

**Internal Revenue Service (IRS)** Estab. by act of July 1, 1862. Administers and enforces internal revenue laws except those relating to alcohol, tobacco, firearms, and explosives. Determines, assesses, and collects federal tax revenues from public. Encourages, assesses, and enforces compliance with tax laws.

**United States Mint** Mint of the United States estab. by act of April 2, 1792. Bureau of the Mint estab. Feb. 12, 1873. Renamed United States Mint Jan. 9, 1984, by Secretarial Order. Manufactures and distributes coins for circulation through Federal Reserve Banks. Mints foreign coins. Processes gold and silver bullion. Manufactures national medals, proof coin sets, and commemorative coins for sale to public.

**Bureau of the Public Debt** Estab. June 30, 1940, by Reorganization Act of 1939. Manages public debt. Offers public-debt securities. Audits retired securities and interest coupons. Maintains accounting control over public-debt receipts and expenditures, securities, and interest costs. Adjudicates claims of lost, stolen, or destroyed securities.

**United States Savings Bonds Division** Estab. Dec. 26, 1945, by Treasury Order. Promotes sale and retention of U.S. Savings Bonds. Encourages support and understanding of Savings Bonds program.

**United States Secret Service** Protects president and vice president (and president-elect and vice president-elect) of U.S. and their families. Protects former presidents and their wives until their death. Protects distinguished foreign visitors and U.S. officials abroad at direction of president. Detects and apprehends counterfeiters. Suppresses forgery of government securities and documents. Provides security at White House complex, vice president's residence, and various foreign diplomatic missions or embassies as directed by president.

**Office of Thrift Supervision (OTS)** 1700 G St. NW, Washington, DC 20552. (202) 906-6913. Estab. by the Financial Institutions Reform, Recovery and Enforcement Act, Aug. 9, 1989. Established by Congress as part of a reorganization of the thrift regulatory structure, the OTS has authority to charter federal thrift institutions, and to serve as the primary regulator of the approximately 2,600 federal and state chartered thrifts belonging to the Savings Association Insurance Fund (SAIF).

**Department of Veterans Affairs** 810 Vermont Ave. NW, Washington, DC 20420. (202) 233-2300. Estab. by Department of Veterans Affairs Act of 1988; predecessor Veterans Administration created 1930. Administers benefit programs for veterans and their families, including military-related death or disability compensation, pensions, education and rehabilitation, home loan guaranty, and medical care programs.

**Veterans Health Services and Research Administration** Provides hospital, nursing home, and domiciliary care and outpatient care to eligible veterans. Operates 172 medical centers, 16 domiciliaries, 226 outpatient clinics, 106 nursing home care units, and 194 Vietnam Veteran Outreach Centers.

**Veterans Benefit Administration** Has responsibility for claims for disability compensation and pension, specially adapted housing and automobiles, special clothing allowances, and emergency officers' retirement pay, survivors' claims for death compensation, dependency and indemnity compensation, burial and plot allowance claims, and reimbursement for headstones.

**Vocational Rehabilitation and Education Service** Responsible for readjustment of veterans of post-Korean and Vietnam era; educational assistance for veterans and members of selected reserve, and for spouses, surviving spouses, and children of veterans who are permanently and totally disabled or die from disability incurred or aggravated in active service, or who are POWs or MIA.

**National Cemetery System** Provides services and monuments for graves of veterans, their spouses, and eligible dependents in 112 national, state, and private veterans' cemeteries and aid to states for establishment and improvement of veterans' cemeteries. Cemeteries are designated national shrines.

## INDEPENDENT ESTABLISHMENTS, CORPORATIONS, AND QUASI-OFFICIAL AGENCIES

**ACTION** 1100 Vermont Ave. NW, Washington, DC 20525. (202) 634-9380. Created July 1, 1971, by Reorganization Plan No. 1 of 1971. Encourages and mobilizes Americans to perform voluntary services and programs for low-income individuals and communities. Identifies and appraises new volunteer grants and programs. Develops volunteer service opportunities for widest possible range of Americans. Included in its programs are Volunteers in Service to America (VISTA), Foster Grandparents Program (FGP), and Retired Senior Volunteer Program (RSVP).

**Administrative Conference of the United States** 2120 L Street NW, Washington, DC 20037. (202) 254-7020. Created in 1964 by Administrative Conference Act. Develops improvements in federal administration of government programs. Agency heads meet with lawyers, university professors, and other experts to exchange ideas, share experiences and judgments, and conduct studies at this forum.

**African Development Foundation** Suite 600, 1625 Massachusetts Ave. NW, Washington, DC 20036. (202) 673-3916. Created in 1984 by African Development Foundation Act. Nonprofit government corporation. Through grants, loans, and loan guarantees, aids self-help efforts by poor people in African countries. Fosters stronger bonds between Africa and U.S. Stimulates and assists expansion and development by Africans in their respective nations.

**American Battle Monuments Commission** 20 Massachusetts Ave. NW, Washington, DC 20314. (202) 272-0533. Created by act of Mar. 4, 1923. Designs, constructs, and maintains federal military cemeteries and memorial sites in the U.S. and abroad.

**AMTRAK (National Railroad Passenger Corporation)** 60 Massachusetts Ave. NE, Washington, DC 20002. (202) 906-3000. Created by Rail Passenger Service Act of 1970. Develops, operates, and improves intercity rail passenger service to create national rail transportation system.

**Appalachian Regional Commission (ARC)** 1666 Connecticut Ave. NW, Washington, DC 20235. (202) 673-7893. Created by Appalachian Regional Development Act of 1965. Federal-state government agency concerned with economic, physical, and social development of 13-state Appalachian region (includes parts of Ala., Ga., Ky., Md., Miss., N.Y., N.C., Ohio, Pa., S.C., Tenn., and Va., and all of W.Va.). Provides aid to counties; constructs Appalachian Development Highway System and local access roads to stimulate industrial and commercial growth and to provide access to community facilities; strengthens local governments to create jobs and industry.

**Board for International Broadcasting** Suite 400, 1201 Connecticut Ave. NW, Washington, DC 20036. (202) 254-8040. Created by Board for International Broadcasting Act of 1973. Oversees content and operations of Radio Liberty and Radio Free Europe.

**Central Intelligence Agency (CIA)** Washington, DC 20505. (703) 482-1100. Created by National Security Act of 1947. Under direction of president and National Security Council. Advises NSC on intelligence matters of national security. Collects, evaluates, and disseminates intelligence information relating to national security and to drug production and trafficking. Collects, produces, and disseminates counterintelligence and foreign intelligence here (in conjunction with FBI) and abroad. Conducts special activities as directed by president. Protects security of its activities, information, and personnel by necessary and appropriate means.

**Commission on the Bicentennial of the United States Constitution** 808 17th St. NW, Washington, DC 20006. (202) USA-1787. Created Sept. 29, 1983, by act of Congress. Continues through 1991. Promotes, coordinates, and develops events and activities commemorating the 200th anniversary of adoption of Constitution on Sept. 17, 1787.

**Commission on Civil Rights (CCR)** 1121 Vermont Ave. NW, Washington, DC 20425. (202) 376-8312; for deaf and hearing impaired (202) 376-8116. Created by Civil Rights Act of 1957. Holds public hearings and collects and studies information on discrimination or denial of equal protection based on race, color, religion, sex, age, handicap, or national origin. Studies in particular fair enforcement of civil rights laws and guarantee of voting rights and equal opportunity in education, employment, and housing.

**Commission of Fine Arts** 708 Jackson Place NW, Washington, DC 20006. (202) 566-1066. Created May 17, 1910, by act of Congress. Advises president, members of Congress, and other governmental agencies on matters pertaining to plans for public buildings, parks, and other architectural elements of Washington, DC

**Commodity Futures Trading Commission (CFTC)** 2033 K St. NW, Washington, DC 20581. (202) 254-8630. Created May 14, 1973, by Commodity Futures Act of 1973. Regulates trading on the 11 U.S. futures exchanges. Regulates activities of commodity exchange members, public brokerage houses, commodity trading advisers, and other related employees. Ensures fair futures trading. Protects rights of customers and financial integrity of marketplace.

**Consumer Product Safety Commission (CPSC)** 5401 Westbard Ave., Bethesda, MD 20207. (301) 492-6580. Created May 14, 1973, by Consumer Product Safety Act. Protects public from unreasonable risk of injury from consumer products. Develops, enforces, and evaluates safety standards for consumer products.

**Defense Nuclear Facilities Board** Ste. 675, 600 E St. NW, Washington, DC 20004. (202) 376-5083. Created Sept. 29, 1988, by Atomic Energy Act of 1954 as amended. Reviews and evaluates content and implementation of standards relating to design, construction, operation, and decommissioning of defense nuclear facilities of the Dept. of Energy.

**Environmental Protection Agency (EPA)** 401 M St. SW, Washington, DC 20460. (202) 382-4361. Created Dec. 2, 1970, by Reorganization Plan No. 3 of 1970. Protects and enhances environment. Controls and reduces pollution of air and water. Regulates solid-waste disposal and use of pesticides, radiation, and toxic substances.

**Equal Employment Opportunity Commission (EEOC)** 1801 L St. NW, Washington, DC 20507. (202) 663-4900; (800) USA-EEOC. Created July 2, 1965, by Title VII of Civil Rights Act of 1964. Protects against discrimination based on race, color, handicap, religion, sex, age, and national origin in hiring, promoting, firing, wages, testing, training, apprenticeship, and all other terms and conditions of employment.

**Export-Import Bank of the United States** 811 Vermont Ave. NW, Washington, DC 20571. (202) 566-8990. Created Feb. 2, 1934, by Executive Order 6581. Facilitates and aids exports of U.S. goods and services through loans, loan guarantees, and insurance to exporters and private banks.

**Farm Credit Administration** 1501 Farm Credit Drive, McLean, VA 22102-5090. (703) 883-4056. Created by Farm Credit Act of 1971. Regulates and examines programs, banks, associations, and organizations of the Farm Credit System, which provides credit to farmers, ranchers, producers of farm products, rural home-owners, and associations and organizations of farmers, ranchers, and farm-equipment producers.

**Federal Communications Commission (FCC)** 1919 M Street NW, Washington, DC 20554.

(202) 632-7000. Created by Communications Act of 1934. Regulates interstate and foreign communications by radio, television, wire, and cable. Oversees development of broadcast services and rapid and efficient provision of telephone and telegraph services nationwide.

**Federal Deposit Insurance Corporation (FDIC)** 550 17th St. NW, Washington, DC 20429. (202) 898-6996. Created June 16, 1933, by Federal Reserve Act. Protects money supply by insuring deposits in and reviewing operations of state-chartered banks that are not members of Federal Reserve System. Assumed responsibility for insuring savings and loan institutions formerly insured by defunct Federal Savings and Loan Insurance Corp. (FSLIC) in 1989.

**Federal Election Commission (FEC)** 999 E St. NW, Washington, DC 20463. (202) 376-3120; (800) 424-9530. Created by Federal Election Campaign Act of 1971. Provides public funding for presidential elections. Ensures public disclosure of campaign finance activities. Administers and enforces contribution and spending limits for federal elections. (See also "U.S. Presidential Elections.")

**Federal Emergency Management Agency (FEMA)** 500 C St. SW, Washington, DC 20472. (202) 646-4600. Created Mar. 31, 1979, by Reorganization Plan No. 3 of 1978. Provides single point of accountability for all federal emergency preparedness, mitigation, and response activities. Facilitates most efficient use of resources in cases of natural or man-made emergencies.

**Federal Housing Finance Board** 1777 F St. NW, Washington, DC 20006. (202) 408-2576. Created Aug. 9, 1989, by Financial Institutions Reform, Recovery, and Enforcement Act of 1989. Succeeds Federal Home Loan Bank Board; administers and enforces Federal Home Loan Bank Act as amended.

**Federal Labor Relations Authority (FLRA)** 500 C St. SW, Washington, DC 20424. (202) 382-0711. Created Jan. 1, 1979, by Reorganization Plan No. 2 of 1978. Protects rights of federal employees to organize, bargain collectively, and participate in labor organizations. Oversees rights and obligations of federal employees and labor organizations that represent them.

**Federal Maritime Commission** 1100 L St. NW, Washington, DC 20573-0001. (202) 523-5725. Created Aug. 12, 1961, by Reorganization Plan No. 7 of 1961. Regulates foreign and domestic maritime offshore commerce. Keeps U.S. international trade open and fair to all nations. Protects against unauthorized activity in U.S. waterborne commerce.

**Federal Mediation and Conciliation Service** 2100 K St. NW, Washington, DC 20427. (202) 653-5290. Created in 1947 by Labor Management Relations Act. Promotes development of stable labor-management relations. Prevents or minimizes work stoppages by helping to settle disputes and by advocating collective bargaining, mediation, and arbitration.

**Federal Mine Safety and Health Review Commission** 1730 K St. NW, Washington, DC 20006. (202) 653-5625. Estab. by Federal Mine Safety and Health Amendments Act of 1977. Quasi-judicial agency that decides cases brought by

Mine Safety and Health Board, mine operators, and miners.

**Federal Reserve System** Board of Governors of Federal Reserve System. 20th St. and Constitution Ave. NW, Washington, DC 20551. (202) 452-3204 or 452-3215. Created Dec. 23, 1913, by Federal Reserve Act. Central bank of U.S. Administers and creates national credit and monetary policy. Regulates money supply. Maintains soundness of banking industry.

**Federal Retirement Thrift Investment Board** 805 15th St. NW, Washington, DC 20005. (202) 523-5660. Created by Federal Employees' Retirement System Act of 1986. Administers Thrift Savings Plan for federal employees.

**Federal Trade Commission (FTC)** Pennsylvania Ave. at Sixth St. NW, Washington, DC 205890. (202) 326-180. Created in 1914 by Federal Trade Commission Act and Clayton Act. Maintains free and fiar competition in free enterprise system. Breaks up monopolies. Seeks to prevent corruption, restraints on trade, and unfair trade practices.

**General Services Administration (GSA)** General Service Building, 18th and F Sts. NW, Washington, DC 20405, (202) 501-0705; (202) 566-0705. Created July 1, 1949 by Federal Property and Administrative Services Act of 1949. Establishes policy for and manages government property and records, construction of buildings, distrubiton of supplies, and other government services. Its services are divided among four service agencies.

*Information Resources Management Services (IRMS)* Coordinates and manages government's information distribution systems and programs. Facilitates use of automated data processing and telecommunications equipment, improves federal records and information, and manages and operates Federal Information Centers.

*Federal Supply Service (FSS)* Contracts and distributes supplies, services, and property to federal agencies worldwide.

*Public Buildings Service (PBS)* Oversees design, building, appraisal, repair, operation, and maintenance of most federally controlled buildings.

*Federal Property Resources Service (FPRS)* Utilizes and disposes of government-owned real estate. Acquires, sells, and manages National Defense Stockpile of strategic and critical materials.

**Inter-American Foundation** 1515 Wilson Boulevard, Rosslyn, VA 22209. (703) 841-3810. Created by Congressin 1969. Supports social and economic development in Latin America and Caribbean. Makes grants to self-help organizations for the poor.

**Interstate Commerce Commission (ICC)** 12th St. and Constitution Ave. NW, Washington, DC 20423. (202) 275-7119. Created by act of Feb. 4, 1887. Regulates interstate transportation involved in commerce. Certifies interstate carriers. Ensures fair rates and services to public.

**Legal Services Corporation** 400 Virginia Ave. SW, Washington, DC 20024-2751. (202) 863-1820. Created by Legal Services Act of 1974. Makes legal assistance for noncriminal proceedings available to those who would otherwise be unable to afford it.

**Merit Systems Protection Board (MSPB)** 1120 Vermont Ave. NW, Washington, DC 20419

(202) 653-7124. Created Jan. 1, 1979, to succeed United States Civil Service Commission (estab. Jan. 16, 1883). Oversees personnel practices of government. Hears and decides charges of wrongdoing and orders corrective and disciplinary action against agencies when necessary. (See also "Office of Special Counsel.")

**National Aeronautics and Space Administration (NASA)** 600 Independence Ave. SW, Washington, DC 20546. (202) 453-1000. Created by National Aeronautics and Space Act of 1958. Develops, constructs, tests, and operates vehicles for in-flight research within and outside Earth's atmosphere. Disseminates information about space exploration and agency's activities.

**National Archives and Records Administration (NARA)** Seventh St. and Pennsylvania Ave. NW, Washington, DC 20408. (202) 501-5400. Created by act of Oct. 19, 1984. Establishes policy for managing records of U.S. government and making them available to public. Maintains 11 regional archives and 14 federal records centers, as well as 11 presidential libraries or collections.

**National Capital Planning Commission (NCPC)** 1325 G St. NW, Washington, DC 20576. (202) 724-0206. Created by National Capital Planning Act of 1952. Coordinates planning and development activities in National Capital region, which includes Washington DC, Montgomery and Prince Georges counties in Maryland, and Fairfax, Loudon, Prince William, and Arlington counties in Virginia.

**National Credit Union Administration (NCUA)** 1776 G St. NW, Washington, DC 20456. (202) 682-9650. Created by act of Mar. 10, 1970. Charters, insures, supervises, and examines federal credit unions. Administers National Credit Union Share Insurance Fund. Supplies emergency loans to credit unions through Central Liquidity Facility. Credit unions are financial cooperatives that encourage thrift and provide credit at reasonable rates to their members.

**National Foundation on the Arts and the Humanities** 1100 Pennsylvania Ave. NW, Washington, DC 20506. (202) 682-5400. Created by National Foundation on the Arts and the Humanities Act of 1965. Its three divisions encourage and support national progress in humanities and arts.

*National Endowment for the Arts (NEA)* 1100 Pennsylvania Ave. NW, Washington, DC 20506. (202) 682-5400. Fosters professional excellence in arts. Creates climate for arts to flourish and be appreciated, experienced, and enjoyed by the public.

*National Endowment for the Humanities (NEH)* 1100 Pennsylvania Ave. NW, Washington, DC 20506. (202) 786-0438. Independent grant-making agency supports research, education, and public programs in humanities.

*Institute of Museum Services (IMS)* Room 510, 1100 Pennsylvania Ave. NW, Washington, DC 20506. (202) 786-0539. Independent grant-making agency assists museums in maintaining, increasing, and improving services to the public.

**National Labor Relations Board (NLRB)** 1717 Pennsylvania Ave. NW, Washington, DC 20570. (202) 632-4950. Created by National

Labor Relations Act of 1935 (also known as Wagner Act). Administers federal labor law. Safeguards employees' rights to organize, conducts elections to determine whether workers want unions as their bargaining representative, and prevents or remedies unfair labor practices.

**National Mediation Board** 1425 K St. NW, Washington, DC 20572. (202) 523-5920. Created June 21, 1934, by amendment to Railway Labor Act. Resolves and investigates representation disputes in railroad and airline industries that could interrupt flow of commerce and endanger national economy. These disputes include grievances over wages, hours, and working conditions. Supervises representation disputes in the two industries.

**National Science Foundation (NSF)** 1800 G St. NW, Washington, DC 20550. (202) 357-9498. Created by National Science Foundation Act of 1950. Promotes progress of science and engineering through support of research and education programs. Educational programs are designed to facilitate increased understanding of science and engineering and to ensure adequate supply of scientists for country's needs.

**National Transportation Safety Board (NTSB)** 800 Independence Ave. SW, Washington, DC 20594. (202) 382-6600. Created Apr. 1, 1975, by Independent Safety Board Act of 1974. Ensures safe operation of all types of transportation in U.S. Investigates accidents, conducts studies, and makes policy recommendations to government agencies, transportation industry, and others on ways to implement and improve safety measures and programs.

**Nuclear Regulatory Commission (NRC)** 1717 H St. NW, Washington, DC 20555. (301) 492-0240. Created by Energy Reorganization Act of 1974. Licenses and regulates uses of civilian nuclear energy to protect public health and environment. Sets licensing regulations, issues licenses for, and inspects construction, ownership, and operation of nuclear reactors and other nuclear materials.

**Occupational Safety and Health Review Commission (OSHRC)** 1825 K St. NW, Washington, DC 20006. (202) 634-7943. Created by Occupational Safety and Health Act of 1970. Adjudicates disputes forwarded by Department of Labor over results of safety and health inspections performed by Occupational Safety and Health Administration (OSHA). Serves as court of both first and last resort for health and safety violations in workplace.

**Office of Government Ethics** Ste. 500, 1201 New York Ave. NW, Washington, DC 20005-3917. (202) 523-5757. Created Oct. 1, 1989, by Ethics in Government Act of 1978, as amended. Provides overall direction for executive branch policies to prevent conflicts of interest on the part of officers and employees of all executive agencies.

**Office of Personnel Management (OPM)** 1900 E St. NW, Washington, DC 20415. (202) 606-1800. Created Jan. 1, 1979, by Reorganization Plan No. 2 of 1978. Recruits, examines, trains, and promotes people for government jobs, regardless of race, religion, sex, political influence, and other nonmerit factors. Provides direct benefits to employees and to retired employees and their survivors.

**Office of Special Counsel** 1120 Vermont Ave. NW, Washington, DC 20005. (202) 653–7188; (800) 872–9855. Investigates allegations of personnel practice violations by federal, state, and local employees; prosecutes individuals who violate civil service rules and regulations before the Merit Systems Protection Board.

**Oversight Board** Ste. 600, 1777 F St. NW, Washington, DC 20232. (202) 786–9672. Estab. by the Federal Home Bank Act amendments of Aug. 9, 1989. Responsible for general oversight of the Resolution Trust Corporation (RTC) and the Resolution Funding Corporation (REFCORP). Develops and establishes strategies, policies, and goals for the RTC's activities; also reviews the RTC's performance relative to approved budget plans pursuant to the terms of the Financial Institutions Reform, Recovery and Enforcement Act.

**Panama Canal Commission** Room 550, 2000 L St. NW, Washington, DC 20036. (202) 634–6441. Created by Panama Canal Act of 1979. Operates, maintains, and improves the Panama Canal to provide safe and economical transit for world shipping. Will perform these functions until expiration of Panama Canal Treaty of 1979 on Dec. 31, 1999, when Republic of Panama will assume full responsibility for canal.

**Peace Corps** 1990 K St. NW, Washington, DC 20526. (202) 606–3010. Created by Peace Corps Act of 1961. Promotes world peace and friendship. Helps people of other countries develop manpower. Promotes understanding of American people by people abroad and vice versa. Special emphasis placed on helping poorest areas of countries served by the Peace Corps.

**Pennsylvania Avenue Development Corporation (PADC)** Suite 1220 North, 1331 Pennsylvania Ave. NW, Washington, DC 20004–1703. (202) 724–9073. Created by act of Oct. 27, 1972. Guides and oversees development and revitalization of Pennsylvania Avenue between White House and Capitol and adjacent blocks north of the avenue.

**Pension Benefit Guaranty Corporation (PBGC)** 2020 K St. NW, Washington, DC 20006. (202) 778–8800. Created Sept. 2, 1974, by Title IV of Employee Retirement Income Security Act of 1974. Guarantees payment of nonforfeitable pension benefits in covered private-sector defined benefit pension plans.

**Postal Rate Commission** 1333 H St. NW, Washington, DC 20268–0001. (202) 789–6840. Created Aug. 12, 1970, by Postal Reorganization Act. Recommends changes in postal rates, fees, services, programs, studies, and mail classification schedules. Hears complaints about postal rates, services, and fees.

**Railroad Retirement Board** 844 Rush St., Chicago, IL 60611. (312) 751–4930. Created by Railroad Retirement Act of 1935. Administers retirement-survivor and unemployment-sickness benefit programs for railroad workers and their families under Railroad Retirement and Railroad Unemployment Insurance Acts.

**Resolution Trust Corporation (RTC)** 801 17th St. NW, Washington, DC 20434. (202) 416–7557. Estab. by the Financial Institutions Reform, Recovery and Enforcement Act, Aug. 9, 1989. The RTC is a federally chartered corporation the sole purpose of which is to

contain, manage, and resolve failed savings associations acquired from the defunct Federal Savings and Loan Insurance Corporation (FSLIC)—or new insolvencies acquired from the Office of Thrift Supervision (OTS)—and to recover funds through the management and ultimate sale of the institutions' assets.

**Securities and Exchange Commission (SEC)** 450 Fifth St. NW, Washington, DC 20549. (202) 272–3100. Created July 2, 1934, by Securities Exchange Act of 1934. Provides fullest possible disclosure to the public of securities sales, operations, and registrations. Protects public against malpractice in securities and financial markets.

**Selective Service System** National Headquarters, Washington, DC 20435. (202) 621–5388. Created June 24, 1948, by Military Selective Service Act. Requires registration, and maintains list of males age 18–26 eligible to serve in armed forces in case of national security emergency.

**Small Business Administration (SBA)** Imperial Building, 1441 L St. NW, Washington, DC 20416. (202) 653–6365 (personnel locator); (202) 653–7561 (answer desk); (800) 368–5855 (toll-free); (202) 653–7557 (fraud-waste). Created by Small Business Act of 1953. Aids, counsels, makes loans to, and protects interests of small businesses; ensures that they receive fair amount of government purchases and contracts and sales of government property.

**Smithsonian Institution** 1000 Jefferson Drive SW, Washington, DC 20560. (202) 357–2700. Created by act of Aug. 10, 1846. Performs fundamental research; publishes results of studies, explorations, and investigations; preserves for study and research more than 100 million items of scientific, cultural, and historical interest. Maintains exhibits representative of arts, American history, technology, aeronautics, and natural history. Many institutions and museums are under direction of Smithsonian. Most prominent are Arthur M. Sackler Gallery (Cambridge, Mass.), Cooper-Hewitt Museum of Design (New York City), National Air and Space Museum, National Zoological Park, Smithsonian Astrophysical Laboratories, National Gallery of Art, and John F. Kennedy Center for the Performing Arts (Washington, DC).

**State Justice Institute** 120 South Fairfax St., Alexandria, VA 22314. (703) 684–6100. Created by State Justice Institute Act of 1984. Directs and ensures protection of fair and effective judicial system, fosters cooperation with federal judiciary, and disseminates information regarding state judicial systems.

**Tennessee Valley Authority (TVA)** 400 West Summit Hill Dr., Knoxville, TN 37902–2003. (615) 632–2101. Capitol Hill Office Building, 412 First St. SE, Washington, DC 20444. (202) 479–4412. Created by act of May 18, 1933. Government-owned corporation. Conducts resource development programs for advancement of growth in Tennessee Valley region. Controls floods, develops navigation, produces electric power, develops fertilizer, improves recreation, and develops forestry and wildlife.

**United States Arms Control and Disarmament Agency (ACDA)** 320 21st St. NW, Washington, DC 20451. (202) 647–8677. Created by act of

Sept. 26, 1961. Formulates and implements arms control and disarmament policies to promote security and foreign relations. Prepares and participates in negotiations on strategic arms limitations, mutual force reductions in central Europe, chemical weapons, worldwide arms trade, and other issues.

**United States Information Agency (USIA)** 301 Fourth St. SW, Washington, DC 20547. (202) 619–4355. Created by United States Information and Educational Exchange Act of 1948 and Mutual Educational and Cultural Exchange Act of 1961. Oversees and administers overseas information and cultural programs, including Voice of America and Fulbright scholarship program. Strengthens foreign understanding of American society and tries to obtain support abroad for U.S. foreign policies. Advises president and National Security Council on worldwide opinion of U.S. policies.

**United States Institute of Peace** 1550 M St. NW, Washington, DC 20005–1708. (202) 457–1700. Created by act of Oct. 19, 1984. Develops and disseminates knowledge about peaceful resolution of international conflicts. Provides grants to other institutions promoting peace through development and dissemination of information.

**United States International Development Cooperation Agency (IDCA)** 320 21st St. NW, Washington, DC 20523–0001. (202) 663–1449. Created Oct. 1, 1979, by Reorganization Plan No. 2 of 1979. Plans, sets, and coordinates policy relevant to international economic issues affecting developing countries. Ensures that development goals are considered in all executive-branch policies regarding trade, financing and monetary affairs, technology, and other economic issues. It is divided into three umbrella agencies.

*Agency for International Development (AID)* Carries out economic assistance and self-help programs for people in developing countries. Improves human and natural resources, quality of life, and political and economic stability.

*Overseas Private Investment Corporation (OPIC)* Facilitates, fosters, and encourages U.S. investments in more than 100 foreign countries that both reap profits for investors and help social and economic development of the countries.

*Trade and Development Program (TDP)* Created July 1, 1980. Promotes economic development. Exports U.S. goods and services to Third World countries. Finances studies for development projects for Third World countries.

**United States International Trade Commission** 500 E St. SW, Washington, DC 20436. (202) 252–1000. Created by act of Sept. 8, 1916. Furnishes studies, reports, and recommendations regarding international trade and tariffs to president, Congress, and other government agencies. Conducts investigations, public hearings, and research projects pertaining to U.S. international economic policies.

**United States Postal Service** 475 L'Enfant Plaza SW, Washington, DC 20260–0010. (202) 268–2143. Created Aug. 12, 1970, by Postal Reorganization Act. Provides mail-processing and delivery service to individuals and businesses in U.S. Protects mail from loss or theft and apprehends violators of postal laws.

# Federal Employees and Budget

## FEDERAL JOBS AND SALARIES

As of Mar. 31, 1990, there were 2,034,846 full-time nonpostal federal civilian employees. Nearly 96% of the federal civilian work force was employed in the United States; 10,841 (0.5%) worked in U.S. territories, and 71,073 (3.5%) worked in foreign countries. Among the states, California had the largest number of government employees (210,276, or 10.3%) and Vermont the fewest (2,557, or 0.1%). The majority of government employees—1,716,711, or 84.4%—worked in metropolitan statistical areas, led by the Washington, D.C., MSA, with 294,466, or 14.5% of the total. The next largest MSAs by government employment were Philadelphia, Pa.-N.J., with 50,739, and Norfolk–Virginia Beach–Portsmouth, Va., with 50,168.

Only four executive departments accounted for more than 70% of the federal civilian work force: Defense (983,962, or 48.4% of the total), Veterans Affairs (203,397, or 10.0%), the Treasury (157,648, or 7.7%), and Health and Human Services (108,400, or 5.3%). The largest percentage increase over 1989 occurred in the Federal Deposit Insurance Corporation, up 66% from 7,895 to 13,039, reflecting in part the assimilation of employees of the defunct Federal Home Loan Bank Board.

Federal government civilian employees are paid according to a number of different systems—the General Schedule (GS), Federal Wage Systems, and other acts and administratively determined systems. Overall, the average salary for full-time civilian government employees was $31,174, a 5.3% increase from the previous year primarily due to a 3.6% "pay comparability increase" effective January 1990, and increases in the number of special pay-rate authorizations. Average salaries by major geographic areas were: United States, $31,191; Washington, D.C., area, $38,927; foreign countries, $31,674; and U.S. territories, $26,177.

### White-collar Employees

**General Schedule** The General Schedule covers 1,505,748 (74.0%) government workers. There are 18 grades broadly defined in terms of responsibility, difficulty, and qualifications. Within each grade there are steps (10 each for GS grades 1–15, nine for GS-16, five for GS-17, and one for GS-18). Within-grade advancement occurs on a fixed schedule, though employees demonstrating "high-quality performance" can receive "quality step increases."

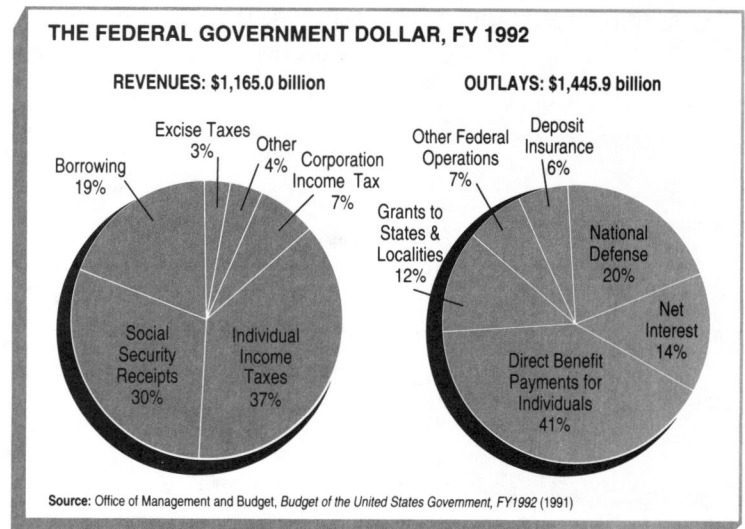

THE FEDERAL GOVERNMENT DOLLAR, FY 1992

REVENUES: $1,165.0 billion

Excise Taxes 3%
Other 4%
Borrowing 19%
Corporation Income Tax 7%
Social Security Receipts 30%
Individual Income Taxes 37%

OUTLAYS: $1,445.9 billion

Other Federal Operations 7%
Deposit Insurance 6%
Grants to States & Localities 12%
National Defense 20%
Net Interest 14%
Direct Benefit Payments for Individuals 41%

**Source:** Office of Management and Budget, *Budget of the United States Government, FY1992* (1991)

## FEDERAL GOVERNMENT OUTLAYS, BY BRANCH AND AGENCY, 1989–92 (millions of dollars)

| Agency | Actual 1989 | Actual 1990 | Estimated 1991 | Estimated 1992 |
|---|---|---|---|---|
| Legislative branch | $ 2,095 | $ 2,230 | $ 2,548 | $ 2,994 |
| Judicial branch | 1,492 | 1,641 | 2,056 | 2,341 |
| Executive branch: | | | | |
| Executive Office of the President | 124 | 157 | 258 | 254 |
| Funds appropriated to the president | 4,280 | 10,087 | 11,254 | 12,044 |
| Dept. of Agriculture | 48,316 | 46,012 | 55,432 | 55,691 |
| Dept. of Commerce | 2,571 | 3,734 | 2,796 | 2,756 |
| Dept. of Defense (military functions) | 294,880 | 287,755 | 287,451 | 283,045 |
| Dept. of Defense (civil functions) | 23,450 | 24,975 | 26,415 | 28,231 |
| Dept. of Education | 21,608 | 23,109 | 24,839 | 27,494 |
| Dept. of Energy | 11,387 | 12,014 | 13,539 | 14,897 |
| Dept. of Health and Human Services (except Social Security) | 172,301 | 193,678 | 222,435 | 242,543 |
| Social Security | 227,473 | 244,998 | 263,837 | 282,785 |
| Dept. of Housing and Urban Development | 19,680 | 20,167 | 23,473 | 24,297 |
| Dept. of the Interior | 5,213 | 5,796 | 6,386 | 6,475 |
| Dept. of Justice | 6,232 | 6,507 | 8,689 | 10,042 |
| Dept. of Labor | 22,654 | 25,316 | 34,503 | 34,759 |
| Dept. of State | 3,722 | 3,979 | 4,306 | 4,509 |
| Dept. of Transportation | 26,607 | 28,637 | 30,768 | 31,862 |
| Dept. of the Treasury | 230,571 | 255,266 | 277,047 | 298,581 |
| Dept. of Veterans Affairs | 30,041 | 28,998 | 31,338 | 32,815 |
| Environmental Protection Agency | 4,906 | 5,108 | 5,776 | 5,896 |
| General Services Administration | −463 | −123 | 756 | 719 |
| National Aeronautics and Space Administration | 11,036 | 12,429 | 13,499 | 14,721 |
| Office of Personnel Management | 29,073 | 31,949 | 35,161 | 37,046 |
| Small Business Administration | 85 | 692 | 529 | 318 |
| Other independent agencies | 33,890 | 73,617 | 125,708 | 102,108 |
| Undistributed offsetting receipts | −89,155 | −99,025 | −109,436 | −118,029 |
| On-budget | (−72,903) | (−77,467) | (−83,445) | (−88,065) |
| Off-budget[1] | (−16,252) | (−21,558) | (−25,991) | (−29,964) |
| **Total outlays** | **$1,144,069** | **$1,251,703** | **$1,409,563** | **$1,445,902** |

**Note:** Outlays are the measure of government spending—payments to liquidate obligations (other than the repayment of debt), net of cash, and offsetting collections. Outlays are generally recorded on a cash basis, but also include many cash-equivalent transactions and interest accrued on public issues of the public debt. 1. The off-budget federal entities consist of the two social security trust funds, old-age and survivors insurance (OASI) and disability insurance (DI), and the Postal Service fund. **Source:** Office of Management and Budget, *Budget of the United States Government, FY 1992* (1991).

## FEDERAL GOVERNMENT PAY SYSTEMS, 1990

| Grade | Employees | Mean salary |
|---|---|---|
| **GENERAL SCHEDULE** | | |
| GS-1 | 921 | $ 10,947 |
| GS-2 | 6,603 | 12,564 |
| GS-3 | 44,523 | 14,284 |
| GS-4 | 140,077 | 16,453 |
| GS-5 | 193,018 | 18,699 |
| GS-6 | 103,033 | 21,075 |
| GS-7 | 146,823 | 23,005 |
| GS-8 | 32,040 | 26,160 |
| GS-9 | 157,679 | 27,793 |
| GS-10 | 29,238 | 31,892 |
| GS-11 | 196,320 | 33,812 |
| GS-12 | 208,574 | 40,801 |
| GS-13 | 138,266 | 49,003 |
| GS-14 | 73,140 | 58,363 |
| GS-15 | 34,787 | 70,316 |
| GS-16 | 572 | 77,605 |
| GS-17 | 88 | 78,200 |
| GS-18 | 46 | 78,200 |
| Total | 1,505,748 | $31,239 |
| **EXECUTIVE SCHEDULE[1]** | | |
| Level I | 35 | $107,300 |
| Level II | 254 | 96,600 |
| Level III | 81 | 89,000 |
| Level IV | 30 | 83,600 |
| Level V | 16 | 78,200 |
| Total | 416 | $86,065 |

**Note**: As of Mar. 31. 1. As of Feb. 1, 1990. **Source**: U.S. Office of Personnel Management, *Pay Structure of the Federal Civil Service* (1990).

## U.S. FEDERAL EMPLOYMENT, 1988–90

| Description | 1988 | 1989 | 1990 |
|---|---|---|---|
| Executive branch employment | 5,229,710 | 5,231,941 | 5,173,611 |
| Executive branch civilian employment[1] | 2,198,856 | 2,207,632 | 2,213,471 |
| Department of Defense (DOD) nonmilitary functions | 1,010,194 | 1,037,626 | 997,197 |
| Non-DOD employment | 1,188,662 | 1,170,006 | 1,216,274 |
| U.S. Postal Service | 832,014 | 826,365 | 816,948 |
| Special categories[2] | 22,904 | 30,123 | 36,748 |
| Military personnel on active duty[3] | 2,175,936 | 2,167,821 | 2,106,444 |
| Dept. of Defense | 2,138,213 | 2,130,229 | 2,069,357 |
| Dept. of Transportation | 37,723 | 37,592 | 37,087 |
| Legislative and judicial personnel[4] | 59,049 | 59,605 | 61,100 |
| **Total federal employment** | **5,288,759** | **5,291,546** | **5,234,711** |

1. Excludes Postal Service employees. 2. Developmental positions under the Worker-Trainee Opportunity Program; participants in the Cooperative Education Program; disadvantaged summer and part-time workers under such Office of Personnel Management programs as Summer Aids, stay-in-school, and junior fellowship; and certain statutory exemptions. 3. Excludes reserve components. 4. Excludes members and officers of Congress. **Source**: Office of Management and Budget, *Budget of the United States Government, FY1992* (1991).

## SALARIES OF FEDERAL OFFICIALS

| Branch/official | Salary |
|---|---|
| **EXECUTIVE BRANCH** | |
| President | $200,000 |
| Expense allowance | 50,000 |
| Travel allowance | 100,000 |
| Vice President | 94,000 |
| Expense allowance | 10,000 |
| **LEGISLATIVE BRANCH** | |
| *Senate[1]:* | |
| President pro tempore | $113,400 |
| Expense allowance | 10,000 |
| Senators | 101,900 |
| Expense allowance for the majority and minority leaders, each | 10,000 |
| Expense allowance for majority and minority whips, each | 5,000 |
| Expense allowance for chairmen of majority and minority conference committees, each | 3,000 |
| *House of Representatives[2]:* | |
| Speaker of the House | $160,600 |
| Expense allowance | 25,000 |
| Minority and majority leaders | 138,900 |
| Expense allowance, each | 10,000 |
| Representatives | 125,100 |
| Expense allowance for majority and minority whips, each | 5,000 |
| **JUDICIAL BRANCH** | |
| Chief Justice | $160,600 |
| Associate justices | 153,600 |
| Circuit judges | 132,700 |
| District and other judges | 125,100 |

1. All Senators have an allowance for hiring personnel that ranges from $814,000 to $1,764,000 per year (actual amounts are determined by the population of the senator's home state), and an official expense allowance (for maintenance of district offices, transportation, etc.) that ranges from $44,000 to $200,000 (determined by the distance between the home state and Washington, D.C.) 2. All Representatives have an allowance for hiring personnel of $515,760 per year, and an official expense allowance that averages $176,000 (actual amounts are determined by the distance between the home state and Washington, D.C.). **Source:** Executive Office of the White House; U.S. Congress; Administrative Office of the U.S. Courts.

## THE FEDERAL GOVERNMENT: EMPLOYEES AND BUDGET, 1901–91

| Year | Number of employees[1] | Budget (millions) | | Surplus or deficit (−) |
|---|---|---|---|---|
| | | Receipts | Outlays | |
| 1901 | 239,476 | $ 588 | $ 525 | $ 63 |
| 1910 | 388,708 | 676 | 694 | −18 |
| 1920 | 655,265 | 6,649 | 6,358 | 291 |
| 1930 | 601,319 | 4,058 | 3,320 | 738 |
| 1940 | 1,042,420 | 6,548 | 9,468 | −2,920 |
| 1945 | 3,816,310 | 45,159 | 92,712 | −47,553 |
| 1950 | 1,960,708 | 39,443 | 42,562 | −3,119 |
| 1960 | 2,398,704 | 92,492 | 92,191 | 301 |
| 1970 | 2,984,574 | 192,807 | 195,649 | −2,842 |
| 1980 | 2,875,866 | 517,112 | 590,920 | −73,808 |
| 1985 | 3,001,000[2] | 734,057 | 946,316 | −212,260 |
| 1990 | 3,053,774 | 1,031,308 | 1,251,703 | −220,396 |
| 1991 | N.A. | 1,091,440 | 1,409,563 | −318,123 |

1. Paid civilians only. 2. Figure rounded in source. **Source:** U.S. Bureau of the Census, *Statistical History of the U.S.* (1976); Office of Management and Budget, *Budget of the United States Government, FY1992* (1991).

**Foreign Service and Veterans Affairs** Foreign Service Personnel and Officers pay systems covers 13,609 employees with an average salary of $44,976. The Foreign Service Compensation system covers 183 employees in defense agencies with average salaries of $58,445. Department of Veterans Affairs pay systems cover 6,847 physicians and dentists with an average salary of $73,777, 130 podiatrists and optometrists ($61,056), and 30,509 nurses ($36,097).

**Executive Schedule and Senior Executive Service (SES)** The Executive Schedule covers top officials in the executive branch above the GS-18 level. Broadly speaking, the five Executive Schedule levels include the following job titles: level I, cabinet members; level II, deputy secretaries of major departments; level III, presidential advisers, chief administrators of major independent agencies, and under secretaries; level IV, assistant secretaries, deputy under secretaries, and general counsels in executive departments; and level V, deputy assistant secretaries, administrators, commissioners, and directors.

The SES covers most managerial and policy positions in the executive branch that are classifiable as GS-16 through GS-18 and that do not require Senate confirmation. In 1990 there were 7,542 employees covered by SES; salaries averaged $78,772.

**Special rates** The government has difficulty recruiting and retaining qualified personnel in certain occupations and for certain locations with higher competitive salaries. To alleviate this problem, the Office of Personnel Management has the authority to establish special rates for certain white-collar positions. As of Mar. 31, 1990, 184,400 white-collar employees were being paid special rate salaries.

### Blue-collar Employees

As of Mar. 31, 1990, the federal government employed 368,582 workers (18.1% of the civilian work force) in blue-collar (trades and labor) occupations. Most of these (92.0%) were employed in the United States outside the Washington, D.C., area; 5.5% were employed in and around Washington, and 2.5% worked overseas. The Department of Defense employed 75% of all blue-collar government workers.

Blue-collar pay rates are governed by Federal Wage Systems and determined on a prevailing rate basis by pay locality. The worldwide average salary for the blue-collar work force in 1990 was $26,565. In 1989 (the latest year for which figures are available), salaries for men averaged $26,342 and salaries for women averaged $21,615. From 1987 to 1989, average salaries for men rose $1,355 (5.4%) but only $996 (4.8%) for women. The highest average salaries were $33,223 for men and $27,764 for women in motion picture, radio, television, and sound equipment operation occupations. The lowest average salaries were $18,303 for men in general services and support work, and $15,876 for women in vessel jobs.

## THE CONGRESSIONAL BUDGET PROCESS

| On or before | Action to be completed |
|---|---|
| First Monday in February | President submits his budget. Congressional committees have six weeks to submit views and estimates to budget committees. |
| February 15 | Congressional Budget Office submits report to budget committees. |
| April 1 | Senate Budget Committee reports concurrent resolution[1] on the budget. |
| April 15 | Congress completes action on concurrent resolution[1] on the budget. |
| May 15 | Annual appropriation bills may be considered in the House. |
| June 10 | House Appropriations Committee reports last annual appropriations bill. |
| June 15 | Congress completes action on reconciliation legislation. |
| June 30 | House completes action on annual appropriation bills. |
| October 1 | Fiscal year begins. |

1. A concurrent resolution sets levels for new budget authority and outlays, direct loan obligations, primary loan guarantee commitments, the amount by which federal revenues should be increased or decreased, the budget surplus or deficit, the public debt, and so on. **Source**: Committee on Ways and Means, U.S. House of Representatives, *Overview of Entitlement Programs, 1991 Green Book* (1991).

### Glossary of Federal Budget Terms

**Budget authority** The authority provided by law to incur financial obligations that result in immediate or future *outlays* involving government funds or to collect offsetting *receipts*.

**Budget deficit/surplus** A budget deficit occurs when government *outlays* exceed government *receipts*; a surplus occurs when receipts exceed outlays. The budget deficit in 1990 was $220.4 billion; the record deficit was $221.2 billion in 1986. The last year in which a budget surplus was recorded was 1969 ($3.2 billion). *The Budget for the U.S. Government FY1992*, published by the Office of Management and Budget, projects a budget surplus of $19.9 billion in 1996. However, government predictions of future budgets are traditionally unreliable.

**Fiscal year** The federal government's fiscal year begins Oct. 1 and ends Sept. 30 of the next calendar year; so, FY1991 began Oct. 1, 1990, and ended Sept. 30, 1991.

**Intergovernmental expenditure/revenue** Amounts paid to or received from other governments either in the form of shared revenues and grants-in-aid, reimbursements for performance of general government activities or for specific services such as care of prisoners for the paying government, or in lieu of taxes.

**Off-budget/on-budget** Some presentations in the federal budget distinguish on-budget totals from off-budget totals. On-budget totals reflect the transactions of all federal government entities except those excluded from the budget totals by law, the two Social Security *trust funds* (old-age and survivors insurance and the federal disability insurance trust funds), and the Postal Service fund. Off-budget totals reflect the transactions of government entities excluded from the on-budget totals by law.

**Offsetting collections** Collections from the public that result from business-type or market-oriented activities and collections; examples include proceeds from the sale of electric power by the Tennessee Valley Authority, voluntary medical insurance premiums paid to the supplementary medical insurance trust fund, and the sale of postage stamps.

**Outlays** Budget outlays are expenditures and net lending of funds under *budget authority* during the fiscal year. They constitute the spending side of the budget.

**Receipts** Budget receipts constitute the income side of the budget and are composed almost entirely of taxes or other compulsory payments to the government.

**Trust fund** In the federal budget, a trust fund means only that the law requires that funds must be accounted for separately and used only for specified purposes. The largest trust funds are those for civil service and military retirement, Social Security, Medicare, and unemployment insurance. These are financed largely by Social Security taxes and contributions and payments from the general fund. There are also major trust funds for transportation and bank deposit insurance which are financed by *user charges*.

**User charges** Charges for services rendered, collected in the form of taxes, such as highway excise taxes to fund the highway trust fund.

## FEDERAL GOVERNMENTAL RECEIPTS BY SOURCE, 1980–92 (millions of dollars)

| Source | Actual | | | Estimated | |
|---|---|---|---|---|---|
| | 1980 | 1985 | 1990 | 1991 | 1992 |
| Individual income taxes | $244,069 | $334,531 | $466,884 | $492,884 | $529,518 |
| Corporation income taxes[1] | 64,600 | 61,331 | 93,507 | 95,866 | 101,913 |
| Social insurance taxes and contributions[2] | 157,803 | 265,163 | 380,047 | 401,955 | 429,363 |
| On-budget | (45,594) | (78,992) | (98,392) | (103,668) | (114,109) |
| Off-budget | (113,209) | (186,171) | (281,656) | (298,287) | (315,254) |
| Excise taxes[3] | 24,329 | 35,992 | 35,345 | 44,810 | 47,768 |
| Other[4] | 25,311 | 37,040 | 55,524 | 56,175 | 56,467 |
| Total | $517,112 | $734,057 | $1,031,308 | $1,091,440 | $1,165,029 |
| On-budget | (403,903) | (547,886) | (749,652) | (793,153) | (849,775) |
| Off-budget | (113,209) | (186,171) | (281,656) | (298,287) | (315,254) |

1. Beginning 1987 includes trust fund receipts for the hazardous substance superfund. 2. Includes employment taxes and contributions, unemployment insurance, and other retirement contributions. 3. Includes taxes on alcohol, tobacco, windfall profits and ozone depletion, and federal trust funds. 4. Includes estate and gift taxes, customs duties and fees, federal reserve deposits, and other. **Source**: Office of Management and Budget, *Budget of the U.S. Government, FY1992* (1991).

## GOVERNMENT EMPLOYMENT AND POPULATION, 1960–90

| Fiscal year | Federal executive branch[1] ('000s) | State and local goverments ('000s) | All governmental units ('000s) | Federal as percent of all governmental units | Federal employment per 1,000 population |
|---|---|---|---|---|---|
| 1960[2] | 2,355 | 6,073 | 8,444 | 28.1% | 13.2 |
| 1965 | 2,496 | 7,683 | 10,179 | 24.5 | 12.8 |
| 1970[2] | 2,944 | 9,869 | 12,813 | 23.0 | 14.4 |
| 1975 | 2,848 | 12,114 | 14,962 | 19.0 | 13.2 |
| 1980[2] | 2,821 | 13,542 | 16,363 | 17.2 | 12.3 |
| 1985 | 2,964 | 13,827 | 16,791 | 17.7 | 12.4 |
| 1990[2] | 3,067 | 15,337 | 18,404 | 16.7 | 12.2 |

1. Covers total year-end civilian employment of full-time permanent, temporary, part-time, and intermittent employees in the executive branch, including the Postal Service, and beginning in 1970, includes various disadvantaged worker-trainee programs. 2. Includes temporary employees in the decennial census. **Source**: Office of Management and Budget, *Budget of the United States Government, FY1992* (1991).

## SOCIAL SECURITY AND THE BUDGET DEFICIT, 1990–95 (billions of dollars)

| Definition | 1990 | 1991 | 1992 | 1993 | 1994 | 1995 |
|---|---|---|---|---|---|---|
| President's policy deficit/surplus | –$121.4 | –$64.0 | $26.0 | $ 4.2 | $ 8.9 | $ 7.4 |
| Less Social Security reserve | 61.9 | 77.7 | 89.5 | 106.1 | 120.8 | 133.2 |
| On-budget policy deficit/surplus | –183.2 | –141.6 | –114.9 | –101.8 | –111.8 | –125.7 |

**Sources:** Office of Management and Budget. *Budget of the United States Government FY1991* (1990). Social Security Administration, unpublished data.

## SUMMARY OF FEDERAL GOVERNMENT FINANCES, 1985/86–1988/89

| Item | Amount 1985–86 (millions) | Amount 1988–89 (millions) | Per capita 1989[1] |
|---|---|---|---|
| **REVENUES** | | | |
| **Revenue, total** | **$847,516** | **$1,092,660** | **$4,401.65** |
| General revenue | 580,611 | 743,359 | 2,994.53 |
| General revenue from own sources | 578,473 | 740,456 | 2,982.84 |
| Taxes | 471,898 | 615,853 | 2,480.89 |
| Income | 412,102 | 548,981 | 2,211.50 |
| Individual | 348,959 | 445,690 | 1,795.41 |
| Corporation | 63,143 | 103,291 | 416.09 |
| Sales, gross receipts, and customs | 47,046 | 52,527 | 211.60 |
| Customs duties | 13,420 | 16,450 | 66.27 |
| Motor fuel | 11,641 | 14,372 | 57.90 |
| Alcoholic beverages | 5,601 | 5,810 | 23.40 |
| Public utilities | 5,047 | 6,390 | 25.74 |
| Air transportation | 2,708 | 3,569 | 14.38 |
| Telephone | 2,339 | 2,821 | 11.36 |
| Tobacco products | 4,608 | 4,290 | 17.28 |
| Other sales and gross receipts taxes | 6,729 | 5,215 | 21.01 |
| Oil windfall profit tax | 3,442 | 30 | 0.12 |
| Motor fuel vehicles, chassis, and body | 1,091 | 1,259 | 5.07 |
| Tires, inner tubes, and tread rubber | 286 | 313 | 1.26 |
| Other categories not shown | 1,910 | 3,613 | 14.55 |
| Other taxes | 12,750 | 14,345 | 57.79 |
| Death and gift | 6,958 | 8,745 | 35.23 |
| All other | 5,792 | 5,600 | 22.56 |
| Charges and miscellaneous general revenue | 106,575 | 124,603 | 501.95 |
| Current charges | 63,291 | 76,332 | 307.45 |
| Postal receipts | 29,099 | 36,965 | 148.91 |
| National defense and international relations | 6,774 | 7,769 | 31.30 |
| Natural resources | 14,705 | 17,236 | 69.43 |
| Commodity Credit Corporation—sale of agricultural products | 2,815 | 3,563 | 14.35 |
| Tennessee Valley Authority | 4,304 | 5,060 | 20.38 |
| Department of Interior—energy sales | 2,252 | 2,371 | 9.55 |
| Mineral ore and product sales | 578 | 631 | 2.54 |
| Timber sales | 468 | 906 | 3.65 |
| All other resource charges | 4,288 | 4,705 | 18.95 |
| Other current charges | 12,713 | 14,352 | 57.82 |
| Sale of property | 2,697 | 5,295 | 21.33 |
| Interest earnings | 13,931 | 13,453 | 54.19 |
| Other miscellaneous general revenue | 26,656 | 29,533 | 118.97 |
| Federal Reserve System—earnings | 18,374 | 19,604 | 78.97 |
| Continental shelf lands—lease and royalty revenues | 4,716 | 2,930 | 11.80 |
| Other | 3,566 | 6,499 | 26.18 |
| Insurance trust revenue | 266,905 | 349,301 | 1,407.12 |
| Social Security and Medicare insurance (OASDHI) | 257,263 | 339,493 | 1,367.61 |
| Employee retirement | 4,451 | 4,424 | 17.82 |
| Railroad retirement | 4,194 | 4,488 | 18.08 |
| Veterans' life insurance | 686 | 695 | 2.80 |
| Unemployment compensation | 221 | 201 | 0.81 |
| **EXPENDITURES** | | | |
| **Expenditure, total** | **$1,096,401** | **$1,270,068** | **$5,116.31** |
| Expenditure, by function: | | | |
| General expenditure | 796,209 | 910,438 | 3,667.59 |
| Intergovernmental expenditure | 115,632 | 127,247 | 512.60 |
| Education[2] | 18,023 | 21,670 | 87.29 |
| Elementary and secondary education | 3,268 | 4,013 | 16.17 |
| School breakfast and lunch | 3,086 | 3,595 | 14.48 |
| Federally affected area assistance | 674 | 732 | 2.95 |

| Item | Amount 1985–86 (millions) | Amount 1988–89 (millions) | Per capita 1989[1] |
|---|---|---|---|
| Public welfare | $ 44,544 | $ 56,410 | $ 227.24 |
| Medical assistance | 26,098 | 36,177 | 145.73 |
| Maintenance assistance | 9,540 | 11,783 | 47.47 |
| Low-income energy assistance | 2,842 | 2,102 | 8.47 |
| Health and hospital | 4,615 | 6,070 | 24.45 |
| Special supplemental food programs—WIC programs | 1,710 | 2,102 | 8.47 |
| National Institutes of Health | 666 | 909 | 3.66 |
| Highways | 14,370 | 13,441 | 54.15 |
| Natural resources, parks, and recreations | 2,424 | 2,298 | 9.26 |
| Housing and community development | 11,237 | 11,814 | 47.59 |
| Other | 20,419 | 15,544 | 62.62 |
| Urban mass transportation | 3,349 | 3,539 | 14.26 |
| Contribution to District of Columbia | 530 | 538 | 2.17 |
| Direct expenditure | 680,577 | 783,191 | 3,154.99 |
| Selected federal programs: | | | |
| National defense and international relations | 312,183 | 346,338 | 1,395.18 |
| Military functions | 288,454 | 320,844 | 1,292.48 |
| Economic assistance | 7,788 | 6,474 | 26.08 |
| Atomic energy | 7,602 | 8,962 | 36.10 |
| Foreign affairs, n.e.c. | 3,383 | 4,237 | 17.07 |
| Food for freedom | 1,095 | 1,098 | 4.42 |
| Military assistance | 3,820 | 4,531 | 18.25 |
| Postal service | 30,985 | 36,472 | 146.92 |
| Space research and technology | 7,275 | 10,806 | 43.53 |
| Education service: | | | |
| Education | 13,581 | 16,815 | 67.74 |
| Veterans' education benefits | 766 | 527 | 2.12 |
| Other | 12,815 | 16,288 | 65.61 |
| Libraries | 316 | 467 | 1.88 |
| Social service and income maintenance: | | | |
| Public welfare | 25,790 | 31,170 | 125.56 |
| Hospitals | 7,573 | 8,187 | 32.98 |
| Public hospitals | 7,032 | 7,578 | 30.53 |
| Veterans | 6,185 | 6,721 | 27.07 |
| Other public hospitals | 847 | 857 | 3.45 |
| Other hospitals | 541 | 609 | 2.45 |
| Health | 7,520 | 9,147 | 36.85 |
| Social insurance administration | 3,871 | 4,405 | 17.74 |
| Veterans' services | 17,139 | 18,669 | 75.21 |
| Transportation: | | | |
| Highways | 568 | 776 | 3.13 |
| Air transportation | 3,599 | 4,428 | 17.84 |
| Water transport and terminals | 1,690 | 2,149 | 8.66 |
| Public safety: | | | |
| Police protection | 3,543 | 4,952 | 19.95 |
| Correction | 798 | 1,303 | 5.25 |
| Environment and housing: | | | |
| Natural resources, parks, and recreation | 60,075 | 54,975 | 221.46 |
| Soil, water, mineral, and electric energy resources | 15,358 | 16,434 | 66.20 |
| Energy programs | 5,995 | 5,490 | 22.12 |
| Tennessee Valley Authority | 3,951 | 3,764 | 15.16 |
| Army Corps of Engineers | 1,891 | 1,966 | 7.92 |
| Soil Conservation Service | 692 | 695 | 2.80 |
| Stabilization of farm prices and income | 28,214 | 19,156 | 77.17 |
| Commodity Credit Corporation | 26,560 | 16,132 | 64.99 |
| Farm credit programs | 9,591 | 11,294 | 45.50 |
| Forestry | 1,864 | 2,497 | 10.06 |
| Other agricultural resources | 1,545 | 1,714 | 6.90 |

| Item | Amount 1985–86 (millions) | Amount 1988–89 (millions) | Per capita 1989[1] | Item | Amount 1985–86 (millions) | Amount 1988–89 (millions) | Per capita 1989[1] |
|---|---|---|---|---|---|---|---|
| Other natural resources | $ 2,049 | $ 2,166 | $ 8.73 | Social Security and Medicare | $ 267,923 | $ 321,335 | $1,294.46 |
| National Oceanographic and Atmospheric Administration (NOAA) | 1,246 | 1,180 | 4.75 | Insurance (OASDHI) | | | |
| | | | | Employee retirement | 24,226 | 29,491 | 118.80 |
| Housing and community development | 7,925 | 13,492 | 54.35 | Railroad retirement | 5,969 | 6,672 | 26.88 |
| | | | | Veterans' life insurance | 1,893 | 2,042 | 8.23 |
| Government administration: | | | | Unemployment compensation | 181 | 90 | 0.36 |
| Federal administration | 5,400 | 7,132 | 28.73 | **DEBT** | | | |
| Judicial and legal | 2,090 | 2,949 | 11.88 | Gross debt outstanding at end of fiscal year | 2,129,506 | 2,881,112 | 11,606.20 |
| Other government administration | 1,129 | 1,209 | 4.87 | Public debt | 2,125,304 | 2,857,431 | 11,510.81 |
| Interest on general debt | 144,167 | 174,288 | 702.10 | Federal agency debt | 4,202 | 23,681 | 95.40 |
| General expenditure, n.e.c. | 23,360 | 33,062 | 133.19 | | | | |
| Insurance trust expenditure | 300,192 | 359,630 | 1,448.72 | Held by federal government | 383,919 | 676,842 | 2,726.57 |
| | | | | Other debt outstanding | 1,745,587 | 2,204,270 | 8,879.63 |

**Note:** n.e.c. = not elsewhere classified. Detail may not add to total due to rounding. 1. Per capita figures are calculated on the basis of amounts rounded to the nearest thousand. 2. Includes amounts not shown in detail. **Source:** U.S. Bureau of the Census, *Government Finances 1988–89* (1991).

# KEY GOVERNMENT FUNCTIONS

# National Defense

Throughout history, the primary goal of every central government has been the protection of its citizens from hostile attacks of foreign enemies. In 1989, the United States spent over $300 billion to keep 2.1 million people in active military service and to maintain the greatest arsenal of weapons ever known.

Since the end of World War II, a large percentage of people and materiel has been committed to regions around the world that the government has determined are vital to U.S. interests. Between 1961 and 1980, the defense budget averaged around $200 billion annually (in 1982 constant dollars)—even during the Vietnam War. In 1981, however, the Reagan administration began a massive defense buildup which swelled successive defense budgets to unprecedented numbers and in the process helped to quadruple the annual federal deficit in less than five years.

Partly in response to the nation's budget deficit, and partly thanks to the lessening of tensions between the United States and the Soviet Union, politicians of all stripes are looking at the defense budget as the likeliest place to make savings, the outstanding question being how much.

While the end of the Cold War has reduced the threat of an all-out confrontation between either conventional or nuclear forces of the Soviet Union and the United States, the U.S. is committed to maintaining active duty and reserve forces sufficient for quick and effective response to crises around the world. In 1990–91, U.S. military forces took part in a broad range of operations, including: the maintenance of Saudi Arabian and restoration of

## CHAIRMEN OF THE JOINT CHIEFS OF STAFF, 1949–90

General of the Army Omar N. Bradley, USA, 1949–53
Adm. Arthur W. Radford, USN, 1953–57
Gen. Nathan F. Twining, USAF, 1957–60
Gen. Lyman L. Lemnitzer, USA, 1960–62
Gen. Maxwell D. Taylor, USA, 1962–64
Gen. Earle G. Wheeler, USA, 1964–70
Adm. Thomas H. Moorer, USN, 1970–74
Gen. George S. Brown, USAF, 1974–78
Gen. David C. Jones, USAF, 1978–82
Gen. John W. Vessey, Jr., USA, 1982–85
Adm. William J. Crowe, USN, 1985–89
Gen. Colin L. Powell, USA, 1989–present

**Source:** U.S. Dept. of Defense, *Defense 90* (1990).

Kuwaiti sovereignty following Iraq's invasion of Kuwait (DESERT STORM/DESERT SHIELD, 1990–91); the evacuation of American and other foreign nationals from civil war–torn Somalia (EASTERN EXIT, 1990) and Liberia (SHARP EDGE, 1990); and the supply of humanitarian assistance to Kurdish refugees in Iraq (PROVIDE COMFORT, 1991) and to victims of flood, famine, and disease in typhoon-lashed Bangladesh (SEA ANGEL, 1991). In addition, the Department of Defense is the lead agency in government for the detection and monitoring of aerial and maritime transportation of illegal drugs into the United States.

**The defense establishment** The Department of Defense (DOD) is a cabinet-level organization responsible for providing the military forces needed to deter war and protect the security of the United States. The major elements of these forces are the Army, Navy, Air Force, and Marine Corps. Under the president, who is also the commander-in-chief, the secretary of defense exercises direction, authority, and control over the Department of Defense, which

includes the three military departments, the Joint Chiefs of Staff and Joint Staff, 10 unified and specified commands, the DOD inspector general, 13 defense agencies, and seven DOD field activities.

The four armed services are subordinate to the military departments, which are responsible for recruiting, training, and equipping their forces. The Marine Corps is the second armed service in the Department of the Navy. (A fifth armed service, the U.S. Coast Guard, reports to the Department of Transportation in peacetime and to the Department of the Navy in wartime.)

The earliest precursor to the Department of Defense was the War Department, established by Congress in 1789; a separate Navy Department was created in 1798. These were merged under the National Security Act of 1947 and subsequent amendments. By 1949 the secretary of defense was established as the principal assistant to the president on defense matters in charge of the Department of Defense.

**Chain of command** Operational command of U.S. combat forces is assigned to the nation's unified and specified commands. The chain of command runs from the president to the secretary of defense, through the Joint Chiefs of Staff to the commanders-in-chief of the unified and specified commands. (The four service secretaries are not part of this chain of command.) A *unified command* is composed of forces from two or more services, has a broad and continuing mission, and is normally organized on a geographical basis. The eight unified commands are: U.S. European Command, U.S. Pacific Command, U.S. Atlantic Command, U.S. Southern Command, U.S. Central Command, U.S. Space Command, U.S. Special Operations Command, and U.S. Transportation Command. A *specified command* also has a broad and continuing mission but is organized on a functional basis and is normally made up of forces from a single service. The two specified commands are the Strategic Air Command (SAC) and the Forces Command.

**U.S. Army** In peacetime, the primary mission of the continental U.S. armies is to train reserves and national guard, plan for mobilization, and coordinate domestic emergency relief efforts. The largest unit is a numbered *army*, such as the Fifth Army. (In time of war, two or three armies may be brought under a single command in an *army group*.) An *army* comprises two or more corps plus a headquarters (HQ) unit; a *corps* is made up of two to five divisions and an HQ.

There are 18 active and 10 reserve divisions in the U.S. Army combat forces. The *division* is a self-sufficient force, typically consisting of three brigades (each comprising three to five battalions) and various combat support elements. A *brigade* is made up of two or more regiments or battalions; a *regiment*, of subordinate units such as battalions, companies, or squadrons; a *battalion*, of four or more companies; a *company* of several platoons; and a *platoon* of four squads. A *squad* consists of about 10 soldiers.

**U.S. Marine Corps** Marine Corps organization emphasizes the close integration of air-ground operations for service with the U.S. fleet and for the conduct of land operations essential to the prosecution of a naval campaign. All marines serve "at the pleasure of the president," and the Corps's mission includes "performing such other duties as the president may direct."

The smallest tactical unit of Marine Corps infantry is the *fire team*, which consists of four marines. A *squad* is made up of three fire teams, and there are three squads to a *platoon*, three platoons to a *company*, three companies to a *battalion*, three battalions to a *regiment*, three regiments to a *brigade*, and three brigades to a *division*.

These components are organized into three basic organizational structures called *Marine air-ground task forces*, or MAGTFs. The largest—about 47,500 personnel—is the *Marine Expeditionary Force* (MEF), which consists of a Marine air wing (330 planes), a Marine division, and a force service support group. The *Marine Expeditionary Brigade* (MEB) consists of a Marine air group (150 planes), a regimental landing group, and a brigade service support group—about 15,000 personnel. The smallest and most responsive Marine force, the *Marine Expeditionary Unit* (MEU), consists of about 2,500 personnel and is made up of a helicopter squadron, a battalion landing team, and a unit service support group. MEUs are sea-based, can be airlifted, and are equipped and trained to be self-sustaining in the field for up to 30 days. There are currently three MEFs, six MEBs, and five MEUs.

**U.S. Navy** The ships of the U.S. Navy are organized into the Pacific Fleet, the Atlantic Fleet, and U.S. Naval Forces Europe. These are composed of numbered fleets which consist of *carrier battle groups, amphibious ready groups,* and one or more *underway replenishment groups*. Smaller subdivisions of naval forces are the *flotilla*, consisting of two or more squadrons; a *squadron*, of two or more divisions; and a *division*, normally made up of four ships.

A naval *task force* designates a collection of ships under a single command designed to accomplish a particular tactical or strategic purpose. An *amphibious squadron* consists of amphibious assault ships, amphibious transport docks, dock landing ships, and tank landing ships and transports troops and equipment necessary for an assault landing from the sea.

## MAJOR U.S. ARMY FORCES

| Unit | Headquarters |
|---|---|
| Forces Command | Ft. McPherson, Ga. |
| I Corps | Ft. Lewis, Wash. |
| 7th infantry (light), "Bayonet" | Ft. Ord, Calif. |
| 9th infantry (motorized), "Old Reliables" | Ft. Lewis, Wash. |
| III Corps, "Phantom Corps" | Ft. Hood, Tex. |
| 2nd armored, "Hell on Wheels" | Ft. Hood, Tex. |
| 1st cavalry, "First Team" | Ft. Hood, Tex. |
| 1st infantry (mech.), "The Big Red One" | Ft. Riley, Kans. |
| 4th infantry (mech.), "The Ivy Division" | Ft. Carson, Colo. |
| 5th infantry (mech.), "Red Diamond" | Ft. Polk, La. |
| XVIII Airborne Corps | Ft. Bragg, N.C. |
| 82nd airborne, "All American" | Ft. Bragg, N.C. |
| 101st airborne (air assault), "Screaming Eagles" | Ft. Campbell, Ky. |
| 24th infantry (mech.), "Victory" | Ft. Stewart, Ga. |
| 10th mountain (light infantry), "Climb to Glory" | Ft. Drum, N.Y. |
| U.S. Army Pacific | Hawaii |
| 6th infantry (light) | Alaska |
| 25th infantry (light), "Tropic Lightning" | Hawaii |
| **National Guard divisions:** | |
| 1st U.S. Army | Ft. George G. Meade, Md. |
| 50th armored, "Jersey Blues" | East Orange, N.J. |
| 26th infantry, "Yankee" | Boston, Mass. |
| 28th infantry, "Keystone" | Harrisburg, Pa. |
| 29th infantry (light), "Blue and Grey" | Ft. Belvoir, Va. |
| 42nd infantry, "Rainbow" | New York, N.Y. |
| 2nd U.S. Army | Ft. Gillem, Ga. |
| 4th U.S. Army | Ft. Sheridan, Ill. |
| 38th infantry, "Cyclone" | Indianapolis, Ind. |
| 47th infantry, "Viking" | St. Paul, Minn. |
| 5th U.S. Army | Ft. Sam Houston, Tex |
| 49th armored, "Lone Star" | Austin, Tex. |
| 35th infantry (mech.), "Santa Fe" | Ft. Leavenworth, Tex. |
| 6th U.S. Army | Presidio of San Francisco, Calif. |
| 40th infantry (mech.), "Sunshine" | Los Alamitos, Calif. |
| **Army Components of Unified Commands:** | |
| 7th Army | Heidelberg, Germany |
| V Corps | Frankfurt, Germany |
| 3rd armored, "Spearhead" | Germany |
| 8th infantry (mech.), "Pathfinder" | Germany |
| VII Corps | Stuttgart, Germany |
| 1st armored, "Old Ironsides" | Germany |
| 3rd infantry (mech.), "Marne" | Germany |
| 8th Army | Youngsan, S. Korea |
| 2nd infantry, "Indianhead" | S. Korea |

**Source:** U.S. Army Force Command.

## MAJOR MARINE CORPS COMPONENTS

| Name | Headquarters |
|---|---|
| Fleet Marine Force, Pacific | Camp H.M. Smith, Hawaii |
| 1st Marine division | Camp Pendleton, Calif. |
| 1st force service support group | Camp Pendleton, Calif. |
| 1st Marine aircraft wing | Marine Air Station El Toro, Calif. |
| 3rd Marine division | Camp Kinser, Okinawa, Japan |
| 3rd force service support group | Camp Kinser, Okinawa, Japan |
| 3rd Marine aircraft wing | Camp Foster, Okinawa, Japan |
| Fleet Marine Force, Atlantic | Norfolk, Va. |
| 2nd Marine division | Camp Lejeune, N.C. |
| 2nd force service support group | Camp Lejeune, N.C. |
| 2nd Marine aircraft wing | Marine Air Station Cherry Point, N.C. |

**Marine reserves** 4th Marine division; 4th Marine aircraft wing; 4th force service support group.

**Source:** U.S. Marine Corps.

## MAJOR NAVAL OPERATING FORCES

| Name/elements | Headquarters/station |
|---|---|
| Pacific Fleet | Pearl Harbor, Hawaii |
| 3rd Fleet (2 carrier battle groups; 1 underway replenishment group) | Pearl Harbor, Hawaii; Eastern Pacific |
| 7th Fleet (4 carrier battle fleets; 2 amphibious ready groups; 4 underway replenishment groups) | Yokusaka, Japan; Western Pacific and Indian Ocean |
| Atlantic Fleet | Norfolk, Va. |
| 2nd Fleet (2 carrier battle groups; 3 underway replenishment groups) | Norfolk, Va.; Atlantic |
| U.S. Naval Forces Europe | London, England |
| 6th Fleet (4 carrier battle groups; 1 amphibious ready group; 2 underway replenishment groups) | Gaeta, Italy; Mediterranean |

**Note:** Wartime disposition. **Source:** U.S. Dept. of Defense, *Annual Report to the President and the Congress* (1991).

## MAJOR COAST GUARD COMMANDS

| Name | Headquarters |
|---|---|
| Coast Guard Headquarters | Washington, D.C. |
| Atlantic Area | New York, N.Y. |
| 1st District | Boston, Mass. |
| 2nd District | St. Louis, Mo. |
| 5th District | Portsmouth, Va. |
| 7th District | Miami, Fla. |
| 8th District | New Orleans, La. |
| 9th District | Cleveland, Ohio |
| Pacific Area | San Francisco, Calif. |
| 11th District | Long Beach, Calif. |
| 13th District | Seattle, Wash. |
| 14th District | Honolulu, Hawaii |
| 17th District | Juneau, Alaska |

**Source:** U.S. Coast Guard.

## MAJOR AIR FORCE UNITS

| Name | Headquarters/location |
|---|---|
| Air Force Communications Command | Scott AFB, Belleville, Ill. |
| Air Force Logistics Command | Wright-Patterson AFB, Dayton, Ohio |
| Air Force Space Command | Peterson AFB, Colorado Springs, Colo. |
| Air Force Special Operations Command | Hurlburt Field, Ft. Walton Beach, Fla. |
| Alaskan Command | Elmendorf AFB, Anchorage, Alaska |
| Military Airlift Command | Scott AFB, Belleville, Ill. |
| 21st Air Force | McGuire AFB, Trenton, N.J. |
| 22nd Air Force | Travis AFB, Fairfield, Calif. |
| Pacific Air Forces | Hickam AFB, Honolulu, Hawaii |
| 5th Air Force | Yokota AFB, Japan |
| 7th Air Force | Osan AB, Osan, South Korea |
| 11th Air Force | Elmendorf AFB, Anchorage, Alaska |
| 13th Air Force | Clark AB, Manila, Philippines |
| Strategic Air Command[1] | Offutt AFB, Omaha, Nebr. |
| 8th Air Force | Barksdale AFB, Bossier City, La. |
| 15th Air Force | March AFB, Riverside, Calif. |
| Tactical Air Command[2] | Langley AFB, Hampton, Va. |
| 1st Air Force | Langley AFB, Hampton, Va. |
| 9th Air Force | Shaw AFB, Sumter, S.C. |
| 10th Air Force (AFRES) | Bergstrom AFB, Austin, Tex. |
| 12th Air Force | Bergstrom AFB, Austin, Tex. |
| U.S. Air Forces, Europe | Ramstein AB, Ramstein, Germany |
| 3rd Air Force | RAF Mildenhall, United Kingdom |
| 16th Air Force | Torrejon AB, Spain |
| 17th Air Force | Sembach AB, Germany |

**Note:** AB = air base; AFB = air force base; RAF = Royal Air Force (UK); AFRES = Air Force Reserve. 1. There are 18 bomber bases in the Strategic Air Command (SAC): 17 in the continental United States and 1 in the Mariana Islands. 2. There are 43 tactical air wings: 28 in the continental United States, 4 in Germany, 3 in the UK, 2 each in Alaska, South Korea, and Japan, and 1 each in the Philippines and Spain, the last scheduled for deactivation. **Source:** Air Force Association, Guide to Major Air Force Installations Worldwide and ANG and AFRES Bases (May 1991).

## STRATEGIC OFFENSIVE FORCES

### Land-based missile forces
**B-1 bomber bases:** McConnell AFB, Kans.; Grand Forks AFB, N.Dak.; Ellsworth AFB, S.Dak.; Dyess AFB, Tex.

**B-2 bomber base:** Whiteman AFB, Mo.

**B-52 bomber bases**[1]**:** Eaker AFB, Ark.; Castle AFB, Calif.; Barksdale AFB, La.; Loring AFB, Maine; K.I. Sawyer AFB, Mich.; Wurtsmith AFB, Mich.; Griffiss AFB, N.Y.; Minot AFB, N.Dak.; Carswell AFB, Tex.; Fairchild AFB, Wash.

**Minuteman bases:** Malmstrom AFB, Mont.; Whiteman AFB, Mo.; Ellsworth AFB, S.Dak.; Grand Forks AFB, N.Dak.; Minot AFB, N.Dak.

**Peacekeeper base:** Francis E. Warren AFB, Wyo.

### Strategic submarine forces[2]
**SSBN**[3] **bases:** Kings Bay, Ga.; Charleston, S.C.; Bangor, Wash.; Holy Loch, UK.

1. The B-52 squadrons at Loring AFB and Barksdale AFB are assigned a conventional bomber role. 2. Includes 31 nuclear-armed submarines. 3. SSBN = ballistic missile submarine, nuclear-powered. **Source:** U.S. Dept. of Defense, Annual Report to the President and the Congress (1991).

## GUARD AND RESERVE FORCES, 1990

| Status | Army National Guard | Army Reserve | Naval Reserve | Marine Corps Reserve | Air National Guard | Air Force Reserve | Total DOD | Coast Guard Reserve |
|---|---|---|---|---|---|---|---|---|
| **SELECTED RESERVE** | | | | | | | | |
| Officer | 49,549 | 62,220 | 29,719 | 3,718 | 14,061 | 17,253 | 176,520 | 1,640 |
| Enlisted | 406,685 | 251,461 | 124,381 | 39,960 | 102,872 | 67,105 | 992,464 | 10,265 |
| Total | 456,234 | 313,681 | 154,100 | 43,678 | 116,933 | 84,358 | 1,168,984 | 11,905 |
| **INDIVIDUAL READY RESERVE/INACTIVE NATIONAL GUARD** | | | | | | | | |
| Officer | 872 | 46,270 | 18,220 | 4,757 | — | 12,345 | 82,464 | 724 |
| Enlisted | 9,346 | 221,470 | 63,997 | 31,098 | — | 51,857 | 377,768 | 4,405 |
| Total | 10,218 | 267,740 | 82,217 | 35,855 | — | 64,202 | 460,232 | 5,129 |
| **TOTAL READY RESERVE** | | | | | | | | |
| Officer | 50,421 | 108,490 | 47,939 | 8,475 | 14,061 | 29,598 | 258,984 | 2,364 |
| Enlisted | 416,031 | 472,931 | 188,378 | 71,058 | 102,872 | 118,962 | 1,370,232 | 14,670 |
| Total | 466,452 | 581,421 | 236,317 | 79,533 | 116,933 | 148,560 | 1,629,216 | 17,034 |
| **STANDBY RESERVE** | | | | | | | | |
| Officer | — | 372 | 7,791 | 1,236 | — | 14,471 | 23,870 | 545 |
| Enlisted | — | 377 | 2,980 | 330 | — | 1,260 | 4,947 | 1 |
| Total | — | 749 | 10,771 | 1,566 | — | 15,731 | 28,817 | 546 |

**Note:** As of Mar. 31. **Source:** U.S. Dept. of Defense, Defense 90 (1990).

**U.S. Air Force** The Air Force is organized into a number of commands. Within commands concerned with the strategic or tactical operation of aircraft, the primary subdivisions are indicated by the term *air force* prefaced by a number, such as the Eighth Air Force. Such an air force is composed of wings; a *wing* consists of two or more groups or squadrons; a *group* of two or more squadrons; and a *squadron* of two or more flights. A *flight* is the basic tactical unit and consists of four or more planes.

**U.S. Coast Guard** The Coast Guard is a branch of the armed forces of the United States at all times. What distinguishes it from the other services is that it is part of the Department of Transportation—not Defense—except during wartime, or at the direction of the president, when it operates as part of the Navy. A successor to the Revenue Marine established in 1790, its primary function is to enforce federal maritime law. In 1989 the Coast Guard's budget was $2.9 billion, and the active duty force consisted of 36,718 personnel.

**Nuclear forces** Nuclear forces are classified as either strategic or nonstrategic. A strategic weapon is a nuclear-armed missile of intermediate or intercontinental range (usually more than 5,500 km or 3,300 mi.) capable of attacking large target areas in another country. The strategic triad—a cornerstone of post–World War II U.S. defense—is composed of land-based missile forces, including intercontinental ballistic missiles (ICBMs); submarine-launched ballistic missiles (SLBMs); and manned aircraft of the strategic bomber force. Nonstrategic nuclear weapons are shorter-range weapons that can be deployed on the battlefield and include sea-launched cruise missiles, artillery-fired atomic projectiles, and dual-capable (conventional and nuclear) aircraft.

**Special Operations Forces (SOF)** A unified command whose elements are drawn from the four major services, the special operations forces are designated to achieve military objectives of a limited and specific nature. Among the various elements of the SOF are: *Army* special forces; Rangers; psychological operations, civil affairs, and special operations aviation units; *Navy* SEAL (sea-air-land) teams and special boat units; and *Air Force* 23rd Air Force special operations force.

### Reserve Forces

The reserve forces constitute the initial and primary augmentation of active forces in any emergency requiring rapid expansion of those forces. The objective of the Department of Defense's "total force policy" is to achieve the most cost-effective mix of active duty, reserve, and contract personnel consistent with the requirements of peacetime deployments and responsiveness to war.

There are seven reserve components: Army National Guard, Army Reserve, Naval Reserve, Marine Corps Reserve, Air National Guard, Air Force Reserve, and Coast Guard Reserve. All National Guard and reserve personnel are assigned to one of three categories: Ready Reserve, Standby Reserve, or Retired Reserve. All National Guard members are in the Ready Reserve. The Ready Reserve consists of the Selected Reserve, Individual Ready Reserve, and Inactive National Guard. Some reservists are organized in units, others train as individuals. All are subject to orders for active duty in time of war or national emergency.

In addition, members of the Selected Reserve may be ordered to active duty under implementation of the presidential call-up authority. The president can activate up to 200,000 members of the Selected Reserve involuntarily, for operational missions of not more than 90 days, without declaring a national emergency.

## U.S. ARMED FORCES WORLDWIDE, 1990

| Location | Army | Navy | Marine Corps | Air Force | Total DOD |
|---|---|---|---|---|---|
| **UNITED STATES[1]** | | | | | |
| Continental U.S. | 443,258 | 267,829 | 142,056 | 391,909 | 1,245,052 |
| Alaska | 9,605 | 2,332 | 160 | 10,678 | 22,775 |
| Hawaii | 18,485 | 12,368 | 9,188 | 5,533 | 45,574 |
| Guam | 38 | 4,448 | 379 | 3,074 | 7,939 |
| Johnston Atoll | 119 | 2 | 0 | 10 | 131 |
| Puerto Rico | 1,142 | 3,197 | 214 | 234 | 4,787 |
| Transients | 14,945 | 13,655 | 8,283 | 9,063 | 36,883 |
| Afloat | — | 194,670 | 1,293 | — | 205,026 |
| Total[2] | 487,669 | 498,539 | 161,573 | 420,522 | 1,568,303 |
| **EUROPE** | | | | | |
| Belgium | 1,493 | 126 | 32 | 607 | 2,258 |
| West Germany[3] | 207,660 | 331 | 113 | 38,546 | 246,650 |
| Greece | 397 | 523 | 16 | 2,161 | 3,097 |
| Greenland | 0 | 0 | 0 | 183 | 183 |
| Iceland | 3 | 1,831 | 91 | 1,334 | 3,259 |
| Italy | 3,928 | 5,900 | 286 | 5,533 | 15,647 |
| Netherlands | 869 | 20 | 10 | 1,948 | 2,847 |
| Norway | 38 | 41 | 23 | 122 | 224 |
| Portugal | 62 | 394 | 13 | 1,194 | 1,663 |
| Spain | 17 | 4,159 | 174 | 4,634 | 8,984 |
| Turkey | 1,149 | 120 | 20 | 3,562 | 4,851 |
| United Kingdom | 288 | 2,385 | 379 | 23,502 | 26,554 |
| Afloat | — | 16,056 | 2,388 | — | 18,444 |
| Total[2] | 215,992 | 31,777 | 3,336 | 83,388 | 344,078 |
| Eastern Europe | 76 | 5 | 119 | 19 | 219 |
| **EAST ASIA AND PACIFIC** | | | | | |
| Australia | 14 | 420 | 10 | 278 | 722 |
| Japan | 1,791 | 7,005 | 21,976 | 16,052 | 46,824 |
| Philippines | 371 | 5,088 | 1,028 | 8,386 | 14,873 |
| South Korea | 31,579 | 379 | 2,240 | 10,985 | 45,183 |
| Thailand | 178 | 10 | 25 | 44 | 257 |
| Afloat | — | 25,502 | 2,460 | — | 27,962 |
| Total[2] | 33,977 | 38,483 | 27,805 | 35,785 | 136,050 |
| **AFRICA, NEAR EAST, AND SOUTH ASIA** | | | | | |
| Bahrain | 7 | 156 | 11 | 9 | 183 |
| British Indian Ocean Territory[4] | 3 | 893 | 38 | 24 | 958 |
| Egypt | 509 | 35 | 37 | 39 | 620 |
| Saudi Arabia | 172 | 46 | 20 | 205 | 443 |
| Afloat | — | 3,357 | 0 | — | 3,357 |
| Total[2] | 933 | 4,527 | 530 | 380 | 6,370 |
| **OTHER WESTERN HEMISPHERE** | | | | | |
| Bermuda | 0 | 1,542 | 72 | — | 1,614 |
| Canada | 10 | 399 | 12 | 135 | 556 |
| Cuba (Guantanamo) | 0 | 2,041 | 470 | 2 | 2,513 |
| Honduras | 1,808 | 4 | 693 | 15 | 2,520 |
| Panama | 9,409 | 532 | 706 | 2,772 | 13,419 |
| Afloat | — | 3,578 | 0 | — | 3,578 |
| Total[2] | 11,556 | 8,248 | 2,189 | 2,997 | 24,970 |
| **WORLDWIDE** | | | | | |
| Ashore | 750,193 | 338,740 | 189,762 | 534,091 | 1,812,723 |
| Afloat | — | 243,163 | 6,141 | 9,063[5] | 258,367 |
| Total | 750,193 | 581,903 | 195,903 | 543,028 | 2,071,090 |

**Note:** Includes countries and regional areas where 100 or more U.S. military members are assigned. 1. Includes territories and special locations. 2. Regional totals include countries with less than 100 assigned U.S. military members. 3. Includes West Berlin. 4. Includes Diego Garcia. 5. Includes transients. **Source:** U.S. Dept. of Defense, Defense 90 (1990).

## MAJOR WEAPON SYSTEMS AND COMBAT FORCES, 1980–91

| Weapon or force | 1980 | 1984 | 1990 | 1991[1] |
|---|---|---|---|---|
| **STRATEGIC FORCES** | | | | |
| **Land-based ICBMs[2]** | | | | |
| Minuteman | 1,000 | 1,000 | 950 | 950 |
| Peacekeeper | 0 | 0 | 50 | 50 |
| **Strategic bombers (PAA)** | | | | |
| B-52G/H[3] | 241 | 241 | 154 | 125 |
| B-1B | 0 | 0 | 90 | 84 |
| **Fleet Ballistic Missile Launchers (SLBMs)[2]** | | | | |
| Poseidon (C-3 and C-4) | 336 | 384 | 368 | 352 |
| Trident | — | 72 | 216 | 264 |
| **Strategic Defense Interceptors (PAA/squadrons)** | | | | |
| Active | 127/7 | 90/5 | 18/1 | 0/0 |
| Reserve | 165/10 | 162/10 | 216/12 | 216/12 |
| **GENERAL PURPOSE FORCES** | | | | |
| **Active land forces** | | | | |
| Army divisions | 16 | 16 | 18 | 16 |
| Marine Corps divisions | 3 | 3 | 3 | 3 |
| Army separate brigades[4] | 8 | 8 | 8 | 8 |
| Army Special Forces groups | 2 | 4 | 5 | 5 |
| Army Ranger regiments | 0 | 0 | 1 | 1 |
| **Active tactical air forces (PAA/squadrons)** | | | | |
| Air Force attack and fighter aircraft | 1,608/74 | 1,734/77 | 1,719/76 | 1,644/76 |
| Conventional bombers | 0 | 0 | 33 | 33 |
| Navy attack and fighter aircraft | 696/60 | 616/63 | 694/93 | 644/59 |
| Marine Corps attack and fighter aircraft | 329/25 | 256/24 | 344/25 | 376/25 |
| **Naval forces** | | | | |
| Strategic forces ships | 48 | 41 | 39 | 40 |
| Battle forces ships | 384 | 425 | 409 | 385 |
| Support forces ships | 41 | 46 | 66 | 66 |
| Reserve forces ships | 6 | 12 | 31 | 37 |
| Total battle forces deployable | 479 | 524 | 545 | 528 |
| Other reserve forces ships | 44 | 24 | 16 | 14 |
| Other auxiliaries | 8 | 9 | 3 | 3 |
| Total other forces | 52 | 33 | 19 | 17 |
| **AIRLIFT AND SEALIFT FORCES** | | | | |
| **Intertheater airlift (PAA)** | | | | |
| C-5 | 70 | 70 | 109 | 109 |
| C-141 | 234 | 234 | 234 | 234 |
| KC-10 | 0 | 25 | 57 | 57 |
| **Intratheater airlift (PAA)** | | | | |
| C-130 | 482 | 520 | 460 | 462 |
| **Sealift ships[5]** | | | | |
| Tankers, active | 21 | 21 | 28 | 31 |
| Cargo, active | 23 | 30 | 40 | 41 |
| Ready Reserve Forces (RRF) | 24 | 51 | 96 | 103 |
| National Defense Reserve Fleet (NDRF)[6] | 0 | 0 | 121 | 121 |

**Note:** PAA = primary aircraft authorized. 1. Estimated. 2. Number on-line. 3. Does not include conventional B-52 force. 4. Does not include roundout brigades; does include the Eskimo scout group and the armored cavalry regiments. 5. Includes fast sealift ships, afloat repositioning force ships, and common user (charter) ships. 6. Beginning in FY 1988, specific NDRF ships were designated militarily useful ships. **Source:** U.S. Dept. of Defense, Annual Report to the President and the Congress (1991).

## DEPARTMENT OF DEFENSE CONTRACT AWARDS, PAYROLL, AND PERSONNEL, BY STATE, 1989

| State | Payroll[1] ('000s) | Contract awards[2] ('000s) | Personnel Military | Personnel Civilian[3] |
|---|---|---|---|---|
| Alabama | $2,099,002 | $1,392,388 | 21,249 | 25,622 |
| Alaska | 850,702 | 539,795 | 22,792 | 5,103 |
| Arizona | 1,493,684 | 2,846,887 | 26,248 | 11,192 |
| Arkansas | 663,700 | 369,592 | 8,963 | 5,155 |
| California | 13,912,641 | 23,124,697 | 204,168 | 131,515 |
| Colorado | 2,039,851 | 2,928,301 | 40,020 | 14,358 |
| Connecticut | 637,516 | 6,082,290 | 6,687 | 5,007 |
| Delaware | 235,042 | 171,036 | 4,636 | 1,813 |
| District of Columbia | 1,115,876 | 1,235,964 | 13,646 | 17,858 |
| Florida | 5,492,485 | 4,452,383 | 77,818 | 33,813 |
| Georgia | 3,773,609 | 1,864,180 | 63,250 | 39,949 |
| Hawaii | 2,234,004 | 578,733 | 43,792 | 20,246 |
| Idaho | 285,497 | 74,789 | 5,167 | 1,324 |
| Illinois | 1,764,713 | 1,249,101 | 38,265 | 21,668 |
| Indiana | 966,580 | 1,763,077 | 5,660 | 15,687 |
| Iowa | 186,720 | 425,910 | 352 | 1,472 |
| Kansas | 1,162,362 | 954,967 | 22,298 | 9,516 |
| Kentucky | 1,757,259 | 332,724 | 38,824 | 14,030 |
| Lousiana | 1,343,788 | 1,693,487 | 25,250 | 8,501 |
| Maine | 639,673 | 370,011 | 5,585 | 10,746 |
| Maryland | 2,956,671 | 3,870,678 | 36,566 | 43,656 |
| Massachusetts | 1,040,842 | 8,757,467 | 9,655 | 12,163 |
| Michigan | 885,377 | 1,265,931 | 8,648 | 13,140 |
| Minnesota | 330,070 | 1,773,974 | 845 | 3,620 |
| Mississippi | 1,016,057 | 1,234,558 | 14,664 | 13,260 |
| Missouri | 1,557,898 | 6,282,649 | 16,752 | 23,529 |
| Montana | 217,309 | 80,536 | 4,576 | 1,351 |
| Nebraska | 620,435 | 221,684 | 13,052 | 4,820 |
| Nevada | 526,962 | 230,148 | 10,292 | 2,179 |
| New Hampshire | 281,047 | 477,798 | 3,614 | 1,849 |
| New Jersey | 1,629,682 | 3,393,371 | 18,029 | 21,476 |
| New Mexico | 950,812 | 625,032 | 14,993 | 9,178 |
| New York | 1,884,187 | 6,552,164 | 28,918 | 20,178 |
| North Carolina | 3,461,629 | 1,103,742 | 92,257 | 15,518 |
| North Dakota | 327,676 | 121,814 | 10,818 | 1,886 |
| Ohio | 1,954,878 | 5,069,368 | 11,715 | 35,805 |
| Oklahoma | 1,815,834 | 659,115 | 28,158 | 24,398 |
| Oregon | 386,962 | 178,526 | 666 | 3,196 |
| Pennsylvania | 2,463,445 | 2,828,032 | 5,954 | 51,972 |
| Rhode Island | 395,694 | 417,484 | 4,059 | 4,512 |
| South Carolina | 2,606,245 | 568,166 | 41,605 | 20,714 |
| South Dakota | 246,627 | 67,426 | 6,960 | 1,479 |
| Tennessee | 898,374 | 1,118,445 | 9,934 | 7,688 |
| Texas | 7,264,089 | 9,262,814 | 127,016 | 62,287 |
| Utah | 974,556 | 982,645 | 5,828 | 22,021 |
| Vermont | 76,631 | 163,359 | 64 | 590 |
| Virginia | 9,378,976 | 5,896,749 | 96,171 | 111,703 |
| Washington | 3,028,727 | 2,951,055 | 40,533 | 29,398 |
| West Virginia | 180,605 | 163,440 | 415 | 1,954 |
| Wisconsin | 415,773 | 1,080,789 | 867 | 3,311 |
| Wyoming | 163,895 | 67,136 | 3,809 | 1,168 |
| Undistributed | N.A. | N.A. | 33,594 | 1,983 |
| **Total U.S.** | **$92,592,669** | **$119,916,607** | **1,375,706** | **966,597** |

**Note**: For year ending Sept. 30. 1. Payroll estimates cover active duty military and direct hire civilian personnel, including Army Corps of Engineers. 2. Military awards for supplies, services, and construction; expenditures relating to awards may extend over several years. Net value of contracts of over $25,000 for work in each state; the state in which the prime contractor is located is not necessarily the state in which the subcontracted work is done. 3. Civilian employees represent direct hire civilian employees. **Source**: U.S. Dept. of Defense, *Defense 90* (1991).

## ACTIVE DUTY, MONTHLY BASIC PAY TABLE

| Pay grade | Rank | 2 | 10 | 20 | 26 |
|---|---|---|---|---|---|
| | | **COMMISSIONED OFFICERS** | | | |
| O-10 | General Admiral | $5,911.80 | $6,138.30 | $7,115.10[1] | $7,558.50[1] |
| O-9 | Lt. General Vice-Admiral | 5,193.90 | 5,439.30 | 6,478.80[1] | 6,875.10[1] |
| O-8 | Maj. General Rear Admiral | 4,721.40 | 5,193.90 | 6,138.30 | 6,289.50 |
| O-7 | Brig. General Commodore | 4,068.00 | 4,496.70 | 5,551.20 | 5,551.20 |
| O-6 | Colonel Captain | 3,102.00 | 3,305.10 | 4,250.40 | 4,877.10 |
| O-5 | Lt. Colonel Commander | 2,651.40 | 2,920.50 | 3,845.10 | 3,979.20 |
| O-4 | Major Lt. Commander | 2,317.80 | 2,808.60 | 3,327.60 | 3,327.60 |
| O-3 | Captain Lieutenant | 1,977.60 | 2,676.30 | 2,877.90 | 2,877.90 |
| O-2 | 1st Lieutenant Lieut. (J.G.) | 1,684.50 | 2,135.40 | 2,135.40 | 2,135.40 |
| O-1 | 2d Lieutenant Ensign | 1,394.10 | 1,684.50 | 1,684.50 | 1,685.40 |
| | | **WARRANT OFFICERS** | | | |
| W-4 | Chief Warrant Comm. Warrant | $1,933.20 | $2,249.10 | $2,762.70 | $3,077.40 |
| W-3 | Chief Warrant Comm. Warrant | 1,776.60 | 2,067.30 | 2,430.00 | 2,606.40 |
| W-2 | Chief Warrant Comm. Warrant | 1,551.90 | 1,844.10 | 2,180.70 | 2,268.60 |
| W-1 | Warrant Officer | 1,370.40 | 1,684.50 | 2,023.50 | 2,023.50 |
| | | **ENLISTED MEMBERS** | | | |
| E-9 | Sgt. Major Master C.P.O. | N.A. | $2,096.10 | $2,337.00 | $2,698.80 |
| E-8 | Master Sgt. Senior C.P.O. | N.A. | 1,808.10 | 2,048.40 | 2,410.20 |
| E-7 | Sgt. Ist Class Chief Petty Officer | $1,324.80 | 1,566.00 | 1,807.20 | 2,168.70 |
| E-6 | Staff Sgt. Petty Officer, 1st Class | 1,150.80 | 1,392.90 | 1,583.10 | 1,583.10 |
| E-5 | Sergeant Petty Officer, 2d Class | 1,008.60 | 1,272.60 | 1,343.40 | 1,343.40 |
| E-4 | Corporal Petty Officer, 3d Class | 912.60 | 1,082.40 | 1,082.40 | 1,082.40 |
| E-3 | Private 1st Class Seaman | 858.90 | 928.80 | 928.80 | 928.80 |
| E-2 | Private Seaman Apprentice | 783.60 | 783.60 | 783.60 | 783.60 |
| E-1 | Recruit[2] Seaman Recruit[2] | 646.20 | 646.20 | 646.20 | 646.20 |

**Note**: Effective Jan. 1, 1989. In addition, military personnel not living on base are provided a basic allowance for quarters, which ranges from approximately $250–600 a month for enlisted members. Officers with dependents receive approximately $400–700 a month, enlisted members $280–500 a month. 1. Basic pay is limited to $6,291.60 per month, to correspond to Level V of the Executive Schedule (as of Apr. 1989). 2. Less than four months' service. **Source**: U.S. Dept. of Defense.

## U.S. SERVICE AND CASUALTIES IN MAJOR WARS AND CONFLICTS

| Division of service | Number serving | Battle deaths | Other deaths | Wounds not mortal |
|---|---|---|---|---|
| **REVOLUTIONARY WAR (1775–83)** | | | | |
| Army | N.A. | 4,044 | N.A. | 6,004 |
| Navy | N.A. | 342 | N.A. | 114 |
| Marines | N.A. | 49 | N.A. | 70 |
| Total | N.A. | 4,435 | N.A. | 6,188 |
| **WAR OF 1812 (1812–15)** | | | | |
| Army | N.A. | 1,950 | N.A. | 4,000 |
| Navy | N.A. | 265 | N.A. | 439 |
| Marines | N.A. | 45 | N.A. | 66 |
| Total | 286,730 | 2,260 | N.A. | 4,505 |
| **MEXICAN WAR (1846–48)** | | | | |
| Army | N.A. | 1,721 | 11,550 | 4,102 |
| Navy | N.A. | 1 | N.A. | 3 |
| Marines | N.A. | 11 | N.A. | 47 |
| Total | 78,718 | 1,733 | 11,550 | 4,152 |
| **CIVIL WAR (1861–65)[1]** | | | | |
| Army | 2,128,948 | 138,154 | 221,374 | 280,040 |
| Navy | 84,415[2] | 2,112 | 2,411 | 1,710 |
| Marines | — | 148 | 312 | 131 |
| Total | 2,213,363 | 140,414 | 224,097 | 281,881 |
| **SPANISH-AMERICAN WAR (1898)** | | | | |
| Army | 280,564 | 369 | 2,061 | 1,594 |
| Navy | 22,875 | 10 | 0 | 47 |
| Marines | 3,321 | 6 | 0 | 21 |
| Total | 306,760 | 385 | 2,061 | 1,662 |
| **WORLD WAR I (1917–1918)** | | | | |
| Army | 4,057,101 | 50,510 | 55,868 | 193,663 |
| Navy | 599,051 | 431 | 6,856 | 819 |
| Marines | 78,839 | 2,461 | 390 | 9,520 |
| Total | 4,734,991 | 53,402 | 63,114 | 204,002 |
| **WORLD WAR II (1941–46)** | | | | |
| Army | 11,260,000 | 234,874 | 83,400 | 565,861 |
| Navy | 4,183,466 | 36,950 | 25,664 | 37,778 |
| Marines | 669,100 | 19,733 | 4,778 | 67,207 |
| Total | 16,112,556 | 291,557 | 113,842 | 670,846 |
| **KOREAN CONFLICT (1950–53)** | | | | |
| Army | 2,834,000 | 27,709 | N.A. | 77,596 |
| Navy | 1,177,000 | 468 | 939 | 1,576 |
| Marines | 424,000 | 4,267 | 1,261 | 23,744 |
| Air Force | 1,285,000 | 1,302 | 243 | 368 |
| Total | 5,720,000 | 33,746 | N.A. | 103,284 |
| **VIETNAM CONFLICT (1964–73)** | | | | |
| Army | 4,368,000 | 30,905 | 7,275 | 96,802 |
| Navy | 1,842,000 | 1,631 | 925 | 4,178 |
| Marines | 794,000 | 13,081 | 1,754 | 51,392 |
| Air Force | 1,740,000 | 1,738 | 842 | 931 |
| Total | 8,744,000 | 47,355 | 10,796 | 153,303 |

**Note:** N.A. = not available. Prior to World War I, dates are approximate. Actual period covered for World War I: Apr. 6, 1917–Nov. 11, 1918; World War II: Dec. 7, 1941–Dec. 31, 1946; Korea: June 25, 1950–July 27, 1953; Vietnam: Aug. 4, 1964–Jan. 27, 1973. 1. Union forces only; authoritative statistics for Confederate forces not available. Estimates of the number who served range from 600,000 to 1.5 million. *The Final Report of the Provost Marshal General, 1863–1866* indicated 133,821 Confederate deaths (74,524 battle and 59,297 other) based upon incomplete returns. In addition, an estimated 26,000–31,000 Confederate prisoners died in prisons. 2. Includes Navy and Marines. **Source:** U.S. Dept. of Defense, *Defense 90* (1990).

## FEDERAL BUDGET OUTLAYS FOR NATIONAL DEFENSE FUNCTIONS, 1970–91
(billions of dollars)

| Function | 1970 | 1975 | 1980 | 1985 | 1990 | 1991[1] |
|---|---|---|---|---|---|---|
| Defense Dept., military | $80.1 | $84.9 | $130.9 | $245.2 | $289.8 | $287.5 |
| Military personnel | 29.0 | 32.2 | 40.9 | 67.8 | 75.4 | 78.9 |
| Percent of military budget | 36.2% | 37.9% | 31.2% | 27.7% | 26.0% | 27.4% |
| Operations and maintenance | $21.6 | $26.3 | $44.9 | $72.4 | $87.2 | $85.1 |
| Procurement | 21.6 | 16.0 | 29.0 | 70.4 | 81.0 | 79.1 |
| Research, development, test, and evaluation | 7.2 | 8.9 | 13.1 | 27.1 | 37.5 | 35.5 |
| Military construction | 1.2 | 1.5 | 2.5 | 4.3 | 5.1 | 4.6 |
| Family housing | 0.6 | 1.1 | 1.7 | 2.6 | 3.5 | 3.3 |
| Other[2] | −1.1 | −1.1 | −1.1 | 0.6 | −0.5 | 0.4 |
| Atomic energy activities[3] | 1.4 | 1.5 | 2.9 | 7.1 | 9.0 | 10.5 |
| Defense-related activities[4] | 0.2 | 0.2 | 0.2 | 0.5 | 0.6 | 0.9 |
| **Total outlays** | **$81.7** | **$86.5** | **$134.0** | **$252.7** | **$299.3** | **$298.9** |
| Annual percent change[5] | 10.1% | 9.0% | 15.2% | 11.1% | −1.4% | −0.1% |

1. Estimated. 2. Includes revolving and management funds, trust funds, special foreign currency programs, allowances, and offsetting receipts. 3. Includes defense activities only. 4. Includes civil defense activities. 5. Change from immediate prior year; except for 1970, change from 1965. **Source:** U.S. Office of Management and Budget, *Budget of the United States Government* (annual).

## MINORITIES IN UNIFORM, 1989

| Service | Black Number | Black Percent | Hispanic Number | Hispanic Percent | Other[1] Number | Other[1] Percent | Total Number | Total Percent |
|---|---|---|---|---|---|---|---|---|
| | | | | **OFFICERS** | | | | |
| Army | 11,435 | 10.7% | 1,858 | 1.7% | 3,291 | 3.1% | 16,548 | 15.6% |
| Navy | 2,776 | 3.8 | 1,617 | 2.2 | 1,980 | 2.7 | 6,373 | 8.8 |
| Marine Corps | 1,013 | 5.1 | 446 | 2.2 | 390 | 2.0 | 1,849 | 9.3 |
| Air Force | 5,671 | 5.5 | 2,097 | 2.0 | 2,896 | 2.8 | 10,664 | 10.4 |
| Total | 20,895 | 6.9 | 6,018 | 2.0 | 8,557 | 2.8 | 35,470 | 11.8 |
| | | | | **ENLISTED** | | | | |
| Army | 205,663 | 31.6% | 27,713 | 4.3% | 29,562 | 4.5% | 262,938 | 40.3% |
| Navy | 86,926 | 17.1 | 28,752 | 5.7 | 28,393 | 5.6 | 14,0717 | 28.3 |
| Marine Corps | 36,877 | 20.8 | 12,362 | 7.0 | 5,494 | 3.1 | 54,733 | 30.9 |
| Air Force | 79,578 | 17.3 | 17,288 | 3.8 | 15,276 | 3.3 | 112,142 | 24.4 |
| Total | 409,044 | 22.8 | 86,115 | 4.8 | 78,725 | 4.4 | 573,884 | 31.9 |

**Note:** As of December 1989. 1. Includes Native Americans, Alaskan Natives, and Pacific Islanders. **Source:** U.S. Dept. of Defense, *Defense 90* (1990).

## WOMEN IN UNIFORM, 1989

| Service | Officers Number | Officers Percent | Enlisted Number | Enlisted Percent |
|---|---|---|---|---|
| Army | 12,134 | 11.4% | 74,335 | 11.4% |
| Navy | 7,557 | 10.5 | 49,735 | 9.9 |
| Marine Corps | 671 | 3.4 | 8,809 | 5.0 |
| Air Force | 13,406 | 13.0 | 63,176 | 13.7 |
| Total | 33,768 | 11.2 | 196,055 | 11.0 |

**Source:** U.S. Dept. of Defense, *Defense 90* (1990).

## U.S. SERVICE ACADEMIES

U.S. Military Academy, West Point, N.Y. 10996 (1802).

U.S. Naval Academy, Annapolis, Md. 21402 (1845).

U.S. Air Force Academy, Colorado Springs, Colo. 80840 (1954).

U.S. Coast Guard Academy, New London, Conn. 06320 (1876).

U.S. Merchant Marine Academy, Kings Point, N.Y. 11024 (1943).

## TOP 10 DEFENSE CONTRACTORS, 1990

In fiscal year 1990, the Department of Defense awarded approximately $131 billion in prime defense contracts (excluding small awards of less than $25,000). The top 10 companies accounted for a third of all contracts awarded.

| Company | Awards ('000s) | Percent of total |
|---|---|---|
| **Total contract awards** | **$130,758,093** | **100.00%** |
| Top 100 contractors | 86,670,694 | 66.28 |
| Top 10 contractors | 43,288,296 | 33.10 |
| McDonnell Douglas Corp. | 8,211,427 | 6.27 |
| General Dynamics Corp. | 6,303,093 | 4.82 |
| General Electric Co. | 5,588,964 | 4.27 |
| General Motors Corp. | 4,106,570 | 3.14 |
| Raytheon | 4,070,955 | 3.11 |
| Lockheed Corp. | 3,552,628 | 2.71 |
| Martin Marietta Corp. | 3,491,992 | 2.67 |
| United Technologies Corp. | 2,855,766 | 2.18 |
| Grumman Corp. | 2,696,966 | 2.06 |
| Tenneco, Inc. | 2,409,935 | 1.84 |

**Source:** U.S. Dept. of Defense, *100 Companies Receiving the Largest Dollar Volume of Prime Contract Awards, FY1990* (1991).

## MILITARY PERSONNEL ON ACTIVE DUTY: SELECTED YEARS 1801–1990

| Year/War | Total[1] | Year/War | Total[1] | Year/War | Total[1] | Year/War | Total[1] |
|---|---|---|---|---|---|---|---|
| 1801 | 7,108 | CIVIL WAR | | 1920 | 343,302 | VIETNAM CONFLICT | |
| 1810 | 11,554 | 1861 | 217,112 | 1930 | 255,648 | 1966 | 3,094,058 |
| WAR OF 1812 | | 1862 | 673,124 | 1940 | 458,365 | 1967 | 3,376,880 |
| 1813 | 25,152 | 1863 | 960,061 | 1941 | 1,801,101 | 1968 | 3,547,902 |
| 1814 | 46,858 | 1864 | 1,031,724 | WORLD WAR II | | 1969 | 3,460,162 |
| 1815 | 40,885 | 1865 | 1,062,848 | 1942 | 3,858,791 | 1970 | 3,066,294 |
| 1820 | 15,113 | 1870 | 50,348 | 1943 | 9,044,745 | 1975 | 2,128,000[2] |
| 1830 | 11,942 | 1880 | 37,894 | 1944 | 11,451,719 | 1980 | 2,051,000[2] |
| 1840 | 21,616 | 1890 | 38,666 | 1945 | 12,123,455 | 1986 | 2,169,000[2] |
| MEXICAN WAR | | SPANISH-AMERICAN WAR | | 1946 | 3,030,088 | 1987 | 2,174,000[2] |
| 1846 | 39,165 | 1898 | 235,785 | 1950 | 1,460,261 | 1988 | 2,138,000[2] |
| 1847 | 57,761 | 1900 | 139,344 | KOREAN CONFLICT | | 1989 | 2,130,200[2] |
| 1848 | 60,308 | 1915 | 174,112 | 1951 | 3,249,455 | 1990 | 2,076,400[3] |
| 1850 | 20,824 | WORLD WAR I | | 1952 | 3,635,912 | | |
| 1860 | 27,958 | 1917 | 643,833 | 1953 | 3,555,067 | | |
| | | 1918 | 2,897,167 | 1960 | 2,476,435 | | |
| | | 1919 | 1,172,602 | | | | |

1. Excludes the Coast Guard. 2. Figures rounded after 1970. 3. Estimated. **Source:** U.S. Bureau of the Census, *Statistical History of the U.S.* (1976) and *Statistical Abstract of the United States, 1991* (1991).

*"In the councils of government, we must guard against the acquisition of unwarranted influence, whether sought or unsought, by the military-industrial complex. The potential for the disastrous rise of misplaced power exists and will persist."*

—Dwight D. Eisenhower, from his farewell address (1961)

# Social Insurance Programs

In order to provide a safety net for disadvantaged, elderly, and disabled persons, the federal government administers a range of social insurance and social assistance programs, including Medicare, unemployment insurance, workers' compensation, and temporary disability insurance. Also included are an array of "income support programs" such as supplemental security income (SSI), aid to families with dependent children (AFDC), Medicaid, food stamps, low-income home-energy assistance, public housing, special nutritional programs, and general assistance. Three additional programs provide for veterans, public employees, and railroad employees.

Social insurance programs were not developed all at once to fulfill a specific agenda of national need. Rather, they are a hodgepodge of legislation passed (and often altered) over the years to meet the needs of particular groups of citizens at particular times. In what the government calls social insurance programs, certain risks—injury, disability, unemployment, old age, and death—are lumped together. "Premiums," usually in the form of a payroll tax, are paid by employees and/or their employers. The benefit is paid, regardless of other financial resources (other than earnings), when one of those "risks" occurs.

## Social Security

The Great Depression proved that traditional support systems—the family, private charities, and local government—failed in nationwide economic hard times. Many old people had exhausted their savings and were desti-

## SOCIAL SERVICE PROGRAMS

Information about social service programs can be obtained from the following government agencies:
**Aid to Families with Dependent Children (AFDC)** Family Support Admin., U.S. Dept. of Health and Human Services.
**Black lung program** Office of Workers Compensation Progs., U.S. Dept. of Labor.
**Food Stamps** Food and Nutrition Service, U.S. Dept. of Agriculture.
**Housing subsidies** Special Needs Assistance Progs., U.S. Dept. of Housing and Urban Development; Farmers Home Admin.
**Medicaid** Health Care Financing Admin., U.S. Dept. of Health and Human Services.
**Medicare (HI)** Health Care Financing Admin., U.S. Dept. of Health and Human Services.
**Social Security (OASDI)** Social Security Admin., U.S. Dept. of Health and Human Services.
**Special nutrition programs** Food and Nutrition Service, U.S. Dept. of Agriculture.
**Supplemental Security Income (SSI)** Social Security Admin., U.S. Dept. of Health and Human Services.
**Temporary disability insurance** Employment and Training Admin., U.S. Dept. of Labor.
**Unemployment insurance** Office of Workers Compensation Progs., U.S. Dept. of Labor.
**Veterans' benefits** U.S. Dept. of Veterans Affairs.

**Note**: For additional information see Part II, "Executive Departments."

tute; during the depression less than 10% of the aged left estates large enough to be probated. This led to the enactment of one of the most comprehensive pieces of legislation ever passed by Congress, the Social Security Act.

Signed into law by Franklin Roosevelt on Aug. 14, 1935, the Social Security Act established two social insurance programs: a federal system of old-age benefits for retired workers in commerce and industry, and a federal-state system of unemployment insurance. The law also

provided for federal matching grants-in-aid to states to help them assist the needy aged, blind persons, and children. Today, in the words of former Social Security Commissioner Dorcas R. Hardy, it is the "most complex government program that God and Congress ever created."

The first payments of monthly benefits were made in 1940; since then, $2.9 trillion in cash benefits have been paid. Major changes in the scope of Social Security were made in 1956, when the program was broadened through the addition of disability insurance; in 1965, through the addition of Medicare and Medicaid; in 1970, when the "black lung" program was developed to provide benefits to coal miners who suffer from black lung disease; in 1972, when Congress authorized cost-of-living increases; and in 1974, when Social Security insurance was taken over by the Social Security Administration. In 1983, amendments provided for the taxing of up to one-half of benefits for certain upper-income beneficiaries.

Workers and their employers each contribute an equal amount to the Social Security program to pay for retirement, disability, and Medicare benefits. The amount deducted from paychecks has increased steadily since 1983, and leveled off in 1990 at 7.65% on earnings up to $51,300. (The cap on earnings can be adjusted for inflation; in 1991 it was $53,400.) Employers must contribute the same amount. Self-employed workers, who are both employee and employer, pay both shares, or a total of 15.3%.

### Old-age, survivors and disability insurance (OASDI)
This program's basic principles are that benefits are related to earnings in covered work, benefits are paid regardless of income from savings, pensions, etc., and universal compulsory coverage is to assure a base of economic security. Monthly benefits are payable at age 65 to workers who are eligible, and lump sum payments are made to the estates of workers who die before reaching 65. The addition of disability insurance in 1956 broadened the program's scope, and in 1972 Congress authorized provisions for cost-of-liv-

ing increases. The 1983 amendments improved the program's financial footing with tax rate increases, permanent increases in self-employment tax rates, and taxing up to one-half of benefits for certain upper-income beneficiaries: single retirees with adjusted gross income (AGI) above $25,000 and married couples with AGI above $32,000.

**Eligibility** Insured status: A worker must have a specific amount of work-covered employment (about 97% of all jobs today are covered by the program, compared with 55% in 1939). Persons reaching age 62 in 1991 or later will need credit for 10 years of work in covered jobs to qualify for retirement benefits. If a worker dies before achieving fully insured status, survivor benefits may be paid to his or her spouse.

**Annual earnings test** Monthly benefits are paid to a worker and to his or her family members and survivors only when they do not have substantial earnings from work. Retirees under 65 may earn up to $7,080. Retirees age 65 to 69 may earn $9,720 in income before benefits are reduced. Retirees over age 70 receive benefits regardless of income.

For beneficiaries under age 65 who have earnings in excess of these amounts, $1 of benefits is lost for each $2 of earnings; for beneficiaries age 65–69, the reduction rate is $1 for every $3 of earnings in excess of the exempt amount.

**Disability requirement** For monthly benefits, the impairment must prohibit the individual from engaging in any kind of substantial gainful work (up to $500 a month). Work is encouraged by referrals to state vocational rehabilitation agencies, and the individual is allowed a trial period of work during which benefits continue.

**Benefit amounts** A worker's Social Security benefit is based on his or her average "covered" earning computed over the period of time he or she could have been expected to work. Workers become eligible for benefits at age 62. However, a worker who retires at 62 receives as little as 80% of the full amount that would have been payable at age 65. The normal retirement age will be increased gradually from 65 to 67, beginning in 2003. The highest basic monthly payment for workers who retired at age 65 in 1991 and who consistently had earnings of at least $51,300 was $1,022.90.

The OASDI programs are financed from tax-es collected on earnings in covered jobs from employees and employers, which are deposited in two separate trust funds. The money received by the trust funds can be used only to pay OASDI benefits and operating expenses.

**Medicare** The Social Security Amendments of 1965 established two contributory health insurance programs designed to provide assistance for medical expenses for the aged and disabled. The first is a compulsory program of hospital insurance (HI) which provides basic protection against the costs of inpatient hospital services and related post-hospital care, including home health services, part-time nursing care, and physical therapy. Persons reaching age 65 without qualifying for HI may voluntarily enroll by paying a monthly premium.

The second health program is supplementary medical insurance (SMI) coverage, a voluntary program in which enrolled individuals pay a monthly premium of $29.90. The program's coverage includes physician's and surgeon's services, outpatient services and laboratory tests, ambulance services, surgical dressings, home health services, and comprehensive outpatient services.

As with OASDI, hospital insurance is financed by a tax on earnings: of the 7.65% tax on earnings (FICA) deducted from employee paychecks, 1.65% is for hospital insurance and the 6.2% is for OASDI.

**Effectiveness of Social Security** According to the government, the Social Security system has achieved its basic goal of helping elderly people maintain a basic standard of living. It has dramatically reduced the poverty rate for the elderly from 35% in 1959 to 11.4% in 1989. The benefits are the primary source of cash income for most elderly Americans, providing 53% of total income for all retirees age

## SOCIAL INSURANCE PROGRAMS: BENEFICIARIES AND BENEFITS

| Program | Beneficiaries | Benefits (billions) |
|---|---|---|
| OASDI | 39.8 mil. (1990) | $230.9 (1988) |
| Medicare | 33.3 mil. (1991[1]) | 80.3 (1991[1]) |
| Medicaid | 23.5 mil. (1989) | 54.4 (1989) |
| Food Stamps | 18.8 mil. (1989) | 11.7 (1989) |
| AFDC | 11.4 mil. (1990) | 18.5 (1990) |
| SSI | 4.8 mil. (1990) | 16.1 (1990) |

**Note:** OASDI = old-age, survivors and disability insurance; AFDC = aid to families with dependent children; SSI = social security insurance. 1. Estimated. **Source:** Social Security Administration, publ. in U.S. House of Representatives, Committee on Ways and Means, *Overview of Entitlement Programs, 1991 Green Book* (1991).

## APPROXIMATE MONTHLY RETIREMENT, DISABILITY, AND SURVIVOR BENEFITS

| Worker's age, 1990 | Worker's family | Insured worker's earnings, 1989 | | | |
|---|---|---|---|---|---|
| | | $15,000 | $25,000 | $35,000 | $48,000 + |
| **Retirement benefits[1]** | | | | | |
| 55 | Retired worker only | $632 | $ 906 | $1,027 | $1,126 |
| | Worker and spouse[2] | 948 | 1,359 | 1,540 | 1,689 |
| 65 | Retired worker only | 582 | 832 | 925 | 975 |
| | Worker and spouse[2] | 873 | 1,248 | 1,387 | 1,463 |
| **Disability benefits[3]** | | | | | |
| 25 | Disabled worker only | $591 | $848 | $992 | $1,149 |
| | Disabled, with dependents[4] | 887 | 1,272 | 1,488 | 1,724 |
| 35 | Disabled worker only | 586 | 839 | 986 | 1,122 |
| | Disabled, with dependents[4] | 879 | 1,258 | 1,479 | 1,683 |
| 45 | Disabled worker only | 585 | 837 | 969 | 1,048 |
| | Disabled, with dependents[4] | 877 | 1,256 | 1,454 | 1,573 |
| 55 | Disabled worker only | 584 | 834 | 937 | 990 |
| | Disabled, with dependents[4] | 877 | 1,251 | 1,406 | 1,486 |
| 64 | Disabled worker only | 573 | 819 | 910 | 957 |
| | Disabled, with dependents[4] | 860 | 1,228 | 1,365 | 1,435 |
| **Survivor benefits[5]** | | | | | |
| 25 | Spouse and 1 child[6] | $892 | $1,280 | $1,494 | $1,736 |
| | Spouse and 2 children[7] | 1,063 | 1,495 | 1,742 | 2,026 |
| | 1 child only | 446 | 640 | 747 | 868 |
| | Spouse at age 60 | 425 | 610 | 712 | 828 |
| 35 | Spouse and 1 child[6] | 878 | 1,260 | 1,480 | 1,712 |
| | Spouse and 2 children[7] | 1,040 | 1,476 | 1,726 | 1,996 |
| | 1 child only | 439 | 630 | 740 | 856 |
| | Spouse at age 60 | 419 | 600 | 705 | 816 |
| 45 | Spouse and 1 child[6] | 876 | 1,256 | 1,460 | 1,586 |
| | Spouse and 2 children[7] | 1,036 | 1,472 | 1,703 | 1,849 |
| | 1 child only | 438 | 628 | 730 | 793 |
| | Spouse at age 60 | 418 | 599 | 696 | 756 |
| 55 | Spouse and 1 child[6] | 876 | 1,300 | 1,406 | 1,486 |
| | Spouse and 2 children[7] | 1,035 | 1,468 | 1,639 | 1,733 |
| | 1 child only | 438 | 625 | 703 | 743 |
| | Spouse at age 60 | 418 | 596 | 670 | 708 |
| 65 | Spouse and 1 child[6] | 872 | 1,248 | 1,386 | 1,462 |
| | Spouse and 2 children[7] | 1,036 | 1,461 | 1,618 | 1,705 |
| | 1 child only | 436 | 624 | 693 | 731 |
| | Spouse at age 60 | 416 | 595 | 661 | 697 |

**Note:** Assumes steady earnings; actual benefits depend on the pattern of past and future earnings. 1. If worker retires at normal retirement age with steady lifetime earnings. 2. Spouse is assumed to be the same age as the worker. Spouse may qualify for a higher retirement benefit based on his or her own work record. 3. For workers with steady earnings and disabled in 1990. 4. Includes spouse and child, the maximum family benefit. 5. For workers with steady earnings who died in 1990. 6. Benefits are the same for two children if no parent survives or if the surviving parent has substantial earnings. 7. Equals maximum family benefit. **Source:** Social Security Administration publications *Retirement* (1990), *Disability* (1990), and *Survivors* (1990).

65 and over. For 23% of the elderly, it constitutes 90% or more of total income. And for 14% of the elderly, Social Security is the only source of income. For all people receiving social insurance benefits (including Social Security)—not just the elderly—the payouts lifted 15.2 million out of poverty, reducing the number of poor to 33.8 million in 1989. Means-tested cash and in-kind transfers reduce the poverty count by an additional 6.2 million individuals.

## Future of Social Security

Originally funded on a "pay-as-you-go" basis, the system was overhauled in 1988 to keep it fiscally sound into the future. In 1988 the program's funds were running down because of an interval in the 1970s when prices outpaced wages and cost-of-living adjustments were not being offset by increased payments into the funds. To bolster the funds and protect today's young generation from large tax hikes when the baby-boom generation retires, the government ordered incremental increases in

## OASDI BENEFICIARIES AND BENEFIT PAYMENTS, 1990

| Beneficiaries | Beneficiaries ('000s) | Percent of all beneficiaries | Average monthly benefit |
|---|---|---|---|
| Retired workers | 24,838 | 62.4% | $603 |
| Wives and husbands of retired workers | 3,101 | 7.8 | 311 |
| Children of retired workers | 422 | 1.1 | 259 |
| Disabled workers | 3,011 | 7.6 | 587 |
| Wives and husbands of disabled workers | 266 | 0.7 | 150 |
| Children of disabled workers | 989 | 2.5 | 164 |
| Widowed mothers and fathers | 304 | 0.8 | 409 |
| Surviving children | 1,776 | 4.5 | 406 |
| Widows and widowers | 5,010 | 12.6 | 556 |
| Disabled widow(er)s | 101 | 0.3 | 389 |
| Parents | 6 | (z) | 482 |
| Special age-72 | 7 | (z) | 167 |
| **Total monthly beneficiaries** | **39,832** | **100.0%** | **$544** |

**Note**: Figures as of December. OASDI = old-age, survivors and disability insurance. z = less than 0.1%. **Source**: Social Security Administration, publ. in U.S. House of Representatives, Committee on Ways and Means, *Overview of Entitlement Programs, 1991 Green Book* (1991).

## MEDICARE RECIPIENTS AND BENEFITS, 1991

| Program | Total enrolled ('000s) | Enrollees served ('000) | Average annual benefit |
|---|---|---|---|
| **AGED ENROLLEES** | | | |
| Total[1] | 33,671 | 7,035 | $2,046 |
| Hospital insurance | 30,332 | 6,330 | 2,148 |
| Supplementary medical insurance | 3,339 | 705 | 2,046 |
| **DISABLED ENROLLEES** | | | |
| Total[1] | 32,732 | 26,263 | $1,361 |
| Hospital insurance | 29,777 | 24,045 | 1,346 |
| Supplementary medical insurance | 2,955 | 2,218 | 1,517 |

**Note**: As of July 1. 1. Unduplicated count of persons enrolled under one or both parts of the program. **Source**: Social Security Administration, publ. in U.S. House of Representatives, Committee on Ways and Means, *Overview of Entitlement Programs, 1991 Green Book* (1991).

the Social Security tax rate. The program quickly began building reserves because there were millions more workers paying into the system than there were retirees and others receiving benefits. Projections indicate annual surpluses reaching $500 million a day or close to $200 billion a year by the start of the next century. Only well into the next century, when the baby boomers retire, do forecasts show the surpluses diminishing. However, the Hospital Insurance Fund (Medicare) will start to run a deficit because of the aging population by the year 2000 unless it receives additional funding. Estimates are that the "nest egg" for retirement benefits will have disappeared by 2050, eaten away by baby boomers who will have started to retire in 2010.

## Other Programs

**Unemployment compensation** The Social Security Act provided an inducement to states to enact unemployment insurance laws. The Department of Labor oversees the system, but each state, as well as the District of Columbia, Puerto Rico, and the Virgin Islands, administers its own program. Covered employers are charged a tax of 6.2% on the first $7,000 of each worker's covered wages annually. About 106 million workers—90% of all wage and salary workers—were covered in 1990.

**Eligibility** Workers must be ready, able, and willing to work and must be registered for work at a state public employment office. A worker's benefit is based on his or her employment in covered work over a prior performance period. No state can deny benefit to a claimant if he or she refuses to accept a new job under substandard labor conditions or where he or she would be required to join a company union.

In 1990, there were 8.1 million beneficiaries. Their average weekly benefit was $161 and the average duration of benefit was 13.5 weeks. The weekly benefit varies from state to state, but the general formula is designed to compensate for between 50% and 70% of average weekly pretax wage, up to a state-determined minimum. All but three states provide a statutory maximum of 26 weeks of benefits in a

benefit year. Minimum benefits—from $5 to $68 a week—are provided in every state. Maximum benefits range from $96 in Indiana to $423 in Massachusetts.

**Workers' compensation** Social insurance began in the United States with workers' compensation. A law covering federal civilian employees engaged in hazardous jobs was enacted in 1908, and the first state compensation law to be held constitutional was enacted in 1911. These laws made industry responsible for the compensation of workers (or their survivors) injured or killed while on the job, and were designed to provide cash benefits and medical care when workers were injured in connection with their jobs. A worker incurring an occupational injury is compensated regardless of fault or blame in the accident. A federal program enacted in 1969 protects coal miners (see "Black lung program"). In 1987, benefits paid under workers' compensation programs totaled more than $27 billion.

Workers' compensation is almost exclusively financed by employers, on the principle that the cost of work-related accidents is part of the expense of production. Employers can use private insurance companies or can qualify as self-insurers.

**Eligibility** The cash benefits for temporary total disability, permanent, total, or partial disability, or death of a breadwinner is usually about 66.6% of weekly earnings at the time of the accident. Most state laws pay temporary disability benefits for as long as the disability lasts and the condition has not been stabilized to the point where no further improvement can result from medical treatment. About 87% of the nation's employed wage and salary labor force are covered by compensation laws. The most usual exempted workers are domestic, agricultural, and casual laborers.

**Permanent partial disability** Compensation for specific, or "schedule," injuries (for clearly measurable matters) is generally subject to different (usually lower) dollar maximums and is determined without regard to loss of earning power. Compensation for "nonschedule" injuries (injuries to head, back, nervous system) is the difference between wages before and after impairment.

**Death benefits** Compensation is related to earnings and is graduated by the number of dependents.

**Medical benefits** are furnished without limit as to time or amount for accidental injuries.

**Black lung program** Established by the Federal Coal Mine Health and Safety Act of 1969, this provides monthly cash benefits to coal miners who are totally disabled because of black lung disease (pneumoconiosis) and to survivors of miners who die from this disease. At the end of 1990, 352,652 disabled workers, dependents, and survivors were receiving cash benefits. The monthly benefit payable to a disabled miner is a flat amount equal to 37.5% of the monthly pay rate for a federal government employee in the first step of Grade GS-2—$387.10 as of January 1991. The benefit is increased based on the number of dependents, up to $774.10 for three or more. Most of the benefits are paid out of a trust fund financed by an excise tax on coal.

**Temporary disability insurance** provides coverage against the risk of lost wages due to short-term nonoccupational disability. The Federal Unemployment Tax Act permits states where employees make contributions under the unemployment insurance program to use some or all of those contributions for disability benefits. It is estimated that in 1986 about two-thirds of the nation's wage and salary earners had some protection through various voluntary and governmental group arrangements. In general the benefit amount for a week is intended to replace at least half the weekly wage loss for a maximum of 26 to 39 weeks per year.

## Income Support Programs

To be eligible for these programs, a person must have income and assets below a certain level and often must meet other eligibility criteria. Today Supplemental Security Income (SSI) and Aid to Families with Dependent Children (AFDC) are the two major cash assistance programs. A number of other programs, including Medicaid and food stamps, provide benefits for special needs and purposes.

**Poverty income guidelines** The poverty income guidelines are used to determine whether a person or family is eligible for assistance under a particular federal program. Since 1973 the poverty income guidelines have been computed from the official poverty-threshold by increasing the weighted average poverty-thresholds by the percentage change in the Consumer Price Index during the preceding year and rounding the value for a family of four up to the next higher $50. Poverty income guidelines for families with fewer or more than four members are derived from that for a family of four.

## Programs for Special Groups

**Veterans' benefits** The tradition of veterans' benefits dates to the 18th century when the Continental Congress provided disability pensions for veterans of the Revolutionary War. Today, the Department of Veterans Affairs (DVA) offers a wide range of services and benefits to eligible veterans, their dependents, and their survivors. In 1990, federal outlays for veterans' benefits and services were $29.1 billion.

While the veteran population as a whole is decreasing in numbers, from about 29.5 million in 1975 to 27.1 million in 1989—the number of veterans age 65 or older is increasing rapidly, from about 2.2 million in 1975 to about 7.1 million in 1990. The use and cost of medical care are expected to grow more rapidly over the next several years than those of other veterans' benefits and services. Compensation and pension caseloads are decreasing steadily due to beneficiary deaths, terminations for excess incomes, and age limitation for dependents. The number of trainees under the Montgomery GI bill will increase as more veterans become eligible.

**Service-connected compensation** is paid to veterans who have incurred injuries or illness

while in service. The amounts of the monthly payments are determined by disability ratings. Death compensation or dependency and indemnity compensation is paid to survivors of veterans who died as a result of service-connected causes. In 1990, about 2.2 million disabled veterans and 321,000 survivors received $11.7 billion in compensation payments.

**Veterans pensions** are means-tested benefits paid to war veterans who have become permanently and totally disabled from non-service-connected causes, and to survivors of war veterans. Benefits are based on family size, and the pensions provide a floor of income. The basic benefit before subtracting other income sources is $9,343 for a veteran with one dependent ($7,133 for a veteran living alone). A surviving spouse with no children could receive two-thirds of the basic benefit amount given a

## FEDERAL POVERTY INCOME GUIDELINES, 1990

| Family size | Contiguous 48 states | Alaska | Hawaii |
|---|---|---|---|
| 1 person | $ 524 | $ 654 | $ 603 |
| 2 people | 702 | 877 | 808 |
| 3 people | 880 | 1,100 | 1,013 |
| 4 people | 1,059 | 1,324 | 1,218 |
| 5 people | 1,237 | 1,547 | 1,423 |
| 6 people | 1,415 | 1,770 | 1,628 |
| 7 people | 1,594 | 1,994 | 1,833 |
| 8 people | 1,772 | 2,217 | 2,038 |
| Increment[1] | 179 | 224 | 205 |

**Note**: Counted (net) monthly income, adjusted for inflation each October; effective October 1990 through September 1991. 1. Amount for each additional family member in family units with more than eight members. **Source**: Social Security Administration, publ. in U.S. House of Representatives, Committee on Ways and Means, *Overview of Entitlement Programs, 1991 Green Book* (1991).

## VETERANS' BENEFITS AND SERVICES: EXPENDITURES AND RECIPIENTS, 1975–89

| Fiscal year | Compensation and pensions | Readjustment, education, job training | Medical programs | Housing loans |
|---|---|---|---|---|
| | **OUTLAYS (billions)** | | | |
| 1975 | $ 7.4 | $4.6 | $3.7 | ([1]) |
| 1980 | 11.0 | 2.3 | 6.5 | ([1]) |
| 1985 | 14.1 | 1.1 | 9.5 | ([1]) |
| 1986 | 14.3 | 0.5 | 9.9 | ([1]) |
| 1987 | 14.3 | 0.5 | 10.3 | ([1]) |
| 1988 | 15.2 | 0.5 | 10.8 | ([1]) |
| 1989 | 15.7 | 0.5 | 11.3 | ([1]) |
| | **RECIPIENTS ('000s)** | | | |
| 1975 | 4,855 | 2,804 | 1,985 | 290 |
| 1980 | 4,646 | 1,232 | 2,671 | 297 |
| 1985 | 4,005 | 491 | 2,963 | 179 |
| 1986 | 3,900 | 388 | 2,942 | 314 |
| 1987 | 3,850 | 312 | 2,900 | 479 |
| 1988 | 3,762 | 273 | 2,922 | 235 |
| 1989 | 3,686 | 330 | 3,344 | 190 |

1. No dollar figures for housing loans are provided because these are revolving funds and are not comparable to program expenditures in the other areas. **Source**: U.S. Dept. of Veterans Affairs, publ. in U.S. House of Representatives, Committee on Ways and Means, *Overview of Entitlement Programs, 1991 Green Book* (1991).

single veteran. About 1.1 million people received $4.0 billion in veterans' pension payments in 1990.

**Medical programs** The DVA operates 172 hospital centers, 126 nursing homes, 32 domiciliaries, and 339 outpatient clinics. In 1990 the DVA's nationwide health system received 3.3 million applications for care. About 1.1 million hospital patients and 97,000 nursing home and domiciliary patients were treated in DVA and non-DVA facilities, and 23 million outpatient visits were provided. In 1990, DVA medical programs cost the federal government $11.4 billion.

The DVA extends free priority care to service-connected disabled veterans, to veterans in special categories, and to needy non-service-connected veterans—in 1991, those with incomes of $21,805 or less if married with one dependent, plus $1,213 for each additional dependent, or $18,171 or less if single. As facilities and other resources permit, the DVA provides care to non-service-connected veterans with incomes that exceed the mandatory care income limits.

**Housing and loan programs** The DVA expects to close about 161,000 guaranteed loans for housing for veterans in 1992. The maximum guaranty is as follows: 50% of the loan amount for loans of $45,000 or less; $22,500 for loans between $45,001 and $56,250; the lesser of $36,000 or 40% of the loan for loans between $56,251 and $144,000; and the lesser of $46,000 or 25% of the loan for loans in excess of $144,000.

**Other veterans' programs** In 1990, the DVA spent $493 million for a variety of education and training programs for eligible veterans and military personnel. The largest program is the Montgomery GI bill, which provides educational assistance. Contributions are required, and veterans can receive a basic educational benefit of up to $300 per month for 36 months while in an educational program.

The veterans' job training act program provides payments to defray training costs of employers who hire certain veterans of the Korean conflict or Vietnam era who have been unemployed for long periods of time.

**Supplemental Security Income (SSI)** In 1972 Congress replaced the federal-state programs for needy aged (over 65 years old), blind, and disabled people with a single federal Supplementary Security Income program. Monthly cash payments are made to eligible persons whose "countable" income (in 1991) is less than $5,124 for individuals receiving only Social Security, or $10,788 for individuals with only wage income. (For married couples, the figures are $10,788 and $15,660 respectively.) Individual assets are limited to $2,000 for an individual and $3,000 for a couple. The qualifying standards for disability benefits are the same as those used for the Social Security disability insurance program. In 1991, the regular federal SSI benefit was $407 for eligible individuals and $610 for eligible couples. To encourage SSI recipients to work, $65 of earned income in any month is excluded from countable income. In 1990, nearly 4.8 million persons were receiving federal SSI payments

## MEDICAID RECIPIENTS AND EXPENDITURES, 1989

| Status | Recipients ('000s) | Expend-itures[1] (mil.) |
|---|---|---|
| Aged | 3,131,620 | $18,558 |
| Blind | 94,844 | 409 |
| Disabled | 3,495,598 | 20,476 |
| Dependent children under 21 | 10,318,231 | 6,892 |
| Adults in families with dependent children | 5,717,380 | 6,897 |
| Other | 1,175,112 | 1,137 |
| **Total** | **23,510,689[2]** | **$54,354** |

1. Does not include Arizona or smaller territories or capitation premium payments. 2. Unduplicated count of recipients. A small number of recipients are in more than one category during the year. **Source**: Social Security Administration, publ. in U.S. House of Representatives, Committee on Ways and Means, *Overview of Entitlement Programs, 1991 Green Book* (1991).

averaging $290 per month. In addition, states have the option of supplementing federal SSI under their own programs or in programs administered by the federal government. Nearly 2.0 million persons received state supplements in 1990; the average payment was $135.75. Total federal and state SSI payments in 1990 were $16.1 billion.

**Medicaid** Enacted jointly with Medicare in 1965, Medicaid provides federal matching funds to states to help pay the cost of medical care and services for low-income persons. Payments are made to suppliers of the care and service. To be eligible for matching funds, a state Medicaid program must cover all persons who receive assistance under AFDC. (Most SSI recipients are also covered.) In 1989, 23.5 million aged, blind, disabled, or poor persons with families received Medicaid benefits at a total cost to state and federal governments of $61.2 billion. Medicaid may also pay the premiums for supplementary medical insurance and the deductible and coinsurance cost of hospital insurance. Medicaid also covers some medical services that Medicare does not.

**Aid to Families with Dependent Children (AFDC)** The Social Security Act of 1935 included a provision authorizing a federal-state program to help needy families with children. Cost of the program is shared by federal, state, and local governments. To qualify for grants, the states must comply with federal guidelines. States may choose whom they will assist, how the assistance will be given, and how much it will be. The states compute "needs standards," taking into account allowances for food, clothing, shelter, utilities, and other necessities. The family's need is theoretically equal to the difference between the amount of the "needs standard" and the family's income. However, states are not required to provide the full amount of the difference. In January 1991 the needs standard for a family of three ranged from a high of $1,029 in Vermont to a low of $310 in New Mexico and only $180 in Puerto Rico. The median maximum state benefit nationwide was $367 (for a family of three), ranging from $124 in Alabama to $891 in Alaska. To qualify, chil-

## VETERANS' COMPENSATION AND BENEFITS, BY PERIOD OF SERVICE AND STATUS, 1980-89

| Veteran status and period of service | Veterans on rolls ('000s) | | | Average payment (annual basis)[1] | | |
|---|---|---|---|---|---|---|
| | 1980 | 1985 | 1989 | 1980 | 1985 | 1989 |
| Total | 4,646 | 4,006 | 3,654 | $2,370 | $3,505 | $4,111 |
| **VETERAN STATUS** | | | | | | |
| Living veterans | 3,195 | 2,931 | 2,776 | $2,600 | $3,666 | $4,126 |
| Service connected | 2,273 | 2,240 | 2,192 | 2,669 | 3,692 | 4,078 |
| Non–service connected | 922 | 690 | 584 | 2,428 | 3,581 | 4,308 |
| Deceased veterans | 1,451 | 1,075 | 878 | 1,863 | 3,066 | 4,062 |
| Service connected | 358 | 336 | 323 | 3,801 | 5,836 | 6,992 |
| Non–service connected | 1,093 | 739 | 555 | 1,228 | 1,809 | 2,358 |
| **PERIOD OF SERVICE** | | | | | | |
| Prior to World War I | 14 | 7 | 4 | $1,432 | $1,855 | $2,388 |
| Living | (z) | (z) | (z) | 2,634 | 4,436 | 8,411 |
| Deceased | 14 | 7 | 4 | 1,403 | 1,822 | 2,296 |
| World War I | 692 | 381 | 228 | 1,683 | 2,461 | 3,181 |
| Living | 198 | 68 | 24 | 2,669 | 4,439 | 6,316 |
| Deceased | 494 | 313 | 204 | 1,288 | 2,029 | 2,808 |
| World War II | 2,520 | 2,097 | 1,796 | 2,307 | 3,317 | 3,851 |
| Living | 1,849 | 1,575 | 1,352 | 2,462 | 3,460 | 3,936 |
| Deceased | 671 | 522 | 445 | 1,880 | 2,888 | 3,594 |
| Korean conflict[2] | 446 | 399 | 391 | 2,691 | 4,114 | 4,836 |
| Living | 317 | 309 | 306 | 2,977 | 4,260 | 4,852 |
| Deceased | 129 | 90 | 85 | 1,990 | 3,615 | 4,776 |
| Peace-time | 312 | 404 | 472 | 3,080 | 3,973 | 4,042 |
| Living | 262 | 352 | 421 | 2,828 | 3,589 | 3,621 |
| Deceased | 50 | 52 | 51 | 4,399 | 6,577 | 7,503 |
| Vietnam era[3] | 662 | 716 | 762 | 2,795 | 4,021 | 4,683 |
| Living | 569 | 626 | 673 | 2,709 | 3,849 | 4,416 |
| Deceased | 93 | 90 | 89 | 3,324 | 5,220 | 6,691 |

**Note**: Living refers to veterans receiving compensation for disability incurred or aggravated while on active duty and war veterans receiving pension and benefits for non-service-connected disabilities. Deceased refers to deceased veterans whose dependents were receiving pensions and compensation benefits. (z) = fewer than 500. 1. Averages based on unrounded expenditures for veterans on the rolls at the end of the fiscal year. 2. Service during period June 27, 1950, to Jan. 31, 1955. 3. Service from Aug. 5, 1964, to May 7, 1975. **Source**: U.S. Dept. of Veterans Affairs, *Annual Report of the Secretary of Veterans Affairs*.

## SUPPLEMENTAL SECURITY INSURANCE, 1990

| Type of payment | Total | Aged | Blind | Disabled |
|---|---|---|---|---|
| **NUMBER OF BENEFICIARIES** | | | | |
| Federal SSI payments | 4,369,502 | 1,257,969 | 74,900 | 3,036,631 |
| Federal SSI only | 2,719,231 | 806,221 | 42,929 | 1,870,081 |
| Federal SSI and state supplementation | 1,650,271 | 451,748 | 31,971 | 1,166,552 |
| State supplementation | 2,045,120 | 645,380 | 40,744 | 1,358,996 |
| State supplementation only | 394,849 | 193,632 | 8,773 | 192,444 |
| **Total** | **4,764,351** | **1,451,601** | **83,673** | **3,229,077** |
| **AVERAGE MONTHLY AMOUNT** | | | | |
| Federal SSI payments | $253.11 | $171.66 | $271.40 | $286.41 |
| State supplementation | 135.75 | 138.41 | 189.10 | 132.89 |
| **Total** | **$290.41** | **$210.30** | **$335.04** | **$325.27** |

**Note**: As of September. **Source**: Social Security Administration, publ. in U.S. House of Representatives, Committee on Ways and Means, *Overview of Entitlement Programs, 1991 Green Book* (1991).

## AFDC BENEFICIARIES AND BENEFITS, 1970-90

| Year | Average monthly beneficiaries ('000s) | | | Average monthly benefit | | Total benefits (millions) |
|---|---|---|---|---|---|---|
| | Families | Recipients | Children | Family | Recipient | |
| 1970 | 1,909 | 7,429 | 5,494 | $178 | $ 46 | $ 4,082 |
| 1975 | 3,342 | 11,067 | 7,928 | 210 | 63 | 8,412 |
| 1980 | 3,642 | 10,597 | 7,320 | 274 | 94 | 11,956 |
| 1985 | 3,692 | 10,813 | 7,165 | 339 | 116 | 14,957 |
| 1990 | 3,967 | 11,439 | 7,744 | 389 | 135 | 18,535 |

**Note**: AFDC = Aid to Families with Dependent Children. **Source**: Social Security Administration, publ. in U.S. House of Representatives, Committee on Ways and Means, *Overview of Entitlement Programs, 1991 Green Book* (1991).

dren generally have to be under the age of 18. AFDC recipients who are employable must register for work in the work incentive program (WIN) and must work a specific number of hours to receive aid.

**Food stamps** By providing eligible applicants with coupons to buy food, this program enables families in need to purchase a nutritionally adequate diet. In general a household is considered eligible if it has less than $2,000 in liquid assets, or if 30% of its countable cash income is insufficient to purchase an adequate low-cost diet, as defined by the U.S. Department of Agriculture's (USDA) "Thrifty Food Plan." As of October 1990, an eligible four-person household with no income received $352 per month in food stamps. (The amount was higher in Alaska, Hawaii, Guam, and the Virgin Islands.)

The Food Stamp Act of 1964 set eligibility requirements for food stamp program participants and provides coupons through state and local agencies that are used to buy food in approved retail stores. The program involved 20.0 million participants in fiscal year 1990, with each participant receiving an average of $59 in monthly coupons. The total value of food stamps issued was $16.5 billion.

States delegate varying degrees of authority to counties and cities, but the federal government finances 100% of the state-issued food benefits and part of the state's administrative costs. The Omnibus Budget Reconciliation Act of 1982 tightened eligibility and authorized pilot projects in which recipients lose their stamps if they don't work at least 20 hours a week.

Although the objective of the food stamp program is to provide benefits equitably to similarly qualified applicants, because of the different state methods of calculating monthly incomes—average or actual—households with monthly incomes close to the eligibility limit can obtain food stamps in some states but not in others.

**Special nutrition programs** The USDA administers a number of programs designed to help safeguard the health and well-being of the nation's children by assisting the states in providing adequate meals to all children at a moderate cost. The programs include the National School Lunch Program, the School Breakfast Program, the Summer Food Service Program, the Child Care Food Program, the Special Milk Program, and the Special Supplemental Food Program for Women, Infants, and Children (WIC) Program. The nutrition program for the elderly requires no income test, but preference is given to those with the greatest need.

**Housing subsidies** The federal government has traditionally provided housing aid directly to lower-income households in the form of rental and mortgage-interest subsidies. The primary purposes are to improve housing quality and to reduce housing costs for lower-income households. Other goals include promoting residential construction, expanding housing opportunities for disadvantaged groups and groups with special housing needs, promoting neighborhood preservation and revitalization, increasing home ownership, and empowering the poor to become home owners.

Most housing aid is targeted to very-low-income renters through two basic types of rental assistance programs. Project-based aid is typically tied to projects specifically produced for lower-income households through new construction or substantial renovation. Almost all project-based aid is provided through production-oriented programs, including the public-housing program, the section 8 new construction and substantial rehabilitation program, and the section 236 mortgage-interest-subsidy program (all administered by the Department of Housing and Urban Development), and the section 515 mortgage-interest-subsidy program administered by the Farmers Home Administration.

Household-based subsidies permit renters to choose from standard housing units in the existing private housing stock. Rental assistance programs generally reduce tenants' rent payments to 30% of their income, with the government paying the balance of the contract rents.

The federal government also assists some lower- and moderate-income householders in becoming home owners by making long-term commitments to reduce their mortgage interest. These generally reduce mortgage payments, property taxes, and insurance costs to a fixed percentage of income, ranging from 20% to 28%.

The total number of households receiving assistance has increased substantially, from 3.2 million at the beginning of fiscal year 1977 to 5.6 million at the beginning of 1991. The number of households receiving rental subsidies increased from 2.1 million to 4.6 million, while the number of home owners receiving assistance in a given year has fluctuated between 1.0 million and 1.2 million, with a steady decline since 1983. Total outlays for housing aid rose from $3.2 billion in 1977 to $18.3 billion in 1990, while per unit outlays rose from $980 to $3,290 in the same period.

**Housing for the homeless** HUD funding for homeless programs is made available to state and local governments, Indian tribes, and nonprofit organizations. In 1991, $234.5 million was appropriated for homeless programs. The specific programs are the Emergency Shelter Grants (ESG) Program, the Supportive Housing Demonstration Program, Shelter-Plus-Care Homeless Rental Housing Assistance, and the HUD-Owned Single Property Disposition Program.

**Head Start** Head Start provides a wide range of services to children of low-income families (and their families) up to the age of 5. Its goals are to improve the social competence, learning skills, and health and nutrition status of low-income children so that they can begin school on an equal footing with their more advantaged peers. The services include cognitive and language development, medical, dental, and mental health services (including screening and immunizations), and nutritional and social services. Parental involvement is extensive, through both volunteer participation and employment of parents as Head Start staff.

At least 90% of Head Start children come from families with incomes at or below the poverty line, and at least 10% of enrollment slots in each state must be available to handicapped children. In 1990, 548,470 children—about 23% of 3-to-5-year old children living in poor families—were served in Head Start programs, at a total federal cost of $1.5 billion. About 70% of Head Start families had incomes below $9,000; only 34% of the heads of households were employed full time, and 45% percent were unemployed; 55% of the families were single-parent families, and 41% were two-parent families.

---

### FEDERAL FOOD ASSISTANCE PROGRAMS, 1970–89

| Program | 1970 | 1980 | 1985 | 1989 |
|---|---|---|---|---|
| **PARTICIPANTS (MILLIONS)** | | | | |
| Food stamps | 4.3 | 21.1 | 19.9 | 18.8 |
| National school lunch program[1] | 22.4 | 26.6 | 23.6 | 24.2 |
| School breakfast[2] | 0.5 | 3.6 | 3.4 | 3.8 |
| Women-infants-children | — | 2.0 | 3.3 | 4.4 |
| Child care feeding[3] | 0.1 | 0.7 | 1.0 | 1.4 |
| Summer feeding[4] | 0.2 | 1.9 | 1.5 | 1.7 |
| Nutrition program for the elderly (meals served) | — | 166 | 225 | 244 |
| **FEDERAL COST (MILLIONS)** | | | | |
| Food stamps | $550 | $8,721 | $10,744 | $11,682 |
| National school lunch program[1] | 300 | 2,279 | 2,578 | 3,005 |
| School breakfast | 11 | 288 | 379 | 512 |
| Women-infants-children | — | 603 | 1,235 | 1,553 |
| Child care feeding[3] | 6 | 207 | 390 | 612 |
| Summer feeding[4] | 2 | 106 | 101 | 132 |
| Nutrition program for the elderly | — | 75 | 134 | 145 |

1. Data are for month in which most pupils participated nationwide. Covers public and private elementary and secondary schools and residential child care institutions. Costs do not include the value of USDA donated commodities. 2. September through May average lunches or breakfasts served, divided by the ratio of average daily attendance to enrollment. 3. Provides year-round subsidies to feed preschool children in child care centers and family day care programs. Number of participants is annual average daily attendance at participating institutions. 4. Provides free meals to poor children in summer months. Number of participants is July average daily attendance at participating institutions. **Source:** U.S. Dept. of Agriculture, *Agricultural Statistics* (annual), and unpublished data.

---

### HEAD START PARTICIPATION AND FUNDING, 1966–91

| Year | Enrollment | Budget authority (millions) |
|---|---|---|
| 1966 | 733,000 | $ 198.9 |
| 1970 | 477,400 | 325.7 |
| 1975 | 349,000 | 403.9 |
| 1980 | 376,300 | 735.0 |
| 1985 | 452,080 | 1,075.0 |
| 1990 | 548,470 | 1,552.0 |
| 1991 | 603,835[1] | 1,951.8 |

**Note:** Since 1982, only full-year services have been provided. 1. Projected. **Source:** U.S. Dept of Health and Human Services, publ. in U.S. House of Representatives, Committee on Ways and Means, *Overview of Entitlement Programs, 1991 Green Book* (1991).

# U.S. Postal Service

At first glance the most compelling facts about today's Postal Service are the sheer size and scope of the operation. With over 800,000 employees moving more than 160 billion pieces of mail annually (656 per capita, and 40% of the world's total), this is surely one of the most vital services the government performs for business and the citizenry alike. What most people don't realize is that it's done at a cost to the consumer significantly less than in any other industrial nation.

First established by the Continental Congress in 1775, the Postal Service was made part of the federal system in the Constitution, and the office of postmaster general was established in George Washington's very first cabinet. In 1969, however, in response to vociferous complaints of mismanagement, waste, unreliable service, and staggering financial losses, the Nixon administration reorganized the service as an independent establishment within the executive branch. The Postal Service Act of 1969 removed the postmaster general from the cabinet and created a self-supporting postal corporation owned by the federal government and vested power in an 11-member board of governors, nine of whom are appointed by the president with the consent of the Senate; these in turn appoint the postmaster general, who serves as the CEO of the Postal Service; the 11th member of the board is chosen by the other 10 and serves as deputy postmaster general.

Finally, the 1969 law established an independent Postal Rate Commission of five members, appointed by the president, to recommend postal rates and classifications for adoption by the board of governors.

Just how well this new arrangement has worked is hard to judge. In the years 1979 to 1988, the Postal Service had five years of losses and five years in the black; in 1989 it had net income of $61 million, followed in 1990 by a net loss of $873 million. In terms of service, an April 1990 Roper poll found that 70% of those interviewed indicated they were satisfied with the Postal Service.

## POSTAL ABBREVIATIONS FOR STATES AND TERRITORIES

| State | Postal abbrev. | State | Postal abbrev. |
|-------|------|-------|------|
| Alabama | AL | New Hampshire | NH |
| Alaska | AK | New Jersey | NJ |
| Arizona | AZ | New Mexico | NM |
| Arkansas | AR | New York | NY |
| California | CA | North Carolina | NC |
| Colorado | CO | North Dakota | ND |
| Connecticut | CT | Ohio | OH |
| Delaware | DE | Oklahoma | OK |
| District of Columbia | DC | Oregon | OR |
| Florida | FL | Pennsylvania | PA |
| Georgia | GA | Rhode Island | RI |
| Hawaii | HI | South Carolina | SC |
| Idaho | ID | South Dakota | SD |
| Illinois | IL | Tennessee | TN |
| Indiana | IN | Texas | TX |
| Iowa | IA | Utah | UT |
| Kansas | KS | Vermont | VT |
| Kentucky | KY | Virginia | VA |
| Louisiana | LA | Washington | WA |
| Maine | ME | West Virginia | WV |
| Maryland | MD | Wisconsin | WI |
| Massachusetts | MA | Wyoming | WY |
| Michigan | MI | American Samoa | AS |
| Minnesota | MN | Canal Zone | CZ |
| Mississippi | MS | Guam | GU |
| Missouri | MO | Northern Mariana Islands | CM |
| Montana | MT | Puerto Rico | PR |
| Nebraska | NE | Trust Territory of the Pacific | TT |
| Nevada | NV | Virgin Islands | VI |

## ZIP CODES

As of April 1990, there were 42,500 separate ZIP Codes designated by the U.S. Postal Service. While the assignment of ZIP Codes seems random, the system is a logical one. ZIP Codes are five-digit or nine-digit (ZIP + 4) codes that identify areas within the United States and its territories for purposes of simplifying delivery of the U.S. mail. The USPS divides the U.S. into 10 geographical areas each consisting of three or more states and/or territories. Key post offices within each area are designated sectional centers. The first number in a ZIP Code indicates its geographical area, and the first three digits stand for either a sectional center or a large city. The last two digits stand for either a particular post office or a postal delivery area.

| ZIP Code beginning | States |
|------|--------|
| 0 – – – – | Connecticut, Maine, New Hampshire, New Jersey, Puerto Rico, Rhode Island, Vermont, Virgin Islands |
| 1 – – – – | Delaware, New York, Pennsylvania |
| 2 – – – – | District of Columbia, Maryland, North Carolina, South Carolina, Virginia, West Virginia |
| 3 – – – – | Alabama, Florida, Georgia, Mississippi, Tennessee |
| 4 – – – – | Indiana, Kentucky, Michigan, Ohio |
| 5 – – – – | Iowa, Minnesota, Montana, North Dakota, South Dakota, Wisconsin |
| 6 – – – – | Illinois, Kansas, Missouri, Nebraska |
| 7 – – – – | Arkansas, Louisiana, Oklahoma, Texas |
| 8 – – – – | Arizona, Colorado, Idaho, Nevada, New Mexico, Utah, Wyoming |
| 9 – – – – | Alaska, American Samoa, California, Federated States of Micronesia, Guam, Hawaii, Marshall Islands, Northern Mariana Islands, Oregon, Palau, Wake, Washington |

## DOMESTIC POSTAGE RATES

### First-class Mail

| Weight | Rate | Weight | Rate |
|--------|------|--------|------|
| 1 oz. | $0.29 | 7 oz. | $1.67 |
| 2 oz. | 0.52 | 8 oz. | 1.90 |
| 3 oz. | 0.75 | 9 oz. | 2.13 |
| 4 oz. | 0.98 | 10 oz. | 2.36 |
| 5 oz. | 1.21 | 11 oz. | 2.59 |
| 6 oz. | 1.44 | | |

For letters more than 11 oz. use priority mail.

### Post Cards

Single post card = $0.19. Post cards cannot exceed 4.25" × 6", nor be smaller than 3.5" × 5".

### Priority Mail

Priority mail is a zone-based domestic service providing two-day delivery between all major business centers in the U.S. For packages up to 2 lb., the rate is $2.40 regardless of the zone to which it is sent. For packages weighing more than 2 lb., different rates apply depending on weight and the zone, up to a maximum of $72.24 for a 70 lb. package sent to zone 7. For details and rates, consult postmaster.

### Express Mail

Express mail is an overnight delivery service available every day of the year for items up to 70 lbs. in weight and 108" in combined length and girth. The post office will pick up packages to be sent express mail for a fee. Call 1-800-333-8777.

| Weight | Rate |
|--------|------|
| Up to 8 oz. | $ 9.95 |
| 8 oz.–2 lb. | 13.95 |
| 2 lb.–70 lb. | Consult postmaster |
| Pickup fee | $4.50 |

### Second-class Mail

Regular and preferred second-class rates are available only to newspapers and periodicals that have been authorized second-class mail privileges. The general public can mail newspapers and periodicals only by first-, third-, or fourth-class mail, express mail, or priority mail.

### Third-class Mail

Third-class rates are for circulars, books, catalogues, and other printed matter; merchandise, seeds, cuttings, bulbs, roots, scions, and plants, weighing less than 16 oz. Bulk rates are also available.

| Weight | Rate | Weight | Rate |
|--------|------|--------|------|
| 1 oz. | $0.29 | 8 oz. | $1.33 |
| 2 oz. | 0.52 | 10 oz. | 1.44 |
| 3 oz. | 0.75 | 12 oz. | 1.56 |
| 4 oz. | 0.98 | 14 oz. | 1.67 |
| 6 oz. | 1.21 | Less than 16 oz. | 1.79 |

### Fourth-class Mail (Parcel Post)

Parcel post is a zone-based class of mail for sending merchandise; written communications having the nature of current and personal correspondence are not permitted. The maximum rate is $32.25 for a 70 lb. package sent to zone 8.

**Source:** U.S. Postal Service, "Postal Rates, Fees, and Information" (1989).

## INTERNATIONAL POSTAL RATES, 1991

| Type/Weight | Canada | Mexico | All other countries Surface | All other countries Airmail |
|---|---|---|---|---|
| **First-class letters:** | | | | |
| 0.5 oz. | $0.40 | $0.35 | $0.70 | $0.50 |
| 1.0 | 0.40 | 0.45 | 0.70 | 0.95 |
| 1.5 | 0.63 | 0.55 | 0.95 | 1.34 |
| 2.0 | 0.63 | 0.65 | 0.95 | 1.73 |
| **Postcards** | $0.30 | $0.30 | $0.35 | $0.40 |
| **Aerogrammes** | 0.45 | 0.45 | 0.45 | 0.45 |

**Source**: U.S. Postal Service (1991).

## POSTAGE STAMPS

In 1990, the Postal Service printed 40 billion stamps—enough to circle the Earth at the equator 25 times. The first stamps issued by the precursor to the U.S. Postal Service were a 5-cent Benjamin Franklin (the nation's first Postmaster General) and a 10-cent George Washington, both in 1847.

There are three main categories of stamps. *Definitive issues* are generally two-color and printed in quantities of hundreds of millions over several years. The Postal Service is committed to always having a definitive flag issue in circulation in the standard first-class (29-cent in 1991) denomination. All stamps supporting third-class mailing rates are definitive issues. These include fractional rate stamps in series such as the Great American and Transportation series used by large companies for sending mass mailings.

*Commemorative issues* generally celebrate historic events or personalities and are more elaborate in their design and printing. They are issued in quantities of about 150 million over the course of three months during which they can be purchased at all post offices. (They are available for up to one year at philatelic windows in main post offices.) *Airmail issues* (for overseas mail) are printed for longer than commemorative issues, although modest demand results in smaller quantities being printed.

In 1989, the Postal Service began test-marketing peel-and-stick postage stamps. These self-adhesive stamps do not have to be torn from a pane or a coil, or licked for affixing to an envelope, and their adhesive produces a bond superior to traditional stamps. The stamps are now available at selected automated teller machines (ATMs) nationwide, where they can be purchased with a bank card, as well as at philatelic windows.

## VOLUME OF MAIL HANDLED, 1989–90

| Service | Thousands of pieces 1989 | Thousands of pieces 1990 | Percent change |
|---|---|---|---|
| First-class | 85,855,458 | 89,269,649 | 4.0% |
| Priority mail | 470,831 | 517,850 | 10.0 |
| Express mail | 53,308 | 58,582 | 9.9 |
| Mailgram | 16,871 | 14,001 | -17.0 |
| Second-class | 10,523,374 | 10,680,469 | 1.5 |
| Third-class | 62,779,116 | 63,725,110 | 1.5 |
| Fourth-class | 625,932 | 662,977 | 5.9 |
| International surface | 165,799 | 165,901 | 0.1 |
| International airmail | 558,056 | 632,364 | 13.3 |
| U.S. Postal Service | 527,791 | 538,427 | 2.0 |
| Free for the blind | 26,728 | 35,440 | 32.6 |
| **Total mail** | **161,603,264** | **166,300,770** | **2.9%** |

**Source**: U.S. Postal Service, *Annual Report of the Postmaster General, Fiscal Year 1990* (1991).

## POSTAL SERVICE EMPLOYEES AND OFFICES, 1989–90

| Employees | 1989 | 1990 |
|---|---|---|
| **HEADQUARTERS** | | |
| Washington, D.C. | 2,278 | 2,291 |
| Field support units | 5,882 | 5,691 |
| Inspection services (field) | 4,276 | 4,259 |
| **FIELD CAREER EMPLOYEES** | | |
| Regional offices | 431 | 542 |
| Postmasters | 27,242 | 26,995 |
| Supervisors | 44,793 | 43,458 |
| Professional, administrative, technical personnel | 10,528 | 9,793 |
| Clerks | 300,908 | 290,380 |
| Nurses | 318 | 286 |
| Mailhandlers | 52,295 | 51,123 |
| City delivery carriers | 240,159 | 236,081 |
| Motor vehicle operators | 7,357 | 7,308 |
| Rural delivery carriers and substitutes on vacant routes | 40,802 | 42,252 |
| Special delivery messengers | 2,142 | 2,012 |
| Building and equipment maintenance personnel | 33,348 | 33,323 |
| Vehicle maintenance personnel | 4,956 | 4,874 |
| Total career employees | 777,715 | 760,668 |
| Noncareer employees | 21,209 | 26,289 |
| **OFFICES, STATIONS, AND BRANCHES** | | |
| Post offices | 29,083 | 28,959 |
| Stations and branches | 10,948 | 11,108 |
| Classified stations and branches | 4,958 | 5,008 |
| Contract stations and branches | 4,297 | 4,397 |
| Community post offices | 1,693 | 1,703 |
| Total offices, branches, and stations | 40,031 | 40,067 |

**Source**: U.S. Postal Service, *Annual Report of the Postmaster General, Fiscal Year 1990* (1991).

# Internal Revenue Service

Founded in 1862, the Internal Revenue Service (IRS) is the office of the Department of the Treasury charged with collecting federal taxes. The Constitution empowers Congress to levy excise taxes and—in emergencies—to raise direct taxes. Congress's right to levy taxes on the income of individuals and corporations was contested throughout the 19th century, but that authority was written into the Constitution with the passage of the 16th Amendment in 1913. Today the source of most of the federal government's revenues is the individual income tax, corporate income tax, excise taxes, estate taxes, and gift taxes. The IRS is responsible for these taxes as well as for collecting employee and employer payments for social insurance and retirement insurance (see "Social Insurance Programs"); since 1986, taxes on alcohol, tobacco, firearms, and explosives have been collected by the Bureau of Alcohol, Tobacco, and Firearms.

In 1990 the IRS processed 201.7 million tax returns totaling $959.1 billion (net). Individual returns made up 56% of the number of returns, and net revenues from individual income taxes constituted 48.3% of total revenues.

## TAX RATE SCHEDULES, 1991

| Taxable income | What you pay |
|---|---|
| **SINGLE INDIVIDUALS** | |
| $0.00–$20,350 | 15% of sum over $0.00 |
| $20,350–$49,300 | $3,052.50 + 28% of sum over $20,350 |
| $49,300 and over | $11,158.50 +31% of sum over $49,300 |
| **HEADS OF HOUSEHOLDS** | |
| $0.00–$27,300 | 15% of sum over $0.00 |
| $27,300–$70,450 | $4,095.00 + 28% of sum over $27,300 |
| $70,450 and over | $16,177.00 + 31% of sum over $70,450 |

| Taxable Income | What you pay |
|---|---|
| **MARRIED INDIVIDUALS FILING JOINTLY, OR QUALIFYING WIDOW(ER)S** | |
| $0.00–$34,000 | 15% of sum over $0.00 |
| $34,000–$82,150 | $5,100.00 + 28% of sum over $34,000 |
| $82,150 and over | $18,582.00 +31% of sum over $82,150 |
| **MARRIED INDIVIDUALS FILING SEPARATE RETURNS** | |
| $0.00–$17,000 | 15% of sum over $0.00 |
| $17,000–$41,075 | $2,550.00 + 28% of sum over $17,000 |
| $41,075 and over | $9,291.00 + 31% of sum over $41,075 |

**Source**: Internal Revenue Service, 1991.

## Principal Deductions

**Personal exemptions** In filing income tax, taxpayers are allowed to claim personal exemptions for themselves and each dependent. Congress determines the amount allowable for deductions on personal and other exemptions. For income earned in 1989, the amount was $2,000, and starting in 1990, the exemption is pegged to the inflation rate.

**Interest expenses** As of 1991, there is no deduction allowed for interest expenses, though in prior years there was. Nonbusiness interest expense falls into four categories: consumer interest (on loans used for personal reasons, such as auto loans, school loans, and insurance); mortgage interest; investment interest; and passive activity interest.

**Medical expenses** Although almost all medical expenses are deductible, it is difficult to take a deduction because your combined expenses for the year must total 7.5% of your adjusted gross income (AGI). So, for a taxpayer with an AGI of $25,000, medical expenses would have to exceed $1,875.

## Examination and Enforcement

A significant portion of the increased tax revenues collected by the government derives from increased efforts by the IRS to identify delinquent taxpayers. Over 80% of all taxpayers pay their taxes voluntarily; but to ensure that appropriate taxes are paid, and to locate delinquent taxpayers, the IRS has a number of examination and enforcement procedures. The most broad-reaching of the IRS's examination systems is the matching document program, formally known as the Information Returns Program (IRP). This matches third-party information on wages, interest, dividends, and certain deductions with the amounts reported by taxpayers on their returns and identifies people who are reported to have received income but did not file returns. When information does not agree with filed documents, taxpayers are asked to explain the discrepancy. In 1990 the IRS received more than 1 billion information returns. They identified 2.95 million people who underreported their earnings, and 1.96 million people who failed to file taxes altogether. The additional taxes and penalties assessed totaled $3.5 billion.

In 1990 the IRS examined 0.53% of all individual federal returns filed. A total of 883,140 individual returns were examined, resulting in $4.9 billion recommended additional taxes and penalties and refunds totaling $189.4 million.

The IRS also examined 71,337 corporate returns, or 2.6% of all returns filed. These resulted in additional taxes and penalties of $13.8 billion—an average of $193.9 million per return examined—and total refunds of $376 million. The IRS's most sophisticated program is the Coordinated Examination Program, which tackles the largest and most complex domestic and foreign-controlled corporations. In 1989 the IRS conducted 1,570 examinations by Coordinated Examination Program specialists, which resulted in recommended additional taxes and penalties of $10.8 billion,

### AVERAGE ITEMIZED DEDUCTIONS BY ADJUSTED GROSS INCOME, 1989

| Adjusted gross income ranges | Average deduction for: | | | |
| --- | --- | --- | --- | --- |
| | Medical expenses | Taxes | Contributions | Interest[1] |
| $25,000–$30,000 | $ 3,128 | $ 1,975 | $ 1,019 | $ 4,314 |
| $30,000–$40,000 | 2,849 | 2,342 | 1,184 | 4,887 |
| $40,000–$50,000 | 3,546 | 2,947 | 1,318 | 5,400 |
| $50,000–$75,000 | 4,713 | 3,943 | 1,607 | 6,271 |
| $75,000–$100,000 | 6,448 | 5,713 | 2,108 | 8,531 |
| $100,000–$200,000 | 10,090 | 9,020 | 3,532 | 12,150 |
| $200,000–$500,000 | 24,134 | 19,645 | 7,213 | 19,853 |
| $500,000–$1 million | 40,556 | 43,499 | 18,374 | 29,788 |
| $1 million or more | 66,478 | 148,529 | 83,929 | 68,303 |

**Note:** Figures, based on preliminary statistics for 1989 returns, average deductions itemized on Schedule A of Form 1040. 1. For 1989, 20% of "personal interest" was deductible. In 1991 there is no deduction. **Source:** Research Institute of America, 1991.

### RETURNS FILED AND EXAMINED, AND ADDITIONAL TAXES AND PENALTIES, 1990

| Type of return | Total filed 1989[1] | Total returns examined | Percent examined | Additional taxes and penalties (mil.)[2] | Average tax and penalty per return[3] |
| --- | --- | --- | --- | --- | --- |
| Individual, total | 109,868,400 | 883,140 | 0.80% | $4,934 | $16,248 |
| 1040-A, TPI < $10,000 | 42,116,300 | 185,935 | 0.44 | 576 | 17,958 |
| Non 1040-A, TPI < $10,000 | 20,464,800 | 115,296 | 0.56 | 225 | 6,243 |
| TPI $25,000–$50,000 | 26,359,200 | 195,818 | 0.76 | 542 | 7,278 |
| TPI $50,000–$100,000 | 11,167,100 | 121,475 | 1.09 | 448 | 9,512 |
| TPI > $100,000 | 2,554,700 | 120,438 | 4.71 | 1,602 | 25,755 |
| Sched. C—TGR < $25,000 | 2,167,800 | 29,384 | 1.36 | 108 | 6,959 |
| Sched. C—TGR $25,000–$100,000 | 2,667,300 | 49,753 | 1.86 | 304 | 9,697 |
| Sched. C—TGR > $100,000 | 1,464,200 | 49,518 | 3.38 | 1,016 | 27,608 |
| Sched. F—TGR < $100,000 | 638,000 | 8,304 | 1.30 | 24 | 5,964 |
| Sched. F—TGR > $100,000 | 269,000 | 7,239 | 2.69 | 88 | 16,560 |
| Fiduciary | 2,625,300 | 2,559 | 0.10 | 110 | 42,992 |
| Partnership | 1,663,200 | 13,227 | 0.80 | — | — |
| Corporation | 2,752,300 | 71,337 | 2.59 | 13,834 | 193,925 |
| Small business corp. (1120S) | 1,351,100 | 9,964 | 0.74 | 13 | 1,338 |
| Form 1120DISC | — | 644 | — | — | — |
| Estate | 55,800 | 11,798 | 21.14 | 1,832 | 15,525 |
| Gift | 123,500 | 1,640 | 1.33 | 247 | 150,526 |
| Excise | 887,200 | 41,258 | 4.65 | 219 | 5,313 |
| Employment | 28,893,100 | 69,971 | 0.24 | 453 | 6,886 |
| Windfall profit | — | 2,983 | — | 556 | 972,264 |

**Note:** < = less than. > = greater than. TPI = total personal income. TGR = total gross receipts. Totals may not add due to rounding. 1. Calendar year. 2. Recommended. 3. Includes only returns reviewed by revenue agents. Additional taxes and penalties were recovered through reviews of individual returns by tax auditors and service centers. **Source:** Internal Revenue Service, *Annual Report 1990* (1991).

### INTERNAL REVENUE COLLECTIONS, 1990 (thousands of dollars)

| Type of return | Gross collections | Refunds[1] | Net collections | |
| --- | --- | --- | --- | --- |
| | | | Amount | Percent of total |
| Corporation income taxes | $110,016,539 | $16,882,913 | $93,133,626 | 9.7% |
| Individual income taxes | 540,228,408 | 76,786,752[2] | 463,441,656 | 48.3 |
| Employment taxes, total | 367,219,321 | 1,278,534 | 365,940,787 | 38.2 |
| OASDHI[3] | 357,545,552 | 1,081,680 | 356,463,872 | 37.2 |
| Railroad retirement | 4,157,771 | 41,046 | 4,116,725 | 0.4 |
| Unemployment insurance | 5,515,998 | 155,809 | 5,360,190 | 0.6 |
| Estate and gift taxes | 11,761,939 | 268,739 | 11,493,200 | 1.2 |
| Excise taxes | 27,139,445 | 2,033,859 | 25,105,586 | 2.6 |
| **Grand total** | **1,056,365,652** | **97,250,797** | **959,114,855** | **100.0** |

**Note:** Detail may not add to totals due to rounding. 1. Does not include interest paid on refunds totaling $1.8 billion. 2. Refunds of forms 1040, 1040A and 1040EZ, including withheld taxes minus FICA. 3. Old-age, survivor's, disability and hospital insurance; includes federal insurance and self-employment insurance contributions not shown separately. **Source:** Internal Revenue Service, *Annual Report 1990* (1991).

approximately $6.9 million per corporation examined. In 1990, the IRS estimated that the CEP again accounted for about half of the $22.3 billion additional taxes and penalties recommended after examination.

## Tax Freedom Day

To gauge the extent of the total tax burden on individual taxpayers, experts have devised a formula to calculate how long a person has to work to pay all his or her obligations to the state. Suppose you began paying your taxes for the year on Jan. 1 and spent no money until these were paid off. The day you started paying for food, rent, schools, and other necessities is called tax freedom day. In 1929, the beginning of the Great Depression, tax freedom day fell on Feb. 9; in 1990 it was May 8. Looked at another way, while you would have spent 52 minutes out of each day to earn enough money for a day's worth of taxes in 1929, you now spend 2 hours and 49 minutes. In other words, you spend 3.25 times more of your annual income on taxes now than you would have 60 years ago.

Taxpayers worked two minutes more to pay federal taxes in 1990 than in 1980 (but two minutes less than in 1982, the worst year for federal taxes). They had to work eight minutes more to pay off state and local taxes.

## TAX FREEDOM DAY, 1929–90

| Year | Tax Freedom Day[1] | Tax bite in the eight-hour day[2] | | |
|------|------|-------|---------|-------------|
| | | Total | Federal | State/local |
| 1929 | Feb. 9 | 0:52 | 0:19 | 0:33 |
| 1940 | Mar. 8 | 1:29 | 0:45 | 0:44 |
| 1950 | Apr. 3 | 2:02 | 1:30 | 0:32 |
| 1960 | Apr. 17 | 2:22 | 1:40 | 0:42 |
| 1970 | Apr. 28 | 2:34 | 1:40 | 0:54 |
| 1980 | May 1 | 2:39 | 1:48 | 0:51 |
| 1985 | May 1 | 2:38 | 1:44 | 0:54 |
| 1990 | May 8 | 2:49 | 1:50 | 0:59 |

1. The date on which the average person would finish paying federal, state, and local taxes if all earnings since Jan. 1 were turned over to government to fulfill annual tax obligations. 2. Reflects the amount of time out of each workday that the average person spends earning enough money to pay tax obligations. **Source**: Tax Foundation (Washington, D.C.), *Facts and Figures on Government Finance* (1991).

## INTERNAL REVENUE COLLECTIONS, COSTS, AND TAX PER CAPITA, 1960–90

| Fiscal year | Collections | Cost of collecting $100 | Tax per capita |
|------|------|------|------|
| 1960 | $ 91,774,802,823 | $0.40 | $ 507.96 |
| 1965 | 114,434,633,721 | 0.52 | 588.95 |
| 1970 | 195,722,096,497 | 0.45 | 955.31 |
| 1975 | 293,822,725,772 | 0.54 | 1,375.84 |
| 1980 | 519,375,273,361 | 0.44 | 2,275.66 |
| 1985 | 742,871,541,283 | 0.48 | 3,098.99 |
| 1986 | 782,251,812,225 | 0.49 | 3,232.51 |
| 1987 | 886,290,589,996 | 0.49 | 3,627.22 |
| 1988 | 935,106,594,222 | 0.54 | 3,792.15 |
| 1989 | 1,013,322,133,000 | 0.51 | 4,073.22 |
| 1990 | 1,056,365,651,631 | 0.52 | 4,203.12 |

**Note**: Current dollars. **Source**: Internal Revenue Service, *Annual Report 1990* (1991).

## INTERNAL REVENUE COLLECTIONS BY PRINCIPAL SOURCES, 1961–90
(thousands of dollars)

| Year | Total internal revenue collections | Corporate income and profits tax | Individual income tax | Employment taxes | Estate and gift taxes | Excise taxes |
|------|------|------|------|------|------|------|
| 1961 | $ 94,401,086 | $ 21,764,940 | $ 46,153,001 | $ 12,502,451 | $ 1,916,392 | $12,064,302 |
| 1965 | 114,434,634 | 26,131,334 | 53,660,683 | 17,104,306 | 2,745,532 | 14,792,779 |
| 1970 | 195,722,096 | 35,036,983 | 103,651,585 | 37,449,188 | 3,680,076 | 15,904,264 |
| 1975 | 293,822,726 | 45,746,660 | 156,399,437 | 70,140,809 | 4,688,079 | 16,847,741 |
| 1980 | 519,375,273 | 72,379,610 | 287,547,782 | 128,330,480 | 6,498,381 | 24,619,021 |
| 1985 | 742,871,541 | 77,412,769 | 396,659,558 | 225,214,568 | 6,579,703 | 37,004,944 |
| 1990 | 1,056,365,652 | 110,016,539 | 540,228,408 | 367,219,321 | 11,761,939 | 27,139,445 |

**Source**: Internal Revenue Service, *Annual Report 1990* (1991).

## INTERNAL REVENUE PERSONNEL SUMMARY, 1990

| Location and type | Employees |
|------|------|
| **LOCATION** | |
| National office | 8,140 |
| Regional offices | 108,285 |
| **Service, total** | **116,425** |
| **TYPE** | |
| Data processing operations | 39,580 |
| Collection | 18,391 |
| Taxpayer service | 8,457 |
| Examination | 28,574 |
| Employee plans/exempt organizations | 2,429 |
| Appeals | 2,930 |
| Tax fraud | 2,930 |
| Executive direction | 158 |
| Management services | 1,204 |
| Resources management | 5,533 |
| Counsel | 2,935 |
| Inspection | 1,319 |
| International | 659 |

**Note**: At close of year. **Source**: Internal Revenue Service, *Annual Report 1990* (1991).

## Special Considerations

Individual federal income tax returns have a box for the presidential election campaign fund. Citizens and aliens who owe at least one dollar in tax can designate one dollar of the tax to go to the fund. Doing so in no way affects the tax you owe or the amount of your refund, if there is any. In 1988, 22.8 million (21%) of all individual returns showed designations to this fund, bringing to $534.8 million the total credited to the fund since it began in 1972.

*"That the power to tax involves the power to destroy; that the power to destroy may defeat and render unless the power to create . . . are propositions not to be denied."*

—Chief Justice John Marshall
*McCulloch* v. *Maryland* (1819)

Since 1982, federal tax forms have also carried a message inviting individuals to make voluntary contributions to reduce the national debt. Under this program taxpayers can send a separate check with their return payable to the Bureau of Public Debt and take a deduction of their tax return for the following year. In 1988 there were 423 contributions totaling $175,000.

## TAX RETURNS PROCESSED, 1990

| Type of return | Number of returns |
|------|------|
| Individual income tax (Form 1040 series) | 112,492,218 |
| Estimated tax (Form 1040ES) | 38,188,206 |
| Fiduciary (Form 1041 series) | 2,701,930 |
| Fiduciary estimated tax (Form 1041ES) | 651,456 |
| Partnership (Form 1065) | 1,741,163 |
| Corporate income tax (Forms 1120 series, 1066) | 4,310,771 |
| Estate tax (Forms 706, 706NA) | 58,629 |
| Gift tax (Form 709) | 146,014 |
| Employment taxes (Forms 94X series, CT-1, 1042) | 28,914,476 |
| Exempt organizations (Forms 990 series, 4720, 5227) | 483,856 |
| Employee plans (Form 5500 series) | 1,015,906 |
| Excise taxes (Forms 720, 730, 2290, 11C) | 839,857 |
| Supplemental documents (1040X, 2688, 4868, 7004, 1041A) | 10,170,156 |
| **Total tax returns** | **201,714,638** |

**Source**: Internal Revenue Service, *Annual Report 1990* (1991).

# STATES, TERRITORIES, AND POSSESSIONS

This section, a compilation of history and statistics about the 50 United States, the District of Columbia, and U.S. territories and possessions, includes a brief history of each state and territory; its official motto and other emblems; a summary of geographic, demographic, and economic facts; and a list of prominent natives, places, and dates.

Statistical sources include the U.S. Census Bureau's 1990 decennial census and *The Statistical Abstract* (annual); the Council of State Governments' *Book of the States 1990–91* and *State Elective Officials and the Legislatures 1991–92*; and the Bureau of Economic Analysis's *Survey of Current Business*, "Gross State Product by Industry 1963–86" (1988).

The headings for demographic statistics in the paragraphs on People and Language conform to U.S. Census Bureau usage, except "Indian" is used as a short form for American Indian, Eskimo, and Aleut, and "Asian" is used for Asian and Pacific Islander.

## Alabama

The memory of the Native American presence is particularly strong in Alabama. Trade with the Northeast via the Ohio River valley began during the Burial Mound Period (1000 B.C.–A.D. 700) and continued until European contact. Meso-American influence is evident in the agrarian Mississippian culture that followed. Pressured by white settlers in the early 19th century, the Creeks warred against the U.S. government until defeated by Gen. Andrew Jackson.

The cradle of the Confederacy during the Civil War, Alabama was center stage in the civil rights movement of the 1950s and 1960s. Although cotton is still a major crop, the northern part of the state around Birmingham is an important industrial area with abundant coal, iron ore, limestone, and electricity from the TVA. Increasingly urban—70 percent of the population lived in rural areas 50 years ago, compared with less than 40 percent today—Alabama's economy is progressing slowly. It still ranks near last in taxes and most services.

NAME Probably after Alabama. Trade with NICKNAME Heart of Dixie. CAPITAL Montgomery. ENTERED UNION Dec. 14, 1819 (22d). MOTTO "We dare defend our rights."
**Emblems** BIRD Yellowhammer. DANCE Square dance. GAME BIRD Wild turkey. FISH Tarpon. FOSSIL *Basilosaurus oetoides*. MINERAL Hematite. NUT Pecan. SONG "Alabama." STONE Marble. TREE Southern (longleaf) pine.
**Land** TOTAL AREA 51,705 sq. mi. (29th), incl. 938 sq. mi. inland water. BORDERS Tenn., Ga., Fla., Gulf of Mexico, Miss. RIVERS Alabama, Chattahoochee, Mobile, Tennessee, Tennessee-Tombigbee Waterway, Tensaw, Tombigbee. LAKES Guntersville, Pickwick, Wheeler, Wilson (all formed by Tennessee Valley Authority [TVA]); Dannelly Res., Martin, Lewis Smith, Weiss. MOUNTAINS Cumberland, Lookout, Raccoon, Sand.

**Elected officials** Gov. Harold Guy Hunt (R, term exp. 1995). Lt. Gov. Jim Folsom, Jr. (D). Sec. State Billy Joe Camp (D). Atty. Gen. Jimmy Evans (D).
**People** (1990) 4,040,587 (22d). RACE/NATIONAL ORIGIN (1990): White 73.6%. Black 25.3%. Indian 0.4%. Asian 0.5%. Other 0.1%. Hispanic 0.6%.
**Cities** (1990) Birmingham 265,968. Mobile 196,278. Montgomery 187,106. Huntsville 159,789. Tuscaloosa 77,759. Dothan 53,589. Decatur 48,761. Gadsden 42,523. Hoover 39,788. Florence 36,426.
**Business** GROSS STATE PRODUCT (GSP, 1986) $55 bil. (24th). Sectors of GSP: Farms 2.06%. Agricultural services, forestry, & fisheries 0.36%. Mining 2.53%. Construction 3.19%. Manufacturing 23.48%. Transportation & public utilities 10.12%. Wholesale 6.56%. Retail 9.54%. Finance, insurance, & real estate 13.16%. Services 13.45%. Federal government 4.62%. Federal military 2.00%. State & local government 8.93%. FORTUNE 500 COMPANIES (1990): 4: Intergraph, Russell, SCI Systems, Vulcan Materials.
**Famous natives** Hank Aaron, baseball player. Tallulah Bankhead, actress. William B. Bankhead, politician. Hugo L. Black, jurist. Wernher von Braun (b. Germany), rocket scientist. Nat ("King") Cole, singer. Red Eagle (William Weatherford), Creek leader. W.C. Handy, musician. Frank M. Johnson, Jr., jurist. Helen Keller, author. Coretta Scott (Mrs. Martin Luther) King, reformer. Harper Lee, author. Joe Louis, boxer. Jesse Owens, runner. Leroy Robert ("Satchell") Paige, baseball player. Walker Percy, author. George Wallace, politician. Hank Williams, singer.
**Noteworthy places** Alabama Deep Sea Fishing Rodeo, Dauphin Island. Alabama Space and Rocket Center, U.S. Space Camp, Huntsville. Battleship USS *Alabama*, Mobile. Birmingham Museum of Art. First White House of the Confederacy, Montgomery. Horseshoe Bend Natl. Military Park. Mound State Monument Archaeological Museum, Moundville. Museum of Natural History, Univ. Alabama, Tuscaloosa. Point Clear (resort). Russell Cave Natl. Monument. Tuskegee Institute.
**Memorable events** Humans first inhabit Russell Cave c. 6000 B.C. Temple Mound culture flourishes around Moundville, A.D. 1200–1500. First Europeans in Mobile Bay 1519. Hernando de Soto's battle with Tuscaloosa possibly bloodiest encounter ever between Europeans and Native Americans in U.S. 1540. Spanish at Mobile Bay 1599. Pierre Le Moyne, sieur d'Iberville, establishes first permanent colony at Mobile 1711. Treaty of Paris gives Mobile to Britain 1763. U.S. control recognized 1783. Chickasaws, Choctaws, and Cherokees cede lands to U.S. 1805. First Baptist Church established 1808. Gen. Andrew Jackson defeats Creek Indian Confederacy at Horseshoe Bend 1814. Cotton principal cash crop 1820s. Beginning of coal and iron mining and steel manufac-

## POPULATION OF THE STATES, 1990

| State | Population 1990 | Rank | Change 1980–90 Number | Percent |
|---|---|---|---|---|
| United States | 248,709,873 | – | 22,165,068 | 9.8% |
| Alabama | 4,040,587 | 22 | 146,699 | 3.8 |
| Alaska | 550,043 | 49 | 148,192 | 36.9 |
| Arizona | 3,665,228 | 24 | 947,013 | 34.8 |
| Arkansas | 2,350,725 | 33 | 64,290 | 2.8 |
| California | 29,760,021 | 1 | 6,092,119 | 25.7 |
| Colorado | 3,294,394 | 26 | 404,430 | 14.0 |
| Connecticut | 3,287,116 | 27 | 179,540 | 5.8 |
| Delaware | 666,168 | 46 | 71,830 | 12.1 |
| Dist. of Columbia[1] | 606,900 | – | –31,433 | –4.9 |
| Florida | 12,937,926 | 4 | 3,191,602 | 32.7 |
| Georgia | 6,478,216 | 11 | 1,015,111 | 18.6 |
| Hawaii | 1,108,229 | 41 | 143,538 | 14.9 |
| Idaho | 1,006,749 | 42 | 62,814 | 6.7 |
| Illinois | 11,430,602 | 6 | 4,084 | 0.0 |
| Indiana | 5,544,159 | 14 | 53,935 | 1.0 |
| Iowa | 2,776,755 | 30 | –137,053 | –4.7 |
| Kansas | 2,477,574 | 32 | 113,895 | 4.8 |
| Kentucky | 3,685,296 | 23 | 24,519 | 0.7 |
| Louisiana | 4,219,973 | 21 | 14,073 | 0.3 |
| Maine | 1,227,928 | 38 | 103,268 | 9.2 |
| Maryland | 4,781,468 | 19 | 564,493 | 13.4 |
| Massachusetts | 6,016,425 | 13 | 279,388 | 4.9 |
| Michigan | 9,295,297 | 8 | 33,219 | 0.4 |
| Minnesota | 4,375,099 | 20 | 299,129 | 7.3 |
| Mississippi | 2,573,216 | 31 | 52,578 | 2.1 |
| Missouri | 5,117,073 | 15 | 200,387 | 4.1 |
| Montana | 799,065 | 44 | 12,375 | 1.6 |
| Nebraska | 1,578,385 | 36 | 8,560 | 0.5 |
| Nevada | 1,201,833 | 39 | 401,340 | 50.1 |
| New Hampshire | 1,109,252 | 40 | 188,642 | 20.5 |
| New Jersey | 7,730,188 | 9 | 365,365 | 5.0 |
| New Mexico | 1,515,069 | 37 | 212,175 | 16.3 |
| New York | 17,990,455 | 2 | 432,383 | 2.5 |
| North Carolina | 6,628,637 | 10 | 746,871 | 12.7 |
| North Dakota | 638,800 | 47 | –13,917 | –2.1 |
| Ohio | 10,847,115 | 7 | 49,485 | 0.5 |
| Oklahoma | 3,145,585 | 28 | 120,295 | 4.0 |
| Oregon | 2,842,321 | 29 | 209,216 | 7.9 |
| Pennsylvania | 11,881,643 | 5 | 17,748 | 0.1 |
| Rhode Island | 1,003,464 | 43 | 56,310 | 5.9 |
| South Carolina | 3,486,703 | 25 | 364,883 | 11.7 |
| South Dakota | 696,004 | 45 | 5,236 | 0.8 |
| Tennessee | 4,877,185 | 17 | 286,065 | 6.2 |
| Texas | 16,986,510 | 3 | 2,757,319 | 19.4 |
| Utah | 1,722,850 | 35 | 261,813 | 17.9 |
| Vermont | 562,758 | 48 | 51,302 | 10.0 |
| Virginia | 6,187,358 | 12 | 840,540 | 15.7 |
| Washington | 4,866,692 | 18 | 734,536 | 17.8 |
| West Virginia | 1,793,477 | 34 | –156,167 | –8.0 |
| Wisconsin | 4,891,769 | 16 | 186,002 | 4.0 |
| Wyoming | 453,588 | 50 | –15,969 | –3.4 |

1. If the District of Columbia were included with the states it would have ranked 48th in 1990 and 47th in 1980. **Source**: U.S. Bureau of the Census release, 1991.

turing 1850s. Alabama secedes from Union; first capital of Confederate States of America at Montgomery 1861. Battle of Mobile Bay 1864. Readmitted to Union 1868. Booker T. Washington founds Tuskegee Institute 1881. Destruction of cotton crops by boll weevils leads to diversification of rural economy 1915. Tennessee Valley Authority enacted by Congress 1933. Montgomery bus boycott 1955. Freedom march from Selma to Montgomery 1965.

**Tourist information** 1-800-ALABAMA or 1-205-242-4169.

## Alaska

One-fifth the size of the entire lower 48 states, Alaska is a vast, geographically varied wilderness. The coast from the Bering Sea to the Arctic was originally inhabited by Eskimos and Aleuts, while inland and to the south were Athapascans and people of the Northwest Indian culture. Russian fur traders in the 1740s were the first Europeans to recognize the region's commercial potential, and the Russian Orthodox faith is still found in the old territorial capital of Sitka (New Archangel).

Russia sold Alaska to the United States in 1867 for $7.2 million—2 cents an acre—and Alaska experienced successive booms in furs, fishing, whaling, and gold. Discovery of oil on the North Slope near Prudhoe Bay in 1968 and completion of an 800-mile trans-Alaska pipeline a decade later made oil production the centerpiece of the state's economy in the 1980s. But in 1989 oil production at Prudhoe Bay declined for the first time. In anticipation of the end of the oil boom, government and industry officials are looking at ways to diversify the state's economy. One possibility, additional exploration at Arctic National Wildlife Refuge, was endangered when the *Exxon Valdez* struck a reef outward bound from Valdez, spilling 10 million gallons of oil into Prince William Sound on March 24, 1989. However, as the public memory of the disaster recedes and the Persian Gulf oil supplies are threatened by regional insecurity, the refuge is once again being considered.

NAME From Aleut *alaska* and Eskimo *alakshak*, both meaning "mainland." NICKNAME None. CAPITAL Juneau. ENTERED UNION Jan. 3, 1959 (49th). MOTTO "North to the future."

**Emblems** BIRD Willow ptarmigan. FISH King salmon. FLOWER Forget-me-not. GEM Jade. MARINE MAMMAL Bowhead whale. MINERAL Gold. SONG "Alaska's Flag." SPORT Mushing (dog-team racing). TREE Sitka spruce.

**Land** TOTAL AREA 591,004 sq. mi. (1st), incl. 20,171 sq. mi. inland water. BORDERS Arctic Ocean (Chukchi Sea, Beaufort Sea), Yukon, British Columbia, Pacific Ocean, and Bering Strait. RIVERS Colville, Porcupine, Noatak, Yukon, Susitna, Copper, Kobuk, Koyukuk, Kuskokwim, Tanana. MOUNTAINS Alaska Range (Mt. McKinley 20,320 ft., highest in North America), Aleutian Range, Brooks Range, Kuskokwim, St. Elias. OTHER NOTABLE FEATURES Aleutian Islands, Alexander Archipelago, Kodiak Island, Nunivak Island, Point Barrow (71°23'N), Pribilof Islands, Seward Peninsula, St. Lawrence Island.

**Elected officials** Gov. Walter J. Hickel (I, term exp. 1994). Lt. Gov. John B. Coghill (I).

**People** (1990) 550,043 (49th). RACE/NATIONAL ORIGIN (1990): White 75.5%. Black 4.1%. Indian 15.6%. Asian 3.6%. Other 1.2%. Hispanic 3.2%.

**Cities** (1990) Anchorage 226,338. Fairbanks 30,843. Juneau 26,751. Sitka 8,588. Ketchikan 8,263. Kodiak 6,365. Kenai 6,327. Bethel 4,674. Valdez 4,068. Wasilla 4,028.

**Business** GROSS STATE PRODUCT (GSP, 1986) $19.6 bil. (38th). SECTORS OF GSP: Farms 0.12%. Agricultural services, forestry, & fisheries 1.50%. Mining 33.36%. Construction 10.12%. Manufacturing 4.99%. Transportation & public utilities 7.64%. Wholesale 2.50%. Retail 5.66%. Finance, insurance, & real estate 3.27%. Federal government 3.27%. Federal military 3.63%. State & local government 9.57%. *FORTUNE* 500 COMPANIES (1990): 0.

**Famous natives** Aleksandr Baranov (b. Russia), 1st governor of Russian America. Vitus Bering (b. Denmark), explorer. Ernest Gruening (b. N.Y.), governor. Carl Ben Eielson, bush pilot. Walter Hickel (b. Kans.), governor.

**Noteworthy places** Aniakchak Natl. Monument. Cape Krusenstern Natl. Monument. Denali Natl. Park (formerly Mt. McKinley Natl. Park). Gates of the Arctic Natl. Park. Glacier Bay Natl. Park. Katmai Natl. Park (Valley of Ten Thousand Smokes). Kenai Fjords Natl. Park. Klondike Gold Rush Natl. Hist. Park. Kobuk Valley Natl. Park. Lake Clark Natl. Park. Little Diomede Island—2.5 mi. from Big Diomede Island (USSR). Sitka Natl. Hist. Park. St. Michael's Cathedral, Sitka. Wrangell–St. Elias Natl. Park.

**Memorable events** Earliest migration from Asia to Americas across Bering Sea land bridge, c. 15,000 years ago. Alaska inhabited by Tlingits, Tinnehs, Aleuts, and Eskimos. Peter the Great sponsors expedition to find land opposite Siberia 1728. Bering expedition lands near Mt. Elias; begins Pacific Northwest fur trade with Europe and Asia 1741. Russians establish first European settlement at Three Saints Bay 1784. Russian-American Company chartered 1799. Baranov's massacre of Tlingits at Sitka 1802. Gold discovered at Stikine Creek (1861), Juneau (1880), Fortymile Creek (1886), Nome (1898), Fairbanks (1903). Russians sell Alaska to U.S. for $7.2 million 1867. First salmon cannery established 1878. Japanese occupy Agattu, Attu, and Kiska islands 1942–43. Alaskans vote for statehood 1946. Statehood 1959. Earthquake destroys Anchorage, Northwest Panhandle, and Cook Inlet; tsunami wipes out Valdez; coast sinks 32 ft. at Kodiak and Seward and rises 16 ft. at Cordova 1964. Oil discovered on North Slope 1968. Alaska Native Claims Settlement Act gives Alaska's Native Americans 44 million acres for native landholdings 1971. Completion of 789-mi. pipeline to Valdez 1977. Population growth of 32.8% highest in U.S. 1980–86. *Exxon Valdez* spills 10 million gallons of oil into Prince William Sound off Valdez—worst oil spill in U.S history 1989.

**Tourist information** 1-907-465-2010.

## Arizona

The Hopi village of Oraibi is the oldest continuously inhabited town in the United States, and today vast tracts of Arizona are reserved for Apaches, Hopis, Navajos, Papagos, and other Native Americans. Last of the 48 conterminous states admitted to the union, Arizona was sparsely settled until the advent of air-conditioning in the post-war years made it habitable and a popular destination for retirees. More recently, there has been a boom in manufacturing and light industry, and in the 1980s population growth was among the highest in the nation. Mexican-Americans are an especially important political force.

As in most southwestern states, water scarcity is a major problem. Arizona draws 2.8 million acre-feet of water from the Colorado River, whose water it shares with five other states and Mexico. The Central Arizona Project (CAP), a 330-mile, $3.5 billion pipeline to Phoenix and Tucson, is under construction.

NAME Probably from the Pima or Papago for "place of small springs." NICKNAME Grand Canyon State. CAPITAL Phoenix. ENTERED UNION Feb. 14, 1912 (48th). MOTTO *Ditat deus* (God enriches).

**Emblems** BIRD Cactus wren. FLOWER Blossom of the saguaro cactus. GEMSTONE Turquoise. OFFICIAL NECK WEAR Bola tie. SONGS "Arizona March Song," "Arizona." TREE Palo verde.

**Land** TOTAL AREA 114,000 sq. mi. (6th), incl. 492 sq. mi. inland water. BORDERS Utah, Colo., N.Mex., Sonora, Baja California Norte, Calif., Nev. RIVERS Colorado, Gila, Little Colorado, Salt, Zuni. LAKES Havasu, Mead, Mohave, Powell, Roosevelt, San Carlos. MOUNTAINS Black, Gila, Hualpai, Mohawk, San Francisco Peaks (Humphreys Peak 12,633 ft.). OTHER NOTABLE FEATURES Grand Canyon, Kaibab Plateau, Painted Desert, Petrified Forest, Sonoran Desert.

**Elected officials** Gov. Fife Symington (R, term exp. 1995). Sec. State Richard Mahoney (D). Atty. Gen. Grant Wood (R).

**People** (1990) 3,665,228 (24th). RACE/NATIONAL ORIGIN (1990): White 80.8%. Black 3.0%. Indian 5.6%. Asian 1.5%. Other 9.1%. Hispanic 18.8%.

**Cities** (1990) Phoenix 983,403. Tucson 405,390. Mesa 288,091. Glendale 148,134. Tempe 141,865. Scottsdale 130,069. Chandler 90,533. Yuma 54,923. Peoria 50,618. Flagstaff 45,857.

**Business** GROSS STATE PRODUCT (GSP, 1986) $53.3 bil. (25th). SECTORS OF GSP: Farms 1.53%. Agricultural services, forestry, & fisheries 0.58%. Mining 1.28%. Construction 10.01%. Manufacturing 13.47%. Transportation & public utilities 8.72%. Wholesale 5.26%. Retail 11.51%. Finance, insurance, & real estate 16.73%. Services 16.99%. Federal government 2.52%. Federal military 1.58%. State & local government 9.83%. *FORTUNE* 500 COMPANIES (1990): 2: Magma Copper, Phelps Dodge.

**Famous natives** Bruce Babbitt, politician. Cesar Chavez, labor leader. Cochise, Apache chief. Andrew Ellicott Douglass (b. Vt.), dendrochronologist. Wyatt Earp (b. Ill.), lawman. Barry Goldwater, politician. Goyathlay (Geronimo), Apache chieftain. Carl T. Hayden, congressman. Eusebio Kino (b. Italy), missionary. Sandra Day O'Connor, jurist. William H. Rehnquist, jurist. Linda Ronstadt, singer. Morris Udall, politician.

**Noteworthy places** Canyon de Chelly Natl. Monument. Casa Grande Ruins Natl. Monument. Chiricahua Natl. Monument. Ft. Bowie. Grand Canyon Natl. Park. Heard Museum, Phoenix. London Bridge, Lake Havasu City. Montezuma Castle Natl. Monument. Navajo Natl. Monument. Organ Pipe Cactus Natl. Monument. Painted Desert. Petrified Forest Natl. Park. Pipe Spring Natl. Monument. Saguaro Natl. Monument. Sunset Crater Natl. Monument. Taliesin West, near Scottsdale. Tonto Natl. Monument. Tumacacori Natl. Monument. Tuzigoot Natl. Monument. Walnut Canyon Natl. Monument. Wupatki Natl. Monument.

**Memorable events** Apaches and Navajos absorb Pueblos c. A.D. 1000. Alvar Núñez Cabeza de Vaca, first Spanish explorer 1536. Marcos de Niza 1539. Ruled as part of New Spain 1598-1821. First missionaries among Hopis 1638. Tubac first European settlement 1752. Tucson founded 1776. Apaches wipe out settlements under Mexican control, except Tucson 1821. Northern part ceded to U.S. following Mexican War 1848. Area south of Gila River to U.S. after Gadsden Purchase 1853. Territory 1863. Southern Pacific Railroad reaches Tucson 1880. Apaches subjugated 1886. Congress refuses to grant statehood 1906. Roosevelt Dam and Reservoir built on Salt River 1911. Native Americans given right to vote 1948. Glen Canyon Dam built on Colorado River 1964. Population growth of 22.1% highest in continental U.S. 1980-86.

**Tourist information** 1-602-542-3618 or 1-602-542-TOUR.

## Arkansas

First inhabited by bluff dwellers 10,000 years ago, the Boston and Ouachita mountains of western Arkansas are the only mountains between the Appalachians and the Rockies. By the time of the Hernando De Soto expedition of 1541, Arkansas was inhabited by a variety of peoples: the agrarian Quapaws to the south, the Caddo to the west and south, the Osage to the north, and the Chickasaw and Choctaw in the northeast. The Arkansas Post, the first permanent settlement in the Mississippi Valley, became the pillar of the French claim to the region of what became the Louisiana Purchase.

Not fully part of the deep south, and cut off geographically from the Midwest, Arkansas has developed slowly. Although cotton was a mainstay of the economy and Arkansas joined the Confederacy during the Civil War, it was the first southern state to have integrated public colleges after World War II, a fact overshadowed by Gov. Orville Faubus's resistance to the integration of the Little Rock public schools. In recent years, Arkansas has attracted manufacturing and industry, but has one of the highest rural populations and ranks low in services, income, and education attainment.

**Name** For term for Quapaw tribe given by other Indians. **Nickname** Land of Opportunity. **Capital** Little Rock. **Entered Union** June 15, 1836 (25th). **Motto** *Regnat populus* (Let the people rule).

**Emblems** BIRD Mockingbird. FLOWER Apple blossom. GEM Diamond. SONG "Arkansas." TREE Pine.

**Land** TOTAL AREA 53,187 sq. mi. (27th), incl. 1,109 sq. mi. inland water. BORDERS Mo., Tenn., Miss., La., Tex., Okla. RIVERS Arkansas, Mississippi, Ouachita, Red, St. Francis, White. LAKES Beaver, Bull Shoals, Chicot, Dardanelle, Greers Ferry, Greeson, Norfolk, Ouachita. OTHER NOTABLE FEATURES Ozark Mts.

**Elected officials** Gov. Bill Clinton (D, term exp. 1995). Lt. Gov. Jim Guy Tucker (D). Sec. State W.J. ("Bill") McCuen (D). Atty. Gen. Winston Bryant (D).

**People** (1990) 2,350,725 (33d). RACE/NATIONAL ORIGIN (1990): White 82.7%. Black 15.9%. Indian 0.5%. Asian 0.5%. Other 0.3%. Hispanic 0.8%.

**Cities** (1990) Little Rock 175,795. Fort Smith 72,798. North Little Rock 61,741. Pine Bluff 57,140. Jonesboro 46,535. Fayetteville 42,099. Hot Springs 32,462. Springdale 29,941. Jacksonville 29,101. West Memphis 28,259.

**Business** GROSS STATE PRODUCT (GSP, 1986) $31.6 bil. (33d). SECTORS OF GSP: Farms 5.56%. Agricultural services, forestry, & fisheries 0.41%. Mining 1.61%. Construction 4.91%. Manufacturing 24.60%. Transportation & public utilities 10.42%. Wholesale 5.43%. Retail 10.43%. Finance, insurance, & real estate 14.16%. Services 12.10%. Federal government 1.44%. Federal military 1.27%. State & local government 7.69%. *FORTUNE* 500 COMPANIES (1990): 4: Hudson Foods, Murphy Oil, Riceland Foods, Tyson Foods.

**Famous natives** Maya Angelou, author. Glen Campbell, singer. Hattie W. Caraway, first woman senator. Johnny Cash, singer. Eldridge Cleaver, author. William Fulbright (b. Mo.), politician. Alan Ladd, actor. Douglas MacArthur, general. Dick Powell, actor. Brooks Robinson, baseball player. Winthrop Rockefeller (b. N.Y.), politician/philanthropist. Edward Durrell Stone, architect. C. Vann Woodward, historian.

**Noteworthy places** Arkansas Post Natl. Monument (1st permanent French settlement in lower Mississippi Valley). Buffalo Natl. River. Crater of Diamonds State Park, Murfreesboro. Eureka Springs. Ft. Smith Natl. Hist. Site. Hot Springs Natl. Park. Pea Ridge Natl. Military Park.

**Memorable events** Bluff-dwellers present c. A.D. 500, followed by mound-building cultures. Hernando de Soto explores for Spain 1541. Jacques Marquette and Louis Jolliet explore for France 1673. René-Robert de La Salle meets Quapaws 1682. Henri de Tonti founds Arkansas Post on Arkansas River 1686. Ceded from France to Spain 1782; to France 1800; to U.S. 1803. Territory 1819. Admitted to Union as slave state, under terms of 1820 Missouri Compromise, 1836. Secedes from Union 1861. Fall of Little Rock to Union army 1863. Readmitted to Union 1868. Bauxite discovered 1887. Oil production begins 1920s. Federal troops called to Little Rock to ensure high school desegregation 1957. McClellan-Kerr Arkansas River Navigation System links Arkansas and Oklahoma to Mississippi River system 1971.

**Tourist information** 1-800-643-8383 or 1-800-482-8999.

## California

Before the arrival of Europeans, no area of comparable size in North America was home to a greater variety of languages and cultures than what is now California, and today the state's population is more diverse than any other. Some demographers expect that within 50 years more than 40 percent of California's population will be of Hispanic origin, a larger proportion than at any time since before the Gold Rush of 1849. But the trend toward a two-tiered society is also increasing, with Caucasians and Asians on top and African-Americans and Hispanics on the bottom.

The largest state by population since the 1960s, California gained seven additional representatives in Congress as a result of the 1990 census, for a total of 52. This factor, as well as plans to hold its presidential primary before that of most other states, will make California more of a bellwether in national affairs than ever. Moreover, by some estimates California is the sixth largest economic power in the world.

Despite these attractions, and the state's rugged terrain and dramatic vistas, California has problems. The state's position as a leader in agriculture masks an alarming lack of water. It already draws off 4.4 million acre-feet from the Colorado River, mostly for irrigating the Imperial Valley—a desert when settlers crossed it 150 years ago. Almost the entire flow of the San Joaquin River is similarly diverted for the Central Valley. This inefficient use of water leaves less and less for consumption by people, whose numbers have leaped from 15 million in 1960 to 29.7 million in 1990.

Of more immediate concern is the threat of earthquakes. California has already suffered eight major earthquakes in this century. The 1906 quake destroyed San Francisco, and the Loma Prieta earthquake on Oct. 17, 1989—the second most powerful in U.S. history—killed 67 people, left 48,000 people homeless, and resulted in $10 billion in property damage. Like surfers waiting for the perfect wave, scientists are still bracing for "the big one."

**Name** Probably from mythical island in García Ordoñez de Montalvo's 16th-century romance, *The Deeds of Esplandián*. **Nickname** Golden State. **Capital** Sacramento. **Entered Union** Sept. 9, 1850 (31st). **Motto** "Eureka" (I have found it).

**Emblems** ANIMAL California grizzly bear (extinct). BIRD California valley quail. FISH California golden trout. FLOWER Golden poppy. FOSSIL California saber-toothed cat. GEMSTONE Benitoite. INSECT California dog-face butterfly. MARINE MAMMAL California gray whale. MINERAL Gold. REPTILE California desert tortoise. ROCK

Serpentine. SONG "I Love You, California." TREE California redwood.

**Land** TOTAL AREA 158,706 sq. mi. (3d), incl. 2,407 sq. mi. inland water. BORDERS Oreg., Nev., Ariz., Baja California Norte, Pacific Ocean. RIVERS American, Colorado, Colorado River Aqueduct, Eel, Friant-Kern Canal, Klamath, Russian, Sacramento, Salinas, San Joaquin. LAKES Clear, Goose, Honey, Mono, Owens, Salton Sea, Shasta, Tahoe. MOUNTAINS Coast Ranges, Klamath, Lassen Peak, Sierra Nevada (Mt. Whitney 14,494 ft.). OTHER NOTABLE FEATURES Catalina Islands, Death Valley (282 ft. below sea level), San Francisco Bay, San Joaquin Valley.

**Elected officials** Gov. Pete Wilson (R, term exp. 1995). Lt. Gov. Leo T. McCarthy (D). Sec. State March Fong Eu (D). Atty. Gen. Daniel E. Lungren (R).

**People** (1990) 29,760,021 (1st). RACE/NATIONAL ORIGIN (1990): White 69.0%. Black 7.4%. Indian 0.8%. Asian 9.6%. Other 13.2%. Hispanic 25.8%.

**Cities** (1990) Los Angeles 3,485,398. San Diego 1,110,549. San Jose 782,248. San Francisco 723,959. Long Beach 429,433. Oakland 372,242. Sacramento 369,365. Fresno 354,202. Santa Ana 293,742. Anaheim 266,406.

**Business** GROSS STATE PRODUCT (GSP, 1986) $533.8 bil. (1st). SECTORS OF GSP: Farms 1.49%. Agricultural services, forestry, & fisheries 0.62%. Mining 1.11%. Construction 4.47%. Manufacturing 18.30%. Transportation & public utilities 7.85%. Wholesale 7.25%. Retail 10.34%. Finance, insurance, & real estate 17.57%. Services 19.37%. Federal government 2.01%. Federal military 1.76%. State & local government 7.85%. FORTUNE 500 COMPANIES (1990): 38: incl. Apple Computer, Atlantic Richfield, Chevron, Clorox, Hewlett-Packard, Litton Industries, Lockheed, Mattel, Northrop, Occidental Petroleum, Rockwell International, Sun-Diamond Growers, Tandem Computers, Teledyne, Times Mirror, UNOCAL.

**Famous natives** Ansel Adams, photographer. Dave Brubeck, musician. Luther Burbank (b. Mass.), horticulturist. John Cage, composer. Joe DiMaggio, baseball player. Robert Frost, poet. Ernest and Julio Gallo (b. Italy), vintners. Pancho Gonzales, tennis player. Samuel Ichiye Hayakawa, politician/educator. William Randolph Hearst, publisher. Steve Jobs, computer scientist. Billie Jean King, tennis player. Allen Lockheed, aviator. Jack London, author. Paul Masson (b. France), vintner. Marilyn Monroe, actress. John Muir (b. Scotland), naturalist. Richard M. Nixon, U.S. president. John Northrop, aviator. Adlai Stevenson, politician. John Steinbeck, author. Levi Strauss (b. Germany), clothier. Edward Teller (b. Hungary), nuclear physicist. Shirley Temple, actress. Earl Warren, politician/jurist.

**Noteworthy places** Big Sur, Monterey. Cabrillo Natl. Monument. California Academy of Sciences, San Francisco. California Palace of the Legion of Honor, San Francisco. Channel Islands Natl. Park. Devils Postpile Natl. Monument. Death Valley Natl. Monument. Disneyland. Fine Arts Museum of San Francisco. Fishermen's Wharf, San Francisco. Hollywood. Huntington Library and Botanical Gardens, San Marino. J. Paul Getty Museum, Malibu. Joshua Tree Natl. Monument. Kings Canyon Natl. Park. Lassen Volcanic Natl. Park. Lava Beds Natl. Monument. Los Angeles Co. Museum of Art. Muir Woods Natl. Monument. Mt. Palomar Observatory. Natl. Maritime Museum, San Francisco. Natural History Museum, Los Angeles. Natural History Museum of San Diego. Norton Simon Museum of Art at Pasadena. Pinnacles Natl. Monument. Redwood Natl. Park. Rosicrucian Egyptian Museum, San José. San Diego Museum of Art. San Diego Museum of Man. San Diego Zoo. San Francisco Museum of Modern Art. Sequoia Natl. Park. Southwest Museum (Casa de Adobe), Los Angeles. Yosemite Natl. Park.

**Memorable events** João Rodrigues Cabrilho lands at San Diego Bay 1542. Francis Drake lands north of San Francisco Bay 1579. Junípero Serra founds missions at San Diego (1769), Monterey (1770), San Luis Obispo (1772), and San Juan Capistrano (1776). California declares allegiance to independent Mexico 1821. First wagon train from Missouri 1841. Gold discovered north of Los Angeles 1842. California declares itself independent republic 1846. Gold found at John Sutter's mill; nine days later, by Treaty of Guadalupe Hidalgo, Mexico cedes California to U.S. 1848. Announcement of gold discovery brings 80,000 'Forty-niners. Gold rush peaks 1852. Transcontinental telegraph completed 1861. Transcontinental railway completed 1869. U.S. Congress enacts Chinese Exclusion Act, prohibiting immigration of Chinese laborers 1882, 1892, and 1902; Act repealed 1943. San Francisco earthquake kills 452, destroys 28,000 buildings 1906. Webb Alien Land Law prohibits Japanese from holding land 1913. Los Angeles has one car for every three people, twice national average, 1925. Dust Bowl immigrants 1930. Hollywood produces bulk of movies for U.S. theaters, which number more than banks 1940. Most populous state 1963. Proposition 13 limits property tax 1978. Loma Prieta earthquake registers 7.1 on Richter scale—second most powerful in U.S. history; 67 dead, 48,000 homeless, and $10 billion in property damage 1989.

**Tourist information** 1–800–862–2543 or 1–916–322–1396.

# Colorado

The native peoples of Colorado were the Plains Indians (Arapahoe and Cheyenne) to the east and the Great Basin Indians (Utes) to the west. This pre-Columbian division of the land is reflected today in Colorado's economy, which is a mix of agriculture and technology in the east and mining and ski tourism in the mountains. Despite a lack of natural sources of water on the Plains, sugar-beet processing has for years been a staple of the agricultural sector. During the oil price shocks of the 1970s, shale-oil production on the Western Slope created a boom comparable to Colorado's silver and lead boom in the late 19th century. Colorado's love of the outdoors is increasingly in conflict with its tradition of unhindered growth. Colorado's cities east of the Rockies sprawl without effective plans for land use. While a state of great natural beauty, it must cope with a high altitude that almost doubles the effect of auto emissions. Economic development means in large part resource extraction and requires more and more water, whose limited supply poses a great question for the future.

NAME Spanish for the color red. NICKNAME Centennial State. CAPITAL Denver. ENTERED UNION Aug. 1, 1876 (38th). MOTTO *Nil sine numine* (Nothing without providence).

**Emblems** ANIMAL Rocky Mountain bighorn sheep. BIRD Lark bunting. FLOWER Rocky Mountain Columbine. GEM Aquamarine. SONG "Where the Columbines Grow." TREE Colorado blue spruce.

**Land** TOTAL AREA 104,091 sq. mi. (8th), incl. 496 sq. mi. inland water. BORDERS Wyo., Nebr., Kans., Okla., N.Mex., Ariz., Utah. RIVERS Arkansas, Colorado, Green, Platte, Rio Grande. LAKES Blue Mesa, Dillon, Granby. MOUNTAINS Front Range, Laramie, Sangre de Cristo, San Juan, Sawatch Range (Mt. Elbert 14,443 ft.).

**Elected officials** Gov. Roy Romer (D, term exp. 1995). Lt. Gov. C. Michael Callihan (D). Sec. State Natalie Meyer (R). Atty. Gen. Gale Norton (R).

**People** (1990) 3,294,394 (26th). RACE/NATIONAL ORIGIN (1990): White 88.2%. Black 4.0%. Indian 0.8%. Asian 1.8%. Other 5.1%. Hispanic 12.9%.

**Cities** (1990) Denver 467,610. Colorado Springs 281,140. Aurora 222,103. Lakewood 126,481. Pueblo 98,640. Arvada 89,235. Fort Collins 87,758. Boulder 83,312. Westminster 74,625. Greeley 60,536.

**Business** GROSS STATE PRODUCT (GSP, 1986) $59.2 bil. (23d). SECTORS OF GSP: Farms 2.15%. Agricultural services, forestry, & fisheries 0.41%. Mining 2.88%. Construction 5.93%. Manufacturing 12.90%. Transportation & public utilities 11.09%. Wholesale 6.39%. Retail 10.62%. Finance, insurance, & real estate 16.37%. Services 17.27%. Federal government 2.97%. Federal military 2.22%. State & local government 8.79%. FORTUNE 500 COMPANIES (1990): 5: Adolph Coors, Cyprus Minerals, Manville, Newmont Mining, Storage Technology.

**Famous natives** Charlie Bent (b. Va.), trapper. "Unsinkable" Molly Brown, *Titanic* survivor. Scott Carpenter, astronaut. Lon Chaney, actor. Jack Dempsey, boxer. Mamie Eisenhower, First Lady. Douglas Fairbanks, actor. Anne Parrish, novelist. Lowell Thomas, journalist. Byron R. White, jurist. Paul Whiteman, conductor.

**Noteworthy Places** Black Canyon of the Gunnison Natl. Monument. Buffalo Bill grave site, Evergreen. Central City Opera House. Colorado Springs Fine Arts Center. Denver Art Museum. Denver Mint. Denver Museum of Natural History. Dinosaur Natl. Monument. Florissant Fossil Beds Natl. Monument. Garden of the Gods, Colorado Springs. Great Sand Dunes Natl. Monument. Hovenweep Natl. Monument. Mesa Verde Natl. Park. Molly Brown House, Denver. Pikes Peak. Red Rocks Amphitheater. Rocky Mountain Natl. Park, Aspen. U.S. Air Force Academy, Colorado Springs. U.S. Olympic Headquarters, Colorado Springs. Yucca

House Natl. Monument.

**Memorable events** Pueblos build cliff dwellings near Mesa Verde through 1200s. Arapahos and Cheyennes settle area after 13th century. France abandons claims 1763. Juan de Uribarri explores area 1786. Spain restores area to France 1801. To U.S. as part of Louisiana Purchase 1803. Zebulon Pike explores for U.S. 1806. Kit Carson and other scouts explore and trade with Native Americans 1810s–20s. Native Americans form alliance at Brent's Fork 1840. John Frémont's explorations 1842–53. Present territorial limits after Mexican War 1848. First permanent settlement at San Luis 1851. Gold found west of Denver—"Pike's Peak or Bust"—1858. Mineral springs bring first tourists 1861. Homestead Act encourages farming 1862. U.S. Army kills 400 Cheyenne at Sand Creek Massacre 1864; Utes and Cheyennes fight white settlement through 1870s. John Wesley Powell and nine others navigate Colorado River from the Green River branch in Wyoming to the end of Grand Canyon in Arizona 1869. Railroad link to Denver 1870. Silver and lead discoveries 1875. Uranium discovered near Grand Junction 1946. U.S. Air Force Academy founded Denver 1954; to Colorado Springs 1958. Shale oil boom on Western Slope 1974 and 1979. Accumulation of nuclear waste threatens suspension of operations at Rocky Flats 1988.

**Tourist information** 1–800–433–2656 or 1–303–592–5510.

## Connecticut

Called the "arsenal of the nation" during the Revolution, Connecticut today leads the 50 states in defense-contract dollars per capita, although population ebb and flow continue to test its manufacturing wealth. Hartford has been the insurance capital of the world since before 1800, and Connecticut's quarries provided much of the red sandstone that became known as "brownstone" after it lined New York City streets.

With conditions favorable for affluent business, Connecticut has the highest per capita income in the country. However, it faced severe budget deficits in 1991; this forced passage of a state income tax after a prolonged budget crisis. The disparities in wealth between the very rich suburbs and the decaying industrial cities were highlighted by the city of Bridgeport's bankruptcy filing in June 1991. Although located in one of the country's wealthiest counties, Bridgeport's 180,000 mostly lower-middle-class inhabitants shoulder all the costs for county-wide health and criminal justice services themselves, in a pattern repeated statewide.

NAME From Mahican word meaning "beside the long tidal river." NICKNAMES Constitution State, Nutmeg State. CAPITAL Hartford. ENTERED UNION Jan. 9, 1788 (5th). MOTTO *Qui transtulit sustinet* (He who transplanted still sustains).

**Emblems** ANIMAL Sperm whale. BIRD American robin. FLOWER Mountain laurel. HERO Nathan Hale. INSECT European praying mantis. MINERAL Garnet. SHIP USS *Nautilus*. SONG "Yankee Doodle." TREE White oak.

**Land** TOTAL AREA 5,018 sq. mi. (48th), incl. 146 sq. mi. inland water. BORDERS Mass., R.I., Long Island Sound, N.Y. RIVERS Connecticut, Housatonic, Mianus, Naugatuck, Thames. LAKES Bantam, Barkhamstead, Candlewood, Waramaug. OTHER NOTABLE FEATURES Berkshire Hills, Long Island Sound.

**Elected officials** Gov. Lowell P. Weicker, Jr. (I, term exp. 1995). Lt. Gov. Eunice Groark (I). Sec. State Pauline R. Kezer (R). Atty. Gen. Richard Blumenthal (D).

**People** (1990) 3,287,116 (27th). RACE/NATIONAL ORIGIN (1990): White 87.0%. Black 8.3%. Indian 0.2%. Asian 1.5%. Other 2.9%. Hispanic 6.5%.

**Cities** (1990) Bridgeport 141,686. Hartford 139,739. New Haven 130,474. Waterbury 108,961. Stamford 108,056. Norwalk 78,331. New Britain 75,491. Danbury 65,585. Bristol 60,640. Meriden 59,479.

**Business** GROSS STATE PRODUCT (GSP, 1986) $70.6 bil. (22d). SECTORS OF GSP: Farms 0.40%. Agricultural services, forestry, & fisheries 0.29%. Mining 0.11%. Construction 4.18%. Manufacturing 24.32%. Transportation & public utilities 7.62%. Wholesale 7.12%. Retail 9.65%. Finance, insurance, & real estate 19.91%. Services 16.66%. Federal government 2.48%. Federal military 0.74%. State & local government 6.53%. *FORTUNE* 500 COMPANIES (1990): 26: incl. American Brands, Champion International, General Electric, Olin, Pitney Bowes, Stanley Works, Union Carbide, United Technologies, XEROX.

**Famous natives** Benedict Arnold, traitor. P.T. Barnum, showman. Lyman Beecher, theologian. John Brown, abolitionist. Samuel Colt, inventor. Jonathan Edwards, theologian. Charles Goodyear, inventor. Nathan Hale, patriot. Katharine Hepburn, actress. Charles Ives, composer. J.P. Morgan, financier. Ralph Nader, consumer advocate. Frederick Law Olmsted, landscape architect. Harriet Beecher Stowe, author. John Trumbell, artist. Noah Webster, lexicographer. Eli Whitney, inventor.

**Noteworthy places** Charles Ives Center, Danbury. Eugene O'Neill Memorial Theater Center, Waterford. Gilette Castle. Housatonic State Park. Mark Twain House, Hartford. Mystic Marinelife Aquarium. Mystic Seaport. Norwalk Maritime Center. U.S. Coast Guard Academy. USS *Nautilus*, New London. Wadsworth Atheneum, Hartford. Whitney Museum of Modern Art, Stamford. Yale Center for British Art, New Haven. Yale University, New Haven.

**Memorable events** Adriaen Block claims for Dutch 1614. First English settlement in Windsor 1633. Royal charter of 1662 hidden in Charter Oak 1687. *Hartford Courant*, oldest continuously published newspaper in U.S., first published 1764. Samuel Colt develops six-shooter 1835. Horace Wells uses first anesthesia 1845. Elias Howe invents sewing machine 1845. U.S. Coast Guard Academy founded New London 1876. First woman governor elected in her own right, Ella T. Grasso 1974.

**Tourist information** 1–800–CT–BOUND or 1–203–258–4290.

## Delaware

The du Pont family has enjoyed a political and economic prominence in Delaware unmatched in the history of the other 49 states. Seven generations ago E.I. du Pont de Nemours and Co. was founded as a gunpowder mill, then grew into a monopoly, and in the wake of World War I diversified into today's giant, with interests in banking, media, and real estate. Only half the size of Los Angeles County, Delaware was called the corporate state by Ralph Nader's "raiders" in 1973. Its liberal incorporation laws have led more than half the *Fortune* 500 companies to incorporate there. It was one of the few states to prosper even during the recession of the early 1980s.

NAME For Thomas West, Lord De La Warre, colonial governor of Virginia. NICKNAMES First State, Diamond State. CAPITAL Dover. ENTERED UNION Dec. 7, 1787 (1st). MOTTO "Liberty and Independence."

**Emblems** BIRD Blue hen chicken. FISH Weakfish. FLOWER Peach blossom. INSECT Ladybug. ROCK Sillimanite. SONG "Our Delaware." TREE American holly.

**Land** TOTAL AREA 2,044 sq. mi. (49th), incl. 112 sq. mi. inland water. BORDERS Pa., N.J., Atlantic Ocean, Md. RIVERS Chesapeake and Delaware Canal, Delaware, Nanticoke.

**Elected officials** Gov. Michael N. Castle (R, term exp. 1993). Lt. Gov. Dale E. Wolf (R). Atty. Gen. Charles M. Oberly III (D).

**People** (1990) 666,168 (46th). RACE/NATIONAL ORIGIN (1990): White 80.3%. Black 16.9%. Indian 0.3%. Asian 1.4%. Other 1.1%. Hispanic 2.4%.

**Cities** (1990) Wilmington 71,529. Dover 27,630. Newark 25,098. Milford 6,040. Elsmere Town 5,935. Seaford 5,689. Smyrna Town 5,231. New Castle 4,837. Middletown Town 3,834. Georgetown Town 3,732.

**Business** GROSS STATE PRODUCT (GSP, 1986) $11.7 bil. (46th). SECTORS OF GSP: Farms 1.86%. Agricultural services, forestry, & fisheries 0.28%. Mining 0.02%. Construction 4.83%. Manufacturing 28.40%. Transportation & public utilities 7.79%. Wholesale 5.61%. Retail 8.41%. Finance, insurance, & real estate 18.19%. Services 13.81%. Federal government 1.41%. Federal military 0.74%. State & local government 7.92%. *FORTUNE* 500 COMPANIES (1990): 3: E.I. Du Pont de Nemours, E.W. Scripps, Hercules.

**Famous natives** Valerie Bertinelli, actress. John Dickinson (b. Md.), Penman of the Revolution. Eleuthère I. du Pont, manufacturer. Pierre S. ("Pete") du Pont, politician. Morgan Edwards, founder of Brown University (R.I.). Thomas Macdonough, navy officer. Howard Pyle, illustrator. Edward R. Squibb, physician/manufacturer. Christopher Ward, historian.

**Noteworthy places** Brandywine Zoo, Wilmington. Delaware Art Museum, Wilmington. Delaware State Museum, Dover. Dover Downs International Speedway. Grand Opera House, Wilmington. Hagley Museum, Wilmington. Rehoboth Beach.

**Memorable events** Dutch arrive 1631. Swedes establish first permanent settlement at Wilmington 1638. Captured by Dutch 1655. To England 1664. Part of territory granted to William Penn 1682. Breaks off from Pennsylvania; first to ratify Constitution 1776. E.I. du Pont de Nemours Co. founded 1802. Railroad connects Wilmington to Philadelphia and Baltimore 1838. Though slave state, sides with Union during Civil War 1861–65. Delaware last state to abolish whipping post (last used 1952) 1972. **Tourist information** 1-800-441-8846 or 1-800-282-8667.

## District of Columbia

Chosen as the site for the nation's capital by George Washington, Washington, D.C., was carved out of land ceded by Maryland and Virginia. Although under federal jurisdiction, the District has petitioned for statehood as New Columbia. In 1961 Congress enacted the 23d Amendment granting citizens of D.C. the right to vote in presidential elections for the first time, and 10 years later gave the District a nonvoting delegate to the House of Representatives. The District's largest employer is the federal government, and printing is the largest industry. President John F. Kennedy called it a city of "Southern efficiency and Northern charm," but since his time, the city has become a leading patron of the arts. The problems of any large city are made worse by the city's largely transient population of government workers. The city, as the seat of the U.S. government, is a mecca for tourists from around the world, and more than 17 million people visit it each year.

NAME After Christopher Columbus; Columbia was commonly used for the U.S. before 1800. NICKNAME None. CAPITAL Washington. BECAME CAPITAL Dec. 1, 1800. MOTTO *Justitia omnibus* (Justice for all).

**Emblems** BIRD Wood thrush. FLOWER American beauty rose. TREE Scarlet oak.

**Land** TOTAL AREA 69 sq. mi., incl. 6 sq. mi. inland water. BORDERS Md., Va. RIVERS Anacostia, Potomac.

**Elected officials** Mayor Sharon Pratt Dixon (D, term exp. 1995).

**People** (1990) 606,900. RACE/NATIONAL ORIGIN (1990): White 29.6%. Black 65.8%. Indian 0.2%. Asian 1.8%. Other 2.5%. Hispanic 5.4%.

**Business** GROSS STATE PRODUCT (GSP, 1986) $28.8 bil. SECTORS OF GSP: Farms 0.00%. Agricultural services, forestry, & fisheries 0.02%. Mining 0.02%. Construction 6.87%. Manufacturing 3.62%. Transportation & public utilities 6.23%. Wholesale 1.84%. Retail 4.40%. Finance, insurance, & real estate 9.23%. Services 28.48%. Federal government 32.33%. Federal military 2.43%. State & local government 3.90%. *FORTUNE* 500 COMPANIES (1990): 3: Danaher, Harman Intl. Industries, Washington Post.

**Famous natives** Edward Albee, playwright. Carl Bernstein, journalist. John Foster Dulles, politician. Duke Ellington, composer. J. Edgar Hoover, FBI director. Marjorie Kinnan Rawlings, novelist. John Philip Sousa, composer.

**Noteworthy places** The Capitol. Chesapeake & Ohio Canal Natl. Hist. Park. Corcoran Gallery of Art. Dumbarton Oaks. Folger Shakespeare Library. Freer Gallery of Art. Hirshhorn Museum. Jefferson Memorial. Kennedy Center. Library of Congress. Lincoln Memorial. Natl. Air and Space Museum. Natl. Gallery of Art. Natl. Museum of African Art. Natl. Museum of American Art. Natl. Museum of American History. Natl. Museum of Natural History. Natl. Portrait Gallery. Naval Observatory. Navy Memorial Museum. Renwick Gallery. Smithsonian Institution. Vietnam Veterans Memorial. Washington Monument. Washington Zoo. White House. Woodrow Wilson House.

**Memorable events** Originally part of Maryland. Congress approves plan to secure land for seat of federal government, no more than 10 miles square, on land in Virginia and Maryland 1787. George Washington commissions Pierre Charles l'Enfant to lay out city 1791. Government moves 1800. British sail up the Potomac and burn capital 1814. Virginia reclaims its half of District 1846. President Abraham Lincoln assassinated 1865. Coxey's Army marches on Washington 1894. The Bonus Army—17,000 veterans—marches on Washington 1932. Led by Martin Luther King, Jr., 200,000 march for Civil Rights 1963. One hundred thousand protest Vietnam War 1971. Democratic party headquarters at Watergate burglarized by men linked to President Richard M. Nixon's reelection effort 1972. Congress grants limited self-rule; mayor and city council elected 1975. Mayor Marion Barry indicted on drug charges 1990.

**Tourist information** 1-202-789-7000.

## Florida

A vast network of swamps, rivers, and lakes, much of Florida is barely above sea level. Florida is home to Disney World, Cypress Gardens, the wealth-laden resort of Palm Beach, the *National Enquirer*, and the Okefenokee Swamp, and the pleasant climate and proximity to the Caribbean and Latin America have attracted large populations of the elderly and immigrants, as well as millions of tourists. One of the fastest-growing states, Florida has been plagued by drug trafficking, racial disturbances, and environmental damage to such wildlife as the crocodile, alligator, and the Florida panther.

NAME By Juan Ponce de León for Pascua Florida (Easter festival of the flowers). NICKNAME Sunshine State. CAPITAL Tallahassee. ENTERED UNION Mar. 3, 1845 (27th). MOTTO "In God We Trust." POET LAUREATE Dr. Edmund Skellings.

**Emblems** ANIMAL Florida panther. BEVERAGE Orange juice. BIRD Mockingbird. FLOWER Orange blossom. FRESHWATER FISH Florida largemouth bass. GEM Moonstone. MARINE MAMMALS Dolphin, manatee. SALTWATER FISH Atlantic sailfish. SHELL Horse conch. SONG "Old Folks at Home" ("Swanee River"). STONE Agatized coral. TREE Sabal palmetto palm.

**Land** TOTAL AREA 58,664 sq. mi. (22d), incl. 4,511 sq. mi. inland water. BORDERS Ga., Atlantic Ocean, Gulf of Mexico, Ala. RIVERS Apalachicola, Caloosahatchee, Indian, Kissim-

mee, Perdido, St. Johns, St. Mary's, Suwanee, Withlacoochee. LAKES Apopka, George, Okeechobee, Seminole. OTHER NOTABLE FEATURES Everglades, Florida Keys, Okefenokee Swamp.

**Elected officials** Gov. Lawton Chiles (D, term exp. 1995). Lt. Gov. Buddy MacKay (D). Sec. State Jim Smith (R). Atty. Gen. Robert A. Butterworth (D).

**People** (1990) 12,937,926 (4th). RACE/NATIONAL ORIGIN (1990): White 83.1%. Black 13.6%. Indian 0.3%. Asian 1.2%. Other 1.8%. Hispanic 12.2%.

**Cities** (1990) Jacksonville 672,971. Miami 358,548. Tampa 280,015. St. Petersburg 238,629. Hialeah 188,004. Orlando 164,693. Ft. Lauderdale 149,377. Tallahassee 124,773. Hollywood 121,697. Clearwater 98,784.

**Business** GROSS STATE PRODUCT (GSP, 1986) $177.7 bil. (6th). SECTORS OF GSP: Farms 1.81%. Agricultural services, forestry, & fisheries 0.69%. Mining 0.87%. Construction 7.25%. Manufacturing 10.80%. Transportation & public utilities 9.29%. Wholesale 7.08%. Retail 12.08%. Finance, insurance, & real estate 18.77%. Services 19.46%. Federal government 1.97%. Federal military 1.93%. State & local government 7.99%. *FORTUNE* 500 COMPANIES (1990): 6: incl. DWG, Harcourt Brace Jovanovich, Knight-Ridder.

**Famous natives** Mary Bethune, educator/reformer. Faye Dunaway, actress. Zora Neale Hurston, writer. James Weldon Johnson, lawyer/novelist. Osceola, Seminole chief. Sidney Poitier, actor. A. Philip Randolph, labor leader. Edmund Kirby Smith, Confederate general. Joseph Warren ("Vinegar Joe") Stillwell, army officer. Ben Vereen, actor/singer.

**Noteworthy places** Biscayne Natl. Park. Castillo de San Marcos, St. Augustine. Everglades Natl. Park. Florida State Museum, Gainesville. Ft. Jefferson Natl. Monument. Ft. Matanzas Natl. Monument. Kennedy Space Center, Cape Canaveral. Ringling Museum, Sarasota. St. Augustine. Walt Disney World/Epcot Center, Orlando.

**Memorable events** Juan Ponce de León claims Florida for Spain 1513. French stake claim for Florida 1562; build Ft. Caroline 1564. Pedro Menéndez de Avilés founds St. Augustine, first permanent European settlement in U.S. 1565. Spain cedes Florida to U.S. 1819. Seminole War 1835–42. State secedes from Union 1861. Readmitted 1868. Carl Fisher begins to develop Miami Beach as resort 1912. Florida's first paper mill opens, expanding forest industry 1931. More than 100,000 Cuban refugees enter U.S., most through Florida, during Mariel boat lift 1980. Army Corps of Engineers announce plans to let Kissimmee River, canalized in 1971, return to natural course to Lake Okeechobee; the largest back-to-nature project ever undertaken in U.S. 1990.

**Tourist information** 1-904-487-1462.

## Georgia

The largest state east of the Mississippi River, Georgia is diverse in its terrain, embracing the woods of the Blue Ridge Mountains to the north and the alligators of the Okefenokee

Swamp in the south. Though two-thirds of the population are urban dwellers, Georgia's farms rank first in poultry production and are leading producers of pecans, cattle, hogs, and peanuts. Up from a past of slavery and separate-but-equal facilities, in the early 1970s Atlanta elected Andrew Young the first black member of the U.S. Congress and Maynard Jackson the first black mayor from the South since Reconstruction. Today divisions linger in Georgia, the cities favoring a progressive stance and the rural areas clinging to some of the ways of the Old South.

**Name** For King George II of England 1732. **Nicknames** Empire State of the South, Peach State. **Capital** Atlanta. **Entered Union** Jan. 2, 1788 (4th). **Motto** "Wisdom, justice, moderation."

**Emblems** **Bird** Brown thrasher. **Fish** Largemouth bass. **Flower** Cherokee rose. **Fossil** Shark tooth. **Gem** Quartz. **Insect** Honeybee. **Songs** "Georgia," "Georgia on My Mind." **Tree** Live oak. **Wildflower** Azalea.

**Land** **Total area** 58,910 sq. mi. (21st), incl. 854 sq. mi. inland water. **Borders** Tenn., N.C., S.C., Atlantic Ocean, Fla., Ala. **Rivers** Altamaha, Apalachicola, Chattahoochee, Flint, Ocmulgee, Oconee, Savannah, Suwanee. **Lakes** Clark Hill, Harding, Hartwell, Seminole, Sidney Lanier, Sinclair, Walter F. George, West Point Lake. **Other notable features** Blue Ridge Mountains (Mt. Enotah 4,784 ft.), Okefenokee Swamp.

**Elected officials** Gov. Zell Miller (D, term exp. 1995). Lt. Gov. Pierre Howland (D). Sec. State Max Cleland (D). Atty. Gen. Michael J. Bowers (D).

**People** (1990) 6,478,216 (11th). **Race/national origin** (1990): White 71.0%. Black 27.0%. Indian 0.2%. Asian 1.2%. Other 0.7%. Hispanic 1.7%.

**Cities** (1990) Atlanta 394,017. Columbus 179,278. Savannah 137,560. Macon 106,612. Albany 78,122. Roswell 47,923. Athens 45,734. Augusta 44,639. Marietta 44,129. Warner Robins 43,726.

**Business** **Gross state product** (GSP, 1986) $102.9 bil. (12th). **Sectors of GSP:** Farms 1.75%. Agricultural services, forestry, & fisheries 0.33%. Mining 0.56%. Construction 5.38%. Manufacturing 20.92%. Transportation & public utilities 10.98%. Wholesale 9.56%. Retail 10.04%. Finance, insurance, & real estate 13.76%. Services 14.17%. Federal government 2.96%. Federal military 2.05%. State & local government 7.55%. *Fortune* 500 companies (1990): 14: incl. Coca-Cola, Georgia Gulf, Georgia-Pacific, West Point–Pepperell.

**Famous natives** James Brown, singer. Erskine Caldwell, author. James Earl ("Jimmy") Carter, U.S. president. Ray Charles, musician. Ty Cobb, baseball player. James Dickey, poet. W.E.B. DuBois, educator/reformer. Martin Luther King, Jr., minister/reformer. Sidney Lanier, author. Little Richard, musician. Carson McCullers, author. Alexander McGillivray, Creek chief. Margaret Mitchell, author. Elijah Muhammad, religious leader. Flannery O'Connor, author. Burt Reynolds, actor. Jackie Robinson, baseball player. Tomochichi, Yamacraw chief. Joanne Woodward, actress.

**Noteworthy places** Chickamauga and Chattanooga Natl. Military Park. Confederate Memorial, Stone Mountain. Ft. Frederica Natl. Monument. Ft. Pulaski Natl. Monument. High Museum of Art, Atlanta. Martin Luther King Natl. Hist. Site., Atlanta. Ocmulgee Natl. Monument. Okefenokee Swamp. Savannah Historic District.

**Memorable events** Hernando de Soto explores region 1540. Cotton gin invented 1793. Georgia expels Cherokee Indian tribes on Trail of Tears 1832–38. Secedes from Union 1860. Gen. William T. Sherman's 60,000 troops cut 60-mi. swath in their "march to the sea" 1864. Formula for Coca-Cola developed by chemist in search of cure for hangover 1886. Cyclone kills 1,000 in Charleston, S.C., and Savannah 1893. Franklin D. Roosevelt dies at the Little White House, Warm Springs 1945. First state to give vote to 18-year-olds 1948. Emory University designated to receive $100-million philanthropic gift from Robert W. Woodruff 1979. Dept. of Justice rules that state's process for electing superior court judges violates 1965 Voting Rights Act 1990.

**Tourist information** 1–800–VISIT–GA or 1–404–656–3590.

# Hawaii

What the air conditioner did for the Sunbelt, the jetliner has done for Hawaii. Because of the jet, Hawaii is a possible vacation spot for millions and welcomes 20 times the air travelers of 25 years ago. Thousands of miles from both California and mainland Asia, Hawaii was originally peopled by Polynesian seafarers around A.D. 500 and has the richest ethnic mix of any state, with the lowest percentage of whites and high percentages of Asians. It was partly fear of this diversity that stalled its statehood. A link between the United States and Asia, Hawaii is the center of U.S. defense in the Pacific and is home to 100,000 veterans, three-quarters of them veterans of Vietnam. Hawaii produces large quantities of pineapples and sugarcane, and efforts are under way to harness thermal electric power from Mauna Loa volcano.

**Name** Of unknown origin, perhaps from Hawaii Loa, traditional discoverer of islands, or from Hawaiki, the traditional Polynesian homeland. **Nicknames** Aloha State, Paradise of the Pacific. **Capital** Honolulu. (21°19'N, 157°52'W). **Entered Union** Aug. 21, 1959 (50th). **Motto** *Ua mau ke ea o ka aina i ke pono* (The life of the land is perpetuated in righteousness).

**Emblems** **Bird** Nene (Hawaiian goose). **Fish** Humuhumunukunukuapuaa. **Flower** Pua aloalo (hibiscus). **Song** "Hawaii Ponoi." **Tree** Kukui (candlenut).

**Land** **Total area** 6,470 sq. mi. (47th), incl. 45 sq. mi. inland water. Surrounded by Pacific Ocean. **Rivers** Kaukonahua Stream, Wailuku Stream. **Lakes** Halulu, Kolekole, Salt Lake, Waiia Res. **Other notable features** Pearl Harbor. Hualalai, Kilauea, Mauna Kea (13,796 ft.), and Mauna Loa volcanoes. **Main islands** Hawaii, Kauai, Maui, Molokai, Oahu.

**Elected officials** Gov. John D. Waihee III (D, term exp. 1994). Lt. Gov. Benjamin J. Cayetano (D).

**People** (1990) 1,108,229 (41st). **Race/national origin** (1990): White 33.4%. Black 2.5%. Indian 0.5%. Asian 61.8%. Other 1.9%. Hispanic 7.3%.

**Cities** (1990) Honolulu 365,272. Hilo 37,808. Kailua 36,818. Kaneohe 35,448. Waipahu 31,435. Pearl City 30,993. Waimatu 29,967. Mililani Town 29,359. Schofield Barracks 19,597. Wahiawa 17,386.

**Business** **Gross state product** (GSP, 1986) $19.3 bil. (40th). **Sectors of GSP:** Farms 2.00%. Agricultural services, forestry, & fisheries 0.35%. Mining 0.01%. Construction 6.12%. Manufacturing 5.18%. Transportation & public utilities 9.89%. Wholesale 4.35%. Retail 11.13%. Finance, insurance, & real estate 17.59%. Services 19.79%. Federal government 6.12%. Federal military 9.57%. State & local government 7.90%. *Fortune* 500 companies (1990): 0.

**Famous natives** Bernice P. Bishop, philanthropist. Sanford B. Dole, statehood advocate. Charlotte (b. Ohio) and Luther Halsey Gulick, Camp Fire Girls founders. Don Ho, singer. Daniel J. Inouye, politician. Duke Kahanamoku, swimmer. Victoria Kaiulani, last heiress presumptive to Hawaiian throne. Kamehameha I, king. Kamehameha III, king. Liliuokalani, queen. Bette Midler, singer.

**Noteworthy places** Bernice P. Bishop Museum, Honolulu. Diamond Head. Haleakala Natl. Park, Maui. Hawaii Volcanoes Natl. Park (Kilauea and Mauna Loa), Hawaii. Iolani Palace, Honolulu. Kaloko-Honokohau Natl. Hist. Park, Molokai. Natl. Cemetery of the Pacific and USS *Arizona* Memorial. Polynesian Cultural Center, Laiea. Pu'uhonua o Honaunau Natl. Hist. Park, Hawaii.

**Memorable events** Polynesians first arrive 6th century. Second wave of Polynesians arrive 10th century. Captain James Cook first European to visit islands 1778; killed on Hawaii 1779. Sugar production begins 1835. Land reform ends feudal system 1848. Monarchy rule ends in revolution 1893. Becomes U.S. Territory 1900. Japanese attack Pearl Harbor 1941. Statehood 1959.

**Tourist information** 1–808–923–1811.

# Idaho

Idaho is 25 percent Mormon, and the Latter-day Saints here have their greatest influence outside Utah. The northern panhandle, where people tend to look west to Washington, and the south, where Mormons look to Utah, are connected by a single highway. The health of Boise's economy, with its large share of homegrown industrial success, unites the two other areas. Home to some of the most isolated and rugged country in the United States, Idaho's diversified economy has traditionally been based on lumber, potatoes, and mining. In the 1980s these were augmented by a number of small high-tech industries fleeing the high cost of business in California.

**Name** Means "gem of the mountains." **Nick-**

NAME Gem State. CAPITAL Boise. ENTERED UNION July 3, 1890 (43d). MOTTO *Esto perpetua* (May it last forever).

**Emblems** BIRD Mountain bluebird. FLOWER Syringa. GEM Star garnet. HORSE Appaloosa. SONG "Here We Have Idaho." TREE Western white pine.

**Land** TOTAL AREA 83,564 sq. mi. (13th), incl. 1,152 sq. mi. inland water. BORDERS British Columbia, Mont., Wyo., Utah, Nev., Oreg., Wash. RIVERS Bear, Clearwater, Payette, Salmon, Snake. LAKES American Falls Res., Coeur d'Alene, Pend Oreille. MOUNTAINS Bitterroot Range, Centennial, Clearwater, Salmon River, Sawtooth Range (Castle Peak 11,820 ft.), Wasatch Range. OTHER NOTABLE FEATURES Grand Canyon of the Snake River.

**Elected officials** Gov. Cecil D. Andrus (D, term exp. 1995). Lt. Gov. C.L. Otter (R). Sec. State Pete T. Cenarussa (R). Atty. Gen. Larry Echottawk (D).

**People** (1990) 1,006,749 (42d): RACE/NATIONAL ORIGIN (1990): White 94.4%. Black 0.3%. Indian 1.4%. Asian 0.9%. Other 3.0%. Hispanic 5.3%.

**Cities** (1990) Boise 125,738. Pocatello 46,080. Idaho Falls 43,929. Nampa 28,365. Lewiston 28,082. Twin Falls 27,591. Coeur d'Alene 24,563. Moscow 18,519. Caldwell 18,400. Rexburg 14,302.

**Business** GROSS STATE PRODUCT (GSP, 1986) $13.2 bil. (44th). SECTORS OF GSP: Farms 8.17%. Agricultural services, forestry, & fisheries 0.90%. Mining 1.29%. Construction 3.31%. Manufacturing 16.34%. Transportation & public utilities 10.48%. Wholesale 5.84%. Retail 10.36%. Finance, insurance, & real estate 15.79%. Services 15.03%. Federal government 2.35%. Federal military 1.57%. State & local government 8.54%. *FORTUNE* 500 COMPANIES (1990): 1: Boise Cascade.

**Famous natives** Joseph, Nez Percé chief. Ezra Taft Benson, politician. Gutzon Borglum, sculptor. Frank Church, politician. Ezra Pound, poet. Harmon Killebrew, baseball player. Jerry Kramer, football player. Sacagawea (Bird Woman), Shoshone interpreter. Lana Turner, actress.

**Noteworthy places** Craters of the Moons Natl. Monument. Hell's Canyon Natl. Recreation Area. Nez Percé Natl. Hist. Park. Sawtooth Natl. Recreation Area. Sun Valley ski resort. Yellowstone Natl. Park.

**Memorable events** Lewis and Clark expedition 1805. Becomes part of U.S. when Idaho Treaty concluded with Britain 1846. Gold Rush 1860. Nez Percé War 1877. Statehood 1890. World's first breeder reactor built at Idaho Falls, 1951. Snake River opened to navigation, linking Lewiston to Pacific Ocean at Astoria, Oregon, 1975. New Teton River Dam collapses as it is being filled for first time; 10 dead, $400 million in damage 1976.

**Tourist information** 1-800-635-7820 or 1-208-334-2470.

## Illinois

The Illinois economy is enormously productive and diverse. While Chicago is a leader in world finance and trade, the southern part of the state has rich farmlands (the state is second to Iowa in corn and soybean exports) and mineral deposits (both coal and gas—there are especially rich coal deposits in the southeast region around Cairo, known as Little Egypt). Manufacturing centers around Chicago, Rockford—the state's second-largest city—and Springfield, the capital. Chicago is also a major transportation hub with extensive rail networks, an international port serving ships from both the Atlantic and Gulf of Mexico, and the largest airport in the country. Another leading industry in Illinois is political patronage, infecting both the Chicago-based Democrats and the downstate Republicans. Reform of the system, which boasted 12,000 patronage positions for the governor and cabinet officials in the 1970s, seems a remote possibility and would take the bite out of the state's tradition of muckraking journalism.

NAME Corruption of *iliniwek* ("tribe of the superior men"), natives of region at time of earliest French explorations. NICKNAME Prairie State. CAPITAL Springfield. ENTERED UNION Dec. 3, 1818 (21st). MOTTO "State sovereignty—national unity." SLOGAN "Land of Lincoln."

**Emblems** ANIMAL White-tailed deer. BIRD Cardinal. FLOWER Violet. INSECT Monarch butterfly. MINERAL Fluorite. SONG "Illinois." TREE White oak.

**Land** TOTAL AREA 56,345 sq. mi. (24th), incl. 700 sq. mi. inland water. BORDERS Wis., Lake Michigan, Ind., Ky., Mo., Iowa. RIVERS Fox, Illinois, Illinois Waterway, Kankakee, Kaskaskia, Mississippi, Ohio, Rock, Vermillion, Wabash. LAKES Carlyle, Crab Orchard. OTHER NOTABLE FEATURES Charles Mound (1,235 ft.), Little Egypt.

**Elected officials** Gov. Jim Edgar (R, term exp. 1995). Lt. Gov. Bob Kustra (R). Sec. State George Ryan (R). Atty. Gen. Roland W. Burris (D).

**People** (1990) 11,430,602 (6th). RACE/NATIONAL ORIGIN (1990): White 78.3%. Black 14.8%. Indian 0.2%. Asian 2.5%. Other 4.2%. Hispanic 7.9%.

**Cities** (1990) Chicago 2,783,726. Rockford 139,426. Peoria 113,504. Springfield 105,227. Aurora 99,581. Naperville 85,351. Decatur 83,885. Elgin 77,010. Joliet 76,836. Arlington Heights Village 75,460.

**Business** GROSS STATE PRODUCT (GSP, 1986) $209.7 bil. (4th). SECTORS OF GSP: Farms 1.61%. Agricultural services, forestry, & fisheries 0.27%. Mining 0.76%. Construction 4.12%. Manufacturing 20.16%. Transportation & public utilities 10.80%. Wholesale 8.48%. Retail 9.39%. Finance, insurance, & real estate 17.52%. Services 17.48%. Federal government 1.73%. Federal military 0.70%. State & local government 6.97%. *FORTUNE* 500 COMPANIES (1990): 47: incl. Amoco, Archer Daniels Midland, Beatrice, Caterpillar, Fruit of the Loom, Morton Thiokol, Motorola, Quaker Oats, Sara Lee, Tribune, Wm. Wrigley, Jr., Zenith Electronics.

**Famous natives** Jane Addams, reformer (Nobel Peace Prize, 1930). Ernie Banks, baseball player. Saul Bellow, author (Nobel Prize, 1976). Harry A. Blackmun, jurist. Ray Bradbury, author. Gwendolyn Brooks, poet. William Jennings Bryan, politician. Edgar Rice Burroughs, novelist. St. Frances Xavier Cabrini (b. Italy). Clarence Darrow, lawyer. Miles Davis, musician. John Dos Passos, novelist. Enrico Fermi (b. Italy), nuclear physicist (Nobel Prize, 1938). Robert Louis ("Bob") Fosse, choreographer. Milton Friedman, economist (Nobel Prize, 1976). Benny Goodman, musician. Ernest Hemingway, novelist. Charlton Heston, actor. William Holden, actor. Vachel Lindsay, poet. Archibald MacLeish, poet. Ludwig Mies van der Rohe (b. Germany), architect. Charles W. Post, cereal manufacturer. Ronald Reagan, U.S. president. Carl Sandburg, poet. Albert G. Spalding, merchant. John Paul Stevens, jurist. Gloria Swanson, actress.

**Noteworthy places** Art Institute of Chicago. Crab Orchard Wildlife Refuge. Dickson Mounds Museum, Lewistown. Field Museum of Natural History, Chicago. Ft. Chartres. Ft. Kaskaskia. Ft. Massac. Frank Lloyd Wright Historic District, Oak Park. Illinois State Museum, Springfield. Lincoln Home Natl. Hist. Park, Springfield. Mormon Settlement, Nauvoo. Morton Arboretum, Lisle. Museum of Science and Industry, Chicago. Shawnee Natl. Forest. Starved Rock State Park.

**Memorable events** French missionary explorers Jacques Marquette and Louis Jolliet in Illinois 1673. Cahokia first European settlement 1699. Territory to England after French and Indian War 1763. Chicago founded by Jean-Baptiste Point du Sable 1779. Illinois and Michigan Canal links Lake Michigan and Mississippi River 1848. Lincoln-Douglas Debates at Springfield 1860. Half of Chicago destroyed by great fire 1871. Terrorist bombing leaves nine dead and 130 wounded in Haymarket affair, Chicago 1886. Columbia Exposition, Chicago 1893. First successful nuclear chain reaction created at University of Chicago 1942. Riots at Democratic National Convention in Chicago 1968. Sears Tower, world's tallest building (1,454 ft.), completed in Chicago 1973.

**Tourist information** 1-800-223-0121, 1-217-782-7137, or 1-800-252-8987.

## Indiana

Indiana is strong in both farms and manufacturing. Its southern half has large coal deposits and produces most of the limestone quarried in the U.S. To the north the fertile land helps make Indiana one of the primary farm-belt states. Indiana is also very much a part of the industrial Midwest, where unemployment is always a threat, especially in the heavily industrial areas of Gary and Indianapolis. These geographic divisions have parallels in the political history of the state, which during the Civil War was Union in the north and Confederate in the south. In 1966 the state's patronage politics were upset by reapportionment, and urban counties increased representation. George Bush recognized the importance of Indiana's votes and value as a home of traditional values when he chose J. Danforth Quayle as his running mate.

NAME For the land of Indians by early set-

tlers, who found many distinct tribes living in region. NICKNAME Hoosier State. CAPITAL Indianapolis. ENTERED UNION Dec. 11, 1816 (19th). MOTTO "The Crossroads of America."
**Emblems** BIRD Cardinal. FLOWER Peony. POEM "Indiana." SONG "On the Banks of the Wabash, Far Away." STONE Indiana limestone. TREE Tulip tree.
**Land** TOTAL AREA 36,185 sq. mi. (38th), incl. 253 sq. mi. inland water. BORDERS Lake Michigan, Mich., Ohio, Ky., Ill. RIVERS Kankakee, Ohio, Tippecanoe, Wabash, White, Whitewater. LAKES Freeman, Shafer.
**Elected officials** Gov. Evan Bayh (D, term exp. 1993). Lt. Gov. Frank L. O'Bannon (D). Sec. State Joseph H. Hogsett (D). Atty. Gen. Linley E. Pearson (R).
**People** (1990) 5,544,159 (14th). RACE/NATIONAL ORIGIN (1990): White 90.6%. Black 7.8%. Indian 0.2%. Asian 0.7%. Other 0.7%. Hispanic 1.8%.
**Cities** (1990) Indianapolis 731,327. Fort Wayne 173,072. Evansville 126,272. Gary 116,646. South Bend 105,511. Hammond 84,236. Muncie 71,035. Bloomington 60,633. Anderson 59,459. Terre Haute 57,483.
**Business** GROSS STATE PRODUCT (GSP, 1986) $84.9 bil. (14th). SECTORS OF GSP: Farms 2.43%. Agricultural services, forestry, & fisheries 0.24%. Mining 0.66%. Construction 4.58%. Manufacturing 29.80%. Transportation & public utilities 9.64%. Wholesale 5.87%. Retail 10.05%. Finance, insurance, & real estate 14.48%. Services 12.90%. Federal government 1.58%. Federal military 0.53%. State & local government 7.25%. FORTUNE 500 COMPANIES (1990): 9: incl. Arvin Industries, Ball, Cummins Engine, Eli Lilly, Great Lakes Chemical.
**Famous natives** Hoagy Carmichael, composer. Eugene V. Debs, politician/organizer. Theodore Dreiser, author. Benjamin Harrison, U.S. president. Jimmy Hoffa, union leader. Michael Jackson, singer. Carole Lombard, actress. Cole Porter, composer. Ernie Pyle, journalist. Knute Rockne (b. Norway), football player. Paul Samuelson, economist (Nobel Prize, 1960). Booth Tarkington, author. Kurt Vonnegut, author. Wendell L. Willkie, politician. Wilbur Wright, aviation pioneer.
**Noteworthy places** Ernie Pyle birthplace, Dana. George Rogers Clark Natl. Hist. Park, Vincennes. Benjamin Harrison home, Indianapolis. Hoosier Natl. Forest. Indiana Dunes Natl. Lakeshore. Indianapolis Motor Speedway and Museum. Indianapolis Museum of Art. New Harmony village. Old state capital, Corydon. Wilbur Wright State Memorial, Millville. Wyandotte Cave. Tippecanoe sites.
**Memorable events** Mound Builders present c. A.D. 1000. René-Robert Cavelier de La Salle explores for French 1679–87. French near Vincennes from c. 1700. French cede territory to British 1763. Gen. Ambrose Clark captures Ft. Vincennes 1779. Territory ceded to U.S. 1783; included in Northwest Territory 1787. Miamis defeat U.S. twice in 1790. Gen. Anthony Wayne defeats Miamis at Battle of Fallen Timbers 1794. Territory included in Indiana Territory 1800. Gen. William Henry Harrison defeats Tecumseh's Indian Confederation at Tippecanoe 1811. Statehood 1816. Studebaker

wagon company founded in South Bend 1852. U.S. Steel establishes mill at company-built town of Gary 1906. First Indianapolis 500 run 1911. Only a dozen car companies producing cars, down from a pre–World War I peak of 375, 1920. Studebaker, last Indiana-based car manufacturer, closes 1963.
**Tourist information** 1–800–289–6646 or 1–317–232–8860.

## Iowa

Iowa lies between the two great rivers of the central United States, the Mississippi and the Missouri, with a quarter of the nation's richest and deepest topsoil. Iowa's farmers lead the country in the production of corn, and Iowa is also a big producer of hogs, cattle, and other livestock. With about 75 percent of Iowans employed in agriculture-related industries and 90 percent of the land farmed, Iowa is deeply affected by natural disasters such as the 1988 drought. Yet more than 120 *Fortune* 500 companies have production facilities in this farm state. Industrial production has risen since World War II, though in the early 1980s many workers were laid off in the Mississippi River cities of Dubuque and Davenport. Iowans send abroad a quarter of the food they produce. As a result, this traditionally Republican state is better attuned to world developments than one might initially suspect.
NAME For Iowa tribe. NICKNAME Hawkeye State. CAPITAL Des Moines. ENTERED UNION Dec. 28, 1846 (29th). MOTTO "Our liberties we prize and our rights we will maintain."
**Emblems** BIRD Eastern goldfinch. FLOWER Wild rose. SONG "The Song of Iowa." STONE Geode. TREE Oak.
**Land** TOTAL AREA 56,275 sq. mi. (25th), incl. 310 sq. mi. inland water. BORDERS Minn., Wis., Ill., Mo., Nebr., S.Dak. RIVERS Big Sioux, Des Moines, Mississippi, Missouri. LAKES Okoboji, Rathbun Res., Red Rock, Saylorville Res., Spirit, Storm. OTHER NOTABLE FEATURES Ocheyedan Mound (1,675 ft.).
**Elected officials** Gov. Terry E. Branstad (R, term exp. 1995). Lt. Gov. Joy C. Corning (R). Sec. State Elaine Baxter (D). Atty. Gen. Bonnie Campbell (D).
**People** (1990) 2,776,755 (30th). RACE/NATIONAL ORIGIN (1990): White 96.6%. Black 1.7%. Indian 0.3%. Asian 0.9%. Other 0.5%. Hispanic 1.2%.
**Cities** (1990) Des Moines 193,187. Cedar Rapids 108,751. Davenport 95,333. Sioux City 80,505. Waterloo 66,467. Iowa City 59,738. Dubuque 57,546. Council Bluffs 54,315. Ames 47,198. Cedar Falls 34,298.
**Business** GROSS STATE PRODUCT (GSP, 1986) $43.8 bil. (29th). SECTORS OF GSP: Farms 10.43%. Agricultural services, forestry, & fisheries 0.58%. Mining 0.21%. Construction 3.19%. Manufacturing 21.05%. Transportation & public utilities 8.11%. Wholesale 6.75%. Retail 9.01%. Finance, insurance, & real estate 17.87%. Services 13.40%. Federal government 0.40%. Federal military 0.23%. State & local government 8.77%. FORTUNE 500 COMPANIES (1990): 4: Bandag, Hon Industries,

Maytag, Meredith.
**Famous natives** Norman E. Borlaug, agronomist (Nobel Peace Prize, 1970). William F. ("Buffalo Bill") Cody, scout/showman. George Gallup, pollster. Josiah B. Grinnell (b. Vt.), abolitionist. Herbert Hoover, U.S. president. Harry L. Hopkins, politician. John L. Lewis, labor leader. John R. Mott, religious leader. Billy Sunday, baseball player/evangelist. John Wayne, actor. Meredith Wilson, composer. Grant Wood, painter.
**Noteworthy places** Amana Colonies. Davenport Art Gallery. Des Moines Art Center. Effigy Mounds Natl. Monument, Marquette. Ft. Dodge Hist. Museum. Herbert Hoover birthplace and library, West Branch. Natl. Rivers Hall of Fame, Dubuque. Putnam Museum, Davenport.
**Memorable events** Mound Builders present c. A.D. 1000. Jacques Marquette and Louis Jolliet claim land for France 1673. Part of Louisiana Purchase 1803. Part of Missouri Territory 1812–21. Black Hawk Wars 1832, 1834–37. First permanent settlement at Dubuque 1833. Organized as Iowa Territory (incl. parts of Minnesota, North Dakota, and South Dakota) 1838. Statehood 1846. Capital moved from Iowa City to Des Moines 1857. Fifty percent of Iowa's farms foreclosed during depression 1929–35. Urban population exceeds rural for first time 1960. Population loss of 2.2% greater than any other state 1980–86.
**Tourist information** 1–800–345–IOWA.

## Kansas

Kansas burst on the American scene as the territory called Bleeding Kansas, seething with conflict over slavery. Victorious New England abolitionists imprinted the state with the Puritan ethic. They were early supporters of prohibition, partly to discourage foreign newcomers. The geographic center of the continental United States is near Lebanon. Kansas has suffered postwar decline with other Plains states, but it is a primary producer of wheat, cattle, and other agricultural products. Its manufacturing base also includes extensive aircraft industries, and it leads the states in the production of helium.
NAME For Kansa or Kaw, "people of the south wind." NICKNAME Sunflower State. CAPITAL Topeka. ENTERED UNION Jan. 29, 1861 (34th). MOTTO *Ad astra per aspera* (To the stars through adversity).
**Emblems** ANIMAL American buffalo. BIRD Western meadowlark. FLOWER Wild native sunflower. MARCH "The Kansas March." SONG "Home on the Range." TREE Cottonwood.
**Land** TOTAL AREA 82,277 sq. mi. (14th), incl. 499 sq. mi. inland water. BORDERS Nebr., Mo., Okla., Colo. RIVERS Arkansas, Kansas, Missouri, Republican, Saline, Smoky Hill, Solomon. LAKES Kanopolis, Malvern, Perry, Pomona, Tuttle Creek, Waconda. OTHER NOTABLE FEATURES Flint Hills.
**Elected officials** Gov. Joan Finney (D, term exp. 1995). Lt. Gov. James L. Francisco (D). Sec. State Bill Graves (R). Atty. Gen. Robert T. Stephan (R).

**People** (1990) 2,477,574 (32d). RACE/NATIONAL ORIGIN (1980): White 90.1%. Black 5.8%. Indian 0.9%. Asian 1.3%. Other 2.0%. Hispanic 3.8%.
**Cities** (1990) Wichita 304,011. Kansas City 149,767. Topeka 119,883. Overland Park 111,790. Lawrence 65,608. Olathe 63,352. Salina 42,303. Hutchinson 39,308. Leavenworth 38,495. Shawnee 37,993.
**Business** GROSS STATE PRODUCT (GSP, 1986) $42.5 bil. (30th). SECTORS OF GSP: Farms 6.65%. Agricultural services, forestry, & fisheries 0.33%. Mining 2.07%. Construction 4.05%. Manufacturing 18.65%. Transportation & public utilities 11.98%. Wholesale 6.94%. Retail 9.00%. Finance, insurance, & real estate 15.47%. Services 13.27%. Federal government 1.23%. Federal military 2.07%. State & local government 8.29%. *FORTUNE* 500 COMPANIES (1990): 3: Doskocil, Mueller Industries, National Coop. Refinery.
**Famous natives** Walter Chrysler, carmaker. Robert Dole, politician. Amelia Earhart, aviator. Dwight David Eisenhower (b. Tex.), general/U.S. president. Nancy Landon Kassebaum, politician. Alf Landon, politician. Edgar Lee Masters, poet. Carry Nation (b. Ky.), prohibitionist. Charlie ("Bird") Parker, musician. Damon Runyon, writer. Gale Sayers, football player. William Allen White, the Sage of Emporia, editor.
**Noteworthy places** Agricultural Hall of Fame, Kansas City. Dodge City. Eisenhower Center, Abilene. Ft. Larned. Ft. Leavenworth. Ft. Riley. Ft. Scott. John Brown's Cabin, Osawatomie. Kansas Cosmosphere and Space Discovery Center, Hutchinson. Kansas State Historical Society Museum, Topeka. Wichita Art Museum.
**Memorable events** First major expedition to region under Francisco Vásquez de Coronado 1540–41. La Salle claims territory including Kansas for France 1682. Part of Louisiana Purchase 1803. Area visited by Meriwether Lewis and George Rogers Clark (1803), Zebulon Pike (1806), and Stephen H. Long (1819). Santa Fe Trail crosses Kansas 1821. Fts. Leavenworth (1827), Scott (1842), and Riley (1853) established to protect pioneers on Santa Fe and Oregon trails. Organized as Territory by Kansas-Nebraska Act 1854, which repealed Missouri Compromise of 1820. "Bleeding Kansas" scene of free vs. slave rivalry 1854–56. Statehood 1861. Introduction of winter wheat makes Kansas leading U.S. wheat producer 1870. Airplane manufacturing starts in Wichita 1919. "Dust Bowl" drought drives thousands of farmers off the land, especially in western Kansas, 1934–35. Murder of Clutter family by Richard E. Hickock and Perry E. Smith at Holcomb (later the subject of Truman Capote's *In Cold Blood*)1959.
**Tourist information** 1–913–296–2009 or 1–800–252–6727.

## Kentucky, Commonwealth of

First pioneered by English immigrants in the mid-17th century, Kentucky's golden age as a choice frontier destination in the early 1800s was brought to an end by the Civil War.

During the Civil War, the Bluegrass gentry supported the Confederacy, while the Appalachian backwoods men enlisted in the Union Army. Many took advantage of their uniforms to settle old accounts, and the social order was often threatened before the turn of the century. Though the state is known today for its bourbon and horse breeding, many Kentuckians make their living from the land as tobacco farmers or coal miners. The Appalachian part of the state in the east delivers about 20 percent of the nation's coal, but its economic problems remain acute, despite vast expenditures during the "war on poverty."

NAME Corruption of Iroquois *kenta-ke* (meadowland) or Wyandot *kah-ten-tah-teh* (land of tomorrow). NICKNAME Bluegrass State. CAPITAL Frankfort. ENTERED UNION June 1, 1792 (15th). MOTTO "United we stand, divided we fall."
**Emblems** BIRD Cardinal. COLORS Blue and gold. FISH Bass. FLOWER Goldenrod. SONG "My Old Kentucky Home." TREE Kentucky coffee tree. WILD ANIMAL Gray squirrel.
**Land** TOTAL AREA 40,409 sq. mi. (37th), incl. 740 sq. mi. inland water. BORDERS Ind., Ohio, W.Va., Va., Tenn., Mo., Ill. RIVERS Cumberland, Kentucky, Licking, Ohio, Tennessee. LAKES Barkley, Barren River Res., Dewey, Grayson Res., Laurel Res., Nolin Res., Rough Res. MOUNTAINS Appalachian (Black Mt. 4,145 ft.), Cumberland. OTHER NOTABLE FEATURES Tennessee Valley.
**Elected officials** Gov. Wallace G. Wilkinson (D, term exp. 1995). Lt. Gov. Brereton C. Jones (D). Sec. of the Commonwealth Bremer Ehrler (D). Atty. Gen. Fredric J. Cowan (D).
**People** (1990) 3,685,296 (23d). RACE/NATIONAL ORIGIN (1990): White 92.0%. Black 7.1%. Indian 0.2%. Asian 0.5%. Other 0.2%. Hispanic 0.6%.
**Cities** (1990) Louisville 269,063. Lexington-Fayette 225,366. Owensboro 53,549. Covington 43,264. Bowling Green 40,641. Hopkinsville 29,809. Paducah 27,256. Frankfort 25,968. Henderson 25,945. Ashland 23,622.
**Business** GROSS STATE PRODUCT (GSP, 1986) $53.1 bil. (26th). SECTORS OF GSP: Farms 3.21%. Agricultural services, forestry, & fisheries 0.39%. Mining 5.66%. Construction 4.93%. Manufacturing 24.02%. Transportation & public utilities 8.73%. Wholesale 4.97%. Retail 9.65%. Finance, insurance, & real estate 14.89%. Services 11.96%. Federal government 2.44%. Federal military 2.10%. State & local government 7.04%. *FORTUNE* 500 COMPANIES (1990): 2: Ashland Oil, Brown-Forman.
**Famous natives** Muhammad Ali, boxer. Alben W. Barkley, politician. Daniel Boone (b. Pa.), frontiersman. Louis D. Brandeis, jurist. Kit Carson, frontiersman. Henry Clay, politician. Jefferson Davis, president of Confederate States of America. D.W. Griffith, director. John Marshall Harlan, jurist. Abraham Lincoln, U.S. president. Col. Harland Sanders, entrepreneur. Frederick M. Vinson, jurist. Robert Penn Warren, author.
**Noteworthy places** Abraham Lincoln birthplace, Hodgenville. Churchill Downs, Louisville. George S. Patton, Jr., Military Museum,

Fort Knox. J.B. Speed Art Museum, Louisville. Land Between the Lakes Natl. Rec. Area. Mammoth Cave Natl. Park. My Old Kentucky Home, Bardstown. Old Ft. Harrod State Park.
**Memorable events** English enter territory through Cumberland Gap 1750. Territory included in area ceded by French 1763. Daniel Boone leads expeditions into region 1769. First settlement Harrodsburg 1774. Daniel Boone blazes Wilderness Trail through Cumberland Gap, establishes Ft. Boonesborough 1775. Organized as a county of Virginia 1776. British support Indian resistance ("Dark and Bloody Wars") until George Rogers Clark captures British forts in Indiana and Illinois 1778. Included as part of U.S. after Revolution 1783. Virginia approves separate statehood, achieved 1792. First steamboat reaches Louisville from New Orleans 1815. Invaded by Confederate armies 1862. Kentucky Derby first run at Louisville 1875. State has highest per capita income of southern states 1900; ranks last among all 48 states in per capita income 1940. Farm population decreases by 76%, and total number of farms by 53%, 1945–80.
**Tourist information** 1–800–225–TRIP or 1–800–255–PARK.

## Louisiana

European influences and ethnic diversity distinguish Louisiana from the rest of the nation. When Louisiana entered the Union in 1812, it brought with it a French legal system and a bilingualism that still survive. African-Americans, Cajuns, and Creoles have all contributed to its distinctive music and cuisine. The state has rich farmland, more oil and gas reserves than any other state but Texas, and in New Orleans an international port that serves the most extensive river system in North America (see also "Transportation").

The "devil's bargain" with the petrochemical industry struck by charismatic populist governor Huey Long (assassinated in 1935) brought needed jobs to the state. But the environmental impact of 100 loosely regulated petrochemical plants on the Mississippi River between New Orleans and Baton Rouge is being assessed only now. The state's reliance on the petroleum industry was felt when a downturn in oil prices in the 1980s led to massive unemployment—15 percent in 1987; in addition, 200,000 people left the state. Another burden from the Long days is the state's property tax—the lowest rate in the nation. With only meager revenues, government has invested little in infrastructure or education, and the state had the highest high school dropout rate in the nation in 1989.

Economic diversification is under way. The Red River should be cleared for commercial navigation as far as Shreveport by 1992, which will make the lumber and farming in the northwest part of the state more profitable. In 1987, 19.3 million tourists, almost 400,000 from abroad, spent almost $4 billion in "the sportsman's paradise," and in an effort to attract foreign tourists, the state allows foreign visitors a rebate on the state sales tax.

NAME For King Louis XIV. NICKNAME Pelican State. CAPITAL Baton Rouge. ENTERED UNION Apr. 30, 1812 (18th). MOTTO "Union, justice, confidence."

**Emblems** BIRD Eastern brown pelican. COLORS Gold, white, and blue. CRUSTACEAN Crawfish. DOG Catahoula leopard. FLOWER Magnolia. FOSSIL Petrified palmwood. GEM Agate. INSECT Honeybee. SONGS "Give Me Louisiana," "You Are My Sunshine." TREE Bald cypress.

**Land** TOTAL AREA 47,751 sq. mi. (31st), incl. 3,230 sq. mi. inland water. BORDERS Ark., Miss., Gulf of Mexico, Tex. RIVERS Atchafalaya, Mississippi, Ouachita, Pearl, Red, Sabine. LAKES Bistineau, Borgne, Caddo, Catahoula, Grand, Maurepas, Pontchartrain, Salvador, White. OTHER NOTABLE FEATURES Bayou Barataria, Bayou Bodcau, Bayou D'Arbonne, Driskill Mt. (535 ft.).

**Elected officials** Gov. Charles E. ("Buddy") Roemer (R, term exp. 1992). Lt. Gov. Paul Hardy (R). Sec. State Walter ("Fox") McKeithen (R). Atty. Gen. William J. Guste, Jr. (D).

**People** (1990) 4,219,973 (21st). RACE/NATIONAL ORIGIN (1990): White 67.3%. Black 30.8%. Indian 0.4%. Asian 1.0%. Other 0.5%. Hispanic 2.2%.

**Cities** (1990) New Orleans 496,938. Baton Rouge 219,531. Shreveport 198,525. Lafayette 94,440. Kenner 72,033. Lake Charles 70,580. Monroe 54,909. Bossier City 52,721. Alexandria 49,188. New Iberia 31,828.

**Business** GROSS STATE PRODUCT (GSP, 1986) $74.4 bil. (20th). SECTORS OF GSP: Farms 0.90%. Agricultural services, forestry, & fisheries 0.31%. Mining 16.82%. Construction 5.25%. Manufacturing 12.99%. Transportation & public utilities 11.15%. Wholesale 5.73%. Retail 8.86%. Finance, insurance, & real estate 14.82%. Services 13.11%. Federal government 1.37%. Federal military 1.25%. State & local government 7.45%. FORTUNE 500 COMPANIES (1990): 4: Avondale Industries, Freeport-McMoran, Louisiana Land and Exploration, McDermott.

**Famous natives** Louis Armstrong ("Satchmo"), jazz musician. Pierre Beauregard, Confederate general. Braxton Bragg, Confederate general. Truman Capote, author. Clyde Cessna, aviator. Michael DeBakey, surgeon. Fats Domino, singer. Lillian Hellman, author. Mahalia Jackson, singer. Jean Baptiste Le Moyne, sieur de Bienville (b. Canada), founded New Orleans. Jerry Lee Lewis, singer. Huey P. Long, senator. Ferdinand Joseph La Menthe ("Jelly Roll") Morton, musician. Leonidas K. Polk, clergyman/Confederate general. Henry Miller Shreve (b. N.J.), riverboat captain. Edward D. White, Jr., jurist.

**Noteworthy places** Avery Island. Cabildo, New Orleans. French Quarter, New Orleans. Garden District, New Orleans. Hodges Gardens, Natchitoches. Jean Lafitte Natl. Hist. Park, Chalmette. Kent House Museum, Alexandria. Longfellow-Evangeline State Commemorative Area, St. Martinsville. Louisiana Maritime Museum, Baton Rouge. New Orleans Museum of Art.

**Memorable events** Area first visited by Alonso Alvarez de Piñeda 1519. Claimed by René-Robert Cavelier de La Salle for France 1682.

New Orleans founded 1718. French crown colony 1731. Four thousand Acadians (Cajuns) from Nova Scotia forcibly transported by British to Louisiana and settled in Bayou Teche 1755. Lands west of Mississippi given to Spain for help in French and Indian War 1763. Lands east of Mississippi ceded to Britain 1763. Same lands retroceded to France 1800. Jefferson negotiates Louisiana Purchase; U.S. acquires 885,000 sq. mi. for $15 million 1803. Statehood 1812. Andrew Jackson beats British at Battle of New Orleans 1815. State secedes 1861. Surrenders to Union forces 1862. Readmitted to Union 1868. Petroleum discovered 1901. Huey "The Kingfish" Long elected to senate 1928; assassinated 1935. Racial designation law of 1970 repealed 1983.

**Tourist information** 1-800-33-GUMBO or 1-504-342-8119.

## Maine

Down-Easters—the original Puritans as well as the later French Canadians—are distinct from the New Englanders of Maine's economically more vital sister states. Their land, especially the coast, is rugged, and the living everywhere is hard. Maine touches only one other state, and it has an end-of-the-line feel to it. Lumbering, fishing, and potato farming were the traditional industries. More than half of the state is still unorganized territory largely owned by paper companies. In the 18th century, canneries, textiles, and shoe factories developed. Recently Maine's economy has combined light industry and tourism that is moving it into the mainstream. The modern Maine entrepreneur, often an out-of-stater, seeks an economy based on small industries and more in keeping with Maine's independent temperament.

NAME Either for Maine in France or to distinguish mainland from islands in Gulf of Maine. NICKNAME Pine Tree State. CAPITAL Augusta. ENTERED UNION Mar. 15, 1820 (23d). MOTTO *Dirigo* (I direct).

**Emblems** ANIMAL Moose. BIRD Chickadee. FISH Landlocked salmon. FLOWER White pinecone and tassel. INSECT Honeybee. MINERAL Tourmaline. SONG "State of Maine Song." TREE Eastern white pine.

**Land** TOTAL AREA 33,265 sq. mi. (39th), incl. 2,270 sq. mi. inland water. BORDERS Quebec, New Brunswick, Atlantic Ocean, N.H. RIVERS Alagash, Androscoggin, Aroostock, Kennebec, Machias, Penobscot, Piscataqua, Salmon Falls, St. John. LAKES Chamberlain, Chesuncook, Grand, Moosehead, Rangeley, Sebago. OTHER NOTABLE FEATURES Longfellow Mts. (Mt. Katahdin 5,268 ft.), Mt. Desert Island, Penobscot Bay.

**Elected officials** Gov. John R. McKernan, Jr. (R, term exp. 1995). Sec. State G. William Diamond (D). Atty. Gen. James E. Tierney (D).

**People** (1990) 1,227,928 (38th). RACE/NATIONAL ORIGIN (1990): White 98.4%. Black 0.4%. Indian 0.5%. Asian 0.5%. Other 0.1%. Hispanic 0.6%.

**Cities** (1990) Portland 64,358. Lewiston 39,757. Bangor 33,181. Auburn 24,309. South

Portland 23,163. Augusta 21,325. Biddeford 20,710. Waterville 17,173. Westbrook 16,121. Saco 15,181.

**Business** GROSS STATE PRODUCT (GSP, 1986) $17.3 bil. (42d). SECTORS OF GSP: Farms 1.09%. Agricultural services, forestry, & fisheries 1.20%. Mining 0.04%. Construction 6.29%. Manufacturing 21.14%. Transportation & public utilities 9.34%. Wholesale 5.95%. Retail 11.48%. Finance, insurance, & real estate 16.31%. Services 14.46%. Federal government 3.09%. Federal military 1.95%. State & local government 7.71%. FORTUNE 500 COMPANIES (1990): 0.

**Famous natives** Cyrus H.K. Curtis, publisher. Hannibal Hamlin, politician. Sarah Orne Jewett, novelist. Henry Wadsworth Longfellow, poet. Sir Hiram and Hudson Maxim, inventors. Edna St. Vincent Millay, poet. Edmund S. Muskie, politician. John Knowles Paine, composer. Kenneth Roberts, novelist. Edward Arlington Robinson, poet. Nelson Rockefeller, politician. Marguerite Yourcenar (b. France), author.

**Noteworthy places** Acadia Natl. Park, Mt. Desert Island. Allagash Natl. Wilderness Waterway. Boothbay Railway Museum. Campobello-Longfellow House, Portland. Maine Maritime Museum, Bath. Portland Art Museum Roosevelt-Campobello Intl. Park, Campobello Island. St. Croix Island Natl. Monument.

**Memorable events** Vikings explore coast c. A.D. 1000. Bartholomew Gosnold sails along coast 1602. French settlers at St. Croix River 1604. Included in grant to Plymouth Company 1606. Monhegan Island and Saco settled 1622. Annexed to Massachusetts Colony 1652. French attack northern territory intermittently through 1713. Statehood 1820. Border with Canada settled 1842. First state prohibition law enacted 1851. Penobscot and Passamaquoddy tribes file claim against state for $300-million compensation for land seized in violation of 1790 Indian Non-Intercourse Act, 1972; settled for $81.5 million 1980. First state to allow inheritance taxes to be paid with works of art 1979.

**Tourist information** 1-207-289-2423 or 1-800-533-9595.

## Maryland

Maryland wraps like a fishhook from the Atlantic Ocean around the fish-rich Chesapeake Bay and into the Cumberland Mountains in the northwest. Baltimore—full of urban problems but newly redeveloped with urban homesteading and shopsteading—holds the center. The suburbs of Baltimore and Washington seem far removed from the Delmarva (DELaware, MARyland, VirginiA) peninsula with its watermen hanging on to an older way of life. Terrain, cultures, and history are a border state's mix of North and South. Founded as a haven for Catholics, Maryland's population is still 20 percent Catholic.

NAME For Henrietta Maria, queen consort of Charles I. NICKNAMES Old Line State, Free State. CAPITAL Annapolis. ENTERED UNION Apr. 28, 1788 (7th). MOTTO *Fatti maschii, parole femine* (Manly deeds, womanly words).

**Emblems** BIRD Baltimore oriole. DOG Chesapeake Bay retriever. FISH Rockfish. FLOWER Black-eyed Susan. FOSSIL *Ecphora quadricostata* (extinct snail). INSECT Baltimore checkerspot butterfly. SONG "Maryland, My Maryland." SPORT Jousting. TREE White oak.
**Land** TOTAL AREA 10,460 sq. mi. (42d), incl. 623 sq. mi. inland water. BORDERS Pa., Del., Atlantic Ocean, Va., D.C., W.Va. RIVERS Chester, Choptank, Nanticoke, Patapsco, Patuxent, Pocomoke, Potomac, Susquehanna. OTHER NOTABLE FEATURES Allegheny Mts., Blue Ridge Mts., Chesapeake Bay.
**Elected officials** Gov. William Donald Schaefer (D, term exp. 1995). Lt. Gov. Melvin A. Steinberg (D). Atty. Gen. J. Joseph Curran, Jr. (D).
**People** (1990) 4,781,468 (19th). RACE/NATIONAL ORIGIN (1990): White 71.0%. Black 24.9%. Indian 0.3%. Asian 2.9%. Other 0.9%. Hispanic 2.6%.
**Cities** (1990) Baltimore 736,014. Rockville 44,835. Frederick 40,148. Gaithersburg 39,542. Bowie 37,589. Hagerstown 35,445. Annapolis 33,187. Cumberland 23,706. College Park 21,927. Greenbelt 21,096.
**Business** GROSS STATE PRODUCT (GSP, 1986) $76.5 bil. (18th). SECTORS OF GSP: Farms 0.81%. Agricultural services, forestry, & fisheries 0.40%. Mining 0.15%. Construction 5.24%. Manufacturing 11.90%. Transportation & public utilities 8.61%. Wholesale 7.15%. Retail 11.46%. Finance, insurance, & real estate 16.76%. Services 20.05%. Federal government 7.06%. Federal military 1.87%. State & local government 8.52%. FORTUNE 500 COMPANIES (1990): 4: Black & Decker, Crown Central Petroleum, McCormick, Martin Marietta.
**Famous natives** Russell Baker, journalist. Benjamin Banneker, surveyor. Eubie Blake, pianist. Rachel Carson, biologist/author. Stephen Decatur, navy officer. Frederick Douglass, abolitionist. Billie Holiday, singer. Johns Hopkins, financier/philanthropist. Francis Scott Key, lawyer/poet. Thurgood Marshall, jurist. H.L. Mencken, writer. Charles Willson Peale, artist. William Pinckney, statesman. James Rouse, urban planner. Babe Ruth, baseball player. Upton Sinclair, author. Roger B. Taney, jurist. Harriet Tubman, abolitionist.
**Noteworthy places** Aberdeen Proving Ground. Antietam Natl. Battlefield, Sharpsburg. Assateague Island Natl. Seashore. Baltimore Aquarium. Baltimore Museum of Art. Baltimore Museum of Industry. Calvert Marine Museum, Solomons. Chesapeake & Ohio Canal Natl. Hist. Park. Chesapeake Bay Maritime Museum, St. Michaels. Ft. McHenry Natl. Monument, Baltimore. Harpers Ferry Natl. Hist. Park. Liberty ship *John W. Brown*, Baltimore. St. Marys City. State House, Annapolis. U.S. Naval Academy, Annapolis. USS *Constellation*, Baltimore. Walters Art Gallery, Baltimore.
**Memorable events** John Smith explores area 1608. William Claiborne sets up trading post on Kent Island 1631. Land granted to Cecilius Calvert, Lord Baltimore, 1632. Leonard Calvert and 200 Roman Catholic settlers land on Blakistone Island 1634. Mason Dixon line establishes northern boundary of state 1763–67; later identified as boundary between slave and nonslave states. Francis Scott Key composes "The Star

Spangled Banner" after British fail to take Ft. McHenry 1814. U.S. Naval Academy founded Annapolis 1845. State under federal military control during Civil War 1861–65. First state to adopt income tax 1938. Alabama Gov. George C. Wallace shot while campaigning in Democratic presidential primary 1972.
**Tourist information** 1–301–263–7940 or 1–301–333–6611.

---

# Massachusetts, Commonwealth of

Massachusetts is rich in the history of the early American republic. The Boston Tea Party, the "shot heard 'round the world" from Lexington and Concord, and the Battle of Bunker Hill are American folklore. So is the feast of Thanksgiving, first celebrated by the Puritans at Plymouth. Fishing, trade, textiles, and leather industries were the backbone of Massachusetts's 19th-century economy. Today Boston's Route 128 is the East Coast's counterpart to California's Silicon Valley, with some of the nation's most advanced computer and electronic research and manufacturing. The state's "economic miracle" of the 1980s is over, and in 1989 unemployment was above the national average for the first time in a decade. In late 1989 its Standard & Poor's credit rating was downgraded to BBB—the lowest ranking of any state.

A staple of the Massachusetts scene is education, in which the state is a national leader. Boston alone boasts such institutions as Harvard University (founded 1636), M.I.T., Northeastern, Brandeis, Boston University, Boston College, Wellesley, and Tufts. To the west are the University of Massachusetts, Amherst, Williams, Smith, and Mt. Holyoke.
NAME For Massachuset tribe, whose name means "at or about the great hill." NICKNAME Bay State. CAPITAL Boston. ENTERED UNION Feb. 6, 1788 (6th). MOTTO *Ense petit placidam sub libertate quietem* (By the sword we seek peace, but peace only under liberty).
**Emblems** BEVERAGE Cranberry juice. BIRD Chickadee. BUILDING & MONUMENT STONE Granite. DOG Boston terrier. EXPLORER ROCK Dighton Rock. FISH Cod. FLOWER Mayflower. FOLK SONG "Massachusetts." GEM Rhodonite. HEROINE Deborah Samson. HISTORICAL ROCK Plymouth Rock. HORSE Morgan. INSECT Ladybug. MARINE MAMMAL Right whale. MINERAL Babingtonite. POEM "Blue Hills of Massachusetts." ROCK Roxbury pudding stone. SONG "All Hail to Massachusetts." STONE Granite. TREE American elm.
**Land** TOTAL AREA 8,284 sq. mi. (45th), incl. 460 sq. mi. inland water. BORDERS Vt., N.H., Atlantic Ocean, R.I., Conn., N.Y. RIVERS Cape Cod Canal, Connecticut, Merrimack, Taunton. OTHER NOTABLE FEATURES Buzzard's Bay, Cape Ann, Cape Cod, Cape Cod Bay, Connecticut Valley, Elizabeth Islands, Martha's Vineyard, Monomoy Island, Nantucket Island.
**Elected officials** Gov. William Weld (R, term exp. 1995). Lt. Gov. Argeo Paul Cellucci (R). Sec. of Commonwealth Michael Joseph Con-

nolly (D). Atty. Gen. L. Scott Harshburger (D).
**People** (1990) 6,016,425 (13th). RACE/NATIONAL ORIGIN (1990): White 89.8%. Black 5.0%. Indian 0.2%. Asian 2.4%. Other 2.6%. Hispanic 4.8%.
**Cities** (1990) Boston 574,283. Worcester 169,759. Springfield 156,983. Lowell 103,439. New Bedford 99,922. Cambridge 95,802. Brockton 92,788. Fall River 92,703. Quincy 84,985. Newton 82,585.
**Business** GROSS STATE PRODUCT (GSP, 1986) $115.5 bil. (10th). SECTORS OF GSP: Farms 0.31%. Agricultural services, forestry, & fisheries 0.42%. Mining 0.06%. Construction 4.71%. Manufacturing 21.73%. Transportation & public utilities 7.14%. Wholesale 4.41%. Retail 9.94%. Finance, insurance, & real estate 17.08%. Services 22.11%. Federal government 1.54%. Federal military 0.56%. State & local government 7.09%. FORTUNE 500 COMPANIES (1990): 14: incl. Digital Equipment, Gillette, Ocean Spray, Polaroid, Raytheon, Wang Laboratories.
**Famous natives** John Adams, U.S. president. John Quincy Adams, U.S. president. Samuel Adams, patriot. Horatio Alger, clergyman/author. Susan B. Anthony, suffragette. Clara Barton, nurse. Leonard Bernstein, composer. George Herbert Walker Bush, U.S. president. John ("Johnny Appleseed") Chapman, pioneer. Richard Cardinal Cushing, prelate. Bette Davis, actress. Emily Dickinson, poet. Ralph Waldo Emerson, author. Marshall Field, merchant. R. Buckminster Fuller, inventor/engineer. John Hancock, patriot. Oliver Wendell Holmes, jurist. Winslow Homer, painter. John F. Kennedy, U.S. president. Jack Kerouac, author. Cotton Mather, theologian. Samuel Eliot Morison, historian. Samuel Morse, inventor. Thomas P. ("Tip") O'Neill, congressman. Edgar Allan Poe, poet/author. Paul Revere, patriot/silversmith. Louis Sullivan, architect. Henry David Thoreau, author.
**Noteworthy places** Addison Gallery of American Art, Andover. Arnold Arboretum, Boston. Arthur M. Sackler Museum, Cambridge. Berkshires Museum, Pittsfield. Boston Museum of Fine Arts. Boston Natl. Hist. Park (incl. Bunker Hill, Charlestown Navy Yard, Old North Church). Busch-Reisinger Museum, Cambridge. Cape Cod Natl. Seashore. Clark Art Institute, Williamsburg. Fogg Art Museum, Boston. Gardner Art Museum, Boston. Lowell Natl. Hist. Park. Minute Man Natl. Hist. Park, Lexington and Concord. Nantucket Hist. Society. Old Sturbridge Village. Peabody Museum, Salem. Plimoth Plantation, Plymouth. Shaker Village. Tanglewood Music Festival, Lenox. USS *Constitution* ("Old Ironsides"), Charlestown. Walden Pond. Woods Hole Oceanographic Institute. Worcester Art Museum.
**Memorable events** Pilgrims land at Plymouth 1620. First Thanksgiving celebrated 1621. Harvard College founded 1636. Region acquires province of Maine 1652. Colonists battle Wampanoags in King Philip's War 1655–56. Boston Massacre 1770. Boston Tea Party protests taxation 1773. Battles at Lexington, Concord, and Bunker Hill 1775. Shays's Rebellion 1785–86. Maine becomes a separate state 1820. Massachusetts receives influx of Irish

immigrants fleeing famine 1845. Textile workers' strike at Lawrence brings International Workers of the World (IWW) to prominence in East 1912. Cape Cod Canal completed 1914. International protest follows trial and execution of anarchists Nicola Sacco and Bartolomeo Vanzetti for robbery and murder 1920; names cleared by governor's proclamation 1970. Eleven robbers steal $2.7 million from Brink's North Terminal Garage 1950. Martha's Vineyard and Nantucket symbolically vote to secede from state 1973.
**Tourist information** 1-617-536-4100 or 1-617-727-3201.

## Michigan

The automobile is the single commodity with which Michigan is most identified, and it is the home of the big three automakers, General Motors, Ford, and Chrysler. More than 50 percent of Michiganders live in the southeastern corner of the state, where the car industry flourishes. In the Upper Peninsula, across the Straits of Mackinac, lumber and copper have been the principal commodities from the 19th century, and the northern part of the Lower Peninsula boasts rich farmland. Michigan's boundaries include parts of four of the five Great Lakes, and it has more coastline than any state except Alaska. Michigan has had an outstanding reputation in higher education, and the University of Michigan at Ann Arbor and Michigan State are helping to foster the state's high-tech industries. But the state's heavy reliance on auto manufacturing makes it vulnerable to economic downturns, as was witnessed in the early 1980s when the state's unemployment was among the very highest in the nation.
**NAME** From Fox *mesikami*, "large lake." **NICKNAMES** Wolverine State, Lake State. **CAPITAL** Lansing. **ENTERED UNION** Jan. 26, 1837 (26th). **MOTTO** *Si quaeris peninsulam amoenam circumspice* (If you are looking for a beautiful peninsula, look around you).
**Emblems** BIRD Robin. FISH Trout. FLOWER Apple blossom. GEM Chlorastrolite. INSECT Dragonfly. SONG "Michigan, My Michigan." STONE Petoskey stone. TREE White pine.
**Land** TOTAL AREA 58,527 sq. mi. (23d), incl. 1,573 sq. mi. inland water. BORDERS Lake Superior, Ontario, Lake Huron, Lake Erie, Ohio, Ind., Lake Michigan, Wis. RIVERS Brule, Detroit, Kalamazoo, Menominee, Montreal, Muskegon, St. Joseph, St. Mary's. LAKES Burt, Higgins, Houghton, Huron, Manistique, Michigan, Mullett, St. Clair, Superior. OTHER NOTABLE FEATURES Isle Royale, Mt. Curwood (1,980 ft.), Saginaw Bay, Traverse Bay, Whitefish Bay.
**Elected officials** Gov. John Engler (R, term exp. 1995). Lt. Gov. Connie Binsfeld (R). Sec. State Richard H. Austin (D). Atty. Gen. Frank J. Kelley (D).
**People** (1990) 9,295,297 (8th). RACE/NATIONAL ORIGIN (1990): White 83.4%. Black 13.9%. Indian 0.6%. Asian 1.1%. Other 0.9%. Hispanic 2.2%.
**Cities** (1990) Detroit 1,027,974. Grand Rapids

189,126. Warren 144,864. Flint 140,761. Lansing 127,321. Sterling Heights 117,810. Ann Arbor 109,592. Livonia 100,850. Dearborn 89,286. Westland 84,724.
**Business** GROSS STATE PRODUCT (GSP, 1986) $153.2 bil. (9th). SECTORS OF GSP: Farms 1.07%. Agricultural services, forestry, & fisheries 0.23%. Mining 0.66%. Construction 3.18%. Manufacturing 31.02%. Transportation & public utilities 7.41%. Wholesale 6.19%. Retail 9.26%. Finance, insurance, & real estate 15.78%. Services 15.13%. Federal government 1.10%. Federal military 0.33%. State & local government 8.65%. *FORTUNE* 500 COMPANIES (1990): 20: incl. Chrysler, Dow Corning, Ford Motor, General Motors, Gerber Products, Kellogg, Thorn Apple Valley, Upjohn, Whirlpool.
**Famous natives** Ralph J. Bunche, statesman (Nobel Peace Prize, 1950). Paul de Kruif, bacteriologist. Thomas Dewey, politician. Herbert H. Dow (b. Canada), chemical manufacturer. Edna Ferber, author. Henry Ford, industrialist. Edgar Guest, journalist/poet. Robert Ingersoll, industrialist. Will Kellogg, businessman/philanthropist. Charles A. Lindbergh, aviator. Antoine de La Mothe, sieur de Cadillac (b. France), founded Detroit. Pontiac, Ottawa chief. William Upjohn, drug manufacturer.
**Noteworthy places** Detroit Historical Society. Detroit Institute of Arts. Dossin Great Lakes Museum, Detroit. Great Lakes Indian Interpretive Museum, Detroit. Greenfield Village, Dearborn. Historic Ft. Wayne, Detroit. Isle Royale Natl. Park. Mackinac Island. Pictured Rocks Natl. Lakeshore, Lake Superior. Sleeping Bear Dunes Natl. Lakeshore, Lake Superior.
**Memorable events** French explorers in region 1634. Jacques Marquette settles Sault Ste. Marie 1668. Detroit founded as French military post 1701. Region ceded to England 1763; to U.S. 1783. Included in Northwest Territory but British maintain control until 1796. Michigan Territory 1805. First steamboat on Great Lakes reaches Detroit 1818. Statehood 1837. First state to outlaw capital punishment 1846. Republican party organized at Jackson 1854. Canals at Sault Ste. Marie link Lakes Superior and Huron 1855. Ransom E. Olds and Henry Ford, working independently, develop gaspowered car 1896. United Auto Workers first to use sit-down strike successfully in contract negotiations 1935. Worst race riot in U.S. history leaves 43 dead and $200 million in damages in Detroit 1967. Congress authorizes $1.5 billion in federal loan guarantees to bail out Chrysler Corporation 1979.
**Tourist information** 1-800-543-2YES or 1-517-373-1195.

## Minnesota

A land of at least 10,000 lakes, Minnesota is a magnet for outdoorsmen, canoers, and fishermen. It is also home to the largest Scandinavian populations in the United States. Originally exploited for its wealth of lumber and iron—the Mesabi Range still produces 60% of the nation's iron ore—Minnesota also has

highly developed agribusinesses (especially dairy products), manufacturing, and transportation industries. Minneapolis and St. Paul are at the north end of the Mississippi River system, and Duluth at the westernmost point of Lake Superior is the largest U.S. inland port. Both self-sufficient and politically liberal, Minnesota has one of the best state school systems.
**NAME** From the Sioux *minisota*, "sky-tinted waters." **NICKNAMES** North Star State, Gopher State. **CAPITAL** St. Paul. **ENTERED UNION** May 11, 1858 (32d). **MOTTO** *L'étoile du nord* (Star of the north).
**Emblems** BIRD Common loon. DRINK Milk. FISH Walleye. FLOWER Pink and white lady's slipper. GEM Lake Superior agate. GRAIN Wild rice. MUSHROOM Morel, or sponge mushroom. SONG "Hail, Minnesota!" TREE Red pine.
**Land** TOTAL AREA 84,402 sq. mi. (12th), incl. 4,854 sq. mi. inland water. BORDERS Manitoba, Ontario, Lake Superior, Wis., Iowa, S.Dak., N.Dak. RIVERS Minnesota, Mississippi, Red River of the North, St. Croix. LAKES Itasca, Lake of the Woods, Leech, Mille Lacs, Red, Winnibigoshish. OTHER NOTABLE FEATURES Mesabi Range.
**Elected officials** Gov. Arne Carlson (R, term exp. 1995). Lt. Gov. Joanell Dyrstad (R). Sec. State Joan Anderson Growe (D). Atty. Gen. Hubert H. Humphrey III (Democratic-Farmer-Labor).
**People** (1990) 4,375,099 (20th). RACE/NATIONAL ORIGIN (1990): White 94.4%. Black 2.2%. Indian 1.1%. Asian 1.8%. Other 0.5%. Hispanic 1.2%.
**Cities** (1990) Minneapolis 368,383. St. Paul 272,235. Bloomington 86,335. Duluth 85,493. Rochester 70,745. Brooklyn Park 56,381. Coon Rapids 52,978. Burnsville 51,288. Plymouth 50,889. St. Cloud 48,812.
**Business** GROSS STATE PRODUCT (GSP, 1986) $75.6 bil. (19th). SECTORS OF GSP: Farms 4.40%. Agricultural services, forestry, & fisheries 0.33%. Mining 0.54%. Construction 3.65%. Manufacturing 20.91%. Transportation & public utilities 9.06%. Wholesale 7.96%. Retail 9.63%. Finance, insurance, & real estate 18.29%. Services 15.43%. Federal government 1.14%. Federal military 0.24%. State & local government 8.43%. *FORTUNE* 500 COMPANIES (1990): 18: incl. Control Data, Cray Research, General Mills, Geo. R. Hormel, Honeywell, Land O'Lakes, Minnesota Mining & Manufacturing (3M), Tonka.
**Famous natives** Warren Burger, jurist. Bob Dylan, musician. F. Scott Fitzgerald, novelist. Judy Garland, actress. J. Paul Getty, businessman. Sinclair Lewis, author (Nobel Prize, 1930). Paul Manship, sculptor. William and Charles Mayo, surgeons. Eugene McCarthy, politician. Walter F. Mondale, politician. Charles Schulz, cartoonist. Ole Edvart Rölvaag (b. Norway), novelist. Richard W. Sears, merchant.
**Noteworthy places** Boundary Waters Canoe Area. Grand Portage Natl. Monument. International Falls. Lake Itasca State Park (headwaters of Mississippi). Mayo Clinic, Rochester. Minneapolis Institute of Arts. Minnehaha Falls, Minneapolis. Minnesota Zoo, Apple Valley. Pipestone Natl. Monument. Tyrone Guthrie Theater, Minneapolis. Voyageurs Natl. Park. Walker Art

Center, Minneapolis.

**Memorable events** Pierre Esprit Radisson and Médard Chouart des Grosselliers visit area 1654–60. René-Robert de La Salle and Louis Hennepin explore upper Mississippi 1680. Daniel Greysolon, sieur Duluth, claims region for France 1679. Area east of Mississippi to Britain 1763; to U.S. 1783. Western region of state as part of Louisiana Purchase 1803. Britain cedes northern strip to U.S. 1818. Ft. Snelling built 1820. Northern border settled by Ashburton Treaty 1842. Minnesota Territory created 1849. Statehood 1858. Sioux driven from state after uprising led by Chief Little Crow 1862. Iron ore deposits discovered in Mesabi Range 1890. Democratic party merges with Farmer-Labor party 1944.

**Tourist information** 1–800–328–1461, 1–612–296–5029 or 1–800–652–9747.

# Mississippi

Mississippi's rank as the poorest state in the nation can be traced to the Civil War. Before the Civil War, Mississippi was the fifth-wealthiest state in the nation. The war cost the state 30,000 men (65% of the Southerners who died). Plantation owners who survived the war were virtually bankrupted by the emancipation of the slaves, and Union troops under Sherman and others left widespread destruction in their wake. The increasingly harsh race laws passed around 1900 also cost the state in the emigration of almost half a million (75% blacks, 25% whites) in the 1940s. Compounding all this was the fact that until World War II, Mississippi had virtually no urban center such as Jackson to attract or sustain major industry. In race relations particularly, Mississippi has made vast improvements, and there have been substantial gains in education and the attraction of out-of-state companies, especially light industry.

NAME From Ojibwa *misi sipi*, "great river." NICKNAME Magnolia State. CAPITAL Jackson. ENTERED UNION Dec. 10, 1817 (20th). MOTTO *Virtute et armis* (By virtue and arms).

**Emblems** BEVERAGE Milk. BIRD Mockingbird. FISH Largemouth or black bass. FLOWER Magnolia. FOSSIL Prehistoric whale. INSECT Honeybee. MAMMAL White-tailed deer. SONG "Go, Mississippi." STONE Petrified wood. TREE Magnolia. WATERFOWL Wood duck. WATER MAMMAL Porpoise.

**Land** TOTAL AREA 47,689 sq. mi. (32d), incl. 456 sq. mi. inland water. BORDERS Tenn., Ala., Gulf of Mexico, La., Ark. RIVERS Big Black, Mississippi, Pearl, Tennessee, Yazoo. LAKES Arkabutla, Grenada, Ross Barnett Res., Sardis. OTHER NOTABLE FEATURES Pontotoc Ridge.

**Elected officials** Gov. Ray Mabus (D, term exp. 1992). Lt. Gov. Brad Dye (D). Sec. State Dick Molpus (D). Atty. Gen. Mike Moore (D).

**People** (1990) 2,573,216 (31st). RACE/NATIONAL ORIGIN (1990): White 63.5%. Black 35.6%. Indian 0.3%. Asian 0.5%. Other 0.1%. Hispanic 0.6%.

**Cities** (1990) Jackson 196,637. Biloxi 46,319. Greenville 45,226. Hattiesburg 41,882. Meridian 41,036. Gulfport 40,775. Tupelo 30,685. Pascagoula 25,899. Columbus 23,799. Clinton 21,847.

**Business** GROSS STATE PRODUCT (GSP, 1986) $31.8 bil. (32d). SECTORS OF GSP: Farms 2.98%. Agricultural services, forestry, & fisheries 0.44%. Mining 2.60%. Construction 4.49%. Manufacturing 27.24%. Transportation & public utilities 8.55%. Wholesale 5.15%. Retail 10.67%. Finance, insurance, & real estate 13.41%. Services 11.24%. Federal government 2.24%. Federal military 2.40%. State & local government 8.58%. *FORTUNE* 500 COMPANIES (1990): 0.

**Famous natives** Medgar Evers, reformer. William Faulkner, novelist. Shelby Foote, historian. Jim Henson, puppeteer. B.B. King, musician. Elvis Presley, singer. Leontyne Price, opera singer. John C. Stennis, politician. Conway Twitty, singer. Muddy Waters, musician. Eudora Welty, novelist. Ben Ames Williams, novelist. Tennessee Williams, playwright. Richard Wright, author.

**Noteworthy places** Delta Blues Museum, Clarksdale. Natchez Trace Natl. Parkway. Seafood Industry Museum, Biloxi. Tupelo Natl. Battlefield. Vicksburg Natl. Military Park.

**Memorable events** Hernando de Soto's expedition travels through Mississippi 1540–41. René-Robert Cavelier de La Salle claims Mississippi Valley for France 1682. Pierre Le Moyne, sieur d'Iberville builds Ft. Maurepas on Biloxi Bay 1699. Natchez (Ft. Rosalie) established 1716. France cedes territory to Britain 1763. Mississippi Territory (including present-day Alabama) created 1798. Statehood (Natchez first capital) 1817. Secedes from Union; Jefferson Davis becomes president of Confederacy 1861. Siege of Vicksburg 1863. Petroleum discovered 1939. Gov. Ross R. Barnett found guilty of contempt in preventing desegregation of University of Mississippi; James H. Meredith first black enrolled at University of Mississippi 1962. Civil rights leader Medgar Evers assassinated in Jackson and buried in Arlington National Cemetery 1963. White civil rights workers James Cheney, Andrew Goodman, and Michael Schwerner killed 1964.

**Tourist information** 1–800–647–2290 or 1–601–359–3414.

# Missouri

Missouri is remarkable for the number and variety of its neighbors—southern states (Arkansas, Kentucky, and Tennessee), midwestern states (Illinois and Iowa), and Plains states (Oklahoma, Nebraska, and Kansas). For Missouri, geography was destiny. Still one of the country's most important inland ports, St. Louis was founded at the confluence of the Missouri and Mississippi rivers and became the gateway to the West; and Independence (now part of metropolitan Kansas City) got its start provisioning wagons for the Oregon and Santa Fe trails. The Pony Express from St. Joseph to Sacramento began in 1860, and the first attempt at airmail service was tried in St. Louis in 1911. While farming and livestock are still important to the state's economy, manufacturing and banking are now the biggest sectors.

NAME From Iliniwek *missouri*, "owner of big

canoes." NICKNAME Show Me State. CAPITAL Jefferson City. ENTERED UNION Aug. 10, 1821 (24th). MOTTO *Salus populi suprema lex esto* (The welfare of the people shall be the supreme law).

**Emblems** BIRD Bluebird. FLOWER Hawthorne. INSECT Honeybee. MINERAL Galena. ROCK Mozarkite. SONG "Missouri Waltz." TREE Dogwood.

**Land** TOTAL AREA 69,697 sq. mi. (19th), incl. 752 sq. mi. inland water. BORDERS Iowa, Ill., Ky., Tenn., Ark., Okla., Kans., Nebr. RIVERS Des Moines, Mississippi, Missouri, Osage, St. Francis. LAKES Bull Shoals, Clearwater, Lake of the Ozarks, Lake of the Woods, Tablerock, Wappapella. OTHER NOTABLE FEATURES Ozark Mts. (Taum Sauk Mt. 1,772 ft.).

**Elected officials** Gov. John Ashcroft (R, term exp. 1993). Lt. Gov. Mel Carnahan (R). Sec. State Roy D. Blunt (R). Atty. Gen. William Webster (R).

**People** (1990) 5,117,073 (15th). RACE/NATIONAL ORIGIN (1990): White 87.7%. Black 10.7%. Indian 0.4%. Asian 0.8%. Other 0.4%. Hispanic 1.2%.

**Cities** (1990) Kansas City 435,146. St. Louis 396,685. Springfield 140,494. Independence 112,301. St. Joseph 71,852. Columbia 69,101. St. Charles 54,555. Florissant 51,206. Lee's Summit 46,418. St. Peters 45,779.

**Business** GROSS STATE PRODUCT (GSP, 1986) $83.5 bil. (15th). SECTORS OF GSP: Farms 2.33%. Agricultural services, forestry, & fisheries 0.30%. Mining 0.35%. Construction 4.14%. Manufacturing 22.64%. Transportation & public utilities 10.96%. Wholesale 7.03%. Retail 10.42%. Finance, insurance, & real estate 15.61%. Services 16.14%. Federal government 2.61%. Federal military 0.83%. State & local government 6.63%. *FORTUNE* 500 COMPANIES (1990): 14: incl. Anheuser-Busch, Emerson Electric, General Dynamics, McDonnell Douglas, Monsanto, Ralston Purina.

**Famous natives** Thomas Hart Benton, painter. Yogi Berra, baseball player. George Caleb Bingham (b. Va.), painter. Omar Bradley, general. Adophus Busch (b. Germany), brewer. George Washington Carver, botanist. Walter Cronkite, journalist. Walt Disney, film producer. T.S. Eliot, author. Walker Evans, photographer. Langston Hughes, poet. Jesse James, outlaw. Marianne Moore, poet. Reinhold Niebuhr, theologian. J.C. Penny, businessman. John J. ("Black Jack") Pershing, soldier. Joseph Pulitzer (b. Hungary), publisher. Ginger Rogers, dancer. Casey Stengel, baseball player. Virgil Thompson, composer. Harry S Truman, U.S. president. Mark Twain, writer. Tom Watson, golfer. Shelley Winters, actress.

**Noteworthy places** Churchill Memorial, St. Aldermanbury Church, Fulton. Gateway Arch, St. Louis. George Washington Carver Natl. Monument, Diamond. Harry S Truman Library, Independence. Mark Twain Area, Hannibal. Nelson-Atkins Museum of Art, Kansas City. Pony Express Museum, St. Joseph. St. Louis Art Museum. Wilson's Creek Natl. Battlefield.

**Memorable events** French miners and hunters settle at Ste. Genevieve 1735. Pierre Laclade settles St. Louis 1765. New Madrid earthquakes (8.6 on Richter scale) rock buildings as far away as Baltimore 1811–12. Statehood 1821. Missouri legislature split over secession: minority party adopts secession ordinance; Missouri admitted to Confederacy; majority party remains loyal to Union 1861. Jesse James killed by fellow gang member at St. Joseph 1882. Lake of the Ozarks formed after completion of Bagnell Dam on Osage River 1931. Winston Churchill delivers "iron curtain" speech at Fulton 1952. Gateway Arch, 630 ft. high, opened at St. Louis 1964. St. Louis population declines 47% 1950–80.

**Tourist information** 1-800-877-1234 or 1-314-751-4133.

# Montana

Mountains account for only the western two-fifths of the state, where copper mining, lumbering, and tourism are the chief industries. The eastern portion of the state is part of the Great Plains. There the "Big Sky Country" is devoted to agriculture and especially ranching. For many years Montana was in the grip of the Anaconda Copper Mining Company, which virtually owned the state government and took most of the company's profits out of the state. After Anaconda's demise in the 1970s, Montana developed some of the most stringent environmental laws in the West. Although the copper mining damage is done, these laws will have a beneficial impact on the southeastern corner of the state, which is now being exploited for its enormous reserves of low-sulphur coal.

NAME From Spanish *montaña*, "mountainous." NICKNAMES Treasure State, Big Sky Country. CAPITAL Helena. ENTERED UNION Nov. 8, 1889 (41st). MOTTO *Oro y plata* (Gold and silver).

**Emblems** BIRD Western meadowlark. FISH Blackspotted cutthroat trout. FLOWER Bitterroot. GEMS Yogo sapphire, Montana agate. GRASS Bluebunch wheatgrass. SONG "Montana." STATE BALLAD "Montana Melody." TREE Ponderosa pine.

**Land** TOTAL AREA 147,046 sq. mi. (4th), incl. 1,658 sq. mi. inland water. BORDERS British Columbia, Alberta, Saskatchewan, N.Dak., S.Dak., Wyo., Idaho. RIVERS Kootenai, Milk, Missouri, Musselshell, Powder, Yellowstone. LAKES Bighorn, Canyon Ferry, Elwell, Flathead, Ft. Peck. MOUNTAINS Absaroka Range, Beartooth Range (Granite Peak 12,799 ft.), Big Belt, Bitterroot Range, Centennial, Crazy, Lewis Range, Little Belt. OTHER NOTABLE FEATURES Continental Divide, Missoula Valley.

**Elected officials** Gov. Stan Stephens (R, term exp. 1993). Lt. Gov. Allen Kolstad (R). Sec. State Mike Cooney (D). Atty. Gen. Marc Racicot (R).

**People** (1990) 799,065 (44th). RACE/NATIONAL ORIGIN (1990): White 92.7%. Black 0.3%. Indian 6.0%. Asian 0.5%. Other 0.5%. Hispanic 1.5%.

**Cities** (1990) Billings 81,151. Great Falls 55,097. Missoula 42,918. Butte–Silver Bow 33,941. Helena 24,569. Bozeman 22,660. Kalispell 11,917. Anaconda–Deer Lodge Co.

10,278. Havre 10,201. Miles City 8,461.

**Business** GROSS STATE PRODUCT (GSP, 1986) $12.2 bil. (45th). SECTORS OF GSP: Farms 7.79%. Agricultural services, forestry, & fisheries 0.50%. Mining 7.30%. Construction 8.40%. Manufacturing 7.24%. Transportation & public utilities 12.23%. Wholesale 5.45%. Retail 8.6%. Finance, insurance, & real estate 16.51%. Services 13.21%. Federal government 2.65%. Federal military 1.22%. State & local government 8.89%. *FORTUNE* 500 COMPANIES (1990): 0.

**Famous natives** Gary Cooper, actor. Marcus Daly (b. Ireland), mine owner. Chet Huntley, journalist. Myrna Loy, actress. Mike Mansfield (b. N.Y.), politician/diplomat. Jeannette Rankin, politician/reformer. Charles M. Russell, artist.

**Noteworthy places** Big Hole Natl. Battlefield. Bob Marshall Wilderness. Charles M. Russell Museum, Great Falls. Custer Battlefield Natl. Monument. Ft. Union Trading Post Natl. Hist. Site. Lewis and Clark Caverns State Park. Museum of the Plains Indian, Browning. Natl. Bison Range. Waterton-Glacier International Peace Park. World Museum of Mining, Butte. Yellowstone Natl. Park.

**Memorable events** French explorers and trappers visit region 1740s. Large part of state in Louisiana Purchase 1803. Lewis and Clark expedition 1805–06. Ft. Benton first permanent settlement 1846. Western part of state included in Washington Territory 1853 and 1859; eastern part in Nebraska (1854) and Dakota (1861) territories. Gold discovered at Bannack (1862) and Alder Gulch (1863). Organized as Montana Territory 1864. Dakota and Cheyenne defeat U.S. troops under Gen. William Armstrong Custer at Battle of Little Bighorn 1876. Under Chief Joseph, Nez Percé beat U.S. Army at Big Hole Basin 1877. Marcus Daly discovers copper near Butte 1880s. Statehood 1889. Homesteaders enter state 1909. Ft. Peck Dam completed 1940. Anaconda Copper Mining, dominant in Montana industry and politics since 1915, closes mining operations at Butte 1983. Elizabeth Prophet (Guru Ma) convinces 3,000 disciples of the Church Universal and Triumphant to await nuclear cataclysm in underground shelters in Paradise Valley while state bureaucrats worried over sewage facilities 1990.

**Tourist information** 1-800-548-3390 or 1-406-444-2654.

# Nebraska

Although set aside as Indian territory in 1834 and made off-limits to white settlement, thousands of whites crossed the region along the Independence, Mormon, and Oregon trails. Eventually Congress opened the land to settlement, which accelerated after the Homestead Act of 1862 and the coming of the railroads. The newcomers took up ranching and farming under hard conditions. The winter of 1886–87 killed thousands of cattle and drove many large-scale ranchers into bankruptcy, while the dust bowl of the 1930s spurred a mass exodus. Significant industry did not develop until

World War II, when many war-related industries and army airfields moved to the center of the country. Nearly half of the work force of the state—among the leading agricultural states, especially in the production of corn for grain and livestock—is in agriculture. A state constitutional amendment passed in 1982 prevents the sale of farmlands and ranch lands to anyone other than a Nebraska family farm corporation.

NAME From Oto *nebrathka*, "flat water." NICKNAME Cornhusker State. CAPITAL Lincoln. ENTERED UNION Mar. 1, 1867 (37th). MOTTO "Equality before the law."

**Emblems** BIRD Western meadowlark. FLOWER Goldenrod. FOSSIL Mammoth. GEM Blue agate. GRASS Little blue stem. INSECT Honeybee. MAMMAL White-tailed deer. ROCK Prairie agate. SOIL Soils of the Holdrege series. SONG "Beautiful Nebraska." TREE Western cottonwood.

**Land** TOTAL AREA 77,355 sq. mi. (15th), incl. 711 sq. mi. inland water. BORDERS S.Dak., Iowa, Mo., Kans., Colo., Wyo. RIVERS Missouri, North Platte, Republican, South Platte. LAKES Harlan Co. Res., Lewis and Clark Lake. OTHER NOTABLE FEATURES Pine Ridge, Sand Hills.

**Elected officials** Gov. Ben Nelson (D, term exp. 1995). Lt. Gov. Maxine Moul (D). Sec. State Allen J. Beermann (R). Atty. Gen. Don Stenberg (R).

**People** (1990) 1,578,385 (36th). RACE/NATIONAL ORIGIN (1990): White 93.8%. Black 3.6%. Indian 0.8%. Asian 0.8%. Other 1.0%. Hispanic 2.3%.

**Cities** (1990) Omaha 335,795. Lincoln 191,972. Grand Island 39,386. Bellevue 30,982. Kearney 24,396. Fremont 23,680. Hastings 22,837. North Platte 22,605. Norfolk 21,476. Columbus 19,480.

**Business** GROSS STATE PRODUCT (GSP, 1986) $26.5 bil. (34th). SECTORS OF GSP: Farms 12.03%. Agricultural services, forestry, & fisheries 0.50%. Mining 0.26%. Construction 3.61%. Manufacturing 13.76%. Transportation & public utilities 11.27%. Wholesale 7.06%. Retail 8.91%. Finance, insurance, & real estate 17.29%. Services 13.45%. Federal government 0.23%. Federal military 2.01%. State & local government 9.62%. *FORTUNE* 500 COMPANIES (1990): 5: AG Processing, Berkshire Hathaway, Conagra, Peter Kiewit Sons', Valmont Industries.

**Famous natives** Fred Astaire, dancer. Marlon Brando, actor. Willa Cather (b. Va.), author. Loren Eiseley, anthropologist. The Rev. Edward J. Flanagan (b. Ireland), reformer. Henry Fonda, actor. Gerald Ford, U.S. president. Rollin Kirby, cartoonist. Melvin Laird, politician. Harold Lloyd, actor. Mahpiua Luta (Red Cloud), Oglala Sioux chief. Malcolm X, religious leader. Roscoe Pound, educator.

**Noteworthy places** Agate Fossil Beds Natl. Monument. Arbor Lodge State Park, Nebraska City. Boys Town, Omaha. Buffalo Bill Ranch State Hist. Park. Chimney Rock Hist. Site. Homestead Natl. Monument, Beatrice. Oregon Trail. Pioneer Village, Minden. Scotts Bluff Natl. Monument. Stuhr Museum of the Prairie Pioneer, Grand Island.

**Memorable events** Acquired as part of Louisiana Purchase 1803. Separate territory created by Kansas-Nebraska Act 1854. Size reduced after creation of Colorado and Dakota territories 1861. Statehood 1867. To encourage tree planting, becomes first state to observe Arbor Day 1872. Adopts unicameral legislature 1937. Oil discovered 1939. Population peaks at 1,605,000 1984–85.

**Tourist information** 1-800-228-4307 or 1-800-742-7595.

## Nevada

Set in the Great Basin desert, Nevada is one of the most barren places in North America, and the state receives less rainfall than any other. First explored by Europeans in 1776, it was 75 years before anyone thought of establishing a town in the area, and it did not last a decade. Miners came to Nevada early, but the discovery of the Comstock Lode in 1859 brought thousands. To add free-state congressional votes, Nevada was hustled into the Union in 1864, three years before its boundaries were settled. The Comstock Lode was depleted by the 1870s, and it took more gold and silver strikes in the early 1900s, as well as the discovery of copper, to get the economy rolling again. The mainstay of the economy since World War II has been the gambling industry, which generates virtually half of all tax revenues; Las Vegas alone can accommodate as many as 150,000 conventioneers and tourists at one time.

Name From Spanish, meaning "snow-covered sierra." Nicknames Sagebrush State, Silver State. Capital Carson City. Entered Union Oct. 31, 1864 (36th). Motto "All for our country."

**Emblems** Animal Desert bighorn sheep. Bird Mountain bluebird. Flower Sagebrush. Fossil Icthyosaur. Grass Indian ricegrass. Metal Silver. Song "Home Means Nevada." Tree Single-leaf piñon.

**Land** Total area 110,561 sq. mi. (7th), incl. 667 sq. mi. inland water. Borders Oreg., Idaho, Utah, Ariz., Calif. Rivers Colorado, Humboldt. Lakes Pyramid, Walker, Winnemucca. Other notable features Black Rock Desert, Carson Sink, Humboldt Salt Marsh, Mojave Desert.

**Elected officials** Gov. Robert J. Miller (D, term exp. 1991). Lt. Gov. vacant. Sec. State Frankie Sue Del Papa (D). Atty. Gen. Brian McKay (R).

**People** (1990) 1,201,833 (39th). Race/national origin (1990): White 84.3%. Black 6.6%. Indian 1.6%. Asian 3.2%. Other 4.4%. Hispanic 10.4%.

**Cities** (1990) Las Vegas 258,295. Reno 133,850. Henderson 64,942. Sparks 53,367. North Las Vegas 47,707. Carson City 40,443. Elko 14,736. Boulder City 12,567. Fallon 6,438. Winnemucca 6,134.

**Business** Gross state product (GSP, 1986) $19.4 bil. (39th). Sectors of GSP: Farms 0.57%. Agricultural services, forestry, & fisheries 0.30%. Mining 2.82%. Construction 7.75%. Manufacturing 4.80%. Transportation & public utilities 9.44%. Wholesale 4.07%. Retail 9.82%. Finance, insurance, & real estate 14.14%. Services 35.53%. Federal gov-

ernment 1.85%. Federal military 1.59%. State & local government 7.34%. Fortune 500 companies (1990): 0.

**Famous natives** Walter Van Tilburg Clark (b. Me.), author. Sarah Winnemucca Hopkins, interpreter/teacher. John William MacKay, miner. William Morris Stewart (b. N.Y.), lawyer/senator.

**Noteworthy places** Death Valley Natl. Monument. Lehman Caves Natl. Monument. Valley of the Fire State Park, Overton.

**Memorable events** Francisco Tomás Garcés explores area 1775–76. Jedediah Smith, trader, crosses region 1826–27. Old Spanish Trail (1830) and California Trail (1833) cross region. John Frémont explores area 1843–45. To U.S. after Mexican War 1846. Genoa, first settlement in Nevada, founded as Mormon Station 1849. Gold of Comstock Lode discovered 1859. Organized as separate territory 1861. Statehood 1864. Nevada legalizes gambling 1931. Hoover Dam built on Colorado River 1935. Nuclear tests begun at Yucca Flats 1951. Population grows more than 550% 1950–88.

**Tourist information** 1-800-NEVADA8 or 1-702-885-3636.

## New Hampshire

New Hampshire has a disproportionate influence on presidential elections because by state law its primary must fall at least one week before any other state's (though Iowa's caucuses can come earlier). Through independence the mainstays of the economy were fishing, trade, and farming. Boston proved more suitable for trade, and New Hampshire's stubborn land was outproduced by the more fertile valleys to the south and west. The state's economy receded until the beginning of the Industrial Revolution, when there was tremendous growth in textile-producing mill towns in the Merrimack River Valley. The mills began to close after World War I, and the economy faltered again. Lately improvement has come as high-tech firms from Boston have sought refuge in New Hampshire's favorable tax climate. Expansion here, too, has threatened New Hampshire's natural spaces.

Name For English county of Hampshire. Nickname Granite State. Capital Concord. Entered Union June 21, 1788 (9th). Motto "Live free or die."

**Emblems** Amphibean Spotted newt. Bird Purple finch. Flower Purple lilac. Gem Smoke quartz. Insect Ladybug. Mineral Beryl. Song "Old New Hampshire." Tree White birch.

**Land** Total area 9,279 sq. mi. (44th), incl. 286 sq. mi. inland water. Borders Quebec, Maine, Atlantic Ocean, Mass., Vt. Rivers Connecticut, Merrimack, Piscataqua, Saco, Salmon Falls. Lakes First Connecticut, Francis, Newfound, Ossipee, Sunapee, Winnipesaukee. Other notable features Isles of Shoals, White Mts. (Mt. Washington 6,288 ft., highest peak in Northeast).

**Elected officials** Gov. Judd Gregg (R, term exp. 1993).

**People** (1990) 1,109,252 (40th). Race/national origin (1990): White 98.0%. Black 0.6%.

Indian 0.2%. Asian 0.8%. Other 0.3%. Hispanic 1.0%.

**Cities** (1990) Manchester 99,567. Nashua 79,662. Concord 36,006. Rochester 26,630. Portsmouth 22,925. Dover 25,042. Keene 22,430. Laconia 15,743. Claremont 13,902. Lebanon 12,183.

**Business** Gross state product (GSP, 1986) $18.5 bil. (41st). Sectors of GSP: Farms 0.46%. Agricultural services, forestry, & fisheries 0.35%. Mining 0.14%. Construction 7.29%. Manufacturing 25.99%. Transportation & public utilities 6.31%. Wholesale 5.67%. Retail 10.64%. Finance, insurance, & real estate 18.70%. Services 15.94%. Federal government 1.42%. Federal military 0.86%. State & local government 6.26%. Fortune 500 companies (1990): 3: Henley Group, Nashua, Tyco Laboratories.

**Famous natives** Salmon P. Chase, jurist. Ralph Adams Cram, architect. Mary Baker Eddy, founder, Church of Christ, Scientist. Daniel Chester French, sculptor. Horace Greeley, journalist. Sarah Buell Hale, author. Franklin Pierce, U.S. president. Augustus Saint-Gaudens (b. Ireland), sculptor. Alan Shepard, astronaut. Daniel Webster, politician. Eleazar Wheelock (b. Conn.), Dartmouth founder.

**Noteworthy places** Currier Gallery of Art, Manchester. The Flume (gorge). Franconia Notch. Isles of Shoals. Lake Winnipesaukee. Mt. Washington. Shaker Village, Canterbury. St. Gaudens Natl. Hist. Site. Strawberry Banke. White Mountains Natl. Forest.

**Memorable events** Martin Pring sails along coast 1603. Champlain explores area 1604. John Smith visits Isles of Shoals 1614. Included in king's grant to John Mason and Sir Ferdinando Gorges 1622. First settlers at Little Harbor, near Portsmouth 1623. Made separate royal province 1679, though under Massachusetts governor 1699–1741. Rogers's Rangers halt Indian raids 1759. New Hampshire patriots seize British fort at Portsmouth and drive out Royal governor 1775. Province relinquishes claims to New Connecticut (Vermont) 1782. First textile mill built 1803. Treaty of Portsmouth ends Sino-Russian War 1905. Bretton Woods conference leads to establishment of International Monetary Fund 1944. First state to adopt lottery to support public education 1963.

**Tourist information** 1-603-271-2666.

## New Jersey

With the entire state population classified as living in metro areas, New Jersey is the most densely populated state, 15 times the national average. The image survives of New Jersey as a chemical-industrial wasteland south of New York Harbor. Pharmaceuticals and chemicals are in fact New Jersey's leading products, but the next most important industry is tourism, because of the money tourists spend at the gaming tables of Atlantic City. What earns New Jersey its nickname, the Garden State, is its extensive small-scale agriculture, which produces tomatoes, dairy products, asparagus, blueberries, corn, and poultry.

New Jersey lies on a plain between Philadelphia and New York City, two larger neighbors that have overshadowed New Jersey on the national scene since colonial days. Yet during the Revolution, more than 100 battles were fought on New Jersey soil, and today the overwhelming majority of containerized shipping in the Port of New York and New Jersey is shipped from New Jersey terminals. Per capita income is always among the top five in the nation.

**NAME** After English Channel Island of Jersey. **NICKNAME** Garden State. **CAPITAL** Trenton. **ENTERED UNION** Dec. 18, 1787 (3d). **MOTTO** "Liberty and prosperity."
**Emblems** **ANIMAL** Horse. **BIRD** Eastern goldfinch. **FLOWER** Violet. **INSECT** Honeybee. **MEMORIAL TREE** Dogwood. **TREE** Red oak.
**Land** **TOTAL AREA** 7,787 sq. mi. (46th), incl. 319 sq. mi. inland water. **BORDERS** N.Y., Atlantic Ocean, Del., Pa. **RIVERS** Delaware, Hackensack, Hudson, Passaic. **LAKES** Greenwood, Hopatcong, Round Valley Res., Spruce Run. **OTHER NOTABLE FEATURES** Delaware Water Gap, Kittatinny Mts., Palisades, Pine Barrens, Ramapo Mts.
**Elected officials** Gov. James J. Florio (D, term exp. 1994).
**People** (1990) 7,730,188 (9th). **RACE/NATIONAL ORIGIN** (1990): White 79.3%. Black 13.4%. Indian 0.2%. Asian 3.5%. Other 3.6%. Hispanic 9.6%.
**Cities** (1990) Newark 275,221. Jersey City 228,537. Paterson 140,891. Elizabeth 110,002. Edison CDP 88,680. Trenton 88,675. Camden 87,492. East Orange 73,552. Clifton 71,742. Cherry Hill 69,319.
**Business** **GROSS STATE PRODUCT** (GSP, 1986) $154.8 bil. (8th). **SECTORS OF GSP:** Farms 0.32%. Agricultural services, forestry, & fisheries 0.30%. Mining 0.06%. Construction 4.90%. Manufacturing 19.73%. Transportation & public utilities 10.50%. Wholesale 8.71%. Retail 8.96%. Finance, insurance, & real estate 18.55%. Services 18.01%. Federal government 1.81%. Federal military 0.52%. State & local government 7.65%. **FORTUNE** 500 **COMPANIES** (1990): 23: incl. Allied Signal, BASF, Campbell Soup, Hoechst Celanese, Ingersoll-Rand, Johnson & Johnson, Merck.
**Famous natives** Count Basie, jazz musician. William J. Brennan, jurist. Aaron Burr, politician. Grover Cleveland, U.S. president. James Fenimore Cooper, novelist/historian. Stephen Crane, author. Albert Einstein (b. Germany), nuclear physicist. Waldo Frank, author. Joyce Kilmer, poet. Jerry Lewis, actor. Jack Nicholson, actor. Zebulon Pike, explorer. Molly Pitcher, Revolutionary War heroine. Paul Robeson, actor/singer. Walter Schirra, astronaut. Frank Sinatra, singer. Alfred Stieglitz, photographer. Meryl Streep, actress. Aaron Montgomery Ward, merchant. William Carlos Williams, poet.
**Noteworthy places** Cape May Historic District. Edison Natl. Hist. Site, West Orange. Lakehurst Naval Air Station. Liberty State Park, Jersey City. Morristown Natl. Hist. Park. Newark Museum. Palisades Interstate Park. Pine Barrens wilderness area. Princeton University. Walt Whitman House, Camden.

**Memorable events** Giovanni de Verrazano explores 1524. Hudson explores up Hudson River 1609. Dutch settlers establish Ft. Nassau 1623. New Jersey taken over by British and organized as colony under Sir George Carteret 1665. Major battles of Revolution at Trenton (1776), Princeton (1777), and Monmouth (1778). Women given vote at Elizabethtown 1800. Voting rights restricted to men 1807. Adopts state constitution 1844. Passenger ship *Morro Castle* burns off Asbury Park; 134 die 1934. Dirigible *Hindenburg* explodes while mooring at Lakehurst; 36 die 1937. New Jersey Turnpike linking New York City and Philadelphia opens 1952. Five days of race riots in Newark leave 26 dead 1967. Gambling legalized in Atlantic City 1978. State enacts strictest gun legislation in U.S. 1990.
**Tourist information** 1–800–JERSEY7 or 1–609–292–2470.

## New Mexico

The development problem of the western states is shared by New Mexico, which of all states has the smallest percentage of its area covered by water. Rich in other resources, it is the uranium capital of the world. The state mineral tax brings in 28 percent of state revenues, some of which goes into permanent endowments. Distribution of wealth in New Mexico remains uneven, but Hispanics, who tend to register as Democrats, vote in roughly the same ways as Anglos. A higher percentage of Native Americans lives in New Mexico than in any other state. Today mining is the biggest industry, though manufacturing is growing. Despite the enormous governmental investment in research at Los Alamos, where the atom bomb was born, the highly classified nature of this work limits the development of related industry.

**NAME** By Spanish explorers after Mexico. **NICKNAME** Land of Enchantment. **CAPITAL** Santa Fe. **ENTERED UNION** Jan. 6, 1912 (47th). **MOTTO** *Crescit eundo* (It grows as it goes).
**Emblems** **ANIMAL** Black bear. **BIRD** Roadrunner (chaparral bird). **FISH** Cutthroat trout. **FLOWER** Yucca. **FOSSIL** *Coelphysis* dinosaur. **GEM** Turquoise. **SONGS** "O, Fair New Mexico," "Así es Nuevo Mejico." **TREE** Piñon.**VEGETABLES** Frijole, chili.
**Land** **TOTAL AREA** 121,593 sq. mi. (5th), incl. 258 sq. mi. inland water. **BORDERS** Colo., Okla., Tex., Chihuahua, Ariz. **RIVERS** Gila, Pecos, Rio Grande, Zuni. **LAKES** Conchas Res., Eagle Nest, Elephant Butte Res., Navajo Res., Ute Res. **MOUNTAINS** Chuska, Guadalupe, Sacramento, San Andres, Sangre de Cristo. **OTHER NOTABLE FEATURES** Carlsbad Caverns, Continental Divide, Staked Plain.
**Elected officials** Gov. Bruce King (D, term exp. 1995). Lt. Gov. Casey Luna (D). Sec. State Stephanie Gonzales (D). Atty. Gen. Tom Udall (D).
**People** (1990) 1,515,069 (37th). **RACE/NATIONAL ORIGIN** (1990): White 75.6%. Black 2.0%. Indian 8.9%. Asian 0.9%. Other 12.6%. Hispanic 38.2%.
**Cities** (1990) Albuquerque 384,736. Las Cruces

62,126. Santa Fe 55,859. Roswell 44,654. Farmington 33,997. Rio Rancho 32,505. Clovis 30,954. Hobbs 29,115. Alamogordo 27,596. Carlsbad 24,952.
**Business** **GROSS STATE PRODUCT** (GSP, 1986) $23.6 bil. (37th). **SECTORS OF GSP:** Farms 1.90%. Agricultural services, forestry, & fisheries 0.27%. Mining 13.48%. Construction 6.68%. Manufacturing 7.97%. Transportation & public utilities 10.29%. Wholesale 4.06%. Retail 9.38%. Finance, insurance, & real estate 14.36%. Services 14.84%. Federal government 3.98%. Federal military 2.49%. State & local government 10.31%. **FORTUNE** 500 **COMPANIES** (1990): 0.
**Famous natives** William ("Billy the Kid") Bonney (b. N.Y.), outlaw. Peter Hurd, artist. Archbishop Jean Baptiste Lamy (b. France), missionary. Georgia O'Keeffe (b. Wis.), artist. Popé, Tewa Pueblo chief.
**Noteworthy places** Aztec Ruins Natl. Monument. Bandelier Natl. Monument. Capulin Mt. Natl. Monument. Carlsbad Caverns Natl. Park. Chaco Culture Natl. Hist. Park. El Morro Natl. Monument. Ft. Union Natl. Monument. Gila Cliff Dwellings Natl. Monument. Museum of New Mexico, Santa Fe. Pecos Mission. Salinas Mission. Santa Fe Opera. Wheelwright Museum of the American Indian, Santa Fe. White Sands Natl. Monument.
**Memorable events** Marcos de Niza enters Zuni country 1539. Juan de Oñate establishes first Spanish settlement on Rio Grande near Española 1598. Santa Fe founded; becomes capital of New Mexico 1710. Santa Fe Trail from Independence, Missouri, completed; Mexico secedes from Spain 1821. Manuel Armijo suppresses revolt against Mexican rule (1837); defeats invasion from Republic of Texas (1841). Land annexed by U.S. after Mexican-American War 1848. Organized as territory with Arizona and part of Colorado 1850. Lincoln County War pits cattlemen against merchants 1878–81. Statehood; 17 killed in raid by Pancho Villa 1912. Los Alamos selected as first research and development facility for nuclear weapons 1942. First atom bomb exploded at Alamagordo Air Base 1945.
**Tourist information** 1–800–545–2040 or 1–505–827–0291.

## New York

New York's greatest and most inviting asset has always been its strategic location and long arteries into the hinterland. New York Bay is one of the great natural harbors of the world, and the broad Hudson River is one of the most fortunately placed. After the opening of the Erie Canal between the Hudson and Lake Erie in 1825, New York City became the trading center for the Midwest as well as the Hudson Valley and the Atlantic Coast. Buffalo also experienced a boom, becoming a major Great Lakes industrial port. New York is still the first state in number of manufacturing establishments and employees. Wall Street alone employs half a million people.

Although New York's population grew by nearly half a million people between 1980 and

1990, its relatively slow rate of growth resulted in a loss of three congressional seats—an indication of the change in the state's political clout. As its place among the 50 states has fallen by some measures, New York City's worldwide importance in business, culture, and communications has risen.

NAME For Duke of York, later James II, of England. NICKNAME Empire State. CAPITAL Albany. ENTERED UNION 26 July, 1788 (11th). MOTTO *Excelsior* (Higher).

**Emblems** ANIMAL Beaver. BEVERAGE Milk. BIRD Bluebird. FISH Brook or speckled trout. FLOWER Rose. FOSSIL Prehistoric crab *(Eurypterus remipes)*. FRUIT Apple. GEM Garnet. SONG "I Love New York." TREE Sugar maple.

**Land** TOTAL AREA 49,108 sq. mi. (30th), incl. 1,731 sq. mi. inland water. BORDERS Lake Ontario, Ontario, Quebec, Vt., Mass., Conn., Atlantic Ocean, N.J., Pa., Lake Erie. RIVERS Allegheny, Delaware, Genesee, Hudson, Mohawk, New York State Barge Canal, Niagara, St. Lawrence, Susquehanna. LAKES Cayuga, Champlain, Chautauqua, Erie, George, Oneida, Ontario, Seneca. MOUNTAINS Adirondack (Mt. Marcy 5,344 ft.), Allegheny, Berkshire Hills, Catskill, Kittatinny, Ramapo. OTHER NOTABLE FEATURES Hudson Valley, Mohawk Valley, Niagara Falls, Palisades, Thousand Islands.

**Elected officials** Gov. Mario M. Cuomo (D, term exp. 1992). Lt. Gov. Stan Lundine (D). Atty. Gen. Robert Abrams (D).

**People** (1990) 17,990,455 (2d). RACE/NATIONAL ORIGIN (1990): White 74.4%. Black 15.9%. Indian 0.3%. Asian 3.9%. Other 5.5%. Hispanic 12.3%.

**Cities** (1990) New York 7,322,564. Buffalo 328,123. Rochester 231,636. Yonkers 188,082. Syracuse 163,860. Albany 101,082. Utica 68,637. New Rochelle 67,265. Mount Vernon 67,153. Schenectady 65,566.

**Business** GROSS STATE PRODUCT (GSP, 1986) $362.7 bil. (2d). SECTORS OF GSP: Farms 0.41%. Agricultural services, forestry, & fisheries 0.18%. Mining 0.14%. Construction 4.11%. Manufacturing 16.51%. Transportation & public utilities 9.18%. Wholesale 8.44%. Retail 8.03%. Finance, insurance, & real estate 22.17%. Services 21.10%. Federal government 1.42%. Federal military 0.30%. State & local government 9.01%. *FORTUNE* 500 COMPANIES (1990): 59: incl. Avon Products, Bristol-Meyers Squibb, Colgate-Palmolive, Coltec Industries, Dow Jones, Eastman Kodak, Grumman, IBM, International Paper, McGraw-Hill, New York Times, Pepsico, Pfizer, Philip Morris, Revlon Group, R.J.R. Nabisco Holdings, Texaco.

**Famous natives** Woody Allen, director. John Jacob Astor (b. Germany), merchant. Humphrey Bogart, actor. George Burns, actor. Aaron Copland, composer. Agnes De Mille, choreographer. George Eastman, camera inventor. Millard Fillmore, U.S. president. Lou Gehrig, baseball player. George Gershwin, composer. Julia Ward Howe, reformer. Washington Irving, author. Henry James, author. Vince Lombardi, football coach. Groucho Marx, comedian. Herman Melville, author. Ogden Nash, poet/humorist. Eugene O'Neill, playwright. Otetiani

(Red Jacket), Seneca chief. Channing E. Phillips, minister/reformer. John D. Rockefeller, industrialist. Norman Rockwell, illustrator. Richard Rodgers, composer. Franklin Delano Roosevelt, U.S. president. Theodore Roosevelt, U.S. president. Jonas Salk, physician. St. Elizabeth Ann Seton. Elizabeth Cady Stanton, suffragette. James Johnson Sweeney, art critic. Martin Van Buren, U.S. president. Mae West, actress. E.B. White, author. Walt Whitman, poet.

**Noteworthy places** Albright-Knox Gallery of American Art, Buffalo. American Merchant Marine Museum, Kings Point. Baseball Hall of Fame, Cooperstown. Bear Mt. State Park. Buffalo Museum of Science. Corning Glass Center, Corning. Erie Canal Museum, Syracuse. Farmers' Museum, Cooperstown. Fenimore House, Cooperstown. Franklin D. Roosevelt Natl. Hist. Site, Hyde Park. Ft. Stanwix Natl. Monument, Rome. Ft. Ticonderoga. Hudson Valley. Mohawk Valley. Niagara Falls. Palisades Interstate Park. Saratoga Natl. Hist. Park. Vanderbilt Museum, Hyde Park. U.S. Military Academy, West Point. Women's Rights Natl. Hist. Park, Seneca Falls. NEW YORK CITY American Academy of Arts & Sciences. American Museum of Natural History. Bronx Zoo. Brooklyn Botanical Garden. Brooklyn Museum. Cathedral of St. John the Divine. Cooper-Hewitt Museum. Federal Hall. Fraunces Tavern. Frick Collection. Guggenheim Museum. Hispanic Society of America. Jewish Museum. Lincoln Center for the Performing Arts. Metropolitan Museum of Art. Museum of Modern Art. Museum of the American Indian. N.Y. Public Library. N.Y. Stock Exchange. Rockefeller Center. South Street Seaport Museum. Statue of Liberty. United Nations.

**Memorable events** Giovanni de Verrazano sails into New York Bay 1524. Samuel de Champlain sails down the St. Lawrence River 1603. Henry Hudson sails up Hudson River 1609. Dutch establish Ft. Orange (Albany) 1614. Peter Minuit buys Manhattan Island and founds colony of New Amsterdam 1625. British take New Amsterdam and name it New York 1664. Ethan Allen takes Ft. Ticonderoga 1775. George Washington inaugurated president New York City 1789. U.S. Military Academy founded West Point 1802. Erie Canal opened 1825. Statue of Liberty dedicated 1886. New York City includes Manhattan, Bronx, Queens, Brooklyn, and Staten Island 1898. President William McKinley assassinated in Buffalo 1901. UN headquarters established at New York City 1945. St. Lawrence Seaway opened 1959.

**Tourist information** 1–800–225–5697 or 1–518–474–4116.

---

# North Carolina

At the time of the Revolution, tobacco and rice plantations dominated the economy of the eastern part of the state, which in turn dominated the legislature. Last to ratify the Constitution, North Carolina was also the last southern state to secede from the Union. The Civil War cost North Carolina dearly; recon-

struction was short-lived, and blacks were effectively disenfranchised again by the turn of the century. Since World War II, the state has grown increasingly prosperous, especially in the "academic triangle" that encloses the University of North Carolina at Chapel Hill, Duke, and North Carolina State. The traditional industries of textiles, furniture, and tobacco still lead, partly because of diversification within them. Although North Carolina benefits from the general Sunbelt boom and from an influx of foreign capital, the state is still burdened by low-skilled jobs and has the lowest industrial index in the United States.

NAME For King Charles I (Carolus is Latin for Charles). NICKNAMES Tarheel State, Old North State. CAPITAL Raleigh. ENTERED UNION Nov. 21, 1789 (12th). MOTTO *Esse quam videri* (To be rather than to seem).

**Emblems** BIRD Cardinal. FISH Channel bass. FLOWER Dogwood. INSECT Honeybee. PRECIOUS STONE Emerald. REPTILE Eastern box turtle. ROCK Granite. SHELL Scotch bonnet. SONG "The Old North State." TREE Pine.

**Land** TOTAL AREA 52, 669 sq. mi. (28th), incl. 3,826 sq. mi. inland water. BORDERS Va., Atlantic Ocean, S.C., Ga., Tenn. RIVERS Albemarle, Pee Dee, Roanoke, Yadkin. LAKES Buggs Island, High Rock, Mattamuskeet, Norman, Waccamaw. MOUNTAINS Black, Blue Ridge, Great Smoky, Unaka. OTHER NOTABLE FEATURES Great Dismal Swamp, Outer Banks, Pamlico Sound.

**Elected officials** Gov. James G. Martin (R, term exp. 1993). Lt. Gov. Jim Gardner (R). Sec. State Rufus L. Edmisten (D). Atty. Gen. Lacy H. Thornburg (D).

**People** (1990) 6,628,637 (10th). RACE/NATIONAL ORIGIN (1990): White 75.6%. Black 22.0%. Indian 1.2%. Asian 0.8%. Other 0.5%. Hispanic 1.2%.

**Cities** (1990) Charlotte 395,934. Raleigh 207,951. Greensboro 183,521. Winston-Salem 143,485. Durham 136,611. Fayetteville 75,695. High Point 69,496. Asheville 61,607. Wilmington 55,530. Gastonia 54,732.

**Business** GROSS STATE PRODUCT (GSP, 1986) $101 bil. (13th). SECTORS OF GSP: Farms 2.05%. Agricultural services, forestry, & fisheries 0.35%. Mining 0.28%. Construction 3.98%. Manufacturing 31.37%. Transportation & public utilities 8.63%. Wholesale 6.38%. Retail 10.14%. Finance, insurance, & real estate 12.66%. Services 11.74%. Federal government 1.64%. Federal military 2.78%. State & local government 8.00%. *FORTUNE* 500 COMPANIES (1990): 5: Burlington-Holdings, Cone Mills, Guilford Mills, Nucor, Standard Commercial.

**Famous natives** Virginia Dare, first English colonist born in North America (1587). Benjamin Newton Duke and James Buchanan Duke, industrialists/philanthropists. Richard J. Gatling, inventor. Billy Graham, minister. O. Henry, writer. Jesse Jackson, minister/reformer. Andrew Johnson, U.S. president. William Rufus King, politician. Meadow Lark Lemon, athlete. Dolley Madison, First Lady. Thelonius Monk, musician. Edward R. Murrow, journalist. James Knox Polk, U.S. president. Moses Waddell, Confederate general.

**Noteworthy places** Bennett Place. Blue Ridge Natl. Parkway. Cape Hatteras and Cape Lookout Natl. Seashore. Carl Sandburg home, Hendersonville. Ft. Raleigh. Great Smoky Mountains Natl. Hist. Park. Guilford Courthouse Natl. Military Park. Mint Museum, Charlotte. Moores Creek Natl. Battlefield. North Carolina Maritime Museum, Beaufort. North Carolina Museum of Art, Raleigh. Roanoke Island. Wright Brothers Natl. Memorial, Kitty Hawk.
**Memorable events** Part of Carolina grant given to eight noblemen by Charles II 1663. Culpeper's Rebellion in reaction to unfair tax collection policies 1677. Tuscarora lose war against European immigrants 1713. Proprietors sell rights to Crown; becomes royal province 1729. Mecklenburg Declaration (1775), forerunner of Declaration of Independence. Becomes first colony to sanction explicitly declaration of independence from Britain in Apr. 1776. Gen. Charles Cornwallis wins Battle of Guilford Courthouse, but British lose control of colony 1781. Ratifies Constitution 1789. Gives up claims to western territories, now part of Tennessee 1790. Establishes first state university system in U.S. 1829. Cherokees driven out of North Carolina to Oklahoma 1838. Secedes 1861. Readmitted to Union 1868. American Tobacco Company founded 1890. Wright brothers launch first successful airplane at Kitty Hawk 1903. Confrontation between Ku Klux Klan and anti-Klan demonstrators leaves five dead; 12 Klansmen charged with first-degree murder 1979.
**Tourist information** 1-800-VISITNC.

## North Dakota

The first permanent settlers in North Dakota were Scots-Canadians who settled at Pembina on the Red River near the Canadian border, and who traded primarily with Winnipeg and St. Paul. The arrival of the Northern Pacific Railway in 1872 created a surge of huge farms, many of which were wiped out by drought and harsh winters in the 1880s. There followed a huge influx of Norwegians and Germans whose influence is still very apparent today. North Dakota's economy is heavily agricultural and leads the nation in production of wheat. Farming is centered in the fertile Red River of the North Valley, with livestock throughout the rest of the state. In recent years this has been augmented by mining—North Dakota has the greatest lignite coal reserves of any state in the United States and some natural gas reserves.

NAME For northern section of Dakota territory; *dakota* is Sioux word for "allies." NICKNAMES Sioux State, Peace Garden State, Flickertail State. CAPITAL Bismarck. ENTERED UNION Nov. 2, 1889 (39th). MOTTO "Liberty and union, now and forever, one and inseparable."
**Emblems** BEVERAGE Milk. BIRD Western meadowlark. FISH Northern pike. FLOWER Wild prairie rose. GRASS Western wheatgrass. M ARCH "Spirit of North Dakota." SONG "North Dakota Hymn." STONE Teredo petrified wood. TREE American elm.

**Land** TOTAL AREA 70,703 sq. mi. (17th), incl. 1,403 sq. mi. inland water. BORDERS Saskatchewan, Manitoba, Minn., S.Dak., Mont. RIVERS Missouri, Red River of the North. LAKES Ashtabula, Devils, Oahe, Sakakawea. OTHER NOTABLE FEATURES Geographical center of North America, Missouri Plateau, Red River Valley, Rolling Drift Prairie.
**Elected officials** Gov. George A. Sinner (R, term exp. 1993). Lt. Gov. Lloyd Omdahl (D). Sec. State Jim Kusler (D). Atty. Gen. Nicholas Spaeth (D).
**People** (1990) 638,800 (47th). RACE/NATIONAL ORIGIN (1990): White 94.6%. Black 0.6%. Indian 4.1%. Asian 0.5%. Other 0.3%. Hispanic 0.7%.
**Cities** (1990) Fargo 74,111. Grand Forks 49,425. Bismarck 49,256. Minot 34,544. Dickinson 16,097. Jamestown 15,571. Mandan 15,177. Williston 13,131. West Fargo 12,287. Wahpeton 8,751.
**Business** GROSS STATE PRODUCT (GSP, 1986) $10.7 bil. (48th). SECTORS OF GSP: Farms 14.39%. Agricultural services, forestry, & fisheries 0.40%. Mining 6.33%. Construction 5.52%. Manufacturing 5.80%. Transportation & public utilities 10.53%. Wholesale 7.84%. Retail 8.32%. Finance, insurance, & real estate 16.89%. Services 12.59%. Federal government 0.08%. Federal military 3.24%. State & local government 8.24%. FORTUNE 500 COMPANIES (1990): 0.
**Famous natives** Angie Dickinson, actress. John Bernard Flannagan, sculptor. Louis L'Amour, novelist. Peggy Lee, singer. Eric Sevareid, broadcaster. Vihjalmur Stefansson (b. Canada), ethnologist. Lawrence Welk, entertainer.
**Noteworthy places** Ft. Abraham Lincoln State Park. Ft. Union Trading Post Natl. Hist. Site. International Peace Garden. Knife River Indian Villages Natl. Hist. Site. Theodore Roosevelt Natl. Park, the Badlands.
**Memorable events** Pierre Gaultier de Varennes, sieur de Vérendrye first European to visit area 1738. U.S. acquires half of territory in Louisiana Purchase 1803. Meriwether Lewis and George Rogers Clark expedition builds Ft. Mandan 1804-05. First permanent settlement at Pembina 1812. Britain cedes western half of state to U.S. 1818. Missouri River steamboats reach territory 1838. First railroad arrives 1873. Statehood 1889. First state to hold presidential primary 1912. Garrison Dam completed, forming Lake Sakakawea; gambling (blackjack) legalized 1981.
**Tourist information** 1-800-437-2077, 1-701-224-2525, or 1-800-472-2100; 1-800-537-8879 (from Canada).

## Ohio

The first settlements in Ohio were Marietta, in 1788, and Cincinnati in 1789, on the Ohio River, but significant migration into the state didn't occur until after the War of 1812. Shipping flourished in the 1820s and 1830s thanks to a network of canals connecting the Ohio and Lake Erie. Since 1959 the St. Lawrence Seaway has helped keep Ohio among the top five

exporting states. Heavy industry also flourished in the northern cities that had access to coal and iron ore from the Lake Superior region. The 1870s saw the development of a manufacturing base that later became an integral part of the automotive industry. Although Ohio's economy has traditionally been well balanced between agriculture, industry, mining, and trade, the recession of the early 1980s weakened manufacturing, triggered flight from the industrial cities, and saw a dramatic shift to a service economy.

NAME From Iroquois *oheo*, "beautiful." NICKNAME Buckeye State. CAPITAL Columbus. ENTERED UNION Mar. 1, 1803 (17th). MOTTO "With God, all things are possible."
**Emblems** BEVERAGE Tomato juice. BIRD Cardinal. FLOWER Scarlet carnation. GEM Ohio flint. INSECT Ladybug. SONG "Beautiful Ohio." TREE Buckeye.
**Land** TOTAL AREA 41,330 sq. mi. (35th), incl. 326 sq. mi. inland water. BORDERS Mich., Lake Erie, Pa., W.Va., Ky., Ind. RIVERS Cuyahoga, Maumee, Miami, Muskingum, Ohio, Sandusky, Scioto. LAKES Berlin Res., Dillon Res., Erie, Mosquito Res., St. Mary's.
**Elected officials** Gov. George Voinovich (D, term exp. 1995). Lt. Gov. Mike DeWine (R). Sec. State Bob Taft (R). Atty. Gen. Lee Fisher (D).
**People** (1990) 10,847,115 (7th). RACE/NATIONAL ORIGIN (1990): White 87.8%. Black 10.6%. Indian 0.2%. Asian 0.8%. Other 0.5%. Hispanic 1.3%.
**Cities** (1990) Columbus 632,910. Cleveland 505,616. Cincinnati 364,040. Toledo 332,943. Akron 223,019. Dayton 182,044. Youngstown 95,732. Parma 87,876. Canton 84,161. Lorain 71,245.
**Business** GROSS STATE PRODUCT (GSP, 1986) $176.1 bil. (7th). SECTORS OF GSP: Farms 1.08%. Agricultural services, forestry, & fisheries 0.25%. Mining 0.82%. Construction 3.16%. Manufacturing 29.20%. Transportation & public utilities 9.26%. Wholesale 6.50%. Retail 9.80%. Finance, insurance, & real estate 15.37%. Services 15.18%. Federal government 1.72%. Federal military 0.41%. State & local government 7.26%. FORTUNE 500 COMPANIES (1990): 37: incl. American Greetings, Dana, Eaton, Goodyear Tire & Rubber, Mead, NCR, Penn Central, Procter & Gamble, Rubbermaid, Sherwin-Williams, TRW.
**Famous natives** Sherwood Anderson, writer. Neil Armstrong, astronaut. George Bellows, artist. Ambrose Bierce, author. George Armstrong Custer, army officer. Paul Laurence Dunbar, poet. Thomas A. Edison, inventor. James A. Garfield, U.S. president. John Glenn, astronaut/politician. Ulysses S. Grant, U.S. president. Zane Grey, author. Warren G. Harding, U.S. president. Benjamin Harrison, U.S. president. Rutherford B. Hayes, U.S. president. Bob Hope, entertainer. William McKinley, U.S. president. Annie Oakley, markswoman. Ransom Eli Olds, carmaker. Eddie Rickenbacker, pilot. William Sherman, army officer. William Howard Taft, U.S. president/chief justice. Art Tatum, pianist. Tecumseh, Shawnee chief. James Thurber, humorist. Orville Wright, airplane inventor.

**Noteworthy places** Air Force Museum, Dayton. Cleveland Museum of Art. Cleveland Museum of Natural History. Columbus Museum of Art. Great Lakes Historical Society Museum, Vermilion. Mound City Group Natl. Monument, Chillicothe. Neil Armstrong Air and Space Museum, Wapakoneta. Ohio River Museum, Marietta. Pro Football Hall of Fame, Canton. Toledo Museum of Art.

**Memorable events** Hopewell Mound-Builders present throughout state prior to arrival of Miamis, Shawnees, Wyandots, and Delawares. Conflicting claims by France, Virginia, Connecticut, and New York 1609–1786. René-Roger Cavelier de La Salle visits region 1669–70. To Britain 1763. To U.S. after 1783. Becomes part of Northwest Territory 1787. First settlement at Marietta 1788. Gen. "Mad" Anthony Wayne beats Tecumseh at Battle of Fallen Timbers 1794. Enters Union 1803. Harrison beats Tecumseh at Battle of Tippecanoe 1811. Oliver Hazard Perry beats British fleet at Battle of Put-in-Bay 1813. Ohio and Erie Canal completed 1832. Dayton flood kills 400 in Miami River Valley; damage put at $100 million 1913. Carl B. Stokes elected mayor of Cleveland, first black mayor of major U.S. city 1967. Four students protesting Vietnam War killed by National Guard at Kent State University 1970.

**Tourist information** 1–800–BUCKEYE.

## Oklahoma

French trappers entered the region of Oklahoma in the 1700s. In 1830 the land was designated the Indian Country, set aside for members of the Cherokees, Chickasaw, Choctaw, Creek, and Seminole deported from the southeast by the Indian Removal Act of 1830. These "Five Civilized Tribes," among others, fared well until the Civil War. They supported the Confederacy (some were actually slaveholders), and in 1868 Col. George Armstrong Custer led a massacre of Cheyenne at the Battle of the Washita. Twenty years later the government abrogated its treaty commitments and opened the territory to settlement. Today the state has a distinctly southern character. The region bordering the Red River is known as "Little Dixie," and as many as two-thirds of all Oklahomans consider themselves born-again Christians.

Oklahoma has a diversified economy. The state led the country in oil and gas production through the 1920s. Agriculture was hit heavily by the dust bowl of the 1930s, and thousands of "Okies" fled west. While agriculture and petroleum are still vital to the economy, manufacturing is increasingly important. The state is crossed by two of the country's longest rivers. The Arkansas links Catoosa (near Tulsa) to the Gulf of Mexico and the Mississippi River system; but the Red River is not navigable in Oklahoma, and dissolved salts make it useless for agriculture, industry, or residential purposes.

NAME From Choctaw *okla humma*, "land of the red people." NICKNAME Sooner State. CAPITAL Oklahoma City. ENTERED UNION Nov. 16, 1907 (46th). MOTTO *Labor omnia vincit* (Work overcomes all obstacles).

**Emblems** ANIMAL American buffalo. BIRD Scissor-tailed flycatcher. COLORS Green and white. FISH White bass. FLORAL EMBLEM Mistletoe. GRASS Indian grass. POEM "Howdy Folks." REPTILE Collared lizard (mountain boomer). SONG "Oklahoma!" STONE Barite rose (rose rock). TREE Redbud. WALTZ "Oklahoma Wind."

**Land** TOTAL AREA 69,956 sq. mi. (18th), incl. 1,301 sq. mi. inland water. BORDERS Kans., Mo., Ark., Tex., N.Mex., Colo. RIVERS Arkansas, Canadian, Cimarron, Red. LAKES Canton, Lake o' the Cherokees, Oologah, Texoma. OTHER NOTABLE FEATURES Ouachita Mts., Ozark Plateau, Staked Plain, Wichita Mts.

**Elected officials** Gov. Dave Walters (D, term exp. 1995). Lt. Gov. Jack Mildren (D). Atty. Gen. Robert Henry (D).

**People** (1990) 3,145,585 (28th). RACE/NATIONAL ORIGIN (1990): White 82.1%. Black 7.4%. Indian 8.0%. Asian 1.1%. Other 1.3%. Hispanic 2.7%.

**Cities** (1990) Oklahoma City 444,719. Tulsa 367,302. Lawton 80,561. Norman 80,071. Broken Arrow 58,043. Edmond 52,315. Midwest City 52,267. Enid 45,309. Moore 40,318. Muskogee 37,708.

**Business** GROSS STATE PRODUCT (GSP, 1986) $49.8 bil. (27th). SECTORS OF GSP: Farms 3.39%. Agricultural services, forestry, & fisheries 0.27%. Mining 10.40%. Construction 4.28%. Manufacturing 14.27%. Transportation & public utilities 10.52%. Wholesale 6.12%. Retail 9.87%. Finance, insurance, & real estate 13.54%. Services 13.07%. Federal government 3.68%. Federal military 2.04%. State & local government 8.54%. *FORTUNE* 500 COMPANIES (1990): 3: Kerr-McGee, Mapco, Phillips Petroleum.

**Famous natives** Ralph Ellison, author. Woody Guthrie, reformer/musician. Patrick J. Hurley, diplomat. Karl Jansky, electrical engineer. Mickey Mantle, baseball player. Wiley Post, aviator. Tony Randall, actor. Oral Roberts, evangelist. Will Rogers, humorist. Maria Tallchief, ballerina. Jim Thorpe, athlete.

**Noteworthy places** American Indian Hall of Fame, Anadarko. Chisholm Trail Museum, Kingfisher. Ft. Gibson Stockade, Muskogee. Natl. Cowboy Hall of Fame, Oklahoma City. Ouachita Natl. Forest. Pioneer Woman Museum, Ponca City. Will Rogers Memorial, Claremore.

**Memorable events** Francisco Vásquez de Coronado expedition in territory 1541. Except for panhandle, becomes part of Louisiana purchase 1803. Region made Indian Territory (not organized) in 1830 and becomes home of "Five Civilized Tribes"—Cherokee, Choctaw, Chickasaw, Creek, and Seminole— after they left the southeast on Trail of Tears 1828–46. U.S. acquires panhandle with annexation of Texas 1845. Territory opened to homesteaders 1889. Commercial oil well at Bartlesville 1897. Indian Territory and Oklahoma Territory merged and granted statehood 1907. Gov. John C. Walton impeached after declaring martial law to quell violence 1923. McClellan-Kerr Arkansas River Navigation System links Oklahoma to Mississippi, making Catoosa (Tulsa) major

inland port 1971.

**Tourist information** 1–800–652–6552 or 1–800–654–8240.

## Oregon

Although the Lewis and Clark expedition reached the mouth of the Columbia River in 1805, interest in the area was kindled by the Hudson's Bay Company and later by Jason Lee, a Methodist minister who settled near Salem in 1834. After the decline of the fur trade, lumbering became the most important industry in Oregon. Though lumbering and related industries are still leading employers—the state is the leading grower of Christmas trees—Oregon has benefited from the arrival of smaller computer and electronics firms leaving California in search of a more favorable business climate. Traditionally progressive, it is one of most active states in the environmental protection movement. Only one-third of the population is affiliated with an organized religion.

NAME Unknown origin, first applied to Columbia River. NICKNAME Beaver State. CAPITAL Salem. ENTERED UNION Feb. 14, 1859 (33d). MOTTO "The Union." POET LAUREATE William E. Stafford.

**Emblems** ANIMAL Beaver. BIRD Western meadowlark. DANCE Square dance. FISH Chinook salmon. FLOWER Oregon grape. INSECT Swallowtail butterfly. SONG "Oregon, My Oregon." STONE Thunderegg. TREE Douglas fir.

**Land** TOTAL AREA 97,073 sq. mi. (10th), incl. 889 sq. mi. inland water. BORDERS Wash., Idaho, Nev., Calif., Pacific Ocean. RIVERS Columbia, Snake, Willamette. MOUNTAINS Cascade Range, Coast Range, Klamath. OTHER NOTABLE FEATURES Willamette Valley.

**Elected officials** Gov. Barbara Roberts (D, term exp. 1995). Sec. State Phil Keisling (D). Atty. Gen. Dave Frohnmayer (R).

**People** (1990) 2,842,321 (29th). RACE/NATIONAL ORIGIN (1990): White 92.8%. Black 1.6%. Indian 1.4%. Asian 2.4%. Other 1.8%. Hispanic 4.0%.

**Cities** (1990) Portland 437,319. Eugene 112,669. Salem 107,786. Gresham 68,235. Beaverton 53,310. Medford 46,951. Corvallis 44,757. Springfield 44,683. Hillsboro 37,520. Lake Oswego 30,576.

**Business** GROSS STATE PRODUCT (GSP, 1986) $41.3 bil. (31st). SECTORS OF GSP: Farms 3.04%. Agricultural services, forestry, & fisheries 0.91%. Mining 0.14%. Construction 3.28%. Manufacturing 19.82%. Transportation & public utilities 10.03%. Wholesale 7.78%. Retail 9.48%. Finance, insurance, & real estate 17.84%. Services 15.46%. Federal government 2.52%. Federal military 0.39%. State & local government 9.31%. *FORTUNE* 500 COMPANIES (1990): 5: Louisiana Pacific, Nerco, Pope & Talbot, Tektronix, Willamette Industries.

**Famous natives** In-mut-too-yah-lat-lat (Joseph), Nez Percé chief. Edwin Markham, poet. Dr. John McLoughlin, fur trader ("Father of Oregon"). Linus Pauling, chemist. John Reed, author. William Simon U'Ren (b. Wis.), lawyer/reformer.

**Noteworthy places** Bonneville Dam, Columbia

River. Columbia River Gorge. Columbia River Museum, Astoria. Crater Lakes Natl. Park. Ft. Clatsop Natl. Monument. Hells Canyon. High Desert Museum, Bend. John Day Fossil Beds Natl. Monument. Mt. Hood. Oregon Caves Natl. Monument. Oregon Dunes Natl. Recreation Area. Point Perpetua. Timberline Lodge.

**Memorable events** Sir Francis Drake turns away from fogbound coast of Pacific Northwest 1578. Capt. James Cook visits 1778. Mouth of Columbia River explored by Capt. Robert Gray, who claims region for U.S. 1792. Meriwether Lewis and George Rogers Clark expedition arrives at mouth of Columbia 1805. Claims to Oregon Territory, from California border to Alaska and east to Montana and Wyoming, relinquished by Spain (1819), Russia (1825), and Britain (1846). First settlers arrive Willamette Valley 1843. Organized as territory 1848. Statehood 1859. Railroad arrives 1883. Bonneville Dam completed 1937. Following severe rain and snow that claim 40 lives, Oregon declared disaster area 1964. First state to enact "bottle law" 1972. Snake River opened to navigation, linking Astoria to Lewiston, Idaho 1975.

**Tourist information** 1-800-547-7842 or 1-800-543-8838.

## Pennsylvania, Commonwealth of

William Penn and his Quakers encouraged settlement and religious tolerance, and Pennsylvania was the first state to abolish slavery. In the late colonial period, Philadelphia was the cultural capital of the colonies. The first Continental Congress convened there in 1774, and it was for some 15 years the U.S. capital. With access to both the Great Lakes and to the Atlantic, Pennsylvanians took a lead in opening up the Midwest. Its resources include large coal deposits—which contribute to its ironmaking capabilities—lumber, textiles, and leather. Leadership in these sectors lasted well into the 20th century, when Pennsylvania lost ground to Sunbelt states. As in many states, there has been growth in tourist and service industries, though machinery production and trade continue to expand significantly.

NAME For Adm. William Penn, father of William Penn, founder of commonwealth. NICKNAME Keystone State. CAPITAL Harrisburg. ENTERED UNION Dec. 12, 1787 (2d). MOTTO "Virtue, liberty and independence."

**Emblems** ANIMAL White-tailed deer. BEAUTIFICATION AND CONSERVATION PLANT Penngift crown vetch. BEVERAGE Milk. BIRD Ruffed grouse. DOG Great dane. FISH Brook trout. FLOWER Mountain laurel. INSECT Firefly. SONG "Pennsylvania." TREE Hemlock.

**Land** TOTAL AREA 45,308 sq. mi. (33d), incl. 420 sq. mi. inland water. BORDERS N.Y., N.J., Del., Md., W.Va., Ohio, Lake Erie. RIVERS Allegheny, Delaware, Juniata, Monongahela, Ohio, Schuylkill, Susquehanna. LAKES Allegheny Res., Erie, Pymatuning Res., Shenango Res. MOUNTAINS Allegheny, Kittatinny, Laurel Hills, Pocono.

**Elected officials** Gov. Robert P. Casey (D, term exp. 1995). Lt. Gov. Mark A. Singel (D). Atty. Gen. Ernest D. Preate, Jr. (R).

**People** (1990) 11,881,643 (5th). RACE/NATIONAL ORIGIN (1990): White 88.5%. Black 9.2%. Indian 0.1%. Asian 1.2%. Other 1.0%. Hispanic 2.0%.

**Cities** (1990) Philadelphia 1,585,577. Pittsburgh 369,879. Erie 108,718. Allentown 105,090. Scranton 81,805. Reading 78,380. Bethlehem 71,428. Lancaster 55,551. Harrisburg 52,376. Altoona 51,881.

**Business** GROSS STATE PRODUCT (GSP, 1986) $183.6 bil. (5th). SECTORS OF GSP: Farms 1.03%. Agricultural services, forestry, & fisheries 0.28%. Mining 1.02%. Construction 4.06%. Manufacturing 22.14%. Transportation & public utilities 10.50%. Wholesale 6.70%. Retail 9.51%. Finance, insurance, & real estate 16.23%. Services 18.49%. Federal government 2.52%. Federal military 0.49%. State & local government 7.02%. FORTUNE 500 COMPANIES (1990): 36: incl. Alcoa, Bethlehem Steel, Hershey Foods, H.J. Heinz, PPG Industries, Quaker State, Scott Paper, Sun, Unisys, USX, Westinghouse Electric.

**Famous natives** Louisa May Alcott, author. Maxwell Anderson, playwright. James Buchanan, U.S. president. Alexander Calder, sculptor. Andrew Carnegie (b. Scotland), industrialist/philanthropist. Mary Cassatt, painter. Wilt Chamberlain, basketball player. Bill Cosby, comedian/philanthropist. Stephen Foster, songwriter. Benjamin Franklin (b. Mass.), inventor/statesman. Robert Fulton, inventor. Milton S. Hershey, chocolatier. George C. Marshall, statesman. Andrew W. Mellon, financier/philanthropist. Robert E. Peary, explorer. Betsy Ross, patriot. Andy Warhol, artist. Johnny Weissmuller, swimmer/actor. Benjamin West, painter.

**Noteworthy places** Academy of Natural Sciences, Philadelphia. Carnegie Institute, Pittsburgh. Delaware Water Gap Natl. Recreation Area. Ft. Necessity Natl. Battlefield. Franklin Institute, Philadelphia. Gettysburg Battlefield. Hugh Moore Hist. Park and Museums, Easton. Independence Natl. Hist. Park, Philadelphia. Liberty Bell, Carpenters Hall, Philadelphia. Pennsylvania Academy of Fine Arts, Philadelphia. Pennsylvania Dutch Country. Philadelphia Museum of Art. Pine Creek Gorge. Valley Forge Natl. Hist. Park.

**Memorable events** Cornelis Jacobssen sails into Delaware Bay 1614. Swedes settle at Tinicum Island 1643. Charles II grants proprietary charter to William Penn 1681. First U.S. hospital established, in Philadelphia, 1751. Mason-Dixon Line establishes southern boundary of state 1763–67—later, boundary between slave and nonslave states. Declaration of Independence (1776) and Constitution (1787) signed in Philadelphia. Becomes first state to abolish slavery 1780. Bank of North America becomes first bank chartered in U.S. 1781. Philadelphia capital of U.S. 1790-1800. First iron furnace in U.S. 1792. Battle of Gettysburg turning point in Civil War; Lincoln's Gettysburg Address 1863. Centennial Exhibition at Philadelphia 1876. Johnstown flood—worst

in U.S. history—kills 2,200 people 1889. Pinkerton detectives kill 9 strikers at Homestead steel works near Pittsburgh 1892. Twenty coal miners killed during strike for eight-hour day and other concessions 1897. More than 500 injured during three-day race riot in Philadelphia 1964. Partial meltdown at Three Mile Island forces closure of nuclear reactor 1979. Storage tank spills 713,000 gallons diesel fuel into Monongahela River, disrupting water supplies in Pennsylvania, West Virginia, and Ohio 1988.

**Tourist information** 1-800-VISITPA.

## Rhode Island and Providence Plantations

Giovanni de Verrazano was the first European to record visiting the area of Narragansett Bay, the prominent inlet that almost splits the eastern third of the state from the rest. The first settlers were followers of Roger Williams, who left the restrictive religious atmosphere of the Puritan Massachusetts Bay Colony to found Providence in 1636. Rhode Island is the site of the first U.S. Baptist church, at Providence, and at Newport the first Quaker meetinghouse and the first synagogue. It was the last of the 13 original colonies to ratify the Constitution, the centralized federalism of which many Rhode Islanders objected to. The development of 19th-century Rhode Island was influenced by immigration and the Industrial Revolution; the state's leading manufacturers are still silver, jewelry, and textiles.

NAME For Rhode Island in Narragansett Bay, named in turn for Mediterranean island of Rhodes. NICKNAMES Ocean State, Little Rhody. CAPITAL Providence. ENTERED UNION May 29, 1790 (13th). MOTTO "Hope."

**Emblems** BIRD Rhode Island red. FLOWER Violet. MINERAL Bowenite. ROCK Cumberlandite. SONG "Rhode Island." TREE Red maple.

**Land** TOTAL AREA 1,212 sq. mi. (50th), incl. 157 sq. mi. inland water. BORDERS Mass., Atlantic Ocean, Conn. RIVERS Blackstone, Pawcatuck, Providence, Sakonnet. OTHER NOTABLE FEATURES Block Island, Narragansett Bay, Rhode Island (Aquidneck Island).

**Elected officials** Gov. Bruce G. Sunlun (D, term exp. 1993). Lt. Gov. Roger N. Begin (D). Sec. State Kathleen S. Connell (D). Atty. Gen. James E. O'Neal (D).

**People** (1990) 1,003,464 (43d). RACE/NATIONAL ORIGIN (1990): White 91.4%. Black 3.9%. Indian 0.4%. Asian 1.8%. Other 2.5%. Hispanic 4.6%.

**Cities** (1990) Providence 160,728. Warwick 85,427. Cranston 76,060. Pawtucket 72,644. East Providence 50,380. Woonsocket 43,877. Newport 28,227. Central Falls 17,637.

**Business** GROSS STATE PRODUCT (GSP, 1986) $15.2 bil. (43d). SECTORS OF GSP: Farms 0.42%. Agricultural services, forestry, & fisheries 0.70%. Mining 0.06%. Construction 2.65%. Manufacturing 24.31%. Transportation & public utilities 6.76%. Wholesale 6.39%. Retail 10.64%. Finance, insurance, & real estate 17.86%. Services 18.22%. Federal government 2.19%. Federal military 1.75%.

State & local government 8.06%. *FORTUNE* 500 COMPANIES (1990): 3: Hasbro, Nortek, Textron.
**Famous natives** George M. Cohan, actor/producer. Nathanael Greene, army officer. Metacomet (King Philip), Wampanoag chief. Oliver H. Perry and Matthew C. Perry, naval officers. Gilbert Stuart, portraitist.
**Noteworthy places** John Carter Brown Library, Providence. First Baptist church in North America (1638), Providence. Ft. Adams State Park, Newport. Nathanael Greene homestead, Coventry. Hoffenreffer Museum of Anthropology, Bristol. Museum of Art of the Rhode Island School of Design, Providence. Naval War College Museum, Newport. Newport mansions. Museum of Yachting, Newport. Tennis Hall of Fame, Newport. Trouro Synagogue (1763, oldest extant in North America), Newport.
**Memorable events** Roger Williams, expelled from Massachusetts Bay Colony, settles in Providence 1636. Other religious exiles settle in Portsmouth (1638), Newport (1639), and Warwick (1642). King Philip's War 1675-76. First Quaker meetinghouse in North America founded 1699. First colony to renounce allegiance to Britain 1776. Last colony to ratify Constitution 1790. Dorr's Rebellion achieves liberalization of state constitution, which had remained unchanged since 1663, 1842. America's Cup race held in Newport for first time 1930. Newport Bridge across Narragansett Bay completed 1969. *Australia II* first non-U.S. boat to win America's Cup in 132 years 1983.
**Tourist information** 1-401-277-2601 or 1-800-556-2484.

## South Carolina

South Carolina's early economy was based on rice—its plantations worked by slaves—though tobacco later played a major role. As was true in North Carolina, many settlers made their way into the back country where they eked out a living as tenant farmers. During the Revolution, Ft. Charlotte was the first British installation to fall to Colonial troops, and at the outbreak of the Civil War, Ft. Sumter was the first Union installation to fall to Confederate forces. While agriculture remained a staple of the state's economy through the close of the 19th century, textile manufacture took over in the early 20th century. The postwar era has seen the rapid expansion of the chemical and paper industries, as well as large-scale development of the Atlantic Coast ports of Charleston, Georgetown, and Port Royal. In September 1989, Hurricane Hugo took 24 lives and caused $6 billion in property damage. According to some officials, relief efforts were hampered by widespread illiteracy, a crisis worsened by—or due to—the doubling of the high school dropout rate between 1986 and 1990.

NAME For King Charles II (Carolus is Latin for Charles). NICKNAME Palmetto State. CAPITAL Columbia. ENTERED UNION May 23, 1788 (8th). MOTTO *Animis opibusque parati* (Prepared in mind and deed); *Dum spiro spero* (While I breathe I hope). POET LAUREATE Helen von Kolnitz Hyer.
**Emblems** ANIMAL White-tailed deer. BEVERAGE Milk. BIRD Carolina wren. DANCE Shag. DOG Boykin spaniel. FISH Striped bass. FLOWER Yellow jessamine. FRUIT Peach. SHELL Lettered olive. SONG "Carolina." STONE Blue granite. TREE Palmetto. WILD GAME BIRD Wild turkey.
**Land** TOTAL AREA 31,113 sq. mi. (40th), incl. 910 sq. mi. inland water. BORDERS N.C., Atlantic Ocean, Ga. RIVERS Congaree, Edisto, Pee Dee, Savannah, Tugalos, Wateree. LAKES Greenwood, Hartwell, Keowee, Marion, Murray, Santee Res., Wylie. OTHER NOTABLE FEATURES Blue Ridge Mts., Congaree Swamp, Sea Islands.
**Elected officials** Gov. Carroll A. Campbell, Jr. (R, term exp. 1995). Lt. Gov. Nick A. Theodore (D). Sec. State Jim Miles (R). Atty. Gen. T. Travis Medlock (D).
**People** (1990) 3,386,703 (25th). RACE/NATIONAL ORIGIN (1990): White 69.0%. Black 29.8%. Indian 0.2%. Asian 0.6%. Other 0.3%. Hispanic 0.9%.
**Cities** (1990) Columbia 98,052. Charleston 80,414. North Charleston 70,218. Greenville 58,282. Spartanburg 43,467. Sumter 41,943. Rock Hill 41,643. Mount Pleasant Town 30,108. Florence 29,813. Anderson 26,184.
**Business** GROSS STATE PRODUCT (GSP, 1986) $44.7 bil. (28th). SECTORS OF GSP: Farms 0.97%. Agricultural services, forestry, & fisheries 0.40%. Mining 0.23%. Construction 4.00%. Manufacturing 26.72%. Transportation & public utilities 8.45%. Wholesale 5.80%. Retail 1.10%. Finance, insurance, & real estate 12.94%. Services 12.46%. Federal government 2.52%. Federal military 4.42%. State & local government 9.99%. *FORTUNE* 500 COMPANIES (1990): 3: JPS Textile Group, Sonoco Products, Springs Industries.
**Famous natives** James F. Byrnes, politician/jurist. John C. Calhoun, politician. Dizzy Gillespie, musician. Althea Gibson, athlete. DuBose Heyward, author. Andrew Jackson, U.S. president. Eartha Kitt, singer. James Longstreet, army officer. Francis Marion, army officer/politician. Charles C. Pinckney and Thomas Pinckney, diplomats. Edward Rutledge and John Rutledge, politicians. Strom Thurmond, politician.
**Noteworthy places** Charleston Museum (1773, oldest in U.S.). Congaree Swamp Natl. Monument. Cowpens Natl. Battlefield. Ft. Moultrie, Ft. Johnson, and Ft. Sumter Natl. Monument, Charleston. Hilton Head Island. Kings Mountain Natl. Military Park. Ninety-Six Natl. Hist. Site, Greenwood. Patriots Point Maritime Museum, Charleston. Sea Islands. Spoleto Music Festival, Charleston.
**Memorable events** Spanish visit 1521. French Huguenots at Port Royal 1562. Included in Carolina grant by Charles II 1663. Charleston founded 1680. Becomes royal province 1729. Ratifies Constitution 1787. *Best Friend of Charleston*, first American steam locomotive built for passenger use 1833. First state to secede from Union Dec. 20, 1860. Confederate forces attack Ft. Sumter Apr. 12, 1861. Secession repealed 1865. Readmitted to Union 1868. Cyclone kills 1,000 in Savannah, Ga., and Charleston 1893. Savannah River nuclear plant begins production near Aiken 1951; closed for safety reasons 1988.
**Tourist information** 1-803-734-0122.

## South Dakota

The United States did not organize the Dakota Territory until 1861, and even then interest in the region was scant until gold was discovered in 1874. The majority of those who remained after the gold rush turned to cattle ranching, which was a mainstay of the economy through the first half of the 20th century. A manufacturing base was developed after four major dams were built on the Missouri River in the 1930s. They provided hydroelectric power and increased irrigation along the Missouri, which cuts the state in half. Concerned especially over the abrogation of 19th-century treaties, the American Indian Movement (AIM) took over the courthouse at Wounded Knee for 10 weeks in 1973. While U.S. courts have found in favor of the Sioux in several cases concerning the earlier treaties, many maintain that the settlements are insufficient, and the disparity in living conditions between whites and Native Americans remains pronounced.

NAME For southern section of Dakota territory; *dakota* is Sioux word for "allies." NICKNAMES Coyote State, Sunshine State. CAPITAL Pierre. ENTERED UNION Nov. 2, 1889 (40th). MOTTO "Under God the people rule."
**Emblems** ANIMAL Coyote. BIRD Chinese ring-necked pheasant. FISH Walleye. FLOWER Pasque flower. GEM Fairburn agate. GRASS Western wheatgrass. INSECT Honeybee. MINERAL Rose quartz. SONG "Hail, South Dakota." TREE Black Hills spruce.
**Land** TOTAL AREA 77,116 sq. mi. (16th), incl. 1,164 sq. mi. inland water. BORDERS N.Dak., Minn., Iowa, Nebr., Wyo., Mont. RIVERS Cheyenne, James, Missouri, Moreau, White. LAKES Belle Fourche Res., Big Stone, Traverse. OTHER NOTABLE FEATURES Badlands, Black Hills (Harney Peak 7,242 ft.).
**Elected officials** Gov. George S. Mickelson (R, term exp. 1995). Lt. Gov. Walter D. Miller (R). Sec. State Joyce Hazeltine (R). Atty. Gen. Mark Barnett (R).
**People** (1990) 696,004 (45th). RACE/NATIONAL ORIGIN (1990): White 91.6%. Black 0.5%. Indian 7.3%. Asian 0.4%. Other 0.2%. Hispanic 0.8%.
**Cities** (1990) Sioux Falls 100,814. Rapid City 54,523. Aberdeen 24,927. Watertown 17,592. Brookings 16,270. Mitchell 13,798. Pierre 12,906. Yankton 12,703. Huron 12,448. Vermillion 10,034.
**Business** GROSS STATE PRODUCT (GSP, 1986) $9.8 bil. (49th). SECTORS OF GSP: Farms 15.32%. Agricultural services, forestry, & fisheries 0.56%. Mining 1.19%. Construction 3.83%. Manufacturing 9.97%. Transportation & public utilities 9.51%. Wholesale 6.27%. Retail 10.37%. Finance, insurance, & real estate 17.53%. Services 13.53%. Federal government 1.79%. Federal military 2.13%. State & local government 7.99%. *FORTUNE* 500 COMPANIES (1990): 0.

**Famous natives** Tom Brokaw, journalist. Martha ("Calamity") Jane Burk (b. Mo.) frontierswoman. Alvin Hansen, economist. Hubert H. Humphrey, politician. Ernest O. Lawrence, physicist (Nobel Prize, 1939). George McGovern, politician. Ta-sunko-witko (Crazy Horse), Oglala Sioux chief. Tatanka Iyotake (Sitting Bull), Sioux chief.

**Noteworthy places** Badlands Natl. Park. Crazy Horse State Memorial, Custer. Custer State Park. Ft. Sisseton. Geographical center of the United States. Jewel Cave Natl. Monument. Mount Rushmore Natl. Memorial. Wind Cave Natl. Park.

**Memorable events** French visit region 1742–43. Region to U.S. in Louisiana Purchase 1803. Ft. Pierre first permanent settlement 1817. Part of Dakota Territory 1861. Gold discovered in Black Hills 1874. Divided from North Dakota; statehood 1889. U.S. troops massacre Sioux at Battle of Wounded Knee 1890.

**Tourist information** 1–800–843–1930 or 1–800–952–2217.

## Tennessee

At first claimed by Virginia and later by North Carolina, Tennessee had its first great pioneer in Daniel Boone, who traversed the region in the 1760s. Political attitudes in the 18th century were shaped by the land, with the cotton and tobacco growers in the fertile western part of the state favoring slavery and the backwoods people of the eastern hills opposed to it. The Cherokees were removed to Oklahoma by the federal government in the 1830s. The state was captured by Union troops in 1862 and put under the governorship of Andrew Johnson, later a U.S. president.

Its economy was radically altered in the 1930s and 1940s by the creation of the Tennessee Valley Authority, which provided abundant energy for industry, and to a lesser extent by the location of the government's first uranium enrichment facility at Oak Ridge during World War II. The state's leading industries are textiles, food processing, and chemicals, and there is considerable lead and coal mining in the east.

**Name** For Tenase, principal village of Cherokees. **Nickname** Volunteer State. **Capital** Nashville. **Entered Union** June 1, 1796. **Motto** "Agriculture and commerce." **Slogan** Tennessee—America at its best. **Poet laureate** Richard M. ("Pek") Gunn.

**Emblems** **Animal** Raccoon. **Bird** Mockingbird. **Folk dance** Square dance. **Cultivated flower** Iris. **Gem** Tennessee pearl. **Insects** Ladybug, firefly. **Poem** "Oh Tennessee, My Tennessee." **Public school song** "My Tennessee." **Rock** Limestone agate. **Songs** "When It's Iris Time in Tennessee," "The Tennessee Waltz," "My Homeland, Tennessee," "Rocky Top." **Tree** Tulip poplar. **Wildflower** Passion flower.

**Land** **Total area** 42,144 sq. mi. (34th), incl. 989 sq. mi. inland water. **Borders** Ky., Va., N.C., Ga., Ala., Miss., Ark., Mo. **Rivers** Clinch, Cumberland, Mississippi, Tennessee. **Lakes** Boone, Center Hill, Cherokee, Dale Hollow, Douglass, J. Percy Priest, Watauga. **Other notable features** Cumberland Mts., Great Smoky Mts., Tennessee Valley, Unaka Mts.

**Elected officials** Gov. Ned Ray McWherter (D, term exp. 1995).

**People** (1990) 4,877,185 (17th). **Race/national origin** (1990): White 83.0%. Black 16.0%. Indian 0.2%. Asian 0.7%. Other 0.2%. Hispanic 0.7%.

**Cities** (1990) Memphis 610,337. Nashville-Davidson (CC) 510,784. Knoxville 165,121. Chattanooga 152,466. Clarksville 75,494. Johnson City 49,381. Jackson 48,949. Murfreesboro 44,922. Kingsport 36,365. Germantown 32,893.

**Business** **Gross state product** (GSP, 1986) $72.3 bil. (21st). **Sectors of GSP:** Farms 1.64%. Agricultural services, forestry, & fisheries 0.28%. Mining 0.49%. Construction 4.41%. Manufacturing 25.02%. Transportation & public utilities 7.76%. Wholesale 7.29%. Retail 11.32%. Finance, insurance, & real estate 14.28%. Services 15.40%. Federal government 4.06%. Federal military 0.63%. State & local government 7.44%. **Fortune** 500 companies (1990): 1: Dixie Yarns.

**Famous natives** James Agee, author. Davy Crockett, frontiersman. David Farragut, naval officer. Aretha Franklin, singer. Cordell Hull, statesman (Nobel Peace Prize, 1945). Dolly Parton, singer. Sikawyi (Sequoya), Cherokee scholar. Alvin York, soldier.

**Noteworthy places** American Museum of Science and Energy, Oak Ridge. Andrew Johnson Natl. Hist. Site, Greenville. Chickamauga and Chattanooga Natl. Military Park. Cumberland Natl. Hist. Park. Ft. Donelson Natl. Military Park. Grand Ole Opry, Nashville. Great Smoky Mountains Natl. Park. The Hermitage (Andrew Jackson home), Nashville. Lookout Mountain, Chattanooga. The Parthenon, Nashville. Shiloh Natl. Military Park, Pittsburg Landing. Stones River Natl. Battlefield, Murfreesboro.

**Memorable events** De Soto expedition passes through region 1540. French claim territory as part of Louisiana; English claim territory as part of Carolina grant 1663. French claim given up after French and Indian War 1763. State of Franklin established in what is now eastern Tennessee 1784–87. Organized as Territory South of the Ohio 1790. Statehood 1796. Secedes from Union 1861. Battles of Shiloh (1862), Chattanooga (1863), Stones River (1863), and Nashville (1864). Readmitted to Union 1866. Clarence Darrow defends John T. Scopes for violating ban on teaching evolution in public schools; loses case 1925. Congress creates Tennessee Valley Authority 1933. First operational nuclear reactor at Oak Ridge 1943. Martin Luther King assassinated at Memphis 1968.

**Tourist information** 1–615–741–2158.

## Texas

The land that is Texas today was originally part of Spain's holdings in Mexico. After Mexico won independence, the new government invited U.S. citizens to settle there. After many clashes between the Mexican and Anglo cultures, Texas broke away and for 10 years was an independent country before becoming a state in 1845. Modern Texas was made by oil, discovered at Spindletop in 1901, and the state's economy has been tied to the oil market ever since. After World War II, the Texas economy soared, bringing both prosperity and an unprecedented population boom. With the oil glut of the early 1980s, growth came to a halt, causing a drastic realignment of economic priorities. Unemployment jumped more than 20 percent between 1980 and 1988, and remained higher than the national average in 1990, a year that saw many bank failures. The economy has been forced to diversify; currently the petroleum industry accounts for only 10 percent of state revenues, down from 25 percent a decade before. Texas has enormous resources ranging from cotton, cattle, and timber to aerospace, computers, and electronics. The largest of the 48 contiguous states, Texas's image as a state of wide-open spaces is understandable, but fully 80 percent of its people live in metropolitan areas, and Dallas, Houston, and San Antonio are among the nation's 10 largest cities. Twenty-five percent of the population is Hispanic, and the majority of those are Mexican-American.

**Name** From Caddo *tavshas*, "friends." **Nickname** Lone Star State. **Capital** Austin. **Entered Union** Dec. 29, 1845 (28th). **Motto** "Friendship."

**Emblems** **Bird** Mockingbird. **Dish** Chili. **Flower** Bluebonnet. **Gem** Topaz. **Grass** Sideoats grama. **Songs** "Texas, Our Texas," "The Eyes of Texas." **Stone** Palmwood. **Tree** Pecan.

**Land** **Total area** 266,807 sq. mi. (2d), incl. 4,790 sq. mi. inland water. **Borders** Okla., Ark., La., Gulf of Mexico, Tamaulipas, Coahuila, Chihuahua, N.Mex. **Rivers** Brazos, Colorado, Natchez, Red, Rio Grande, Sabine, Trinity. **Lakes** Sam Rayburn Res., Texoma, Toledo Bend Res. **Other notable features** Balcomes Escarpment, Diablo Sierra, Edwards Plateau, Guadalupe Mts., Staked Plain, Stockton Plateau.

**Elected officials** Gov. Ann Richards (D, term exp. 1995). Lt. Gov. Bob Bullock (D). Atty. Gen. Dan Morales (D).

**People** (1990) 16,986,510 (3d). **Race/national origin** (1990): White 75.2%. Black 11.9%. Indian 0.4%. Asian 1.9%. Other 10.6%. Hispanic 25.5%.

**Cities** (1990) Houston 1,630,553. Dallas 1,006,877. San Antonio 935,933. El Paso 515,342. Austin 465,622. Ft. Worth 447,619. Arlington 261,721. Corpus Christi 257,453. Lubbock 186,206. Garland 180,650.

**Business** **Gross state product** (GSP, 1986) $303.5 bil. (3d). **Sectors of GSP:** Farms 1.60%. Agricultural services, forestry, & fisheries 0.33%. Mining 10.25%. Construction 5.35%. Manufacturing 16.05%. Transportation & public utilities 10.96%. Wholesale 7.64%. Retail 9.31%. Finance, insurance, & real estate 13.64%. Services 14.23%. Federal government 1.95%. Federal military 1.42%. State & local government 7.26%. **Fortune** 500 companies (1990): 36: incl. American Petrofina, Compaq Computer, Kimberly-Clark, Pennzoil, Shell Oil, Temple-Inland, Tenneco,

Texas Instruments, Vista Chemical.
**Famous natives** Stephen Austin (b. Va.), pioneer. James ("Jim") Bowie (b. Ky.), army officer. Carol Burnett, comedian. J. Frank Dobie, folklorist. Dwight D. Eisenhower, U.S. president/general. Samuel Houston (b. Va.), president Republic of Texas/governor state of Texas. Howard Hughes, industrialist/aviator. Lyndon Baines Johnson, U.S. president. Janis Joplin, singer. Barbara Jordan, politician. Audie Murphy, soldier/actor. Chester Nimitz, navy officer. Katherine Anne Porter, author. Samuel T. Rayburn, politician. Mildred ("Babe") Didrikson Zaharias, athlete.
**Noteworthy places** The Alamo, San Antonio. Alibates Flint Quarries Natl. Monument. Big Bend Natl. Park. Ft. Davis. Galveston Historical Foundation. Guadalupe Mountains Natl. Park. Houston Museum of Fine Arts. Lyndon B. Johnson Natl. Hist. Park, Johnson City. Lyndon B. Johnson Space Center, Houston. Old Stone Ft., Nacogdoches. Padre Island Natl. Seashore. San Antonio Missions Natl. Hist. Park. Texas Ranger Museum, Waco.
**Memorable events** Alonso Alvarez de Piñeda sails along coast 1519. Estevanico blazes trail through West Texas 1539. Spanish establish settlement at Ysleta near El Paso 1682. René-Robert Cavelier de La Salle attempts to found colony on Matagorda Bay, establishing claim to region for France 1685. Effective Spanish occupation 1715. U.S. acquires French claim to region with Louisiana Purchase 1803. U.S. relinquishes claim to Spain 1819. Americans move into region in early 19th century. Mexico, of which Texas is a province, wins independence from Spain 1821. Declaration of Independence from Mexico; Santa Anna victor at Battle of the Alamo; Sam Houston victor at Battle of San Jacinto; founding of Republic of Texas 1836. Texas granted statehood by U.S. 1845. Secedes from Union 1861; readmitted 1870. Hurricane kills 6,000 at Galveston 1900. NASA Space Center opens at Houston 1962. President John F. Kennedy assassinated at Dallas 1963.
**Tourist information** 1–800–888–8TEX.

## Utah

In the middle of the Great Basin between the Rocky Mountains and the Sierra Nevada, Utah was an arid and uninviting region. After Joseph Smith, the founder of the Church of Jesus Christ of Latter-day Saints (Mormons), was lynched in Illinois, Brigham Young led his people west, ultimately to the Salt Lake Valley in 1847. The chief obstacle to statehood was polygamy, which the church eventually renounced. There was an influx of non-Mormons after the discovery of silver in 1863, but Mormons still comprise two-thirds of the state's population, and the state remains conservative in outlook. Although the federal government is a major employer, government policy has lately been challenged by increased concern over the issues of chemical weapons testing, the MX missile, and disposal of nuclear waste from the Rocky Mountain Arsenal in neighboring Colorado.

NAME For Ute Indians. NICKNAMES Beehive State, Mormon State. CAPITAL Salt Lake City. ENTERED UNION Jan. 4, 1896 (45th). MOTTO "Industry."
**Emblems** ANIMAL Elk. BIRD Seagull. EMBLEM Beehive. FISH Rainbow trout. FLOWER Sego lily. GEM Topaz. SONG "Utah, We Love Thee." TREE Blue spruce.
**Land** TOTAL AREA 84,899 sq. mi. (11th), incl. 2,826 sq. mi. inland water. BORDERS Idaho, Wyo., Colo., Ariz., Nev. RIVERS Bear, Colorado, Green, Sevier. LAKES Bear, Great Salt, Utah. MOUNTAINS La Sal, Uinta (Kings Peak 13,528 ft.), Wasatch Range. OTHER NOTABLE FEATURES Great Salt Lake Desert (Bonneville Salt Flats), Kaibab Plateau.
**Elected officials** Gov. Norman H. Bangerter (R, term exp. 1993). Lt. Gov. W. Val Oveson (R). Atty. Gen. R. Paul Van Dam (D).
**People** (1990) 1,722,850 (35th). RACE/NATIONAL ORIGIN (1990): White 93.8%. Black 0.7%. Indian 1.4%. Asian 1.9%. Other 2.2%. Hispanic 4.9%.
**Cities** (1990) Salt Lake City 159,936. West Valley City 86,976. Provo 86,835. Sandy 75,058. Orem 67,561. Ogden 63,909. Taylorsville-Bennion 52,351. West Jordan 42,892. Layton 41,784. Bountiful 36,659.
**Business** GROSS STATE PRODUCT (GSP, 1986) $24 bil. (36th). SECTORS OF GSP: Farms 1.45%. Agricultural services, forestry, & fisheries 0.21%. Mining 2.60%. Construction 5.08%. Manufacturing 16.62%. Transportation & public utilities 12.64%. Wholesale 6.56%. Retail 10.01%. Finance, insurance, & real estate 14.89%. Services 14.58%. Federal government 5.18%. Federal military 1.18%. State & local government 9.01%. FORTUNE 500 COMPANIES (1990): 1: Thiokol.
**Famous natives** Maude Adams, actress. John Moses Browning, inventor. Philo Farnsworth, engineer. Merlin Olsen, football player/actor. Ivy Baker Priest, U.S. treasurer. Brigham Young (b. Vt.), religious leader. Loretta Young, actress.
**Noteworthy places** Arches Natl. Park. Bryce Canyon Natl. Park. Canyonlands Natl. Park. Capitol Reef Natl. Park. Cedar Breaks Natl. Monument. Dinosaur Natl. Monument. Flaming Gorge Dam Natl. Monument. Great Salt Lake. Lake Powell Natl. Monument. Monument Valley. Mormon Tabernacle, Salt Lake City. Natural Bridges Natl. Monument. Promontory Point. Rainbow Bridge Natl. Monument. Temple Square, Salt Lake City. Timpanogas Cave Natl. Monument. Zion Natl. Park.
**Memorable events** First visited probably by explorers from Coronado expedition 1540. Silvestre Vélez de Escalante and Francisco Atanasio Dominguez explore for Spain 1776. James Bridger discovers Great Salt Lake 1824. Led by Brigham Young, Mormons reach Great Salt Lake 1847. U.S. acquires Utah region from Mexico 1848. Mormons organize state of Deseret 1849; Congress refuses to recognize and instead organizes Territory of Utah 1850. Silver discovered at Little Cottonfield Canyon 1868. First transcontinental railroad completed with driving of golden spike at Promontory Point 1869. Mormon church renounces polygamy 1890, paving way to statehood

1896. Uranium discovered near Moab 1952.
**Tourist information** 1–801–538–1030.

## Vermont

Originally claimed by both New Hampshire and New York, Vermont's independence was asserted by Ethan Allen. His Green Mountain Boys rid the state of New Yorkers in 1770, fought well against the British in the Revolution, and declared the independent republic of New Connecticut in 1777. Allen was eventually overthrown, and Vermont joined the Union in 1791.

Vermont traditionally has strong ties to Canada, and there was an influx of French-Canadians as Vermont began to develop its manufacturing base in the mid-19th century. Vermont's politics have always been characterized by tolerance and progressivism. As New Connecticut, it abolished slavery and allowed universal male suffrage. More recently, Bernard Sanders, Socialist mayor of Burlington from 1981 to 1989, was elected to Congress in 1990, where he serves as an Independent. Vermont's environmental concerns focus on acid rain and the degree to which development (especially by the tourist industry) should infringe on the state's remaining unspoiled land.

NAME From French *vert mont*, "green mountain." NICKNAME Green Mountain State. CAPITAL Montpelier. ENTERED UNION Mar. 4, 1791 (14th). MOTTO "Freedom and unity."
**Emblems** ANIMAL Morgan horse. BEVERAGE Milk. BIRD Hermit thrush. COLD-WATER FISH Brook trout. FLOWER Red clover. INSECT Honeybee. SONG "Hail, Vermont!" TREE Sugar maple. WARM-WATER FISH Walleye pike.
**Land** TOTAL AREA 9,614 sq. mi. (43d), incl. 341 sq. mi. inland water. BORDERS Quebec, N.H., Mass., N.Y. RIVERS Connecticut, Lamoille, Otter Creek, Poultney, White, Winooski. LAKES Bomoseen, Champlain, Memphremagog, Willoughby. OTHER NOTABLE FEATURES Grand Isle, Green Mts. (Mt. Mansfield 4,393 ft.), Taconic Mts.
**Elected officials** Gov. Howard Dean (R, term exp. 1993). Lt. Gov. vacant. Sec. State James H. Douglas (R). Atty. Gen. Jeffrey L. Amestoy (R).
**People** (1990) 562,758 (48th). RACE/NATIONAL ORIGIN (1990): White 98.6%. Black 0.2%. Indian 0.1%. Asian 0.2%. Other 0.2%. Hispanic 0.5%.
**Cities** (1990) Burlington 37,712. Rutland 18,436. South Burlington 10,679. Barre 9,824. Essex Junction 7,033. Montpelier 8,241. St. Albans 7,308. Winooski 6,318. Newport 4,756. Bellows Falls 3,456.
**Business** GROSS STATE PRODUCT (GSP, 1986) $8.6 bil. (50th) SECTORS OF GSP: Farms 2.73%. Agricultural services, forestry, & fisheries 0.44%. Mining 0.27%. Construction 6.23%. Manufacturing 22.94%. Transportation & public utilities 8.00%. Wholesale 5.54%. Retail 10.11%. Finance, insurance, & real estate 18.20%. Services 15.90%. Federal government 1.83%. Federal military 0.38%. State & local government 7.45%. FORTUNE 500 COMPANIES (1990): 0.

**Famous natives** Ethan Allen (b. Conn.), army officer. Chester Arthur, U.S. president. Calvin Coolidge, U.S. president. John Deere, industrialist. George Dewey, naval officer. John Dewey, philosopher. Stephen Douglas, politician. James Fisk, financier. Rudy Vallee, singer.
**Noteworthy places** Bennington Battleground/Monument. Calvin Coolidge Homestead, Plymouth. Maple Grove Maple Museum, Rock of Ages Tourist Center, Graniteville. Shelburne Museum. St. Johnsbury. Vermont Marble Exhibit, Proctor.
**Memorable events** Samuel de Champlain explores for France 1609. First French settlement at Ste. Anne 1666. First English settlers build Ft. Drummer near Brattleboro 1724. Bennington settled 1761. Ethan Allen organizes Green Mountain Boys 1764. Green Mountain Boys capture Ft. Ticonderoga and Ft. Crown Point 1775. Gen. John Stark defeats British Gen. John Burgoyne near Bennington; constitution abolishes slavery and grants universal male suffrage 1777. Claims to area relinquished by Massachusetts (1781), New Hampshire (1782), and New York (1790). First state admitted after original 13 1791. MacDonough defeats British Lake Champlain fleet 1814. Canal between Hudson River and Lake Champlain gives Vermont direct access to port of New York 1823. Confederate soldiers steal $400,000 from St. Albans bank 1864. Blue law repealed, allowing stores to open on Sundays 1982.
**Tourist information** 1-802-828-3236.

## Virginia, Commonwealth of

The first successful English settlement in America was at Jamestown in 1607. The differences between the Virginia colonists and those of Massachusetts were pronounced, and the commercial southern planter class shared little of their New England counterparts' religious zeal. Virginia bred its own strain of independence, and it was the fiery Patrick Henry who heralded the American Revolution with the cry "Give me liberty or give me death." Seven of the first 12 presidents were from Virginia. With an economy very dependent on labor-intensive tobacco in the mid-19th century, Virginia seceded from the Union over the slavery issue, despite the misgivings of many, including Robert E. Lee. After the war Virginia developed an increasingly diversified industrial and manufacturing base that survives today, with food products, tobacco, and chemicals leading the way. Despite the dramatic decline of the American merchant marine, Virginia's shipbuilding industry in Newport News flourished in the 1980s, thanks to the Pentagon's commitment to a 600-ship navy. Norfolk is also one of the country's leading commercial ports.
NAME For Elizabeth I, called Virgin Queen. NICKNAMES Old Dominion, Mother of Presidents, Mother of States. CAPITAL Richmond. ENTERED UNION June 25, 1788 (10th). MOTTO *Sic semper tyrannis* (Thus always to tyrants).
**Emblems** BEVERAGE Milk. BIRD Cardinal. DOG Foxhound. FLOWER Dogwood. SHELL Oyster. SONG "Carry Me Back to Old Virginia." TREE Dogwood.

**Land** TOTAL AREA 40,767 sq. mi. (36th), incl. 1,063 sq. mi. inland water. BORDERS Md., D.C., Atlantic Ocean, N.C., Tenn., Ky., W.Va. RIVERS James, Potomac, Rappahannock, Roanoke, Shenandoah, York. LAKES Buggs Island, Claytor, Gaston, Leesville. MOUNTAINS Allegheny, Blue Ridge, Cumberland, Unaka. OTHER NOTABLE FEATURES Great Dismal Swamp, Shenandoah Valley.
**Elected officials** Gov. L. Douglas Wilder (D, term exp. 1994). Lt. Gov. Donald Beyer (D). Atty. Gen. Mary Sue Terry (D).
**People** (1990) 6,187,358 (12th). RACE/NATIONAL ORIGIN (1990): White 77.4%. Black 18.8%. Indian 0.2%. Asian 2.6%. Other 0.9%. Hispanic 2.6%.
**Cities** (1990) Virginia Beach 393,069. Norfolk 261,229. Richmond 203,056. Newport News 170,045. Chesapeake 151,976. Hampton 133,793. Alexandria 111,183. Portsmouth 103,907. Roanoke 96,397. Lynchburg 66,049.
**Business** GROSS STATE PRODUCT (GSP 1986) $104.2 (11th). SECTORS OF GSP: Farms 0.93%. Agricultural services, forestry, & fisheries 0.33%. Mining 1.07%. Construction 5.77%. Manufacturing 17.86%. Transportation & public utilities 9.20%. Wholesale 5.47%. Retail 9.41%. Finance, insurance, & real estate 14.74%. Services 15.74%. Federal government 6.04%. Federal military 5.96%. State & local government 7.49%. FORTUNE 500 COMPANIES (1990): 13: incl. Gannett, James River Corp. of Virginia, Media General, Mobil, Reynolds Metals, Smithfield Foods, Universal.
**Famous natives** Richard E. Byrd, explorer/aviator. William Clark, explorer. Jerry Falwell, evangelist. William Henry Harrison, U.S. president. Patrick Henry, Revolutionary patriot. Thomas Jefferson, U.S. president. Joseph E. Johnston, Confederate general. John Paul Jones (b. Scotland), navy officer. Robert E. Lee, Confederate general. Meriwether Lewis, explorer. James Madison, U.S. president. John Marshall, jurist. Cyrus Hall McCormick, inventor. James Monroe, U.S. president. Walter Reed, doctor. Pat Robertson, evangelist/politician. Bill ("Bojangles") Robinson, dancer. George C. Scott, actor. Thomas Sumter, army officer. Zachary Taylor, U.S. president. John Tyler, U.S. president. Booker T. Washington, educator. George Washington, U.S. president. Woodrow Wilson, U.S. president.
**Noteworthy places** Appomattox Courthouse Natl. Hist. Park. Arlington Natl. Cemetery. Booker T. Washington Natl. Monument, Roanoke. Colonial Natl. Hist. Park (incl. Jamestown, Yorktown, and Williamsburg). Fredericksburg and Spotsylvania Natl. Military Park. George Washington birthplace, Frederick Co. Harpers Ferry Natl. Hist. Site. The Mariners' Museum, Newport News. Monticello, Charlottesville. Mount Vernon. Petersburg Natl. Battlefield. Robert E. Lee Memorial, Lexington. Shenandoah Natl. Park. Virginia Beach. Virginia Museum of Fine Arts. Wolf Trap Farm for the Performing Arts, Reston.
**Memorable events** John Smith founds Jamestown, first permanent settlement in North America, 1607. John Rolfe marries Pocahontas, daughter of Powhatan, leader of so-called Powhatan Confederacy 1614. First English women arrive at Jamestown; House of Bur-

gesses established 1619. Northampton Declaration first resistance to taxation without representation 1653. College of William and Mary founded 1693. First state to establish Committee of Correspondence 1773. American Revolution ends with Charles Cornwallis's surrender to George Washington at Yorktown 1781. Nat Turner's slave revolt 1831. State secedes from Union 1861. Civil War ends with Robert E. Lee's surrender to Ulysses S. Grant at Appomattox Courthouse 1865. Readmitted to Union 1870. Norfolk Naval Base founded 1917. John D. Rockefeller, Jr., undertakes restoration of Colonial Williamsburg 1926. E. Claiborne Robins donates $50 million to University of Richmond 1969.
**Tourist information** 1-800-VISITVA.

## Washington

The northwest corner of the continental United States was originally the locus of a rich Native American culture noted today primarily for its ornately carved canoes and totem poles. In 1792, Boston merchant Capt. Robert Gray began a trade in sea otter pelts, but the first permanent settlers in the region did not establish themselves for almost 50 years. Agriculture and lumbering were, and remain, mainstays of the state's economy—the farming regions in the east, rich in dairy products, fruit and wheat, and the lumber industry in the western part of the state rely heavily on exports to the Far East. This geographic split reflects the weather patterns: eastern Washington rarely gets more than 10 inches of rain in a year, while on the Pacific Coast it rains almost every day.

Since World War I, Puget Sound has been a center of heavy industry and shipbuilding, and 60% of the population is concentrated in the region. Boeing maintains one of the country's largest airplane-manufacturing plants in the Seattle-Tacoma area. The industrial work force was open to progressive and sometimes radical unionism, and the International Workers of the World (Wobblies) had their national headquarters at Seattle. Before statehood the territorial government pioneered women's suffrage, but Congress declared the women's right to vote unconstitutional.
NAME For George Washington. NICKNAME Evergreen State. CAPITAL Olympia. ENTERED UNION Nov. 11, 1889 (42d). MOTTO *Alki* (By and by).
**Emblems** BIRD Willow goldfinch. FISH Steelhead trout. FLOWER Western rhododendron. GEM Petrified wood. SONG "Washington, My Home." TREE Western hemlock.
**Land** TOTAL AREA 68,138 sq. mi. (20th), incl. 1,627 sq. mi. inland water. BORDERS British Columbia, Idaho, Oreg., Pacific Ocean. RIVERS Chehalis, Columbia, Pend Oreille, Snake, Yakima. LAKES Baker, Bank, Chelan, Franklin D. Roosevelt, Ross, Rufus Woods. MOUNTAINS Cascade Range, Coast Range, Kettle River Range, Olympic. OTHER NOTABLE FEATURES Puget Sound, San Juan Islands, Strait of Juan de Fuca.
**Elected officials** Gov. Booth Gardner (D, term

exp. 1993). Lt. Gov. Joel Pritchard (R). Sec. State Ralph Munro (R). Atty. Gen. Kenneth O. Eikenberry (R).

**People** (1990) 4,866,692 (18th). RACE/NATIONAL ORIGIN (1990): White 88.5%. Black 3.1%. Indian 1.7%. Asian 4.3%. Other 2.4%. Hispanic 4.4%.

**Cities** (1990) Seattle 516,259. Spokane 177,196. Tacoma 176,664. Bellevue 86,874. Everett 69,961. Yakima 54,827. Bellingham 52,179. Vancouver 46,380. Kennewick 42,155. Renton 41,668.

**Business** GROSS STATE PRODUCT (GSP, 1986) $77.7 bil. (16th). SECTORS OF GSP: Farms 2.61%. Agricultural services, forestry, & fisheries 1.05%. Mining 0.22%. Construction 5.75%. Manufacturing 17.27%. Transportation & public utilities 8.58%. Wholesale 8.04%. Retail 10.72%. Finance, insurance, & real estate 15.66%. Services 15.04%. Federal government 2.96%. Federal military 2.25%. State & local government 9.85%. *FORTUNE* 500 COMPANIES (1990): 5: Boeing, Burlington Resources, Longview Fibre, Paccar, Weyerhaeuser.

**Famous natives** Harry L. ("Bing") Crosby, singer. Merce Cunningham, choreographer. Jimi Hendrix, guitarist. Henry M. ("Scoop") Jackson, politician. Robert Joffrey, choreographer. Marcus Whitman (b. N.Y.), missionary/pioneer.

**Noteworthy places** Klondike Gold Rush Natl. Hist. Park, Seattle. Mount Rainier Natl. Park. Mount Saint Helens Natl. Monument. North Cascades Natl. Park. Olympic Natl. Park. San Juan Islands Natl. Hist. Park. Seattle Art Museum.

**Memorable events** Sir Francis Drake skirts coast of Pacific Northwest 1579. Juan de Fuca sails into straits now bearing his name. Bruno de Heceta lands at Hoh River 1775. Capt. James Cook arrives 1778. Capt. Robert Gray discovers mouth of Columbia River, which he names for his ship; George Vancouver explores Puget Sound 1792. Lewis and Clark expedition winters at Columbia River 1805. Marcus Whitman, Protestant Mission Board, settles near Walla Walla 1836. Territorial status 1853. Northern Pacific railroad reaches Puget Sound 1883. Alaska-Yukon-Pacific Exposition at Seattle 1909. Grand Coulee Dam, largest concrete hydroelectric dam in U.S., completed 1941. Hanford Works atomic energy plant opens 1943. Upholding treaty provisions from Washington's days as a territory, a decision awards Native Americans half the catch of Northwest salmon and steelhead 1974. Mt. Saint Helens erupts, killing 60 1980. Washington Public Power Supply System (known as "whoops") defaults on $8.25 billion bond issue 1983. Reports linking growth-enhancing chemical Alar to cancer generate $140 million loss for Washington's apple growers 1988.

**Tourist information** 1-800-544-1800.

## West Virginia

When Virginia seceded in 1861, its western counties reorganized and in 1863 were admitted to the Union as a separate state. Despite the rugged terrain, through which transportation has always been difficult, farming remained the backbone of the economy until the close of the 19th century, when coal mining and other extractive industries developed. After World War II, the manufacturing base developed to include steel and chemical manufacturing. The Monongahela, Kanawha, and Little Kanawha rivers are all navigable tributaries of the Ohio River, which forms West Virginia's western border, but the state's internal transportation needs have not been met. Even with vast natural resources, West Virginia has long been one of the poorest states in the union. Population losses since the 1950s have been pronounced, and the 8% loss between 1980 and 1990 was the highest in the country. There is low participation in the work force by women, and educational achievements are well below the national average.

NAME for western part of Virginia. NICKNAME Mountain State. CAPITAL Charleston. ENTERED UNION June 20, 1863 (35th). MOTTO *Montani semper liberi* (Mountaineers are always free).

**Emblems** ANIMAL Black bear. BIRD Cardinal. COLORS Old gold and blue. FISH Brook trout. FLOWER *Rhododendron maximum* (big laurel). FRUIT Apple. SONGS "The West Virginia Hills," "West Virginia, My Home Sweet Home," "This Is My West Virginia." TREE Sugar maple.

**Land** TOTAL AREA 24,231 sq. mi. (41st), incl. 112 sq. mi. inland water. BORDERS Ohio, Pa., Md., Va., Ky. RIVERS Big Sandy, Guayandotte, Kanawha, Little Kanawha, Monongahela, Ohio, Potomac. LAKES Summersville Dam. MOUNTAINS Allegheny, Blue Ridge, Cumberland.

**Elected officials** Gov. Gaston Caperton (D, term exp. 1993). Sec. State Ken Hechler (D). Atty. Gen. Mario Palumbo (D).

**People** (1990) 1,793,477 (34th). RACE/NATIONAL ORIGIN (1990): White 96.2%. Black 3.1%. Indian 0.1%. Asian 0.4%. Other 0.1%. Hispanic 0.5%.

**Cities** (1990) Charleston 57,287. Huntington 54,844. Wheeling 34,882. Parkersburg 33,862. Morgantown 25,879. Weirton 22,124. Fairmont 20,210. Beckley 18,296. Clarksburg 18,059. Martinsburg 14,073.

**Business** GROSS STATE PRODUCT (GSP, 1986) $24.1 bil. (35th). SECTORS OF GSP: Farms 0.77%. Agricultural services, forestry, & fisheries 0.16%. Mining 13.19%. Construction 4.79%. Manufacturing 14.46%. Transportation & public utilities 13.64%. Wholesale 5.11%. Retail 9.36%. Finance, insurance, & real estate 14.56%. Services 12.48%. Federal government 1.75%. Federal military 0.29%. State & local government 9.45%. *FORTUNE* 500 COMPANIES (1990): 2: Weirton Steel, Wheeling-Pittsburgh Steel.

**Famous natives** Newton D. Baker, politician. Pearl Buck, novelist (Nobel Prize, 1938). John W. Davis, politician. Thomas ("Stonewall") Jackson, Confederate general. Dwight Whitney Morrow, lawyer/diplomat. Michael Owens, manufacturer. Walter Reuther, labor leader. Cyrus Vance, statesman. Charles ("Chuck") Yeager, pilot.

**Noteworthy places** Cass Scenic Railroad. Harpers Ferry Natl. Hist. Park. Monongahela Natl. Forest. New River Gorge Bridge. Science and Cultural Center, Charleston.

**Memorable events** First permanent settlement by Morgan Morgan at Mill Creek 1731. Coal discovered on Coal River 1742. Wheeling Convention repudiates act of secession; forms new state of Kanawha 1861. Enters Union as West Virginia 1863. Population peaks at 2.5 million 1950. Unemployment jumps 8.6% to 18.0%, highest in nation, 1980–83.

**Tourist information** 1-800-CALLWVA.

## Wisconsin

The indigenous people of the region had a largely agricultural economy, but the fur trade drew Europeans into the region. Native resistance to white settlement was strong and not overcome until the Black Hawk Wars of 1832. In the early 19th century, German, Scandinavian, and Dutch farmers immigrated to the region in large numbers. Many social welfare policies now common to the nation as a whole—including aid to dependent children, workmen's compensation, and old-age assistance—were pioneered in Wisconsin. Although manufacturing accounts for the lion's share of Wisconsin's profits, agriculture is extremely important, and the state is the nation's leading producer of dairy products. There are major shipping facilities at Superior, Green Bay, and Milwaukee.

NAME From Ojibwa *wishkonsing*, "place of the bearer." NICKNAME Badger State. CAPITAL Madison. ENTERED UNION May 29, 1848 (30th). MOTTO "Forward."

**Emblems** ANIMAL Badger. BIRD Robin. DOMESTIC ANIMAL Dairy cow. FISH Muskellunge. FLOWER Wood violet. INSECT Honeybee. MINERAL Galena. ROCK Red granite. SOIL Antigo silt loam. SONG "Oh, Wisconsin!" SYMBOL OF PEACE Mourning dove. TREE Sugar maple. WILDLIFE ANIMAL White-tailed deer.

**Land** TOTAL AREA 56,153 sq. mi. (26th), incl. 1,727 sq. mi. inland water. BORDERS Minn., Lake Superior, Mich., Lake Michigan, Ill., Iowa. RIVERS Black, Chippewa, Menominee, Mississippi, St. Croix, Wisconsin. LAKES Chippewa, Du Bay, Mendota, Michigan, Superior, Winnebago. OTHER NOTABLE FEATURES Apostle Islands, Door Peninsula, Green Bay.

**Elected officials** Gov. Tommy G. Thompson (R, term exp. 1995). Lt. Gov. Scott McCallum (R). Sec. State Douglas LaFollette (D). Atty. Gen. James Doyle (D).

**People** (1990) 4,891,769 (16th). RACE/NATIONAL ORIGIN (1990): White 92.2%. Black 5.0%. Indian 0.8%. Asian 1.1%. Other 0.9%. Hispanic 1.9%.

**Cities** (1990) Milwaukee 628,088. Madison 191,262. Green Bay 96,466. Racine 84,298. Kenosha 80,352. Appleton 65,695. West Allis 63,221. Waukesha 56,958. Eau Claire 56,856. Oshkosh 55,006.

**Business** GROSS STATE PRODUCT (GSP, 1986) $76.9 bil. (17th). SECTORS OF GSP: Farms 4.02%. Agricultural services, forestry, & fisheries 0.38%. Mining 0.11%. Construction 3.05%. Manufacturing 27.69%. Transportation & public utilities 7.90%. Wholesale 5.98%. Retail 9.19%. Finance, insurance, & real estate 17.57%. Services 13.85%. Federal government 1.09%. Federal military 0.39%. State & local government 8.79%. FORTUNE 500 COMPANIES (1990): 12: incl. Harley-Davidson, Harnischfeger Industries, Johnson Controls, Snap-On-Tools, Universal Foods.

**Famous natives** King Camp Gillette, inventor/businessman. Harry Houdini (b. Hungary), magician. Robert La Follette, politician. Liberace (Wladziu Valentino), pianist. Alfred Lunt, actor. Joseph R. McCarthy, politician. Spencer Tracy, actor. Thorstein Veblen, economist. Orson Welles, director. Laura Ingalls Wilder, novelist. Thornton Wilder, author. Frank Lloyd Wright, architect.

**Noteworthy places** Apostle Island Natl. Lakeshore. Chequamegon Natl. Forest. Circus World Museum, Baraboo. Door County Peninsula. Ice Age Natl. Scientific Reserve. Manitowoc Maritime Museum. Milwaukee Art Museum. Milwaukee Public Museum. Nicolet Natl. Forest. Old Wade House and Carriage Museum, Greenbush. Old World Wisconsin, Eagle. Villa Louis, Prairie du Chien. Wisconsin Dells.

**Memorable events** Jean Nicolet lands at Green Bay 1634. French establish mission and trading post near Ashland 1634. British take control of region 1763. Land ceded to U.S. 1787, but U.S. control not established until after War of 1812. Becomes independent Territory 1836. Statehood 1848. More than 800 die in forest fire near Peshtigo 1871. First hydroelectric plant completed at Appleton 1882. Ringling Brothers circus formed at Baraboo 1884. First state to enact income tax 1911.

**Tourist information** 1-800-372-2737, 1-800-432-8747, 1-608-266-2161.

## Wyoming

Tens of thousands of migrants traveled through the region of Wyoming along the Oregon Trail, which was pioneered in 1812-13, but few settled the land until Ft. Laramie was built in 1834. Territorial status came in 1869. Wyoming was the first state to give the vote to women, and in 1925 Nellie Tayloe Ross became the first woman governor following the

death of her husband. Cattle ranching is the traditional mainstay of the economy. The state ranks second in uranium output and has 35 percent of the country's deposits. In the last 20 years, petroleum and coal production have become increasingly important. Wyoming is best known for its natural wonders. Yellowstone National Park—the site of Old Faithful—is the oldest and largest national park in the country. Following a decade-long mining boom in the 1970s and 1980s, Wyoming's population declined, and it has fallen behind even Alaska in total population.

**NAME** From Delaware *maugh-wau-wa-ma*, "large plains" or "mountains and valleys alternating." **NICKNAME** Equality State. **CAPITAL** Cheyenne. **ENTERED UNION** July 10, 1890 (44th). **MOTTO** "Equal rights."

> *"The great social adventure of America is no longer the conquest of the wilderness, but the absorption of fifty different peoples."*
>
> —Walter Lippman (1889–1974)

**Emblems** BIRD Meadowlark. FLOWER Indian paintbrush. GEM Jade. SONG "Wyoming." TREE Cottonwood.

**Land** TOTAL AREA 97,809 sq. mi. (9th), incl. 820 sq. mi. inland water. BORDERS Mont., S.Dak., Nebr., Colo., Utah, Idaho. RIVERS Bighorn, Green, North Platte, Powder, Snake, Yellowstone. LAKES Bighorn, Yellowstone. MOUNTAINS Absaroka, Bighorn, Black Hills, Laramie, Owl Creek, Teton Range, Wind River Range, Wyoming Range.

**Elected officials** Gov. Michael J. Sullivan (D, term exp. 1992). Sec. State Kathy Karpan (D). Atty. Gen. Stan Smith (R).

**People** (1990) 453,588 (50th). RACE/NATIONAL ORIGIN (1990): White 94.2%. Black 0.8%. Indian 2.1%. Asian 0.6%. Other 2.3%. Hispanic 5.7%.

**Cities** (1990) Cheyenne 50,008. Casper 46,742.

Laramie 26,687. Rock Springs 19,050. Gillette 17,635. Sheridan 13,900. Green River 12,711. Evanston 10,903. Rawlins 9,380. Riverton 9,202.

**Business** GROSS STATE PRODUCT (GSP, 1986) $11.7 bil. (47th). SECTORS OF GSP: Farms 1.61%. Agricultural services, forestry, & fisheries 0.27%. Mining 26.38%. Construction 11.8%. Manufacturing 2.84%. Transportation & public utilities 13.57%. Wholesale 3.45%. Retail 6.56%. Finance, insurance, & real estate 13.89%. Services 7.77%. Federal government 1.83%. Federal military 1.15%. State & local government 8.88%. FORTUNE 500 COMPANIES (1990): 0.

**Famous natives** James Bridger (b. Va.), pioneer. Jackson Pollock, painter. Nellie Tayloe Ross (b. Mo.), politician.

**Noteworthy places** Buffalo Bill Museum, Cody. Devil's Tower Natl. Monument. Ft. Bridger State Park. Ft. Laramie Natl. Hist. Site. Fossil Butte Natl. Monument. Grand Teton Natl. Park. Natl. Elk Refuge. Yellowstone Natl. Park (Old Faithful).

**Memorable events** Part of Louisiana Territory claimed for France 1682. Pierre Gaultier de Varennes, sieur de Vérendrye explores region for France 1743. Region to U.S. with Louisiana Purchase 1803. John Colter crosses area of Yellowstone 1807–08. Part of region under joint Anglo-American occupation 1818–46. Indian Wars follow massacre of army detachments 1854 and 1866. Wyoming Territory organized 1868. Women's suffrage adopted permanently (first instance in U.S.) 1869. Union Pacific railroad crosses state 1869. Yellowstone, world's first national park, opens 1872. White mob kills 28 Chinese miners and burns Chinatown in Rock Springs 1885. Statehood 1890. Nellie Tayloe Ross first woman governor 1925. First Intercontinental Ballistic Missile (ICBM) base opens near Cheyenne 1951. Fires consume 1.6 million acres of land in and around Yellowstone Park—the worst fire to hit the nation's (and the world's) oldest national park—but the land has undergone intense rejuvenation 1988.

**Tourist information** 1-800-CALLWYO.

## U.S. TERRITORIES AND POSSESSIONS

Today the United States administers a number of overseas territories and commonwealth states under a variety of circumstances. The provisions of the Northwest Ordinance of 1787 established the system under which U.S. territories can achieve statehood. In order to elect a territorial legislature and send a nonvoting delegate to Congress, a territory must contain 5,000 inhabitants of voting age; it is eligible for statehood when the population numbers 60,000.

In 1947 the United Nations created the Trust Territory of the Pacific Islands—comprising what are known today as the Federated States of Micronesia (FSM), the Republic of the Marshall Islands, the Commonwealth of the Northern Mariana Islands, and the Republic of

Palau. Only Palau is still administered as a Trust Territory. The Marshall Islands and FSM are now self-governing states with close ties to the United States defined by a compact of free association under which their defense is the responsibility of the United States, they receive extensive U.S. economic assistance, and their conduct of foreign affairs must be consistent with the terms of the compact.

The territories of American Samoa, Guam, and the Virgin Islands of the United States (USVI) have nonvoting representatives in Congress, and Puerto Rico is represented by a nonvoting resident commissioner. Residents of American Samoa are U.S. nationals, and those of Guam, Puerto Rico, and the USVI, U.S. citizens.

In addition to these territories, the United States has a number of possessions whose population is too small to make local government practicable, or which are uninhabited altogether.

## American Samoa
### Territory of American Samoa

**Geography Location:** seven islands (Tutuila, Ta'u, Olosega, Ofu, Aunun, Rose, Swain's) in southern central Pacific Ocean; Pago Pago 14°17'S, 170°41'W. **Boundaries:** Hawaii about 2,300 mi. (3,700 km) to NNE, Cook Islands to E, Tonga to SW, Western Samoa to W. **Total land area:** 76.1 sq. mi. (199 sq km). **Coastline:** 72 mi. (116 km). **Comparative area:** slightly larger than Washington, D.C. **Land use:** 10% arable land; 5% permanent crops; 0% meadows and pastures; 75% forest and woodland; 10% other. **Major cities:** (1990 census) Pago Pago (capital; Ma'oputasi Co.) 10,640.

**People Population:** 46,773 (1990 census). Nationality: noun—American Samoan(s); adjective—American Samoan. **Ethnic groups:** 90% Samoan (Polynesian), 2% Caucasian, 2% Tongan,

6% other. **Languages:** Samoan (closely related to Hawaiian and other Polynesian languages) and English; most people are bilingual. **Religions:** 50% Christian Congregationalist, 20% Roman Catholic, 30% mostly Protestant denominations and other.

**Government Type:** unincorporated and unorganized territory of U.S. **Constitution:** ratified 1966, in effect 1967. **National holiday:** Flag Day, Apr. 17 (1900). **Heads of government:** Peter T. Coleman, governor (since Nov. 1988). **Structure:** executive—governor is popularly elected to four-year term and exercises authority under direction of U.S. Secretary of Interior; legislative—bicameral legislature (Fono) with 18-member Senate chosen by county councils to serve four-year terms and House of Representatives with 20 members popularly elected to serve two-year terms, plus a nonvoting delegate from Swain's Island; judicial—high court with chief justice and associate justices appointed by U.S. Secretary of Interior.

**Economy Monetary unit:** U.S. dollar. **Budget:** (1986 est.) *income:* $90.3 mil.; *expend.:* $93.2 mil. **GNP:** $190 mil., $5,210 per capita (1985). **Chief crops:** bananas, coconuts, vegetables, taro, breadfruit, yams, copra, pineapples, papayas. **Natural resources:** pumice and pumicite. **Major industries:** tuna canneries (largely dependent on foreign supplies of raw tuna), meat canning, handicrafts, dairy farming, tourism. **Labor force:** 10,000 (1986 est.); 48% government, 33% tuna canneries, 19% other. **Exports:** $288 mil. (f.o.b., 1987); 93% canned tuna. **Imports:** $346 mil. (c.i.f., 1987); 18% building materials, 17% food, 14% petroleum products. **Major trading partners:** *exports:* 99.7% U.S.; *imports:* 72% U.S., 7% Japan, 7% New Zealand, 5% Australia, 9% other.

American Samoa consists of seven islands between 14° and 15° south, and 168° and 171° west. First peopled by Polynesians in the first millennium B.C., the islands had as their first European visitor Louis Antoine de Bougainville, who visited in 1768 and called them the "Islands of the Navigators," in recognition of the islanders' seamanship. American whalers and missionaries began arriving in the 1830s, and the United States secured trading privileges by treaty in 1878. In 1889 the United States, Britain, and Germany established tripartite control of the islands. After 10 years of warring among the islanders, the British withdrew their claim, and Germany and the United States divided responsibility for the islands along longitude 171° west. The high chiefs of Tutuila ceded the islands of Tutuila and Aunun to the United States in 1900, and the high chiefs of the Manu'a islands ceded those of Ta'u, Ofu, Olosega, and Rose in 1904. Swain's Island became part of American Samoa in 1925.

Administered by the U.S. Department of the Interior since 1904, American Samoa is an unincorporated and unorganized territory, with its own government but under the plenary authority of the Department of the Interior. There is no congressional intent to grant statehood to the island. American Samoans will reconsider their relationship with the United States in 1994. The people have their own con-stitution and elect their own governor and representatives to the Fono; but the justices of the high court are appointed by the secretary of the interior. The population is more than 80% rural.

## Baker and Howland Islands

About 1,600 miles (2,575 km) southwest of Hawaii and 1,000 miles west of Jarvis Island are Baker Island (0°48′N, 176°38′W) and Howland Island (0°14′N, 176°28′W, 40 mi. north of Baker). Discovered in 1842, the two coral atolls were worked for guano until about 1890. Great Britain claimed them in 1889, but the United States made them territories in 1935 and sent colonists to them. With an area of about one square mile each, neither is inhabited today. Both are unincorporated territories administered by the U.S. Fish and Wildlife Service as part of the National Wildlife Refuge.

## Guam
### Territory of Guam
**Geography Location:** southernmost and largest of Mariana Islands in western North Pacific Ocean; Agaña 13°28′N, 144°45′E. **Boundaries:** Tokyo, Japan, about 1,350 mi. (2,170 km) to N; Honolulu, Hawaii 3,300 mi. (5,955 km) to ENE; Federated States of Micronesia to S, Philippines to W across Philippine Sea. **Total land area:** 209 sq. mi. (541 sq km). **Coastline:** 78 mi. (125.5 km). **Comparative area:** slightly more than 3 times size of Washington, D.C. **Land use:** 11% arable land; 11% permanent crops; 15% meadows and pastures; 18% forest and woodland; 45% other. **Major cities:** Agaña (capital).

**People Population:** 141,039 (1990 census). **Nationality:** noun—Guamanian(s); adjective—Guamanian. **Ethnic groups:** 50% Chamorro, 25% Filipino, 10% Caucasian, 15% Chinese, Japanese, Korean, other. **Languages:** English and Chamorro; most people bilingual; Japanese also widely spoken. **Religions:** 98% Roman Catholic, 2% other.

**Government Type:** organized, unincorporated territory of U.S. **Constitution:** Organic Act of Aug. 1, 1950. **National holiday:** Guam Discovery Day, first Monday in March. **Heads of government:** Joseph A. Ada, governor (since 1986). **Structure:** executive—governor elected to 4-year term; legislative—Senate has 21 members elected for 2-year terms; judicial—U.S. District Court, Guam Superior Court.

**Economy Monetary unit:** U.S. dollar. **Budget:** (1987 est.) *income:* $208.0 mil.; *expend.:* $175 mil. **GNP:** $1.0 bil., $7,675 per capita. **Chief crops:** fruits, vegetables, eggs, copra; relatively undeveloped with most food imported. **Livestock:** poultry, pigs. **Natural resources:** fishing (largely undeveloped), tourism (especially from Japan). **Major industries:** U.S. military, tourism, petroleum refining. **Labor force:** 42,000 (1986); 45% government, 55% other. **Exports:** $39 mil. (f.o.b., 1983); mostly transshipments of refined petroleum and petroleum products, copra, fish. **Imports:** $61 mil. (c.i.f., 1983); mostly crude petroleum and petroleum products; food, manufactured goods. **Major trading partners:** *exports:* 25% U.S., 75% other; *imports:* 77% U.S., 23% other.

Guam was inhabited by Chamorros from the Malay Peninsula as early as 1500 B.C.; the first European to stop at Guam was Ferdinand Magellan in 1521. Spanish colonization began with the arrival of Jesuit missionaries in 1668. By 1700 pestilence and insurrection had reduced the Chamorro population from 50,000 to about 2,000. Guam was ceded to the United States in 1899. In 1941 it was occupied by Japan—the only inhabited U.S. territory to be seized by enemy forces during World War II—and was retaken by the Americans in 1944. (Congress designated 1,960 acres as the War in the Pacific National Historic Park in 1978.) In 1950 it received its first nonmilitary administration in more than 200 years. Though Guam is unincorporated, the congressionally approved Guam Organic Act provides for a republican form of government with executive, legislative, and judicial branches. The Guam Commonwealth Act has been approved by plebiscite and is awaiting congressional ratification. Although Chamorros represent a significant portion of the population, Guam is a multiethnic state.

## Jarvis Island, Kingman Reef, and Palmyra Atoll

Jarvis Island (0°23′S, 160°02′W; about 1,300 mi. (2,090 km) S of Hawaii), Kingman Reef (6°24′N,162°22′W; about 995 mi. (1,600 km) SSW of Hawaii), and Palmyra Atoll (5°52′N, 162°05′W; about 995 mi. (1,600 km) SSW of Hawaii) are in the Line Island group. Discovered in 1798, Kingman Reef (0.4 sq. mi.; 1 sq km) was annexed by the United States in 1922 and used as an aviation station during the 1930s. Discovered in 1802, Palmyra Atoll consists of about 50 islets with a combined area of four square miles. It was annexed by the Kingdom of Hawaii in 1862, by Great Britain in 1889, and claimed by the United States in 1912. Privately owned, it is administered by the Department of the Navy, as is Kingman Reef. Jarvis Island (1.8 sq. mi.; 4.5 sq km) was claimed by the United States in 1857, annexed by Great Britain in 1889, and reclaimed by the United States in 1935. Its rich guano deposits were worked by U.S. and British companies in the late 19th century.

## Johnston Atoll
**Geography Location:** Johnston Island (16°45′N, 169°32′W) and three uninhabited islands in central Pacific Ocean. **Boundaries:** Honolulu, Hawaii, about 825 mi. (1,330 km) to ENE; Marshall Islands to SW. **Total land area:** 1.1 sq. mi. (2.8 sq km). **Coastline:** 6.21 mi. (10 km). **Comparative area:** about 4.7 times size of the Mall in Washington, D.C. **Land use:** 0% arable land; 0% permanent crops; 0% meadows and pastures; 0% forest and woodland; 100% other. **Major cities:** none.

**People Population:** 1,203 (1989), all U.S. government personnel and contractors.

**Government Type:** unincorporated territory of U.S.

Johnston Atoll (16°45′N, 169°32′W) includes Johnston, Sand, Hikina, and Akan islands, with a total area of 1.1 square miles. Claimed by the United States in 1858, Johnston Atoll is manned and administered by the Defense Nuclear Agency

(DNA), and managed jointly as a National Wildlife Refuge by the DNA and the Fish and Wildlife Service.

## Midway Islands

**Geography** **Location:** Sand Island and Eastern Island in northern Pacific Ocean; 28°15′N, 177°25′W. **Boundaries:** Honolulu about 1,460 mi. (2,350 km) to SE, Marshall Islands to SW. **Total land area:** 2.0 sq. mi. (5.2 sq km). **Coastline:** 9.3 mi. (15 km). **Comparative area:** about nine times size of the Mall in Washington, D.C. **Land use:** 0% arable land; 0% permanent crops; 0% meadows and pastures; 0% forest and woodland; 100% other. **Major cities:** none.

**People** **Population:** 453 U.S. military personnel (1989). **Nationality:** noun—Midway Islander(s); adjective—Midway Island. **Languages:** English. **Religions:** Christianity.

**Government Type:** unincorporated territory of U.S.

**Economy** **Monetary unit:** U.S. dollar. **Major industries:** support of U.S. naval air facility.

Midway (28°13′N, 177°26′W) consists of Midway Atoll, Eastern Island, and Sand Island. Although they are part of the Leeward Islands—the westernmost islands of the Hawaiian chain—they are not part of the state of Hawaii. They were the site of the Battle of Midway, June 1942, a turning point in the Pacific theater of World War II. Today they are administered by the Department of the Navy, which maintains a naval air station there. The navy and the Fish and Wildlife Service jointly manage the islands as a National Wildlife Refuge.

## Navassa

Located in the Caribbean between the islands of Jamaica and Haiti and 100 mi. (160 km) south of the U.S. naval base at Guantánamo, Cuba. Navassa was claimed by the U.S. in 1856. It is uninhabited except for a lighthouse under U.S. Coast Guard administration. The island is about 2 sq. mi. (5.2 sq km).

## Northern Mariana Islands
### Commonwealth of the
### Northern Mariana Islands

**Geography** **Location:** nine major islands (incl. Saipan, Rota, Tinian) in western central Pacific Ocean; Saipan 15°13′N, 145°44′E. **Boundaries:** Japan to N; Honolulu, Hawaii, about 3,500 mi. (5,635 km) to E; Guam to SW; Philippines to W across Philippine Sea. **Total land area:** 293 sq. mi. (759 sq km). **Coastline:** undetermined. **Comparative area:** slightly more than 2.5 times size of Washington, D.C. **Land use:** 1% arable land; N.A.% permanent crops; 19% meadows and pastures; N.A.% forest and woodland; N.A.% other. **Major cities:** (1990 census) Saipan (capital) 38,896.

**People** **Population:** 43,345 (1990 census). **Nationality:** undetermined. **Ethnic groups:** Chamorro majority, Carolinians, other Micronesians; Spanish, German, Japanese admixtures. **Languages:** English, Chamorro, Carolinian. **Religions:** Chris-

tian with Roman Catholic majority; some traditional beliefs.

**Government Type:** commonwealth. **Constitution:** Covenant Agreement effective Nov. 3, 1986. **National holiday:** Commonwealth Day, Jan. 8. **Heads of government:** Pedro P. Tenorio, governor (since 1978). **Structure:** executive—governor elected by popular vote; legislative—bicameral legislature (nine-member Senate elected for four-year term, 15-member House of Representatives elected for two-year term); judiciary—U.S. District Court, U.S. Commonwealth Trial Court, Commonwealth Appeals Court.

**Economy** **Monetary unit:** U.S. dollar. **Budget:** (1987) *income:* $N.A.; *expend.:* $70.6 mil. **GNP:** $165 mil., $9,170 per capita (1982). **Chief crops:** coffee, coconuts, fruits, tobacco. **Livestock:** cattle, pigs. **Natural resources:** arable land, fish. **Major industries:** tourism, construction, light industry, handicrafts. **Labor force:** 17,533, incl. 10,000 foreign workers (1988 est.). **Exports:** vegetables, beef, pork. **Imports:** N.A. **Major trading partners:** N.A.

Running north from the island of Guam across a 600-mile-long archipelago in the Pacific Island group known as Micronesia, the islands of the Northern Marianas (CNMI) were originally settled by Pacific argonauts as early as 1500 B.C. Ferdinand Magellan landed at Saipan in 1521, introducing Western culture to the region. The Spanish took control of the archipelago in 1565 and ruled until 1898, when Germany took over the islands. After World War I, the League of Nations mandated the Marianas to Japan, which developed extensive sugar-processing works on Saipan. Allied forces took the Marianas in 1944.

In 1947 the islands were included in the UN Trust Territory of the Pacific and placed under U.S. administration. In 1976 the CNMI adopted its own constitution. A mutually approved Covenant to Establish a Commonwealth was implemented by the Marianas and the United States in 1986. The Northern Marianas are subject to provisions of U.S. law, except regarding customs, minimum wages, immigration, and taxation. The people are, as a rule, U.S. citizens.

The CNMI benefits substantially from U.S. assistance. A seven-year agreement to end in 1992 allocates $288 million for development, government operations, and other programs, and the CNMI is also eligible for other federal programs provided to the 50 states. Tourism—which has registered a yearly increase of 7.5% since 1980—accounts for approximately 37% of the island's gross product. The government is the largest employer.

## Trust Territory of the Pacific Islands
### (Republic of Palau)

**Geography** **Location:** more than 200 islands, in a chain about 400 mi. (650 km) long, in western central Pacific Ocean; Koror 7°21′N, 134°31′E. **Boundaries:** Guam 720 mi. (1,160 km) to NE, Federated States of Micronesia to E, island of New Guinea to S, Philippines 530 mi. (850 km) to NW. **Total land area:** 177 sq. mi. (458 sq km). **Coastline:**

944 mi. (1,519 km). **Comparative area:** slightly more than 2.5 times size of Washington, D.C. **Land use:** N.A.% arable land; N.A.% permanent crops; N.A.% meadows and pastures; N.A.% forest and woodland; N.A.% other. **Major cities:** (1990 census) Koror state 10,501; Koror is the capital; a new capital is being built at Babelthuap, 20 km northeast.

**People** **Population:** 15,122 (1990 census). **Nationality:** noun—Palauan(s); adjective—Palauan. **Ethnic groups:** composite of Polynesian, Malayan, and Melanesian races. **Languages:** Palauan (official), English, Trukese dialect. **Religions:** predominantly Christian, mainly Roman Catholic.

**Government Type:** constitutional government, which signed Compact of Free Association with U.S. Jan. 10, 1986. **Constitution:** Jan. 11, 1981. **National holiday:** Constitution Day, July 9 (1979). **Heads of government:** Ngiratkel Etpison, president (since 1988). **Structure:** executive—president and vice president popularly elected; legislative—bicameral legislature (Olbiil Era Kelulu); judicial—supreme court headed by chief justice.

**Economy** **Monetary unit:** U.S. dollar. **Budget:** (1986) *income:* $6.0 mil.; *expend.:* $N.A. **GDP:** $31.6 mil., $2,260 per capita (1986). **Chief crops:** subsistence level production of coconut, copra, cassava, sweet potatoes. **Livestock:** N.A. **Natural resources:** forests, minerals (especially gold), marine products, deep-seabed minerals. **Major industries:** tourism, craft items (shell, wood, pearl, some commercial fishing and agriculture. **Labor force:** N.A. **Exports:** $0.5 mil. (f.o.b.,1986). **Imports:** $27.2 mil. (c.i.f., 1986). **Major trading partners:** *exports:* U.S., Japan; *imports:* U.S.

The first inhabitants of Palau (or Belau) probably arrived from Indonesia and the Philippines about 1500 B.C. The first European to visit the area was Ferdinand Magellan, in 1521. However, it was the British who dominated trade to Palau until 1885, when Pope Leo XIII acknowledged Spain's claims to the Carolines. Spain controlled Palau from 1885 to 1899, when Palau was sold to Germany. The Germans introduced coconut planting and phosphate mining, and introduced sanitary measures that arrested the deadly epidemics of dysentery and influenza, which in 120 years reduced the population from 40,000 to 4,000.

Japan occupied Palau in 1914 and over the next 30 years, increased the mining, agriculture, and fishing industries; in 1938 Palau became a closed military area and was the site of heavy fighting during World War II, especially on Peleliu. Although Palau has had its own government and constitution since 1980, Palauans have not approved a Compact of Free Association with the United States by the requisite 75 percent majority, and it continues to be administered by the United States under the auspices of the UN Trusteeship Council.

## Puerto Rico
### Commonwealth of Puerto Rico

**Geography** **Location:** large island of Puerto Rico, together with Vieques, Culebra, and many smaller islands, in northeastern Caribbean Sea; San Juan 18°29′N, 66°08′W. **Boundaries:** between Atlantic Ocean to N and Caribbean Sea to S; Virgin Islands to E, Dominican Republic 50 mi. (80 km) to W. **Total land area:** 3,459 sq. mi. (8,959 sq km). **Coastline:** 310 mi. (500 km). **Comparative area:** slightly less than three times size of Rhode Island. **Land use:** 8% arable land; 9% permanent crops; 51% meadows and pastures; 25% forest and woodland; 7% other. **Major cities:** (1990 census) San Juan (capital) 437,745; Bayamón 220,262; Ponce 187,749; Carolina 177,806; Caguas 133,447.

**People  Population:** 3,522,037 (1990 census). **Nationality:** noun—Puerto Rican(s); adjective—Puerto Rican. **Ethnic groups:** almost entirely Hispanic. **Languages:** Spanish (official), English. **Religions:** mostly Christian, 85% Roman Catholic, 15% Protestant and other.

**Government  Type:** commonwealth associated with U.S. **Constitution:** effective July 25, 1952. **National holiday:** Constitution Day, July 25. **Heads of government:** Rafael Hernandez Colón, governor. **Structure:** executive—governor elected by direct vote to four-year term; legislative—bicameral legislature (Senate with 27 members, House of Representatives with 51 members, all elected by popular vote to four-year terms); judiciary—Supreme Court appointed by governor.

**Economy  Monetary unit:** U.S. dollar. **Budget:** (1988) *income:* $4.9 bil.; *expend.:* $4.9 bil. **GNP:** $14.8 bil., $4,520 per capita (1985). **Chief crops:** sugarcane, coffee, bananas, yams, pineapples; more than 50% of food requirements are imported. **Livestock:** chickens, cattle, pigs. **Natural resources:** some copper and nickel; potential for onshore and offshore crude oil. **Major industries:** manufacturing, pharmaceuticals, chemicals. **Labor force:** 1,062,000 (1988); 23% government, 20% trade, 18% manufacturing, 4% agriculture, 35% other. **Exports:** $13.2 bil. (f.o.b., FY 1988) sugar, coffee, petroleum products, chemicals, metal products, textiles, electronic equipment. **Imports:** $11.8 bil. (c.i.f., FY 1988); chemicals, apparel, fish products, metal products, electronic equipment. **Major trading partners: exports:** 87% U.S.; *imports:* 60% U.S.

Initially peopled by Igneris and Taínos, Puerto Rico had as its first European visitor Christopher Columbus, in 1493. In 1508 Juan Ponce de Léon led the first European settlers to San Juan, and by 1514 the Taíno population had dropped from an estimated 30,000 to 4,000. In the 17th and 18th centuries, Puerto Rico was invaded by both English and Danish forces, and though San Juan was captured or burned several times, the Spanish maintained their control of the island.

The Spanish constitution granted Puerto Ricans citizenship in 1812, but a revolution was put down in 1868. Spain granted Puerto Rico self-government in 1897, but this was repealed when sovereignty was transferred to the United States after the Spanish-American War. Despite early attempts to Americanize

Puerto Rico, including an effort to make English the official language and granting citizenship in 1917, the Popular Democratic party, founded in 1938, brought about a change in political status from that of a U.S. colony to an autonomous commonwealth in 1952.

Governed under the Puerto Rican Federal Relations Act and a constitution modeled on that of the United States, Puerto Rico is nonetheless an autonomous political entity in voluntary association with the United States. Despite dramatic increases in industrial development since the 1950s, Puerto Rico suffered from net outward migration until 1988.

Puerto Ricans remain divided between those who favor statehood and those who favor maintaining commonwealth status. (Those seeking independence are a vocal but small minority.) In the November 1988 election, pro-commonwealth Gov. Hernandez Colón won only 48.7% of the vote, against the pro-statehood Baltasar Corrada del Rio's 45.8%.

# Virgin Islands
### Virgin Islands of the United States

**Geography  Location:** three main inhabited islands (St. Croix, St. Thomas, and St. John) and about 50 smaller islands, mostly uninhabited, in northeastern Caribbean Sea; Charlotte Amalie 18°22′N, 64°56′W. **Boundaries:** British Virgin Islands to N, Netherlands Antilles to E, Caribbean Sea to S, Puerto Rico about 40 mi. (64 km) to W. **Total land area:** 136 sq. mi. (352 sq km). **Coastline:** undetermined. **Comparative area:** slightly less than twice size of Washington, D.C. **Land use:** 15% arable land; 6% permanent crops; 26% meadows and pastures; 6% forest and woodland; 47% other. **Major cities:** (1990 census) Charlotte Amalie (capital) 12,331; Christiansted 2,555; Frederiksted 1,064.

**People  Population:** 101,809 (1990 census). **Nationality:** noun—Virgin Islander(s); adjective—Virgin Islander. **Ethnic groups:** 74% West Indian (45% born in Virgin Islands, 29% born elsewhere in West Indies), 13% U.S. mainland, 5% Puerto Rican, 8% other; 80% black, 15% white, 5% other; 14% of Hispanic origin. **Languages:** English (official), Spanish, Creole. **Religions:** 42% Baptist, 34% Roman Catholic, 17% Episcopalian, 7% other.

**Government  Type:** organized, unincorporated territory of U.S. **Constitution:** Revised Organic Act of July 22, 1954, serves as constitution. **National holiday:** Transfer Day (from Denmark to U.S.), Mar. 31. **Heads of government:** Alexander Farrelly, governor. **Structure:** executive—governor elected to four-year term; legislative—unicameral legislature (senate with 15 members elected to two-year terms); judiciary—two U.S. district courts.

**Economy  Monetary unit:** U.S. dollar. **Budget:** (1988) *income:* $315 mil.; *expend.:* $322 mil. **GDP:** $1.03 bil., $9,030 per capita (1985). **Chief crops:** truck gardens, fruit, sorghum. **Livestock:** cattle. **Natural resources:** sun, sand, sea, surf.

**Major industries:** tourism, government service, petroleum refining. **Labor force:** 45,000 (1987). **Exports:** $3.4 bil. (f.o.b., 1985); 94% refined petroleum products. **Imports:** $3.7 bil. (c.i.f., 1985); crude oil, foodstuffs, consumer goods, building material. **Major trading partners: exports:** U.S., Puerto Rico; *imports:* U.S., Puerto Rico.

The Virgin Islands of the United States (USVI) consist of more than 50 islands located about 40 miles east of Puerto Rico and about 1,730 miles east-southeast of Miami. Excavations have revealed evidence of human habitation in the Virgin Islands (both British and U.S.) from as early as A.D. 100. By 1493, when Christopher Columbus landed on the islands—which he named Virgin Islands for the virgin martyr St. Ursula—they were inhabited by Carib Indians who were driven out by the Spanish in 1555.

In 1672 St. Thomas was settled by the Danish West India Company. The Danes laid claim to St. John in 1683 and purchased St. Croix from the French in 1733. The United States purchased the Virgin Islands from Denmark for $25 million in 1917, making them a territory under the jurisdiction of the navy. U.S. citizenship was granted in 1927, and the Department of the Interior assumed administration of the islands in 1931. The first governor elected by popular vote was installed in 1970, and an independent constitution was voted down by the electorate in 1979.

The primary industry is tourism, which accounts for 70 percent of GDP and employs 70 percent of the work force. International business and financial services are increasingly important. The world's largest petroleum refinery is at St. Croix.

# Wake Islands

**Geography  Location:** three islands (Wake, Wilkes, and Peale) in western Pacific Ocean; Wake 19°18′N, 166°36′E. **Boundaries:** Honolulu 2,300 mi. (3,700 km) to E, Marshall Islands to S, Guam about 1,280 mi. (2,060 km) to W. **Total land area:** 2.5 sq. mi. (6.5 sq km). **Coastline:** 12 mi. (19.3 km). **Comparative area:** about 11 times size of the Mall in Washington, D.C. **Land use:** 0% arable land; 0% permanent crops; 0% meadows and pastures; 0% forest and woodland; 100% other. **Major cities:** none.

**People  Population:** 302 (1989); no indigenous inhabitants; temporary population consists of U.S. Air Force personnel and about 225 U.S. and Thai contractors.

**Government  Type:** unincorporated territory of U.S., administered by U.S. Air Force.

The Wake Island group was first discovered by the British Capt. William Wake in 1796. It was charted by Capt. Charles Wilkes's surveying expedition, which was accompanied by a naturalist named Peale. Annexed by the United States in 1898, Wake became a civil aviation station in the 1930s and was captured by the Japanese shortly after Pearl Harbor. It was retaken in 1944. Formerly an important commercial aviation base, it is now used only by U.S. military and some commercial cargo planes.

## STATE GOVERNMENT FINANCES

**Revenues** Revenue of state governments from all sources in 1989 was $586.6 billion, an 8.2% increase over the year before. Taxes accounted for 48.4%, or $284.0 billion, of the total state general revenue, up 7.5% from 1988. Sales taxes and gross receipts accounted for 24% and individual income taxes for 15% of general revenue. Charges and miscellaneous general revenue increased 11.2%, to $82.5 billion. The 30 state lotteries in operation (for more than in 1988) provided $7.0 billion in net revenue, 25% more than in 1988. Sales revenue from liquor stores, which are operated in 17 states, totaled $2.8 billion. (Liquor store expenditures amounted to only $2.4 billion.)

**Expenditures** State government expenditures in 1989 amounted to $525.1 billion, an increase of 8.3% from the amount spent in 1988. State general expenditures amounted to $469.3 billion, 8.3% more than in 1988. The leading expenditure categories, by function, were education services (29.6%) and social services and income maintenance (22.9%). Note that state governments spend more on interest on general debt (3.5% of the total) than on environment and housing (2.8%).

## U.S. TERRITORIAL EXPANSION

| Accession | Acquisition date | Gross area (land and water) Sq. mi. | Sq km |
|---|---|---|---|
| The 50 states | (X) | 3,618,770 | 9,372,614 |
| Territory in 1790[1] | (X) | 891,364 | 2,308,633 |
| Louisiana Purchase | 1803 | 831,321 | 2,153,121 |
| Purchase of Florida | 1819 | 69,866 | 180,953 |
| Texas | 1845 | 384,958 | 997,041 |
| Oregon | 1846 | 283,439 | 734,107 |
| Mexican Cession | 1848 | 530,706 | 1,374,529 |
| Gadsden Purchase | 1853 | 29,640 | 76,768 |
| Alaska | 1867 | 591,004 | 1,530,700 |
| Hawaii | 1898 | 6,471 | 16,760 |
| Other areas | | | |
| Puerto Rico | 1898 | 3,515 | 9,104 |
| Guam | 1898 | 209 | 541 |
| American Samoa | 1899 | 77 | 199 |
| Virgin Islands, U.S. | 1917 | 132 | 342 |
| Trust Territory of the Pacific Islands | 1947 | 533[2] | 1,380 |
| Northern Mariana Is. | 1947 | 184 | 477 |
| All other | (X) | 14 | 36 |
| **Total U.S. territory** | **(X)** | **3,623,434** | **9,384,694** |

**Note:** Boundaries of all U.S. territories listed here were indefinite, at least in part, at the time of acquisition. Area figures shown here represent precise determinations of specific territories that have been marked on maps, based on interpretations of the several treaties of cession, which are necessarily debatable. These determinations were made by a committee of representatives of various governmental agencies in 1912. Subsequently, these figures were adjusted to bring them into agreement with remeasurements made in 1980. 1. Includes that part of the drainage basin of the Red River of the North south of the 49th parallel, sometimes considered part of the Louisiana Purchase. 2. Land area only. **Source:** U.S. Bureau of the Census, *Statistical Abstract of the United States 1990* (1990).

## STATES RANKED ACCORDING TO SELECTED TAX AMOUNTS, 1990

| State | Total tax collections ('000s) | Rank | Per capita tax amounts (dollars) Total sales tax | Rank | General sales tax | Rank | Individual income tax | Rank |
|---|---|---|---|---|---|---|---|---|
| Alabama | $ 3,819,513 | 26 | $ 945.29 | 44 | $ 256.85 | 42 | $277.55 | 35 |
| Alaska | 1,546,441 | 40 | 2,811.49 | 1 | (X) | — | (X) | — |
| Arizona | 4,376,761 | 21 | 1,194.13 | 20 | 523.21 | 7 | 290.24 | 33 |
| Arkansas | 2,260,936 | 34 | 961.80 | 42 | 357.08 | 27 | 314.46 | 31 |
| California | 43,419,164 | 1 | 1,458.98 | 9 | 457.89 | 10 | 565.33 | 8 |
| Colorado | 3,069,428 | 29 | 931.71 | 45 | 250.51 | 43 | 407.27 | 18 |
| Connecticut | 5,286,014 | 19 | 1,602.62 | 4 | 743.33 | 3 | 185.71 | 38 |
| Delaware | 1,129,551 | 44 | 1,695.59 | 3 | (X) | — | 684.98 | 3 |
| Florida | 13,289,492 | 4 | 1,027.17 | 37 | 633.13 | 5 | (X) | — |
| Georgia | 7,078,197 | 13 | 1,092.62 | 31 | 407.31 | 19 | 442.70 | 15 |
| Hawaii | 2,334,797 | 33 | 2,106.78 | 2 | 1,061.77 | 1 | 627.21 | 6 |
| Idaho | 1,138,748 | 43 | 1,131.11 | 25 | 380.52 | 22 | 400.36 | 19 |
| Illinois | 12,890,512 | 6 | 1,127.72 | 27 | 356.67 | 28 | 375.17 | 25 |
| Indiana | 6,101,619 | 18 | 1,100.55 | 30 | 460.21 | 9 | 376.89 | 23 |
| Iowa | 3,313,094 | 28 | 1,193.15 | 21 | 339.81 | 32 | 457.98 | 13 |
| Kansas | 2,668,998 | 31 | 1,077.26 | 32 | 352.20 | 30 | 345.81 | 28 |
| Kentucky | 4,260,691 | 22 | 1,156.13 | 24 | 295.11 | 39 | 328.41 | 29 |
| Louisiana | 4,086,693 | 24 | 968.42 | 40 | 299.26 | 38 | 174.68 | 39 |
| Maine | 1,560,869 | 39 | 1,271.14 | 16 | 414.50 | 17 | 472.80 | 12 |
| Maryland | 6,450,139 | 17 | 1,348.99 | 11 | 328.74 | 35 | 599.06 | 7 |
| Massachusetts | 9,369,108 | 10 | 1,557.26 | 7 | 325.19 | 36 | 816.05 | 2 |
| Michigan | 11,343,403 | 8 | 1,220.34 | 19 | 342.93 | 31 | 422.47 | 17 |
| Minnesota | 6,819,254 | 14 | 1,558.65 | 6 | 427.31 | 12 | 657.50 | 4 |
| Mississippi | 2,395,876 | 32 | 931.08 | 46 | 423.06 | 15 | 167.26 | 40 |
| Missouri | 4,939,169 | 20 | 965.23 | 41 | 371.08 | 23 | 349.92 | 27 |
| Montana | 857,685 | 45 | 1,073.36 | 33 | (X) | — | 349.96 | 26 |
| Nebraska | 1,512,928 | 41 | 958.53 | 43 | 321.88 | 37 | 313.97 | 32 |
| Nevada | 1,583,282 | 38 | 1,317.39 | 15 | 667.32 | 4 | (X) | — |
| New Hampshire | 595,299 | 49 | 536.67 | 50 | (X) | — | 37.31 | 42 |
| New Jersey | 10,433,910 | 9 | 1,349.76 | 10 | 425.78 | 14 | 381.89 | 21 |
| New Mexico | 2,014,040 | 36 | 1,329.34 | 14 | 551.78 | 6 | 238.25 | 37 |
| New York | 28,614,593 | 2 | 1,590.54 | 5 | 333.67 | 33 | 849.85 | 1 |
| North Carolina | 7,864,737 | 11 | 1,186.48 | 22 | 267.46 | 41 | 511.48 | 10 |
| North Dakota | 677,112 | 46 | 1,059.97 | 35 | 361.57 | 24 | 165.45 | 41 |
| Ohio | 11,436,367 | 7 | 1,054.32 | 36 | 330.88 | 34 | 380.31 | 22 |
| Oklahoma | 3,476,859 | 27 | 1,105.31 | 29 | 268.46 | 40 | 318.19 | 30 |
| Oregon | 2,785,890 | 30 | 980.15 | 39 | (X) | — | 642.66 | 5 |
| Pennsylvania | 13,219,655 | 5 | 1,112.61 | 28 | 355.59 | 29 | 271.06 | 36 |
| Rhode Island | 1,233,305 | 42 | 1,229.05 | 18 | 396.05 | 21 | 425.11 | 16 |
| South Carolina | 3,934,383 | 25 | 1,128.40 | 26 | 415.25 | 16 | 395.84 | 20 |
| South Dakota | 500,093 | 50 | 718.52 | 49 | 358.75 | 25 | (X) | — |
| Tennessee | 4,245,024 | 23 | 870.38 | 47 | 480.59 | 8 | 21.11 | 43 |
| Texas | 14,716,513 | 3 | 866.36 | 48 | 448.91 | 11 | (X) | — |
| Utah | 1,767,991 | 37 | 1,026.20 | 38 | 410.43 | 18 | 375.44 | 24 |
| Vermont | 665,743 | 47 | 1,183.00 | 23 | 241.72 | 44 | 445.85 | 14 |
| Virginia | 6,600,489 | 15 | 1,066.77 | 34 | 218.68 | 45 | 498.14 | 11 |
| Washington | 7,423,096 | 12 | 1,525.29 | 8 | 918.68 | 2 | (X) | — |
| West Virginia | 2,229,745 | 35 | 1,243.25 | 17 | 426.28 | 13 | 288.19 | 34 |
| Wisconsin | 6,557,746 | 16 | 1,340.57 | 13 | 405.54 | 20 | 536.59 | 9 |
| Wyoming | 611,613 | 48 | 1,348.39 | 12 | 357.74 | 26 | (X) | — |

**Note:** (X) = State collects no tax for that item. **Source:** U.S. Bureau of the Census, *State Government Tax Collections, 1990* (1991).

## SUMMARY OF STATE GOVERNMENT FINANCES, 1989

| Item | Amount 1989 (millions) | Percent change 1988–89 | Per capita 1989[1] |
|---|---|---|---|
| **REVENUES** | | | |
| **Revenue, total** | **$586,560** | **8.2%** | **$2,368.65** |
| General revenue | 482,351 | 8.3 | 1,947.83 |
| Intergovernmental revenue | 115,765 | 7.9 | 467.48 |
| From federal government | 108,235 | 7.7 | 437.08 |
| Public welfare | 51,934 | 8.4 | 209.72 |
| Education | 19,547 | 8.8 | 78.93 |
| Highways | 14,404 | 7.0 | 58.17 |
| Health and hospitals | 4,769 | 14.8 | 19.26 |
| Employment security administration | 2,968 | 2.5 | 11.99 |
| Housing and community development | 1,762 | 2.3 | 7.11 |
| Natural resources | 1,430 | -10.7 | 5.77 |
| Transit subsidies | 867 | 6.0 | 3.50 |
| Other from federal government | 10,556 | 6.2 | 42.63 |
| From local governments | 7,530 | 11.3 | 30.41 |
| Taxes | 284,042 | 7.5 | 1,147.02 |
| Sales and gross receipts | 138,249 | 6.1 | 558.28 |
| General | 93,414 | 7.3 | 377.23 |
| Selective | 44,834 | 3.7 | 181.05 |
| Motor fuels | 18,029 | 4.8 | 72.81 |
| Tobacco products | 5,039 | 4.1 | 20.35 |
| Alcoholic beverages | 3,115 | -2.3 | 12.58 |
| Insurance | 7,341 | 6.3 | 29.64 |
| Public utilities | 6,108 | -1.1 | 24.67 |
| Parimutuels | 663 | -2.1 | 2.68 |
| Other selective sales | 4,539 | 6.9 | 18.33 |
| License taxes | 17,666 | 3.9 | 71.34 |
| Motor vehicles | 9,351 | 5.7 | 37.76 |
| Corporations in general | 2,997 | -5.4 | 12.10 |
| Motor vehicle operators | 794 | 3.8 | 3.20 |
| Hunting and fishing | 773 | 5.5 | 3.12 |
| Alcoholic beverages | 248 | 1.6 | 1.00 |
| Other licenses | 3,504 | 7.9 | 14.15 |
| Individual income | 88,693 | 10.7 | 358.16 |
| Corporate net income | 23,861 | 10.4 | 96.36 |
| Death and gift | 3,486 | 7.6 | 14.08 |
| Property | 5,417 | 7.9 | 21.88 |
| Severance | 4,147 | -4.2 | 16.75 |
| Documentary and stock transfer | 2,398 | 1.4 | 9.68 |
| Other | 125 | 13.6 | 0.51 |
| Charges and miscellaneous general revenue | 82,543 | 11.2 | 333.33 |
| Current charges | 38,553 | 12.0 | 155.68 |
| Education | 21,502 | 11.3 | 86.83 |
| Higher education | 21,166 | 11.2 | 85.47 |
| Other education | 336 | 15.5 | 1.36 |
| Hospitals | 8,526 | 14.7 | 34.43 |
| Highways | 2,434 | 6.3 | 9.83 |
| Toll facilities | 2,205 | 7.6 | 8.90 |
| Other | 230 | -3.8 | 0.93 |
| Miscellaneous commercial activities | 239 | 52.2 | 0.97 |
| Natural resources | 954 | 14.0 | 3.85 |
| Parks and recreation | 708 | 12.7 | 2.86 |
| Other charges | 4,188 | 11.1 | 16.91 |
| Miscellaneous general revenue | 43,990 | 10.6 | 177.64 |
| Interest earnings | 25,218 | 9.7 | 101.83 |
| Rents and royalties | 2,028 | -28.7 | 8.19 |
| Donations | 3,147 | 17.7 | 12.71 |
| Fines and forfeits | 1,288 | 14.8 | 5.20 |
| Sale of property | 184 | -12.8 | 0.74 |
| Other | 12,124 | 22.2 | 48.96 |
| Utility revenue[2] | 3,248 | 7.2 | 13.12 |
| Water | 89 | 23.6 | 0.36 |
| Electric | 2,114 | 6.2 | 8.54 |
| Transit | 1,039 | 7.3 | 4.19 |

| Item | Amount 1989 (millions) | Percent change 1988–89 | Per capita 1989[1] |
|---|---|---|---|
| Insurance trust revenue | 98,174 | 8.5 | 396.45 |
| Employee retirement | 67,964 | 6.9 | 274.45 |
| Unemployment compensation | 19,640 | 14.3 | 79.31 |
| Workers' compensation | 8,251 | 11.9 | 33.32 |
| Other | 2,320 | -2.4 | 9.37 |
| Liquor stores revenue | 2,788 | 0.8 | 11.26 |
| **EXPENDITURE, BY FUNCTION** | | | |
| **Expenditure, total** | **$525,077** | **8.3%** | **$2,120.37** |
| General expenditure | 469,269 | 8.6 | 1,895.00 |
| Intergovernmental expenditure | 165,506 | 9.1 | 668.35 |
| State payments to federal government | 2,930 | 10.4 | 11.83 |
| Direct expenditure | 303,763 | 8.3 | 1,226.65 |
| Education services | | | |
| Education | 173,184 | 8.6 | 699.35 |
| Intergovernmental expenditure | 104,601 | 9.7 | 422.40 |
| Direct expenditure | 68,583 | 7.0 | 276.95 |
| Higher education | 55,988 | 6.8 | 226.09 |
| Elementary and secondary | 1,417 | 1.4 | 5.72 |
| Other | 11,177 | 8.5 | 45.14 |
| Libraries | 660 | 6.1 | 2.66 |
| Social services and income maintenance | | | |
| Public welfare | $92,750 | 10.1% | $374.54 |
| Intergovernmental expenditure | 19,614 | 11.0 | 79.21 |
| Supplementary Security Income program | 2,916 | 10.8 | 11.78 |
| Direct expenditure | 73,136 | 9.9 | 295.34 |
| Vendor payments | 48,871 | 11.9 | 197.35 |
| Cash assistance payments | 11,180 | 2.0 | 45.15 |
| Other | 13,085 | 9.6 | 52.84 |
| Hospitals | 21,414 | 8.9 | 86.48 |
| Intergovernmental expenditure | 104 | 23.8 | 0.42 |
| Direct expenditure | 21,311 | 8.8 | 86.06 |
| State hospitals | 21,206 | 8.8 | 85.63 |
| Other hospitals (nongovernmental) | 105 | 8.2 | 0.42 |
| Health | 17,188 | 13.1 | 69.41 |
| Employment security administration | 2,937 | 3.3 | 11.86 |
| Veterans' services | 146 | 9.0 | 0.59 |
| Transportation | | | |
| Highways | 42,694 | 4.9 | 172.41 |
| Intergovernmental expenditure | 7,376 | 6.1 | 29.79 |
| Direct expenditure | 35,318 | 4.7 | 142.62 |
| Regular highway facilities | 33,039 | 4.9 | 133.42 |
| Toll highway facilities | 2,279 | 2.6 | 9.20 |
| Airports | 711 | 8.2 | 2.87 |
| Water transport and terminals | 664 | 31.5 | 2.68 |
| Transit subsidies | 2,651 | 4.4 | 10.71 |
| Public safety | | | |
| Police protection | 4,746 | 5.3 | 19.16 |
| Correction | 15,018 | 12.9 | 60.64 |
| Protective inspection and regulation, not elsewhere classified | 3,389 | 9.9 | 13.69 |
| Environment and housing | | | |
| Sewerage | 1,293 | -9.3 | 5.22 |
| Solid waste management | 635 | 151.0 | 2.57 |
| Natural resources | 9,070 | 9.1 | 36.63 |
| Parks and recreation | 2,589 | 9.3 | 10.46 |
| Housing and community development | 2,943 | 15.4 | 11.88 |
| Governmental administration | | | |
| Financial administration | 7,672 | 10.1 | 30.98 |
| Judicial and legal | 5,439 | 12.4 | 21.96 |
| General public buildings | 1,251 | 11.7 | 5.05 |

| Item | Amount 1989 (millions) | Percent change 1988–89 | Per capita 1989[1] |
|---|---|---|---|
| Other governmental administration | 2,251 | 8.1 | 9.09 |
| Interest on general debt | 20,355 | 5.1 | 82.20 |
| Other and unallocable | 37,619 | 6.2 | 151.91 |
| Utility expenditure[2] | 6,410 | 2.9 | 25.88 |
| Water | 128 | 21.9 | 0.52 |
| Electric | 2,346 | 2.9 | 9.47 |
| Transit | 3,931 | 2.2 | 15.88 |
| Insurance trust expenditure | 46,995 | 6.3 | 189.77 |
| Employee retirement | 26,966 | 11.4 | 108.90 |
| Unemployment compensation | 12,791 | -1.8 | 51.65 |
| Workers' compensation | 5,318 | 2.6 | 21.48 |
| Other | 1,919 | 5.9 | 7.75 |
| Liquor stores expenditure | 2,403 | 1.1 | 9.71 |

**INDEBTEDNESS AND DEBT TRANSACTIONS**

| Item | Amount 1989 (millions) | Percent change 1988–89 | Per capita 1989[1] |
|---|---|---|---|
| **Debt at end of fiscal year** | **$295,618** | **6.8%** | **$1,193.76** |
| Long-term | 293,368 | 6.5 | 1,184.68 |
| Public debt for private purpose | 138,974 | 13.4 | 561.21 |
| Higher education | 28,383 | -2.9 | 114.62 |

| Item | Amount 1989 (millions) | Percent change 1988–89 | Per capita 1989[1] |
|---|---|---|---|
| Elementary and secondary education | 3,662 | 12.2 | 14.79 |
| Electric power | 7,514 | -4.2 | 30.34 |
| Transit system | 3,920 | 11.2 | 15.83 |
| Water supply | 753 | -5.9 | 3.04 |
| Other and unallocable | 110,161 | 1.8 | 444.85 |
| Short-term | 2,250 | 68.2 | 9.09 |
| Long-term debt issued | 41,955 | 15.3 | 169.42 |
| Long-term debt retired | 26,916 | 3.1 | 108.69 |

**CASH AND SECURITY HOLDINGS**

| Item | Amount 1989 (millions) | Percent change 1988–89 | Per capita 1989[1] |
|---|---|---|---|
| **Total** | **$880,994** | **14.1%** | **$3,557.63** |
| Cash and security holdings of insurance trust systems | 563,182 | 19.3 | 2,274.24 |
| Employment retirement | 505,664 | 19.4 | 2,041.97 |
| Unemployment compensation | 34,342 | 25.3 | 138.68 |
| Workers compensation | 21,789 | 10.5 | 87.99 |
| Other insurance trust systems | 1,387 | 19.7 | 5.60 |
| Cash and security holdings, other than insurance trust systems | 317,811 | 5.9 | 1,283.39 |

Note: Percent and per capita figures are calculated on the basis of amounts rounded to the nearest thousand. 1. Based on population as of July 1, 1989. 2. May include minor amounts for gas supply that are not included in the detail.
Source: U.S. Bureau of the Census, State Government Finances in 1989 (1990).

## STATE EXCISES ON GENERAL SALES, CIGARETTES, AND MOTOR FUEL, 1990

| State | General sales and gross receipts — Percentage rate | Food exempt[1] | Drugs exempt[2] | Cigarettes (cents per package) | Gasoline (cents per gallon) |
|---|---|---|---|---|---|
| Alabama | 4.0%[3] | No | Yes | 16.5¢ | 11¢ |
| Alaska | (X) | (X) | (X) | 29 | 8 |
| Arizona | 5.0[3] | Yes | Yes | 15 | 17 |
| Arkansas | 4.0[3] | No | Yes | 21 | 13.5 |
| California | 4.75[3] | Yes | Yes | 35 | 14 |
| Colorado | 3.0[3] | Yes | Yes | 20 | 20 |
| Connecticut | 8.0 | Yes | Yes | 40 | 22 |
| Delaware | (X) | (X) | (X) | 19 | 16 |
| District of Columbia | 6.0 | Yes | Yes | 17 | 18 |
| Florida | 6.0[3] | Yes | Yes | 33.9 | 4 |
| Georgia | 4.0[3] | No | Yes | 12 | 7.5[4] |
| Hawaii | 4.0 | No | Yes | (5) | 11[6] |
| Idaho | 5.0 | No | Yes | 18 | 18 |
| Illinois | 5.0[3] | No[7] | No[7] | 30 | 19 |
| Indiana | 5.0 | Yes | Yes | 15.5 | 15 |
| Iowa | 4.0 | Yes | Yes | 31 | 20 |
| Kansas | 4.25[3] | No | Yes | 24 | 16 |
| Kentucky | 5.0[3] | Yes | Yes | 3 | 15 |
| Louisiana | 4.0 | No[8] | Yes | 20 | 20 |
| Maine | 5.0 | Yes | Yes | 31 | 17 |
| Maryland | 5.0 | Yes | Yes | 13 | 18.5 |
| Massachusetts | 5.0 | Yes | Yes | 26 | 17 |
| Michigan | 4.0 | Yes | Yes | 25 | 15 |
| Minnesota | 6.0[3] | Yes | Yes | 38 | 20 |
| Mississippi | 6.0 | No | Yes | 18 | 18 |
| Missouri | 4.225[3] | No | Yes | 13 | 11 |
| Montana | (X) | (X) | (X) | 18¢ | 20¢ |
| Nebraska | 4.0%[3] | Yes | Yes | 27 | 21.9 |
| Nevada | 5.75[3] | Yes | Yes | 35 | 16.25 |
| New Hampshire | (X) | (X) | (X) | 25 | 16 |
| New Jersey | 6.0 | Yes | Yes | 40 | 10.5 |
| New Mexico | 4.75[3] | No | No | 15 | 16.2 |
| New York | 4.0[3] | Yes | Yes | 39 | 8 |
| North Carolina | 3.0[3] | No | Yes | 2 | 21.5 |
| North Dakota | 6.0 | Yes | Yes | 30 | 17 |
| Ohio | 5.0[3] | Yes | Yes | 18 | 18 |
| Oklahoma | 4.0[3] | No | Yes | 23 | 17 |
| Oregon | (X) | (X) | (X) | 28 | 18 |
| Pennsylvania | 6.0 | Yes | Yes | 18 | 12 |
| Rhode Island | 6.0 | Yes | Yes | 37 | 20 |
| South Carolina | 5.0 | No | Yes | 7 | 16 |
| South Dakota | 4.0[3] | No | Yes | 23 | 18 |
| Tennessee | 5.5[3] | No | Yes | 13 | 20 |
| Texas | 6.25[3] | Yes | Yes | 41 | 15 |
| Utah | 5.0[3] | No | Yes | 23 | 19 |
| Vermont | 4.0 | Yes | Yes | 17 | 16 |
| Virginia | 3.5[3] | No | Yes | 2.5 | 17.5 |
| Washington | 6.5 | Yes | Yes | 34 | 22 |
| West Virginia | 6.0 | No | Yes | 17 | 15.5 |
| Wisconsin | 5.0[3] | Yes | Yes | 30 | 21.5 |
| Wyoming | 3.0[3] | No | Yes | 12 | 9 |

Note: X = no tax levied. 1. Reflects the status as of the end of the fiscal year for the sale of most food products for consumption off premises; federal statute prohibits states from taxing food purchased with USDA food stamps. 2. Reflects the status as of the end of the fiscal year. 3. State authorizes state collection of combined state and local sales taxes in those jurisdictions that approve supplemental local sales taxes under state-enabling legislation. 4. An additional tax is levied at the rate of 3% of the retail sales price of the motor fuel, less the current 7.5 per gallon tax. This tax is levied, collected, and administered in the same manner as the sales and use tax. 5. Rate is 40% of the wholesale price. 6. Combined state and county rates are: Hawaii, 19.8¢; Honolulu, 27.5¢; Kauai, 21¢; and Maui, 20¢. 7. Subject to a 1% state sales tax effective Jan. 1, 1990. In addition, these items may be subject to a 1% local tax. 8. Subject to a 2% state tax. **Source:** U.S. Bureau of the Census, State Government Tax Collection, 1990 (1991).

## DISTRIBUTION OF FEDERAL FUNDS TO STATES AND TERRITORIES, 1990

| State | Total (millions) | Per capita Amount | Rank |
|---|---|---|---|
| United States | $1,002,703 | $3,974.31 | — |
| Alabama | 17,261 | 4,271.79 | 12 |
| Alaska | 3,227 | 5,866.65 | 2 |
| Arizona | 15,072 | 4,112.18 | 16 |
| Arkansas | 8,250 | 3,509.46 | 36 |
| California | 115,802 | 3,891.19 | 23 |
| Colorado | 14,586 | 4,427.63 | 10 |
| Connecticut | 14,739 | 4,483.79 | 9 |
| Delaware | 2,149 | 3,225.57 | 43 |
| District of Columbia | 17,353 | 28,592.06 | — |
| Florida | 51,359 | 3,969.61 | 19 |
| Georgia | 21,149 | 3,264.57 | 42 |
| Hawaii | 5,461 | 4,927.28 | 6 |
| Idaho | 3,888 | 3,861.51 | 24 |
| Illinois | 36,696 | 3,210.31 | 44 |
| Indiana | 16,915 | 3,050.92 | 49 |
| Iowa | 9,962 | 3,587.48 | 34 |
| Kansas | 9,538 | 3,849.64 | 26 |
| Kentucky | 13,524 | 3,669.70 | 32 |
| Louisiana | 15,116 | 3,581.97 | 35 |
| Maine | 4,925 | 4,010.67 | 18 |
| Maryland | 27,118 | 5,671.41 | 4 |
| Massachusetts | 29,778 | 4,949.43 | 5 |
| Michigan | 29,205 | 3,141.86 | 47 |
| Minnesota | 15,073 | 3,445.13 | 40 |
| Mississippi | 10,066 | 3,911.71 | 22 |
| Missouri | 24,258 | 4,740.65 | 7 |
| Montana | 3,345 | 4,186.40 | 13 |
| Nebraska | 6,092 | 3,859.53 | 25 |
| Nevada | 4,144 | 3,448.17 | 39 |
| New Hampshire | 3,559 | 3,208.56 | 45 |
| New Jersey | 28,322 | 3,663.76 | 33 |
| New Mexico | 8,640 | 5,702.65 | 3 |
| New York | 70,493 | 3,918.35 | 21 |
| North Carolina | 20,172 | 3,043.19 | 50 |
| North Dakota | 2,910 | 4,554.95 | 8 |
| Ohio | 37,920 | 3,495.86 | 37 |
| Oklahoma | 11,804 | 3,752.69 | 29 |
| Oregon | 9,826 | 3,457.19 | 38 |
| Pennsylvania | 45,424 | 3,823.04 | 27 |
| Rhode Island | 4,318 | 4,302.99 | 11 |
| South Carolina | 13,664 | 3,918.80 | 20 |
| South Dakota | 2,863 | 4,113.69 | 15 |
| Tennessee | 18,049 | 3,700.71 | 30 |
| Texas | 58,237 | 3,428.43 | 41 |
| Utah | 6,511 | 3,779.23 | 28 |
| Vermont | 1,772 | 3,147.99 | 46 |
| Virginia | 36,346 | 5,874.30 | 1 |
| Washington | 20,149 | 4,140.11 | 14 |
| West Virginia | 6,609 | 3,684.86 | 31 |
| Wisconsin | 14,928 | 3,051.63 | 48 |
| Wyoming | 1,855 | 4,089.12 | 17 |
| American Samoa | 103 | 2,717.03 | — |
| Guam | 895 | 6,882.38 | — |
| Northern Marianas | 68 | 3,424.90 | — |
| Puerto Rico | 7,699 | 2,338.63 | — |
| U.S. Virgin Islands | N.A. | 4,972.48 | — |

**Note**: Includes grants to state and local governments, salaries and wages, direct payments for individuals, and procurement contract awards. **Source**: U.S. Bureau of the Census, *Federal Expenditures by State for Fiscal Year 1990* (1991).

## STATE GOVERNMENT TAX REVENUE, BY TYPE OF TAX, 1989 (in thousands)

| State | Total[1] | Sales and gross receipts | Licenses | Individual income | Corporate net income | Property | Death and gift |
|---|---|---|---|---|---|---|---|
| States using tax[2] | 51 | 51 | 51 | 45 | 47 | 43 | 51 |
| All states | $284,412,634 | $138,569,077 | $17,702,540 | $88,817,680 | $23,865,597 | $5,292,776 | $3,485,608 |
| Alabama | 3,662,563 | 1,916,314 | 296,931 | 1,063,321 | 215,817 | 85,964 | 11,469 |
| Alaska | 1,410,330 | 80,954 | 80,109 | (X) | 459,686 | 89,713 | 669 |
| Arizona | 4,060,582 | 2,470,297 | 260,957 | 913,344 | 200,027 | 191,877 | 240,080 |
| Arkansas | 2,172,464 | 1,179,715 | 162,884 | 681,935 | 111,671 | 6,036 | 8,676 |
| California | 41,213,784 | 16,205,198 | 1,761,806 | 15,815,364 | 5,062,844 | 2,004,209 | 335,083 |
| Colorado | 2,903,821 | 1,241,925 | 168,883 | 1,272,854 | 171,176 | 8,520 | 16,237 |
| Connecticut | 4,808,456 | 3,057,099 | 246,436 | 450,737 | 799,953 | 12 | 188,679 |
| Delaware | 1,130,196 | 158,817 | 329,958 | 427,396 | 155,400 | (X) | 15,723 |
| Dist. of Columbia | 2,243,115 | 643,849 | 38,517 | 603,469 | 156,414 | 710,766 | 24,678 |
| Florida | 12,455,553 | 9,878,661 | 770,546 | (X) | 725,364 | 259,858 | 190,282 |
| Georgia | 6,347,203 | 2,812,473 | 185,198 | 2,732,045 | 525,015 | 22,647 | 37,326 |
| Hawaii | 2,217,039 | 1,315,214 | 33,832 | 768,004 | 88,099 | (X) | 6,675 |
| Idaho | 1,035,025 | 521,382 | 93,036 | 346,674 | 71,621 | 78 | 1,853 |
| Illinois | 11,760,588 | 5,997,812 | 840,635 | 3,510,059 | 1,073,022 | 229,010 | 95,764 |
| Indiana | 5,902,572 | 3,390,994 | 219,277 | 1,944,900 | 282,022 | 3,189 | 61,203 |
| Iowa | 3,167,409 | 1,443,362 | 278,998 | 1,172,573 | 202,685 | (X) | 66,510 |
| Kansas | 2,496,343 | 1,159,738 | 138,607 | 844,369 | 198,305 | 30,291 | 45,310 |
| Kentucky | 4,072,935 | 1,872,719 | 244,360 | 1,111,707 | 310,803 | 281,890 | 53,397 |
| Louisiana | 3,969,193 | 2,069,706 | 401,715 | 676,843 | 344,584 | 28,068 | 36,743 |
| Maine | 1,590,423 | 774,754 | 96,364 | 571,263 | 96,333 | 28,479 | 10,255 |
| Maryland | 6,195,976 | 2,640,580 | 245,738 | 2,655,228 | 331,079 | 163,225 | 60,175 |
| Massachusetts | 9,118,183 | 3,027,564 | 308,785 | 4,286,689 | 1,189,321 | 1,188 | 258,560 |
| Michigan | 11,124,073 | 4,329,932 | 652,445 | 3,789,065 | 1,862,126 | 332,290 | 102,989 |
| Minnesota | 6,400,520 | 2,952,207 | 422,085 | 2,496,790 | 487,818 | 7,922 | 27,290 |
| Mississippi | 2,277,058 | 1,520,385 | 154,024 | 400,207 | 142,787 | 269 | 14,303 |
| Missouri | 4,685,374 | 2,365,602 | 346,359 | 1,688,344 | 243,226 | 11,241 | 28,853 |
| Montana | 727,969 | 179,330 | 80,410 | 265,538 | 56,140 | 36,569 | 10,092 |
| Nebraska | 1,449,994 | 781,194 | 101,561 | 474,100 | 80,624 | 4,118 | 3,777 |
| Nevada | 1,356,233 | 1,177,523 | 156,895 | (X) | (X) | 15,838 | 5,591 |
| New Hampshire | 613,232 | 268,582 | 86,156 | 36,255 | 152,005 | 9,857 | 30,977 |
| New Jersey | 10,501,352 | 5,330,708 | 656,704 | 2,896,266 | 1,309,625 | 24,926 | 204,343 |
| New Mexico | 1,892,961 | 1,077,544 | 126,634 | 349,239 | 76,542 | 275 | 6,556 |
| New York | 26,576,039 | 8,663,676 | 752,082 | 13,844,385 | 2,008,913 | (X) | 511,979 |
| North Carolina | 7,369,389 | 2,916,047 | 473,153 | 3,030,765 | 789,261 | 86,892 | 71,747 |
| North Dakota | 666,140 | 378,918 | 56,973 | 105,524 | 42,433 | 1,135 | 1,658 |
| Ohio | 10,807,392 | 5,400,602 | 787,769 | 3,809,492 | 730,510 | 13,228 | 56,992 |
| Oklahoma | 3,312,359 | 1,501,553 | 343,603 | 932,616 | 112,851 | (X) | 35,983 |
| Oregon | 2,586,262 | 363,268 | 292,535 | 1,725,324 | 157,816 | 183 | 8,983 |
| Pennsylvania | 12,692,593 | 6,368,268 | 1,284,556 | 3,058,526 | 1,169,237 | 147,015 | 446,708 |
| Rhode Island | 1,159,113 | 580,077 | 45,892 | 421,460 | 77,624 | 8,590 | 19,360 |
| South Carolina | 3,718,568 | 1,997,468 | 195,328 | 1,248,058 | 220,379 | 7,990 | 35,986 |
| South Dakota | 472,409 | 379,435 | 44,137 | (X) | 26,490 | (X) | 13,099 |
| Tennessee | 4,066,459 | 3,083,461 | 399,929 | 95,463 | 371,545 | (X) | 43,613 |
| Texas | 13,974,361 | 10,962,405 | 1,734,888 | (X) | (X) | (X) | 104,880 |
| Utah | 1,623,563 | 882,395 | 72,420 | 541,173 | 92,207 | 322 | 4,416 |
| Vermont | 634,459 | 309,904 | 48,825 | 213,337 | 38,310 | 400 | 4,020 |
| Virginia | 6,621,017 | 2,607,580 | 373,296 | 3,106,916 | 347,447 | 15,747 | 44,678 |
| Washington | 6,510,602 | 4,897,079 | 353,857 | (X) | (X) | 1,006,528 | 17,328 |
| West Virginia | 1,912,859 | 969,431 | 123,067 | 467,420 | 206,487 | 1,801 | 5,022 |
| Wisconsin | 6,407,675 | 2,902,667 | 310,188 | 2,576,112 | 448,367 | 45,132 | 98,012 |
| Wyoming | 581,971 | 206,558 | 61,714 | (X) | (X) | 80,254 | 1,704 |

1. Includes severance, documentary and stock transfer, and other taxes not shown separately. 2. Figures include District of Columbia. **Source**: U.S. Bureau of the Census, *State Government Tax Collections, 1989* (1990).

## COMPOSITION OF STATE LEGISLATURES, 1991

| State or other jurisdiction | Senate Demo-crats | Repub-licans | Total | House Demo-crats | Repub-licans | Total | State or other jurisdiction | Senate Demo-crats | Repub-licans | Total | House Demo-crats | Repub-licans | Total |
|---|---|---|---|---|---|---|---|---|---|---|---|---|---|
| Alabama | 28 | 7 | 35 | 83 | 22 | 105 | New Jersey | 22 | 17 | 40[4] | 43 | 37 | 80 |
| Alaska | 10 | 10 | 20 | 23 | 17 | 40 | New Mexico | 26 | 16 | 42 | 49 | 21 | 70 |
| Arizona | 17 | 13 | 30 | 27 | 33 | 60 | New York | 26 | 35 | 61 | 95 | 55 | 150 |
| Arkansas | 31 | 4 | 35 | 91 | 9 | 100 | North Carolina | 36 | 14 | 50 | 81 | 39 | 120 |
| California | 26 | 11 | 40[1] | 47 | 32 | 80[2] | North Dakota | 27 | 26 | 53 | 48 | 58 | 106 |
| Colorado | 12 | 23 | 35 | 27 | 38 | 65 | Ohio | 12 | 21 | 33 | 61 | 38 | 99 |
| Connecticut | 20 | 16 | 36 | 89 | 62 | 151 | Oklahoma | 37 | 11 | 48 | 69 | 32 | 101 |
| Delaware | 15 | 6 | 21 | 17 | 24 | 41 | Oregon | 20 | 10 | 30 | 28 | 32 | 60 |
| Florida | 23 | 17 | 40 | 74 | 46 | 120 | Pennsylvania | 24 | 26 | 50 | 107 | 96 | 203 |
| Georgia | 45 | 11 | 56 | 145 | 35 | 180 | Rhode Island | 45 | 5 | 50 | 89 | 11 | 100 |
| Hawaii | 22 | 3 | 25 | 45 | 6 | 51 | South Carolina | 34 | 11 | 46[2] | 80 | 41 | 124[1] |
| Idaho | 21 | 21 | 42 | 28 | 56 | 84 | South Dakota | 17 | 18 | 35 | 24 | 46 | 70 |
| Illinois | 31 | 28 | 59 | 72 | 46 | 118 | Tennessee | 20 | 13 | 33 | 56 | 43 | 99 |
| Indiana | 24 | 26 | 50 | 52 | 48 | 100 | Texas | 22 | 8 | 31[2] | 92 | 56 | 150[9] |
| Iowa | 28 | 22 | 50 | 55 | 45 | 100 | Utah | 10 | 19 | 29 | 31 | 44 | 75 |
| Kansas | 18 | 22 | 40 | 63 | 62 | 125 | Vermont | 16 | 14 | 30 | 73 | 75 | 150[10] |
| Kentucky | 27 | 11 | 38 | 68 | 32 | 100 | Virginia | 30 | 10 | 40 | 59 | 39 | 100[10] |
| Louisiana | 33 | 6 | 39 | 84 | 17 | 105[3] | Washington | 24 | 25 | 49 | 58 | 40 | 98 |
| Maine | 22 | 13 | 35 | 97 | 54 | 151 | West Virginia | 33 | 1 | 34 | 74 | 26 | 100 |
| Maryland | 38 | 9 | 47 | 117 | 24 | 141 | Wisconsin | 19 | 14 | 33 | 58 | 41 | 99 |
| Massachusetts | 26 | 14 | 40 | 121 | 38 | 160[4] | Wyoming | 10 | 20 | 30 | 22 | 42 | 64 |
| Michigan | 18 | 20 | 38 | 61 | 49 | 110 | All states | 1,209 | 731 | 1,995[11] | 3,273 | 2,174 | 5,466[12] |
| Minnesota | 46[5] | 21[6] | 67 | 80[5] | 54[6] | 134 | District of Columbia[13] | 11 | 0 | 13[14] | Unicameral | | |
| Mississippi | 44 | 8 | 52 | 102 | 19 | 122[7] | American Samoa | Nonpartisan | | 18[15] | Nonpartisan | | 21 |
| Missouri | 23 | 11 | 34 | 97 | 65 | 163[2] | Guam | 11 | 10 | 21 | Unicameral | | |
| Montana | 29 | 21 | 50 | 61 | 39 | 100 | Northern Mariana Islands | 3 | 6 | 9 | 9 | 6 | 15 |
| Nebraska | Nonpartisan | | 49 | Unicameral | | | Puerto Rico | 18[16] | 8[17] | 27[18] | 36[16] | 15[17] | 53[18] |
| Nevada | 11 | 10 | 21 | 22 | 20 | 42 | U.S. Virgin Islands | 6 | 2 | 15[19] | Unicameral | | |
| New Hampshire | 11 | 13 | 24 | 128 | 270 | 400[8] | | | | | | | |

**Note:** As of Mar. 31. 1. Includes one Independent and two vacancies. 2. Includes one vacancy. 3. Includes one Independent and three vacancies. 4. Includes one Independent. 5. Democrat-Farmer-Labor. 6. Independent-Republican. 7. Includes one Independent-Democrat. 8. Includes one Independent and one Independent-Democrat. 9. Includes two vacancies. 10. Includes two Independents. 11. Includes 49 nonpartisan (Nebraska), two Independents, and four vacancies. 12. Includes eight Independents, two Independent-Democrats, and nine vacancies. 13. Council of the District of Columbia. 14. Includes one Independent and one vacancy. 15. Includes four vacancies. 16. Popular Democratic Party. 17. New Progressive Party. 18. Includes one Puerto Rican Independent Party. 19. Includes three Independents and four Citizens Movement. **Source:** Council of State Governments, *State Elective Officials and the Legislatures, 1991–92* (1991).

## SALARIES OF MAJOR STATE ADMINISTRATIVE OFFICIALS, 1990

| State | Governor | Lieutenant governor | Secretary of state | Attorney general | State | Governor | Lieutenant governor | Secretary of state | Attorney general |
|---|---|---|---|---|---|---|---|---|---|
| Alabama | $ 70,233 | $ 43,860 | $ 36,234 | $ 77,420 | Nebraska | $ 58,000 | $ 40,000 | $ 40,000 | $ 57,500 |
| Alaska | 81,648 | 66,816[1] | 66,816[1] | 66,816[1] | Nevada | 70,857 | 12,500 | 50,500 | 62,500 |
| Arizona | 75,000 | (2) | 50,000 | 70,000 | New Hampshire | 75,753 | (2) | 60,410 | 67,625 |
| Arkansas | 35,000 | 14,000 | 22,500 | 46,785 | New Jersey | 85,000 | 46,667 | 95,000 | 95,000 |
| California | 85,000 | 72,500 | 72,500 | 77,500 | New Mexico | 90,000 | 40,425 | 40,425 | 46,200 |
| Colorado | 70,000 | 48,500 | 48,500 | 60,000 | New York | 130,000 | 110,000 | 87,338 | 110,000 |
| Connecticut | 78,000 | 55,000 | 50,000 | 60,000 | North Carolina | 123,000 | 70,992 | 70,992 | 70,992 |
| Delaware | 80,000 | 35,100 | 69,900 | 81,400 | North Dakota | 65,196 | 53,496 | 49,300 | 55,704 |
| Florida | 100,883 | 91,301 | 52,762 | 91,301 | Ohio | 65,000 | 46,883 | 66,997 | 66,997 |
| Georgia | 88,872 | 57,702 | 71,184 | 72,824 | Oklahoma | 70,000 | 40,000 | 37,500 | 55,000 |
| Hawaii | 94,780 | 90,041 | 90,041 | 85,302 | Oregon | 77,500 | (3) | 59,500 | 64,000 |
| Idaho | 55,000 | 15,000 | 45,000 | 48,000 | Pennsylvania | 85,000 | 67,500 | 58,000 | 84,000 |
| Illinois | 93,266 | 65,835 | 82,294 | 82,294 | Rhode Island | 69,000 | 52,000 | 52,000 | 55,000 |
| Indiana | 77,194 | 63,986 | 45,994 | 59,202 | South Carolina | 84,897 | 37,142 | 72,161 | 72,161 |
| Iowa | 72,500 | 25,100 | 55,700 | 69,600 | South Dakota | 60,819 | 52,915 | 41,309 | 51,626 |
| Kansas | 73,137 | 20,688 | 56,400 | 65,345 | Tennessee | 85,000 | 49,500 | 65,000 | 65,650 |
| Kentucky | 69,731 | 59,263 | 59,263 | 59,263 | Texas | 93,432 | 7,200 | 72,549 | 74,698 |
| Louisiana | 66,096 | 63,367 | 60,169 | 66,566 | Utah | 69,992 | 52,499 | 52,499 | 56,014 |
| Maine | 70,000 | (2) | 47,154 | 56,366 | Vermont | 75,800 | 31,600 | 47,700 | 57,300 |
| Maryland | 85,000 | 72,500 | 45,000 | 72,500 | Virginia | 85,000 | 28,000 | 59,247 | 75,000 |
| Massachusetts | 75,000 | 60,000 | 60,000 | 65,000 | Washington | 96,700 | 51,100 | 52,600 | 75,700 |
| Michigan | 106,690 | 80,300 | 89,000 | 89,000 | West Virginia | 72,000 | (2) | 43,200 | 50,400 |
| Minnesota | 103,860 | 57,125 | 57,125 | 81,138 | Wisconsin | 86,149 | 46,360 | 42,098 | 73,903 |
| Mississippi | 75,600 | 40,800 | 54,000 | 61,200 | Wyoming | 70,000 | 52,500 | 52,500 | 63,147 |
| Missouri | 88,541 | 53,277 | 70,909 | 76,786 | **U.S. average** | **$79,336** | **$45,570** | **$57,246** | **$67,657** |
| Montana | 51,713 | 37,098 | 35,031 | 47,166 | | | | | |

1. Minimum figure in the salary range; top of the range is $92,676. 2. No specific chief administrative official or agency is in charge of this function. 3. Functions of lieutenant governor are the responsibility of the secretary of state. **Source:** Council of State Governments, *The Book of the States 1990–91* (1990).

## STATE GOVERNMENT INDIVIDUAL INCOME TAXES, 1989

| State | Taxable income rate range | Taxable income brackets Lowest: amount under | Taxable income brackets Highest: amount over | Federal income tax deductible[1] | State | Taxable income rate range | Taxable income brackets Lowest: amount under | Taxable income brackets Highest: amount over | Federal income tax deductible[1] |
|---|---|---|---|---|---|---|---|---|---|
| Alabama[2,3] | 2.0–5.0% | $ 500 | $ 3,000 | Yes | Mississippi | 3.0–5.0% | $ 5,000 | $ 10,000 | No |
| Arizona[4] | 2.0–8.0 | 1,290 | 7,740 | Yes[5] | Missouri[2,11] | 1.5–6.0 | 1,000 | 9,000 | Yes |
| Arkansas | 1.0–7.0 | 3,000 | 25,000 | No | Montana[4] | 2.0–11.0 | 1,500 | 52,500 | Yes |
| California[4] | 1.0–9.3 | 4,020 | 26,380 | No | Nebraska | 2.0–5.9 | 1,800 | 27,000 | No |
| Colorado | 5% of modified federal taxable income | | | No | New Hampshire | Limited income tax[12] | | | |
| Connecticut | Very limited income tax[6] | | | | New Jersey | 2.0–3.5[13] | 20,000 | 50,000 | No |
| Delaware[2] | 3.2–7.7 | 1,000 | 40,000 | No | New Mexico | 1.8–8.5 | 5,200 | 64,000 | No |
| Dist. of Columbia | 6.0–9.5 | 10,000 | 20,000 | No | New York[2] | 4.0–7.5 | 5,500 | 13,000 | No |
| Georgia | 1.0–6.0 | 750 | 7,000 | No | North Carolina | 6.0–7.0[14] | 12,750 | 12,750 | No |
| Hawaii[2] | 2.0–10.0 | 1,500 | 20,500 | No | North Dakota | 2.6–12.0[15] | 3,000[15] | 50,000[15] | Yes |
| Idaho | 2.0–8.2 | 1,000 | 20,000 | No | Ohio[2] | 0.743–6.9 | 5,000 | 100,000 | No |
| Illinois | 3.0 | Flat rate | | No | Oklahoma | 0.5–6.0[16] | 1,000[16] | 7,500[16] | Yes[16] |
| Indiana[2] | 3.4 | Flat rate | | No | Oregon[2,4] | 5.0–9.0 | 2,000 | 5,000 | Yes[17] |
| Iowa[2,4] | 0.4–9.98 | 1,000[7] | 45,720[7] | Yes | Pennsylvania[2] | 2.1 | Flat rate | | No |
| Kansas | 4.5–5.9[8] | 27,500[8] | 27,500[8] | Yes | Rhode Island | 22.96% of federal income tax liability | | | No |
| Kentucky[2] | 2.0–6.0 | 3,000 | 8,000 | Yes | South Carolina | 3.0–7.0 | 4,000 | 10,000 | No |
| Louisiana | 2.0–6.0 | 10,000 | 50,000 | Yes | Tennessee | Limited income tax[18] | | | |
| Maine | 2.0–8.5 | 4,000 | 16,000 | No | Utah | 2.55–7.22 | 750 | 3,750 | Yes[19] |
| Maryland[2,9] | 2.0–5.0 | 1,000 | 3,000 | No | Vermont | 25% of federal income tax liability | | | |
| Massachusetts | 5.0–10.0 | Flat rate[10] | | No | Virginia | 2.0–5.75 | 3,000 | 16,000 | No |
| Michigan[2] | 4.6 | Flat rate | | No | West Virginia | 3.0–6.5 | 10,000 | 60,000 | No |
| Minnesota[4] | 6.0–8.0 | 13,000 | 13,000 | No | Wisconsin | 4.9–6.93 | 7,500 | 15,000 | No |

**Note**: Alaska, Florida, Nevada, South Dakota, Texas, Washington, and Wyoming have no state income tax. 1. A state provision that allows the taxpayer to deduct fully the federal income tax payment reduces the effective marginal tax rate for persons in the highest state and federal tax brackets by approximately one-half the nominal tax rate—the deduction is a lesser benefit to other taxpayers. 2. States in which one or more local governments levy a local income tax. 3. Social Security (FICA) taxes are included in itemized deductions. 4. Indexed by an inflation factor. 5. An additional deduction from income is allowed in the amount of 65% of federal income tax liability or $600, whichever is greater, but not to exceed $10,000 for married filing jointly or $5,000 for all other filers. 6. There is an income tax on interest and dividend income only. The rate of this tax ranges from 1% of interest and dividend income for taxpayers with an adjusted gross income (AGI) of $54,000 to $57,999 to 12% of such income of taxpayers with an AGI over $100,000. Capital gains are taxed at 7% after an exemption of $100 is applied. 7. Tax cannot reduce after tax income of taxpayer to below $5,000. 8. Income below $27,500 taxed at 4.5% rate, income above $27,500 taxed at 5.95% rate. 9. All counties have a local income tax surcharge of at least 20% of state tax liability; most counties have a surcharge of 50%. 10. There is a 10% (flat rate) tax imposed on capital gains, interest, and dividends of residents, and Massachusetts business income of nonresidents. All other net income is taxed at 5%. No taxes are imposed on single persons with gross income of $8,000 or less ($12,000 married). 11. FICA taxes deductible when itemizing deductions. 12. There is a 5% tax on dividend and interest income (excluding income from savings bank deposits) in excess of $1,200 ($2,400 married). 13. No taxpayer is subject to tax if gross income is $3,000 or less ($1,500 married, filing separately). 14. Taxable income brackets are for single taxpayers. Breaking point for higher marginal tax rate varies according to filing status. 15. Taxpayers have the option of paying a tax of 14% of adjusted federal income tax liability or using the long form with a separate schedule; taxpayers using the long form may deduct federal income tax paid. 16. These tax rates and brackets apply to single persons not deducting federal income tax. For individuals deducting federal income tax, rates range from 0.5% of the first $1,000 to 10% on income over $15,250. 17. Federal tax deduction limited to $3,000 ($1,500 married, filing separately). 18. Interest and dividends taxed at 6%. 19. One-half of federal tax liability is deductible. **Source**: Advisory Commission on Intergovernmental Relations (Washington, D.C.), *Significant Features of Fiscal Federalism* (1990).

# CITIES AND COUNTIES IN THE U.S.

## CITIES AND COUNTIES IN THE UNITED STATES

Included here is basic information about population change, cost of living, and government finances in major U.S. cities, metropolitan statistical areas, and counties. In addition there are brief descriptions and statistics for each of the 50 largest cities—from Albuquerque to Washington, D.C. Statistical sources include the U.S. Census Bureau's 1990 decennial census, *City Government Finances in 1988–89*, *County Government Finances in 1988–89*, and the *Statistical Abstract of the United States 1991*.

## FORMS OF LOCAL GOVERNMENT

In addition to the one federal and 50 state governments, the Bureau of the Census recog-

nizes five basic types of organized local government. In addition to these, which are authorized in state constitutions and statutes, some local governments operate under "home-rule charters," the form and organization of which are specified by locally approved charters rather than by general or special state law. In 1987 there were a total of 83,236 state and local governments and 497,155 elected officials.

**Counties** County governments are established to provide general government, and include those governments designated as boroughs in Alaska, parishes in Louisiana, and counties in the other states. In 1987 there were 3,042 county governments; the most common forms are:

**Council-commission** A county government without a chief executive but with an elected governing body that shares administrative responsibility with officials elected or appointed to specific positions.

**Council-administrator** A county government with an elected governing body responsible for overall policy, and an appointed administrator (sometimes called a county manager, county commissioner, or county judge) responsible for administration. The powers of the administrator under this form of government may vary widely. **Council-elected executive** A county government with an elected governing body and an elected chief executive—sometimes called a president or a chairperson of the board. The powers of the executive under this form of government may vary widely.

**Municipalities** Municipal governments are established to provide general government for a specific concentration of population in a defined area and include those governments designated as cities, villages, boroughs (except in Alaska), and towns (except in the six New England states, Minnesota, New York, and Wisconsin). In 1987 there were 19,200 municipal governments; the most common forms are:

**Mayor-council** A municipal government with an elected mayor and an elected council or other governing body. In some mayor-council municipalities, the mayor is the chief executive, with broad powers. In some other mayor-council cities, the mayor has limited powers.

**Council-manager** A municipal government with an elected council or other governing body responsible for overall policy, and an appointed manager responsible for administration. The council may select a chairperson from among their own number who may be designated as the mayor.

**Commission** A municipal government with an elected board of commissioners responsible for overall policy. Each commissioner is responsible for administration of one or more departments of the municipal government. The board may select a chairperson from among their own number who may be designated as the mayor.

**Towns** Township governments are established to provide general government for areas defined without regard to population concentration and include those governments designated as towns in Connecticut, Maine (including organized plantations), Massachusetts, Minnesota, New Hampshire (including organized locations), New York, Rhode Island, Vermont, and Wisconsin, and townships in other states. In 1987 there were 16,691 township governments; the most common forms are:

**Town meeting** A township government in which an annual meeting of resident voters makes basic policy. An elected board (often called "a board of selectmen" or "township supervisors") is responsible for day-to-day administration of the township.

**Representative town meeting** A township government in which a town meeting composed of elected representatives of the resident voters makes basic policy. This form of government is usually found in more populous towns or townships. An elected board (often called "a board of selectmen" or "township supervisors") is responsible for day-to-day administration of the township.

**School districts** School district governments are organized local entities providing public elementary, secondary, and/or higher education which, under state law, have sufficient administrative and fiscal autonomy to qualify as separate governments. Excludes "dependent public school systems" of county, township, or state governments. In 1987 there were 14,721 school district governments.

**Special district governments** All organized local entities other than the four categories listed above, authorized by state law to provide only one or a limited number of designated functions, and with sufficient administrative and fiscal autonomy to qualify as separate governments; known by a variety of titles, including districts, authorities, boards, commissions, etc., as specified in the state legislation. In 1987 there were 29,532 special district governments.

**Source:** U.S. Bureau of the Census, *1987 Census of Governments: Popularly Elected Officials* (1990).

## 50 LARGEST CITIES

### Albuquerque, New Mexico

Seventy million years ago, earthquakes and volcanoes pushed the land that is now Albuquerque above the sea, forming the Rio Grande valley and a ring of mountain ranges. Even today the 10,000-foot-high Sandia Mountains are rising slowly, and the Rio Grande Valley continues gradually to deepen. During the Ice Age, Sandia Man roamed the area hunting mastodon and buffalo, and some 3,000 years ago the Anasazi built stone and adobe cities, which still stand. The 1530s marked the arrival of Spanish conquistadors and missionaries.

Founded as a Spanish villa in 1706, when 35 families moved to the land along the Rio Grande, Albuquerque was named by Don Francisco Cuervo y Valdez in honor of the duke of Albuquerque, King Phillip's viceroy of New Spain. Indian raids arrested the villa's expansion, and 100 years after its founding its population numbered a mere 2,200. Benefiting from their proximity to the Santa Fe trail, the people farmed; raised cattle; marketed adobe, for building, and wool; and ran trading posts, military supply depots, saloons, hotels, and mercantile businesses. The introduction of the railroad in 1880 spurred Albuquerque's growth, and the 1940 population of 35,000 has since grown more than tenfold.

Albuquerque occupies a central position along the Rio Grande Research Corridor, which stretches from Los Alamos to Las Cruces, and is home to the University of New Mexico and such major high-tech installations as Sandia National Laboratories, GTE Communications Systems, Unisys, and General Electric. Albuquerque's cultural and historic attractions include the Albuquerque Museum, the Indian Pueblo Cultural Center, the Maxwell Museum of Anthropology, the National Atomic Museum, the Spanish History Museum, and Petroglyph National Monument.

**Population** 384,736 (1990). Rank: 38. Pop. density: 3,025/sq. mi. (1,167/sq km).
**Location** 35°05′N, 106°39′W. County: Bernalillo.
**Terrain and climate** Elev.: 5,300 ft. Area: 127.2 sq. mi. (329.4 sq km). Avg. daily min. temp.: Jan.: 22.3°F/–5.3°C; avg. daily max.: July: 92.8°F/33.7°C. Avg. annual rainfall: 8.12″; snowfall: 11″; clear days: 71; precipitation days: 135.
**Government** Form: mayor and council. Mayor: Louis Saavedra. Election: Nov. 1993. Municipal tel. number: (505) 768–3000.
**Finances** (1988–89) Revenue: $450,741,000. Expenditure: $503,901,000. Debt outstanding: $1,063,658,000; per capita: $2,810.34.
**Visitor info.:** (505) 243–3696.

### Atlanta, Georgia

Atlanta, the capital and largest city of Georgia, lies at the base of the Blue Ridge Mountains near the Chattahoochee River. First settled in 1836, the area became the terminus for the Georgia Railroad in 1845 and took the name Atlanta. The population grew to 15,000 by 1861, and during the Civil War Atlanta became a strategic Confederate depot and collection point for recruits, establishing it as one of the most important cities of the Confederacy and making it a vital objective during Gen. William Tecumseh Sherman's infamous march to the sea in 1864. After two months of bitter battle, Sherman took the city on Sept. 1. After the war the ravaged city was rebuilt, and it became the state capital in 1878.

The chief commercial, industrial, insurance, telecommunications, and distributing center of the Southeast, Atlanta includes among its wide cross-section of industries railroad shops, large printing and publishing operations, automobile assembly plants, telecommunications equipment manufacturing, and numerous factories producing items ranging from foods and beverages to furniture.

An important educational and cultural center, the city boasts more than 20 institutions of higher learning, including Georgia Tech, Emory University, and Oglethorpe University, and is the site of the Atlanta Historical Society Library and exhibition, the Cyclorama (a three-dimension painting re-creating the battle of Atlanta during the Civil War), the Atlanta Science and Technology Museum, High Museum of Art, and the Fernbank Science Center, featuring the nation's third-largest planetarium.

**Population** 394,017 (1990). Rank: 36. Pop. density: 3,003/sq. mi. (1,160/sq km).
**Location** 33°45′N, 84°23′W. Counties: DeKalb, Fulton.
**Terrain and climate** Elev.: 1,034 ft. Area: 131.2 sq. mi. (339.80 sq km). Avg. daily min. temp.: Jan.: 32.6°F/0.3°C; avg. daily max.: July: 87.9°F/31°C. Avg. annual rainfall: 48.61″; snowfall: 2″; clear days: 108; precipitation days: 116.
**Government** Form: mayor and council. Mayor: Maynard Jackson. Election: Nov. 1993. Municipal tel. number: (404) 330–6000.
**Finances** (1988–89) Revenue: $715,813,000. Expenditure: $692,306,000. Debt outstanding: $1,195,576,000; per capita: $2,845.12.
**Visitor info:** (404) 521–6688.

### Austin, Texas

Austin, the capital of Texas, lies about 80 miles northeast of San Antonio on the banks of the Colorado River. First inhabited by nomadic Indian tribes, the area had as its first permanent European settler Jacob Harrell, in 1835, who, with the three families who joined him a few years later, established the town of Waterloo. In 1838 it was chosen as the site of the Texas Republic's capital and was renamed Austin after Stephen F. Austin, who brought the first Anglo settlers to Texas in the 1820s. After 1845, when Texas gained admission into the Union, Austin began to flourish, and by 1930 it had grown into a major regional center with a population of 75,000.

Austin was originally a business and distribution center serving the farmers of the Blackland Prairies to the east; its farmers now produce cotton, maize, corn, livestock, and poultry. Traditional industries such as meat packing, canning, and furniture manufacturing have been outstripped by the high-tech companies that have helped to nearly double the population since 1970. The University of Texas, founded in 1881 in Austin, boasts the highest endowment of any U.S. university—a legacy of the Texas oil fields. As the university developed into a first-class institution feeding the city's cultural and economic life, and with the influx of electronics and computer companies, Austin has prospered into a metropolis of national, even worldwide, scope.

**Population** 465,622 (1990). Rank: 27. Pop. density: 2,007/sq. mi. (775/sq km).
**Location** 30°17'N, 97°45'W. Counties: Travis, Williamson.
**Terrain and climate** Elev.: 570 ft. Area: 232 sq. mi. (600.9 sq km). Avg. daily min. temp.: Jan.: 38.8°F/3.8°C; avg. daily max.: July: 95.4°F/35.2°C. Avg. annual rainfall: 31.50"; snowfall: 1"; clear days: 115; precipitation days: 82.
**Government** Form: council and manager. Mayor: Bruce Todd. Election: May 1994. Municipal tel. number: (512) 499–2000.
**Finances** (1988–89) Revenue: $1,033,815,000. Expenditure: $1,194,061,000. Debt outstanding: $3,031,797,000; per capita: $6,524.34.
**Visitor info.:** (512) 478–0098.

## Baltimore, Maryland

One of America's most active seaports since Colonial days and chartered in 1729 as a major conduit of tobacco exportation, Baltimore was named after the founder of the colony of Maryland, George Calvert, Lord Baltimore. By the time of the Revolutionary War, it earned fame as an important commercial and maritime center, and ships sailing from Baltimore plied their trade with northern Europe, the Mediterranean, and the Caribbean. Chartered as a city in 1797, Baltimore saw its commercial activity surge with the burgeoning of its iron and copper industries, its proximity to the nation's capital, and the arrival of the Baltimore and Ohio Railroad, which developed links to the Midwest. However, the deep, divisive passions of the Civil War stunted growth, and it was years before the city recovered.

A fire in 1904 destroyed almost every building in the downtown area, providing impetus for needed revitalization. The two world wars renewed demands for Baltimore's port facilities and fostered development of a solid heavy-industrial base. But following World War II, the city's infrastructure aged and decayed. Today Baltimore remains a large port and industrial city with one of the largest steel plants in the world (Bethlehem Steel's Sparrow Point works). Much of the city has been rebuilt through urban renewal efforts, and its population seems to have stabilized after a loss of almost 20 percent in the 1960s.

Among the city's historic sites is Fort Mc-Henry, where Francis Scott Key wrote "The Star-Spangled Banner." Baltimore is home to St. Mary's Seminary and University (1791), Johns Hopkins University (1876), and the University of Baltimore (1925), among other noted institutions of higher learning.

**Population** 736,014 (1990). Rank: 13. Pop. density: 9,166/sq. mi. (3,539/sq km).
**Location** 39°17'N, 76°37'W. County: independent city.

**Terrain and climate** Elev.: 155 ft. Area: 80.3 sq. mi. (208 sq km). Avg. daily min. temp.: Jan.: 24.3°F/-4.2°C; avg. daily max.: July: 87.1°F/30.6°C. Avg. annual rainfall: 43.39"; snowfall: 22"; clear days: 106; precipitation days: 112.
**Government** Form: mayor and council. Mayor: Kurt L. Schmoke. Election: Nov. 1991. Municipal tel. number: (301) 396–3100.
**Finances** (1988–89) Revenue: $1,777,828,000. Expenditure: $1,519,732,000. Debt outstanding: $1,249,346,000; per capita: $1,662.69.
**Visitor info.:** (800) 282–6632.

## Boston, Massachusetts

Named for the English port from which many Puritan immigrants came to America, Boston was first settled in 1630 under the leadership of John Winthrop. As the capital of the Massachusetts Bay Colony, it quickly became the cultural and mercantile capital of the New England colonies. Bostonians never wholly embraced British authority, and they provided the earliest challenges to British rule in their reaction to the Stamp Act (1765) and through the Boston Tea Party (1783). The colonists killed in the Boston Massacre (1770) were the first to fall in the years immediately preceding the American Revolution.

With the end of the Revolution, Boston merchants found themselves shut out of English ports by prohibitive tariffs, and in their quest for new markets for American goods opened American trade to the Orient and India. In the 19th century, Boston benefited early from the Industrial Revolution and from several waves of immigration, particularly blacks from the Southern states, and Irish and Italians from Europe.

Although Boston's preeminence in trade and industry did not survive the 19th century, the city continues to be a major center for banking and financial services. Since World War II, its suburbs have flourished as centers of research and development and of the computer industry—Route 128 is the East Coast's answer to California's "Silicon Valley"—spurring investment in downtown Boston. As the gateway to New England and the birthplace of the Revolution, Boston is also a center for tourism.

Perhaps most important to its identity is Boston's wealth of diverse educational, cultural, and religious institutions. Harvard (across the Charles River in Cambridge, 1636) is the country's oldest college, and Roxbury Latin (1645) the country's oldest privately endowed secondary school. Today Boston embraces more than 20 colleges and universities, as well as some of the finest cultural institutions in the country, including the American Academy of Arts and Sciences (1780), the Massachusetts Historical Society (1791), the Boston Athenaeum (1807), the Boston Public Library (the nation's first, 1854), the Boston Museum of Fine Arts (1870), and the Boston Symphony (1881). The *Boston Globe* is one of the nation's oldest and most distinguished daily and Sunday newspapers.

**Population** 574,283 (1990). Rank: 20. Pop. density: 12,167/sq. mi. (4,700/sq km).
**Location** 39°17'N, 76°37'W. County: Suffolk.

**Terrain and climate** Elev.: 10 ft. Area: 47.2 sq. mi. (122.2 sq km). Avg. daily min. temp.: Jan.: 22.8°F/-5.1°C; avg. daily max.: July: 81.8°F/27.6°C. Avg. annual rainfall: 43.81"; snowfall: 42"; clear days: 99; precipitation days: 128.
**Government** Form: mayor and council. Mayor: Raymond L. Flynn. Election: Nov. 1991. Municipal tel. number: (617) 725–4000.
**Finances** (1988–89) Revenue: $1,683,383,000. Expenditure: $1,602,629,000. Debt outstanding: $818,002,000; per capita: $1,415.64.
**Visitor info.:** (617) 536–4100.

## Buffalo, New York

Bordering Lake Erie and located on the Niagara River where the Peace Bridge connects the United States to Canada, Buffalo, the second-largest city in New York State, offers a wide variety of commercial activity. An international inland port via the St. Lawrence Seaway and the Erie Canal, one of the busiest railroad systems in the country, and its position as the western terminus for the New York State Thruway, all make Buffalo an important transportation center. While the city's manufacturing base declined from 32 percent of total commerce in 1971 to 19 percent in 1987, the emergence of service businesses and financial organizations, particularly banks, has bolstered the local economy. The proximity to Niagara Falls lures thousands of tourists to the city every year.

The Erie Canal made Buffalo a strategic gateway to the West. The town dates back to the 1700s when the Holland Land Company acquired tracts of land in western New York, and after a plan was drawn up in 1800, the residents chose the name Buffalo, probably after the Indians' mispronunciation of the French *beau fleuve* (beautiful river)—the Niagara. After completion of the Erie Canal in 1825, the city evolved into a heavy manufacturing center, the biggest ship-to-rail grain-transfer point in the country, and in 1932 the "Queen City of the Great Lakes" was incorporated.

Buffalo was the birthplace of Presidents Millard Fillmore and Grover Cleveland; the Wilcox Mansion, where Theodore Roosevelt was sworn in as president after the assassination of William McKinley, stands as a national historic site.

**Population** 328,123 (1990). Rank: 50. Pop. density: 7,850/sq. mi. (3,030/sq km).
**Location** 42°53'N, 78°53'W. County: Erie.
**Terrain and climate** Elev.: 706 ft. Area: 41.8 sq. mi. (108.3 sq km). Avg. daily min. temp.: Jan.: 17°F/-8°C; avg. daily max.: July: 80.2°F/26.7°C. Avg. annual rainfall: 37.52"; snowfall: 90"; clear days: 55; precipitation days: 168.
**Government** Form: mayor and council. Mayor: James D. Griffin. Election: Nov. 1993. Municipal tel. number: (716) 851–4841.
**Finances** (1988–89) Revenue: $661,926,000. Expenditure: $677,704,000. Debt outstanding: $336,689,000; per capita: $1,073.73.
**Visitor info.:** (716) 852–0511.

## Charlotte, North Carolina

An area of lush green foothills lying at the southernmost tip of the Carolina Piedmont, Charlotte has long been a crossroads city and an important distribution point for the surrounding farmlands. About 250 years ago, Scottish and Irish settlers retracing old Catawba Indian trading routes established a settlement where the paths crossed, and in 1762 it was named Charlotte, after the new bride of King George III. Remembering General Cornwallis's reference to Charlotte as a "hornet's nest" while his army briefly occupied it during the American Revolution, the city adopted the symbol as its emblem. The discovery of a 17-pound gold nugget in 1799 triggered a gold rush, and although the mines dotting the landscape boosted business, the California gold rush in the mid-1800s lured away prospectors, putting Charlotte on its future course as a top cotton producer. A leading city of the Confederacy in the Civil War, Charlotte hosted the last full meeting of the Confederate cabinet in 1865.

Recently, the city's economy has diversified to include the production of chemicals, foodstuffs, machinery, metals, and textiles. The city has matured into a major center of world trade and technology, with more than 160 multinational companies engaging in such businesses as microelectronics, insurance, machining, and biomedical supplies. Located equidistant from the northeastern, midwestern, and southern Florida markets, with an inland port of entry for goods and a foreign trade zone where items may be held without duty, Charlotte remains a key distribution conduit. A midsize city at the heart of a rapidly expanding metropolitan region, Charlotte ranks as the nation's fifth-largest urban area with a population of more than 5 million living within a 100-mile radius of the city. The Charlotte Motor Speedway, and the Charlotte Hornets, one of the expansion teams added to the NBA in 1988, are sources of civic pride.

**Population** 395,934 (1990). Rank: 35. Pop. density: 2,603/sq. mi. (1,005/sq km).

**Location** 35°13′N, 80°51′W. County: Mecklenburg.

**Terrain and climate** Elev.: 665 ft. Area: 152.1 sq. mi. (393.9 sq km). Avg. daily min. temp.: Jan.: 42°F/6°C; avg. daily max.: July: 79°F/26°C. Avg. annual rainfall: 43.16″; snowfall: 6″; clear days: 111; precipitation days: 111.

**Government** Form: council-mayor and manager. Mayor: Sue Myrick. Election: Nov. 1991. Municipal tel. number: (704) 336–2244.

**Finances** (1988–89) Revenue: $365,857,000. Expenditure: $450,994,000. Debt outstanding: $730,197,000; per capita: $1,984.99.

**Visitor info.:** (704) 371–8700.

## Chicago, Illinois

Chicago extends roughly 26 miles along the southwestern shoreline of Lake Michigan. The city has historically been a major transportation hub and gateway to the Great Plains and continues to be one today, with major air, rail, and highway hubs. Nineteen trunk-line railroad routes converge at Chicago, linking it with every major U.S. and Canadian city. The city has three major airports, including O'Hare, the busiest in the nation. It is also a hub for major interstate highways running east-west and north-south.

Historically, Chicago's rise parallels the westward expansion of the American republic. Chicago was first settled in 1779, when Jean Baptiste Point de Sable built a house on the site. In 1803 federal troops built a stockade named Fort Dearborn, but by 1830 only 12 families had settled in the area. In the 1830s, however, the population grew rapidly as Americans spread westward, and the city of Chicago was incorporated in 1837 with a population of 4,170. Chicago then began to grow into a bustling Great Lakes port, connected to the Mississippi via a system of rivers and canals.

Chicago has maintained its strategic importance despite changes in transportation technology and remains today a prosperous city. Over the years Chicago has been noted as a hotbed of labor reform, the center of violent organized-crime gang wars during the Prohibition era, and a prime example of the good and the bad of American city machine-politics. Despite its checkered past, however, it has grown into the wealthiest and most vibrant city in the Midwest, with hardly a sign of the rust-belt malaise plaguing many of its sister cities. Chicago ranks first among American cities in the number of employed chemists and second in engineers. It has grown into a financial center with three of the nation's four largest futures exchanges and the world's largest listed-stock-options exchange.

Major attractions include the Museum of Science and Industry, the Field Museum of Natural History, the Chicago Historical Society, the Lincoln Park Zoo, the Chicago Lyric Opera Company, the Chicago Symphony Orchestra, and the Chicago Art Institute. Downtown Chicago currently has three of the five tallest manmade structures in the world—the Sears Tower (110 stories, 1,454 ft. high), the Amoco building (1,136 ft.), and the John Hancock building (1,127 ft.). It is also home to the world's tallest apartment complex, the 70-story Lake Point Tower, and the world's largest commercial building, the Merchandise Mart.

**Population** 2,783,726 (1990). Rank: 3. Pop. density: 12,204/sq. mi. (4,712/sq km).

**Location** 41°53′N, 87°38′W. County: Cook.

**Terrain and climate** Elev.: 623 ft. Area: 228.1 sq. mi. (590.8 sq km). Avg. daily min. temp.: Jan.: 13.6°F/–10.2°C; avg. daily max.: July: 83.3°F/28.5° Avg. annual rainfall: 33.34″; snowfall: 40″; clear days: 94; precipitation days: 123.

**Government** Form: mayor and council. Mayor: Richard M. Daley. Election: Apr. 1995. Municipal tel. number: (312) 744–4000.

**Finances** (1988–89) Revenue: $3,237,022,000. Expenditure: $3,211,760,000. Debt outstanding: $3,639,333,000; per capita: $1,222.27.

**Visitor info.:** (312) 793-2094.

## Cincinnati, Ohio

Cincinnati's origins can be traced to 1788, when the town of Columbia was founded between the Little Maumee and Great Maumee rivers where they meet the Ohio. In 1790 it was renamed Cincinnati, after the Society of the Cincinnati, an organization of Revolutionary War veterans. Settlement of the city increased after the Battle of Fallen Timbers (1794) put down Miami resistance to European-settler control of the region.

In 1811 the *New Orleans*, the first steamboat on the Western rivers, arrived from Pittsburgh, and thereafter Cincinnati became a major inland port. The city's commercial status was consolidated in the 1840s after the opening of the Miami and Erie Canal, which joined the Ohio River at Cincinnati with Lake Erie at Toledo, and the arrival of the first railroads in 1843. Large numbers of German immigrants gave the city a European flavor. By mid-century Cincinnati had reached its zenith as a commercial and manufacturing center, well deserving of Longfellow's epithet, "Queen City of the West." Cincinnati continued to prosper after the Civil War, though it was beset by problems ranging from perennial flooding to extensive government corruption. By 1910 its population had reached 360,000, about what it is today.

Cincinnati continues to be a hub of transportation and industry, particularly strong in the manufacture of transportation equipment and industrial machinery, food and beverage production, steel, and printing. It is one of the nation's largest inland coal ports and a regional center for wholesaling, retailing, insurance, and finance.

Among its many colleges and universities are the University of Cincinnati, Cincinnati Technical College, the Athenaeum of Ohio, Hebrew Union College-Jewish Institute of Religion (founded in 1875 and the oldest rabbinic college in the U.S.), and Cincinnati Bible Seminary. It is the home of the William Howard Taft birthplace, the Harriet Beecher Stowe House State Memorial, Tyler-Davidson Fountain, and the Cincinnati Zoo, the second-oldest zoo in the country. Cincinnati is also home port of the restored historic riverboats *Delta Queen* and *Mississippi Queen*.

**Population** 364,040 (1990). Rank: 45. Pop. density: 4,667/sq. mi. (1,802/sq km).

**Location** 41°53′N, 84°01′W. County: Hamilton.

**Terrain and climate** Elev.: 540 ft. Area: 78 sq. mi. (202 sq km). Avg. daily min. temp.: Jan.: 20.4°F/–6.4°C; avg. daily max.: July: 85.8°F/29.8°C. Avg. annual rainfall: 40.10″; snowfall: 19″; clear days: 80; precipitation days: 131.

**Government** Form: council and manager. Mayor: David Mann. Election: Nov. 1991. Municipal tel. number: (513) 352-3000.

**Finances** (1988–89) Revenue: $556,405,000. Expenditure: $505,786,000. Debt outstanding: $221,093,000, per capita: $596.77.

**Visitor info.:** (513) 621-2142.

## Cleveland, Ohio

The heart of the largest metropolitan area in Ohio, Cleveland was founded in 1795 and named after Moses Cleaveland, a surveyor with the Connecticut Land Company, which administered the state of Connecticut's lingering claim on 3.5 million acres of what is now Ohio (the Western Reserve). A frontier village at the mouth of the Cuyahoga River on Lake Erie, Cleveland was transformed into the business and manufacturing center of northern Ohio by the opening of the Erie Canal in 1825, and the Ohio and Erie Canal, which linked Cleveland with Portsmouth on the Ohio River. When the Soo Locks opened Lake Superior to trade with the Lower Lakes in 1855, Cleveland became a major shipping center for ore, lumber, copper, coal, and farm produce.

During the Civil War, the city's iron ore and coal deposits were mined for steel production, and commercial activity increased to meet the Union's increased demands for heavy machinery, railroad equipment, and ships. In the postwar years, Cleveland's mills and factories expanded even further to satisfy the increased needs of new cities and farms springing up in the wake of westward migration.

Although heavy manufacturing employs 22.5 percent of the city's work force (more than the national average), the national trend toward a service economy has had a severe impact on the local economy. Nonetheless, heavy industry is a cornerstone of the city's economy, with many large industrial companies located there. In addition, there are many medical and industrial research firms, most notably the world-famous Cleveland Clinic and NASA's Lewis Research Center.

Cleveland's industrial strength manifests itself in its flourishing cultural institutions. University Circle, a nearly 500-acre site near Case Western Reserve University (a merger of Western Reserve University and Case Institute of Technology), is home to the Cleveland Play House, the nation's oldest repertory theater; the world-famous Cleveland Orchestra; the Cleveland Museum of Natural History; Western Reserve Historical Society; the Cleveland Health Museum; Allen Memorial Medical Library; and the Cleveland Zoo. In the revitalized downtown area, centered on the Mall are the Cleveland Institute of Art, the Cleveland Institute of Music, and the Karamu Center for interracial cultural events.

**Population** 505,616 (1990). Rank: 24. Pop. density: 6,400/sq. mi. (2,471/sq km).
**Location** 41°30′N, 81°42′W. County: Cuyahoga.
**Terrain and climate** Elev.: 805 ft. Area: 79 sq. mi. (204.6 sq km). Avg. daily min. temp.: Jan.: 18.5°F/-7.5°C; avg. daily max.: July: 81.7°F/27.6°C. Avg. annual rainfall: 35.40″; snowfall: 54″; clear days: 70; precipitation days: 156.
**Government** Form: mayor and council. Mayor: Michael R. White. Election: Nov. 1994. Municipal tel. number: (216) 664-2000.
**Finances** (1988–89) Revenue: $645,712,000. Expenditure: $639,061,000. Debt outstanding: $700,435,000; per capita: $1,343.45.
**Visitor info.:** (216) 621-3300

### Columbus, Ohio

The Ohio legislature designated a site along the banks of the Scioto River in the center of the state as the capital in 1812 and named it Columbus in honor of the famous explorer of the New World. From the first, the city exploited its status as the seat of government and its prime location in the middle of the nation's growing network of roads, canals, and highways. Incorporated in 1834, Columbus became a thriving hub of agricultural trade.

Between 1850 and 1900, its population grew from 17,800 to more than 100,000. Because of the many carriage factories, in the 19th century Columbus was known as the Buggy Capital of the World. Five railroads

passed through the city, so banks soon began to spring up, making Columbus a financial center for the surrounding farm counties.

As in the 19th century, Columbus's modern economy is built on government, agriculture, local finance, and education. In 1950, to counter the trend of suburbanization, the city developed a policy of annexation of surrounding communities. Because it is less reliant on heavy industry than other Midwestern cities, it has weathered the decline of the rust belt better than most, remaining a bustling metropolis. In the 1980s the city realized the creation of more than $780 million in new development and 97,550 new jobs.

Ohio State University, one of the nation's large state universities, opened as the Ohio Agricultural and Mechanical College in 1870, and the city today has a rich academic community that includes the Ohio Dominican College (whose origins date to 1868), the Columbus College of Art and Design, and the Ohio Institute of Technology. Business leaders and politicians have joined in an effort to make the city a center for the arts, refurbishing three theaters and building a complex of three more.

**Population** 632,910 (1990). Rank: 16. Pop. density: 3,388/sq. mi. (1,308/sq km).
**Location** 39°58′W, 83°00′W. Counties: Fairfield, Franklin.
**Terrain and climate** Elev.: 833 ft. Area: 186.8 sq. mi. (483.8 sq km). Avg. daily min. temp.: Jan.: 19.4°F/-7°C; avg. daily max.: July: 84.4°F/29.1°C. Avg. annual rainfall: 36.97″; snowfall: 28″; clear days: 75; precipitation days: 136.
**Government** Form: mayor and council. Mayor: Dana G. Rinehart. Election: Nov. 1991. Municipal tel. number: (614) 645-8100.
**Finances** (1988–89) Revenue: $521,575,000. Expenditure: $572,467,000. Debt outstanding: $1,043,756,000; per capita: $1,832.53.
**Visitor info.:** (614) 221-6623.

### Dallas, Texas

First settled in 1841 by John Neely Bryan, a Tennessee trader and lawyer, Dallas stretches about 30 miles east of Fort Worth on the Trinity River. Named in 1846 after James K. Polk's vice president, George Mifflin Dallas, it was chartered as a city in 1871. Though it grew substantially with the arrival of railroads in 1872, the population numbered a mere 92,000 in 1910.

Located in the heart of the northern Texas oil belt, Dallas today thrives on a diverse economic base, which, in addition to oil and natural gas, includes production of brick clay and the raw materials for Portland cement, and cotton, grains, fruits, beef, dairy cattle, hogs, sheep, and poultry from surrounding farms. One of the largest inland cotton markets, and a leading distributor of farm goods and machinery, Dallas also serves as the Southwest's banking center, with major banks, insurance companies, and the Federal Reserve Bank for the 11th District. Key manufacturing industries include aerospace, electronics, transportation equipment, machinery, food and related products, and apparel.

Some of Dallas's distinguished universities

are Southern Methodist, Southwestern Medical School of the University of Texas, Dallas Theological Seminary and Graduate School of Theology, and the Baylor University Schools of Dentistry and Nursing. The Dallas Symphony Orchestra, Dallas Theater Center, Dallas Civic Opera, Dallas Historical Society Museum in the Texas Hall of State, and the Dallas Garden Center contribute to the city's rich cultural life. Fair Park, the site of the annual State Fair of Texas, remains the most widely attended state fair in the country.

**Population** 1,006,877 (1990). Rank: 8. Pop. density: 3,038/sq. mi. (1,173/sq km).
**Location** 32°47′N, 96°49′W. Counties: Collin, Dallas, Denton, Kaufman, Rockwall.
**Terrain and climate** Elev.: 596 ft. Area: 331.4 sq. mi. (858.3 sq km). Avg. daily min. temp.: Jan.: 33.9°F/1°C; avg. daily max.: July: 97.8°F/36.5°C. Avg. annual rainfall: 34.16″; snowfall: 3″; clear days: 138; precipitation days: 79.
**Government** Form: council and manager. Mayor: Annette Strauss. Election: Nov. 1991. Municipal tel. number: (214) 670-4054.
**Finances** (1988–89) Revenue: $971,445,000. Expenditure: $1,057,238,000. Debt outstanding: $1,525,357,000; per capita: $1,544.88.
**Visitor info.:** (214) 746-6600.

### Denver, Colorado

Denver was born during the great "Pike's Peak or Bust" gold rush of 1859, when small flakes of placer gold were found where the South Platte River meets Cherry Creek. In its first few years, the city survived a flood, several major fires, Indian attacks, and an invasion by Confederate soldiers during the Civil War. With the discovery of more gold in the Rocky Mountains, Denver became a boom town. Saloons, gambling halls, and wagon trains lined the mud-filled streets, and just about every outlaw, desperado, and lawman in the West made at least one visit to the city. The turn of the century brought respectability, and the wealth of the mountains was poured into parks, fountains, tree-lined streets, and elaborate mansions.

During the oil crisis of the late 1970s and early 1980s, Denver experienced a second boom when it became a corporate center for oil-from-shale companies working the western slope of the Rockies. Then one of the fastest-growing cities in the United States, in 1983 it doubled its office space as part of a five-year building campaign that added 16 skyscrapers, a $76-million pedestrian mall, and an $80-million performing arts center. Although expansion was slowed by the energy glut of the mid-1980s, the city is planning the construction of a new airport, convention center, and billion-dollar light-rail system. In 1991, Major League Baseball awarded the city one of two expansion team franchises.

Denver's population is among the youngest in the nation. The youthful flavor of the city is very evident; Denver leads the nation in movie attendance and has more sporting goods stores per resident than any other city in the world. The city's 205 parks are so active that a speed limit was recently instituted—for bicycles.

**Population** 467,610 (1990). Rank: 26. Pop.

density: 4,378/sq. mi. (1,691/sq km).
**Location** 39°44'N, 104°59'W. County: Denver.
**Terrain and climate** Elev.: 5,280 ft. Area: 106.8 sq. mi. (276.6 sq km). Avg. daily min. temp.: Jan.: 15.9°F/-8.9°C; avg. daily max: July: 88°F/31°C. Avg. annual rainfall: 15.31"; snowfall: 60"; clear days: 115; precipitation days: 88.
**Government** Form: mayor and council. Mayor: Wellington Webb. Election: May 1995. Municipal tel. number: (303) 575-2721.
**Finances** (1988-89) Revenue: $949,509,000. Expenditure: $1,003,120,000. Debt outstanding: $1,302,061,000; per capita: $2,645.44.
**Visitor Info.:** (303) 892-1112.

## Detroit, Michigan

Founded in 1701 by Antoine de La Mothe, sieur de Cadillac, Detroit lies on the Detroit River between Lake Erie and Lake Huron. Named Fort Pontchartrain-du-Détroit (of the strait), the oldest permanent settlement on the Great Lakes flourished as a trading post for trappers, under French control (to 1760), then British (to 1796), and then American.

The first steamboat reached Detroit from Buffalo in 1818, but it was the easy access to Eastern markets via the Erie Canal in 1825 that allowed Detroit to exploit the abundant natural resources in the Michigan peninsula and fostered its emergence as a modern industrial giant in the post-Civil War years. Tenth among cities in the value of its manufactures by 1899, Detroit's main exports included iron ore, copper, lead, salt, and fish. The development of the automotive industry, which eventually became centered in Detroit, propelled Detroit to number three by the 1920s. While Detroit is the home of General Motors, Chrysler, and Ford, recently the automotive industry has been as much a curse as a blessing, for every setback to any of the "Big Three" is felt throughout the Motor City.

Despite the fact that it remains third in industrial manufacturing in the country, Detroit has been plagued by urban decline. The relatively low standard of living among the predominantly black inhabitants ignited riots in the 1940s and 1960s, and the city's crime rate is today among the highest in the nation. However, it was Detroit blacks who gave rise to one of the most sensational expressions of popular culture in the 1960s. Founded in 1960, the Tamla Motown label propelled the Jackson 5, the Supremes, and Stevie Wonder—among others—to world renown, and in the process created the largest black-owned business in the country.

The city's rich and diverse cultural institutions include the Detroit Institute of Arts, which houses one of the largest collections of American art in the world, in addition to extensive European holdings; the Detroit Symphony; the Cranbrook Academy of Art; and the 1,000-acre Belle Isle Park, situated on an island in the Detroit River and including beaches, a yacht basin, a zoo, an aquarium, and a botanical garden.
**Population** 1,027,974 (1990). Rank: 7. Pop. density: 7,581/sq. mi. (2,927/sq km).
**Location** 42°20'N, 83°03'W. County: Wayne.

**Terrain and climate** Elev.: 581 ft. Area: 135.6 sq. mi. (351.2 sq km). Avg. daily min. temp.: Jan.: 16.1°F/-8.8°C; avg. daily max.: July: 83.1°F/28.3°C. Avg. annual rainfall: 30.97"; snowfall: 39"; clear days: 75; precipitation days: 133.
**Government** Form: mayor and council. Mayor: Coleman A. Young. Election: Nov. 1993. Municipal tel. number: (313) 224-3400.
**Finances** (1988-89) Revenue: $2,009,765,000. Expenditure: $2,021,372,000. Debt outstanding: $1,334,332,000; per capita: $1,288,06.
**Visitor info.:** (313) 259-4333.

## El Paso, Texas

The largest Texas city bordering Mexico, El Paso sits in the western part of the state on the northern bank of the Rio Grande across from Juarez. A major port of entry, with the biggest commercial and manufacturing base in the area, the city encompasses a region of mines, oil fields, livestock ranches, and farms (principal crops: pecans, fruit, cotton, alfalfa, onions, lettuce, chilies). Important industries include metals smelting and refining, oil and gas refining, textiles, meat packing, and food processing. The city is also home to the University of Texas, at El Paso.

In 1536 Alvar Núñez Cabeza de Vaca crossed the Rio Grande, becoming the first European to step foot in the area, but settlement did not follow until 1659, with the establishment of both El Paso del Norte on the southern bank of the Rio Grande, and the Mission of Guadalupe. In 1682 settlers from New Mexico founded Yselta, an area within the current city limits of El Paso, but permanent settlement did not begin until the arrival of Juan Maria Ponce de Léon in 1827. Incorporated as a city in 1873, El Paso grew into a major industrial center with the introduction of the railroads in 1881.

El Paso's access to sources of cheap labor complemented its mining, refining, and agricultural activities and helped build the city's manufacturing base. Its proximity to Juarez, Mexico, makes it a vibrant tourist haven, and its pleasant climate, combined with its position on the immigration route from Latin America, have made El Paso one of the fastest-growing cities in the country. El Paso also has the highest percentage of citizens with Hispanic ancestry of any American city.
**Population** 515,342 (1990). Rank: 22. Pop. density: 2,150/sq. mi. (830/sq km).
**Location** 31°45'N, 106°29'W. County: El Paso.
**Terrain and climate** Elev.: 3,700 ft. Area: 239.7 sq. mi. (620.8 sq km). Avg. daily min. temp.: Jan.: 30.4°F/-0.8°C; avg. daily max.: July: 95.3°F/35.1°C. Avg. annual rainfall: 7.82"; snowfall: 5"; clear days: 194; precipitation days: 45.
**Government** Form: mayor and council. Mayor: William S. Tilney. Election: May 1993. Municipal tel. number: (915) 541-4145.
**Finances** (1988-89) Revenue: $272,798,000. Expenditure: $246,271,000. Debt outstanding: $436,539,000; per capita: $854.33.
**Visitor info.:** (915) 541-4948.

## Fort Worth, Texas

Named in 1849 after Gen. William J. Worth, commander of the U.S. Army in Texas, Fort Worth originally served to protect settlers from Indian attacks. It grew slowly, mainly as a stopover on the cattle drives along the Chisolm Trail, until the Texas and Pacific Railroad reached the city in 1871. Stockyards sprang up, making Fort Worth a conduit of cattle shipping, and with the building of a grain elevator it developed into a milling center as well. By the turn of the century, it had also emerged as a successful meat-packing market. Oil was discovered in 1917, bringing prosperity and transforming the city into a major refining center with a dozen operating facilities. The two world wars introduced military installations (particularly airfields) to the area. Fort Worth is the sixth-largest city in Texas, boasting three of the state's finest art museums and a network of parks with total acreage second only to Chicago's. In 1990 it was announced that Fort Worth would become the first city outside of Washington, D.C., where paper money is printed.
**Population** 447,619 (1990). Rank: 28. Pop. density: 1,732/sq. mi. (668/sq km).
**Location** 32°45'N, 97°18'W. County: Tarrant.
**Terrain and climate** Elev.: 670 ft. Area: 258.5 sq. mi. (670.3 sq km). Avg. daily min. temp.: Jan.: 33.9°F/1°C; avg. daily max.: July: 97.8°F/36.5°C. Avg. annual rainfall: 29.45"; snowfall: 1.4"; clear days: 137; precipitation days: 78.
**Government** Form: council and manager. Mayor: Kay Ranger. Election: May 1993. Municipal tel. number: (817) 870-6117.
**Finances** (1988-89) Revenue: $463,907,000. Expenditure: $444,161,000. Debt outstanding: $962,279,000; per capita: $2,255.64.
**Visitor info.:** (817) 336-8791.

## Fresno, California

Fresno grew up around a train station established in 1872 for what became the Southern Pacific Railway. The city was incorporated in 1874. With the introduction of irrigation to the fertile San Joaquin Valley in the 1880s, the small city thrived at the center of a healthy agricultural economy. Today Fresno County is the number one producer of agricultural products in the nation—and the world—and averages more than $2 billion a year in the production and processing of 200 commercial crops, including grapes (for wine and raisins), melon, cotton, alfalfa, barley, grains, cattle, sheep, and poultry.

Fresno's population grew 63 percent between 1980 and 1990, and in the 1980s it was the ninth fastest growing city in the United States and by far the fastest growing of the nation's 50 largest cities.

Located in central California, Fresno—the name is Spanish for ash tree—is a gateway to the Sierra Nevadas, and it is less than 90 minutes from three national parks—Kings Canyon (55 miles), Sequoia (85 miles), and Yosemite (92 miles). Among the attractions to be found within the city limits are the Fresno Art Museum, the Fresno Zoo, the Kearney Mansion Museum (restored home of Theo Kearney, "Raisin King of California"), the Fresno Metropolitan Museum, and the Discovery Center. There are also 10 colleges and universities, including a campus of California State University and Fresno City College.

**Population** 354,202 (1990). Rank: 47. Population density: 3,564/sq. mi. (1,378/sq km).

**Location** 36°44′N, 119°46′W. County: Fresno.

**Terrain and climate** Elev. 328 ft. Area: 99.4 sq. mi. (257 sq km). Avg. daily min. temp. Jan.: 37.4°/3°C; avg. daily max. July: 98.7°F/37°C. Avg. annual rainfall: 10″; snowfall 0″; clear days: 200; precipitation days: 44.

**Government** Form: council manager. Mayor: Karen Humphrey. Election: May 1993. Municipal tel.: (209) 498-1560.

**Finances** (1988–89) Revenue: $240,321,000. Expenditure: $193,499,000. Debt outstanding: $256,541,000; per capita: $835.39.

**Visitor info.:** (209) 233-0836.

## Honolulu, Hawaii

Discovered by Europeans in 1794, Honolulu, meaning "sheltered harbor," has attracted droves of visitors ever since. Situated on Oahu Island, it benefits from a large bay fully protected by coral reefs and its large port facilities. Because of its hospitable climate—it is the southernmost city in the U.S.—the beaches of Waikiki, its majestic mountains, and exotic locale, Honolulu's major industry is tourism; several million visitors come annually, mainly from the U.S. mainland and the Far East, particularly from Japan.

The defense industry is the second mainstay of Honolulu's economy; the United States has long maintained major installations around the island, including the naval base at Pearl Harbor, Hickam Air Force Base, and the U.S. Army's Schofield Barracks and Fort Shafter. Honolulu also serves as the center for Hawaii's export crops—sugar, pineapple, and molasses—and is the principal port for the import of much of the island-state's necessities.

**Population** 365,272 (1990). Pop. density: 14,438/sq. mi. (5,575/sq km).

**Location** 21°19′N, 155°42′W. County: Honolulu.

**Terrain and climate** Elev.: 15 ft. Area: 25.3 sq. mi. (65.52 sq km). Avg. daily min. temp.: Jan.: 65.3°F/18.5°C; avg. daily max.: July: 87.1°F/30.6°C. Avg. annual rainfall: 23.47″; snowfall: 0″; clear days: 90; precipitation days: 102.

**Government** Form: mayor and council. Mayor: Frank F. Fasi. Election: Nov. 1992. Municipal tel. number: (808) 523-4141.

**Finances** (1988–89) Revenue: $636,433,000. Expenditure: $789,252,000. Debt outstanding: $593,466,000; per capita: $707.77.

**Visitor info.:** (808) 923-1811.

## Houston, Texas

On Aug. 30, 1836, brothers August C. and John K. Allen founded this city, naming it after Sam Houston, the first president of the Republic of Texas. The Allens paid just over $1.40 per share for 6,642 acres of land near the headwaters of Buffalo Bayou about 50 miles inland from the Gulf of Mexico. Houston's proximity

to Stephen Austin's central Texas colonies gave it great potential as a marketing and distribution site. Incorporated in 1837, the city served as capital of the Republic of Texas until 1840. When the first railroad in Texas began operating out of Houston in 1853, the city developed into a major agricultural center, while the discovery of oil in southeast Texas at Spindletop in 1901 and the opening of the man-made Houston Ship Channel in 1914 stimulated petroleum refining and metal fabricating. During World War II, petrochemical production began on a large scale, and with the building of NASA's $761-million complex in the early 1960s (now known as the Johnson Space Center), Houston took center stage as the main player in manned spacecraft.

A major corporate and international business center—13 *Fortune*-500 companies are based there—present-day Houston has successfully limited its dependence on the energy economy. It rank's third nationally in number of trade offices, fifth in foreign consulates, and sixth in international air passengers. With more than half the Port of Houston's cargo in foreign trade in 1987, Houston ranked second among U.S. ports in foreign tonnage.

The presence of the Texas Medical Center also makes Houston a vital U.S. center for the practice and progress of modern high-tech medicine. The center's 39 institutions occupy in excess of 550 acres, and as of 1987 employed over 522,000 workers, with a student enrollment exceeding 10,000.

**Population** 1,630,553 (1990). Rank: 4. Pop. density: 2,847/sq. mi. (1,099/sq km).

**Location** 29°46′N, 95°22′W. Counties: Fort Bend, Harris, Montgomery.

**Terrain and climate** Elev.: 49 ft. Area: 572.7 sq. mi. (1,483.3 sq km). Avg. daily min. temp.: Jan.: 40.8°F/4.8°C; avg. daily max.: July: 93.6°F/34.2°C. Avg. annual rainfall: 44.77″; snowfall: 0″; clear days, 94; precipitation days: 107.

**Government** Form: mayor and council. Mayor: Kathryn J. Whitmire. Election: Nov. 1992. Municipal tel. number: (713) 247-2200.

**Finances** (1988–89) Revenue: $1,618,645,000. Expenditure: $1,643,022,000. Debt outstanding: $3,434,078,000; per capita: $2,022.32.

**Visitor info.:** (713) 523-5050.

## Indianapolis, Indiana

Indianapolis, the capital of Indiana and a major commercial center in the country's heartland, is intersected by more highways than any other city in the nation, earning it the name the Crossroads of America. Fifty percent of America's population is within a day's drive of the city, a geographic asset that makes it a focal point of transportation and manufacturing.

The Euro-American settlement, established in 1820 where Fall Creek meets the White River, was chosen as the location of Indiana's capital in 1825. The state government created jobs triggering an expanding population that further swelled with the routing of the National Road (U.S. 40) in 1830. Development mushroomed in 1839 with the building of the Central Canal on the White River, providing a vital

transportation link and the necessary water power to run factories, sawmills, and paper mills. Maintenance of the canal, however, proved impossible, and the town declined until the introduction of the railroad. By 1853 railroad lines fed into Indianapolis from every corner of the nation, and at one point nearly 200 trains passed through daily. At the turn of the century, Indianapolis had emerged as a sophisticated city with sidewalks and streetcars. The city's economy prospered during early stages of the automotive industry, producing more than 50 types of cars—including the Dusenberg, the Marmon, and the Stutz—before Detroit gained ascendancy.

Having survived the decline in heavy industry and the flight of the affluent to the suburbs, Indianapolis remains a hub of manufacturing and transportation, with a bustling wheat, soybean, and livestock market. Key industries include electronics, metal fabrication, pharmaceuticals, and transportation equipment. Downtown Indianapolis has enjoyed a renaissance with the construction of a convention center, the Hoosier Dome, Market Square Arena, and the refurbishment of Union Station. The city has also built a number of amateur sports arenas and in 1987 hosted the Pan Am Games. But the city's premier attraction remains the Indianapolis 500, the annual Memorial Day race first held in 1911.

**Population** 741,952 (1990). Rank: 12. Pop. density: 2,109/sq. mi. (814/sq km).

**Location** 39°46′N, 86°09′W. County: Marion.

**Terrain and climate** Elev.: 808 ft. Area: 352 sq. mi. (911.7 sq km). Avg. daily min. temp.: Jan.: 17.8°F/-7.8°C; avg. daily max.: July: 85.2°F/29.5°C. Avg. annual rainfall: 39.12″; snowfall: 21″; clear days: 90; precipitation days: 122.

**Government** Form: mayor and council. Mayor: William H. Hudnut III. Election: Nov. 1991. Municipal tel. number: (317) 236-3600.

**Finances** (1988–89) Revenue: $815,735,000. Expenditure: $846,385,000. Debt outstanding: $950,046,000; per capita: $1,306.57.

**Visitor info.:** (317) 237-5200.

## Jacksonville, Florida

The first Europeans to visit the area were French Huguenots, who in 1564 established a colony at Fort Caroline on the Saint Johns River in northeast Florida. The Spanish destroyed the fort in the following year. Permanent settlement began in 1816, and in 1822 Jacksonville was laid out and named for then Maj. Gen. Andrew Jackson, who had led the U.S. campaign to take Florida from the Spanish. Growth was slow until after the Civil War, but by 1960 the population was more than 200,000. In 1968 the population jumped to more than 500,000 when it was consolidated with Duval County, and Jacksonville became the largest city by area in the nation.

Presently Florida's largest city, Jacksonville is a major regional center for commerce, industry, finance, and medicine. After years of improvements on its harbor, 25 miles west from the mouth of the Saint Johns, it has grown into a major port of entry and is the primary distribution center for the region. Jacksonville has also emerged as a leading resort with extensive recreational and convention facilities. Among its amenities are the Haydon Burns Library, Cummer Gallery of Art, Jacksonville Art Museum, Jacksonville Zoological Park, Saint Johns River Park, and Fort Caroline National Memorial, site of the first European colony in Florida. Among its leading educational institutions are Jacksonville University and the University of Northern Florida.

**Population** 672,971 (1990). Rank: 15. Pop. density: 801/sq. mi. (342/sq km).

**Location** 30°20′N, 81°39′W. County: Duval.

**Terrain and climate** Elev.: 31 ft. Area: 840 sq. mi. (1,967.6 sq km). Avg. daily min. temp.: Jan.: 41.7°F/°C; avg. daily max.: July: 90.7°F/29.5°C. Avg. annual rainfall: 52.77″; snowfall: 0″; clear days: 98; precipitation days: 116.

**Government** Form: mayor and council. Mayor: Ed Austin. Election: May 1995. Municipal tel. number: (904) 630–1776.

**Finances** (1988–89) Revenue: $1,279,911,000. Expenditure: $1,344,441,000. Debt outstanding: $4,016,130,000; per capita: $6,320.33.

**Visitor info.**: (904) 353–9736.

## Kansas City, Missouri

Kansas City's Euro-American beginnings were as a trading outpost established by the French fur trader François Chouteau in 1821. In 1833 the town of Westport was founded nearby, and in 1850 the City of Kansas received its first charter. (Its name was changed to Kansas City in 1889.)

Situated at the confluence of the Kansas and Missouri rivers, Kansas City prospered early on as a river port and as the terminus of the Santa Fe and Oregon trails. With the arrival of the railroad in 1866, Kansas City's status as a major commercial hub was assured. Thanks to its central location and the development of excellent and diversified transportation and storage facilities, Kansas City is one of the nation's key markets for agricultural and livestock products, as well as for the distribution of heavy agricultural machinery. The Kansas City Board of Trade is one of the largest grain and commodities trading markets in the world. Other major industries are greeting card publishing, telecommunications, and high-tech manufacturing, especially instrument-landing systems for airplanes. Kansas City is also home to the 10th Federal Reserve Bank.

An early oasis of culture in the midst of an unsettled (by Euro-Americans), "untamed" prairie (the city once boasted two opera houses), Kansas City remains a mecca of the arts, with such cultural offerings as the Kansas City Art Institute, the Nelson-Atkins Museum of Art, the Kansas City Symphony, the Lyric Opera, and the Missouri Repertory Theatre. The city's beginnings are preserved in the Lone Jack Civil War Museum and in Missouri Town 1855, and it is the site of the annual American Royal Livestock, Horse Show, and Rodeo, held as part of the annual convention of the Future Farmers of America. Among its institutes of higher learning are Rockhurst College (1916), the University of Missouri–Kansas City, and the DeVry Institute of Technology.

**Population** 435,146 (1990). Rank: 31. Pop. density: 1,375/sq. mi. (531/sq km).

**Location** 39°07′N, 94°38′W. Counties: Cass, Clay, Jackson, Platte.

**Terrain and climate** Elev.: 744 ft. Area: 316.4 sq. mi. (819.5 sq km). Avg. daily min. temp.: Jan.: 17.2°F/–8.2°C; avg. daily max.: July: 88.5°F/31.3°C. Avg. annual rainfall: 29.27″; snowfall: 5.9″; clear days: 132; precipitation days: 97.

**Government** Form: council and manager. Mayor: Emanuel Cleaver. Election: Mar. 1995. Municipal tel. number: (816) 274–2595.

**Finances** (1988–89) Revenue: $581,125,000. Expenditure: $550,430,000. Debt outstanding: $549,817,000; per capita: $1,252.57.

**Visitor info.**: (816) 274–2533.

## Long Beach, California

Originally the site of an Indian trading camp, by the end of the 18th century the area that is now Long Beach was part of the Spanish Ranchos Los Alamitos and Cerritos. In 1882 William E. Willmore began development of the land as a resort (which he named for himself). When first incorporated in 1888, it was named Long Beach after its 8.5 miles of Pacific beachfront. Content to remain a resort community, Long Beach had its fortunes rewritten in 1921 when extensive petroleum deposits were first discovered at Signal Hill. Today industry is a major presence in Long Beach—especially ship repair, transportation, oil refining, and marine research; in addition the navy maintains a large base with dry dock facilities.

Among its cultural and recreational attractions are Long Beach's own Museum of Art; the Terrace Theater, home of the Long Beach Symphony Orchestra; and the Long Beach Community Playhouse. Popular tourist attractions include Los Cerritos, a Spanish adobe house dating to 1844; the magnificent ocean liner *Queen Mary*, which today serves as a floating maritime museum, convention center, and hotel; and the *Spruce Goose*, Howard Hughes's unflyable plane of gigantic proportions. Long Beach is also the site of a Formula 1 Grand Prix every spring. Disneyland is in nearby Anaheim.

**Population** 429,433 (1990). Rank: 32. Pop. density: 8,623/sq. mi. (3,329/sq km).

**Location** 33°47′N, 118°11′W. County: Los Angeles.

**Terrain and climate** Elev.: 35 ft. Area: 49.8 sq. mi. (129 sq km). Avg. daily min. temp.: Jan.: 44.3°F/6.8°C; avg. daily max.: July: 83°F/28.3°C. Avg. annual rainfall: 12″; snowfall: 0″; clear days: 143; precipitation days: 35.

**Government** Form: council and manager. Mayor: Ernie Kell. Election: June 1994. Municipal tel. number: (213) 590–6555.

**Finances** (1988–89) Revenue: $685,190,000. Expenditure: $697,840,000. Debt outstanding: $567,536,000; per capita: $1,367.42.

**Visitor info.**: (213) 436–3645.

## Los Angeles, California

In pre-Spanish days, the area of Los Angeles was inhabited by approximately 4,000 Indian peoples, representing some 30 different groups. The Uto-Aztecan village of Yang-na, with a population of 300, was located in what is now downtown Los Angeles, in the vicinity of Alameda and Commercial streets. In October 1542 Joao Rodrigues Cabrilho, a Portuguese explorer in the employ of Spain, became the first European to set foot on Los Angeles soil, but 200 years passed before a land expedition under the command of Gaspar de Portola crossed the territory on the way from Monterey to San Diego in 1769.

The establishment of the Mission of San Gabriel (destined to become the largest of the Franciscan Missions) followed, and in 1781 Spanish Gov. Felipe Neve founded the city of El Pueblo de Nuestra Señora de los Angeles de Porciuncula (The Village of Our Lady of the Angels) as part of a plan to colonize California. Spanish rule continued until 1822, when Spain relinquished her holdings in western America, prompting California to pledge her allegiance to the Mexican empire. With the Treaty of Guadalupe Hidalgo (1848), the United States acquired all of California from Mexico, and in 1850 Los Angeles was incorporated as a city. Introduction of the Southern Pacific Railroad in 1876 sparked a 12-year land boom, promoting the city's growth. By 1892 Los Angeles thrived as a center of oil production, and in 1899 work began on the largest man-made deep-water facility in the world. It had emerged as the motion picture capital of the world by 1910. Industry accelerated in the 1920s, and today L.A. ranks as one of the three great industrial cities in the country.

A thriving metropolis, Los Angeles boasts one of the finest highway systems in the world, handling over 4.9 million cars registered in the Los Angeles metropolitan area—1.6 cars per household, the highest ratio in the world. Three transcontinental railway systems terminate in L.A., 37 certified air carriers fly to all parts of the world, its harbors have 46 miles of waterfront, and the city has the largest trucking center in the West. L.A. remains the world's movie mecca, teeming with studios, stars, and the starstruck.

Los Angelinos live with daily problems of smog, traffic jams, spectacular traffic accidents, and the everpresent threats of mud slides, fires, floods, high winds, and earthquakes. But the year-round sunshine, and the abundance of beaches and mountain areas, all within an easy drive, tend to ameliorate one's anxiety.

**Population** 3,485,398 (1990). Rank: 2. Pop. density: 7,481/sq. mi. (2,888/sq km).

**Location** 34°04′N, 118°15′W. County: Los Angeles.

**Terrain and climate** Elev.: 104 ft. Area: 465.9 sq. mi. (1,206.7 sq km). Avg. daily min. temp.: Jan.: 47.3°F/8.5°C; avg. daily max.: July: 75.3°F/24°C. Avg. annual rainfall: 14.85″; snowfall: 0″; clear days: 143; precipitation days: 35.

**Government** Form: mayor and council. Mayor: Tom Bradley. Election: June 1993. Municipal tel. number: (213) 485–2121.

**Finances** (1988–89) Revenue: $5,968,047,000. Expenditure: $5,392,880,000. Debt outstanding: $5,468,207,000; per capita: $1,630.98.

**Visitor info.**: (213) 485–4423.

## Memphis, Tennessee

The first settlers in the area of Memphis arrived on the bluffs overlooking the Mississippi River more than a thousand years ago. The Chickasaw forcibly displaced these people—about whom little is known, including their name—and lived there for eight centuries until 1838, when the U.S. government scattered the entire tribe to Oklahoma and parts further west so that Euro-Americans could develop the land. The Spanish explorer Hernando de Soto first set eyes on the bluffs in 1541. Other explorers passed through over the next century, and in 1739 the French built Fort Assumption. The French, Spanish, and Chickasaw fought over the land for the balance of the 18th century until it became a part of the United States in 1797. The area's original American owners, Gen. James Winchester, Judge John Overton, and Gen. Andrew Jackson (who later sold his share and went on to become president), established the town in 1819 and named it Memphis, after the ancient Egyptian city on the Nile.

River boatmen gave young Memphis a reputation for brawls and bawdiness, while mosquitoes gave it a history of yellow fever epidemics, which in the 1880s claimed more than half the city's population and jeopardized its charter. A sewage system, the first of its kind, finally helped conquer the epidemic. Between the river traffic and cotton crops, the city prospered, attracting Irish and German immigrants, and by the 20th century was on its way to becoming the unofficial capital of the mid-South. Elvis Presley, who expanded on the city's rhythm and blues tradition to become the world's first rock and roll idol, remains the city's single most enduring contribution to popular culture.

In 1991, the Lorraine Motel, where civil rights leader Dr. Martin Luther King, Jr., was assassinated in 1968, was opened as the National Civil Rights Museum.

**Population** 610,337 (1990). Rank: 18. Pop. density: 2,311/sq. mi. (892/sq km).
**Location** 35°08′N, 90°03′W. County: Shelby.
**Terrain and climate** Elev.: 307 ft. Area: 264.1 sq. mi. (684 sq km). Avg. daily min. temp.: Jan.: 30.9°F/–0.6°C; avg. daily max.: July: 91.5°F/ 33°C. Avg. annual rainfall: 51.57″; snowfall: 6″; precipitation days: 106.
**Government** Form: mayor and council. Mayor: Richard C. Hackett. Election: Oct. 1991. Municipal tel. number: (901) 576-6000.
**Finances** (1988–89) Revenue: $1,629,319,000. Expenditure: $1,505,754,000. Debt outstanding: $749,420,000; per capita: $1,161.55.
**Visitor info.**: (901) 576-8181.

## Miami, Florida

Miami, the most southerly major city in the continental United States, sits about two degrees north of the Tropic of Cancer, a location that has made it a long-standing resort haven. Miami in the 1980s also thrived as a major hub of commerce and as a population center for Latin American immigrants, particularly those arriving from Cuba, whose ambition and business acumen contributed to the city's prosperity. While tourists still generate over 60 percent of the area's economic activity, many other areas of enterprise, such as construction, light industry, and agriculture (limes, tomatoes, avocados, mangoes, and beans) have flourished.

Miami (whose name is thought to derive from the Indian *mayami*, meaning "big water"), dates back to the 16th century when Native Americans occupied the southern part of Florida. Fort Dallas, built near the mouth of the Miami River in 1836 as a base of war against the Seminoles, became the first permanent Euramerican settlement. The building of the Florida East Coast Railroad, coinciding with Miami's incorporation as a city in 1896 (population 343), offered ready access to the area. Resort hotels quickly cropped up, and Miami, along with the rest of Florida, enjoyed great success. In 1926 a severe hurricane submerged much of its land under water, abruptly ending Miami's prosperity, but the city managed to grow steadily by draining and developing swampland. After World War II, new resorts rose up, and Miami thrived. In 1991, Major League Baseball awarded the city one of two expansion team franchises.

The relative success of the large influx of Hispanics—especially Cubans—since the 1960s is a source of ill feelings, especially to many in the black community, and the city has been wracked by rioting in recent years.

**Population** 358,548 (1990). Rank: 46. Pop. density: 10,453/sq. mi. (4,038/sq km).
**Location** 25°47′N, 80°11′W. County: Dade.
**Terrain and climate** Elev.: 12 ft. Area: 34.3 sq. mi. (88.8 sq km). Avg. daily min. temp.: Jan.: 59.2°F/15.1°C; avg. daily max.: July: 88.7°F/ 31.5°C. Avg. annual rainfall: 57.55″; snowfall: 0″; clear days: 76; precipitation days: 129.
**Government** Form: council and manager. Mayor: Xavier L. Suarez. Election: Nov. 1993. Municipal tel. number: (305) 250-5300.
**Finances** (1988–89) Revenue: $315,861,000. Expenditure: $359,678,000. Debt outstanding: $503,152,000; per capita: $1,355.84.
**Visitor info.**: (305) 539-3000.

## Milwaukee, Wisconsin

During the 1670s the French explorers Jacques Marquette and Louis Jolliet were the first Europeans to visit the site of present-day Milwaukee, an area on the western shore of Lake Michigan at the confluence of the Menomonee and Kinnickinnic rivers. In 1795 Jacques Vicau of the North West Company established a trading post, and in 1818 Solomon Laurent Juneau, the first permanent Euro-American settler, founded Milwaukee (from the Indian term *millioke*, meaning "beautiful land"). From the 1840s on, large numbers of German immigrants came to the city, making up more than 60 percent of the 1850 population; today an estimated one-third of the city's residents are of German descent.

A flourishing agricultural center, Milwaukee had by the Civil War become the largest wheat market in the world. Its industrial base expanded after the war, and by 1940 the city ranked fourth in manufacturing among U.S. cities. Still one of the most vigorous producers of durable goods—especially automotive parts, construction and road-building equipment, diesel and gasoline engines, tractors, and outboard motors—Milwaukee has also emerged as a major meat-packing center. Reflecting its German heritage, the city developed a successful brewing industry, with two of the largest beer-producing companies in the country—Schlitz and Pabst. A major Great Lakes and, since the opening of the St. Lawrence Seaway, international port, Milwaukee handles 12 international steamship lines.

**Population** 628,088 (1990). Rank: 17. Pop. density: 6,556/sq. mi. (2,532/sq km).
**Location** 43°02′N, 87°55′W. County: Milwaukee.
**Terrain and climate** Elev.: 581 ft. Area: 95.8 sq. mi. (248.1 sq km). Avg. daily min. temp.: Jan.: 11.3°F/–11.5°C; avg. daily max.: July: 79.8°F/ 26.5°C. Avg. annual rainfall: 30.94″; snowfall: 45″; clear days: 96; precipitation days: 122.
**Government** Form: mayor and council. Mayor: John O. Norquist. Election: Nov. 1992. Municipal tel. number: (414) 278-3200.
**Finances** (1988–89) Revenue: $707,684,000. Expenditure: $604,844,000. Debt outstanding: $491,923,000; per capita: $820.72.
**Visitor info.**: (800) 231-0903.

## Minneapolis, Minnesota

Despite its arctic winters, Minneapolis is one of the most desirable cities in the United States. It sits astride the Mississippi River, near the headwaters of the Minnesota River, about 350 miles northwest of Chicago. While it is the largest commercial metropolis in the north between Milwaukee and Seattle, no single industry dominates, although many large computer and electronics companies make Minneapolis their home. A regional banking center and the site of the Federal Reserve Bank for the Ninth District, Minneapolis has the world's largest cash grain exchange and the world's four largest wheat-flour-milling companies, and provides the upper Midwest with truck, barge, and air transport.

In 1682 Father Louis Hennepin, the French priest who explored the Mississippi, was the first European to set eyes on the Falls of St. Anthony, the future site of Minneapolis. Unsettled until Fort Snelling was built in 1819 to protect fur traders from the Sioux and Chippewa, the town of St. Anthony began growing up on one side of the Mississippi and a second settlement on the other. The two were consolidated in 1872; the new name was a hybrid of the Indian word *minne*, meaning "water," and the Greek word for "city," *polis*. Minneapolis blossomed on the basis of its flour and lumber milling. By century's end, the forests to the north had been depleted, but flour milling continues as a thriving industry to this day.

Long considered a center of progressive political and social thinking, Minneapolis is a mecca of education and culture. It is the site of the main campus of the University of Minnesota, the Minnesota Orchestra, and the Minneapolis Institute of the Arts. A haven for outdoor enthusiasts, the park system numbers 153 parks encompassing 6,000 acres, and with 10 percent of its surface covered by water, Minneapolis has 12 lakes within its city limits.

**Population** 368,383 (1990). Rank: 42. Pop. density: 6,686/sq. mi. (2,582/sq km).

**Location** 44°59′N, 98°16′W. County: Hennepin.

**Terrain and climate** Elev.: 828 ft. Area: 55.1 sq. mi. (142.7 sq km). Avg. daily min. temp.: Jan.: 2.4°F/-16.4°C; avg. daily max.: July: 83.4°F/ 28.5°C. Avg. annual rainfall: 26.36″; snowfall: 46″; clear days: 100; precipitation days: 113.

**Government** Form: mayor and council. Mayor: Donald McKay Fraser. Election: Nov. 1993. Municipal tel. number: (612) 348-2100.

**Finances** (1988–89) Revenue: $739,047,000. Expenditure: $714,043,000. Debt outstanding: $1,901,697,000; per capita: $5,517.44.

**Visitor info.**: (612) 348-7000.


## Nashville, Tennessee

In the winter of 1779–80, settlers from North Carolina, led by James Robertson, arrived at a place on the Cumberland River called Big Salt Lick, and built forts on both sides of the river, one of which they named Nashborough, after Gen. Francis Nash of the Revolutionary Army. Adopting the name Nashville in 1784, the settlement was chartered as a city in 1806, became state capital in 1843, and prospered until the Civil War as the northern terminus of the Natchez Trace, a 500-mile road to Natchez, Mississippi. The site of one of the war's last major battles in December 1864, the city underwent a long period of rebuilding, and by the end of the century the population reached 81,000. The city continued to grow, doubling in population by World War II, and has experienced even greater expansion since that time.

While best known as a major center of both the recording and music-publishing industries, Nashville enjoys a widely diversified economic foundation and serves as a distribution and marketing point for the upper southern region of the country. Several religious organizations and their publishing operations are headquartered there, and the city comprises more than a dozen institutions of higher learning, including Vanderbilt University, Fisk University, and Tennessee State University. With a growing base of manufacturing, insurance, and banking, Nashville, as home of the Grand Ole Opry, has also developed into a regional tourist and convention attraction. A full-scale replica of the Greek temple the Parthenon is a noted site.

**Population** 510,784 (1990). Rank: 23. Pop. density: 1,065 sq. mile (411/sq km).

**Location** 36°10′N, 86°47′N. County: Davidson.

**Terrain and climate** Elev.: 605 ft. Area: 479.5 sq. mi. (1,241.9 sq km). Avg. daily min. temp.: Jan.: 27.8°F/-2.3°C; avg. daily max.: July: 89.8°F/32.1°C. Avg. annual rainfall: 48.49″; snowfall: 10.7″; clear days: 103; precipitation days: 119.

**Government** Form: mayor and council. Mayor: Phil Bredesen. Election: Aug. 1994. Municipal tel. number: (615) 862-6000.

**Finances** (1988–89) Revenue: $1,508,916,000. Expenditure: $1,477,785,000. Debt outstanding: $2,389,915,000; per capita: $4,964.72.

**Visitor info.**: (615) 259-4755.


## New Orleans, Louisiana

Founded in 1718 by Jean Baptiste le Moyne and named Ville d'Orléans after the regent of France, the city of New Orleans is one of the nation's most distinctive cities. Situated only 110 miles from the mouth of the Mississippi River, it has long been a major international port (it ranks second in the nation today), and thanks to overlapping waves of French, Spanish, African-American, and Anglo-American immigrants, it has one of the most richly textured cultures of any city in North America. It is geographically distinct, too, in that much of it is below sea level; the almost constant threat of flooding is mitigated by an intricate network of canals and levees.

After half a century under French rule, New Orleans became the capital of Spanish Louisiana in 1763. It was briefly under French rule again (1800–03) before being acquired by the United States as part of the Louisiana Purchase. Although Louisiana was admitted as a state in 1815, New Orleans continues to reflect its Spanish and French heritage in its architecture, cuisine, and its flamboyant Mardi Gras celebration at the beginning of Lent. African-American traditions are strong here, too, and Dixieland jazz—long heralded as a uniquely American music—is a fusion of African and European styles.

In addition to being a major port for the export of cotton, rice, petroleum products, iron, steel, and corn and the import of sugar, bananas, coffee, bauxite, and molasses, New Orleans is a major center for offshore drilling in the Gulf of Mexico. In recent years its industrial sector, with an emphasis on aerospace research and technology, petroleum refinement, and shipbuilding, has been strong.

A major tourist attraction in its own right, the city includes among its special points of interest St. Louis Cathedral, the French Market, Preservation Hall and Dixieland Hall, and the Presbytère—all in the French Quarter—the celebrated residential architecture of the Garden District, the New Orleans Museum of Art, the Confederate Museum, and Audubon Park Zoo. Among its educational institutions are Tulane University, Sophie Newcomb College, and Dillard University.

**Population** 496,938 (1990). Rank: 25. Pop. density: 2,492/sq. mi. (962/sq km).

**Location** 29°58′W, 90°04′W. Parish: Orleans.

**Terrain and climate** Elev.: 30 ft. Area: 199.4 sq. mi. (516.4 sq km). Avg. daily min. temp.: Jan.: 43°F/6.1°C; avg. daily max.: July: 90.7°F/ 32.6°C. Avg. annual rainfall: 59.74″; snowfall: 0.2″; clear days: 109; precipitation days: 113.

**Government** Form: mayor and council. Mayor: Sidney J. Barthelemy. Election: Feb. 1994. Municipal tel. number: (504) 586-4000.

**Finances** (1988–89) Revenue: $685,383,000. Expenditure: $739,402,000. Debt outstanding: $1,182,178,000; per capita: $2,223.35.

**Visitor info.**: (504) 566-5011.


## New York City, New York

Even before the arrival of Europeans in North America, the waters that today make New York one of the world's foremost ports— and the foremost city in the United States— were the scene of lively trade between the predominant Algonquian tribes in the region. The city's modern history dates to 1524, when the Florentine explorer Giovanni de Verrazano sailed into New York Bay. In 1609 Henry Hudson, an English navigator sailing for the Dutch East India Company, explored the river that bears his name today. In 1625 the Dutch West India Company purchased Manhattan and established Nieuw Amsterdam, which quickly became a profitable trading post. Dutch settlers soon expanded beyond the original colony, settling Breukelen, Nieuw Harlem, Bronx, and Staaten Eylandt. Taken by the British in 1664 (the Dutch briefly regained control in 1673-74), and renamed for the duke of York, the town continued to prosper.

As resentment of British authority grew, New York became a seat of colonial discontent, participating in actions against the Stamp Act (1763) and tea tax (1773). But after the Battle of Long Island and Washington's retreat in August 1776, the British held New York through the end of the war. Yet Washington was inaugurated president at Federal Hall (today the site of the second Federal Reserve Bank) on Wall Street, and in 1789-90 New York was the nation's capital.

Industry and trade expanded dramatically after the opening of the Erie Canal from Troy (150 miles up the Hudson River) and Buffalo (350 miles west of Troy) gave New York direct access to raw materials and markets of the Great Lakes states. In the mid-19th century, New York became the country's primary port of immigration, and many of the millions of immigrants who came to America carved out distinctly ethnic neighborhoods throughout the city in a patchwork that survives to the present.

In 1898 an act of the state legislature created "Greater New York," and today New York's population is greater than that of Los Angeles and Chicago (the second- and third-largest cities in the country) combined. Even if they were separate cities, four of New York's boroughs would rank in the top 10—Brooklyn fourth (2.3 million), Queens fifth (1.9 million), Manhattan eighth (1.5 million), and the Bronx ninth (1.2 million).

New York's attractions are almost innumerable—enough to draw over 17 million visitors per year—but they include 150 museums, 400 art galleries, 38 Broadway theaters, and scores of concert halls, clubs, and dance halls. In addition there are 780 landmark buildings, 50 landmark interiors, and 51 historic districts. (A list of attractions can be found under "New York State.") The city leads the nation in the arts, fashion, advertising, banking and financial services, publishing, broadcasting, and certain of the service industries; it is the home of the UN General Assembly; and there are 87 colleges and universities, including Columbia University, New York University, Long Island University, Brooklyn College, St. Johns University, the Pratt Institute of Technology, the Juilliard School, and the School of Visual Arts. Manufactured products comprise apparel, chemicals, metal products, and printing.

**Population** 7,322,564 (1990). Rank: 1. Pop. density: 24,287/sq. mi. (9,377/sq km).
**Location** 40°43′N, 74°00′W. Counties: Bronx, Kings, New York, Queens, Richmond.
**Terrain and climate** Elev.: 87 ft. Area: 301.5 sq. mi. (780.9 sq km). Avg. daily min. temp.: Jan.: 25.6°F/–3.5°C; avg. daily max.: July: 85.3°F/29.6°C. Avg. annual rainfall: 44.12″; snowfall: 29″; clear days: 107; precipitation days, 121.
**Government** Form: mayor and council. Mayor: David N. Dinkins. Election: Nov. 1993. Municipal tel. number: (212) 566–5700.
**Finances** (1988–89) Revenue: $34,637,806,000. Expenditure: $34,159,738,000. Debt outstanding: $23,360,078,000; per capita: $3,177.07.
**Visitor info.:** (212) 397–8222.

## Oakland, California

The first Euramerican to settle present-day Oakland was Dom Luis Maria Peralta, in 1820, who established the 44,000-acre settlement called Rancho San Antonio in 1820. Its first real growth began with the establishment of ferry service to San Francisco in 1852, though the ferry was dramatically superceded by Oakland's selection as the western terminus of the first transcontinental railroad in 1869. The city remained in the economic shadow of its more sophisticated neighbor across the Bay until the San Francisco earthquake of 1906 drove 100,000–150,000 people to Oakland for shelter. An estimated 65,000 of these are thought to have settled there permanently, providing an impetus for Oakland's long period of growth as an international port and industrial center.

A major commercial and cultural center with a container port ranked 10th in the world, Oakland is also the major northern hub of the California freeway system, which is integrated with the Bay Area Rapid Transit (BART) System. It has also become the premier biotechnology center in the region, and regional and international headquarters for firms in finance, medicine, telecommunications, international trade, and heavy industry are located there.

Long a primarily industrial urban center, Oakland has pumped hundreds of millions of dollars into development of its downtown area and the Jack London waterfront—named for the author who spent his youth on the Oakland docks. More artists reside in Oakland than anywhere else in the country with the exception of New York's Greenwich Village. Oakland embraces a racially and culturally diverse populace, and a 1980 University of Wisconsin study found it the most integrated city in the nation.
**Population** 372,242 (1990). Rank: 39. Pop. density: 6,906/sq. mi. (2,666/sq km).
**Location** 37°49′N, 122°16′W. County: Alameda.
**Terrain and climate** Elev.: 42 ft. Area: 53.9 sq. mi. (139.6 sq km). Avg. daily min. temp.: Jan.: 43.4°F/6.3°C; avg. daily max.: July: 70.6°F/29.6°C. Avg. annual rainfall: 18.03″; snowfall: N.A.; clear days: N.A.; precipitation days: N.A.
**Government** Form: council and manager. Mayor: Elihu Harris. Election: Nov. 1995. Municipal tel. number: (415) 273–3141.
**Finances** (1988–89) Revenue: $471,951,000.

Expenditure: $412,563,000. Debt outstanding: $1,025,244,000; per capita: $2,872.96.
**Visitor info.:** (415) 839–9000.

## Oklahoma City, Oklahoma

Oklahoma City sprang up during the Great Land Rush of 1889 and, by presidential proclamation, opened for Euro-American settlement officially on April 22 of that year. At day's end approximately 10,000 settlers had moved in—the greatest one-day nonannexation population increase in the history of cities. Oklahoma became a state in 1907 and Oklahoma City its capital in 1910, by which time the population had swelled to about 64,000. Since then, it has become Oklahoma's largest city, its leading commercial center, and home to the National Cowboy Hall of Fame.

Oklahoma City's economy, based on oil and livestock, thrives on petroleum production, meat processing, and the breeding of stocker and feeder cattle. The city hosts a flourishing printing and publishing industry and manufactures a diversity of products, including automobiles, electronics equipment, computers, communications switches, and oil well supplies. As a vital banking center serving the central and western regions of the state, Oklahoma City is home to a Federal Reserve branch bank. On a somewhat less positive note, Oklahoma City reportedly sparked the "go-go" banking syndrome that characterized the 1970s oil boom, when the Penn Square Bank's ill-advised oil patch loans nearly devastated the U.S. banking system.
**Population** 444,719 (1990). Rank: 29. Pop. density: 736/sq. mi. (284/sq km).
**Location** 35°03′N, 97°30′W. Counties: Canadian, Cleveland, McClain, Oklahoma.
**Terrain and climate** Elev.: 1,304 ft. Area: 604 sq. mi. (1,564.4 sq km). Avg. daily min. temp.: Jan.: 25.2°F/–3.7°C; avg. daily max.: July: 93.5°F/34.1°C. Avg. annual rainfall: 30.89″; snowfall: 9″; clear days: 141; precipitation days: 81.
**Government** Form: council and manager. Mayor: Ronald J. Norick. Election: Mar. 1995. Municipal tel. number: (405) 297–2424.
**Finances** (1988–89) Revenue: $324,102,000. Expenditure: $403,420,000. Debt outstanding: $516,765,000; per capita: $1,189.66.
**Visitor info.:** (405) 278–8912.

## Omaha, Nebraska

Permanent settlement in what is now Omaha began with a fur-trading post established shortly after the Lewis and Clark expedition passed through the area in 1804. In 1820 the U.S. government built Ft. Atkinson, and the surrounding community became a major stop on both the Mormon and the Lewis and Clark trails, and was incorporated as a city in 1854. After strong lobbying by citizens of Council Bluffs, Iowa, just across the Missouri River to the east, Omaha (the name means "above all others on the stream") became the eastern terminus of the Union-Pacific transcontinental railroad, the country's first railroad, in 1869. Within six years the population grew to 39,000, and by the turn of the century had passed the 100,000 mark.

As a major transportation hub of the Midwest—Omaha today boasts seven major railroads, and the recently expanded Port of Omaha services a dozen barge lines—the city became a major distribution center for meat and grain, living up to its motto We Feed the World. Its major food products include pasta, potato chips, coffee, pancake mixes, frozen dinners, and Omaha steaks. With 44 *Fortune*-500 manufacturing operations and a healthy publishing industry (roughly one out of every four manufacturers is either a publisher or printer), Omaha's diversified economy also has strong roots in insurance; communications; sophisticated medical facilities, centered around the medical schools of Creighton University and the University of Nebraska; and Offutt Air Force Base, headquarters of the Strategic Air Command.

Among its performing arts institutions are the Omaha Symphony, Opera/Omaha, the Omaha Ballet, the Orpheum Theater, and the Omaha Community Playhouse. Museums and historic sites include the Boys Town Hall of Fame, the Henry Doorly Zoo and Aquarium, the Great Plains Black Museum, the historic ships USS *Hazard* and USS *Marlin*, and the Old Market, a mixed-use National Historic District on the Missouri River.
**Population** 335,795 (1990). Rank: 48. Pop. density: 3,382/sq. mi. (1,306/sq km).
**Location** 41°17′N, 96°01′W. County: Douglas.
**Terrain and climate** Elev.: 982 ft. Area: 99.3 sq. mi. (257.2 sq km). Avg. daily min. temp.: Jan.: 10.2°F/–12.1°C; avg. daily max.: July: 88.5°F/31.3°C. Avg. annual rainfall: 30.34″; snowfall: 32″; clear days: 113; precipitation days: 99.
**Government** Form: mayor and council. Mayor: P.J. Morgan. Election: May 1993. Municipal tel. number: (402) 444–5000.
**Finances** (1988–89) Revenue: $232,682,000. Expenditure: $218,209,000. Debt outstanding: $185,498,000; per capita: $525.24.
**Visitor info.:** (402) 444–4660.

## Philadelphia, Pennsylvania

In 1632 a small contingent of Swedes and Finns came to the land where the Schuylkill River meets the Delaware and founded New Sweden. In 1655 Peter Stuyvesant seized New Sweden for the Dutch, inciting conflict with the British until the Dutch relinquished their rights to the territory in 1673. Nine years later William Penn established a town between the Schuylkill and the Delaware rivers, naming it Philadelphia, the "city of brotherly love," and in two years it evolved into an active settlement of about 2,500 people, most of them Quakers.

In the mid-1700s, Benjamin Franklin began shaping the destiny of Philadelphia by presiding over the founding of the University of Pennsylvania (America's first university), Pennsylvania Hospital, and a fire insurance company (both also firsts). Under his guidance Philadelphia became the premier colonial city for the arts and the home of many famous educators, scientists, authors, and painters. In addition a total of 17 libraries were founded at this time. The meeting place of the

Continental Congress and the site of the signing of the Declaration of Independence, Philadelphia was the nation's capital from 1790 to 1800, the year the federal government moved permanently to Washington, D.C.

Throughout the l9th century, the influx first of Irish and German, then Jewish, Italian, Polish, and Slavic immigrants from Europe, and blacks from the South, helped build the city's industrial base. Today Philadelphia ranks second among U.S. cities in oil refining; other principal industries are electrical machinery, automobile and truck bodies, petrochemicals, metalworking, and scientific instruments.

**Population** 1,585,577 (1990). Rank: 5. Pop. density: 11,659/sq. mi. (4,502/sq km).
**Location** 39°57′N, 75°10′W. County: Philadelphia.
**Terrain and climate** Elev.: 28 ft. Area: 136 sq. mi. (352.2 sq km). Avg. daily min. temp.: Jan.: 23.8°F/–4.5°C; avg. daily max.: July: 86.1°F/30°C. Avg. annual rainfall: 41.42″; snowfall: 20″; clear days: 92; precipitation days: 116.
**Government** Form: mayor and council. Mayor: W. Wilson Goode. Election: Nov. 1991. Municipal tel. number: (215) 686–7116.
**Finances** (1988–89) Revenue: $3,162,404,000. Expenditure: $3,288,399,000. Debt outstanding: $3,909,482,000; per capita: $2,373.70.
**Visitor info.:** (215) 636–1666.

### Phoenix, Arizona

Phoenix, the capital of Arizona and its largest city, sits in the Salt River valley in a former desert that has become a prosperous agricultural area because of a network of irrigated dams located northeast of the city. Long a resort area owing to its mild climate, Phoenix has recently emerged as a lively commercial and agricultural center as well. A prospering high-tech haven attracting businesses engaged in electronics, communications, and research and development, the city also has a strong manufacturing base, which includes airport parts, electronic equipment, agricultural chemicals, radios, air conditioners, and leather goods. Among its agricultural products are lettuce, melons, vegetables, grapefruit, oranges, lemons, and olives.

While Phoenix benefits from modern irrigation efforts, the Hohokam Indian people dug the area's first irrigation ditches in the third century B.C. and developed an extensive network of canals during their culture's decline in A.D. 1400. The area was not resettled until 1864, when a hay camp was established to supply Camp McDowell 30 miles away. Jack Weilling and "Lord Darrell" Dupa rebuilt the old Indian irrigation ditches in 1867 and named the site Phoenix, after the mythical bird that rose from its own ashes. The settlement grew as a trading post, was incorporated as a city in 1881, and became capital of the territory in 1889 and state capital when Arizona was admitted to the Union in 1912.

With the westward exodus from the snowbelt states, and the perfecting of air conditioning to make the summer heat bearable, the small 1950s resort city of 106,818 people has since swelled almost ninefold.

**Population** 983,403 (1990). Rank: 9. Pop. density: 2,622/sq. mi. (1,012/sq km).
**Location** 33°27′N, 112°04′W. County: Maricopa.
**Terrain and climate** Elev.: 1,117 ft. Area: 375 sq. mi. (971.3 sq km). Avg. daily min. temp.: Jan.: 44.4°F/6.8°C; avg. daily max.: July: 107.5°F/41°C. Avg. annual rainfall: 7.11″; snowfall: 0″; clear days: 214; precipitation days: 34.
**Government** Form: Mayor and council. Mayor: Paul Johnson. Election: Nov. 1991. Municipal tel. number: (602) 262-7111.
**Finances** (1988–89) Revenue: $1,059,974,000. Expenditure: $1,119,333,000. Debt outstanding: $1,964,379,000; per capita: $2,126.53.
**Visitor info.:** (602) 254–6500.

### Pittsburgh, Pennsylvania

Long one of the leading urban industrial areas in the country, Pittsburgh sits at the confluence of the Allegheny and Monongahela rivers, which join to form the Ohio River. In 1754 the British chose the site for its access to this extensive river network (which today reaches to the Gulf of Mexico, the Great Lakes, and up the Missouri River) and began building Fort Pitt, named for Prime Minister William Pitt. Pittsburgh is also situated in the midst of extensive deposits of oil, coal, and natural gas; the production of steel and iron began in the 1790s. In the 19th century, Pittsburgh was one of the nation's largest producers of steel and iron, and in 1881 its industrial workers formed the American Federation of Labor.

After the boom years of the 1940s and 1950s, the city's fortunes began to shrivel with the decline of heavy industry, a dwindling population, and high unemployment in the 1980s. Yet with 40 miles of riverfront, Pittsburgh remains the country's largest inland port, and is still a leader in the manufacture of petrochemicals and glass products, as well as the home of more than 150 industrial research companies.

Moreover, Pittsburgh's industrial past has left a rich cultural legacy, which contributed to its recent ranking as number one in the country by *Places Rated Almanac*. Its cultural institutions include Phipps Conservatory, Buhl Planetarium, Carnegie Institute, Carnegie Music Hall, and Carnegie Museum of Natural History (the latter three named for the Scots-born industrialist and philanthropist Andrew Carnegie), as well as the Pittsburgh Symphony Orchestra, the Pittsburgh Public Theater, and Pittsburgh Dance Theater. Its universities include the University of Pittsburgh, Pittsburgh Theological Seminary, Duquesne University, and Carnegie-Mellon University.

**Population** 369,879 (1990). Rank: 40. Pop. density: 6,677/sq. mi. (2,578/sq km).
**Location** 40°26′N, 80°01′W. County: Allegheny.
**Terrain and climate** Elev.: 1,223 ft. Area: 55.4 sq. mi. (143.5 sq km). Avg. daily min. temp.: Jan.: 19.2°F/–7.1°C; avg. daily max.: July: 86.1°F/30°C. Avg. annual rainfall: 36.29″; snowfall: 45″; clear days: 59; precipitation days: 152.
**Government** Form: mayor and council. Mayor: Sophie Masloff. Election: Nov. 1994. Municipal tel. number: (412) 255–2100.

**Finances** (1988–89) Revenue: $397,919,000. Expenditure: $360,810,000. Debt outstanding: $551,805,000; per capita: $1,470.58.
**Visitor info.:** (412) 281–7711.

### Portland, Oregon

Portland's renowned beauty is a result of its unique natural setting, which offers a view of the Cascade Mountains and Mt. Hood to the east, Mt. Adams to the northeast, and Mt. St. Helens and Mt. Rainier to the north. Eleven bridges span the Willamette River, which divides the city into east and west sections.

Indian traders traveling between Oregon City and Vancouver carved out an acre of land by the Willamette River 12 miles north of Oregon City, which became known as The Clearing. In 1884 William Overton claimed the 640 acres surrounding the area, which he then sold to Asa Lovejoy and Francis W. Pettygrove, who set out to build a city. Winning a coin toss, Pettygrove named the city-to-be after his hometown in Maine.

As a vital port of entry (the coast's only freshwater port) with a large inland harbor, Portland is a leader in the shipping of lumber, flour, and grain and has blossomed into Oregon's largest city. Main industries also include paper and pulp, mining, high-tech equipment, and aerospace. Portland enjoys an active arts community, and its residents partake of the beaches and ski slopes within easy driving distance.

**Population** 437,319 (1990). Rank: 30. Pop. density: 3,839/sq. mi. (1,482/sq km).
**Location** 45°32′N, 122°37′W. Counties: Clackamas, Multnomah, Washington.
**Terrain and climate** Elev.: 39 ft. Area: 113.9 sq. mi. (295 sq km). Avg. daily min. temp.: Jan.: 33.5°F/0.8°C; avg. daily max.: July: 79.5°F/26.3°C. Avg. annual rainfall: 37.39″; snowfall: 7″; clear days: 69; precipitation days: 152.
**Government** Form: commission. Mayor: J.E. Bud Clark. Election: Nov. 1992. Municipal tel. number: (503) 248–4120.
**Finances** (1988–89) Revenue: $423,633,000. Expenditure: $419,735,000. Debt outstanding: $596,457,000; per capita: $1,425.33.
**Visitor info.:** (503) 222–2223.

### Sacramento, California

The capital of California and its seventh-largest city, Sacramento sits 75 miles northwest of San Francisco at the confluence of the American and Sacramento rivers. A wholesale and retail center for the surrounding rich farmland, the city includes among its main commercial enterprises food processing and canning and one of the world's largest almond-shelling plants.

Receiving a land grant from the Mexican government in 1839, Swiss-American John Augustus Sutter founded a colony called New Helvetia, and when Fort Sutter was constructed in 1844, it became one of California's chief trading posts. Established soon after the discovery of gold in 1848, Sacramento grew to 7,000 residents by 1850, became state capital in 1854, and in 1863 was incorporated as a city.

The "Gateway to the Goldfields," "Old Sacramento" became a pivotal point of commerce in the 1860s, connected to the mining towns by the American River and transporting produce from the farms and orchards lining the banks of the Sacramento River. Sailors stopping in San Francisco visited Sacramento to replenish their stocks of fresh produce and to entertain themselves in the saloons and gambling halls. The wealthy lived in great mansions by the river, and cobblestone streets, gaslights, and wood sidewalks imbued the town with a touch of civility. Today's Sacramento, appreciated for its subtle, quiet charms, embraces 120 parks; hiking and biking trails along the American River Parkway; a large collection of art galleries; two symphony orchestras; ballet, theater and opera companies; and a number of jazz clubs and coffeehouses.

**Population** 369,365 (1990). Rank: 41. Pop. density: 3,796/sq. mi. (1,466/sq km).

**Location** 38°35′N, 121°29′W. County: Sacramento.

**Terrain and climate** Elev.: 25 ft. Area: 97.3 sq. mi. (252 sq km). Avg. daily min. temp.: Jan.: 37.9°F/3.2°C; avg. daily max.: July: 93.3°F/34°C. Avg. annual rainfall: 17.87″; snowfall: 0.1″; clear days: 193; precipitation days: 57.

**Government** Form: council and manager. Mayor: Anne Rudin. Election: Nov. 1992. Municipal tel. number: (916) 449-5706.

**Finances** (1988–89) Revenue: $294,978,000. Expenditure: $288,633,000. Debt outstanding: $218,505,000; per capita: $646.04.

**Visitor info.:** (916) 442-5542.

## St. Louis, Missouri

St. Louis is one of the nation's major centers of transportation, manufacturing, commerce, and education. With abundant water and electric power, with a work force of over a million people in the metropolitan area, and in an area rich in mineral resources, St. Louis ranks as one of the top 10 industrial areas in the country. It is also one of the nation's busiest river ports, the third-largest rail center, and the eighth-largest trucking center, and has the sixth-busiest airport. Aircraft, automobiles, printing, beer, and chemicals are among the principal products. The metropolitan area boasts five universities, 23 colleges, and seven junior colleges. St. Louis University, the oldest university west of the Mississippi, founded in 1818, and Washington University are world famous for their medical schools and research programs and their Nobel Prize winners.

For the 40 years after its founding in 1764 by Pierre Laclade, St. Louis was a French settlement and trading post, outfitting fur trading expeditions up the Missouri River. With the Louisiana Purchase in 1803, St. Louis came under American control. The city was incorporated in 1823 with a population of almost 5,000 people. The first steamboat docked at St. Louis in 1817, and steamboats then became a vital part of the city's growth. Fueled by settlers from the east and especially Irish and German immigrants attracted by the prosperity of the river trade, the city's population grew rapidly. In 1870 St. Louis had a population of 311,000, and it was the country's third-largest city after New York and Philadelphia. The pop-

ulation grew to a peak of 856,800 in 1950, but the post–World War II flight to the suburbs hit St. Louis hard, reducing its population by almost half.

The downtown St. Louis area has many landmarks and historic buildings. The Old Cathedral, completed in 1834, and the Old Courthouse, where the Dred Scott case was first tried, have been preserved as part of the Jefferson National Expansion Memorial. Atop the famous Gateway Arch, the observation room provides a panoramic view of St. Louis. Kiel Auditorium contains a 3,500-seat opera house and a 10,000-seat convention hall. Forest Park, site of the 1904 Louisiana Purchase Exposition (also known as the St. Louis World's Fair), comprises the St. Louis Zoo, McDonnell Planetarium, and the Jewel Box, an all-glass floral display house. St. Louis is also the home of the Missouri Botanical Gardens, which features the Climatron—a geodesic dome with rare orchids and other tropical plants— and the nation's largest Japanese garden. The St. Louis Symphony (founded in 1880) is the country's second oldest and is housed in Powell Symphony Hall.

**Population** 396,685 (1990). Rank: 34. Pop. density: 6,461/sq. mi. (2,495/sq. km).

**Location** 38°37′N, 90°12′W. County: independent city.

**Terrain and climate** Elev.: 564 ft. Area: 61.4 sq. mi. (159 sq km). Avg. daily min. temp.: Jan.: 19.9°F/–6.7°C; avg. daily max.: July: 89°F/31°C. Avg. annual rainfall: 33.91″; snowfall: 18″; clear days: 105; precipitation days: 108.

**Government** Form: mayor and council. Mayor: Vincent C. Schoemehl, Jr. Election: Apr. 1993. Municipal tel. number: (314) 622-3201.

**Finances** (1988–89) Revenue: $604,564,000. Expenditure: $563,084,000. Debt outstanding: $744,314,000; per capita: $1,843.73.

**Visitor info.:** (314) 421-1023.

## San Antonio, Texas

San Antonio, the third-largest city in Texas, lies in the state's south-central region at the edge of the Gulf Coastal Plain 140 miles from the Gulf of Mexico. One of the fastest-growing cities in the nation with a projected population of 1 million by or before the 1990 census, its economy thrives on agriculture, livestock, and the activity of wholesale traders who dominate the commerce of southwestern Texas and northern Mexico. Adding further stimulus to the economy are five major military installations—Fort Sam Houston, Randolph Air Force Base, Kelly Air Force Base, Lackland Air Force Base, and Brooks Air Force Base.

The founding of the mission of San Antonio de Valero (later known as the Alamo) and the Presidio of San Antonio in 1718 represented the area's first permanent Euro-American settlement. When 56 settlers from the Canary Islands joined the original coterie of ranchers, missionaries, and soldiers, they formed the first municipal organization in Texas, called the villa of San Fernando de Bexar, which became a city in 1809. They remained under Mexican rule until the battle of San Jacinto in 1836. With the influx of American pioneers and German immigrants following Texas state-

hood, the population grew to more than 96,000 by 1910, and has since increased nearly tenfold.

Today San Antonio is a popular haven for vacationers, with over 10 million visitors per year. San Antonio's attractions include the Alamo and its four sister missions; the Riverwalk along the San Antonio River; Breckenridge Park, home of one of America's largest zoos; Sea World of Texas; La Villita; the Tower of the Americas; and the Spanish Governor's Palace.

**Population** 935,933 (1990). Rank: 10. Pop. density: 3,074/sq. mi. (1,187/sq km).

**Location** 29°25′N, 98°30′W. County: Bexar.

**Terrain and climate** Elev.: 701 ft. Area: 304.5 sq. mi. (788.7 sq km). Avg. daily min. temp.: Jan.: 39°F/3.8°C; avg. daily max.: July: 96.3°F/35.7°C. Avg. annual rainfall: 29.13″; snowfall: 0.5″; clear days: 110; precipitation days: 81.

**Government** Form: council and manager. Mayor: Nelson Wolff. Election: May 1993. Municipal tel. number: (512) 299-7060.

**Finances** (1988–89) Revenue: $1,311,739,000. Expenditure: $1,517,526,000. Debt outstanding: $3,670,655,000; per capita: $3,900.18.

**Visitor info.:** (512) 270-8700.

## San Diego, California

Sixty years after João Rodrigues Cabrilho first sailed into San Diego Bay, Sebastian Vizcaino embarked from Spain with three ships to explore the coast of California, and in November 1602 anchored on the lee of what is now known as Point Loma. When he finished charting the bay two days later, he changed its original name, San Miguel, to San Diego, in honor of San Diego de Alcalal de Henares. In 1769 Father Junipero Serra established California's first mission, the Mission San Diego de Alcala.

Compared to its sister cities to the north— Los Angeles and San Francisco—San Diego developed slowly, despite its large and hospitable harbor. In 1887 the city became the southern terminus for the Santa Fe Railroad, but floods soon washed out the tracks and track beds, and the railroad was rebuilt to terminate in L.A. This, along with L.A.'s man-made harbor, put San Diego at an almost insurmountable disadvantage. With its industrial developppment stunted, San Diego welcomed the establishment of a U.S. Navy base during World War I; since then, about a quarter of the navy's seagoing vessels and roughly 20 percent of the marine corps's forces have located there. Jonas Salk's work on polio and the emergence of the University of California at San Diego has earned the city the reputation as a premier biomedical research center, luring billions of dollars in development and research grants.

San Diego, a picturesque city with many tourist attractions, enjoys an average of 350 days of sunshine, enticing both residents and visitors to its 70 beaches and the parks, resorts, and health spas lining its great bay. Balboa Island is the site of both Balboa Park, host to international expositions in 1915 and 1935, and the San Diego Zoo, one of the finest in the nation. The pleasure boats berthed at the city's numerous yacht clubs offer a curious contrast to the naval warships moored nearby.

**Population** 1,110,549 (1990). Rank: 6. Pop. density: 3,376/sq. mi. (1,303/sq km).

**Location** 32°43′N, 117°09′W. County: San Diego.

**Terrain and climate** Elev.: 13 ft. Area: 329 sq. mi. (852.1 sq km). Avg. daily min. temp.: Jan.: 48.4°F/9.1°C; avg. daily max.: July: 75.6°F/24.2°C. Avg. annual rainfall: 9.32″; snowfall: 0″; clear days: 150; precipitation days: 41.

**Government** Form: council and manager. Mayor: Maureen O'Connor. Election: Dec. 1992. Municipal tel. number: (619) 236-6363.

**Finances** (1988–89) Revenue: $1,161,712,000. Expenditure: $1,027,173,000. Debt outstanding: $1,467,746,000; per capita: $1,371.33.

**Visitor info.:** (619) 236-1212.

## San Francisco, California

Located near the Golden Gate, the strait between San Francisco Bay and the Pacific Ocean, fog-bound San Francisco hid from some of the greatest European navigators to explore the West Coast. João Rodrigues Cabrilho discovered the Farrallon Islands just off the coast in 1542, and Sir Francis Drake landed a few miles north of the Golden Gate in 1579. Yet it was another 200 years before Don Gasper de Portola sailed into the bay, followed six years later by Don Juan Manuel Ayala, who established a town and mission.

Neither the Spanish nor (after 1821) the Mexican governments were very keen on capitalizing on San Francisco's temperate and strategic location, and when Capt. John Montgomery raised the American flag there on July 9, 1846, the community consisted of only 840 people. The discovery of gold at Sutter's mill in 1848, and the gold rush of 1849—which brought 40,000 of the hopeful to California, most by ship—catapulted San Francisco onto the world map, and the following year it was incorporated as a city.

San Francisco continued to prosper as a major transportation and industrial center, but in 1906 an earthquake registering 8.6 on the Richter scale claimed 452 lives, 28,000 buildings, and losses totaling approximately $350 million. San Francisco rose from the ashes to become a thriving, multifaceted, cosmopolitan city and one of the country's leaders in world trade. It is a port of call for more than 40 steamship lines, which import approximately $25 billion worth of goods from more than 300 ports around the world. A major international financial center, it is the headquarters of three of the nation's largest banks, the 12th Federal Reserve District, and the Pacific Stock Exchange. There are also more than 650 insurance companies, and the city is a haven for venture capitalists and entrepreneurs: More than 90 percent of its businesses have fewer than 25 employees. Several U.S. military installations are based in the area.

Well known for its spirit of individualism, San Francisco was a haven for the beat movement of the 1950s, and the capital of the 1960s hippie movement was the Haight-Ashbury district. The city's more traditional arts institutions include the San Francisco Ballet, the San Francisco Opera, the San Francisco Symphony, and the American Conservatory Theater. Among its leading educational institutions are the University of San Francisco, the Heald Institute of Technology, the University of California, the San Francisco Art Institute, the San Francisco Conservatory of Music, and the San Francisco College of Mortuary Science. Among its many museums are the National Maritime Historic Park, the Fine Arts Museum, and the California Palace of the Legion of Honor. Other attractions include its historic cable cars (first used in 1873), Chinatown, and Fisherman's Wharf.

**Population** 723,959 (1990). Rank: 14. Pop. density: 15,603/sq. mi. (6,023/sq km).

**Location** 37°47′N, 122°25′W. County: San Francisco.

**Terrain and climate** Elev.: 155 ft. Area: 46.4 sq. mi. (120.2 sq km). Avg. daily min. temp.: Jan.: 41.5°F/5.2°C; avg. daily max.: July: 71°F/21°C. Avg. annual rainfall: 19.71″; snowfall: 0″; clear days: 162; precipitation days: 67.

**Government** Form: mayor and council. Mayor: Art Agnos. Election: Nov. 1991. Municipal tel. number: (415) 554-6141.

**Finances** (1988–89) Revenue: $2,626,443,000. Expenditure: $2,260,293,000. Debt outstanding: $2,286,617,000; per capita: $3,125.29.

**Visitor info:** (415) 974-6900.

## San Jose, California

Located at the southern end of San Francisco Bay, about 45 miles south of San Francisco, San Jose was the first nonreligious European community founded in California. Pueblo de San Jose de Guadalupe was settled in 1777 by enterprising farmers who sought to make themselves and the region independent of Mexico and the Spanish-mission network for their supplies. Fruit and olive trees, hides, tallow, livestock, grain, and lively retail activity all contributed to San Jose's early prosperity, and it was the first state capital (1849–52).

San Jose remained an agricultural center until World War II, when industry and technology began to expand. The rapid growth of innovative industry over the last 20 years, taking its lead from research and development begun at nearby Stanford University in the 1930s, changed the area dramatically. With the revolution in high technology, Santa Clara County became known as Silicon Valley, excelling in the production of information systems, personal computers, and peripherals, and fostering a burgeoning semiconductor industry. At the same time, financial services, real estate, construction, and retail industries all flourished.

More than 2,600 high-tech companies employing 250,000 people are located in San Jose, and one-third of the labor force works in manufacturing, a very high proportion in postindustrial America. Santa Clara County has the highest median family income in California, and according to a 1987 survey of buying power by *Sales and Marketing* magazine, the San Jose metropolitan area is third in the nation in median household "effective buying power." The same survey ranks it second in California, and fifth in the nation, in manufacturing as measured by value of shipments—$30.5 billion in 1986.

**Population** 782,248 (1990). Rank: 11. Pop. density: 4,623/sq. mi. (1,785/sq km).

**Location** 37°10′N, 121°53′W. County: Santa Clara.

**Terrain and climate** Elev.: 65 ft. Area: 169.2 sq. mi. (438.2 sq km). Avg. daily min. temp.: Jan.: 41.1°F/5°C; avg. daily max.: July: 81.5°F/27.5°C. Avg. annual rainfall: 13.86″; snowfall: 0″; clear days: N.A.; precipitation days: N.A.

**Government** Form: council and manager. Mayor: Susan Hammer. Election: Nov. 1994. Municipal tel. number: (408) 277-4237.

**Finances** (1988–89) Revenue: $636,623,000. Expenditure: $618,256,000. Debt outstanding: $991,411,000; per capita: $1,342.61.

**Visitor info:** (408) 295-9600.

## Seattle, Washington

Located on the protected waters of Puget Sound, Seattle was the first Euro-American settlement established in the Pacific Northwest north of the Columbia River. Starting out at Alki Point in 1851, the settlers moved to what is now known as Pioneer Square. Befriended by the Suquamish chief Sealth (Seattle is a loose approximation of his name), the people turned to lumber harvesting and log milling, which formed the backbone of the city's economy.

With the completion of the Great Northern Railway in 1893 and with the Alaska gold rush of 1897, when Seattle became the "Gateway to the Klondike," the city was transformed into a metropolis of merchants and entrepreneurs. Even as gold fever abated, and despite a devastating fire in 1899, the city prospered as a major port to the Orient and as an industrial center. In 1909 Seattle was the site of the Alaska-Yukon-Pacific Exposition. The completion of the Panama Canal in 1914 brought even more business to the already bustling port. Two years later a small company began building two-seater biplanes, marking the start of Seattle's enduring link with the aerospace industry. In time the little company became Boeing, the world's largest producer of commercial planes, employing more than 85,000 people in the Seattle area.

Endowed with spectacular natural beauty, with the broad expanse of Puget Sound before it and the snow-capped peaks of the Cascade Mountains and Mt. Rainier visible to the south and east, the Seattle area offers a wide variety of outdoor activities, from skiing and hiking to fishing and boating. A second international exposition, the Seattle World's Fair in 1962, helped establish the city's reputation as a center of technology, trade, industry, and tourism. The leading cultural programs are put on by the Seattle Symphony Orchestra, the Seattle Opera Association, and the Seattle Repertory Theater. Other attractions include the Seattle Art Museum, Pioneer Square, Pike Place Market, the historic ships on Lake Union, and Woodland Park and Zoo, as well as the many events at the 74-acre Seattle Center, whose buildings and parklike grounds and fountains are legacies of the World's Fair. Among the 20 universities and colleges in the area are the University of Washington and Seattle Pacific University.

**Population** 516,259 (1990). Rank: 21. Pop. density: 6,175/sq. mi. (2,385/sq km).
**Location** 47°36′N, 122°20′W. County: King.
**Terrain and climate** Elev.: 450 ft. Area: 83.6 sq. mi. (216.5 sq km). Avg. daily min. temp.: Jan.: 34.3°F/1.2°C; avg. daily max.: July: 75.2°F/24°C. Avg. annual rainfall: 38.85″; snowfall: 15″; clear days: 57; precipitation days: 160.
**Government** Form: mayor and council. Mayor: Norman B. Rice. Election: Nov. 1993. Municipal tel. number: (206) 684-4000.
**Finances** (1988–89) Revenue: $929,803,000. Expenditure: $974,435,000. Debt outstanding: $896,800,000; per capita: $1,785.74.
**Visitor info:** (206) 461-5840.

## Toledo, Ohio

Toledo's origins can be traced to late 18th-century speculators who purchased tracts of land on either side of the Maumee River near its mouth, at the western end of Lake Erie. Although the smaller upriver towns of Perrysburg and Maumee were settled earlier, the twin towns of Port Lawrence and Vistula, laid out in 1832, were right on the lake. When it was found that steamers could navigate the river, the newer towns merged, adopting an anonymous suggestion to name itself for the city in Spain.

Toledo's early history and prosperity were tied to plans for the Miami and Erie Canal, which when completed in 1845 linked the Ohio River and Lake Erie. The border between Ohio (statehood, 1803) and Michigan (1837) was ill-defined. In the Toledo War (1835–36), Michigan held that Toledo was theirs. But Toledans opted for Ohio, figuring that Ohio would not finance a canal to the benefit of another state. (In exchange Michigan received the Upper Peninsula and admission to the Union.)

Though the canal was only moderately successful, Toledo benefited from the railroads that superceded it, and by the Civil War it was a major rail center. Toledo is a major shipper of coal, grain, iron ore, and general cargo. The city's manufactures include automotive components, plastics, and glass. In 1887, Edward Libbey relocated his New England Glass Company in Toledo, and Toledo's nickname is "Glass Capital of the World." Although unemployment reached a high of 11.9 percent in 1982, it has dropped considerably as new companies have been taking root, especially medical research companies drawn by the Medical College of Ohio's development of the Health Technology Park.

Toledo's cultural attractions include the Toledo Opera, Toledo Symphony Orchestra, Toledo Ballet, and the Toledo Repertoire Theatre. In addition there is the excellent Toledo Museum of Art as well as the Glass Apple, which exhibits glass pieces by local and international artists. Toledo's major educational institutions include the University of Toledo, Bowling Green State University, and the Medical College of Ohio.

**Population** 332,943 (1990). Rank: 49. Pop. density: 3,954/sq. mi. (1,527/sq km).
**Location** 41°39′N, 83°33′W. County: Lucas.
**Terrain and climate** Elev.: 692 ft. Area: 84.2 sq. mi. (218.1 sq km). Avg. daily min. temp.: Jan.: 15.5°F/-9.1°C; avg. daily max.: July: 83.4°F/28.5°C. Avg. annual rainfall: 31.77″; snowfall: 37″; clear days: 71; precipitation days: 136.
**Government** Form: city manager. Mayor: John McHugh. Election: Nov. 1991. Municipal tel. number: (419) 245-1010.
**Finances** (1988–89) Revenue: $260,521,000. Expenditure: $246,960,000. Debt outstanding: $203,043,000; per capita: $595.85.
**Visitor info:** (800) 243-4667.

## Tucson, Arizona

The first European to travel through the area that is now Tucson was the Jesuit missionary Eusebio Kino in 1692. In 1700 the mission of San Xavier del Bac was established among the Papago Indians nearby. It was not until 1776, however, that the Spanish established a permanent settlement, taking its name from the Papago *Stjukshon* (or *Chuk Shon*), meaning "village of the dark spring at the foot of the mountain." Tucson remained under Spanish and Mexican control until it was acquired by the U.S. government as part of the Gadsden Purchase in 1853. During the Civil War it was under Confederate control, but from 1867 to 1877 it was the territorial capital.

Despite the arrival of the Southern Pacific railroad in 1880 and the discovery of extensive copper deposits in southern Arizona, neither Tucson's location nor its natural resources much stimulated its economy. It was best known as a winter and health resort and as a commercial hub for the surrounding agricultural and mining industries. In 1950 the population was only 45,500.

The last 40 years have seen a dramatic change. One of the many beneficiaries of the exodus from the industrial states to the Sunbelt, Tucson has seen its population grow almost tenfold in that period, and in the last decade, Tucson added 20,000 manufacturing jobs. Surrounded by a wealth of natural beauty, the city is still appealing to retirees and tourists, as is reflected in the many golf courses, ranches, and resorts in and around Tucson. It is surrounded by four mountain ranges: the Rincon, Santa Catalina, Tucson, and Santa Rita. Other natural wonders include Sabino Canyon (which has the only year-round stream in the region), the Saguaro National Monument (a preserve for Saguaro cacti), and Tucson Mountain Park, site of the Arizona-Sonora Desert Museum. The University of Arizona is located in Tucson, and the Davis-Mothan Air Force Base and Kitts Peak Observatory are nearby.

**Population** 405,390 (1990). Rank: 33. Pop. density: 3,243/sq. mi. (1,248/sq km).
**Location** 32°13′N, 110°58′W. County: Pima.
**Terrain and climate** Elev.: 2,584 ft. Area: 125 sq. mi. (324.8 sq km). Avg. daily min. temp.: Jan.: 38.1°F/3.3°C; avg. daily max.: July: 98.5°F/3.3°C. Avg. annual rainfall: 11.14″; snowfall: 2″; clear days: 198; precipitation days: 50.
**Government Form:** council and manager. Mayor: Thomas J. Volgy. Election: Nov. 1991. Municipal tel. number: (602) 791-4201.
**Finances** (1988–89) Revenue: $428,877,000. Expenditure: $455,571,000. Debt outstanding: $797,365,000; per capita: $2,067.21.
**Visitor info:** (602) 624-1817.

## Tulsa, Oklahoma

Tulsa was first settled by Indian nations forced out of the South Atlantic states by the Indian Removal Act of 1830. The name they chose for their new home was Tulsey Town, a corruption of *Tullahassee,* meaning "Old Town." The name Tulsa was made official with the establishment of a post office in 1879. In 1900, Tulsa's population numbered less than 2,000, but the discovery of extensive oil fields at the turn of the century, beginning with the Glenn Pool and Red Ford strikes, started Tulsa on its way from a small Indian settlement to a sizable metropolis. By 1907 its population had increased to 7,298, and by 1920 it was 10 times that. Soon Tulsa was "Oil Capital of the World."

While still heavily involved in the oil and gas industry—it remains the home of about 500 oil-related companies—modern Tulsa is a far more diverse city than is its oil patch origins. Among Tulsa's top employees are regional, national, and international firms involved in aviation and aerospace, energy, computer technology, insurance, telecommunications, health care, and electronic equipment. The Port of Catoosa, which opened in 1971 after completion of the 445-mile Arkansas-Mississippi Waterway, is a major inland port, providing Tulsa with a direct link to the Mississippi River system and the Gulf of Mexico.

While growing in business, Tulsa has preserved the cultural heritage of its early oil barons and workers as well as that of its original Indian settlers. Thomas Gilcrease, a Creek Indian, became a millionaire with the Glenn Pool oil strike, and founded the Thomas Gilcrease Institute of American History and Art, devoted to American Indian heritage. The Tulsa Opera Company was founded in the early 1900s, and along with the city's philharmonic, ballet, and theaters, it gives Tulsa just cause to lay claim to being the cultural capital of Oklahoma. Tulsans also honor their roots through rodeos and regional music festivals. In addition representatives of the state's 65 Indian tribes gather in Tulsa each summer for their annual powwow. Among Tulsa's eight colleges and universities are the University of Tulsa, Oral Roberts University, and University Center at Tulsa, a consortium of Langston University, Northeastern State University, Oklahoma State University, and the University of Oklahoma.

**Population** 367,302 (1990). Rank: 43. Pop. density: 1,974/sq. mi. (762/sq km).
**Location** 36°10′N, 95°55′W. Counties: Osage, Tulsa.
**Terrain and climate** Elev.: 676 ft. Area: 186.1 sq. mi. (482 sq km). Avg. daily min. temp.: Jan.: 24.8°F/-4°C; avg. daily max.: July: 93.9°F/34.3°C. Avg. annual rainfall:

38.77"; snowfall: 9"; clear days: 127; precipitation days: 90.
**Government** Form: commission. Mayor: Roger A. Randle. Election: Mar. 1994. Municipal tel. number: (918) 596-7411.
**Finances** (1988–89) Revenue: $417,616,000. Expenditure: $448,402,000. Debt outstanding: $1,504,860,000; per capita: $4,085.63.
**Visitor info:** (918) 585-1201.

## Virginia Beach, Virginia

Throughout much of its history—which dates to the landing of the Jamestown colonists at Point Henry in 1607–Virginia Beach was overshadowed by its northern neighbor, Norfolk, which with its magnificent harbor was long the home of many shipping and naval enterprises at the mouth of Chesapeake Bay. But Virginia Beach has seen remarkable change in the last two decades.

In 1970 Virginia Beach's population was 172,000, only slightly more than half that of Norfolk. By 1990 it had grown 128 percent, to 393,000, and it is one of fastest-growing of the country's 50 largest cities. Local initiative accounts for most of this growth; in the same period, Norfolk's population fell 11 percent. A dominant presence is the U.S. Navy, which has three bases—Oceana Naval Air Station, Little Creek Naval Amphibious Base, and the Dam Neck Fleet Training Center—and which, together with the U.S. Army's Fort Story, employs 36,000 military and civilian personnel.

With 38 miles of Atlantic shoreline, 28 miles of public beaches, and the Seashore State Park—2,700 acres of shady upland woods, cypress swamps, and Spanish moss—the city continues to depend on tourism as a major factor in its economy and attracts 2.5 million visitors a year. The city's main industries, which include marine and engineering services, construction, communications, and electronics, occupy 10 industrial/business parks, including four built by the Virginia Beach Development Authority.

Among Virginia Beach's outstanding historic and recreational attractions are the Virginia Marine Science Museum; the Adam Thoroughgood House (c. 1680, one of the oldest brick houses in North America); the Old Cape Henry Lighthouse, authorized by the first Congress in 1790; and the statue of Adm. Compte de Grasse, whose defeat of the British at the Battle of the Virginia Capes brought about the defeat of Gen. Cornwallis at Yorktown and the end of the American Revolution in 1781.
Population 393,069 (1990). Rank: 37. Pop. density: 1,740/sq. mi. (672/sq km).
**Location** 36°51′N, 75°59′W. County: independent city.
**Terrain and climate** Elev.: 12 ft. Area: 225.9 sq. mi. (585.1 sq km). Avg. daily min. temp.: Jan.:

31.7°F/–0.1°C; avg. daily max.: July: 86.9°F/30.5°C. Avg. annual rainfall: 45.22"; snowfall: 7"; clear days: 110; precipitation days: 115.
**Government** Form: council and manager. Mayor: Meyera E. Oberndorf. Election: May 1992. Municipal tel. number: (804) 427-4581.
**Finances** (1988–89) Revenue: $642,309,000. Expenditure: $610,722,000. Debt outstanding: $447,834,000; per capita: $1,225.93.
**Visitor info:** (800) VA-BEACH (822-3224).

## Washington, D.C.

(For description, see "States, Territories, and Possessions.")
**Population** 606,900 (1990). Rank: 19. Pop. density: 9,679/sq. mi. (3,737/sq km).
**Location** 38°54′N, 77°02′W. County: independent city.
**Terrain and climate** Elev.: 30 ft. Area: 62.7 sq. mi. (162.4 sq km). Avg. daily min. temp.: Jan.: 27.5°F/–2.5°C; avg. daily max.: July: 87.9°F/31°C. Avg. annual rainfall: 39"; snowfall: 16"; clear days: 101; precipitation days: 111.
**Government** Form: mayor and council. Mayor: Sharon Pratt Dixon. Election: Nov. 1994. Municipal tel. number: (202) 727-2980.
**Finances** (1988–89) Revenue: $4,120,270,000. Expenditure: $4,146,592,000. Debt outstanding: $3,043,072,000; per capita: $4,932.05.
**Visitor info:** (202) 789-7000.

## Cities in America

Since 1960 the growth of the urban population has occurred primarily in cities of under 250,000. In that year there were five cities of a million or more people; in 1990 there were eight. Over the same time period, the number of cities of between 500,000 and 1 million inhabitants remained unchanged at 16, while the number of cities of 250,000 to 500,000 inhabitants grew 33%, from 30 to 40.

The 1990 census recorded 29 new cities joining the ranks of those with populations over 100,000. Eighteen were in California, four in Texas, two in Arizona, and one each in Florida, Kansas, Massachusetts, Oregon, and South Dakota. Two of the California cities over

100,000, Santa Clarita in Los Angeles County, and Moreno Valley in Riverside County, were not incorporated cities in 1980.

Five cities fell from the ranks of 100,000+ cities since 1980: Columbia, S.C.; Davenport, Iowa; Pueblo, Colo.; Roanoke, Va.; and Youngstown, Ohio.

## MAJOR U.S. CITIES: POPULATION, POPULATION CHANGE, POPULATION DENSITY, AND LAND AREA, 1970–90

| City | Population ('000s) 1970 | 1980 | 1990 | Rank 1990 | Percent change 1980–90 | Per sq. mi. 1988 | Land area (sq. mi.) 1987[1] | City | Population ('000s) 1970 | 1980 | 1990 | Rank 1990 | Percent change 1980–90 | Per sq. mi. 1988 | Land area (sq. mi.) 1987[1] |
|---|---|---|---|---|---|---|---|---|---|---|---|---|---|---|---|
| Abilene, Tex. | 90 | 98 | 107 | 179 | 8.5% | 1,106 | 96.4 | Boston, Mass. | 641 | 563 | 574 | 20 | 2.0% | 12,242 | 47.2 |
| Akron, Ohio | 275 | 237 | 223 | 71 | –6.0 | 3,567 | 62.1 | Bridgeport, Conn. | 157 | 143 | 142 | 123 | –0.6 | 9,508 | 14.7 |
| Albany, N.Y. | N.A. | 102 | 101 | 192 | –0.6 | N.A. | N.A. | Brownsville, Tex. | 53 | 85 | 105 | 174 | 23.0 | 3,616 | 28.9 |
| Albuquerque, N.Mex. | 245 | 332 | 385 | 38 | 15.6 | 2,952 | 128.2 | Buffalo, N.Y. | 463 | 358 | 328 | 50 | –8.3 | 7,502 | 41.8 |
| Alexandria, Va. | 111 | 103 | 111 | 164 | 7.7 | 7,228 | 15.0 | Cedar Rapids, Iowa | 111 | 110 | 109 | 174 | –1.4 | 1,995 | 55.3 |
| Allentown, Pa. | 110 | 104 | 105 | 184 | 1.3 | 6,011 | 17.5 | Charlotte, N.C. | 241 | 315 | 396 | 35 | 25.5 | 2,314 | 159.0 |
| Amarillo, Tex. | 127 | 149 | 158 | 110 | 5.6 | 1,904 | 87.2 | Chattanooga, Tenn. | 120 | 170 | 152 | 113 | –10.1 | 1,314 | 123.8 |
| Anaheim, Calif. | 166 | 219 | 266 | 59 | 21.4 | 5,486 | 44.6 | Chesapeake, Va. | 90 | 114 | 152 | 114 | 32.7 | 435 | 340.0 |
| Anchorage, Alaska[2] | 48 | 174 | 226 | 69 | 29.8 | 126 | 1,732.0 | Chicago, Ill. | 3,369 | 3,005 | 2,784 | 3 | –7.4 | 13,054 | 228.1 |
| Ann Arbor, Mich. | 100 | 108 | 110 | 170 | 1.5 | 4,187 | 25.9 | Chula Vista, Calif. | 68 | 84 | 135 | 131 | 61.0 | 4,641 | 27.2 |
| Arlington, Tex. | 90 | 160 | 262 | 61 | 63.5 | 2,823 | 91.2 | Cincinnati, Ohio | 454 | 385 | 364 | 45 | –5.5 | 4,750 | 78.0 |
| Atlanta, Ga. | 495 | 425 | 394 | 36 | –7.3 | 3,203 | 131.2 | Cleveland, Ohio | 751 | 574 | 506 | 24 | –11.9 | 6,600 | 79.0 |
| Aurora, Colo. | 75 | 159 | 222 | 72 | 40.1 | 1,838 | 119.0 | Colorado Springs, Colo. | 136 | 215 | 281 | 54 | 30.7 | 1,981 | 142.9 |
| Austin, Tex. | 254 | 346 | 466 | 27 | 34.6 | 1,884 | 246.6 | Columbus, Ga.[3] | 155 | 169 | 179 | 93 | 5.4 | 817 | 217.5 |
| Bakersfield, Calif. | 70 | 106 | 175 | 97 | 65.5 | 1,863 | 84.6 | Columbus, Ohio | 540 | 565 | 633 | 16 | 12.0 | 3,001 | 189.8 |
| Baltimore, Md. | 905 | 787 | 736 | 13 | –6.4 | 9,357 | 80.3 | Concord, Calif. | 85 | 104 | 111 | 163 | 7.3 | 3,687 | 29.3 |
| Baton Rouge, La. | 166 | 220 | 220 | 73 | –0.4 | 3,223 | 73.0 | Corpus Christi, Tex. | 205 | 232 | 257 | 64 | 10.9 | 2,202 | 118.5 |
| Beaumont, Tex. | 118 | 118 | 114 | 155 | –3.2 | 1,533 | 74.5 | Dallas, Tex. | 844 | 905 | 1,007 | 8 | 11.3 | 2,965 | 333.0 |
| Berkeley, Calif. | 114 | 103 | 103 | 189 | –0.6 | 9,510 | 10.9 | Dayton, Ohio | 243 | 194 | 182 | 89 | –5.9 | 3,225 | 55.2 |
| Birmingham, Ala. | 301 | 284 | 266 | 60 | –6.5 | 1,863 | 148.8 | Denver, Colo. | 515 | 493 | 467 | 26 | –5.1 | 4,609 | 106.8 |
| Boise City, Idaho | 75 | 102 | 126 | 145 | 23.0 | 2,377 | 46.7 | Des Moines, Iowa | 201 | 191 | 193 | 80 | 1.1 | 2,905 | 66.4 |

| City | Population ('000s) 1970 | 1980 | 1990 | Rank 1990 | Percent change 1980–90 | Per sq. mi. (sq. mi.) 1988 | Land area (sq. mi.) 1987[1] |
|---|---|---|---|---|---|---|---|
| Detroit, Mich. | 1,514 | 1,203 | 1,023 | 7 | -14.6% | 7,639 | 135.6 |
| Durham, N.C. | 95 | 101 | 137 | 130 | 35.1 | 1,725 | 66.9 |
| Elizabeth, N.J. | 113 | 106 | 110 | 168 | 3.6 | 8,987 | 11.7 |
| El Monte, Calif. | N.A. | 79 | 106 | 181 | 33.6 | N.A. | N.A. |
| El Paso, Tex. | 322 | 425 | 515 | 22 | 21.2 | 2,066 | 247.3 |
| Erie, Pa. | 129 | 119 | 109 | 175 | -8.7 | 5,198 | 21.7 |
| Escondido, Calif. | N.A. | 64 | 109 | 176 | 68.8 | N.A. | N.A. |
| Eugene, Oreg. | 79 | 106 | 113 | 159 | 6.6 | 3,009 | 35.9 |
| Evansville, Ind. | 139 | 130 | 126 | 144 | -3.2 | 3,045 | 42.1 |
| Flint, Mich. | 193 | 160 | 141 | 125 | -11.8 | 4,331 | 32.7 |
| Fort Lauderdale, Fla. | 140 | 153 | 149 | 116 | -2.5 | 4,903 | 29.7 |
| Fort Wayne, Ind. | 178 | 172 | 173 | 99 | 0.4 | 2,924 | 61.5 |
| Fort Worth, Tex. | 393 | 385 | 448 | 28 | 16.2 | 1,581 | 269.8 |
| Fremont, Calif. | 101 | 132 | 173 | 98 | 31.4 | 2,125 | 78.4 |
| Fresno, Calif. | 166 | 217 | 354 | 47 | 62.9 | 3,153 | 97.4 |
| Fullerton, Calif. | 86 | 102 | 114 | 156 | 11.6 | 4,943 | 22.2 |
| Garden Grove, Calif. | 121 | 123 | 143 | 120 | 16.0 | 7,644 | 17.7 |
| Garland, Tex. | 81 | 139 | 181 | 91 | 30.1 | 3,188 | 56.6 |
| Gary, Ind. | 175 | 152 | 117 | 154 | -23.2 | 3,362 | 39.4 |
| Glendale, Ariz. | 36 | 97 | 148 | 117 | 52.4 | 2,781 | 50.4 |
| Glendale, Calif. | 133 | 139 | 180 | 92 | 29.5 | 5,268 | 30.6 |
| Grand Rapids, Mich. | 198 | 182 | 189 | 83 | 4.0 | 4,271 | 43.4 |
| Greensboro, N.C. | 144 | 156 | 184 | 88 | 17.9 | 2,300 | 79.1 |
| Hampton, Va. | 121 | 123 | 138 | 133 | 9.1 | 2,549 | 51.3 |
| Hartford, Conn. | 158 | 136 | 140 | 127 | 2.5 | 7,376 | 17.8 |
| Hayward, Calif. | 93 | 94 | 111 | 162 | 19.1 | 2,328 | 44.5 |
| Hialeah, Fla. | 102 | 145 | 188 | 85 | 29.4 | 8,355 | 19.4 |
| Hollywood, Fla. | 107 | 121 | 122 | 148 | 0.3 | 4,748 | 25.3 |
| Honolulu, Hawaii[4] | 325 | 365 | 365 | 44 | 0.1 | 4,323 | 87.0 |
| Houston, Tex. | 1,234 | 1,595 | 1,631 | 4 | 2.2 | 2,936 | 578.3 |
| Huntington Beach, Calif. | 116 | 171 | 182 | 90 | 6.5 | 6,871 | 27.2 |
| Huntsville, Ala. | 139 | 143 | 160 | 109 | 12.1 | 1,057 | 150.9 |
| Independence, Mo. | 112 | 112 | 112 | 160 | 0.5 | 1,428 | 80.6 |
| Indianapolis, Ind.[5] | 737 | 712 | 742 | 12 | 4.3 | 2,066 | 351.9 |
| Inglewood, Calif. | 90 | 94 | 110 | 169 | 16.4 | 11,677 | 8.9 |
| Irvine, Calif. | (6) | 62 | 110 | 167 | 77.6 | 2,286 | 43.8 |
| Irving, Tex. | 97 | 110 | 155 | 112 | 41.0 | 1,973 | 67.4 |
| Jackson, Miss. | 154 | 203 | 197 | 78 | -3.1 | 1,895 | 106.2 |
| Jacksonville, Fla.[5] | 504 | 571 | 673 | 15 | 17.9 | 837 | 759.2 |
| Jersey City, N.J. | 260 | 224 | 229 | 67 | 2.2 | 16,487 | 13.2 |
| Kansas City, Kans. | 168 | 161 | 150 | 115 | -7.1 | 1,496 | 107.4 |
| Kansas City, Mo. | 507 | 448 | 435 | 31 | -2.9 | 1,383 | 317.4 |
| Knoxville, Tenn. | 175 | 175 | 165 | 102 | -5.7 | 2,195 | 78.4 |
| Lakewood, Colo. | 93 | 114 | 126 | 143 | 11.1 | 2,876 | 41.5 |
| Lansing, Mich. | 131 | 130 | 127 | 142 | -2.4 | 3,560 | 35.1 |
| Laredo, Tex. | 69 | 91 | 123 | 147 | 34.4 | 4,200 | 29.7 |
| Las Vegas, Nev. | 126 | 165 | 258 | 63 | 56.9 | 2,659 | 79.2 |
| Lexington-Fayette, Ky.[7] | 108 | 204 | 225 | 70 | 10.4 | 793 | 284.7 |
| Lincoln, Nebr. | 150 | 172 | 192 | 81 | 11.7 | 3,075 | 61.1 |
| Little Rock, Ark. | 132 | 159 | 176 | 96 | 10.5 | 1,857 | 97.0 |
| Livonia, Mich. | 110 | 105 | 101 | 193 | -3.8 | 2,905 | 34.8 |
| Long Beach, Calif. | 359 | 361 | 429 | 32 | 18.8 | 8,334 | 49.8 |
| Los Angeles, Calif. | 2,812 | 2,969 | 3,485 | 2 | 17.4 | 7,175 | 467.3 |
| Louisville, Ky. | 362 | 299 | 269 | 58 | -9.9 | 4,613 | 61.1 |
| Lowell, Mass. | N.A. | 92 | 103 | 188 | 11.9 | N.A. | N.A. |
| Lubbock, Tex. | 149 | 174 | 186 | 87 | 6.8 | 1,768 | 106.4 |
| Macon, Ga. | 122 | 117 | 106 | 180 | -8.8 | 2,373 | 49.7 |
| Madison, Wis. | 172 | 171 | 191 | 82 | 12.1 | 3,199 | 55.7 |
| Memphis, Tenn. | 624 | 646 | 610 | 18 | -5.5 | 2,443 | 264.1 |
| Mesa, Ariz. | 63 | 152 | 288 | 53 | 89.0 | 2,579 | 108.7 |

| City | Population ('000s) 1970 | 1980 | 1990 | Rank 1990 | Percent change 1980–90 | Per sq. mi. (sq. mi.) 1988 | Land area (sq. mi.) 1987[1] |
|---|---|---|---|---|---|---|---|
| Mesquite, Tex. | N.A. | 67 | 101 | 190 | 51.3% | N.A. | N.A. |
| Miami, Fla. | 335 | 347 | 359 | 46 | 3.4 | 10,819 | 34.3 |
| Milwaukee, Wis. | 717 | 636 | 628 | 17 | -1.3 | 6,257 | 95.8 |
| Minneapolis, Minn. | 434 | 371 | 368 | 42 | -0.7 | 6,255 | 55.1 |
| Mobile, Ala. | 190 | 200 | 196 | 79 | -2.1 | 1,526 | 136.8 |
| Modesto, Calif. | 62 | 107 | 165 | 103 | 54.0 | 5,291 | 28.1 |
| Montgomery, Ala. | 133 | 178 | 187 | 86 | 5.2 | 1,456 | 132.9 |
| Moreno Valley, Calif.[8] | N.A. | N.A. | 118 | 151 | N.A. | N.A. | N.A. |
| Nashville-Davidson, Tenn. | 426 | 478 | 511 | 23 | 6.9 | 1,004 | 479.5 |
| Newark, N.J. | 382 | 329 | 275 | 56 | -16.4 | 13,021 | 24.1 |
| New Haven, Conn. | 138 | 126 | 130 | 138 | 3.5 | 6,552 | 18.9 |
| New Orleans, La. | 593 | 558 | 497 | 25 | -10.9 | 2,667 | 199.4 |
| Newport News, Va. | 138 | 145 | 170 | 100 | 17.4 | 2,451 | 65.3 |
| New York, N.Y. | 7,896 | 7,072 | 7,322 | 1 | 3.5 | 24,387 | 301.5 |
| Norfolk, Va. | 308 | 267 | 261 | 62 | -2.2 | 5,385 | 53.2 |
| Oakland, Calif. | 362 | 339 | 372 | 39 | 9.7 | 6,621 | 53.9 |
| Oceanside, Calif. | 40 | 77 | 128 | 141 | 67.4 | 2,802 | 40.2 |
| Oklahoma City, Okla. | 368 | 404 | 445 | 29 | 10.1 | 688 | 631.1 |
| Omaha, Nebr. | 347 | 314 | 336 | 48 | 7.0 | 3,532 | 100.0 |
| Ontario, Calif. | 64 | 89 | 133 | 134 | 49.9 | 3,344 | 36.9 |
| Orange, Calif. | 77 | 91 | 111 | 165 | 21.0 | 4,677 | 22.6 |
| Orlando, Fla. | 99 | 128 | 165 | 104 | 28.4 | 2,396 | 65.1 |
| Overland Park, Kans. | 78 | 82 | 112 | 161 | 36.7 | 2,020 | 52.9 |
| Oxnard, Calif. | 71 | 108 | 142 | 121 | 31.4 | 5,331 | 24.4 |
| Pasadena, Calif. | 113 | 118 | 132 | 137 | 11.4 | 5,690 | 23.2 |
| Pasadena, Tex. | 90 | 113 | 119 | 150 | 6.0 | 3,060 | 38.2 |
| Paterson, N.J. | 145 | 138 | 141 | 124 | 2.1 | 16,701 | 8.3 |
| Peoria, Ill. | 127 | 124 | 114 | 157 | -8.6 | 2,560 | 42.8 |
| Philadelphia, Pa. | 1,949 | 1,688 | 1,586 | 5 | -6.1 | 12,110 | 136.0 |
| Phoenix, Ariz. | 584 | 790 | 983 | 9 | 24.5 | 2,352 | 392.8 |
| Pittsburgh, Pa. | 520 | 424 | 370 | 40 | -12.8 | 6,773 | 55.4 |
| Plano, Tex. | 18 | 72 | 129 | 140 | 77.9 | 1,891 | 62.8 |
| Pomona, Calif. | 87 | 93 | 132 | 136 | 42.0 | 5,261 | 22.9 |
| Portland, Oreg. | 380 | 368 | 437 | 30 | 18.8 | 3,467 | 120.7 |
| Portsmouth, Va. | 111 | 105 | 104 | 186 | -0.6 | 3,597 | 29.9 |
| Providence, R.I. | 179 | 157 | 161 | 107 | 2.5 | 8,263 | 18.9 |
| Raleigh, N.C. | 123 | 150 | 208 | 75 | 38.4 | 2,239 | 83.4 |
| Rancho Cucamonga, Calif. | N.A. | 55 | 101 | 191 | 83.5 | N.A. | N.A. |
| Reno, Nev. | 73 | 101 | 134 | 132 | 32.8 | 3,013 | 37.1 |
| Richmond, Va. | 249 | 219 | 203 | 76 | -7.4 | 3,549 | 60.1 |
| Riverside, Calif. | 140 | 171 | 227 | 68 | 32.8 | 2,743 | 76.8 |
| Rochester, N.Y. | 295 | 242 | 232 | 66 | -4.2 | 6,719 | 34.2 |
| Rockford, Ill. | 147 | 140 | 139 | 128 | -0.2 | 3,128 | 43.0 |
| Sacramento, Calif. | 257 | 276 | 369 | 41 | 34.0 | 3,458 | 97.8 |
| Salem, Oreg. | N.A. | 89 | 108 | 178 | 21.0 | N.A. | N.A. |
| St. Louis, Mo. | 622 | 453 | 397 | 34 | -12.4 | 6,574 | 61.4 |
| St. Paul, Minn. | 310 | 270 | 272 | 57 | 0.7 | 4,945 | 52.4 |
| St. Petersburg, Fla. | 216 | 239 | 239 | 65 | 0.0 | 4,145 | 56.8 |
| Salinas, Calif. | 59 | 80 | 109 | 173 | 35.2 | 5,711 | 17.7 |
| Salt Lake City, Utah | 176 | 163 | 160 | 108 | -1.9 | 1,520 | 100.5 |
| San Antonio, Tex. | 654 | 786 | 936 | 10 | 19.1 | 2,860 | 329.1 |
| San Bernardino, Calif. | 107 | 119 | 164 | 105 | 38.2 | 2,674 | 55.5 |
| San Diego, Calif. | 697 | 876 | 1,111 | 6 | 26.8 | 3,257 | 328.8 |
| San Francisco, Calif. | 716 | 679 | 724 | 14 | 6.6 | 15,768 | 46.4 |
| San Jose, Calif. | 460 | 629 | 782 | 11 | 24.3 | 4,331 | 170.5 |
| Santa Ana, Calif. | 156 | 204 | 294 | 52 | 44.0 | 8,742 | 27.4 |
| Santa Clarita, Calif.[8] | N.A. | N.A. | 111 | 166 | N.A. | N.A. | N.A. |
| Santa Rosa, Calif. | 50 | 83 | 113 | 158 | 37.1 | 3,164 | 34.2 |
| Savannah, Ga. | 118 | 142 | 138 | 129 | -2.9 | 2,393 | 61.0 |
| Scottsdale, Ariz. | 68 | 89 | 130 | 139 | 46.8 | 667 | 182.5 |

| City | Population ('000s) | | | Rank 1990 | Percent change 1980–90 | Per sq. mi. 1988 | Land area (sq. mi.) 1987[1] |
|---|---|---|---|---|---|---|---|
| | 1970 | 1980 | 1990 | | | | |
| Seattle, Wash. | 531 | 494 | 516 | 21 | 4.5% | 6,000 | 83.7 |
| Shreveport, La. | 182 | 206 | 199 | 77 | -4.1 | 2,290 | 95.2 |
| Simi Valley, Calif. | N.A. | 78 | 100 | 195 | 29.3 | N.A. | N.A. |
| Sioux Falls, S.Dak. | N.A. | 81 | 101 | 194 | 23.9 | N.A. | N.A. |
| South Bend, Ind. | 126 | 110 | 106 | 182 | -3.8 | 2,901 | 36.6 |
| Spokane, Wash. | 171 | 171 | 177 | 94 | 3.4 | 3,041 | 56.2 |
| Springfield, Ill. | N.A. | 100 | 105 | 183 | 5.2 | N.A. | N.A. |
| Springfield, Mass. | 164 | 152 | 157 | 111 | 3.1 | 4,742 | 31.7 |
| Springfield, Mo. | 120 | 133 | 140 | 126 | 5.2 | 2,024 | 70.5 |
| Stamford, Conn. | 109 | 102 | 108 | 177 | 5.5 | 2,631 | 38.1 |
| Sterling Heights, Mich. | 61 | 109 | 118 | 152 | 8.1 | 3,135 | 36.6 |
| Stockton, Calif. | 110 | 148 | 211 | 74 | 42.3 | 3,948 | 48.3 |
| Sunnyvale, Calif. | 96 | 107 | 117 | 153 | 10.0 | 4,965 | 23.4 |
| Syracuse, N.Y. | 197 | 170 | 164 | 106 | -3.7 | 6,454 | 23.8 |
| Tacoma, Wash. | 154 | 159 | 176 | 95 | 11.5 | 3,430 | 47.8 |
| Tallahassee, Fla. | 73 | 82 | 125 | 146 | 53.0 | 2,140 | 58.7 |
| Tampa, Fla. | 278 | 272 | 280 | 55 | 3.1 | 2,699 | 104.4 |

| City | Population ('000s) | | | Rank 1990 | Percent change 1980–90 | Per sq. mi. 1988 | Land area (sq. mi.) 1987[1] |
|---|---|---|---|---|---|---|---|
| | 1970 | 1980 | 1990 | | | | |
| Tempe, Ariz. | 64 | 107 | 142 | 122 | 32.7% | 3,592 | 39.1 |
| Thousand Oaks, Calif. | 36 | 77 | 104 | 185 | 35.4 | 2,098 | 48.4 |
| Toledo, Ohio | 383 | 355 | 333 | 49 | -6.1 | 4,047 | 84.2 |
| Topeka, Kans. | 125 | 119 | 120 | 149 | 1.0 | 2,249 | 54.4 |
| Torrance, Calif. | 135 | 130 | 133 | 135 | 2.5 | 6,729 | 20.5 |
| Tucson, Ariz. | 263 | 331 | 405 | 33 | 22.6 | 2,655 | 145.3 |
| Tulsa, Okla. | 330 | 361 | 367 | 43 | 1.8 | 1,927 | 191.1 |
| Vallejo, Calif. | 72 | 80 | 109 | 171 | 36.0 | 3,889 | 25.9 |
| Virginia Beach, Va. | 172 | 262 | 393 | 37 | 49.9 | 1,428 | 255.8 |
| Waco, Tex. | 95 | 101 | 104 | 187 | 2.3 | 1,324 | 78.1 |
| Warren, Mich. | 179 | 161 | 145 | 118 | -10.1 | 4,227 | 34.4 |
| Washington, D.C. | 757 | 638 | 607 | 19 | -4.9 | 9,840 | 62.7 |
| Waterbury, Conn. | 108 | 103 | 109 | 172 | 5.5 | 3,654 | 28.6 |
| Wichita, Kans. | 277 | 280 | 304 | 51 | 8.6 | 2,524 | 117.0 |
| Winston-Salem, N.C. | 134 | 132 | 143 | 119 | 8.8 | 2,118 | 70.2 |
| Worcester, Mass. | 177 | 162 | 170 | 101 | 4.9 | 4,176 | 37.4 |
| Yonkers, N.Y. | 204 | 195 | 188 | 84 | -3.7 | 10,000 | 18.3 |

**Note**: Cities over 100,000 population. N.A. = Not available. 1. As of December 31; reflects estimates of areas annexed or detached since January 1, 1980, as provided by the municipalities. 2. Anchorage city consolidated with Anchorage Borough Sept. 15, 1975. 3. Columbus, Ga., and the unincorporated balance of Muscogee Co. consolidated on Jan. 1, 1971. 4. Data represent the census-designated place of Honolulu, as delineated by the State of Hawaii. 5. Consolidated city. 6. Not incorporated in 1970. 7. Lexington and Fayette Co. consolidated Jan. 1, 1974. 8. Not incorporated in 1980. **Source**: U.S. Bureau of the Census, *Statistical Abstract of the United States 1990* (1990), and release (1991).

## 25 FASTEST-GROWING MAJOR CITIES IN THE U.S., 1980–90

| Rank/City | Population | | Percent change | Rank | |
|---|---|---|---|---|---|
| | 1980 | 1990 | | 1980 | 1990 |
| 1. Mesa, Ariz. | 152,404 | 288,091 | 89.0% | 102 | 53 |
| 2. Rancho Cucamonga, Calif. | 55,250 | 101,409 | 83.5 | N.A. | 191 |
| 3. Plano, Tex. | 72,331 | 128,713 | 77.9 | N.A. | 140 |
| 4. Irvine, Calif. | 62,134 | 110,330 | 77.6 | N.A. | 167 |
| 5. Escondido, Calif. | 64,355 | 108,635 | 68.8 | N.A. | 176 |
| 6. Oceanside, Calif. | 76,698 | 128,398 | 67.4 | N.A. | 141 |
| 7. Bakersfield, Calif. | 105,611 | 174,820 | 65.5 | 152 | 97 |
| 8. Arlington, Tex. | 160,113 | 261,721 | 63.5 | 94 | 61 |
| 9. Fresno, Calif. | 217,491 | 354,202 | 62.9 | 65 | 47 |
| 10. Chula Vista, Calif. | 83,927 | 135,163 | 61.0 | N.A. | 131 |
| 11. Las Vegas, Nev. | 164,674 | 258,295 | 56.9 | 89 | 63 |
| 12. Modesto, Calif. | 106,963 | 164,730 | 54.0 | 147 | 103 |
| 13. Tallahassee, Fla. | 81,548 | 124,773 | 53.0 | N.A. | 146 |
| 14. Glendale, Ariz. | 97,172 | 148,134 | 52.4% | N.A. | 117 |
| 15. Mesquite, Tex. | 67,053 | 101,484 | 51.3 | N.A. | 190 |
| 16. Ontario, Calif. | 88,820 | 133,179 | 49.9 | N.A. | 134 |
| 17. Virginia Beach, Va. | 262,199 | 393,069 | 49.9 | 56 | 37 |
| 18. Scottsdale, Ariz. | 88,622 | 130,069 | 46.8 | N.A. | 139 |
| 19. Santa Ana, Calif. | 204,023 | 293,742 | 44.0 | 69 | 52 |
| 20. Stockton, Calif. | 148,283 | 210,943 | 42.3 | 107 | 74 |
| 21. Pomona, Calif. | 92,742 | 131,723 | 42.0 | N.A. | 136 |
| 22. Irving, Tex. | 109,943 | 155,037 | 41.0 | 142 | 112 |
| 23. Aurora, Colo. | 158,588 | 222,103 | 40.1 | 97 | 72 |
| 24. Raleigh, N.C. | 150,255 | 207,951 | 38.4 | 105 | 75 |
| 25. San Bernardino, Calif. | 118,794 | 164,164 | 38.2 | 131 | 105 |

**Note**: Cities over 100,000 population. **Source**: U.S. Bureau of the Census release (1991).

## 25 MAJOR U.S. CITIES WITH LARGEST DECLINES IN POPULATION, 1980–90

| Rank/City | Population | | Percent change | Rank | |
|---|---|---|---|---|---|
| | 1980 | 1990 | | 1980 | 1990 |
| 1. Gary, Ind. | 151,968 | 116,646 | -23.2% | 104 | 154 |
| 2. Newark, N.J. | 329,248 | 275,221 | -16.4 | 46 | 56 |
| 3. Detroit, Mich. | 1,203,368 | 1,027,974 | -14.6 | 6 | 7 |
| 4. Pittsburgh, Pa. | 423,959 | 369,879 | -12.8 | 30 | 40 |
| 5. St. Louis, Mo. | 452,801 | 396,685 | -12.4 | 26 | 34 |
| 6. Cleveland, Ohio | 573,822 | 505,616 | -11.9 | 18 | 24 |
| 7. Flint, Mich. | 159,611 | 140,761 | -11.8 | 95 | 125 |
| 8. New Orleans, La. | 557,927 | 496,938 | -10.9 | 22 | 25 |
| 9. Warren, Mich. | 161,134 | 144,864 | -10.1 | 93 | 118 |
| 10. Chattanooga, Tenn. | 169,514 | 152,466 | -10.1 | 88 | 113 |
| 11. Louisville, Ky. | 298,694 | 269,063 | -9.9 | 49 | 58 |
| 12. Macon, Ga. | 116,896 | 106,612 | -8.8 | 135 | 180 |
| 13. Erie, Pa. | 119,123 | 108,718 | -8.7 | 130 | 175 |
| 14. Peoria, Ill. | 124,160 | 113,504 | -8.6% | 126 | 157 |
| 15. Buffalo, N.Y. | 357,870 | 328,123 | -8.3 | 39 | 50 |
| 16. Richmond, Va. | 219,214 | 203,056 | -7.4 | 64 | 76 |
| 17. Chicago, Ill. | 3,005,072 | 2,783,726 | -7.4 | 2 | 3 |
| 18. Atlanta, Ga. | 425,022 | 394,017 | -7.3 | 29 | 36 |
| 19. Kansas City, Kans. | 161,148 | 149,767 | -7.1 | 92 | 115 |
| 20. Birmingham, Ala. | 284,413 | 265,968 | -6.5 | 50 | 60 |
| 21. Baltimore, Md. | 786,741 | 736,014 | -6.4 | 10 | 13 |
| 22. Toledo, Ohio | 354,635 | 332,943 | -6.1 | 40 | 49 |
| 23. Philadelphia, Pa. | 1,688,210 | 1,585,577 | -6.1 | 4 | 5 |
| 24. Akron, Ohio | 237,177 | 223,019 | -6.0 | 59 | 71 |
| 25. Dayton, Ohio | 193,536 | 182,044 | -5.9 | 73 | 89 |

**Note**: Cities over 100,000 population. **Source**: U.S. Bureau of the Census release (1991).

## POPULATION CHANGE IN THE 50 LARGEST U.S. CITIES, RANKED BY PERCENTAGE CHANGE 1980-90

| Rank/City | Population 1980 | Population 1990 | Change 1980-90 Number | Change 1980-90 Percent | Pop. Rank 1990 | Rank/City | Population 1980 | Population 1990 | Change 1980-90 Number | Change 1980-90 Percent | Pop. Rank 1990 |
|---|---|---|---|---|---|---|---|---|---|---|---|
| 1. Fresno, Calif. | 217,491 | 354,202 | 136,711 | 62.9% | 47 | 26. Indianapolis, Ind. | 711,539 | 741,952 | 30,413 | 4.3% | 12 |
| 2. Virginia Beach, Va. | 262,199 | 393,069 | 130,870 | 49.9 | 37 | 27. New York, N.Y. | 7,071,639 | 7,322,564 | 250,925 | 3.5 | 1 |
| 3. Austin, Tex. | 345,890 | 465,622 | 119,732 | 34.6 | 27 | 28. Miami, Fla. | 346,681 | 358,548 | 11,867 | 3.4 | 46 |
| 4. Sacramento, Calif. | 275,741 | 369,365 | 93,624 | 34.0 | 41 | 29. Houston, Tex. | 1,595,138 | 1,630,553 | 35,415 | 2.2 | 4 |
| 5. San Diego, Calif. | 875,538 | 1,110,549 | 235,011 | 26.8 | 6 | 30. Boston, Mass. | 562,994 | 574,283 | 11,289 | 2.0 | 20 |
| 6. Charlotte, N.C. | 315,474 | 395,934 | 80,460 | 25.5 | 35 | 31. Tulsa, Okla. | 360,919 | 367,302 | 6,383 | 1.8 | 43 |
| 7. Phoenix, Ariz. | 789,704 | 983,403 | 193,699 | 24.5 | 9 | 32. Honolulu, Hawaii | 365,048 | 365,272 | 224 | 0.1 | 44 |
| 8. San Jose, Calif. | 629,400 | 782,248 | 152,848 | 24.3 | 11 | 33. Minneapolis, Minn. | 370,951 | 368,383 | -2,568 | -0.7 | 42 |
| 9. Tucson, Ariz. | 330,537 | 405,390 | 74,853 | 22.6 | 33 | 34. Milwaukee, Wis. | 636,297 | 628,088 | -8,209 | -1.3 | 17 |
| 10. El Paso, Tex. | 425,259 | 515,342 | 90,083 | 21.2 | 22 | 35. Kansas City, Mo. | 448,028 | 435,146 | -12,882 | -2.9 | 31 |
| 11. San Antonio, Tex. | 785,940 | 935,933 | 149,993 | 19.1 | 10 | 36. Washington, D.C. | 638,432 | 606,900 | -31,532 | -4.9 | 19 |
| 12. Portland, Oreg. | 368,148 | 437,319 | 69,171 | 18.8 | 30 | 37. Denver, Colo. | 492,686 | 467,610 | -25,076 | -5.1 | 26 |
| 13. Long Beach, Calif. | 361,498 | 429,433 | 67,935 | 18.8 | 32 | 38. Memphis, Tenn. | 646,174 | 610,337 | -35,837 | -5.5 | 18 |
| 14. Jacksonville, Fla. | 571,003 | 672,971 | 101,968 | 17.9 | 15 | 39. Cincinnati, Ohio | 385,409 | 364,040 | -21,369 | -5.5 | 45 |
| 15. Los Angeles, Calif. | 2,968,528 | 3,485,398 | 516,870 | 17.4 | 2 | 40. Philadelphia, Pa. | 1,688,210 | 1,585,577 | -102,633 | -6.1 | 5 |
| 16. Fort Worth, Tex. | 385,164 | 447,619 | 62,455 | 16.2 | 28 | 41. Toledo, Ohio | 354,635 | 332,943 | -21,692 | -6.1 | 49 |
| 17. Albuquerque, N.Mex. | 332,920 | 384,736 | 51,816 | 15.6 | 38 | 42. Baltimore, Md. | 786,741 | 736,014 | -50,727 | -6.4 | 13 |
| 18. Columbus, Ohio | 565,021 | 632,910 | 67,889 | 12.0 | 16 | 43. Atlanta, Ga. | 425,022 | 394,017 | -31,005 | -7.3 | 36 |
| 19. Dallas, Tex. | 904,599 | 1,006,877 | 102,278 | 11.3 | 8 | 44. Chicago, Ill. | 3,005,072 | 2,783,726 | -221,346 | -7.4 | 3 |
| 20. Oklahoma City, Okla. | 404,014 | 444,719 | 40,705 | 10.1 | 29 | 45. Buffalo, N.Y. | 357,870 | 328,123 | -29,747 | -8.3 | 50 |
| 21. Oakland, Calif. | 339,337 | 372,242 | 32,905 | 9.7 | 39 | 46. New Orleans, La. | 557,927 | 496,938 | -60,989 | -10.9 | 25 |
| 22. Omaha, Nebr. | 313,939 | 335,795 | 21,856 | 7.0 | 48 | 47. Cleveland, Ohio | 573,822 | 505,616 | -68,206 | -11.9 | 24 |
| 23. Nashville-Davidson, Tenn. | 477,811 | 510,784 | 32,973 | 6.9 | 23 | 48. St. Louis, Mo. | 452,801 | 396,685 | -56,116 | -12.4 | 34 |
| 24. San Francisco, Calif. | 678,974 | 723,959 | 44,985 | 6.6 | 14 | 49. Pittsburgh, Pa. | 423,959 | 369,879 | -54,080 | -12.8 | 40 |
| 25. Seattle, Wash. | 493,846 | 516,259 | 22,413 | 4.5 | 21 | 50. Detroit, Mich. | 1,203,368 | 1,027,974 | -175,394 | -14.6 | 7 |

**Source**: U.S. Bureau of the Census release, 1991.

## CITIES, BY POPULATION SIZE, 1960-88

| Population size | Number of cities 1960 | Number of cities 1970 | Number of cities 1988 | Population (mil.) 1960 | Population (mil.) 1970 | Population (mil.) 1988 | Percent of total 1960 | Percent of total 1970 | Percent of total 1988 |
|---|---|---|---|---|---|---|---|---|---|
| Total | 18,088 | 18,666 | 19,252 | 115.9 | 131.9 | 152.2 | 100.0% | 100.0% | 100.0% |
| 1 million or more | 5 | 6 | 7 | 17.5 | 18.8 | 19.1 | 15.1 | 14.2 | 12.6 |
| 500,000-1 million | 16 | 20 | 17 | 11.1 | 13.0 | 11.5 | 9.6 | 9.8 | 7.6 |
| 250,000-500,000 | 30 | 30 | 37 | 10.8 | 10.5 | 13.2 | 9.3 | 7.9 | 8.7 |
| 100,000-250,000 | 79 | 97 | 125 | 11.4 | 13.9 | 18.4 | 9.8 | 10.5 | 12.1 |
| 50,000-100,000 | 180 | 232 | 300 | 12.5 | 16.2 | 20.6 | 10.8 | 12.2 | 13.6 |
| 25,000-50,000 | 366 | 455 | 575 | 12.7 | 15.7 | 19.9 | 11.0 | 11.9 | 13.1 |
| 10,000-25,000 | 978 | 1,127 | 1,323 | 15.1 | 17.6 | 20.7 | 13.1 | 13.3 | 13.6 |
| Under 10,000 | 16,434 | 16,699 | 16,868 | 24.9 | 26.4 | 28.7 | 21.5 | 20.0 | 18.8 |

**Source:** U.S. Bureau of the Census, *Statistical Abstract of the United States 1990* (1990).

## 10 BEST-PAID U.S. MAYORS, 1991

| Rank/Mayor | City | Salary |
|---|---|---|
| 1. Kathryn J. Whitmire | Houston | $130,516 |
| 2. Coleman A. Young | Detroit | 130,000 |
| 3. Art Agnos | San Francisco | 129,090 |
| 4. David N. Dinkins | New York City | 123,500 |
| 5. Tom Bradley | Los Angeles | 117,884 |
| 6. Richard M. Daley | Chicago | 115,000 |
| 7. Raymond L. Flynn | Boston | 100,000 |
| Maynard Jackson | Atlanta | 100,000 |
| 9. Ed Austin | Jacksonville | 96,377 |
| 10. Norman B. Rice | Seattle | 95,398 |

**Source:** *City & State*, Sept. 23-Oct. 6, 1991 (Crain Communications, Inc.).

## City Finances

**General revenues** The primary source of funds for municipalities in 1988-89 was intergovernmental aid—monies received from other governments mostly in the form of grants or shared revenues. Intergovernmental aid accounted for $40.2 billion, or 28% of all city revenues. The second largest source of city funds was property taxes, which made up $32.3 billion, or 22.5% of the total. Sales, income, and other taxes combined accounted for another 22.1% of city revenue, while utility and other charges contributed 15.3% to county coffers.

Municipalities in the United States received $184.7 billion from all revenue sources and made expenditures totaling $182.7 billion in 1988-89. Since 1975-76, city governments have received a greater share of general revenue from their own sources and a smaller share from revenues provided by other governments.

### CITY EXPENDITURES BY FUNCTION, 1989

| Function | Amount (billions) | Percent of total |
|---|---|---|
| Environment and housing | $28.7 | 25.2% |
| Public safety | 27.9 | 24.5 |
| Education services | 17.9 | 15.7 |
| Transportation | 15.5 | 13.6 |
| Social services and income maintenance | 14.0 | 12.3 |
| Government administration | 9.9 | 8.7 |

# SUMMARY OF CITY GOVERNMENT FINANCES, 1988–89

| Item | Amount 1988–89 (millions) | Percent distri-bution 1988–89 | Percent change over 1987–88 | Item | Amount 1988–89 (millions) | Percent distri-bution 1988–89 | Percent change over 1987–88 |
|---|---|---|---|---|---|---|---|
| **REVENUES** | | | | Own | $ 5,576 | 4.0% | 2.8% |
| **Revenue, total** | **$184,770** | **—** | **4.6%** | Other | 521 | 0.4 | 17.6 |
| General revenue | 143,496 | 100.0% | 5.6 | Health | 2,221 | 1.6 | 2.1 |
| Intergovernmental revenue | 40,205 | 28.0 | 4.6 | Transportation: | | | |
| From state governments | 29,457 | 20.6 | 5.2 | Highways | 11,003 | 7.8 | 2.2 |
| General local government support | 8,222 | 5.7 | 5.5 | Air transportation | 2,508 | 1.8 | -0.2 |
| From federal government | 7,348 | 5.1 | 0.8 | Parking facilities | 601 | 0.4 | -9.4 |
| From local governments | 3,310 | 2.3 | 7.9 | Water transport | 424 | 0.3 | -17.8 |
| General revenue from own sources | 103,290 | 72.0 | 6.1 | Transit subsidies | 1,098 | 0.8 | 12.4 |
| Taxes | 63,930 | 44.6 | 6.9 | Public safety: | | | |
| Property | 32,324 | 22.5 | 7.9 | Police protection | 16,370 | 11.7 | 4.1 |
| General sales | 10,551 | 7.4 | 3.7 | Fire protection | 8,726 | 6.2 | 5.7 |
| Selective sales | 6,992 | 4.9 | 7.3 | Correction | 1,798 | 1.3 | 6.2 |
| Income | 9,033 | 6.3 | 7.2 | Protective inspection and regulation | 1,290 | 0.9 | 3.5 |
| Other | 5,030 | 3.5 | 6.3 | Environment and housing: | | | |
| Charges and miscellaneous | 39,360 | 27.4 | 4.7 | Sewerage | 9,895 | 7.1 | -2.1 |
| Current charges | 22,409 | 15.6 | 4.8 | Solid waste management | 5,178 | 3.7 | 9.1 |
| Sewerage | 7,351 | 5.1 | 8.0 | Parks and recreation | 6,743 | 4.8 | 4.4 |
| Hospitals | 3,612 | 2.5 | 1.9 | Housing and community development | 7,082 | 5.0 | 7.5 |
| Interest earnings | 10,424 | 7.3 | 10.1 | Natural resources | 148 | 0.1 | 4.2 |
| Special assessments | 1,021 | 0.7 | -17.1 | Government administration: | | | |
| Sale of property | 631 | 0.4 | -3.2 | Financial administration | 3,775 | 2.7 | 11.9 |
| Other and unallocable | 4,876 | 3.4 | -0.1 | Judicial and legal | 1,825 | 1.3 | 10.9 |
| Utility revenue | 31,838 | 100.0 | 5.1 | General public buildings | 1,682 | 1.2 | 2.1 |
| Electric power | 16,599 | 52.1 | 5.3 | Other | 2,867 | 2.0 | -1.2 |
| Water supply | 11,158 | 35.0 | 6.9 | Interest on general debt | 10,611 | 7.6 | 6.4 |
| Transit system | 1,782 | 5.6 | 1.2 | General expenditure not elsewhere classified | 13,236 | 9.4 | 0.7 |
| Gas supply | 2,299 | 7.2 | -0.6 | Utility expenditure | 36,186 | 100.0 | 5.0 |
| Liquor store revenue | 276 | — | 1.1 | Electric power | 16,659 | 46.0 | 4.1 |
| Insurance trust revenue | 9,161 | 100.0 | -10.8 | Water supply | 12,598 | 34.8 | 4.2 |
| Employment retirement | 9,096 | 99.3 | -10.7 | Transit system | 4,717 | 13.0 | 14.2 |
| Unemployment compensation[1] | 64 | 0.7 | -25.6 | Gas supply | 2,213 | 6.1 | -1.7 |
| | | | | Liquor store expenditure | 249 | — | 2.9 |
| **EXPENDITURE** | | | | Insurance trust expenditure | 6,057 | 100.0 | -0.1 |
| **Expenditure, total** | **$182,763** | **100.0%** | **4.6%** | Employee retirement | 5,986 | 98.8 | -0.2 |
| Expenditure by function: | | | | Unemployment compensation[1] | 71 | 1.2 | 2.9 |
| General expenditure | 140,271 | 100.0 | 4.8 | Exhibit: Salaries and wages | 63,352 | 34.7 | 6.8 |
| Intergovernmental expenditure | 4,409 | 3.1 | -5.2 | **INDEBTEDNESS AND DEBT TRANSACTIONS** | | | |
| Direct general expenditure | 135,862 | 96.9 | 5.1 | **Debt outstanding at end of fiscal year** | **$198,914** | **100.0%** | **5.0%** |
| Capital outlay | 21,768 | 15.5 | 0.1 | Long-term debt outstanding | 193,668 | 97.4 | 4.7 |
| Other | 114,094 | 81.3 | 6.1 | Short-term debt outstanding | 5,247 | 2.6 | 18.4 |
| Education services: | | | | | | | |
| Education | 16,208 | 11.6 | 11.1 | Long-term debt issued | 25,957 | 100.0 | 17.1 |
| Libraries | 1,757 | 1.3 | 6.2 | Long-term debt retired | 15,838 | 100.0 | 5.4 |
| Social services and income maintenance: | | | | **CASH AND SECURITY HOLDINGS** | | | |
| Public welfare | 7,129 | 5.1 | 9.1 | **Total, end of fiscal year** | **$227,251** | **100.0%** | **7.4%** |
| Cash assistance payments | 2,099 | 1.5 | 2.7 | Employment retirement | 86,134 | 37.9 | 7.2 |
| Medical vendor payments | 361 | 0.3 | 4.9 | Unemployment compensation[1] | 81 | — | -4.7 |
| Other | 4,669 | 3.3 | 12.5 | Other | 141,036 | 62.1 | 7.5 |
| Hospitals | 6,097 | 4.3 | 3.9 | | | | |

1. Washington, D.C., only. **Source**: U.S. Bureau of the Census, *City Government Finances in 1988–89* (1991).

Municipalities received $28.1 billion from state governments in fiscal 1986–87. This, together with sums received directly from the federal government and from other local governments (mainly counties), made the total of city intergovernmental revenues $40.2 billion, or 28% of general revenue from all sources. Included in this total are $1.2 billion in general revenue sharing funds distributed by the federal government to municipalities under the State and Local Fiscal Assistance Act of 1972. Current charges and miscellaneous sources supplied $39.4 billion of general revenue in 1988–89.

**General expenditures** About $128 billion, or 70%, of all municipal expenditures in fiscal 1988–89 (including amounts for utilities, insurance trusts, and governmental administration) was for current operation. By function, environment and housing accounted for one-fifth of municipal expenditures, as did public safety. Education services accounted for 8.8%. (In most cities, public schools are administered by independent school districts. In 1988–89, total school district government expenditures amounted to $163.0 billion, as against $15.8 billion expended by municipalities on education.) Transportation, social services, and income maintenance together accounted for 17%, and government administration for 5.5% of municipal government expenditures.

## TAX BURDENS IN MAJOR U.S. CITIES

Tax rates differ widely not only from state to state and city to city, but also from one income level to another. Any tax system in which the percentage of taxes paid rises with the income level is said to be *progressive*. A system where the percentage tax burden is the same at all income levels is said to be *proportional*. And a system in which the percentage of taxes paid decreases as income rises is said to be *regressive*. Because progressivity is measured as the ratio of one tax rate to another, progressivity does not necessarily reflect the actual tax burden.

### TAX BURDEN BY INCOME LEVEL IN SELECTED CITIES, 1989

| City | $25,000 Percent[1] | Amount | $50,000 Percent[1] | Amount | $75,000 Percent[1] | Amount | $100,000 Percent[1] | Amount | Progressivity index[2] |
|---|---|---|---|---|---|---|---|---|---|
| Albuquerque, N.Mex. | 8.3% | $2,074 | 8.2% | $4,166 | 9.2% | $6,880 | 9.7% | $9,679 | 0.857 |
| Anchorage, Alaska | 5.6 | 1,407 | 5.2 | 2,581 | 5.2 | 3,880 | 4.9 | 4,885 | 1.152 |
| Atlanta, Ga. | 10.6 | 2,651 | 10.4 | 5,181 | 11.3 | 8,478 | 11.2 | 11,202 | 0.947 |
| Baltimore, Md. | 11.4 | 2,861 | 11.5 | 5,758 | 11.8 | 8,832 | 11.7 | 11,701 | 0.978 |
| Billings, Mont. | 7.1 | 1,763 | 7.5 | 3,770 | 8.5 | 6,377 | 8.6 | 8,626 | 0.818 |
| Birmingham, Ala. | 8.4 | 2,092 | 7.2 | 3,614 | 7.4 | 5,576 | 7.2 | 7,233 | 1.157 |
| Boise City, Idaho | 7.9 | 1,976 | 9.4 | 4,682 | 10.8 | 8,097 | 11.3 | 11,253 | 0.702 |
| Boston, Mass. | 7.5 | 1,886 | 7.7 | 3,847 | 9.0 | 6,747 | 8.8 | 8,825 | 0.855 |
| Bridgeport, Conn. | 11.0 | 2,754 | 9.0 | 4,484 | 10.2 | 7,653 | 9.7 | 9,717 | 1.134 |
| Burlington, Vt. | 8.1 | 2,024 | 8.1 | 4,075 | 9.2 | 6,888 | 9.4 | 9,446 | 0.857 |
| Casper, Wyo. | 4.7 | 1,182 | 3.6 | 1,790 | 4.2 | 3,158 | 3.9 | 3,875 | 1.220 |
| Charleston, W.Va. | 7.5 | 1,877 | 7.1 | 3,560 | 8.7 | 6,514 | 8.8 | 8,834 | 0.850 |
| Charlotte, N.C. | 9.2 | 2,309 | 9.1 | 4,558 | 9.9 | 7,416 | 9.9 | 9,909 | 0.932 |
| Chicago, Ill. | 7.7 | 1,931 | 7.6 | 3,791 | 7.9 | 5,910 | 7.8 | 7,722 | 0.994 |
| Cleveland, Ohio | 9.7 | 2,429 | 10.1 | 5,049 | 10.7 | 8,051 | 11.1 | 11,126 | 0.873 |
| Columbia, S.C. | 9.4 | 2,352 | 9.9 | 4,928 | 11.0 | 8,226 | 10.9 | 10,862 | 0.866 |
| Denver, Colo. | 9.7 | 2,413 | 9.0 | 4,504 | 9.8 | 7,358 | 9.6 | 9,579 | 1.008 |
| Des Moines, Iowa | 10.4 | 2,610 | 10.7 | 5,331 | 11.0 | 8,287 | 11.0 | 10,951 | 0.953 |
| Detroit, Mich. | 12.1 | 3,016 | 12.2 | 6,091 | 12.5 | 9,363 | 12.5 | 12,478 | 0.967 |
| Fargo, N. Dak. | 7.8 | 1,957 | 7.5 | 3,766 | 8.1 | 6,084 | 8.2 | 8,211 | 0.953 |
| Honolulu, Hawaii | 9.1 | 2,282 | 10.0 | 5,002 | 10.9 | 8,200 | 11.2 | 11,222 | 0.813 |
| Houston, Tex. | 5.4 | 1,356 | 4.6 | 2,284 | 4.6 | 3,437 | 4.4 | 4,375 | 1.240 |
| Indianapolis, Ind. | 8.8 | 2,197 | 7.7 | 3,834 | 8.5 | 6,361 | 8.2 | 8,202 | 1.072 |
| Jackson, Miss. | 8.0 | 1,988 | 7.9 | 3,951 | 9.3 | 7,010 | 9.2 | 9,178 | 0.867 |
| Jacksonville, Fla. | 4.3 | 1,067 | 4.5 | 2,234 | 4.8 | 3,606 | 4.8 | 4,769 | 0.895 |
| Las Vegas, Nev. | 6.3 | 1,570 | 5.0 | 2,521 | 5.4 | 4,078 | 5.1 | 5,088 | 1.234 |
| Little Rock, Ark. | 7.6 | 1,888 | 7.8 | 3,904 | 8.8 | 6,611 | 9.0 | 8,978 | 0.841 |
| Los Angeles, Calif. | 7.2 | 1,801 | 7.9 | 3,958 | 10.0 | 7,505 | 10.7 | 10,666 | 0.675 |
| Louisville, Ky. | 9.5 | 2,380 | 9.4 | 4,696 | 9.5 | 7,110 | 9.3 | 9,288 | 1.025 |
| Manchester, N.H. | 5.5 | 1,381 | 4.7 | 2,365 | 5.2 | 3,905 | 4.8 | 4,825 | 1.145 |
| Memphis, Tenn. | 7.4 | 1,849 | 6.1 | 3,036 | 6.1 | 4,546 | 5.8 | 5,840 | 1.267 |
| Milwaukee, Wis. | 14.2 | 3,546 | 14.8 | 7,409 | 15.2 | 11,405 | 15.1 | 15,063 | 0.942 |
| Minneapolis, Minn. | 8.8 | 2,195 | 11.1 | 5,556 | 12.8 | 9,625 | 13.0 | 13,008 | 0.675 |
| New Orleans, La. | 5.1 | 1,276 | 7.3 | 3,643 | 8.3 | 6,253 | 8.4 | 8,389 | 0.608 |
| New York, N.Y. | 10.6 | 2,654 | 12.3 | 6,154 | 13.7 | 10,272 | 14.0 | 14,001 | 0.758 |
| Newark, N.J. | 9.7 | 2,418 | 9.8 | 4,878 | 10.2 | 7,636 | 10.1 | 10,117 | 0.956 |
| Norfolk, Va. | 8.5 | 2,120 | 8.6 | 4,317 | 9.9 | 7,396 | 9.6 | 9,618 | 0.882 |
| Oklahoma City, Okla. | 7.5 | 1,874 | 7.4 | 3,708 | 8.4 | 6,272 | 8.4 | 8,386 | 0.894 |
| Omaha, Nebr. | 9.2 | 2,306 | 8.7 | 4,351 | 9.8 | 7,377 | 9.9 | 9,856 | 0.936 |
| Philadelphia, Pa. | 12.3 | 3,067 | 11.6 | 5,803 | 11.4 | 8,529 | 11.1 | 11,135 | 1.102 |
| Phoenix, Ariz. | 7.3 | 1,815 | 6.9 | 3,467 | 7.9 | 5,910 | 7.6 | 7,642 | 0.950 |
| Portland, Maine | 8.2 | 2,047 | 9.2 | 4,622 | 11.3 | 8,455 | 11.4 | 1,409 | 0.718 |
| Portland, Oreg. | 14.0 | 3,496 | 14.6 | 7,288 | 15.2 | 11,429 | 15.1 | 15,139 | 0.924 |
| Providence, R.I. | 10.4 | 2,595 | 9.8 | 4,904 | 11.2 | 8,364 | 11.1 | 11,125 | 0.933 |
| Salt Lake City, Utah | 9.3 | 2,313 | 9.6 | 4,784 | 10.1 | 7,593 | 10.1 | 10,083 | 0.917 |
| Seattle, Wash. | 7.8 | 1,961 | 6.3 | 3,127 | 6.7 | 4,991 | 6.2 | 6,231 | 1.259 |
| Sioux Falls, S.Dak. | 9.2 | 2,312 | 7.7 | 3,869 | 7.7 | 5,790 | 7.4 | 7,396 | 1.250 |
| St. Louis, Mo. | 8.7 | 2,164 | 8.6 | 4,303 | 9.1 | 6,804 | 8.9 | 8,883 | 0.975 |
| Washington, D.C. | 10.4 | 2,602 | 10.8 | 5,381 | 11.6 | 8,732 | 11.9 | 11,941 | 0.872 |
| Wichita, Kans. | 8.1 | 2,024 | 7.2 | 3,594 | 8.9 | 6,689 | 8.7 | 8,730 | 0.927 |
| Wilmington, Del. | 5.3 | 1,330 | 6.4 | 3,207 | 7.2 | 5,402 | 7.6 | 7,596 | 0.701 |
| **51 city average** | **8.6** | **2,146** | **8.5** | **4,267** | **9.3** | **7,001** | **9.3** | **9,301** | **0.948** |

**Note**: This table deals only with individual tax burdens. The four major taxes compared are the individual income tax, real property taxes on residential property, general sales and use taxes, and various automobile taxes, including the gasoline tax, registration fees, excise taxes, and personal property taxes. 1. Percentage of income. 2. An index coefficient of less than 1.000 indicates a progressive tax system; an index coefficient of greater than 1.000 indicates a regressive tax system; an index coefficient of 1.000 indicates a proportional tax system. **Source**: Government of the District of Columbia, Dept. of Finance and Revenues, *Tax Rates and Tax Burdens in the District of Columbia: A Nationwide Comparison* (1990).

## Tax Progressivity

Several factors contribute to the progressivity of a tax system. A graduated individual income tax rate combined with exemptions and credits to lessen the regressiveness of the property tax will increase the progressivity of a tax system. Progressivity can be lessened by lack of an individual income tax as well as by reliance on regressive taxes such as the sales tax and certain automobile taxes. The upper and lower income levels chosen for comparison also affect progressiveness.

The following table shows the percentage tax burden at various income levels in the five most and least progressive cities in the table "Tax Burdens by Income Level." (The 51 city average is 0.938.) The most progressive systems are found in New Orleans, Minneapolis, Los Angeles, Wilmington, and Boise City, Idaho. Each of these five cities is characterized

## TAX PROGRESSIVITY IN SELECTED CITIES, 1989

| Most progressive | | Least progressive | |
|---|---|---|---|
| City | Index | City | Index |
| New Orleans, La. | 0.608 | Memphis, Tenn. | 1.267 |
| Los Angeles, Calif. | 0.675 | Seattle, Wash. | 1.259 |
| Minneapolis, Minn. | 0.675 | Sioux Falls, S.Dak. | 1.250 |
| Wilmington, Del. | 0.701 | Houston, Tex. | 1.240 |
| Boise City, Idaho | 0.702 | Las Vegas, Nev. | 1.234 |

**Note**: An index coefficient of less than 1.000 indicates a progressive tax system; an index coefficient of greater than 1.000 indicates a regressive tax system; a proportional system is indicated by a coefficient of 1.000. **Source**: Government of the District of Columbia, Dept. of Finance and Revenues, *Tax Rates and Tax Burdens in the District of Columbia: A Nationwide Comparison* (1990).

by graduated individual income tax rates, and all but Wilmington have some type of exemption or credit to lessen the regressiveness of the real property tax. The four cities with the most regressive state and local tax systems are Memphis, Seattle, Sioux Falls, and Houston. None of these cities levies an individual income tax, and in Sioux Falls and Memphis the sales and use tax burden is substantially above the 51 city average.

## The Cost of Living Index

The cost of living index, compiled by the American Chamber of Commerce Researchers Association, measures relative price levels for consumer goods and services. The nationwide average equals 100 and each area's index is read as a percentage of the nationwide average. So, Philadelphia is significantly above the national average in every category, while Tulsa is below the average in all but one category. The index reflects differentials for a mid-manager standard of living by its weighting structure. Housing costs, for example, are more heavily weighted than they would be if the index were structured to reflect average costs for a clerical worker, or for all urban consumers. Tax burdens are not included in the cost of living index.

## METROPOLITAN STATISTICAL AREAS (MSAs)

For statistical purposes, the Office of Management and Budget (OMB) divides the population of the United States into metropolitan and nonmetropolitan populations. The OMB distinguishes between metropolitan statistical areas (MSAs), consolidated metropolitan statistical areas (CMSAs), primary metropolitan statistical areas (PMSAs), and in the Northeast, New England county metropolitan areas (NECMAs).

An MSA is either one city of 50,000 or more inhabitants, or an urbanized area (as defined by the Census Bureau) of at least 50,000 inhabitants and a total MSA population of at least 100,000 (in New England, 75,000). An MSA includes the county in which the central city is located plus any adjacent counties in which at least 50% of the population lives in the urbanized area. Within metropolitan complexes of one million or more population, separate component areas—PMSAs—are defined if specified criteria are met; and any area containing PMSAs is designated a CMSA. Although the 283 metropolitan areas of the United States make up only about 16% of the country's land area, they are home to 77.5% of all Americans.

According to the 1990 census, the U.S. population living in all metropolitan areas totaled 192,725,741, an increase of just over 20 million (11.6%) since 1980. The same areas grew 10.6% in the 1970s. The population living outside metropolitan areas totaled only 55,984,132 people, increasing by only about 2.1 million (3.9%) since 1980.

The 1990 census indicated that there were 39 metropolitan areas of at least 1 million population; these areas have a combined population of 124.8 million people, or 50.2% of the national total. By contrast, the 1950 census showed only 14 metropolitan areas of this size, and their combined population of about 45 million people amounted to less than 30% of the total U.S. population.

## THE COST OF LIVING INDEX IN SELECTED U.S. CITIES, 1991

| Urban area | Composite index (100%) | Grocery items (17%) | Housing (22%) | Utilities (11%) | Transportation (13%) | Health care (7%) | Misc. goods & services (30%) | Urban area | Composite index (100%) | Grocery items (17%) | Housing (22%) | Utilities (11%) | Transportation (13%) | Health care (7%) | Misc. goods & services (30%) |
|---|---|---|---|---|---|---|---|---|---|---|---|---|---|---|---|
| Albuquerque, N.Mex. | 101.7 | 94.3 | 103.9 | 95.4 | 101.9 | 111.8 | 104.3 | Memphis, Tenn. | 94.3 | 101.0 | 85.9 | 90.4 | 103.0 | 85.4 | 96.4 |
| Atlanta, Ga. | 100.9 | 98.9 | 101.4 | 115.1 | 102.1 | 112.3 | 93.2 | Miami/Dade Co., Fla. | 113.9 | 98.1 | 120.7 | 133.1 | 111.3 | 126.5 | 109.1 |
| Austin, Tex. | 99.9 | 97.0 | 89.9 | 109.5 | 97.2 | 91.6 | 108.3 | Milwaukee, Wis. PMSA | 103.3 | 102.0 | 122.9 | 97.7 | 98.2 | 101.1 | 94.6 |
| Buffalo, N.Y. | 111.8 | 105.4 | 121.8 | 134.7 | 113.3 | 104.9 | 100.8 | Nassau-Suffolk, N.Y. PMSA | 152.1 | 118.9 | 207.4 | 217.6 | 129.0 | 134.4 | 120.5 |
| Charlotte, N.C. | 101.3 | 97.8 | 101.0 | 95.4 | 96.1 | 108.5 | 106.1 | New Orleans, La. | 97.7 | 101.3 | 88.1 | 123.2 | 98.6 | 87.8 | 95.3 |
| Cincinnati, Ohio | 104.7 | 102.4 | 111.6 | 101.9 | 104.0 | 94.6 | 104.7 | Oklahoma City, Okla. | 95.8 | 101.2 | 77.8 | 109.2 | 97.7 | 97.3 | 99.7 |
| Cleveland, Ohio | 105.9 | 97.0 | 104.2 | 125.2 | 111.6 | 109.4 | 101.7 | Omaha, Nebr. | 90.4 | 94.9 | 84.3 | 91.6 | 103.4 | 82.7 | 87.9 |
| Columbus, Ohio | 105.9 | 99.5 | 116.6 | 107.0 | 110.0 | 103.4 | 100.0 | Philadelphia, Pa. | 127.6 | 113.4 | 139.3 | 178.5 | 111.7 | 134.4 | 113.6 |
| Dallas, Tex. | 103.7 | 100.1 | 102.2 | 116.9 | 106.4 | 108.4 | 99.8 | Phoenix, Ariz. | 102.0 | 95.8 | 98.0 | 101.9 | 108.4 | 116.9 | 102.3 |
| Denver, Colo. | 101.6 | 96.3 | 103.6 | 95.6 | 107.8 | 119.0 | 98.5 | Pittsburgh, Pa. | 110.4 | 101.0 | 115.1 | 125.5 | 119.1 | 105.0 | 104.3 |
| El Paso, Tex. | 95.8 | 99.0 | 85.9 | 81.5 | 109.1 | 96.5 | 100.4 | Portland, Oreg. | 109.2 | 104.8 | 131.0 | 71.7 | 109.6 | 132.2 | 103.8 |
| Fort Worth, Tex. | 99.0 | 104.0 | 81.8 | 108.0 | 114.8 | 99.4 | 98.7 | Sacramento, Calif. | 106.3 | 102.2 | 118.9 | 82.6 | 110.1 | 116.7 | 104.1 |
| Fresno, Calif. | 115.1 | 110.2 | 126.4 | 109.8 | 105.1 | 119.9 | 114.8 | San Antonio, Tex. | 94.9 | 101.6 | 86.5 | 78.1 | 110.3 | 96.1 | 96.4 |
| Houston, Tex. PMSA | 101.5 | 107.1 | 89.3 | 93.8 | 118.8 | 104.1 | 101.9 | San Diego, Calif. | 131.4 | 103.5 | 211.7 | 71.4 | 127.8 | 135.4 | 111.1 |
| Indianapolis, Ind. | 97.7 | 95.8 | 98.0 | 94.4 | 97.9 | 98.8 | 99.4 | Seattle, Wash. | 115.1 | 117.9 | 144.9 | 62.6 | 119.1 | 140.9 | 103.4 |
| Jacksonville, Fla. | 96.3 | 97.6 | 89.7 | 97.4 | 104.3 | 101.2 | 95.5 | St. Louis, Mo.-Ill. MSA | 97.8 | 97.6 | 99.1 | 107.2 | 98.6 | 101.0 | 92.5 |
| Kansas City, Mo.-Kans. | 94.6 | 94.4 | 97.8 | 85.9 | 91.3 | 103.7 | 94.8 | St. Paul, Minn. | 98.8 | 87.4 | 99.7 | 97.1 | 104.1 | 111.3 | 100.0 |
| Los Angeles-Long Beach, Calif. | 120.9 | 104.9 | 185.3 | 73.7 | 108.8 | 129.0 | 103.4 | Tucson, Ariz. | 100.9 | 95.7 | 92.7 | 84.0 | 121.0 | 113.9 | 104.4 |
| | | | | | | | | Tulsa, Okla. | 92.8 | 101.2 | 78.6 | 88.4 | 99.1 | 97.0 | 96.5 |

**Note**: Percentage figures in parentheses show relative weight of component indexes used in calculating composite cost of living index. **Source**: American Chamber of Commerce Researchers Association, *Cost of Living Index: Comparative Data for 291 Urban Areas, First Quarter 1991* (1991). Reprinted by permission.

## POPULATION OF METROPOLITAN STATISTICAL AREAS, 1980–90

| Metropolitan statistical area | 1980 | 1990 | Change 1980–90 Number | Percent | CMSA/MSA rank 1980 | 1990 |
|---|---|---|---|---|---|---|
| Abilene, Tex. MSA | 110,932 | 119,655 | 8,723 | 7.9% | 235 | 235 |
| Albany, Ga. MSA | 112,394 | 112,561 | 167 | 0.1 | 232 | 248 |
| Albany-Schenectady-Troy, N.Y. MSA | 835,880 | 874,304 | 38,424 | 4.6 | 46 | 48 |
| Albuquerque, N.Mex. MSA | 420,261 | 480,577 | 60,316 | 14.4 | 80 | 77 |
| Alexandria, La. MSA | 135,282 | 131,556 | -3,726 | -2.8 | 196 | 210 |
| Allentown-Bethlehem, Pa.-N.J MSA | 635,481 | 686,688 | 51,207 | 8.1 | 54 | 58 |
| Altoona, Pa. MSA | 136,621 | 130,542 | -6,079 | -4.4 | 195 | 219 |
| Amarillo, Tex. MSA | 173,699 | 187,547 | 13,848 | 8.0 | 157 | 164 |
| Anchorage, Alaska MSA | 174,431 | 226,338 | 51,907 | 29.8 | 156 | 143 |
| Anderson, Ind. MSA | 139,336 | 130,669 | -8,667 | -6.2 | 189 | 217 |
| Anderson, S.C. MSA | 133,235 | 145,196 | 11,961 | 9.0 | 199 | 197 |
| Anniston, Ala. MSA | 119,761 | 116,034 | -3,727 | -3.1 | 218 | 241 |
| Appleton-Oshkosh-Neenah, Wis. MSA | 291,369 | 315,121 | 23,752 | 8.2 | 107 | 114 |
| Asheville, N.C. MSA | 160,934 | 174,821 | 13,887 | 8.6 | 171 | 171 |
| Athens, Ga. MSA | 130,015 | 156,267 | 26,252 | 20.2 | 204 | 182 |
| Atlanta, Ga. MSA | 2,138,136 | 2,833,511 | 695,375 | 32.5 | 16 | 12 |
| Atlantic City, N.J. MSA | 276,385 | 319,416 | 43,031 | 15.6 | 113 | 112 |
| Augusta, Ga.-S.C. MSA | 345,923 | 396,809 | 50,886 | 14.7 | 95 | 91 |
| Austin, Tex. MSA | 536,688 | 781,572 | 244,884 | 45.6 | 63 | 52 |
| Bakersfield, Calif. MSA | 403,089 | 543,477 | 140,388 | 34.8 | 84 | 68 |
| Baltimore, Md. MSA | 2,199,497 | 2,382,172 | 182,675 | 8.3 | 15 | 18 |
| Bangor, Maine MSA | 83,919 | 88,745 | 4,826 | 5.8 | 270 | 268 |
| Baton Rouge, La. MSA | 494,151 | 528,264 | 34,113 | 6.9 | 69 | 71 |
| Battle Creek, Mich. MSA | 141,579 | 135,982 | -5,597 | -4.0 | 186 | 205 |
| Beaumont-Port Arthur, Tex. MSA | 373,211 | 361,226 | -11,985 | -3.2 | 88 | 102 |
| Bellingham, Wash. MSA | 106,701 | 127,780 | 21,079 | 19.8 | 242 | 221 |
| Benton Harbor, Mich. MSA | 171,276 | 161,378 | -9,898 | -5.8 | 161 | 177 |
| Billings, Mont. MSA | 108,035 | 113,419 | 5,384 | 5.0 | 240 | 246 |
| Biloxi-Gulfport, Miss. MSA | 182,161 | 197,125 | 14,964 | 8.2 | 153 | 156 |
| Binghamton, N.Y. MSA | 263,460 | 264,497 | 1,037 | 0.4 | 123 | 127 |
| Birmingham, Ala. MSA | 883,993 | 907,810 | 23,817 | 2.7 | 42 | 46 |
| Bismarck, N.Dak. MSA | 79,988 | 83,831 | 3,843 | 4.8 | 275 | 273 |
| Bloomington, Ind. MSA | 98,787 | 108,978 | 10,191 | 10.3 | 253 | 251 |
| Bloomington-Normal, Ill. MSA | 119,149 | 129,180 | 10,031 | 8.4 | 219 | 220 |
| Boise City, Idaho MSA | 173,125 | 205,775 | 32,650 | 18.9 | 158 | 154 |
| Boston-Lawrence-Salem, Mass.-N.H. CMSA | 3,971,792 | 4,171,643 | 199,851 | 5.0 | 7 | 7 |
|   Boston, Mass. PMSA | 2,805,911 | 2,870,669 | 64,758 | 2.3 | N.A. | N.A. |
|   Brockton, Mass. PMSA | 182,891 | 189,478 | 6,587 | 3.6 | N.A. | N.A. |
|   Lawrence-Haverhill, Mass.-N.H. PMSA | 339,090 | 393,516 | 54,426 | 16.1 | N.A. | N.A. |
|   Lowell, Mass.-N.H. PMSA | 243,142 | 273,067 | 29,925 | 12.3 | N.A. | N.A. |
|   Nashua, N.H. PMSA | 142,527 | 180,557 | 38,030 | 26.7 | N.A. | N.A. |
|   Salem-Gloucester, Mass. PMSA | 258,231 | 264,356 | 6,125 | 2.4 | N.A. | N.A. |
| Bradenton, Fla. MSA | 148,445 | 211,707 | 63,262 | 42.6 | 181 | 152 |
| Bremerton, Wash. MSA | 147,152 | 189,731 | 42,579 | 28.9 | 182 | 160 |
| Brownsville-Harlingen, Tex. MSA | 209,727 | 260,120 | 50,393 | 24.0 | 138 | 129 |
| Bryan-College Station, Tex. MSA | 93,588 | 121,862 | 28,274 | 30.2 | 259 | 229 |
| Buffalo-Niagara Falls, N.Y. CMSA | 1,242,826 | 1,189,288 | -53,538 | -4.3 | 29 | 33 |
|   Buffalo, N.Y. PMSA | 1,015,472 | 968,532 | -46,940 | -4.6 | N.A. | N.A. |
|   Niagara Falls, N.Y. PMSA | 227,354 | 220,756 | -6,598 | -2.9 | N.A. | N.A. |
| Burlington, N.C. MSA | 99,319 | 108,213 | 8,894 | 9.0 | 251 | 253 |
| Burlington, Vt. MSA | 115,308 | 131,439 | 16,131 | 14.0 | 225 | 212 |
| Canton, Ohio MSA | 404,421 | 394,106 | -10,315 | -2.6 | 83 | 93 |
| Casper, Wyo. MSA | 71,856 | 61,226 | -10,630 | -14.8 | 278 | 283 |
| Cedar Rapids, Iowa MSA | 169,775 | 168,767 | -1,008 | -0.6 | 163 | 174 |
| Champaign-Urbana-Rantoul, Ill. MSA | 168,392 | 173,025 | 4,633 | 2.8 | 164 | 172 |
| Charleston, S.C. MSA | 430,346 | 506,875 | 76,529 | 17.8 | 77 | 73 |
| Charleston, W.Va. MSA | 269,595 | 250,454 | -19,141 | -7.1 | 118 | 134 |
| Charlotte-Gastonia-Rock Hill, N.C.-S.C. MSA | 971,447 | 1,162,093 | 190,646 | 19.6 | 36 | 34 |
| Charlottesville, Va. MSA | 113,568 | 131,107 | 17,539 | 15.4 | 226 | 214 |
| Chattanooga, Tenn.-Ga. MSA | 426,443 | 433,210 | 6,767 | 1.6 | 78 | 82 |
| Cheyenne, Wyo. MSA | 68,649 | 73,142 | 4,493 | 6.5% | 281 | 281 |
| Chicago-Gary-Lake County, Ill.-Ind.-Wis. CMSA | 7,937,290 | 8,065,633 | 128,343 | 1.6 | 3 | 3 |
|   Aurora-Elgin, Ill. PMSA | 315,607 | 356,884 | 41,277 | 13.1 | N.A. | N.A. |
|   Chicago, Ill. PMSA | 6,060,383 | 6,069,974 | 9,591 | 0.2 | N.A. | N.A. |
|   Gary-Hammond, Ind. PMSA | 642,733 | 604,526 | -38,207 | -5.9 | N.A. | N.A. |
|   Joliet, Ill. PMSA | 355,042 | 389,650 | 34,608 | 9.7 | N.A. | N.A. |
|   Kenosha, Wis. PMSA | 123,137 | 128,181 | 5,044 | 4.1 | N.A. | N.A. |
|   Lake County, Ill. PMSA | 440,388 | 516,418 | 76,030 | 17.3 | N.A. | N.A. |
| Chico, Calif. MSA | 143,851 | 182,120 | 38,269 | 26.6 | 185 | 167 |
| Cincinnati-Hamilton, Ohio-Ky.-Ind. CMSA | 1,660,257 | 1,744,124 | 83,867 | 5.1 | 20 | 23 |
|   Cincinnati, Ohio-Ky.-Ind. PMSA | 1,401,470 | 1,452,645 | 51,175 | 3.7 | N.A. | N.A. |
|   Hamilton-Middletown, Ohio PMSA | 258,787 | 291,479 | 32,692 | 12.6 | N.A. | N.A. |
| Clarksville-Hopkinsville, Tenn.-Ky. MSA | 150,220 | 169,439 | 19,219 | 12.8 | 179 | 173 |
| Cleveland-Akron-Lorain, Ohio CMSA | 2,834,062 | 2,759,823 | -74,239 | -2.6 | 11 | 13 |
|   Akron, Ohio PMSA | 660,328 | 657,575 | -2,753 | -0.4 | N.A. | N.A. |
|   Cleveland, Ohio PMSA | 1,898,825 | 1,831,122 | -67,703 | -3.6 | N.A. | N.A. |
|   Lorain-Elyria, Ohio PMSA | 274,909 | 271,126 | -3,783 | -1.4 | N.A. | N.A. |
| Colorado Springs, Colo. MSA | 309,424 | 397,014 | 87,590 | 28.3 | 105 | 90 |
| Columbia, Mo. MSA | 100,376 | 112,379 | 12,003 | 12.0 | 250 | 249 |
| Columbia, S.C. MSA | 409,953 | 453,331 | 43,478 | 10.6 | 82 | 79 |
| Columbus, Ga.-Ala. MSA | 239,196 | 243,072 | 3,876 | 1.6 | 131 | 136 |
| Columbus, Ohio | 1,243,827 | 1,377,419 | 133,592 | 10.7 | 28 | 29 |
| Corpus Christi, Tex. | 326,228 | 349,894 | 23,666 | 7.3 | 99 | 105 |
| Cumberland, Md.-W.Va. | 107,782 | 101,643 | -6,139 | -5.7 | 241 | 259 |
| Dallas-Fort Worth, Tex. CMSA | 2,930,568 | 3,885,415 | 954,847 | 32.6 | 10 | 9 |
|   Dallas, Tex. PMSA | 1,957,430 | 2,553,362 | 595,932 | 30.4 | N.A. | N.A. |
|   Fort Worth-Arlington, Tex. PMSA | 973,138 | 1,332,053 | 358,915 | 36.9 | N.A. | N.A. |
| Danville, Va. MSA | 111,789 | 108,711 | -3,078 | -2.8 | 233 | 252 |
| Davenport-Rock Island-Moline, Iowa-Ill. MSA | 384,749 | 350,861 | -33,888 | -8.8 | 86 | 104 |
| Dayton-Springfield, Ohio MSA | 942,083 | 951,270 | 9,187 | 1.0 | 39 | 44 |
| Daytona Beach, Fla. MSA | 258,762 | 370,712 | 111,950 | 43.3 | 124 | 96 |
| Decatur, Ala. MSA | 120,401 | 131,556 | 11,155 | 9.3 | 217 | 211 |
| Decatur, Ill. MSA | 131,375 | 117,206 | -14,169 | -10.8 | 210 | 239 |
| Denver-Boulder, Colo. CMSA | 1,618,461 | 1,848,319 | 229,858 | 14.2 | 21 | 22 |
|   Boulder-Longmont, Colo. PMSA | 189,625 | 225,339 | 35,714 | 18.8 | N.A. | N.A. |
|   Denver, Colo. PMSA | 1,428,836 | 1,622,980 | 194,144 | 13.6 | N.A. | N.A. |
| Des Moines, Iowa MSA | 367,561 | 392,928 | 25,367 | 6.9 | 89 | 94 |
| Detroit-Ann Arbor, Mich. CMSA | 4,752,764 | 4,665,236 | -87,528 | -1.8 | 6 | 6 |
|   Ann Arbor, Mich. PMSA | 264,740 | 282,937 | 18,197 | 6.9 | N.A. | N.A. |
|   Detroit, Mich. PMSA | 4,488,024 | 4,382,299 | -105,725 | -2.4 | N.A. | N.A. |
| Dothan, Ala. MSA | 122,453 | 130,964 | 8,511 | 7.0 | 214 | 215 |
| Dubuque, Iowa MSA | 93,745 | 86,403 | -7,342 | -7.8 | 258 | 271 |
| Duluth, Minn.-Wis. MSA | 266,650 | 239,971 | -26,679 | -10.0 | 119 | 140 |
| Eau Claire, Wis. MSA | 130,932 | 137,543 | 6,611 | 5.0 | 203 | 204 |
| El Paso, Tex. MSA | 479,899 | 591,610 | 111,711 | 23.3 | 70 | 66 |
| Elkhart-Goshen, Ind. MSA | 137,330 | 156,198 | 18,868 | 13.7 | 193 | 183 |
| Elmira, N.Y. MSA | 97,656 | 95,195 | -2,461 | -2.5 | 255 | 266 |
| Enid, Okla. MSA | 62,820 | 56,735 | -6,085 | -9.7 | 284 | 284 |
| Erie, Pa. MSA | 279,780 | 275,572 | -4,208 | -1.5 | 111 | 124 |
| Eugene-Springfield, Oreg. MSA | 275,226 | 282,912 | 7,686 | 2.8 | 115 | 119 |
| Evansville, Ind.-Ky. MSA | 276,252 | 278,990 | 2,738 | 1.0 | 114 | 121 |
| Fargo-Moorhead, N.Dak.-Minn. MSA | 137,574 | 153,296 | 15,722 | 11.4 | 191 | 185 |
| Fayetteville, N.C. MSA | 247,160 | 274,566 | 27,406 | 11.1 | 127 | 125 |
| Fayetteville-Springdale, Ark. MSA | 100,494 | 113,409 | 12,915 | 12.9 | 249 | 247 |
| Fitchburg-Leominster, Mass. MSA | 94,018 | 102,797 | 8,779 | 9.3 | 257 | 258 |
| Flint, Mich. MSA | 450,449 | 430,459 | -19,990 | -4.4 | 73 | 84 |
| Florence, Ala. MSA | 135,065 | 131,327 | -3,738 | -2.8 | 197 | 213 |
| Florence, S.C. MSA | 110,163 | 114,344 | 4,181 | 3.8 | 236 | 245 |
| Fort Collins-Loveland, Colo. MSA | 149,184 | 186,136 | 36,952 | 24.8 | 180 | 165 |
| Fort Myers-Cape Coral, Fla. MSA | 205,266 | 335,113 | 129,847 | 63.3 | 140 | 110 |

| Metropolitan statistical area | 1980 | 1990 | Change 1980–90 Number | Percent | CMSA/MSA rank 1980 | 1990 |
|---|---|---|---|---|---|---|
| Fort Pierce, Fla. MSA | 151,196 | 251,071 | 99,875 | 66.1% | 178 | 133 |
| Fort Smith, Ark.-Okla. MSA | 162,813 | 175,911 | 13,098 | 8.0 | 169 | 169 |
| Fort Walton Beach, Fla. MSA | 109,920 | 143,776 | 33,856 | 30.8 | 237 | 198 |
| Fort Wayne, Ind. MSA | 354,156 | 363,811 | 9,655 | 2.7 | 93 | 100 |
| Fresno, Calif. MSA | 514,621 | 667,490 | 152,869 | 29.7 | 67 | 59 |
| Gadsden, Ala. MSA | 103,057 | 99,840 | –3,217 | –3.1 | 245 | 260 |
| Gainesville, Fla. MSA | 171,392 | 204,111 | 32,719 | 19.1 | 160 | 155 |
| Glens Falls, N.Y. MSA | 109,649 | 118,539 | 8,890 | 8.1 | 238 | 238 |
| Grand Forks, N.Dak. MSA | 66,100 | 70,683 | 4,583 | 6.9 | 283 | 282 |
| Grand Rapids, Mich. MSA | 601,680 | 688,399 | 86,719 | 14.4 | 56 | 57 |
| Great Falls, Mont. MSA | 80,696 | 77,691 | –3,005 | –3.7 | 274 | 279 |
| Greeley, Colo. MSA | 123,438 | 131,821 | 8,383 | 6.8 | 212 | 209 |
| Green Bay, Wis. MSA | 175,280 | 194,594 | 19,314 | 11.0 | 155 | 158 |
| Greensboro-Winston-Salem-High Point, N.C. MSA | 851,444 | 942,091 | 90,647 | 10.6 | 44 | 45 |
| Greenville-Spartanburg, S.C. MSA | 570,210 | 640,861 | 70,561 | 12.4 | 59 | 62 |
| Hagerstown, Md. MSA | 113,086 | 121,393 | 8,307 | 7.3 | 227 | 230 |
| Harrisburg-Lebanon-Carlisle, Pa. MSA | 556,242 | 587,986 | 31,744 | 5.7 | 62 | 67 |
| Hartford-New Britain-Middletown, Conn. CMSA | 1,013,508 | 1,085,837 | 72,329 | 7.1 | 35 | 36 |
| Bristol, Conn. PMSA | 73,762 | 79,488 | 5,726 | 7.8 | N.A. | N.A. |
| Hartford, Conn. PMSA | 715,923 | 767,841 | 51,918 | 7.3 | N.A. | N.A. |
| Middletown, Conn. PMSA | 81,582 | 90,320 | 8,738 | 10.7 | N.A. | N.A. |
| New Britain, Conn. PMSA | 142,241 | 148,188 | 5,947 | 4.2 | N.A. | N.A. |
| Hickory-Morganton, N.C. MSA | 202,711 | 221,700 | 18,989 | 9.4 | 142 | 148 |
| Honolulu, Hawaii MSA | 762,565 | 836,231 | 73,666 | 9.7 | 47 | 51 |
| Houma-Thibodaux, La. MSA | 176,876 | 182,842 | 5,966 | 3.4 | 154 | 166 |
| Houston-Galveston-Brazoria, Tex. CMSA | 3,099,942 | 3,711,043 | 611,101 | 19.7 | 9 | 10 |
| Brazoria, Tex. PMSA | 169,587 | 191,707 | 22,120 | 13.0 | N.A. | N.A. |
| Galveston-Texas City, Tex. PMSA | 195,738 | 217,399 | 21,661 | 11.1 | N.A. | N.A. |
| Houston, Tex. PMSA | 2,734,617 | 3,301,937 | 567,320 | 20.7 | N.A. | N.A. |
| Huntington-Ashland, W.Va.-Ky.-Ohio MSA | 336,410 | 312,529 | –23,881 | –7.1 | 97 | 115 |
| Huntsville, Ala. MSA | 196,966 | 238,912 | 41,946 | 21.3 | 144 | 141 |
| Indianapolis, Ind. MSA | 1,166,575 | 1,249,822 | 83,247 | 7.1 | 30 | 31 |
| Iowa City, Iowa MSA | 81,717 | 96,119 | 14,402 | 17.6 | 273 | 265 |
| Jackson, Mich. MSA | 151,495 | 149,756 | –1,739 | –1.1 | 177 | 191 |
| Jackson, Miss. MSA | 362,038 | 395,396 | 33,358 | 9.2 | 92 | 92 |
| Jackson, Tenn. MSA | 74,548 | 77,982 | 3,436 | 4.6 | 277 | 278 |
| Jacksonville, Fla. MSA | 722,252 | 906,727 | 184,475 | 25.5 | 50 | 47 |
| Jacksonville, N.C. MSA | 112,784 | 149,838 | 37,054 | 32.9 | 229 | 190 |
| Jamestown-Dunkirk, N.Y. MSA | 146,925 | 141,895 | –5,030 | –3.4 | 183 | 202 |
| Janesville-Beloit, Wis. MSA | 139,420 | 139,510 | 90 | 0.1 | 188 | 203 |
| Johnson City-Kingsport-Bristol, Tenn.-Va. MSA | 433,638 | 436,047 | 2,409 | 0.6 | 76 | 81 |
| Johnstown, Pa. MSA | 264,506 | 241,247 | –23,259 | –8.8 | 121 | 138 |
| Joplin, Mo. MSA | 127,513 | 134,910 | 7,397 | 5.8 | 209 | 207 |
| Kalamazoo, Mich. MSA | 212,378 | 223,411 | 11,033 | 5.2 | 136 | 146 |
| Kankakee, Ill. MSA | 102,926 | 96,255 | –6,671 | –6.5 | 246 | 264 |
| Kansas City, Mo.-Kans. MSA | 1,433,464 | 1,566,280 | 132,816 | 9.3 | 25 | 25 |
| Killeen-Temple, Tex. MSA | 214,587 | 255,301 | 40,714 | 19.0 | 135 | 131 |
| Knoxville, Tenn. MSA | 565,970 | 604,816 | 38,846 | 6.9 | 60 | 65 |
| Kokomo, Ind. MSA | 103,715 | 96,946 | –6,769 | –6.5 | 243 | 263 |
| La Crosse, Wis. MSA | 91,056 | 97,904 | 6,848 | 7.5 | 262 | 262 |
| Lafayette, La. MSA | 190,231 | 208,740 | 18,509 | 9.7 | 150 | 153 |
| Lafayette-West Lafayette, Ind. MSA | 121,702 | 130,598 | 8,896 | 7.3 | 215 | 218 |
| Lake Charles, La. MSA | 167,223 | 168,134 | 911 | 0.5 | 165 | 175 |
| Lakeland-Winter Haven, Fla. MSA | 321,652 | 405,382 | 83,730 | 26.0 | 101 | 87 |
| Lancaster, Pa. MSA | 362,346 | 422,822 | 60,476 | 16.7 | 91 | 85 |
| Lansing-East Lansing, Mich. MSA | 419,750 | 432,674 | 12,924 | 3.1 | 81 | 83 |
| Laredo, Tex. MSA | 99,258 | 133,239 | 33,981 | 34.2 | 252 | 208 |
| Las Cruces, N.Mex. MSA | 96,340 | 135,510 | 39,170 | 40.7 | 256 | 206 |
| Las Vegas, Nev. MSA | 463,087 | 741,459 | 278,372 | 60.1 | 72 | 53 |
| Lawrence, Kans. MSA | 67,640 | 81,798 | 14,158 | 20.9% | 282 | 275 |
| Lawton, Okla. MSA | 112,456 | 111,486 | –970 | –0.9 | 231 | 250 |
| Lewiston-Auburn, Maine MSA | 84,864 | 88,141 | 3,277 | 3.9 | 268 | 269 |
| Lexington-Fayette, Ky. MSA | 317,548 | 348,428 | 30,880 | 9.7 | 103 | 106 |
| Lima, Ohio MSA | 154,795 | 154,340 | –455 | –0.3 | 175 | 184 |
| Lincoln, Nebr. MSA | 192,884 | 213,641 | 20,757 | 10.8 | 147 | 151 |
| Little Rock-North Little Rock, Ark. MSA | 474,463 | 513,117 | 38,564 | 8.1 | 71 | 72 |
| Longview-Marshall, Tex. MSA | 151,760 | 162,431 | 10,671 | 7.0 | 176 | 176 |
| Los Angeles-Anaheim-Riverside, Calif., CMSA | 11,497,549 | 14,531,529 | 3,033,980 | 26.4 | 2 | 2 |
| Anaheim-Santa Ana, Calif. PMSA | 1,932,921 | 2,410,556 | 477,635 | 24.7 | N.A. | N.A. |
| Los Angeles-Long Beach, Calif. PMSA | 7,477,239 | 8,863,164 | 1,385,925 | 18.5 | N.A. | N.A. |
| Oxnard-Ventura, Calif. PMSA | 529,174 | 669,016 | 139,842 | 26.4 | N.A. | N.A. |
| Riverside-San Bernardino, Calif. PMSA | 1,558,215 | 2,588,793 | 1,030,578 | 66.1 | N.A. | N.A. |
| Louisville, Ky.-Ind. MSA | 956,426 | 952,662 | –3,764 | –0.4 | 38 | 43 |
| Lubbock, Tex. MSA | 211,651 | 222,636 | 10,985 | 5.2 | 137 | 147 |
| Lynchburg, Va. MSA | 141,289 | 142,199 | 910 | 0.6 | 187 | 200 |
| Macon-Warner Robins, Ga. MSA | 263,591 | 281,103 | 17,512 | 6.6 | 122 | 120 |
| Madison, Wis. MSA | 323,545 | 367,085 | 43,540 | 13.5 | 100 | 99 |
| Manchester, N.H. MSA | 129,305 | 147,809 | 18,504 | 14.3 | 205 | 193 |
| Mansfield, Ohio MSA | 131,205 | 126,137 | –5,068 | –3.9 | 202 | 223 |
| McAllen-Edinburg-Mission, Tex. MSA | 283,323 | 383,545 | 100,222 | 35.4 | 110 | 95 |
| Medford, Oreg. MSA | 132,456 | 146,389 | 13,933 | 10.5 | 200 | 196 |
| Melbourne-Titusville-Palm Bay, Fla. MSA | 272,959 | 398,978 | 126,019 | 46.2 | 116 | 89 |
| Memphis, Tenn.-Ark.-Miss. MSA | 913,472 | 981,747 | 68,275 | 7.5 | 40 | 41 |
| Merced, Calif. MSA | 134,558 | 178,403 | 43,845 | 32.6 | 198 | 168 |
| Miami-Fort Lauderdale, Fla. CMSA | 2,643,766 | 3,192,592 | 548,816 | 20.8 | 12 | 11 |
| Fort Lauderdale-Hollywood-Pompano Beach, Fla. PMSA | 1,018,257 | 1,255,488 | 237,231 | 23.3 | N.A. | N.A. |
| Miami-Hialeah, Fla. PMSA | 1,625,509 | 1,937,094 | 311,585 | 19.2 | N.A. | N.A. |
| Midland, Tex. MSA | 82,636 | 106,611 | 23,975 | 29.0 | 272 | 255 |
| Milwaukee-Racine, Wis. CMSA | 1,570,152 | 1,607,183 | 37,031 | 2.4 | 23 | 24 |
| Milwaukee, Wis. PMSA | 1,397,020 | 1,432,149 | 35,129 | 2.5 | N.A. | N.A. |
| Racine, Wis. PMSA | 173,132 | 175,034 | 1,902 | 1.1 | N.A. | N.A. |
| Minneapolis-St. Paul, Minn.-Wis. MSA | 2,137,133 | 2,464,124 | 326,991 | 15.3 | 17 | 16 |
| Mobile, Ala. MSA | 443,536 | 476,923 | 33,387 | 7.5 | 74 | 78 |
| Modesto, Calif. MSA | 265,900 | 370,522 | 104,622 | 39.3 | 120 | 97 |
| Monroe, La. MSA | 139,241 | 142,191 | 2,950 | 2.1 | 190 | 201 |
| Montgomery, Ala. MSA | 272,687 | 292,517 | 19,830 | 7.3 | 117 | 117 |
| Muncie, Ind. MSA | 128,587 | 119,659 | –8,928 | –6.9 | 206 | 234 |
| Muskegon, Mich. MSA | 157,589 | 158,983 | 1,394 | 0.9 | 173 | 181 |
| Naples, Fla. MSA | 85,971 | 152,099 | 66,128 | 76.9 | 266 | 186 |
| Nashville, Tenn. MSA | 850,505 | 985,026 | 134,521 | 15.8 | 45 | 40 |
| New Bedford, Mass. MSA | 166,699 | 175,641 | 8,942 | 5.4 | 166 | 170 |
| New Haven-Meriden, Conn. MSA | 500,642 | 530,180 | 29,718 | 5.9 | 68 | 69 |
| New London-Norwich, Conn.-R.I. MSA | 250,839 | 266,819 | 15,980 | 6.4 | 125 | 126 |
| New Orleans, La. MSA | 1,256,668 | 1,238,816 | –17,852 | –1.4 | 27 | 32 |
| New York-Northern New Jersey-Long Island, N.Y.-N.J.-Conn. CMSA | 17,539,532 | 18,087,251 | 547,719 | 3.1 | 1 | 1 |
| Bergen-Passaic, N.J. PMSA | 1,292,970 | 1,278,440 | –14,530 | –1.1 | N.A. | N.A. |
| Bridgeport-Milford, Conn. PMSA | 438,557 | 443,722 | 5,165 | 1.2 | N.A. | N.A. |
| Danbury, Conn. PMSA | 170,369 | 187,867 | 17,498 | 10.3 | N.A. | N.A. |
| Jersey City, N.J. PMSA | 556,972 | 553,099 | –3,873 | –0.7 | N.A. | N.A. |
| Middlesex-Somerset-Hunterdon, N.J. PMSA | 886,383 | 1,019,835 | 133,452 | 15.1 | N.A. | N.A. |
| Monmouth-Ocean, N.J. PMSA | 849,211 | 986,327 | 137,116 | 16.1 | N.A. | N.A. |
| Nassau-Suffolk, N.Y. PMSA | 2,605,813 | 2,609,212 | 3,399 | 0.1 | N.A. | N.A. |
| New York, N.Y. PMSA | 8,274,961 | 8,546,846 | 271,885 | 3.3 | N.A. | N.A. |
| Newark, N.J. PMSA | 1,879,147 | 1,824,321 | –54,826 | –2.9 | N.A. | N.A. |
| Norwalk, Conn. PMSA | 126,692 | 127,378 | 686 | 0.5 | N.A. | N.A. |
| Orange County, N.Y. PMSA | 259,603 | 307,647 | 48,044 | 18.5 | N.A. | N.A. |
| Stamford, Conn. PMSA | 198,854 | 202,557 | 3,703 | 1.9 | N.A. | N.A. |

| Metropolitan statistical area | 1980 | 1990 | Change 1980–90 Number | Percent | CMSA/MSA rank 1980 | 1990 |
|---|---|---|---|---|---|---|
| Norfolk-Virginia Beach-Newport News, Va. MSA | 1,160,311 | 1,396,107 | 235,796 | 20.3% | 31 | 28 |
| Ocala, Fla. MSA | 122,488 | 194,833 | 72,345 | 59.1 | 213 | 157 |
| Odessa, Tex. MSA | 115,374 | 118,934 | 3,560 | 3.1 | 224 | 236 |
| Oklahoma City, Okla. MSA | 860,969 | 958,839 | 97,870 | 11.4 | 43 | 42 |
| Olympia, Wash. MSA | 124,264 | 161,238 | 36,974 | 29.8 | 211 | 178 |
| Omaha, Nebr.-Iowa MSA | 585,122 | 618,262 | 33,140 | 5.7 | 57 | 63 |
| Orlando, Fla. MSA | 699,904 | 1,072,748 | 372,844 | 53.3 | 51 | 37 |
| Owensboro, Ky. MSA | 85,949 | 87,189 | 1,240 | 1.4 | 267 | 270 |
| Panama City, Fla. MSA | 97,740 | 126,994 | 29,254 | 29.9 | 254 | 222 |
| Parkersburg-Marietta, W.Va.-Ohio MSA | 157,893 | 149,169 | -8,724 | -5.5 | 172 | 192 |
| Pascagoula, Miss. MSA | 118,015 | 115,243 | -2,772 | -2.3 | 221 | 243 |
| Pensacola, Fla. MSA | 289,782 | 344,406 | 54,624 | 18.9 | 109 | 107 |
| Peoria, Ill. MSA | 365,864 | 339,172 | -26,692 | -7.3 | 90 | 108 |
| Philadelphia-Wilmington-Trenton, Pa.-N.J.-Del.-Md. CMSA | 5,680,509 | 5,899,345 | 218,836 | 3.9 | 4 | 5 |
| Philadelphia, Pa.-N.J. PMSA | 4,716,559 | 4,856,881 | 140,322 | 3.0 | N.A. | N.A. |
| Vineland-Millville-Bridgeton, N.J. PMSA | 132,866 | 138,053 | 5,187 | 3.9 | N.A. | N.A. |
| Trenton, N.J. PMSA | 307,863 | 325,824 | 17,961 | 5.8 | N.A. | N.A. |
| Wilmington, Del.-N.J.-Md. PMSA | 523,221 | 578,587 | 55,366 | 10.6 | N.A. | N.A. |
| Phoenix, Ariz. MSA | 1,509,175 | 2,122,101 | 612,926 | 40.6 | 24 | 20 |
| Pine Bluff, Ark. MSA | 90,718 | 85,487 | -5,231 | -5.8 | 263 | 272 |
| Pittsburgh-Beaver Valley, Pa. CMSA | 2,423,311 | 2,242,798 | -180,513 | -7.4 | 13 | 19 |
| Beaver County, Pa. PMSA | 204,441 | 186,093 | -18,348 | -9.0 | N.A. | N.A. |
| Pittsburgh, Pa.PMSA | 2,218,870 | 2,056,705 | -162,165 | -7.3 | N.A. | N.A. |
| Pittsfield, Mass. MSA | 83,490 | 79,250 | -4,240 | -5.1 | 271 | 277 |
| Portland, Maine MSA | 193,831 | 215,281 | 21,450 | 11.1 | 145 | 150 |
| Portland-Vancouver, Oreg.-Wash. CMSA | 1,297,977 | 1,477,895 | 179,918 | 13.9 | 26 | 27 |
| Portland, Oreg. PMSA | 1,105,750 | 1,239,842 | 134,092 | 12.1 | N.A. | N.A. |
| Vancouver, Wash. PMSA | 192,227 | 238,053 | 45,826 | 23.8 | N.A. | N.A. |
| Portsmouth-Dover-Rochester, N.H.-Maine MSA | 190,938 | 223,578 | 32,640 | 17.1 | 148 | 145 |
| Poughkeepsie, N.Y MSA | 245,055 | 259,462 | 14,407 | 5.9 | 129 | 130 |
| Providence-Pawtucket-Fall River, R.I.-Mass. CMSA | 1,083,139 | 1,141,510 | 58,371 | 5.4 | 33 | 35 |
| Fall River, Mass.-R.I. PMSA | 157,222 | 157,272 | 50 | 0.0 | N.A. | N.A. |
| Pawtucket-Woonsocket-Attleboro, R.I.-Mass. PMSA | 307,403 | 329,384 | 21,981 | 7.2 | N.A. | N.A. |
| Providence, R.I. PMSA | 618,514 | 654,854 | 36,340 | 5.9 | N.A. | N.A. |
| Provo-Orem, Utah MSA | 218,106 | 263,590 | 45,484 | 20.9 | 134 | 128 |
| Pueblo, Colo. MSA | 125,972 | 123,051 | -2,921 | -2.3 | 210 | 226 |
| Raleigh-Durham, N.C. MSA | 560,774 | 735,480 | 174,706 | 31.2 | 61 | 54 |
| Rapid City, S.Dak. MSA | 70,361 | 81,343 | 10,982 | 15.6 | 279 | 276 |
| Reading, Pa. MSA | 312,509 | 336,523 | 24,014 | 7.7 | 104 | 109 |
| Redding, Calif. MSA | 115,613 | 147,036 | 31,423 | 27.2 | 223 | 194 |
| Reno, Nev. MSA | 193,623 | 254,667 | 61,044 | 31.5 | 146 | 132 |
| Richland-Kennewick-Pasco, Wash. MSA | 144,469 | 150,033 | 5,564 | 3.9 | 184 | 189 |
| Richmond-Petersburg, Va. MSA | 761,311 | 865,640 | 104,329 | 13.7 | 48 | 49 |
| Roanoke, Va. MSA | 220,393 | 224,477 | 4,084 | 1.9 | 133 | 144 |
| Rochester, Minn. MSA | 92,006 | 106,470 | 14,464 | 15.7 | 261 | 256 |
| Rochester, N.Y. MSA | 971,230 | 1,002,410 | 31,180 | 3.2 | 37 | 39 |
| Rockford, Ill. MSA | 279,514 | 283,719 | 4,205 | 1.5 | 112 | 118 |
| Sacramento, Calif. MSA | 1,099,814 | 1,481,102 | 381,288 | 34.7 | 32 | 26 |
| Saginaw-Bay City-Midland, Mich. MSA | 421,518 | 399,230 | -22,198 | -5.3 | 79 | 88 |
| Salem, Oreg. MSA | 249,895 | 278,024 | 28,129 | 11.3 | 126 | 122 |
| Salinas-Seaside-Monterey, Calif. MSA | 290,444 | 355,660 | 65,216 | 22.5 | 108 | 103 |
| Salt Lake City-Ogden, Utah MSA | 910,222 | 1,072,227 | 162,005 | 17.8 | 41 | 38 |
| San Angelo, Tex. MSA | 84,784 | 98,458 | 13,674 | 16.1 | 269 | 261 |
| San Antonio, Tex. MSA | 1,072,125 | 1,302,099 | 229,974 | 21.5 | 34 | 30 |
| San Diego, Calif. MSA | 1,861,846 | 2,498,016 | 636,170 | 34.2 | 19 | 15 |
| San Francisco-Oakland-San Jose, Calif. CMSA | 5,367,900 | 6,253,311 | 885,411 | 16.5 | 5 | 4 |
| Oakland, Calif. PMSA | 1,761,710 | 2,082,914 | 321,204 | 18.2 | N.A. | N.A. |
| San Francisco, Calif. PMSA | 1,488,895 | 1,603,678 | 114,783 | 7.7% | N.A. | N.A. |
| San Jose, Calif. PMSA | 1,295,071 | 1,497,577 | 202,506 | 15.6 | N.A. | N.A. |
| Santa Cruz, Calif. PMSA | 188,141 | 229,734 | 41,593 | 22.1 | N.A. | N.A. |
| Santa Rosa-Petaluma, Calif. PMSA | 299,681 | 388,222 | 88,541 | 29.5 | N.A. | N.A. |
| Vallejo-Fairfield-Napa, Calif. PMSA | 334,402 | 451,186 | 116,784 | 24.9 | N.A. | N.A |
| Santa Barbara-Santa Maria-Lompoc, Calif. PMSA | 298,694 | 369,608 | 70,914 | 23.7 | 106 | 98 |
| Santa Fe, N.Mex. MSA | 93,118 | 117,043 | 23,925 | 25.7 | 260 | 240 |
| Sarasota, Fla. MSA | 202,251 | 277,776 | 75,525 | 37.3 | 143 | 123 |
| Savannah, Ga. MSA | 220,553 | 242,622 | 22,069 | 10.0 | 132 | 137 |
| Scranton-Wilkes-Barre, Pa. MSA | 728,796 | 734,175 | 5,379 | 0.7 | 49 | 55 |
| Seattle-Tacoma, Wash. CMSA | 2,093,285 | 2,559,164 | 465,879 | 22.3 | 18 | 14 |
| Seattle, Wash. PMSA | 1,607,618 | 1,972,961 | 365,343 | 22.7 | N.A. | N.A. |
| Tacoma, Wash. PMSA | 485,667 | 586,203 | 100,536 | 20.7 | N.A. | N.A. |
| Sharon, Pa. MSA | 128,299 | 121,003 | -7,296 | -5.7 | 208 | 231 |
| Sheboygan, Wis. MSA | 100,935 | 103,877 | 2,942 | 2.9 | 248 | 257 |
| Sherman-Denison, Tex. MSA | 89,796 | 95,021 | 5,225 | 5.8 | 264 | 267 |
| Shreveport, La. MSA | 333,158 | 334,341 | 1,183 | 0.4 | 98 | 111 |
| Sioux City, Iowa-Nebr. MSA | 117,457 | 115,018 | -2,439 | -2.1 | 222 | 244 |
| Sioux Falls, S.Dak. MSA | 109,435 | 123,809 | 14,374 | 13.1 | 239 | 224 |
| South Bend-Mishawaka, Ind. MSA | 241,617 | 247,052 | 5,435 | 2.2 | 130 | 135 |
| Spokane, Wash. MSA | 341,835 | 361,364 | 19,529 | 5.7 | 96 | 101 |
| Springfield, Ill. MSA | 187,770 | 189,550 | 1,780 | 0.9 | 151 | 161 |
| Springfield, Mass. MSA | 515,259 | 529,519 | 14,260 | 2.8 | 66 | 70 |
| Springfield, Mo. MSA | 207,704 | 240,593 | 32,889 | 15.8 | 139 | 139 |
| St. Cloud, Minn. MSA | 163,256 | 190,291 | 27,665 | 16.9 | 168 | 159 |
| St. Joseph, Mo. MSA | 87,888 | 83,803 | -4,805 | -5.5 | 265 | 274 |
| St. Louis, Mo.-Ill. MSA | 2,376,968 | 2,444,099 | 67,131 | 2.8 | 14 | 17 |
| State College, Pa. MSA | 112,760 | 123,786 | 11,026 | 9.8 | 230 | 225 |
| Steubenville-Weirton, Ohio-W.Va. MSA | 163,734 | 142,523 | -21,211 | -13.0 | 167 | 199 |
| Stockton, Calif. MSA | 347,342 | 480,628 | 133,286 | 38.4 | 94 | 76 |
| Syracuse, N.Y. MSA | 642,971 | 659,864 | 16,893 | 2.6 | 53 | 61 |
| Tallahassee, Fla. MSA | 190,329 | 233,598 | 43,269 | 22.7 | 149 | 142 |
| Tampa-St. Petersburg-Clearwater, Fla. MSA | 1,613,600 | 2,067,959 | 454,359 | 28.2 | 22 | 21 |
| Terre Haute, Ind. MSA | 137,247 | 130,812 | -6,435 | -4.7 | 194 | 216 |
| Texarkana, Tex.-Ark. MSA | 113,067 | 120,132 | 7,065 | 6.2 | 228 | 233 |
| Toledo, Ohio MSA | 616,864 | 614,128 | -2,736 | -0.4 | 55 | 64 |
| Topeka, Kans. MSA | 154,916 | 160,976 | 6,060 | 3.9 | 174 | 179 |
| Tucson, Ariz. MSA | 531,443 | 666,880 | 135,437 | 25.5 | 64 | 60 |
| Tulsa, Okla. MSA | 657,173 | 708,954 | 51,781 | 7.9 | 52 | 56 |
| Tuscaloosa, Ala. MSA | 137,541 | 150,522 | 12,981 | 9.5 | 192 | 188 |
| Tyler, Tex. MSA | 128,366 | 151,309 | 22,943 | 17.9 | 207 | 187 |
| Utica-Rome, N.Y. MSA | 320,180 | 316,633 | -3,547 | -1.1 | 102 | 113 |
| Victoria, Tex. MSA | 68,807 | 74,361 | 5,554 | 8.1 | 280 | 280 |
| Visalia-Tulare-Porterville, Calif. MSA | 245,738 | 311,921 | 66,183 | 26.9 | 128 | 116 |
| Waco, Tex. MSA | 170,755 | 189,123 | 18,368 | 10.8 | 162 | 162 |
| Washington, D.C.-Md.-Va. MSA | 3,250,921 | 3,923,574 | 672,653 | 20.7 | 8 | 8 |
| Waterbury, Conn. MSA | 204,968 | 221,629 | 16,661 | 8.1 | 141 | 149 |
| Waterloo-Cedar Falls, Iowa MSA | 162,781 | 146,611 | -16,170 | -9.9 | 170 | 195 |
| Wausau, Wis. MSA | 111,270 | 115,400 | 4,130 | 3.7 | 234 | 242 |
| West Palm Beach-Boca Raton-Delray Beach, Fla. MSA | 576,758 | 863,518 | 286,760 | 49.7 | 58 | 50 |
| Wheeling, W.Va.-Ohio MSA | 185,566 | 159,031 | -26,265 | -14.2 | 152 | 180 |
| Wichita Falls, Tex. MSA | 121,082 | 122,378 | 1,296 | 1.1 | 216 | 228 |
| Wichita, Kans. MSA | 442,401 | 485,270 | 42,869 | 9.7 | 75 | 75 |
| Williamsport, Pa. MSA | 118,416 | 118,710 | 294 | 0.2 | 220 | 237 |
| Wilmington, N.C. MSA | 103,471 | 120,284 | 16,813 | 16.2 | 244 | 232 |
| Worcester, Mass. MSA | 402,918 | 436,905 | 33,987 | 8.4 | 85 | 80 |
| Yakima, Wash. MSA | 172,508 | 188,823 | 16,315 | 9.5 | 159 | 163 |
| York, Pa. MSA | 381,255 | 417,848 | 36,593 | 9.6 | 87 | 86 |
| Youngstown-Warren, Ohio MSA | 531,350 | 492,619 | -38,731 | -7.3 | 65 | 74 |
| Yuba City, Calif. MSA | 101,979 | 122,643 | 20,664 | 20.3 | 247 | 227 |
| Yuma, Ariz. MSA | 76,205 | 106,895 | 30,690 | 40.3 | 276 | 254 |

**Note:** CMSA = consolidated metropolitan statistical area; MSA = metropolitan statistical area; N.A. = not applicable. **Source:** U.S. Bureau of the Census release, 1991.

## TOP 25 METROPOLITAN STATISTICAL AREAS BY POPULATION, 1980–90

| Metropolitan statistical area | Population 1980 | Population 1990 | Change 1980–90 Number | Change 1980–90 Percent | Metropolitan statistical area | Population 1980 | Population 1990 | Change 1980–90 Number | Change 1980–90 Percent |
|---|---|---|---|---|---|---|---|---|---|
| 1. New York–Northern New Jersey–Long Island, N.Y.–N.J.–Conn. CMSA | 17,539,532 | 18,087,251 | 547,719 | 3.1% | 12. Atlanta, Ga. MSA | 2,138,136 | 2,833,511 | 695,375 | 32.5% |
| | | | | | 13. Cleveland–Akron–Lorain, Ohio CMSA | 2,834,062 | 2,759,823 | −74,239 | −2.6 |
| 2. Los Angeles–Anaheim–Riverside, Calif. CMSA | 11,497,549 | 14,531,529 | 3,033,980 | 26.4 | 14. Seattle–Tacoma, Wash. CMSA | 2,093,285 | 2,559,164 | 465,879 | 22.3 |
| | | | | | 15. San Diego, Calif. MSA | 1,861,846 | 2,498,016 | 636,170 | 34.2 |
| 3. Chicago–Gary–Lake County, Ill.–Ind.–Wis. CMSA | 7,937,290 | 8,065,633 | 128,343 | 1.6 | 16. Minneapolis–St. Paul, Minn.–Wis. MSA | 2,137,133 | 2,464,124 | 326,991 | 15.3 |
| 4. San Francisco–Oakland–San Jose, Calif. CMSA | 5,367,900 | 6,253,311 | 885,411 | 16.5 | 17. St. Louis, Mo.–Ill. MSA | 2,376,968 | 2,444,099 | 67,131 | 2.8 |
| | | | | | 18. Baltimore, Md. MSA | 2,199,497 | 2,382,172 | 182,675 | 8.3 |
| 5. Philadelphia–Wilmington–Trenton, Pa.–N.J.–Del.–Md. CMSA | 5,680,509 | 5,899,345 | 218,836 | 3.9 | 19. Pittsburgh–Beaver Valley, Pa. CMSA | 2,423,311 | 2,242,798 | −180,513 | −7.4 |
| | | | | | 20. Phoenix, Ariz. MSA | 1,509,175 | 2,122,101 | 612,926 | 40.6 |
| 6. Detroit–Ann Arbor, Mich. CMSA | 4,752,764 | 4,665,236 | −87,528 | −1.8 | 21. Tampa–St. Petersburg–Clearwater, Fla. MSA | 1,613,600 | 2,067,959 | 454,359 | 28.2 |
| 7. Boston–Lawrence–Salem, Mass.–N.H. CMSA | 3,971,792 | 4,171,643 | 199,851 | 5.0 | 22. Denver–Boulder, Colo. | 1,618,461 | 1,848,319 | 229,858 | 14.2 |
| 8. Washington, D.C.–Md.–Va. MSA | 3,250,921 | 3,923,574 | 672,653 | 20.7 | 23. Cincinnati–Hamilton, Ohio–Ky.–Ind. CMSA | 1,660,257 | 1,744,124 | 83,867 | 5.1 |
| 9. Dallas–Fort Worth, Tex. CMSA | 2,930,568 | 3,885,415 | 954,847 | 32.6 | 24. Milwaukee–Racine, Wis. CMSA | 1,570,152 | 1,607,183 | 37,031 | 2.4 |
| 10. Houston–Galveston–Brazoria, Tex. CMSA | 3,099,942 | 3,711,043 | 611,101 | 19.7 | 25. Kansas City, Mo.–Kans. MSA | 1,433,464 | 1,566,280 | 132,816 | 9.3 |
| 11. Miami–Fort Lauderdale, Fla. CMSA | 2,643,766 | 3,192,592 | 548,816 | 20.8 | | | | | |

**Note:** CMSA = consolidated metropolitan statistical area; MSA = metropolitan statistical area. **Source:** U.S. Bureau of the Census release, 1991.

## 25 FASTEST-GROWING MSAs, 1980–90

| Metropolitan statistical area | Population 1980 | Population 1990 | Change 1980–90 Number | Change 1980–90 Percent |
|---|---|---|---|---|
| 1. Naples, Fla. MSA | 85,971 | 152,099 | 66,128 | 76.9% |
| 2. Fort Pierce, Fla. MSA | 151,196 | 251,071 | 99,875 | 66.1 |
| 3. Fort Myers–Cape Coral, Fla. MSA | 205,266 | 335,113 | 129,847 | 63.3 |
| 4. Las Vegas, Nev. MSA | 463,087 | 741,459 | 278,372 | 60.1 |
| 5. Ocala, Fla. MSA | 122,488 | 194,833 | 72,345 | 59.1 |
| 6. Orlando, Fla. MSA | 699,904 | 1,072,748 | 372,844 | 53.3 |
| 7. West Palm Beach–Boca Raton–Delray Beach, Fla. MSA | 576,758 | 863,518 | 286,760 | 49.7 |
| 8. Melbourne–Titusville–Palm Bay, Fla. MSA | 272,959 | 398,978 | 126,019 | 46.2 |
| 9. Austin, Tex. MSA | 536,688 | 781,572 | 244,884 | 45.6 |
| 10. Daytona Beach, Fla. MSA | 258,762 | 370,712 | 111,950 | 43.3 |
| 11. Bradenton, Fla. MSA | 148,445 | 211,707 | 63,262 | 42.6 |
| 12. Las Cruces, N.Mex. MSA | 96,340 | 135,510 | 39,170 | 40.7 |
| 13. Phoenix, Ariz. MSA | 1,509,175 | 2,122,101 | 612,926 | 40.6 |
| 14. Yuma, Ariz MSA | 76,205 | 106,895 | 30,690 | 40.3 |
| 15. Modesto, Calif. MSA | 265,900 | 370,522 | 104,622 | 39.3 |
| 16. Stockton, Calif. MSA | 347,342 | 480,628 | 133,286 | 38.4 |
| 17. Sarasota, Fla. MSA | 202,251 | 277,776 | 75,525 | 37.3 |
| 18. McAllen–Edinburg–Mission, Tex. MSA | 283,323 | 383,545 | 100,222 | 35.4 |
| 19. Bakersfield, Calif. MSA | 403,089 | 543,477 | 140,388 | 34.8 |
| 20. Sacramento, Calif. MSA | 1,099,814 | 1,481,102 | 381,288 | 34.7 |
| 21. San Diego, Calif. MSA | 1,861,846 | 2,498,016 | 636,170 | 34.2 |
| 22. Laredo, Tex. MSA | 99,258 | 133,239 | 33,981 | 34.2 |
| 23. Jacksonville, N.C. MSA | 112,784 | 149,838 | 37,054 | 32.9 |
| 24. Dallas–Fort Worth, Tex. CMSA | 2,930,568 | 3,885,415 | 954,847 | 32.6 |
| 25. Merced, Calif. MSA | 134,558 | 178,403 | 43,845 | 32.6 |

**Note:** CMSA = consolidated metropolitan statistical area; MSA = metropolitan statistical area. **Source:** U.S. Bureau of the Census release, 1991.

## 25 FASTEST-DECLINING MSAs, 1980–90

| Metropolitan statistical area | Population 1980 | Population 1990 | Change 1980–90 Number | Change 1980–90 Percent |
|---|---|---|---|---|
| 1. Casper, Wyo. MSA | 71,856 | 61,226 | −10,630 | −14.8% |
| 2. Wheeling, W.Va.–Ohio MSA | 185,566 | 159,031 | −26,265 | −14.2 |
| 3. Steubenville–Weirton, Ohio–W.Va. MSA | 163,734 | 142,523 | −21,211 | −13.0 |
| 4. Decatur, Ill. MSA | 131,375 | 117,206 | −14,169 | −10.8 |
| 5. Duluth, Minn.–Wis. MSA | 266,650 | 239,971 | −26,679 | −10.0 |
| 6. Waterloo–Cedar Falls, Iowa MSA | 162,781 | 146,611 | −16,170 | −9.9 |
| 7. Enid, Okla. MSA | 62,820 | 56,735 | −6,085 | −9.7 |
| 8. Davenport–Rock Island–Moline, Iowa–Ill. MSA | 384,749 | 350,861 | −33,888 | −8.8 |
| 9. Johnstown, Pa. MSA | 264,506 | 241,247 | −23,259 | −8.8 |
| 10. Dubuque, Iowa MSA | 93,745 | 86,403 | −7,342 | −7.8 |
| 11. Pittsburgh–Beaver Valley, Pa. CMSA | 2,423,311 | 2,242,798 | −180,513 | −7.4 |
| 12. Youngstown–Warren, Ohio MSA | 531,350 | 492,619 | −38,731 | −7.3 |
| 13. Peoria, Ill. MSA | 365,864 | 339,172 | −26,692 | −7.3 |
| 14. Huntington–Ashland, W.Va.–Ky.–Ohio MSA | 336,410 | 312,529 | −23,881 | −7.1 |
| 15. Charleston, W.Va. MSA | 269,595 | 250,454 | −19,141 | −7.1 |
| 16. Muncie, Ind. MSA | 128,587 | 119,659 | −8,928 | −6.9 |
| 17. Kokomo, Ind. MSA | 103,715 | 96,946 | −6,769 | −6.5 |
| 18. Kankakee, Ill. MSA | 102,926 | 96,255 | −6,671 | −6.5 |
| 19. Anderson, Ind. MSA | 139,336 | 130,669 | −8,667 | −6.2 |
| 20. Benton Harbor, Mich. MSA | 171,276 | 161,378 | −9,898 | −5.8 |
| 21. Pine Bluff, Ark. MSA | 90,718 | 85,487 | −5,231 | −5.8 |
| 22. Sharon, Pa. MSA | 128,299 | 121,003 | −7,296 | −5.7 |
| 23. Cumberland, Md.–W.Va. | 107,782 | 101,643 | −6,139 | −5.7 |
| 24. Parkersburg–Marietta, W.Va.–Ohio MSA | 157,893 | 149,169 | −8,724 | −5.5 |
| 25. St. Joseph, Mo. MSA | 87,888 | 83,803 | −4,805 | −5.5 |

**Note:** CMSA = consolidated metropolitan statistical area; MSA = metropolitan statistical area. **Source:** U.S. Bureau of the Census release, 1991.

## PERCENTAGE OF POPULATION IN METROPOLITAN AREAS, 1987

| Most metropolitan states | Percent | Least metropolitan states | Percent |
|---|---|---|---|
| New Jersey | 100.0% | Idaho | 19.6% |
| California | 95.7 | Vermont | 23.1 |
| Maryland | 92.9 | Montana | 24.2 |
| Connecticut | 92.6 | South Dakota | 28.7 |
| Rhode Island | 92.6 | Wyoming | 29.0 |
| Florida | 90.8 | Mississippi | 30.3 |
| Massachusetts | 90.7 | Maine | 36.1 |
| New York | 90.5 | West Virginia | 36.3 |
| Pennsylvania | 84.7 | North Dakota | 38.0 |
| Nevada | 82.7 | Arkansas | 39.5 |

**Note:** Shows 10 most- and 10 least-metropolitan states. **Source:** U.S. Bureau of the Census, *Current Population Reports, Patterns of Metropolitan Area and County Population Growth, 1980 to 1987* (1990).

## COUNTIES IN AMERICA

In 1990 there were 3,141 counties in the United States. While 50% of Americans live in cities, almost every American lives in a county. Counties were originally the creation of state governments, which saw them as the local arm of state authority, with special responsibility for rural areas. Counties were intended more for the administrative convenience of the state than to meet the immediate needs of county residents and were not designed to have the intimate relationship with or understanding of the needs of localities theoretically characteristic of municipalities. But most states have loosened the reins on county governments in recent years, giving them more authority to meet the needs of population centers that have pushed beyond municipal limits. (Note that in Louisiana, counties are called parishes, and in Alaska they are known as boroughs. The five boroughs of New York City are counties.)

### County Government Finances

**Expenditures** County governments spent $119.3 billion on revenues of $119.8 billion in fiscal year 1988–89. Among the major programs counties spent their money on were public welfare, education, health, and transportation. Counties also have responsibilities involving law enforcement, jails and detention facilities, electoral and judicial administration, public-record-keeping, tax assessment and collection, issuance of licenses, building and upkeep of roads and highways, and programs to promote agriculture and rural areas, public health, and welfare. Many counties also run community colleges.

**Revenues** The primary source of funds for counties in 1988–89 was intergovernmental aid, monies received from other governments mostly in the form of grants or shared revenues. Intergovernmental aid accounted for $41.6 billion, or 36.1% of all county revenues. The second-largest source of county funds was property taxes, which made up $32.2 billion, or

## THE 50 LARGEST U.S. COUNTIES, 1990

| Rank/County | Population 1990 | Population 1980 | Change 1980–90 Number | Change 1980–90 Percent | Pop. Rank 1980 |
|---|---|---|---|---|---|
| 1. Los Angeles County, Calif. | 8,863,164 | 7,477,238 | 1,385,926 | 18.5% | 1 |
| 2. Cook County, Ill. | 5,105,067 | 5,253,628 | −148,561 | −2.8 | 2 |
| 3. Harris County, Tex. | 2,818,199 | 2,409,547 | 408,652 | 17.0 | 3 |
| 4. San Diego County, Calif. | 2,498,016 | 1,861,846 | 636,170 | 34.2 | 8 |
| 5. Orange County, Calif. | 2,410,556 | 1,932,921 | 477,635 | 24.7 | 6 |
| 6. Kings County, N.Y. | 2,300,664 | 2,231,028 | 69,636 | 3.1 | 5 |
| 7. Maricopa County, Ariz. | 2,122,101 | 1,509,175 | 612,926 | 40.6 | 12 |
| 8. Wayne County, Mich. | 2,111,687 | 2,337,843 | −226,156 | −9.7 | 4 |
| 9. Queens County, N.Y. | 1,951,598 | 1,891,325 | 60,273 | 3.2 | 7 |
| 10. Dade County, Fla. | 1,937,094 | 1,625,509 | 311,585 | 19.2 | 10 |
| 11. Dallas County, Tex. | 1,852,810 | 1,556,419 | 296,391 | 19.0 | 11 |
| 12. Philadelphia County, Pa. | 1,585,577 | 1,688,210 | −102,633 | −6.1 | 9 |
| 13. King County, Wash. | 1,507,319 | 1,269,898 | 237,421 | 18.7 | 20 |
| 14. Santa Clara County, Calif. | 1,497,577 | 1,295,071 | 202,506 | 15.6 | 18 |
| 15. New York County, N.Y. | 1,487,536 | 1,428,285 | 59,251 | 4.1 | 15 |
| 16. San Bernardino County, Calif. | 1,418,380 | 895,016 | 523,364 | 58.5 | 30 |
| 17. Cuyahoga County, Ohio | 1,412,140 | 1,498,400 | −86,260 | −5.8 | 13 |
| 18. Middlesex County, Mass. | 1,398,468 | 1,367,034 | 31,434 | 2.3 | 16 |
| 19. Allegheny County, Pa. | 1,336,449 | 1,450,195 | −113,746 | −7.8 | 14 |
| 20. Suffolk County, N.Y. | 1,321,864 | 1,284,231 | 37,633 | 2.9 | 19 |
| 21. Nassau County, N.Y. | 1,287,348 | 1,321,582 | −34,234 | −2.6 | 17 |
| 22. Alameda County, Calif. | 1,279,182 | 1,105,379 | 173,803 | 15.7 | 22 |
| 23. Broward County, Fla. | 1,255,488 | 1,018,257 | 237,231 | 23.3 | 23 |
| 24. Bronx County, N.Y. | 1,203,789 | 1,168,972 | 34,817 | 3.0 | 21 |
| 25. Bexar County, Tex. | 1,185,394 | 988,971 | 196,423 | 19.9 | 26 |
| 26. Riverside County, Calif. | 1,170,413 | 663,199 | 507,214 | 76.5 | 52 |
| 27. Tarrant County, Tex. | 1,170,103 | 860,880 | 309,223 | 35.9 | 34 |
| 28. Oakland County, Mich. | 1,083,592 | 1,011,793 | 71,799 | 7.1 | 25 |
| 29. Sacramento County, Calif. | 1,041,219 | 783,381 | 257,838 | 32.9 | 40 |
| 30. Hennepin County, Minn. | 1,032,431 | 941,411 | 91,020 | 9.7 | 29 |
| 31. St. Louis County, Mo. | 993,529 | 974,180 | 19,349 | 2.0 | 27 |
| 32. Erie County, N.Y. | 968,532 | 1,015,472 | −46,940 | −4.6 | 24 |
| 33. Franklin County, Ohio | 961,437 | 869,126 | 92,311 | 10.6 | 32 |
| 34. Milwaukee County, Wis. | 959,275 | 964,988 | −5,713 | −0.6 | 28 |
| 35. Westchester County, N.Y. | 874,866 | 866,599 | 8,267 | 1.0 | 33 |
| 36. Hamilton County, Ohio | 866,228 | 873,203 | −6,975 | −0.8 | 31 |
| 37. Palm Beach County, Fla. | 863,518 | 576,758 | 286,760 | 49.7 | 70 |
| 38. Hartford County, Conn. | 851,783 | 807,766 | 44,017 | 5.4 | 37 |
| 39. Pinellas County, Fla. | 851,659 | 728,531 | 123,128 | 16.9 | 45 |
| 40. Honolulu County, Hawaii | 836,231 | 762,565 | 73,666 | 9.7 | 43 |
| 41. Hillsborough County, Fla. | 834,054 | 646,939 | 187,115 | 28.9 | 57 |
| 42. Fairfield County, Conn. | 827,645 | 807,143 | 20,502 | 2.5 | 38 |
| 43. Shelby County, Tenn. | 826,330 | 777,113 | 49,217 | 6.3 | 41 |
| 44. Bergen County, N.J. | 825,380 | 845,385 | −20,005 | −2.4 | 36 |
| 45. Fairfax County, Va. | 818,584 | 595,754 | 222,830 | 37.4 | 66 |
| 46. New Haven County, Conn. | 804,219 | 761,325 | 42,894 | 5.6 | 44 |
| 47. Contra Costa County, Calif. | 803,732 | 656,331 | 147,401 | 22.5 | 54 |
| 48. Marion County, Ind. | 797,159 | 765,233 | 31,926 | 4.2 | 42 |
| 49. DuPage County, Ill. | 781,666 | 658,858 | 122,808 | 18.6 | 53 |
| 50. Essex County, N.J. | 778,206 | 851,304 | −73,098 | −8.6 | 35 |

**Source:** U.S. Bureau of the Census release, 1991.

28% of the total. Sales, income, and other taxes contributed 10.4% to county coffers.

Most of the intergovernmental aid received by counties was contributed by state governments, which accounted for $37.4 billion, or 90% of all intergovernmental aid. In 1986 the Reagan administration ended the Federal General Revenue Sharing program, established in 1972 to distribute funds directly to county governments to meet locally identified needs. The end of federal revenue sharing and cut-

backs in other federal programs aiding local governments have forced state governments to find new sources of funds for local governments to continue providing needed services. This has been done mostly through increases in direct financial assistance to the counties by the states and by the states granting counties more authority to raise local taxes.

According to a study by the National Association of Counties, 39% of the country's 443 counties with populations greater than 100,000

## SUMMARY OF COUNTY GOVERNMENT FINANCES, 1988–89

| Item | Amount 1988–89 (millions) | Percent distri- bution 1988–89 | Percent change over 1987–88 | Item | Amount 1988–89 (millions) | Percent distri- bution 1988–89 | Percent change over 1987–88 |
|---|---|---|---|---|---|---|---|
| **REVENUES** | | | | Own | $ 11,284 | 9.8% | 11.1% |
| **Revenue, total** | **$119,836** | **—** | **8.7%** | Other | 510 | 0.4 | -2.9 |
| General revenue | $115,459 | 100.0% | 8.9% | Health | 7,161 | 6.2 | 11.7 |
| Intergovernmental revenue | 41,647 | 36.1 | 7.8 | Transportation: | | | |
| From state governments | 37,401 | 32.4 | 8.7 | Highways | 8,872 | 7.7 | 5.6 |
| General local government support | 4,424 | 3.8 | 12.6 | Air transportation | 1,243 | 1.1 | 22.0 |
| From federal government | 2,546 | 2.2 | -3.7 | Parking facilities | 60 | 0.1 | 66.7 |
| From local governments | 1,700 | 1.5 | 7.7 | Water transport and terminals | 72 | 0.1 | 5.9 |
| General revenue from own sources | 73,812 | 63.9 | 9.5 | Transit subsidies | 579 | 0.5 | 15.8 |
| Taxes | 44,196 | 38.3 | 8.9 | Public safety: | | | |
| Property | 32,232 | 27.9 | 8.6 | Police protection | 6,082 | 5.3 | 9.3 |
| General sales | 6,884 | 6.0 | 8.6 | Fire protection | 1,456 | 1.3 | 16.4 |
| Selective sales | 1,494 | 1.3 | 9.6 | Correction | 5,695 | 4.9 | 8.7 |
| Income | 1,303 | 1.1 | 8.9 | Protective inspection and regulation | 367 | 0.3 | 9.9 |
| Other | 2,283 | 2.0 | 14.2 | Environment and housing: | | | |
| Charges and miscellaneous | 29,617 | 25.7 | 10.3 | Sewerage | 1,945 | 1.7 | 8.0 |
| Current charges | 17,831 | 15.4 | 10.4 | Solid waste management | 1,763 | 1.5 | 19.0 |
| Sewerage | 1,071 | 0.9 | 3.6 | Parks and recreation | 2,207 | 1.9 | 13.4 |
| Hospitals | 8,214 | 7.1 | 11.0 | Housing and community development | 963 | 0.8 | 12.8 |
| Education | 899 | 0.8 | 9.4 | Natural resources | 1,119 | 1.0 | 0.9 |
| Interest earnings | 8,155 | 7.1 | 13.4 | Government administration: | | | |
| Special assessments | 605 | 0.5 | -9.0 | Financial administration | 3,213 | 2.8 | 8.6 |
| Sale of property | 165 | 0.1 | 39.8 | Judicial and legal | 5,686 | 4.9 | 13.7 |
| Other and unallocable | 2,859 | 2.5 | 4.8 | General public buildings | 1,927 | 1.7 | 10.4 |
| | | | | Other | 2,502 | 2.2 | 8.3 |
| Utility revenue | 1,412 | 100.0 | 10.2 | Interest on general debt | 7,502 | 6.5 | 4.6 |
| Electric power | 115 | 8.1 | 5.5 | General expenditure not elsewhere classified | 8,802 | 7.6 | 5.9 |
| Water supply | 1,151 | 81.5 | 11.4 | Utility expenditure | 2,601 | 100.0 | 9.5 |
| Transit system | 133 | 9.4 | 5.6 | Electric power | 139 | 5.3 | 3.0 |
| Gas supply | 14 | 1.0 | 7.7 | Water supply | 1,786 | 68.7 | 16.1 |
| Liquor store revenue | 252 | — | 0.4 | Transit system | 661 | 25.4 | -3.9 |
| Employment retirement | 2,713 | — | 2.7 | Gas supply | 15 | 0.6 | — |
| | | | | Liquor store expenditure | 219 | — | 0.9 |
| **EXPENDITURE** | | | | Employee retirement | 1,342 | — | 6.9 |
| **Expenditure, total** | **$119,274** | **100.0%** | **9.1%** | | | | |
| Expenditure by function: | | | | Exhibit: Salaries and wages | $43,461 | 36.4% | 8.6% |
| General expenditure | $115,112 | 100.0% | 9.2% | | | | |
| Intergovernmental expenditure | 5,311 | 4.6 | 4.5 | **INDEBTEDNESS AND DEBT TRANSACTIONS** | | | |
| Direct general expenditure | 109,801 | 95.4 | 9.4 | **Debt outstanding at end of fiscal year** | **$110,036** | **100.0%** | **7.0%** |
| Capital outlay | 12,014 | 10.4 | 10.7 | Long-term debt outstanding | 107,174 | 97.4 | 6.9 |
| Other | 97,787 | 84.9 | 9.2 | Short-term debt outstanding | 2,862 | 2.6 | 10.9 |
| Education services: | | | | | | | |
| Education | 16,677 | 14.5 | 9.5 | Long-term debt issued | 13,446 | 100.0 | 10.3 |
| Libraries | 1,039 | 0.9 | 7.9 | Long-term debt retired | 7,985 | 100.0 | -12.1 |
| Social services and income maintenance: | | | | | | | |
| Public welfare | 16,387 | 14.2 | 8.7 | **CASH AND SECURITY HOLDINGS** | | | |
| Cash assistance payments | 7,448 | 6.5 | 8.3 | **Total, end of fiscal year** | **$126,844** | **100.0%** | **6.6%** |
| Medical vendor payments | 652 | 0.6 | 8.8 | Employment retirement | 25,310 | 20.0 | 8.4 |
| Other | 8,287 | 7.2 | 9.1 | Other | 101,534 | 80.0 | 6.2 |
| Hospitals | 11,793 | 10.2 | 10.4 | | | | |

**Source:** U.S. Bureau of the Census, *County Government Finances: 1988–89* (1991).

faced budget deficits in 1991. The average budget shortfall was $8.3 mil. with the worst hit being Philadelphia Co. ($219 million), New York Co. (Manhattan: $100 mil.), and bordering Washington, D.C., Maryland's Montgomery Co. ($85 million), and Prince Georges Co. ($80 million). The worst hit states were California, where 74% of all counties reported a deficit, Maryland (73%), New York (73%), Virginia (61%), North Carolina (44%), and Ohio (28%).

From 1972 to 1986, local governments received annual payments of as much as $6.8 billion from the federal government through the General Revenue Sharing program. Of this, approximately 30% was allocated to counties. As a consequence of fiscal federalism—a cornerstone of "Reaganomics"—general revenue sharing was eliminated in 1986. This resulted in a drop in federal assistance as a percentage of total county revenues of 73% between 1980 and 1986. This coincided with rapid population growth in the counties and the necessity for developing costly infrastructure and services such as public health and safety, coupled with a number of unfunded states and federal mandates.

While state aid to counties increased 15.5% over the period 1978-86, revenues from their own sources increased 52%. Most of this increase came from real property tax, both from increased tax revenues as property values went up and from hikes in property tax rates.

# THE AMERICAN PEOPLE TODAY

The United States is the fourth most populous nation in the world, ranking behind only China, India, and the Soviet Union. According to the U.S. Census Bureau, on March 6, 1990, the resident population of the United States reached the 250 million mark, more than three times the 1900 figure of 76 million, about double what it was in 1930, and almost 100 million more than the 1950 total. The Census Bureau predicts that this kind of rapid growth, based mainly as it was on high birth rates and, during the first two decades of the century, extraordinarily high immigration rates, cannot occur during the next century. In fact the underlying shifts in social behavior that will cause dramatic changes in the nature of the population have been in place for 20 years or so, just at the end of a most prolific period of population expansion.

Between 1946 and 1964, just over 75 million babies were born in America, a demographic achievement so noteworthy that those born during this time have their own collective designation, the "Baby Boom generation." During these years the crude birth rate soared to as high as 24 live births (per 1,000 population) in some years, compared to 20 or so in the years before the war; fertility rates, too, reached exceptional levels, ranging from 101 to 121 (per 1,000 women ages 15–44), as compared with an average of about 75 in earlier years. As a result the population grew at an annual rate of between 1.4% and 1.8%.

Quite remarkably, however, this population burst came to a sudden unexpected halt, so sudden that by 1968 the population growth had sunk to 1%, the birth rate to under 18, and fertility rates to about 85, levels that have sunk much farther since. As a result projected population growth over the next few decades is extremely low: 7.1% for the 1990s and 5.3% for the first decade of the new century. By way of comparison, between 1950 and 1960, the population grew 19%.

That period of unparalleled growth has affected many aspects of daily life and will continue to do so for another 50 years. Demographers sometimes refer to the Baby Boomers, somewhat inelegantly perhaps, as the "Pig in the Python" in order to explain how this group has continued to distort the normal contours of the general body of the population. During the fifties their numbers required great capital outlays for new schools and later for expanding colleges and universities. In the seventies they jammed the labor market, causing higher unemployment rates, but helped the economy by increasing consumption and expanding the housing market. After the turn of the century, the Baby Boom generation will begin to enter the retirement years, and even here they will cause a strain on existing structures. What will happen is that the ratio of people working—those born during the 1970s and 1980s, now being called the Baby Bust—to those retired

will shrink dramatically. Today that ratio is 5-1, but by 2020 or so, it will be 2.5-1.

If the Baby Boomers and those in much smaller numbers who followed them represent, demographically speaking, the most significant group among the American people, it is the immigrant group that has caused the most interest in recent years. Because their numbers have increased greatly since the 1960s, many see them as the key to preventing future population decline, as current U.S. birth and fertility rates stabilize at a very low level. In recent years immigration has accounted for over 25% of the nation's growth. Over the last 20 years, the origins of most immigrants have been Asian and Latin American nations, so the ethnic composition of the American people is clearly going to change and become even more diverse than today.

In the pages that follow, all of these matters are taken up—fertility, race, immigration—to create a statistical portrait of the population both past and present, with a glimpse at the future as well:

## THE 1990 CENSUS

Article I, section 2 of the U.S. Constitution requires Congress to undertake a census of the population every 10 years for the purpose of apportioning seats in the House of Representatives. Today the decennial census is also used to apportion federal and state funds totaling as much as $100 billion a year, so it is vitally important to local governments and individuals throughout the country. City and county planners and health care administrators, as well as the entire marketing and advertising industries, are strongly dependent on census data for their day-to-day operations. So it's not surprising that the 1990 census, officially taken on Apr. 1, was the largest undertaking of its kind in our history. The first results—state population figures—were released in December 1990, as required by law.

### Highlights of the Census

**Population growth** Since the 1980 census, the resident population of the United States increased by 22,164,873, from 226,545,805 to 248,709,873—a growth rate of 9.8%, the second lowest in census history. Only the Depression decade of the 1930s was lower (7.3%), while by contrast the Baby Boom era of the 1950s reached a growth rate of 18.5%. (Between 1790 and 1910 the rate was never less than 21%.)

**Regional growth** During the 1980s, the South and the West together accounted for 89% of national population growth, about the same as they did in the 1970s. As of 1990 their combined share of the U.S. population was 55.6%, up from 52.3% in 1980 and 48.0% in 1970.

The West had the highest growth rate (22.3%) in the 1980s, a slight decline from the 1970s (23.9%) but still more than twice the national rate. The South's growth rate fell sharply to 13.4% from 20.0%, but was still significantly higher than the national rate. Growth rates rose in the Northeast (from 0.2% to 3.4%), but fell in the Midwest (from 4.0% to 1.4%).

**State population growth** For the first time in census history, only three states accounted for over half the national population growth. The combined increases in California (6.1 million), Florida (3.2 million), and Texas (2.8 million) totaled 12.0 million, or 54%, of the 22.2 million national population increase.

California continued to grow at record levels during the 1980s, so that by 1990 12.0% of all Americans lived there. In addition its numerical growth of 6.1 million and its 26% share of national population growth are unprecedented in census history.

The five fastest growing states during the 1980–90 decade were Nevada (50.1% increase), Alaska (36.9%), Arizona (34.8%), Florida (32.7%), and California (25.7%). Over the last 50 years Arizona, Florida, and Nevada have been on every such list while Alaska and California only missed once.

Only two states in the Northeast had growth rates higher than the national average, New Hampshire (20.5%) and Vermont (10.0%); none of the Midwest states did. Four states lost population during the eighties: West Virginia (–8.0%), Iowa (–4.7%), Wyoming (–3.4%), and North Dakota (–2.1%).

**Population growth in metropolitan areas** The 1990 census revealed that 77.5% of all U.S. residents (192,725,741) lived in one of the 284 metropolitan areas in the U.S., an increase of 11.6%, or more than 20 million. The number of 1-million-plus metropolitan areas rose from 35 to 39, and the population in these areas rose to 124.8 million, or 50.2% of the total U.S. population. About 90% of population growth in the 1980s took place in metropolitan areas.

A total of 46 metropolitan areas grew by more than 25% (Florida dominated the list with nine of the 11 top areas). The Los Angeles–Anaheim–Riverside metropolitan area gained about 3 million people in the 1980s, by far the largest numerical increase of any area (in fact the increase alone was greater than the total population of 272 metropolitan areas).

The population living outside metropolitan areas totaled 55,984,132, an increase of only 2.1 million (3.9%) over the decade.

**Congressional representation** As a result of population changes between 1980 and 1990 eight states will have more representatives and 13 will have fewer when the 103rd Congress convenes in January 1993.

## U.S. RESIDENT POPULATION AND POPULATION CHANGE, BY STATE, 1980–90

| State | 1980 Population | Rank | 1990 Population | Rank | Number change | Percent change |
|---|---|---|---|---|---|---|
| United States | 226,545,805 | — | 248,709,873 | — | 22,165,068 | 9.8% |
| Alabama | 3,893,888 | (22) | 4,040,587 | (22) | 146,699 | 3.8 |
| Alaska | 401,851 | (50) | 550,043 | (49) | 148,192 | 36.9 |
| Arizona | 2,718,215 | (29) | 3,665,228 | (24) | 947,013 | 34.8 |
| Arkansas | 2,286,435 | (33) | 2,350,725 | (33) | 64,290 | 2.8 |
| California | 23,667,902 | (1) | 29,760,021 | (1) | 6,092,119 | 25.7 |
| Colorado | 2,889,964 | (28) | 3,294,394 | (26) | 404,430 | 14.0 |
| Connecticut | 3,107,576 | (25) | 3,287,116 | (27) | 179,540 | 5.8 |
| Delaware | 594,338 | (47) | 666,168 | (46) | 71,830 | 12.1 |
| Dist. of Columbia[1] | 638,333 | — | 606,900 | — | −31,433 | −4.9 |
| Florida | 9,746,324 | (7) | 12,937,926 | (4) | 3,191,602 | 32.7 |
| Georgia | 5,463,105 | (13) | 6,478,216 | (11) | 1,015,111 | 18.6 |
| Hawaii | 964,691 | (39) | 1,108,229 | (41) | 143,538 | 14.9 |
| Idaho | 943,935 | (41) | 1,006,749 | (42) | 62,814 | 6.7 |
| Illinois | 11,426,518 | (5) | 11,430,602 | (6) | 4,084 | 0.0 |
| Indiana | 5,490,224 | (12) | 5,544,159 | (14) | 53,935 | 1.0 |
| Iowa | 2,913,808 | (27) | 2,776,755 | (30) | −137,053 | −4.7 |
| Kansas | 2,363,679 | (32) | 2,477,574 | (32) | 113,895 | 4.8 |
| Kentucky | 3,660,777 | (23) | 3,685,296 | (23) | 24,519 | 0.7 |
| Louisiana | 4,205,900 | (19) | 4,219,973 | (21) | 14,073 | 0.3 |
| Maine | 1,124,660 | (38) | 1,227,928 | (38) | 103,268 | 9.2 |
| Maryland | 4,216,975 | (18) | 4,781,468 | (19) | 564,493 | 13.4 |
| Massachusetts | 5,737,037 | (11) | 6,016,425 | (13) | 279,388 | 4.9 |
| Michigan | 9,262,078 | (8) | 9,295,297 | (8) | 33,219 | 0.4 |
| Minnesota | 4,075,970 | (21) | 4,375,099 | (20) | 299,129 | 7.3 |
| Mississippi | 2,520,638 | (31) | 2,573,216 | (31) | 52,578 | 2.1 |
| Missouri | 4,916,686 | (15) | 5,117,073 | (15) | 200,387 | 4.1% |
| Montana | 786,690 | (44) | 799,065 | (44) | 12,375 | 1.6 |
| Nebraska | 1,569,825 | (35) | 1,578,385 | (36) | 8,560 | 0.5 |
| Nevada | 800,493 | (43) | 1,201,833 | (39) | 401,340 | 50.1 |
| New Hampshire | 920,610 | (42) | 1,109,252 | (40) | 188,642 | 20.5 |
| New Jersey | 7,364,823 | (9) | 7,730,188 | (9) | 365,365 | 5.0 |
| New Mexico | 1,302,894 | (37) | 1,515,069 | (37) | 212,175 | 16.3 |
| New York | 17,558,072 | (2) | 17,990,455 | (2) | 432,383 | 2.5 |
| North Carolina | 5,881,766 | (10) | 6,628,637 | (10) | 746,871 | 12.7 |
| North Dakota | 652,717 | (46) | 638,800 | (47) | −13,917 | −2.1 |
| Ohio | 10,797,630 | (6) | 10,847,115 | (7) | 49,485 | 0.5 |
| Oklahoma | 3,025,290 | (26) | 3,145,585 | (28) | 120,295 | 4.0 |
| Oregon | 2,633,105 | (30) | 2,842,321 | (29) | 209,216 | 7.9 |
| Pennsylvania | 11,863,895 | (4) | 11,881,643 | (5) | 17,748 | 0.1 |
| Rhode Island | 947,154 | (40) | 1,003,464 | (43) | 56,310 | 5.9 |
| South Carolina | 3,121,820 | (24) | 3,486,703 | (25) | 364,883 | 11.7 |
| South Dakota | 690,768 | (45) | 696,004 | (45) | 5,236 | 0.8 |
| Tennessee | 4,591,120 | (17) | 4,877,185 | (17) | 286,065 | 6.2 |
| Texas | 14,229,191 | (3) | 16,986,510 | (3) | 2,757,319 | 19.4 |
| Utah | 1,461,037 | (36) | 1,722,850 | (35) | 261,813 | 17.9 |
| Vermont | 511,456 | (48) | 562,758 | (48) | 51,302 | 10.0 |
| Virginia | 5,346,818 | (14) | 6,187,358 | (12) | 840,540 | 15.7 |
| Washington | 4,132,156 | (20) | 4,866,692 | (18) | 734,536 | 17.8 |
| West Virginia | 1,949,644 | (34) | 1,793,477 | (34) | −156,167 | −8.0 |
| Wisconsin | 4,705,767 | (16) | 4,891,769 | (16) | 186,002 | 4.0 |
| Wyoming | 469,557 | (49) | 453,588 | (50) | −15,969 | −3.4 |

1. If the District of Columbia were included with the states it would have ranked 48th in 1990 and 47th in 1980. **Source:** U.S. Bureau of the Census release, 1991.

| Congressional seats gained | | | |
|---|---|---|---|
| California | 7 | Arizona | 1 |
| Florida | 4 | Georgia | 1 |
| Texas | 3 | North Carolina | 1 |
| Washington | 1 | Virginia | 1 |

| Congressional seats lost | | | |
|---|---|---|---|
| New York | −3 | Kentucky | −1 |
| Illinois | −2 | Louisiana | −1 |
| Michigan | −2 | Massachusetts | −1 |
| Ohio | −2 | Montana | −1 |
| Pennsylvania | −2 | New Jersey | −1 |
| Iowa | −1 | West Virginia | −1 |
| Kansas | −1 | | |

**Race and Hispanic origin** Between 1980 and 1990 the number of whites in the U.S. population increased from 188.4 million to 199.7 million, a growth rate of 6.0%, significantly below the 9.8% national rate. Since 1970, the white population of the U.S. has decreased from 87.5% of the total to 80.3%.

The black population increased by 13.2% during the 1980s, from 26.5 million to 29.1 million, and now comprises 12.1% of the total population, up from 11.1% in 1970.

The Hispanic population continued its dramatic growth—53%—during the last census decade, as their numbers increased from 14.6 million in 1980 to 22.4 million in 1990. Hispanics now comprise 9.0% of the U.S. population, up from an estimated 4.5% in 1970, and 6.4% in 1980.

The fastest growing population group in the U.S. is the Census Bureau category Asian or Pacific Islander. With literally millions of Asian immigrants coming to the U.S., the number in this category has grown by an extraordinary 108% in only one decade, from 3.5 million to 7.3 million. While the Asian or Pacific Islander group made up just under 3% of the total U.S. population in 1990, this was about twice what it was in 1980 (1.5%).

## The Accuracy of the Census

According to the Census Bureau's own estimates, the 1990 census missed between 4.3 million and 6.3 million persons, an undercount of 1.7% to 2.5%. (In 1980, the estimate was 3 million persons, or 1.2%.) The postcensus survey, based on a sampling of 165,000 households and released in April 1991, indicated that the total population was between 252.9 million and 254.9 million, not the 248.7 million who were actually counted. Moreover, the most severe cases of undercounting were found in large cities and among minority groups.

Despite the fact that the postcensus survey was instituted because several cities (including New York and Los Angeles) had filed lawsuits against the Census Bureau in 1987, Secretary of Commerce Robert A. Mosbacher refused to adjust the census counts. After taking advice from demographers both in and out of the Census Bureau—who reportedly split evenly on the question—he came to the conclusion that an adjustment would improve the figures for the nation as a whole and for 29 of the 50 states but not for the localities where the majority of Americans live. Most Democrats and the leaders of every major city denounced the decision as politically motivated.

### DIMENSIONS OF THE 1990 CENSUS

In 1790 the first census report contained 56 pages. In contrast, the 1990 results totaled approximately 420,000 pages, with statistics for every geographic area, including the 50 states, over 3,000 counties, 16,000 townships, 20,000 municipalities, and 6.9 million city and county blocks. The Census Bureau also produced 90,000 maps for the states to use in redrawing congressional and state legislative districts. Here are some statistics that show what was involved in putting this together:

**Number of questionnaires**: 106 million.

**Total cost**: $2.6 billion, or $10.40 per U.S. resident.

**Personnel**: Approximately 480,000, all of whom must sign a secrecy oath. (The normal Census Bureau staff is 9,000.)

**Facilities**: 7 processing centers, 13 regional census centers, 484 temporary field offices.

**Equipment**: 9.4 million pencils, 530 minicomputers and microcomputers, 12 laser sorters, 72 camera/page turners, 21 microfilm processors, and 21 FOSDICs (Film Optical Sensing Device for Input to Computer).

**Source**: U.S. Bureau of the Census release, 1990.

## POPULATION GROWTH, BY REGION, 1790–2000 (in thousands)

| Year | Northeast | Midwest[1] | South[2] | West |
|---|---|---|---|---|
| 1790 | 1,968 | N.A. | 1,961 | N.A. |
| 1800 | 2,636 | 51 | 2,622 | N.A. |
| 1810 | 3,487 | 292 | 3,461 | N.A. |
| 1820 | 4,360 | 859 | 4,419 | N.A. |
| 1830 | 5,542 | 1,610 | 5,708 | N.A. |
| 1840 | 6,761 | 3,352 | 6,951 | N.A. |
| 1850 | 8,627 | 5,404 | 8,983 | 179 |
| 1860 | 10,594 | 9,097 | 11,133 | 619 |
| 1870 | 12,299 | 12,981 | 12,288 | 991 |
| 1880 | 14,507 | 17,364 | 16,517 | 1,801 |
| 1890 | 17,407 | 22,410 | 20,028 | 3,134 |
| 1900 | 21,047 | 26,333 | 24,524 | 4,309 |
| 1910 | 25,869 | 29,889 | 29,389 | 7,082 |
| 1920 | 29,662 | 34,020 | 33,126 | 9,214 |
| 1930 | 34,427 | 38,594 | 37,858 | 12,324 |
| 1940 | 35,977 | 40,143 | 41,666 | 14,379 |
| 1950 | 39,478 | 44,461 | 47,197 | 20,190 |
| 1960 | 44,678 | 51,619 | 54,973 | 28,053 |
| 1970 | 49,041 | 56,572 | 62,795 | 34,804 |
| 1980 | 49,135 | 58,866 | 75,372 | 43,172 |
| 1990 | 50,809 | 59,669 | 85,446 | 52,786 |
| 2000[3] | 51,800 | 59,600 | 96,900 | 59,400 |

1. Called North Central prior to 1980. 2. Includes black slave population through 1860. 3. Projections. **Sources:** U.S. Bureau of the Census, *The Statistical History of the U.S.* (1976) and *Statistical Abstract of the United States 1991* (1991).

## U.S. POPULATION, POPULATION DENSITY, AND AREA OF RESIDENCE, 1790–1990

| Year | Total population | Percent increase | Pop. per sq. mi. | Percent urban | Percent rural |
|---|---|---|---|---|---|
| 1790 | 3,929,214 | N.A. | 4.5 | 5.1% | 94.9% |
| 1800 | 5,308,483 | 35.1% | 6.1 | 6.1 | 93.9 |
| 1810 | 7,239,881 | 36.4 | 4.3 | 7.3 | 92.7 |
| 1820 | 9,638,453 | 33.1 | 5.5 | 7.2 | 92.8 |
| 1830 | 12,866,020 | 33.5 | 7.4 | 8.8 | 91.2 |
| 1840 | 17,069,453 | 32.7 | 9.8 | 10.8 | 89.2 |
| 1850 | 23,191,876 | 35.9 | 7.9 | 15.3 | 84.7 |
| 1860 | 31,443,321 | 35.6 | 10.6 | 19.8 | 80.2 |
| 1870 | 39,818,449 | 26.6 | 13.4 | 25.7 | 74.3 |
| 1880 | 50,155,783 | 26.0 | 16.9 | 28.2 | 71.8 |
| 1890 | 62,947,714 | 25.5 | 21.2 | 35.1 | 64.9 |
| 1900 | 75,994,575 | 20.7 | 25.6 | 39.6 | 60.4 |
| 1910 | 91,972,266 | 21.0 | 31.0 | 45.6 | 54.4 |
| 1920 | 105,710,620 | 14.9 | 35.6 | 51.2 | 48.8 |
| 1930 | 122,775,046 | 16.1 | 41.2 | 56.1 | 43.9 |
| 1940 | 131,669,275 | 7.2 | 44.2 | 56.5 | 43.5 |
| 1950 | 150,697,361 | 14.5 | 50.7 | 64.0 | 36.0 |
| 1960 | 179,323,175 | 18.5 | 50.6 | 69.9 | 30.1 |
| 1970 | 203,302,031 | 13.4 | 57.4 | 73.5 | 26.5 |
| 1980 | 226,545,805 | 11.4 | 64.0 | 73.7 | 26.3 |
| 1990 | 248,709,873 | 9.8 | 70.2[1] | 72.8[2] | 27.2[2] |

1. Estimated. 2. Figures are for 1989. **Sources:** U.S. Bureau of the Census, *The Statistical History of the U.S.* (1976) and *Statistical Abstract of the United States 1991* (1991).

## U.S. POPULATION BY STATE, 1790–1990

| State | 1790 | 1800 | 1810 | 1820 | 1830 | 1840 | 1850 | 1860 |
|---|---|---|---|---|---|---|---|---|
| Total U.S. | 3,929,214 | 5,308,483 | 7,239,881 | 9,638,453 | 12,860,702 | 17,063,353 | 23,191,876 | 31,443,321 |
| Alabama | — | 1,250 | 9,046 | 127,901 | 309,527 | 590,756 | 771,623 | 964,201 |
| Alaska | — | — | — | — | — | — | — | — |
| Arizona | — | — | — | — | — | — | — | — |
| Arkansas | — | — | 1,062 | 14,273 | 30,388 | 97,574 | 209,897 | 435,450 |
| California | — | — | — | — | — | — | 92,597 | 379,994 |
| Colorado | — | — | — | — | — | — | — | 34,277 |
| Connecticut | 237,946 | 251,002 | 261,942 | 275,248 | 297,675 | 309,978 | 370,792 | 460,147 |
| Delaware | 59,096 | 64,273 | 72,674 | 72,749 | 76,748 | 78,085 | 91,532 | 112,216 |
| District of Columbia | — | 8,144 | 15,471 | 23,336 | 30,261 | 33,745 | 51,687 | 75,080 |
| Florida | — | — | — | — | 34,730 | 54,477 | 87,445 | 140,424 |
| Georgia | 82,548 | 162,686 | 252,433 | 340,989 | 516,823 | 691,392 | 906,185 | 1,057,286 |
| Hawaii | — | — | — | — | — | — | — | — |
| Idaho | — | — | — | — | — | — | — | — |
| Illinois | — | — | 12,282 | 55,211 | 157,445 | 476,183 | 851,470 | 1,711,951 |
| Indiana | — | 5,641 | 24,520 | 147,178 | 343,031 | 685,866 | 988,416 | 1,350,428 |
| Iowa | — | — | — | — | — | 43,112 | 192,214 | 674,913 |
| Kansas | — | — | — | — | — | — | — | 107,206 |
| Kentucky | 73,677 | 220,955 | 406,511 | 564,317 | 687,917 | 779,828 | 982,405 | 1,155,684 |
| Louisiana | — | — | 76,556 | 153,407 | 215,739 | 352,411 | 517,762 | 708,002 |
| Maine | 96,540 | 151,719 | 228,705 | 298,335 | 399,455 | 501,793 | 583,169 | 628,279 |
| Maryland | 319,728 | 341,548 | 380,546 | 407,350 | 447,040 | 470,019 | 583,034 | 687,049 |
| Massachusetts | 378,787 | 422,845 | 472,040 | 523,287 | 610,408 | 737,699 | 994,514 | 1,231,066 |
| Michigan | — | — | 4,762 | 8,896 | 31,369 | 212,267 | 397,654 | 749,113 |
| Minnesota | — | — | — | — | — | — | 6,077 | 172,023 |
| Mississippi | — | 7,600 | 31,306 | 75,448 | 136,621 | 375,651 | 606,526 | 791,305 |
| Missouri | — | — | 19,783 | 66,586 | 140,455 | 383,702 | 682,044 | 1,182,012 |
| Montana | — | — | — | — | — | — | — | — |
| Nebraska | — | — | — | — | — | — | — | 28,841 |
| Nevada | — | — | — | — | — | — | — | 6,857 |
| New Hampshire | 141,885 | 183,858 | 214,460 | 244,161 | 269,328 | 284,574 | 317,976 | 326,073 |
| New Jersey | 184,139 | 211,149 | 245,562 | 277,575 | 320,823 | 373,306 | 489,555 | 672,035 |
| New Mexico | — | — | — | — | — | — | 61,547 | 93,516 |
| New York | 340,120 | 589,051 | 959,049 | 1,372,812 | 1,918,608 | 2,428,921 | 3,097,394 | 3,880,735 |
| North Carolina | 393,751 | 478,103 | 555,500 | 638,829 | 737,987 | 753,419 | 869,039 | 992,622 |
| North Dakota | — | — | — | — | — | — | — | — |
| Ohio | — | 45,365 | 230,760 | 581,434 | 937,903 | 1,519,467 | 1,980,329 | 2,339,511 |
| Oklahoma | — | — | — | — | — | — | — | — |
| Oregon | — | — | — | — | — | — | 12,093 | 52,465 |
| Pennsylvania | 434,373 | 602,365 | 810,091 | 1,049,458 | 1,348,233 | 1,724,033 | 2,311,786 | 2,906,215 |
| Rhode Island | 68,825 | 69,122 | 76,931 | 83,059 | 97,199 | 108,830 | 147,545 | 174,620 |
| South Carolina | 249,073 | 345,591 | 415,115 | 502,741 | 581,185 | 594,398 | 668,507 | 703,708 |
| South Dakota | — | — | — | — | — | — | — | 4,837 |
| Tenneesee | 35,691 | 105,602 | 261,727 | 422,832 | 681,904 | 829,210 | 1,002,717 | 1,109,801 |
| Texas | — | — | — | — | — | — | 212,592 | 604,215 |
| Utah | — | — | — | — | — | — | 11,380 | 40,273 |
| Vermont | 85,425 | 154,465 | 217,895 | 235,981 | 280,652 | 291,948 | 314,120 | 315,098 |
| Virginia[2] | 747,610 | 880,200 | 974,600 | 1,065,366 | 1,211,405 | 1,239,797 | 1,421,661 | 1,596,318 |
| Washington | — | — | — | — | — | — | 1,201 | 11,594 |
| West Virginia | — | — | — | — | — | — | — | — |
| Wisconsin | — | — | — | — | — | 30,945 | 305,391 | 775,881 |
| Wyoming | — | — | — | — | — | — | — | — |

**Note:** Excludes military and overseas population. Populations of regions, areas, and territories prior to statehood are wherever possible that of 1980 area of state. 1. 1980 figures are revised estimates issued by the Census Bureau in 1987. 2. The figures for Virginia through 1860 are from the 1960 census; in

## U.S. POPULATION BY STATE, 1790–1990

| 1870 | 1880 | 1890 | 1900 | 1910 | 1920 | 1930 | 1940 | 1950 | 1960 | 1970 | 1980[1] | 1990 | State |
|---|---|---|---|---|---|---|---|---|---|---|---|---|---|
| 38,558,371 | 50,189,209 | 62,979,766 | 76,212,168 | 92,228,496 | 106,021,537 | 123,202,624 | 132,164,569 | 151,325,798 | 179,323,175 | 203,302,031 | 226,542,203 | 248,709,873 | **United States** |
| 996,992 | 1,262,505 | 1,513,401 | 1,828,697 | 2,138,093 | 2,348,174 | 2,646,248 | 2,832,961 | 3,061,743 | 3,266,740 | 3,444,354 | 3,894,025 | 4,040,587 | Alabama |
| – | 33,426 | 32,052 | 63,592 | 64,356 | 55,036 | 59,278 | 72,524 | 128,643 | 226,167 | 302,583 | 401,851 | 550,043 | Alaska |
| 9,658 | 40,440 | 88,243 | 122,931 | 204,354 | 334,162 | 435,573 | 499.261 | 749,587 | 1,302,161 | 1,775,399 | 2,716,546 | 3,665,228 | Arizona |
| 484,471 | 802,525 | 1,128,211 | 1,311,564 | 1,574,449 | 1,752,204 | 1,854,482 | 1,949,387 | 1,909,511 | 1,786,272 | 1,923,322 | 2,286,357 | 2,350,725 | Arkansas |
| 560,247 | 864,694 | 1,213,396 | 1,485,053 | 2,377,549 | 3,426,861 | 5,677,251 | 6,907,387 | 10,586,223 | 15,717,204 | 19,971,069 | 23,667,764 | 29,760,021 | California |
| 39,864 | 194,327 | 413,249 | 539,700 | 799,024 | 939,629 | 1,035,791 | 1,123,296 | 1,325,089 | 1,753,947 | 2,209,596 | 2,889,735 | 3,294,394 | Colorado |
| 537,454 | 622,700 | 746,258 | 908,420 | 1,114,756 | 1,380,631 | 1,606,903 | 1,709,242 | 2,007,280 | 2,535,234 | 3,032,217 | 3,107,564 | 3,287,116 | Connecticut |
| 125,015 | 146,608 | 168,493 | 184,735 | 202,322 | 223,003 | 238,380 | 266,505 | 318,085 | 446,292 | 548,104 | 594,338 | 666,168 | Delaware |
| 131,700 | 177,624 | 230,392 | 278,718 | 331,069 | 437,571 | 486,869 | 663,091 | 802,178 | 763,956 | 756,668 | 638,432 | 606,900 | District of Columbia |
| 187,748 | 269,493 | 391,422 | 528,542 | 752,619 | 968,470 | 1,468,211 | 1,897,414 | 2,771,305 | 4,951,560 | 6,791,418 | 9,746,961 | 12,937,926 | Florida |
| 1,184,109 | 1,542,180 | 1,837,353 | 2,216,331 | 2,609,121 | 2,895,832 | 2,908,506 | 3,123,723 | 3,444,578 | 3,943,116 | 4,587,930 | 5,462,982 | 6,478,216 | Georgia |
| – | – | – | 154,001 | 191,874 | 255,881 | 368,300 | 422,770 | 499,794 | 632,772 | 769,913 | 964,691 | 1,108,229 | Hawaii |
| 14,999 | 32,610 | 88,548 | 161,772 | 325,594 | 431,866 | 445,032 | 524,873 | 588,637 | 667,191 | 713,015 | 944,127 | 1,006,749 | Idaho |
| 2,539,891 | 3,077,871 | 3,826,352 | 4,821,550 | 5,638,591 | 6,485,280 | 7,630,654 | 7,897,241 | 8,712,176 | 10,081,158 | 11,110,285 | 11,427,409 | 11,430,602 | Illinois |
| 1,680,637 | 1,978,301 | 2,192,404 | 2,516,462 | 2,700,876 | 2,930,390 | 3,238,503 | 3,427,796 | 3,934,224 | 4,662,498 | 5,195,392 | 5,490,214 | 5,544,159 | Indiana |
| 1,194,020 | 1,624,615 | 1,912,297 | 2,231,853 | 2,224,771 | 2,404,021 | 2,470,939 | 2,538,268 | 2,621,073 | 2,757,537 | 2,825,368 | 2,913,808 | 2,776,755 | Iowa |
| 364,399 | 996,096 | 1,428,108 | 1,470,495 | 1,690,949 | 1,769,257 | 1,880,999 | 1,801,028 | 1,905,299 | 2,178,611 | 2,249,071 | 2,364,236 | 2,477,574 | Kansas |
| 1,321,011 | 1,648,690 | 1,858,635 | 2,147,174 | 2,289,905 | 2,416,630 | 2,614,589 | 2,845,627 | 2,944,806 | 3,038,156 | 3,220,711 | 3,660,324 | 3,685,296 | Kentucky |
| 726,915 | 939,946 | 1,118,588 | 1,381,625 | 1,656,388 | 1,798,509 | 2,101,593 | 2,363,880 | 2,683,516 | 3,257,022 | 3,644,637 | 4,206,116 | 4,219,973 | Louisiana |
| 626,915 | 648,936 | 661,086 | 694,466 | 742,371 | 768,014 | 797,423 | 847,226 | 913,774 | 969,265 | 993,722 | 1,125,043 | 1,227,928 | Maine |
| 780,894 | 934,943 | 1,042,390 | 1,188,044 | 1,295,346 | 1,449,661 | 1,631,526 | 1,821,244 | 2,343,001 | 3,100,689 | 3,923,897 | 4,216,933 | 4,781,468 | Maryland |
| 1,457,351 | 1,783,085 | 2,238,947 | 2,805,346 | 3,366,416 | 3,852,356 | 4,249,614 | 4,316,721 | 4,690,514 | 5,148,578 | 5,689,170 | 5,737,093 | 6,016,425 | Massachusetts |
| 1,184,059 | 1,636,937 | 2,093,890 | 2,420,982 | 2,810,173 | 3,668,412 | 4,842,325 | 5,256,106 | 6,371,766 | 7,823,194 | 8,881,826 | 9,262,044 | 9,295,297 | Michigan |
| 439,706 | 780,773 | 1,310,283 | 1,751,394 | 2,075,708 | 2,387,125 | 2,563,953 | 2,792,300 | 2,982,483 | 3,413,864 | 3,806,103 | 4,075,970 | 4,375,099 | Minnesota |
| 827,922 | 1,131,597 | 1,289,600 | 1,551,270 | 1,797,114 | 1,790,618 | 2,009,821 | 2,183,796 | 2,178,914 | 2,178,141 | 2,216,994 | 2,520,770 | 2,573,216 | Mississippi |
| 1,721,295 | 2,168,380 | 2,679,185 | 3,106,665 | 3,293,335 | 3,404,055 | 3,629,367 | 3,784,664 | 3,954,653 | 4,319,813 | 4,677,623 | 4,916,762 | 5,117,073 | Missouri |
| 20,595 | 39,159 | 142,924 | 243,329 | 376,053 | 548,889 | 537,606 | 559,456 | 591,024 | 674,767 | 694,409 | 786,690 | 799,065 | Montana |
| 122,993 | 452,402 | 1,062,656 | 1,066,300 | 1,192,214 | 1,296,372 | 1,377,963 | 1,315,834 | 1,325,510 | 1,411,330 | 1,485,333 | 1,569,825 | 1,578,385 | Nebraska |
| 42,491 | 62,266 | 47,355 | 42,335 | 81,875 | 77,407 | 91,058 | 110,247 | 160,083 | 285,278 | 488,738 | 800,508 | 1,201,833 | Nevada |
| 318,300 | 346,991 | 376,530 | 411,588 | 430,572 | 443,083 | 465,293 | 491,524 | 533,242 | 606,921 | 737,681 | 920,610 | 1,109,252 | New Hampshire |
| 906,096 | 1,131,116 | 1,444,933 | 1,883,669 | 2,537,167 | 3,155,900 | 4,041,334 | 4,160,165 | 4,835,329 | 6,066,782 | 7,171,112 | 7,365,011 | 7,730,188 | New Jersey |
| 91,874 | 119,565 | 160,282 | 195,310 | 327,301 | 360,350 | 423,317 | 531,818 | 681,187 | 951,023 | 1,017,055 | 1,303,302 | 1,515,069 | New Mexico |
| 4,382,759 | 5,082,871 | 6,003,174 | 7,268,894 | 9,113,614 | 10,385,227 | 12,588,066 | 13,479,142 | 14,830,192 | 16,782,304 | 18,241,391 | 17,558,165 | 17,990,455 | New York |
| 1,071,361 | 1,399,750 | 1,617,949 | 1,893,810 | 2,206,287 | 2,559,123 | 3,170,276 | 3,571,623 | 4,061,929 | 4,556,155 | 5,084,411 | 5,880,095 | 6,628,637 | North Carolina |
| 2,405 | 36,909 | 190,983 | 319,146 | 577,056 | 646,872 | 680,845 | 641,935 | 619,636 | 632,446 | 617,792 | 652,717 | 638,800 | North Dakota |
| 2,665,260 | 3,198,062 | 3,672,329 | 4,157,545 | 4,767,121 | 5,759,394 | 6,646,697 | 6,907,612 | 7,946,627 | 9,706,397 | 10,657,423 | 10,797,603 | 10,847,115 | Ohio |
| – | – | 258,657 | 790,371 | 1,657,155 | 2,028,283 | 2,396,040 | 2,336,434 | 2,233,351 | 2,328,284 | 2,559,463 | 3,025,487 | 3,145,585 | Oklahoma |
| 90,923 | 174,768 | 317,704 | 413,536 | 672,765 | 783,389 | 953,786 | 1,089,684 | 1,521,341 | 1,768,687 | 2,091,533 | 2,633,156 | 2,842,321 | Oregon |
| 3,521,951 | 4,282,891 | 5,258,113 | 6,302,115 | 7,665,111 | 8,720,017 | 9,631,350 | 9,900,180 | 10,498,012 | 11,319,366 | 11,800,766 | 11,864,720 | 11,881,643 | Pennsylvania |
| 217,353 | 276,531 | 345,506 | 428,556 | 542,610 | 604,397 | 687,497 | 713,346 | 791,896 | 859,488 | 949,723 | 947,154 | 1,003,464 | Rhode Island |
| 705,606 | 995,577 | 1,151,149 | 1,340,316 | 1,515,400 | 1,683,724 | 1,738,765 | 1,899,804 | 2,117,027 | 2,382,594 | 2,590,713 | 3,120,729 | 3,486,703 | South Carolina |
| 11,776 | 98,268 | 348,600 | 401,570 | 583,888 | 636,547 | 692,849 | 642,961 | 652,740 | 680,514 | 666,257 | 690,768 | 696,004 | South Dakota |
| 1,258,520 | 1,542,359 | 1,767,518 | 2,020,616 | 2,184,789 | 2,337,885 | 2,616,556 | 2,915,841 | 3,291,718 | 3,567,089 | 3,926,018 | 4,591,023 | 4,877,185 | Tennessee |
| 818,579 | 1,591,749 | 2,235,527 | 3,048,710 | 3,896,542 | 4,663,228 | 5,824,715 | 6,414,824 | 7,711,194 | 9,579,677 | 11,198,655 | 14,225,513 | 16,986,510 | Texas |
| 86,786 | 143,963 | 210,779 | 276,749 | 373,351 | 449,396 | 507,847 | 550,310 | 688,862 | 890,627 | 1,059,273 | 1,461,037 | 1,722,850 | Utah |
| 330,551 | 332,286 | 332,422 | 343,641 | 355,956 | 352,428 | 359,611 | 359,231 | 377,747 | 389,881 | 444,732 | 511,456 | 562,758 | Vermont |
| 1,225,163 | 1,512,565 | 1,655,980 | 1,854,184 | 2,061,612 | 2,309,187 | 2,421,851 | 2,677,773 | 3,318,680 | 3,966,949 | 4,651,448 | 5,346,797 | 6,187,358 | Virginia |
| 23,955 | 75,116 | 357,232 | 518,103 | 1,141,990 | 1,356,621 | 1,563,396 | 1,736,191 | 2,378,963 | 2,853,214 | 3,413,244 | 4,132,353 | 4,866,692 | Washington |
| 442,014 | 618,457 | 762,794 | 958,800 | 1,221,119 | 1,463,701 | 1,729,205 | 1,901,974 | 2,005,552 | 1,860,421 | 1,744,237 | 1,950,186 | 1,793,477 | West Virginia |
| 1,054,670 | 1,315,497 | 1,693,330 | 2,069,042 | 2,333,860 | 2,632,067 | 2,939,006 | 3,137,587 | 3,434,575 | 3,951,777 | 4,417,821 | 4,705,642 | 4,891,769 | Wisconsin |
| 9,118 | 20,789 | 62,555 | 92,531 | 145,965 | 194,402 | 225,565 | 250,742 | 290,529 | 330,066 | 332,416 | 469,557 | 453,588 | Wyoming |

the 1980 summary, the Census Bureau gave separate figures for West Virginia between 1790 and 1860, even though it did not become a state until 1863. Since the result diminishes Virginia's population by over 300,000 in 1850 and 1860, a crucial period, we decided to keep the earlier breakdowns. **Sources:** U.S. Bureau of the Census, *1980 Census of Population: U.S. Summary, Number of Inhabitants* (1981), and Release (1990).

## RESIDENT POPULATION OF THE STATES BY RACE AND HISPANIC ORIGIN, 1990

| State | Total | White | Black | American Indian, Eskimo, or Aleut | Asian or Pacific Islander | Other | Hispanic origin[1] |
|---|---|---|---|---|---|---|---|
| United States | 248,709,873 | 199,686,070 | 29,986,060 | 1,959,234 | 7,273,662 | 9,804,847 | 22,354,059 |
| Alabama | 4,040,587 | 2,975,797 | 1,020,705 | 16,506 | 21,797 | 5,782 | 24,629 |
| Alaska | 550,043 | 415,492 | 22,451 | 85,698 | 19,728 | 6,674 | 17,803 |
| Arizona | 3,665,228 | 2,963,186 | 110,524 | 203,527 | 55,206 | 332,785 | 688,338 |
| Arkansas | 2,350,725 | 1,944,744 | 373,912 | 12,773 | 12,530 | 6,766 | 19,876 |
| California | 29,760,021 | 20,524,327 | 2,208,801 | 242,164 | 2,845,659 | 3,939,070 | 7,687,938 |
| Colorado | 3,294,394 | 2,905,474 | 133,146 | 27,776 | 59,862 | 168,136 | 424,302 |
| Connecticut | 3,287,116 | 2,859,353 | 274,269 | 6,654 | 50,698 | 96,142 | 213,116 |
| Delaware | 666,168 | 535,094 | 112,460 | 2,019 | 9,057 | 7,538 | 15,820 |
| Dist. of Columbia | 606,900 | 179,667 | 399,604 | 1,466 | 11,214 | 14,949 | 32,710 |
| Florida | 12,937,926 | 10,749,285 | 1,759,534 | 36,355 | 154,302 | 238,470 | 1,574,143 |
| Georgia | 6,478,216 | 4,600,148 | 1,746,565 | 13,348 | 75,781 | 42,374 | 108,922 |
| Hawaii | 1,108,229 | 369,616 | 27,195 | 5,099 | 685,236 | 21,083 | 81,390 |
| Idaho | 1,006,749 | 950,451 | 3,370 | 13,780 | 9,365 | 29,783 | 52,927 |
| Illinois | 11,430,602 | 8,952,978 | 1,694,273 | 21,836 | 285,311 | 476,204 | 904,446 |
| Indiana | 5,544,159 | 5,020,700 | 432,092 | 12,720 | 37,617 | 41,030 | 98,788 |
| Iowa | 2,776,755 | 2,683,090 | 48,090 | 7,349 | 25,476 | 12,750 | 32,647 |
| Kansas | 2,477,574 | 2,231,986 | 143,076 | 21,965 | 31,750 | 48,797 | 93,670 |
| Kentucky | 3,685,296 | 3,391,832 | 262,907 | 5,769 | 17,812 | 6,976 | 21,984 |
| Louisiana | 4,219,973 | 2,839,138 | 1,299,281 | 18,541 | 41,099 | 21,914 | 93,044 |
| Maine | 1,227,928 | 1,208,360 | 5,138 | 5,998 | 6,683 | 1,749 | 6,829 |
| Maryland | 4,781,468 | 3,393,964 | 1,189,899 | 12,972 | 139,719 | 44,914 | 125,102 |
| Massachusetts | 6,016,425 | 5,405,374 | 300,130 | 12,241 | 143,392 | 155,288 | 287,549 |
| Michigan | 9,295,297 | 7,756,086 | 1,291,706 | 55,638 | 104,983 | 86,884 | 201,596 |
| Minnesota | 4,375,099 | 4,130,395 | 94,944 | 49,909 | 77,886 | 21,965 | 53,884 |
| Mississippi | 2,573,216 | 1,633,461 | 915,057 | 8,525 | 13,016 | 3,157 | 15,931 |
| Missouri | 5,117,073 | 4,486,228 | 548,208 | 19,835 | 41,277 | 21,525 | 61,702 |
| Montana | 799,065 | 741,111 | 2,381 | 47,679 | 4,259 | 3,635 | 12,174 |
| Nebraska | 1,578,385 | 1,480,558 | 57,404 | 12,410 | 12,422 | 15,591 | 36,969 |
| Nevada | 1,201,833 | 1,012,695 | 78,771 | 19,637 | 38,127 | 52,603 | 124,419 |
| New Hampshire | 1,109,252 | 1,087,433 | 7,198 | 2,134 | 9,343 | 3,144 | 11,333 |
| New Jersey | 7,730,188 | 6,130,465 | 1,036,825 | 14,970 | 272,521 | 275,407 | 739,861 |
| New Mexico | 1,515,069 | 1,146,028 | 30,210 | 134,355 | 14,124 | 190,352 | 579,224 |
| New York | 17,990,455 | 13,385,255 | 2,859,055 | 62,651 | 693,760 | 989,734 | 2,214,026 |
| North Carolina | 6,628,637 | 5,008,491 | 1,456,323 | 80,155 | 52,166 | 31,502 | 76,726 |
| North Dakota | 638,800 | 604,142 | 3,524 | 25,917 | 3,462 | 1,755 | 4,665 |
| Ohio | 10,847,115 | 9,521,756 | 1,154,826 | 20,358 | 91,179 | 58,996 | 139,696 |
| Oklahoma | 3,145,585 | 2,583,512 | 233,801 | 252,240 | 33,563 | 42,289 | 86,160 |
| Oregon | 2,842,321 | 2,636,787 | 46,178 | 38,496 | 69,269 | 51,591 | 112,707 |
| Pennsylvania | 11,881,643 | 10,520,201 | 1,089,795 | 14,733 | 137,438 | 119,476 | 232,262 |
| Rhode Island | 1,003,464 | 917,375 | 38,861 | 4,071 | 18,325 | 24,832 | 45,752 |
| South Carolina | 3,486,703 | 2,406,974 | 1,039,884 | 8,246 | 22,382 | 9,217 | 30,551 |
| South Dakota | 696,004 | 637,515 | 3,258 | 50,575 | 3,123 | 1,533 | 5,252 |
| Tennessee | 4,877,185 | 4,048,068 | 778,035 | 10,039 | 31,839 | 9,204 | 32,741 |
| Texas | 16,986,510 | 12,774,762 | 2,021,632 | 65,877 | 319,459 | 1,804,780 | 4,339,905 |
| Utah | 1,722,850 | 1,615,845 | 11,576 | 24,283 | 33,371 | 37,775 | 84,597 |
| Vermont | 562,758 | 555,088 | 1,951 | 1,696 | 3,215 | 808 | 3,661 |
| Virginia | 6,187,358 | 4,791,739 | 1,162,994 | 15,282 | 159,053 | 58,290 | 160,288 |
| Washington | 4,866,692 | 4,308,937 | 149,801 | 81,483 | 210,958 | 115,513 | 214,570 |
| West Virginia | 1,793,477 | 1,725,523 | 56,295 | 2,458 | 7,459 | 1,742 | 8,489 |
| Wisconsin | 4,891,769 | 4,512,523 | 244,539 | 39,387 | 53,583 | 41,737 | 93,194 |
| Wyoming | 453,588 | 427,061 | 3,606 | 9,479 | 2,806 | 10,636 | 25,751 |

1. Persons of Hispanic origin may be of any race. **Source:** U.S. Bureau of the Census release, 1991.

## U.S. POPULATION ABROAD BY SELECTED COUNTRY, 1989

| Country | Resident U.S. citizens ('000s) | Country | Resident U.S. citizens ('000s) |
|---|---|---|---|
| Australia | 67.0 | Japan | 34.9 |
| Belgium | 12.8 | Jerusalem | 30.0 |
| Brazil | 41.5 | Mexico | 425.4 |
| Canada | 259.7 | Netherlands | 22.5 |
| Colombia | 20.8 | Panama | 7.5 |
| Costa Rica | 23.7 | Philippines | 120.6 |
| Dominican Republic | 48.8 | Portugal | 20.8 |
| Egypt | 17.8 | Spain | 61.4 |
| | | Switzerland | 24.1 |
| France | 44.6 | Turkey | 11.2 |
| Greece | 54.0 | United Kingdom | 170.1 |
| Hong Kong | 17.3 | Venezuela | 20.3 |
| Ireland | 31.8 | West Germany | 152.3 |
| Israel | 77.2 | **Total[1]** | **2,241.7** |
| Italy | 83.4 | | |

1. Includes other countries not shown separately. **Source:** U.S. Bureau of the Census, *Statistical Abstract of the United States 1991* (1991), from unpublished data of the U.S. Dept. of State.

were brought here that just before the Civil War blacks constituted 15% of the population.

After the war, however, the proportion of whites rapidly increased as millions of immigrants from northern Europe settled throughout the country. The relentless movement of the population westward deprived the Native Americans of their lands and—with the assistance of several bloody wars—helped to reduce their numbers in 1900 to a small fraction (less than 100,000 perhaps) of what they were estimated to have been only a century before.

The black population, with 9–10% of the total, remained the only significant minority group until the 1960s, when a surge of new immigrants from Puerto Rico, Mexico, and Cuba made the Hispanic presence felt in very short order. So rapid and strong an impression did these groups make that the Census Bureau created a new population category, "Hispanic Origin"; since some Hispanics are black, some white, and still others Indian, this designation has nothing to do with race.

During the 1970s and 1980s, the arrival of hundreds of thousands of Asians again caused a noticeable change in the composition of the population. The 1990 census was the first one to include a separate category for Asians and Pacific Islanders; in previous years they had been included, together with American Indians, Aleuts, and Eskimos, in the "Other Races" grouping.

## The Black Population

Ever since the Founding Fathers reached their famous "compromise" declaring a slave the equivalent of three-fifths of a person, the black population has had a less-than-equal standing in relation to the majority of Americans. Over the last two centuries, the struggle for equality, even in a nation pledged to that ideal, has proven long, hard, and in many cases

## THE POPULATION BY RACE AND HISPANIC ORIGIN

It is important to note that the Census Bureau's classification of the population by race, in its words, "reflects common usage, not an attempt to define biological stock." Only since 1960, however, have the Census Bureau's race figures been based on self-identification.

The people of the United States are predominantly white, accounting for an estimated 80.3% of the total population in 1990. This dominance has been true since colonial days, although even then the indigenous peoples and the African slaves were significant racial minorities. In fact, as slave labor became essential to the Southern economy, so many slaves

intractable, as so many contemporary facts and figures in this book make all too evident. From higher infant mortality rates and poverty rates to lower life expectancy and family income levels, the black population continues to reap the effects of two centuries of slavery and one of institutionalized segregation.

In 1990 the black population numbered 29,986,070 million, an estimated 12.1% of all Americans, by far the nation's largest minority group. Since 1980 the black population has grown 13.2%, more than twice the rate of growth for whites (6.0%); the Census Bureau projections indicate that this trend will continue through the 1990s. So too will the age differences between the races. In 1989 the median age for blacks was 27.7, about six years below the white population's 33.6. Other indications of the youthful nature of the black population are the proportion over 65 (only 8% compared with 13% for whites) and the percentage under 18 (33% to 25%).

Most black people (52.8%) continue to live in the South, where they made up 18.5% of the population in 1990; in the Northeast, blacks were 11% of the population, 9.6% in the Midwest, and only 5.4% in the West. In 1988 the majority of blacks (57%) lived in central cities of metropolitan areas, more than twice the proportion for whites (27%); the ratios in the suburban parts of metropolitan areas were just the

## RESIDENT POPULATION DISTRIBUTION FOR THE U.S., BY RACE AND HISPANIC ORIGIN, 1980–90

| Race/Hispanic origin[1] | 1980 Number | 1980 Percent | 1990 Number | 1990 Percent | Change Number | Change Percent |
|---|---|---|---|---|---|---|
| **Total population** | **226,545,805** | **100.0%** | **248,709,873** | **100.0%** | **22,164,068** | **9.8%** |
| White | 188,371,622 | 83.1 | 199,686,070 | 80.3 | 11,314,448 | 6.0 |
| Black | 26,495,025 | 11.7 | 29,986,060 | 12.1 | 3,491,035 | 13.2 |
| American Indian, Eskimo, or Aleut | 1,420,400 | 0.6 | 1,959,234 | 0.8 | 538,834 | 37.9 |
| Asian or Pacific Islander | 3,500,439 | 1.5 | 7,273,662 | 2.9 | 3,773,223 | 107.8 |
| Other race | 6,758,319 | 3.0 | 9,804,847 | 3.9 | 3,046,528 | 45.1 |
| Hispanic origin | 14,608,673 | 6.4 | 22,354,059 | 9.0 | 7,745,386 | 53.0 |

1. Persons of Hispanic origin may be of any race. **Source:** U.S. Bureau of the Census release, 1991.

## BLACK POPULATION OF THE U.S. BY REGION AND PERCENT OF TOTAL POPULATION, 1985–2010 (in thousands)

| Region | 1985 Number | 1985 Percent | 1990 Number | 1990 Percent | 2000[1] Number | 2000[1] Percent | 2010[1] Number | 2010[1] Percent |
|---|---|---|---|---|---|---|---|---|
| Northeast | 4,848 | 9.9% | 5,613 | 11.0% | 6,363 | 12.3% | 6,941 | 13.2% |
| Midwest | 5,337 | 9.1 | 5,716 | 9.6 | 6,542 | 11.0 | 7,013 | 11.9 |
| South | 14,048 | 18.6 | 15,829 | 18.5 | 18,546 | 19.1 | 20,630 | 19.7 |
| West | 2,262 | 5.2 | 2,262 | 5.4 | 3,555 | 6.0 | 4,126 | 6.3 |
| **Total U.S.** | **26,495** | **11.7** | **29,986** | **12.1** | **35,006** | **13.1** | **38,710** | **13.7** |

1. Projections. **Source:** U.S. Bureau of the Census, *1990 Census Profile (Number 2), Race and Hispanic Origin* (1991); *Projections of the Population of States By Age, Sex, and Race: 1988 to 2010* (1989).

## BLACK POPULATION OF METROPOLITAN AREAS, 1980–90

| Rank/Metropolitan area | 1980 | 1990 | Number change | Percent change |
|---|---|---|---|---|
| 1. New York-Northern New Jersey-Long Island, N.Y.-N.J.-Conn. CMSA | 2,825,102 | 3,289,465 | 464,363 | 16.4% |
| 2. Chicago-Gary-Lake County, Ill.-Ind.-Wis. CMSA | 1,557,287 | 1,547,725 | –9,562 | –0.6 |
| 3. Los Angeles-Anaheim-Riverside, Calif. CMSA | 1,059,124 | 1,229,809 | 170,685 | 16.1 |
| 4. Philadelphia-Wilmington-Trenton, Pa.-N.J.-Del.-Md. CMSA | 1,032,882 | 1,100,347 | 67,465 | 6.5 |
| 5. Washington, D.C.-Md.-Va. MSA | 870,657 | 1,041,934 | 171,277 | 19.7 |
| 6. Detroit-Ann Arbor, Mich. CMSA | 921,168 | 975,199 | 54,031 | 5.9 |
| 7. Atlanta, Ga. MSA | 525,676 | 736,153 | 210,477 | 40.0 |
| 8. Houston-Galveston-Brazoria, Tex. CMSA | 564,838 | 665,378 | 100,540 | 17.8 |
| 9. Baltimore, Md. MSA | 560,952 | 616,065 | 55,113 | 9.8 |
| 10. Miami-Fort Lauderdale, Fla. CMSA | 394,042 | 591,440 | 197,398 | 50.1 |
| 11. Dallas-Fort Worth, Tex. CMSA | 419,030 | 554,616 | 135,586 | 32.4 |
| 12. San Francisco-Oakland,San Jose, Calif. CMSA | 468,477 | 537,753 | 69,276 | 14.8 |
| 13. Cleveland-Akron-Lorain, Ohio CMSA | 425,861 | 441,940 | 16,079 | 3.8 |
| 14. New Orleans, La. MSA | 409,076 | 430,470 | 21,394 | 5.2 |
| 15. St. Louis, Mo.-Ill. MSA | 407,918 | 423,182 | 15,264 | 3.7 |
| 16. Memphis, Tenn-Ark.-Miss. MSA | 364,253 | 399,011 | 34,758 | 9.5 |
| 17. Norfolk-Virginia Beach-Newport News, Va. MSA | 326,102 | 398,093 | 71,991 | 22.1 |
| 18. Richmond-Petersburg, Va. MSA | 221,456 | 252,340 | 30,884 | 13.9 |
| 19. Birmingham, Ala. MSA | 240,271 | 245,726 | 5,455 | 2.3 |
| 20. Boston-Lawrence-Salem, Mass.-N.H. MSA | 176,265 | 239,059 | 62,794 | 35.6 |
| 21. Charlotte-Gastonia-Rock Hill, N.C.-S.C. MSA | 194,056 | 231,654 | 37,598 | 19.4 |
| 22. Milwaukee-Racine, Wis. CMSA | 164,571 | 214,182 | 49,611 | 30.1 |
| 23. Cincinnati-Hamilton, Ohio-Ky.-Ind. CMSA | 185,728 | 203,607 | 17,879 | 9.6% |
| 24. Kansas City, Mo.-Kans. MSA | 180,161 | 200,508 | 20,347 | 11.3 |
| 25. Tampa-St. Petersburg-Clearwater, Fla. MSA | 148,465 | 185,503 | 37,038 | 24.9 |
| 26. Raleigh-Durham, N.C. MSA | 146,624 | 183,447 | 36,823 | 25.1 |
| 27. Greensboro-Winston-Salem-High Point, N.C. MSA | 162,134 | 182,284 | 20,150 | 12.4 |
| 28. Jacksonville, Fla. MSA | 156,025 | 181,265 | 25,240 | 16.2 |
| 29. Pittsburgh-Beaver Valley, Pa. CMSA | 181,644 | 178,857 | –2,787 | –1.5 |
| 30. Indianapolis, Ind. MSA | 157,254 | 172,326 | 15,072 | 9.6 |
| 31. Jackson, Miss. MSA | 149,457 | 167,899 | 18,442 | 12.3 |
| 32. Columbus, Ohio MSA | 137,287 | 164,602 | 27,315 | 19.9 |
| 33. San Diego, Calif. MSA | 104,452 | 159,306 | 54,854 | 52.5 |
| 34. Baton Rouge, La. MSA | 137,581 | 156,509 | 18,928 | 13.8 |
| 35. Charleston, S.C. MSA | 133,478 | 153,227 | 19,749 | 14.8 |
| 36. Nashville, Tenn. MSA | 137,348 | 152,349 | 15,001 | 10.9 |
| 37. Columbia, S.C. MSA | 117,906 | 137,906 | 20,000 | 17.0 |
| 38. Orlando, Fla. MSA | 90,595 | 133,308 | 42,713 | 47.1 |
| 39. Mobile, Ala. MSA | 126,835 | 130,512 | 3,677 | 2.9 |
| 40. Dayton-Springfield, Ohio MSA | 118,294 | 126,238 | 7,944 | 6.7 |
| 41. Louisville, Ky.-Ind. MSA | 120,610 | 124,761 | 4,151 | 3.4 |
| 42. Augusta, Ga.-S.C. MSA | 106,729 | 123,482 | 16,753 | 15.7 |
| 43. Seattle-Tacoma, Wash. CMSA | 87,976 | 123,266 | 35,290 | 40.1 |
| 44. Buffalo-Niagara Falls, N.Y. CMSA | 113,975 | 121,956 | 7,981 | 7.0 |
| 45. Shreveport, La. MSA | 110,478 | 116,892 | 6,414 | 5.8 |
| 46. Greenville-Spartanburg, S.C. MSA | 97,561 | 111,334 | 13,773 | 14.1 |
| 47. West Palm Beach-Boca Raton-Delray Beach, Fla. MSA | 77,576 | 107,705 | 30,129 | 38.8 |
| 48. Montgomery, Ala. MSA | 94,494 | 105,196 | 10,702 | 11.3 |
| 49. Sacramento, Calif. MSA | 61,594 | 101,940 | 40,346 | 65.5 |
| 50. Little Rock-North Little Rock, Ark. MSA | 90,783 | 101,862 | 11,079 | 12.2 |

**Source:** U.S. Bureau of the Census release, 1991.

opposite with 50% of the white population living there and only 25% of blacks.

Significant differences between the races also exist in other demographic categories, most notably in the high divorce rates for blacks and the related numbers of married-couple families and households run by women. Between 1970 and 1989, in the category "female householder, no spouse present," the percentage for blacks rose from 28.3% to 43.5%, while the percentage of black married-couple families declined to 50.2% from 68.1% in 1970.

(See also "The U.S. Economy" for information about black employment, income, wealth, and poverty.)

## BLACK POPULATION OF THE U.S., 1790–1990

| Year | Number ('000s) | Percent of total pop. | Year | Number ('000s) | Percent of total pop. |
|------|------|------|------|------|------|
| 1790 | 757 | 19.3% | 1920 | 10,463 | 9.9% |
| 1800 | 1,002 | 18.9 | 1930 | 11,891 | 9.7 |
| 1850 | 3,639 | 15.7 | 1940 | 12,866 | 9.8 |
| 1860 | 4,442 | 14.1 | 1950 | 15,042 | 10.0 |
| 1870 | 4,880 | 12.7 | 1960[1] | 18,872 | 10.5 |
| 1880 | 6,581 | 13.1 | 1970 | 22,581 | 11.1 |
| 1890 | 7,489 | 11.9 | 1980 | 26,683 | 11.8 |
| 1900 | 8,834 | 11.6 | 1985 | 28,994 | 12.1 |
| 1910 | 9,828 | 10.7 | 1990 | 29,986 | 12.1 |

1. Includes Alaska and Hawaii for first time. **Source:** U.S. Bureau of the Census release, 1991, and *Statistical Abstract of the United States 1990* (1990).

## 10 STATES WITH THE LARGEST BLACK POPULATION, 1990

| State | Black population | Percent of total population |
|------|------|------|
| 1. New York | 2,859,055 | 15.9% |
| 2. California | 2,208,801 | 7.4 |
| 3. Texas | 2,021,632 | 11.9 |
| 4. Florida | 1,759,534 | 13.6 |
| 5. Georgia | 1,746,565 | 27.0 |
| 6. Illinois | 1,694,273 | 14.8 |
| 7. North Carolina | 1,456,323 | 22.0 |
| 8. Louisiana | 1,299,281 | 30.8 |
| 9. Michigan | 1,291,706 | 13.9 |
| 10. Maryland | 1,189,899 | 24.9 |

**Source:** U.S. Bureau of the Census release, 1991.

## 10 STATES WITH HIGHEST PERCENTAGE OF BLACK POPULATION, 1990

| Rank/State | Total population | Black population | Percent black |
|------|------|------|------|
| 1. Mississippi | 2,573,216 | 915,057 | 35.6% |
| 2. Louisiana | 4,219,973 | 1,299,281 | 30.8 |
| 3. South Carolina | 3,486,703 | 1,039,884 | 29.8 |
| 4. Georgia | 6,478,216 | 1,746,565 | 27.0 |
| 5. Alabama | 4,040,587 | 1,020,705 | 25.3 |
| 6. Maryland | 4,781,468 | 1,189,899 | 24.9 |
| 7. North Carolina | 6,628,637 | 1,456,323 | 22.0 |
| 8. Virginia | 6,187,358 | 1,162,994 | 18.8 |
| 9. Delaware | 666,168 | 112,460 | 16.9 |
| 10. Tennessee | 4,877,185 | 778,035 | 16.0 |

**Source:** U.S. Bureau of the Census release, 1991.

## The Hispanic Population

Between 1980 and 1990, the U.S. population grew by 9.8%, but the number of Hispanics increased by 53% (7.8 million), making them one of the fastest growing segments of the U.S. population. In the 1990 census, the Census Bureau counted a total of 22.4 million Hispanics in the United States.

A look at earlier population statistics reveals a pattern of tremendous growth among U.S. Hispanics. In 1970 there were approximately 9 million Hispanics in the United States. By 1980 the number had increased to 14.6 million. Prior to 1970, Census Bureau surveys were conducted differently from the way they are now. Spanish-surnamed Americans and people who were born, or whose parents were born, in a Hispanic country were identified, but non-Spanish-surnamed Hispanics and third- or fourth-generation Hispanics were not. Therefore, government data on Hispanics compiled before 1970 are highly inaccurate.

The rapid growth of the Hispanic population is due to immigration and a higher fertility rate than that of the non-Hispanic population. According to the National Center for Health Statistics, between 1983 and 1985 the birth rate among Hispanic women rose 11% as compared with 3% for non-Hispanics. In 1985 Hispanic births accounted for 17% of all births in the United States, although Hispanics only composed about 7% of the population.

Within the next 25 years, the Hispanic population will become the largest minority in the United States, surpassing blacks. The number of Hispanics is likely to exceed 31.2 million by the year 2000. If this projection proves correct, Hispanics will then make up 11.6% of the total U.S. population, while blacks will constitute 13.3%. The Census Bureau forecasts that by 2025 the number of Hispanics could reach 60.9 million, or 20.2% of the population, although these figures may prove high if fertility and immigration rates decrease. A more conservative estimate places the Hispanic population at 39.3 million by 2025.

**Geographical distribution** Over half of all U.S. Hispanics (53.8%) live in California or Texas. In 1990, 7.7 million (25.8%) of the residents of California and 4.3 million (25.5%) of the residents of Texas were Hispanic. The great majority of the Hispanics in these two states are of Mexican origin. New York, with 2.2 million (12.3%), is the state with the third-largest number of Hispanics, the majority of whom are Puerto Rican. Florida, where 2.2 million (12.2%) Hispanics reside, has the fourth-largest Hispanic population; the majority are of Cuban background. Florida had the highest growth rate (83%) since 1980, with Texas second at 45%.

As the accompanying table demonstrates, the growth of the Hispanic population in metropolitan areas reflects the high concentration of Hispanics in Texas and California. Since 1980 the Los Angeles area has witnessed a 73.4% increase, adding over 2 million Hispanics, and Dallas–Fort Worth has more than doubled its Hispanic population (109%) with an increase of 271,000.

## STATES WITH LARGEST HISPANIC POPULATIONS, 1990

| State | Hispanics (millions) | Percent of U.S. Hispanics | Percent of state's population |
|------|------|------|------|
| California | 7.7 | 34.4% | 25.8% |
| Texas | 4.3 | 19.4 | 25.5 |
| New York | 2.2 | 9.9 | 12.3 |
| Florida | 1.6 | 7.0 | 12.2 |
| Illinois | 0.9 | 4.0 | 7.9 |
| Arizona | 0.7 | 3.1 | 18.8 |
| New Jersey | 0.7 | 3.3 | 9.6 |
| New Mexico | 0.6 | 2.6 | 38.2 |
| Colorado | 0.4 | 1.9 | 12.9 |

**Source:** U.S. Bureau of the Census release, 1991.

**Who is Hispanic?** Broadly understood, the term Hispanic refers to people of Spanish or Spanish-American origin. American Hispanics are of diverse backgrounds. The majority trace their roots to Mexico, Puerto Rico, or Cuba; however, every Spanish-speaking country is represented in the U.S. Hispanic population. (People of Brazilian origin are not included because Brazil is a Portuguese-speaking country.) In recent years extreme poverty and upheaval have led political Salvadorans and other Central Americans to emigrate to the United States in increasing numbers.

Contrary to popular opinion, Spanish-speaking countries are not culturally homogeneous but varied and complex, incorporating Spanish and other European influences as well as Indian and African traits. In the Caribbean area, Panama, and the coasts of Venezuela, Colombia, Ecuador, and sections of Peru, African culture has left a strong legacy. In Mexico, most of Central America, and the Andean countries, diverse Indian cultures have had a major impact. Latin American society varies greatly according to social class, and vast differences exist between urban and rural areas. Since American Hispanics come from different countries and social backgrounds, they do not compose a uniform, cohesive population group.

U.S. Hispanics are of many races, since every race is represented in Spanish America. In some areas intermingling has made it impossible to distinguish one race from another, but in others, races are clearly defined. In Argentina, for example, there is a white majority of 99.6%—mostly of Italian, German, or English extraction. Cuba, the Dominican Republic, Panama, Venezuela, and the coastal areas of Colombia, Ecuador, and Peru all have significant black populations. In Bolivia about one-half of the population is Indian and a third is mestizo (of mixed white and Indian ancestry). Both Peru and Cuba have concentrations of persons of Chinese ancestry, and Peru has a growing Japanese population. About 63% of U.S. Hispanics trace their roots to Mexico, where about 55% of the population is mestizo, 30% Indian, and 15% white.

Despite their diversity there are many factors that unite the Hispanic peoples, among them language, religion, customs, and attitudes to-

## HISPANIC POPULATION OF METROPOLITAN AREAS, 1980–90

| Rank/Metropolitan area | 1980 | 1990 | Number change | Percent change | Rank/Metropolitan area | 1980 | 1990 | Number change | Percent change |
|---|---|---|---|---|---|---|---|---|---|
| 1. Los Angeles-Anaheim-Riverside, Calif. CMSA | 2,755,914 | 4,779,118 | 2,023,204 | 73.4% | 12. McAllen-Edinburg-Mission, Tex. MSA | 230,212 | 326,972 | 96,760 | 42.0 |
| | | | | | 13. Fresno, Calif. MSA | 150,790 | 236,634 | 85,844 | 56.9% |
| 2. New York-Northern New Jersey-Long Island, N.Y.-N.J.-Conn. CMSA | 2,050,998 | 2,777,951 | 726,953 | 35.4 | 14. Denver-Boulder, Colo. CMSA | 173,687 | 226,200 | 52,513 | 30.2 |
| | | | | | 15. Philadelphia-Wilmington-Trenton, Pa.-N.J.-Del.-Md. CMSA | 147,902 | 225,868 | 77,966 | 52.7 |
| 3. Miami-Fort Lauderdale, Fla. CMSA | 621,309 | 1,061,846 | 440,537 | 70.9 | 16. Washington, D.C.-Md.-Va. MSA | 94,968 | 224,786 | 129,818 | 136.7 |
| 4. San Francisco-Oakland, San Jose, Calif. CMSA | 660,190 | 970,403 | 310,213 | 47.0 | 17. Brownsville-Harlingen, Tex. MSA | 161,654 | 212,995 | 51,341 | 31.8 |
| 5. Chicago-Gary-Lake County, Ill.-Ind.-Wis. CMSA | 632,443 | 893,422 | 260,979 | 41.3 | 18. Boston-Lawrence-Salem, Mass.-N.H. CMSA | 92,463 | 193,199 | 100,736 | 108.9 |
| 6. Houston-Galveston-Brazoria, Tex. CMSA | 448,460 | 772,295 | 323,835 | 72.2 | 19. Corpus Christi, Tex. MSA | 158,119 | 181,860 | 23,741 | 15.0 |
| | | | | | 20. Albuquerque, N.Mex. MSA | 154,620 | 178,310 | 23,690 | 15.3 |
| 7. San Antonio, Tex. MSA | 481,511 | 620,290 | 138,779 | 28.8 | 21. Sacramento, Calif. MSA | 105,665 | 172,374 | 66,709 | 63.1 |
| 8. Dallas-Fort Worth, Tex. CMSA | 247,823 | 518,917 | 271,094 | 109.4 | 22. Tucson, Ariz. MSA | 111,418 | 163,262 | 51,844 | 46.5 |
| 9. San Diego, Calif. MSA | 275,177 | 510,781 | 235,604 | 85.6 | 23. Austin, Tex. MSA | 94,367 | 159,942 | 65,575 | 69.5 |
| 10. El Paso, Tex. MSA | 297,001 | 411,619 | 114,618 | 38.6 | 24. Bakersfield, Calif. MSA | 87,026 | 151,995 | 64,969 | 74.7 |
| 11. Phoenix, Ariz. MSA | 199,003 | 345,498 | 146,495 | 73.6 | 25. Tampa-St. Petersburg-Clearwater, Fla. MSA | 80,265 | 139,248 | 58,983 | 73.5 |

**Source:** U.S. Bureau of the Census release, 1991.

ward self, family, and society. In the United States, these factors vary in importance according to the degree to which an individual has assimilated into the mainstream. For example, although language has traditionally been an important unifying factor, large numbers of second-generation Hispanics are English-dominant. About 85% of U.S. Hispanics speak English. Although the Spanish language continues to exert a strong emotional pull among U.S. Hispanics, it is difficult to assess to what extent Spanish will remain a unifying force among future generations.

**Origins of U.S. Hispanics** The majority of U.S. Hispanics are of Mexican origin. Mexicans and Mexican-Americans compose 60.3% of the total U.S. Hispanic population. The number of people of Mexican background living in the United States grew from about 8.4 million in 1980 to 13.5 million in 1990.

About 12.2% of U.S. Hispanics are Puerto Rican. This group has increased from about 2 million to 2.7 million between 1980 and 1990. (These figures do not include Puerto Ricans living in Puerto Rico, which is a U.S. territory but for which a separate census report is issued.) In recent years the flow of Puerto Ricans to U.S. cities has been reversed, with more Puerto Ricans emigrating from the mainland to the island than the other way around.

The U.S. Central and South American populations showed the highest growth rate between 1980 and 1987. At the beginning of the decade, the number of Central Americans living in the United States was small. In census data Central Americans were included in the general category "Other," which was composed of persons of Spanish or South American origin, as well as Hispanics who did not specify their origin on census surveys. By 1982 the U.S. Central American population had increased so significantly that the Census Bureau created a new category: Central and South American. In the 1990 census, Central and South American Hispanics were asked to specify their country of origin, thereby enabling the government to compile

## SELECTED CHARACTERISTICS OF PERSONS OF HISPANIC AND NON-HISPANIC ORIGINS IN THE U.S., 1990

| Characteristic | Total non-Hispanic origin | Hispanic origin | Hispanic origin Mexican | Puerto Rican | Cuban | South America | Other Hispanic |
|---|---|---|---|---|---|---|---|
| Number ('000s)[1] | 225,413 | 20,779 | 13,305 | 2,180 | 1,014 | 2,842 | 1,437 |
| Percent of total | N.A. | 100.0% | 64.0% | 10.5% | 4.9% | 13.7% | 6.9% |
| Median age | 33.5 | 26.0 | 24.1 | 27.0 | 39.1 | 28.0 | 31.1 |
| Percent male | 48.5% | 50.2% | 51.2% | 47.7% | 48.4% | 48.8% | 48.1% |
| **MARITAL STATUS[2]** | | | | | | | |
| Never married | 25.7% | 32.2% | 33.1% | 34.9% | 20.0% | 33.0% | 28.2% |
| Married | 58.8 | 57.5 | 57.8 | 52.3 | 62.8 | 58.3 | 57.3 |
| Widowed | 7.5 | 3.8 | 3.4 | 4.5 | 7.1 | 2.8 | 5.2 |
| Divorced | 8.0 | 6.5 | 5.7 | 8.3 | 10.0 | 5.8 | 9.3 |
| **TYPE OF HOUSEHOLD** | | | | | | | |
| Number of households ('000s)[1] | 87,414 | 5,933 | 3,447 | 747 | 397 | 806 | 537 |
| Married-couple families | 56.0% | 57.2% | 60.5% | 45.9% | 58.7% | 57.1% | 50.9% |
| Female householder, no husband present | 11.2 | 18.8 | 16.3 | 31.2 | 14.4 | 20.8 | 17.9 |
| Male householder, no wife present | 2.9 | 5.5 | 6.7 | 3.1 | 2.8 | 5.3 | 4.2 |
| Nonfamily households | 29.9 | 18.4 | 16.5 | 19.8 | 24.1 | 16.8 | 27.0 |
| **SIZE OF HOUSEHOLD** | | | | | | | |
| Average number of persons | 2.58 | 3.48 | 3.84 | 2.91 | 2.55 | 3.51 | 2.65 |
| One person | 25.3% | 14.4% | 12.5% | 16.3% | 20.7% | 12.8% | 22.2% |
| Two persons | 33.0 | 21.8 | 18.9 | 26.7 | 28.5 | 19.3 | 31.8 |
| Three persons | 17.1 | 19.2 | 18.6 | 20.8 | 19.9 | 20.5 | 18.6 |
| Four persons | 15.2 | 19.8 | 19.8 | 18.9 | 17.7 | 24.2 | 15.8 |
| Five persons | 6.2 | 12.7 | 14.4 | 9.9 | 8.1 | 13.4 | 7.8 |
| Six or more persons | 3.1 | 12.2 | 15.9 | 7.4 | 5.1 | 9.7 | 3.7 |

1. Estimate. 2. Age 15 and over. **Source:** U.S. Bureau of the Census, Current Population Reports, *The Hispanic Population in the U.S., March 1990* (1991).

more accurate figures on Salvadorans and other groups (that data will not be available for another year). According to the Census Bureau's annual survey, the Current Population Reports, in 1982 there were approximately 1.5 million persons in the Central and South American category; by 1990 there were over 2.8 million, an increase of over 50%. Central and South Americans now make up 13.7% of the total U.S. Hispanic population.

Most Central American immigrants are from Nicaragua and El Salvador, although a significant number are from Guatemala. Statistical data on Salvadorans is uncertain, since the 1980 census did not break down the Central American category according to country or origin, and since many Salvadorans arrived here illegally after 1980 and do not figure in any subsequent census update. During the latter part of the 1980s, large numbers of Nicaraguans entered the country as political refugees. In Miami, where between 150 and 200 Central American immigrants arrive every week, Central Americans compose nearly 17% of the entire Hispanic population; in 1970, they composed less than 1%. There are an estimated 250,000 Nicaraguans presently living in the United States.

Cubans and Cuban-Americans make up 4.9% of the total number of Hispanics in the United States. Large numbers of Cubans arrived in 1961 during the Cuban airlift and again in 1980 during the Mariel boat lift. Between 1980 and 1989, the number of Americans of Cuban origin increased from 800,000 to just over one million. Since 1985 the Cuban

population has shown little fluctuation or perhaps a very slight decrease.

The remaining 6.9% of the U.S. Hispanic population is of "Other Spanish" origin. This group grew from approximately 1.2 million in 1982 to 1.4 million in 1990.

## The Asian and Pacific Islander Population

In 1970 the Census Bureau counted about 1.5 million Asians and Pacific Islanders living in the United States. By the 1980 census, that figure had more than doubled to 3.5 million, thanks in large part to the more than 400,000 Southeast Asian refugees who came to America during 1975–80 under the Refugee Resettlement Program. Between 1980 and 1989, 2.4 million more Asian immigrants entered the United States, resulting in a 1990 census count of 7,273,662 Asians and Pacific Islanders, or a 107.8% increase over 1980. In 1990 this group represented 2.9% of the total U.S. population, as compared to 1.5% a decade earlier.

## ASIAN POPULATION OF THE U.S., 1980–90

| Group | 1980 Census Number | 1980 Census Percent | 1990 Census Number | 1990 Census Percent | Number change | Percent change |
|---|---|---|---|---|---|---|
| Asian Indian | 361,531 | 0.2% | 815,447 | 0.3% | 453,916 | 125.6% |
| Chinese | 806,040 | 0.4 | 1,645,472 | 0.7 | 839,432 | 104.1 |
| Filipino | 774,652 | 0.3 | 1,406,770 | 0.6 | 632,118 | 81.6 |
| Guamanian | 32,158 | 0.0 | 49,345 | 0.0 | 17,187 | 53.4 |
| Hawaiian | 166,814 | 0.1 | 211,014 | 0.1 | 44,200 | 26.5 |
| Japanese | 700,974 | 0.3 | 847,562 | 0.3 | 146,588 | 20.9 |
| Korean | 354,593 | 0.2 | 798,849 | 0.3 | 444,256 | 125.3 |
| Samoan | 41,948 | 0.0 | 62,964 | 0.0 | 21,016 | 50.1 |
| Vietnamese | 261,729 | 0.1 | 614,547 | 0.2 | 352,818 | 134.8 |
| Other Asian or Pacific Islander | N.A. | N.A. | 821,692 | 0.3 | N.A. | N.A. |
| **Total Asian or Pacific Islander** | **3,500,439**[1] | **1.5** | **7,273,662** | **2.9** | **3,773,223** | **107.8** |

**Note**: N.A. = Not available from 1980 tabulations. 1. Figures for 1980 are not strictly comparable with those for 1990. The total for 1980 includes only the nine specific groups listed. **Source**: U.S. Bureau of the Census release, 1991.

## ASIAN AND PACIFIC ISLANDER POPULATION OF METROPOLITAN AREAS, 1980–90

| Rank/Metropolitan area | 1980 | 1990 | Number change | Percent change | Rank/Metropolitan area | 1980 | 1990 | Number change | Percent change |
|---|---|---|---|---|---|---|---|---|---|
| 1. Los Angeles-Anaheim-Riverside, Calif. CMSA | 561,876 | 1,339,048 | 777,172 | 138.3% | 5. Chicago-Gary-Lake County, Ill.-Ind.-Wis. CMSA | 144,626 | 256,050 | 111,424 | 77.0% |
| 2. San Francisco-Oakland-San Jose, Calif. CMSA | 454,647 | 926,961 | 472,314 | 103.9 | 6. Washington, D.C.-Md.-Va. MSA | 83,008 | 202,437 | 119,429 | 143.9 |
| | | | | | 7. San Diego, Calif. MSA | 89,861 | 198,311 | 108,450 | 120.7 |
| 3. New York-Northern New Jersey-Long Island, N.Y.-N.J.-Conn. CMSA | 370,731 | 873,213 | 502,482 | 135.5 | 8. Seattle-Tacoma, Wash. CMSA | 78,255 | 164,286 | 86,031 | 109.9 |
| | | | | | 9. Houston-Galveston-Brazoria, Tex. CMSA | 53,056 | 132,131 | 79,075 | 149.0 |
| 4. Honolulu, Hawaii MSA | 456,465 | 526,459 | 69,994 | 15.3 | 10. Philadelphia-Wilmington-Trenton, Pa.-N.J.-Del.-Md. CMSA | 53,291 | 123,458 | 70,167 | 131.7 |

**Source**: U.S. Bureau of the Census release, 1991.

## POPULATION OF SELECTED RESERVATIONS AND TRUST LANDS, 1990

| Rank/Reservation or Trust Land | Total population | American Indian, Eskimo, or Aleut Population | American Indian, Eskimo, or Aleut Percent of total | Rank/Reservation or Trust Land | Total population | American Indian, Eskimo, or Aleut Population | American Indian, Eskimo, or Aleut Percent of total |
|---|---|---|---|---|---|---|---|
| 1. Navajo and Trust Lands, Ariz., N.Mex., Utah | 148,451 | 143,405 | 96.6% | 14. Fort Peck, Mont. | 10,595 | 5,782 | 54.6% |
| 2. Pine Ridge and Trust Lands, Nebr.-S.Dak. | 12,215 | 11,182 | 91.5 | 15. Wind River, Wyo. | 21,851 | 5,676 | 26.0 |
| 3. Fort Apache, Ariz. | 10,394 | 9,825 | 94.5 | 16. Eastern Cherokee, N.C. | 6,527 | 5,388 | 82.5 |
| 4. Gila River, Ariz. | 9,540 | 9,116 | 95.6 | 17. Flathead, Mont. | 21,259 | 5,130 | 24.1 |
| 5. Papago, Ariz. | 8,730 | 8,480 | 97.1 | 18. Cheyenne River, S.Dak. | 7,743 | 5,100 | 65.9 |
| 6. Rosebud and Trust Lands, S.Dak. | 9,696 | 8,043 | 83.0 | 19. Standing Rock, N.Dak.-S.Dak. | 7,956 | 4,870 | 61.2 |
| 7. San Carlos, Ariz. | 7,294 | 7,110 | 97.5 | 20. Crow and Trust Lands, Mont. | 6,370 | 4,724 | 74.2 |
| 8. Zuni Pueblo, Ariz.-N.Mex. | 7,412 | 7,073 | 95.4 | 21. Mississippi Choctaw and Trust Lands, Miss. | 4,073 | 3,932 | 96.5 |
| 9. Hopi and Trust Lands, Ariz. | 7,360 | 7,061 | 95.9 | 22. Colville, Wash. | 6,957 | 3,788 | 54.4 |
| 10. Blackfeet, Mont. | 8,549 | 7,025 | 82.2 | 23. Laguna Pueblo and Trust Lands, N.Mex. | 3,731 | 3,634 | 97.4 |
| 11. Turtle Mountain and Trust Lands, N.Dak.-S.Dak. | 7,106 | 6,772 | 95.3 | 24. Red Lake, Minn. | 3,699 | 3,602 | 97.4 |
| 12. Yakima and Trust Lands, Wash. | 27,668 | 6,307 | 22.8 | 25. Northern Cheyenne and Trust Lands, Mont.-S.Dak. | 3,923 | 3,542 | 90.3 |
| 13. Osage, Okla.[1] | 41,645 | 6,161 | 14.8 | | | | |

**Note**: Ranked by total American Indian, Eskimo, or Aleut population. 1. The Osage Reservation is coextensive with Osage County. **Source**: U.S. Bureau of the Census release, 1991.

## The American Indian, Eskimo, and Aleut Population

According to the 1990 census, there are currently 1,878,285 American Indians and 80,949 Alaska Natives (Eskimos and Aleuts) living in the United States. This represents a significant increase since the 1960 census, when only 524,000 (42,500 Alaska Natives) were counted. About 46% of American Indians live in the West, 29.7% in the South, 17.8% in the Midwest, and only 6.5% in the Northeast. According to the 1990 census, four states had over 100,000 Native Americans: Oklahoma (252,089), California (236,078), Arizona (203,009), and New Mexico (134,097).

The 1990 census reported that 37.7% (739,108) of the American Indian, Eskimo, and Aleut populations lived inside federally "identified areas," including reservations (home to 1,411,435 in 1990) that the federal government recognizes as territory in which American Indian tribes have jurisdiction. (State reservations are lands held in trust by state governments for the use and benefit of a given tribe.) Another 25,996 lived on "trust lands" that are held in trust by the federal government but that consist of property associated with a particular tribe or reservation.

The federal government's Bureau of Indian Affairs recognizes 503 distinct Native American communities, including numerous Alaska Native villages; 278 reservations, where about 25% of the population (340,000) still resides; and the so-called historic areas of Oklahoma, former reservations whose boundaries were legally established during the 1900–1907 period (9% of the total population, or 116,000, lived there in 1980).

## NUMBER OF PERSONS AND PERCENT OF TOTAL POPULATION, BY AGE GROUP, 1960–2020 (numbers in thousands)

| Age in years | 1960 ('000s) | 1960 Percent | 1970 ('000s) | 1970 Percent | 1980 ('000s) | 1980 Percent | 1990 ('000s) | 1990 Percent | 2000 ('000s) | 2000 Percent | 2010 ('000s) | 2010 Percent | 2020 ('000s) | 2020 Percent |
|---|---|---|---|---|---|---|---|---|---|---|---|---|---|---|
| Under 5 | 20,341 | 11.3% | 17,166 | 8.4% | 16,458 | 7.2% | 18,408 | 7.4% | 16,898 | 6.3% | 16,899 | 6.0% | 17,095 | 5.8% |
| 5–13 | 32,965 | 18.2 | 36,672 | 17.9 | 31,095 | 13.7 | 32,393 | 12.9 | 33,483 | 12.5 | 31,001 | 11.0 | 31,697 | 10.8 |
| 14–17 | 11,219 | 6.2 | 15,924 | 7.8 | 16,142 | 7.1 | 13,237 | 5.3 | 15,332 | 5.7 | 14,746 | 5.2 | 14,074 | 4.8 |
| 18–24 | 16,128 | 8.9 | 24,712 | 12.1 | 30,350 | 13.3 | 26,140 | 10.4 | 25,231 | 9.4 | 27,155 | 9.6 | 25,018 | 8.5 |
| 25–34 | 22,919 | 12.7 | 25,323 | 12.3 | 37,626 | 16.5 | 43,925 | 17.5 | 37,149 | 13.8 | 37,572 | 13.3 | 39,100 | 13.3 |
| 35–44 | 24,221 | 13.4 | 23,150 | 11.3 | 25,868 | 11.4 | 37,897 | 15.1 | 43,911 | 16.4 | 37,202 | 13.2 | 37,591 | 12.8 |
| 45–64 | 36,203 | 20.0 | 41,999 | 20.5 | 44,515 | 19.5 | 46,851 | 18.7 | 61,381 | 22.9 | 78,637 | 27.8 | 77,722 | 26.4 |
| 65+ | 16,675 | 9.2 | 20,107 | 9.8 | 25,704 | 11.3 | 31,559 | 12.6 | 34,882 | 13.0 | 39,362 | 13.9 | 52,067 | 17.7 |
| 85+ | 940 | 0.5 | 1,430 | 0.7 | 2,269 | 1.0 | 3,254 | 1.3 | 4,622 | 1.7 | 6,115 | 2.2 | 6,651 | 2.3 |
| 100+ | 3 | — | 5 | — | 15 | — | 56 | — | 100 | — | 171 | 0.1 | 266 | 0.1 |
| Total U.S. pop. | 180,671 | | 205,052 | | 227,757 | | 250,410 | | 268,266 | | 282,575 | | 294,364 | |
| Median age | 29.4 | | 27.9 | | 30.0 | | 33.0 | | 36.4 | | 38.9 | | 40.2 | |

**Note:** Figures for 1990 and after are the projections the Census Bureau calls the "middle" or "most likely" series. **Sources:** U.S. Bureau of the Census, *Projections of the Population of the U.S. by Age, Sex, and Race 1988 to 2040* (1989) and *Statistical Abstract of the United States 1989* (1989).

## The U.S. Population by Age

With birth rates and fertility rates declining rapidly since 1965, it should come as no surprise that the median age of the U.S. population has been rising almost as quickly. It will continue to rise for the foreseeable future in part because of the aging of the Baby Boom generation.

During the Baby Boom years of the 1950s and 1960s, the median age of the population actually declined, the only time in U.S. history it has done so. Since then, however, the steady decline in the number of young people, especially those under 18 years of age (from 34.1% in 1970 to 25.6% in 1990), combined with the increase of those between 25 and 44 (23.6% of the population in 1970 but 32.6% in 1990) has driven the median age from 28 in 1970 to 33 in 1990. A five-year increase in 20 years is unprecedented in our history, but what's more remarkable is that we will most likely duplicate that feat over the next 20 years.

The other major factor in the so-called "graying of America" is the increased life expectancy for older people. The Census Bureau estimates that 31.7 million Americans (12.3% of the population) were over the age of 65 in 1990; this represents a 24.1% increase since 1980. By the year 2000, the bureau projects another increase of 10.2%, or 34.9 million people over the age of 65. Over the first decade of the 21st century, the over-65 population will grow at about the same rate—from 10–12%—but between 2010 and 2020, the projected increase jumps to 31.2%, and to 25.6% between 2020 and 2030, as the members of the Baby Boom generation finally become senior citizens. In the year 2030, 21% of the population, or 65 million Americans, will be 65 years old or older. That's 40 years from now, a demographic stone's throw away. By comparison, bear in mind that 40 years ago, in 1950, the over-65 population totaled 7% of all Americans and numbered 9 million.

## The U.S. Population by Sex

According to census records, males always outnumbered females in the United States until 1950. Since then, however, the ratio of males to females has been declining every decade, especially in the older age brackets. Because women live so much longer on average than men do, there are currently over 30% more women in the over-65 category. In the crucial mating and marrying years (14–44), however, the numbers are not significantly different.

## U.S. POPULATION BY SEX: TOTALS AND RATIO OF MALES TO FEMALES, 1920–89

| Year | Male ('000s) | Female ('000s) | Males per 100 females All ages | 14–24 | 25–44 | 65+ |
|---|---|---|---|---|---|---|
| 1920 | 53,900 | 51,810 | 104.0 | 97.3 | 105.1 | 101.3 |
| 1930 | 62,137 | 60,638 | 102.5 | 98.4 | 101.8 | 100.5 |
| 1940 | 66,062 | 65,608 | 100.7 | 98.9 | 98.5 | 95.5 |
| 1950 | 74,833 | 75,864 | 98.6 | 98.2 | 96.4 | 89.6 |
| 1960 | 88,331 | 90,992 | 97.1 | 98.7 | 95.7 | 82.8 |
| 1970 | 98,926 | 104,309 | 94.8 | 98.7 | 95.5 | 72.1 |
| 1980 | 110,053 | 116,493 | 94.5 | 101.9 | 97.4 | 67.6 |
| 1989[1] | 120,982 | 127,258 | 95.1 | 102.5 | 99.0 | 68.9 |

1. Estimated figures. **Source:** U.S. Bureau of the Census, *Statistical Abstract of the United States 1991* (1991).

## CHARACTERISTICS OF THE POPULATION OVER AGE 65, 1989

| Characteristic | Male | Female |
|---|---|---|
| Total (millions) | 12.1 | 16.9 |
| White | 10.8 | 15.2 |
| Black | 1.0 | 1.5 |
| **PERCENT DISTRIBUTION** | | |
| Marital status: | | |
| Single | 4.7% | 5.0% |
| Married | 77.0 | 41.7 |
| Spouse absent | 2.7 | 1.6 |
| Widowed | 14.0 | 48.7 |
| Divorced | 4.3 | 4.5 |
| Family status: | | |
| In families[1] | 82.0% | 57.0% |
| Nonfamily householders | 16.6 | 41.8 |
| Secondary individuals | 1.4 | 1.2 |
| Living arrangements: | | |
| Living in household | 99.7% | 99.6% |
| Living alone | 15.9 | 40.9 |
| Spouse present | 74.3 | 40.1 |
| Living with someone else | 9.5 | 18.6 |
| Not in household | 0.3 | 0.4 |
| Labor force participation: | | |
| Employed | 16.2% | 8.1% |
| Not in labor force | 83.4 | 91.6 |
| Unemployed | 0.4 | 0.2 |
| Percent below poverty level: | | |
| Family householders | 5.4% | 13.9% |
| Unrelated individuals | 19.5 | 25.5 |

1. Excludes those living in unrelated subfamilies. **Source:** U.S. Bureau of the Census, *Statistical Abstract of the United States 1991* (1991).

## THE MEDIAN AGE OF THE U.S. POPULATION 1820–2030

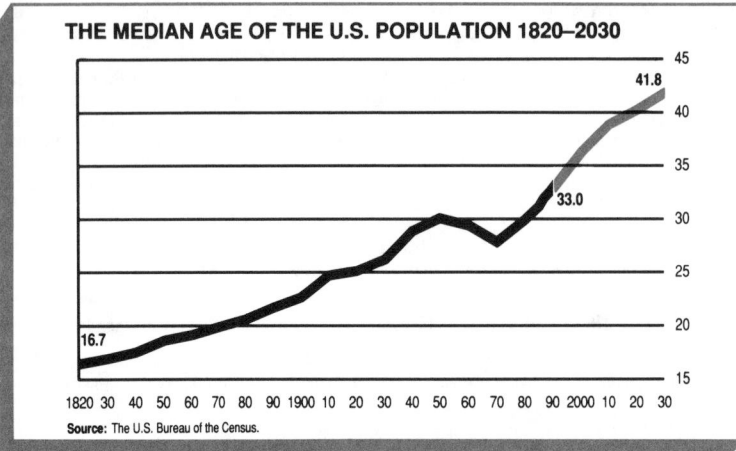

**Source:** The U.S. Bureau of the Census.

## GROWTH OF THE POPULATION AGE 65 AND OVER, BY NUMBER AND PERCENT, 1900–2030

| Year | Population 65 and over ('000s) | Percent increase by decade | Percent of population 65 and over |
|------|------|------|------|
| 1900 | 3,099 | N.A. | 4.1% |
| 1910 | 3,986 | 28.6% | 4.3 |
| 1920 | 4,929 | 23.7 | 4.7 |
| 1930 | 6,705 | 36.0 | 5.5 |
| 1940 | 9,031 | 34.7 | 6.9 |
| 1950 | 12,397 | 37.3 | 8.1 |
| 1960 | 16,675 | 34.5 | 9.2 |
| 1970 | 20,107 | 20.6 | 9.8 |
| 1980 | 25,549 | 27.1 | 11.3 |
| 1990 | 29,835 | 24.1 | 12.7 |
| 2000 | 31,697 | 10.2 | 13.0 |
| 2010 | 34,921 | 12.2 | 13.8 |
| 2020 | 39,195 | 31.2 | 17.3 |
| 2030 | 51,422 | 25.6 | 21.2 |

**Note:** Figures for 1990 through 2030 are Census Bureau projections based on their "most likely" series of estimates. **Source:** Population Reference Bureau, Beth J. Soldo and Emily Agree, *America's Elderly* (1988), based on U.S. Bureau of the Census data.

## VITAL STATISTICS: BIRTHS, DEATHS, MARRIAGES, DIVORCES

The National Center for Health Statistics does a month-by-month tracking of four sets of numbers that both it and the Census Bureau refer to as "vital": births, deaths, marriages, and divorces.

**Births** An estimated 4.18 million babies were born in the United States in 1990, 4% more than the provisional number reported in 1989. While this is the largest number of live births reported since 1964, the crude birth rate—the number of live births per 1,000 total population—of 16.7 remained substantially smaller than at any time before 1970 (although it was 3% higher than in 1989). The Census Bureau attributes the increase in the absolute number of births since 1975 to the increased number of women of childbearing age, i.e., the women of the Baby Boom era. In 1987 and 1988, the increase was the result, in part, of that same group having babies at a much later age than women of previous generations. Now there is some preliminary evidence that women are actually having more children.

**Deaths** An estimated 2.16 million deaths occurred in 1990, one of the largest numbers ever recorded. The death rate of 8.6 per 1,000 population was 1% lower than in the previous year. (For infant mortality figures and for more specific information about death rates by cause, see "Health and Medicine.")

In 1990 there were 2,017,000 more births than deaths; this figure is called the *natural increase*, meaning the growth in population without immigration (which has accounted for another 600,000 people per year in recent years).

**Marriages** An estimated 2.45 million couples married during 1990, an increase of 1% from 1988 and 1989; the marriage rate increased to 9.8 per 1,000 population. Until 1987 the rate had not fallen below 10 during the 1970s or the 1980s. Whether or not this represents any kind of trend is difficult to determine,

## BIRTHS AND DEATHS IN THE U.S., 1910–90 (in thousands)

| Year | Live births | Birth rate[1] | Deaths[2] | Death rate[1] |
|------|------|------|------|------|
| 1910 | 2,777 | 30.1 | N.A. | 14.7 |
| 1920 | 2,950 | 27.7 | N.A. | 13.0 |
| 1930 | 2,618 | 21.3 | N.A. | 11.3 |
| 1935 | 2,377 | 18.7 | 1,393 | 10.9 |
| 1940 | 2,559 | 19.4 | 1,417 | 10.8 |
| 1945 | 2,858 | 20.4 | 1,402 | 10.6 |
| 1950 | 3,632 | 24.1 | 1,452 | 9.6 |
| 1955 | 4,097 | 25.0 | 1,529 | 9.3 |
| 1960 | 4,258 | 23.7 | 1,712 | 9.5 |
| 1965 | 3,760 | 19.5 | 1,828 | 9.4 |
| 1970 | 3,731 | 18.4 | 1,921 | 9.5 |
| 1975 | 3,144 | 14.6 | 1,893 | 8.8 |
| 1980 | 3,612 | 15.9 | 1,990 | 8.8 |
| 1981 | 3,629 | 15.8 | 1,978 | 8.6 |
| 1982 | 3,681 | 15.9 | 1,975 | 8.5 |
| 1983 | 3,639 | 15.5 | 2,019 | 8.6 |
| 1984 | 3,669 | 15.5 | 2,039 | 8.6 |
| 1985 | 3,761 | 15.8 | 2,086 | 8.7 |
| 1986 | 3,757 | 15.6 | 2,105 | 8.7 |
| 1987 | 3,829 | 15.7 | 2,127 | 8.7 |
| 1988 | 3,913 | 15.9 | 2,171 | 8.8 |
| 1989 | 4,021 | 16.2 | 2,155 | 8.7 |
| 1990 | 4,179 | 16.7 | 2,162 | 8.6 |

1. Per 1,000 total population. 2. Excludes fetal deaths. **Sources:** U.S. Bureau of the Census, *The Statistical History of the U.S. (1976)*; U.S. National Center for Health Statistics, *Vital Statistics of the United States 1987* (1988) and *Monthly Vital Statistics Report, April 1991* (1991).

since so many people are postponing marriage until they are much older than what was once the norm. In 1960, for example, about 40% of all 19-year-old women were married, but by 1990 only 11% were. Also in 1960, about 92% of all women were married before they reached age 30, but by 1990 only 81% were. Moreover, between 1970 and 1990, the proportion of 30-to-34-year-olds who had never married almost tripled, rising from 6% to 16% for women, and from 9% to 27% for men; for those age 35 to 39, the proportion of never married doubled over the two decades, from 5% to 10% for women and from 7% to 15% for men.

## MEDIAN AGE AT FIRST MARRIAGE, BY SEX, 1890–1990

| Year | Male | Female | Year | Male | Female |
|------|------|------|------|------|------|
| 1890 | 26.1 | 22.0 | 1960 | 22.8 | 20.3 |
| 1900 | 25.9 | 21.9 | 1970 | 23.2 | 20.8 |
| 1910 | 25.1 | 21.6 | 1980 | 24.7 | 22.0 |
| 1920 | 24.6 | 21.2 | 1985 | 25.5 | 23.3 |
| 1930 | 24.3 | 21.3 | 1988 | 25.9 | 23.6 |
| 1940 | 24.3 | 21.5 | 1989 | 26.2 | 23.8 |
| 1950 | 22.8 | 20.3 | 1990 | 26.1 | 23.9 |

**Sources:** U.S. Bureau of the Census, *The Statistical History of the U.S.* (1976) and *Marital Status and Living Arrangements: March 1990* (1991).

## THE UNMARRIED: IS THERE A SHORTAGE OF MEN?

In 1990, according to the Census Bureau, there were 36 million men and 43 million women who had never married or who were currently widowed or divorced, a ratio of 84 unmarried men per 100 unmarried women. The popular interpretation of these figures—that there is a shortage of eligible men—fails to consider that women are more likely to live longer (and so be counted among the widowed) and less likely to remarry after a divorce. So in fact, during the peak marrying ages, unmarried men outnumber unmarried women: among persons under age 25 there were 111 unmarried men for every 100 unmarried women; and in the 25-to-29 age group, there were 127 men for every 100 women. It's not until the 40-to-44 group that the reversal begins, and among the 65-and-over group there is a dramatic change, with only 29 unmarried men for every 100 unmarried women.

**Source:** U.S. Bureau of the Census, *Marital Status and Living Arrangements: March 1990* (1991).

## MARITAL STATUS OF THE POPULATION BY SEX AND AGE, 1990

| Age | Total number ('000s) | Percent distribution by marital status | | | | | Age | Total number ('000s) | Percent distribution by marital status | | | | |
|---|---|---|---|---|---|---|---|---|---|---|---|---|---|
| | | Single, never married | Married, spouse present | Married, spouse absent[1] | Widowed | Divorced | | | Single, never married | Married, spouse present | Married, spouse absent[1] | Widowed | Divorced |
| | | **MALE** | | | | | | | **FEMALE** | | | | |
| 18–19 | 3,639 | 96.8% | 2.8% | 0.3% | N.A. | N.A. | 18–19 | 3,683 | 90.3% | 8.2% | 1.1% | N.A. | 0.4% |
| 20–24 | 8,811 | 79.3 | 18.4 | 1.3 | N.A. | 1.1% | 20–24 | 9,117 | 62.8 | 31.1 | 3.2 | 0.1% | 2.8 |
| 25–29 | 10,515 | 45.2 | 47.4 | 2.7 | 0.1% | 4.7 | 25–29 | 10,685 | 31.1 | 56.6 | 4.8 | 0.4 | 7.1 |
| 30–34 | 10,947 | 27.0 | 61.2 | 3.8 | 0.2 | 7.9 | 30–34 | 11,094 | 16.4 | 67.0 | 5.3 | 0.8 | 10.5 |
| 35–39 | 9,844 | 14.7 | 70.0 | 4.0 | 0.4 | 10.9 | 35–39 | 10,047 | 10.4 | 69.7 | 4.6 | 1.4 | 13.8 |
| 40–44 | 8,487 | 10.5 | 74.0 | 3.6 | 0.5 | 11.3 | 40–44 | 8,817 | 8.0 | 69.1 | 4.8 | 2.3 | 15.8 |
| 45–54 | 12,292 | 6.3 | 77.8 | 3.6 | 1.2 | 11.1 | 45–54 | 13,012 | 5.0 | 70.7 | 4.6 | 5.3 | 14.4 |
| 55–64 | 10,002 | 5.8 | 79.5 | 3.3 | 3.3 | 8.1 | 55–64 | 11,230 | 3.9 | 66.1 | 2.9 | 17.2 | 9.9 |
| 65–74 | 8,013 | 4.7 | 78.2 | 2.0 | 9.2 | 6.0 | 65–74 | 9,966 | 4.6 | 51.1 | 2.1 | 36.1 | 6.2 |
| 75–84 | 3,562 | 3.3 | 71.2 | 2.6 | 19.5 | 3.3 | 75–84 | 5,792 | 5.2 | 27.7 | 1.4 | 62.0 | 3.6 |
| 85+ | 758 | 3.5 | 46.9 | 4.2 | 43.4 | 2.0 | 85+ | 1,475 | 6.2 | 10.1 | 0.5 | 79.8 | 3.4 |
| Total 18+ | 86,872 | 25.8 | 61.3 | 3.0 | 2.7 | 7.2 | Total 18+ | 94,977 | 18.9 | 56.0 | 3.7 | 12.1 | 9.3 |

1. Includes separated, other reasons for absence, and for females, husband in armed forces. **Source**: U.S. Bureau of the Census, *Marital Status and Living Arrangements: March 1990* (1991).

## BLACK-WHITE MARRIED COUPLES IN THE U.S., 1970–89 (in thousands)

| Characteristic | 1970 | 1980 | 1989 |
|---|---|---|---|
| Total married couples | 44,597 | 49,714 | 52,924 |
| Total black-white | 65 | 167 | 219 |
| Husband black, wife white | 41 | 122 | 155 |
| Wife black, husband white | 24 | 45 | 64 |

**Source**: U.S. Bureau of the Census, *Statistical Abstract of the United States 1991* (1991).

**Divorces** An estimated 1.17 million divorces were granted in 1990. The divorce rate per 1,000 population remained at 4.7, down from the 1986–88 rate of 4.8, and down from its peak of 5.3 in 1979. (In that year the divorce rate per 1,000 married women reached 22.8, up from 9.2 in 1960.) While the divorce rate has stabilized, the ratio of divorced persons to married persons (with spouse present) has skyrocketed. Between 1970 and 1990 the proportion tripled from 47 divorced per 1,000 married to 142 per 1,000. For blacks, the rise was even greater, going from 83 per 1,000 to 282 per 1,000 in the same period.

In 1988, the most recent year for which final divorce statistics (as opposed to estimates) are available, divorce rates were highest for teenage wives (56.3 per 1,000), about twice the rate of wives age 30 to 34.

Divorce is generally more prevalent among the young. In 1988, 53% of men and 50% of women divorcing were under 25, figures that reflect the early demise of a sizable portion of all marriages: over one-third of all divorces in 1988 were for couples married less than five years, and almost two-thirds for couples married less than 10 years.

In 1990, there were 15.1 million currently divorced persons in the U.S., 8% of the total adult population. There are more divorced women (8.8 million) than men (6.3 million) because women are less likely to remarry.

## PERCENT OF POPULATION NEVER MARRIED, BY AGE AND SEX, 1960–90

| Sex and age | 1960 | 1970 | 1980 | 1990 | Sex and age | 1960 | 1970 | 1980 | 1990 |
|---|---|---|---|---|---|---|---|---|---|
| | **MEN** | | | | | **WOMEN** | | | |
| **Total: 15 and over** | 23.2% | 28.1% | 29.6% | 29.9% | **Total: 15 and over** | 17.3% | 22.1% | 22.5% | 22.8% |
| 15–17 | 98.8 | 99.4 | 99.4 | 99.8 | 15–17 | 93.2 | 97.3 | 97.0 | 98.5 |
| 18 | 94.6 | 95.1 | 97.4 | 98.5 | 18 | 75.6 | 82.0 | 88.0 | 92.0 |
| 19 | 87.1 | 89.9 | 90.9 | 95.3 | 19 | 59.7 | 68.8 | 77.6 | 88.7 |
| 20–24 | 53.1 | 54.7 | 68.8 | 79.3 | 20–24 | 28.4 | 35.8 | 50.2 | 62.8 |
| 25–29 | 20.8 | 19.1 | 33.1 | 45.2 | 25–29 | 10.5 | 10.5 | 20.9 | 31.1 |
| 30–34 | 11.9 | 9.4 | 15.9 | 27.0 | 30–34 | 6.9 | 6.2 | 9.5 | 16.4 |
| 35–39 | 8.8 | 7.2 | 7.8 | 14.7 | 35–39 | 6.1 | 5.4 | 6.2 | 10.4 |
| 40–44 | 7.3 | 6.3 | 7.1 | 10.5 | 40–44 | 6.1 | 4.9 | 4.8 | 8.0 |
| 45–54 | 7.4 | 7.5 | 6.1 | 6.3 | 45–54 | 7.0 | 4.9 | 4.7 | 5.0 |
| 55–64 | 8.0 | 7.8 | 5.3 | 5.8 | 55–64 | 8.0 | 6.8 | 4.5 | 3.9 |
| 65 and over | 7.7 | 7.5 | 4.9 | 4.2 | 65 and over | 8.5 | 7.7 | 5.9 | 4.9 |

**Source**: U.S. Bureau of the Census, *Marital Status and Living Arrangements: March 1990* (1991).

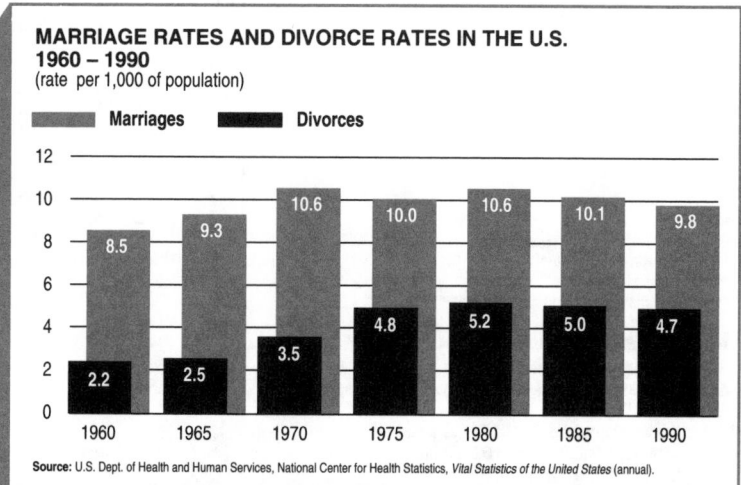

### MARRIAGE RATES AND DIVORCE RATES IN THE U.S. 1960 – 1990
(rate per 1,000 of population)

■ Marriages   ■ Divorces

| | 1960 | 1965 | 1970 | 1975 | 1980 | 1985 | 1990 |
|---|---|---|---|---|---|---|---|
| Marriages | 8.5 | 9.3 | 10.6 | 10.0 | 10.6 | 10.1 | 9.8 |
| Divorces | 2.2 | 2.5 | 3.5 | 4.8 | 5.2 | 5.0 | 4.7 |

**Source**: U.S. Dept. of Health and Human Services, National Center for Health Statistics, *Vital Statistics of the United States* (annual).

## MARRIAGES AND DIVORCES IN THE U.S., 1920–90

| Year | Marriages ('000s) | Rate per 1,000 of population | Divorces ('000s) | Rate per 1,000 of population |
|---|---|---|---|---|
| 1920 | 1,274 | 12.0 | 171 | 1.6 |
| 1925 | 1,188 | 10.3 | 175 | 1.5 |
| 1930 | 1,127 | 9.2 | 196 | 1.6 |
| 1935 | 1,327 | 10.4 | 218 | 1.7 |
| 1940 | 1,596 | 12.1 | 264 | 2.0 |
| 1945 | 1,613 | 12.2 | 485 | 3.5 |
| 1950 | 1,667 | 11.1 | 385 | 2.6 |
| 1955 | 1,531 | 9.3 | 377 | 2.3 |
| 1960 | 1,523 | 8.5 | 393 | 2.2 |
| 1965 | 1,800 | 9.3 | 479 | 2.5 |
| 1970 | 2,163 | 10.6 | 708 | 3.5 |
| 1975 | 2,153 | 10.0 | 1,036 | 4.8 |
| 1980 | 2,390 | 10.6 | 1,189 | 5.2 |
| 1981 | 2,422 | 10.6 | 1,213 | 5.3 |
| 1982 | 2,456 | 10.6 | 1,170 | 5.0 |
| 1983 | 2,446 | 10.5 | 1,158 | 4.9 |
| 1984 | 2,477 | 10.5 | 1,169 | 5.0 |
| 1985 | 2,413 | 10.1 | 1,190 | 5.0 |
| 1986 | 2,400 | 10.0 | 1,159 | 4.8 |
| 1987 | 2,421 | 9.9 | 1,157 | 4.8 |
| 1988[1] | 2,389 | 9.7 | 1,183 | 4.8 |
| 1989[1] | 2,404 | 9.7 | 1,163 | 4.7 |
| 1990[1] | 2,448 | 9.8 | 1,175 | 4.7 |

1. Estimated figures. **Sources:** U.S. Bureau of the Census, *The Statistical History of the U.S.* (1976); U.S. National Center for Health Statistics, *Vital Statistics of the United States* (annual) and *Monthly Vital Statistics Report, March 1991* (1991).

## DIVORCED PERSONS PER 1,000 MARRIED PERSONS, BY SEX AND RACE, 1960–90

| Sex/race | 1960 | 1970 | 1980 | 1990 |
|---|---|---|---|---|
| | **BOTH SEXES** | | | |
| All races | 35 | 47 | 100 | 142 |
| White | 33 | 44 | 92 | 133 |
| Black | 62 | 83 | 203 | 282 |
| Hispanic[1] | N.A. | 61 | 98 | 129 |
| | **MALE** | | | |
| All races | 28 | 35 | 79 | 118 |
| White | 27 | 32 | 74 | 112 |
| Black | 45 | 62 | 149 | 208 |
| Hispanic | N.A. | 40 | 64 | 103 |
| | **FEMALE** | | | |
| All races | 42 | 60 | 120 | 166 |
| White | 38 | 56 | 110 | 153 |
| Black | 78 | 104 | 258 | 358 |
| Hispanic | N.A. | 81 | 132 | 155 |

**Note:** Per 1,000 married persons with spouse present. 1. Persons of Hispanic origin may be of any race. **Source:** U.S. Bureau of the Census, *Marital Status and Living Arrangements: March 1990* (1991).

## Women and Childbearing: Current Trends

According to the Census Bureau's latest (1990) Current Population Survey, there were 58.4 million women in the United States ages 15 to 44; of these, 3.9 million reported having a birth in the preceding 12 months, resulting in an estimated fertility rate of 67.0 births per 1,000 women ages 15 to 44. These figures have not fluctuated a great deal over the last decade, despite the increased number of women of childbearing age in the population.

**Minorities** Significantly higher fertility rates were reported among minorities: 93 per 1,000 Hispanic women and 78.4 for black women, as compared with 65.2 for white women. It should be noted, however, that there were no significant differences between black and white fertility rates among women over 24; only in the 15–24 category do black women have significantly more births per 1,000 women.

Hispanic women ages 15 to 44 accounted for 13% of all births in the Census Bureau survey, although they represented only 8% of all women in the United States. The fertility rate among Hispanic women was 93.0 births per 1,000 women ages 15–44, as compared with 67.0 per 1,000 for all women. Hispanic women ages 15–44 have an average of 1.5 children each, as compared with 1.2 for non-Hispanic women.

**Women over 29** The Census Bureau noted again, as it had in previous reports, that a significant number of women in their thirties were having children or were planning to. In the 12

## FERTILITY RATES OF U.S. WOMEN, 1930–90

| Year | General fertility rate[1] | Total fertility rate | Year | General fertility rate[1] | Total fertility rate |
|---|---|---|---|---|---|
| 1930 | 89.2 | 2,600 | 1961 | 117.2 | 3,629 |
| 1931 | 84.6 | 2,467 | 1962 | 112.2 | 3,474 |
| 1932 | 81.7 | 2,383 | 1963 | 108.5 | 3,333 |
| 1933 | 76.3 | 2,235 | 1964 | 105.0 | 3,208 |
| 1934 | 78.5 | 2,294 | 1965 | 96.6 | 2,928 |
| 1935 | 77.2 | 2,250 | 1966 | 91.3 | 2,736 |
| 1936 | 75.8 | 2,207 | 1967 | 87.6 | 2,573 |
| 1937 | 77.1 | 2,236 | 1968 | 85.7 | 2,477 |
| 1938 | 79.1 | 2,288 | 1969 | 86.5 | 2,465 |
| 1939 | 77.6 | 2,238 | 1970 | 87.9 | 2,480 |
| 1940 | 79.9 | 2,301 | 1971 | 81.6 | 2,267 |
| 1941 | 83.4 | 2,399 | 1972 | 73.1 | 2,010 |
| 1942 | 91.5 | 2,628 | 1973 | 68.8 | 1,879 |
| 1943 | 94.3 | 2,718 | 1974 | 67.8 | 1,835 |
| 1944 | 88.8 | 2,568 | 1975 | 66.0 | 1,774 |
| 1945 | 85.9 | 2,491 | 1976 | 65.0 | 1,738 |
| 1946 | 101.9 | 2,943 | 1977 | 66.8 | 1,790 |
| 1947 | 113.3 | 3,274 | 1978 | 65.5 | 1,760 |
| 1948 | 107.3 | 3,109 | 1979 | 67.2 | 1,808 |
| 1949 | 107.1 | 3,110 | 1980 | 68.4 | 1,840 |
| 1950 | 106.2 | 3,091 | 1981 | 67.4 | 1,815 |
| 1951 | 111.4 | 3,267 | 1982 | 67.3 | 1,829 |
| 1952 | 113.8 | 3,355 | 1983 | 65.8 | 1,803 |
| 1953 | 115.0 | 3,418 | 1984 | 65.4 | 1,806 |
| 1954 | 117.9 | 3,537 | 1985 | 66.2 | 1,843 |
| 1955 | 118.3 | 3,574 | 1986 | 65.4 | 1,836 |
| 1956 | 121.0 | 3,682 | 1987 | 65.7 | 1,871 |
| 1957 | 122.7 | 3,760 | 1988 | 67.3 | 1,932 |
| 1958 | 120.0 | 3,693 | 1989 | 68.0 | 2,000 |
| 1959 | 119.9 | 3,705 | 1990 | 67.0 | 2,090[2] |
| 1960 | 118.0 | 3,654 | | | |

1. Figures through 1989 are based on all women ages 18 to 44; 1990 figure includes all women 15–44. 2. Estimated. **Sources:** U.S. Bureau of the Census, *U.S. Population Estimates and Components of Change 1970–87* (1988); *U.S. Population Estimates, by Age, Sex, Race, and Hispanic Origin: 1989* (1990); *The Fertility of American Women: 1990* (1991); U.S. National Center for Health Statistics, *Vital Statistics* (annual).

months ending June 1990, the birth rate per 1,000 women ages 30–34 was 80.4, as compared with 60.0 in 1980 and 56.4 in 1976; for women 35–39 the birth rate was 37.3 in 1990, as against 22.6 in 1976. (There has also been a relatively sharp increase in the birth rate for women ages 40–44, from 6.5 per 1,000 in 1976 to 8.6 in the 1990 survey.)

**Pregnancies of unmarried women** The Census Bureau reports that the number of out-of-wedlock and premaritally conceived births continued to increase. In the year ending June 1990, over 913,000 unmarried women ages 15–44 gave birth, 23% of the total number of women who had a birth. Among white women it was 17.2%, among Hispanic women 23.2%, and among black women 56.7%. Among teenagers ages 15 to 19, there were 229,000 births to unmarried women, or 67.8% of all births to women in that age group; the rates were 59.0% for whites, 65.1% for Hispanics, and 89.6% for blacks.

## The Fertility Rates of American Women

Population experts predict future trends in population growth by studying many factors, including the crude birth rate (see "Vital Statistics") and two significant fertility rates. The *general fertility rate*, as defined by the Census Bureau, measures the ratio of live births to the total number of women ages 18 to 44. (In 1990 the Census Bureau began reporting based on women ages 15 to 44, thereby lowering the fertility rate but more accurately measuring the increasing number of teenage pregnancies.)

The *total fertility rate*, as used by the National Center for Health Statistics, is the number of births 1,000 women ages 10 to 50 would have in their lifetimes if at each year of age they experienced the birth rates occurring to women of that age in the specified calendar year. The total fertility rate is sometimes defined in the popular media as the number of *likely* births

## WOMEN AND CHILDBEARING IN THE U.S., BY AGE, 1976–90

| Characteristic | 1976 | 1980 | 1985 | 1990 |
|---|---|---|---|---|
| Total number of women, 18–44 years | 41,618 | 45,652 | 50,951 | 53,520 |
| Percent childless | 35.0% | 36.7% | 38.1% | 36.6% |
| Births per 1,000 women | 67.2 | 71.1 | 68.6 | 71.2 |
| | **PERCENT OF CHILDLESS WOMEN** | | | |
| 18–24 years | 69.0% | 70.0% | 71.4% | 70.7% |
| 25–29 years | 30.8 | 36.8 | 41.5 | 42.1 |
| 30–34 years | 15.6 | 19.8 | 26.2 | 25.7 |
| 35–39 years | 10.5 | 12.1 | 16.7 | 17.7 |
| 40–44 years | 10.2 | 10.1 | 11.4 | 16.0 |
| | **BIRTHS PER 1,000 WOMEN** | | | |
| 18–24 years | 92.2 | 96.6 | 95.4 | 99.5 |
| 25–29 years | 104.8 | 114.8 | 109.2 | 112.1 |
| 30–34 years | 56.4 | 60.0 | 69.9 | 80.4 |
| 35–39 years | 22.6 | 26.9 | 25.9 | 37.3 |
| 40–44 years | 6.5 | 9.9 | 7.1 | 8.6 |

**Source:** U.S. Bureau of the Census, *Fertility of American Women: June 1990* (1991).

one woman will have in her lifetime. In 1988, for example, the official total fertility rate was 1,930 per 1,000 women, but it often appeared in the media as 1.9 per woman.

The total fertility rate is most helpful in measuring long-term trends, especially in determining whether or not the nation is sustaining a level of reproduction necessary for maintaining current population levels. That level, generally regarded as 2,100 per 1,000 women, has not been achieved in the United States since 1971. Since 1987 the figure has been moving upward, reflecting both the large number of women in their thirties who are having babies and the fact that women are having more babies. Still, the Census Bureau predicts that the rates will not reach 2,100 again in the foreseeable future. It is this fact that has made the topic of immigration policy such a crucial one for the future. (See also the section "Immigration.")

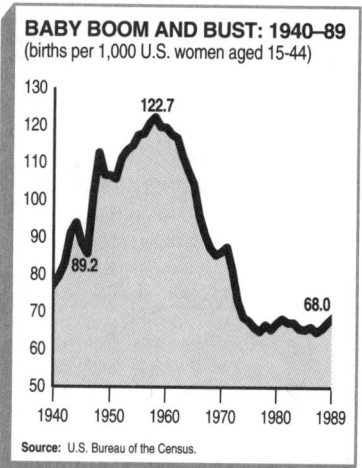

**BABY BOOM AND BUST: 1940–89**
(births per 1,000 U.S. women aged 15-44)

122.7

89.2

68.0

1940  1950  1960  1970  1980  1989

**Source:** U.S. Bureau of the Census.

**COHABITATION**
According to researchers at the University of Wisconsin, cohabitation without benefit of the marriage vow has become so commonplace that it may actually offset the declining marriage rate. In the late 1960s and early 1970s only about 11% of adults lived together before their first marriage, but by the early 1980s an estimated 44% did. Adults under the age of 30 are about twice as likely to be currently cohabitating. So although the percent of women married before the age of 25 has dropped dramatically (from 82% for women born in the 1940s, to 61% for those born in the 1960s) the percent cohabitating before their 25th birthday increased from 3% for women born in the early 1940s, to 37% for women born in the early 1960s.

**Source:** American Demographics.

## HOUSEHOLDS AND FAMILIES

Since the very first census in 1790, the federal government has not only attempted to count every individual, it has also tried to determine where those individuals live and with whom. While the definition of *household* has changed somewhat over the years, it has remained a central element in understanding the basic structure of American society. Since 1970 the size and composition of the household unit has revealed the extent of social change more clearly than any other measure.

**Households** Virtually all Americans are part of a household. As of March 1990, the Census Bureau determined that 245.8 million persons—out of a total population of 249 million—belonged to some form of household unit (the remainder were in institutions or other kinds of group living arrangements). According to the official Census Bureau definition, a household consists of "all persons who occupy a housing unit. A house, an apartment or other group of rooms, or a single room is regarded as a housing unit when it is occupied or intended for occupancy as separate living quarters; that is, when the occupants do not live and eat with any other persons in the structure, and there is direct access from the outside or through a common hall."

There are two major categories of households identified by the Census Bureau: family and nonfamily. A family or family household requires the presence of at least two persons, the householder (i.e., the person in whose name the housing unit is owned or rented) and one or more additional family members related to the householder through birth, adoption, or marriage. A nonfamily household consists of a householder who either lives alone or exclusively with persons who are not related to the householder. Since 1970 the rapid growth of nonfamily households has led to a continuous increase in the number of households and a fall in the average number of persons in each.

As of March 1990, there was a total of 93.3

### HOUSEHOLDS AND FAMILIES: GROWTH AND CHANGE, 1960–90
(numbers in thousands)

| Type of unit | 1960 | 1970 | 1980 | 1985 | 1990 | Percent change 1970–80 | Percent change 1980–90 |
|---|---|---|---|---|---|---|---|
| **Households** | **52,799** | **63,401** | **80,776** | **86,789** | **93,347** | **27.4%** | **15.5%** |
| Average size | 3.33 | 3.14 | 2.76 | 2.69 | 2.63 | — | — |
| Family households | 44,905 | 51,456 | 59,550 | 62,706 | 66,090 | 15.7 | 10.9 |
| Married couple | 39,254 | 44,728 | 49,112 | 50,350 | 52,317 | 9.8 | 6.6 |
| Male householder[1] | 1,228 | 1,228 | 1,733 | 2,228 | 2,884 | 41.1 | 66.4 |
| Female householder[1] | 4,422 | 5,500 | 8,705 | 10,129 | 10,890 | 58.3 | 25.1 |
| Nonfamily households | 7,895 | 11,945 | 21,226 | 24,082 | 27,257 | 77.7 | 28.4 |
| Male householder | 2,716 | 4,063 | 8,807 | 10,114 | 11,606 | 116.8 | 31.8 |
| Female householder | 5,179 | 7,882 | 12,419 | 13,968 | 15,651 | 57.6 | 26.0 |
| One person | 6,896 | 10,851 | 18,296 | 20,602 | 22,999 | 68.6 | 25.7 |
| **Families** | **45,111** | **51,586** | **59,550** | **62,706** | **66,090** | **15.4%** | **11.0%** |
| Average size | 3.67 | 3.58 | 3.29 | 3.23 | 3.17 | — | — |
| Married couple | 39,329 | 44,755 | 49,112 | 50,350 | 52,317 | 9.7 | 6.5 |
| Male householder[1] | 1,275 | 1,239 | 1,733 | 2,228 | 2,884 | 39.9 | 66.4 |
| Female householder[1] | 4,507 | 5,591 | 8,705 | 10,129 | 10,890 | 55.7 | 25.1 |
| **Unrelated subfamilies** | **207** | **130** | **360** | **526** | **534** | **176.9%** | **48.3%** |
| Married couple | 75 | 27 | 20 | 46 | 68 | N.A.[2] | N.A.[2] |
| Father-child[1] | 47 | 11 | 36 | 85 | 45 | N.A.[2] | N.A.[2] |
| Mother-child[1] | 85 | 91 | 304 | 395 | 421 | 234.1 | 38.5 |
| **Related subfamilies** | **1,514** | **1,150** | **1,150** | **2,228** | **2,403** | **0%** | **109.0%** |
| Married couple | 871 | 617 | 582 | 719 | 871 | -5.7 | 49.7 |
| Father-child[1] | 115 | 48 | 54 | 116 | 153 | N.A.[2] | 183.0 |
| Mother-child[1] | 528 | 484 | 512 | 1,392 | 1,378 | 5.8 | 169.1 |

1. No spouse present. 2. Not shown; base less than 75,000. **Sources:** U.S. Bureau of the Census. *Household and Family Characteristics: March 1990* (1991) and *The Statistical History of the U.S.* (1976).

million households in the United States, the largest number ever, with an average of 2.63 persons in each, significantly lower than the figures for 1970 (3.14) and for 1980 (2.76). While the U.S. population grew by 8.5% between 1980 and 1988, the number of households increased 13.9%, or 11.1 million units (1 million more were added in 1989). This continues a trend begun during the 1970s when the number of households increased by more than 20%, or over 17.3 million units, nearly double the 1940s and 1950s growth and over 60% more than the relatively explosive 1960s.

The most significant change helping to ignite this surge was the unprecedented increase in the number of nonfamily households, which grew by 77.7% in the 1970s and 28.4% during the 1980s.

Several factors help to account for this sudden change, including the rapid rise in the divorce rate and an increase in the number of young single people living on their own and deciding to postpone marriage. The demographic results can be found in the increasing number of people living alone (up 54% in the 1970s and 25.7% in the 1980s); in 1989 some

22.7 million people lived alone, a total of 84% of the 26.9 million nonfamily households.

An additional 2.9 million unmarried-couple households make up the largest proportion of the remaining number; while they compose only about 5% of the 55.2 million couples in the United States who maintain their own households, their sudden appearance on the American social landscape during the 1970s—they increased by about 120% during that decade—made them the subject of widespread media coverage. They grew another 80% in the 1980s (1.6 million to 2.9 million). As currently defined by the Census Bureau, an unmarried-couple household is two persons of the opposite sex who share living quarters; although a close personal relationship is implied, other types—including tenancy—are included. But no more than two unrelated adults are present in an unmarried-couple household, although children under age 15 may be present (31%, or 891,000, did contain such children in 1990).

Despite all the attention given to the growth of nonfamily households, the fact remains that the overwhelming majority of Americans—212.5 million in 1990—live in some kind of family situation. This is not to say that the size and structure of the family hasn't undergone major revamping in recent decades, but rather to emphasize its inherent strength as the basic social unit despite the presence of powerful forces for change.

**Families** In 1990 there were 66.1 million family households in the United States; almost 80% (52.3 million) were married couples, and almost half of those had children of their own

under age 18. But since 1970 significant changes in the basic structure of the American family have taken place. The proportion of two-parent households, for example, has declined from 40% of the total in 1970 to only 26% in 1990, while the number of single-parent family groups more than doubled, from 3.8 million to 9.7 million (8.4 million of these were maintained by women). In addition, average family size declined dramatically from 3.58 in 1970 to 3.17 in 1990, and the percentage of families without children rose from 44.1% to 51.1%.

Another important, though less vital, sign of change is the growth in the number of so-called *subfamilies*. These are families who live in a household and are either related to or not related to the householder. The Census Bureau describes a *related subfamily* as a married couple with or without children, or one parent with one or more of his or her own single (never married) children under 18 living in a household and related to the person who maintains the household. Related subfamilies have grown dramatically between 1980 and 1990 (109%) to 2.4 million, and almost all of them are made up of mothers with children. They are not counted in the total number of families. An *unrelated subfamily* is a group of two persons or

## FAMILIES: NUMBER, AVERAGE SIZE, AND PERCENT DISTRIBUTION, BY NUMBER OF CHILDREN, 1970–90

| Year | No. of families ('000s) | Avg. size of family | Percent distribution by number of own children under 18 | | | | |
|---|---|---|---|---|---|---|---|
| | | | None | 1 | 2 | 3 | 4 or more |
| 1970 | 51,586 | 3.58 | 44.1% | 18.2% | 17.4% | 10.6% | 9.8% |
| 1975 | 55,712 | 3.42 | 46.0 | 19.7 | 18.0 | 9.3 | 6.9 |
| 1980 | 59,550 | 3.29 | 47.9 | 20.9 | 19.3 | 7.8 | 4.1 |
| 1985 | 62,706 | 3.23 | 50.4 | 20.9 | 18.6 | 7.2 | 3.0 |
| 1988 | 65,133 | 3.17 | 51.0 | 21.0 | 18.2 | 7.0 | 2.8 |
| 1990 | 66,090 | 3.17 | 51.1 | 20.5 | 18.5 | 7.0 | 2.8 |

**Sources:** U.S. Bureau of the Census, *Household and Family Characteristics: March 1990* (1990) and *Statistical Abstract of the United States 1989* (1989).

## UNMARRIED COUPLE HOUSEHOLDS, 1960–90 (in thousands)

| Characteristic | 1960 | 1970 | 1980 | 1990 |
|---|---|---|---|---|
| **Total** | **439** | **523** | **1,589** | **2,856** |
| Without children under 15 | 242 | 327 | 1,159 | 1,966 |
| With children under 15 | 197 | 196 | 431 | 891 |

**Note:** Figures may not add to total due to rounding. **Source:** U.S. Bureau of the Census, *Marital Status and Living Arrangements: March 1990* (1991).

## NUMBER OF U.S. HOUSEHOLDS AND AVERAGE NUMBER OF PERSONS PER HOUSEHOLD, 1940–90

| Year | Number of households ('000s) | Average number per household | | |
|---|---|---|---|---|
| | | All ages | Under 18 yrs. | 18 yrs. and older |
| 1940 | 34,949 | 3.67 | 1.14 | 2.53 |
| 1950 | 43,544 | 3.37 | 1.06 | 2.31 |
| 1955 | 47,874 | 3.33 | 1.14 | 2.19 |
| 1960 | 52,799[1] | 3.33 | 1.21 | 2.12 |
| 1965 | 57,436 | 3.29 | 1.21 | 2.09 |
| 1970 | 63,401 | 3.14 | 1.09 | 2.05 |
| 1975 | 71,120 | 2.94 | 0.93 | 2.01 |
| 1980 | 80,776 | 2.76 | 0.79 | 1.97 |
| 1985 | 86,789 | 2.69 | 0.72 | 1.97 |
| 1990 | 93,347 | 2.63 | 0.69 | 1.94 |

1. Alaska and Hawaii included for first time. **Sources:** U.S. Bureau of the Census, *The Statistical History of the U.S.* (1976) and *Household and Family Characteristics: March 1990 and 1989* (1990).

## LIVING ARRANGEMENTS OF CHILDREN UNDER 18, BY RACE, 1970–90
(numbers in thousands)

| Living arrangement | 1970 | | 1980 | | 1990 | |
|---|---|---|---|---|---|---|
| | Number | Percent | Number | Percent | Number | Percent |
| **ALL CHILDREN[1]** | | | | | | |
| Children under 18 | 69,162 | 100.0% | 63,427 | 100.0% | 64,137 | 100.0% |
| Living with: | | | | | | |
| Two parents | 58,939 | 85.2% | 48,624 | 76.7% | 46,503 | 72.5% |
| One parent | 8,199 | 11.9 | 12,466 | 19.7 | 15,867 | 24.7 |
| Mother only | 7,452 | 10.8 | 11,406 | 18.0 | 13,874 | 21.6 |
| Father only | 748 | 1.1 | 1,060 | 1.7 | 1,993 | 3.1 |
| Other relatives | 1,547 | 2.2 | 1,949 | 3.1 | 1,422 | 2.2 |
| Nonrelatives only | 477 | 0.7 | 388 | 0.6 | 346 | 0.5 |
| **WHITE CHILDREN** | | | | | | |
| Children under 18 | 58,790 | 100.0% | 52,242 | 100.0% | 51,390 | 100.0% |
| Living with: | | | | | | |
| Two parents | 52,624 | 89.5% | 43,200 | 82.7% | 40,593 | 79.0% |
| One parent | 5,109 | 18.9 | 7,901 | 15.1 | 9,870 | 19.2 |
| Mother only | 4,581 | 16.0 | 7,059 | 13.5 | 8,321 | 16.2 |
| Father only | 528 | 0.9 | 842 | 1.6 | 1,549 | 3.0 |
| Other relatives | 696 | 1.6 | 887 | 1.7 | 708 | 1.4 |
| Nonrelatives only | 362 | 0.6 | 254 | 0.5 | 220 | 0.4 |
| **BLACK CHILDREN** | | | | | | |
| Children under 18 | 9,422 | 100.0% | 9,375 | 100.0% | 10,018 | 100.0% |
| Living with: | | | | | | |
| Two parents | 5,508 | 58.5% | 3,956 | 42.2% | 3,781 | 37.7% |
| One parent | 2,996 | 31.8 | 4,297 | 45.8 | 5,485 | 54.8 |
| Mother only | 2,783 | 29.5 | 4,117 | 43.9 | 5,132 | 51.2 |
| Father only | 213 | 2.3 | 180 | 1.9 | 353 | 3.5 |
| Other relatives | 820 | 8.7 | 999 | 10.7 | 654 | 6.5 |
| Nonrelatives only | 97 | 1.0 | 123 | 1.3 | 98 | 1.0 |
| **HISPANIC CHILDREN** | | | | | | |
| Children under 18 | 4,006 | 100.0% | 5,459 | 100.0% | 7,174 | 100.0% |
| Living with: | | | | | | |
| Two parents | 3,111 | 77.7% | 4,116 | 75.4% | 4,789 | 66.8% |
| One parent | N.A. | N.A. | 1,152 | 21.1 | 2,154 | 30.0 |
| Mother only | N.A. | N.A. | 1,069 | 19.6 | 1,943 | 2.9 |
| Father only | N.A. | N.A. | 83 | 1.5 | 211 | 2.5 |
| Other relatives | N.A. | N.A. | 183 | 3.4 | 177 | 2.5 |
| Nonrelatives only | N.A. | N.A. | 8 | 0.1 | 54 | 0.8 |

1. Includes other children not shown separately. **Source:** U.S. Bureau of the Census, *Marital Status and Living Arrangements: March 1990* (1991).

more who are related to each other by birth, marriage, or adoption, but who are not related to the householder. Unrelated subfamilies currently number 534,000, a more than 200% increase since 1970; often they are guests or boarders or resident employees.

## Living Arrangements of Children and Young Adults

Among the important social changes of the last 20 years, two of the most revealing concern whom children live with and how soon young people get to live on their own. Since 1970, the number of children under 18 living with only one parent has doubled both in number and as a percentage of all children under 18. In 1990, over 25% lived with only one parent, as compared to just under 12% in 1970. This increase reflects the soaring divorce rate of the period. For black children, of whom 54.8% lived with only one parent in 1990, the number of one-parent situations has risen from 3 million in 1970 to 5.5 million in 1990, with slightly more than half of them born to unmarried mothers, a 50% increase since 1980.

Inflation, soaring housing costs, and stagnant wage rates have helped to keep people ages 18 to 34 living at home with their parents for an increasingly long period. This applies to both sexes and is related to the postponement of marriage by large numbers of both. In 1970, for example, 38% of all people 18 to 24 had their own family household or were married to someone who did; by 1990, only 22% were. Among the same age group, the percentage still living in their parents' household rose from 48% to 53% between 1980 and 1990. Among those ages 25 to 34, the percentage of family householders or people married to one dropped from 83% to 64% between 1970 and 1990. Among these older young adults, too, the number living in nonfamily households grew from 5% to almost 13% in the same period.

## HOUSING

According to the U.S. Bureau of the Census, *Current Housing Reports*, there were 107.2 million housing units in the U.S. in the first quarter of 1991, the latest period for which data were available. Of these units:
• 95.0 million (88.6%) were occupied.
• 60.7 million (56.6%) were occupied by home owners.
• 34.3 million (32%) were occupied by renters.
• 12.2 million (11.4%) were vacant (the rental vacancy rate was 7.5%; the home-owner vacancy rate was 1.7%; the remaining 2.2% were off the market for various reasons).
**Housing units** The American ideal of the intact nuclear family may be somewhat tarnished in these days of high divorce rates and growing single-parent households, but U.S. housing patterns still reflect traditional values. About 69.3 million homes—65% of U.S. housing—were single-unit structures (72% if mobile homes are included) according to the 1989 *American Housing Survey* of the Census Bureau. About 29.4

million units were in multiple dwellings, ranging from two- to four-family houses to large apartment buildings. (Included were 4.5 million condominiums and 871,000 co-ops.)
**Size of housing units** In 1989 one-half of 105.6 million units contained more than 5.3 rooms and half had fewer; the overwhelming majority of units, 79.3 million, had four to seven rooms, while only 13.1 million had eight or more, and 13.2 million had three or less.

The median size of all single, detached one-family houses (including mobile homes) was 1,639 square feet; for those that were owner-occupied the figure was 1,766 square feet. About 15.4% (10.6 million) had more than 2,500 square feet, and 44.4% (28.8 million) had less than 1,500 square feet. In recent years the size of new, privately owned one-family houses had skyrocketed from an average of 1,500 square feet in 1970 to 2,035 square feet in 1989.
**Growth of housing** In 1989 the median age of all U.S. housing structures was 27 years (1962). Only 10.9 million units built before 1919 were still in use. This reflects the extraordinary growth of the housing industry during the last 30 years when 55.3 million units were built, almost 20 million more than in the 40 previous years. Between 1920 and 1989 approximately 90 million housing units (still in use) were built while the population increased by only 140 million; or, a new unit was built per 1.5 persons.

**Home ownership** Of the 59.2 million owner-occupied housing units listed by the Census Bureau in 1989, just over 90.4% (54.2 million) were owned by whites, 8% (4.6 million) by blacks, and 4% (2.5 million) by Hispanics. Among white householders, 67.4% were owners, and among minority householders 43.3% were.

During the 1980s the home ownership rate—the percentage of householders who were home owners—declined for the first time since the 1930s. In 1989 the home ownership rate was 63.9%, significantly lower than the 65.6% recorded in 1980. Much of the decline occurred because of an increasing number of non-married-couple family households and also because skyrocketing home prices prevented many married-couple families under 50 from purchasing homes. The home ownership rates for home owners over 60 actually increased slight-

### GROWTH OF HOUSING BY DECADE, 1920–89

| Decade | Millions of units built |
|---|---|
| 1920–29 | 6.1 |
| 1930–39 | 7.0 |
| 1940–49 | 9.0 |
| 1950–59 | 14.2 |
| 1960–69 | 16.8 |
| 1970–79 | 24.8 |
| 1980–89 | 13.7 |

**Source:** U.S. Bureau of the Census, *1987 American Housing Survey for the United States* (1989).

### HOUSING UNITS BY TYPE, 1989

| Housing units per structure | Millions of units | Percent of units |
|---|---|---|
| Single, detached | 63.6 | 60.1% |
| Single, attached | 5.7 | 5.4 |
| Mobile home or trailer | 6.9 | 6.5 |
| 2 to 4 | 11.3 | 10.7 |
| 5 to 9 | 5.6 | 5.2 |
| 10 to 19 | 4.9 | 4.6 |
| 20 to 49 | 3.8 | 3.5 |
| 50 or more | 4.0 | 3.8 |
| **Total housing units** | **105.7** | **100.0** |

**Note:** Figures may not add to totals due to rounding. **Source:** U.S. Bureau of the Census, *1989 American Housing Survey* (1991).

### MEDIAN SALES PRICE OF EXISTING ONE-FAMILY HOUSES IN SELECTED METROPOLITAN AREAS, 1988–91
(in thousands)

| Metropolitan statistical area | 1988 | 1989 | 1991[1] |
|---|---|---|---|
| Atlanta, Ga. | N.A. | $ 84.0 | $ 86.2 |
| Baltimore, Md. | $ 88.7 | 96.3 | 103.0 |
| Boston, Mass. | 181.2 | 181.9 | 160.1 |
| Chicago, Ill. | 98.9 | 107.0 | 109.0 |
| Cincinnati, Ohio | 69.7 | 75.8 | 83.6 |
| Cleveland, Ohio | 69.2 | 75.2 | 81.1 |
| Dallas, Tex. | 90.8 | 92.4 | 86.1 |
| Denver, Colo. | 81.8 | 85.5 | 83.1 |
| Detroit, Mich. | 73.1 | 73.7 | 78.4 |
| Houston, Tex. | 61.8 | 66.7 | 71.4 |
| Kansas City, Mo.-Kans. | 70.5 | 71.6 | 73.2 |
| Los Angeles area, Calif. | 179.4 | 214.1 | 203.9 |
| Miami-Hialeah, Fla. | 82.9 | 86.9 | 88.0 |
| Milwaukee, Wis. | 74.5 | 79.6 | 87.1 |
| Minneapolis–St. Paul, Minn. | 85.2 | 87.2 | 90.5 |
| New York–New Jersey–Long Island, N.Y.-N.J.-Conn. | 183.8 | 183.2 | 166.4 |
| Philadelphia, Pa. | 102.4 | 103.9 | 106.1 |
| Phoenix, Ariz. | 80.0 | 78.8 | 84.0 |
| Pittsburgh, Pa. | 63.2 | 65.8 | 69.0 |
| San Diego, Calif. | 147.8 | 181.8 | 181.9 |
| San Francisco Bay area, Calif. | 212.6 | 260.2 | 244.8 |
| Seattle-Tacoma, Wash. | 88.7 | 115.0 | 139.1 |
| St. Louis, Mo. | 78.1 | 76.9 | 78.9 |
| Tampa–St. Petersburg–Clearwater, Fla. | 65.6 | 71.9 | 68.1 |
| Washington, D.C.-Md.-Va. | 132.5 | 144.4 | 145.5 |

1. First quarter only. **Source:** National Association of Realtors, *Home Sales* (May 1991).

## FAIR MARKET RENTS FOR EXISTING HOUSING FOR SELECTED METROPOLITAN AREAS, 1991

| Metropolitan area | 1 Bed-room | 2 Bed-rooms | 3 Bed-rooms |
|---|---|---|---|
| Anaheim-Santa Ana, Calif. | $732 | $863 | $1,078 |
| Atlanta, Ga. | 479 | 564 | 705 |
| Baltimore, Md. | 465 | 547 | 684 |
| Boston, Mass. | 739 | 869 | 1,087 |
| Chicago, Ill. | 543 | 635 | 799 |
| Cincinnati, Ohio | 389 | 458 | 572 |
| Cleveland, Ohio | 396 | 466 | 583 |
| Dallas, Tex. | 450 | 529 | 661 |
| Denver, Colo. | 404 | 476 | 594 |
| Detroit, Mich. | 425 | 499 | 625 |
| Fort Lauderdale-Hollywood-Pompano Beach, Fla. | 513 | 604 | 756 |
| Fresno, Calif. | 447 | 526 | 657 |
| Honolulu, Hawaii | 591 | 695 | 875 |
| Houston, Tex. | 364 | 429 | 537 |
| Indianapolis, Ind. | 408 | 480 | 600 |
| Kansas City, Mo. | 378 | 444 | 555 |
| Las Vegas, Nev. | 540 | 636 | 797 |
| Los Angeles-Long Beach, Calif. | 642 | 747 | 957 |
| Memphis, Tenn. | 361 | 425 | 529 |
| Miami-Hialeah, Fla. | 491 | 578 | 722 |
| Milwaukee, Wis. | 407 | 482 | 603 |
| Minneapolis-St. Paul, Minn. | 464 | 550 | 688 |
| New Orleans, La. | 423 | 498 | 622 |
| New York, N.Y.[1] | 531 | 625 | 783 |
| Oklahoma City, Okla. | 352 | 414 | 518 |
| Philadelphia, Pa. | 495 | 583 | 729 |
| Phoenix, Ariz. | 490 | 575 | 720 |
| Pittsburgh, Pa. | 373 | 439 | 549 |
| Portland, Oreg. | 418 | 492 | 650 |
| Sacramento, Calif. | 463 | 554 | 805 |
| San Diego, Calif. | 583 | 684 | 857 |
| San Francisco, Calif. | 775 | 919 | 1,144 |
| San Jose, Calif. | 716 | 844 | 1,054 |
| Seattle, Wash. | 507 | 592 | 765 |
| St. Louis, Mo. | 413 | 487 | 608 |
| Tampa-St. Petersburg-Clearwater, Fla. | 427 | 503 | 627 |
| Washington, D.C.-Md.-Va. | 621 | 731 | 914 |
| West Palm Beach-Boca Raton-Delray Beach, Fla. | 449 | 523 | 640 |

**Note:** Figures are projections for 1991 made in 1990. 1. Figures include areas outside Manhattan. **Source:** U.S. Dept. of Housing and Urban Development, Office of the Federal Housing Commissioner, as recorded in *The Federal Register*, Oct. 1, 1990.

## AVERAGE SALES PRICES OF NEW ONE-FAMILY HOUSES, BY REGION, 1965–90 (in current dollars)

| Year | United States | Northeast | Midwest | South | West |
|---|---|---|---|---|---|
| 1965 | $21,500 | $22,900 | $22,800 | $18,900 | $23,200 |
| 1970 | 26,600 | 32,800 | 28,000 | 24,000 | 26,900 |
| 1975 | 42,600 | 47,000 | 43,400 | 39,600 | 44,300 |
| 1980 | 76,400 | 80,300 | 74,400 | 69,100 | 89,400 |
| 1985 | 100,800 | 121,900 | 95,400 | 88,900 | 111,800 |
| 1988 | 138,300 | 179,300 | 123,700 | 114,800 | 155,700 |
| 1990 | 149,800 | 190,500 | 133,000 | 123,500 | 180,600 |

**Source:** U.S. Bureau of the Census, *New One-Family Houses Sold and For Sale, 1990* (1991).

## MEDIAN SALES PRICES OF NEW ONE-FAMILY HOUSES IN SELECTED METROPOLITAN AREAS, 1987–89 (in thousands)

| Metropolitan statistical area | 1987 | 1988 | 1989 |
|---|---|---|---|
| Atlanta, Ga. | $ 94.6 | $ 91.5 | $ 94.9 |
| Baltimore, Md. | 113.6 | 127.9 | 149.3 |
| Chicago, Ill. | 147.2 | 169.1 | 192.3 |
| Dallas, Tex. | 89.5 | 92.7 | 100.2 |
| Denver, Colo. | 111.0 | 126.5 | 144.9 |
| Houston, Tex. | 95.9 | 101.7 | 120.9 |
| Kansas City, Mo. | 75.2 | 79.0 | 80.1 |
| Las Vegas, Nev. | 91.2 | 102.7 | 110.7 |
| Los Angeles–Anaheim–Riverside, Calif. | 133.6 | 145.8 | 172.4 |
| Miami–Ft. Lauderdale, Fla. | 91.7 | 93.3 | 108.5 |
| Minneapolis–St. Paul, Minn. | 99.6 | 99.6 | 103.7 |
| New York–New Jersey–Long Island, N.Y.-N.J.-Conn. | 195.1 | 195.7 | 202.2 |
| Phoenix, Ariz. | 98.4 | 107.3 | 101.5 |
| St. Louis, Mo. | 96.1 | 104.3 | 113.3 |
| San Antonio, Tex. | 87.3 | 86.0 | 83.8 |
| San Diego, Calif. | 156.9 | 190.2 | 243.6 |
| Seattle-Tacoma, Wash. | 114.7 | 112.2 | 131.8 |
| Tampa–St. Petersburg–Clearwater, Fla. | 85.2 | 87.1 | 92.3 |
| Washington, D.C.-Md.-Va. | 135.6 | 158.8 | 182.3 |
| West Palm Beach–Boca Raton–Delray Beach, Fla. | 105.3 | 106.8 | 154.2 |

**Note:** Figures are for houses sold. **Source:** U.S. Bureau of the Census, *New One-Family Houses Sold and For Sale, 1990* (1991).

## HOME OWNERSHIP RATES IN THE U.S., BY AGE AND FAMILY STATUS, 1982–90

| Age of householder | 1982 | 1985 | 1988 | 1990 |
|---|---|---|---|---|
| All households | 64.8% | 63.9% | 63.8% | 63.9% |
| Less than 25 years | 19.3 | 17.2 | 15.8 | 15.7 |
| 25–29 | 38.6 | 37.7 | 35.9 | 35.2 |
| 30–34 | 57.1 | 54.0 | 53.2 | 51.8 |
| Less than 35 years | 41.2 | 39.9 | 39.3 | 38.5 |
| 35–39 | 67.6 | 65.4 | 63.6 | 63.0 |
| 40–44 | 73.0 | 71.4 | 70.7 | 69.8 |
| 45–49 | 76.0 | 74.3 | 74.4 | 73.9 |
| Less than 50 years | 55.3 | 54.4 | 54.5 | 54.3 |
| 50 years and over | 77.2 | 76.9 | 77.1 | 77.4 |
| 65 years and over | 74.4 | 74.8 | 75.6 | 76.3 |
| Married-couple families | 78.5 | 78.2 | 78.9 | 78.1 |
| Less than 25 years | 32.6 | 31.0 | 29.1 | 27.3 |
| Less than 35 years | 58.2 | 57.6 | 58.0 | 56.0 |
| Less than 50 years | 71.3 | 70.9 | 71.8 | 70.8 |
| 50 years and over | 88.1 | 88.3 | 88.9 | 89.2 |
| **NON-MARRIED-COUPLE HOUSEHOLDS** | | | | |
| Male householder | | | | |
| Less than 25 years | 21.6% | 18.2% | 17.6% | 19.3% |
| Less than 35 years | 35.8 | 34.4 | 31.8 | 31.8 |
| Less than 50 years | 49.4 | 48.6 | 46.1 | 45.9 |
| 50 years and over | 76.1 | 75.0 | 76.4 | 75.8 |
| 65 years and over | 75.3 | 78.3 | 80.0 | 80.7 |
| Female householder | | | | |
| Less than 25 years | 8.9% | 7.1% | 8.4% | 8.7% |
| Less than 35 years | 20.9 | 19.2 | 18.5 | 17.2 |
| Less than 50 years | 35.2 | 33.5 | 33.2 | 32.5 |
| 50 years and over | 70.9 | 71.7 | 71.4 | 70.2 |
| 65 years and over | 75.1 | 76.7 | 78.3 | 76.9 |
| **ONE-PERSON HOUSEHOLDS** | | | | |
| One-person households | 45.6% | 45.8% | 46.3% | 49.0% |
| Male householder | 38.0 | 38.8 | 39.9 | 42.4 |
| Less than 50 years | 28.5 | 29.6 | 30.8 | 33.0 |
| 50 years and over | 52.9 | 53.9 | 54.9 | 57.4 |
| Female householder | 51.2 | 51.3 | 51.8 | 53.6 |
| Less than 50 years | 23.3 | 25.8 | 27.8 | 30.2 |
| 50 years and over | 61.6 | 61.2 | 61.8 | 63.3 |

**Note:** Rate is the percentage of householders who were home owners. **Source:** U.S. Bureau of the Census, *Housing Vacancies and Homeownership, Annual Statistics: 1990* (1991).

regional tax burdens and energy supplies. Only 9% (3.0 million) of all renters paid over $700 a month. Monthly housing costs for owners was $397 including mortgage payment, taxes, and maintenance costs.

ly during the 1980s and stood at 76.3% in 1990.

Married-couple families own most of the homes in the U.S. In 1989, over 40.8 million (68%) of the 59.9 million owner-occupied units were in this category; one-person households accounted for 11 million (up about 24% since 1980), and so-called other two-or-more-person households for the remaining 7 million.

In 1990, the average cost of a new one-family house in the U.S. was $149,800, about double the average price ($76,400) in 1980. Prices in the Northeast and the West were significantly higher than in other regions (see the accompanying table).

**Housing costs** According to an annual survey by the Chicago Title Insurance Company the average price paid by first-time home-buyers was $97,100 in 1988, and for buyers who previously owned a home $141,400. Average monthly mortgage payments were $1,008, 32.8% of owners' incomes. Although 82% of the 1.08 million new homes bought in 1988 were mortgaged, only 56.9% of all total owner-occupied homes, including condominiums, still had mortgages in 1987 (5.9% had two or more). The 43.1% of so-called "free and clear" homes represents the high proportion of elderly Americans who are homeowners.

The monthly cost of running a house or apartment can vary dramatically based on

## THE HOMELESS

Although homeless people have become a common sight in almost every community, their plight is always surrounded by some kind of controversy, one that is fueled by a wide range of opinions, some based on fact and others on stereotypes. The often shrill debate about just who the homeless are and what can or should be done for them has been hampered by a lack of reliable information on everything from the causes of homelessness to the actual number of people living on the streets or in shelters.

## ESTIMATES OF THE HOMELESS POPULATION IN SELECTED U.S. CITIES, 1990

| Rank/City | Total | Number in shelters | Number visible on street |
|---|---|---|---|
| 1. New York | 33,830 | 23,383 | 10,447 |
| 2. Los Angeles | 7,706 | 4,597 | 3,109 |
| 3. Chicago | 6,764 | 5,180 | 1,584 |
| 4. San Francisco | 5,569 | 4,003 | 1,566 |
| 5. San Diego | 4,947 | 2,846 | 2,101 |
| 6. Washington, D.C. | 4,813 | 4,682 | 131 |
| 7. Philadelphia | 4,485 | 3,416 | 1,069 |
| 8. Newark | 2,816 | 1,974 | 842 |
| 9. Seattle | 2,539 | 2,170 | 360 |
| 10. Atlanta | 2,491 | 2,431 | 60 |
| 11. Boston | 2,463 | 2,245 | 218 |
| 12. Houston | 1,931 | 1,780 | 151 |
| 13. Phoenix | 1,786 | 1,710 | 276 |
| 14. Portland | 1,702 | 1,553 | 149 |
| 15. Sacramento | 1,552 | 1,287 | 265 |
| 16. Baltimore | 1,531 | 1,144 | 387 |
| 17. Dallas | 1,493 | 1,200 | 293 |
| 18. Denver | 1,269 | 1,169 | 100 |
| 19. Oklahoma City | 1,250 | 1,016 | 234 |
| 20. Minneapolis | 1,080 | 1,052 | 28 |

**Source**: U.S. Bureau of the Census release, 1991.

**The number of homeless** Estimates of the total number vary depending on the group doing the counting. The total ranges from about 50,000 (the U.S. Department of Housing and Urban Development) to 3 million (homeless advocacy groups).

A 1988 study by the National Alliance to End Homelessness calculated that on a given night there are about 735,000 homeless in the United States, and that during the course of the year between 1.3 and 2 million people will be homeless for one or more nights. Another study, released in 1989 by the Urban Institute, concluded that there were about 600,000 Americans living in shelters or on the streets on a given night.

The first comprehensive federal effort to count the homeless was done as part of the 1990 census count. The Census Bureau hired approximately 22,000 people who, armed with flashlights and survey questionnaires, attempted to locate every homeless person they could find between 6 p.m. and 4 a.m. on Mar. 20–21. They visited 11,000 shelters and 24,000 street sites and reported a total of 228,621 homeless persons—178,828 in emergency shelters and 49,793 at "preidentified street locations." Among the states, California (48,887) and New York (43,204) ranked first and second; the next two, Florida and Pennsylvania, were far behind with 10,299 and 9,549 respectively. Among the major cities none came remotely close to New York's 33,830.

No one, not even the Census Bureau, believes that nearly all the homeless were counted. In fact, census officials claim they never believed they could count all the homeless but that a strong effort was needed to help estimate the total population of the country. Despite this disclaimer, every advocacy group for the homeless feared the low count would be used to lower the amount of federal funding currently allocated.

**Who are the homeless?** While a 1988 study of 27 major cities by the U.S. Conference of Mayors did not give a figure for the total number of homeless, the study did pinpoint a number of characteristics. Contrary to common belief, not all homeless are single men. The number of middle-age men has been shrinking, while families with young children are the fastest-growing group. And the demographics of the homeless differ dramatically from city to city.

The composition of the cities' homeless population was, on average: 49% single men, 34% members of families, 13% single women, and 5% runaway and so-called "throwaway" youth (children rejected by parents). Children—both in families and runaways—account for about 25% of the population; persons considered mentally ill account for about 25%; substance abusers account for 34%. The survey also found that 21% of homeless people are employed in full- or part-time jobs; 26% are veterans.

Another study found that the average age of single homeless men and women was between 34 and 37, which is much lower than found in previous decades. Homeless adults are likely to have never been married; they also usually don't have strong family ties.

The Institute of Medicine (part of the National Academy of Sciences) looked at a number of surveys and found that minorities composed the largest number of homeless in major cities like New York, Detroit, Chicago, Baltimore, and St. Louis. Whites accounted for the highest percentage in Milwaukee, Phoenix, Portland, and the state of Ohio.

Cities in which single men accounted for 60% or more of the homeless population included Charleston, Minneapolis, Nashville, Phoenix, Saint Paul, Salt Lake City, San Francisco, and San Juan. Cities where single men accounted for 30% or less of the population included Detroit, Kansas City, Mo., Norfolk, and Portland.

Unaccompanied youths—runaways and throwaways—account for 10% or more of the population in Denver, Los Angeles, New Orleans, Providence, San Antonio, San Francisco, and San Juan.

Thirty percent or more of the homeless were considered severely mentally ill in Boston, Charleston, Cleveland, Denver, Kansas City, Los Angeles, Nashville, Providence, San Francisco, San Juan, and Seattle. A survey funded by the Robert Wood Johnson Foundation estimated that a third of homeless adults are mentally ill.

Forty percent or more of the homeless were considered to be substance abusers in Cleveland, Hartford, Minneapolis, Providence, San Juan, Seattle, and Trenton.

**Homeless families** Families with children account for more than half the homeless population in Detroit, New York City, Norfolk, Portland, and Trenton. They compose one-fifth or less in Charleston, Minneapolis, New Orleans, Phoenix, Saint Paul, San Francisco, and San Juan. Among homeless families 23% were headed by two parents; the rest by single parents, usually a woman with two to three children under the age of five. A 1988 U.S. Department of Education survey estimated that there were 220,000 homeless school-age children; of those children, more than 65,000 do not attend school regularly.

**Causes of homelessness** Every city surveyed by the Conference of Mayors cited lack of affordable housing for low-income people as the main cause of homelessness. Other causes frequently cited were unemployment, mental illness, substance abuse, poverty, teen pregnancy, and domestic violence.

A 1988 Institute of Medicine review of data on the causes of homelessness found three patterns: temporary, episodic, and chronic. In the first category fell people displaced from their homes by natural and man-made disasters, like hurricanes and fires. Once a low-income or poor person or family is temporarily homeless, it often becomes difficult to resettle in permanent housing because of other problems like loss of possessions, family breakup, and substance abuse. Episodically homeless people are frequently welfare recipients who run out of funds halfway into the month, as well as runaway or throwaway youths who move in and out of family situations. They are also abused wives and children who may move in with relatives or friends from time to time. The chronically homeless—who live on the streets for long periods of time—are more likely to suffer from substance abuse and mental illness than members of the other groups.

The institute study also found that there appears to be a direct correlation between the reduced availability of low-cost housing and the increased number of homeless. The number of low-cost housing units has decreased, because as many as half a million are lost annually through conversion, abandonment, fire, or demolition. Moreover, since 1980 the federal government has reduced its subsidies for the construction and maintenance of such units by 60%. According to the institute, approximately 2.5 million low-cost units have been lost since 1980.

The institute also pointed to the jump in the number of poor Americans, about 10 million over the last decade, as a reason for the growing number of homeless.

The institute also noted that in several studies there was general agreement that deinstitutionalization from large mental facilities contributed to the increased number of homeless in the 1980s. They cited the lack of local community mental health services, such as group homes, as one of the primary reasons mentally ill people end up homeless.

**Federal funding** The various federal government programs to assist the homeless are grouped under the Stewart B. McKinney Homeless Assistance Act, which became law in July 1987. The act includes nearly 20 different provisions for emergency shelter, food, health care, mental health care, housing, educational programs, job training, and other community services. Federal agencies providing services include HUD, Health and Human Resources, the Federal Emergency Management Agency, and the Labor, Education, and Veterans' departments. Although the bill authorized $634 million in payments in fiscal 1989, Congress appropriated only $388 million. President George Bush's proposed 1990 budget included full funding for the McKinney program at $676 million. Congress has appropriated $1.1 billion total for McKinney Act programs. However, states and cities still pick up the major part of the bill for caring for the homeless. New York City, for example, budgeted $475 million to help the homeless in fiscal 1989.

## IMMIGRATION

Over the last two centuries, the mingling of peoples from all parts of the world has been a vital element in the formation of the United States, both as a land of opportunity and in its emergence as a world power. In one relatively brief period, between 1880 and 1920, the massive influx of more than 20 million European immigrants provided the inexhaustible and indefatigable labor supply necessary to transform the nation from an agricultural society to an industrialized one with unparalleled rapidity.

Over the next 40 years, however, the flow of immigration was reduced dramatically by a governmental decision to close the doors to most foreign groups. Motivated at first by a disconcerting kind of nativism, anti-immigration sentiments were later bolstered by the Great Depression and the need to provide work for those already living here. World War II and the subsequent national readjustment limited immigration for several decades.

Since 1960 a steadily increasing number of immigrants—both legal and illegal—has had a very noticeable impact on both the size and ethnic composition of the American population. The startling upsurge in the number of Asian and Hispanic immigrants during the 1970s and 1980s has been caused by a variety of factors, from wars and political upheaval to the mundane fact of geographical proximity in the case of Mexico. Currently, over half a million new legal immigrants are arriving annually, and well over half are from those two ethnic backgrounds.

While immigration is higher today than in the recent past, it is hard to predict what the future holds. Many demographers argue that if the immigration rate falls much below current levels, the effect on American population growth could be severe. With the dramatic decline in its birth rates and fertility rates, the United States might very well begin to experience negative population growth by the year 2030; by 2020, immigration will most likely add more population than natural increase will. According to the Office of Population Research at Princeton University, the United States will need 464,000 immigrants each year over the next century just to keep total population in 2100 at the same size as in 1980.

### ESTIMATED NUMBER OF U.S. IMMIGRANTS, BY REGION AND SELECTED COUNTRY OF LAST RESIDENCE, 1820–1990

| Region/country | Total 1820–1990[1] | 1990 | Region/country | Total 1820–1990[1] | 1990 |
|---|---|---|---|---|---|
| **Europe** | **37,101,060** | **124,026** | Israel | 137,540 | 5,906 |
| Austria-Hungary | 4,342,782 | 4,733 | Japan | 462,244 | 6,431 |
| Austria | 1,828,946[2] | 3,774 | Korea | 642,248 | 30,964 |
| Hungary | 1,667,760[2] | 959 | Philippines | 1,026,653 | 71,279 |
| Belgium | 210,556 | 827 | Turkey | 412,327 | 3,205 |
| Czechoslovakia[3] | 145,801 | 578 | Vietnam | 458,277 | 14,755 |
| Denmark | 370,412 | 674 | Other Asia | 1,030,718 | 90,619 |
| France | 787,587 | 4,265 | **North America** | **13,067,548** | **1,050,527** |
| Germany | 7,083,465 | 12,152 | Canada | 4,295,585 | 24,642 |
| Greece | 703,904 | 3,887 | Mexico | 3,888,729 | 680,186[10] |
| Ireland[4] | 4,725,133 | 9,740 | **Caribbean** | **2,703,177** | **112,635** |
| Italy | 5,373,108 | 16,246 | Cuba | 748,710 | 9,436 |
| Netherlands | 374,232 | 1,515 | Dominican Republic | 510,136 | 42,136 |
| Norway-Sweden | 2,145,954 | 1,930 | Haiti | 234,757 | 19,869 |
| Norway | 801,224[5] | 552 | Jamaica | 429,500 | 23,667 |
| Sweden | 1,284,475[5] | 1,378 | Other Caribbean | 780,074 | 17,527 |
| Poland | 606,336 | 18,364 | **Central America** | **819,628** | **146,243** |
| Portugal | 501,261 | 4,066 | El Salvador | 274,667 | 79,601 |
| Romania[6] | 204,841 | 3,496 | Other Central America | 544,961 | 66,642 |
| Spain | 285,148 | 2,744 | **South America** | **1,250,303** | **86,821** |
| Switzerland | 359,439 | 1,288 | Argentina | 131,118 | 5,953 |
| USSR | 3,443,706 | 14,779 | Colombia | 295,353 | 23,783 |
| United Kingdom[7] | 5,119,150 | 19,054 | Ecuador | 155,767 | 12,474 |
| Yugoslavia[8] | 136,271 | 2,778 | Other South America | 668,065 | 44,611 |
| Other Europe | 181,974 | 910 | Other America | 110,126 | 0 |
| **Asia** | **6,019,180** | **321,879** | **Africa** | **334,145** | **32,797** |
| China[9] | 914,376 | 40,639 | **Oceania** | **204,622** | **6,804** |
| Hong Kong | 302,230 | 14,367 | **Not specified** | **267,459** | **450** |
| India | 455,716 | 28,809 | | | |
| Iran | 176,851 | 14,905 | **All countries** | **56,994,014** | **1,536,483** |

1. Because of changes in boundaries, changes in lists of countries, and lack of data for specified countries for various periods, data for certain countries are not comparable throughout. Data for specified countries are included with countries to which they belonged prior to World War I. 2. Data for Austria and Hungary not reported until 1861 and not reported separately for all years. 3. Data begin in 1920. 4. Prior to 1926, data for N. Ireland included in Ireland. 5. Data for Norway and Sweden not reported separately until 1871. 6. Data begin in 1880. 7. Since 1925, data for UK refer to England, Wales, Scotland, and N. Ireland. 8. Since 1922, the Serb, Croat, and Slovene Kingdom has recorded as Yugoslavia. 9. Beginning in 1957, China includes Taiwan. 10. For 1989 and 1990 the number of immigrants was about five times higher than previous years because illegal aliens were granted resident status in 1989 under the Immigration Reform and Control Act of 1986. **Source**: U.S. Dept. of Justice, *1990 Statistical Yearbook of the Immigration and Naturalization Service* (1991).

**Who is eligible today?** Prior to 1875 anyone from any foreign country could enter the U.S. freely and take up permanent residence here. Over the next 60 years, however, Congress passed laws restricting immigration on the basis of morality (no prostitutes or convicts), race (the Chinese Exclusion Act of 1882 was the first), and national origin (immigrants from Southern and Central Europe as well as Asia were severely limited during the 1920s). In 1952 Congress passed the Immigration and Nationality Act which reaffirmed national origin as the central criterion for eligibility and established a preferential system for skilled workers and relatives of U.S. citizens.

As defined by law today, immigrants are persons granted legal permanent residence in the United States. Current law limits the total number of immigrants by restricting visas to 270,000 annually (no more than 20,000 from any one independent country, 5,000 from a dependency). Visas are allocated on the basis of six preference categories based on the immigrant's relationship to a U.S. citizen or the possession of desirable job skills. Since the U.S. admits many more than 270,000 immigrants,

there are clearly exceptions to these limitations. The accompanying tables detail both the preference categories and the major exceptions that make up current U.S. immigration policy.

### Illegal Immigrants

By the very nature of how they enter the United States, it is impossible to know with any accuracy just how many illegal immigrants reside here (estimates range from 4 to 12 million. Many illegals cross the border from Mexico for only a brief period to find temporary work (usually in agriculture) and then return. Mexico remains the primary source of illegal immigrants, with perhaps 55-60% of the total.

During the 1980s the federal government stepped up its efforts to seal off the 2,000-mile U.S.-Mexican border. Apprehensions of illegals rose from about 1 million a year in 1980 to almost 2 million by 1987. But, obviously, the government can't incarcerate such large numbers of people for any protracted period of time so many illegals just keep trying until they are successful.

## IMMIGRATION AS A PERCENTAGE OF TOTAL U.S. POPULATION GROWTH, 1901 – 1990

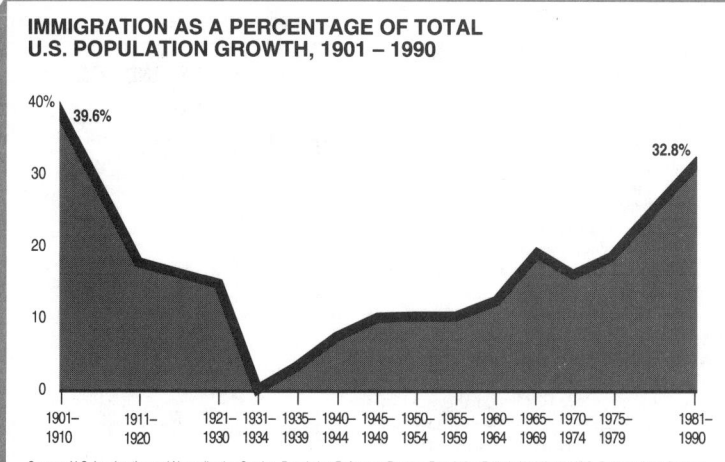

Source: U.S. Immigration and Naturalization Service, Population Reference Bureau, *Population Bulletin* (1986), and U.S. Bureau of the Census, *1990 Census Profile* (1991).

## U.S. IMMIGRATION RATE BY DECADE, 1820–1990

| Period | Total number ('000s) | Rate per 1,000 U.S. pop. |
|---|---|---|
| 1820–30 | 152 | 1.2 |
| 1831–40 | 599 | 3.9 |
| 1841–50 | 1,713 | 8.4 |
| 1851–60 | 2,598 | 9.3 |
| 1861–70 | 2,315 | 6.4 |
| 1871–80 | 2,812 | 6.2 |
| 1881–90 | 5,247 | 9.2 |
| 1891–1900 | 3,688 | 5.3 |
| 1901–10 | 8,795 | 10.4 |
| 1911–20 | 5,736 | 5.7 |
| 1921–30 | 4,107 | 3.5 |
| 1931–40 | 528 | 0.4 |
| 1941–50 | 1,035 | 0.7 |
| 1951–60 | 2,515 | 1.5 |
| 1961–70 | 3,322 | 1.7 |
| 1971–80 | 4,493 | 2.1 |
| 1981–90 | 7,338 | 2.9 |

Source: U.S. Immigration and Naturalization Service, *1990 Statistical Yearbook* (1991).

## IMMIGRATION AS A PERCENTAGE OF TOTAL POPULATION GROWTH, 1901–90

| Period | Percent | Period | Percent |
|---|---|---|---|
| 1901–10 | 39.6% | 1950–54 | 10.6% |
| 1911–20 | 17.7 | 1955–59 | 10.7 |
| 1921–30 | 15.0 | 1960–64 | 12.5 |
| 1930–34 | –0.1 | 1965–69 | 19.7 |
| 1935–39 | 3.2 | 1971–80 | 19.4 |
| 1940–44 | 7.4 | 1981–90 | 32.8 |
| 1945–49 | 10.2 | | |

Sources: U.S. Immigration and Naturalization Service, Population Reference Bureau, *Population Bulletin,* "Immigration to the U.S.: The Unfinished Story" (1986); U.S. Bureau of the Census, *1990 Census Profile* (1991).

## NATIONS SENDING LARGEST PERCENTAGE OF TOTAL U.S. IMMIGRANTS, 1820–1990

| Country | Percent |
|---|---|
| Germany | 12.4% |
| Italy | 9.4 |
| United Kingdom | 9.0 |
| Ireland | 8.3 |
| Austria-Hungary | 7.6 |
| Canada | 7.5 |
| Mexico | 6.8 |
| USSR | 6.0 |

Source: U.S. Immigration and Naturalization Service, *1990 Statistical Yearbook* (1991).

## THE STATUE OF LIBERTY

The Statue of Liberty Enlightening the World was conceived and designed by Frédéric-Auguste Bartholdi (with Gustave Eiffel's help) and given to the United States by the French government in honor of the centennial of American independence in 1876. Funded by subscriptions from the French people, it was dedicated by President Grover Cleveland in 1886 and became a national monument in 1924.

Measuring 151 feet (46 m) to the top of her torch, Miss Liberty still stands guard over the entrance to New York harbor, the inscription on her base a poignant reminder of the vision Americans once had of their country:

"... Give me your tired, your poor
Your huddled masses yearning to breathe free,
The wretched refuse of your teeming shore.
Send these, the homeless, tempest-tost to me,
I lift my lamp beside the golden door!"

—Emma Lazarus,
"The New Colossus"

## IMMIGRATION TO THE U.S. IN THE 1980s

The following nations sent the most legal immigrants to the U.S. between 1981 and 1989. Note that Mexico's total jumped dramatically in 1989 because of the large number of illegal immigrants (338,700) granted permanent legal residence under the 1986 Immigration Reform and Control Act.

| Country | Legal immigrants |
|---|---|
| Mexico | 975,657 |
| Philippines | 477,485 |
| China (mainland and Taiwan) | 306,108 |
| South Korea | 302,782 |
| Vietnam | 266,027 |
| India | 221,977 |
| Dominican Republic | 209,899 |
| Jamaica | 184,481 |
| United Kingdom | 140,119 |
| Cuba | 135,142 |
| El Salvador | 133,938 |
| Canada | 132,296 |
| Haiti | 118,510 |
| Iran | 101,267 |

Source: U.S. Dept. of Justice, *1989 Statistical Yearbook of the Immigration and Naturalization Service* (1990).

## PERCENT OF IMMIGRANTS ADMITTED BY REGION, 1955–89

| Region | 1955 –64 | 1965 –74 | 1975 –84 | 1985 –89 |
|---|---|---|---|---|
| Europe | 50.2% | 29.8% | 13.4% | 9.9% |
| Asia | 7.7 | 22.4 | 43.3 | 40.7 |
| Africa | 0.7 | 1.5 | 2.4 | 2.8 |
| Oceania | 0.4 | 0.7 | 0.8 | 0.6 |
| North America | 36.0 | 39.6 | 33.6 | 39.4 |
| Caribbean | 7.1 | 18.0 | 15.1 | 14.8 |
| Central A. | 2.5 | 2.6 | 3.7 | 5.6 |
| Other N. A. | 26.4 | 19.0 | 14.8 | 18.9 |
| South America | 5.1 | 6.0 | 6.6 | 6.6 |

Note: Data are for fiscal years. Source: U.S. Dept. of Justice, *1989 Statistical Yearbook of the Immigration and Naturalization Service* (1990).

## EXEMPTIONS TO VISA LIMITATIONS AND NUMBER ADMITTED, 1990

The major categories of immigrants exempt from the 270,000 limit are:

• Immediate relatives of U.S. citizens (spouses, children, parents of children over 21): 231,680.
• Refugees and asylee adjustments: 97,364.
• Special immigrants (including certain ministers of religion, certain former employees of the U.S. government abroad): 4,463.
• Amerasians born in Vietnam (and their parents or guardians or spouses): 13,059.
• Babies born abroad to legal permanent residents: 2,410.
• Aliens who have unlawfully resided in the U.S. since Jan. 1, 1982 (a provision of the Immigration Reform and Control Act, 1986): 880,372.

Source: U.S. Dept. of Justice, *1990 Statistical Yearbook of the Immigration and Naturalization Service* (1991).

Both the cost and the futility of trying to stop the flow of illegal immigration with force led Congress to pass the Immigration Reform and Control Act of 1986. This bill proposed to curb illegal immigration by imposing severe fines and possible prison terms on any employer who knowingly hires someone not authorized to work in the United States. Supporters of the bill believe that without the incentive of available jobs illegals will cease their efforts to come here.

The law also recognized that the government can't deport millions of illegals as it did in the 1930s and 1950s, so the bill provided for amnesty to all aliens who entered the United States before Jan. 1, 1982; they also received temporary resident status, with the right to apply for permanent resident alien status, and in five years, for citizenship status. Aliens who worked at least 90 days in U.S. agriculture for three years qualified for permanent resident status after one year; those who worked at least 90 days between May 1985 and May 1986 were given temporary resident status, and they could become permanent residents after two years. An estimated 3.1 million illegal aliens were able to gain legal status; in 1989, 479,000 received permanent status, and in 1990 over 880,000 did.

In May 1989 the U.S. General Accounting Office (GAO), making its first public assessment of the 1986 act, determined that the U.S. Immigration and Naturalization Service had provided 1.7 million employers with information about the law, issued warnings to over 4,000, and fined 1,700. A follow-up report by the GAO, issued in March 1990, found that the law had caused "widespread discrimination" against legal job applicants who appear foreign. There is little or no indication, moreover, that the flow of illegal immigrants has slowed down. Some experts believe that those granted amnesty are encouraging relatives to enter illegally, since they now have someone who can provide for them legally.

## SEX IN AMERICA

Pollsters scrutinize every angle of American life, including what goes on beyond closed bedroom doors. The research ranges from the statistical—like the survey done by the National Center for Health Statistics—to the anecdotal, such as reader polls taken by popular magazines. Here's a summary of the two most serious studies, one conducted by the federal government, the other by a leading university.

**Women and sex** The National Survey of Family Growth is conducted periodically by the National Center for Health Statistics, with a national sample of women ages 15 to 44 years old. The most recent report, issued in July 1987, used data compiled in 1982. Some findings from the report:

• By age 25, 97% of women have had sexual intercourse.
• Of women ages 15 to 19, 47% have had intercourse.

• Nearly 70% of all married women had premarital intercourse.
• Women in their early 20s began having intercourse earlier than women who are presently in their early 30s.
• Patterns of first intercourse were affected by educational level and family life-style. College-educated women were likely to begin having intercourse later (and to marry later) than high school dropouts. Women who came from single-parent families were more likely to begin having intercourse (and to marry) at earlier ages than women who had lived with both parents.

Among women who had intercourse in the three months before the National Survey of Family Growth interview, more than two-thirds reported having intercourse once a week or more, and over two-fifths said they had intercourse at least several times a week. Women ages 25–29 were more likely than either older or younger women to have intercourse several times a week. The data suggest a pattern in which intercourse becomes more frequent as age increases, reaches a peak in the mid-to-late 20s, and then declines.

**Number of sexual partners** The National Opinion Research Center (NORC) at the University of Chicago looked at the sexual behavior of 1,481 adults (a representative nationwide sample) in 1988 and found that most adults were either monogamous or abstained from sex. The survey's findings:

• 60% of men and women claimed only one sexual partner.
• 22% claimed no sexual partner.
• 11% claimed two to four.
• 2% five or more.
• 6% didn't respond.

In reference to gender of partners, 91.3% of the male respondents said their partners were exclusively female; 3% said partners were exclusively male; 0.4% said they were bisexual; and 5.3% did not answer the question. Of the female respondents, 95.4% said their partners were exclusively male; 0.2% said their partners

## ADULTS REPORTING SEXUAL PARTNERS IN PAST 12 MONTHS, BY MARITAL STATUS, SEX, AND AGE, 1988

| Number of sex partners | Age of respondents | | | | |
|---|---|---|---|---|---|
| | 18–29 | 30–44 | 45–60 | 61+ | Total |
| **ALL MEN** | | | | | |
| 0 | 9.7% | 8.2% | 16.4% | 30.3% | 14.6% |
| 1 | 46.1 | 71.0 | 64.6 | 60.6 | 61.3 |
| 2 | 9.1 | 5.6 | 6.4 | 0.8 | 5.6 |
| 3 | 9.7 | 3.9 | 1.8 | 2.3 | 4.7 |
| 4 | 6.1 | 2.6 | 0.9 | 2.3 | 3.1 |
| 5–10 | 8.5 | 1.3 | 0.9 | – | 2.8 |
| 10+ | 3.0 | 0.9 | 1.8 | – | 1.4 |
| No answer | 7.9 | 6.5 | 7.3 | 3.8 | 6.4 |
| **ALL WOMEN** | | | | | |
| 0 | 7.3% | 7.1% | 28.5% | 60.8% | 26.7% |
| 1 | 66.0 | 77.8 | 62.9 | 29.8 | 58.2 |
| 2 | 13.1 | 5.2 | 2.6 | 0.8 | 5.2 |
| 3 | 4.2 | 4.8 | 0.7 | – | 2.6 |
| 4 | 2.1 | 0.8 | – | – | 0.7 |
| 5–10 | 1.0 | 0.4 | – | 0.4 | 0.5 |
| 10+ | – | 0.4 | 0.7 | – | 0.2 |
| No answer | 6.3 | 3.6 | 4.6 | 8.2 | 5.9 |
| **MARRIED MEN, SPOUSE IN HOUSEHOLD** | | | | | |
| 0 | 0% | 3.8% | 8.9% | 20.4% | 8.5% |
| 1 | 80.0 | 87.2 | 78.5 | 74.2 | 81.2 |
| 2 | 2.0 | 2.6 | 3.8 | – | 2.1 |
| 3 | 4.0 | – | 1.3 | 1.1 | 1.1 |
| 4 | 2.0 | – | – | 1.1 | 0.5 |
| 5–10 | – | 0.6 | 1.3 | – | 0.5 |
| 10+ | – | – | 1.3 | – | 0.3 |
| No answer | 12.0 | 5.8 | 5.1 | 3.2 | 5.8 |
| **MARRIED WOMEN, SPOUSE IN HOUSEHOLD** | | | | | |
| 0 | 0% | 3.5% | 7.3% | 24.5% | 8.8% |
| 1 | 89.3 | 91.6 | 85.4 | 65.3 | 82.9 |
| 2 | 3.6 | – | – | 1.0 | 1.0 |
| 3 | 2.4 | – | – | – | 0.5 |
| 4 | – | – | – | – | – |
| 5–10 | – | – | – | 1.0 | 0.2 |
| 10+ | – | – | 1.2 | – | 0.2 |

**Note:** Dash (–) indicates zero. **Source:** National Opinion Research Center, *General Social Survey, 1988* (1988).

## METHODS OF CONTRACEPTION, BY AGE, RACE, AND MARITAL STATUS OF U.S. WOMEN, 1988

| Age, race, and marital status | Women ('000s) | Using any method | Female sterilization | Male sterilization | Pill | IUD | Dia-phragm | Con-dom | Other methods |
|---|---|---|---|---|---|---|---|---|---|
| All women | 57,900 | 60.3% | 27.5% | 11.7% | 30.7% | 2.0% | 5.7% | 14.6% | 7.7% |
| **BY AGE** | | | | | | | | | |
| 15–24 | 18,592 | 45.7% | 3.6% | 1.3% | 64.9% | 0.2% | 2.7% | 20.8% | 6.5% |
| 25–34 | 21,726 | 66.3 | 25.0 | 10.2 | 32.6 | 2.1 | 7.3 | 13.7 | 9.1 |
| 35–44 | 17,582 | 68.3 | 47.6 | 20.8 | 4.3 | 3.1 | 6.0 | 11.2 | 6.9 |
| **BY RACE** | | | | | | | | | |
| White | 47,077 | 61.8% | 26.1% | 13.6% | 29.8% | 1.8% | 6.2% | 14.9% | 7.5% |
| Black | 7,679 | 56.7 | 38.1 | 0.9 | 38.0 | 3.1 | 1.9 | 10.3 | 7.8 |
| **BY MARITAL STATUS** | | | | | | | | | |
| Never married | 21,058 | 41.9% | 6.4% | 1.8% | 59.0% | 1.3% | 4.9% | 19.6% | 7.0% |
| Currently married | 29,147 | 74.3 | 31.4 | 17.3 | 20.4 | 2.0 | 6.2 | 14.3 | 8.4 |
| Formerly married | 7,695 | 57.6 | 50.7 | 3.6 | 25.3 | 3.6 | 5.3 | 5.9 | 5.7 |

**Source:** U.S. Dept. of Health and Human Services, *Advance Data from Vital and Health Statistics of the National Center for Health Statistics* (Mar. 20, 1990).

were exclusively female; and 4.4% did not answer the question.

In addition, 6% of the men and 1% of the women indicated that at least one partner was a casual date or a "pickup."

In an effort to collect accurate data, the NORC included a number of questions about sexual behavior in its General Social Surveys for the first time in 1988 and 1989. The surveys cover a broad range of topics and poll about 1,500 adults (a representative national sample). The survey's 1988 and 1989 findings:

**Sex partners** The average American has 1.16 sex partners over the course of one year, with the widowed reporting the fewest (0.21), and the never married (1.84) and separated (2.41) reporting the most. Over a lifetime, the average American adult will have had 7.14 sex partners since age 18. The numbers are lowest among the widowed (3.01) and rise according to marital status: currently married (5.72), never married (8.67), separated (11.75), and divorced (13.30). The number of partners was highest in the 40–49 age group.

**Abstinence** According to the NORC survey, about 22% of adult Americans had no sex partners in 1989. Abstinence is reported twice as frequently by women (28%) as by men (14%); 9.2% of married couples reported abstinence in the past year, while 25.9% of divorced and 20% of separated adults did; 85.9% of the widowed reported no sex partners for the year. The survey claims there is no connection between abstinence and religious beliefs, race, or region, but found that it is higher among the less educated.

**Marital fidelity** About 75% of Americans consider sexual relations with someone other than one's spouse as always wrong. Over a given year, only about 1.5% of married people have a sex partner other than their spouse. In this survey, men and women did not vary in their levels of fidelity. The survey found, however, that infidelity does seem to increase with age and, presumably, the age of the marriage.

**Sexual orientation** The survey found that 98.5% of sexually active adults have been exclusively heterosexual during the last year. The survey acknowledges that the number is considerably below the 10% adult homosexuals that the Kinsey report claimed (see "Homosexuality") and argues that a 2% homosexual figure is "in line with the best available figures" found in other 1988 studies. The survey also found that 80% of Americans "strongly disapprove" of homosexuality, up from 75% a decade ago.

**Frequency of sexual intercourse** American adults report engaging in sexual intercourse 57 times a year, with the greatest frequency among married couples and separated individuals. Sexual activity appears strongly related to general and marital happiness. Among the married, the "very happy" report having intercourse 75 times annually, while those rating marriages as "not too happy" have intercourse 43 times a year. Although men reported more sexual activity (66 times a year compared to 51 times for women), there was no significant difference reported by married men and women. Not surprisingly, married people under 30 have sex most frequently, 105 times a year.

**Teenage sex** A 1988 nationwide survey of 1,880 boys ages 15–19 found the notion of male teenagers as "sexual adventurers" to be more myth than reality. While 60% of teen boys reported experiencing intercourse at least once during the past year, the majority had relatively few partners and infrequent intercourse. On the average, the sexually active teen spent at least six months with no sexual partners. Only about 20% report multiple relationships within the same month. On the average, teen boys said they had intercourse 2.66 times a month, with the lowest average reported by 15-year-olds (1.79 times monthly) and the highest by 19-year-olds (3.45 times a month).

About 11% of American teens said they had their first sexual experience by age 14; 21% by age 15; 58% by age 17; 66% by age 18; and 79% by age 19. The study, done by the Urban Institute of Washington, D.C., also found significant differences in sexual activity according to race. Black teens had intercourse at earlier ages, more frequently, and with more sexual partners than white and Hispanic males.

The survey also found that due to fear of AIDS and other sexually transmitted diseases, 57% of the boys said they used condoms, more than double the number of a similar survey done in 1979.

# THE UNITED STATES ECONOMY

## GROSS NATIONAL PRODUCT AND INCOME

The goal of an economic system is to transform resources into final products, by way of business enterprises, for society's consumption. This includes the manufacture of tangible goods such as cars, bread, furniture, and so on, and the provision of services (intangible goods) such as health care, education, or motion pictures. The most commonly used measure associated with this goal is the Gross National Product (GNP). The GNP is the total value of all final goods and services (not including illegal transactions) currently produced in the economy measured at prices established in the market. The word *final* serves to exclude intermediate goods sold to producers and used to make finished products eventually sold to consumers in the market. Auto parts such as batteries and tires sold to automakers are examples of intermediate goods and are included in the GNP only through the price of the car when it is sold. In terms of expenditure categories, the GNP comprises purchases of goods and services by consumers and government, gross private domestic investment (or business purchases), and net exports.

Assessment of the GNP in current dollars is referred to as a nominal measure. Nominal measures may be misleading because the economy appears to grow as average prices rise with inflation. An alternative method is to evaluate the GNP by measuring the value of goods and services using constant prices for a given year; the government currently uses 1982 as the base year. Assessments based on constant prices are referred to as real measures because they indicate the change in quantity of output of the economy.

An important criticism of the GNP as an indicator of progress is that it may not be an accurate assessment of the standard of living an economy provides. Not all goods and services are equally important, for example, but all are counted equally in the GNP. Similarly, many of the characteristics that reflect the quality of life in an economy, such as education levels, the availability of health services, and leisure, may not be captured by GNP measures. For example, the fact that an economy generates high levels of pollution would not show up in a measure of the GNP. Two economies might be otherwise identical except for one being pollution free, while the other generates industrial wastes and poisons. Because the latter might demand many services to clean up the pollution and treat those exposed to it, the GNP would be higher in that economy. Yet most people would prefer to live in the pollution-free economy.

Because the GNP is simply a measure of economic activity and not of general welfare, one might turn to income distribution statistics such as the change in the percentage of population below the poverty level to assess the quality of life in the economy.

By some measures, since 1979 the poor in the United States have gotten poorer and the rich richer. In 1989 the overall proportion of Americans living in poverty was 12.8%, or 31.5 million people. This is down from a peak of 15.2% in 1983 but higher than for all years between 1969 and 1979, a period when GNP growth was very slow. As the income share of the highest fifth of all families increased from 41.1% of all national income in 1973 to 44.6% in 1989, the income share of the lowest fifth declined from 5.5% to 4.6%.

By race and Hispanic origin, there are wide disparities in income levels. In 1989 the percentage of whites below the poverty line was only 10%, as against 26% for Hispanics and 31% for blacks. These differences are even more pronounced when broken down by age groups. While the percentage of all children under 18 living in poverty was 19.6% in

1989—the highest child poverty rate of any industrialized nation in the world—for whites the rate was 14.8%, for Hispanics it was 36.2%, and for blacks 43.7%.

Among the elderly, whose poverty rate is lower than the national average (11.4% vs. 12.8%), there are also disparities by race and Hispanic origin. In the period 1980–89, the rate for whites decreased by more than 3% from 13.6% to 9.6%; among elderly blacks the poverty rate decreased from 38.1% to 30.8%; and among elderly Hispanics the poverty rate decreased from 30.8% to 20.6%.

## GNP IN CURRENT AND CONSTANT (1982) DOLLARS, 1929–90 (billions of dollars)

| Item | 1929 | 1935 | 1940 | 1945 | 1950 | 1955 | 1960 | 1965 | 1970 | 1975 | 1980 | 1985 | 1987 | 1988 | 1989 | 1990 |
|---|---|---|---|---|---|---|---|---|---|---|---|---|---|---|---|---|
| **Current dollars** | | | | | | | | | | | | | | | | |
| Gross national product (GNP) | $103.9 | $72.8 | $100.4 | $213.4 | $288.3 | $405.9 | $515.3 | $705.1 | $1,015.5 | $1,598.4 | $2,732.0 | $4,014.9 | $4,526.7 | $4,864.3 | $5,200.8 | $5,465.1 |
| Personal consumption expenditures | 77.3 | 55.8 | 71.0 | 119.6 | 192.1 | 257.9 | 330.7 | 440.7 | 640.0 | 1,012.8 | 1,732.6 | 2,629.0 | 3,012.1 | 3,227.5 | 3,450.1 | 3,657.3 |
| Durable goods | 9.2 | 5.1 | 7.8 | 8.0 | 30.8 | 38.9 | 43.5 | 63.5 | 85.7 | 135.4 | 219.3 | 372.2 | 421.9 | 451.1 | 474.6 | 480.3 |
| Nondurable goods | 37.7 | 29.3 | 37.0 | 71.9 | 98.2 | 124.7 | 153.2 | 191.9 | 270.3 | 416.2 | 681.4 | 911.2 | 997.9 | 1,046.9 | 1,130.0 | 1,193.7 |
| Services | 30.4 | 21.3 | 26.2 | 39.7 | 63.2 | 94.3 | 134.0 | 185.4 | 284.0 | 461.2 | 831.9 | 1,345.6 | 1,592.3 | 1,729.6 | 1,845.5 | 1,983.3 |
| Gross private domestic investment | 16.7 | 6.6 | 13.4 | 11.3 | 55.1 | 69.7 | 78.2 | 116.2 | 148.8 | 219.6 | 437.0 | 643.1 | 712.9 | 766.5 | 771.2 | 741.0 |
| Fixed investment | 14.9 | 5.6 | 11.2 | 12.3 | 48.3 | 64.0 | 75.1 | 106.2 | 145.7 | 225.2 | 445.3 | 631.8 | 673.7 | 718.1 | 742.9 | 746.1 |
| Nonresidential | 11.0 | 4.3 | 7.7 | 10.6 | 27.8 | 39.0 | 48.8 | 73.1 | 105.2 | 162.9 | 322.8 | 442.9 | 446.8 | 488.4 | 511.9 | 524.1 |
| Residential | 4.0 | 1.3 | 3.5 | 1.7 | 20.5 | 25.0 | 26.3 | 33.1 | 40.5 | 62.3 | 122.5 | 188.8 | 226.9 | 229.7 | 231.0 | 222.0 |
| Change in business inventories | 1.7 | 1.1 | 2.2 | –1.0 | 6.8 | 5.7 | 3.1 | 9.9 | 3.1 | –5.6 | –8.3 | 11.3 | 39.2 | 48.4 | 28.3 | –5.0 |
| Net exports of goods and services | 1.1 | 0.1 | 1.8 | –0.5 | 2.2 | 3.0 | 5.9 | 9.7 | 8.5 | 31.1 | 32.1 | –78.0 | –123.0 | –94.6 | –46.1 | –31.2 |
| Exports | 7.1 | 3.3 | 5.4 | 7.4 | 14.5 | 21.1 | 29.9 | 42.9 | 68.9 | 161.3 | 351.0 | 370.9 | 428.0 | 519.7 | 626.2 | 672.8 |
| Imports | 5.9 | 3.2 | 3.7 | 7.9 | 12.3 | 18.1 | 24.0 | 33.2 | 60.5 | 130.3 | 318.9 | 448.9 | 551.1 | 614.4 | 672.3 | 704.0 |
| Government purchases[1] | 8.9 | 10.2 | 14.2 | 83.0 | 38.8 | 75.3 | 100.6 | 138.6 | 218.2 | 335.0 | 530.3 | 820.8 | 924.7 | 964.9 | 1,025.6 | 1,098.1 |
| Federal | 1.5 | 3.1 | 6.1 | 74.8 | 19.1 | 44.9 | 54.4 | 68.7 | 98.8 | 129.2 | 208.1 | 355.2 | 382.0 | 381.0 | 400.0 | 424.0 |
| National defense | N.A. | N.A. | 2.3 | 73.7 | 14.3 | 39.0 | 45.3 | 51.0 | 76.8 | 89.6 | 142.7 | 259.1 | 295.3 | 298.4 | 301.0 | 313.6 |
| State and local | 7.4 | 7.2 | 8.1 | 8.2 | 19.8 | 30.3 | 46.1 | 69.9 | 119.4 | 205.9 | 322.2 | 465.6 | 542.8 | 583.9 | 625.6 | 674.1 |
| **Constant (1982) dollars** | | | | | | | | | | | | | | | | |
| Gross national product (GNP) | $709.6 | $580.2 | $772.9 | $1,354.8 | $1,203.7 | $1,494.9 | $1,665.3 | $2,087.6 | $2,416.2 | $2,695.0 | $3,187.1 | $3,618.7 | $3,847.0 | $3,996.1 | $4,117.7 | $4,157.3 |
| Personal consumption expenditures | 471.4 | 412.1 | 502.6 | 592.7 | 733.2 | 873.8 | 1,005.1 | 1,236.4 | 1,492.0 | 1,711.9 | 2,000.4 | 2,354.8 | 2,521.0 | 2,592.2 | 2,656.8 | 2,681.6 |
| Durable goods | 40.3 | 28.9 | 40.6 | 28.7 | 80.7 | 96.9 | 98.0 | 134.6 | 162.5 | 205.6 | 245.9 | 355.1 | 390.9 | 409.7 | 428.0 | 427.4 |
| Nondurable goods | 211.4 | 201.5 | 259.4 | 323.5 | 352.8 | 413.2 | 463.3 | 543.2 | 632.5 | 676.5 | 762.6 | 847.4 | 890.5 | 899.6 | 919.9 | 911.1 |
| Services | 219.7 | 181.7 | 202.7 | 240.5 | 299.8 | 363.6 | 443.9 | 558.5 | 697.0 | 829.8 | 991.9 | 1,152.3 | 1,239.5 | 1,283.0 | 1,309.0 | 1,343.1 |
| Gross private domestic investment | 139.2 | 60.9 | 111.8 | 76.5 | 234.9 | 259.8 | 260.5 | 367.0 | 381.5 | 383.3 | 509.3 | 637.0 | 674.8 | 721.8 | 716.9 | 688.7 |
| Fixed investment | 128.4 | 54.7 | 97.4 | 84.9 | 210.8 | 243.5 | 252.7 | 341.8 | 373.3 | 396.1 | 516.2 | 627.9 | 640.4 | 679.3 | 693.1 | 692.3 |
| Nonresidential | 93.0 | 40.0 | 65.0 | 74.2 | 124.0 | 151.0 | 159.4 | 227.6 | 264.0 | 281.2 | 379.2 | 453.5 | 445.1 | 487.5 | 506.1 | 515.4 |
| Residential | 35.4 | 14.7 | 32.5 | 10.7 | 86.7 | 92.4 | 93.3 | 114.2 | 109.3 | 114.9 | 137.0 | 174.4 | 195.2 | 191.8 | 187.0 | 176.8 |
| Change in business inventories | 10.8 | 6.2 | 14.4 | –8.4 | 24.2 | 16.3 | 7.7 | 25.2 | 8.2 | –12.8 | –6.9 | 9.1 | 34.4 | 42.5 | 23.8 | –3.6 |
| Net exports of goods and services | 4.7 | –5.9 | 8.2 | –18.9 | 4.7 | — | –4.0 | –2.7 | –30.0 | 18.9 | 57.0 | –104.3 | –128.9 | –100.2 | –54.1 | –33.8 |
| Exports | 42.1 | 26.6 | 40.0 | 35.2 | 59.2 | 76.9 | 98.4 | 132.0 | 178.3 | 259.7 | 388.9 | 367.2 | 427.8 | 504.8 | 593.3 | 631.5 |
| Imports | 37.4 | 32.5 | 31.7 | 54.1 | 54.6 | 76.9 | 102.4 | 134.7 | 208.3 | 240.8 | 332.0 | 471.4 | 556.7 | 605.0 | 647.4 | 665.3 |
| Government purchases[1] | 94.2 | 113.0 | 150.2 | 704.5 | 230.8 | 361.3 | 403.7 | 487.0 | 572.6 | 580.9 | 620.5 | 731.2 | 780.2 | 782.3 | 798.1 | 820.8 |
| Federal | 18.3 | 34.1 | 63.6 | 634.0 | 116.7 | 217.9 | 220.6 | 244.4 | 268.3 | 226.3 | 246.9 | 326.0 | 339.0 | 328.7 | 334.9 | 343.7 |
| National defense | N.A. | N.A. | N.A. | N.A. | N.A. | N.A. | N.A. | N.A. | N.A. | N.A. | 161.1 | 171.2 | 237.2 | 264.9 | 261.8 | 258.7 |
| State and local | 75.9 | 79.0 | 86.6 | 70.5 | 114.2 | 143.4 | 183.1 | 242.5 | 304.3 | 354.6 | 373.6 | 405.2 | 441.2 | 453.6 | 463.2 | 477.1 |

1. Purchases of goods and services. **Sources:** U.S. Bureau of Economic Analysis, *The National Income and Product Accounts of the United States, 1929–1982* and *Survey of Current Business* (July issues and April 1991).

## GNP, BY INDUSTRY, IN CONSTANT (1982) DOLLARS, 1980–89

| Industry | GNP by industry (billions) 1980 | 1985 | 1987 | 1989 | Average annual percent change 1980–85 | 1985–89 | 1980–89 | Industry | GNP by industry (billions) 1980 | 1985 | 1987 | 1989 | Average annual percent change 1980–85 | 1985–89 | 1980–89 |
|---|---|---|---|---|---|---|---|---|---|---|---|---|---|---|---|
| **Gross national product (GNP)** | **$3,187.1** | **$3,618.7** | **$3,845.3** | **$4,117.7** | **2.6%** | **3.4%** | **3.2%** | Machinery, except electrical | $ 84.6 | $ 134.5 | $ 138.1 | $ 174.9 | 9.7% | 6.0% | 11.9% |
| Domestic industries (GDP) | 3,131.7 | 3,581.9 | 3,820.0 | 4,087.6 | 2.7 | 2.8 | 3.4 | Electric and electronic equipment | 62.7 | 79.7 | 82.9 | 90.8 | 4.9 | 2.8 | 5.0 |
| Private industries | 2,739.5 | 3,183.1 | 3,442.7 | 3,710.9 | 3.0 | 3.3 | 3.9 | Motor vehicles and equipment | 33.7 | 50.9 | 44.8 | 47.3 | 8.6 | –1.4 | 4.5 |
| Agriculture, forestry, and fisheries | 76.2 | 93.8 | 105.1 | 100.5 | 4.2 | 1.4 | 3.5 | Other transportation equipment | 38.1 | 43.8 | 55.7 | 63.8 | 2.8 | 9.1 | 7.5 |
| Farms | 64.2 | 79.4 | 83.8 | 78.8 | 4.3 | –0.2 | 2.5 | Instruments and related products | 21.8 | 24.7 | 25.7 | 26.6 | 2.5 | 1.5 | 2.4 |
| Mining | 135.6 | 130.1 | 127.5 | 127.2 | –0.8 | –0.4 | –0.7 | Nondurable goods[1] | 263.9 | 293.0 | 336.6 | 345.4 | 2.1 | 3.6 | 3.4 |
| Construction | 161.6 | 165.4 | 177.5 | 179.0 | 0.5 | 1.8 | 1.2 | Food and kindred products | 56.7 | 63.1 | 66.7 | 70.3 | 2.2 | 2.3 | 2.7 |
| Manufacturing[1] | 665.4 | 786.8 | 852.2 | 929.0 | 3.4 | 3.6 | 4.4 | Tobacco manufactures | 9.5 | 6.9 | 5.2 | 3.1 | –6.2 | –11.0 | –7.5 |
| Durable goods[1] | 401.5 | 493.7 | 515.6 | 583.7 | 4.2 | 3.6 | 5.0 | Textile mill products | 16.1 | 16.3 | 17.4 | 16.7 | 0.2 | 0.5 | 0.4 |
| Lumber and wood products | 20.4 | 20.1 | 25.0 | 25.6 | –0.3 | 5.5 | 2.8 | Apparel and other textile products | 20.1 | 19.9 | 22.0 | 22.4 | –0.2 | 2.5 | 1.3 |
| Furniture and fixtures | 10.2 | 12.2 | 12.8 | 12.2 | 3.6 | 0.0 | 2.2 | Paper and allied products | 24.6 | 30.2 | 33.7 | 33.0 | 4.2 | 1.9 | 3.8 |
| Stone, clay, and glass products | 21.1 | 22.6 | 22.0 | 23.6 | 1.4 | 0.9 | 1.3 | Printing and publishing | 36.9 | 43.0 | 44.7 | 45.1 | 3.1 | 1.0 | 2.5 |
| Primary metal industries | 46.4 | 34.2 | 34.8 | 36.9 | –5.9 | 1.6 | –2.3 | | | | | | | | |
| Fabricated metal products | 52.5 | 56.8 | 58.9 | 65.8 | 1.6 | 3.2 | 2.8 | | | | | | | | |

| Industry | GNP by industry (billions) | | | | Average annual percent change | | |
|---|---|---|---|---|---|---|---|
| | 1980 | 1985 | 1987 | 1989 | 1980–85 | 1985–89 | 1980–89 |
| Chemicals and allied products | $ 50.1 | $ 59.1 | $ 71.9 | $ 76.1 | 3.4% | 5.8% | 5.8% |
| Petroleum and coal products | 26.7 | 24.9 | 42.6 | 44.9 | -1.4 | 16.1 | 7.6 |
| Rubber and misc. plastic products | 18.9 | 26.2 | 29.5 | 30.8 | 6.8 | 3.5 | 7.0 |
| Leather and leather products | 4.3 | 3.4 | 3.0 | 2.9 | -4.6 | -2.9 | -3.6 |
| Transportation and public utilities | 293.4 | 326.0 | 371.3 | 402.3 | 2.1 | 4.7 | 4.1 |
| Transportation | 129.5 | 125.4 | 149.8 | 156.3 | -0.6 | 4.9 | 2.3 |
| Railroad transportation | 27.2 | 19.3 | 25.8 | 28.0 | -6.6 | 9.0 | 0.3 |
| Local interurban passenger transit | 7.0 | 6.3 | 6.1 | 6.3 | -2.1 | 0.0 | -1.1 |
| Trucking and warehousing | 51.5 | 52.6 | 65.8 | 68.6 | 0.4 | 6.1 | 3.7 |
| Water transportation | 8.3 | 7.8 | 3.7 | 4.0 | -1.2 | -9.7 | -5.8 |
| Transportation by air | 23.1 | 24.4 | 33.0 | 31.7 | 1.1 | 6.0 | 4.1 |
| Pipelines, except natural gas | 5.1 | 4.9 | 4.4 | 5.5 | -0.8 | 2.4 | 0.9 |
| Transportation services | 7.2 | 10.0 | 10.9 | 12.2 | 6.8 | 4.4 | 7.7 |
| Communications | 78.4 | 95.2 | 102.1 | 109.4 | 4.0 | 3.0 | 4.4 |
| Telephone and telegraph | 71.1 | 85.8 | 93.2 | 98.8 | 3.8 | 3.0 | 4.3 |
| Radio and television broadcasting | 7.3 | 9.4 | 8.9 | 10.6 | 5.2 | 2.6 | 5.0 |
| Electric, gas, and sanitary services | 85.5 | 105.3 | 119.4 | 136.6 | 4.3 | 5.9 | 6.6 |
| Wholesale trade | 213.5 | 268.5 | 284.3 | 304.7 | 4.7 | 2.7 | 4.7 |
| Retail trade | 286.9 | 341.8 | 371.6 | 412.0 | 3.6 | 4.1 | 4.8 |
| Finance, insurance, and real estate | 464.3 | 524.3 | 560.6 | 604.0 | 2.5 | 3.0 | 3.3 |
| Banking | 56.7 | 61.9 | 62.8 | 63.1 | 1.8 | 0.4 | 1.3 |
| Credit agencies other than banks | 5.2 | 7.0 | 8.3 | 8.3 | 6.1 | 0.5 | 6.6 |
| Security and commodity brokers, and services | 10.7 | 16.9 | 29.8 | 37.9 | 9.6 | 24.9 | 28.2 |
| Insurance carriers | $ 28.6 | $ 33.5 | $ 34.4 | $ 36.7 | 3.2% | 1.9% | 3.1% |
| Insurance agents and brokers, and services | 17.3 | 20.0 | 20.0 | 22.1 | 2.9 | 2.1 | 3.1 |
| Real estate | 339.6 | 376.0 | 394.5 | 424.4 | 2.1 | 2.6 | 2.8 |
| Holding and other investment companies | 6.3 | 9.0 | 10.9 | 11.5 | 7.4 | 5.6 | 9.2 |
| Services[1] | 442.6 | 546.4 | 592.6 | 652.3 | 4.3 | 3.9 | 5.3 |
| Hotels and other lodging places | 22.6 | 23.5 | 28.2 | 32.5 | 0.8 | 7.7 | 4.9 |
| Personal services | 22.2 | 25.4 | 26.3 | 30.3 | 2.7 | 3.9 | 4.1 |
| Business services | 84.0 | 120.8 | 139.7 | 158.7 | 7.5 | 6.3 | 9.9 |
| Auto repair, services, and garages | 24.4 | 30.1 | 28.4 | 28.8 | 4.3 | -0.9 | 2.0 |
| Motion pictures | 5.7 | 7.5 | 8.9 | 9.8 | 5.6 | 6.1 | 8.0 |
| Amusement and recreation services | 13.7 | 17.9 | 20.1 | 22.8 | 5.5 | 5.5 | 7.4 |
| Health services | 129.4 | 158.9 | 158.0 | 164.4 | 4.2 | 0.7 | 3.0 |
| Legal services | 28.9 | 35.0 | 36.9 | 41.8 | 3.9 | 3.9 | 5.0 |
| Educational services | 18.1 | 21.5 | 22.7 | 24.1 | 3.5 | 2.4 | 3.7 |
| Social services and membership organizations | 30.2 | 33.3 | 36.5 | 40.9 | 2.0 | 4.6 | 3.9 |
| Misc. professional services | 47.1 | 53.6 | 67.4 | 76.4 | 2.6 | 8.5 | 6.9 |
| Private households | 7.4 | 8.8 | 8.7 | 9.5 | 3.5 | 1.6 | 3.2 |
| Government and government enterprises | 382.7 | 400.8 | 415.6 | 430.5 | 0.9 | 1.5 | 1.4 |
| Federal | 138.3 | 146.5 | 149.2 | 152.5 | 1.2 | 0.8 | 1.5 |
| State and local | 244.4 | 254.4 | 266.4 | 278.0 | 0.8 | 1.9 | 1.5 |
| Statistical discrepancy | 5.9 | -4.3 | -9.1 | -13.8 | — | — | — |
| Rest of the world[2] | 55.5 | 36.9 | 25.3 | 30.2 | -7.8 | -3.6 | -5.1 |

1. Includes items not shown separately. 2. Net property income from abroad, including profits, dividends, and interest on assets held overseas by domestic residents, minus profits, dividends, and interest paid to foreigners on assets held in the United States. **Sources:** U.S. Bureau of Economic Analysis, *The National Income and Product Accounts of the United States, 1929–82*, and *Survey of Current Business* (July issues, and April 1991).

## NATIONAL INCOME, BY TYPE OF INCOME, 1970–90 (billions of current dollars)

| Type of income | 1970 | 1975 | 1980 | 1985 | 1990 |
|---|---|---|---|---|---|
| **National Income** | **$832.6** | **$1,289.1** | **$2,203.5** | **$3,234.0** | **$4,418.4** |
| Compensation of employees | 618.3 | 948.7 | 1,638.2 | 2,367.5 | 3,244.2 |
| Wages and salaries | 551.5 | 814.7 | 1,372.0 | 1,975.2 | 2,705.3 |
| Government and government enterprise | 117.1 | 176.1 | 260.1 | 371.8 | 508.0 |
| Other | 434.3 | 638.6 | 1,111.8 | 1,603.4 | 2,197.2 |
| Supplements to wages and salaries | 66.8 | 134.0 | 266.3 | 392.4 | 538.9 |
| Employer contributions for social insurance | 34.3 | 68.0 | 127.9 | 204.8 | 280.8 |
| Other labor income | 32.5 | 65.9 | 138.4 | 187.6 | 258.1 |
| Proprietors' income[1] | 80.2 | 125.4 | 180.7 | 255.9 | 402.5 |
| Farm | 14.7 | 25.4 | 20.5 | 30.2 | 49.9 |
| Nonfarm | $ 65.4 | $100.0 | $160.1 | $225.6 | $352.6 |
| Rental income of persons[2] | 18.2 | 13.5 | 6.6 | 9.2 | 6.9 |
| Corporate profits[1] | 74.7 | 117.6 | 177.2 | 282.3 | 298.3 |
| Corporate profits[3] | 69.5 | 123.9 | 194.0 | 222.6 | 293.3 |
| Profits before tax | 76.0 | 134.8 | 237.1 | 224.3 | 304.7 |
| Profits tax liability | 34.4 | 50.9 | 84.8 | 96.4 | 132.1 |
| Profits after tax | 41.7 | 83.9 | 152.3 | 127.8 | 172.5 |
| Dividends | 22.5 | 29.6 | 54.7 | 83.3 | 133.9 |
| Undistributed profits | 19.2 | 54.3 | 97.6 | 44.6 | 38.7 |
| Inventory valuation adjustment | -6.6 | -11.0 | -43.1 | -1.7 | -11.4 |
| Capital consumption adjustment | 5.2 | -6.2 | -16.8 | 59.7 | 4.9 |
| Net interest | 41.2 | 83.8 | 200.9 | 319.0 | 466.7 |

1. With inventory valuation and capital consumption adjustments. 2. With capital consumption adjustment. 3. With inventory valuation adjustment. **Sources:** U.S. Bureau of Economic Analysis, *The National Income and Product Accounts of the United States, 1929–82* and *Survey of Current Business* (July issues and April 1991).

## PERCENT DISTRIBUTION OF NATIONAL INCOME, BY TYPE, 1970–90

| Type of income | 1970 | 1975 | 1980 | 1985 | 1990 |
|---|---|---|---|---|---|
| **National income, total** | **100.0%** | **100.0%** | **100.0%** | **100.0%** | **100.0%** |
| Compensation of employees | 74.3 | 73.6 | 74.3 | 73.2 | 73.4 |
| Wages and salaries | 66.2 | 63.2 | 62.3 | 61.1 | 61.2 |
| Supplements to wages, salaries | 8.0 | 10.4 | 12.1 | 12.1 | 12.1 |
| Proprietors' income[1] | 9.6 | 9.7 | 8.2 | 7.9 | 9.1 |
| Farm | 1.8 | 2.0 | 0.9 | 0.9 | 1.1 |
| Nonfarm | 7.9 | 7.8 | 7.3 | 7.0 | 8.0 |
| Rental income of persons[2] | 2.2% | 1.0% | 0.3% | 0.3% | 0.2% |
| Corporate profits[1] | 9.0 | 9.1 | 8.0 | 8.7 | 6.8 |
| Profits before tax | 9.1 | 10.5 | 10.8 | 6.9 | 6.9 |
| Profits after tax | 5.0 | 6.5 | 6.9 | 4.0 | 3.9 |
| Inventory valuation adjustment | -0.8 | -0.9 | -2.0 | -(Z) | -0.3 |
| Capital consumption adjustment | 0.6 | -0.5 | -0.8 | 1.8 | 0.1 |
| Net interest | 4.9 | 6.5 | 9.1 | 9.9 | 10.6 |

**Note:** Z = less than 0.05%. 1. With inventory valuation and capital consumption adjustments. 2. With capital consumption adjustment. **Sources:** U.S. Bureau of the Census, based on data from U.S. Bureau of Economic Analysis, *The National Income and Product Accounts of the United States, 1929–82* and *Survey of Current Business* (July issues and April 1991).

## MONEY INCOME OF HOUSEHOLDS—PERCENT DISTRIBUTION BY MONEY INCOME LEVEL, BY SELECTED CHARACTERISTICS, 1989

| Characteristic | Total ('000s) | Percent distribution of households by income level | | | | | | | | | Median income |
| --- | --- | --- | --- | --- | --- | --- | --- | --- | --- | --- | --- |
| | | Under $5,000 | $5,000–$9,999 | $10,000–14,999 | $15,000–24,999 | $25,000–34,999 | $35,000–49,999 | $50,000–74,999 | $75,000–99,999 | $100,000 & over | |
| **All households** | **93,347** | **5.3%** | **10.3%** | **9.7%** | **17.9%** | **15.9%** | **17.3%** | **14.5%** | **5.1%** | **3.9%** | **$28,906** |
| **AGE OF HOUSEHOLDER** | | | | | | | | | | | |
| Under 65 | 73,191 | 4.8% | 6.6% | 7.7% | 16.8% | 16.9% | 19.7% | 16.9% | 6.0% | 4.5% | $33,019 |
| 15–24 | 5,121 | 12.1 | 13.7 | 13.5 | 26.5 | 17.6 | 11.2 | 4.3 | 0.6 | 0.3 | 18,663 |
| 25–34 | 20,472 | 4.5 | 6.7 | 8.3 | 20.5 | 19.9 | 21.0 | 13.8 | 3.4 | 1.8 | 29,823 |
| 35–44 | 20,554 | 3.4 | 5.1 | 5.9 | 14.1 | 16.7 | 22.3 | 20.8 | 7.0 | 4.8 | 37,635 |
| 45–54 | 14,514 | 4.0 | 4.6 | 5.8 | 12.2 | 14.0 | 19.9 | 21.6 | 9.9 | 8.0 | 41,523 |
| 55–64 | 12,529 | 5.7 | 8.6 | 9.4 | 16.7 | 15.5 | 16.9 | 15.4 | 6.0 | 5.8 | 30,819 |
| 65 + | 20,156 | 7.1 | 23.6 | 17.1 | 22.0 | 12.2 | 8.6 | 5.6 | 2.0 | 1.8 | 15,771 |
| 65–74 | 11,733 | 5.4 | 18.1 | 15.7 | 23.3 | 14.7 | 10.6 | 7.2 | 2.7 | 2.3 | 18,959 |
| 75 + | 8,423 | 9.3 | 31.4 | 19.0 | 20.1 | 8.8 | 5.8 | 3.2 | 1.2 | 1.1 | 12,101 |
| **RACE AND HISPANIC ORIGIN OF HOUSEHOLDER** | | | | | | | | | | | |
| White | 80,163 | 4.2% | 9.4% | 9.4% | 17.8% | 16.2% | 18.1% | 15.2% | 5.4% | 4.2% | $30,406 |
| Black | 10,486 | 14.1 | 17.2 | 11.9 | 19.6 | 13.8 | 12.0 | 8.5 | 2.2 | 0.8 | 18,083 |
| Hispanic[1] | 5,933 | 8.1 | 13.4 | 12.3 | 21.9 | 15.8 | 14.7 | 9.6 | 2.6 | 1.6 | 21,921 |
| **REGION** | | | | | | | | | | | |
| Northeast | 19,127 | 4.3% | 9.9% | 8.4% | 15.9% | 14.4% | 17.6% | 17.2% | 6.7% | 5.7% | $32,643 |
| Midwest | 22,760 | 5.2 | 10.3 | 9.5 | 18.1 | 16.6 | 18.5 | 14.4 | 4.3 | 3.0 | 28,750 |
| South | 32,262 | 7.0 | 11.4 | 11.1 | 18.9 | 16.1 | 15.9 | 12.3 | 4.2 | 3.0 | 25,870 |
| West | 19,197 | 3.7 | 8.9 | 9.0 | 18.3 | 16.2 | 18.1 | 15.5 | 5.9 | 4.6 | 31,086 |
| **SIZE OF HOUSEHOLD** | | | | | | | | | | | |
| 1 person | 22,999 | 11.4% | 23.6% | 15.4% | 21.8% | 13.3% | 8.9% | 3.7% | 0.9% | 1.0% | $14,829 |
| 2 persons | 30,114 | 3.6 | 7.2 | 10.1 | 20.0 | 17.6 | 18.3 | 14.4 | 4.9 | 4.0 | 29,862 |
| 3 persons | 16,128 | 3.7 | 5.7 | 6.6 | 15.2 | 16.5 | 21.1 | 19.2 | 7.1 | 4.8 | 36,277 |
| 4 persons | 14,456 | 2.7 | 4.1 | 5.3 | 12.3 | 16.0 | 22.7 | 22.8 | 8.2 | 5.8 | 40,744 |
| 5 persons | 6,213 | 2.4 | 4.7 | 5.9 | 14.5 | 15.8 | 22.0 | 21.1 | 7.4 | 6.2 | 39,281 |
| 6 persons | 2,143 | 3.6 | 6.1 | 7.3 | 17.5 | 15.0 | 17.4 | 18.8 | 8.3 | 6.0 | 35,304 |
| 7 persons + | 1,295 | 3.8 | 6.3 | 8.4 | 18.3 | 15.5 | 15.6 | 18.8 | 8.6 | 4.8 | 32,644 |
| **TYPE OF HOUSEHOLD** | | | | | | | | | | | |
| Family households | 66,090 | 3.4% | 6.1% | 7.9% | 16.6% | 16.5% | 20.0% | 18.0% | 6.6% | 4.9% | $34,633 |
| Married-couple families | 52,317 | 1.4 | 3.8 | 6.6 | 15.4 | 16.8 | 21.8 | 20.6 | 7.7 | 5.8 | 38,664 |
| Male householder, no wife present | 2,884 | 3.5 | 7.1 | 8.1 | 20.7 | 18.7 | 19.2 | 14.7 | 5.0 | 3.0 | 30,336 |
| Female householder, no husband present | 10,890 | 13.1 | 16.8 | 14.3 | 21.2 | 14.5 | 11.2 | 6.4 | 1.6 | 0.9 | 17,383 |
| Nonfamily households | 27,257 | 10.0 | 20.5 | 14.0 | 21.2 | 14.4 | 11.0 | 6.0 | 1.5 | 1.5 | 17,115 |
| Male householder | 11,606 | 7.3 | 13.5 | 12.0 | 21.8 | 16.9 | 15.1 | 8.7 | 2.2 | 2.5 | 22,423 |
| Living alone | 9,049 | 8.7 | 16.2 | 13.9 | 23.3 | 15.8 | 13.0 | 5.6 | 1.6 | 2.0 | 19,617 |
| Female householder | 15,651 | 12.0 | 25.8 | 15.4 | 20.8 | 12.5 | 7.9 | 4.0 | 0.9 | 0.7 | 13,755 |
| Living alone | 13,950 | 13.2 | 28.4 | 16.5 | 20.8 | 11.6 | 6.3 | 2.4 | 0.5 | 0.4 | 12,190 |
| **EDUCATIONAL ATTAINMENT OF HOUSEHOLDER[2]** | | | | | | | | | | | |
| 8 yrs. or less | 10,695 | 13.4% | 26.9% | 16.2% | 20.8% | 10.5% | 7.3% | 3.6% | 0.9% | 0.5% | $12,696 |
| High school, total | 41,318 | 5.4 | 11.4 | 11.7 | 20.3 | 17.7 | 17.4 | 11.9 | 2.8 | 1.5 | 25,608 |
| 1–3 yrs. | 10,091 | 9.7 | 17.9 | 15.0 | 21.9 | 14.7 | 11.7 | 6.9 | 1.5 | 0.7 | 17,767 |
| 4 yrs. | 31,227 | 4.0 | 9.3 | 10.6 | 19.8 | 18.6 | 19.2 | 13.6 | 3.3 | 1.8 | 28,060 |
| College, total | 36,214 | 1.9 | 3.7 | 5.0 | 13.2 | 15.2 | 21.1 | 22.1 | 9.6 | 8.1 | 42,153 |
| 1–3 yrs. | 15,842 | 2.6 | 5.8 | 6.9 | 16.8 | 17.7 | 22.3 | 18.9 | 5.5 | 3.4 | 35,083 |
| 4 yrs. + | 20,372 | 1.4 | 2.1 | 3.5 | 10.4 | 13.3 | 20.3 | 24.5 | 12.7 | 11.8 | 49,180 |
| 4 yrs. | 11,189 | 1.7 | 2.4 | 4.1 | 11.8 | 14.7 | 21.1 | 24.3 | 10.9 | 9.1 | 45,814 |
| 5 yrs. + | 9,183 | 1.0 | 1.8 | 2.8 | 8.8 | 11.7 | 19.3 | 24.7 | 14.9 | 15.1 | 53,969 |

**Note:** Percentage figures calculated by *Universal Almanac*. 1. Hispanic persons may be of any race. 2. 25 years old and over. **Source:** U.S. Bureau of the Census, *Current Population Reports: Money Income of Households, Families, and Persons in the United States, 1988 and 1989* (1991).

## PERSONAL INCOME PER CAPITA FOR SELECTED METROPOLITAN AREAS (MSAs), 1986–89

| Metropolitan area, ranked by 1989 personal income | 1987 | 1988 | 1989 | Percent of national average 1989 |
|---|---|---|---|---|
| United States | $15,425 | $16,510 | $17,592 | N.A. |
| **LOWEST PER CAPITA INCOME** | | | | |
| 1. McAllen-Edinburg-Mission, Tex. | $ 6,881 | $ 7,309 | $ 7,814 | 44% |
| 2. Laredo, Tex. | 6,959 | 7,482 | 8,043 | 46 |
| 3. Brownsville-Harlingen, Tex. | 7,360 | 7,835 | 8,435 | 48 |
| 4. Las Cruces, N.M. | 9,580 | 9,851 | 10,389 | 59 |
| 5. El Paso, Tex. | 9,507 | 10,016 | 10,735 | 61 |
| 6. Provo-Orem, Utah | 9,204 | 10,203 | 11,171 | 64 |
| 7. Pascagoula, Miss. | 10,262 | 10,928 | 11,342 | 64 |
| 8. Houma-Thibodaux, La. | 10,524 | 11,162 | 11,850 | 67 |
| 9. Lawton, Okla. | 11,096 | 11,485 | 11,945 | 68 |
| 10. Pine Bluff, Ark. | 10,770 | 11,546 | 12,134 | 69 |
| 11. Jacksonville, N.C. | 10,856 | 11,386 | 12,157 | 69 |
| 12. Biloxi-Gulfport, Miss. | 10,816 | 11,495 | 12,209 | 69 |
| 13. Charleston, S.C. | 11,816 | 12,597 | 12,351 | 70 |
| 14. Anniston, Ala. | 11,019 | 11,696 | 12,353 | 70 |
| 15. Clarksville-Hopkinsville, Tenn.-Ky. | 11,186 | 11,829 | 12,495 | 71 |
| 16. Gadsden, Ala. | 11,267 | 11,985 | 12,514 | 71 |
| 17. Florence, S.C. | 11,200 | 12,093 | 12,635 | 72 |
| 18. Florence, Ala. | 11,033 | 11,966 | 12,691 | 72 |
| 19. Ocala, Fla. | 11,463 | 12,003 | 12,699 | 72 |
| 20. Yuma, Ariz. | 11,801 | 12,664 | 12,725 | 72 |
| 21. Fort Smith, Ark.-Okla. | 11,571 | 12,228 | 12,749 | 72 |
| 22. Huntington-Ashland, W.Va.-Ky.-Ohio | 11,173 | 11,930 | 12,755 | 73 |
| 23. Bryan-College Station, Tex. | 10,646 | 11,584 | 12,760 | 73 |
| 24. Monroe, La. | 11,450 | 12,158 | 12,783 | 73 |
| 25. Alexandria, La. | 11,288 | 12,061 | 12,865 | 73 |

| Metropolitan area, ranked by 1989 personal income | 1987 | 1988 | 1989 | Percent of national average 1989 |
|---|---|---|---|---|
| **HIGHEST PER CAPITA INCOME** | | | | |
| 1. Bridgeport-Stamford-Norwalk-Danbury, Conn. | $26,519 | $29,315 | $31,438 | 179% |
| 2. San Francisco, Calif. | 24,442 | 26,453 | 28,170 | 160 |
| 3. Bergen-Passaic, N.J. | 22,969 | 25,499 | 27,374 | 156 |
| 4. Middlesex-Somerset-Hunterdon, N.J. | 22,964 | 25,308 | 26,716 | 152 |
| 5. Lake County, Ill. | 22,388 | 24,037 | 25,804 | 147 |
| 6. Nassau-Suffolk, N.Y. | 22,140 | 24,076 | 25,628 | 146 |
| 7. Washington, D.C.-Md.-Va. | 21,508 | 23,249 | 24,845 | 141 |
| 8. Anchorage, Alaska | 20,810 | 21,699 | 24,773 | 141 |
| 9. Newark, N.J. | 20,960 | 23,056 | 24,729 | 141 |
| 10. San Jose, Calif. | 21,547 | 23,120 | 24,581 | 140 |
| 11. West Palm Beach-Boca Raton-Delray Beach, Fla. | 21,636 | 22,739 | 24,319 | 138 |
| 12. Anaheim-Santa Ana, Calif. | 21,406 | 22,790 | 24,288 | 138 |
| 13. Sarasota, Fla. | 20,639 | 22,023 | 24,039 | 137 |
| 14. Trenton, N.J. | 20,633 | 22,425 | 23,913 | 136 |
| 15. Boston-Lawrence-Salem-Lowell-Brockton, Mass. (NECMA) | 20,330 | 22,354 | 23,746 | 135 |
| 16. Hartford-New Britain-Middletown-Bristol, Conn. (NECMA) | 20,438 | 22,269 | 23,695 | 135 |
| 17. Monmouth-Ocean, N.J. | 20,482 | 22,278 | 23,456 | 133 |
| 18. Naples, Fla. | 20,547 | 21,504 | 23,322 | 133 |
| 19. Atlantic City, N.J. | 20,105 | 21,647 | 23,001 | 131 |
| 20. Ann Arbor, Mich. | 19,975 | 21,110 | 22,512 | 128 |
| 21. Oakland, Calif. | 19,706 | 21,106 | 22,249 | 126 |
| 22. New York, N.Y. | 18,920 | 20,609 | 22,064 | 125 |
| 23. Manchester-Nashua, N.H. (NECMA) | 19,671 | 21,185 | 22,010 | 125 |
| 24. Fort Lauderdale-Hollywood-Pompano Beach, Fla. | 19,101 | 20,425 | 21,898 | 124 |
| 25. New Haven-Waterbury-Meriden, Conn. (NECMA) | 18,733 | 20,490 | 21,736 | 124 |

**Note**: NECMA = New England county metropolitan area. See "Metropolitan Statistical Areas" for definitions. **Source**: Bureau of Economic Analysis, *Survey of Current Business* (April 1991).

## Definitions of Output, Income, and Expenditure Terms

**Capital consumption adjustment** Used for corporations, nonfarm sole proprietorships, and partnerships, this is the difference between capital consumption claimed on income tax returns and capital consumption allowances measured at straight-line depreciation, consistent-service lives, and replacement cost. The tax return data are valued at historical costs and reflect changes over time in service lives and depreciation patterns as permitted by tax regulations.

**Consumer expenditure** Consumer expenditure statistics presented in the accompanying tables are arrived at from the findings of the Consumer Expenditure Survey program, designed to provide a continuous flow of data on the buying habits of American consumers, necessary for future revisions of the Consumer Price Index. One group of 5,000 consumers in 85 urban areas around the country keeps diaries of expenditures on small, frequently purchased items, such as food and beverages, tobacco, housekeeping supplies, nonprescription drugs,

and personal care products and services. Another 5,000 consumers are interviewed quarterly for information about large expenditures, such as those for property, automobiles, and major appliances, or about expenditures occurring on a fairly regular basis, such as rent, utilities, and insurance premiums.

**Discretionary income** Households with spendable (after-tax) income at least 30% higher than that needed for average expenditures for their income group are considered to have discretionary income, allowing them to maintain a living standard comfortably higher than the average for similar households. According to the U.S. Census Bureau's March 1987 Current Population Survey, discretionary income totaled nearly $320 billion, or about 15% of total after-tax income received by households. This is an increase of 22% over 1983. Some interesting statistics about discretionary income:

• Households with two or more people earning a paycheck account for 65% of all U.S. discretionary dollars.
• While only about 17% of households have pretax incomes of $50,000 or more, they control close to 80% of all discretionary income.
• While slightly more than one-fifth of all

householders have a college degree, they account for more than half of all discretionary income.
• Both blacks and Hispanics are only half as likely as whites to have discretionary income.
• 34% of all homes in the New England states have discretionary income.
• Homes in the suburbs of major metropolitan areas are one-and-a-half times as likely to be in the discretionary income class as households in central cities.

**Disposable personal income** is that income after personal tax and nontax payments; this is the income available to persons for spending and saving. Personal tax and nontax payments are tax payments (except personal contributions for social insurance, net of refunds) by persons that are not chargeable to business expense, and also include certain personal payments to general government that are treated like taxes. Personal taxes include income, estate, gift, and personal property taxes and motor vehicle licenses. Nontax payments include passport fees, fines and penalties, donations, and tuitions and fees paid to schools and hospitals operated mainly by government.

**Family income** The term *family* refers to

## PERSONAL INCOME PER CAPITA IN CURRENT DOLLARS, BY STATE, 1970–90

| State | Personal income | | | | Income rank | | State | Personal income | | | | Income rank | |
|---|---|---|---|---|---|---|---|---|---|---|---|---|---|
| | 1970 | 1980 | 1985 | 1990[1] | 1980 | 1990 | | 1970 | 1980 | 1985 | 1990[1] | 1980 | 1990 |
| Alabama | $2,945 | $ 7,704 | $10,698 | $14,826 | 47 | 44 | Montana | $3,528 | $ 8,924 | $11,015 | $15,110 | 33 | 41 |
| Alaska | 5,073 | 13,835 | 18,785 | 21,761 | 1 | 6 | Nebraska | 3,759 | 9,274 | 12,967 | 17,221 | 30 | 27 |
| Arizona | 3,789 | 9,172 | 12,957 | 16,297 | 32 | 34 | Nevada | 4,878 | 11,421 | 14,693 | 19,416 | 5 | 13 |
| Arkansas | 2,827 | 7,465 | 10,525 | 14,218 | 49 | 47 | New Hampshire | 3,890 | 9,788 | 15,367 | 20,789 | 23 | 8 |
| California | 4,746 | 11,603 | 16,035 | 20,795 | 3 | 7 | New Jersey | 4,805 | 11,573 | 17,618 | 24,968 | 4 | 2 |
| Colorado | 4,025 | 10,598 | 14,699 | 18,794 | 13 | 16 | New Mexico | 3,145 | 8,169 | 11,197 | 14,228 | 41 | 46 |
| Connecticut | 5,037 | 12,112 | 18,227 | 25,358 | 2 | 1 | New York | 4,855 | 10,721 | 15,773 | 21,975 | 10 | 4 |
| Delaware | 4,587 | 10,249 | 14,547 | 20,039 | 14 | 11 | North Carolina | 3,236 | 7,999 | 11,662 | 16,203 | 44 | 35 |
| District of Columbia | 5,250 | 12,322 | 17,811 | 24,181 | — | — | North Dakota | 3,129 | 8,538 | 11,951 | 15,255 | 37 | 39 |
| Florida | 3,943 | 9,764 | 13,935 | 18,586 | 24 | 19 | Ohio | 4,033 | 9,723 | 13,176 | 17,473 | 25 | 24 |
| Georgia | 3,377 | 8,348 | 12,616 | 16,944 | 38 | 30 | Oklahoma | 3,436 | 9,393 | 12,139 | 15,444 | 28 | 38 |
| Hawaii | 4,944 | 10,617 | 13,900 | 20,254 | 11 | 10 | Oregon | 3,889 | 9,866 | 12,628 | 17,156 | 19 | 29 |
| Idaho | 3,467 | 8,569 | 10,817 | 15,160 | 36 | 40 | Pennsylvania | 4,042 | 9,891 | 13,554 | 18,672 | 18 | 18 |
| Illinois | 4,563 | 10,837 | 14,730 | 20,303 | 7 | 9 | Rhode Island | 4,050 | 9,518 | 13,779 | 18,841 | 27 | 15 |
| Indiana | 3,771 | 9,245 | 12,424 | 16,864 | 31 | 31 | South Carolina | 3,004 | 7,589 | 10,729 | 15,099 | 48 | 42 |
| Iowa | 3,804 | 9,537 | 12,619 | 17,249 | 26 | 26 | South Dakota | 3,200 | 8,217 | 11,029 | 15,872 | 40 | 36 |
| Kansas | 3,770 | 9,941 | 13,812 | 17,986 | 17 | 21 | Tennessee | 3,151 | 8,030 | 11,252 | 15,798 | 42 | 37 |
| Kentucky | 3,141 | 8,022 | 10,768 | 14,929 | 43 | 43 | Texas | 3,629 | 9,798 | 13,476 | 16,759 | 22 | 32 |
| Louisiana | 3,071 | 8,682 | 11,302 | 14,391 | 34 | 45 | Utah | 3,297 | 7,952 | 10,653 | 14,083 | 45 | 48 |
| Maine | 3,405 | 8,218 | 11,903 | 17,200 | 39 | 28 | Vermont | 3,604 | 8,577 | 12,373 | 17,436 | 35 | 25 |
| Maryland | 4,475 | 10,790 | 15,970 | 21,864 | 8 | 5 | Virginia | 3,743 | 9,827 | 14,468 | 19,746 | 21 | 12 |
| Massachusetts | 4,514 | 10,612 | 16,305 | 22,642 | 12 | 3 | Washington | 4,165 | 10,725 | 14,076 | 18,858 | 9 | 14 |
| Michigan | 4,133 | 10,165 | 14,001 | 18,346 | 15 | 20 | West Virginia | 3,078 | 7,915 | 10,073 | 13,747 | 46 | 49 |
| Minnesota | 3,995 | 10,062 | 14,144 | 18,731 | 16 | 17 | Wisconsin | 3,889 | 9,845 | 13,234 | 17,503 | 20 | 22 |
| Mississippi | 2,597 | 6,926 | 9,249 | 12,735 | 50 | 50 | Wyoming | 3,797 | 11,339 | 12,726 | 16,398 | 6 | 33 |
| Missouri | 3,809 | 9,298 | 13,250 | 17,497 | 29 | 23 | | | | | | | |

1. Preliminary data. **Source:** U.S. Bureau of Economic Analysis, *Survey of Current Business* (April 1991) and unpublished data.

a group of two or more persons related by birth, marriage, or adoption who reside together; all such persons are considered members of one family. Family income refers to the sum of all income of the family members.

**Gross domestic product (GDP)** is the measure of the output of production attributable to all factors of production (labor and property) physically located in a country. The GDP therefore excludes net property income from abroad (such as the earnings of U.S. nationals working overseas), which is included in the GNP.

**Gross national product (GNP)** is the total national output of goods and services valued at market prices. The GNP in this broad context measures the output attributable to the factors of production—labor and property—supplied by U.S. residents. The GNP differs from "national income" mainly in that the GNP includes allowances for depreciation and for indirect business taxes (sales and property taxes).

**Gross state product (GSP)** is the gross market value of the goods and services attributable to labor and property located in a state. It is the state counterpart of the nation's GDP.

**Household income** A household includes related family members and all unrelated persons, if any—such as lodgers, foster children, wards, or employees—who share a house, an apartment, or a single room when it is occupied or intended for occupancy as separate living quarters by that household; that is, when the members of the household do not live and eat with any other persons in the structure and there is direct access from the outside or

## PERSONAL INCOME PER CAPITA FOR SELECTED COUNTIES, 1989

| Rank/County | Per capita income 1989 |
|---|---|
| United States average | $17,592 |
| Metropolitan portion | 18,771 |
| Nonmetropolitan portion | 13,557 |
| **HIGHEST PER CAPITA INCOME** | |
| 1. Haines Borough, Alaska | $37,548 |
| 2. Loving, Tex. | 37,122 |
| 3. New York, N.Y. | 35,193 |
| 4. Marin, Calif. | 34,983 |
| 5. Pitkin, Colo. | 33,108 |
| 6. Arlington, Va. | 33,039 |
| 7. Wheeler, Nebr. | 32,706 |
| 8. Somerset, N.J. | 32,469 |
| 9. Fairfield, Conn. | 31,438 |
| 10. Alexandria, Va.[1] | 31,264 |
| 11. Westchester, N.Y. | 31,188 |
| 12. Cheyenne, Colo. | 31,117 |
| 13. Bergen, N.J. | 30,967 |
| 14. Hunterdon, N.J. | 30,301 |
| 15. Morris, N.J. | 29,981 |
| 16. Bristol Bay Borough, Alaska | 29,755 |
| 17. Montgomery, Md. | 29,639 |
| 18. Nassau, N.Y. | 28,678 |
| 19. Fairfax, Fairfax City, and Falls Church, Va.[2] | 28,366 |
| 20. Howard, Md. | 28,252 |
| 21. Valdez-Cordova, Alaska | 27,727 |
| 22. San Mateo, Calif. | 27,659 |
| 23. Kiowa, Colo. | 26,916 |
| 24. Sherman, Tex. | 26,900 |
| 25. Nantucket, Mass. | 26,652 |

| Rank/County | Per capita income 1989 |
|---|---|
| **LOWEST PER CAPITA INCOME** | |
| 1. Starr, Tex. | $4,549 |
| 2. Shannon, S.Dak. | 5,294 |
| 3. Maverick, Tex. | 6,155 |
| 4. Dimmit, Tex. | 6,576 |
| 5. Zavala, Tex. | 6,739 |
| 6. McCreary, Ky. | 6,834 |
| 7. Sioux, N.Dak. | 7,052 |
| 8. Todd, S.Dak. | 7,053 |
| 9. Madison, La. | 7,096 |
| 10. Menifee, Ky. | 7,107 |
| 11. Elliott, Ky. | 7,181 |
| 12. Willacy, Tex. | 7,199 |
| 13. Jackson, S.Dak. | 7,303 |
| 14. Owsley, Ky. | 7,334 |
| 15. Zapata, Tex. | 7,334 |
| 16. Apache, Ariz. | 7,406 |
| 17. Clay, W.Va. | 7,427 |
| 18. Jackson, Ky. | 7,479 |
| 19. Perry, Ala. | 7,643 |
| 20. Buffalo, S.Dak. | 7,695 |
| 21. Corson, S.Dak. | 7,731 |
| 22. Magoffin, Ky. | 7,772 |
| 23. St. Helena, La. | 7,777 |
| 24. Summers, W.Va. | 7,791 |
| 25. Jefferson, Miss. | 7,813 |

1. Independent city. 2. Combination area consisting of two independent cities with populations less than 100,000 combined with an adjacent county. The county name appears first, followed by the city names. Separate estimates for the jurisdictions making up the combined area are not available. **Source:** U.S. Bureau of Economic Analysis, *Survey of Current Business* (April 1991).

## MONEY INCOME OF FAMILIES—MEDIAN FAMILY INCOME, BY RACE AND HISPANIC ORIGIN, 1989

| | Number ('000s) | | | | Median family income (dollars) | | | |
|---|---|---|---|---|---|---|---|---|
| Characteristic | All families | White | Black | Hispanic[1] | All families | White | Black | Hispanic[1] |
| All families | 66,090 | 56,590 | 7,470 | 4,840 | $34,213 | $35,975 | $20,209 | $23,446 |
| **TYPE OF FAMILY** | | | | | | | | |
| Married-couple families | 52,317 | 46,981 | 3,750 | 3,395 | $38,547 | $39,208 | $30,650 | $27,382 |
| Wife in paid labor force | 30,188 | 26,829 | 2,400 | 1,763 | 45,266 | 45,803 | 37,787 | 34,821 |
| Wife not in paid labor force | 22,129 | 20,153 | 1,350 | 1,633 | 28,747 | 29,689 | 18,727 | 20,717 |
| Male HHer, no wife present | 2,884 | 2,303 | 446 | 329 | 27,847 | 30,487 | 18,395 | 25,176 |
| Female HHer, no husband present | 10,890 | 7,306 | 3,275 | 1,116 | 16,442 | 18,946 | 11,630 | 11,745 |
| **NUMBER OF EARNERS[2]** | | | | | | | | |
| No earners | 9,439 | 7,816 | 1,396 | 615 | $14,285 | $16,360 | $ 6,166 | $ 7,486 |
| One earner | 18,146 | 14,970 | 2,601 | 1,554 | 25,226 | 27,145 | 15,440 | 17,250 |
| Two earners | 29,235 | 25,737 | 2,609 | 1,860 | 40,658 | 41,429 | 32,171 | 29,420 |
| Three earners | 6,724 | 5,832 | 659 | 541 | 51,758 | 52,582 | 43,693 | 40,480 |
| Four or more earners | 2,546 | 2,236 | 205 | 271 | 65,722 | 66,890 | 53,258 | 46,858 |

**Note:** HH = household. HHer = householder. Families as of March 1989. 1. Hispanic persons may be of any race. 2. Excludes families with members who are in the Armed Forces. **Source:** U.S. Bureau of the Census, *Current Population Reports.*

through a common hall. Household income, therefore, is the sum of all income of household members. The "householder" (which replaced the term *head of household* beginning with the 1980 Current Population Survey) is the person in whose name the home is owned or rented. In the case of joint ownership, one person in each household is designated as the householder for statistical purposes.

**Inventory valuation adjustment** This represents the difference between the book value of inventories used in production and the cost of replacing them.

**Mean vs. median income** Mean (or average) income refers to the sum of all incomes of a group divided by the number of incomes in that group. Median income is the middle income when they are arranged in order of size—that is, there are the same number of incomes above and below the median. For example, consider incomes of $2,000, $3,000, $4,000, $15,000 and $95,000: the mean income is the sum of these divided by five, or $23,800; the median income is $4,000.

**Money income** This refers to income received (exclusive of certain money receipts such as capital gains) before payments for such things as personal income taxes, Social Security, union dues, and Medicare deductions. Money income does not include income in the form of noncash benefits such as food stamps, health benefits, and subsidized housing; rent-free housing and goods produced and consumed on farms; or the use of business transportation and facilities, full or partial payments by business for retirement programs, medical and educational expenses, and so on. These elements should be considered when comparing income levels. None of the aggregate income concepts (GNP, national income, or personal income) is exactly comparable with money income, although personal income is the closest.

**National income,** the aggregate of labor and property earnings derived from the current production of goods and services, is the sum of employee compensation, proprietors' income, rental income, corporate profits, and net interest. It measures the total factor costs of the

## PERSONS BELOW POVERTY LEVEL, BY RACE, 1960–89

| | Number below poverty level (millions) | | | | Percent below poverty level | | | | Average income cutoffs for family of four at poverty level[3] |
|---|---|---|---|---|---|---|---|---|---|
| Year | All races[1] | White | Black | Hispanic[2] | All races[1] | White | Black | Hispanic[2] | |
| 1960 | 39.9 | 28.3 | N.A. | N.A. | 22.2% | 17.8% | N.A. | N.A. | $ 3,022 |
| 1970 | 25.4 | 17.5 | 7.5 | N.A. | 12.6 | 9.9 | 33.5% | N.A. | 3,968 |
| 1975 | 25.9 | 17.8 | 7.5 | 3.0 | 12.3 | 9.7 | 31.3 | 26.9% | 5,500 |
| 1980 | 29.3 | 19.7 | 8.6 | 3.5 | 13.0 | 10.2 | 32.5 | 25.7 | 8,414 |
| 1985 | 33.1 | 22.9 | 8.9 | 5.2 | 14.0 | 11.4 | 31.3 | 29.0 | 10,989 |
| 1989 | 31.5 | 20.8 | 9.3 | 5.4 | 12.8 | 10.0 | 30.7 | 26.2 | 12,675 |

1. Includes other races not shown separately. 2. Hispanic persons may be of any race. 3. Prior to 1980, income cutoffs are for nonfarm families only. **Source:** U.S. Bureau of the Census, *Current Population Reports* (series).

goods and services produced by the economy. Income is measured before deduction of taxes.

**Personal income** is the current income received by persons from all sources minus their personal contributions for social insurance. *Persons* include individuals (including owners of unincorporated firms), nonprofit institutions serving individuals, private trust funds, and private noninsured welfare funds. Personal income includes transfers (payments not resulting from current production) from government and business, such as Social Security benefits and public assistance, but excludes transfers among persons. Also included are certain nonmonetary types of income: estimated net rental value to owner-occupants of their home, the value of services furnished without payment by financial intermediaries, and food and fuel produced and consumed on farms.

**Poverty level** is an estimate of the income necessary to purchase what society defines as a minimally acceptable standard of living. Families and unrelated individuals are classified as being above or below the poverty level according to their money income as a group and the number of people in the group (e.g., in 1989 a family of four with total money income below $12,675 lived below the poverty level). Classification is based on the poverty index originated by the Social Security Administration in 1964 and revised in 1969 and 1980. The poverty index is based solely on money income and does not reflect the fact that many low-income

persons receive noncash benefits such as food stamps, Medicaid, and public housing. The poverty thresholds are updated every year to reflect changes in the Consumer Price Index.

**Private domestic investment** This consists of (1) nonresidential fixed investment, i.e., firms' purchases of capital goods such as plants and equipment; (2) residential fixed investment (the building of single- and multifamily housing units); and (3) the change in business inventories, which are stocks on hand of raw materials and finished goods.

## POVERTY LEVELS BASED ON MONEY INCOME FOR FAMILIES AND UNRELATED INDIVIDUALS, 1989

| Size of unit | 1989 |
|---|---|
| 1 person (unrelated individual) | $ 6,311 |
| Under 65 years | 6,452 |
| 65 years and over | 5,947 |
| 2 persons | 8,076 |
| Householder under 65 years | 8,343 |
| Householder 65 years and over | 7,501 |
| 3 persons | 9,885 |
| 4 persons | 12,675 |
| 5 persons | 14,990 |
| 6 persons | 16,921 |
| 7 persons | 19,162 |
| 8 persons | 21,328 |
| 9 persons or more | 25,480 |

**Note:** Weighted averages. **Source:** U.S. Bureau of the Census, *Current Population Reports* (series).

## ECONOMIC INDICATORS

All market economies regularly go through cycles of recession—when output declines and unemployment rises—and expansion—when output and employment rise. These "business cycles" are one of the most important factors determining the socioeconomic conditions in any society. Although economists still have very little idea what actually causes recessions and what leads the economy to begin expanding again, they have had some success in predicting business cycles. Economic forecasting is the science of making these predictions. It is especially useful to be able to predict recessions sufficiently far in advance so that governments can take actions to stimulate the economy and reduce the severity of these downturns.

Economic indicators track developments in areas of the economy that are thought to be crucial to the future health of the economy, just as a barometer measures changes in air pressure that are crucial to changes in the weather. The development of economic indicators began around World War I but suffered a setback when the early forecasters failed to predict the Great Depression in 1929. During the depression the government asked a private research group, the National Bureau of Economic Research, to develop a set of measures that would help predict changes in business cycles. The group devised a list of measures based on analyses of previous business cycles. Since then, the list has been revised several times—most recently in March 1989—to reflect changes in the way the economy is structured.

### Leading Indicators

There are currently 11 leading economic indicators, representing a broad spectrum of economic activity. These indicators are said to "lead" because their numbers change months in advance of a change in the general level of economic activity. They are as follows:

1. Average length of work week of production workers in manufacturing.
2. Average weekly state unemployment insurance claims.
3. New orders for consumer goods and materials in 1982 dollars.
4. Vendor performance (percent of companies receiving slower deliveries from suppliers).
5. Contracts and orders for plant and equipment in 1982 dollars.
6. Index of new private housing units authorized by local building permits.
7. Change in manufacturers' unfilled orders of durable goods in 1982 dollars. (See "Note" below.)
8. Change in sensitive materials prices.
9. Index of stock prices, i.e., of 500 common stocks (Standard and Poor's 500).
10. Money supply-M2 in 1982 dollars. (See "Money and Banking" section.)
11. Index of consumer expectations. (See "Note" below.)

(Note: Numbers 7 and 11 of the above list were added to the index in March 1989, while "change in business and consumer credit outstanding" and "change in manufacturing and trade inventories on hand and on order" were dropped, owing to untimely data availability. In addition the base year of the index was changed from 1972 to 1982.)

This composite of leading economic indicators is published by the U.S. Department of Commerce, Bureau of Economic Analysis. The composite has a noteworthy record: since 1948 it has accurately predicted every downturn and upswing in the economy. One major reason for this success is that many of the indicators represent commitments to economic activity in the coming months. The average lead for the index is 9.5 months at business cycle peaks (indicating the end of a business cycle expansion and the beginning of a recession) and 4.5 months at business cycle troughs (indicating the end of a business cycle recession and the beginning of an expansion).

### Coincident and Lagging Indicators

In addition to the leading economic indicators, two other sets of measures are used to track business cycles and the state of the economy. One set includes the coincident indicators, which measure how well the economy is doing at that moment (roughly, within three months of the business cycle turning points). These include the number of employees on nonagricultural payrolls; manufacturing and trade sales in 1982 dollars; index of industrial production; and personal income less transfer payments in 1982 dollars. The second set includes lagging economic indicators. These are the ratio of consumer installment credit outstanding to personal income; commercial and industrial loans outstanding in 1982 dollars; the average prime interest rate charged by banks; the ratio of manufacturing and trade inventories to sales in 1982 dollars; the average duration of unemployment in weeks (inverted); the change in index of labor cost per unit of output in manufacturing; and the change in the Consumer Price Index for services per unit labor costs. At business cycle peaks, the average lag of the index is 4.5 months, and at business cycle troughs 8.5 months. It seems reasonable to wonder what use there is for an indicator that tells you where you have already been. But in fact that is exactly their use: they provide another way of measuring whether turning points in the business cycle truly have occurred.

The government produces a wide variety of economic indicators in addition to those discussed here for use in tracking more specific aspects of the economy, such as labor or capital markets.

## PRICES AND INFLATION

### Inflation

Inflation is a sustained rise in the general price level in the economy. It affects the level and timing of spending in the economy since it indicates the extent to which income will cover the purchase of a consumer's basket of goods (food, clothes, entertainment, medical services, housing, gasoline, and so on). For example, if a consumer is considering purchasing a televi-

## COMPOSITE INDEX OF LEADING, COINCIDENT, AND LAGGING INDICATORS, 1969–91 (1982 = 100)

| Year | Leading indicators | Coincident indicators | Lagging indicators |
|---|---|---|---|
| 1969 | 83.1 | 82.0 | 87.6 |
| 1970 | 79.0 | 83.5 | 93.2 |
| 1971 | 79.8 | 81.5 | 89.3 |
| 1972 | 88.1 | 85.4 | 85.4 |
| 1973 | 97.3 | 94.4 | 87.6 |
| 1974 | 95.5 | 96.3 | 97.7 |
| 1975 | 78.0 | 87.2 | 102.5 |
| 1976 | 93.0 | 89.8 | 88.0 |
| 1977 | 98.5 | 95.3 | 86.9 |
| 1978 | 101.9 | 101.1 | 92.5 |
| 1979 | 105.3 | 110.5 | 98.8 |
| 1980 | 101.2 | 111.0 | 108.3 |
| 1981 | 102.8 | 108.5 | 101.2 |
| 1982 | 97.2 | 102.1 | 104.9 |
| 1983 | 106.8 | 97.9 | 91.9 |
| 1984 | 123.5 | 109.1 | 94.1 |
| 1985 | 121.5 | 114.7 | 105.5 |
| 1986 | 127.9 | 117.8 | 111.0 |
| 1987 | 136.2 | 119.4 | 112.2 |
| 1988 | 138.7 | 125.6 | 114.0 |
| 1989 | 145.9 | 132.4 | 117.6 |
| 1990 | 145.4 | 131.9 | 119.2 |
| 1991 | 138.8 | 127.4 | 119.9 |

**Note:** Figures are for January of the year shown. See accompanying text for a description of specific indicators. **Source:** U.S. Dept. of Commerce, unpublished data, 1991.

## PURCHASING POWER OF THE DOLLAR, 1950–90 (PPI, 1982 = $1.00; CPI, 1982–84 = $1.00)

As indicated below, a 1982 dollar would have bought $4.15 worth of merchandise in 1950, while in 1990 only $0.77 worth of merchandise could be purchased with the same dollar.

| | Annual average as measured by: | |
|---|---|---|
| Year | Producer prices | Consumer prices |
| 1950 | $3.546 | $4.151 |
| 1955 | 3.279 | 3.732 |
| 1960 | 2.994 | 3.373 |
| 1965 | 2.933 | 3.166 |
| 1970 | 2.545 | 2.574 |
| 1975 | 1.718 | 1.859 |
| 1980 | 1.136 | 1.215 |
| 1985 | 0.955 | 0.928 |
| 1989 | 0.880 | 0.807 |
| 1990 | 0.839 | 0.766 |

**Note:** PPI = Producer Price Index; CPI = Consumer Price Index. **Source:** U.S. Bureau of Labor Statistics and U.S. Bureau of Economic Analysis, Survey of Current Business (monthly data).

sion and inflation is high (that is, prices are rising rapidly), he or she will buy the television as soon as possible since savings may not cover the cost a month or a year from now. Inflation is closely watched to determine wage contracts and Social Security benefits that contain cost-of-living adjustment clauses. If wage contracts cover a long period of time and inflation is rapid, consumers' standard of living will fall in the interim before new contracts can be negoti-

## CONSUMER PRICE INDEXES FOR SELECTED METROPOLITAN STATISTICAL AREAS, 1990 (1982–84 = 100)

| Area | All items | Food and beverages | Food | Housing | Apparel and upkeep | Transportation | Medical care | Entertainment | Fuel and utilities |
|---|---|---|---|---|---|---|---|---|---|
| **U.S. city average** | **130.7** | **132.1** | **132.4** | **128.5** | **124.1** | **120.5** | **162.8** | **132.4** | **111.6** |
| Baltimore, Md. | 130.8 | 136.9 | 137.9 | 125.2 | 128.1 | 122.8 | 158.4 | 138.3 | 102.7 |
| Boston-Lawrence-Salem, Mass.-N.H. | 138.9 | 138.6 | 139.0 | 137.0 | 138.2 | 119.7 | 181.6 | 144.2 | 104.9 |
| Chicago-Gary-Lake County, Ill.-Ind.-Wis. | 131.7 | 130.3 | 130.4 | 131.4 | 124.3 | 118.7 | 163.0 | 139.2 | 108.9 |
| Cleveland-Akron-Lorain, Ohio | 129.0 | 130.6 | 131.2 | 127.7 | 117.8 | 119.4 | 156.6 | 133.6 | 112.0 |
| Dallas-Ft. Worth, Tex. | 125.1 | 131.1 | 131.5 | 114.3 | 137.5 | 117.2 | 161.9 | 137.5 | 109.3 |
| Detroit-Ann Arbor, Mich. | 128.6 | 126.5 | 126.3 | 126.4 | 127.9 | 124.0 | 159.8 | 128.1 | 112.4 |
| Houston-Galveston-Brazoria, Tex. | 120.6 | 128.7 | 129.2 | 104.8 | 132.5 | 116.0 | 161.2 | 134.9 | 101.9 |
| Los Angeles-Anaheim-Riverside, Calif. | 135.9 | 130.9 | 130.3 | 139.3 | 126.4 | 126.5 | 163.3 | 125.4 | 124.5 |
| Miami-Ft. Lauderdale, Fla. | 128.0 | 134.3 | 135.9 | 120.4 | 135.6 | 121.6 | 151.8 | 121.0 | 109.3 |
| New York-Northern New Jersey-Long Island, N.Y.-N.J.-Conn. | 138.5 | 139.6 | 139.7 | 139.3 | 121.8 | 123.1 | 172.4 | 135.6 | 102.8 |
| Philadelphia-Wilmington-Trenton, Pa.-N.J.-Del.-Md. | 135.8 | 131.2 | 130.8 | 138.7 | 101.4 | 127.7 | 167.4 | 133.5 | 112.9 |
| Pittsburgh-Beaver Valley, Pa. | 126.2 | 124.3 | 123.8 | 124.8 | 125.0 | 112.1 | 160.6 | 138.8 | 123.7 |
| St. Louis-East St. Louis, Mo.-Ill. | 128.1 | 134.9 | 135.4 | 124.9 | 120.9 | 117.4 | 159.0 | 124.4 | 113.7 |
| San Francisco-Oakland-San Jose, Calif. | 132.1 | 134.7 | 135.7 | 137.3 | 107.5 | 114.7 | 160.5 | 140.7 | 125.1 |
| Washington, D.C.-Md.-Va. | 135.6 | 133.4 | 132.9 | 136.6 | 139.4 | 120.7 | 162.4 | 135.6 | 110.5 |

**Source**: U.S. Bureau of Labor Statistics, *Monthly Labor Review and CPI Detailed Report* (January issues).

---

ated. Savings will tend to fall as consumers store their wealth in the form of commodities

The cause of inflation is often described as "too much money chasing too few goods," brought about by the money supply rising rapidly or production of goods falling behind demand for them. Inflation may be due to (1) cost-push factors—that is, if the cost of inputs such as labor, raw materials, or other intermediate goods rises, the cost of the final product also rises; or (2) demand-pull factors—that is, if the demand for goods and services rises above the full employment level, wages rise as employers compete for labor, and the general price level of goods and services rises.

### Consumer Price Index (CPI)

Often referred to as the "cost of living index," the Consumer Price Index is the most commonly used measure of inflation. The index measures the average change in prices relative to an arbitrary base year of a common bundle of goods and services bought by the average consumer on a regular basis. The Bureau of Labor Statistics publishes two CPIs: (1) CPI-U for All Urban Consumers, which includes wage earners and clerical workers; professional, managerial, and technical workers; the self-employed; short-term workers; the unemployed; retirees and others not in the labor force—altogether covering 80% of the population—and (2) CPI-W for Urban Wage Earners and Clerical Workers, covering 32% of the population. Prices (including direct taxes) are collected from over 57,000 housing units and 19,000 establishments in 85 areas across the country. In calculating the index number, based on 100,000 price quotes a month, larger weights are assigned to goods that represent larger proportions of consumer expenditure. The index costs $26 million a year to produce and requires 40 economists and analysts tracking price changes in 365 categories.

### Producer Price Index

The Producer Price Index measures average changes in prices received by producers of all commodities, at all stages of processing, produced in the United States. Prices used in con-

## CONSUMER PRICE INDEX (CPI-U), 1947–90 (1982–84 = 100)

| Year | CPI | Year | CPI |
|---|---|---|---|
| 1947 | 22.3 | 1982 | 96.5 |
| 1950 | 24.1 | 1983 | 99.6 |
| 1955 | 26.8 | 1984 | 103.9 |
| 1960 | 29.6 | 1985 | 107.6 |
| 1965 | 31.5 | 1986 | 109.6 |
| 1970 | 38.8 | 1987 | 113.6 |
| 1975 | 53.8 | 1988 | 118.3 |
| 1980 | 82.4 | 1989 | 124.0 |
| 1981 | 90.9 | 1990 | 130.7 |

**Note:** Indicates annual averages for all urban consumers. **Source:** U.S. Bureau of the Census, *Current Population Reports* (series).

## PRODUCER PRICE INDEXES— MAJOR COMMODITY GROUPS, 1950–90 (1982 = 100)

| Year | All commods. | Farm products[1] | Industrial commods. | Energy[2] | Metals and metal products |
|---|---|---|---|---|---|
| 1950 | 27.3 | 37.7 | 25.0 | 12.6 | 22.0 |
| 1955 | 29.3 | 36.6 | 27.8 | 13.2 | 27.2 |
| 1960 | 31.7 | 37.7 | 30.5 | 13.9 | 30.6 |
| 1965 | 32.3 | 39.0 | 30.9 | 13.8 | 32.0 |
| 1970 | 38.1 | 44.9 | 35.2 | 15.3 | 38.7 |
| 1975 | 58.4 | 74.0 | 54.9 | 35.4 | 61.5 |
| 1980 | 89.8 | 98.3 | 88.0 | 82.8 | 95.0 |
| 1985 | 103.2 | 100.7 | 103.7 | 91.4 | 104.4 |
| 1990 | 116.3 | 118.6 | 115.8 | 82.2 | 123.0 |

1. Processed foods and feeds. 2. Fuels, related products, and power.
**Source:** U.S. Bureau of Labor Statistics, *Producer Price Indexes* (monthly and annual).

structing the index are collected from sellers and generally apply to the first significant large-volume commercial transaction for each commodity—i.e., the manufacturer's or other producer's selling price or the selling price on an organized exchange or at a central market. The weights used in the index represent the total net selling value of commodities produced

## PRODUCER PRICE INDEXES— SELECTED COMMODITIES, 1970–90 (1982 = 100)

| Commodity group | 1970 | 1975 | 1980 | 1985 | 1990 |
|---|---|---|---|---|---|
| **All commodities** | **38.1** | **58.4** | **89.8** | **103.2** | **116.3** |
| **Farm products and processed foods and feeds** | **44.9** | **74.0** | **98.3** | **100.7** | **118.6** |
| Farm products | 45.8 | 77.0 | 102.9 | 95.1 | 112.2 |
| Processed foods and feeds | 44.6 | 72.6 | 95.9 | 103.5 | 121.9 |
| **Industrial commodities** | **35.2** | **54.9** | **88.0** | **103.7** | **115.8** |
| Textile products and apparel | 52.4 | 67.4 | 89.7 | 102.9 | 114.9 |
| Hides, skins, leather, related products | 42.0 | 56.5 | 94.7 | 108.9 | 141.7 |
| Fuels, related products, power | 15.3 | 35.4 | 82.8 | 91.4 | 82.2 |
| Chemicals and allied products | 35.0 | 62.0 | 89.0 | 103.7 | 123.6 |
| Rubber and plastic products | 44.9 | 62.2 | 90.1 | 101.9 | 113.6 |
| Lumber and wood products | 39.9 | 62.1 | 101.5 | 106.6 | 129.7 |
| Pulp, paper, and allied products | 37.5 | 59.0 | 86.3 | 113.3 | 141.3 |
| Metals and metal products | 38.7 | 61.5 | 95.0 | 104.4 | 123.0 |
| Machinery and equipment | 40.0 | 57.9 | 86.0 | 107.2 | 120.7 |
| Furniture and household durables | 51.9 | 67.5 | 90.7 | 107.1 | 119.1 |
| Nonmetallic mineral products | 35.3 | 54.4 | 88.4 | 108.6 | 114.7 |
| Transportation equipment | 41.9 | 56.7 | 82.9 | 107.9 | 121.5 |

**Source:** U.S. Bureau of Labor Statistics, *Producer Price Indexes* (monthly and annual).

or processed in the country. Values are f.o.b. (free on board) at the production point and are exclusive of excise taxes.

### Implicit Price Deflator

The implicit price deflator (also called the GNP deflator) is derived from the ratio of current- to constant-dollar GNP (multiplied by 100) and measures the value of current production in current prices relative to the value of the same goods and services in prices for the base year. For example, in 1990, GNP in current dollars was $5,465.1 billion, and GNP in constant (1982) dollars was $4,157.3 billion. Therefore, the GNP deflator for 1990 was (5,465.1/4,157.3) x 100, or 131.4, which is simply a comparison of 1982 and 1990 prices. It is a weighted average of the detailed price indexes used in the deflation of GNP, but the indexes are combined using weights that reflect the composition of GNP in each period. Thus, changes in the implicit price deflator reflect not only changes in prices but also changes in the composition of GNP.

## MONEY AND BANKING

### Federal Reserve System

The government's interest in monitoring and controlling the banking industry and managing the money supply led to the Federal Reserve Act of 1913. The act created the Federal Reserve System (or the "Fed," as it is popularly known), the nation's central bank. There are 12 regional Fed banks located in major cities throughout the country (Boston, New York, Philadelphia, Cleveland, Richmond, Atlanta, Chicago, St. Louis, Minneapolis, Kansas City, Dallas, and San Francisco). Commercial banks within each region select a majority of the directors who run each regional Fed bank. The president of the United States appoints a board of governors for the whole system, and the board is responsible for coordinating policies across the system. But the regional Feds play an important role in shaping those policies by representing regional interests and decentralizing the decision-making process.

The Fed has three main policy tools in managing the overall economy. First, it controls the *reserve requirements* at all depository institutions. These requirements determine what per-

### CONSUMER CREDIT OUTSTANDING, 1970–88 (billions of dollars)

| Type of credit | 1970 | 1975 | 1980 | 1985 | 1988 |
|---|---|---|---|---|---|
| **Credit outstanding** | **$131.6** | **$204.9** | **$349.4** | **$592.4** | **$728.9** |
| Ratio to disposable personal income[1] | 18.3% | 17.9% | 18.2% | 20.8% | 21.0% |
| **Installment** | **$103.9** | **$167.0** | **$297.6** | **$517.8** | **$659.5** |
| By type of credit: | | | | | |
| Automobile paper | $36.3 | $56.9 | $111.9 | $209.6 | $281.2 |
| Revolving | 4.9 | 14.5 | 54.8 | 122.0 | 174.8 |
| Mobile-home paper | 2.4 | 15.3 | 18.6 | 26.8 | 25.7 |
| All other loans | 60.2 | 80.1 | 112.1 | 159.2 | 177.8 |
| By major holder: | | | | | |
| Commercial banks | $48.6 | $82.9 | $145.5 | $241.6 | $318.9 |
| Finance companies | 27.2 | 32.7 | 61.9 | 111.0 | 145.2 |
| Credit unions | 12.8 | 25.4 | 43.6 | 71.9 | 86.1 |
| Retailers[2] | 12.9 | 16.6 | 26.1 | 39.1 | 43.5 |
| Other[3] | 2.3 | 9.2 | 20.3 | 53.9 | 65.8 |
| **Noninstallment** | **$27.7** | **$37.9** | **$51.8** | **$74.7** | **$69.4** |
| Single-payment loans | 18.9 | 26.8 | 39.6 | 59.1 | 49.0 |
| Charge accounts | 8.7 | 11.0 | 12.1 | 15.6 | 20.4 |

**Note:** Data represent estimated amounts of credit outstanding as of end of year; seasonally adjusted. 1. Based on fourth-quarter seasonally adjusted disposable personal income at annual rates as published by the U.S. Bureau of Economic Analysis. 2. Excludes 30-day charge credit held by travel and entertainment companies. 3. Comprises savings institutions and gasoline companies. **Sources:** Board of Governors of the Federal Reserve System, *Federal Reserve Bulletin* (monthly), *Annual Statistical Digest*, and unpublished data.

### FEDERAL RESERVE BANK OF NEW YORK—DISCOUNT RATES, 1976–91

| Effective date | Rate per year[1] | Effective date | Rate per year[1] |
|---|---|---|---|
| Jan. 19, 1976 | 5.50% | Nov. 2, 1981 | 13.00% |
| Nov. 22, 1976 | 5.25 | Dec. 4, 1981 | 12.00 |
| Aug. 31, 1977 | 5.75 | July 20, 1982 | 11.50 |
| Oct. 26, 1977 | 6.00 | Aug. 2, 1982 | 11.00 |
| Jan. 9, 1978 | 6.50 | Aug. 16, 1982 | 10.50 |
| May 11, 1978 | 7.00 | Aug. 27, 1982 | 10.00 |
| July 3, 1978 | 7.25 | Oct. 12, 1982 | 9.50 |
| Aug. 21, 1978 | 7.75 | Nov. 22, 1982 | 9.00 |
| Sept. 22, 1978 | 8.00 | Dec. 15, 1982 | 8.50 |
| Oct. 16, 1978 | 8.50 | Apr. 9, 1984 | 9.00 |
| Nov. 1, 1978 | 9.50 | Nov. 21, 1984 | 8.50 |
| July 20, 1979 | 10.00 | Dec. 24, 1984 | 8.00 |
| Aug. 17, 1979 | 10.50 | May 20, 1985 | 7.50 |
| Sept. 19, 1979 | 11.00 | Mar. 7, 1986 | 7.00 |
| Oct. 8, 1979 | 12.00 | Apr. 21, 1986 | 6.50 |
| Feb. 15, 1980[2] | 13.00 | July 11, 1986 | 6.00 |
| May 30, 1980 | 12.00 | Aug. 21, 1986 | 5.50 |
| June 13, 1980 | 11.00 | Sept. 4, 1987 | 6.00 |
| July 28, 1980 | 10.00 | Aug. 9, 1988 | 6.50 |
| Sept. 26, 1980 | 11.00 | Feb. 24, 1989 | 7.00 |
| Nov. 17, 1980 | 12.00 | Dec. 19, 1990 | 6.50 |
| Dec. 5, 1980 | 13.00 | Feb. 1, 1991[3] | 6.00 |
| May 5, 1981 | 14.00 | | |

1. Rates for short-term adjustment credit. 2. Discount rates for 1980 and 1981 do not include the surcharge applied to frequent borrowings by large institutions. The surcharge reached 3% in 1980 and 4% in 1981 and was eliminated in November 1981. 3. In effect as of July 1, 1991. **Source:** Board of Governors of the Federal Reserve System, *Federal Reserve Bulletin* (monthly) and *Annual Statistical Digest*.

### DEPOSIT-TAKING INSTITUTIONS: NUMBER AND PERCENTAGE SHARE OF DEPOSITS, 1990

| Type of institution | Number of institutions | Percent share | Deposits[1] (billions) | Percent share |
|---|---|---|---|---|
| Commercial banks | 12,509 | 41.4% | $2,270.7 | 63.5% |
| Savings banks[2] | 469 | 1.6 | 214.4 | 6.0 |
| Savings institutions[3] | 2,700 | 8.9 | 890.5 | 24.9 |
| Credit unions | 14,544 | 48.1 | 201.2 | 5.6 |
| **Total** | **30,232** | **100.0%** | **$3,576.8** | **100.0%** |

1. Includes deposits gathered both domestically and internationally by U.S. institutions. 2. Savings banks include state-chartered savings banks. 3. Savings institutions include federally chartered savings banks and savings and loans. **Sources:** Federal Deposit Insurance Corp., *FDIC Data Book* (June 30, 1991); Office of Thrift Supervision (unpublished data); Credit Union National Association (unpublished data).

centage of a bank's deposits must be held in reserve in the form of either deposits with Federal Reserve banks or vault cash—currently 3% (as of Dec. 18, 1990) for depository institutions with net transaction accounts of under $41.1 million and 1.5% for nonpersonal time deposits that mature in less than 1.5 years. Raising the reserve requirements reduces the amount of loans available to borrowers and helps slow down the economy. In an attempt to boost economic activity, in 1991 the Fed lowered reserve requirements for various types of deposits. For example, for institutions that report quarterly there is no reserve requirement for nonpersonal time deposits that mature in less than 1.5 years. The reserve ratios are rarely adjusted, however.

A more frequently used instrument is *the discount rate*, the interest rate the Federal Reserve banks charge their commercial bank customers to borrow money. The Fed is known as the lender of last resort because of its responsibility to lend to banks in need, and it thus maintains the stability of the banking system. Raising the discount rate generally leads commercial banks to raise the interest rates

they charge their customers. This raises the costs of borrowing in the private sector and slows the economy. (Cutting the discount rate does the reverse and stimulates the economy.)

Most important, the Fed can also control the level of bank reserves through *open market operations*; that is, the direct sale and purchase of Treasury securities and other government debt instruments. When the Fed sells securities, it takes money from the buyer and holds it in its reserves, reducing the money supply; when it buys these instruments, it pays for them by taking money from its reserves, which then goes into circulation, increasing the money supply. The Fed increased its holdings by $24 billion in 1990, for example, since it bought more securities than it sold by that amount, thereby increasing the money supply. In 1989, the Fed decreased the money supply by $10 billion.

Controlling the money supply through open market operations is certainly the most common and, many would argue, the most important function of the Fed. The money supply shapes interest rates, through the supply and demand of money. Because the Fed is constantly involved in these open market operations (in order to keep the size of the money supply in proportion with a growing economy, for example), adjustments can be made subtly.

In addition, the Federal Reserve regulates banks through the Federal Deposit Insurance Corporation, influences foreign-currency exchange rates through the sale or purchase of foreign currencies, and coordinates international financial policy.

**The money supply** Money provides a medium of exchange as well as a way to store value, and traditionally, currency (paper money and coins) served that role exclusively. But over time, new financial instruments have developed that serve at least some of the functions of money; checking accounts serve exactly the same role as currency, and to an extent money-

## THE MONEY SUPPLY: MONEY STOCK AND LIQUID ASSETS, 1970–90 (in billions of dollars)

| Item | 1970 | 1975 | 1980 | 1985 | 1990 | Item | 1970 | 1975 | 1980 | 1985 | 1990 |
|---|---|---|---|---|---|---|---|---|---|---|---|
| **M1, TOTAL** | **$215** | **$288** | **$412** | **$620** | **$825** | Small time-deposits[7] | $266 | $338 | $728 | $880 | $1,165 |
| Currency[1] | 47 | 73 | 115 | 168 | 246 | Commercial banks | 117 | 142 | 286 | 383 | 598 |
| Traveler's checks[2] | 1 | 2 | 4 | 6 | 8 | Thrift institutions | 149 | 196 | 442 | 496 | 567 |
| Demand deposits[3] | 165 | 212 | 261 | 267 | 277 | | | | | | |
| Other checkable deposits[4] | (Z) | 1 | 31 | 179 | 294 | **M3, TOTAL** | **$677** | **$1,172** | **$1,991** | **$3,196** | **$4,114** |
| | | | | | | M2 | 628 | 1,023 | 1,633 | 2,563 | 3,330 |
| **M2, TOTAL** | **$628** | **$1,023** | **$1,633** | **$2,563** | **$3,330** | Nontransaction components in M3[5] | 49 | 149 | 358 | 633 | 784 |
| M1 | 215 | 288 | 412 | 620 | 825 | Large time-deposits[8] | 45 | 130 | 260 | 436 | 506 |
| Nontransaction components in M2[5] | 414 | 736 | 1,221 | 1,943 | 2,505 | Commercial banks[9] | 45 | 123 | 215 | 285 | 385 |
| Overnight repurchase (RP) agreements and Eurodollars[6] | 1 | 6 | 28 | 70 | 74 | Thrift institutions | 1 | 6 | 45 | 152 | 121 |
| Money market funds, general-purpose broker/dealer[6] | (Z) | 3 | 62 | 177 | 348 | Term RPs and term Eurodollars[6,10] | 4 | 18 | 84 | 142 | 162 |
| Money market deposit accounts[6] | (Z) | (Z) | (Z) | 514 | 506 | Money-market funds, institution only[6] | (Z) | (Z) | 15 | 65 | 126 |
| Commercial banks | (Z) | (Z) | (Z) | 333 | 378 | | | | | | |
| Thrift institutions | (Z) | (Z) | (Z) | 181 | 128 | **L, TOTAL** | **$816** | **$1,367** | **$2,328** | **$3,825** | **$4,979** |
| Savings deposits | 327 | 389 | 400 | 301 | 411 | M3 | 677 | 1,172 | 1,991 | 3,196 | 4,114 |
| Commercial banks | 128 | 161 | 186 | 125 | 199 | Savings bonds | 52 | 67 | 72 | 79 | 125[11] |
| Thrift institutions | 199 | 228 | 214 | 177 | 211 | Short-term Treasury securities[12] | 49 | 68 | 134 | 301 | 349[11] |
| | | | | | | Bankers acceptances | 4 | 10 | 32 | 43 | 34[11] |
| | | | | | | Commercial paper[13] | 35 | 94 | 99 | 207 | 358[11] |

**Note:** As of December of year shown. Seasonally adjusted. Z = less than $500 million. 1. Currency outside U.S. Treasury, Federal Reserve banks, and the vaults of depository institutions. 2. Outstanding amount of nonbank issuers. 3. At commercial banks and foreign-related institutions. 4. Consists of negotiable order of withdrawal (NOW) and automatic transfer service (ATS) accounts at all depository institutions, plus credit union share draft balances and demand deposits at thrift institutions. 5. This sum is seasonally adjusted as a whole. 6. Not seasonally adjusted. 7. Issued in amounts of less than $100,000. Includes retail repurchase agreements. Excludes individual retirement accounts (IRAs) and Keogh accounts. 8. Issued in amounts of $100,000 or more. Excludes those booked at international banking facilities. 9. Excludes those held by money-market mutual funds, depository institutions, and foreign banks and official institutions. 10. Excludes those held by depository institutions and money-market mutual funds. 11. Preliminary data, November 1990. 12. U.S. Treasury bills and coupons with remaining maturities of less than 11 months held by other than depository institutions, Federal Reserve banks, money-market mutual fund, and foreign entities. 13. Excludes commercial paper held by money-market mutual funds. **Source:** Board of Governors of the Federal Reserve System, *Money Stock, Liquid Assets, and Debt Measures, Federal Reserve Statistical Release H.6* (weekly).

## TOP 25 U.S. COMMERCIAL BANKS RANKED BY ASSETS AND BY DEPOSITS, 1990

| Rank by assets/Bank | Assets ('000s) | Deposits ('000s) | Rank by deposits | Rank by assets/Bank | Assets ('000s) | Deposits ('000s) | Rank by deposits |
|---|---|---|---|---|---|---|---|
| 1. Citibank NA, New York | $157,821,000 | $112,586,000 | 1 | 15. Republic National Bank, New York | $22,914,176 | $15,750,448 | 18 |
| 2. Bank of America NT&SA, San Francisco | 96,281,000 | 77,027,000 | 2 | 16. NBD Bank, NA, Detroit | 21,858,195 | 16,864,551 | 14 |
| 3. Chase Manhattan Bank NA, New York | 73,360,000 | 59,862,000 | 3 | 17. Marine Midland Bank NA, Buffalo | 19,546,106 | 16,356,546 | 16 |
| 4. Morgan Guaranty Trust Co., New York | 68,645,842 | 37,847,005 | 7 | 18. NCNB National Bank of North Carolina, Charlotte | 19,070,326 | 11,802,446 | 27 |
| 5. Manufacturers Hanover Trust Co., New York | 57,753,000 | 41,384,000 | 6 | 19. First Interstate Bank of California, Los Angeles | 19,068,021 | 15,831,927 | 17 |
| 6. Security Pacific National Bank, Los Angeles | 55,681,500 | 45,376,676 | 4 | 20. First Union National Bank, Charlotte | 18,738,779 | 12,076,946 | 22 |
| 7. Wells Fargo Bank NA, San Francisco | 53,823,569 | 42,716,399 | 5 | 21. Mellon Bank NA, Pittsburgh | 17,381,784 | 11,834,294 | 25 |
| 8. Bankers Trust Co., New York | 53,681,000 | 28,844,000 | 10 | 22. Wachovia Bank & Trust Co. NA, Winston-Salem, N.C. | 16,844,993 | 11,889,754 | 24 |
| 9. Chemical Bank, New York | 48,160,000 | 30,667,000 | 9 | 23. First Union National Bank of Florida, Jacksonville | 16,682,706 | 12,468,080 | 19 |
| 10. Bank of New York | 42,383,461 | 33,468,870 | 8 | 24. CoreStates Bank, NA, Philadelphia | 16,537,098 | 11,796,851 | 28 |
| 11. First National Bank, Chicago | 35,994,285 | 25,289,561 | 12 | 25. Pittsburgh National Bank | 16,529,301 | 10,910,127 | 31 |
| 12. NCNB Texas National Bank, Dallas | 32,729,399 | 26,593,824 | 11 | | | | |
| 13. Continental Bank NA, Chicago | 26,737,000 | 16,455,000 | 15 | | | | |
| 14. First National Bank, Boston | 24,866,576 | 20,079,100 | 13 | | | | |

**Note:** NA = national association; NT&SA = national trust and savings association. Federal regulatory report of condition for December 31, 1990, and various state banking departments. With respect to mergers, *American Banker* follows the bank of charter in determining the surviving bank. **Source:** *American Banker* (Mar. 28, 1991).

market funds and other instruments can do so as well. In fact in 1986, 48% of household expenditures were paid for with checking accounts, and only 34% were paid for with cash.

The Fed uses four different measures of the money supply, which include different monetary instruments:

M1 is the original and most commonly reported measure of the money supply, which embraces currency and coins, demand deposits, traveler's checks, and other checkable deposits.

M2 is M1 plus overnight repurchasement agreements, overnight Eurodollars, money-market mutual-fund balances, money-market deposit accounts, and savings and small time-deposits.

M3 is M2 plus money-market mutual-fund balances held by financial institutions, term re-

purchase agreements and term Eurodollars, and large time-deposits.

L is M3 plus Treasury bills, commercial paper, and other very liquid assets such as savings bonds.

## The U.S. Banking System

**Commercial banks** are the largest financial institutions in the country and are the principal vehicles for exchanging money. The nation's first commercial bank was the Bank of America (now First Pennsylvania Bank), established in Philadelphia in 1782. Commercial banks hold about two-thirds of the nation's money deposits. Savings and loans, the next-largest source of deposits, hold about half as much.

There are approximately 12,400 commercial

banks in the country. They may be chartered either by the federal government or by individual states. While banks themselves may not operate across states, they may be owned by holding companies that can operate interstate, if state laws permit. Fifteen of the nation's largest 100 banks have foreign owners.

Commercial banks can make loans to individuals and to commercial operations, establish checking or demand deposits, maintain "trust" departments that make investments for customers, and perform a variety of other functions such as issuing credit cards. Until the deregulation of the 1980s, commercial banks were the only ones permitted to issue checking accounts. Regulations that developed after bank failures in the Great Depression still keep these banks out of the investment business—

## TOP 25 U.S. THRIFTS RANKED BY ASSETS AND BY DEPOSITS, 1990

| Rank by assets/Bank | Assets ('000s) | Deposits ('000s) | Rank by deposits | Rank by assets/Bank | Assets ('000s) | Deposits ('000s) | Rank by deposits |
|---|---|---|---|---|---|---|---|
| 1. Home Savings of America, FA, Irwindale, Calif.[1] | $51,253,405 | $38,955,434 | 1 | 13. Coast Federal Bank, Los Angeles | $10,247,415 | $8,708,233 | 10 |
| 2. Great Western Bank, FSB, Beverly Hills, Calif. | 39,230,339 | 29,150,284 | 2 | 14. First Federal Bank of Michigan, Detroit | 9,962,317 | 3,659,139 | 35 |
| 3. Glendale Federal Bank, FSB, Calif. | 23,439,196 | 15,628,356 | 4 | 15. Standard Federal Bank, Troy, Mich. | 9,297,253 | 5,897,087 | 16 |
| 4. World Savings, FS&LA, Oakland | 22,042,045 | 14,129,588 | 5 | 16. First Gibraltar Bank, FSB, Dallas | 8,860,438 | 7,425,344 | 13 |
| 5. California Federal Bank, FSB, Los Angeles | 21,504,990 | 16,762,762 | 3 | 17. Anchor Savings Bank, FSB, Northport, N.Y. | 8,825,543 | 7,074,802 | 14 |
| 6. First Nationwide Bank, FSB, San Francisco | 20,429,452 | 12,026,543 | 8 | 18. Sunbelt Savings, FSB, Dallas | 8,354,072 | 4,341,038 | 29 |
| 7. Homefed Bank, FSB, San Diego | 18,260,755 | 13,739,425 | 7 | 19. Household Bank, FSB, Newport Beach, Calif | 7,887,017 | 5,030,077 | 20 |
| 8. American Savings Bank, FA, Irvine, Calif. | 16,490,794 | 13,955,956 | 6 | 20. Pacific First Bank, FSB, Seattle | 7,040,547 | 4,803,885 | 22 |
| 9. Goldome, Buffalo | 11,310,969 | 7,855,637 | 11 | 21. People's Bank, Bridgeport, Conn. | 6,917,710 | 5,720,680 | 17 |
| 10. CrossLand Savings FSB, Brooklyn, N.Y. | 11,177,977 | 7,761,024 | 12 | 22. Citibank, FSB, San Francisco | 6,728,237 | 4,764,337 | 23 |
| 11. Dime Savings Bank of New York FSB, Garden City | 10,841,836 | 8,831,889 | 9 | 23. Imperial Federal Savings Assn., San Diego[2] | 6,583,515 | 4,393,306 | 28 |
| | | | | 24. Meritor Savings Bank, Philadelphia | 6,519,714 | 4,819,880 | 21 |
| 12. Great American Bank, SSB, San Diego | 10,551,690 | 6,682,556 | 15 | 25. Manhattan Savings Bank, New York[3] | 5,909,720 | 5,282,558 | 19 |

**Note**: FA = federal association; FSB = federal savings bank; FS&LA = federal savings and loan association; SSB = state savings bank. 1. Consolidated to include Bowery Savings Bank and Home Savings Bank of New York, acquired in November 1990. 2. Thrift was in RTC conservatorship at year end. 3. On May 2, 1990, Williamsburgh Savings Bank, Brooklyn, a subsidiary of Republic New York Corp., acquired The Manhattan Savings Bank. Williamsburgh then changed its title and location. **Source**: *American Banker* (May 17, 1991).

largely to protect depositors and the solvency of banks from potential effects of bad investments. But deregulation of the banking industry in the 1980s is blurring many of these distinctions. In particular, investment companies are now permitted to issue demand deposits and to compete with banks in other areas as well. (As a result these companies are sometimes referred to as nonbanks.)

**Bank failures** The failure of a commercial bank is an especially serious problem because of the domino effect it may have on other financial institutions and businesses. Banks, and indeed all depository institutions, ultimately fail when many of their loans go bad and cannot be repaid. But even before that happens, depositors may get nervous about the security of their accounts and withdraw them all at once—a "run on the bank." Because banks loan out deposits and hold in reserve only a small percentage of the value of those deposits, banks experiencing a run would have to call in some of their loans (mainly those already due), putting sudden pressure on many commercial borrowers and causing some to fail. In addition the withdrawal of deposits and of loans reduces the money supply sharply. This process was an important cause of the Great Depression. Following the banking failures during the depression (2,293 banks failed in 1931, and 4,000 banks failed in 1933), the Federal Deposit Insurance Corporation (FDIC) was created in 1933 to protect the accounts of depositors and, more important, to help prevent bank failures. The FDIC charges banks a premium to pay for this coverage. The corporation is designed to prevent runs on banks by insuring deposits and lending to banks to prevent the need to call in loans.

But banks still fail because of bad loans. Since 1945 U.S. banks have failed at the rate of about six per year. That number escalated rapidly in the 1980s, however—up to 207 failures in 1989. In 1990, 168 failed, and an additional 440 banks are expected to fail by the end of 1992. Most of these failures occurred in agricultural states where the failure of farms led to defaults on loans; more than half of all bank failures can be attributed to agriculture loans. Fraud also played an important role, especially in Tennessee, where more than 30 banks have failed since 1982. When a bank fails, the FDIC pays off each depositor (currently, up to $1,000,000 in banks that are members of the Federal Reserve System and in such nonmember banks as join the insurance fund) and then sells the bank's assets. Sometimes the FDIC arranges for another bank's acquisition of the failed bank by subsidizing the sale. On December 31, 1990, the FDIC made its largest payout—$424.4 million—to depositors of the failed Capital Bank and Trust Co. in Boston.

**Thrifts** are depository institutions including savings and loans (S&Ls), savings banks, and credit unions. Of the 17,244 thrifts in the country, the largest and most important are the S&Ls, which were created to provide home mortgages for borrowers and long-term savings deposits for individual investors. Until recently, thrifts were prohibited from engaging in riskier loans—including most commercial loans—and issuing checking deposits, and a ceiling was placed on the rate of interest they

## FDIC/BIF-INSURED BANKS—NUMBER, BANKING OFFICES, AND DEPOSITS, 1990

| Charter class | Banks | Offices | Deposits (millions) | | |
|---|---|---|---|---|---|
| | | | IPC[1] | Other[2] | Total |
| Commercial banks | 12,509 | 61,763 | $2,086,297 | $180,194 | $2,266,491 |
| National banks | 4,063 | 30,574 | 1,219,208 | 104,686 | 1,323,894 |
| State banks (Federal Reserve members) | 1,019 | 6,754 | 270,210 | 26,016 | 296,226 |
| State banks (Non–Federal Reserve members) | 7,427 | 24,435 | 596,879 | 49,492 | 646,372 |
| Savings banks | 479 | 3,693 | 211,983 | 2,425 | 214,409 |
| U.S. branches of foreign banks | 0 | 54 | 4,177 | 67 | 4,244 |
| **All banks** | **12,988** | **65,510** | **$2,302,457** | **$182,686** | **$2,485,144** |

**Note:** The Financial Institutions Reform, Recovery, and Enforcement Act (FIRREA) of 1989 transferred deposit insurance for savings associations from the Federal Savings and Loan Corporation (FSLIC) to the FDIC's Savings Association Insurance Fund (SAIF). The FDIC's Deposit Insurance Fund was renamed the Bank Insurance Fund (BIF). FIRREA regulations Permit BIF-insured institution to absorb or purchase SAIF-insured thrift offices. 1. IPC = individuals, partnerships, and corporations. 2. Includes federal government public funds and official checks. **Source:** Federal Deposit Insurance Corp., *FDIC Data Book, Operating Banks and Branches*, (June 30, 1990)

could pay depositors. Congress lifted the ceiling on interest payments to depositors in 1980 and in 1982 allowed the S&Ls to issue commercial loans and to invest directly in real estate developments.

The Federal Home Loan Bank System was established in 1932 to serve some of the same functions for S&Ls that the Federal Reserve provides for banks. It has now been succeeded by the Office of Thrift Supervision (OTS), which identifies institutions that may be financially distressed or likely to fail. All federally chartered S&Ls are regulated by the system (and must have the word *Federal* in their name). Less than half the thrifts are federally chartered, however; the rest are chartered by states, although most of these have joined the system as well. The FSLIC (Federal Savings and Loan Insurance Corporation) insured deposits at member S&Ls until 1989, when it became insolvent and was dismantled.

**The savings and loan crisis** The S&Ls came under enormous economic pressure in the 1970s, when interest rates paid by banks and other financial institutions rose well above the rate ceiling for thrifts, and they started losing depositors. Further, they were in a financial

## MONEY-MARKET INTEREST RATES AND MORTGAGE RATES, 1970–90 (percent per year)

| Type | 1970 | 1975 | 1980 | 1985 | 1990 |
|---|---|---|---|---|---|
| Federal funds, effective rate[1] | 7.18% | 5.82% | 13.36% | 8.10% | 8.10% |
| Commercial paper, 3-month[1, 2] | N.A. | 6.25 | 12.66 | 7.95 | 8.06 |
| Prime rate charged by banks | 7.91 | 7.86 | 15.27 | 9.93 | 10.01 |
| Eurodollar deposits, 3-month | 8.52 | 7.03 | 14.00 | 8.27 | 8.16 |
| Finance paper, 3-month[2, 3] | 7.18 | 6.15 | 11.49 | 7.77 | 7.87 |
| Bankers acceptances, 90-day[2, 4] | 7.31 | 6.29 | 12.72 | 7.92 | 7.93 |
| Large negotiable certificates of deposit, 3-month, secondary market | 7.56 | 6.44 | 13.07 | 8.05 | 8.15 |
| Federal Reserve discount rate[5] | 5.5–6.00 | 6.00–7.75 | 10.00–13.00 | 7.5–8.00 | 6.5–7.00 |
| U.S. Government securities:[6] | | | | | |
| 3-month Treasury bill | 6.39 | 5.78 | 11.43 | 7.48 | 7.50 |
| 6-month Treasury bill | 6.51 | 6.09 | 11.37 | 7.65 | 7.46 |
| 1-year Treasury bill | 6.48 | 6.28 | 10.89 | 7.81 | 7.35 |
| Prime 1-year municipals[7] | 4.35 | 3.91 | 6.14 | 5.10 | 5.85 |
| Home mortgages (HUD series):[8] | | | | | |
| FHA insured, secondary market[9] | 9.03 | 9.19 | 13.44 | 12.24 | 10.17 |
| Conventional, new-home[10, 11] | 8.52 | 9.10 | 13.95 | 12.28 | 9.68 |
| Conventional, existing-home[10] | 8.56 | 9.14 | 13.95 | 12.29 | 9.73 |

1. Based on daily offering rates of dealers. 2. Yields are quoted on a bank-discount basis, rather than an investment-yield basis (which would give a higher figure). 3. Placed directly; averages of daily offering rates quoted by finance companies. 4. Based on the most representative daily offering rates of dealers. Beginning Aug. 15, 1974, closing rates were used, and from Jan. 1, 1981, rates of top-rated banks only. 5. Federal Reserve Bank of New York, low and high. The discount rates for 1980 and 1981 do not include the surcharge applied to frequent borrowings by large institutions. The surcharge reached 3% in 1980 and 4% in 1981; it was eliminated in November 1981. 6. Averages based on daily closing bid yields in secondary market bank discount basis. 7. Averages based on quotation for one day each month. **Source:** Salomon Brothers, Inc., New York, *An Analytical Record of Yields and Yield Spreads.* 8. HUD = Housing and Urban Development. 9. Averages based on quotations for one day each month as compiled by the Federal Housing Administration. 10. Primary market. 11. Average contract rate on new commitments. **Sources:** Except as noted, Board of Directors of the Federal Reserve System, *Federal Reserve Bulletin* (monthly) and *Annual Statistical Digest,* and U.S. Dept of Commerce, *Survey of Current Business* (April and May 1991).

## BOND AND STOCK YIELDS, 1970–90 (percent per year)

| Type | 1970 | 1975 | 1980 | 1985 | 1990 |
|---|---|---|---|---|---|
| U.S. Treasury, constant maturities:[1, 2] | | | | | |
| 3-year | 7.29% | 7.49% | 11.55% | 9.64% | 8.26% |
| 5-year | 7.38 | 7.77 | 11.48 | 10.13 | 8.37 |
| 10-year | 7.35 | 7.99 | 11.46 | 10.62 | 8.55 |
| U.S. Govt., long-term bonds[2, 3] | 6.58 | 6.98 | 10.81 | 10.75 | 8.74 |
| State and local govt. bonds, Aaa[4] | 6.12 | 6.42 | 7.86 | 8.60 | 6.96 |
| State and local govt. bonds, Baa[4] | 6.75 | 7.62 | 9.02 | 9.58 | 7.29 |
| High-graded municipal bonds (Standard & Poor's)[5] | 6.51 | 6.89 | 8.51 | 9.18 | 7.76[6] |
| Municipal (Bond Buyer, 20 bonds) | 6.35 | 7.05 | 8.59 | 9.11 | 7.27 |
| Corporate Aaa seasoned[4] | 8.04 | 8.83 | 11.94 | 11.37 | 9.32 |
| Corporate Baa seasoned[4] | 9.11 | 10.61 | 13.67 | 12.72 | 10.31 |
| Corporate Aaa utility bonds[7] | 8.72 | 9.17 | 12.57 | 11.79 | 9.58 |
| Corporate (Moody's)[4] | 8.51 | 9.57 | 12.75 | 12.05 | 9.77 |
| Industrials (37 bonds)[8] | 8.26 | 9.25 | 12.35 | 11.80 | 9.77 |
| Public utilities (40 bonds) | 8.68 | 9.88 | 13.15 | 12.29 | 9.76 |
| Stocks (Standard & Poor's):[5] | | | | | |
| Preferred (10 stocks)[9] | 7.22 | 8.36 | 10.60 | 10.49 | 8.96 |
| Common: Composite (500 stocks) | 3.83 | 4.31 | 5.26 | 4.25 | 3.61 |
| Industrials (400 stocks) | 3.62 | 3.96 | 4.95 | 3.76 | 3.16 |

1. Yields on the more actively traded issues adjusted to constant maturities by the U.S. Treasury. 2. Yields are based on closing bid prices quoted by at least five dealers. 3. Averages (to maturity or call) for all outstanding bonds neither due nor callable in less than 10 years, including several very low yielding "flower" bonds. 4. **Source:** Moody's Investors Service, New York, N.Y. 5. **Source:** Standard & Poor's Corp., New York, N.Y., *Standard & Poor's Outlook* (weekly). 6. Data are for 1989. 7. Based on first trading day of each month, deferred call, new issue estimate. **Source:** Salomon Brothers, Inc., New York, N.Y., *An Analytical Record of Yields and Yield Spreads.* 8. Covers 40 bonds for period 1970–83 and 38 bonds for 1984–86. 9. Yields based on 10 stocks, 4 yields. Issues converted to a price equivalent to $100 par and a 7% annual dividend before averaging. **Sources:** Except as noted, U.S. Dept. of Commerce, *Survey of Current Business* (monthly) and Board of Governors of the Federal Reserve System, *Federal Reserve Bulletin* (monthly).

bind because their outstanding loans were all in mortgages—long-term, 30-year loans issued at low interest. In part because of this, the thrifts were deregulated, released from many of the restrictions on their activities and allowed to pursue a more diverse market for loans. With this new freedom, however, many S&Ls took on loans that were at a higher level of risk in order to earn a higher rate of return. Some argue that the insurance on deposits provided by the Federal Home Loan Bank encouraged the S&Ls to make loans that were too risky.

Lending institutions fail mainly if a large percentage of their loans go bad and cannot be collected. And mortgage loans fail, not just because buyers cannot make their payments, but also because the collateral (the buildings) may decline in price so that it is less than the value of the loan. Especially in the Southwest, many of the loans for real estate development failed when the oil industry declined in the 1980s, taking local economies with it. S&Ls started to collapse at an alarming rate—517 thrifts closed between 1980 and 1988. With liabilities of $100 billion in excess of assets, the FSLIC ran out of money. Its insurance obligations passed to the FDIC, and the Resolution Trust Corporation (RTC) was formed to dispose of (sell) approximately $400 billion of insolvent thrifts' assets. The government dealt with 205 insolvent S&Ls in 1988 alone by subsidizing their sale to more secure institutions.

As of July 1991, the RTC had resolved 458 institutions, and there were 173 institutions

## MEDIAN MONEY INCOME OF YEAR-ROUND, FULL-TIME CIVILIAN WORKERS, BY SEX AND AGE, 1970–89

| Age[1] | Female | | | | Male | | | |
|---|---|---|---|---|---|---|---|---|
| | 1970 | 1980 | 1985 | 1989 | 1970 | 1980 | 1985 | 1989 |
| Total with income | $5,440[2] | $11,591 | $16,252 | $19,612 | $9,184[2] | $19,173 | $24,999 | $28,511 |
| 15–19 yrs. | 3,783[3] | 6,779 | 8,372 | — | 3,950[3] | 7,753 | 9,050 | — |
| 20–24 yrs. | 4,928 | 9,407 | 11,757 | 13,653[4] | 6,655 | 12,109 | 13,827 | 15,501[4] |
| 25–34 yrs. | 5,923 | 12,190 | 16,740 | 19,706 | 9,126 | 17,724 | 22,321 | 24,991 |
| 35–44 yrs. | 5,531 | 12,239 | 18,032 | 21,498 | 10,258 | 21,777 | 28,966 | 32,370 |
| 45–54 yrs. | 5,588 | 12,116 | 17,009 | 20,905 | 9,931 | 22,323 | 29,880 | 35,356 |
| 55–64 yrs. | 5,468 | 11,931 | 16,761 | 19,895 | 9,071 | 21,053 | 28,387 | 34,505 |
| 65 and over | 4,884 | 12,342 | 18,336 | 21,505 | 6,754 | 17,307 | 26,146 | 34,110 |

1. Age as of March of following year. 2. 14 years old and over. 3. 14 to 19 years old. 4. Includes 15–24 years old. **Source:** U.S. Bureau of the Census, *Current Population Reports* (series).

## PER CAPITA MONEY INCOME, BY RACE AND HISPANIC ORIGIN, 1970–89

| Year | Current dollars | | | | Constant (1989) dollars | | | |
|---|---|---|---|---|---|---|---|---|
| | All races | White | Black | Hispanic[1] | All races | White | Black | Hispanic[1] |
| 1970 | $ 3,177 | $ 3,354 | $1,869 | N.A. | $10,153 | $10,719 | $5,973 | N.A. |
| 1975 | 4,818 | 5,072 | 2,972 | $2,847 | 11,505 | 11,690 | 6,850 | $6,562 |
| 1980 | 7,787 | 8,233 | 4,804 | 4,865 | 11,718 | 12,389 | 7,229 | 7,321 |
| 1985 | 11,013 | 11,671 | 6,840 | 6,613 | 12,692 | 13,450 | 7,883 | 7,621 |
| 1989 | 14,056 | 14,896 | 8,747 | 8,390 | 14,056 | 14,896 | 8,747 | 8,390 |

**Note:** N.A. = Not available. 1. Hispanic persons may be of any race. **Source:** U.S. Bureau of the Census, *Current Population Reports: Money Income of Households, Families, and Persons in the United States: 1988 and 1989* (1991).

under conservatorship. Under the conservatorship program, the RTC assigns a managing agent and a credit specialist to each participating institution to oversee its operations and ensure that management adheres to RTC policies and procedures and that no fraudulent practices are in evidence. In addition, the OTS has identified (as of July 1991) another 164 institutions that are "likely failures" and 378 undercapitalized institutions classified as "distressed." From the program's inception through September 1991, the OTS had spent $80 billion to bail out S&Ls. Government estimates suggest that it will cost American taxpayers $500 billion over the coming years to bail them out. Some estimates conclude that fraud contributed to more than one-third of these insolvent cases, suggesting that FSLIC monitoring and enforcement of regulations were hopelessly inadequate.

**Credit unions** are employer-sponsored cooperative organizations that provide consumer and mortgage credit to their members. Employers often arrange for payroll-deduction savings plans through the credit union.

**Mortgage loans** Mortgages are loans backed by buildings—either private dwellings or commercial buildings. In 1989 the value of mortgage debt outstanding in the country amounted to $3.5 trillion. Traditionally, virtually all mortgages had fixed-interest payments and 30-year terms. With the escalation of interest rates beginning in the late 1970s, however, a range of alternative arrangements has been developed, including reducing the period of the loan, typically to 15 years—in order to reduce interest payments—and making the interest rate vary with market rates—*adjustable rate mortgages*. Some mortgages that hold payments in the first few years and then increase them rapidly for the remaining term of the mortgage are known as balloon mortgages.

## Financial Instruments

**Money instruments** Treasury bills are securities sold by the U.S. Treasury in denominations of $10,000 that mature at various dates, but all in less than one year. Treasury bills pay an interest rate that is adjusted by the Treasury according to supply and demand. The Treasury bill rate is thought to be the highest risk-free rate of return among all investments.
**Federal funds** are the reserves the Fed requires depository institutions such as commercial banks to hold on deposit at their regional Federal Reserve Bank as protection against withdrawals. Banks and other depository institutions can loan reserves in excess of those required by the Fed to each other. These Fed Fund loans can provide institutions with large amounts of liquid assets on very short notice, and most loans are for no more than one day.
**Commercial paper** consists of debt or promissory notes (similar to an I.O.U.) issued by corporations as a way to borrow money in the short-term, generally less than one year. Commercial paper provides an alternative, generally cheaper way of raising money than taking a commercial bank loan. The rate of interest paid on commer-

cial paper is higher than that on Treasury bills because of the greater risk; the risk that even large, secure companies such as IBM will default on their debts is still greater than the risk that the U.S. government will. Commercial paper is one of the most important investments made by money-market accounts.
**Certificates of deposit (CDs)** Customers who make these deposits at commercial banks or thrift institutions receive a certificate describing the maturity date of the deposit (e.g., a five-year CD). CDs guarantee a rate of return for as long as 10 years into the future. In addition, the fact that they can be purchased at local banks also makes them easy to secure. These factors make them appealing to the general public. The interest paid on CDs is set by the market and is generally the same across large institutions. However, some institutions that are not as strong financially may have to pay a higher rate of return in order to compensate for the greater risk (although still perhaps negligible in an absolute sense) of default.
**Money-market accounts** Customers pool their money into a fund that then purchases short-term debt such as Treasury bills and commercial paper in order to earn a high rate of return while maintaining liquidity (i.e., being able to convert assets quickly into cash). Customers typically can write checks on their money-market accounts, which are processed through cooperating banks, but checks generally have to be in large denominations—greater than $250—to prevent customers from using them as demand deposit accounts with the high administrative costs associated with them.

**Capital instruments** Stock, or equity, the most important source of capital for firms, represents a claim on the assets or equity of a business as well as on its earnings. The owners of stock are literally the owners of the firm and vote on issues affecting it, most importantly voting to elect the directors who control the firm's management. The claims of stockholders are subordinate to the claims of bondholders. There is also a distinction between preferred stock and common stock; the claims of those holding the former must be paid first. The price of stock depends heavily on expectations about the firm's earnings. Stock prices vary with the state of the economy because the earnings prospects of firms vary depending on whether the economy is in an expansion or recession. Unlike debt instruments that come due at a fixed point in the future, stock never comes due; it represents a permanent claim on future earnings, and that is why changes in even the most long-term prospects for a firm will affect the price of its stock.
**Treasury bonds,** or notes, have longer-term dates of maturity, from one to 10 years, than do Treasury bills. They are sold by the Treasury in denominations of $1,000 and are the principal means of funding government borrowing and the national debt. The interest on these bonds is paid out regularly and is known as coupons. (Historically, owners of the bonds had to send in coupons that were then redeemed for interest payments, hence the phrase *clipping coupons*).

**Other government securities** Some agencies of the government that are involved in lending are permitted to sell securities in order to raise funds. The most important of these is the Federal National Mortgage Association—FNMA, or "Fanny Mae." It buys and sells mortgages insured by the federal government and stabilizes the market for those mortgages in the process.
**Corporate bonds** are sold by corporations to dealers called underwriters and then to the public in order to raise long-term funds for investment. Corporate bonds are the alternative to issuing stock for raising funds. Bondholders are not the owners of the corporation the way stockholders are, and one advantage of issuing bonds therefore is that ownership and control over the corporation is not affected. So-called "junk bonds" are a type of corporate bond with very high risk—for example, where there is not enough collateral to back the value of the bonds.
**Municipal bonds** are issued by state and local governments to raise funds, usually to provide public works and other facilities. The federal government is prohibited by the Constitution from interfering in the ability of state and local governments to raise revenue, so income from municipal bonds is not subject to federal taxes. So-called revenue bonds are paid for by user fees—for example, tolls collected on a parkway are used to pay for the bonds used to build it. General-obligation bonds are paid for through general taxes. Municipal bonds tend to be very safe, although there have been occasions on which some state and local governments have had to take extraordinary actions to avoid default—most notably, New York City in 1975, which received a federal loan and sold new bonds to its municipal employee unions in order to avoid default.

## GOVERNMENT DEBT

One of the most debated economic issues is the importance of the government's budget deficit, usually called the national debt. The national debt totaled over $3.5 trillion as of June 1991 and was increasing by approximately $500,000 every minute. Each family's proportionate share equalled just over $54,000. The government raises most of its resources through taxes, but it can also raise money by borrowing or by selling bonds (e.g., Treasury bonds and savings bonds)—which increasingly have been purchased by investors outside the country, who held 18% of the privately held U.S. public debt securities in 1990. The bonds raise money now but must be repaid in the future through revenues from taxes. The budget deficit in any year indicates the difference between what the government takes in through taxes and other forms of revenues and what it expends. The deficit therefore suggests how much the government needs to borrow to fill that gap. The total amount of present and past borrowing, plus interest, constitutes the total government debt. In 1990, interest on the public debt amounted to $264.9 billion, or 21.2% of federal outlays. This is only partially

## PUBLIC DEBT OF, AND INTEREST PAID BY, THE FEDERAL GOVERNMENT, 1940–90

| | Public debt | | | Interest paid | |
|---|---|---|---|---|---|
| | | Average annual | | | Percent of |
| Year | Total[1] (billions) | percent change[2] | Per capita[3] | Total (billions) | federal outlays[4] |
| 1940 | $ 43.0 | 8.4% | $ 325 | $ 1.0 | 10.5% |
| 1945 | 258.7 | 43.0 | 1,849 | 3.8 | 4.1 |
| 1950 | 256.1 | -0.1 | 1,688 | 5.7 | 13.4 |
| 1955 | 272.8 | 1.3 | 1,651 | 6.4 | 9.4 |
| 1960 | 284.1 | 0.9 | 1,572 | 9.2 | 10.0 |
| 1965 | 313.8 | 2.0 | 1,613 | 11.3 | 9.6 |
| 1970 | 370.1 | 3.3 | 1,814 | 19.3 | 9.9 |
| 1971 | 397.3 | 7.4 | 1,921 | 21.0 | 10.0 |
| 1972 | 426.4 | 7.3 | 2,037 | 21.8 | 9.4 |
| 1973 | 457.3 | 7.2 | 2,164 | 24.2 | 9.8 |
| 1974 | 474.2 | 3.7 | 2,223 | 29.3 | 10.9 |
| 1975 | 533.2 | 12.4 | 2,475 | 32.7 | 9.8 |
| 1976 | 620.4 | 16.4 | 2,852 | 37.1 | 10.0 |
| 1977 | 698.8 | 10.1 | 3,170 | 41.9 | 10.2 |
| 1978 | 771.5 | 10.4 | 3,463 | 48.7 | 10.6 |
| 1979 | 826.5 | 7.1 | 3,669 | 59.8 | 11.9 |
| 1980 | 907.7 | 9.8 | 3,985 | 74.9 | 12.7 |
| 1981 | 997.9 | 9.9 | 4,338 | 95.6 | 14.1 |
| 1982 | 1,142.0 | 14.4 | 4,913 | 117.4 | 15.7 |
| 1983 | 1,377.2 | 20.6 | 5,870 | 128.8 | 15.9 |
| 1984 | 1,572.3 | 14.2 | 6,640 | 153.8 | 18.1 |
| 1985 | 1,823.1 | 16.0 | 7,616 | 178.9 | 18.9 |
| 1986 | 2,125.3 | 16.6 | 8,793 | 187.1 | 18.9 |
| 1987 | 2,350.3 | 10.6 | 9,630 | 195.4 | 19.5 |
| 1988 | 2,602.3 | 10.9 | 10,556 | 214.1 | 20.1 |
| 1989 | 2,857.4 | 9.8 | N.A. | 241.0 | 21.1 |
| 1990 | 3,233.3 | 13.2 | N.A. | 264.9 | 21.2 |

**Note:** For fiscal years ending in year shown. Total public debt is restricted to borrowing by the Treasury and the value of savings bonds at current redemption value. 1. Adjusted to exclude nonmarketable issues to the International Monetary Fund and other international institutions for 1950, 1955, 1960, 1965, and 1970–74. 2. From preceding year shown; for 1940, change is from 1935. 3. For 1940–76, based on estimated July 1 population; thereafter, based on Oct. 1 resident population; prior to 1960, excludes Alaska and Hawaii. 4. Calculated on total expenditures not reduced by interfund transactions representing interest and certain other payments to Treasury through 1950. Beginning 1955, total budget outlays. **Sources:** Through U.S. fiscal 1980—U.S. Dept. of the Treasury, *Statistical Appendix to the Annual Report of the Secretary of the Treasury on the State of the Finances*; thereafter—U.S. Dept. of the Treasury, *Monthly Statement of the Public Debt of the United States* and *Final Monthly Treasury Statement of Receipts and Outlays of the U.S. Government.*

offset by interest earnings received by trust funds such as the civil service retirement and disability fund, Medicare, and Social Security, which bring the total of net interest paid by the federal government to $202.6 billion.

Governments routinely borrow to pay for long-term projects that will benefit the community both immediately and in the future. It can be argued that because much of the benefit from projects such as highways and other public works will be enjoyed by the next generation of taxpayers, the latter should also bear much of the cost. And they can do that by paying off the government debt (paying the premiums on government bonds) through taxes in the future. Controversy arises when the government borrows to pay for its more routine expenditures. One justification for such borrowing is that it can be used to manage business cycles in the

## FEDERAL RECEIPTS, OUTLAYS, AND DEBT, 1977–90 (billions of dollars)

| Fiscal year | Total receipts | Total outlays | Deficit | Gross federal debt (end of period) Total | Held by the public |
|---|---|---|---|---|---|
| 1977 | $ 355.6 | $ 409.2 | $-53.6 | $ 709.1 | $ 551.8 |
| 1978 | 399.6 | 458.7 | -59.2 | 780.4 | 610.9 |
| 1979 | 463.3 | 503.5 | -40.2 | 833.8 | 644.6 |
| 1980 | 517.1 | 590.9 | -73.8 | 914.3 | 715.1 |
| 1981 | 599.3 | 678.2 | -78.9 | 1,003.9 | 794.4 |
| 1982 | 617.8 | 745.7 | -127.9 | 1,147.0 | 929.4 |
| 1983 | 600.6 | 808.3 | -207.8 | 1,381.9 | 1,141.8 |
| 1984 | 666.5 | 851.8 | -185.3 | 1,576.7 | 1,312.6 |
| 1985 | 734.1 | 946.3 | -212.3 | 1,827.5 | 1,509.9 |
| 1986 | 769.1 | 989.8 | -220.7 | 2,129.5 | 1,745.6 |
| 1987 | 854.1 | 1,002.1 | -148.0 | 2,354.3 | 1,896.1 |
| 1988 | 909.0 | 1,064.1 | -155.1 | 2,614.6 | 2,063.9 |
| 1989 | 990.8 | 1,142.8 | -152.0 | 2,881.1 | 2,204.3 |
| 1990 | 1,031.2 | 1,251.6 | -220.4 | 3,190.5 | 2,186.7 |

**Source:** U.S. Office of Management and Budget, *Budget of the United States Government* (annual) and *Monthly Treasury Statement of Receipts and Outlays of the United States Government.*

economy; in other words, during recessions the government can borrow in order to increase expenditures and expand the economy without raising taxes, which would slow it down.

When the total amount of government debt becomes large, some economists believe that it damages the economy in a number of ways. First, the fact that the government is selling large amounts of debt means that it is competing for limited investor dollars with private borrowers, driving up the cost of borrowing and making it harder for private-sector businesses to make investments for future growth. Second, the future taxes needed to pay off large amounts of government debt may place a serious drain on the future economy, again diverting resources from investment in the private sector. Politicians are concerned because debt payments must be funded from tax revenues, so they must either raise taxes or reduce government spending in other areas (e.g., in defense and entitlement programs).

The debate over debt really turns on how much is "too much." Between 1935 and 1981, the only two significant increases in the deficit occurred during World War II and certain years of the Vietnam War when deficits were about $25 billion; between 1981 and 1988, however, the Reagan administration ran annual deficits averaging $167 billion and increased the nation's total outstanding gross debt from just over $1 trillion to over $2.6 trillion. In 1990, the national debt topped $3 trillion for the first time ever.

## THE LABOR FORCE

**Labor force participation rate** The labor force (or Labor Force Participation Rate—LFPR) is that proportion of the population that is either employed or actively seeking employment, 66.6% in 1990. It represents the supply of labor available for the economy. The LFPR is

lower for young people because many are in school, and also for older people because many have retired. It is highest for married men and for women who are heads of households.

**Women in the work force** One of the most important developments in the labor force has been the sharp increase in the LFPR of women, which has virtually doubled since the early 1960s. This increase can be attributed in part to changing attitudes toward appropriate roles for women as many have left traditional homemaking roles for careers in the labor force. Moreover, women are now attaining higher levels of education, delaying childbearing, having fewer children, and returning to work sooner than ever before. Women are also branching out into occupations traditionally dominated by men (lawyers, physicians, and managers).

Women have joined the labor force at an astounding rate since 1960. A few highlights of this trend:

• In 1990, 56.7 million women were in the U.S. civilian labor force (57.5% of all women). Of those, 29.8 million were married, 2.7 million separated, and 6.2 million divorced.

• In 1990 over half of all married women (58.4%) were either employed or actively seeking employment, compared to less than one-third (30.5%) in 1960.

• While there has been a smaller percentage increase among separated and divorced women, their LFPRs in 1988 were 60.9% and 75.7%, respectively, compared with 52.1% and 71.5% in 1970 (statistics for 1960 are not available).

• Unemployment rates have dropped from 1960 to 1990 for married and divorced women. In other words, of the women who want to work, a greater percentage can successfully find employment, reflecting the increased acceptance of women's roles in the labor force.

• For married women with children under six years of age, the increase in labor participation during 1960–88 is even more dramatic—it more than tripled, from 18.6% to 57.1%.

• Of all married women, black women with children between the ages of 6 and 13 had the highest LFPR in 1988—81.4%.

• During the recession of 1982–83, when overall unemployment reached 9.7%, women who were separated and had children under the age of six were particularly hard hit, with an unemployment rate of 27.6%.

• Median weekly earnings for women working full-time (74% of all working women) were $348 (as opposed to $485 for men) per week in 1990, up 2.9% from one year earlier, but still only 70% of men's median weekly earnings. Median weekly earnings for white women were $355, for black women $308, and $280 for Hispanic women.

• The number of firms owned by women increased by 57% from 1982 to 1987; 55.1% of all service businesses are owned by women.

**Government employment** Of the 119.6 million people employed in 1990, civilian employees in all levels of government totaled 17.7 million, or 14.8% of the employed labor force in the nation. The inclusion of military personnel (1.6 million) raises total government employment to 19.3 million.

**Unemployment rate** One of the most closely watched labor force statistics is the unemployment rate, which was 5.5% in 1990. Contrary to popular opinion, the unemployment rate is only an indirect measure of the people without jobs. In fact, the unemployment rate measures, as a proportion of the total labor force, those people without jobs who are actively seeking employment (within the last four weeks). So the unemployment rate may rise as new job seekers enter the labor force; every spring, for example, it rises slightly as school graduates enter the labor force and look for jobs. It may also fall as workers retire or otherwise leave the labor force. Further, when the economy is in a prolonged recession, the unemployment rate may actually drop slightly simply because some of the job seekers may give up trying to find a job and withdraw from the labor force.

The unemployment rate over time for the United States is a measure associated with identifying periods of expansion and recession. It reached a peak of 9.6% during the 1982–83 recession. The relatively high periods of unemployment beginning in the mid-1970s are in part due to the expansion of the labor force as the "baby boom" generation left school and began looking for work.

**Hispanics** One of the most interesting developments in the U.S. labor force is the rise of Hispanic workers and firms. They are the fastest-growing population group in the labor force, in large part due to immigration, with Mexicans making up the largest share. By the year 2000, the number of Hispanic workers in the labor force will account for 10% of the total labor force. Most of this projected increase can be attributed to the rise in the proportion of Hispanic women working (historically, these

women were more likely to stay at home). Overall, however, Hispanic workers earn only 74% as much as the average for all workers. They also have a significantly higher unemployment rate: in 1990, it was 8.0%, which, while much lower than in recent years, was still higher than the 5.4% for the non-Hispanic population. Hispanic-owned firms in the U.S. increased by 81% from 1982 to 1987, when they numbered 422,373. During the same period, the overall number of firms rose by only 14%.

**Productivity** measures how much output an economy or organization can generate from a given amount of input. Higher levels of productivity suggest greater efficiency—doing more with the same amount of resources, just as an efficient or economical car goes farther on a gallon of gasoline. Increases in productivity, as the result of better tools or improved methods, provide the main mechanism for increas-

## CIVILIAN EMPLOYMENT IN OCCUPATIONS WITH THE LARGEST JOB GROWTH AND IN THE FASTEST-GROWING AND FASTEST-DECLINING OCCUPATIONS, 1988 AND 2000

| Occupation[1] | Employment ('000s) 1988 | Employment ('000s) 2000[2] | Percent change 1988–2000 |
|---|---|---|---|
| Total[3] | 118,104 | 136,211 | 15% |
| **Largest job growth[4]** | | | |
| Salespersons, retail | 3,834 | 4,564 | 19% |
| Registered nurses | 1,577 | 2,190 | 39 |
| Janitors and cleaners | 2,895 | 3,450 | 19 |
| Waiters and waitresses | 1,786 | 2,337 | 31 |
| General managers and top executives | 3,030 | 3,509 | 16 |
| General office clerks | 2,519 | 2,974 | 18 |
| Secretaries, except legal and medical | 2,903 | 3,288 | 13 |
| Nursing aides, orderlies, and attendants | 1,184 | 1,562 | 32 |
| Truck drivers, light and heavy | 2,399 | 2,768 | 15 |
| Receptionists and information clerks | 833 | 1,164 | 40 |
| Cashiers | 2,310 | 2,614 | 13 |
| Guards | 795 | 1,050 | 32 |
| Computer programmers | 519 | 769 | 48 |
| Food counter, fountain, and related workers | 1,626 | 1,866 | 15 |
| Food preparation workers | 1,027 | 1,260 | 23 |
| Licensed practical nurses | 626 | 855 | 37 |
| Teachers, secondary school | 1,164 | 1,388 | 19 |
| Computer systems analysts | 403 | 617 | 53 |
| Accountants and auditors | 963 | 1,174 | 22 |
| Teachers, kindergarten and elementary | 1,359 | 1,567 | 1 |
| Maintenance repairers, general utility | 1,080 | 1,282 | 19 |
| Child care workers | 670 | 856 | 28 |
| Gardeners and groundskeepers, except farm | 760 | 943 | 24 |
| Lawyers | 582 | 763 | 31 |
| Electrical and electronics engineers | 430 | 615 | 40 |
| Carpenters | 1,081 | 1,257 | 16 |
| Stock clerks, sales floor | 1,166 | 1,340 | 15 |
| Food service and lodging managers | 560 | 721 | 29 |
| Home health aides | 236 | 397 | 68 |
| Cooks, restaurant | 572 | 728 | 27 |
| Physicians | 535 | 684 | 28 |
| Teachers aides and educational assistants | 682 | 827 | 21 |
| Clerical supervisors and managers | 1,183 | 1,319 | 12 |
| Blue collar worker supervisors | 1,797 | 1,930 | 7 |

| Occupation[1] | Employment ('000s) 1988 | Employment ('000s) 2000[2] | Percent change 1988–2000 |
|---|---|---|---|
| Electrical and electronic engineering technicians | 341 | 471 | 38% |
| Dining room and cafeteria attendants and bar helpers | 448 | 578 | 29 |
| Financial managers | 673 | 802 | 19 |
| Automotive mechanics | 771 | 898 | 16 |
| Medical secretaries | 207 | 327 | 58 |
| Social workers | 385 | 495 | 29 |
| **Fastest-growing occupations** | | | |
| Medical assistants | 149 | 253 | 70% |
| Home health aides | 236 | 397 | 68 |
| Radiologic technologists and technicians | 132 | 218 | 66 |
| Medical secretaries | 207 | 327 | 58 |
| Securities and financial services sales workers | 200 | 309 | 55 |
| Travel agents | 142 | 219 | 54 |
| Computer systems analysts | 403 | 617 | 53 |
| Computer programmers | 519 | 769 | 48 |
| Human services workers | 118 | 171 | 45 |
| Correction officers and jailers | 186 | 262 | 41 |
| Electrical and electronics engineers | 439 | 615 | 40 |
| Receptionists and information clerks | 833 | 1,164 | 40 |
| **Fastest-declining occupations** | | | |
| Electrical and electronic equipment assemblers, precision | 161 | 91 | −44% |
| Electrical and electronic assemblers | 237 | 134 | −44 |
| Farmers | 1,141 | 875 | −23 |
| Stenographers | 159 | 122 | −23 |
| Telephone and cable TV line installers and repairers | 127 | 100 | −21 |
| Sewing machine operators, garment | 620 | 531 | −14 |
| Crushing and mixing machine operators and tenders | 136 | 117 | −14 |
| Textile draw-out and winding machine operators and tenders | 227 | 197 | −13 |
| Machine feeders and offbearers | 249 | 218 | −13 |
| Hand packers and packagers | 635 | 560 | −12 |
| Packaging and filling machine operators and tenders | 286 | 254 | −11 |

1. For occupations employing 100,000 or more in 1988. Includes wage and salary jobs, self employed, and unpaid family members. 2. Based on moderate trend assumptions. 3. Includes other occupations, not shown separately. 4. Based on absolute employment change 1988-2000. **Source**: U.S. Bureau of Labor Statistics, *Monthly Labor Review* (Nov. 1989).

## AVERAGE HOURLY AND WEEKLY EARNINGS IN CURRENT AND CONSTANT (1977) DOLLARS, BY PRIVATE INDUSTRY GROUP, 1970–90

Although it is true that average hourly and weekly nominal wages (in current dollars) have risen over the past two decades—by 210% and 268%, respectively—when inflation is accounted for, real weekly earnings (in constant dollars) have actually fallen an average of 11.2% since 1970. Paychecks may be getting bigger, but a 1990 paycheck doesn't go as far as a 1970 paycheck in covering living expenses.

| Private industry group | Current dollars | | | | | | Constant (1977) dollars | | | | | |
|---|---|---|---|---|---|---|---|---|---|---|---|---|
| | 1970 | 1975 | 1980 | 1985 | 1988 | 1990 | 1970 | 1975 | 1980 | 1985 | 1988 | 1989 |
| **Average hourly earnings** | **$3.23** | **$4.53** | **$6.66** | **$ 8.57** | **$ 9.29** | **$10.03** | **$5.04** | **$5.10** | **$4.89** | **$4.88** | **$4.84** | **$4.90** |
| Manufacturing | 3.35 | 4.83 | 7.27 | 9.54 | 10.18 | 10.84 | 5.23 | 5.44 | 5.34 | 5.44 | 5.30 | 5.20 |
| Mining | 3.85 | 5.95 | 9.17 | 11.98 | 12.75 | 13.65 | 6.01 | 6.70 | 6.74 | 6.83 | 6.64 | 6.53 |
| Construction | 5.24 | 7.31 | 9.94 | 12.32 | 13.01 | 13.73 | 8.17 | 8.23 | 7.30 | 7.02 | 6.77 | 6.64 |
| Transportation, public utilities | 3.85 | 5.88 | 8.87 | 11.40 | 12.32 | 12.95 | 6.01 | 6.62 | 6.52 | 6.50 | 6.41 | 6.24 |
| Wholesale trade | 3.44 | 4.73 | 6.96 | 9.16 | 9.94 | 10.80 | 5.37 | 5.33 | 5.11 | 5.22 | 5.17 | 5.16 |
| Retail trade | 2.44 | 3.36 | 4.88 | 5.94 | 6.31 | 6.78 | 3.81 | 3.78 | 3.59 | 3.38 | 3.28 | 3.26 |
| Finance, insurance, real estate | 3.07 | 4.06 | 5.79 | 7.94 | 9.09 | 9.99 | 4.79 | 4.57 | 4.25 | 4.52 | 4.73 | 4.75 |
| Services | 2.81 | 4.02 | 5.85 | 7.90 | 8.91 | 9.86 | 4.38 | 4.53 | 4.30 | 4.50 | 4.64 | 4.66 |
| **Average weekly earnings** | **$120** | **$164** | **$235** | **$299** | **$322** | **$346** | **$187** | **$184** | **$173** | **$170** | **$169**[1] | **$166**[2] |
| Manufacturing | 133 | 191 | 289 | 386 | 418 | 442 | 208 | 215 | 212 | 220 | 221[1] | 215[2] |
| Mining | 164 | 249 | 397 | 520 | 539 | 601 | 256 | 280 | 292 | 296 | 285[1] | 286[2] |
| Construction | 195 | 266 | 368 | 464 | 493 | 524 | 304 | 300 | 270 | 265 | 251[1] | 247[2] |
| Transportation, public utilities | 156 | 233 | 351 | 450 | 484 | 504 | 243 | 262 | 258 | 257 | 251[1] | 243[2] |
| Wholesale trade | 137 | 183 | 267 | 352 | 379 | 411 | 214 | 206 | 197 | 200 | 198[1] | 198[2] |
| Retail trade | 82 | 109 | 147 | 175 | 184 | 195 | 128 | 123 | 108 | 100 | 97[1] | 95[2] |
| Finance, insurance, real estate | 113 | 148 | 210 | 289 | 326 | 358 | 176 | 167 | 154 | 165 | 171[1] | 170[2] |
| Services | 97 | 135 | 191 | 257 | 290 | 321 | 151 | 152 | 140 | 146 | 153[1] | 154[2] |

1. Figures for December. 2. Preliminary figures for December. **Source:** U.S. Bureau of Labor Statistics, *Employment and Earnings* (monthly).

## EMPLOYMENT STATUS OF THE POPULATION BY RACE AND HISPANIC ORIGIN, 1975–90 (numbers in thousands)

| Year/race and Hispanic origin | Civilian non-institutional population[1] | Civilian labor force | | | | |
|---|---|---|---|---|---|---|
| | | Total | Percent of population | Number employed | Employment/ population ratio[2] | Percent unemployed |
| | | | White | | | |
| 1975 | 134,790 | 82,831 | 61.5% | 76,411 | 56.7% | 7.8% |
| 1980 | 146,122 | 93,600 | 64.1 | 87,715 | 60.0 | 6.3 |
| 1983 | 150,805 | 97,021 | 64.3 | 88,893 | 58.9 | 8.4 |
| 1985 | 153,679 | 99,926 | 65.0 | 93,736 | 61.0 | 6.2 |
| 1990 | 160,415 | 107,177 | 66.8 | 102,087 | 63.6 | 4.7 |
| | | | Black | | | |
| 1975 | 15,751 | 9,263 | 58.8% | 7,894 | 50.1% | 14.8% |
| 1980 | 17,824 | 10,865 | 61.0 | 9,313 | 52.2 | 14.3 |
| 1983 | 18,925 | 11,647 | 61.5 | 9,375 | 49.5 | 19.5 |
| 1985 | 19,664 | 12,364 | 62.9 | 10,501 | 53.4 | 15.1 |
| 1990 | 21,300 | 13,493 | 63.3 | 11,966 | 56.2 | 11.3 |
| | | | Hispanic[3] | | | |
| 1975 | N.A. | N.A. | N.A. | N.A. | N.A. | N.A. |
| 1980 | 9,598 | 6,146 | 64.0% | 5,527 | 57.6% | 10.1% |
| 1983 | 11,029 | 7,033 | 63.8 | 6,072 | 55.1 | 13.7 |
| 1985 | 11,915 | 7,698 | 64.6 | 6,888 | 57.8 | 10.5 |
| 1990 | 14,297 | 9,576 | 67.0 | 8,808 | 63.9 | 8.0 |

1. Age 16 and over. 2. Civilians employed as a percentage of the civilian noninstitutional population. 3. Hispanic persons may be of any race. **Source:** U.S. Bureau of Labor Statistics, *Employment and Earnings* (monthly).

## EMPLOYMENT STATUS OF THE POPULATION BY SEX, 1960–90 (numbers in thousands)

| Year and sex | Civilian non-institutional population[1] | Civilian labor force | | | | |
|---|---|---|---|---|---|---|
| | | Total | Percent of population | Number employed | Employment/ population ratio[2] | Percent unemployed |
| | | | Total | | | |
| 1960 | 117,245 | 69,628 | 59.4% | 65,778 | 56.1% | 5.5% |
| 1965 | 126,513 | 74,455 | 58.9 | 71,088 | 56.2 | 4.5 |
| 1970 | 137,085 | 82,771 | 60.4 | 78,678 | 57.4 | 4.9 |
| 1975 | 153,153 | 93,775 | 61.2 | 85,846 | 56.1 | 8.5 |
| 1980 | 167,745 | 106,940 | 63.8 | 99,303 | 59.2 | 7.1 |
| 1985 | 178,206 | 115,461 | 64.8 | 107,150 | 60.1 | 7.2 |
| 1990 | 188,049 | 124,787 | 66.4 | 117,914 | 62.7 | 5.5 |
| | | | Male | | | |
| 1960 | 55,662 | 46,388 | 83.3% | 43,904 | 78.9% | 5.4% |
| 1965 | 59,782 | 48,255 | 80.7 | 46,340 | 77.5 | 4.0 |
| 1970 | 64,304 | 51,228 | 79.7 | 48,990 | 76.2 | 4.4 |
| 1975 | 72,291 | 56,299 | 77.9 | 51,857 | 71.7 | 7.9 |
| 1980 | 79,398 | 61,453 | 77.4 | 57,186 | 72.0 | 6.9 |
| 1985 | 84,469 | 64,411 | 76.3 | 59,891 | 70.9 | 7.0 |
| 1990 | 89,650 | 68,234 | 76.1 | 64,435 | 71.9 | 5.6 |
| | | | Female | | | |
| 1960 | 61,582 | 23,240 | 37.7% | 21,874 | 35.5% | 5.9% |
| 1965 | 66,731 | 26,200 | 39.3 | 24,748 | 37.1 | 5.5 |
| 1970 | 72,782 | 31,543 | 43.3 | 29,688 | 40.8 | 5.9 |
| 1975 | 80,860 | 37,475 | 46.3 | 33,989 | 42.0 | 9.3 |
| 1980 | 88,348 | 45,487 | 51.5 | 42,117 | 47.7 | 7.4 |
| 1985 | 93,736 | 51,050 | 54.5 | 47,259 | 50.4 | 7.4 |
| 1990 | 98,399 | 56,554 | 57.5 | 53,479 | 54.3 | 5.4 |

1. Age 16 and over. 2. Civilians employed as a percentage of the civilian noninstitutional population. **Source:** U.S. Bureau of Labor Statistics, *Employment and Earnings* (monthly).

ing output in an economy and ultimately for raising standards of living. Productivity is usually measured in terms of labor—output per worker or per hour of labor—not only because labor is the most important resource but also because it is one of the easiest to measure.

**Wages** vary not only among the different professions but also between sexes and regions of the country. For example, women in year-round, full-time executive, administrative, and managerial positions have a median yearly income of only 61% of the median income for men in the same occupation group. This percentage is higher in the field of laborers, precision production, craft, and repair; but for all major occupation groups reported by the U.S. Bureau of the Census, women receive only a fraction of that received by their male counterparts. This may be due, in part, to the fact that women enter and leave the work force more times throughout their lives than do men and spend a smaller percentage of their lives economically active.

Another factor influencing the discrepancy between men's and women's wages is the concentration of women in occupations that pay less. In 1985, 70% of all women were employed in occupations in which 75% of employees were women. Five of the top 10 occupations employing women were sales clerk, clerical worker, bookkeeper, cashier, and social worker. The next two most popular were registered nurse and elementary school teacher.

Minimum wage in the nation was first enacted by the state of Massachusetts in 1912, covered only women, and was designed to shorten hours and raise pay in the covered industries. Nationwide a minimum wage was established during the Great Depression, but the amount varied among industries, usually around $0.35 per hour. The minimum wage rose from $3.35 to $4.25 per hour in April 1991, although employers may pay a special subminimum training wage of $3.35 (or 85% of the minimum wage) for a period of 90 days. States may require higher minimum wages, and 10 do so; 6.5% of all workers receive wages no higher than the minimum wage.

**Unions** A labor union is an organization of workers who engage in collective bargaining with employers for higher wages, better working conditions, and increased benefits. In the United States, unions are organized at three levels: (1) labor federations or voluntary associations of national unions, which settle disputes between national unions, lobby for favorable labor legislation, and engage in public relations. There is only one labor foundation in the country—the American Federation of Labor and Congress of Industrial Organizations, or AFL-CIO—to which virtually all union members belong; (2) national unions, which coordinate agreements across local unions and conduct collective bargaining negotiations with industry employers; and (3) local unions, which administer labor contracts, serving individual members, employers, and in some cases, establishments directly. Unions can be divided into two groups: (1) industrial unions, representing workers of a particular firm or industry, such as autoworkers and steelworkers, and (2) craft

## EFFECTIVE FEDERAL MINIMUM HOURLY WAGE RATES, 1950–91

| In effect | Minimum rate for nonfarm workers | Percent of avg. earnings[1] | Minimum rate for farm workers[2] |
|---|---|---|---|
| 1950 | $0.75 | 54% | N.A. |
| 1956 | 1.00 | 52 | N.A. |
| 1961 | 1.15 | 50 | N.A. |
| 1963 | 1.25 | 51 | N.A. |
| 1967 | 1.40 | 50 | $1.00 |
| 1968 | 1.60 | 54 | 1.15 |
| 1974 | 2.00 | 46 | 1.60 |
| 1975 | 2.10 | 45 | 1.80 |
| 1976 | 2.30 | 46 | 2.00 |
| 1978 | 2.65 | 44 | 2.65 |
| 1979 | 2.90 | 45 | 2.90 |
| 1980 | 3.10 | 44 | 3.10 |
| 1981 | 3.35 | 43 | 3.35 |
| 1989 | 3.35 | 32 | 3.35 |
| 1991 | 4.25[3] | 39 | 4.25[3] |

**Note:** N.A. = not applicable. 1. Percent of gross average hourly earnings of production workers in manufacturing. 2. Not included until 1966. 3. In effect June 1, 1991. **Source:** U.S. Dept. of Labor.

## PERCENT OF FEMALE WORKERS IN SELECTED OCCUPATIONS, 1975–90

| Occupation | Percentage of women employed within occupation | | |
|---|---|---|---|
| | 1975 | 1985 | 1990 |
| Airline pilot | — | 2.6% | 5.1% |
| Auto mechanic | 0.5% | 0.6 | 0.8 |
| Bartender | 35.2 | 47.9 | 55.6 |
| Bus driver | 37.7 | 49.2 | 51.6 |
| Cab driver, chauffeur | 8.7 | 10.9 | 9.5 |
| Carpenter | 0.6 | 1.2 | 1.3 |
| Child care worker | 98.4 | 96.1 | 97.0 |
| Computer programmer | 25.6 | 34.3 | 36.0 |
| Computer systems analyst | 14.8 | 28.0 | 34.5 |
| Data entry keyer | 92.8 | 90.7 | 87.2 |
| Data-processing equipment repairer | 1.8 | 10.4 | 11.4 |
| Dental assistant | 100.0 | 99.0 | 98.7 |
| Dentist | 1.8 | 6.5 | 9.5 |
| Economist | 13.1 | 34.5 | 43.8 |
| Editor, reporter | 44.6 | 51.7 | 52.0 |
| Garage gas station attendant | 4.7 | 6.8 | 4.7 |
| Lawyer, judge | 7.1 | 18.2 | 20.8 |
| Librarian | 81.1 | 87.0 | 83.3 |
| Mail carrier | 8.7 | 17.2 | 24.9 |
| Office machine repairer | 1.7 | 5.7 | 5.4 |
| Physician | 13.0 | 17.2 | 19.3 |
| Registered nurse | 97.0 | 95.1 | 94.5 |
| Social worker | 60.8 | 66.7 | 68.2 |
| Teacher, college/university | 31.1 | 35.2 | 37.7 |
| Teacher, elementary school | 85.4 | 84.0 | 85.2 |
| Telephone installer/repairer | 4.8 | 12.8 | 11.3 |
| Telephone operator | 93.3 | 88.8 | 89.0 |
| Waiter/waitress | 91.1 | 84.0 | 80.8 |
| Welder | 4.4 | 4.8 | 4.0 |

**Source:** U.S. Dept. of Labor, Bureau of Labor Statistics, *Employment and Earnings* (monthly).

## U.S. MEMBERSHIP IN AFL-CIO–AFFILIATED UNIONS, BY SELECTED UNION, 1979–89 (thousands of workers)

| Labor organization | 1979 | 1985 | 1989 |
|---|---|---|---|
| Total[1] | 13,621 | 13,109 | 14,100 |
| Actors and artists | 75 | 100 | 97 |
| Automobile, aerospace, and agriculture (UAW) | (X) | 974 | 917 |
| Bakery, confectionery, and tobacco | 131 | 115 | 103 |
| Boilermakers, iron shipbuilders[2,3] | 129 | 110 | 75 |
| Bricklayers | 106 | 95 | 84 |
| Carpenters[2] | 626 | 616 | 613 |
| Clothing and textile workers (ACTWU)[2] | 308 | 228 | 180 |
| Communications workers (CWA) | 485 | 524 | 492 |
| Electrical workers (IBEW) | 825 | 791 | 744 |
| Electronic, electrical, and salaried[2,4] | 243 | 198 | 171 |
| Operating engineers | 313 | 330 | 330 |
| Firefighters | 150 | 142 | 142 |
| Food and commercial workers (UFCW)[2] | 1,123 | 989 | 999 |
| Garment workers (ILGWU) | 314 | 210 | 153 |
| Glass, molders, pottery, and plastics[2] | 50 | 104 | 86 |
| Government, American federation (AFGE) | 236 | 199 | 156 |
| Graphic communications[2] | 171 | 141 | 124 |
| Hotel and restaurant employees | 373 | 327 | 278 |
| Ironworkers | 146 | 140 | 111 |
| Laborers | 475 | 383 | 406 |
| Letter carriers (NALC) | 151 | 186 | 201 |
| Machinists and aerospace (IAM)[2] | 688 | 537 | 517 |
| Office and professional employees | 83 | 90 | 84 |
| Oil, chemical, atomic workers (OCAW) | 146 | 108 | 71 |
| Painters | 160 | 133 | 128 |
| Paperworkers international | 262 | 232 | 210 |
| Plumbing and pipefitting | 228 | 226 | 220 |
| Postal workers | 245 | 232 | 213 |
| Retail, wholesale, department store | 122 | 106 | 137 |
| Rubber, cork, linoleum, plastic | 158 | 106 | 92 |
| Seafarers | 84 | 80 | 80 |
| Service employees (SEIU)[2,5] | 537 | 688 | 762 |
| Sheet metal workers | 120 | 108 | 108 |
| State, county, municipal (AFSCME)[5] | 889 | 997 | 1,090 |
| Steelworkers | 964 | 572 | 481 |
| Teachers (AFT) | 423 | 470 | 544 |
| Teamsters[6] | (X) | (X) | 1,161 |
| Transit union | 94 | 94 | 96 |
| Transport workers | 85 | 85 | 85 |
| Transportation/communications intl. | 127 | 102 | 86 |

**Note:** X = Not applicable. Figures represent the labor organizations as constituted in 1989 and reflect past merger activity. Membership figures based on average per capita paid membership to the AFL-CIO–for the two-year period ending in June of the year shown and reflect only actively employed members. Labor unions shown had a membership of 70,000 or more in 1989. 1. Includes other AFL-CIO–affiliated unions, not shown separately. 2. Figures reflect mergers with one or more unions since 1979. 3. Includes blacksmiths, forgers, and helpers. 4. Includes machine and furniture workers. 5. Excludes hospital and health care employees which merged into both unions on June 1, 1989 (membership of 23,000 in 1985, and 58,000 in 1989). 6. Includes chauffeurs, warehousemen, and helpers. **Source:** American Federation of Labor and Congress of Industrial Organizations, *Report of the AFL CIO Executive Council* (annual).

## WORK STOPPAGES, 1960–90

| Year | Number of work stoppages[1] | Workers involved[2] ('000s) | Days idle Number[3] ('000s) | Percent estimated working time[4] |
|------|-----|-----|-----|-----|
| 1960 | 222 | 896 | 13,260 | 0.09% |
| 1965 | 268 | 999 | 15,140 | 0.10 |
| 1970 | 381 | 2,468 | 52,761 | 0.29 |
| 1975 | 235 | 965 | 17,563 | 0.09 |
| 1980 | 187 | 795 | 20,844 | 0.09 |
| 1985 | 54 | 324 | 7,079 | 0.03 |
| 1988 | 40 | 118 | 4,364 | 0.02 |
| 1989 | 51 | 452 | 16,996 | 0.07 |
| 1990 | 44 | 185 | 5,926 | 0.03 |

**Note:** Excludes work stoppages involving fewer than 1,000 workers and lasting less than one day. 1. Beginning in the year indicated. 2. Workers are counted more than once if involved in more than one stoppage during the year. 3. Resulting from all stoppages in effect in a year, including those that began in an earlier year. 4. Agricultural and government employees are included in the total working time; private household, forestry, and fishery employees are excluded. **Source:** U.S. Bureau of Labor Statistics, *Current Wage Developments* (monthly), and *Monthly Labor Review* (January 1991).

unions, representing employees with a specific skill, such as pilots and musicians.

Many workers choose not to unionize because of the potential costs involved in membership, such as dues, lost pay during strikes, and possible retribution by employers. Union membership in the nation declined between 1983 and 1990 by one million members (17.7 million to 16.7 million). In 1990, 16.1% of the total labor force and 36.5% of government employees belonged to unions. This is down from a peak of around 25.4% of the total labor force in 1954. Notable examples of membership decline are among steelworkers, garment workers, and oil, chemical, and atomic workers, which each fell by about 50% during 1979–90. Virtually all of these losses are due to the loss of jobs in unionized firms. A number of factors may have contributed to this decline, such as changes in technology that displace workers, as in the music industry, and increased factor costs and international competition that make production less economically feasible, as in the steel industry.

**Working hours** Average weekly hours worked differ between industries, with the highest average in mining (44 hours) and the lowest average in the retail trade industries (28.8 hours). The Fair Labor Standards Act (FLSA) of 1938 specifies that nonsupervisory or "nonexempt" (i.e., not exempt from the FLSA) employees receive overtime pay at the rate of 1.5 times their hourly rate of pay for all hours over 40 worked. The overtime provisions of the FLSA were designed to make it costly for employers to use overtime, not only to prevent a burdensome lengthening of the work week but also to encourage them to hire additional workers as opposed to working their current employees longer hours.

Of the 1989 full-time work force, it is estimated that 24% spent 49 or more hours per week working, up from 18% in 1979. Consequently, Americans' leisure hours fell from

## 30 METROPOLITAN AREAS WITH HIGHEST JOB GROWTH, 1990-2010
(in thousands)

| Rank/Metropolitan statistical area | Number of jobs 1990 | Number of jobs 2010 | Change in employment 1990–2010 |
|------|-----|-----|-----|
| 1. Los Angeles-Long Beach, Calif. | 5,292 | 6,620 | 1,328 |
| 2. Washington, D.C.-Md.-Va. | 2,795 | 3,958 | 1,163 |
| 3. Anaheim-Santa Ana, Calif. | 1,563 | 2,664 | 1,102 |
| 4. Atlanta, Ga. | 1,857 | 2,765 | 907 |
| 5. Houston, Tex. | 1,914 | 2,776 | 862 |
| 6. Dallas, Tex. | 1,676 | 2,462 | 785 |
| 7. San Diego, Calif. | 1,417 | 2,117 | 700 |
| 8. Phoenix, Ariz. | 1,233 | 1,931 | 698 |
| 9. Boston-Lawrence-Salem-Lowell-Brockton, Mass. | 2,493 | 3,180 | 686 |
| 10. Chicago, Ill. | 3,683 | 4,301 | 618 |
| 11. Seattle, Wash. | 1,350 | 1,918 | 568 |
| 12. Tampa-St. Petersburg-Clearwater, Fla. | 1,111 | 1,675 | 564 |
| 13. Minneapolis-St. Paul, Minn.-Wis. | 1,634 | 2,196 | 562 |
| 14. Philadelphia, Pa.-N.J. | 2,676 | 3,198 | 522 |
| 15. Denver, Colo. | 1,076 | 1,580 | 503 |
| 16. Riverside-San Bernardino, Calif. | 993 | 1,456 | 462 |
| 17. Nassau-Suffolk, N.Y. | 1,427 | 1,889 | 462 |
| 18. San Jose, Calif. | 1,016 | 1,475 | 459 |
| 19. Orlando, Fla. | 692 | 1,139 | 447 |
| 20. Sacramento, Calif. | 829 | 1,240 | 411 |
| 21. Fort Lauderdale-Hollywood-Pompano Beach, Fla. | 656 | 1,057 | 401 |
| 22. San Francisco, Calif. | 1,264 | 1,660 | 396 |
| 23. Baltimore, Md. | 1,423 | 1,800 | 377 |
| 24. Oakland, Calif. | 1,154 | 1,528 | 374 |
| 25. West Palm Beach-Boca Raton-Delray Beach, Fla. | 488 | 851 | 364 |
| 26. Detroit, Mich. | 2,246 | 2,604 | 358 |
| 27. New York, N.Y. | 4,795 | 5,152 | 357 |
| 28. Miami-Hialeah, Fla. | 1,108 | 1,444 | 336 |
| 29. St. Louis, Mo.-Ill. | 1,454 | 1,762 | 308 |
| 30. Las Vegas, Nev. | 447 | 733 | 286 |
| Total 30 MSAs | – | – | 17,366 |
| **U.S. Total** | **–** | **–** | **38,877** |

**Source:** NPA Data Services, Inc., 1991.

26.2 per week in 1973 to 16.6 in 1987.

**Absenteeism** Of the full-time, nonagricultural workforce, in 1989, 5.1% were absent at any given time:
• 2.9% were on vacation;
• 1.2% were ill;
• 0.09% could not get to work due to bad weather;
• 0.05% were absent due to industrial disputes.

**Moonlighting** Over 6.2% of all employees worked more than one job in 1989, up from 4.7% in 1975. More men moonlight (6.4%); but the percentage of women holding two jobs has nearly tripled since 1970—from 2.2% to 5.9%—and is fast approaching the figure for men. Among the reasons cited for working long hours are to help pay regular living expenses, to build up savings, and to get a jump on the competition.

**Temporary workers** In 1987, approximately 900,000 people worked for firms that provide temporary help to employers, with the largest percentage (52%) providing administrative support, most notably general office clerks (11.4%) and typists and word processors (9.8%). Operators, fabricators, and laborers (that is, assemblers and construction laborers) made up 25.6% of the temporary work force. The highest paid temporary workers were engineers, who averaged $24.74 per hour, and the lowest were construction laborers, at $3.72 per hour.

**Benefits** Employee benefits are the non-wage aspects of compensation; in 1988, benefits accounted for approximately 29% of total employee compensation. Certain benefits are required legally, such as Social Security, benefits, workers' compensation, and state unemployment insurance; others are offered at the option of the employer. On average, employee compensation can be broken down as follows:
• Basic pay: pay for hours worked or units of output, 71%;
• Supplemental pay: reimbursement accounts, shift-differential pay, overtime premiums, and nonproduction (for example, Christmas) bonuses, 5%;
• Paid leave: holiday, vacation, personal, sick, jury duty, funeral, and military leave, 7%;
• Life, health, and disability insurance, 6%;
• Legally required benefits: Social Security, workers' compensation, and unemployment insurance, 9%.

In recent years flexible benefit plans (also called cafeteria plans) have been available to more workers—from 5% in 1986 to 13% in 1988. These plans allow workers to choose from a menu of benefits according to their individual needs. For example, a married couple might select a benefit plan that covers the cost of child care; later on, after the child is grown, they could elect to cover nursing home expenses for their parents under the same plan. Such schemes are attractive because the worker receives higher compensation, and the benefits are usually taxable at a lower rate than wages and salaries.

Another form of nonwage benefit is a reimbursement account to which employees—and in some cases employers—make contributions to cover expenses not covered by regular benefit packages, such as care for dependents, health care deductibles, and insurance premiums. Instead of giving an employee a cash raise, for instance, the employer would put a like amount in the reimbursement fund. (Because this is for the benefit of the individual employee only and not for a general fund, it is known as an employee contribution.) What makes this scheme attractive is that while the cost of the benefit chosen is covered by the fund, the employee doesn't pay taxes on the money compensation as he or she would on cash wages or salaries.

Benefits such as employer-subsidized child care and maternity and paternity leave are also on the rise. In 1988 unpaid maternity leave was available to 33% of employees in medium and large firms, unpaid paternity leave to 16%, with an average of four months. But paid leave was very rare.

# U.S. BUSINESS

The Office of Management and Budget (OMB) classifies the entire national economy into industries, based on principal product or activity. There are nine industrial divisions, which are further classified into groups and subgroups. For example, under "manufacturing" would fall "food and kindred products," and beneath that, "meat-packing plants." The nine industrial divisions listed in the OMB's Standard Industry Classification (SIC) are agriculture, forestry, and fishing; mining; construction; manufacturing; transportation and public utilities; finance, insurance, and real estate; wholesale trade; retail trade; and services. In 1988, 6.0 million establishments employed 87.9 million workers, with payrolls totaling $1.9 trillion.

## Services and Manufacturing

Another way to view the economy is to divide it into manufacturing industries, producing such tangible goods as cars, shoes, and furniture, and services industries, producing such intangible products as entertainment, tourism, and banking. The manufacturing industries are further broken down into those producing durable goods—that is, goods consumed over time, such as cars and houses—and nondurable goods consumed in the short run, such as food and soap. Services have played an increasingly important role in the economy, partly because manufacturing companies increasingly contract for services, such as transportation, accounting, marketing, and communications, previously performed in-house.

The service sector, which includes government, accounted for approximately 72% of U.S. GNP and 74% of employment in 1987. In the three years ended 1988 the service sector

## NUMBER OF BUSINESS ESTABLISHMENTS WITH EMPLOYEES AND PAYROLL, BY MAJOR GROUP, 1988

| Major group | Number of establishments | Number of employees | Annual payroll ('000s) |
|---|---|---|---|
| **Total** | **6,018,600** | **87,881,632** | **$1,859,529,932** |
| **Agricultural services, forestry, and fishing** | **73,764** | **461,768** | **$7,161,195** |
| Agricultural services | 70,291 | 432,453 | 6,589,097 |
| Forestry | 1,699 | 17,875 | 273,171 |
| Fishing, hunting, and trapping | 1,679 | 9,067 | 216,523 |
| Administrative and auxiliary | 95 | 2,373 | 82,404 |
| **Mining** | **30,755** | **734,953** | **$24,769,489** |
| Metal mining | 1,010 | 45,033 | 1,515,520 |
| Coal mining | 3,412 | 152,001 | 5,265,585 |
| Oil and gas extraction | 19,636 | 301,579 | 8,666,134 |
| Nonmetallic minerals | 5,362 | 103,333 | 2,864,359 |
| Administrative and auxiliary | 1,335 | 133,007 | 6,457,891 |
| **Construction** | **533,842** | **4,938,977** | **$121,573,914** |
| General contractors and operative builders | 157,503 | 1,279,815 | 31,051,785 |
| Heavy construction contractors | 31,583 | 704,748 | 21,035,247 |
| Special trade contractors | 344,343 | 2,932,592 | 68,634,165 |
| Administrative and auxiliary | 413 | 21,822 | 852,717 |
| **Manufacturing** | **362,905** | **19,261,691** | **$514,310,757** |
| Food and kindred products | 20,323 | 1,438,668 | 31,961,362 |
| Tobacco manufactures | 144 | 46,619 | 1,526,020 |
| Textile mill products | 6,325 | 682,674 | 11,985,237 |
| Apparel and other textile products | 22,143 | 1,070,973 | 14,552,008 |
| Lumber and wood products | 32,860 | 712,498 | 13,758,210 |
| Furniture and fixtures | 11,564 | 519,911 | 9,607,505 |
| Paper and allied products | 6,328 | 625,238 | 18,109,060 |
| Printing and publishing | 60,434 | 1,524,887 | 36,365,784 |
| Chemicals and allied products | 12,027 | 831,621 | 26,906,026 |
| Petroleum and coal products | 2,217 | 118,263 | 4,382,661 |
| Rubber and miscellaneous plastics products | 14,632 | 869,856 | 19,262,549 |
| Leather and leather products | 2,123 | 129,561 | 1,891,582 |
| Stone, clay, and glass products | 15,872 | 518,820 | 13,046,269 |
| Primary metal industries | 6,715 | 725,201 | 21,827,991 |
| Fabricated metal products | 35,743 | 1,491,640 | 38,168,438 |
| Machinery, except electrical | 51,101 | 1,924,409 | 56,601,634 |
| Electric and electronic equipment | 16,110 | 1,595,832 | 42,255,152 |
| Transportation equipment | 10,389 | 1,847,865 | 61,836,358 |
| Instruments and related products | 10,196 | 1,002,522 | 30,752,721 |
| Miscellaneous manufacturing industries | 16,393 | 386,761 | 7,708,735 |
| Administrative and auxiliary | 9,267 | 1,197,872 | 51,805,455 |
| **Transportation and other public utilities** | **220,564** | **5,270,318** | **$146,799,151** |
| Local and interurban passenger transit | 14,250 | 303,501 | 4,012,647 |
| Trucking and warehousing | 98,017 | 1,482,680 | 33,442,446 |
| Water transportation | 6,939 | 155,579 | 4,266,337 |
| Transportation by air | 8,944 | 622,522 | 18,931,610 |
| Pipe lines, except natural gas | 661 | 16,857 | $ 650,017 |
| Transportation services | 39,004 | 321,424 | 6,664,103 |
| Communication | 30,617 | 1,210,665 | 37,516,314 |
| Electric, gas, and sanitary sevices | 18,169 | 853,591 | 29,627,891 |
| Administrative and auxiliary | 3,963 | 303,499 | 11,687,786 |
| **Wholesale trade** | **462,173** | **5,981,378** | **$160,225,619** |
| Wholesale trade—durable goods | 289,967 | 3,390,497 | 93,305,831 |
| Wholesale trade—nondurable goods | 166,615 | 2,283,536 | 55,473,838 |
| Administrative and auxiliary | 5,591 | 307,345 | 11,445,950 |
| **Retail trade** | **1,472,878** | **18,801,521** | **$215,884,994** |
| Building materials and garden supplies | 71,422 | 679,445 | 10,832,509 |
| General merchandise stores | 35,054 | 2,066,306 | 20,101,279 |
| Food stores | 183,226 | 2,886,034 | 31,688,950 |
| Automotive dealers and service stations | 208,343 | 2,075,912 | 38,748,142 |
| Apparel and accessory stores | 148,310 | 1,156,594 | 10,953,557 |
| Furniture and home furnishings stores | 104,990 | 711,571 | 11,154,544 |
| Eating and drinking places | 378,450 | 6,097,450 | 43,161,453 |
| Miscellaneous retail | 326,645 | 2,317,288 | 28,457,215 |
| Administrative and auxiliary | 16,438 | 810,921 | 20,787,345 |
| **Finance, insurance, and real estate** | **518,150** | **6,659,618** | **$177,202,919** |
| Banking | 76,314 | 1,959,784 | 42,931,981 |
| Credit agencies other than banks | 43,576 | 542,186 | 13,783,418 |
| Security, commodity brokers, and services | 21,559 | 426,626 | 27,517,549 |
| Insurance carriers | 39,900 | 1,326,450 | 35,432,109 |
| Insurance agents, brokers, and services | 105,133 | 685,969 | 17,999,193 |
| Real estate | 207,965 | 1,286,615 | 25,398,464 |
| Holding and other investment offices | 21,491 | 239,589 | 8,572,824 |
| Administrative and auxiliary | 2,212 | 192,399 | 5,567,381 |
| **Services** | **1,937,547** | **25,142,715** | **$477,823,583** |
| Hotels and other lodging places | 48,951 | 1,384,565 | 15,836,786 |
| Personal services | 177,926 | 1,101,272 | 11,747,274 |
| Business services | 250,527 | 4,385,365 | 77,999,320 |
| Auto repair, services, and garages | 145,497 | 812,538 | 13,223,609 |
| Miscellaneous repair services | 61,615 | 356,096 | 7,315,792 |
| Motion pictures | 33,527 | 369,632 | 6,700,603 |
| Amusement and recreation services | 70,545 | 909,289 | 13,224,063 |
| Health services | 417,183 | 7,221,951 | 159,061,465 |
| Legal services | 135,709 | 848,507 | 30,270,241 |
| Educational services | 33,225 | 1,630,888 | 25,019,650 |
| Social services | 104,757 | 1,532,276 | 16,561,277 |
| Museums, botanical, zoological gardens | 2,992 | 56,503 | 880,883 |
| Membership organizations | 214,302 | 1,778,170 | 19,367,879 |
| Engineering and management services | 199,037 | 2,301,991 | 67,674,611 |
| Miscellaneous services | 34,181 | 122,267 | 2,937,631 |
| Administrative and auxiliary | 7,973 | 331,405 | 10,002,499 |
| **Unclassified establishments** | **406,021** | **638,693** | **$13,796,311** |

**Note:** Excludes government employees, railroad employees, and self-employed persons. **Source:** U.S. Bureau of the Census, *Country Business Patterns 1988* (1991).

added the equivalent of 6.64 million full-time employees, or 92% of all new jobs in that period.

In 1991, U.S. industries are expected to grow for a ninth straight year, but at a slower rate (1.13%) than 1990 (1.38%). Services will continue to grow at a faster rate than manufacturing, at rates comparable to those of 1990. Export growth accounted for 70% of GNP growth during the first three quarters of 1990, although exports constitute only 10% of GNP, and the trend is expected to continue.

## GROWTH RATES FOR SELECTED SERVICE INDUSTRIES, 1991

| Industry | Unit of measure | Rate of growth |
|---|---|---|
| Electronic information services | Revenues | 20.0% |
| Computer software | Revenues | 20.0 |
| Computer professional services | Revenues | 17.3 |
| Data processing | Revenues | 16.0 |
| Accounting | Receipts | 12.7 |
| Health services | Revenues | 12.0 |
| Cable television | Revenues | 12.0 |
| Management, consulting, and public relations | Receipts | 10.3 |
| Leasing | Equipment cost added | 8.1 |
| Life insurance | Premiums | 8.0 |
| Property-casualty insurance | Net premiums written | 6.2 |
| Total retail trade | Sales | 6.0 |
| Food retailing | Sales | 7.7 |
| Eating and drinking places | Sales | 6.2 |
| Department stores | Sales | 6.2 |
| Apparel and accessories stores | Sales | 6.1 |
| Advertising | Receipts | 5.6 |
| Banking | Assets | 5.5 |
| Prerecorded music | Manufacturers' dollar value | 5.0 |
| Legal services | Receipts | 4.8 |
| Home entertainment | Revenues | 4.0 |
| Motion picture theaters | Receipts | 1.6 |
| Space commerce | Revenues | 0.0 |

**Source**: U.S. Dept. of Commerce, *U.S. Industrial Outlook, 1991* (1991)

## 10 FASTEST GROWING INDUSTRIES, 1987–91

| Industry | Annual compound rate of change |
|---|---|
| X-ray apparatus and tubes | 10.9% |
| Electromedical equipment | 10.7 |
| Medicinals and botanicals | 9.8 |
| Semiconductors and related devices[1] | 8.9 |
| Machine tools | 8.1 |
| Farm machinery and equipment | 8.0 |
| Oil and gas field machinery | 7.8 |
| Computers and peripherals[1] | 7.7 |
| Surgical appliances and supplies | 7.7 |
| Surgical and medical instruments | 7.3 |

**Note**: Based on constant dollar shipments, except as noted. 1. Current dollars. **Source**: U.S. Dept. of Commerce, *U.S. Industrial Outlook 1991* (1991).

Strong industries include information economy related services (computer equipment, radio and television communications equipment, electronic information services, and data processing); health care services (health and medical services, medical equipment, and drugs); export industries (aircraft and parts, computers, motor vehicles, electronic components, medicinals, plastic products, and petrochemicals); and travel services. The travel industry has shown steady growth during the late 1980s and early 1990s. Payments by outbound U.S. travelers grew by 50% from 1985 to 1990, while receipts from foreign visitor spending rose 129%. Growth in machine tools, which traditionally reflects the growth rate of the overall economy, is growing at a stronger than expected rate (8.1% for the period 1987–91) due to heavy investment in increased productivity by businesses.

Slowest growing industries are industries related to construction/residential housing (steel, construction materials, wood products, and household consumer durables) and to motor vehicles (steel, glass, and a variety of other basic materials), cigars, and chewing tobacco.

## FINANCING BUSINESS

When an individual or a group of individuals decides to start a new company, they need money to rent or buy office space and equipment and to pay workers. Since there is a time lag between the day a business opens and the day a business sells its first good or service, funds must be borrowed from a bank or other finan-

## GROWTH RATE ESTIMATES AND PROJECTIONS FOR SELECTED MANUFACTURING INDUSTRY GROUPS, 1989–91

| Industry group | 1989 | 1990 | 1991 |
|---|---|---|---|
| New construction | -1.5% | -1.6% | -2.8% |
| Construction materials | 1.5 | -0.8 | -3.2 |
| Food and beverages | 1.4 | 1.3 | 1.3 |
| Wood products | -0.3 | -1.6 | -3.5 |
| Paper and allied products | 1.3 | 1.6 | 2.2 |
| Printing and publishing | 2.1 | 1.0 | 2.1 |
| Chemicals and allied products | 2.0 | 1.6 | 1.0 |
| Rubber and plastic products | 1.1 | 1.0 | 0.8 |
| Steel mill products | 0.3 | -1.0 | -4.8 |
| Machine tools | 18.6 | 5.3 | 5.0 |
| Computers and peripherals[1] | 6.1 | 4.4 | 5.6 |
| Industrial machinery | 4.7 | 2.5 | 1.9 |
| Telephone and communication equipment | 2.6 | 1.9 | 1.9 |
| Electronic components and accessories | 6.7 | 1.8 | 6.2 |
| Electrical equipment | 0.7 | -1.1 | -2.3 |
| Motor vehicles and parts | 0.0 | -2.6 | -1.4 |
| Aircraft and parts | -14.0 | 17.9 | 4.6 |
| Scientific and medical equipment | 7.0 | 2.1 | 2.9 |
| Household consumer durables | 1.3 | -2.0 | -2.0 |

**Note**: Based on constant dollar shipments except as noted. 1. Current dollars. **Source**: U.S. Dept. of Commerce, *U.S. Industrial Outlook 1991* (1991).

cial institution or from individual investors to meet costs before revenues are generated. Additional funds may be needed throughout the life of the business to finance research and development of a new product or service or for the construction of new factories. Financing can take many forms, from short-term bank loans, commercial paper, or trade credit to long-term stocks and bonds.

Trade credit, the largest category of short-term financing, is an arrangement between a company and its suppliers whereby materials and supplies are delivered to the company with a promise to pay the invoice, plus interest, usually within a specified number of weeks. Commercial bank lending may take the form of a single loan with repayment in a lump sum or in installments over the life of the loan, or it may be a line of credit up to a maximum the bank will allow the company to overdraw on its account. Commercial paper is a promissory note of a well-established firm sold primarily to other business firms, with repayments made in two to six months. The only problem with commercial paper is that its resources are limited to the liquidity that corporations have at any given time for lending to other firms.

Intermediate-term financing (with a timeframe of 1 to 15 years) may take the form of lease financing, whereby a company rents, rather than buys, the assets it uses; conditional sales contracts, by which equipment is bought over a period of time (the seller continues to have title of ownership until payment is completed); or term loans or business credit supplied by commercial banks and life insurance companies, repaid by amortization payments over the life of the loan (1 to 15 years).

The issuance of stocks and bonds constitute the long-term source of finance for firms. Bonds are debt instruments (IOUs issued by a company to the bondholder) that obligate the firm to pay interest at specific times. Alternatively, firms can raise money by issuing preferred and common stocks. Unlike bonds, stocks entitle the holder to share in ownership and profits made by the firm through dividends paid out for the entire period the investor owns the stock. However, if the business has low profits or limited funds, bondholders are paid first, preferred stockholders next, and common stockholders last.

### Wall Street

The U.S. stock market, commonly known as Wall Street, began in the late 18th century as a merchant-organized public auction in stocks and government bonds for the purpose of financing the government and expanding business and trade. At that time brokers handed over securities to auctioneers who sold securities to the highest bidder. Today, while the form of the stock exchange has changed dramatically, the purpose remains the same.

The most commonly cited index of Wall Street's performance is the Dow Jones average (see "Glossary of Financial Terms"). The Dow rose dramatically in the 1980s, passing the 2,000 mark in January 1987 and reaching over 2,700 by August, only to drop by over 500 points on "Black Monday," Oct. 19, 1987, losing over 22% of its value in one day (nearly 10 percentage points more than the day of the Great Crash of 1929) and closing around 1,700. Black Monday was precipitated by investors' fear of a falling dollar and increased interest rates in order to attract external funds to finance the enormous U.S. trade deficit ($15.7 billion for the month of August 1987 alone). For corporations and consumers, this translates into increased borrowing costs, lower investment and spending, recession, and a decrease in corporate earnings, culminating in the heavy sales of equities on Oct. 19, 1987. Since then the Dow Jones Industrial Average has surpassed 1987 levels, and on Aug. 28, 1991, closed at 3,055.23, an all-time high as of Sept. 15, 1991.

### New York Stock Exchange (NYSE)

In 1990, 39.7 billion shares with a value of $1.3 trillion were traded on the New York Stock Exchange (NYSE), which was formally founded in 1817, when less than 100 shares were traded each day.

### The American Stock Exchange (Amex)

The American Stock Exchange, located a few blocks from the New York Stock Exchange in New York's financial district, is known as the stock market for the small investor and small companies. The stock issues of organizations that do not meet the listing and size requirements of the NYSE typically are traded there. For years the Amex was known as the "New York Curb Exchange" because its trading was conducted on the street outside the office buildings of many brokers. The exchange moved indoors in 1921.

Trading volume continued to increase on the Amex in 1990. Average daily trading volume was 13.2 million shares, up from 12.4 million in 1989 and 9.9 million in 1988. There were 859 companies listed on the Amex at the end of 1990, about the same as the year before. New issues rose by 46%, as more companies went public and transfer activity increased. In 1990, 3.3 billion shares changed hands on the Amex, the second highest level ever behind 1987; the number of shares outstanding reached a new record of 9.8 billion, rising for the tenth consecutive year, with an aggregate market value of $102.3 billion and an average price per share of $10.47, the lowest since 1980; and Amex's dollar volume of trading was $37.7 billion.

### NASDAQ

The most heavily traded over-the-counter stocks are exchanged through the NASDAQ National Market system, the second-largest stock market in the United States and the fifth largest in the world in terms of the dollar value of shares. Founded in 1971, NASDAQ—the National Association of Securities Dealers Automated Quotations—uses computers and high-technology telecommunications systems to trade—and to monitor the trading of—millions of securities daily.

More than 33.3 billion shares were traded through NASDAQ in 1990, down slightly from 33.5 billion shares in 1989. The dollar value of this trading was $452.4 billion, the fifth largest worldwide, behind the NYSE ($1.33 trillion), Tokyo ($1.31 trillion), London ($544.3 billion), and Germany ($539.4 billion).

The average number of shares traded daily on NASDAQ in 1990 was 131.9 million, nearly a five-fold increase over the 1980 average of 26.5 million. In 1980, when 19.7 billion shares were traded on the NASDAQ, NYSE, and Amex market combined, NASDAQ accounted for 34.4% of the total. Ten years later, with 76.4 billion shares traded on those same markets, NASDAQ's share of the total had risen to 43.7%. In 1990, 4,132 companies were listed with NASDAQ with a total share volume of 33.4 billion, an 81% increase in the number of companies traded on NASDAQ and a 78% jump in the number of issues offered over 1981. The total share volume of the 1,769 companies listed on the NYSE in 1990 was 39.7 billion; that of the 859 companies traded through Amex was 3.3 billion.

## NYSE LISTED STOCKS, 1924–90
(figures in millions)

| Year-end | Number of shares | Market value | Average price[1] |
|---|---|---|---|
| 1924 | 433 | $ 27,072 | $62.45 |
| 1945 | 1,592 | 73,765 | 46.33 |
| 1950 | 2,353 | 93,807 | 39.86 |
| 1960 | 6,458 | 306,967 | 47.53 |
| 1970 | 16,065 | 636,380 | 39.61 |
| 1975 | 22,478 | 85,110 | 30.48 |
| 1980 | 33,709 | 1,242,803 | 36.87 |
| 1985 | 52,427 | 1,950,332 | 37.20 |
| 1990 | 90,732 | 2,819,778 | 31.08 |

1. This average cannot be used as an index of price trend owing to changes in shares listed caused by new listings, suspensions, stock splits, and stock dividends. **Source:** New York Stock Exchange, *Fact Book 1991* (1991).

## NYSE MEMBERSHIP PRICES, 1875–1990

| Year | High | Low | Year | High | Low |
|---|---|---|---|---|---|
| 1875 | $ 6,800 | $ 4,300 | 1955 | $ 90,000 | $ 80,000 |
| 1895 | 20,000 | 17,000 | 1965 | 250,000 | 190,000 |
| 1905 | 85,000 | 72,000 | 1970 | 320,000 | 130,000 |
| 1915 | 74,000 | 38,000 | 1975 | 138,000 | 55,000 |
| 1925 | 150,000 | 99,000 | 1980 | 275,000 | 175,000 |
| 1935 | 140,000 | 65,000 | 1985 | 480,000 | 310,000 |
| 1945 | 95,000 | 49,000 | 1990 | 430,000 | 250,000 |

**Source:** New York Stock Exchange, *Fact Book 1991* (1991).

## NYSE: SHARES TRADED, 1900–90
(in thousands)

| Year | Daily Average | Record High | Record Low |
|---|---|---|---|
| 1900 | 505 | 1,627 | 89 |
| 1910 | 601 | 1,656 | 111 |
| 1920 | 828 | 2,008 | 227 |
| 1930 | 2,959 | 8,279 | 1,090 |
| 1940 | 751 | 3,940 | 130 |
| 1950 | 1,980 | 4,859 | 1,061 |
| 1955 | 2,578 | 7,717 | 1,230 |
| 1960 | 3,042 | 5,303 | 1,894 |
| 1965 | 6,176 | 11,434 | 3,028 |
| 1970 | 11,564 | 21,345 | 6,660 |
| 1975 | 18,551 | 35,158 | 8,670 |
| 1980 | 44,871 | 84,297 | 16,132 |
| 1985 | 109,169 | 181,027 | 62,055 |
| 1990 | 156,777 | 292,364 | 56,853 |

**Source:** New York Stock Exchange, *Fact Book 1991* (1991).

## GLOSSARY OF FINANCIAL TERMS

**Arbitrage** Simultaneous purchase and sale of a commodity or currency in at least two markets where price discrepancies exist. The arbitrageur makes a profit by buying an asset with a low price in one market and selling it in another market where the asset carries a higher price.

**Bear/bull** A bear is a speculator who expects prices to fall and sells stocks or *bonds* in order to buy them later at a lower price. A bull expects prices to rise and therefore buys now for resale later. Thus, a bearish (bullish) market is one in which prices are generally falling (rising).

**Blue chip stock** A stock that is considered a safe investment, with a low *yield* and a high price per share, issued by companies that are well known and have a history of good management and increasing profit levels.

**Bond** A debt obligation requiring the issuer to pay a fixed sum of money annually until maturity (interest payments) and then, at maturity, a fixed sum of money to repay the initial amount borrowed (principal). (See "Corporate bond").

**Capital gain** An increase in the market value of an asset above the price originally paid for it, realized when the asset is sold.

**Capital loss** A decrease in the market value of an asset below the price originally paid for it, realized when the asset is sold.

**Common stock/equity** A piece of paper that entitles the owner to a share of the *firm's* profits and a share of the voting power in shareholder elections. In other words, a shareholder is part owner of the firm. If he owns 50% of the issued shares of common stock (when no *preferred stock* is issued), he owns 50% of the company, and will receive 50% of profits paid out in *dividends*. Over 40 million Americans invest in common stocks.

**Convertible bond** A debt instrument that carries an option for the holder to convert it into a specified amount of company stock.

**Corporate bond** A debt obligation requiring the corporation to pay a fixed sum of money annually until maturity (interest payments) and then, at maturity, a fixed sum of money to repay the initial amount borrowed (principal). *Bonds* carry no claim to ownership and therefore pay no *dividends*, but payments to bondholders take priority over payments to stockholders.

**Debenture** A debt *security* that pays a fixed interest rate, issued by a company in order to raise finance for commercial or industrial operations.

**Divestiture** The sale by a company of a product line, subsidiary, or division. (See section "Mergers and Acquisitions.")

**Dividend** A payment made to *common* and *preferred stock* holders out of a *firm's* profits either in the form of cash or additional shares.

**Dow Jones Industrial Average** Dating back to

1893, this index of 30 *blue chip stocks* in industry traded on the New York Stock Exchange (and determined by the editors of the *Wall Street Journal*) is the most widely cited indicator of how the stock market is doing.

**Establishment** A physical place of business activity such as a factory, assembly plant, retail store, or warehouse, where goods are made, stored, or processed or where services are performed.

**Eurocurrency** A currency deposited outside its country of origin for use as a medium of international credit. The Eurocurrency market developed in the late 1950s and constitutes a vast international pool of highly mobile money. Eurocurrencies are used to facilitate international trade and the payment of deficits and for currency speculation.

**Firm** A business organization that owns and/or operates one or more *establishments*. Also called a company, enterprise, or business venture. Firms can be of three types: (1) sole proprietorships—firms owned directly by one person; (2) partnerships—firms whose ownership is shared by a fixed number of proprietors; and (3) corporations—firms created by a government charter, which grants them greater accessibility to financial capital through the selling of *common* or *preferred stock*, greater accessibility to debt capital through the selling of *bonds*, and limited liability in the event of bankruptcy.

**Futures market/forward market** A market in which commodities or *securities* are bought and sold at prices fixed now, for delivery at specified future date. Futures are traded on the American Stock Exchange; the Chicago Board of Trade; Chicago Board Options Exchange; Chicago Mercantile Exchange; Chicago Rice and Cotton Exchange; Commodity Exchange, New York (COMEX); Kansas City Board of Trade; MidAmerica Commodity Exchange, Chicago; Minneapolis Grain Exchange; New York Coffee, Sugar, and Coca Exchange (including the Citrus Associates); New York Cotton Exchange; New York Futures Exchange; New York Mercantile Exchange; New York Stock Exchange; Pacific Stock Exchange, Los Angeles and San Francisco; and Philadelphia Stock Exchange.

**Greenmail** Analogous to blackmail, the practice of purchasing enough shares in a *firm* or trading company to threaten a takeover, thereby forcing the owners to buy them back at a higher rate in order to retain control of the business.

**Insider trading** Trading in the stock market based on information that has not been made public and that is intended to remain confidential—for example, information that a small company is about to become part of a national corporation. The penalties paid by individuals and corporations for such activities in recent years have reached into the hundreds of millions of dollars.

**Junk bond/high yield bond** *Bonds* with a *rating* below investment grade—that is, at or below Ba1 (Moody's Investors Service), at or below BB+ (Standard & Poor's), or unrated. Issuers of junk bonds are usually small companies who in the past have been limited to borrowing from banks to raise capital for corporate growth.

Despite the fact that the major ratings services consider junk bonds risky (hence their name), they have a historically low default rate—only 1.5% between the mid-1970s and mid-1980s. The junk market grew considerably in the 1980s, and by 1987 accounted for over 25% of the value of all *corporate bonds* outstanding.

**Leveraged buyout** The purchase of a company by one of its employee groups (usually upper management) or a large shareholder with borrowed funds, usually using the company's assets as security for the loans. Leveraged buyouts have been used to combat hostile takeover bids.

**Mutual fund** A pool of financial assets in which investors may buy shares and derive the benefits or share the losses, depending on the performance of the collective *securities*. Shares are sold publicly and can be redeemed at any time. Funds can consist of stocks, *bonds*, gold, government securities, or other assets, and their names are descriptive of their primary purpose; for example, bonds funds, equity-fund portfolios, income funds, money market–mutual funds, and municipal funds. (See "Money Market Accounts" under "Money and Banking" in the section "The Economy.")

**Option** A contract to buy or sell commodities or *securities* within a given time period at a fixed price. For stocks, this period is usually three months. A contract to sell is a *put option* (or put); to buy, a *call option* (or call); and one to buy or sell is a *double option*. A buyer (seller) will gain if the trading price rises (falls) by more than the cost of entering into the contract. Options are traded on the same exchanges as *futures* contracts.

**Over-the-counter (OTC) stock** A *security* not listed on a *stock exchange* that is traded between two individuals. The name stems from the 18th century practice of merchants selling stocks directly to investors over the counter in their own shops, without the use of *stockbrokers* or auctioneers.

**Pension fund** A scheme whereby private- or public-sector employers, unions, and—as in the case of individual retirement accounts (IRAs) and Keogh plans—individuals contribute to a fund from which money is paid out to the employees, union members, or contributors (or their dependents) upon death, disability, or retirement. Contributions can be based on a percentage of salary or corporate profits; in some cases employees may make voluntary or mandatory contributions to the fund. Pension fund assets are usually held in the form of *securities* or property with a preference for long-term assets.

**Preferred stock** Similar to *common stock*, except that owners of preferred stock have no voting rights and are paid their *dividends* at a fixed rate, before common-stock holders receive any dividends.

**Rating** An agency evaluation of the quality of a debt instrument or a company issuing debt. Standard & Poor's and Moody's Investment Service are the two major credit ratings agencies in the United States. The ratings measure the safety of interest and principal payments of bonds. S&P bond ratings are, from most to least secure, AAA, AA, A, BBB, BB, B, CCC,

CC, C. Moody's ratings are Aaa, Aa, A, Baa, Ba, B, Caa, Ca, C.

**Securities** Financial assets (usually long-term), such as equities or stocks and *debentures* or *bonds;* may also refer to shorter-term assets such as U.S. Treasury bills.

**Securities and Exchange Commission (SEC)** U.S. government agency that regulates the *securities* industry by requiring registration of *stockbrokers*, dealers, and *stock exchanges*. The SEC also reviews the financial position of companies issuing securities for public sale and investigates illegal activities such as *insider trading*.

**Standard & Poor's 500 Composite Stock Price Index (S&P 500)** A widely used measure of the movement of the U.S. stock market. The S&P 500 was introduced in 1957 and is one of 12 leading economic indicators used by the U.S. Commerce Department. The 500 issues include 400 industrial, 40 utility, 20 transportation, and 40 financial companies—primarily those listed on the New York Stock Exchange (NYSE). The index is considered to be value-weighted because each stock is weighted according to its market value; calculated on a total return basis with *dividends* reinvested.

**Stock exchange** A market in which *securities* (other than bills and similar short-term instruments) issued by central and local government bodies and public companies are traded (e.g., the New York Stock Exchange, the American Stock Exchange, the London Stock Exchange). Only members of a stock exchange may deal on it, and membership and arrangements for trading are strictly regulated. Stock exchanges in the United States are the American Stock Exchange (New York); Boston Stock Exchange; Cincinnati Stock Exchange; Intermountain Stock Exchange (Salt Lake City); Midwest Stock Exchange (Chicago); New York Stock Exchange; Pacific Stock Exchange (Los Angeles, San Francisco); Philadelphia Stock Exchange; and Spokane Stock Exchange.

**Stock market** An institution in which stocks and shares are traded, existing in all advanced Western countries. Stock markets enable companies to raise equity or loan capital more easily from the public, since investors can quickly realize their holdings because of the stock exchange share quotation. The principal overseas stock markets are located in Amsterdam, Brussels, Frankfurt, Hong Kong, Johannesburg, London, Milan, Paris, Singapore, Stockholm, Sydney, Tokyo, Toronto, and Zurich.

**Stockbroker** An individual who acts as an adviser and an agent (working on commission) to buy and sell stocks on behalf of a client on a particular *stock exchange* of which the stockbroker is a member.

**Wilshire 5000 Index** The broadest measure of the U. S. stock market, containing some 5,000 issues, including all publicly traded U.S. stocks for which daily pricing is available (i.e., includes all Amex, NYSE, and *OTC stocks*).

**Yield** The annual return on a *security*, as a percentage of its current market price. A stock's *dividend* yield is the annual dividend divided by its current stock price.

## SMALL BUSINESS

Small businesses account for 99% of the 19 million nonfarm businesses in the United States today. Sole proprietorships make up 13.2 million of these small businesses, while 1.8 million are partnerships and 4 million corporations. Small businesses employ 55% of the private work force, make 44% of all sales in America, and produce 38% of the nation's gross national product. Since 1978 the number of small businesses has increased 56%.

Most Americans—nearly 67%—get their first employment experience through small firms. Small businesses lead the way in the creation of new jobs in the American economy. Between 1981 and 1986, small businesses with fewer than 500 employees created 62% of the 8.9 million new jobs in the country. Between September 1987 and September 1988 alone, 2.3 million new jobs were generated in small-business dominated industries. During the first six months of 1987, the most recent period for which statistics are available, small business income was $320.1 billion—up 12.9% from the same period of 1986.

Small businesses are twice as likely as large firms to produce innovations relative to the number of persons they employ, and they have created more than half of the new products and service innovations developed since World War II. Among the fastest-growing small businesses today are eating and drinking establishments, trucking firms, doctors' offices, computer and data services, and amusements and recreation services.

The standards used by the U.S. Small Business Administration to determine whether a business is small vary from industry to industry and are relative within an industry. In manufacturing, a firm with 500 to 1,500 employees is classified a small business. In construction, this classification applies to companies with gross annual receipts between $7 million and $14.7 million. A company in the services and retail industry with gross annual receipts between $2.5 million and $14 million is considered a small business. A wholesaler with as many as 100 employees also will be classified as a small business. Thus a steel mill with 1,200 employees is considered to be a small business right along with a mom-and-pop candy store.

**Franchising**, a century-old tradition, has never been more popular in the United States than it is now. Franchises did more than $600 million in business in 1989, accounting for one-third of all consumer purchases; projections for the future are even greater.

Today franchised business represents nearly 40% of all U.S. retail sales. The Department of Commerce estimates that by the year 2000, franchising will account for more than half of all sales. Franchising has grown by more than 72% since 1984, and more than 7.0 million people are employed in over a half-million American franchise outlets across the country and around the world.

The appeal of franchising is universal. The franchiser can expand a business without borrowing huge amounts of capital. He also receives an up-front fee from the franchisee and a steady flow of income from each franchised unit, usually 2–5% of the franchise's gross income. The franchisees get to own their own businesses with a national reputation already built in. Typically they also receive training, financial assistance, help in choosing sites, and other business expertise from the parent company. Franchisees also pay a portion of their income to nationwide advertising.

## TOP 50 FRANCHISES, BY NUMBER OF FRANCHISES, 1990

| Rank/Franchise | Business | Franchise fees | Number of franchises |
| --- | --- | --- | --- |
| 1. McDonald's | Fast food restaurants | $22,500 | 7,919 |
| 2. Century 21 Real Estate | Real estate brokers | 11,000–25,000 | 7,009 |
| 3. Kentucky Fried Chicken | Fast food restaurants | 20,000 | 5,828 |
| 4. Dairy Queen | Ice cream stores | 30,000 | 5,214 |
| 5. Burger King, Inc. | Fast food restaurants | 40,000 | 5,101 |
| 6. H & R Block | Tax preparation | 600–1,200 | 4,837 |
| 7. Subway Sandwiches & Salads | Fast food restaurants | 10,000 | 4,760 |
| 8. Jazzercise | Dance fitness centers | 500 | 4,407 |
| 9. Servicemaster | Commercial cleaning services | 8,000–19,000 | 4,069 |
| 10. Domino's Pizza | Pizza delivery and takeout | 1,320–3,250 | 3,699 |
| 11. Electronic Realty Associates | Real estate brokers | 18,900 | 3,247 |
| 12. Baskin-Robbins Ice Cream | Ice cream stores | 0 | 3,157 |
| 13. Budget Rent A Car | Car rental | 15,000 | 3,049 |
| 14. 7-Eleven Store | Convenience stores | varies | 3,010 |
| 15. Chem-Dry | Carpet and upholstery cleaning | 7,700–19,000 | 2,506 |
| 16. Wendy's | Fast food restaurants | 25,000 | 2,451 |
| 17. Hardee's Food Systems | Fast food restaurants | 15,000 | 2,359 |
| 18. Merle Norman Cosmetics | Cosmetics studios | 0 | 2,343 |
| 19. Radio Shack | Electronics retailers | 15,000–40,000 | 2,246 |
| 20. Little Caesars Pizza | Pizza takeout | 20,000 | 2,202 |
| 21. Arby's | Fast food restaurants | 25,000–37,500 | 2,121 |
| 22. Midas Muffler & Brake Shops | Auto maintenance centers | 10,000 | 2,115 |
| 23. Jani-King International | Janitorial services | 14,500 | 2,071 |
| 24. Diet Center | Weight loss centers | 30,000 | 1,800 |
| 25. Dunkin' Donuts | Donut shops | 30,000–40,000 | 1,733 |
| 26. Re/Max Intl. Inc. | Real estate brokers | 10,000–20,000 | 1,711 |
| 27. Realty World | Real estate brokers | 14,000–16,000 | 1,702 |
| 28. TCBY Yogurt | Frozen yogurt stores | 20,000 | 1,651 |
| 29. Dollar Rent A Car | Car rental | N.A. | 1,600 + |
| 30. Rainbow International | Carpet dyeing and cleaning | $15,000 | 1,573 |
| 31. Success Motivation Institute Inc. | Human resources development/ managerial training | 20,000 | 1,448 |
| 32. Holiday Inns | Hotel/motel | varies | 1,396 |
| 33. Packy the Shipper | Packaging/shipping centers | 395 | 1,390 |
| 34. Nutri-System | Weight loss centers | 13,000 | 1,343 |
| 35. Fantastic Sam's | Discount hair cutters | 25,000 | 1,325 |
| 36. Choice Hotels Intl. | Hotels/motels/resorts | 35,000 | 1,311 |
| 37. Coverall North America Inc. | Commercial office cleaning | 3,250–33,360 | 1,260 |
| 38. American Intl. Rent-a-Car | Car rental and leasing | 25,000 + | 1,239 |
| 39. Mail Boxes Etc. | Postal services | 19,500 | 1,187 |
| 40. PIP Printing | Business printing | 40,000 | 1,126 |
| 41. Decorating Den | Home decorating services | 7,000–19,000 | 1,100 |
| 42. Taco Bell | Mexican fast food restaurants | 35,000 | 1,035 |
| 43. Days Inn of America | Hotels/motels | varies | 1,025 |
| 44. Ben Franklin Stores, Inc. | Variety/craft stores | 24,000 | 1,018 |
| 45. Minuteman Press International | Printing centers | 32,500 | 1,000 + |
| 46. Kwik-Kopy Printing Centers | Printing services | 22,000 | 1,000 + |
| 47. Leadership Management Inc. | Human resource development/ managerial training | 30,000 | 982 |
| 48. Jiffy Lube | Auto maintenance | 35,000 | 947 |
| 49. Sonic Drive In Restaurants | Fast food drive-in restaurants | 15,000 | 944 |
| 50. Coast to Coast Total Hardware | Hardware retailers | 5,000 | 933 |

**Source:** *Entrepreneur* (Jan. 1991).

## BIG BUSINESS: THE *FORTUNE* 500

The goal of almost all new companies is to make it onto *Fortune* magazine's annual list of the 500 largest corporations in America. Industrial companies are ranked overall and by industry according to their volume of sales. For example, although Philip Morris is best known for its tobacco products, it is included in the food industry where its sales volume is largest. Industry groups are based on categories established by the U.S. Office of Management and Budget and issued by the Federal Statistical Policy and Standards Office.

After a record-breaking year in 1988 with profits up 55% over 1987, overall profits among the *Fortune* 500 fell 8.2% in 1989 and another 11.7% in 1990 in the face of recessionary pressures. Sales of *Fortune* 500 industrials rose 6.4%, to $2.3 trillion, a new record. Sales of the 500 ranged from $126 billion to $546 million, with a median of $1.6 billion.

Topping the *Fortune* 500 list once again was General Motors, with sales of $126 billion. But the motor vehicle industry was the poorest performer by nearly every measure, with profits down by up to 81%. Pharmaceuticals outperformed other industries for the fifth consecutive year, with a median return on investment

*"One aspect of modern life which has gone far to stifle men is the rapid growth of tremendous corporations. . . . The disappearance of free enterprise has led to a submergence of the individual in the impersonal corporation in much the same manner as he has been submerged in the state in other lands."*

—William O. Douglas (1939)

(ROE) of 26.4% due largely to price increases and strong international sales.

The *Fortune* Service 500 consists of eight different lists: the 100 largest diversified service companies; the 100 largest banks; the 50 largest savings institutions; the 50 largest diversified financial companies; the 50 largest retailers; the 50 largest life insurers; the 50 largest utilities; and the 50 largest transportation companies. They are ranked according to

sales or assets depending on the industry.

Profits for companies on the *Fortune* Service 500 for 1990 were $61 billion, down 12% from 1989 and 23% from 1988. The economy-wide recession and low productivity growth rates (negative 1% since 1982) contributed to the decrease in profits. Of the eight categories on the list, only commercial banking companies and retailing companies showed positive profits, 60% and 36% respectively. The diversified service companies, including a wide range of services from movies and broadcasting to waste processing, reported a decline in profits of over 25%. Diversified financial companies, including casualty and property insurers and consumer finance companies, also did poorly in 1990, with profits down 27.7%.

The woes of the S&L crisis continued in 1990. Overall, the 50 largest savings institutions lost $1.8 billion, up from a loss of $3.1 billion in 1989, and all 50 showed a negative return to shareholders. Many were taken over by the Resolution Trust Corporation, the successor to the FSLIC.

The worst performance came from the transportation sector, led by the airline industry with profits down by 88%. The Persian Gulf War made air travel less popular, and while fare wars tried to counter that trend, they lowered revenues and profits.

---

## LEADING *FORTUNE* SERVICE 500 COMPANIES, BY INDUSTRY, 1990 (in millions)

### DIVERSIFIED SERVICE COMPANIES, BY SALES

| Company (1989 rank) | Sales | Profits |
|---|---|---|
| 1. American Telephone & Telegraph (1) | $37,479.0 | $2,735.0 |
| 2. Enron (4) | 13,201.8 | 202.2 |
| 3. Fleming Cos. (2) | 11,932.8 | 97.3 |
| 4. Time Warner (—) | 11,517.0 | (227.0) |
| 5. Super ValuStores (3) | 11,160.2 | 147.7 |
| 6. United Telecommunications (6) | 8,345.1 | 308.7 |
| 7. American Financial (8) | 7,890.1 | 22.3 |
| 8. McKesson (7) | 7,790.9 | 98.7 |
| 9. MCI Communications (11) | 7,701.0 | 299.0 |
| 10. Marriott (5) | 7,693.0 | 47.0 |

### RETAILING COMPANIES, BY SALES

| Company (1989 rank) | Sales | Profits |
|---|---|---|
| 1. Sears Roebuck (1) | $55,971.7 | $ 902.2 |
| 2. Wal-Mart Stores (3) | 32,601.6 | 1,291.0 |
| 3. K Mart (2) | 32,080.0 | 756.0 |
| 4. American Stores (5) | 22,155.5 | 182.4 |
| 5. Kroger (4) | 20,261.0 | 82.4 |
| 6. J.C. Penney (6) | 17,410.0 | 577.0 |
| 7. Safeway Stores (7) | 14,873.6 | 87.1 |
| 8. Dayton Hudson (8) | 14,739.0 | 412.0 |
| 9. Great Atlantic & Pacific Tea (10) | 11,164.2 | 146.7 |
| 10. May Department Stores (9) | 11,027.0 | 500.0 |

### UTILITIES, BY ASSETS

| Company (1989 rank) | Assets | Operating revenues |
|---|---|---|
| 1. GTE (1) | $33,769.0 | $18,374.0 |
| 2. BellSouth (2) | 30,206.8 | 14,436.0 |
| 3. Bell Atlantic (3) | 27,998.5 | 12,298.0 |
| 4. US West (5) | 27,050.2 | 9,957.3 |
| 5. Nynex (4) | 26,650.7 | 13,585.3 |
| 6. Southwestern Bell (8) | 22,195.5 | 9,112.9 |
| 7. Pacific Gas & Electric (6) | 21,958.4 | 9,597.5 |
| 8. American Information Tech. (10) | 21,715.1 | 10,662.5 |
| 9. Pacific Telesis Group (7) | 21,581.0 | 9,716.0 |
| 10. Southern (9) | 19,955.0 | 8,003.0 |

### LIFE INSURANCE COMPANIES, BY ASSETS

| Company (1989 rank) | Assets | Premium/ annuity income |
|---|---|---|
| 1. Prudential of America (1) | $133,456.0 | $24,108.2 |
| 2. Metropolitan Life (2) | 103,228.4 | 19,527.4 |
| 3. Aetna Life (4) | 52,342.6 | 9,591.4 |
| 4. Equitable Life Assurance (3) | 50,301.6 | 4,029.8 |
| 5. Teachers Insurance & Annuity (5) | 49,894.1 | 2,978.9 |
| 6. New York Life (6) | 39,876.3 | 7,709.6 |
| 7. Connecticut General Life (7) | 37,407.3 | 4,418.7 |
| 8. John Hancock Mutual Life (9) | 33,749.5 | 6,822.8 |
| 9. Travelers (8) | 33,027.6 | 4,866.1 |
| 10. Northwestern Mutual Life (10) | 31,377.1 | 4,166.2 |

### TRANSPORTATION COMPANIES, BY REVENUES

| Company (1989 rank) | Revenues | Profits |
|---|---|---|
| 1. United Parcel Service (1) | $13,628.6 | $ 596.8 |
| 2. AMR (2) | 11,803.6 | (39.6) |
| 3. UAL (3) | 11,160.1 | 94.5 |
| 4. Delta Air Lines (4) | 8,582.2 | 302.8 |
| 5. CSX (5) | 8,306.0 | 416.0 |
| 6. NWA (8) | 7,257.1 | (10.4) |
| 7. Union Pacific (7) | 7,059.2 | 618.1 |
| 8. Federal Express (10) | 7,026.2 | 115.8 |
| 9. USAir Group (9) | 6,562.8 | (454.4) |
| 10. Continental Airlines Holdings (6) | 6,283.6 | (2,343.9) |

### DIVERSIFIED FINANCIAL COMPANIES, BY ASSETS

| Company (1989 rank) | Assets | Revenues |
|---|---|---|
| 1. American Express (1) | $137,682.0 | $24,332.0 |
| 2. Federal National Mortgage Association (2) | 133,113.0 | 12,612.0 |
| 3. Salomon (3) | 109,877.0 | 8,946.0 |
| 4. Aetna Life & Casualty (4) | 89,300.7 | 19,428.3 |
| 5. Merrill Lynch (5) | 68,129.5 | 11,213.4 |
| 6. Cigna (6) | 63,691.0 | 18,344.0 |
| 7. American International Group (9) | 58,143.1 | 15,702.1 |
| 8. Travelers (7) | 55,356.0 | 12,150.0 |
| 9. Morgan Stanley Group (8) | 53,526.5 | 5,869.6 |
| 10. ITT (10) | 49,043.0 | 20,604.0 |

**Note**: Dollar figures in parentheses indicate losses. **Source**: *Fortune Magazine* (June 3, 1991); reprinted by permission of Time-Life Inc.

## LEADING *FORTUNE* 500 INDUSTRIAL COMPANIES, BY INDUSTRY AND SALES, 1990 (in millions)

### AEROSPACE (18 companies)

| | |
|---|---|
| 1. Boeing (13) | $27,595.0 |
| 2. United Technologies (17) | 21,783.2 |
| 3. McDonnell Douglas (24) | 16,351.0 |
| 4. Allied-Signal (36) | 12,396.0 |
| 5. General Dynamics (48) | 10,182.0 |
| 6. Lockheed (50) | 9,977.0 |
| 7. Textron (61) | 7,917.6 |
| 8. Martin Marietta (83) | 6,142.7 |
| 9. Northrop (96) | 5,502.6 |
| 10. Grumman (122) | 4,041.3 |

### APPAREL (13 companies)

| | |
|---|---|
| 1. Levi Strauss Assoc. (116) | $4,247.1 |
| 2. VF (171) | 2,624.0 |
| 3. Liz Claiborne (237) | 1,754.7 |
| 4. Fruit of the Loom (272) | 1,426.8 |
| 5. Hartmarx (293) | 1,310.1 |
| 6. Crystal Brands (370) | 876.1 |
| 7. Leslie Fay (376) | 858.8 |
| 8. Gitano Group (395) | 806.6 |
| 9. Kellwood (402) | 779.9 |
| 10. Phillips–Van Heusen (411) | 734.5 |

### BEVERAGES (7 companies)

| | |
|---|---|
| 1. Pepsico (23) | $17,802.7 |
| 2. Anheuser-Busch (44) | 10,750.6 |
| 3. Coca-Cola (47) | 10,406.3 |
| 4. Coca-Cola Enterprises (123) | 4,040.6 |
| 5. J.E. Seagram (142) | 3,411.6 |
| 6. Adolph Coors (225) | 1,867.5 |
| 7. Brown-Forman (342) | 1,023.8 |

### BUILDING MATERIALS (10 companies)

| | |
|---|---|
| 1. PPG Industries (86) | $6,118.4 |
| 2. Owens-Illinois (121) | 4,070.6 |
| 3. American Standard (134) | 3,646.6 |
| 4. Owens-Corning Fiberglas (148) | 3,111.0 |
| 5. Corning (154) | 2,980.4 |
| 6. Armstrong World Ind. (177) | 2,535.6 |
| 7. USG (206) | 2,102.0 |
| 8. Lafarge (256) | 1,598.1 |
| 9. Holnam (334) | 1,074.6 |
| 10. Southdown (487) | 565.9 |

### CHEMICALS (42 companies)

| | |
|---|---|
| 1. E.I. Du Pont de Nemours (9) | $39,839.0 |
| 2. Dow Chemical (18) | 20,005.0 |
| 3. Monsanto (53) | 9,047.0 |
| 4. Union Carbide (65) | 7,621.0 |
| 5. W.R. Grace (71) | 6,774.7 |
| 6. Lyondell Petrochemical (76) | 6,508.0 |
| 7. Bayer USA (89) | 5,903.7 |
| 8. Hoechst Celanese (90) | 5,881.0 |
| 9. BASF (99) | 5,381.2 |
| 10. American Cyanamid (108) | 4,821.5 |

### COMPUTERS[1] (22 companies)

| | |
|---|---|
| 1. IBM (4) | $69,018.0 |
| 2. Hewlett-Packard (29) | 13,233.0 |
| 3. Digital Equipment (30) | 13,084.5 |
| 4. UNISYS (49) | 10,111.3 |
| 5. NCR (79) | 6,395.0 |
| 6. Apple Computer (95) | 5,558.4 |
| 7. Compaq Computer (136) | 3,625.7 |
| 8. Pitney Bowes (145) | 3,267.0 |
| 9. Wang Laboratories (169) | 2,634.7 |
| 10. Sun Microsystems (181) | 2,480.7 |

### ELECTRONICS (43 companies)

| | |
|---|---|
| 1. General Electric (6) | $58,414.0 |
| 2. Westinghouse Electric (33) | 12,915.0 |
| 3. Rockwell International (35) | 12,442.5 |
| 4. Motorola (42) | 10,885.0 |
| 5. Raytheon (52) | 9,362.3 |
| 6. TRW (58) | 8,169.0 |
| 7. Emerson Electric (66) | 7,573.4 |
| 8. Whirlpool (72) | 6,647.0 |
| 9. Texas Instruments (74) | 6,567.0 |
| 10. Cooper-Industries (81) | 6,222.2 |

### FOOD (49 companies)

| | |
|---|---|
| 1. Philip Morris (7) | $44,323.0 |
| 2. Occidental Petroleum (16) | 21,947.0 |
| 3. Conagra (25) | 15,517.7 |
| 4. Sara Lee (38) | 11,652.0 |
| 5. Archer-Daniels-Midland (60) | 7,925.3 |
| 6. Borden (64) | 7,632.8 |
| 7. Ralston Purina (67) | 7,133.2 |
| 8. General Mills (77) | 6,486.7 |
| 9. Campbell Soup (80) | 6,223.4 |
| 10. H.J. Heinz (87) | 6,112.4 |

### FOREST PRODUCTS (36 companies)

| | |
|---|---|
| 1. International Paper (32) | $12,960.0 |
| 2. Georgia-Pacific (34) | 12,665.0 |
| 3. Weyerhaeuser (54) | 9,024.3 |
| 4. Kimberly-Clark (78) | 6,447.9 |
| 5. Stone Container (92) | 5,770.4 |
| 6. James River Corp. of Va. (97) | 5,442.7 |
| 7. Scott Paper (98) | 5,390.9 |
| 8. Champion Intl. (104) | 5,159.0 |
| 9. Mead (109) | 4,796.1 |
| 10. Boise Cascade (118) | 4,189.5 |

### FURNITURE (9 companies)

| | |
|---|---|
| 1. Johnson Controls (112) | $4,515.3 |
| 2. Interco (201) | 2,224.5 |
| 3. Leggett & Platt (330) | 1,088.6 |
| 4. Lear Seating (337) | 1,067.9 |
| 5. Herman Miller (374) | 869.5 |
| 6. Hon Industries (438) | 668.0 |
| 7. Sealy Holdings (449) | 641.6 |
| 8. Kimball International (457) | 619.9 |
| 9. La-Z-Boy Chair (473) | 594.8 |

### INDUSTRIAL AND FARM EQUIPMENT (36 companies)

| | |
|---|---|
| 1. Tenneco (26) | $14,893.0 |
| 2. Caterpillar (39) | 11,540.0 |
| 3. Deere (62) | 7,881.0 |
| 4. Black & Decker (107) | 4,876.9 |
| 5. Dresser Industries (111) | 4,528.1 |
| 6. Ingersoll-Rand (132) | 3,737.8 |
| 7. Cummins Engine (140) | 3,461.8 |
| 8. Baker Hughes (173) | 2,614.3 |
| 9. Parker Hannifin (179) | 2,512.3 |
| 10. Great Amer. Mgmt.& Invt. (186) | 2,435.4 |

### JEWELRY, SILVERWARE (1 company)

| | |
|---|---|
| 1. Jostens (399) | $387.5 |

### METAL PRODUCTS (23 companies)

| | |
|---|---|
| 1. Peter Kiewit Sons' (105) | $5,086.7 |
| 2. Gillette (113) | 4,394.0 |
| 3. Masco (146) | 3,234.6 |
| 4. Crown Cork & Seal (150) | 3,080.1 |
| 5. Illinois Tool Works (176) | 2,550.8 |
| 6. McDermott (193) | 2,327.3 |
| 7. Sequa (198) | 2,243.0 |
| 8. Tyco Laboratories (205) | 2,102.7 |
| 9. Stanley Works (215) | 1,977.0 |
| 10. Harsco (236) | 1,766.7 |

### METALS (30 companies)

| | |
|---|---|
| 1. Aluminum Co. of America (43) | $10,865.1 |
| 2. LTV (84) | 6,138.3 |
| 3. Reynolds Metals (88) | 6,075.7 |
| 4. Bethlehem Steel (106) | 4,929.1 |
| 5. Inland Steel Industries (125) | 3,870.4 |
| 6. Amax (128) | 3,810.5 |
| 7. Phelps Dodge (168) | 2,655.7 |
| 8. National Steel (180) | 2,507.6 |
| 9. Maxxam (191) | 2,360.7 |
| 10. Penn Central (204) | 2,154.3 |

### MINING, CRUDE-OIL PRODUCTION (13 companies)

| | |
|---|---|
| 1. Hanson Industries NA (75) | $6,558.3 |
| 2. Asarco (199) | 2,241.7 |
| 3. Oryx Energy (211) | 2,041.0 |
| 4. Burlington Resources (221) | 1,880.6 |
| 5. Freeport-McMoran (251) | 1,618.1 |
| 6. Union Texas (290) | 1,332.5 |
| 7. Vulcan Materials (326) | 1,105.3 |
| 8. Louisiana Land & Explor. (366) | 884.8 |
| 9. Nerco (387) | 827.7 |
| 10. Newmont Mining (426) | 700.3 |

### MOTOR VEHICLES AND PARTS (17 companies)

| | |
|---|---|
| 1. General Motors (1) | $126,017.0 |
| 2. Ford Motor (3) | 98,274.7 |
| 3. Chrysler (11) | 30,868.0 |
| 4. Dana (101) | 5,225.5 |
| 5. Eaton (120) | 4,102.0 |
| 6. Navistar International (126) | 3,854.2 |
| 7. Paccar (161) | 2,817.7 |
| 8. Arvin Industries (235) | 1,769.6 |
| 9. Echlin (253) | 1,607.2 |
| 10. Fleetwood Enterprises (257) | 1,563.2 |

### PETROLEUM REFINING (27 companies)

| | |
|---|---|
| 1. Exxon (2) | $105,885.0 |
| 2. Mobil (5) | 58,770.0 |
| 3. Texaco (8) | 41,235.0 |
| 4. Chevron (10) | 39,262.0 |
| 5. Amoco (12) | 28,277.0 |
| 6. Shell Oil (14) | 24,423.0 |
| 7. USX (19) | 19,462.0 |
| 8. Atlantic Richfield (21) | 18,819.0 |
| 9. Phillips Petroleum (27) | 14,032.0 |
| 10. SUN (37) | 11,909.0 |

### PHARMACEUTICALS (14 companies)

| | |
|---|---|
| 1. Johnson & Johnson (41) | $11,232.0 |
| 2. Bristol-Myers Squibb (46) | 10,509.0 |
| 3. Merck (63) | 7,824.1 |
| 4. Amer. Home Prod. (70) | 6,917.2 |
| 5. Pfizer (73) | 6,559.7 |
| 6. Abbott Laboratories (82) | 6,210.3 |
| 7. Eli Lilly (103) | 5,191.6 |
| 8. Warner-Lambert (110) | 4,769.1 |
| 9. Schering-Plough (144) | 3,322.9 |
| 10. Upjohn (153) | 3,032.7 |

### PUBLISHING, PRINTING (21 companies)

| | |
|---|---|
| 1. Times Mirror (135) | $3,633.2 |
| 2. R.R. Donnelley & Sons (139) | 3,497.9 |
| 3. Gannett (141) | 3,445.5 |
| 4. Berkshire Hathaway (170) | 2,625.0 |
| 5. Tribune (192) | 2,353.0 |
| 6. Knight-Ridder (194) | 2,305.2 |
| 7. Reader's Digest Assoc. (209) | 2,055.8 |
| 8. McGraw-Hill (218) | 1,938.6 |
| 9. New York Times (234) | 1,776.8 |
| 10. Dow Jones (240) | 1,727.6 |

### RUBBER PRODUCTS (11 companies)

| | |
|---|---|
| 1. Goodyear Tire & Rubber (40) | $11,453.0 |
| 2. Premark International (163) | 2,721.4 |
| 3. Rubbermaid (259) | 1,539.4 |
| 4. Raychem (317) | 1,135.6 |
| 5. M.A. Hanna (320) | 1,119.7 |
| 6. Cooper Tire & Rubber (364) | 896.8 |
| 7. A. Schulman (433) | 681.1 |
| 8. Standard Products (446) | 653.3 |
| 9. Carlisle (454) | 625.4 |
| 10. Bandag (472) | 595.9 |

### SCIENTIFIC AND PHOTOGRAPHIC EQUIPMENT (18 companies)

| | |
|---|---|
| 1. Eastman Kodak (20) | $19,075.0 |
| 2. Xerox (22) | 18,382.0 |
| 3. Minnesota Mining (31) | 13,021.0 |
| 4. Baxter International (59) | 8,148.0 |
| 5. Honeywell (69) | 6,985.2 |
| 6. EG&G (182) | 2,478.5 |
| 7. Becton Dickinson (212) | 2,012.7 |
| 8. Polaroid (213) | 2,006.4 |
| 9. Tektronix (276) | 1,412.3 |
| 10. Bausch & Lomb (280) | 1,386.3 |

### SOAPS, COSMETICS (12 companies)

| | |
|---|---|
| 1. Procter & Gamble (15) | $24,376.0 |
| 2. Unilever U.S. (55) | 8,680.0 |
| 3. Colgate-Palmolive (94) | 5,740.2 |
| 4. Avon Products (138) | 3,508.8 |
| 5. Clorox (262) | 1,501.7 |
| 6. International Flavors (350) | 962.8 |
| 7. Alberto-Culver (396) | 795.8 |
| 8. Helene Curtis (409) | 736.0 |
| 9. Stanhome (434) | 675.7 |
| 10. NCH (453) | 628.4 |

### TEXTILES (13 companies)

| | |
|---|---|
| 1. Wickes (133) | $3,649.0 |
| 2. Burlington Holdings (195) | 2,290.5 |
| 3. Springs Industries (222) | 1,879.1 |
| 4. West Point–Pepperell (238) | 1,753.6 |
| 5. Shaw Industries (264) | 1,475.4 |
| 6. Amoskeag (297) | 1,276.5 |
| 7. DWG (300) | 1,239.0 |
| 8. JPS Textile Group (391) | 821.7 |
| 9. Cone Mills (432) | 683.7 |
| 10. Interface (455) | 623.5 |

### TOBACCO (7 companies)

| | |
|---|---|
| 1. RJR Nabisco Holdings (28) | $13,879.0 |
| 2. American Brands (57) | 8,270.3 |
| 3. Universal (162) | 2,815.1 |
| 4. Lorillard (254) | 1,605.3 |
| 5. Standard Commercial (353) | 945.1 |
| 6. Dibrell Brothers (403) | 768.4 |
| 7. UST (404) | 755.4 |

### TOYS, SPORTING GOODS (3 companies)

| | |
|---|---|
| 1. Hasbro (260) | $1,520.0 |
| 2. Mattel (265) | 1,470.6 |
| 3. Tonka (398) | 788.5 |

### TRANSPORTATION EQUIPMENT (5 companies)

| | |
|---|---|
| 1. Brunswick (183) | $2,477.6 |
| 2. Trinity Industries (292) | 1,310.9 |
| 3. Outboard Marine (314) | 1,145.6 |
| 4. Harley-Davidson (375) | 864.6 |
| 5. Avondale Industries (405) | 755.0 |

**Note:** Figures in parentheses indicate overall *Fortune* 500 rank. 1. Includes office equipment. **Source:** *Fortune* (Apr. 22, 1991); reprinted by permission of Time-Life Inc.

## MERGERS AND ACQUISITIONS

A merger is a joint decision by two or more firms to combine their assets; an acquisition refers to the purchase of one company by another. There are several reasons for firms to merge or acquire each other. In merging their operations, two companies might make better use of their assets—a pool company busy in the summer might combine with a ski company busy in the winter to make year-round use of facilities and staff. In acquiring another firm, a company may believe that the business it is buying is worth more than the current price if, for example, it can manage the business more efficiently.

Firms may also decide to use the acquisition process to purchase themselves. If management believes that the current price of its firm's stock is lower than it could be, it may purchase the firm's outstanding stock and "take the firm private," one advantage being that the government places fewer restrictions and regulations on privately held companies. Also, the firm is protected from unwanted ("hostile") takeovers because there are no outside shareholders from whom corporate raiders can purchase stock and thereby gain control.

Acquisitions and mergers receive attention because ownership of enormous productive assets changes hands very quickly. Despite the reasons offered for merging or acquiring companies, the generally poor showing of so many firms following mergers and acquisitions casts doubt on the efficiency arguments. The process often leads to reorganizations and profound changes—sharp reductions in some functions and employment, expansions in others—which influence people both inside and outside the firm. One such result is *divestiture*, the sale of a company's product line, division, or subsidiary because it no longer fits well with the expanded firm's overall goal or because the business may need a quick infusion of cash to pay off debt incurred in the merger or acquisition. Divestments can provide an opportunity for leveraged buyouts, in which a group of employees, typically upper-level management, purchases the division and operates it themselves, preserving their jobs in the process.

Another concern is the extent to which acquisitions, especially, have transferred ownership of U.S. industries to foreign interests. The pace of foreign acquisitions as measured by dollar value has increased sharply in recent years; the leading buyers of U.S. firms have been British concerns.

The rapid growth of mergers and acquisitions in the 1980s was due in part to the deregulation of banking (making consolidations in that industry easier); the government's more lenient antitrust policy and its allowing mergers even of direct competitors; and the 1982–83 recession, which left many firms weak and searching for stronger ownership. From 1980 to 1989, 31,105 deals were transacted with a collective value of $1.34 trillion. The trend peaked in 1986 with 4,448 mergers, acquisitions, and divestitures. In 1989 there were 3,412 deals,

### LARGEST U.S. MERGERS AND ACQUISITIONS, LEVERAGED BUYOUTS, AND FOREIGN ACQUISITIONS IN THE U.S. (in millions)

| Buyer | Target | Price | Year |
|---|---|---|---|
| **Mergers and acquisitions** | | | |
| Standard Oil Co. of California[1] | Gulf. Corp. | $13,300 | 1984 |
| Phillip Morris Cos. | Kraft Inc. | 12,644 | 1988 |
| Time Inc. | Warner Communications, Inc. | 12,636 | 1990 |
| Bristol-Myers Co. | Squibb Corp. | 12,526 | 1989 |
| Texaco Inc. | Getty Oil Co. | 10,125 | 1984 |
| Dow Chemical Co. | Marion Laboratories Inc. (67% acquisition of majority interest) | 7,079 | 1989 |
| Du Pont Co. | Conoco Inc. | 6,924 | 1981 |
| GTE Corp. | Contel Corp. | 6,421 | 1990 |
| United States Steel Corp.[2] | Marathon Oil Co. | 6,150 | 1982 |
| General Electric Co. | RCA Corp | 6,142 | 1986 |
| **Leveraged buyouts** | | | |
| Kohlberg Kravis Roberts & Co. | RJR Nabisco Inc. | $24,717 | 1989 |
| Kohlberg Kravis Roberts & Co. | Beatrice Cos. | 6,250 | 1986 |
| Kohlberg Kravis Roberts & Co. | Safeway Stores Inc. | 4,235 | 1986 |
| Thompson Co. | Southland Corp. | 4,004 | 1987 |
| AV Holdings Corp. | Borg-Warner Corp. | 3,760 | 1987 |
| Wings Holdings Inc. | NWA Inc. | 3,759 | 1989 |
| Kohlberg Kravis Roberts & Co. | Owens-Illinois Inc. | 3,688 | 1987 |
| TF Investments Inc. | Hospital Corp. of America | 3,686 | 1989 |
| FH Acquisitions Corp. | Fort Howard Corp. | 3,589 | 1988 |
| Macy Acquiring Corp. | R.H. Macy & Co. | 3,501 | 1986 |
| **Foreign acquisitions in the U.S.** | | | |
| Beecham Group PLC (UK) | SmithKline Beckman Corp. | $8,279 | 1989 |
| British Petroleum Corp. (UK) | Standard Oil Co. | 7,565 | 1987 |
| Matsushita Electric Industrial Co. (Japan) | MCA Inc. | 6,589 | 1990 |
| Campeau Corp. (Canada) | Federated Department Stores Inc. | 6,506 | 1988 |
| Grand Metropolitan (UK) | Pillsbury Co. | 5,758 | 1989 |
| Royal Dutch/Shell Group (Netherlands-UK) | Shell Oil Co. | 5,657 | 1985 |
| B.A.T. Industries PLC (UK) | Farmers Group Inc. | 5,169 | 1988 |
| Campeau Corp. (Canada) | Allied Signal Corp. | 3,597 | 1986 |
| Sony Corp. (Japan) | Columbia Pictures Entertainment, Inc. | 3,478 | 1989 |
| Unilever NV (Netherlands) | Chesebrough-Pond's Inc. | 3,095 | 1987 |

**Note:** As of July 1, 1991. 1. Now known as Chevron Corp. 2. Now known as USX Corp. **Source:** *Mergers and Acquisitions* (Philadelphia, Pa.); reprinted by permission.

valued at $230.7 billion, including the largest transaction in mergers and acquisitions history—the leveraged buyout of RJR Nabisco, Inc. for $24.7 billion. In 1990, however, merger and acquisition activity slowed considerably, reflecting the downturn of the U.S. economy.

## ADVERTISING

If they wish to make a profit, both large and small purveyors of consumer products and services must find ways to let their potential customers know about their business. Since the U.S. media (newspapers, radio, television, magazines) also are run as profit-earning enterprises, it seems natural that the two forces would be joined by their common needs. This in fact happened about 150 years ago, when whole pages of newspapers were jammed with the unadorned but paid announcements of everything from patent medicines to clothing and hardware. By 1900 so many large businesses had sprung up (Procter & Gamble and

Kellogg's, for example) that nationally distributed magazines (including *Ladies' Home Journal*) became enormously profitable ventures based on the advertising placed by these firms. By 1910 over $1 billion a year was being spent on advertising, which was itself now entrenched as a business of its own with established practices and with dozens of schools specially designed to teach the most persuasive selling techniques.

Throughout the 20th century, advertising expanded along with the economy, and it provided businesses with a distinctly American voice that moved the merchandise in an unprecedented manner. Few facts reveal the extraordinary growth of the so-called mass-consumption society as vividly as those dealing with the advertising business. In 1950, as the postwar economy began to heat up, American business spent $5.7 billion to advertise its goods and services; by 1960 that figure would double, and then almost double again by 1970. Between 1970 and 1990, as the Baby Boom generation entered the marketplace and the

## TOTAL U.S. ADVERTISING VOLUME BY MEDIUM, 1989–90 (millions of dollars)

| Medium | 1989 Expenditures | 1989 Percent share | 1990 Expenditures | 1990 Percent share | Percent change 1989–90 | Medium | 1989 Expenditures | 1989 Percent share | 1990 Expenditures | 1990 Percent share | Percent change 1989–90 |
|---|---|---|---|---|---|---|---|---|---|---|---|
| Newspapers, total | $32,368 | 26.1% | $32,280 | 25.1% | -0.3% | Spot (national) | $ 1,547 | 1.2% | $ 1,635 | 1.3% | 5.7% |
| National | 3,948 | 3.2 | 4,122 | 3.2 | 4.4 | Local (spot) | 6,300 | 5.1 | 6,609 | 5.1 | 4.9 |
| Local | 28,420 | 22.9 | 28,158 | 21.9 | -0.9 | Direct mail | 21,945 | 17.7 | 23,370 | 18.2 | 6.5 |
| Magazines, total | 6,716 | 5.4 | 6,803 | 5.3 | 1.3 | Business papers | 2,763 | 2.2 | 2,875 | 2.2 | 4.1 |
| Weeklies | 2,813 | 2.3 | 2,864 | 2.2 | 1.8 | Outdoor | 1,111 | 0.9 | 1,084 | 0.8 | -2.4 |
| Women's | 1,710 | 1.4 | 1,713 | 1.3 | 0.2 | National | 653 | 0.5 | 640 | 0.5 | -2.0 |
| Monthlies | 2,193 | 1.8 | 2,226 | 1.7 | 1.5 | Local | 458 | 0.4 | 444 | 0.3 | -3.1 |
| Farm publications | 212 | 0.2 | 215 | 0.2 | 1.4 | Yellow pages | 8.330 | 6.7 | 8,926 | 6.9 | 7.2 |
| Television, total | 26,891 | 21.7 | 28,405 | 22.1 | 5.6 | National | 1,011 | 0.8 | 1,132 | 0.9 | 12.0 |
| Network | 9,110 | 7.4 | 9,383 | 7.3 | 3.0 | Local | 7,319 | 5.9 | 7,794 | 6.1 | 6.5 |
| Spot (national) | 7,354 | 5.9 | 7,788 | 6.1 | 5.9 | Miscellaneous, total[1] | 15,271 | 12.3 | 15,955 | 12.4 | 4.5 |
| Cable (national) | 1,197 | 1.0 | 1,393 | 1.1 | 16.4 | National | 10,998 | 8.9 | 11,608 | 9.0 | 5.5 |
| Syndication | 1,288 | 1.0 | 1,589 | 1.2 | 23.4 | Local | 4,273 | 3.4 | 4,347 | 3.4 | 1.7 |
| Local (spot) | 7,612 | 6.1 | 7,856 | 6.1 | 3.2 | Total national | 69,218 | 55.9 | 73,035 | 56.8 | 5.5 |
| Cable (local) | 330 | 0.3 | 396 | 0.3 | 20.0 | Total local | 54,712 | 44.1 | 55,604 | 43.2 | 1.6 |
| Radio, total | 8,323 | 6.7 | 8,726 | 6.8 | 4.8 | **Grand total** | **$123,930** | **100.0%** | **$128,639** | **100.0%** | **3.8%** |
| Network | 476 | 0.4 | 482 | 0.4 | 1.3 | | | | | | |

**Note:** Estimates include all costs, including time, talent, space, and production. 1. Includes weeklies, shoppers, pennysavers, bus, and cinema advertising. **Source:** Newspaper Advertising Bureau, Inc. (1991).

## ADVERTISING EXPENDITURES IN THE U. S.,1776–1990 (millions of dollars)

| Year | Amount[1] | Year | Amount[1] |
|---|---|---|---|
| 1776 | $ 0.2 | 1955 | $ 9,150.0 |
| 1800 | 1.0 | 1960 | 11,960.0 |
| 1820 | 3.0 | 1965 | 15,250.0 |
| 1840 | 7.0 | 1970 | 19,550.0 |
| 1850 | 12.0 | 1975 | 28,160.0 |
| 1860 | 22.0 | 1980 | 54,780.0 |
| 1867 | 40.0 | 1981 | 60,430.0 |
| 1876 | 150.0 | 1982 | 66,580.0 |
| 1880 | 175.0 | 1983 | 75,850.0 |
| 1890 | 300.0 | 1984 | 88,100.0 |
| 1900 | 450.0 | 1985 | 94,750.0 |
| 1909 | 1,000.0 | 1986 | 102,140.0 |
| 1915 | 1,100.0 | 1987 | 109,787.0 |
| 1940 | 2,110.0 | 1988 | 118,050.0 |
| 1945 | 2,840.0 | 1989 | 125,550.0[2] |
| 1950 | 5,700.0 | 1990 | 132,640.0[2] |

1. These are estimated figures of the monies spent on placing advertising in all media; the costs of producing the advertising are not included. 2. Preliminary estimates. **Sources:** McCann-Erickson, N.Y.; figures through 1975 were compiled for *Advertising Age* and reprinted July 5, 1976.

economy expanded, advertising expenditures grew at a spiraling rate, reaching $132 billion by 1990.

Over 60% of all advertising dollars are spent to place ads in newspapers or magazines or to run commercials on radio and television. Most of that money in turn is spent by the nation's largest manufacturers of automobiles, food, soft drinks, and beer.

Most advertising dollars are filtered through about 6,000 advertising agencies, who create the ads and buy the space or time from the media. The agency business has undergone a

## TOP 25 U.S.-BASED AD AGENCIES, BY GROSS DOMESTIC INCOME, 1989 (millions of dollars)

| U.S. rank / Agency, headquarters | U.S. gross income | U.S. billings | U.S. employees | Worldwide gross income | World rank |
|---|---|---|---|---|---|
| 1. Young & Rubicam Inc., N.Y. | $409.5 | $3,114.8 | 4,066 | $865.4 | 3 |
| 2. Saatchi & Saatchi Advertising, N.Y. | 395.2 | 2,778.9 | 1,760 | 890.0 | 2 |
| 3. BBDO Worldwide, N.Y. | 373.6 | 2,656.0 | 3,375 | 656.6 | 7 |
| 4. Backer Spielvogel Bates Worldwide, Inc., N.Y. | 310.7 | 2,158.0 | 1,370 | 759.8 | 4 |
| 5. Ogilvy & Mather Worldwide, Inc., N.Y. | 305.1 | 2,104.4 | 2,636 | 699.7 | 6 |
| 6. DDB Needham Worldwide, N.Y. | 302.9 | 2,386.3 | 3,025 | 552.9 | 11 |
| 7. Leo Burnett Co. Inc., Chicago | 288.8 | 1,945.3 | 2,222 | 483.8 | 14 |
| 8. Foote, Cone & Belding Communications, Inc., Chicago | 280.5 | 1,871.2 | 2,832 | 510.9 | 12 |
| 9. J. Walter Thompson Co., N.Y. | 266.5 | 1,851.0 | 2,484 | 626.4 | 8 |
| 10. Grey Advertising Inc., N.Y. | 240.7 | 1,605.3 | 2,067 | 498.9 | 13 |
| 11. D'Arcy Masius Benton & Bowles, Inc., N.Y. | 232.3 | 2,055.3 | 2,341 | 471.5 | 15 |
| 12. Lintas: Worldwide, N.Y. | 224.9 | 1,499.9 | 1,781 | 593.3 | 9 |
| 13. McCann-Erickson Worldwide, N.Y. | 209.1 | 1,394.8 | 1,767 | 715.5 | 5 |
| 14. Bozell Inc., N.Y. | 155.4 | 1,165.0 | 1,643 | 190.7 | 19 |
| 15. Wells, Rich, Greene, Inc., N.Y. | 132.5 | 883.0 | 860 | 132.5 | 26 |
| 16. NW Ayer Inc., N.Y. | 128.8 | 859.1 | 980 | 210.5 | 18 |
| 17. Campbell-Mithun-Esty, Minneapolis (BSBW) | 115.9 | 859.8 | 1,155 | (1) | (1) |
| 18. Ketchum Communications, Pittsburgh | 112.9 | 854.9 | 1,229 | 117.8 | 29 |
| 19. Chiat/Day/Mojo, Venice, Calif. | 106.0 | 785.0 | 935 | 150.0 | 24 |
| 20. Ross Roy Group, Bloomfield Hills, Mich. | 97.7 | 651.1 | 1,046 | 97.7 | 32 |
| 21. Della Femina, McNamee EWDB, Inc., N.Y. | 87.8 | 728.7 | 851 | (1) | (1) |
| 22. Scali, McCabe, Sloves, Inc., N.Y. | 79.0 | 590.3 | 717 | 127.0 | 27 |
| 23. Tracy-Locke, Dallas (BBDO) | 55.6 | 404.6 | 625 | (1) | (1) |
| 24. AC&R Advertising Inc., N.Y. (S&SAW) | 45.8 | 369.1 | 436 | (1) | (1) |
| 25. Admarketing, Inc., Los Angeles | 44.9 | 252.0 | 133 | 44.9 | 47 |

1. Ranks lower than 100 in worldwide gross income. **Source:** *Advertising Age* (1990), reprinted by permission of Crain Communications, Inc.

dramatic restructuring recently as the corporate-raider mentality invaded Madison Avenue with a vengeance. Many of the largest agencies, most with worldwide connections, have merged with others to form enormous corpora-

tions, so the names of the top 25 change rapidly from year to year. The largest advertising agency in the world is Dentsu, Inc. in Tokyo; in 1989 it had a gross income of $1.3 billion and billings of over $10 billion.

## THE 100 LEADING U.S. ADVERTISERS, 1990 (millions of dollars)

| Rank/Company | Total spending | Rank/Company | Total spending | Rank/Company | Total spending |
|---|---|---|---|---|---|
| 1. Philip Morris Cos. | $2,072.0 | 35. R.H. Macy & Co. | $312.7 | 69. Subaru of America | $159.5 |
| 2. Procter and Gamble Co. | 1,779.3 | 36. U.S. Government | 309.5 | 70. Mobil Corp. | 156.3 |
| 3. Sears, Roebuck & Co. | 1,432.1 | 37. Nissan Motor Co. | 300.6 | 71. Hasbro Inc. | 151.9 |
| 4. General Motors Corp. | 1,363.8 | 38. Honda Motor Co. | 298.8 | 72. Schering-Plough Corp. | 150.2 |
| 5. Grand Metropolitan PLC | 823.3 | 39. Campeau Corp. | 294.9 | 73. Citicorp | 146.3 |
| 6. PepsiCo Inc. | 786.1 | 40. Mars Inc. | 293.3 | 74. Loews Corp. | 143.0 |
| 7. McDonald's Corp. | 774.4 | 41. Hershey Foods Corp. | 288.2 | 75. Paramount Communications | 141.2 |
| 8. Eastman Kodak Co. | 718.8 | 42. American Express Co. | 267.9 | 76. Hallmark Cards | 138.2 |
| 9. RJR Nabisco | 703.5 | 43. Colgate-Palmolive Co. | 246.3 | 77. Seagram Co. | 136.8 |
| 10. Kellogg Co. | 611.6 | 44. General Electric Co. | 243.2 | 78. E.I. du Pont de Nemours | 133.2 |
| 11. Nestlé SA | 608.4 | 45. Pfizer Inc. | 235.3 | 79. Bell-Atlantic Corp. | 132.0 |
| 12. Unilever NV | 604.1 | 46. Tandy Corp. | 232.7 | 80. Volkswagen AG | 131.9 |
| 13. Ford Motor Co. | 602.1 | 47. American Stores Co. | 220.0 | 81. Circuit City Stores | 131.2 |
| 14. Anheuser-Busch Cos. | 591.5 | 48. MCA Inc. | 219.9 | 82. AMR Corp. | 131.0 |
| 15. Warner-Lambert Co. | 585.9 | 49. Montgomery Ward & Co. | 213.6 | 83. News Corp. | 128.9 |
| 16. AT&T Co. | 567.7 | 50. Hyundai Group | 212.8 | 84. ITT Corp. | 128.5 |
| 17. Time Warner | 567.5 | 51. ConAgra | 211.3 | 85. UAL Corp. | 127.3 |
| 18. K Mart Corp. | 561.4 | 52. U.S. Dairy Farmers | 205.9 | 86. Wal-Mart Stores | 127.1 |
| 19. Chrysler Corp. | 532.5 | 53. American Brands | 204.2 | 87. Carter Hawley Hale Stores | 126.6 |
| 20. Johnson & Johnson | 487.1 | 54. SmithKline Beecham PLC | 203.2 | 88. Kroger Co. | 125.5 |
| 21. General Mills | 471.0 | 55. Adolph Coors Co. | 201.0 | 89. Wm. Wrigley Jr. Co. | 124.3 |
| 22. American Home Products Corp. | 456.1 | 56. IBM Corp. | 196.9 | 90. Levi Strauss & Co. | 123.1 |
| 23. Bristol-Myers Squibb Co. | 451.6 | 57. Campbell Soup Co. | 196.7 | 91. Wendy's International | 122.4 |
| 24. Ralston Purina Co. | 429.5 | 58. Revlon Group | 196.5 | 92. United Communications | 121.3 |
| 25. Toyota Motor Corp. | 417.6 | 59. B.A.T. Industries PLC | 196.4 | 93. NYNEX Corp. | 120.7 |
| 26. J.C. Penney Co. | 407.5 | 60. Mazda Motor Corp. | 196.3 | 94. Continental Airlines Holdings | 119.6 |
| 27. May Department Stores Co. | 385.7 | 61. Gillette Co. | 185.1 | 95. Delta Air Lines | 116.0 |
| 28. Coca-Cola Co. | 385.3 | 62. Phillips NV | 182.3 | 96. Daimler-Benz AG | 115.5 |
| 29. Sara Lee Corp. | 367.9 | 63. Clorox Co. | 179.9 | 97. Bayer AG | 112.0 |
| 30. Quaker Oats Co. | 357.8 | 64. Goodyear Tire & Rubber Co. | 168.3 | 98. Whitman Corp. | 108.4 |
| 31. Sony Corp. | 356.5 | 65. CPC International | 168.2 | 99. Nike Inc. | 104.6 |
| 32. H.J. Heinz Co. | 342.3 | 66. Marriott Corp. | 162.0 | 100. Dr. Pepper/Seven Up Cos. | 104.3 |
| 33. Walt Disney Co. | 338.7 | 67. Dow Chemical Co. | 160.2 | | |
| 34. Dayton Hudson Corp. | 314.2 | 68. S.C. Johnson & Son | 160.1 | | |

Source: *Advertising Age* (1991), reprinted by permission of Crain Communications, Inc.

# THE MEDIA

## THE PRINT MEDIA

### Newspapers

The mutual distrust between government and the media dates back to the very first American newspaper in 1690, when a three-page publication called *Publick Occurrences, Both Foreign and Domestick* was suppressed by the government after one issue. A number of newspapers sprang up during the pre–Revolutionary War period, and by 1775 the colonies, with a population of 2.5 million people, were served by 48 weekly newspapers, small in both size and circulation. The first daily, the *Pennsylvania Evening Post and Daily Advertiser*, was not published until 1783. By 1800 there were 20 daily newspapers and more than 1,000 small-town and frontier weeklies. Most of the dailies, filled with political and business news, were expensive and aimed at educated, affluent readers. The first of the mass-circulation dailies, known as the penny press, was the *New York Sun*, started in 1833 and sold for the bar-

## NEWSPAPERS—NUMBER AND CIRCULATION, 1900–90

| Year | Total Number of papers | Total Daily circulation ('000s) | Morning Number of papers | Morning Daily circulation ('000s) | Evening Number of papers | Evening Daily circulation ('000s) | Sunday Number of papers | Sunday Daily circulation ('000s) |
|---|---|---|---|---|---|---|---|---|
| 1900 | 2,226 | 15,102 | — | — | — | — | — | — |
| 1915 | 2,580 | 28,777 | — | — | — | — | 571 | 16,480 |
| 1920 | 2,042 | 27,791 | 437 | — | 1,605 | — | 522 | 17,084 |
| 1925 | 2,008 | 33,739 | 427 | — | 1,581 | — | 548 | 23,355 |
| 1930 | 1,942 | 39,589 | 388 | — | 1,554 | — | 521 | 26,413 |
| 1935 | 1,950 | 38,156 | 390 | — | 1,560 | — | 518 | 28,147 |
| 1940 | 1,878 | 41,132 | 380 | 16,114 | 1,498 | 25,018 | 525 | 32,371 |
| 1945 | 1,749 | 48,384 | 330 | 19,240 | 1,419 | 29,144 | 485 | 39,680 |
| 1950 | 1,772 | 53,829 | 322 | 21,266 | 1,450 | 32,563 | 549 | 46,582 |
| 1955 | 1,760 | 56,147 | 316 | 22,183 | 1,454 | 33,964 | 541 | 46,448 |
| 1960 | 1,763 | 58,882 | 312 | 24,029 | 1,459 | 34,853 | 563 | 47,699 |
| 1965 | 1,751 | 60,358 | 320 | 24,107 | 1,444 | 36,251 | 562 | 48,600 |
| 1970 | 1,748 | 62,108 | 334 | 25,934 | 1,429 | 36,174 | 586 | 49,217 |
| 1975 | 1,756 | 60,655 | 339 | 25,490 | 1,436 | 36,165 | 639 | 51,096 |
| 1980 | 1,745 | 62,202 | 387 | 29,414 | 1,388 | 32,787 | 735 | 54,672 |
| 1985 | 1,676 | 62,766 | 482 | 36,362 | 1,220 | 26,405 | 798 | 58,826 |
| 1990 | 1,611 | 62,324 | 559 | 41,308 | 1,084 | 21,015 | 865 | 62,409 |

Sources: American Newspaper Publishers Assn., *Editor and Publisher* (1991); U.S. Bureau of the Census, *The Statistical History of the United States* (1976).

## TOP 100 DAILY NEWSPAPERS IN THE U.S., BY CIRCULATION, 1990

| Rank | Newspaper | Average daily paid circulation | Rank | Newspaper | Average daily paid circulation | Rank | Newspaper | Average daily paid circulation |
|---|---|---|---|---|---|---|---|---|
| 1. | Wall Street Journal | 1,857,131 | 35. | New Orleans Times-Picayune | 278,990 | 68. | Baltimore Evening Sun | 166,684 |
| 2. | USA Today | 1,347,450 | 36. | San Jose Mercury News | 278,676 | 69. | Pittsburgh Post-Gazette | 162,520 |
| 3. | Los Angeles Times | 1,196,323 | 37. | Milwaukee Journal | 265,461 | 70. | San Antonio Light | 162,431 |
| 4. | New York Times | 1,108,447 | 38. | San Diego Union | 265,246 | 71. | Fort Worth Star-Telegram | 161,698 |
| 5. | New York Daily News | 1,097,693 | 39. | Sacramento Bee | 264,462 | 72. | Asbury Park (N.J.) Press | 159,629 |
| 6. | Washington Post | 780,582 | 40. | Columbus Dispatch | 250,572 | 73. | Hackensack (N.J.) Record | 159,550 |
| 7. | Chicago Tribune | 721,067 | 41. | Baltimore Sun | 243,609 | 74. | Riverside (Calif.) Press-Enterprise | 154,764 |
| 8. | Long Island/New York Newsday | 714,128 | 42. | Denver Post | 243,292 | 75. | Akron Beacon Journal | 154,134 |
| 9. | Detroit Free Press | 636,182 | 43. | Charlotte Observer | 236,802 | 76. | Norfolk Virginian-Pilot | 153,181 |
| 10. | San Francisco Chronicle | 562,887 | 44. | Fort Lauderdale Sun-Sentinel | 235,556 | 77. | Toledo Blade | 153,023 |
| 11. | Chicago Sun-Times | 527,238 | 45. | Seattle Times | 233,995 | 78. | Raleigh News & Observer | 150,267 |
| 12. | Boston Globe | 521,354 | 46. | Louisville Courier-Journal | 233,714 | 79. | Columbia (S.C.) State | 145,528 |
| 13. | Philadelphia Inquirer | 519,895 | 47. | Pittsburgh Press | 231,910 | 80. | Fresno Bee | 145,169 |
| 14. | New York Post | 510,219 | 48. | Indianapolis Star | 228,582 | 81. | Grand Rapids Press | 144,800 |
| 15. | Detroit News | 500,980 | 49. | Hartford Courant | 228,075 | 82. | Richmond (Va.) Times-Dispatch | 143,141 |
| 16. | Newark Star-Ledger | 476,257 | 50. | Philadelphia Daily News | 225,063 | 83. | Allentown (Pa.) Morning Call | 136,435 |
| 17. | Houston Chronicle | 442,044 | 51. | Daily Oklahoman (Oklahoma City) | 221,595 | 84. | San Francisco Examiner | 136,346 |
| 18. | Miami Herald | 428,931 | | | | 85. | Las Vegas Review-Journal | 135,314 |
| 19. | Cleveland Plain Dealer | 428,012 | 52. | Dallas Times Herald | 219,329 | 86. | Rochester (N.Y.) Democrat & Chronicle | 132,603 |
| 20. | Minneapolis Star Tribune | 407,441 | 53. | Memphis Commercial Appeal | 210,477 | | | |
| 21. | Dallas Morning News | 385,366 | 54. | Des Moines Register | 207,126 | 87. | Arkansas Democrat (Little Rock) | 130,024 |
| 22. | St. Louis Post-Dispatch | 382,381 | 55. | Seattle Post-Intelligencer | 205,357 | 88. | Long Beach Press-Telegram | 129,195 |
| 23. | Boston Herald | 358,925 | 56. | Providence Journal | 204,337 | 89. | Nashville Tennessean | 127,936 |
| 24. | Orange County-Santa Ana Register | 353,637 | 57. | St. Paul Pioneer Press | 202,705 | 90. | Arkansas Gazette (Little Rock) | 126,547 |
| | | | 58. | Los Angeles Daily News | 199,589 | 91. | Tulsa World | 125,037 |
| 25. | St. Petersburg Times | 353,130 | 59. | Cincinnati Enquirer | 199,012 | 92. | Lexington Herald-Leader | 124,000 |
| 26. | Rocky Mountain News (Denver) | 351,996 | 60. | Atlanta Journal | 191,811 | 93. | Omaha World-Herald | 123,901 |
| 27. | Arizona Republic (Phoenix) | 330,706 | 61. | San Antonio Express-News | 185,589 | 94. | Sarasota Herald-Tribune | 122,403 |
| 28. | Houston Post | 328,671 | 62. | Dayton Daily News | 183,633 | 95. | Oakland Tribune | 121,537 |
| 29. | Portland Oregonian | 324,163 | 63. | Florida Times-Union (Jacksonville) | 179,047 | 96. | Albuquerque Journal | 121,030 |
| 30. | Atlanta Constitution | 316,793 | | | | 97. | Wichita Eagle | 120,828 |
| 31. | Buffalo News | 308,714 | 64. | West Palm Beach Post | 178,115 | 98. | Wilmington News Journal | 120,653 |
| 32. | Tampa Tribune | 289,999 | 65. | Milwaukee Sentinel | 176,549 | 99. | Worcester Telegram & Gazette | 118,192 |
| 33. | Kansas City Star | 287,345 | 66. | Austin American-Statesman | 173,368 | 100. | Tacoma Morning News Tribune | 117,881 |
| 34. | Orlando Sentinel | 279,393 | 67. | Birmingham News | 169,660 | | | |

**Source**: *Editor and Publisher International Year Book* (1991).

gain price of one cent. The *Sun*, with its crime stories and soft features, marked a dramatic change in newspaper coverage.

The next major change in newspapers came in the era during and after the Civil War. Dramatic technological improvements such as the transatlantic cable, the telephone, the electric light bulb, typewriters, web-fed presses, and the typesetting machine made possible cheap, mass-circulation newspapers. By 1900 the number of daily newspapers had jumped to 2,226. Over the next half-century, the number of newspapers steadily declined while readership increased owing in part to the popularity of Sunday editions.

**Newspapers today** In 1990, 1,611 daily newspapers were published in the United States— 1,084 afternoon publications and 559 morning papers. The number of newspapers has been slowly declining for decades, in part because of radio and television, but also because, in the fight for readers and advertising, competing papers have battled until a single winner emerged. Only 41 cities have competing newspapers today, a major change from the turn of the century when most major cities had more than two newspapers.

Daily circulation has hovered around 60 million

for 15 years or so, with a total of 62,324,156 in 1990. The average paper sells under 50,000 copies a day, and 156 have a daily circulation of more than 100,000. However, the 20 largest newspaper chains account for more than 80% of total daily circulation, reflecting a trend that started in the 1970s.

> *". . . Were it left to me to decide whether we should have a government without newspapers, or newspapers without government, I should not hesitate for a moment to prefer the latter."*
>
> —Thomas Jefferson, (1787).

### Magazines

In 1989, 11,556 consumer and trade magazines were published. Consumer magazines range from the very specialized (*Fly Fisherman*) to general interest (*People*) and are sold either by subscription or through retail outlets (supermarkets, newsstands, etc.). The Audit Bureau of Circulations (A.B.C.) monitors the sales of about 500 of the most popular consumer magazines. While single-copy sales of A.B.C. magazines have decreased steadily since 1978, subscriptions have increased about 50 percent during the same period, more than offsetting the single-copy decline. Trade publications are magazines with a narrow focus in a particular area of business (e.g. trucking, restaurants, computers). There are about 3,700 trade publications; they are sold either by subscription or distributed free.

Almost all magazines make money through revenues from both circulation and advertising. The most financially successful magazines are not necessarily the largest sellers, the difference being in the advertising fees they are able to obtain. *The New Yorker*, for example, is in the top 30 of all magazines in revenues but does not even make the top-100 list in circulation.

## TOP 100 U.S. MAGAZINES, BY CIRCULATION, 1990

| Rank | Magazine | Combined circulation | Percent change 1989–90 |
|---|---|---|---|
| **Total, Top 100** | | **261,688,396** | **–1.3%** |
| 1. | Modern Maturity | 22,430,894 | 4.7% |
| 2. | NRTA/AARP Bulletin | 22,103,887 | 4.8 |
| 3. | Reader's Digest | 16,264,547 | –0.5 |
| 4. | TV Guide | 15,604,267 | –1.7 |
| 5. | National Geographic Magazine | 10,189,703 | –6.4 |
| 6. | Better Homes and Gardens | 8,007,222 | 0.0 |
| 7. | Family Circle | 5,431,779 | –0.6 |
| 8. | Good Housekeeping | 5,152,521 | 0.0 |
| 9. | McCall's | 5,020,127 | –1.4 |
| 10. | Ladies' Home Journal | 5,001,739 | –0.7 |
| 11. | Woman's Day | 4,802,842 | 2.1 |
| 12. | Time | 4,094,935 | –5.6 |
| 13. | Redbook | 3,907,221 | 0.2 |
| 14. | National Enquirer | 3,803,607 | –7.3 |
| 15. | Playboy | 3,488,006 | 2.0 |
| 16. | Star | 3,431,453 | –4.4 |
| 17. | Sports Illustrated | 3,220,016 | –6.0 |
| 18. | Newsweek | 3,211,958 | 1.0 |
| 19. | People Weekly | 3,208,668 | –1.9 |
| 20. | Prevention | 3,002,108 | –3.6 |
| 21. | The American Legion Magazine | 2,956,342 | 4.5 |
| 22. | First For Women | 2,649,810 | –24.5 |
| 23. | Cosmopolitan | 2,600,971 | –3.7 |
| 24. | AAA World | 2,573,424 | — |
| 25. | Southern Living | 2,341,074 | 1.0 |
| 26. | U.S. News & World Report | 2,311,534 | 4.6 |
| 27. | Smithsonian | 2,234,706 | –4.6 |
| 28. | Glamour | 2,156,157 | –3.1 |
| 29. | Field & Stream | 2,016,298 | 0.0 |
| 30. | V.F.W. Magazine | 2,013,256 | 1.7 |
| 31. | NEA Today | 1,978,641 | 3.1 |
| 32. | Motorland | 1,957,583 | 4.9 |
| 33. | Money | 1,915,053 | 4.4 |
| 34. | Home & Away | 1,877,949 | 4.8 |
| 35. | Life | 1,844,482 | 5.4 |
| 36. | Ebony | 1,810,668 | 1.0 |
| 37. | Popular Science | 1,807,540 | –0.6 |
| 38. | Country Living | 1,803,867 | 0.1 |
| 39. | Seventeen | 1,772,362 | 0.4 |
| 40. | Parents Magazine | 1,743,424 | –0.5 |
| 41. | 1,001 Home Ideas | 1,662,102 | 3.7 |
| 42. | Popular Mechanics | 1,651,064 | 0.0 |
| 43. | Discovery | 1,644,044 | 2.3 |
| 44. | Penthouse | 1,612,574 | –11.9 |
| 45. | Outdoor Life | 1,512,464 | 0.3 |
| 46. | Woman's World | 1,505,312 | –3.5 |
| 47. | Adventure Road | 1,493,624 | 1.0 |
| 48. | The Elks Magazine | 1,472,652 | –1.9 |
| 49. | Soap Opera Digest | 1,447,041 | –1.3 |
| 50. | Sunset, The Magazine of Western Living | 1,409,587 | 1.0 |
| 51. | Bon Appetit | 1,397,559 | 3.1% |
| 52. | The American Rifleman | 1,378,042 | –4.5 |
| 53. | Golf Digest | 1,357,433 | –0.5 |
| 54. | Boys' Life | 1,357,173 | 1.7 |
| 55. | New Woman | 1,340,540 | –3.6 |
| 56. | The Family Handyman | 1,331,696 | –3.7 |
| 57. | US | 1,326,410 | –2.9 |
| 58. | Sesame Street Magazine | 1,249,565 | 1.1 |
| 59. | Rolling Stone | 1,229,280 | 1.0 |
| 60. | The American Hunter | 1,226,402 | –11.2 |
| 61. | Vogue | 1,215,767 | –2.6 |
| 62. | Home Mechanix | 1,215,178 | 0.5 |
| 63. | The Workbasket | 1,215,175 | –6.2 |
| 64. | Globe | 1,200,484 | –9.7 |
| 65. | Mademoiselle | 1,178,116 | 1.4 |
| 66. | 'Teen | 1,175,037 | 6.8 |
| 67. | Changing Times | 1,139,738 | –12.3 |
| 68. | Discover | 1,121,855 | 6.5 |
| 69. | Travel & Leisure | 1,117,412 | 0.2 |
| 70. | Self | 1,100,897 | –9.3 |
| 71. | Golf Magazine | 1,088,999 | 6.8 |
| 72. | Organic Gardening | 1,034,842 | –0.2 |
| 73. | Country Living | 1,029,342 | 6.9 |
| 74. | Michigan Living | 1,027,443 | 0.1 |
| 75. | Weight Watchers Magazine | 1,020,248 | 1.2 |
| 76. | YM | 1,008,522 | 4.3 |
| 77. | Yankee | 1,000,784 | –0.2 |
| 78. | House Beautiful | 985,129 | 4.8 |
| 79. | Scouting | 980,638 | 3.3 |
| 80. | Jet | 968,545 | 12.5 |
| 81. | Car and Driver | 959,395 | 2.7 |
| 82. | Home | 942,159 | 1.8 |
| 83. | Sport | 925,984 | –3.6 |
| 84. | Cooking Light | 924,499 | 34.1 |
| 85. | Popular Photography | 911,117 | –1.8 |
| 86. | Gourmet | 899,549 | 11.4 |
| 87. | Business Week (North America) | 894,043 | 0.5 |
| 88. | Motor Trend | 892,930 | 9.2 |
| 89. | Health | 878,994 | –19.3 |
| 90. | Hot Rod | 876,938 | –3.8 |
| 91. | Consumers Digest | 873,704 | 7.4 |
| 92. | Workbench | 862,985 | –5.1 |
| 93. | Nation's Business | 860,120 | 0.2 |
| 94. | Essence | 850,607 | –0.1 |
| 95. | Omni | 838,420 | –9.4 |
| 96. | Elle | 836,556 | 1.2 |
| 97. | American Legion Auxiliary National News | 828,027 | 12.5 |
| 98. | Food & Wine | 818,165 | –0.7 |
| 99. | Weekly World News | 816,676 | –3.8 |
| 100. | American Health—Fitness Body & Mind | 806,172 | –19.4 |

**Note**: Leading Audit Bureau of Circulation magazines by average paid combined circulation per issue, second six months of 1990. **Source**: Magazine Publishers of America, 1991.

## TOP 50 MAGAZINES RANKED BY REVENUES, 1990

| Rank | Magazine | Revenues | Percent change 1989–90 |
|---|---|---|---|
| 1. | Time | $381,852,410 | 2.3% |
| 2. | People Weekly | 345,791,839 | 6.0 |
| 3. | Sports Illustrated | 335,690,172 | –0.3 |
| 4. | TV Guide | 320,308,116 | –0.8 |
| 5. | Newsweek | 253,253,187 | –1.0 |
| 6. | Business Week | 245,886,035 | –5.6 |
| 7. | Forbes | 169,455,846 | 7.5 |
| 8. | Good Housekeeping | 163,240,991 | 10.3 |
| 9. | Fortune | 161,774,642 | –3.3 |
| 10. | U.S. News & World Report | 159,338,356 | 4.2 |
| 11. | Better Homes & Gardens | 143,544,885 | –5.8 |
| 12. | Family Circle | 137,273,222 | –10.4 |
| 13. | Cosmopolitan | 129,913,724 | 3.3 |
| 14. | Ladies' Home Journal | 109,404,461 | 4.5 |
| 15. | Reader's Digest | 108,592,492 | –4.4 |
| 16. | Vogue | 108,081,835 | 7.0 |
| 17. | Woman's Day | 99,101,166 | –26.9 |
| 18. | Glamour | 94,877,938 | 6.8 |
| 19. | Rolling Stone | 76,037,112 | 7.0 |
| 20. | Money | 75,779,599 | –4.9 |
| 21. | Redbook | 75,689,905 | 0.9 |
| 22. | McCall's | 73,433,029 | –1.8 |
| 23. | Elle | 67,721,832 | 8.1 |
| 24. | Golf Digest | 66,702,279 | 4.2 |
| 25. | Southern Living | 63,930,677 | 4.4 |
| 26. | The New Yorker | 61,232,176 | 13.3 |
| 27. | Parents | 59,636,244 | –1.2 |
| 28. | Travel & Leisure | 58,631,236 | 9.9 |
| 29. | Bride's | 56,176,029 | 1.6 |
| 30. | Modern Maturity | 51,254,738 | 8.0 |
| 31. | Vanity Fair | 49,894,916 | 19.9 |
| 32. | Car and Driver | 49,674,355 | –8.5 |
| 33. | Gentlemen's Quarterly | 49,573,439 | –0.7 |
| 34. | Mademoiselle | 48,951,987 | 0.5 |
| 35. | Architectural Digest | 48,183,194 | 4.6 |
| 36. | Inc. | 48,085,758 | 3.1 |
| 37. | Playboy | 47,814,982 | 2.8 |
| 38. | Self | 46,849,170 | 10.7 |
| 39. | Sunset | 45,916,902 | 3.5 |
| 40. | Life | 45,883,293 | –19.3 |
| 41. | Country Living | 44,414,547 | 4.2 |
| 42. | New York Magazine | 43,434,140 | –8.4 |
| 43. | Modern Bride | 41,107,014 | 6.9 |
| 44. | Smithsonian | 40,994,931 | –6.3 |
| 45. | Esquire | 39,414,127 | 3.7 |
| 46. | Town & Country | 39,218,588 | 8.1 |
| 47. | National Geographic | 38,473,200 | 9.1 |
| 48. | Ebony | 37,716,243 | –0.8 |
| 49. | Golf | 37,554,994 | 14.5 |
| 50. | Harper's Bazaar | 37,433,759 | 4.1 |

### MAGAZINE SUPPLEMENTS

| Rank | Magazine | Revenues | Percent change 1989–90 |
|---|---|---|---|
| 1. | Parade | $355,170,972 | 12.9% |
| 2. | New York Times Magazine | 128,146,797 | 1.0 |
| 3. | USA Weekend | 119,042,581 | 14.6 |
| 4. | Los Angeles Times | 26,392,772 | –11.0 |

**Source**: Publishers Information Bureau, 1991.

## Books

### NEW BOOKS PUBLISHED, BY SUBJECT, 1980–90

| Subject | 1980 | 1985 | 1990[1] |
|---|---|---|---|
| Agriculture | 461 | 536 | 469 |
| Art | 1,691 | 1,545 | 1,320 |
| Biography | 1,891 | 1,953 | 1,886 |
| Business | 1,185 | 1,518 | 1,361 |
| Education | 1,011 | 1,085 | 892 |
| Fiction | 2,835 | 5,105 | 5,103 |
| General works | 1,643 | 2,905 | 1,939 |
| History | 2,220 | 2,327 | 2,227 |
| Home economics | 879 | 1,228 | 814 |
| Juvenile | 2,859 | 3,801 | 4,735 |
| Language | 529 | 632 | 504 |
| Law | 1,102 | 1,349 | 915 |
| Literature | 1,686 | 1,964 | 1,991 |
| Medicine | 3,292 | 3,579 | 2,939 |
| Music | 357 | 364 | 335 |
| Philosophy/ psychology | 1,429 | 1,559 | 1,776 |
| Poetry and drama | 1,179 | 1,166 | 992 |
| Religion | 2,055 | 2,564 | 2,151 |
| Science | 3,109 | 3,304 | 2,795 |
| Sociology, economics | 7,152 | 7,441 | 6,835 |
| Sports, recreation | 971 | 1,154 | 905 |
| Technology | 2,337 | 2,526 | 2,251 |
| Travel | 504 | 465 | 586 |
| **Total** | **42,377** | **50,070[2]** | **45,718** |

**Note**: Comprises new books (published for the first time), and new editions (with changes in text or format). Excludes government publications, books sold only by subscription, dissertations, periodicals, quarterlies, and pamphlets under 49 pages. 1. Preliminary. 2. Increase is due largely to a major improvement in the recording of paperbound books between 1980 and 1985. **Source**: R.R. Bowker Co., New York, N.Y., *Publishers Weekly*. (Copyright by Reed Publishing, 1991, used with permission.)

### NUMBER AND VALUE OF U.S. BOOKS SOLD, 1985–90 (in millions)

| Type of publication and market area | Publishers units | | Consumer expenditures | |
|---|---|---|---|---|
| | 1985 | 1990 | 1985 | 1990 |
| **TYPE OF PUBLICATION** | | | | |
| Trade | 576.6 | 730.7 | $3,660.0 | $6,497.8 |
| Adult trade | 376.7 | 420.4 | 2,871.2 | 4,776.8 |
| Juvenile trade | 199.9 | 310.3 | 788.8 | 1,721.0 |
| Religious | 141.5 | 137.7 | 925.6 | 1,361.9 |
| Professional | 125.7 | 148.6 | 2,043.4 | 2,956.8 |
| Book clubs | 132.9 | 110.6 | 581.5 | 704.7 |
| Mail order publications | 125.2 | 142.6 | 650.1 | 751.7 |
| Mass market paperback | 429.8 | 488.8 | 1,244.5 | 1,775.4 |
| University press | 16.1 | 15.8 | 172.8 | 284.1 |
| ELHI[1] | 245.0 | 218.7 | 1,415.3 | 1,947.9 |
| College | 120.2 | 149.7 | 1,575.3 | 2,319.0 |
| Subscription reference | 1.0 | 1.1 | 342.0 | 443.6 |
| **All books** | **1,914.0** | **2,144.3** | **$12,610.2** | **$19,042.9** |
| Hardbound total[2] | 605.2 | 721.9 | 6,976.6 | 10,593.9 |
| Paperbound total[2] | 1,182.6 | 1,278.7 | 4,641.8 | 7,253.7 |
| **MARKET AREA** | | | | |
| Domestic | 1,787.7 | 2,005.0 | $12,610.2 | $19,042.9 |
| General retailers | 829.1 | 1,009.8 | 5,102.6 | 8,465.4 |
| Colleges | 225.1 | 254.6 | 2,308.9 | 3,403.2 |
| Libraries and institutions | 79.8 | 88.4 | 1,090.1 | 1,591.8 |
| School | 259.8 | 244.1 | 1,685.3 | 2,365.0 |
| Direct to consumer | 299.9 | 304.1 | 2,213.5 | 2,901.0 |
| Other | 94.2 | 104.1 | 209.8 | 316.5 |
| Export | 126.2 | 139.4 | N.A. | N.A. |
| **Total** | **1,914.0** | **2,144.3** | **$12,610.2** | **$19,042.9** |

**Note**: Includes all titles released by publishers in the United States, and imports that appear under the imprint of American publishers. Multivolume sets such as encyclopedias are counted as one unit. 1. Elementary and high school textbooks. 2. Does not include mail order or subscription reference publications. **Source**: Book Industry Study Group, Inc., *Book Industry Trends*, annual (1991), reprinted by permission.

> ## "Libraries should be open to all—except the censor."
> —John F. Kennedy, *Saturday Review* (Oct. 29, 1960).

### BEST-SELLERS IN AMERICA, 1960–90

**Year  Fiction**

1960 *Advise and Consent*, Allen Drury
1961 *The Agony and the Ecstasy*, Irving Stone
1962 *Ship of Fools*, Katherine Anne Porter
1963 *The Shoes of the Fisherman*, Morris L. West
1965 *The Source*, James A. Michener
1966 *Valley of the Dolls*, Jacqueline Susann
1967 *The Arrangement*, Elia Kazan
1968 *Airport*, Arthur Hailey
1969 *Portnoy's Complaint*, Philip Roth
1970 *Love Story*, Erich Segal
1971 *Wheels*, Arthur Hailey
1972 *Jonathan Livingston Seagull*, Richard Bach
1973 *Jonathan Livingston Seagull*, Richard Bach
1974 *Centennial*, James A. Michener
1975 *Ragtime*, E. L. Doctorow
1976 *Trinity*, Leon Uris
1977 *The Silmarillion*, J.R.R. Tolkien
1978 *Chesapeake*, James A. Michener
1979 *The Matarese Circle*, Robert Ludlum
1980 *The Covenant*, James Michener
1981 *Noble House*, James Clavell
1982 *E.T. The Extra-Terrestrial Storybook*, William Kotzwinkle
1983 *Return of the Jedi Storybook*, Joan D. Vinge

**Sources**: Alice Payne Hackett, *70 Years of Best Sellers*; *Publishers Weekly*.

**Year  Fiction**

1984 *The Talisman*, Stephen King, Peter Straub
1985 *The Mammoth Hunters*, Jean M. Auel
1986 *It*, Stephen King
1987 *Tommy Knocker*, Stephen King
1988 *The Cardinal of the Kremlin*, Tom Clancy
1989 *Clear and Present Danger*, Tom Clancy
1990 *The Plains of Passage*, Jean Auel

**Year  Nonfiction**

1960 *Folk Medicine*, D.C. Jarvis
1961 *The New English Bible: The New Testament*
1962 *Calories Don't Count*, Dr. Herman Taller
1963 *Happiness Is a Warm Puppy*, Charles M. Schulz
1965 *How To Be a Jewish Mother*, Dan Greenburg
1966 *How to Avoid Probate*, Norman F. Dacey
1967 *Death of a President*, William Manchester
1968 *Better Homes and Gardens New Cook Book*
1969 *American Heritage Dictionary of the English Language*, ed. William Morris
1970 *Everything You Wanted to Know About Sex but Were Afraid to Ask*, David Reuben, M.D.
1971 *The Sensuous Man*, "M."

**Year  Nonfiction**

1972 *The Living Bible*, Kenneth Taylor
1973 *The Living Bible*, Kenneth Taylor
1974 *The Total Woman*, Marabel Morgan
1975 *Angels: God's Secret Agents*, Billy Graham
1976 *The Final Days*, Bob Woodward, Carl Bernstein
1977 *Roots*, Alex Haley
1978 *If Life is a Bowl of Cherries—What Am I Doing in the Pits?* Erma Bombeck
1979 *Aunt Erma's Cope Book*, Erma Bombeck
1980 *Crisis Investing*, Douglas R. Casey
1981 *The Beverly Hills Diet*, Judy Mazel
1982 *Jane Fonda's Workout Book*, Jane Fonda
1983 *In Search of Excellence*, Thomas J. Peters, Robert H. Waterman, Jr.
1984 *Iacocca: An Autobiography*, Lee Iacocca with William Novak
1985 *Iacocca: An Autobiography*, Lee Iacocca with William Novak
1986 *Fatherhood*, Bill Cosby
1987 *Time Flies*, Bill Cosby
1988 *The Eight-Week Cholesterol Diet*, Robert Kowalski
1989 *All I Really Need to Know I Learned in Kindergarten*, Robert Fulghum
1990 *A Life on the Road*, Charles Kuralt

## THE ELECTRONIC MEDIA

### Television

### TOP 50 U.S. TV SHOWS, BY RATING

| Rank/Program | Date | Net-work | Rating |
|---|---|---|---|
| 1. M*A*S*H* Special | 2/28/83 | CBS | 60.2% |
| 2. Dallas | 11/21/80 | CBS | 53.3 |
| 3. Roots, part 8 | 1/30/77 | ABC | 51.1 |
| 4. Super Bowl XVI game | 1/24/82 | CBS | 49.1 |
| 5. Super Bowl XVII game | 1/30/83 | NBC | 48.6 |
| 6. Super Bowl XX game | 1/26/86 | NBC | 48.3 |
| 7. Gone with the Wind, pt. 1 | 11/7/76 | NBC | 47.7 |
| 8. Gone with the Wind, pt. 2 | 11/8/76 | NBC | 47.4 |
| 9. Super Bowl XII game | 1/15/78 | CBS | 47.2 |
| 10. Super Bowl XIII game | 1/21/79 | NBC | 47.1 |
| 11. Bob Hope Christmas Show | 1/15/70 | NBC | 46.6 |
| 12. Super Bowl XVIII game | 1/22/84 | CBS | 46.4 |
| 13. Super Bowl XIX game | 1/20/85 | ABC | 46.4 |
| 14. Super Bowl XIV game | 1/20/80 | CBS | 46.3 |
| 15. ABC Theater "The Day After" | 1/20/83 | ABC | 46.0 |
| 16. The Fugitive | 8/29/67 | ABC | 45.9 |
| 17. Roots, part 6 | 1/28/77 | ABC | 45.9 |
| 18. Super Bowl XXI game | 1/25/87 | CBS | 45.8 |
| 19. Roots, part 5 | 1/27/77 | ABC | 45.7 |
| 20. The Ed Sullivan Show | 2/9/64 | CBS | 45.3 |
| 21. Bob Hope Christmas Show | 1/14/71 | NBC | 45.0 |
| 22. Roots, part 3 | 1/25/77 | ABC | 44.8 |
| 23. Super Bowl XI game | 1/9/77 | NBC | 44.4 |
| 24. Super Bowl XV game | 1/25/81 | NBC | 44.4 |
| 25. Super Bowl VI game | 1/16/72 | CBS | 44.2 |
| 26. Roots, part 2 | 1/24/77 | ABC | 44.1 |
| 27. The Beverly Hillbillies | 1/8/64 | CBS | 44.0 |
| 28. The Ed Sullivan Show | 2/16/64 | CBS | 43.8 |
| 29. Roots, part 4 | 1/26/77 | ABC | 43.8 |
| 30. Super Bowl XXIII game | 1/22/89 | NBC | 43.5 |
| 31. Academy Awards | 4/7/70 | ABC | 43.4 |
| 32. Thorn Birds, part 3 | 3/29/83 | ABC | 43.2 |
| 33. Thorn Birds, part 4 | 3/30/83 | ABC | 43.1 |
| 34. NFC Championship game | 1/10/82 | CBS | 42.9 |
| 35. The Beverly Hillbillies | 1/15/64 | CBS | 42.8 |
| 36. Super Bowl VII game | 1/14/73 | NBC | 42.7 |
| 37. Thorn Birds, part 2 | 3/28/83 | ABC | 42.5 |
| 38. The Beverly Hillbillies | 2/26/64 | CBS | 42.4 |
| 39. Super Bowl IX game | 1/12/75 | NBC | 42.4 |
| 40. Cinderella | 2/22/65 | CBS | 42.3 |
| 41. Love Story (Sunday Night Movie) | 10/1/72 | ABC | 42.3 |
| 42. Airport (Movie Special) | 11/11/73 | ABC | 42.3 |
| 43. Super Bowl X game | 1/18/76 | CBS | 42.3 |
| 44. Roots, part 7 | 1/29/77 | ABC | 42.3 |
| 45. The Beverly Hillbillies | 3/25/64 | CBS | 42.2 |
| 46. The Beverly Hillbillies | 2/5/64 | CBS | 42.0 |
| 47. The Beverly Hillbillies | 1/29/64 | CBS | 41.9 |
| 48. Super Bowl XXII game | 1/31/88 | ABC | 41.9 |
| 49. Miss America Pageant | 9/9/61 | CBS | 41.8 |
| 50. The Beverly Hillbillies | 1/1/64 | CBS | 41.8 |

**Note:** As of Apr. 20, 1990; does not include programs broadcast on more than one network, e.g., the Apollo moon landing, or programs under 30 minutes scheduled duration. **Source:** Nielsen Media Research, 1990.

### TELEVISION FACTS, 1991

- TV is in **98.2%** of all U.S. households.
- Of households with TV, **98.1%** have color, while **64.5%** have two or more sets.
- Cable TV is in **58.9%** of all households; pay cable is at the **29.0%** level, and VCR penetration is up to **71.9%**.
- TV set sales continued to grow in 1989, topping the **23 million** mark for the first time.
- The number of commercial TV stations continued to grow. As of Jan. 1, 1990, there were **1,092 stations** on the air: 547 VHF, 545 UHF.
- At least one TV was on in each household an average of **7 hrs. and 1 min.** per day in 1989 (up about one full hour since 1971, when the average was 6 hrs. and 2 min.).

**Source:** Television Bureau of Advertising, 1991.

### TOP 10 TV SHOWS, 1990–91

| Rank/Program | Network | Rating[1] | Share[2] |
|---|---|---|---|
| 1. Cheers | NBC | 21.6 | 34 |
| 2. 60 Minutes | CBS | 20.5 | 34 |
| 3. Roseanne | ABC | 18.2 | 28 |
| 4. A Different World | NBC | 17.9 | 29 |
| 5. The Cosby Show | NBC | 17.4 | 28 |
| 6. NFL Monday Night Football | ABC | 17.2 | 30 |
| 7. America's Funniest Home Videos | ABC | 17.0 | 26 |
| 8. Murphy Brown | CBS | 16.9 | 26 |
| 9. America's Funniest People | ABC | 16.7 | 25 |
| 9. Designing Women | CBS | 16.7 | 26 |
| 9. Empty Nest | NBC | 16.7 | 30 |

**Note:** For the period from Sept. 17, 1990, to Apr. 14, 1991. 1. The percentage of all TV households tuned to a particular program. 2. The percentage of households using TVs at a given time tuned to a particular program. **Source:** Nielsen Media Research, 1991.

### MOST POPULAR TV SHOWS, BY DECADE

These charts are based on a show's average rating throughout each decade, and are thus an indication of both popularity and longevity.

| Decade and program | Network | Average rating | Decade and program | Network | Average rating |
|---|---|---|---|---|---|
| **1950–59** | | | **1960–69** | | |
| 1. A. Godfrey's Talent Scouts | CBS | 32.9% | 1. Bonanza | NBC | 29.6% |
| 2. I Love Lucy | CBS | 31.6 | 2. The Red Skelton Show | CBS | 26.4 |
| 3. You Bet Your Life | NBC | 30.1 | 3. The Andy Griffith Show | CBS | 22.4 |
| 4. Dragnet | NBC | 24.6 | 4. The Beverly Hillbillies | CBS | 21.9 |
| 5. The Jack Benny Show | CBS | 22.3 | 5. The Ed Sullivan Show | CBS | 21.7 |
| 6. A. Godfrey and Friends | CBS | 19.5 | 6. The Lucy Show/Here's Lucy | CBS | 21.3 |
| 7. Gunsmoke | CBS | 15.6 | 7. The Jackie Gleason Show | CBS | 16.5 |
| 8. The Red Skelton Show | NBC | 15.2 | 8. Bewitched | ABC | 14.8 |
| 9. December Bride | CBS | 13.8 | 9. Gomer Pyle | CBS | 13.4 |
| 10. I've Got a Secret | CBS | 12.9 | 10. Candid Camera | CBS | 11.2 |
| 11. $64,000 Question | CBS | 11.2 | 11. The Dick Van Dyke Show | CBS | 11.1 |
| 12. Disneyland | ABC | 10.8 | 12. The Danny Thomas Show | CBS | 10.7 |
| 13. The Ed Sullivan Show | CBS | 10.6 | 13. Family Affair | CBS | 9.8 |
| 14. Have Gun—Will Travel | CBS | 10.3 | 14. Laugh-In | NBC | 7.9 |
| 15. The Danny Thomas Show | CBS | 9.9 | 15. Rawhide | CBS | 7.5 |
| **1970–79** | | | **1980–89** | | |
| 1. All in the Family | CBS | 23.1% | 1. 60 Minutes | CBS | 23.5% |
| 2. M*A*S*H | CBS | 17.6 | 2. Dallas | CBS | 21.0 |
| 3. Hawaii Five-O | CBS | 16.5 | 3. The Cosby Show | NBC | 16.9 |
| 4. Happy Days | ABC | 15.9 | 4. Dynasty | ABC | 14.5 |
| 5. The Waltons | CBS | 14.0 | 5. Knots Landing | CBS | 14.2 |
| 6. The Mary Tyler Moore Show | CBS | 13.7 | 6. Cheers | NBC | 14.0 |
| 7. Sanford & Son | NBC | 13.4 | 7. Magnum, P.I. | CBS | 13.7 |
| 8. One Day at a Time | CBS | 11.4 | 8. Murder, She Wrote | CBS | 12.9 |
| 9. Three's Company | ABC | 10.8 | 9. Who's the Boss? | ABC | 12.2 |
| 10. 60 Minutes | CBS | 10.0 | 10. Family Ties | NBC | 11.8 |
| 11. Maude | CBS | 9.8 | 11. Falcon Crest | CBS | 11.6 |
| 12. Gunsmoke | CBS | 9.7 | 12. The Golden Girls | NBC | 11.0 |
| 13. Charlie's Angels | ABC | 9.6 | 13. Kate & Allie | CBS | 10.6 |
| 14. The Jeffersons | CBS | 9.4 | 14. Night Court | NBC | 9.8 |
| 15. Laverne & Shirley | ABC | 9.3 | 15. Newhart | CBS | 8.7 |

**Source:** Baseline II, Inc.; basic data, Nielsen Media Research.

## U.S. TV STATIONS AND HOUSEHOLDS WITH TV, 1950–91

| Year | Commercial TV stations on air | Households with TV ('000s) | Percent of U.S. households |
|---|---|---|---|
| 1950 | 98 | 3,800 | 9% |
| 1955 | 411 | 32,000 | 67 |
| 1960 | 515 | 45,200 | 86 |
| 1965 | 569 | 53,800 | 95 |
| 1970 | 677 | 60,100 | 96 |
| 1975 | 706 | 71,500 | 97 |
| 1980 | 734 | 77,800 | 98 |
| 1981 | 756 | 79,900 | 98 |
| 1982 | 777 | 81,500 | 98 |
| 1983 | 813 | 83,300 | 98 |
| 1984 | 841 | 83,800 | 98 |
| 1985 | 883 | 84,900 | 98 |
| 1986 | 919 | 85,900 | 98 |
| 1987 | 968 | 87,400 | 98 |
| 1988 | 1,028 | 88,600 | 98 |
| 1989[1] | 1,064 | 90,400 | 98 |
| 1990 | 1,092 | 92,100 | 98 |
| 1991 | N.A. | 92,100 | 98 |

**Note:** Includes commercial stations only. 1. TV household figures from 1989 include Alaska and Hawaii. **Sources:** Nielsen Media Research, 1991; *Television Digest* (1991).

## LONGEST-RUNNING NATIONAL NETWORK SERIES OF ALL TIME

| Program | Number of seasons | Years[1] |
|---|---|---|
| *Walt Disney* | 34 | 1954– |
| *The Ed Sullivan Show* | 24 | 1948–71 |
| *60 Minutes* | 22 | 1968– |
| *Gunsmoke* | 20 | 1955–75 |
| *The Red Skelton Show* | 20 | 1951–71 |
| *Meet the Press* | 18 | 1947–65 |
| *What's My Line?* | 18 | 1950–67 |
| *I've Got a Secret* | 17 | 1952–76 |
| *Lassie* | 17 | 1954–71 |
| *The Lawrence Welk Show* | 17 | 1955–71 |

**Note:** Includes prime-time (6–11 p.m.) shows only; sports broadcasts and movie series are not included. 1. These dates reflect the first and last broadcasts of each show. Programs did not necessarily run continuously throughout this period. **Source:** Baseline II, Inc., 1991.

## Cable Television

Cable television was originally designed as a means of improving TV reception in some rural areas. In the 1960s operators realized that viewers were willing to pay for commercial-free programming, but their efforts to capitalize on the idea were hampered by stringent Federal Communications Commission restrictions. Not until 1975, when RCA put its first communications satellite into operation, did the industry really bloom. Under the name Home Box Office, the company started to transmit programming that could be received by independent operators around the country and then relayed to subscribers at minimal cost. With the dismissal of most of the FCC's regulations by a federal court in 1977, the door was opened for the development of what is now a multibillion-dollar industry.

## TOP 10 CABLE TELEVISION NETWORKS, 1990

| Rank/Network | Subscribers ('000s) | Number of systems | Launch date | Content |
|---|---|---|---|---|
| 1. Cable News Network (CNN) | 58,900 | 10,748 | 1980 | 24-hour news, special-interest reports |
| 2. Entertainment and Sports Programming Network (ESPN) | 58,800 | 24,000 | 1979 | Sports events, business news |
| 3. Superstation TBS | 57,600 | 14,815 | 1976 | Movies, sports, original and syndicated shows |
| 4. USA Network | 56,700 | 10,100 | 1980 | Sports, family entertainment |
| 5. Music Television (MTV) | 56,600 | 6,405 | 1981 | Music videos, concerts, interviews |
| 6. The Discovery Channel | 55,800 | 9,326 | 1985 | Nonfiction, nature, science |
| 7. Nickelodeon/Nick at Nite | 55,500 | 8,668 | 1979 | Children's programming, young adults |
| 8. Turner Network Television (TNT) | 54,600 | 7,208 | 1988 | Movies, sports, children's programming |
| 9. The Nashville Network (TNN) | 54,000 | 12,329 | 1983 | Country music, talk shows, sports |
| 10. Cable Satellite Public Affairs Network (C-SPAN) | 54,000 | 4,081 | 1979 | Public affairs |

**Source:** National Cable Television Assn., *Cable TV Developments* (Aug. 1991).

## BASIC CABLE TV SYSTEMS AND SUBSCRIBERS, 1952–91

| Year | Number of systems[1] | Subscribers ('000s) | Percent of U.S. households with TV |
|---|---|---|---|
| 1952 | 70 | 14 | 0.1% |
| 1955 | 400 | 150 | 0.5 |
| 1960 | 640 | 650 | 1.4 |
| 1965 | 1,325 | 1,300 | 2.3 |
| 1970 | 2,490 | 3,900 | 6.7 |
| 1975 | 3,506 | 8,600 | 12.6 |
| 1980 | 4,225 | 15,200 | 19.9 |
| 1981 | 4,375 | 17,830 | 22.3 |
| 1982 | 4,825 | 24,290 | 29.8 |
| 1983 | 5,600 | 28,320 | 34.0 |
| 1984 | 6,200 | 32,930 | 39.3 |
| 1985 | 6,600 | 36,340 | 42.8 |
| 1986 | 7,500 | 39,160 | 45.6 |
| 1987 | 7,900 | 41,690 | 47.7 |
| 1988 | 8,500 | 43,790 | 49.4 |
| 1989 | 9,050 | 47,770 | 52.8 |
| 1990 | 9,612 | 51,900 | 56.4 |
| 1991 | 10,704 | 55,560 | 58.5 |

1. As of April 1. **Sources:** A.C. Nielsen, 1991; *TV & Cable Fact Book* (1991).

## TOP 5 PAY-CABLE TELEVISION SERVICES, 1990

| Rank/Network | Subscribers ('000s) | Content |
|---|---|---|
| 1. Home Box Office | 17,300 | Movies, variety, sports, documentaries |
| 2. Showtime | 6,500 | Movies, variety, comedy specials |
| 3. Cinemax | 6,400 | Movies, comedy, music specials |
| 4. The Disney Channel | 5,000 | Movies, cartoons |
| 5. The Movie Channel | 3,500 | Movies, film festivals |

**Source:** National Cable Television Assoc., *National Cable Network Directory* (1991).

## PAY-CABLE SUBSCRIBERS, 1975–90

| Year | Pay-cable households ('000s) | Percent of U.S. TV households |
|---|---|---|
| 1975 | 140 | 0.2% |
| 1976 | 470 | 0.7 |
| 1977 | 980 | 1.4 |
| 1978 | 1,600 | 2.2 |
| 1979 | 3,100 | 4.2 |
| 1980 | 5,200 | 6.8 |
| 1981 | 8,100 | 10.1 |
| 1982 | 12,600 | 15.5 |
| 1983 | 16,160 | 19.4 |
| 1984 | 19,820 | 23.7 |
| 1985 | 21,840 | 25.7 |
| 1986 | 22,840 | 26.6 |
| 1987 | 22,850 | 26.1 |
| 1988 | 24,290 | 27.4 |
| 1989 | 26,100 | 28.9 |
| 1990 | 26,530 | 29.1 |

**Source:** Nielsen Media Research, 1991.

## Video

## TOP-RENTING PRERECORDED VIDEOS, 1990

| Rank/Title | Distributor |
|---|---|
| 1. *Look Who's Talking* | RCA/Columbia |
| 2. *When Harry Met Sally. . .* | Nelson Home Entertainment |
| 3. *Parenthood* | MCA/Universal |
| 4. *K-9* | MCA/Universal |
| 5. *Dead Poets Society* | Touchstone |
| 6. *Steel Magnolias* | RCA/Columbia |
| 7. *Sea of Love* | MCA/Universal |
| 8. *Turner & Hooch* | Touchstone |
| 9. *Black Rain* | Paramount |
| 10. *Internal Affairs* | Paramount |

**Source:** *Billboard* (1991).

## BEST-SELLING PRERECORDED VIDEOS, 1990

| Rank/Title | Distributor | Units sold ('000s) |
|---|---|---|
| 1. *The Little Mermaid* | Disney | 9,000 |
| 2. *Teenage Mutant Ninja Turtles* | LIVE | 8,800 |
| 3. *Peter Pan (animated)* | Disney | 7,000 |
| 4. *Pretty Woman* | Paramount | 6,200 |
| 5. *Honey, I Shrunk the Kids* | Disney | 5,800 |
| 6. *Indiana Jones and the Last Crusade* | Paramount | 5,500 |
| 7. *All Dogs Go to Heaven* | MGM/UA | 3,800 |
| 8. *Total Recall* | LIVE | 3,400 |
| 9. *Peter Pan (live-action)* | Good Times | 3,100 |
| 10. *Lethal Weapon II* | Warner | 3,000 |

**Source:** *Video Store* (1991).

## BEST-SELLING PRERECORDED VIDEOS OF ALL TIME

| Rank/Title | Distributor | Units sold (millions) |
|---|---|---|
| 1. *E.T.—The Extra-Terrestrial* | MCA | 15.1 |
| 2. *Batman* | Warner | 11.5 |
| 3. *Bambi* | Disney | 10.5 |
| 4. *The Little Mermaid* | Disney | 9.0 |
| 5. *Teenage Mutant Ninja Turtles* | LIVE | 8.8 |
| 6. *Who Framed Roger Rabbit* | Touchstone | 8.5 |
| 7. *Cinderella* | Disney | 7.6 |
| 8. *Peter Pan (animated)* | Disney | 7.0 |
| 9. *Pretty Woman* | Paramount | 6.2 |
| 10. *Honey, I Shrunk the Kids* | Disney | 5.8 |

**Note:** As of April 1991. **Source:** *Video Store* (1991).

## U.S. HOUSEHOLDS WITH VIDEO-CASSETTE RECORDERS, 1978–90

| Year | U.S. households with VCRs ('000s) | Percent of U.S. households with TVs |
|---|---|---|
| 1978 | 200 | 0.3% |
| 1979 | 400 | 0.5 |
| 1980 | 840 | 1.1 |
| 1981 | 1,440 | 1.8 |
| 1982 | 2,530 | 3.1 |
| 1983 | 4,580 | 5.5 |
| 1984 | 8,880 | 10.6 |
| 1985 | 17,600 | 20.8 |
| 1986 | 30,920 | 36.0 |
| 1987 | 42,560 | 48.7 |
| 1988 | 51,390 | 58.0 |
| 1989 | 58,400 | 64.6 |
| 1990 | 66,940 | 73.4 |

**Source:** Nielsen Media Research, 1991.

## Radio

According to statistics compiled by the Radio Advertising Bureau, 99% of all U.S. households have at least one radio. Of Americans over age 12, 96.3% listen to radio for an average of 2 hours and 29 minutes each workday. There are a total of 541.1 million radios in the U.S., 19% more than in 1980, distributed as follows: 349.3 million are in homes, 131.4 million in cars, 37.8 million in trucks and vans, and 22.6 million in the workplace.

## U.S. RADIO STATIONS AND RADIO SALES, 1946–90

| Year | Radio stations on air[1] | Unit sales to dealers ('000s)[2] |
|---|---|---|
| 1946 | 961 | N.A. |
| 1950 | 2,773 | N.A. |
| 1955 | 3,211 | 7,327 |
| 1960 | 4,133 | 18.031 |
| 1965 | 5,249 | 31,689 |
| 1970 | 6,760 | 34,049 |
| 1975 | 7,744 | 25,276 |
| 1980 | 8,566 | 28,104 |
| 1981 | 9,361 | 31,476 |
| 1982 | 9,461 | 31,782 |
| 1983 | 9,678 | 39,496 |
| 1984 | 10,021 | 46,453 |
| 1985 | 10,359 | 21,575 |
| 1986 | 9,824 | 25,364 |
| 1987 | 10,074 | 28,110 |
| 1988 | 10,244 | 23,623 |
| 1989 | 10,674 | 25,254 |
| 1990 | 10,819 | 21,585 |

1. Includes AM and FM, commercial and noncommercial. 2. Includes table, clock, and portable—but not auto—radios. **Sources:** National Association of Broadcasters; Electronic Industries Assn., 1991.

## U.S. COMMERCIAL RADIO STATIONS, BY FORMAT, 1989–90

| Format | 1989 | 1990 |
|---|---|---|
| Country | 2,304 | 2,314 |
| Adult contemporary | 1,965 | 1,898 |
| Golden oldies | 690 | 729 |
| Contemporary hits | 740 | 705 |
| Religious | 676 | 661 |
| Nostalgia | 464 | 457 |
| News/talk | 357 | 404 |
| Album-oriented rock | 305 | 339 |
| Easy listening | 331 | 268 |
| Spanish | 213 | 214 |
| Urban contemporary | 191 | 191 |
| Soft contemporary | 150 | 182 |
| Classic rock | 121 | 127 |
| Black/R&B | 87 | 87 |
| Variety | 71 | 66 |
| Business news | 31 | 57 |
| Classical | 50 | 51 |
| News | 28 | 40 |
| Ethnic | 38 | 34 |
| New age | 28 | 31 |
| Jazz | 30 | 28 |
| Educational | 5 | 2 |
| **Total** | **8,875** | **8,945** |

**Note:** Includes AM and FM stations. **Source:** Radio Information Center, New York, 1991.

## Film

## U.S. FILM BOX-OFFICE RECEIPTS, ADMISSIONS, AND ADMISSION CHARGES, 1926–90

| Year | Box office receipts (millions) Current dollars | Box office receipts (millions) Constant dollars[1] | Admissions ('000s) | Average admission charge |
|---|---|---|---|---|
| 1926 | $720.0 | $4,621.0 | 2,600,000 | N.A. |
| 1930 | 732.0 | 4,979.4 | 4,680,000 | N.A. |
| 1935 | 566.0 | 4,693.3 | 3,900,000 | $0.24 |
| 1940 | 735.0 | 5,964.0 | 4,160,000 | 0.24 |
| 1945 | 1,450.0 | 9,151.1 | 4,680,000 | 0.35 |
| 1950 | 1,376.0 | 6,486.0 | 3,120,000 | 0.53 |
| 1955 | 1,326.0 | 5,620.7 | 3,392,000 | 0.50 |
| 1960 | 951.0 | 3,649.8 | 2,080,000 | 0.69 |
| 1965 | 927.0 | 3,343.1 | 2,288,000 | 1.01 |
| 1970 | 1,162.0 | 3,402.1 | 920,400 | 1.55 |
| 1975 | 2,115.0 | 4,465.9 | 988,000 | 2.05 |
| 1980 | 2,748.5 | 3,789.2 | 1,021,500 | 2.69 |
| 1981 | 2,965.6 | 3,706.2 | 1,060,000 | 2.78 |
| 1982 | 3,452.7 | 4,064.5 | 1,175,400 | 2.94 |
| 1983 | 3,766.0 | 4,925.4 | 1,196,900 | 3.15 |
| 1984 | 4,030.6 | 4,406.9 | 1,199,100 | 3.36 |
| 1985 | 3,749.4 | 3,958.5 | 1,056,100 | 3.55 |
| 1986 | 3,778.0 | 3,915.9 | 1,017,200 | 3.71 |
| 1987 | 4,252.9 | 4,252.9 | 1,088,500 | 3.91 |
| 1988 | 4,458.4 | 4,282.7 | 1,084,800 | 4.11 |
| 1989 | 5,033.4 | 4,611.2 | 1,132,500 | 4.45 |
| 1990 | 5,021.8 | 4,354.8 | 1,057,900 | 4.75 |

1. 1987. **Sources:** Baseline II, Inc., 1991; Motion Picture Association of America, 1991; U.S. Dept. of Commerce, *Film Daily Yearbook* (annual).

## MOST POPULAR FILMS, BY DECADE

| Title | Year | Director | Rental (millions) |
|---|---|---|---|
| **Pre-1930** | | | |
| *The Birth of a Nation* | 1915 | D.W. Griffith | $10.0 |
| *The Big Parade* | 1925 | K. Vidor | 5.5 |
| *The Singing Fool* | 1928 | L. Bacon | 4.0 |
| **1930–39** | | | |
| *Gone with the Wind* | 1939 | V. Fleming | $77.6 |
| *Snow White and the Seven Dwarfs* | 1937 | (Animated) | 62.8 |
| *King Kong* | 1933 | M. Cooper | 5.0 |
| *The Wizard of Oz* | 1939 | V. Fleming | 4.5 |
| *San Francisco* | 1936 | W.S. Van Dyke | 4.0 |
| **1940–49[1]** | | | |
| *Cinderella* | 1949 | (Animated) | $38.5 |
| *Pinocchio* | 1940 | (Animated) | 32.9 |
| *Song of the South* | 1946 | H. Foster/ W. Jackson | 29.2 |
| *Fantasia* | 1940 | (Animated) | 28.5 |
| *Bambi* | 1942 | (Animated) | 28.4 |

## MOST POPULAR FILMS, BY DECADE

| Title | Year | Director | Rental (millions) |
|---|---|---|---|
| **1950–59** | | | |
| The Ten Command-ments | 1956 | C.B. DeMille | $43.0 |
| Lady and the Tramp | 1955 | (Animated) | 40.2 |
| Ben Hur | 1959 | W. Wyler | 36.7 |
| Around the World in 80 Days | 1956 | M. Anderson | 23.1 |
| Sleeping Beauty | 1959 | (Animated) | 21.5 |
| **1960–69** | | | |
| The Sound of Music | 1965 | R. Wise | $79.7 |
| Doctor Zhivago | 1965 | D. Lean | 47.1 |
| Butch Cassidy and the Sundance Kid | 1969 | G.R. Hill | 46.0 |
| Mary Poppins | 1964 | R. Stevenson | 45.0 |
| The Graduate | 1968 | M. Nichols | 43.4 |
| **1970–79** | | | |
| Star Wars | 1977 | G. Lucas | $193.50 |
| Jaws | 1975 | S. Spielberg | 129.50 |
| Grease | 1978 | R. Kleiser | 96.30 |
| The Exorcist | 1973 | W. Friedkin | 89.00 |
| The Godfather | 1972 | F.F. Coppola | 86.30 |
| Superman | 1978 | R. Donner | 82.80 |
| Close Encounters of the Third Kind | 1977 | S. Spielberg | 82.80 |
| Saturday Night Fever | 1977 | J. Badham | 74.10 |
| The Sting | 1973 | G.R. Hill | 71.40 |
| American Graffiti | 1973 | G. Lucas | 55.10 |
| **1980–89** | | | |
| E.T.—The Extra-Terrestrial | 1982 | S. Spielberg | $228.62 |
| Return of the Jedi | 1983 | R. Marquand | 168.00 |
| Batman | 1989 | T. Burton | 150.50 |
| The Empire Strikes Back | 1980 | J. Kershner | 141.60 |
| Ghostbusters | 1984 | I. Reitman | 128.30 |
| Raiders of the Lost Ark | 1981 | S. Spielberg | 115.60 |
| Indiana Jones and the Last Crusade | 1989 | S. Spielberg | 115.50 |
| Indiana Jones and the Temple of Doom | 1984 | S. Spielberg | 109.00 |
| Beverly Hills Cop | 1984 | M. Brest | 108.00 |
| Back to the Future | 1985 | R. Zemeckis | 104.41 |

1. All films listed for this decade were made by Disney studios and have been rereleased on a regular basis ever since. Their dominance on this chart is partly due to the fact that they are "continually" generating revenue. **Source:** *Variety.*

## 20 TOP-GROSSING FEATURE FILMS, 1990

| Rank/Title | Distributor | Box-office gross (millions) |
|---|---|---|
| 1. Ghost | Paramount | $206.1 |
| 2. Pretty Woman | BV/Touchstone | 178.4 |
| 3. Home Alone | 20th Century Fox | 152.1 |
| 4. Teenage Mutant Ninja Turtles | New Line | 133.1 |
| 5. The Hunt for Red October | Paramount | 120.7 |
| 6. Total Recall | Tri-Star | 118.3 |
| 7. Die Hard 2 | 20th Century Fox | 115.3 |
| 8. Driving Miss Daisy | Warner Bros. | 105.0 |
| 9. Dick Tracy | BV/Touchstone | 103.7 |
| 10. Back to the Future III | Universal | 86.5 |
| 11. Presumed Innocent | Warner Bros. | 86.0 |
| 12. Days of Thunder | Paramount | 82.7 |
| 13. Another 48 Hrs. | Paramount | 80.8 |
| 14. Bird on a Wire | Universal | 70.2 |
| 15. Born on the Fourth of July | Universal | 69.1 |
| 16. Dances With Wolves | Orion | 61.6 |
| 17. Flatliners | Columbia | 61.2 |
| 18. Three Men and a Little Lady | BV/Touchstone | 54.0 |
| 19. Arachnophobia | BV/Hollywood | 53.1 |
| 20. Problem Child | Universal | 50.3 |

**Note:** As of Jan. 3, 1991. Box office gross represents total receipts from all North American ticket sales. **Source:** Baseline II, Inc., 1991.

## The Recording Industry

Prerecorded cassettes accounted for 51% of unit disc/tape sales in 1990 and have been the most popular format for recorded music since 1983. The success of the format is undoubtedly linked to that of the personal cassette player, first introduced by the Sony Corporation in 1979. Sony estimated 1988 sales of its popular "Walkman" model at 10 million units. Compact disc shipments outstripped those of LPs for the first time in 1988.

## U.S. SHIPMENTS OF SINGLES, LPs, CDs, AND CASSETTES, 1975–90
(in thousands)

| Year | Singles | LPs/EPs | CDs | Cassettes |
|---|---|---|---|---|
| 1975 | 164,000 | 257,000 | N.A. | 16,200 |
| 1976 | 190,000 | 273,000 | N.A. | 21,800 |
| 1977 | 190,000 | 344,000 | N.A. | 36,900 |
| 1978 | 190,000 | 341,300 | N.A. | 61,300 |
| 1979 | 195,500 | 318,300 | N.A. | 82,800 |
| 1980 | 164,300 | 322,800 | N.A. | 110,200 |
| 1981 | 154,700 | 295,200 | N.A. | 137,000 |
| 1982 | 137,200 | 243,900 | N.A. | 182,300 |
| 1983 | 124,800 | 209,600 | 800 | 236,800 |
| 1984 | 131,500 | 204,600 | 5,800 | 332,000 |
| 1985 | 120,700 | 167,000 | 22,600 | 339,100 |
| 1986 | 93,900 | 125,200 | 53,000 | 344,500 |
| 1987 | 82,000 | 107,000 | 102,100 | 410,000 |
| 1988 | 65,600 | 72,400 | 149,700 | 450,100 |
| 1989 | 36,600 | 34,600 | 207,200 | 446,200 |
| 1990 | 27,600 | 11,700 | 286,500 | 442,200 |

**Note:** Net figures (rounded) after returns from retailers. **Source:** Recording Industry Association of America, Inc., *Inside the Recording Industry: A Statistical Overview–1991 Update* (1991).

## THE ELECTRONIC HOME, 1991

| Facility | Percent of U.S. homes |
|---|---|
| Radio | 98% |
| Television set | 98 |
| Color television set | 96 |
| Audio system | 93 |
| Videocassette recorder (VCR) | 72 |
| Two or more television sets | 63 |
| Basic cable | 58 |
| Prerecorded videocassettes | 52 |
| Telephone answering device | 39 |
| One or more pay channels | 29 |
| Cordless telephone | 34 |
| Home computer | 28 |
| Compact disc player | 25 |
| Color TV with MTS[1] | 24 |
| Home alarm system | 15 |
| Camcorder | 13 |
| Projection television | 7 |
| LCD television | 6 |
| Satellite dish | 3 |

1. MTS = equipped for stereo sound. **Source:** Television Bureau of Advertising, 1991; Electronic Industries Assoc., 1991.

## SALES OF TELEPHONES, ANSWERING MACHINES, FAX MACHINES, AND MODEMS, 1983–91

Unit sales to dealers ('000s)

| Year | Cellular phones[1] | All other phones[1] | Answering machines[1] | Fax machines | Modems[2] |
|---|---|---|---|---|---|
| 1983 | N.A. | N.A. | 2,200 | 95.4 | 770 |
| 1984 | N.A. | N.A. | 3,000 | 115.5 | 960 |
| 1985 | N.A. | N.A. | 4,220 | 139.5 | 1,220 |
| 1986 | 280 | 22,200 | 6,450 | 218.5 | 1,380 |
| 1987 | 300 | 22,300 | 8,800 | 583.8 | 1,810 |
| 1988 | 500 | 23,400 | 11,100 | 1,260.9 | 2,020 |
| 1989 | 870 | 29,000 | 12,500 | 1,640.0 | 2,520 |
| 1990 | 2,100 | 27,250 | 11,000 | 1,800.0 | 2,740 |
| 1991 | 2,600 | 27,025 | 11,625 | N.A. | N.A. |

1. Estimated figures. 2. A modem is a device that transmits computer files and other information via phone lines. **Sources:** Electronic Industries Assn., 1991; Computer and Business Equipment Manufacturers Assn., 1991.

*"The new electronic interdependence recreates the world in the image of a global village."*

—Marshall McLuhan, *Guttenberg Galaxy* (1962).

# CRIME AND PUNISHMENT

National crime statistics are maintained by the Federal Bureau of Investigation (FBI) and the Bureau of Justice Statistics, two divisions of the U.S. Department of Justice. The FBI compiles annual figures from law enforcement agencies around the country that it publishes in *Uniform Crime Reports*. The most serious crimes—called crime index offenses—are divided into violent crimes (murder and non-negligent manslaughter, forcible rape, robbery, and aggravated assault) and property crimes (burglary, larceny and theft, motor vehicle theft, and arson).

Between 1980 and 1989, the number of crime index offenses committed grew 6.3%. After a high of 13.4 million crime index offenses in 1981, there was a steady decline until 1984, when there were only 11.8 million. From 1985 to 1989, however, crime grew at a fast rate, with 14.3 million crime index offenses reported in 1989. The rate of crime per 100,000 inhabitants followed similar trends. In 1980 there were 5,950 crime index offenses per 100,000 inhabitants, compared to 5,031 in 1984, and 5,741 in 1989. The number and rate of murders declined slightly from 1986 to 1987. But in 1988 and 1989 the number of murders rose 4.0% and the rate per 100,000 inhabitants rose 3.6%. The rate of serious crime by location was 7,232.0 per 100,000 inhabitants in cities, 4,984.1 per 100,000 in suburban counties, and 2,061.7 per 100,000 rural counties.

**Value of stolen property** While the taxpayer cost of fighting crime can be easily calculated, the emotional cost to victims and their families, and the overall burden to society,

## SERIOUS CRIME IN THE U.S., BY OFFENSE, 1980–89

| Serious crimes | Crime 1989 | | Change over 1988 | | Change over 1980 | |
|---|---|---|---|---|---|---|
| | Number | Rate per 100,000 | Percent | Rate per 100,000 | Percent | Rate per 100,000 |
| **VIOLENT CRIME** | **1,646,040** | **663.1** | **5.1%** | **4.1** | **22.4%** | **11.1** |
| Murder | 21,500 | 8.7 | 4.0 | 3.6 | –6.7 | –14.7 |
| Forcible rape | 94,500 | 38.1 | 2.2 | 1.3 | 13.9 | 3.5 |
| Robbery | 578,330 | 233.0 | 6.5 | 5.5 | 2.2 | –7.2 |
| Aggravated assault | 951,710 | 383.4 | 4.6 | 3.6 | 41.5 | 28.4 |
| **PROPERTY CRIME** | **12,605,400** | **5,077.9** | **2.0%** | **1.0** | **4.5%** | **–5.1** |
| Burglary | 3,168,400 | 1,276.3 | –1.6 | –2.5 | –16.5 | –24.2 |
| Larceny/theft | 7,872,400 | 3,171.3 | 2.2 | 1.2 | 10.3 | 0.1 |
| Motor vehicle theft | 1,564,800 | 630.4 | 9.2 | 8.1 | 38.3 | 25.5 |
| **Total serious crimes[1]** | **14,251,400** | **5,741.0** | **2.4** | **1.4** | **6.3** | **–3.5** |

**Note**: Does not include arson data due to insufficient data. 1. May not add to total due to rounding. **Source**: Federal Bureau of Investigation, *Uniform Crime Reports 1989: Crime in the United States* (1990).

is inestimable. The most obvious measurable cost is the value of property or goods stolen from the victim. In 1989, this amounted to $13.5 billion, of which only $5.3 billion, or 40%, was recovered. By type of property stolen, motor vehicle thefts had the highest cumulative value of $7.2 billion, an average value per incident of $5,284. The average value of property stolen during the course of murders and rapes was only $113 and $35, respectively. Of property recovered, motor vehicles ranked first by value—$4.9 billion—and as a percentage of property stolen—67%; televisions, radios, and stereos ranked last at 5%.

**Law enforcement personnel** As of October 1989, there were approximately 496,000 officers and 180,000 civilians employed in law enforcement nationwide. Cities over 250,000 employed roughly 3.5 law enforcement personnel per 1,000 inhabitants, compared with rates of 3.3 and 3.6 per 1,000 in suburban and rural counties respectively.

was responsible for 46% of all violent crime arrests and 59% of all property crime arrests.

By sex, 82% of all those arrested were males, who accounted for 79% of crime index offense arrests—89% of those for violent crimes, and 76% of those for property crime. Females were most often arrested for larceny/theft. This crime accounted for 19% of all arrests of women, and for 77% of all crime index offense arrests of women; 51% of all female larceny/theft arrestees were under 25 years old. Overall, female arrests in 1989 were up 8% from the year before, compared to a 6% increase for males.

By race, 67% of all those arrested were white, 31% were black, and 2% were of other races. Whites accounted for 61% of crime index offense arrests, 51% of violent crime arrests, and 64% of property crime arrests.

## VALUE OF PROPERTY STOLEN AND RECOVERED, BY TYPE, 1989

| | Value of property | | |
|---|---|---|---|
| Type of property | Stolen ('000s) | Recovered ('000s) | Percent recovered |
| Motor vehicles | $7,244,136 | $4,870,921 | 67.2% |
| Consumable goods | 83,479 | 11,732 | 14.1 |
| Livestock | 22,814 | 6,059 | 26.6 |
| Clothing and furs | 290,311 | 32,822 | 11.3 |
| Firearms | 112,167 | 12,503 | 11.1 |
| Household goods | 215,829 | 14,010 | 6.5 |
| Office equipment | 243,977 | 21,763 | 8.9 |
| Currency, notes, etc. | 773,440 | 56,604 | 7.3 |
| Jewelry and precious metals | 1,093,773 | 60,449 | 5.5 |
| Televisions, stereos, etc. | 1,022,005 | 50,596 | 5.0 |
| Miscellaneous | 2,371,462 | 207,256 | 8.7 |
| **Total[1]** | **$13,473,393** | **$5,344,716** | **39.7%** |

**Note**: Based on a survey of 12,636 law enforcement agencies representing 219,021,000 inhabitants. Data for 1989 were not available for Florida. 1. All totals and percentages calculated before rounding. **Source**: Federal Bureau of Investigation, *Uniform Crime Reports 1989: Crime in the United States* (1990).

## ARRESTS

U.S. law enforcement agencies made an estimated 14.3 million arrests in 1989 for all criminal infractions except traffic violations. This represents a rate of 5,625 arrests per 100,000 population. In cities with populations of 250,000 or more, the arrest rate was 7,792 per 100,000 (down 1.4% from 1988); for suburban counties, 4,339 per 100,000 (up 11.8%); and for rural counties, 3,501 per 100,000 (up 0.7%).

The total number of arrests increased 7% over 1988. Arrests of adults rose 7%, while arrests of juveniles (under age 18) increased 2%. For the eight crime index offenses (the most serious crimes), arrests increased 6% overall—7% for adults and 3% for juveniles. Arrests for violent crimes increased 9%, and 5% for property crimes.

By age, 5% of all people arrested were under age 15; 15% under 18; 30% under 21; and 46% under 25. Of people arrested for crime index offenses, 27% were under age 18, 42% under 21, and 56% under 25. The under-25 age group

## ARRESTS IN THE U.S., 1989

| | Arrests | |
|---|---|---|
| Crime | Number | Rate per 100,000 |
| Violent crime | 537,084 | 268.6 |
| Murder | 17,975 | 9.0 |
| Forcible rape | 30,544 | 15.3 |
| Robbery | 133,830 | 66.9 |
| Aggravated assault | 354,735 | 177.4 |
| Property crime | 1,808,414 | 904.4 |
| Burglary | 356,717 | 178.4 |
| Larceny/theft | 1,254,220 | 627.4 |
| Motor vehicle theft | 182,810 | 91.4 |
| Arson | 14,667 | 7.3 |
| All serious crimes[1] | 2,345,498 | 1,173.1 |
| Other crimes | 8,901,929 | 4,452.1 |
| **Total arrests** | **11,247,427** | **5,625.2** |

**Note**: Arrest figures based on information supplied by 10,503 agencies. 1. May not add to total due to rounding. **Source**: Federal Bureau of Investigation, *Uniform Crime Reports 1989: Crime in the United States* (1990).

## SERIOUS CRIME PER 100,000 POPULATION, BY STATE, 1989

| State | All serious crime | Murder | Forcible rape | Robbery | Aggra-vated assault | Burglary | Larceny/ theft | Motor vehicle theft |
|---|---|---|---|---|---|---|---|---|
| Ala. | 4,627.8 | 10.2 | 31.0 | 133.9 | 415.7 | 1,146.8 | 2,592.8 | 297.5 |
| Alaska | 4,779.9 | 8.0 | 52.9 | 67.6 | 369.3 | 826.9 | 3,000.2 | 455.0 |
| Ariz. | 8,059.7 | 6.7 | 36.2 | 139.0 | 417.7 | 1,667.2 | 5,106.1 | 686.9 |
| Ark. | 4,555.7 | 8.4 | 38.4 | 110.6 | 316.3 | 1,194.4 | 2,621.9 | 265.6 |
| Calif. | 6,763.4 | 10.9 | 41.2 | 331.8 | 593.8 | 1,412.3 | 3,346.5 | 1,026.9 |
| Colo. | 6,039.4 | 4.4 | 36.2 | 90.0 | 340.8 | 1,250.4 | 3,864.8 | 452.9 |
| Conn. | 5,270.0 | 5.9 | 27.5 | 214.8 | 263.6 | 1,236.0 | 2,824.4 | 697.8 |
| Del. | 4,865.2 | 5.1 | 84.5 | 138.8 | 328.1 | 902.2 | 3,015.5 | 391.1 |
| D.C. | 10,293.4 | 71.9 | 30.8 | 1,083.1 | 956.1 | 1,950.3 | 4,828.5 | 1,372.7 |
| Fla. | 8,804.5 | 11.1 | 49.7 | 404.0 | 644.6 | 2,282.8 | 4,606.6 | 805.7 |
| Ga. | 7,073.1 | 12.7 | 48.9 | 271.1 | 403.0 | 1,712.5 | 3,971.1 | 653.7 |
| Hawaii | 6,270.4 | 4.8 | 44.6 | 83.2 | 137.6 | 1,343.4 | 4,260.3 | 396.6 |
| Idaho | 3,931.0 | 2.6 | 23.3 | 15.0 | 213.8 | 872.1 | 2,645.5 | 158.8 |
| Ill. | 5,639.2 | 9.0 | 35.7[1] | 335.7 | 465.4 | 1,076.0 | 3,109.9 | 607.4 |
| Ind. | 4,440.0 | 6.3 | 32.3 | 101.4 | 266.5 | 969.1 | 2,673.2 | 391.1 |
| Iowa | 4,081.4 | 1.9 | 16.2 | 39.0 | 209.2 | 846.9 | 2,809.9 | 158.3 |
| Kans.[2] | 4,982.8 | 5.5 | 36.5 | 99.8 | 259.1 | 1,188.7 | 3,096.0 | 297.4 |
| Ky. | 3,317.1 | 7.9 | 24.6 | 76.1 | 248.3 | 819.1 | 1,921.4 | 219.8 |
| La. | 6,241.3 | 14.9 | 38.2 | 237.3 | 491.4 | 1,464.7 | 3,473.5 | 521.3 |
| Maine | 3,583.6 | 3.2 | 18.7 | 24.0 | 91.2 | 802.8 | 2,460.5 | 183.2 |
| Md. | 5,526.6 | 11.6 | 38.0 | 332.1 | 473.7 | 1,123.5 | 2,919.5 | 664.2 |
| Mass. | 5,136.0 | 4.3 | 31.8 | 202.6 | 436.3 | 1,065.5 | 2,484.8 | 910.7 |
| Mich. | 5,968.3 | 10.7 | 71.4 | 222.3 | 404.7 | 1,224.8 | 3,311.7 | 722.6 |
| Minn. | 4,383.2 | 2.5 | 31.3 | 94.8 | 159.6 | 896.9 | 2,818.1 | 379.9 |
| Miss. | 3,515.3 | 9.7 | 38.8 | 78.3 | 184.4 | 1,145.3 | 1,879.7 | 179.2 |
| Mo. | 5,127.1 | 7.9 | 30.8 | 195.0 | 398.9 | 1,135.8 | 2,835.2 | 523.6 |
| Mont. | 3,997.5 | 2.9 | 18.0 | 17.0 | 78.2 | 691.7 | 2,964.3 | 225.6 |
| Nebr. | 4,091.6 | 2.5 | 23.6 | 52.0 | 201.4 | 745.5 | 2,880.4 | 186.2 |
| Nev. | 6,271.7 | 8.2 | 59.6 | 250.6 | 306.9 | 1,404.8 | 3,662.1 | 579.6 |
| N.H. | 3,596.2 | 3.3 | 29.5 | 23.8 | 111.8 | 736.9 | 2,446.9 | 244.0 |
| N.J. | 5,269.4 | 5.1 | 31.7 | 273.3 | 299.0 | 976.6 | 2,764.7 | 919.2 |
| N.Mex. | 6,573.8 | 8.6 | 45.9 | 105.2 | 544.1 | 1,711.1 | 3,809.0 | 349.9 |
| N.Y. | 6,293.2 | 12.5 | 29.2 | 579.3 | 510.1 | 1,176.2 | 3,033.2 | 952.7 |
| N.C. | 5,253.8 | 8.9 | 29.9 | 133.5 | 374.1 | 1,503.5 | 2,918.6 | 285.3 |
| N.Dak. | 2,560.9 | 0.6 | 11.8 | 9.2 | 41.5 | 358.9 | 2,025.8 | 113.0 |
| Ohio | 4,733.2 | 6.0 | 44.7 | 170.9 | 247.1 | 1,018.2 | 2,811.1 | 435.3 |
| Okla. | 5,502.6 | 6.5 | 37.5 | 126.2 | 321.3 | 1,563.6 | 2,862.0 | 585.5 |
| Oreg. | 6,161.1 | 4.8 | 46.6 | 151.8 | 315.4 | 1,425.4 | 3,677.0 | 540.1 |
| Pa. | 3,360.4 | 6.3 | 24.6 | 149.7 | 198.0 | 713.7 | 1,798.7 | 469.4 |
| P.R. | 3,277.0 | 13.9 | 15.2 | 394.0 | 227.8 | 1,004.3 | 1,131.1 | 490.7 |
| R.I. | 5,224.8 | 4.9 | 26.7 | 112.4 | 234.0 | 1,206.9 | 2,715.8 | 924.1 |
| S.C. | 5,619.2 | 9.1 | 46.5 | 130.2 | 627.8 | 1,392.8 | 3,070.8 | 342.1 |
| S.Dak. | 2,685.2 | 1.3 | 32.0 | 11.7 | 90.5 | 474.7 | 1,966.0 | 109.0 |
| Tenn. | 4,513.6 | 8.4 | 46.0 | 160.4 | 334.1 | 1,206.9 | 2,224.9 | 532.9 |
| Tex. | 7,926.9 | 11.9 | 46.8 | 223.1 | 376.6 | 2,014.9 | 4,365.0 | 888.5 |
| Utah | 5,682.1 | 2.6 | 28.6 | 52.6 | 174.9 | 897.0 | 4,288.8 | 237.6 |
| Vt. | 4,088.5 | 1.9 | 23.1 | 18.0 | 89.8 | 1,029.1 | 2,727.7 | 198.9 |
| Va. | 4,211.4 | 7.9 | 26.9 | 106.5 | 171.3 | 756.9 | 2,831.2 | 310.9 |
| Wash. | 6,593.8 | 4.4 | 61.7 | 140.1 | 265.5 | 1,545.1 | 4,119.3 | 457.6 |
| W.Va. | 2,362.8 | 6.5 | 18.7 | 42.7 | 78.8 | 626.5 | 1,432.8 | 156.8 |
| Wis. | 4,164.8 | 3.6 | 20.4 | 75.2 | 123.4 | 733.2 | 2,877.3 | 311.7 |
| Wyo. | 3,889.1 | 4.4 | 28.2 | 17.1 | 208.6 | 631.8 | 2,861.7 | 137.3 |
| **Total U.S.** | **5,741.0** | **8.7** | **38.1** | **233.0** | **383.4** | **1,276.3** | **3,171.3** | **630.4** |

1. Forcible rape data by the state-level Uniform Crime Reporting Program administered by the Illinois Department of State Police were not in accordance with national guidelines and the FBI estimated Illinois 1988 rape totals using the national rate of forcible rapes when grouped by like agencies. 2. Data are not included in U.S. totals. **Source:** Federal Bureau of Investigation, *Uniform Crime Reports: Crime in the United States 1989* (1990).

## SERIOUS CRIME IN THE 50 LARGEST CITIES, RANKED BY RATE PER 1,000 POPULATION, 1989

| City[1] | Crime index offenses | Rate per 1,000[2] | Murder | Forcible rape | Robbery | Aggra-vated assault | Property crimes |
|---|---|---|---|---|---|---|---|
| Atlanta | 88,241 | 207.6 | 246 | 691 | 6,796 | 9,119 | 71,684 |
| Miami | 70,226 | 184.2 | 132 | 285 | 7,289 | 6,387 | 56,133 |
| Dallas | 167,849 | 168.5 | 351 | 1,185 | 9,442 | 10,250 | 146,621 |
| Fort Worth | 67,912 | 157.8 | 113 | 454 | 2,525 | 3,576 | 61,244 |
| St. Louis | 62,683 | 154.7 | 158 | 330 | 4,220 | 7,936 | 50,039 |
| Charlotte | 49,702 | 133.4 | 73 | 325 | 2,369 | 4,873 | 42,062 |
| Seattle | 66,713 | 129.7 | 38 | 478 | 2,448 | 3,914 | 59,835 |
| Portland, Oreg. | 54,860 | 128.8 | 38 | 415 | 2,667 | 4,932 | 46,808 |
| Kansas City, Mo. | 56,505 | 128.3 | 140 | 507 | 3,824 | 4,525 | 47,509 |
| San Antonio | 121,667 | 128.1 | 168 | 477 | 2,710 | 1,898 | 116,414 |
| Oakland | 46,280 | 126.3 | 129 | 442 | 3,224 | 4,760 | 40,725 |
| Detroit | 127,218 | 122.4 | 624 | 1,424 | 11,902 | 11,006 | 102,262 |
| Boston[2] | 70,003 | 120.7 | 99 | 483 | 5,866 | 6,471 | 57,084 |
| Fresno | 37,085 | 117.6 | 42 | 234 | 1,525 | 2,488 | 32,796 |
| Oklahoma City | 48,786 | 112.9 | 61 | 352 | 1,617 | 2,277 | 44,479 |
| New Orleans | 59,534 | 112.6 | 251 | 388 | 5,449 | 4,115 | 49,331 |
| Phoenix | 103,016 | 109.4 | 126 | 399 | 2,615 | 5,341 | 94,535 |
| Houston | 187,308 | 109.3 | 459 | 1,152 | 9,820 | 8,097 | 167,780 |
| Austin | 50,512 | 107.7 | 31 | 235 | 1,019 | 1,320 | 47,907 |
| El Paso | 55,113 | 106.9 | 41 | 241 | 1,139 | 3,301 | 50,391 |
| Minneapolis | 42,459 | 106.5 | 46 | 462 | 2,524 | 2,335 | 37,092 |
| Columbus | 60,184 | 105.2 | 90 | 543 | 3,127 | 2,226 | 54,198 |
| Sacramento | 36,057 | 103.9 | 44 | 187 | 1,654 | 1,773 | 32,399 |
| Jacksonville | 67,996 | 103.9 | 165 | 609 | 3,940 | 4,735 | 58,547 |
| Washington, D.C. | 62,338 | 103.2 | 434 | 186 | 6,541 | 5,775 | 49,402 |
| Chicago[3] | 300,134 | 100.4 | 742 | N.A. | 31,588 | 37,615 | 230,189 |
| Albuquerque | 38,594 | 100.3 | 41 | 178 | 1,032 | 3,445 | 33,898 |
| New York | 718,534 | 97.5 | 1,905 | 3,254 | 93,377 | 70,951 | 579,047 |
| Toledo | 33,283 | 97.2 | 41 | 392 | 1,583 | 1,273 | 29,994 |
| Long Beach | 40,621 | 95.3 | 85 | 247 | 3,763 | 3,074 | 33,452 |
| Baltimore | 72,021 | 94.4 | 262 | 541 | 7,966 | 6,849 | 56,403 |
| Los Angeles | 324,734 | 94.4 | 877 | 1996 | 31,063 | 43,361 | 247,437 |
| San Diego | 103,287 | 94.0 | 121 | 410 | 3,585 | 6,008 | 93,163 |
| Tulsa | 33,863 | 92.4 | 32 | 307 | 1,416 | 2,595 | 29,513 |
| San Francisco | 68,121 | 90.7 | 73 | 380 | 5,005 | 4,606 | 58,057 |
| Pittsburgh | 33,909 | 90.1 | 31 | 219 | 2,471 | 1,858 | 29,330 |
| Memphis | 58,464 | 89.8 | 141 | 781 | 3,781 | 3,327 | 50,434 |
| Milwaukee | 53,106 | 88.4 | 112 | 461 | 2,415 | 1,281 | 48,837 |
| Buffalo | 27,379 | 87.1 | 37 | 268 | 1,829 | 2,345 | 22,900 |
| Cleveland | 44,555 | 85.0 | 144 | 837 | 4,045 | 2,939 | 36,590 |
| Denver | 38,072 | 77.0 | 55 | 325 | 1,267 | 1,925 | 34,500 |
| Philadelphia[2] | 115,602 | 70.0 | 475 | 784 | 10,233 | 6,562 | 97,548 |
| Nashville[2] | 34,950 | 69.7 | 69 | 478 | 1,608 | 3,075 | 29,720 |
| Omaha[2] | 23,345 | 65.7 | 23 | 188 | 639 | 1,901 | 20,594 |
| Indianapolis | 31,770 | 65.6 | 41 | 483 | 1,806 | 3,529 | 25,911 |
| Honolulu | 52,909 | 62.3 | 43 | 412 | 815 | 1,027 | 50,612 |
| Virginia Beach | 20,983 | 56.7 | 17 | 133 | 318 | 294 | 20,221 |
| San Jose | 39,315 | 51.9 | 38 | 399 | 995 | 3,103 | 34,780 |
| Cincinnati | 28,325 | 46.1 | 45 | 351 | 1,428 | 1,866 | 24,635 |
| Tucson | N.A. | N.A. | N.A. | N.A. | N.A. | N.A. | N.A. |

1. Rates per 1,000 inhabitants were computed by the editors on the basis of figures supplied by the Federal Bureau of Investigation. 2. Arson is not included in the figures for either Property Crimes or Crime Index Offenses. 3. Forcible rape figures supplied by the Illinois Department of State police are not in accordance with the Federal Bureau of Investigation's Uniform Crime Report guidelines. 4. Tucson, Ariz., did not report crime figures for 1989 to the FBI. **Source:** Federal Bureau of Investigation, *Uniform Crime Reports 1989: Crime in the United States* (1990).

## ARRESTS, BY SEX AND AGE, 1989

| Offense charged | Male Total | Male Under 18 | Female Total | Female Under 18 | Total All Ages | Total Under 18 | Total Over 18 |
|---|---|---|---|---|---|---|---|
| All arrests | 6,950,843 | 1,027,567 | 1,544,336 | 289,399 | 8,495,179 | 1,316,966 | 7,178,213 |
| Percent distribution | 81.8% | 12.1% | 18.2% | 3.4% | 100.0% | 15.5% | 84.5% |
| Crime index offenses | 1,431,853 | 396,357 | 387,143 | 96,193 | 1,818,996 | 492,550 | 1,326,446 |
| Percent distribution | 16.9% | 4.7% | 4.6% | 1.1% | 21.4% | 5.8% | 15.6% |
| **VIOLENT CRIME** | | | | | | | |
| Murder | 12,434 | 1,619 | 1,676 | 114 | 14,110 | 1,733 | 12,377 |
| Forcible rape | 23,352 | 3,514 | 254 | 66 | 23,606 | 3,580 | 20,026 |
| Robbery | 101,385 | 22,812 | 9,567 | 2,105 | 110,952 | 24,917 | 86,035 |
| Aggravated assault | 242,399 | 30,852 | 36,553 | 5,135 | 278,952 | 35,987 | 242,965 |
| Total | 379,570 | 58,797 | 48,050 | 7,420 | 427,620 | 66,217 | 361,403 |
| Percent distribution | 4.5% | 0.7% | 0.6% | 0.1% | 5.0% | 0.8% | 4.3% |
| **PROPERTY CRIME** | | | | | | | |
| Burglary | 252,673 | 79,020 | 25,747 | 7,094 | 278,420 | 86,114 | 192,306 |
| Larceny/theft | 660,274 | 201,295 | 297,334 | 75,239 | 957,608 | 276,534 | 681,074 |
| Motor vehicle theft | 129,483 | 52,770 | 14,424 | 5,984 | 143,907 | 58,718 | 85,189 |
| Arson | 9,853 | 4,475 | 1,588 | 492 | 11,441 | 4,967 | 6,474 |
| Total | 1,052,283 | 337,560 | 339,093 | 88,773 | 1,391,376 | 426,333 | 965,043 |
| Percent distribution | 12.4% | 4.0% | 4.0% | 1.0% | 16.4% | 5.0% | 11.4% |

**Source**: Federal Bureau of Investigation, *Uniform Crime Reports 1989: Crime in the United States* (1990).

## CORRECTIONS

**Jails and prisons** Although the terms tend to be used synonymously, "jails" and "prisons" differ in the inmates they house and their locations, physical size, and programs. Jails are locally administered facilities that house inmates after arraignment, prisoners serving terms of less than one year, and prisoners who cannot be housed in state prisons due to overcrowding. Jail populations are calculated based on a daily population. As of June 30, 1990, the adult jail population of 405,320 included 49% convicted and 51% unconvicted inmates.

Prisons are administered by state or federal government authority. Typically they hold convicted offenders sentenced to more than one year of confinement. They tend to be located away from dense population centers, and they are usually larger than jails and have more rehabilitation programs. Between 1980 and 1990, the number of prison inmates skyrocketed both in absolute numbers—134%, from 329,821 to 771,243—and in rate per 100,000 population—111%, from 139 to 293. The female prison population has grown faster than the male population each year since 1981, causing the female share of the nation's prison population to increase from 4.2% in 1981 to 5.7% in 1989. Overall, the ratio of men to women behind bars is about 17:1, and the rate of prisoners per 100,000 population by sex is 566 for men and 31 for women.

Prisoners are demographically distinct from the general population. They are younger, less educated, and more than two-and-a-half times as likely never to have married.

**Prison capacity** is measured by the number of beds a corrections rating authority assigns it, the number of prisoners the staff can accommodate, or the number of prisoners the facility was built to house. In 1990, U.S. prisons were housing between 18% and 29% more inmates than they were intended to hold.

## ADULT PRISONERS UNDER CORRECTIONAL SUPERVISION, 1985–89

| Correctional population | 1985 Number | 1985 Percent of pop.[1] | 1989 Number | 1989 Percent of pop.[1] | Percent change 1985–89 |
|---|---|---|---|---|---|
| Probation | 1,968,712 | 1.12% | 2,520,479 | 1.37% | 28.0% |
| Jail | 254,986 | 0.15 | 393,303 | 0.21 | 54.2 |
| Prison | 487,593 | 0.28 | 683,367 | 0.37 | 40.2 |
| Parole | 300,203 | 0.17 | 456,797 | 0.25 | 52.2 |
| Total[2] | **3,011,494** | **1.71%** | **4,053,946** | **2.20%** | **34.6%** |

1. Includes U.S. resident population age 18 or over. 2. Percentages may not add to total due to rounding. **Source**: U.S. Bureau of Justice Statistics, *Probation and Parole 1989* (1990).

## U.S. PRISON CAPACITY, 1989–90

| Category | 1990 prison pop. as percent of: Highest capacity | 1990 prison pop. as percent of: Lowest capacity | 1989–90 net change in: Highest capacity | 1989–90 net change in: Lowest capacity |
|---|---|---|---|---|
| Federal | 151% | 151% | 10,818 | 10,818 |
| State[1] | 115 | 127 | 9,845 | 44,068 |
| **Total** | **118** | **129** | **20,664** | **54,886** |

1. Excludes inmates held in local jails because of crowding in state facilities. **Source**: U.S. Bureau of Justice Statistics, *Prisoners in 1990* (1991).

## PRISONERS IN THE U.S., 1990

| Category | All prisoners Prisoners | All prisoners Percent change 1989–90 | Sentenced to more than 1 year Prisoners | Sentenced to more than 1 year Percent change 1989–90 | Incarceration rate 1990[1] |
|---|---|---|---|---|---|
| **BY SYSTEM** | | | | | |
| Federal | 65,526 | 10.7% | 52,208 | 10.7% | 21 |
| State[2] | 705,717 | 8.0 | 687,555 | 8.5 | 272 |
| **BY SEX** | | | | | |
| Male | 727,398 | 8.3% | 699,443 | 8.7% | 566 |
| Female | 43,845 | 7.9 | 40,320 | 8.2 | 31 |
| **Total** | **771,243** | **8.2%** | **739,763** | **8.6%** | **293** |

1. The number of prisoners sentenced to more than one year per 100,000 resident population. 2. Includes 18,380 state prisoners in 20 states and the District of Columbia held in local jails because of crowding in state facilities. **Source**: U.S. Bureau of Justice Statistics, *Prisoners in 1990* (1991).

## JAIL EXPENDITURES, BY STATE, 1988

| State | Total expenditures ('000s) | Operating expenditures ('000s) | Capital expenditures ('000s) | Operating expenditures per inmate[1] | State | Total expenditures ('000s) | Operating expenditures ('000s) | Capital expenditures ('000s) | Operating expenditures per inmate[1] |
|---|---|---|---|---|---|---|---|---|---|
| Alabama | $ 47,380 | $ 33,835 | $ 13,545 | $ 6,905 | Nebraska | $ 15,594 | $ 14,184 | $ 1,410 | $12,778 |
| Alaska | 4,257 | 1,227 | 3,030 | 43,836 | Nevada | 37,044 | 35,135 | 1,909 | 16,087 |
| Arizona | 48,233 | 48,086 | 147 | 8,279 | New Hampshire | 16,054 | 11,852 | 4,202 | 15,098 |
| Arkansas | 25,684 | 17,311 | 8,373 | 8,837 | New Jersey | 137,619 | 127,876 | 9,743 | 11,648 |
| California | 659,718 | 523,498 | 136,220 | 8,262 | New Mexico | 25,474 | 25,121 | 353 | 11,657 |
| Colorado | 97,214 | 71,863 | 25,351 | 15,998 | New York | 872,290 | 578,439 | 293,851 | 22,698 |
| District of Columbia | 14,113 | 13,563 | 550 | 8,745 | North Carolina | 51,756 | 41,956 | 9,800 | 7,556 |
| Florida | 360,767 | 316,730 | 44,037 | 11,718 | North Dakota | 7,119 | 4,788 | 2,331 | 17,099 |
| Georgia | 144,876 | 97,237 | 47,639 | 6,013 | Ohio | 140,206 | 104,199 | 36,007 | 11,498 |
| Idaho | 7,323 | 6,831 | 492 | 8,331 | Oklahoma | 21,239 | 19,427 | 1,812 | 7,150 |
| Illinois | 106,562 | 100,471 | 6,092 | 10,628 | Oregon | 65,366 | 38,906 | 26,460 | 13,861 |
| Indiana | 60,322 | 34,514 | 25,808 | 6,820 | Pennsylvania | 216,127 | 204,067 | 12,060 | 15,046 |
| Iowa | 29,214 | 16,778 | 12,436 | 15,798 | South Carolina | 24,076 | 23,340 | 736 | 6,629 |
| Kansas | 23,775 | 19,092 | 4,683 | 10,243 | South Dakota | 5,061 | 4,423 | 639 | 8,604 |
| Kentucky | 46,479 | 37,899 | 8,580 | 8,045 | Tennessee | 106,467 | 71,707 | 34,760 | 7,112 |
| Louisiana | 84,485 | 65,242 | 19,243 | 5,882 | Texas | 280,381 | 215,108 | 65,273 | 7,386 |
| Maine | 16,334 | 9,415 | 6,918 | 14,463 | Utah | 14,149 | 13,908 | 241 | 10,272 |
| Maryland | 97,842 | 88,031 | 9,811 | 12,059 | Virginia | 114,467 | 103,561 | 10,906 | 11,367 |
| Massachusetts | 88,576 | 75,564 | 13,011 | 13,962 | Washington | 65,667 | 64,901 | 766 | 11,178 |
| Michigan | 128,311 | 116,605 | 11,706 | 12,347 | West Virginia | 12,211 | 11,793 | 417 | 8,388 |
| Minnesota | 62,401 | 44,349 | 18,052 | 14,778 | Wisconsin | 84,325 | 50,889 | 33,436 | 11,001 |
| Mississippi | 21,148 | 17,342 | 3,806 | 5,341 | Wyoming | 19,088 | 7,440 | 11,648 | 15,276 |
| Missouri | 41,160 | 39,010 | 2,150 | 9,081 | **Total U.S.** | **$4,555,650** | **$3,574,941** | **$980,709** | **$10,639** |
| Montana | 7,696 | 7,428 | 269 | 12,463 | | | | | |

**Note:** There were no locally operated jails in Connecticut, Delaware, Hawaii, Rhode Island, or Vermont in 1988. 1. Determined by dividing the amount spent on salaries, wages, supplies, utilities, transportation, contractual services, and other current items paid for during the fiscal year by the average daily inmate population. **Source:** U.S. Bureau of Justice Statistics, *Census of Local Jails 1988* (1991).

## U.S. JAIL POPULATION, 1990

| Sex and legal status | Number of inmates 1989 | Number of inmates 1990 | Percent change 1989–90 |
|---|---|---|---|
| **ONE DAY COUNT[1]** | | | |
| All inmates | 395,553 | 405,320 | 2.5% |
| Adults | 393,303 | 403,019 | 2.5 |
| Male | 356,050 | 305,821 | 2.7 |
| Female | 37,253 | 37,198 | — |
| Juveniles[2] | 2,250 | 2,301 | 2.3 |
| **AVERAGE DAILY POPULATION** | | | |
| All inmates | 386,845 | 408,075 | 5.5% |
| Adults | 384,954 | 405,935 | 5.5 |
| Male | 349,180 | 368,091 | 5.4 |
| Female | 35,774 | 37,644 | 5.8 |
| Juveniles[2] | 1,891 | 2,140 | 13.2 |

1. Data for June 30 of year shown. 2. Juveniles are persons defined by state statute as being under a certain age, usually 18, and subject initially to juvenile court authority even if tried as adults in criminal court. Because less than 1% of the jail population was juveniles, caution must be used in interpreting any changes over time. **Source:** U.S. Bureau of Justice Statistics Bulletin, *Jail Inmates, 1990* (1991).

**Probation and parole** In the five years 1985–89, the number of people under "correctional supervision" in the United States—in jail or prison, on parole or probation—jumped 35%, from 3.01 million to 4.05 million. If the entire correctional population of the United States comprised a separate state, it would rank 22nd in the nation by number of inhabitants—between Minnesota and Alabama. The strain has been felt at every level of the criminal justice system. When an offender is convicted, the primary sentencing alternatives are incarcera-

tion or probation. Once imprisoned, the offender may become eligible for parole, a form of conditional release. As prison space has decreased in proportion to the number of criminals, the number of conditional releases has increased to alleviate overcrowding. Of the offenders under correctional supervision in 1989, 2.5 million—62%—were on probation, and 456,797—11%—were on parole from prison.

**Recidivism** In 1986, the last year for which data are available, 82% of all state and federal prisoners were recidivists, that is, inmates who had committed crimes after serving a previous prison term or being on probation or parole. Of all inmates, 60% had been imprisoned two or more times, 45% three or more, and 20% six or more.

## CAPITAL PUNISHMENT

In the period 1930–89, 3,979 executions were carried out under state or federal authority. Overall, the number of prisoners executed each year declined steadily between 1930 and 1968. There were 1,667 executions in the 1930s, 1,284 in the 1940s, 717 in the 1950s, and 191 between 1960 and 1967. There were none between 1968 and 1978—the Supreme Court ruled the death penalty unconstitutional in 1972, and reinstated it in 1976. But between 1977 and 1989, 120 executions were carried out, all but one for murder, and all but one male.

Fourteen states have carried out 100 or more executions since 1930; but as of 1989, 14 states and the District of Columbia did not authorize the death penalty for any crime. In

Maine, Minnesota, and Wisconsin, there has been no death penalty statute in force since 1930, and Alaska and Hawaii have had no death penalty statute since 1960. The death penalty was either abolished or declared unconstitutional in Michigan (1963), Iowa and West Virginia (1965), Kansas (1973), the District of Columbia (1973), Rhode Island (1979), Oregon (1981), Massachusetts and New York (1984), and Vermont (1989). South Dakota abolished the death penalty in 1915, restored it in 1939, abolished it again in 1977, and restored it again in 1979. In California the death penalty was found "partially unconstitutional" in 1984.

**Race and capital punishment** Apart from the broad question of whether it is right for the state to take the life of an individual, the major issues of concern to those opposed to capital punishment are whether it is a deterrent to crime, a violation of the Eighth Amendment prohibiting "cruel and unusual punishment," or used fairly with respect to race.

Historically, blacks have been more likely to be executed than whites in proportion to both the general population and prison population. Blacks represent 53% of prisoners executed between 1930 and 1989, as against 46% whites and 1% classified as other. (It is worth noting, however, that of the 33 women executed in the same period, 21 were white and 12 were black.) Since 1977, 59% of all those executed were white, and 41% were black.

**Automatic review** Of the 36 states with capital punishment statutes in 1988, 34 provided for automatic review of all death penalty sentences. Arkansas and Ohio had no specific

## NUMBER OF PRISONERS EXECUTED, BY SYSTEM, 1930–89 (ranked by executions since 1977)

| System | Number executed Since 1930 | Since 1977 | In 1989 | On death row 1989[1] | Method of execution |
|--------|------|------|------|------|------|
| Texas | 330 | 33 | 4 | 304 | Injection |
| Florida | 191 | 21 | 2 | 289 | Electrocution |
| Louisiana | 151 | 18 | 0 | 35 | Electrocution |
| Georgia | 380 | 14 | 1 | 90 | Electrocution |
| Virginia | 100 | 8 | 1 | 43 | Electrocution |
| Alabama | 142 | 7 | 4 | 106 | Electrocution |
| Nevada | 33 | 4 | 2 | 52 | Injection |
| Mississippi | 158 | 4 | 1 | 44 | Injection; gas |
| North Carolina | 266 | 3 | 0 | 88 | Injection; gas |
| Utah | 16 | 3 | 0 | 11 | Injection; firing squad |
| South Carolina | 164 | 2 | 0 | 42 | Electrocution |
| Indiana | 43 | 2 | 0 | 48 | Electrocution |
| Missouri | 63 | 1 | 1 | 72 | Injection; gas |
| California | 292 | 0 | 0 | 254 | Gas |
| Ohio | 172 | 0 | 0 | 98 | Electrocution |
| Pennsylvania | 152 | 0 | 0 | 112 | Electrocution |
| Arkansas | 118 | 0 | 0 | 33 | Injection; electrocution |
| Kentucky | 103 | 0 | 0 | 29 | Electrocution |
| Tennessee | 93 | 0 | 0 | 75 | Electrocution |
| Illinois | 90 | 0 | 0 | 115 | Injection |
| New Jersey | 74 | 0 | 0 | 18 | Injection |
| Maryland | 68 | 0 | 0 | 16 | Gas |
| Oklahoma | 60 | 0 | 0 | 109 | Injection |
| Washington | 47 | 0 | 0 | 7 | Injection; hanging |
| Colorado | 47 | 0 | 0 | 3 | Injection |

| System | Number executed Since 1930 | Since 1977 | In 1989 | On death row 1989[1] | Method of execution |
|--------|------|------|------|------|------|
| Arizona | 38 | 0 | 0 | 84 | Gas |
| Federal system | 33 | 0 | 0 | 0 | Method of state of execution |
| Connecticut | 21 | 0 | 0 | 2 | Electrocution |
| Oregon | 19 | 0 | 0 | 23 | Injection |
| Delaware | 12 | 0 | 0 | 7 | Injection |
| New Mexico | 8 | 0 | 0 | 1 | Injection |
| Wyoming | 7 | 0 | 0 | 2 | Injection |
| Montana | 6 | 0 | 0 | 8 | Injection; hanging |
| Nebraska | 4 | 0 | 0 | 12 | Electrocution |
| Idaho | 3 | 0 | 0 | 18 | Injection; firing squad |
| South Dakota | 1 | 0 | 0 | 0 | Injection |
| New Hampshire | 1 | 0 | 0 | 0 | Injection; hanging |
| New York | 329 | 0 | | | No death penalty statute |
| Massachusetts | 27 | 0 | | | No death penalty statute |
| Iowa | 18 | 0 | | | No death penalty statute |
| Vermont | 4 | 0 | | | No death penalty statute |
| Rhode Island | 0 | 0 | | | No death penalty statute |
| West Virginia | 40 | | | | No death penalty statute |
| Dist. of Columbia | 40 | | | | No death penalty statute |
| Kansas | 15 | | | | No death penalty statute |
| North Dakota | 0 | | | | No death penalty statute |
| Michigan | 0 | | | | No death penalty statute |
| **Total U.S.** | **3,979** | **140** | **16** | **2,250** | |

**Note:** Alaska, Hawaii, Maine, Minnesota, and Wisconsin have not had death penalty statutes on the books since 1930. 1. As of Dec. 31. **Source:** U.S. Bureau of Justice Statistics, *Capital Punishment 1989* (1990).

provisions for automatic review; nor did the federal government. While most states authorize automatic review of both the conviction and the sentence, Illinois and Indiana require review of the sentence only. Typically, the review is undertaken regardless of the defendant's wishes and is conducted by the state's highest appellate court. If either the conviction or the sentence is vacated, the case may be remanded to the trial court for additional proceedings or for retrial. The death penalty may be reimposed as a result of retrial or resentencing.

## VICTIMS OF VIOLENT CRIME

**Violence by intimates** Women are generally less likely than men to be crime victims except in two categories of crime: violence between intimates and rape. Women were victims of violent intimates at a rate three times that of men—6.3 per 1,000 women, compared to 1.8 per 1,000 men. Among victims of violence by a stranger, the rate for women was 61% lower than that for men (11.4 per 1,000 compared with 29.4 per 1,000). Among violent crime victims, 25% of women and 4% of men were victimized by persons whom they knew intimately. Women were six times more likely than men to be victimized by a spouse, ex-spouse, boyfriend, or girlfriend.

Of the intimates' violent crimes that female victims reported, 85% were assaults, 11% were robberies, and 3% were rapes. Those women victimized by intimates were more likely to experience assaults and less likely to be robbed

than female victims of nonintimates.

Three out of four offenders committing domestic violence against women were spouses, ex-spouses, or current or ex-boyfriends. When only spousal abuse is considered, divorced or separated men committed 79% of such violence, and husbands 21%. About one in five women victimized by a spouse or ex-spouse reported that she had previously been the victim of similar crimes. On average these women had sustained three assaults in the six months prior to being interviewed, and the assaults were so similar that they could not remember them distinctly.

**Rape** According to data gathered in more than half a million interviews conducted by the Bureau of Justice Statistics's (BJS) National Crime Survey, only 53% of all rapes attempted or completed between 1973 and 1987 were reported to the police. (The BJS acknowledges that some victims do not even report rapes to the survey interviewer and that the exact

## PRISONERS EXECUTED, BY RACE, 1930–89

| Race | 1930–89 Number | Percent | 1930–77 Number | Percent | 1977–89 Number | Percent |
|------|------|------|------|------|------|------|
| White | 1,822 | 45.8% | 1,751 | 45.4% | 71 | 59.2% |
| Black | 2,115 | 53.2 | 2,066 | 53.5 | 49 | 40.8 |
| Other | 42 | 1.1 | 42 | 1.1 | 0 | 0.0 |
| **Total** | **3,979** | **100.0%** | **3,859** | **100.0%** | **120** | **100.0%** |

**Note:** Executions under civil authority only. Does not include 160 executions carried out under military authority since 1930. There were no executions carried out between 1968 and 1976. **Source:** U.S. Bureau of Justice Statistics, *Sourcebook of Criminal Justice Statistics 1989* (1990), and *Capital Punishment 1989* (1990).

## HOMICIDE RATES BY RACE, SEX, AND AGE OF VICTIMS, 1986

| Age of victim | Total White | Black | Male White | Black | Female White | Black |
|------|------|------|------|------|------|------|
| **Total** | 5.4 | 31.2 | 7.9 | 52.3 | 2.9 | 12.3 |
| 1–11 | 1.4 | 6.1 | 1.4 | 6.6 | 1.3 | 5.5 |
| 12–15 | 1.8 | 6.3 | 1.8 | 9.2 | 1.7 | 3.3 |
| 16–19 | 6.1 | 33.6 | 8.7 | 54.3 | 3.4 | 12.6 |
| 20–24 | 10.1 | 59.3 | 15.0 | 100.0 | 5.1 | 21.4 |
| 25–34 | 9.0 | 60.9 | 13.6 | 104.3 | 4.3 | 22.4 |
| 35–49 | 6.7 | 39.8 | 10.1 | 71.6 | 3.4 | 13.5 |
| 50–64 | 4.1 | 21.5 | 6.2 | 39.0 | 2.1 | 7.2 |
| 65 or older | 3.2 | 16.5 | 4.2 | 28.5 | 2.6 | 8.4 |

**Note:** Rates per 100,000 resident population. **Source:** U.S. Bureau of Justice Statistics Special Report, *Black Victims* (1990).

amount of the undercount is impossible to ascertain.)

Serious injury or the presence of a weapon increased the likelihood of the crime being reported to the police: approximately 70% of rapes were reported when a weapon was involved, while less than 50% were reported when no weapon was involved. When police were not informed of a completed rape, victims gave three main reasons for not reporting the crime: 25% said they considered the rape a private or personal matter or one they wanted to solve themselves; 23% feared reprisals by the offender or his friends or family; and 23% thought the police would be inefficient, ineffective, or insensitive.

## VICTIM-OFFENDER RELATIONSHIP IN CRIMES OF VIOLENCE, 1979–87

| Victim-offender relationship | Percent of violent crimes | |
|---|---|---|
| | Female victims | Male victims |
| Intimate | 24.5% | 3.9% |
| Spouse | 2.2 | 0.2 |
| Ex-spouse | 8.5 | 0.6 |
| Parent | 0.8 | 0.3 |
| Child | 0.7 | 0.1 |
| Brother/sister | 1.3 | 0.5 |
| Other relative | 2.4 | 1.1 |
| Boyfriend/girlfriend | 7.8 | 0.4 |
| Unspecified | 0.9 | 0.7 |
| Other person known to victim | 27.3 | 26.8 |
| Stranger | 44.4 | 65.3 |
| Unknown relationship | 3.7 | 4.0 |

**Note:** Detail may not add to total due to rounding. Victimization with multiple offenders (4% of victimizations by intimates) is classified according to closest relative involved. **Source:** U.S. Bureau of Justice Statistics, *Female Victims of Violent Crime* (1991).

## REPORTING OF RAPE BY WOMEN, BY CHARACTERISTICS OF THE CRIME AND THE VICTIM, 1973–87

| Characteristics of crime or victim | Average annual number of rapes | Percent of incidents reported to police |
|---|---|---|
| All rapes | 154,500 | 53% |
| Attempted | 101,600 | 50 |
| Completed | 52,900 | 59 |
| Victim-offender relationship: | | |
| Nonstranger | 58,800 | 47% |
| Stranger | 89,900 | 57 |
| Presence of weapon: | | |
| No weapon | 101,600 | 47% |
| Weapon | 36,500 | 71 |
| Presence of injury: | | |
| No injury | 93,900 | 48% |
| Injury | 60,700 | 61 |
| Minor injury[1] | 41,200 | 55 |
| Serious injury[2] | 19,300 | 74 |
| Race of victim: | | |
| White | 121,400 | 52% |
| Black | 29,900 | 56 |
| Other | 3,200 | 50 |
| Age of victim: | | |
| 12–15 | 16,800 | 70% |
| 16–19 | 37,600 | 48 |
| 20–24 | 41,000 | 48 |
| 25–34 | 41,600 | 51 |
| 35–49 | 11,800 | 56 |
| 50–64 | 3,800 | 74 |
| 65 or older | 1,800 | 55 |
| Marital status of victim: | | |
| Married | 27,100 | 54% |
| Widowed | 3,900 | 62 |
| Separated/divorced | 36,500 | 51 |
| Never married | 86,500 | 53 |

1. Includes bruises, black eyes, cuts, scratches, swelling, and undetermined injuries requiring less than two days of hospitalization. 2. Includes gunshot wounds, broken bones, loss of teeth, internal injuries, lacerations, loss of consciousness, and undetermined injuries requiring two or more days of hospitalization. **Source:** U.S. Bureau of Justice Statistics, *Female Victims of Violent Crime* (1991).

## ILLEGAL DRUGS

The number of Americans who feel drugs and drug abuse constitute a real threat to the nation has risen dramatically in recent years. Part of this perception has been fueled by the media and the federal government's declaration of a "war on drugs." According to a series of Gallup Polls taken between 1985 and 1989, respondents describing drug abuse as the most important problem facing our country today has grown steadily, from 2% in 1985 to 27% in May 1989. The largest increase was in the nine months between September 1988—when only 11% thought drug abuse was the country's most serious problem—and May 1989. (In contrast, in the 26 months between July 1986 and September 1988, the increase was only from 8% to 11%.)

Among the strategies proposed for combatting drug abuse, the most controversial is the call for legalization, a tactic employed with mixed results in various European countries for years. Proponents of legalization run the gamut of the political spectrum. Public opinion research and surveys conducted by the National Institute on Drug Abuse indicate less enthusiasm from the general public, and the decrease in drug use seems to validate the belief that education is the best solution.

When asked to consider what strategies would do the most to "halt the drug epidemic in the United States," respondents indicated the following preferences:

—47% "educating young people and other nonusers about the dangers of drug abuse";

—35% "making it harder for illegal drugs to get into the country";

—6% "helping drug users obtain treatment to overcome their dependency."

In addition, 13% volunteered "all" of the above, and 1% percent volunteered "none."

# HEALTH AND MEDICINE

## MILESTONES IN THE HISTORY OF MEDICINE

*B.C.*

**c. 2700** Chinese emperor Shen Nung develops principles of herbal medicine and acupuncture.

**c. 1700** The Code of Hammurabi, king of Babylon, comprises regulations concerning physicians, including what they may treat and what their fees should be.

**c. 1500** The Ebers Papyrus describes many remedies used in Ancient Egypt to treat dental ailments.

**c. 400** Hippocrates of Cos (Greek: c. 460–c. 377), teacher and medical practitioner known as Father of Medicine, writes Hippocratic Oath, which sets ethical standards still followed by physicians throughout the world.

**c. 300** Herophilus (Greek: c. 355–280) pioneers dissection of human body and founds first school of anatomy.

*A.D.*

**c. 20** Aulus Cornelius Celsus (Roman: 1st cent.) writes first-known medical textbook.

**c. 100** Romans develop a public medical service and appoint physicians to provide medical help to poor.

**c. 180** Galen (Greek: c. 130–c. 201) writes *Methodus Medando*, which summarizes medical knowledge of ancient times. Galen's views on human physiology and disease would influence medical thought for more than 1500 years.

**c. 450** Susruta (Indian) notes relationship of malaria to mosquitoes and of bubonic plague to rats.

**c. 900** Rhazes (Persian: c.865–923/35) is first to describe smallpox and establish criteria for diagnosing and treating it.

**1030** Ibn Sina (Avicenna; Persian: 980–1037), publishes *Canon of Medicine*, which becomes leading medical encyclopedia for centuries.

**c. 1270** Spectacles are introduced by Venetian –80 glassmakers.

**1403** Venice imposes world's first quarantine of infected areas as safeguard against Black Death (bubonic plague).

**1530** First book devoted to dentistry published anonymously in Germany.

**1543** Andreas Vesalius (Flemish: 1514–64)

publishes first accurate anatomy text and establishes foundations of modern anatomy.

**1597** Gasparo Tapliacossi (Italian) publishes first textbook of plastic surgery and revives operation of rhinoplasty (nose surgery).

**1601** Sir James Lancaster (English: c. 1554–1618) writes that lemon juice helps prevent scurvy.

**1628** William Harvey (English: 1578–1657) describes functions of the heart and how blood circulates throughout the body.

**1658** Jan Swammerdam (Dutch: 1637–80) discerns red blood cells.

**1670** Thomas Willis (English: 1621–75) rediscovers connection between sugar in urine and diabetes (known in antiquity by Greeks, Chinese, and Indians).

**1751** Pennsylvania Hospital, first general hospital in U.S., founded in Philadelphia by Quakers.

**1761** Leopold Auenbrugger von Auenbrugg (Austrian: 1722–1809) discovers that fluid in chest cavity and other health problems can be detected by tapping gently on the chest. Giovanni B. Morgagni (Italian: 1682–1771) establishes modern pathological anatomy with publication of *On the Seats and Causes of Disease.*

**1796** Edward Jenner (English: 1749–1823) develops smallpox vaccine from cowpox serum.

**1816** René T.H. Laënnec (French: 1781–1826) invents stethoscope and introduces practice of auscultation (monitoring sounds made by internal organs).

**1818** James Blundel (English) performs first successful human blood transfusion.

**1831** Samuel Guthrie (American: 1782–1848) discovers chloroform.

**1833** William Beaumont (American: 1785–1853) provides first clear insight into nature of gastric digestion.

**1839** Horace Hayden (American: 1769–1844) and Chapin Harris (1806–60) found world's first dental school, Baltimore College of Dental Surgery.

**1842** Crawford Long (American: 1815–78) removes tumor from patient inhaling ether—first known operation under general anesthesia; publishes his findings in 1849, three years after William Morton (American: 1819–68) demonstrates effectiveness of ether as anesthetic.

**1850** Hermann Helmholtz (German: 1821–94) invents ophthalmoscope, instrument used to examine interior of the eye.

**1855** Manuel Garcia (Spanish: 1805–1906) invents modern laryngoscope, device used to inspect the throat, especially the larynx and vocal cords.

**1863** International Red Cross established at Geneva, Switzerland.

**1865** Joseph Lister (English: 1827–1912) revolutionizes surgery when he introduces use of disinfectants to reduce infection. Louis Pasteur (French: 1822–95) shows that spoilage of wine can be prevented by partial heat-sterilization; process, called pasteurization, soon applied to milk and other foods.

**1866** Sir Thomas C. Allbutt (English: 1836–1925) invents clinical thermometer.

**1868** Carl Wunderlich (German: 1815–77) establishes that fever is a symptom, not a disease, and introduces use of thermometer for taking body temperature.

**1876** Robert Koch (German: 1843–1910) demonstrates that anthrax is caused by rod-shaped bacterium—the first time a microorganism is proved cause of a disease.

**1881** Pasteur produces vaccine that successfully prevents anthrax—first disease prevented by vaccine.

**1890** Emil von Behring (German: 1854–1917) and Shibasaburo Kitasato (Japanese: 1852–1931) independently discover antitoxins.

**1892** Dmitri Ivanovski (Russian: 1864–1920) discovers filterable viruses (viruses tiny enough to pass through fine filters previously believed to trap all living organisms).

**1893** Felix Hofmann (German) develops a process for production of acetylsalicylic acid, the form of aspirin used today.

**1895** Wilhelm Röntgen (German: 1845–1923) discovers X rays, which soon leads to their use as diagnostic tools for medicine and surgery.

**1900** Sigmund Freud (Austrian: 1856–1955), founder of psychoanalysis, publishes *The Interpretation of Dreams.* Karl Landsteiner (Austrian-American: 1868–1943) discovers three blood groups, later named A, B, and O; fourth group, to be named AB, discovered in 1902. Walter Reed (American: 1851–1902) establishes that yellow fever virus is transmitted by mosquitoes.

**1901** Jokichi Takamine (Japanese-American: 1854–1922) isolates adrenaline, first hormone to be isolated.

**1902** Eugene Opie (American) establishes that diabetes results from destruction of specific portions of pancreatic tissue—the islets of Langerhans.

**1905** Albert Einhorn (American) synthesizes procaine (novocaine), which becomes the most widely used dental anesthetic.

**1906** August von Wassermann (German: 1866–1925) develops blood test for syphilis.

**1910** Marie Curie (French: 1867–1934) isolates pure radium metal, which came to be used to treat cancer.

**1913** Elmer McCollum (American: 1879–1967) and Marguerite Davis discover fat-soluble factor in butterfat, later named vitamin A. Béla Schick (Hungarian-American: 1877–1967) perfects test for determining susceptibility to diphtheria.

**1915** Death certificates come into general use in U.S.

**1918** Francis Benedict (American: 1870–1957) devises basal metabolism test for measuring rate at which metabolism (total of all chemical reactions) occurs in the body.

**1921** Sir Frederick G. Banting (Canadian: 1891–1941) and Charles H. Best (1899–1978) extract insulin from the pancreas.

**1928** Sir Alexander Fleming (Scottish: 1881–1955) discovers penicillin, a substance in green mold *Penicillium notatum* that destroys certain bacteria.

**1935** Gerhard Domagk (German: 1895–1964) announces discovery of protosil (sulfanomide–crysoidin), the first useful sulfa drug.

**1937** Bernard Fantus (American) establishes first blood bank, in Chicago.

**1937** Alton Ochsner (American: 1896–1981) and Michael De Bakey (1908– ) suggest that cigarette smoking is cause of lung cancer.

**1943** Selman Waksman (American: 1888–1973) isolates streptomycin, an antibiotic effective against bacterium that causes tuberculosis.

**1944** Willem Kolff (Dutch-American: 1911–) develops first kidney dialysis machine. Oswald Avery (Canadian: 1877–1955), Colin MacLeod, and Maclyn McCarty prove that DNA (deoxyribonucleic acid) is blueprint of heredity that determines how an organism develops. First eye bank, Eye-Bank for Sight Restoration, founded in New York.

**1945** Alfred Blalock (American: 1899–1964) introduces first operation to enable blue, or cyanotic, babies to survive (cyanosis, caused by poor circulatory flow or other problems, results in diminished oxygen in blood, causing bluish discoloration of the skin).

**1947** Eugene Payne (American) uses chloromycetin, developed by Parke-Davis researchers, to treat typhus patients; first use of "broad-spectrum" antibiotic.

**1948** Philip S. Hench (American: 1896–1965) and Edward C. Kendall (1886–1972) synthesize cortisone and use it to treat arthritis victims.

**1952** Jonas Salk (American: 1914– ) develops first vaccine against polio.

**1953** John H. Gibbon, Jr. (American: 1903– ) uses heart-lung machine he invented in successful open-heart operation.

**1954** Surgeons led by Joseph Murray (American) perform first successful kidney transplant. E. Cuyler Hammond (American: 1912–86) and Daniel Horn (American) present dramatic evidence of dangers in smoking.

**1957** Alick Isaacs (Scottish: 1921–67) and Jean Lindenmann (English) discover interferon, a protein that interferes with viral reproduction.

**1961** Scientists at Bell Laboratories announce first continuously operating laser, a tool having many surgical uses.

**1963** Thomas Starzl (American: 1926– ) performs first human liver transplant operation.

**1964** James Hardy (American: 1918– ) performs first human lung transplant.

**1966** Paul Parkman and Harry Myer (Americans) develop vaccine for rubella (German measles). Insulin synthesized independently by Michael Katsoyannis (American) and scientists in the People's Republic of China—first hormone to be synthesized.

**1967** Christiaan Barnard (South African: 1922– ) performs world's first heart transplant. Rene Favaloro (Argenti-

nian) performs first successful coronary bypass operation. First modern hospice founded in London.

**1969** Denton Cooley (American: 1920– ) implants first temporary artificial heart in human being.

**1972** Computerized axial tomography (CAT scan) is introduced in Great Britain.

**1975** First cases of what comes to be known as Lyme disease are reported in Lyme, Connecticut.

**1976** First recognized outbreak of "Legionnaires' disease" occurs at American Legion convention in Philadelphia.

**1977** Scientists at Genentech Corporation (U.S.) induce bacteria to make humanbrain hormone somatostatin—first human chemical produced by recombinant-DNA techniques.

**1978** First "test-tube baby" (person conceived outside human body) is born, in

England.

**1981** Scientists identify previously unknown disease, acquired immune deficiency syndrome (AIDS). Surgeons at University of California at San Francisco perform first successful operation on a fetus.

**1982** William DeVries (American) performs first complete replacement of human heart with artificial heart on Dr. Barney B. Clark at University of Utah.

**1984** First baby produced from frozen embryo is born, in Melbourne, Australia. Luc Montagnier (French) discovers virus believed to cause AIDS.

**1990** R Michael Blaese, W. French Anderson, and Kenneth W. Culver (Americans) develop procedure to infuse genetically engineered blood cells for treatment of immune system disorder—first gene therapy used in a human.

## HEALTH CARE EXPENDITURES

Health care costs are soaring, increasing much faster than the general inflation rate. During the 1980s, the health care component of the Consumer Price Index (CPI) increased at an annual rate of 8.3%, compared to 5.5% for the overall CPI. Health care costs are expected to continue to rise through the 1990s. According to testimony presented to the Senate Finance Committee by Budget Director Richard G. Darman in 1991, "Total health spending . . . is currently projected to reach 17% by the year 2000 and 37% of GNP by 2030."

The increases reflect higher prices for medical services, plus greater use of these services. Many factors contribute including: the rapidly increasing elderly population, who use medical care more intensely than younger people; more sophisticated, higher-priced medical equipment; specialization and labor intensiveness in the health care industry; an absence of appropriate and less expensive alternatives to hospital care; costly treatments for cancer, AIDS, and other ailments; abuses of Medicare and Medicaid programs; services needed by victims of crime, drugs, and accidents.

Health care expenditures continued to accelerate in 1989, reaching $604.1 billion, an increase of 11.1% over 1988. These moneys amounted to 11.6% of the GNP for 1989, up from 11.2% in 1988. Expenditures averaged $2,354 per capita, of which $2,068 was for personal health care; the remainder went to research, construction, program administration, the net cost of private health insurance, and public health activities. The $2,068 per capita amount for personal health care represented an increase of 10.6% over 1988 and was primarily due to economywide and industry-specific price inflation.

According to data compiled from statistics of the Organization for Economic Cooperation and Development, the United States spends more than any other developed nation on health care relative to its economy.

### NATIONAL EXPENDITURES FOR HEALTH CARE, 1960–1989

| Category | 1960 | 1965 | 1970 | 1975 | 1980 | 1985 | 1989 |
|---|---|---|---|---|---|---|---|
| **AMOUNT IN BILLIONS OF DOLLARS** | | | | | | | |
| Total expenditures | $27.1 | $41.6 | $74.4 | $132.9 | $249.1 | $420.1 | $604.1 |
| Private | 20.5 | 31.3 | 46.7 | 77.8 | 143.9 | 245.0 | 350.9 |
| Public | 6.7 | 10.3 | 27.7 | 55.1 | 105.2 | 175.1 | 253.3 |
| Federal | 2.9 | 4.8 | 17.7 | 36.4 | 72.0 | 123.6 | 174.4 |
| State and local | 3.7 | 5.5 | 9.9 | 18.7 | 33.2 | 51.5 | 78.8 |
| **PER CAPITA AMOUNT** | | | | | | | |
| Total expenditures | $143 | $204 | $346 | $592 | $1,059 | $1,700 | $2,354 |
| Private | 108 | 154 | 217 | 346 | 612 | 992 | 1,367 |
| Public | 35 | 50 | 129 | 245 | 447 | 708 | 987 |
| Federal | 15 | 24 | 83 | 162 | 306 | 500 | 680 |
| State and local | 20 | 27 | 46 | 83 | 141 | 208 | 307 |
| **PERCENT DISTRIBUTION** | | | | | | | |
| Total expenditures | 100.0% | 100.0% | 100.0% | 100.0% | 100.0% | 100.0% | 100.0% |
| Private | 75.5 | 75.3 | 62.8 | 58.5 | 57.8 | 58.3 | 58.1 |
| Public | 24.5 | 24.7 | 37.2 | 41.5 | 42.2 | 41.7 | 41.9 |
| Federal | 10.7 | 11.6 | 23.9 | 27.4 | 28.9 | 29.4 | 28.9 |
| State and local | 13.8 | 13.2 | 13.3 | 14.1 | 13.3 | 12.3 | 13.0 |
| **PERCENT OF GNP** | | | | | | | |
| National Health expenditures | 5.3% | 5.9% | 7.3% | 8.3% | 9.1% | 10.5% | 11.6% |

**Source:** U.S. Dept. of Health and Human Services, Health Care Financing Administration.

## Hospital Care

Hospital care has long claimed the biggest share of health care dollars—and the percentage is growing. In 1950 hospital care accounted for 30.4% of personal health care costs. By 1987 the percentage had reached 43.9%.

Costs vary markedly depending on the care required and the locale. For example, according to the Health Insurance Association of America, surgical costs of a hysterectomy averaged $4,165 in New York City in 1989, as compared to $1,885 in Atlanta; a triple coronary bypass averaged $5,624 in Philadelphia versus $4,425 in Dallas.

## Nursing-Home Care

People who reach age 65 have a 44% chance of spending some time in a nursing home before they die. The cost for such care is high . . . and rising rapidly. It currently averages close to $30,000 a year in the United States, though it is significantly higher in some parts of the country than in others.

At the beginning of 1987, there were 1.5 million nursing-home residents in the United States. More than 90% were age 65 or older, and over 45% were age 85 or older. Females accounted for 73.4% of the patients, reflecting the tendency for women to outlive men.

Americans spent $1 billion on nursing-home care in 1960, $4.9 billion in 1970, and $20 bil-

## HEALTH CARE SPENDING, BY CATEGORY, 1989

| Category | Amount in billions | Percent |
|---|---|---|
| Hospital care | $232.8 | 38.5% |
| Physicians' services | 117.6 | 19.5 |
| Drugs, other aids and supplies | 58.1 | 9.6 |
| Nursing-home care | 47.9 | 7.9 |
| Administration and net cost of private health insurance | 35.3 | 5.9 |
| Dentists' services | 31.4 | 5.2 |
| Other professional services | 27.0 | 4.5 |
| Government public health activities | 17.5 | 2.9 |
| Research | 11.0 | 1.8 |
| Other personal health care | 10.5 | 1.7 |
| Construction | 9.6 | 1.6 |
| Home health care | 5.4 | 0.9 |
| **Total** | **$604.1** | **100.0%** |

**Source:** U.S. Dept. of Health and Human Services, Health Care Financing Administration.

## HEALTH EXPENDITURES AS A PERCENTAGE OF GNP FOR SELECTED COUNTRIES, 1960–89

| Nation | 1960 | 1970 | 1980 | 1989 |
|---|---|---|---|---|
| United States | 5.2% | 7.4% | 9.3% | 11.8% |
| Sweden | 4.7 | 7.2 | 9.5 | 8.8 |
| Canada | 5.5 | 7.1 | 7.4 | 8.7 |
| France | 4.2 | 5.8 | 7.6 | 8.7 |
| Netherlands | 3.9 | 6.0 | 8.2 | 8.3 |
| Germany | 4.7 | 5.9 | 8.5 | 8.2 |
| Switzerland | 3.3 | 5.2 | 7.3 | 7.8 |
| Italy | 3.3 | 5.2 | 6.8 | 7.6 |
| Australia | 4.6 | 4.9 | 6.5 | 7.0 |
| Japan | 2.9 | 4.4 | 6.4 | 6.7 |
| Spain | 2.3 | 3.7 | 5.6 | 6.3 |
| United Kingdom | 3.9 | 4.5 | 5.8 | 5.8 |
| Greece | 3.2 | 4.0 | 4.3 | 5.1 |

**Sources:** Organization for Economic Cooperation and Development, *Measuring Health Care 1960–1983*; OECD, *Facts and Trends* (1991).

lion in 1980. By 1989, the figure reached $47.9 billion. Out-of-pocket payments, including personal savings and social security benefits, covered 44.4% of this cost; Medicaid paid 43.1%; other government and private funds, including private health insurance, were responsible for the remaining costs.

### Paying for Health Care

Medical care is generally paid for in one of three ways:

1. By patients; according to a 1990 report from the U.S. Dept. of Health and Human Services, 21% of the nation's medical costs in 1989 were paid directly by patients.

2. By an insurance plan; 33% of personal health care expenditures are financed by private insurers. Much of this in turn is paid by employer health plans. General Motors Corp. spent $2.9 billion for employee health benefits in 1987; AT&T spent about $1 billion.

3. As a public charge, which means that the government—and, ultimately, the taxpayer—pays the bill; 42% of medical costs are paid for by federal, state, and local governments. In some

## THE BOOMING COST OF HOSPITAL CARE, BY STATE, 1980–89

| State | Average daily room charge | | | Average cost per day[1] | | | Average cost per stay[1] | | |
|---|---|---|---|---|---|---|---|---|---|
| | 1980 | 1985 | 1989 | 1980 | 1985 | 1988 | 1980 | 1985 | 1988 |
| **U.S. Total** | **$127** | **$212** | **$262** | **$245** | **$460** | **$586** | **$1,851** | **$3,245** | **$4,207** |
| Alabama | 96 | 161 | 195 | 209 | 389 | 596 | 1,459 | 2,653 | 3,471 |
| Alaska | 189 | 295 | 363 | 408 | 693 | 961 | 2,276 | 3,742 | 5,615 |
| Arizona | 106 | 191 | 230 | 290 | 591 | 760 | 2,013 | 3,547 | 4,527 |
| Arkansas | 86 | 140 | 161 | 185 | 381 | 463 | 1,172 | 2,292 | 2,994 |
| California | 161 | 281 | 382 | 362 | 654 | 804 | 2,395 | 4,050 | 5,061 |
| Colorado | 124 | 211 | 262 | 247 | 486 | 627 | 1,760 | 3,221 | 4,432 |
| Connecticut | 127 | 206 | 354 | 271 | 502 | 685 | 2,039 | 3,610 | 5,065 |
| Delaware | 125 | 214 | 284 | 238 | 474 | 628 | 1,937 | 3,357 | 4,391 |
| Dist. of Columbia | 170 | 274 | 418 | 358 | 612 | 811 | 3,189 | 4,962 | 6,150 |
| Florida | 109 | 181 | 240 | 247 | 494 | 646 | 1,803 | 3,381 | 4,506 |
| Georgia | 92 | 150 | 190 | 218 | 386 | 516 | 1,380 | 2,501 | 3,488 |
| Hawaii | 127 | 231 | 303 | 245 | 420 | 517 | 1,868 | 3,522 | 4,651 |
| Idaho | 110 | 197 | 254 | 208 | 373 | 457 | 1,251 | 2,402 | 3,151 |
| Illinois | 144 | 248 | 283 | 277 | 498 | 633 | 2,183 | 3,607 | 4,645 |
| Indiana | 107 | 184 | 239 | 214 | 446 | 572 | 1,620 | 2,942 | 3,750 |
| Iowa | 107 | 179 | 213 | 199 | 359 | 432 | 1,465 | 2,735 | 3,547 |
| Kansas | 104 | 183 | 232 | 207 | 401 | 448 | 1,592 | 2,954 | 3,498 |
| Kentucky | 92 | 175 | 214 | 189 | 367 | 485 | 1,268 | 2,323 | 3,108 |
| Louisiana | 89 | 154 | 208 | 233 | 475 | 605 | 1,492 | 2,842 | 3,784 |
| Maine | 124 | 208 | 291 | 217 | 394 | 475 | 1,707 | 2,870 | 3,808 |
| Maryland | 119 | 186 | 248 | 251 | 443 | 579 | 2,136 | 3,237 | 3,997 |
| Massachusetts | 151 | 229 | 301 | 294 | 500 | 671 | 2,578 | 4,194 | 5,225 |
| Michigan | 151 | 267 | 311 | 267 | 507 | 644 | 2,087 | 3,666 | 4,712 |
| Minnesota | 105 | 187 | 240 | 203 | 369 | 458 | 1,818 | 3,302 | 4,103 |
| Mississippi | 67 | 113 | 167 | 174 | 319 | 375 | 1,178 | 2,037 | 2,593 |
| Missouri | 107 | 185 | 243 | 230 | 457 | 578 | 1,848 | 3,383 | 4,288 |
| Montana | 113 | 201 | 275 | 160 | 312 | 354 | 1,321 | 2,658 | 3,312 |
| Nebraska | 100 | 155 | 189 | 194 | 347 | 414 | 1,526 | 2,892 | 4,093 |
| Nevada | 125 | 243 | 256 | 343 | 677 | 763 | 2,201 | 3,953 | 4,840 |
| New Hampshire | 125 | 200 | 280 | 203 | 422 | 546 | 1,432 | 2,644 | 3,685 |
| New Jersey | 146 | 183 | 249 | 212 | 400 | 509 | 1,850 | 2,914 | 3,774 |
| New Mexico | 115 | 193 | 241 | 263 | 501 | 670 | 1,549 | 2,837 | 3,793 |
| New York | 157 | 228 | 291 | 257 | 419 | 530 | 2,469 | 3,930 | 5,070 |
| North Carolina | 87 | 139 | 174 | 187 | 356 | 487 | 1,397 | 2,416 | 3,538 |
| North Dakota | 93 | 173 | 217 | 177 | 322 | 377 | 1,528 | 2,918 | 3,869 |
| Ohio | 139 | 228 | 269 | 241 | 493 | 612 | 1,907 | 3,428 | 4,173 |
| Oklahoma | 101 | 162 | 204 | 239 | 455 | 547 | 1,527 | 2,814 | 3,632 |
| Oregon | 133 | 225 | 333 | 277 | 549 | 703 | 1,671 | 2,879 | 3,833 |
| Pennsylvania | 132 | 255 | 327 | 234 | 468 | 583 | 1,947 | 3,412 | 4,370 |
| Rhode Island | 138 | 206 | 297 | 260 | 447 | 546 | 2,162 | 3,432 | 4,396 |
| South Carolina | 80 | 145 | 201 | 186 | 358 | 474 | 1,367 | 2,508 | 3,347 |
| South Dakota | 96 | 161 | 190 | 189 | 282 | 360 | 1,265 | 2,442 | 3,214 |
| Tennessee | 91 | 140 | 181 | 204 | 397 | 517 | 1,427 | 2,709 | 3,545 |
| Texas | 91 | 159 | 212 | 226 | 461 | 628 | 1,491 | 2,799 | 3,884 |
| Utah | 112 | 173 | 279 | 271 | 556 | 737 | 1,462 | 2,799 | 3,879 |
| Vermont | 116 | 209 | 304 | 183 | 343 | 491 | 1,472 | 2,705 | 3,588 |
| Virginia | 101 | 165 | 194 | 211 | 399 | 529 | 1,647 | 2,862 | 3,690 |
| Washington | 125 | 229 | 327 | 262 | 546 | 708 | 1,502 | 3,062 | 3,984 |
| West Virginia | 110 | 166 | 202 | 195 | 399 | 494 | 1,393 | 2,520 | 3,319 |
| Wisconsin | 104 | 166 | 194 | 218 | 392 | 484 | 1,765 | 2,974 | 3,583 |
| Wyoming | 98 | 173 | 200 | 242 | 367 | 416 | 1,189 | 2,357 | 3,107 |

1. These are costs to the hospital. **Sources:** Health Insurance Association of America, *Source Book of Health Insurance Data, 1989*, and *Survey of Semi-Private Room Charges* (semiannual); American Hospital Association, *Hospital Statistics* (annual).

instances the percentage is even greater. For example, injuries caused by firearms cost an estimated $429 million annually in hospital expenses alone. According to a University of California study published in 1988, 85.6% of this is borne by taxpayers. The cost would top $1 billion if expenses such as ambulance services, doctors' fees, follow-up care, and rehabilitation were included.

**Health insurance** Americans spend more than 3% of their disposable income for health insurance premiums. There are five basic types of insurance:

1. Hospital expense insurance—pays costs of hospital room, X rays, medicines, etc.

2. Surgical expense insurance—pays costs of an operation.

3. Medical expense insurance—pays for visits to a physician's office.

4. Major medical expense insurance—pays costs associated with extended sickness or injury.

5. Disability income insurance—pays a benefit when the person is unable to work because of illness or injury.

**Federal insurance plans** Two government health programs, Medicare and Medicaid, pay approximately 27% of U.S. health costs. (The remaining federal health spending covers military and veterans' health care.)

Medicare is a federal health insurance plan for people age 65 and older and for severely disabled people under age 65. Medicaid is a health care program for poor people. It is funded jointly by federal and state agencies. (See also Part II, "Social Insurance Programs.")

**Health maintenance organizations (HMOs)** An HMO is a prepaid health care plan that provides comprehensive health care services to enrolled members on a prepaid basis. In other words, it integrates insurance and health care delivery within one organization. Between 1976 and 1990 the number of HMOs increased from 174 to 572, and enrollment rose from 6 million to approximately 33 million. There are two basic types of HMOs:

1. Individual practice associations, which contract with an association of physicians from various settings (a mixture of solo and group practices) to provide health care in their own offices. In 1990, 360 of all HMOs, with 13.7 million enrollees, were of this type.

2. Group practices, which contract with a group of physicians to provide medical services at one or more sites. In 1990, 212 HMOs, with 19.3 million enrollees, were of this type.

**The uninsured** The Census Bureau reported in 1990 that an estimated 31.5 million Americans—one person in eight—have no health insurance. The study concluded that 26.5% of Hispanic Americans were not covered in 1988, while the figure was 20.2% for blacks and 11.7% for whites. The age group least likely to have insurance protection was 16 to 24, with 21.9% lacking coverage. Because of the Medicare program, only 0.3% of people over 65 lacked coverage.

A study conducted by the U.S. Bipartisan Commission on Comprehensive Health Care indicated that in addition to the millions of people without any insurance coverage, as many as 20 million have inadequate health coverage. The Commission and Census Bureau reports came at a time when the government was under increasing pressure to consider proposals for universal health coverage.

## SURGERY

Increases in the number of surgical operations during the past decade have been accompanied by dramatic changes in the rates of some procedures. An excellent example is the growing incidence of cesarean sections—surgical incisions through the abdomen and uterus for removal of a baby, performed when normal vaginal delivery is deemed hazardous for the mother or child. Cesareans accounted for 10.4% of all live births in 1975, 16.5% in 1980, 22.7% in 1985, and 24.4% in 1988, decreasing slightly to 23.8% in 1989.

The frequency of certain procedures varies according to age, but, surprisingly, there may also be variations from one geographical region

to another. For example, 32% of the 1985 births in New Orleans covered by Blue Cross and other commercial insurers were cesareans—10% higher than the national average. Hysterectomies are performed on fewer than 5 out of 1,000 women per year in the Northeast but on more than 8 per 1,000 in the South.

### Eliminating the Need for Exploratory Surgery

Technological advances are creating new milestones in the art of medicine. Nowhere is this more apparent—or welcome—than in the diagnosis of people's health. Thanks to sophisticated electronics and other tools, physicians can obtain highly detailed views of internal organs without surgery. This often can be done on an outpatient basis, thereby lowering costs and avoiding risks associated with exploratory surgery. Furthermore, the techniques enable physicians to detect cancers and other problems in their earliest stages, allowing them to take preventive action that will decrease

chances of severe damage or death. New imaging techniques include the following:

**CAT** Computerized Axial Tomography—Uses X rays to take pictures, or tomograms, of the patient's body. The pictures are reconstructed by a computer to produce a crisp, 3-D image. CAT scans are particularly helpful in locating tumors, including ones deep in the brain.

**DSA** Digital Subtraction Angiography—An iodine-containing substance that is opaque to X rays is injected into blood vessels. Before and after X-ray images create a sharp picture of the vessels and the flow of blood.

**MRI** Magnetic Resonance Imaging—Uses a combination of a strong magnetic field and radio waves to measure the distribution and chemical bonds of the protons in the body's hydrogen atoms. A computer translates measurements into 3-D images. MRI is frequently used to view the brain and other soft tissues.

**PET** Positron-Emission Tomography—Small amounts of positron-emitting isotopes are injected into the blood to study the flow of blood

## HOSPITAL FACILITIES AND THEIR USE, 1946–89

| Year | Number of hospitals | Number of beds ('000s) | Admissions ('000s) | Occupancy rate | Outpatient visits ('000s) |
|---|---|---|---|---|---|
| 1946 | 6,125 | 1,436 | 15,675 | 79.5% | N.A. |
| 1950 | 6,788 | 1,456 | 18,483 | 86.0 | N.A. |
| 1955 | 6,956 | 1,604 | 21,073 | 85.0 | N.A. |
| 1960 | 6,876 | 1,658 | 25,027 | 84.6 | N.A. |
| 1965 | 7,123 | 1,704 | 28,812 | 82.3 | 125,793 |
| 1970 | 7,123 | 1,616 | 31,759 | 80.3 | 181,370 |
| 1975 | 7,156 | 1,466 | 36,157 | 76.7 | 254,844 |
| 1980 | 6,965 | 1,365 | 38,892 | 77.7 | 262,951 |
| 1985 | 6,872 | 1,318 | 36,304 | 69.0 | 282,140 |
| 1988 | 6,780 | 1,248 | 34,107 | 69.2 | 336,208 |
| 1989 | 6,720 | 1,226 | 33,742 | 69.6 | 352,248 |

**Note**: N.A. = not available. **Source**: American Hospital Association, *Hospital Statistics* (annual).

## MOST COMMON SURGICAL PROCEDURES, 1980–89

| Sex and procedure | Procedures ('000s) | | | Procedures per 1,000 population | | |
|---|---|---|---|---|---|---|
| | 1980 | 1985 | 1989 | 1980 | 1985 | 1989 |
| **Males, all ages[1]** | **8,505** | **8,805** | **8,886** | **78.1** | **76.3** | **72.8** |
| Cardiac catheterization | 228 | 439 | 601 | 2.2 | 3.9 | 5.1 |
| Prostatectomy | 335 | 367 | 376 | 3.1 | 3.2 | 3.0 |
| Reduction of fracture (excluding skull, nose, and jaw) | 325 | 339 | 342 | 2.9 | 2.8 | 2.8 |
| Coronary bypass | 108 | 172 | 271 | 1.0 | 1.6 | 2.3 |
| Repair of inguinal hernia | 483 | 370 | 220 | 4.6 | 3.3 | 1.8 |
| Operations on muscles, tendons, fascia, and bursa | 210 | 194 | 191 | 1.9 | 1.7 | 1.6 |
| **Females, all ages[1]** | **15,989** | **15,994** | **14,484** | **126.1** | **117.2** | **101.0** |
| Procedures to assist delivery | 2,391 | 2,494 | 2,446 | 18.4 | 18.0 | 17.1 |
| Cesarean section | 619 | 877 | 938 | 4.8 | 6.3 | 6.6 |
| Repair of lacerations due to giving birth | 355 | 548 | 762 | 2.8 | 3.9 | 5.3 |
| Hysterectomy | 649 | 670 | 541 | 5.2 | 5.0 | 3.9 |
| Removal of one or both ovaries | 483 | 525 | 421 | 3.9 | 4.0 | 3.1 |
| Destruction or closing off of fallopian tubes | 641 | 466 | 389 | 4.9 | 3.3 | 2.7 |
| Diagnostic dilation and curettage of uterus | 923 | 349 | 137 | 7.3 | 2.6 | 1.0 |

**Note:** Data is for inpatients discharged from non-federal, short-stay hospitals, based on a sample of hospital records. Beginning in 1989, the definition of some procedures was revised, thus causing a discontinuity in the trends for the totals. 1. Includes procedures not listed. Rates are age adjusted. **Source:** U.S. Dept. of Health and Human Services, National Center for Health Statistics, *Health United States 1990* (1991).

and its distribution to heart muscles or other tissues.

**SPECT** Single Photo Emission Computer Tomography—Uses radioisotopes to measure blood flow in small vessels. SPECT is particularly well suited to imaging the brain and is used to study such disorders as epilepsy, schizophrenia, Parkinson's disease, and strokes.

**Thermographic imaging** Data on the body's heat gathered by an infrared camera is converted by a computer into a temperature map, which is useful in detecting cancers and studying blood flow into limbs.

**Ultrasound imaging, or sonography** High-frequency sound waves are beamed at the body's organs. The echoes that bounce back are translated into computer images. Because it doesn't use X rays, sonography is recommended for use on pregnant women. It also is well suited for examining the gall bladder, liver, heart, and prostate gland.

## Organ Transplantation

Transplant surgery is more successful than ever, thanks to improved surgical techniques, a better understanding of the body's immune system, and the development of drugs that combat rejection of implanted organs. Kidney transplants, for instance, enjoy a high rate of success and are much less expensive—and much more convenient—than maintaining a patient on dialysis.

Unfortunately, a scarcity of donor organs keeps thousands of patients waiting, sometimes in vain. According to the United Network for Organ Sharing, as of Apr. 15, 1991, there were 22,909 Americans waiting for donor organs: 18,366 for kidneys, 2,007 for hearts, 1,386 for livers, 570 for pancreases, 411 for lungs, and 169 for heart-lung.

In addition to organs, tissues—cornea, bone, and skin—can be transplanted. In fact, corneal transplants are the most frequently performed transplant surgery; in 1989 there were 38,464 such operations, with a success rate averaging about 90%. As with organs, the need for tissues frequently exceeds the supply.

There are 71 organ procurement programs in the United States. Many have toll-free telephone numbers. The United Network for Organ Sharing operates the national waiting list (1-800-24-DONOR).

**Leading transplant centers** To perform transplants, hospitals must be licensed. Of the 6,174 hospitals reporting to the American Hospital Association's 1989 Annual Sur-

vey, 507 (8.2%) had facilities for performing organ or tissue transplants. The largest percentage of these (36%) were hospitals with 500 or more beds. California (41), Wisconsin (40), and Texas (35) led the states with the most organ-transplant facilities.

The following medical centers are leading transplant facilities that perform all or most transplant procedures.

**Alabama** The University of Alabama Hospital, 619 South 19 St., Birmingham, AL 35233; (205) 934-4011.

**California** University of California Medical Center, 10833 Le Conte Ave., Los Angeles, CA 90024; (213) 825-9111.

**Florida** Shands Hospital, University of Florida, Gainesville, FL 32610; (904) 395-0111.

**Illinois** University of Chicago Medical Center, 5841 Maryland Ave., Chicago, IL 60637; (312) 702-1000.

**Maryland** Johns Hopkins Medical Institutions, 600 North Wolfe St., Baltimore, MD 21205; (301) 955-5000.

**Massachusetts** Massachusetts General Hospital, 32 Fruit St., Boston, MA 02114; (617) 726-2000.

**Minnesota** The Mayo Clinic and Hospitals, 220 First St., S.W., Rochester, MN 55901; (507) 284-2511. The University of Minnesota Hospital and Clinics, Harvard Street at East River Road, Minneapolis, MN 55455; (612) 626-3000.

**Missouri** Barnes Hospital, Barnes Hospital Plaza, St. Louis, MO 63110; (314) 362-5000.

**New York** The Presbyterian Hospital, Columbia-Presbyterian Medical Center, New York, NY 10032-3784; (212) 305-5156.

**North Carolina** Duke University Medical Center, Durham, NC 27710; (919) 684-8111.

**Ohio** The Cleveland Clinic Foundation, 9500 Euclid Avenue, Cleveland, OH 44106; (216) 444-2200.

**Pennsylvania** Presbyterian-University Hospital, DeSoto at O'Hara St., Pittsburgh, PA 15213; (412) 647-2345.

**Texas** The Texas Medical Center, 6565 Fannin, Houston, TX 77030; (713) 790-3311.

**Utah** University Hospital and Clinics, The University of Utah Health Sciences Center, 50 N. Medical Drive, Salt Lake City, UT 84132; (801) 581-2121.

**Virginia** Medical College of Virginia Hospitals, 401 North 12 St., Richmond, VA 23298; (804) 786-4682.

**Wisconsin** University of Wisconsin Hospital and Clinics, 600 Highland Ave., Madison, WI 53792; (608) 263-6400.

## WHO HAS ABORTIONS?

Estimates based on a national survey of approx. 10,000 women who had abortions in 1987.

**MARITAL STATUS**

- Separated 6.4%
- Married 18.5%
- Single 63.3%
- Divorced 11.2%
- Widowed 0.6%

**AGE**

- 40 and over 1.7%
- 35-39 5.7%
- 30-34 11.7%
- 25-29 22.9%
- Under 18 11.7%
- 18-19 13.8%
- 20-24 33.1%

**Note:** Estimates based on a national survey of approximately 10,000 women who had abortions in 1987. **Source:** Alan Guttmacher Institute. Published in "Family Planning Perspectives" and *New York Times.*

## Abortion

The deliberate termination of a pregnancy before the fetus is capable of living outside the womb has generally been legal in the United States since 1973, when the Supreme Court ruled (in *Roe* v. *Wade*) that abortion cannot be prohibited during the first three months of pregnancy. From 1973 through 1982, the reported number of legal abortions increased every year. Since 1983, however, the numbers, as well as the ratio of abortions to live births, have remained relatively stable.

According to a 1990 report from the Centers for Disease Control, women who obtained abortions in 1988 were predominantly 24 years of age or younger, white, unmarried, and had no live-born children. As in previous years, about half of the abortions were performed during the first eight weeks of gestation; 88% were performed in the first 12 weeks. Curettage was the primary abortion procedure, accounting for 97% of all abortions.

The rate of abortion among American women is greater than among women in many other industrialized nations. The Alan Guttmacher Institute of New York indicates that the abortion rate—the number of abortions per 1,000 women aged 15 to 44—was 28 in 1985. Based on abortion rates, the institute projects that among every 100 women in the United States there will be 76 abortions, with some women having more than one.

## NUMBER AND COST OF TRANSPLANT OPERATIONS, 1989

| Organ | Year first performed | Number | Cost range | Mean cost | Success rate (1988) |
|---|---|---|---|---|---|
| Heart | 1967 | 1,689 | $50,000–287,000 | $148,000 | 82.8% |
| Heart-Lung | 1981 | 67 | 135,000–250,000 | 210,000 | 56.9[1] |
| Kidney | 1954 | 8,942 | 25,000–130,000 | 51,000 | 91.9, 96.6[2] |
| Liver | 1963 | 2,191 | 66,000–367,000 | 235,000 | 76.0 |
| Lung | 1963 | 91 | N.A. | 225,000 | 48.4[1] |
| Pancreas | 1966 | 418 | 51,000–135,000 | 70,000 | 89.1[1] |

1. Based on a comparatively small number of operations. 2. Success rates for cadaver and living related donor kidneys. **Source:** United Network for Organ Sharing; cost data prepared for the Network by Roger Evans, Battelle Institute.

## REPORTED ABORTIONS, 1972–88

| Category | 1972 | 1976 | 1980 | 1988[1] |
|---|---|---|---|---|
| **NUMBER OF ABORTIONS** | | | | |
| Reported abortions | 586,760 | 988,267 | 1,297,606 | 1,371,285 |
| Number per 1,000 live births | 180 | 312 | 359 | 352 |
| **PERCENT OF TOTAL** | | | | |
| Race | | | | |
| White | 77.0% | 66.6% | 69.9% | 65.3% |
| Other | 23.0 | 33.4 | 30.1 | 34.8 |
| Marital Status | | | | |
| Married | 29.7 | 24.6 | 23.1 | 20.4 |
| Unmarried | 70.3 | 75.4 | 76.9 | 79.6 |
| Age | | | | |
| Under 20 | 32.6 | 32.1 | 29.2 | 25.1 |
| 20–24 | 32.5 | 33.3 | 35.5 | 32.8 |
| 25 or older | 34.9 | 34.6 | 35.3 | 42.1 |
| Weeks of gestation | | | | |
| Up to 8 | 34.0 | 47.0 | 51.7 | 49.6 |
| 9–10 | 30.7 | 28.0 | 26.2 | 26.1 |
| 11–12 | 17.5 | 14.4 | 12.2 | 12.5 |
| 13–15 | 8.4 | 4.5 | 5.2 | 6.4 |
| 16–20 | 8.2 | 5.1 | 3.9 | 4.4 |
| 21 or more | 1.3 | 0.9 | 0.9 | 1.0 |

1. Preliminary. **Source:** U.S. Dept. of Health and Human Services, Centers for Disease Control, *Morbidity and Mortality Weekly Report* (Nov. 23, 1990).

## REPORTED CASES OF COMMON INFECTIOUS DISEASES, 1950–90

| Disease | 1950 | 1960 | 1970 | 1980 | 1985 | 1990 |
|---|---|---|---|---|---|---|
| Aseptic meningitis | N.A. | 1,593 | 6,480 | 8,028 | 10,619 | 11,178 |
| Brucellosis (undulant fever) | 3,510 | 751 | 213 | 183 | 153 | 77 |
| Diphtheria | 5,796 | 918 | 435 | 3 | 3 | 4 |
| Encephalitis | 1,135 | 2,341 | 1,950 | 1,402 | 1,537 | 1,250 |
| Legionnellosis | N.A | N.A. | N.A. | N.A. | 830 | 1,284 |
| Leprosy | 44 | 54 | 129 | 223 | 361 | 203 |
| Malaria | 2,184 | 72 | 3,051 | 2,062 | 1,049 | 1,185 |
| Meningococcal infections | 3,788 | 2,259 | 2,505 | 2,840 | 2,479 | 2,349 |
| Mumps ('000s) | N.A. | N.A. | 105 | 8.6 | 3 | 5.1 |
| Pertussis (whooping cough) ('000s) | 120.7 | 14.8 | 4.2 | 1.7 | 3.6 | 4.2 |
| Plague[1] | N.A. | 2 | 13 | 18 | 17 | 2 |
| Poliomyelitis | 33,300 | 3,190 | 33 | 9 | 7 | 0 |
| Rabies, in animals | 7,901 | 3,567 | 3,224 | 6,421 | 5,565 | 4,219 |
| Rubella (German measles) ('000s) | N.A. | N.A. | 56.6 | 3.9 | 0.6 | 1.1 |
| Tetanus | 486 | 368 | 148 | 95 | 83 | 60 |
| Toxic shock syndrome | N.A | N.A. | N.A. | N.A. | 384 | 293 |
| Trichinosis | 327 | 160 | 109 | 131 | 61 | 30 |
| Tularemia[2] | 927 | 390 | 172 | 234 | 177 | 137 |
| Typhoid fever | 2,484 | 816 | 346 | 510 | 402 | 503 |
| Typhus fever, tick-borne | 464 | 204 | 380 | 1,163 | 714 | 654 |
| Venereal disease[3] | | | | | | |
| Gonorrhea ('000s) | 286.7 | 258.9 | 600.1 | 1,004 | 911 | 664.2 |
| Syphilis ('000s) | 217.6 | 122 | 91.4 | 69 | 68 | 48.1 |

1. Plague: disease caused by the bite of fleas infected with the bacterium *Yersinia pestis*. 2. Tularemia: disease caused by the bacterium *Pasturella tularensis*, transmitted to humans by insects or direct contact with infected animals. 3. Civilian cases only. **Source:** U.S. Dept. of Health and Human Services, Centers for Disease Control, *Morbidity and Mortality Weekly Report*.

## DISEASE

Five of the most common categories of disease are:

1. Hereditary diseases—transferred from parent to child by genes. Examples: hemophilia, Down's syndrome, cystic fibrosis, sickle cell anemia.

2. Deficiency diseases—caused by lack of vitamins or other essential nutrients. Examples: scurvy, pellagra.

3. Infectious diseases—caused by viruses, bacteria, fungi, and other organisms and transferred from person to person. Examples: common cold, influenza, chicken pox, measles.

4. Diseases caused by chemical and physical agents such as radiation, smoke, drugs, and poisons. Examples: allergies, asbestosis, byssinosis, lead poisoning.

5. Degenerative diseases—resulting from natural aging processes. In some cases, cancer and high blood pressure are degenerative diseases.

### Heart Disease

Cardiovascular diseases (diseases of the heart and blood vessels) are America's number one killer. During 1989 an estimated 934,300 people died from these diseases. This represented approximately 43% of all deaths.

Death rates vary according to age, sex, race, even geographical location. Rates increase with age and are about 77% higher among men than among women. For both sexes, death rates are significantly higher among blacks than among whites, though the disparity has narrowed substantially in the past 20 years.

A study that divided the nation into nine geographic areas found that, on the average, people in the Mountain states have the lowest death rates from cardiovascular diseases, while those in the east south-central states (Kentucky, Tennessee, Alabama, and Mississippi) have the highest.

Death rates from heart disease have declined. This is due in part to improved drug treatments and other medical advancements. Another factor has been improved personal health habits: people have stopped smoking, decreased the amount of fat in their diets, and taken other steps that reduce their risks of cardiovascular disease.

**Heart attacks** A heart attack occurs when the blood supply to the heart muscles is blocked. An uncomfortable pressure, fullness, squeezing, or pain in the center of the chest that lasts for two minutes or more may be a sign of a heart attack. Sweating, dizziness, nausea, fainting, or shortness of breath may also occur. Some 1,500,000 people suffer heart attacks annually. One-third of these people do not survive. Of the survivors, 100,000 will have a second heart attack within two years.

**Strokes and bypass surgery** A stroke occurs when the blood supply to the brain is blocked, usually by a clot. The primary signal of a stroke is a sudden, temporary weakness or numbness of the face, arm, or leg on one side of the body. Other signals include temporary loss of speech, difficulty in speaking or understanding speech, temporary vision problems (particularly in one eye), unsteadiness, or unexplained dizziness.

Some 230,000 bypass operations at an estimated cost of $6 billion are performed annually in the country, more than double the number performed in 1980. In this operation a blood vessel from elsewhere in the body is used to reroute blood around a blocked coronary artery. The purpose: to reduce the person's risk of a stroke. Studies have indicated, however, that for a significant percentage of patients such surgery does not significantly improve their chances of survival over the following six years. Other research found that up to 44% of bypass operations are unnecessary or inappropriate.

## HEART DISEASE DEATH RATES, 1960–88 (per 100,000 population)

| Age | 1960[1] | 1970 | 1980 | 1988 |
|---|---|---|---|---|
| All ages | | | | |
| Age adjusted | 286.2 | 253.6 | 202.2 | 166.3 |
| Crude | 369.0 | 362.0 | 336.0 | 311.3 |
| Under 1 year | 6.6 | 13.1 | 22.8 | 22.6 |
| 1-4 years | 1.3 | 1.7 | 2.6 | 2.4 |
| 5-14 years | 1.3 | 0.8 | 0.9 | 0.9 |
| 15-24 years | 4.0 | 3.0 | 2.9 | 2.9 |
| 25-34 years | 15.6 | 11.4 | 8.3 | 8.2 |
| 35-44 years | 74.6 | 66.7 | 44.6 | 34.2 |
| 45-54 years | 271.8 | 238.4 | 180.2 | 131.4 |
| 55-64 years | 737.9 | 652.3 | 494.1 | 400.9 |
| 65-74 years | 1,740.5 | 1,558.2 | 1,218.6 | 984.1 |
| 75-84 years | 4,089.4 | 3,683.8 | 2,993.1 | 2,542.7 |
| 85 and older | 9,317.8 | 7,891.3 | 7,777.1 | 7,098.1 |

1. Includes deaths of nonresidents of the U.S. **Source:** U.S. Dept. of Health and Human Services, National Center for Health Statistics. *Health United States, 1990* (1991).

## 5-YEAR SURVIVAL RATES FOR CANCER, BY RACE AND SITE, 1960–86

| Cancer site | 1960–63 | 1970–73 | 1981–86 |
|---|---|---|---|
| **WHITES** | | | |
| **All sites** | **39%** | **43%** | **52%** |
| Bladder | 53 | 61 | 79 |
| Breast (females) | 63 | 68 | 78 |
| Cervix | 58 | 64 | 67 |
| Colon | 43 | 49 | 57 |
| Leukemia | 14 | 22 | 36 |
| Liver | 2 | 3 | 5 |
| Lung and bronchus | 8 | 10 | 13 |
| Ovary | 32 | 36 | 39 |
| Pancreas | 1 | 2 | 3 |
| Prostate | 50 | 63 | 75 |
| Rectum | 38 | 45 | 54 |
| Stomach | 11 | 13 | 16 |
| Thyroid | 83 | 86 | 94 |
| **BLACKS** | | | |
| **All sites** | **27%** | **31%** | **38%** |
| Bladder | 24 | 36 | 59 |
| Breast (females) | 46 | 51 | 64 |
| Cervix | 47 | 61 | 57 |
| Colon | 34 | 37 | 48 |
| Leukemia | N.A. | N.A. | 29 |
| Liver | N.A. | N.A. | 4 |
| Lung and bronchus | 5 | 7 | 11 |
| Ovary | 32 | 32 | 38 |
| Pancreas | 1 | 2 | 4 |
| Prostate | 35 | 55 | 62 |
| Rectum | 27 | 30 | 41 |
| Stomach | 8 | 13 | 18 |
| Thyroid | N.A. | N.A. | 96 |

**Note:** Rates are an average of cases diagnosed in years shown. **Source:** U.S. Dept. of Health and Human Services, National Cancer Institute; published in American Cancer Society, Cancer Facts and Figures—1991 (1991).

## CANCER DEATH RATES, 1950–88

### (per 100,000 population)

| Age | 1950[1] | 1960[1] | 1970 | 1980 | 1988 |
|---|---|---|---|---|---|
| **All ages** | | | | | |
| Age adjusted | 125.3 | 125.8 | 129.8 | 132.8 | 132.7 |
| Crude | 139.8 | 149.2 | 162.8 | 183.9 | 197.3 |
| Under 1 year | 8.7 | 7.2 | 4.7 | 3.2 | 2.3 |
| 1–4 years | 11.7 | 10.9 | 7.5 | 4.5 | 3.7 |
| 5–14 years | 6.7 | 6.8 | 6.0 | 4.3 | 3.3 |
| 15–24 years | 8.6 | 8.3 | 8.3 | 6.3 | 5.1 |
| 25–34 years | 20.0 | 19.5 | 16.5 | 13.7 | 11.9 |
| 35–44 years | 62.7 | 59.7 | 59.5 | 48.6 | 44.2 |
| 45–54 years | 175.1 | 177.0 | 182.5 | 180.0 | 160.4 |
| 55–64 years | 392.9 | 396.8 | 423.0 | 436.1 | 447.3 |
| 65–74 years | 692.5 | 713.9 | 751.2 | 817.9 | 842.7 |
| 75–84 years | 1,153.3 | 1,127.4 | 1,169.2 | 1,232.3 | 1,313.3 |
| 85 and older | 1,451.0 | 1,450.0 | 1,320.7 | 1,594.6 | 1,638.9 |

1. Includes deaths of nonresidents of the U.S. **Source:** U.S. Dept. of Health and Human Services, National Center for Health Statistics, Health United States, 1990 (1991).

## Cancer

The nation's second leading cause of death is a group of diseases characterized by the unrestrained growth of cells. It afflicts people of all ages and races, and it varies greatly in cause, symptoms, response to treatment, and

## ESTIMATED CANCER DEATHS BY SITE AND SEX, 1991

| Site | New cases | | | Deaths | | |
|---|---|---|---|---|---|---|
| | Total | Male | Female | Total | Male | Female |
| Skin | 32,000[1] | 17,000[1] | 15,000[1] | 8,500[2] | 5,400 | 3,100 |
| Oral | 30,800 | 20,600 | 10,200 | 8,150 | 5,275 | 2,875 |
| Lung, bronchus, and other respiratory | 178,000 | 114,000 | 64,000 | 148,025 | 95,800 | 52,225 |
| Breast | 175,900[3] | 900[3] | 175,000[3] | 44,800 | 300 | 44,500 |
| Esophagus | 10,900 | 7,600 | 3,300 | 9,800 | 7,300 | 2,500 |
| Stomach | 23,800 | 14,500 | 9,300 | 13,400 | 8,100 | 5,300 |
| Liver and bile passages | 15,000 | 7,800 | 7,200 | 12,100 | 6,300 | 5,800 |
| Pancreas | 28,200 | 13,700 | 14,500 | 25,200 | 12,000 | 13,200 |
| Colon and rectum | 157,500 | 79,000 | 78,500 | 60,500 | 30,000 | 30,500 |
| Other digestive plus unspecified digestive | 2,500 | 1,200 | 1,300 | 1,050 | 500 | 550 |
| Urinary (bladder, kidney, etc.) | 75,500 | 52,800 | 22,700 | 20,100 | 12,700 | 7,400 |
| Leukemias | 28,000 | 15,800 | 12,200 | 18,100 | 9,800 | 8,300 |
| Other blood plus lymph tissues | 56,900 | 30,000 | 26,900 | 29,400 | 15,200 | 14,200 |
| Bone | 2,000 | 1,100 | 900 | 1,050 | 550 | 500 |
| Connective tissue | 5,800 | 3,100 | 2,700 | 3,300 | 1,600 | 1,700 |
| Endocrine glands | 13,900 | 4,100 | 9,800 | 1,675 | 700 | 975 |
| Eye | 1,700 | 900 | 800 | 300 | 150 | 150 |
| Brain and central nervous system | 16,700 | 9,000 | 7,700 | 11,500 | 6,200 | 5,300 |
| Ovary | 20,700 | — | 20,700 | 12,500 | — | 12,500 |
| Uterus | 46,000 | — | 46,000 | 10,000 | — | 10,000 |
| Other genital, female | 5,000 | — | 5,000 | 1,000 | — | 1,000 |
| Prostate | 122,000 | 122,000 | — | 32,000 | 32,000 | — |
| Testis | 6,100 | 6,100 | — | 375 | 375 | — |
| Other genital, male | 1,200 | 1,200 | — | 250 | 250 | — |
| All other plus unspecified sites | 41,000 | 21,000 | 20,000 | 40,000 | 21,000 | 19,000 |

1. Melanoma only. 2. Melanoma 6,500; other skin 2,000. 3. Invasive cancer only. **Source:** American Cancer Society, Cancer Facts and Figures—1991 (1991).

possibility of cure.

Overall, cancer incidence and mortality rates have increased steadily. In part this is due to an increasingly aging population. Also, some cancers, particularly lung cancer, have a long latency period, developing after years of exposure to tobacco smoke or other cancer-causing agents.

The incidence of cancer varies from state to state. According to the American Cancer Society, the highest cancer death rates during 1991 will occur in the District of Columbia (222 cancer deaths per 100,000 population), Maryland (194), Delaware (190), Alaska (189), and Louisiana (187). The states with the lowest cancer death rates will be Utah (122), Hawaii (138), Colorado (144), New Mexico (144), and Idaho (146).

**Cancer survival rates** According to the American Cancer Society, more than 7 million Americans are alive who have a history of cancer, 3 million of them with diagnosis made five or more years ago. Chances of surviving cancer have steadily improved. In the 1930s, fewer than two out of 10 American cancer patients survived at least five years after diagnosis. In contrast, four out of 10 who get cancer this year will be alive five years after diagnosis.

Survival depends on many factors. Two of the most important are the site of the tumor and how much the cancer has spread before treatment is begun. The American Cancer Society estimated that of people diagnosed with cancers of the breast, tongue, mouth, colon,

rectum, cervix, prostate, testis, and melanoma (skin cancer) during 1991, nearly 100,000 more would survive if their cancers had been detected in a localized stage and treated promptly. In addition, the Society estimates that 155,000 lives would be lost in 1991 to cancer because of tobacco smoking.

**Cancer death rates** Since the 1950s, cancer death rates have fallen dramatically for children and young adults. Slighter declines have occurred among adults age 45–55, while death rates for older adults have increased somewhat. The pattern also varies according to sex and race. For white males, the age-adjusted rate rose from 130.9 cancer deaths per 100,000 population in 1950 to 157.6 in 1988. The rise was much greater for black males, from 126.1 to 227.0. For white females, the rate fell from 119.4 to 110.1, and for black females it fell from 131.9 to 131.2.

The American Cancer Society estimates that 514,000 Americans will die of cancer in 1991—about 1,400 people a day. Lung cancer is the leading cause of cancer deaths, killing an estimated 92,000 men and 51,000 women in 1991. Among women, breast cancer is the second most common killer, though if detected early and treated properly, it has a very high cure rate. Among men, prostate cancer causes the second greatest number of deaths. It, too, has a high survival rate if discovered while still localized within the general region of the prostate.

**Cancer warning signs** Early detection is the key in fighting cancer. See your doctor if one of the following symptoms lasts longer than two weeks.

1. Unusual bleeding or discharge.
2. A sore that does not heal.
3. A change in a wart or mole.
4. A lump or thickening in the breast or elsewhere.
5. A change in bowel or bladder habits.
6. Nagging cough or hoarseness.
7. Indigestion or difficulty in swallowing.

## AIDS

Acquired immune deficiency syndrome (AIDS) has been called "the most alarming disease of our times." By March 1991, the disease had claimed more than 105,000 lives just in the United States. Researchers at the Centers for Disease Control (CDC) project that 165,000 to 215,000 more Americans will die of AIDS by the end of 1993. Yet this devastating disease was unknown until 1981.

AIDS is caused by the human immunodeficiency virus (HIV), which is spread through contact with infected body fluids such as blood and semen. Infected people may harbor the virus within their bodies for several years or even longer before developing any symptoms. Though symptomless, they can still infect others. The CDC estimates that approximately 1 million persons in the United States are infected with HIV.

The illness suppresses the body's immune system, making patients very susceptible to deadly "opportunistic diseases" that strike when body defenses are down. Among these are Kaposi's Sarcoma, a rare form of skin cancer, and pneumocystis, a parasitic lung infection.

AIDS is apparently fatal: no one has recovered from the disease. No cure has yet been developed—nor do researchers anticipate development in the near future of a vaccine to pre-

## AIDS CASES AND DEATHS IN THE U.S., 1981–90

| Year | Cases diagnosed | Cases diagnosed to date | Known deaths | Known deaths to date |
|---|---|---|---|---|
| Pre-1981 | 83 | 83 | 31 | 31 |
| 1981 | 309 | 392 | 132 | 163 |
| 1982 | 1,110 | 1,502 | 449 | 612 |
| 1983 | 2,974 | 4,476 | 1,465 | 2,077 |
| 1984 | 5,994 | 10,470 | 3,343 | 5,420 |
| 1985 | 11,263 | 21,733 | 6,623 | 12,043 |
| 1986 | 18,277 | 40,010 | 11,356 | 23,399 |
| 1987 | 27,172 | 67,182 | 15,279 | 38,678 |
| 1988 | 32,699 | 99,851 | 19,350 | 58,280 |
| 1989 | 36,110 | 135,961 | 25,013 | 83,041 |
| 1990 | 30,704 | 166,665 | 22,236 | 105,277[1] |

Note: Reporting of diagnosed cases and deaths, particularly in more recent years, is incomplete. 1. In addition, through February 1991, there were 191 people known to have died but whose dates of death are unknown. Source: U.S. Dept. of Health and Human Services, Centers for Disease Control, HIV/AIDS Surveillance Report (March 1991).

## AIDS IN THE CITIES, 1991

| City | Number of cases |
|---|---|
| New York, N.Y. | 31,082 |
| Los Angeles, Calif. | 11,062 |
| San Francisco, Calif. | 9,717 |
| Houston, Tex. | 5,010 |
| Washington, D.C. | 4,770 |
| Miami, Fla. | 4,509 |
| Newark, N.J. | 4,497 |
| Chicago, Ill. | 4,170 |
| Philadelphia, Pa. | 3,468 |
| Atlanta, Ga. | 3,424 |
| Dallas, Tex. | 2,856 |
| Boston, Mass. | 2,715 |
| Ft. Lauderdale, Fla. | 2,687 |
| San Diego, Calif. | 2,421 |
| Oakland, Calif. | 2,078 |
| Baltimore, Md. | 2,013 |
| Jersey City, N.J. | 1,815 |
| Nassau-Suffolk, N.Y. | 1,733 |
| Seattle, Wash. | 1,697 |
| Tampa-St. Petersburg, Fla. | 1,650 |
| New Orleans, La. | 1,496 |
| West Palm Beach, Fla. | 1,488 |
| Detroit, Mich. | 1,465 |
| Bergen-Passaic, N.J. | 1,386 |
| Anaheim, Calif. | 1,373 |

Source: U.S. Dept. of Health and Human Services, Centers for Disease Control, HIV/AIDS Surveillance Report (March 1991).

## AIDS CASES BY REGION AND SELECTED COUNTRIES, 1991

| Region/Country | Reported cases | Region/Country | Reported cases | Region/Country | Reported cases |
|---|---|---|---|---|---|
| African region | 85,728 | Jamaica | 183 | Netherlands | 1,597 |
| Benin | 124 | Mexico | 5,907 | Norway | 203 |
| Burundi | 3,305 | Nicaragua | 11 | Poland | 51 |
| Ghana | 1,732 | Panama | 220 | Portugal | 586 |
| Ivory Coast | 6,836 | Trinidad and Tobago | 736 | Romania | 1,226 |
| Kenya | 9,139 | **United States** | **167,803** | Spain | 7,489 |
| Mozambique | 162 | Venezuela | 1,061 | Sweden | 510 |
| Nigeria | 149 | Eastern Mediterranean region | 675 | Switzerland | 1,730 |
| Rwanda | 3,407 | Afghanistan | 0 | United Kingdom | 4,228 |
| South Africa | 650 | Cyprus | 19 | U.S.S.R. | 48 |
| Tanzania | 8,163 | Egypt | 27 | Southeast Asia region | 162 |
| Uganda | 17,422 | Iran | 19 | Bangladesh | 1 |
| Zambia | 4,036 | Lebanon | 24 | India | 60 |
| Zimbabwe | 5,249 | Morocco | 70 | Indonesia | 9 |
| American region | 207,364 | Pakistan | 14 | Mongolia | 0 |
| Argentina | 710 | Somalia | 13 | Nepal | 4 |
| Bahamas | 599 | Syria | 9 | Sri Lanka | 8 |
| Barbados | 172 | Tunisia | 66 | Thailand | 80 |
| Bermuda | 147 | European region | 48,329 | Western Pacific region | 3,275 |
| Brazil | 16,015 | Belgium | 824 | Australia | 2,457 |
| Canada | 4,768 | Czechoslovakia | 24 | China | 5 |
| Chile | 255 | Denmark | 759 | Hong Kong | 42 |
| Colombia | 1,285 | France | 13,145 | Japan | 374 |
| Costa Rica | 232 | Germany | 6,022 | Malaysia | 16 |
| Cuba | 73 | Greece | 412 | New Zealand | 229 |
| Dominican Republic | 1,485 | Ireland | 179 | Philippines | 42 |
| El Salvador | 323 | Israel | 141 | Singapore | 22 |
| Honduras | 1,098 | Italy | 8,227 | Taiwan | 24 |

Source: World Health Organization, Update: AIDS Cases Reported to Surveillance, Forecasting and Impact Assessment Unit (SFI) Global Programme on AIDS (April 1991).

vent infection. Numerous drugs to combat AIDS are being tested, and several are being used to suppress the AIDS virus and combat the infections that afflict AIDS patients. Only azidothymidine (AZT) has thus far been demonstrated to extend life.

**AIDS patients** In the United States, homosexual and bisexual males make up approximately 59% of all adolescent adult AIDS patients. The other major group afflicted with AIDS is intravenous drug abusers—both men and women—who constitute 22% of the total. New infections are increasing at a much higher rate among drug users than among homosexuals.

Cases are not limited to these high-risk groups. Anyone may become infected by having sex with someone who is infected with the AIDS virus. Babies of infected women may be born with the disease because it can be transmitted from the mother to the baby before or during birth. Also, prior to blood screening that began in 1985, some hemophiliacs and other people were infected when they received blood contaminated with the HIV virus.

The overwhelming majority of AIDS cases are found in large cities and metropolitan areas. Through February 1991, 25 metropolitan areas accounted for 65% of all reported AIDs cases, as shown in the accompanying table.

**Heterosexuals and AIDS** New cases of AIDS attributed to heterosexual contacts represented 6% of the total number of new U.S. cases reported in 1990. Despite the comparatively low percentage, the disease is spreading faster among heterosexuals than among any other group. Heterosexuals most at risk are those with venereal disease and multiple sex partners. A 1989 study of patients at two clinics in Baltimore found that heterosexuals who had syphilis were seven to nine times more likely to have AIDS than other patients at the clinic. (Sores caused by syphilis and other venereal diseases are believed to make it easier for AIDS viruses to enter the body.)

Of the adult and adolescent AIDS cases reported through December 1990, only 2% of all AIDS cases in men were attributed to heterosexual contact. Almost all of these cases occurred among men either born in countries where transmission is predominantly heterosexual or among men who had had sex with female intravenous drug users. In contrast, 33% of all AIDS cases among women have been attributed to heterosexual contact; the majority resulted from sex with male intravenous drug users.

Many women infected with the AIDS virus give birth to babies that are also infected. In 1990 there were 681 cases of AIDS transmission from mothers to newborns—an increase of 21% over 1989.

**AIDS: A global problem** As of April 1, 1991, a global total of 345,533 cases of AIDS from 162 countries had been reported to the World Health Organization (WHO). The actual number of AIDS cases is believed to be considerably higher, however. The shortfall results from incomplete case detection and reporting, and delays in reporting cases to WHO. Some experts estimate under-reporting to be as high as 90% in Africa, compared to about 20% under-reporting in the U.S.

Furthermore, WHO experts believe that 8 million to 10 million people are infected with the AIDS virus worldwide. This will result in up to 3 million cases of AIDS by 1993—just among people now carrying the virus.

AIDS cases and infections have been reported from all continents, but there are significant differences in incidence and patterns of infection. Incidence has been lowest in Asia, while Africa, particularly Central and East Africa, has been hardest hit. In cities such as Lusaka, Zambia, and Kampala, Uganda, more than 20% of the adults are infected.

There are three patterns of AIDS spread. In Africa, parts of Latin America, and the Caribbean, AIDS spread has been predominantly among heterosexuals, and the disease affects both sexes fairly equally. In the United States and Western Europe, the disease appeared first in homosexuals and bisexuals, though heterosexual transmission is growing in those areas. The remainder of the world—Eastern Europe, the Middle East, North Africa, and most countries in Asia and the Pacific—is experiencing a "delayed" spread, having only about 1% of the AIDS cases reported to WHO.

## ADULTS AND ADOLESCENTS WITH AIDS, 1981–90

| Characteristic | Males | | Females | | Total | |
|---|---|---|---|---|---|---|
| | Cases | Percent | Cases | Percent | Cases | Pecent |
| Homosexual/bisexual males | 94,126 | 66% | — | — | 94,126 | 59% |
| Intravenous (IV) drug abusers | 26,540 | 19 | 7,858 | 51% | 34,398 | 22 |
| Homosexual male and IV drug abusers | 10,557 | 7 | — | — | 10,557 | 7 |
| Hemophilia/coagulation disorder | 1,352 | 1 | 34 | 0 | 1,386 | 1 |
| Heterosexuals | 3,367 | 2 | 5,073 | 33 | 8,440 | 5 |
| Blood transfusion | 2,252 | 2 | 1,432 | 9 | 3,684 | 2 |
| Other/Undetermined[1] | 4,600 | 3 | 1,096 | 7 | 5,696 | 4 |
| **Total** | **142,794** | **100%** | **15,493** | **100%** | **158,287** | **100%** |

Note: Provisional data. Cases with more than one risk factor other than the combinations listed are tabulated only in the category listed first. 1. Includes patients on whom risk information is incomplete, patients still under investigation, men reported only to have had heterosexual contact with a prostitute, and patients for whom no specific risk was identified; also includes one health care worker who developed AIDS after documented needlestick to blood. **Source:** U.S. Dept. of Health and Human Services, Centers for Disease Control, *HIV/AIDS Surveillance Report* (January 1991).

## CHILDREN WITH AIDS, 1981–90

| Characteristic | 1990 | | Cumulative 1981–90 | |
|---|---|---|---|---|
| | Total | Percent | Total | Percent |
| Hemophilia/coagulation disorder | 31 | 4% | 139 | 5% |
| Mother with/at risk of AIDS[1] | 681 | 87 | 2,327 | 84 |
| Blood transfusion | 39 | 5 | 252 | 9 |
| Undetermined[2] | 31 | 4 | 68 | 2 |
| **Total** | **782** | **100%** | **2,786** | **100%** |

Note: Provisional data. Includes all patients under 13 years of age at time of diagnosis. Cases with more than one risk factor other than the combinations are tabulated only in the category listed first. 1. Data suggest transmission from an infected mother to her fetus or infant during the perinatal period. 2. Includes patients on whom risk information is incomplete and patients still under investigation. **Source:** U.S. Dept. of Health and Human Services, Centers for Disease Control, *HIV/AIDS Surveillance Report* (January 1991).

## Sexually Transmitted Diseases

The most common sexually transmitted diseases (STDs) include genital warts, herpes, chlamydia, gonorrhea, and syphilis. STDs have been around since the beginning of recorded history, and while the prevalence of some have declined, rates for others have exploded. Today, millions of people suffer from STDs. The ubiquity of these diseases can be attributed in part to the fact that more people have been engaging in sex, and with more than one partner. The increased awareness of safe-sex practices, including the use of condoms and other "barrier" contraceptives (which is due to the fear of

## REPORTED CASES OF VENEREAL DISEASES, 1970-90

| Year | Syphilis | Gonorrhea |
|---|---|---|
| 1970 | 91,382 | 600,072 |
| 1974 | 83,771 | 906,121 |
| 1980 | 68,832 | 1,004,029 |
| 1984 | 69,886 | 879,587 |
| 1988 | 40,430 | 699,587 |
| 1989 | 42,857 | 700,751 |
| 1990 | 48,363 | 672,738 |

Note: Includes both civilian and military cases. **Source:** U.S. Dept. of Health and Human Services, Centers for Disease Control, *Morbidity and Mortality Weekly Report* (January issues).

contracting AIDS) will probably lead to decline in the number of STD cases.

Many STDs have similar symptoms. Some have no symptoms at all, particularly in women. The following may indicate the presence of an STD: vaginal or penile discharge; inflammation, itching, or pain in the genital or anal area; pain during intercourse; burning during urination; sores, blisters, bumps, or rashes; fever or swollen glands; lower abdominal or testicular pain.

Immediate, proper treatment is urged for all STDs. Failure to do so can have serious consequences, resulting in infertility, blindness, cancer, and death. Children born to women afflicted with STDs may suffer brain damage and other disorders.

Only cases of syphilis and gonorrhea are currently reported to the Centers for Disease Control. Even with these, the actual number of cases is believed to be significantly higher than reported. Estimates for new cases of gonorrhea approach 2 million annually; for syphilis the estimates are approximately 100,000.

It is estimated that as many as 40 million Americans suffer from genital warts, with some 500,000 to 750,000 new cases annually. Herpes is believed to afflict up to 20 million people, with 200,000 to 500,000 new cases each year. And each year there may be more than 5 million new cases of chlamydia, a disease caused by the bacterium *Chlamydia trachomatis* and perhaps the fastest-spreading STD in the country today.

## Hepatitis: A Growing Cause of Liver Disease

One of today's most serious health problems caused by viruses is viral hepatitis, a disease that attacks the liver. Of particular concern is hepatitis B, which is generally transmitted via contact with the blood of an infected person during sex, during birth, or through contaminated needles or syringes. People at high risk are intravenous drug users who share needles, homosexual men, and heterosexuals with multiple partners.

According to the Centers for Disease Control, new infections increased from about 200,000 cases in 1978 to 300,000 in 1988. Some of those infected become chronic carriers. An estimated one million Americans are believed to be chronic carriers, capable of transmitting the virus to other people. Furthermore, chronic carriers are at high risk of developing cirrhosis or liver cancer. Each year in the United States, about 4,000 hepatitis B patients die of cirrhosis and 1,000 die of liver cancer. The World Health Organization estimates that 2 billion people worldwide are infected with hepatitis B, and that the disease causes 1.2 million deaths each year. The toll is particularly high in developing countries, where the virus often is passed from mothers to their newborn infants. Even in the United States, some 3,500 infants become infected each year.

Two vaccines for hepatitis B became available in the 1980s, but both are costly and as a result few people have been vaccinated.

## CHANGES IN THE LEADING CAUSES OF DEATH, 1900–87

| Cause of death | Percent of deaths | | | | | |
|---|---|---|---|---|---|---|
| | 1900 | 1920 | 1940 | 1960 | 1980 | 1987[1] |
| **NATURAL CAUSES** | | | | | | |
| Ischemic heart disease; other myocardial insufficiencies | 7.9% | 12.2% | 26.5% | 28.9% | 28.8% | 24.1% |
| Hypertensive heart disease and hypertension | [2] | [2] | [2] | [2] | 1.5 | 1.4 |
| Other heart diseases | [2] | [2] | [2] | 7.8 | 8.2 | 10.6 |
| Cerebrovascular disease | 4.7 | 6.6 | 7.4 | 11.3 | 8.6 | 7.0 |
| Diseases of the arteries, arterioles, capillaries | 0.3 | 1.8 | 1.8 | 2.1 | 2.5 | 2.2 |
| Cancer | 3.8 | 6.6 | 11.5 | 15.6 | 20.9 | 22.4 |
| Diabetes | 0.6 | 1.2 | 2.5 | 1.7 | 1.8 | 1.8 |
| Influenza and pneumonia | 10.4 | 11.7 | 6.5 | 3.9 | 2.7 | 3.2 |
| Chronic liver disease and cirrhosis | 1.3 | 0.8 | 0.9 | 1.2 | 1.5 | 1.2 |
| Other diseases | 65.9 | 52.3 | 34.1 | 20.4 | 15.3 | 19.3 |
| **Total natural causes** | **94.9%** | **93.2%** | **91.2%** | **92.9%** | **91.9%** | **93.2%** |
| **EXTERNAL CAUSES** | | | | | | |
| Motor vehicle accidents | — | 0.8% | 2.4% | 2.2% | 2.7% | 2.2% |
| Other accidents | 4.4 | 4.7 | 4.4 | 3.3 | 2.8 | 2.3 |
| Suicide | 0.6 | 0.8 | 1.4 | 1.1 | 1.4 | 1.4 |
| Homicide | 0.1 | 0.5 | 0.6 | 0.5 | 1.2 | 0.9 |
| **Total external causes** | **5.1%** | **6.8%** | **8.8%** | **7.1%** | **8.1%** | **6.8%** |

1. Preliminary figures. 2. Included with "Other Diseases." **Source:** U.S. Dept. of Health and Human Services, National Center for Health Statistics.

## Resurgence of Old Diseases

A number of diseases once thought to be under control are now on the upswing.

**Tuberculosis** By the late 1970s, public health experts were predicting that this chronic bacterial disease would be almost completely eliminated in the United States by the end of the century. In the past few years, however, the number of cases has been increasing, especially in cities such as Newark, Miami, Atlanta, San Diego, and New York. The resurgence appears to result in part from the fact that people infected with the AIDS virus are very susceptible to tuberculosis. Other high-risk groups include drug users, alcoholics, the homeless, and people living in crowded conditions. According to the World Health Organization (WHO), some 1.7 billion people are infected with tuberculosis worldwide, and the disease kills 3 million people annually. A tuberculosis vaccine exists, but it is designed for children and is not effective on adults.

**Measles** cases jumped to a ten-year high in the United States in 1990, with 26,527 cases (including 97 deaths) reported to the Centers for Disease Control (CDC). The resurgence of the disease was blamed on the failure of many parents to get their children immunized. Also, the effectiveness of the measles vaccine appeared to decrease over time. The CDC recommends a second dose of the vaccine for children who are beginning kindergarten or first grade. According to the WHO, about 49 million people are infected worldwide, and the disease kills about 1.5 million annually.

**Malaria** is caused by a parasite transmitted by the anopheles mosquito. The number of infected people rose steadily during the 1980s, in part because developing equatorial countries are encouraging development in swampy, anopheles-infected regions. According to WHO estimates, malaria affects more than 270 million and kills 1.2 million people worldwide yearly.

## LEADING CAUSES OF DEATH, 1989

| Cause of death | Deaths in 1989 | | Death rate per 100,000 | |
|---|---|---|---|---|
| | Number | Percent | 1979 | 1989 |
| **All causes** | **2,155,000** | **100.0%** | **852.2** | **868.1** |
| Heart diseases | 735,450 | 34.1 | 326.5 | 296.3 |
| Cancer | 497,220 | 23.1 | 179.6 | 200.3 |
| Cerebrovascular diseases | 147,470 | 6.8 | 75.5 | 59.4 |
| Accidents | 94,780 | 4.4 | 46.9 | 38.2 |
| Pulmonary diseases | 84,350 | 3.9 | 22.2 | 34.0 |
| Pneumonia and influenza | 75,240 | 3.5 | 20.1 | 30.3 |
| Diabetes mellitus | 46,560 | 2.2 | 14.8 | 18.8 |
| Suicide | 31,210 | 1.4 | 12.1 | 12.6 |
| Liver disease and cirrhosis | 26,380 | 1.2 | 13.2 | 10.6 |
| Homicide and legal intervention | 23,020 | 1.1 | 10.0 | 9.3 |
| AIDS | 21,360 | 1.0 | — | 8.6 |
| Kidney diseases | 21,230 | 1.0 | 7.0 | 8.6 |
| Atherosclerosis | 19,120 | 0.9 | 12.8 | 7.7 |
| Septicemia | 19,080 | 0.9 | 3.6 | 7.7 |
| Perinatal-related conditions | 18,540 | 0.9 | 10.4 | 7.5 |
| All other causes | 293,940 | 13.6 | — | 118.4 |

**Source:** U.S. Dept. of Health and Human Services, National Center for Health Statistics, *Monthly Vital Statistics Report* (Aug. 30, 1990).

## DEATH

Provisional data indicate that 2,162,000 deaths occurred in the United States in 1990, about 7,000 more deaths than in the previous year. The death rate of 8.6 per 1,000 population was 1% lower than the rate of 8.7 for 1989.

## DEATHS AND DEATH RATES, 1990

| Age | Total deaths | Rate per 100,000 population Both sexes | Male | Female |
|---|---|---|---|---|
| All ages | 2,175,000 | 867.7 | 922.0 | 816.1 |
| Under 1 year | 38,200 | 944.0 | 1,042.9 | 839.7 |
| 1–4 years | 6,859 | 45.7 | 50.7 | 40.4 |
| 5–14 years | 8,600 | 24.1 | 28.8 | 19.2 |
| 15–24 years | 37,280 | 103.7 | 154.3 | 51.7 |
| 25–34 years | 60,910 | 139.2 | 204.4 | 73.9 |
| 35–44 years | 83,790 | 221.9 | 307.2 | 138.5 |
| 45–54 years | 118,550 | 465.4 | 603.6 | 334.4 |
| 55–64 years | 253,280 | 1,181.7 | 1,516.7 | 880.8 |
| 65–74 years | 483,490 | 2,624.8 | 3,384.1 | 2,013.4 |
| 75–84 years | 611,220 | 6,137.4 | 7,992.3 | 4,999.8 |
| 85 and older | 471,090 | 14,974.3 | 17,743.4 | 13,897.8 |
| Not stated | 1,440 | — | — | — |

**Note:** For the 12 months ending November 1990. Data are provisional, estimated from a 10% sample of deaths. **Source:** U.S. Dept. of Health and Human Services, National Center for Health Statistics, *Monthly Vital Statistics Report* (Apr. 8, 1991).

Males experience greater number of deaths and higher death rates than females, with black males having significantly higher numbers and rates than white males. Provisional data reported by the National Center for Health Statistics indicate that age-adjusted death rates (which take into account changes and variations in the age composition of the population) for 1989 were: white females, 378.8 deaths per 100,000 population; black females, 564.6; white males, 647.9; and black males, 1,010.0.

**Causes of death** For the purpose of national mortality statistics, every death is attributed to one underlying condition. The 15 leading causes of death in 1989 accounted for 86.4% of all deaths in the United States. The leading causes of death from 1979 through 1989 have generally been the same, but the order has often varied. The exception is AIDS, which ranked as a cause of death for the first time in 1987.

Over the years the leading causes of death have changed significantly. In 1900, infectious diseases took many lives, a fact reflected in the five leading causes of death: (1) pneumonia and influenza, (2) tuberculosis, (3) gastritis, (4) heart disease, and (5) cerebrovascular diseases. Today none of the top five causes of death is an infectious disease.

### Life Expectancy

Life expectancy figures represent the average number of years that infants are expected to live. Life expectancy has improved steadily over the years, largely due to a decline in deaths during childhood. The development of drugs to combat infectious diseases, plus improved nutrition and better environmental sanitation, have all played major roles in combating early deaths.

## AVERAGE REMAINING LIFE EXPECTANCY (in years)

| Age in 1986 | All races M | All races F | Whites M | Whites F | Other races M | Other races F |
|---|---|---|---|---|---|---|
| At birth | 71.3 | 78.3 | 72.0 | 78.8 | 67.2 | 75.1 |
| 1 | 71.1 | 78.0 | 71.7 | 78.4 | 67.4 | 75.1 |
| 2 | 70.2 | 77.0 | 70.8 | 77.5 | 66.4 | 74.2 |
| 3 | 69.2 | 76.1 | 69.8 | 76.5 | 65.5 | 73.2 |
| 4 | 68.2 | 75.1 | 68.8 | 75.5 | 64.5 | 72.3 |
| 5 | 67.3 | 74.1 | 67.8 | 74.6 | 63.6 | 71.3 |
| 6 | 66.3 | 73.1 | 66.9 | 73.6 | 62.6 | 70.3 |
| 7 | 65.3 | 72.2 | 65.9 | 72.6 | 61.6 | 69.4 |
| 8 | 64.3 | 71.2 | 64.9 | 71.6 | 60.6 | 68.4 |
| 9 | 63.3 | 70.2 | 63.9 | 70.6 | 59.7 | 67.4 |
| 10 | 62.4 | 69.2 | 62.9 | 69.6 | 58.7 | 66.4 |
| 11 | 61.4 | 68.2 | 61.9 | 68.6 | 57.7 | 65.4 |
| 12 | 60.4 | 67.2 | 61.0 | 67.7 | 56.7 | 64.4 |
| 13 | 59.4 | 66.2 | 60.0 | 66.7 | 55.7 | 63.4 |
| 14 | 58.4 | 65.2 | 59.0 | 65.7 | 54.8 | 62.5 |
| 15 | 57.5 | 64.3 | 58.0 | 64.7 | 53.8 | 61.5 |
| 16 | 56.5 | 63.3 | 57.1 | 63.7 | 52.8 | 60.5 |
| 17 | 55.6 | 62.3 | 56.1 | 62.8 | 51.9 | 59.5 |
| 18 | 54.6 | 61.3 | 55.2 | 61.8 | 51.0 | 58.6 |
| 19 | 53.7 | 60.4 | 54.3 | 60.8 | 50.0 | 57.6 |
| 20 | 52.8 | 59.4 | 53.4 | 59.9 | 49.1 | 56.6 |
| 21 | 51.9 | 58.4 | 52.5 | 58.9 | 48.2 | 55.7 |
| 22 | 51.0 | 57.5 | 51.5 | 57.9 | 47.3 | 54.7 |
| 23 | 50.1 | 56.5 | 50.6 | 56.9 | 46.4 | 53.7 |
| 24 | 49.2 | 55.5 | 49.7 | 56.0 | 45.5 | 52.8 |
| 25 | 48.2 | 54.6 | 48.8 | 55.0 | 44.7 | 51.8 |
| 26 | 47.3 | 53.6 | 47.9 | 54.0 | 43.8 | 50.9 |
| 27 | 46.4 | 52.6 | 47.0 | 53.1 | 42.9 | 49.9 |
| 28 | 45.5 | 51.7 | 46.0 | 52.1 | 42.0 | 49.0 |
| 29 | 44.6 | 50.7 | 45.1 | 51.1 | 41.1 | 48.0 |
| 30 | 43.7 | 49.7 | 44.2 | 50.1 | 40.3 | 47.1 |
| 31 | 42.7 | 48.8 | 43.2 | 49.2 | 39.4 | 46.1 |
| 32 | 41.8 | 47.8 | 42.3 | 48.2 | 38.5 | 45.2 |
| 33 | 40.9 | 46.8 | 41.4 | 47.2 | 37.7 | 44.3 |
| 34 | 40.0 | 45.9 | 40.5 | 46.3 | 36.8 | 43.3 |
| 35 | 39.1 | 44.9 | 39.5 | 45.3 | 36.0 | 42.4 |
| 36 | 38.2 | 44.0 | 38.6 | 44.3 | 35.1 | 41.5 |
| 37 | 37.3 | 43.0 | 37.7 | 43.4 | 34.3 | 40.6 |
| 38 | 36.4 | 42.1 | 36.8 | 42.4 | 33.5 | 39.7 |
| 39 | 35.5 | 41.1 | 35.9 | 41.5 | 32.6 | 38.7 |
| 40 | 34.5 | 40.2 | 34.9 | 40.5 | 31.8 | 37.8 |
| 41 | 33.6 | 39.2 | 34.0 | 39.6 | 31.0 | 36.9 |
| 42 | 32.8 | 38.3 | 33.1 | 38.6 | 30.2 | 36.0 |

| Age in 1986 | All races M | All races F | Whites M | Whites F | Other races M | Other races F |
|---|---|---|---|---|---|---|
| 43 | 31.9 | 37.3 | 32.2 | 37.7 | 29.4 | 35.1 |
| 44 | 31.0 | 36.4 | 31.3 | 36.7 | 28.6 | 34.3 |
| 45 | 30.1 | 35.5 | 30.4 | 35.8 | 27.8 | 33.4 |
| 46 | 29.2 | 34.6 | 29.5 | 34.9 | 27.0 | 32.5 |
| 47 | 28.4 | 33.7 | 28.7 | 33.9 | 26.2 | 31.6 |
| 48 | 27.5 | 32.8 | 27.8 | 33.0 | 25.4 | 30.8 |
| 49 | 26.6 | 31.8 | 26.9 | 32.1 | 24.6 | 29.9 |
| 50 | 25.8 | 31.0 | 26.1 | 31.2 | 23.9 | 29.1 |
| 51 | 25.0 | 30.1 | 25.2 | 30.3 | 23.1 | 28.2 |
| 52 | 24.1 | 29.2 | 24.4 | 29.4 | 22.4 | 27.4 |
| 53 | 23.3 | 28.3 | 23.6 | 28.6 | 21.7 | 26.6 |
| 54 | 22.5 | 27.5 | 22.7 | 27.7 | 21.0 | 25.8 |
| 55 | 21.8 | 26.6 | 21.9 | 26.8 | 20.3 | 25.0 |
| 56 | 21.0 | 25.8 | 21.2 | 26.0 | 19.6 | 24.2 |
| 57 | 20.2 | 24.9 | 20.4 | 25.1 | 19.0 | 23.4 |
| 58 | 19.5 | 24.1 | 19.6 | 24.3 | 18.3 | 22.7 |
| 59 | 18.8 | 23.3 | 18.9 | 23.4 | 17.7 | 21.9 |
| 60 | 18.0 | 22.5 | 18.2 | 22.6 | 17.0 | 21.2 |
| 61 | 17.3 | 21.7 | 17.5 | 21.8 | 16.4 | 20.5 |
| 62 | 16.7 | 20.9 | 16.8 | 21.0 | 15.8 | 19.8 |
| 63 | 16.0 | 20.1 | 16.1 | 20.2 | 15.3 | 19.1 |
| 64 | 15.3 | 19.4 | 15.4 | 19.5 | 14.7 | 18.4 |
| 65 | 14.7 | 18.6 | 14.8 | 18.7 | 14.1 | 17.7 |
| 66 | 14.1 | 17.9 | 14.1 | 18.0 | 13.6 | 17.1 |
| 67 | 13.4 | 17.1 | 13.5 | 17.2 | 13.1 | 16.4 |
| 68 | 12.8 | 16.4 | 12.9 | 16.5 | 12.5 | 15.7 |
| 69 | 12.2 | 15.7 | 12.3 | 15.8 | 12.0 | 15.1 |
| 70 | 11.7 | 15.0 | 11.7 | 15.1 | 11.5 | 14.5 |
| 71 | 11.1 | 14.3 | 11.1 | 14.4 | 11.0 | 13.8 |
| 72 | 10.6 | 13.7 | 10.6 | 13.7 | 10.5 | 13.2 |
| 73 | 10.1 | 13.0 | 10.1 | 13.0 | 10.1 | 12.7 |
| 74 | 9.6 | 12.4 | 9.6 | 12.4 | 9.6 | 12.1 |
| 75 | 9.1 | 11.7 | 9.1 | 11.8 | 9.2 | 11.5 |
| 76 | 8.6 | 11.1 | 8.6 | 11.1 | 8.7 | 11.0 |
| 77 | 8.2 | 10.5 | 8.1 | 10.5 | 8.3 | 10.4 |
| 78 | 7.7 | 9.9 | 7.7 | 9.9 | 7.9 | 9.9 |
| 79 | 7.3 | 9.4 | 7.3 | 9.4 | 7.5 | 9.4 |
| 80 | 6.9 | 8.8 | 6.9 | 8.8 | 7.1 | 8.9 |
| 81 | 6.5 | 8.3 | 6.5 | 8.3 | 6.8 | 8.4 |
| 82 | 6.1 | 7.8 | 6.1 | 7.8 | 6.5 | 7.9 |
| 83 | 5.8 | 7.3 | 5.7 | 7.3 | 6.2 | 7.5 |
| 84 | 5.5 | 6.8 | 5.4 | 6.8 | 5.9 | 7.1 |
| 85 | 5.2 | 6.4 | 5.1 | 6.4 | 5.7 | 6.8 |

**Note:** Based on an individual's age in 1986. For example, a black female age 40 in 1986 would be expected to live 37.8 more years, or to about 77 or 78 years old. A white male born in 1986 would expect to live to age 72. **Source:** U.S. Dept. of Health and Human Services, National Center for Health Statistics.

In 1988, the average life expectancy at birth was 74.9 years. Life expectancy for the white population was 75.6, the same as the record high in 1987, while the black population experienced a decrease to 69.2 years from a life expectancy of 69.4 in 1987.

The difference in life expectancy between the white and black populations narrowed from 7.6 years in 1970 to 5.6 years in 1983 and 1984. Thereafter, it increased, to 6.4 years in 1988. Increases in death rates from homicides, killings in police confrontations, auto accidents, AIDS, tuberculosis, and other categories had a disproportionate impact on the races in the latest years, affecting blacks more than whites.

## LIFE EXPECTANCY AT BIRTH, 1920–88

| Year[1] | All races Male | All races Female | Whites Male | Whites Female | Others Male | Others Female |
|---|---|---|---|---|---|---|
| 1920 | 53.6 | 54.6 | 54.4 | 55.6 | 45.5 | 45.2 |
| 1930 | 58.1 | 61.6 | 59.7 | 63.5 | 47.3 | 49.2 |
| 1940 | 60.8 | 65.2 | 62.1 | 66.6 | 51.5 | 54.9 |
| 1950 | 65.6 | 71.1 | 66.5 | 72.2 | 59.1 | 62.9 |
| 1960 | 66.6 | 73.1 | 67.4 | 74.1 | 61.1 | 66.3 |
| 1970 | 67.1 | 74.7 | 68.0 | 75.6 | 60.0 | 68.3 |
| 1980 | 70.0 | 77.4 | 70.7 | 78.1 | 63.8 | 72.5 |
| 1988 | 71.5 | 78.3 | 72.3 | 78.9 | 64.9 | 73.4 |

1. Data prior to 1960 exclude Alaska and Hawaii. Data prior to 1940 are for death-registration states only. **Source:** U.S. Dept. of Health and Human Services, National Center for Health Statistics, *Health United States 1990* (1991).

## Infant Mortality

In 1990 there were 38,100 deaths of infants age one year or less. The most commonly used index for measuring the risk of dying during the first year of life are infant mortality rates, which are calculated by dividing the number of infant deaths by the number of live births registered for the same period. The 1990 rate of 9.1 infant deaths per 1,000 live births was the lowest ever recorded for the United States. The number of infants deaths decreased only 2% from 1989, but the number of births increased 4%, resulting in a 6% decrease in the infant mortality rate from 1989 to 1990.

The rate among white infants is less than half that of black infants: 8.5 infants deaths per 1,000 live births for whites in 1988, versus 17.6 per 1,000 for blacks. The reasons for this discrepancy are not clear, although an important factor is believed to be the quality of medical care received by people of different socioeconomic groups. For example, several studies

### U.S. INFANT MORTALITY RATE,
1940–90 (per 1,000 live births)

| Race | 1940 | 1950 | 1960 | 1970 | 1980 | 1986 | 1990[1] |
|---|---|---|---|---|---|---|---|
| All races | 47.0 | 29.2 | 26.0 | 20.0 | 12.6 | 10.4 | 9.1 |
| White | 43.2 | 26.8 | 22.9 | 17.8 | 11.0 | 8.9 | N.A. |
| Black | 72.9 | 43.9 | 44.3 | 32.6 | 21.4 | 18.0 | N.A. |

1. Provisional data for 12 months ending November 1990. **Source**: U.S. Dept of Health and Human Services, National Center for Health Statistics, *Monthly Vital Statistics Report* (April 1991).

### INFANT MORTALITY RATES IN SELECTED INDUSTRIALIZED NATIONS, 1982–87

| Rank/nation | Infant deaths per 1,000 births[1] | |
|---|---|---|
| | 1982 | 1987 |
| 1. Japan | 6.6 | 5.0 |
| 2. Sweden | 6.9 | 5.7 |
| 3. Finland | 6.8 | 6.2 |
| 4. Switzerland | 7.7 | 6.9 |
| 5. Canada | 9.1 | 7.3 |
| 6. Singapore | 10.7 | 7.3 |
| 7. Hong Kong | 9.9 | 7.5 |
| 8. Netherlands | 8.3 | 7.6 |
| 9. France | 9.5 | 7.8 |
| 10. Ireland | 10.5 | 7.9 |
| 11. West Germany | 10.9 | 8.2 |
| 12. Denmark | 8.2 | 8.3 |
| 13. Norway | 8.1 | 8.4 |
| 14. Scotland | 11.4 | 8.5 |
| 15. Australia | 10.3 | 8.7 |
| 16. Northern Ireland | 13.7 | 8.7 |
| 17. East Germany | 11.4 | 8.8 |
| 18. Spain | 11.3 | 9.0 |
| 19. England & Wales | 10.8 | 9.2 |
| 20. Belgium | 11.1 | 9.7 |
| 21. Austria | 12.8 | 9.8 |
| 22. Italy | 13.1 | 9.8 |
| 23. New Zealand | 12.0 | 10.0 |
| 24. United States | 11.5 | 10.1 |

1. Babies who die before one year of age. **Source**: U.S. Dept. of Health and Human Services, National Center for Health Statistics, *Health United States, 1990* (1991).

of infant deaths have shown that adequate prenatal care is strongly associated with higher infant birth weight and survival. Many black mothers, who are far more likely to be poor than white mothers, do not have access to proper prenatal care. Poor nutrition, alcohol and drug abuse, and other social factors also play significant roles.

Disproportionate poverty among minority groups is not the whole story, however. Studies have shown that even black infants born to college-educated mothers had nearly twice the mortality rate of comparable white infants.

## Suicide

Each year, some 30,000 Americans kill themselves—about one person every 20 minutes. In addition, an estimated 400,000 unsuccessful attempts are made. Although more attempts are made by women, more completed suicides are by men. In 1988, there were 24,078 suicides committed by men and 6,329 committed by women.

Particularly troublesome is the suicide rate for people age 15 to 23, which has almost tripled since 1950. The causes of youth suicide are not yet known, although some evidence suggests that suicide is not as frequently associated with depression in young people as it is in adults. Many young suicide victims had a history of impulsive, aggressive, or antisocial behavior, often complicated by drug abuse. Having a parent who committed suicide also seems to increase a person's vulnerability.

Significant differences in suicide rates exist among the states. For 1988, the highest rates were reported for Nevada (26.0), New Mexico (22.8), Arizona (19.5), Colorado (18.1), and Montana (18.0). The lowest were for New York (6.7), New Jersey (7.0), Massachusetts (8.6), South Carolina (9.9), and Rhode Island (10.0).

Most Americans who commit suicide shoot themselves, usually with handguns. Other common methods, in decreasing order of frequency, include drug overdose (primarily drugs prescribed by physicians), cutting and stabbing, jumping from high places, inhaling poisonous gas, hanging, and drowning.

Many experts believe that suicide statistics are grimmer than reported. They contend that numerous suicides are categorized as accidents or other deaths to spare families.

### SUICIDE IN THE U.S., 1950–88

| Age | Total 1988 | Rate per 100,000 population | |
|---|---|---|---|
| | | 1950 | 1988 |
| All ages | 30,407[1] | 11.4 | 12.7 |
| 0–4 years | — | — | — |
| 5–14 years | 243 | 0.2 | 0.7 |
| 15–24 years | 4,929 | 4.5 | 13.2 |
| 25–34 years | 6,710 | 9.1 | 15.4 |
| 35–44 years | 5,205 | 14.3 | 14.8 |
| 45–54 years | 3,532 | 20.9 | 14.6 |
| 55–64 years | 3,406 | 27.0 | 15.6 |
| 65–74 years | 3,296 | 29.3 | 18.4 |
| 75–84 years | 2,462 | 31.1 | 25.9 |
| 85 and older | 605 | 28.8 | 20.5 |

1. Includes 19 people of unknown age. **Source**: U.S. Dept. of Health and Human Services, National Center for Health Statistics, *Monthly Vital Statistics Report* (November 1990).

## ACCIDENTS

Every 10 minutes, two people are killed and about 170 are disabled in accidents in the United States. Accidents are the nation's fourth most common cause of death. But for people between the ages of 1 and 37, accidents are *the* leading cause of death. And among youths age 15 to 24, accidents claim more lives than all other causes combined. More than three out of four accident victims in this age group are males.

Accident rates vary significantly from one place to another. The accidental death rate for the U.S. in 1989 was 38.1 deaths per 100,000 population. The highest death rates were in New Mexico (64.1) and South Carolina (54.2); the lowest were in Ohio (27.0) and New York (27.8).

The costs incurred from accidents total almost $150 billion annually—for medical care, wage loss, insurance administration, property damage, fire loss, and so on.

Approximately 20 million home injuries occurred in 1988. Some 3.4 million of these disabled people for one or more days. About 90,000 resulted in permanent impairment.

### TYPES OF ACCIDENTAL DEATHS, 1989

| Type | Number of deaths | Age group (years) | | | | | | |
|---|---|---|---|---|---|---|---|---|
| | | 0–4 | 5–14 | 15–24 | 25–44 | 45–64 | 65–74 | 75 + |
| All accidents | 94,500 | 4,000 | 4,100 | 16,000 | 28,300 | 15,400 | 8,500 | 18,200 |
| Motor vehicle | 46,900 | 1,400 | 2,300 | 12,400 | 16,100 | 7,500 | 3,300 | 3,900 |
| Falls | 12,400 | 100 | 50 | 300 | 1,000 | 1,600 | 1,750 | 7,600 |
| Poisoning by solids and liquids[1] | 5,600 | 40 | 20 | 700 | 3,500 | 900 | 210 | 230 |
| Drowning | 4,600 | 600 | 600 | 900 | 1,300 | 650 | 280 | 270 |
| Fires and burns | 4,400 | 650 | 350 | 300 | 1,000 | 750 | 450 | 900 |
| Suffocation | 3,900 | 350 | 50 | 50 | 350 | 500 | 600 | 2,000 |
| Firearms | 1,600 | 40 | 210 | 500 | 500 | 230 | 60 | 60 |
| Poisoning by gases | 900 | 20 | 20 | 150 | 350 | 170 | 50 | 140 |
| All other[2] | 14,200 | 800 | 500 | 700 | 4,200 | 3,100 | 1,800 | 3,100 |

1. Deaths from poisons, drugs, medicines, mushrooms, and shellfish. Excludes poisonings from spoiled foods, salmonella, etc., which are classified as disease deaths. 2. Medical complications, air and water transport, machinery, excessive cold, etc. **Source**: National Safety Council, *Accident Facts* (1990).

## Motor Vehicle Deaths, 1989

Since the nation's first motor vehicle death—reportedly in New York City on September 14, 1899—nearly 2,800,000 people have died in motor vehicle accidents. Over the years, however, the numbers of deaths per 100,000 population and per 100,000 registered vehicles have declined drastically. For example, according to the National Safety Council, there were 3,100 motor vehicle deaths in 1912, when the number of registered vehicles totaled only 950,000. In 1989 there were 46,900 fatalities, but registered vehicles had risen to 193 million. Here's how people died in motor vehicle accidents in 1989:

19,900—collisions between two or more motor vehicles

13,100—collisions with guardrails and other fixed objects

## ACCIDENTS BY SITE, 1989

| Site | Deaths | Disabling injuries | Cost (billions) |
|---|---|---|---|
| Total[1] | 94,500 | 9,000,000 | $148.5 |
| Motor vehicle | 46,900 | 1,700,000 | 72.2 |
| Home | 22,500 | 3,400,000 | 18.2 |
| Work | 10,400 | 1,700,000 | 48.5 |
| Other | 19,000 | 2,400,000 | 12.5 |

1. Deaths and injuries for the four separate classes total more than national figures due to rounding and because some deaths and injuries are included in more than one class. For example, 3,900 work deaths involved motor vehicles and are in both the work and motor vehicle totals. **Source**: National Safety Council, *Accident Facts* (1990).

7,200—pedestrians struck by motor vehicles
4,900—noncollision accidents
1,000—collisions with cyclists
700—collisions with railroad trains
100—other types of collisions, usually ones involving animals or animal-drawn vehicles.

## ESTIMATED NUMBER OF INJURIES IN U.S., SELECTED PRODUCTS, 1990

| Product | Estimated injuries | Product | Estimated injuries |
|---|---|---|---|
| Stairs, steps | 998,871 | Hammers | 49,469 |
| Bicycles, accessories | 580,119 | Razors, shavers | 46,274 |
| Knives | 446,317 | Jewelry | 44,343 |
| Tables | 316,530 | Wheelchairs | 42,578 |
| Chairs | 275,100 | Chain saws | 39,331 |
| Nails, screws, tacks | 253,873 | Bunk beds | 36,908 |
| Windows, window glass | 169,734 | Hot water | 36,240 |
| Bathtubs, showers | 136,616 | Contact lenses | 35,311 |
| Drinking glasses | 133,375 | Trampolines | 32,553 |
| Ladders | 126,653 | Pens, pencils | 32,340 |
| Fences, fence posts | 120,865 | Televisions | 32,303 |
| Bottles, jars | 117,786 | Paper money, coins | 29,612 |
| Drugs, medications | 114,345 | Refrigerators | 28,343 |
| Carpets, rugs | 86,269 | Scissors | 26,342 |
| Skateboards | 82,428 | Sleds | 24,095 |
| Footwear | 75,870 | Pins, needles | 23,369 |
| Lawn mowers | 75,351 | Gasoline | 20,002 |
| Sinks, toilets | 57,203 | Baby strollers | 12,748 |

**Note**: These national estimates are based on injuries treated in hospital emergency rooms participating in the National Electronic Injury Surveillance System. Patients said their injuries were related to the products; this does not necessarily mean the injuries were caused by the products. **Source**: Consumer Product Safety Commission, National Electronic Injury Surveillance System, *Product Summary Report* (1990).

## ACCIDENTAL DEATHS AND DEATH RATES BY NATION, 1987–88
### (per 100,000 population)

| Nation | Year reported | Accidental deaths | Rate per 100,000 pop. |
|---|---|---|---|
| Australia | 1988 | 5,751 | 34.8 |
| Austria | 1988 | 3,976 | 52.3 |
| Canada | 1987 | 9,492 | 37.0 |
| Chile | 1987 | 3,038 | 24.2 |
| Costa Rica | 1988 | 902 | 31.5 |
| Cuba | 1987 | 7,612 | 73.9 |
| Czechoslovakia | 1988 | 8,584 | 55.0 |
| Denmark | 1988 | 2,598 | 50.7 |
| England, Wales | 1988 | 11,322 | 22.5 |
| France | 1988 | 33,101 | 59.2 |
| Hong Kong | 1987 | 776 | 13.8 |
| Hungary | 1988 | 7,619 | 71.9 |
| Iceland | 1988 | 77 | 30.8 |
| Japan | 1988 | 30,212 | 24.8 |
| Kuwait | 1987 | 535 | 28.6 |
| Poland | 1988 | 18,169 | 48.0 |
| Portugal | 1988 | 4,630 | 45.0 |
| Singapore | 1987 | 431 | 16.5 |
| Sweden | 1987 | 2,893 | 34.4 |
| Switzerland | 1988 | 3,352 | 50.8 |
| Thailand | 1987 | 14,009 | 26.1 |
| United States | 1987 | 95,020 | 39.0 |
| West Germany | 1988 | 19,778 | 32.2 |

**Note**: Accidental deaths are classified on the basis of a World Health Organization standard. However, differences in reporting among nations affect comparisons. **Source**: World Health Organization.

# RELIGION IN AMERICA

As of 1987, the most recent year for which figures are available, 147.5 million Americans claimed affiliation with a religious group. This represents about 61 percent of the population. The following table shows that 94 percent of the religiously affiliated were members of Christian or quasi-Christian denominations. Non-Christian religions—primarily Judaism and Islam—account for the other 6 percent.

Christians in the United States are members of a bewildering variety of denominations, each independent of the next. The *Yearbook of American and Canadian Churches* lists about 220 Christian denominations, and other sources list more than 1,000. For simplicity's sake the following table groups the denominations into 20 major families. Denominations listed in the same family nearly always share common historical roots and some principal doctrines. They may disagree violently about other doctrines and issues, however. The following are brief descriptions of each of the Christian denominational families and of major non-Christian faiths. (See also Part III, "World Religions.")

## Roman Catholic Church

The Roman Catholic church is the largest single Christian denomination in the United States. It claims nearly 36 percent of all religiously affiliated people—22 percent of the total population. Worldwide, there are nearly 900 million Roman Catholics (see "World Religion").

Many U.S. Catholics—descendants of immigrants from Ireland, Germany, Poland, Italy, and France—are concentrated in the Northeast and the industrial Midwest. Hispanic-Americans in Florida and the Southwest are also predominantly Catholic.

The church is hierarchically organized. Bishops, who administer church affairs in a given region, are appointed by higher authority. The world leader of the Roman church is the pope, who directs the church from Vatican City in Rome.

Priests are male and in most parts of the church must be and remain unmarried. Orders of nuns and monks provide many educational and charitable services. Many local churches operate parochial elementary schools. Regional bodies and religious orders operate high schools and help administer many seminaries and church-related colleges. In recent years the number of applicants for the priesthood and for religious orders has sharply decreased, even as membership in the church has continued to increase.

Catholic leaders have taken strong stands on many contemporary issues. The National Conference of Catholic Bishops has taken relatively liberal positions on efforts to bring about world peace and economic justice. In areas of personal conduct, the church is more conservative. It leads the campaign to outlaw abortion and opposes mechanical means of birth control.

## Baptist Churches

The Baptist family of churches is the largest Protestant family in the United States. Baptists trace their theological roots back to radical reformers in Europe in the 1500s, but the number of Baptists in the world was tiny until the 1800s, when Baptist faith and practice became predominant in the American South (both for whites and for blacks). Baptists are still most heavily represented in the southern and border states.

Local Baptist congregations have great independence, determining many of their own policies. At the same time, these churches share many practices. They agree that the rite of baptism should be administered only to those who have reached an age of independent judgment. Consequently, children are baptized no earlier than the age of 6 or 7, often by total immersion in the baptismal water. A Baptist child is not counted as a member until after baptism, which means that small children are not included in the membership totals reported above.

Most Baptists take a strong stand on the authority of the Bible, and many (though not all) believe that it should be interpreted literally. Baptists have traditionally been strong supporters of separation of church and state. Many Baptist denominations have mounted energetic missionary campaigns to bring the Christian message to people around the world.

The Southern Baptist Convention, a predominantly white church, is the largest Protestant denomination in the United States. The two National Baptist Conventions and the Progressive National Baptist Convention are predominantly black churches. Together they account for the religious affiliation of more blacks than any other family of churches.

### Methodist Churches

Methodist churches trace their origins to John Wesley (1703–91), a minister in the Church of England who sought to bring a new sense of warmth and commitment to individuals' religious life. He urged his followers to set aside regular times to study the Bible and pray together. Wesley's opponents laughingly called his followers Methodists because of their discipline and seriousness. Wesley himself remained in the Church of England his whole life, but his followers began to develop independent organizations, both in England and the United States.

On the American frontier, Methodist "circuit riders" traveled from settlement to settlement, preaching and marrying, baptizing and burying members of pioneer families. Methodism grew with astonishing swiftness. By 1820 it was the largest religious family in the United States, and it remained the largest Protestant family until the 1920s.

The United Methodist Church accounts for more than two-thirds of the Methodist family's total membership. This denomination is made up of not only traditional Methodists but also several churches of German origin whose beliefs and spirit accorded well with Methodism. The two "African" churches and the Christian Methodist Church are predominantly black churches, and they account for nearly all of the remaining third of the Methodist group.

### Lutheran Churches

Lutherans trace their churches back to the German reformer Martin Luther (1483–1546). Luther sought to reform the doctrine and practice of the Roman Christian Church in Europe. He complained about corruption among the clergy and advocated worship in the language of the people rather than in Latin. He also came to favor a married, rather than a celibate, clergy. The Church of Rome considered Luther disloyal and eventually drove him out. He then helped establish independent churches in northern Germany.

Immigrants from Germany and Scandinavia brought the Lutheran faith to North America, concentrating first in Pennsylvania. Later immigrants settled in the upper Midwest. By 1900 scores of small Lutheran Church bodies were divided from one another by language,

theology, and degree of assimilation into American society. The Evangelical Lutheran Church in America represents a uniting of many of those earlier churches. The Lutheran Church–Missouri Synod, a national church despite its name, is more conservative theologically.

### Pentecostal Churches

The Pentecostal churches share a belief that God grants believers special spiritual gifts—especially the experience called "speaking in tongues," a common feature of Pentecostal services.

Pentecostal churches trace their origin to the day of Pentecost, described in the biblical book of Acts, when early Christians received ecstatic or mystical powers. Modern Pentecostalism began in the early 1900s, when members of some Holiness churches received the gift of tongues (see "Holiness Churches" following).

Pentecostal congregations tend to be small. They may meet in storefronts or in rented quarters on upper floors. Yet the Pentecostal faith, with its immediacy and emotional power, is perhaps the fastest-growing in the nation, attracting thousands of new adherents each year. In addition Pentecostal beliefs have had an impact on Roman Catholic, Lutheran, Episcopal, and other denominations. These denominations report a growth among adherents of "charismatic renewal," a movement based on spiritual gifts.

The two Churches of God in Christ and the United Pentecostal Church are predominantly black denominations. The Assemblies of God is the largest predominantly white denomination. Many Pentecostal organizations are regional or purely local. Because of this loose organization, there are likely to be thousands of Pentecostal believers not counted here because their local congregations are not affiliated with a regional or national group.

### Reformed Churches

The Reformed churches are those that trace their descent to the French-Swiss reformer John Calvin (1509–64). These churches were especially significant in the early settlement of the present-day United States. The Pilgrims and Puritans who settled in New England established the Congregational Church, which is a main component of today's United Church of Christ. New York was settled by the Dutch, who established the present-day Reformed Church in America. Later, immigrants of Scottish and Scotch-Irish descent established a strong Presbyterian Church. Presbyterians differed from Congregationalists in matters of church governance but shared many points of theology and practice.

Reformed church buildings are generally simple and sparsely adorned. Similarly, worship in these churches is austere and simple. Reformed churches generally value a well-educated clergy. In the past they helped found Harvard, Yale, and Princeton. Direct ties to these universities have ended, but Reformed organizations still support many colleges.

The Presbyterian Church (USA) is the result of several mergers between smaller Pres-

byterian churches that had been separated by regional and doctrinal differences. The United Church of Christ includes, in addition to Congregational churches, descendants of German Reformed churches and of the Evangelical and Reformed Church (also of German descent). The Reformed Church in America and the Christian Reformed Church are both of Dutch descent.

### Orthodox Churches

The first great schism in the Christian church occurred in A.D. 1054 between the Western church, centered at Rome, and the Eastern church, centered at Constantinople (present-day Istanbul). In 1054 Eastern Christianity was predominant in Greece and the Middle East, and missionaries had already introduced the faith in Russia. The Russian church celebrated its 1,000th anniversary in 1988. Immigrants from these countries brought Orthodox churches to the United States.

The two largest Orthodox churches in the United States today are Greek and Russian, respectively. The next largest represent Armenians (whose homeland straddles the border between Iran and the Soviet Union) and Syrians. Together these four churches have more than 80 percent of the Orthodox membership.

Orthodox churches are organized hierarchically. Archbishops and bishops possess special spiritual authority and administer church affairs. Religious observances tend to be solemn and elaborate. Ancient liturgies in the ancient languages have been carefully preserved. Orthodox clergy are male, and in most churches they are allowed to marry. Because of differences in calculating feast days, Easter and other movable feasts may occur on different dates in the Orthodox church than in the Western churches.

In the United States, many Orthodox churches have served as cultural centers for immigrants seeking to preserve their own ethnic heritage. At the same time, however, many denominations are active members of ecumenical groups such as the National Council of Churches.

### Latter-day Saints (Mormons)

The churches of the Latter-day Saints, known popularly as Mormon churches, were founded by a 19th-century American prophet named Joseph Smith (1805–44). Smith, who grew up in western New York State, reported direct revelations from God. His religious vision included both traditional Christian elements and new accounts of God's visitations to pre-Columbian America.

Smith assembled a community of believers that settled first in western New York and later in Ohio, Missouri, and Illinois. Wherever it went, it aroused the antagonism of neighboring non-Mormons. Persecution came to a climax with the murder of Smith himself in 1844.

The next great leader of the church was Brigham Young (1801–77), who led the majority of Mormons westward to settle in the then-uninhabited basin by the Great Salt Lake. There the church grew and prospered. Even

# RELIGIOUS AFFILIATIONS IN THE UNITED STATES

| FAMILY/Denomination | Local congregations | Total clergy | Total membership | % of total affiliated |
|---|---|---|---|---|
| ALL RELIGIOUSLY AFFILIATED | 346,092 | 532,697 | 147,499,662 | 100.0% |
| CHRISTIAN CHURCHES | 342,576 | 526,082 | 138,585,662 | 94.0% |
| ROMAN CATHOLIC CHURCH | 23,561 | 53,382 | 52,893,217 | 35.9% |
| BAPTIST CHURCHES | 97,004 | 146,818 | 28,224,395 | 19.1% |
| Southern Baptist Convention | 37,072 | 63,200 | 14,613,618 | |
| National Baptist Convention, USA, Inc. | 26,000 | 27,500 | 5,500,000 | |
| National Baptist Convention of America | 11,398 | 28,574 | 2,668,799 | |
| American Baptist Churches in the USA | 5,864 | 7,678 | 1,576,483 | |
| Baptist Bible Fellowship International | 3,449 | 4,500 | 1,405,900 | |
| Progressive Natl. Baptist Convention, Inc. | 655 | 863 | 521,692 | |
| General Assoc. of Regular Baptist Churches | 1,571 | 2,045 | 300,839 | |
| American Baptist Association | 1,705 | 1,760 | 250,000 | |
| National Primitive Baptist Convention, Inc. | 606 | 636 | 250,000 | |
| Baptist Missionary Association of America | 1,359 | 2,450 | 228,125 | |
| Conservative Baptist Assoc. of America | 1,140 | — | 225,000 | |
| Free Will Baptists, Natational Assoc. of | 2,483 | 2,895 | 205,546 | |
| Baptist General Conference | 762 | 1,700 | 131,480 | |
| Liberty Baptist Fellowship | 267 | 374 | 130,000 | |
| Others (10 denominations) | 2,673 | 2,643 | 216,913 | |
| METHODIST CHURCHES | 52,704 | 53,554 | 13,343,996 | 9.0% |
| United Methodist Church | 37,876 | 37,808 | 9,192,172 | |
| African Methodist Episcopal Church | 6,200 | 6,550 | 2,210,000 | |
| African Methodist Episcopal Zion Church | 6,057 | 6,396 | 1,195,173 | |
| Christian Methodist Episcopal Church | 2,340 | 2,650 | 718,922 | |
| Others (4 denominations) | 231 | 150 | 27,729 | |
| LUTHERAN CHURCHES | 18,739 | 27,153 | 8,455,747 | 5.7% |
| Evangelical Lutheran Church in America | 11,041 | 16,929 | 5,318,844 | |
| Lutheran Church—Missouri Synod | 5,897 | 8,044 | 2,630,588 | |
| Wisconsin Evangelical Lutheran Synod | 1,180 | 1,497 | 416,493 | |
| Others (9 denominations) | 621 | 683 | 89,822 | |
| PENTECOSTAL CHURCHES | 41,501 | 80,431 | 7,901,625 | 5.4% |
| Church of God in Christ | 9,982 | 10,425 | 3,709,661 | |
| Assemblies of God | 10,886 | 26,837 | 2,135,104 | |
| Church of God (Cleveland, Tenn.) | 5,346 | 9,638 | 505,775 | |
| United Pentecostal Church International | 3,410 | 6,984 | 500,000 | |
| Church of God in Christ, International | 300 | 1,600 | 200,000 | |
| International Church of the Foursquare Gospel | 1,250 | 3,482 | 186,213 | |
| Pentecostal Holiness Church, International | 1,461 | 3,422 | 113,000 | |
| Others (24 denominations) | 8,866 | 18,043 | 551,872 | |
| REFORMED CHURCHES | 22,513 | 36,527 | 5,733,828 | 3.9% |
| Presbyterian Church (USA) | 11,531 | 19,514 | 3,007,322 | |
| United Church of Christ | 6,406 | 10,071 | 1,676,105 | |
| Reformed Church in America | 928 | 1,636 | 340,359 | |
| Christian Reformed Church in North America | 650 | 1,077 | 219,988 | |
| Presbyterian Church in America | 913 | 1,702 | 188,083 | |
| Others (12 denominations) | 2,085 | 2,527 | 301,971 | |
| ORTHODOX CHURCHES | 1,746 | 2,236 | 4,459,177 | 3.0% |
| Greek Orthodox Archdiocese of North and South America | 535 | 655 | 1,950,000 | |
| Orthodox Church in America | 440 | 531 | 1,000,000 | |
| Armenian Church of Amer., Diocese of the | 66 | 61 | 450,000 | |
| Antiochan Orthodox Christian Archdiocese of North America | 120 | 180 | 280,000 | |
| Coptic Orthodox Church | 28 | 28 | 115,000 | |
| American Carpatho-Russian Orthodox Greek Catholic Church | 70 | 66 | 100,000 | |
| Others (14 denominations) | 487 | 715 | 564,177 | |
| LATTER-DAY SAINTS CHURCHES | 9,575 | 45,614 | 4,057,131 | 2.8% |
| Church of Jesus Christ of Latter-day Saints | 8,396 | 28,598 | 3,860,000 | |
| Reorganized Church of Jesus Christ of Latter-day Saints | 1,094 | 16,585 | 192,077 | |
| Others (2 denominations) | 85 | 431 | 5,054 | |

| FAMILY/Denomination | Local congregations | Total clergy | Total membership | % of total affiliated |
|---|---|---|---|---|
| CHRISTIAN CHURCHES AND CHURCHES OF CHRIST | 23,151 | 12,282 | 3,793,915 | 2.6% |
| Churches of Christ | 13,364 | — | 1,623,754 | |
| Christian Church (Disciples of Christ) | 4,221 | 6,806 | 1,106,692 | |
| Christian Churches and Churches of Christ | 5,566 | 5,476 | 1,063,469 | |
| EPISCOPAL CHURCHES | 7,175 | 14,235 | 2,516,240 | 1.7% |
| Episcopal Church | 7,054 | 14,111 | 2,504,507 | |
| Others (2 denominations) | 121 | 124 | 11,733 | |
| HOLINESS CHURCHES | 14,843 | 22,395 | 1,398,557 | 0.9% |
| Church of the Nazarene | 5,018 | 8,667 | 530,912 | |
| Christian and Missionary Alliance | 1,691 | 2,154 | 238,734 | |
| Church of God (Anderson, Ind.) | 2,296 | 3,313 | 188,662 | |
| Wesleyan Church | 1,704 | 2,596 | 109,196 | |
| Christian Congregation, Inc. | 1,450 | 1,455 | 105,478 | |
| Others (13 denominations) | 2,684 | 4,210 | 225,575 | |
| JEHOVAH'S WITNESSES | 8,336 | — | 752,404 | 0.5% |
| CHURCH OF CHRIST, SCIENTIST | — | — | 700,000[1] | 0.5% |
| ADVENTIST CHURCHES | 4,641 | 6,236 | 698,521 | 0.5% |
| Seventh-Day Adventists | 4,055 | 5,481 | 666,199 | |
| Others (4 denominations) | 586 | 755 | 32,322 | |
| SALVATION ARMY | 1,092 | 5,195 | 432,893 | 0.3% |
| ROMAN RITE CHURCHES | 308 | 316 | 347,092 | 0.2% |
| Polish National Catholic Church of Amer. | 162 | 141 | 282,411 | |
| North American Old Roman Catholic Church | 133 | 150 | 62,611 | |
| Others (2 denominations) | 13 | 25 | 2,070 | |
| MENNONITE CHURCHES | 2,365 | 3,168 | 239,681 | 0.2% |
| Mennonite Church | 989 | 2,399 | 91,167 | |
| Old Order Amish Church | 696 | — | 62,640 | |
| Others (9 denominations) | 680 | 769 | 85,874 | |
| BRETHREN CHURCHES | 1,545 | 2,718 | 216,217 | 0.1% |
| Church of the Brethren | 1,059 | 1,963 | 155,967 | |
| Others (3 denominations) | 486 | 755 | 60,250 | |
| UNITARIAN UNIVERSALIST ASSOCIATION | 956 | 1,069 | 173,167 | 0.1% |
| FRIENDS (QUAKER) CHURCHES (5 denominations) | 1,395 | 1,095 | 120,320 | 0.1% |
| MISCELLANEOUS CHURCHES | 9,426 | 11,658 | 1,127,539 | 0.8% |
| Community Churches, International Confederation of | 350 | 350 | 200,000 | |
| Independent Fundamental Churches of America | 1,019 | 1,366 | 120,446 | |
| Congregational Christian Churches, National Association of | 464 | 826 | 108,115 | |
| Christian Brethren (also known as The Plymouth Brethren) | 1,150 | 500 | 98,000 | |
| Evangelical Free Church of America | 880 | 1,484 | 95,722 | |
| Evangelical Covenant Church | 570 | 930 | 86,079 | |
| Others (37 denominations) | 4,993 | 6,202 | 419,177 | |
| OTHER CHRISTIANS (UNREPORTED) | — | — | 1,000,000[1] | 0.7% |
| OTHER RELIGIONS | 3,516 | 6,615 | 8,914,000 | 6.0% |
| JEWS | 3,416 | 6,500 | 5,814,000 | 3.9% |
| MUSLIMS | — | — | 2,500,000[1] | 1.7% |
| BUDDHIST CHURCHES OF AMERICA | 100 | 115 | 100,000 | 0.1% |
| OTHER NON-CHRISTIANS (UNREPORTED) | — | — | 500,000[1] | 0.3% |

1. Estimates—denominations/organizations do not report membership. **Sources:** Christianity—*Yearbook of American and Canadian Churches 1988.* An estimated 1 million people are members of very small denominations or independent congregations not accounted for in the YACC. Judaism—*Yearbook of American and Canadian Churches 1988.* Number represents the total of all who are considered members of the Jewish cultural community. Islam—based on *The World Christian Encyclopedia,* 1985 estimate for North America. Number represents the total of all who are considered members of the Islamic cultural community. Other—*Universal Almanac* estimate. Number includes 100,000 Buddhists not affiliated with Buddhist Churches of America and members of other non-Christian religious organizations.

today the majority of religiously affiliated people in Utah belong to the Church of the Latter-day Saints. There are also many adherents in surrounding states, and the Mormons pursue a worldwide campaign of proselytizing.

The Reorganized Church is the largest of the groups that did not make the trek to the Great Salt Lake. Its headquarters are in Independence, Missouri, which Smith had designated as the site of a great future temple.

## Christian Churches and Churches of Christ

This family of churches traces its origins to a great religious awakening in 1800 on the Pennsylvania and Kentucky frontiers. Discouraged by sectarian competition among Methodists, Presbyterians, and others, leaders of the revival did not seek to form a denomination but to reestablish a single nondenominational Christian church. In time they became a denomination themselves.

In the 1870s the Churches of Christ and the Christian Church (Disciples) split over questions of using musical instruments in worship and over the issue of centralizing one church functions. The Churches of Christ opposed both instrumental music and national organization. The Disciples allowed instrumental music and established a central missionary board to coordinate mission work. They are ecumenically minded and have a long history of cooperation and discussion with other denominations.

The third group, the Christian Churches and Churches of Christ, split from the Disciples in the 1920s and 1930s. They do allow instrumental music but are theologically more conservative than the Disciples.

## Episcopal Family of Churches

The Episcopal churches are descendants of the Church of England, which was established as a separate church by King Henry VIII in 1534. Churches descending from the English church make up the worldwide Anglican Communion. The American church takes its name from the word *bishop*, which suggests its hierarchical organization.

In colonial times the Church of England was established in the southern colonies and had some influence in the middle colonies, but it was not welcome in New England, where Reformed churches were predominant. During the American Revolution, most Church of England members and clergy remained loyal to England. Thousands emigrated to Canada. Those who remained were under suspicion, and some were persecuted. The church almost ceased to function.

After the revolution, a small group of Anglicans loyal to the United States gradually revived the church. It never grew as rapidly as the Methodist and Baptist families, but it did gain considerable influence. Especially in eastern cities, many families of wealth and power were Episcopalian.

The Episcopal Church accommodates a wide spectrum of belief and practice. It is usually considered Protestant and shares much with other Protestant denominations, yet its worship services retain much of pre-Reformation Catholic tradition. One wing of the church retains a strong emphasis on the church's Catholic heritage.

## Holiness Churches

The Holiness churches grew from a religious revival in the late 1800s, primarily in Methodist congregations. The originators of the movement objected to the excessive bureaucracy of established denominations and sought to refocus attention on the need for deep personal change. They placed great emphasis on the teachings of Methodism's founder, John Wesley, that those who are saved may aspire to the gift of complete sanctification, or holiness.

Around 1900, groups of especially intense Holiness worshipers began experiencing further "gifts of the Spirit." From these experiences grew the first Pentecostal churches with their emphasis on speaking in tongues. Many who began as adherents of Holiness churches became Pentecostalists. The Holiness churches rejected what they considered the extremism of Pentecostal worship.

## Jehovah's Witnesses

Jehovah's Witnesses are a remarkably active and dynamic sect, visible to most from street-corner or door-to-door encounters. They were founded by Charles Taze Russell (1852–1916) in western Pennsylvania in the 1870s. The Witnesses preach a slightly unorthodox form of the Christian message and look intently for the end of the present world. They claim 3 million members worldwide, of whom about a quarter live in the United States.

## Church of Christ, Scientist

Christian Scientists, as adherents are often known, follow the teachings of Mary Baker Eddy (1821–1910), who founded the church in 1879 in Boston and wrote *Science and Health with a Key to the Scriptures*, which remains a major sourcebook for the church. Christian Science asserts that sickness and other adversities exist only in the mind and that disciplined spiritual thinking can correct them. Thus, Christian Scientists avoid most or all medical treatment. Christian Science practitioners help adherents deal with illness but do not serve as clergy. The church operates many reading rooms open to the public.

## The Adventist Family of Churches

Adventist churches sprang up in the United States in the 1840s with a wave of concern about prophecies of the end of the world. Adventists anticipate and prepare for the world's end and the second coming of Jesus Christ. The largest Adventist group, the Seventh-Day Adventists, is one of the most dynamic religious groups in the world today, claiming a worldwide membership of 5 million and a growth rate of more than 7 percent annually. As their name suggests, they worship on Saturday rather than Sunday. They operate parochial schools, colleges, medical schools, and hospitals.

## The Salvation Army

The Salvation Army is familiar to outsiders through its work among the homeless and the poor and its fund-raising on the streets, especially before Christmas. The church, which originated in England in 1865, is organized in quasi-military style, and many of its members devote their lives to its service.

## Roman Rite Churches

The Roman Rite churches are those that have split from the Roman Catholic church in recent times but have maintained many of its rituals and doctrines. The Polish church was established in Scranton, Pennsylvania, in the 1890s by church leaders of Polish descent. The Old Catholic churches had their origin in Europe after 1870.

## Mennonite Churches

Mennonites trace their roots to a small group of Christians after 1530 who sought a reformation even more radical than those advocated by Lutherans and Calvinists. They were called Mennonites after Menno Simons (1469–1561), one of their early leaders. Their most distinctive practice is adult baptism, offered only to those who have made a decision to follow Christ's teachings.

Because they would not swear oaths and would not bear arms in the service of their temporal leaders, Mennonites were severely persecuted. Small bands were scattered to many corners of the world. Some settled in Pennsylvania beginning in the late 1600s. In the 1870s other groups arrived from Russia. Today more than 40 percent of the world's Mennonites live in the United States. The next-largest group (estimated to be 150,000) lives in the Soviet Union. In recent times Mennonites have become well known for their world relief work.

The Amish are groups with Mennonite beliefs who seek to remain quite aloof from the surrounding culture. The Old Order Amish, centered in Pennsylvania, wear "plain" clothing and still drive horses and buggies rather than automobiles.

## Churches of the Brethren

The Brethren, founded as a dissenting group in Germany in the early 1700s, immigrated to Pennsylvania in the 1720s to escape persecution. There they have remained. Brethren share many doctrinal points with their neighbors, the Mennonites. They practice adult baptism, refuse to swear oaths, and will not serve as combatants in war. The various Brethren denominations agree in basic theology but differ on less significant matters of interpretation.

## Unitarian Universalist Association

Unitarianism was an outgrowth of New England Congregationalism in the late 1700s and early 1800s. Unitarians asserted God's unity and repudiated the doctrine of the Trinity. They also interpreted other Christian beliefs in a liberal, figurative manner. Universalism was a separate movement emphasizing the availability of God's care to all people, not only to a small chosen group. In 1961 Unitarian and Universalist organizations merged.

## Friends (Quaker) Churches

Known popularly as Quakers, the Friends were established by the English religious mystic George Fox (1624–91), in the mid-1600s. They were persecuted in England for refusing to take oaths or to serve as combatants in war. Under the protection of William Penn (1644–1718), many settled in Pennsylvania. According to Fox, they were called Quakers because they were admonished to "tremble at the word of the Lord." In Pennsylvania the Quakers set themselves apart, dressing plainly and avoiding worldly amusements. In Philadelphia they became influential business people.

The most distinctive doctrine of the Friends is that of the Inner Light, the spark of God in each individual. Friends have avoided setting up formal church structures, and many groups have no clergy. Friends have organized remarkable world relief and peace organizations, by which they are perhaps best known to outsiders.

## Other Christian Churches

Among the other denominations reported by the *Yearbook of American and Canadian Churches*, there is a wide variety of religious belief and practice. Many of the groups are radically congregational, making generalizations risky. Other groups are heterodox offshoots from the Pentecostal family. In many cases they depend on a single strong leader. The smallest denominations listed may actually be a single local congregation that reports as a separate church body.

Among the miscellaneous groups are spiritualist and other "New Age" groups. Some of these mix spiritualism with Christianity; others may not consider themselves Christian in any sense.

The estimated one million adherents of unlisted organizations are primarily members of independent Christian congregations. These may be Baptist, Methodist, Holiness, or Pentecostal in belief or practice; they may be unaffiliated because of disputes with a regional or national body or simply by long-standing tradition. Many such congregations are remote and isolated.

# OTHER RELIGIONS

## Judaism

Judaism is the largest non-Christian religious family in the United States. As descendants of the Jews of biblical times, Jews worship one God and follow the religious precepts in the Hebrew scriptures, the writings called the Old Testament by Christians. Jews recognize Jesus as a religious teacher but do not acknowledge him as the Messiah or Son of God. Jews still await the coming of the Messiah as foretold by the prophets.

A handful of Jews arrived in North America in the 1600s. In the 1800s, Jews from Germany arrived with other immigrants. Then between 1890 and 1920, several million Jews arrived from eastern Europe, fleeing persecution and hard times in Russia and Poland. In the 1930s and 1940s, Jews reached America as refugees

| RELIGIOUS AFFILIATION IN THE U.S. | | |
|---|---|---|
| Religion | Members | Percent of affiliated |
| Christianity | 138,585,662 | 94.0% |
| Judaism | 5,814,000 | 3.9 |
| Islam | 2,500,000 | 1.7 |
| Other | 600,000 | 0.4 |
| Total affiliated | 147,499,662 | 100.0% |

from the Nazi extermination campaigns. The slaughter of some 6 million Jews by the Germans, called the Holocaust, is one of two central facts of modern Jewish experience. The second is the establishment of Israel as an independent state in 1948. Today more Jews live in Israel than in any other country except the United States.

Jewish organizations report that there are 5.8 million Americans Jews. Of these, perhaps 3.8 million are religiously affiliated or observant. The remaining 2 million consider their Judaism to be more ethnic or cultural than religious.

There are three main branches of religious Judaism—Reform, Conservative, and Orthodox. Reform Judaism flowered in the United States in the late 1800s, especially among immigrants from Germany. In some respects it resembles liberal Protestantism in the spectrum of Christian churches. Reform temples may have stained glass windows and large pipe organs. A Sabbath service may include choral music and a sermon. About 1.4 million Jews are affiliated with Reform temples.

Conservative Judaism rose in response to Reform. It sought to preserve more of the ancient observances of old orthodoxy but without losing touch with American culture and

> *"The day this country ceases to be free for irreligion it will cease to be free for religion—except for the sect that can win political power."*
>
> —Associate Justice Robert H. Jackson, dissenting in *Zorach* v. *Clauson* (1952).

behavior. As a middle road between Reform and Orthodox Judaism, Conservative Judaism has gained numerical superiority. About 2 million Jews are affiliated with Conservative institutions.

Orthodox Judaism is by far the smallest of the three branches, with an estimated 400,000 adherents. Orthodox Jews are known for their distinctive dress and their tendency to remain apart from the larger community. The majority of Orthodox Jews live in New York City in small self-contained communities. Orthodox Judaism consists of scores of small groups, each with its own history and slightly differing patterns of belief and ritual.

## Islam

The Islamic faith, whose followers are called Muslims, is the third of the great theistic world religions, along with Judaism and Christianity. Each of these religions worships the same God (for whom the Muslim name is Allah), and each has its holiest places in the Middle East. Jerusalem is a holy city for all three faiths. (see "World Religions.")

The first sizable group of Muslims arrived in the United States from Lebanon in the early 1900s. Later waves of immigration have brought Pakistanis, Indians, Arabs, and Iranians, among others. Some have been refugees from political or religious persecution. Some came as students and remained. Perhaps one million engage in at least some religious observance during the year. Many of the rest consider themselves loyal supporters of Islam even if they do not participate regularly.

There are about 600 Islamic centers in the United States, many of which include a mosque for worship. The largest concentrations of Muslims are in cities in the Northeast and industrial Midwest. Observances may vary from one center to another, depending on the nationality of its adherents and their length of residence in the United States. In general, recent immigrants are more conservative and follow Islamic ritual and custom more closely.

## Buddhist Churches of America

The Buddhist Churches of America is the oldest and largest U.S. Buddhist group. It represents the Jodo Shinshu sect of Buddhism, and many of its members are of Japanese descent.

There are many other Buddhist organizations in the United States and may be as many as 100,000 additional Americans who subscribe to Buddhist tenets. They are included under the heading "not separately listed."

## Other Non-Christians

This category includes other Buddhists (not members of Buddhist Churches of America), Hindus, followers of tribal religions, and adherents of recent quasi-religious sects such as est and Scientology.

# EDUCATION

The American people's unwavering commitment to public education dates back more than 150 years. Fueled by a demand for literacy from two different creeds, one described in the Bible, the other in the Declaration of Independence, the American system of education grew to be an essential element in Americans' faith that their nation was uniquely the land of opportunity.

Today that belief has evolved into what is called equality of opportunity, and this vital idea has helped create a school system whose size and scope is unrivaled by any Western democracy.

Over 59 million students and more than 7 million teachers, administrators, and support staff are directly involved in education. The cost of this undertaking is, of course, staggering: over $350 billion annually—about $5,200 per student—or almost 7% of the gross national product (GNP), virtually all of it for public education. And while some may complain bitterly about the quality of the results, or about overt waste, mismanagement, and even fraud, no one any longer questions the essential role of education in American life today.

## PUBLIC EDUCATION EXPENDITURES, 1940–90

| School year ending | Expenditures (billions) | Expenditure per student | As percentage of GNP |
|---|---|---|---|
| 1940 | $ 3.3 | $ 106 | 3.6% |
| 1950 | 8.9 | 259 | 3.5 |
| 1960 | 23.9 | 472 | 4.8 |
| 1970 | 68.5 | 955 | 7.1 |
| 1980 | 165.6 | 2,491 | 6.6 |
| 1985 | 247.7 | 3,760 | 6.6 |
| 1986 | 269.5 | 4,070 | 6.7 |
| 1987 | 290.9[1] | 4,300 | 6.9 |
| 1988 | 313.6[1] | 4,642[2] | 6.9[1] |
| 1989 | 337.0[2] | 4,927[2] | 6.9[2] |
| 1990 | 358.7[2] | 5,247[2] | 6.9[2] |

1. Preliminary figure. 2. Estimated. **Source:** U.S. Dept. of Education, National Center for Education Statistics, *Digest of Education Statistics 1990.*

### Expenditures in Public Elementary and Secondary Schools

Between 1978 and 1982, expenditures per student remained stable after adjustment for inflation. Prior to 1978 and after 1982, they increased faster than inflation. Annual expenditures per student in public elementary and secondary schools rose to a record high of $4,931 in 1988–89.

Total expenditures on education now account for almost 7% of the U.S. gross national product. After rising rapidly from 1959 to 1969, the proportion of GNP spent on education declined as enrollment in elementary and secondary schools declined.

## EDUCATIONAL ATTAINMENT OF THE POPULATION, AGE 25 + , 1989

| Characteristic | Number of persons ('000s) | 4 or more years of high school | 1 or more years of college | 4 or more years of college |
|---|---|---|---|---|
| All persons | 154,155 | 76.9% | 38.4% | 21.1% |
| **SEX** | | | | |
| Male | 73,225 | 77.2 | 41.0 | 24.5 |
| Female | 80,930 | 76.6 | 35.3 | 18.1 |
| **RACE** | | | | |
| White | 132,903 | 78.4 | 39.3 | 21.8 |
| Black | 16,395 | 64.6 | 28.1 | 11.8 |
| Other[1] | 4,857 | 76.1 | 48.6 | 34.2 |
| Hispanic origin | 10,438 | 50.9 | 23.0 | 9.9 |
| **REGION** | | | | |
| Northeast | 33,064 | 77.9 | 37.9 | 23.1 |
| Midwest | 37,217 | 78.8 | 35.6 | 18.9 |
| South | 52,559 | 72.5 | 35.7 | 19.3 |
| West | 31,315 | 80.8 | 46.7 | 24.8 |
| **RESIDENCE** | | | | |
| Metropolitan area | 119,716 | 78.8 | 41.6 | 23.4 |
| Nonmetropolitan area | 34,439 | 70.2 | 27.4 | 13.2 |
| **AGE GROUP** | | | | |
| 25 to 34 | 43,240 | 86.6 | 45.2 | 24.2 |
| 35 to 44 | 35,873 | 86.6 | 49.4 | 27.9 |
| 45 to 54 | 24,621 | 78.4 | 37.9 | 22.0 |
| 55 to 64 | 21,399 | 69.1 | 29.5 | 16.2 |
| 65 to 74 | 17,747 | 60.4 | 23.3 | 11.7 |
| 75 or older | 11,276 | 46.2 | 19.2 | 10.1 |

1. Includes Orientals and Native Americans. **Source:** U.S. Bureau of the Census, *Current Population Survey, March 1989* (1991).

## EDUCATIONAL ATTAINMENT OF POPULATION 25 + YEARS, 1940–89

| Year | Both sexes | Male | Female |
|---|---|---|---|
| **Completed 4 years of high school or more** | | | |
| 1940 | 24.5% | 22.7% | 26.3% |
| 1950 | 34.3 | 32.6 | 36.0 |
| 1959 | 43.7 | 42.2 | 45.2 |
| 1970 | 55.2 | 55.0 | 55.4 |
| 1980 | 68.6 | 69.1 | 68.1 |
| 1989 | 76.9 | 77.2 | 76.6 |
| **Completed 4 years of college or more** | | | |
| 1940 | 4.6% | 5.5% | 3.8% |
| 1950 | 6.2 | 7.3 | 5.2 |
| 1959 | 8.1 | 10.3 | 6.0 |
| 1970 | 11.0 | 14.1 | 8.2 |
| 1980 | 17.1 | 20.8 | 13.5 |
| 1989 | 22.1 | 24.5 | 18.1 |

**Source:** U.S. Bureau of the Census, *Current Population Survey* (Mar. 1989).

In 1979 a historic shift occurred in the source of money to operate the American public school system. That was the year the state share of revenues rose above the local share for the first time. The federal share for elementary and secondary schools has always been relatively small.

## SCHOOL ENROLLMENT, KINDERGARTEN THROUGH UNIVERSITY LEVEL

| Category | Fall enrollment (students in millions) | | | | |
|---|---|---|---|---|---|
| | 1970 | 1975 | 1980 | 1985 | 1990[1] |
| **ELEMENTARY (K–8)** | | | | | |
| Public | 32.6 | 30.5 | 27.7 | 27.0 | 29.5 |
| Private | 4.1 | 3.7 | 4.0 | 4.2 | 4.2 |
| **SECONDARY (9–12)** | | | | | |
| Public | 13.3 | 14.3 | 13.2 | 12.4 | 11.3 |
| Private | 1.3 | 1.3 | 1.3 | 1.4 | 1.2 |
| **HIGHER EDUCATION** | | | | | |
| Public | 6.4 | 8.8 | 9.5 | 9.5 | 10.5 |
| Private | 2.2 | 2.4 | 2.6 | 2.8 | 3.0 |
| Total | 59.9 | 61.0 | 58.3 | 57.3 | 59.7 |

1. Projected. **Source:** U.S. Dept. of Education, National Center for Education Statistics, *Digest of Education Statistics 1990.*

## NUMBER OF SCHOOLS IN THE U.S., 1988–89

| Elementary and secondary | Public | Private[1] |
|---|---|---|
| Elementary | 59,296 | 17,087 |
| Secondary | 20,550 | 2,425 |
| Combined | 2,235 | 7,296 |
| Other schools[2] | 1,084 | — |
| Total | 83,165 | 26,608 |

| Colleges and universities | Total | Public | Private |
|---|---|---|---|
| 4-year colleges | 2,129 | 598 | 1,531 |
| 2-year colleges | 1,436 | 984 | 452 |
| Total | 3,565 | 1,582 | 1,983 |

1. 1987–88. 2. Includes special, alternative schools, and others not reported by grade span. **Source:** U.S. Dept. of Education, National Center for Education Statistics, *Digest of Education Statistics 1990.*

## REVENUES FOR PUBLIC ELEMENTARY AND SECONDARY SCHOOLS, 1920–88

| School year ending | Total revenues (billions) | Source by percent | | |
|---|---|---|---|---|
| | | Federal | State | Local |
| 1920 | $ 1.0 | 0.3% | 16.5% | 83.2% |
| 1930 | 2.1 | 0.4 | 16.9 | 82.7 |
| 1940 | 2.3 | 1.8 | 30.3 | 68.0 |
| 1950 | 5.4 | 2.9 | 39.8 | 57.3 |
| 1960 | 14.7 | 4.4 | 39.1 | 56.5 |
| 1970 | 40.3 | 8.0 | 39.9 | 52.1 |
| 1975 | 64.4 | 9.0 | 42.2 | 48.8 |
| 1980 | 96.9 | 9.8 | 46.8 | 43.4 |
| 1985 | 137.3 | 6.6 | 48.9 | 44.4 |
| 1986 | 149.1 | 6.7 | 49.4 | 43.9 |
| 1987 | 158.8 | 6.4 | 49.8 | 43.9 |
| 1988 | 169.6 | 6.3 | 49.5 | 44.1 |

**Source:** U.S. Dept. of Education, National Center for Education Statistics, *Digest of Education Statistics 1990.*

## NUMBER OF CATHOLIC SCHOOLS, PUPILS, AND TEACHERS, 1960–90

| Category | 1960 | 1970 | 1980 | 1990 |
|---|---|---|---|---|
| **ELEMENTARY** | | | | |
| Number | 10,501 | 9,362 | 8,043 | 7,291 |
| Pupils enrolled | 4,373,000 | 3,355,000 | 2,269,000 | 1,883,906 |
| Teachers, total | 108,000 | 112,000 | 97,000 | 91,039 |
| Religious | 79,000 | 52,000 | 25,000 | 10,837 |
| Lay | 29,000 | 60,000 | 72,000 | 80,202 |
| **SECONDARY** | | | | |
| Number | 2,392 | 1,981 | 1,516 | 1,296 |
| Pupils enrolled | 880,000 | 1,008,000 | 837,000 | 591,533 |
| Teachers, total | 44,000 | 55,000 | 49,000 | 40,159 |
| Religious | 33,000 | 29,000 | 14,000 | 6,579 |
| Lay | 11,000 | 26,000 | 35,000 | 33,580 |

**Sources:** National Catholic Education Assn., *United States Catholic Elementary and Secondary Schools (annual).*

## PRIVATE SCHOOLS

Data concerning private elementary and secondary schools are not as readily available as for public institutions. According to the Department of Education:

- There are 25,616 private schools: 15,303 elementary, 2,438 secondary, 4,949 combined, and 2,926 other types.
- 9,911, or almost 40%, are affiliated with the Roman Catholic church, 10,771 with all other religious groups, and 4,934 have no religious affiliation.
- Private schools employ 404,000 teachers (92,000 in nonreligious schools), who are paid average base salaries of $13,600 to $16,500.
- Overall, 76% of all private school teachers are female, but only 51.5% of private secondary school teachers are female.
- Nearly 40% of private schools enroll less than 5% minority students, while 72% of private schools enroll less than 24% minority students.

**Source:** U.S. Dept. of Education, National Center for Education Statistics, *Digest of Education Statistics 1989.*

## AVERAGE SAT SCORES BY GROUPS

| Group | 1980 | 1985 | 1990 | Total test-takers, class of 1990 |
|---|---|---|---|---|
| White | 924 | 939 | 933 | 694,976 |
| Mexican-American | 785 | 808 | 809 | 26,073 |
| Black | 690 | 722 | 737 | 94,311 |
| **National average** | **890** | **906** | **900** | **1,025,523** |
| Men | 919 | 936 | 928 | 490,420 |
| Women | 863 | 877 | 874 | 535,103 |

**Source:** College Board.

## MOST POPULAR MAJORS AMONG INCOMING FRESHMEN, 1989–90

| | Percentage | |
|---|---|---|
| Major | 1989 | 1990 |
| Business administration | 6.5% | 5.5% |
| Accounting | 6.1 | 5.3 |
| Elementary education | 4.6 | 5.1 |
| Nursing | 2.8 | 4.2 |
| Psychology | 4.2 | 4.2 |
| Management | 4.5 | 4.0 |
| Premedicine, predental, preveterinary | 3.0 | 3.2 |
| Political science | 3.1 | 3.0 |
| Electrical engineering | 3.0 | 2.5 |
| Marketing | 3.0 | 2.5 |
| Communications | 2.7 | 2.3 |
| Therapy | 2.3 | 2.3 |
| Arts | 2.1 | 2.0 |
| Mechanical engineering | 2.0 | 2.0 |
| Architecture, urban planning | 1.3 | 1.9 |
| Secondary education | 1.8 | 1.9 |
| General Biology | 1.8 | 1.8 |
| Computer science | 1.6 | 1.7 |
| Law enforcement | 1.5 | 1.7 |
| Aeronautical engineering | 1.5 | 1.4 |

**Note:** Tie percentages are ranked the same and listed in alphabetical order. **Source:** Higher Education Research Institute, University of California, Los Angeles, *The American Freshman, National Norms for Fall, 1990.*

## AVERAGE COST OF 4-YEAR COLLEGES, 1978–91
(tuition and fees, per year)

| Year | Public | Private |
|---|---|---|
| 1978–79 | $ 688 | $2,958 |
| 1979–80 | 738 | 3,225 |
| 1980–81 | 804 | 3,617 |
| 1981–82 | 909 | 4,113 |
| 1982–83 | 1,031 | 4,639 |
| 1983–84 | 1,148 | 5,093 |
| 1984–85 | 1,228 | 5,556 |
| 1985–86 | 1,318 | 6,121 |
| 1986–87 | 1,414 | 6,658 |
| 1987–88 | 1,537 | 7,116 |
| 1988–89 | 1,646 | 7,722 |
| 1989–90 | 1,781 | 8,446 |
| 1990–91 | 1,809 | 9,391 |

**Source:** U.S. Dept. of Education, National Center for Education Statistics, *Digest of Education Statistics 1990*; College Board.

## AVERAGE ACT SCORES BY GROUPS

| Group | 1989 | 1990 | Total test-takers, class of 1990 |
|---|---|---|---|
| White | 21.3 | 21.2 | 605,361 |
| Mexican-American | 18.1 | 18.3 | 22,806 |
| Black | 16.6 | 17.0 | 71,197 |
| **National average** | **20.6** | **20.6** | **817,096** |
| Men | 21.2 | 21.0 | 373,310 |
| Women | 20.1 | 20.3 | 443,786 |

**Source:** The American College Testing Program.

## HOW THE STATES RANK IN PUBLIC EDUCATION, 1989–90

| State | Enrollment (rank) | Expenditures per pupil (rank) | Average teacher salary (rank) | High school graduation rate (rank) |
|---|---|---|---|---|
| **U.S.** | **40,569,542 —** | **$4,890 —** | **$31,166 —** | **71.1% —** |
| Ala. | 728,254 (21) | $3,314 (46) | $25,500 (40) | 74.9 (23) |
| Alaska | 107,487 (47) | 7,252 (5) | 43,153 (1) | 65.5 (43) |
| Ariz. | 679,310 (23) | 3,853 (39) | 29,402 (24) | 61.1 (48) |
| Ark. | 434,960 (33) | 3,272 (48) | 22,009 (50) | 77.2 (17) |
| Calif. | 4,771,978 (1) | 4,598 (24) | 36,418 (6) | 65.9 (42) |
| Colo. | 562,755 (27) | 4,580 (26) | 30,758 (20) | 74.7 (24) |
| Conn. | 465,602 (31) | 7,934 (3) | 40,461 (2) | 84.9 (7) |
| Del. | 97,808 (48) | 5,848 (9) | 33,377 (11) | 71.7 (32) |
| D.C. | 81,301 (51) | 7,407 (4) | 37,950 (4) | 58.2 (50) |
| Fla. | 1,789,944 (5) | 5,051 (19) | 28,806 (26) | 58.0 (51) |
| Ga. | 1,126,535 (9) | 4,456 (28) | 27,892 (30) | 61.0 (49) |
| Hawaii | 169,193 (42) | 4,504 (27) | 32,047 (15) | 69.1 (38) |
| Idaho | 214,571 (38) | 3,037 (50) | 23,861 (45) | 75.4 (22) |
| Ill. | 1,797,355 (4) | 4,853 (21) | 32,794 (13) | 75.6 (21) |
| Ind. | 955,611 (13) | 4,126 (36) | 30,493 (22) | 76.3 (19) |
| Iowa | 478,486 (29) | 4,590 (25) | 26,747 (37) | 85.8 (5) |
| Kans. | 430,864 (34) | 4,706 (22) | 28,671 (28) | 80.2 (9) |
| Ky. | 630,688 (24) | 3,824 (40) | 26,275 (38) | 69.0 (39) |
| La. | 775,300 (19) | 3,457 (45) | 24,300 (44) | 61.4 (47) |
| Maine | 208,384 (39) | 5,577 (12) | 26,881 (36) | 74.4 (25) |
| Md. | 698,806 (22) | 5,887 (8) | 36,601 (5) | 74.1 (26) |
| Mass. | 825,579 (15) | 6,170 (7) | 34,175 (10) | 75.0 (35) |
| Mich. | 1,566,030 (8) | 5,073 (18) | 36,010 (8) | 73.6 (29) |
| Minn. | 739,553 (20) | 5,114 (16) | 32,190 (14) | 90.9 (1) |
| Miss. | 502,020 (28) | 3,151 (49) | 24,363 (43) | 66.9 (40) |
| Mo. | 807,934 (17) | 4,226 (32) | 27,229 (33) | 74.0 (28) |
| Mont. | 150,991 (43) | 4,147 (34) | 25,081 (42) | 87.3 (4) |
| Nebr. | 269,861 (37) | 3,874 (38) | 25,522 (39) | 85.4 (6) |
| Nev. | 186,800 (40) | 4,387 (30) | 30,590 (21) | 75.8 (20) |
| N.H. | 171,696 (41) | 5,149 (15) | 28,986 (25) | 74.1 (26) |
| N.J. | 1,076,005 (11) | 8,439 (1) | 35,676 (9) | 77.4 (15) |
| N.Mex. | 279,219 (36) | 4,180 (33) | 25,120 (41) | 71.9 (31) |
| N.Y. | 2,565,841 (3) | 8,094 (2) | 38,925 (3) | 62.3 (46) |
| N.C. | 1,078,153 (10) | 4,386 (31) | 27,814 (31) | 66.7 (41) |
| N.Dak. | 117,134 (46) | 3,581 (42) | 23,016 (46) | 88.3 (2) |
| Ohio | 1,764,500 (6) | 4,394 (29) | 31,200 (17) | 79.6 (10) |
| Okla. | 577,000 (26) | 3,484 (44) | 23,070 (47) | 71.7 (32) |
| Oreg. | 472,400 (30) | 5,085 (17) | 30,840 (19) | 73.0 (30) |
| Pa. | 1,655,271 (7) | 5,670 (11) | 33,338 (12) | 78.4 (14) |
| R.I. | 135,035 (44) | 6,523 (6) | 36,057 (7) | 69.8 (36) |
| S.C. | 616,805 (25) | 3,731 (41) | 27,200 (34) | 64.6 (45) |
| S.Dak. | 127,100 (45) | 3,312 (47) | 21,300 (51) | 79.6 (10) |
| Tenn. | 828,688 (14) | 3,503 (43) | 27,052 (35) | 69.3 (37) |
| Tex. | 3,316,785 (2) | 4,056 (37) | 27,496 (32) | 65.3 (44) |
| Utah | 435,762 (32) | 2,733 (51) | 23,735 (46) | 79.4 (12) |
| Vt. | 94,779 (50) | 5,418 (13) | 28,798 (27) | 78.7 (13) |
| Va. | 985,031 (12) | 5,000 (20) | 30,926 (18) | 71.6 (34) |
| Wash. | 810,232 (16) | 4,638 (23) | 30,475 (23) | 77.1 (18) |
| W.Va. | 328,069 (35) | 4,146 (35) | 22,842 (49) | 77.3 (16) |
| Wisc. | 782,905 (18) | 5,703 (10) | 31,921 (16) | 84.9 (7) |
| Wyo. | 97,172 (49) | 5,281 (14) | 28,188 (29) | 88.3 (2) |

**Note:** Enrollment figures are as of fall 1989; graduation as of June 1988; expenditures and average salary are for 1989–90 school year. **Sources:** National Education Association, *Rankings of the States, 1990*; U.S. Dept. of Education, 1990.

## PROFILES OF SAT SCORES, BY SEX, 1990

| Score | Male Number | Male Percent | Female Number | Female Percent |
|---|---|---|---|---|
| **VERBAL** | | | | |
| 750–800 | 676 | (1) | 550 | (1) |
| 700–740 | 4,981 | 1% | 4,041 | 1% |
| 650–690 | 11,977 | 2 | 9,862 | 2 |
| 600–640 | 23,562 | 5 | 20,514 | 4 |
| 550–590 | 36,831 | 8 | 34,799 | 7 |
| 500–540 | 54,612 | 10 | 55,147 | 10 |
| 450–490 | 76,374 | 16 | 83,126 | 16 |
| 400–440 | 86,149 | 18 | 98,803 | 18 |
| 350–390 | 77,747 | 16 | 89,044 | 17 |
| 300–340 | 58,658 | 12 | 69,265 | 13 |
| 250–290 | 36,270 | 7 | 43,276 | 8 |
| 200–240 | 22,583 | 5 | 26,676 | 5 |
| Total | 490,420 | 100 | 535,103 | 100 |
| Mean score | 429 | – | 419 | – |
| **MATH** | | | | |
| 750–800 | 9,792 | 2% | 2,343 | – |
| 700–740 | 22,247 | 5 | 8,979 | 2% |
| 650–690 | 38,634 | 8 | 21,950 | 4 |
| 600–640 | 48,980 | 10 | 35,887 | 7 |
| 550–590 | 61,073 | 12 | 53,584 | 10 |
| 500–540 | 68,435 | 14 | 71,084 | 13 |
| 450–490 | 68,166 | 14 | 80,683 | 15 |
| 400–440 | 60,939 | 12 | 81,151 | 15 |
| 350–390 | 51,814 | 11 | 77,848 | 15 |
| 300–340 | 36,642 | 7 | 61,437 | 11 |
| 250–290 | 19,581 | 4 | 32,916 | 6 |
| 200–240 | 4,117 | 1 | 7,241 | 1 |
| Total | 490,420 | 100 | 535,103 | 100 |
| Mean score | 499 | – | 455 | – |

1. Less than 0.5%. **Source**: College Board (1991).

**Enrollment** Public elementary school enrollment declined between 1975 and 1985 as the number of young people decreased, but it began rising again in 1987. Higher-education enrollment has increased during the past two decades despite a drop, which began in 1981, in the traditional college-age population.

## DEGREES CONFERRED IN U.S., BY TYPE, 1950–88

| Year | All degrees[1] | Bachelor's | First professional[2] | Master's[3] | Doctorates |
|---|---|---|---|---|---|
| 1949–50 | 496,661 | | 432,058[4] | 58,183 | 6,420 |
| 1959–60 | 476,704 | | 392,440[4] | 74,435 | 9,829 |
| 1969–70 | 1,064,385 | 792,656 | 34,578 | 208,291 | 29,866 |
| 1979–80 | 1,330,244 | 929,417 | 70,131 | 298,081 | 32,615 |
| 1984–85 | 1,373,734 | 979,417 | 75,063 | 286,251 | 32,943 |
| 1985–86 | 1,383,953 | 987,823 | 73,910 | 288,567 | 33,653 |
| 1986–87 | 1,387,766 | 991,339 | 72,750 | 289,557 | 34,120 |
| 1987–88 | 1,397,349 | 993,362 | 70,415 | 298,733 | 34,839 |

1. Does not include associate of arts (A.A.) or associate of science (A.S.) degrees; more than 400,000 of these have been given each year since 1980. 2. Degrees are medical doctor, law, dentistry, optometry, podiatry, pharmacy, theology, chiropractic, and veterinary medicine. 3. Until 1965–66 some master's degrees (e.g., library science and social work) were listed in first-professional category. 4. Prior to 1961 bachelor's and first-professional degrees were listed together. **Source**: National Center for Education Statistics, *Digest of Education Statistics 1990*.

## College Entrance Examination Scores

SATs (Scholastic Aptitude Tests) measure verbal and mathematical reasoning abilities. These tests are developed and administered by the Educational Testing Service, Princeton, N.J., for the College Board, headquartered in New York City. The College Board is a non-profit organization that provides tests and many other educational services for students, schools, and colleges.

In 1990 some 1,025,523 students took the SATs. The mean score of the combined math and verbal tests was 900. Because males consistently outscore females on these tests, some groups have raised the issue of gender bias, i.e., that the tests may be inherently unfair to women students.

ACTs are administered by the American College Testing Program, a nonprofit educational organization, which has its national headquarters in Iowa City, Iowa. The ACT composite score is the average of four tests that measure academic abilities in English, mathematics, social studies, and natural sciences.

Improvements have been modest in national average scores for all groups on college entrance examinations given by the College Board (SAT) and the American College Testing Program (ACT). Men continue to score higher than women. And, despite steady improvement by minority test-takers, white students still score higher than other racial/ethnic groups by a substantial margin.

## Higher Education: Growth and Change

The accompanying figures give a startling picture of just how the coming of age of the Baby Boom generation transformed U.S. higher education. In just one decade (the 1960s), the number of undergraduate degrees conferred more than doubled, while the number of doctorates actually tripled. These extraordinary changes were matched in kind by dramatic shifts in what students wanted to study: during the late 1960s, for example, the number of degrees in sociology and psychology jumped by more than 15,000 each in just a few years (1966–70), while interest in business and management soared during the 1980s.

Between 1980 and 1988, the population age 18 to 24 fell by 11% (to 27 million), but college enrollment rose almost 8% to 13.1 million; by 1996 it should top 13.7 million.

# U.S. ENERGY

Energy is usually measured in millions or larger quantities of British thermal units (Btu). One Btu is approximately the energy released in burning a wooden match. An engine burning eight gallons of gasoline releases 1 million ($10^6$) Btu. One quadrillion ($10^{15}$) Btu is the energy released from an engine burning 8 billion gallons of gasoline.

Historically, three fossil fuels have accounted for the bulk of U.S. energy production, which totaled 66 quadrillion Btu in 1989. Coal accounted for the largest share of domestic energy production in 1949-51 and 1984-89. In the interim, first crude oil and then natural gas dominated domestic production.

The relationship between total energy consumption and real gross national product (GNP) is a primary indicator of the energy intensity of the economy. Energy consumption more than doubled between 1949 and 1973 (from 30 quadrillion to 74 quadrillion Btu), increasing at approximately the same rate as GNP. But although energy consumption reached a record high 81.23 quadrillion Btu in 1989, energy consumption per (1982) dollar of GNP was only 19,600 Btu—a 29% decline since 1970.

A second indicator of energy intensity is per capita consumption. In the 1960s and early 1970s, per capita end-use consumption rose from 212 million Btu in 1960 to a peak of 285 million Btu in 1973. Thereafter, per capita consumption dropped to 226 million Btu in 1983, rising again to 246 million Btu in 1988 and 1989.

A third indicator is energy consumption per household, which declined from 138 million Btu in 1978 to 101 million Btu in 1987. In 1987, household energy consumption totaled 9 quadrillion Btu. Energy consumed by households is primarily used for space and water

## U.S. ENERGY CONSUMPTION, 1950–89

| | Total energy consumption (quadrillion Btu) | | Per capita consumption (million Btu) | |
|---|---|---|---|---|
| Year | Total | End-use[1] | Total | End-use[1] |
| 1950 | 33.08 | 29.37 | 219 | 194 |
| 1955 | 38.82 | 34.02 | 235 | 206 |
| 1960 | 43.80 | 37.96 | 244 | 212 |
| 1965 | 52.68 | 44.93 | 272 | 232 |
| 1970 | 66.43 | 54.91 | 327 | 270 |
| 1975 | 70.55 | 56.16 | 327 | 261 |
| 1980 | 75.96 | 58.60 | 335 | 259 |
| 1985 | 73.95 | 55.40 | 310 | 232 |
| 1989 | 81.23 | 61.01 | 327 | 246 |

1. Total energy consumption less losses from generation, transmission, and distribution of electricity, power plant use, and unaccounted for losses. **Source**: U.S. Dept. of Energy, *Annual Energy Review 1989* (1990).

## U.S. FUEL CONSUMPTION, BY TYPE AND END-USE SECTOR, 1950–89

| Year | Resi-dential and commercial | Indus-trial | Trans-porta-tion | Electric utilities | Total | Year | Resi-dential and commercial | Indus-trial | Trans-porta-tion | Electric utilities | Total | Year | Resi-dential and commercial | Indus-trial | Trans-porta-tion | Electric utilities | Total |
|---|---|---|---|---|---|---|---|---|---|---|---|---|---|---|---|---|---|
| | PETROLEUM (million barrels/day) | | | | | | NATURAL GAS (trillion cubic feet/year) | | | | | | COAL (million short tons/year) | | | | |
| 1950 | 1.07 | 1.82 | 3.36 | 0.21 | 6.46 | 1950 | 1.59 | 3.43 | 0.13 | 0.63 | 5.77 | 1950 | 114.6 | 224.6 | 63.0 | 91.9 | 494.1 |
| 1955 | 1.40 | 2.39 | 4.46 | 0.21 | 8.46 | 1955 | 2.75 | 4.54 | 0.25 | 1.15 | 8.69 | 1955 | 68.4 | 217.8 | 17.0 | 143.8 | 447.0 |
| 1960 | 1.71 | 2.71 | 5.14 | 0.24 | 9.80 | 1960 | 4.12 | 5.77 | 0.35 | 1.72 | 11.97 | 1960 | 40.9 | 177.4 | 3.0 | 176.7 | 398.1 |
| 1965 | 1.91 | 3.25 | 6.04 | 0.32 | 11.51 | 1965 | 5.34 | 7.11 | 0.50 | 2.32 | 15.28 | 1965 | 25.7 | 200.8 | 0.7 | 244.8 | 472.0 |
| 1970 | 2.18 | 3.81 | 7.78 | 0.93 | 14.70 | 1970 | 7.24 | 9.25 | 0.72 | 3.93 | 21.14 | 1970 | 16.1 | 186.6 | 0.3 | 320.2 | 523.2 |
| 1975 | 1.95 | 4.04 | 8.95 | 1.39 | 16.32 | 1975 | 7.43 | 8.36 | 0.58 | 3.16 | 19.54 | 1975 | 9.4 | 147.2 | (2) | 406.0 | 562.6 |
| 1980 | 1.52 | 4.84 | 9.55 | 1.15 | 17.06 | 1980 | 7.36 | 8.20 | 0.63 | 3.68 | 19.88 | 1980 | 6.5 | 127.0 | (2) | 569.3 | 702.7 |
| 1985 | 1.35 | 4.02 | 9.87 | 0.48 | 15.73 | 1985 | 6.86 | 6.87 | 0.50 | 3.04 | 17.28 | 1985 | 7.8 | 116.4 | (2) | 693.8 | 818.0 |
| 1989[1] | 1.40 | 4.26 | 10.85 | 0.74 | 17.24 | 1989[1] | 7.57 | 8.02 | 0.59 | 2.77 | 18.95 | 1989[1] | 6.2 | 117.8 | (2) | 765.8 | 889.6 |

1. Preliminary. 2. Less than 0.05 million short tons; quantities are included in "industrial" column. **Source**: U.S. Dept. of Energy, *Annual Energy Review 1989* (1990).

heating, air conditioning, and appliances.

The transportation and residential and commercial sectors accounted for most of the growth in energy consumption during 1949-89. Residential and commercial consumption leveled off in response to higher energy prices, but following the price declines in 1986 and 1988, grew to a record 29.6 quadrillion Btu. Transportation consumption increased more slowly over the same 40-year period but peaked at 22.19 quadrillion Btu in 1988 before declining slightly to 22.15 quadrillion Btu in 1989.

### Fossil Fuels

**Petroleum** Since 1958 the United States has consumed more energy than it produces; energy imports make up the difference. Net imports of energy (primarily petroleum) grew rapidly through 1973, when they totaled 13 quadrillion Btu, or 20% of consumption. Despite the Arab oil embargo of 1973-74 and increases in the price of crude oil, petroleum net imports continued to grow, climbing to 18 quadrillion Btu in 1977. That year, U.S. dependence on petroleum net imports peaked at 47% of consumption. A second round of price increases in 1979-81 suppressed demand for foreign oil. In 1985 petroleum net imports totaled 9 quadrillion Btu, and U.S. dependence on foreign oil fell to 27% of consumption. That was the last year the ratio of petroleum net imports to petroleum consumption declined. In 1989 as the price of crude oil continued to be depressed, U.S. dependence on foreign oil reached 41%, and dependence on net imports from members of OPEC had risen from 12% of consumption in 1985 to 24%.

**Natural gas** Natural gas is the primary source of energy for space heating in 50 million U.S. households. U.S. natural gas trade was limited to the border countries of Mexico and Canada until shipping natural gas in liquified form emerged as an alternative to pipelines. In 1969, the first shipments of liquified natural gas (LNG) were sent to Japan, and U.S. imports from Algeria began the following year. In 1989 U.S. net imports of natural gas by all routes totaled 1.3 trillion cubic feet. This represents a 7% increase over 1988 net imports. Imports make up 6.9% of domestic LNG consumption, up slightly from 6.8% in 1988.

**Coal** Since World War II coal has been the

### U.S. ENERGY OVERVIEW, 1960–89 (quadrillion Btu)

| Activity and energy source | 1960 | 1970 | 1975 | 1980 | 1985 | 1989[1] |
|---|---|---|---|---|---|---|
| PRODUCTION | | | | | | |
| Crude oil[2] | 14.93 | 20.40 | 17.73 | 18.25 | 18.99 | 16.15 |
| Natural gas plant liquids | 1.46 | 2.51 | 2.37 | 2.25 | 2.24 | 2.16 |
| Natural gas[3] | 12.66 | 21.67 | 19.64 | 19.91 | 16.91 | 17.53 |
| Coal | 10.82 | 14.61 | 14.99 | 18.60 | 19.33 | 21.23 |
| Nuclear electric power | 0.01 | 0.24 | 1.90 | 2.74 | 4.15 | 5.69 |
| Hydroelectric power | 1.61 | 2.63 | 3.15 | 2.90 | 2.94 | 2.74 |
| Other[4] | (5) | 0.02 | 0.07 | 0.11 | 0.21 | 0.22 |
| **Total** | **41.49** | **62.07** | **59.86** | **64.76** | **64.77** | **65.71** |
| IMPORTS | | | | | | |
| Crude oil[6] | 2.20 | 2.81 | 8.72 | 11.19 | 6.81 | 12.51 |
| Petroleum products[7] | 1.80 | 4.66 | 4.23 | 3.46 | 3.80 | 4.47 |
| Natural gas | 0.16 | 0.85 | 0.98 | 1.01 | 0.95 | 1.38 |
| Other[8] | 0.07 | 0.07 | 0.19 | 0.31 | 0.54 | 0.38 |
| **Total** | **4.23** | **8.39** | **14.11** | **15.97** | **12.10** | **18.74** |
| EXPORTS | | | | | | |
| Coal | 1.02 | 1.94 | 1.76 | 2.42 | 2.44 | 2.65 |
| Crude oil and petroleum products | 0.43 | 0.55 | 0.44 | 1.16 | 1.66 | 1.84 |
| Other[9] | 0.03 | 0.18 | 0.16 | 0.14 | 0.14 | 0.23 |
| **Total** | **1.48** | **2.66** | **2.36** | **3.72** | **4.23** | **4.72** |
| CONSUMPTION | | | | | | |
| Petroleum products[10] | 19.92 | 29.52 | 32.73 | 34.20 | 30.92 | 34.02 |
| Natural gas | 12.39 | 21.79 | 19.95 | 20.39 | 17.83 | 19.50 |
| Coal | 9.84 | 12.26 | 12.66 | 15.42 | 17.48 | 18.92 |
| Nuclear power | 0.01 | 0.24 | 1.90 | 2.74 | 4.15 | 5.69 |
| Hydroelectric power[11] | 1.66 | 2.65 | 3.22 | 3.12 | 3.36 | 2.85 |
| Other[12] | (5) | -0.04 | 0.09 | 0.08 | 0.20 | 0.25 |
| **Total** | **43.80** | **66.43** | **70.55** | **75.96** | **73.95** | **81.23** |

**Note**: Data do not include consumption of wood energy (other than that consumed by electric utilities) which totaled about 2.6 quadrillion Btu in 1984. This table also does not include small quantities of other energy forms for which consistent historical data are not available, such as geothermal, waste, wind, photovoltaic, or solar thermal energy sources except that consumed by electric utilities. Sum of components may not equal total due to independent rounding. 1. Preliminary. 2. Includes lease condensate. 3. Dry natural gas. 4. Includes electricity produced from geothermal, wood, waste, wind, photovoltaic, and solar thermal energy sources connected to electric utility distribution systems. 5. Less than 0.005 quadrillion Btu. 6. Includes imports of crude oil for the Strategic Petroleum Reserve which began in 1977. 7. Includes imports of unfinished oils and natural gas plant liquids. 8. Includes coal, coal coke, and hydroelectric power. 9. Includes natural gas, coal coke, and hydroelectric power. 10. Petroleum products supplied include natural gas plant liquids and crude oil burned as fuel. 11. Includes industrial generation of hydroelectric power and net electricity imports. 12. Includes electricity produced from geothermal, wood, waste, wind, photovoltaic, and solar thermal sources connected to electric utility distribution systems, and net imports of coal coke. **Source**: U.S. Dept. of Energy, *Annual Energy Review 1989* (1990).

major U.S. energy export. Throughout most of the 1960s and 1970s, U.S. exports of coal increased, reaching 113 million short tons in 1981. Exports were significantly lower during the rest of the decade, though they were up in 1989, to 100.8 million short tons. Canada, Japan, and Italy are the largest markets and

together accounted for 41% of total exports in 1989. However, Japan's 1989 purchases were only a little more than half what they were in 1981, and U.S. exports to major European markets also were down markedly from 1981.

Electric utilities are the primary domestic consumers of coal. Their consumption grew from a 17% share in 1949 to an 86% share in 1989. Over the same period, consumption in all other sectors declined, most dramatically in the transportation sector, where railroads switched to petroleum, and in the residential and commercial sector. In 1949, the two sectors accounted for 39% of coal consumption, and by 1989 less than 1%.

The Department of Energy estimates that the demonstrated reserve base of coal was 473 billion short tons in 1989. With an overall recoverability rate of 50%, coal production could be sustained at current levels for more than 200 years.

## Nuclear Power

Between 1980 and 1989 the number of U.S. nuclear power plants in operation grew by more than half, from 70 units to 110 units, and net nuclear generation of electricity grew 111%, from 251 billion kilowatt-hours (kWh) to 529 billion kWh in 1989. Most (85) nuclear power plants in the United States are located in the eastern half of the country. In addition to the operating units, 1 unit had reached the start-up stage and 10 units had received construction permits by the end of 1989. Although the number of operable units reached an all-time high in 1989, the total of 121 units in all stages of planning, construction, or operation

was well below the total of 236 in 1975. Since then many planned units have been canceled, and no orders for new units have been announced since 1978.

Several factors have contributed to the decline in the number of planned nuclear units. Growth in electricity demand has been slower than expected; longer lead times for licensing and construction coupled with higher financing expenses have increased costs; and rising interest rates and an uncertain economic environment have eroded electric utilities' willingness to commission new plants.

A further deterrent has been increased public opposition to nuclear power plants because

## U.S. COMMERCIAL NUCLEAR PLANTS IN OPERATION, 1989

In 1989 there were 110 operable nuclear reactors in 32 states. This table lists the total number of reactors in each state, the names of individual units, and their locations.

**Alabama = 5**
Browns Ferry 1, 2, & 3, Decatur
Joseph M. Farley 1 & 2, Dothan
**Arizona = 3**
Palo Verde 1, 2, & 3, Wintersburg
**Arkansas = 2**
Arkansas Nuclear 1 & 2, Russellville
**California = 6**
Diablo Canyon 1 & 2, Avila Beach
Rancho Seco, Clay Station[1]
San Onofre 1, 2, & 3, San Clemente
**Connecticut = 4**
Connecticut Yankee, Haddam Neck
Millstone 1, 2, & 3, Waterford
**Florida = 5**
Crystal River 3, Red Level
St. Lucie 1 & 2, Ft. Pierce
Turkey Point 3 & 4, Florida City
**Georgia = 4**
Hatch 1 & 2, Baxley
Vogtle 1 & 2, Waynesboro
**Illinois = 13**
Braidwood 1 & 2, Braidwood
Byron 1 & 2, Byron
Clinton 1, Clinton
Dresden 2 & 3, Morris

La Salle 1 & 2, Seneca
Quad Cities 1 & 2, Cordova
Zion 1 & 2, Zion
**Iowa = 1**
Duane Arnold, Palo
**Kansas = 1**
Wolf Creek, Burlington
**Louisiana = 2**
River Bend 1, St. Francisville
Waterford 3, Taft
**Maine = 1**
Maine Yankee, Wiscasset
**Maryland = 2**
Calvert Cliffs 1 & 2, Lusby
**Massachusetts = 2**
Pilgrim 1, Plymouth
Yankee Rowe 1, Rowe
**Michigan = 5**
Big Rock Point, Charlevoix
Donald C. Cook 1 & 2, Bridgman
Fermi 2, Newport
Palisades, South Haven
**Minnesota = 3**
Monticello, Monticello
Prairie Island 1 & 2, Red Wing

**Mississippi = 1**
Grand Gulf 1, Port Gibson
**Missouri = 1**
Callaway 1, Fulton
**Nebraska = 2**
Cooper, Brownville
Fort Calhoun 1, Fort Calhoun
**New Jersey = 4**
Hope Creek 1, Salem
Oyster Creek 1, Forked River
Salem 1 & 2, Salem
**New York = 6**
Indian Point 2 & 3, Buchanan
James A. Fitzpatrick, Scriba
Nine Mile Point 1 & 2, Oswego
Robert E. Ginna, Rochester
**North Carolina = 5**
Brunswick 1 & 2, Southport
McGuire 1 & 2, Cowens Ford Dam
Shearon Harris 1, New Hill
**Ohio = 2**
Davis-Besse 1, Oak Harbor
Perry 1, North Perry
**Oregon = 1**
Trojan, Prescott

**Pennsylvania = 9**
Beaver Valley 1 & 2, Shippingport
Limerick 1 & 2, Pottstown
Peach Bottom 2 & 3, Lancaster
Susquehanna 1 & 2, Berwick
Three Mile Island 1, Middletown
**South Carolina = 7**
Catawba 1 & 2, Clover
H.B. Robinson 2, Hartsville
Oconee 1, 2, & 3, Seneca
Summer 1, Jenkinsville
**Tennessee = 2**
Sequoyah 1 & 2, Daisy
**Texas = 2**
South Texas 1 & 2, Bay City
**Vermont = 1**
Vermont Yankee, Vernon
**Virginia = 4**
North Anna 1 & 2, Mineral
Surrey 1 & 2, Surrey
**Washington = 1**
WNP 2, Richland
**Wisconsin = 3**
Kewaunee, Carlton
Point Beach 1 & 2, Two Creeks

1. Rancho Seco was shut down by the Sacramento Municipal Utility District following a referendum on its continued operation. There are no plans to operate it as a nuclear unit; however, it retains an operating license. **Source:** U.S. Dept. of Energy, *Commercial Nuclear Power 1990: Prospects for the United States and the World* (1990).

## U.S. NET GENERATION OF ELECTRICITY BY UTILITIES, BY ENERGY SOURCE, 1950–89 (billion kilowatthours)

| Year | Coal | Natural gas | Petroleum[1] | Nuclear power | Hydroelectric power | Geothermal and other[2] | Total |
|------|------|------|------|------|------|------|------|
| 1950 | 155 | 45 | 34 | 0 | 96 | (3) | 329 |
| 1955 | 301 | 95 | 37 | 0 | 113 | (3) | 547 |
| 1960 | 403 | 158 | 48 | 1 | 146 | (3) | 756 |
| 1965 | 571 | 222 | 65 | 4 | 194 | (3) | 1,055 |
| 1970 | 704 | 373 | 184 | 22 | 248 | 1 | 1,532 |
| 1975 | 853 | 300 | 289 | 173 | 300 | 3 | 1,918 |
| 1980 | 1,162 | 346 | 246 | 251 | 276 | 6 | 2,286 |
| 1985 | 1,402 | 292 | 100 | 384 | 281 | 11 | 2,470 |
| 1988 | 1,541 | 253 | 149 | 527 | 223 | 12 | 2,704 |
| 1989[4] | 1,551 | 264 | 158 | 529 | 264 | 11 | 2,779 |

1. Includes distillate fuel oil, residual fuel oil (including crude oil burned as fuel), jet fuel, and petroleum coke. 2. Other is wood, waste, photovoltaic, and solar thermal energy used to generate electricity for distribution. 3. Less than 0.5 billion kilowatthours. 4. Preliminary. **Source:** U.S. Dept. of Energy, *Annual Energy Review 1989* (1990).

## GASOLINE AND HEATING OIL RETAIL PRICES, 1950–89 (cents per gallon)

| Year | Motor gasoline[1] | | | | Residential heating oil[2] | |
|------|------|------|------|------|------|------|
| | Leaded regular | | Unleaded regular | | | |
| | Current | Constant[3] | Current | Constant[3] | Current | Constant[3] |
| 1950 | 26.8¢ | 112.1¢ | N.A. | N.A. | N.A. | N.A. |
| 1955 | 29.1 | 107.0 | N.A. | N.A. | N.A. | N.A. |
| 1960 | 31.1 | 100.6 | N.A. | N.A. | 15.0¢ | 48.5¢ |
| 1965 | 31.2 | 92.3 | N.A. | N.A. | 16.0 | 47.3 |
| 1970 | 35.7 | 85.0 | N.A. | N.A. | 18.5 | 44.0 |
| 1975 | 56.7 | 95.6 | N.A. | N.A. | 37.7 | 63.6 |
| 1980 | 119.1 | 139.0 | 124.5¢ | 145.3¢ | 97.4 | 113.7 |
| 1985 | 111.5 | 100.5 | 120.2 | 108.4 | 105.3 | 95.0 |
| 1988 | 89.9 | 74.1 | 94.6 | 78.0 | 81.3 | 67.0 |
| 1989 | 99.8 | 79.0 | 102.1 | 80.8 | 90.0[4] | 71.3[4] |

1. Prices include taxes and are calculated from a sample of stations providing all types of services (i.e., full-, mini-, and self-serve). Geographic coverage: 1950-70, 55 representative cities; 1975, 56 urban areas; 1980-88, 85 urban areas. 2. Prices derived by dividing sum of estimated national retail sales for residential heating oil (No. 2 fuel oil) by the estimated volume of retail sales for residential heating. Data for 1980-88 exclude taxes. 3. Constant 1982 dollars. 4. Preliminary. **Source:** U.S. Dept. of Energy, *Annual Energy Review 1989* (1990).

## U.S. NUCLEAR GENERATION OF ELECTRICITY, 1957–89

| Year | Operable units | Net generation of electricity | |
|---|---|---|---|
| | | Billion net kilo-watthours | Percent of total U.S. generation |
| 1957 | 1 | (1) | (2) |
| 1960 | 3 | 0.5 | 0.1% |
| 1965 | 6 | 3.7 | 0.3 |
| 1970 | 18 | 21.8 | 1.4 |
| 1975 | 54 | 172.5 | 9.0 |
| 1980 | 70 | 251.1 | 11.0 |
| 1985 | 95 | 383.7 | 15.5 |
| 1986 | 100 | 414.0 | 16.6 |
| 1987 | 107 | 455.3 | 17.7 |
| 1988 | 108 | 527.0 | 19.5 |
| 1989[3] | 110 | 529.4 | 19.1 |

1. Less than 0.05 billion kilowatthours. 2. Less than 0.05%. 3. Preliminary. **Source:** U.S. Dept. of Energy, *Annual Energy Review 1989* (1990).

of concerns about their safety and the disposal of spent nuclear fuel. These concerns were heightened in the wake of the accident at Three Mile Island near Harrisburg, Pennsylvania, in 1979, and the far more devastating one at Chernobyl in the Soviet Union in 1986.

### Electricity

Net generation of electricity by electric utilities reached 2.8 trillion kilowatthours (kWh) in 1989, up 2.7% from 1987. Coal accounted for 1,551 billion kWh, compared to 264 billion kWh for natural gas and 159 billion kWh for petroleum. Nuclear-based generation reached an all-time high of 529 billion kWh. Due to two consecutive years of drought, hydroelectric generation declined to 223 billion kWh in 1988, 23% below the level in 1986, but rose again to 264 billion kWh. Geothermal and other alternative energy sources accounted for 11 billion kWh.

The weighted average of the real price of electricity to all sectors in 1989 was $0.06 per kWh, 13% below the price in 1960. Although

## U.S. NUCLEAR GENERATING UNITS WITH LEAST UNSCHEDULED DOWNTIME

| Rank/unit | Utility | Year built | Lifetime forced outage rate[1] |
|---|---|---|---|
| 1. Point Beach 2 | Wisconsin Electric Power | 1972 | 1.2% |
| 2. Point Beach 1 | Wisconsin Electric Power | 1970 | 1.9 |
| 3. Kewaunee | Wisconsin Public Service | 1974 | 2.6 |
| 4. Diablo Canyon 1 | Pacific Gas and Electric | 1984 | 2.8 |
| 5. Prairie Island 2 | Northern States Power (Minn.) | 1974 | 3.0 |
| 6. Fort Calhoun 1 | Omaha Public Power District | 1973 | 3.0 |
| 7. Callaway 1 | Union Electric (Mo.) | 1984 | 3.3 |
| 8. St. Lucie 1 | Florida Power and Light | 1976 | 3.4 |
| 9. Monticello 1 | Northern States Power (Minn.) | 1971 | 4.0 |
| 10. Joseph M. Farley 2 | Alabama Power | 1981 | 4.6 |

1. Unscheduled downtime as a percentage of time since the unit was put in operation. Does not include scheduled downtime for maintenance and refueling, although in general the units with low forced outage rates also had the highest overall performance rate. **Source:** U.S. Dept. of Energy, *Commercial Nuclear Power 1990: Prospects for the United States and the World* (1990).

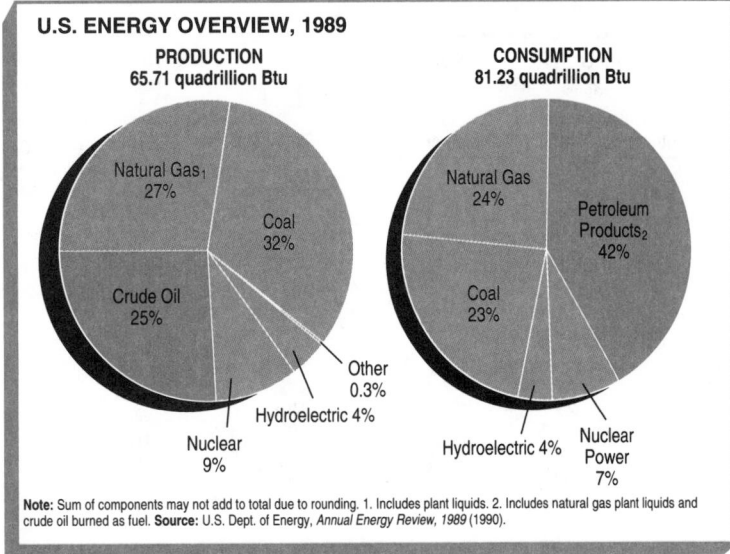

### U.S. ENERGY OVERVIEW, 1989

**PRODUCTION**
65.71 quadrillion Btu

Natural Gas₁ 27%
Coal 32%
Crude Oil 25%
Nuclear 9%
Hydroelectric 4%
Other 0.3%

**CONSUMPTION**
81.23 quadrillion Btu

Natural Gas 24%
Petroleum Products₂ 42%
Coal 23%
Hydroelectric 4%
Nuclear Power 7%

**Note:** Sum of components may not add to total due to rounding. 1. Includes plant liquids. 2. Includes natural gas plant liquids and crude oil burned as fuel. **Source:** U.S. Dept. of Energy, *Annual Energy Review, 1989* (1990).

prices of other major energy sources increased significantly during the same period, electricity

remained by far the most expensive source of energy per Btu.

# Transportation

Americans spend nearly $800 billion for transportation products and services annually. In 1988, the United States recorded 3.6 trillion passenger-miles of travel and 3.6 million ton-miles of freight traffic. Transportation and transportation-related businesses employ one-tenth of the American work force. As a share of consumer spending, transportation accounts for almost 20 percent of the total.

The government has traditionally played a leading role in the development of the nation's transportation infrastructure. Technological, economic, and demographic changes all help to shape the government's priorities. In the 19th and early 20th centuries, for instance, the gov-

ernment made enormous direct and indirect contributions to the development of the nation's railroads. Today, the nation's 135,000-mile-long rail network is the second largest in the world after the Soviet Union; but in terms of passenger-miles per person carried (50 miles per person per year) the U.S. doesn't even rank in the top 50, and today the government spends vastly more on highways and aviation than on railroad transportation. In 1991, the government sought $14.1 billion for highway and highway safety programs, $9.3 billion for aviation, and $2.4 billion for mass transit.

**Costs** Transportation costs vary dramatically among the primary carrier types. In 1988 the average revenue per passenger-mile—that is, the revenue generated from carrying one passenger one mile—was $0.20 for first-class and $0.12 for coach and economy air carrier; $0.12 for commuter rail; $0.11 for Amtrak; and $0.11 for intercity bus. By comparison, the

## RAILROAD NETWORKS AND PASSENGER MILES PER PERSON, SELECTED NATIONS

| Country | Railway network (thousands of miles) | Country | Passenger miles per person |
|---|---|---|---|
| USSR | 148.3 | Japan | 1,647.0 |
| United States | 135.2 | Switzerland | 913.8 |
| Canada | 39.5 | East Germany | 811.8 |
| India | 37.1 | Czechoslovakia | 771.6 |
| China | 31.6 | Poland | 769.2 |
| Australia | 23.6 | USSR | 765.6 |
| France | 20.8 | France | 644.4 |
| Argentina | 20.5 | Austria | 582.6 |
| West Germany | 16.4 | Denmark | 562.2 |
| Poland | 14.5 | Hungary | 543.6 |

**Note:** Latest available figures, 1986–88. **Source:** Union Internationale des Chemins de Fer, *Statistiques Internationales des Chemins de Fer.*

average cost of operating a car in 1989 (including variable costs for gas and oil, maintenance, and tires and fixed costs for insurance, registration, depreciation, and finance charges) was $0.38 per mile.

**A nation on the move** Of the 3.8 trillion intercity passenger-miles traveled in 1988, 3.4 trillion—89%—were by passenger car or taxi. Certificated airlines accounted for 334 billion miles, or 9%. Intercity buses accounted for 23.1 million (0.6%), general aviation for 12.1 million (0.3%), and railroads (not including commuter rail) for 7 million (0.2%) of all passenger-miles traveled.

In 1988 there were 64,013 vehicles engaged in local mass transit. (This figure does not include taxi cabs, which numbered 144,000). Passengers logged 38.2 billion miles on 8.1 billion trips. Buses accounted for 60% of pas-

senger trips and 46% of passenger miles traveled, and rapid rail accounted for 31% of passenger trips taken and 31% of passenger miles traveled. The length of an average trip was 21.9 miles by commuter rail, 5.8 miles by ferryboat, 4.7 miles by rapid rail, and 3.7 miles by bus.

The change in price of average passenger fares between 1980 and 1988 varied hugely by mode of transportation. Air fares increased only 6%, intercity bus fares rose 35%, and Amtrak fares 55%. Average fares for local transit and commuter rail service more than doubled. In the same period, the cost-per-mile of operating a passenger car increased 19%, despite an 11% drop in the cost-per-mile of gas and oil due to low energy prices and increased fuel efficiency.

**Commerce** In 1988 the average freight rev-

enue per ton-mile—that is, the revenue generated from carrying one ton of freight one mile—was $1.14 for an air carrier, $0.14 for a common carrier truck, $0.03 for railroad, $0.01 for pipeline, and 0.8 cents for inland waterway carriers. Of the 3.3 trillion revenue ton-miles of freight traveled in 1989, 37% went by water, 27% by rail, 19% by motor vehicles, 17% by oil pipeline, and a mere 0.2% by air.

**Maritime transportation** Waterborne commerce remains especially vital to the U.S. economy. In 1989, 48 U.S. ports handled over 10 million tons of cargo. Of these, three handled more than 100 million tons: New Orleans, 177.5 million; New York, 148.6 million; and Houston, 125.6 million. Of the 148 U.S. ports that handled more than 1 million tons of commerce in 1989, 46 were located on the Atlantic coast, 20 on the Gulf of Mexico, 34 on

## U.S. ROADS AND STREETS, 1904–88

| | Surfaced mileage ('000s) | | | Total mileage ('000s) | | | |
|---|---|---|---|---|---|---|---|
| Year | State control | County and local control | Total | State control | County and local control | Total | Percent surfaced |
| 1904 | 0 | — | 204 | — | — | 2,351 | 8.7% |
| 1921 | 84 | 363 | 447 | 203 | 2,957 | 3,160 | 14.1 |
| 1930 | 227 | 627 | 854 | 324 | 2,935 | 3,259 | 26.2 |
| 1935 | 374 | 881 | 1,255 | 523 | 2,787 | 3,310 | 37.9 |
| 1940 | 449 | 1,108 | 1,557 | 551 | 2,736 | 3,287 | 47.4 |
| 1945 | 482 | 1,239 | 1,721 | 574 | 2,745 | 3,319 | 51.9 |
| 1950 | 542 | 1,397 | 1,939 | 609 | 2,704 | 3,313 | 58.5 |
| 1955 | 610 | 1,663 | 2,273 | 651 | 2,767 | 3,418 | 66.5 |
| 1960 | 660 | 1,897 | 2,557 | 694 | 2,852 | 3,546 | 72.1 |
| 1965 | 701 | 2,075 | 2,776 | 728 | 2,962 | 3,690 | 75.2 |
| 1970 | 748 | 2,198 | 2,946 | 781 | 2,949 | 3,730 | 79.0 |
| 1975 | 763 | 2,338 | 3,101 | 796 | 3,042 | 3,838 | 80.8 |
| 1980 | 753 | 2,605 | 3,358 | 781 | 3,174 | 3,955 | 84.9 |
| 1985 | 612 | 2,868 | 3,480 | 613 | 3,249 | 3,862 | 90.1 |
| 1988 | 618 | 2,873 | 3,491 | 619 | 3,252 | 3,871 | 90.2 |

**Source:** Motor Vehicle Manufacturers Association of the United States, Inc., *MVMA Motor Vehicle Facts & Figures '90* (1990).

## PASSENGER-MILES AND REVENUE TON-MILES OF FREIGHT, BY MODE OF TRANSPORTATION, 1980–88

| Mode of transport | 1980 | 1985 | 1988 |
|---|---|---|---|
| **PASSENGER-MILES (millions)** | | | |
| Air carrier[1] | 204,367 | 277,836 | 334,291 |
| General aviation, intercity | 14,700 | 13,000 | 12,100 |
| Highway: | | | |
| Passenger car and taxi | 2,556,671 | 2,899,300 | 2,429,805 |
| Intercity bus | 27,400 | 23,800 | 23,100 |
| Class I rail[2] | 6,516 | 6,547 | 6,941 |
| Amtrak | 4,503 | 4,785 | 5,686 |
| **REVENUE TON-MILES OF FREIGHT (millions)** | | | |
| Air carrier[1,3] | 4,528 | 5,156 | 8,169 |
| Oil pipeline | 588,000 | 564,000 | 605,000 |
| Class I rail | 918,958 | 876,984 | 996,182 |
| Motor vehicle, intercity | 555,000 | 610,000 | 699,000 |
| Water transport: | | | |
| Inland waterways and Great Lakes | 406,879 | 381,693 | 438,185 |
| Domestic waterways | 921,836 | 892,970 | 890,028 |

1. Includes domestic operations, certificated, all services. 2. Includes commuter rail. 3. Includes revenue ton-miles, U.S. and foreign mail, and express as reported on AIM Form 41. **Source:** U.S. Dept. of Transportation, *National Transportation Statistics Annual Report* (1990).

## NUMBER OF VEHICLES IN THE U.S., 1980–88

| Mode of transport | 1980 | 1985 | 1988 |
|---|---|---|---|
| Air carrier, certificated, all services[1] | 2,718 | 3,100 | 4,188 |
| General aviation | 211,045 | 210,654 | 210,266 |
| Passenger car and taxi ('000s) | 121,601 | 131,864 | 141,252 |
| Motorcycle ('000s) | 5,694 | 5,444 | 4,584 |
| Intercity bus | 21,400 | 20,200 | 19,887 |
| Local transit, total | 75,388 | 88,691 | 96,490[2] |
| Motor bus | 59,411 | 57,285 | 60,388[2] |
| Heavy rail | 9,641 | 9,326 | 10,539[2] |
| Light rail | 1,013 | 699 | 831[2] |
| Trolley bus | 823 | 676 | 710[2] |
| Commuter rail | 4,500 | 4,035 | 4,649[2] |
| Demand response | N.A. | 15,545 | 18,190[2] |
| Other | N.A. | 1,006 | 1,183[2] |
| Class I rail, total | 1,198,310 | 890,302 | 744,691 |
| Freight cars | 1,168,114 | 867,070 | 724,840 |
| Locomotives | 27,977 | 22,548 | 19,364 |
| Passenger-train cars | 2,219 | 684 | 487 |
| Amtrak, total | 2,547 | 2,200 | 2,236 |
| Passenger-train cars | 2,128 | 1,818 | 1,845 |
| Locomotives | 419 | 382 | 391 |
| Truck, total ('000s) | 33,667 | 39,196 | 42,529 |
| Water transport, total | 37,149 | 39,230 | 36,952 |
| Inland water vessels | 36,285 | 38,493 | 36,277 |
| Oceangoing ships[3] | 864 | 737 | 675 |

**Note:** As of December of year shown. 1. Domestic and international certificated aircraft, all services. 2. Preliminary figures. 3. Vessels 1,000 gross tons and over. **Source:** U.S. Dept. of Transportation, *National Transportation Statistics Annual Report* (1990).

## U.S. MASS TRANSIT, 1989

| | Passenger trips | | | Average | |
|---|---|---|---|---|---|
| Mode | Total 1989 (millions) | Percent change 1988–89 | Passenger miles (millions) | length of trip (miles) | Vehicles operated[1] |
| Motor bus | 4,838.5 | 1.2% | 17,746.7 | 3.7 | 42,700 |
| Rapid rail | 2,541.9 | 10.1 | 12,030.0 | 4.7 | 8,306 |
| Streetcar | 161.0 | 5.5 | 507.3 | 3.2 | 531 |
| Trolley bus | 129.6 | –4.6 | 199.2 | 1.5 | 495 |
| Commuter rail | 329.6 | 5.5 | 7,211.9 | 21.9 | 4,111 |
| Demand response | 37.2 | 10.7 | 246.8 | 6.6 | 7,280 |
| All other[2] | 56.0 | –11.5 | 292.9 | 5.2 | 590 |
| **All modes** | **8,093.8** | **4.0%** | **38,234.4** | **4.7** | **64,013** |

1. Includes purchased transportation, transit services provided by public agencies, and/or private carriers under contract to public agencies. 2. Includes aerial tramway, automated guideway, cable car, ferry service, inclined plane, jitney, and van-pool. **Source:** U.S. Dept. of Transportation, *National Urban Mass Transportation Statistics, 1989 Section 15 Annual Report* (1990).

## U.S. MOTOR-VEHICLE REGISTRATIONS BY STATE, 1989

| State | Automobiles | Buses | Trucks | Total motor vehicles | Percent change 1988–89 | Automobiles per capita |
|---|---|---|---|---|---|---|
| Ala. | 2,670,443 | 8,370 | 944,391 | 3,623,204 | −6.6% | 0.65 |
| Alaska | 230,608 | 2,118 | 131,017 | 363,743 | 0.5 | 0.43 |
| Ariz. | 1,958,341 | 4,309 | 812,620 | 2,775,270 | 2.6 | 0.55 |
| Ark. | 924,063 | 5,262 | 503,743 | 1,433,068 | 0.4 | 0.38 |
| Calif. | 16,718,380 | 38,854 | 4,913,899 | 21,671,133 | 1.6 | 0.57 |
| Colo. | 2,289,827 | 5,515 | 858,496 | 3,153,838 | 7.9 | 0.69 |
| Conn. | 2,492,238 | 8,812 | 150,093 | 2,651,143 | 0.0 | 0.77 |
| Del. | 402,666 | 1,715 | 117,210 | 521,591 | 1.9 | 0.59 |
| D.C. | 242,228 | 2,781 | 13,925 | 258,934 | −1.9 | 0.40 |
| Fla. | 8,972,724 | 36,247 | 2,197,933 | 11,206,904 | 2.0 | 0.70 |
| Ga. | 3,711,699 | 18,696 | 1,540,092 | 5,270,487 | 1.4 | 0.57 |
| Hawaii | 641,204 | 4,226 | 90,963 | 736,393 | 4.5 | 0.57 |
| Idaho | 616,496 | 3,632 | 418,917 | 1,039,045 | 10.5 | 0.60 |
| Ill. | 6,436,253 | 17,680 | 1,567,762 | 8,021,695 | 2.0 | 0.55 |
| Ind. | 3,176,080 | 21,224 | 1,124,998 | 4,322,302 | 3.7 | 0.56 |
| Iowa | 1,845,275 | 9,062 | 728,933 | 2,583,270 | 0.6 | 0.65 |
| Kans. | 1,390,764 | 3,760 | 592,123 | 1,986,647 | −10.1 | 0.55 |
| Ky. | 1,881,057 | 9,816 | 952,160 | 2,843,033 | 1.7 | 0.50 |
| La. | 1,986,561 | 19,566 | 969,970 | 2,976,097 | 1.3 | 0.45 |
| Maine | 717,581 | 2,835 | 218,885 | 939,301 | 0.1 | 0.58 |
| Md. | 2,901,912 | 11,013 | 614,502 | 3,527,427 | 1.7 | 0.61 |
| Mass. | 3,305,207 | 11,044 | 488,207 | 3,804,458 | −0.4 | 0.56 |
| Mich. | 5,576,753 | 22,706 | 1,539,124 | 7,138,583 | 0.0 | 0.60 |
| Minn. | 2,567,455 | 13,215 | 702,622 | 3,283,292 | 2.3 | 0.59 |
| Miss. | 1,427,136 | 8,682 | 431,263 | 1,867,081 | 4.5 | 0.54 |
| Mo. | 2,725,908 | 11,576 | 1,106,498 | 3,843,982 | 1.3 | 0.53 |
| Mont. | 441,264 | 1,967 | 297,966 | 741,197 | 2.6 | 0.54 |
| Nebr. | 896,340 | 4,928 | 460,456 | 1,361,724 | 2.5 | 0.55 |
| Nev. | 580,872 | 1,744 | 243,107 | 825,723 | 2.2 | 0.46 |
| N.H. | 739,347 | 1,670 | 194,625 | 935,642 | 0.8 | 0.66 |
| N.J. | 5,154,365 | 17,784 | 464,181 | 5,636,330 | −1.8 | 0.66 |
| N.Mex. | 805,599 | 3,427 | 464,181 | 1,294,521 | 2.2 | 0.52 |
| N.Y. | 8,705,834 | 30,093 | 1,284,612 | 10,020,539 | 1.9 | 0.48 |
| N.C. | 3,646,514 | 34,455 | 1,432,255 | 5,113,224 | 1.8 | 0.55 |
| N.Dak. | 374,458 | 2,183 | 259,554 | 636,195 | −2.9 | 0.56 |
| Ohio | 7,766,905 | 33,020 | 1,713,993 | 9,513,918 | 10.5 | 0.71 |
| Okla. | 1,668,691 | 12,958 | 886,605 | 2,568,454 | 0.6 | 0.51 |
| Oreg. | 1,790,574 | 10,261 | 577,916 | 2,378,751 | 2.7 | 0.63 |
| Pa. | 6,347,133 | 30,818 | 1,531,428 | 7,909,379 | 1.8 | 0.52 |
| R.I. | 555,665 | 1,554 | 113,357 | 670,576 | 0.0 | 0.55 |
| S.C. | 1,840,479 | 13,853 | 614,608 | 2,468,940 | 2.3 | 0.57 |
| S.Dak. | 417,105 | 2,049 | 286,232 | 705,386 | 1.8 | 0.58 |
| Tenn. | 3,451,763 | 13,191 | 850,748 | 4,315,702 | 2.1 | 0.70 |
| Tex. | 8,561,270 | 60,411 | 3,942,874 | 12,564,555 | 1.3 | 0.50 |
| Utah | 796,102 | 1,157 | 377,602 | 1,174,861 | 1.3 | 0.46 |
| Vt. | 341,377 | 1,435 | 118,792 | 461,604 | 1.9 | 0.60 |
| Va. | 3,736,193 | 17,097 | 1,106,438 | 4,859,728 | 4.1 | 0.61 |
| Wash. | 2,876,438 | 7,581 | 1,206,111 | 4,090,130 | 5.2 | 0.60 |
| W.Va. | 822,395 | 3,823 | 387,732 | 1,213,950 | −5.6 | 0.43 |
| Wisc. | 2,669,060 | 12,484 | 789,464 | 3,471,008 | −11.0 | 0.55 |
| Wyo. | 286,841 | 2,381 | 197,367 | 486,589 | 1.0 | 0.59 |
| **Total** | **143,081,443** | **625,040** | **43,554,064** | **187,260,547** | **1.6** | **0.57** |

**Note**: Includes privately owned vehicles and federal, state, and municipal vehicles; does not include vehicles owned by the military services. **Source**: U.S. Dept. of Transportation, *Highway Statistics 1989* (1990).

## U.S. MOTOR-VEHICLE FACTORY SALES AND REGISTRATIONS, 1900–89

| | Factory sales | | |
|---|---|---|---|
| Year | Passenger cars | Trucks and buses | Motor vehicle registrations[1] |
| 1900 | 4,192 | — | 8,000 |
| 1905 | 24,250 | 750 | 78,800 |
| 1910 | 181,000 | 6,000 | 468,500 |
| 1915 | 895,930 | 74,000 | 2,490,932 |
| 1920 | 1,905,560 | 321,789 | 9,239,161 |
| 1925 | 3,735,171 | 530,659 | 19,940,724 |
| 1930 | 2,787,456 | 575,364 | 26,531,990 |
| 1935 | 3,273,874 | 697,367 | 26,229,743 |
| 1940 | 3,717,385 | 754,901 | 32,453,233 |
| 1945 | 69,552 | 655,683 | 31,035,420 |
| 1950 | 6,665,863 | 1,337,193 | 49,161,691 |
| 1955 | 7,920,186 | 1,249,106 | 62,688,792 |
| 1960 | 6,674,796 | 1,194,475 | 73,857,768 |
| 1965 | 9,305,561 | 1,751,805 | 90,357,667 |
| 1970 | 6,546,817 | 1,692,440 | 108,418,197 |
| 1975 | 6,712,852 | 2,272,160 | 132,948,709 |
| 1980 | 6,400,026 | 1,667,283 | 155,796,219 |
| 1985 | 8,002,259 | 3,356,905 | 171,653,675 |
| 1989 | 6,807,416 | 4,061,950 | 188,669,000[2] |

1. Through 1935, privately owned vehicles only; 1940–89, privately and publicly owned vehicles, excluding military vehicles. Data exclude farm trucks registered at a nominal fee in certain states and restricted to use in the vicinity of owners' farms; in 1988, there were 64,120 such trucks. 2. Preliminary. **Source**: Motor Vehicle Manufacturers Association of the United States, Inc., *MVMA Motor Vehicle Facts & Figures '90* (1990).

## FUEL EFFICIENCY OF U.S. PASSENGER CARS, 1955–89

| | | New car, model year basis | |
|---|---|---|---|
| Year | Average U.S. passenger car | Domestic cars | Domestic and imported cars |
| 1955 | 14.53 mpg | 16.0 mpg | 16.1 mpg |
| 1960 | 14.28 | 15.5 | 16.1 |
| 1965 | 14.27 | 15.4 | 15.9 |
| 1970 | 13.52 | 14.1 | 15.2 |
| 1975 | 13.52 | 15.1 | 16.2 |
| 1980 | 15.46 | 22.6 | 24.3 |
| 1985 | 18.20 | 26.4 | 27.6 |
| 1989 | 19.95[1] | 27.1 | 28.3 |

**Note**: mpg = miles per gallon; calculated on the basis of 55% city and 45% highway miles sales weighted harmonic average. 1. Figure for 1988. **Source**: U.S. Dept. of Transportation, *National Transportation Statistics Annual Report* (1990).

## WORLD MOTOR VEHICLE PRODUCTION, 1950–89
### (in thousands)

| Year | United States | Canada | Europe | Japan | Other | World total | U.S. share of total |
|---|---|---|---|---|---|---|---|
| 1950 | 8,006 | 391 | 2,128 | 32 | 20 | 10,577 | 76.2% |
| 1955 | 9,204 | 452 | 3,742 | 68 | 162 | 13,628 | 67.5 |
| 1960 | 7,905 | 398 | 6,824 | 482 | 879 | 16,488 | 47.9 |
| 1965 | 11,138 | 847 | 9,549 | 1,876 | 858 | 24,267 | 45.9 |
| 1970 | 8,284 | 1,187 | 13,154 | 5,289 | 1,352 | 29,267 | 28.3 |
| 1975 | 8,987 | 1,424 | 13,590 | 6,942 | 2,056 | 32,998 | 27.2 |
| 1980 | 8,010 | 1,374 | 15,530 | 11,043 | 2,538 | 38,495 | 20.8 |
| 1985 | 11,653 | 1,933 | 15,988 | 12,271 | 2,938 | 44,782 | 26.0 |
| 1989 | 10,852 | 1,940 | 18,983 | 13,026 | 4,090 | 48,891 | 22.2 |

**Source**: Motor Vehicle Manufacturers Association of the United States, Inc., *MVMA Motor Vehicle Facts & Figures '90* (1990).

the Pacific, 31 on the Great Lakes, and 17 on the Mississippi River and its tributaries.

All told, at the end of 1989 there were 39,209 U.S.-flag self-propelled and non-self-propelled (for instance, barges) passenger and cargo vessels operating or available for operation. This represented a combined capacity of 68.7 million short tons, 181,329 passengers, and 326 railroad cars. Of these, 57 vessels were classified as sailing vessels—a small but notable minority.

As of 1990, the American oceangoing merchant marine—often billed as the fourth arm of

national defense—ranked 8th in number of oceangoing ships with only 635 ships of more than 1,000 gross tons; of these, only 380 ships were in active service. In peacetime, many shippers in industrialized nations chose to register their oceangoing ships under "flags of convenience" to avoid the high costs of labor, stringent safety regulations, and shipbuilding in their own countries. About a dozen countries are considered flags of convenience, and the leading two—Liberia and Panama—together account for 27% of total deadweight tonnage and 20% of all merchant ships over 1,000 gross

register tons.

**Aviation** Thirty of the world's 50 busiest airports in terms of passengers enplaned, deplaned, and transferred are in the United States, including seven of the top 10. By region, 13 of the top 50 are in Asia and Oceania. By country, Japan and Britain have three of the busiest airports, while Germany and France each have two. Toronto's Lester B. Pearson International Airport ranks 22nd, and Mexico City International Airport—the largest airport in Latin America—ranks 47th.

## WORLD MOTOR VEHICLE PRODUCTION, 1988–89

| Country | 1988 Total | 1988 Percent of total | 1989 Total | 1989 Percent of total | Percent change 1988–89 | Country | 1988 Total | 1988 Percent of total | 1989 Total | 1989 Percent of total | Percent change 1988–89 |
|---|---|---|---|---|---|---|---|---|---|---|---|
| Argentina | 164,162 | 0.3% | 127,824 | 0.3% | −22.1 | Italy | 2,111,019 | 4.4 | 2,220,774 | 4.5 | 5.2 |
| Australia | 339,500 | 0.7 | 358,264 | 0.7 | 5.5 | Japan | 12,699,803 | 26.3 | 13,025,678 | 26.6 | 2.6 |
| Austria | 10,500 | — | 11,664 | — | 10.0 | Korea | 1,083,655 | 2.2 | 1,129,470 | 2.3 | 4.2 |
| Belgium | 399,102 | 0.8 | 388,579 | 0.8 | −2.6 | Mexico | 512,776 | 1.1 | 641,779 | 1.3 | 25.2 |
| Brazil | 1,068,900 | 2.2 | 1,011,983 | 2.1 | −5.3 | Netherlands | 139,111 | 0.3 | 163,330 | 0.3 | 17.4 |
| Canada | 2,043,124 | 4.2 | 1,939,502 | 4.0 | −5.1 | Poland | 350,639 | 0.7 | 338,600 | 0.7 | −3.4 |
| China | 647,000 | 1.3 | 489,475 | 1.0 | −24.3 | Spain | 1,866,464 | 3.9 | 2,045,557 | 4.2 | 9.6 |
| Czechoslovakia | 230,000 | 0.4 | 239,181 | 0.5 | 4.0 | Sweden | 483,623 | 1.0 | 465,876 | 1.0 | −3.7 |
| France | 3,698,465 | 7.7 | 3,919,776 | 8.0 | 6.0 | UK | 1,544,848 | 3.2 | 1,625,672 | 3.3 | 5.2 |
| Germany, East | 262,190 | 0.5 | 257,000 | 0.5 | 2.0 | U.S. | 11,190,452 | 23.2 | 10,852,055 | 22.2 | −3.0 |
| Germany, West | 4,625,314 | 9.6 | 4,851,647 | 9.9 | 4.9 | USSR | 2,180,000 | 4.5 | 2,100,000 | 4.3 | −3.7 |
| Hungary | 13,043 | — | 11,930 | — | −8.5 | Yugoslavia | 330,423 | 0.7 | 342,934 | 0.7 | 3.8 |
| India | 311,362 | 0.6 | 332,515 | 0.7 | 6.8 | **Total** | **48,305,475** | **100.0%** | **48,891,065** | **100.0%** | **1.2%** |

**Note:** Includes passenger vehicles, trucks, and buses. **Source:** Motor Vehicle Manufacturers Association of the United States, Inc., *Motor Vehicle Facts & Figures '90* (1990).

> *"In America there are two classes of travel— first class and with children."*
> —Robert Benchley (1889–1945).

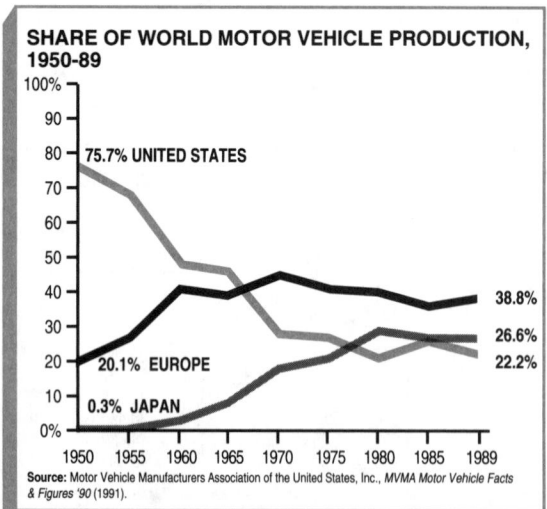

## SHARE OF WORLD MOTOR VEHICLE PRODUCTION, 1950-89

75.7% UNITED STATES

20.1% EUROPE

0.3% JAPAN

38.8%

26.6%

22.2%

**Source:** Motor Vehicle Manufacturers Association of the United States, Inc., *MVMA Motor Vehicle Facts & Figures '90* (1991).

## WORLD MOTOR VEHICLE REGISTRATIONS, 1960–88

| Year | Cars | Trucks and buses | Population Per car | Population Per vehicle |
|---|---|---|---|---|
| 1960 | 98,317,475 | 28,637,342 | 29.2 | 22.6 |
| 1965 | 139,779,540 | 38,127,320 | 22.7 | 17.9 |
| 1970 | 193,515,717 | 52,851,828 | 18.4 | 14.4 |
| 1975 | 260,207,459 | 67,693,176 | 14.6 | 11.6 |
| 1980 | 320,539,030 | 90,573,495 | 13.5 | 10.8 |
| 1985 | 374,727,233 | 112,816,433 | 12.6 | 10.5 |
| 1988 | 412,907,178 | 126,882,443 | 12.0 | 9.3 |

**Source:** Motor Vehicle Manufacturers Association of the United States, Inc., *MVMA Motor Vehicle Facts & Figures '90* (1990).

## TOP 15 U.S. CARGO AIRLINES, 1989

| Rank/Airline | Freight ton-miles ('000s)[1] | Rank/Airline | Freight ton-miles ('000s)[1] |
|---|---|---|---|
| 1. Federal Express | 2,511,808 | 9. Trans World | 493,567 |
| 2. Northwest | 1,665,815 | 10. Challenge Air Cargo | 108,325 |
| 3. Flying Tiger | 1,640,092 | 11. Eastern | 71,438 |
| 4. United | 1,006,579 | 12. USAir | 56,958 |
| 5. Pan American | 727,519 | 13. Rosenbalm | 45,182 |
| 6. American | 637,956 | 14. Piedmont | 41,667 |
| 7. Continental | 520,108 | 15. Alaska | 41,088 |
| 8. Delta | 518,793 | | |

**Note:** Carriers certificated under Section 401, Federal Aviation Act. 1. One ton of freight traveling one mile generates one freight-ton mile. **Source:** Air Transport Association of America, *Air Transport 1990: The Annual Report of the U.S. Scheduled Airline Industry* (1990).

## U.S.-FLAG PASSENGER AND CARGO VESSELS, 1989

| Type of vessel | Total | Atlantic, Pacific, Gulf coasts | Mississippi River[1] | Great Lakes system |
|---|---|---|---|---|
| **SELF-PROPELLED VESSELS** | | | | |
| Dry cargo and/or passenger vessels | 2,468 | 867 | 1,383 | 218 |
| Cargo capacity[2] | 6,935,078 | 4,358,587 | 391,657 | 2,184,834 |
| Passengers | 177,955 | 96,869 | 47,905 | 33,181 |
| Ferries, railroad car | 134 | 113 | 5 | 16 |
| RR car capacity | 78 | 0 | 0 | 78 |
| Tankers | 227 | 223 | 0 | 4 |
| Cargo capacity[2] | 12,962,289 | 12,925,136 | 0 | 37,153 |
| Towboats | 5,242 | 1,752 | 3,293 | 197 |
| Sailing vessels | 57 | 11 | 45 | 1 |
| Cargo capacity[2] | 8,097 | 5,188 | 2,909 | 0 |
| Passengers | 3,374 | 1,343 | 1,781 | 250 |
| **NON-SELF-PROPELLED VESSELS[3]** | | | | |
| Number of vessels | 31,081 | 4,388 | 26,365 | 328 |
| Cargo capacity[2] | 48,835,117 | 8,819,075 | 39,489,219 | 526,923 |
| RR car capacity | 248 | 107 | 0 | 141 |
| **TOTAL VESSELS** | | | | |
| Number of vessels | 39,209 | 7,354 | 31,091 | 764 |
| Cargo capacity[2] | 68,740,581 | 26,107,986 | 39,883,785 | 2,748,810 |
| Passengers | 181,329 | 98,212 | 49,686 | 33,431 |
| RR car capacity | 326 | 107 | 0 | 219 |

**Note:** Includes vessels operating or ready for operation as of Dec. 31. Does not include general ferries, fishing and excursion vessels, or floating equipment used in construction such as dredges, piledrivers, derricks, and flats. 1. Includes Mississippi River system and Gulf Intracoastal Waterway. 2. Short tons. 3. Includes barges and scows (dry cargo), tank barges (liquid cargo), and railroad float cars. **Source:** U.S. Army Corps of Engineers, *Waterborne Transportation Lines of the United States, 1989* (1990).

## MAJOR MERCHANT FLEETS OF THE WORLD, BY TONNAGE AND NUMBER OF SHIPS, 1989

| Rank/Country | Deadweight tons ('000s) | Number of ships[1] | Rank |
|---|---|---|---|
| 1. Liberia | 89,200 | 1,405 | 3 |
| 2. Panama | 72,977 | 3,304 | 1 |
| 3. Japan | 39,699 | 1,118 | 6 |
| 4. Greece | 37,130 | 974 | 7 |
| 5. Cyprus | 31,832 | 1,140 | 5 |
| 6. USSR | 25,481 | 2,434 | 2 |
| 7. British Independent Territories | 24,180 | 545 | 9 |
| 8. United States[2] | 21,601 | 424 | 13 |
| 9. Norway | 19,335 | 366 | 15 |
| 10. China | 18,437 | 1,235 | 4 |
| 11. Nassau, Bahamas | 16,547 | 430 | 12 |
| 12. Philippines | 14,770 | 562 | 8 |
| 13. Singapore | 11,752 | 417 | 14 |
| 14. Korea, South | 11,382 | 434 | 11 |
| 15. Italy | 10,765 | 500 | 10 |
| All others[3] | 156,831 | 8,180 | — |
| **Total** | **601,919** | **23,468** | — |

1. Oceangoing merchant ships of 1,000 gross tons and over. 2. Privately owned. 3. Includes 251 U.S. government-owned ships of 3,975,000 deadweight tons. **Source:** U.S. Dept. of Transportation, Maritime Administration, *Marad '89* (1990).

## 50 LARGEST U.S. PORTS BY COMMERCIAL TONNAGE, 1989

| Rank/Port | Total | Domestic | Foreign |
|---|---|---|---|
| 1. New Orleans, La. | 177,522,833 | 108,092,611 | 69,430,222 |
| 2. New York, N.Y. | 148,590,443 | 94,291,078 | 54,299,365 |
| 3. Houston, Tex. | 125,583,156 | 62,059,763 | 63,523,393 |
| 4. Valdez Harbor, Alaska | 95,436,011 | 95,425,052 | 10,959 |
| 5. Baton Rouge, La. | 82,399,896 | 48,133,860 | 34,266,036 |
| 6. Corpus Christi, Tex. | 60,478,858 | 22,772,616 | 37,706,242 |
| 7. Long Beach, Calif. | 54,807,692 | 31,241,280 | 23,566,412 |
| 8. Norfolk Harbor, Va. | 52,055,188 | 10,342,760 | 41,712,428 |
| 9. Tampa Harbor, Fl. | 49,280,790 | 28,163,821 | 21,116,969 |
| 10. Los Angeles, Calif. | 47,272,062 | 22,518,507 | 24,753,555 |
| 11. Baltimore Harbor, Md. | 44,883,667 | 14,532,097 | 30,351,570 |
| 12. Texas City, Tex. | 41,272,401 | 19,168,660 | 22,103,741 |
| 13. Lake Charles, La. | 40,813,125 | 17,095,761 | 23,717,364 |
| 14. Duluth-Superior, Minn. | 40,802,541 | 33,763,865 | 7,038,676 |
| 15. Mobile, Ala. | 39,980,262 | 21,526,657 | 18,435,605 |
| 16. Philadelphia, Pa. | 36,060,212 | 13,155,307 | 22,904,905 |
| 17. Pittsburgh, Pa. | 33,416,374 | 33,416,374 | 0 |
| 18. Beaumont, Tex. | 31,668,257 | 21,050,046 | 10,618,211 |
| 19. Pascagoula, Miss. | 31,545,792 | 12,288,028 | 19,257,764 |
| 20. Port Arthur, Tex. | 31,127,913 | 11,488,984 | 19,638,929 |
| 21. Portland, Oreg. | 30,029,747 | 11,984,498 | 18,045,249 |
| 22. Marcus Hook, Pa. | 29,903,912 | 15,057,174 | 14,846,738 |
| 23. St. Louis, Mo. | 26,037,347 | 26,037,347 | 0 |
| 24. Richmond, Calif. | 25,103,335 | 18,792,293 | 6,311,042 |
| 25. Chicago, Ill. | 23,445,821 | 19,204,573 | 4,241,248 |
| 26. Tacoma Harbor, Wash. | 22,450,622 | 4,506,907 | 17,943,715 |
| 27. Newport News, Va. | 21,851,818 | 2,568,239 | 19,283,579 |
| 28. Seattle, Wash. | 21,763,451 | 7,229,522 | 14,533,929 |
| 29. Paulsboro, N.J. | 21,445,977 | 8,471,206 | 12,974,771 |
| 30. Detroit, Mich. | 20,700,867 | 16,897,152 | 3,803,715 |
| 31. Boston, Mass. | 18,989,416 | 6,844,998 | 12,144,418 |
| 32. Huntington, W.Va. | 15,707,397 | 15,707,397 | 0 |
| 33. Freeport, Tex. | 15,176,018 | 8,471,820 | 6,704,198 |
| 34. Indiana Harbor, Ind. | 15,054,899 | 14,385,047 | 669,852 |
| 35. Jacksonville, Fla. | 15,002,231 | 8,135,398 | 6,866,833 |
| 36. Toledo Harbor, Ohio | 14,805,833 | 8,384,414 | 6,421,419 |
| 37. Cleveland, Ohio | 14,687,619 | 10,698,352 | 3,989,267 |
| 38. Port Everglades, Fla. | 14,684,674 | 9,854,936 | 4,829,738 |
| 39. Lorain Harbor, Ohio | 14,568,175 | 14,553,284 | 14,891 |
| 40. San Juan, P.R. | 13,873,968 | 9,085,277 | 4,788,691 |
| 41. Anacortes, Wash. | 13,169,491 | 10,455,086 | 2,714,405 |
| 42. Savannah, Ga. | 12,830,333 | 2,438,113 | 10,392,220 |
| 43. Presque Isle, Mich. | 12,155,757 | 8,582,975 | 3,572,782 |
| 44. Memphis, Tenn. | 11,843,550 | 11,843,274 | 276 |
| 45. Galveston, Tex. | 11,837,611 | 4,164,886 | 7,672,725 |
| 46. Cincinnati, Ohio | 11,556,801 | 11,556,801 | 0 |
| 47. Honolulu, Hawaii | 10,360,134 | 9,351,725 | 1,008,409 |
| 48. Ashtabula, Ohio | 10,322,455 | 5,969,575 | 4,352,880 |
| 49. Oakland, Calif. | 9,999,668 | 2,655,793 | 7,343,875 |
| 50. Charleston, S.C. | 9,633,632 | 3,312,629 | 6,321,003 |

**Source:** U.S. Army Corps of Engineers, *Principal Ports CY 1989 by Total Tonnage* (1991).

## WORLD'S 50 BUSIEST AIRPORTS, 1989

| Rank/Airport | Total passengers[1] | Total cargo (tons) | | Total operations | |
|---|---|---|---|---|---|
| 1. Chicago O'Hare Intl. | 59,130,007 | 958,430 | (5) | 780,658 | (1) |
| 2. Dallas/Ft. Worth Intl. | 47,579,046 | 502,212 | (17) | 698,870 | (2) |
| 3. Los Angeles Intl. | 44,967,221 | 1,130,050 | (4) | 637,117 | (4) |
| 4. Hartsfield Atlanta Intl. | 43,312,285 | 540,749 | (15) | 665,930 | (3) |
| 5. Heathrow Airport, London | 39,905,200 | 765,600 | (7) | 368,600 | (22) |
| 6. Tokyo-Haneda Intl. | 36,567,738 | 581,940 | (13) | 178,992 | (79) |
| 7. J.F. Kennedy Intl., New York | 30,323,077 | 1,372,243 | (1) | 305,058 | (34) |
| 8. San Francisco Intl. | 29,939,835 | 558,078 | (14) | 427,475 | (12) |
| 9. Stapleton Intl., Denver | 27,568,033 | 273,388 | (29) | 463,797 | (8) |
| 10. Frankfurt, West Germany | 26,006,900 | 1,223,207 | (3) | 325,472 | (30) |
| 11. Orly, Paris | 24,288,440 | 280,177 | (27) | 196,066 | (70) |
| 12. Miami Intl. | 23,385,010 | 796,690 | (6) | 385,135 | (17) |
| 13. La Guardia, New York | 23,158,317 | 107,237 | (59) | 349,116 | (26) |
| 14. Honolulu Intl. | 22,617,340 | 363,790 | (21) | 403,635 | (14) |
| 15. Logan Intl., Boston | 22,272,690 | 340,903 | (24) | 388,792 | (16) |
| 16. Osaka Intl. | 21,873,831 | 454,201 | (18) | 64,675 | (217) |
| 17. Detroit Metropolitan Wayne Co. | 21,495,159 | 179,279 | (40) | 374,520 | (20) |
| 18. Gatwick, London | 21,293,200 | 225,000 | (34) | 206,200 | (64) |
| 19. Newark Intl. | 20,927,946 | 448,776 | (19) | 365,106 | (23) |
| 20. Sky Harbor Airport, Phoenix | 20,710,790 | 94,506 | (65) | 484,940 | (6) |
| 21. Charles de Gaulle, Paris | 20,669,542 | 609,995 | (10) | 206,394 | (62) |
| 22. Lester B. Pearson Intl., Toronto | 20,418,094 | 291,311 | (26) | 354,996 | (25) |
| 23. Lambert-St. Louis Intl. | 20,015,015 | 91,998 | (68) | 428,875 | (11) |
| 24. Minneapolis-St. Paul Intl. | 19,400,815 | 242,483 | (33) | 364,030 | (24) |
| 25. Hong Kong Intl. | 17,431,124 | 751,060 | (8) | 94,300 | (161) |
| 26. Orlando Intl. | 17,232,351 | 128,531 | (53) | 282,657 | (37) |
| 27. Greater Pittsburgh Intl. | 17,145,272 | 114,340 | (55) | 376,786 | (19) |
| 28. New Tokyo Intl.—Narita | 16,982,055 | 1,352,837 | (2) | 118,883 | (123) |
| 29. McCarran Intl., Las Vegas | 16,684,036 | 40,509 | (98) | 385,077 | (18) |
| 30. Fiumicino, Rome | 16,177,277 | 248,239 | (32) | 165,179 | (88) |
| 31. Houston Intercontinental | 16,007,355 | 204,256 | (37) | 313,298 | (32) |
| 32. Schipol, Amsterdam | 15,998,174 | 609,672 | (11) | 235,969 | (48) |
| 33. Charlotte/Douglas Intl. | 15,348,542 | 112,187 | (57) | 430,718 | (10) |
| 34. Sea-Tac Intl., Seattle | 15,241,072 | 293,939 | (25) | 334,924 | (27) |
| 35. Washington, D.C., National | 15,139,975 | 60,236 | (84) | 311,207 | (33) |
| 36. Philadelphia Intl. | 14,808,721 | 262,654 | (30) | 374,410 | (21) |
| 37. Arlanda, Stockholm | 14,278,156 | 94,206 | (67) | 253,890 | (46) |
| 38. Singapore Changi Airport | 12,973,237 | 587,153 | (12) | 98,791 | (155) |
| 39. Bangkok Intl. | 12,669,102 | 349,998 | (23) | 116,770 | (126) |
| 40. Copenhagen, Denmark | 12,436,654 | 161,944 | (44) | 212,979 | (57) |
| 41. Zurich, Switzerland | 12,150,558 | 274,258 | (28) | 210,464 | (59) |
| 42. Salt Lake City Intl. | 11,898,847 | 96,684 | (63) | 296,186 | (36) |
| 43. San Diego Intl. | 11,111,080 | 53,572 | (90) | 207,388 | (60) |
| 44. Athens, Greece | 10,514,367 | 94,372 | (66) | 113,048 | (132) |
| 45. Baltimore/Washington Intl. | 10,356,548 | 163,356 | (43) | 303,759 | (35) |
| 46. Dulles Intl., Washington | 10,178,671 | 156,928 | (46) | 224,949 | (51) |
| 47. Munich-Riem, West Germany | 10,100,858 | 72,106 | (77) | 189,964 | (73) |
| 48. Manchester, UK | 10,069,860 | 72,865 | (76) | 154,864 | (95) |
| 49. Tampa Intl. | 9,692,975 | 78,853 | (72) | 206,351 | (63) |
| 50. Kansas City Intl. | 9,541,506 | 77,407 | (73) | 220,118 | (54) |

1. Enplaned, deplaned, and transferred. **Source:** Airport Operators Council International, *Worldwide Airport Traffic Report-Calendar Year 1989* (1990).

## U.S. AIR TRAVEL ARRIVALS FROM AND DEPARTURES TO FOREIGN COUNTRIES, 1980–89 (thousands of passengers)

| Country | Arrivals from 1980 | Arrivals from 1989 | Departures to 1980 | Departures to 1989 |
|---|---|---|---|---|
| Australia | 227 | 433 | 245 | 466 |
| Bahamas, The | 1,123 | 1,596 | 1,006 | 1,288 |
| Barbados | 135 | 220 | 126 | 221 |
| Belgium | 242 | 305 | 231 | 294 |
| Bermuda | 497 | 451 | 467 | 283 |
| Brazil | 300 | 501 | 291 | 495 |
| China/Taiwan | 113 | 229 | 90 | 245 |
| Colombia | 315 | 284 | 299 | 291 |
| Denmark | 267 | 356 | 254 | 313 |
| Dominican Republic | 468 | 934 | 443 | 838 |
| France | 689 | 1,570 | 635 | 1,494 |
| Germany, West | 1,175 | 2,135 | 1,178 | 2,064 |
| Grand Cayman | 121 | 226 | 112 | 199 |
| Greece | 208 | 128 | 190 | 124 |
| Haiti | 133 | 234 | 124 | 224 |
| Hong Kong | 228 | 347 | 152 | 315 |
| Ireland | 220 | 436 | 212 | 299 |
| Israel | 189 | 206 | 186 | 256 |
| Italy | 537 | 749 | 495 | 691 |
| Jamaica | 429 | 899 | 382 | 798 |
| Japan | 1,624 | 4,117 | 1,602 | 4,081 |
| Korea, Republic of | 234 | 666 | 186 | 559 |
| Mexico | 2,886 | 3,816 | 2,886 | 3,656 |
| Netherlands | 427 | 763 | 409 | 714 |
| Netherlands Antilles | 327 | 593 | 282 | 494 |
| Panama | 150 | 111 | 142 | 131 |
| Philippines | 194 | 239 | 160 | 209 |
| Spain | 312 | 503 | 273 | 484 |
| Switzerland | 312 | 648 | 306 | 655 |
| United Kingdom | 2,973 | 4,638 | 2,840 | 4,528 |
| Venezuela | 533 | 415 | 518 | 395 |
| All other | 2,674 | 4,469 | 2,534 | 4,049 |
| U.S. carrier | 10,031 | 17,174 | 9,369 | 15,687 |
| Foreign carrier | 10,231 | 16,044 | 9,886 | 15,466 |
| **Total passengers** | **20,262** | **33,217** | **19,256** | **31,153** |

**Note:** Covers passengers on international commercial flights arriving at or departing from U.S. airports. Excludes traffic between U.S. and Canada, border crossers, crewmen, and military personnel. Travelers between U.S. ports in the 50 states, territories, and possessions are included. **Source:** U.S. Dept. of Transportation, *National Transportation Statistics Annual Report* (1990).

## TOP 25 U.S. AIRLINES, 1989

| Rank | Airline | Passengers ('000s) | Revenue passenger miles ('000s)[1] | Rank[2] | Rank | Airline | Passengers ('000s) | Revenue passenger miles ('000s)[1] | Rank[2] |
|---|---|---|---|---|---|---|---|---|---|
| 1. | American | 72,359 | 73,480,582 | 1 | 14. | Alaska | 4,963 | 4,021,835 | 13 |
| 2. | Delta | 68,200 | 59,348,135 | 3 | 15. | Midway | 4,681 | 3,485,191 | 15 |
| 3. | United | 54,919 | 69,591,003 | 2 | 16. | Braniff | 4,316 | 3,654,099 | 14 |
| 4. | USAir | 44,495 | 25,132,053 | 8 | 17. | Aloha | 4,002 | 533,476 | 18 |
| 5. | Northwest | 38,627 | 45,663,048 | 4 | 18. | Air Wisconsin | 2,195 | 434,262 | 19 |
| 6. | Continental | 34,957 | 38,771,729 | 5 | 19. | West Air | 1,819 | 388,879 | 22 |
| 7. | Trans World | 25,150 | 35,046,235 | 6 | 20. | Horizon Air | 1,587 | 314,650 | 24 |
| 8. | Southwest | 20,241 | 9,278,940 | 10 | 21. | Trump Shuttle | 880 | 184,545 | 27 |
| 9. | Pan American | 17,174 | 29,359,723 | 7 | 22. | Aspen | 798 | 189,335 | 26 |
| 10. | Piedmont | 16,657 | 8,565,386 | 11 | 23. | Presidential | 660 | 270,142 | 25 |
| 11. | Eastern | 14,517 | 11,592,456 | 9 | 24. | Midwest Express | 615 | 394,733 | 21 |
| 12. | America West | 13,300 | 7,802,119 | 12 | 25. | Markair | 394 | 165,309 | 28 |
| 13. | Hawaiian | 5,277 | 2,808,565 | 16 | | | | | |

1. One paying passenger traveling one mile generates one revenue passenger mile. 2. Tower ranks 17, American Trans Air 20, and Air America 23 in terms of revenue passenger miles. **Source:** Air Transport Association of America, *Air Transport 1990: The Annual Report of the U.S. Scheduled Airline Industry* (1990).

## TOP 25 DOMESTIC AIRLINE ROUTES, 1989

| Rank | Metropolitan areas | | Number of passengers |
|---|---|---|---|
| 1. | New York | Boston | 3,171,150 |
| 2. | New York | Los Angeles | 3,113,880 |
| 3. | New York | Washington | 2,971,540 |
| 4. | New York | Chicago | 2,445,930 |
| 5. | New York | Miami | 2,200,570 |
| 6. | Los Angeles | San Francisco | 2,197,210 |
| 7. | Dallas/Ft. Worth | Houston | 2,139,130 |
| 8. | New York | San Francisco | 2,066,510 |
| 9. | Honolulu | Kahului, Maui | 1,986,880 |
| 10. | Chicago | Detroit | 1,745,290 |
| 11. | New York | Orlando | 1,709,590 |
| 12. | New York | Ft. Lauderdale | 1,692,520 |
| 13. | Los Angeles | Phoenix | 1,684,640 |
| 14. | Honolulu | Lihue, Kauai | 1,668,420 |
| 15. | New York | San Juan | 1,582,740 |
| 16. | Los Angeles | Honolulu | 1,408,630 |
| 17. | New York | Atlanta | 1,269,530 |
| 18. | New York | West Palm Beach | 1,231,650 |
| 19. | Chicago | Los Angeles | 1,158,990 |
| 20. | Honolulu | Kona, Hawaii | 1,110,140 |
| 21. | San Franciso | San Diego | 1,108,060 |
| 22. | Chicago | St. Louis | 1,049,790 |
| 23. | New York | Tampa | 1,019,930 |
| 24. | New York | Dallas/Ft. Worth | 1,014,890 |
| 25. | Phoenix | San Diego | 967,640 |

**Note:** For 12 months ended December 1989. Passengers inbound plus outbound. Includes all commercial airports in a metropolitan area. Does not include connecting passengers. **Source:** Air Transport Association of America, *Air Transport 1990: The Annual Report of the U.S. Scheduled Airline Industry* (1990).

## COMMUTER AND RAPID RAIL SYSTEMS IN THE U.S., 1989

| System | Passenger trips ('000s) | Passenger miles ('000s) | Sta- tions | Route miles | Vehicles operated |
|---|---|---|---|---|---|
| **COMMUTER RAIL** | | | | | |
| New York-Long Island RR | 96,171.0 | 2,117,068.4 | 134 | 623.3 | 1,040 |
| New York-Metro North | 57,343.7 | 1,535,405.1 | 105 | 535.9 | 664 |
| Newark-New Jersey Transit | 42,332.6 | 997,596.1 | 153 | 793.4 | 613 |
| Chicago, Commuter Rail Board | 29,884.7 | 612,715.7 | 121 | 417.0 | 391 |
| Philadelphia SEPTA | 26,806.2 | 361,883.1 | 181 | 415.6 | 275 |
| Chicago & NW Transit | 23,231.1 | 514,791.3 | 62 | 309.4 | 331 |
| Boston, Amtrak/MBTA | 18,620.3 | 330,133.9 | 99 | 529.2 | 245 |
| Chicago, Burlington Northern | 12,988.2 | 260,019.8 | 27 | 75.0 | 163 |
| Staten Island RT | 6,222.8 | 42,937.5 | 22 | 28.6 | 36 |
| San Francisco, CALTRANS | 5,632.9 | 131,074.5 | 26 | 93.8 | 67 |
| **RAPID RAIL** | | | | | |
| New York City TA | 1,702,610.8 | 7,376,120.5 | 469 | 492.9 | 5,024 |
| Washington Metro Area TA | 183,479.6 | 978,315.0 | 64 | 139.1 | 576 |
| Chicago TA | 168,658.8 | 1,050,921.7 | 143 | 191.0 | 923 |
| Metro Boston TA | 157,937.6 | 480,184.7 | 53 | 76.7 | 449 |
| Philadelphia, SEPTA | 94,099.9 | 415,800.4 | 76 | 75.8 | 297 |
| Metro Atlanta RTA | 65,603.0 | 359,269.8 | 29 | 67.0 | 139 |
| San Francisco, BART | 64,064.5 | 757,350.0 | 0 | 142.0 | 346 |
| New York, PATH | 60,494.6 | 294,983.4 | 13 | 27.6 | 297 |
| Baltimore MTA | 13,983.6 | 66,871.0 | 12 | 26.6 | 60 |
| Miami/Dade Co. TA | 12,127.9 | 95,449.9 | 21 | 42.2 | 70 |
| New Jersey Port Authority TC | 11,025.3 | 96,730.9 | 13 | 31.5 | 90 |
| Cleveland RTA | 7,860.1 | 58,041.8 | 18 | 38.2 | 35 |

**Note:** Rapid rail includes subways, elevated trains, and metros. BART = Bay Area Rapid Transit Authority; CALTRANS = California Transportation Authority; MBTA = Metropolitan Boston Transit Authority; PATH = Port Authority Trans Hudson; SEPTA = Southeastern Pennsylvania Transit Authority. **Source:** U.S. Dept of Transportation, *National Urban Mass Transportation Statistics, 1989 Section 15 Annual Report* (1990).

## AMTRAK OPERATING STATISTICS, 1985–90

| Category | 1985 | 1986 | 1987 | 1988 | 1989 | 1990 |
|---|---|---|---|---|---|---|
| **SYSTEM** | | | | | | |
| Route miles ('000s) | 24 | 24 | 24 | 24 | 24 | 24 |
| Stations | 503 | 491 | 487 | 498 | 504 | 516 |
| Train miles operated (mil.) | 30 | 29 | 30 | 30 | 31 | 33 |
| **ON-TIME PERFORMANCE** | | | | | | |
| Systemwide | 81% | 74% | 74% | 71% | 75% | 76% |
| Short distance | 82 | 76 | 78 | 76 | 81 | 82 |
| Long distance | 78 | 69 | 62 | 54 | 54 | 53 |
| **RIDERSHIP** | | | | | | |
| Passengers (mil.) | 20.8 | 20.3 | 20.4 | 21.5 | 21.4 | 22.2 |
| Northeast corridor | 11.2 | 10.7 | 10.7 | 11.2 | 11.1 | 11.2 |
| Short distance | 4.5 | 4.4 | 4.5 | 4.8 | 4.7 | 5.2 |
| Long distance | 5.0 | 5.1 | 5.2 | 5.4 | 5.5 | 5.8 |
| Passenger miles (mil.)[1] | 4,582 | 5,013 | 5,221 | 5,678 | 5,859 | 6,057 |
| **LOCOMOTIVE UNITS** | | | | | | |
| Operating fleet | 291 | 291 | 289 | 298 | 312 | 318 |
| Available for service | 93.2% | 92.0% | 89.0% | 88.0% | 87.0% | 84.0% |
| Average age (years) | 7 | 8 | 9 | 10 | 11 | 12 |
| New units | 10 | 0 | 0 | 10 | 13 | 0 |
| **PASSENGER-TRAIN CARS** | | | | | | |
| Operating fleet[2] | 1,854 | 1,835 | 1,831 | 1,853 | 1,912 | 1,983 |
| Average age (years) | 14.2 | 14.6 | 15.6 | 16.6 | 17.5 | 20.0 |
| **FINANCIAL** | | | | | | |
| Revenues (mil.) | $ 825 | $ 861 | $ 973 | $1,106 | $1,269 | $1,308 |
| Expenses (mil.) | 1,600 | 1,563 | 1,672 | 1,757 | 1,934 | 2,012 |

1. Not including commuter service under contract to the Massachusetts Bay Transport Authority. 2. Includes some older or damaged cars awaiting overhaul, conversion to head-end power, or sale. **Source:** Amtrak—National Railroad Passenger Corporation, *Annual Report 1990* (1990).

## U.S. RAILROADS AND TRAIN-MILES OPERATED, 1989

| Rank/Railroad class and company | Train-miles operated |
|---|---|
| **CLASS I RAILROADS, TOTAL** | **532,861,687** |
| 1. Burlington Northern Inc. | 87,973,832 |
| 2. Union Pacific Railroad Co. | 73,542,594 |
| 3. CSX Transportation | 68,005,329 |
| 4. Norfolk Southern Corp. | 51,388,959 |
| 5. Atchison, Topeka and Santa Fe Railway Co. | 50,262,154 |
| 6. Consolidated Rail Corp. (Conrail) | 48,153,848 |
| 7. Southern Pacific Transportation Co. | 42,852,553 |
| 8. Amtrak (National Railroad Passenger Corp.) | 38,976,550 |
| 9. Chicago and North Western | 18,561,983 |
| 10. Kansas City Southern Railway Co. | 10,462,531 |
| 11. St. Louis Southwestern Railway Co. | 9,133,486 |
| 12. Illinois Central Gulf Railroad Co. | 9,108,322 |
| 13. Soo Line Railroad Co. | 8,680,071 |
| 14. Denver and Rio Grande Western Railroad Co. | 7,058,487 |
| 15. Grand Trunk Western Railroad Co. | 5,809,803 |
| 16. Louisiana and Arkansas Railway Co. | 4,890,761 |
| 17. Florida East Coast Railway Co. | 3,219,300 |
| 18. Elgin, Joliet and Eastern Railway Co. | 1,660,343 |
| 19. Delaware and Hudson Railway | 1,484,500 |
| 20. Springfield Terminal Railway Co. | 1,349,580 |
| CLASS II RAILROADS | 6,352,462 |
| CLASS III RAILROADS | 71,671,483 |
| **Total, all railroads** | **620,598,940** |

**Note:** Railroads are classified according to total annual gross operating revenue (in 1978 dollars): class I, more than $50 million; class II, $10–$50 million; class III, less than $10 million. **Source:** U.S. Dept. of Transportation, *Accident/Incident Bulletin, No. 158, Calendar Year 1989* (1990).

# Agriculture

In the United States during the colonial period and the early years of the Republic, agriculture, while vital (involving 95% of the population), remained relatively small-scale and in economic terms primitive, with the exception of large plantations in the South devoted to cotton, tobacco, and rice. The Civil War brought higher food prices and increased mechanization throughout the farming industry. It also led to federal legislation aimed at encouraging farming; the Homestead Act of 1862 and the Morrill Land Grant College Act were especially important. The decision to build a transcontinental rail system—undertaken by private enterprise abetted by government grants—opened up large areas of the Great Plains to farming, and the railroad companies recruited immigrants to buy and farm the land the government had given the companies.

In the early 20th century, machinery gradually replaced animal power. In 1910, for example, U.S. farms used 24.2 million horses and mules and only about a thousand tractors; by 1959 the figures had changed to 4.7 million tractors and only 3.2 million draft animals. World War I stimulated agriculture, but the stimulus led to overproduction, which, with the coming of peace, depressed prices and land values. This decline both contributed to and was intensified by the Great Depression, one of the most paralyzing aspects of which was a near total cessation of world agricultural trade. The plight of farmers during the 1930s prompted considerable government remedies, including various forms of credit, price supports, rural electrification, and serious efforts at soil conservation. World War II again gave impetus to agriculture.

After the war, new machinery, new chemicals, and hybrid crops, more resistant to weather and biological enemies, significantly increased crop yields. By the end of the 1940s, the United States had become the world's largest single producer of wheat, corn, and soybeans. One byproduct of this success was the creation of huge surpluses. U.S. agriculture proved a potent force in the world economy and in foreign policy, and in 1954, Public Law 480 provided for the export of surplus grains to poorer nations both to prevent starvation and stimulate economic development, and to alleviate the pressures on the domestic agriculture sector caused by the surpluses.

Research into developing ever hardier strains of food crops and livestock continues. Yet the number of American farms has declined as small units lose out to huge agribusinesses owned by corporations with assets that smaller farmers cannot match. Between 1980 and 1990, the number of farms fell from 2.4 million to 2.1 million (a decline of 13%), while average acreage per farm rose from 426 to 461 (an increase of 9%). Overall, the total land area devoted to farming dropped from 1,039,000

## U.S. FARMS, ACREAGE, AND POPULATION, 1850–1990

| | | Acreage | | | Population | |
|---|---|---|---|---|---|---|
| Year | Farms ('000s) | Total ('000s) | Per farm | Percent of U.S. | Total ('000s) | Percent of U.S. |
| 1850 | 1,449 | 293,561 | 203 | 15.6% | — | — |
| 1860 | 2,044 | 407,213 | 199 | 21.4 | — | — |
| 1870 | 2,660 | 407,735 | 153 | 21.4 | — | — |
| 1880 | 4,009 | 536,082 | 134 | 28.2 | 21,973 | 43.8% |
| 1890 | 4,565 | 623,219 | 137 | 32.7 | 24,771 | 42.3 |
| 1900 | 5,740 | 841,202 | 147 | 37.0 | 29,835 | 41.9 |
| 1910 | 6,366 | 881,431 | 139 | 38.8 | 32,077 | 34.9 |
| 1920 | 6,454 | 958,677 | 149 | 42.2 | 31,974 | 30.1 |
| 1930 | 6,295 | 990,112 | 157 | 43.6 | 30,529 | 24.9 |
| 1940 | 6,102 | 1,065,114 | 175 | 46.8 | 30,547 | 23.2 |
| 1950 | 5,388 | 1,161,420 | 216 | 51.1 | 23,048 | 15.3 |
| 1960 | 3,962 | 1,176,946 | 297 | 49.5[1] | 15,635 | 8.7 |
| 1970 | 2,954 | 1,102,769 | 373 | 47.0[2] | 9,712 | 4.8 |
| 1980 | 2,440 | 1,039,000[3] | 426 | 44.8 | 6,051 | 2.7 |
| 1990[4] | 2,143 | 988,000[3] | 461 | 42.7 | 4,801 | 1.9 |

1. Figure for 1959. 2. Figure for 1969. 3. Figure rounded in source. 4. Preliminary. **Source:** U.S. Bureau of the Census, *Statistical History of the United States* (1970); *Statistical Abstract of the United States 1991* (1991).

## FARMS: NUMBER AND ACREAGE, BY STATE, 1980–90

| State | Farms ('000s) 1980 | Farms ('000s) 1990 | Acreage (millions) 1980 | Acreage (millions) 1990 | Acreage per farm 1980 | Acreage per farm 1990 | State | Farms ('000s) 1980 | Farms ('000s) 1990 | Acreage (millions) 1980 | Acreage (millions) 1990 | Acreage per farm 1980 | Acreage per farm 1990 |
|---|---|---|---|---|---|---|---|---|---|---|---|---|---|
| Alabama | 59 | 47 | 12 | 10 | 207 | 219 | Montana | 24 | 25 | 62 | 61 | 2,601 | 2,449 |
| Alaska | (Z) | (Z) | 2 | 1 | 3,378 | 1,724 | Nebraska | 65 | 57 | 48 | 47 | 734 | 826 |
| Arizona | 8 | 8 | 38 | 36 | 5,080 | 4,615 | Nevada | 3 | 3 | 9 | 9 | 3,100 | 3,560 |
| Arkansas | 59 | 47 | 17 | 16 | 280 | 330 | New Hampshire | 3 | 3 | 1 | (Z) | 160 | 163 |
| California | 81 | 85 | 34 | 31 | 417 | 362 | New Jersey | 9 | 8 | 1 | 1 | 109 | 107 |
| Colorado | 27 | 27 | 36 | 33 | 1,358 | 1,249 | New Mexico | 14 | 14 | 47 | 45 | 3,467 | 3,296 |
| Connecticut | 4 | 4 | (Z) | (Z) | 117 | 108 | New York | 47 | 39 | 9 | 8 | 200 | 218 |
| Delaware | 4 | 3 | 1 | 1 | 186 | 197 | North Carolina | 93 | 62 | 12 | 10 | 126 | 156 |
| Florida | 39 | 41 | 13 | 11 | 344 | 266 | North Dakota | 40 | 34 | 42 | 41 | 1,043 | 1,191 |
| Georgia | 59 | 49 | 15 | 13 | 254 | 255 | Ohio | 95 | 84 | 16 | 16 | 171 | 187 |
| Hawaii | 4 | 5 | 2 | 2 | 458 | 372 | Oklahoma | 72 | 70 | 35 | 33 | 481 | 471 |
| Idaho | 24 | 22 | 15 | 14 | 623 | 628 | Oregon | 35 | 37 | 18 | 18 | 517 | 488 |
| Illinois | 107 | 83 | 29 | 29 | 269 | 343 | Pennsylvania | 62 | 53 | 9 | 8 | 145 | 153 |
| Indiana | 87 | 68 | 17 | 16 | 193 | 240 | Rhode Island | 1 | 1 | (Z) | (Z) | 87 | 92 |
| Iowa | 119 | 104 | 34 | 34 | 284 | 322 | South Carolina | 34 | 25 | 6 | 5 | 188 | 212 |
| Kansas | 75 | 69 | 48 | 48 | 644 | 694 | South Dakota | 39 | 35 | 45 | 44 | 1,169 | 1,266 |
| Kentucky | 102 | 93 | 15 | 14 | 143 | 152 | Tennessee | 96 | 89 | 14 | 12 | 142 | 139 |
| Louisiana | 37 | 34 | 10 | 9 | 273 | 265 | Texas | 196 | 186 | 138 | 132 | 705 | 710 |
| Maine | 8 | 7 | 2 | 1 | 195 | 199 | Utah | 14 | 13 | 12 | 11 | 919 | 856 |
| Maryland | 18 | 15 | 3 | 2 | 157 | 148 | Vermont | 8 | 7 | 2 | 2 | 226 | 216 |
| Massachusetts | 6 | 7 | 1 | 1 | 116 | 99 | Virginia | 58 | 46 | 10 | 9 | 169 | 193 |
| Michigan | 65 | 54 | 11 | 11 | 175 | 200 | Washington | 38 | 37 | 16 | 16 | 429 | 432 |
| Minnesota | 104 | 89 | 30 | 30 | 291 | 337 | West Virginia | 22 | 21 | 4 | 4 | 191 | 180 |
| Mississippi | 55 | 40 | 15 | 13 | 265 | 325 | Wisconsin | 93 | 80 | 19 | 18 | 200 | 220 |
| Missouri | 120 | 108 | 31 | 30 | 261 | 281 | Wyoming | 9 | 9 | 35 | 35 | 3,846 | 3,910 |
| | | | | | | | **U.S. total** | **2,440** | **2,143** | **1,039** | **988** | **426** | **461** |

**Note:** Z = less than 500 farms or 500,000 acres. **Source:** U.S. Dept. of Agriculture, *Farms and Land in Farms, Final Estimates by State 1979–87*, and *Crop Production* (1990).

## FARM INCOME: MARKETINGS AND GOVERNMENT PAYMENTS, BY STATE, 1989 (millions of dollars)

| State | Total | Farm marketings Crops | Farm marketings Live-stock and products | Government payments | State | Total | Farm marketings Crops | Farm marketings Live-stock and products | Government payments |
|---|---|---|---|---|---|---|---|---|---|
| U.S. total | $159,173 | $75,449 | $83,724 | $10,887 | Montana | $ 1,610 | $ 710 | $ 899 | $ 289 |
| Alabama | 2,628 | 696 | 1,932 | 121 | Nebraska | 8,521 | 2,878 | 5,643 | 542 |
| Alaska | 29 | 20 | 9 | 1 | Nevada | 235 | 94 | 141 | 6 |
| Arizona | 1,902 | 1,158 | 744 | 85 | New Hampshire | 142 | 79 | 63 | 2 |
| Arkansas | 4,131 | 1,470 | 2,661 | 440 | New Jersey | 660 | 463 | 197 | 21 |
| California | 17,515 | 12,422 | 5,093 | 372 | New Mexico | 1,424 | 450 | 974 | 65 |
| Colorado | 3,899 | 1,250 | 2,649 | 183 | New York | 2,857 | 911 | 1,946 | 76 |
| Connecticut | 404 | 218 | 188 | 2 | North Carolina | 4,551 | 2,046 | 2,505 | 94 |
| Delaware | 663 | 160 | 503 | 5 | North Dakota | 2,108 | 1,465 | 642 | 475 |
| Florida | 6,203 | 4,982 | 1,221 | 38 | Ohio | 3,812 | 2,114 | 1,698 | 274 |
| Georgia | 3,869 | 1,598 | 2,270 | 173 | Oklahoma | 3,594 | 1,185 | 2,409 | 235 |
| Hawaii | 587 | 495 | 92 | (Z) | Oregon | 2,297 | 1,558 | 739 | 60 |
| Idaho | 2,715 | 1,670 | 1,046 | 99 | Pennsylvania | 3,581 | 986 | 2,595 | 68 |
| Illinois | 6,710 | 4,458 | 2,252 | 726 | Rhode Island | 79 | 66 | 13 | (Z) |
| Indiana | 4,318 | 2,502 | 1,817 | 334 | South Carolina | 1,225 | 675 | 551 | 73 |
| Iowa | 9,119 | 3,911 | 5,209 | 981 | South Dakota | 2,992 | 884 | 2,108 | 340 |
| Kansas | 6,324 | 2,079 | 4,245 | 588 | Tennessee | 1,921 | 861 | 1,060 | 141 |
| Kentucky | 2,928 | 1,258 | 1,670 | 118 | Texas | 10,760 | 3,897 | 6,863 | 1,249 |
| Louisiana | 1,661 | 1,048 | 614 | 250 | Utah | 748 | 174 | 574 | 35 |
| Maine | 447 | 233 | 215 | 7 | Vermont | 426 | 51 | 375 | 7 |
| Maryland | 1,346 | 476 | 870 | 24 | Virginia | 2,058 | 685 | 1,372 | 39 |
| Massachusetts | 429 | 317 | 112 | 4 | Washington | 3,639 | 2,438 | 1,201 | 131 |
| Michigan | 2,940 | 1,627 | 1,313 | 262 | West Virginia | 314 | 64 | 250 | 12 |
| Minnesota | 6,526 | 2,809 | 3,716 | 600 | Wisconsin | 5,278 | 941 | 4,337 | 522 |
| Mississippi | 2,292 | 1,000 | 1,292 | 325 | Wyoming | 856 | 186 | 669 | 34 |
| Missouri | 3,900 | 1,732 | 2,168 | 356 | | | | | |

**Note:** Z = less than $500,000. **Source:** U.S. Dept. of Agriculture, *Economic Indicators of the Farm Sector: State Financial Summary, 1989* (1990).

## PRINCIPAL FARM COMMODITIES BY STATE, RANKED BY VALUE OF FARM MARKETINGS, 1989

| State | Principal commodities in order of marketing receipts and as a percentage of total marketings | State | Principal commodities in order of marketing receipts and as a percentage of total marketings |
|---|---|---|---|
| United States | Cattle, dairy products, soybeans, corn (52%) | | |
| 1. California | Dairy products, cattle, greenhouse, grapes (39%) | 26. Idaho | Cattle, dairy products, potatoes, wheat (64%) |
| 2. Iowa | Hogs, corn, cattle, soybeans (92%) | 27. Tennessee | Cattle, dairy products, greenhouse, soybeans (57%) |
| 3. Texas | Cattle, cotton, dairy products, greenhouse (69%) | 28. Mississippi | Broilers, cotton, soybeans, cattle (69%) |
| 4. Nebraska | Cattle, corn, hogs, soybeans (87%) | 29. Oregon | Cattle, greenhouse, dairy products, wheat (47%) |
| 5. Illinois | Corn, soybeans, hogs, cattle (90%) | 30. Virginia | Cattle, dairy products, broilers, turkeys (57%) |
| 6. Minnesota | Dairy products, corn, cattle, hogs (65%) | 31. Arizona | Cattle, cotton, dairy products, lettuce (64%) |
| 7. Kansas | Cattle, wheat, sorghum grain, soybeans (83%) | 32. Louisiana | Soybeans, cotton, cattle, sugar (50%) |
| 8. Wisconsin | Dairy products, cattle, corn, hogs (85%) | 33. Montana | Cattle, wheat, barley, hay (85%) |
| 9. Florida | Greenhouse, oranges, tomatoes, sugar (51%) | 34. Maryland | Broilers, dairy products, greenhouse, cattle (71%) |
| 10. Indiana | Corn, hogs, soybeans, cattle (75%) | 35. New Mexico | Cattle, dairy products, hay, chili peppers (74%) |
| 11. North Carolina | Tobacco, broilers, hogs, turkeys (57%) | 36. South Carolina | Tobacco, cattle, soybeans, dairy products (43%) |
| 12. Ohio | Corn, soybeans, dairy products, hogs (68%) | 37. New Jersey | Greenhouse, dairy products, eggs, peaches (49%) |
| 13. Missouri | Soybeans, cattle, hogs, corn (71%) | 38. Hawaii | Sugar, pineapples, greenhouse, nuts (74%) |
| 14. Georgia | Broilers, peanuts, eggs, cattle (60%) | 39. Utah | Cattle, dairy products, turkeys, hay (71%) |
| 15. Pennsylvania | Dairy products, cattle, greenhouse, eggs (68%) | 40. Wyoming | Cattle, sheep, sugar beets, hay (86%) |
| 16. Colorado | Cattle, wheat, corn, dairy products (80%) | 41. Delaware | Broilers, soybeans, corn, greenhouse (82%) |
| 17. Arkansas | Broilers, soybeans, rice, cattle (67%) | 42. Massachusetts | Greenhouse, cranberries, dairy products, eggs (75%) |
| 18. Washington | Dairy products, cattle, apples, wheat (56%) | 43. Vermont | Dairy products, cattle, hay, apples (93%) |
| 19. Michigan | Dairy products, corn, cattle, hogs (56%) | 44. Connecticut | Eggs, greenhouse, dairy products, tobacco (76%) |
| 20. Oklahoma | Cattle, wheat, dairy products, broilers (78%) | 45. Maine | Dairy products, potatoes, eggs, cattle (75%) |
| 21. New York | Dairy products, greenhouse, cattle, eggs (74%) | 46. Nevada | Cattle, hay, dairy products, potatoes (89%) |
| 22. South Dakota | Cattle, corn, wheat (73%) | 47. West Virginia | Dairy products, broilers, apples, cattle (70%) |
| 23. Kentucky | Tobacco, horses, cattle, dairy products (70%) | 48. New Hampshire | Dairy products, greenhouse, apples, cattle (77%) |
| 24. North Dakota | Wheat, cattle, barley, sunflowers (69%) | 49. Rhode Island | Greenhouse, dairy products, eggs, potatoes (67%) |
| 25. Alabama | Broilers, cattle, eggs, peanuts (69%) | 50. Alaska | Greenhouse, dairy products, hay, potatoes (82%) |

**Source:** U.S. Dept of Agriculture, *Economic Indicators of the Farm Sector: State Financial Summary, 1989* (1990).

acres to 988,000 acres, a decline of 5%. Because agribusinesses are much less labor intensive, the total farm population has declined also, 21% between 1980 and 1990. This diminishing opportunity for farm work has accelerated internal migration from country to city. The surpluses created by expanded and more efficient production require governments to prop up prices, often at the consumer's expense. Complaints are now heard that the programs initiated in the country during the 1930s to help farmers have become wasteful and counterproductive. And the worldwide nature of agricultural progress—the "green revolution"—has increased competition for markets, in some cases hurting farmers who depend upon exporting a large share of their crop.

## FOREIGN OWNERSHIP OF U.S. AGRICULTURAL LAND, 1989
### (thousands of acres)

| Characteristic | Acreage owned Total | Acreage owned Percent | Acreage acquired[1] Total | Acreage acquired[1] Percent |
|---|---|---|---|---|
| Total[2] | 12,876 | 100.0% | 306 | 100.0% |
| Country of foreign owner | | | | |
| Canada | 1,658 | 12.9 | 94 | 30.7 |
| Netherlands Antilles | 385 | 3.0 | 1 | 0.3 |
| Switzerland | 216 | 1.7 | 8 | 2.6 |
| United Kingdom | 295 | 2.3 | 6 | 2.0 |
| West Germany | 740 | 5.7 | 24 | 7.8 |
| Through U.S. interest[3] | | | | |
| Canada | 1,385 | 10.8 | 31 | 10.1 |
| France | 828 | 8.4 | 23 | 7.5 |
| Luxembourg | 233 | 1.8 | — | — |
| Netherlands | 340 | 2.6 | 7 | 2.3 |
| Netherlands Antilles | 230 | 1.8 | 1 | 0.3 |
| Switzerland | 281 | 2.2 | 8 | 2.7 |
| United Kingdom | 2,427 | 18.8 | 14 | 4.6 |
| West Germany | 417 | 3.2 | 1 | 0.3 |

**Note**: As of Dec. 31. Covers "foreign persons"—including individuals, corporations, and governments—reporting under the Agricultural Foreign Investment Disclosure Act of 1978. Acreage figures reported do not necessarily mean that they are wholly owned by foreign investors. 1. Acquisitions made Jan. 1-Dec. 31, 1989. 2. Includes other countries not shown separately. 3. Reports filed by U.S. corporations with foreign shareholders. **Source**: U.S. Dept. of Agriculture, *Foreign Ownership of U.S. Agricultural Land through Dec. 31, 1989* (1990).

## FOREST AND RANGE FIRES: ACRES BURNED, 1980–90
### (in millions)

| Year | Acreage | Year | Acreage |
|---|---|---|---|
| 1980 | 5.3 | 1986 | 3.2 |
| 1981 | 4.8 | 1987 | 4.4 |
| 1982 | 2.3 | 1988 | 6.0 |
| 1983 | 5.1 | 1989 | 1.8 |
| 1984 | 3.0 | 1990 | 4.6 |
| 1985 | 5.3 | | |

**Source**: Boise Interagency Fire Center, 1990.

## LUMBER PRODUCTION, BY KIND OF WOOD, 1960–88 (millions of board feet)

| Item | 1960 | 1970 | 1980 | 1985 | 1988 |
|---|---|---|---|---|---|
| **Total production** | **32,926** | **34,668** | **35,354** | **36,445** | **44,730** |
| Softwoods[1,2] | 26,672 | 27,530 | 28,239 | 30,479 | 37,003 |
| Cedar | N.A. | 633 | 722 | 759 | 883 |
| Douglas fir | 8,832 | 7,727 | 6,853 | 7,751 | 10,092 |
| Hemlock | 2,032 | 1,980 | 1,855 | N.A. | N.A. |
| Ponderosa pine | 3,169 | 3,429 | 3,269 | 3,773 | 3,943 |
| Redwood | 1,000 | 1,078 | 770 | 1,155 | 1,172 |
| Southern yellow pine[2] | 5,660 | 7,063 | 8,217 | 10,230 | 12,471 |
| White fir | 2,224 | 2,063 | 1,643 | 2,272 | 2,888 |
| Hardwoods[1,2] | 6,254 | 7,138 | 7,115 | 5,966 | 7,727 |
| Ash | 125 | 159 | N.A. | 218 | 296 |
| Beech | 195 | 188 | 183 | 89 | 117 |
| Cottonwood and aspen | 206 | 229 | 303 | 216 | 239 |
| Elm | 195 | 155 | 149 | N.A. | N.A. |
| Maple | 602 | 742 | 225[3] | 532 | 630 |
| Oak | 2,789 | 3,250 | 3,356 | 2,793 | 3,684 |
| Sweet gum[4] | 331 | 376 | 371 | 293 | 354 |
| Tupelo and black gum | 292 | 335 } | 661 | 544 | 836 |
| Yellow poplar | 592 | 606 } | | | |

**Notes:** Figures for 1960 do not include Alaska and Hawaii. 1. Includes types not shown separately. 2. Beginning in 1986, data are not directly comparable to previous years due to the inclusion of 200 sawmills in the survey for the first time. 3. Excludes hard maple. 4. Red and sap. **Source:** U.S. Bureau of the Census, *Current Industrial Reports* (annual).

## FISHERIES—QUANTITY OF CATCH, BY STATE, 1980–90 (millions of pounds, live weight)

| Region/State | 1980 | 1985 | 1990 |
|---|---|---|---|
| **U.S. total** | **6,482** | **6,258** | **8,463** |
| New England | 788 | 590 | 565 |
| Maine | 245 | 175 | 151 |
| New Hampshire | 19 | 8 | 11 |
| Massachusetts | 438 | 296 | 269 |
| Rhode Island | 81 | 104 | 125 |
| Connecticut | 5 | 7 | 9 |
| Middle Atlantic | 244 | 151 | 172 |
| New York | 39 | 39 | 37 |
| New Jersey | 201 | 108 | 128 |
| Delaware | 4 | 5 | 7 |
| Chesapeake Bay | 717 | 815 | 778 |
| Maryland | 80 | 92 | 85 |
| Virginia | 637 | 723 | 693 |
| South Atlantic | 473 | 311 | 256 |
| North Carolina | 356 | 215 | 164 |
| South Carolina | 21 | 13 | 20 |

| Region/State | 1980 | 1985 | 1990 |
|---|---|---|---|
| Georgia | 19 | 17 | 16 |
| Florida (east coast) | 77 | 66 | 56 |
| Gulf States | 1,979 | 2,412 | 1,789 |
| Florida (west coast) | 115 | 117 | 141 |
| Alabama | 25 | 30 | 25 |
| Mississippi | 232 | 471 | 298 |
| Louisiana | 1,412 | 1,693 | 1,228 |
| Texas | 94 | 103 | 96 |
| Great Lakes[1] | 44 | 54 | 38 |
| Pacific Coast | 2,140 | 1,816 | 4,840 |
| Washington | 156 | 167 | 163 |
| Oregon | 126 | 101 | 170 |
| California | 804 | 363 | 418 |
| Alaska | 1,054 | 1,185 | 4,089 |
| Hawaii | 11 | 17 | 24 |
| Mississippi River and tributaries | 85 | 92 | N.A. |

1. Includes, in addition to the Great Lakes, small amounts for Lake St. Clair (Mich.), Lake of the Woods, Namakan Lake, and Rainy Lake (Minn.). **Source:** U.S. National Oceanic and Atmospheric Administration, National Marine Fisheries Service, *Fishery Statistics of the United States* (annual) and *Fisheries of the United States* (annual).

## FISHERIES: DOMESTIC CATCH AT SELECTED U.S. PORTS, 1989 (by quantity of catch)

| Port | Catch (mil. lb.) | Value (mil.) | Port | Catch (mil. lb.) | Value (mil.) |
|---|---|---|---|---|---|
| Dutch Harbor-Unalaska, Alaska | 504.3 | $107.0 | Beaufort-Morehead City, N.C. | 95.0 | 25.0 |
| Cameron, La. | 352.7 | 20.5 | Ketchikan, Alaska | 91.6 | 45.6 |
| Pascagoula-Moss Point, Miss. | 282.1 | 16.9 | New Bedford, Mass. | 90.4 | 141.0 |
| Empire-Venice, La. | 272.7 | 49.2 | Morgan City-Berwick, La. | 68.1 | 17.8 |
| Kodiak, Alaska | 213.2 | 100.2 | Cordova, Alaska | 55.3 | 35.3 |
| Dulac-Chauvin, La. | 210.9 | 50.0 | Cape May-Wildwood, N.J. | 54.0 | 30.8 |
| Intercoastal City, La. | 207.2 | 9.5 | Astoria, Oreg. | 51.0 | 20.0 |
| Los Angeles, Calif. | 177.6 | 20.3 | Port Hueneme-Oxnard-Ventura, Calif. | 50.9 | 7.9 |
| Petersburg, Alaska | 113.5 | 61.4 | Portland, Maine | 49.0 | 34.4 |
| Gloucester, Mass. | 98.5 | 30.0 | Point Judith, R.I. | 48.3 | 23.6 |

**Source**: U.S. National Oceanic and Atmospheric Administration, National Marine Fisheries Service, *Fishery Statistics of the United States* (annual) and *Fisheries of the United States* (annual).

# PART III THE WORLD

## WORLD GEOGRAPHY

### GLOSSARY OF GEOGRAPHICAL WORDS AND TERMS

(*Note:* See also Part IV: "Earth Sciences: Composition of the Earth.")

**Altitude** How high a place or a thing is, usually measured from sea level or from the surface of the land.

**Archipelago** A cluster of islands.

**Arctic Circle** An imaginary line drawn along approximately latitude 66½° N. The climate north of the Arctic Circle is very cold, and relatively few people live there.

**Atoll** A coral reef that partially or completely surrounds a lagoon.

**Basin** A portion of land that is lower than the surrounding area. Basins are created when vertical movement causes the Earth's crust to warp. Also, the area drained by a river and its tributaries.

**Bay** Part of an ocean, sea, or other body of water that extends inland. Bays are generally smaller than gulfs.

**Bight** A bay formed by a bend in the coastline.

**Caldera** A huge crater formed when the top of a volcano collapses or is exploded away.

**Canyon** A narrow, deep valley with steep sides. Many canyons have a river on their floor.

**Continent** A large unbroken land mass, distinguished from an island or peninsula. The seven continents are North America, South America, Europe, Asia, Africa, Australia, and Antarctica, though Europe and Asia are a continuous land mass divided along the spine of the Ural mountains running south from the Arctic Ocean.

**Continental drift theory** The theory, proposed in 1915 by Alfred Wegener, that all of the continents used to be joined in one supercontinent, Pangaea. Some 200 million years ago, Pangaea began to break up, and the continents "drifted" through the oceans to their present locations. The continental drift theory has now largely been replaced by the plate tectonics theory.

**Continental shelf** The edge of a continent covered by shallow ocean water, up to about 100 fathoms (600 feet), beyond which is the continental slope, which descends to the deep-sea plain, about 13,000–20,000 feet (4,000–6,000 m).

**Cove** A small and sheltered bay or inlet. Also, a small valley in a mountain.

**Crater** The bowl-shaped depression at the top of a volcano. Also, the depression made when a meteorite hits the Earth. (See *Caldera*.)

**Delta** A triangular-shaped piece of land formed by sediment at the mouth of a river.

**Desert** (See "The Great Deserts.")

**Dune** A hill or ridge of sand that has been deposited by wind.

**Equator** An imaginary line that circles the Earth halfway between the Poles. The equator is at latitude 0°.

**Equinox** The two times during the year (on or about Mar. 21 and Sept. 23) when the sun's rays strike the equator vertically. At equinox, day and night are the same length everywhere in the world. (See *Solstice*.)

**Erosion** The gradual wearing away of the surface of the land. For example, soil is eroded by wind and water; rock is eroded by freezing and thawing.

**Estuary** A valley at the mouth of a river where fresh water and sea water mix. Estuaries are created either when the land sinks or when the sea level rises and are generally shaped like a funnel.

**Fjord** A long, narrow inlet of the ocean with steeply sloping sides.

**Floodplain** Flat, low-lying land along either side of a river that is subject to flooding.

**Geyser** A jet of hot water or steam periodically

## WORLD AREA AND POPULATION BY SELECTED REGION, 1991

| Region | Area Square miles | Area Square kilometers | Area Percent of world total | Population[1] Total (mil.) | Population[1] Percent of total | Population[1] Per square mile | Population[1] Per square kilometer |
|---|---|---|---|---|---|---|---|
| World total | 65,251,120 | 169,000,401 | 100.0% | 5,384 | 100.0% | 82.5 | 31.8 |
| Africa | 11,647,720 | 30,167,594 | 17.9 | 677 | 12.5 | 58.1 | 22.4 |
| Antarctica | 14,000,000 | 36,260,000 | 21.5 | (2) | (2) | (2) | (2) |
| Asia[3] | 10,428,300 | 27,009,297 | 15.9 | 3,155 | 58.6 | 302.5 | 116.8 |
| Australia | 2,967,900 | 7,686,861 | 4.5 | 18 | 0.3 | 6.1 | 2.3 |
| Caribbean | 90,850 | 235,302 | 0.1 | 34 | 0.6 | 374.2 | 144.5 |
| Central America[4] | 963,840 | 2,496,346 | 1.5 | 116 | 2.2 | 120.4 | 46.5 |
| Europe[5] | 1,879,810 | 4,868,708 | 2.9 | 502 | 9.3 | 264.5 | 103.1 |
| North America[6] | 7,466,890 | 19,339,245 | 11.4 | 280 | 5.2 | 37.4 | 14.5 |
| Oceania | 316,420 | 819,528 | 0.5 | 10 | 0.2 | 31.6 | 12.2 |
| South America | 6,839,890 | 17,715,315 | 10.5 | 302 | 5.6 | 44.2 | 17.0 |
| USSR | 8,649,500 | 22,402,205 | 13.3 | 292 | 5.4 | 33.7 | 13.0 |

1. Mid-1990 estimate. 2. Antarctica has no indigenous population. 3. Not including that part of the USSR lying east of the Ural Mts. 4. Includes Mexico. 5. Not including that part of the USSR lying west of the Ural Mts. 6. Not including Mexico. **Sources:** Population Reference Bureau, Inc., *World Population Data Sheet 1991* (1991), and Central Intelligence Agency, *World Factbook 1991* (1990).

## THE CONTINENTS: HIGHEST AND LOWEST ELEVATIONS

| Continent | Highest point | Location | Distance above sea level Feet | Distance above sea level Meters | Lowest point | Location | Distance below sea level Feet | Distance below sea level Meters |
|---|---|---|---|---|---|---|---|---|
| Asia | Mt. Everest | Nepal-China | 29,028 | 8,848 | Dead Sea | Israel-Jordan | 1,312 | 400 |
| S. America | Mt. Aconcagua | Argentina | 22,834 | 6,960 | Valdes Peninsula | Argentina | 131 | 40 |
| N. America | Mt. McKinley | U.S. (Alaska) | 20,320 | 6,194 | Death Valley | U.S. (California) | 282 | 86 |
| Africa | Mt. Kilimanjaro | Tanzania | 19,340 | 5,895 | Lake Assal | Djibouti | 512 | 156 |
| Europe | Mt. Elbrus | USSR | 18,510 | 5,642 | Caspian Sea | USSR | 92 | 28 |
| Antarctica | Vinson Massif | Ellsworth Mts. | 16,864 | 5,140 | Unknown | — | — | — |
| Australia | Mt. Kosciusko | New South Wales | 7,310 | 2,228 | Lake Eyre | South Australia | 52 | 16 |

**Source:** *National Geographic Atlas of the World* (1981).

## THE WORLD'S LARGEST ISLANDS

| Island | Location | Flags | Area Sq. mi. | Area Sq km | Island | Location | Flags | Area Sq. mi. | Area Sq km |
|--------|----------|-------|--------------|------------|--------|----------|-------|--------------|------------|
| Greenland | N. Atlantic Ocean | Denmark | 840,000 | 2,175,600 | Cuba | Caribbean Sea | Cuba | 44,218 | 114,525 |
| New Guinea | S. Pacific Ocean | Indonesia, Papua New Guinea | 306,000 | 792,540 | North Island | S. Pacific Ocean | New Zealand | 44,035 | 114,051 |
| | | | | | Newfoundland | N. Atlantic Ocean | Canada | 42,030 | 108,858 |
| Borneo | S. Pacific Ocean | Indonesia, Malaysia, Brunei | 280,100 | 725,459 | Luzon | N. Pacific Ocean | Philippines | 40,880 | 105,879 |
| | | | | | Iceland | N. Atlantic Ocean | Iceland | 39,769 | 103,002 |
| Madagascar | Indian Ocean | Madagascar | 226,658 | 587,044 | Mindanao | N. Pacific Ocean | Philippines | 36,775 | 95,247 |
| Baffin | Arctic Ocean | Canada | 195,928 | 507,454 | Novaya Zemlya | Arctic Ocean | USSR | 35,000 | 90,650 |
| Sumatra | Indian Ocean, S. Pacific Ocean | Indonesia | 165,000 | 427,350 | Ireland | N. Atlantic Ocean | Ireland, UK | 32,599 | 84,431 |
| | | | | | Hokkaido | S. Pacific Ocean | Japan | 30,144 | 78,073 |
| Honshu | N. Pacific Ocean | Japan | 87,805 | 227,415 | Hispaniola | Caribbean Sea | Haiti, Dominican Republic | 29,530 | 76,483 |
| Great Britain | N. Atlantic Ocean | United Kingdom | 84,200 | 218,078 | | | | | |
| Victoria | Arctic Ocean | Canada | 83,896 | 217,291 | Sakhalin | N. Pacific Ocean | USSR | 29,500 | 76,405 |
| Ellesmere | Arctic Ocean | Canada | 75,767 | 196,237 | Banks | Arctic Ocean | Canada | 27,033 | 70,015 |
| Celebes | Pacific Ocean | Indonesia | 69,000 | 178,710 | Tasmania | S. Pacific Ocean | Australia | 26,178 | 67,801 |
| South Island | S. Pacific Ocean | New Zealand | 58,305 | 151,010 | Sri Lanka | Indian Ocean | Sri Lanka | 25,332 | 65,610 |
| Java | Indian Ocean, S. Pacific Ocean | Indonesia | 48,900 | 126,651 | Devon | Arctic Ocean | Canada | 21,331 | 55,247 |

**Source:** National Geographic Society.

## OCEANS OF THE WORLD

| Name | Area ('000s) Sq. mi. | Area ('000s) Sq km | Maximum depth Feet | Maximum depth Meters | Name | Area ('000s) Sq. mi. | Area ('000s) Sq km | Maximum depth Feet | Maximum depth Meters |
|------|----------------------|--------------------|--------------------|----------------------|------|----------------------|--------------------|--------------------|----------------------|
| **Pacific Ocean:** | **63,800** | **165,250** | **36,200** | **11,034** | **Atlantic Ocean:** | **31,830** | **82,440** | **30,246** | **9,219** |
| with marginal seas | 69,370 | 179,680 | — | — | with marginal seas | 41,100 | 106,460 | — | — |
| South China Sea | 1,331 | 3,447 | 18,241 | 5,560 | Arctic Ocean | 5,400 | 14,090 | 17,881 | 5,450 |
| Sea of Okhotsk | 610 | 1,580 | 11,063 | 3,372 | Caribbean Sea | 1,063 | 2,754 | 25,197 | 7,680 |
| Bering Sea | 876 | 2,270 | 13,750 | 4,191 | Mediterranean Sea | 967 | 2,505 | 16,470 | 5,020 |
| Sea of Japan | 389 | 1,007 | 12,280 | 3,733 | Norwegian Sea | 597 | 1,547 | 13,189 | 4,020 |
| East China Sea | 290 | 752 | 9,126 | 2,782 | Gulf of Mexico | 596 | 1,544 | 14,370 | 4,380 |
| Yellow Sea | 161 | 417 | 300 | 91 | Hudson Bay | 475 | 1,230 | 850 | 259 |
| **Indian Ocean:** | **28,360** | **73,440** | **24,442** | **7,450** | Greenland Sea | 465 | 1,205 | 15,899 | 4,846 |
| with marginal seas | 28,930 | 74,920 | — | — | North Sea | 222 | 575 | 2,170 | 659 |
| Arabian Sea | 1,492 | 3,863 | 19,029 | 5,800 | Black Sea | 178 | 461 | 7,360 | 2,237 |
| Bay of Bengal | 839 | 2,172 | 17,251 | 5,258 | Baltic Sea | 163 | 422 | 1,440 | 437 |
| Red Sea | 169 | 438 | 7,370 | 2,240 | | | | | |

**Source:** International Hydrographic Organization.

---

thrown up by a hot spring.

**Glacier** A large mass of slowly moving ice. Glaciers are formed on land when snow is compacted and recrystallizes.

**Gorge** An especially narrow and steep-walled canyon.

**Gulf** Part of an ocean or sea that extends inland. Gulfs are generally larger than bays.

**Hemisphere** One-half of the Earth's surface, whether divided latitudinally or longitudinally. For example, the Northern Hemisphere lies north of the equator, the Southern Hemisphere south of the equator. By convention, the Eastern Hemisphere consists of the continents of Europe, Asia, and Africa; the Western Hemisphere, of North America and South America.

**Inlet** An indentation in the shore of a sea, an ocean, or the bank of a river. Also, a narrow waterway that connects a lagoon to a larger body of water or that passes between two peninsulas.

**Island** A landmass completely surrounded by water.

**Isthmus** A narrow strip of land that connects two larger land masses.

**Lagoon** A shallow pool or pond completely, or

almost completely, separated from the sea.

**Lake** A body of water, often of considerable size, surrounded by land.

**Latitude and longitude** Latitude is the angle (measured in degrees, minutes, and seconds) between a point on the Earth's surface north or south of the equator, the center of the Earth, and the equator (0°0'0" latitude). Longitude is the angle between a point on the Earth's surface, the center of the Earth, and the prime meridian (0°0'0" longitude). There are 90 degrees of latitude between the equator and each of the poles (shown on a globe as parallel horizontal lines). There are 360 degrees of longitude (shown as vertical lines) divided into 180° east and west of the prime meridian (180°E and 180°W are thus the same). Since 1884 Greenwich, England (near London), has been universally recognized as the point through which the prime meridian passes. A degree (°) is 1/360 of a circle, a minute (') 1/60 of a degree, and a second (") 1/60 of a minute.

**Lava** Magma that reaches the surface of the Earth and from which most of the gases have escaped. (See *Volcano*.)

**Leeward** The direction or side sheltered from the wind. (See *Windward*.)

**Lithosphere** The outer layer of the Earth composed of rock; about 50 miles thick.

**Magma** Molten rock that lies deep within the Earth. In a volcanic eruption, magma bursts through the outer surface of the Earth's crust. (See *Lava, Volcano*.)

**Mountain** Land that rises above its surroundings. Mountains are higher than hills. Older mountain ranges, like the Appalachians, are rounded because they are old and worn down; younger ranges, like the Andes or the Himalayas, have jagged peaks because they are still rising.

**North Pole** The northernmost point on the Earth, or the northern axis on which the Earth spins. The North Pole, at latitude 90°N, lies in the middle of the Arctic Circle.

**Ocean** (See "The Oceans of the World.")

**Peninsula** A portion of land almost entirely surrounded by water.

**Plain** A large portion of level or rolling land that is treeless.

**Plate tectonics theory** The theory, first proposed in 1968, that the lithosphere is made up of some 20 sections, each of which consists of continental and ocean crust. The plates shift, moving continents, changing the size and

## MAJOR RIVERS OF THE WORLD, BY LENGTH

| River | Length Miles | Km | Source | Outflow |
|---|---|---|---|---|
| Nile | 4,145 | 6,673 | Tributaries of Lake Victoria, E. Africa | Mediterranean Sea |
| Amazon | 4,000 | 6,440 | Andes Mts., Peru | Atlantic Ocean |
| Mississippi-Missouri | 3,740[1] | 6,021[1] | Confluence of Jefferson, Madison, and Galatin R., Montana | Gulf of Mexico |
| Changjiang (Yangtze) | 3,720 | 5,989 | Kunlun Mts., China | China Sea |
| Yenisei-Angara | 3,650[2] | 5,877[2] | Lake Baikal, USSR | Kara Sea (Arctic) |
| Amur-Argun | 3,590[2] | 5,780[2] | Khingan Mts., China | Sea of Japan |
| Ob-Irtysh | 3,360[2] | 5,410[2] | Altai Mts., China | Gulf of Ob (Arctic) |
| Plata-Parana | 3,030[2] | 4,878[2] | Confluence of Paranaiba and Grande R., Brazil | Atlantic Ocean |
| Huang He (Yellow) | 2,903 | 4,674 | Kunlun Mts., China | Yellow Sea |
| Congo (Zaire) | 2,900 | 4,669 | Confluence of Luapula and Lualaba R., Zaire | Atlantic Ocean |
| Lena | 2,730 | 4,395 | Baikal Mts., USSR | Laptev Sea (Arctic) |
| MacKenzie | 2,635[2] | 4,242[2] | Headwaters of Finlay R., British Columbia | Beaufort Sea (Arctic) |
| Mekong | 2,600 | 4,186 | T'ang-ku-la Mts., Tibet | South China Sea |
| Niger | 2,600 | 4,186 | Guinea | Atlantic Ocean |
| Missouri | 2,533 | 4,078 | Confluence of Jefferson, Madison, and Galatin R., Montana | Mississippi River |
| Mississippi | 2,348[3] | 3,780[3] | Lake Itasca, Minnesota | Gulf of Mexico |
| Murray-Darling | 2,330 | 3,751 | Great Dividing Range, Australia | Indian Ocean |
| Volga | 2,290 | 3,687 | Valdai Hills, USSR | Caspian Sea |
| Madeira | 2,013 | 3,241 | Confluence of Mamore and Beni R., Bolivia/Brazil | Amazon River |
| Sao Francisco | 1,988 | 3,201 | Minas Gerais State, Brazil | Atlantic Ocean |
| Yukon | 1,979 | 3,186 | Confluence of Lewes and Pelly R., Yukon Terr. | Bering Sea |
| Rio Grande | 1,885 | 3,035 | San Juan Mts., Colorado | Gulf of Mexico |

| River | Length Miles | Km | Source | Outflow |
|---|---|---|---|---|
| Purus | 1,860 | 2,995 | Andes Mts., Peru | Amazon River |
| Tunguska, Lower | 1,860 | 2,995 | North of Lake Baikal, USSR | Yenesei River |
| Indus | 1,800 | 2,898 | Himalayas, Tibet | Arabian Sea |
| Danube | 1,776 | 2,859 | Confluence of Breg and Brigach R., Germany | Black Sea |
| Brahmaputra | 1,770 | 2,850 | Himalayas, Tibet (China) | Ganges River |
| Salween | 1,750 | 2,818 | Tibetan Plateau, Tibet | Bay of Bengal |
| Para-Tocantins | 1,710[2] | 2,753[2] | Goias State, Brazil | Atlantic Ocean |
| Zambezi | 1,700 | 2,737 | Zambia | Indian Ocean |
| Paraguay | 1,610 | 2,592 | Mato Grosso State, Brazil | Parana River |
| Nelson-Saskatchewan | 1,600 | 2,576 | Rocky Mts., Canada | Hudson Bay |
| Amu Darya | 1,578 | 2,541 | Pamir Mts., USSR | Aral Sea |
| Ural | 1,575 | 2,536 | Ural Mts., USSR | Caspian Sea |
| Ganges | 1,560 | 2,512 | Himalayas, India | Bay of Bengal |
| Euphrates | 1,510 | 2,431 | Confluence of Murat Nehri and Kara Su R., Turkey | Shatt-al-Arab |
| Arkansas | 1,450 | 2,335 | Colorado | Mississippi River |
| Colorado | 1,450 | 2,335 | Colorado | Gulf of California |
| Dneiper | 1,420 | 2,286 | Valdai Hills, USSR | Black Sea |
| Atchafalaya-Red | 1,400 | 2,254 | New Mexico | Gulf of Mexico |
| Syr Darya | 1,370 | 2,206 | Tien Shan, China/USSR | Aral Sea |
| Kasai | 1,338 | 2,154 | Angola | Congo (Zaire) River |
| Kolyma | 1,320 | 2,130 | Kolyma Mts., USSR | Arctic Ocean |
| Irrawaddy | 1,300 | 2,093 | Confluence of Mali and Nmai R., Myanmar | Bay of Bengal |
| Ohio-Allegheny | 1,300 | 2,093 | Pennsylvania | Mississippi River |
| Orange | 1,300 | 2,093 | Lesotho | Atlantic Ocean |
| Orinoco | 1,280 | 2,060 | Sierra Parima Mts., Venezuela | Atlantic Ocean |
| Columbia | 1,243 | 2,001 | Columbia L., British Columbia | Pacific Ocean |
| Tigris | 1,180 | 1,900 | Turkey | Shatt-al-Arab |
| Rhine | 820 | 1,320 | Confluence of Hinterrhein and Vorderrhein R., Switzerland | North Sea |
| St. Lawrence | 800 | 1,288 | L. Ontario | Gulf of St. Lawrence |

1. From the mouth of the Mississippi up the Missouri to the Red Rock River in Montana. 2. Includes the length of tributaries that are part of the main trunk stream. 3. From the mouth of the Mississippi up to its source in Minnesota.
**Source:** U.S. Dept. of Commerce, National Oceanic and Atmospheric Admin., *Principal Rivers and Lakes of the World* (1982).

shape of oceans, causing earthquakes, and creating volcanos and mountains. The plate tectonics theory has largely replaced the continental drift theory.

**Plateau** A portion of land, generally large and with a level surface, that is sharply elevated above the surrounding land. Plateaus are created when vertical movement causes the Earth's crust to warp.

**Pond** A small body of water surrounded by land.

**Prairie** Level or rolling land generally covered with grasses, with few trees.

**River** A large stream.

**Sahel** The Arabic word for "shore," the Sahel is a dry region separating the Sahara desert from tropical West and Central Africa running from Senegal to the Sudan. The meager rainfall (4–8 in. per year) supports limited crops and grazing.

**Savanna** A portion of land in the tropics or subtropics with only scattered trees but whose grasses can survive with scant rainfall.

**Sea** A large body of salt water, generally considered smaller than an ocean.

**Solstice** The time when the sun's rays strike vertically the Tropic of Cancer or the Tropic of Capricorn. At solstice the daylight hours reach their maximum or minimum. In the Northern Hemisphere, the summer solstice occurs on or about June 22; that is the "longest day of the year" and signals the beginning of summer. The winter solstice occurs on or about Dec. 22; that is the "shortest day of the year" and signals the beginning of winter. In the Southern Hemisphere, the longest and shortest days of the year occur on Dec. 22 and June 22, respectively. (See *Equinox*.)

**Sound** A body of water that separates an island from the mainland, or that connects two oceans, seas, or other bodies of water. Sounds are generally long and narrow.

## MAJOR NATURAL LAKES OF THE WORLD

| Lake | Surface area Sq. mi. | Sq km | Location | Maximum depth Feet | Meters | Elevation Feet | Meters | Lake | Surface area Sq. mi. | Sq km | Location | Maximum depth Feet | Meters | Elevation Feet | Meters |
|---|---|---|---|---|---|---|---|---|---|---|---|---|---|---|---|
| Caspian Sea¹ | 143,240 | 370,992 | USSR, Iran | 3,363 | 1,025 | -92 | -28 | Mai-Ndombe | 3,100² | 8,029² | Zaire | 36 | 11 | 1,116 | 340 |
| Superior | 31,700 | 82,103 | Ontario, Can.; Mich., Wis., Minn. | 1,333 | 406 | 600 | 183 | Athabasca | 3,064 | 7,936 | Saskatchewan, Alberta, Can. | 407 | 124 | 700 | 213 |
| Victoria | 26,820 | 69,464 | Uganda, Kenya, Tanzania | 279 | 85 | 3,720 | 1,134 | Eyre¹ | 2,970² | 7,692² | Australia | 4 | 1 | -52 | -16 |
| Aral Sea¹ | 24,904 | 64,501 | USSR | 220 | 67 | 174 | 53 | Reindeer | 2,568 | 6,651 | Saskatchewan, Manitoba, Can. | 720 | 219 | 1,106 | 337 |
| Huron | 23,000 | 59,570 | Ontario, Can.; Mich. | 750 | 229 | 576 | 176 | Tonle Sap | 2,500² | 6,475² | Cambodia | 39 | 12 | (⁴) | (⁴) |
| Michigan | 22,300 | 57,757 | Mich., Ind., Ill., Wis. | 923 | 281 | 579 | 176 | Rudolf¹ | 2,473 | 6,405 | Kenya, Ethiopia | 240 | 73 | 1,401 | 427 |
| Tanganyika | 12,350 | 31,987 | Burundi, Tanzania, Zambia, Zaire | 4,800 | 1,463 | 2,543 | 775 | Issyk-Kul¹ | 2,355 | 6,099 | USSR | 2,303 | 702 | 5,279 | 1,609 |
| Baikal | 12,160 | 31,494 | USSR | 5,315 | 1,620 | 1,493 | 455 | Torrens¹ | 2,230² | 5,776² | Australia | 0.5 | 0.2 | 92 | 28 |
| Great Bear | 12,028 | 31,153 | Northwest Terr., Can. | 1,356 | 413 | 512 | 156 | Albert | 2,160 | 5,594 | Uganda, Zaire | 168 | 51 | 2,030 | 619 |
| Nyasa (Malawi) | 11,150 | 28,879 | Tanzania, Mozambique, Malawi | 2,280 | 695 | 1,550 | 472 | Vanern | 2,156 | 5,581 | Sweden | 325 | 99 | 144 | 44 |
| Great Slave | 11,030 | 28,568 | Northwest Terr., Can. | 2,015 | 614 | 513 | 156 | Nettilling | 2,140 | 5,543 | Baffin Is., Can. | (⁴) | (⁴) | 95 | 29 |
| Erie | 9,910 | 25,667 | Ontario, Can.; N.Y., Pa., Ohio, Mich. | 210 | 64 | 570 | 174 | Winnipegosis | 2,075 | 5,374 | Manitoba, Can. | 39 | 12 | 830 | 253 |
| | | | | | | | | Bangweulu | 1,930 | 4,999 | Zambia | 16 | 5 | 3,500 | 1,067 |
| Winnipeg | 9,417 | 24,390 | Manitoba, Can. | 92 | 28 | 713 | 217 | Nipigon | 1,872 | 4,848 | Ontario, Can. | 541 | 165 | 1,050 | 320 |
| Ontario | 7,540 | 19,529 | Ontario, Can.; N.Y. | 802 | 244 | 245 | 75 | Gairdner¹ | 1,840² | 4,763² | Australia | 0.5 | 0.2 | 112 | 34 |
| Balkhash¹ | 7,115² | 18,428² | USSR | 87 | 27 | 1,115 | 340 | Urmia¹ | 1,815² | 4,701² | Iran | 49 | 15 | 4,180 | 1,274 |
| Ladoga | 6,835 | 17,703 | USSR | 755 | 230 | 13 | 4 | Manitoba | 1,800 | 4,662 | Manitoba, Can. | 92 | 28 | 813 | 248 |
| Chad | 6,300 | 16,317 | Chad, Nigeria, Niger | 36 | 11 | 787 | 240 | Kyoga | 1,710 | 4,429 | Uganda | 26 | 8 | 3,400 | 1,036 |
| | | | | | | | | Khanka | 1,700 | 4,403 | China, USSR | 33 | 10 | 226 | 69 |
| Maracaibo³ | 5,200 | 13,468 | Venezuela | 115 | 35 | sea level | sea level | Lake of the Woods | 1,695 | 4,390 | Minn.; Ontario, Manitoba, Can. | 69 | 21 | 1,060 | 323 |
| Patos³ | 3,920 | 10,153 | Brazil | 15 | 5 | (⁴) | (⁴) | Great Salt¹ | 1,680 | 4,351 | Utah | 48 | 15 | 4,200 | 1,280 |
| Onega | 3,720 | 9,635 | USSR | 394 | 120 | 108 | 33 | Mweru | 1,680 | 4,351 | Zambia, Zaire | 10 | 3 | 3,008 | 917 |
| Titicaca | 3,200 | 8,288 | Bolivia, Peru | 990 | 302 | 12,500 | 3,810 | Peipus | 1,660 | 4,299 | USSR | 41 | 12 | 98 | 30 |
| Nicaragua | 3,150 | 8,159 | Nicaragua | 230 | 70 | 102 | 31 | Koko Nor (Tsing Hai) | 1,650 | 4,274 | China | 125 | 38 | 10,515 | 3,205 |
| | | | | | | | | Dubawnt | 1,600 | 4,144 | Northwest Terr., Can. | (⁴) | (⁴) | 774 | 236 |
| | | | | | | | | Tung-t'ing Hu | 1,430² | 3,704² | China | (⁴) | (⁴) | 36 | 11 |
| | | | | | | | | Van Golu¹ | 1,420 | 3,678 | Turkey | 82 | 25 | 5,643 | 1,720 |
| | | | | | | | | Tana | 1,390 | 3,600 | Ethiopia | 30 | 9 | 6,003 | 1,830 |

1. Saltwater. A lake is a body of water surrounded by land; the Caspian Sea is thus a lake. It was called a sea by the Romans because of its salty water. 2. Subject to large seasonal variation in surface area. 3. Lagoon. 4. No information available. **Source:** U.S. National Oceanic and Atmospheric Administration, *Principal Rivers and Lakes of the World* (1982).

**South Pole** The southernmost point on the Earth, or the southern axis on which the Earth spins. The South Pole, at latitude 90°S, lies in the middle of the Antarctic Circle.

**Steppe** A portion of land with little rainfall, extreme temperature variations, and drought-resistant vegetation.

**Strait** A narrow body of water that connects two large bodies of water.

**Stream** Any body of running water that flows on or under the surface of the Earth. Brooks and creeks are small streams; rivers are large streams.

**Swamp** A portion of wet, waterlogged, or flooded land.

**Tide** The rise and fall of the surface of the ocean and of bays, gulfs, and other bodies of water connected to the ocean. Tides are caused by the gravitational pull of the moon, which passes over the same meridian of the Earth about once every 24 hours and 50 minutes. The length of time between successive high (or low) tides is about 12 hours and 25 minutes.

**Tributary** A stream or river that flows into a larger stream or river.

**Tropic of Cancer** Latitude 23½°N, which marks

the northernmost limit of the sun's vertical rays. The area between the Tropic of Cancer and the Tropic of Capricorn is known as the "tropics." (See *Equinox*.)

**Tropic of Capricorn** Latitude 23½°S, which marks the southernmost limit of the sun's vertical rays.

**Tundra** An area of treeless plain near or above the Arctic Circle. Tundra subsoil is permanently frozen, but the soil thaws enough to support the growth of mosses, lichens, and some small flowering shrubs.

**Valley** A long and sometimes narrow depression on the surface of the Earth, usually between two mountain ridges or ranges.

**Volcano** A mountain formed by lava and/or other materials that have burst forth from deep within the Earth. (See *Caldera, Crust, Lava, Magma*.)

**Windward** The direction or side facing the wind.

# OCEANS OF THE WORLD

The water of the world's oceans covers more than 70 percent of the world's surface. While for many years the so-called World Ocean was divided into five parts—the Pacific, Atlantic, Indian, Arctic, and Antarctic—scientists today commonly recognize only the first three as separate and distinct oceans. The Arctic and Antarctic, as well as other large bodies of water such as the Caribbean Sea, the Gulf of Mexico, Hudson Bay, the Mediterranean and Black seas, and the South China Sea are termed marginal seas. The International Hydrographic Organization identifies 66 seas, gulfs, bays, bights, straits, channels, and passages, many of which are further subdivided. For instance, the Mediterranean Sea is divided into western and eastern basins, and the western basin is subdivided into the Strait of Gibraltar, the Balearic Sea, Ligurian Sea, Tyrrhenian Sea, Ionian Sea, Adriatic Sea, and Aegean Sea. The accompanying table gives the area and maximum depths of the world's three major oceans and selected marginal seas.

# THE WORLD'S HIGHEST MOUNTAIN PEAKS

| Mountain peak | Range | Location | Feet | Meters | Mountain peak | Range | Location | Feet | Meters |
|---|---|---|---|---|---|---|---|---|---|
| Everest | Himalayas | Nepal-China | 29,028 | 8,848 | Pyramid | Himalayas | Nepal-India | 23,400 | 7,132 |
| K2 (Godwin Austen) | Karakoram | Kashmir | 28,250 | 8,611 | Api | Himalayas | Nepal | 23,399 | 7,132 |
| Kanchenjunga | Himalayas | Nepal-India | 28,208 | 8,598 | Pauhunri | Himalayas | India-China | 23,385 | 7,128 |
| Lhotse I | Himalayas | Nepal-China | 27,923 | 8,511 | Trisul | Himalayas | India | 23,360 | 7,120 |
| Makalu I | Himalayas | Nepal-China | 27,824 | 8,481 | Korzhenevski Peak | Pamirs | USSR | 23,310 | 7,105 |
| Lhotse II | Himalayas | Nepal-China | 27,560 | 8,400 | Kangto | Himalayas | India-China | 23,260 | 7,090 |
| Dhaulagiri | Himalayas | Nepal | 26,810 | 8,172 | Nyainqentanglha | Nyainqentanglha Shan | China | 23,255 | 7,088 |
| Manaslu I | Himalayas | Nepal | 26,760 | 8,156 | Trisuli | Himalayas | India | 23,210 | 7,074 |
| Cho Oyu | Himalayas | Nepal-China | 26,750 | 8,153 | Dunagiri | Himalayas | India | 23,184 | 7,066 |
| Nanga Parbat | Himalayas | Kashmir | 26,660 | 8,126 | Revolution Peak | Pamirs | USSR | 22,880 | 6,974 |
| Annapurna | Himalayas | Nepal | 26,504 | 8,078 | Aconcagua | Andes | Argentina | 22,834 | 6,960 |
| Gasherbrum | Karakoram | Kashmir | 26,470 | 8,068 | Ojos del Salado | Andes | Argentina-Chile | 22,572 | 6,880 |
| Broad | Karakoram | Kashmir | 26,400 | 8,047 | Bonete | Andes | Argentina | 22,546 | 6,872 |
| Gosainthan | Himalayas | China | 26,287 | 8,012 | Tupungato | Andes | Argentina-Chile | 22,310 | 6,800 |
| Annapurna II | Himalayas | Nepal | 26,041 | 7,937 | Moscow Peak | Pamirs | USSR | 22,260 | 6,785 |
| Gyachung Kang | Himalayas | Nepal-China | 25,910 | 7,897 | Pissis | Andes | Argentina | 22,241 | 6,779 |
| Disteghil Sar | Karakoram | Kashmir | 25,858 | 7,882 | Mercedario | Andes | Argentina | 22,211 | 6,770 |
| Himalchuli | Himalayas | Nepal | 25,801 | 7,864 | Huascaran | Andes | Peru | 22,205 | 6,768 |
| Nuptse | Himalayas | Nepal-China | 25,726 | 7,841 | Llullaillaco | Andes | Argentina-Chile | 22,057 | 6,723 |
| Masherbrum | Karakoram | Kashmir | 25,660 | 7,821 | El Libertador | Andes | Argentina | 22,047 | 6,720 |
| Nanda Devi | Himalayas | India | 25,645 | 7,817 | Cachi | Andes | Argentina | 22,047 | 6,720 |
| Rakaposhi | Karakoram | Kashmir | 25,550 | 7,788 | Kailas | Himalayas | China | 22,027 | 6,714 |
| Kanjut Sar | Karakoram | Kashmir | 25,461 | 7,761 | Incahuasi | Andes | Argentina-Chile | 21,720 | 6,620 |
| Kamet | Himalayas | India-China | 25,447 | 7,756 | Yerupaja | Andes | Peru | 21,709 | 6,617 |
| Namcha Barwa | Himalayas | China | 25,445 | 7,756 | Kurumda | Pamirs | USSR | 21,686 | 6,610 |
| Kua·la·man·ta·t'a (Gurla Mandhata) | Himalayas | China | 25,355 | 7,728 | Galan | Andes | Argentina | 21,654 | 6,600 |
| Wu·lu·k'o·mu·shih (Ulugh Muztagh) | Kunlun | China | 25,340 | 7,724 | El Muerto | Andes | Argentina-Chile | 21,457 | 6,540 |
| Kung·ko·erh (Kungur) (Muztagh Ata) | Mu·ssu·t'a·ko·a·t'e (Muztagh Ata) | China | 25,325 | 7,719 | Sajama | Andes | Bolivia | 21,391 | 6,520 |
|  |  |  |  |  | Nacimiento | Andes | Argentina | 21,302 | 6,493 |
| Tirich Mir | Hindu Kush | Pakistan | 25,230 | 7,690 | Illimani | Andes | Bolivia | 21,201 | 6,462 |
| Saser Kangri | Karakoram | Kashmir | 25,172 | 7,672 | Coropuna | Andes | Peru | 21,083 | 6,426 |
| Makalu II | Himalayas | Nepal-China | 25,120 | 7,657 | Laudo | Andes | Argentina | 20,997 | 6,400 |
| Minya Konka (Gonggashan) | Daxue Shan | China | 24,900 | 7,590 | Ancohuma | Andes | Bolivia | 20,958 | 6,388 |
| Kula Kangri | Himalayas | Bhutan-China | 24,784 | 7,554 | Ausangate | Andes | Peru | 20,945 | 6,384 |
| Chang·tzu | Himalayas | Nepal-China | 24,780 | 7,553 | Toro | Andes | Argentina-Chile | 20,932 | 6,380 |
| Mu·ssu·t'a·ko·a·t'e (Muztagh Ata) | Mu·ssu·t'a·ko·a·t'e (Muztagh Ata) | China | 24,757 | 7,546 | Illampu | Andes | Bolivia | 20,873 | 6,362 |
| Skyang Kangri | Himalayas | Kashmir | 24,750 | 7,544 | Tres Cruces | Andes | Argentina-Chile | 20,853 | 6,356 |
| Communism Peak | Pamirs | USSR | 24,590 | 7,495 | Huandoy | Andes | Peru | 20,852 | 6,356 |
| Jongsong Peak | Himalayas | Nepal-India | 24,472 | 7,459 | Parinacota | Andes | Bolivia-Chile | 20,768 | 6,330 |
| Pobeda Peak | Tian Shan | USSR-China | 24,406 | 7,439 | Tortolas | Andes | Argentina-Chile | 20,745 | 6,323 |
| Sia Kangri | Himalayas | Kashmir | 24,350 | 7,422 | Ampato | Andes | Peru | 20,702 | 6,310 |
| Haramosh Peak | Karakoram | Kashmir | 24,270 | 7,397 | El Condor | Andes | Argentina | 20,669 | 6,300 |
| Istoro Nal | Hindu Kush | Pakistan | 24,240 | 7,388 | Salcantay | Andes | Peru | 20,574 | 6,271 |
| Tent Peak | Himalayas | Nepal-India | 24,165 | 7,365 | Chimborazo | Andes | Ecuador | 20,561 | 6,267 |
| Chomo Lhari | Himalayas | Bhutan-China | 24,040 | 7,327 | Huancarhuas | Andes | Peru | 20,531 | 6,258 |
| Chamlang | Himalayas | Nepal | 24,012 | 7,319 | Famatina[1] | Andes | Argentina | 20,505 | 6,250 |
| Kabru | Himalayas | Nepal-India | 24,002 | 7,316 | Pumasillo | Andes | Peru | 20,492 | 6,246 |
| Alung Gangri | Himalayas | China | 24,000 | 7,315 | Solo | Andes | Argentina | 20,492 | 6,246 |
| Baltoro Kangri | Himalayas | Kashmir | 23,990 | 7,312 | Polleras | Andes | Argentina | 20,456 | 6,235 |
| Muztagh Ata | Kunlun | China | 23,890 | 7,282 | Pular | Andes | Chile | 20,423 | 6,225 |
| Mana | Himalayas | India | 23,860 | 7,273 | Chani | Andes | Argentina | 20,341 | 6,200 |
| Baruntse | Himalayas | Nepal | 23,688 | 7,220 | McKinley | Alaska | U.S. (Alaska) | 20,320 | 6,194 |
| Nepal Peak | Himalayas | Nepal-India | 23,500 | 7,163 | Aucanquilcha | Andes | Chile | 20,295 | 6,186 |
| Amne Machin | Kunlun | China | 23,490 | 7,160 | Juncal | Andes | Argentina-Chile | 20,276 | 6,180 |
| Gauri Sankar | Himalayas | Nepal-China | 23,440 | 7,145 | Negro | Andes | Argentina | 20,184 | 6,152 |
| Badrinath | Himalayas | India | 23,420 | 7,138 | Quela | Andes | Argentina | 20,128 | 6,135 |
| Nunkun | Himalayas | Kashmir | 23,410 | 7,135 | Condoriri | Andes | Bolivia | 20,095 | 6,125 |
| Lenin Peak | Pamirs | USSR | 23,405 | 7,134 | Palermo | Andes | Argentina | 20,079 | 6,120 |
|  |  |  |  |  | Solimana | Andes | Peru | 20,068 | 6,117 |
|  |  |  |  |  | San Juan | Andes | Argentina-Chile | 20,049 | 6,111 |
|  |  |  |  |  | (Sierra) Nevada | Andes | Argentina-Chile | 20,023 | 6,103 |
|  |  |  |  |  | Antofalla | Andes | Argentina | 20,013 | 6,100 |
|  |  |  |  |  | Marmolejo | Andes | Argentina-Chile | 20,013 | 6,100 |

1. Formerly General Manuel Belgrano. **Note:** Mountains over 20,000 feet. **Source:** National Geographic Society.

North Pole

ARCTIC OCEAN

80°   80°

70°   GREENLAND   70°
(Den.)

ALASKA   ICELAND   60°
60°   (U.S.)

CANADA
50°   50°

40°   NORTH AMERICA   40°

UNITED STATES   30°
30°   AZORES
(Port.)

BERMUDA
(UK)   ATLANTIC   20°
HAWAII   BAHAMAS
20°   (U.S.)   Gulf of   CUBA   DOMINICAN
MEXICO   Mexico   REPUBLIC   PUERTO RICO
(U.S.) ST. KITTS AND NEVIS   CAPE VERDE
JAMAICA   DOMINICA   ISLANDS   OCEAN
BELIZE   HAITI   ST. LUCIA
GUATEMALA   Caribbean Sea   BARBADOS
HONDURAS   GRENADA   TRINIDAD AND   10°
EL SALVADOR   TOBAGO
PACIFIC   OCEAN   NICARAGUA   VENEZUELA   GUYANA
10°   COSTA RICA   SURINAME
PANAMA   COLOMBIA   FR. GUIANA
GALAPAGOS
ISLANDS   0°
0°   (Ecu.)   ECUADOR

SOUTH AMERICA

10°   WESTERN   PERU   BRAZIL   10°
SAMOA
FRENCH   BOLIVIA
FIJI   AMERICAN   POLYNESIA
20°   SAMOA   PARAGUAY   20°

PITCAIRN ISLAND   EASTER
(UK)   ISLAND   CHILE   URUGUAY   30°
30°   (Chile)   ARGENTINA

HOMOLOSINE
40°   PROJECTION   40°

50°   FALKLAND   50°
ISLANDS
(UK)
60°   60°
165°   150°   135°   120°   105°   100°   90°   75°   60°   45°   30°   20°
ANTARCTICA   70°
70°   ANTARCTICA
80°   80°

0   2000 miles

0   3000 km
South Pole   South Pole

THE WORLD: WESTERN HEMISPHERE

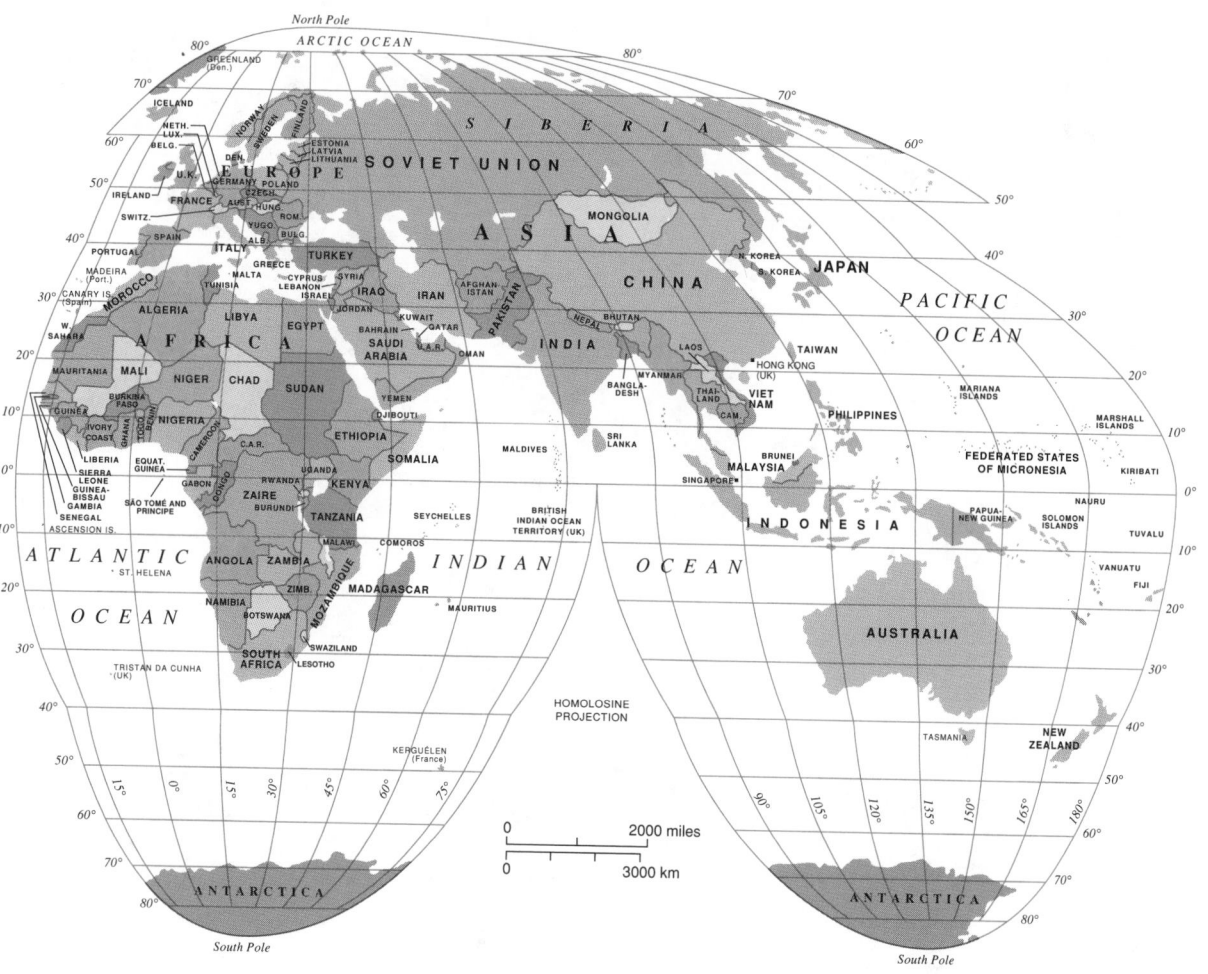

North Pole

80° ARCTIC OCEAN 80°

70° GREENLAND (Den.) 70°

ICELAND

NETH. LUX. NORWAY SWEDEN FINLAND ESTONIA LATVIA LITHUANIA S I B E R I A 60°

60° EUROPE SOVIET UNION 70°

IRELAND BELG. DEN. U.K. GERMANY POLAND CZECH. 50°

50° FRANCE SWITZ. AUST. HUNG. YUGO ROM. BULG. A S I A MONGOLIA 50°

PORTUGAL SPAIN ITALY GREECE ALB. TURKEY CHINA N. KOREA S. KOREA JAPAN 40°

40° MADEIRA (Port.) CYPRUS SYRIA PACIFIC

30° CANARY IS. (Spain) MOROCCO MALTA TUNISIA LEBANON ISRAEL IRAQ JORDAN AFGHAN-ISTAN IRAN PAKISTAN OCEAN 30°

ALGERIA LIBYA EGYPT BAHRAIN KUWAIT QATAR NEPAL BHUTAN TAIWAN

20° W. SAHARA AFRICA SAUDI ARABIA U.A.E. OMAN INDIA LAOS HONG KONG (UK) 20°

MAURITANIA MALI NIGER CHAD SUDAN YEMEN MYANMAR THAI-LAND VIET NAM MARIANA ISLANDS

10° GUINEA BURKINA FASO NIGERIA DJIBOUTI BANGLA-DESH CAM. PHILIPPINES MARSHALL ISLANDS 10°

IVORY COAST GHANA TOGO BENIN CAMEROON C.A.R. ETHIOPIA SRI LANKA BRUNEI FEDERATED STATES OF MICRONESIA KIRIBATI

LIBERIA SIERRA LEONE GUINEA-BISSAU GAMBIA SENEGAL EQUAT. GUINEA GABON CONGO ZAIRE UGANDA SOMALIA MALDIVES SINGAPORE MALAYSIA NAURU

0° SAO TOMÉ AND PRINCIPE RWANDA BURUNDI KENYA SEYCHELLES INDONESIA PAPUA-NEW GUINEA SOLOMON ISLANDS 0°

ASCENSION IS. TANZANIA BRITISH INDIAN OCEAN TERRITORY (UK) TUVALU

10° ATLANTIC MALAWI COMOROS INDIAN OCEAN VANUATU 10°

ANGOLA ZAMBIA MOZAMBIQUE MADAGASCAR FIJI

20° OCEAN ST. HELENA NAMIBIA ZIMB. MAURITIUS AUSTRALIA 20°

BOTSWANA SWAZILAND

30° TRISTAN DA CUNHA (UK) SOUTH AFRICA LESOTHO NEW ZEALAND 30°

HOMOLOSINE PROJECTION

40° KERGUÉLEN (France) TASMANIA 40°

50° 50°

15° 0° 15° 30° 45° 60° 75° 90° 105° 120° 135° 150° 165° 180°

60° 0 2000 miles 60°

70° 0 3000 km 70°

80° ANTARCTICA ANTARCTICA 80°

South Pole South Pole

THE WORLD: EASTERN HEMISPHERE

AFRICA AND MIDDLE EAST

EUROPE

## WORLD'S LARGEST CAPACITY RESERVOIRS

| Reservoir | Capacity (mil.) | | River or basin, and location | Year (to be) completed | Reservoir | Capacity (mil.) | | River or basin, and location | Year (to be) completed |
| | Cubic yards[1] | Cubic meters[1] | | | | Cubic yards[1] | Cubic meters[1] | | |
|---|---|---|---|---|---|---|---|---|---|
| Owen Falls | 3,537,000[2] | 2,700,000[2] | Lake Victoria/Nile, Uganda | 1954 | Ust-Ilim | 77,683 | 59,300 | Angara, USSR | 1977 |
| Kariba | 236,216 | 180,600 | Zambezi, Zimbabwe/Zambia | 1959 | Volga–V.I. Lenin (Kuibyshev) | 75,980 | 58,000 | Volga, USSR | 1955 |
| Bratsk | 221,744 | 169,270 | Angara, USSR | 1964 |  |  |  |  |  |
| Aswan (High) | 221,259 | 168,900 | Nile, Egypt | 1970 | Serra de Mesa | 70,629 | 54,000 | Tocantins, Brazil | (1993) |
| Akosombo | 193,880 | 148,000 | Volta, Ghana | 1965 | Caniapiscau (3, 4, 5) | 70,478 | 53,800 | Caniapiscau, Quebec | 1981 |
| Daniel Johnson | 185,826 | 141,852 | Manicouagan, Quebec | 1968 | Bukhtarma | 65,238 | 49,800 | Irtysh, USSR | 1960 |
| Guri (Raul Leoni) | 180,780 | 138,000 | Caroni, Venezuela | 1986 | Atatürk | 63,797 | 48,700 | Euphrates, Turkey | (1995) |
| Krasnoyarsk | 96,023 | 73,300 | Yenesei, USSR | 1967 | Upper Wainganga | 63,313 | 50,700 | Wainganga, India | 1987 |
| Bennett W.A.C. | 92,105 | 70,309 | Peace, British Columbia | 1967 | Irkutsk | 59,904 | 45,800 | Angara, USSR | 1956 |
| Zeya | 89,604 | 68,400 | Zeya, USSR | 1978 | Tucurui (Raul G. Lhano) | 59,904 | 45,800 | Tocantins, Brazil | 1984 |
| Cabora Bassa | 82,530 | 63,000 | Zambezi, Mozambique | 1974 |  |  |  |  |  |
| La Grande 2 | 80,847 | 61,715 | La Grande, Quebec | 1978 | Turukhansk | 58,950 | 45,000 | Lower Tunguska, USSR | (1994) |
| Chapeton | 79,386 | 60,600 | Parana, Argentina | (1998) | Lower Kamskaya | 58,858 | 45,000 | Kama, USSR | 1987 |
| La Grande 3 | 78,626 | 60,020 | La Grande, Quebec | 1981 | Bakun | 57,378 | 43,800 | Rajang, Malaysia | (1995) |
| Boguchany | 78,123 | 58,200 | USSR | UC |  |  |  |  |  |

**Note:** UC = under construction. 1. One acre foot equals approximately 2,110 m$^3$ or 1,613 yd$^3$. 2. Includes a natural lake. **Source:** *International Water Power & Dam Construction Handbook 1990* (1990).

## WORLD'S LARGEST VOLUME DAMS

| Dam | Volume ('000s) | | River or basin, and location | Year (to be) completed | Dam | Volume ('000s) | | River or basin, and location | Year (to be) completed |
| | Cubic yards | Cubic meters | | | | Cubic yards | Cubic meters | | |
|---|---|---|---|---|---|---|---|---|---|
| Syncrude Tailings[1] | 707,400 | 540,000 | Alberta, Canada | (1992) | Mangla | 85,646 | 65,379 | Jhelum, Pakistan | 1967 |
| Chapeton | 388,022 | 296,200 | Parana, Argentina | (1998) | Gardiner | 85,020 | 65,400 | South Saskatchewan, Saskatchewan | 1968 |
| Pati | 301,536 | 230,180 | Parana, Argentina | 1990 |  |  |  |  |  |
| New Cornelia Tailings[1] | 274,445 | 209,500 | Ten Mile Wash, Arizona | 1973 | Afsluitdijk | 83,093 | 63,430 | Zuider Zee, Netherlands | 1932 |
|  |  |  |  |  | Oroville | 78,122 | 59,635 | Feather, California | 1968 |
| Tarbela | 136,919 | 105,922 | Indus, Pakistan | 1976 | San Luis | 78,022 | 59,559 | San Luis, California | 1967 |
| Fort Peck | 125,825 | 96,050 | Missouri, Montana | 1937 | Nurek | 75,980 | 58,000 | Vakhsh, USSR | 1980 |
| Lower Usuma | 121,830 | 93,000 | Usuma, Nigeria | 1990 | Tucurui | 71,500 | 55,000 | Tocantins, Brazil | 1984 |
| Cipasang | 117,900 | 90,000 | Cimanuk, Indonesia | UC | Garrison | 66,607 | 50,845 | Missouri, North Dakota | 1956 |
| Atatürk | 109,850 | 84,500 | Euphrates, Turkey | 1990 | Cochiti | 65,801 | 50,230 | Grande, New Mexico | 1975 |
| Yacyreta-Apipe | 105,300 | 81,000 | Parana, Paraguay/Argentina | 1991 | Oosterschelde | 65,500 | 50,000 | Vense Gat Oosterschelde, Neth. | 1986 |
| Guri (Raul Leoni) | 102,142 | 77,971 | Caroni, Venezuela | 1986 | Tahqua (Thawra) | 60,260 | 46,000 | Euphrates, Syria | 1976 |
| Rogun | 98,905 | 75,500 | Vakhsh, USSR | 1987 | Aswan (High) | 58,033 | 44,300 | Nile, Egypt | 1970 |
| Oahe Tailings | 86,472 | 66,517 | Missouri, South Dakota | 1960 |  |  |  |  |  |

**Note:** Volume refers to amount of material (earth, concrete, etc.) used in construction of dam. UC = under construction. 1. Dams formed from waste ore (tailings) from mining. **Source:** *International Water Power & Dam Construction Handbook 1990* (1990).

## THE GREAT DESERTS

To many people, the word *desert* brings to mind images of shifting sand dunes, scorching sun, and occasional lush oases. But there are actually many kinds of deserts, because a desert is simply an area that receives little precipitation and has little plant cover. Thus polar areas can be considered deserts, for their precipitation is locked into ice and snow. So are places such as the Taklimakan, which lies in a rain shadow on the leeward side of mountain ranges, and the Atacama, which is near cold ocean currents that cool the air and prevent the formation of rain clouds. But most deserts are found in the tropics, where giant high-pressure cells keep rain from forming. Some deserts are indeed flat and sandy, but others are solid rock, loose pebbles, or even mountain plateaus. One of the many fascinating characteristics of deserts is their strangely shaped rock formations,

## DESERT EXTREMES

• The Sahara is the largest desert, with an area greater than the continental United States.
• The driest place on earth is in the Atacama desert of Chile, where no rainfall at all was recorded between 1570 and 1971.
• The highest temperature ever recorded—136°F (58°C)—was at Al-Aziziya, in the Libyan desert.
• The lowest point in the world—1,302 feet (397 m) below sea level—is on the shores of the Dead Sea in the Negev desert.
• The lowest point in the Western Hemisphere—282 feet (86 m) below sea level—is in Death Valley, California.

created by wind-whipped sand.

Altogether, arid lands cover about a fifth of the Earth's total land surface—a third, if semi-

arid areas are also included. About a billion people live in arid and semiarid areas, and more than 100 countries are facing problems associated with expanding deserts.

**Uses of the desert** Even the hot, sandy, tropical deserts are not necessarily, as their name implies, deserted. Traders, herders, and farmers have called the desert home for thousands of years. Settlements have grown up around oases or in irrigated areas, from ancient times to the present. Deserts are important to historians, archaeologists, paleontologists, and other scientists for the relics of the past that are preserved there. Dinosaur eggs have been found in the Gobi desert, for instance, and whole cities are said to lie buried beneath the Taklimakan desert.

Deserts are also important for extractive industries. The Negev was the site of the fabled King Solomon's Mines. In the 19th century, borax was mined in Death Valley. Petroleum is found in the Sahara (Arabic for "wilderness")

## GREAT DESERTS OF THE WORLD

| Desert | Location | Approximate size | | Desert | Location | Approximate size | |
|--------|----------|---------|---------|--------|----------|---------|---------|
| | | Sq. mi. | Sq km | | | Sq. mi. | Sq km |
| An Nafud[1] | N Saudi Arabia | 40,000 | 103,600 | Mojave | S California, W Arizona | 15,000 | 38,900 |
| Atacama | N Chile | 70,000 | 181,300 | Namib | Namibia | 800[4] | 1,290[4] |
| Black Rock | NW Nevada | 1,000 | 2,600 | Negev | S Israel | 4,700 | 12,200 |
| Chihuahuan | Texas, New Mexico, Arizona; Mexico | 140,000 | 362,600 | Nubian[3] | NE Sudan | 100,000 | 259,000 |
| Dasht-e-Kavir | Central Iran | 300 x 100 | 485 x 160 | Painted Desert | N Arizona | 200[5] | 320[5] |
| Dasht-e-Lut | E Iran | 20,000 | 51,800 | Rub al-Khali | S Saudi Arabia | 250,000 | 647,500 |
| Death Valley | E California, SW Nevada | 3,000 | 7,800 | ("Empty Quarter")[1] | | | |
| Gibson[2] | W Australia | 120,000 | 310,800 | Sahara | N Africa | 3,500,000 | 9,065,000 |
| Gobi | Mongolia; China | 500,000 | 1,295,000 | Simpson[2] | Central Australia | 40,000 | 103,600 |
| Great Sandy[2] | NW Australia | 150,000 | 338,500 | Sonoran | SW Arizona, SE California; NW Mexico | 70,000 | 181,300 |
| Great Victoria[2] | SW Australia | 150,000 | 338,500 | Syrian[1] | N Saudi Arabia; E Jordan; S Syria; | 100,000 | 259,000 |
| Kalahari | S Africa | 225,000 | 582,800 | | W Iraq | | |
| Kara Kum (Turkestan) | Turkmen SSR (Asiatic USSR) | 120,000 | 310,800 | Taklimakan | Xinjiang Uygur Autonomous Region, | 140,000 | 362,600 |
| Kyzyl Kum | Kazakh SSR, Uzbek SSR | 100,000 | 259,000 | | China | | |
| | (Asiatic USSR) | | | Thar (Great Indian) | NW India; Pakistan | 100,000 | 259,000 |
| Libyan[3] | Libya; SW Egypt; Sudan | 450,000 | 1,165,500 | | | | |

1. Part of Great Arabian Desert. 2. Part of Great Australian Desert. 3. Part of Sahara Desert. 4. Length; width varies from 30–100 mi. (48–160 km). 5. Length; width varies from 15–30 mi. (24–48 km).

and in the deserts of the Arabian peninsula. The Atacama is famed for its deposits of nitrate and copper. The Rub al-Khali, or "Empty Quarter," of Saudi Arabia is thought to contain deposits of limestone and gravel, but no one is certain because it has not yet been fully explored.

# THE POLAR REGIONS

## Antarctica

**Geography** **Location:** centered on the South Pole and situated almost entirely within the Antarctic Circle at 66½°S. **Land:** total area: about 5,404,000 sq. mi. (14,000,000 sq km). **Land boundary:** none; bordered by South Atlantic, Indian, and South Pacific oceans. **Temperature:** varies with location and altitude. East Antarctica is coldest; Antarctic peninsula in the west is mildest; mean annual temperature of the interior regions is –57°C (–71°F); mean temperatures at the coastal McMurdo station range from –28°C (–18°F) in August to –3°C (27°F) in January. **Daylight/darkness:** six months of continuous daylight from mid-September to mid-March; six months of continuous darkness from mid-March to mid-September. **Coastline:** undetermined. **Comparative area:** slightly less than 1.5 times size of U.S.; second smallest continent, after Australia. **Land use:** 0% cultivated, 0% forests, 0% lakes. **Major cities:** none.

**People** **Population:** no indigenous inhabitants; staffing of research stations varies seasonally; summer (January) pop.: approx. 3,300; winter (July) pop.: approx. 1,148.

**Government** **Type:** Antarctic Treaty (see below). **Natural Resources:** estimates are imprecise. May contain some 900 major mineral deposits, but only about 20 are in ice-free areas. Quantities of iron ore, coal, and offshore deposits of oil and natural gas are basically inaccessible. Small amounts of copper, chromium, platinum, nickel, gold, and hydrocarbons. **The Land:** Some 200 million years ago, Ant-

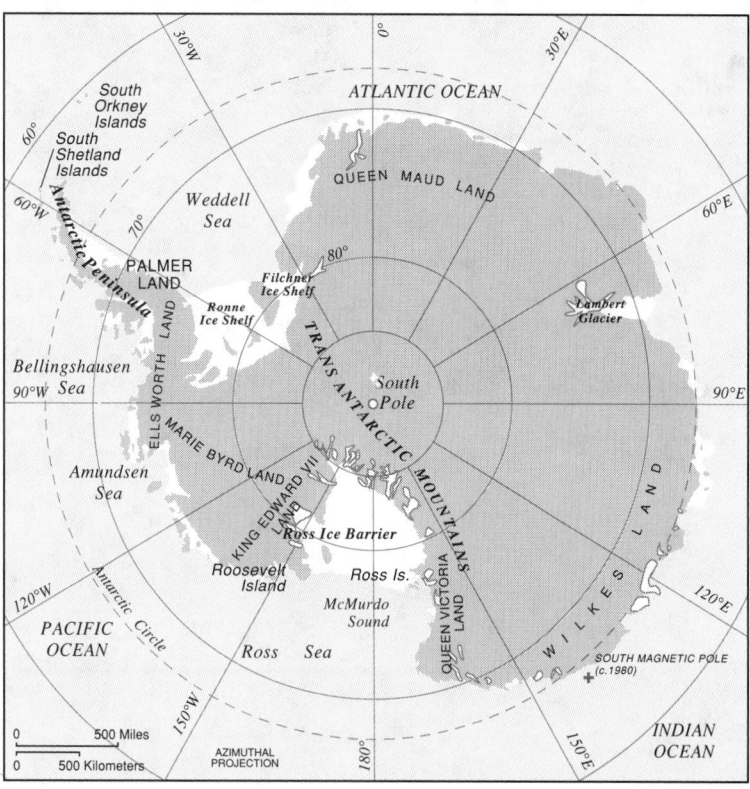

ANTARCTICA

arctica was joined to South America, Africa, India, and Australia as one large continent. Geological changes caused the breakup into separate continents. Studies indicate that Antarctica once had a tropical environment, but that its present ice form is at least 20 million years old. Approximately 98% of the continent

is covered by ice; it contains about 90% of the world's ice and 70% of the fresh water.

Elevations average from 6,600–13,200 ft. (2,000–4,000 m); mountain ranges, up to 16,500 ft. (5,000 m) high. Ice-free coastal areas include parts of southern Victoria Land, Wilkes Land, and Ross Island. The Antarctic

ATLANTIC
OCEAN

North Pole
○
ARCTIC
OCEAN

Chukchi
Sea

Bering
Sea

Barents
Sea

Kara
Sea

Laptev
Sea

Kamchatka
Peninsula

Arctic Circle

Sea of
Okhotsk

Moscow

SOVIET UNION
(U.S.S.R.)

Yakutsk

Sakhalin

URAL MTS.

Lena

Ekaterinburg
Chelyabinsk

Angara

Krasnoyarsk

Lake
Baikal

Amur

Harbin

Vladivostok

JAPAN

Omsk

Novosibirsk

Irkutsk

Sea Of
Japan

Tokyo

Yokohama

Black Sea

Ankara

Ural

Irtysh

Ob

NORTH
KOREA

Kyoto

TURKEY

CYPRUS

Caspian Sea

Aral
Sea

Lake
Balkhash

Ulan Bator

MONGOLIA

Pyongyang

Seoul

Osaka

LEBANON

SYRIA

Syr Darya

Tashkent

Alma-Ata

Beijing

SOUTH
KOREA

ISRAEL

IRAQ

Amu Darya

Frunze

Yellow
Sea

JORDAN

Ashkhabad

TAKLIMAKAN
DESERT

CHINA

Shanghai

IRAN

AFGHANISTAN

Dushanbe

East
China
Sea

Dushanbe

KUWAIT

Kabul

Hwang He
(Yellow)

Chungking

Wuhan

Yangtze

Taipei

BAHRAIN

Islamabad

Tibet

Salween

TAIWAN

Tropic of Cancer

QATAR

Lahore

Hsi
Chiang

Guangzhou
(Canton)

SAUDI
ARABIA

UNITED
ARAB
EMIRATES

OMAN

PAKISTAN

Delhi

NEPAL

Brahmaputra

BHUTAN

HONG KONG (UK)

MACAU
(Port.)

Karachi

New
Delhi

Kathmandu

Timphu

Dhaka

Hanoi

Manila

Calcutta

Mandalay

LAOS

YEMEN

INDIA

BANGLA-
DESH

MYANMAR

Vientiane

VIETNAM

PHILIPPINES

Gulf of Aden

Arabian
Sea

Bombay

THAILAND

South
China
Sea

Davao

SOMALIA

Yangon

Bangkok

CAMBODIA

Madras

Andaman
Islands
(India)

Phnom
Penh

Ho Chi Minh City
(Saigon)

Bandar Seri
Bagawan

BRUNEI

Laccadive
Islands
(India)

SRI LANKA

Nicobar
Islands
(India)

Medan

MALAYSIA

Celebes

Colombo
Male

Kuala Lumpur

SINGAPORE

Borneo

MALDIVES

INDONESIA

SEYCHELLES

Sumatra

Jakarta

Surabaya

Java

Bali

COMOROS

BRITISH INDIAN
OCEAN TERRITORY
(UK)

CHRISTMAS ISLAND
(Australia)

MADAGASCAR

INDIAN OCEAN

COCOS ISLANDS
(Australia)

0         1000 miles

RÉUNION
(France)

MAURITIUS

AZIMUTHAL EQUAL-AREA PROJECTION

0      1500 km

AUSTRALIA

PACIFIC
OCEAN

Equator

ice sheet averages 7,090 ft. (2,160 m) in depth and is 15,670 ft. (4,776 m) deep at its thickest point. Altitude at the South Pole is about 9,800 ft. (3,000 m).

**Land/sea life:** Land life includes bacteria, lichens, mosses, two kinds of flowering plants in the ice-free areas, penguins, and some flying birds. Sea life includes several types of seals and whales, many of which were hunted to near extinction, but are now protected by international conventions.

**Exploration:** In 1772–75 British Capt. James Cook circumnavigated the continent without sighting land. U.S. Capt. John Davis made the first known landing on the continent on Feb. 7, 1821. In 1908 the United Kingdom became the first nation to claim a "slice" of the continent, subsequently followed by claims from New Zealand (1923), France (1924), Australia (1933), Norway (1939), Chile (1940), and Argentina (1943). The United States and the USSR have never claimed any Antarctica territory. Claims made by other nations are not recognized by other countries or the United Nations.

In 1911 Capt. Robert F. Scott and Roald Amundsen of Norway began a "race to the pole." Amundsen's party arrived at the South Pole on Dec. 14, 1911, while Scott located the pole on Jan. 18, 1912.

**Scientific research:** The greatest scientific study ever conducted in Antarctica occurred in 1957–58, when 67 nations participated in the International Geophysical Year (IGY). Twelve countries established more than 50 stations to study the effects of the continent's huge ice mass on global weather, the oceans, the aurora australis, and the ionosphere. During the late 1980s, research was focused on the study of the ozone depletion in the stratosphere—called the ozone hole—which allows high levels of potentially harmful ultraviolet radiation to reach the Earth's surface.

In 1987 the following countries maintained research stations year-round: USSR (7), Argentina (6), UK (4), Chile (3), Australia (3), United States (3), Japan (2), and one each by Brazil, China, West Germany, France, India, Italy, New Zealand, Poland, and South Africa.

**Antarctica Treaty:** Signed in 1959 by the 12 International Geophysical Year nations (in force as of June 23, 1961), it establishes a legal framework for exploration and research; the treaty is to be reviewed and revised in the fall of 1991. The treaty states that the area is to be used for peaceful purposes only, and military activity such as weapons testing is prohibited; calls for freedom of scientific investigation and cooperation, and a free exchange of information and personnel; nuclear explosions or disposal of radioactive wastes is forbidden; and treaty-state observers have free access, including aerial observation, to any area and may inspect all stations, installations, and equipment.

Two types of members: consultative (voting) members conduct research programs and acceding (nonvoting) members agree to the terms of the treaty. The original 12 signatories: Argentina, Australia, Belgium, Chile, France, Japan, New Zealand, Norway, South Africa,

United Kingdom, United States, and the USSR. Other consultative members that conduct Antarctic research: Poland (1977), West Germany (1981), Brazil (1983), India (1983), China (1985), Uruguay (1985), Italy (1987), and East Germany (1987). As of May 1989, there were also 24 acceding (nonvoting) members.

> *"Great God!*
> *This is an*
> *awful place."*
>
> —Capt. Robert Falcon Scott,
> *Journal,* upon reaching
> the South Pole (1912)

## The Arctic

**Geography    Total area:** The Arctic Regions comprise all the lands north of the Arctic Circle—66°30′N—including the northern reaches of Asia, Europe, and North America, the Arctic Ocean, and its islands. In terms of climate, geography, and culture this demarcation is relatively insignificant, but within the Arctic Circle there is at least one 24-hour period during which the sun never sets (summer solstice), and one in which it never rises (winter solstice). The Arctic Ocean is the fourth largest after the Pacific, Atlantic, and Indian; its primary marginal seas are the Beaufort Sea, Baffin Bay, Greenland Sea, Barents Sea, Kara Sea, Laptev Sea, East Siberian Sea, and Chukchi Sea. The main island groups are the Canadian Arctic Archipelago (550,000 sq. mi.; 1,424,483 sq km), Greenland (840,000 sq. mi.; 2,175,590 sq km), Novaya Zemlya (31,000 sq. mi.; 80,290 sq km), and Svalbard (24,000 sq. mi.; 62,160 sq km). Governments with territory north of the Arctic Circle are Canada, the U.S., the USSR, Finland, Sweden, Norway, and Denmark (Greenland). The Arctic Ocean is 5,430,505 sq. mi. (14,068,000 sq km), slightly more than 1.5 times the size of the U.S. **Coastline:** 17,525 mi. (45,389 km).

**Climate:** The dominant fact of life is the frigid conditions: persistent cold and relatively modest annual temperature ranges; winters characterized by continuous darkness, cold and stable weather conditions, and clear skies; summers characterized by continuous daylight, damp and foggy weather, and weak cyclones with rain or snow. Between 60°N and 75°N there is seasonal freezing, while north of 75°N there is permanent ice. In North America, temperatures during the colder months average −25°F (−31°C), while Siberia is somewhat colder at −35°F (−37°C). **Terrain:** The central surface is covered by a perennial drifting polar ice cap which averages about three meters thick, although pressure ridges may be three times that size. It drifts in a clockwise pattern in the Beaufort Gyral Stream, but exhibits nearly straight-line movement from the New Siberian Islands (USSR) to the Denmark Strait (between Greenland and Iceland). The ice pack is surrounded by open

seas during the summer, but more than doubles in size during the winter and extends to the encircling land masses. The ocean floor is about 50% continental shelf (the highest percentage of any ocean) with the remainder a central basin interrupted by three submarine ridges (the Alpha Cordillera, Nansen Cordillera, and Lomosov Ridge). The maximum depth is 15,670 ft. (4,776 m) in the Fram Basin. **Natural resources:** In the Arctic Ocean there are sand and gravel aggregates, placer deposits, polymetallic nodules, oil and gas fields, fish, marine mammals (seals and whales). **Environment:** Endangered marine species include walruses and whales; ice islands occasionally break away from northern Ellesmere Island; icebergs calved from western Greenland and extreme northeastern Canada; snow cover over the frozen ocean lasts about 10 months, with maximum coverage of 20–50 cm in March or April; permafrost in islands; virtually ice-locked from October to June; fragile ecosystem slow to change and slow to recover from disruptions or damage.

**Population** Ethnologists distinguish three native cultural areas—the Western Arctic, including Eskimo peoples (from the east coast of Greenland to Alaska) and Aleuts; Paleo-Siberian, including the Chukchi and Eskimo of Eastern Asia; and Eurasian Arctic, including some Chukchi, Yakut, Nenets, and Lapps. Today, however, the vast majority of the people living and working within the Arctic Circle are non-native peoples in industry or scientific enterprises.

**Economy Overview:** While there is a fair amount of economic activity in the continental portions of the Arctic—principally extractive industries in Siberia, northern Canada, and Alaska's North Slope—conditions in the numerous Arctic islands all but prevent significant development there. Norwegian and Soviet miners extract about 1 million tons of coal per year from mines on Svalbard, and in Greenland there are large deposits of cryolite, lead, and other minerals, but only lead can be mined economically. Economic activity in the Arctic Ocean is limited to the exploitation of natural resources including crude oil, natural gas, fishing, and sealing.

**Communications Ports:** Churchill (Canada), Narvik (Norway), Murmansk (USSR), Prudhoe Bay (U.S.). **Telecommunications:** No submarine cables. **Transportation:** There is a sparse network of air, ocean, river, and land routes. The Arctic provides the shortest marine link between the extremes of eastern and western USSR. The two major waterways are the Northwest Passage, in North America, and the Northern Sea Route, in Asia, but ships are subject to superstructure icing from October to May. The U.S. and the USSR operate floating research stations. Access to the Arctic Ocean from the Pacific Ocean is through the Bering Strait; from the Atlantic, through the Davis Strait (bet. Canada and Greenland), the Denmark Strait (bet. Greenland and Iceland), or the Norwegian Sea (bet. Iceland and Norway).

SOUTH AMERICA

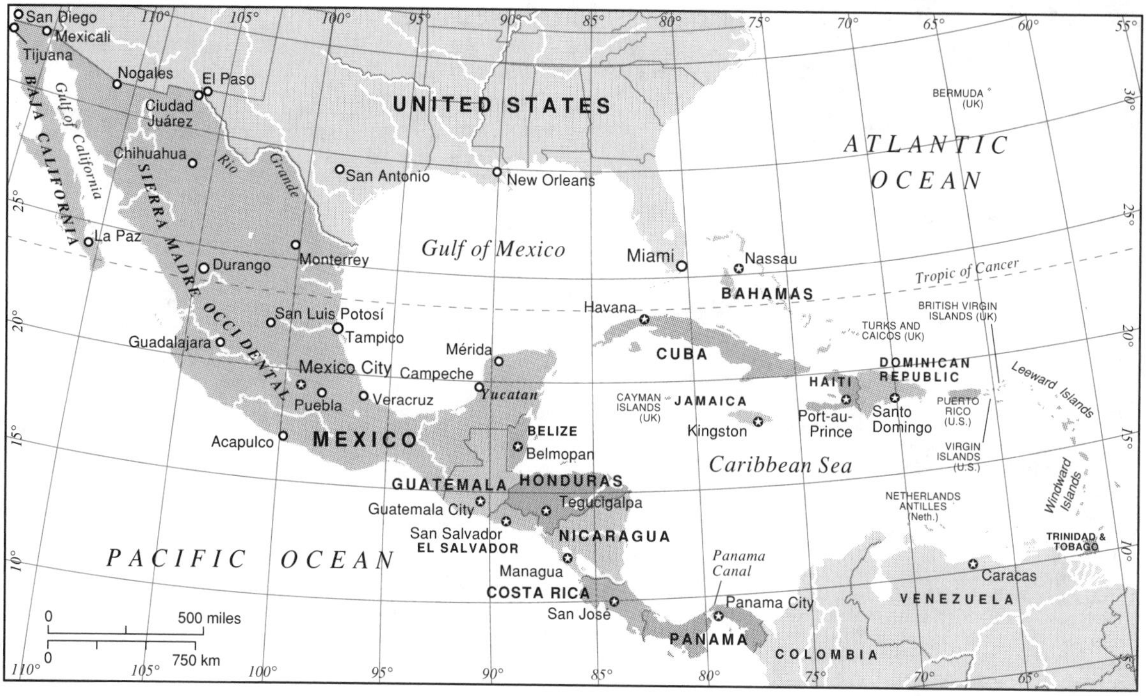

**Top map:**

San Diego
Mexicali
Tijuana
Nogales
El Paso
Ciudad Juárez
Chihuahua
San Antonio
New Orleans
UNITED STATES
BERMUDA (UK)
ATLANTIC OCEAN
BAJA CALIFORNIA
Gulf of California
SIERRA MADRE OCCIDENTAL
Rio Grande
La Paz
Durango
Monterrey
Gulf of Mexico
Miami
Nassau
Tropic of Cancer
BAHAMAS
Havana
BRITISH VIRGIN ISLANDS (UK)
TURKS AND CAICOS (UK)
Leeward Islands
San Luis Potosí
Tampico
Guadalajara
Mérida
CUBA
HAITI
DOMINICAN REPUBLIC
Mexico City
Campeche
Yucatan
CAYMAN ISLANDS (UK)
JAMAICA
Port-au-Prince
Santo Domingo
PUERTO RICO (U.S.)
Puebla
Veracruz
Acapulco
MEXICO
BELIZE
Belmopan
Kingston
VIRGIN ISLANDS (U.S.)
Caribbean Sea
Windward Islands
GUATEMALA
HONDURAS
Tegucigalpa
NETHERLANDS ANTILLES (Neth.)
TRINIDAD & TOBAGO
Guatemala City
San Salvador
EL SALVADOR
NICARAGUA
Panama Canal
PACIFIC OCEAN
Managua
COSTA RICA
San José
Panama City
VENEZUELA
Caracas
PANAMA
COLOMBIA

0 — 500 miles
0 — 750 km

POLYCONIC PROJECTION

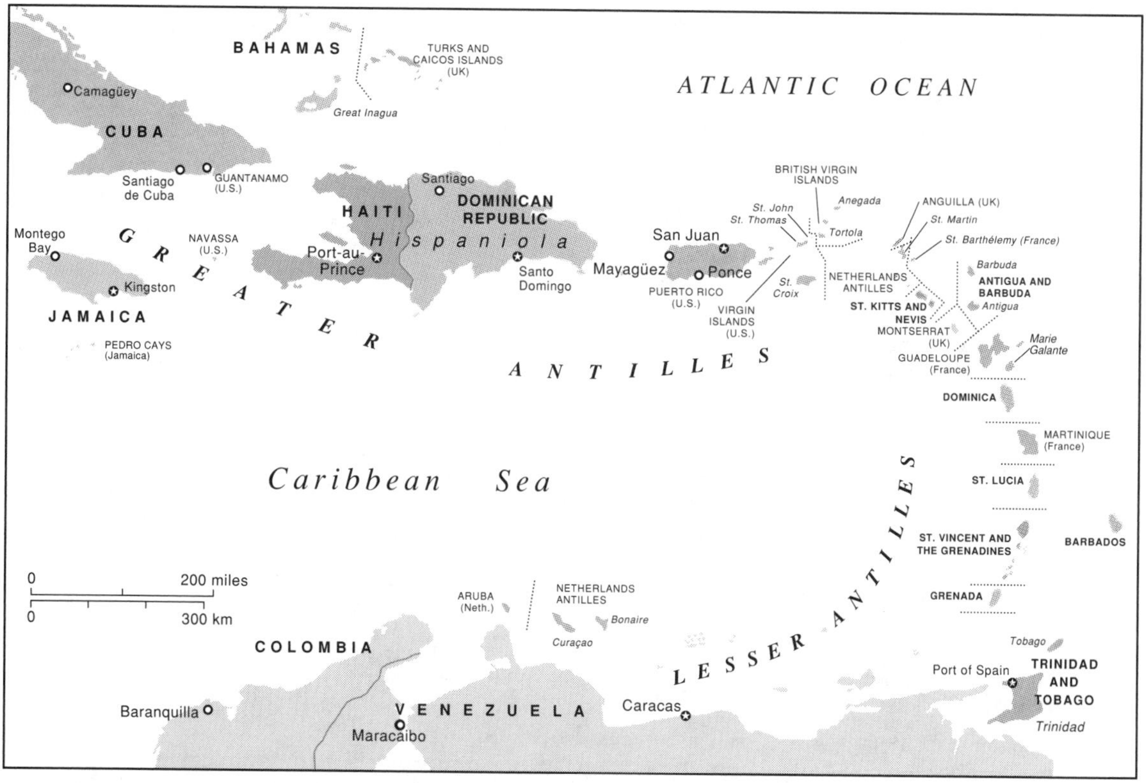

**Bottom map:**

BAHAMAS
TURKS AND CAICOS ISLANDS (UK)
ATLANTIC OCEAN
Camagüey
CUBA
Great Inagua
Santiago de Cuba
GUANTANAMO (U.S.)
Santiago
HAITI
DOMINICAN REPUBLIC
Hispaniola
San Juan
BRITISH VIRGIN ISLANDS
Anegada
ANGUILLA (UK)
St. John
St. Thomas
Tortola
St. Martin
St. Barthélemy (France)
Montego Bay
NAVASSA (U.S.)
Port-au-Prince
Santo Domingo
Mayagüez
Ponce
PUERTO RICO (U.S.)
St. Croix
NETHERLANDS ANTILLES
Barbuda
ANTIGUA AND BARBUDA
Kingston
G R E A T E R
VIRGIN ISLANDS (U.S.)
Antigua
ST. KITTS AND NEVIS
MONTSERRAT (UK)
Marie Galante
JAMAICA
PEDRO CAYS (Jamaica)
A N T I L L E S
GUADELOUPE (France)
DOMINICA
MARTINIQUE (France)
Caribbean Sea
ST. LUCIA
ST. VINCENT AND THE GRENADINES
BARBADOS
L E S S E R   A N T I L L E S
GRENADA
0 — 200 miles
0 — 300 km
ARUBA (Neth.)
NETHERLANDS ANTILLES
Bonaire
Curaçao
Tobago
Port of Spain
TRINIDAD AND TOBAGO
COLOMBIA
VENEZUELA
Caracas
Baranquilla
Maracaibo
Trinidad

CENTRAL AMERICA AND CARIBBEAN

# Climate and Weather

## CLIMATES OF THE WORLD

Knowing the similarities and differences between climates in various parts of the world helps us understand many things about our planet: why people live where they do; how they make their living; the problems and potentials of their land. Climates are very complex, however, and no climatic classification is ideal. The most commonly used classification was developed more than 50 years ago by a German climatologist, Wladimir Koppen. The Koppen system uses temperature and precipitation as the major criteria for grouping climates. Boundaries between climatic zones are determined by the limits of where certain plants grow.

The five major climatic zones are known by the capital letters **A, B, C, D,** and **E**; each major zone has subzones. High-altitude areas are sometimes shown with the letter **H** because their climates are so complex that small maps cannot show all the detail. (In the text that follows, **R** stands for the annual rainfall in centimeters; **T** is the average annual temperature in degrees Celsius.)

**A Humid tropical climates** The average temperature of every month is 64°F (18°C) or higher. There is no winter.
**Af** *Rain forest.* The driest month has at least 2.4 inches (6 cm) of rain. The Amazon basin is an example of an **Af** climate.
**Am** *Monsoon.* Similar to **Af**, but with a short dry season. The amount of rainfall in the driest month is less than 2.4 inches (6 cm), but equal to or greater than 10 – (R/25). The southwestern coast of India is an example of an **Am** climate.
**Aw** *Savanna.* There is a well-defined dry season in the winter. The amount of rainfall in the driest month is less than 10 – (R/25). The Brazilian highlands are a large area with an **Aw** climate.
**As** (Rare) There is a well-defined dry season in the summer.

**B Dry climates** Annual rainfall is less than annual potential evaporation. The boundary between dry areas and humid areas is R < 2T + 28 when at least 70% of the rainfall occurs in the warmer six months; R < 2T when at least 70% of the rainfall occurs in the cooler six months; or R < 2T + 14 when neither half of the year receives at least 70% of the total annual rainfall.
**BS** *Steppe.* The boundary between steppe and desert is half of the dry/humid boundary. Steppes border many of the world's large deserts.
**BSh** *Low-latitude steppe.* The average annual temperature is at least 64°F (18°C).
**BSk** *Mid-latitude steppe.* The average annual

## CLIMATE OF SELECTED WORLD CITIES

Average highest and lowest temperatures for selected months in degrees Fahrenheit. Precipitation is the average monthly amount in inches of rainfall equivalent.

| City | January Temp. Max. | January Temp. Min. | January Avg. precip. | April Temp. Max. | April Temp. Min. | April Avg. precip. | July Temp. Max. | July Temp. Min. | July Avg. precip. | October Temp. Max. | October Temp. Min. | October Avg. precip. |
|---|---|---|---|---|---|---|---|---|---|---|---|---|
| Accra, Ghana | 87° | 73° | 0.6" | 88° | 76° | 3.2" | 81° | 73° | 1.8" | 85° | 74° | 2.5" |
| Amsterdam, Netherlands | 40 | 34 | 2.0 | 52 | 43 | 1.6 | 69 | 59 | 2.6 | 56 | 48 | 2.8 |
| Athens, Greece | 54 | 42 | 2.2 | 67 | 52 | 0.8 | 90 | 72 | 0.2 | 74 | 60 | 1.7 |
| Baghdad, Iraq | 60 | 39 | 0.9 | 85 | 57 | 0.5 | 110 | 76 | trace | 92 | 61 | 0.1 |
| Bangkok, Thailand | 89 | 67 | 0.2 | 95 | 78 | 2.3 | 90 | 76 | 6.9 | 88 | 76 | 9.9 |
| Beirut, Lebanon | 62 | 51 | 7.5 | 72 | 58 | 2.2 | 87 | 73 | trace | 81 | 69 | 2.0 |
| Belfast, United Kingdom | 42 | 34 | 4.2 | 53 | 38 | 2.4 | 65 | 52 | 3.5 | 55 | 44 | 3.8 |
| Berlin, Germany | 35 | 26 | 1.9 | 55 | 38 | 1.7 | 74 | 55 | 3.1 | 55 | 41 | 1.7 |
| Bombay, India | 88 | 62 | 0.1 | 93 | 74 | trace | 88 | 75 | 24.3 | 93 | 73 | 2.5 |
| Budapest, Hungary | 35 | 26 | 1.5 | 62 | 44 | 2.0 | 82 | 61 | 2.0 | 61 | 45 | 2.1 |
| Buenos Aires, Argentina | 85 | 63 | 3.1 | 72 | 54 | 3.5 | 57 | 42 | 2.2 | 69 | 50 | 3.4 |
| Cairo, Egypt | 65 | 47 | 0.2 | 83 | 57 | 0.1 | 96 | 70 | 0.0 | 86 | 65 | trace |
| Calcutta, India | 80 | 55 | 0.4 | 97 | 76 | 1.7 | 90 | 79 | 12.8 | 89 | 74 | 4.5 |
| Canton (Guangzhov), China | 65 | 49 | 0.9 | 77 | 65 | 6.8 | 91 | 77 | 8.1 | 85 | 67 | 3.4 |
| Cape Town, South Africa | 78 | 60 | 0.6 | 72 | 53 | 1.9 | 63 | 45 | 3.5 | 70 | 52 | 1.2 |
| Casablanca, Morocco | 63 | 48 | 2.1 | 69 | 52 | 1.4 | 79 | 65 | 0.0 | 76 | 58 | 1.5 |
| Christchurch, New Zealand | 70 | 53 | 2.2 | 62 | 45 | 1.9 | 50 | 35 | 2.7 | 62 | 44 | 1.7 |
| Colombo, Sri Lanka | 86 | 72 | 3.5 | 88 | 76 | 9.1 | 85 | 77 | 5.3 | 85 | 75 | 13.7 |
| Copenhagen, Denmark | 36 | 29 | 1.6 | 50 | 37 | 1.7 | 72 | 55 | 2.2 | 53 | 42 | 2.1 |
| Dakha, Bangladesh | 77 | 56 | 0.3 | 92 | 74 | 5.4 | 85 | 77 | 5.3 | 85 | 75 | 13.7 |
| Dakar, Senegal | 79 | 64 | trace | 81 | 65 | trace | 88 | 76 | 3.5 | 89 | 76 | 1.5 |
| Dublin, Ireland | 47 | 35 | 2.7 | 54 | 38 | 1.9 | 67 | 51 | 2.8 | 57 | 43 | 2.7 |
| Edinburgh, United Kingdom | 43 | 35 | 2.5 | 50 | 39 | 1.6 | 65 | 52 | 3.1 | 53 | 44 | 2.9 |
| Geneva, Switzerland | 39 | 29 | 1.9 | 58 | 41 | 2.5 | 77 | 58 | 2.9 | 58 | 44 | 3.8 |
| Hanoi, Vietnam | 68 | 58 | 0.8 | 80 | 79 | 3.6 | 92 | 79 | 11.9 | 94 | 72 | 3.5 |
| Hong Kong | 64 | 56 | 1.3 | 75 | 67 | 5.4 | 87 | 78 | 15.0 | 81 | 73 | 4.5 |
| Istanbul, Turkey | 45 | 36 | 3.7 | 61 | 45 | 1.9 | 81 | 65 | 1.7 | 67 | 54 | 3.8 |
| Jakarta, Indonesia | 84 | 74 | 11.8 | 87 | 75 | 5.8 | 87 | 73 | 2.5 | 87 | 74 | 4.4 |
| Jerusalem, Israel | 55 | 41 | 5.1 | 73 | 50 | 0.9 | 87 | 63 | 0.0 | 81 | 59 | 0.3 |
| Kabul, Afghanistan | 36 | 18 | 1.3 | 66 | 43 | 3.3 | 92 | 61 | 0.1 | 73 | 64 | 0.4 |
| Karachi, Pakistan | 77 | 55 | 0.5 | 90 | 73 | 0.1 | 91 | 81 | 3.2 | 91 | 72 | 0.1 |
| Kinshasa, Zaire | 87 | 70 | 5.3 | 89 | 71 | 7.7 | 81 | 64 | 0.1 | 88 | 70 | 4.7 |
| Lagos, Nigeria | 88 | 74 | 1.1 | 89 | 77 | 5.9 | 83 | 74 | 11.0 | 85 | 74 | 8.1 |
| Leningrad, USSR | 23 | 12 | 1.0 | 45 | 31 | 1.0 | 71 | 57 | 2.5 | 45 | 37 | 1.8 |
| Lima, Peru | 82 | 66 | 0.1 | 80 | 63 | trace | 67 | 57 | 0.3 | 71 | 58 | 0.1 |
| Lisbon, Portugal | 56 | 46 | 3.3 | 64 | 52 | 2.4 | 79 | 63 | 0.2 | 69 | 57 | 3.1 |
| London, United Kingdom | 44 | 35 | 2.0 | 56 | 40 | 1.8 | 73 | 55 | 2.0 | 58 | 44 | 2.3 |
| Madrid, Spain | 47 | 33 | 1.1 | 64 | 44 | 1.7 | 87 | 62 | 0.4 | 66 | 48 | 1.9 |
| Manila, Philippines | 87 | 72 | 4.8 | 91 | 73 | 5.8 | 88 | 73 | 6.5 | 89 | 73 | 7.9 |
| Melbourne, Australia | 78 | 57 | 1.9 | 68 | 51 | 2.3 | 56 | 42 | 1.9 | 67 | 48 | 2.6 |
| Mexico City, Mexico | 66 | 42 | 0.2 | 78 | 52 | 0.7 | 74 | 54 | 4.5 | 70 | 50 | 1.6 |
| Montreal, Canada | 21 | 6 | 3.8 | 50 | 33 | 2.6 | 78 | 61 | 3.7 | 54 | 40 | 3.4 |
| Moscow, USSR | 21 | 9 | 1.5 | 47 | 31 | 1.9 | 76 | 55 | 3.0 | 46 | 34 | 2.7 |
| Nairobi, Kenya | 77 | 54 | 1.5 | 75 | 58 | 8.3 | 69 | 51 | 0.6 | 76 | 55 | 2.1 |
| Oslo, Norway | 30 | 20 | 1.7 | 50 | 34 | 1.6 | 73 | 56 | 2.9 | 49 | 37 | 2.9 |
| Paris, France | 42 | 32 | 1.5 | 60 | 41 | 1.7 | 76 | 55 | 2.1 | 59 | 44 | 2.2 |
| Prague, Czechoslovakia | 34 | 25 | 0.9 | 55 | 40 | 1.5 | 74 | 58 | 2.6 | 54 | 44 | 1.2 |
| Reykjavik, Iceland | 36 | 28 | 4.0 | 43 | 33 | 2.1 | 58 | 48 | 2.0 | 44 | 36 | 3.4 |
| Rio de Janeiro, Brazil | 84 | 73 | 4.9 | 80 | 69 | 4.2 | 75 | 63 | 1.6 | 77 | 66 | 3.1 |
| Riyadh, Saudi Arabia | 70 | 46 | 0.1 | 89 | 64 | 1.0 | 107 | 78 | 0.0 | 94 | 61 | 0.0 |
| Rome, Italy | 54 | 39 | 3.3 | 68 | 46 | 2.0 | 88 | 64 | 0.4 | 73 | 53 | 4.3 |
| Santiago, Chile | 85 | 53 | 0.1 | 74 | 45 | 0.5 | 59 | 37 | 3.0 | 72 | 45 | 0.6 |
| Seoul, South Korea | 32 | 15 | 1.2 | 62 | 41 | 3.0 | 84 | 70 | 14.8 | 67 | 45 | 1.6 |
| Shanghai, China | 47 | 32 | 1.9 | 67 | 49 | 3.6 | 91 | 75 | 5.8 | 75 | 56 | 2.9 |
| Singapore | 86 | 73 | 9.9 | 88 | 75 | 7.4 | 88 | 75 | 6.7 | 87 | 74 | 8.2 |
| Stockholm, Sweden | 31 | 23 | 1.5 | 45 | 32 | 1.5 | 70 | 55 | 2.8 | 48 | 39 | 2.1 |
| Sydney, Australia | 78 | 65 | 3.5 | 71 | 58 | 5.3 | 60 | 46 | 4.6 | 71 | 56 | 2.8 |
| Tahiti, French Polynesia | 89 | 72 | 13.2 | 89 | 72 | 6.8 | 86 | 68 | 2.6 | 87 | 70 | 3.4 |
| Taipei, Taiwan | 66 | 53 | 3.8 | 77 | 64 | 5.3 | 92 | 76 | 8.8 | 80 | 68 | 5.5 |
| Tehran, Iran | 45 | 27 | 1.8 | 71 | 49 | 1.4 | 99 | 72 | 0.1 | 76 | 53 | 0.3 |
| Tokyo, Japan | 47 | 29 | 1.9 | 63 | 46 | 5.3 | 83 | 70 | 5.6 | 69 | 55 | 8.2 |
| Toronto, Canada | 30 | 16 | 2.7 | 50 | 34 | 2.5 | 79 | 59 | 3.0 | 56 | 40 | 2.4 |
| Warsaw, Poland | 30 | 21 | 1.2 | 54 | 38 | 1.5 | 75 | 56 | 3.0 | 54 | 41 | 1.7 |
| Wellington, New Zealand | 69 | 56 | 3.2 | 63 | 51 | 3.8 | 53 | 42 | 5.4 | 60 | 48 | 4.0 |

**Source:** U.S. Dept. of Commerce, *Climates of the World* (1972).

## CLIMATES OF SELECTED U.S. CITIES

If you plan to travel or move to a different city, it is helpful to know the normal daily high temperature for each month (in degrees Fahrenheit) and the normal monthly rain or snow (precipitation). Precipitation data are based on rain and melted snow or ice. The third line shows snow and ice pellets.

| City | Jan. | Feb. | Mar. | Apr. | May | June | July | Aug. | Sept. | Oct. | Nov. | Dec. |
|---|---|---|---|---|---|---|---|---|---|---|---|---|
| Baltimore, Md. | 41° | 44° | 53° | 65° | 74° | 83° | 87° | 86° | 79° | 68° | 56° | 45° |
| | 3.0" | 3.0" | 3.7" | 3.4" | 3.4" | 3.8" | 3.9" | 4.6" | 3.5" | 3.1" | 3.1" | 3.4" |
| | 6.1" | 7.2" | 3.9" | 0.1" | T | — | — | — | — | — | 1.1" | 3.5" |
| Boston, Mass. | 36° | 38° | 45° | 57° | 67° | 77° | 82° | 80° | 72° | 63° | 52° | 40° |
| | 4.0" | 3.7" | 4.1" | 3.7" | 3.5" | 2.9" | 2.7" | 3.7" | 3.4" | 3.4" | 4.2" | 4.5" |
| | 12.5" | 11.4" | 7.6" | 1.0" | — | — | — | — | — | — | 1.4" | 7.6" |
| Chicago, Ill. | 29° | 34° | 44° | 59° | 70° | 79° | 83° | 82° | 76° | 64° | 48° | 35° |
| | 1.6" | 1.3" | 2.6" | 3.7" | 3.2" | 4.1" | 3.6" | 3.5" | 3.4" | 2.3" | 2.1" | 2.1" |
| | 11.4" | 7.8" | 7.1" | 1.9" | 0.1" | — | — | — | — | T | 2.1" | 9.1" |
| Cleveland, Ohio | 33° | 35° | 45° | 58° | 69° | 78° | 82° | 80° | 74° | 63° | 49° | 38° |
| | 2.5" | 2.2" | 3.0" | 3.3" | 3.5" | 3.4" | 3.4" | 3.4" | 2.9" | 2.5" | 2.8" | 2.8" |
| | 12.6" | 11.5" | 10.2" | 2.3" | 0.1" | — | — | — | T | 0.7" | 5.1" | 11.6" |
| Columbus, Ohio | 35° | 38° | 49° | 62° | 73° | 81° | 84° | 83° | 77° | 65° | 51° | 39° |
| | 2.8" | 2.2" | 3.2" | 3.4" | 3.8" | 4.0" | 4.0" | 3.7" | 2.8" | 1.9" | 2.6" | 2.6" |
| | 8.6" | 6.3" | 4.5" | 1.0" | T | — | — | — | — | T | 2.5" | 5.6" |
| Dallas–Ft. Worth, Tex. | 54° | 59° | 67° | 77° | 84° | 93° | 98° | 97° | 90° | 80° | 66° | 58° |
| | 1.7" | 1.9" | 2.4" | 3.6" | 4.3" | 2.6" | 2.0" | 1.8" | 3.3" | 2.5" | 1.8" | 1.7" |
| | 1.4" | 1.0" | 0.2" | — | — | — | — | — | — | — | 0.1" | 0.3" |
| Denver, Colo. | 43° | 47° | 51° | 61° | 71° | 82° | 88° | 86° | 78° | 67° | 52° | 46° |
| | 0.5" | 0.7" | 1.2" | 1.8" | 2.5" | 1.6" | 1.9" | 1.5" | 1.2" | 1.0" | 0.8" | 0.6" |
| | 7.8" | 7.5" | 12.8" | 9.3" | 1.8" | — | — | — | 1.7" | 3.7" | 8.4" | 7.3" |
| Detroit, Mich. | 31° | 34° | 43° | 58° | 69° | 79° | 83° | 82° | 74° | 63° | 48° | 35° |
| | 1.9" | 1.7" | 2.5" | 3.2" | 2.8" | 3.4" | 3.1" | 3.2" | 2.3" | 2.1" | 2.3" | 2.5" |
| | 10.4" | 8.7" | 7.0" | 1.8" | T | — | — | — | — | 0.1" | 3.3" | 10.7" |
| El Paso, Tex. | 58° | 63° | 70° | 79° | 87° | 96° | 95° | 93° | 88° | 79° | 66° | 58° |
| | 0.4" | 0.5" | 0.3" | 0.2" | 0.2" | 0.6" | 1.6" | 1.2" | 1.4" | 0.7" | 0.3" | 0.4" |
| | 1.4" | 0.8" | 0.4" | 0.4" | — | — | — | — | — | — | 1.0" | 1.8" |
| Houston, Tex. | 62° | 66° | 72° | 79° | 85° | 91° | 94° | 93° | 89° | 82° | 72° | 65° |
| | 3.2" | 2.3" | 3.3" | 2.7" | 4.2" | 4.7" | 4.1" | 3.3" | 4.9" | 3.7" | 3.4" | 3.7" |
| | 0.2" | 0.2" | — | — | — | — | — | — | — | — | T | T |
| Indianapolis, Ind. | 34° | 39° | 49° | 63° | 73° | 82° | 85° | 84° | 78° | 66° | 51° | 39° |
| | 2.7" | 2.5" | 3.6" | 3.7" | 3.7" | 4.0" | 4.3" | 3.5" | 2.7" | 2.5" | 3.0" | 3.0" |
| | 6.3" | 5.9" | 3.5" | 0.5" | T | — | — | — | — | T | 1.9" | 4.8" |
| Jacksonville, Fla. | 65° | 67° | 73° | 79° | 85° | 89° | 91° | 90° | 87° | 80° | 72° | 66° |
| | 3.1" | 3.5" | 3.6" | 3.1" | 3.5" | 5.3" | 6.5" | 7.3" | 7.6" | 3.9" | 1.9" | 2.6" |
| | T | | | | | | | | | | | |

| City | Jan. | Feb. | Mar. | Apr. | May | June | July | Aug. | Sept. | Oct. | Nov. | Dec. |
|---|---|---|---|---|---|---|---|---|---|---|---|---|
| Los Angeles, Calif. | 67° | 69° | 69° | 71° | 73° | 78° | 84° | 84° | 83° | 79° | 73° | 68° |
| | 3.7" | 3.0" | 2.4" | 1.2" | 0.2" | — | — | 0.1" | 0.3" | 0.2" | 1.9" | 2.0" |
| | — | T | — | — | — | — | — | — | — | — | — | T |
| Memphis, Tenn. | 48° | 53° | 61° | 73° | 81° | 88° | 92° | 92° | 90° | 84° | 75° | 61° |
| | 4.6" | 4.3" | 5.4" | 5.8" | 5.1" | 3.6" | 4.0" | 3.7" | 3.6" | 2.4" | 4.2" | 4.9" |
| | 2.5" | 1.5" | 0.9" | T | — | — | — | — | — | — | 0.1" | 0.7" |
| Milwaukee, Wis. | 26° | 30° | 39° | 54° | 65° | 75° | 80° | 78° | 71° | 60° | 45° | 32° |
| | 1.7" | 1.3" | 2.6" | 3.4" | 2.7" | 3.6" | 3.5" | 3.1" | 2.9" | 2.3" | 2.0" | 2.0" |
| | 13.1" | 9.3" | 8.9" | 1.8" | — | — | — | — | — | T | 2.8" | 10.7" |
| New Orleans, La. | 62° | 65° | 71° | 79° | 85° | 90° | 91° | 90° | 87° | 79° | 70° | 64° |
| | 5.0" | 5.2" | 4.7" | 4.5" | 5.1" | 4.6" | 6.7" | 6.0" | 5.9" | 2.7" | 4.1" | 5.3" |
| | — | 0.1" | T | — | — | — | — | — | — | — | T | 0.1" |
| New York, N.Y. | 38° | 40° | 49° | 61° | 72° | 80° | 85° | 84° | 76° | 66° | 54° | 42° |
| | 3.2" | 3.1" | 4.2" | 3.8" | 3.8" | 3.2" | 3.8" | 4.0" | 3.7" | 3.4" | 4.1" | 3.8" |
| | 7.6" | 8.7" | 5.0" | 0.9" | T | — | — | — | — | — | 0.9" | 5.5" |
| Phoenix, Ariz. | 65° | 70° | 75° | 83° | 92° | 102° | 105° | 102° | 98° | 88° | 74° | 66° |
| | 0.7" | 0.6" | 0.8" | 0.3" | 0.1" | — | 0.7" | 1.0" | 0.6" | 0.6" | 0.5" | 0.8" |
| | T | — | T | T | — | — | — | — | — | — | — | — |
| Philadelphia, Pa. | 39° | 41° | 51° | 63° | 73° | 82° | 86° | 85° | 79° | 67° | 55° | 43° |
| | 3.2" | 2.8" | 3.9" | 3.5" | 3.2" | 3.9" | 3.9" | 4.1" | 3.4" | 2.8" | 3.3" | 3.5" |
| | 6.6" | 6.9" | 3.8" | 0.3" | T | — | — | — | — | — | 0.6" | 3.6" |
| San Antonio, Tex. | 62° | 66° | 74° | 80° | 86° | 92° | 95° | 95° | 89° | 82° | 71° | 65° |
| | 1.6" | 1.9" | 1.3" | 2.7" | 3.7" | 3.0" | 1.9" | 2.7" | 3.8" | 2.9" | 2.3" | 1.4" |
| | 1.6" | 0.7" | 0.2" | T | — | — | — | — | — | — | 0.5" | 0.2" |
| San Diego, Calif. | 65° | 66° | 66° | 68° | 69° | 71° | 76° | 78° | 77° | 75° | 70° | 66° |
| | 2.1" | 1.4" | 1.6" | 0.8" | 0.2" | 0.1" | — | 0.1" | 0.2" | 0.3" | 1.1" | 1.4" |
| | T | — | T | — | — | — | — | — | — | — | T | T |
| San Francisco, Calif. | 56° | 59° | 60° | 61° | 63° | 64° | 64° | 65° | 69° | 68° | 63° | 57° |
| | 4.5" | 2.8" | 2.6" | 1.5" | 0.4" | 0.2" | — | 0.1" | 0.2" | 1.1" | 2.5" | 3.5" |
| | T | T | T | — | — | — | — | — | — | — | T | T |
| Seattle, Wash. | 45° | 50° | 53° | 58° | 65° | 69° | 75° | 74° | 69° | 60° | 51° | 47° |
| | 5.9" | 4.2" | 3.7" | 2.5" | 1.7" | 1.5" | 0.9" | 1.4" | 2.0" | 3.4" | 5.4" | 6.3" |
| | 3.3" | 0.8" | 0.6" | T | — | — | — | — | — | T | 0.8" | 1.9" |
| Washington, D.C. | 43° | 46° | 55° | 67° | 76° | 84° | 88° | 86° | 80° | 69° | 57° | 47° |
| | 2.8" | 2.6" | 3.5" | 2.9" | 3.5" | 3.4" | 3.9" | 4.4" | 3.9" | 2.9" | 2.8" | 3.2" |
| | 5.5" | 5.8" | 2.1" | — | T | — | — | — | — | — | 0.9" | 3.1" |

**Note:** — = no precipitation; T = trace. **Source:** U.S. National Oceanic and Atmospheric Administration, *Comparative Climatic Data for the United States through 1987* (1988).

temperature is less than 64°F (18°C).

**BW** *Desert.* The boundary between desert and steppe is half of the dry/humid boundary. The Sahara desert is the largest area with a **BW** climate.

**BWh** *Low-latitude desert.* The average annual temperature is at least 64°F (18°C).

**BWk** *Mid-latitude desert.* The average annual temperature is less than 64°F (18°C).

**C Subtropical climates** The average temperature of the coldest month is between 64°F (18°C) and 27°F (−3°C). These are mainly humid mid-latitude areas with mild winters. The principal natural vegetation is broad-leaved forest.

**Cw** (Rare) The wettest month occurs in summer and has at least 10 times as much rainfall as the driest month in winter. **Cw** zones are mainly areas of evergreen forest in mountainous **Aw** zones.

**Cs** *Dry summer.* The wettest month occurs in winter and has at least three times as much rainfall as the driest month in summer. Less than 1.5 inches (4 cm) of rain falls during the driest summer month.

**Csa** *Warm, dry summer.* The average temperature of the warmest month is more than 72°F (22°C), and for at least four months the average temperature is more than 50°F (10°C). Italy and other Mediterranean countries have a **Csa** climate.

**Csb** *Cool, dry summer.* In no month is the average temperature more than 72°F (22°C), but for at least four months the average temperature is more than 50°F (10°C). **Csb** climates are found near San Francisco, California; on the coast near Santiago, Chile; and in Portugal.

**Cf** *Humid summer.* Areas that cannot meet the criteria for **Cw** and **Cs**.

**Cfa** *Humid, warm summer.* The average temperature of the warmest month is more than 72°F (22°C), and for at least four months the average temperature is more than 50°F (10°C). Much of the eastern United States is in a **Cfa** zone.

**Cfb** *Marine west coast.* In no month is the average temperature more than 72°F (22°C), but for at least four months the average temperature is more than 50°F (10°C). Great Britain, New Zealand, and the west coast of Alaska are all examples of **Cfb** climates.

**D Continental climates** The average temperature of the warmest month is more than 50°F (10°C), and the average temperature of the coldest month is 27°F (−3°C) or below. Forests are the principal natural vegetation.

**Dfa** *Humid, warm summer.* All seasons have some precipitation. The average temperature of the warmest month is more than 72°F (22°C), and for at least four months the average temperature is more than 50°F (10°C). The northern Great Plains of the United States have a **Dfa** climate.

**Dwa** *Humid, warm summer.* The wettest month occurs in summer and has at least 10 times as much rainfall as the driest month in winter. The average temperature of the warmest month is more than 72°F (22°C), and for at least four months the average temperature is more than

50°F (10°C). The land around the northern part of the Yellow Sea has a **Dwa** climate.

**Dfb** *Humid, cool summer.* All seasons have some precipitation. In no month is the average temperature more than 72°F (22°C), but for at least four months the average temperature is more than 50°F (10°C). A large **Dfb** area stretches from eastern Europe into Asia.

**Dwb** *Humid, cool summer.* The wettest month occurs in summer and has at least 10 times as much rainfall as the driest month in winter. In no month is the average temperature more than 72°F (22°C), but for at least four months the average temperature is more than 50°F (10°C). Much of the area between Manchuria and the Sea of Okhotsk has a **Dwb** climate.

**Dfc** *Subpolar.* All seasons have some precipitation. For one to three months, the average temperature is 50°F (10°C) or more. A huge **Dfc** area is in Siberia and adjacent parts of the Soviet Union.

**E Polar climates** The average temperature of the warmest month is less than 50°F (10°C). There is no summer, and no trees grow.

**ET** *Tundra.* The average temperature of the warmest month is less than 50°F (10°C) but more than 32°F (0°C). Vast areas of northern North America, Europe, and Asia lie in the **ET** climate zone.

**EF** *Ice cap.* The average temperature of the warmest eight months is 32°F (0°C) or less. The **EF** climate is found at the North and South poles and in interior Greenland.

## WEATHER WORDS

**Air mass** A large body of air that, at a given elevation, has about the same temperature and humidity throughout.

**Barometric pressure** The weight of a column of air at a particular place is determined by measuring the height of a column of mercury under a vacuum. The instrument for making such a measurement is called a barometer. At sea level the average barometric pressure measured this way is 29.92 inches (75 cm). In the International System, air pressure is measured in bars or in kiloPascals. A bar is slightly less than the standard air pressure at sea level, and a kiloPascal is one hundredth of a bar. At any location, however, barometric pressure is affected by changes in temperature, humidity, or elevation. When the "barometer is falling," the air pressure is decreasing, often a sign of a storm.

**Climate** General weather conditions over a long period of time.

**Cold front** The place where cold air that is advancing meets warm air that is retreating before it. This kind of weather not only lowers temperature as it passes but also causes high winds and may cause thunderstorms.

**Cyclone** A region of low atmospheric pressure (see "Depression"). Severe cyclones are known as hurricanes, tropical cyclones, and typhoons.

**Degree-days** A degree-day is one degree of deviation of the daily mean temperature from a given norm, usually 65°F. Cooling degree-days are the number of degrees Fahrenheit by which the mean temperature exceeds 65°F, while heating degree-days are the number of degrees the mean temperature is below 65°F. During a year, keeping track of the total number of degree-days (adding the ones for each day) is used to keep track of cooling or heating needs. For example, oil companies use heating degree-days to estimate how much oil their customers have used and when they might need a refill.

**Depression** Any region of low air pressure. In temperate regions over land, the typical depression is a *low*. The often more powerful depression occurring over tropical waters is called a *tropical depression*. If the air pressure in a tropical depression continues to fall, it becomes a tropical storm or, lower still, a *hurricane*.

**Dew point** The temperature at which dew (drops of water) begins to form as air cools. Air can hold only a certain amount of water vapor at a given temperature. When the temperature falls, excess water vapor must turn into a liquid.

**El Niño** A change in the circulation and temperature of the waters off the west coast of South America that occurs every few years. Water that is normally cold is replaced by warmer water, disrupting the local environment in many ways (e.g., moving fish away from the surface, which results in less food for water fowl, and causing rain in normally dry regions). Because El Niño is linked to other weather systems, a strong El Niño can affect weather worldwide.

**Front** The boundary between two different air masses.

**High** An air mass characterized hy higher-than-normal air pressure; usually this is a fair-weather system. Some highs are typically found in the same place each year, such as one that occurs over Bermuda in most summers.

**Hurricane** A huge tropical rainstorm with winds that swirl rapidly around a calm, dry, central "eye." To be classified a hurricane, a tropical storm must have wind speeds of more than 64 mph (103 km/hour). The average hurricane is 375 miles (600 km) in diameter and extends up 40,000 feet (12,000 m) above the surface of the ocean. The eye averages 12.5 miles (20 km) in diameter. When a hurricane hits land, its fierce winds and floods can do great damage. On average five hurricanes each year threaten the eastern and southern United States.

**Jet stream** A strong river or two of high winds in the upper atmosphere (but below the stratosphere) that travels from west to east at between 75 and 150 mph (120–240 km/hour), most often in the middle latitudes. Discovered by American bomber pilots in World War II, it is now known to have significant effects on weather.

**Low** An air mass characterized by lower-than-normal air pressure; usually this is the heart of a storm system. Some lows are found in the same region most of the year, such as the low in the Pacific just off the coast of Alaska.

**Mean temperature** Technically, this should be the average of all temperatures during the day; sometimes it is the average of 24 temperatures taken once each hour; but most often the mean temperature is simply the average of the high and low for the day.

**Monsoon** A wind system in which the prevailing direction of the wind reverses itself from season to season. Southeast Asia is the most typical monsoon region. The summer (southwest) monsoon, characterized by hot, moist air and heavy rains, last from April to September. The winter (northeast) monsoon lasts from October to March and is characterized by cool, dry air.

**Occluded front** When a cold front overtakes a warm front, the denser cold air flows under the less dense warm air.

**Prevailing winds** Throughout the world, winds follow regular patterns. In some places winds are so light and infrequent as to scarcely exist, such as in the doldrums along the equator and in the horse latitudes near latitude 30° north and south. In other places the winds tend to come from a particular direction and are called prevailing winds.

**Rain shadow** An area on the leeward side of a mountain range that receives little rainfall.

**Relative humidity** The amount of moisture (water vapor) in the air compared with the total amount it can hold expressed as a percent. Warm air can hold more water vapor than cold air, so a relative humidity of 75% on a warm summer day is moister than a relative humidity of 75% on a cool winter day. However, because evaporation is greater on warm days, the relative humidity in summer is generally higher than in winter.

**Secondary cold front** A cold front that sometimes forms behind another cold front and that is often even colder than the first front.

**Secondary depression** A low that forms to the south or east of a low that is a storm center.

**Squall line** A line of instability that often precedes a cold front, marked by wind gusts and often by heavy rain.

**Stationary front** A front that stays in the same place.

**Storm surge** The rise in water levels in the ocean or a large lake that comes from a combination of wind and low pressure during a storm, especially pronounced during a hurricane.

**Temperature-humidity index** A number derived from a formula relating temperature and humidity to discomfort. When it is 75, many are uncomfortable, while at 80 or above, almost everyone is uncomfortable. Temperatures are less comfortable at high humidities because cooling by sweating is less efficient.

## TORNADOES, FLOODS, AND TROPICAL CYCLONES IN THE U.S., 1980–89

| Item | 1980 | 1981 | 1982 | 1983 | 1984 | 1985 | 1986 | 1987 | 1988 | 1989 |
|---|---|---|---|---|---|---|---|---|---|---|
| Tornadoes, number | 866 | 783 | 1,046 | 931 | 907 | 684 | 764 | 656 | 702 | 858 |
| Lives lost, total | 28 | 24 | 64 | 34 | 122 | 94 | 15 | 59 | 32 | 49 |
| Most in a single tornado | 5 | 5 | 10 | 3 | 16 | 18 | 3 | 30 | 5 | 20 |
| Floods: lives lost | 97 | 90 | 155 | 200 | 126 | 304 | 80 | 82 | 29 | 61 |
| Property loss (mil.) | $1,500 | $1,000 | $3,500 | $4,100 | $4,000 | $3,000 | $4,000 | $1,490 | $114 | $415 |
| North Atlantic tropical cyclones and hurricanes: | | | | | | | | | | |
| Number reaching U.S. coast | 2 | 2 | 1 | 2 | 2 | 11 | 6 | 7 | 12 | 4 |
| Hurricanes only | 1 | — | — | 1 | 1 | 7 | 4 | 2 | 5 | 3 |
| Lives lost in U.S. | 2 | — | — | 22 | 4 | 30 | 9 | — | — | 55 |

**Note:** A tornado is a violent, rotating column of air descending from a cumulonimbus cloud in the form of a tubular or funnel-shaped cloud, usually characterized by movements along a narrow path and wind speeds from 100 to 300 miles per hour; also known as a twister or waterspout. Tropical cyclones have maximum winds of 39 to 73 miles per hour; hurricanes have maximum winds of 74 miles per hour or higher. **Source:** U.S. National Oceanic and Atmospheric Administration, data for 1980, *Climatological Data: National Summary* (monthly with annual summary); thereafter, *Storm Data* (monthly).

**Tornado** A small and short-lived but very severe windstorm. Tornadoes are whirling columns of air that reach down from a cloud, and they often accompany thunderstorms, rain, and hail. With wind speeds up to 300 mph (480 km/hr) tornadoes can do tremendous damage. The diameter of the average tornado is between 500 and 2,000 feet (150–600m). The average tornado moves along the ground at 28 mph (45 km/hr) and has a "path" that is 16 miles (26 km) long. In the United States some 750 tornadoes are reported every year, most frequently between April and June.

**Tropical storm** A storm that forms over the ocean in the tropics and often moves onto land, where it loses strength. Technically, a storm is designated a tropical storm only when winds are between 39 and 73 miles per hour. If winds become greater, a tropical storm becomes a hurricane.

**Trough** A low that is long, rather than nearly circular.

**Typhoon** A hurricane formed in the western Pacific Ocean.

**Warm front** The boundary of a moving warm-air mass.

**Weather** The condition of the atmosphere—temperature, rain, and wind, for example—in a particular place. A climate is defined by weather conditions over a long period of time.

**Wind** Any current of air, measured on land in miles per hour and at sea in knots. The direction of a given wind is determined from the point of the compass from which it blows (e.g., northeast, south). In various regions of the world, names are given to seasonal winds of particular quality. Among these are the *bora*, a cold, usually dry north/northeast wind along the eastern Adriatic; *brickfielder*, a hot north wind of southeastern Australia; *buran*, a cold, violent north/northeast wind of Siberia and central Asia, common in winter; *chinook*, a dry winter or spring wind that blows down the eastern slopes of the Rocky mountains, often warm enough to melt the snow; *harmattan*, a hot, dry north wind in West Africa that cools as it evaporates the moist air of the coast; *mistral*, a cold, strong north/northwest wind of the western Mediterranean, with a surface strength of 60 km/hour, frequent in winter; *pampero*, a sudden, cold south or west wind in Argentina and Uruguay, frequent in summer; *Santa Ana*, a hot, dry wind that blows from the north or east in Southern California; *sirocco*, a hot south wind of North Africa and southern Italy; *southerly burster*, a cold, violent south wind of southeastern Australia; *williwaw*, a violent squall that blows in the Strait of Magellan (South America); and *zonda*, a hot, dry north wind of Argentina and Uruguay.

> *"Everybody talks about the weather, but nobody does anything about it."*
>
> —Charles Dudley Warner, editorial, *The Hartford Courant* (1897)

## BEAUFORT WIND SCALE

In 1806, Admiral Sir Francis Beaufort devised a scale for recording wind force at sea based on the effect of the wind on a full-rigged ship of war. In 1838 this scale was adopted by the British Admiralty, and in 1874 it was adopted for international use. It is now the chief scale for specifying the force of the wind and is used in all parts of the world, both on land and sea. Originally there were no specific wind speeds corresponding to various force numbers on the Beaufort scale. Since 1946, wind speed has been determined according to measurements made by an anemometer (a device for measuring wind) at 10 m (30 ft.) above the ground.

| Force | Description of wind | Mean wind speed in knots[1] | Specification for use on land and at sea |
|---|---|---|---|
| Force 0 | Calm | Less than 1 | Calm, smoke rises vertically. Sea like a mirror. |
| Force 1 | Light air | 1–3 | Direction of wind shown by smoke drift, but not by wind vanes. Ripples with appearance of scales are formed, but without foam crests. |
| Force 2 | Light breeze | 4–6 | Wind felt on face; leaves rustle; ordinary vane moved by wind. Small wavelets, still short but more pronounced; crests have a glassy appearance and do not break. |
| Force 3 | Gentle breeze | 7–10 | Leaves and small twigs in constant motion; wind extends light flag. Large wavelets; crests begin to break; foam of glassy appearance; perhaps scattered white horses. |
| Force 4 | Moderate breeze | 11–16 | Raises dust and loose paper; small branches are moved. Small waves becoming longer; fairly frequent white horses. |
| Force 5 | Fresh breeze | 17–21 | Small trees in leaf begin to sway; crested wavelets form on inland waters. Moderate waves, taking a more pronounced long form; many white horses are formed (chance of some spray). |
| Force 6 | Strong breeze | 22–27 | Large branches in motion; whistling heard in telegraph wires; umbrellas used with difficulty. Large waves begin to form; the white foam crests are more extensive everywhere (probably some spray). |
| Force 7 | Moderate gale, Near gale | 28–33 | Whole trees in motion; inconvenience felt when walking against wind. Sea heaps up and white foam from breaking waves begins to be blown in streaks along the direction of the wind. |
| Force 8 | Fresh gale, Gale | 34–40 | Breaks twigs off trees; generally impedes progress. Moderately high waves of greater length; edges of crests begin to break into spindrift; foam is blown in well-marked streaks. |
| Force 9 | Strong gale | 41–47 | Slight structural damage occurs (chimney pots and slate removed). High waves; dense streaks of foam; crests of waves begin to topple, tumble, and roll over. |
| Force 10 | Whole gale, Storm | 48–55 | Seldom experienced inland; trees uprooted; considerable structural damage occurs. Very high waves with long overhanging crests; the resulting foam, in great patches, is blown in dense white streaks; the sea takes a white appearance; the tumbling of the sea becomes heavy and shocklike; visibility affected. |
| Force 11 | Storm, Violent storm | 56–63 | Very rarely experienced; accompanied by widespread damage. Exceptionally high waves at sea (medium-sized ships might be lost to view behind the waves); the sea is completely covered with white patches of foam; visibility affected. |
| Force 12 + | Hurricane[2] | 64 and above | The air is filled with foam and spray; sea completely white with driving spray; visibility very seriously affected. |

1. Nautical miles-per-hour; 1 nautical mile = 1.151 statute miles. 2. Force 13: 72–80 knots; force 14: 81–89; force 15: 90–99; force 16: 100–108; force 17: 109–118. **Sources:** Smithsonian Institution, *Smithsonian Meteorological Tables* (1966); Hydrographer of the Navy (UK), *Ocean Passages for the World* (1977).

### Wind-Chill Factor

Sometimes called a wind-chill index, this is a measure of the cooling power of air movement and low temperature on the human body. Because heat passes directly from a warm body to the cooler air surrounding it—a process known as convection—wind produces a continuing source of cooler air and a chilling effect that is equivalent to a lower temperature. The effect of wind on a warm day is pleasant, but as temperatures approach freezing, wind chill is not only unpleasant but can be dangerous. As the table below shows, a temperature of 5°F combined with a breeze of 10 mph produces a wind-chill temperature of −15°F—a temperature at which frostbite occurs much sooner than at 5°F. Wind speeds above 45 mph have little additional cooling effect.

## DETERMINING THE WIND-CHILL FACTOR

| Wind speed | 35°F | 30°F | 25°F | 20°F | 15°F | 10°F | 5°F | 0°F | −5°F | −10°F | −15°F | −20°F | −25°F | −30°F | −35°F | −40°F | −45°F | Wind speed |
|---|---|---|---|---|---|---|---|---|---|---|---|---|---|---|---|---|---|---|
| 5 mph | 33° | 27° | 21° | 16° | 12° | 7° | 0° | −5° | −10° | −15° | −21° | −26° | −31° | −36° | −42° | −47° | −52° | 5 mph |
| 10 mph | 22 | 16 | 10 | 3 | −3 | −9 | −15 | −22 | −27 | −34 | −40 | −46 | −52 | −58 | −64 | −71 | −77 | 10 mph |
| 15 mph | 16 | 9 | 2 | −5 | −11 | −18 | −25 | −31 | −38 | −45 | −51 | −58 | −65 | −72 | −78 | −85 | −92 | 15 mph |
| 20 mph | 12 | 4 | −3 | −10 | −17 | −24 | −31 | −39 | −46 | −53 | −60 | −67 | −74 | −81 | −88 | −95 | −102 | 20 mph |
| 25 mph | 8 | 1 | −7 | −15 | −22 | −29 | −36 | −44 | −51 | −59 | −66 | −74 | −81 | −88 | −96 | −103 | −110 | 25 mph |
| 30 mph | 6 | −2 | −10 | −18 | −25 | −33 | −41 | −49 | −56 | −64 | −71 | −79 | −86 | −93 | −101 | −109 | −116 | 30 mph |
| 35 mph | 4 | −4 | −12 | −20 | −27 | −35 | −43 | −52 | −58 | −67 | −74 | −82 | −89 | −97 | −105 | −113 | −120 | 35 mph |
| 40 mph | 3 | −5 | −13 | −21 | −29 | −37 | −45 | −53 | −60 | −69 | −76 | −84 | −92 | −100 | −107 | −115 | −123 | 40 mph |
| 45 mph | 2 | −6 | −14 | −22 | −30 | −38 | −46 | −54 | −62 | −70 | −78 | −85 | −93 | −102 | −109 | −117 | −125 | 45 mph |

## TIME ZONES AND AREA CODES FOR SELECTED NATIONS

| Country | Hours from EST | Country code | City code |
|---|---|---|---|
| Afghanistan | +9.5 | | Direct dialing not available |
| Algeria | +6 | 213 | Not required |
| American Samoa | −6 | 684 | Not required |
| Angola | +6 | | Direct dialing not available |
| Argentina | +2 | 54 | Buenos Aires 1, Cordoba 51, Rosario 41 |
| Australia | +15 | 61 | Adelaide 8, Brisbane 7, Canberra 62, Melbourne 3, Sydney 2 |
| Austria | +6 | 43 | Graz 316, Linz 731, Vienna 1 |
| Bahrain | +8 | 973 | Not required |
| Bangladesh | +11 | 880 | Chittagong 31, Dhaka 2, Khulna 41 |
| Belgium | +6 | 32 | Antwerp 3, Brussels 2, Ghent 91, Liege 41 |
| Belize | −1 | 501 | Belize City 2, Belmopan 8 |
| Bolivia | +1 | 591 | La Paz 2, Santa Cruz 33 |
| Botswana | +7 | 267 | Francistown 21, Gaborone 31 |
| Brazil[1] | +2 | 55 | Belo Horizonte 31, Brasília 61, Rio de Janeiro 21, Sao Paulo 11 |
| Brunei | +13 | 673 | Bandar Seri Begawan 2, Kuala Belait 3 |
| Bulgaria | +7 | 359 | Plovdiv 32, Sofia 2, Varna 52 |
| Burkina Faso | +5 | 226 | Not required |
| Burundi | +7 | | Direct dialing not available |
| Cameroon | +6 | 237 | Not required |
| Canada | Similar to U.S. | | See "Area Codes of the United States, Canada, and the Caribbean" |
| Central African Rep. | +6 | | Direct dialing not available |
| Chad | +6 | | Direct dialing not available |
| Chile | +1 | 56 | Santiago 2, Valparaíso 32, Viña del Mar 32 |
| China (PRC) | +13 | 86 | Beijing 1, Fuzhou 591, Ghuangzhou (Canton) 20, Shanghai 21 |
| Colombia | 0 | 57 | Barranquilla 58, Bogotá 1, Cali 23, Medellín 4 |
| Congo | +6 | | Direct dialing not available |
| Costa Rica | −1 | 506 | Not required |
| Cuba | 0 | | Direct dialing not available |
| Cyprus[2] | +7 | 357 | Larnaca 41, Limassol 51, Nicosia 2 |
| Czechoslovakia | +6 | 42 | Bratislava 7, Brno 5, Prague 2 |
| Denmark | +6 | 45 | Árhus 6, Copenhagen 3, Odense 7 |
| Ecuador | 0 | 593 | Ambato 2, Cuenca 7, Guayaquil 4, Quito 2 |
| Egypt | +7 | 20 | Alexandria 3, Cairo 2, El Mansoura 50 |
| El Salvador | −1 | 503 | Not required |
| Ethiopia | +8 | 251 | Addis Ababa 1, Asmara 4, Dire Dawa 5 |
| Fiji | +17 | 679 | Not required |
| Finland | +7 | 358 | Epoo 15, Helsinki 0, Tampere 31 |
| France[3] | +6 | 33 | Lyon 7, Marseilles 91, Nice 93, Paris 1 |
| Gabon | +6 | 241 | Not required |
| Gambia | +5 | 220 | Not required |
| Germany (East)[4] | +6 | 37 | Berlin 2, Dresden 51, Leipzig 41 |
| Germany (West)[4] | +6 | 49 | Berlin 30, Bonn 228, Frankfurt 69, Munich 89 |
| Ghana | +5 | 233 | Accra 21, Kumasi 51, Takoradi 31 |
| Greece | +7 | 30 | Athens 1, Piraeus 1, Thessaloniki 31 |
| Guadeloupe | +1 | 590 | Not required |
| Guam | +15 | 671 | Not required |
| Guatemala | −1 | 502 | Guatemala City 2; all other cities 9 |
| Guinea | +5 | 224 | Conakry 4, Kindia 61, Labe 51, Mamou 68 |
| Guyana | +2 | 592 | Georgetown 2, New Amsterdam 3 |
| Haiti | 0 | 509 | Cap-Haïtien 3, Gonaïves 2, Port-au-Prince 1 |
| Honduras | −1 | 504 | Not required |
| Hong Kong | +13 | 852 | Hong Kong 5, Kowloon 3, New Territories 0 |
| Hungary | +6 | 36 | Budapest 1, Debrecen 52, Miskolc 46 |
| Iceland | +5 | 354 | Akureyri 6, Keflavik 2, Reykjavik 1 |
| India | +10.5 | 91 | Ahmadabad 272, Bangalore 812, Bombay 22, Calcutta 33, Madras 44, New Delhi 11 |
| Indonesia[5] | +12 | 62 | Jakarta 21, Medan 61, Surabaya 31 |
| Iran | +8.5 | 98 | Isfahan 31, Mashad 51, Tehran 21 |
| Iraq | +8 | 964 | Baghdad 1, Basrah 40, Mosul 60 |
| Ireland | +5 | 353 | Cork 21, Dublin 1, Galway 91, Limerick 61 |
| Israel | +7 | 972 | Haifa 4, Jerusalem 2, Tel Aviv 3 |
| Italy | +6 | 39 | Florence 55, Genoa 10, Milan 2, Naples 81, Rome 6, Turin 11 |
| Ivory Coast | +5 | 225 | Not required |
| Japan | +14 | 81 | Kyoto 75, Nagoya 52, Osaka 6, Sapporo 11, Tokyo 33, Yokohama 45 |
| Jordan | +7 | 962 | Amman 6, Irbid 2, Sult 5, Zagra 9 |
| Kenya | +8 | 254 | Mombasa 11, Nairobi 2, Nakuru 37 |
| Kiribati | +17 | 686 | Not required |
| Korea, South | +14 | 82 | Inchon 32, Kwangju 62, Pusan 51, Seoul 2, Taegu 53 |
| Kuwait | +8 | 965 | Not required |
| Lebanon | +7 | | Direct dialing not available |
| Lesotho | +7 | 266 | Not required |
| Liberia | +5 | 231 | Not required |
| Libya | +7 | 218 | Benghazi 61, Misuratha 51, Tripoli 21 |
| Luxembourg | +6 | 352 | Not required |
| Madagascar | +8 | | Direct dialing not available |
| Malawi | +7 | 265 | Blantyre, Lilongwe: not required |
| Malaysia[6] | +13 | 60 | Ipoh 5, Johore Bahru 7, Kuala Lumpur 3 |
| Mali | +5 | 223 | Not required |

| Country | Hours from EST | Country code | City code |
|---|---|---|---|
| Marshall Is. | +17 | 692 | Ebeye 871, Majuro 9 |
| Mauritania | +5 | Direct dialing not available | |
| Mauritius | +9 | 230 | Not required |
| Mexico[7] | +1 | 52 | Guadalajara 36, Monterrey 83, Mexico City 5, Puebla 22 |
| Micronesia | +16 | 691 | Kosrae 370, Ponape 320, Truk 330, Yap 350 |
| Mongolia | +13 | Direct dialing not available | |
| Morocco | +5 | 212 | Casablanca, not required; Rabat 7 |
| Mozambique | +7 | Direct dialing not available | |
| Myanmar | +11.5 | Direct dialing not available | |
| Namibia | +7 | 264 | Grootfontein 673, Windhoek 61 |
| Nepal | +10.5 | 977 | Not required |
| Netherlands | +6 | 31 | Amsterdam 20, Rotterdam 10, The Hague 70 |
| Neth. Antilles | +1 | 599 | Bonaire 7, Curacao 9, St. Maarten 5 |
| New Zealand | +17 | 64 | Auckland 9, Christchurch 3, Wellington 4 |
| Nicaragua | −1 | 505 | Granada 55, León 311, Managua 2 |
| Niger | +6 | 227 | Not required |
| Nigeria | +6 | 234 | Lagos 1 |
| No. Mariana Is. | +15 | 670 | Rota Is. 532, Susupe City 234, Tinian Is. 433 |
| Norway | +6 | 47 | Bergen 5, Oslo 2, Stavanger 4, Trondheim 7 |
| Oman | +9 | 968 | Not required |
| Pakistan | +10 | 92 | Islamabad 51, Karachi 21, Lahore 42 |
| Panama | 0 | 507 | Not required |
| Papua New Guinea | +15 | 675 | Not required |
| Paraguay | +2 | 595 | Asuncion 21, Pedro Juan Caballero 36 |
| Peru | 0 | 51 | Arequipa 54, Callao 14, Lima 14, Trujillo 44 |
| Philippines | +13 | 63 | Cebu 32, Davao 82, Iloilo 33, Manila 2 |
| Poland | +6 | 48 | Gdansk 58, Lodz 42, Warsaw 22 |
| Portugal | +5 | 351 | Coimbra 39, Lisbon 1, Porto 2, Sebutal 65 |
| Qatar | +8 | 974 | Not required |
| Romania | +7 | 40 | Brasov 21, Bucharest 0, Constanta 16 |

| Country | Hours from EST | Country code | City code |
|---|---|---|---|
| Saudi Arabia | +8 | 966 | Jeddah 2, Mecca 2, Riyadh 1, Taif 2 |
| Senegal | +5 | 221 | Not required |
| Sierra Leone | +5 | 232 | Freetown 22; all other points 232 |
| Singapore | +13 | 65 | Not required |
| Somalia | +8 | Direct dialing not available | |
| South Africa | +7 | 27 | Cape Town 21, Durban 31, Johannesburg 11 |
| Spain | +6 | 34 | Barcelona 3, Madrid 1, Seville 54, Valencia 6 |
| Sri Lanka | +10.5 | 94 | Colombo 1, Kandy 8, Trincomalee 26 |
| Sudan | +7 | Direct dialing not available | |
| Sweden | +6 | 46 | Göteburg 31, Malmö 40, Stockholm 8 |
| Switzerland | +6 | 41 | Basel 61, Berne 31, Geneva 22, Zurich 1 |
| Syria | +7 | Direct dialing not available | |
| Taiwan | +13 | 886 | Kaohsiung 7, Tainin 6, Taipei 2 |
| Tanzania | +8 | 255 | Dar Es Salaam 51, Mwanza 68, Tanga 53 |
| Thailand | +12 | 66 | Bangkok 2, Burirum 44, Chanthaburi 39 |
| Togo | +5 | 228 | Not required |
| Tunisia | +6 | 216 | Bizerte 2, Kairouan 7, Tunis 1 |
| Turkey | +7 | 90 | Adana 711, Ankara 4, Istanbul 1, Izmir 51 |
| Uganda | +8 | 256 | Entebbe 42, Jinja 43, Kampala 41, Kyambogo 41 |
| United Arab Emirates | +9 | 971 | Abu Dhabi 2, Dubai 4, Sharjah 6 |
| United Kingdom | +5 | 44 | Birmingham 21, Glasgow 41, Manchester 61, London: inner 71, outer 81 |
| Uruguay | +2 | 598 | Montevideo 2, Paysandu 722 |
| USSR[8] | +8 | 7 | Moscow 095; elsewhere consult operator |
| Vatican City | +6 | 39 | All points 6 |
| Venezuela | +1 | 58 | Caracas 2, Maracaibo 61, Valencia 41 |
| Yemen | +8 | 967 | Amran 2, Sanaa 2, Taiz 4, Yarim 4, Zabid 3 |
| Yugoslavia | +6 | 38 | Belgrade 11, Skopje 91, Zagreb 41 |
| Zaire | +6 | 243 | Kinshasa 12, Lubumbashi 222 |
| Zambia | +7 | 260 | Kitwe 2, Lusaka 1, Ndola 26 |
| Zimbabwe | +7 | 263 | Bulawayo 9, Harare 4, Mutare 20 |

1. More than one time zone; difference based on Rio de Janeiro. 2. Turkish-occupied Cyprus uses the country code for Turkey (90), plus: Famagusta 536, Kyrenia 581. 3. All codes in Paris are 1 + 8 digits beginning with 3, 4, or 6. 4. The German telephone system remains divided along pre-unification lines. 5. More than one time zone; difference based on Jakarta. 6. More than one time zone; difference based on Kuala Lumpur. 7. More than one time zone; difference based on Mexico City. International code applies for calls made from international direct dial areas. From other areas, to call Mexico City dial 90 + 5; consult operator for other calls. 8. More than one time zone; difference based on Moscow. **Source:** AT&T, *International Telecommunications Guide* (1990).

## THE 50 TALLEST BUILDINGS IN THE WORLD

| Rank/Building | City | Year built | Stories | Height Meters | Feet |
|---|---|---|---|---|---|
| 1. Sears Tower | Chicago | 1974 | 110 | 443 | 1,454 |
| 2. World Trade Center, North | New York | 1972 | 110 | 417 | 1,368 |
| 3. World Trade Center, South | New York | 1973 | 110 | 415 | 1,362 |
| 4. Empire State | New York | 1931 | 102 | 381 | 1,250 |
| 5. Central Plaza | Hong Kong | UC92 | 78 | 374 | 1,227 |
| 6. Bank of China Tower | Hong Kong | 1988 | 72 | 368 | 1,209 |
| 7. Amoco | Chicago | 1973 | 80 | 346 | 1,136 |
| 8. John Hancock | Chicago | 1968 | 100 | 344 | 1,127 |
| 9. Chrysler Building | New York | 1930 | 77 | 319 | 1,046 |
| 10. First Interstate World Center | Los Angeles | 1989 | 75 | 310 | 1,018 |
| 11. Texas Commerce Plaza | Houston | 1982 | 79 | 305 | 1,000 |
| 12. Allied Bank Plaza | Houston | 1983 | 71 | 296 | 970 |
| 13. 311 S. Wacker Drive | Chicago | UC90 | 65 | 296 | 970 |
| 14. Columbia Center | Seattle | 1984 | 76 | 291 | 954 |
| 15. American International | New York | 1932 | 67 | 290 | 950 |
| 16. One Liberty Place | Philadelphia | 1987 | 60 | 287 | 945 |
| 17. First Bank Tower | Toronto | 1975 | 72 | 285 | 935 |
| 18. 40 Wall Tower | New York | 1966 | 71 | 283 | 927 |
| 19. Interfirst Plaza Tower | Dallas | 1985 | 70 | 281 | 921 |
| 20. Citicorp Center | New York | 1977 | 59 | 280 | 919 |
| 21. Overseas Union Bank | Singapore | 1986 | 63 | 280 | 919 |
| 22. Two Prudential Plaza | Chicago | UC90 | 64 | 278 | 912 |
| 23. Scotia Plaza | Toronto | 1988 | 68 | 275 | 901 |
| 24. Transco Tower | Houston | 1983 | 64 | 275 | 901 |
| 25. Society Center | Cleveland | UC92 | 57 | 271 | 888 |
| 26. Landmark Tower | Yokohama | UC93 | — | 268 | 882 |
| 27. 900 N. Michigan | Chicago | 1989 | 69 | 267 | 875 |
| 28. AT&T Corp. Center | Chicago | 1988 | 64 | 267 | 875 |
| 29. NCNB Corporate Ctr. | Charlotte | UC92 | 60 | 267 | 875 |
| 30. Water Tower Place | Chicago | 1976 | 74 | 262 | 859 |
| 31. United California Bank | Los Angeles | 1974 | 62 | 262 | 858 |
| 32. Transamerica Pyramid | San Francisco | 1972 | 48 | 260 | 853 |
| 33. Parque Central Torres de Oficinas | Caracas | 1978 | 62 | 260 | 853 |
| 34. RCA Rockefeller Center | New York | 1933 | 70 | 259 | 850 |
| 35. Messeturm | Frankfurt | UC90 | 70 | 259 | 850 |
| 36. First National Bank | Chicago | 1969 | 60 | 259 | 850 |
| 37. USX Tower | Pittsburgh | 1970 | 64 | 256 | 841 |
| 38. Atlantic Center (IBM) | Atlanta | 1988 | 50 | 250 | 820 |
| 39. City Spire | New York | 1987 | 72 | 248 | 814 |
| 40. One Chase Manhattan Plaza | New York | 1961 | 60 | 248 | 813 |
| 41. Pan American | New York | 1963 | 59 | 246 | 808 |
| 42. M.L.C. Centre | Sydney | 1978 | 67 | 244 | 801 |
| 43. City Hall Tower | Tokyo | UC91 | 48 | 243 | 798 |
| 44. Momentum Place | Dallas | 1987 | 60 | 243 | 797 |
| 45. Tokyo Metropolitan Govt. | Tokyo | UC91 | 48 | 243 | 797 |
| 46. Rialto Center | Melbourne | 1986 | 70 | 242 | 794 |
| 47. Woolworth | New York | 1913 | 57 | 241 | 792 |
| 48. Mellon Bank | Philadelphia | UC90 | 56 | 241 | 792 |
| 49. 1 Palac Kultury I Nauki | Warsaw | 1955 | 42 | 241 | 790 |
| 50. John Hancock Tower | Boston | 1973 | 64 | 241 | 790 |

**Note:** UC = under construction. **Source:** Council on Tall Buildings and Urban Habitat, Lehigh University (1991).

# Languages of the World

The function of language is to enable people to communicate ideas to one another, primarily through audible speech, and secondarily through written words. The number of languages, to say nothing of dialects, is impossible to compute specifically, but estimates put the number at between 4,000 and 10,000 worldwide. Dialects are variations within languages. Estimates of the number of dialects in the world vary from about 20,000 to more than 50,000. There is some disagreement regarding what represents a dialect and what represents a language. Generally, most linguists would accept "the criterion of mutual intelligibility" and decide that two varieties—for example, the "King's English" and "Brooklynese"—are dialects of the same language if their speakers can understand each other. The number of writing systems used to transcribe these languages is considerably less, because not all spoken languages have a written form.

In order to simplify their study of the world's languages, linguists group languages (in groups, families, phyla, complexes, dialects, and so on) according to various similarities of vocabulary, grammar, and other features. A language that has no known relationship to any other is called a language isolate. The accompanying list shows the primary language families and languages, and the regions or countries where they are most commonly found.

## Language Families and Languages

**Afro-Asiatic** *Berber* (Cen. Sahara). *Chadic* inc. Hausa (W. Cen. Africa). *Cushitic* (Ethiopia, Somalia). *Semitic* inc. Amharic, Arabic, Hebrew, Maltese, Tigrinya (N. Africa, E. Africa, Mideast, Malta).
**Australian aboriginal langs.** (Australia).
**Austro-Asiatic** *Mon-Khmer* inc. Khmer, Viet-Muong (Cambodia, Malaysia, Thailand, Vietnam). *Munda* (India). *Nicobarese* (Nicobar Is.).
**Austronesian** *Western Malayo-Polynesian* inc. Javanese, Malay, Achinese, Batak, Minangkabau, Sundanese, Madurese, Balinese, Iban, Ngadju, Macasserese, Buginese, Malagasay (Madagascar, Indonesia, S. Asia, Papua–New Guinea, Philippines). *Oceanic* inc. Samoan, Tongan, Fijian, Tahitian, Hawaiian, Maori (Oceania). *S. Halmahera-W. New Guinea* langs. *Central Malayo-Polynesian* langs. *Formosan* langs. *Chamic* langs. (S.E. Asia).
**Dravidian** inc. Tamil, Malayalam, Kannada, Telugu (S. India, Pakistan, Nepal, Sri Lanka, Maldives).
**Eurasiatic stock: Altaic** *Turkic* inc. Turkish, Azerbaidjani, Kazakh, Kirghiz, Tatar, Turkmen, Uighur, Uzbek (Turkey, Cyprus, Soviet Asia, Iran, China). *Mongolian* inc. Buryat, Mongolian

(Mongolia, China, USSR). *Tungusic* inc. Manchu (China, USSR). Some linguists also include Japanese and Korean, though these may be language isolates. **Uralic** inc. Hungarian, Finnish, Estonian, Lappish, and *Samoyedic* langs. (N.E. Europe, N. Asia).
**Indo-European** *Armenian. Celtic* langs. (N.W. Europe). *Germanic* inc. Dutch, English, German, Scandinavian langs., Yiddish (N. Europe, N. America, Caribbean, S. Africa). *Greek. Italic* inc. Latin. *Romance* inc. French, Italian, Portuguese, Romanian, Spanish (Europe, Latin America, N. America). *Slavonic* inc. Bulgarian, Czech, Polish, Russian, Serbo-Croat, Slovak (E. Europe, Soviet Asia). *Indo-Aryan* inc. Bengali, Gujarati, Hindi, Punjabi, Sanskrit, Urdu (Pakistan, India, Bangladesh). *Iranian* inc. Baluchi, Farsi, Kurdish, Pashto (Turkey, Iraq, Iran, Afghanistan, Pakistan, Soviet Asia).
**Indo-Pacific** *Papuan* langs., *Tasmanian* langs. (Papua, Tasmania).
**Khoisan** inc. !Khung (S.W. Africa, Tanzania).
**Meso-American Indian: Mayan** inc. Quich, Yucatec, Cakchiquel, Mam, Kekchi, Tzotzil, Tzeltal, Chol, Huastec, (Guatemala, Mexico, Belize, Honduras). **Misumalpan** inc. Mosquito (Nicaragua, El Salvador). **Mixtecan** inc. Mixtec (Mexico). **Oto-Pamean** inc. Otomian, Mazahua (Mexico). **Popolocan** inc. Mazatec (Mexico). **Totonacan** inc. Totonac (Mexico). **Uto-Aztecan** inc. Aztec (Mexico, U.S.). **Zapotecan** inc. Zapotec (Mexico).
**Niger-Kordofanian group: Niger-Congo** *West Atlantic* inc. Fulani, Serer, Wolof, Dyola (W. Africa). *Mande* inc. Malinke, Mende (W. Africa). *Gur (Voltaic)* inc. Mossi. *Kwa* inc. Yoruba, Akan, Ibo (coastal W. Africa). *Adamawa-Eastern* inc. Sango, Baya (Cen. Africa). *Benue-Congo* inc. Bantu langs. Fang, Kongo, Luba, Luganda, Rwanda, Shona, Sotho, Swahili, Xhosa, Zulu. (S. Cen. Africa). **Kordofanian** langs. (Sudan).
**Nilo-Saharan** inc. *Chari-Nile* langs., Fur, Koma, Songhai (Cen. Africa).
**North American: Na-Dené** inc. Navajo (U.S.).
**Sino-Tibetan** *Baric* langs. (India). *Bodish-Himalyish* Tibetan (Himalayas). *Burmese-Lolo* Burmese, Naga, Kachin (Burma, S.E. Asia, Bangladesh, Himalayas). *Chinese* Mandarin, Wu, Xiang, Kan, Hakka, Yue, Min (China, S.E. Asia, Indonesia).
**South American Indian: Quechumaran** inc. Quechua, Aymara, (Bolivia, Peru). **Tupian** inc. Guaraní, Tupi (Paraguay, Brazil, Bolivia).
**Tai** inc. Thai (Thailand, China).
**Language isolates** inc. Ainu (N. Japan). Basque (N. Spain, S.W. France). Georgian (Caucasus Mts.).

## Principal Languages of the World

Exact data on language use are notoriously difficult to compile. National censuses are conducted at different intervals, and not all include questions about language. When they do, they can refer either to the language spoken in the home (the language one speaks best), or to the language spoken most often, or to all the languages one might speak. Even without uniform and precise data, about half the world's population speak one of a dozen or so languages, and

the general geography of the most widely used languages is fairly clear.

**Chinese** is the mother tongue of more than 1 billion people. Although the spoken dialects of Chinese are not mutually intelligible, they share the same writing system (*hanzi*) and two people can speak different dialects and still be able to read each other's writing. This is possible because *hanzi* uses symbols to represent objects and ideas, not sounds.

The principal dialect is *Mandarin*, based on the dialect spoken in northern China around Beijing, and is the official language of China, Taiwan, and Singapore. The mother tongue of some 500–825 million people, its use is expected to grow rapidly because it is now being taught in all Chinese schools. The other principle dialects are *Cantonese* (or *Yue*), spoken in southern China and Hong Kong (where it is an official language); *Wu*, spoken in Shanghai and nearby provinces in eastern China; *Min*, found in southeastern China, Taiwan, and Malaysia; and *Xiang, Kan,* and *Hakka,* all spoken in southeastern China and Taiwan.

**English**, although it is the mother tongue of only 300–450 million people, is spoken by perhaps as many as one third of the world's people. From the island kingdom of England, it spread throughout the British Empire to the Americas, Africa, India, and throughout the Pacific. Today, English is an official language in 87 nations and territories. The main concentrations of English speakers are found in the United States, Great Britain, India, Nigeria, Canada, Australia, and Ireland.

**Hindi** is spoken by more than 250–300 million people. One of India's two official languages (with English), Hindi also has significant numbers of speakers in Trinidad, Guyana, South Africa, Mauritius, and other countries. Hindi and Urdu (see below) have a common spoken form, Hindustani; but as literary languages, they remain distinct, Hindi being written in Devanagari script, Urdu in Perso-Arabic.

**Arabic** is the mother tongue of at least 165 million people. In addition to its being an official language in 18 countries in North Africa and the Middle East, it is also the language of the Koran—and thus, for Muslims, of God—and it is the second language of many Indians, Indonesians, Iranians, and other inhabitants of largely Muslim nations.

**Russian** is spoken by 250–300 million people. Although it is the official language of the USSR, according to a 1979 census only 59% of the population claimed it as a mother tongue. There are large numbers of non-native Russian speakers throughout the Soviet Union as well as in Eastern Europe.

**Malay** variants and dialects of Malay are used as an official language in Indonesia (where it is known as *Bahasa Indonesia*), Malaysia (*Bahasa Malaysia*), and Singapore and Brunei (*Bahasa Melayu*). Although this represents a population of more than 180 million people, it is not the mother tongue of a majority in any of these countries. The most widely spoken single language is Javanese, spoken by more than 70 million Indonesians.

**Bengali** is spoken by more than 150 million people in Bangladesh, where it is the official language and the mother tongue of almost the whole country, and in the Indian state of West Bengal.

**Spanish** is spoken by 125–320 million people worldwide, and is the official language of 20 nations, territories, and colonies, including Spain and former Spanish colonies of the Americas. It is also the first language of many immigrants from these countries to the United States.

**French** is spoken by 100–150 million people. Though there are fewer native speakers of French than of other major languages, its significance lies in the fact that it is the official language of 37 countries, colonies, and territories in Europe, Africa, the Americas, and the Pacific.

**Japanese** is the mother tongue of virtually all Japanese, more than 125 million people, almost all of whom live in Japan; there are significant minorities in the United States and Brazil. Modern Japanese employs four writing systems, *kanji* (adapted from the Chinese *hanzi*) *hiragana*, *katakana*, and *romaji*.

**Portuguese** is spoken by 100–170 million people, the majority of whom live in Brazil. It is the official language there, in Portugal, and in six other countries (most in Southern Africa).

**German** is spoken by 90–150 million people. It is an official language of six European countries—Germany, Austria, Switzerland, Luxembourg, Liechtenstein, and Belgium—and is spoken by significant minorities especially in Eastern Europe, Latin America, the United States, and elsewhere.

**Urdu** is spoken by more than 50–90 million people in Pakistan (where it is the official but by no means most widely spoken language), and India, where there are more than 40 million speakers. (See "Hindi" above.)

# World Population

World population has now surpassed 5.3 billion and continues to increase, although at a diminishing rate. The world's population growth rate now stands at 1.7% (it averaged 2% in the 1960s) and is projected to continue dwindling in the next century when it could drop to 1.4%. Still, because the current population is so large (2.2 billion larger than in 1960), even a slower growth rate will result in enormous numbers of people being added—an estimated 3 billion between 1990 and 2020.

This section examines world population in terms of countries and areas classified by development categories according to the UN format. While the United Nations does not issue a precise definition, "developed" countries and regions are considered to be the industrialized nations, those with a high gross national product (GNP) and a high per capita GNP, and those with high levels of science and technology. The developed countries and areas include all of North America and Europe, as well as the Soviet Union, Japan, Australia, and New Zealand.

"Developing" countries are also not defined, but are generally understood to be nations whose populations are poorer, whose economy is based on agricultural production, whose GNP and per capita GNP are low, and who lack advanced technologies. In general, developing countries are members of the Group of 77 (G-77), currently 125 countries (see "International Organizations," "Group of 77"). Developing countries and areas include all of sub-Saharan Africa, the Near East and North Africa, Latin America and the Caribbean, Asia (except Japan), and Oceania (except Australia and New Zealand).

In 1950 two-thirds of the world's population lived in developing countries; by 1987 the share had increased to three-fourths. Asia has the world's largest landmass and holds just over half of the world's people. The other half are about evenly distributed between the developed nations and the remaining developing regions.

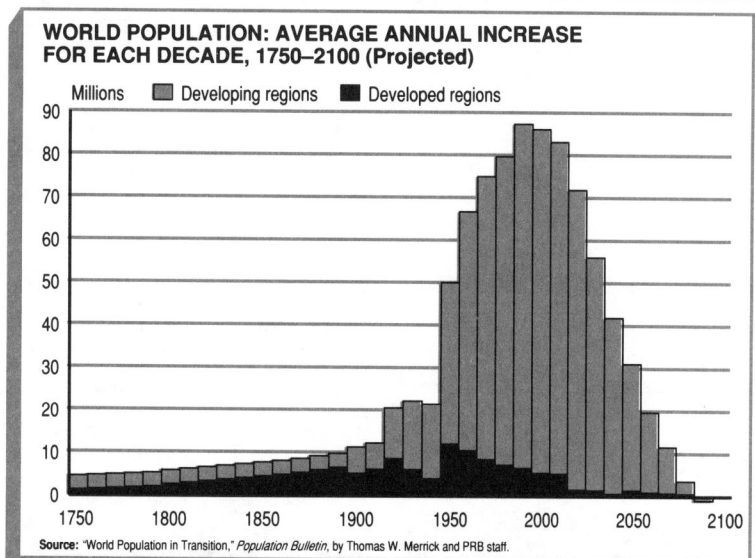

## WORLD POPULATION: AVERAGE ANNUAL INCREASE FOR EACH DECADE, 1750–2100 (Projected)

Millions — Developing regions — Developed regions

Source: "World Population in Transition," *Population Bulletin*, by Thomas W. Merrick and PRB staff.

## NUMBER OF YEARS BETWEEN EACH BILLION ADDED TO WORLD POPULATION

| Year | World population | Number of years for next billion |
|------|------------------|-----------------------------------|
| 1801 | 1 billion | N.A. |
| 1925 | 2 billion | 124 |
| 1959 | 3 billion | 34 |
| 1974 | 4 billion | 15 |
| 1986 | 5 billion | 12 |
| 1997 | 6 billion | 11 |
| 2008 | 7 billion | 11 |
| 2018 | 8 billion | 10 |
| 2028 | 9 billion | 10 |
| 2040 | 10 billion | 12 |

**Source:** U.S. Bureau of the Census, *World Population Profile: 1987* (1987).

## WORLD BIRTHS, DEATHS, AND POPULATION GROWTH, 1990

| | |
|---|---|
| Births | 141,542,000 |
| Deaths | 50,255,000 |
| Natural increase | 91,287,000 |
| Births per 1,000 population | 27.0 |
| Deaths per 1,000 population | 9.0 |
| Growth rate (percent) | 1.7% |

**Source:** U.S. Bureau of the Census.

as family planning.

**Death rate** The average annual number of deaths during a year per 1,000 population at midyear; also known as crude death rate.

**Demography** The statistical study of the characteristics of human populations including size and density, growth, distribution, migration, and vital statistics, and the effect of these factors on social and economic conditions.

**Growth rate** The average annual percent change in the population, resulting from a surplus (or deficit) of births over deaths and the balance of migrants entering and leaving a country. The rate may be positive or negative; also known as population growth rate or average annual rate of growth.

## Glossary of Demographic Terms

**Birth rate** The average annual number of births during a year per 1,000 population at midyear; also known as crude birth rate.

**Contraception** Deliberate use of methods to prevent conception or pregnancy; also known

## AVERAGE ANNUAL GROWTH RATE, BY REGION AND DEVELOPMENT CATEGORY, 1950–2010

| Region | 1950 | 1960 | 1970 | 1980 | 1990 | 2000 |
|---|---|---|---|---|---|---|
| **World** | **1.7%** | **2.0%** | **1.8%** | **1.8%** | **1.7%** | **1.4%** |
| Developed | 1.3 | 1.0 | 0.8 | 0.6 | 0.5 | 0.3 |
| Developing | 1.9 | 2.4 | 2.2 | 2.1 | 2.0 | 1.7 |
| Sub-Saharan Africa | 2.1 | 2.5 | 2.8 | 3.1 | 3.1 | 2.9 |
| Near East and North Africa | 2.6 | 2.5 | 2.8 | 2.8 | 2.6 | 2.3 |
| Asia | 1.7 | 2.2 | 2.0 | 1.9 | 1.7 | 1.3 |
| Developed | 1.2 | 1.0 | 1.1 | 0.5 | 0.4 | 0.2 |
| Developing | 1.8 | 2.3 | 2.1 | 1.9 | 1.7 | 1.3 |
| Latin America and the Caribbean | 2.7 | 2.7 | 2.4 | 2.0 | 1.8 | 1.5 |
| North America | 1.8 | 1.3 | 1.1 | 0.9 | 0.7 | 0.5 |
| Europe | 0.8 | 0.8 | 0.5 | 0.3 | 0.2 | 0.1 |
| Soviet Union | 1.7 | 1.2 | 0.9 | 0.9 | 0.7 | 0.7 |
| Oceania | 2.3 | 2.1 | 1.6 | 1.4 | 1.3 | 1.1 |
| Developed | 2.2 | 1.9 | 1.4 | 1.1 | 1.0 | 0.7 |
| Developing | 2.3 | 2.7 | 2.5 | 2.3 | 2.2 | 1.9 |
| Excluding China | | | | | | |
| World | 1.8 | 1.9 | 1.9 | 1.8 | 1.7 | 1.6 |
| Developing | 2.2 | 2.4 | 2.4 | 2.3 | 2.2 | 2.0 |
| Asia | 1.9 | 2.2 | 2.2 | 2.0 | 1.9 | 1.6 |
| Developing | 2.0 | 2.3 | 2.3 | 2.1 | 1.9 | 1.7 |

**Source:** U.S. Bureau of the Census, International Data Base (1989).

---

### 3 MORE PEOPLE EACH SECOND

Every 2 seconds, 9 babies are born and 3 people die. The net increase of 3 people each second results in a growth in world population of 10,600 per hour, 254,000 per day, 1.8 million per week, 7.7 million per month, and 93 million per year. Eighty-seven million of the annual increase occurs in developing countries, 6 million in developed countries.

By the year 2000, annual growth will increase to 94 million, and by 2020 it will be 98 million. In 2020, 98% of the increase will be in developing countries.

**Source:** U.S. Bureau of the Census, World Population Profile: 1989 (1989).

---

**Infant mortality rate** The number of deaths to infants under 1 year of age in a given year per 1,000 live births occurring in the same year.

**Projections** Data on population and vital rates derived for future years based on statistics from population censuses, vital registration systems, or sample surveys pertaining to the recent past, and on assumptions about future trends.

**Total fertility rate** The average number of children who would be born per woman if all women lived to the end of their childbearing years and bore children according to a given fertility rate at each age.

**Vital events** Births and deaths.

**Vital rates** Birth rates and death rates.

## 30 MOST POPULOUS NATIONS BY POPULATION, 1950–2050

Shifting population size in developed and developing nations is causing dramatic changes in the ranking of countries by population. As populations in developing countries continue to increase, populations in developed regions have already begun to decline and are projected to continue decreasing.

| 1950 | 1987 | 2025 | 2050 |
|---|---|---|---|
| 1. China | 1. China | 1. China | 1. India |
| 2. India | 2. India | 2. India | 2. China |
| 3. Soviet Union | 3. Soviet Union | 3. Soviet Union | 3. Nigeria |
| 4. United States | 4. United States | 4. Indonesia | 4. Pakistan |
| 5. Japan | 5. Indonesia | 5. Nigeria | 5. Soviet Union |
| 6. Indonesia | 6. Brazil | 6. United States | 6. Brazil |
| 7. Brazil | 7. Japan | 7. Brazil | 7. Indonesia |
| 8. United Kingdom | 8. Nigeria | 8. Pakistan | 8. United States |
| 9. West Germany | 9. Bangladesh | 9. Bangladesh | 9. Bangladesh |
| 10. Italy | 10. Pakistan | 10. Iran | 10. Iran |
| 11. Bangladesh | 11. Mexico | 11. Ethiopia | 11. Ethiopia |
| 12. France | 12. Vietnam | 12. Mexico | 12. Philippines |
| 13. Nigeria | 13. Philippines | 13. Philippines | 13. Mexico |
| 14. Pakistan | 14. West Germany | 14. Vietnam | 14. Vietnam |
| 15. Mexico | 15. Italy | 15. Japan | 15. Kenya |
| 16. Spain | 16. United Kingdom | 16. Egypt | 16. Zaire |
| 17. Vietnam | 17. France | 17. Turkey | 17. Egypt |
| 18. Poland | 18. Thailand | 18. Zaire | 18. Tanzania |
| 19. Egypt | 19. Turkey | 19. Kenya | 19. Turkey |
| 20. Philippines | 20. Egypt | 20. Thailand | 20. Japan |
| 21. Turkey | 21. Iran | 21. Tanzania | 21. Saudi Arabia |
| 22. South Korea | 22. Ethiopia | 22. Burma | 22. Thailand |
| 23. Ethiopia | 23. South Korea | 23. South Africa | 23. Uganda |
| 24. Thailand | 24. Spain | 24. Sudan | 24. Sudan |
| 25. Burma | 25. Burma | 25. South Korea | 25. Burma |
| 26. East Germany | 26. Poland | 26. France | 26. South Africa |
| 27. Argentina | 27. South Africa | 27. United Kingdom | 27. Syria |
| 28. Iran | 28. Zaire | 28. Italy | 28. Morocco |
| 29. Yugoslavia | 29. Argentina | 29. West Germany | 29. Algeria |
| 30. Romania | 30. Colombia | 30. Uganda | 30. Iraq |

**Note:** Developing countries are shown in bold. **Source:** U.S. Bureau of the Census, World Population Profile: 1987 (1987).

---

## WORLD POPULATION TRENDS

Currently, about 90 million people are added each year to the world's total population, more than the present population of Mexico. During the period 2015–20, the annual increment is projected to be nearly 100 million. In 1987 the world's population reached over 5 billion for the first time. Latest population projections indicate that it will take just over 50 years for the second 5 billion to be added. Although the population growth rate is projected to decline from 1.7% in 1987 to 1.3% in the period 2015–20, the average net number of people will continue to rise because the percentage increase of population is larger than the percentage decline of the growth rate.

During the next half-century, all regions of Europe and Japan are anticipated to have declining populations. In fact, the process has already begun. Between 1980 and 1985 the populations of Denmark, East Germany, West Germany, and Hungary declined, and that trend is expected to continue into the next century.

But in other areas, Africa specifically, the trend is quite different. Africa's infant mor-

## WORLD POPULATION PROJECTIONS

| Year | Population |
|---|---|
| 1990 | 5,333,000,000 |
| 2000 | 6,291,000,000 |
| 2010 | 7,255,000,000 |
| 2020 | 8,281,000,000 |

**Source:** U.S. Bureau of the Census, World Population Profile: 1989 (1989).

tality rate is 42% higher than the world average, its overall death rate 58% higher, its birth rate 68% higher, and its population growth rate 82% higher. According to the most recent projections, from 1950 to 2050, the population of Africa south of the Sahara will have grown from just 7% to nearly 21% of the world total. During this period the world population will have experienced a fourfold increase, from 2.56 billion to 10.81 billion, while that of sub-Saharan Africa will have experienced a twelvefold increase, from 186 million to 2.26 billion.

## POPULATION INDICATORS BY REGION AND NATION, 1990

| Region/Country | Population estimate ('000s) 1990 | 2025 | Birth rate per 1,000 1990 | Death rate per 1,000 1990 | Life expectancy 1990 | Percent urban 1990 | Fertility rate per woman 1990 |
|---|---|---|---|---|---|---|---|
| **World total** | **5,292,177** | **8,466,516** | **26** | **9** | **63** | **43%** | **3.3** |
| More Developed Regions | 1,205,192 | 1,352,086 | 13 | 9 | 74 | 72 | 1.9 |
| Less Developed Regions | 4,086,985 | 7,114,429 | 29 | 9 | 61 | 33 | 3.7 |
| **AFRICA** | **647,518** | **1,580,984** | **43** | **13** | **53** | **34** | **5.1** |
| **Eastern Africa** | **194,822** | **523,024** | **47** | **15** | **51** | **22** | **6.6** |
| Burundi | 5,451 | 13,099 | 44 | 15 | 51 | 7 | 6.1 |
| Ethiopia | 46,743 | 112,268 | 46 | 21 | 43 | 12 | 6.3 |
| Kenya | 25,129 | 77,615 | 50 | 9 | 60 | 23 | 7.6 |
| Madagascar | 11,979 | 32,983 | 44 | 12 | 55 | 25 | 6.5 |
| Malawi | 8,427 | 22,804 | 51 | 18 | 48 | 14 | 6.9 |
| Mauritius | 1,103 | 1,479 | 17 | 5 | 70 | 42 | 1.9 |
| Mozambique | 15,663 | 34,368 | 43 | 16 | 48 | 26 | 6.2 |
| Rwanda | 7,231 | 18,079 | 49 | 15 | 50 | 7 | 8.0 |
| Somalia | 7,554 | 18,903 | 46 | 18 | 46 | 36 | 6.5 |
| Tanzania | 27,328 | 84,783 | 49 | 12 | 54 | 32 | 7.0 |
| Uganda | 18,441 | 55,198 | 49 | 13 | 53 | 10 | 6.8 |
| Zambia | 8,455 | 25,465 | 49 | 12 | 55 | 55 | 7.0 |
| Zimbabwe | 9,720 | 22,620 | 39 | 8 | 60 | 27 | 5.3 |
| **Middle Africa** | **69,563** | **179,645** | **44** | **14** | **52** | **39** | **6.0** |
| Angola | 10,020 | 24,730 | 46 | 18 | 46 | 28 | 6.3 |
| Cameroon | 11,245 | 26,177 | 41 | 14 | 52 | 49 | 5.7 |
| Central African Rep. | 2,912 | 6,814 | 43 | 18 | 47 | 46 | 5.8 |
| Chad | 5,678 | 13,244 | 43 | 17 | 47 | 33 | 5.8 |
| Congo | 1,994 | 4,963 | 43 | 15 | 50 | 42 | 5.8 |
| Gabon | 1,170 | 2,927 | 43 | 15 | 53 | 45 | 5.3 |
| Zaire | 35,990 | 99,512 | 44 | 12 | 54 | 39 | 6.0 |
| **Northern Africa** | **142,648** | **275,020** | **34** | **9** | **61** | **44** | **4.8** |
| Algeria | 25,363 | 50,590 | 36 | 7 | 64 | 44 | 5.2 |
| Egypt | 54,059 | 93,976 | 30 | 8 | 63 | 48 | 4.2 |
| Libya | 4,544 | 12,846 | 43 | 8 | 63 | 70 | 6.7 |
| Morocco | 25,138 | 44,367 | 31 | 8 | 63 | 48 | 4.2 |
| Sudan | 25,195 | 59,594 | 43 | 14 | 51 | 22 | 6.3 |
| Tunisia | 8,168 | 13,283 | 26 | 6 | 67 | 54 | 3.4 |
| **Southern Africa** | **40,972** | **78,022** | **31** | **8** | **62** | **55** | **4.4** |
| Botswana | 1,285 | 3,363 | 44 | 9 | 60 | 23 | 5.9 |
| Lesotho | 1,773 | 4,272 | 39 | 10 | 58 | 20 | 5.6 |
| Namibia | 1,875 | 4,948 | 41 | 10 | 58 | 56 | 5.7 |
| South Africa | 35,248 | 63,232 | 29 | 8 | 62 | 58 | 4.2 |
| **Western Africa** | **199,511** | **525,271** | **47** | **14** | **51** | **33** | **6.7** |
| Benin | 4,740 | 12,987 | 49 | 17 | 48 | 41 | 6.9 |
| Burkina Faso | 9,006 | 22,677 | 46 | 17 | 49 | 9 | 6.4 |
| Ghana | 15,020 | 37,031 | 42 | 11 | 56 | 33 | 6.2 |
| Guinea | 6,875 | 15,710 | 45 | 20 | 44 | 25 | 6.1 |
| Ivory Coast | 12,595 | 39,842 | 50 | 12 | 54 | 46 | 7.3 |
| Liberia | 2,553 | 7,240 | 44 | 12 | 56 | 44 | 6.4 |
| Mali | 9,361 | 24,141 | 48 | 19 | 46 | 19 | 6.6 |
| Mauritania | 2,024 | 4,962 | 45 | 17 | 48 | 42 | 6.4 |
| Niger | 7,109 | 18,940 | 50 | 18 | 46 | 19 | 7.0 |
| Nigeria | 113,016 | 301,312 | 48 | 14 | 52 | 35 | 6.8 |
| Senegal | 7,369 | 16,364 | 44 | 17 | 47 | 38 | 6.2 |
| Sierra Leone | 4,150 | 9,640 | 47 | 21 | 43 | 32 | 6.4 |
| Togo | 3,454 | 9,500 | 43 | 12 | 55 | 25 | 6.0 |
| **LATIN AMERICA** | **448,096** | **760,378** | **26** | **7** | **67** | **72** | **3.3** |
| **Caribbean** | **33,639** | **48,758** | **23** | **7** | **67** | **59** | **2.8** |
| Cuba | 10,324 | 11,967 | 15 | 7 | 74 | 74 | 1.7 |
| Dominican Rep. | 7,169 | 11,447 | 28 | 6 | 67 | 60 | 3.3 |
| Haiti | 6,504 | 11,534 | 33 | 11 | 56 | 30 | 4.4 |
| Jamaica | 2,520 | 3,758 | 22 | 5 | 74 | 52 | 2.4 |
| Puerto Rico | 3,708 | 5,177 | 19 | 6 | 75 | 73 | 2.3 |
| Trinidad and Tobago | 1,282 | 1,918 | 21 | 6 | 71 | 69 | 2.5 |
| **Central America** | **117,669** | **213,186** | **28** | **5** | **69** | **66** | **3.5** |
| Costa Rica | 3,014 | 5,250 | 25 | 4 | 75 | 53 | 3.0 |
| El Salvador | 5,251 | 11,299 | 36 | 6 | 66 | 44 | 4.5 |
| Guatemala | 9,196 | 21,668 | 38 | 7 | 64 | 41 | 5.4 |
| Honduras | 5,138 | 11,510 | 37 | 7 | 65 | 43 | 4.9 |
| Mexico | 88,597 | 150,061 | 26 | 5 | 70 | 72 | 3.1 |
| Nicaragua | 3,870 | 9,219 | 38 | 6 | 66 | 59 | 5.0 |
| Panama | 2,417 | 3,861 | 24 | 5 | 72 | 54 | 2.9 |
| **South America** | **296,786** | **498,433** | **26** | **7** | **66** | **76** | **3.3** |
| Argentina | 32,321 | 45,504 | 20 | 8 | 71 | 86 | 2.8 |
| Bolivia | 7,313 | 18,294 | 41 | 12 | 55 | 51 | 5.8 |
| Brazil | 150,367 | 245,808 | 26 | 7 | 66 | 76 | 3.2 |
| Chile | 13,173 | 19,773 | 22 | 6 | 71 | 85 | 2.7 |
| Colombia | 31,819 | 51,718 | 26 | 7 | 65 | 70 | 3.3 |
| Ecuador | 10,781 | 22,909 | 33 | 7 | 66 | 56 | 4.3 |
| Guyana | 1,039 | 1,569 | 21 | 5 | 70 | 34 | 2.4 |
| Paraguay | 4,276 | 9,182 | 33 | 6 | 67 | 47 | 4.3 |
| Peru | 22,332 | 41,006 | 31 | 7 | 64 | 70 | 4.0 |
| Uruguay | 3,128 | 3,875 | 18 | 10 | 71 | 85 | 2.5 |
| Venezuela | 19,735 | 38,000 | 28 | 5 | 70 | 90 | 3.5 |
| **NORTH AMERICA** | **275,880** | **332,997** | **13** | **8** | **76** | **74** | **1.8** |
| Canada | 26,525 | 32,051 | 12 | 7 | 77 | 76 | 1.7 |
| United States | 249,235 | 300,796 | 14 | 8 | 76 | 74 | 1.9 |
| **ASIA** | **3,108,475** | **4,889,451** | **26** | **8** | **63** | **29** | **3.2** |
| **Eastern Asia** | **1,334,018** | **1,728,571** | **19** | **6** | **71** | **29** | **2.1** |
| China | 1,135,495 | 1,492,550 | 19 | 6 | 70 | 21 | 2.2 |
| Hong Kong | 5,840 | 6,952 | 13 | 6 | 76 | 93 | 1.6 |
| Japan | 123,456 | 128,595 | 12 | 7 | 78 | 76 | 1.8 |
| Korea, North | 22,936 | 39,606 | 26 | 4 | 70 | 67 | 3.2 |
| Korea, South | 43,582 | 54,626 | 16 | 6 | 70 | 72 | 1.8 |
| Mongolia | 2,226 | 5,419 | 37 | 7 | 65 | 51 | 5.2 |
| **Southeastern Asia** | **440,830** | **700,544** | **26** | **8** | **61** | **29** | **3.2** |
| Cambodia | 8,245 | 13,988 | 36 | 14 | 50 | 11 | 4.4 |
| Indonesia | 180,513 | 263,250 | 25 | 10 | 58 | 28 | 2.9 |
| Laos | 4,070 | 7,735 | 38 | 14 | 50 | 18 | 5.3 |
| Malaysia | 17,339 | 27,886 | 25 | 5 | 70 | 42 | 3.1 |
| Myanmar | 41,675 | 72,619 | 29 | 8 | 62 | 24 | 3.7 |
| Singapore | 2,701 | 3,238 | 15 | 5 | 73 | 99 | 1.7 |
| Thailand | 55,701 | 80,911 | 20 | 6 | 67 | 22 | 2.2 |
| Vietnam | 67,170 | 117,971 | 30 | 8 | 63 | 21 | 3.7 |
| **Southern Asia** | **1,202,857** | **2,173,800** | **33** | **10** | **59** | **27** | **4.5** |
| Afghanistan | 16,556 | 41,062 | 52 | 21 | 43 | 21 | 6.8 |
| Bangladesh | 115,593 | 234,986 | 40 | 13 | 52 | 13 | 5.1 |
| Bhutan | 1,516 | 3,069 | 38 | 15 | 49 | 5 | 5.5 |
| India | 853,372 | 1,445,570 | 31 | 10 | 60 | 28 | 4.1 |
| Iran | 56,585 | 122,169 | 39 | 6 | 67 | 54 | 5.4 |
| Nepal | 19,143 | 34,972 | 36 | 12 | 53 | 9 | 5.5 |
| Pakistan | 122,666 | 267,088 | 41 | 10 | 59 | 31 | 5.9 |
| Sri Lanka | 17,209 | 24,448 | 20 | 5 | 71 | 21 | 2.5 |
| **Western Asia** | **130,769** | **286,534** | **33** | **7** | **65** | **58** | **4.7** |
| Iraq | 18,919 | 49,992 | 40 | 6 | 66 | 74 | 5.9 |
| Israel | 4,580 | 6,932 | 20 | 6 | 76 | 91 | 2.7 |
| Jordan | 4,269 | 13,129 | 45 | 5 | 67 | 68 | 6.9 |
| Kuwait | 2,090 | 4,350 | 28 | 2 | 73 | 95 | 4.3 |
| Lebanon | 2,965 | 4,950 | 27 | 7 | 68 | 83 | 3.1 |
| Oman | 1,468 | 4,308 | 44 | 10 | 58 | 10 | 7.1 |
| Saudi Arabia | 14,131 | 44,780 | 41 | 6 | 65 | 77 | 7.1 |
| Syria | 12,500 | 32,270 | 41 | 5 | 67 | 51 | 6.3 |
| Turkey | 55,616 | 89,646 | 26 | 7 | 66 | 48 | 3.2 |

| Region/Country | Population estimate ('000s) 1990 | 2025 | Birth rate per 1,000 1990 | Death rate per 1,000 1990 | Life expectancy 1990 | Percent urban 1990 | Fertility rate per woman 1990 |
|---|---|---|---|---|---|---|---|
| United Arab Emirates | 1,588 | 2,692 | 20 | 3 | 71 | 77 | 4.3 |
| Yemen, Republic of | 10,506 | 29,739 | 47 | 10 | 59 | 30 | 5.7 |
| **EUROPE** | **497,740** | **512,290** | **12** | **10** | **75** | **73** | **1.7** |
| **Eastern Europe** | **113,573** | **123,291** | **13** | **10** | **72** | **63** | **1.9** |
| Bulgaria | 9,010 | 8,944 | 12 | 11 | 73 | 70 | 1.8 |
| Czechoslovakia | 15,667 | 17,181 | 13 | 11 | 72 | 68 | 2.0 |
| Germany, East | 16,649 | 16,155 | 11 | 11 | 74 | 77 | 1.7 |
| Hungary | 10,551 | 10,199 | 11 | 12 | 71 | 60 | 1.8 |
| Poland | 38,423 | 45,065 | 14 | 9 | 71 | 63 | 2.1 |
| Romania | 23,271 | 25,744 | 15 | 10 | 71 | 50 | 2.0 |
| **Northern Europe** | **83,793** | **85,751** | **13** | **11** | **76** | **87** | **1.8** |
| Denmark | 5,120 | 4,971 | 11 | 11 | 76 | 86 | 1.5 |
| Finland | 4,974 | 5,120 | 11 | 10 | 75 | 67 | 1.7 |
| Ireland | 3,719 | 4,958 | 17 | 8 | 75 | 59 | 2.4 |
| Norway | 4,211 | 4,504 | 12 | 10 | 77 | 74 | 1.7 |
| Sweden | 8,339 | 8,135 | 11 | 12 | 77 | 83 | 1.7 |
| United Kingdom | 56,926 | 57,463 | 13 | 11 | 76 | 92 | 1.8 |
| **Southern Europe** | **144,534** | **150,270** | **12** | **9** | **75** | **64** | **1.7** |
| Albania | 3,245 | 5,010 | 21 | 5 | 72 | 35 | 2.7 |
| Greece | 10,047 | 10,080 | 11 | 10 | 76 | 62 | 1.7 |

| Region/Country | Population estimate ('000s) 1990 | 2025 | Birth rate per 1,000 1990 | Death rate per 1,000 1990 | Life expectancy 1990 | Percent urban 1990 | Fertility rate per woman 1990 |
|---|---|---|---|---|---|---|---|
| Italy | 57,321 | 54,919 | 11 | 10 | 76 | 68 | 1.5 |
| Portugal | 10,284 | 10,934 | 13 | 10 | 74 | 33 | 1.7 |
| Spain | 39,332 | 42,530 | 12 | 9 | 77 | 78 | 1.7 |
| Yugoslavia | 23,848 | 26,291 | 13 | 8 | 73 | 50 | 1.9 |
| **Western Europe** | **155,838** | **152,975** | **12** | **10** | **76** | **80** | **1.6** |
| Austria | 7,492 | 7,042 | 11 | 11 | 75 | 57 | 1.5 |
| Belgium | 9,938 | 9,920 | 11 | 11 | 75 | 96 | 1.6 |
| France | 56,173 | 60,442 | 13 | 9 | 76 | 74 | 1.8 |
| Germany, West | 60,539 | 53,965 | 10 | 11 | 75 | 86 | 1.4 |
| Netherlands | 14,751 | 15,081 | 11 | 8 | 77 | 88 | 1.5 |
| Switzerland | 6,520 | 6,117 | 11 | 10 | 77 | 59 | 1.6 |
| **OCEANIA** | **26,476** | **38,964** | **19** | **7** | **69** | **70** | **2.5** |
| **Australia-New Zealand** | **20,124** | **26,752** | **14** | **7** | **76** | **85** | **1.8** |
| Australia | 16,745 | 22,686 | 14 | 7 | 76 | 85 | 1.8 |
| New Zealand | 3,378 | 4,066 | 15 | 8 | 75 | 84 | 1.8 |
| Melanesia | 5,417 | 10,913 | 34 | 9 | 59 | 21 | 4.9 |
| Papua New Guinea | 4,011 | 8,600 | 36 | 10 | 56 | 15 | 5.3 |
| **USSR** | **287,990** | **351,450** | **16** | **9** | **70** | **67** | **2.3** |

**Source:** United Nations Population Fund (UNFPA), *The State of World Population 1990* (1990).

## WORLD POPULATION BY REGION AND DEVELOPMENT CATEGORY, 1950–2010 (in millions)

| Region | 1950 | 1960 | 1970 | 1980 | 1990 | 2000 | 2010 |
|---|---|---|---|---|---|---|---|
| **WORLD** | **2,565** | **3,050** | **3,721** | **4,477** | **5,333** | **6,291** | **7,255** |
| Developed | 832 | 945 | 1,049 | 1,137 | 1,211 | 1,270 | 1,315 |
| Developing | 1,733 | 2,105 | 2,672 | 3,340 | 4,122 | 5,021 | 5,940 |
| Sub-Saharan Africa | 194 | 239 | 305 | 403 | 542 | 739 | 992 |
| Near East and North Africa | 87 | 112 | 144 | 191 | 253 | 328 | 414 |
| Asia | 1,368 | 1,628 | 2,037 | 2,494 | 2,994 | 3,536 | 4,027 |
| Developed | 84 | 94 | 104 | 117 | 124 | 129 | 133 |
| Developing | 1,284 | 1,533 | 1,933 | 2,377 | 2,870 | 3,406 | 3,895 |
| Latin America and the Caribbean | 166 | 218 | 286 | 364 | 450 | 540 | 630 |

| Region | 1950 | 1960 | 1970 | 1980 | 1990 | 2000 | 2010 |
|---|---|---|---|---|---|---|---|
| North America | 166 | 199 | 226 | 252 | 277 | 296 | 312 |
| Europe | 392 | 425 | 460 | 484 | 499 | 511 | 513 |
| Soviet Union | 180 | 214 | 243 | 266 | 291 | 312 | 334 |
| Oceania | 12 | 16 | 19 | 23 | 26 | 30 | 33 |
| Developed | 10 | 13 | 15 | 18 | 20 | 22 | 24 |
| Developing | 2 | 3 | 4 | 5 | 6 | 8 | 9 |
| Excluding China | | | | | | | |
| World | 2,002 | 2,399 | 2,901 | 3,494 | 4,203 | 5,000 | 5,856 |
| Developing | 1,170 | 1,454 | 1,852 | 2,357 | 2,992 | 3,730 | 4,541 |
| Asia | 805 | 977 | 1,217 | 1,511 | 1,864 | 2,244 | 2,629 |
| Developing | 721 | 883 | 1,113 | 1,394 | 1,740 | 2,115 | 2,497 |

**Note:** Figures may not add to totals owing to rounding. **Source:** U.S. Bureau of the Census, *World Population Profile: 1989* (1989).

## WORLD'S LARGEST URBAN AREAS PROJECTED FOR 2000 (in thousands)

| City | Projection |
|---|---|
| 1. Tokyo-Yokohama, Japan | 29,971 |
| 2. Mexico City, Mexico | 27,872 |
| 3. São Paulo, Brazil | 25,354 |
| 4. Seoul, South Korea | 21,976 |
| 5. Bombay, India | 15,357 |
| 6. New York, United States | 14,648 |
| 7. Osaka-Kobe-Kyoto, Japan | 14,287 |
| 8. Tehran, Iran | 14,251 |
| 9. Rio de Janeiro, Brazil | 14,169 |
| 10. Calcutta, India | 14,088 |
| 11. Buenos Aires, Argentina | 12,911 |
| 12. Manila, Philippines | 12,846 |
| 13. Jakarta, Indonesia | 12,804 |
| 14. Lagos, Nigeria | 12,528 |
| 15. Cairo, Egypt | 12,512 |
| 16. Delhi, India | 11,849 |
| 17. Karachi, Pakistan | 11,299 |
| 18. Moscow, Soviet Union | 11,121 |
| 19. Los Angeles, United States | 10,714 |

**Source:** U.S. Bureau of the Census, International Data Base (1989).

## WORLD'S LARGEST URBAN AREAS, 1990 (in thousands)

| City | Population |
|---|---|
| 1. Tokyo-Yokohama, Japan | 26,952 |
| 2. Mexico City, Mexico | 20,207 |
| 3. São Paulo, Brazil | 18,052 |
| 4. Seoul, South Korea | 16,268 |
| 5. New York, United States | 14,622 |
| 6. Osaka-Kobe-Kyoto, Japan | 13,826 |
| 7. Bombay, India | 11,777 |
| 8. Calcutta, India | 11,663 |
| 9. Buenos Aires, Argentina | 11,518 |
| 10. Rio de Janeiro, Brazil | 11,428 |
| 11. Moscow, Soviet Union | 10,367 |
| 12. Los Angeles, United States | 10,060 |

**Source:** U.S. Bureau of the Census, International Data Base (1989).

## WORLD CITIES WITH GREATEST POPULATION DENSITY, 1989

| Urban area | Population per sq. mi. |
|---|---|
| 1. Hong Kong, Hong Kong | 247,004 |
| 2. Lagos, Nigeria | 129,705 |
| 3. Dhaka, Bangladesh | 125,511 |
| 4. Jakarta, Indonesia | 122,033 |
| 5. Bombay, India | 120,299 |
| 6. Ho Chi Minh City, Vietnam | 114,914 |
| 7. Ahmadabad, India | 108,618 |
| 8. Shenyang, China | 108,080 |
| 9. Tianjin, China | 97,291 |
| 10. Chengdu, China | 93,242 |
| 11. Cairo, Egypt | 92,168 |

**Source:** U.S. Bureau of the Census, International Data Base (1989).

## POPULATION OF THE WORLD'S LARGEST URBAN AREAS, 1960–2000, RANKED BY 1985 POPULATION (in millions)

The following urban areas had populations of 2 million or more in 1985. An urban area is a central city, or several cities, and the surrounding urbanized areas; also called a metropolitan area.

| Urban area | 1960 | 1970 | 1985 | 1990[1] | 2000[1] | Urban area | 1960 | 1970 | 1985 | 1990[1] | 2000[1] |
|---|---|---|---|---|---|---|---|---|---|---|---|
| 1. Tokyo-Yokohama, Japan | 10.69 | 14.91 | 18.82 | 19.28 | 20.22 | 51. Belo Horizonte, Brazil | 0.89 | 1.63 | 3.25 | 3.89 | 5.11 |
| 2. Mexico City, Mexico | 5.22 | 9.12 | 17.30 | 20.25 | 25.82 | 52. Barcelona, Spain | 1.94 | 2.66 | 3.20 | 3.24 | 3.35 |
| 3. São Paulo, Brazil | 4.84 | 8.22 | 15.88 | 18.77 | 23.97 | 53. Toronto, Canada | 1.76 | 2.55 | 3.16 | 3.33 | 3.58 |
| 4. New York, United States | 14.23 | 16.29 | 15.64 | 15.69 | 15.78 | 54. Melbourne, Australia | 1.88 | 2.34 | 3.15 | 3.23 | 3.41 |
| 5. Shanghai, China | 10.67 | 11.41 | 11.96 | 12.35 | 14.30 | 55. Ahmadabad, India | 1.21 | 1.74 | 3.14 | 3.76 | 5.28 |
| 6. Calcutta, India | 5.62 | 7.12 | 10.95 | 12.54 | 16.53 | 56. Hyderabad, India | 1.27 | 1.80 | 3.12 | 3.70 | 5.13 |
| 7. Buenos Aires, Argentina | 6.93 | 8.55 | 10.88 | 11.71 | 13.18 | 57. Istanbul, Turkey | 1.45 | 2.78 | 2.94 | 2.98 | 3.29 |
| 8. Rio de Janeiro, Brazil | 5.07 | 7.17 | 10.37 | 11.37 | 13.26 | 58. Alexandria, Egypt | 1.51 | 2.02 | 2.93 | 3.35 | 4.40 |
| 9. London, United Kingdom | 10.73 | 10.59 | 10.36 | 10.40 | 10.51 | 59. Washington, D.C., United States | 1.83 | 2.50 | 2.91 | 3.03 | 3.22 |
| 10. Seoul, South Korea | 2.39 | 5.42 | 10.28 | 11.66 | 13.77 | 60. Ankara, Turkey | 0.64 | 1.27 | 2.90 | 3.63 | 5.20 |
| 11. Bombay, India | 4.15 | 5.98 | 10.07 | 11.79 | 16.00 | 61. Birmingham, United Kingdom | 2.67 | 2.81 | 2.87 | 2.89 | 2.93 |
| 12. Los Angeles, United States | 6.56 | 8.43 | 10.05 | 10.48 | 10.99 | 62. Montreal, Canada | 2.04 | 2.70 | 2.84 | 2.86 | 2.90 |
| 13. Osaka-Kobe, Japan | 5.75 | 7.61 | 9.45 | 9.82 | 10.49 | 63. Houston, United States | 1.16 | 1.70 | 2.83 | 3.19 | 3.65 |
| 14. Beijing, China | 7.31 | 8.29 | 9.25 | 9.59 | 11.17 | 64. Guadalajara, Mexico | 0.93 | 1.58 | 2.77 | 3.20 | 4.11 |
| 15. Moscow, USSR | 6.29 | 7.07 | 8.97 | 9.54 | 10.40 | 65. Pôrto Alegre, Brazil | 1.04 | 1.55 | 2.74 | 3.18 | 4.02 |
| 16. Paris, France | 7.23 | 8.34 | 8.68 | 8.68 | 8.72 | 66. Recife, Brazil | 1.24 | 1.82 | 2.74 | 3.04 | 3.65 |
| 17. Jakarta, Indonesia | 2.81 | 4.48 | 7.94 | 9.48 | 13.25 | 67. Rangoon, Burma[2] | 0.96 | 1.42 | 2.73 | 3.17 | 4.32 |
| 18. Tianjin, China | 5.98 | 6.87 | 7.89 | 8.25 | 9.70 | 68. Boston, United States | 2.43 | 2.67 | 2.71 | 2.74 | 2.83 |
| 19. Cairo/Giza, Egypt | 4.46 | 5.69 | 7.69 | 8.64 | 11.13 | 69. Chongqing, China | 2.15 | 2.46 | 2.70 | 2.81 | 3.33 |
| 20. Tehran, Iran | 1.79 | 3.29 | 7.52 | 9.38 | 13.58 | 70. Casablanca, Morocco | 1.10 | 1.54 | 2.69 | 3.24 | 4.49 |
| 21. Delhi, India | 2.33 | 3.64 | 7.40 | 9.13 | 13.24 | 71. Kinshasa, Zaire | 0.50 | 1.23 | 2.69 | 3.30 | 5.04 |
| 22. Milan, Italy | 4.51 | 5.52 | 7.22 | 7.53 | 8.15 | 72. Dallas, United States | 1.16 | 2.04 | 2.68 | 2.87 | 3.13 |
| 23. Manila/Quezon City, Philippines | 2.32 | 3.60 | 7.03 | 8.26 | 11.07 | 73. Athens, Greece | 1.81 | 2.10 | 2.68 | 2.80 | 3.04 |
| 24. Chicago, United States | 6.00 | 6.76 | 6.84 | 6.90 | 7.03 | 74. Chengdu, China | 1.12 | 1.58 | 2.67 | 3.02 | 3.87 |
| 25. Karachi, Pakistan | 1.82 | 3.14 | 6.70 | 8.16 | 12.00 | 75. Algiers, Algeria | 0.87 | 1.19 | 2.66 | 3.38 | 5.09 |
| 26. Bangkok, Thailand | 2.19 | 3.27 | 6.07 | 7.38 | 10.71 | 76. Ho Chi Minh City, Vietnam | 1.53 | 2.30 | 2.62 | 2.85 | 3.75 |
| 27. Lima/Callao, Peru | 1.75 | 2.92 | 5.68 | 6.78 | 9.14 | 77. Kiev, USSR | 1.19 | 1.65 | 2.61 | 2.92 | 3.44 |
| 28. Madras, India | 1.74 | 3.12 | 5.19 | 6.03 | 8.15 | 78. Harbin, China | 1.55 | 2.00 | 2.61 | 2.82 | 3.46 |
| 29. Hong Kong, Hong Kong | 2.74 | 3.53 | 5.13 | 5.62 | 6.37 | 79. Singapore, Singapore | 1.27 | 1.58 | 2.56 | 2.70 | 2.95 |
| 30. Leningrad, USSR | 3.46 | 3.96 | 5.11 | 5.43 | 5.93 | 80. Monterrey, Mexico | 0.93 | 1.28 | 2.53 | 3.01 | 3.97 |
| 31. Dhaka, Bangladesh | 0.66 | 1.54 | 4.89 | 6.53 | 11.16 | 81. Manchester, United Kingdom | 2.53 | 2.53 | 2.50 | 2.51 | 2.53 |
| 32. Madrid, Spain | 2.22 | 3.37 | 4.71 | 4.95 | 5.36 | 82. Taipei, Taiwan | 0.97 | 1.50 | 2.50 | 2.84 | 3.68 |
| 33. Bogotá, Colombia | 1.32 | 2.37 | 4.49 | 5.27 | 6.53 | 83. Zibo, China | 0.80 | 1.30 | 2.39 | 2.78 | 3.66 |
| 34. Baghdad, Iraq | 1.02 | 2.10 | 4.42 | 5.34 | 7.42 | 84. Surabaja, Indonesia | 0.98 | 1.53 | 2.37 | 2.73 | 3.68 |
| 35. Philadelphia, United States | 3.66 | 4.05 | 4.18 | 4.24 | 4.36 | 85. Turin, Italy | 1.25 | 1.62 | 2.26 | 2.40 | 2.61 |
| 36. Santiago, Chile | 2.12 | 3.01 | 4.16 | 4.55 | 5.26 | 86. Xi'an, China | 1.34 | 1.73 | 2.26 | 2.44 | 3.00 |
| 37. Naples, Italy | 3.20 | 3.59 | 4.11 | 4.15 | 4.30 | 87. Salvador, Brazil | 0.73 | 1.16 | 2.24 | 2.65 | 3.45 |
| 38. Pusan, South Korea | 1.17 | 1.85 | 4.11 | 4.90 | 6.20 | 88. Bucharest, Romania | 1.40 | 1.69 | 2.23 | 2.37 | 2.64 |
| 39. Shenyang, China | 2.47 | 3.14 | 4.08 | 4.39 | 5.35 | 89. Liupanshui, China | 1.19 | 1.66 | 2.19 | 2.37 | 2.92 |
| 40. Bangalore, India | 1.20 | 1.66 | 3.97 | 5.14 | 7.96 | 90. Hamburg, West Germany | 2.09 | 2.20 | 2.19 | 2.19 | 2.19 |
| 41. Detroit, United States | 3.56 | 3.99 | 3.83 | 3.86 | 3.96 | 91. Nanjing, China | 1.45 | 1.78 | 2.14 | 2.28 | 2.75 |
| 42. Sydney, Australia | 2.14 | 2.68 | 3.78 | 3.93 | 4.23 | 92. Poona, India | 0.74 | 1.13 | 2.13 | 2.58 | 3.69 |
| 43. Caracas, Venezuela | 1.31 | 2.12 | 3.74 | 4.18 | 5.03 | 93. Tashkent, USSR | 1.00 | 1.40 | 2.13 | 2.36 | 2.74 |
| 44. Lahore, Pakistan | 1.24 | 1.97 | 3.70 | 4.35 | 6.16 | 94. Munich, West Germany | 1.33 | 1.71 | 2.11 | 2.18 | 2.22 |
| 45. Rome, Italy | 2.33 | 3.07 | 3.69 | 3.75 | 3.87 | 95. Medan, Indonesia | 0.47 | 0.64 | 2.09 | 3.01 | 5.36 |
| 46. Lagos, Nigeria | 0.70 | 1.44 | 3.65 | 4.79 | 8.34 | 96. Kitakyushu, Japan | 1.31 | 1.60 | 2.06 | 2.13 | 2.22 |
| 47. Wuhan, China | 2.17 | 2.73 | 3.38 | 3.60 | 4.35 | 97. Budapest, Hungary | 1.81 | 1.95 | 2.06 | 2.06 | 2.09 |
| 48. Guangzhou (Canton), China | 1.93 | 2.50 | 3.30 | 3.57 | 4.37 | 98. Kanpur, India | 0.97 | 1.29 | 2.03 | 2.35 | 3.17 |
| 49. San Francisco, United States | 2.45 | 3.01 | 3.30 | 3.40 | 3.55 | 99. Nagoya, Japan | 1.50 | 1.85 | 2.03 | 2.03 | 2.03 |
| 50. Katowice, Poland | 2.44 | 2.77 | 3.27 | 3.46 | 3.77 | | | | | | |

1. Projected figures. 2. Now known as Yangon, Myanmar. **Source:** United Nations, Department for International Economic and Social Affairs, *The Prospects of World Urbanization: Revised as of 1984–85* (1987).

## URBANIZATION

According to the U.S. Census Bureau, 29% of the world's population lived in urban areas in 1950; by 1970, 37% did. The movement of millions of people from rural to urban areas then continued with even greater intensity, so that by 1985, 45% of the world's population were urban dwellers.

In 1950, 54% of the people in developed regions lived in urban areas; in developing regions, 17% were urban dwellers. By 1985 urbanization had reached 72% in the developed areas and 36% in developing countries. In other words, from 1950 to 1985, nearly 1.5 billion people were added to urban areas in developing regions, while the developed urban areas added 400 million people.

In 1970 there were 62 urban areas of 2 million or more inhabitants; by 1985 there were 99, 12 with 10 million or more inhabitants, and 8 of these were in less-developed regions. The 9 countries containing the world's 12 largest urban areas constitute 52% of the world's population. Among the 99 urban areas, 35 were in developed countries in 1985.

The U.S. Census Bureau projects that from 1985 to 2000, the urban areas in developing regions will add 1 billion inhabitants, while those in the developed urban areas will add 200 million. At that point, 52% of the world's total population will be living in urban centers; the developed regions will be 75% urbanized and the developing areas 47%.

By 2000, 23 urban areas are expected to have more than 10 million people, 17 of these areas in less-developed countries and 6 in more-developed regions.

## POPULATION GROWTH FOR SELECTED COUNTRIES

| Nation | Years to double population |
|---|---|
| Nigeria | 23 |
| Bangladesh | 25 |
| Pakistan | 26 |
| Brazil | 35 |
| India | 35 |
| Indonesia | 36 |
| China (mainland) | 44 |
| United States | 79 |
| Soviet Union | 89 |
| Japan | 150 |

**Source:** U.S. Bureau of the Census, *World Population Profile: 1989* (1989).

## COUNTRIES WITH HIGHEST AND LOWEST INFANT MORTALITY RATES, 1989

| Country | Infant mortality rate[1] | Country | Infant mortality rate[1] |
|---|---|---|---|
| **Highest infant mortality** | | **Lowest infant mortality** | |
| Western Sahara | 176 | Japan | 5 |
| Afghanistan | 173 | Liechtenstein | 5 |
| The Gambia | 172 | Finland | 6 |
| Angola | 161 | Hong Kong | 6 |
| Sierra Leone | 157 | Iceland | 6 |
| Mali | 151 | Ireland | 6 |
| Guinea | 149 | Sweden | 6 |
| Central African Rep. | 143 | Switzerland | 6 |
| Mozambique | 142 | Canada | 7 |
| Bhutan | 139 | Denmark | 7 |
| Chad | 139 | West Germany | 7 |
| Bangladesh | 138 | Netherlands | 7 |
| Burkina Faso | 138 | Norway | 7 |
| Niger | 137 | Andorra | 8 |
| Malawi | 132 | Aruba | 8 |
| Cambodia | 131 | Austria | 8 |
| Guinea-Bissau | 130 | Australia | 8 |
| | | Belgium | 8 |
| | | Cyprus | 8 |
| | | Italy | 8 |
| | | Luxembourg | 8 |
| | | Malta | 8 |

1. Rate per 1,000 live births. **Source:** U.S. Bureau of the Census, *World Population Profile: 1989* (1989).

## INFANT MORTALITY

Infant mortality rates vary greatly among countries of the world. Infant deaths account for about 1 out of 4 deaths in developing countries; in developed nations, infant deaths account for only 2% of all deaths. Whether or not a newborn survives the first year of life depends on the age of the mother, the order of birth, nutritional level of the mother, medical care provided during pregnancy and at birth, and supplying basic needs after birth.

There is a strong correlation between high birth rates and high infant death rates, caused,

in part, by children being born too close together, the mother being too young or too old, and the difficulties of providing sufficient food and medical services for a number of children. The developed nations have the lowest birth rates and the lowest infant death rates. The developing nations with the highest birth rates also have high infant death rates.

Sub-Saharan Africa has the highest birth rate of any region and also the highest infant mortality rate. Nine of the 10 countries having the world's highest infant mortality rates are in Africa.

## INFANT MORTALITY RATES BY REGION, 1989

| Region | Infant mortality rate (per 1,000 live births) |
|---|---|
| Sub-Saharan Africa | 110 |
| Near East and North Africa | 77 |
| Asia | 72 |
| Latin America and Caribbean | 55 |
| Oceania | 34 |
| North America, Europe, USSR | 16 |

**Source:** U.S. Bureau of the Census, *World Population Profile: 1989* (1989).

# World Religions

In 1985, of an estimated 4.8 billion people on Earth, about four out of five were identified as adherents of a religion. The remainder were either nonreligious (agnostic) or atheistic (actively opposed to theistic religion). This section describes the major religions of the world, their basic tenets, scriptures, schools and sects, and their history. (Additional detail may be found in the section "Religion in America.") The primary source of information in this section is *The World Christian Encyclopedia*.

## CHRISTIANITY

**Founder** Jesus Christ, who is seen by most Christians as the Son of God. The Julian and

Gregorian calendars are dated from the traditional year of his birth. Scholars today believe he was actually born about 3 B.C. and died about A.D. 30. Jesus was born and raised a Jew, and became a rabbi, or teacher. According to Christian scripture, he was the Messiah awaited by the Jewish people. He took up preaching and healing at the age of 30. Three years later he was sentenced to death in Jerusalem and was executed by crucifixion. The scriptures further report that he soon rose from the dead.

**Scripture** The Bible, which consists of the Old Testament, a collection of books originally written in Hebrew (which are also the holy books of Judaism), and the New Testament, writings in Greek about the life and teachings of Jesus and his early followers.

**Beliefs** Orthodox belief is in one God as revealed in three persons—God the Father (the Creator), God the Son (Jesus Christ, the Redeemer), and God the Holy Spirit (the Sanctifier). Christians believe that Jesus restored a right relationship between God and human beings through his death by crucifixion and his

resurrection from the dead.

**Practice** Most Christian denominations observe the rite of baptism, administered to children and to newly converted members, and the Eucharist, or Communion, in which members partake of bread and wine in commemoration of Jesus Christ.

Christians are organized into congregations and gather for worship in churches. Most denominations have designated Sunday (the day Jesus rose from the dead) as the day for special observance and worship. A few have designated Saturday, the Jewish Sabbath, instead.

In most Christian denominations, men and women observe monogamy, and divorce is forbidden or discouraged. There are many different standards of personal conduct, ranging from the ascetic to the celebratory.

**Schools and sects** There are two historic divisions in Christianity. In A.D. 1054 the Eastern (or Orthodox) church and Western (or Roman) church separated. Then, in the 1500s, reformers including Martin Luther and John Calvin broke from the Roman church to form a

## CHRISTIANS, BY SECT AND REGION

| Region | Roman Catholic | Orthodox | Protestants and others[1] | Crypto-Christians[2] | Total | Percent of all Christians |
|---|---|---|---|---|---|---|
| Europe | 251,100,000 | 35,800,000 | 115,700,000 | 18,300,000 | 420,900,000 | 27.2% |
| Latin America | 369,100,000 | 400,000 | 21,500,000 | 1,200,000 | 392,200,000 | 25.3 |
| Africa | 89,700,000 | 22,000,000 | 118,100,000 | 6,500,000 | 236,300,000 | 15.3 |
| North America | 86,500,000 | 5,800,000 | 134,900,000 | 0 | 227,200,000 | 14.7 |
| South Asia | 72,800,000 | 3,200,000 | 30,800,000 | 19,100,000 | 125,900,000 | 8.1 |
| USSR | 3,900,000 | 63,000,000 | 4,500,000 | 30,800,000 | 102,200,000 | 6.6 |
| East Asia | 3,600,000 | 100,000 | 16,400,000 | 2,200,000 | 22,300,000 | 1.4 |
| Oceania | 7,400,000 | 500,000 | 13,600,000 | 0 | 21,500,000 | 1.4 |
| **Total** | **884,100,000** | **130,800,000** | **455,500,000** | **78,100,000** | **1,548,500,000** | **100.0%** |

1. Includes some Christian groups not traditionally classified as Protestant.   2. People who identify themselves as Christian but who (often for reasons of personal safety or prudence) are not included in membership lists of any Christian organization.

number of separate denominations that together are called Protestant. The Orthodox churches remain dominant in Greece, the Soviet Union, and in parts of eastern Europe. The Roman church (known today as the Roman Catholic or simply the Catholic church) predominates in southern Europe and Latin America. Protestant churches predominate in northern Europe (including Great Britain), North America, and Australia. Both Catholic and Protestant churches have conducted industrious mission programs in Africa and Asia and share influence in those regions. In addition to the three main groups are many small denominations and sects that do not fit comfortably into any of the three main groups.

**History** At the time of his death, Jesus had only a small handful of followers. Within a century, however, they had spread the new teaching to much of the Roman Empire. There were small communities of worshipers in the cities of Greece, Asia Minor, and Palestine and in Rome itself. Christians were persecuted cruelly by the Roman state and in many places were driven underground. By A.D. 300, however, Christians had attained some influence. In 313 the emperor Constantine decreed toleration for Christianity and reportedly was baptized on his deathbed. By the end of the century, Christianity was the official religion of the empire.

This marked the beginning of a newly militant phase. Missionaries were sent to the far reaches of Europe to establish churches. Christianity gradually triumphed throughout Europe, from Ireland to the plains of Poland.

During the Middle Ages, the Eastern and Western churches divided. The Western church was a major preserver and extender of learning at home. Abroad it sought to dislodge, in a series of Crusades, the Muslim Turks who had control of the Holy Land.

A long period of religious strife began with the Reformation after 1517. Brutal religious wars convulsed Europe, causing untold suffering. At the same time, European exploration and conquests were spreading Christianity to the Americas and to Asia. Roman Catholics and Protestants proselytized wherever they predominated.

From the mid-1800s to the mid-1900s, the Western churches (Catholic and Protestant) carried out energetic missionary programs to Africa and East Asia. Although they failed in their aim to Christianize the world, they did contribute to the growth of vigorous and independent churches in Africa and Asia. Today there are more Christians in Africa than in North America.

**Geography and numbers** Although Christianity began in the Middle East, the lands of its origin are now dominated by Judaism and Islam. Yet it has spread quite literally to every continent of the world and claims more than 1.5 billion adherents—about one person in every three in the world population. The accompanying table shows adherents by world region.

Christianity is the predominant religion in Europe, North and South America, and Oceania (Australia, New Zealand, and the Pacific Islands). It is also a major force in sub-Saharan Africa and in parts of South Asia. It is least significant in the Middle East and East Asia.

## ISLAM

**Founder** Muhammad, who is seen as a special prophet of the one God. Muhammad was born about A.D. 570 at Mecca (now in western Saudi Arabia) and died in 632 in the nearby city of Medina.

**Scripture** The Koran (original language: Arabic). Muslims believe the Koran to be the word of the one God, spoken to Muhammad by angels.

**Beliefs** Muhammad began preaching about A.D. 610 and established Islam as a powerful new force before his death in 632. His teachings were based in part on those of Judaism and Christianity. In agreement with these, Muhammad recognized one God. He acknowledged Hebrew history and its religious teachers and recognized Jesus as a prophet. However, Muhammad's was a distinct new revelation. His teachings are contained in the Islamic holy book, the Koran.

**Practice** A Muslim has five main religious duties:

1. To profess faith in a statement that may be translated, "There is only one God and Muhammad is his prophet."

2. To pray five times each day, facing Mecca. In Islamic countries criers in tall minarets call the times of prayer.

3. To give alms for the support of the faith and of the poor.

4. To observe a solemn fast during Ramadan, the ninth month in the Islamic calendar.

5. To make, at least once in a lifetime, a pilgrimage to Mecca.

Devout Muslims maintain strict rules of conduct. Women are expected to dress modestly, even to cover their faces in public. Sale and consumption of alcohol is forbidden. As in orthodox Judaism, eating pork is forbidden. Muslim places of worship are called mosques. The principal weekly worship is on Friday at midday.

**Schools and sects** The largest division in Islam is between the Sunnites (often called orthodox Muslims), and the Shiites, who have about 20 million members (less than 3% of all Muslims). Most Shiites live in Iran and Iraq; the two Muslim countries recently were involved in a bitter and protracted war against each other. The original cause of the break between Sunnites and Shiites was disagreement about the transferal of power from Muhammad to his descendants. Today Shiites follow somewhat different rituals than those of the Sunnites and recognize additional holy days and holy places (mainly in Iraq and Iran).

**History** From its earliest days, Islam was a militant faith. During the first 100 years, the leaders established an empire that stretched from Spain to India. In 732 a Muslim army aiming to conquer Europe was defeated at Tours, in central France, but Muslims were not overthrown in Spain until 1492.

Muslim leaders often allowed practice of other religions in their territories, but eventually many people in the conquered lands became Muslims. The empire broke into smaller units as leaders fought against each other. During the Middle Ages, Christian Europe mounted several attacks on Islamic states, seeking to free the Christian holy lands. These were known as the Crusades. The Europeans had brief successes, but the Middle East remained predominantly Muslim.

In 1453 the Ottoman Turks conquered the important Christian capital of Constantinople. Eventually the city's name was changed to Istanbul. The Turks pushed north and westward into Europe but were finally defeated near Vienna, Austria, in 1683.

## ADHERENTS OF MAJOR WORLD RELIGIONS, BY REGION (in thousands)

| Region | Christianity | | Islam | | Hinduism | | Buddhism | | Judaism | |
|---|---|---|---|---|---|---|---|---|---|---|
| | Adherents | Percent | Adherents | Percent | Adherents | Percent | Adherents | Percent | Adherents | Percent |
| Africa | 236,300 | 15.3% | 215,800 | 26.4% | 1,300 | 0.2% | z | z | 300 | 1.7% |
| Asia, East | 22,300 | 1.4 | 22,300 | 2.7 | z | z | 143,400 | 48.5% | z | z |
| Asia, South[1] | 125,900 | 8.1 | 534,900 | 65.5 | 644,000 | 99.5 | 150,900 | 51.0 | 3,900 | 21.9 |
| Europe | 420,300 | 27.2 | 9,200 | 1.1 | 600 | 0.1 | 200 | 0.1 | 1,500 | 8.4 |
| Latin America | 392,200 | 25.3 | 600 | 0.1 | 600 | 0.1 | 500 | 0.2 | 1,000 | 5.6 |
| North America | 227,200 | 14.7 | 2,600 | 0.3 | 700 | 0.1 | 200 | 0.1 | 7,900 | 44.4 |
| Oceania | 21,500 | 1.4 | 100 | z | 300 | z | z | z | 100 | 0.6 |
| USSR | 102,200 | 6.6 | 31,500 | 3.9 | z | z | 400 | 0.1 | 3,100 | 17.4 |
| **Total** | **1,548,500** | **100.0** | **817,000** | **100.0** | **647,500** | **100.0** | **295,600** | **100.0** | **17,800** | **100.0** |

**Note**: z = less than 100,000 or 0.1%. 1. Includes Middle East. **Source**: *The World Christian Encyclopedia* (1985).

From 1700 to the mid-1900s, many Islamic nations fell under the control of European powers. Europeans brought modern technology and business and, for the most part, a strong prejudice against Islamic laws and ways.

In Muslim countries after World War II, modernist politicians (with strong support from the West) fought many battles against Muslim traditionalists. Beginning in the 1970s, traditionalists, often appealing to the national pride of their people, began a powerful counteroffensive. Muslim traditionalists overthrew the shah of Iran, a major ally of the United States.

**Geography and numbers** With an estimated 800 million adherents, Islam is the second largest of the major world religions after Christianity. The center of Islam is the Arabian peninsula, where the new faith was established. Mecca and Medina in Saudi Arabia are its holiest places. Predominantly Islamic countries stretch from Morocco in the west to Indonesia in the Far East; these include Egypt, Iran, Pakistan, Bangladesh, and Indonesia. Saudi Arabia and other oil-producing states of the Arabian peninsula are also influential. Muslims are an important minority in sub-Saharan Africa and the Soviet Union.

# HINDUISM

**Founder** No single teacher founded Hinduism. Its origins are lost in the mists of time. Some elements date to 3000 B.C. Other elements may have been brought by Aryan peoples who invaded India about 1500 B.C. Hinduism has gone through many stages and changed its form many times.

**Scripture** Many writings are considered part of Hindu scriptures. They include four Vedas, among the oldest religious writings known to humankind; two long epic poems, the *Ramayana* and the *Mahabharata;* and the *Bhagavadgita,* a philosophical part of the *Mahabharata.* Indian holy books include ancient prayers and hymns, instructions for religious rituals, philosophy, and elaborate stories about gods and humans. They were first written down in Sanskrit, an ancient language still learned by devoted Hindus.

**Beliefs** Hinduism is polytheistic, recognizing not just a handful of gods, but thousands of gods. Among the more important are Brahma, the creator; Vishnu, who preserves the world and may appear as the Hindu hero Krishna; and Siva, the god of destruction. Many Hindus are devoted to Siva's wife, who is known by several names. As Uma, she is a protector and goddess of motherhood. As Kali or Durga, she is a destroyer. Many Hindu deities have mixed powers—they are both good and bad, creative and destructive.

Hindus have a deep respect for all living things—even insects. The holiest animal is the cow. In India cattle roam freely, and killing them for their meat is considered a grave offense. From this respect for life grew the philosophy of Mahatma Gandhi, the hero of Indian independence in the mid-1900s. Gandhi's life and writings inspired people in many parts of the world.

Hindus believe in reincarnation. They believe that when a person dies, his or her soul lives on and appears in a new body. If the person has done good things, the soul may appear in an individual at a higher level of existence. An evil person's soul might reappear in the body of a lowly animal.

One of the schools of Hindu philosophy is called yoga. A student of yoga learns bodily and mental exercises to help create readiness for meditation. Yoga has become popular in Western countries, often as a nonreligious discipline to enhance physical and emotional health.

**Practice** Hindu devotion is largely an individual and family matter. Hindus do not form congregations that meet regularly for worship. Many homes have a shrine to honor particularly important gods.

Hindu temples are buildings devoted to a particular god or group of gods. Many Hindus believe that a statue in a temple is the god himself. Priests at a temple may bathe and dress the statue each day and bring it food. A Hindu priest may serve at a particular temple and be devoted to a particular god. Once or twice a year, a temple may celebrate a holy day in honor of its god. Thousands or even millions may come to see or participate in the festival and to give honor to the god. Some of the most famous temples are on the banks of the Ganges and other rivers in India.

Traditional Hinduism observed caste, the division of people into rigid groups by occupation and social standing. The four traditional castes are (1) Brahmans—priestly leaders and their families, (2) Kshatriyas—princes and soldiers, (3) Vaisyas—merchants and landowners, and (4) Sudras—farmers and workers. In addition there was a large group of outcasts—people with no caste and no standing. Known as untouchables, they were ignored and mistreated until modern times. In 1950 the government of India outlawed the caste system. Still, many Hindus prefer to mix primarily with members of their own caste.

**Schools and sects** Through its long history, Hinduism has seen many sects. Tantrism, which grew up after A.D. 600, emphasized special rituals as a means of enlightenment. They used mystical diagrams (mandalas) and chants (mantras) in their search. Bhakti, a sect begun after A.D. 1300, emphasized the primacy of love for a deity and used love between humans as an illustration. This sect rejected caste, ritual, and creeds, emphasizing the need for sincerity. Today sects that have melded elements of Hinduism, Christianity, and Islam are seeking converts in India. One of these so-called new religions may develop into a new and distinct world religion.

**History** From its prehistoric beginnings, Hinduism developed into the first great world religion, extending its influence through the Indian subcontinent and many surrounding regions—especially Sri Lanka, Burma, and parts of Indonesia.

With the rise of Buddhism after 600 B.C., however, Hinduism sank gradually into eclipse. Buddhism dominated India and spread through most of the rest of Asia, where it remained a dominant force until recent times. In India, Hinduism gradually regained its primary position. Similarly, after A.D. 650 Islam swept into India from the west. It gained many converts at the expense of Hinduism. Again Hinduism gradually regained its earlier dominance. (Islam remained dominant in the northwestern and northeastern extremities of the subcontinent—now Pakistan and Bangladesh.)

Hinduism has had great influence on distant parts of the world. The founders of Buddhism, Jainism, and Sikhism were all Hindus. The influence of Hinduism in modern times has been mostly indirect. Traditional Hinduism is not a proselytizing religion, and its deep ties to India make it difficult to transport. Still, Hindu doctrines and disciplines promoting meditation have become well known by many in Western countries.

**Geography and numbers** Hinduism is the traditional religion of India. Its almost 650 million adherents make it the third-largest religious group in the world after Christianity and Islam. Nearly all practicing Hindus in the world live in India itself or in neighboring South Asia. Outside Asia, Hinduism flourishes mainly in expatriate communities of Indians.

## BUDDHISM

**Founder** Siddhartha Gautama (c. 563–483 B.C.), who came to be known as Buddha. According to Buddhist scriptures, Siddhartha Gautama was born into a princely family on the Indian subcontinent (in the present-day country of Nepal). At the age of 29, he had a series of visions that persuaded him to leave his wife and young son. He wandered for some years seeking enlightenment. One day, while sitting under a bo tree in a village, he gained enlightenment. Soon his followers called him Enlightened One, or Buddha. For the rest of his life (he lived to be perhaps 80 years old), Buddha wandered through northern India teaching.

**Scripture** The Tripitika, or "three baskets," is a collection of sayings and rules for conduct collected by Buddha's early followers. Nearly all Buddhists reverence the Tripitika, although many treasure other works as well.

**Beliefs** Buddhists share with Hinduism a belief in the cycle of reincarnation. When a person's body dies, the soul is reborn in another person or animal. Buddha believed there was a way to end this cycle of death and rebirth. He taught that a person should seek a state of detachment from worldly things and desires. Achieving this state, called nirvana, could bring contentment and would be the end of the reincarnation cycle for the soul.

Buddha rejected extreme asceticism and extreme self-indulgence. He recommended a Middle Way. The Buddhist discipline is summarized in the Eightfold Path, which consists of right knowledge, right thought, right action, right livelihood, right effort, right mindfulness, right concentration, and right speech.

**Practice** From early times Buddhists established orders of monks. The monks withdraw from the everyday world and live austere lives of meditation. They live on alms contributed by lay Buddhists. Although many monks devote their lives to their orders, others may spend a year or two as monks before taking up responsibility as laymen. Early monks served as missionaries, carrying the tenets of Buddhism through all of Asia.

Collective rituals play a smaller part in the life of a Buddhist than in the lives of Jews, Christians, or Muslims. Buddhist temples are primarily for individual meditation.

**Schools and sects** The most significant division in Buddhism is between the Therevada and Mahayana schools. Therevada Buddhism, which remains most influential in Sri Lanka, Burma, Thailand, and Cambodia, is most traditional in seeking to concentrate on the life and teachings of Gautama. Mahayana Buddhism, which became predominant in China and Japan, offers a more liberal interpretation of Buddhist teachings. It reveres other enlightened teachers, or Buddhas, and emphasizes the importance of each person's seeking to become a bodhisattva, one who seeks Buddhahood through compassion and action as well as contemplation.

A more recent school, Zen, has received particular attention in the Western world. This "meditation" school began in the A.D. 700s. One branch emphasizes mental meditation, finding wisdom in the paradoxical statements (koans) of earlier Zen masters. A second branch emphasizes physical discipline as an aid to true meditation.

**History** The original teachings of Buddhism were spoken and written in Pali, a language of India. Therevada Buddhists still study Buddhist writings in this language. Therevada missionaries carried Buddhism eastward to the rest of South Asia.

Between 200 B.C. and A.D. 200, Mahayana Buddhism spread widely in China. Chinese missionaries carried the teachings to Korea and Japan. The flowering of Buddhism in China provided a second center for the religion, one in which language and practice differed.

After A.D. 700, in a remarkable shift, Buddhism began to lose its influence in India. Islamic conquests claimed many converts, and Hinduism (having absorbed some Buddhist thinking) reawakened. By 1000, Buddhism was virtually nonexistent in India, but it continued to prosper among India's neighbors to the east.

**Geography and numbers** Although Buddhism originated in India, today the vast majority of Buddhists are outside India in neighboring countries to the east and in East Asia. Recent estimates are that 300 million people adhere to Buddhist beliefs and practices. Many of these may also observe rituals in other religions, such as folk religion (in China) or Shinto (in Japan).

## JUDAISM

**Founder** Judaism was not founded by a single religious leader. It developed among wandering Semitic tribes who came to be known variously as Hebrews, Israelites, and eventually, Jews. The traditional patriarch of the Jewish people is Abraham, to whom God promised a land of plenty. The lawgiver, some centuries later, was Moses, who received God's commandments at Mount Sinai. The Jewish nation reached its height of power under the kings David and Solomon. The latter built an elaborate and beautiful temple at Jerusalem.

**Scripture** The Jewish scriptures, originally written and still often read and studied in

| WORLD RELIGIONS | | |
|---|---|---|
| **Group** | **Adherents** | **Percent of world pop.** |
| Major World Religions | | |
| Christianity | 1,548,500,000 | 32.4% |
| Islam | 817,000,000 | 17.1 |
| Hinduism | 647,500,000 | 13.5 |
| Buddhism | 295,600,000 | 6.2 |
| Judaism | 17,800,000 | 0.4 |
| Total | 3,326,400,000 | 69.6% |
| Other Broad Religious Groupings | | |
| Chinese folk religions | 188,000,000 | 3.9% |
| New Asian religions | 106,400,000 | 2.2 |
| Tribal religions | 91,200,000 | 1.9 |
| Total | 385,600,000 | 8.0% |
| Regional and Smaller Religious Groups | | |
| Sikhism | 16,100,000 | 0.34% |
| Shamanism | 12,200,000 | 0.26 |
| Spiritism | 6,700,000 | 0.14 |
| Confucianism | 5,200,000 | 0.11 |
| Bahaism | 4,400,000 | 0.09 |
| Jainism | 3,300,000 | 0.07 |
| Shintoism | 3,200,000 | 0.07 |
| Parsiism (Zoroastrianism) | 500,000 | 0.01 |
| Total | 51,600,000 | 1.1% |
| Unaffiliated | | |
| Nonreligious | 805,900,000 | 16.9% |
| Atheist | 210,500,000 | 4.4 |
| Total | 1,026,400,000 | 21.3% |
| **Total** | **4,781,200,000** | **100.0%** |

Hebrew, are the same books Christians call the Old Testament. The first five books, known to Jews as the Torah, have special significance. These books tell of the Covenant God made with the Jewish people and outline the laws (including the Ten Commandments) by which they were to live. The remaining books provide additional history, the exhortations of the prophets, hymns and songs for worship (especially the Psalms), and other poetry and wisdom writings.

**Beliefs** The early Jews, in contrast to neighboring peoples, worshiped one God, whom they recognized as the Creator of all things and the God of all. Among God's characteristics were both judgment and mercy. His Covenant with the Jews promised them his care and protection; they were to follow his laws. During the time of the prophets, when the Jewish states had declined, the prophets told of the coming of a leader anointed by God—the Messiah. Jews still await the coming of the Messiah.

**Practice** Jews worship in synagogues, often modest places of worship for a small congregation. Saturday, the seventh day of the week, is the Sabbath, a special day of rest and worship. Worship consists of readings from the scriptures, the chanting or singing of psalms or other songs of praise, and prayer.

## NONRELIGIOUS AND ATHEISTS

| Region | Nonreligious | Atheist | Total | Percent |
|---|---|---|---|---|
| East Asia | 618,900,000 | 123,400,000 | 742,300,000 | 73.0% |
| USSR | 83,100,000 | 60,600,000 | 143,700,000 | 14.1 |
| Europe | 49,400,000 | 17,400,000 | 66,800,000 | 6.6 |
| South Asia | 18,400,000 | 5,100,000 | 23,500,000 | 2.3 |
| North America | 19,000,000 | 1,000,000 | 20,000,000 | 2.0 |
| Latin America | 12,900,000 | 2,400,000 | 15,300,000 | 1.5 |
| Oceania | 2,900,000 | 500,000 | 3,400,000 | 0.3 |
| Africa | 1,300,000 | 100,000 | 1,400,000 | 0.1 |
| **Total** | **805,900,000** | **210,500,000** | **1,016,400,000** | **100.0%** |

**Schools and sects** There are three main branches of modern Judaism. Orthodox Judaism is the most conservative branch, observing laws concerning clean and unclean foods, purification, and other ancient rituals. One part of orthodoxy is the Hasidim, fundamentalist sects that grew up in eastern Europe in the 1700s and 1800s.

Reform Judaism, strong in the United States, is the most liberal of the three main branches. Reform Jews seek to follow the spirit of Judaism and are free to disregard part of the ancient rules of conduct and ritual. Reform places of worship are called temples. Some temples resemble Christian churches in their design and in their observances, which may include, for example, music from a pipe organ and choir.

Conservative Judaism seeks a middle road between Orthodox and Reform. It is the most recent of the three branches and is strong in the United States.

**History** After wealth and influence during the reigns of David and Solomon (c. 1000 B.C.), the Jewish state was divided by dynastic feuds into a northern and a southern kingdom. Both kingdoms eventually fell victim to neighboring peoples. In 587 the southern kingdom (Judah) was overrun by the Babylonians, and many Jews were taken as slaves to Babylon. Solomon's Temple at Jerusalem was destroyed. Fifty years later the Jews were freed, and they rebuilt the temple. In the 100s B.C., the whole region was conquered by Rome. The Jews mounted a revolt against Rome in A.D. 66. This resulted in Roman reprisals, including the destruction of the second temple in A.D. 70. Jews were dispersed in all directions and were to have no land of their own for nearly 1,900 years.

Judaism and the Jewish people survived in many parts of the world. Some lived in Palestine, some in Babylon. Many moved to Europe—especially to Spain, France, Germany, Poland, and western Russia.

Christians of Europe often persecuted the Jews. They passed laws against Jews owning land or engaging in certain businesses. Sometimes mobs of angry people destroyed Jewish settlements and killed the inhabitants. In the 1930s Adolf Hitler and his Nazi party blamed Jews for Germany's defeats and sufferings. He planned to exterminate all the Jews in Europe and succeeded in killing an estimated 6 million. This event is known as the Holocaust.

Even before the Holocaust, Jewish leaders had begun a campaign for the establishment of a Jewish state in the Middle East. After World War II, they received the support of Britain and the United States, and a new country called Israel was carved from Palestine. Since Israel's beginning in 1948, it has often been attacked and harassed by its neighbors, who are Muslim and never agreed to the new state.

**Geography and numbers** The largest number of Jews live in North America, to which they emigrated in large numbers between 1880 and 1920. They are concentrated in and near large cities, especially New York. The Jews in South Asia are nearly all residents of Israel. Jews in the USSR have been harassed in recent years, and many are seeking to emigrate to Israel or the United States.

## OTHER RELIGIONS

According to scholars who helped assemble *The World Christian Encyclopedia*, three types of religion (in addition to those listed above) claim tens of millions of adherents in the world. These they call Chinese Folk Religion, New Religions, Tribal Religions. In addition there are many smaller religious groups, some of which have had influence far beyond their present numbers.

**Chinese Folk Religion,** estimated to be a primary faith for about 180 million people (about 20% of China's population), consists of a blend of ancient ancestor worship with some elements of Buddhism, Confucianism, and Taoism. Confucius, a great Chinese philosopher and teacher, lived in the sixth century B.C. He taught respect for family and ruler. Taoism is a philosophy or religion based on the teachings of Lao-tzu, another great teacher of Confucian times. Chinese folk religion is also followed by many in scattered Chinese settlements in other parts of the world.

**New Religions** are those that have grown up in the past century, principally in Asia. A new religion typically blends elements of (a) local religious tradition and practice; (b) Hinduism, Buddhism, or Islam; and (c) modern Western thought. Whether any of these new religions will develop a truly international following remains to be seen. But together they account for an estimated 100 million adherents, mainly in such Asian countries as Indonesia, the Philippines, and Japan.

**Tribal Religions** are animistic religions practiced by isolated peoples, primarily in Africa and South Asia.

The more important smaller groups are the following:

**Sikhism** and **Jainism** are developments from certain strands of Hinduism. There are an estimated 16 million Sikhs and more than 3 million Jains, predominantly in India.

**Confucianism** is based on the teachings of Confucius, a Chinese teacher of the 500s B.C. Confucianism has had a powerful influence on Chinese history and philosophy. An estimated 5 million people in East Asia consider themselves Confucianists.

**Baha'i** is an independent religion that teaches that the revealed religions of the world are in agreement and that each of the prophet-founders of the religions revealed the will of God for a particular time and place in history. The Baha'i faith began in 1844 in Iran. Its prophet-founder is Baha'Ullah, meaning "glory of God." The Baha'i faith has an estimated 5 million adherents worldwide. Its headquarters are in Haifa, Israel. A major U.S. temple in Wilmette, Illinois, attracts many visitors.

**Parsees,** a people who emigrated centuries ago from Persia (Iran) to India, follow the teachings of the Persian prophet Zoroaster, who lived in the 500s B.C. They are a prosperous sect centered on Bombay, marrying only among themselves and seeking no converts. Estimates of their number range from 200,000 to 500,000.

## NONRELIGIOUS AND ATHEISTS

According to *The World Christian Encyclopedia*, more than a billion of the world's people consider themselves nonreligious (agnostic about religious claims) or atheistic (actively opposed to religion). Nearly three-quarters of these people live in East Asia, where they are a majority of the population of China. Nonreligious persons and atheists also make up a majority of people in the Soviet Union.

If the estimates of non- and antireligious peoples are correct, these peoples make up the largest religious bloc in the world after Christianity.

## WORLD RELIGIONS: A Brief Chronology

*B.C.*

**c. 3000** Earliest elements of Hinduism develop in India.

**c. 2500** Egyptian pyramids at Giza completed.

**c. 1500** Aryan peoples invade India; bring additional elements of Hinduism.

**c. 1290** Moses leads Jewish people out of Egypt.

**1010–ebrero
922** Reigns of Jewish kings David and Solomon. A great temple built at Jerusalem.

**740** Jewish prophet Isaiah flourishes.

**628** Traditional birth date of Zoroaster, religious teacher in Persia. Followers today are Parsees in India.

**604** Traditional birth date of Chinese teacher Lao-tzu, a founder of Taoism.

**587** Babylonians destroy Jewish temple at Jerusalem and take many Jews as slaves. Fifty years later, Jews are freed; begin to rebuild temple.

**560** Birth of Siddhartha Gautama in northern India; later known as Buddha. Dies c. 480. His teachings, on which Buddhism is based, gain many followers in India; later spread to Southeast Asia.

**551** Birth of Chinese teacher Confucius. Dies c. 479.

**200** Mahayana Buddhism begins to spread in China and Japan.

**100s** Jewish lands conquered by Roman Empire.

**3** Birth of Jesus Christ; Western calendar dated from supposed year of his birth.

*A.D.*

**30** Death and resurrection of Jesus Christ. By 100, Christians are in many parts of present-day Greece, Turkey, Syria, Lebanon, Israel, Egypt, despite active persecution by Romans.

**66–** Jewish revolt against Romans ends in
**70** destruction of second temple and scattering of Jews in all directions.

**175** Apostles' Creed, a brief statement of Christian beliefs, formulated.

**303–** In final organized program of persecu-
**12** tion, Romans kill estimated 500,000 Christians.

**313** The emperor Constantine decrees toleration for Christianity in Roman Empire. In 325 he calls synod of Nicaea, which formulates Nicene Creed. By end of 300s, Christianity is official religion of empire.

**354** Birth of St. Augustine, influential Christian teacher, in North Africa. Dies 430.

**570** Muhammad, founder of Islam, born at Mecca (now in Saudi Arabia). Dies in 632 in nearby city of Medina.

**600 +** Tantrism, a Hindu school, grows up, emphasizing special rituals as means of enlightenment; uses mystical diagrams (mandalas) and chants (mantras).

**650 +** Islam sweeps into India; gains many converts.

**700 +** Development in China of Zen, a school of Buddhism, which has received particular attention in the modern Western world.

**732** A Muslim army aiming to conquer Europe defeated by Franks at Tours in central France.

**988** Christianity reaches Russia through missionaries from eastern churches.

**1054** Eastern (or Orthodox) and Western (or Roman) churches go separate ways after disputes about doctrine and authority.

**1096** Christians in Europe go on first Crusade to take Holy Land from Muslims.

Seven other major Crusades pursued between 1100 and 1300. Christian warriors temporarily occupy Jerusalem and other cities but soon lose them again to Muslims.

**1227** Birth of Thomas Aquinas, great Christian theologian, in Italy.

**1300 +** Bhakti, a Hindu sect, develops, emphasizing primacy of love for a deity and using love between humans as illustration; rejects caste, ritual, and creeds and emphasizes need for sincerity.

**1377** English theologian and religious reformer John Wycliffe accused of heresy by Pope Gregory XI for attacks on worldliness of the church.

**1415** Excommunication and execution of Czech religious leader Jan Hus, who protested sale of indulgences and other papal excesses, sets off Hussite Wars, which end with Compactata of Prague (1436).

**1452** Ottoman Turks (Muslims) conquer capital of Eastern Christian church, Constantinople. Eventually, city's name changed to Istanbul. Turks push westward into Europe.

**1469** Birth of Nanak, founder of Sikhism, in Punjab region of India.

**1517** Martin Luther, a German priest, posts 95 theses on cathedral door, questioning church teachings. Luther refuses to recant; is excommunicated from Catholic church. With cooperation of north German princes, he forms new Protestant churches. This begins Reformation, which ultimately divides European Christianity into two warring camps.

**1534** King Henry VIII of England denies power of pope over church in England and establishes Church of England responsible to monarch. New church gradually adopts Protestant beliefs but maintains many practices of earlier Catholic era.

**1536** John Calvin, a young French scholar, born in 1509, publishes *Institutes of the Christian Religion*, and becomes second major leader of Protestant Christianity, helping to create Presbyterian and other Reformed churches.

**1540** Ignatius Loyola, a Spaniard, establishes the Jesuits (Society of Jesus) with papal approval. This order becomes powerful instrument of Catholic church in disputes with Protestants, in missionary efforts around world, and in education.

**1545–** Council of Trent makes major reforms
**63** in Catholic church and defines disagreements with Protestants. Its work begins Catholic Reformation, or Counter-Reformation.

**1618–** Thirty Years War, caused in part by
**48** Protestant-Catholic hatreds, decimates central Europe. Calvinist leaders in England overthrow monarchy and execute king in civil war (1642–49). Monarchy is restored in 1660.

**1620** Pilgrims, a small group of English Calvinists, establish colony at Plymouth in North America to escape persecution in England. They are first of thousands of Calvinists to settle in present-day New England.

**1683** Muslim Turks defeated near Vienna, Austria, in their last attempt to establish foothold in western Europe.

**1734** The Great Awakening, a religious revival, sweeps New England, begun by prominent Massachusetts preacher Jonathan Edwards. English evangelist George Whitefield tours American colonies beginning in 1738, preaching to outdoor gatherings.

**1738** Christian conversion experienced by brothers John and Charles Wesley in England. They begin evangelical activities, leading to development of independent Methodist church.

**1792** Second Awakening sweeps new United States, lasting more than 20 years. Revivals in Kentucky in 1800 result in formation of new denominations, ancestors of Disciples of Christ, Churches of Christ, and Christian churches.

**1830** American Joseph Smith has religious visions that lead him to organize the Church of Jesus Christ of the Latter-Day Saints (Mormons). Movement grows rapidly but generates intense opposition. Smith murdered by anti-Mormons in 1844.

**1844** Baha'i established in Iran.

**1869–** Vatican Council I, convened by Pope
**79** Pius IX, declares that teachings of pope in matters of faith and morals are infallible.

**1875** Mary Baker Eddy publishes *Science and Health with Key to the Scriptures*, in Boston; it becomes basis of Church of Christ, Scientist.

**1900** First documented modern Pentecostal experience—worshipers speak in unknown tongues during prayer meeting in Kansas. Within 20 years, Pentecostal churches form major new Christian denomination.

**1938–** German government carries out de-
**45** struction of estimated 6 million European Jews. This event known as the Holocaust.

**1948** Allied powers guarantee new state of Israel in Middle East for settlement by Jews.

**1948** World Council of Churches established at huge assembly in Amsterdam. This ecumenical organization supported by many Protestant, Anglican, and Orthodox denominations. Headquarters are in Geneva, Switzerland.

**1962–** Vatican Council II, convened by Pope
**65** John XXIII, announces many liberalizing changes in Roman Catholic liturgy and practice; supports cautious involvement in ecumenical discussions with other Christians.

# THE INTERNATIONAL ECONOMY

## INTERNATIONAL TRADE

International trade takes place because no single country can produce efficiently all of the commodities it needs, and some nations enjoy an advantage in producing certain kinds of products, either because of a comparative wealth of resources (capital, labor, natural resources) or more efficient production techniques. Even an economy with the most efficient technology has a limit on its resources, however, and rather than using them to produce all kinds of products, it concentrates its resources on what it makes most efficiently. It then trades those goods for other commodities, importing those it produces least efficiently. As a result, all countries are better off; specialization results in the expansion of the total supply of goods, and the cost of acquiring them falls accordingly.

Efficiency can be measured by output per hour of production. The comparative output-per-hour measure shows how slow the increase in U.S. productivity has been relative to its competitors. While U.S. productivity more than doubled since 1960, productivity tripled in most of Europe and rose more than eightfold in Japan. In part these improvements in other countries reflect their low starting points, especially in Japan and West Germany, where their economies were recovering from the devastation of World War II. However, productivity has risen by nearly the same rate in the United States, Japan, and Europe since 1982.

Just which commodities a country will export and import depends on the relative prices of the factors used in production. A country such as India has abundant labor and low wages. It therefore exports labor-intensive products, such as garments. A country such as Canada, which has abundant natural resources, specializes in agriculture and raw materials. Countries such as Canada and India then import goods for which the factors of production are in relatively short supply.

The relative price of labor depends in part on the labor force participation rate, which has been rising owing largely to women leaving homemaking for the work force. Unemployment is also on the rise, especially in the United States, Canada, and Great Britain, where economic activity has taken a downturn. The ability of the Japanese and Swedish economies to keep unemployment rates low, even in the middle of the recession, is certainly impressive and represents the commitment and active efforts of their governments to that goal.

Of course, there are political reasons why countries do not completely specialize their production. No country, for example, wants to import all of its military equipment for fear that supplies would be cut off in the event of international conflict. Similarly, even inefficient pro-

ducers, such as farmers in Japan where land is scarce and expensive, may have political power that forces their governments to subsidize them.

**Tariffs, Quotas, and GATT** One way to protect a country's own producers, especially where they are inefficient compared with the international competition, is with import tariffs—taxes on goods that are produced abroad. Import tariffs raise the price of imports relative to domestic alternatives and discourage demand for the former. If one country is the sole importer or even the main importer of another's exports, it is possible that an import tariff will simply force the exporter to cut its selling price (in order to keep the price to consumers—including the tariff—from rising sharply and cutting off demand). In this case, the exporter pays virtually the whole cost of the tariff. If, on the other hand, the importer badly needs the import and there are few substitutes, raising the tariff simply raises the costs to one's own consumers. Critics of U.S. trade policy point out that because Japan is now virtually the sole supplier of many consumer electronic products in the United States, tariffs against those products simply raise their prices and fuel U.S. inflation. Import quotas attempt to achieve a restriction on imports, without the price rises associated with tariffs, by setting direct limits on the number of items imported. Perhaps the most important import quota in recent years was when Japan agreed in the 1980s to abide by a limit on the number of cars it exports to the United States. As a result Japanese automakers are now exporting larger, more expensive cars, and 22% of the U.S. auto market now goes to Japanese cars.

So-called trade wars start when one country imposes a tariff on imports from a second country, and the latter responds with tariffs of its own against the first country. The arguments presented above about the benefits of trade have led to efforts to restrict the use of tariffs and maintain free trade. The General Agreement on Tariffs and Trade (GATT) is an agreement among 84 signatory and an additional 27 countries under special arrangement (together accounting for more than 85% of world trade) to apply all reductions in tariffs and other measures to liberalize trade achieved between member countries. The European Common Market is a trading group whose members (West Germany, Italy, France, Belgium, the Netherlands, Luxembourg, Spain, Portugal, and Greece) will have abolished by 1992 all tariffs and trade restrictions between them. (See "The European Community.")

**Dumping** Sometimes exporters sell commodities abroad at prices below those they charge for the same item in their home market. This situation is known as dumping. It may

## TOP 10 U.S. MERCHANDISE TRADE PARTNERS, 1990 (millions of dollars)

| Rank/Country | Exports | Imports | Net balance |
|---|---|---|---|
| 1. Canada | $83,498 | $92,934 | –$9,436 |
| 2. Japan | 47,857 | 89,657 | –41,820 |
| 3. Mexico | 28,275 | 30,530 | –2,255 |
| 4. United Kingdom | 22,922 | 19,955 | 2,967 |
| 5. Germany[1] | 18,292 | 27,973 | –9,681 |
| 6. South Korea | 13,967 | 18,447 | –4,480 |
| 7. France | 13,664 | 13,024 | 640 |
| 8. Netherlands | 12,765 | 4,983 | 7,827 |
| 9. Taiwan | 11,134 | 23,223 | –12,089 |
| 10. Belgium and Luxembourg | 10,367 | 4,567 | 5,800 |

**Note:** Preliminary data. 1. Prior to fourth quarter 1990, data for West Germany only. **Source:** U.S. Dept. of Commerce, *Survey of Current Business* ( Mar. 1991).

## 10 LARGEST U.S. MERCHANDISE EXPORTS, 1990 (billions of dollars)

| Rank/ Product name | Volume | |
|---|---|---|
| | 1989 | 1990[1] |
| 1. Aircraft and spacecraft | $31.1 | $38.2 |
| 2. Computers and peripherals | 21.5 | 24.7 |
| 3. Petrochemicals | 20.8 | 21.4 |
| 4. Motor vehicles and car bodies | 12.3 | 16.0 |
| 5. Electronic components and accessories | 13.4 | 14.3 |
| 6. Automotive parts and accessories | 13.8 | 13.1 |
| 7. Synthetic resin, rubber, and plastics | 11.1 | 12.8 |
| 8. Organic chemicals | 10.2 | 10.1 |
| 9. Drugs | 4.4 | 5.3 |
| 10. Laboratory instruments and apparatus | 4.3 | 4.7 |

1. Estimated. **Source:** U.S. Dept. of Commerce, *U.S. Industrial Outlook, 1991* (1991).

occur sporadically because of overproduction for home markets; the excess is then sold abroad cheaply, or "dumped." It also may occur more regularly because of government subsidies to maintain production in the face of declining demand in the home country (e.g., to maintain jobs). Finally, it may be part of an anticompetitive strategy to crush the domestic competition in one's foreign markets and then to raise prices once competitors have been eliminated. Consumers may benefit from dumping in the short run, but it may also do long-term damage to domestic producers.

**Trends in U.S. exports** The top U.S. merchandise exports account for about one-third of the total, and high-technology exports (computers, electronic components, radiological apparatus, electrical apparatus) account for

## 10 FASTEST GROWING U.S. MERCHANDISE EXPORTS, 1985–89

(Percent change, annual rates)

| Rank/Product group | 1985–88 | 1989[1] |
|---|---|---|
| 1. Musical instruments (36) | 34.0% | 18.9% |
| 2. Tobacco manufactures (27) | 31.0 | 18.6 |
| 3. Fresh, chilled, and frozen meat (35) | 28.8 | 65.5 |
| 4. Pulp and waste paper (23) | 27.7 | 22.3 |
| 5. Electronic components and parts (5) | 25.2 | 23.3 |
| 6. Synthetic resins, rubber, and plastics (10) | 24.4 | 49.0 |
| 7. Animal feedstuffs except unmilled cereal (25) | 21.9 | N.A. |
| 8. Wood in the rough (37) | 21.1 | 4.5 |
| 9. Electro-medical and radiological apparatus (39) | 20.4 | 46.5 |
| 10. Electrical apparatus (22) | 18.1 | 33.1 |

**Note:** Numbers in parentheses indicate their rank in 1984. 1. As of June. Product categories for 1989 are not strictly comparable with those of earlier periods. **Sources:** U.S. Dept. of Commerce, *U.S. Foreign Trade Highlights, 1988*; U.S. Dept. of Commerce, *Harmonized Trade Data Time Series* (Oct., 1989).

about 60% of total exports. Exports of agriculture will probably never reach the growth levels of the 1970s, since the green revolution and trading policies, particularly of the European Community, have created worldwide food surpluses that are not likely to be eliminated soon.

## INTERNATIONAL FINANCE

Because countries have their own currencies, trade between them also involves exchanging or trading currencies. In order for Americans to buy Japanese cars, for example, dollars must first be converted to Japanese yen in order to pay for them. The exchange rate between currencies represents the ratio at which they can be exchanged or the price of one currency in terms of the other. For example, if the exchange rate between the British pound and the U.S. dollar is $1.50/£, then one British pound can be purchased for $1.50.

The exchange rate for most world currencies is determined by the market. Some Eastern bloc countries can maintain fixed exchange rates because by law all sales take place through the government. The exchange rate of a currency rises, or appreciates, when the demand for it rises and/or the supply falls. This may happen because foreign buyers want to buy more of its goods or because consumers within the country decide to buy fewer imports. It may also happen because the country reduces its money supply. Finally, the central banks of countries can manipulate their exchange rates slightly by buying and selling their own and other currencies (see "The Federal Reserve"). The dollar depreciated by 15% in 1990 due to declining U.S. interest rates and economic growth rates lower than in other countries, notably Germany and Japan, which made the dollar a less attractive currency in which to invest.

## FOREIGN EXCHANGE RATES: CURRENCY UNITS PER DOLLAR

| Country/currency | 1986 | 1987 | 1988 | 1989 | 1990 |
|---|---|---|---|---|---|
| Australia/dollar[1] | 67.09 | 70.14 | 78.41 | 79.19 | 78.07 |
| Austria/schilling | 15.26 | 12.65 | 12.36 | 13.24 | 11.33 |
| Belgium/franc | 44.66 | 37.36 | 36.78 | 39.41 | 33.42 |
| Canada/dollar | 1.39 | 1.33 | 1.23 | 1.18 | 1.17 |
| China/yuan | 3.46 | 3.73 | 3.73 | 3.77 | 4.79 |
| Denmark/krone | 8.10 | 6.85 | 6.74 | 7.32 | 6.19 |
| Finland/markka | 5.07 | 4.40 | 4.19 | 4.30 | 3.83 |
| France/franc | 6.93 | 6.01 | 5.96 | 6.38 | 5.45 |
| Germany/deutsche mark | 2.17 | 1.80 | 1.76 | 1.88 | 1.62 |
| Greece/drachma | 139.93 | 135.47 | 142.00 | 162.60 | 158.59 |
| Hong Kong/dollar | 7.80 | 7.80 | 7.81 | 7.80 | 7.79 |
| India/rupee | 12.60 | 12.94 | 13.90 | 16.21 | 17.49 |
| Ireland/punt[1] | 134.14 | 148.79 | 152.49 | 141.80 | 165.76 |
| Italy/lira | 1,491.16 | 1,297.03 | 1,302.39 | 1,372.28 | 1,198.27 |
| Japan/yen | 168.35 | 144.60 | 128.17 | 138.07 | 145.00 |
| Malaysia/ringgit | 2.58 | 2.52 | 2.62 | 2.71 | 2.71 |
| Netherlands/guilder | 2.45 | 2.03 | 1.98 | 2.12 | 1.82 |
| New Zealand/dollar[1] | 52.46 | 59.33 | 65.56 | 59.35 | 59.62 |
| Norway/krone | 7.40 | 6.74 | 6.52 | 6.91 | 6.25 |
| Portugal/escudo | 149.80 | 141.20 | 144.26 | 157.53 | 142.70 |
| Singapore/dollar | 2.18 | 2.11 | 2.01 | 1.95 | 1.81 |
| South Africa/rand | 2.29 | 2.04 | 2.19 | 2.62 | 2.59 |
| South Korea/won | 884.61 | 825.93 | 734.51 | 674.29 | 710.64 |
| Spain/peseta | 140.04 | 123.54 | 116.52 | 118.44 | 101.96 |
| Sri Lanka/rupee | 27.93 | 29.47 | 31.85 | 35.95 | 40.08 |
| Sweden/krona | 7.13 | 6.35 | 6.14 | 6.46 | 5.92 |
| Switzerland/franc | 1.80 | 1.49 | 1.46 | 1.63 | 1.39 |
| Taiwan/dollar | 37.84 | 31.76 | 28.64 | 26.41 | 26.92 |
| Thailand/baht | 26.31 | 25.77 | 25.31 | 25.73 | 25.61 |
| United Kingdom/pound[1] | 146.77 | 163.98 | 178.13 | 163.82 | 178.41 |
| United States/dollar[2] | 112.22 | 96.94 | 92.72 | 98.60 | 89.09 |

**Note:** Averages of certified noon buying rates in New York for cable transfers. 1. Value in U.S. cents. 2. Index of weighted-average exchange value of U.S. dollar against the currencies of 10 industrial countries. The weight for each of the 10 countries is 1972–76 average world trade of that country divided by the average world trade of all 10 countries combined. Series revised as of Aug. 1978 (see *Federal Reserve Bulletin*, vol. 64, Aug. 1978). **Source:** Board of Directors of the Federal Reserve System, *Federal Reserve Bulletin* (monthly).

**The Gold standard** Before World War I, exchange rates for world currencies were fixed, artificially, by tying them to a certain amount of gold—$32, for example, might equal one ounce of gold. Central banks would then buy and sell gold in order to equalize supply and demand for the currencies and maintain the fixed exchange rates. For this reason the central banks maintained enormous gold stockpiles, such as the United States had at Fort Knox. People therefore referred to currencies as being "backed by gold." Long-term changes in trading relationships and in the demand for various currencies eventually made the fixed exchange rates of the gold standard impossible to support. In 1944, the Bretton Woods agreement established the U.S. dollar as the world standard, but the United States still backed its dollars with gold and used gold to settle its debts. After 1973 the United States abandoned that role, and most of the world's exchange rates were set by market forces.

**Balance of payments** The balance of payments accounts are the list of transactions between a country and the rest of the world. This account comprises three parts: the current account—a record of exports and imports of goods (e.g., oil, clothing), services (e.g., tourism), net investment income, and unilateral transfers (the trade balance includes the export and import of goods alone); the capital account—a record of exports and imports of assets such as bank loans and corporate stock purchases; and the official-reserves accounts—a record of a country's sales and purchases of official reserve assets at the central bank.

**Trade balance** When a country imports goods from another country worth more than the value of its exports to that country, there is said to be a deficit in the balance of trade between the countries. Changes in exchange rates tend to equalize the supply and demand for currencies and the balance of trade; in the case above, the exchange rate for the first country's currency should fall relative to the second country's, reducing imports by making them more expensive and encouraging exports by making them cheaper. But this equalization may take a long time to occur (consumers and producers in the two countries must change their behavior). And central banks may want to slow the pace at which exchange rates adjust to slow the effects on trading sectors within their economies.

The balance of trade indicates something about how an economy is changing and, ultimately, about its competitiveness vis-à-vis other countries. A rising balance-of-trade deficit indicates that an economy is not able to sell its goods abroad, and that consumers are favoring imports over domestically produced goods. Al-

## WORLD'S 50 LARGEST BANKS, RANKED BY ASSETS, 1990

| Rank/Company | Country | Assets (mil.) | Rank/Company | Country | Assets (mil.) |
|---|---|---|---|---|---|
| 1. Dai-Ichi Kangyo Bank | Japan | $428,167 | 26. Citibank | U.S. | $155,394 |
| 2. Sumitomo Bank | Japan | 490,161 | 27. Swiss Bank Corp. | Switzerland | 151,260 |
| 3. Mitsui Taiyo Kobe Bank | Japan | 408,754 | 28. Hongkong & Shanghai Banking Corp. | Hong Kong | 148,488 |
| 4. Sanwa Bank | Japan | 402,699 | 29. Commerzbank | Germany | 144,166 |
| 5. Fuji Bank | Japan | 399,545 | 30. Toyo Trust & Banking Co. | Japan | 141,744 |
| 6. Mitsubishi Bank | Japan | 391,528 | 31. Bayerische Vereinsbank | Germany | 137,747 |
| 7. Credit Agricole Mutuel | France | 305,206 | 32. Banca Nazionale del Lavoro | Italy | 137,714 |
| 8. Banque Nationale de Paris | France | 291,873 | 33. Deutsche Genossenschaftsbank | Germany | 136,453 |
| 9. Industrial Bank of Japan | Japan | 290,067 | 34. Westdeutsche Landesbank Girozentrale | Germany | 135,824 |
| 10. Credit Lyonnais | France | 287,330 | 35. Istituto Bancario San Paolo di Torino | Italy | 133,487 |
| 11. Deutsche Bank | Germany | 266,286 | 36. Nippon Credit Bank | Japan | 128,321 |
| 12. Barclays Bank | UK | 258,983 | 37. Algemene Bank Nederland[1] | Netherlands | 122,042 |
| 13. Tokai Bank | Japan | 249,751 | 38. Rabobank Nederland | Netherlands | 119,728 |
| 14. Norinchukin Bank | Japan | 249,667 | 39. Credit Suisse | Switzerland | 117,346 |
| 15. Mitsubishi Trust & Banking Corp. | Japan | 237,696 | 40. Bayerische Hypothekenbank·und Wechsel-Bank | Germany | 116,411 |
| 16. National Westminster Bank | UK | 232,512 | 41. Midland Bank | UK | 114,501 |
| 17. Bank of Tokyo | Japan | 223,185 | 42. Amsterdam-Rotterdam Bank[1] | Netherlands | 112,461 |
| 18. Societe Generale | France | 219,983 | 43. Banque Paribas[2] | France | 111,555 |
| 19. Sumitomo Trust & Banking Co. | Japan | 218,916 | 44. Kyowa Bank[3] | Japan | 111,547 |
| 20. Mitsui Trust & Banking Co. | Japan | 210,935 | 45. Lloyds Bank | UK | 105,988 |
| 21. Long-Term Credit Bank of Japan | Japan | 200,679 | 46. Saitama Bank[3] | Japan | 105,635 |
| 22. Dresdner Bank | Germany | 186,936 | 47. Bayerische Landesbank Girozentrale | Germany | 103,722 |
| 23. Union Bank of Switzerland | Switzerland | 183,443 | 48. NMB Postbank Group | Netherlands | 102,894 |
| 24. Yasuda Trust & Banking Co. | Japan | 175,552 | 49. Shoko Chukin Bank | Japan | 102,673 |
| 25. Daiwa Bank | Japan | 171,239 | 50. Cassa di Risparmio delle Provincie Lombarde | Italy | 99,946 |

1. A subsidiary of the $231.4 billion-asset ABN Amro Holding, N.V., Amsterdam, Netherlands, the 17th largest banking company in the world. 2. A subsidiary of the $185.6 billion-asset Compagnie Financiere de Paribas, Paris, the 25th largest banking company in the world. 3. On April 1, Kyowa Bank and Saitama Bank merged to form Kyowa Saitama Bank, Ltd. Had the merger taken place on March 31, the new bank would have ranked 20th with combined assets of $217 billion. **Source:** American Banker (July 26, 1991).

though U.S. exports constitute only about 10% of GNP, in the first three quarters of 1990 export growth accounted for 70% of GNP growth. The U.S. economy ran a current account deficit of $99.3 billion in 1990, down from $110 billion in 1989, due to a decrease in the merchandise trade deficit, an increase in services surplus (to $22.9 billion), and a surplus of investment income.

**Capital account and Official Reserves Account** The U.S. economy ran a net deficit in assets equaling $26.3 billion at the end of 1990, 70% less than a year earlier. The decrease can again be attributed to the declining value of the dollar, lower U.S. investment returns, increased demand for capital abroad, and a decline in stock markets, all of which resulted in substantial swings to net outflows on securities transactions and on net direct investment transactions. The United States became a debtor nation in 1985, when the U.S. net international investment deficit was $110.7 billion, down from a $3.5-billion surplus the previous year. At least part of the explanation was that the Federal Reserve was operating a tight-money policy in order to reduce inflation, driving up interest rates and exchange rates (by reducing the supply of dollars and the attractiveness of interest-paying instruments in dollars). The fact that the exchange rate was held higher in this fashion in turn made the balance of payments situation worse, since in the future the United States must pay dividends and interest to foreigners who invest, some estimate $40–50 billion a year by 1992. In 1980 the United States funded all of its investments with its own savings, but now the economy's investment needs are met using at least 50% foreign

funds, since U.S. savings levels have been insufficient to meet these needs.

Foreign direct investment in U.S. companies and factories totaled $25.7 billion in 1990 (a decrease of 64%), 75% of which came from Western Europe. A weakened and declining U.S. economy, repayment by U.S. affiliates of large amounts of debt acquired in recent years, interest in European investment opportunities in anticipation of a single market in 1992, and to a lesser extent, opportunities in Eastern Europe, contributed to the dramatic decline.

**International Lending: The World Bank and the IMF** As a part of the Bretton Woods Conference in 1944, the 42 countries represented created two important international financial institutions: the International Monetary Fund (IMF) and the International Bank for Reconstruction and Development (IBRD), commonly known as the World Bank. Each of the 151 IMF members contributes resources to the fund; financial contributions and voting rights are proportional to the size of their international payments. (The United States, Japan, West Germany, France, the United Kingdom, Belgium, the Netherlands, and Canada are the largest members.) The IMF makes loans to member countries having difficulty paying foreign debts and establishes many of the guidelines through which international financial transactions take place. The IBRD, together with its affiliates the International Development Association (IDA) and the International Finance Corporation (IFC), makes longer-term loans to developing countries to promote economic growth and development. Funds for the World Bank are raised by subscription

## 20 MOST HIGHLY INDEBTED DEVELOPING COUNTRIES, 1988–89
(millions of U.S. dollars)

| Country | Total external debt | | Percent change 1988–89 |
|---|---|---|---|
| | 1988 | 1989 | |
| Brazil | $115,646 | $111,290 | –3.77% |
| Mexico | 100,752 | 95,641 | –5.07 |
| Argentina | 58,706 | 64,745 | 10.29 |
| India | 57,254 | 62,509 | 9.18 |
| Indonesia | 52,797 | 53,111 | 0.59 |
| Egypt | 49,485 | 48,799 | –1.39 |
| China | 42,406 | 44,857 | 5.78 |
| Poland | 42,146 | 43,324 | 2.80 |
| Turkey | 40,864 | 41,600 | 1.80 |
| Venezuela | 35,473 | 33,144 | –6.57 |
| South Korea | 35,694 | 33,111 | 7.24 |
| Nigeria | 31,947 | 32,832 | 2.77 |
| Philippines | 29,161 | 28,902 | –0.90 |
| Algeria | 25,074 | 26,067 | 3.96 |
| Thailand | 21,827 | 23,466 | 6.98 |
| Morocco | 20,334 | 20,851 | 2.54 |
| Hungary | 19,625 | 20,605 | 4.76 |
| Peru | 18,999 | 19,876 | 4.41 |
| Yugoslavia | 21,002 | 19,651 | –6.87 |
| Chile | 19,578 | 18,241 | –6.83 |

**Source:** The World Bank, World Debt Tables 1990–1991 (1991).

from its members among Western industrialized countries. In recent years, however, there has been a reversal of the flow of funds between developed and developing countries, due to a drastic reduction in new lending and the large debt service payments. Developing countries are usually characterized by low average real per capita income, low life expectancy and literacy rates, high rates of population growth, a high proportion of the labor force in primary activities such as agriculture and mining, and low growth rates of per capita income.

International debt of developing economies, an issue that has been front-page news since the debt crisis in 1982 when Mexico suspended all loan repayments, now totals $1.3 trillion. Reducing this enormous debt is important to the United States for a number of reasons. Beyond philanthropic considerations, the United States relies on a number of developing countries as trading partners and thus buyers of U.S. goods. If these economies are strapped with large loan repayments, there will be less money for investment (unless new money is printed—fueling inflation and further destabilizing the economy), economic activity will likely slow, and demand for imports will fall, thereby reducing employment in the United States, something the United States cannot afford considering its slowing domestic demand. Decreased exports to Latin America since 1982 resulted in the loss of 340,000 U.S. jobs.

The most recent debt reduction plan, put forth by Treasury Secretary Nicholas Brady in 1989, encompasses large debt conversion of loans made by American banks—up to 35% in the case of Mexico (whose total debt to governments and commercial banks now hovers around $95 billion, $50 billion to banks alone). By October 1990, Brady Initiative operations concluded in Mexico, the Philippines, and Costa Rica had reduced commercial bank debt in these three countries by $9.5 billion through debt reduction and buy-backs.

Japan has recently joined the ranks of large donor countries involved in international development. In mid-1989 Japan announced its plan to use $38 billion of its current account surplus to help Third World countries, in the form of grants and loans. This makes Japan the world's largest donor of foreign aid, contributing 32% of total Western giving in 1987 (as compared to 9% in 1980). However, as a percentage of gross national product, this amounted to 0.75% in 1986. Along with this increased lending comes a greater voting strength in policy issues at the World Bank, which has gone from 4.5% in 1984 to 6.5% in 1988.

## THE EUROPEAN COMMUNITIES (EC)

"Europe without frontiers"—shorthand for a vision of an economic superpower, a single European market of 350 million people prosperous beyond past dreams—is the goal for 1992. Whether the full vision of "1992" proves to be a will-o'-the-wisp or an attainable goal, there is no doubt that the Europeans have moved very far indeed since the bleak days of 1945.

Out of the wreckage of World War II, with generous American aid under the Marshall Plan after 1948, western Europe commenced reconstruction, and between 1948 and 1954 various "economic miracles" occurred. Yet without economic integration the recoveries of these separate nations appeared to mean duplications, inefficiencies, diminished competition, and the threat of gluts and shortages in different industries in the separate countries.

One measure of economic integration—a small one but a sign of what might be achieved—was Benelux, the customs union constructed even before war's end in 1944 by Holland, Belgium, and Luxembourg. Despite difficulties rooted in the unequal status of the three economies, Benelux was by 1948 a going concern, with free movement of capital and labor and rapidly rising production.

In 1950, France's foreign minister, Robert Schuman, suggested that coal and steel production in France and West Germany be placed under a supranational (not intergovernmental) "high authority." That very evening the West German chancellor, Konrad Adenauer, announced his government's willingness to negotiate with France on Schuman's proposal. Other European countries were invited to join, while Britain, fearing loss of sovereignty, demurred. Italy and the Benelux countries joined the negotiations, hammering out by April 1951 the treaty that established the European Coal and Steel Community (ECSC), effective July 1, 1952.

In the common market for coal and steel, import and export duties were abolished, as were government subsidies. While the tonnage of coal mined grew slowly (due to high production costs and the availability of petroleum and hydropower as attractive energy alternatives), the distribution of coal supplies was rationalized with customers able to buy from nearby ECSC mines rather than distant national mines. It was otherwise with iron ore and steel. Between 1952 and 1958 France increased its production of iron ore by one-half and its sales to other ECSC members by two-thirds. In the same period steel production in the community grew by one-half while trade in steel grew two-and-a-half times.

These successes led the six nations ("the Six") to discuss during 1955 and 1956 further steps in economic integration. Negotiations culminated in March of 1957 in the Treaty of Rome, actually a pair of treaties establishing the European Economic Community (EEC, or Common Market) and the European Atomic Energy Community (Euratom). The EEC was designed for a number of ends: to reduce and eventually abolish all tariffs among its members and establish a single external tariff system for the Community (these goals were not realized until July 1968); eventually to coordinate transportation systems, agricultural policies, and general economic policies; to remove private and public measures restricting free competition; and to foster the free movement of labor, entrepreneurship, and capital. Euratom was intended for the common development of peaceful uses of atomic energy and to establish a nuclear energy industry on a European scale. Denmark, Ireland, and the UK joined Euratom, the ECSC, and the EEC in 1973, Greece in 1981, and Portugal and Spain in 1986.

The advent of Charles DeGaulle as president of the new (Fifth) French Republic had a powerful effect upon the communities. When the United Kingdom suggested in 1958 expanding the EEC into an Atlantic free-trade area, France exercised its veto. In response Britain fostered in 1959 the European Free Trade Association (EFTA) whose members, besides Britain, were Denmark, Norway, Sweden, Portugal, Austria, and Switzerland. Finland joined in 1961 and Iceland joined in 1970. Britain and Denmark withdrew in 1973 to join the EEC. A free-trade association however was not a common market, since it established no common external tariff, leaving its members free to maintain their own tariffs with respect to nonmembers; and it aimed simply at eliminating trade barriers among members on nonagricultural goods.

Then began the second stage in the development of the EC. When Britain sought entry in 1961 into the Common Market, DeGaulle, fearing American influence and objecting to the special terms that Britain sought for the Commonwealth countries, exercised France's veto in 1963. He then pushed for agricultural integration, a thorny issue since each of the Six had its own system of protectionist duties, agricultural subsidies, and crop controls. The huge German market beckoned for France's chronic farm surpluses, yet Germany hesitated to sacrifice her own farmers in return for cheaper food.

A serious crisis impended, a crisis averted by the Dutch ("Mansholt") proposals to integrate agricultural policies by 1970: a common market with common prices, duties upon imports into the Community and subsidies for exporters, and a fair living standard for farmers. This Common Agricultural Policy, adopted in 1962, has meant protection for farmers through managed (higher-than-market) prices, overproduction (especially of butter and wine), and direction not by the market but by Brussels' so-called "Eurocrats."

The third stage came with the 1967 formation, by the Brussels Treaty of 1965 (often called the "Second Treaty of Rome"), of the Commission of European Communities—the EC—a merger of the EEC, the ECSC, and Euratom into one, with a four-part structure: commission, council, parliament, and court.

It was the "refounded" EC that the United Kingdom was at last permitted to join in 1973 (after another Gaullist veto in 1967). As in its earlier attempts it was accompanied by Ireland, Denmark, and Norway. (Norwegian voters subsequently rejected by referendum the terms of the treaty, so that the Six became the Nine.) The Community was further enlarged subsequently by the accession of Greece in 1981 and Spain and Portugal in 1986.

Member states' restrictions on the movement of capital have prevented creation of an EC financial market. But in 1979 the European Monetary System (EMS) was founded. It consisted of four main components: a European Currency Unit (ECU), credit facilities, transfer arrangements, and exchange-rate stabilization mechanisms. The UK, and later Greece (1981), declined to participate in the EMS.

**Europe 1992** "Europe without frontiers"—this is the Commission's favored slogan to summarize the Single European Act of 1986, which sets 1992 as the target date for establishing what the Treaty of Rome envisioned, a single market free of barriers to the free movement of goods, services, capital, and labor. Brainchild of Commission President Jacques Delors, the Single European Act is a compendium of almost 300 rules and directives assembled in a white paper by Britain's Lord Cockfield and made law by the Commission in 1987. But like the Soviet Union's slogan of "perestroika," the meaning of "Europe without frontiers" is not quite clear.

The fundamental difference as to its meaning concerns the extent to which "harmonization" among the members of the Community will be the result of Commission directives or the result of market forces. More precisely, what will be the mix of the two?

Each of the member states relies upon a Value Added Tax (a hidden sales tax) for revenue; but rates vary widely. Without Commission directives, business should shift to the low-tax states, imperiling the revenue, and the social services therefore, of the high-tax states. On the other hand, Commission directives establishing a permissible range of rates would represent the Comunity's setting tax rates for the member states, a serious diminution of national sovereignty. Similar difficult questions have arisen for myriad areas of economic life: wage differences; varying safety laws; banking regulations, and taxes on investment income; the existence of certain import quotas—and perhaps hundreds more.

All these actual and potential areas of dispute cast an air of uncertainty upon "1992." Since the more serious disputes will almost certainly be referred to the Community's Court of Justice, the Court is expected to play a crucial role in establishing a body of "case law" through precedents and may thereby grow to be a major force among the four institutions of the Community.

All that can confidently be predicted is that the twelve national markets will, in varying ways and degrees, become easier for other EC members to enter. As the chairman of Olivetti expressed it, 1992 will prove to be "a trend not a task."

### Structure of EC

*The Commission* is composed of 17 commissioners appointed by member governments; the five largest countries, France, Germany, Italy, Spain, and the United Kingdom, appoint two commissioners each. The EC treaties direct Commission members to act independently of their governments and represent the entire community's interests. The Commission supervises implementation of EC treaties, initiates and implements EC policy, transacts negotiations with nonmember states, and manages EC funds. The Commission can be forced to resign by two-thirds majority vote of the European Parliament. The Commission headquarters are in Brussels. The president, who is appointed by the Council of Ministers, serves a two-year term.

*The Council of Ministers* consists of the foreign ministers of the 12 member governments and is the chief decision-making body of the EC, passing legislation on the major issues affecting all members. Votes are by majority. The Council meets in Brussels (usually three times a year), and its presidency alternates among the member countries for six-month terms.

*The European Parliament* The 518 deputies of the European Parliament are elected directly by the citizens of the individual countries. The Parliament oversees the EC budget and passes on Commission proposals to the Council of Ministers. The Parliament also passes on new applications to the EC. Deputies are elected to five-year terms and meet monthly in Strasbourg.

*The Court of Justice* is the court of last resort for the EC, interpreting EC treaties and legislation and hearing complaints about member-government violations. The Court also resolves differences between EC legislation and national laws. The 11 judges and five advocates-general are appointed by the member governments and serve six-year terms. Decisions are made by simple majority but always announced unanimously. The Court is located in Luxembourg.

*The Economic and Social Committee* is composed of 156 members representing employers' organizations, trade unions, and "special interests" (small businesses, consumers, agriculturalists, and professions). Through consultation, the Committee presents its views to the Council of Ministers and the EC Commission.

# World Energy

The world's primary energy sources in 1989 were crude oil and natural gas liquids, natural gas, coal, and electricity from hydroelectric and nuclear power. Measured in British thermal units (Btu), world production of these energy sources exceeded 338 quadrillion ($10^{15}$) Btu. Crude oil and natural gas liquids accounted for 40% of total output, coal 27%, dry natural gas 21%, hydroelectric power 6%, and nuclear power 6%.

**Crude oil** World production of crude oil and natural gas liquids was 64.3 million barrels per day in 1989—down 3% from 1988. The United States, the USSR, and Saudi Arabia produced 42% of the world's crude oil. In the Middle East and Africa, crude oil and natural gas liquids production rose 8% from 21.2 million barrels per day in 1988 to 23.1 million barrels per day in 1989; this was still below the 25.2 million barrels per day produced in 1980. World petroleum consumption exceeded 66 million barrels per day in 1989, the highest level in 10 years. Production of natural gas liquids rose 27% from 1980 to 1989. The U.S. accounted for 32% of total production in 1989.

**Dry natural gas** World production of dry natural gas increased 36% between 1980 and 1989. The USSR accounted for 39% and the U.S. for 24% of world production in 1989. North America accounted for 30% of total natural gas consumption in 1989.

**Coal** World coal production increased from

## TOP 10 PRODUCERS OF PRIMARY ENERGY, BY SOURCE, 1989[1]

| Crude oil[2] | (thousand barrels/day) |
|---|---|
| 1. USSR | 11,420 |
| 2. United States | 7,613 |
| 3. Saudi Arabia | 5,064 |
| 4. Iran | 2,863 |
| 5. Iraq | 2,822 |
| 6. China | 2,760 |
| 7. Mexico | 2,513 |
| 8. United Arab Emirates | 1,960 |
| 9. Venezuela | 1,907 |
| 10. Kuwait | 1,802 |

| Natural gas plant liquids[3] | (thousand barrels/day) |
|---|---|
| 1. United States | 1,546 |
| 2. USSR | 720 |
| 3. Saudi Arabia | 421 |
| 4. Canada | 411 |
| 5. Mexico | 376 |
| 6. United Kingdom | 140 |
| 7. Algeria | 130 |
| 8. United Arab Emirates | 127 |
| 9. Kuwait | 110 |
| 10. Venezuela | 108 |

| Dry natural gas | (trillion cubic feet) |
|---|---|
| 1. USSR | 28.14 |
| 2. United States | 17.26 |
| 3. Canada | 3.59 |
| 4. Netherlands | 2.53 |
| 5. United Kingdom | 1.67 |
| 6. Algeria | 1.64 |
| 7. Indonesia | 1.39 |
| 8. Romania | 1.33 |
| 9. Norway | 1.09 |
| 10. Saudi Arabia | 1.06 |

| Coal[4] | (million short tons) |
|---|---|
| 1. China | 1,063 |
| 2. United States | 980 |
| 3. USSR | 816 |
| 4. Germany, East | 336 |
| 5. Poland | 275 |
| 6. India | 210 |
| 7. Germany, West | 206 |
| 8. Australia | 201 |
| 9. South Africa | 194 |
| 10. Czechoslovakia | 138 |

| Hydroelectric power[5] | (billion kWh) |
|---|---|
| 1. Canada | 287.6 |
| 2. United States | 268.2 |
| 3. USSR | 221.9 |
| 4. Brazil | 211.2 |
| 5. Norway | 117.4 |
| 6. China | 105.8 |
| 7. Japan | 83.5 |
| 8. Sweden | 70.8 |
| 9. India | 55.6 |
| 10. France | 50.3 |

**Note:** Sum of components may not add to total due to rounding. 1. Preliminary; per year except as indicated. 2. Includes lease condensate. 3. Does not include China, for which data are unavailable. 4. Includes anthracite, semianthracite, bituminous, subbituminous, lignite, and brown coal. 5. Net generation; data consist of utility and nonutility sources. Excludes generation from pumped storage. **Source:** U.S. Dept. of Energy, *International Energy Annual 1989* (1991).

4.2 billion short tons in 1980 to 5.2 billion short tons in 1989. China, the U.S., and the USSR together accounted for 55% of total coal production in 1989.

**Hydroelectric power** Generation of hydroelectric power worldwide rose 12% between 1980 and 1989. Canada, the U.S., the USSR, Brazil, and Norway produced 54% of the total in 1989.

**Nuclear electric power** Between 1980 and 1989, world generation of nuclear electric power increased 157%. The five leading producers in 1989 were the U.S., France, the USSR,

## WORLD PRIMARY ENERGY PRODUCTION BY SOURCE, 1980–89
(quadrillion Btu)

| Source | 1980 | 1985 | 1989[1] |
|---|---|---|---|
| Crude oil[2] | 127.59 | 114.68 | 127.45 |
| Natural gas plant liquids | 5.48 | 6.23 | 6.99 |
| Dry natural gas | 52.79 | 61.37 | 71.11 |
| Coal | 75.02 | 86.09 | 91.90 |
| Hydroelectric power[3] | 18.21 | 20.67 | 21.23 |
| Nuclear power[3] | 7.51 | 15.15 | 19.66 |
| Total[4] | 286.61 | 304.19 | 338.34 |

Note: Sum of components may not equal total due to rounding. 1. Preliminary. 2. Includes lease condensate. 3. Net generation; does not include energy consumed by the generating unit. 4. Total excludes wood, waste, wind, photovoltaic, and solar thermal energy. Source: U.S. Dept. of Energy, *International Energy Annual 1989* (1991).

## PRIMARY ENERGY DEPENDENCY BY REGION, 1989 (quadrillion Btu)

| Region | Production | Consumption | Net |
|---|---|---|---|
| North America | 86.21 | 96.80 | –10.59 |
| Central and South America | 15.33 | 13.62 | 1.71 |
| Western Europe | 36.66 | 60.25 | –23.59 |
| Eastern Europe and USSR | 85.24 | 79.49 | 5.75 |
| Middle East | 39.55 | 10.39 | 29.16 |
| Africa | 20.24 | 9.72 | 10.52 |
| Far East and Oceania | 55.12 | 70.20 | –15.08 |
| World | 338.35 | 340.47 | 2.12 |

Source: U.S. Dept. of Energy, *International Energy Annual 1989* (1991).

## WORLD PRIMARY ENERGY PRODUCTION BY REGION, 1989 (quadrillion Btu)

| Region | Crude oil[1] | Natural gas plant liquids | Dry natural gas | Coal[2] | Hydro-electric power | Nuclear power | Total |
|---|---|---|---|---|---|---|---|
| North America | 24.94 | 3.25 | 22.30 | 23.33 | 5.94 | 6.56 | 86.21 |
| Central and South America | 8.82 | 0.28 | 2.09 | 0.63 | 3.43 | 0.07 | 15.33 |
| Western Europe | 8.27 | 0.41 | 7.17 | 8.74 | 4.80 | 7.27 | 36.66 |
| Eastern Europe and USSR | 25.08 | 1.14 | 28.42 | 25.02 | 2.58 | 3.01 | 85.24 |
| Middle East | 34.57 | 1.24 | 3.62 | 0.02 | 0.10 | 0.00 | 39.55 |
| Africa | 12.56 | 0.37 | 2.40 | 4.33 | 0.46 | 0.11 | 20.24 |
| Far East and Oceania | 13.22 | 0.28 | 5.12 | 29.93 | 3.92 | 2.64 | 55.12 |
| World total | 127.45 | 6.99 | 71.11 | 91.90 | 21.23 | 19.66 | 338.34 |

Note: Figures reported are for net generation and exclude energy consumed by the generating plants. Sum of components may not add to total due to independent rounding. 1. Includes lease condensate. 2. Includes anthracite, subanthracite, bituminous, lignite, and brown coal. Source: U.S. Dept. of Energy, *International Energy Annual 1989* (1991).

## WORLD PRIMARY ENERGY CONSUMPTION BY REGION, 1989 (quadrillion Btu)

| Region | Petroleum | Dry natural gas | Coal[1] | Hydro-electric power | Net nuclear power | Total |
|---|---|---|---|---|---|---|
| North America | 41.26 | 22.56 | 20.47 | 5.94 | 6.57 | 96.80 |
| Central and South America | 7.39 | 2.10 | 0.63 | 3.43 | 0.07 | 13.62 |
| Western Europe | 26.65 | 9.71 | 11.77 | 4.80 | 7.32 | 60.25 |
| Eastern Europe and USSR | 22.32 | 27.02 | 24.58 | 2.58 | 2.99 | 79.49 |
| Middle East | 6.57 | 3.59 | 0.14 | 0.10 | 0.00 | 10.39 |
| Africa | 4.16 | 1.40 | 3.58 | 0.46 | 0.11 | 9.72 |
| Far East and Oceania | 26.67 | 5.24 | 31.73 | 3.92 | 2.64 | 70.20 |
| World total | 135.01 | 71.62 | 92.89 | 21.23 | 19.71 | 340.37 |

Note: Figures reported are for net generation and exclude energy consumed by the generating plants. Sum of components may not add to total due to independent rounding. 1. Includes anthracite, subanthracite, bituminous, lignite, and brown coal. Source: U.S. Dept. of Energy, *International Energy Annual 1989* (1991).

## WORLD ENERGY PRODUCTION BY REGION, 1980–89

| Region | Dry natural gas[1] 1980 | 1985 | 1989[4] | Coal[2] 1980 | 1985 | 1989[4] | Hydroelectric power[3] 1980 | 1985 | 1989[4] |
|---|---|---|---|---|---|---|---|---|---|
| North America | 23.06 | 20.31 | 21.81 | 878 | 960 | 1,071 | 546.9 | 611.0 | 575.2 |
| Central and South America | 1.30 | 1.76 | 2.01 | 16 | 21 | 28 | 199.1 | 278.3 | 329.7 |
| Western Europe | 7.02 | 6.75 | 7.04 | 543 | 570 | 563 | 442.4 | 463.2 | 461.3 |
| Eastern Europe and USSR | 17.34 | 24.96 | 30.40 | 1,566 | 1,671 | 1,687 | 209.8 | 239.7 | 248.3 |
| Middle East | 1.33 | 2.38 | 3.45 | 1 | 1 | 1 | 9.6 | 9.6 | 9.6 |
| Africa | 0.69 | 1.86 | 2.27 | 133 | 198 | 202 | 62.4 | 46.1 | 44.4 |
| Far East and Oceania | 2.38 | 3.98 | 4.91 | 1,036 | 1,422 | 1,602 | 281.3 | 342.5 | 377.1 |
| World total | 53.11 | 62.00 | 71.88 | 4,173 | 4,844 | 5,154 | 1,751.6 | 1,990.4 | 2,045.6 |

Note: Sum of components may not equal total due to independent rounding. 1. Trillions of cubic feet. 2. Millions of short tons. 3. Billions of kilowatthours. 4. Preliminary. Source: U.S. Dept. of Energy, *International Energy Annual 1989* (1991).

## WORLD CRUDE OIL PRODUCTION, 1960–89 (million barrels per day)

| Country | 1960 | 1970 | 1975 | 1980 | 1985 | 1989[1] |
|---|---|---|---|---|---|---|
| **Organization of Oil Producing Countries (OPEC)[2]** | | | | | | |
| Indonesia | 0.41 | 0.85 | 1.31 | 1.58 | 1.33 | 1.37 |
| Iran | 1.07 | 3.83 | 5.35 | 1.66 | 2.25 | 2.86 |
| Iraq | 0.97 | 1.55 | 2.26 | 2.51 | 1.43 | 2.82 |
| Nigeria | 0.02 | 1.08 | 1.78 | 2.06 | 1.50 | 1.69 |
| Saudi Arabia[3] | 1.31 | 3.80 | 7.08 | 9.90 | 3.39 | 5.15 |
| Venezuela | 2.85 | 3.71 | 2.35 | 2.17 | 1.68 | 1.88 |
| Other OPEC | 2.07 | 8.59 | 7.03 | 7.11 | 5.05 | 6.86 |
| Total OPEC | 8.70 | 23.41 | 27.15 | 26.99 | 16.63 | 22.63 |

| Country | 1960 | 1970 | 1975 | 1980 | 1985 | 1989[1] |
|---|---|---|---|---|---|---|
| **Non-OPEC countries** | | | | | | |
| Canada | 0.52 | 1.26 | 1.43 | 1.44 | 1.47 | 1.58 |
| China | 0.10 | 0.60 | 1.49 | 2.11 | 2.51 | 2.78 |
| Mexico | 0.27 | 0.49 | 0.71 | 1.94 | 2.75 | 2.51 |
| United Kingdom | ([4]) | ([4]) | 0.01 | 1.62 | 2.53 | 1.79 |
| United States | 7.04 | 9.64 | 8.38 | 8.60 | 8.97 | 7.63 |
| USSR | 2.91 | 6.97 | 9.47 | 11.46 | 11.25 | 11.36 |
| Other non-OPEC | 1.42 | 3.50 | 4.14 | 5.20 | 7.54 | 9.24 |
| World total | 20.96 | 45.87 | 52.78 | 59.35 | 53.65 | 59.52 |

1. Preliminary. 2. In addition to those listed separately, current OPEC members are: Algeria, Ecuador, Gabon, Kuwait, Libya, Qatar, and United Arab Emirates. 3. Includes about one-half of the production in the Neutral Zone between Kuwait and Saudi Arabia. 4. Less than 5,000 barrels per day. Source: U.S. Dept. of Energy, *Annual Energy Review 1989* (1991).

Japan, and West Germany, generating 73% of the world total. Although the number of nuclear reactors in operation worldwide remained unchanged, there were regional gains in North America and the Far East, offset by the closure of seven reactors in the USSR.

**Energy consumption** By region, North America, Europe, and the Far East all consumed more energy than they produced. Imports as a percentage of production were 12.3% for North America, 64% for Western Europe, and 27% for the Far East and Oceania.

Japan, which uses 25% of all energy consumed in the Far East and Oceania, imports 4.7 times more energy than it produces. Net exporters of energy, by region, were the Middle East, Africa, Central and South America, and Eastern Europe and the USSR.

## WORLD NUCLEAR POWER GENERATION, BY REGION AND COUNTRY, 1980–89 (billion kilowatt-hours)

| Region and country | Net power generation 1980 | Net power generation 1985 | Net power generation 1989[1] | Operable reactors[2] | Region and country | Net power generation 1980 | Net power generation 1985 | Net power generation 1989[1] | Operable reactors[2] |
|---|---|---|---|---|---|---|---|---|---|
| North America | 287.0 | 440.8 | 604.7 | 129 | Yugoslavia | 0.0 | 4.0 | 3.9 | 1 |
| Canada | 35.9 | 57.1 | 75.4 | 18 | Eastern Europe and USSR | 90.7 | 200.9 | 263.2 | 66 |
| Mexico | — | — | — | 1 | Bulgaria | 5.9 | 12.5 | 15.1 | 5 |
| United States | 251.1 | 383.7 | 529.4 | 110 | Czechoslovakia | 4.3 | 11.2 | 21.9 | 8 |
| Central and South America | 2.2 | 8.7 | 6.3 | 3 | Germany, East | 11.3 | 12.1 | 11.1 | 6 |
| Argentina | 2.2 | 5.5 | 4.8 | 2 | Hungary | 0.0 | 6.1 | 13.1 | 4 |
| Brazil | 0.0 | 3.2 | 1.5 | 1 | USSR | 69.3 | 159.0 | 202.0 | 43 |
| Western Europe | 207.4 | 559.8 | 695.3 | 159 | Middle East | 0.0 | 0.0 | 0.0 | 0 |
| Belgium | 11.9 | 32.8 | 38.2 | 7 | Africa | 0.0 | 5.5 | 11.1 | 2 |
| Finland | 6.6 | 17.8 | 18.0 | 4 | South Africa | 0.0 | 5.5 | 11.1 | 2 |
| France | 63.4 | 211.2 | 286.4 | 55 | Far East and Oceania | 92.6 | 192.2 | 249.7 | 62 |
| Germany, West | 43.7 | 125.9 | 140.8 | 22 | India | 2.7 | 4.3 | 3.8 | 7 |
| Italy[3] | 2.1 | 6.7 | 0.0 | 2 | Japan | 78.7 | 144.4 | 174.6 | 39 |
| Netherlands | 4.0 | 3.7 | 3.8 | 2 | Korea, South | 3.3 | 15.9 | 44.6 | 9 |
| Spain | 5.2 | 28.0 | 52.9 | 10 | Pakistan | 0.1 | 0.2 | 0.1 | 1 |
| Sweden | 25.3 | 55.8 | 61.8 | 12 | Taiwan | 7.8 | 27.3 | 26.6 | 6 |
| Switzerland | 12.9 | 20.1 | 21.4 | 5 | **World total** | **679.9** | **1,407.8** | **1,830.2** | **421** |
| United Kingdom | 32.3 | 53.8 | 68.0 | 39 | | | | | |

**Note:** Net generation; does not include energy consumed by the generating unit. Sum of components may not equal total due to independent rounding. 1. Preliminary. 2. As of Dec. 31, 1989. 3. Under Italy's new National Energy Plan, existing nuclear plants have been mothballed or decommissioned and nuclear plants under construction are being converted to burn gas or coal. **Source:** U.S. Dept. of Energy, *International Energy Annual 1989* (1991) and *Commercial Nuclear Power 1990: Prospects for the United States and the World* (1990).

# World Commodity Production

This section presents information about production of major world commodities: nonfuel minerals and ores, food, livestock, fish, and forestry. Virtually all of the information is from the United Nations.

For energy-related commodities, see also "U.S. Energy" and "World Energy."

## Food and Livestock Production

According to the Food and Agricultural Organization of the United Nations (FAO), global agricultural production stagnated in both 1987 and 1988—the most recent years for which figures are available. Overall output remained at approximately 1986 levels. Production fell by about 5% in the developed nations. Nearly two-thirds of African countries suffered setbacks, compared to just over half in Latin America and the Caribbean, a third in the Near East, and a quarter in the Far East.

Cereal (wheat, rice, barley, corn, millet, and sorghum) production declined worldwide in 1988 to an estimated 1,743 million tons—3.3% less than the already low level of 1987. The sharpest

drop occurred in North America, where drought reduced output by 27%. Production in Eastern Europe and the USSR dropped a slight 5%. In the Far East, however, cereal production increased by nearly 9% because of an excellent crop in India. China's cereal output declined by nearly 2%. African cereal production staged a strong and much-needed recovery of about 12% from 1987 shortfalls. Cereal crops, particularly wheat, fared poorly in Latin America, but Oceania registered significantly large harvests.

The FAO estimated a 2% increase in global meat production. Beef output increased substantially in Latin America, the Caribbean, and in North America, but these gains were largely offset by declines in Western Europe. Milk production, which had declined in 1987 for the first time in 24 years, expanded modestly in 1988 with Third World increases offsetting reductions in Western Europe.

Coffee production declined sharply in 1988 as a result of bad weather in Brazil and other Latin American and Caribbean areas, where output dropped nearly 30%. Cocoa production rose, as did that of pulses (including beans such as chickpeas, dry beans, and dry peas), in the main producing areas.

### WORLD FOOD PRODUCTION: PAST, PRESENT, FUTURE

- Many developing countries are losing the battle to keep food production commensurate with high population growth. For the 94 developing countries reporting to the UN, cereal production per person actually fell in 51 and rose in only 43 between 1979–87.
- Developing countries as a whole are less able to be self-sufficient in food. In 1969–71 they imported only 20 million tons of cereal; by 1983–85 imports rose to 69 million tons and are projected to total 112 million tons by 2000. These deficits have thus far been balanced by corresponding surpluses in the industrialized countries—mainly North America.
- World food security now depends shakily on the production of North American farmers. After the drought-hit U.S. harvest of 1988, world cereal surpluses dropped from 451 million tons in 1986–87 to only 290 million tons in 1989, down from a safe 24% of annual consumption to the danger level of 17%.
- By the year 2000 at least 36 countries, with a combined population of 486 million, will be unable to feed their populations from their own lands.

**Source:** United Nations Population Fund (UNFPA), *The State of World Population 1990* (1990).

## LEADING PRODUCERS OF SELECTED GRAINS, 1989
(thousands of metric tons)

| Country | Total | Percent of world total | Country | Total | Percent of world total |
|---|---|---|---|---|---|
| **Cereals[1]** | | | **Rice** | | |
| China | 365,472 | 19.5% | China | 179,403 | 35.0% |
| United States | 284,248 | 15.2 | India | 107,500 | 21.0 |
| USSR | 203,460 | 10.9 | Indonesia | 43,566 | 8.6 |
| India | 192,516 | 10.3 | Bangladesh | 26,600 | 5.2 |
| France | 57,140 | 3.0 | Thailand | 21,300 | 4.2 |
| Indonesia | 49,893 | 2.7 | Viet Nam | 18,100 | 3.5 |
| Canada | 47,955 | 2.6 | Myanmar | 13,581 | 2.6 |
| Brazil | 43,701 | 2.3 | Japan | 12,934 | 2.5 |
| Bangladesh | 27,518 | 1.5 | Brazil | 11,107 | 2.1 |
| Poland | 26,958 | 1.4 | Philippines | 9,459 | 1.9 |
| **Corn** | | | **Wheat** | | |
| United States | 191,197 | 40.0% | China | 91,002 | 16.9% |
| China | 75,840 | 16.1 | USSR | 90,500 | 16.8 |
| Brazil | 26,508 | 5.6 | United States | 55,407 | 10.2 |
| USSR | 17,000 | 3.6 | India | 53,995 | 10.0 |
| France | 12,926 | 2.7 | France | 31,817 | 5.9 |
| Romania | 11,800 | 2.5 | Canada | 24,383 | 4.5 |
| South Africa | 11,700 | 2.4 | Turkey | 15,729 | 2.9 |
| Mexico | 9,900 | 2.1 | Pakistan | 14,419 | 2.6 |
| Yugoslavia | 9,415 | 2.0 | Australia | 14,200 | 2.6 |
| India | 7,800 | 1.7 | UK | 13,900 | 2.5 |

1. Includes wheat, rice, barley, corn, millet, and sorghum. **Source:** Food and Agricultural Organization of the UN, *FAO Production Yearbook 1989* (1990).

## PRODUCTION OF SELECTED GRAINS BY REGION AND DEVELOPMENT CATEGORY, 1989
(thousands of metric tons)

| Region and development category | Cereals[1] | Corn | Rice | Wheat |
|---|---|---|---|---|
| **World total** | **1,864,852** | **470,318** | **506,291** | **538,056** |
| Africa | 90,845 | 36,414 | 10,505 | 13,218 |
| North America[2] | 356,741 | 210,964 | 9,255 | 83,738 |
| South America | 77,800 | 36,737 | 17,191 | 18,429 |
| Asia | 821,740 | 108,630 | 463,889 | 192,429 |
| Europe | 291,806 | 60,212 | 2,140 | 125,406 |
| Oceania | 22,460 | 361 | 786 | 14,335 |
| USSR | 203,460 | 17,000 | 2,525 | 90,500 |
| Developed countries | 879,682 | 286,885 | 25,358 | 313,937 |
| Developing countries | 985,170 | 183,433 | 480,934 | 224,119 |

1. Includes wheat, rice, barley, corn, millet, and sorghum. 2. Includes Central America. **Source:** Food and Agricultural Organization of the UN, *FAO Production Yearbook 1989* (1990).

## LEADING PRODUCERS OF SELECTED LIVESTOCK, 1989
(thousands of head[1])

| Country | Total | Percent of world total | Country | Total | Percent of world total |
|---|---|---|---|---|---|
| **Cattle** | | | **Pigs** | | |
| India | 195,500 | 15.2% | China | 348,954 | 41.0% |
| Brazil | 136,814 | 10.6 | USSR | 78,100 | 9.2 |
| USSR | 119,600 | 9.3 | United States | 55,499 | 6.5 |
| United States | 99,180 | 7.7 | Brazil | 33,200 | 3.9 |
| China | 77,141 | 6.0 | West Germany | 22,589 | 2.6 |
| Argentina | 50,782 | 4.0 | Poland | 18,835 | 2.2 |
| Mexico | 34,999 | 2.7 | Spain | 16,100 | 1.9 |
| Ethiopia | 28,900 | 2.3 | Romania | 15,400 | 1.8 |
| Colombia | 24,671 | 1.9 | Mexico | 14,080 | 1.6 |
| Bangladesh | 23,000 | 1.8 | Netherlands | 13,820 | 1.6 |
| **Goats** | | | **Sheep** | | |
| India | 107,000 | 20.0% | Australia | 165,000 | 14.0% |
| China | 77,883 | 14.7 | USSR | 139,500 | 11.8 |
| Pakistan | 34,194 | 6.4 | China | 102,655 | 8.7 |
| Nigeria | 26,000 | 4.9 | New Zealand | 60,569 | 5.2 |
| Somalia | 20,300 | 3.8 | India | 53,486 | 4.5 |
| Ethiopia | 18,000 | 3.4 | Turkey | 34,850 | 3.0 |
| Sudan | 14,000 | 2.6 | Iran | 34,000 | 2.9 |
| Iran | 13,500 | 2.5 | South Africa | 29,850 | 2.5 |
| Turkey | 13,100 | 2.4 | Argentina | 29,345 | 2.5 |
| Indonesia | 10,600 | 2.0 | UK | 29,046 | 2.5 |
| **Chickens (mil.)** | | | | | |
| China | 1,981 | 18.7% | Japan | 330 | 3.1% |
| United States | 1,550 | 14.6 | India | 270 | 2.6 |
| USSR | 1,160 | 10.9 | Mexico | 226 | 2.1 |
| Brazil | 600 | 5.7 | Nigeria | 200 | 1.9 |
| Indonesia | 444 | 4.2 | France | 190 | 1.8 |

1. Except as indicated. **Source:** Food and Agricultural Organization of the UN, *FAO Production Yearbook 1989* (1990).

## LEADING PRODUCERS OF SELECTED MEATS, 1989
(thousands of metric tons)

| Country | Total | Percent of world total | Country | Total | Percent of world total |
|---|---|---|---|---|---|
| **Beef and veal** | | | **Pork** | | |
| United States | 10,655 | 21.0% | China | 22,070 | 32.0% |
| USSR | 8,600 | 17.3 | United States | 7,176 | 10.6 |
| Argentina | 2,600 | 5.2 | USSR | 6,750 | 10.0 |
| Brazil | 2,478 | 5.0 | West Germany | 3,300 | 4.8 |
| Mexico | 1,796 | 3.6 | France | 1,840 | 2.7 |
| France | 1,716 | 3.4 | Poland | 1,753 | 2.5 |
| West Germany | 1,585 | 3.2 | Spain | 1,720 | 2.5 |
| Australia | 1,491 | 3.0 | Netherlands | 1,632 | 2.4 |
| Italy | 1,166 | 2.3 | Japan | 1,570 | 2.3 |
| UK | 958 | 1.9 | East Germany | 1,368 | 2.0 |
| **Lamb and mutton** | | | **Poultry** | | |
| USSR | 850 | 13.1% | United States | 10,088 | 26.0% |
| New Zealand | 572 | 8.8 | USSR | 3,250 | 8.5 |
| Australia | 542 | 8.3 | China | 2,767 | 7.3 |
| China | 420 | 6.4 | Brazil | 2,140 | 5.6 |
| UK | 347 | 5.3 | Japan | 1,475 | 3.9 |
| Turkey | 304 | 4.6 | France | 1,426 | 3.7 |
| Iran | 241 | 3.7 | UK | 1,102 | 2.9 |
| Spain | 200 | 3.0 | Italy | 1,080 | 2.8 |
| Pakistan | 193 | 2.9 | Mexico | 846 | 2.2 |
| India | 158 | 2.4 | Spain | 806 | 2.1 |

**Source:** Food and Agricultural Organization of the UN, *FAO Production Yearbook 1989* (1990).

## PRODUCTION OF SELECTED MEATS BY REGION AND DEVELOPMENT CATEGORY, 1989 (metric tons)

| Region and development category | Beef and veal | Lamb | Pork | Poultry |
|---|---|---|---|---|
| World total | 49,436 | 6,473 | 67,460 | 37,817 |
| Africa | 3,455 | 850 | 488 | 1,708 |
| North America[1] | 14,028 | 200 | 9,547 | 12,087 |
| South America | 7,100 | 277 | 1,930 | 3,471 |
| Asia | 3,532 | 1,866 | 26,606 | 8,587 |
| Europe | 10,500 | 1,316 | 21,745 | 8,254 |
| Oceania | 2,021 | 1,114 | 395 | 460 |
| USSR | 8,600 | 850 | 6,750 | 3,250 |
| Developed countries | 34,680 | 3,581 | 38,914 | 24,731 |
| Developing countries | 14,785 | 2,892 | 28,546 | 13,086 |

1. Includes Central America. **Source:** Food and Agricultural Organization of the UN, *FAO Production Yearbook 1989* (1990).

## PRODUCTION OF SELECTED LIVESTOCK BY REGION AND DEVELOPMENT CATEGORY, 1989 (thousands of head[1])

| Region and development category | Cattle | Pigs | Sheep | Goats | Chickens (mil.) |
|---|---|---|---|---|---|
| World total | 1,281,472 | 846,174 | 1,175,524 | 526,440 | 10,574 |
| Africa | 185,794 | 13,097 | 200,711 | 169,467 | 854 |
| North America[2] | 166,999 | 87,864 | 19,182 | 15,058 | 2,022 |
| South America | 261,096 | 55,658 | 113,647 | 21,875 | 942 |
| Asia | 391,556 | 420,136 | 325,643 | 296,342 | 4,234 |
| Europe | 125,569 | 185,925 | 151,264 | 15,135 | 1,291 |
| Oceania | 30,858 | 5,393 | 225,577 | 2,064 | 71 |
| USSR | 119,600 | 78,100 | 139,500 | 6,500 | 1,160 |
| Developed countries | 403,695 | 346,706 | 558,172 | 31,343 | 4,562 |
| Developing countries | 877,777 | 499,467 | 617,353 | 495,098 | 6,012 |

1. Except as indicated. 2. Includes Central America. **Source:** Food and Agricultural Organization of the UN, *FAO Production Yearbook 1989* (1990).

## PRODUCTION OF SELECTED BEVERAGES AND BEVERAGE CROPS BY REGION AND DEVELOPMENT CATEGORY, 1989 (thousands of metric tons)

| Region and development category | Cocoa beans | Coffee, green | Tea | Wine |
|---|---|---|---|---|
| World total | 2,467 | 5,775 | 2,475 | 29,055 |
| Africa | 1,384 | 1,261 | 303 | 1,117 |
| North America[1] | 125 | 1,041 | 1 | 2,049 |
| South America | 568 | 2,527 | 54 | 2,860 |
| Asia | 338 | 877 | 1,966 | 253 |
| Europe | N.A. | N.A. | N.A. | 20,333 |
| Oceania | 52 | 69 | 8 | 543 |
| USSR | N.A. | N.A. | 143 | 1,900 |
| Developed countries | N.A. | 1 | 243 | 25,629 |
| Developing countries | 2,467 | 5,775 | 2,231 | 3,426 |

**Note:** N.A. means not applicable because the food is not grown or is not grown in significant amounts. 1. Includes Central America. **Source:** Food and Agricultural Organization of the UN, *FAO Production Yearbook 1989* (1990).

## PRODUCTION OF SELECTED DAIRY PRODUCTS BY REGION AND DEVELOPMENT CATEGORY, 1989 (metric tons)

| Region and development category | Cow milk ('000s) | Butter and ghee[1] | Cheese | Hen eggs |
|---|---|---|---|---|
| World total | 474,020 | 7,611,826 | 14,475,276 | 34,714,112 |
| Africa | 13,787 | 175,896 | 472,221 | 1,470,246 |
| North America[2] | 86,273 | 745,695 | 3,487,670 | 5,478,690 |
| South America | 30,025 | 157,722 | 524,589 | 2,056,980 |
| Asia | 49,882 | 1,634,937 | 743,977 | 13,513,568 |
| Europe | 172,450 | 2,762,500 | 6,838,084 | 7,266,833 |
| Oceania | 14,004 | 355,076 | 318,784 | 247,804 |
| USSR | 107,600 | 1,780,000 | 2,089,950 | 4,680,000 |
| Developed countries | 378,990 | 5,682,065 | 12,748,820 | 19,179,424 |
| Developing countries | 95,031 | 1,929,762 | 1,726,455 | 15,534,690 |

1. A semifluid clarified butter used especially in India. 2. Includes Central America. **Source:** Food and Agricultural Organization of the UN, *FAO Production Yearbook 1989* (1990).

## LEADING PRODUCERS OF SELECTED BEVERAGES AND BEVERAGE CROPS, 1988 (thousands of metric tons)

| Country | Total | Percent of world total | Country | Total | Percent of world total | Country | Total | Percent of world total | Country | Total | Percent of world total |
|---|---|---|---|---|---|---|---|---|---|---|---|
| **Cocoa beans** | | | **Tea** | | | **Coffee, green** | | | **Wine** | | |
| Ivory Coast | 680 | 30.4% | India | 690 | 27.6% | Brazil | 1,321 | 23.0% | Italy | 6,390 | 23.3% |
| Brazil | 347 | 15.5 | China | 566 | 22.6 | Colombia | 780 | 12.6 | France | 6,379 | 23.3 |
| Ghana | 290 | 13.0 | Sri Lanka | 225 | 9.0 | Indonesia | 358 | 6.4 | Spain | 2,267 | 8.2 |
| Malaysia | 220 | 9.8 | Kenya | 164 | 6.5 | Mexico | 283 | 5.1 | Argentina | 1,800 | 6.5 |
| Nigeria | 140 | 6.2 | USSR | 160 | 6.4 | Ivory Coast | 187 | 3.2 | United States | 1,740 | 6.3 |
| Cameroon | 130 | 5.8 | Indonesia | 144 | 5.7 | Uganda | 184 | 3.2 | USSR | 1,540 | 5.6 |
| Ecuador | 77 | 3.5 | Turkey | 140 | 5.6 | Ethiopia | 180 | 3.2 | Romania | 1,000 | 3.6 |
| Colombia | 55 | 2.5 | Japan | 96 | 3.8 | Guatemala | 162 | 2.9 | West Germany | 985 | 3.6 |
| Mexico | 50 | 2.2 | Iran | 46 | 1.8 | El Salvador | 152 | 2.7 | South Africa | 850 | 3.1 |
| Indonesia | 44 | 2.0 | Bangladesh | 41 | 1.6 | Philippines | 141 | 2.5 | Yugoslovia | 576 | 2.1 |

**Source:** Food and Agricultural Organization of the UN, *FAO Production Yearbook 1988* (1989).

## LEADING PRODUCERS OF SELECTED DAIRY PRODUCTS, 1989 (metric tons)

| Country | Total | Percent of world total | Country | Total | Percent of world total | Country | Total | Percent of world total | Country | Total | Percent of world total |
|---|---|---|---|---|---|---|---|---|---|---|---|
| **Butter and ghee** | | | **Cow milk, whole fresh ('000s)** | | | **Cheese** | | | **Hen eggs** | | |
| USSR | 1,780,000 | 23.0% | USSR | 107,600 | 22.0% | United States | 3,016,000 | 20.8% | China | 6,800,000 | 19.5% |
| India | 840,000 | 11.0 | United States | 65,432 | 13.8 | USSR | 2,089,950 | 14.4 | USSR | 4,680,000 | 13.4 |
| United States | 571,700 | 7.5 | France | 27,250 | 5.7 | France | 1,388,000 | 9.5 | United States | 3,973,600 | 11.4 |
| France | 539,193 | 7.0 | West Germany | 24,200 | 5.1 | West Germany | 1,039,650 | 7.1 | Japan | 2,408,249 | 6.9 |
| West Germany | 380,000 | 4.9 | India | 23,000 | 4.8 | Italy | 706,051 | 4.9 | Brazil | 1,100,000 | 3.1 |
| Pakistan | 331,761 | 4.3 | Poland | 15,700 | 3.3 | Netherlands | 561,275 | 3.9 | India | 1,072,000 | 3.0 |
| East Germany | 315,000 | 4.1 | UK | 14,550 | 3.0 | Poland | 446,903 | 3.1 | France | 891,000 | 2.6 |
| Poland | 289,727 | 3.8 | Brazil | 13,609 | 2.8 | Egypt | 315,500 | 2.2 | Mexico | 847,200 | 2.4 |
| Netherlands | 177,000 | 2.3 | Netherlands | 11,250 | 2.3 | UK | 284,000 | 2.0 | Spain | 772,600 | 2.2 |
| Czechoslovakia | 150,000 | 1.9 | Italy | 10,650 | 2.2 | Argentina | 281,000 | 2.0 | West Germany | 726,000 | 2.1 |

**Source:** Food and Agricultural Organization of the UN, *FAO Production Yearbook 1989* (1990).

## Fish Production

After 10 years of steady growth, world fish catch leveled off in 1987. The world harvest in 1987, 92.7 million tons, exceeded only marginally the previous record 92.4 million tons of 1986. This leveling off had been expected. New quota controls limited the output of a number of important fisheries, and more importantly, El Niño warm currents in the southeastern Pacific substantially reduced catches of small pelagic species in South America.

Japan and the USSR, the world's two largest producers, reported catches of 11.8 and 11.2 million tons respectively—very close to their 1986 levels. China, the world's third largest producer, increased its catch by 16%, mainly as a result of its continuing development of long-distance marine fisheries. U.S. production surged 16%, aided by the expansion of at-sea transshipment operations in the North Pacific. Joint venture enterprises were also a major factor behind a further 25% increase in landings by New Zealand, whose production has now risen nearly fivefold over the last 10 years.

Latin American fish production fell by some 2 million tons. Production fell by 32% in Ecuador, by 30% in Peru, and by 14% in Chile. In other parts of Latin America, output continued to expand, especially in Argentina,

which boosted its production by 33%, Panama by 30%, and Mexico by 9%.

Catches off the coast of southern and southwest Africa almost tripled. While output in Ghana and Senegal increased by 16% and 5% respectively, Morocco and the Ivory Coast experienced declines of 18% and 3% respectively. In Asia, the Philippines, Malaysia, Indonesia, Pakistan, and Sri Lanka all reported

bigger catches. Only Thailand saw its output fall—by 15%. Elsewhere in Asia, catches were generally stable. Output declined or remained stable in most European and Scandinavian countries. Norway maintained its 1986 production. Production fell from between 2% and 4% in all EC nations except Ireland, where output rose by 8%, and the United Kingdom, where it increased by 12%.

### FISH CATCHES BY REGION, 1988
(in metric tons, live weight catches)

| Region | Catch by marine areas | Catch by inland fishing areas |
|---|---|---|
| **World total** | **84,560,700** | **13,424,700** |
| Africa | 3,508,100 | 1,802,200 |
| Asia | 34,413,600 | 9,187,600 |
| Europe | 12,390,500 | 483,900 |
| North America | 9,004,200 | 563,700 |
| Oceania | 863,100 | 24,200 |
| South America | 14,044,700 | 367,500 |
| USSR | 10,336,500 | 995,600 |

**Note:** Includes fish, crustaceans, mollusks, etc. **Source:** Food and Agricultural Organization of the UN, *FAO Yearbook of Fishery Statistics, Catches and Landings, 1988* (1989).

### LEADING PRODUCERS OF FISH CATCHES, 1988

| Country | Live weight (metric tons) | Percent of world total |
|---|---|---|
| Japan | 11,896,935 | 12.0% |
| USSR | 11,332,101 | 11.0 |
| China | 10,358,678 | 10.0 |
| Peru | 6,637,106 | 6.7 |
| United States | 5,965,598 | 6.0 |
| Chile | 5,210,201 | 5.3 |
| India | 3,145,650 | 3.2 |
| South Korea | 2,727,059 | 2.7 |
| Indonesia | 2,703,260 | 2.7 |
| Thailand | 2,350,000 | 2.3 |

**Note:** Includes fish, crustaceans, mollusks, etc. **Source:** Food and Agricultural Organization of the UN, *FAO Yearbook of Fishery Statistics, Catches and Landings, 1988* (1989).

## World Production of Selected Minerals and Ores

According to the United Nations Conference on Trade and Development (UNCTAD), the world's production of basic nonfuel minerals and ores increased steadily during the 1970s and 1980s. In 1988 the world's leading producers of basic nonfuel minerals and ores were the Soviet Union, China, Australia, Canada, Brazil, and the United States.

From 1975 to 1988, China tripled production of nickel and sulfur and doubled its output of lead ore, phosphate rock, and tungsten ore. Although the U.S. was the leading producer of sulfur and phosphate rock in the 1980s, actual production decreased from 11,866,000 metric tons in 1980

to 10,746,000 metric tons in 1988 for sulfur and from 53,362,800 metric tons to 46,596,100 metric tons for phosphate rock.

In 1975 the U.S. produced 1,282,200 metric tons of copper ore, Chile produced 828 metric tons, and the USSR 950 metric tons. Chile surpassed U.S. production in 1982 and is now the world's leading producer of copper ore, accounting for 17% of the world total. By 1988 U.S. production was 16% of the world total, while USSR production was 11%.

Iron ore production in the U.S. was 75,456,000 metric tons (12% of the world total) in 1981 and fell to 57,515,000 metric tons (6%) in 1988. During this same time period, iron ore production in the USSR increased from 242,000,000

metric tons to 248,000,000 metric tons and output from China, Brazil, and Australia also increased. Throughout the decade the USSR was the world's leading producer of iron ore, accounting for 25% of the global supply in 1988. Producing 16% and 15% respectively, China and Brazil ranked second and third in production of iron ore in 1988.

Producing 36% of the world's bauxite and 27% of the world's alumina, Australia is the leading producer of both minerals. Australia also produces 13% of the world's lead ore, 10% of the iron ore, and ranks fifth in production of manganese ore and sixth in production of tungsten ore.

## LEADING PRODUCERS OF SELECTED MINERALS AND ORES, 1988 (thousands of metric tons)

| ALUMINA (Actual weight) | |
|---|---|
| **World total** | **19,557.0** |
| Australia | 5,255.5 |
| United States | 2,552.5 |
| USSR | 2,300.0 |
| Suriname | 816.0 |
| China | 765.0 |
| Jamaica | 757.0 |
| Brazil | 708.5 |
| Venezuela | 642.0 |
| India | 595.0 |
| Yugoslavia | 587.0 |

| BAUXITE (Actual weight) | |
|---|---|
| **World total** | **100,924.0** |
| Australia | 36,192.0 |
| Guinea | 16,834.0 |
| Jamaica | 8,515.0 |
| Brazil | 7,728.0 |
| USSR | 5,900.0 |
| Suriname | 3,434.0 |
| India | 3,415.0 |
| Yugoslavia | 3,034.0 |
| Hungary | 2,906.0 |
| China | 2,850.0 |

| COPPER ORE (Copper content) | |
|---|---|
| **World total** | **8,791.8** |
| Chile | 1,451.0 |
| United States | 1,419.7 |
| USSR | 990.0 |
| Canada | 756.5 |
| Zambia | 480.1 |
| Zaire | 467.0 |
| Poland | 441.0 |
| China | 370.0 |
| Peru | 298.3 |
| Mexico | 273.5 |

| GOLD (metric tons) | |
|---|---|
| **World total** | **N.A.** |
| South Africa | 621.0 |
| United States | 205.3 |
| Australia | 152.0 |
| Canada | 128.5 |
| Brazil | 100.2 |
| Philippines | 42.7 |
| Colombia | 33.4 |
| Papua New Guinea | 32.6 |
| Chile | 22.7 |
| Venezuela | 16.0 |

| IRON ORE (Actual weight) | |
|---|---|
| **World total** | **956,557.0** |
| USSR | 248,000.0 |
| China | 154,780.0 |
| Brazil | 146,000.0 |
| Australia | 96,084.0 |
| India | 50,390.0 |
| United States | 57,515.0 |
| Canada | 40,409.0 |
| Sweden | 20,447.0 |
| Venezuela | 18,473.0 |
| Liberia | 12,808.0 |

| LEAD ORE (Lead content) | |
|---|---|
| **World total** | **3,455.6** |
| USSR | 520.0 |
| Australia | 465.5 |
| United States | 395.7 |
| Canada | 366.6 |
| China | 311.6 |
| Mexico | 171.3 |
| Peru | 149.0 |
| Yugoslavia | 95.5 |
| South Africa | 91.3 |
| Bulgaria | 90.0 |

| MANGANESE ORE (Actual weight) | |
|---|---|
| **World total** | **23,684.9** |
| USSR | 9,200.0 |
| South Africa | 3,453.0 |
| China | 2,750.0 |
| Gabon | 2,254.0 |
| Australia | 1,985.5 |
| Brazil | 1,670.0 |
| India | 1,320.1 |
| Mexico | 443.8 |
| Ghana | 230.9 |
| Yugoslavia | 107.0 |

| NICKEL ORE (Nickel content) | |
|---|---|
| **World total** | **849.9** |
| USSR | 205.0 |
| Canada | 203.3 |
| New Caledonia | 67.0 |
| Australia | 62.4 |
| Indonesia | 59.8 |
| Cuba | 43.8 |
| South Africa | 34.8 |
| Dominican Republic | 29.3 |
| China | 28.6 |
| Botswana | 22.5 |

| PHOSPHATE ROCK (Actual weight) | |
|---|---|
| **World total** | **164,956.9** |
| United States | 46,596.1 |
| USSR | 38,820.0 |
| Morocco | 24,783.3 |
| China | 15,000.0 |
| Tunisia | 6,103.3 |
| Jordan | 5,666.2 |
| Brazil | 4,671.6 |
| Israel | 3,479.0 |
| Togo | 3,464.0 |
| South Africa | 2,850.2 |

| SULFUR (Actual weight) | |
|---|---|
| **World total** | **58,398.0** |
| United States | 10,746.0 |
| USSR | 10,700.0 |
| Canada | 6,907.0 |
| Poland | 5,090.0 |
| China | 4,750.0 |
| Mexico | 2,393.0 |
| Japan | 2,447.0 |
| West Germany | 1,795.0 |
| Saudi Arabia | 1,450.0 |
| Spain | 1,340.0 |

| TIN ORE (Tin content) | |
|---|---|
| **World total** | **203.8** |
| Brazil | 42.8 |
| Indonesia | 30.6 |
| China | 30.0 |
| Malaysia | 28.9 |
| USSR | 15.0 |
| Thailand | 14.2 |
| Bolivia | 10.5 |
| Australia | 7.0 |
| Peru | 4.4 |
| Canada | 3.8 |

| TUNGSTEN ORE (Tungsten content) | |
|---|---|
| **World total** | **46.0** |
| China | 25.0 |
| USSR | 7.5 |
| Mongolia | 2.0 |
| South Korea | 1.8 |
| Austria | 1.5 |
| Australia | 1.3 |
| Portugal | 1.4 |
| Bolivia | 0.9 |
| Brazil | 0.7 |
| Thailand | 0.7 |

**Source:** UN Conference on Trade and Development, *UNCTAD Commodity Yearbook 1990* (1990); and Consolidated Gold Fields, *Gold 1989* (1989).

## World Lumber Production

The volume of wood removed from forests and from trees outside forests (collectively called roundwood) increased throughout the 1970s and 1980s; growth in 1989 was 3%. Since 1978 the United States has felled more trees annually than any other country; the U.S. share of world roundwood production rose from 13% in 1977 to 15.3% in 1989.

Although awareness of the fragility of the world's forests and their importance for food production has improved significantly, deforestation proceeds at an alarming rate in many parts of the world. Developing countries in the tropics are losing an estimated 11 million hectares (27.2 million acres) of forest each year. Conserving forests and reforesting felled forests are slowly but increasingly becoming part of national forestry development plans in many countries.

### LUMBER PRODUCTION BY REGION AND DEVELOPMENT CATEGORY, 1989

| Region and development category | Cubic meters ('000s) |
|---|---|
| **World total** | **3,462,962** |
| Africa | 498,508 |
| North America[1] | 771,385 |
| South America | 335,575 |
| Asia | 1,067,347 |
| Europe | 368,251 |
| Oceania | 39,796 |
| USSR | 382,100 |
| Developed countries | 1,542,507 |
| Developing countries | 1,920,455 |

1. Includes Central America. **Source:** Food and Agricultural Organization of the UN, *FAO Yearbook of Forest Products 1989* (1991).

### LEADING LUMBER PRODUCERS, 1989

| Country | Cubic meters ('000s) | Percent of world total |
|---|---|---|
| United States | 533,168 | 15.3% |
| USSR | 382,100 | 11.0 |
| China | 274,590 | 7.9 |
| India | 269,451 | 7.7 |
| Brazil | 255,455 | 7.3 |
| Canada | 176,976 | 5.1 |
| Indonesia | 175,730 | 5.0 |
| Nigeria | 108,298 | 3.1 |
| Sweden | 55,704 | 1.6 |
| Finland | 46,262 | 1.3 |

**Source:** Food and Agricultural Organization of the UN, *FAO Yearbook of Forest Products 1989* (1991).

# INTERNATIONAL ORGANIZATIONS

Only those states having full official membership are listed as members; states having special relations and observer status to an organization are not included. Membership is as of July 1990. Contact headquarters to obtain publications produced by the organization.

## Association of South East Asian Nations (ASEAN) HQ: Jalan Sisingamangaraja, POB 2072, Jakarta, Indonesia. **Estab.**: Aug. 9, 1967, in Bangkok, to promote political and economic cooperation among non-Communist states of region by coordinating policies in trade, transportation, communications, agriculture, science, finance, and culture. **Members** (6): Brunei, Indonesia, Malaysia, Philippines, Singapore, Thailand.

## Colombo Plan for Co-operative Economic and Social Development in Asia and the Pacific (the Colombo Plan) HQ: 12 Melbourne Ave, POB 596, Colombo 4, Sri Lanka. **Estab.**: 1950, by seven Commonwealth nations to promote development by newly independent Asian members. Plan has expanded to fostering international effort to aid economic and social development of Asian members. Developed member states provide assistance to developing nations, and countries within region promote economic and technical cooperation among themselves. **Members** (26): Afghanistan, Australia, Bangladesh, Bhutan, Cambodia, Canada, Fiji, India, Indonesia, Iran, Japan, Laos, Malaysia, Maldives, Myanmar, Nepal, New Zealand, Pakistan, Papua New Guinea, Philippines, South Korea, Singapore, Sri Lanka, Thailand, UK, U.S.

## Commonwealth HQ: Marlborough House, Pall Mall, London, SW1Y 5HX, England. **Estab.**: By some members of British Empire through evolutionary process formalized by Statute of Westminster on Dec. 31, 1931. Modern Commonwealth was born in 1949, when member countries accepted India's intention of becoming republic while continuing "her full membership of the Commonwealth of Nations." Created to promote cooperation among countries presently or formerly part of British Empire, Commonwealth is voluntary association of independent states and has no written constitution and no rigid contractual obligations. Emphasis is on consultation and exchange of views for cooperation, especially in economic affairs, drug trafficking, international terrorism, and technical assistance to less developed states. Some countries that were part of British Empire are not part of Commonwealth. Observer at the UN. **Members** (48) (year of entry): Antigua and Barbuda (1981), Australia (1931), Bahamas (1973), Bangladesh (1972), Barbados (1966), Belize (1981), Botswana (1966), Brunei (1984), Canada (1931), Cyprus (1961), Dominica (1978), Gambia (1965), Ghana (1957), Grenada (1974), Guyana (1966), India (1947), Jamaica (1962), Kenya (1963), Kiribati (1979), Lesotho (1966), Malawi (1964), Malaysia (1957), Maldives (1982), Malta (1964), Mauritius (1968), Namibia (1990), New Zealand (1931), Nigeria

(1960), Pakistan (1989), Papua New Guinea (1975), Seychelles (1976), Sierra Leone (1961), Singapore (1965), Solomon Islands (1978), Sri Lanka (1948), St. Kitts and Nevis (1983), St. Lucia (1979), St. Vincent and the Grenadines (1979), Swaziland (1968), Tanzania (1961), Tonga (1970), Trinidad and Tobago (1962), Uganda (1962), UK (1931), Vanuatu (1980), Western Samoa (1970), Zambia (1964), Zimbabwe (1980).

## European Communities (EC, the Common Market) HQ: None. Meetings of principal organs in Brussels, Luxembourg, and Strasbourg. (Publications available from Office for the Official Publications of the EC, 5 rue du Commerce, 2985 Luxembourg.) **Estab.**: By treaty signed at Brussels, effective July 1, 1967. EC is composed of European Coal and Steel Community (ECSC), established Apr. 8, 1965; European Economic Community (EEC), also known as Common Market, created by Treaty of Rome, effective Jan. 1, 1958; and European Atomic Energy Community (Euratom), created in 1957. The three organizations are united under one secretariat and work to integrate their economies and coordinate social development. **Members** (12): Belgium, Denmark, France, Germany, Greece, Ireland, Italy, Luxembourg, Netherlands, Portugal, Spain, UK. Approximately 60 nations in Africa, Caribbean, and Pacific are affiliated under Lome Convention.

## European Free Trade Association (EFTA) HQ: 9–11 rue de Varembé, 1211 Geneva 20, Switzerland. **Estab.**: May 3, 1960, to achieve free trade in industrial products between members, to assist in creation of single market of Western European countries, and to contribute to expansion of world trade in general. First goal achieved in 1966, three years ahead of schedule. EFTA created as response to six-state European Economic Community (EEC) when attempts to establish one all-European, free-trade organization encompassing both groups broke down. EFTA entered into free-trade agreements with EC Jan. 1, 1973, and trade barriers were removed July 1, 1976. **Members** (6): Austria, Finland, Iceland, Norway, Sweden, Switzerland. Liechtenstein is participant because of its customs union with Switzerland.

## Group of 77 (G-77) Correspondence: c/o Permanent Representative UN, UN Plaza, Box 20, New York, NY 10017. **Estab.**: Oct. 1967, in Algiers following first session of UN Conference on Trade and Development (UNCTAD) in 1964. Orginally ad hoc group of 77 developing countries that coordinated their negotiating positions on matters of trade and development within UNCTAD sessions, Group now functions as negotiating Third World block in international community. Group aims to promote mutual cooperation in trade, technology, food, agriculture, energy, raw materials, finance, industrialization, and technical development and works cooperatively for establishment of "New Economic Order"—

briefly, the position that developing countries should have negotiating power in dialogues with industrialized nations. **Members** (127): (asterisk indicates original 77 members): Afghanistan,* Algeria,* Angola, Antigua and Barbuda, Argentina,* Bahamas, Bahrain, Bangladesh, Barbados, Belize,* Bhutan, Bolivia,* Botswana, Brazil,* Brunei,* Burkina Faso,* Burundi,* Cambodia,* Cameroon,* Cape Verde, Central African Republic,* Chad,* Chile,* Colombia,* Comoros, Congo,* Costa Rica,* Cuba, Cyprus,* Djibouti, Dominica, Dominican Republic,* Ecuador,* Egypt,* El Salvador,* Equatorial Guinea, Ethiopia,* Fiji, Gabon,* Gambia, Ghana,* Grenada, Guatemala,* Guinea,* Guinea-Bissau, Guyana, Haiti,* Honduras,* India,* Indonesia,* Iran,* Iraq,* Ivory Coast, Jamaica,* Jordan,* Kenya,* Kuwait,* Laos,* Lebanon, Lesotho,* Liberia, Libya,* Madagascar,* Malawi, Malaysia,* Maldives,* Mali,* Malta, Mauritania,* Mauritius, Mexico,* Mongolia,* Morocco,* Mozambique, Myanmar,* Nepal,* Nicaragua,* Niger, Nigeria,* North Korea, Oman, Pakistan,* Palestine (PLO), Panama,* Papua New Guinea, Paraguay,* Peru,* Philippines,* Qatar, Romania, Rwanda,* Samoa, São Tomé and Príncipe, Saudia Arabia,* Senegal,* Seychelles, Sierra Leone,* Singapore, Solomon Islands, Somalia,* South Korea,* Sri Lanka,* St. Kitts and Nevis,* St. Lucia, St. Vincent and the Grenadines, Sudan,* Suriname, Swaziland, Syria,* Tanzania,* Thailand,* Togo,* Tonga, Trinidad and Tobago,* Tunisia,* Uganda,* United Arab Emirates, Uruguay,* Vanuatu, Venezuela,* Vietnam,* Yemen,* Yugoslavia,* Zaire,* Zambia, Zimbabwe.

## International Criminal Police Organization (ICPO/INTERPOL) HQ: 26 rue Armengaud, 92210 Saint-Cloud, France. **Estab.**: By Second International Criminal Police Congress at Vienna in 1923, "to ensure and promote the widest possible mutual assistance between all criminal police authorities within the limits of the law existing in the different countries and in the spirit of the Universal Declaration of Human Rights." **Members** (146): Algeria, Angola, Andorra, Antigua and Barbuda, Argentina, Aruba, Australia, Austria, Bahamas, Bahrain, Bangladesh, Barbados, Belgium, Belize, Benin, Bolivia, Botswana, Brazil, Brunei, Burkina Faso, Burundi, Cambodia, Cameroon, Canada, Central African Republic, Chad, Chile, China, Colombia, Congo, Costa Rica, Cuba, Cyprus, Denmark, Djibouti, Dominica, Dominican Republic, Ecuador, Egypt, Equatorial Guinea, Ethiopia, Fiji, Finland, France, Gabon, Gambia, Germany, Ghana, Greece, Grenada, Guatemala, Guinea, Guyana, Haiti, Honduras, Hungary, Iceland, India, Indonesia, Iran, Iraq, Ireland, Israel, Ivory Coast, Italy, Jamaica, Japan, Jordan, Kenya, Kiribati, Kuwait, Laos, Lebanon, Lesotho, Liberia, Libya, Liechtenstein, Luxembourg, Madagascar, Malawi, Malaysia, Maldives, Mali, Malta, Mauritania, Mauritius, Mexico, Monaco, Morocco, Myanmar, Nauru,

Nepal, Netherlands, Netherlands Antilles, New Zealand, Nicaragua, Niger, Nigeria, Norway, Oman, Pakistan, Panama, Papua New Guinea, Paraguay, Peru, Philippines, Portugal, Qatar, Romania, Rwanda. Saudi Arabia, Senegal, Seychelles, Sierra Leone, Singapore, Somalia, South Korea, Spain, Sri Lanka, St. Kitts and Nevis, St. Lucia, St. Vincent, Sudan, Suriname, Swaziland, Sweden, Switzerland, Syria, Tanzania, Thailand, Togo, Tonga, Trinidad and Tobago, Tunisia, Turkey, Uganda, United Arab Emirates, UK, Uruguay, U.S., Venezuela, Yemen, Yugoslavia, Zaire, Zambia, Zimbabwe.

## International Telecommunication Satellite Organization (INTELSAT)

HQ: 3400 Internal Drive, NW, Washington, DC 20008. **Estab.**: Feb. 12, 1973, by two international agreements to maintain and operate the global satellite system used by public international telecommunication services. Operates space equipment and Earth stations owned by telecommunication entities in each country. INTELSAT's 13-satellite system provides about two-thirds of world's international telecommunication services to more than 140 countries. Services include telephone, television, facsimile, data, and telex transmissions. **Members** (120): Afghanistan, Algeria, Angola, Argentina, Australia, Austria, Bangladesh, Bahamas, Barbados, Belgium, Benin, Bolivia, Burkina Faso, Brazil, Cameroon, Canada, Cape Verde, Central African Republic, Chad, Chile, China, Colombia, Congo, Costa Rica, Cyprus, Denmark, Dominican Republic, Ecuador, Egypt, El Salvador, Ethiopia, Fiji, Finland, France, Gabon, Germany, Ghana, Greece, Guatemala, Guinea, Haiti, Honduras, Iceland, India, Indonesia, Iran, Iraq, Ireland, Israel, Italy, Ivory Coast, Jamaica, Japan, Jordan, Kenya, Kuwait, Lebanon, Libya, Liechtenstein, Luxembourg, Madagascar, Malawi, Malaysia, Mali, Mauritania, Mauritius, Mexico, Monaco, Morocco, Mozambique, Nepal, Netherlands, New Zealand, Nicaragua, Niger, Nigeria, Norway, Oman, Pakistan, Panama, Papua New Guinea, Paraguay, Peru, Philippines, Portugal, Qatar, Romania, Rwanda, Saudi Arabia, Senegal, Singapore, Somalia, South Africa, South Korea, Spain, Sri Lanka, Sudan, Swaziland, Sweden, Switzerland, Syria, Tanzania, Thailand, Togo, Trinidad and Tobago, Tunisia, Turkey, Uganda, United Arab Emirates, United Kingdom, Uruguay, U.S., Vatican City, Venezuela, Vietnam, Yugoslavia, Yemen, Zaire, Zambia, Zimbabwe.

## League of Arab States (Arab League)

HQ: 37 avenue Khereddine Pacha, Tunis, Tunisia. **Estab.**: By treaty signed on Mar. 22, 1945, at Cairo, Egypt, to promote cultural, economic, and communication ties among members and to mediate internal disputes. Because Egypt signed peace treaty with Israel, its membership was suspended in Mar. 1979, and league's headquarters moved from Cairo to Tunis. Egypt was readmitted to league on May 23, 1989. Observer at UN. **Members** (21): Algeria, Bahrain, Djibouti, Egypt, Iraq, Jordan, Kuwait, Lebanon, Libya, Mauritania, Morocco, Oman, Palestine (PLO), Qatar, Saudi Arabia, Somalia, Sudan, Syria, Tunisia, United

Arab Emirates, Yemen.

## Nonaligned Movement (NAM)

HQ: None. Chairship on three-year rotating basis. Yugoslavia is 1989–92 chair. Mission of Yugoslavia to the United Nations, 854 Fifth Ave., New York, NY 10021. **Estab.**: Through series of conferences, first of which met in Belgrade, Yugoslavia, Sept. 1–6, 1961, to ensure national independence and security of nonaligned countries in their "struggle against imperialism, colonialism, neocolonialism, apartheid, racism, including Zionism, and all forms of foreign aggression, occupation, domination, interference or hegemony, as well as against great power and bloc politics." In mid-1970s NAM called for "New International Economic Order"—briefly, the position that developing countries should have negotiating power in dialogues with industrialized nations. **Members** (101): Afghanistan, Algeria, Angola, Argentina, Bahamas, Bahrain, Bangladesh, Barbados, Belize, Benin, Bhutan, Bolivia, Botswana, Burkina Faso, Burundi, Cambodia, Cameroon, Cape Verde Islands, Central African Republic, Chad, Colombia, Comoro Islands, Congo, Cuba, Cyprus, Djibouti, Ecuador, Egypt, Equatorial Guinea, Ethiopia, Gabon, Gambia, Ghana, Grenada, Guinea, Guinea-Bissau, Guyana, India, Indonesia, Iran, Iraq, Ivory Coast, Jamaica, Jordan, Kenya, Kuwait, Laos, Lebanon, Lesotho, Liberia, Libya, Madagascar, Malawi, Malaysia, Maldives, Mali, Malta, Mauritania, Mauritius, Morocco, Mozambique, Namibia, Nepal, Nicaragua, Niger, Nigeria, North Korea, Oman, Pakistan, Palestine (PLO), Panama, Peru, Qatar, Rwanda, São Tomé and Principe, Saudia Arabia, Senegal, Seychelles, Sierra Leone, Singapore, Somalia, Sri Lanka, St. Lucia, Sudan, Suriname, Swaziland, Syria, Tanzania, Togo,

---

### THE IRON CURTAIN FALLS

In 1991, two multilateral organizations that symbolized the Communist side of the Cold War went out of business.

**Council for Mutual Economic Cooperation** (CMEA, or COMECON) was established by seven Eastern European countries in April 1949 to assist members in economic and technological development. Upon its dissolution on June 28, 1991, its members were: Bulgaria, Cuba (joined in 1972), Czechoslovakia, East Germany (1950), Hungary, Mongolia (1962), Poland, Romania, the USSR, and Vietnam (1978). Albania was a member from 1949 to 1961.

**The Warsaw Treaty Organization** (Warsaw Pact) was established by a treaty signed May 14, 1955, as a mutual defense alliance among Communist countries in Eastern Europe, specifically as a balance to NATO. It later became an instrument of Soviet political control over Eastern Europe. Upon its dissolution on July 1, 1991, its members were: Bulgaria, Czechoslovakia, East Germany, Hungary, Poland, Romania, and the USSR. (See also Part I, "The Year in Review.")

---

Trinidad and Tobago, Tunisia, Uganda, United Arab Emirates, Vanuatu, Vietnam, Yemen, Yugoslavia, Zaire, Zambia, Zimbabwe.

## North Atlantic Treaty Organization (NATO)

HQ: 1110 Brussels, Belgium. **Estab.**: By North Atlantic Treaty on Aug. 24, 1949, as international defense organization composed of European countries, Canada, and U.S. Members agree to settle disputes among each other by peaceful means and regard attack on one as attack on all. Members develop joint defense plans, consult on political problems, share science and technology, and organize joint training. NATO attempts to maintain military balance with countries of Warsaw Pact. NATO forces comprise three elements: conventional forces, intermediate and short-range nuclear forces, and strategic nuclear forces of UK and U.S. NATO consists of three commands: European Command, HQ in Casteau, Belgium; Atlantic Ocean Command, HQ in Norfolk, Virginia, U.S.; and Channel Command, HQ in Northwood, UK. **Members** (16): Belgium, Canada, Denmark, France, Germany, Greece, Iceland, Italy, Luxembourg, Netherlands, Norway, Portugal, Spain, Turkey, UK, U.S.

## Organization of African Unity (OAU)

HQ: POB 3243, Addis Ababa, Ethiopia. **Estab.**: By charter on May 25, 1963 at Addis Ababa, to promote unity and solidarity among African states. OAU works to eradicate all forms of colonialism from Africa and to defend their sovereignty, territorial integrity, and independence. Observer at UN. **Members** (51): Algeria, Angola, Benin, Botswana, Burkina Faso, Burundi, Cameroon, Cape Verde, Central African Republic, Chad, Comoros, Congo, Djibouti, Egypt, Equatorial Guinea, Ethiopia, Gabon, Gambia, Ghana, Guinea, Guinea-Bissau, Ivory Coast, Kenya, Lesotho, Liberia, Libya, Madagascar, Malawi, Mali, Mauritania, Mauritius, Mozambique, Namibia, Niger, Nigeria, Rwanda, Sahrawi Arab Democratic Republic (Western Sahara), São Tomé and Principe, Senegal, Seychelles, Sierra Leone, Somalia, Sudan, Swaziland, Tanzania, Togo, Tunisia, Uganda, Zaire, Zambia, Zimbabwe.

## Organization of American States (OAS)

HQ: 1889 F St., NW, Washington, DC 20006, U.S. **Estab.**: By charter signed at Bogota, Colombia, effective Dec. 13, 1951, to work for "order of peace and justice, promoting solidarity among the American states," and to establish "new objectives and standards for the promotion of the economic, social and cultural development of the peoples of the Hemisphere, and to speed the process of economic integration." Programs include promotion of human rights, education, economic and social development, and scientific exchanges. Observer at UN. **Members** (32): Antigua and Barbuda, Argentina, Bahamas, Barbados, Bolivia, Brazil, Chile, Colombia, Costa Rica, Cuba (was suspended from OAS activities but not membership in 1962), Dominica, Dominican Republic, Ecuador, El Salvador, Grenada, Guatemala, Haiti, Honduras, Jamaica, Mexico, Nicaragua, Panama, Paraguay, Peru, St. Kitts and Nevis, St. Lucia,

St. Vincent and the Grenadines, Suriname, Trinidad and Tobago, Uruguay, U.S., Venezuela.

## Organization for Economic Cooperation and Development (OECD)
**HQ:** 2 rue André Pascal, 75775 Paris Cedex 16, France. **Estab.:** By convention signed at Paris, effective Sept. 30, 1961, to help "member countries promote economic growth, employment, and improved standards of living through the coordination of policy [and] to help promote the sound and harmonious development of the world economy and improve the lot of the developing countries, particularly the poorest." **Members** (24): Australia, Austria, Belgium, Canada, Denmark, Finland, France, Germany, Greece, Iceland, Ireland, Italy, Japan, Luxembourg, Netherlands, New Zealand, Norway, Portugal, Spain, Sweden, Switzerland, Turkey, UK, U.S.

## Organization of the Petroleum Exporting Countries (OPEC)
**HQ:** Obere Donaustrasse 93, 1020 Vienna, Austria. **Estab.:** Nov. 14, 1960, by resolution adopted at Baghdad, Iraq, to attempt to set world oil prices by coordinating members' oil production. OPEC countries conduct research on all areas affecting oil, from uses and development to economic and financial issues. In 1985 it was estimated that OPEC members possessed 67.3% of world's known reserves of crude petroleum and 34.7% of known reserves of natural gas. Observer at UN. **Members** (13): Algeria, Ecuador, Gabon, Indonesia, Iran, Iraq, Kuwait, Libya, Nigeria, Qatar, Saudia Arabia, United Arab Emirates, Venezuela. (See also "World Energy.")

# The United Nations

## Establishment
President Franklin D. Roosevelt coined the name United Nations, which was first used in the "Declaration by United Nations," Jan. 1, 1942, during World War II, when representatives of 26 countries pledged their governments to continue fighting together against the Axis Powers. From August to October 1944, representatives of China, the Soviet Union, the United Kingdom, and the United States met at Dumbarton Oaks, a mansion in Washington, D.C., to discuss creating an international peacekeeping organization. Out of these meetings came a general outline for the UN.

At the UN Conference on International Organization, which met at San Francisco from Apr. 25 to June 26, 1945, representatives from 50 countries drew up the UN Charter and signed it on June 26, 1945. Poland, not present at the conference, signed on Oct. 15, 1945, and is considered one of the 51 founding member states.

The UN officially came into existence on Oct. 24, 1945, when the charter was ratified by China, France, the Soviet Union, the United Kingdom, the United States and by a majority of the other signatories.

## UN Charter
Full text of the charter may be purchased for $1 from the United Nations, Sales Section, New York, NY 10017 U.S. The preamble to the charter sets forth the hopes for the UN:

WE THE PEOPLES OF THE UNITED NATIONS DETERMINED
- to save succeeding generations from the scourge of war . . .
- to reaffirm faith in fundamental human rights, in the dignity and worth of the human person, in the equal rights of men and women and of nations large and small, and
- to establish conditions under which justice and respect for the obligations arising from treaties and other sources of international law can be maintained, and
- to promote social progress and better standards of life in larger freedom,

AND FOR THESE ENDS
- to practice tolerance and live together in peace with one another as good neighbors, and
- to unite our strength to maintain international peace and security, and
- to ensure, by the acceptance of principles and the institution of methods, that armed force shall not be used, save in the common interest, and
- to employ international machinery for the promotion of the economic and social advancement of all peoples,

HAVE RESOLVED TO COMBINE OUR EFFORTS TO ACCOMPLISH THESE AIMS. Accordingly, our respective Governments, through representatives assembled in the city of San Francisco, who have exhibited their full powers found to be in good and due form, have agreed to the present Charter of the United Nations and do hereby establish an international organization to be known as the United Nations.

## Purposes
The purposes of the United Nations as set forth in the Charter are: 1. To maintain international peace and security. 2. To develop friendly relations among nations based on respect for the principle of equal rights and self-determination of peoples. 3. To cooperate in solving international problems of an economic, social, cultural, or humanitarian character, and in promoting respect for human rights and fundamental freedoms for all. 4. To be a center for harmonizing the actions of nations in the attainment of these common ends.

## Official Languages
Originally, there were five official languages of the UN: Chinese, English, French, Russian, and Spanish. Arabic was added to the General Assembly in 1973, to the Security Council in 1982, and to the Economic and Social Council in 1983. All major UN documents and all meetings of the General Assembly, the Security Council, and the Economic and Social Council are translated into the six working languages.

## United Nations Headquarters
United Nations, New York, NY 10017. The UN Headquarters covers a 16-acre site in New York City along the East River from 42d to 48th streets. It consists of the interconnected General Assembly, Secretariat, and Dag Hammarskjold Library buildings. Across the street are other UN office buildings: One, Two, and Three UN Plaza. Acquisition of the site was made possible by a gift of $8.5 million from John D. Rockefeller, Jr., and one-third of that amount from New York City. The Board of Design who drew the architectural plans consisted of an international team of architects from 10 countries. In the spring of 1951, the 39-story Secretariat building was complete and began functioning as the official UN home. The interiors of the buildings have been decorated by many gifts from governments and peoples from all over the world.

## Geneva Office
United Nations, Palais des Nations, 1211 Geneva 10, Switzerland. The Palais des Nations houses the European offices of the UN. Located in Geneva, Switzerland, and built in 1936, the complex was the headquarters for the League of Nations.

## Vienna Office
United Nations International Centre, A-1400 Vienna, Austria. The Austrian government built the Vienna International Centre at a cost of $700 million and offers the space rent-free to the UN and its agencies.

## Permanent Observers
to the UN at the New York Headquarters cannot vote and do not have diplomatic privileges or immunities. They do have free access to the public meetings and distribution of relevant documentation.

## Nonmember Observer States
are the Holy See, Monaco, San Marino, and Switzerland.

## U.S. REPRESENTATIVES TO THE UN
The U.S. representative to the UN holds the title Ambassador Extraordinary and Plenipotentiary and heads the U.S. Mission to the UN.

| Year | Ambassador |
| --- | --- |
| 1946 | Edward R. Stetinius, Jr. |
| 1946–47 | Herschel V. Johnson (acting) |
| 1947–53 | Warren R. Austin |
| 1953–60 | Henry Cabot Lodge, Jr. |
| 1960–61 | James J. Wadsworth |
| 1961–65 | Adlai E. Stevenson |
| 1965–68 | Arthur J. Goldberg |
| 1968 | George W. Ball |
| 1968–69 | James Russell Wiggins |
| 1969–71 | Charles W. Yost |
| 1971–73 | George Bush |
| 1973–75 | John A. Scali |
| 1975–76 | Daniel P. Moynihan |
| 1976–77 | William W. Scranton |
| 1977–79 | Andrew Young |
| 1979–81 | Donald McHenry |
| 1981–85 | Jeane J. Kirkpatrick |
| 1985–89 | Vernon A. Walters |
| 1989–present | Thomas R. Pickering |

## UNITED NATIONS MEMBER STATES (166 member states as of October 1991)

| Country | Joined U.N. | Country | Joined U.N. | Country | Joined U.N. | Country | Joined U.N. |
|---|---|---|---|---|---|---|---|
| Afghanistan | 1946 | Dominican Republic | 1945 | Libyan Arab Jamahiriya | 1955 | Saint Vincent and the Grenadines | 1980 |
| Albania | 1955 | Ecuador | 1945 | Liechtenstein | 1990 | São Tomé and Principe | 1975 |
| Algeria | 1962 | Egypt[2] | 1945 | Lithuania | 1991 | Saudi Arabia | 1945 |
| Angola | 1976 | El Salvador | 1945 | Luxembourg | 1945 | Senegal | 1960 |
| Antigua and Barbuda | 1981 | Equatorial Guinea | 1968 | Madagascar | 1960 | Seychelles | 1976 |
| Argentina | 1945 | Estonia | 1991 | Malawi | 1964 | Sierra Leone | 1961 |
| Australia | 1945 | Ethiopia | 1945 | Malaysia[3] | 1957 | Singapore[5] | 1965 |
| Austria | 1955 | Fiji | 1970 | Maldives | 1965 | Solomon Islands | 1978 |
| Bahamas | 1973 | Finland | 1955 | Mali | 1960 | Somalia | 1960 |
| Bahrain | 1971 | France | 1945 | Malta | 1964 | South Africa | 1945 |
| Bangladesh | 1974 | Gabon | 1960 | Marshall Islands | 1991 | South Korea | 1991 |
| Barbados | 1966 | Gambia | 1965 | Mauritania | 1961 | Spain | 1955 |
| Belgium | 1945 | Germany | 1973 | Mauritius | 1968 | Sri Lanka | 1955 |
| Belize | 1981 | Ghana | 1957 | Mexico | 1945 | Sudan | 1956 |
| Benin | 1960 | Greece | 1945 | Micronesia | 1991 | Suriname | 1975 |
| Bhutan | 1971 | Grenada | 1974 | Mongolia | 1961 | Swaziland | 1968 |
| Bolivia | 1945 | Guatemala | 1945 | Morocco | 1956 | Sweden | 1946 |
| Botswana | 1966 | Guinea | 1958 | Mozambique | 1975 | Syrian Arab Republic[2] | 1945 |
| Brazil | 1945 | Guinea-Bissau | 1974 | Myanmar | 1948 | Tanzania[4] | 1961 |
| Brunei Darussalam | 1984 | Guyana | 1966 | Namibia | 1990 | Thailand | 1946 |
| Bulgaria | 1955 | Haiti | 1945 | Nepal | 1955 | Togo | 1960 |
| Burkina Faso | 1960 | Honduras | 1945 | Netherlands | 1945 | Trinidad and Tobago | 1962 |
| Burundi | 1962 | Hungary | 1955 | New Zealand | 1945 | Tunisia | 1956 |
| Byelorussian Soviet Socialist Rep. | 1945 | Iceland | 1946 | Nicaragua | 1945 | Turkey | 1945 |
| Cambodia | 1955 | India | 1945 | Niger | 1960 | Uganda | 1962 |
| Cameroon | 1960 | Indonesia | 1950 | Nigeria | 1960 | Ukrainian Soviet Socialist Republic | 1945 |
| Canada | 1945 | Iran | 1945 | North Korea | 1991 | Union of Soviet Socialist Republics | 1945 |
| Cape Verde | 1975 | Iraq | 1945 | Norway | 1945 | United Arab Emirates | 1971 |
| Central African Republic | 1960 | Ireland | 1955 | Oman | 1971 | United Kingdom | 1945 |
| Chad | 1960 | Israel | 1949 | Pakistan | 1947 | United States | 1945 |
| Chile | 1945 | Italy | 1955 | Panama | 1945 | Uruguay | 1945 |
| China[1] | 1945 | Ivory Coast | 1960 | Papua New Guinea | 1975 | Vanuatu | 1981 |
| Colombia | 1945 | Jamaica | 1962 | Paraguay | 1945 | Venezuela | 1945 |
| Comoros | 1975 | Japan | 1956 | Peru | 1945 | Vietnam | 1977 |
| Congo | 1960 | Jordan | 1955 | Philippines | 1945 | Western Samoa | 1976 |
| Costa Rica | 1945 | Kenya | 1963 | Poland | 1945 | Yemen | 1947 |
| Cuba | 1945 | Kuwait | 1963 | Portugal | 1955 | Yugoslavia | 1945 |
| Cyprus | 1960 | Laos | 1955 | Qatar | 1971 | Zaire | 1960 |
| Czechoslovakia | 1945 | Latvia | 1991 | Romania | 1955 | Zambia | 1964 |
| Denmark | 1945 | Lebanon | 1945 | Rwanda | 1962 | Zimbabwe | 1980 |
| Djibouti | 1977 | Lesotho | 1966 | Saint Kitts and Nevis | 1983 | | |
| Dominica | 1978 | Liberia | 1945 | Saint Lucia | 1979 | | |

1. By resolution 2758 (XXVI) of Oct. 25, 1971, the General Assembly decided "to restore all its rights to the People's Republic of China and to recognize the representatives of its Government as the only legitimate representatives of China to the United Nations, and to expel forthwith the representatives of Chiang Kai-shek from the place they unlawfully occupy at the United Nations and in all the organizations related to it." 2. Egypt and Syria were original UN members from Oct. 24, 1945. Following a plebiscite on Jan. 21, 1958, the United Arab Republic was established by a union of Egypt and Syria and continued as a single member. On Oct. 13, 1961, Syria resumed its status as an independent state and simultaneously its UN membership. On Sept. 2, 1971, the United Arab Republic changed its name to Arab Republic of Egypt. 3. The Federation of Malaya joined the UN on Sept. 17, 1957. On Sept. 16, 1963, its name was changed to Malaysia, following the admission to the new federation of Singapore, Sabah (North Borneo), and Sarawak. Singapore became an independent state on Aug. 9, 1965 and a UN member on Sept. 21, 1965. 4. Tanganyika was a UN member from Dec. 14, 1961, and Zanzibar was a member from Dec. 16, 1963. Following the ratification on Apr. 26, 1964, of Articles of Union between Tanganyika and Zanzibar, the United Republic of Tanganyika and Zanzibar continued as a single member, changing its name to the United Republic of Tanzania on Nov. 1, 1964.

---

**Intergovernmental and Other Observer Organizations** are the following: African, Caribbean, and Pacific Group of States; African Development Bank (ADB); Agency for Cultural and Technical Cooperation; Agency for the Prohibition of Nuclear Weapons in Latin America and the Caribbean; Asian-African Legal Consultative Committee; Commonwealth Secretariat; Council of Europe; European Economic Community (EEC); International Committee of the Red Cross; Latin American Economic System; League of Arab States; Organization of African Unity (OAU); Organization of American States (OAS); Organization of the Islamic Conference; Palestine Liberation Organization (PLO).

## PRINCIPAL ORGANS

The charter established six principal organs of the UN.

### General Assembly

The Assembly is the world's forum for discussing major issues facing the world community, including world peace and security, human rights, global environment, disarmament, health issues, and the rights of women and children.

The Assembly consists of all 159 member states, each having one vote. On important issues a two-thirds majority of those present and voting is required; other questions require a simple majority vote. It usually holds annual sessions from September to December and may call for extra sessions when needed. Its agenda

of more than 150 matters for discussion is first dealt with in seven main committees: First Committee—disarmament and related security issues; Second Committee—economic and financial matters; Third Committee—social, humanitarian, and cultural areas; Fourth Committee—decolonization; Fifth Committee—administrative and budgetary issues; Sixth Committee—legal matters; and the Special Political Committee. The Assembly discusses reports from each committee as well as reports from each UN program, other UN bodies, and the secretary-general. It conducts studies and makes recommendations (called resolutions) but has no power to enforce its decisions (resolutions), except the power of world opinion.

The Assembly considers and approves the UN budget and assesses member states according to their ability to pay.

## Security Council

The Council may investigate any dispute or situation that might lead to international friction, and may recommend methods for adjusting such disputes or terms for their settlement. While other UN organs make recommendations to governments, the Council alone has the power to make decisions that member states are obligated under the charter to carry out.

The Security Council has 15 members. The charter designated five permanent members, and the General Assembly elects 10 other members for two-year terms. They are not eligible for immediate reelection. The presidency of the General Assembly rotates monthly among each of the members in turn, according to English alphabetical order. The Council may be called into session at any time, and a representative of each member state must be present at UN Headquarters at all times.

The five permanent members are China, France, the Soviet Union, the United Kingdom, and the United States.

The terms of office of each current (1991) nonpermanent member end on Dec. 31 of the year indicated in parentheses: Austria (1992), Belgium (1992), Cuba (1991), Ecuador (1992), India (1992), Ivory Coast (1991), Romania (1991), Yemen (1991), Zaire (1991), Zimbabwe (1992).

Decisions on matters of procedure require the approval of at least nine of the 15 members. Decisions on all other matters also require nine votes, including the concurring votes of all five permanent members. A negative vote by any permanent member on a nonprocedural matter is often referred to as the veto, which results in the rejection of the proposal.

## Economic and Social Council (ECOSOC)

The ECOSOC is the principal organ that coordinates the economic and social work of the UN and its specialized agencies. It makes recommendations and initiates activities relating to world trade, industrialization, natural resources, human rights, the status of women, population, social welfare, education, health and related matters, science and technology, and many other economic and social questions.

The ECOSOC has 54 members elected for three-year terms by the General Assembly. The term of office of current (1991) members expires on Dec. 31 of the year indicated in parentheses:

Algeria (1992); Argentina (1993); Austria (1993); Bahamas (1991); Bahrain (1992); Botswana (1993); Brazil (1991); Bulgaria (1992); Burkina Faso (1992); Cameroon (1991); Canada (1992); Chile (1993); China (1992); Czechoslovakia (1991); Ecuador (1992); Finland (1992); France (1993); Germany (1993); Guinea (1993); Indonesia (1991); Iran (1992); Iraq (1991); Italy (1991); Jamaica (1992); Japan (1993); Jordan (1991); Kenya (1991); Malaysia (1993); Mexico (1992); Morocco (1993); Netherlands (1991); New Zealand (1991); Nicaragua (1991); Niger (1991); Pakistan (1992); Peru (1993); Rwanda (1992); Somalia (1993); Spain (1993); Sweden (1992); Syria (1993); Thailand (1991); Togo (1993);

Trinidad and Tobago (1993); Tunisia (1991); Turkey (1993); Ukraine (1991); United Kingdom (1992); United States (1991); USSR (1992); Yugoslavia (1993); Zaire (1992); Zambia (1991).

The Council generally holds two month-long sessions each year, one in New York and the other in Geneva. Its subsidiary bodies carry out year-round work. They consist of six Functional Commissions: Statistical Commission, Population Commission, Commission for Social Development, Commission on Human Rights, Commission on the Status of Women, and Commission on Narcotic Drugs. There are also five Regional Commissions: Economic Commission for Africa (ECA), in Addis Ababa, Ethiopia; Economic and Social Commission for Asia and the Pacific (ESCAP) in Bangkok, Thailand; Economic Commission for Europe (ECE) in Geneva, Switzerland; Economic Commission for Latin America and the Caribbean (ECLAC) in Santiago, Chile; Economic and Social Commission for Western Asia (ESCWA) in Baghdad, Iraq.

### Relations with Nongovernmental Organizations (NGOs)

Under the charter, the ECOSOC may consult with nongovernmental organizations (NGOs) concerned with matters within the Council's competence. Over 750 NGOs have consultative status with the Council and may send observers to public meetings of the Council and its subsidiary bodies and may submit written statements relevant to the Council's work. Examples of NGOs affiliated with ECOSOC include Amnesty International, Catholic Relief Services, Greenpeace International, Rotary International, The Hunger Project, the Sierra Club, and the Salvation Army.

## Trusteeship Council

Supervising the administration of trust territories, the Council's goal is to promote the development of a territory toward self-government or independence.

As of 1991, only one Trust Territory of the original 11 trusteeships remained—the Trust Territory of the Pacific Islands (Republic of Palau), administered by the United States. The Council has five members: the United States (as the administering state) and the other permanent members of the Security Council—China, France, the Soviet Union, and the United Kingdom.

## International Court of Justice (World Court)

Created under the UN Charter as the UN's official judicial organ, the ICJ, or World Court, has its seat at The Hague, Netherlands. All UN member states are automatically members of the Court. Three countries that are not UN members are parties to the Court—Switzerland (1948), Liechtenstein (1950), and San Marino (1954).

The Court is not open to individuals. It issues judgments on all questions that states refer to it and all matters provided for in the UN Charter or in treaties or conventions in force. Both the General Assembly and the Security Council can ask the Court for an advisory opinion on any legal question, as can other organs

of the UN or its specialized agencies when authorized to do so by the Assembly.

The Court has dealt with a wide variety of subjects, including territorial rights, the delimitation of territorial waters and continental shelves, fishing jurisdiction, questions of nationality and the right of individuals to asylum, territorial sovereignty, and the right of passage through foreign territory.

The judgment of the Court is final and without appeal. However, a revision may be applied for within 10 years from the date of the judgment on the ground of a new decisive factor. If a party rejects the judgment, the other party may take the issue to the Security Council.

**Judges**   The International Court of Justice has 15 independent judges, of different nationalities, elected by both the General Assembly and the Security Council. Judges hold nine-year terms and may be reelected. The Court itself elects its president and vice president for three-year terms and is in permanent session, except during vacations. All questions are decided by a majority of the judges present; the president votes only in case of a tie.

The judges, listed in their official order of precedence, are the following (terms end on Feb. 5 of the year indicated in parentheses): *president:* Sir Robert Y. Jennings of the United Kingdom (2000); *vice president:* Shigeru Oda of Japan (1994); *judges:* Manfred Lachs of Poland (1994); Taslim Olawale Elias of Nigeria (1994); Roberto Ago of Italy (1997); Mohammed Shahabuddeen of Guyana (1997), Stephen M. Schwebel of the United States (1997); Mohammed Bedjaoui of Algeria (2000); Ni Zhengyu of China (1994); Jens Evensen of Norway (1997); Nikolai K. Tarassov of the Soviet Union (1997); Gilbert Guillaume of France (2000); Christopher G. Weeramantry of Sri Lanka (2000); Raymond Ranjeva of Madagascar (2000).

## Secretariat

Servicing the other UN organs and administering the programs and policies they develop, the UN Secretariat is headed by the secretary-general. It consists of an international staff of more than 25,000 men and women from over 150 countries whose work includes administering peacekeeping operations; organizing international conferences on problems of worldwide concern; surveying world economic and social trends and problems; preparing studies on such subjects as human rights, disarmament, and development; interpreting speeches, translating documents, and supplying the world's communications media with information about the UN.

**Secretary-General**   The General Assembly elects the secretary-general who may be reelected to terms of office of five years. The secretary-general cannot be from one of the permanent member states of the Security Council. Those who have served in this post are: Trygve Lie, Norway, Feb. 1, 1946, to Nov. 10, 1952; Dag Hammarskjold, Sweden, Apr. 11, 1953, to Sept. 17, 1961; U Thant, Burma, Nov. 3, 1961, to Dec. 31, 1971; Kurt Waldheim, Austria, Jan. 1, 1972, to Dec. 31, 1981; Javier Pérez de Cuéllar, Peru, Jan. 1, 1982, to present.

# UNITED NATIONS PROGRAMS

Each UN program was created by the General Assembly and reports to it through the Economic and Social Council (ECOSOC).

UN programs, agencies, and commissions are headquartered around the world.

## International Research and Training Institute for the Advancement of Women (INSTRAW) Estab.: 1979 (made UN program in 1985); HQ: Calle César Nicolas Penson, 102-A, Santo Domingo, Dominican Republic. Carries out research, training, and information activities worldwide to show and increase women's key role in development.

## UN Centre for Human Settlements (Habitat) Estab.: 1978; HQ: P.O. Box 30030, Nairobi, Kenya. Works to provide models and tools so people can improve their housing. Major concerns are planning, financing, and management of human settlements—especially in developing countries.

## UN Children's Fund (UNICEF) Estab.: 1946; HQ: UNICEF House, Three UN Plaza, New York, NY 10017, U.S. Provides care for children in developing countries by working in both rural and urban settings to provide low-cost, community-based services in interrelated fields of maternal and child health, applied nutrition, clean water and sanitation, formal and nonformal education, and supporting services for women and girls. UNICEF has brought about a virtual revolution in child survival at low cost and in relatively short time, by emphasizing immunization, breast-feeding, growth monitoring, and a simple oral rehydration method.

## UN Conference on Trade and Development (UNCTAD) Estab.: 1964; HQ: Place des Nations, 1211 Geneva 10, Switzerland. Formulates international trade policies, mediates multilateral trade agreements, and coordinates trade and development policies of governments and regional economic groups. Seeks to make international financial and monetary system more responsive to needs of developing countries.

## UN Development Programme (UNDP) Estab.: 1965; HQ: One UN Plaza, New York, NY 10017, U.S. Coordinates all development activities within UN system. Operates over 5,000 projects in 150 countries and territories to facilitate development in economic and social sectors, including farming, fishing, forestry, mining, manufacturing, power, transport, communications, housing, trade, health and environmental sanitation, economic planning, and public administration.

## UN Disaster Relief Co-ordinator, Office of the (UNDRO) Estab.: 1972; HQ: Place des Nations, 1211 Geneva 10, Switzerland. Acts as focal point and clearinghouse for information on relief needs and on supplies sent by donors to meet those needs. Promotes study, prevention, control, and prediction of natural disasters and provides governments requesting it with assistance in predisaster planning.

## UN Environment Programme (UNEP) Estab.: 1972; HQ: P.O. Box 30552, Nairobi, Kenya. Monitors significant changes in environment and encourages and coordinates sound environmental practices. Programs include Earthwatch, an international surveillance network with three main components: (1) Global Environmental Monitoring System, which monitors selected environmental factors and reports them to governments; (2) INFO-TERRA, a computerized referral service to 20,000 sources in some 100 countries for environmental information; and (3) International Register of Potentially Toxic Chemicals, which works to provide scientific and regulatory information on chemicals.

## UN High Commissioner for Refugees, Office of the (UNHCR) Estab.: 1950; HQ: Place des Nations, 1211 Geneva 10, Switzerland. Provides food, clothing, and shelter for refugees and works with governments to establish safe conditions whereby refugees may return home, and when that is not possible, seeks to ensure that refugees receive asylum. In 1988 UNHCR provided services for more than 12 million refugees worldwide.

## UN Institute for Training and Research (UNITAR) Estab.: 1965; HQ: 801 UN Plaza, New York, NY 10017, U.S. Provides training for members of UN's permanent missions, including courses on international economics, workshops in drafting and negotiating international legal instruments and in dispute settlement, and training in peace, security, human rights, and humanitarian assistance issues.

## UN Population Fund (UNFPA) Estab.: 1969; HQ: 220 E. 42d St., New York, NY 10017, U.S. Provides assistance to population programs in developing countries; promotes understanding of key population factors—population growth, fertility, mortality, spatial distribution, and migration.

## UN University (UNU) Estab.: 1973; HQ: Toho Seimei Building, 15–1, Shibuya 2-chome, Shibuya-ku, Tokyo 150, Japan. Has no students of its own, no campus, and no faculty. It is an international community of scholars engaged in research operating through worldwide networks of academic research institutions and is concerned with nine program areas, including peace and conflict resolution; global economy; energy systems and policy; resource policy and management; food-energy nexus; food, nutrition, biotechnology, and poverty; human and social development; and regional perspectives. Operates two research and training centers, one for development economics research, in Finland, and one for natural resources, on the Ivory Coast.

## World Food Council (WFC) Estab.: 1974; HQ: Via delle Terme di Caracalla, 00100 Rome, Italy. Encourages developing countries to adopt national food strategy whereby they assess their food situation—needs, supply, potential for increasing production, storage, processing, transportation, and distribution; not engaged in field operations.

## World Food Programme (WFP) Estab.: 1963; HQ: Via Cristoforo Colombo, 426, 00145 Rome, Italy. (Joint program operated by United Nations and Food and Agriculture Organization [FAO]). Provides food to support development activities and in times of emergencies. Operates projects in forestry, soil erosion control, irrigation, land rehabilitation, and rural settlements.

# SPECIALIZED AGENCIES OF THE UNITED NATIONS

The specialized agencies associated with the United Nations are self-governing, independent organizations that work with the UN system and each other through the coordination machinery of the Economic and Social Council (ECOSOC). Each country affiliates with each agency on an individual basis. Membership in an agency is separate from UN membership.

## Food and Agriculture Organization (FAO) Member states: 158; Estab.: Oct. 16, 1945; HQ: Via delle Terme di Caracalla, 00100 Rome, Italy. Works to increase output of farmlands, forests, and fisheries and to raise nutritional levels. Cosponsors World Food Programme, which uses food, cash, and services donated by member states for programs of social and economic development and for emergency situations.

## General Agreement on Tariffs and Trade (GATT) Member states: 94 are contracting parties, 30 apply Agreement on de facto basis, and one acceded provisionally; Estab.: Jan. 1, 1948; HQ: Centre William Rappard, 154 rue de Lausanne, 1211 Geneva 21, Switzerland. (Not UN specialized agency in formal sense.) Principal international body concerned with reduction of trade barriers and other measures that distort competition, and with conciliation of trade disputes. Contracting parties account for four-fifths of world trade. Major negotiating conferences, called Rounds, last for several years. In September 1986 GATT trade ministers launched the Uruguay Round in Uruguay.

## International Atomic Energy Agency (IAEA) Member states: 113; Estab.: July 29, 1957; HQ: Vienna International Centre, P.O. Box 100, A-1400 Vienna, Austria. (Not regular specialized agency in that it does not report through ECOSOC but directly to General Assembly.) To foster and guide development of peaceful uses of atomic energy, it establishes standards for nuclear safety and environmental protection, aids member countries through technical cooperation, and fosters exchange of scientific and technical information on nuclear energy.

## International Civil Aviation Organization (ICAO) Member states: 156; Estab.: Apr. 4, 1947; HQ: 1000 Sherbrooke St. West, Suite 400, Montreal, Quebec H3A 2R2, Canada. Works for safer air travel conditions

worldwide. Establishes visual and instrument flight rules for pilots and crews, develops aeronautical charts for navigation, coordinates aircraft radio frequencies, and works with customs procedures.

### International Fund for Agricultural Development (IFAD) Member states: 139; Estab.: Nov. 30, 1977; HQ: Via del Serafico 10, 00142 Rome, Italy. Lends money to peoples in developing countries for agricultural development projects, including livestock, fisheries, processing and storage, irrigation, research, and training.

### International Labour Organisation (ILO) Member states: 150; Estab.: 1919, under Treaty of Versailles, became UN specialized agency Dec. 14, 1946; HQ: 4, route des Morillons, CH-1211 Geneva 22, Switzerland. Promotes social justice for working people everywhere by formulating international policies and programs to help improve working and living conditions; creates international labor standards to serve as guidelines for governments and assists in vocational training, management techniques, occupational safety, and health.

### International Maritime Organization (IMO) Member states: 127; Estab.: Mar. 17, 1958; HQ: 4 Albert Embankment, London SE1 SR, England. Works to improve international shipping procedures and encourages highest standards in maritime safety; seeks to prevent and control marine pollution from ships and sets standards for training and certification of seafarers.

### International Monetary Fund (IMF) Member states: 151; Estab.: Dec. 27, 1945; HQ: 700 19th St., NW, Washington, DC 20431. Makes financing available to members in balance-of-payments difficulties and provides technical assistance to improve their economic management.

### International Telecommunication Union (ITU) Member states: 160; Estab.: 1865 (became UN specialized agency Jan. 1949); HQ: Place des Nations, 1211 Geneva 20, Switzerland. Coordinates use of radio frequencies, tracks positions assigned by countries to geostationary satellites, creates telecommunication equipment, promotes safety measures, and conducts studies.

### UN Educational, Scientific and Cultural Organization (UNESCO) Member states: 158; Estab.: Nov. 4, 1946; HQ: 7, Place de Fontenoy, 75007 Paris, France. Promotes literacy through programs in teacher training, building schools, and developing textbooks. Natural-science programs include Man and the Biosphere; Intergovernmental Oceanographic Commission; and International Hydrological and International Geological Correlation programs. Other activities include study and development of cultures, and conservation of world's inheritance of books, art, and monuments.

### UN Industrial Development Organization (UNIDO) Member states: 118; Estab.: 1966 (became a UN specialized agency Jan. 1, 1986); HQ: Wagramerstrasse 5, Vienna XXII, Austria. Promotes and accelerates industrialization of developing countries by providing technical assistance, training programs, and advisory services. Serves as clearinghouse for industrial information; collects, analyzes, publishes, standardizes, and improves industrial statistics.

### Universal Postal Union (UPU) Member states: 168; Estab.: July 1, 1875 (became UN specialized agency July 1, 1948); HQ: Weltpoststrasse 4, Berne, Switzerland. Establishes regulations for smooth exchange of mail worldwide.

### World Bank Group of three institutions sharing one address. HQ: 1818 H St., NW, Washington, DC 20433. *International Bank for Reconstruction and Development (IBRD)* Member states: 151; Estab.: Dec. 27, 1945, to provide loans and technical assistance to developing countries to assist in their reconstruction and development. *International Finance Corporation (IFC)* Member states: 131 (membership open only to World Bank members); Estab.: July 20, 1956, to stimulate flow of private capital into productive investment in member countries. While closely associated with Bank, IFC is separate legal entity and its funds are distinct from those of Bank. *International Development Association (IDA)* Member states: 135; Estab.: Sept. 24, 1960. (Affiliate of Bank, IDA has same directors and staff as Bank.) Lends money to poor countries on easier terms than Bank alone could give.

### World Health Organization (WHO) Member states: 166; Estab.: Apr. 7, 1948; HQ: 20, avenue Appia, 1211 Geneva 27, Switzerland. Coordinates programs aimed at solving health problems by working with governments, other UN agencies, and nongovernmental organizations. In 1977 WHO set "Health for All by the Year 2000" as overriding priority and developed eight-point strategy for implementation, including education on current health issues; proper food supply and nutrition; safe water and sanitation; maternal and child health; immunization against major infectious diseases; and prevention and control of local diseases. WHO is coordinating global strategy to control and prevent AIDS (acquired immune deficiency syndrome).

### World Intellectual Property Organization (WIPO) Member states: 112; Estab.: 1883 (became a UN specialized agency Dec. 17, 1974); HQ: 34, chemin des Colombettes, 121 Geneva 20, Switzerland. Promotes protection of intellectual property and cooperation in enforcement of agreements on matters such as copyrights, trademarks, industrial designs, and patents.

### World Meteorological Organization (WMO) Member states: 158; Estab.: 1873 (became UN specialized agency Mar. 23, 1950); HQ: 41, avenue Giuseppe-Motta, 1211 Geneva 20, Switzerland. Facilitates exchange of weather reports among countries; established World Weather Watch to track global weather conditions.

# PEACEKEEPING OPERATIONS

UN peacekeeping is the use of multinational forces, under UN command, to keep disputing countries or communities from fighting while efforts are made to help them negotiate a solution. It is undertaken only with the agreement of both hostile parties. UN Peacekeeping Forces received the Nobel Peace Prize in 1988. The following list is of current peacekeeping operations. Size of each operation is as of May 1, 1991.

### UN Truce Supervision Organization (UNTSO) Estab.: 1948. Mandate has evolved. Currently UN observers (294) assist peacekeeping operations in Middle East and small detachments are in Beirut and Amman.

### UN Military Observer Group in India and Pakistan (UNMOGIP) Estab.: 1948. UN observers (39) are stationed on both sides of Line of Control agreed on by India and Pakistan under Simla agreement of July 1972.

### UN Peacekeeping Force in Cyprus (UNFICYP) Estab.: 1964. UN troops (2,130) and civilian police (37) control 112-mi.-(180-km-) long buffer zone on Cyprus between cease-fire lines agreed on by Cyprus National Guard and Turkish forces, and ensure that status quo along the lines is maintained.

### UN Disengagement Observer Force (UNDOF) Estab.: 1974. UN troops and observers (1,314) maintain "area of separation" on Golan Heights between Israel and Syria.

### UN Interim Force in Lebanon (UNIFIL) Estab.: 1978. UN troops (5,885) are in southern Lebanon to confirm withdrawal of Israeli forces, restore international peace and security, and assist Lebanese government in ensuring return of its authority in area.

### UN Angola Verification Mission (UNAVEM) Estab.: 1989. Observer mission of 60 observers verifies withdrawal of Cuban troops from Angola.

### UN Observer Group in Central America (ONUCA) Estab.: 1989. UN observers (200) and troops (826) verify that the five Central American governments comply with security undertakings under the Guatemala agreement.

### UN Iraq-Kuwait Obersvation Mission (UNIKOM) Estab.: 1991. Comprises military observers (300)—including for the first time observers from the five permanent members of the Security Council serving together—support units (460), and infantry companies to monitor the demilitarized zone set up by the Security Council on the Iraq-Kuwait border as well as along the Khor Abdullah waterway.

### UN Mission for the Referendum in Western Sahara (MINURSO) Estab.: 1991. To comprise civilian, security, and military observers (approx. 2,900) for supervision of a cease-fire between POLISARIO and Moroc-

can forces and to organize and supervise a referendum by which the people of Western Sahara are to choose between independence and integration with Morocco.

## KEY EVENTS IN UN HISTORY

**1946** (Jan. 10) First session of General Assembly begins at London with delegates of 51 member states.

**1947** (Nov. 29) General Assembly passes Plan of Partition with Economic Union concerning the future government of Palestine, thereby paving way for government of Tel Aviv to declare State of Israel on May 14, 1948.

**1948** (Dec. 10) Universal Declaration of Human Rights adopted by General Assembly.

UN pioneers concept of peacekeeping observer missions and peacekeeping forces (1956).

UN technical assistance to developing countries begins with appropriation of $350,000. Today UN Development Program alone helps finance development activities valued at over $2 billion a year.

**1949** Mediates cease-fire between India and Pakistan, ending two years of fighting over control of Kashmir.

Mediates cease-fire between Israel and Arab states.

**1950** Security Council calls member states to help South Korea repel invasion from North Korea. (USSR absent from Council, protesting exclusion of People's Republic of China from UN.)

Economic and Social Council adopts Standard International Trade Classification as basis for gathering world trade statistics.

**1953** UN coordinates first global-census effort and establishes earth's population for first time in history—2.4 billion people.

Signs truce with North Korea ending conflict with South Korea.

**1955** First of ongoing congresses of criminologists and police officials draws up international principles and standards of criminal justice.

**1959** UN General Assembly adopts Declaration on the Rights of the Child.

**1960** Under decolonization program seventeen territories become newly independent States, 16 in Africa, and join UN.

UN Educational, Scientific and Cultural Organization coordinates aid from 50 nations to move Egyptian temples at Abu Simbel to higher ground while Aswan High Dam being built.

**1962** Secretary-general plays key role in resolving U.S.-Soviet confrontation over issue of nuclear missiles in Cuba.

**1963** Security Council calls for voluntary arms embargo against South Africa. (Made mandatory in 1977.)

**1964** Having restored law and order, peacekeeping troops withdraw from Congo (now Zaire).

**1967** After war erupts in Middle East, Security Council adopts Resolution 242, calling for withdrawal of forces from occupied territories, and recognizes right of all states in area to security.

UN begins international standardization of geographical names and publishes international geographical dictionaries. Mediates settlement of Six-Day Arab-Israeli War.

**1970** General Assembly adopts first internationally agreed-on set of principles on seabed and ocean floor beyond national jurisdiction. Declares area "common heritage" of humanity.

Commission on Human Rights establishes procedure whereby citizens may bring human rights violations by governments to commission; accused governments notified and invited to respond.

**1972** UN Environment Conference meets at Stockholm; adopts declaration to coordinate environmental issues internationally.

**1973** Security Council orders cease-fire in 17-day-old Middle East War and sends peacekeeping force to prevent further fighting between Israel and Arab states.

**1975** UN conference at Mexico City launches Decade for Women to begin major effort toward women's equality worldwide.

**1979** World Health Organization announces smallpox eradicated from all peoples on earth.

**1982** Convention on Law of the Sea covers navigational rights, definition of territorial jurisdiction in coastal regions, economic exploitation of continental shelf and deep seabed, and protection of marine environment.

**1983** Commission on Status of Women establishes procedure to receive and respond to citizens' complaints of sex discrimination by governments.

**1985** General Assembly establishes Program of Action for African Recovery and Development, 1986–90.

UN Decade for Women culminates in conference at Nairobi that launches Forward-looking Strategies for the Advancement of Women to the Year 2000.

**1987** First International Conference on Drug Abuse and Illicit Trafficking (at Vienna) develops program on international coordination of illicit-drug issues.

General Assembly receives Report of World Commission on Environment and Development ("Our Common Future")—describes environmental threats and plan for "sustainable development."

**1988** All UN programs and specialized agencies incorporate environmental factors into their programs.

UN mediates ending of Iran and Iraq war.

UN mediates Soviet withdrawal from Afghanistan and establishes Operation Salam to rebuild country.

**1989** UN mediates withdrawal of Cuban troops from Angola and South African troops from Namibia.

UN sends peacekeeping troops and advisers to Namibia to supervise elections aimed at setting up self-government.

UN sends peacekeeping operation to Nicaragua to monitor free elections.

General Assembly adopts Convention on the Rights of the Child.

General Assembly calls for International Conference on Environment and Development for June 1992 in Brazil.

**1990** Security Council votes unanimously for international boycott against Iraq until it withdraws from Kuwait.

(Nov.) Security Council votes for use of force to expel Iraq from Kuwait.

**1991** (Apr.) Security Council calls for cease-fire and sets terms of peace settlement in Iraq-Kuwait conflict. Security Council establishes peacekeeping force along Iraq-Kuwait border.

## MODEL UNITED NATIONS

The Model United Nations (MUN) is a simulation of the activities of the UN conducted by high school and college students worldwide. The MUN introduces students to important concepts in international relations and global diplomacy by having them assume the roles of nations' delegates in simulated sessions of the General Assembly, the Security Council, and various UN committees. Current situations are simulated, and the participants must use accurate documentation.

In the United States, more than 60,000 students in approximately 2,000 high schools and colleges participate in MUN simulations, and approximately 100 major annual conferences are held at colleges and universities.

While teachers and students can conduct their simulations informally, the United Nations Association–USA provides coordinating services to those who chose to affiliate. UNA-USA provides a calendar of conferences, teacher and student guides, and training sessions. UNA-USA, 485 Fifth Avenue, New York, NY 10017; (212) 697-3232.

UN documents are provided by the Public Inquiries Unit. Cost is $15 for postage.

## FURTHER UN INFORMATION

**General Information** UN Information Center, 1889 F St., NW, Washington, DC 20006; (202) 289-8670—free materials, loans UN films, interlibrary loan program, library. Public Inquiries Unit, UN, Room GA-57, New York, NY 10017; (212) 963-4475—general information, free charts, booklets, and study kits on work of the UN.

**Sales Publications** UN Sales, UN, Room DC2-853, New York, NY 10017; (212) 963-8302—free publications catalog describing materials for sale.

**Computer Database** United Nations Information Service (UNISER), Global Education Motivators, Inc., Chestnut Hill College, Chestnut Hill, PA 19118-2695; (215) 248-1150—includes daily UN press releases, news highlights, Spanish and French language news, and environment database. Cost is on-line time.

# Nations of the World

The following section presents major facts about all the nations of the world, including statistics on each nation's geography, people, government, economy, membership in major interational organizations, and written text describing highlights of the country's history.

The commonly used name for each country is listed first, followed by the formal name. A list of colonial and other former names is found in the following section, "Territories of the World." Geographical descriptions are listed in both miles and kilometers, and the latitude and longitude of most islands are given. Government leaders are accurate as of Sept. 6, 1991.

Organizations to which a nation is a party are abbreviated under the category "Intl. Orgs." (For more about these, see "The United Nations" and "International Organizations.")

Sources of information include the Central Intelligence Agency of the United States, the United Nations, the U.S. Bureau of the Census, and the U.S. Department of State. Names of heads of government are from the United Nations official protocol office.

## Afghanistan
### Republic of Afghanistan
**Geography Location:** landlocked country in southwestern Asia. **Boundaries:** USSR to N, China to NE, Pakistan to E and S, Iran to W. **Total land area:** 251,773 sq. mi. (652,225 sq km). **Coastline:** none. **Comparative area:** slightly smaller than Texas. **Land use:** 12% arable land; negl. % permanent crops; 46% meadows and pastures; 3% forest and woodland; 39% other; includes negl. % irrigated. **Major cities:** (1982 est.) Kabul (capital) 1,036,407; Qandahar 191,345; Herat 150,497; Mazar-i-Sharif 110,367; Jalalabad 57,824.

**People Population:** 15,862,293 (1990). **Nationality:** noun—Afghan(s); adjective—Afghan. **Ethnic groups:** 50% Pashtun, 25% Tajik, 9% Uzbek, 9% Hazara. **Languages:** 50% Pashtu, 35% Afghan Persian (Dari), 11% Turkic langs. (primarily Uzbek and Turkmen), 4% minor langs. (30, primarily Baluchi and Pashai); much bilingualism. **Religions:** 74% Sunni Muslim, 15% Shia Muslim, 11% other.

**Government Type:** communist regime backed by multidivisional Soviet force. **Independence:** Aug. 1919 (from UK). **Constitution:** adopted Nov. 30, 1987. **National holiday:** Apr. 27. **Heads of government:** Mohammad Najibullah, president (since Nov. 1987); Fazl-Ul Haq Khaliqyar, prime minister (since May 1990). **Structure:** president elected by legislature; cabinet and judiciary responsible to president; Council of Ministers has full authority when legislature is not in session; Revolutionary Council acting as legislature and final court of appeal to be replaced eventually by bicameral legislature.

**Economy Monetary unit:** afghani. **Budget:** (1987 est.) *income:* N.A.; *expend.:* $646.7 mil. **GDP:** $3 bil., $220 per capita (1989 est.). **Chief crops:** subsistence farming and animal husbandry; wheat, fruits, nuts, karakul pelts, wool; illegal producer of opium poppy and cannabis for international drug trade. **Livestock:** sheep, cattle, goats, asses, horses. **Natural resources:** natural gas, crude oil, coal, copper, talc. **Major industries:** small-scale production of textiles, soap, furniture, shoes, fertilizer, and cement for domestic use; handwoven carpets for export; extractive industries (oil and copper). **Labor force:** 4.98 mil. (1980 est.); 67.8% agriculture and animal husbandry, 10.7% services and other, 10.2% industry; current figures unavailable because of fighting (1986). **Exports:** $512 mil. (f.o.b., 1988); 55% natural gas, 24% fruits and nuts, handwoven carpets, wool, cotton. **Imports:** $996 mil. (c.i.f., 1988); food supplies, petroleum products. **Major trading partners: exports:** USSR, Eastern Europe; *imports:* USSR, Eastern Europe.

**Intl. Orgs.** Colombo Plan, FAO, G-77, IAEA, IBRD, ICAO, IDA, IFAD, IFC, ILO, IMF, INTELSAT, ITU, NAM, UN, UNESCO, UPU, WHO, WMO.

Mountainous and landlocked, Afghanistan has been a crossroads of trans-Asian trade and conquest since antiquity. A part of the Persian Empire, Bactria was conquered by Alexander the Great, and became independent in the third century B.C. before falling to the Parthians in the next century. In the seventh century A.D., a flourishing Buddhist civilization there fell to Islamic conquests. Genghis Khan overthrew the 11th-century empire of Mahmud of Gazni in the early 13th century, and Afghanistan was the center of Tamerlane's empire in the late 14th century. Thereafter, the region was divided among various tribes and petty kingdoms.

Modern Afghan history began with the establishment of a united emirate by Ahmed Shah Durrani in 1747. In the 19th century, Russia and Great Britain contested domination of Afghanistan. The British Afghan Wars of 1838–42 and 1878–80 left Afghanistan unconquered but within Britain's sphere of influence. Afghanistan achieved full independence from Britain in 1919 under Amanullah Khan, who proclaimed himself king in 1926. Modern reforms were instituted by Amanullah and his successors Mohammed Nadir Shah (1929–33) and Mohammed Zahir Shah (1933–73).

The monarchy fell to a military coup in 1973, and Mohammed Daud Khan established a republic. In 1978 pro-Soviet leftists took power in a coup, and, ostensibly at the government's invitation, Soviet troops invaded Afghanistan in December 1979 to put down widespread popular revolts against Communist rule. In the ensuing civil war, the government's forces and their Soviet allies (with an eventual troop strength of more than 100,000) controlled the cities and main transportation routes, but guerrilla forces contested the countryside. In 1988 the Soviet Union began a withdrawal of its troops, completed by February 1989. The rebel factions failed to achieve a united front and the government confounded predictions that it would fall soon after the Soviet departure. The USSR continues to support the Kabul government, and sporadic fighting continues.

## Albania
### People's Socialist Republic of Albania
**Geography Location:** southeastern Europe. **Boundaries:** Yugoslavia to N and E, Greece to S, and Adriatic and Ionian seas (parts of Mediterranean Sea) to W. **Total land area:** 11,100 sq. mi. (28,748 sq km). **Coastline:** 225 mi. (362 km). **Comparative area:** slightly larger than Maryland. **Land use:** 21% arable land; 4% permanent crops; 15% meadows and pastures; 38% forest and woodland; 22% other; includes 1% irrigated. **Major cities:** (1987) Tiranë (Tirana; capital) 225,700; Durrës (Durazzo) 78,700; Elbasan 78,300; Shkodër (Scutari) 76,300; Vlorë (Vlonë or Valona) 67,600.

**People Population:** 3,273,131 (1990). **Nationality:** noun—Albanian(s); adjective—Albanian. **Ethnic groups:** 96% Albanian, 4% Greek, Vlach, Gypsy, Serb, and Bulgarian. **Languages:** Albanian (Tosk is official dialect), Greek. **Religions:** Albania claims to be world's first atheist state; all churches and mosques were closed in 1967 and religious observances prohibited; pre-1967 estimates of religious affiliation—70% Muslim, 20% Albanian Orthodox, 10% Roman Catholic.

**Government Type:** communist state (Stalinist). **Independence:** Nov. 28, 1912 (from Turkey). **Constitution:** Dec. 27, 1976. **National holiday:** Liberation Day, Nov. 29. **Heads of government:** Ramiz Alia, president (since Nov. 1982); Ylli Bufi, prime minister (since June 1991). **Structure:** Council of Ministers; legislature (People's Assembly); judiciary.

**Economy Monetary unit:** lek. **Budget:** (1989) *income:* $2.3 bil.; *expend.:* $2.3 bil. **GNP:** $3.8 bil., about $1,200 per capita (1986). **Chief crops:** vegetables, wheat, potatoes, tobacco, sugar beets, cotton, corn. **Livestock:** sheep, goats, cattle, pigs, asses. **Natural resources:** crude oil, natural gas, coal, chromium, copper. **Major industries:** food processing, textiles and clothing, lumber. **Labor force:** 1.5 mil. (1987); about 60% agriculture, 40% industry and commerce (1986). **Exports:** $378 mil. (1987 est.); asphalt, bitumen, petroleum products, metals and metallic ores, electricity, oil, vegetables, fruits, tobacco. **Imports:** $255 mil. (f.o.b., 1987 est.); machinery, machine tools, iron and steel products, textiles, chemicals. **Major trading partners:** (1986) *exports:* Italy, Greece, Czechoslovakia, Yugoslavia, W. Germany. *imports:* Italy, Czechoslovakia, Yugoslavia, Romania, W. Germany.

**Intl. Orgs.** FAO, IAEA, ITU, UN, UNESCO, UPU, WHO, WMO.

The city of Epidamnus (Durrës) was colonized by Greeks from Corinth and Corcyra in 625 B.C. Later the Roman province of Illyricum, Albania was a much-coveted area after the fall of Rome and was in turn ruled by Byzantines, Normans, Venetians, Slavs, and the kings of Naples. Under the leadership of Skanderbeg (1405-68), Albania repulsed repeated Turkish invasions. But Albania was part of the Ottoman Empire from 1478 until 1912. Ottoman rule succeeded in converting most of the populace to Islam (with Catholic minorities in the north and Greek Orthodox in the south) but did not destroy the Albanian sense of national identity, based on ties of tribe, clan, and family.

Independence came in 1912 as a result of the First Balkan War, when Austria-Hungary and Italy fostered the creation of an Albanian state. Occupied by its sponsors during World War I, Albania emerged from the war in a state of near-anarchy. With Yugoslav support, a tribal chief, Ahmed Zogu, became president of the republic in 1924; he proclaimed himself King Zog I in 1928.

In 1939 Italy invaded and annexed Albania. During World War II, partisan resistance was dominated by a leftist force under the leadership of Enver Hoxha. Allied forces liberated Albania in 1944, and Hoxha seized control of the government. A socialist republic was established in 1946: foreigners were expelled and their assets nationalized; churches were closed; agriculture and industry were collectivized. Albania under Hoxha became one of the world's most thoroughly totalitarian states.

A doctrinaire Stalinist, Hoxha broke with Nikita Khruschev's Soviet Union in 1961 and became a client state of China. But with liberalization in China after 1977, Hoxha broke that link as well. Albania became almost totally isolated from world affairs.

Hoxha died in April 1985 and was succeeded as president and first secretary of the Albanian Communist party by Ramiz Alia. In 1989, Alia began to ease curbs on religion, tourism, and foreign investment, and to expand foreign trade. In December 1990, he allowed the formation of the opposition Democratic party, which lost to the Communists in elections in March 1991. Civil unrest grew in the spring, and neighboring countries, especially Greece and Italy, had to contend with tens of thousands of refugees. Meanwhile, the government also supports an ethnic Albanian separatist movement in Yugoslavia's Kosovo province.

With Chinese aid, the Albanian economy developed some basic industry and an export trade in chromium and processed foodstuffs. Despite industrialization, more than half the population remains in the agricultural sector.

## Algeria

**Democratic and Popular Republic of Algeria**
**Geography** **Location:** northern coast of Africa. **Boundaries:** Mediterranean Sea to N, Tunisia and Libya to E, Mali and Niger to S, Morocco, Western Sahara, Mauritania to W. **Total land area:** 919,595 sq. mi. (2,381,741 sq km). **Coastline:** 620 mi. (998 km). **Comparative area:** slightly less than 3.5 times size of Texas. **Land use:** 3% arable land; negl. % permanent crops; 13% meadows and pastures; 2% forest and woodland; 82% other; includes negl. % irrigated. **Major cities:** (1984 est.) Algiers (capital) 1,721,607; Oran 663,504; Constantine 448,578; Annaba 348,322; Blida 191,314.

**People** **Population:** 25,566,507 (1990). **Nationality:** noun—Algerian(s); adjective—Algerian. **Ethnic groups:** 99% Arab-Berber, less than 1% European. **Languages:** Arabic (official), French, Berber dialects. **Religions:** 99% Sunni Muslim (state religion), 1% Christian and Jewish.

**Government** **Type:** republic. **Independence:** July 5, 1962 (from France). **Constitution:** Nov. 19, 1976, effective Nov. 22, 1976. **National holiday:** Anniversary of the Revolution, Nov. 1. **Heads of government:** Col. Chadli Bendjedid, president (since Feb. 1979); Sid Ahmed Ghozali, prime minister (since June 1991). **Structure:** executive; unicameral legislature (National People's Assembly); judiciary.

**Economy** **Monetary unit:** Algerian dinar. **Budget:** (1988) *income:* $17.4 bil.; *expend.:* $22.0 bil. **GDP:** $54.1 bil., $2,235 per capita (1987 est.). **Chief crops:** wheat, barley, oats, grapes, olives. **Livestock:** chickens, sheep, goats, cattle, horses. **Natural resources:** crude oil, natural gas, iron ore, phosphates, uranium. **Major industries:** petroleum, light industries, natural gas, mining. **Labor force:** 3.7 mil. (1984); 40% industry and commerce, 30% agriculture, 17% government, 10% services. **Exports:** $9.1 bil. (f.o.b., 1989 est.); 98% petroleum and natural gas. **Imports:** $7.8 bil. (f.o.b., 1989 est.); 36% consumer goods, 35% capital goods, 20% food. **Major trading partners:** *exports:* Netherlands, Czechoslovakia, Romania, Italy, France, U.S.; *imports:* 25% France, 8% Italy, 8% West Germany, 6% U.S.

**Intl. Orgs.** Arab League, FAO, G-77, GATT (de facto), IAEA, IBRD, ICAO, IDA, IFAD, ILO, IMF, IMO, INTELSAT, INTERPOL, ITU, NAM, OAU, OPEC, UN, UNESCO, UPU, WHO, WIPO, WMO.

From around 3000 B.C. nomadic ancestors of the Berbers inhabited Algeria, as the expanding Sahara desert displaced prehistoric grasslands and forests. The Phoenicians established trading centers in the Mediterranean coastal plain around 1200 B.C. Those centers were taken over by the Romans beginning around 200 B.C. With Roman support the Berber chief Masinissa formed the kingdom of Numidia in what is now northern Algeria. From 46 B.C. to about A.D. 640, the area was controlled successively by the Romans, Germanic Vandal tribes, and the Byzantine Empire.

In the eighth century A.D., the Islamic conquests spread Arab culture to Numidia. Most of the Berbers converted to Islam. The blend of Berber and Arab culture in Algeria gave rise to a flourishing and rich Islamic civilization in the coastal plain, while Tuareg and other nomadic peoples controlled the sparsely inhabited interior.

Around 1500 the Christian kingdom of Spain captured Algiers and other coastal cities. In 1518 Barbarossa, a Turkish sea captain, captured Algiers and drove the Spanish out. In so doing, he joined Algeria to the expanding Turkish Ottoman Empire. Piracy became a key source of income for the Ottoman cities of Algeria. In the early 1800s, France, along with England and the United States, began military operations to suppress piracy in the Mediterranean. In 1830 France invaded Algeria, putting an end to Ottoman rule and establishing their own administration. Algeria was ruled as part of France itself. Many French settlers (*colons*) migrated to Algeria. Both they and the native Algerians were considered citizens of France, but the colons were granted substantial political and economic advantages over the indigenous population.

In 1847 a rebellion led by Abd-al-Qadir, a powerful Muslim leader, was suppressed by the French, but the spirit of Algerian nationalism remained alive. In 1848, in the wake of the rebellion, all of Algeria was conquered by the French and legally confirmed as an integral part of France. During World War II, many Algerians joined the Free French, hoping that their display of loyalty would be rewarded with greater self-rule after the war. Those hopes were disappointed, as French administration was resumed in 1945.

In 1954 the Front de Liberation Nationale (FLN) began a guerrilla war against the French in Algeria. They were opposed by French police and military forces and by the Secret Army Organization (OAS), an underground movement of colons who favored continued French rule. As the FLN gained strength, by 1958 French Premier Charles de Gaulle established a policy designed to prepare Algeria for self-rule.

Algerian independence was proclaimed on July 3, 1962; a million colons fled to France. A power struggle within the new Algerian government was resolved when Ahmed Ben Bella became the country's first premier in 1963. In 1965 Ben Bella was deposed by Col. Houari Boumidienne, who ruled as the head of a military government. In 1967 Algeria declared war on Israel, broke with the West, and established close relations with the USSR. Since the early 1970s, relations with the West, and particularly with France, have improved, but Algeria remains a member of the hard-line anti-Israel block of the Arab League.

Algeria's economic mainstay is petroleum. Agriculture (grain, wine grapes, dates, vegetables) is the principal economic activity in coastal areas, while pastoralism and mining dominate in the interior. Despite attempts at industrialization (steel, textiles, fertilizer, plastics, light manufacturing), the economy is plagued by instability and high unemployment.

The first free, multiparty elections since independence were held on June 12, 1990. The Islamic Salvation Front, which advocates turning Algeria into an Islamic Republic, won overwhelming control of provincial and local assemblies.

## Andorra
### Principality of Andorra

**Geography** **Location:** Pyrenees Mountains, southwestern Europe. **Boundaries:** France to N and E, Spain to S and W. **Total land area:** 180 sq. mi. (467 sq km). **Coastline:** none. **Comparative area:** slightly more than 2.5 times size of Washington, D.C. **Land use:** 2% arable land; 0% permanent crops; 56% meadows and pastures; 22% forest and woodland; 20% other. **Major cities:** Andorra la Vella (capital).

**People** **Population:** 51,895 (1990). **Nationality:** noun—Andorran(s); adjective—Andorran. **Ethnic groups:** Catalan stock; 61% Spanish, 30% Andorran, 6% French, 3% other. **Languages:** Catalan (official); many also speak some French and Castilian. **Religions:** virtually all Roman Catholic.

**Government** **Type:** unique co-principality under formal sovereignty of president of France and Spanish bishop of Seo de Urgel, who are represented locally by officials called verguers. **Independence:** N.A. **Constitution:** none; some decrees, mostly custom and usage. **National holiday:** N.A. **Heads of government:** French co-prince François Mitterrand, president of France (since 1981) and Spanish Episcopal co-prince Msgr. Juan Marti y Alanís, bishop of Seo de Urgel, Spain (since 1971). **Structure:** legislative—General Council of the Valleys (28 members); executive—syndic (manager) and deputy sub-syndic chosen by General Council; judiciary—chosen by co-princes, who appoint two civil judges, judge of appeals, and two battles (court prosecutors); final appeal to Supreme Court of Andorra at Perpignan, France, or to Ecclesiastical Court of Bishop of Seo de Urgel, Spain.

**Economy** **Monetary unit:** French franc and Spanish peseta. **Budget:** N.A. **GNP:** N.A. **Chief crops:** sheep raising; small quantities of tobacco, rye, wheat, barley, oats, and some vegetables. **Livestock:** N.A. **Natural resources:** hydropower, mineral water, timber, iron ore, lead. **Major industries:** tourism (particularly skiing), sheep, timber, tobacco, smuggling. **Labor force:** largely shepherds and farmers. **Exports:** N.A. **Imports:** N.A. **Major trading partners:** France, Spain.

**Intl. Orgs.** UNESCO.

Set high in the Pyrenees, the tiny state of Andorra is both a medieval relic and a modern capitalist land. Since 1278 Andorra has owed feudal allegiance to two co-rulers, the bishop of Seo de Urgel in Spain and, now, the president of France. Andorra has no constitution, so the exact rights of the co-rulers remain vague. Foreign affairs are handled by France.

Andorra has no customs department, no registration or regulation of businesses, and no penal code. Its traditional economic mainstay has been the "transshipment of goods" (i.e., smuggling) between France and Spain. Andorra attracts tourists drawn by bargain shopping, and it is a banking center. These activities have fueled a seemingly endless economic boom in the postwar period. However, Spain's entry into the EC threatens Andorra's advantages as a duty-free haven; unrestrained currency movements

invite intervention by the country's co-rulers; and the tourist boom poses a danger of over-development and environmental destruction.

## Angola
### People's Republic of Angola

**Geography** **Location:** southwestern Africa. **Boundaries:** Zaire to N and NE, Zambia to E, Namibia to S, South Atlantic Ocean to W; Cabinda district separated from rest of country by Congo to N, Zaire to S. **Total land area:** 481,354 sq. mi. (1,246,700 sq km). **Coastline:** 994 mi. (1,600 km). **Comparative area:** slightly less than twice size of Texas. **Land use:** 2% arable land; negl. % permanent crops; 23% meadows and pastures; 43% forest and woodland; 32% other. **Major cities:** Luanda (capital) 1,200,000 (1982 est.); Huambo (Nova Lisboa) 61,885; Lobito 59,258; Benguela 40,996; Lubango (São da Bandeira) 31,674 (1970 census).

**People** **Population:** 8,534,483 (1990). **Nationality:** noun—Angolan(s); adjective—Angolan. **Ethnic groups:** 37% Ovimbundu, 25% Kimbundu, 13% Bakongo, 2% Mestiço, 1% European, 22% other. **Languages:** Portuguese (official), various Bantu dialects. **Religions:** 68% Roman Catholic, 20% Protestant, 12% indigenous beliefs.

**Government** **Type:** Marxist people's republic. **Independence:** Nov. 11, 1975 (from Portugal). **Constitution:** Nov. 11, 1975. **National holiday:** Independence Day, Nov. 11. **Heads of government:** José Eduardo dos Santos, president (since Sept. 1979). **Structure:** legislative—National People's Assembly; official party is supreme political institution.

**Economy** **Monetary unit:** kwanza. **Budget:** (1986 est.) *income:* N.A.; *expend.:* $2.7 bil. **GDP:** $5.0 bil., $600 per capita (1988 est.). **Chief crops:** cash crops—coffee, sisal, corn, cotton, sugar; food crops—cassava, corn, vegetables, plantains, bananas and other local foodstuffs; disruptions caused by civil war require food imports. **Livestock:** cattle, goats, pigs, sheep. **Natural resources:** petroleum, diamonds, iron ore, phosphates, copper. **Major industries:** petroleum, mining (phosphate rock, diamonds), fish processing. **Labor force:** 2.8 mil. (1985 est.); 85% agriculture, 15% industry. **Exports:** $2.9 bil. (f.o.b., 1989 est.); oil, coffee, diamonds, sisal, fish and fish products. **Imports:** $2.5 bil. (f.o.b., 1989 est.); capital equipment (machinery, electrical equipment), food, vehicles and spare parts, textiles and clothing, medicines; substantial military deliveries. **Major trading partners:** U.S., USSR, Cuba, Portugal, Brazil.

**Intl. Orgs.** FAO, G-77, GATT (de facto), ICAO, IFAD, ILO, IMO, INTELSAT, ITU, NAM, OAU, UN, UNESCO, UPU, WHO, WMO.

Bantu peoples have occupied Angola for at least 2,000 years. Portuguese explorers searching for a sea route to India founded Luanda (1575) and Benguela (1617). Portugal, at first in alliance with the north Angolan kingdom of Bakongo, engaged in an extensive trade of slaves to Brazil—3 million in 300 years.

In the late 19th century, Angola was organized as a Portuguese colony, sometimes called Portuguese West Africa. Portuguese settlers dominated local government, trade, and small-scale industry in addition to organizing plantation-style cultivation of cotton, palm oil, bananas, and coffee. A railroad was built to transport exports of metal from the Katanga region of the Belgian Congo (now Zaire) to the coast.

By the 1950s non-Portuguese Angolans began to agitate for independence. The National Front spearheaded the liberation movement. Guerrilla warfare began in 1961, with several feuding factions fighting the Portuguese. Following the Portuguese revolution of 1974, factional warfare intensified and most Portuguese settlers fled the country, leaving it seriously lacking in trained administrative and commercial personnel. Independence came on Nov. 11, 1975.

Civil war between the National Front, the Popular Movement for the Liberation of Angola (MPLA), and the National Union for the Total Independence of Angola (UNITA) led, in 1976, to the victory of the MPLA, which organized a Marxist state with Soviet backing and Cuban technical support including 37,000 soldiers. Large portions of the country remained in the hands of UNITA, which continued the civil war with Chinese and American support through the 1980s.

Direct clashes between Angolan and South African troops occurred during the 1980s, as Angola gave shelter to SWAPO guerrilla forces seeking independence for Namibia.

Cuban troops withdrew from Angola between January 1989 and May 1991, and a cease-fire between the government and UNITA was also concluded in May 1991. While agreeing to recognize the dos Santos government in the interim, UNITA has called for elections to be held by May 1992.

Much of Angola consists of an arid plateau. The densely forested northeastern region yields hardwoods and also produces diamonds. Most agriculture is confined to a narrow coastal strip. Angola is rich in mineral resources and there is some industrial development, including food processing, paper, textiles, shoes, and other light manufacturing. Despite the civil war and economic mismanagement, which have caused widespread poverty, Angola's long-term economic prospects are promising.

## Antigua and Barbuda

**Geography** **Location:** eastern Caribbean Sea approximately 300 mi. (480 km) SE of Puerto Rico. Antigua 17°06'N, 61°50'W; Barbuda 17°38'N, 61°48'W. **Boundaries:** Atlantic Ocean to N and E, Caribbean Sea to S and W. **Total land area:** 171 sq. mi. (441.6 sq km). **Coastline:** 95 mi. (153 km). **Comparative area:** slightly less than 2.5 times size of Washington, D.C. **Land use:** 18% arable land; 0% permanent crops; 7% meadows and pastures; 16% forest and woodland; 59% other; includes N.A. % irrigated. **Major cities:** St. John's (capital) 36,000.

**People** **Population:** 63,726 (1990). **Nationality:** noun—Antiguan(s); adjective—Antiguan. **Ethnic groups:** almost entirely of black-

African origin; some of British, Portuguese, Lebanese, and Syrian origin. **Languages:** English (official), local dialects. **Religions:** Anglican (predominant), other Protestant sects, some Roman Catholic.

**Government** **Type:** independent state recognizing Elizabeth II as chief of state. **Independence:** Nov. 1, 1981 (from UK). **Constitution:** Nov. 1, 1981. **National holiday:** Nov. 1. **Heads of government:** Sir Wilfred Ebenezer Jacobs, governor-general (since 1967); Vere C. Bird, prime minister (since 1976). **Structure:** executive—prime minister and cabinet; bicameral legislature—17-member popularly elected House of Representatives and 17-member Senate; judiciary—court of appeals.

**Economy** **Monetary unit:** East Caribbean (EC) dollar. **Budget:** (1988 est.) **income:** $77 mil.; **expend.:** $81 mil. **GDP:** $353.5 mil., $5,550 per capita (1985). **Chief crops:** cotton (main crop), sugar. **Livestock:** cattle, sheep, goats, pigs. **Natural resources:** negl.; pleasant climate fosters tourism. **Major industries:** tourism, construction, light manufacturing (clothing, alcohol, household appliances). **Labor force:** 30,000 (1983); 82% commerce and services, 11% agriculture, 7% industry; 20% unemployment (1983). **Exports:** $30.4 mil. (f.o.b., 1988 est) 46% petroleum products, 29% manufactures, 14% food and live animals, 11% machinery and transportation equipment. **Imports:** $302.1 mil. (c.i.f., 1988 est.): food and live animals, machinery and transport equipment, manufactures, chemicals. **Major trading partners: exports:** 40% Trinidad and Tobago, 8% Barbados, 0.3% U.S.; **imports:** 27% U.S., 14% UK, 7% Caribbean Community and EC.

**Intl. Orgs.** Commonwealth, FAO, G-77, IBRD, ICAO, ILO, IMF, OAS, UN, UNESCO, WHO, WMO.

Columbus visited and claimed Antigua for Spain in 1493. It was settled by the British in 1632, who grew tobacco and, later, sugar. The island's economy was hobbled by abolition of slavery in 1834, a succession of natural disasters in the 1840s, and the closing of the Royal Dockyard in 1854. Today, tourism is a mainstay of the economy. Residents of Barbuda have been intent on severing political relations between the two islands as a result of cultural and political differences with Antiguans. Government officials have been implicated in the transshipment of Israeli weapons to the Medellín drug cartel.

## Argentina
### Argentine Republic

**Geography** **Location:** southern South America. **Boundaries:** Bolivia, Paraguay, Brazil to N.; Uruguay, South Atlantic Ocean to E.; Chile to W. **Total land area:** 1,068,302 sq. mi. (2,766,889 sq km) (figures exclude Falkland Islands and Antarctic territory claimed by Argentina). **Coastline:** 3,099 mi. (4,986 km). **Comparative area:** about 1.8 times size of Alaska. **Land use:** 9% arable land; 4% permanent crops; 52% meadows and pastures; 22%

forest and woodland; 13% other; includes 1% irrigated. **Major cities:** (1980 census) Buenos Aires (capital) 2,922,829; Córdoba 983,969; Rosario 957,301; Mendoza 605,623; La Plata 564,750.

**People** **Population:** 32,290,966 (1990). **Nationality:** noun—Argentine(s); adjective—Argentine. **Ethnic groups:** 85% white, 15% mestizo, Indian, and other nonwhite groups. **Languages:** Spanish (official), English, Italian, German, French. **Religions:** 90% nominally Roman Catholic (less than 20% practicing), 2% Protestant, 2% Jewish, 6% other.

**Government** **Type:** republic. **Independence:** July 9, 1816 (from Spain). **Constitution:** May 1, 1853. **National holiday:** Independence Day, May 25. **Head of government:** Carlos Saúl Menem, president (since July 1989). **Structure:** executive (president, vice president, cabinet); legislative (National Congress—Senate, Chamber of Deputies); national judiciary.

**Economy** **Monetary unit:** austral. **Budget:** (1988) **income:** $11.5 bil.; **expend.:** $13 bil. **GNP:** $72 bil., $2,217 per capita (1987). **Chief crops:** cereals, oilseed, livestock products; major world exporter of temperate-zone foodstuffs. **Livestock:** cattle, sheep, pigs, horses, goats. **Natural resources:** fertile plains of the pampas, lead, zinc, copper. **Major industries:** food processing (especially meat packing), motor vehicles, consumer durables. **Labor force:** 10.9 mil. (1985 est.); 57% services, 31% industry, 12% agriculture; 6.5% unemployment (1988 est.). **Exports:** $9.6 bil. (f.o.b., 1989); meat, wheat, corn, oilseed, hides. **Imports:** $4.3 bil. (c.i.f., 1989); machinery and equipment, chemicals, metals, fuel, lubricants. **Major trading partners: exports:** 14% U.S., USSR, Italy, Brazil, Japan; **imports:** 25% U.S., Brazil, W. Germany, Bolivia, Japan.

**Intl. Orgs.** FAO, G-77, GATT, IAEA, IBRD, ICAO, IDA, IFAD, IFC, ILO, IMF, IMO, INTELSAT, INTERPOL, ITU, NAM, OAS, UN, UNESCO, UPU, WHO, WMO.

The indigenous nomads of the area around the river La Plata resisted Spanish intrusion, which began with the first founding of Buenos Aires by Pedro de Mendoza in 1536. Argentina was part of Spain's Viceroyalty of Peru until reforms in the Bourbon dynasty and a need to defend against Portuguese encroachment from Brazil led to the formation of the Viceroyalty of La Plata, including Argentina, Bolivia, Paraguay, and Uruguay, in 1776. Following the relaxation of trade restrictions two years later, Buenos Aires grew from a small town to a city of 50,000 by 1800. A provisional junta of the Provinces of Río de la Plata was established in 1810 after the Napoleonic occupation of Spain, and in 1816 the United Provinces of the Río de la Plata declared their independence.

After independence the question of political relations among the United Provinces was settled by a federalist solution in which the provinces dissolved into a number of practically independent republics. In 1824, a constituent assembly created the office of president, first held by Bernardino Rivadavia. However, the failure to ratify a workable constitution caused

Rivadavia to resign.

Juan Manuel de Rosas became governor of Buenos Aires in 1829 and presided over the construction of a federal agreement between the provinces in 1831. Rosas governed Buenos Aires with an iron hand until his expulsion in 1852. The other provinces formed the Argentine Federation, based on a federal constitution of 1853, but Buenos Aires refused to join. Buenos Aires and the Argentine Federation entered into war between 1859 and 1861; they reached an agreement on the inclusion of Buenos Aires in the Argentine Republic in 1862.

Argentina joined Brazil and Uruguay in a war (1865–70) against Paraguay. During the latter part of the 1870s, the government took the initiative against the indigenous populations of Patagonia and Tierra del Fuego, which were partitioned with Chile. Immigration from Europe, especially Spain and Italy, resulted in enormous growth from the mid-19th century. In 1869, there were 2 million inhabitants; by 1914, 8 million; by 1955, 19 million; and by 1990, 32 million. Prior to World War II, Argentina was acutely Eurocentric, with an eye to British finance and French culture; this has changed since.

The Argentine military, led by Lt. Gen. José F. Uriburu, ousted the civilian government of the Radical party in 1930 with the intention of following the European model of politics. In 1946 Juan Domingo Perón won the presidential election and constructed a populist political alliance that included workers, industrialists, and the armed forces. The Perón-inspired populist ideology of *justicialismo* included extension of the franchise to women and redistribution of income to workers and the poor. The activities of Perón's charismatic wife, Eva, bolstered justicialismo through her effort to distribute goods to the poor through the Social Aid Foundation.

Tied in with Perón's populist strategy was his policy of nationalist economic development, whereby state-led development was financed through extraction of capital from the old export-agricultural elite and politically supported through populism. The Perón government incurred great expense to gain control over foreign-owned economic infrastructure. A number of events led to Perón's downfall in 1955. The market for Argentine goods deteriorated after World War II. As Perón shifted his strategy to encourage foreign investment and impose economic austerity, repression against the political opposition grew. The death of Eva Perón in 1952 robbed Perón of an important political resource, and when the government challenged the Catholic church on a number of issues, the military ousted Perón.

After a brief period of military rule, in which an attempt was made to roll back "Peronism," Arturo Frondizi of the "Intransigent" faction of the Radical party won the presidency and assumed office in 1958. In the following years, the military repeatedly attempted to keep the Peronistas from returning to power on the basis of their electoral support. When Frondizi refused to annul a Peronist victory in 1962, the armed forces withdrew their support and removed him from office. Pres. Arturo Illía was ousted from office in 1966 for the same reason:

his failure to tame Perón's followers.

A military bureaucratic authoritarian regime led by a series of Argentine officers was established during 1966–73. The political arena was undergoing polarization, and extreme violence by factions on the left and right led the military to accept Perón's return to the presidency in 1973. Perón died the following year, and his second wife, Isabel, replaced him in office; she was unable to retain power, and the military removed her in 1976.

Determined to deal with what they saw as a leftist threat, the military again opted for a bureaucratic authoritarian solution. As part of this "solution," the armed forces launched what was later called the "dirty war" against leftists, during which up to 20,000 people lost their lives. The authoritarian government collapsed after the ill-starred 1982 Falkland/Malvinas Islands War against Britain led to the resignation of the junta and the holding of elections. Raúl Alfonsín, of the Radical Union party, was elected president in the wake of these events in 1983. In 1989, he was succeeded by Carlos Saúl Menem. Widely proclaimed as the political heir of Juan Perón, Menem has nonetheless encouraged free enterprise and good relations with the United States. Government controls on foreign investment and trade have been relaxed, and the government has sold off the state airline and telephone company, television and radio stations, and other enterprises. The country still struggles with high inflation and unemployment.

## Australia
### Commonwealth of Australia
**Geography** **Location:** continent of Australia, between Indian and Pacific oceans. **Boundaries:** nearest neighbor is Papua New Guinea, to N. **Total land area:** 2,966,151 sq. mi. (7,682,300 sq km). **Coastline:** 16,010 mi. (25,760 km). **Comparative area:** slightly smaller than U.S. **Land use:** 6% arable land; negl. % permanent crops; 58% meadows and pastures; 14% forest and woodland; 22% other; includes negl. % irrigated. **Major cities:** (1985 est.) Canberra (capital) 273,600; Sydney 3,391,600; Melbourne 2,916,600; Brisbane 1,157,200; Perth 1,001,000.

**People** **Population:** 16,923,478 (1990). **Nationality:** noun—Australian(s); adjective—Australian. **Ethnic groups:** 95% Caucasian, 4% Asian, 1% aboriginal and other. **Languages:** English, native langs. **Religions:** 26.1% Anglican, 26.0% Roman Catholic, 24.3% other Christian.

**Government** **Type:** federal parliamentary state recognizing Elizabeth II as sovereign or head of state. **Independence:** Jan. 1, 1901 (from federation of UK colonies). **Constitution:** July 9, 1900; effective Jan. 1, 1901. **National holiday:** Australia Day, Jan. 26. **Heads of government:** William G. Hayden, governor general (since Feb. 1989); Robert Hawke, prime minister (since Mar. 1983). **Structure:** prime minister and cabinet responsible to House; bicameral legislature (Federal Parliament—Senate and House of Representatives); independent judiciary.

**Economy** **Monetary unit:** Australian dollar. **Budget:** (1990) *income:* $76.3 bil; *expend.:* $69.1 bil. **GNP:** $240.8 bil., $14,300 per capita (1989 est.). **Chief crops:** large areas devoted to grazing; 60% of area used for crops is planted in wheat; major products—wool, lamb, beef, wheat, fruits; self-sufficient in food. **Livestock:** sheep, cattle, pigs. **Natural resources:** bauxite, coal, iron ore, copper, tin. **Major industries:** mining, industrial and transportation equipment, food processing. **Labor force:** 7.7 mil. (1987); 33.8% finance and services, 22.3% public and community services, 20.1% wholesale and retail trade, 16.2% manufacturing and industry, 6.9% unemployment rate (1988). **Exports:** $43.2 bil. (f.o.b., 1989); wheat, barley, beef, lamb, dairy products. **Imports:** $48.6 bil. (c.i.f., 1989); manufactured raw materials, capital equipment, consumer goods. **Major trading partners:** *exports:* 26% Japan, 11% U.S., 6% New Zealand, 4% S. Korea, 4% Singapore; *imports:* 22% U.S., 22% Japan, 7% UK, 6% W. Germany, 4% New Zealand.

**Intl. Orgs.** Colombo Plan, Commonwealth, FAO, GATT, IAEA, IBRD, ICAO, IDA, IFAD, IFC, ILO, IMF, IMO, INTELSAT, INTERPOL, ITU, OECD, UN, UNESCO, UPU, WHO, WIPO, WMO.

The continent-nation of Australia is distinguished by its geographical isolation and by the unique flora and fauna which that isolation has fostered. The ancestors of today's aborigines arrived from Southeast Asia as much as 40,000 years ago. Thereafter, aborigine culture evolved in isolation except for some contact between the peoples of the northern coast and New Guinea. Australia was first sighted by Europeans at the beginning of the 17th century. In the 18th century, it was visited by the Dutch, who named it New Holland. The eastern coast was systematically explored in 1770 by Capt. James Cook, who claimed it for Great Britain.

British settlement began in 1788, with the landing of about 700 convicts near Sydney. Australia remained a penal colony during the first half of the 19th century, during which time the continent was explored and separate colonies were established. Aboriginal populations were displaced and in some areas (most notably the island Tasmania) they were totally exterminated. Discovery of gold in Victoria in 1851 created a gold rush that greatly accelerated immigration. By the end of the 19th century, the three mainstays of the Australian economy—livestock (beef and sheep), mining, and wheat growing—were firmly established.

In 1901, a commonwealth was established consisting of a confederation of the various states except for the Northern Territory, which was added in 1911. The British Crown is represented by an appointed governor-general; the national government is a parliamentary system, but much local authority resides in the separate states. Comprehensive social welfare legislation was passed by the state and national governments soon after the commonwealth's formation. The population is highly educated and enjoys a generally high standard of living, but most aborigines are detribalized and live in considerable poverty.

Australian troops fought with distinction in both world wars. A Japanese threat to Australia in 1942 was averted by Allied victory in the Battle of the Coral Sea. Australia and the United States are firm allies, and Australian troops joined U.S. forces in Korea, Vietnam, and the Persian Gulf War. Australia administers several external island groups and claims territory in Antarctica. (See "Territories of the World.")

The abandonment of discriminatory immigration practices in 1973 led to a new wave of immigration, particularly from Asia. In the process Australian economic ties to Asia and the Pacific Rim have expanded considerably. New exploitation of mineral and hydrocarbon resources has in many cases been accomplished with Japanese investment or with long-term export contracts to Japan. Australia has also undergone considerable industrial development in the past two decades. However, once the richest nation in the world in per capita GNP, it is no longer even in the top 10. After a century in power, the Labor party is seeking to privatize some state-owned industries and to trim some of its more lavish benefit programs.

## Austria
### Republic of Austria
**Geography** **Location:** landlocked country in central Europe. **Boundaries:** Germany and Czechoslovakia to N, Hungary to E, Yugoslavia and Italy to S, Switzerland and Liechtenstein to W. **Total land area:** 32,377 sq. mi. (83,855 sq km). **Coastline:** none. **Comparative area:** between South Carolina and Maine. **Land use:** 17% arable land; 1% permanent crops; 24% meadows and pastures; 39% forest and woodland; 19% other; includes negl. % irrigated. **Major cities:** (1981 census) Vienna (capital) 1,531,346; Graz 243,166; Linz 199,910; Salzburg 139,426; Innsbruck 117,287.

**People** **Population:** 7,644,275 (1990). **Nationality:** noun—Austrian(s); adjective—Austrian. **Ethnic groups:** 99.4% German, 0.3% Croatian, 0.2% Slovene, 0.1% other. **Languages:** German. **Religions:** 85% Roman Catholic, 6% Protestant, 9% none or other.

**Government** **Type:** federal republic. **Constitution:** 1920; revised 1929; reinstated Dec. 1945. **National holiday:** Oct. 26. **Heads of government:** Kurt Waldheim, president (since July 1986); Franz Vranitzky, chancellor (since June 1986). **Structure:** bicameral legislature (Federal Assembly—Federal Council, National Council); directly elected president whose functions are largely representational; independent federal judiciary.

**Economy** **Monetary unit:** schilling. **Budget:** (1988) *income:* $34.2 bil.; *expend.:* $39.5 bil. **GDP:** $103.2 bil., $13,600 per capita (1989 est.). **Chief crops:** forest products, cereals, potatoes, sugar beets; 84% self-sufficient. **Livestock:** chickens, pigs, cattle, turkeys, sheep. **Natural resources:** iron ore, crude oil, timber, magnesite, aluminum. **Major industries:** foods, iron, steel, machinery. **Labor force:** 3.0 mil. (1988); foreign laborers number 177,840,

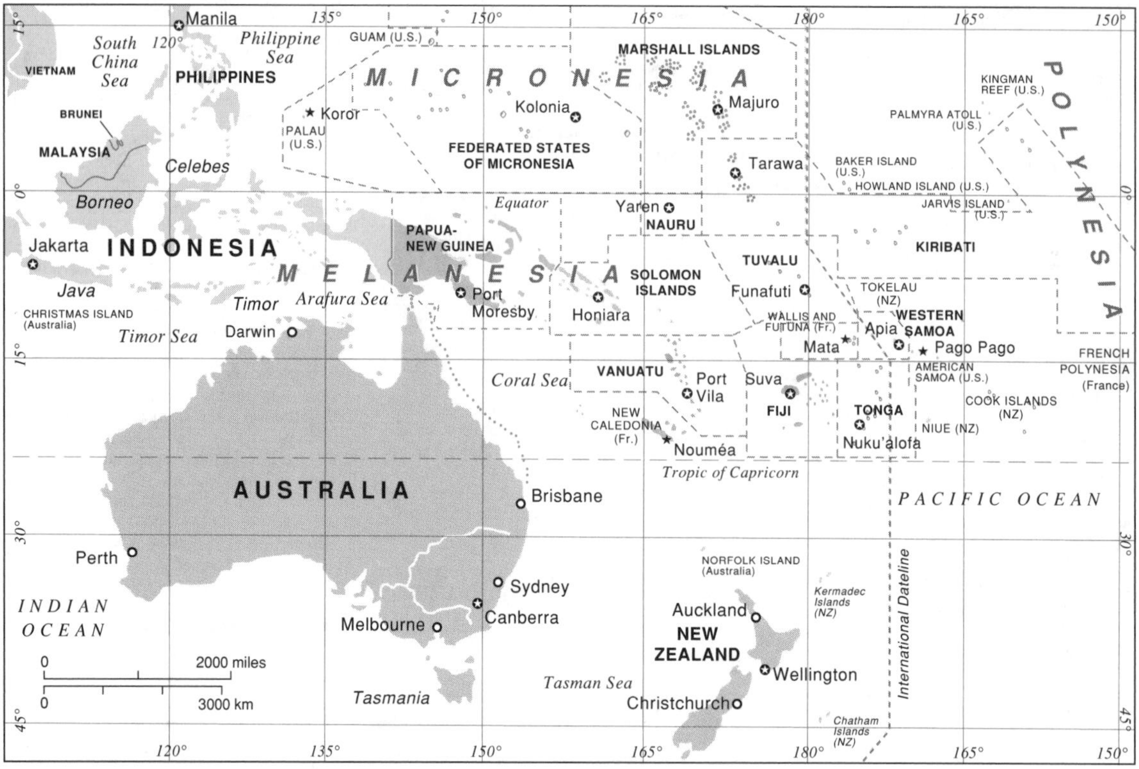

## Top Map (Miller Projection)

VIETNAM

Manila

_South China Sea_

_Philippine Sea_

GUAM (U.S.)

M I C R O N E S I A

MARSHALL ISLANDS

KINGMAN REEF (U.S.)

BRUNEI

PALAU (U.S.)

★ Koror

Kolonia ⊙

⊙ Majuro

PALMYRA ATOLL (U.S.)

MALAYSIA

_Celebes_

FEDERATED STATES OF MICRONESIA

⊙ Tarawa

BAKER ISLAND (U.S.)

HOWLAND ISLAND (U.S.)

_Borneo_

_Equator_

Yaren ⊙

NAURU

JARVIS ISLAND (U.S.)

Jakarta

INDONESIA

_Java_

M E L A N E S I A

PAPUA-NEW GUINEA

⊙ Port Moresby

TUVALU

Funafuti ⊙

SOLOMON ISLANDS

Honiara ⊙

KIRIBATI

TOKELAU (NZ)

WALLIS AND FUTUNA (Fr.)

⊙ Apia

WESTERN SAMOA

Pago Pago ⊙

P O L Y N E S I A

CHRISTMAS ISLAND (Australia)

_Timor_

_Arafura Sea_

_Timor Sea_

Darwin ⊙

Mata ★

AMERICAN SAMOA (U.S.)

FRENCH POLYNESIA (France)

_Coral Sea_

VANUATU

Port Vila ⊙

Suva ⊙

FIJI

TONGA

Nuku'alofa ⊙

COOK ISLANDS (NZ)

NIUE (NZ)

NEW CALEDONIA (Fr.)

Nouméa ⊙

_Tropic of Capricorn_

AUSTRALIA

Brisbane ⊙

_PACIFIC OCEAN_

Perth ⊙

NORFOLK ISLAND (Australia)

_Kermadec Islands (NZ)_

Sydney ⊙

Melbourne ⊙

Canberra ⊙

Auckland ⊙

NEW ZEALAND

⊙ Wellington

_INDIAN OCEAN_

0 — 2000 miles

0 — 3000 km

_Tasmania_

_Tasman Sea_

Christchurch ⊙

_Chatham Islands (NZ)_

_International Dateline_

MILLER PROJECTION

## Bottom Left Map (Lambert's Azimuthal Equal-Area Projection)

LAMBERT'S AZIMUTHAL EQUAL-AREA PROJECTION

_Arafura Sea_

INDONESIA

Darwin ⊙

_Gulf of Carpentaria_

_Great Barrier Reef_

_Coral Sea_

_Timor Sea_

NORTHERN TERRITORY

AUSTRALIA

_Great Sandy Desert_

_Hamersley Range_

_Gibson Desert_

⊙ Alice Springs

QUEENSLAND

_Great Dividing Range_

WESTERN AUSTRALIA

_Great Victoria Desert_

SOUTH AUSTRALIA

_Lake Eyre_

_Great Artesian Basin_

Brisbane ⊙

_Nullarbor Plain_

_Lake Gairdner_

_Lake Torrens_

_Darling R._

Perth ⊙

_Great Australian Bight_

Adelaide ⊙

NEW SOUTH WALES

Sydney ⊙

_Murray R._

Canberra ⊙

_INDIAN OCEAN_

VICTORIA

Melbourne ⊙

0 — 400 miles

0 — 600 km

_Bass Strait_

_Tasman Sea_

TASMANIA

Hobart ⊙

## Bottom Right Map (New Zealand)

_PACIFIC OCEAN_

NORTH ISLAND

Auckland ⊙

Hamilton ⊙

_Tasman Sea_

Palmerston North ⊙

Nelson ⊙

⊙ Wellington

SOUTH ISLAND

_SOUTHERN ALPS_

Christchurch ⊙

Dunedin ⊙

NEW ZEALAND

Invercargill ⊙

0 — 200 miles

0 — 300 km

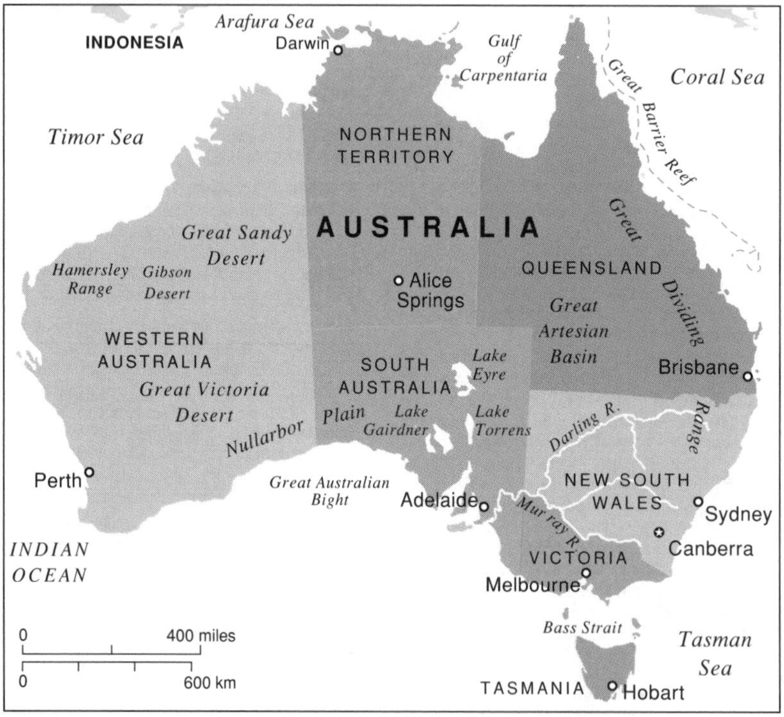

about 6% of the labor force; 56.4% services, 35.4% industry and crafts; 5.4% unemployment (1988); estimated 200,000 Austrians are employed in other European countries; foreign laborers in Austria number 138,700, about 4.3% of labor force (1984). **Exports:** $31.2 bil. (f.o.b., 1989); machinery, equipment, iron, steel, lumber. **Imports:** $37.9 bil. (c.i.f., 1989); petroleum, foodstuffs, machinery, equipment, vehicles. **Major trading partners:** *exports:* 35% W. Germany, 10% Italy, 8% Eastern Europe (excluding USSR), 7% Switzerland, 4% U.S., 3% OPEC; *imports:* 44% W. Germany, 9% Italy, 6% Eastern Europe (excluding USSR), 5% Switzerland, 3% U.S., 2% USSR.

**Intl. Orgs.** EFTA, FAO, GATT, IAEA, IBRD, ICAO, IDA, IFAD, IFC, ILO, IMF, IMO, INTELSAT, INTERPOL, ITU, OECD, UN, UNESCO, UPU, WHO, WIPO, WMO.

The Celtic tribes in what is now Austria were conquered by Rome under Emperor Augustus. After the fall of Rome, it was overrun by Huns, Lombards, Ostrogoths, and Bavarians. In 788 it was incorporated into the empire of Charlemagne. From the ninth to the 13th century, its territory was divided among a variety of feudal domains. In the late 13th century, Austria was reunited under Rudolph I of Habsburg, whose dynasty became synonymous with Austrian history for the next seven centuries. Rudolph's successors steadily enlarged their domain by conquest and marital diplomacy until, by the reign of Charles V (1500–58), they ruled not only the Holy Roman Empire, encompassing most of central Europe, but also Spain, the Netherlands, and all of Spain's colonial possessions.

After the reign of Charles V, the Habsburg empire was split into two branches, one governing Spain, the other the Holy Roman Empire. Habsburg power in Germany declined after the Thirty Years' War (1618–48) but was affirmed in the Danube valley after the defeat of the Turkish siege of Vienna in 1683. The marriage of Maria Teresa to Francis of Lorraine gave rise to the House of Habsburg–Lorraine in 1745. In 1804 the Austrian empire was founded, and two years later, the defunct Holy Roman Empire was abolished. The Ausgleich ("compromise") of 1867 transformed the empire into the Dual Monarchy of Austria-Hungary.

In 1914 the assassination of Archduke Franz Ferdinand, the heir to the Austrian throne, led to the outbreak of World War I, which resulted in a wholesale redrawing of national boundaries in Central Europe. Austria emerged as a small Alpine republic, with about 12 percent of the territory of the old Dual Monarchy. The new republic faced a severe postwar economic crisis, as well as a political stalemate between the Christian Social party and the Social Democratic party, each with the support of about half of the electorate, and each with its own paramilitary organization.

In 1933, as Hitler's National Socialists rose to power in Germany, Austrian Chancellor Engelbert Dollfuss, leader of the Christian Social party, instituted rule by decree and began building a corporate state modeled on Italian fascism. His attempt to disarm the Social Democratic militia led to civil war. The government triumphed, but Dollfuss was assassinated in an attempted coup by Austrian Nazis in July 1934. Hitler finally forced Austrian union with Germany (the Anschluss) in 1938, after which Austria was considered a part of Greater Germany.

Conquered by American and Soviet troops early in 1945, Austria, after World War II, was divided into French, British, American, and Russian zones of occupation, but the occupying powers permitted the formation of a unified national government. A coalition government was formed in November 1945 and recognized by the Western powers in 1946. The occupation ended in 1955 with the signing of the Austrian State Treaty. The four powers withdrew their forces, and Austria pledged itself to a policy of permanent neutrality, with no foreign military alliances or military bases on Austrian territory.

A coalition government continued to 1966, when the People's party under Josef Klaus gained a parliamentary majority. In 1970 the Socialist party under Bruno Kreisky came to power. Socialist dominance continued until 1983, when the Socialists had to form a coalition with the right-wing Freedom party in order to stay in power. Kreisky resigned and was succeeded by Fred Sinowatz.

The titular post of president of Austria became a focus of controversy when former UN secretary general Kurt Waldheim was elected to that post. Campaign revelations linking him to Nazi atrocities in the Balkans brought soul-searching at home and a storm of protest from abroad.

The Austrian economy, decimated after World War I, has flourished in the post–World War II period under a mild form of socialism and with a boost from the American Marshall Plan. Tourism, a highly developed manufacturing sector, and substantial petroleum reserves have contributed to the country's prosperity; economic agreements with the EEC have made Austria a well-integrated participant in the Western European economy.

# Bahamas
## Commonwealth of the Bahamas
**Geography Location:** nearly 700 islands in an archipelago that extends 590 mi. (950 km) SE–NW between Florida and Haiti. Nassau 25°05′N, 77°20′W. **Boundaries:** western Atlantic Ocean to N, E, S, and W. **Total land area:** 5,382 sq. mi. (13,939 sq km). **Coastline:** 2,200 mi. (3,542 km). **Comparative area:** slightly larger than Connecticut. **Land use:** 1% arable land; negl. % permanent crops; negl. % meadows and pastures; 32% forest and woodland; 67% other; includes N.A. % irrigated. **Major cities:** (1980 est.) Nassau (capital) 110,000.

**People Population:** 246,491 (1990). **Nationality:** noun—Bahamian(s); adjective—Bahamian. **Ethnic groups:** 85% black, 15% white. **Languages:** English, some Creole among Haitian immigrants. **Religions:** 29% Baptist, 23% Anglican, 22% Roman Catholic; smaller groups of other Protestants, of Greek Orthodox and Jews.

**Government Type:** independent commonwealth recognizing Elizabeth II as chief of state. **Independence:** July 10, 1973 (from UK). **Constitution:** July 10, 1973. **National holiday:** Independence Day, July 10. **Heads of government:** Sir Henry Milton Taylor, governor-general (since June 1988); Lynden O. Pindling, prime minister (since Jan. 1967). **Structure:** executive (prime minister and cabinet); bicameral legislature (Parliament—16-member appointed Senate, 49-member elected House of Assembly); judiciary.

**Economy Monetary unit:** Bahamian dollar. **Budget:** (1989 est.) *income:* $555.0 mil.; *expend.:* $702.0 mil. **GDP:** $2.4 bil., $9,875 per capita (1988 est.) **Chief crops:** vegetables, tomatoes, pineapples, bananas, citrus fruits; food importer. **Livestock:** sheep, pigs, goats, cattle. **Natural resources:** salt, argonite, timber. **Major industries:** banking, tourism, cement. **Labor force:** 132,600 (1986); 30% government, 25% hotels and restaurants, 10% business services; 30% unemployment (1986). **Exports:** $733 mil. (f.o.b., 1987); pharmaceuticals, cement, rum, crawfish. **Imports:** $1.7 bil. (f.o.b., 1987); foodstuffs, manufactured goods, mineral fuels. **Major trading partners:** (1988); *exports:* 90% U.S., 10% UK; *imports:* 30% Iran, 20% Nigeria, 10% U.S., 10% EC, 10% Gabon.

**Intl. Orgs.** Commonwealth, FAO, G-77, GATT (de facto), IBRD, ICAO, ILO, IMF, IMO, INTERPOL, ITU, NAM, OAS, UN, UNESCO, UPU, WHO, WIPO, WMO.

Christopher Columbus made his first landfall in the Americas in the Bahamas Oct. 12, 1492. Though the Spanish never settled the islands, they enslaved and removed to Hispaniola 40,000 of the indigenous Arawaks by 1508. Their shallow seas (*baja mar*) made the islands a haven for pirates in the 17th century—as well as during the Civil War, Prohibition, and for drug smugglers today.

British colonization of the Bahamas began in 1629 and continued slowly over the next two centuries, though it got a big boost from loyalists and their slaves—freed in 1834—during the American Revolution. High unemployment continues to be a problem, and parliament is expected to relax restrictions on offshore banking to stem the flight of international capital prompted by allegations of government corruption and involvement in drug trafficking.

# Bahrain
## State of Bahrain
**Geography Location:** group of 35 islands in western Persian Gulf. Manama 26°17′N, 50°33′E. **Boundaries:** Saudi Arabia about 15 mi. (24 km) to W and Qatar about 17 mi. (28 km) to SE. **Total land area:** 267 sq. mi. (691 sq km). **Coastline:** 161 mi. (259 km). **Comparative area:** slightly less than 3.5 times size of Washington, D.C. **Land use:** 2% arable land; 2% per-

manent crops; 6% meadows and pastures; 0% forest and woodland; 90% other; includes negl. % irrigated. **Major cities:** (1981 census) Manama (capital) 121,986; Muharraq Town 61,853.

**People Population:** 520,186 (1990). **Nationality:** noun—Bahraini(s); adjective—Bahraini. **Ethnic groups:** 63% Bahraini, 13% Asian, 10% other Arab, 8% Iranian, 6% other. **Languages:** Arabic (official), Farsi, Urdu; English widely spoken. **Religions:** 70% Shia Muslim, 30% Sunni Muslim.

**Government Type:** traditional monarchy. **Independence:** Aug. 15, 1973 (from UK). **Constitution:** May 26, 1973 (effective Dec. 1973). **National holiday:** Dec. 16. **Heads of government:** Isa bin Sulman al-Khalifa, amir (since Nov. 1961); Khalifa bin Sulman al-Khalifa, prime minister (since Jan. 1970). **Structure:** amir rules with help of cabinet led by prime minister; amir dissolved National Assembly (Aug. 1975) and suspended constitutional provision for election of assembly; independent judiciary.

**Economy Monetary unit:** Bahrain dinar. **Budget:** (1987) *income:* $1,136 mil.; *expend.:* $880 mil. **GDP:** $3.5 bil., $7,550 per capita. **Chief crops:** not self-sufficient in food production; produces some fruits and vegetables; engages in dairy and poultry farming and in shrimping and fishing. **Livestock:** goats, sheep, cattle. **Natural resources:** oil, associated and nonassociated natural gas, fish. **Major industries:** petroleum processing and refining, aluminum smelting and fabrication. **Labor force:** 140,000 (1982); 85% industry and commerce (note: 42% of labor force is Bahraini). **Exports:** $2.4 bil. (f.o.b., 1988); 80% petroleum, 7% aluminum. **Imports:** $2.5 bil. (f.o.b., 1988); 59% nonoil, 41% crude oil. **Major trading partners:** *exports:* U.S., UAE, Japan, Singapore, Saudi Arabia; *imports:* UK, Saudi Arabia, U.S., Japan.

**Intl. Orgs.** Arab League, FAO, G-77, GATT (de facto), IBRD, ICAO, ILO, IMF, IMO, INTERPOL, NAM, UN, UNESCO, UPU, WHO.

Bahrain has been an entrepôt of trade between Arabia and India since the second millenium B.C. The Portuguese fortified Bahrain in the 16th century but were driven out by the Persian Shah Abbas I early in the 17th century. At the end of the 18th century, it became an Arab sheikhdom within the Ottoman Empire.

Bahrain entered into treaty relations with Great Britain in 1820 and became a British protectorate in 1861. After British forces withdrew from the gulf, the nation became an independent emirate, in August 1971, under Amir Isa bin Sulman al-Khalifa, who came to the throne in 1961.

Oil reserves—first discovered in 1932—were largely depleted by the mid-1970s. The economy now has diversified to include oil refining, aluminum smelting, international banking, and shipping services. Bahrain has close relations with Saudi Arabia; a causeway permits direct-road communication between the two countries.

---

# Bangladesh
## People's Republic of Bangladesh

**Geography Location:** southern Asia. **Boundaries:** India to N, E, and W; Myanmar to E, Bay of Bengal to S. **Total land area:** 55,598 sq. mi. (143,998 sq km). **Coastline:** 360 mi. (580 km). **Comparative area:** between Arkansas and Wisconsin. **Land use:** 67% arable land; 2% permanent crops; 4% meadows and pastures; 16% forest and woodland; 11% other; includes 14% irrigated. **Major cities:** (1981 census) Dhaka (formerly Dacca) (capital) 3,430,312; Chittagong 1,391,877; Khulna 646,359; Rajshahi 253,740; Comilla 184,132.

**People Population:** 118,433,062 (1990). **Nationality:** noun—Bangladeshi(s); adjective—Bangladesh. **Ethnic groups:** 98% Bengali, 250,000 Biharis, less than 1 mil. tribals. **Languages:** Bangla (official); English widely used. **Religions:** 83% Muslim, 16% Hindu, less than 1% Buddhist, Christian, and other.

**Government Type:** republic. **Independence:** Dec. 16, 1971 (from Pakistan). **Constitution:** Nov. 4, 1972, effective Dec. 16, 1972, suspended following coup of Mar. 24, 1982, restored Nov. 10, 1986; civil liberties curtailed under Nov. 27, 1987, State of Emergency Declaration. **National holiday:** National Day, Mar. 26; Victory Day, Dec. 16. **Heads of government:** Ms. Begum Khaleda Zia, prime minister (since Feb. 1991). **Structure:** presidential system of government, 330-member unicameral legislature (parliament), and independent judiciary; president has substantial control over judiciary; parliament dissolved on Dec. 6, 1987.

**Economy Monetary unit:** taka. Budget: (1989) *income:* $1.8 bil.; *expend.:* $3.3 bil. **GDP:** $20.6 bil., $180 per capita. **Chief crops:** large-scale subsistence farming, heavily dependent on Monsoon rain; main crops are jute, tea, and rice; grain, cotton, and oilseed shortages. **Livestock:** chickens, ducks, cattle, goats, buffalo. **Natural resources:** natural gas, uranium, arable land, timber. **Major industries:** jute manufactures, food processing, cotton textiles. **Labor force:** 35.1 mil. (1986); extensive export of labor to Saudi Arabia, UAE, Oman, and Kuwait; 74% agriculture, 15% services, 11% industry and commerce, unemployment 30% (est.). **Exports:** $1.3 bil. (f.o.b., 1989 est.); jute, shrimp, manufacturing, leather, tea. **Imports:** $3.1 bil. (c.i.f., 1989 est.); food, petroleum and other energy, nonfood consumer goods, semiprocessed goods. **Major trading partners:** *exports:* 24% U.S., 22% Western Europe, 9% Middle East, 8% Japan, 7% Eastern Europe; *imports:* 18% Western Europe, 14% Japan, 9% Middle East, 8% U.S.

**Intl. Orgs.** Colombo Plan, Commonwealth, FAO, G-77, GATT, IAEA, IBRD, ICAO, IDA, IFAD, IFC, ILO, IMF, IMO, INTELSAT, INTERPOL, ITU, NAM, UN, UNCTAD, UNESCO, UPU, WHO, WMO.

Located on the alluvial plain of the Ganges River northeast of India, Bengal was ruled by Buddhist kings from the eighth to 12th cen-

turies. Conquered by Muslim invaders around 1200, many inhabitants converted to Islam and Bengal became part of the Moghul empire in the 16th century. The British East India Company established a settlement in 1642, and by 1750 all of Bengal was under British rule. The formerly diverse agricultural economy became dominated by export crops of opium and jute, while rice continued to be grown in the fertile delta. The region's trade flowed through the British-built city of Calcutta.

With Indian independence in 1947, Bengal was partitioned along religious lines, Hindu West Bengal (including Calcutta) remaining with India and Muslim East Bengal becoming the eastern province of Pakistan. In the elections of 1971, the Bengali Awami League gained control of Pakistan's National Assembly. Seating of the new National Assembly was postponed, and riots broke out in East Pakistan. Troops from West Pakistan were sent to quell the riots on May 25; the following day East Pakistan declared its independence as Bangladesh. Civil war followed; 10 million refugees fled to India. Following Indian intervention, Pakistan acknowledged Bangladesh's independence on Dec. 15.

Politics in Bangladesh have been dominated by coups and a series of military governments; the first president, Sheik Mujibur Rahman, was assassinated in 1974. Opposition unrest in December 1990 forced the resignation of Hussain Mohammad Ershad, president since a 1982 military coup. In national elections in February 1991, the Bangladesh Nationalist party (BNP) of Begum Khaleda Zia, widow of former president Ziaur Rahman (assassinated in 1981), won 138 of 330 parliamentary seats. The BNP promotes an Islamic state, free enterprise and privatization, and supports a constitutional change that would put the prime minister in charge of the legislative agenda and make the presidency a ceremonial post.

A secessionist guerrilla movement in the Chittagong Hill tracts was defused in 1989 after 15 years of warfare when the government granted the region greater local autonomy.

Plagued by overpopulation, a decline in the world market for jute, and frequent catastrophic floods—one in 1975 killed an estimated 500,000 people, and another in 1991 approximately 130,000—Bangladesh remains one of the world's poorest countries and depends heavily on foreign aid.

---

# Barbados

**Geography Location:** easternmost of Caribbean islands, about 200 mi. (320 km) NE of Trinidad. Bridgetown 13°06′N, 59°36′W. **Boundaries:** Atlantic Ocean. **Total land area:** 166 sq. mi. (430 sq km). **Coastline:** 60 mi. (97 km). **Comparative area:** slightly less than 2.5 times size of Washington, D.C. **Land use:** 77% arable land; 0% permanent crops; 9% meadows and pastures; 0% forest and woodland; 14% other; includes N.A. % irrigated. **Major cities:** (1980 census) Bridgetown (capital) 7,517.

**People Population:** 262,688 (1990). **Nationality:** noun—Barbadian(s); adjective—Barbadian. **Ethnic groups:** 80% African, 16%

mixed, 4% European. **Languages:** English. **Religions:** 70% Anglican, 9% Methodist, 4% Roman Catholic, 17% other, including Moravian.

**Government Type:** independent sovereign state within commonwealth recognizing Elizabeth II as chief of state. **Independence:** Nov. 30, 1966 (from UK). **Constitution:** Nov. 30, 1966. **National holiday:** Independence Day, Nov. 30. **Heads of government:** Dame Ruth Nita Barrow, governor-general (since June 1990); Erskine Sandiford, prime minister (since June 1987). **Structure:** cabinet headed by prime minister; bicameral legislature (Parliament—21-member appointed Senate and 27-member elected House of Assembly).

**Economy Monetary unit:** Barbados dollar. **Budget:** (1986) *income:* $476 mil.; *expend.:* $543 mil. **GDP:** $1.3 mil., $5,250 per capita (1988 est.). **Chief crops:** sugarcane, subsistence foods. **Livestock:** sheep, pigs, goats, cattle. **Natural resources:** crude oil, fishing, natural gas. **Major industries:** tourism, sugar, light manufacturing. **Labor force:** 112,300 (1985 est.); 37% services and government, 22% commerce, 22% manufacturing and construction. **Exports:** $173 mil. (f.o.b., 1988); sugar and molasses, rum, electrical components, clothing. **Imports:** $582 mil. (f.o.b., 1988); foodstuffs, consumer durables, machinery, fuels. **Major trading partners:** (1984) *exports:* 30% U.S., 30% CARICOM, UK, Puerto Rico, Canada. *imports:* 34% U.S., CARICOM, UK, Canada, Japan.

**Intl. Orgs.** Commonwealth, FAO, G-77, GATT, IBRD, ICAO, IFAD, IFC, ILO, IMF, IMO, INELSAT, INTERPOL, ITU, NAM, OAS, UN, UNESCO, UPU, WHO, WMO.

Barbados is the only Caribbean island not to have changed hands prior to independence. Although the Spanish removed virtually all the indigenous Arawaks of Barbados by the mid-1500s, the island was not claimed until the British arrived in the 1620s. Tobacco, cotton, and sugarcane—harvested with slave labor until 1833—were mainstays of the economy. The 1966 constitution mandates the promotion of economic equality among Barbadians, and the country is fairly prosperous relative to other Caribbean states. The government actively supports multilateral trade and investment with the Caribbean Community (CARICOM).

## Belgium
### Kingdom of Belgium

**Geography Location:** northwestern Europe. **Boundaries:** Netherlands to N, Luxembourg and Germany to E, France to S, and North Sea to W. **Total land area:** 11,783 sq. mi. (31,519 sq km). **Coastline:** 40 mi. (64 km). **Comparative area:** slightly larger than Maryland. **Land use:** 24% arable land; 1% permanent crops; 20% meadows and pastures; 21% forest and woodland; 34% other; includes negl. % irrigated. **Major cities:** (1987) Bruxelles (Brussels—capital) 970,346; Antwerpen (Anvers, Antwerp) 476,044; Gent (Gand, Ghent)

232,620; Charleroi 208,938; Liège (Luik) 200,312.

**People Population:** 9,909,285 (1990). **Nationality:** noun—Belgian(s); adjective—Belgian. **Ethnic groups:** 55% Fleming, 33% Walloon, 12% mixed or other. **Languages:** 56% Flemish (Dutch), 32% French, 1% German; 11% legally bilingual; divided along ethnic lines. **Religions:** 75% Roman Catholic; remainder Protestant or other.

**Government Type:** constitutional monarchy. **Independence:** Oct. 4, 1830 (from Netherlands). **Constitution:** Feb. 7, 1831; last revised Aug. 8–9, 1980. **National holiday:** National Day, July 21. **Heads of government:** Baudouin I, king (since Aug. 1950); Wilfried Martens, prime minister (since Apr. 1979, with 10–month interruption in 1981). **Structure:** executive branch consists of king and cabinet; cabinet responsible to bicameral parliament (Senate and Chamber of Representatives); independent judiciary; coalition governments are usual.

**Economy Monetary unit:** Belgian franc. **Budget:** (1989) *income:* $45.0 bil.; *expend.:* $55.3 bil. **GDP:** $136 bil., $13,700 per capita. **Chief crops:** grains, sugar beets, flax, potatoes, other vegetables; livestock production predominates. **Livestock:** pigs, cattle, sheep, horses, goats. **Natural resources:** coal, natural gas. **Major industries:** engineering, metal products, processed food, beverages, chemicals. **Labor force:** 4 mil. (1987); 58% services, 37% industry; 10.8% unemployment. **Exports:** (Belgium-Luxembourg Economic Union) $100.3 bil. (f.o.b., 1989); iron, steel, transportation equipment, tractors, diamonds. **Imports:** (Belgium-Luxembourg Economic Union) $100.1 bil. (c.i.f., 1989); fuels, grains, chemicals. **Major trading partners:** (Belgium-Luxembourg Economic Union, 1988) *exports:* 74% EC, 5% U.S., 2% communist countries; *imports:* 72% EC, 5% U.S., 4% oil-exporting developing countries, 3% communist countries.

**Intl. Orgs.** EC, FAO, GATT, IAEA, IBRD, ICAO, IDA, IFAD, IFC, ILO, IMF, IMO, INTELSAT, INTERPOL, ITU, NATO, OAS (observer), OECD, UN, UNESCO, UPU, WHO, WIPO, WMO.

The country now known as Belgium was, during the Middle Ages, part of the powerful duchy of Burgundy. By marriage and diplomacy, the "Low Countries" became part of the Habsburg empire in 1482 (see "Austria"). In a struggle lasting from the late 16th century to the Treaty of Westphalia in 1648, the northern part of that region (Netherlands) became independent, but the southern portion remained part of the Habsburg empire—under the Spanish branch until 1715, then under the Austrian branch until the defeat of Napoleon in 1815. The Congress of Vienna attached the lands to an enlarged Kingdom of the Netherlands.

In 1830 the Belgians revolted against the Dutch, and in 1831 the Treaty of London recognized an independent Kingdom of Belgium. Throughout the 19th century, its unity was precarious, as the country was bitterly divided politically between Catholic and Liberal parties, and ethnically between Dutch-speaking Flemings and French-speaking Walloons.

In 1885 Belgium became a colonial power in Africa with Leopold II's establishment of the Congo Free State (later the Belgian Congo), which gained independence in 1960 as Zaire.

Belgium was a major battleground during World War I. Its boundaries were reestablished in 1919 by the Treaty of Versailles. When German troops of Hitler's Third Reich overran Belgium in May 1940, King Leopold III quickly signed an armistice, hoping to placate Hitler and avert further fighting. But the Belgian government fled to England, repudiated the armistice, and joined the Allies. The Germans controlled Belgium until the liberation of Brussels in September 1944.

Belgium made a swift postwar recovery. But the political atmosphere was poisoned by the issue of what to do about wartime collaborators up to and including the king. A referendum in 1950 narrowly approved Leopold III's return to the throne, but he was persuaded to abdicate in 1951 in favor of his son, Baudouin I. Belgium became a founding member of the United Nations, the Benelux Pact, NATO, and the EC (Brussels is the seat of the European Parliament).

Belgium has a flourishing economy with a highly modernized industrial sector complemented by tourism and agriculture. The issue of language dominates politics; since the 1960s, Belgium has devolved into a de facto confederation of Flemish-, French-, and German-speaking regions, with Brussels a multilingual region unto itself. The country's complex coalition politics are dominated by three major parties: Christian Socialists, Socialists, and Liberals.

## Belize

**Geography Location:** northeastern coast of Central America. **Boundaries:** Mexico to N, Caribbean Sea to E and S and W, Guatemala to S and W. **Total land area:** 8,867 sq. mi. (22,965 sq km). **Coastline:** 240 mi. (386 km). **Comparative area:** between Massachusetts and New Hampshire. **Land use:** 2% arable land; negl. % permanent crops; 2% meadows and pastures; 44% forest and woodland; 52% other; includes negl. % irrigated. **Major cities:** (1985 est.) Belmopan (capital) 4,500; Belize City 47,000; Corozal 10,000; Orange Walk 9,600; Dangringa 7,700.

**People Population:** 219,737 (1990). **Nationality:** noun—Belizean(s); adjective—Belizean. **Ethnic groups:** 39.7% Creole, 33.1% mestizo, 9.5% Maya, 7.6% Garifuna. **Languages:** English (official), Spanish, Maya, Garifuna (Carib). **Religions:** 60% Roman Catholic, 40% Protestant (Anglican, Seventh-Day Adventist, Methodist, Baptist, Jehovah's Witnesses, Mennonite).

**Government Type:** parliamentary. **Independence:** Sept. 21, 1981 (from UK). **Constitution:** Sept. 21, 1981. **National holiday:** N.A. **Heads of government:** Dame Minita Gordon, governor-general (since Dec. 1981); George Cadle Price, prime minister (since Sept. 1989).

**Structure:** cabinet; bicameral legislature (National Assembly—electoral redistricting in Oct. 1984 expanded House of Representatives from 18 to 28 seats; eight-member appointed Senate; either house may choose its speaker or president, respectively, from outside its membership); judiciary.

**Economy** Monetary unit: Belizean dollar. **Budget:** (1988 est.) *income:* $94.6 mil.; *expend.:* $74.3 mil. **GDP:** $225.6 mil., $1,285 per capita (1989 est.). **Chief crops:** sugarcane, citrus fruits, corn, molasses, rice, beans, bananas; net importer of food; illegal producer of cannabis for international drug trade. **Livestock:** cattle, pigs, horses, mules, sheep, goats. **Natural resources:** arable land potential, timber, fish. **Major industries:** sugar refining, clothing, timber, and forest products. **Labor force:** 51,500 (1985); 30% agriculture, 16% services, 15.4% government, 11.2% commerce; shortage of skilled labor and all types of technical personnel; over 14% unemployment. **Exports:** $75 mil. (1986); sugar, garments, seafood, molasses, citrus. **Imports:** $110 mil. (1986); machinery and transportation equipment, food, manufactured goods, fuels, chemicals. **Major trading partners:** (1987) *exports:* 47% U.S., UK, Trinidad and Tobago, Canada; *imports:* 55% U.S., UK, Netherlands Antilles, Mexico.

**Intl. Orgs.** Commonwealth, FAO, G-77, GATT, IBRD, IDA, IFAD, IFC, ILO, IMF, ITU, UN, UNESCO, UPU, WHO, WMO.

During the 1700s, Spain held sovereignty over Belize but never attempted to settle it. The British gradually did settle there, however, and in 1862, British Honduras, as it was called, became a Crown colony. Although Britain granted Belize independence in 1981, Guatemala claims sovereignty over the area. Due to the threat of hostilities between the two countries, Belize's government, headed by Prime Minister Manuel Esquivel, is currently backed by British troops. High unemployment rates continue to be a problem for Belize.

## Benin
### People's Republic of Benin
**Geography** Location: western coast of Africa. **Boundaries:** Burkina Faso and Niger to N, Nigeria to E, Gulf of Guinea to S, Togo to W. **Total land area:** 43,484 sq. mi. (112,622 sq km). **Coastline:** 75 mi. (121 km). **Comparative area:** between Tennessee and Pennsylvania. **Land use:** 12% arable land; 4% permanent crops; 4% meadows and pastures; 35% forest and woodland; 45% other; includes negl. % irrigated. **Major cities:** (1981 est.) Porto-Novo (capital) 144,000; Cotonou 383,250.

**People** Population: 4,673,964 (1990). **Nationality:** noun—Beninese (sing., pl.); adjective—Beninese. **Ethnic groups:** 99% African (Fon, Adja, Yoruba, Bariba); 5,500 Europeans. **Languages:** French (official); Fon and Yoruba in south; six major tribal languages in north. **Religions:** 70% indigenous beliefs, 15% Muslim, 15% Christian.

**Government** Type: Soviet-modeled civilian government. **Independence:** Aug. 1, 1960 (from France). **Constitution:** Nov. 1990. **National holiday:** Nov. 30. **Heads of government:** Nicéphore Soglo, president (since Apr. 1991). **Structure:** National Executive Council; National Assembly.

**Economy** Monetary unit: Communauté Financière Africaine (CFA) franc. **Budget:** (1989) *income:* $168 mil.; *expend.:* $317 mil. **GNP:** $1.7 bil., $335 per capita (1988). **Chief crops:** cash crops—palm oil, peanuts, cotton, coffee, shea nuts, tobacco; food crops—corn, cassava, yams, rice, sorghum, millet. **Livestock:** sheep, goats, cattle, pigs, horses. **Natural resources:** small offshore oil deposits, limestone, marble, timber. **Major industries:** palm oil and palm kernel oil processing, textiles, beverages. **Labor force:** 1.9 mil. (1987); 60% agriculture, 2% industrial sector, remainder employed in transport, commerce, and public services; 49% of population of working age. **Exports:** $226 mil. (f.o.b., 1988); palm products, cotton, crude oil, cocoa. **Imports:** $413 mil. (f.o.b., 1988); foodstuffs, beverages, tobacco, petroleum products. **Major trading partners:** *exports:* 36% W. Germany, 16% France, 14% Spain, 8% Italy, 7% UK; *imports:* 34% France, 10% Netherlands, 7% Japan, 6% Italy, 5% U.S.

**Intl. Orgs.** FAO, G-77, GATT, IBRD, ICAO, IDA, IFAD, ILO, IMF, IMO, INTERPOL, ITU, NAM, UN, UNESCO, UPU, WHO, WIPO, WMO.

Although the early history of Benin is sketchy, a number of kingdoms had appeared in the region by the 11th century, and it was a center of wealth and power by the 1300s. In the 16th century, the Allada kingdom was founded in the south. In 1625, three brothers divided their power between Allada, Adjatché (Porto Novo), and Abomey. Under Ouegbadja (r. 1645–85) the latter, known as Dahomey, predominated. Much of its wealth derived from contact with Europeans, and especially the slave trade, which continued until 1885.

European contact began with the arrival of the Portuguese in 1485. Although traders and missionaries were established at Ouidah and Porto Novo in the 1500s, European influence remained slight. Dahomey expansion continued well into the 19th century. A commercial treaty with the French was signed in 1842, and relations between Dahomeyans and European soon worsened. Outright hostilities began under Behanzin (r. 1858–89), who was defeated by the French, and in 1893 the French assimilated Abomey, Allada, and Porto Novo into the colony of Dahomey.

Independence from French rule came in 1960, followed by more than a decade of coups until Mathieu Kerekou came to power in 1972. Kerekou established a Marxist regime, nationalizing large private businesses and abolishing opposition parties. By 1989, the economy was a shambles and most trade was conducted on the black market.

In December, there were demonstrations calling for Kerekou's resignation. The government abandoned Marxism and former World Bank official Nicéphore Soglo was named

prime minister. A new constitution was approved in a referendum in November 1990, and legislative elections were held in February 1991. In March, Soglo defeated Kerekou for the presidency. Kerekou was the first president in 30 years of postcolonial African history removed from office by the electorate.

## Bhutan
### Kingdom of Bhutan
**Geography** Location: Himalaya mountains in southern Asia. **Boundaries:** China to N and W, India to S and E. **Total land area:** 17,954 sq. mi. (46,500 sq km). **Coastline:** none. **Comparative area:** between Maryland and West Virginia. **Land use:** 2% arable land; negl. % permanent crops; 5% meadows and pastures; 70% forest and woodland; 23% other. **Major cities:** (1985 est.) Timphu (capital) 30,000; Phuntsholing 30,000.

**People** Population: 1,565,969 (1990). **Nationality:** noun—Bhutanese (sing., pl.); adjective—Bhutanese. **Ethnic groups:** 60% Bhote, 25% ethnic Nepalese, 15% indigenous or migrant tribes. **Languages:** Dzongkha (official), various Tibetan dialects, various Nepalese dialects. **Religions:** 75% Lamaistic Buddhism, 25% Indian- and Nepalese-influenced Hinduism.

**Government** Type: monarchy; special treaty relationship with India. **Independence:** Aug. 8, 1949 (from India). **Constitution:** no written constitution or bill of rights. **National holiday:** Dec. 17. **Heads of government:** Jigme Singye Wangchuk, king (since July 1972). **Structure:** appointed ministers; 150-member indirectly elected National Assembly consisting of 110 village elders or heads of family, 10 monastic representatives, and 30 senior government administrators.

**Economy** Monetary unit: ngultrums and rupees are legal tender. **Budget:** (1989 est.) *income:* $99.0 mil.; *expend.:* $128.0 mil. **GDP:** $273 mil., $199 per capita (1988 est.). **Chief crops:** rice, corn, barley, wheat, potatoes. **Livestock:** cattle, poultry, pigs, sheep, yaks. **Natural resources:** timber, hydropower, gypsum, calcium carbide. **Major industries:** cement, chemical products, mining. Labor force: (1983) 95% agriculture, 1% industry and commerce, massive lack of skilled labor. **Exports:** $70.9 mil. (f.o.b., 1989); cardamom, gypsum, timber, handicrafts. **Imports:** $138.3 mil. (1989 est.); fuels and lubricants, grain, machinery and parts, vehicles. **Major trading partner:** India (93% of exports, 67% of imports).

**Intl. Orgs.** Colombo Plan, FAO, G-77, IBRD, IDA, IFAD, IMF, NAM, UN, UNESCO, UPU, WHO.

A Tibetan-style Lamaistic Buddhist theocracy was established in this Himalayan enclave in the 16th century. The region came under the domination of the British raj in India in 1865, and Britain established a protectorate in 1910. A 1949 treaty with India granted independence to Bhutan. The present Druk Gyalpo, or Precious Ruler of the Dragon People, is the fourth in a dynasty dating from 1907. He is slowly introducing reforms into his feudal, medieval country by broadening educational opportunities and compelling Buddhist monks to take up social work outside their monasteries.

## Bolivia
### Republic of Bolivia

**Geography Location:** landlocked country in central South America. **Boundaries:** Brazil to N and E, Paraguay and Argentina to S, Chile and Peru to W. **Total land area:** 424,164 sq. mi. (1,098,581 sq km). **Coastline:** none. **Comparative area:** between Texas and Alaska. **Land use:** 3% arable land; negl. % permanent crops; 25% meadows and pastures; 52% forest and woodland; 20% other; includes negl. % irrigated. **Major cities:** (1987 est.) La Paz (administrative capital) 1,013,688; Sucre (legal capital and seat of judiciary) 92,917; Santa Cruz de la Sierra 577,803; Cochabamba 360,446; Oruro 189,278; Potosí 111,215.

**People Population:** 6,706,854 (1990). **Nationality:** noun—Bolivian(s); adjective—Bolivian. **Ethnic groups:** 30% Quechua, 25% Aymara, 25–30% mixed, 5–15% European. **Languages:** Spanish, Quechua, and Aymara (all official). **Religions:** 95% Roman Catholic; active Protestant minority, especially Methodist.

**Government Type:** republic. **Independence:** Aug, 6, 1825 (from Spain). **Constitution:** Feb. 2, 1967. **National holiday:** Independence Day, Aug. 6. **Heads of government:** Jaime Paz Zamora, president (since Aug. 1989); **Structure:** executive; bicameral legislature (National Congress—Senate and Chamber of Deputies); congress began meeting again in Oct. 1982; judiciary.

**Economy Monetary unit:** boliviano. **Budget:** (1987) *income:* $2.8 bil.; *expend.:* $2.8 bil. **GNP:** $4.6 bil., $680 per capita (1987 est.) **Chief crops:** potatoes, corn, rice, sugarcane, yucca, bananas, coffee; imports significant quantities of wheat; illegal producer of coca for international drug trade. **Livestock:** sheep, cattle, goats, pigs, asses. **Natural resources:** tin, natural gas, crude oil, zinc, tungsten. **Major industries:** mining, smelting, petroleum refining. **Labor force:** 1.7 mil. (1983); 50% agriculture, 26% services and utilities, 10% manufacturing, 10% other; 11% unemployment (1988). **Exports:** $634 mil. (f.o.b., 1989); 45% metals, 32% natural gas, coffee, soybeans, sugar. **Imports:** $786 mil. (c.i.f., 1989); food, petroleum, consumer goods, capital goods. **Major trading partners:** *exports:* 23% U.S., Argentina. *imports:* 15% U.S.

**Intl. Orgs.** FAO, G-77, IAEA, IBRD, ICAO, IDA, IFAD, IFC, ILO, IMF, INTELSAT, INTERPOL, ITU, NAM, OAS, UN, UNESCO, UPU, WHO, WMO.

The Incan empire conquered the region that is now Bolivia in the 13th century. The Spanish discovered the fabulous silver deposits of the region and established their presence in the area in the cities of Sucre (1538) and Potosí (1545). From the early colonial period on, Bolivia—then called Upper Peru and part of the Viceroyalty of Peru—depended heavily on the export of minerals. The exploitation of tin and later oil and natural gas has had an important economic and political impact on the country's development.

In 1776, Upper Peru was transferred to the new Viceroyalty of La Plata centered in Buenos Aires. Upper Peru began agitating for independence in 1809, but it was not until liberation by Símon Bolívar (for whom the country was renamed) in 1825 that Bolivia became the last Spanish possession in South America to achieve independence. During 1836–39, Peru formed a brief union with Bolivia, until Chile broke up the confederation.

Bolivia has lost much of its original territory to its neighbors. The dictator Mariano Melgarejo sold large chunks of territory from 1865 to 1871. After the War of the Pacific (1879–84), Bolivia lost its access to the sea. And in the 1932–35 Chaco War with Paraguay, Bolivia lost more territory in the east.

In addition to its topographical and economic fragmentation, Bolivia has suffered from Indian/non-Indian racial and cultural divisions, and political rivalry between the elites from the Potosí region and those from La Paz and Santa Cruz. Conservatives of the silver-mining southern region of Potosí controlled the government until their ouster in 1898 by the Liberal tin interests of the La Paz region, who presided over a period of stable republican politics that lasted until the Great Depression and the Chaco War.

One of the results of the Chaco War was the fragmentation of the Bolivian military into competing factions as the factions took sides in the struggle for power between conservative landowners and middle-class reformers; this caused extreme instability of the political order right up until the Bolivian National Revolution in 1952. In 1941 the National Revolutionary Movement (MNR) was formed with the aim of transferring control of the country from conservative landowning elites to the middle sectors. The leadership of the movement found itself outpaced by revolts sponsored by workers and peasants; the MNR therefore incorporated these elements into its program. When the 1952 revolution brought the MNR to power, its leadership, which included the future four-time president Victor Paz Estenssoro, embarked on a reformist political program. The military overthrew the MNR in 1964, and it has since fragmented, but Paz Estenssoro was again elected to the presidency in 1985. Jaime Paz Zamora, leader of the Movement of the Revolutionary Left, gained the presidency in 1989.

Although tin used to be a major export, the mines have closed and the country is heavily reliant on foreign aid—$300 million in 1990. Exports of coca leaves to Colombian drug processors are thought to amount to $1.5 billion annually.

## Botswana
### Republic of Botswana

**Geography Location:** landlocked country in southern Africa. **Boundaries:** Namibia to N and W, Zimbabwe to NE, South Africa to SE and S. **Total land area:** 224,711 sq. mi. (582,000 sq km). **Coastline:** none. **Comparative area:** about size of Texas. **Land use:** 2% arable land; 0% permanent crops; 75% meadows and pastures; 2% forest and woodland; 21% other; includes negl. % irrigated. **Major cities:** (1981 census) Gaborone (capital) 59,657; Francistown 31,065; Selebi-Pikwe 29,469; Serowe 23,661; Mahalapye 20,712.

**People Population:** 1,224,527 (1990). **Nationality:** noun and adjective—Motswana (sing.), Batswana (pl.). **Ethnic groups:** 95% Batswana; 4% Kalanga, Basarwa, and Kgalagadi; 1% white. **Languages:** English (official), Setswana. **Religions:** 50% Christian, 50% indigenous beliefs.

**Government Type:** parliamentary republic. **Independence:** Sept. 30, 1966 (from UK). **Constitution:** Mar. 1965, effective Sept. 30, 1966. **National holiday:** Botswana Day, Sept. 30. **Heads of government:** Quett K.J. Masire, president (since July 1980). **Structure:** executive—president appoints and presides over cabinet; legislative—bicameral legislature (National Assembly with 34 popularly elected members and four members elected by the 34 representatives; House of Chiefs with deliberative powers only); judiciary—local courts administer customary law; high court and subordinate courts have criminal jurisdiction; court of appeal.

**Economy Monetary unit:** pula. **Budget:** (1990 est.) *income:* $1.2 bil.; *expend.:* $1.0 bil. **GDP:** $1.87 bil., $1,600 per capita. **Chief crops:** corn, sorghum, millet, cowpeas; heavy dependence on imported food. **Livestock:** cattle, goats, sheep, donkeys, horses. **Natural resources:** diamonds, copper, nickel, salt, soda ash. **Major industries:** livestock processing; mining of diamonds, copper, nickel, coal, salt, soda ash, potash; tourism. **Labor force:** 400,000; 163,000 formal-sector employees (1988 est.); most others engaged in cattle raising and subsistence agriculture; 40,000 formal-sector employees spend at least six to nine months per year as wage earners in South Africa (1980); 25% unemployment (1987). **Exports:** $1.3 bil. (f.o.b., 1988); 88% diamonds, 5% copper and nickel, 4% meat, cattle, and animal products. **Imports:** $1.1 bil. (c.i.f., 1988); foodstuffs, vehicles, textiles, petroleum products. **Major trading partners:** Switzerland, U.S., UK, other EC-associated members of Southern African Customs Union.

**Intl. Orgs.** Commonwealth, FAO, G-77, GATT (de facto), IBRD, ICAO, IDA, IFAD, IFC, ILO, IMF, INTERPOL, ITU, NAM, UN, UNESCO, UPU, WHO, WMO.

Botswana, occupying a high and relatively arid tableland in southern Africa, was traditionally occupied by diverse groups of farmers, pastoralists, and hunter-gatherers. European missionaries arrived from South Africa in the early 19th century. In the late 19th century, native peoples resisted the encroachment of Afrikaners from the Transvaal; in response the British government established a protectorate in what was then called Bechuanaland in 1886. The southern part of the protectorate was organized as a Crown Colony and ultimately passed under the control of South Africa. During the 20th century, the territory remaining in the protectorate saw a steady evolution of local rule.

In 1920 two advisory councils were established to represent the interests of native and European inhabitants. In 1934 British authorities promulgated regulations establishing the powers and jurisdictions of native chiefs and the functions of native councils and courts. Local fiscal powers were established soon thereafter. In 1951 a joint (native-European) advisory council was set up, and 10 years later an elected legislature met under the provisions of a constitution promulgated on May 2, 1961.

In 1963–64 the British government accepted Botswanan proposals for self-government. A new capital was established at Gaborone in February 1965; a new constitution came into effect in the following month, and Botswana became fully independent on Sept. 30, 1966. Since independence, Botswana has been a multiparty, multiracial democracy that has remained untouched by the political turmoil affecting most of its neighbors.

Botswana is also one of the most prosperous countries in Africa. It is the world's largest producer of diamonds; revenues from diamond exports have been wisely managed, leading to significant budgetary surpluses in recent years. Gold and soda ash are also mined. Tourism, bolstered by Botswana's large herds of big game, is the country's major nonmining industry. About 75 percent of the population is engaged in agriculture and herding; Botswana is one of Africa's largest exporters of meat and animal products.

## Brazil
### Federative Republic of Brazil

**Geography Location:** central and northeastern South America. **Boundaries:** Colombia, Venezuela, Guyana, Suriname, French Guiana to N; Atlantic Ocean to E; Uruguay, Argentina, Paraguay to S; Peru, Bolivia to W. **Total land area:** 3,286,488 sq. mi. (8,511,965 sq km). **Coastline:** 4,652 mi. (7,491 km). **Comparative area:** slightly smaller than U.S. **Land use:** 7% arable land; 1% permanent crops; 19% meadows and pastures; 67% forest and woodland; 6% other; includes negl. % irrigated. **Major cities:** Brasília (capital) 1,567,709; São Paulo 10,063,110; Rio de Janeiro 5,603,388; Belo Horizonte 2,114,429; Salvador 1,804,438.

**People Population:** 152,505,077 (1990). **Nationality:** noun—Brazilian(s); adjective—Brazilian. **Ethnic groups:** Portuguese, Italian, German, Japanese, black, Amerindian; 55% white, 38% mixed, 6% black, 1% other. **Languages:** Portuguese (official), Spanish, English, French. **Religions:** 90% Roman Catholic (nominal).

**Government Type:** federal republic; democratically elected president since 1985. **Independence:** Sept. 7, 1822 (from Portugal). **Constitution:** Jan. 24, 1967, extensively amended in 1969; Senate and Chamber of Deputies combined to form Constituent Assembly in 1987 to draft new constitution. **National holiday:** Inde-

pendence Day, Sept. 7. **Heads of government:** Fernando Collor de Mello, president (since Mar. 1990). **Structure:** strong executive with broad powers; bicameral legislature (National Congress) with growing powers, composed of Senate and Chamber of Deputies; 11-member Supreme Court.

**Economy Monetary unit:** novo cruzado. **Budget:** (1986) *income:* $27.8 bil.; *expend.:* $40.1 bil. **GDP:** $377 bil., $2,500 per capita (1989 est.). **Chief crops:** coffee, rice, corn, sugarcane, cocoa, soybeans; nearly self-sufficient except for wheat. **Livestock:** cattle, pigs, sheep, goats, horses, mules, asses. **Natural resources:** iron ore, manganese, bauxite, nickel, uranium. **Major industries:** textiles and other consumer goods, shoes, chemicals. **Labor force:** 57 mil. (1989 est.); 42% services, 31% agriculture, 27% industry; 2% unemployment (1989). **Exports:** $34.2 bil. (f.o.b., 1989 est.); coffee, metallurgical products, chemical products, foodstuffs, iron ore. **Imports:** $18 bil. (f.o.b., 1989 est.); crude oil, capital goods, chemical products, foodstuffs, coal. **Major trading partners:** (1987) *exports:* 28% U.S., 26% EC, 12% Latin America, 7% Japan, 27% other; *imports:* 24% Middle East and Africa, 22% EC, 21% U.S., 12% Latin America, 6% Japan.

**Intl. Orgs.** FAO, G-77, GATT, IAEA, IBRD, ICAO, IDA, IFAD, IFC, ILO, IMF, IMO, INTELSAT, ITU, OAS, UN, UNESCO, UPU, WHO, WIPO, WMO.

The Portuguese arrived on the coast of what would become Brazil with the expedition of Pedro Alvares Cabral in 1500 and found an indigenous population of semisedentary and nonsedentary cultures. Many of the semisedentary Indians spoke the Tupian language and shared similar cultural features. The Tupians quickly formed economic relationships with the first Europeans, who were interested in the valuable dyewood that was so abundant in Brazil.

The transition of Indian-European economic relations from barter to slavery was given momentum by the introduction of sugar export agriculture, a trend that began in the region in the 1540s. The 1560s saw epidemics of smallpox and measles in the coastal areas, which greatly reduced the indigenous population. Although the European sugar growers initially favored the use of indigenous peoples over imported African slave labor (owing to the lower price of Indian slaves), the shortage of labor resulting from the epidemics led to increasing use of African slave labor by the Portuguese.

The Portuguese vied with other European powers for control of Brazilian territory, and in 1630 the Dutch briefly seized the northeastern sugar-growing area. Brazil's southern regions were underpopulated during the early colonial period, and Portuguese activity was largely limited to cattle raising. With the discovery of gold (1690s) and diamonds (1729), European interest in and settlement of the Minas Gerais area in the southeast quickened.

In 1808, the Portuguese royal court escaped Napoleon's armies with the help of the British fleet, and the prince regent, Dom João VI, sought refuge in Brazil and made it the seat of the Portuguese empire. Dom João returned to a

Portugal liberated from Napoleonic occupation in 1821, leaving his son Dom Pedro behind as prince regent. In 1822, defying orders to return to Portugal and opposed to the imminent reversion of Brazil to colonial status, Dom Pedro declared Brazil's independence and was crowned emperor. In 1825 an agreement mediated by the British led to Portuguese recognition of Brazil as a separate kingdom.

The early years of independence were rocky. Dom Pedro became increasingly estranged from his people and began losing control of the Brazilian political situation owing to a continuing series of landowner revolts and to the loss of a war with the United Provinces of Rio de la Plata over what would become Uruguay. In 1831 Dom Pedro abdicated in favor of his 5-year-old son, Dom Pedro II; a regency governed Brazil until his accession to the throne in 1840.

The Brazilian empire found itself continually involved in the wars and internal politics of Uruguay, Argentina, and Paraguay in the 1850s and 1860s. The bloody five-year war with Paraguay that began in 1865 resulted in Paraguay's eventual defeat, but the process of the war had important consequences for the future of Brazil: the expansion of the military in numbers and power, the fragmentation of the political party system, and the undermining of the legitimacy of slavery. Slavery was abolished in 1888, and the following year, a military coup overthrew the emperor.

The "Old Republic," which lasted between 1889 and 1930, was a federal system in which much of the political control in Brazilian society was relegated to state-based political networks with local bosses. The presidency was assigned in a de facto rotation system called the politics of the governors, in which the president's office was controlled in turn by the most important state power networks. The world depression of 1929 hit the Brazilian agricultural export economy hard, and in 1930 the military overthrew the elected president; Getúlio Vargas, a politician from the state of Rio Grande do Sul, took over the office.

Vargas proceeded to centralize power in the presidency, diminishing states' rights dramatically. Civil unrest allowed Vargas to declare a state of siege with military backing, and in 1937 he declared the establishment of the Estado Novo, a state wherein Vargas had absolute power, in imitation of Portuguese and Italian regimes of the period. The military ousted Vargas in 1945, ushering in the period of the "Second Republic." Vargas again won reelection in 1950 but committed suicide in 1954. Juscelino Kubitschek, elected president in 1955, sought to develop the country and led the way for construction of the new capital of Brasília in the previously undeveloped interior.

His successor, Jânio da Silva Quadros, resigned in 1961, and the presidency passed to populist Vice Pres. João Goulart. The populist mobilization of peasants and workers endorsed by the Goulart government led to his overthrow by the military in 1964.

The Brazilian military governed the country until 1985. Military rule was not maintained in the form of a dictatorship; rather, the military ruled as a more or less cohesive institution. The succession of generals and their technocratic allies attempted to develop the country through a pattern of state-led growth from which civilian politics were excluded. The tendency for the military to become institutionally divided through its involvement in political governance combined with social groups' increasing demands to be included in the political process led to the transition toward civilian leadership in Brazil.

In 1985, Tancredo Neves, a civilian, was elected president, but he died before taking office. José Sarney, the vice presidential candidate, became Brazil's first civilian president since 1964.

Promising to revitalize the economy with a free-market revolution, less government, and more growth, conservative Fernando Collor de Mello became president in March 1990. Although there have been tentative steps—the military's share of the budget was reduced from 6% to 2.2%, and some companies have been privatized—inflation and debt still strain the economy.

The 1988 murder of environmental activist Chico Mendes focused world attention on the rapidly accelerating deforestation of the Amazon River basin. Pres. Collor has campaigned actively to halt the destruction in Amazonia—including protecting the stone age Yanomami Indians—and in 1992 Rio De Janeiro will host a UN-sponsored conference on development and the environment.

## Brunei
### Negara Brunei Darussalam

**Geography** **Location:** southeastern Asia, Kalimantan (Borneo) island. Bandar Seri Begawan 4°56′N, 114°58′E. **Boundaries:** surrounded on landward side by Sarawak, state, of Malaysia; South China Sea to N. **Total land area:** 2,226 sq. mi. (5,765 sq km). **Coastline:** 100 mi. (161 km). **Comparative area:** slightly larger than Delaware. **Land use:** 1% arable land; 1% permanent crops; 1% meadows and pastures; 79% forest and woodland; 18% other; includes negl. % irrigated. **Major cities:** Bandar Seri Begawan (formerly Brunei Town) (capital) 55,070 (1985 est.); Seria, Kuala Belait, Tutong.

**People** **Population:** 345,048 (1989). **Nationality:** noun—Bruneian(s); adjective—Bruneian. **Ethnic groups:** 64% Malay, 20% Chinese, 16% other. **Languages:** Malay (official), English, Chinese. **Religions:** 60% Muslim (official), 32% Buddhist and indigenous beliefs, 8% Christian.

**Government** **Type:** constitutional sultanate. **Independence:** Jan. 1, 1984 (from UK). **Constitution:** Sept. 29, 1959 (some provisions suspended since Dec. 1962, others since independence). **National holiday:** National Day, Feb. 23. **Heads of government:** Sir Hassanal Bolkiah, sultan and prime minister (since Aug. 1968). **Structure:** chief of state is sultan (advised by appointed privy council), who appoints executive council and legislative council.

**Economy** **Monetary unit:** brunei dollar. **Budget:** (1987) *income:* $1.2 bil.; *expend.:* $1.1 bil. **GDP:** $3.3 bil., $9,600 per capita (1989 est.).

**Chief crops:** rice, pepper. **Livestock:** pigs, buffalo, cattle, goats. **Natural resources:** crude oil, natural oil, natural gas, timber. **Major industries:** crude petroleum, liquefied natural gas, construction. **Labor force:** 68,128 (1984; includes members of army); 50.4% production of oil and natural gas, construction; 47.6% trade, services, and other; 2.0% agriculture, forestry, and fishing. **Exports:** $2.07 bil. (1987); 98–99% crude oil, liquefied natural gas, petroleum products. **Imports:** $800 mil. (1987); includes machinery and transport equipment, manufactured goods, beverages, tobacco; most consumer goods and food imported. **Major trading partners:** (1985) *exports:* (crude petroleum and liquefied natural gas) roughly two-thirds to Japan; *imports:* 24% Singapore, 20% Japan, 16% U.S.

**Intl. Orgs.** ASEAN, ICAO, IMO, INTERPOL, ITU, UN, UPU, WHO, WMO.

The Islamic sultanate of Brunei became dominant in northern Borneo in the 16th century but declined in power after the 17th century under pressure from the Dutch and other foreign powers. An Anglo-Dutch agreement of 1824 assigned North Borneo to Great Britain's sphere of influence in Asia. In 1841 a British adventurer, James Brooke, aided the sultan of Brunei in putting down a rebellion and was rewarded by being given the province of Sarawak, comprising more than half of the sultanate's area. Britain established a protectorate over Sabah, the eastern portion of Brunei, in 1881. That left the sultan with a tiny realm on the Brunei River, which was ultimately placed under British protection in 1888. The discovery of Southeast Asia's richest oilfield in Brunei and its offshore waters made the sultanate an enclave of tremendous wealth from the late 1920s onward.

Following Japanese occupation during World War II, British rule resumed in North Borneo. Sarawak and Sabah became part of Malaysia in 1963. Brunei was granted independence from Great Britain on Dec. 1, 1984. The sultan of Brunei, an absolute monarch, rules from the world's largest royal palace in Bandar Seri Begawan, the nation's capital. The economy is centered almost entirely on petroleum and international banking and investments.

## Bulgaria
### People's Republic of Bulgaria

**Geography** **Location:** southeastern Europe. **Boundaries:** Romania to N, Black Sea to E, Turkey and Greece to S, Yugoslavia to W. **Total land area:** 42,823 sq. mi. (110,912 sq km). **Coastline:** 220 mi. (354 km). **Comparative area:** between Tennessee and Pennsylvania. **Land use:** 34% arable land; 3% permanent crops; 18% meadows and pastures; 35% forest and woodland; 10% other; includes 11% irrigated. **Major cities:** (1987 est.) Sofia (capital) 1,128,859; Plovdiv 356,596; Varna 305,891; Burgas 197,555; Ruse 190,450.

**People** **Population:** 8,933,544 (1990). **Nationality:** noun—Bulgarian(s); adjective—Bulgarian. **Ethnic groups:** 85.3% Bulgarian, 8.5% Turk, 2.6% Gypsy, 2.5% Macedonian, 0.3% Armenian, 0.2% Russian, 0.6% other. **Languages:** Bulgarian; secondary languages closely correspond to ethnic breakdown. **Religions:** regime promotes atheism; religious background of population is 85% Bulgarian Orthodox, 13% Muslim, 0.8% Jewish, 0.7% Roman Catholic, 0.5% Protestant, Gregorian-Armenian, and other.

**Government** **Type:** republic. **Independence:** Sept. 22, 1908 (from Ottoman Empire). **Constitution:** new constitution being written. **National holiday:** National Liberation Day, Mar. 3. **Heads of government:** Zheliu Zhelev, president (since Aug. 1990); Dimitar Popov, prime minister (since Dec. 1990). **Structure:** Executive branch—president (elected by National Assembly), 11 ministers; Legislative—National Assembly with 400 popularly elected members; Judiciary—Supreme Court, Court of Appeals, regional courts.

**Economy** **Monetary unit:** lev. **Budget:** (1988) *income:* $26.0 bil.; *expend:* $28.0 bil. **GNP:** $51.2 bil., $5,710 per capita (1989 est.). **Chief crops:** grain, tobacco, fruits, vegetables, cheese, sunflower seeds; mainly self-sufficient. **Livestock:** poultry, sheep, pigs, goats, horses. **Natural resources:** bauxite, copper, lead, zinc, coal. **Major industries:** food processing, machine and metal building, electronics. **Labor force:** 4.3 mil. (1987); 33% industry, 20% agriculture, 47% other; N.A. unemployment. **Exports:** $20.3 bil. (f.o.b., 1988); 60.5% machinery and equipment; 14.7% agricultural products; 10.6% manufactured consumer goods; 8.5% fuels, minerals, raw materials, metals; 5.7% other. **Imports:** $21.0 bil. (f.o.b., 1988); 45.2% fuels, minerals, raw materials; 39.8% machinery and equipment; 4.6% manufactured consumer goods; 3.8% agricultural products; 6.6% other. **Major trading partners:** *exports:* 61% USSR, 5.5% E. Germany, 4.9% Czechoslovakia, 3.5% Libya, 2.9% Iraq, 1.2% W. Germany, 1% Greece; *imports:* 57.5% USSR, 5.7% E. Germany, 4.8% W. Germany, 1.6% Austria, 1% Libya, 0.9% Brazil.

**Intl. Orgs.** FAO, IAEA, ICAO, ILO, IMO, ITU, UN, UNESCO, UPU, WHO, WIPO, WMO.

Turkic Bulgars arrived at the west shore of the Black Sea in the seventh century, mingling with the indigenous Slavic population. The Bulgars accepted Eastern Orthodox Christianity in the ninth century and were conquered and incorporated into the Byzantine Empire by Basil II in the late 10th century. With the decline of Byzantium, Bulgaria became an independent kingdom, but it was conquered by the Ottoman Turks in 1396 and remained part of the Ottoman Empire for the next 500 years.

In the Treaty of San Stefano, ending the Russo-Turkish War in 1878, a Bulgarian state was promised that was to stretch from the Adriatic to the Black Sea. But the Great Powers would not permit so large a Russian client state, and instead the Berlin Conference of 1878 sanctioned the creation of a much smaller Bulgarian state, under a German dynasty with the Ottoman sultan as nominal overlord. Bulgaria gained full independence in 1908.

The Balkan Wars of 1912 and 1913 led to an expansion of Bulgarian territory, but after World War I, Bulgaria, which had been allied with the Central Powers, lost its Aegean coastline to Greece. A series of weak parliamentary governments under King Boris III (r. 1918–43) ended when the king established a personal dictatorship in 1935. Bulgaria joined the Axis powers in 1941 and declared war against the Western powers but not against Russia. Under occupation by its German allies, Bulgaria once again expanded to the Aegean during the war.

Russian troops entered Bulgaria in 1944 and organized a communist government on the basis of the leftist anti-Nazi resistance. The boy-king Simeon II remained on the throne until 1946, when the monarchy was abolished by a popular referendum. The People's Republic of Bulgaria was established in 1946.

Until the end of World War II, Bulgaria was a peasant society, with 80 percent of the population engaged in agriculture; industrial development was rudimentary. The People's Republic established a planned economy on the Soviet model; Russian credits and trade agreements permitted a rapid industrialization focused on machinery and equipment for export.

In 1954 Todor Zhivkov became first secretary of the Bulgarian Communist party. He served as premier in the 1960s and president from 1971 to 1990.

In the 1960s Zhivkov promoted a certain amount of decentralization and responsiveness to market forces, but with the 1968 Russian invasion of Czechoslovakia, he returned the economy to central planning, collective farming, and giant state-industrial enterprises. In October 1985 Zhivkov met with Mikhail Gorbachev and reforms based on Gorbachev's "self-management" policies were instituted in 1986.

Democratic reform began with Zhivkov's sudden resignation in November 1989. (He was later tried for misappropriating state property, inciting ethnic violence, and other crimes.) There followed a year of popular unrest and political turmoil with a succession of dramatic changes in the ruling hierarchy, culminating in the August election of Zheliu Zhelev of the reform Union of Democratic Forces as president (Bulgaria's first non-Communist leader in 40 years), and the appointment of political independent Dimitar Popov as prime minister in December.

A new constitution is being drafted, and the country's Turkish minority is enjoying a measure of religious and cultural freedom not seen since the 1950s. Economic reforms have been introduced, but Bulgaria's economy has been so closely tied to that of the USSR and other eastern bloc nations that its future rests in part on the fate of reform in its neighbor countries.

## Burkina Faso

**Geography**   **Location:** landlocked country in western Africa. **Boundaries:** Mali to N and W, Niger to E, Benin, Togo, Ghana, Ivory Coast to S. **Total land area:** 105,870 sq. mi. (274,200 sq km). **Coastline:** none. **Comparative area:** between Colorado and Nevada. **Land use:** 10% arable land; negl. % permanent crops; 37% meadows and pastures; 26% forest and woodland; 27% other; includes negl. % irrigated. **Major cities:** (1985 census) Ouagadougou (capital) 441,514; Bobo-Dioulasso 228,668; Koudougou 51,926; Ouahigouya 38,902; Banfora 35,319.

**People**   **Population:** 9,077,828 (1990). **Nationality:** noun—Burkinabe (sing., pl.); adjective—Burkinabe. **Ethnic groups:** Mossi (about 2.5 mil.), Gurunsi, Senufo, Lobi, Bobo, Mande, Fulani. **Languages:** French (official); tribal lan guages spoken by 90% of population. **Religions:** 65% indigenous beliefs, 25% Muslim, 10% Christian (mainly Roman Catholic).

**Government**   **Type:** military; established by coup on Aug. 4, 1983. **Independence:** Aug. 5, 1960 (from France). **Constitution:** none; Constitution of Nov. 1977 was abolished following coup of Nov. 25, 1980. **National holiday:** Independence Day, Aug. 4. **Heads of government:** Capt. Blaise Compaore, president (since Oct. 1987). **Structure:** executive—president; military council of unknown number; 21-member military and civilian cabinet; judiciary.

**Economy**   **Monetary unit:** Communauté Financière Africaine (CFA) franc. **Budget:** (1987) *income:* $422 mil.; *expend.:* $516 mil. **GDP:** $1.43 bil., $170 per capita (1988). **Chief crops:** cash crops—peanuts, shea nuts, sesame, cotton; food crops—sorghum, millet, corn, rice; food shortages. **Livestock:** cattle, goats, sheep, pigs, asses. **Natural resources:** manganese, limestone, marble; small deposits of gold, antimony, copper, nickel, bauxite. **Major industries:** agricultural processing plants; brewery, cement, and brick plants. **Labor force:** 3.3 mil. (1984); 82% agriculture, 13% industry, 5% other; 20% of male labor force migrates annually to neighboring countries for seasonal employment; 30,000 are wage earners; 44% of population of working age. **Exports:** $249 mil. (f.o.b., 1988); livestock, oilseeds, gold, cotton. **Imports:** $591 mil. (f.o.b., 1988); machinery, grain, dairy products, petroleum. **Major trading partners:** *exports:* (1985) 42% EC (30% France), 17% Taiwan, 15% Ivory Coast. *imports:* 37% EC (23% France), 31% Africa, 15% U.S.

**Intl. Orgs.**   FAO, G-77, GATT, IBRD, ICAO, IDA, IFAD, IFC, ILO, IMF, INTELSAT, INTERPOL, ITU, NAM, UN, UNESCO, UPU, WHO, WIPO, WMO.

The Mossi empire dominated the area of what is now Burkina Faso, a landlocked nation in western Africa with few natural resources and poor agricultural conditions, from as early as the 11th century. They ruled the region, often resisting Muslim invaders, until modern times.

The region was hardly visited by Europeans before the 1880s, but by 1896 the French had captured the Mossi capital city of Ouagadougou and established a protectorate over the area. The French created Upper Volta in 1919, naming it for the upper basin of the Volta River. Upper Volta became a self-governing state with the French Overseas Community in 1958 and gained independence Aug. 5, 1960.

After a brief period of military rule, the nation ratified a new constitution on June 14, 1970, and made a peaceful transition to civilian rule based on the French model. In 1980 the constitution was overthrown and a military government was set up. There was another coup on Aug. 4, 1983, and a government was established patterned after the Libyan government of Muammar al-Qaddafi. On Aug. 14, 1984, Upper Volta officially changed its name to Burkina Faso.

Two attempted coups against the government of Capt. Blaise Compaore, in September and December 1989, were put down and the leaders executed.

## Burundi
### Republic of Burundi

**Geography**   **Location:** landlocked country on northeastern shore of Lake Tanganyika in central Africa. **Boundaries:** Rwanda to N, Tanzania to E and S, Zaire to W. **Total land area:** 10,747 sq. mi. (27,834 sq km). **Coastline:** none. **Comparative area:** slightly larger than Maryland. **Land use:** 43% arable land; 8% permanent crops; 35% meadows and pastures; 2% forest and woodland; 12% other; includes negl. % irrigated. **Major cities:** Bujumbura (capital) 172,201 (1979 census); Gitega 15,943 (1978).

**People**   **Population:** 5,645,997 (1990). **Nationality:** noun—Burundian(s); adjective—Burundi. **Ethnic groups:** 85% Hutu (Bantu), 14% Tutsi (Hamitic), 1% Twa (Pygmy); 70,000 refugees, mostly Rwandans and Zairians; 3,000 Europeans and 2,000 South Asians. **Languages:** Kirundi and French (both official), Swahili (along Lake Tanganyika and in Bujumbura area). **Religions:** 67% Christian (62% Roman Catholic, 5% Protestant), 32% indigenous beliefs, 1% Muslim.

**Government**   **Type:** republic. **Independence:** July 1, 1962 (from UN trusteeship under Belgian administration). **Constitution:** Nov. 20, 1981; on taking power Maj. Pierre Buyoya suspended Constitution and formed Military Council for National Redemption. **National holiday:** Independence Day, July 1. **Heads of government:** Maj. Pierre Buyoya, president (since Sept. 1987); Adrien Sibomana, prime minister (since Oct. 1988). **Structure:** executive—president and cabinet; legislature—National Assembly reestablished in 1982; judiciary.

**Economy**   **Monetary unit:** Burundi franc. **Budget:** (1988 est.) *income:* $213.0 mil.; *expend.:* $292.0 mil. **GDP:** $1.3 bil., $255 per capita (1988). **Chief crops:** cash crops—coffee, cotton, tea; food crops—manioc, yams, peas, corn, sorghum. **Livestock:** goats, cattle, sheep, pigs. **Natural resources:** nickel, uranium, rare earth oxide, peat, cobalt. **Major industries:** light consumer goods such as blankets, shoes, soap; assembly of imports; public works construction. **Labor force:** 1.9 mil. (1983); 93% agriculture, 7% other. **Exports:** $128 mil. (f.o.b., 1988); 87% coffee; tea, cotton, hides, skins. **Imports:** $204 mil. (1988); 31% capital goods, 15% petroleum products, foodstuffs. **Major trading partners:** *exports:* 83% EC, 5% U.S.,

2% Asia; *imports:* 57% EC, 23% Asia, 3% U.S.

**Intl. Orgs.** FAO, G-77, GATT, IBRD, ICAO, IDA, IFAD, IFC, ILO, IMF, INTERPOL, ITU, NAM, UN, UNESCO, UPU, WHO, WIPO, WMO.

Burundi's population is divided between two ethnic groups, the majority Hutu and the minority, but politically powerful, Tutsi. The Hutu were the original settlers of the country and practiced agriculture; the cattle-herding Tutsi arrived several hundred years ago and established a form of feudal overlordship over the Hutu. The traditional government was monarchical, with a king (*mwami*) chosen from among a group of aristocratic families (*ganwa*).

European exploration of Burundi began in 1858, and the territory was incorporated into German East Africa in 1899. It was occupied by Belgian troops in 1916. Following World War I, the League of Nations in 1923 awarded Burundi, along with neighboring Rwanda, to Belgium as a mandated territory. Belgian rule over the Territory of Ruanda-Urundi, as it was then called, continued under a UN trusteeship after World War II.

Burundi became independent on July 1, 1962, as a constitutional monarchy under the traditional mwami. The country rapidly lapsed into political chaos. In 1966, with the backing of the army, Capt. Michel Micombero overthrew the monarchy and proclaimed a republic. A Hutu rebellion in 1972 against Tutsi political domination left 10,000 Tutsi dead; Tutsi reprisals in 1972–73 resulted in the slaughter of 150,000 Hutu. The Micombero government was overthrown in a bloodless coup, and on Nov. 1, 1976, Lt. Col. Jean-Baptiste Bagaza took control of the government.

Bagaza was overthrown in September, 1987, while attending a conference of French-speaking African nations in Quebec. His successor is Maj. Pierre Buyoya. The Buyoya government has proclaimed a policy of nonalignment in foreign affairs, seeking closer links with the West, while maintaining relations with Libya and the Eastern bloc. Domestically, the government has pledged to eradicate Bagaza's record of persecution of the Catholic church (62% of Burundians are Catholic) and to seek ethnic reconciliation between Hutu and Tutsi. The latter policy was threatened, however, by renewed outbreaks of ethnic violence in 1988.

Burundi's economy is based primarily on agriculture; the country's dense population is distributed throughout the land on small farms. Overpopulation and soil impoverishment have overwhelmed the country's once-prosperous rural economy, and Burundi is now one of the world's poorest countries. The principal export crop is coffee; tea and cotton are also exported. The recent discovery of substantial nickel deposits promises to enhance Burundi's export sector.

## Cambodia
### State of Cambodia

**Geography** **Location:** on Indochinese peninsula in Southeast Asia. **Boundaries:** Thailand to W and N, Laos to N, Gulf of Thailand to S, Vietnam to E. **Total land area:** 69,898 sq. mi.

(181,035 sq km). **Coastline:** 275 mi. (443 km). **Comparative area:** between Missouri and Oklahoma. **Land use:** 16% arable land; 1% permanent crops; 3% meadows and pastures; 76% forest and woodland; 4% other; includes 1% irrigated. **Major cities:** (1989 est.) Phnom Penh (capital) 800,000.

**People** **Population:** 6,991,107 (1990). **Nationality:** noun—Kampuchean(s); adjective—Kampuchean. **Ethnic groups:** 90% Khmer (Cambodian), 5% Chinese, 5% other minorities. **Languages:** Khmer (official), French. **Religions:** 95% Theravada Buddhism, 5% other.

**Government** **Type:** disputed. **Independence:** Nov. 9, 1953 (from France). **Constitution:** June 27, 1981. **National holiday:** Apr. 17. **Heads of government:** Heng Samrin, president (since Jan. 1979); Hun Sen, prime minister. [The UN recognizes Prince Norodom Sihanouk, president (since July 1982); Son Sann, prime minister (since June 1982).] **Structure:** Council of Ministers, comprising an inner cabinet and a number of coordination committees.

**Economy** **Monetary unit:** riel. **Budget:** N.A. **GDP:** $890 mil., $130 per capita (1989 est.). **Chief crops:** mainly subsistence farming except for rubber plantations; main crops—rice, rubber, corn; food shortages—rice, meat, vegetables, dairy products, sugar, flour. **Livestock:** cattle, pigs, buffalo, horses. **Natural resources:** timber, gemstones, some iron ore, manganese, phosphates, hydropower potential. **Major industries:** rice milling, fishing, wood and wood products. **Labor force:** 2.5–3 mil.; 80% agriculture (1988 est.). **Exports:** $32 mil. (1988); natural rubber, rice, pepper, wood. **Imports:** $147 mil. (1988); international food aid, fuels, consumer goods. **Major trading partners:** Vietnam, USSR, Eastern Europe, Japan, India.

**Intl. Orgs.** Colombo Plan, FAO, G-77, GATT (de facto), IAEA, IBRD, ICAO, IDA, ILO, IMF, IMO, INTERPOL, ITU, NAM, UN, UNESCO, UPU, WHO, WMO.

The dominant power in Indochina from the eighth through the 13th centuries, the Khmer empire encompassed present-day Cambodia and much of western Thailand, southern Laos, and central and southern Vietnam. It built magnificent Buddhist temple cities at Angkor Wat and Angkor Thon. From the 14th century onward, the Khmer empire came under increasing pressure from the expansionist Vietnamese state of Annam, which absorbed the territories east of the Mekong River. In the 18th century, the kingdom of Siam (Thailand) annexed three western provinces of the Khmer empire. The remaining Khmer territory became the French protectorate of Cambodia in 1863, and a French colony as part of the Union of Indochina in 1887. In 1907 France forced Siam to return some territory to Cambodia.

During World War II, Cambodia was occupied by Japan from 1942 to 1945, when French control was restored. After the French defeat in Indochina, Cambodia became independent in 1953 under Prince Norodom Sihanouk, who had ascended the throne in 1941. In 1960 Sihanouk was named head of state under a constitutional monarchy. Shaken by the Vietnam War in the 1960s, Cambodia broke relations with the United States in 1965 because of South Vietnamese incursions across the border. In 1969 relations were restored when Sihanouk charged North Vietnam with arming the Khmer Rouge Cambodian Communist rebels. In the same year, American planes began secret bombing raids in Cambodia. In 1970 Sihanouk was ousted by a coup led by pro-U.S. Gen. Lon Nol; the monarchy was abolished, and Prince Sihanouk went into exile.

In April 1975 the Khmer Rouge, led by Pol Pot, captured the capital, Phnom Penh, and established a new government, the Kampuchean People's Republic. In an ensuing reign of terror, an estimated 3 million people died and hundreds of thousands more fled to refugee camps in Thailand. In 1978, Vietnamese troops invaded, capturing Phnom Penh on Jan. 7, 1979, and installing a new government led by Heng Samrin. The Kampuchean People's Republic continued to be recognized as the legal government of Cambodia in the United Nations and by most non-Soviet-bloc nations. A coalition dominated by the Khmer Rouge resisted the Vietnamese takeover, but by 1985 almost all of the country was under Vietnamese control.

Most Vietnamese troops withdrew in 1989, and Prince Sihanouk emerged as the leader of a coalition of antigovernment forces. Starting in late 1988 conferences including representatives from all Cambodian factions were held to forge a political settlement to end the 20-year-old civil war, and by the fall of 1991, an agreement between the government and the antigovernment coalition seemed near.

## Cameroon
### Republic of Cameroon

**Geography** **Location:** western coast of central Africa. **Boundaries:** Nigeria to NW, Chad to NE, Central African Republic to E, Congo to SE, Gabon, Equatorial Guinea to S, Gulf of Guinea to W. **Total land area:** 183,569 sq. mi. (475,442 sq km). **Coastline:** 250 mi. (402 km). **Comparative area:** slightly larger than California. **Land use:** 13% arable land; 2% permanent crops; 18% meadows and pastures; 54% forest and woodland; 13% other; includes negl. % irrigated. **Major cities:** (1986 est.) Yaoundé (capital) 653,670; Douala 1,029,731; Nkongsamba (and environs) 123,149; Maroua (and environs) 103,653.

**People** **Population:** 11,092,470 (1990). **Nationality:** noun—Cameroonian(s); adjective—Cameroonian. **Ethnic groups:** 31% Cameroon Highlanders, 19% Equatorial Bantu, 11% Kirdi, 10% Fulani, 8% Northwestern Bantu, 7% Eastern Nigritic, 13% other African; less than 1% non-African; over 200 ethnic groups of widely differing background. **Languages:** English and French (both official); 24 major African language groups. **Religions:** 51% indigenous beliefs, 33% Christian, 16% Muslim.

**Government** **Type:** unitary republic; one-party presidential regime. **Independence:** Jan. 1, 1960 (from UN trusteeship under French administration). **Constitution:** May 20, 1972. **National holiday:** National Day, May 20. **Heads of government:** Paul Biya, president (since Nov. 1982). **Structure:** executive—president; legislative—National Assembly; judiciary—Supreme Court has power of judicial review when questions of constitutionality are referred to it by president.

**Economy** **Monetary unit:** Communauté Financière Africaine (CFA) franc. **Budget:** (1988) *income:* $2.17 bil.; *expend.:* $2.17 bil. **GDP:** $12.9 bil., $955 per capita. **Chief crops:** coffee, cocoa, timber, cotton, rubber. **Livestock:** poultry, cattle, goats, sheep, pigs. **Natural resources:** crude oil, bauxite, iron ore, timber, hydropower potential. **Major industries:** crude oil production, small aluminum plant, food processing. **Labor force:** (1983) 74.4% agriculture, 11.4% industry and transport, 14.2% other services; 50% of population of working age (1985). **Exports:** $2 bil. (f.o.b., 1988); 56% petroleum products, cocoa, coffee, timber. **Imports:** $2.3 bil. (c.i.f., 1988 est.); machines and electrical equipment, chemical products, consumer goods, transport equipment. **Major trading partners: exports:** EC (50% Netherlands), 3% U.S. *imports:* 42% France, 7% Japan, 4% U.S.

**Intl. Orgs.** FAO, G-77, GATT, IAEA, IBRD, ICAO, IDA, IFAD, IFC, ILO, IMF, IMO, INTELSAT, INTERPOL, ITU, NAM, UN, UNESCO, UPU, WHO, WIPO, WMO.

Cameroon was settled by the Sao people about 1,000 years ago. In later times others, including the Bamileke, Bassa, Douala, and Fulani, migrated into the region. Portuguese trading stations were established along the coast beginning in the 15th century, and between 1500 and the early 19th century, the population was severely depleted by the slave trade in the hands of various European nations. European rivalries for domination in Cameroon were settled temporarily in 1884 when Germany established a protectorate.

British and French troops invaded German Cameroon during World War I, and following the war the League of Nations divided the protectorate into two mandated territories—French in the eastern sector and British in the west. French Cameroon rejected the Vichy government in World War II and became an important African base for Charles de Gaulle's Free French. In 1946 British and French rule in western and eastern Cameroon was reaffirmed under UN trusteeships.

In 1958 the French trusteeship was abolished, and the Republic of Cameroon became independent on Jan. 1, 1960. In February 1961 a UN-supervised plebiscite was held in British Cameroon, allowing the people of that region to choose between union with Nigeria and union with the Republic of Cameroon. The northern two-thirds of the British territory elected union with Nigeria; the southern portion joined the Republic of Cameroon on Oct. 1, 1961, to form the Federal Republic of Cameroon. In 1972 the federal structure was abolished by a national referendum, and the United Republic of Cameroon was established. In 1984 the nation's name reverted to the Republic of Cameroon.

During the federal period, Cameroon had a multiparty political system, with party divisions coinciding with the old distinctions between west and east Cameroon. In 1966 all political parties were amalgamated to form the Cameroon National Union, which, with various changes in name, has dominated the political life of Cameroon ever since. In 1980 Pres. Ahidjo, the long-time political leader of Cameroon, was elected without opposition to a fifth five-year term in office. He resigned in 1982 and was replaced by Prime Minister Paul Biya. Pres. Biya was reelected in his own right in 1984; he retained the backing of the military in putting down an attempted coup in April of that year. He abolished the office of prime minister, thus strengthening presidential government, and has instituted political reforms whereby multiple candidates stand for office within the structure of the country's single-party system.

The economy of Cameroon is based primarily on agriculture. The country is self-sufficient in food and exports coffee, cocoa, rubber, cotton, palm oil, and timber. Oil is the principal export, however, accounting for 60 percent of export earnings. Overreliance on oil export earnings in the 1970s led to the growth of government bureaucracy, corruption, and excessive spending; the fall in oil prices in the 1980s thus led to economic turmoil and dislocation. These negative effects were cushioned to some extent by the health of the agricultural sector of the economy; austerity measures in the 1980s have allowed the government to begin to adjust to an era of shrinking petroleum revenues.

# Canada

**Geography** **Location:** northern North America (excluding Alaska and Greenland); second-largest country in the world. **Boundaries:** Arctic Ocean to N, Greenland to NE across Baffin Bay, Atlantic Ocean to E, United States to S, Pacific Ocean and Alaska to W. **Total land area:** 3,990,456 sq. mi. (9,976,140 sq km). **Coastline:** 151,492 mi. (243,791 km). **Comparative area:** slightly larger than U.S. **Land use:** 5% arable land; negl. % permanent crops; 3% meadows and pastures; 35% forest and woodland; 57% other; includes negl. % irrigated. **Major cities:** (1986 census) Ottawa (capital) 819,263; Toronto 3,427,168; Montréal 2,921,357; Vancouver 1,380,729; Edmonton 785,465.

**People** **Population:** 26,538,229 (1990). **Nationality:** noun—Canadian(s); adjective—Canadian. **Ethnic groups:** 40% British Isles origin, 27% French origin, 20% other European, 1.5% indigenous Indian or Eskimo. **Languages:** English, French. **Religions:** 46% Roman Catholic, 16% United Church, 10% Anglican.

**Government** **Type:** federal state recognizing Elizabeth II as sovereign. **Independence:** July 1, 1867 (from UK). **Constitution:** amended British North America Act of 1867 transferred power and rights to Canada, Apr. 17, 1982; charter of rights and unwritten customs. **National holiday:** Canada Day, July 1. **Heads of government:** Brian Mulroney, prime minister (since Sept. 1984); Ramon John Hnatyshyn, governor-general (since Jan. 1990). **Structure:** executive—cabinet collectively responsible to House of Commons and headed by prime minister; legislative—282-seat Parliament with queen represented by governor-general, Senate, and House of Commons; judiciary—judges appointed by governor-general with Supreme Court as highest tribunal.

**Economy** **Monetary unit:** Canadian dollar. **Budget:** (1988 est.) *income:* $79.2 bil.; *expend.:* $102.0 bil. **GDP:** $513.6 bil., $19,600 per capita (1989 est.). **Chief crops:** grain (principally wheat), feedgrains, oilseeds, tobacco. **Livestock:** cattle, pigs, sheep. **Natural resources:** nickel, zinc, copper, gold, lead. **Major industries:** processed and unprocessed minerals, food products, wood and paper products. **Labor force:** 13.38 mil.; 75% services, 14% manufacturing; 7.8% unemployment. **Exports:** $127.2 bil. (f.o.b., 1989); newsprint, wood pulp, timber, grain, crude petroleum. **Imports:** $116.5 bil. (c.i.f., 1989); processed foods, beverages, crude petroleum, chemicals, industrial machinery. **Major trading partners: exports:** U.S., Japan, UK, W. Germany, other EC, USSR; *imports:* U.S., Japan, UK, W. Germany, other EC, Taiwan, S. Korea, Mexico.

**Intl. Orgs.** Colombo Plan, Commonwealth, FAO, GATT, IAEA, IBRD, ICAO, IDA, IFAD, IFC, ILO, IMF, IMO, INTELSAT, INTERPOL, ITU, NATO, OAS, OECD, UNESCO, UPU, WHO, WIPO, WMO.

Canada is geographically the second-largest country in the world, but most of its territory is very sparsely settled. The vast majority of the country's 26 million people live in a narrow band along the border with the United States. Despite a long tradition of national independence, Canada's history has been dominated by relations with Great Britain, the United States, and, to a lesser extent, France.

Canada's earliest inhabitants arrived via the Bering land bridge from Asia around 15,000 years ago and diversified to form the various Inuit (Eskimo), Northwest Indian, Plains Indian, and forest Indian cultures that still contribute significantly to Canada's national identity. The earliest-known European settlers of Canada were Vikings, who established a short-lived colony in Newfoundland around A.D. 1000. British, French, and other European explorers made numerous voyages to Canada during the 16th century, stimulated by Canada's rich resources of fish, forest products, and furs.

The first permanent European settlement in Canada was the French trading station at Quebec, founded by Samuel de Champlain in 1608. Fur traders rapidly spread into the interior along the St. Lawrence River and the Great Lakes; European diseases, particularly smallpox, decimated Native American populations as the explorers advanced. In 1663 New France was organized as a French Crown Colony, and royal governors replaced private commercial interests in governing Quebec.

The Hudson Bay Company was chartered by the British Crown in 1670, inaugurating a long period of commercial and territorial rivalry in Canada between Britain and France. In general, France sought to expand New France northward and westward, while Britain sought to

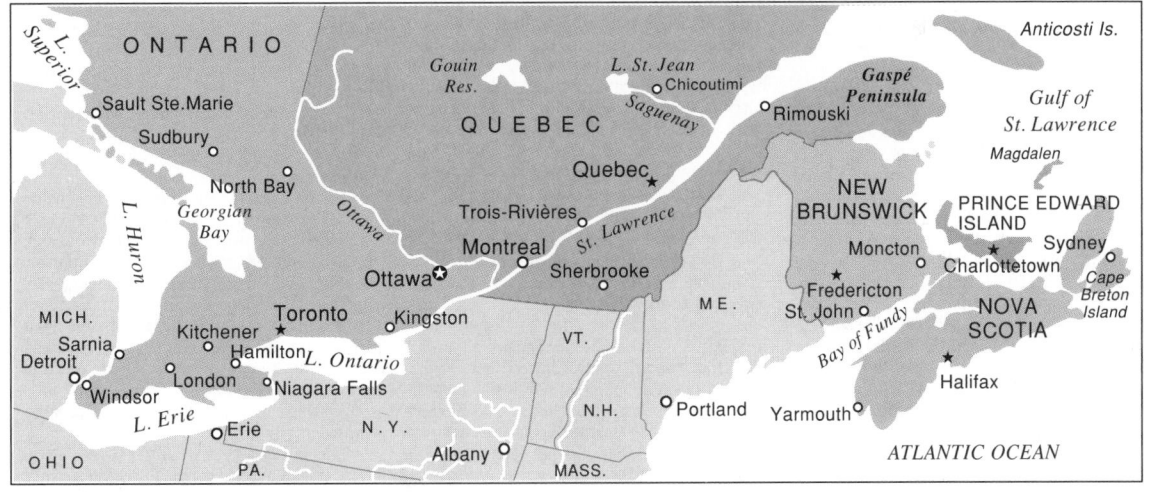

## Main map labels

ARCTIC OCEAN
ICELAND
Arctic Circle
Beaufort Sea
Prince Patrick
Melville  Bathurst
NORTH MAGNETIC POLE (c.1980)
Devon
Ellesmere
GREENLAND (Den.)
Banks
Parry Channel
Somerset
Baffin Bay
Porcupine
Yukon
ALASKA (U.S.)
Inuvik
DISTRICT OF FRANKLIN
Prince of Wales
Victoria
Boothia Pen.
Baffin
Davis Strait
Dawson
YUKON
Port Radium
Great Bear L.
Coppermine
Prince Charles
Foxe Basin
L. Amadjuak
Whitehorse
Juneau
NORTHWEST TERRITORIES
DISTRICT OF MACKENZIE
Yellowknife
Great Slave L.
Thelon
Dubawnt L.
DISTRICT OF KEEWATIN
Hudson Strait
Ungava Bay
Cape Chidley
Nain
Labrador Sea
NEWFOUNDLAND
Queen Charlotte Islands
Prince Rupert
Prince George
BRITISH COLUMBIA
ROCKY MOUNTAINS
Athabasca L.
Uranium City
Reindeer L.
Churchill
Churchill
Hudson Bay
Fort Severn
Fort Chima
Schefferville
Goose Bay
LABRADOR
L. Nueltin
Nelson
James Bay
Kamloops
Fraser
Banff
Columbia
ALBERTA
Edmonton
Assiniboine
SASKATCHEWAN
Saskatoon
Saskatchewan
MANITOBA
Severn
ONTARIO
L. Mistassini
QUEBEC
Anticosti Is.
Gulf of St. Lawrence
Newfoundland
St. John's
ST. PIERRE AND MIQUELON (France)
PACIFIC OCEAN
Vancouver
Victoria
Calgary
Regina
L. Winnipeg
L. Manitoba
Winnipeg
L. Nipigon
Thunder Bay
Superior
Sault Ste.Marie
Gaspé Pen.
NEW BRUNSWICK
Quebec
Fredericton
PRINCE EDWARD ISLAND
Charlottetown
NOVA SCOTIA
Halifax
WASH.
ORE.
MONT.
N.D.
MINN.
Lake of the Woods
Trois-Rivières
Montreal
ME.
Bay of Fundy
ATLANTIC OCEAN
CALIF.
NEV.
IDAHO
WYO.
S.D.
NEB.
IOWA
WIS.
UNITED STATES
Ottawa
Toronto
L. Ontario
VT.
N.H.
MASS.
R.I.
CONN.
N.J.
N.Y.
MICH.
L. Michigan
L. Huron
L. Erie
UTAH
ILL.
IND.
OHIO
PA.

CHAMBERLIN TRIMETRIC PROJECTION

0   500 miles
0   750 km

## Inset map labels

L. Superior
ONTARIO
Gouin Res.
L. St. Jean
Chicoutimi
Gaspé Peninsula
Anticosti Is.
Gulf of St. Lawrence
Sault Ste.Marie
Sudbury
QUEBEC
Saguenay
Rimouski
Magdalen
North Bay
Georgian Bay
L. Huron
Ottawa
Quebec
Trois-Rivières
Montreal
St. Lawrence
Sherbrooke
NEW BRUNSWICK
Moncton
Fredericton
St. John
PRINCE EDWARD ISLAND
Charlottetown
Sydney
Cape Breton Island
NOVA SCOTIA
Ottawa
Toronto
Kingston
ME.
Bay of Fundy
Halifax
MICH.
Sarnia
Detroit
Kitchener
Hamilton
L. Ontario
VT.
Windsor
London
Niagara Falls
L. Erie
Erie
N.Y.
N.H.
Portland
Yarmouth
ATLANTIC OCEAN
OHIO
PA.
Albany
MASS.

expand its domination southward and westward from Hudson Bay. French and British interests clashed directly along the Atlantic coast, where both British and French settlements were established. Local and regional wars between the French and the British were endemic in Canada throughout the 17th and 18th centuries; each side enlisted Native American allies. These wars were often inconclusive, but in Queen Anne's War (1702–13), Britain gained a significant advantage by winning control of Acadia and Newfoundland, and by driving the French from Hudson Bay.

The French and Indian Wars of 1756–63, a North American extension of Europe's Seven Years' War, proved to be the decisive turning point in the Anglo-French rivalry in Canada. Prior to the outbreak of full-scale war, in 1755 the British deported some 7,000–10,000 French settlers from Acadia, in Nova Scotia, to the West Indies; many later settled in Louisiana. When war broke out in Europe in 1756, Britain employed its superior sea power to cut New France off from Europe and captured Quebec in the Battle of the Plains of Abraham in 1759. Montreal capitulated in 1760, leaving Britain in control of New France.

Faced with the difficult problem of governing New France's large and rapidly growing French population (which far outnumbered the English-speaking population of Canada), the British in 1774 passed the Quebec Act, which recognized the French's legal code and manorial system of land tenure, and granted legal status to the Roman Catholic church. The act also extended Canadian territory south to the Ohio river, which enraged the inhabitants of the 13 American colonies and helped fuel the American Revolution.

During the American Revolution, nearly 40,000 loyalists fled to Canada from the rebellious colonies, establishing English-speaking settlements in New Brunswick and in western Quebec. Friction between English- and French-speaking Canadians led the British in 1791 to divide Canada (west of the Atlantic maritime provinces) into two provinces, Upper Canada and Lower Canada. Each was granted a legislature; that of Upper Canada was based on British institutions, while that of Lower Canada retained the French forms established by the Quebec Act of 1774.

During the War of 1812 between Great Britain and the United States, Canada became a battleground; Toronto was captured and pillaged by the Americans in 1813. Many Americans hoped to expand the territory of the United States at the expense of Canada, or even to entice Canada into a continental American union, but Canadians, whether English- or French-speaking, showed no enthusiasm for joining the United States. A small British garrison, with the support of Native American irregular forces, kept the Americans at bay. The Convention of 1818 established the border between Canada and the United States at latitude 49° north, as far west as the Rocky Mountains, and provided for joint U.S.-British control of Oregon (i.e., the entire Columbia River basin).

Following the War of 1812, British authorities actively encouraged British immigration

to Canada, and between 1815 and 1855, one million Britons answered the call. This immigration radically altered the ethnic balance of Canada, making French-speaking Canadians a minority population for the first time. The francophones of Lower Canada, hemmed in on all sides by English speakers, rose in rebellion under the leadership of the Parti Patriote in 1837–38. In response, Lord Durham recommended in 1839 that Canada be united under a single government, and the Union of Canada was enacted in 1841. This move did not, however, quell the growing nationalism of French Canadians.

Oregon became an issue in the American presidential election of 1844, with the United States claiming the entire Columbia River basin north to 54°40' ("fifty-four forty or fight"). War threatened but diplomacy triumphed; in 1846 the boundary at 49° was extended westward to the Pacific Ocean. Gold was discovered in British Columbia in 1856, leading to a gold rush and a substantial increase in the population of western Canada.

Growing trade between Canada and the United States from the 1840s onward, and the development of a continental system of railroads in both Canada and the United States in the 1850s, led to a relative decline in British influence in Canada. The American Civil War had the indirect effect of prompting Canadians to seek self-government in a federal union. Previously, there had been little contact between the Canadas (Upper and Lower) and the maritime provinces, while the vast territories of the west were still privately administered by the Hudson Bay Company. A federal union was forged in a series of conferences beginning in 1864, and the federation of Quebec, Ontario, Nova Scotia, and New Brunswick was recognized by the British North America Act of July 1, 1867.

The Dominion of Canada thus established in 1867 became a self-governing entity within the British Empire; Sir J.A. Macdonald became Canada's first prime minister (1867–73). The dominion rapidly expanded. In 1869 it purchased the western territories of the Hudson Bay Company, and in 1870, in response to a rebellion of French-speaking Métis in Manitoba, Manitoba was granted provincial status within the federation. In 1871 the union of British Columbia with Canada was secured with the promise of a transcontinental railway within 10 years; the Canadian Pacific Railway was completed in 1885. Prince Edward Island joined the federation in 1873, but neighboring Newfoundland remained a British colony outside the Canadian federation until 1949.

A second francophone rebellion broke out in Manitoba in 1885. Its leader, Louis Riel, was executed and became a symbol of French Canadian grievances against the English-speaking majority. Wilfred Laurier became Canada's first francophone prime minister in 1896, but he was unable to achieve a solution to the problem of the rights of Catholics and French-speakers outside Quebec. Legislation restricting those rights had already been enacted in Manitoba in 1890.

The Klondike Gold Rush of 1897–98 brought Canada to worldwide attention and indirectly helped promote the settlement of rich agricultural lands in the Canadian west. Immigrants to the prairie region came not only from eastern Canada, but also from Europe, notably Germany, Scandinavia, and the Ukraine. Japanese farmers and Chinese railroad and mining workers settled west of the Rockies, further increasing Canada's ethnic diversity, though Asian immigrants were denied citizenship through discriminatory legislation. Alberta and Saskatchewan were granted provincial status in 1905; the Yukon Territory and the Northwest Territories continued to be governed by controllers appointed by the federal government and patrolled by the famous Royal Canadian Mounted Police.

Urbanization and industrialization were stimulated in the early 20th century by the exploitation of extensive mineral resources in western Canada and in northern Quebec, and by the development of hydroelectric projects and transportation facilities throughout the country. The long-lived Laurier government fell in 1911, when his proposal for free trade with the United States evoked widespread fears that Canada's nascent industries would suffer without protective tariffs.

Laurier's Conservative successor, Robert Borden, sent Canadian volunteer troops to fight in World War I in 1914 and, over the objections of most French Canadian leaders, bolstered Canada's war efforts in Europe through national conscription in 1917. The distinguished performance of Canada's armed forces in the war bought the country renewed international respect and appreciation.

Borden's wartime English-speaking Conservative-Liberal coalition collapsed in 1921. He was succeeded by the Liberal leader William L. Mackenzie King, who was to be Canada's prime minister for over 20 years (1921–30, 1935–48). Mackenzie King faced a challenge from the Progressive party, based in the agricultural plains provinces, but he managed to outwit and neutralize the Progressive leadership; the party disappeared as a political force after the mid-1920s. Mackenzie King skillfully managed the economic prosperity of the 1920s, which saw the establishment in Canada of branch plants of many American industrial firms.

The Statute of Westminster, which created the British Commonwealth in 1931, had the effect of granting full self-government to Canada within the Commonwealth.

Canada's federal structure was ill-equipped to manage the economic collapse of the 1930s, which brought both industrial depression and a drought-induced agricultural crisis. Efforts to deal with unemployment, land foreclosures, and other economic ills fell almost entirely to the provincial governments, which were not up to the task. The growth of private cooperative movements brought some relief to the maritime provinces and the plains provinces, while interest grew in constitutional reform to strengthen the federal government.

Canada's recovery from the Great Depression was stimulated primarily by the advent of

World War II, which Canada entered in 1939. Although the war years brought price controls, rationing, and other emergency measures, the overall effect of the war was to strengthen all sectors of Canada's economy and to enhance Canada's international status as a leading military and industrial power. Canada's overseas troops during the war were almost entirely volunteers; conscription for overseas service was not imposed until late in 1944. This policy proved highly popular in both English- and French-speaking Canada and contributed to the Liberal electoral victory of 1945 that gave Mackenzie King a renewed mandate for the postwar era.

The two decades following the war saw the gradual expansion of federal financial responsibility for national welfare measures, including pensions, unemployment insurance, and comprehensive medical care, though the administration of such programs remained a provincial matter. These developments coincided with an increase in urbanization and industrialization in the major centers of Vancouver, Toronto, and Montreal. Formal "equalization payments" were enacted in the 1950s to reduce economic disparities between rich and poor provinces. The early stages of these developments played a part in persuading Newfoundland to join the federation as Canada's 10th province in 1949.

A landslide Conservative victory in 1958 brought John Diefenbaker to the prime ministership, but the Conservatives proved unable to offer a coherent political program for the nation and were ousted in the elections of 1963, which returned the Liberals to power. Canadian politics since the 1960s have been marked by increasing regionalization; the Liberal party is based largely in the east, while the New Democratic party, organized in 1961, has little support east of Ontario. The Conservatives offer a broad but insecure national alternative. Regional politics revolve in part around the different responses of agricultural and industrial provinces to the political and economic impact of the American colossus to the south.

The language issue has continued to divide Canada politically and ideologically in the postwar period. The rise of an aggressive Quebecois nationalism in the 1960s led directly to the Liberal prime ministership of Pierre Trudeau, a Quebecois who was known as a supporter of a strong federal constitution. Trudeau's efforts toward conciliation and for constitutional guarantees for Quebec within a strong federal structure proved unavailing, however. In 1970 he invoked the War Measures Act to send troops to Quebec to put down a wave of separatist terrorism, leaving the province subdued but sullen.

The 1976 electoral victory in Quebec of the Parti Québécois under René Lévesque provoked fears that Quebec would secede from Canada. Lévesque's plan for a separate "sovereignty-association" status for Quebec was rejected by a popular referendum in 1980, but only because of Trudeau's pledge to seek full autonomy for Canada in order to secure constitutional protection for Quebec's special interests.

In November 1981, despite Lévesque's protests that the measures did not go far enough, Canada's provincial governments reached agreement on proposals for constitutional change. The result was the passage by the British Parliament of the Canada Act, which came into effect on Apr. 17, 1982, granting full independence and constitutional autonomy to Canada and severing its last colonial ties to the British government. Canada's new 1982 Constitution more clearly delineated the powers of the federal and provincial governments, provided for Supreme Court review of legislation, and included a Charter of Rights to protect civil liberties.

A national recession in the late 1970s and early 1980s led to the fall of Trudeau's Liberal government and to the election of the Conservative party leader Brian Mulroney (also a native of Quebec) as prime minister in 1984. The Mulroney government has encouraged foreign investment and privatization as a means of revitalizing Canada's economy, with considerable success. A notable development has been an influx of immigrants from Hong Kong—110,000 between 1984 and 1991—who have pumped an estimated $2–$3 billion a year into the economy.

The Meech Lake Agreement, containing a number of articles clarifying the 1982 Constitution, was worked out between Mulroney and Quebec's Liberal Premier Robert Bourassa, along with the leaders of Canada's nine other provinces, and signed on June 23, 1987. In general, its provisions enhanced the power of the provinces as against that of the federal government; a key provision grants constitutional protection to Quebec's efforts to remain a "distinct society," linguistically and culturally French. The aggressive measures of the Quebec government to eradicate the use of English in the public affairs of the province provoked a backlash from Quebec's English-speaking minority, while bilingualism continues to be widely resented in Canada's English-speaking provinces. The Meech Lake Agreement failed to become law when the legislatures of Newfoundland and Manitoba declined to ratify it by the June 23, 1990, deadline. Canada thereupon was plunged into the most serious constitutional crisis in its history. Quebec has since called for a redistribution of power to the provinces that would severely weaken federal authority except for defense and management of the national debt.

The most significant achievement of the Mulroney government has been the negotiation and passage, in 1988–89, of a free-trade agreement with the United States, to be implemented in stages during the 1990s. It promises to create a North American free-trade zone that should strengthen Canada's economy, but at the cost, some Canadians fear, of further eroding Canada's sovereignty and distinctive national identity.

## Cape Verde
### Republic of Cape Verde

**Geography** **Location:** archipelago of 15 islands in Atlantic Ocean, off northern Africa. Praia 14°54′N, 23°31′W. **Boundaries:** Senegal about 300 mi. (500 km) to E. **Total land area:** 1,557 sq. mi. (4,033 sq km). **Coastline:** 600 mi. (965 km). **Comparative area:** slightly larger than Rhode Island. **Land use:** 9% arable land; negl. % permanent crops; 6% meadows and pastures; negl. % forest and woodland; 85% other; includes 1% irrigated. **Major cities:** (1980 census) Cidade de Praia (capital) 57,748.

**People** **Population:** 374,984 (1990). **Nationality:** noun—Cape Verdean(s); adjective—Cape Verdean. **Ethnic groups:** 71% Creole (mulatto), 28% African, 1% European. **Languages:** Portuguese and Crioulo (blend of Portuguese and West African). **Religions:** Roman Catholicism fused with indigenous beliefs.

**Government** **Type:** republic. **Independence:** July 5, 1975 (from Portugal). **Constitution:** Sept. 7, 1980, amended Feb. 12, 1981. **National holiday:** Independence Day, July 5. **Heads of government:** Antonio M. Monteiro, president (since Mar. 1991); Dr. Carlos Alberto de Carvalho Veiga, prime minister (since Feb. 1991). **Structure:** executive—president; legislative—56-member National People's Assembly.

**Economy** **Monetary unit:** escudo. **Budget:** (1988) *income:* $80.0 mil.; *expend.:* $87.0 mil. **GDP:** $158 mil., $494 per capita (1987). **Chief crops:** bananas, coffee, sugarcane, corn, beans. **Livestock:** goats, pigs, cattle, asses. **Natural resources:** salt, basalt rock, pozzolana, limestone, kaolin, fish. **Major industries:** salt mining. **Labor force:** 57% agriculture, 29% services, 14% industry (1981); 50% of population of working age (1983). **Exports:** $8.9 mil. (f.o.b., 1987); fish, bananas, salt, flour. **Imports:** $124 mil. (c.i.f., 1987); petroleum, foodstuffs, consumer goods, industrial products. **Major trading partners:** *exports:* Portugal, Angola, Algeria, Belgium/Luxembourg, Italy; *imports:* Portugal, Netherlands, Spain, France, U.S., W. Germany.

**Intl. Orgs.** FAO, G-77, GATT (de facto), IBRD, ICAO, IDA, IFAD, ILO, IMF, IMO, ITU, NAM, UN, UNESCO, UPU, WHO, WMO.

In 1462 the Portuguese founded the first European city in the tropics at Ribeira Grande on Santiago, one of the 15 islands that compose the Republic of Cape Verde. Located 385 miles off the west coast of Africa, the Cape Verde Islands prospered during the slave trade in the 16th century and later served as supply stations on sea routes and trading lanes. The rise of whaling in the 19th century led to contact with the United States, as American ships recruited crews from the islands. The United States set up an American consulate, headquarters for the U.S. Navy African Squadron, and a transatlantic cable station in the islands.

Portugal changed the status of the archipelago from colony to overseas province in 1951; five years later, citizens of Cape Verde and Portuguese Guinea organized the African Party for the Independence of Guinea-Bissau and Cape Verde (PAIGC) to petition Portugal to improve living conditions. Beginning as a clandestine organization, the PAIGC became an overt political movement on the islands after the 1974 revolution in Portugal. An agreement between the PAIGC and Portugal, providing for a transitional government in Cape Verde, paved the way for full independence in 1975.

In 1980 the PAIGC became the PAICV, which remained the "supreme expression" of Cape Verdeans' political will until the opposition won a parliamentary majority in the nation's first multiparty elections in January 1991.

## Central African Republic

**Geography** **Location:** landlocked country in central Africa. **Boundaries:** Chad to N, Sudan to E, Zaire, Congo to S, Cameroon to W. **Total land area:** 240,535 sq. mi. (622,984 sq km). **Coastline:** none. **Comparative area:** slightly smaller than Texas. **Land use:** 3% arable land; negl. % permanent crops; 5% meadows and pastures; 64% forest and woodland; 28% other. **Major cities:** Bangui (capital) 473,817 (1984 est.); Berbérati 100,000; Bouar 55,000 (1982 est.).

**People** **Population:** 2,877,365 (1990). **Nationality:** noun—Central African(s); adjective—Central African. **Ethnic groups:** 34% Baya, 27% Banda, 21% Mandija, 10% Sara, 4% Mboum, 4% M'Baka; 6,500 Europeans, of which 3,600 are French. **Languages:** French (official), Sangho (lingua franca and national language), Arabic, Hunsa, Swahili. **Religions:** 25% Protestant, 25% Roman Catholic, 24% indigenous beliefs, 15% Muslim, 11% other; indigenous beliefs and practices strongly influence Christian majority.

**Government** **Type:** republic; one-party presidential regime since 1986. **Independence:** Aug. 13, 1960 (from France). **Constitution:** Nov. 21, 1986. **National holiday:** Independence Day, Aug. 13. **Heads of government:** Gen. André-Dieudonné Kolingba, president (since Sept. 1981). **Structure:** executive—chief of state; legislative—parliament, includes National Assembly and Social and Economic Council; judiciary.

**Economy** **Monetary unit:** Communauté Financière Africaine (CFA) franc. **Budget:** (1989 est.) **income:** $132.0 mil.; **expend.:** $305.0 mil. **GDP:** $1.27 bil., $453 per capita (1988 est.). **Chief crops:** cash crops—cotton, coffee, peanuts, sesame, tobacco; food crops—manioc, corn, millet, sorghum, peanuts. **Livestock:** cattle, goats, pigs, sheep. **Natural resources:** diamonds, uranium, timber, gold, oil. **Major industries:** sawmills, breweries, diamond mining. **Labor force:** 775,413 (1986 est.); 85.0% agriculture, 8.9% commerce and services, 6.1% other. **Exports:** $138.0 mil. (f.o.b., 1988 est.); diamonds, cotton, coffee, timber, tobacco. **Imports:** $285 mil. (f.o.b., 1988 est.); food, textiles, petroleum products, machinery, electrical equipment, motor vehicles. **Major trading partners:** *exports:* France, Belgium, Japan, U.S.; *imports:* France, other EC countries, Japan, Algeria, Yugoslavia.

**Intl. Orgs.** FAO, G-77, GATT, IBRD, ICAO, IDA, IFAD, ILO, IMF, INTELSAT, INTER-

POL, ITU, NAM, UN, UNESCO, UPU, WHO, WIPO, WMO.

A landlocked country in Africa's central region, the Central African Republic is one of the least-developed countries in the world. Most of its people are farmers, and the nation has little manufacturing, few reliable roads, and no railroad. Europeans first came to the area in the early 1800s in their search for slaves, but it was not until 1889 that the French established an outpost as the current capital city of Bangui. The region was organized as the territory of Ubangi-Shari five years later. In 1910 Ubangi-Shari was incorporated into French Eqitorial Africa along with what are now the countries of Chad, the Congo, and Gabon.

The country was granted internal self-government by the French under its present name in 1958 and became a member of the French Overseas Community. Independence was achieved on Aug. 13, 1960. The first prime minister, Barthelemy Boganda, was killed in an airplane crash in 1959 and was succeeded by his nephew, David Dacko. Dacko was elected to a seven-year term in January 1964, but an army coup in 1966 overthrew his government. The head of the army, Jean-Bedel Bokassa, was installed as president. Named president for life in 1972, in 1976 Bokassa declared himself emperor and changed the name of the country to the Central African Empire.

Dacko returned to power in 1979, however, and Bokassa went into exile in France. The name of the country was changed back to the Central African Republic. A multiparty political system was reinstated in March 1981, but army officers threw Dacko out of office once again six months later and banned all political parties. Though the military was again in control, the government put Bokassa on trial for a variety of crimes, including murder and torture, after his return in 1986, and he was ultimately sentenced to life in prison.

## Chad
### Republic of Chad

**Geography** **Location:** landlocked country in north central Africa. **Boundaries:** Libya to N, Sudan to E, Central African Republic to S, Cameroon, Nigeria to SE, Niger to W. **Total land area:** 486,180 sq. mi. (1,259,200 sq km). **Coastline:** none. **Comparative area:** between Texas and Alaska. **Land use:** 2% arable land; negl. % permanent crops; 36% meadows and pastures; 11% forest and woodland; 51% other; includes negl. % irrigated. **Major cities:** (1979 est.) N'Djamena (capital) 402,000; Sarh 124,000; Moundou 87,000; Bongor 69,000; Doba 64,000.

**People** **Population:** 5,017,431 (1990). **Nationality:** noun—Chadian(s); adjective—Chadian. **Ethnic groups:** 200 distinct ethnic groups, most of whom are Muslims (Arabs, Toubou, Fulbe, Kotoko, Hausa, Kanembou, Baguirmi, Boulala, and Maba) in north and center and non-Muslims (Sara, Ngambaye, Mbake, Goulaye, Moudang, Moussei, Massa) in south; some

15,000 nonindigenous, of whom 1,000 are French. **Languages:** French and Arabic (both official); Sara and Sango in south; more than 100 different languages and dialects. **Religions:** 44% Muslim, 33% Christian, 23% indigenous beliefs.

**Government** **Type:** republic. **Independence:** Aug. 11, 1960 (from France). **Constitution:** Apr. 14, 1962 (currently suspended); National Charter, promulgated March 1991, serves as basis for government. **National holiday:** Independence Day, Aug. 11. **Heads of government:** Idriss Deby, president (since Dec. 1990); Jean Alingue Bawoyen, prime minister (since Mar. 1991). **Structure:** executive—president; Council of Ministers; National Consultative Council; judiciary—court of appeal.

**Economy** **Monetary unit:** Communauté Financière Africaine (CFA) franc. **Budget:** (1988 est.) **income:** $61.0 mil.; **expend.:** $85.0 mil. **GDP:** $902 mil., $190 per capita (1986 est.). **Chief crops:** cash crops—cotton, gum arabic, peanuts, fish; food crops—millet, sorghum, rice, sweet potatoes, yams, cassava, dates. **Livestock:** goats, sheep, cattle, asses, camels. **Natural resources:** small quantities of crude oil (unexploited but exploitation beginning), uranium, natron (sodium carbonate), kaolin, fish (Lake Chad). **Major industries:** cotton textile mills, slaughterhouses, brewery, natron. **Labor force:** 85% agriculture—unpaid subsistence farming, herding and fishing, 15% other. **Exports:** $432 mil. (f.o.b., 1988); 43% cotton, 35% cattle, 5% textiles, fish. **Imports:** $214 mil. (f.o.b., 1988); 39% machinery and transport equipment, 20% industrial goods, 13% petroleum products, 9% foodstuffs. **Major trading partners:** *exports:* France, Nigeria, Cameroon; *imports:* U.S., France.

**Intl. Orgs.** EC (associate), FAO, G-77, GATT, IBRD, ICAO, IDA, IFAD, IFC, ILO, IMF, INTELSAT, INTERPOL, ITU, NAM, UN, UNESCO, UPU, WHO, WIPO, WMO.

The Sao and other ancient peoples built centers of civilization near Lake Chad that flourished for many centuries until they were displaced by the medieval kingdoms of Kanem-Bornu, Baguirmi, and Ouaddai. From about 1400 onward, Chad became a meeting-ground between the Muslim cultures of the Sahara and the Sahel and the black African societies of the tropics. Between 1500 and 1800, Arab slave raiders were active around Lake Chad, supplying slaves for European traders on Africa's west coast.

French military forces reached Chad from West Africa in 1891 and fought a series of battles over the next two decades with the Arab rulers of the region. A French governorship of Chad was established in 1905 (based in Brazzaville, the Congo), but the country was not brought entirely under French control until 1914. Chad was incorporated into the federation of French Equatorial Africa in 1910 and was organized as a colony within the federation in 1920.

French Equatorial Africa was dissolved in 1959, and Chad became an autonomous member of the French Community. Full independence followed on Aug. 11, 1960; François Tombalbage became Chad's first president. In 1965 the Muslim northern and eastern parts of the country rebelled against the southern-led government; despite the aid of French troops, the government was unable to suppress the rebellion, and civil war became endemic.

Tombalbage was overthrown in 1975 in a military coup led by another southerner, Gen. Felix Malloum. Efforts to broaden the composition of the national government broke down, and in 1979 Prime Minister Hissein Habre broke with the government and led northern forces against the national army. A cease-fire was negotiated under international auspices, and a National Unity Transitional Government (GUNT) was installed in November 1979, but civil war broke out again in March 1980. Pres. Goukouni Oueddei sought Libyan aid in restoring order; a contingent of 7,000 Libyan troops occupied the country until 1981. They were replaced by an international peacekeeping force organized by the Organization of African Unity.

Civil war broke out again in February 1982, and in June, northern forces occupied the capital. A new republican government under the presidency of Hissein Habre was proclaimed on June 7. OAU forces withdrew, and Habre's government soon controlled all of the country except for a few northern areas held by GUNT. In 1983 GUNT launched a counterattack and regained some territory with the aid of Libyan forces. French and Zairian troops were sent to aid Habre's forces. In September 1984 France and Libya agreed to the withdrawal of all foreign forces from Chad, but Libyan forces remained. GUNT forces controlled the country north of the 16th parallel; Libyan forces occupied the Aozou Strip, along the border, with the apparent intention of annexing it to Libya.

Between 1984 and 1986 Habre persuaded most Chadean dissident forces to rejoin the national government, and in November 1986 he launched a campaign to recapture the north. The lightly armed but highly mobile Chadean forces won a series of victories in 1987, but Libyan forces continue to occupy the Aozou Strip. In May 1988 Libya's Col. Qaddafi declared an end to the 20-year war with Chad, but did not relinquish Libya's claim to the Aozou Strip, the dispute over which is before the International Court of Justice.

On Nov. 10, 1990, rebel forces led by renegade Gen. Idriss Deby launched attacks from Sudan and advanced toward the capital. On Dec. 1, Pres. Habre and his cabinet fled the country, and Deby, who seeks the transformation of the political system to a multiparty democracy, proclaimed a provisional government and suspended the constitution. A national charter calling for a new constitution and national elections to be held within 30 months came into force in March 1991. At the same time, Jean Alingue was named prime minister.

Chad, largely arid and lacking natural resources, is overwhelmingly an agricultural and pastoral country; the national economy remains at the subsistence level with only rudimentary industrial development. The country is pre-cariously self-sufficient in food; principal exports are cotton and livestock.

## Chile
### Republic of Chile

**Geography Location:** South Pacific coast of South America. **Boundaries:** Peru, Bolivia to N, Argentina to E, Pacific Ocean to W. **Total land area:** 292,132 sq. mi. (756,626 sq km). **Coastline:** 3,999 mi. (6,435 km). **Comparative area:** slightly larger than Texas. **Land use:** 7% arable land; negl. % permanent crops; 16% meadows and pastures; 21% forest and woodland; 56% other; includes 2% irrigated. **Major cities:** (1990) Gran Santiago (capital) 4,385,481; Concepción 306,464; Viña del Mar 281,063; Valparaíso 276,756; Talcahuano 246,853.

**People Population:** 13,082,842 (1990). **Nationality:** noun—Chilean(s); adjective—Chilean. **Ethnic groups:** 95% European and European-Indian, 3% Indian, 2% other. **Languages:** Spanish. **Religions:** 89% Roman Catholic, 11% Protestant, small Jewish population.

**Government Type:** republic. **Independence:** Sept. 18, 1810 (from Spain). **Constitution:** Sept. 11, 1980, effective Mar. 11, 1981; modified by public referendum on July 31, 1989. **National holiday:** Independence Day, Sept. 18. **Heads of government:** Patricio Aylwin Azocar, president (since Mar. 1990). **Structure:** Executive branch headed by president and cabinet of 20 ministers; legislature consists of Senate of elected and appointed members (47 in June 1990), and Chamber of Deputies, fixed at 102 members; Judicial branch consists of Supreme Court, Courts of Appeals and lower-level tribunals. New Congress first met on Mar. 11, 1990.

**Economy Monetary unit:** Chilean peso. **Budget:** (1986) **income:** $4.9 bil.; **expend.:** $5.1 bil. **GDP:** $25.3 bil., $1,970 per capita (1989). **Chief crops:** wheat, potatoes, corn, sugar beets, onions, beans, fruit; net agricultural importer. **Livestock:** sheep, cattle, pigs, goats, horses. **Natural resources:** copper, timber, iron ore, nitrates, precious metals. **Major industries:** copper, other minerals, foodstuffs, fish processing. **Labor force:** 3.84 mil. (1985); 38.6% services (including 12% government), 31.3% industry and commerce, 15.9% agriculture, forestry, fishing; 7.1% unemployment (1988 est.). **Exports:** $7.0 bil. (f.o.b., 1988); 48% copper, 33% industrial products, molybdenum, iron ore, wood pulp, fishmeal. **Imports:** $4.7 bil. (f.o.b., 1988); petroleum, wheat, capital goods, spare parts, raw materials. **Major trading partners:** **exports:** 34% EC, 22% U.S., 10% Japan, 7% Brazil; **imports:** 23% EC, 20% U.S., 10% Japan, 9% Brazil.

**Intl. Orgs.** FAO, G-77, GATT, IAEA, IBRD, ICAO, IDA, IFAD, IFC, ILO, IMF, IMO, INTELSAT, INTERPOL, ITU, OAS, UN, UNESCO, UPU, WHO, WIPO, WMO.

Before the arrival of Europeans in the mid-1530s, indigenous habitation of the territory that would become Chile included the Araucanian population in the south and peo-ples under the influence of the Inca empire in the north.

The Spanish founded the cities of Valparaiso in 1536, Santiago in 1541, and Concepción in 1550. Chile was under the authority of the Viceroyalty of Peru, established in 1544. Between 1810 and 1818, fortunes of the Chilean independence movement ebbed and flowed, culminating in the victory of Bernardo O'Higgins and the separatist forces in 1817. Independence was finally achieved in 1818.

From 1818 to 1833, Chile underwent a period of political instability, the roots of which can be traced to power struggles among elite Chilean families. In 1833 a strong presidential-dominant constitution was written under the influence of leading political figure Diego Portales that set the form of government in Chile until 1891. Chile expanded its territory at the expense of Peru and Bolivia, first in a war with the Peruvian-Bolivian Confederation (1836–39) and later as a result of the War of the Pacific (1879–83).

A civil war was fought in 1890–91 between forces of the president, José Balmaceda, and the Chilean Congress over the issue of the limits of presidential authority. The defeat of the presidential forces led to the establishment of a congressional-dominant parliamentary system. The checks on policy initiative resulting from the parliamentary system left government deadlocked in the face of mounting social and political problems arising at the turn of the century. The occurrence of a number of bloody strike actions crystallized political debate around social issues such as better wages and working conditions. The immobilized parliamentary system was unable to respond to these problems. In 1925, when Congress failed to allocate funds for military pay, the forces overthrew the parliamentary government.

A new constitution was drawn up that same year that moved governmental structure toward presidential dominance. Nevertheless, political instability continued until 1933, when the new constitution was implemented. The Chilean balance of political power from 1958 until 1973 remained almost equally divided among parties representing the right, the center, and the left of the political spectrum. In order to prevent an electoral victory for the leftist parties, forces on the right allied themselves with the centrist Christian Democrats in the 1964 election, and this resulted in the victory of Christian Democratic presidential candidate Eduardo Frei Montalva.

The program of the Christian Democrats, based on ideology and political strategy, included an ambitious agrarian reform and attempts to organize Chile's urban poor. It was believed that these stances would benefit the Christian Democrats at the polls in the 1970 presidential election. As in 1958, the 1970 election fielded three presidential candidates who represented the political right, center, and left. The candidate of the leftist Popular Unity coalition, Dr. Salvador Allende Gossens, won with 36.3 percent of the vote, and the Congress recognized Dr. Allende's victory after a bitter debate.

The Allende government nationalized the

foreign-owned copper industry, but the resulting international boycott of Chilean copper imposed in retaliation for this action left Chile unable to market her copper. Other nationalizations by the government included the coal and steel industries and 60 percent of private banking. The Popular Unity government found itself unable to control peasant seizures of land and factory takeovers by workers. The copper embargo, land and factory seizures, government subsidies to the poor for basic goods, and runaway inflation resulted in a deterioration of the national economy that particularly affected the middle classes. Members of Congress from the center and right had hoped to gain enough seats in the 1973 congressional elections to impeach Allende, but instead the Popular Unity made impressive electoral gains, just as it had in the municipal elections of 1971. As political struggle intensified, the president resorted to inclusion of military officers in the government in order to bolster the legitimacy of the Popular Unity administration in the eyes of political opponents.

On Sept. 11, 1973, segments of the military led by commanders of three of Chile's four armed forces took control of the government, killing Allende in the process. Gen. Augusto Pinochet Ugarte emerged from the junta as the new president. The junta announced the arrest of some 13,000 persons, many of whom then lost their lives in a wave of brutal repression. (Mass graves were discovered in the desert in 1990, and in 1991 a commission reported that between 1973 and 1990, 2,279 people were killed, more than 2,000 by the government.) In March 1974 the dictatorship published its Declaration of Principles, the essential elements of which included a laissez-faire economic orientation, anti-Marxism, and nationalism.

A new constitution was approved by plebiscite in 1980. The two-phase evolution of Chile's political structure included an authoritarian "transitional period" between 1980 and 1989 and implementation of a new political structure thereafter. The constitution created a presidential system with very extensive executive powers and a "guardian" role for the military.

In an October 1988 plebiscite, Chileans rejected continuation of Pinochet rule and called for an end to the dictatorship. On Dec. 14, 1989, Patricio Aylwin Azocar of the Christian Democratic party (one of a 17-party alliance) was elected president with over 55 percent of the vote; he took office in March 1990, thereby ending 17 years of military dictatorship.

In recent years, Chile's economy has expanded, exports have increased, and it has succeeded in lowering its large external debt; but inflation remains high. Although exports are still dominated by the copper industry—more than 40%—other minerals and manufactures are gaining in importance.

## China
### People's Republic of China

**Geography Location:** covers vast area of eastern Asia. **Boundaries:** USSR to N and W;

Mongolia to N; N. Korea to NE; Pacific Ocean to E; India, Nepal, Bhutan, Myanmar, Laos, and Vietnam to S; Afghanistan and Pakistan to W. **Total land area:** 3,838,784 sq. mi. (9,596,960 sq km). **Coastline:** 9,112 mi. (14,500 km). **Comparative area:** between U.S. and Canada. **Land use:** 10% arable land; negl. % permanent crops; 31% meadows and pastures; 14% forest and woodland; 45% other; includes 5% irrigated. **Major cities:** (1987 est.) Beijing (capital) 6,710,000; Shanghai 7,220,000; Tianjin 5,540,000; Shenyang 4,370,000; Wuhan 3,570,000.

**People Population:** 1,133,682,501 (1990 census). **Nationality:** noun—Chinese (sing., pl.); adjective—Chinese. **Ethnic groups:** 93.3% Han Chinese, 6.7% Zhuang, Uygur, Hui, Yi, Tibetan, Miao, Manchu, Mongol, Buyi, Korean, and numerous lesser nationalities. **Languages:** Standard Chinese (Putonghua) or Mandarin (based on the Beijing dialect); also Yue (Cantonese), Wu (Shanghainese), Minbei (Fuzhou), Minnan (Hokkien-Taiwanese), Xiang, Gan, Hakka dialects, and minority langs. (see "Ethnic groups" above). **Religions:** officially atheist, but traditionally pragmatic and eclectic; most important elements of religion are Confucianism, Taoism, and Buddhism; about 2–3% Muslim, 1% Christian.

**Government Type:** communist state; real authority lies with Communist party's politburo; National People's Congress, in theory the highest organ of government, usually ratifies party's programs; State Council actually directs government. **Constitution:** Dec. 4, 1982. **National holiday:** National Day, Oct. 1. **Heads of government:** Gen. Yang Shangkun, president (since Apr. 1988); Li Peng, premier (since Nov. 1987). **Structure:** control is exercised by Chinese Communist party, through State Council, which supervises ministries, commissions, and bureaus; all are technically under Standing Committee of National People's Congress.

**Economy Monetary unit:** yuan. **Budget: income:** N.A.; **expend.:** N.A. **GNP:** $350 bil., $320 per capita (1988). **Chief crops:** rice, wheat, corn, other grains, oilseed; mainly subsistence agriculture. **Livestock:** pigs, sheep, cattle and buffalo, goats, horses. **Natural resources:** coal, iron ore, crude oil, mercury, tin; world's largest hydropower potential. **Major industries:** iron, steel, coal. **Labor force:** 513 mil. (1986 est.); 61.1% agriculture and forestry, 25.2% industry and commerce; **Exports:** $52.5 bil. (f.o.b., 1989); manufactured goods, agricultural products, grain (rice and corn), oil, minerals. **Imports:** $59.1 bil. (c.i.f., 1989); grain (mostly wheat), chemical fertilizer, steel, industrial raw materials, machinery. **Major trading partners:** (1989) *exports:* Hong Kong, Japan, U.S., USSR, Singapore; *imports:* Hong Kong, Japan, U.S., W. Germany, USSR.

**Intl. Orgs.** FAO, IAEA, IBRD, ICAO, IDA, IFAD, IFC, ILO, IMF, IMO, INTELSAT, ITU, UN, UNESCO, UPU, WHO, WIPO, WMO.

China is one of the world's oldest civilizations. Dynastic rule in the North China Plain

began around 2000 B.C. The unifying Qin (221 B.C.) and Han (206 B.C.) dynasties greatly expanded the territory of the empire and established the basic pattern of imperial bureaucratic government that would endure until the beginning of the 20th century. Major dynasties during that period include the Han (206 B.C.–A.D. 220), Tang (618–907), Song (960–1279), Yuan or Mongol (1279–1368), Ming (1368–1644), and Qing (1644–1911).

By the late 18th century, the Qing dynasty faced increasingly dangerous problems of explosive population growth, bureaucratic stagnation, and trade pressure from the West. Opium—introduced by Great Britain to balance its trade in tea, silk, porcelain, and other goods—created severe social problems. Western demands for free trade resulted in the Opium War (1839–42), in which China was humiliatingly defeated by the British. The treaties of Nanjing (1842) and Tianjin (1858) opened China to Western merchants and missionaries and created foreign-ruled enclaves on Chinese soil. At the same time, the Taiping Rebellion and other popular uprisings led to the deaths of at least 20 million Chinese between 1850 and 1870.

Such reform efforts as the Self-Strengthening Movement (1870s) and the 1898 Reform Movement proved inadequate to the task of strengthening and modernizing China's dynastic government. Japan, modernizing rapidly after the Meiji Restoration of 1868, joined the race for commercial access to China, decisively winning the Sino-Japanese War of 1894–95. The antiforeign Boxer Uprising of 1900 was put down by a joint foreign military force, dealing a mortal blow to Qing rule. On Oct. 10, 1911, the dynasty fell to a coalition of forces led by the veteran revolutionary nationalist Sun Yat-sen.

China's first attempt at republican government, under Pres. Yuan Shikai and subsequent presidents, quickly degenerated into factionalism and warlord control in the provinces. In 1915 Japan successfully demanded further concessions, provoking public outcries. When news reached China on May 4, 1919, that the Treaty of Versailles granted Japan all of Germany's former concessions in China, students rioted throughout the country, demanding reforms and modernization (the May Fourth Movement). Sun Yat-sen's Nationalist party (Kuomintang, or KMT) and the Chinese Communist party (CCP, founded in 1921 by Mao Zedong) joined forces in 1922 in an attempt to create a second republican revolution.

Sun Yat-sen died in 1925. His successor, Chiang Kai-shek, consolidated KMT forces in Guangzhou and mounted the Northern Expedition (1927–29) to defeat or co-opt the various provincial warlords and reunify the country. In the course of this successful effort, Chiang turned on his Communist allies. A series of failed Communist uprisings and KMT anti-Communist extermination campaigns between 1927 and 1934 nearly wiped out the CCP. Remnants of the party broke out of encirclement in Jiangxi Province in 1934 and undertook the 6,000-mile Long March to a secure base in Yan'an, Shanxi Province. There, under Mao,

## CHINA'S POPULATION

China historically has had the largest population of any country in the world. In line with trends throughout the world, China's population grew slowly until about 1700, and accelerated thereafter. Civil wars and natural disasters have occasionally led to sharp population decreases, but the overall trend has been steadily upward.

| | | |
|---|---|---|
| **A.D. 2** | 60,000,000 (household census) | |
| **1000** | 100,000,000 (est.) | |

**Mongol invasions, 1220–1270; fall of Yuan Dynasty, 1368**

| | |
|---|---|
| **1390** | 75,000,000 (est.) |
| **1573** | 150,000,000 (est.) |

**Fall of Qing Dynasty, 1644**

| | |
|---|---|
| **1685** | 100,000,000 (est.) |
| **1749** | 177,495,000 (census) |
| **1790** | 301,487,000 (census) |
| **1850** | 450,000,000 (est.) |

**Taiping Rebellion, 1851–1863**

| | |
|---|---|
| **1870** | 370,000,000 (est.) |
| **1910** | 450,000,000 (est.) |

**War with Japan, 1937–1945**

| | |
|---|---|
| **1945** | 450,000,000 (est.) |
| **1953** | 583,600,000 (census) |
| **1957** | 646,500,000 (census) |

**Great Leap Forward, 1959–60; mass starvation**

| | |
|---|---|
| **1966** | 750,000,000 (est.) |
| **1972** | 870,000,000 (est.) |
| **1976** | 925,000,000 (est.) |
| **1982** | 1,008,152,137 (census) |
| **1988** | 1,088,169,192 (census) |
| **1990** | 1,133,682,501 (census) |
| **2000** | 1,300,000,000 (projected) |

Family planning programs introduced in 1966 resulted in a sharp downturn in fertility, particularly with the promulgation of the "one child per family" policy in 1980. The privatization of agriculture in 1983 has, however, produced a sharp increase in fertility in rural areas, imperiling efforts to control China's future population growth.

**Live births per 1,000 population**

| | |
|---|---|
| **1974** | 42.0 (est.) |
| **1976** | 32.0 (est.) |
| **1980** | 22.0 (est.) |
| **1988** | 14.30 urban, 24.94 rural (census) |

Zhou Enlai, and Zhu De, the CCP recovered its strength. In the Xi'an Incident of December 1936, Chiang was kidnapped by mutinous KMT allies and forced at gunpoint to agree to forming a United Front with the CCP against Japan.

Meanwhile Japan continued its penetration of China, with the assassination of Manchurian warlord and KMT ally Jiang Zuolin in 1928, the invasion of Manchuria on Sept. 18, 1931, and the establishment of the puppet state of Manchuguo in 1934. On July 7, 1937, fighting erupted between Japanese and Chinese troops near Beijing. The Japanese rapidly moved south to the Yangtse Valley, bombing and capturing Shanghai. The Nationalist capital at

Nanjing fell in November 1937, amid widespread atrocities against civilians. The KMT army and government retreated to a wartime capital at Chongqing. The remainder of World War II in China was largely a stalemate, with Japan occupying most of the country. KMT-held areas opposed the Japanese with conventional forces (supported, after 1941, by the Americans), while the Communists harassed the Japanese with guerrilla tactics.

At the end of World War II, American forces ensured that the KMT would receive Japan's surrender throughout most of China, giving the Nationalists a commanding position while U.S. Gen. George Marshall attempted to mediate the creation of a KMT-CCP coalition government. That effort failed, and civil war broke out. The KMT advantage was dissipated by ruinous inflation, corruption, mismanagement, and military ineffectiveness. At the end of 1947, with the Communist forces making continual advances, the United States pulled out of China. After losing several major battles throughout 1948–49, KMT forces retreated to Taiwan; in Beijing, Mao Zedong proclaimed the establishment of the People's Republic of China (PRC) on Oct. 1, 1949.

With American backing, the Republic of China established a temporary capital at Taipei (see "Taiwan") and continued to claim sovereignty over all of China, retaining China's seat in the United Nations. The PRC was quickly granted diplomatic recognition by Soviet bloc nations and some Western nations, notably Great Britain, but was effectively isolated in most international affairs by American support for Nationalist China. Chinese troops entered the Korean War in November 1950, as UN forces approached the Sino-Korean border at the Yalu River. This direct confrontation between China and the U.S. forestalled any possibility of normal contacts for more than two decades thereafter, as U.S.-Chinese relations were held in the grip of the Cold War.

Within China the CCP rapidly consolidated its control of the country and began the task of rebuilding the nation after decades of internal and external warfare. Priority was given to land reform. Land was confiscated from landlords and returned to peasant ownership; landlords and other "class enemies" were tried and condemned by People's Courts set up under party auspices. Under the first five-year plan, announced in 1953, peasants were urged to set up rural cooperatives, while industrial recovery began with Soviet assistance. Artists, writers, and intellectuals were ordered to devote themselves to the service of the party and the nation. In 1956 Mao announced a policy of "let a hundred flowers bloom, let a hundred schools of thought contend," inviting criticism of the party and government. He was shocked by the vigor of the criticism thus produced; many critics were sent to labor camps in the ensuing Anti-Rightist Campaign of 1957.

Angered by the arrogance of Soviet advisers and by Soviet refusal to share nuclear weapons technology with China, Mao broke with the Soviet Union and expelled all Soviet personnel in 1958. At the same time, he announced the policy of the Great Leap Forward, under which

China was to make rapid progress on all fronts without outside aid. Huge rural communes took the place of peasant smallholdings and cooperatives, and agriculture was placed under the direction of centralized planning. In industry, labor and enthusiasm were expected to make up for a shortage of capital and technical expertise. The Great Leap was a catastrophic failure, causing widespread famine and social dislocation, as Mao admitted in a forced self-criticism in 1960. Mao temporarily withdrew into the background as a group of party pragmatists led by Liu Shaoqi assumed power in the early 1960s.

In foreign affairs Chinese shelling of the Nationalist-held offshore islands of Quemoy and Matsu in 1958 led to a crisis in the Taiwan Straits, patrolled by the U.S. Seventh Fleet to prevent a recurrence of China's civil war. A rebellion in Tibet in 1959 was suppressed with much bloodshed, and the dalai lama fled to India. Chinese troop movements into Tibet contributed to the outbreak in 1960 of a border war with India. Throughout the 1960s China worried about being drawn into the Vietnam war.

In late 1965 Mao made a bid to return to full power. His vehicle was the Great Proletarian Cultural Revolution, formally launched in 1966. Shock troops of teenage Red Guards were used to attack the entrenched party bureaucracy; Liu Shaoqi was placed under house arrest, and other prominent officials, including Deng Xiaoping, were exiled to rural areas. By 1968 internal disorder was so great that the military intervened to restore control in many areas. Most established organs of power were replaced under the Cultural Revolution by Revolutionary Committees; intellectuals, technical workers, and bureaucrats were severely persecuted. In 1971 Mao's second-in-command, Marshal Lin Biao, staged an abortive coup and died while attempting to flee the country. With Mao increasingly old and ill, most of his power was exercised by his wife, Jiang Qing, and her associates. Her rival, Premier Zhou Enlai, attempted to maintain orderly government functions in the face of this turmoil.

The 1968 Soviet invasion of Czechoslovakia convinced Mao that the USSR was potentially a greater threat to China than America, and he quietly encouraged the growth of better relations with the U.S. With tacit American approval, the PRC replaced the Republic of China (Taiwan) in the UN on Oct. 25, 1971. During Feb. 21–28, 1972, U.S. Pres. Richard Nixon visited China. The Shanghai Communiqué, issued at the end of that visit, clarified the positions of both sides and paved the way for the resumption of U.S.-China relations short of formal diplomatic recognition.

Zhou Enlai died in January 1976, and Deng Xiaoping became acting premier. In April 1976 a rally in Beijing commemorating Zhou's birthday was dispersed by police on orders from Jiang Qing, and a riot ensued (the Tienanmen Square Incident). Deng was dismissed from office. But when Mao died on Sept. 9, 1976, Deng reemerged as China's paramount leader, behind the new acting premier and acting party chairman, figurehead Hua Guofeng. Jiang Qing and three associates were arrested along with many of their allies. Labeled the Gang of Four, Jiang Qing's clique was blamed for all the ills of the Cultural Revolution; they were tried and convicted for crimes against the state in 1981.

China's post-Mao transformation took a decisive turn in 1978, with the announcement of the policy of the Four Modernizations (agriculture, industry, science and technology, and defense). Foreign investment and technology transfer were encouraged, and thousands of students were sent to study abroad. For a few months in the winter of 1978–79, the authorities tolerated the public posting of written critiques of the government ("Democracy Wall"). Deng consolidated power in his own hands, still acting behind the scenes; Hua Guofeng was dismissed from office, while Deng's allies Hu Yaobang and Zhao Ziyang were promoted to leadership of the party and government in 1982.

On Jan. 1, 1979, China and the United States entered into formal diplomatic relations; the United States rescinded its recognition of the Republic of China as China's legal government but maintained separate nongovernmental relations with the ROC under the Taiwan Relations Act. China's relations with Vietnam deteriorated in 1978 following Vietnam's invasion of Cambodia. In February 1979, China attempted, with little success, to "teach Vietnam a lesson" in a brief but violent border war. A conflict with Great Britain was resolved in 1984 as both sides agreed that Hong Kong would be returned to Chinese sovereignty, but with considerable local autonomy, in 1997. Relations with the Soviet Union remained strained, China insisting that no improvement could come before the USSR reduced its troop concentrations on the Sino-Soviet border, withdrew from Afghanistan, and pressured Vietnam into withdrawing from Cambodia. China's overall foreign-policy stance in the post-Mao era has been low-key and nonconfrontational.

In the 1980s, China achieved spectacular improvements in agricultural production through dismantling rural communes and returning land to individual peasant holdings under long-term leases. Small-scale private enterprise has been encouraged in both rural and urban areas. Reform in industry and in the centrally controlled price structure has been harder to achieve and has led to such side-effects as inflation and increased corruption. Within the overall context of reform, factions of relatively more conservative and reformist leaders have coexisted uneasily. A conservative drive against "spiritual pollution" in 1986 was quickly blunted by Deng, but in January 1987, the reformist party-secretary Hu Yaobang was ousted after student demonstrations calling for more democracy. The CCP 12th Party Congress in October 1987 forced the retirement of some older conservatives, named the reformist Zhao Ziyang as party secretary, and elevated the conservative pragmatist Li Peng as premier.

In April 1989 student demonstrators in Beijing mourning the death of Hu Yaobang launched a general movement for greater democracy. Demonstrators began a hunger strike and disrupted a summit visit by Soviet President Gorbachev. Martial law was proclaimed in May as demonstrations spread to other cities. Troops opened fire in Tienanmen Square on June 3–4, killing hundreds of demonstrators. In the aftermath, Zhao Ziyang was replaced as party secretary by Jiang Zemin, thousands of protesters and suspected dissidents were arrested (and an unknown number executed), and hard-liners in the government took firm control of the country. Noted dissident Fang Lizhi and his wife took refuge in the American embassy.

World opinion was outraged by the Tienanmen incident; the United States and many other countries instituted sanctions against China, tourism plummeted, and the economy went into general decline. International trade gradually resumed during 1989–90, and the United States renewed China's most-favored-nation status in June 1990 after several hundred dissidents were released from prison. Fang Lizhi and his wife were allowed to emigrate to England in July 1990; Western leaders at the July summit of economic powers promised to lift sanctions in 1991 if China's political climate continued to improve.

China has strived to put Tienanmen Square behind it by holding speedy trials of those charged in connection with demonstrations. The government has also made overtures to the USSR, and from its permanent seat on the UN Security Council supported coalition efforts against Iraq in the Persian Gulf conflict.

## Colombia
### Republic of Colombia

**Geography Location:** northwestern coast of South America. **Boundaries:** Caribbean Sea to N, Venezuela, Brazil to E, Peru, Ecuador to S, Panama, Pacific Ocean to W. **Total land area:** 440,831 sq. mi. (1,141,748 sq km). **Coastline:** 1,992 mi. (3,208 km). **Comparative area:** between Texas and Alaska. **Land use:** 4% arable land; 2% permanent crops; 29% meadows and pastures; 49% forest and woodland; 16% other; includes negl. % irrigated. **Major cities:** (1985) Bogotá (capital) 3,982,941; Medellín 1,468,089; Cali 1,350,565; Barranquilla 899,781; Cartagena 531,426.

**People Population:** 33,076,188 (1990). **Nationality:** noun—Colombian(s); adjective—Colombian. **Ethnic groups:** 58% mestizo, 20% white, 14% mulatto, 4% black, 4% other. **Languages:** Spanish. **Religions:** 95% Roman Catholic.

**Government Type:** republic; executive branch dominates government structure. **Independence:** July 20, 1810 (from Spain). **Constitution:** Aug. 4, 1886, with amendments codified in 1946 and 1968. **National holiday:** Independence Day, July 20. **Heads of government:** César Gaviria Trujillo, president (since Aug. 1990). **Structure:** president; bicameral legislature (Congress—Senate, House of Representatives); judiciary.

**Economy Monetary unit:** Colombian peso. **Budget:** (1987) *income:* $3.6 bil.; *expend.:* $3.7 bil. **GDP:** $33 bil., $1,140 per capita (1987). **Chief crops:** coffee, rice, corn, sugarcane, plantains, cotton, tobacco, bananas;

illegal producer of coca and cannabis for international drug trade. **Livestock:** cattle, sheep, pigs, horses, goats. **Natural resources:** crude oil, natural gas, coal, iron ore, nickel. **Major industries:** textiles, food processing, oil. **Labor force:** 11 mil. (1986); 53% services, 26% agriculture, 21% industry (1981); 12% unemployment (1987). **Exports:** $4.6 bil. (f.o.b., 1987); 30% coffee, 24% petroleum, coal, bananas, fresh cut flowers. **Imports:** $4.3 bil. (c.i.f., 1987); industrial equipment, transportation equipment, foodstuffs, chemicals. **Major trading partners: exports:** 36% U.S., 21% EC, 5% Japan, 4% Netherlands, 3% Sweden; **imports:** 34% U.S., 16% EC, 4% Brazil, 3% Venezuela, 3% Japan.

**Intl. Orgs.** FAO, G-77, GATT, IAEA, IBRD, ICAO, IDA, IFAD, IFC, ILO, IMF, IMO, INTELSAT, INTERPOL, ITU, NAM, OAS, UN, UNESCO, UPU, WHO, WIPO, WMO.

The territory that is now Colombia was home to various sedentary and semisedentary cultures prior to the arrival of Europeans. The Chibcha population of the Andean region might have numbered about one million prior to European contact. Portions of the area that make up modern Colombia fell under the authority of the Inca empire.

In 1538 the colony of New Granada was established with its capital at Bogotá, and for most of the period up until 1740, the area was within the jurisdiction of the Viceroyalty of Peru. In that year a new viceroyalty was established that included modern-day Colombia, Ecuador, Panama, and Venezuela. During the wars of independence against Spain, forces under Simón Bolívar were victorious over the royalists at the Battle of Boyacá in 1819, and the region gained its independence in 1821.

Colombian territory was a part of the federation of Gran Colombia until the collapse of the federal arrangement in 1830. Thereafter, the country—called New Granada—remained a separate political entity (which included the area of Panama). By the 1850s a federal system had been adopted for the country. But this arrangement rapidly disintegrated, and the practically semisovereign states were involved in a constant struggle with the central government for autonomy. The effort to define the political structure was largely resolved with the constitution of 1886, which ended federalist regional autonomy and made Colombia a unitary republic.

Colombian political struggle since the 1850s had been characterized by a rivalry between two groups that coalesced into the Liberal and Conservative parties. During much of the 19th century, the Liberal-Conservative ideological battle was influenced to a great extent by the definition of the role of the Roman Catholic church in the country's political and social life. The 1887–88 Concordat represented a settlement on the role of the church in which the church was to have "official protection," while the state was to have authority over public education. The settlement left a central position for the church in Colombian society that was not substantially altered by the Concordat of 1942.

The Liberal-Conservative struggle led to at least six civil wars, which often ended in inter-party compromise. A struggle in 1854 involved the issue of the future direction of the country's economic development and was followed by a settlement among elites. The Liberal-Conservative war of 1860–63 led to a Liberal victory and a period of Liberal political hegemony that lasted until 1886. The period of Conservative rule from 1886 until 1930 was punctuated by the "War of a Thousand Days" (1899–1902), in which the Conservatives defeated the Liberals. In 1903 the Colombian government rejected a U.S. offer for construction of a canal in Panama. As a result Panama (backed by the U.S.) revolted against the Colombian government, ending in the separation of Panama from Colombia.

The world depression of 1929 seriously disrupted both the economy and the politics of Colombia. The loss of popularity of the ruling Conservatives due to both the overall economic collapse and their increasingly brutal repression of the labor movement led to a Liberal victory in 1930. A new civil war between peasants loyal to the two parties also broke out that year. By 1934 Liberal Pres. Alfonso López Pumarejo had inaugurated his "Revolution on the March" program of socioeconomic reform.

During the 1946 presidential election, Conservatives won the presidency with a minority of the overall vote, defeating a split Liberal party. Armed conflict originally instigated by the two party elites erupted. The political violence, however, soon took on a momentum of its own, expanding in scope. This marked the beginning of La Violencia (1948–57) during which more than 200,000 people died. In the summer of 1957, leaders of the Liberal and Conservative parties reached an agreement on constitutional reform in an attempt to end the violence. The agreement, known as the National Front, was to be in force for 16 years and included provisions for regular alternation of the presidency between the parties, as well as an accord on equal staffing of all political positions by both parties. The Liberal and Conservative parties agreed they alone would monopolize the arena of legitimate political competition for the 16-year period. The agreement held up until 1968 constitutional revisions allowed for other organized political groups to be officially recognized.

The emergence of terrorist and paramilitary groups on both the right and left—some with ties to the drug trade—in the 1960s and 1970s weakened the two-party power-sharing monopoly. In March 1990, one of the most notorious left-wing groups, M-19, elected to lay down its arms and enter the political mainstream and immediately captured 19 of 70 seats in a constitutional convention called to rewrite the constitution. Other groups followed suit in 1991.

Colombia has also had to cope with a burgeoning narcotics trade. Throughout the 1980s, narco-terrorists murdered government officials (including judges and legislators), journalists, and innocent bystanders with impunity. Despite the assassination of four presidential candidates prior to the May 1990 election, the Liberal party's ultimate candidate, Carlos Gaviria Trujillo, won the election campaigning vigorously against the drug traffickers.

## Comoros
### Federal Islamic Republic of the Comoros

**Geography** **Location:** part of archipelago in Mozambique Channel; three main islands, Njazidja, Nzwami, and Mwali (formerly Grande-Comore, Anjouan and Mohéli). Moroni, Njazidja Is., 11°40'S, 43°16'E. **Boundaries:** between Madagascar and southeast Africa. **Total land area:** 719 sq. mi. (1,862 sq km). **Coastline:** 211 mi. (340 km). **Comparative area:** slightly more than 12 times size of Washington, DC. **Land use:** 35% arable land; 8% permanent crops; 7% meadows and pastures; 16% forest and woodland; 34% other. **Major cities:** (1980 census) Moroni (capital) 17,267; Mutsamudu 13,000; Fomboni 5,400.

**People** **Population:** 460,188 (1990). **Nationality:** noun—Comoran(s); adjective—Comoran. **Ethnic groups:** Antalote, Cafre, Makoa, Oimatsaha, Sakalava. **Languages:** Shaafi Islam (Swahili dialect), Malagasy, French. **Religions:** 86% Sunni Muslim, 14% Roman Catholic.

**Government** **Type:** republic. **Independence:** July 6, 1975 (from France). **Constitution:** Oct. 1, 1978, amended Oct. 1982 and Jan. 1985. **National holiday:** N.A. **Heads of government:** Said Mohamed Djohar, president (since Mar. 1990); Ali Mroudjae, prime minister (since Feb. 1982). **Structure:** executive—president; legislative—38-member Federal Assembly.

**Economy** **Monetary unit:** Comoran franc. **Budget:** (1988 est.) *income:* $75.2 mil.; *expend.:* $77.9 mil. **GDP:** $207 mil., $475 per capita. **Chief crops:** cash crops—essential oils for perfumes (mainly ylang-ylang), vanilla, copra, cloves; food crops—rice, manioc, maize, fruits, vegetables. **Livestock:** poultry, cattle, sheep. **Natural resources:** negligible. **Major industries:** perfume distillation. **Labor force:** 140,000 (1982); 80% agriculture, 3% government, 17% other; significant unemployment; 51% of population of working age (1985). **Exports:** $12 mil. (f.o.b., 1987); perfume oils, vanilla, copra, cloves. **Imports:** $52 mil. (c.i.f., 1987); rice and other foodstuffs, cement, fuels, chemicals, textiles. **Major trading partners:** *exports:* 53% U.S., 41% France, 4% Africa, 2% Germany; *imports:* 62% Europe (22% France), 5% Africa, Pakistan, China.

**Intl. Orgs.** FAO, G-77, IBRD, IDA, IFAD, ILO, IMF, ITU, NAM, UN, UNESCO, UPU, WHO, WMO.

The Federal Islamic Republic of Comoros is part of an archipelago composed of four prominent islands (the fourth, Mayotte, is a French dependency) and several smaller islands. Numerous groups from Africa, Europe, and Asia invaded the islands over the centuries. Shirazi Arabs introduced Islam to Comoros around the turn of the 16th century, and the French established colonial rule over the archipelago between 1841 and 1912 and developed a plantation-based economy. The islands remained a French territory until 1961 when political

autonomy was granted. Comoros gained independence in 1975. (Representatives from the island of Mayotte abstained on the vote for unilateral independence, and it remains under French administration.) Although overthrown by foreign mercenaries in 1975, Pres. Ahmed Abdallah Abderemane returned to power in 1978 and helped establish the country's first constitution. In November 1989 he was assassinated by a small group of rebels who quickly dispersed under pressure from the French government. The nation's first contested presidential election was held in March 1990.

Much of the nation's soil is laden with lava, making it unsuitable for farming, especially on the island of Njazidja (Grand Comore), which is dominated by Mount Kartala, an active volcano. This obstacle to agriculture hinders the growth of Comoros, one of the poorest and least developed nations in the world. Poor transportation links between the islands and a harsh cyclone season add further to the country's problems. But Comoros has invested heavily in its tourism industry.

## Congo
### People's Republic of the Congo

**Geography** **Location:** equatorial country on western coast of Africa. **Boundaries:** Cameroon to NW, Central African Republic to NE, Zaire to E and S, Angolan district of Cabinda to S, Gulf of Guinea to SW, Gabon to W. **Total land area:** 132,047 sq. mi. (342,000 sq km). **Coastline:** 105 mi. (169 km). **Comparative area:** between New Mexico and Montana. **Land use:** 2% arable land; negl. % permanent crops; 29% meadows and pastures; 62% forest and woodland; 7% other. **Major cities:** (1974 census) Brazzaville (capital) 456,383; Pool 219,329; Pointe-Noire 214,466; Bouenza 135,999; Cuvette 127,558.

**People** **Population:** 2,242,274 (1990). **Nationality:** noun—Congolese (sing., pl.); adjective—Congolese or Congo. **Ethnic groups:** 75 groups, almost all Bantu—48% Kongo, 20% Sangha, 17% Teke, 12% M'Bochi; about 8,500 Europeans, mostly French. **Languages:** French (official); many African languages with Lingala and Kikongo most widely used. **Religions:** 50% Christian, 42% indigenous beliefs, 2% Muslim.

**Government** **Type:** people's republic. **Independence:** Aug. 15, 1960 (from France). **Constitution:** July 8, 1979. **National holiday:** National Day, Aug. 15. **Heads of government:** Col. Denis Sassou-Nguesso, president (since Feb. 1979); André Milongo, prime minister (since June 1991). **Structure:** executive—president; Council of State; judiciary.

**Economy** **Monetary unit:** Communauté Financière Africaine (CFA) franc. **Budget:** (1988) *income:* $382 mil.; *expend.:* $575 mil. **GDP:** $2.2 bil., $1,000 per capita (1988 est.). **Chief crops:** cash crops—sugarcane, wood, coffee, cocoa beans, palm kernels; food crops—root crops, rice, corn, bananas, manioc. **Livestock:** goats, cattle, sheep, pigs. **Natural resources:** petroleum, timber, potash, lead, zinc. **Major industries:** crude oil, cement, sawmills. **Labor force:** 79,100 (1985); 75% agriculture, 25%

commerce, industry, government; 51% of population of working age with 40% economically active; 40,000–60,000 unemployed. **Exports:** $912 mil. (f.o.b., 1987); 72% crude petroleum, lumber, plywood, coffee, cocoa. **Imports:** $494.4 mil. (c.i.f., 1987); foodstuffs, consumer goods, intermediate manufactures, capital equipment. **Major trading partners:** *exports:* U.S., France, other EC; *imports:* France, Italy, other EC, U.S., W. Germany.

**Intl. Orgs.** FAO, G-77, GATT, IBRD, ICAO, IDA, IFAD, IFC, ILO, IMF, IMO, INTELSAT, INTERPOL, ITU, NAM, UN, UNESCO, UPU, WHO, WIPO, WMO.

Beginning around 1,500 years ago, the lower reaches of the Congo River formed the focus of a number of well-organized states. The Kongo and Ndonga flourished south of the river; north of the river, in what is now the Congo, the Loango, Teke, and Bobangi were dominant. Some of these states were weakened beginning in the 16th century by the Portuguese slave trade, although the Loango benefited from the trade through the 19th century.

With the weakening of Portuguese power, the French became the dominant European power in western Africa. In 1883 they established a protectorate over the Teke kingdom, which they renamed Middle Congo. The treaty with the Teke king was concluded by Pierre Savorgnan de Brazza, for whom the capital was—and is—named.

In 1910 the French confederated their protectorates of Gabon, Middle Congo, Ubangi-Shari (later the Central African Republic), and Chad to form French Equatorial Africa. The territory became an important base of Free French activity during World War II, in acknowledgment of which Gen. Charles de Gaulle granted French citizenship to the territory's inhabitants in 1946, and local power was devolved upon advisory assemblies. The Republic of the Congo attained full autonomy upon the dissolution of the confederation of French Equatorial Africa in 1959, and the nation gained full independence on Apr. 15, 1960.

In August 1963 Pres. Fulbert Youlou was driven from office by violent labor unrest; the military took control and then installed a provisional civilian government led by Alphonse Massamba-Debat. He was subsequently elected president for a five-year term.

In 1968 Massamba-Debat was overthrown in a military coup and replaced by Capt. Marien Ngouabi. In 1969 Ngouabi reorganized the Congo as a People's Republic and changed the name of the ruling party from the National Revolutionary Movement party to the Congolese Labor party. Both China and the USSR vied for influence in the new People's Republic which, despite its Marxist-Leninist stance, remained strongly linked to France—its main source of trade, aid, and foreign investment.

Ngouabi was assassinated on Mar. 18, 1977, and replaced by an 11-man military committee of the Congolese Labor party, led by Gen. Joachim Yhomby-Opango. Yhomby-Opango resigned and was arrested for treason in 1979. He was replaced as president by Denis Sassou-Nguesso who was reelected to a third five-year term in 1989. Opposition parties were legalized as of Jan. 1, 1991, following mounting calls for liberalization and labor strikes.

The topography of the Congo consists of fertile plains and thick forests. The country is primarily agricultural; palm oil, coffee, cocoa, and tobacco are cultivated for export. The country is rich in minerals, including oil, natural gas, potash, lead, copper, and zinc. Much of the nation's mineral and petroleum earnings has been spent on ill-conceived and unproductive state projects. Corruption and economic mismanagement are rampant, and unemployment remains over 20%, a problem aggravated by the fact that 70% of the population is under age 35.

## Costa Rica
### Republic of Costa Rica

**Geography** **Location:** Central American isthmus. **Boundaries:** Nicaragua to N, Caribbean Sea to E, Panama to S, and Pacific Ocean to W. **Total land area:** 19,730 sq. mi. (51,100 sq km). **Coastline:** 801 mi. (1,290 km). **Comparative area:** slightly smaller than West Virginia. **Land use:** 6% arable land; 7% permanent crops; 45% meadows and pastures; 34% forest and woodland; 8% other; includes 1% irrigated. **Major cities:** (1984 census) San José (capital) 245,370; Puntarenas 47,851; Limón 43,158; Alajuela 33,929; Cartago 23,884.

**People** **Population:** 3,032,795 (1990). **Nationality:** noun—Costa Rican(s); adjective—Costa Rican. **Ethnic groups:** 96% white, 3% black, 1% Indian. **Languages:** Spanish (official), Jamaican dialect of English spoken around Puerto Limón. **Religions:** 95% Roman Catholic.

**Government** **Type:** democratic republic. **Independence:** Sept. 15, 1821 (from Spain). **Constitution:** Nov. 9, 1949. **National holiday:** Independence Day, Sept. 18. **Heads of government:** Rafael Angel Calderón, president (since May 1990). **Structure:** executive—president (head of government and chief of state), elected for single four-year term; two vice presidents; legislative—57-delegate unicameral Legislative Assembly elected at four-year intervals (legislator may not serve consecutive terms); judiciary—Supreme Court of Justice (17 magistrates elected by Legislative Assembly at eight-year intervals).

**Economy** **Monetary Unit:** colón. **Budget:** (1988) *income:* $719 mil.; *expend.:* $808 mil. **GDP:** $4.7 bil., $1,630 per capita. **Chief crops:** coffee, bananas, sugarcane, rice, corn, cocoa; illegal producer of cannabis for international drug trade. **Livestock:** cattle, pigs, horses. **Natural resources:** hydropower potential. **Major industries:** food processing, textiles, clothing, construction materials. **Labor force:** 868,300 (1985 est.); 35.1% industry and commerce, 27% agriculture, 26.1% government and services, 11.8% other; 6.2% unemployment (1987). **Exports:** $1.3 bil. (f.o.b., 1988); coffee, bananas, textiles, sugar. **Imports:** $1.4 bil. (c.i.f., 1988); petroleum, machinery, consumer durables, chemicals, fertilizer. **Major trading partners:** *exports:* 75% U.S., W. Germany, Guatemala, Netherlands, UK, Japan; *imports:* 35% U.S., Japan, Guatemala, W. Germany.

**Intl. Orgs.** FAO, G-77, IAEA, IBRD, ICAO, IDA, IFAD, IFC, ILO, IMF, IMO, INTELSAT, INTERPOL, ITU, UN, UNESCO, UPU, WHO, WMO.

Costa Rica was under the jurisdiction of the Spanish colonial kingdom of Guatemala until it broke with Spain in 1821, along with other parts of Central America. With the collapse of the United Provinces of Central America in 1838, Costa Rica became an independent republic, and the country held its first democratic elections in 1889.

An attempt at electoral fraud in 1948 led to a brief civil war, which was won by the National Liberation forces under "Don Pepé" Jose Figueres Ferrer. The Costa Rican army was subsequently abolished.

In the 1980s, under Pres. Oscar Arias Sánchez, Costa Rica vigorously promoted the settlement of civil strife in Nicaragua and El Salvador. Though he was awarded the 1987 Nobel Peace Prize for his Central American peace plan, Arias was critized for neglecting domestic issues, and inflation hit 25% in 1989.

## Cuba
### Republic of Cuba

**Geography** **Location:** largest island in Caribbean Sea, about 100 mi. (160 km) S of Florida. **Boundaries:** North Atlantic Ocean to N, Windward Passage to E, Caribbean Sea to S, Yucatan Channel to W. **Total land area:** 42,803 sq. mi. (110,860 sq km). **Coastline:** 2,319 mi. (3,735 km). **Comparative area:** between Tennessee and Pennsylvania. **Land use:** 23% arable land; 6% permanent crops; 23% meadows and pastures; 17% forest and woodland; 31% other; includes 10% irrigated. **Major cities:** (1989 est.) Havana (capital) 2,096,054; Santiago de Cuba 405,354; Camagüey 283,008; Holguin 228,053; Guantánamo 200,381.

**People** **Population:** 10,620,099 (1990). **Nationality:** noun—Cuban(s); adjective—Cuban. **Ethnic groups:** 51% mulatto, 37% white, 11% black, 1% Chinese. **Languages:** Spanish. **Religions:** at least 85% nominally Roman Catholic before Castro assumed power.

**Government** **Type:** Communist state. **Independence:** May 20, 1902 (from Spain). **Constitution:** Feb. 24, 1976. **National holiday:** Anniversary of the Revolution, Jan. 1. **Heads of government:** Fidel Castro Ruz, prime minister from Feb. 1959, president (since Dec. 1976). **Structure:** executive; legislative (National Assembly of the People's Power); controlled judiciary.

**Economy** **Monetary unit:** Cuban peso. **Budget:** (1989 est.) *income:* $11.7 bil.; *expend.:* $13.5 bil. **GNP:** $20.9 bil., $2,000 per capita. **Chief crops:** sugar, tobacco, rice, potatoes, tubers, citrus, coffee. **Livestock:** cattle, pigs, horses, sheep. **Natural resources:** cobalt, nickel, iron ore, copper, manganese. **Major industries:** sugar milling, petroleum refining, food and tobacco processing. **Labor force:** 3.3 mil. (1987); 30% services and government,

29% industry, 13% agriculture, 11% commerce; 7% unemployment (1988). **Exports:** $5.5 bil. (f.o.b., 1988); sugar, nickel, shellfish, citrus, tobacco, coffee. **Imports:** $7.6 bil. (c.i.f., 1988); capital goods, industrial raw materials, food, petroleum. **Major trading partners:** *exports:* 67% USSR, 6% E. Germany, 4% China; *imports:* 71% USSR, 15% other communist countries.

**Intl. Orgs.** FAO, G-77, GATT, IAEA, ICAO, IFAD, ILO, IMO, ITU, NAM, OAS (nonparticipant), UN, UNESCO, UNIDO, UPU, WHO, WIPO, WMO.

At the time of Christopher Columbus's arrival in 1492, Cuba was home to Arawak, Ciboney, and Guanahatabey Indian people. Cuba served as a launching point for Spanish imperial conquests in the Americas, and the early 19th century wars of independence that swept the rest of Spanish America did not overthrow the imposing Spanish garrison there. Slavery was abolished in 1886, but Spanish colonialism lingered in Cuba until the 1890s.

Spanish control of the island began to deteriorate in the late 1860s with the beginning of the "Ten Years War" (1868-78), and Cuba finally separated from Spain as a result of the Cuban-U.S.-Spanish war, which ended with the signing of the Treaty of Paris in 1898. Cuba became a U.S. protectorate by virtue of the U.S.-sponsored Platt Amendment (1901) to the new Cuban constitution. The Platt Amendment gave the United States the right to intervene in Cuban affairs, and after the initial occupation of the island, U.S. troops repeatedly invaded and occupied the former Spanish colony.

Corruption and political repression plagued Cuban politics during the first half of the 20th century. Gerardo Machado won election to the presidency in 1925, but he quickly turned his administration of the island into a dictatorship that lasted until his ouster by a progressive coalition of students and labor in 1933. The "revolution" of 1933 installed Ramón Grau San Martín as the new head of the government, but the United States supported Grau's ouster, and army Sgt. Fulgencio Batista replaced him. Batista ruled the country either directly or indirectly for the next quarter century.

In 1953 Fidel Castro Ruz lead a failed attack on the Moncada army barracks in Santiago. In December 1956 Fidel and Raúl Castro, Argentine physician Ernesto "Che" Guevara, and 79 others returned to Cuba and waged a guerrilla campaign against the government. Batista's military failed to defeat the guerrillas, and in the wake of increasing demonstrations of public antipathy for his government, the dictator fled the country. The communist Fidelistas took control Jan. 1, 1959.

By mid-1959, revolutionary tribunals had tried and executed more than 500 political "enemies." The leaders announced an agrarian reform, and by 1960 the nationalization of the economy was in full swing. In 1961 U.S.-Cuban diplomatic relations were severed, and the U.S.-sponsored Bay of Pigs invasion by Cuban exiles was a failure. In 1962 the Cuban missile crisis brought the world to the brink of nuclear war when U.S. spy planes uncovered Soviet

intentions to place nuclear weapons on the island. The Soviets agreed to the withdrawal of missiles in exchange for a U.S. pledge not to invade Cuba.

In its active foreign policy, Cuba has provided technical assistance to a number of left-wing regimes in Africa and Latin America. Between 1975 and 1991 it maintained an extensive military presence in Angola, and it has also supported communist insurgencies throughout Latin America.

Castro has balked at Soviet pressure to institute economic and political reforms; cutbacks in Soviet aid and trade have led to a severe economic downturn.

## Cyprus
### Republic of Cyprus

**Geography** **Location:** eastern Mediterranean Sea. Nicosia 35°11′N, 33°23′E. **Boundaries:** 62 mi. (100 km) S of Turkey, Syria to E. **Total land area:** 3,572 sq. mi. (9,521 sq km). **Coastline:** 403 mi. (648 km). **Comparative area:** between Delaware and Connecticut. **Land use:** 40% arable land; 7% permanent crops; 10% meadows and pastures; 18% forest and woodland; 25% other; includes 10% irrigated. **Major cities:** Nicosia (capital) 149,100 (excludes Turkish-occupied portion); Limassol 107,200; Larnaca 48,300 (1982); Famagusta (Gazi Magusa) 39,500 (mid-1974); Phaphos 20,800 (1982).

**People** **Population:** 707,776 (1990). **Nationality:** noun—Cypriot(s); adjective—Cypriot. **Ethnic groups:** 78% Greek, 18% Turkish, 4% other. **Languages:** Greek, Turkish, English. **Religions:** 78% Greek Orthodox, 18% Muslim, 4% Maronite, Armenian, Apostolic, and other.

**Government** **Type:** republic. **Independence:** Aug. 16, 1960 (from UK). **Constitution:** Aug. 16, 1960; negotiations have been held intermittently to create basis for new or revised constitution to govern the island and relations between Greek and Turkish Cypriots. **National holiday:** Independence Day, Oct. 1. **Heads of government:** George Vassiliou, president (since Feb. 1988); Turkish sector—Rauf Denktash, president (since 1975). **Structure:** currently, government of Cyprus has effective authority over only Greek Cypriot community; headed by president of republic and comprising Council of Ministers, House of Representatives, and Supreme Court; Turkish Cypriots declared their own Constitution and governing bodies within Turkish Federated State of Cyprus in 1975; state renamed Turkish Republic of Northern Cyprus in 1983.

**Economy** **Monetary unit:** Cypriot pound. **Budget:** (1989 est.) *income:* $1.2 bil.; *expend.:* $1.4 bil. **GDP:** $4.2 bil., $6,100 per capita (1988 est.). **Chief crops:** potatoes and other vegetables, grapes, citrus, wheat, carob beans. **Livestock:** chickens, sheep, goats, pigs, cattle. **Natural resources:** copper, pyrites, asbestos, gypsum, timber. **Major industries:** mining (iron pyrites, gypsum, asbestos), manufactures principally for local consumption (beverages, footwear, clothing, cement). **Labor force:** Greek

area—251,406 (1986); 42% services, 33% industry, 22% agriculture; 3.4% unemployment; **Exports:** $767 mil. (f.o.b., 1988); principal items—food and beverages, including citrus, raisins, potatoes, wine; also, cement, clothing. **Imports:** $1.9 bil. (c.i.f., 1988); 23% consumer goods, 12% petroleum and lubricants, foodstuffs, feed grains, machinery. **Major trading partners:** (1987) *exports:* 37% Middle East and N. Africa, 27% UK, 11% other EC, 2% U.S.; *imports:* 60% EC, 7% Middle East and N. Africa, 4% U.S.

**Intl. Orgs.** Commonwealth, FAO, G-77, GATT, IAEA, IBRD, ICAO, IDA, IFAD, IFC, ILO, IMF, IMO, INTELSAT, INTERPOL, ITU, NAM, UN, UNESCO, UPU, WHO, WMO.

Recent excavations on Cyprus indicate a human presence at least 10,000 years ago. Mycenean (Greek) culture flourished in the second millenium B.C. Phoenicians colonized the island in the 900s, and it remained a major entrepôt for eastern Mediterranean trade. Annexed to Rome in 58 B.C. it was later part of the Byzantine Empire until the English Richard I (Lion Hearted) established a crusader state in A.D. 1191. The Lusignan dynasty ruled until 1489, when Cyprus was annexed by Venice. It was subsequently conquered by the Ottoman Empire in 1571.

In 1878 the Congress of Berlin placed Cyprus under British administration. In 1914 it was annexed outright by Great Britain and was made a British colony in 1925. From 1945 to 1948, the British used Cyprus as a detention area for "illegal" Jewish immigrants to Palestine.

After 1947 the Greek Cypriot community continued its long-standing agitation for union (*enosis*) with Greece, a policy strongly opposed by the Turkish Cypriot community. Communal violence broke out in 1954–55. In 1960 Cyprus was granted full independence under an agreement that forbade either enosis or partition and included guarantees of the rights of both Greeks and Turks. Attempts by the president, Archbishop Makarios, to alter the constitution to favor the Greek majority provoked further communal clashes in 1964, when a UN peacekeeping force was sent to the island. On July 15, 1974, a military coup by officers favoring union with Greece deposed the Makarios government. On July 20 Turkey invaded Cyprus and, after the collapse of cease-fire talks in August, occupied the northern two-fifths of the island. In 1975 the Turkish government announced a de facto partition of Cyprus; the northern territory was proclaimed the Turkish Federated State of Cyprus, under Pres. Rauf Denktash.

Makarios returned as president of the Republic of Cyprus, which was thus reduced in size, and remained in office until his death in 1977. He was succeeded by Spyros Kyprianou. Some 200,000 Greek Cypriots were expelled from the Turkish sector to the Republic; many Turks fled from the Republic to the Turkish sector. With a return of political stability, renewed foreign investment, and a customs union negotiated with the EEC, the Republic's economy has prospered, led by agriculture, light manufacturing, and tourism.

In the Turkish sector, the economy remains stagnant, hampered by the loss of population, wartime damage, and stringent economic controls. The Turkish sector proclaimed its independence as the Turkish Republic of Northern Cyprus in 1983, but the new republic has not gained international recognition.

In 1988 George Vassiliou was elected president of the Republic of Cyprus. Talks aimed at achieving a federation of Cyprus's two republics remain stalemated.

# Czechoslovakia
## Czech and Slovak Federal Republic

**Geography Location:** landlocked country in central Europe. **Boundaries:** Poland to N, USSR to E, Hungary to SE, Austria to SW, Germany to W. **Total land area:** 49,384 sq. mi. (127,905 sq km). **Coastline:** none. **Comparative area:** between New York and Alabama. **Land use:** 40% arable land; 1% permanent crops; 13% meadows and pastures; 37% forest and woodland; 9% other; includes 1% irrigated. **Major cities:** (1989 est.) Prague (capital) 1,211,207; Bratislava 435,710; Brno 389,789; Ostrava 330,602; Košice 232,362.

**People Population:** 15,682,243 (1990). **Nationality:** noun—Czechoslovak(s); adjective—Czechoslovak. **Ethnic groups:** 64.3% Czech, 30.5% Slovak, 3.8% Hungarian, 0.4% German, 0.4% Polish, 0.3% Ukrainian, 0.1% Russian, 0.2% other (Jewish, Gypsy). **Languages:** Czech and Slovak (both official), Hungarian. **Religions:** 77% Roman Catholic, 20% Protestant, 2% Orthodox, 1% other.

**Government Type:** republic. **Independence:** Oct. 28, 1918 (from Austro-Hungarian empire). **Constitution:** constitution of July 11, 1960 is being revised: a new constitution is expected at the end of 1991. **National holiday:** Liberation Day, May 9. **Heads of government:** Václav Havel, president (since July 1990); Dr. Marián Calfa, prime minister (since July 1990). **Structure:** Executive branch—president elected by National Assembly and Ministers (specific titles are being revised); Legislative—parliament or National Assembly has two houses elected by the people in June 1990; Judicial—Supreme Court and regional courts.

**Economy Monetary unit:** kčs or koruna. **Budget:** (1986) *income:* $22.4 bil.; *expend:* $21.9 bil. **GNP:** $123.2 bil., $7,878 per capita (1989 est.). **Chief crops:** diversified agriculture; main crops—wheat, rye, oats, corn, barley; net food importer—meat, wheat, vegetable oils, fresh fruits and vegetables. **Livestock:** pigs, cattle, sheep, goats, horses. **Natural resources:** coal, coke, timber, lignite, uranium. **Major industries:** iron and steel, machinery and equipment, cement. **Labor force:** 8.2 mil. (1987); 50.8% construction and communications, 36.9% industry, 12.3% agriculture (1982). **Exports:** $24.5 bil. (f.o.b., 1988); 58.5% machinery and equipment, 15.2% industrial consumer goods, 10.6% minerals and metals, 6.1% agricultural and forestry products. **Imports:** $23.5 bil. (f.o.b., 1988);

41.6% machinery and equipment, 32.2% fuels, minerals, and metals, 11.5% agricultural and forestry products, 6.7% consumer goods. **Major trading partners:** USSR, E. Germany, Poland, Hungary, W. Germany, Yugoslavia, Austria, Bulgaria, Romania; 80% with communist countries, 20% with noncommunist countries.

**Intl. Orgs.** CMEA, FAO, GATT, IAEA, ICAO, ILO, IMO, ITU, UN, UNESCO, UPU, Warsaw Pact, WHO, WIPO, WMO.

Bohemia, Moravia, and Slovakia— "lands of the Crown of St. Vaclav"—were formed into the Moravian empire in the ninth century. Slovakia was later conquered by the Magyars, while Bohemia and Moravia remained an independent kingdom under the Přemyslid dynasty, within the Holy Roman Empire. Prague became a great university city in the 14th century. After the Battle of Mohacs in 1526, Bohemia came under Habsburg control. An unsuccessful Bohemian revolt in 1618 initiated the Thirty Years' War.

Bohemia and Moravia were among the richest lands in the Austro-Hungarian Empire. Agriculture prospered in the lowlands and plains, while the hills and mountains, settled by ethnic Germans in the 13th century, were rich in minerals. After 1648 the Czech majority was dominated by German nobility, in Bohemia, Moravia, and Silesia, and Hungarian nobility in Slovakia. The growth of industry in the 19th century led to great prosperity for the urban elite, whereas the nobility became relatively stagnant.

The Habsburg monarchy crumbled during World War I, and in 1918 a new multi-ethnic state of Czechoslovakia emerged, including not only Czechs but also Germans, Slovaks, Magyars, Poles, and Ukrainians. Its founders, Eduard Beneš and Thomas Masaryk, managed to forge a national identity, and it became the most democratic state in Central Europe in the interwar period.

Following the Munich Pact of September 1938, Hitler annexed the German-speaking regions of the "Sudetenland," and in 1939 he absorbed the Czech lands, while establishing a "protectorate" over Slovakia. The Nazis ruled Czechoslovakia with great severity, but the economy boomed with wartime production for the German army. Prague was occupied by Russian troops in 1945.

After World War II, Beneš returned as president. Czechoslovakia ceded its easternmost lands, Carpatho-Ruthenia, to the USSR and expelled or executed over 3 million Germans, along with all German-speaking Jews who had survived the war. In 1948 a Communist coup forced Beneš to resign; he was replaced by the Communist leader Klement Gottwald. Jan Masaryk, the foreign minister, committed suicide or was murdered. Purges and persecutions followed.

With Stalin's death in 1953, Gottwald was replaced as party first secretary by Stalinist hard-liner Antonin Novotny, who also became president in 1957. In 1968 Novotny was replaced as first secretary by a liberal, Alexander Dubcek. Czechoslovakia suddenly was in the vanguard of communist reform. The new

regime abolished censorship, denounced Stalin, decentralized economic decision-making, and granted real power to the national assembly.

The brief "Prague Spring" ended in August 1968, when Warsaw Pact troops invaded. In 1969 Dubcek was replaced by Gustáv Husak. The party was purged, censorship restored, dissent repressed, and the centralized economy restored.

The 1970s brought inflation and economic stagnation but produced no change in policy. The rise of the Solidarity movement in Poland in the early 1980s provoked a backlash of preventive repression in Czechoslovakia, aimed especially at Charter 77, a human-rights organization, and at the Catholic church.

The prodemocracy movement began in earnest in October 1989, inspired by a lack of confidence in Communist rule and by reform movements throughout Eastern Europe. The resignation of Communist leaders throughout December culminated in the parliamentary elections of Vaclav Havel, a dissident playwright and head of a loose coalition of opposition groups called Civic Forum, as president, and the vindicated Alexander Dubcek as chairman of parliament.

Despite severe economic difficulties, revelations of state security abuses, environmental pollution, and other problems inherited from the Communist era, Czechoslovakia's "Velvet Revolution" was a resounding political and popular success. Soviet troops left by March; and in June Civic Forum and its Slovakian ally, Public Against Violence, won 47% of the vote in parliamentary elections, against 14% for the Communists and 12% for the Christian Democrats. Vaclav Havel was elected president, and Marian Calfa became prime minister.

Slovak resentment of the Czech majority remains an issue. While some Slovaks are calling for a federal government of more or less sovereign Slovak and Czech states, others seek the creation of an independent state.

# Denmark
## Kingdom of Denmark

**Geography Location:** northern Europe. **Boundaries:** Skagerrak channel to N, Baltic Sea to E, Germany to S, North Sea to W. **Total land area:** 16,638 sq. mi. (43,092 sq km). **Coastline:** 2,100 mi. (3,379 km). **Comparative area:** between Maryland and West Virginia. **Land use:** 61% arable land; negl. % permanent crops; 6% meadows and pastures; 12% forest and woodland; 21% other; includes 9% irrigated. **Major cities:** (1986) København (Copenhagen—capital) 1,351,999; Århus (Aarhus) 195,152; Odense 137,286; Alborg (Aalborg) 113,650; Esbjerg 71,112.

**People Population:** 5,131,217 (1990). **Nationality:** noun—Dane(s); adjective—Danish. **Ethnic groups:** Scandinavian, Eskimo, Faeroese, Greenlandic. **Languages:** Danish, Faeroese, German. Greenlandic (Eskimo dialect); small German-speaking minority. **Religions:** 97% Evangelical Lutheran, 2% other Protestant and Roman Catholic, 1% other.

**Government Type:** constitutional monarchy. **Constitution:** June 5, 1953. **National holiday:** Birthday of the Queen, Apr. 16. **Heads of government:** Margrethe II, queen (since Jan. 1972); Poul Schlüter, prime minister (since Sept. 1982). **Structure:** executive power vested in Crown but exercised by cabinet responsible to parliament; legislative authority rests jointly with Crown and parliament (Folketing); Supreme Court, two superior courts, 106 lower courts.

**Economy Monetary unit:** krone. **Budget:** (1988) *income:* $34 bil.; *expend.:* $34 bil. **GDP:** $73.7 bil., $14,300 per capita (1989 est.). **Chief crops:** highly intensive, specializes in dairying and animal husbandry; main crops—cereals, root crops; food imports—oilseed, grain, animal foodstuffs. **Livestock:** chickens, pigs, cattle, ducks, turkeys. **Natural resources:** crude oil, natural gas, fish, salt, limestone. **Major industries:** food processing, machinery and equipment, textiles, clothing. **Labor force:** 2.76 mil. (1988); 51% services, 34% industry, 8% government, 7% agriculture, forestry, fishing: 9.6% unemployment (1989). **Exports:** $27.7 bil. (f.o.b., 1989 est.); meat and meat products, dairy products, transport equipment, fish. **Imports:** $26.4 bil. (c.i.f., 1989 est.); petroleum, machinery and equipment, chemicals, grain and foodstuffs. **Major trading partners:** *exports:* 6% U.S., W. Germany, Norway, Sweden, UK, other EC, Japan; *imports:* 7% U.S., W. Germany, Netherlands, Sweden, UK, other EC.

**Intl. Orgs.** EC, FAO, GATT, IAEA, IBRD, ICAO, IDA, IFAD, IFC, ILO, IMF, IMO, INTELSAT, INTERPOL, ITU, NATO, OECD, UN, UNESCO, UPU, WHO, WIPO, WMO.

The obscure Norse kingdom of Denmark made its debut in world history in the eighth century, when Viking raiders began to plunder northwestern Europe. The Danish overseas possessions of the Faeroe Islands and Greenland are a modern reminder of the high point of Viking exploration and conquest. King Harold Bluetooth (d. 985) was Denmark's first Christian monarch; his son, King Canute, ruled an empire that included Denmark, England, Norway, and southern Sweden. Danish royal power reached its high point in the late 14th century but began to wane with the establishment of an independent Swedish monarchy in 1523. In the 16th century, Copenhagen was an important center of European intellectual life.

Further losses of territory were imposed by the Treaty of Copenhagen (1660). Denmark lost control of Norway at the Congress of Vienna (1815) and of Schleswig-Holstein after a civil war in 1864. Iceland, part of Denmark since the 14th century, was granted home rule in 1874, becoming independent in 1944.

In the 19th century, Denmark was transformed from a poor peasant society to one of Europe's richest agricultural nations by means of reforms that established agricultural cooperatives and emphasized intensive specialization in the production of dairy products and pork. These products remain a mainstay of the Danish economy.

Denmark remained neutral during World War I. In 1939 Denmark signed a 10-year non-aggression pact with Germany, but Germany nevertheless invaded Denmark in April 1940; the country surrendered without a fight. In 1941 Denmark's ambassador in Washington transferred defense of Greenland to the United States, and much of Denmark's merchant fleet joined the Allied war effort. Denmark was placed under German martial law in August 1943 and treated as an enemy nation. Danish resistance succeeded in evacuating 7,000 Jews to neutral Sweden. Denmark was liberated by British troops in May 1945.

Although Denmark was not technically a participant on the Allied side in World War II, it received favorable treatment in the postwar period, becoming a UN member in 1946 and a founding member of NATO in 1949. By the latter year, the postwar recovery was complete, with industrial levels exceeding those of the prewar period. High taxes, unemployment, and inflation remained problems, but the economy was aided by the growth of trade with West Germany, which was just beginning its "economic miracle."

In 1953 the king assented to a constitutional reform that abolished the upper house of the legislature, leaving the Folketing as the sole legislative body. Proportional representation meant that it was virtually impossible for any political party to gain a parliamentary majority; Denmark is always governed by coalition regimes. In the postwar period, these normally have been led by the Social Democrats.

In the 1950s Denmark adopted a characteristically Scandinavian program of free enterprise, high taxes, and extensive social welfare systems. A high rate of economic growth, spurred by agricultural exports, continued throughout the 1960s. Denmark joined the EC in 1972. The 1970s brought economic difficulties, as Danish oil exploration in the North Sea yielded disappointing results, and inflation reached double digits annually.

The elections of 1982 installed Denmark's first Conservative government since 1905. A Conservative four-party coalition formed in 1984 has remained in office to the present. The general revival of the world economy in the 1980s coupled with government austerity measures has led to renewed growth and lowered inflation, with both figures now averaging 3 percent annually.

The Faeroe Islands were granted self-rule n 1948; the economy is based on fishing and sheep-raising. Greenland was granted self-rule in 1979. Geographically huge but with a population of under 60,000, the island bases its economy on fishing, tourism, and revenues from military bases.

## Djibouti
### Republic of Djibouti

**Geography Location:** northeastern Africa. **Boundaries:** Red Sea to N, Gulf of Aden to E, Somalia to SE, Ethiopia to S, W, and NW. **Total land area:** 8,958 sq. mi. (23,200 sq km). **Coastline:** 195 mi. (314 km). **Comparative area:** between Massachusetts, and New Hamp-

shire. **Land use:** 0% arable land; 0% permanent crops; 9% meadows and pastures; negl. % forest and woodland; 91% other. **Major cities:** Djibouti (capital) 200,000 (1981); Dikhil, Ali-Sabieh, Tadjourah, Obock.

**People Population:** 337,386 (1990). **Nationality:** noun—Djiboutian(s); adjective—Djiboutian. **Ethnic groups:** 60% Somali (Issa), 35% Afar, 5% French, Arab, Ethiopian, and Italian. **Languages:** French (official); Arabic, Somali, and Afar widely used. **Religions:** 94% Muslim, 6% Christian.

**Government Type:** republic. **Independence:** June 27, 1977 (from France). **Constitution:** partial Constitution ratified Jan. 1981 by National Assembly. **National holiday:** June 27. **Heads of government:** Hassan Gouled Aptidon, president (since June 1977); Barkat Gourad Hamadou, prime minister (since Nov. 1990). **Structure:** executive; legislative—65-member parliament (National Assembly); judiciary.

**Economy Monetary unit:** Djibouti franc. **Budget:** (1987 est.) *income:* $117 mil., *expend.:* $163 mil. **GNP:** $333 mil., $1,070 per capita (1986). **Chief crops:** livestock; limited commercial crops, including fruits and vegetables. **Livestock:** goats, sheep, camels, cattle, asses. **Natural resources:** geothermal areas. **Major industries:** limited to a few small-scale enterprises, such as dairy products and mineral-water boiling. **Labor force:** small number of semiskilled workers at port; 3,000 railway workers; 52% of population of working age (1983). **Exports:** $128 mil. (f.o.b., 1986); hides and skins and transit of coffee; a large portion consists of reexports to foreign residents of Djibouti. **Imports:** $198 mil. (c.i.f., 1986); foods, machinery, transport equipment, chemicals, petroleum. **Major trading partners:** *exports:* 50% Middle East, 43% Africa, 7% W. Europe; *imports:* 36% EC, 21% Africa, 14% Bahrain, 12% Asia, 2% U.S.

**Intl. Orgs.** Arab League, FAO, G-77, IBRD, ICAO, IDA, IFAD, IFC, ILO, IMF, IMO, INTERPOL, ITU, NAM, OAU, UN, UPU, WHO, WMO.

This small, arid region on the Horn of Africa near the southern mouth of the Red Sea became the object of British-French rivalry with the opening of the Suez Canal in 1869. The French sphere of influence, called French Somaliland, was affirmed by agreements with Ethiopia in 1897, 1945, and 1954. In the early 20th century, the French constructed a railroad from Addis Ababa to Djibouti, adding to the colony's strategic value.

French and Italian forces clashed at the border of Ethiopia and French Somaliland with the Italian invasion of Ethiopia in the 1930s. During World War II, the territorial administration at first sided with the Vichy government but in December 1942 established ties with the Free French and the Allies.

The colony was reorganized in 1957 and in 1958 became, by referendum, a French Overseas Territory. In July 1967 its name was changed to the Territory of the Afars and Issas. Growing nationalist sentiment led to a referendum in favor of complete independence. The

Republic of Djibouti became independent on June 27, 1977.

Djibouti's only significant natural resource is its geothermal areas. Shipping provides some income in the port city of Djibouti, but overall the economy depends heavily on French aid and on income derived from the French garrisons that remain stationed there.

## Dominica
### Commonwealth of Dominica

**Geography** **Location:** eastern Caribbean Sea, between Guadeloupe to N and Martinique to S. Roseau 15°18′N, 61°23′W. **Boundaries:** Dominica Passage to N, Atlantic Ocean to E, Martinique Passage to S, Caribbean Sea to W. **Total land area:** 290 sq. mi. (751 sq km). **Coastline:** 92 mi. (148 km). **Comparative area:** slightly more than four times size of Washington, D.C. **Land use:** 9% arable land; 13% permanent crops; 3% meadows and pastures; 41% forest and woodland; 34% other; includes N.A. % irrigated. **Major cities:** (1981 census) Roseau (capital) 8,279; Portsmouth 2,200.

**People** **Population:** 84,854 (1990). **Nationality:** noun—Dominican(s); adjective—Dominican. **Ethnic groups:** mostly black, some Carib-Indians. **Languages:** English (official), French patois widely spoken. **Religions:** 80% Roman Catholic, some Anglican and Methodist.

**Government** **Type:** independent state within commonwealth. **Independence:** Nov. 3, 1978 (from UK). **Constitution:** Nov. 3, 1978. **National holiday:** Nov. 3. **Heads of government:** Sir Clarence Seignoret, president (since Dec. 1983); Mary Eugenia Charles, prime minister (since July 1980). **Structure:** executive—cabinet headed by prime minister; legislative—31-member bicameral House of Assembly (1 ex-officio member, 9 appointed members, and 21 popularly elected members); judicial—magistrate's courts and regional court of appeals.

**Economy** **Monetary unit:** East Caribbean (EC) dollar. **Budget:** (1988) *income:* $60.0 mil.; *expend.:* $52.0 mil. **GDP:** $137 mil., $1,408 per capita. **Chief crops:** bananas, citrus, coconuts, cocoa, yams, essential oils. **Livestock:** pigs, goats, cattle, sheep. **Natural resources:** timber. **Major industries:** agricultural processing, tourism, soap and other coconut-based products. **Labor force:** 25,000 (1984); 40% agriculture, 32% industry and commerce, 28% services; 15–20% unemployment. **Exports:** $46 mil. (f.o.b., 1987); bananas, coconuts, lime juice and oil, cocoa, re-exports. **Imports:** $66 mil. (c.i.f., 1987); machinery and equipment, foodstuffs, manufactured articles, cement. **Major trading partners:** (1985) *exports:* 72% UK, 10% Jamaica, 6% OECS, 3% U.S.; *imports:* 23% U.S., 18% UK, 15% CARICOM, 15% OECS, 5% Japan, 3% Canada.

**Intl. Orgs.** Commonwealth, FAO, G-77, GATT (de facto), IBRD, IDA, IFAD, IFC, ILO, IMF, IMO, INTERPOL, OAS, UN, UNESCO, UPU, WHO, WMO.

Pre-Columbian Dominica was a stronghold of Carib Indians, who had expelled the Arawaks in the 14th century, and today it is the only island in the Caribbean with a native Carib population. Dominica was visited by Columbus on his second American voyage; but though frequented by Spanish ships, it was not settled until French missionaries arrived in the 1630s. Carib resistance was so strong that the French and British agreed to consider the island neutral territory, until it passed under British control in 1763.

Later it was administratively joined to the Leeward and then the Windward Islands, and then became part of the West Indies Federation. It entered into political association with the United Kingdom in 1967. In 1978 Dominica gained independence from Britain. Prime Minister Mary Eugenia Charles's Freedom party has held power since 1980 on a program of economic reconstruction. Hurricanes in 1979–80 largely destroyed the island's agriculture. The government has attempted to effect economic diversification policies, including tourism, since the disaster.

## Dominican Republic

**Geography** **Location:** eastern Hispaniola, in Caribbean Sea. Santo Domingo 19°30′N, 70°42′W. **Boundaries:** North Atlantic to N, Mona Passage to E, Caribbean Sea to S, Haiti to W. **Total land area:** 18,680 sq. mi. (48,380 sq km). **Coastline:** 800 mi. (1,288 km). **Comparative area:** slightly more than four times size of Washington, D.C. **Land use:** 23% arable land; 7% permanent crops; 43% meadows and pastures; 13% forest and woodland; 14% other; includes 4% irrigated. **Major cities:** (1981) Santo Domingo (capital) 1,313,172; Santiago de los Caballeros 278,638; La Romana 91,571; San Pedro de Macorís 78,562; San Francisco de Macorís 64,906.

**People** **Population:** 7,240,793 (1990). **Nationality:** noun—Dominican(s); adjective—Dominican. **Ethnic groups:** 73% mixed, 16% white, 11% black. **Languages:** Spanish. **Religions:** 95% Roman Catholic.

**Government** **Type:** republic. **Independence:** Feb. 27, 1844 (from Haiti). **Constitution:** Nov. 28, 1966. **National holiday:** Independence Day, Feb. 27. **Heads of government:** Joaquín Balaguer Ricardo, president (since Aug. 1986). **Structure:** president popularly elected for four-year term; bicameral legislature (National Congress—30-seat Senate and 120-seat Chamber of Deputies elected for four-year terms); Supreme Court.

**Economy** **Monetary unit:** Dominican peso. **Budget:** (1988) *income:* $413 mil.; *expend.:* $522 mil. **GDP:** $5.1 bil., $790 per capita (1987 est.). **Chief crops:** sugarcane, coffee, rice, cocoa, tobacco, corn. **Livestock:** cattle, pigs, goats, horses, asses, mules, sheep. **Natural resources:** nickel, bauxite, gold, silver. **Major industries:** tourism, sugar processing, ferro-nickel and gold mining. **Labor force:** 2.3–2.6 mil. (1986); 49% agriculture, 33% services, 18% industry. **Exports:** $711 mil. (f.o.b., 1988); sugar, coffee, cocoa, gold, ferro-nickel. **Imports:**

$1.8 bil. (c.i.f., 1988); foodstuffs, petroleum, cotton and manufactures, chemicals and pharmaceuticals. **Major trading partners:** (1987) *exports:* 74% U.S., including Puerto Rico; *imports:* 37% U.S., including Puerto Rico.

**Intl. Orgs.** FAO, G-77, GATT, IAEA, IBRD, ICAO, IDA, IFAD, IFC, ILO, IMF, IMO, INTELSAT, INTERPOL, ITU, UN, UNESCO, UPU, WHO, WMO.

The Dominican Republic takes up the eastern two-thirds of the island of Hispaniola, which it shares with Haiti. Christopher Columbus visited the island in 1492, and Santo Domingo is the oldest continually inhabited European settlement in the Americas, with the oldest cathedral, hospital, and monastery in the Western hemisphere.

Western Hispaniola (Haiti) was ceded to France in 1697, and the eastern part of the island in 1795. Liberated with the Haitian slave revolts of 1801, it fell under Haitian rule from 1804 to 1808 (when it reverted to Spanish rule), and again from 1822 to 1844. It was again occupied by Spain from 1861 to 1865. Under Ulises Heureux (1882–99), the Dominican Republic enjoyed a period of independence and prosperity. The United States occupied the Dominican Republic between 1916 and 1924. In 1930 Rafael Trujillo set up a dictatorship lasting 31 years. Dominican political strife triggered another U.S. invasion (1965–66) to end the revolution. Reformist party candidate Joaquín Balaguer Ricardo, president from 1966 to 1978, regained the presidency in 1986, and was reelected in 1990.

## Ecuador
### Republic of Ecuador

**Geography** **Location:** northwestern South America. **Boundaries:** Colombia to N, Peru to E and S, Pacific Ocean to W. **Total land area:** 106,860 sq. mi. (276,840 sq km); incl. Galapagos Islands, 0°45′S, 90°19′W. **Coastline:** 1,389 mi. (2,237 km). **Comparative area:** between Colorado and Nevada. **Land use:** 6% arable land; 3% permanent crops; 17% meadows and pastures; 51% forest and woodland; 23% other; includes 2% irrigated. **Major cities:** (1986 est.) Quito (capital) 1,093,278; Guayaquil 1,509,108; Cuenca 193,012; Machala 137,321; Portoviejo 134,393.

**People** **Population:** 10,506,668 (1990). **Nationality:** noun—Ecuadorian(s); adjective—Ecuadorian. **Ethnic groups:** 55% mestizo, 25% Indian, 10% Spanish, 10% black. **Languages:** Spanish (official), Indian languages, especially Quechua. **Religions:** 95% Roman Catholic.

**Government** **Type:** republic. **Independence:** May 24, 1822 (from Spain). **Constitution:** Aug. 10, 1979. **National holiday:** Independence Day, Aug. 10. **Heads of government:** Rodrigo Borja-Cevallos, president (since Aug. 1988). **Structure:** executive; unicameral legislature (Chamber of Representatives); independent judiciary.

**Economy** **Monetary unit:** sucre. **Budget:** (1988 est.) *income:* $2.2 bil.; *expend.:* $2.7 bil.

GDP: $9.8 bil., $935 per capita (1989). **Chief crops:** bananas, coffee, cocoa, sugarcane, corn, potatoes, rice; illegal producer of coca for international drug trade. **Livestock:** pigs, cattle, sheep. **Natural resources:** petroleum, fish, timber. **Major industries:** food processing, textiles, chemicals. **Labor force:** 2.8 mil. (1983); 52% agriculture, 20% services, 13% manufacturing; 8.5% unemployment. **Exports:** $2.2 bil. (f.o.b., 1988); 47% petroleum, coffee, bananas, cocoa products, shrimp. **Imports:** $1.6 bil. (c.i.f., 1988); transport equipment, vehicles, machinery, chemicals, petroleum. **Major trading partners:** *exports:* (1988) 58% U.S., Latin America, Caribbean, EC; *imports:* (1987) 28% U.S., Latin America, Caribbean, EC, Japan.

**Intl. Orgs.** FAO, G-77, IAEA, IBRD, ICAO, IDA, IFAD, IFC, ILO, IMF, IMO, INTELSAT, INTERPOL, ITU, NAM, OAS, OPEC, UN, UNESCO, UPU, WHO, WMO.

The Inca empire maintained control over the territory that is now Ecuador until the arrival of Spanish conqueror Francisco Pizarro in 1532. The Spanish conquistadores quickly dismantled the indigenous political structure, which had been weakened by a series of wars between the Inca chief Atahualpa and his half brother Huáscar. The Spaniards arrived in the Quito region in 1533 and established the city of Guayaquil shortly thereafter. The administrative center of Spanish rule was originally established through the viceroyalty of Peru in 1544, and an *audiencia* (a regional high court under the nominal authority of the viceroy) was established at Quito in 1563. Administrative control of the region was transferred to Bogotá and the viceroyalty of New Granada in 1718.

The local junta of Quito ousted the audiencia in 1809, but they did not achieve independence for the region until after the military victory of the rebel forces over the royalists at the battle of Pichincha in 1822. Ecuador formed a part of the Confederation of Gran Colombia until the confederation's collapse in 1830. The leader of the forces for independence, Gen. Juan José Flores, removed the country from the Gran Colombian confederation and ruled as dictator until his ouster in 1845. A political rivalry existed between the Liberals of Guayaquil and the Conservatives of Quito, but Conservative dominance of the government lasted until 1895.

During the rule of Conservative Pres. Gabriel García Moreno (1861–75), the Roman Catholic church gained a central place in the political and cultural life of the country. García Moreno tied citizenship requirements to Catholic religious affiliation, brought in the Jesuits to "purify" the country through a new educational program, and dedicated the country to the Sacred Heart of Jesus. He was assassinated in 1875.

In 1895 the Radical Liberal (anticlerical) party seized power and held it until 1944. José María Velasco Ibarra, who was in and out of power until 1972, dominated the political scene. Political stability within the country had much to do with the state of the economy. The traditional reliance on cacao production was superseded in the 1950s by a "banana boom," and the discovery of large oil deposits

by U.S. corporations in the 1960s led to a shift toward reliance on oil revenues by the following decade. A Peruvian invasion in 1941 led to the loss of almost half of Ecuador's national territory; a simmering hostility has remained between the two countries ever since.

Military factions kidnapped Pres. León Febres Cordero in 1987, releasing him in exchange for amnesty for two-time coup leader Lt. Gen. Frank Vargas Pazos. In 1988 Rodrigo Borja, of the Democratic Left party (ID), was elected to the presidency.

In 1990, the previously ignored Indian minority emerged as a political force, boycotting the decennial census and staging a series of peaceful demonstrations known simply as "The Uprising." Among their demands were land redistribution, official recognition of Ecuador as a multinational state, Indian control of archaeological sites, funding for bilingual education, research into traditional medicine, and the expulsion of an American evangelical group.

Stuck between Peru and Columbia (the largest coca leaf grower and largest cocaine refiner in the world, respectively), Ecuador struggles to supress the drug trade but managed to reduce coca leaf production 90% in 1990. Heavily dependent on oil, it benefited from oil price increases during the Persian Gulf War.

# Egypt
## Arab Republic of Egypt
**Geography Location:** northeastern Africa and Asia (Sinai peninsula). **Boundaries:** Mediterranean Sea to N, Israel to NE, Red Sea to E, Sudan to S, and Libya to W. **Total land area:** 385,229 sq. mi. (997,739 sq km)—inhabited and cultivated territory accounts for 13,587 sq. mi. (35,189 sq km). **Coastline:** 1,523 mi. (2,450 km). **Comparative area:** about 1.4 times size of Texas. **Land use:** 3% arable land; 2% permanent crops; 0% meadows and pastures; negl. % forest and woodland; 95% other; includes 2% irrigated. **Major cities:** (1986 census) El-Qahira (Cairo) (capital) 6,052,800; El-Iskandriyah (Alexandria) 2,917,300; Giza 3,700,100; Mansoura 3,500,500; Zagazig 3,420,100.

**People Population:** 54,705,746 (1990). **Nationality:** noun—Egyptian(s); adjective—Egyptian. **Ethnic groups:** 90% Eastern Hamitic stock, 10% Greek, Italian, Syro-Lebanese. **Languages:** Arabic (official), English and French widely understood by educated classes. **Religions:** (official estimate) 94% Muslim (mostly Sunni), 6% Coptic Christian and other.

**Government Type:** republic. **Independence:** Feb. 28, 1922 (from UK). **Constitution:** Sept. 11, 1971. **National holiday:** National Day, July 23. **Heads of government:** Mohammed Hosni Mubarak, president (since 1981); Dr. Atef Sidky, prime minister (since Nov. 1986). **Structure:** executive power vested in president, who appoints cabinet; People's Assembly is principal legislative body, with Shura Council having consultative role; independent judiciary administered by minister of justice.

**Economy Monetary unit:** Egyptian pound. **Budget:** (1989 est.) *income:* $7 bil. *expend.:* $11.5 bil.. **GDP:** $38.3 bil., $700 per capita. **Chief crops:** fodder, maize, wheat, cotton, rice; not self-sufficient in food. **Livestock:** chickens, ducks, buffalo, cattle, goats. **Natural resources:** crude oil, natural gas, iron ore, phosphates, manganese. **Major industries:** textiles, food processing, tourism. **Labor force:** about 15 mil. (1989 est.); 40–45% agriculture, 36% government (local and national), public sector enterprises and armed forces, 20% privately owned service and manufacturing enterprises (1984); shortage of skilled labor; unemployment about 7% (official est.); about 2 million Egyptians work abroad, mostly in Iraq and Gulf Arab states (1988 est.). **Exports:** $2.55 bil. (f.o.b., 1989); raw cotton, crude and refined petroleum, cotton yarn, textiles. **Imports:** $10.1 bil. (c.i.f., 1988); foodstuffs, machinery and equipment, fertilizers, wood products, durable consumer goods. **Major trading partners:** U.S., EC, Japan, Eastern Europe.

**Intl. Orgs.** Arab League, FAO, G-77, GATT, IAEA, IBRD, ICAO, IDA, IFAD, IFC, ILO, IMF, IMO, INTELSAT, INTERPOL, ITU, NAM, OAU, UN, UNESCO, UPU, WHO, WIPO, WMO.

Civilization began in the fertile valley of the Nile River around 5000 B.C. In about 3200 B.C., King Menes established the first of many dynasties of pharaohs that unified the country from the Nile Delta to Upper Egypt, creating a distinctive ancient civilization of great wealth and cultural brilliance.

The last pharaonic dynasty was overthrown by the Persians in 341 B.C. The Persians in turn were replaced by the Alexandrian and Ptolemaic Greek dynasties and then by the rule of the Roman Empire. Egypt was part of the Byzantine Empire from the third to the seventh centuries A.D., when it was conquered by the Arab Islamic expansion. Arab rule was ended around 1250 when the Mameluke dynasty, of Caucasian origin, established control. The Mamelukes were defeated by the Turks in 1517, and Egypt was incorporated into the Ottoman Empire.

The Suez Canal was built by a French corporation during 1859–69 but was taken over by the British in 1875. This, together with the expansion of the British Empire in East Africa and the Sudan, led to the establishment of de facto British rule in Egypt in 1882, although Egypt remained nominally part of the Ottoman Empire until 1914. A British protectorate in Egypt was established in that year, replaced by a League of Nations Mandate in 1922. The autonomy of the Egyptian monarchy was strengthened in an Anglo-Egyptian treaty of 1936, but Great Britain continued to maintain military forces in Egypt and controlled the Sudan as an Anglo-Egyptian condominium.

Egypt saw heavy fighting between British and Axis forces during World War II. After the war, a nationalist movement gained strength. The 1936 treaty was abrogated by Egypt in 1951. An uprising of the Society of Free Officers on July 23, 1952, forced King Farouk to abdicate. A republic was proclaimed on June 18, 1953. Lt. Col. Gamal Abdel Nasser became premier in 1954 and president in 1956.

British troops were withdrawn from the Suez Canal zone in June 1956. On July 26, 1956, Egypt announced the nationalization of the canal. Israel invaded the Sinai Peninsula at the end of October 1956. France and Great Britain landed forces and bombed Egyptian positions; a cease-fire went into effect under UN supervision on Nov. 17. A UN peacekeeping force patrolled the border between Egypt and Israel from 1957 to 1967.

Increasing Soviet involvement in Egypt was confirmed with its aid to Egypt in the construction of the Aswan High Dam. The dam, completed in 1971, provides both irrigation and hydropower but at the cost of extensive environmental damage.

Egypt and Syria joined together as the United Arab Republic in 1958. Later joined by Yemen, the union was dissolved in 1961.

Egyptian incursions into the Gaza Strip and the Sharm el Sheikh in early June 1967 led to the outbreak of full-scale war with Israel on June 5. The Six-Day War ended on June 10 with Israel in full control of Gaza and the Sinai peninsula to the banks of the Suez Canal. Sporadic fighting between Egyptian and Israeli forces continued throughout 1969–70. The Suez Canal remained closed to shipping until 1975.

Nasser died in 1970 and was succeeded by Vice Pres. Anwar Sadat, who concluded a treaty of friendship with the USSR, but expelled all Soviet troops and advisers in 1972.

On Oct. 6, 1973, Egyptian forces crossed the Suez Canal and attacked Israeli positions in the Sinai (Syrian forces also attacked Israeli positions in the Golan Heights). Israel drove back the attackers, and the Yom Kippur War ended in a cease-fire on Oct. 24.

In 1974 Sadat's government became increasingly friendly to the West, welcoming foreign investment and American aid. In 1974 and 1975 disengagement accords were signed with Israel, providing for the return of the Sinai to Egypt in stages. In November 1977 Sadat visited Jerusalem as a gesture of peace, and a peace treaty between Israel and Egypt was signed (after a series of talks mediated by Pres. Jimmy Carter at Camp David, Md.) on Mar. 26, 1979. Formal diplomatic relations were established in 1982. As a result of the peace treaty with Israel, Egypt was suspended from the Arab League—it was readmitted in 1989—and attacked by Libyan forces on several occasions along the Egyptian-Libyan border.

Popular unrest fomented by the Muslim Brotherhood in September 1981 led to a military crackdown. Pres. Sadat was assassinated by members of a military conspiracy on Oct. 6, 1981, and was succeeded by Vice Pres. Mohammed Hosni Mubarak. The government has remained on friendly terms with Israel and the United States and has gradually improved relations with the rest of the Arab world. During the Persian Gulf War, it was a staunch member of the anti-Iraq coalition, in return for which the United States forgave $7 billion in debt, and other governments were expected to negotiate terms for an additional $40 billion.

Egypt has a mixed and rapidly developing economy. The industrial sector is dominated by textiles, petrochemicals, cement, fertilizer, chemicals, mining, and light manufacturing. Egypt is one of the world's largest producers of cotton, and the agricultural sector also includes grain, dates, sugar, citrus fruits, and vegetables. The economy has been hampered by unrestrained population growth, especially in the Cairo megalopolis.

---

# El Salvador
## Republic of El Salvador

**Geography Location:** Pacific coast of Central America. **Boundaries:** Honduras to N and E, Pacific Ocean to S, Guatemala to W. **Total land area:** 8,260 sq. mi. (21,393 sq km). **Coastline:** 191 mi. (307 km). **Comparative area:** about size of Massachusetts. **Land use:** 27% arable land; 8% permanent crops; 29% meadows and pastures; 6% forest and woodland; 30% other; includes 5% irrigated. **Major cities:** (1985 est.) San Salvador (capital) 462,652.

**People Population:** 5,309,865 (1990). **Nationality:** noun—Salvadoran(s); adjective—Salvadoran. **Ethnic groups:** 89% mestizo, 10% Indian, 1% white. **Languages:** Spanish, Nahua (among some Indians). **Religions:** 97% Roman Catholic; activity by Protestant groups throughout country.

**Government Type:** republic. **Independence:** Sept. 15, 1821 (from Spain). **Constitution:** Dec. 20, 1983. **National holiday:** Independence Day, Sept. 15. **Heads of government:** Alfredo Cristiani-Burkard, president (since June 1989). **Structure:** executive; Legislative Assembly (60 seats); Supreme Court.

**Economy Monetary unit:** Salvadoran colón. **Budget:** (1988) *income:* $688 mil.; *expend.:* $725 mil. **GDP:** $5.5 bil., $1,020 per capita (1989 est.). **Chief crops:** coffee, cotton, corn, sugar, beans, rice, sorghum, wheat. **Livestock:** cattle, pigs, horses, mules, goats, sheep. **Natural resources:** hydropower and geothermal power, crude oil. **Major industries:** food processing, textiles, clothing. **Labor force:** 1.7 mil. (1982 est.); 40% agriculture, 16% manufacturing, 16% commerce, 13% government; shortage of skilled labor and large pool of unskilled labor, but manpower-training programs improving situation; 30% unemployment (1987 est.). **Exports:** $497 mil. (f.o.b., 1989); 60% coffee, sugar, cotton, shrimp. **Imports:** $1.1 bil. (c.i.f., 1989); petroleum products, consumer goods, foodstuffs, machinery, construction materials. **Major trading partners:** *exports:* 49% U.S., 24% W. Germany, 7% Guatemala, 4% Costa Rica, 4% Japan; *imports:* 40% U.S., 12% Guatemala, 7% Venezuela, 7% Mexico, 5% W. Germany, 4% Japan.

**Intl. Orgs.** FAO, G-77, IAEA, IBRD, ICAO, IDA, IFAD, IFC, ILO, IMF, IMO, INTELSAT, INTERPOL, ITU, OAS, UN, UNESCO, UPU, WIPO, WMO.

A number of Indian tribes, of which the Pipil were dominant, originally inhabited the area now called El Salvador. The native population resisted the first attempt at Spanish colonization, begun in 1524, for almost 15 years. In 1821 El Salvador gained its independence from Spain, first as a jurisdiction under the Mexican empire and two years later as a member of the United Provinces of Central America. The Central American Federation collapsed in 1838, and in 1840 El Salvador emerged from a bloody two-year struggle as an independent republic.

The Salvadoran economy came to be dominated by coffee production from the 1860s onward, and a series of laws in the 1880s allowed for concentration of both land ownership and political power in the hands of a coffee oligarchy. In 1931 a reformist president won election, but the military subsequently dismissed him. A revolt ensued (1932) in which 10,000 to 20,000 Salvadorans—mostly peasants—were killed. The apparent result of the massacre, which was called La Matanza, was a period of relative political stability that lasted until the 1970s.

In 1979 a political coup led by a group of junior military officers overthrew Pres. Gen. Carlos Humberto Romero. Owing to the polarization between conservative and reformist political groups, the first two civilian-military juntas resigned as a result of their failure to have their programs implemented by the military. A third government, which included Christian Democrat José Napoleón Duarte, took over on Mar. 5, 1980, on the basis of an armed forces' pledge to carry out an agrarian reform program. In 1980 the coalition of opposition political organizations became the Democratic Revolutionary Front (FDR), and five revolutionary military organizations consolidated under the banner of the Farabundo Marti Front for National Liberation (FMLN). Six social-democratic political leaders were assassinated in November 1980, further cementing the political opposition around the FMLN-FDR coalition. Although the revolutionary opposition called for a "final offensive" to overthrow the political-military structure of rule, this action ultimately failed.

A three-part agrarian reform program was initiated in 1980 in El Salvador, but the central part of the program—to redistribute most of the land involved in export agriculture—was dropped as a result of opposition from the agricultural elite.

In March 1982 elections for a constituent assembly, a majority of seats went to the rightist ARENA coalition. In December 1983 a new constitution went into effect, and in 1984 Christian Democrat José Napoleón Duarte assumed the presidency. Christian Democrats also gained in congressional and municipal elections in 1985.

In 1989, Alfredo Cristiani of the conservative Alliance for National Renovation was elected president. On Nov. 11, 1989, FMLN guerrillas launched a new offensive that lasted for several weeks before fading away. Immediately thereafter Cristiani faced a new crisis when military officers were implicated in the murder of six Jesuit priests in San Salvador. The government's failure to prosecute the officers involved jeopardized U.S. military aid to El Salvador, with which the army grew from 15,000 to 55,000 between 1980 and 1989.

Although negotiations between the rebels

and the government were initiated in 1986, they proceeded fitfully. In 1991, though, rebel groups began to renew the peace process, meeting with European foreign ministers in Mexico, calling a cease-fire for national elections in March 1991, and dropping political reforms as a prerequisite for a permanent cease-fire. Though even foreign observers thought the election was rigged in favor of ARENA, it did less well than expected against the Christian Democrats and the new nonrevolutionary leftist party, Democratic Convergence.

## Equatorial Guinea
### Republic of Equatorial Guinea
**Geography** **Location:** mainland territory of Río Muni in western Africa and five inhabited islands: Bioko (3°45′N, 8°50′E), Corisco, Great Elobey, Small Elobey, and Pagalu (Annabon). **Boundaries:** Cameroon to N, Gabon to E and S, Gulf of Guinea to W. **Total land area:** 10,831 sq. mi. (28,051 sq km). **Coastline:** 184 mi. (296 km). **Comparative area:** slightly larger than Maryland. **Land use:** 5% arable land; 4% permanent crops; 4% meadows and pastures; 61% forest and woodland; 26% other. **Major cities:** (1983 census) Malabo (capital) 15,323; Bata 24,100.

**People** **Population:** 368,935 (1990). **Nationality:** noun—Equatorial Guinean(s); adjective—Equatorial Guinean. **Ethnic groups:** indigenous population of Bioko, primarily Bubi, some Fernandinos; Río Muni, primarily Fang; less than 1,000 Europeans, mostly Spanish. **Languages:** Spanish (official), pidgin English, Fang. **Religions:** nominally Christian, predominantly Roman Catholic, indigenous practices.

**Government** **Type:** republic. **Independence:** Oct. 12, 1968 (from Spain). **Constitution:** Aug. 15, 1982. **National holiday:** Oct. 12. **Heads of government:** Col. Teodoro Obiang Nguema Mbasogo, president (since Aug. 1979); Don Cristino Seriche Bioco Malabo, prime minister (since Aug. 1982). **Structure:** executive—president with broad powers, prime minister; unicameral legislature—House of Representatives of the People; free judiciary.

**Economy** **Monetary unit:** Communauté Financière Africaine (CFA) franc. **Budget:** (1988) *income:* $23.0 mil.; *expend.:* $31.0 mil. **GNP:** $103 mil., $293 per capita (1986); economy destroyed during regime of former Pres. Masie Nguema. **Chief crops:** cash crops—timber and coffee from Río Muni, cocoa from Bioko; food crops—rice, yams, cassava, bananas, oil palm nuts. **Livestock:** sheep, goats, pigs, cattle. **Natural resources:** timber, crude oil, small unexploited deposits of gold, manganese, uranium. **Major industries:** fishing, sawmilling. **Labor force:** (1981) 76% agriculture, 16% services, 8% other; labor shortages on plantations; 58% of population of working age. **Exports:** $30.0 mil. (1988 est.); cocoa beans, coffee, timber. **Imports:** $50.0 mil. (1988 est.); foodstuffs, petroleum, beverages, clothing, machinery. **Major trading partners:** (1987) *exports:* 44% Spain, 19% W. Germany,

12% Italy, 11% Netherlands; *imports:* 34% Spain, 16% Italy, 14% France, 8% Netherlands.

**Intl. Orgs.** FAO, G-77, GATT (de facto), IBRD, ICAO, IDA, IFAD, ILO, IMF, IMO, INTERPOL, ITU, NAM, UN, UNESCO, UPU, WHO.

Equatorial Guinea consists of the Mbini River basin on the West African coast, and a number of offshore islands, chiefly Bioko and Pagalu (Annobón). Indigenous Pygmies were displaced beginning in the 17th century by migrations of various peoples that now inhabit the coastal region and by the Fang, who comprise 80 percent of the present population.

Bioko was discovered in 1473 by the Portuguese explorer Fernando Po, and until modern times the island bore his name. Portugal controlled the islands and adjacent mainland, exploiting them for the slave trade, until 1778 when the territory was ceded to Spain. Equatorial Guinea remained underdeveloped because of conflicting territorial claims and a lack of Spanish investment. Eventually, however, a plantation system was developed for the cultivation of cocoa, particularly on Bioko, using workers imported from Nigeria.

In 1959 the Spanish territories in the Gulf of Guinea were given status equivalent to a province of Spain. Investment in education, health care facilities, and other social programs, combined with the flourishing plantation economy, made the territory one of the most prosperous and best educated in West Africa. Local autonomy was granted in 1963 and full independence in 1968.

Francisco Macias Nguema was elected Equatorial Guinea's first president in 1968. In 1970 he dissolved all opposition parties and declared a one-party state, and in 1972 proclaimed himself president for life and commenced rule by decree. During the next seven years, a reign of terror resulted in the death or exile of one-third of the country's people. Nigerian workers, along with other foreigners, were expelled from the country in 1976; without their labor and technical skills, the economy was quickly ruined.

Macias Nguema was overthrown in August 1979 in a military coup led by his nephew, Lt. Col. Teodoro Obiang Nguema Mbasogo. Macias Nguema was tried and executed a month later. The Spanish-educated Nguema Mbasogo moved to reduce Soviet influence and to improve relations with Spain. A new constitution was approved in a referendum in August 1982.

## Ethiopia
### People's Democratic Republic of Ethiopia
**Geography** **Location:** northeastern Africa. **Boundaries:** Red Sea and Djibouti to NE, Somalia to E and SE, Kenya to S, Sudan to W and NW. **Total land area:** 483,123 sq. mi. (1,251,282 sq km). **Coastline:** 680 mi. (1,094 km). **Comparative area:** between Texas and Alaska. **Land use:** 12% arable land; 1% permanent crops; 41% meadows and pastures; 24% forest and woodland; 22% other; includes negl. % irrigated. **Major cities:** (1984 census) Addis Ababa (capital) 1,412,577; Asmara 275,385; Dire

Dawa 98,104; Gondar (including Azeso) 80,886; Nazret 76,284.

**People** **Population:** 51,666,622 (1990). **Nationality:** noun—Ethiopian(s); adjective—Ethiopian. **Ethnic groups:** 40% Oromo, 32% Amhara and Tigrean, 9% Sidamo, 6% Shankella. **Languages:** Amharic (official), Tigrinya, Orominga, Arabic; English is major foreign language taught in schools. **Religions:** 40–45% Muslim, 35–40% Ethiopian Orthodox, 15–20% Animist, 5% other.

**Government** **Type:** communist state. **Constitution:** Sept. 1987. **National holiday:** Popular Revolution Commemoration Day, Sept. 12. **Heads of government:** Meles Zenawi, president (since 1991); Tamirat Layene, prime minister (since 1991). **Structure:** executive power exercised by president, elected for five-year term by National Assembly (Shengo); 835-member legislature has nominal powers, elected every five years; cabinet selected by prime minister, appointed by president; judiciary at higher levels based on Western pattern, at lower levels on traditional pattern.

**Economy** **Monetary unit:** Ethiopian birr. **Budget:** (1987) *income:* $1.4 bil.; *expend.:* $1.9 bil. **GNP:** $6.6 bil., $130 per capita (1989 est.). **Chief crops:** main crop—coffee; also cereals, pulses, oilseed, meat, hides and skins. **Livestock:** cattle, sheep, goats, asses, horses. **Natural resources:** small reserves of gold, platinum, copper, potash. **Major industries:** cement, textiles, food processing. **Labor force:** 90% agriculture and animal husbandry, 10% government, military, and quasigovernment; 51% of population of working age (1985). **Exports:** $418 mil. (f.o.b., 1988 est.); 60% coffee. **Imports:** $1.1 bil. (c.i.f., 1988); foodstuffs, fuels, capital goods. **Major trading partners:** *exports:* U.S., W. Germany, Djibouti, Japan, Yemen. *imports:* USSR, Italy, W. Germany, Japan, UK.

**Intl. Orgs.** FAO, G-77, IAEA, IBRD, ICAO, IDA, IFAD, IFC, ILO, IMF, IMO, INTELSAT, INTERPOL, ITU, NAM, OAU, UN, UNESCO, UPU, WHO, WMO.

Ethiopia played an important role in the Red Sea trade of the classical world and was mentioned by the Greek historian Herodotus in the fifth century B.C. According to legend, the Ethiopian monarchy was founded by Melelik I, son of Israel's King Solomon and the Queen of Sheba (Sab'a, i.e. North Yemen). Coptic Christianity became Ethiopia's dominant religion in the fourth century A.D. Ethiopia successfully resisted Islamic invasions in the seventh century except in areas along the Red Sea coast but was cut off from the rest of the Christian world by the Islamic states of North Africa and the Middle East.

Portugal established forts and trading stations on the Red Sea coast beginning in 1493, strengthening their domination of trade in the Indian Ocean. The Portuguese also sponsored Roman Catholic missionaries but with little success. A century of religious strife ended with the expulsion of all foreign missionaries in the 1630s. Ethiopia successfully resisted an attempted Italian invasion in 1880.

Ethiopia began to emerge into the modern world under Melelik II (r. 1889–1913). A period of instability after his death ended with the accession in 1930 of Haile Selassie. Italy invaded again in 1936 and soon conquered the entire country. Protests by the League of Nations had no effect; Haile Selassie fled to exile in England. The Italians were driven out during World War II by British and Ethiopian forces, and Haile Selassie returned to his throne.

Civil unrest broke out in February 1974, and Haile Selassie was deposed on Sept. 13, 1974. A coalition of urban elites and the armed forces took over, abolishing the monarchy in 1975 and curbing the power of the Coptic church. Land reform was instituted, and a socialist state proclaimed. In 1977–78 a period of "red terror" resulted in the arrest and execution of thousands of the new regime's opponents. A provisional military council, the Dergue, was confirmed in power under the leadership of Col. Mengistu Haile-Mariam.

A military assistance agreement in 1976 between Ethiopia and the USSR ended an earlier military relationship with the United States; American military advisers were expelled. In 1977 Somalia, taking advantage of Ethiopia's shifting military situation, attacked across the Ogaden desert, aiming to restore certain disputed areas of Ethiopia to Somalia. A massive infusion of Soviet arms and Cuban troops expelled the Somalis in March 1978, but border clashes continued thereafter.

After the expulsion of the Italians during World War II, the province of Eritrea, under a UN plan, was to have become autonomous in a federation with Ethiopia. Instead, Eritrea was made a province of the Ethiopian Empire in 1962. A coalition of Marxist and non-Marxist liberation forces—most prominent among them the Eritrean People's Liberation Front (EPLF)—resisted the annexation from the beginning. By the spring of 1991, Eritrean forces had gained control of all of Eritrea, including Ethiopia's only outlets to the sea.

Another rebel group, the Ethiopian People's Revolutionary Democratic Front (EPRDF), sought autonomy for Tigre, a northern region between Ethiopia and Eritrea. In February 1991, the EPRDF launched a major offensive that culminated in Mengistu Haile Mariam's flight in May, a week before scheduled ceasefire talks were to start in London. The talks proceeded quickly under the auspices of the United States, and rebel forces under the leadership of the EPRDF entered Addis Ababa virtually unopposed at the end of May.

The best organized of the three rebel groups (the third, the Oromo Liberation Front, seeks autonomy for the country's largest ethnic group in the southwest), the once doctrinaire Marxist EPRDF took the lead in installing a transitional government and pledged to hold free, democratic elections by May 1992. They also claimed to favor a UN-sponsored referendum on Eritrean independence.

Ethiopia faced unparalleled destruction during its civil war and a succession of devastating famines, and securing famine relief from the international community was a priority of the transitional government as it assumed power in May 1991. (See Part I, "The Year in Review.")

## Fiji
### Republic of Fiji

**Geography Location:** more than 300 islands (100 inhabited), in South Pacific Ocean. Suva 18°08′S, 178°25′E. **Boundaries:** South Pacific Ocean to N, S, and W; Koro Sea to E; nearest neighbor is Vanuatu, about 600 mi. (1,000 km) to W. **Total land area:** 7,095 sq. mi. (18,376 sq km). **Coastline:** 702 mi. (1,129 km). **Comparative area:** slightly smaller than New Jersey. **Land use:** 8% arable land; 5% permanent crops; 3% meadows and pastures; 65% forest and woodland; 19% other; includes negl. % irrigated. **Major cities:** (1986) Suva (capital) 69,481.

**People Population:** 759,567 (1990). **Nationality:** noun—Fijian(s); adjective—Fijian. **Ethnic groups:** 49% Indian; 46% Fijian, 5% European, other Pacific Islanders, overseas Chinese, and others. **Languages:** English (official), Fijian, Hindustani. **Religions:** Fijians are mainly Christian, Indians are Hindu with Muslim minority.

**Government Type:** military coup leader Col. Sitiveni Rabuka formally declared Fiji a republic Oct. 6, 1987. **Independence:** Oct. 10, 1970 (from UK). **Constitution:** Oct. 10, 1970 (suspended 1987). **National holiday:** Fiji Day, Oct. 10. **Heads of government:** Ratu Sir Penaia Ganilau, president; Ratu Sir Kamisese Mara, prime minister; both appointed by coup leader Gen. Sitiveni Rabuka in Dec. 1987. **Structure:** executive—prime minister and cabinet; judicial—Supreme Court, court of appeal, magistrate's courts.

**Economy Monetary unit:** Fiji dollar. **Budget:** (1988) *income:* $260 mil.; *expend.:* $233 mil. **GDP:** $1.32 bil., $1,750 per capita (1989 est.). Chief crops: sugar, copra, ginger, rice; major deficiency, grains. **Livestock:** cattle, goats, horses, pigs. **Natural resources:** timber, fish, gold, copper, offshore oil potential. **Major industries:** sugar, copra, tourism. **Labor force:** 176,000 (1979); 40% paid employees; remainder involved in subsistence agriculture. **Exports:** $312 mil. (1988); 49% sugar, copra, processed fish, lumber. **Imports:** $454 mil. (1988); 15% foodstuffs, petroleum products, machinery, consumer goods. **Major trading partners:** 45% UK, 21% Australia, 5% U.S.; *imports:* 5% U.S., New Zealand, Australia, Japan.

**Intl. Orgs.** Colombo Plan, EC (associate), FAO, G-77, GATT (de facto), IBRD, ICAO, IDA, IFAD, IFC, ILO, IMF, IMO, INTELSAT, INTERPOL, ITU, UN, UNESCO, UPU, WHO, WIPO, WMO (resigned from Commonwealth Oct. 1986).

First reported to the West by the Dutch navigator Abel Tasman in 1643, the Fiji Islands were annexed as a British Crown Colony in 1874. Between 1879 and 1916, large numbers of Indian indentured laborers were imported to work on sugar plantations; eventually the original Melanesian inhabitants were outnumbered by persons of Indian descent. Fiji became an independent parliamentary democracy on Oct. 10, 1970, with most land ownership and political power vested in the Fijian minority. A parliamentary election in 1987 brought the Indian party to power; the elected government was ousted in a military coup, and Lt. Col. Sitiveni Rabuka assumed control of the government on May 21, 1987. The coup and its aftermath provoked a constitutional crisis that remains unresolved.

Fiji's economy is based largely on agriculture. Rice, vegetables, and livestock are produced for local consumption; sugar, copra, and ginger are important export crops. Gold and silver mining and limestone quarrying are economically important, as is tourism. There is some light industry. Fuel and most manufactured goods are imported, leading to a persistent balance-of-payments deficit.

## Finland
### Republic of Finland

**Geography Location:** northern Europe. **Boundaries:** Norway to N, USSR to E, Baltic Sea to S, Gulf of Bothnia, Sweden to W. **Total land area:** 130,559 sq. mi. (338,145 sq km). **Coastline:** 700 mi. (1,126 km) excluding islands and coastal indentations. **Comparative area:** between New Mexico and Montana. **Land use:** 8% arable land; 0% permanent crops; negl. % meadows and pastures; 76% forest and woodland; 16% other; includes negl. % irrigated. **Major cities:** (1988) Helsinki (capital) 489,965; Tampere 171,068; Espoo 167,734; Turku 159,917; Vantaa 151,157.

**People Population:** 4,977,325 (1990). **Nationality:** noun—Finn(s); adjective—Finnish. **Ethnic groups:** Finn, Swede, Lapp, Gypsy. **Languages:** 93.5% Finnish, 6.3% Swedish (both official); small Lapp- and Russian-speaking minorities. **Religions:** 97% Evangelical Lutheran, 1.2% Eastern Orthodox, 1.8% other.

**Government Type:** republic. **Independence:** Dec. 6, 1917 (from USSR). **Constitution:** July 17, 1919. **National holiday:** Independence Day, Dec. 6. **Heads of government:** Dr. Mauno Koivisto, president (since Nov. 1981); Esko Aho, prime minister (since Apr. 1991). **Structure:** executive power is vested in president and coalition cabinet responsible to parliament; legislative authority rests jointly with president and unicameral legislature (Eduskunta); Supreme Court, four superior courts, 193 lower courts.

**Economy Monetary unit:** markka. **Budget:** (1988 est.) *income:* $28.1 bil.; *expend.:* $28.1 bil. **GDP:** $74.4 bil., $15,000 per capita (1989 est.). **Chief crops:** cereals, sugar beets, potatoes; 85% self-sufficient, but short of food and fodder grains. **Livestock:** poultry, cattle, pigs, reindeer, sheep. **Natural resources:** timber, copper, zinc, iron ore, silver. **Major industries:** metal manufacturing and shipbuilding, forestry and wood processing (pulp, paper), copper refining; shortages—fossil fuels; industrial raw materials (except wood, iron ore); food and fodder grains. **Labor force:** 2.56 mil. (1988 est.); 33.1% services; 22.9% mining and manufacturing; 13.8% commerce; 10.3% agriculture, forestry, and fishing; 3.4% unemployment. **Exports:** $22.2 bil. (f.o.b., 1987); timber, paper and pulp, ships, machinery, clothing, footwear. **Imports:** $22.0 bil. (c.i.f., 1987); foodstuffs, petroleum and petroleum products, chemicals, transport equipment, iron, steel. **Major trading partners:** *exports:* 44% EC (13% UK, 11% W. Germany), 15% USSR, 14% Sweden, 6% U.S.; *imports:* 44% EC (17% W. Germany, 7% UK), 13% Sweden, 12% USSR, 6% U.S.

**Intl. Orgs.** EC (free trade agreement), EFTA (associate), FAO, GATT, IAEA, IBRD, ICAO, IDA, IFAD, IFC, ILO, IMF, IMO, INTERPOL, ITU, OECD, UN, UNESCO, UPU, WHO, WIPO, WMO.

The Finns originated in the Ural Mountains, and their language is akin to Hungarian and closely similar to Estonian. Migrating from western Siberia to what is now Finland in the eighth century, they drove the indigenous Lapps to northernmost Scandinavia. Finland was conquered and Christianized by the Swedes in the 12th century and in the 16th century, became a Swedish grand duchy. Ethnic Swedes make up about 7 percent of the present population. Finland was frequently a battleground in wars between Sweden and Russia; about one-third of the population perished in a war-induced famine in 1696. In 1721 Sweden ceded the province of Viborg to Russia, and all of Finland was taken over by Russia in 1809.

Under the Russians the czars became simultaneously grand dukes of Finland and ruled it as a semiautonomous province. Attempts to "russify" Finland in the later 19th century provoked great popular resistance. When the Russian empire and then the Russian Republic fell in the 1917 Revolution, Finland lapsed into a fierce civil war between Communists and non-Communists. The "whites" under Baron Gustaf Mannerheim were the victors, and Finland became an independent country for the first time in its history.

In 1939 the USSR attacked the Finnish Republic; Finland's resistance in the "Winter War" was heroic but unavailing. Defeated, it was forced to cede Western Keralia to the USSR. After the German invasion of Russia in 1941, fighting between Finland and Russia resumed; England, but not America, declared war on Finland as a cocombatant with Germany. Russia again defeated Finland in 1944 and obliged the Finns to wage war against the German occupying army in northern Finland; much of the country was devastated.

The terms of the 1944 armistice between Finland and the USSR were very harsh: Finland ceded the Petsamo region to the Soviet Union, and thus was cut off from the Barents Sea; the Porkkala peninsula was leased to the Soviets for 50 years, and reparations amounting to 80 percent of Finland's exports were paid in kind. Soviet pressure forced Finland to reject Marshall Plan aid after World War II, but Finland

benefited indirectly from the rapid postwar recovery of the Scandinavian region. The gross national product returned to prewar levels by 1947.

Finland's economy had traditionally been centered on timber and other forest products, including pulp and paper, and on small-scale, highly productive agriculture. In the postwar period, industrial development was emphasized; the production of heavy machinery is now the country's leading industry.

In 1948 the Finns signed a mutual defense pact with the USSR, renewed in 1955, 1970, and 1983. Finland's presidents, Juho Paasikivi (1946–56) and Urho Kekkonen (1956–81), although conservative and nationalistic, realized that the country's independence required the avoidance of any appearance of anti-Soviet moves in foreign policy.

With the establishment of good Soviet-Finnish relations, the Porkkala peninsula was returned to Finland in 1956. Russia has not opposed Finland's gradual development of economic ties with the West. Finland joined the Nordic Council and the United Nations in 1955. It became an associate member of the European Free Trade Association in 1961 and a full member in 1985, and negotiated a free-trade agreement with the EEC in 1973.

With a strong presidency providing stability despite revolving-door coalition governments in the Eduskunta (parliament), and a prudent foreign policy in the shadow of the USSR, Finland has preserved its free economy and civil liberties. Though its prosperity is sufficient to support a typically Scandinavian social welfare state, in 1991 Finland was suffering its worst recession since 1945, and unemployment was rising.

# France
## French Republic

**Geography Location:** western Europe. **Boundaries:** English Channel to N, Belgium, Luxembourg, Germany, Switzerland, Italy to E, Mediterranean Sea, Spain to S, Atlantic Ocean to W. **Total land area:** 210,026 sq. mi. (543,965 sq km). **Coastline:** 2,130 mi. (3,427 km). **Comparative area:** between California and Texas. **Land use:** 32% arable land; 2% permanent crops; 23% meadows and pastures; 27% forest and woodland; 16% other; includes 2% irrigated. **Major cities:** (1982 census) Paris (capital) 2,188,918; Marseille (Marseilles) 878,689; Lyon (Lyons) 418,476; Toulouse 354,289; Nice 338,486.

**People Population:** 56,358,331 (1990). **Nationality:** noun—Frenchman (men), Frenchwoman (women); adjective—French. **Ethnic groups:** Celtic and Latin with Teutonic, Slavic, North African, Indochinese, and Basque minorities. **Languages:** French (100% of population); rapidly declining regional dialects (Provençal, Breton, Alsacian, Corsican, Catalan, Basque, Flemish). **Religions:** 90% Roman Catholic, 2% Protestant, 1% Jewish, 1% Muslim (North African workers), 6% unaffiliated.

**Government Type:** republic, with president whose previously wide powers have been

somewhat curtailed by current power-sharing arrangement with prime minister. **Constitution:** Sept. 28, 1958, amended concerning election of president in 1962. **National holiday:** National Day, July 14. **Heads of government:** François Mitterrand, president (since May 1988); Edith Cresson, prime minister (since May 1991). **Structure:** presidentially appointed prime minister heads Council of Ministers, which is formally responsible to National Assembly; bicameral legislature—National Assembly (577 members), Senate (317 members)—restricted by a delaying action; judiciary independent in principle.

**Economy Monetary unit:** French franc. **Budget:** (1989 est.) *income:* $197.0 bil.; *expend.:* $213.4 bil. **GDP:** $819.6 bil., $14,600 per capita. **Chief crops:** cereals, sugar beets, potatoes, wine grapes (western Europe's foremost producer); self-sufficient for most temperate foodstuffs; agricultural shortages include fats and oils, tropical produce. **Livestock:** cattle, pigs, sheep, goats, horses, asses. **Natural resources:** coal, iron ore, bauxite, fish, timber. **Major industries:** steel, machinery and equipment, textiles and clothing. **Labor force:** 24.04 mil. (1987); 61.5% services, 31.3% industry, 7.3% agriculture; 10.5% unemployment. **Exports:** $183.1 bil. (f.o.b., 1989 est.); machinery and transport equipment, chemicals, foodstuffs, agricultural products, iron and steel products. **Imports:** $194.5 bil. (c.i.f., 1989 est.); crude petroleum, machinery and equipment, agricultural products, chemicals, iron and steel products. **Major trading partners:** *exports:* 15.8% W. Germany, 12.2% Italy, 10% UK, 8.9% Belgium-Luxembourg, 8.7% Netherlands, 6.7% U.S.; *imports:* 19.4% W. Germany, 11.5% Italy, 9.2% Belgium-Luxembourg, 7.7% U.S., 7.2% UK, 5.2% Netherlands.

**Intl. Orgs.** EC, FAO, GATT, IAEA, IBRD, ICAO, IDA, IFAD, IFC, ILO, IMF, IMO, INTELSAT, INTERPOL, ITU, NATO (signatory), OAS (observer), OECD, UN, UNESCO, UPU, WHO, WIPO, WMO.

Pre-Roman France, known as Gaul, was populated by Celtic and Germanic tribes. The Mediterranean coast had been colonized by Phoenician and Greek traders and was conquered by Rome in the second century B.C. The Roman conquest of all of Gaul was carried out by Julius Caesar between 58 and 51 B.C. Gaul became a prosperous and thoroughly Latinized province of the Roman Empire and Christianity was introduced in the first century A.D.

Barbarian invaders including Visigoths, Franks, and Burgundii swept through France in the fifth century. In 486 Clovis, chief of the Franks, unified the country, accepted Christianity, and established the Merovingian dynasty. France was invaded by Muslim Saracens in the seventh century, but in 732 Charles Martel defeated the Saracens. His son, Pepin the Short, overthrew the last Merovingian ruler in 751 and proclaimed himself king. Pepin's son, Charlemagne, greatly expanded his kingdom and was crowned emperor of the West by the pope in 800.

The rise of feudalism greatly weakened the power of the Carolingians and France broke up into estates, some of them effectively independent countries, ruled by great aristocrats. Among the most important were the dukedoms of Aquitaine and Burgundy and the counties of Flanders, Blois, and Anjou. In 911 the Vikings, who had repeatedly raided the Atlantic coast of France, established the duchy of Normandy.

In 987 the Carolingian dynasty died out in France (although it survived in the Holy Roman Empire) and was replaced by a new line, the Capetians. Steadily expanding in both territory and power from their base in Paris, the Capetians solidified the foundations of the French monarchy. Paris became a great monastic and university city as well as a center of trade and manufacturing. Under the crusader-king Louis IX (St. Louis), France also became an international power.

During the 14th century, the Black Death, peasant rebellions, and the beginning of the Hundred Years' War (1337–1453) with England further weakened the French monarchy. The Norman conquest of England in 1066 had entwined the fortunes of the French and English monarchies, and with the Capetian line in decline, England pursued its claims in France. Henry V of England defeated the French at Agincourt in 1415, and in 1420 Charles IV made Henry heir to the throne of France. Henry's forces were defeated by French armies inspired by Joan of Arc, and in 1429 his claim to the French throne was overturned. In 1435 Burgundy allied itself with France, and in 1453 the English were driven out of France, except for an enclave at Calais.

Louis XI completed the consolidation of France under the French monarchy. France prospered as a center of commerce, industry, agriculture, learning, and culture throughout the 16th century but was disrupted by religious disputes stemming from the Reformation. The Protestant Henry of Navarre, heir to the throne, was obliged to accept Catholicism before being crowned in 1594; he became founder of the Bourbon monarchy.

The consolidation of power under a highly centralized monarchy continued under Henry's heirs. With a foreign policy shaped by the powerful prime ministers Cardinal Richelieu and Cardinal Mazarin, France under Louis XIII and Louis XIV enhanced its stature in Europe by defeating the Habsburgs in the Thirty Years' War (1618–48). Louis XIV—the Sun King—moved the court from Paris to his new palace at Versailles and presided over the wealthiest and most powerful monarchy in Europe.

Louis XIV's persecution of the Huguenots resulted in a great emigration of Protestants from France. A grand alliance of European states thwarted France's expansionist aims on the continent, but France became a major colonial power in North America, controlling Canada and Louisiana (including most of the Mississippi-Missouri valley), and pursued overseas ventures in Africa and Asia as well.

In the mid-18th century, France was weakened internationally by the expensive and fruitless Wars of the Austrian Succession and the Seven Years' War. Under the Treaty of Paris (1763), France ceded control of Canada to Great Britain. The Enlightenment made France a world center of intellectual activity but also led to the questioning of the political and social bases of the French monarchy. An increasingly wealthy and politically active bourgeoisie chafed under the restrictions of an archaic socioeconomic order.

France under Louis XVI supported the American colonies in the Revolutionary War, incurring a large public debt in the process. Combined with unrestrained extravagance on the part of the court and the aristocracy, poverty increased among the rural peasantry and the urban working class, while the bourgeoisie demanded a greater voice in government. These trends came to a head with the storming of the Bastille on July 14, 1789; soon thereafter, the Estates-General took control of the country, and France was in the throes of revolution.

Revolutionary leaders at first allowed Louis XVI to remain on the throne in a limited monarchy, but the king and Marie Antoinette were subsequently tried for treason and executed in 1793. Thousands died during the Reign of Terror which continued until July 1794, ending with the execution of its primary architects, the revolutionary leaders Augustin Robespierre and Georges Danton. The Directory, with five heads of each division of government (1795–99), failed to maintain public order and suffered military reverses in foreign wars in which successive revolutionary governments had been embroiled since 1792. On Nov. 9, 1799, the Directory was overthrown by the Consulate, with Napoleon Bonaparte named first consul.

Napoleon proclaimed himself emperor of France in 1804. He transformed French law through the Code Napoleon and initially expanded the French empire in Europe and the Middle East. Suffering repeated reverses against British naval forces and disastrous losses in his 1812 invasion of Russia, Napoleon was defeated by the British under Wellington at Waterloo in 1815, and the French empire collapsed.

Emerging from the revolution as a modern, bureaucratized state dominated by the bourgeoisie, France restored its monarchy in 1815 but not its monarchical absolutism. Charles X, successor to Louis XVIII, was ousted in a coup d'état in 1830 and replaced by the moderate Louis Philippe. The monarchy came to an end in the wave of popular revolt that swept France, along with most of Europe, in 1848; Louis Napoleon (nephew of Bonaparte) became president of the Second Republic. In 1852 he created the Second Empire, ruling as Napoleon III and presiding over a court that set the standards of fashion for the wealthy bourgeois society of 19th-century Europe.

During the 19th century, France again became a major colonial power, acquiring important possessions in North and West Africa and Indochina. It also became a world leader in art, science, and literature and was transformed into a major industrial power. Politically, however, France suffered from endemic weakness. The Second Empire ended disastrously with defeat in the Franco-Prussian War of 1870–71; the Paris Commune, formed during that war, was overthrown with great bloodshed. The Third Republic (1871–1914), despite the glittering pleasures of the Belle Epoque and France's considerable prestige as a world power, was shaken by the Dreyfus Affair of 1894–1906 and ill-served by both its political and military leaders.

France joined with Great Britain and Russia in forming the Triple Entente of 1907, a defensive agreement against the Triple Alliance of Germany, Italy, and the Austro-Hungarian empire. During World War I—in effect a war between these two alliances—France suffered millions of casualties and severe damage in the north. Although its role as a leader of the victorious alliance was confirmed at the Versailles Conference of 1919, France was seriously weakened by the war and played a diminished role as a world power in the postwar era.

France suffered badly in the world depression of the 1930s and could muster neither political nor military energy to offer effective opposition to the rise of Nazi Germany and fascist Italy. France was a participant in the Munich Agreement of 1938, which sealed the fate of central Europe. When World War II broke out in 1939, Hitler initially held off his attack on France, but when it came in May–June 1940, France was swiftly and ignominiously defeated.

During World War II, northern France was under German occupation, while in the south a collaborationist, semifascistic state was organized, with its capital at Vichy. Meanwhile, in London, Gen. Charles de Gaulle rallied the Free French forces, which fought on the allied side in various campaigns. During the war de Gaulle's followers drew up a Constitution for a Fourth Republic; following France's liberation and the war's end, the Free French forces assumed power, and the Constitution was ratified in 1946.

Although it suffered from inherent political weaknesses and often failed to provide stable cabinets, the Fourth Republic presided over postwar recovery, aided by the Marshall Plan; it promoted a mixed socialist–free enterprise economy and instituted social reforms such as women's suffrage and social security. It also led the way toward a united Europe, playing a leading role in the organization of the EEC in 1957. Despite a 20-year alliance with the Soviet Union concluded in 1944, France became a founding member of NATO in 1949.

The Fourth Republic was unable, however, to withstand the strains of the dismantling of France's empire during the postwar wave of decolonization. France's recovery of Indochina in 1945 set off a war of national liberation there that lasted until France withdrew from the colony in 1954. Morocco and Tunisia won their independence in 1956; in Algeria, regarded as part of France itself, the rebels fought on.

The Algerian war seriously polarized French public opinion, and, threatened with an army coup, the National Assembly voted in 1958 to grant Pres. Charles de Gaulle emergency powers for six months. De Gaulle outmaneuvered his army backers and negotiated to turn Algeria over to the Algerians, a process completed in

1962. Meanwhile he also restored order at home and presided over the drafting of a new constitution that created the Fifth Republic in 1958.

The new Constitution created a strong presidency, with powers to name the premier and the Council of Ministers and to preside over their meetings. The legislature was required to give priority to government initiatives and lacked authority over national defense, education, labor, and local government. Under the governments of premiers Michel Debré and Georges Pompidou, the Gaullist regime further advanced modernization of French industry and greatly benefited French agriculture by expanding the Common Market to include agricultural as well as industrial goods.

De Gaulle followed an independent foreign policy, pursuing European integration as well as closer relations with the Communist bloc and the Third World. He blocked British entry into the Common Market; developed an independent nuclear force, refusing to sign nuclear test-ban and nonproliferation treaties; pursued a historic rapprochement with Germany; recognized the People's Republic of China; established a leading French role in the former French colonies of Africa; and withdrew French forces from the NATO military command.

Reelected president in 1965, after a runoff election against the Socialist-Communist alliance candidate François Mitterrand, de Gaulle continued his independent policy until student riots in early 1968 provoked police repression, which led to further popular support for the students, especially in Paris. De Gaulle dissolved the National Assembly and, in an emotional campaign on behalf of national stability, won a new electoral majority. In 1969, however, following political reverses, de Gaulle resigned as president.

The elections of June 1969 gave the presidency to former premier Georges Pompidou, who died in office in April 1974. He was succeeded by the Independent Republican Valery Giscard d'Estaing, who served until May 1981. During these years the Gaullist heritage was developed and consolidated. In foreign policy the movement toward European unity continued with the development of the European Parliament and, in a reversal of policy in 1973, French support for British membership in the EEC. The economic shock of the OPEC price rises of 1973–74 led to a decision to stress new industrial ventures in high-technology fields, symbolized by the Anglo-French Concorde supersonic transport.

An aging population and the expansion of welfare provisions put a strain on the economy. The 1970s were years of social ferment, with a relaxation of divorce laws and the legalization of contraception and abortion, and a decline in church membership and attendance. In 1978 disillusionment stemming from inflation and social difficulties under Giscard d'Estaing brought about a leftist electoral victory for the first time under the Fifth Republic.

The Gaullist era came to an end in 1981, when Socialist François Mitterrand defeated Giscard in a presidential election. Giscard

immediately dissolved the National Assembly, and in the ensuing election, the Gaullists won a popular majority and formed a coalition cabinet with the Communists. Mitterrand's government pursued an aggressive program of nationalization of banks and major industries and reform of local government. Continued economic difficulties led to a loss of popular support for Mitterrand's policies. In the elections of 1986, Jacques Chirac's coalition of Gaullists and Giscardists won an absolute majority in the National Assembly, and Chirac became premier—the first time since 1958 that the president and the premier were of opposing parties. An accommodation was worked out in which Mitterrand concentrated on foreign affairs, and Chirac on domestic matters. Mitterrand oversaw a restoration of French military cooperation with NATO and a continuation of Franco-German cooperation, supported Chad in its war with Libya, and attempted to find a settlement of an armed separatist movement of native Kanaks against French settlers (who form a majority of the island's population) in the overseas territory of New Caledonia.

At home Chirac and his party reversed Mitterrand's policy of nationalization of banking and industry, cut taxes, and brought about a significant reduction in the inflation rate. Chirac ran for president against Mitterrand in 1988 but was defeated, leading to a continuation of the leftist-rightist "cohabitation government."

Despite postwar decolonization, France continues to control a far-flung, though geographically small, empire around the world. It has five "overseas departments" that are politically an integral part of France (French Guiana, Guadeloupe, Martinique, St. Pierre and Miquelon, and Mayotte), and a number of "overseas territories," including New Caledonia, French Polynesia, and Wallis and Futuna. (See "Territories of the World.")

# Gabon
## Gabonese Republic

**Geography** **Location:** western coast of Africa. **Boundaries:** Equatorial Guinea to NW, Cameroon to N, Congo to E and S, Atlantic Ocean to W. **Total land area:** 103,347 sq. mi. (267,667 sq km). **Coastline:** 550 mi. (885 km). **Comparative area:** slightly smaller than Colorado. **Land use:** 1% arable land; 1% permanent crops; 18% meadows and pastures; 78% forest and woodland; 2% other. **Major cities:** (1985 est.) Libreville (capital) 350,000; Port-Gentil 165,000.

**People** **Population:** 1,068,240 (1990). **Nationality:** noun—Gabonese (sing., pl.); adjective—Gabonese. **Ethnic groups:** about 40 Bantu groups, including four major tribal groupings (Fang, Eshira, Bapounou, Bateke); about 100,000 expatriate Africans and Europeans, including 27,000 French. **Languages:** French (official), Fang, Myene, Bateke, Bapounou/Eschira, Bandjabi. **Religions:** 55–75% Christian, less than 1% Muslim, remainder indigenous beliefs.

**Government** **Type:** republic; one-party

presidential regime since 1964. **Independence:** Aug. 17, 1960 (from France). **Constitution:** Feb. 21, 1961, revised Apr. 15, 1975. **National holiday:** Renovation Day, Mar. 12; Independence Day, Aug. 17. **Heads of government:** El Hadj Omar Bongo, president (since Dec. 1967); Casimir Oye-Mba, prime minister (since Nov. 1990). **Structure:** power centralized in president, elected by universal suffrage for seven-year term; unicameral legislature—93-member National Assembly, including nine members chosen by Omar Bongo, has limited powers; constitution amended in 1979 so that assembly deputies will serve five year terms; independent judiciary.

**Economy** **Monetary unit:** Communauté Financière Africaine (CFA) franc. **Budget:** (1988) **income:** $927 mil.; **expend.:** $1.2 bil. **GDP:** $3.2 bil., $3,200 per capita (1986). **Chief crops:** cash crops—cocoa, coffee, wood, palm oil, rice; food crops—pineapples, bananas, manioc, peanuts, root crops; imports food. **Livestock:** pigs, sheep, goats, cattle. **Natural resources:** crude oil, manganese, uranium, gold, timber, iron ore. **Major industries:** sawmills, petroleum, food, beverages; mining of increasing importance, especially for manganese and uranium. **Labor force:** 120,000 (1983); 65% agriculture, 30% industry and commerce; 58% of population of working age. **Exports:** $1.14 bil. (f.o.b., 1989 est.); 70% crude oil, 12% wood, 11% manganese, 6% uranium. **Imports:** $76 mil. (c.i.f., 1989 est.); foodstuffs, chemical products, petroleum products, construction materials, manufactures. **Major trading partners:** **exports:** 53% France, 22% U.S., W. Germany, Japan; **imports:** 48% France, 3% U.S., W. Germany, U.K.

**Intl. Orgs.** FAO, G-77, GATT, IAEA, IBRD, ICAO, IDA, IFAD, IFC, ILO, IMF, IMO, INTELSAT, INTERPOL, ITU, NAM, OPEC, UN, UNESCO, UPU, WHO, WIPO, WMO.

Gabon, an equatorial nation largely covered by dense rain forest, is inhabited by a highly diverse mixture of people who migrated into the region over the course of the past 700 years; the now-dominant Fang arrived during the 19th century. The first Europeans to reach the area were the Portuguese in the 15th century; they were followed by Dutch, French, and British traders in the 16th century. All engaged in the slave trade.

France established an informal protectorate in 1839–41 and set about suppressing the slave trade. In 1849 a group of freed slaves settled near the American mission station at Baraka and renamed the town Libreville. France established a colonial administration in 1903 and in 1910 made it part of French Equatorial Africa. The territory became an important base of Free French activity during World War II, and in 1946 Gen. Charles de Gaulle granted French citizenship to the territory's inhabitants, and local power was devolved upon advisory assemblies. In 1959 French Equatorial Africa was dissolved; Gabon became fully independent on Aug. 17, 1960.

Gabon has remained politically stable under its 1961 constitution. Gabon's first president,

Leon M'Ba, was briefly deposed by a military coup in 1964 but quickly reinstated with the aid of French troops. He died in 1967 and was succeeded by the vice president, Omar Bongo. Bongo combined all political parties into the Gabonese Democratic party in 1968, was elected president in his own right in 1975, and was reelected in 1979 and 1986.

Gabon is rich in natural resources, including petroleum, manganese, uranium, and timber. Petroleum exports account for 80 percent of foreign earnings. The country was badly hit by the fall in petroleum prices in the early 1980s, but the economy remained fundamentally sound, and in 1988 foreign creditors agreed to a restructuring of the country's external debt. Prospects for increased petroleum production, as well as expanded exploitation of other resources, seem bright. The country is under-developed agriculturally, however, and imports 90 percent of its food.

Unlike many African countries, Gabon is rel-atively underpopulated. It has a large corps of well educated people, and its French population (18,000) has more than tripled since 1959. Plans for future economic development revolve around expanding the country's infrastruc-ture, notably the TransGabon Railway (the third stage of which was completed in 1986) and a national highway network, as well as attracting increased foreign investment.

## The Gambia
### Republic of The Gambia
**Geography Location:** narrow territory around Gambia River on northwestern coast of Africa. **Boundaries:** Senegal to N, E, and S, Atlantic Ocean to W. **Total land area:** 4,361 sq. mi. (11,295 sq km). **Coastline:** 50 mi. (80 km). **Comparative area:** between Delaware and Con-necticut. **Land use:** 16% arable land; 0% per-manent crops; 9% meadows and pastures; 20% forest and woodland; 55% other; includes 3% irrigated. **Major cities:** (1983 census) Banjul (capital) 44,188; Serrekunda 68,433; Brikama 19,584; Bakau 19,309; Farafenni 10,168.

**People Population:** 848,147 (1990). **Nationality:** noun—Gambian(s); adjective—Gambian. **Ethnic groups:** 42% Mandinka, 18% Fula, 16% Wolof, 10% Jola, 9% Serahuli, 1% non-Gambian, 4% other. **Languages:** English (official), Mandinka, Wolof, Fula, and others. **Religions:** 90% Muslim, 9% Christian, 1% indigenous beliefs.

**Government Type:** republic; on Feb. 1, 1982, The Gambia and Senegal formed a loose confederation named Senegambia that calls for eventual integration of their armed forces and economic cooperation. **Independence:** Feb. 18, 1965 (from UK). **Constitution:** Apr. 24, 1970; formally signed agreement of confederation with Senegal Dec. 12, 1981 (effective Feb. 1, 1982) named Senegambia. **National holiday:** Independence Day, Feb. 18. **Heads of govern-ment:** Alhaji Sir Dawda Kairaba Jawara, presi-dent (since Feb. 1970). **Structure:** unicameral legislature—43-member parliament in which four seats are reserved for tribal chiefs, four are

government-appointed, 35 are elected for five-year terms; judiciary.

**Economy Monetary unit:** dalasi. **Budget:** (1989) **income:** $75 mil.; **expend.:** $67 mil. **GDP:** $195 mil., $250 per capita. **Chief crops:** peanuts, millet, sorghum, rice, maize. **Live-stock:** cattle, goats, sheep, pigs, asses. **Natural resources:** fish. **Major industries:** peanut pro-cessing, tourism, beverages. **Labor force:** 165,000 (1983 est.); 75% agriculture, 18.9% industry, commerce, and services; 55% of population of working age. **Exports:** $133 mil. (f.o.b., 1989); peanuts and peanut products, fish, palm ker-nels. **Imports:** $105 mil. (c.i.f., 1989); textiles, foodstuffs, tobacco, machinery, petroleum products, chemicals. **Major trading partners:** (1986) **exports:** 49% Ghana, 27% Europe, 12% Japan, 1% U.S.; **imports:** 55% Europe (39% EC, 16% other), 20% Asia, 11% U.S., 4% Senegal.

**Intl. Orgs.** Commonwealth, FAO, G-77, GATT, IBRD, ICAO, IDA, IFAD, IFC, IMF, IMO, ITU, NAM, UN, UNESCO, UPU, WHO, WMO.

Thirty miles across at its widest point, and 295 miles long, the serpentine republic of The Gambia was gerrymandered into being out of competing French and British colonial inter-ests. Once the westernmost part of the King-dom of Mali, The Gambia was visited by the Portuguese in 1455. In 1588, they sold British traders exclusive rights to the Gambia River, and in 1660 British merchants established a trading fort. England and France struggled for two hundred years to gain political and eco-nomic control over the territory, but in 1783 the French ceded to Great Britain possession of The Gambia. Its present boundaries were established in 1889 when it became a British Crown Colony. Between 1901 and 1906, legis-lative councils were established to encourage self-government, and slavery was abolished.

During World War II, Gambian troops fought with the British in Burma and The Gam-bia was an important airbase. After World War II the country moved quickly toward constitu-tional government, achieving independence as a constitutional monarchy within the British Commonwealth of Nations in 1965. The Gam-bia became a republic on Apr. 24, 1970.

In 1982, The Gambia and Senegal, which surrounds the country on three sides, estab-lished the confederation of Senegambia under which the two countries retained their inde-pendence but united their military, monetary systems, and parliament. Proving ineffective, the confederation was abolished in 1989.

## Germany
### Federal Republic of Germany
**Geography Location:** north central Europe. **Boundaries:** Denmark, Baltic Sea to N, Poland, Czechoslovakia to E, Austria, Switzerland to S, France, Luxembourg, Belgium, Netherlands, North Sea to W. **Total land area:** 137,855 sq. mi. (357,041 sq km). **Coastline:** 1,385 mi. (2,389 km). **Comparative area:** between New Mexico and Montana. **Land use:** 34% arable land; 2% permanent crops; 17% meadows and

pastures; 29% forest and woodland; 17% other; includes 1% irrigated. **Major cities:** (1988 est.) Berlin (capital) 3,299,975; Bonn (seat of gov-ernment) 290,800; Hamburg 1,594,190; München (Munich) 1,201,479; Köln (Cologne) 930,907; Essen 621,436; Leipzig 547,308; Dresden 519,527; Chemnitz (Karl-Marx-Stadt) 313,095; Magdeburg 290,381.

**People Population:** 78,475,370 (1990). **Nationality:** noun—German(s); adjective—Ger-man. **Ethnic groups:** Predominantly German; small Slavic and Danish minorities. **Lan-guages:** German, Sorbian. **Religions:** 45% Protestant, 37% Roman Catholic, 18% unaffili-ated and other.

**Government Type:** federal republic. **Con-stitution:** May 23, 1949; provisional constitu-tion known as Basic Law. **National holiday:** Oct. 3. **Heads of government:** Dr. Richard von Weizsäcker, president (since July 1984); Dr. Helmut Kohl, chancellor (since Oct. 1982). **Structure:** president (titular head of state), chancellor (executive head of government); bicameral parliament—Bundesrat (Federal Council, upper house), Bundestag (National Assembly, lower house); independent judiciary.

**Intl. Orgs.** EC, FAO, GATT, IAEA, IBRD, ICAO, IDA, IFAD, IFC, ILO, IMF, IMO, INTEL-SAT, INTERPOL, ITU, NATO, OAS (observer), OECD, UN, UNESCO, UPU, WHO, WIPO, WMO.

**Note:** On Oct 3, 1990, East Germany acceded to West Germany and ceased to exist as a sepa-rate nation by dissolving its constitution and accepting that of West Germany. The following economic statistics are for the separate states prior to unification.

### East Germany
**Economy Monetary unit:** deutsche mark. **Budget:** (1986) **income:** $123.5 bil.; **expend.:** $123.2 bil. **GNP:** $159.5 bil., $9,679 per capita (1988). **Chief crops:** potatoes, rye, wheat, bar-ley, oats; shortages—grain, vegetables, vegeta-ble oil. **Livestock:** poultry, pigs, cattle, sheep, beehives. **Natural resources:** brown coal, potash, uranium, copper, natural gas. **Major industries:** metal fabrication, chemicals, brown coal. **Labor force:** 8.96 mil. (1987); 37.7% industry, 21.1% services, 10.8% agriculture and forestry, 10.3% commerce. **Exports:** $30.7 bil. (f.o.b., 1988); 47% machinery and transport equipment, 16% consumer goods, 13% chem-ical products and building materials. **Imports:** $31 bil. (c.i.f., 1988); 40% fuels and metals, 29% machinery and transport equipment, 9% chemical products and building materials. **Major trading partners: exports:** USSR, Czechoslovakia, Poland, W. Germany, Hungary, Bulgaria, Switzerland, Romania; **imports:** 65% CMEA, 33% non-communist countries.

Even before the fighting in Germany sub-sided in 1945, the Soviet Air Force brought Walter Ulbricht, the exiled leader of the Ger-man Communist party, back to the USSR's zone of occupation in Germany. Backed by 20 Soviet divisions, Ulbricht and the party com-menced the communization of the eastern zone.

After local and state elections embarrassed the Communists, Stalin and Ulbricht forced all other parties into the National Front. With no other electoral lists permitted, voters gave a 99.7% approval to the National Front in the first elections to East Germany's "People's Chamber" in 1950.

While Ulbricht attempted to collectivize agriculture and plan industrial development in the eastern zone, the Soviet Union extracted heavy reparations payments, bringing on an acute economic crisis. In June 1953, shortly after Stalin's death, strikes and riots erupted; order was quickly restored. The USSR renounced further reparation payments and declared East Germany a sovereign state.

By 1963 East Germany had become the second-largest industrial power in Eastern Europe, and in 1968 it surpassed Czechoslovakia in output. A significant shift of labor to industry reduced the farm population to under 20 percent of total population by 1960. Though farming became mechanized and more productive, it remained relatively inefficient.

Although East Germany enjoyed prestige within the Eastern bloc as an industrial power, the steady stream of emigrants to West Germany told a different story. After a renewed collectivization policy was implemented in 1960, the stream became a flood, and East Germany responded by building the Berlin Wall. The wall was a visible sign of political failure, but it did slow the stream of emigration to a trickle.

An aging Ulbricht was replaced in May 1971 as party first secretary by Erich Honecker, who also became head of state in 1976. Honecker completed state ownership of all industry in 1972. Industries were grouped into 133 giant monopolies known as Kombinate, each covering one industrial sector and vertically integrated from research to sales.

After the "opening to the east" (Ostpolitik) of Willi Brandt the two Germanies grew closer, at least economically. East Germany's trade with West Germany, regarded as "intranational" by Bonn, gave it access to the EC. However, East Germany resisted Mikhail Gorbachev's reform policies in the 1980s, trying to establish itself as a model of old-style communism in Eastern Europe.

In the fall of 1989 tens of thousands of East Germans fled to West Germany through Hungary and Czechoslovakia, triggering a series of dramatic demonstrations and the dismantling of the Berlin Wall in December. Honecker's government collapsed, as did that of his successor, as the momentum for unification became unstoppable. In March 1990 Christian Democrat Lothar de Maizière was elected prime minister on a unification platform. Monetary union occurred on July 1, 1990, with the deutsche mark replacing the ostmark. Unification came on Oct. 2.

## West Germany

**Economy** **Monetary unit:** deutsche mark. **Budget:** (1988) *income:* $539 bil.; *expend.:* $563 bil. **GDP:** $945.7 bil., $15,300 per capita (1989 est.). **Chief crops:** grains, potatoes, sugar beets; 75% self-sufficient. **Livestock:** chickens, pigs, cattle, ducks, sheep. **Natural resources:** iron ore, coal, potash, timber. **Major industries:** among world's largest producers of iron, steel, coal, cement, chemicals, machinery, ships, vehicles, machine tools, electronics, food and beverages; shortages—fats and oils, pulses, tropical products, sugar, cotton, wool, rubber, petroleum, iron ore, bauxite, nonferrous metals, sulfur. **Labor force:** 27.79 mil. (1987); 41.6% industry, 34.7% services and other, 18.2% trade and transport; 8.7% unemployment (1987). **Exports:** $323.4 bil. (f.o.b., 1988); 86.6% manufactures (includes machines and machine tools, chemicals, motor vehicles, iron and steel products), 5.1% agricultural products, 4.9% raw materials, 2.3% fuels, 4.9% other. **Imports:** $250.6 bil. (f.o.b., 1988); 68.5% manufactures, 12% agricultural products, 9.7% fuels, 7.1% raw materials. **Major trading partners:** (1987) *exports:* 52.7% EC (12% France, 9% Netherlands, 9% Italy, 9% UK, 7% Belgium-Luxembourg), 18% other Western Europe, 10% U.S., 4% Eastern Europe, 3% OPEC. *imports:* 52.7% EC (12% France, 11% Netherlands, 10% Italy, 7% UK, 7% Belgium-Luxembourg), 15% other Western Europe, 6% U.S., 6% Japan.

The ancient tribes of Germany resisted Roman conquest with mixed success. German mercenaries served in the Roman legions, and Germanic invasions contributed to the fall of Rome. Most of Germany was united within the empire of Charlemagne. Divided among his three sons in 843, the empire's eastern regions became the heart of the Germanies. The Holy Roman Empire, founded in 962, gave some unity to the politically fragmented German territories, but its boundaries included more than Germany, and some Germans remained outside it. But that unity was fragile; the Holy Roman emperor was a feudal overlord rather than a ruler, and hundreds of separate political bodies coexisted within the imperial domain. Along the North Sea and Baltic coasts, the Hanseatic League controlled much of the commerce of northern Europe.

With the Reformation in the 16th century, religious divisions added to Germany's existing political fragmentation and local allegiances. The Thirty Years' War (1618–48) resulted in the virtual extinction of the Holy Roman Empire and left Germany without even a shadow of unity.

After the Napoleonic Wars, in which much of Germany was conquered by France, the Congress of Vienna (1814–15) sanctioned the creation of a German League to succeed the Holy Roman Empire. The league consisted of 39 states, including five substantial kingdoms and the Austro-Hungarian empire. Prussia, one of the five kingdoms, had already risen to prominence under Frederick the Great in the 18th century. In a series of wars in the mid-19th century, Prussia conquered the other German states; after defeating France in the Franco-Prussian War of 1870–71, Prussia declared the establishment of the German empire. Under its chancellor, Otto von Bismarck, Germany became a major European power in the late 19th century, with a booming industrial economy, flourishing agriculture, an expanding colonial empire, and growing military might.

The German empire reached its height under Kaiser Wilhelm II on the eve of World War I. Germany's disastrous defeat in that war was compounded by the harsh terms of the Treaty of Versailles (1919), which stripped Germany of its colonial empire, awarded part of Schlesswig to Denmark, Alsace-Lorraine to France, and part of Prussia to Poland, and abolished the German monarchy.

The Weimar Republic, established in 1919, gradually overcame economic difficulties, including ruinous inflation, to achieve a measure of postwar recovery in the 1920s. The republic was, however, disrupted by labor strife, political fragmentation, and the rise of armed extremist political movements on both left and right. After the onset of the world economic depression in 1929, Adolf Hitler's National Socialist movement gained increasing power, both at the polls and through open thuggery against its opponents. Hitler's appointment as chancellor in 1933 effectively put an end to the Weimar Republic as a functioning democracy.

The onset of World War II in Europe was presaged by Hitler's annexation of Austria and Czechoslovakia in 1938 and precipitated by the German invasion of Poland in 1939. Early military successes gave Germany control of most of Europe, but the eventual victory of the Allied powers in 1945 left the country exhausted and in ruins. Much of the Jewish population of Germany, and of other territories under German control, had been killed during the Holocaust of World War II. German cities were reduced to rubble, and a quarter of the country's homes were uninhabitable. Famine and fuel shortages added to the general misery.

Politically, Germany had essentially ceased to exist in 1945. The Allies divided the country into four zones of occupation, with a similar four-part division of Berlin. As the Cold War rift between the Western powers and the USSR intensified during the late 1940s, so too the division of Germany hardened. In 1948 the USSR imposed a blockade on West Berlin; the city was supplied by a massive airlift from the West for several months. In 1949 two Germanies were created: the German Democratic Republic in the Russian zone in the east, and the Federal Republic of Germany in the Allied zone in the west.

The Federal Republic was largely the creation of one man, Konrad Adenauer. A veteran pre-Hitler politician, he founded the Federation of Christian Democratic Parties (CDU-CSU) in 1945, and as president of the Parliamentary Council formed during the occupation, he virtually wrote the new constitution for West Germany. In the first elections held in the Federal Republic (August 1949), the "bourgeois coalition" led by the CDU-CSU won a parliamentary majority in the Bundestag, and Adenauer became chancellor, a post he held for 14 years. In 1951 the Western powers granted the new state autonomy in foreign affairs, and recognized its full sovereignty in 1954.

In foreign affairs Adenauer relied heavily on friendship with the United States and reconciliation with France. He also supported European integration: In 1951 West Germany joined both the Council of Europe and the Coal and Steel Community. West Germany was admitted to NATO in 1955 and in 1957 became one of the six founding members of the EEC.

In domestic affairs the political alliance between Adenauer and Ludwig Erhard led to political stability and the creation of a market-driven economy. With a currency reform program and Marshall Plan aid in place by 1948 under occupation administration, the stage was set for Germany's "economic miracle" of the 1950s. Between 1949 and 1964, industrial production increased by 60 percent and gross national product tripled, while unemployment fell to 1 percent, even as millions of refugees from East Germany were integrated into the West German economy. In the same period, over 8 million houses and apartments were constructed.

In the early 1960s, tensions between West and East Germany increased, as East Germany constructed the Berlin Wall (1961) to stem the flow of refugees to the West. In 1963 Erhard succeeded Adenauer as chancellor. Economic growth slowed to an annual 3 percent rate, but West Germany was already one of Europe's strongest economic powers, even providing jobs for hundreds of thousands of "guest workers" from southern Europe and Turkey.

Erhard resigned in 1966 when his coalition fell apart over the issue of a planned tax increase. He was succeeded by Kurt Kiesinger, who presided over a historic "great coalition" of Christian Democrats and Social Democrats. Under Willi Brandt (who served as deputy chancellor and foreign minister), the Social Democrats had shifted their orientation from a Marxist party to a reformist, market-oriented stance.

Elections in 1969 produced a majority for the coalition headed by the Social Democrats, a coalition that governed until 1982. Brandt succeeded Kiesinger and pursued an *Ostpolitik* ("opening to the east"), regularizing relations with East Germany, signing a nonaggression pact with the USSR, and recognizing the border between East Germany and Poland. But domestically, West Germany suffered serious dislocations from the OPEC oil price increases of the early 1970s; inflation reached almost 8 percent. Revelations that a Brandt aide was an East German spy led to his replacement as chancellor by Helmut Schmidt in 1974.

Schmidt continued Brandt's eastern policy but also pursued improved relations with the West. Economic difficulties persisted, however, and Schmidt's government fell in 1982. The Christian Democrats returned to power under chancellor Helmut Kohl. The general improvement of the world economy in the 1980s led to economic recovery in Germany, boosting Kohl's popularity. The 1980s saw the rise to political prominence (though not to power) of the pacifist-environmentalist Green party.

Since the 1970s, Germany has been disrupted by terrorism, both homegrown and foreign, most notably the massacre of Israeli athletes by PLO terrorists at the 1972 Munich Olympics. German leftists have killed a number of leading industrialists and economists.

Kohl won widespread international admiration for his handling of the collapse of the East German regime and for pressing for rapid German unification. Although united Germany was expected to be the dominant power in Europe by the time the European Community formally unites in 1992, the costs and difficulties of unification have proven greater than anticipated, and the economic differences between eastern and western halves of Germany seem likely to persist for a few years.

(For recent key events, see Part I, "The Year in Review.")

## Ghana
### Republic of Ghana

**Geography Location:** western Africa. **Boundaries:** Burkina Faso to N, Togo to E, Gulf of Guinea to S, Ivory Coast to W. **Total land area:** 92,100 sq. mi. (238,537 sq km). **Coastline:** 335 mi. (539 km). Comparative area: slightly smaller than Oregon. **Land use:** 5% arable land; 7% permanent crops; 15% meadows and pastures; 37% forest and woodland; 36% other; includes negl. % irrigated. **Major cities:** (1984 census) Accra (capital) 964,879; Kumasi 348,880; Tamale 136,828; Tema 99,608; Takoradi 61,527.

**People Population:** 15,167,243 (1990). **Nationality:** noun—Ghanaian(s); adjective—Ghanaian. **Ethnic groups:** 99.8% black African (major groups—44% Akan, 16% Moshi-Dagomba, 13% Ewe, 8% Ga), 0.2% European and other. **Languages:** English (official), Akan, Moshi-Dagomba, Ewe, Ga. **Religions:** 38% indigenous beliefs, 30% Muslim, 24% Christian, 8% other.

**Government Type:** military. **Independence:** Mar. 6, 1957 (from UK). **Constitution:** Sept. 24, 1979; suspended Dec. 31, 1981. **National holiday:** Independence Day, Mar. 6. **Heads of government:** Flt. Lt. (Ret.) Jerry John Rawlings, chairman of PNDC (since Dec. 1981). **Structure:** executive—seven-member Provisional National Defense Council (PNDC); on Jan. 21, 1982, PNDC appointed secretaries to head most ministries.

**Economy Monetary unit:** cedi. **Budget:** (1988 est.) *income:* $769 mil.; *expend.:* $749 mil. **GNP:** $5.2 bil., $400 per capita. **Chief crops:** cocoa, coffee, root crops, corn, sorghum, millet, peanuts; not self-sufficient in food production but has that potential; an illegal producer of cannabis for international drug trade. **Livestock:** goats, sheep, cattle, pigs, asses. **Natural resources:** gold, timber, industrial diamonds, bauxite, manganese. **Major industries:** mining, lumbering, light manufacturing. **Labor force:** 3.7 mil. (1983); 54.7% agriculture and fishing, 18.7% industry, 15.2% sales and clerical; 400,000 unemployed; 48% of population of working age. **Exports:** $977 mil. (f.o.b., 1987); 60% cocoa; wood, gold, diamonds, manganese, bauxite, aluminum (aluminum regularly excluded from balance-of-payments data). **Imports:** $988 mil. (c.i.f., 1987); textiles and other manufactured goods, food, fuels, transport equipment. **Major trading partners:** *exports:* 23% U.S., UK, other EC; *imports:* 10% U.S., UK, W. Germany, France, Japan, S. Korea.

**Intl. Orgs.** Commonwealth, FAO, G-77, GATT, IAEA, IBRD, ICAO, IDA, IFAD, IFC, ILO, IMF, IMO, INTELSAT, INTERPOL, ITU, NAM, UN, UNESCO, UPU, WHO, WIPO, WMO.

The connection between modern Ghana and the 10th century Ghana empire of southern Mali is obscure. By the 13th century the Akan around the city of Kumasi were trading gold and other commodities with the Mande to the north. The number of competing states in the region grew rapidly after European contact. The Asante empire began in the early 17th century under Osei Tutu. By 1750 it controlled the northern part of Ghana, and by 1820 it had brought the coastal Fante empire, with its access to the European trade, under its control.

The Portuguese first explored the area, on Africa's west coast, in 1471, naming it the Gold Coast because of its gold deposits and its reserves of "black gold"—slaves. In the 16th and 17th centuries, the British, Danes, and Dutch established slave trading posts there, which is where most American slaves came from. The slave trade ended in the 1850s, and the British gained control of the Gold Coast, making it a protectorate in 1871 and a colony in 1886.

Great Britain gave the colony a new constitution in 1946 under which Africans held a majority of seats in the legislature. Kwame Nkrumah became prime minister of the colony in 1952 and the first prime minister of the nation when it became independent.

At independence, Ghana boasted Africa's largest man-made deep-water port and the most productive gold mine in the world, and it was the second largest producer of industrial diamonds in the world. Nkrumah began to limit the freedom of opposition parties, court Communist bloc nations, and exert absolute authority. In January 1964 all opposition parties were outlawed. A military council seized power in February 1966 and ousted Nkrumah.

Civilian governments ran the country briefly (1969–72, 1979–81), but in 1981, Flt. Lt. Jerry Rawlings took power in a coup and has ruled ever since. Ghana suffered severe economic problems throughout the 1970s and 1980s, and many of Ghana's people left for Nigeria to find work. In 1983 Nigeria ousted more than one million of these migrant workers, returning them to their homeland and increasing Ghana's economic woes.

After five years of stagnation, Ghana achieved a 6 percent economic growth rate in 1989 under a World Bank restructuring program. But political unrest remains, and Chairman Rawlings survived an assassination attempt in February 1990.

## Greece
### Hellenic Republic

**Geography Location:** southeastern Europe. **Boundaries:** Albania, Yugoslavia, Bulgaria to N, Turkey to NE, Aegean Sea to E, Mediterranean Sea to S, Ionian Sea to W, Albania to NW; numerous islands surround mainland. **Total land area:** 50,949 sq. mi. (131,957 sq km). **Coastline:** 8,500 mi. (13,676 km). **Comparative area:** slightly larger than New York. **Land use:** 23% arable land; 8% permanent crops; 40% meadows and pastures; 20% forest and woodland; 9% other; includes 7% irrigated. **Major cities:** (1981 census) Athinai (Athens, capital) 885,737; Thessaloniki (Salonika) 406,413; Piraeus 196,389; Patras 142,163; Larissa 102,426.

**People Population:** 10,028,171 (1990). **Nationality:** noun—Greek(s); adjective—Greek. **Ethnic groups:** 97.7% Greek, 1.3% Turkish, 1.0% Vlach, Slav, Albanian, Pomach (note: Greek government states there are no ethnic divisions in Greece). **Languages:** Greek (official); English and French widely understood. **Religions:** 98% Greek Orthodox, 1.3% Muslim, 0.7% other.

**Government Type:** presidential parliamentary government; monarchy rejected by referendum Dec. 8, 1974. **Constitution:** June 11, 1975. **National holiday:** Independence Day, Mar. 25. **Heads of government:** Constantine Karamanlis, president (since May 1990); Constantine Mitsotakis, prime minister (since Apr. 1990). **Structure:** executive—president elected by Vouli (parliament), prime minister, and cabinet; legislative—unicameral legislature (300-member Vouli); judiciary—independent.

**Economy Monetary unit:** Greek drachma. **Budget:** (1988) *income:* $15.5 bil.; *expend.:* $23.9 bil. **GDP:** $56.3 bil., $5,605 per capita (1989 est.). **Chief crops:** wheat, olives, tobacco, cotton, raisins, fruit; nearly self-sufficient. **Livestock:** chickens, sheep, goats, pigs, cattle. **Natural resources:** bauxite, lignite, magnesite, crude oil, marble. **Major industries:** food and tobacco processing, textiles, chemicals. **Labor force:** 3.86 mil. (1985); 43% services, 27% agriculture, 20% manufacturing and mining; 7.4% unemployment (1986). **Exports:** $5.9 bil. (f.o.b., 1988); manufactured goods, food, live animals, fuels, lubricants, raw materials. **Imports:** $13.5 bil. (c.i.f., 1988); machinery and transport equipment, light manufactures, fuels, lubricants, foodstuffs, chemicals. **Major trading partners:** *exports:* 24% W. Germany, 14% Italy, 11.8% non-oil developing countries, 9.5% France, 7.1% U.S., 6.8% UK; *imports:* 22% W. Germany, 14% non-oil developing countries, 13% oil-exporting countries, 12% Italy, 8% France, 3.2% U.S.

**Intl. Orgs.** EC, FAO, GATT, IAEA, IBRD, ICAO, IDA, IFAD, IFC, ILO, IMF, IMO, INTELSAT, INTERPOL, ITU, NATO, OECD, UN, UNESCO, UPU, WHO, WIPO, WMO.

The Bronze Age and Iron Age cultures of Greece evolved to create the most glorious civilization of the ancient world. During their high point, from the fifth to the third century B.C., the city-states of Greece led the world in art, philosophy, political culture, and science. Greece vied with the Persian empire for control of Asia Minor and competed with the Phoenicians in maritime commerce in the Mediterranean. Alexander the Great, king of Macedonia, spread Greek civilization widely by conquering much of the Middle East and western Asia,

but his empire did not long outlast his death in 323 B.C.

Greece was absorbed into the Roman Empire during the second and first centuries B.C. In the fourth century A.D., with the division of the Roman Empire, Greece became part of the Byzantine (Eastern Roman) Empire. Seven years after the Ottoman Turks captured Constantinople in 1453, they overran Greece and ruled it as part of the Ottoman Empire for 350 years.

Under Ottoman rule, much of the administration of Greece was left in local hands, keeping alive a sense of Greek nationhood and a tradition of Greek leadership, particularly through the clergy of the Greek Orthodox church. Inspired by the French Revolution, a romanticized ideal of the classical past, and religious nationalism, in 1821 Greece rebelled against Turkish rule. With the support of England, France, and Russia, Greek independence was won in 1827, although the country included only about half of its present territory.

The Western powers sponsored a monarchical government in Greece, ruled by a German prince. Deposed in a revolt, he was succeeded by King George I, a Danish prince who ruled from 1863 until his assassination in 1913. In the three Balkan Wars of 1912, 1913, and 1914, Greece expanded its borders to reach approximately its present size.

In 1923 a Greek Republic was established, but in 1935 King George II returned to his throne, placing government control in the hands of the patriotic but semifascistic Gen. Ioannis Metaxas. In 1940 Metaxas resisted Italy's attempt to conquer Greece, defeating Mussolini's armies so badly that Hitler sent crack troops to his ally's assistance. The German occupation of Greece was complete by June 1941. The Germans pillaged the country and massacred Jews; their Bulgarian allies colonized Macedonia.

During World War II, resistance grew among both Communist and anti-Communist groups, both beyond the reach of the government-in-exile in London. With the German withdrawal in October 1944, resistance groups battled each other; this led to full-scale civil war by 1946. British, and then American assistance (under the Truman Doctrine), enabled the Greek government to defeat the Communist forces when Stalin refused to intervene.

King George II died in 1947, succeeded by his brother, King Paul I. Political instability—16 governments during 1946–52—prevailed until, under American pressure, the Greeks adopted a new constitution designed to ensure stable government.

Until the postwar period, Greece's economy had been dominated by agriculture and livestock raising. Industry was limited largely to textiles and food processing; shipping was the major service industry. Under policies instituted in 1952 by the government of Marshall Alexandros Papagos, the industrial sector led a period of vigorous economic growth lasting into the 1960s. A market-oriented economy, tariff protection for Greek industry, tight internal security, and close ties with the West

formed the mainstays of Greek policy.

Greece joined NATO in 1951, as did Turkey. Conflict over Cyprus divided the two nominal allies, however. The failure of the government of Constantine Karamanlis to resolve the Cyprus situation eroded his popularity, and he was replaced in 1964 by George Papandreou, who governed at the head of a left-center coalition. King Constantine, who succeeded his father in 1963, forced Papandreou to resign in 1964, after he and members of his government were accused of various improprieties. A military coup, led by Col. George Papadopoulos, toppled the government in 1967. A countercoup by the king on Dec. 13, 1967, failed, and the king fled the country.

A military dictatorship ruled from 1967 to 1974. Its failed attempt to intervene in Cyprus in 1974 provoked a Turkish invasion of the island and led to the military regime's collapse. Karamanlis headed the government once again; his party won a large majority in parliamentary elections in November, and a republic was formally established with the promulgation of a new constitution in 1975. Karamanlis's New Democracy party received a renewed but smaller majority in parliamentary elections in 1977.

Greece, an associate member of the EC since 1961, became a full member in 1981. Full military membership in NATO was restored in 1980. In 1981 the Panhellenic Socialist Movement under Andreas Papandreou won a parliamentary majority, renewed in 1984. The left-wing Papandreou government was outspokenly anti-NATO, anti-EC, and anti-American, but its policy was more moderate than its rhetoric, extending even to modest cooperation with Turkey in the Aegean. The Papandreou government was shaken by several pro-Palestinian terrorist incidents in Greece, and by a scandal involving the married Papandreou's relationship with a younger woman.

During 1989–90 Greece struggled through three parliamentary elections in less than a year. In the first two no major party won a clear victory, leading to weak, short-lived coalition governments. The third, in the spring of 1990, resulted in a slim majority for the center-right party and the apparent decline of Papandreou's stature as a national leader.

The Greek economy, now more industrial than agricultural, has been hurt by persistent inflation, severe environmental problems, and the fluctuating fortunes of the shipping industry.

## Grenada

**Geography Location:** southeastern Caribbean Sea, about 100 mi. (160 km) N of Trinidad. St. George's 12°03′N, 61°45′W. **Boundaries:** Atlantic Ocean to NE, E, and SE.; Caribbean Sea to SW, W, and NW. **Total land area:** 133 sq. mi. (344 sq km). **Coastline:** 75 mi. (121 km). **Comparative area:** about twice size of Washington, D.C. **Land use:** 15% arable land; 26% permanent crops; 3% meadows and pastures; 9% forest and woodland; 47% other; includes N.A. irrigated. **Major cities:** (1980 est.) St.

George's (capital) 7,500.

**People Population:** 84,175 (1990). **Nationality:** noun—Grenadian(s); adjective—Grenadian. **Ethnic groups:** mainly of black African descent. **Languages:** English (official), some French patois. **Religions:** largely Roman Catholic, some Anglican and other Protestant sects.

**Government Type:** independent state; recognizes Elizabeth II as chief of state. **Independence:** Feb. 7, 1974 (from UK). **Constitution:** Dec. 19, 1973. **National holiday:** Independence Day, Feb. 7. **Heads of government:** Sir Paul Scoon, governor-general (since Sept. 1978); Nicholas Braithwaite, prime minister (since Mar. 1990). **Structure:** executive (cabinet led by prime minister); bicameral legislature (15-member elected House of Representatives and 13-member appointed Senate); judiciary (Grenada Supreme Court, composed of High Court of Justice and two-tier court of appeals).

**Economy Monetary unit:** East Caribbean (EC) dollar. **Budget:** (1989 est.) *income:* $74.2 mil.; *expend.:* $82.3 mil. **GDP:** $129.7 mil., $1,535 per capita (1988). **Chief crops:** cocoa, nutmeg, mace, bananas. **Livestock:** sheep, goats, pigs, cattle, asses. **Natural resources:** none. **Major industries:** tourism, fish, beverages. **Labor force:** 36,000 (1985); 31% services, 24% agriculture, 45% other. **Exports:** $31.8 mil. (f.o.b., 1988 est.); 35% nutmeg, 15% coca beans, 13% bananas, 7% mace. **Imports:** $92.6 mil. (c.i.f., 1988 est.); 24% machinery, 22% food, 19% manufactured goods, 8% petroleum. **Major trading partners:** (1985) *exports:* 4% U.S., UK, Netherlands, W. Germany; *imports:* 32% U.S., UK, Trinidad and Tobago.

**Intl. Orgs.** FAO, G-77, GATT (de facto), IBRD, ICAO, IDA, IFAD, IFC, ILO, IMF, ITU, NAM, OAS, UN, UNESCO, UPU, WHO.

Dominated in the early 1600s by the warlike Carib Indians, Grenada alternated between French and British possession between 1650 and 1783, when British rule was established. Independence came in 1974. The leftist New Jewel Movement seized power in a 1979 coup, but its leader, Maurice Bishop, was assassinated during a military coup in 1983. Shortly thereafter, the United States invaded and returned power to the governor-general until 1984. In elections held on Mar. 13, 1990, no party gained a parliamentary majority. Prime Minister Nicholas Braithwaite of the National Democratic Congress party formed a coalition government in April 1990.

## Guatemala
### Republic of Guatemala
**Geography Location:** northern part of Central American isthmus. **Boundaries:** Mexico to N and W, Honduras and Belize to E, El Salvador to S. **Total land area:** 42,042 sq. mi. (108,889 sq km). **Coastline:** 248 mi. (400 km). **Comparative area:** slightly smaller than Tennessee. **Land use:** 12% arable land; 4% permanent crops; 12% meadows and pastures; 40% forest and woodland; 32% other; includes 1% irrigated. **Major cities:** (1986 est.) Guatemala

City (capital) 1,800,000; Escuintla 87,000; Quezaltenango 72,000; Totonicapón 54,000.

**People Population:** 9,097,636 (1990). **Nationality:** noun—Guatemalan(s); adjective—Guatemalan. **Ethnic groups:** 56% Ladino (mestizo and westernized Indian), 44% Indian. **Languages:** Spanish, but over 40% of population speaks an Indian language as primary tongue (18 Indian dialects, including Quiche, Cakchiquel, Kekchi). **Religions:** predominantly Roman Catholic, some Protestant and traditional Mayan.

**Government Type:** republic. **Independence:** Sept. 15, 1821 (from Spain). **Constitution:** May 31, 1985, effective Jan. 1986. **National holiday:** Independence Day, Sept. 15. **Heads of government:** Jorge Serrano Elias, president (since Jan. 1991). **Structure:** traditionally dominant executive; new 100-member congress installed Jan. 14, 1986; power vested in office of president; seven-member (minimum) Supreme Court.

**Economy Monetary unit:** quetzal. **Budget:** (1988) *income:* $771 mil.; *expend.:* $957 mil. **GDP:** $10.8 bil., $1,185 per capita (1989 est.). **Chief crops:** coffee, cotton, corn, beans, sugarcane, bananas; illegal producer of opium poppy and cannabis for international drug trade. **Livestock:** cattle, pigs, sheep, horses, goats. **Natural resources:** crude oil, nickel, rare woods, fish, chicle. **Major industries:** sugar, textiles and clothing, furniture. **Labor force:** 2.5 mil. (1985); 57% agriculture, 14% manufacturing, 13% services, 7% commerce; 12% unemployment and underemployment (1987 est.). **Exports:** $1.02 bil. (f.o.b., 1988); 38% coffee, 7% bananas, 7% sugar, 4% cardamom. **Imports:** $1.5 bil. (c.i.f., 1988); fuel and petroleum products, machinery, grain, fertilizers, motor vehicles. **Major trading partners:** *exports:* 29% U.S., El Salvador, W. Germany, Costa Rica; *imports:* 38% U.S., Mexico, Japan, W. Germany, El Salvador.

**Intl. Orgs.** FAO, G-77, IAEA, IBRD, ICAO, IDA, IFAD, IFC, ILO, IMF, IMO, INTELSAT, INTERPOL, ITU, UN, UNESCO, UPU, WHO, WMO.

Modern Guatemala was the heart of the Maya civilization that began early in the Christian era and flourished from the fourth to the 10th centuries. From the 11th century on there were two major powers, the Cakchiquel and the Quiché. They were overthrown by the Spanish who invaded from the north in 1524.

The captaincy general of Guatemala was the seat of Spanish military authority in Central America until the 19th century. After an earthquake destroyed Antiqua in 1773, the capital was moved to Guatemala City. Despite a lack of economic or commercial prosperity, Guatemala was the center of the United Provinces of Central America after independence was gained from Spain (1821) and Mexico (1823). The United Provinces collapsed after an uprising by Rafael Carrera, and Guatemala became a separate country in 1838.

The Liberal party held power from 1851 to 1944. There was considerable economic development under Manuel Estrada Cabrera (1898–

1920) and Jorge Ubico (1931–44), but their regimes were repressive. Juan José Arévalo was elected president in 1945. He was succeeded, with strong Communist support, by Jacobo Arbenz, who was deposed in 1954 by a U.S.-backed coup led by Col. Carlos Castillo Armas. The military has ruled either directly or indirectly since then.

Antigovernment guerrilla activity began in 1960, and in 1982 three groups formed the Guatemalan National Revolutionary Union (URNG). The guerrillas, the army, and right-wing death squads have been responsible for an estimated 100,000 deaths, mostly civilians. Although the United States suspended $2.8 million in military aid due to the government's failure to resolve the murder of a U.S. citizen in June 1990, substantive change in government policy is not soon likely.

## Guinea
### Republic of Guinea
**Geography Location:** western Africa. **Boundaries:** Guinea-Bissau to NW, Senegal to N, Mali to NE, Ivory Coast to SE, Liberia, Sierra Leone to S, Atlantic Ocean to W. **Total land area:** 94,926 sq. mi. (245,857 sq km). **Coastline:** 199 mi. (320 km). **Comparative area:** between Utah and Oregon. **Land use:** 6% arable land; negl. % permanent crops; 12% meadows and pastures; 42% forest and woodland; 40% other; includes negl. % irrigated. **Major cities:** (1983 est.) Conakry (capital) 656,000.

**People Population:** 7,269,240 (1990). **Nationality:** noun—Guinean(s); adjective—Guinean. **Ethnic groups:** Fulani, Malinke, Sousou, 15 smaller groups. **Languages:** French (official), tribal languages. **Religions:** 85% Muslim, 10% Christian, 5% indigenous beliefs.

**Government Type:** republic. **Independence:** Oct. 2, 1958 (from France). **Constitution:** May 14, 1982, suspended after coup of Apr. 3, 1984. **National holiday:** Independence Day, Oct. 2. **Heads of government:** Gen. Lansana Conté, president (since Dec. 1984). **Structure:** coup on Apr. 3, 1984, established 17-member Military Committee for National Redressment (CMRN) to determine government policy; highest-ranking CMRN member became president, with other CMRN members assuming most cabinet portfolios.

**Economy Monetary unit:** Guinean franc. **Budget:** (1988 est.) *income:* $357 mil.; *expend.:* $400 mil. **GDP:** $2.5 bil., $350 per capita (1987 est.). **Chief crops:** cash crops—coffee, bananas, palm products, peanuts, citrus fruits, pineapples; food crops—cassava, rice, millet, corn, sweet potatoes. **Livestock:** cattle, sheep, goats, pigs, asses. **Natural resources:** bauxite, iron ore, diamonds, gold, uranium. **Major industries:** bauxite mining, alumina, diamond mining. **Labor force:** 2.4 mil. (1983); 82% agriculture, 11% industry and commerce; 88,112 civil servants (1987); 52% of population of working age (1985). **Exports:** $553 mil. (f.o.b., 1988 est.); bauxite, alumina, diamonds, coffee, pineapples. **Imports:** $509 mil. (c.i.f., 1988 est.); petroleum products, metals, machinery and transport equipment, foodstuffs, textiles. **Major trading partners:** *exports:* 33% U.S., 33% EC, 20% USSR and Eastern Europe; *imports:* 16% U.S., France, Brazil.

**Intl. Orgs.** FAO, G-77, IBRD, ICAO, IDA, IFAD, ILO, IMF, IMO, INTELSAT, INTERPOL, ITU, NAM, UN, UNESCO, UPU, WHO, WMO.

Guinea was formed out of the remains of a series of empires that flourished in West Africa between the 10th and 15th centuries. Situated to the southwest of the Sahara desert on the west coast of Africa, Guinea was a crossroads of West African trade long before Europeans arrived.

French merchants began trading in what is now Guinea in the early 17th century. France began acquiring land in the area in the mid-19th century, and in 1845 the territories were organized as a separate colony. The colony received the name French Guinea in 1893.

Most high political posts were held by Europeans until after World War II. In 1946 French Guinea became a territory in the federation of French West Africa. Colonial reforms gradually allowed Guineans greater autonomy. In September 1958 Guinea became the only French colony to reject membership in the Fifth French Republic, resulting in the severance of political ties with France. The territorial assembly proclaimed Guinean independence on Oct. 2, 1958, and a new government headed by Sékou Touré was formed on the same day.

Touré was adamant in his rejection of French colonialism, severing ties with France (1960-63) and soliciting economic and other assistance from the USSR, China, and the United States. Touré remained in power until his death in April 1984. A military government gained power a week after his death. By the end of 1987, relations with France improved, and free-market mechanisms were implemented. Proposals for multiparty democracy, to be phased in over five years, and a free-market economy were announced in late 1989.

## Guinea-Bissau
### Republic of Guinea-Bissau
**Geography** **Location:** northwestern coast of Africa. **Boundaries:** Senegal to N, Guinea to E and S, Atlantic Ocean to W. **Total land area:** 10,811 sq. mi. (28,000 sq km). **Coastline:** 217 mi. (350 km). **Comparative area:** about size of Maryland. **Land use:** 9% arable land; 1% permanent crops; 46% meadows and pastures; 38% forest and woodland; 6% other. **Major cities:** (1979 census) Bissau (capital) 109,214; Bafatá 13,429; Gabú 7,803; Mansoa 5,390; Catió 5,170.

**People** **Population:** 998,963 (1990). **Nationality:** noun—Guinea-Bissauan(s); adjective—Guinea-Bissauan. **Ethnic groups:** about 99% African (30% Balanta, 20% Fula, 14% Manjaca, 13% Mandinga, 7% Papel); less than 1% European and mulatto. **Languages:** Portuguese (official), Criolo, numerous African languages. **Religions:** 65% indigenous beliefs, 30% Muslim, 5% Christian.

**Government** **Type:** republic; highly centralized one-party regime since Sept. 1974. **Independence:** Sept. 24, 1973 (from Portugal). **Constitution:** May 16, 1984. **National holiday:** Independence Day, Sept. 24. **Heads of government:** Gen. João Bernardo Vieira, president (since Nov. 1980). **Structure:** executive—president and cabinet; legislature—50-member National Popular Assembly, overseen by 15-member Council of State.

**Economy** **Monetary unit:** Guinea Bissauan pesos. **Budget:** (1987) *income:* $20 mil.; *expend.:* $25 mil. **GDP:** $152 mil., $160 per capita. **Chief crops:** rice, palm products, root crops, coconuts, peanuts. **Livestock:** cattle, goats, pigs, sheep. **Natural resources:** unexploited deposits of petroleum, bauxite, phosphates; fish, timber. **Major industries:** agricultural processing, beer, soft drinks. **Labor force:** (1983) 90% agriculture; 53% of population of working age. **Exports:** $15 mil. (1987); peanuts, cashews, palm kernels, fish. **Imports:** $49 mil. (1987); capital equipment, consumer goods, semiprocessed goods, foods, petroleum. **Major trading partners:** *exports:* Portugal, Spain, Switzerland, Cape Verde, China; *imports:* Portugal, USSR, EC countries, other European, Senegal, U.S.

**Intl. Orgs.** FAO, G-77, GATT (de facto), IBRD, ICAO, IDA, IFAD, IFC, ILO, IMF, IMO, ITU, NAM, UN, UNESCO, UPU, WHO, WMO.

The Portuguese began exploring and trading in what is now Guinea-Bissau in the 15th century and in 1630 began to exert administrative control over the territory. The area became the center of the Portuguese slave trade. When the slave trade declined in the 19th century, the coastal port of Bissau became a major commercial center. Later in the 19th century, the Portuguese began to conquer the interior of the territory and in 1879 consolidated the region into a territory called Portuguese Guinea which in 1952 became an overseas province of Portugal.

A nationalist movement began in 1956 under the leadership of Amilcar Cabral and the African Party for the Independence of Guinea and Cape Verde (PAIGC). Armed insurrection broke out in 1961. By 1972 the PAIGC exerted influence over much of the country. Civilian rule was established in the territory that it controlled, and elections were held for a national assembly. Cabral was assassinated in 1973, but soon after the PAIGC National Assembly declared the independence of Guinea-Bissau from Portugal. Portugal acknowledged the country's new status on Sept. 24, 1973, after it received U.S. recognition.

The civilian government was overthrown by a military coup in 1980, and the country was run by a Revolutionary Council headed by Brig. Gen. João Bernardo Vieira until a new constitution was adopted in May 1984. Under the new constitution, a new national assembly was selected, and Vieira was elected president in 1984 and 1989.

## Guyana
### Co-operative Republic of Guyana
**Geography** **Location:** northeastern South America. **Boundaries:** North Atlantic Ocean to N, Suriname to E, Brazil to S, Venezuela to W. **Total land area:** 83,000 sq. mi. (214,969 sq km). **Coastline:** 285 mi. (459 km). **Comparative area:** between Kansas and Idaho. **Land use:** 3% arable land; negl. % permanent crops; 6% meadows and pastures; 83% forest and woodland; 8% other; includes 1% irrigated. **Major cities:** (1976 est.) Georgetown (capital) 72,049.

**People** **Population:** 764,649 (1990). **Nationality:** noun—Guyanese (sing., pl.); adjective—Guyanese. **Ethnic groups:** 51% East Indian, 43% black and mixed, 4% Amerindian, 2% European and Chinese. **Languages:** English, Amerindian dialects. **Religions:** 57% Christian, 33% Hindu, 9% Muslim, 1% other.

**Government** **Type:** republic within Commonwealth. **Independence:** May 26, 1966 (from UK). **Constitution:** Oct. 6, 1980. **National holiday:** Republic Day, Feb. 23. **Heads of government:** Hugh Desmond Hoyte, president (since Aug. 1985); Hamilton Green, prime minister (since Aug. 1985). **Structure:** executive—president, who appoints and heads cabinet; unicameral legislature (53-member National Assembly) elected by proportional representation every five years.

**Economy** **Monetary unit:** Guyanese dollar. **Budget:** (1988 est.) *income:* $173.0 mil.; *expend.:* $414.0 mil. **GDP:** $323.0 mil., $420.0 per capita (1986). **Chief crops:** sugarcane, rice, other food crops; food shortages—wheat flour, cooking oil, processed meat, dairy products. **Livestock:** pigs, cattle, sheep, goats. **Natural resources:** bauxite, gold, diamonds, hardwood timber, shrimp, fish. **Major industries:** bauxite mining, sugar, rice milling. **Labor force:** 268,000 (1985); public-sector employment amounts to 60-80% of total labor force; 44.5% industry and commerce, 33.8% agriculture, 21.7% services; unemployment and underemployment 30% (1985 est.). **Exports:** $215.0 mil. (f.o.b., 1988 est.); bauxite, sugar, rice, shrimp, molasses. **Imports:** $216.0 mil. (f.o.b., 1988 est.); manufactures, machinery, food, petroleum. **Major trading partners:** (1986): *exports:* 37% UK, 12% U.S., 10.6% Canada, 4.8% CARICOM; *imports:* (1984) 41% CARICOM, 18% U.S., 9% UK, 3% Canada.

**Intl. Orgs.** FAO, G-77, GATT, IBRD, ICAO, IDA, IFAD, IFC, ILO, IMF, IMO, INTERPOL, ITU, NAM, OAS (observer), UN, UNESCO, UPU, WHO, WMO.

Although the region was visited by Europeans in the 15th century, Guyana was only colonized in the early 1600s by the Dutch. Rule in the area was later contested by the French and the British, and it became the colony of British Guiana in 1831. After slavery was abolished, indentured servants from the East Indies were brought to work the land, and their descendants are in the majority today.

The People's National Congress (East

Indian) has been in power since 1964, and socialist policies have dominated the political landscape since independence in 1966. Most of the country's large companies are nationalized, so despite its having the purest bauxite in the world, some gold, and conditions favorable to agriculture, it remains poor, dependent on foreign aid and remittances from overseas workers for much of its revenue.

## Haiti
### Republic of Haiti

**Geography Location:** western part of Hispaniola in northern Caribbean Sea. Port-au-Prince 18°33'N, 72°20'W. **Boundaries:** North Atlantic Ocean to N, Dominican Republic to E, Caribbean Sea to S, Windward Passage to W. **Total land area:** 10,714 sq. mi. (27,750 sq km). **Coastline:** 1,100 mi. (1,771 km). **Comparative area:** slightly larger than Maryland. **Land use:** 20% arable land; 13% permanent crops; 18% meadows and pastures; 4% forest and woodland; 45% other; includes 3% irrigated. **Major cities:** (1984 est.) Port-au-Prince (capital) 738,342.

**People Population:** 6,143,141 (1990). **Nationality:** noun—Haitian(s); adjective—Haitian. **Ethnic groups:** 95% black, 5% mulatto and European. **Languages:** French (official, but spoken by only 10% of population); all speak Creole. **Religions:** 75–80% Roman Catholic—of which majority also practice voodoo (called vodun)—10% Protestant.

**Government Type:** republic. **Independence:** Jan. 1, 1804 (from France). **Constitution:** Aug. 27, 1983, suspended Feb. 1986; draft constitution approved Mar. 1987. **Heads of government:** The Rev. Jean Bertrand Aristide, president (since Feb. 1991). **Structure:** Consultative Council (45-member civilian advisory body); judiciary appointed by president.

**Economy Monetary unit:** gourde. **Budget:** (1988) *income:* $252 mil.; *expend.:* $357 mil. **GDP:** $2.4 bil., $380 per capita. **Chief crops:** coffee, sugarcane, rice, corn, sorghum. **Livestock:** cattle, goats, pigs, horses, asses, sheep, mules. **Natural resources:** bauxite. **Major industries:** sugar refining, textiles, flour milling. **Labor force:** 2.3 mil. (1982); 66% agriculture, 25% services, 9% industry; shortage of skilled labor, unskilled labor abundant; significant unemployment. **Exports:** $200 mil. (f.o.b., 1988); 65% light manufactures, 17% coffee, 8% other agriculture. **Imports:** $344 mil. (c.i.f., 1988); 36% machines and manufactures, 21% food and beverages, 12% fats and fuels, 11% petroleum products. **Major trading partners:** *exports:* 77% U.S., 5% France, 4% Italy; *imports:* 65% U.S., 6% Netherlands Antilles, 5% Japan, 4% France.

**Intl. Orgs.** FAO, G-77, GATT, IAEA, IBRD, ICAO, IDA, IFAD, IFC, ILO, IMF, IMO, INTELSAT, INTERPOL, ITU, UN, UNESCO, UPU, WHO, WMO.

The Arawak island of Haiti was discovered by Christopher Columbus, who renamed it Hispaniola, in December 1492. In the next century the Arawaks were worked to death, murdered, or killed by disease. The western third of the island was harassed by French pirates and was ceded to France in 1697. With a diverse slave-based agricultural economy, the colony accounted for two-thirds of French overseas investment.

A slave revolt in 1791 led to abolition in 1794, and the whole island came under French rule the same year. Toussaint Louverture, an ex-slave, became governor-general in 1801, but he was deposed by the French. In 1803 a black army under Jean-Jacques Dessalines (Emperor Jacques I, 1804–06) and Henry Christophe (Henry I, 1806–20) defeated the French in 1803. Independence was declared in 1804. Under Jean-Pierre Boyer (1820–43), Haiti invaded and occupied Santo Domingo (which had been restored to Spain in 1808) from 1822 to 1844.

The next century was marked by political instability and an increased U.S. business and military presence in Haitian affairs. From 1905 to 1947, the United States had direct or indirect control of Haitian finances, and from 1915 to 1934 the country was under U.S. military occupation.

François "Papa Doc" Duvalier became president in 1957. He later transferred power to his son, Jean-Claude, who ruled until his ouster in a 1986 coup. He was followed by a succession of short-lived, brutal, and incompetent military regimes. In 1989 supreme court justice Ertha-Pascal Troillot was named interim president. In December 1990, Haiti held its first democratic national elections, and the Rev. Jean-Bertrand Aristide, a 37-year-old Roman Catholic priest, was elected president for a five-year term.

Haiti is the poorest country in the western hemisphere. Its population is largely illiterate, the better educated elite having fled the country's authoritarian rule, and it is overwhelmingly dependent on foreign aid.

## Holy See
### Vatican City

**Geography Location:** entirely within city of Rome, Italy; outside Vatican City, 13 buildings in Rome and Castel Gandolfo (the pope's summer residence) enjoy extraterritorial rights. **Boundaries:** surrounded by Italian territory. **Total land area:** 0.17 sq. mi. (0.44 sq km). **Coastline:** none. **Comparative area:** about ⁷⁄₁₀ size of the Mall in Washington, D.C. **Land use:** 0% arable land; 0% permanent crops; 0% meadows and pastures; 0% forest and woodland; 100% other. **Major cities:** Vatican City (capital).

**People Population:** 774 (1990). **Nationality:** N.A. **Ethnic groups:** primarily Italians, but also many other nationalities. **Languages:** Italian, Latin, various other languages. **Religions:** Roman Catholic.

**Government Type:** monarchical-sacerdotal state, seat of Holy See. **Independence:** Feb. 11, 1929 (from Italy). **Constitution:** Apostolic Constitution of 1967 (effective Mar. 1, 1968). **National holiday:** installation day of Pope John Paul II, Oct. 22. **Heads of government:** John Paul II, supreme pontiff (Karol Wojtylla, elected pope Oct. 16, 1978). Archbishop Angelo Sodano, Pro-Secretary of State of the Holy See. **Structure:** pope possesses full executive, legislative, and judicial powers; he delegates these powers to president of Pontifical Commission, who is subject to pontifical appointment and recall; Secretariat of State and Council of Public Affairs (which handles Vatican diplomacy) and Prefecture of Economic Affairs; College of Cardinals acts as chief papal adviser.

**Economy Monetary unit:** Vatican issues its own coinage called Vatican lira, which is interchangeable with Italian lira. **Budget:** (1986) *income:* $57 mil.; *expend.:* $113.7 mil., supported financially by contributions (known as Peter's Pence) from Roman Catholics throughout world; some income derived from sale of Vatican postage stamps and tourist mementos, fees for admission to museums, and sale of publications. **GDP:** N.A. **Chief crops:** N.A. **Livestock:** N.A. **Natural resources:** N.A. **Major industries:** consists of printing and production of small amount of mosaics and staff uniforms; worldwide banking and financial activities. **Labor force:** about 1,500; Vatican City employees are divided into three categories—executives, office workers, and salaried employees. **Exports:** N.A. **Imports:** N.A. **Major trading partners:** N.A.

**Intl. Orgs.** IAEA, INTELSAT, ITU, UPU, WIPO; permanent observer status at FAO, OAS, UN, UNESCO.

The Holy See is the smallest sovereign state in the world both in size and in population. It is a remnant of the "Patrimony of St. Peter," the secular state donated to the popes in the eighth century by Pepin the Short, father of Charlemagne. One of the major political powers on the Italian peninsula throughout the Middle Ages and into modern times, the States of the Church were conquered in 1870 by the new Kingdom of Italy, which made Rome its capital.

In 1929 Mussolini's government made peace with the papacy in the Lateran Treaty, which recognized the Holy See as an independent state. The treaty was incorporated into the Italian Constitution of 1947. Under the terms of the treaty, the pope is pledged to perpetual neutrality and may intervene in international affairs as a mediator only upon request.

The pope is the sovereign of the Holy See in his capacity as bishop of Rome, and in that capacity, he accepts the credentials of foreign ambassadors assigned to the Holy See. The United States opened diplomatic relations with the Holy See in 1984, following the repeal of an 1867 law forbidding such relations. Pope John Paul II, a native of Poland, has been a source of spiritual leadership especially for Catholics in Eastern Europe. Since the collapse of communism in Eastern Europe, many countries there have renewed diplomatic relations with the Holy See.

As sovereign of the Holy See, the pope is an elected absolute monarch who appoints a Pontifical Council to govern the city on his behalf. The council meets only a few times each year.

The economy is based on service industries, including printing; its revenues come from museum fees, philatelic sales, and sales of publications.

# Honduras
## Republic of Honduras

**Geography Location:** Central America. **Boundaries:** Caribbean Sea to N, Nicaragua to E, El Salvador, Nicaragua to S, Guatemala, El Salvador to W. **Total land area:** 43,277 sq. mi. (112,088 sq km). **Coastline:** 509 mi. (820 km). **Comparative area:** between Tennessee and Pennsylvania. **Land use:** 14% arable land; 2% permanent crops; 30% meadows and pastures; 34% forest and woodland; 20% other; includes 1% irrigated. **Major cities:** (1989 est.) Tegucigalpa (capital) 608,100; San Pedro Sula 309,900; La Ceiba 71,600; El Progreso 63,400.

**People Population:** 5,259,699 (1990). **Nationality:** noun—Honduran(s); adjective—Honduran. **Ethnic groups:** 90% mestizo, 7% Indian, 2% black, 1% white. **Languages:** Spanish, Indian dialects. **Religions:** 97% Roman Catholic, small Protestant minority.

**Government Type:** republic. **Independence:** Sept. 15, 1821 (from Spain). **Constitution:** Jan. 11, 1982 (effective Jan. 20, 1982). **National holiday:** Independence Day, Sept. 15. **Head of government:** Rafael Leonardo Callejas Romero, president (since Jan. 1990). **Structure:** constitution provides for elected president, unicameral legislature (134-member National Congress), and national judicial branch.

**Economy Monetary unit:** lempira. **Budget:** (1989) *income:* $1.1 bil.; *expend.:* $0.9 bil. **GDP:** $4.4 bil.; $890 per capita (1988). **Chief crops:** bananas, coffee, corn, beans, sugarcane, rice, tobacco. **Livestock:** cattle, pigs, horses, mules. **Natural resources:** timber, gold, silver, copper, lead. **Major industries:** agricultural processing (sugar and coffee), textiles, clothing. **Labor force:** 1.3 mil. (1985); 62% agriculture, 20% services, 9% manufacturing, 3% construction; 13-22% unemployment (1989). **Exports:** $1 bil. (f.o.b., 1988); bananas, shrimp, lobster, coffee, lumber, meat, metals, sugar. **Imports:** $1.4 bil. (f.o.b., 1988 est.); petroleum, chemicals, basic manufactures, machinery and transport equipment. **Major trading partners:** *exports:* 52% U.S., 11% W. Germany, Belgium, Japan, Italy; *imports:* 39% U.S., 9% Japan, CACM (Central American Common Market), Venezuela, Mexico.

**Intl. Orgs.** FAO, G-77, IBRD, ICAO, IDA, IFAD, IFC, ILO, IMF, IMO, INTELSAT, INTERPOL, ITU, UN, UNESCO, UPU, WHO, WMO.

Early in the Christian era, the Mayan civilization extended south to the pre-Columbian city of Copán in what is now northwestern Honduras. The territory was also home to the Lenca Indians and the indigenous people of the Moskitia area.

A silver strike in the 1570s prompted the first major influx of Spanish. The region was also celebrated for its tropical hardwood for-ests. Although the British controlled the Caribbean coast in the late 1700s, Honduras was a province of the Spanish captaincy of Guatemala. It became a member of the United Provinces of Central America after independence from Spain and Mexico, and an independent republic after the 1838 collapse of the Central American Federation.

Conservatives dominated Honduran politics until the 1870s, when the Liberals came to power and adopted a new constitution that reduced the influence of the church, among other things. Economic development came especially from a number of U.S. firms whose efforts were regarded as exploitative rather than beneficial; in 1912, U.S. Pres. William Taft sent marines to protect U.S. interests.

Political unrest continued until the presidency of Gen. Tuburcio Carías Andino (1932–49), who was followed by a succession of pro-labor presidents. In 1963, a coup led by Col. Osvaldo López Arellano deposed the civilian president, and the military ruled almost uninterrupted until 1982. In 1969, the expulsion of thousands of Salvadoran peasants who had immigrated during the 1950s and 1960s led to the Soccer War with El Salvador. An armistice was negotiated by the OAS.

During the 1980s, Honduras was threatened by civil wars in El Salvador and Nicaragua. Honduran territory was used by Nicaraguan Contras, for which Honduras received substantial U.S. military and other aid. Demobilization of the Contras has alleviated tensions between left and right within the country, but the country faces enormous economic problems.

# Hungary
## Republic of Hungary

**Geography Location:** landlocked country in eastern Europe. **Boundaries:** Czechoslovakia to N, USSR to NE, Romania to E, Yugoslavia to S, Austria to W. **Total land area:** 35,920 sq. mi. (93,033 sq km). **Coastline:** none. **Comparative area:** about size of Indiana. **Land use:** 54% arable land; 3% permanent crops; 14% meadows and pastures; 18% forest and woodland; 11% other; includes 2% irrigated. **Major cities:** (1989) Budapest (capital) 2,113,645; Debrecen 219,251; Miskolc 207,826; Szeged 189,484; Pécs 183,082.

**People Population:** 10,568,686 (1990). **Nationality:** noun—Hungarian(s); adjective—Hungarian. **Ethnic groups:** 96.6% Hungarian, 1.6% German, 1.1% Slovak, 0.3% Southern Slav, 0.2% Romanian. **Languages:** 98.2% Hungarian, 1.8% other. **Religions:** 67.5% Roman Catholic, 20.0% Calvinist, 5.0% Lutheran, 7.5% atheist and other.

**Government Type:** republic. **Constitution:** Aug. 18, 1949; effective Aug. 20, 1949; revised Apr. 19, 1972. **National holiday:** Aug 20. **Heads of government:** Dr. Arpád Göncz, president (since May 1990); Dr. Jozsef Antall, prime minister (since May 1990). **Structure:** executive—Presidential Council (elected by parliament); unicameral legislature—National Assembly (elected by direct suffrage); judicial—Supreme Court (elected by parliament).

**Economy Monetary unit:** forint. **Budget:** (1988) *income:* $14.0 bil.; *expend.:* $14.2 bil. **GNP:** $64.6 bil., $6,108 per capita (1989 est.). **Chief crops:** corn, wheat, potatoes, sugar beets, barley; normally, self-sufficient. **Livestock:** chickens, pigs, sheep, ducks, cattle. **Natural resources:** bauxite, coal, natural gas, fertile soils. **Major industries:** mining, metallurgy, engineering industries. **Labor force:** 4.86 mil. (1987); 43.2% services, trade, government, and other; 18.3% agriculture; N.A. unemployment. **Exports:** $19.1 bil. (f.o.b., 1988); 36% capital goods, 24% foods, 18% consumer goods, 11% fuels and minerals. **Imports:** $18.3 bil. (c.i.f., 1988); 28% machinery and transport equipment, 20% fuels, 16% manufactured consumer goods, 14% chemical products, 6% agriculture. **Major trading partners:** (1987) *exports:* 48% USSR, 25% Eastern Europe, 16% developed countries, 8% less-developed countries; *imports:* 43% USSR, 28% Eastern Europe, 23% less-developed countries, 3% U.S.

**Intl. Orgs.** FAO, GATT, IAEA, IBRD, ICAO, ILO, IMF, IMO, ITU, UN, UNESCO, UPU, WHO, WIPO, WMO.

The Magyars, a tribe of Central Asian horsemen, invaded Europe in the ninth century A.D. and settled in the Hungarian Plain where, under their chieftain Arpad, they displaced earlier Germanic and Slavic settlers and organized a kingdom in 896. The Hungarians converted to Christianity during the 10th century, and King Stephen (later St. Stephen) received a royal crown from Pope Sylvester II in 1001.

After the Battle of Mohacs in 1526, most of Hungary fell under Ottoman rule. The Turks were driven out in a series of battles with the Habsburg Holy Roman emperors at the end of the 17th century. Thereafter Hungary was part of the Habsburg empire until 1867, when the Dual Monarchy of Austria-Hungary was organized, making Hungary independent of Austria in all but finance, the military, and foreign affairs.

During the 18th century, Hungary experienced extensive immigration of Romanians from the east and Slovaks from the north; by 1900 Magyars formed only a bare majority of the population. The pre–World War I economy was largely agricultural, with most of the population living in rural poverty. Agriculture-related industry (beet sugar factories, breweries, tanneries, textile mills) developed in the late 19th century, along with some heavy industry.

In the dismemberment of Austria-Hungary following the defeat of the Central Powers in World War I, Hungary surrendered extensive territories to Romania, Yugoslavia, and Czechoslovakia. With the Treaty of Trianon ("Bloody Trianon") in 1920, the country lost 70 percent of its territory and 60 percent of its population; one-third of the Magyar people lived on foreign soil.

Short-lived governments—a republic under Michael Karolyi, and a Bolshevist state under Bela Kun—were replaced in 1920 by a new monarchy, with Adm. Miklós Horthy serving as regent. The Horthy regime was authoritarian but not fascist; its main objective was the recovery of Hungary's lost territories. Hungary established common cause with Germany in 1938, recovering some territory from Czechoslovakia and Romania in the bargain, but at the price of participating in Hitler's war with the Soviet Union. Germany occupied Hungary in 1944 and set up a Hungarian Nazi regime. Late in 1944 the Russian army drove out the Germans and set up their own occupation.

The establishment of a full-scale Soviet-satellite regime was relatively slow. A republic was declared in February 1946, and the non-Communist Zoltan Tildy was elected president. Tildy was forced out in 1947, however, and replaced by the Stalinist dictator, Matias Rakosi. After the death of Stalin in 1953, the moderate Imre Nagy became premier and introduced some economic reforms. Nagy was forced out of office in 1955.

Nikita Khrushchev's denunciation of Stalin in 1956, combined with an atmosphere of rising expectations for further reforms in Hungary, led to a popular uprising in October 1956. Nagy, backed by the army, formed a coalition government on Oct. 23, proclaimed Hungary's neutrality, ended censorship, opened the country's borders, and withdrew from the Warsaw Pact. The ousted Communist party secretary, Erno Gero, called for Soviet support; on Nov. 4, Soviet troops launched a massive invasion that soon crushed the rebellion. The Soviet army then installed János Kadar as premier; Nagy was executed. About 200,000 Hungarians fled the country, and many more were imprisoned.

After several years of repressive rule, the Kadar regime announced, in 1963, amnesty for participants in the 1956 rebellion. Stalinists were gradually removed from the government, economic reforms emphasizing profit and productivity were introduced, and trade with the West was expanded. Hungary reluctantly took part in the suppression of Czechoslovakia's "Prague Spring" in 1968. In the same year, it announced the New Economic Mechanism (NEM) policy, ending central economic planning and introducing semifree enterprise under bureaucratic control.

After a brief return to central planning in the 1970s, the NEM was reintroduced in 1979 and expanded in 1982, when Hungary joined the World Bank and the IMF. Private ownership of subsidiaries of state-owned enterprises was permitted. In 1987 a pro-Gorbachev premier, Karoly Grosz, took office and in 1988 became head of the Communist party as well.

Hungary, often regarded as a model of perestroika, remains a society troubled by its socialist/free enterprise and authoritarian/democratic dualities. Economic growth became less robust in the late 1980s; social problems such as suicide, alcoholism, and divorce are on the rise. Relations with Romania have become tense as a result of Romanian destruction of ethnic Hungarian villages in that country and Romanian claims that the Hungarian government discriminates against ethnic Romanians within its borders.

The Grosz government collapsed in the fall of 1989, and the Hungarian Communist party abolished itself. Free elections were held in March and April of 1990, and the Democratic Forum, led by Jozsef Antall, won a plurality and formed a coalition government with the Smallholders and Christian Democratic parties. Having already achieved substantial perestroika-style economic reforms under communism, Hungary was well-placed to make a rapid transition to free enterprise and was seeking admission to the EC.

## Iceland
### Republic of Iceland
**Geography Location:** near Arctic Circle in North Atlantic Ocean. Reykyavík 64°09′N, 21°58′W. **Boundaries:** Greenland about 190 mi. (300 km) to NW, Norway about 620 mi. (1,000 km) to E, UK 500 mi. (800 km) to S. **Total land area:** 39,679 sq. mi. (103,000 sq km). **Coastline:** 3,100 mi. (4,988 km). **Comparative area:** slightly smaller than Kentucky. **Land use:** negl. % arable land; 0% permanent crops; 23% meadows and pastures; 1% forest and woodland; 76% other. **Major cities:** (1983) Reykjavík (capital) 87,309.

**People Population:** 257,023 (1990). **Nationality:** noun—Icelander(s); adjective—Icelandic. **Ethnic groups:** homogeneous mixture of descendants of Norwegians and Celts. **Languages:** Icelandic (official). **Religions:** 95% Evangelical Lutheran, 3% other Protestant and Roman Catholic, 2% no affiliation.

**Government Type:** republic. **Independence:** June 7, 1944 (from Denmark). **Constitution:** June 16, 1944; effective June 17, 1944. **National holiday:** Anniversary of the Establishment of the Republic, June 17. **Heads of government:** Mrs. Vigdís Finnbogadottir, president (since July 1980); David Oddsson, prime minister (since Apr. 1991). **Structure:** executive power vested in president but exercised by cabinet responsible to parliament; legislative authority rests jointly with president and parliament (Althing); Supreme Court and 29 lower courts.

**Economy Monetary unit:** króna. **Budget:** (1988) *income:* $1.5 bil.; *expend.:* $1.7 bil. **GDP:** $4.0 bil., $16,200 per capita (1989 est.). **Chief crops:** dairying, hay, potatoes, turnips. **Livestock:** cattle, sheep, horses, pigs, poultry. **Natural resources:** fish, hydroelectric and geothermal power, diatomite. **Major industries:** fish processing, aluminum smelting, ferrosilicon production. **Labor force:** 122,800 (1986); 55.4% commerce, finance, and services; 5.8% agriculture; 14.3% other manufacturing; 7.9% fishing and fish processing; 1.3% unemployment. **Exports:** $1.4 bil. (f.o.b., 1988); fish and fish products, animal products, aluminum, diatomite. **Imports:** $1.6 bil. (c.i.f., 1988); machinery and transport equipment, petroleum, foodstuffs, textiles. **Major trading partners:** (1987) *exports:* 58.9% EC (23.3% UK, 10.3% W. Germany), 13.6% U.S., 3.6% USSR; *imports:* 58% EC (16% W. Germany), 10.4% Denmark, 9.2% UK), 8.5% U.S., 3.9% USSR

**Intl. Orgs.** EC (free-trade agreement pending resolution of fishing limits issue), EFTA, FAO, GATT, IAEA, IBRD, ICAO, IDA, IFC, ILO, IMF, IMO, INTELSAT, INTERPOL, ITU, NATO, OECD, UN, UNESCO, UPU, WHO, WMO.

The volcanic island of Iceland was settled in the ninth century A.D. by Vikings, who established Europe's oldest body of representative government, the Althing, in 930. Christianity was introduced around 1000. In the 13th century, Iceland acknowledged Norwegian rule. In 1380 Denmark, by then in control of all of Scandinavia, conquered Iceland as well. Iceland gained its independence in 1918 but shared a common king, Christian X, with the Danes. During World War II, first British, and then American, troops garrisoned the island; in 1944, with Denmark occupied by the Nazis, Iceland deposed its king and proclaimed itself a republic.

Iceland became a UN member in 1946 and a member of NATO in 1949. Lacking its own armed forces, it grudgingly tolerated the presence of an American air base at Keflavik. The republic developed a Scandinavian-style welfare state, with comprehensive social benefits that have produced one of the world's healthiest and best-educated peoples.

Less than 1 percent of Iceland's territory is arable; the island imports grain and vegetables but is self-sufficient in meat and dairy products. Fishing is the principal industry, accounting for 75 percent of exports and engaging one-seventh of the work force. Between 1958 and 1976, Iceland carried on "cod wars" with the United Kingdom, Norway, and Denmark, involving disputes over Iceland's claim to extensive territorial waters.

Multiparty representation in the Althing has created a trend of government by coalitions or minority cabinets. Politically stable, the republic faces economic problems brought on by high taxes, chronic inflation, and a huge national debt. Iceland maintains close ties with Scandinavia and actively participates in the Nordic Council.

## India
### Republic of India
**Geography Location:** Asian subcontinent, with Himalayan mountain range to N. **Boundaries:** Pakistan to NW; China, Bhutan, Nepal to N; Myanmar to NE; Bangladesh to E (surrounded by Indian territory except for short frontier with Myanmar); Bay of Bengal to E; Sri Lanka to SE across Palk Strait; Arabian Sea to W. **Total land area:** 1,269,219 sq. mi. (3,287,263 sq km). **Coastline:** 4,350 mi. (7,000 km). **Comparative area:** slightly more than one-third the size of U.S. **Land use:** 55% arable land; 1% permanent crops; 4% meadows and pastures; 23% forest and woodland; 17% other; includes 13% irrigated. **Major cities:** (1981 census) New Delhi (capital) 273,036; Greater Bombay 8,243,405; Delhi 4,884,234; Calcutta 3,305,006; Madras 3,276,622.

**People Population:** 849,746,001 (1990). **Nationality:** noun—Indian(s); adjective—Indian.

**Ethnic groups:** 72% Indo-Aryan, 25% Dravidian, 3% Mongoloid and other. **Languages:** Hindi, English, and 14 other official languages; 24 languages spoken by million or more persons each; numerous other languages and dialects; Hindi is national language and primary tongue of 30% of people; English enjoys associate status but is the most important language for national, political, and commercial communication; Hindustani, a variant of Hindi/Urdu, is spoken throughout northern India. **Religions:** 82.6% Hindu, 11.4% Muslim, 2.4% Christian, 2.0% Sikh.

**Government Type:** federal republic. **Independence:** Aug. 15, 1947 (from UK). **Constitution:** Jan. 26, 1950. **National holiday:** Republic Day, Jan. 26. **Heads of government:** Ramaswamy Venkataraman, president (since July 1987); P.V. Narasimha Rao, prime minister (since June 1991). **Structure:** bicameral parliament—Government Assembly (Rajya Sabha) and People's Assembly (Lok Sabha); relatively independent judiciary.

**Economy Monetary unit:** rupee. **Budget:** (1989) *income:* $48.0 bil.; *expend.:* $53.0 bil. **GNP:** $333 bil., $400 per capita. **Chief crops:** rice, other cereals, pulses, oilseed, cotton; legal producer of opium poppy for pharmaceutical trade but also illegal producer of opium poppy and cannabis for international drug trade. **Livestock:** cattle, goats, buffalo, sheep, pigs. **Natural resources:** coal (4th largest reserves in world), iron ore, manganese, mica, bauxite. **Major industries:** textiles, food processing, steel. **Labor force:** 284.4 mil. (1985); 67% agriculture, more than 10% unemployed and underemployed (1987). **Exports:** $17.2 bil. (f.o.b., 1989); tea, coffee, iron ore, fish products. **Imports:** $24.7 bil. (c.i.f., 1989); petroleum, edible oils, textiles, clothing. **Major trading partners:** *exports:* 25% EC, 19% U.S., 17% USSR and Eastern Europe, 10% Japan; *imports:* 33% EC, 19% Middle East, 10% Japan, 9% U.S., 8% USSR and Eastern Europe.

**Intl. Orgs.** Colombo Plan, Commonwealth, FAO, G-77, GATT, IAEA, IBRD, ICAO, IDA, IFAD, IFC, ILO, IMF, IMO, INTELSAT, INTERPOL, ITU, NAM, UN, UNESCO, UPU, WHO, WIPO, WMO.

Indian civilization is one of the oldest in the world. Neolithic agricultural communities had appeared in the Indus River valley by 3000 B.C. and cities at Harappa and Mohenjo-Daro were founded around 2500 B.C. Around 1500 B.C. Indo-Europeans (Aryans) from Central Asia imposed their own religion, culture, and political system on the indigenous population and generated population movements toward southern India.

Indo-European civilization was characterized by caste; everyone was a member of one of four fundamental divisions of society: Brahmins, hereditary priests responsible for higher learning and rituals; Ksatrias, warriors and administrators; Vaisas, merchants; and Sudras, farmers and subjugated peoples. At the bottom were casteless people, known later as untouchables.

By the mid-first millennium B.C., Brahminism had declined into a state of religious formal-ism. That situation prompted two reformations around 600 B.C., the first of which produced the Jain religion, the second, Buddhism. Jainism remained confined largely to India, while Buddhism eventually influenced most of the cultures of Asia, though it died out in India itself. Buddhism was adopted as a state religion by Asoka, third and greatest emperor of the Mauryan empire (325–184 B.C) under which much of India was united for the first time. Following the collapse of the Mauryan empire, Hinduism evolved out of Buddism, Brahminism, and other local cults and became the dominant religion of India.

South India in the post-Mauryan period was divided into numerous states, the most prominent of which was Chola, a Tamil kingdom in the southeast that had extensive trade connections throughout the Indian Ocean.

The Gupta dynasty (c. A.D. 320–544), based in the Ganges River valley, established its rule over most of northern India and created what is generally regarded as a golden age of north Indian culture, with flourishing cities and significant achievements in art, literature, and science.

In the seventh century, King Sri Harsha created a short-lived feudal empire that united most of the petty states in the upper Ganges valley, while the Chalyuka dynasty dominated southern India. In the early eighth century, the Indus River valley was invaded by Arabs who introduced Islam to the region. The empire of Sri Harsha fell apart, to be replaced by the numerous petty kingdoms of the Rajputs, while political power became fragmented in the south as well.

The 11th century saw the ascendency of Islam throughout northern India, which came under the shadow of the empire of Mamud of Ghazni, based in Afghanistan. In 1192 the Ghaznavid general Kutb ud-din Aibak defeated a coalition of Rajput states; in 1206 he founded the Sultanate of Delhi, which in the 13th century held off Mongol invasions in northwestern India and brought all of the subcontinent, except for the southernmost states, under its control. While the rulers of the sultanate were Muslims, most of their subjects remained Hindu.

Internal rebellions combined with the sacking of Delhi by Timur Leng (Tamerlane) in 1398 weakened the Sultanate of Delhi. In 1526 Babur, a descendant of Timur Leng, conquered all of northern India and established the Moghul empire. Under Akbar the Great, the empire flourished; Moghul culture gave rise to new styles of architecture, painting, and music.

In the 17th century, the Moghul emperors were threatened by the Hindu Marathas, whose kingdom on the west-central coast rapidly encompassed most of south India. By the late 18th century, Maratha power had spread to the north, and most of the petty kingdoms of the Moghul empire became part of a Maratha confederacy, owing only nominal allegiance to Delhi. By that time all of India was threatened by the expansion of the European powers.

Vasco Da Gama had landed at Calicut in 1498, and in 1510 the Portuguese founded a colony at Goa. Dutch traders competed with the Portuguese during the 16th century, and Brit-ish and French merchants followed in the 17th century. British trading stations were established at Surat (1612), Bombay (1661), and Calcutta (1690). In the mid-18th century, warfare broke out between British and French forces in India, and the French were confined to a few small enclaves. The growing instability of the Moghul empire in the face of Marathan and Rajput revolts and the expansion of the southern kingdom of Mysore encouraged the British to seek further control of Indian territory. Robert Clive's victory at Plassey in 1757 brought Orissa, Bihar, and Bengal under British control; British rule was extended to the upper Ganges in 1775. Victory over the maharaja of Mysore in 1792 paved the way for British control over much of the south.

British parliamentary acts of 1773 and 1784 placed these acquisitions firmly under government control, and in 1803 the Moghul emperor accepted the offer of a protectorate, and British suzerainty in India was assured. After a protracted war, 1812–23, Marathan resistance to British control was broken. The first Anglo-Afghan War, 1838–42, was inconclusive in Afghanistan but led to consolidation of British control of the Punjab.

In 1833 Parliament assumed political control of British interests in South Asia, while private merchants had unrestricted access to the economy. Plantation crops, such as opium and cotton, began to displace subsistence agriculture, which made India more dependent on imported goods.

In 1857 Indian troops in the British colonial forces staged a mutiny in north-central India that lasted 14 months. In 1858 the Moghul empire was dissolved, as was the East India Company. The government of India was made directly subject to the British Crown, which exercised control through a viceroy and through the British Colonial Office. Queen Victoria was crowned empress of India in 1877.

British sovereignty in India—the raj—was a patchwork of direct and indirect rule. In general, coastal areas, major river valleys, and strategic frontier regions were ruled by British authorities, while interior states continued as British protectorates controlled by British advisers to native princes. In 1861 Indians were appointed to advisory councils of the viceroy and provincial governors.

The Indian National Congress was organized in 1885. In the wake of popular demonstrations in 1905, elections were instituted to choose Indian members of the viceroy's legislative council. Separate electorates were created for the Muslim and Hindu communities, formalizing a divisive force in Indian politics and weakening opposition to British rule.

In 1914, with Chinese loss of control in Tibet, India's northern boundary was pushed forward to the McMahon Line, following the highest peaks in the Himalayas. This set the stage for numerous later boundary disputes between China and India, Pakistan, and Burma.

The Government of India Act of 1919 transferred some political power to elected provincial officials but left the appointed British governors firmly in control. In that year Mohandas K. Gandhi organized the first passive-resistance campaigns and was imprisoned. In 1935 the Government of India Act created elected provincial legislatures. In the first elections (1937) the Congress party under Jawaharlal Nehru won control of seven of the 11 provinces. Nehru's goal of a united Indian opposition to British rule was thwarted by Mohammed Ali Jinnah's Moslem League, which demanded the creation of a separate Muslim state.

During World War II, the British military position in South Asia was complicated by calls for Indian independence. An offer of local autonomy, with independence to follow, was spurned by Nehru, and an Indian National army under Subhas Bose fought with the Japanese. Jinnah's call for an independent Pakistan was greatly enhanced by his wholehearted support of the British.

In 1947, the British raj became two independent nations, predominantly Hindu India and predominantly Muslim Pakistan. Despite its considerable stature in the international community at large, India has been troubled by a number of disputes with its neighbors and separatist movements within its own borders. Following independence hundreds of semiautonomous princely states were brought under control of the central government. The French ceded their remaining trading colonies in the 1950s, and Portugal gave up Goa in 1961. In 1962, India warred with China in a still unresolved dispute over their border along Kashmir and Assam. The state of Bhutan was granted independence in 1971, and in 1974 Sikkim was annexed and its monarchy abolished.

India's most intractable disputes have been with Pakistan. Immediately after independence, Hindus in Pakistan and Muslims in India were set upon by the majority populations; hundreds of thousands were killed, and at least 12 million refugees fled over the border in both directions. On Jan. 30, 1948, Gandhi was assassinated by a Hindu extremist who blamed him for partition.

In granting independence, Britain had divided states of Bengal and Punjab between the two countries, but fighting erupted over the status of Jammu and Kashmir, and a cease-fire line negotiated by the UN in 1949 has never been ratified as a formal national boundary. In 1989, separatists in the Indian part of Kashmir began calling for an end to Indian rule, and relations with Pakistan have worsened as India accused its neighbor of providing support for the guerrillas. In 1971, after 10 million refugees poured across its border, India intervened in the Pakistani civil war in an action that prompted an almost immediate cease-fire and the creation of an independent Bangladesh. India and Bangladesh have long-standing disputes over sharing water from the Ganges River watershed.

India's main separatist movement involves Sikh separatists in the Punjab who seek the formation of an independent state of Khalistan, but who are thought to be supported by Pakistan. The government is also contending with increasingly determined separatist movements in the northeastern states of Assam and its neighbor Nagaland.

The British legacy in India included a sizable national elite, well educated and committed to principles of parliamentary democracy. The English language linked the elites of India's linguistically diverse regions, easing minorities' fears of domination by a Hindi-speaking majority. India's economy had seen some industrial development under the British, but its infrastructure was geared to integration in a colonial empire rather than to independence. Port cities, heavy industry, and plantation agriculture coexisted with widespread rural poverty in subsistence-level villages, and the years following independence saw a massive migration of the rural poor into overburdened cities.

Under Prime Minister Jawaharlal Nehru, India assumed a leadership role in the world movement of nonaligned nations and followed a policy of neutrality in international affairs. The gradual development of good relations between the United States and Pakistan led to correspondingly difficult U.S.-India relations. In August 1971 India signed a 20-year friendship treaty with the Soviet Union.

Nehru died on May 27, 1964, and was succeeded by Lal Bahadur Shastri. Nehru's daughter, Mrs. Indira Gandhi, was named prime minister on Jan. 19, 1966. In 1967 the dominant Congress party faced electoral setbacks; in 1969 it split into "Old" and "New" wings. Mrs. Gandhi's New Congress party won control of the legislature.

Faced with protests and strikes after the New Congress party was convicted of voting irregularities in 1975, Mrs. Gandhi declared a state of emergency in June; censorship was imposed, thousands were arrested for political offenses, and various economic-control measures were adopted. An opposition coalition led by the Janata Dal party won a massive victory in parliamentary elections in 1977. Mrs. Gandhi was driven from office, and the state of emergency was annulled. Mrs. Gandhi's party was returned to power in 1980, and she resumed the prime ministership. After an army attack on the Sikhs' Golden Temple in Amritsar, Gandhi was assassinated by Sikh bodyguards in October 1984. She was succeeded in office by her son, Rajiv, who placed the Punjab under direct control of the federal government.

On Dec. 3, 1984, methyl isocyanate gas leaked from a Union Carbide plant in Bhopal, killing over 2,500 people. The accident prompted a broad inquiry into industrial safety standards in India.

Indian troops, in July 1987, intervened in the growing civil war in Sri Lanka between the government and Tamil separatists. A negotiated truce under Indian auspices broke down, and Indian troops were involved in the conflict until their withdrawal in late 1989.

In November 1989, Rajiv Gandhi's Congress party was voted out of office in general elections after people close to the government were accused of taking kickbacks in a government arms purchase scandal. Gandhi was succeeded by V.P. Singh of the Janata Dal party, whose government collapsed after 11 months over a dispute involving Hindu plans to build a temple on the site of a mosque in Ayodhya. (Hindus contend the mosque was built on the site of Rama's birthplace.) Middle-class Hindus also protested an affirmative action policy to set aside federal government jobs for members of lower castes.

Singh was followed by Chandra Shekhar, whose minority government controlled 60 of 525 seats in the house and served only with the backing of the Congress party. After a parliamentary boycott by the Congress party instigated by Rajiv Gandhi, Shekhar quit the government in March 1991, agreeing to stay on as a caretaker until the May election. The election, postponed two weeks following the assassination of Gandhi, was won by the Congress party, and P.V. Narasimha Rao became prime minister.

India has enjoyed significant domestic and international achievements in the 40 years since independence. The nation's territory has been consolidated, and separatist movements in various provinces have been successfully resisted. The federal parliamentary system has proved workable, and the federal government has established its constitutional right to intervene in state affairs under some conditions. India's armed forces are large, well trained, and well equipped, with some nuclear capability. India has maintained watchful, but generally peaceful, relations with two unfriendly neighbors, Pakistan and China, and continues to play a leading role in the nonaligned movement. The Green Revolution of the 1970s has made the country self-sufficient in food for the first time since the 19th century. The country has a large, well-educated middle class and a growing industrial economy.

Nevertheless, the nation faces persistent problems, including separatist movements, regional grievances, and communal conflicts. Much of the population (65%) consists of illiterate people living in rural and urban poverty or near-poverty; the benefits of modernization have been unevenly distributed. Corruption is rife in politics and business. The national economy continues to be hampered by government intervention and controls on international trade and finance. Measures to control population growth have been generally unsuccessful. India's historical legacy of diversity and disunity continues to complicate the country's transformation into a modern nation-state.

## Indonesia
### Republic of Indonesia

**Geography Location:** archipelago of about 13,700 islands stretching from Malay peninsula to New Guinea between mainland of Southeast Asia and Australia. Jakarta 6°08'S, 106°45'E. **Boundaries:** land borders with Papua New Guinea, to E of Irian Jaya, and with Malaysian states of Sarawak and Sabah in northern Borneo. **Total land area:** 735,538 sq. mi. (1,904,569 sq km). **Coastline:** 34,006 mi. (54,716 km). **Comparative area:** slightly less than three times the size of Texas. **Land use:** 8% arable land; 3% permanent crops; 7% meadows and pastures; 67% forest and woodland; 15% other; includes 3% irrigated. **Major cities:** (1983 est.) Jakarta (capital) 7,347,800; Surabaya 2,223,600; Medan 1,805,500; Bandung 1,566,700; Semarang 1,205,800.

**People Population:** 190,136,221 (1990). **Nationality:** noun—Indonesian(s); adjective—Indonesian. **Ethnic groups:** majority of Malay stock comprising 45% Javanese, 14% Sudanese, 7.5% Madurese, 7.5% coastal Malays. **Languages:** Indonesian (modified form of Malay; official); English and Dutch, leading foreign languages; local dialects, most widely spoken of which is Javanese. **Religions:** 88% Muslim, 6% Protestant, 3% Roman Catholic, 2% Hindu.

**Government Type:** republic. **Independence:** Aug. 17, 1945 (from Netherlands). **Constitution:** Aug. 1945, abrogated by Federal Constitution of 1949 and Provisional Constitution of 1950, restored July 5, 1959. **National holiday:** Independence Day, Aug. 17. **Heads of government:** Gen. (ret.) Suharto, president (since Mar. 1968). **Structure:** executive—headed by president who is chief of state and head of cabinet; cabinet selected by president; unicameral legislature (DPR, or House of Representatives) of 500 members (100 appointed, 400 elected); second body (MPR, or People's Consultative Assembly) of 1,000 members includes legislature and 500 other members (chosen by several processes but not directly elected); MPR elects president and vice president and theoretically determines national policy; judicial—Supreme Court is highest court.

**Economy Monetary unit:** Indonesian rupiah. **Budget:** (1989) *income:* $20.9 bil.; *expend.:* $20.9 bil. **GNP:** $80.0 bil., $430 per capita. **Chief crops:** subsistence food production, and smallholder and plantation production for export; rice, cassava, peanuts, rubber, cocoa; illegal producer of cannabis for international drug trade. **Livestock:** goats, cattle, sheep, pigs, buffalo. **Natural resources:** crude oil, tin, natural gas, nickel, timber. **Major industries:** petroleum, textiles, mining. **Labor force:** 67 mil. (1985 est.); 55% agriculture, 10% manufacturing, 4% construction, 3% transport and communication; 2.9% unemployment. **Exports:** $21.0 bil. (f.o.b., 1989 est.); 40% petroleum and liquefied natural gas, 15% timber, 7% textiles, 5% rubber, 3% coffee. **Imports:** $13.2 bil. (c.i.f., 1989 est.); 39% machinery, 19% chemical products, 16% manufactured goods. **Major trading partners:** (1988) *exports:* 42% Japan, 16% U.S., 11% EC, 9% Singapore; *imports:* 26% Japan, 19% EC, 13% U.S., 7% Singapore.

**Intl. Orgs.** ASEAN, FAO, G-77, GATT, IAEA, IBRD, ICAO, IDA, IFAD, IFC, ILO, IMF, IMO, INTELSAT, INTERPOL, ITU, NAM, OPEC, UN, UNESCO, UPU, WHO, WIPO, WMO.

The precolonial East Indies consisted of several Islamic and Hindu kingdoms in the western islands and tribal societies in the easterly ones. The Portuguese established trading posts in the 16th century; by the 17th century, control had largely passed to the Dutch East India Company. With the company's bankruptcy in 1799, the Dutch established direct colonial rule. Several 19th-century anticolonial uprisings, though costly to the Dutch, failed to dislodge them. Nationalist sentiment grew in the early 20th century, organized around Islamic groups, the Indonesian Communist party (PKI, founded 1920), and the Indonesian Nationalist party (PNI, founded 1927). Sukarno, founder of the PNI, achieved prominence as a nationalist leader and was jailed by the Dutch.

The Dutch East Indies fell quickly to the Japanese early in 1942. Some nationalists at first hailed the Japanese as liberators but quickly turned against their harsh occupation. On Aug. 17, 1945, Sukarno proclaimed Indonesia's independence. With British aid, the Dutch returned and tried to reestablish colonial rule; in 1949, threatened with a cutoff of American Marshall Plan aid, they withdrew and acknowledged Indonesia's independent status. Under Sukarno Indonesia took a leading role in international affairs among the nonaligned nations of the Third World.

In 1963 Indonesia gained control of the last Dutch outpost in the Indies, Irian Jaya (western New Guinea). Sukarno then launched a disastrous policy of "confrontation" with Malaysia in North Borneo. Sukarno's politics moved steadily to the left, and Indonesia became hostile to the West and friendly with China. The influence of the PKI grew steadily. On Sept. 30, 1965, the army crushed an attempted coup by the PKI, setting off a popular reaction in which several hundred thousand people were killed as suspected Communists. Sukarno was shunted aside, and power devolved to Gen. Suharto, who became president in 1968. Indonesia played an instrumental role in founding the Association of Southeast Asian Nations (ASEAN) in 1967. The PKI was banned, and Indonesian policy swung sharply in favor of the West and the non-Communist states of Southeast Asia.

The economy grew rapidly, aided by oil revenue, timber exports to Japan, and the Green Revolution in rice agriculture. Foreign investment aided industrial development, which was hampered, however, by domestic content laws and other trade restrictions. A policy of "transmigration" attempted, with mixed success, to move farmers from overcrowded Java and Bali to underdeveloped areas in Sumatra, Borneo, Sulawesi, and Irian Jaya. In 1975 Indonesia invaded the former Portuguese colony of East Timor, which was annexed in 1976. More than 100,000 East Timorese have been killed and the annexation is not recognized internationally.

In recent years declining oil revenues have been partly offset by the growth of industry and tourism. Pres. Suharto remains in power, at the head of the Golkar united-front party, but in 1990 the government lifted restrictions on the press and released a leading dissident, Hartono Dharsono, who may run against Suharto in 1993.

---

# Iran
## Islamic Republic of Iran

**Geography Location:** western Asia. **Boundaries:** USSR and Caspian Sea to N, Pakistan and Afghanistan to E, Persian (Arabian) Gulf and Gulf of Oman to S, and Turkey and Iraq to W. **Total land area:** 636,296 sq. mi. (1,648,000 sq km). **Coastline:** 1,976 mi. (3,180 km). **Comparative area:** slightly larger than Alaska. **Land use:** 8% arable land; negl. % permanent crops; 27% meadows and pastures; 11% forest and woodland; 54% other; includes 2% irrigated. **Major cities:** (1986) Tehran (Teheran) (capital) 5,770,000; Mashad (Meshed) 1,500,000; Isfahan (Esfahan) 1,000,000 (1986 census); Tabriz 925,000; Shiraz 800,000 (1982 est.).

**People Population:** 55,647,001 (1990). **Nationality:** noun—Iranian(s); adjective—Iranian. **Ethnic groups:** 63% ethnic Persian, 18% Turkic, 13% other Iranian, 3% Kurdish. **Languages:** Farsi, Turki, Kurdish, Arabic, English, French. **Religions:** 93% Shia Muslim; 5% Sunni Muslim; 2% Zoroastrian, Jewish, Christian, and Baha'i.

**Government Type:** theocratic republic. **Constitution:** Dec. 2-3, 1979. **National holidays:** Shia Islam religious holidays observed nationwide; Victory of the Islamic Revolution, Feb. 11; Islamic Republic Day, April 1. **Heads of government:** Ali-Akbar Hahsemi Rafsanjani, president (since Sept. 1989). **Structure:** executive, unicameral legislature (Islamic Consultative Assembly), and judicial branches.

**Economy Monetary unit:** Iranian rial. **Budget:** (1988 est.) *income:* N.A.; *expend.:* $55.1 bil. **GNP:** $93.5 bil., $1,800 per capita. **Chief crops:** wheat, barley, rice, sugar beets; illegal producer of opium poppy for international drug trade. **Livestock:** sheep, goats, cattle, asses, horses. **Natural resources:** petroleum, natural gas, coal, chromium. **Major industries:** petroleum, petrochemicals, textiles. **Labor force:** 15.4 mil. (1988 est.); 33% agriculture, 21% manufacturing; shortage of skilled labor; 30% unemployment. **Exports:** $12.3 bil. (f.o.b., 1988); 90% petroleum; carpets, fruits, nuts, hides. **Imports:** $12.0 bil. (c.i.f., 1988); machinery, military supplies, metal works, foodstuffs, pharmaceuticals. **Major trading partners: *exports:*** Japan, Turkey, Italy, Netherlands, Spain; ***imports:*** W. Germany, Japan, Turkey, UK, Italy.

**Intl. Orgs.** FAO, G-77, IAEA, IBRD, IDA, IFC, ILO, IMO, INTELSAT, OPEC, UN, UNESCO, UNIDO, WHO.

In 549 B.C. Cyrus the Great established the Persian empire by uniting Persia and conquered Babylonia. His successors Darius and Xerxes tried unsuccessfully to conquer Greece. Alexander the Great conquered Persia in 333 B.C., but the Persians regained their independence after his death. The Persian Sassanian empire, established in A.D. 226, was the principal eastern rival of the Roman Empire. In 641 the Sassanians were defeated by invading Arabs, and Islam replaced the indigenous Zoroastrian religion. Persia reasserted its national identity—though not its political independence—under Islam and became a major center of Shia Muslim culture. In the early 13th century, Persia was conquered by the Mongols, who ruled the country until 1502.

The brilliant Safavid dynasty (1499–1736) was followed by two centuries of decline. During the 19th century, Persia lost control over Afghanistan and the Caucasus, while internal affairs came increasingly under British and Russian control. In 1907 an Anglo-Russian agreement formally divided Persia into spheres of influence. Following World War I, Persia was recognized as an independent nation, but was virtually a British protectorate. The Soviet Union renounced all claims to Persia in 1921.

In 1921 Reza Khan established a military dictatorship and had himself declared a hereditary monarch, Reza Shah Pahlavi, in 1925. In March 1935, the country's name was formally changed to Iran. In 1941 Great Britain, anxious over access to Iran's rich oil fields, charged Iran with pro-Axis activity, occupied Iran, and forced the abdication of Reza Shah in favor of his son, Mohammad Reza Shah Pahlavi. In 1945 Iran became a charter member of the United Nations, and in 1946–47, the Soviets tentatively backed the creation of the autonomous Republic of Iranian Azerbaijan (in the north) and the Kurdish Republic of Mahabad (between Lake Urmia and Iraq).

Under Mohammed Mossadegh the National Front gained power in 1951. With Mossadegh as premier, parliament nationalized the oil industry; Britain responded with an economic blockade. The shah was briefly driven from power, but in August 1953, monarchist elements with clandestine British and American support ousted Mossadegh and restored the shah to the throne. The shah pursued a pro-Western policy of modernization and anticommunism and was rewarded with massive military and economic aid. His combination of secular, authoritarian rule and economic and social modernization was popular with the urban business sector but deeply resented by the rural population and the urban poor. Unrestrained use of the secret police to suppress any sign of dissent led to widespread popular disaffection.

Religiously inspired protests resulted in widespread violence in late 1978. A military government was installed by the shah on Nov. 6, with Prime Minister Shahpur Bakhtiar given sweeping powers. The shah went into exile on Jan. 16, 1979. On Jan. 31 Iran's dominant religious leader, Ayatollah Ruhollah Khomeini, returned to Iran from his exile in France. Government forces were routed by Khomeini's supporters, and Bakhtiar's government fell on Feb. 11. Throughout 1979 clashes took place between rival religious factions, between religious parties and secular leftists, and between the urban middle class and the disenfranchised poor. Thousands of people were arrested and executed by the religious militia forces.

On Nov. 4, 1979, militants seized the U.S. embassy in Tehran and held 62 Americans hostage, provoking a long international crisis. An American military raid in April 1980 failed in an attempt to free the hostages. The hostages were finally freed on Jan. 21, 1981, minutes after Ronald Reagan was inaugurated as president of the United States. The following day Iran's president, Abolhassan Bani-Sadr, was dismissed from office, and the Ayatollah Khomeini took over direct executive powers. This was followed by a new wave of executions, with political moderates and non-Islamic religious believers among the principal victims.

On Sept. 22, 1980, a dispute between Iran and Iraq over the Shatt al-Arab waterway flared into open warfare. The war severely crippled Iran. Estimates on casualties range from 450,000 to more than a million dead on both sides, and the war absorbed nearly all Iran's revenue from oil exports, leaving the country nearly bankrupt. The United States was also drawn into the conflict. In 1986, Reagan administration officials attempted to secure the release of hostages in Lebanon by trading arms to the Iranians; and on July 3, 1988, an American ship patrolling in the Persian Gulf accidently shot down an Iranian civilian airliner, killing all aboard.

In September 1988, a UN initiative led to a cease-fire between Iran and Iraq and to the opening of negotiations to find a permanent settlement to the war. Largely isolated from the world community, Iran's domestic priority in the wake of the war is the rebuilding of the nation's economy.

In February 1989, Ayatollah Khomeini pronounced death sentences on Indian-born British author Salman Rushdie and the publishers of his novel *Satanic Verses* because of its alleged insults to Muhammad and Islam. The book was banned in several Muslim countries, and Britain and the EC nations broke diplomatic relations with Iran over the incident.

On June 3, 1989, Ayatollah Khomeini died, but the dire predictions that his death would cause turmoil within the Iranian political hierarchy proved wrong. In September 1989 Ali-Akbar Rafsanjani assumed the presidency and has so far kept the disparate political factions at bay.

Although Iran condemned the presence of Western troops in the Middle East during the Persian Gulf conflict, it abided by UN sanctions against Iraq and grounded Iraqi planes that sought refuge from allied bombing raids during the war.

Iran is located in an area of frequent earthquake activity. On June 21, 1990, a severe earthquake struck the Caspian Sea coast near Rasht, killing some 30,000 people and bringing enormous devastation to two provinces.

(See "Major News Stories of the Year.")

# Iraq
## Republic of Iraq

**Geography Location:** western Asia with narrow outlet to Persian (Arabian) Gulf. **Boundaries:** Turkey to N, Iran to E, Saudi Arabia and Kuwait to S, Syria and Jordan to W. **Total land area:** 169,190 sq. mi. (438,317 sq km). **Coastline:** 36 mi. (58 km). **Comparative area:** slightly larger than California. **Land use:** 12% arable land; 1% permanent crops; 9% meadows and pastures; 3% forest and woodland; 75% other; includes 4% irrigated. **Major cities:** Baghdad (capital) 3,236,000 (1987 census); Basra (Basia) 1,540,000; Mosul 1,220,000; Kirkuk 535,000 (1977 census).

**People Population:** 18,781,770 (1990). **Nationality:** noun—Iraqi(s); adjective—Iraqi. **Ethnic groups:** 75–80% Arab, 15-20% Kurdish, 5% Turkoman, Assyrian, and other. **Languages:** Arabic (official), Kurdish (official in Kurdish areas), Assyrian, Armenian. **Religions:** 97% Muslim (60–65% Shia, 32–37% Sunni), 3% Christian and other.

**Government Type:** republic. **Independence:** Oct. 3, 1932 (from League of Nations mandate under British administration). **Constitution:** Sept. 22, 1968, effective July 16, 1970 (interim constitution). **National holidays:** anniversaries of 1958 and 1968 revolutions celebrated July 14 and 17; various religious holidays. **Heads of government:** Saddam Hussein, president (since July 1979); Dr. Saadon Humadi, prime minister (since 1991). **Structure:** Ba'ath party of Iraq has been in power since 1968 coup; unicameral legislature (National Assembly).

**Economy Monetary unit:** Iraqi dinar. **Budget:** (1989) *income:* N.A.; *expend.:* $35 bil. **GNP:** $35 bil., $1,940 per capita (1989 est.). **Chief crops:** dates, wheat, barley, rice, cotton. **Livestock:** sheep, goats, asses, camels. **Natural resources:** crude oil, natural gas, phosphates, sulphur. **Major industries:** petroleum, textiles, shoes. **Labor force:** 3.5 mil. (1980); 39% services, 33% agriculture, 28% industry, severe labor shortage; about 1 mil. Iraqis work abroad (1987). **Exports:** $12.5 bil. (f.o.b., 1988); crude oil and refined products, dates. **Imports:** $10.2 bil. (f.o.b., 1988); food, manufactures, consumer goods. **Major trading partners:** (1987) *exports:* U.S., Brazil, USSR, Italy, Turkey, France, Japan; *imports:* Turkey, U.S., W. Germany, UK, France, Japan, Romania.

**Intl. Orgs.** Arab League, FAO, G-77, IAEA, IBRD, ICAO, IDA, IFAD, IFC, ILO, IMF, IMO, INTELSAT, INTERPOL, ITU, NAM, OPEC, UN, UNESCO, UPU, WHO, WIPO, WMO.

The fertile lands of Mesopotamia, between the Tigris and Euphrates rivers, were the site of one of the world's oldest civilizations. The city-states of Sumer were founded before 3000 B.C. and later became the heart of the Babylonian empire. Babylon became subject to the Assyrian empire after 1350 B.C. and was conquered by the Persians under Cyrus and Darius in the mid-sixth century B.C. Mesopotamia remained under the control of various Persian dynasties for the next 1,000 years.

In the seventh century A.D., the region was rapidly incorporated into the expanding Islamic world. The battle of Basra in 656 decisively established Arab control. In 762 the Caliphate, the center of Islamic rule, was moved from Damascus to the newly founded city of Baghdad, near the ruins of ancient Babylon. Mongol invaders sacked Baghdad in 1258 and destroyed its irrigation works; thereafter the region entered a period of long-term decline. Baghdad fell to the Ottoman Turks in 1534, and Iraq remained a province of the Ottoman Empire until the 20th century.

British troops occupied Iraq in 1915, and Great Britain governed the country under a League of Nations mandate after World War I. A Hashemite monarchy was organized under British protection in 1921. The kingdom of Iraq was granted independence in 1932 but remained closely tied to Great Britain by treaties guaranteeing British interests in petroleum and regional defense. Iraqi oil flowed through British-controlled pipelines traversing Jordan to Haifa (in Israel) and through a French-controlled pipeline traversing Syria to Latakia.

After 1932 several attempted coups by anti-British factions were put down with the aid of British troops. One such coup in April 1941 sought aid from Italy and Germany; British troops landed at Basra in May and restored the pro-British monarchy. Iraq declared war against the Axis powers in 1943. In 1948 Iraq joined the Arab League and participated in the first Arab-Israeli War. Most of Iraq's 85,000 Jews emigrated to Israel after the war ended.

In 1952 a new agreement with Great Britain gave the Iraq Petroleum Company greater control over the country's oil, and a greater share of oil revenues. While remaining part of the Arab League, Iraq in 1955 broke ties with Egypt and also expelled the Soviet ambassador. Iraq signed a mutual defense treaty with Turkey.

A leftist pan-Arab revolutionary coup overthrew the monarchy in 1958 and established a republic, reversing Iraq's former pro-Western stance in international affairs. Oil resources and other industries were nationalized, and large landholdings were broken up. In 1968 a local branch of the international Ba'ath Socialist party came to power and established rule by decree within the republican framework of government. In 1972 the Soviet Union sent arms and advisors to Iraq. In the 1973 Arab-Israeli War, Iraq sent troops to aid Syrian forces on the front lines.

Iranian aid to a long-standing Kurdish rebellion in Iraq's northern mountains strained relations between the two countries. The Kurds were defeated in a bloody campaign in 1975, though the rebellion continued, leading to Iraq's bombing of Kurdish villages in 1979 and other subsequent incidents.

The execution of 21 alleged Communist conspirators in 1978 disrupted relations between Iraq and the USSR. Trade relations with the West were resumed. On July 16, 1979, Gen. Saddam Hussein at-Takriti assumed control of the government and immediately purged leftist elements in the Ba'ath movement.

Several months of intermittent fighting in 1980 between Iraq and Iran for control of the Shatt al-Arab waterway in southern Iraq led to the outbreak of open warfare on Sept. 22, when each country launched bombing attacks on the other's cities. Warfare quickly spread along the entire Iraq-Iran border. The Iran-Iraq War produced eight years of fierce but generally stalemated fighting, with reports of the use of poison gas by both sides. The war spread to the gulf in 1984, as both Iran and Iraq attacked tankers using each other's ports. On June 7, 1981, Israeli war planes destroyed a nuclear reactor near Baghdad, claiming it was capable of producing nuclear weapons.

On May 17, 1987, the USS Stark, an American frigate on station in the gulf, was struck by missiles fired by an Iraqi fighter; 37 American sailors were killed. Iraq claimed that the attack was inadvertent and apologized to the U.S. government.

In September 1988, a UN conference led to a cease-fire in the Iran-Iraq War. In the autumn of 1988, refugees in Turkey reported that poison gas had been used against Kurdish villages in northeastern Iraq as the Kurdish rebellion there continued. During 1989–90 Iraq's re-

## A GLOSSARY OF ARABIC WORDS AND ISLAMIC CONCEPTS

**Ahl al-Kitab** "People of the book"; Jews, Christian and others who have received revelation from God

**Assassins** clandestine order of Muslims who terrorized Crusaders and others by secret murders

**Ayatollah** religious leader among Shia Muslims

**Ba'ath** "renaissance"; refers to Arab Socialist Renaissance party, which calls for pan-Arab socialist state; leading party in Iraq and Syria

**Caliph** "successor"; temporal and spiritual head of Islam

**Dar al-harb** "land at war (with God)"; non-Islamic country

**Dar al-Islam** "land at peace (with God)"; Islamic country (also Dar es-Salaam, Dar al-Salaam)

**Druse** Islamic heresy; now an independent sect mostly in Lebanon

**Fatwa** a binding theologically based legal opinion (Shiite)

**Hadith** sayings and acts attributed to Muhammad

**Hajj** pilgrimage to Mecca

**Hakim** Muslim judge, ruler, or governor; doctor

**Halal** food prepared according to Islamic law

**Hegira** exodus; flight of Muhammad from Mecca to Medina in 622

**Hizbullah** "party of Allah"; name of a political party

**Ijma** consensus

**Ikhwan** brotherhood

**Imam** prayer leader of a Mosque (Sunni); divinely appointed, sinless, infallible successor of Muhammad (Shiite)

**Intifada** "uprising"; refers to Palestinian resistance to Israeli occupation of West Bank and Gaza

**Islam** "submission"

**Jihad** holy war waged as a religious duty

**Koran** word of God divinely revealed to Muhammad

**Mahdi** one rightly guided; Muslim leader who assumes a Messianic role

**Majlis al-ummah** "session of Islamic community"; National Assembly, parliament, council

**Mosque** place of public worship for Muslims

**Muezzin** one who calls Muslim faithful to prayer

**Mujahid** "soldier of God"; mujahiddun (pl.) refers to anti-Communist guerrillas in Afghanistan

**Mullah** member of a quasi-clerical class trained in Islamic law and tradition

**Muslim** "one who surrenders to God"; adherent of Islam

**Salat** daily ritual prayer

**Shahadah** confession of faith

**Shahid** "martyr"; especially in Shia Islam

**Sharia** "path"; Islamic law

**Shiite** (also Shia) Muslim believing Ali and Imams to be only rightful successors to Muhammad (mostly in Iraq and Iran); shia = "sect"

**Shurah** "consultation"

**Sunni** orthodox Muslims adhering to Sunna, i.e. custom and practice based on Muhammad's words and deeds

**Ulama** religious leadership; specialists in Islamic theology

pressive internal policies and continued arms buildup provoked widespread international criticism. Iraqi agents were caught attempting to smuggle several components of nuclear weapons from the United States and Great Britain.

On Aug. 2, 1990, 120,000 Iraqi troops invaded, occupied, and later annexed neighboring Kuwait. The invasion was met with almost universal disapproval, led by the UN Security Council, and U.S. troops were deployed to Saudi Arabia to defend it against a possible invasion. Total coalition forces in and around Saudi Arabia eventually totalled 500,000 troops from 13 countries.

After a six-week air war that destroyed Iraq's offensive and defensive capabilities, as well as much of the country's infrastructure, allied ground forces liberated Kuwait and occupied much of southern Iraq in only four days. Emboldened by the proximity of such overwhelming force, Kurdish and Sunni minorities in Iraq began a civil war that was put down with surprising speed and resulted in the displacement of hundreds of thousands of refugees to Turkey and Iran.

Iraq's economy is dominated by production of oil in the Mosul and Kirkuk oil fields in the northern part of the country, carried by pipelines to terminals at Basra and Fao. Cotton and dates are produced in the south, while wheat and vegetables are important crops in the fertile lands between the Tigris and Euphrates near Baghdad.

(See also Part I, "The Year in Review.")

## Ireland

**Geography** **Location:** 26 of 32 counties comprising island of Ireland, in North Atlantic Ocean. Dublin 53°20′N, 6°15′W. **Boundaries:** Northern Ireland (UK) to N, Great Britain 50 mi (80 km) to E. **Total land area:** 26,593 sq. mi. (68,895 sq km). **Coastline:** 900 mi. (1,448 km). **Comparative area:** slightly larger than W. Virginia. **Land use:** 14% arable land; negl. % permanent crops; 71% meadows and pastures; 5% forest and woodland; 10% other. **Major cities:** (1986 census) Dublin (capital) 920,956; Cork 173,694; Limerick 76,557; Galway 47,104; Waterford 41,054.

**People** **Population:** 3,550,352 (1989). **Nationality:** noun—Irishman (men), Irishwoman (women), Irish (collective pl.); adjective—Irish. **Ethnic groups:** Celtic, with English minority. **Languages:** Irish (Gaelic) and English (official); English widely spoken. **Religions:** 94% Roman Catholic, 4% Anglican, 2% other.

**Government** **Type:** republic. **Independence:** Dec. 6, 1921 (from UK). **Constitution:** Dec. 29, 1937. **National holiday:** St. Patrick's Day, Mar. 17. **Heads of government:** Mary Robinson, president (since Dec. 1990); Charles J. Haughey, prime minister (since Apr. 1987). **Structure:** elected president; bicameral parliament (Seanad, Dail) reflecting proportional and vocational representation; judiciary appointed by president on advice of government.

**Economy** **Monetary unit:** Irish pound. **Budget:** (1989) *income:* $10.9 bil.; *expend.:* $11.2 bil. **GDP:** $31.4 bil., $8,900 per capita. **Chief crops:** turnips, barley, potatoes, sugar beets, wheat; food shortages—grains, fruits, vegetables. **Livestock:** cattle, sheep, pigs. **Natural resources:** zinc, lead, natural gas, crude oil, barite. **Major industries:** food products, brewing, textiles, clothing. **Labor force:** 1.3 mil. (1986); 46.5% services, 21.4% manufacturing and construction, 12.9% agriculture, forestry, fishing; 18.5% unemployment (1988). **Exports:** $20.3 bil. (f.o.b., 1989); live animals, animal products, chemicals, data processing equipment, industrial machinery. **Imports:** $17.3 bil. (c.i.f., 1989); food, animal feed, chemicals, petroleum and petroleum products, machinery, textiles. **Major trading partners:** *exports:* 74% EC (34% UK, 11% W. Germany, 9% France), 8% U.S.; *imports:* 66% EC (42% UK, 8% W. Germany, 4% France), 17% U.S.

**Intl. Orgs.** EC, FAO, GATT, IAEA, IBRD, ICAO, IDA, IFAD, IFC, ILO, IMF, IMO, INTELSAT, INTERPOL, ITU, OECD, UN, UNESCO, UPU, WIPO, WMO.

Ireland, a collection of warring Celtic chieftainships, was converted to Christianity by St. Patrick in the fifth century. Over the next two centuries, Ireland became a great center of monastic Christianity, sending missionaries to Scotland, England, and the continent. While the Roman Empire decayed, Ireland was a center of peace, culture, and learning. Viking invasions in the ninth and 10th centuries caused substantial damage and overturned the rule of the great monasteries and their secular allies. By the time an Irish monarchy was reestablished by Brian Boru in 1014 and the surviving invaders were integrated into Irish society, Ireland had become an isolated, poor backwater on the periphery of Europe.

Trade gave rise to English commercial interests in Ireland and to Henry II's claim to overlordship of Ireland in the 12th century. Henry VIII declared himself king of Ireland and introduced the Reformation there. Large-scale Scottish immigration to Ulster began during the reign of Elizabeth I. Penal laws were applied, banning Catholics from public life and making the Mass an act of treason. A rebellion in 1641 was crushed by Oliver Cromwell over the course of a decade, ending with a massacre of thousands of Irish at Drogheda. After William of Orange's "Glorious Revolution" of 1688, the Irish supported James II, who was defeated at the Battle of the Boyne in 1690.

Following these events, British economic sanctions destroyed Ireland's flourishing export trade in wool. "Plantations" were established by British and Scottish Presbyterian landlords and farmers on lands seized from Irish Catholics. Much of the native aristocracy fled into exile, and the Gaelic language declined to near extinction.

A separate Irish Parliament, dominated by the Anglo-Irish establishment, was instituted in 1782, but it had little power. In 1798 a popular uprising led by Wolf Tone, with inspiration and aid from revolutionary France, was put down with great loss of life.

In 1800 Ireland and England were joined by the Act of Union, whereby Ireland was ineffectively represented in the British Parliament. After popular agitation led by Daniel O'Connell, the Catholic Emancipation Act was enacted by Parliament in 1829, though mandatory tithes continued to support the established Anglican church until 1869.

Under absentee landlords, the Irish population had been reduced to a subsistence diet based largely on potatoes. When a potato blight struck the country in the 1840s, disaster ensued. Between 1846 and 1851, one million people starved to death, and 1.6 million emigrated, most of them to America.

In the late 19th century, a home-rule movement under Charles Stewart Parnell won wide popular support. A Home Rule Act finally was passed by Parliament in 1914, but its effect was postponed for the duration of World War I. Meanwhile the separatist Sinn Fein movement gained momentum, aided by an Irish literary and cultural renaissance in the early 20th century. The Land Purchase Acts of the early 20th century enabled dispossessed peasants to buy land from absentee landlords, creating a rural economic basis for an independent Ireland. The country's economy, based largely on agriculture and pasturage, began to recover. (Industry, principally shipbuilding and textiles, was largely confined to Northern Ireland.)

The postponement of home rule led to the Easter Rebellion of 1916; brutally suppressed, it was followed by the "Troubles," a period of guerrilla warfare lasting to 1920. In that year the Government of Ireland Act established six of Ulster's nine counties as Northern Ireland, an integral part of the United Kingdom but with its own home-rule Parliament. The south's refusal of similar status led to the passage on Dec. 11, 1922, of the Irish Free State Act, by which Ireland became an independent dominion within the British Commonwealth.

The Fine Gael (People of Ireland) party governed until 1932, when Eamon De Valera, as the head of the Fianna Fail (Soldiers of Destiny) party, was elected president, holding that office until 1948. In 1938 the Constitution was revised to sever all connections with the British government except for an "external association" with the British monarchy. The outlawed Irish Republican Army (IRA) pressed for forcible reunification of Ireland and carried out attacks on British interests in both Ireland and Northern Ireland.

Ireland remained neutral during World War II, and its government objected to British military activities in Northern Ireland. But it was generally sympathetic to the Allied war effort, especially after the United States entered the war in 1941. Ireland's wartime neutrality, and its refusal to recognize the USSR, led to its being denied UN membership after the war; Ireland was admitted to the UN in 1955.

In 1949 Ireland severed all ties to the British Crown, becoming a fully independent republic. The Fianna Fail, normally the majority party since 1932, won a majority in the republic's first elections, and De Valera became prime minister. In 1954 a coalition government under John Costello took power. De Valera was elected president of the republic in 1959, as a new generation of parliamentary leadership arose.

During the 1950s, Ireland developed a moderate welfare state with the support of both the Fianna Fail and Fine Gael. In the 1960s attention turned to industrial development: zinc and lead mining, and export-oriented production of textiles, ceramics, and machinery. Ireland was admitted to the EC in 1973. Ireland also became more active in international affairs; as a small nonaligned state, it frequently contributed troops to UN peacekeeping forces.

Beginning in the late 1960s, civil rights demonstrations led frequently to civil disorders and an increase in IRA guerrilla activity in the north. While the 1970s were a boom period for the Irish Republic, sectarian violence and terrorism in the north left over 2,500 dead. The 1980s saw the establishment of an Anglo-Irish Intergovernmental Council (1981) and the Hillsborough accords (1985) between the Thatcher government and the Fine Gael-Labour coalition, which gave Ireland a consultative role in Northern Irish disputes.

The government of Charles Haughey, elected in 1987, continued to face severe economic problems, including high tax rates, high inflation and unemployment, and a high level of public debt through mid-1990. The government is also preoccupied with events in the north.

In the spring of 1989, Haughey's party lost ground in a hastily called general election, and he was forced to form a coalition government. In November 1990, Mary Robinson, a liberal lawyer backed by the Labour party and the Workers party, beat the Fianna Fail candidate in a bid for the presidency.

# Israel
## State of Israel

**Geography** **Location:** western Asia, on eastern shore of Mediterranean Sea; has outlet to Red Sea via Gulf of Aqaba. **Boundaries:** Lebanon to N, Syria to NE, Jordan to E, Egypt to SW, Mediterranean Sea to W. **Total land area:** 8,302 sq. mi. (21,501 sq km). **Coastline:** 170 mi. (273 km). **Comparative area:** slightly larger than Massachusetts. **Land use:** 17% arable land; 5% permanent crops; 40% meadows and pastures; 6% forest and woodland; 32% other; includes 11% irrigated. **Major cities:** (1983) Jerusalem (capital) 428,668; Tel Aviv–Jaffa 327,625; Haifa 235,775; Holon 133,460; Petach-Tikva 123,868.

**People** **Population:** 4,409,218 (1990). **Nationality:** noun—Israeli(s); adjective—Israeli. **Ethnic groups:** 83% Jewish, 17% non-Jewish (mostly Arab). **Languages:** Hebrew (official), Arab (official for Arab minority); English most widely used foreign language. **Religions:** 83% Judaism, 13.1% Islam (mostly Sunni Muslim), 2.3% Christian, 1.6% Druze.

**Government** **Type:** republic. **Indepen-**

**dence:** May 14, 1948 (from League of Nations Mandate under British administration). **Constitution:** no formal constitution; some functions of constitution are filled by Declaration of Establishment (1948), the basic laws of the Knesset (legislature)—relating to the Knesset, Israeli lands, the president, government—and Israeli citizenship law. **National holidays:** Israel declared independence on May 14, 1948; because Jewish calendar is lunar, however, holiday varies from year to year; all major Jewish religious holidays are also observed as national holidays. **Heads of government:** Chaim Herzog, president (since May 1983); Yitzhak Shamir, prime minister (since Oct. 1986). **Structure:** president has largely ceremonial functions, except for authority to decide which political leader should try to form ruling coalition following election or fall of previous government; executive power vested in cabinet; unicameral parliament (Knesset) of 120 members elected under system of proportional representation; legislation provides fundamental laws in absence of written constitution; two distinct court systems (secular and religious).

**Economy** **Monetary unit:** new shekel. **Budget:** (1989 est.) *income:* $24.2 bil.; *expend.:* $26.3 bil. **GNP:** $38 bil., $8,700 per capita (1988). **Chief crops:** citrus and other fruits, vegetables, cotton, beef, and dairy products. **Livestock:** poultry, cattle, sheep, goats. **Natural resources:** copper, phosphates, bromide, potash, clay. **Major industries:** food processing, diamond cutting and polishing, textiles and clothing. **Labor force:** 1,400,000 (1984 est.); 29.5% public services; 22.8% industry, mining, and manufacturing; 12.8% commerce; 8% unemployment (1988). **Exports:** $10.4 bil. (f.o.b., 1989 est.); polished diamonds, citrus and other fruits, textiles and clothing, processed foods, fertilizer and chemical products. **Imports:** $12.4 bil. (c.i.f., 1989 est.); military equipment, rough diamonds, oil, chemicals, machinery. **Major trading partners:** *exports:* U.S., UK, W. Germany, France, Belgium; *imports:* U.S., W. Germany, UK, Switzerland, Italy.

**Intl. Orgs.** FAO, GATT, IAEA, IBRD, ICAO, IDA, IFAD, IFC, ILO, IMF, IMO, INTELSAT, INTERPOL, ITU, OAS (observer), UN, UNESCO, UPU, WHO, WIPO, WMO.

In ancient times called the Land of Canaan, the region between the Jordan River and the Mediterranean Sea was one of the earliest sites of agricultural civilization in the Middle East. Hebrew exiles from Egypt arrived c. 1200 B.C.; their kingdom, Eretz Israel, was well established by 1000 B.C., with its capital at Jerusalem. The kingdom expanded under Kings Saul and David, who extended domination over the Philistines, a local seafaring people, and established the norms of Jewish religious worship at the great temple of Jerusalem.

After the reign of King Solomon, the kingdom split into two parts, Israel and Judah. Israel was conquered by the Assyrians in 722 B.C., and Judah by the Babylonians in 586 B.C. A locally autonomous state was reestablished under the Persian empire in the fifth century

B.C. And in the fourth century B.C., Alexander the Great conquered the region, beginning a period of Hellenizing influence.

A new Jewish state was established in 141 B.C. after the revolt of the Maccabees against Hellenic rule, the state falling to the Roman Empire around 70 B.C. Roman rule was exerted through the puppet kings of the Herodian dynasty. Christianity, a messianic religion centering on the teachings of Jesus of Nazareth, was suppressed in Israel by both the Herodian kings and the Jewish priesthood but spread widely in the eastern Mediterranean in the early first century A.D.

A Jewish rebellion against Rome in A.D. 66 was forcibly suppressed, and the temple at Jerusalem was destroyed by the Romans in A.D. 70. Large numbers of Jews were expelled from Judea, beginning the Jewish Diaspora throughout the Roman world and beyond. A second rebellion of Jews in Israel was quelled in A.D. 132. The territory of the former kingdoms of Israel and Judah became generally known as Palestine, after the name of its ancient inhabitants, the Philistines.

With the official toleration of Christianity in the Roman Empire under Constantine I (early 4th century), Palestine became a major center of Christian pilgrimage. Politically, Palestine was administered as part of the Byzantine Empire.

Expansion of Islam from Arabia brought Palestine under Islamic rule in 636. Thereafter the region was ruled by the Caliphates of Damascus (661–750) and Baghdad (762–1258). Part of Palestine was captured in 1099 by European Crusaders, who established the short-lived Latin Kingdom of Jerusalem. The region was briefly conquered by the Mongols in 1258; defeat of the Mongols in 1260 at the battle of Ain Jalyut, near Nazareth, prevented a Mongol invasion of Egypt.

Palestine next became part of the Mamluk empire and in turn was incorporated into the Ottoman Empire in 1516. The later Ottoman period was one of administrative decline, although the holy places of Judaism, Christianity, and Islam were maintained by local religious authorities.

The emigration of Jews from Europe to the homeland of Israel began around 1870, under the influence of the Zionist movement. Zionism, traceable in part to the thought of Moses Mendelssohn (1729–86), originally emphasized the need to maintain Jewish identity and religious consciousness as well as to promote Jewish assimilation into European culture. By the time of the First World Zionist Congress, convened in Basel by Theodor Herzl in 1897, emphasis had shifted to the need for a specific Jewish homeland. After 1905, under the leadership of Chaim Weizmann, Jewish emigration to Palestine increased as Weizmann attempted to win Turkish approval for a new state of Israel.

With the collapse of the Ottoman Empire during World War I, Palestine came under British rule in 1917. In that year the British government issued the Balfour Declaration, committing Britain to aiding the establishment of a Jewish homeland in Palestine. After Brit-

ain received a League of Nations Mandate to govern Palestine (as well as Transjordan) in 1923, Jewish immigration into Palestine increased significantly. Faced with rising Palestinian Arab opposition to a further increase in Jewish immigration, Britain reinterpreted the Balfour Declaration in greatly restricted terms and attempted to limit the number of Jewish arrivals.

The crisis thus provoked lasted until the outbreak of World War II. During the war the Palestinian Jewish community (then about 500,000) generally supported the British war effort, while some Palestinian Arab leaders translated anti-Zionist sentiments into sympathy for the Axis. In 1946 British authorities refused a recommendation of the Anglo-American Committee of Inquiry that they permit resettlement of 100,000 European Jews in Palestine and that limited further immigration to 2,000 per month. Jewish leaders pressed their cause at the United Nations, while in Palestine, Zionist terrorist organizations waged covert war against the British authorities.

In 1947 a UN Special Committee on Palestine, boycotted by Palestinian Arabs, recommended the partition of Palestine into Jewish and Arab sectors, with Jerusalem to be administered under international control. The United Nations adopted the recommendations on Nov. 29, 1947, and the British began to withdraw their forces, while Palestinian Jews and Arabs prepared for war.

On May 14, 1948, the independent state of Israel was established, with its capital at Tel Aviv. On the same day, troops from the Arab League nations attacked Israel. Fighting and cease-fires alternated throughout 1948; Israel lost control of the Old City of Jerusalem but retained the New City, and elsewhere consolidated its territorial control. Separate armistices between Israel and the Arab nations were concluded in 1949; Jordan retained control of the West Bank, and Egypt occupied Gaza. Large numbers of Palestinian Arab refugees departed for camps in Jordan, Lebanon, and Syria, while equally large numbers of Jews from Arab countries resettled in Israel.

Elections to the Knesset (parliament) were held in January 1949 and resulted in a coalition government. Chaim Weizmann was elected president, and David Ben-Gurion became prime minister. Laws were enacted to ensure religious control of education and civil law and to affirm the "Right of Return" of all Jews to Israel. The role of labor (organized in the Histadrut) was protected by law, as was the establishment of agricultural collectives (kibbutzim).

Taking advantage of the Suez Crisis between Great Britain, France, and Egypt, Israel invaded Egypt's Sinai Peninsula on Oct. 29, 1956. Israeli forces withdrew under the terms of a UN cease-fire on Nov. 6 but retained control of Gaza. Thereafter an uneasy peace prevailed for 11 years under UN supervision.

Throughout this period Israel's population continued to swell with immigrants from Europe, the United States, and other Western countries, and also from the dwindling Jewish communities of the Arab world. Israel's economy, aided by foreign aid and private remittances, grew rapidly, while foreign military aid and the growth of a substantial domestic armaments industry increased its military preparedness.

On May 19, 1967, UN peacekeeping forces withdrew from the Egypt-Israel border on the insistence of Egypt's Pres. Gamal Abdel Nasser. Egyptian forces then reoccupied Gaza and closed the Gulf of Aqaba to Israeli shipping. In the Six-Day War, June 5-10, Israel recaptured Gaza, occupied the Sinai Peninsula to the Suez Canal, and captured the West Bank and the Old City of Jerusalem from Jordan and the Golan Heights from Syria. Another UN-supervised cease-fire went into effect.

Egypt and Syria, backed by Soviet airlifts, invaded Israel on Yom Kippur, Oct. 6, 1973. Israel, with strong U.S. support, counterattacked, driving back the Syrian forces and crossing the Suez Canal from the Sinai into Egypt. Fighting ceased on Oct. 24, and a disengagement agreement was signed on Jan. 18, 1974. Israeli forces withdrew from the west bank of the Suez Canal and, following further agreements, withdrew in stages from the Sinai Peninsula, completing the withdrawal in 1982.

The government of Prime Minister Golda Meir fell after the Yom Kippur War, and a new coalition took power. A period of domestic and international difficulties followed, with severe inflation in the economy and a marked rise in Palestinian and other terrorist attacks against Israeli targets. Israeli forces repeatedly attacked Palestinian bases in southern Lebanon and aided the Christian militia forces in the Lebanese civil war of 1975-76. On July 3, 1976, Israeli commandos raided the airport at Entebbe, Uganda, to rescue 103 hostages held by Arab and German hijackers.

The 1977 parliamentary elections brought a conservative coalition to power, with Menachem Begin elected prime minister. Egypt's president Anwar Sadat visited Jerusalem in November 1977, and Begin and Sadat met at a conference with U.S. Pres. Jimmy Carter at Camp David in 1979. On Mar. 26, 1979, Egypt and Israel signed a formal peace treaty ending 30 years of war and establishing diplomatic relations between the two nations.

In July 1980 Israel affirmed the transfer of its national capital from Tel Aviv to Jerusalem and the incorporation of the (formerly Jordanian) Old City into Israeli territory. The Israeli government decided in 1980 to promote increased Jewish settlement in the West Bank, provoking protest from Palestinian leaders.

Israeli forces invaded southern Lebanon in March 1978. After a brief occupation, most Israeli forces withdrew and were replaced by a UN peacekeeping force, but Israel continued to cooperate with Lebanese Christian militia forces in anti-Palestinian operations. Israeli forces again reoccupied southern Lebanon for five days in April 1980.

Israeli and Syrian forces clashed briefly in April 1981. On June 7, 1981, Israeli jets destroyed a nuclear reactor near Baghdad, Iraq, that Israel claimed could have been used to manufacture materials for nuclear weapons. Prime Minister Begin was returned to office in a close election on June 30, 1981, and he retired in 1983.

Attacking Palestine Liberation Organization strongholds in Lebanon in May, 1982, Israel mounted a full-scale invasion of Lebanon on June 6. Israeli and Syrian forces fought in Lebanon's Bekaa Valley on June 9 but disengaged after a few days. On June 14 Israeli forces surrounded and shelled Beirut, forcing the PLO to evacuate the city. On Sept. 14 Israeli forces occupied West Beirut, following the assassination of the newly elected Lebanese president, Bashir Gemayel. Lebanese Christian militia, with tacit Israeli permission, entered two Palestinian refugee camps at Sabra and Shatila on Sept. 16 and massacred hundreds of civilians, provoking an international outcry against Israel's occupation of Lebanon. Israeli forces withdrew from Lebanon in June 1985, except for a narrow "security zone" along the border.

Parliamentary elections in 1984 resulted in a stalemate between the conservative Likud party and the Labor party, and increased the strength of several splinter right-wing religious parties. A grand-coalition government was formed, with power shared by Likud leader Yitzhak Shamir and Labor leader Shimon Peres. The coalition proved unable to undertake any serious initiatives in foreign or domestic policy. Shamir vetoed an agreement negotiated by Peres with Jordan's King Hussein I to attend a UN-sponsored peace conference in April 1987.

In December 1987, Palestinian residents of Gaza and the West Bank launched a series of violent demonstrations against Israeli authorities. The *intifada*, or uprising, continued into 1991 in a cycle of protest and police reaction that has led to the deaths of hundreds of demonstrators and a crisis of Israeli control in the occupied territories. Tensions have been exacerbated by the immigration of hundreds of thousands of Soviet Jews to Israel since 1989.

Parliamentary elections in November 1988 continued the Likud-Labor stalemate and brought increased power to the minor religious parties. A new grand-coalition government announced in January 1989, with Yitzhak Shamir as prime minister and Shimon Peres as minister of finance, collapsed in mid-March because of disagreements over an American-backed plan for peace talks with the Palestinians. This plunged the country into a crisis, resolved in June 1990 with the formation of a coalition government of Likud and several right-wing religious parties. Shamir managed to survive several no-confidence votes, and his alliance with the religious party Agudat Israel in November solidified his party's power as the Persian Gulf crisis unfolded.

Despite a near-constant condition of war or threat of war since 1948, Israel's economy is thriving in comparison with the other nations of the Middle East. Advanced irrigation techniques have led to abundant production of cotton, vegetables, dates, olives, and fruit. Israel has few mineral or petroleum resources, but the industrial sector is diverse, including textiles, diamond cutting, electronics, plastics, machinery, and pharmaceuticals. There is a large and sophisticated armaments industry. Nevertheless, the economy is hampered by chronic inflation and is heavily dependent on foreign (mostly U.S.) aid from both the public and private sectors.

(See also Part I, "The Year in Review.")

# Italy
## Italian Republic

**Geography  Location:** peninsula, extending from southern Europe into Mediterranean Sea, with a number of adjacent islands, principally Sicily to SW, and Sardinia to W. **Boundaries:** Switzerland and Austria to N, Yugoslavia to NE, Adriatic Sea to E, Ionian Sea to SE, Mediterranean Sea to W, France to NW. **Total land area:** 116,324 sq. mi. (301,277 sq km). **Coastline:** 3,105 mi. (4,996 km). **Comparative area:** slightly larger than Arizona. **Land use:** 32% arable land; 10% permanent crops; 17% meadows and pastures; 22% forest and woodland; 19% other; includes 10% irrigated. **Major cities:** (1988) Roma (Rome; capital) 2,816,474; Milano (Milan) 1,464,127; Napoli (Naples) 1,202,582; Torino (Turin) 1,012,180.

**People  Population:** 57,664,405 (1990). **Nationality:** noun—Italian(s); adjective—Italian. **Ethnic groups:** primarily Italian, but includes small clusters of German-, French-, and Slovene-Italians in north and Albanian-Italians in south; Sicilians. **Languages:** Italian; parts of Trentino-Alto Adige region (e.g., Bolzano) are predominantly German-speaking; significant French-speaking minority in Valle d'Aosta region; Slovene-speaking minority in Trieste-Gorizia area. **Religions:** almost 100% nominally Roman Catholic.

**Government  Type:** republic. **Independence:** N.A. **Constitution:** Jan. 1, 1948. **National holiday:** Anniversary of the Republic, June 2. **Heads of government:** Francesco Cossiga, president (since July 1985); Guilio Andreotti, prime minister (since July 1989). **Structure:** executive—president empowered to dissolve parliament and call national election; commander of armed forces presides over Supreme Defense Council; otherwise, authority to govern invested in Council of Ministers; bicameral legislature—popularly elected parliament (315–member Senate, 630–member Chamber of Deputies); judiciary—independent.

**Economy  Monetary unit:** lire. **Budget:** (1989) *income:* $355 bil.; *expend.:* $448 bil. **GDP:** $803.3 bil., $14,000 per capita (1988). **Chief crops:** fruits, wine, vegetables, cereals, potatoes, olives; 95% self-sufficient; food shortages—fats, meat, fish, eggs. **Livestock:** sheep, pigs, cattle, goats, horses. **Natural resources:** mercury, potash, marble, sulfur, dwindling natural gas and crude oil reserves. **Major industries:** machinery and transport equipment, iron, steel, chemicals. **Labor force:** 23.67 mil. (1987); 56.7% services, 37.9% industry, 5.4% agriculture. **Exports:** $141.6 bil. (f.o.b., 1989); textiles, clothing, metals, transport equipment, chemicals. **Imports:** $143.1 bil. (c.i.f., 1989); petroleum, industrial machinery, chemicals, metals, food, agricultural products. **Major trading partners: exports:** 57% EC, 9%

U.S., 4% OPEC; *imports:* 57% EC, 6% OPEC, 6% U.S.

**Intl. Orgs.** EC, FAO, GATT, IAEA, IBRD, ICAO, IDA, IFAD, IFC, ILO, IMF, IMO, INTEL-SAT, INTERPOL, ITU, NATO, OAS (observer), OECD, UN, UNESCO, UPU, WHO, WIPO, WMO.

Rome became the major power in Italy around 500 B.C., dominating the Etruscans in the north and Greek settlements in the south. The Roman Republic already dominated most of the Mediterranean and western Europe by the time imperial rule was established under Julius Caesar. The empire was divided between Rome and Byzantium in the fourth century A.D. The Roman Empire in the west was severely weakened by Germanic invasions in the fifth century and thereafter gradually dissolved, so that Italy became a disunited collection of aristocratic holdings and independent cities.

By the 10th century, the city-states, especially in the north, emerged as major powers, rivaling the Papal States of the central peninsula. Venice and Genoa emerged as major maritime powers during the medieval period, while Florence, Siena, and other cities developed into centers of agricultural and commercial wealth, impelling the successive renaissances of the 12th and 15th centuries. With the rise of the Habsburg empire, the monarchical powers of northern Europe vied for power in Italy, and the peninsula's small states became pawns of France, Spain, and Austria.

At the turn of the 19th century, Napoleon created the short-lived Kingdom of Italy as a French satellite, but after his fall, there was a general return to the old pattern, with Austria dominating the north. Metternich in 1815 called Italy a "geographic expression."

The 19th century saw the spread of revolutionary ideals, accompanied by a growing sense of nationalism in both politics and culture. The revolutionary military leader, Giuseppe Garibaldi, and the statesman, Conte Camillo di Cavour, brought about the establishment of the Kingdom of Italy in 1861. The kingdom wrested Venice away from Austria and absorbed the Papal States in 1870.

Although united territorially, the kingdom was divided by conflict between church and state, north and south, modern urban industry versus semifeudal rural poverty. Parliamentary politics under the constitutional monarchy created a regime that was weak and venal, inspiring little popular support.

Italy joined the Allied powers in World War I, but its minor gains from the Treaty of Versailles scarcely seemed to justify its wartime suffering and one million dead. Postwar economic dislocation, fear of communism, and political disillusionment abetted the rise of fascism. Benito Mussolini took over the Italian government at the invitation of the king in 1922 and soon acquired dictatorial powers. Papal secular authority in Vatican City was reestablished by the Lateran Agreement of 1929. In the late 1920s and early 1930s, Italy appeared to be a major power, defending Austria from Germany, colonizing Ethiopia, supporting Francisco Franco in the Spanish civil war, and joining in an "axis" with Hitler's Germany.

Mussolini, the senior partner in the fascist axis, soon was eclipsed by Hitler, and Italy was drawn into the disaster of World War II in 1939. Italy annexed Albania and invaded Greece, but that campaign turned into a fiasco from which German troops had to save the Italian army. In 1943 Allied attacks on Italy began; the fascist Grand Council restored to power the king, Victor Emmanuel III, who then had Mussolini arrested. Hitler intervened in September 1943 and began the war in Italy anew, rescuing Mussolini who established another fascist regime in northern Italy, while the legal Italian government in the south switched sides and welcomed Italy's liberation.

The head of the first postwar government was a Christian Democrat, Alcide de Gasperi. The monarchy was abolished by plebiscite in 1946, and the Republic of Italy was established. The north supported the republic, while monarchism retained significant support in the south.

This division reflected a roughly accurate generalization that sees Italy as comprising a progressive commercial and industrial north and a backward agricultural/pastoral south. Despite such industrial giants of the north as Fiat and Pirelli, however, Italy's manufacturing is primarily carried on by medium-size and small firms, while agriculture is characteristic of the whole country. As late as 1956, there were more Italian workers in agriculture than in industry. Agriculture in the north is generally more prosperous than in the south, with its more arid climate and impoverished soil. Italy is a net food importer.

In the first elections under the republic, in 1948, the Christian Democrats benefited from obvious American patronage and a split in the ranks of the Left to win a clear parliamentary majority. Italy accepted Marshall Plan aid and membership in NATO; reintegration into the European mainstream found expression in membership in the Council of Europe and the Coal and Steel Community.

Domestically, reconstruction was the major task, with both industrial and agricultural output severely hampered by social and physical damage from the war; inflation was rampant and basic social services impaired. The Christian Democrats, normally in Center-Right coalitions in the 1950s and Center-Left coalitions in the 1960s, adopted a policy directed at creating a stable currency, a free market, comprehensive social welfare programs, and occasional state intervention in the economy. This created an Italian "economic miracle," with industrial production doubling between 1953 and 1961 and increasing an additional 40 percent by 1966, led by steel, automobiles, machinery, and electrical equipment.

State holding companies have been dominant in banking and energy production and have had a leading role in other large enterprises. An important goal has been to direct investment to the south, including the islands of Sardinia and Sicily. That program has had only marginal success. The south remains relatively poor and increasingly depopulated by migration from rural to urban areas.

Since the 1970s the Christian Democrats have gradually declined in political influence, normally gaining less than 40 percent of the popular vote while continuing to provide premiers in often short-lived coalition cabinets. Left-wing terrorism became a major national problem. The Christian Democratic leader and former prime minister Aldo Moro was kidnapped and murdered in 1978, and U.S. Brig. Gen./NATO officer James Dozier was kidnapped (and subsequently rescued) in 1981. The government of Bettino Craxi, Italy's first Socialist premier, was severely shaken after it refused to cooperate with the United States in apprehending and trying the hijackers of the *Achille Lauro* in 1985. Craxi resigned in 1987 and was replaced by Giovanni Goria.

Throughout the 1980s, Italy, like the rest of Europe, contended with slowed economic growth, higher inflation, and increased unemployment. By 1990 the fertility rate had declined to the lowest level in western Europe. Lacking effective political unity, Italy's coalition governments have tended to muddle along in the face of these problems.

# Ivory Coast
## Republic of Côte d'Ivoire

**Geography Location:** western coast of Africa. **Boundaries:** Mali and Burkina Faso to N, Ghana to E, Gulf of Guinea to S, Liberia and Guinea to W. **Total land area:** 122,780 sq. mi. (318,000 sq km). **Coastline:** 320 mi. (515 km). **Comparative area:** slightly larger than New Mexico. **Land use:** 9% arable land; 4% permanent crops; 9% meadows and pastures; 26% forest and woodland; 52% other; includes negl. % irrigated. **Major cities:** (1979) Yamoussoukro (capital—not recognized by U.S., which recognizes Abidjan); Abidjan 1,423,323; Bouaké 272,640.

**People Population:** 12,478,024 (1990). **Nationality:** noun—Ivorian(s); adjective—Ivorian. **Ethnic groups:** 23% Baoule, 18% Bete, 15% Senoufou, 11% Malinke and Agni; over 60 ethnic groups; 2 million foreign Africans, mostly Burkinabe; about 130,000–330,000 non-Africans (100,000–300,000 Lebanese, 30,000 French). **Languages:** French (official); over 60 African languages and dialects with Dioula most widely spoken. **Religions:** 63% indigenous beliefs, 25% Muslim, 12% Christian.

**Government Type:** republic. **Independence:** Aug. 7, 1960 (from France). **Constitution:** Nov. 3, 1960. **National holiday:** Dec. 7. **Heads of government:** Félix Houphouet-Boigny, president (since 1960); Alassane D. Ouattara, prime minister (since Nov. 1990). **Structure:** executive—president has broad powers; unicameral legislature—175-member National Assembly; judiciary.

**Economy Monetary unit:** Communauté Financière Africaine (CFA) franc. **Budget:** (1986) *income:* $1.6 bil.; *expend.:* $2.3 bil. **GDP:** $10.3 bil., $960 per capita (1988). **Chief crops:** cash crops—coffee, cocoa, wood, bananas, pineapples, palm oil; food crops—corn, millet, yams, rice; other commodities—cotton, rubber, tobacco. **Livestock:** goats, sheep, cattle, pigs.

**Natural resources:** crude oil, diamonds, manganese, iron ore, cobalt. **Major industries:** foodstuffs, wood processing, oil refinery. **Labor force:** (1985) over 85% agriculture, forestry, livestock raising; 11% wage earners, nearly half in agriculture and remainder in government, industry, commerce, and professions; 54% of working age. **Exports:** $2.2 bil. (f.o.b., 1988); 30% cocoa, 20% coffee, 11% tropical woods; cotton, bananas. **Imports:** $1.3 bil. (c.i.f., 1988); 50% manufactured goods and semifinished products, 40% consumer goods, 10% raw materials and fuels. **Major trading partners:** (1985) France, Nigeria, W. Germany, Netherlands, U.S., Japan.

**Intl. Orgs.** FAO, G-77, GATT, IAEA, IBRD, ICAO, IDA, IFAD, IFC, ILO, IMF, IMO, INTELSAT, INTERPOL, ITU, NAM, UN, UNESCO, UPU, WHO, WIPO, WMO.

The peoples of the Ivory Coast belong to various tribes that had established small and mutually hostile kingdoms prior to the 18th century. The dominant Baule migrated to the Ivory Coast from Ghana about 200 years ago. European contact began with the Portuguese, who established coastal trading stations in the 15th century. They were followed in rapid succession by the Dutch, British, and finally the French, who landed at Assinie in 1637. Dense tropical forests and a lack of good harbors retarded European exploration.

France established a protectorate over the coastal zone in 1842 and during the remainder of the 19th century expanded its control, by conquest and diplomacy, into the interior. In 1893 the Ivory Coast was organized as a French colony, and in 1904 it was made part of French West Africa.

France's Vichy government controlled French West Africa during World War II and harshly suppressed the region's growing nationalist movements. In 1946 a group of West African leaders, inspired by Félix Houphouet-Boigny, formed the African Democratic Assembly, which later cooperated with the French in the implementation of reforms, including, by 1956, universal suffrage and the formation of locally autonomous assemblies. Complete independence for the Ivory Coast came on Aug. 4, 1960.

Félix Houphouet-Boigny was unanimously elected the first president of the Ivory Coast and has been repeatedly reelected ever since. He played a key role in forming the Organization of African Unity in 1963. Under his presidency, the Ivory Coast has enjoyed both political stability and economic prosperity. The Ivory Coast maintains strong commercial and cultural ties to France and is on good terms with other Western-bloc nations.

In the country's first multiparty elections since independence, Houphouet-Boigny's Democratic party captured 82% of the vote against a single opposition candidate, Laurent Gbagbo. In voting for the legislature, the Democrats won 163 of 175 seats.

In February 1990 students rioted to protest government economic policies. Despite the government's efforts to restrain immigration of short-term foreign workers, about one-third of the country's population is made up of migrants from neighboring West African nations. The Liberian civil war also drove about 250,000 refugees into the country.

## Jamaica

**Geography Location:** northern Caribbean Sea. Kingston 17°58′N, 76°48′W. **Boundaries:** Cuba 87 mi. (145 km) to N. **Total land area:** 4,244 sq. mi. (10,991 sq km). **Coastline:** 635 mi. (1,022 km). **Comparative area:** between Delaware and Connecticut. **Land use:** 19% arable land; 6% permanent crops; 18% meadows and pastures; 28% forest and woodland; 29% other; includes 3% irrigated. **Major cities:** Kingston (capital) 104,000 (1980 census); Montego Bay 42,800 (1970 census); Spanish Town 41,600 (1970 census).

**People Population:** 2,441,396 (1990). **Nationality:** noun—Jamaican(s); adjective—Jamaican. **Ethnic groups:** 76.3% African, 15.1% Afro-European, 3.4% East Indian and Afro-East Indian, 3.2% white, 2% other. **Languages:** English, Creole. **Religions:** predominantly Protestant (including Anglican and Baptist), some Roman Catholic, some spiritualist cults.

**Government Type:** independent state within Commonwealth, recognizing Elizabeth II as head of state. **Independence:** Aug. 6, 1962 (from UK). **Constitution:** Aug. 6, 1962. **National holiday:** Independence Day, first Monday in August. **Heads of government:** Michael Manley, prime minister (since Feb. 1989); Gov. Gen. Howard F.H. Cooke, governor-general (since Aug. 1991). **Structure:** cabinet headed by prime minister; bicameral legislature—21-member Senate (13 nominated by prime minister, 8 by opposition leader, if any), 60-member elected House of Representatives; judiciary follows British tradition under chief justice.

**Economy Monetary unit:** Jamaican dollar. **Budget:** (1988 est.) *income:* $1.1 bil.; *expend.:* $1.5 bil. **GDP:** $3.8 bil., $1,529 per capita (1986). **Chief crops:** sugarcane, citrus fruits, bananas, pimientos, coconuts, coffee, cocoa, tobacco; illegal producer of cannabis for international drug trade. **Livestock:** goats, cattle, pigs, asses, mules, horses, sheep. **Natural resources:** bauxite, gypsum, limestone. **Major industries:** tourism, bauxite mining, textiles. **Labor force:** 728,700 (1984); 32% agriculture, 28% industry and commerce, 27% services, 13% government; shortage of technical and managerial personnel; 22% unemployment. **Exports:** $948 mil. (f.o.b., 1989 est.); alumina, bauxite, sugar, bananas, citrus fruits and fruit products. **Imports:** $1.6 bil. (c.i.f., 1989 est.); fuels, machinery, transportation and electrical equipment, food, fertilizer. **Major trading partners:** *exports:* 40% U.S., UK, Canada, Trinidad and Tobago; *imports:* 46% U.S., Venezuela, UK, Japan, Trinidad and Tobago.

**Intl. Orgs.** Commonwealth, FAO, GATT, G-77, IAEA, IBRD, ICAO, IFAD, IFC, ILO, IMF, IMO, INTERPOL, ITU, NAM, OAS, UN, UNESCO, UPU, WHO, WIPO, WMO.

Christopher Columbus visited Jamaica in 1494, and the Spanish ruled the island—exterminating the native Arawaks in the process—until it fell to British control in 1655. A haven for buccaneers, by the 18th century Jamaica was a major sugar producer and the site of one of the busiest slave markets in the world. Emancipation of the slaves in 1833 and abolition of tariff protection in 1846 contributed strongly to the subsequent downfall of the plantation economy.

In 1962 the island gained its independence. The country has been plagued by racial and class division set within the context of an underdeveloped economy. Michael Manley of the People's National party became prime minister in 1972. He nationalized some industry and established closer ties with Cuba. Edward Seaga's Jamaica Labor party came to power in 1980 and encouraged more private-sector involvement in developing the economy. Through Manley was reelected to office in 1989, he has not reversed this general trend.

## Japan

**Geography Location:** chain of more than 3,000 islands extending 1,300 mi. (2,200 km) NE to SW between Sea of Japan and western Pacific Ocean; southern Japan about 93 mi. (150 km) E of S. Korea; islands of Hokkaido, Honshu, Shikoku, and Kyushu account for 98% of land area. Tokyo 35°40′N, 139°45′E. **Boundaries:** Sea of Okhotsk to N, Pacific Ocean to E, East China Sea to SW, and Sea of Japan to W. **Total land area:** 145,870 sq. mi. (377,657 sq km). **Coastline:** 8,505 mi. (13,685 km). **Comparative area:** slightly larger than Montana. **Land use:** 11% arable land; 2% permanent crops; 2% meadows and pastures; 68% forest and woodland; 17% other; includes 9% irrigated. **Major cities:** (1988) Tokyo (capital) 8,155,781; Yokohama 3,121,601; Osaka 2,543,520; Nagoya 2,099,564; Sapporo 1,582,073.

**People Population:** 123,642,641 (1990). **Nationality:** noun—Japanese (sing., pl.); adjective—Japanese. **Ethnic groups:** 99.4% Japanese, 0.6% other (mostly Korean). **Languages:** Japanese. **Religions:** most Japanese observe both Shinto and Buddhist rites; about 16% belong to other faiths, including 0.8% Christian.

**Government Type:** constitutional monarchy. **Constitution:** May 3, 1947. **National holiday:** Foundation Day, Feb. 11. **Heads of government:** Akihito, emperor (since Jan. 1989); Toshiki Kaifu, prime minister (since Aug. 1989). **Structure:** Emperor is symbol of state; executive power is vested in cabinet appointed by prime minister, chosen by lower house of bicameral, elective legislature—diet (House of Councillors, House of Representatives); judiciary is independent.

**Economy Monetary unit:** yen. **Budget:** (1989) *income:* $392 bil.; *expend.:* $464 bil. **GNP:** $1,914.1 bil., $15,600 per capita (1988). **Chief crops:** land intensively cultivated; rice, sugar, vegetables, fruits; 71% self-sufficient in food (1985); food shortages—wheat, corn, beans. **Livestock:** chickens, pigs, cattle, goats, sheep.

**Natural resources:** negl. mineral resources, fish. **Major industries:** metallurgical and engineering industries, electrical and electronic industries, textiles. **Labor force:** 63.3 mil. (1988); 54% trade and services, 33% manufacturing, mining, and construction; **Exports:** $270.0 bil. (f.o.b., 1989); 97% manufactures (including 38% machinery, 17% motor vehicles, 10% consumer electronics). **Imports:** $210 bil. (c.i.f., 1989); 42% manufactures, 30% fossil fuels, 15% foodstuffs, 13% nonfuel raw materials. **Major trading partners:** *exports*: 34% U.S., 22% Southeast Asia, 21% Western Europe; *imports*: 23% Southeast Asia, 23% U.S., 16% Western Europe, 15% Middle East.

**Intl. Orgs.** Colombo Plan, FAO, GATT, IAEA, IBRD, ICAO, IDA, IFAD, IFC, ILO, IMF, IMO, INTELSAT, INTERPOL, ITU, UN, UNESCO, UPU, WHO, WIPO, WMO.

Japan's ancient Jomon civilization was displaced by proto-Japanese Yayoi migrants from mainland northeast Asia beginning in the fourth century B.C. In the early Yayoi period, a mounted military aristocracy dominated rice-growing commoners. The shamanic religion of the time was ancestral to Japan's later indigenous religion, Shinto. Yayoi society evolved into the Yamato protostate, C. A.D. 250–500. The Yamato kings were buried in large, elaborate tomb mounds together with haniwa clay sculptures. From the third century A.D., contact with the mainland increased. Korean missionaries introduced Buddhism and Chinese writing in the mid-sixth century. A centralized monarchy developed in the Yamato Plain, central Honshu Island; Prince Shotoku, a great patron of Buddhism, founded the Horyuji and other great temples in the early seventh century.

In 710 the Yamato kings established a permanent capital for the first time, at Nara; the city was modeled on the contemporary Chinese capital. In 785 the court, split by factionalism and dominated by Nara's large and wealthy Buddhist temples, abandoned the capital; in 794 the new capital at Heian (Kyoto) was completed. The ensuing Heian period was one of the most brilliant in Japanese history. A small civil aristocracy, dominated by the Fujiwara family, drew great wealth from provincial estates and created a metropolitan culture of extreme refinement. From the ninth through the 11th centuries, strong Chinese influences were incorporated into Japanese culture.

In the 12th century the power of the Heian court waned as the influence of the provincial military aristocracy (samurai) grew stronger. In 1156 the capital was seized by the Taira family; in 1185 the Taira were overthrown by their rivals, the Minamoto. The Minamoto established a military government under a shogun (generalissimo) at Kamakura; the emperor remained at Kyoto, stripped of all governmental authority. In Kamakura the Minamoto were soon displaced by their former vassals, the Hojo. During the Kamakura period, the Japanese drew away from Chinese influence in art, architecture, literature, and religion in the process of creating a more distinctively Japanese culture. In 1274 and again in 1281, attempted Mongol invasions were repulsed with the aid of timely typhoons (*kamikaze*, "divine winds").

In the course of a failed attempt at imperial restoration, the Kamakura shogunate was overthrown, in the 1330s, by the Ashikaga family, which in 1338 established a new shogunal government at Muromachi, a precinct of Kyoto. The Muromachi period saw the flowering of a new warrior culture, marked by such military virtues as bravery, loyalty, personal honor, and skill with weapons and by adherence to Zen Buddhism and its associated arts (tea ceremony, flower arranging, calligraphy, etc.). With the Onin Wars of the mid-15th century, the Muromachi shogunate lost most of its power, and the country fell into a century of civil war.

The civil wars were brought to an end during the second half of the 16th century by three successive unifiers, Oda Nobunaga, Hideyoshi, and Tokugawa Ieyasu. At the same time, the Jesuit Francis Xavier and his successors established a short-lived Japanese Christian community. Hideyoshi made several attempts (1592–98) to conquer and annex Korea. In 1601 Tokugawa Ieyasu defeated his rivals in the Battle of Sekigahara. He established a shogunal government at Edo (later Tokyo) in 1603; he and his successors formalized the structure of Japanese feudalism, created a rigid class structure, suppressed Christianity, and enforced the isolation of Japan from virtually all outside influence. Some trade with the mainland and a small Dutch trading station at Nagasaki provided Japan's only windows to the outside world for the next 250 years. The Edo period was marked by urbanization and the development of urban culture (Kabuki theater, wood-block prints, etc.) as the merchant class prospered from internal trade.

The Tokugawa shogun's inability to repel the 1854 visit of American Commodore Matthew Perry and subsequently to avoid establishing commercial and diplomatic relations with Western nations deeply shocked the samurai class. Patriotic young samurai from Choshu, Satsuma, and other outlying feudal domains began to call for the abolition of the shogunate and the restoration of imperial rule in order to confront the threat of contact with the West. Quickly realizing that isolationism was doomed, the young radicals' program changed from "respect the emperor, expel the barbarians" to "enrich the state, strengthen the military." With the accession of the Meiji emperor in 1868, shogunal government ended.

Under direct imperial rule, feudalism was abolished and a wide-ranging program of military, industrial, commercial, and social modernization was implemented. The Meiji Constitution of 1889 created a constitutional monarchy and a parliamentary system of government. Having avoided domination by Western nations, Japan itself became an imperialist power. Defeating China in the Sino-Japanese War of 1894–95 and Russia in the Russo-Japanese War of 1904–05, Japan gained a dominant position in Manchuria and in Korea, which became a Japanese colony in 1910.

Under the ineffectual Taisho emperor (reigned 1912–26), parliamentary government flourished. Japan sided with the Allied Powers in World War I, and the Treaty of Versailles advanced Japan's international interests, particularly in China. The general prosperity of the 1920s was threatened by the Tokyo earthquake of 1923, by labor strife, and by a stagnant agricultural economy. Militant right-wing nationalism began to play an important role in domestic politics.

During the international economic depression of the early 1930s, right-wing militants gained the upper hand; they assassinated many moderate political figures. Japan invaded Manchuria in 1931 and established the puppet state of Manchuguo in 1934. An attempted military coup in 1936 failed in its immediate objectives but led to the establishment of martial law, under which the Showa emperor (Hirohito; reigned 1926–89) became a pawn of the ultranationalists. An invasion and military takeover of eastern China in 1937 was seen as the first step in the creation of a "Greater East Asian Co-prosperity Sphere," designed to unite Asia under Japanese control.

In 1940 Japan entered the Tripartite Alliance with Italy and Nazi Germany. Japan occupied French Indochina in June 1941, provoking increased Allied resistance to Japanese imperial ambitions. Gen. Hideki Tojo became prime minister in October 1941 and ordered simultaneous preemptive strikes against Pearl Harbor, the Philippines, and Malaya on Dec. 7–8. By mid-1942, Japan controlled most of Southeast Asia and the western Pacific, but American victories at the Battle of the Coral Sea in May 1942 and the Battle of Midway in June 1942 halted further Japanese expansion. Thereafter, Japanese forces were steadily pushed back in "island-hopping" campaigns in the central Pacific and along the western Pacific rim, and by Allied counterattacks in Burma. Air attacks on Japan itself culminated in the nuclear bombing of Hiroshima and Nagasaki in August 1945.

Following Japan's formal surrender on Sept. 2, 1945, an American army in Japan under Gen. Douglas MacArthur took control of the country. A new constitution was promulgated, relegating the emperor to purely symbolic status, renouncing the use of military force, and guaranteeing the civil rights of citizens. The industrial combines that had lent strength to Japan's empire were partially dismantled. An international tribunal tried many wartime leaders as war criminals in 1948. In 1949 considerable authority was returned to the conservative government of Premier Shigeru Yoshida. Japan served as a base for American forces during the Korean War, 1950–53, greatly accelerating Japan's postwar economic recovery. On Apr. 28, 1952, a peace treaty between Japan and the United States went into effect, ending the Occupation. On Mar. 8, 1954, the two nations signed a mutual defense assistance pact. Protests over an extension of that treaty, under which substantial U.S. forces were based in Japan, led to the cancellation of a planned visit to Japan by Pres. Dwight Eisenhower in 1960.

Japan was admitted to the United Nations in 1956. The success of Japan's postwar recovery was symbolized by the Tokyo Olympic Games of 1964 and Expo '70 at Osaka. Violent student-protest movements in 1968–69 had no clear political goals and no lasting effect. Politically stable under an unbroken succession of Liberal Democratic party governments, Japan emerged as a major and steadily expanding world industrial power.

In general, Japan has shown reluctance to play an international political role consistent with its vast economic power. From the mid-1970s onward, the balance of trade between Japan and the United States has weighed heavily in Japan's favor, leading to strains in U.S.-Japan relations and American charges that Japan engages in unfair trade practices. In a series of conferences of the noncommunist world's seven leading economic powers in the 1980s, Japan has pledged to take various measures to improve foreign access to Japan's domestic economy. In 1986–87 the Japanese yen appreciated markedly against the U.S. dollar. This has had relatively little effect on the balance of trade but has led to a marked increase in Japanese economic investment in the United States.

Domestically, Japan in the 1980s enjoyed a very high standard of living, marred by the extremely high cost and relatively low quality of housing, and by underinvestment in the public infrastructure. A real estate boom that led prices of commercial property in downtown Tokyo to increase as much as 200-fold in the span of a decade showed signs of softening in 1988.

Japan has been essentially a one-party state in the postwar period. National politics centers on factions within the ruling Liberal Democratic party (LDP). The government is run by political professionals operating according to a system of consensus. A resurgence of nationalism, seen in recent official revisions of school textbooks justifying Japan's role in World War II and in visits of government leaders to the Yasukuni Shrine to pay respects to Japan's war dead, has provoked protests from other Asian nations but little comment at home.

Emperor Hirohito died on Jan. 7, 1989, and was immediately succeeded by his son, Akihito.

Prime Minister Noboru Takeshita was forced to resign in May 1989 as a result of the so-called Recruit Scandal, involving bribery and corruption of senior LDP figures. His successor, Sousuke Uno, lasted only two months before resigning in a scandal over his sexual conduct. Public opinion turned sharply against the LDP, which lost control of the upper house of the Diet in July 1989 elections; the Socialist party, led by Takako Doi, posted significant gains.

Uno's successor, Toshiki Kaifu, expected to be a mere caretaker, has emerged as a skillful leader. Financial aid to Eastern Europe and the Soviet Union and the pledge of billions of dollars to support the Persian Gulf War mark a significant shift in Japan's role in world affairs.

Despite an agreement reached in early 1990 on "structural issues" relating to U.S.-Japan economic relations, trade tensions between the two countries remained strong.

# Jordan
## Hashemite Kingdom of Jordan

**Geography Location:** western Asia. **Boundaries:** Syria to N, Iraq to NE, Saudi Arabia to SE, Israel to W. **Total land area:** 37,738 sq. mi. (97,740 sq km). **Coastline:** 16 mi. (26 km). **Comparative area:** between Indiana and Kentucky. **Land use:** 4% arable land; 0.5% permanent crops; 1% meadows and pastures; 0.5% forest and woodland; 94% other; includes 0.5% irrigated. **Major cities:** (1986) Amman (capital) 972,000; Zagra 392,220; Irbid 271,000; Salt 134,100.

**People Population:** 3,064,508 (1990). **Nationality:** noun—Jordanian(s); adjective—Jordanian. **Ethnic groups:** 98% Arab, 1% Circassian, 1% Armenian. **Languages:** Arabic (official); English widely understood among upper and middle classes. **Religions:** 95% Sunni Muslim, 5% Christian.

**Government Type:** constitutional monarchy. **Independence:** May 25, 1946 (from League of Nations Mandate under British administration). **Constitution:** Jan. 8, 1952. **National holiday:** Independence Day, May 25. **Heads of government:** Hussein ibn Talal, king (since Aug. 1952); Modar Badran, prime minister (since Dec. 1989). **Structure:** king holds balance of power; prime minister exercises executive authority in name of king; cabinet appointed by king and responsible to parliament; bicameral parliament with House of Representatives, dissolved by king in Feb. 1976 and reconvened Jan. 1984, following national elections; Senate last appointed by king in Jan. 1984; secular court system based on differing legal systems of former Transjordan and Palestine; law western in concept and structure; Sharia (religious) courts for Muslims, and religious community council courts for non-Muslim communities; desert police carry out quasi-judicial functions in desert areas.

**Economy Monetary unit:** Jordanian dinar. **Budget:** (1989 est.) *income:* $920 mil.; *expend.:* $1.6 bil. **GNP:** $5.2 bil., $1,760 per capita (1986). **Chief crops:** vegetables, fruits, olive oil, wheat; self-sufficient in only a few foodstuffs. **Livestock:** poultry, goats, sheep, cattle, camels. **Natural resources:** phosphates, potash, shale oil. **Major industries:** phosphate mining, petroleum refining, cement. **Labor force:** 550,000 (1987 est.); 20% agriculture, 20% mining and manufacturing. **Exports:** $910 mil. (f.o.b., 1989 est.); fruits, vegetables, phosphates, fertilizers. **Imports:** $1.7 bil. (c.i.f., 1989 est.); crude oil, textiles, capital goods, motor vehicles, foodstuffs. **Major trading partners:** *exports:* Iraq, Saudi Arabia, India, Kuwait, Japan, China, Yugoslavia, Indonesia; *imports:* EC, U.S., Saudi Arabia, Japan, Turkey, Romania, China, Taiwan.

**Intl. Orgs.** Arab League, FAO, G-77, IAEA, IBRD, ICAO, IDA, IFAD, IFC, ILO, IMF, IMO, INTELSAT, INTERPOL, ITU, NAM, UN, UNESCO, UPU, WHO, WIPO, WMO.

The present territory of the Kingdom of Jordan corresponds to the biblical lands of Edom, Gilead, and Moab. The ancient rock city of Petra was the capital of the Edomite and Nabataean kingdoms. The region was incorporated into the Roman Empire, and later the Latin Kingdom of Jerusalem; it was an important early center of Christianity.

In the 630s Jordan became one of the first areas outside Arabia to fall to the expansion of Islam. It became subject to the Caliphate, located at Damascus and later at Baghdad, and in the 11th century became part of the empire of the Seljuk Turks. The Crusades brought European invaders, but with little lasting impact. The Mongols conquered Jordan in the mid-13th century, and it later passed into the control of the Mamluk sultanate. In 1517 Jordan was incorporated into the Ottoman Empire.

Following the post–World War I breakup of the Ottoman Empire, Jordan came under British control as part of a League of Nations Mandate of Palestine. In 1921 Great Britain sponsored the establishment of a monarchy by Abdullah, son of Hussein ibn Ali, ruler of the Hejaz in Arabia. Britain recognized the independence of the Hashemite Kingdom of Transjordan in 1923; a 1928 treaty gave Britain the unrestricted right to station troops in the kingdom.

Transjordan supported the Allies in World War II and was rewarded with full independence in 1946, though, by treaty, strong military ties to Great Britain were maintained. In 1948 the kingdom joined the Arab League, changed its name to Jordan, and joined other Arab states in the first Arab-Israeli War. The war resulted in the occupation by Jordanian troops of the West Bank and the Old City of Jerusalem, which were formally annexed in 1950.

The present ruler, King Hussein I, came to the throne on Aug. 11, 1952. All British military forces were withdrawn from the kingdom in 1957.

Israel recaptured the West Bank and the Old City of Jerusalem in the Six-Day War of 1967, and large numbers of Palestinian refugees fled to Jordan. Jordan played no substantial role in the October 1974 Arab-Israeli War. In 1974 Jordan accepted the decision of an Arab summit conference designating the Palestine Liberation Organization the sole representative of Palestinians in the West Bank. Jordan's role as a front-line opponent of Israel has won it a large annual subvention from Arab oil states; King Hussein's reputation as an Arab moderate has led to significant American economic and military support.

King Hussein strongly opposed the 1979 Camp David Accords and the Egypt-Israeli peace treaty; Jordan broke off diplomatic relations with Egypt in March 1979 but resumed full relations in 1984.

In July 1971 King Hussein, charging the Palestine Liberation Organization with subversion, had forced withdrawal of PLO troops and political headquarters from Jordan. While some hoped that Hussein would represent the Palestinians in talks with Israel, in 1988 the king flatly rejected any such role, implied that the PLO should declare an independent state on the West Bank and in the Gaza Strip, and declared that any future settlement would require direct talks between Israel and the PLO.

The Persian Gulf War had a drastic impact on Jordan's economy. King Hussein actively backed Iraq, thus jeopardizing direct aid from Kuwait and Saudi Arabia. The return of Jordanian workers from those countries, and the loss of trade with Iraq, also contributed to high unemployment.

Most of Jordan's territory is arid, and the kingdom has no petroleum reserves. The economy depends in part on subsidies from Arab oil states. Grain, olives, dates, fruit, and vegetables are grown in the fertile western region of the country; potassium and potash are mined, and cement is produced. Other industries include textiles, food processing, and light manufacturing.

# Kenya
## Republic of Kenya

**Geography** **Location:** eastern Africa. **Boundaries:** Sudan to NW, Ethiopia to N, Somalia to E, Indian Ocean to SE, Tanzania to SW, Lake Victoria, Uganda to W. **Total land area:** 219,788 sq. mi. (569,250 sq km). **Coastline:** 333 mi. (536 km). **Comparative area:** between California and Texas. **Land use:** 3% arable land; 1% permanent crops; 7% meadows and pastures; 4% forest and woodland; 85% other; includes negl. % irrigated. **Major cities:** (1969 census) Nairobi (capital) 1,103,554; Mombasa 247,073 (1984 est.); Nakuru 47,151; Kisumu 32,431; Thika 18,387.

**People** **Population:** 24,639,261 (1990). **Nationality:** noun—Kenyan(s); adjective—Kenyan. **Ethnic groups:** 21% Kikuyu, 14% Luhya, 13% Luo, 11% Kalenjin, 11% Kamba, 6% Kisii, 6% Meru, 1% Asian, European, Arab; 17% other. **Languages:** English and Swahili (both official), indigenous languages. **Religions:** 38% Protestant, 28% Catholic, 26% indigenous beliefs, 6% Muslim, 2% other.

**Government** **Type:** republic within Commonwealth. **Independence:** Dec. 12, 1963 (from UK). **Constitution:** Dec. 12, 1963. **National holiday:** Jamhuri Day, Dec. 12. **Heads of government:** Daniel T. arap Moi, president (since Oct. 1978). **Structure:** executive—president and cabinet; legislative—unicameral National Assembly of 200 seats, 188 elected by constituencies and 12 appointed by president; judiciary—high court, with chief justice and at least 11 justices, has unlimited original jurisdiction to hear and determine any civil or criminal proceeding; provision for courts of appeal.

**Economy** **Monetary unit:** Kenyan shilling. **Budget:** (1987) *income:* $2.3 bil.; *expend.:* $2.6 bil. **GDP:** $8.5 bil., $360 per capita (1989 est.). **Chief crops:** cash crops—coffee, tea, sisal, pyrethrum, cotton; food crops—corn, wheat, sugarcane, rice, cassava; largely self-sufficient in food; an illegal producer of cannabis for international drug trade. **Livestock:** cattle, goats, sheep, camels, pigs. **Natural resources:** gold, limestone, diatomite, salt barytes, magnesite. **Major industries:** small-scale consumer goods (plastic, furniture, batteries, textiles, soap, cig-

arettes, flour), agricultural processing, oil refining. **Labor force:** 7.4 mil. (1985); 50% public sector, 18% industry and commerce, 17% agriculture, 13% services; 1.1 mil. wage earners; 45% of population of working age. **Exports:** $1 bil. (f.o.b., 1988); 20% coffee, 18% tea, 15% manufactures, 10% petroleum products. **Imports:** $1.8 bil. (f.o.b., 1988); 36% machinery and transport equipment, 33% raw materials, 20% fuels and lubricants, 11% food and consumer goods. **Major trading partners:** (1987) *exports:* 45% Western Europe, 22% Africa, 10% Far East, 4% U.S., 3% Middle East; *imports:* 49% Western Europe, 20% Far East, 19% Middle East, 7% U.S.

**Intl. Orgs.** Commonwealth, FAO, G-77, GATT, IAEA, IBRD, ICAO, IDA, IFAD, IFC, ILO, IMF, IMO, INTELSAT, INTERPOL, ITU, NAM, UN, UNESCO, UPU, WHO, WIPO, WMO.

Kenya formed part of an ancient network of trade between the Red Sea and the coast of East Africa as early as the fourth century B.C. Persian and Arab trading posts were established on the coast by the eighth century A.D. At about the same time, the indigenous Cushitic people of Kenya had been joined by Bantu and Nilotic immigrants. Swahili, a mixture of Bantu and Arabic, developed as a language of trade throughout the region.

Portuguese explorers reached Kenya in 1498. Portuguese control of the coastal area ended in 1729, when the region came under the control of the sultans of Oman. British adventurers explored Kenya in the late 19th century. In 1885 the Berlin Conference divided East Africa into European spheres of influence. The British East Africa Company established a protectorate over the coastal region in 1890 and extended its control into the interior in 1895. British settlers established farms, mission stations, and towns, and Kenya was given colonial status in 1920.

During World War II, northern Kenya was briefly occupied by troops from the Italian colony of Ethiopia. After the British reasserted control, Africans were granted the right to participate in local government in 1944.

From 1952 to 1959, a state of emergency was declared in Kenya because of the "Mau Mau" rebellion against British colonial rule. In response to local unrest, British authorities widened African participation in government and Africans were elected to the Legislative Council in 1957.

Kenya became independent on Dec. 12, 1963, and in 1964 assumed the status of a republic within the British Commonwealth. Jomo Kenyatta, a member of the dominant Kikuyu population and leader of the main political party, the Kenya African National Union (KANU), was elected Kenya's first president. The minority Kenya African Democratic Union (KADU) voluntarily amalgamated itself with KANU in 1964. A leftist party, the Kenya People's Union (KPU) was organized in 1966, led by Oginga Odinga. In 1969 it was implicated in the assassination of Tom Mboya, a prominent political leader; its leaders were imprisoned and the party dissolved. Since 1969 KANU has

been Kenya's sole political party.

Kenyatta died on Aug. 22, 1978, and Vice Pres. Daniel arap Moi succeeded him. In 1982 the constitution was amended to make Kenya a one-party state. Moi was reelected president in 1983 and again in 1988. The latter election was controversial because, for the first time since independence, it was conducted without the use of secret ballots. In recent years foreign observers have accused the Moi government of widespread human rights abuses, and in 1989 the government banned several publications critical of its policies and cracked down on dissent. Unrest spread after Foreign Minister Robert Ouko died under mysterious circumstances, and riots broke out in several cities in 1990. In 1991, Odinga announced plans to form an opposition in direct defiance of the government.

Despite numerous changes in the form of government (federation to republic, parliamentary to presidential, multiparty to single-party, bicameral to unicameral legislature), Kenya has enjoyed a degree of political stability since independence. This could change as Moi refuses to open the political process. Kenya enjoyed a high rate of economic growth in the 1960s, but the growth rate slowed in the 1970s, while the population increased at the highest rate in the world. Most of Kenya's people are engaged in agriculture and animal husbandry. Unemployment is estimated at 30 percent, and even higher in urban areas.

Kenya's economy began to recover somewhat in the mid-1980s, bolstered by high international prices for its chief export, coffee, by excellent grain harvests, and by a burgeoning tourist industry. Industrial development remains slow and plagued by inefficiencies, while the country's basic infrastructure remains underdeveloped.

Kenya's tourist industry has been hurt by reports of poaching and banditry in the national parks. Kenya was a leader in obtaining a ban on world trade in ivory in 1989.

# Kiribati
## Republic of Kiribati

**Geography** **Location:** 33 atolls, in three main groups (E to W: Line Is., Phoenix Is., Gilbert Is.) in mid-Pacific Ocean; about 2,400 mi. (3,870 km) E to W and 1,275 mi. (2,050 km) N to S. Tarawa (Gilberts) 1°30′N, 173°00′E. **Boundaries:** surrounded by Pacific Ocean; nearest neighbors are Nauru to W, and Tuvalu and Tokelau to S. **Total land area:** 332 sq. mi. (861 sq km). **Coastline:** 710 mi. (1,143 km). **Comparative area:** about five times size of Washington, D.C. **Land use:** 0% arable land; 51% permanent crops; 0% meadows and pastures; 3% forest and woodland; 46% other. **Major cities:** Tarawa (capital).

**People** **Population:** 70,012 (1990). **Nationality:** noun—Kiribatian(s); adjective—Kiribati. **Ethnic groups:** Micronesian. **Languages:** English (official), Gilbertese. **Religions:** 48% Roman Catholic, 45% Protestant (Congregational), some Seventh-Day Adventist and Baha'i.

**Government Type:** republic. **Independence:** July 12, 1979 (from UK). **Constitution:** July 12, 1979. **National holiday:** none. **Heads of government:** Ieremia T. Tabai, president (since July 1979). **Structure:** nationally elected president; unicameral legislature—National Assembly (composed of 39 elected members and one nominated representative of Banaban community).

**Economy Monetary unit:** Australian dollar. **Budget:** (1988) *income:* $22 mil.; *expend.:* $12.7 mil. **GDP:** $34 mil., $500 per capita (1985). **Chief crops:** coconuts, copra; subsistence crops of roots and tubers, vegetables, melons, bananas; pigs and chickens; domestic fishing. **Livestock:** chickens, pigs. **Natural resources:** phosphate (production discontinued in 1979). **Major industries:** fishing and handicrafts. **Labor force:** 7,870 economically active (1985 est.). **Exports:** $5.1 mil. (1988); 55% fish, 42% copra. **Imports:** $21.5 mil. (c.i.f., 1988); foodstuffs, fuel, transportation equipment. **Major trading partners:** (1985) *exports:* 20% EC, 12% Marshall Islands, 8% U.S., 4% American Samoa; *imports:* 39% Australia, 21% Japan, 6% New Zealand, 6% UK, 3% U.S.

**Intl. Orgs.** Commonwealth, GATT (de facto), ICAO, IMF, WHO.

In 1892 the British established a protectorate over the Gilbert Islands, inhabited principally by Micronesians. In 1915 Britain joined the islands administratively with the Polynesian-speaking Ellice Islands to the south to form a British colony, the Gilbert and Ellice Islands (later expanded to include other islands). The Japanese occupied the Gilberts in 1942; in 1943 the Allied forces recaptured them, and Tarawa was the scene of some of the fiercest combat in the Pacific.

In 1971 Britain granted the colony self-rule. The Ellice Islands broke away in 1975, becoming the independent nation of Tuvalu in 1978. On July 12, 1979, the Gilbert Islands became independent as Kiribati. United States claims to portions of the Line and Phoenix islands were settled by a friendship treaty in 1979.

Kiribati's economy is based on subsistence farming and on fishing. Copra exports and the sale of fishing rights (principally to Japan) are the main earners of hard currency. The islands remain heavily dependent on foreign aid, principally from the United Kingdom.

## Korea, North
### Democratic People's Republic of Korea
**Geography Location:** northern part of Korean peninsula in eastern Asia. **Boundaries:** China to NW, Sea of Japan to E, Republic of Korea to S, Yellow Sea to SW. **Total land area:** 46,540 sq. mi. (120,538 sq km). **Coastline:** 1,551 mi. (2,495 km). **Comparative area:** between Pennsylvania and Mississippi. **Land use:** 18% arable land; 1% permanent crops; negl. % meadows and pastures; 74% forest and woodland; 7% other; includes 9% irrigated. **Major cities:** (1976 est.) Pyongyang (capital) 1,500,000; Chongjin 300,000; Hungnam 260,000; Kaesong 240,000.

**People Population:** 21,292,649 (1990). **Nationality:** noun—Korean(s); adjective—Korean. **Ethnic groups:** racially homogeneous. **Languages:** Korean. **Religions:** Buddhism and Confucianism; religious activities now almost nonexistent.

**Government Type:** communist state; one-man rule. **Constitution:** adopted 1948, revised Dec. 27, 1972. **National holiday:** Sept. 9. **Heads of government:** Kim Il Sung, president (since Dec. 1972); Yon Hyong Muk, prime minister (since Dec. 1988). **Structure:** Supreme People's Assembly theoretically supervises legislative and judicial functions; State Administration Council (cabinet) oversees ministerial operations.

**Economy Monetary unit:** won. **Budget:** (1989) *income:* $15.6 bil.; *expend.:* $15.6 bil.; **GNP:** $28 bil., $1,240 per capita (1986). **Chief crops:** corn, rice, vegetables; food shortages—meat, fish, cooking oils; production of foodstuffs adequate for domestic needs. **Livestock:** pigs, cattle, sheep, goats, horses. **Natural resources:** coal, lead, tungsten, zinc, graphite. **Major industries:** machine building, military products, electric power, chemicals. **Labor force:** 6.1 mil. (1980); 48% agricultural, 52% nonagricultural; shortage of skilled and unskilled labor. **Exports:** $2.4 bil. (1988); minerals, metallurgical products, agricultural products, manufactures. **Imports:** $3.1 bil. (1988); petroleum, machinery and equipment, coking coal, grain. **Major trading partners:** *exports:* USSR, China, Japan, W. Germany, Hong Kong, Singapore; *imports:* USSR, Japan, China, W. Germany, Hong Kong, Singapore.

**Intl. Orgs.** FAO, G-77, IAEA, ICAO, ITU, NAM, UNCTAD, UNESCO, UPU, WHO, WIPO, WMO; official observer status at UN.

(For pre-1945 history, see "Republic of Korea.")

The Soviet Union's declaration of war against Japan in the waning days of World War II strengthened its position in northeast Asia, and particularly in Korea. After Japan's surrender, Korea was arbitrarily divided into zones of Soviet and American occupation, north and south of latitude 38° north. The Korean Communist party (KCP), founded in 1922, had functioned in exile in the USSR during the Japanese occupation, and KCP workers were quickly moved into the Soviet zone in 1945.

U.S.-Soviet talks aimed at Korean reunification broke down, and in 1948 the establishment of separate regimes in North and South Korea formalized the postwar occupation zones. The Korean Democratic People's Republic was proclaimed on May 1, 1948, and its government was organized in September of that year. It inherited most of the industrial and hydroelectric power infrastructure built during the Japanese colonial period and enjoyed strong Soviet backing.

On June 25, 1950, North Korean troops crossed the 38th parallel in an effort to force the reunification of Korea under a communist regime. UN troops under American leadership came to the defense of the South. (For the Korean War, see "South Korea.") The war was fought to a stalemate, and a truce was signed on July 27, 1953.

North Korea has had a single leader throughout its national history: Kim Il Sung, chairman of the KCP since 1945 and president of the DPRK since 1972. Under Kim Il Sung, North Korea has been a typically Stalinist soviet nation, concentrating its economic energies on heavy industry and imposing a strictly regimented political and social life on its citizens. Economic development has been strongly supported by aid from the Soviet Union, and to a lesser degree, China. After an impressive program of postwar reconstruction in the 1950s and 1960s, the country has fallen into economic stagnation.

Until recently, relations between North and South Korea have been implacably hostile; the North has made numerous attempts to infiltrate and sabotage the South. On Oct. 9, 1983, 17 people, including four South Korean cabinet ministers, were killed in Rangoon, Burma, by a bomb planted by North Korean agents. Since 1985, occasional North-South discussions on such matters as permitting contacts between families divided by the war have produced little result. North Korea originally agreed to co-sponsor the 1988 Summer Olympics with South Korea but later boycotted the games. In 1990 the leaders of both countries held three cordial but unproductive meetings, although they agreed to field all-Korea teams at two international sporting events in 1991.

Current concerns center on new Soviet economic overtures to South Korea, and on attracting Japanese investment to stem its own economic decline.

## Korea, South
### Republic of Korea
**Geography Location:** southern part of Korean peninsula in eastern Asia. **Boundaries:** North Korea to N, separated by frontier roughly following 38th parallel; Sea of Japan to E, East China Sea to S, and Yellow Sea to W. **Total land area:** 38,291 sq. mi. (99,173 sq km). **Coastline:** 1,500 mi. (2,413 km). **Comparative area:** between Indiana and Kentucky. **Land use:** 21% arable land; 1% permanent crops; 1% meadows and pastures; 67% forest and woodland; 10% other; includes 12% irrigated. **Major cities:** (1985 census) Seoul (capital) 9,639,110; Pusan 3,514,798; Taegu 2,029,853; Inchon 1,386,911; Kwangju 905,896.

**People Population:** 43,045,098 (1990). **Nationality:** noun—Korean(s); adjective—Korean. **Ethnic groups:** homogeneous; small Chinese minority (about 20,000). **Languages:** Korean; English widely taught in high school. **Religions:** strong Confucian tradition; vigorous Christian minority (28% of total population); Buddhism; pervasive folk religion (shamanism); Chondokyo (religion of the heavenly way), eclectic religion with nationalist overtones founded in 19th century, claiming about 1.5 mil. adherents.

**Government Type:** republic; power centralized in strong executive. **Constitution:** approved by voters on Oct. 27, 1987, effective

Feb. 25, 1988; requires direct presidential elections and protects human rights. **National holiday:** Independence Day, Aug. 15. **Heads of government:** Roh Tae Woo, president (since Feb. 1988); Won S. Chung, prime minister (since May 1991). **Structure:** unicameral legislature (National Assembly), judiciary.

**Economy Monetary unit:** won. **Budget:** (1990) *income:* $33.6 bil.; *expend.:* $33.6 bil. **GNP:** $200 bil., $4,600 per capita (1989). **Chief crops:** 9 mil. people (22% of population) live in farm households, but agriculture, forestry, and fishing constitute 15% of GNP; main crops— rice, barley, vegetables, legumes. **Livestock:** chickens, pigs, cattle, ducks, rabbits. **Natural resources:** coal (limited), tungsten, graphite, molybdenum. **Major industries:** textiles and clothing, footwear, food processing. **Labor force:** 16.9 mil. (1987); 52% services and other, 21% agriculture, fishing, and forestry; 3% unemployment. **Exports:** $62.3 bil. (f.o.b., 1989); textiles and clothing, electrical machinery, footwear, steel, automobiles. **Imports:** $61.3 bil. (c.i.f., 1989); machinery, oil, steel, transport equipment, textiles. **Major trading partners:** *exports:* 33% U.S., 21% Japan; *imports:* 28% Japan, 25% U.S.

**Intl. Orgs.** Colombo Plan, FAO, G-77, GATT, IAEA, IBRD, ICAO, IDA, IFAD, IFC, IMF, IMO, INTELSAT, INTERPOL, ITU, UNCTAD, UNDP, UNESCO, UNICEF, UNIDO, UPU, WHO, WIPO, WMO; official observer status at UN.

From ancient times Korea has struggled successfully to preserve its national independence. To the native culture—marked by a warrior aristocracy, shamanic religion, and a subject class of rice cultivators—was added, under continuous Chinese influence, a strong adherence to Buddhism and a system of government modeled on Chinese Confucian bureaucratism. The three rival kingdoms of Silla, Paekche, and Koguryo were united, through Chinese intervention, in the seventh century A.D.; unified dynastic rule was maintained thereafter.

The Yi dynasty (1392–1910), under which Korea was known as the Kingdom of Choson, was a staunch tributary ally of China under both the Ming (1368–1644) and Qing (1644–1911) dynasties. A Japanese invasion of Korea in 1592 conquered most of the country but was finally repelled by combined Chinese and Korean forces. From the late 17th century to the 1870s, all non-Chinese foreign influence was rigorously excluded from the country.

Korea's isolation, and its status as a Chinese tributary, ended in 1874, when Japan imposed on it the Treaty of Kwanghwa, guaranteeing Japanese commercial access and other interests. The Sino-Japanese War of 1894–95 was fought primarily over the status of Korea; following Japan's victory in that war, Korea was made a Japanese protectorate and was annexed as a Japanese colony in 1910. A harsh colonial regime was established with the aim of eradicating Korean culture and incorporating Korea entirely into the Japanese empire. During the colonial period, Korean resistance to the Japanese regime was violently suppressed, but resistance movements survived in exile—notably the Korean Communist party in the Soviet Union and a republican movement in China. During World War II, tens of thousands of Koreans were conscripted as forced laborers to work in Japan and in Japanese-occupied territories.

Following Japan's surrender, Korea was arbitrarily divided into zones of Soviet and American occupation, north and south of 38° north latitude. The dividing line split Korea economically as well as geographically and politically; Korea's industry and hydroelectric power was concentrated in the north, while the south was primarily agricultural. In contrast to well-laid Soviet plans for installing a communist government in the north (see "North Korea"), American attempts to reunify the country under a republican regime were inept. By 1948 it had become clear that plans for reunification were hopeless. In May of that year, the Republic of Korea was organized in the south, with Dr. Syngman Rhee as president. The United States withdrew its occupation forces in June 1949.

On June 25, 1950, North Korean troops invaded the south in an apparent attempt to unify the country forcibly under the communist regime. An emergency session of the UN Security Council voted to send troops to Korea; the USSR, having boycotted the session, was unable to exercise its veto on North Korea's behalf. UN troops, dominated by American forces and commanded by Gen. Douglas MacArthur, launched a counterattack in September with a landing at Inchon and swept north, reaching the Chinese border by Nov. 20. On Nov. 26 the tide turned again when Chinese troops entered the war, ostensibly to defend the Chinese border but also to aid their North Korean allies in driving the UN forces south again. Seoul fell once more on Jan. 4, 1951. In February and March another UN counteroffensive drove the combined Chinese and North Korean forces back to the 38th parallel again. Thereafter, the battle lines remained generally stable, although fierce fighting continued at intervals for another two years. On Apr. 11, 1951, Gen. MacArthur was relieved of the Korean command for making unauthorized policy statements and was replaced by Gen. Matthew Ridgway.

Armistice talks began in July 1951 but broke down repeatedly. A truce was signed on July 27, 1953, creating a demilitarized zone along the 38th parallel and establishing a framework for talks on a permanent settlement of the war. Negotiations have continued fruitlessly at the Panmunjom armistice conference headquarters ever since.

Postwar reconstruction, with significant U.S. aid, was overseen by the government of Syngman Rhee. Pres. Rhee resigned in 1960 after a wave of student demonstrations charging him with corruption and undemocratic practices. On May 16, 1961, Gen. Park Chung Hee seized power in a military coup. The military government was given democratic trappings when in 1972 a referendum was passed allowing Gen. Park to run for an unlimited series of six-year presidential terms. Gen. Park was assassinated on Oct. 26, 1979, by the chief of intelligence of the Korean government. In the aftermath of this event, Gen. Chun Doo Hwan rose to power, continuing the military-rule policies of Gen. Park. Gen. Chun's regime was marked by widespread and violent political protest demonstrations.

Despite political repression, South Korea's economy made great strides under Gen. Chun's regime. The traditionally agrarian country was transformed into a modernized, urban, industrial nation. The industrial economy developed a dual structure, dominated by a few conglomerates but also with a very large number of small-scale firms. In 1986 South Korea for the first time achieved a favorable balance-of-payments ratio in foreign trade, and since then the favorable balance has increased rapidly, led by exports of automobiles, textiles and clothing, and consumer electronic goods.

After weeks of widespread demonstrations in mid-1987, Gen. Chun agreed to allow direct presidential elections to choose his successor. The elections, held in November 1987, were generally regarded as fair; the government candidate, Roh Tae Woo, achieved a plurality over the sharply divided opposition parties. Under Pres. Roh, the political situation has calmed, although student demonstrations have continued, calling for greater efforts for Korean reunification and protesting the presence of large numbers of American troops in the country.

The 1988 summer Olympics were held in South Korea, bringing widespread, favorable international attention. However, violent student protests have continued. Slower economic growth has led to labor unrest as well. On the positive side for Pres. Roh, South Korea's relations with China, Japan, and the Soviet Union have improved steadily, and all four nations are promoting better understanding between the two Koreas. Mikhail Gorbachev visited South Korea in 1990 and 1991 and indicated his willingness to enter into bilateral trade and diplomatic contacts despite the protests of North Korea. High-level talks between North and South began in 1990.

## Kuwait
### State of Kuwait

**Geography Location:** northeastern Arabian peninsula. **Boundaries:** Iraq to N, Saudi Arabia to S, Persian Gulf to E. **Total land area:** 6,880 sq. mi. (17,818 sq km). **Coastline:** 310 mi. (499 km). **Comparative area:** between Connecticut and New Jersey. **Land use:** negl. % arable land; 0% permanent crops; 8% meadows and pastures; negl. % forest and woodland; 92% other; includes negl. % irrigated. **Major cities:** (1985 census); Kuwait City (capital) 44,335; Salmiya 153,369; Hawalli 145,126; Faranawiya 68,701; Abraq Kheetan 45,120.

**People Population:** 2,123,711 (1990). **Nationality:** noun—Kuwaiti(s); adjective— Kuwaiti. **Ethnic groups:** 39% Kuwaiti, 39% other Arab, 9% South Asian, 4% Iranian, 9% other. **Languages:** Arabic (official), English widely spoken. **Religions:** 85% Muslim (30%

Shi'a, 45% Sunni, 10% other), 15% Christian, Hindu, Parsi, and other.

**Government** Type: nominal constitutional monarchy. **Independence:** June 19, 1961 (from UK). **Constitution:** Nov. 16, 1962 (some provisions suspended since Aug. 29, 1962). **National holiday:** National Day, Feb. 25. **Head of government:** Jaber al-Ahmad al-Jaber al Sabah, amir (since Dec. 1977); Salem Sabah al-Salem, prime minister (since Apr. 1991). **Structure:** executive—Council of Ministers; legislature—National Assembly (suspended since July 1986).

**Economy** Monetary unit: Kuwaiti dinar. **Budget:** (1988) *income:* $7.1 bil.; *expend.:* $10.5 bil. **GDP:** $20.5 bil., $10,500 per capita (1988). **Chief crops:** virtually none; dependent on imports for food; about 75% of potable water must be distilled or imported. **Livestock:** goats, sheep, cattle, camels. **Natural resources:** petroleum, fish, shrimp, natural gas. **Major industries:** petroleum, petrochemicals, desalination. **Labor force:** 566,000 (1986); 45% services, 20% construction, 12% trade; 70% of labor force is non-Kuwaiti. **Exports:** $7.1 bil. (f.o.b., 1988); 90% oil. **Imports:** $5.2 bil. (c.i.f., 1988); food, construction material, vehicles and parts, clothing. **Major trading partners:** *exports:* Japan, Italy, W. Germany, U.S.; *imports:* Japan, U.S., W. Germany, UK.

**Intl. Orgs.** Arab League, FAO, G-77, GATT, IAEA, IBRD, ICAO, IDA, IFAD, IFC, ILO, IMF, IMO, INTELSAT, INTERPOL, ITU, NAM, OPEC, UN, UNESCO, UPU, WHO, WMO.

Kuwait, at the head of the Persian Gulf, was part of the Abbasid empire from the eighth century and was absorbed into the Ottoman Empire in the late 16th century. It was organized as a principality under the al-Sabah dynasty in 1756, but the Ottomans continued to assert sovereignty. Increasing British influence during the 19th century was formalized in 1899, when Kuwait became a British protectorate.

The discovery of oil, first exported from Kuwait after World War II, rapidly made the principality one of the wealthiest in the Middle East. The British protectorate ended in 1961, when Kuwait gained full independence. The great majority of oil field workers in Kuwait are non-Kuwaiti Arabs, including many Palestinians. Oil revenues have made possible a total welfare state for Kuwaiti citizens, who pay no taxes and enjoy a wide range of free social services.

Kuwait allied itself with Iraq in the Iran-Iraq War of 1980–88; Kuwaiti tankers came under heavy attack from Iranian warships in the gulf. In July 1987, Kuwaiti tankers were reflagged with the U.S. flag and placed under escort of American warships in an operation that continued into 1989. Most of Kuwait's territory is barren and sparsely inhabited.

On Aug. 2, 1990, Kuwait was invaded, and later annexed, by Iraq. In February 1991 it was liberated by a coalition of Arab, non-Arab Muslim, and Western nations led by the United States. Much of the country was destroyed or looted by the Iraqis, who also ignited fires at

more than 500 oil wells, thereby causing one of the worst environmental disasters in history. Since its return to power, the ruling al-Sabah family has come under strong pressure both at home and abroad to institute democratic reforms. (See Part I, "The Year in Review.")

## Laos
### Lao People's Democratic Republic
**Geography** Location: landlocked country in Southeast Asia. **Boundaries:** Myanmar to NW, China to N, Vietnam to E, Cambodia to S, and Thailand to W. **Total land area:** 91,400 sq. mi. (236,800 sq km). **Coastline:** none. **Comparative area:** slightly larger than Utah. **Land use:** 4% arable land; negl. % permanent crops; 3% meadows and pastures; 58% forest and woodland; 35% other; includes 1% irrigated. **Major cities:** (1973) Vientiane (capital) 176,637; Savannaket 50,690; Pakse 44,860; Luang Prabang 44,244; Saya Bury 13,775.

**People** Population: 4,023,736 (1990). **Nationality:** noun—Lao (sing. and pl.); adjective—Laotian or Lao. **Ethnic groups:** 50% Lao, 20% ethnic Thai, 15% Phouteung (Kha), 15% Meo, Hmong, Yao, and other. **Languages:** Lao (official), French, English. **Religions:** 85% Buddhist, 15% animist and other.

**Government** Type: communist state. **Independence:** July 19, 1949 (from France). **Constitution:** draft constitution under discussion since 1976. **National holiday:** Dec. 2. **Heads of government:** Souphanouvong, president (since 1975); Phoumi Vongvichit, acting president (since Oct. 1986); Kaysone Phomvihane, prime minister (since Dec. 1975). **Structure:** president; Supreme People's Assembly; cabinet; cabinet is totally Communist but council contains a few nominal neutralists and non-Communists; National Congress of People's Representatives established current government structure in Dec. 1975.

**Economy** Monetary unit: new kip. **Budget:** (1988 est.) *income:* $71.0 mil.; *expend.:* $198 mil. **GDP:** $585 mil., $150 per capita (1989 est.). **Chief crops:** rice (overwhelmingly dominant), corn, vegetables, tobacco, coffee; formerly self-sufficient; food shortages (due in part to distribution deficiencies) include rice; illegal producer of opium poppy and cannabis for international drug trade. **Livestock:** pigs, buffalo, cattle, goats, horses. **Natural resources:** tin, timber, gypsum, hydropower potential. **Major industries:** tin mining, timber, electric power. **Labor force:** about 1–1.5 mil.; 85–90% in agriculture, est.; 17% unemployment. **Exports:** $57.5 mil. (f.o.b., 1989 est.); electricity, wood products, coffee, tin. **Imports:** $219.0 mil. (c.i.f., 1989 est.); food, fuel oil, consumer goods, manufactures. **Major trading partners:** *exports:* Thailand, Malaysia, Vietnam, USSR, U.S.; *imports:* Thailand, USSR, Japan, France, Vietnam.

**Intl. Orgs.** Colombo Plan, FAO, G-77, IBRD, ICAO, IDA, IFAD, ILO, IMF, INTERPOL, ITU, NAM, UN, UNCTAD, UNESCO, UPU, WHO, WMO.

Inhabited by the Thai-speaking Lao people in the river valleys and by Hmong and other tribal people in the highlands, Laos historically had little national cohesion and was dominated by its more powerful neighbors, Siam (Thailand) to the west and Vietnam to the east. In 1893 France forced Siam to recognize Laos as a French protectorate; the country was thereafter incorporated into the French Union of Indochina. Laos was occupied by Japan during World War II but saw little major fighting.

In 1946 Laos was united under the Luang Prabang dynasty and was granted local autonomy as a constitutional monarchy in 1949. During the final phases of the Indochina War against French colonialism in 1953–54, Vietnamese Communist (Vietminh) incursions reinforced the position of the Laotian Communist party (Pathet Lao) in Laotian politics. Following the French withdrawal in December 1954, Laos became an independent nation and was admitted to the United Nations in 1955.

The creation of a coalition government under Prince Souvana Phouma in 1962 temporarily resolved a turbulent political situation; an international agreement signed in Geneva in that year guaranteed Laos's neutrality. The Pathet Lao withdrew from the coalition in 1964 and renewed its armed uprising against the government, with North Vietnamese support. American planes bombed Vietnamese supply lines along the Ho Chi Minh trail, and American agents recruited Hmong tribesmen as irregular troops to attack Pathet Lao positions. The Pathet Lao nevertheless made steady gains, especially after 1970. In 1973, Prince Souvana Phouma ordered a cease-fire, and in 1975 the Pathet Lao took control of the capital, Vientiane. The Lao People's Democratic Republic was proclaimed on Dec. 3, 1975. Large numbers of Hmong and other tribal people fled to Thailand.

Subsequently, Laos has been strongly dominated by Vietnam, which has stationed significant numbers of troops in the country. Attempts to collectivize the economy have had only partial success. Economic activity continues to be limited mainly to small-scale agriculture and some tin mining and small industry.

## Lebanon
### Republic of Lebanon
**Geography** Location: western Asia. **Boundaries:** Syria to N and E, Israel to S, Mediterranean Sea to W. **Total land area:** 4,036 sq. mi. (10,452 sq km). **Coastline:** 140 mi. (225 km). **Comparative area:** between Delaware and Connecticut. **Land use:** 21% arable land; 9% permanent crops; 1% meadows and pastures; 8% forest and woodland; 61% other; includes 7% irrigated. **Major cities:** (1975 est.) Beirut (capital) 1,500,000; Tarabulus (Tripoli) 160,-000; Zahleh 45,000; Saida (Sidon) 38,000; Sur (Tyre) 14,000.

**People** Population: 3,300,802 (1989). **Nationality:** noun—Lebanese (sing., pl.); adjective—Lebanese. **Ethnic groups:** 93% Arab, 6% Armenian, 1% other. **Languages:** Arabic and French (both official), Armenian, English.

**Religions:** 75% Islam, 25% Christian, negl. Judaism.

**Government Type:** republic. **Independence:** Nov. 22, 1943 (from League of Nations Mandate under French administration). **Constitution:** May 25, 1926 (amended). **National holiday:** Independence Day, Nov. 22. **Heads of government:** M. Elias Hraoui, president (since Nov. 1989); Omar Karame, prime minister (since Dec. 1990). **Structure:** power lies with president, who is elected by unicameral legislature (National Assembly); cabinet appointed by president, approved by legislature; independent secular courts on French pattern; religious courts for matters of marriage, divorce, inheritance, etc.; by custom, president is Maronite Christian, prime minister is Sunni Muslim, and president of legislature is Shia Muslim; parliament seats 108 members, half Christian and half Muslim.

**Economy Monetary unit:** Lebanese pound. **Budget:** (1988 est.) *income:* $50 mil.; *expend.:* $650 mil. **GDP:** $2.3 bil., $700 per capita (1989 est.). **Chief crops:** fruits, wheat, corn, barley, potatoes; not self-sufficient in food; illegal producer of opium poppy and cannabis for international drug trade. **Livestock:** goats, sheep, cattle, asses, pigs. **Natural resources:** limestone, iron ore, salt; water-surplus state in water-deficit region. **Major industries:** banking, food processing, textiles. **Labor force:** 650,000 (1985); 79% industry, commerce, and services, 11% agriculture, 10% government; 33% unemployment (1987 est.). **Exports:** $1 bil. (f.o.b., 1987); agricultural products, chemicals, textiles, precious and semiprecious metals, and jewelry. **Imports:** $1.5 bil. (f.o.b., 1987); N.A. **Major trading partners:** *exports:* 16% Saudi Arabia, 8% Switzerland, 6% Jordan, 6% Kuwait, 5% U.S.; *imports:* 14% Italy, 12% France, 6% U.S., 5% Turkey, 3% Saudi Arabia.

**Intl. Orgs.** Arab League, FAO, G-77, IAEA, IBRD, ICAO, IDA, IFAD, IFC, ILO, IMF, IMO, INTELSAT, INTERPOL, ITU, NAM, UN, UNESCO, UPU, WHO, WMO.

The ancient history of Lebanon is essentially coextensive with that of Syria, of which it was long a part. The port cities of Tripoli, Tyre, and Sidon were important centers of the Phoenician empire. The parallel ranges of the Lebanon and Anti-Lebanon mountains, crowned with the country's famous cedar trees, enclose the fertile Bekaa Valley. The coastal cities became strongholds of early Christianity, later fragmented into numerous sects, including Maronites (Syrian Catholic), Roman Catholic, Greek Orthodox, Syrian Orthodox, and others. The mountains of the south became the center of the Druze sect of Islam, while orthodox Sunni Islam dominated in the Bekaa Valley.

Lebanon came under French influence in the late 18th century, as France claimed the role of protector of Syria's Christian community. France intervened in Lebanon in 1841 and again in 1860 when fighting between Maronite and Druze communities led to the massacre of many Christians. Under pressure from France, the Ottoman Empire granted some local autonomy to the Maronites of greater Lebanon.

In the dismemberment of the Ottoman Empire after World War I, France was granted a League of Nations Mandate over the Levant States (Lebanon and Syria), ensuring French control of the Iraq Petroleum Company pipeline from Iraq to Tripoli. In 1926 Lebanon became a self-governing republic under the mandate, but internal unrest and anti-French sentiment continued. In 1936 France promised to grant full independence to Lebanon in three years, but the agreement was not implemented.

In June 1940 the French administration in Lebanon declared its allegiance to the Vichy government. British and Free French forces occupied Lebanon in June 1941 and declared it an independent republic; but the French retained control, and full independence did not come until Jan. 1, 1944.

Under a National Covenant declared in 1943, political power in the Lebanese parliament was apportioned among the nation's various communities. The president was always to be a Maronite Christian, the prime minister a Sunni Muslim. This provided a workable formula for power sharing but also ensured that the national government would always be hostage to the considerable political, economic, and even military power of separate communities and clans.

The years from the end of World War II to the early 1970s were a brief golden age for Lebanon. Beirut developed into a wealthy, cosmopolitan city, the center of Middle Eastern banking and trade, while agriculture, pastoralism, and small-scale industry flourished in the rest of the country. A Syrian-backed Muslim uprising in 1958 had no significant impact; U.S. Marines landed in May 1958 to protect American interests and remained until October. By the late 1960s, however, Lebanon's stability was threatened by PLO attacks on Israel from Palestinian refugee camps in southern Lebanon and by a shift in the country's demographic balance. Muslims had become a majority in Lebanon by the late 1960s and demanded a revision of the National Covenant, while Maronite Christians continued to cling to their position of political dominance.

Throughout the 1970s, Palestinian raids from Lebanon into Israel brought Israeli retaliatory strikes in southern Lebanon. Israeli troops occupied southern Lebanon in March 1978 and again in April 1980. The Palestinian-Israeli conflict polarized opinion within Lebanon, inflaming nationalist and anti-Western feelings among Lebanon's Sunni Muslims.

Civil war broke out in 1975, with Palestinian and leftist Muslim militias battling militias of the Maronite community, the Christian Phalange party, and other groups. More than 60,000 died, and damage ranged into the billions of dollars. Syrian troops intervened in 1976, battling Palestinian forces in an attempt to restore the status quo. Arab League efforts to negotiate a cease-fire produced an unstable peace at the end of 1976, though Syrian troops remained in Lebanon.

Fighting broke out between Syrian forces and Christian militiamen near Zahle on Apr. 1, 1981. Other groups joined the fighting in a general war of each against all. Israel staged commando raids against Palestinian positions in Tyre and Tulin. Israeli air raids on Beirut caused extensive loss of life and property damage. A Palestinian-Israeli cease-fire went into effect on July 24, but hostilities continued within Lebanon.

Israel invaded Lebanon in a full-scale air and sea assault on June 6, 1982, in an attempt to drive out the PLO. Israeli and Syrian forces came into direct conflict in the Bekaa Valley. Israeli forces surrounded Beirut and began a heavy bombardment of the city. On Aug. 1, Palestinian forces withdrew from Beirut under international supervision. On Sept. 14 newly elected Pres. Bashir Gemayel, a Maronite Christian, was assassinated; Israeli troops occupied the Muslim quarters of West Beirut in response. With tacit Israeli approval, Christian militiamen invaded two refugee camps on Sept. 16 and slaughtered hundreds of Palestinian civilians.

Beirut remained a battle zone in 1983, divided by the "Green Line" into Christian and Muslim sectors. Terrorist bombings were common. The United States, France, Italy, and other Western nations stationed troops in Beirut in an attempt to enforce a cease-fire. Fifty people were killed when a bomb partly destroyed the U.S. embassy on Apr. 18; separate attacks on military installations on Oct. 23 killed 241 U.S. Marines and 58 French soldiers.

Rashid Karami became premier with Syrian support on Apr. 26, 1984. Meanwhile, the civil war continued, with fighting among various groups of Christian, Druze, Sunni, Shiite, and Palestinian militias. Full-scale war between Shiite and Palestinian forces broke out in May 1985. Israeli forces withdrew from most of Lebanon in June, but maintained a "security zone" in the southern part of the country.

Kidnappings of foreign nationals at the hands of various terrorist factions became commonplace in the late 1980s. Premier Karami was assassinated on June 1, 1987, when a bomb destroyed his helicopter.

At an October 1989 Arab League-sponsored meeting, Christian and Muslim leaders agreed on a new national charter. The Taif accord was condemned by Christian militants, led by Gen. Michel Aoun, and Muslim militia leaders. Newly elected Pres. René Mowad, a Syrian-backed Christian, was assassinated on Nov. 22 and succeeded by Elias Hrawi. A revolt by Aoun was put down in October with the help of Syrian forces.

In November 1990, rival Shiite militias—the Syrian-backed Amal and Iranian-backed Party of God—signed an agreement ending three years of fighting. In February 1991 Lebanese troops moved to defend the area for the first time in 13 years and called for Israel to abandon its "security zone" in southern Lebanon. Palestinian guerrillas and Israelis continued to harrass each other across the border.

In addition to leaving 150,000 dead, the civil war severely disrupted the national economy, virtually wiping out the international sector and causing significant damage to the domestic sector.

## Lesotho
### Kingdom of Lesotho

**Geography** **Location:** landlocked country in southern Africa. **Boundaries:** entirely surrounded by South African territory. **Total land area:** 11,720 sq. mi. (30,355 sq km). **Coastline:** none. **Comparative area:** slightly larger than Maryland. **Land use:** 10% arable land; 0% permanent crops; 66% meadows and pastures; 0% forest and woodland; 24% other. **Major cities:** (1976) Maseru (capital) 45,000.

**People** **Population:** 1,711,072 (1989). **Nationality:** noun—Mosotho (sing.), Basotho (pl.); adjective—Basotho. **Ethnic groups:** 99.7% Sotho; 1,600 Europeans, 800 Asians. **Languages:** Sesotho and English (official); Zulu, Xhosa. **Religions:** 80% Christian, 20% indigenous beliefs.

**Government** **Type:** constitutional monarchy; independent member of Commonwealth. **Independence:** Oct. 4, 1966 (from UK). **Constitution:** Oct. 4, 1966, suspended Jan. 1970. **National holiday:** Oct. 4. **Heads of government:** Letsie III, king (since Nov. 1990); Maj. Gen. Elias P. Ramaema, prime minister (since May 1991). **Structure:** executive and legislative authority nominally vested in king; real power rests with Military Council, established after Jan. 1986 coup; 20-member Council of Ministers responsible for administrative duties; judiciary—63 Basotho courts administer customary law, high court and subordinate courts have criminal jurisdiction, court of appeal at Maseru has appellate jurisdiction.

**Economy** **Monetary unit:** maloti. **Budget:** (1989 est.) **income:** $159 mil.; **expend.:** $224 mil. **GDP:** $412 mil., $245 per capita. **Chief crops:** corn, wheat, pulses, sorghum, barley; mostly subsistence farming and livestock. **Livestock:** sheep, goats, cattle, horses, asses. **Natural resources:** some diamonds and other minerals, water, agricultural and grazing land. **Major industries:** tourism. **Labor force:** 662,000 economically active (1985 est.); 86.2% subsistence agriculture; 150,000-250,000 spend from six months to many years as wage earners in South Africa. **Exports:** labor to South Africa (remittances $300 mil. est. in 1985); $55 mil. (f.o.b., 1989 est.); wool, mohair, wheat, cattle, peas. **Imports:** $526 mil. (f.o.b., 1989 est.); mainly corn, building materials, clothing, vehicles, machinery. **Major trading partners:** (1985) **exports:** 87% South Africa, 10% EC; **imports:** 95% South Africa, 2% EC.

**Intl. Orgs.** Commonwealth, FAO, G-77, GATT (de facto), IBRD, ICAO, IDA, IFAD, IFC, ILO, IMF, INTERPOL, ITU, NAM, UN, UNESCO, UPU, WHO, WMO.

Lesotho, formerly known as Basutoland, is an independent kingdom surrounded entirely by the Republic of South Africa. The area was sparsely populated by Bushmen until the 16th century when refugees from tribal wars in surrounding areas began to move in, an influx that continued through the 19th century. These immigrants eventually coalesced into a fairly homogenous cultural group, the Basothos.

Under King Moshoeshoe, who ruled from 1823 to 1870, several Basotho groups were consolidated. But during his reign much land was lost in a series of wars with South Africa, and Moshoeshoe appealed to Queen Victoria for aid. In 1868 the nation became a British protectorate. Between 1884 and 1959 all executive and legislative authority was in the hands of a British high commissioner. In 1903 a Basotho consultative body was established, and in 1959 a new constitution gave the council power to legislate on internal affairs.

The British began to move the country toward full independence, and on Oct. 4, 1966, Basutoland achieved full independence as the Kingdom of Lesotho. The first elections after independence, held in January 1970, were nullified by the leader of the ruling Basutoland National Party (BNP) when early returns indicated that the party might lose. A state of emergency was declared, the constitution was suspended, and parliament dissolved.

Elections in 1985 were boycotted by opposition parties, and in 1986 the BNP government was ousted in a coup. The nation is now run by a military council, which in Feb. 1990 stripped King Moshoeshoe II of his remaining powers. Although critical of apartheid, Lesotho has long had close economic ties with South Africa. In late 1982 South African troops entered Lesotho, claiming that the African National Congress was launching raids from inside Lesotho. But the new military regime has worked to improve relations with South Africa, lessening its criticism of apartheid and increasing economic ties.

## Liberia
### Republic of Liberia

**Geography** **Location:** western Africa. **Boundaries:** Sierra Leone, Guinea to N, Ivory Coast to E, Atlantic Ocean to S and W. **Total land area:** 37,743 sq. mi. (97,754 sq km). **Coastline:** 360 mi. (579 km). **Comparative area:** between Indiana and Kentucky. **Land use:** 1% arable land; 3% permanent crops; 2% meadows and pastures; 39% forest and woodland; 55% other; includes negl. % irrigated. **Major cities:** (1984) Monrovia (capital) 421,058.

**People** **Population:** 2,639,809. **Nationality:** noun—Liberian(s); adjective—Liberian. **Ethnic groups:** 95% indigenous peoples, including Kpelle, Bassa, Gio, Kru, Grebo, Mano, Krahn, Gola, Gbandi, Loma, Kissi, Vai, Bella; 5% descendants of repatriated slaves known as Americo-Liberians. **Languages:** 20% English (official); more than 20 languages of Niger-Congo language group. **Religions:** 70% indigenous beliefs, 20% Muslim, 10% Christian.

**Government** **Type:** republic. **Independence:** July 26, 1847. **Constitution:** Jan. 6, 1986. **National holiday:** Independence Day, July 26. **Heads of government:** Dr. Amos Sawyer, president (since Apr. 1991). **Structure:** executive—president, assisted by appointed cabinet; legislative—bicameral legislature; judiciary.

**Economy** **Monetary unit:** uses U.S. dollar and Liberian dollar. **Budget:** (1989) **income:** $242.1 mil.; **expend.:** $435.4 mil. **GDP:** $988 mil., $395 per capita (1988). **Chief crops:** rubber, rice, oil palm, cassava, coffee, cocoa; imports rice and wheat. **Livestock:** sheep, goats, pigs, cattle; imports livestock. **Natural resources:** iron ore, timber, diamonds, gold. **Major industries:** rubber processing, food processing, construction materials. **Labor force:** 510,000; 70.5% agriculture, 10.8% services, 4.5% industry and commerce, 14.2% other; 220,000 wage earners; non-Africans hold about 95% of top-level management and engineering jobs; 52% of population of working age. **Exports:** $550.0 mil. (f.o.b., 1989); 61% iron ore, 20% rubber, 11% timber. **Imports:** $335 mil. (c.i.f., 1989); machinery, transportation equipment, rice, mineral fuels, chemicals, foodstuffs. **Major trading partners:** **exports:** U.S., EC, Netherlands; **imports:** U.S., EC, Japan, China, Netherlands.

**Intl. Orgs.** FAO, G-77, IAEA, IBRD, ICAO, IDA, IFAD, IFC, ILO, IMF, IMO, INTERPOL, ITU, NAM, UN, UNESCO, UPU, WHO, WMO.

Liberia was populated by migrants from the north and east beginning in the 12th century, but it remained relatively isolated from the remainder of West Africa and was not incorporated into any of the region's premodern kingdoms and empires. Portuguese explorers first reached the Liberian coast in 1461 to be followed by other European traders. Until the 19th century, Liberia was largely ignored by the world except for a small-scale coastal trade in slaves and forest products.

In 1816 the U.S. Congress granted a charter to the American Colonization Society, ACS, a private organization dedicated to the African repatriation of freed slaves. The first settlers landed in 1822 at the town that was later to become Monrovia. In 1838 the settlers organized the Commonwealth of Liberia under a governor appointed by the ACS. The commonwealth declared its independence as the Republic of Liberia in 1847 and adopted a constitution modeled after that of the United States. The new government, Africa's first independent republic, was granted diplomatic recognition by Great Britain in 1848, France in 1852, and the United States in 1862.

Bolstered by the moral backing of the United States, Liberia in its first 100 years of independence succeeded, with difficulty, in fending off British and French attempts to encroach on its territory from their neighboring colonies. Although descendants of freed American slaves are a minority in Liberia's ethnically diverse population, they have consistently dominated the country's political (and to a lesser extent, economic) life.

William V.S. Tubman was elected president in 1944 and served until his death in 1971, successfully steering Liberia through the post-World War II age of African nationalism and decolonization. He was succeeded by William R. Tolbert, Jr. On Apr. 12, 1980, Tolbert was deposed in a military coup led by Master Sgt. Samuel K. Doe. Doe suspended the Constitution and imposed martial law but pledged a new constitution and the resumption of civilian rule by 1985.

Presidential elections were held on Oct. 15, 1985, under the terms of a provisional constitution that for the first time enacted universal suffrage. Samuel Doe was elected president, and his party won 80 percent of the seats in the national legislature. Despite allegations of fraud that led to a violent but unsuccessful coup attempt in November 1985, the Second Republic, under the new constitution, was inaugurated on Jan. 6, 1986, and the Doe government assumed office.

On Dec. 24, 1989, about 150 antigovernment guerrillas of the National Patriotic Forces of Liberia (NPFL), led by Charles Taylor, crossed the border from Ivory Coast. The fighting quickly degenerated into ethnic warfare between the Krahn and Mandingo, in support of the government, and the Gio and Mano, who supported the rebels. In February Prince Johnson split from Taylor's forces and took up fighting both government troops and Taylor. By August there were 5,000 civilian dead, and at least 375,000 refugees had fled to neighboring countries. A peacekeeping force of the Economic Community of West African States (ECOWAS) landed at Monrovia on Aug. 24 to mediate a cease-fire and prepare for free elections. On Sept. 10 Pres. Doe was captured and killed by Prince Johnson, but a cease-fire was not agreed to until Nov. 28, 1990. By some estimates, in 1991 there were as many as 1.3 million displaced persons and refugees. (See Part I, "The Year in Review.")

The national economy is based primarily on rubber, iron ore, and timber, as well as gold, diamonds, coffee, cocoa, and palm oil. Liberia also derives substantial revenue from flag-of-convenience shipping registration and is a major recipient of American economic and military aid, as well as of private American investment.

## Libya

**Socialist People's Libyan Arab Jamahiriya**
**Geography Location:** along Mediterranean coast of North Africa. **Boundaries:** Mediterranean Sea to N, Egypt to E, Sudan to SE, Niger, Chad to S, Tunisia, Algeria to W. **Total land area:** 685,524 sq. mi. (1,775,500 sq km). **Coastline:** 1,100 mi. (1,770 km). **Comparative area:** Alaska plus Oregon. **Land use:** 1% arable land; 0% permanent crops; 8% meadows and pastures; 0% forest and woodland; 91% other; includes negl. % irrigated. **Major cities:** in Jan. 1987, Col. Qaddafi designated Hun, a town 404 mi. (650 km) SE of Tripoli, as administrative capital of country (population N.A.); (1985) Tripoli 858,000; Benghazi 368,000; Misurata 117,000.

**People Population:** 4,221,141 (1990). **Nationality:** noun—Libyan(s); adjective—Libyan. **Ethnic groups:** 97% Berber and Arab; some Greeks, Maltese, Italians, Egyptians, Pakistanis, Turks, Indians, Tunisians. **Languages:** Arabic, Italian, and English widely understood in major cities. **Religions:** 97% Sunni Muslim.

**Government Type:** Jamahiriya, or a state of the masses; in theory, governed by populace. **Independence:** Dec. 24, 1951 (from Italy). **Constitution:** Dec. 11, 1969, amended Mar. 2, 1977. **National holidays:** Revolution Day, Sept. 1; British Evacuation Day, Mar. 28; U.S. Evacuation Day, June 16; Declaration of People's Power, Mar. 2. **Heads of government:** Col. Muammar al-Qaddafi (no official title; runs country and is treated as chief of state) (since Sept. 1969). **Structure:** officially, paramount political power and authority rests with General People's Congress, which theoretically functions as a parliament with a cabinet called General People's Committee.

**Economy Monetary unit:** Libyan dinar. **Budget:** (1986 est.) *income:* $6.4 bil.; *expend.:* $11.3 bil. **GNP:** $20 bil., $5,410 per capita (1988 est.). **Chief crops:** wheat, barley, olives, dates, citrus fruits; 75% of food is imported. **Livestock:** chickens, sheep, goats, cattle, camels. **Natural resources:** crude oil, natural gas, gypsum. **Major industries:** petroleum, food processing, textiles. **Labor force:** 1 mil., of which about 280,000 are resident foreigners; 31% industry, 27% services, 24% government, 18% agriculture; **Exports:** $6.1 bil. (f.o.b., 1988); petroleum; **Imports:** $5 bil. (f.o.b., 1988). **Major trading partners: exports:** Italy, USSR, W. Germany, Spain, France; *imports:* Italy, USSR, W. Germany, UK, Japan.

**Intl. Orgs.** Arab League, FAO, G-77, IAEA, IBRD, ICAO, IDA, IFAD, IFC, ILO, IMF, IMO, INTELSAT, INTERPOL, ITU, NAM, OAU, OPEC, UN, UNESCO, UPU, WHO, WIPO, WMO.

The coastal cities of Libya played an important cultural and commercial role in the Mediterranean in antiquity and were prized possessions of numerous empires. The Libyan coast was successively ruled by Phoenicians, Carthaginians, Berbers, Romans, and Vandals before being incorporated into the Byzantine Empire in the fourth century A.D.; nomadic tribes in the interior were beyond the reach of any government. The Islamic conquests of the seventh and eighth centuries brought Libya into the Muslim world.

Libya was incorporated into the Ottoman Empire shortly after the Ottoman conquest of Egypt in 1517 and was ruled by local Ottoman vassals until 1835 when direct Ottoman government was established. In 1911 Libya was invaded and conquered by Italy. After World War I, local resistance to Italian colonial rule was led by King Idris I, Emir of Cyrenaica. British troops drove Italian and German forces from Libya in 1943. King Idris returned from exile in 1944. Following World War II, most of Libya was ruled as a British protectorate with a smaller portion under French administration.

Libya became an independent constitutional monarchy on Dec. 24, 1951. In 1959 significant oil reserves were discovered, rapidly transforming Libya from one of the poorest states in North Africa to one of the wealthiest.

A military coup on Sept. 1, 1969, led by Col. Muammar al-Qaddafi, deposed the monarchy and declared the establishment of the Libyan Arab Republic. Qaddafi moved rapidly to nationalize foreign assets, expel foreign troops, and close foreign libraries and cultural centers. He also assumed full dictatorial powers under a political system that gives equal weight to Islamic law and his own political philosophy. Popular participation in elections is mandatory, although no government organization outside Qaddafi and his circle of advisers exerts any real authority.

Libya has given strong political and financial aid to various radical Palestinian groups and other enemies of Israel and its supporters, sponsoring terrorist activities throughout Europe and the Middle East in real or putative support of the Palestinian cause. Numerous anti-Qaddafi Libyan exiles have been assassinated in Europe. Libya has also engaged in sporadic military campaigns against Egypt and the Sudan, and has supported both the government and antigovernment forces in Chad, where it has occupied the northern Aouzou Strip since 1984.

Relations between Libya and the United States have been very hostile in the 1980s. On May 6, 1981, the United States closed the Libyan "People's Bureau" (embassy) in Washington, D.C. On Aug. 2, 1981, American jets shot down two attacking Libyan warplanes as U.S. naval forces conducted exercises in the Gulf of Sidra, which Libya claims as national waters. In 1986 the United States imposed economic sanctions on Libya, ordered all Americans to leave the country, and froze Libyan assets in the United States. Another clash in March 1986 ended with the loss of two Libyan ships.

On Apr. 5, 1986, Libyan-sponsored terrorists bombed a nightclub in West Berlin, killing two U.S. soldiers; in response, American bombers attacked Tripoli and Benghazi on Apr. 14 in an apparent attempt to kill Col. Qaddafi himself. In 1990, investigators announced they had linked Libyan agents to the bombing of a Pan Am Jet over Lockerbie, Scotland, in 1988.

Great Britain broke off diplomatic relations with Libya in April 1984 after machine-gun fire from the Libyan "People's Bureau" in London killed a policeman and wounded 10 Libyan exiles demonstrating against Qaddafi's government. In May 1984 an attempted coup against Qaddafi was foiled; this was followed by a purge in which thousands of people were imprisoned or executed. In January 1989 an international outcry arose when a West German company admitted selling equipment to Libya for a chemical weapons plant.

The Libyan economy depends heavily on petroleum and natural gas. Other industrial activities include gypsum mining and light manufacturing, including textiles and carpets. A narrow strip of fertile land along the coast supports mixed agriculture, and sheep, goats, and camels are raised in the desert interior.

## Liechtenstein
### Principality of Liechtenstein

**Geography** **Location:** landlocked country in central Europe. **Boundaries:** Austria to N and E, Switzerland to S and W. **Total land area:** 61.8 sq. mi. (160 sq km). **Coastline:** none. **Comparative area:** about size of Washington, D.C. **Land use:** 25% arable land; 0% permanent crops; 38% meadows and pastures; 19% forest and woodland; 18% other. **Major cities:** (1988 est.) Vaduz (capital) 4,191; Schaan 4,836; Balzers 3,581.

**People** **Population:** 28,292 (1990). **Nationality:** noun—Liechtensteiner(s); adjective—Liechtenstein. **Ethnic groups:** 95% Alemannic, 5% Italian and other. **Languages:** German (official), Alemannic dialect. **Religions:** 82.7% Roman Catholic, 7.1% Protestant, 10.2% other.

**Government** **Type:** hereditary constitutional monarchy. **Independence:** N.A. **Constitution:** Oct. 5, 1921. **National holiday:** N.A. **Heads of government:** Hans-Adam II, prince (since Nov. 1989); Hans Brunhart, prime minister (since May 1978); prince transferred most of his executive powers to his son, Prince Hans Adam, in Aug. 1984. **Structure:** executive—hereditary prince; legislative—unicameral legislature (diet; 15 deputies elected to four-year terms); judiciary—independent.

**Economy** **Monetary unit:** Swiss franc. **Budget:** (1986); *income:* $171 mil.; *expend.:* $189 mil. **GNP:** about $15,000 per capita (1984). Note: Liechtenstein has prosperous economy based primarily on small-scale light industry and some farming; sale of postage stamps to collectors, estimated at $10 mil. annually, provides 10% of state budget; companies incorporated in Liechtenstein solely for tax purposes provide additional 30% of state budget; low business taxes (maximum tax rate 20%) and easy incorporation rules have induced about 25,000 holding, or so-called letter box, companies to establish nominal offices there; economy is tied closely to that of Switzerland in customs union; no national accounts data available. **Chief crops:** vegetables, corn, wheat, potatoes, grapes. **Livestock:** cattle, pigs, horses, sheep, goats. **Natural resources:** hydroelectric potential. **Major industries:** electronics, metal manufacturing, textiles. **Labor force:** 12,258; 5,078 foreign workers (mostly from Switzerland and Austria); 54.4% industry, trade, and building; 41.6% services; 4% agriculture, fishing, forestry, and horticulture; no unemployment. **Exports:** $807 mil. (f.o.b., 1986); small specialty machinery, dental products, stamps, hardware, pottery. **Imports:** N.A.; machinery, metal goods, textiles, foodstuffs, motor vehicles. **Major trading partners:** *exports:* 40% EC, 26% EFTA (19% Switzerland); *imports:* N.A.

**Intl. Orgs.** EFTA, IAEA, INTELSAT, INTERPOL, ITU, UN, UNCTAD, UNICEF, UNIDO, UPU, WIPO.

The alpine principality of Liechtenstein, bordered by Austria and Switzerland, is a remnant of the Holy Roman Empire, an ancient constitutional monarchy with a modern industrial economy. The current dynasty was established in 1699; Prince Franz Josef II came to the throne in 1938, yielding his executive powers to his heir apparent, Hans Adam, in 1984.

Liechtenstein was tied to the Austro-Hungarian monarchy until 1918. Since then it has remained in a customs union with Switzerland, which also handles its foreign affairs. The single-chamber diet, the Landtag is elected by universal suffrage, women having won the right to vote in 1984. The relatively conservative Progressive Citizen's party ruled continuously during 1928-70. From 1970 to 1974, and since 1978, the relatively liberal Fatherland Union has controlled the government.

The economy, dominated by dairy farming before 1945, has since been radically transformed by industrialization and the development of service industries. Liechtenstein is a corporate haven, with some 25,000 corporations maintaining nominal headquarters there. Foreign workers constitute about 40 percent of the work force.

## Luxembourg
### Grand Duchy of Luxembourg

**Geography** **Location:** landlocked country in western Europe. **Boundaries:** Belgium to N and W, Germany to E, France to S. **Total land area:** 999 sq. mi. (2,586 sq km). **Coastline:** none. **Comparative area:** slightly smaller than Rhode Island. **Land use:** 24% arable land; 1% permanent crops; 20% meadows and pastures; 21% forest and woodland; 34% other. **Major cities:** (1988 est.) Luxembourg-Ville (capital) 75,500; Esch-sur-Alzette 23,800; Differdange 15,900; Dudelange 14,100; Petange 11,800.

**People** **Population:** 383,813 (1990). **Nationality:** noun—Luxembourger(s); adjective—Luxembourg. **Ethnic groups:** Celtic base, with French and German blend; also, guest and worker residents from Portugal, Italy, and European countries. **Languages:** Luxembourgish, German, French. **Religions:** 97% Roman Catholic, 3% Protestant and Jewish.

**Government** **Type:** constitutional monarchy. **Independence:** N.A. **Constitution:** Oct. 17, 1868, occasional revisions. **National holiday:** Grand Duke's birthday, June 23. **Heads of government:** Jean de Luxembourg, grand duke (since Nov. 1964); Jacques Santer, prime minister (since June 1984). **Structure:** parliamentary democracy; seven ministers compose Council of Government, headed by president, which constitutes executive; it is responsible to unicameral legislature (Chamber of Deputies); Council of State, appointed for indefinite term, exercises some powers of an upper house; judicial power exercised by independent courts; coalition governments are usual.

**Economy** **Monetary unit:** Luxembourg franc. **Budget:** (1988) *income:* $2.5 bil.; *expend.:* $2.3 bil. **GDP:** $6.3 bil., $17,200 per capita. **Chief crops:** mixed farming, wine. **Live-stock:** cattle, horses, pigs, sheep, poultry. **Natural resources:** iron ore (no longer exploited). **Major industries:** banking, iron and steel, food processing. **Labor force:** 161,000 (1984); 48.9% services, 24.7% industry, 13.2% government; one-third of work force is foreign, comprising mostly workers from Portugal, Italy, France, Belgium, and W. Germany; 1.6% unemployment (1987). **Exports:** $4.7 bil. (f.o.b., 1988); iron and steel products, chemicals, rubber products, glass, aluminum. **Imports:** $5.9 bil. (c.i.f., 1988 est.); minerals, metals, foodstuffs, machinery, quality consumer goods. **Major trading partners:** *exports:* 75% EC, 6% U.S.; *imports:* 40% W. Germany, 35% Belgium, 15% France, 3% U.S.

**Intl. Orgs.** EC, FAO, GATT, IAEA, IBRD, ICAO, IDA, IFAD, IFC, ILO, IMF, INTELSAT, INTERPOL, ITU, NATO, UN, UNESCO, UPU, WHO, WIPO, WMO.

One of hundreds of small principalities in the Holy Roman Empire, Luxembourg joined the German league when the empire was abolished in 1806. It shared a monarchy with the Netherlands, but the two countries remained distinct under a single sovereign. In 1831 Luxembourg lost its French-speaking territory to Belgium. The Treaty of London granted sovereignty to Luxembourg in 1867. When King William III died in 1890, different rules of succession severed the dual monarchy; Queen Wilhelmina succeeded him in the Netherlands, while Adolf of Nassau became grand duke of Luxembourg. The nation's full independence dates from that event.

During the 19th century, Luxembourg developed a balanced modern economy, with prosperous small farms being complemented by industry, particularly mining and steel production. As late as 1970, steel accounted for over 25 percent of the nation's GDP and five-eighths of export earnings, although rising international competition has led to a decline since then.

Luxembourg was overrun by Germany during World War I and again in May 1940, in the early stages of World War II. Archduchess Charlotte fled to London and returned with the Allied armed forces in 1944. The constitutional monarchy has enjoyed political stability since the war, with the Christian Social party normally the senior partner in a three-way coalition.

Luxembourg formed a customs union with Belgium in 1921 and joined the Benelux (Belgium, Netherlands, Luxembourg) union even before World War II had ended. A founding member of the United Nations in 1945, Luxembourg abandoned its traditional neutrality in 1948 and joined NATO in 1949. It was a founding member of the EEC under the 1954 Treaty of Rome and is now home to numerous Common Market institutions, including the Secretariat of the European Parliament and the European Investment Bank; international banking accounts for over half of its gross national product. The country's chief problem is a shrinking and aging citizenry, leading to strains on social services and dependence on foreign workers.

## Madagascar
### Democratic Republic of Madagascar
**Geography  Location:** off southeast Africa in western Indian Ocean. Antananarivo: 18°52′S, 47°30′E. **Boundaries:** about 300 mi. (500 km) E of Mozambique. **Total land area:** 224,532 sq. mi. (581,540 sq km). **Coastline:** 3,000 mi. (4,828 km). **Comparative area:** between California and Texas. **Land use:** 4% arable land; 1% permanent crops; 58% meadows and pastures; 26% forest and woodland; 11% other; includes 1% irrigated. **Major cities:** Antananarivo (capital) 662,585 (1985 est.); Antsirabé 78,941; Toamasina (Tamatave) 77,395; Fianarantsoa 68,054; Mahajanga (Majunga) 65,864 (1975 census).

**People  Population:** 11,800,524 (1990). **Nationality:** noun—Malagasy (sing., pl.); adjective—Malagasy. **Ethnic groups:** highlanders of predominantly Malayo-Indonesian origin (Merina 1,643,000 and related Betsileo 760,000); coastal peoples collectively termed Cotiers, with mixed African, Malayo-Indonesian, and Arab ancestry (Betsimisaraka 941,000; Tsimihety 442,000; Antaisaka 415,000; Sakalava 375,000); 11,000 European French, 5,000 Indians of French nationality, 5,000 Creoles. **Languages:** French and Malagasy (both official). **Religions:** 52% indigenous beliefs, 41% Christian, 7% Muslim.

**Government  Type:** real authority in hands of president, although Supreme Revolutionary Council is theoretically ultimate executive authority. **Independence:** June 26, 1960 (from France). **Constitution:** Dec. 21, 1975. **National holiday:** Independence Day, June 26. **Heads of government:** Adm. Didier Ratsiraka, president (since June 1975); Guy W. Razanamasy, prime minister (since Aug. 1991). **Structure:** executive—president, Supreme Revolutionary Council (made up of military and political leaders) assisted by cabinet (Council of Ministers); unicameral legislature—Popular National Assembly; judiciary—courts patterned after French system, High Council of Institutions has power of constitutional review.

**Economy  Monetary unit:** Malagasy franc. **Budget:** (1988) **income:** $337 mil; **expend.:** $245 mil. **GDP:** $1.7 bil., $155 per capita. **Chief crops:** cash crops—coffee, vanilla, cloves, sugar, tobacco; food crops—rice, cassava, cereals, potatoes, corn. **Livestock:** cattle, pigs, goats, sheep. **Natural resources:** graphite, chromite, coal, bauxite, salt. **Major industries:** agricultural processing (meat canneries, soap factories, brewery, tanneries, sugar refining), light consumer goods industries (textiles, glassware), cement. **Labor force:** 4.9 mil. (1985); 95% nonsalaried family workers engaged in subsistence agriculture; 175,000 wage and salary earners (26% agriculture, 17% domestic service, 15% industry, 14% commerce, 11% construction); 51% of population of working age. **Exports:** $284 mil. (f.o.b., 1988); 45% coffee, 15% vanilla, 11% cloves. **Imports:** $319 mil. (c.i.f., 1988); 30% intermediate manufactures, 28% capital goods, 15% petroleum,

14% consumer goods, 13% food. **Major trading partners:** **exports:** France, W. Germany, Japan, Italy, U.S.; **imports:** France, W. Germany, UK, other EC, U.S.

**Intl. Orgs.** FAO, G-77, GATT, IAEA, IBRD, ICAO, IDA, IFAD, IFC, ILO, IMF, IMO, INTELSAT, INTERPOL, ITU, NAM, UN, UNESCO, UPU, WHO, WMO.

The largest island nation, and fourth largest island, in the world, Madagascar was settled by Malayo-Indonesian migrants some 2,000 years ago. Although later waves of African and Arab migrants were absorbed into the population, to a large extent it is still ethnically and culturally Asian. A Portuguese attempt to colonize the island in the 16th century failed, and during the 18th and 19th centuries, a unified kingdom backed by the British ruled the country. Foreign interests—largely British and French—developed extensive coffee plantations, and the French made Madagascar a protectorate in 1885 and a colony in 1896.

During World War II Madagascar sided with the Free French, and French colonial rule was reestablished after the war. The Malagasy Republic was founded as an independent nation on June 26, 1960. A coup in 1972 brought an anti-French and generally anti-Western government to power. Repression and economic stagnation characterized the 1970s, and in recent years the Malagasy government has become more moderate. Madagascar's unique wildlife—a mixture of African species and others of domestic evolution—makes it of unique scientific interest. In 1990, scientists announced the discovery of the smallest mammal known to science, the dwarf lemur.

## Malawi
### Republic of Malawi
**Geography  Location:** landlocked country in southern central Africa. **Boundaries:** Tanzania to N, Mozambique to E, S, and SW, Zambia to W; Lake Malawi forms much of eastern boundary. **Total land area:** 45,747 sq. mi. (118,484 sq km). **Coastline:** none. **Comparative area:** slightly larger than Pennsylvania. **Land use:** 25% arable land; negl. % permanent crops; 20% meadows and pastures; 50% forest and woodland; 5% other; includes negl. % irrigated. **Major cities:** Lilongwe (capital) 75,000 (1976 est.); Blantyre 219,011 (1977 census).

**People  Population:** 9,157,528 (1990). **Nationality:** noun—Malawian(s); adjective—Malawian. **Ethnic groups:** Chewa, Nyanja, Tumbuko, Yao, Lomwe, Sena, Tonga, Ngoni, Asian, European. **Languages:** English and Chichewa (both official); Tombuka. **Religions:** 55% Protestant, 20% Roman Catholic, 20% Muslim, indigenous beliefs.

**Government  Type:** one-party state. **Independence:** July 6, 1964 (from UK). **Constitution:** July 6, 1964. **National holiday:** Republic Day, July 6. **Heads of government:** Dr. Hastings Kamuzu Banda, president for life (since 1966). **Structure:** executive—strong presidential system with cabinet appointed by presi-

dent; legislative—unicameral National Assembly of 87 elected and up to 15 nominated members; judiciary—high court with chief justice and at least two justices.

**Economy  Monetary unit:** Malawi kwacha. **Budget:** (1988 est.) **income:** $245 mil.; **expend.:** $390.0 mil. **GDP:** $1.4 bil., $180 per capita. **Chief crops:** cash crops—tobacco, tea, sugar, peanuts, cotton; subsistence crops—corn, sorghum, millet, pulses, root crops; self-sufficient in food production. **Livestock:** cattle, goats, pigs, sheep. **Natural resources:** limestone; unexploited deposits of uranium, coal, bauxite. **Major industries:** agricultural processing (tea, tobacco, sugar), sawmilling, cement. **Labor force:** 344,052 (1982); 52% agriculture, 16% personal services, 9% manufacturing. **Exports:** $292 mil. (f.o.b., 1988); tobacco, tea, sugar, peanuts, cotton. **Imports:** $402 mil. (c.i.f., 1988); manufactured goods, machinery and transport equipment, building and construction materials, fuel, fertilizer. **Major trading partners:** **exports:** UK, U.S., South Africa, Zambia; **imports:** South Africa, UK, Japan, U.S., Zimbabwe.

**Intl. Orgs.** Commonwealth, EC (associated member), FAO, G-77, GATT, IBRD, ICAO, IDA, IFAD, IFC, ILO, IMF, INTELSAT, INTERPOL, ITU, NAM, UN, UNESCO, UPU, WHO, WIPO, WMO.

Malawi derives its name from the Maravi, a Bantu people that settled in the region in the 13th century and whose descendants, the Chewas, comprise a significant segment of the current population. In the 1830s, the Ngoni, driven from what is now South Africa by the Zulus, arrived in the area around Lake Nyasa. The arrival of the Scottish missionary David Livingstone in 1859 led to the establishment of the British-controlled Nyasaland Protectorate in 1891. In 1953 Nyasaland formed a federation with Northern and Southern Rhodesia (Zambia and Zimbabwe) and began to organize an independence movement. The fight for independence was led by Dr. H. Kamuzu Banda, an expatriate who assumed the presidency of the Nyasaland African Congress, later the Malawi Congress party, upon his return in 1958. The British granted Nyasaland self-governing status in 1962, and Banda was elected prime minister the following year. Malawi achieved full independence under its present name in 1964.

Malawi currently hosts one of the largest refugee populations in Africa due to political and social strife in neighboring Mozambique. The influx of nearly 650,000 refugees has placed a great strain on the Malawian economy. The nonagenarian Banda, president for life since 1966, faces strong domestic opposition but remains in power with the support of the military.

## Malaysia
**Geography  Location:** 13 states in Southeast Asia; 11 are in Peninsular Malaysia and two, Sabah and Sarawak, lie about 400 mi. (640 km) across South China Sea on northern coast of island of Borneo (Kalimantan). **Bound-**

**aries:** Peninsular Malaysia—Thailand to N, South China Sea to E, Island of Singapore to S across Johor Strait, and Indonesian island of Sumatra to W across Strait of Malacca; Sabah and Sarawak—South China Sea to NW, Sulu Sea to NE, Celebes Sea to E, Indonesia to S; Brunei is enclosed withing Sarawak on coast of South China Sea. **Total land area:** 127,320 sq. mi. (329,757 sq km). **Coastline:** 2,905 mi. (4,675 km). **Comparative area:** between New Mexico and Montana. **Land use:** 3% arable land; 10% permanent crops; negl. % meadows and pastures; 63% forest and woodland; 24% other; includes 1% irrigated. **Major cities:** (1980 census) Kuala Lumpur (capital) 919,610; Ipoh 293,849; George Town (Penang) 248,241; Johore Bahru 246,395; Petaling Jaya 207,805.

**People Population:** 17,510,546 (1990). **Nationality:** noun—Malaysian(s); adjective—Malaysian. **Ethnic groups:** 59% Malay and other indigenous, 32% Chinese, 9% Indian. **Languages:** Peninsular Malaysia—Malay (official); English, Chinese dialects, Tamil; Sabah—English, Malay, numerous tribal dialects, Mandarin and Hakka dialects predominate among Chinese; Sarawak—English, Malay, Mandarin, numerous tribal languages. **Religions:** Peninsular Malaysia—Malays nearly all Muslim, Chinese predominantly Buddhist, Indians predominantly Hindu; Sabah—38% Muslim, 17% Christian, 45% other; Sarawak—35% tribal religion, 24% Buddhist and Confucianist, 20% Muslim, 16% Christian, 5% other.

**Government Type:** Federation of Malaysia formed July 9, 1963; constitutional monarchy nominally headed by paramount ruler (king); bicameral Parliament; Peninsular Malaysian states—hereditary rulers in all but Penang and Melaka, where governors are appointed by Malaysian government, with powers of state governments limited by federal constitution; Sabah—self-governing state, holding 20 seats in House of Representatives, with foreign affairs, defense, internal security, and other powers delegated to federal government; Sarawak—self-governing state, which holds 24 seats in House of Representatives, with foreign affairs, defense, internal security, and other powers delegated to federal government. **Independence:** Aug. 31, 1957 (from UK). **Constitution:** Aug. 31, 1957, amended Sept. 6, 1963, when Federation of Malaya became Federation of Malaysia. **National holiday:** Independence Day, Aug. 31. **Heads of government:** Azlan Shah, king (since Apr. 1989); Dr. Mahathir Mohamad, prime minister (since July 1981). **Structure:** nine state rulers alternate as "king" for five-year terms; locus of executive power vested in prime minister and cabinet, who are responsible to bicameral Parliament (58-member Senate, 177-member House of Representatives); Peninsular Malaysia—executive branches in 11 states vary in detail but are similar in design, with chief minister, appointed by hereditary ruler or governor, heading an executive council (cabinet), which is responsible to elected, unicameral legislature; Sarawak—executive branch headed by governor, appointed by central government,

having largely ceremonial role; executive power exercised by chief minister who heads parliamentary cabinet responsible to unicameral legislature; judiciary is part of Malaysian judicial system.

**Economy Monetary unit:** Malaysian ringgit. **Budget:** (1989) *income:* $8.8 bil. *expend.:* $11.2 bil. **GDP:** $37.9 bil., $2,270 per capita. **Chief crops:** Peninsular Malaysia—natural rubber, palm oil, rice; 10–15% of rice requirements imported; Sabah—mainly subsistence, main crops are rubber, timber, coconut, rice (rice is also food deficit); Sarawak—main crops are rubber, timber, pepper (rice is food deficit). **Livestock:** pigs, cattle, goats, buffalo, sheep. **Natural resources:** tin, crude oil, timber, copper, iron ore. **Major industries:** Peninsular Malaysia—rubber and oil-palm processing and manufacturing, light manufacturing industry, electronics; Sabah—logging, petroleum production; Sarawak—agriculture processing, petroleum production and refining, logging. **Labor force:** 5.95 mil. (1985); 34.5% agriculture; trade, hotels, and restaurants; 15.6% manufacturing, 14.9% government. **Exports:** $24.0 bil. (f.o.b., 1989 est.); natural rubber, palm oil, tin, timber, petroleum. **Imports:** $20.0 bil. (c.i.f., 1989 est.). **Major trading partners:** *exports:* Japan, Singapore, U.S., USSR, Australia, EC; *imports:* Japan, EC, Singapore, W. Germany, UK, Thailand, China.

**Intl. Orgs.** ASEAN, Colombo Plan, Commonwealth, FAO, G-77, GATT, IAEA, IBRD, ICAO, IDA, IFC, ILO, IMF, IMO, INTELSAT, INTERPOL, ITU, NAM, UN, UNESCO, UPU, WHO, WMO.

From ancient times a group of petty principalities in the southern part of the Malay Peninsula, bordering the Strait of Malacca, maintained extensive ties of maritime commerce throughout Southeast Asia. The early Malay states were Hindu, under Indian influence; with the rise of the Kingdom of Malacca in the 15th century, conversion to Islam was widespread. European influence in the Spice Islands began in the 16th century; the Portuguese, initially dominant, gave way to the Dutch, who seized Malacca in 1641.

British influence grew during the 18th century, with the founding of a trading settlement at Penang in 1789. Singapore was founded in 1819, and the Dutch ceded Malacca to Great Britain in 1824. By a series of treaties in the late 19th century, the various Malay states became British protectorates; Britain controlled the entire southern peninsula after 1909. Under British rule, commercial tin mining and the establishment of extensive rubber plantations led to the importation of many Indian and Chinese laborers; eventually ethnic Chinese dominated most of Malaya's domestic economy.

In the 19th century, Great Britain also gained a dominant position in northern Borneo. (Borneo is divided between Brunei, Indonesia, and Malaysia.)

Japan overran Malaya by February 1942. Following World War II, the various Malay states (excluding Singapore) organized into a

federation, which replaced the confusing prewar regime of federated and unfederated protectorates. A Communist rebellion disrupted the country throughout the early 1950s. Following the suppression of the Communist movement, elections were held in mid-1955 for a home-rule government. The elections brought the Alliance party of Tungku Abdul Rahman to power, and the Federation of Malaya became independent in 1957.

The nation expanded on Sept. 16, 1963, with the creation of Malaysia, incorporating the Federation of Malaya as well as Singapore and the former British colonies of North Borneo (thereafter called Sabah) and Sarawak. Singapore seceded from Malaysia in 1965 and became an independent nation. Malaysia is a constitutional monarchy with a parliamentary system; monarchs are chosen for five-year terms from among the hereditary rulers of the nine Malay states.

Ethnic concerns dominate Malaysian politics. Muslim Malays have enacted various laws to restrict the economic power and ethnic cohesion of the non-Islamic Chinese and Indian minorities. On Dec. 2, 1989, Malaysia's Communist party signed a cease-fire and lay down its arms after 41 years of conflict along the Malaysia-Thailand border.

By the mid-1980s exports of oil and natural gas had surpassed Malaysia's traditional principal exports of rubber, tin, and other natural-resource-based commodities (palm oil, timber, spices); modernization has created an export-oriented industrial sector producing textiles, electronic equipment, and other manufactured goods.

---

## Maldives
### Republic of Maldives

**Geography Location:** chain of more than 1,200 small coral islands (about 220 inhabited), 475 mi. (764 km) from N to S and 80 mi. (207 km) from W to E in Indian Ocean; northernmost atoll about 370 mi. (960 km) southwest of India. Malé 4°00'N, 73°28'E. **Boundaries:** Laccadive Sea to NE, Arabian Sea to N, Indian Ocean to S and W. **Total land area:** 115 sq. mi. (298 sq km). **Coastline:** 400 mi. (644 km). **Comparative area:** about 1.5 times size of Washington, D.C. **Land use:** 10% arable land; 0% permanent crops; 3% meadows and pastures; 3% forest and woodland; 84% other. **Major cities:** (1985) Malé (capital) 46,334.

**People Population:** 217,945 (1990). **Nationality:** noun—Maldivian(s); adjective—Maldivian. **Ethnic groups:** admixtures of Sinhalese, Dravidian, Arab, and black. **Languages:** Divehi (dialect of Sinhala; script derived from Arabic); English spoken by most government officials. **Religions:** Sunni Muslim.

**Government Type:** republic. **Independence:** July 26, 1965 (from UK). **Constitution:** June 4, 1964. **National holidays:** Independence Day, July 26; Republic Day, Nov. 11. **Heads of government:** Maumoon Abdul Gayoom, president (since Nov. 1978). **Structure:** elected president, chief executive; popularly elected unicameral national legislature, People's Council (members elected for five-year terms); appointed chief justice responsible for administration of Islamic law.

**Economy** **Monetary unit:** Maldivian rufiya. **Budget:** (1988 est.) *income:* $51.0 mil.; *expend.:* $50.0 mil. **GDP:** $136.0 mil., $670 per capita. **Chief crops:** coconut, limited production of millet, corn, pumpkins, sweet potatoes; shortages—rice, sugar, flour. **Livestock:** N.A. **Natural resources:** fish. **Major industries:** fishing, tourism, some coconut processing. **Labor force:** about 66,000; fishing industry employs about 80% of labor force. **Exports:** $47.0 mil. (f.o.b., 1988 est.); 57% fish, 39% clothing. **Imports:** $90.0 mil. (c.i.f., 1988 est.); 47% intermediate and capital goods, 42% consumer goods, 11% petroleum products. **Major trading partners:** *exports:* Thailand, Western Europe, Sri Lanka; *imports:* Japan, Western Europe, Thailand.

**Intl. Orgs.** Colombo Plan, Commonwealth (special member), FAO, G-77, GATT (de facto), IBRD, ICAO, IDA, IFAD, IFC, IMF, IMO, ITU, NAM, UN, UNESCO, UPU, WHO, WMO.

The small sultanate of the Maldive Islands, with an Islamic population of Sinhalese descent, was made a British protectorate in 1887. The islands' tiny area and poor soil limited development; fishing and fish processing are the main industries, and copra (dried coconut meat for coconut oil) is the only significant crop. The Maldives became an independent nation on July 26, 1965. In 1968 the sultanate was abolished and replaced by a republic. Since independence, tourism has become economically important and now accounts for 10 percent of the gross national product. Protests over the concentration of development on the island of Malé in recent years have led to political unrest in the other islands, while attempts to address the basic needs of those islands have strained the nation's tiny economic base.

The current president, Maumoon Abdul Gayoom, was elected to office in 1978 and subsequently reelected twice. The elections of September 1988 were marked by considerable unrest and demonstrations. An attempted coup against the Gayoom government on Nov. 4, 1988, was put down with the intervention of Indian troops.

## Mali
### Republic of Mali

**Geography** **Location:** northwestern Africa. **Boundaries:** Algeria to N, Niger to E, Burkina Faso, Ivory Coast, Guinea to S, Senegal and Mauritania to W. **Total land area:** 471,042 sq. mi. (1,220,000 sq km). **Coastline:** none. **Comparative area:** between Texas and Alaska. **Land use:** 2% arable land; negl. % permanent crops; 25% meadows and pastures; 7% forest and woodland; 66% other; includes negl. % irrigated. **Major cities:** (1976 census) Bamako (capital) 404,000; Ségou 65,000; Mopti 54,000; Sikasso 47,000; Kayes 45,000.

**People** **Population:** 8,142,373 (1990). **Nationality:** noun—Malian(s); adjective—Mal-

ian. **Ethnic groups:** 50% Mande (Bambara, Malinke, Sarakole), 17% Peul, 12% Voltaic, 6% Songhai, 5% Tuareg and Moor. **Languages:** French (official); Bambara spoken by 80% of population. **Religions:** 90% Muslim, 9% indigenous beliefs, 1% Christian.

**Government** **Type:** republic; single-party constitutional government. **Independence:** Sept. 22, 1960 (from France). **Constitution:** June 2, 1974, effective June 19, 1979. **National holiday:** Independence Day, Sept. 22. **Heads of government:** Lt. Col. Amadou T. Toure, president (since Mar. 1991); Soumana Sako, prime minister (since Apr. 1991). **Structure:** executive—cabinet composed of civilians and army officers; unicameral legislature—National Council; judiciary.

**Economy** **Monetary unit:** Communauté Financière Africaine (CFA) franc. **Budget:** (1987) *income:* $338 mil.; *expend.:* $559 mil. **GDP:** $1.2 bil., $220 per capita. **Chief crops:** millet, sorghum, rice, corn, peanuts; cash crops—peanuts, cotton. **Livestock:** goats, sheep, cattle, asses, camels. **Natural resources:** gold, phosphates, kaolin, salt, limestone, uranium; bauxite, iron ore, manganese, tin, and copper deposits are known but not exploited. **Major industries:** small local consumer goods and processing, construction, phosphate, gold, fishing. **Labor force:** 3.1 mil. (1981); 80% agriculture, 19% services; 50% of population of working age (1985). **Exports:** $260.0 mil. (f.o.b., 1987); livestock, peanuts, dried fish, cotton, skins. **Imports:** $493.0 mil. (f.o.b., 1987); textiles, vehicles, petroleum products, machinery, sugar, cereals. **Major trading partners:** mostly franc zone and Western Europe.

**Intl. Orgs.** FAO, G-77, GATT (de facto), IAEA, IBRD, ICAO, IDA, IFAD, IFC, ILO, IMF, INTELSAT, INTERPOL, ITU, NAM, UN, UNESCO, UPU, WHO, WMO.

Mali has been a center of West African civilization for over 4,000 years. Iron Age civilizations flourished on the middle reaches of the Niger River from about 200 B.C. The kingdom of Ghana arose about A.D. 750 on the strength of the gold trade with North African Berbers. Ghana was overthrown by the Muslim Almoravids, who ruled only 11 years, though Islam remained a major influence from that time. From 1200 to 1400, the Kingdom of Mali was dominant in the region and was renowned throughout Islam and even in Christian Europe for its wealth and power; when Mansa Musa's retinue stopped in Cairo en route to Mecca, it carried so much gold that the price of gold fell 20 percent. By the end of the 14th century, the Mali empire had been eclipsed by the Songhai (Soyinka) empire, centered on the Niger River cities of Gao and Timbuktu.

The Songhai empire collapsed after Timbuktu was sacked by Moroccans in 1591. It fragmented into a series of smaller states, and power shifted from the desert fringe back to the Niger valley, bringing with it a further spread of Islam.

French exploration of Mali led to conquest in 1896 and the creation of the colony of French Sudan in 1898, governed from Dakar, Senegal. Timbuktu continued to decline in importance,

and Bamako became the country's principal urban center.

Malians were granted French citizenship and limited self-rule in 1946. In 1958 the territory became autonomous within the French Overseas Community. In 1959, with French support, the French Sudan and Senegal formed the Federation of Mali, which became independent on June 20, 1960. Senegal seceded from the federation almost immediately, and Mali became an independent republic on Sept. 22, 1960. Modibo Keita was elected the country's first president.

Keita's program of radical control of society and the economy by the central government provoked discontent, and he was overthrown in 1968 by military officers led by Lt. Moussa Traore. Traore's Military Committee of National Liberation ruled until 1979 when it was reorganized under a new constitution as the Malian People's Democratic Union. Traore remains president; his military-backed government has made little progress in bringing political unity to the country or in solving its pressing economic problems.

Mali is primarily agricultural in the south and west, pastoral in the north and east. Principal crops are millet, rice, peanuts, and cotton. The livestock sector has been repeatedly devastated by drought and spreading desertification. The country has some mineral resources, including bauxite, iron, and gold. Mali maintains close ties with France, and the economy remains heavily dependent on foreign assistance.

## Malta
### Republic of Malta

**Geography** **Location:** archipelago (largest islands are Malta, Gozo, and Comino) in central Mediterranean. Valletta 35°54'N, 14°32'E. **Boundaries:** Sicily 58 mi. (93 km) to N, Libya 180 mi. (290 km) to S, Tunisia to W. **Total land area:** 122 sq. mi. (316 sq km). **Coastline:** 87 mi. (140 km). **Comparative area:** slightly less than twice size of Washington, D.C. **Land use:** 38% arable land; 3% permanent crops; 0% meadows and pastures; 0% forest and woodland; 59% other; includes 3% irrigated. **Major cities:** (1988 est.) Valletta (capital) 9,210; Birkirkara 20,711; Qormi 18,841; Sliema 13,558.

**People** **Population:** 353,465 (1990). **Nationality:** noun—Maltese (sing., pl.); adjective—Maltese. **Ethnic groups:** mixture of Arab, Sicilian, Norman, Spanish, Italian, English. **Languages:** Maltese and English. **Religions:** 98% Roman Catholic.

**Government** **Type:** parliamentary democracy, independent republic within Commonwealth. **Independence:** Sept. 21, 1964 (from UK). **Constitution:** Apr. 26, 1974; effective June 2, 1974. **National holiday:** Freedom Day, Mar. 31. **Heads of government:** Dr. Vincent Tabone, president (since Apr. 1989); Eddie Fenech Adami, prime minister (since May 1987). **Structure:** executive—prime minister and cabinet; legislature—65-member House of Representatives; judiciary—independent.

**Economy Monetary unit:** Maltese lire. **Budget:** (1989 est.) *income:* $844 mil.; *expend.:* $938 mil. **GDP:** $1.9 bil., $5,100 per capita (1988). **Chief crops:** potatoes, cauliflower, grapes, wheat, barley; adequate supplies of vegetables, milk, and pork products; seasonal or periodic shortages in grain, animal fodder, fruits, other basic foodstuffs; 20% self-sufficient overall. **Livestock:** pigs, cattle, goats, sheep. **Natural resources:** limestone, salt. **Major industries:** tourism, ship repair yard, clothing. **Labor force:** 125,674 (1987); 30% services (except government), 24% manufacturing, 21% government (except job corps); 4.6% registered unemployment. **Exports:** $710.0 mil. (f.o.b., 1988); clothing, textiles, ships, printed matter. **Imports:** $1.4 bil (c.i.f., 1988); food, petroleum, nonfood raw materials. **Major trading partners:** *exports:* 31% W. Germany, 14% Italy, 14% UK; *imports:* 19% W. Germany, 17% Italy, 17% UK, 11% U.S.

**Intl. Orgs.** Commonwealth, FAO, G-77, GATT, IBRD, ICAO, IFAD, ILO, IMF, IMO, INTERPOL, ITU, NAM, UN, UPU, WHO, WIPO, WMO.

Malta, an ancient crossroads of Mediterranean trade, was ruled successively by Phoenicians, Carthaginians, Greeks, Romans, and Byzantines before being conquered by Islamic Saracens from North Africa in the ninth century. In 1090 the Norman kings of Sicily conquered it and made it a way station for the First Crusade. In 1530 Charles V gave the island to the Knights Hospitalers (the Knights of Malta). The island withstood a siege by the Ottoman Turks in 1565 and fell only to Napoleon in 1798.

The Maltese opted for British rule in 1800, and it was annexed in 1814. Limited self-rule was granted under the constitutions of 1921 and 1939. During World War II, Malta suffered devastating air raids by German and Italian forces; the entire population was awarded the George Cross for bravery.

In 1964 Malta was granted independence within the British Commonwealth, with Elizabeth II as its sovereign. Abrogating its mutual defense treaty with Great Britain in 1971, the Maltese government severed all ties to the British Crown, becoming a fully independent republic. British forces withdrew from the island in 1979.

Malta was governed by the leftist, anticlerical, and neutralist Labour party from 1971 to 1987, whose leader, the ardent nationalist Dominic Mintoff, was prime minister from 1971 to 1984. He was succeeded by Mifsud Bonnici. In 1987 the Catholic and pro-Western Nationalist party won a popular electoral majority but not a majority in the parliament. Under the terms of a 1987 constitutional amendment, it was granted sufficient extra seats in the parliament to allow it to organize a government, under Prime Minister Eddie Fenech Adami.

In 1983 the Labour party government passed a law confiscating 75 percent of the wealth of the Catholic church and attempted to ban religiously sponsored schools. Resolution of the church-state issue is the key problem facing the Nationalist government. In foreign affairs it is faced with the need both to maintain good relations with its close neighbor Libya and to pursue improved relations with the West. In early December, 1989, Mikhail Gorbachev and President George Bush held a summit meeting aboard U.S. and Soviet naval ships in Valetta harbor.

Following the closing of the British naval base, which had been a principal source of revenue, the government pursued a policy of industrialization, led by textiles, furniture, and paper products. The port of Marsaxlokk is an important transshipment point for Mediterranean trade.

## Marshall Islands
### Republic of the Marshall Islands

**Geography Location:** two groups of islands, the Ratak and Ralik chains, comprising 31 atolls in western Pacific. Majuro 7°09′N, 171°12′E. **Boundaries:** Guam about 1,300 mi. (2,100 km) to NW, Hawaii about 2,000 mi. (3,200 km) to NE, Kiribati to S, Federated States of Micronesia to W. **Total land area:** 70 sq. mi. (180 sq km). **Coastline:** undetermined. **Comparative area:** slightly larger than Washington, D.C. **Land use:** 0% arable land; 60% permanent crops; 0% meadows and pastures; 0% forest and woodland; 40% other. **Major cities:** Majuro (capital—pop. N.A.).

**People Population:** 43,417 (1990). **Nationality:** noun—Marshallese; adjective—Marshallese. **Ethnic groups:** almost entirely Micronesian. **Languages:** English (official), two major dialects from Malayo-Polynesian family, Japanese. **Religions:** predominantly Christian, mostly Protestant.

**Government Type:** constitutional government in free association with U.S.; Compact of Free Association entered into force Oct. 21, 1986. **Independence:** Oct. 21, 1986 (from U.S.-administered UN trusteeship). **Constitution:** May 1, 1979. **National holiday:** May 1. **Heads of government:** Amata Kabua, president (since 1979). **Structure:** parliamentary-type government with legislative authority vested in 33-member parliament (Nitijela) and Council of Chiefs (Iroj), a consultative body; supreme court, high court.

**Economy Monetary unit:** U.S. dollar. **Budget:** (1987 est.) $55 mil. **GDP:** $63.0 mil., $1,500 per capita. **Chief crops:** coconuts, cacao, taro, breadfruit, fruits, copra. **Livestock:** pigs, cattle, goats. **Natural resources:** phosphate deposits, marine products, deep seabed minerals. **Major industries:** copra, fish, tourism. **Labor force:** 4,800 (1986); 22% males and 27% females unemployed (1980). **Exports:** $2.5 mil. (f.o.b., 1985); copra, copra oil, agricultural products, handicrafts. **Imports:** $29.2 mil. (c.i.f., 1985); foodstuffs, beverages, building materials. **Major trading partners:** U.S., Japan.

The Marshall Islands, part of the geographic region known as Micronesia, are made up of 31 atolls of the Ratak (Sunrise) and Ralik (Sunset) chains located between 4° and 14°N and 160° and 173°E. Although claimed by Spain in 1592, the islands were left undisturbed by the Spanish empire for 300 years. In 1885, Germany took over the administration on the islands of Jaluit and Ebon. At that time copra (dried coconut meat) trade was the primary industry. Japan assumed control of the Marshalls at the beginning of World War I and held them until 1944, when Allied forces occupied the islands. In 1947 the islands were included in the UN Trust Territory of the Pacific and placed under U.S. administration. In 1946 the U.S. government resettled the inhabitants of Bikini and Enewetak in order to begin nuclear tests, which continued through 1958. Residents began returning to Enewetak in 1980; but the estimated cost of a complete clean-up of Bikini is put at $100 million.

## Mauritania
### Islamic Republic of Mauritania

**Geography Location:** northwestern Africa. **Boundaries:** territory of Western Sahara to N, Algeria to NE, Mali to E and S, Senegal to S, Atlantic Ocean to W. **Total land area:** 397,840 sq. mi. (1,030,400 sq km). **Coastline:** 469 mi. (754 km). **Comparative area:** between Texas and Alaska. **Land use:** negl. % arable land; negl. % permanent crops; 38% meadows and pastures; 15% forest and woodland; 47% other; includes negl. % irrigated. **Major cities:** Nouakchott (capital) 350,000 (1984 est.); Nouadhibou (Port Etienne) 21,961; Kaédi 20,848; Zouérate 17,474; Rosso 16,466 (1977 census).

**People Population:** 1,934,549 (1990). **Nationality:** noun—Mauritanian(s); adjective—Mauritanian. **Ethnic groups:** 40% mixed Moor/black, 30% Moor, 30% black. **Languages:** French (official), Hasaniya Arabic (national), Toucouleur, Fula, Sarakole. **Religions:** nearly 100% Muslim.

**Government Type:** republic; military first seized power in bloodless coup July 10, 1978; palace coup on Dec. 24, 1984, brought president to power. **Independence:** Nov. 28, 1960 (from France). **Constitution:** May 20, 1961, abrogated after coup of July 10, 1978; provisional constitution published Dec. 17, 1980 but abandoned in 1981; new constitutional charter published Feb. 27, 1985. **National holiday:** Independence Day, Nov. 28. **Heads of government:** Col. Maawiya Ould Sid' Ahmed Taya, president (since Dec. 1984). **Structure:** executive—Military Committee for National Salvation rules by decree; national assembly and judiciary suspended pending restoration of civilian rule.

**Economy Monetary unit:** ouguiya. **Budget:** (1988 est.) *income:* $358 mil.; *expend.:* $334 mil. **GDP:** $1.0 bil., $520 per capita. **Chief crops:** most Mauritanians were nomads or subsistence farmers until drought forced them into cities; cash crop—gum arabic; cereals, vegetables, dates. **Livestock:** sheep, goats, cattle, camels, asses. **Natural resources:** iron ore, gypsum, fish, copper, phosphate. **Major industries:**

fishing, fish processing, mining of iron ore and gypsum. **Labor force:** 465,000 (1981 est.); 47% agriculture, 29% services, 14% industry and commerce, 10% government; 45,000 wage earners (1980); considerable unemployment; 53% of population of working age. **Exports:** $424 mil. (f.o.b., 1988); iron ore, processed fish, small amounts of gum arabic and gypsum; also unrecorded but numerically significant cattle exports to Senegal. **Imports:** $365 mil. (c.i.f., 1988); foodstuffs and other consumer goods, petroleum products, capital goods. **Major trading partners: *exports:*** 57% EC, 39% Japan, 2% Ivory Coast; ***imports:*** 79% EC, 5% Africa, 4% U.S., 2% Japan.

**Intl. Orgs.** FAO, G-77, GATT, IBRD, ICAO, IDA, IFAD, IFC, ILO, IMF, IMO, INTELSAT, INTERPOL, ITU, NAM, UN, UNESCO, UPU, WHO, WIPO, WMO.

The population of Mauritania is divided between an Arab and Berber majority in the north and various black African peoples in the south and southwest. From the ninth through the 15th centuries, southern Mauritania was part of the kingdoms of, successively, Ghana, Mali, and Sanghay. In the 1050s, a puritanical Muslim sect, the Almoravids, arose in the Tidra Islands, Between 1054 and 1086 they conquered Ghana, Morocco, Western Algeria, and Spain; they were eclipsed in the next century.

Portuguese trade on the Mauritania coast began in the early 15th century; the Portuguese remained dominant until about 1600 when their control was contested by the British, French, and Dutch. France established a protectorate in 1903, and the area was made a French colony in 1920.

In 1958 Mauritania became a self-governing republic within the French Overseas Community. In 1959 Mokhtar Ould Daddah was elected prime minister, and the country became fully independent on Nov. 28, 1960. A new constitution was adopted in 1961, establishing a presidential form of government. The four major political parties were combined into a single party in 1965.

Morocco claimed Mauritania as part of its sphere of influence; after talks about unifying the two countries broke down, Morocco recognized Mauritanian independence in 1970.

Spain relinquished its claim to the Spanish Sahara in 1976. The southern part of that territory was annexed by Mauritania, while the larger northern section was annexed by Morocco. Rebels of the Polisario Front proclaimed the independent state of Western Sahara, and in 1980 Mauritania relinquished its claims to its portion of the Western Sahara, signed a treaty with Polisario, and resumed relations with Algeria, Polisario's chief backer.

In 1978 Ould Daddah was removed from office in a military coup and was replaced as president by Lt. Col. Haidalla. He in turn was overthrown on Dec. 12, 1984, by Chief of Staff Maawiva Ould Sid' Ahmed Taya. Taya normalized relations with Morocco and held regional and local elections in 1986 and 1987 in a first step toward the restoration of democracy.

Border incidents erupted between Maur-

itania and Senegal in 1989. Mauritania expelled 40,000 black Senegalese workers in July 1989. Racial and religious strife has severely hampered the country's economy.

Mauritania maintains close ties to France and is heavily dependent on French aid. The country has little arable land; some grain is produced, and dates are grown in oases. Most of the economy depends on livestock, which has been severely depleted in droughts during the past decade. Mineral resources include iron ore and gypsum.

## Mauritius

**Geography Location:** southwestern Indian Ocean. Port Louis 20°09'S, 57°29'E. **Boundaries:** nearest neighbor is Réunion to SW. **Total land area:** 788 sq. mi. (2,040 sq km). **Coastline:** 110 mi. (177 km). **Comparative area:** two-thirds size of Rhode Island. **Land use:** 54% arable land; 4% permanent crops; 4% meadows and pastures; 31% forest and woodland; 7% other; includes 9% irrigated. **Major cities:** (1985) Port Louis (capital) 136,323; Beau Bassin/Rose Hill 91,786; Quatre Bornes 64,506; Curepipe 63,181; Vacoas-Phoenix 54,430.

**People Population:** 1,070,005 (1990). **Nationality:** noun—Mauritian(s); adjective—Mauritian. **Ethnic groups:** 68% Indo-Mauritian, 27% Creole, 3% Sino-Mauritian, 2% Franco-Mauritian. **Languages:** English (official), Creole, French, Hindi, Urdu, Hakka, Bojpoori. **Religions:** 51% Hindu, 30% Christian (mostly Roman Catholic with a few Anglicans), 17% Muslim.

**Government Type:** independent state, recognizing Elizabeth II as chief of state. **Independence:** Mar. 12, 1968 (from UK). **Constitution:** Mar. 12, 1968. **National holiday:** Independence Day, Mar. 12. **Heads of government:** Veerasamy Ringadoo, governor-general (since Jan. 1986); Anerood Jugnauth, prime minister (since Oct. 1982). **Structure:** executive power exercised by prime minister and 19-member Council of Ministers; unicameral legislature (Legislative Assembly) with 62 members elected by direct suffrage, eight specially elected by so-called best-loser system.

**Economy Monetary unit:** Mauritian rupee. **Budget:** (1987 est.) *income:* $351 mil.; *expend.:* $414 mil. **GDP:** $1.9 bil., $1,910 per capita (1988). **Chief crops:** about 90% of cultivated land area planted in sugar; also sugar derivatives, tea, tobacco; most food imported. **Livestock:** cattle, goats, pigs, sheep. **Natural resources:** cultivated land, fish. **Major industries:** food processing (largely sugar milling), textiles, and wearing apparel. **Labor force:** 335,000 (1985); 29% government services, 27% agriculture and fishing, 22% manufacturing, 22% other; 15–20% unemployed; 43% of working age. **Exports:** $1.0 bil. (f.o.b., 1988); 44% textiles, 40% sugar, 10% light manufactures. **Imports:** $1.3 bil. (c.i.f., 1988); 50% manufactured goods, 17% capital equipment, 13% foodstuffs, 8% petroleum products, 7% chemicals. **Major trading partners: *exports:*** (EC

countries and U.S. have preferential treatment) 77% EC, 15% U.S.; ***imports:*** EC, U.S., South Africa, Japan.

**Intl. Orgs.** Commonwealth, FAO, G-77, GATT, IAEA, IBRD, ICAO, IDA, IFAD, IFC, ILO, IMF, IMO, INTERPOL, ITU, NAM, OAU, UN, UNESCO, UPU, WHO, WIPO, WMO.

The volcanic island of Mauritius and its seven smaller neighbors lie about 500 miles east of Madagascar and 2,400 miles southwest of India. They were uninhabited when discovered by the Dutch in 1507. Following sporadic Dutch settlement in the 17th century, the French took over in 1721, establishing sugarcane plantations worked by slaves imported from Africa. Mauritius was captured by the British in 1810. Following the abolition of slavery in the British Empire (1834), Indian workers were imported to labor in the cane fields. A majority of the population now is of Indian descent. On Mar. 12, 1968, Mauritius became an independent parliamentary democracy within the British Commonwealth.

The present government is controlled by an alliance of Prime Minister Anerood Jugnauth's Mauritius Socialist Movement and two smaller parties. The country has experienced rapid economic growth in the 1980s, led by exports of woolen knitwear. About 35 percent of the labor force is engaged in manufacturing, principally of clothing and textiles. Sugar remains the most important agricultural crop.

## Mexico
### United Mexican States

**Geography Location:** southernmost state in North America. **Boundaries:** U.S. to N, Gulf of Mexico to E, Belize and Guatemala to S, Pacific Ocean to W. **Total land area:** 756,066 sq. mi. (1,958,201 sq km). **Coastline:** 5,798 mi. (9,329 km). **Comparative area:** about 1.25 times size of Alaska. **Land use:** 12% arable land; 1% permanent crops; 39% meadows and pastures; 24% forest and woodland; 24% other; includes 3% irrigated. **Major cities:** (1979 est.) Ciudad de México (Mexico City—capital) 9,191,295; Netzahualcóyotl 2,331,351; Guadalajara 1,906,145; Monterrey 1,064,629; Heróica Puebla de Zaragoza (Puebla) 710,833.

**People Population:** 87,870,154 (1990). **Nationality:** noun—Mexican(s); adjective—Mexican. **Ethnic groups:** 60% mestizo, 30% Amerindian or predominantly Amerindian, 9% white or predominantly white, 1% other. **Languages:** Spanish. **Religions:** 97% nominally Roman Catholic, 3% Protestant.

**Government Type:** federal republic operating under centralized government. **Independence:** Sept. 16, 1910 (from Spain). **Constitution:** Feb. 5, 1917. **National holiday:** Independence Day, Sept. 16. **Heads of government:** Carlos Salinas de Gortari, president (since Dec. 1988). **Structure:** dominant executive; bicameral legislature (National Congress—Senate, Federal Chamber of Deputies); Supreme Court.

**Economy Monetary unit:** peso. **Budget:** (1988) *income:* $36.1 bil.; *expend.:* $56.1 bil.

**GDP:** $187.0 bil., $2,165 per capita. **Chief crops:** corn, cotton, wheat, coffee, sugarcane. **Livestock:** cattle, pigs, goats, sheep, horses. **Natural resources:** crude oil, silver, copper, gold, lead. **Major industries:** food and beverages, tobacco, chemicals. **Labor force:** 24.7 mil. (1986); 31.4% services; 26% agriculture, forestry, hunting, fishing; 13.9% commerce; 12.8% manufacturing; 9.5% construction; 19% unemployment (1988). **Exports:** $23.0 bil. (f.o.b., 1989); crude oil, oil products, coffee, shrimp, engines, cotton. **Imports:** $23.3 bil. (f.o.b., 1989); grain, metal manufactures, agricultural machinery, electrical equipment. **Major trading partners:** *exports:* 66% U.S., 16% EC, 11% Japan; *imports:* 62% U.S., 18% EC, 10% Japan.

**Intl. Orgs.** FAO, G-77, GATT, IAEA, IBRD, ICAO, IDA, IFAD, IFC, ILO, IMF, IMO, INTELSAT, INTERPOL, ITU, NAM, OAS, UN, UNESCO, UPU, WHO, WIPO, WMO.

The pre-Columbian history of indigenous Mexican cultures is very rich and includes the high civilizations of the Olmecs, Mayas, Toltecs, and Aztecs, in addition to numerous nomadic cultures. In 1519 Hernán Cortés and several hundred Spanish soldiers entered Tenochtitlán (now Mexico City). A two-year campaign against the Aztecs under Montezuma II ended with the Spanish capture of the city. The Viceroyalty of New Spain—with its center at Mexico City—was proclaimed in 1535. At its height it encompassed the lands from California to Panama, Florida, Spain's Caribbean holdings, and the Philippines.

As was the case with the rest of Spanish America, the movement for independence in New Spain coincided with the weakening of the authority of the Spanish Crown as a result of the Napoleonic takeover of Spain in 1808. In 1810 Miguel Hidalgo led a failed uprising and was executed. Following in Hidalgo's footsteps, José María Morelos led another uprising in the south, and he in turn was captured and put to death. Agustín de Iturbide, leader of the royalist forces, defected to the side of those struggling for independence in 1821. Envisioning independent Mexico as a monarchy, military groups proclaimed Iturbide emperor of Mexico in 1822.

The Mexican empire did not last long, and the Central American counties seceded after Iturbide's ouster by Antonio de Santa Anna in 1823. A republic was declared and Guadalupe Victoria was the first president (1824–29). In 1836, Texas seceded from Mexico in a revolution that cost Santa Anna the presidency. Between 1845 and 1848, Mexico fought the United States over U.S. annexation of Texas, and in 1847 U.S. troops occupied Mexico City. Under the Treaty of Guadalupe Hidalgo (1848), Mexico sold about half its territory—including California, Nevada, Utah, most of Arizona, and parts of New Mexico, Colorado, and Wyoming to the United States—for $15 million.

Santa Anna ruled again, as dictator, from 1853 to 1855, before being toppled by the liberal movement, La Reforma. A new constitution was proclaimed in 1857, but Conservatives declared it void. Following the War of Reform

(1858–61), France, Britain, and Spain all claimed compensation for destruction of their nations' property, and in 1862 they landed troops at Veracruz. Britain and Spain withdrew, but Napoleon III attempted to establish a dependent empire in Mexico and installed Archduke Ferdinand Maximilian of Austria on the Mexican throne in 1864. In the face of Mexican resistance and U.S. threats, France ended its Mexican adventure, and in 1867 Maximilian was captured and executed by Liberal forces.

Benito Juárez, who served as provisional president during the War of Reform, was a major force behind the liberal movement called La Reforma, which stressed the promotion of capitalism and the destruction of what were seen as vestiges of feudalism (abolition of *fueros*, traditional corporatist privileges) in Mexico. Juárez won a third presidential term in 1871 but died in office and was succeeded in office by Sebastián Lerdo de Tejada, who was in turn overthrown by Gen. Porfirio Díaz. During the stable dictatorship known as the Porfiriato (1876–1911), Mexico experienced economic growth, though wealthy landowners and the church benefited at the expense of the poor.

The Mexican Revolution began in 1910 after Porfirio Díaz had his electoral opponent, Francisco I. Madero, jailed. In response, Madero formulated his Plan of San Luis Potosí, calling for armed resistance to the dictatorship. Rebellions broke out in the northern state of Chihuahua under the leadership of Pancho Villa and in the southern state of Morelos led by Emiliano Zapata. The two states soon came under rebel control, and in 1911 Díaz left Mexico. Madero was elected president, but his failure to carry through promised reforms resulted in the continuation of the rebellion.

Backed by the U.S., Gen. Victoriano Huerta overthrew Madero in 1913. But the fighting continued, and Huerta lost the support of the U.S. and was forced from office by Zapata, Villa, and Venustiano Carranza, who became president (1914–20). Zapata and Villa continued their resistance, but by 1916 Gen. Alvaro Obregón had driven Villa back to Chihuahua and Zapata's armies had been contained. Carranza called for the election of delegates to a constitutional convention in 1916, and by the following year, the progressive Mexican Constitution of 1917 was in place.

Obregón deposed Carranza in 1920 and served as president until 1924. He was re-elected to succeed Plutarco Elías Calles in 1928 but was assassinated before he could take office. In 1929 Calles founded the National Revolutionary party, which became the Institutional Revolutionary party (PRI) in 1946.

Lázaro Cárdenas won the presidency in 1934, sending Calles, the long-time power behind the scene, into exile. This, coupled with Cárdenas's decision to remove himself from politics at the end of his term, greatly stabilized the institutional structure created by the Mexican Revolution. Cárdenas was the last of the "revolutionary" leaders to make good on the promises to labor and the peasantry. He presided over extensive redistribution of land and in 1938 reorganized the ruling PRI into four

constituencies: peasants, labor, the military, and the popular sector (middle class, professionals). Cárdenas also used the national ownership of subsoil rights enshrined in the Mexican constitution to nationalize U.S. oil companies, thus assuring his credentials as a hero of Mexican nationalism.

The political movement of Mexican presidents since Cárdenas has been away from its peasant and labor constituencies toward business and the popular sector, beginning with Miguel Alemán's election in 1946.

The stability of the PRI was seriously challenged in the 1980s as a result of the economic crisis stemming from the severe decline in the price of oil. Mexico borrowed heavily from foreign creditors during the 1970s on the expectation that oil prices would remain high. The debt problem led to cutbacks in government spending, a catastrophic drop in the value of the currency, and capital and human flight out of the country. The political repercussions of this could be seen in the elections of 1988, in which the ruling PRI had its worst showing ever. Although its candidate, Carlos Salinas de Gortari, won the election, the narrow margin was disputed by the opposition Revolutionary Democratic party (PRD) and National Action party (PAN). Pres. Salinas has vigorously pursued economic reform and sought a free-trade agreement with the United States and Canada.

## Micronesia
### Federated States of Micronesia

**Geography Location:** forms (with Palau) archipelago of Caroline Islands, Ponape (6°52′N, 158°15′E), Yap (9°32′N, 138°08′E), Kosrae (5°19′N, 162°59′E), and Truk (7°22′N, 151°54′E), in western Pacific Ocean. **Boundaries:** Guam to NW, Marshall Islands to E, Papua New Guinea to S, Philippines about 497 mi. (800 km) to W. **Total land area:** 271 sq. mi. (702 sq km). **Coastline:** undetermined. **Comparative area:** about four times size of Washington, D.C. **Land use:** N.A. **Major cities:** Kolonia (capital—population N.A.).

**People Population:** 104,937 (1990). **Nationality:** noun—Micronesian(s); adjective—Micronesian. **Ethnic groups:** nine ethnic Micronesian and Polynesian groups. **Languages:** English (official), Trukese, Pohnpeian, Yapese, Kosrean. **Religions:** predominantly Christian, divided between Roman Catholic and Protestant; also, Assembly of God, Jehovah's Witnesses, Seventh-Day Adventists, Latter-day Saints, and Baha'i.

**Government Type:** constitutional government in free association with U.S.; Compact of Free Association entered into force Nov. 3, 1986. **Independence:** Nov. 3, 1986 (from U.S.-administered UN Trusteeship). **Constitution:** May 10, 1979. **National holiday:** May 10. **Heads of government:** John R. Haglelgam, president (since 1986). **Structure:** executive—national president and vice president elected from ranks of popularly elected senators; legislative—National Congress (unicameral); judicial—national Supreme Court headed by chief justice.

**Economy Monetary unit:** U.S. dollar. **Budget:** (1987 est.) *income:* $110.8 mil.; *expend.:* N.A. **GNP:** $150 mil., $1,500 per capita (1989 est.). **Chief crops:** copra, black pepper, tropical fruits and vegetables, coconuts, cassava, sweet potatoes; mainly subsistence economy. **Livestock:** pigs, chickens. **Natural resources:** forests, marine products, deep seabed minerals. **Major industries:** tourism, craft items from shell, wood, pearl. **Labor force:** undetermined. **Exports:** $1.6 mil. (f.o.b., 1983); copra. **Imports:** $48.9 mil. (c.i.f., 1983). **Major trading partners:** U.S., Japan.

The Federated States of Micronesia extend 1,800 miles across an archipelago of the Caroline Islands in the larger island group of Micronesia. Ethnically diverse (there are eight primary languages, not including dialects), the islands are thought to be the first in the Pacific settled by argonauts from the Philippines and Indonesia, about 1500 B.C. Ferdinand Magellan landed in the Marianas in 1521, and Spain claimed sovereignty from 1565 to 1899, when the Caroline Islands were sold to Germany. After World War I, the League of Nations mandated the islands to Japan, which developed agriculture (especially sugarcane), mining, and fishing. After World War II, the islands were included in the UN Trust Territory of the Pacific and placed under U.S. administration. A compact of free association between Micronesia and the United States was signed in 1986, and Micronesia's trust territory status with the UN trusteeship council was officially dissolved in December 1990.

# Monaco
## Principality of Monaco

**Geography Location:** small enclave in southeastern France. **Boundaries:** France to N, E, and W; Mediterranean Sea to S. **Total land area:** 1.21 sq. mi. (1.95 sq km). **Coastline:** 2.6 mi. (4.1 km). **Comparative area:** about three times size of the Mall in Washington, D.C. **Land use:** 0% arable land; 0% permanent crops; 0% meadows and pastures; 0% forest and woodland; 100% other. **Major cities:** Monaco (capital).

**People Population:** 29,453 (1990). **Nationality:** noun—Monacan(s) or Monegasque(s); adjective—Monacan or Monegasque. **Ethnic groups:** 47% French, 16% Monegasque, 16% Italian, 21% other. **Languages:** French (official), English, Italian, Monegasque. **Religions:** 95% Roman Catholic.

**Government Type:** constitutional monarchy. **Constitution:** Dec. 17, 1962. **National holiday:** Nov. 19. **Heads of government:** Prince Ranier III, chief of state (since Nov. 1949). **Structure:** executive—prince, minister of state (senior French civil servant appointed by prince), and Council of Government as cabinet; legislative—prince and National Council of 18 members; judicial—authority delegated by prince to Supreme Tribunal.

**Economy Monetary unit:** French franc. **Budget:** (1988 est.) *income:* $386 mil.; *expend:*

N.A. **GNP:** N.A. **Chief crops:** N.A. **Livestock:** N.A. **Natural resources:** none. **Major industries:** pharmaceuticals, food processing, precision instruments. **Labor force:** N.A. **Exports:** N.A. **Imports:** N.A. **Major trading partners:** full customs integration with France, which collects and rebates Monacan trade duties; also participates in EC market system through customs union with France.

**Intl. Orgs.** IAEA, ICAO, INTELSAT, INTERPOL, ITU, UN (permanent observer), UPU, WHO, WIPO.

Known to Phoenicians and Greeks from the beginning of the first millenium B.C., the history of the port of Monaco is coextensive with that of southeastern France for much of its history. A western colony of the great trading city-state of Genoa in the 13th century, Monaco in 1368 became an independent principality under the rule of the Grimaldi family. At various points it became a protectorate of Spain, France, and Sardinia, it was restored to independence in 1861 by the Franco-Monegasque treaty.

In 1911 Monaco became a constitutional monarchy under the Matignon-Grimaldi dynasty. In 1918 France required the principality to conform to its national interests in all respects; by an agreement of 1919, should the dynasty fail to produce a male heir, Monaco would be absorbed into France. However, the family is allowed to adopt an heir if they so choose. The marriage of Prince Ranier III to the U.S film star Grace Kelly produced an heir apparent for this generation.

Despite the fame of the Monte Carlo casino, gambling accounts for only 4 percent of the principality's revenues. The principal industry is tourism, followed by light manufacturing. Monaco also supports a prominent institute of oceanography. Land reclamation projects, impelled by a real estate boom, have added about 20 percent to the nation's territory since World War II.

# Mongolia
## Mongolian People's Republic

**Geography Location:** landlocked country in central Asia. **Boundaries:** USSR to N, China to E, S, and W. **Total land area:** 604,250 sq. mi. (1,565,000 sq km). **Coastline:** none. **Comparative area:** slightly larger than Alaska. **Land use:** 1% arable land; 0% permanent crops; 79% meadows and pastures; 10% forest and woodland; 10% other; includes negl. % irrigated. **Major cities:** (1989) Ulan Bator (capital) 548,400; Darhan 85,800; Erdenet 56,100; Baga Nuur 25,000 (1984).

**People Population:** 2,125,463 (1989). **Nationality:** noun—Mongolian(s) adjective—Mongolian. **Ethnic groups:** 90% Mongol, 4% Kazakh, 2% Chinese, 2% Russian, 2% other. **Languages:** Khalkha Mongol used by over 90% of population; Turkic, Russian, Chinese. **Religions:** predominantly Tibetan Buddhist, about 4% Muslim.

**Government Type:** communist state.

**Independence:** Mar. 13, 1921 (from China). **Constitution:** July 6, 1960. **National holiday:** People's Revolution Day, July 11. **Heads of government:** Punsalmaagiin Ochirbat, president (since Mar. 1990); Dashiin Byambasuren, prime minister (since Sept. 1990). **Structure:** executive—Council of Ministers; legislative—unicameral Great People's Hural; judicial—court system; Supreme Court elected by Great People's Hural.

**Economy Monetary unit:** tugrik. **Budget:** (1987 est.) *income:* $2.2 bil.; *expend:* $2.2 bil. **GDP:** $1.7 bil., $880 per capita (1985 est.). **Chief crops:** livestock raising predominates; wheat, oats, barley. **Livestock:** sheep, goats, cattle, horses, camels. **Natural resources:** coal, copper, molybdenum, tungsten, phosphates. **Major industries:** processing of animal products, building materials, foods and beverages. **Labor force:** primarily agricultural; over half adult population is in labor force, including large percentage of women; shortage of skilled labor. **Exports:** $388 mil. (f.o.b., 1985); livestock, animal products, wool, hides, fluorospar, nonferrous metals. **Imports:** $1.0 bil. (c.i.f., 1988); machinery and equipment, fuels, food products, industrial consumer goods, chemicals. **Major trading partners:** nearly all trade with communist countries (about 80% with USSR); total turnover about $1 bil.

**Intl. Orgs.** FAO, IAEA, IBRD, ICAO, IDA, IFAD, IFC, ILO, IMF, IMO, ITU, UN, UNESCO, UNIDO, UPU, WHO, WIPO, WMO.

Mongols under Genghis Khan conquered most of Eurasia in the early 13th century. The Mongol empire broke up in the mid-14th century, and Mongolia lapsed into tribal disunion and political insignificance. Chinese rule was established thereafter in Inner Mongolia (ruled directly) and, in 1691, in Outer Mongolia (a province under local rule). With the 1911 Chinese Revolution, Outer Mongolia unsuccessfully proclaimed its independence from China. The nationalist religious leader the Bogdo Lama sought Russian support in 1920. Under the revolutionary leaders Sukhe Bataar and Khorloin Choibalsan, a "provisional people's government" again declared independence in 1921. Sukhe Bataar died in 1923; on Nov. 26, 1924, the Mongolian People's Republic (MPR) was established with Soviet sponsorship. The early years of the republic were marked by repeated Stalinist purges of Mongol revolutionary leaders and by disastrous attempts at centralized planning.

Choibalsan emerged as party leader in the late 1930s and was confirmed as premier in 1940. In 1939 combined Soviet and Mongolian armies prevented a Japanese conquest of Mongolia. In 1945 the Republic of China recognized the MPR; recognition was reaffirmed by the People's Republic of China in 1949 but abrogated by the Republic of China (on Taiwan) in 1953. In 1948 the first of a new series of five-year plans began to bring industrial and agricultural development to Mongolia, with extensive Soviet aid and support. Choibalsan died in 1952 and was succeeded as premier by Yumjaagiyn Tsedenbal. Following the Sino-Soviet split of 1958, heavy concentrations of

Soviet troops and missiles were stationed along the Chinese-Mongolian border. On Oct. 27, 1961, the MPR was admitted to the United Nations; diplomatic relations with various other non–Soviet bloc nations developed gradually thereafter. Tsedenbal was ousted as party chairman and premier in 1984; he was replaced by Jambyn Batmunkh as party chairman and by Dumaagiin Sodnom as premier. The United States and the MPR established diplomatic relations on Jan. 27, 1987.

Following widespread demonstrations calling for human rights, religious freedom, and an end to special privileges for Communist officials, the Communist party voted to give up its constitutional power in March 1990. After the resignation of Pres. Zhambyn Batmonh, the parliament elected Punsalmaagiin Ochirbat as president; in May he visited Beijing to improve relations and strengthen economic ties; it was the first visit by a Mongolian head of state since 1962.

Mongolia's economy remains concentrated on livestock raising and animal-product processing, with some agriculture, mining, and heavy industry. Half of the population is under 25 years of age.

## Morocco
### Kingdom of Morocco

**Geography Location:** northwestern Africa. **Boundaries:** North Atlantic Ocean to W and NW, Strait of Gibraltar to N, Mediterranean Sea to NE, Algeria to E and SE, Western Sahara to SW. **Total land area:** 274,461 sq. mi. (710,850 sq km). **Coastline:** 1,140 mi. (1,835 km). **Comparative area:** slightly larger than California. **Land use:** 18% arable land; 1% permanent crops; 28% meadows and pastures; 12% forest and woodland; 41% other; includes 1% irrigated. **Major cities:** (1987 est.) Rabat (including Sale; capital) 1,287,000; Casablanca 2,904,000; Marrakech (Marrakesh) 1,425,000; Fes (Fez) 933,000; Oujda 895,000.

**People Population:** 25,648,214 (1990). **Nationality:** noun—Moroccan(s); adjective—Moroccan. **Ethnic groups:** 99.1% Arab-Berber, 0.7% non-Moroccan, 0.2% Jewish. **Languages:** Arabic (official), several Berber dialects; French is language of business, government, diplomacy, and postprimary education. **Religions:** 98.7% Muslim, 1.1% Christian, 0.2% Jewish.

**Government Type:** constitutional monarchy. **Independence:** Mar. 2, 1956 (from France). **Constitution:** Mar. 10, 1972. **National holiday:** Independence Day, Nov. 18. **Heads of government:** Hassan II, king (since Feb. 1961); Azedine Laraki, prime minister (since Sept. 1986). **Structure:** king has paramount executive powers; Constitution provides for prime minister and ministers named by and responsible to king; unicameral legislature (Cf Representatives) of which two-thirds of members are directly elected and one-third are indirectly elected; judiciary independent of other branches.

**Economy Monetary unit:** dirham. **Budget:** (1988) *income:* $5.1 bil.; *expend.:* $6 bil. **GDP:** $21.9 bil., $880 per capita. **Chief crops:** not self-sufficient in food; cereal farming and livestock raising predominant; barley, wheat, citrus fruit, wine, vegetables; illegal producer of cannabis for international drug trade. **Livestock:** sheep, goats, cattle, asses, mules. **Natural resources:** phosphates, iron ore, manganese, lead, zinc, fish, salt. **Major industries:** phosphate rock mining and processing, food processing, leather goods. **Labor force:** 7.4 mil. (1985); 50% agriculture, 26% services, 15% industry; 15% unemployment (1988). **Exports:** $3.1 bil. (f.o.b., 1989); 30% food and beverages, 23% semiprocessed goods, 21% consumer goods. **Imports:** $5.1 bil. (c.i.f., 1989); 24% capital goods, 22% semiprocessed goods, 16% raw materials, 16% fuel and lubricants. **Major trading partners:** *exports:* 58% EC, 7% India, 5% Japan, 5% USSR, 2% U.S.; *imports:* 53% EC, 11% U.S., 4% Canada, 3% Iraq, 3% USSR, 2% Japan.

**Intl. Orgs.** Arab League, EC (associate), FAO, G-77, GATT, IAEA, IBRD, ICAO, IDA, IFAD, IFC, ILO, IMF, IMO, INTELSAT, INTERPOL, ITU, NAM, UN, UNESCO, UPU, WHO, WIPO, WMO.

Neolithic inhabitants of Morocco were displaced by Berbers around 1000 B.C. Phoenician and Carthaginian settlements were established along the Mediterranean coast. Morocco came under Roman rule around 40 A.D. and was invaded via Spain by Germanic Vandals in the fifth century. The Islamic invasions of the mid-seventh century established Arab rule in Morocco, and most of the indigenous Berbers converted to Islam. Ethnic tension between Berbers and Arabs has been a basic element of Moroccan politics and society ever since.

In the late eighth century, King Idris ibn Adballah united Berbers and Arabs in a monarchy that lasted for 200 years and made the capital city of Fez one of the major religious and cultural centers of the Islamic world. In the 11th century, the Almoravid dynasty from Mauritania conquered Morocco, western Algeria, and Spain. It was ousted by another Muslin sect, the Almohads, led by Ibn Tumart. After about 1200 the tide of Moorish expansion in the Iberian Peninsula turned; in 1492 Ferdinand and Isabella expelled the last Moors from Grenada.

Naval conflict between Morocco, Spain, and Portugal continued in the western Mediterranean and along the Atlantic coast of northwestern Africa for several centuries more. In the mid-17th century, Morocco was reunited under the present Alawid dynasty. In the early 19th century, American and British forces combatted Moroccan piracy in the Mediterranean, and Spain established colonies in Tangier in the north and along the Atlantic coast between Morocco and Mauritania.

The attempts of Sultan Hassan I (r. 1873–94) to implement reforms to strengthen Morocco's independence were thwarted by European interests. By the early 20th century, France, securely established in Algeria, began exerting increasing control in Morocco. A multipower conference at Algeciras in 1906 affirmed Moroccan independence but upheld the special rights claimed by Spain and France. The Treaty of Fez, signed in 1912 between France and Sultan Abd-al-Hafidn, ended Moroccan independence by granting the country to France and reaffirming a Spanish sphere of influence in the southwest.

Nationalist unrest and tribal uprisings disrupted French administration in Morocco throughout the 1920s and 1930s. Morocco became a battleground during World War II between the Axis-supported Vichy French government and the Free French and their Allied backers. In 1943 Churchill and Roosevelt met at Casablanca to discuss wartime strategy; in the same year, the Istiqlal (Independence) party was founded to fight for independence from the French in the postwar era.

In 1947 Moroccan liberation forces began open warfare against the French. The exiled Sultan Mohammad V was allowed to return, and France promised independence by 1955.

With the withdrawal of French forces, Morocco became independent on Mar. 2, 1956. Tangier (under international administration since 1923) was incorporated into the newly independent state in October 1956, and the Spanish enclave of Ifni was ceded to Morocco in 1969.

A period of instability ensued after 1957 as newly formed political parties vied for power. King Mohammad I died in 1961 and was succeeded by his son, Hassan II. In 1962 an elected parliamentary government took power under the constitutional monarchy. Political unrest and economic difficulties led to the declaration of states of emergency in 1965 and 1970 and a new constitution in 1977.

Spain withdrew from its former territory of Spanish (now Western) Sahara, a phosphate-rich desert territory on Morocco's southern border, in February 1976. On Apr. 14, 1976, Morocco annexed the northern two-thirds of the territory, while Mauritania claimed the remainder. The Polisario Spanish Saharan liberation movement, backed by Algeria and Libya, conducted guerrilla operations against Moroccan and Mauritanian forces. In 1979 Mauritania gave up its claims, and Morocco claimed the entire region.

In April 1987, Morocco completed construction of a 2,000-mile sand wall completely enclosing Western Sahara. Polisario forces, partly cut off from Algerian aid, nevertheless control much of the Western Saharan countryside, while Morocco holds the cities and towns. In May 1987 a Moroccan-Algerian summit was held under the sponsorship of Saudi Arabia, which offered King Hassan $260 million to rebuild Morocco's war-torn economy in return for allowing a self-determination referendum in the Western Sahara. The king refused. But in 1991, Morocco allowed a UN mission to make preparations in the Western Sahara for a referendum on self-determination.

The Moroccan economy nevertheless has shown rapid development, led by mining, mixed light industry, tourism, and the export of fresh winter fruit and vegetables to Europe.

The Persian Gulf crisis made an already weak economy weaker, and riots during a general strike protesting low wages, economic hardship, and poor job prospects in Fez left 100 dead and hundreds more injured in January 1991. Although Morocco was an active member of the allied coalition against Iraq, Moroccans also staged huge demonstrations in support of Saddam Hussein in February.

## Mozambique
### Republic of Mozambique

**Geography** **Location:** eastern coast of Africa. **Boundaries:** Zambia and Malawi to NW, Tanzania to N, Indian Ocean to E and SE, South Africa and Swaziland to SW, Zimbabwe to W. **Total land area:** 302,739 sq. mi. (784,090 sq km). **Coastline:** 1,535 mi. (2,470 km). **Comparative area:** slightly less than twice size of California. **Land use:** 4% arable land; negl. % permanent crops; 56% meadows and pastures; 20% forest and woodland; 20% other; includes negl. % irrigated. **Major cities:** (1987 est.) Maputo (capital) 1,006,765.

**People** **Population:** 14,565,656 (1990). **Nationality:** noun—Mozambican(s); adjective—Mozambican. **Ethnic groups:** Majority from indigenous tribal groups; about 35,000 Euro-Africans, 15,000 Indians, 10,000 Europeans. **Languages:** Portuguese (official), indigenous languages. **Religions:** 60% indigenous beliefs, 30% Christian, 10% Muslim.

**Government** **Type:** republic. **Independence:** June 25, 1975 (from Portugal). **Constitution:** Nov. 30, 1990. **National holiday:** Independence Day, June 25. **Heads of government:** Joachím Alberto Chissano, president (since Nov. 1986); Mario de Graca Machungo, prime minister (since July 1986). **Structure:** unicameral Assembly, supreme court.

**Economy** **Monetary unit:** meticai. **Budget:** (1988 est.) **income:** $186 mil.; **expend:** $239 mil. **GDP:** $1.6 bil., $110 per capita. **Chief crops:** cash crops—cotton, cashew nuts, sugar, tea, copra; other crops—corn, wheat, peanuts, potatoes, beans; imports—corn. **Livestock:** cattle, goats, pigs, sheep, asses. **Natural resources:** coal, natural gas, copper, bauxite, titanium. **Major industries:** food and beverages, chemicals (fertilizer, soap, paints), petroleum. **Labor force:** 95% agriculture, 5% other. **Exports:** $100 mil. (f.o.b., 1988); 48% shrimp, 21% cashews, 10% sugar. **Imports:** $764 mil. (c.i.f., 1988); food, clothing, farm equipment, petroleum. **Major trading partners:** *exports:* U.S., Western Europe, E. Germany, Japan; *imports:* U.S., Western Europe, USSR.

**Intl. Orgs.** FAO, G-77, GATT (de facto), IBRD, ICAO, IFAD, ILO, IMF, IMO, ITU, NAM, UN, UNESCO, UPU, WHO, WMO.

Mozambique has been inhabited since prehistoric times by a variety of Bantu peoples. Portuguese trading stations were established starting in 1505, and Portugal developed an extensive coastal trade in gold and ivory. Mozambique also served as a way station for Portuguese trade to East Asia.

Despite competition from other European nations, Portugal maintained control of the Mozambique coast. Settlement by sizable numbers of Portuguese immigrants began in the late 19th century. Mozambique was organized as a colony, sometimes called Portuguese East Africa, in 1885; boundaries in the interior were defined in 1891.

Economic development of Mozambique in the 20th century remained almost entirely in Portuguese hands. By the 1950s native peoples began to protest Portuguese rule; a rebellion of the Frelimo (Front for the Liberation of Mozambique) guerrilla movement began in 1961. Rebels controlled most of the northern part of the country by 1964. Fighting continued for another decade.

Following the Portuguese revolution of 1974, Portugal agreed to independence for Mozambique, and many Portuguese settlers returned to Portugal, leaving the country bereft of administrative personnel and infrastructure support. Mozambique became fully independent on June 25, 1975. A Marxist Frelimo government took office, with Samora Michel as the country's first president. The new government formed agricultural collectives and nationalized most private land and industry as well as all social services.

In the late 1970s, fighting broke out between Mozambique and Rhodesia. With the independence of Rhodesia as Zimbabwe in 1980, relations between the two governments improved. Mozambique is to some extent politically and economically dependent on the goodwill of South Africa, despite the ideological differences between the two countries. At the same time, Mozambique has accused South Africa of aiding a rebel movement, Renamo (Mozambique National Resistance), dedicated to overthrowing the Frelimo government.

In 1986, following the death of Samora Michel, Joachím Chissano became president. The Chissano government reintroduced some private small-scale agriculture, loosened ties to the Eastern bloc, and appealed to the West for economic assistance. In 1987 a UN-led relief effort began. In 1989 Mozambique signed a cooperation agreement with South Africa, which cut off its aid to the Renamo insurgents. But fighting continued into 1990.

In November 1990, Mozambique adopted a new constitution widening individual rights and freedoms, including abolition of the death penalty, freedom of the press and speech, and an independent judiciary, as well as establishing multiparty democracy, a presidential regime, and free-market economy. Mozambique is rich in agricultural land and mineral resources. Nevertheless, 15 years of communism, drought, and civil war have left the country poor and dependent on foreign aid.

## Myanmar
### Union of Myanmar

**Geography** **Location:** NW region of Southeast Asia. **Boundaries:** China and Laos to NE, Bangladesh, India to NW, Thailand to SE, Andaman Sea to S, and Bay of Bengal to SW. **Total land area:** 261,218 sq. mi. (676,552 sq km). **Coastline:** 1,902 mi. (3,060 km). **Comparative area:** slightly smaller than Texas. **Land use:** 15% arable land; 1% permanent crops; 1% meadows and pastures; 49% forest and woodland; 34% other; includes 2% irrigated. **Major cities:** (1983 census) Yangon (formerly Rangoon) (capital) 2,458,712; Mandalay 532,895; Bassein 335,000; Moulmein 219,991; Akyab 143,000.

**People** **Population:** 41,277,389 (1990). **Nationality:** noun—Burmese (sing., pl.); adjective—Burmese. **Ethnic groups:** 68% Burman, 9% Shan, 7% Karen, 4% Raljome, 3% Chinese, 2% Indian, 7% other. **Languages:** Burmese, minority ethnic languages. **Religions:** 85% Buddhist, 15% indigenous beliefs, Muslim, Christian, and other.

**Government** **Type:** republic. **Independence:** Jan. 4, 1948 (from UK). **Constitution:** Jan. 3, 1974. **National holiday:** Independence Day, Jan. 4. **Heads of government:** Gen. Saw Maung, chairman (since Sept. 1988). **Structure:** Council of State rules through Council of Ministers; National Assembly (Pyithu Hluttaw, or People's Congress) has legislative power.

**Economy** **Monetary unit:** kyat. **Budget:** (1989 est.) *income:* $4.9 bil.; *expend.:* $5.0 bil. **GDP:** $11.0 bil., $280 per capita. **Chief crops:** paddy, beans, pulses, maize, oilseeds; most rice grown in deltaic land; illegal producer of opium poppy and cannabis for international drug trade. **Livestock:** cattle, pigs, buffalo, goats, sheep. **Natural resources:** crude oil, timber, tin, copper, tungsten. **Major industries:** agricultural processing, textiles and footwear, wood and wood products. **Labor force:** 15.8 mil. (1988); 65.6% agriculture, 13.7% industry, 9.8% trade, 6.6% government; 10.4% unemployment in urban areas (1986–87). **Exports:** $311 mil. (f.o.b., 1988 est.); teak, rice, oilseed, metals, rubber, gems. **Imports:** $536 mil. (c.i.f., 1988 est.); machinery, transport equipment, chemicals, food products. **Major trading partners:** *exports:* U.S., Japan, EC, India, Africa; *imports:* U.S., Japan, EC, China, Thailand.

**Intl. Orgs.** Colombo Plan, FAO, G-77, GATT, IAEA, IBRD, ICAO, IDA, IFC, ILO, IMF, IMO, INTERPOL, ITU, UN, UNESCO, UPU, WHO, WMO.

(Until the summer of 1989 this country was known as Burma.)

Burma, an independent Buddhist monarchy from the 11th century, fell to the Mongol empire in the 13th century, and after the 14th century was a satellite state of China. Anglo-French rivalry over trade left Burma under French influence in the early 19th century, but in a series of three wars (1824–26, 1852, 1885), Great Britain succeeded in bringing all of Burma into the British raj of India. The country became self-governing under a British protectorate in 1937.

Japanese occupation of Burma in early 1942 made the country a major theater of fighting during World War II. The Burma Road, built by the Allies to connect northeastern India with southwestern China, was a key link in bringing supplies to the Chinese Nationalist army during the war.

Burma achieved independence as the Union of Burma on Jan. 4, 1948. Promises of autonomy for ethnic minority regions such as the Shan and Karen States have not been fulfilled, leading to armed separatist movements in those areas ever since. In 1962 a coup led by Gen. Ne Win overthrew the democratic government and established a one-party state under the Burmese Socialist Program party. The party's "Burmese Path to Socialism" resulted in self-imposed international isolation and economic stagnation at home despite the country's potential wealth in agriculture, timber, minerals, and gems.

In July 1988 Ne Win resigned from office in the face of mounting popular demonstrations. A series of short-lived successor governments were unable to restore public order and normal governmental functions; direct military rule was announced in September 1988 as demonstrations continued.

In the general election held on May 27, 1990 (the first multiparty free elections in three decades), the opposition National League for Democracy won a decisive victory, but the results were nullified by the military junta, and the League's leaders remained under arrest. In December 1990, members of the League, now loosely allied with the Karen guerrillas, formed a rival government with U Sein Win as prime minister; his eight cabinet ministers all won seats in the parliamentary elections.

## Namibia
### Republic of Namibia
**Geography Location:** southwest Africa. **Boundaries:** Angola to N, Botswana to E, South Africa to S, Atlantic Ocean to W. **Total land area:** 317,873 sq. mi. (823,290 sq km). **Coastline:** 925 mi. (1,489 km). **Comparative area:** between Texas and Alaska. **Land use:** 1% arable land; negl. % permanent crops; 64% meadows and pastures; 22% forest and woodland; 13% other; includes negl. % irrigated. **Major cities:** (1988 est.) Windhoek (capital) 114,500.

**People Population:** 1,452,951 (1990). **Nationality:** noun—Namibian(s); adjective—Namibian. **Ethnic groups:** 85.6% black (half of whom are Ovambos), 7.5% white, 6.9% mixed. **Languages:** white population—60% speak Afrikaans, 33% German, and 7% English (all official); several indigenous languages. **Religions:** whites predominantly Christian, nonwhites either Christian or indigenous beliefs.

**Government Type:** republic. **Independence:** Mar. 21, 1990 (from South Africa). **Constitution:** Feb. 16, 1990. **National holiday:** Independence Day, Mar. 21. **Heads of government:** Sam Nujoma, president (since Mar. 1990); Hage G. Geingob, prime minister (since Mar. 1990). **Structure:** Executive Branch—president and cabinet of ministers; Legislative—National Assembly composed of 72 members; Judicial—Supreme court and regional courts. (Note: President and 72 members of National Assembly elected in Nov. 1989 in Namibia's first free election; election supervised by United Nations.)

**Economy Monetary unit:** South African rand. **Budget:** (1988) *income:* $781 mil.; *expend.:* $932 mil. **GNP:** $1.54 bil., $1,245 per capita (1986). **Chief crops:** subsistence crops (millet, sorghum, corn, and some wheat) are raised, but most food must be imported. **Livestock:** sheep, cattle, goats, poultry, horses. **Natural resources:** diamonds, copper, uranium, lead, tin. **Major industries:** meat packing, fish processing, dairy products, mining (copper, lead, zinc, diamonds, and uranium). **Labor force:** about 500,000 (1981); 60% agriculture, 19% industry and commerce; 15–17% unemployment. **Exports:** $935 mil. (f.o.b., 1988); diamonds, uranium, zinc, copper, meat, processed fish. **Imports:** $856 mil. (f.o.b., 1988); foodstuffs, manufactured consumer goods, machinery. **Major trading partners:** *exports:* South Africa; *imports:* South Africa, W. Germany, UK, U.S..

**Intl. Orgs.** FAO, ILO, UN, UNESCO, WHO.

The Kalahari desert, on the Namibian plateau, has been inhabited since ancient times by San hunter-gatherers. Various Nama and Bantu peoples migrated into the area more recently. British and Dutch explorers and traders began to penetrate Namibia in the 18th century.

In 1872 Great Britain occupied the area around Walvis Bay and in 1884 annexed it to the Cape Colony. Also in 1884 Germany claimed most of South-West Africa; negotiations between the two powers resulted in German acceptance of Britain's claim of Walvis Bay and British acceptance of Germany's claim to the rest of the coastal region with a sphere of influence in the interior.

During World War I, British troops from South Africa occupied South-West Africa in 1915. In 1920 South Africa received a League of Nations mandate to administer the area. In 1946 when the United Nations succeeded the League, the United Nations proposed that South Africa continue its administration under a UN trusteeship. South Africa refused and annexed South-West Africa.

The proposed UN trusteeship was revoked by the United Nations in 1966. At the same time, the South-West Africa People's Organization (SWAPO), operating from bases in Zambia and Angola, began guerrilla actions against South African troops in the region. In 1968 the United Nations formally renamed the territory Namibia and appointed an 11-nation council to supervise its affairs and devise a plan leading to independence.

In 1971 the International Court of Justice upheld the UN's authority over Namibia and ruled that South Africa's continued occupation of the territory was illegal. In 1975 South Africa convened the Turnhalle Conference, which proposed a plan for Namibian independence based on the racial-separation principles of apartheid. This was rejected by the United Nations, and in 1978 the UN Security Council approved Resolution 435, which called for a general cease-fire to be followed by UN-supervised elections.

In response, South Africa unilaterally held elections in Namibia, which were boycotted by

SWAPO and other African organizations and rejected by the United Nations. In 1982 South Africa declared that it would enter into talks about the future of Namibia only after Cuban troops were withdrawn from Angola. In 1983 South Africa launched a major military operation against SWAPO forces in Angola.

In October 1984 Angolan Pres. dos Santos agreed to work out a plan for withdrawal of Cuban troops as part of a settlement in Namibia. In June 1985 South Africa granted limited local authority to a Namibian government made up of a coalition of parties, excluding SWAPO. In 1987 South African troops occupied southern Angola (to aid Angolan rebels), and in early 1988, fighting between South African troops and Namibian rebels in northern Namibia and southern Angola intensified.

A new round of talks on the future of Namibia between South Africa, Cuba, and Angola, mediated by the United States, began in May 1988, and on Dec. 13, 1988, the three parties agreed on a plan for Namibian independence and a pullout of Cuban troops from Angola.

In January 1989 the Cuban withdrawal from Angola began. On Apr. 1 UN Resolution 435 went into effect in Namibia, and a UN peacekeeping force arrived to supervise the transition to independence. Elections were held in November 1989: SWAPO leader Sam Nujoma won an overwhelming victory, and opposition leaders pledged their support. A Western-style democratic constitution was adopted Feb. 16, 1990, and full independence came on Mar. 21.

Most of Namibia consists of a high, semiarid to desert plateau. The country is sparsely inhabited and supports little agriculture; most of the rural population is engaged in raising livestock. Namibia is rich in minerals, including diamonds, copper, lead, and zinc.

## Nauru
### Republic of Nauru
**Geography Location:** central Pacific Ocean (0°32′S, 166°56′E), about 2,800 mi. (4,500 km) southwest of Hawaii. **Boundaries:** nearest neighbor is Banaba (Ocean Island), in Kiribati, about 185 mi. (300 km) to E. **Total land area:** 8.2 sq. mi. (21.3 sq km). **Coastline:** 15 mi. (24 km). **Comparative area:** about 1/10 size of Washington, D.C. **Land use:** 0% arable land; 0% permanent crops; 0% meadows and pastures; 0% forest and woodland; 100% other. **Major cities:** none as such; government offices in Yaren district.

**People Population:** 9,208 (1990). **Nationality:** noun—Nauruan(s) adjective—Nauruan. **Ethnic groups:** 58% Nauruan, 26% other Pacific Islander, 8% Chinese, 8% European. **Languages:** Nauruan, a distinct Pacific Island language (official); English widely understood and spoken and used for most government and commercial purposes. **Religions:** Christian (two-thirds Protestant, one-third Catholic).

**Government Type:** republic. **Independence:** Jan. 31, 1968 (from UN trusteeship under Australia, New Zealand, and UK). **Con-**

stitution: Jan. 29, 1968. **National holiday:** Independence Day, Jan. 31; Constitution Day, May 17; Angram Day, Oct. 26. **Heads of government:** Hammer DeRoburt, president (since May 1968). **Structure:** president elected from and by Parliament for unfixed term; popularly elected 18-member unicameral legislature (Parliament); four-member cabinet to assist president, appointed by him from Parliament members.

**Economy Monetary unit:** Australian dollar. **Budget:** (1986 est.) *income:* $69.7 mil.; *expend.:* $51.5 mil. **GNP:** over $90 mil., $10,000 per capita (1989). **Chief crops:** negl.; almost completely dependent on imports for food and water. **Livestock:** pigs. **Natural resources:** phosphates. **Major industries:** phosphate mining (about 2 mil. tons per year), financial services, coconuts. **Labor force:** N.A. **Exports:** $93 mil. (1984). **Imports:** $73 mil. (1984): food, fuel, manufactures, machinery. **Major trading partners:** *exports:* Australia, New Zealand; *imports:* Australia, UK, New Zealand, Japan.

**Intl. Orgs.** Commonwealth (special member), ICAO, INTERPOL, ITU, UPU.

Nauru, formerly known as Pleasant Island, is an isolated island lying west of the Gilbert Islands. It became a German protectorate in 1888. After World War I, Nauru was administered by Australia under a League of Nations mandate. It was occupied by Japan throughout World War II. In 1947 it became a UN Trust Territory administered by Australia, and on Jan. 31, 1968, an independent republic. Nauru has a parliament of 18 members, who elect a prime minister and a cabinet. Most of the island's assets are owned by the state-controlled Nauru Phosphate Corporation and by the Nauru Cooperative Society.

Much of the island is covered by phosphate deposits. Phosphate mining and exports, under leases largely controlled by Australian interests, have given Nauru one of the world's highest per-capita incomes. Currently, national attention is focused on attempts to renegotiate the terms of long-term phosphate export contracts, and on the administration of a national trust fund in preparation for a new era, in the relatively near future, when phosphate deposits will have been exhausted.

# Nepal
## Kingdom of Nepal

**Geography Location:** central Asia, in Himalayan mountain range. **Boundaries:** China to N, India to E, S, and W. **Total land area:** 56,827 sq. mi. (147,181 sq km). **Coastline:** none. **Comparative area:** between Illinois and Michigan. **Land use:** 17% arable land; negl. % permanent crops; 13% meadows and pastures; 33% forest and woodland; 37% other; includes 2% irrigated. **Major cities:** (1981 census) Kathmandu (capital) 235,160.

**People Population:** 19,145,800 (1990). **Nationality:** noun—Nepalese (sing. and pl.); adjective—Nepalese. **Ethnic groups:** Newars,

Indians, Tibetans, Gurungs, Magars, Tamangs, Bhotias, Rais, Limbus, Sherpas, as well as many smaller groups. **Languages:** Nepali (official); 20 languages. divided into numerous dialects. **Religions:** only official Hindu kingdom in world, although no sharp distinction between many Hindu (about 88%) and Buddhist groups; small groups of Muslims and Christians.

**Government Type:** nominally, constitutional monarchy; king exercises autocratic control over multitiered system of government. **Constitution:** Dec. 16, 1962. **National holiday:** Birthday of the king and National Day, Dec. 28. **Heads of government:** Birendra Bir Bikram Shah Dev, king (since Jan. 1972); Girija P. Koirala, prime minister (since May 1991). **Structure:** Council of Ministers, appointed by king; Rastriya Panchayat, or National Assembly (140 members serving five-year terms, including 112 directly elected and 28 appointed by king).

**Economy Monetary unit:** Nepalese rupee. **Budget:** (1989 est.) *income:* $296 mil.; *expend.:* $635 mil. **GDP:** $2.9 bil., $158 per capita (1987). **Chief crops:** over 90% of population engaged in agriculture; rice, corn, wheat, sugarcane, oilseeds; illegal producer of cannabis for international drug trade. **Livestock:** cattle, goats, buffalo, sheep, pigs. **Natural resources:** quartz, water, timber, hydroelectric potential, scenic beauty. **Major industries:** small rice, jute, sugar, and oilseed mills; cigarette and brick factories; tourism. **Labor force:** 4.1 mil.; 93% agriculture, 5% services, 2% industry; great lack of skilled labor. **Exports:** $374 mil. (f.o.b., 1989 est.); clothing, carpets, leather goods, grain. **Imports:** $724 mil. (c.i.f., 1989 est.); 20% petroleum products, 11% fertilizer, 10% machinery. **Major trading partners:** (1988) *exports:* 38% India, 23% U.S., 6% UK, 9% other Europe; *imports:* 36% India, 13% Japan, 4% Europe, 1% U.S.

**Intl. Orgs.** Colombo Plan, FAO, G-77, IBRD, ICAO, IDA, IFAD, IFC, ILO, IMF, IMO, INTERPOL, ITU, NAM, UN, UNESCO, UPU, WHO, WMO.

The birthplace of Gautama Buddha (c. 600 B.C.), Nepal was for many centuries a collection of petty principalities, inhabited by various Tibeto-Burman peoples who mostly practiced Lamaistic Buddhism. In 1769 the country's three geographical zones—floodplain, foothills, and high mountains—were united under an ascendant group, the Gurkhas, who made Hinduism the country's official religion. Nepal established treaty relations with Great Britain in 1792 and fought a border war with British India in 1814–16, but it was never incorporated into the British Empire.

An armed revolution in 1950 overthrew a government of heriditary rulers that had overthrown the Shah dynasty in the 19th century. King Tribuhavan (a Shah) was restored and tried to introduce democratic reforms, but his son Mahendra dissolved parliament and introduced a tiered system of town, district, and national councils. Road and air links to India, Pakistan, and Tibet were improved, and Nepal began to emerge from its customary isolation.

The successful climb of Mt. Everest by Sir Edmund Hillary and Tenzing Norgay in 1953 focused international attention on Nepal.

Antigovernment demonstrations in the spring of 1990 culminated in the shooting deaths of 63 civilians on Apr. 6, and three days later the king lifted a 30-year ban on political parties. A new constitution enshrining multiparty democracy and human rights as essentials of the political system was promulgated Nov. 9. The king remains a constitutional monarch and head of the military, but executive power is vested in the prime minister and his cabinet.

In recent years tourism, especially mountaineering and trekking, have increased the country's prosperity but also have created new ecological problems. Additionally, a rapidly increasing population and drastic deforestation have had severe impacts on the country. The economy remains largely in the stage of small-scale agriculture and craft industries. During 1989–90, India blocked the flow of imported goods to Nepal in order to curtail the smuggling of consumer goods and the evasion of Indian duties.

# Netherlands
## Kingdom of The Netherlands

**Geography Location:** western Europe. **Boundaries:** North Sea to N and W, Germany to E, Belgium to S. **Total land area:** 13,103 sq. mi. (33,937 sq km). **Coastline:** 280 mi. (451 km). **Comparative area:** 1.3 times size of Maryland. **Land use:** 25% arable land; 1% permanent crops; 34% meadows and pastures; 9% forest and woodland; 31% other; includes 15% irrigated. **Major cities:** (1989) Amsterdam (capital) 694,680; Rotterdam 576,232; The Hague 443,845; Utrecht 230,634; Eindhoven 190,736. The Hague is seat of government.

**People Population:** 14,936,032 (1990). **Nationality:** noun—Dutchman (men), Dutchwoman (women); adjective—Dutch. **Ethnic groups:** 99% Dutch, 1% Indonesian and other. **Languages:** Dutch (official). **Religions:** 40% Roman Catholic, 31% Protestant, 24% unaffiliated, 5% none.

**Government Type:** constitutional monarchy. **Independence:** N.A. **Constitution:** Feb. 17, 1983. **National holiday:** Queen's Day, Apr. 30. **Heads of government:** Beatrix Wilhelmina Armgard, queen (since Apr. 1980); Ruud Lubbers, prime minister (since Nov. 1982). **Structure:** executive (queen and Cabinet of Ministers), which is responsible to bicameral parliament (States General) consisting of First Chamber (75 indirectly elected members) and Second Chamber (150 directly elected members); independent judiciary; coalition governments are usual.

**Economy Monetary unit:** guilder. **Budget:** (1989) *income:* $71.0 bil.; *expend.:* $82.0 bil. **GDP:** $205.9 bil., $13,900 per capita. **Chief crops:** horticultural crops, grains, potatoes, sugar beets; food shortages—grains, fats, oils. **Livestock:** chickens, pigs, cattle, sheep, horses, ponies. **Natural recources:** natural gas, crude oil, fertile soil. **Major industries:** agro-industries, metal and engineering products, electrical machinery and equipment. **Labor force:** 5.3 mil. (1986); 50.1% services, 28.2% manufacturing and construction, 15.9% government; 11.1% unemployment (1988). **Exports:** $110.3 bil. (f.o.b., 1989); agricultural products, processed foods and tobacco, natural gas, chemicals, metal products. **Imports:** $100.9 bil. (c.i.f., 1989); raw materials and semifinished products, consumer goods, transport equipment, crude oil. **Major trading partners:** (1988) *exports:* 74.9% EC (28.3% W. Germany, 14.2% Belgium-Luxembourg, 10.7% France, 10.2% UK), 4.7% U.S., 0.9% communist countries; *imports:* 63.8% EC (26.5% W. Germany, 23.1% Belgium-Luxembourg, 8.1% UK), 7.9% U.S.

**Intl. Orgs.** EC, FAO, GATT, IAEA, IBRD, ICAO, IDA, IFAD, IFC, ILO, IMF, IMO, INTELSAT, INTERPOL, ITU, NATO, OAS (observer), OECD, UN, UNESCO, UPU, WHO, WIPO, WMO.

Historically, the name Netherlands referred to the low-lying areas of the Holy Roman Empire near the mouths of the Rhine, Meuse, and Scheldt rivers. The Habsburg emperor Charles V willed these territories to his son Philip II of Spain in 1555, but by the end of the 16th century, the northern provinces—the Union of Utrecht, formed in 1579 by William the Silent, of the House of Orange—won their independence in a war that was both religious (Calvinist vs. Catholic) and constitutional (aristocratic/patrician vs. foreign monarchy). The independence of the Netherlands was recognized in the Treaty of Westphalia, which ended the Thirty Years' War in 1648.

Dutch prosperity, founded on the woolen trade with England, grew tremendously through trade and seafaring under the 17th-century republic. The Netherlands amassed a world empire, including the Indonesian archipelago, the island of Sri Lanka (then Ceylon), South Africa, Surinam, parts of the West Indies, and the Hudson valley in New Amsterdam (later New York); in addition it monopolized Western trade with Japan after 1637.

The Netherlands were incorporated into the Napoleonic empire. At the Congress of Vienna in 1815, a Dutch monarchy was established, which included Belgium until 1830. Land drainage and reclamation programs maintained the prosperity of the country's small-scale agriculture, while trade and colonial revenues were increasingly supplemented by industrial development in the 19th century. Dutch prosperity and the country's strategic position gave the Netherlands extraordinary influence and prestige in European affairs into the 20th century, despite the country's small size. It remained neutral in World War I.

Germany invaded the Netherlands in May 1940, taking control of the country after five days of fighting. Preparing to incorporate Holland into the Third Reich, Hitler installed a Nazi civilian government that ruled through totalitarian exploitation and cooperated in the persecution of Jews. But Queen Wilhelmina and the Dutch government escaped to England and maintained a government-in-exile throughout the war.

The final stages of fighting on the western front inflicted severe damage on the country, while in Asia the recovery of Indonesia from Japan led immediately to a declaration of independence under Sukarno. Marshall Plan aid was intended to support a domestic postwar recovery; an equal amount was spent by the Dutch government in an attempt to recapture control of Indonesia before that country's independence was recognized in 1949.

Devastated by World War II and the loss of its empire (except in the Caribbean; see "Territories of the World"), the country faced a bleak future in the postwar years. Forced to turn its attention to recovery at home, the Netherlands worked through the Benelux (Belgium, Netherlands, Luxembourg) union (founded in 1944) and the Common Market to create another European "economic miracle" between the early 1950s and the 1970s. The older bases of the economy—commerce, maritime industry, dairy farming, and flower farming—were expanded and modernized; Rotterdam was rebuilt to become Europe's most important port. Newer industries, such as chemicals and oil refining, electronics, and steel, relied on the country's highly skilled and productive labor force to turn imported raw materials into finished high-value exports. A huge impoundment project turned the Zuider Zee into a new province, increasing the country's land area by 10 percent. Tourism also contributes substantially to the economy.

This postwar prosperity has been based in large part on political stability. A coalition of the Catholic State party and the Labor (formerly Social Democratic) party governed for 10 years under Premier Willem Drees. After 1958 cabinets normally were formed from coalitions headed by three Christian parties (merged in 1980 to form the United Christian Appeal) or by the Liberal party; all pursued essentially the same policies of free enterprise, comprehensive social welfare programs, high taxation, and social liberalism.

Queen Juliana was succeeded in 1980 by Queen Beatrix. Since 1982 a coalition of Christian Democrats and Liberals has provided a cabinet headed by Prime Minister Ruud Lubbers. Government support for the deployment in Holland of NATO cruise missiles has provoked a popular backlash and the growth of the Green party; an antimissile petition was signed by 4 million Dutch citizens.

---

## New Zealand

**Geography** **Location:** South Pacific Ocean about 1,100 mi. (1,750 km) SE of Australia. **Boundaries:** South Pacific Ocean to N, E, and S; Tasman Sea to W. **Total land area:** 103,883 sq. mi. (269,057 sq km). **Coastline:** 9,406 mi. (15,134 km). **Comparative area:** about size of Colorado. **Land use:** 2% arable land; 0% permanent crops; 53% meadows and pastures; 38% forest and woodland; 7% other; includes 1% irrigated. **Major cities:** (1988) Wellington (capital) 325,200; Auckland 841,700; Christ-church 300,700; Napier-Hastings 107,500; Dunedin 106,600.

**People** **Population:** 3,295,866 (1990). **Nationality:** noun—New Zealander(s); adjective—New Zealand. **Ethnic groups:** 88% European, 8.9% Maori, 2.9% Pacific Islander, 0.2% other. **Languages:** English (official), Maori. **Religions:** 81% Christian; 18% none or unspecified; 1% Hindu, Confucian, and other.

**Government** **Type:** independent state within Commonwealth, recognizing Elizabeth II as head of state. **Independence:** Sept. 26, 1907 (from UK). **Constitution:** no formal, written constitution; consists of various documents, including certain acts of UK and New Zealand parliaments; Constitution Act 1986 was to have come into effect Jan. 1, 1987, but has not been enacted. **National holiday:** Waitangi Day, Feb. 6. **Heads of government:** Sir Paul Reeves, governor-general (since Nov. 1985); James D. Bolger, prime minister (since Nov. 1990). **Structure:** unicameral legislature (97-member House of Representatives, commonly called Parliament); three-level court system (magistrates and courts, Supreme Court, and court of appeal).

**Economy** **Monetary unit:** New Zealand dollar. **Budget:** (1990 est.) *income:* $18.6 bil.; **expend.:** $19.1 bil. **GDP:** $39.1 bil., $11,600 per capita (1989 est.). **Chief crops:** fodder and silage crops, wool; food-surplus country. **Livestock:** sheep, cattle, goats, pigs, horses. **Natural resources:** natural gas, iron ore, sand, coal, timber. **Major industries:** food processing, wood and paper products, textiles. **Labor force:** 1,591,900 (1987); 67.4% services, 19.8% manufacturing, 9.3% primary production; 11.3% unemployment (1988). **Exports:** $8.9 bil. (f.o.b., 1989 est.); wool, lamb, mutton, beef, fruit, fish. **Imports:** $7.5 bil. (c.i.f., 1989); petroleum, consumer goods, motor vehicles, industrial equipment. **Major trading partners:** *exports:* 18% EC, 18% Japan, 18% Australia, 14% U.S., 4% China; *imports:* 20% Australia, 17% Japan, 17% EC, 15% U.S., 3% Taiwan.

**Intl. Orgs.** Colombo Plan, Commonwealth of Nations, FAO, GATT, IAEA, IBRD, ICAO, IDA, IFAD, IFC, ILO, IMF, IMO, INTELSAT, INTERPOL, ITU, UN, UNESCO, UPU, WHO, WMO.

Settled by Maori migrants from Polynesia around the 14th century A.D., New Zealand was first brought to Europe's attention by the Dutch explorer Abel Tasman in 1642. In 1769 it was visited and claimed for Great Britain by Capt. James Cook. The first British missionaries arrived in 1814. By the Treaty of Waitangi in 1840, the Maoris were guaranteed possession of their ancestral lands in return for permission to admit British settlers. New Zealand was organized as a full-fledged British colony in 1841. In a series of bloody wars lasting until 1870, the Maoris were defeated and displaced from lands devoted to the expanding British settlements.

In 1907 New Zealand was elevated to the status of a British Dominion. It is an independent member of the British Commonwealth; the crown is represented by a governor-general, while government is vested in a parliament headed by a prime minister. The nation's 250,000 Maoris remain a cohesive culture and directly elect four members of Parliament.

New Zealand is remarkable for having been one of the world's first nations to create a comprehensive welfare state; a legislative history dating back to 1898 has regulated labor practices and mandated universal old-age pensions, public-sector medical care, and other social services. Most mines, forests, transportation facilities, power plants, and communications facilities are publicly owned.

New Zealand troops fought on the side of the allies in both world wars and with UN forces in the Korean War. In 1951 New Zealand joined with Australia and the United States in the ANZUS mutual-defense treaty, dissolved in 1986 after New Zealand's denial of port facilities to U.S. ships carrying nuclear weapons. New Zealand has also objected strenuously to French testing of nuclear weapons in the South Pacific. In July 1985 the *Rainbow Warrior*, a ship owned by the Greenpeace organization that had engaged in antinuclear protests, was bombed and sunk in Auckland harbor by French secret service agents.

New Zealand's economy is dominated by livestock raising; principal exports are dairy products, meat, and wool. Timber and minerals are also exported, along with some manufactured goods. Fisheries and tourism are also economically important.

New Zealand administers the foreign affairs and defense of several Pacific island dependencies (see "Territories of the World") and the Ross Dependency in Antarctica.

# Nicaragua
### Republic of Nicaragua

**Geography Location:** Central American isthmus. **Boundaries:** Honduras to N, Caribbean Sea to E, Costa Rica to S, Pacific Ocean to W. **Total land area:** 46,430 sq. mi. (120,254 sq km). **Coastline:** 565 mi. (910 km). **Comparative area:** between Pennsylvania and Mississippi. **Land use:** 9% arable land; 1% permanent crops; 43% meadows and pastures; 35% forest and woodland; 12% other; includes 1% irrigated. **Major cities:** (1983) Managua (capital) 682,111; (1985 est.) León 100,982; Granada 88,636; Masaya 74,946; Chinandega 67,792.

**People Population:** 3,722,683 (1990). **Nationality:** noun—Nicaraguan(s); adjective—Nicaraguan. **Ethnic groups:** 69% mestizo, 17% white, 9% black, 5% Indian. **Languages:** Spanish (official); English- and Indian-speaking minorities on Atlantic coast. **Religions:** 95% Roman Catholic.

**Government Type:** republic. **Independence:** Sept. 28, 1821 (from Spain). **Constitution:** Jan. 1987. **National holidays:** Independence Day, Sept. 15; Anniversary of the Revolution, July 19. **Head of government:** Mrs. Violeta Barrios de Chamorro, president (since Apr. 1990). **Structure:** Executive branch—president and cabinet of ministers; Legislative—

National Assembly composed of 92 members; Judicial—Supreme Court and regional courts. (Note: President and 92 members of National Assembly elected in Apr. 1990 in free elections supervised by the United Nations and other international observers.)

**Economy Monetary unit:** córdoba. **Budget:** (1987) *income:* $0.9 bil.; *expend.:* $1.4 bil. **GDP:** $1.7 bil., $470 per capita (1989 est.). **Chief crops:** cotton, coffee, sugarcane, rice, corn, beans. **Livestock:** cattle, pigs, horses, mules, sheep, goats. **Natural resources:** gold, silver, copper, tungsten, lead. **Major industries:** food processing, chemicals, metal products. **Labor force:** 1.08 mil. (1987); 44% agriculture, 43% service, 13% industry; 22% unemployment. **Exports:** $250 mil. (f.o.b., 1989 est.); coffee, cotton, sugar, bananas, seafood, meat. **Imports:** $550 mil. (c.i.f., 1989 est.); petroleum, food, chemicals, machinery, clothing. **Major trading partners:** *exports:* 75% OECD, 15% CMEA; *imports:* 55% CMEA, 20% EC, 10% Latin America.

**Intl. Orgs.** FAO, G-77, GATT, IAEA, IBRD, ICAO, IDA, IFAD, IFC, ILO, IMF, IMO, INTELSAT, INTERPOL, ITU, NAM, OAS, UN, UNESCO, UPU, WHO, WMO.

Nicaragua gained independence from Spain in 1821 and formed a constituent part of the United Provinces of Central America in 1823. With the dissolution of the federation in 1838, Nicaragua became an independent republic. Throughout the territory of the United Provinces, an intra-elite struggle between Liberal and Conservative factions defined the political arena during the early part of the 19th century. Nicaraguan Liberals invited the adventurer William Walker of Tennessee to take their part against their Conservative rivals in 1855. Walker took control of the country in 1856 but was driven out by a combined Central American force the following year.

The Conservatives held power in Nicaragua until 1893, when a planters' revolt brought Liberal José Santos Zelaya to the presidency. Because of Zelaya's intention to pursue an isthmian canal project, the U.S. government intervened in support of a Conservative uprising. The United States sent marines to Nicaragua in 1909, and Zelaya resigned in 1910. The marines occupied the country during 1909–25 and 1926–33.

Refusing to abide by a political settlement between the U.S. government and Nicaraguan Liberal forces in 1927, a Liberal officer, Augusto César Sandino, led a guerrilla war against U.S. occupation forces until 1933. Anastasio Somoza García, head of the Nicaraguan National Guard, had Sandino assassinated in 1934 and took over the presidency in 1937. Somoza and his sons Luis and Anastasio Somoza Debayle controlled Nicaragua until 1979.

A broad coalition of groups led by the Sandinista National Liberation Front (FSLN) overthrew the Somoza dictatorship in 1979. The FSLN comprised three groups, or "tendencies," each represented equally on a Sandinista governing board called the National Directorate. Elections were held in 1984 for the presidency,

vice presidency, and a constituent assembly. The Sandinistas won the election for the presidency and vice presidency as well as receiving a working majority in the National Assembly, and a new constitution was promulgated for the country in 1987.

Between 1981 and 1990 the United States actively, but covertly, supported Contra rebels fighting the Sandinista regime in a civil war that cost the country dearly. In 1989, Pres. Daniel Ortega announced elections for early 1990, which he lost in a stunning upset to Violeta Barrios de Chamorro, who headed a 17-party coalition, the United Nicaraguan Opposition (UNO). Although the transition has been relatively peaceful, the government faces dissent from labor, former Contras angry at continued Sandinista control of the army and police, and the business community discouraged by the slow pace of economic recovery.

# Niger
### Republic of Niger

**Geography Location:** landlocked country in western Africa. **Boundaries:** Algeria and Libya to N, Chad to E, Nigeria to S, Benin, Burkina Faso to SW, Mali to W. **Total land area:** 489,076 sq. mi. (1,266,700 sq km). **Coastline:** none. **Comparative area:** between Texas and Alaska. **Land use:** 3% arable land; 0% permanent crops; 7% meadows and pastures; 2% forest and woodland; 88% other; includes negl. % irrigated. **Major cities:** Niamey (capital) 225,314; Zinder 75,000 (1981 est.); Marodi 45,852; Tahoua 31,265; Agadez 20,475 (1977).

**People Population:** 7,969,309 (1990). **Nationality:** noun—Nigerien(s); adjective—Nigerien. **Ethnic groups:** 56% Hausa, 22% Djerma, 8.5% Fula, 8% Tuareg, 4.3% Beri Beri (Kanouri); 1.2% Arab, Toubou, and Gourmantche; about 4,000 French expatriates. **Languages:** French (official), Hausa, Djerma. **Religions:** 80% Muslim, 20% indigenous beliefs and Christians.

**Government Type:** republic; military regimes in power since Apr. 1974. **Independence:** Aug. 3, 1960 (from France). **Constitution:** Sept. 24, 1989. **National holiday:** Independence Day, Aug. 3. **Heads of government:** Col. Ali Saibou, president (since Nov. 1987); Aliou Mahamidou, prime minister (since Mar. 1991). **Structure:** executive—president; 93-seat national assembly.

**Economy Monetary unit:** Communauté Financière Africaine (CFA) franc. **Budget:** (1988 est.) *income:* $254.0 mil.; *expend.:* $510.0 mil. **GDP:** $2.4 bil., $330 per capita. **Chief crops:** cash crops—cowpeas, groundnuts, cotton; food crops—millet, sorghum, rice. **Livestock:** goats, sheep, cattle, asses, camels. **Natural resources:** uranium, coal, iron ore, tin, phosphates. **Major industries:** cement, brick, rice mill. **Labor force:** 2.5 mil. (1982); 90% agriculture; 51% of population of working age. **Exports:** $250.6 mil. (f.o.b., 1985); uranium, livestock, cowpeas, onions, hides, skins; exports understated because much regional trade not recorded. **Imports:** $309.4 mil. (f.o.b.,

1985); petroleum products, primary materials, machinery, vehicles and parts, electronic equipment. **Major trading partners:** N.A.

**Intl. Orgs.** FAO, G-77, GATT, IAEA, IBRD, ICAO, IDA, IFAD, IFC, ILO, IMF, INTELSAT, INTERPOL, ITU, NAM, UN, UNESCO, UPU, WHO, WIPO, WMO.

Most of Niger's territory is dominated by the Sahara and the Sahel (the "shore" of the desert), which have spread southward since prehistoric times. Much of the population lives in the narrow fertile belt south of the Niger River. Much of Niger was incorporated during medieval times in large empires centered in neighboring Mali, Chad, and Nigeria.

In the 18th century, Tuaregs migrating from the northern desert began to form tribal confederations in Niger. They united with local Hausa peoples to wage war against the Fulani Empire.

In the 19th century, British and German explorers seeking the source of the Niger River explored the region. In the European rivalry that followed, the French, from bases in Mali and Chad, began to dominate Niger by 1900; Niger became a French colony in 1922, administered from Dakar, Senegal.

In 1946 the people of Niger, in common with other peoples in French Africa, were granted French citizenship, and limited self-rule began. This local autonomy was expanded in 1956, and in 1958 Niger became an autonomous state within the French Overseas Community. Full independence followed on Aug. 3, 1960; Niger maintained close ties to France.

Hamani Diori was elected Niger's first president in 1960 and was reelected in 1965 and 1970. He was overthrown in 1974 in a military coup led by Lt. Col. Seyni Kountche, who became Niger's next president. In 1987 Pres. Kountche died and was succeeded by Col. Ali Saibou, who was elected president by the Supreme Military Council. Ratification of a new constitution and National Assembly elections were held in December 1989.

Since 1988 the United States and France have pursued closer relations with Niger; an increase in aid is designed in part to offset Libyan influence.

In its limited arable lands Niger grows some peanuts and cotton, and uranium is mined, but livestock-raising remains the mainstay of the economy. In recent years the country has been devastated by drought, which has killed off much of the country's cattle, sheep, and goats and led to widespread famine.

---

## Nigeria
### Federal Republic of Nigeria
**Geography Location:** western coast of Africa. **Boundaries:** Niger to N, Cameroon to E, Gulf of Guinea to S, Benin to W. **Total land area:** 351,649 sq. mi. (910,770 sq km). **Coastline:** 530 mi. (853 km). **Comparative area:** about 1.3 times size of Texas. **Land use:** 31% arable land; 3% permanent crops; 23% meadows and pastures; 15% forest and woodland; 28% other; includes negl. % irrigated. **Major cities:** (1986 est.) Lagos (capital) 5,500,000; Ibadan

2,000,000; Kano 1,000,000; Enugu 500,000.

**People Population:** 118,819,377 (1990). **Nationality:** noun—Nigerian(s); adjective—Nigerian. **Ethnic groups:** 250 tribal groups; Hausa and Fulani in north, Yoruba in southwest, and Ibos in southeast make up 65% of population; 27,000 non-Africans. **Languages:** English (official); Hausa, Yoruba, Fulani, and several other languages also widely used. **Religions:** 50% Muslim, 40% Christian, 10% indigenous beliefs.

**Government Type:** military government since Dec. 31, 1983. **Independence:** Oct.1, 1960 (from UK). **Constitution:** Oct. 1, 1979, amended Feb. 9, 1984. **National holiday:** Independence Day, Oct. 1. **Heads of government:** Ibrahim Babangida, president (since Aug. 1985). **Structure:** Armed Forces Ruling Council; National Council of Ministers and National Council of States; judiciary headed by Supreme Court.

**Economy Monetary unit:** naira. **Budget:** (1988 est.) **income:** $6.5 bil.; **expend:** $7.4 bil. **GNP:** $30 bil., $270 per capita. **Chief crops:** peanuts, cotton, cocoa, rubber, yams; illegal producer of cannabis for international drug trade. **Livestock:** goats, sheep, cattle, pigs, asses. **Natural resources:** crude oil, tin, columbite, iron ore, coal. **Major industries:** mining—crude oil, natural gas, coal, tin, columbite; processing industries—palm oil, peanuts, cotton, rubber, petroleum; manufacturing industries—textiles, cement, building materials, food products, footwear. **Labor force:** 45–50 mil.; 54% agriculture; 19% industry, commerce, and services; 15% government; 49% of population of working age (1985); 7.5% unemployment (1988 est.). **Exports:** $8.4 bil. (f.o.b., 1989 est.); 95% oil, cocoa, palm products, rubber. **Imports:** $5.7 bil. (c.i.f., 1989 est.); consumer goods, capital equipment, chemicals, raw materials. **Major trading partners:** exports: 51% EC, 32% U.S.; imports: EC, U.S.

**Intl. Orgs.** Commonwealth, FAO, G-77, GATT, IAEA, IBRD, ICAO, IDA, IFAD, IFC, ILO, IMF, IMO, INTELSAT, INTERPOL, ITU, NAM, OPEC, UN, UNESCO, UPU, WHO, WMO.

The Nok culture of central Nigeria (500–200 B.C.) was one of the richest and most advanced ancient civilizations in western Africa. Around A.D. 1000, the Muslim Kanem civilization expanded into northern Nigeria; by the 14th century, the amalgamated kingdom of Kanem-Bornu took northern Nigeria as its political center, from which it dominated the Sahel and developed trade routes stretching throughout northern Africa and as far as Europe and the Middle East.

During the 15th and 16th centuries, the Hausa Songhai empire rose to power. It was overthrown by the Fulani Muslim leader Uthman Dan Fodio, who created the Sokoto caliphate.

Southern Nigeria is dominated by the Yoruba, whose Oyo kingdom, centered at Ife, became a major power by A.D. 1000. Oyo gave rise to the Benin civilization, which flourished

from the 15th to the 18th centuries and is famous for its brass, bronze, and ivory sculpture.

The Portuguese established trading stations on the Benin coast in the 15th century; initially, trade relations were cordial, and Benin became well-known in Europe as a powerful and advanced kingdom. With the rise of the slave trade (which began with the cooperation of the Benin kings, who brought slaves from the interior), relations became hostile, and Benin declined under European pressure. The Dutch, British, and other Europeans competed strenuously with Portugal for control of the slave trade, and by the 18th century, most of the coastal region of Nigeria was under British control. By the turn of the 19th century, Britain suppressed the slave trade; slaves captured aboard European ships were transported by the British to Freetown in Sierra Leone.

With the slave trade ended, the British traded with Nigerians for agricultural and forest products and commenced exploration of the Niger River. Lagos came under British control in 1851, and in 1861 Nigeria was made a British colony. Despite native resistance the colony was expanded in 1906 to include territory east of the Niger River, which was called the Protectorate of Southern Nigeria, The two areas were administratively joined in 1914.

During the 1920s Britain began to respond to Nigerian demands for local self-rule. In 1946 the colony was divided into three regions, each with an advisory assembly. In 1954 the colony was reorganized as the Nigerian Federation, and the assemblies were given more authority. Sir Akubar Tafawa Balewa became Nigeria's first prime minister.

In 1961 a UN-supervised referendum in British Cameroon led to the joining with Nigeria of the northern part of that territory, while the southern part joined the new nation of Cameroon.

The 1960s were marked by a struggle for political dominance among the major ethnic groups of Nigeria, including the Ibo (or Igbo), Yoruba, Hausa, and Fulani. Attempts to partition the country on tribal lines for administrative purposes provoked controversy, and charges of corruption and fraud in elections held in 1964 and 1965 led to violence and rioting.

In January 1966 civil war broke out when a group of Ibo army officers overthrew the central government and several of the regional governments. Prime Minister Balewa was killed, along with many other political leaders in the northern and western parts of the country. Gen. Johnson Aguiyi-Ironsi, leader of the Ibo forces, took control of the government. Aguiyi-Ironsi abolished the country's federal structure and set up a strong central government, dominated by the Ibo. Anti-Ibo riots broke out in the north, and many Ibo were massacred. In July 1966 Aguiyi-Ironsi was assassinated by a group of northern army officers. Army Chief of Staff Yakubu Gowon became head of a new military government. The Eastern Region refused to acknowledge Gowon's government.

In 1967 Gowon reapportioned Nigeria into 12 states. The Eastern Region rejected this plan and seceded from Nigeria to form the independent state of Biafra, provoking a civil war that lasted until January 1970, when Biafra was rejoined with Nigeria. An estimated one million Biafrans, mostly Ibos, died from military action or starvation.

The Gowon government tried, with limited success, to aid in the reconstruction of the Eastern Region and to create a harmonious multitribal government. Gowon was overthrown in a coup in 1975. His successor was assassinated in 1976 and succeeded by Lt. Gen. Olusegun Obasanjo. The Obasanjo government increased the number of states from 12 to 19 and promised a return to civilian rule.

Shehu Shagari was elected president in October 1979 and reelected in 1983, but in December 1983 the military again intervened. On Aug. 30, 1985, Maj. Gen. Ibrahim Gbadamosi Babangida came to power.

Despite political difficulties, Nigeria's recovery from the Biafran War was greatly aided in the 1970s by revenues from petroleum exports. Corruption, mismanagement, and overspending of projected petroleum revenues led to a major economic crisis in the early 1980s with the collapse of world crude oil prices. Petroleum export earnings declined from $26 billion in 1980 to $5 billion in 1986. With a high foreign debt, high inflation rate, unemployment, and shortages of basic goods, riots broke out in major population centers. Industrial and infrastructure development stagnated.

In addition, in March 1987 religious violence broke out between the Christian south and the Muslim north; numerous churches and mosques were destroyed or vandalized.

The Babangida government in 1987 announced various economic austerity measures and promoted a campaign to lower the birth rate and control the population—the largest in Africa and the eighth largest in the world. The government also announced plans for a new constitution and to restore civilian rule by 1992.

The Nigerian economy, now dominated by petroleum, is one of the richest in Africa, with substantial mineral resources, export crops, forest products, and a productive offshore fishing industry, as well as a sound industrial base.

# Norway
## Kingdom of Norway

**Geography** **Location:** western Scandinavian peninsula, northern Europe. **Boundaries:** Norwegian Sea to N and W, USSR, Finland to NE, Sweden to E, North Sea to S and W. **Total land area:** 125,050 sq. mi. (323,878 sq km). **Coastline:** 13,626 mi. (21,925 km)—2,125 mi. (3,419 km) mainland; 1,500 mi. (2,413 km) large islands; 10,002 mi. (16,093 km) long fjords, numerous small islands, and minor indentations. **Comparative area:** slightly larger than New Mexico. **Land use:** 3% arable land; 0% permanent crops; negl. % meadows and pastures; 27% forest and woodland; 70% other; includes negl. % irrigated. **Major cities:** (1989) Oslo (capital) 456,124; Bergen 211,095; Trondheim 136,601; Stavanger 96,948; Kristiansand 64,395.

**People** **Population:** 4,252,806 (1990). **Nationality:** noun—Norwegian(s); adjective—Norwegian. **Ethnic groups:** Germanic (Nordic, Alpine, Baltic) and racial-cultural minority of 20,000 Lapps. **Languages:** Norwegian (official), small Lapp- and Finnish-speaking minorities. **Religions:** 94% Evangelical Lutheran (state church), 4% other Protestant and Roman Catholic, 2% other.

**Government** **Type:** constitutional monarchy. **Independence:** Oct. 26, 1905 (from Sweden). **Constitution:** May 17, 1814 and modified in 1884. **National holiday:** Constitution Day, May 17. **Heads of government:** Harold V, king (since Jan. 1991); Mrs. Gro Harlem Brundtland, prime minister (since Nov. 1990). **Structure:** executive power vested in Crown but exercised by cabinet responsible to parliament; legislative authority rests jointly with Crown and parliament (Storting-Lagting, upper house; Odelsting, lower house); Supreme Court, five superior courts, 104 lower courts.

**Economy** (1989) **Monetary unit:** Norwegian krone. **Budget:** *income:* $40.6 bil.; *expend.:* $41.3 bil. **GDP:** $75.8 bil., $17,900 per capita. **Chief crops:** feed grains, potatoes, fruits, vegetables; 40% self-sufficient; food shortages—food grains, sugar. **Livestock:** sheep, cattle, pigs, goats, horses. **Natural resources:** crude oil, copper, natural gas, pyrites, nickel. **Major industries:** petroleum and gas, food processing, shipbuilding. **Shortages:** most raw materials except timber, petroleum, iron, copper, and ilmenite ore. **Labor force:** 2.13 mil.; 33% services, 17.4% commerce, 17.2% mining and manufacturing; 2.1% unemployment (1987). **Exports:** $22.2 bil. (f.o.b., 1989); 25% petroleum and petroleum products, 11% natural gas, 7% fish, 6% aluminum. **Imports:** $18.7 bil. (c.i.f. 1989); machinery, fuels and lubricants, transport equipment, chemicals, foodstuffs. **Major trading partners:** (1986) *exports:* 26% UK, 16% EFTA, 14% less developed countries, 12% Sweden; *imports:* 18% Sweden, 18% less developed countries, 14% W. Germany, 8% Denmark.

**Intl. Orgs.** EC (free-trade agreement), EFTA, FAO, GATT, IAEA, IBRD, ICAO, IDA, IFAD, IFC, ILO, IMF, IMO, INTELSAT, INTERPOL, ITU, NATO, OECD, UN, UNESCO, UPU, WHO, WIPO, WMO.

The Viking age began in 793 with the sack of Lindisfarne in Ireland. By the 10th century, Norse and Danish Vikings had touched in almost every navigable river of Western Europe from Germany to Spain. In addition to coastal raiding, the Norse were beginning the first open-ocean voyages from Europe, sailing direct to Iceland (800 miles) and even to Greenland (2,200 miles), which they colonized in the 10th century.

At the beginning of the 10th century, Harold I united the petty kingdoms of western Scandinavia and extended his realm as far as the Orkney and Shetland islands. Viking nobles fleeing from his conquests consolidated the Norse duchy of Normandy in France. Christianity was established under Olaf II at the beginning of the 11th century.

Under Magnus VI (1263–80), medieval Norway reached the height of its power and prosperity. Norwegian independence ended with the accession in 1319 of Magnus VII, who was king of Sweden as well. Under the Kalmar Union of 1397, the three kingdoms of Scandinavia were merged under Danish control; Norway ceased to exist as a nation-state and was governed by the Danes for the following four centuries.

In 1814 Denmark, which had sided with France in the Napoleonic wars, was forced by the victorious powers to cede Norway to Sweden. Under Sweden's military control, but with a growing sense of nationalism, Norway attempted to establish its own monarchy. The attempt failed, but in 1815 Sweden acknowledged the independence of Norway in perpetual union with the Swedish Crown.

Relations between Norway and Sweden remained strained throughout the 19th century. In 1905 the Norwegian legislature, the Storting, declared the union void and deposed Swedish King Oscar II as king of Norway. Sweden acquiesced, and Prince Charles of Denmark was enthroned as king of Norway, ruling as Haakon VII.

During the 19th century, large numbers of Norwegians emigrated to North America. A rising tide of cultural nationalism was expressed in the flourishing Norwegian literature and art, as well as in a tradition of Arctic exploration. In the 20th century, industrialization, aided by the development of hydroelectric power, began to supplement Norway's traditional economic mainstays of fishing and seafaring.

Norway remained neutral during World War I and was relatively unaffected by the postwar upheavals. Industrialization led to the rise of the Labor party in 1927.

Norway attempted to remain neutral in World War II as well but was invaded by German troops in April 1940; the country fell after a brief resistance aided by a Franco-British expeditionary force. The king and government fled to London and established a government-in-exile there. The Norwegian merchant marine fleet was also largely transferred to Great Britain and contributed to the Allied cause in the North Atlantic. At home, resistance grew to the collaborationist government of the Fascist leader Vidkun Quisling. As the Nazis retreated in 1945, King Haakon and his government returned home in triumph. Within three years the Norwegian economy had returned to prewar levels.

Elections in 1945 returned a majority Labor government in the Storting. Labor set about establishing a characteristic Scandinavian welfare state, emphasizing privately owned, free-market industry, publicly owned utilities, state planning to ensure ample housing as well as full employment through export-oriented industries, a comprehensive social welfare system, and—to pay for the latter—high taxes.

Norway was a founding member of the United Nations and provided that body with its first secretary-general, Trygve Lie. With the hardening of the Cold War, Norway's foreign policy took on a clear pro-Western stance; Norway joined the NATO alliance in 1949. In 1959 Norway became one of the original members of the European Free Trade Association. Through the 1960s industrial development and exports continued to fuel an economic boom that led to great national prosperity and stability.

The 1970s were the decade of oil and gas, with extensive development of North Sea oil and gas fields at the beginning of the decade. As international energy prices rose, the government's petroleum monopoly, Statoil, seemed to provide an endless source of funds. Because Norway's hydroelectric plants made the country self-sufficient in electric power, almost all of the oil and gas was available for export; by 1981 energy exports amounted to one-third, and by 1985 one-half, of Norway's total exports. The government expanded the welfare state and encouraged large wage increases. Public spending swelled, inflation outpaced wages, and government debt mounted; meanwhile Norway became an economic hostage to OPEC oil prices.

In the 1981 elections, the Conservative party formed a government for the first time since 1928; its austerity policy of holding down government spending while increasing taxes on consumer goods aroused popular opposition, and the government fell in 1986. The new Socialist coalition government faced even greater drops in oil revenues, combined with labor unrest and continued inflation. But in 1987 Norway negotiated the sale of gas to EC countries, and the recovery of energy prices in that year brought a partial return to economic stability and prosperity.

## Oman
### Sultanate of Oman

**Geography** **Location:** southeastern Arabian peninsula. **Boundaries:** Gulf of Oman to N, Arabian Sea to E and S, Yemen to SW, Saudi Arabia to W, United Arab Emirates to NW; detached portion of Oman lies at tip of Musandam peninsula, on Strait of Hormuz. **Total land area:** 120,000 sq. mi. (300,000 sq km). **Coastline:** 1,299 mi. (2,092 km). **Comparative area:** about size of New Mexico. **Land use:** negl. % arable land; negl. % permanent crops; 5% meadows and pastures; 0% forest and woodland; 95% other; includes negl. % irrigated. **Major cities:** (1981 est.) Muscat (capital) 50,000.

**People** **Population:** 1,457,064 (1990). **Nationality:** noun—Omani(s); adjective—Omani. **Ethnic groups:** almost entirely Arab, with small Baluchi, Zanzibari, and Indian groups. **Languages:** Arabic (official), English, Baluchi, Urdu, Indian dialects. **Religions:** 75% Ibadhi Muslim, remainder Sunni Muslim, Shia Muslim, some Hindu.

**Government** **Type:** absolute monarchy; independent, with residual UK influence. **Constitution:** none. **National holiday:** National Days, Nov. 18–19. **Head of government:** Qaboos bin Said, sultan and prime minister (since July 1970). **Structure:** executive—sultan appoints 45-member State Consultative Assembly to advise him; judicial—traditional Islamic judges and nascent civil court system.

**Economy** **Monetary unit:** rial. **Budget:** (1989 est.) *income:* $3.1 bil.; *expend.:* $4.2 bil. **GDP:** $7.8 bil., $6,006 per capita (1986 est.). **Chief crops:** based on subsistence farming—fruits, dates, cereals. **Livestock:** cattle, camels. **Natural resources:** crude oil, copper, asbestos, some marble, limestone. **Major industries:** crude oil production and refining, natural gas production, construction. **Labor force:** 430,000; 58% are non-Omani; est. 60% agriculture. **Exports:** $3.6 bil. (f.o.b., 1988 est.); mostly petroleum; nonoil consist mostly of reexports, processed copper, and some agricultural goods. **Imports:** $1.9 bil. (c.i.f., 1988 est.); machinery, transportation equipment, manufactured goods, food, livestock. **Major trading partners:** *exports:* Japan, South Korea, Thailand, UAE; *imports:* Japan, UAE, UK, W. Germany, U.S.

**Intl. Orgs.** Arab League, FAO, G-77, IBRD, ICAO, IDA, IFAD, IFC, IMF, IMO, INTELSAT, INTERPOL, ITU, NAM, UN, UNESCO, UPU, WHO, WMO.

Oman occupies the southeastern corner of Arabia. From ancient times an important center of trade in the Persian Gulf and the Indian Ocean, Oman was frequently dominated by Persia prior to the mid-18th century. The principal port, Muscat, was captured by the Portuguese in 1508 and held by them until 1659, when the Ottoman Turks took possession. They were driven out in 1741 by Ahmed ibn Said of Yemen, who consolidated the sultanate of Oman in 1744 and founded the present royal line.

In the early 19th century, Oman was the most powerful state in Arabia, controlling Zanzibar in East Africa, the southern coast of Iran, and much of Baluchistan (between Pakistan and Iran). Zanzibar was separated from Oman in 1856, and the Persian coast and much of Baluchistan was detached from Oman during the latter half of the 19th century. In 1958 Oman's sole remaining Baluchi possession, the city-state of Gwadar, was ceded to Pakistan in return for a monetary settlement.

Growing British influence was consolidated by the formation of a British protectorate in 1891, reconfirmed in 1951. In the 1950s Britain aided the sultanate in putting down rebellions in the desert interior. The British protectorate ended with Britain's withdrawal from the gulf in 1971.

On July 23, 1970, Sultan Said ibn Taimur was overthrown by his son, Sultan Qaboos bin Said, who instituted a national development program and in 1975 defeated a leftist uprising in the western desert.

Petroleum makes up 95 percent of exports. Banking and shipping services are also important. The country is generally barren, with scattered flocks of sheep and camels. A narrow coastal strip supports some agriculture, chiefly groves of dates and other fruits. Fishing is also commercially important.

## Pakistan
### Islamic Republic of Pakistan

**Geography** **Location:** southern Asia. **Boundaries:** Afghanistan to N, China to far NE, India to E, Arabian Sea to S, and Iran to W. **Total land area:** 310,403 sq. mi. (803,943 sq km). **Coastline:** 650 mi. (1,046 km). **Comparative area:** about twice size of California. **Land use:** 26% arable land; negl. % permanent crops; 6% meadows and pastures; 4% forest and woodland; 64% other; includes 19% irrigated. **Major cities:** (1981 census) Islamabad (capital) 204,364; Karachi 5,180,562; Lahore 2,952,689; Faisalabad (Lyallpur) 1,104,209; Rawalpindi 794,843.

**People** **Population:** 114,649,406 (1990). **Nationality:** noun—Pakistani(s); adjective—Pakistani. **Ethnic groups:** Punjabi, Sindhi, Pashtun (Pathan), Baluch, Muhajir (immigrants from India and their descendants). **Languages:** Urdu and English (official); total spoken languages—64% Punjabi, 12% Sindhi, 8% Pashtu, 7% Urdu, 9% Baluchi and other; English is lingua franca of Pakistani elite and most government ministries, however, official policies are promoting its gradual replacement by Urdu. **Religions:** 97% Muslim (77% Sunni, 20% Shi'a); 3% Christian, Hindu, and other.

**Government** **Type:** parliamentary with strong executive; federal republic. **Independence:** Aug. 15, 1947 (from UK). **Constitution:** Apr. 10, 1973; suspended July 5, 1977; restored Dec. 30, 1985. **National holiday:** Pakistan Day, Mar. 23. **Heads of government:** Ghulam Isheq Khan, president (since Dec. 1988); Muhammad Nawaz Sharif, prime minister (since Nov. 1990). **Structure:** based on English common law but gradually being transformed to correspond to Koranic injunction; former president Mohammad Zia's government established Islamic sharia courts paralleling secular courts and introduced Koranic punishments for some criminal offenses; martial law courts abolished Dec. 30, 1985, and all cases, including those concerning national security, now tried by civilian judiciary under due process safeguards.

**Economy** **Monetary unit:** rupee. **Budget:** (1989 est.) *income:* $7.5 bil.; *expend.:* $10.3 bil. **GNP:** $43.2 bil., $409 per capita (1988). **Chief crops:** wheat, rice, sugarcane, cotton; illegal producer of opium poppy and cannabis for international drug trade. **Livestock:** goats, sheep, cattle, buffalo, asses. **Natural resources:** land, extensive natural gas reserves, limited crude oil, poor quality coal, iron ore. **Major industries:** cotton textiles, food processing. **Labor force:** 28.9 mil. (est.); 54% agriculture, 33% services, 13% mining and manufacturing; extensive export of labor; 3.6% unemployment (1987). **Exports:** $4.5 bil. (f.o.b., 1989); rice, cotton, textiles. **Imports:** $7.2 bil. (f.o.b., 1989); petroleum, petroleum products, machinery, transport equipment, cooking oils. **Major trading partners:** *exports:* 31% EC, 11% U.S., 11% Japan; *imports:* 26% EC, 15% Japan, 11% U.S.

**Intl. Orgs.** Colombo Plan, FAO, G-77, GATT, IAEA, IBRD, ICAO, IDA, IFAD, IFC, ILO, IMF, IMO, INTELSAT, INTERPOL, ITU, NAM, UN, UNESCO, UPU, WHO, WIPO, WMO.

Pakistan occupies the heartland of ancient South Asian civilization, in the Indus River Valley. Agricultural settlements in that area arose by 3000 B.C., and the great cities at Harappa and Mohenjo-Daro were founded some 500 years later. Indo-European (Aryan) invaders from Central Asia overthrew the ancient civilization around 1500 B.C. and established a new culture that spread throughout Pakistan and northern India. Brahmanism, the religious culture of the early Indo-European invaders, gave rise to Buddhism and Jainism around the sixth century B.C., and evolved into Hinduism in the early centuries A.D. The Indus Valley was incorporated into the empire of Alexander the Great, c. 350 B.C., and then into the Mauryan empire of Asoka, which by the third century B.C. controlled all of South Asia except for the southernmost portion of India.

Under various rulers the Indus Valley and the areas to its northwest were a great center of Buddhist culture until the beginning of the eighth century, when the area fell to Muslim Arab invaders. Thereafter, Islam was firmly established throughout the region. But Baluchistan and the Northwest Frontier region became culturally allied to the Persian civilization of Iran and Afghanistan, while Sind and the Punjab were more closely akin to the culture of northern India.

Northern Pakistan was incorporated into the empire of Mahmud of Gazni in the 11th century, and fell to the Mongols in the 13th century. The Indus River became the boundary between the Mongol Inkhanate of Persia and the Sultanate of Delhi. The region was conquered by Timur Leng at the end of the 14th century, and after the fall of the Timurid empire was divided between the Kingdoms of Sind and Multan, in southern and central Pakistan, and the Sultanate of Delhi, in the Punjab. All of Pakistan and northern India was reunited after 1526, when the conquests of Babur established the Mogul empire.

The expansion of British power in India during the 18th century left Pakistan largely untouched; the area was divided among various states, including Sind, the Punjab, Kashmir, and the western reaches of Rajputana. In the first half of the 19th century, British rule extended to the northwest; after the defeat of the Indian Mutiny of 1857, the entire Indus Valley came under British rule. Sind and the Punjab were ruled directly by the British, while the native states were ruled as British protectorates.

From the beginning of the 20th century, various nationalist movements arose throughout British India. The Moslem League, under the leadership of Mohammad Ali Jinnah after 1916, advocated greater popular political participation, dominion status for India, and a strong Muslim voice in Indian administration. Muslims and Hindus were allied in the Non-Cooperation movement of the 1920s, but the alliance soon broke down and degenerated into communal frictions. With growing power of the Congress party in Hindu areas and Gandhi's civil disobedience movement in the 1930s, Jinnah's Moslem League charted an increasingly separate course and called for the creation of a separate Muslim state in 1940.

With the British withdrawal from India in 1947, Hindus in the Muslim majority areas of the Indus Valley and in East Bengal fled to Hindu northern India, while Muslims in Hindu areas fled in the opposite direction. These massive population movements were accompanied by widespread violence leading to the loss of hundreds of thousands of lives. Jinnah, the father of modern Pakistan, died in 1948. Pakistan, encompassing Sind, the Punjab, Baluchistan, the Northwest Frontier Territories, part of Jammu and Kashmir, and adjacent areas in the west and East Bengal in the east, was granted dominion status within the British Commonwealth in 1947, becoming an independent republic in 1956.

Pakistan joined the Central Treaty Organization and became allied with the West, in contrast to the Soviet-leaning nonalignment of India. In 1958 Gen. Mohammad Ayub Khan seized power in a coup; he was elected president in 1960 and reelected in 1965. Following border clashes with India in 1962, Pakistan entered into friendly relations with China, which also had engaged in border warfare with India. Ayub Khan resigned as president in early 1969 after failing to put down widespread demonstrations in East Pakistan. A new government was formed under Gen. Yahya Khan, and martial law was declared. A parliamentary victory by the East Pakistani Awami League in December 1970 led to civil war and the secession of East Pakistan in 1971 (see "Bangladesh").

India's intervention on behalf of East Bengal had led to war on a western front with Pakistan. On July 3, 1972, India and Pakistan agreed to a mutual withdrawal of troops and entered into negotiations designed to settle border disputes and other outstanding problems. Diplomatic relations between India and Pakistan were resumed in 1976.

The elections of 1970 that had precipitated the civil war also brought Zulfikar Ali Bhutto to the presidency. He remained in office until July 1977, when he was overthrown in a military coup led by Gen. Mohammad Zia ul-Haq. He was convicted of complicity in a 1974 political murder and hanged in April 1979. Under Pres. Zia, Pakistan moved toward the implementation of Islamic law in parallel with the constitutional law of Pakistan's parliamentary system. In 1986 Bhutto's daughter, Benazir Bhutto, returned to Pakistan from exile in Europe to organize opposition parties against Pres. Zia; this movement led to widespread rioting in the months that followed.

On Aug. 17, 1988, Pres. Zia, several senior government officials, and the American ambassador were killed in an airplane crash, the cause of which remains under investigation. Zia's death left the government of Pakistan severely weakened, at least temporarily.

Following the invasion of Afghanistan by Soviet troops in 1979, more than two million Afghan refugees entered Pakistan. The government, with American and Chinese support, gave shelter and substantial assistance to the various Afghan resistance movements.

Benazir Bhutto was elected prime minister in 1988. Her government faced a serious challenge from a violent separatist movement in Sind, and in the spring of 1990 war with India threatened as India accused Pakistan of supporting separatist rebels in Kashmir.

On Aug. 6, 1990, Pres. Isheq Khan dismissed the government of Prime Minister Benazir Bhutto, accusing her administration of corruption and nepotism. In November Nawaz Sharif became prime minister. He is the first person to hold that post who is not a feudal landowner from Sind province.

Pakistan's economy is largely agricultural; wheat, rice, and tobacco are grown in the Indus Valley, while pastoralism predominates in the drier areas of the north and west. Urban areas support considerable industry, including textiles, food processing, and manufacturing. Pakistan remains a major recipient of American foreign aid.

# Panama
## Republic of Panama

**Geography Location:** southern Central America. **Boundaries:** Caribbean Sea to N, Colombia to E, Pacific Ocean to S, Costa Rica to W. **Total land area:** 29,762 sq. mi. (77,082 sq km). **Coastline:** 1,546 mi. (2,490 km). **Comparative area:** slightly smaller than South Carolina. **Land use:** 6% arable land; 2% permanent crops; 15% meadows and pastures; 54% forest and woodland; 23% other; includes negl. % irrigated. **Major cities:** (1980 census) Panamá (Panama City–capital) 389,172; Colón 59,840; David 50,016.

**People Population:** 2,425,400 (1990). **Nationality:** noun–Panamanian(s); adjective–Panamanian. **Ethnic groups:** 70% mestizo, 14% West Indian, 10% white, 6% Indian. **Languages:** Spanish (official), 14% speak English as native tongue; many Panamanians bilingual. **Religions:** over 90% Roman Catholic, 6% Protestant.

**Government Type:** republic. **Independence:** Nov. 3, 1903 (from Colombia); became independent from Spain Nov. 28, 1821. **Constitution:** Oct. 11, 1972, with major reforms adopted in Apr. 1983. **National holiday:** Independence Day, Nov. 3. **Head of government:** Guillermo Endara Galimany, president (since Dec. 1989). **Structure:** Executive branch–president, two vice presidents, cabinet; Legislative–one-house National Assembly of 67 members elected by popular vote; Judicial–Supreme Court and lesser courts.

**Economy Monetary unit:** balboa. **Budget:** (1989 est.) **income:** $598 mil.; **expend.:** $750 mil. **GDP:** $3.9 bil., $1,648 per capita. **Chief crops:** bananas, rice, sugarcane, coffee, corn; self-sufficient in basic foods. **Livestock:** cattle, pigs. **Natural resources:** copper, mahogany forests, shrimp. **Major industries:** manufacturing and construction, petroleum refining, brewing, cement and other construction material. **Labor force:** 770,472 (1987); 27.9% government and community services, 26.2% agriculture, hunting, and fishing, 16% commerce, restaurants, and hotels, 10.5% manufacturing and mining; shortage of skilled labor, but over supply of unskilled labor; 23% unemployment (1988 est.). **Exports:** $220 mil. (f.o.b., 1989 est.); 40% bananas, 27% shrimp, 4% coffee, sugar, petroleum products. **Imports:** $830 mil. (c.i.f., 1989 est.); 16% foodstuffs, 16% crude oil, 9% consumer goods. **Major trading partners:** *exports:* 90% U.S., Central America and Caribbean, EC; *imports:* 35% U.S., Central America and Caribbean, Mexico, EC, Venezuela.

**Intl. Orgs.** FAO, G-77, IAEA, IBRD, ICAO, IDA, IFAD, IFC, ILO, IMF, INTELSAT, INTERPOL, ITU, NAM, OAS, UN, UNESCO, UPU, WHO, WMO.

The Spanish first arrived in what is now Panama in 1501. Vasco Nuñez de Balboa returned in 1510, and Pedro Arias Dávila founded the City of Panama in 1519. Panama became attached to the viceroyalty of New Granada after 1739 and left the Spanish empire with the rest of New Granada in 1821, becoming a part of Gran Colombia. The first canal company proposing the construction of a trans-isthmian passageway was formed in 1825–26. The completion of a U.S.-financed railway from Colón to Panama City by 1855 enhanced Panama's importance as a transoceanic passage.

Panamanian nationalists waged a "War of a Thousand Days" against the Bogotá government between 1899 and 1902. In 1903 Panama gained independence from Colombia with U.S. complicity. Within a month Panamanian officials accepted an agreement with the United States that created a canal zone under the control of the U.S. government "in perpetuity," and the Panama Canal was completed and opened in 1914.

Panama experienced protectorate status under U.S. control after independence insofar as the United States "guaranteed the independence" of Panama. The United States explicitly upheld its right of unilateral military intervention in Panama when in 1918 it sent troops there without the permission of the Panamanian government. The 1936 Hull-Alvaro Treaty eliminated protectorate status, and the United States dropped its claim to a right of intervention in the cities of Panama and Colón.

In 1968 a power struggle between Pres. Arnulfo Arias and the Panamanian National Guard led to the ouster of the president. A National Guard junta took control of the government, and Col. (later Gen.) Omar Torrijos Herrera became the ruler of the country the following year. In 1972 a new Assembly under Torrijos's control offered him the title of Jefe Maximo (chief executive) in addition to drafting a new constitution for the country. Torrijos constructed a populist following through the creation of housing projects, a new labor code, an agrarian reform, and an increase in tax rates imposed on foreign banana-interests.

The Panamanian government and the United States concluded a new canal treaty in 1977 the key provisions of which included integration of the Canal Zone with the rest of Panamanian territory and full Panamanian control of the canal in the year 2000. In 1981 Omar Torrijos died in an air accident.

In 1988 the head of the Panamanian military and de facto ruler of the country, Gen. Manuel Noriega, was indicted in the United States on narcotics charges. Gen. Noriega refused to submit to U.S. demands for his resignation. When Panama's Pres. Eric Arturo Delvalle ordered Noriega to resign, the general refused. Pres. Delvalle was forced to go into hiding, and Manuel Solis Palma replaced him in the presidency. The United States responded by freezing Panamanian assets in the United States, thus creating severe economic hardship.

In May 1989 Gen. Noriega annulled election results that showed him losing to Guillermo Endara and assumed the role of dictator. After an unsuccessful coup attempt in October 1989, the United States invaded Panama on Dec. 20, captured Noriega, and brought him to Miami to stand trial on narcotics charges.

Panama remains frustrated by its dependence on the United States and by the fact that the country is still a conduit for South American drugs. The government is ineffective and losing popularity; in December 1990 U.S. forces helped put down a rebellion led by Noriega's former chief of the national police.

## Papua New Guinea

**Geography Location:** eastern section of island of New Guinea and about 600 smaller islands in Bismarck Archipelago (New Britain, New Ireland, and Manus) and northern part of Solomon Islands. Port Moresby 9°30′S, 147°07′E. **Boundaries:** Bismarck Sea to N, Solomon Sea to E, Australia to S, and Indonesia to W. **Total land area:** 178,704 sq. mi. (462,840 sq km). **Coastline:** 3,202 mi. (5,152 km). **Comparative area:** slightly larger than California. **Land use:** negl. % arable land; 1% permanent crops; negl. % meadows and pastures; 71% forest and woodland; 28% other. **Major cities:** (1987 est.) Port Moresby (administrative capital) 145,300.

**People Population:** 3,822,875 (1990). **Nationality:** noun—Papua New Guinean(s); adjective—Papua New Guinean. **Ethnic groups:** predominantly Melanesian and Papuan; some Negrito, Micronesian, and Polynesian. **Languages:** 715 indigenous languages; English spoken by 1–2%, pidgin English widespread; Motu spoken in Papua region. **Religions:** over half of population nominally Christian (490,000 Catholic, 320,000 Lutheran and other Protestant sects); remainder indigenous beliefs.

**Government Type:** independent parliamentary state within Commonwealth recognizing Elizabeth II as head of state. **Independence:** Sept. 16, 1975 (from UN trusteeship under Australian administration). **Constitution:** Sept. 16, 1975. **National holiday:** Independence Day, Sept. 16. **Heads of government:** Vincent Eri, governor-general (since Jan. 1990); Rabbie Namaliu, prime minister (since July 1988). **Structure:** executive—National Executive Council; legislature—House of Assembly (109 members); judiciary—court system consists of Supreme Court of Papua New Guinea and various inferior courts (district courts, local courts, children's courts, wardens' courts).

**Economy Monetary unit:** kina. **Budget:** (1988) *income:* $962 mil.; *expend.:* $988 mil. **GDP:** $3.26 bil., $890 per capita (1985). **Chief crops:** copra, cocoa, coffee, rubber, oil palm. **Livestock:** pigs, cattle, goats, chickens, sheep. **Natural resources:** gold, copper, silver, natural gas, timber. **Major industries:** copra crushing, oil-palm processing, plywood processing. **Labor force:** 1.66 mil.; 732,806 in salaried employment (1980); 54% agriculture, 25% government. **Exports:** $1.4 mil. (f.o.b., 1988); gold, copper ore, coffee, copra, palm oil, timber. **Imports:** $1.2 bil. (c.i.f., 1988); machinery and transport equipment, food, fuels, chemicals. **Major trading partners:** *exports:* W. Germany, Japan, Australia, UK, Spain, U.S.; *imports:* Australia, Singapore, Japan, U.S., New Zealand.

**Intl. Orgs.** Commonwealth, FAO, G-77, GATT (de facto), IBRD, ICAO, IDA, IFAD, IFC, ILO, IMF, IMO, INTELSAT, INTERPOL, ITU, UN, UNESCO, UPU, WHO, WMO.

The island of New Guinea, the world's second-largest, was settled many thousands of years ago by waves of Papuan and Melanesian migrants who developed large numbers of linguistically diverse and mutually hostile tribes of hunters and small cultivators. In the 19th century, the island was divided between the Dutch (to the west, in what is now the Indonesian province of Irian Jaya), Germany, and the British. The German sector was occupied by Australia in 1914 and administered under a League of Nations Mandate after World War I.

Japanese attempts to occupy New Guinea in 1942 met with only partial success. In a series of counteroffensives, the Allies regained control over the entire island by mid-1944.

Beginning in 1949 the former German and British colonies were administered jointly by Australia under a UN mandate. The territories were made self-governing in 1973 and achieved full independence as Papua New Guinea on Sept. 16, 1975. The nation maintains close ties with Australia. Relations are strained with Indonesia, which accuses Papua New Guinea of giving shelter to an Irian Jaya liberation movement.

Papua New Guinea's economy remains largely in the stage of small-scale agriculture. The national economy was badly hurt in 1989 when a vital copper mine on the island of Bougainville was forced to close by separatist guerrillas. The resulting loss of international confidence in Papua New Guinea's economy has led to a decline in foreign investment.

## Paraguay
### Republic of Paraguay
**Geography Location:** landlocked country in central South America. **Boundaries:** Bolivia

to N, Brazil to E, Argentina to S and W. **Total land area:** 157,048 sq. mi. (406,752 sq km). **Coastline:** none. **Comparative area:** about size of California. **Land use:** 20% arable land; 1% permanent crops; 39% meadows and pastures; 35% forest and woodland; 5% other; includes negl. % irrigated. **Major cities:** (1982 census) Asunción (capital) 455,517; Pedro Juan Caballero 37,331; Puerto Presidente Stroessner 36,676; Encarnación 27,632; Villarrica 21,203.

**People Population:** 4,660,270 (1990). **Nationality:** noun—Paraguayan(s); adjective—Paraguayan. **Ethnic groups:** 95% mestizo, 5% white and Indian. **Languages:** Spanish (official), Guaraní. **Religions:** 97% Roman Catholic, Mennonite and other Protestant denominations.

**Government Type:** republic under authoritarian rule. **Independence:** May 14, 1811 (from Spain). **Constitution:** Aug. 25, 1967. **National holiday:** Independence Days, May 14-15. **Heads of government:** Gen. Andrés Rodriguez, president (since Feb. 1989). **Structure:** president heads executive; bicameral legislature (Senate, Chamber of Deputies); judiciary headed by Supreme Court.

**Economy Monetary unit:** guaraní. **Budget:** (1988) **income:** $609 mil.; **expend.:** $1,098 mil. **GDP:** $8.9 bil., $1,970 per capita (1989 est.). **Chief crops:** oilseed, soybeans, cotton, wheat, manioc, sweet potatoes, tobacco, corn, rice, sugarcane; self-sufficient in most foods; illegal producer of cannabis for international drug trade. **Livestock:** cattle, pigs, sheep, horses, goats. **Natural resources:** iron ore, manganese, limestone, hydropower, timber. **Major industries:** meat packing, oilseed crushing, milling. **Labor force:** 1.3 mil. (1986); 44% agriculture, 34% industry and commerce, 18% services; 11% unemployment (1988 est.). **Exports:** $1.0 bil. (f.o.b., 1989 est.); cotton, soybeans, timber, vegetable oils, coffee, tung oil. **Imports:** $1.0 bil. (c.i.f., 1989 est.); 35% capital goods, 20% consumer goods, 19% fuels and lubricants, 16% raw materials, 10% foodstuffs, beverages, tobacco. **Major trading partners: exports:** 37% EC, 25% Brazil, 10% Argentina, 6% Chile, 6% U.S.; **imports:** 30% Brazil, 20% EC, 18% U.S., 8% Argentina, 7% Japan.

**Intl. Orgs.** FAO, G-77, IAEA, IBRD, ICAO, IDA, IFAD, IFC, ILO, IMF, INTELSAT, INTERPOL, ITU, OAS, UN, UNESCO, UPU, WHO, WMO.

When Europeans arrived in what is now Paraguay in the early 16th century, they encountered various groups of semisedentary and nonsedentary indigenous peoples. The Spanish entered into alliances with the Tupian semisedentary Guaraní against the nomadic Guaycuru Indians in the west of the region. Asunción, founded in 1537, was little more than a Spanish defense outpost against the Portuguese and a trading stopover between the silver mines of Potosí and Buenos Aires.

From early in the 17th century, the Jesuits established an extensive network of missions in the southern portion of the colony, and a rivalry grew between the Jesuits and the elites of Asunción over who would determine the colony's social and economic structure. The isolation of the settlers from the mainstream of Spanish colonial society combined with the lack of valuable resources led to the evolution of a relatively egalitarian social structure in Spanish imperial terms. The political elite of Asunción deposed Spanish authority in 1811, and Paraguayan independence was declared in 1813.

Stable authoritarian rule marked the period from independence until 1870. José Gaspar Rodríguez de Francia was declared ruler for life in 1816 and remained in power until his death in 1840. A period of political turmoil followed the death of Francia but was resolved in the election of Carlos Antonio López in 1844; in 1857 he was named president for life. López chose his son Francisco Solano López to succeed him in office in 1862. Francisco Solano intervened in a Brazilian attempt to control the fate of Uruguay, beginning the Paraguayan War, or the War of the Triple Alliance (Brazil, Argentina, Uruguay) from 1865 to 1870. The war was catastrophic for Paraguay, reducing the population from 450,000 to 220,000; almost the entire male population was killed, and Paraguay lost 60,000 square miles of territory while being saddled with a war debt of 19 million gold pesos ($200,000,000). The Brazilian government later dropped the unrealistic payment demand.

After the war the Colorado and Liberal parties developed, although the real political distinctions were dependent more on individuals and families than political ideology. Colorado-party Gen. Bernardino Caballero, backed by Brazil, was the power behind the scenes of frequent changes in government personnel between 1874 and 1904. The Liberals, backed by Argentina, were in power from 1904 until 1936.

After 18 years of authoritarian rule by a number of military officers, Gen. Alfredo Stroessner, with the backing of Colorado-party factions, began his rule in 1954. Stroessner held power until 1989, when Gen. Andrés Rodríguez overthrew him.

# Peru
## Republic of Peru

**Geography Location:** western coast of South America. **Boundaries:** Ecuador, Colombia to N, Brazil, Bolivia to E, Chile to S, Pacific Ocean to W. **Total land area:** 496,225 sq. mi. (1,285,216 sq km). **Coastline:** 1,546 mi. (2,414 km). **Comparative area:** slightly smaller than Alaska. **Land use:** 3% arable land; negl. % permanent crops; 21% meadows and pastures; 55% forest and woodland; 21% other; includes 1% irrigated. **Major cities:** (1985 est.) Lima (capital) 5,330,800; Arequipa 531,829; Callao 515,200; Trujillo 438,709; Chiclayo 347,702.

**People Population:** 21,905,605 (1990). **Nationality:** noun—Peruvian(s); adjective—Peruvian. **Ethnic groups:** 45% Indian, 37% mestizo, 15% white, 3% black, Japanese, Chinese, and other. **Languages:** Spanish and Quechua (official), Aymara. **Religions:** predominantly Roman Catholic.

**Government Type:** republic. **Independence:** July 28, 1821 (from Spain). **Constitution:** July 28, 1980; often referred to as 1979 Constitution because constituent assembly met in 1979, but Constitution actually took effect following year; reestablished civilian government with popularly elected president and bicameral legislature. **National holiday:** Independence Day, July 28. **Heads of government:** Alberto Fujimori, president (since July 1990); Dr. Carlos Torres y Torres Lara, prime minister (since Feb. 1991). **Structure:** executive; bicameral legislature (Senate, Chamber of Deputies); judicial.

**Economy Monetary unit:** inti. **Budget:** (1986) **income:** $3.2 bil.; **expend.:** $3.7 bil. **GDP:** $18.9 bil., $880 per capita. **Chief crops:** wheat, potatoes, beans, rice, barley, coffee, cotton, sugarcane; imports wheat, meat, lard and oils, rice, corn; illegal producer of coca for international drug trade. **Livestock:** sheep, cattle, pigs, goats, horses. **Natural resources:** copper, silver, gold, petroleum, timber. **Major industries:** mining of metals, petroleum, fishing. **Labor force:** 6.8 mil. (1986); 44% government and other services, 37% agriculture, 19% industry; 9.5% unemployment. **Exports:** $3.6 bil. (f.o.b., 1989); fish meal, cotton, sugar, coffee, copper. **Imports:** $2.5 bil. (f.o.b., 1989); foodstuffs, machinery, transport equipment, iron and steel semimanufactures, chemicals. **Major trading partners: exports:** 22% EC, 20% U.S., 11% Japan, 8% Latin America, 4% USSR; **imports:** 23% U.S., 16% Latin America, 12% EC, 7% Japan, 3% Switzerland.

**Intl. Orgs.** FAO, G-77, GATT, IAEA, IBRD, ICAO, IDA, IFAD, IFC, ILO, IMF, IMO, INTELSAT, INTERPOL, ITU, NAM, OAS, UN, UNESCO, UPU, WHO, WMO.

Peru was the site of the civilization of the Inca empire before the arrival of Europeans. The Incas had extended their control over most of the Andean region by the late 15th century. The civilization was advanced in terms of its ability to provide for the welfare of its subjects and was in possession of sophisticated knowledge in a number of fields, including medicine. By the time of the arrival of the Spanish conqueror Francisco Pizarro in 1532, the empire seems already to have been in decline, and a combination of plague and civil war in the decade prior to the appearance of Europeans no doubt made the empire more vulnerable to Spanish conquest. Despite Spanish victories, Inca resistance to Spanish domination was not effectively quelled until the execution of Tupac Amarú in 1571. European-borne diseases such as smallpox and measles devastated the Indian population of the region.

Because of the great wealth of precious metals discovered by the Spanish and the adaptability of a sedentary indigenous civilization to the imposition of Spanish imperial control, Peru quickly became a major focal point of Spanish colonialism in the Americas; they founded Lima in 1535. The viceroyalty of Peru, established in 1544, originally served as the political and administrative nerve center of Spanish colonization of South America. For nearly two centuries, Lima was the seat of power and wealth for the whole region and the focal point of entrenched imperial interests. Peru was "liberated" by Simón Bolívar and José de San Martín in 1821 when Bolívar's army defeated the royalist forces at the battles of Junín and Ayacucho.

In the 40 years after independence, the presidency changed hands 35 times, and the country generated at least 15 different constitutions. Only four of the presidents of the period were constitutionally chosen, and the vast majority of the chief executives were military figures. In 1829 Peru tried and failed to annex Ecuador; in the 1830s an attempt at political federation between Peru and Bolivia collapsed with the Chilean invasion of 1839.

A political movement in favor of civilian rule, the Civilistas, began to organize by the 1860s. Chile defeated Peru in the War of the Pacific (1879–83), and Chileans occupied Lima and its port city of Callao for two years. The Peruvian government was deeply in debt after the war, resulting in the loss of ownership of much of Peru's infrastructure and natural resources to foreigners.

Peru experienced a period of civilian leadership between 1895 and 1930. Pres. Augusto B. Leguía (1908–12, 1919–30) extended his rule in an extraconstitutional manner until 1930, when Col. Luis Sánchez Cerro seized power; he ruled until his assassination in 1933. Gen. Oscar Benavides succeeded Cerro and managed to restore confidence in the economy. In 1939 civilian banker Manuel Prado was elected to the presidency, and the military allowed him to complete his term in office, which expired in 1945. During Prado's administration, Peru went to war with Ecuador and was victorious, seizing a great deal of territory.

Víctor Raúl Haya de la Torre founded Peru's most prominent political party, the American Popular Revolutionary Alliance (APRA), in 1924. As initiated, the party put forward an "antiimperialist" platform aiming at nationalization of land and reconstruction of society in favor of oppressed people. Haya de la Torre was apparently fraudulently deprived of a presidential electoral victory in 1931. The following year Apristas (APRA supporters) seized Trujillo and killed some military personnel. By way of revenge, the army massacred 6,000 Apristas. The result was a continuing enmity between the Peruvian armed forces and the APRA party lasting until the 1980s. Although APRA clearly had majority support from the Peruvian electorate in the intervening period, the party was not allowed to take power directly until 1985.

The Peruvian military, led by Gen. Juan Velasco Alvarado, seized power in 1968 and proceeded to embark upon a nationalist course of reform that included the nationalization of Standard Oil's International Petroleum Company holdings. The Peruvian military took steps to restructure economic and political power in the country by joining the Andean Pact and undermining the power of the tradi-

tional agricultural elite in the country by sponsoring an agrarian reform that mobilized peasant sectors of the population and changed the relations between landlord and peasant. By the late 1970s, however, the military government began to move toward the Right.

The presidency of Peru returned to civilian leadership under the administration of Fernando Belaúnde Terry (1980–85). In 1985, for the first time since its founding, the military allowed the APRA presidential candidate, Alan García Pérez, to take office. García Pérez promised to spend no more than 10 percent of the country's export earnings on payment of Peru's huge outstanding foreign debt and he was enormously popular during his first years in office. His public support was undermined by a growing insurgency sponsored by the Sendero Luminoso ("Shining Path") Maoist guerrillas and runaway inflation.

On June 10, 1990, political novice Alberto Fujimori, the son of Japanese immigrants, defeated the well-known writer Mario Vargas Llosa for the presidency. Fujimori won by opposing Vargas's proposals for economic austerity programs that would have adversely affected Peru's poor and middle classes, but once in office began advocating more conservative economic policies.

In January, the World Health Organization announced that a cholera epidemic had broken out in Peru, and a number of neighboring countries tightened border controls. (See "Major News Stories of the Year.")

# Philippines
## Republic of the Philippines

**Geography Location:** archipelago of some 7,100 islands about 500 mi. (800 km) off southeastern Asia; about 1,100 mi. (2,800 km) from N to S and 650 mi. (1,684 km) from W to E; Luzon in N and Mindanao in S account for 66% of land area. Manila 14°36′N, 120°59′E. **Boundaries:** Luzon Strait to N, Philippine Sea to E, Celebes Sea to S, Sulu Sea to SW, and South China Sea to W. **Total land area:** 115,831 sq. mi. (300,000 sq km). **Coastline:** 22,554 mi. (36,289 km). **Comparative area:** slightly larger than Arizona. **Land use:** 26% arable land; 11% permanent crops; 4% meadows and pastures; 40% forest and woodland; 19% other; includes 5% irrigated. **Major cities:** (1980 census) Manila (capital) 1,630,485; Quezon City 1,165,865; Davao City 610,375; Cebu City 490,281; Caloocan City 467,816.

**People Population:** 66,117,284 (1990). **Nationality:** noun—Filipino(s); adjective—Philippine. **Ethnic groups:** 91.5% Christian Malay, 4% Muslim Malay, 1.5% Chinese, 3% other. **Languages:** Pilipino (based on Tagalog) and English (both official). **Religions:** 83% Roman Catholic, 9% Protestant, 5% Muslim, 3% Buddhist and other.

**Government Type:** republic. **Independence:** July 4, 1946 (from U.S.). **Constitution:** Feb. 2, 1987, effective Feb. 11, 1987. **National holiday:** Independence Day, June 12. **Heads of government:** Mrs. Corazon Aquino, president

(since Feb. 1986). **Structure:** constitution provides for presidential form of government with directly elected president and vice president and U.S.-style bicameral legislature (24-seat Senate and 200-member House of Representatives); judicial branch headed by Supreme Court with descending authority in three-tiered system of local, regional trial, and intermediate appellate courts.

**Economy Monetary unit:** peso. **Budget:** (1989 est.) *income:* $7.2 bil.; *expend.:* $8.1 bil. **GNP:** $40.5 bil., $625 per capita (1987). **Chief crops:** rice, corn, coconut, sugarcane, bananas; illegal producer of cannabis for international drug trade. **Livestock:** pigs, buffalo, goats, cattle, horses. **Natural resources:** timber, crude oil, nickel, cobalt, silver. **Major industries:** textiles, pharmaceuticals, chemicals. **Labor force:** 22.9 mil. (1987); 47% agriculture, 20% industry and commerce, 13.5% services, 10% government; 11.3% unemployment; much underemployment. **Exports:** $8.1 bil. (f.o.b., 1989); 19% electrical equipment, 16% textiles, 11% minerals and ores, 10% farm products, 10% coconut. **Imports:** $10.5 bil. (c.i.f., 1989); 53% raw materials, 17% capital goods, 17% petroleum products. **Major trading partners:** *exports:* 36% U.S., 19% EC, 18% Japan, 9% ESCAP (Economic and Social Commission for Asia and the Pacific), 7% ASEAN; *imports:* 25% U.S., 17% Japan, 13% ESCAP, 11% EC, 10% ASEAN, 10% Middle East.

**Intl. Orgs.** ASEAN, Colombo Plan, FAO, G-77, GATT, IAEA, IBRD, ICAO, IDA, IFAD, IFC, ILO, IMF, IMO, INTELSAT, INTERPOL, ITU, UN, UNESCO, UPU, WHO, WIPO, WMO.

The Philippines were anciently settled by various Malayan peoples in several waves of migration from Southeast Asia. Tribal societies coexisted with petty principalities that had trade links to China, the East Indies, and countries in the Indian Ocean. The Philippines were visited by Magellan (who was killed there) in 1521, and Spanish conquest of the islands began in 1564. The Spanish colonial capital at Manila was founded in 1571 and became a key transit point for trade between Mexico and the Far East. Under Spanish rule a majority of Filipinos became Christian except in the southwestern islands, which remained Muslim. The Spanish period as a whole was marked by a torpid colonial administration and a gradual rise in the power and wealth of the Catholic church.

In the late 19th century, a nationalist movement led by José Rizal gained a wide following. In 1896 an armed uprising began, led by Emilio Aguinaldo. The 1898 victory of Adm. George Dewey at the Battle of Manila Bay during the Spanish-American War led Spain to cede the Philippines to the United States in return for a payment of $20 million. Expecting immediate independence with U.S. support, Aguinaldo declared the islands a republic. When this was not recognized by the United States, Aguinaldo led a new war for independence, which was bloodily suppressed by American troops in a six-year campaign, 1899–1905.

American policy in the Philippines combined military control with an expressed desire to encourage home rule leading to eventual independence. In 1935 the Commonwealth of the Philippines was established, with Manuel Quezon as its first president, beginning what was conceived of as a 10-year period of controlled autonomy leading to full independence on July 4, 1946. In November 1941, Quezon was reelected to the presidency. On Dec. 8, 1941, Japan attacked Manila and destroyed the American bases there. American and Filipino troops, after weeks of fierce fighting, evacuated the islands in March 1942. Quezon went into exile in America. The battle to recapture the Philippines began with the Battle of Leyte Gulf in October 1944 and was completed by July 1945.

In April 1946, Manuel Roxas was elected president of the Commonwealth. Independence came as scheduled on July 4 of that year, with the United States retaining military bases by treaty and establishing a special economic relationship with the Philippines. The leftist Hukbalahap Rebellion, originally a partisan campaign against the Japanese, caused severe difficulties for the new nation until it was finally defeated in military campaigns led by Ramon Magsaysay. Magsaysay was elected to the presidency in November 1953; the last Huk leaders surrendered in 1954.

The early years of independence were marked by some economic development, but also great economic inequality. Most land was held by huge estates, and the economy depended primarily on plantation crops (sugar, copra), mining, and timber. Villagers fleeing the rural subsistence economy poured into the cities, leading to huge slums and a climate of urban poverty and violence. Many Filipinos emigrated to America.

In 1966 Ferdinand Marcos was elected president on a reform platform. Overwhelmed in the early 1970s by demonstrations, a new leftist guerrilla movement, and a separatist rebellion by Islamic Moros in Mindinao, Marcos declared martial law on Sept. 21, 1972. On Jan. 17, 1973, Marcos promulgated a new constitution giving unprecedented power to the presidency. His wife, Imelda, began to wield considerable influence, and the climate of unrest, poverty, and corruption worsened throughout the 1970s. Martial law was lifted, however, on Jan. 17, 1981, and Marcos was reelected to a new six-year term as president.

The airport assassination of opposition leader Benigno Aquino on his return to the Philippines on Aug. 21, 1983, led to a new phase in opposition to Marcos's rule. Marcos retained a majority in elections to the National Assembly in 1984, amid widespread reports of electoral fraud. In a bitterly contested presidential election in February 1986, Marcos was officially declared the winner over Corazon Aquino, widow of Benigno Aquino. Mrs. Aquino also declared herself the winner, and her supporters took to the streets in massive anti-Marcos demonstrations. Deserted by key supporters in the military, church, and middle class, Marcos fled the country on Feb. 25, 1986. Mrs. Aquino took office pledging land reform, a new constitution, and a commission to recover the corruptly gained wealth of the Marcos family.

Under Pres. Aquino the situation in the Philippines has remained unsettled. Her former ally and vice president, Salvadore Laurel, formed an opposition party, and a key military supporter, Juan Ponce Enrile, has been implicated in several pro-Marcos coup attempts. Military and political measures aimed at putting down the Communist insurrection have yielded mixed results. Corruption remains widespread in politics and the economy. Progress in instituting land reform has been slow. The economy of the Philippines continues to be dependent on U.S. and international assistance.

During 1989–90, the Aquino government experienced a steady erosion of power in the face of failure to confront the country's continuing political and economic problems. Sentiment against the continued presence of U.S. military bases (Clark Air Base, Subic Bay Naval Base, and four smaller installations) is also very strong, and as of May 1991, no agreement on the status of the bases after September 1991 had been reached.

Ferdinand Marcos died in Hawaii in September 1989 after a long illness. In July 1990 Imelda Marcos was acquitted in a New York court of larceny and conspiracy charges stemming from her ownership (with her husband) of several office buildings.

# Poland
## Republic of Poland

**Geography** **Location:** eastern Europe. **Boundaries:** Baltic Sea to N, USSR to E, Czechoslovakia to S, Germany to W. **Total land area:** 120,727 sq. mi. (312,683 sq km). **Coastline:** 305 mi. (491 km). **Comparative area:** between Arizona and New Mexico. **Land use:** 48% arable land; 1% permanent crops; 13% meadows and pastures; 29% forest and woodland; 9% other; includes negl. % irrigated. **Major cities:** (1988 est.) Warszawa (Warsaw; capital) 1,651,200; Lödz 851,500; Krakow (Cracow) 743,700; Wroclaw 637,400; Poznan 586,500.

**People** **Population:** 37,776,725 (1990). **Nationality:** noun—Pole(s); adjective—Polish. **Ethnic groups:** 98.7% Polish, 0.6% Ukrainian, 0.5% Byelorussian. **Languages:** Polish. **Religions:** 95% Roman Catholic (about 75% practicing), 5% Uniate, Russian Orthodox, Protestant, and other.

**Government** **Type:** republic. **Independence:** N.A. **Constitution:** constitution of July 22, 1952 was revised and adopted in Jan. 1990. **National holiday:** Constitution Day, May 3. **Heads of government:** Lech Walesa, president (since Dec. 1990); Krzysztof Bielecki, prime minister (since Jan. 1991). **Structure:** Executive branch—president elected by parliament; Legislative—parliament (Sejm) has two houses, upper Senate and lower chamber elected by the people in June 1989; Judicial—Supreme Court, Administrative Supreme Court, Courts of Appeals.

**Economy** **Monetary unit:** zloti. **Budget:** (1988) *income:* $23 bil.; *expend.:* $24 bil. **GNP:** $172.4 bil., $4,565 per capita (1989 est.). **Chief crops:** grain, sugar beets, oilseed, potatoes; exporter of livestock products and sugar; importer of grains; self-sufficient for minimum requirements. **Livestock:** chickens, pigs, cattle, sheep, ducks. **Natural resources:** coal, sulfur, copper, natural gas, silver. **Major industries:** machine building, iron and steel, extractive industries. **Labor force:** 17.1 mil. (1988); 37% industry and construction, 29% agriculture, 15% trade, transport, and communications. **Exports:** $24.7 bil. (f.o.b., 1987 est.); 63% machinery and equipment; 14% fuels, minerals, metals, 14% manufactured consumer goods. **Imports:** $24.7 bil. (c.i.f., 1987 est.); 36% machinery and equipment, 35% fuels, minerals, metals, 12% agricultural and forestry products, 9% manufactured consumer goods. **Major trading partners:** (1988) *exports:* 25% USSR, 12% W. Germany, 6% Czechoslovakia; *imports:* 23% USSR, 13% W. Germany, 6% Czechoslovakia.

**Intl. Orgs.** FAO, GATT, IAEA, ICAO, ILO, IMO, ITU, UN, UNESCO, UPU, WHO, WIPO, WMO.

The Slavic people known as Polonians accepted Christianity in the second half of the 10th century, during the reign of Duke Mieszko, whose close relationship with the papacy prevented the Byzantine Empire from absorbing Poland. A strong and united Polish kingdom existed under the Piast dynasty until 1370. With that dynasty's extinction, the Anjou king of Hungary succeeded to the throne, followed by his daughter Jadwiga, who in 1386 married the grand duke of Lithuania. Thus was formed the great Commonwealth of Poland-Lithuania. Cracow became one of the great cities of late medieval Europe.

With the extinction of the Jagiellonian line in 1572, the monarchy became elective. With a large nobility, equaling about 10 percent of the population, the monarchy grew weak, and Poland increasingly was subject to foreign intervention. The rise of the expansionist powers of Sweden, Prussia, Russia, and Austria came in part at the expense of the Poles. Jan Sobieski (1624–96), who ruled Poland as John III, saved Vienna from the Turks and briefly revived the Polish monarchy, but Polish royal power ended with his death. In a series of partitions in 1772, 1793, and 1795, Poland was dismembered and finally obliterated as a state.

Napoleon revived a Polish national entity with the Grand Duchy of Warsaw; with Napoleon's fall, the Congress of Vienna re-created a Kingdom of Poland in 1815, under the rule of the czar of Russia. After 1830 Poland was subjected to systematic Russification.

The fall of Russia in World War I led to Poland's revival. The Lithuanian Socialist Jósef Pilsudski led Poland in war against the new Bolshevik government of Russia until, in the 1921 Treaty of Riga, Poland emerged with its boundaries restored to approximately those after the partition of 1793. It was ethnically about 70 percent Polish, a triumph for Polish nationalism but the end of Pilsudski's dream of a federation of northeastern Europe. Poland also had the largest Jewish population of any country in Europe.

With a strong legislature and a weak president, the new state seemed to Pilsudski too weak for its own defense. He assumed dictatorial powers in 1926 and ruled by fiat until his death in 1935. After his death a weak parliamentary government was controlled by military officers; the tentative revival of republicanism was halted by Hitler's aggression in 1939.

Like other countries of east-central Europe, Poland was primarily an agricultural country, with grains, sugar beets, and potatoes its principal crops. The postwar republic attempted land reform, with some success; about 750,000 new private farm holdings were created by 1938. Mining—of coal and copper—was the principal traditional industrial activity in the 20th century, supplemented by extraction of natural gas. In the mid-1930s shipbuilding and railroad construction led the way toward a modern economy.

World War II commenced in September 1939, with attacks on Poland by Germany and the Soviet Union. The war brought severe destruction to Poland and the extermination of virtually its entire Jewish population. A government-in-exile was established in London, but the Soviet Union broke relations with it in 1943 when it requested a Red Cross investigation into the murder of 14,000 Polish officers whose bodies were discovered in Katyn Forest. (The Soviet government acknowledged responsibility for the massacre in 1990.) The Soviets established a puppet government in Lublin in 1944. In August the Red Army paused in its western advance on the outskirts of Warsaw, permitting the Nazis to obliterate the Polish Home Army. On Jan. 1, 1945, the USSR recognized the Lublin regime as Poland's provisional government.

By the time of the Allied Powers Conference in Yalta in February 1945, the Red Army was only 40 miles from Berlin and had total control of Poland. The Allies agreed to Stalin's proposal concerning the eastern boundary of Poland (allowing Russia to incorporate the eastern half of the country) and agreed that the government should be constituted from an enlargement of the Lublin regime. At Potsdam in August 1945, it was further agreed that Poland should absorb the eastern portion of Germany. Poland's borders were shifted approximately 200 miles westward from the prewar configuration, becoming once again those of the 10th century. The border with Germany was guaranteed by a treaty of November 1990.

The free elections promised in the Yalta Agreement were postponed until 1947, by which time a Communist victory could be assured. In 1948 the Socialists were forcibly merged into the Communist party; in 1949 Premier Boleslaw Bierut requested that Soviet Gen. Konstantin Rokossovski be appointed minister of defense and commander in chief of the Polish army. In the same year, all cultural periodicals and all writers' and artists' associations were taken over by the Communist party.

But there was little collectivization of Polish agriculture or forced industrialization on the Stalinist model. Intellectuals, bolstered by the Catholic church (which deeply resented a 1953 law requiring government approval for ap-

pointment of bishops), questioned the regime with some boldness. In 1956 both Bierut and Party Secretary Minc died, and the party refused to reelect Rokossovski to the politburo. Wladislaw Gomulka was elected party chairman in October 1956. As Soviet warships sailed through the Baltic toward Poland, Nikita Khrushchev flew to Poland with a delegation of Soviet generals, where Gomulka assured them that Poland would follow the Soviet lead in foreign policy. Distracted by the crisis in Hungary, the Russians left Gomulka in power and even canceled Poland's debt and allowed the dismantling of agricultural collectives.

For a short time Gomulka permitted cultural and educational freedom, gaining the support of intellectuals and artists. But by 1958 he had reverted to Stalinist form, imposing controls and pursuing a somewhat anti-Semitic Polish nationalism. Gomulka ruled until 1970, when he was replaced as party secretary by Edward Gierek. But moral leadership within Poland had clearly passed to Stefan Cardinal Wyszynski, leader of the increasingly vocal Catholic church; Gierek was forced to improve relations with the church in order to maintain his own credibility as a national leader.

Gierek presided over a decade of increasing unrest, with rising prices and growing discontent. Polish exports of ham and furniture to the West under liberalized terms earned some hard currency but were insufficient to curb the rising national debt. The most significant event in Poland in the 1970s was the election of Karol Wojtyla, bishop of Krakow, as Pope John Paul II in October 1978. His visit to Poland in 1979 set the stage for the extraordinary events of the 1980s.

Gierek's austerity program of February 1980 sent meat prices soaring—60 percent in July alone. Strikes for wage adjustments, especially at the Lenin Shipyards in Gdansk, thrust into a position of national leadership the greatest statesman of postwar Poland, the shipyard worker Lech Walesa. Walesa was elected chairman of the national coordinating committee of independent labor unions, Solidarity. Solidarity demands went far beyond lower prices and higher wages; they included independent labor unions with the right to strike, freedom for political prisoners, and an end to censorship. In September 1980 Gierek resigned as party secretary and was replaced by Stanislaw Kania.

By December, 40 independent trade unions had been formed, and a "rural Solidarity" movement was growing. In February 1981 Soviet Army Gen. Wojciech Jaruzelski was named prime minister, and in October he replaced Kania as party secretary. When in December Solidarity announced plans to hold a referendum on the Jaruzelski regime, martial law was declared; Solidarity leaders were arrested, all its activities were banned, and the right to strike was abolished.

But the government was never able to suppress Solidarity as a popular force, and it was legalized in 1989. In June 1989 elections Solidarity won 99 of 100 senate seats and 299 of 460 seats in the lower house, although 65 percent of these had been reserved for the Commu-

nist party. Jaruzelski was elected acting president by parliament and Solidarity leader Tadeusz Mazowiecki became prime minister.

The Communist party voted to disband itself on Jan. 28, 1990, and the Mazowiecki government announced a program of radical economic reform, winning promises of foreign aid and increased investment from Western governments. Despite the ensuing hardships and sporadic strikes and protests, the policy enjoyed widespread popular support.

In June 1990, a commission was appointed to draft a new constitution. Jaruzelski resigned in September, and in presidential elections held in November and December, Walesa, at the head of Solidarity's labor/Catholic faction, defeated Mazowiecki, representing Solidarity's political/technocrat faction. Mazowiecki resigned as prime miniser, and Walesa was sworn in as president on Dec. 22.

## Portugal
### Republic of Portugal

**Geography Location:** Iberian Peninsula in southwest Europe; also two archipelagos in Atlantic Ocean: Azores (37°29′N, 25°40′W) and Madeira Islands (32°40′N, 16°55′W). **Boundaries:** Spain to N and E, Atlantic Ocean to S and W. **Total land area:** 33,549 sq. mi. (92,072 sq km). **Coastline:** 1,114 mi. (1,793 km). **Comparative area:** between Maine and Indiana. **Land use:** 32% arable land; 6% permanent crops; 6% meadows and pastures; 40% forest and woodland; 16% other; includes 7% irrigated. **Major cities:** (1981 census) Lisboa (Lisbon, capital) 807,937; Porto (Oporto) 327,368; Amadora 95,518; Setubal 77,885; Coimbra 74,616.

**People Population:** 10,354,497 (1990). **Nationality:** noun—Portuguese (sing., pl.); adjective—Portuguese. **Ethnic groups:** homogeneous Mediterranean stock on mainland, in Azores, and on Madeira Islands; citizens of black African descent who immigrated during decolonization number less than 100,000. **Languages:** Portuguese. **Religions:** 97% Roman Catholic, 1% Protestant, 2% other.

**Government Type:** republic. **Independence:** N.A. **Constitution:** Apr. 25, 1976, revised Oct. 1982; new discussions on constitutional revisions began Oct. 1987. **National holiday:** Apr. 25. **Heads of government:** Mário Soàres, president (since March 1986); Anibal Cavaco Silva, prime minister (since Nov. 1985). **Structure:** executive—president and prime minister; legislative—unicameral legislature (popularly elected 250-seat Assembly of the Republic); judiciary—independent.

**Economy Monetary unit:** escudo. **Budget:** (1989 est.) *income:* $19.0 bil.; *expend.:* $22.2 bil. **GDP:** $72.1 bil., $6,900 per capita. **Chief crops:** generally underdeveloped; grains, potatoes, olives, grapes for wine; deficit foods—sugar, grain, meat, fish, oilseed. **Livestock:** sheep, pigs, cattle, goats, asses. **Natural resources:** fish, forests (cork), tungsten, iron ore, uranium ore, marble. **Major industries:** textiles, footwear, wood pulp, paper, cork. **Labor**

**force:** 4.58 mil. (1987); 44% services, 34% industry, 22% agriculture; 8% unemployment. **Exports:** $11 bil. (f.o.b., 1988); cotton textiles, cork and cork products, canned fish, wine, timber and timber products. **Imports:** $17.7 bil. (c.i.f., 1988); petroleum, cotton, food grains, industrial machinery, iron and steel. **Major trading partners:** *exports:* 72% EC, 13% other developed countries, 6% U.S.; *imports:* 67% EC, 15% less developed countries, 13% other developed countries, 4% U.S.

**Intl. Orgs.** EC, EFTA, FAO, GATT, IAEA, IBRD, ICAO, IFAD, IFC, ILO, IMF, IMO, INTELSAT, INTERPOL, ITU, NATO, OECD, UN, UNESCO, UPU, WHO, WIPO, WMO.

Portugal traces its origins back to the warlike Lusitanian tribes of Roman times. The nation-state originated as a county of the Kingdom of Castile, reconquered from the Moors in the 11th century. Portugal won recognition as an independent kingdom in 1143, and conquered Lisbon four years later. In 1250 the Algarve was conquered, and by then Portugal had expanded to its modern boundaries. Except for the period 1580-1640, when it was ruled by the Spanish Habsburgs, the Portuguese dynasty maintained its independence into the 20th century.

Portuguese fishermen had probably frequented the Grand Banks from before the time of Columbus, and the nation's tradition of seafaring gave rise to a world empire in the 15th and 16th centuries. Prince Henry the Navigator (1394-1460) colonized the Azores and the Madeiras and sponsored voyages of exploration along the west coast of Africa. Under his successors, Portugal controlled the west African coast, the shores of the Indian Ocean, and large stretches of southern Asia, as well as, in the Western Hemisphere, Brazil. Yet the rise of the empires of Spain and the Netherlands quickly reduced the Portuguese to second-rank status, leaving only Macao, Goa, and Timor in Asia; Portuguese Guinea (Guinea Bissau), Mozambique, and Angola in Africa; and the great territory of Brazil in Latin America.

In the 19th century, a series of dynastic civil wars weakened the monarchy, allowing Britain to gain control of the country's foreign policy (in addition to the wine trade of Oporto, long in British hands). Brazil declared its independence in 1822.

In 1910 Portugal became the first kingdom in Europe to be transformed into a republic. But in the next 15 years, chaos ensued: eight presidents, 44 governments, and a near-collapse of the economy. Finally, the military stepped in and established a dictatorship, lasting until recent times. In 1928 the military installed a civilian dictator, a professor of economics, Antonio Salazar. A firm believer in law and order, he managed to control the turbulence of political life and made the escudo one of Europe's most stable currencies, yet he could do nothing to alter Portugal's fundamental poverty. Although he ruled through civilian governments, his essential power always came from the army.

Portugal has long been Western Europe's poorest country. As late as 1960, almost half of the country's work force was engaged in agriculture, forestry, and fishing. In the north, agriculture was traditionally carried on in smallholdings; the south was characterized by large estates, remnants of feudal fiefs. Even today half of the country's food is imported. Exports were traditionally based on agricultural products (cork, olive oil, port wine) and fish. Industrialization came late to Portugal, and today manufacturing is mostly carried on by small firms engaged in textile and clothing production and other labor-intensive production.

World War II affected Portugal very little. Salazar deftly managed to remain Britain's ally while keeping his country out of the war as a neutral state. In the postwar period, Portugal accepted Marshall Plan aid and became a member of NATO in 1949. Portugal was a founding member of the European Free Trade Association in 1959 and negotiated a special relationship with the EC in 1972 (when its trading partner and ally, Great Britain, joined that body).

Portugal joined the United Nations in 1955 (having been vetoed until then by the Soviet Union), just in time to become embroiled in the worldwide movement for decolonization. Protesting that Portugal had, not colonies, but "overseas provinces," Salazar refused to bow to the pressure of world opinion. In 1961 India forcibly annexed Goa and other Portuguese enclaves on the subcontinent. In the same year, nationalist revolts broke out in Angola, with Guinea and Mozambique following soon after.

The colonial wars of the 1960s placed a terrible strain on Portugal's economy and resulted in severe military losses, and had the unintended effect of spreading Marxist ideas in the armed forces and the universities. And in the end, the colonies gained their independence. Salazar, gravely ill, retired in 1968 and was replaced by Marcelo Caetano. In 1974 Caetano was deposed in a bloodless coup staged by the secret Armed Forces Movement. The coup's leader, Antonio de Spinola, after reaching agreements on the independence of most of Portugal's old colonies, resigned as head of government in September 1974. Costa Gomez replaced Spinola, as a Revolutionary Council was instituted. The council survived two coup attempts, one by right-wing soldiers, the other by Communists, and it promulgated a socialist constitution in 1976. Through a series of unstable governments (16 between 1974 and 1987), the old agrarian estates were expropriated, and banking, insurance, and large industrial concerns were nationalized. The shock of this economic transformation, along with the OPEC price rises, created an economic recession in the 1970s. In addition Portugal had to absorb about a million ethnic Portuguese refugees from the former colonies.

Attempts by center-right coalitions in the 1980s to undo the nationalizations of the 1970s have been thwarted by vetoes of the Constitutional Tribunal (successor to the Revolutionary Council), even when the free-market Social Democratic party holds an absolute majority in the assembly. Portugal entered the EC on Jan. 1, 1986, pledging to reduce tariffs and end agricultural subsidies over a 10-year transitional period.

---

# Qatar
## State of Qatar

**Geography Location:** occupies a peninsula, projecting northward from Arabian mainland, into western part of Persian (Arabian) Gulf. **Boundaries:** Persian Gulf to N, E, and W; Saudi Arabia and United Arab Emirates to S. **Total land area:** 4,416 sq. mi. (11,437 sq km). **Coastline:** 350 mi. (563 km). **Comparative area:** between Delaware and Connecticut. **Land use:** negl. % arable land; 0% permanent crops; 5% meadows and pastures; 0% forest and woodland; 95% other. **Major cities:** (1986) Doha (capital) 217,294; Rayyan 91,996; Wakrah 23,682.

**People Population:** 490,897 (1990). **Nationality:** noun—Qatari(s); adjective—Qatari. **Ethnic groups:** 40% Arab, 18% Pakistani, 18% Indian, 10% Iranian, 14% other. **Languages:** Arabic (official), English commonly used as second language. **Religions:** 95% Muslim.

**Government Type:** traditional monarchy. **Independence:** Sept. 3, 1971 (from UK). **Constitution:** provisional constitution enacted Apr. 2, 1970. **National holiday:** Independence Day, Sept. 3. **Head of government:** Khalifa bin Hamad al-Thani, amir (since Feb. 1972). **Structure:** executive—amir and Council of Ministers; legislature—State Advisory Council.

**Economy Monetary unit:** Qatari riyal. **Budget:** (1988 est.) *income:* $1.7 bil.; *expend.:* $3.4 bil. **GDP:** $5.4 bil., $17,070 per capita (1987). **Chief crops:** farming and grazing on small scale; commercial fishing increasing in importance; most food imported; rice and dates are staple diet. **Livestock:** sheep, goats, camels, cattle, horses. **Natural resources:** crude oil, natural gas, fish. **Major industries:** crude oil production and refining, fertilizers, petrochemicals. **Labor force:** 104,000 (1983); 85% non-Qatari in private sector. **Exports:** $2.2 bil. (f.o.b., 1988 est.); 90% petroleum products, steel, fertilizers. **Imports:** $1.0 bil. (f.o.b., 1988 est.); excluding military equipment—foodstuffs, beverages, animal and vegetable oils. **Major trading partners:** *exports:* France, W. Germany, Italy, Japan, Spain; *imports:* EC, Japan, Arab countries, U.S., Australia.

**Intl. Orgs.** Arab League, FAO, G-77, GATT (de facto), IBRD, ICAO, IFAD, ILO, IMF, IMO, INTELSAT, INTERPOL, ITU, NAM, OPEC, UN, UNESCO, UPU, WHO, WIPO, WMO.

The Qatar peninsula was ruled as part of the sheikhdom of Bahrain from the late 18th century until the mid-19th century. An informal British protectorate was established in 1868; the Ottoman Empire also asserted authority over the sheikhs of Qatar from 1872 to 1916. The Ottomans ceded authority to the British in that year, and a formal British protectorate was organized. When British forces withdrew from the Persian Gulf region in 1971, Qatar entered into negotiations with the emirates of the Trucial Coast to join the federation of the

United Arab Emirates. When those negotiations broke down, Qatar declared its independence on Sept. 3, 1971.

Qatar's economy, formerly limited to fishing, maritime trade, and pastoralism, is now almost entirely dominated by oil, banking, and shipping services in the port of Doha.

## Romania

**Geography Location:** southeastern Europe. **Boundaries:** USSR to N and NE, Black Sea to E, Bulgaria to S, Yugoslavia to SW, Hungary to NW. **Total land area:** 91,699 sq. mi. (237,500 sq km). **Coastline:** 140 mi. (225 km). **Comparative area:** between Utah and Oregon. **Land use:** 43% arable land; 3% permanent crops; 19% meadows and pastures; 28% forest and woodland; 7% other; includes 11% irrigated. **Major cities:** (1986) Bucuresti (Bucharest, capital) 1,989,823; Braşov 351,493; Constanta 327,676; Timisoara 325,272; Iasi 313,060.

**People Population:** 23,273,285 (1990). **Nationality:** noun—Romanian(s); adjective—Romanian. **Ethnic groups:** 89% Romanian, 7.8% Hungarian, 1.5% German, 1.6% Ukrainian, Serb, Croat, Russian, Turk, and Gypsy. **Languages:** Romanian, Hungarian, German. **Religions:** 80% Romanian Orthodox, 6% Roman Catholic, 4% Calvinist, Lutheran, Jewish, Baptist.

**Government Type:** republic. **Independence:** N.A. **Constitution:** new constitution is being written. Constitution of Aug. 21, 1965 will be dissolved when new constitution is adopted by legislature. **National holiday:** National Day, Dec. 1. **Heads of government:** Ion Iliescu, president of National Front of Liberation, a provisional government (since Dec. 1989), elected president of Romania on May 20, 1990. Petre Roman, prime minister of National Front of Liberation, a provisional government (since Dec. 1989), elected prime minister of Romania on May 20, 1990. **Structure:** Executive branch consists of president and cabinet: legislature is parliament having upper Senate chamber and lower Chamber of Deputies; judicial branch consists of Supreme Court and Courts of Appeals.

**Economy** (1987) **Monetary unit:** lei. **Budget:** *income:* $26 bil.; *expend.:* $21.6 bil. **GNP:** $79.8 bil., $3,445 per capita. **Chief crops:** corn, wheat, oilseed; consumer and food supplies weak; net exporter. **Livestock:** poultry, sheep, pigs, cattle, horses. **Natural resources:** crude oil, timber, construction materials. **Major industries:** mining, timber, construction materials. **Labor force:** 10.6 mil.; 34% industry, 28% agriculture, 38% other. **Exports:** $11.5 bil. (f.o.b., 1988); 34.7% machinery and equipment; 24.7% fuels, minerals, and metals; 16.9% manufactured consumer goods; 11.9% agricultural materials and forestry products; 11.6% other. **Imports:** $8.75 bil. (f.o.b., 1988); 51.0% fuels, minerals, and metals, 26.7% machinery and equipment; 11.0% agricultural and forestry products; 4.2% manufactured consumer goods; 7.1% other. **Major trading partners:** (1987) *exports:* 27% USSR, 23% Eastern Europe, 15% EC, 5% U.S., 4% China. *imports:*

60% communist countries, 40% noncommunist countries.

**Intl. Orgs.** FAO, G-77, GATT, IAEA, IBRD, ICAO, IFAD, ILO, IMF, IMO, INTERPOL, ITU, UN, UNESCO, UPU, WHO, WIPO, WMO.

The Roman province of Dacia was sufficiently Latinized to retain the name of Rome long after the empire collapsed in A.D. 286. Overrun by invading Bulgars in the eighth century, the Romanians retained their Latinate language and orthodox Christianity; Romania remained beyond the borders of the Byzantine Empire but was in close contact with it. The country was conquered by the Mongols in the 13th century and formed the independent principalities of Moldavia and Walachia after the Mongols withdrew at the end of that century.

By the 15th century, Moldavia and Walachia had become vassal states of the Ottoman Empire, though with some local autonomy that permitted retention of orthodox Christianity and the creation of a rich local culture. Attempts at national unity against Ottoman rule in 1601 and 1711 failed; in 1861 the provinces united as an autonomous state under the name Romania, within the Ottoman Empire, under Greek administration.

Romania was for centuries the poorest country in Europe. Thoroughly agricultural, it was a land of unfree peasants working the great estates of landowners who were generally wealthy, usually absentee, and often Greek. The peasants not only paid taxes but also were required to perform feudal labor services for the estate owners. Neither industry nor a middle class existed before the 20th century.

After enlarging itself at Bulgaria's expense in the Second Balkan War (1913) on the eve of World War I, Romania switched sides three times, joining the Allies just before the war's end. Its reward was a huge expansion in size, doubling its territory with lands taken from Austria, Russia, and Bulgaria.

The interwar period was one of political turbulence, marked by violence and assassinations. Twice King Carol II went into exile, leaving his throne to his son Prince Michael; the second time was in 1940, when Russia (in accordance with the Hitler-Stalin pact) reclaimed the territories of Bessarabia and northern Bukovina that it had lost to Romania in 1920, while Hitler required Romania to return about half of Transylvania to Hungary.

During World War II, the pro-Hitler dictator Marshall Ion Antonescu took power, supported by a semifascist "Iron Guard," but when the latter attempted a coup, the military crushed the uprising. Romanian troops participated in Hitler's invasion of Russia in 1941, and the country paid the price in 1944 when Russian troops "liberated" the country, with devastating results. King Michael arrested Antonescu and switched to the Allied side, but to no avail. The country was quickly transformed into a Soviet satellite through rigged elections in which the communist National Democratic Front replaced the Peasant Alliance in power; a People's Republic was proclaimed on Dec. 30, 1947, and King Michael was forced to abdicate. A peace treaty in 1947 confirmed the loss of

Bessarabia to Russia but returned Transylvania to Romania.

Under Russian occupation Romania was a virtual Soviet colony. The occupying armies did not leave until after reparation payments were completed in 1958, leaving the dictator Gheorghe Gheorghiu-Dej in power. Despite COMECON plans for Romania to become a major food supplier to the Soviet bloc, Gheorghiu-Dej pursued industrialization on the Stalinist model, in the process ruining Romanian agriculture while creating large, labor-intensive, and highly inefficient factories. The result was an economic depression; politically, however, it produced a de facto independence for Romania within the Soviet bloc. Russian troops were forbidden on Romanian soil, and Romania declined to participate in COMECON policies.

With the death of Gheorghiu-Dej in 1965, power passed to Nicolae Ceauşescu. He promulgated a new constitution and instituted a series of purges, lasting to 1968; he became successively party leader in 1965, prime minister in 1967, and president of the republic in 1974. Ceauşescu continued his predecessor's economic policy, deepening the country's misery; he also pursued a policy of "independence" from the USSR, refusing to go along with Soviet policies of de-Stalinization and liberalization.

Romania's "national communism" was expressed in intense and militant nationalism, coupled with severe repression of ethnic minorities, especially Germans and Magyars in Transylvania. Hundreds of ethnically Hungarian villages were bulldozed into oblivion in the name of agricultural collectivization, leading to increased tensions with Hungary. The damage was compounded by a major earthquake in 1977 that caused extensive damage to Bucharest and surrounding areas.

Ceauşescu's ambitions included the creation of a family dynasty in the Romanian leadership. In 1979 his wife Elena was named first deputy premier and elevated to the Council of Ministers. Her brothers were given important government positions, Ceauşescu's son, despite his reputation as a decadent playboy, was groomed to replace his father.

Romania's transition from Communist rule was sudden and violent. On Dec. 16–18, 1989, demonstrations in Timisoara calling for Ceauşescu's ouster were put down with brute force by the Securitate (secret-police), but they spread and citizens and regular army troops fought pitched battles with Securitate forces in Bucharest. Ceauşescu and his wife fled Bucharest but were captured, tried, and executed by Christmas day. The newly organized Council of National Salvation established a provisional government with former Communist party official Ion Iliescu as president.

The Communist party was outlawed on Jan. 12, 1990. Despite the Council's domination by former Communists, no effective opposition movement emerged, and in elections on May 20, Iliescu was elected president in a landslide and the Council won 233 of 296 seats in the lower house.

On June 13, many anti-Communist demonstrators were beaten and several killed by troops and armed miners brought to Bucharest by the government, an action that was condemned internationally. Calls for Iliescu's resignation and a purge of Communists from government continued into the fall. Tensions were further aggravated when the government's abrupt move to a market economy resulted in food shortages and sharp price increases for consumer goods.

## Rwanda
### Republic of Rwanda

**Geography** **Location:** landlocked country in central Africa. **Boundaries:** Uganda to N, Tanzania to E, Burundi to S, Zaire to W. **Total land area:** 10,169 sq. mi. (26,338 sq km). **Coastline:** none. **Comparative area:** about size of Maryland. **Land use:** 29% arable land; 11% permanent crops; 18% meadows and pastures; 10% forest and woodland; 32% other; includes negl. % irrigated. **Major cities:** (1978 census) Kigali (capital) 117,749; Butare 21,691; Ruhengeri 16,025; Gisenyi 12,436.

**People** **Population:** 7,609,119 (1990). **Nationality:** noun—Rwandan(s); adjective—Rwandan. **Ethnic groups:** 90% Hutu, 9% Tutsi, 1% Twa (Pygmy). **Languages:** Kinyarwanda, French (both official); Kiswahili used in commercial centers. **Religions:** 65% Catholic, 9% Protestant, 9% Muslim; indigenous beliefs.

**Government** **Type:** republic; presidential system in which military leaders hold key offices. **Independence:** July 1, 1962 (from UN trusteeship under Belgian administration). **Constitution:** Dec. 17, 1978. **National holiday:** National Day, July 1. **Heads of government:** Maj. Gen. Juvénal Habyarimana, president (since Sept. 1973). **Structure:** executive—president, 16-member cabinet; unicameral legislature—National Development Council; judiciary—four senior courts, magistrates.

**Economy** **Monetary unit:** Rwanda franc. **Budget:** (1988 est.) *income:* $413 mil.; *expend.:* $522 mil. **GNP:** $2.3 bil., $325 per capita (1987). **Chief crops:** cash crops—coffee, tea, pyrethrum; food crops—bananas, cassava; self-sufficiency declining; country imports foodstuffs. **Livestock:** goats, cattle, sheep, pigs. **Natural resources:** gold, cassiterite (tin ore), wolframite (tungsten ore), natural gas, hydropower. **Major industries:** mining of cassiterite and wolframite, tin, cement. **Labor force:** 3.6 mil. (1985); 93% agriculture, 7% other. **Exports:** $118 mil. (f.o.b., 1988); 85% coffee, tea, tin, cassiterite, wolframite. **Imports:** $278 mil. (c.i.f., 1988); textiles, foodstuffs, machines, equipment, capital goods. **Major trading partners:** *exports:* W. Germany, Belgium, Italy, Uganda, UK; *imports:* U.S., Belgium, W. Germany, Kenya, Japan.

**Intl. Orgs.** FAO, G-77, GATT, IBRD, ICAO, IDA, IFAD, IFC, ILO, IMF, INTERPOL, ITU, NAM, UN, UNESCO, UPU, WHO, WMO.

Tutsi cattle-breeders came to Rwanda, on Africa's east coast, in the late 15th century and slowly conquered the native Hutu farmers. The Tutsi established a monarchy, forcing the Hutus into serfdom. Germans were the first Europeans to arrive in Rwanda and declared it a protectorate in 1899. After World War I Belgium was given a League of Nations mandate over the territory, which became a UN trusteeship after World War II.

Tutsi traditionalists resisted Belgian attempts in the 1950s to institute democratic political institutions. In 1959 the Hutus revolted against the monarchy in a bloody conflict which led to a mass exodus of Tutsis. Two years later the Hutus won a UN-supervised referendum and were granted internal autonomy by Belgium on Jan. 1, 1962. Full independence came on July 1, 1962. Political unrest led to the overthrow of the government in 1973. Maj. Gen. Juvénal Habyarimana dissolved the national assembly and banned all political activity.

In 1990, under pressure from the Tutsi opposition, which seeks the repatriation of approximately 500,000 who have been living in neighboring countries for as long as 30 years, Pres. Habyarimana permitted opposition parties to form and abolished tribal names from identification cards.

## Saint Kitts and Nevis
### Federation of Saint Kitts and Nevis

**Geography** **Location:** two islands in eastern Caribbean Sea, about 45 mi. (72 km) NW of Antigua. Nevis 17°08'N, 62°37'W; St. Kitts 17°17'N, 62°43'W. **Boundaries:** Caribbean Sea to N, E, S, and W. **Total land area:** 101 sq. mi. (261 sq km). **Coastline:** 84 mi. (135 km). **Comparative area:** slightly more than twice size of Washington, D.C. **Land use:** 22% arable land; 17% permanent crops; 3% meadows and pastures; 17% forest and woodland; 41% other; includes N.A. % irrigated. **Major cities:** (1980 est.) Basseterre (capital) 14,161.

**People** **Population:** 40,157 (1990). **Nationality:** noun—Kittian(s), Nevisian(s); adjective—Kittian, Nevisian. **Ethnic groups:** mainly of black African descent. **Languages:** English. **Religions:** Anglican, other Protestant sects, Roman Catholic.

**Government** **Type:** independent state within Commonwealth, recognizing Elizabeth II as chief of state. **Independence:** Sept.19, 1983 (from UK). **Constitution:** Sept. 19, 1983. **National holiday:** Independence Day, Sept 19. **Heads of government:** Sir Clement Arrindell, governor-general (since Nov. 1981); Dr. Kennedy Alphonse Simmonds, prime minister (since Feb. 1980). **Structure:** executive (cabinet headed by prime minister); legislative (11-member popularly elected House of Assembly; separate Nevis Island Legislature and Nevis Island Assembly headed by premier).

**Economy** **Monetary unit:** East Caribbean (EC) dollar. **Budget:** (1988) *income:* $38.5 mil.; *expend.:* $45 mil. **GDP:** $119 mil., $3,240 per capita (1986 est.). **Chief crops:** sugar on St. Kitts, cotton on Nevis. **Livestock:** sheep, pigs, goats, cattle. **Natural resources:** negl. **Major industries:** sugar processing, tourism, cotton. **Labor force:** 20,000 (1981). **Exports:** $30.3 mil. (1988); sugar. **Imports:** $94.7 mil. (c.i.f.,

1988); foodstuffs, manufactures, fuel. **Major trading partners:** (1987) *exports:* 44% U.S., 30% UK, 12% Trinidad and Tobago; *imports:* 33% U.S., 18% UK, 10% Trinidad and Tobago, 6% Canada, 4% Japan.

**Intl. Orgs.** Commonwealth, FAO, IBRD, IMF, OAS, UN.

The French settled St. Kitts in 1627; the English settled Nevis in 1628. In 1783 both became British possessions, and the two islands were united in 1882. Britain granted them independence in 1983, and Prime Minister Kennedy Alphonse Simmonds, who pledges national economic diversification, currently heads the government of this twin-island state. Ninety percent of the country's economy is based on sugar exports, thus leaving the welfare of the citizenry dependent on the fluctuating international sugar market. Damage from Hurricane Hugo devastated 1990 sugar yields, and this hardship, combined with labor disputes over the importation of foreign harvest workers, has led to some highly visible political protests.

## Saint Lucia

**Geography** **Location:** southeastern Caribbean Sea, between Martinique to N and St. Vincent to SW. Castries 14°01'N, 60°59'W. **Boundaries:** St. Lucia Channel to N, Atlantic Ocean to E, St. Vincent Passage to S, Caribbean Sea to W. **Total land area:** 238 sq. mi. (616 sq km). **Coastline:** 98 mi. (158 km). **Comparative area:** about 3.5 times size of Washington, D.C. **Land use:** 8% arable land; 20% permanent crops; 5% meadows and pastures; 13% forest and woodland; 54% other; includes 2% irrigated. **Major cities:** (1986 est.) Castries (capital) 52,868; Vieux Fort; Soufrière; Gros Islet.

**People** **Population:** 153,196 (1990). **Nationality:** noun—St. Lucian(s); adjective—St. Lucian. **Ethnic groups:** 90.3% African descent, 5.5% mixed, 3.2% East Indian, 0.8% Caucasian. **Languages:** English (official), French patois. **Religions:** 90% Roman Catholic, 7% Protestant, 3% Church of England.

**Government** **Type:** independent state within Commonwealth, recognizing Elizabeth II as chief of state. **Independence:** Feb. 22, 1979 (from UK). **Constitution:** Feb. 22, 1979. **National holiday:** Independence Day, Feb. 22. **Heads of government:** Stanislaus James, governor-general (since Oct. 1988); John Compton, prime minister (since May 1982). **Structure:** executive (cabinet headed by prime minister); bicameral legislature (Senate, House of Representatives).

**Economy** **Monetary unit:** East Caribbean (EC) dollar. **Budget:** (1987) *income:* $71.7 mil.; *expend.:* $79.3 mil. **GDP:** $172 mil., $1,258 per capita (1986). **Chief crops:** bananas, coconuts, sugar, cocoa, spices. **Livestock:** sheep, cattle, goats, pigs. **Natural resources:** forests, sandy beaches, minerals (pumice), mineral springs, geothermal potential. **Major industries:** clothing, assembly of electronic components, beverages. **Labor force:** 43,800 (1983 est.); 43.4% agriculture, 38.9% services, 17.7% industry and commerce; 30% unemployment (1984). **Exports:** $76.8 mil. (f.o.b., 1987); 67% bananas, cocoa, vegetables, fruits. **Imports:** $178.1 mil. (f.o.b., 1987); 22% manufactured goods, 21% machinery and transport equipment, 20% food and live animals.**Major trading partners:** *exports:* 55% UK, 21% CARICOM, 18% U.S.; *imports:* 33% U.S., 16% UK, 15% CARICOM, 7% Japan.

**Intl. Orgs.** FAO, G-77, GATT (de facto), IBRD, ICAO, IDA, IFAD, IFC, ILO, IMF, IMO, NAM, OAS, UN, UNESCO, UPU, WHO, WMO.

In 1650 the French settled St. Lucia, which was ceded to Britain in 1814. A member of the Federation of the West Indies from 1958 to 1962, St. Lucia became internally self-governing in 1967 but was still under Great Britain's protection. In 1979 St. Lucia gained full independence and now enjoys stable competitive politics. Hurricane Allen destroyed many of the country's banana plantations in 1980, and the economy is still recovering from the disaster. The current government of Prime Minister John Compton of the United Workers party has pledged agrarian reform and proposed legalizing gambling to stimulate tourism.

## Saint Vincent and the Grenadines

**Geography Location:** large island of St. Vincent (13°12′N, 61°14′W). and about 50 smaller islands in southeastern Caribbean Sea about 21 mi. (34 km) SW of St. Lucia and 100 mi. (160 km) W of Barbados. **Boundaries:** St. Vincent Passage to N, Atlantic Ocean to E and SE, Caribbean Sea to SW and W. **Total land area:** 150 sq. mi. (389 sq km). **Coastline:** 52 mi. (84 km). **Comparative area:** about twice size of Washington, D.C. **Land use:** 38% arable land; 12% permanent crops; 6% meadows and pastures; 41% forest and woodland; 3% other; includes 3% irrigated. **Major cities:** (1987 est.) Kingstown (capital) 19,028.

**People Population:** 112,646 (1990). **Nationality:** noun—St. Vincentian(s) or Vincentian(s); adjective—St. Vincentian or Vincentian. **Ethnic groups:** mainly of black African descent, remainder mixed, with some white, East Indian, and Carib Indian. **Languages:** English, French patois. **Religions:** Anglican, Methodist, Roman Catholic, Seventh-Day Adventist.

**Government Type:** independent state within Commonwealth, recognizing Elizabeth II as chief of state. **Independence:** Oct. 27, 1979 (from UK). **Constitution:** Oct. 27, 1979. **National holiday:** Independence Day, Oct. 27. **Heads of government:** David Jack, governor-general (since Sept. 1989); James Mitchell, prime minister (since July 1984). **Structure:** bicameral legislature—13-member elected House of Representatives and 6-member appointed Senate; judiciary—Supreme Court.

**Economy Monetary unit:** East Caribbean (EC) dollar. **Budget:** (1988) *income:* $42.7 mil.;

*expend.:* $67.5 mil. **GDP:** $136 mil., $1,305 per capita (1986 est.). **Chief crops:** bananas, arrowroot. **Livestock:** sheep, cattle, pigs, goats. **Natural resources:** negl. **Major industries:** food processing (sugar, flour), cement, furniture. **Labor force:** 67,000 (1984 est.); 35% unemployed (1986). **Exports:** $63.8 mil. (f.o.b., 1986); bananas, arrowroot, copra. **Imports:** $87.3 mil. (c.i.f., 1986); foodstuffs, machinery and equipment, chemicals and fertilizers, minerals and fuels. **Major trading partners:** (1985) *exports:* 60% CARICOM, 27% UK, 11% U.S.; *imports:* 37% U.S., 18% CARICOM, 13% UK, 5% Canada.

**Intl. Orgs.** FAO, G-77, GATT (de facto), IBRD, ICAO, IDA, IFAD, IMF, IMO, OAS, UN, UNESCO, UPU, WHO.

Although ceded to Britain in 1763, St. Vincent was inhabited by the fierce Carib Indians, who continued fighting for control of the island until 1796, when they had all been either killed or deported. Just prior to its independence in 1979, St. Vincent and the Grenadines was a self-governing state in association with Great Britain. It is one of the poorest countries in the West Indies. Several natural disasters have plagued the economy, including a 1979 volcanic eruption and two destructive hurricanes in 1980 and 1986. Prime Minister James Mitchell of the New Democratic party currently governs the country.

## San Marino
### Republic of San Marino

**Geography Location:** on slopes of Mt. Titano, in the Apennines, within central Italian region of Emilia-Romagna. **Boundaries:** surrounded by Italian territory. **Total land area:** 23.4 sq. mi. (60.5 sq km). **Coastline:** none. **Comparative area:** about 3/10 size of Washington, D.C. **Land use:** 17% arable land; 0% permanent crops; 0% meadows and pastures; 0% forest and woodland; 83% other. **Major cities:** (1988 est.) San Marino (capital) 4,178.

**People Population:** 23,123 (1990). **Nationality:** noun—Sanmarinese (sing., pl.); adjective—Sanmarinese. **Ethnic groups:** N.A. **Languages:** Italian. **Religions:** Roman Catholic.

**Government Type:** republic. **Independence:** N.A. **Constitution:** Oct. 8, 1600; electoral law of 1926 serves some of functions of constitution. **National holiday:** Anniversary of the Liberation of the Republic, Feb. 5. **Heads of government:** Bernardini Domenico I, secretary of state for foreign and political affairs and for information (since Apr. 1991); Podeschi Claudio I, secretary of state for internal affairs and justice (since Apr. 1991). **Structure:** executive—two captain-regents with six-month terms; actual power wielded by secretary of state for foreign affairs and secretary of state for internal affairs; legislative—Grand and General Council elected by popular vote for five-year terms; Congress of State whose members head administrative departments; judicial—Council of Twelve is supreme judicial body.

**Economy Monetary unit:** Italian lire. **Budget:** (1983) *income:* $99.2 mil; *expend:* N.A. **GNP:** N.A. **Chief crops:** wheat, grapes, other grains, fruits, vegetables. **Livestock:** N.A. **Natural resources:** building stones. **Major industries:** wine, olive oil, cement. **Labor force:** about 4,300. **Exports:** trade data included with Italian statistics; commodity trade consisting primarily of exchanging building stone, lime, wood, chestnuts, wheat, and wine for a wide variety of consumer manufactures. **Imports:** see exports. **Major trading partners:** N.A.

**Intl. Orgs.** ITU, NAM (observer status), UNESCO, UPU, WHO.

The "Most Serene Republic" of San Marino, entirely surrounded by Italy near the city of Rimini, is the oldest republic in the world, with communitarian roots dating to the fourth century A.D. While Piedmont-Sardinia was conquering all of the rest of the Italian peninsula during the period 1860–70, it left San Marino independent; the new Kingdom of Italy signed a treaty of friendship and cooperation with the republic in 1862.

Leftist coalitions governed from 1978 through 1986, giving San Marino the only communist government west of the Soviet bloc. Since 1986 the government has been controlled by a coalition of Communists and Christian Democrats.

The economy is balanced between small-scale agriculture (primarily wine grapes and livestock) and industry, including textiles, ceramics, and furniture. Philatelic sales and tourism are important sources of revenue. Lacking extremes of wealth and poverty and with low unemployment, the republic enjoys general prosperity.

## São Tomé and Príncipe
### Democratic Republic of São Tomé and Príncipe

**Geography Location:** two main islands, São Tomé (0°19′N, 6°43′E) and Príncipe, and Caroço, Pedras, Tinhosas (off Príncipe), and Rolas (off São Tomé), off west coast of Africa. **Boundaries:** west of Gabon in Gulf of Guinea. **Total land area:** 372 sq. mi. (964 sq km). **Coastline:** 130 mi. (209 km). **Comparative area:** about 5.5 times size of Washington, D.C. **Land use:** 1% arable land; 36% permanent crops; 1% meadows and pastures; 0% forest and woodland; 62% other. **Major cities:** São Tomé (capital).

**People Population:** 124,765 (1990). **Nationality:** noun—São Toméan(s); adjective—São Toméan. **Ethnic groups:** Mestiço, Angolares (descendants of Angolan slaves), Servicais (contract laborers from Angola, Mozambique, and Cape Verde), Tongas (children of Servicais born on the islands), and Europeans (primarily Portuguese). **Languages:** Portuguese (official). **Religions:** Roman Catholic, Evangelical, Protestant, Seventh-Day Adventist.

**Government Type:** republic. **Independence:** July 12, 1975 (from Portugal). **Constitution:** Nov. 5, 1975, approved Dec. 15, 1982.

**National holiday:** Independence Day, July 12.
**Heads of government:** Miguel dos Anjos da Cunha Trovoada, president (since Apr. 1991); Daniel Lima dos Santos Diao, prime minister (since Jan. 1991). **Structure:** executive–president assisted by cabinet of ministers; unicameral legislature–40-member National People's Assembly, elected for five years.

**Economy Monetary unit:** dobra. **Budget:** (1987) *income:* $19.2 mil.; *expend.:* $25.1 mil. **GDP:** $37.9 mil., $340 per capita (1986 est.). **Chief crops:** cash crops–cocoa, copra, coconuts, coffee, palm oil, bananas. **Livestock:** goats, pigs, cattle, sheep. **Natural resources:** fish. **Major industries:** small processing factories producing shirts, soap, beer; fish and shrimp processing. **Labor force:** 21,096 (1981); subsistence agriculture and fishing; some unemployment; labor shortages on plantations and for skilled workers; 56% of population of working age (1983). **Exports:** $9.1 mil. (f.o.b., 1988 est.); 90% cocoa, 7% copra, coffee, palm oil. **Imports:** $17.3 mil. (c.i.f., 1988 est.); food products, machinery and electrical equipment, fuels. **Major trading partners:** *exports:* Portugal, U.S., W. Germany, E. Germany, Netherlands, China; *imports:* Portugal, E. Germany, Angola, China.

**Intl. Orgs.** FAO, G-77, GATT (de facto), IBRD, ICAO, IDA, IFAD, IFC, ILO, IMF, ITU, NAM, UN, UNESCO, UPU, WHO, WMO.

The islands of São Tomé and Príncipe, located in the Atlantic Ocean 275 and 125 miles, respectively, off the northern coast of Gabon, make up one of Africa's smallest nations. They were uninhabited when first discovered by the Portuguese in 1470 but by the mid-1500s became Africa's foremost exporter of sugar. As the sugar market declined, the islands became a major slave-trading center and producer of coffee and cocoa. By 1908 São Tomé was the world's largest cocoa producer.

Portugal did not abolish slavery until 1876, and abusive labor practices continued until well into the 20th century. In 1953 hundreds of workers were killed in clashes with the Portuguese. Soon after, a small number of São Toméans formed the Movement for the Liberation of São Tomé and Príncipe (MLSTP) with its base in Gabon. But the islands did not gain independence until July 12, 1975, one year after the dictatorship in Portugal was overthrown.

The MLSTP took over after independence and became the country's only official party. By 1986 the country relied on foreign aid for approximately 41 percent of its gross national product. Although in the past it received military advisers from the Soviet Union and economic advisers from Cuba, São Tomé and Príncipe has announced a foreign policy based upon nonalignment.

## Saudi Arabia
### Kingdom of Saudi Arabia
**Geography Location:** occupies ⁴/₅ of Arabian peninsula in southwestern Asia. **Bound-**

aries: Jordan, Iraq, and Kuwait to N, Persian Gulf, Qatar, and United Arab Emirates to E, Oman to SE, Yemen to S and SE, Red Sea to W. **Total land area:** 864,869 sq. mi. (2,240,000 sq km). **Coastline:** 1,559 mi. (2,510 km). **Comparative area:** about size of Texas and Alaska combined. **Land use:** 1% arable land; negl. % permanent crops; 39% meadows and pastures; 1% forest and woodland; 59% other; includes negl. % irrigated. **Major cities:** (1980 est.) Riyadh (capital) 1,250,000; Jeddah 900,000; Makkah (Mecca) 400,000; Ta'If 203,000; Al-Madinah (Medina) 200,000.

**People Population:** 17,115,728 (1990). **Nationality:** noun–Saudi(s); adjective–Saudi or Saudi Arabian. **Ethnic groups:** 90% Arab, 10% Afro-Asian. **Languages:** Arabic. **Religions:** 100% Muslim.

**Government Type:** monarchy. **Constitution:** none; governed according to Sharia or Islamic law. **National holiday:** Sept. 23. **Head of government:** Fahd ibn Abdul-Aziz al-Saud, king (since June 1982). **Structure:** king rules in consultation with royal family and Council of Ministers.

**Economy Monetary unit:** Saudi riyal. **Budget:** (1990) *income:* $31.5 bil.; *expend.:* $38.1 bil. **GDP:** $73 bil., $4,720 per capita (1988). **Chief crops:** dates, grains, livestock; not self-sufficient in food except for wheat. **Livestock:** sheep, goats, cattle, asses, camels. **Natural resources:** crude oil, natural gas, iron ore, gold, copper. **Major industries:** crude oil production, petroleum refining, basic petrochemicals. **Labor force:** 4.2 mil.; 34% government, 28% industry and oil, 22% services, 16% agriculture; about 60% are foreign workers; 0% unemployment (1987). **Exports:** $24.5 bil. (f.o.b., 1989 est); 89% petroleum and petroleum products. **Imports:** $21.8 bil. (f.o.b., 1989 est.) manufactured goods, transport equipment, construction materials, processed food products. **Major trading partners:** *exports and re-exports:* 26% Japan, 26% U.S., 6% France, 6% Bahrain; *imports:* 20% U.S., 18% Japan, 16% UK, 11% Italy.

**Intl. Orgs.** Arab League, FAO, G-77, IAEA, IBRD, ICAO, IDA, IFAD, IFC, ILO, IMF, IMO, INTELSAT, INTERPOL, ITU, NAM, OPEC, UN, UNESCO, UPU, WHO, WMO.

In ancient times various cultures flourished in parts of the Arabian peninsula, particularly along the western rim, in cities devoted to trade between the Gulf of Aden and the eastern Mediterranean, and in such agricultural and trading centers as Yemen and Oman. Cultural and political unity was lacking, however, until the rise of Mohammed, the prophet of Islam. In A.D. 622 Mohammed fled from Mecca, the holy city of Arabian paganism, to the nearby city of Medina; the Islamic era dates from that year. Preaching from Medina, Mohammed soon gained converts to Islam throughout Arabia. His army captured Mecca in 630, converting its sacred shrine, the Kaaba, to an Islamic place of worship. By 632, when Mohammed died, all of Arabia was unified under Islamic rule.

In 661 the Caliphate, the ruling body of early

Islam, moved from Medina to Damascus. Thereafter Arabia was nominally unified under Islamic rule—but in practice was usually divided among various principalities in the arable areas and trading centers, and under tribal rule in the arid interior. Mecca fell to the Ottoman Empire in 1517, but Ottoman control of Arabia was never complete. The rise of the Wahabi sect of Islam in the 18th century posed a challenge to Ottoman rule. In the 19th century, the Saud family rose to leadership in the Wahabi movement and established a kingdom in Nejd, the central region of Arabia, with a capital at Riyadh.

In 1902 Ibn Saud (1880–1953) consolidated his family's control at Riyadh and in 1912–13 led a new Wahabi revolt against the Ottoman Turks. During World War I, the British aided Ibn Saud's rebellion in the Nejd, along with that of Ibn Saud's rival Hussein ibn Ali in the Hejaz, in the mountains of western Arabia along the coast of the Red Sea. A British protectorate was established in both regions in 1915, and Great Britain maintained a dominant position in Arabia immediately after World War I.

In 1924 Ibn Saud captured Hussein ibn Ali's capital at Mecca, and he proclaimed himself king of Hejaz in 1926 and of Nejd in 1927. Ibn Saud consolidated his control over the following two years, and his kingdom was formally recognized by Great Britain in 1927. The country was renamed Saudi Arabia in 1932.

Saudi Arabia is an absolute monarchy based on Islamic law; it has no written constitution and no parliament. The king exercises sole authority and rules in consultation with a Council of Ministers. Islamic law is enforced; alcohol is prohibited and the public activities of women severely restricted. The Saudi kings have great power within the Islamic world through their control over the holy cities of Mecca and Medina and their administration of the annual Muslim pilgrimages to those cities.

The discovery of oil in eastern Arabia in the early 1930s rapidly transformed Saudi Arabia from an impoverished nation to a center of great wealth. In 1933 an exclusive concession for the exploitation of Saudi Arabian oil was granted to an American-chartered corporation, the Arabian-American Oil Company (Aramco). For many years wealth remained concentrated in the hands of the Saudi clan, and little change was felt in the desert interior, where Bedouin nomads continued to raise sheep and camels, little affected by modernization. Large numbers of Yemenis, Palestinians, Pakistanis, and other foreign workers are employed in the oil fields.

Saudi Arabia remained neutral during most of World War II but declared war on the Axis powers in March 1945; in the same year, it became a founding member of both the United Nations and the Arab League.

Ibn Saud became a leader of Arab anti-Zionism and contributed a small contingent of troops to the 1948 Arab-Israeli War. That policy was maintained by Ibn Saud's second son and successor, King Faisal, who instituted a policy of providing large annual subsidies to Egypt and other Arab League states following the 1967 Arab-Israeli War. In 1973 King

Faisal sent Saudi units to fight in the Arab-Israeli War of that year. He played a leading role in organizing the 1973–74 Arab oil embargo in an effort to force the United States and its allies to take a harder line with Israel.

King Faisal was assassinated by his nephew, Prince Faisal, on Mar. 25, 1975, and was succeeded by King Khalid. Little change in policy resulted. In 1979 Saudi Arabia denounced the Camp David talks and the Egyptian-Israeli peace treaty and led the Arab League effort to ostracize Egypt within the Arab world.

At the same time, Saudi Arabia has consistently opposed leftist and radical movements in the Arab world, sending troops to help put down leftist rebellions in North Yemen and Oman in the 1970s. The Saudi kings have also taken a generally cautious and moderate approach toward Arab relations with the West. Following the transfer of Aramco assets to full Saudi Arabian ownership during 1973–76, Saudi Arabia has used its leading position within the Organization of Petroleum Exporting Countries (OPEC) to argue for a policy of stable production and prices.

This antileftist and moderate policy has been rewarded by the willingness of the United States, Great Britain, France, and other Western nations to sell arms—including jet fighters, tanks, and other sophisticated weapons—to Saudi Arabia despite Israeli protests. The multi-billion-dollar arms trade has helped to offset the Western oil trade deficit with Saudi Arabia.

Saudi Arabia experienced repeated disturbances in the 1980s. Muslim fundamentalist terrorists seized the Grand Mosque at Mecca on Nov. 20, 1979, provoking a crisis for the Saudi monarchy. On July 31, 1987, Iranian pilgrims rioted in Mecca and were fired upon by Saudi security forces; 402 persons died, including 275 Iranians. Iran's Ayatollah Khomeini denounced the Saudi government and said it was unworthy of being the guardian of Islam's sacred shrines.

A long-time supporter of the Palestine Liberation Organization, the Saudi government gave the PLO $850 million during the 1980s, including $12 million in 1990—before the PLO backed Saddam Hussein's invasion of Kuwait.

On Aug. 5, 1990, U.S. Defense Secretary Dick Cheney met with King Fahd and secured his permission to station U.S. troops in Saudi Arabia to guard against a possible Iraqi attack. The Saudis promised the United States $16.8 billion and Egypt $1.5 billion to defray the costs of their military presence in the Persian Gulf. While little ground fighting took place on Saudi soil, there were missile attacks on Riyadh, Dhahran, and elsewhere, and massive oil spills threatened the operation of crucial desalination plants in the Persian Gulf.

In September 1990, Saudi Arabia restored full diplomatic relations with the Soviet Union after 50 years. They also invited Soviet troops to join coalition forces on Saudi soil and made substantial loans to shore up the Soviet economy. (See Part I, "The Year in Review.")

## Senegal
### Republic of Senegal

**Geography Location:** northwestern coast of Africa. **Boundaries:** Mauritania to N, Mali to E, Guinea and Guinea-Bissau to S, Atlantic Ocean to W; The Gambia forms narrow enclave extending 200 mi. (320 km) inland from Atlantic coast. **Total land area:** 74,206 sq. mi. (192,192 sq km). **Coastline:** 330 mi. (531 km). **Comparative area:** between North Dakota and South Dakota. **Land use:** 27% arable land; 0% permanent crops; 30% meadows and pastures; 31% forest and woodland; 12% other; includes 1% irrigated. **Major cities:** (1979 est.) Dakar (capital) 850,000; Thiès 120,000; Kaolack 110,000.

**People Population:** 7,506,197 (1989). **Nationality:** noun—Senegalese (sing., pl.); adjective—Senegalese. **Ethnic groups:** 36% Wolof, 17% Fulani, 17% Serer, 9% Toucouleur, 9% Diola, 9% Mandingo, 1% European and Lebanese. **Languages:** French (official), Wolof, Pulaar, Diola, Mandingo. **Religions:** 92% Muslim, 6% indigenous beliefs, 2% Christian (mostly Roman Catholic).

**Government Type:** republic under multiparty democratic rule; on Feb. 1, 1982, Senegal and The Gambia formed loose confederation named Senegambia that calls for eventual integration of their armed forces and economic cooperation. **Independence:** Apr. 4, 1960 (from France). **Constitution:** Mar. 3, 1963 (formally signed agreement of confederation with The Gambia Dec. 12, 1981, effective Feb. 1, 1982 as Senegambia). **National holiday:** Independence Day, Apr. 4. **Heads of government:** Abdou Diouf, president (since Jan. 1981); Habib Thiam, prime minister (since Apr. 1991). **Structure:** executive—president; legislative—unicameral 120-member National Assembly, elected for five-year term by universal suffrage; judiciary—Supreme Court, members appointed by president.

**Economy Monetary unit:** Communauté Financière Africaine (CFA) franc. **Budget:** (1986) *income:* $443 mil.; *expend.:* $474 mil. **GDP:** $2.0 bil., $290 per capita (1987). **Chief crops:** peanuts (primary cash crop), millet, sorghum, manioc, maize, rice; deficit production of food. **Livestock:** sheep, cattle, goats, asses, horses. **Natural resources:** fish, phosphates, iron ore. **Major industries:** fishing, agricultural processing, phosphate mining. **Labor force:** 2.5 mil. (1985); 77% subsistence agricultural workers; 175,000 wage earners—60% government and parapublic, 40% private sector; 52% of working age. **Exports:** $761 mil. (f.o.b., 1988); 30% manufactures, 27% fish products, 11% peanuts, 11% petroleum products, 10% phosphates. **Imports:** $1.1 bil. (c.i.f., 1988); 30% semimanufactures, 27% food, 17% durable consumer goods, 14% capital goods, 12% petroleum. **Major trading partners:** *exports:* U.S., France, other EC countries, Ivory Coast, India; *imports:* U.S. France, other EC countries, Nigeria, Algeria, China, Japan.

**Intl. Orgs.** FAO, G-77, GATT, IAEA, IBRD, ICAO, IDA, IFAD, IFC, ILO, IMF, IMO, INTEL-SAT, INTERPOL, ITU, NAM, UN, UNESCO, UPU, WHO, WIPO, WMO.

Inhabited since ancient times, Senegal was dominated in the 13th and 14th centuries by the Mandingo and Jolof empires. Portuguese traders and explorers arrived in Senegal in the early 15th century and later competed with the British, Dutch, and French for domination in Senegal. The French established a trading station at Saint-Louis in 1659 and maintained possession thereafter, except for the British enclave along the Gambia River.

In the early 19th century, the French began a series of campaigns to bring the entire country under their control; the last independent sultanate surrendered in 1893. Senegal became a French colony in 1920, and Dakar became the capital of French West Africa. Senegal became a major contributor of African troops to the French armed forces.

In 1946 a territorial assembly was established, with a limited electorate and advisory powers, which were gradually expanded in subsequent years. With the creation of the French Community of Nations in 1958, Senegal achieved local self-rule within the community.

In 1959, with the encouragement of France, Senegal and French Sudan (now Mali) formed the Federation of Mali, which became fully independent on June 20, 1960. Senegal seceded from the federation on Aug. 20 and declared itself the Republic of Senegal. Leopold Sedar Senghor, one of Africa's leading statesmen, became Senegal's first president.

In 1962 Prime Minister Mamdou Dia attempted a coup against the Senghor government; it failed, and Dia was imprisoned. A new constitution was subsequently adopted, strengthening the power of the presidency. Senghor retired from office in 1981 and was succeeded by Adbou Diouf. He encouraged political pluralism and has presided over a generally stable and democratic government. Diouf was elected in his own right in 1983 and reelected in 1988. Following the 1988 elections, riots broke out over charges of electoral fraud, and a state of emergency was declared. There was military tension on the border with Mauritania in 1989, and continued riots in Dakar and other cities, leading to further political tension and economic decline.

In 1982, Senegal established the confederation of Senegambia with The Gambia, which it surrounds on three sides. Under the terms of the confederation the countries retained their independence but united their military, monetary systems, and parliament. The confederation was abolished at Senegal's instigation in 1989.

Senegal remains closely tied to France commercially, culturally, and in foreign affairs. Beginning in the mid-1980s, there has been a surge in illegal immigration of Senegalese to the United States.

Senegal's economy is primarily agricultural. Industries include fishing and fish processing (the principal source of export earnings), food processing, light manufacturing, and phosphate mining. Senegalese merchants are active in commercial networks throughout West Africa.

## Seychelles
### Republic of Seychelles

**Geography** **Location:** more than 90 widely scattered islands in western Indian Ocean about 1,000 mi. (1,600 km) E of Kenya and Tanzania. Victoria (Mahé Is.) 4°37′S, 55°28′E. **Boundaries:** surrounded by Indian Ocean; nearest neighbor is Madagascar about 130 mi. (210 km) S of southernmost island group. **Total land area:** 175 sq. mi. (454 sq km). **Coastline:** 305 mi. (491 km). **Comparative area:** about 2.5 times the size of Washington, D.C. **Land use:** 4% arable land; 18% permanent crops; 0% meadows and pastures; 18% forest and woodland; 60% other. **Major cities:** (1977 census) Victoria (capital) 23,334 (includes suburbs).

**People** **Population:** 68,336 (1990). **Nationality:** noun—Seychellois (sing., pl.); adjective—Seychelles. **Ethnic groups:** Seychellois (mixture of Asians, Africans, Europeans). **Languages:** English, French (official); Creole. **Religions:** 90% Roman Catholic, 8% Anglican, 2% other.

**Government** **Type:** republic; member of Commonwealth. **Independence:** June 29, 1976 (from UK). **Constitution:** June 5, 1979. **National holiday:** June 5 and 29. **Head of government:** France Albert René, president (since June 1977). **Structure:** president; Council of Ministers; People's Assembly (25 members—23 elected and two appointed by president for four-year terms).

**Economy** **Monetary unit:** Seychelles rupee. **Budget:** (1987) *income*: $106.0 mil.; *expend.*: $130 mil. **GDP:** $255 mil., $3,720 per capita (1988 est.). **Chief crops:** islands depend largely on coconut production and export of copra; cinnamon, vanilla, green leaf tea, and patchouli (used for perfumes) are other cash crops; food crops—small quantities of sweet potatoes, cassava, sugarcane, and bananas; islands not self-sufficient in foodstuffs and bulk of supply must be imported. **Livestock:** pigs, goats, cattle. **Natural resources:** fish, copra, cinnamon trees. **Major industries:** tourism is largest industry; processing of coconut and vanilla, fishing. **Labor force:** formal employment (all sectors)—38.4% government, 30.7% parastatal, 30.8% private; formal employment (by sector)—49.0% industry and commerce, 39.0% services, 11.5% agriculture, forestry, and fishing (1984 est.); 57% of population of working age (1983). **Exports:** $17 mil. (f.o.b., 1988 est.); fish, copra, cinnamon bark; reexports—petroleum products. **Imports:** $116 mil. (c.i.f., 1988 est.); manufactured goods, food, tobacco, beverages, machinery and transport equipment. **Major trading partners:** *exports:* 63% France, 12% Pakistan, 10% Réunion, 7% UK; *imports*: 20% UK, 14% France, 13% South Africa, 13% South Yemen, 8% Singapore, 6% Japan.

**Intl. Orgs.** FAO, G-77, GATT (de facto), IBRD, ICAO, IFAD, IFC, ILO, IMF, IMO, INTERPOL, NAM, UN, UNESCO, UPU, WHO, WMO.

The Seychelles Islands were occupied by France in the 18th century and seized by Great Britain in 1794. They were administered along with Mauritius until 1903, when the Seychelles became a separate British colony. African and Indian workers were brought in to work in coconut and spice plantations and in guano mining. The present population is of mixed African, Indian, and European descent.

In the post–World War II period, a home-rule government rejected independence as impractical. At the urging of the Organization of African Unity and the United Nations, the Seychelles declared independence on June 29, 1976. Its first president was ousted in a socialist coup in 1977 led by Prime Minister France Albert René. A new constitution, promulgated in March 1979, formalized one-party rule.

Since independence, the economy of the Seychelles has become heavily dependent on the tourist industry, which accounts for 90 percent of the country's foreign exchange earnings. Fishing, controlled by the Seychelles National Fishing Company, accounts for 40 percent of exports.

## Sierra Leone
### Republic of Sierra Leone

**Geography** **Location:** west central Africa. **Boundaries:** Guinea to N and E, Liberia to S, Atlantic Ocean to W. **Total land area:** 27,653 sq. mi. (71,620 sq km). **Coastline:** 250 mi. (402 km). **Comparative area:** between West Virginia and South Carolina. **Land use:** 23% arable land; 2% permanent crops; 31% meadows and pastures; 29% forest and woodland; 15% other; includes negl. % irrigated. **Major cities:** Freetown (capital) 469,776 (1985 census); Koidu 80,000; Bo 26,000; Kenema 13,000; Makeni 12,000.

**People** **Population:** 4,165,953 (1990). **Nationality:** noun—Sierra Leonean(s); adjective—Sierra Leonean. **Ethnic groups:** over 99% African (30% Temne, 30% Mende, 2% Creole), rest European and Asian. **Languages:** English (official); regular use limited to literate minority; principal languages are Mende in south and Temne in north; Krio is language of resettled ex-slave population of Freetown area and is lingua franca. **Religions:** 30% Muslim, 30% indigenous beliefs, 10% Christian, 30% other or none.

**Government** **Type:** republic under presidential regime since Apr. 1971. **Independence:** Apr. 27, 1961 (from UK). **Constitution:** June 14, 1978. **National holiday:** Republic Day, Apr. 19. **Heads of government:** Gen. Joseph S. Momoh, president (since Nov. 1985). **Structure:** executive—president; legislature—unicameral parliament consists of 104 authorized seats, 85 of which are filled by elected representatives of constituencies and 12 by Paramount Chiefs elected by fellow Paramount Chiefs in each district; president authorized to appoint up to seven members; judiciary.

**Economy** **Monetary unit:** leone. **Budget:** (1990 est.) *income*: $86.0 mil.; *expend.*: $128.0 mil. **GDP:** $965 mil., $250 per capita (1987). **Chief crops:** palm kernels, coffee, cocoa, rice, yams; much of cultivated land devoted to subsistence farming; food crops insufficient for domestic consumption. **Livestock:** cattle, sheep, goats, pigs. **Natural resources:** diamonds, titanium ore, bauxite, iron ore, gold, chromite. **Major industries:** mining (diamonds, iron ore, bauxite, rutile), small-scale manufacturing (beverages, textiles, cigarettes, footwear), petroleum refinery. **Labor force:** about 1.5 mil. (1981); 65% agriculture, 19% industry, 16% services; only small minority, some 65,000, earn wages; 55% of population of working age (1985). **Exports:** $106 mil. (f.o.b., 1988); 50% rutile, 17% bauxite, 11% cocoa, 3% diamonds. **Imports:** $167 mil. (c.i.f., 1988); 40% capital goods, 32% foods, 12% petroleum, 7% consumer goods. **Major trading partners:** *exports:* U.S., UK, Netherlands, W. Germany, other Western European countries; *imports:* U.S., EC, Japan, China.

**Intl. Orgs.** Commonwealth, FAO, G-77, GATT, IAEA, IBRD, ICAO, IDA, IFAD, IFC, ILO, IMF, IMO, INTERPOL, ITU, NAM, UN, UNESCO, UPU, WHO, WMO.

Portuguese domination of the Sierra Leone coast began in 1462. English explorers, including Francis Drake, arrived in the late 16th century. Europeans traded for slaves in Sierra Leone, but in 1787 Freetown was founded by the British Sierra Leone Co. as a haven for freed slaves. The settlement was populated by former slaves from Great Britain, North America, and the Caribbean, and later by slaves liberated from slave trading ships by the British navy.

Sierra Leone was reorganized as a British colony in 1808. The ex-slave population, from diverse tribal and national backgrounds, developed an English-speaking Creole culture unique in Africa. Freetown became the center of British colonial administration and trade in West Africa and was the focus of missionary-supported projects in education, health care, and economic development.

The native peoples of Sierra Leone staged numerous rebellions against the British and the Creole elite; resentment focused on the tax system and on the privileges of the English-speaking descendents of ex-slaves.

During the 20th century, home rule developed through an elected advisory legislature. In 1951 a constitutional framework had been developed as the basis of decolonization. Sir Milton Margei became chief minister in 1953, and prime minister in 1961. Full independence came on Apr. 27, 1971. The last ties with the British Crown were cut in 1971, when Sierra Leone became a republic. A referendum in 1978, implemented in 1979, created a one-party state. In 1984 and 1985 student and public employee protests against the government led to riots and the restoration of multiparty elections.

Sierra Leone has a mixed economy. Cocoa, coffee, palm oil, ginger, and other crops are grown for export; rice is the dietary staple. Mining, particularly for diamonds, bauxite, chrome, and gold, is the most important industry. Tourism is a major foreign exchange earner. Despite political stability and relatively abundant resources, the Sierra Leone economy has been burdened by inflation, corruption, and mismanagement, leading to heavy dependence on foreign borrowing.

## Singapore
### Republic of Singapore

**Geography Location:** Singapore Island and some 57 islets off southern Malay peninsula (linked by a causeway). **Boundaries:** Johor Strait to N; Pacific Ocean to E; Strait of Malacca to SW, separating Singapore from Indonesian island of Sumatra; and Indian Ocean to W. **Total land area:** 240 sq. mi. (622 sq km). **Coastline:** 120 mi. (193 km). **Comparative area:** about 3.5 times size of Washington, D.C. **Land use:** 4% arable land; 7% permanent crops; 0% meadows and pastures; 5% forest and woodland; 84% other. **Major cities:** Singapore (capital).

**People Population:** 2,720,915 (1990). **Nationality:** noun—Singaporean(s); adjective—Singapore. **Ethnic groups:** 76.4% Chinese, 14.9% Malay, 6.4% Indian, 2.3% other. **Languages:** Chinese, Malay, Tamil, and English (official); Malay (national). **Religions:** majority of Chinese are Buddhists or atheists; Malays nearly all Muslim; minorities include Christians, Hindus, Sikhs, Taoists, Confucianists.

**Government Type:** republic. **Independence:** Aug. 9, 1965 (from Malaysia). **Constitution:** June 3, 1959, amended 1965; based on preindependence State of Singapore constitution. **National holiday:** Aug. 9. **Heads of government:** Wee Kim Wee, president (since Sept. 1965); Goh Chok Tong, prime minister (since Nov. 1990). **Structure:** ceremonial president; executive power exercised by prime minister and cabinet responsible to unicameral legislature (Parliament).

**Economy Monetary unit:** Singapore dollar. **Budget:** (1988) *income:* $6.6 bil.; *expend.:* $5.9 bil. **GDP:** $27.5 bil., $10,300 per capita (1989 est.). **Chief crops:** agriculture occupies position of minor importance in economy; self-sufficient in pork, poultry, and eggs; must import much of its other food requirements; major crops—rubber, copra, fruits, vegetables. **Livestock:** N.A. **Natural resources:** negl. **Major industries:** petroleum refining, electronics, oil drilling equipment. **Labor force:** 1.25 mil.; 29% services, 22.4% trade; 3.3% unemployment (1988 est.). **Exports:** $46 bil. (f.o.b., 1989 est.); includes transshipments to Malaysia—petroleum products, rubber, electronics, manufactured goods. **Imports:** $53 bil. (c.i.f., 1989 est.); includes transshipments to Malaysia—capital equipment, petroleum, chemicals, manufactured goods. **Major trading partners:** *exports:* 24% U.S., 13% Malaysia, 9% Japan, 6% Hong Kong, 6% Thailand, 3% Australia; *imports:* 22% Japan, 16% U.S., 14% Malaysia, 12% EC.

**Intl. Orgs.** ASEAN, Colombo Plan, Commonwealth, G-77, GATT, IAEA, IBRD, ICAO, IFC, ILO, IMF, IMO, INTELSAT, INTERPOL, ITU, NAM, UN, UNESCO, UPU, WHO, WMO.

Singapore was founded in 1819 by Sir Thomas Stamford Raffles on land ceded to the East India Company by the sultanate of Johore (see "Malaysia"). An Anglo-Dutch treaty turned Singapore over to the British Crown in 1824, and eventually it was administered as part of the Straits Settlements. With its excellent harbor, Singapore quickly eclipsed Penang and Malacca as the dominant port for trade through the Straits of Malacca.

Fortified as a bastion of British defense in Southeast Asia, Singapore was overrun from the rear by Japanese troops in February 1942. The British reoccupied the city of Singapore in September 1945 and reorganized Singapore as a British colony in 1946. On June 5, 1959, Singapore became a self-governing parliamentary democracy within the British Commonwealth. Its first prime minister, Lee Kwan Yew, has been in office ever since as head of the People's Action party. On Sept. 16, 1963, Singapore, along with Malaya, Sarawak, and Sabah, formed the Malaysian Federation. Singapore, ethnically Chinese, was uncomfortable within the Malay-dominated federation and seceded after two years, becoming an independent nation on Aug. 9, 1965.

Independent Singapore has enjoyed orderly, if authoritarian, government, steady economic growth, and a high standard of living. Still a major port, its economy now also encompasses international banking, finance, communications, high-technology manufacturing, and tourism. The reporting of financial and political scandals in the international press in the 1980s led to restrictions on the domestic circulation of some foreign periodicals. On Nov. 26, 1990, Lee Kuan Yew, Singapore's only prime minister since independence and the longest serving prime minister in the world, resigned after 31 years in office.

## Solomon Islands

**Geography Location:** archipelago in South Pacific E of Papua New Guinea. Honiara (Guadalcanal Is.) 9°28′S, 159°57°E. **Boundaries:** South Pacific Ocean to N, E, and S, Solomon Sea to W; nearest neighbor is Santa Cruz Islands to SE. **Total land area:** 10,639 sq. mi. (27,556 sq km). **Coastline:** 3,302 mi. (5,313 km). **Comparative area:** about size of Maryland. **Land use:** 1% arable land; 1% permanent crops; 1% meadows and pastures; 93% forest and woodland; 4% other. **Major cities:** (1986 census) Honiara (capital) 30,499.

**People Population:** 335,082 (1990). **Nationality:** noun—Solomon Islander(s); adjective—Solomon Islander. **Ethnic groups:** 93% Melanesian, 4% Polynesian, 1.5% Micronesian, 0.8% European. **Languages:** 120 indigenous languages; Melanesian pidgin in much of country is lingua franca; English spoken by 1–2% of population. **Religions:** almost all at least nominally Christian; Anglican, Seventh-Day Adventist, and Roman Catholic churches dominant.

**Government Type:** independent parliamentary state within Commonwealth. **Inde-**

**pendence:** July 7, 1978 (from UK). **Constitution:** July 7, 1978. **National holiday:** Independence Day, July 7. **Heads of government:** George G.D. Lepping, governor-general (since July 1988); Soloman Mamaloni, prime minister (since Mar. 1989). **Structure:** executive authority in governor-general; unicameral legislature (38-member National Parliament).

**Economy Monetary unit:** Solomon Island dollar. **Budget:**(1986) *income:* $139.0 mil.; *expend.:* $154.4 mil. **GDP:** $156 mil., $500 per capita (1988). **Chief crops:** copra, cocoa, palm oil, rice, fruits, vegetables. **Livestock:** pigs and cattle. **Natural resources:** fish, forests, gold, bauxite, phosphates. **Major industries:** copra, fish (tuna). **Labor force:** 23,448 economically active (1984); 32.4% agriculture, forestry, and fishing. **Exports:** $80.1 mil. (f.o.b., 1988); 46% fish, 31% timber, 5% copra, 5% palm oil. **Imports:** $101.7 mil. (c.i.f., 1988); 30% plant and machinery, 19% fuel, 16% food. **Major trading partners:** (1985) *exports:* 51% Japan, 12% UK, 9% Thailand, 8% Netherlands, 2% Australia; *imports:* 36% Japan, 23% U.S., 9% Singapore, 9% UK, 9% New Zealand.

**Intl. Orgs.** Commonwealth, G-77, GATT (de facto), IBRD, IDA, IFAD, IFC, ILO, IMF, UN, UPU, WHO.

In 1893 Great Britain established a protectorate over the South Solomon Islands, including the large islands of Guadalcanal, San Cristobal, and Malata; the protectorate was extended to the smaller easterly islands of the chain in 1898. In 1900 Germany relinquished to Great Britain its claim to the North Solomons, including Choiseul and Santa Isabel; Bougainville Island was retained by Germany (see "Papua New Guinea"). The major islands were occupied by Japan in 1942 and retaken by the Allies in a series of bloody battles in 1943.

The Solomon Islands were made self-governing in January 1976 and became an independent nation on July 7, 1978. The domestic economy is based on subsistence agriculture and fishing. A number of light manufacturing and craft industries have been established in recent years. Copra, cocoa, palm oil, and lumber are the principal exports. The sale of tuna fishing rights in the waters surrounding the Solomon Islands has given the nation a favorable balance of payments.

## Somalia
### Somali Democratic Republic

**Geography Location:** eastern coast of Africa. **Boundaries:** short frontier with Djibouti to NW, Gulf of Aden to N, long coastline on Indian Ocean to E, Kenya to SW, Ethiopia to W. **Total land area:** 246,201 sq. mi. (637,657 sq km). **Coastline:** 1,880 mi. (3,025 km). **Comparative area:** slightly smaller than Texas. **Land use:** 2% arable land; negl. % permanent crops; 46% meadows and pastures; 14% forest and woodland; 38% other; includes 3% irrigated. **Major cities:** (1981 est.) Mogadishu (capital) 500,000; Hargeish 70,000; Kismayu 70,000; Berbera 65,000; Merca 60,000.

**People Population:** 8,424,269 (1990). **Na-**

tionality: noun—Somali(s); adjective—Somali. **Ethnic groups:** 85% Somali, rest mainly Bantu; 30,000 Arabs, 3,000 Europeans, 800 Asians. **Languages:** Somali (official), Arabic, Italian, English. **Religions:** almost entirely Sunni Muslim.

**Government Type:** republic. **Independence:** July 1, 1960 (from a merger of British Somaliland, which became independent from UK June 26, 1960, and Italian Somaliland, which became independent from Italian-administered UN trusteeship July 1, 1960, to form Somali Republic). **Constitution:** Aug. 25, 1979, presidential approval Sept. 23, 1979. **National holiday:** Oct. 21. **Heads of government:** Ali Mahdi Moammad, president (since Aug. 1991); Omar Galeb, prime minister (since Aug. 1991). **Structure:** president dominates political system; cabinet carries out day-to-day government functions; unicameral legislature (National People's Assembly) exists but has little power.

**Economy Monetary unit:** Somali shilling. **Budget:** (1986 est. in percent of GDP) *income:* 5.3%; *expend.:* 17.3%. **GDP:** $1.4 bil., about $200 per capita (1982 est.); no reliable figures of national income data. **Chief crops:** mainly a pastoral country, raising livestock; crops—bananas, sugarcane, cotton, cereals. **Livestock:** goats, sheep, camels, cattle, asses. **Natural resources:** uranium, largely unexploited reserves of iron ore, tin, gypsum, bauxite. **Major industries:** a few small industries, including sugar refining, textiles, petroleum refining. **Labor force:** about 2.2 mil. (1985); very few are skilled laborers; 70% pastoral nomads, 30% agricultural, government, traders, fishermen, handicraftsmen, other; 53% of population of working age. **Exports:** $99 mil. (f.o.b., 1986); livestock, hides, skins, bananas. **Imports:** $363 mil. (c.i.f.,1986); textiles, cereals, transport equipment, machinery, construction materials and equipment. **Major trading partners:** (1985) *exports:* 34.6% Saudi Arabia, 19.6% Italy; *imports:* 26% Italy, 17% U.S., 12% Saudi Arabia.

**Intl. Org.** Arab League, FAO, G-77, IBRD, ICAO, IDA, IFAD, IFC, ILO, IMF, IMO, INTELSAT, INTERPOL, ITU, NAM, OAU, UN, UNESCO, UPU, WHO, WMO.

Arab trading settlements in Somalia were established in the seventh century and gradually evolved into independent sultanates. Portuguese traders established settlements and forts along the coast during the 15th and 16th centuries.

In the early 19th century, Great Britain arranged through local treaties to use harbors along the Somali coast and gained control over the northern part of the country by 1840. The border between Somalia and Ethiopia was demarcated by a treaty between Great Britain and Ethiopia in 1897. In 1885 the sultan of Zanzibar granted commercial advantages to Italy, and by further agreements in 1897 and 1908 Italy gained control over southern Somalia.

During the early 20th century, an uprising against British rule was led by Mohamed Abdullah. Abdullah was defeated by the British with help from his local rivals but is now regarded as the father of Somali nationalism.

The Italian invasion of Ethiopia in 1936 gave Italy a dominant position in the Horn of Africa. In the early phases of World War II, Italian troops drove the British from British Somaliland, but a 1940 counterattack led to British occupation of all of Somalia by 1941. After World War II, as discussions of Somalia's future continued, Britain handed over the Ogaden and neighboring territories to Ethiopia.

A UN pact of 1949 created an Italian trusteeship in the former Italian Somaliland. Italy terminated its trusteeship and British Somaliland, a UK protectorate, achieved independence on June 26, 1960. On July 1 the two entities joined to become Somalia.

The new country was plagued by regional clan-based rivalries, with the Somali Youth League emerging as a unifying national force. In 1969 Maj. Gen. Mohamed Siad Barre took control in a bloodless coup, abolished the national assembly, established a ruling Supreme Revolutionary Council, instituted a socialist regime, and established friendly relations with the USSR.

In 1972 Somali forces began border raids into Ethiopia's Ogaden region, peopled largely by ethnic Somalis. The Somali army mounted a full-scale invasion of the Ogaden in 1977. The Soviet Union switched its support to Ethiopia, and with Soviet aid and Cuban troops, Ethiopia drove back the Somali invasion. Over a million refugees fled from Ethiopia into Somalia, placing a severe burden on the country's fragile economy. The United States has been Somalia's principal source of military and economic aid since 1978.

In May 1988, the Somali National Movement captured a number of cities in the northwest part of the country and held them against the army. In the summer of 1990, the United Somali Congress began a peaceful antigovernment movement around Mogadishu. In December 1990, this flared into a brief but bloody civil war that resulted in the ouster of Pres. Barre on Jan. 26. The Somali National Congress proclaimed a provisional government, but it was not recognized either by the United Somali Movement, which has threatened secession, or the Somali Patriotic Movement, which controls much of central and southern Somalia.

The continued unrest has made it difficult to deliver humanitarian aid despite the efforts of western governments (especially Italy and the United States) and nongovernment organizations to do so. An estimated 50,000 people have been killed since 1988.

(See Part I, "The Year in Review.")

## South Africa
### Republic of South Africa
**Geography Location:** southern Africa. **Boundaries:** Namibia to NW, Botswana, Zimbabwe to N, Mozambique to NE, Swaziland, Indian Ocean to E, Atlantic Ocean to W; Lesotho entirely surrounded by South African territory. **Total land area:** 471,445 sq. mi. (1,221,037 sq km). **Coastline:** 1,791 mi. (2,881 km). **Comparative area:** between Texas and Alaska. **Land use:** 10% arable land; 1% perma-

nent crops; 65% meadows and pastures; 3% forest and woodland; 21% other; includes 1% irrigated. **Major cities:** (1985 census) Cape Town (legislative capital) 1,911,521; Pretoria (administrative capital) 822,925; Johannesburg 1,609,408; Durban 982,075; Port Elizabeth 651,993.

**People Population:** 39,549,941 (1990). **Nationality:** noun—South African(s); adjective—South African. **Ethnic groups:** 69.9% black, 17.8% white, 2.9% Indian; 9.4% other. **Languages:** Afrikaans, English (official); Zulu, Xhosa, North and South Sotho, Tswana. **Religions:** most whites and about 60% of blacks are Christian; roughly 60% of Indians are Hindu, 20% Muslim.

**Government Type:** republic. **Independence:** May 31, 1910 (from UK). **Constitution:** Sept. 3, 1984. **National holiday:** Republic Day, May 31. **Heads of government:** Frederik W. de Klerk, president (since Oct. 1989). **Structure:** executive—president is head of government and chairman of cabinet; tricameral legislature—House of Assembly (whites), House of Representatives (coloreds), and House of Delegates (Indians) elected directly by respective racial electorates; judiciary—courts maintain substantial independence from government influence.

**Economy Monetary unit:** South African rand. **Budget:** (1991) *income:* $24.3 bil.; *expend.:* $27.3 bil. **GDP:** $83.5 bil., $2,380 per capita (1987). **Chief crops:** corn, wheat, sugarcane, tobacco, citrus fruits; self-sufficient in foodstuffs. **Livestock:** sheep, cattle, goats, pigs, horses. **Natural resources:** gold, chromium, antimony, coal, iron ore. **Major industries:** mining (world's largest producer of diamonds, gold, chrome), automobile assembly, metalworking. **Labor force:** 11 mil. economically active (1985); 34% services, 30% agriculture, 29% industry and commerce, 7% mining; 19% unemployment (1987). **Exports:** $21.5 bil. (f.o.b., 1988 est.); 40% gold, 23% minerals and metals, 6% food, 3% chemicals. **Imports:** $18.5 bil. (c.i.f., 1989 est.); 27% machinery, 11% chemicals, 11% vehicles and aircraft, textiles, scientific instruments, base metals. **Major trading partners:** *exports:* U.S., UK, W. Germany, Japan, other EC, Hong Kong. *imports:* U.S., W. Germany, Japan, UK, France, Italy, Switzerland.

**Intl. Orgs.** GATT, IAEA, IBRD, ICAO, IDA, IFC, IMF, INTELSAT, ITU, UN, UPU, WHO, WIPO, WMO (membership rights in IAEA, ICAO, ITU, WHO, and WIPO suspended or restricted).

South Africa was originally inhabited by San and related peoples. Bantu peoples, including the Zulu and Xhosa, migrated to the region beginning around the 15th century and established large native kingdoms.

The Portuguese explorer Bartholomew Diaz discovered and named the Cape of Good Hope in 1488. The Dutch East India Company established a permanent settlement at Cape Town in 1652, which served as a supply and transshipment point for Dutch trade to the East Indies and which attracted Protestant settlers from throughout Western Europe. In a series of wars, the Xhosa people were expelled from the area under Dutch rule.

Great Britain began to dispute Dutch control of the Cape of Good Hope region in the late 18th century. To escape increasing British hegemony, in 1836 many Dutch farmers undertook the Great Trek, a northward migration to lands not under the control of any European power. These Afrikaner pioneers later became known as Boers (farmers). They came into conflict with the Zulu kingdom that, under King Shaka, had recently widened its dominion in the South African interior. The Zulus were defeated at the Battle of Blood River in 1838, but they retained substantial power and territory for another 40 years.

Great Britain formally took control of the Cape Colony in 1841 and annexed Natal in 1843. The other two Afrikaner provinces, the Orange Free State and the Transvaal, remained temporarily free of British control. But when diamonds were discovered in the Orange Free State in 1867 and gold in the Transvaal in 1886, an influx of British miners and entrepreneurs provoked Boer rebellions.

In 1878 the Zulu Kingdom under its last great king, Cetewayo, rebelled against British rule in Natal. British troops attacked Zululand in 1878 and crushed the rebellion in 1879.

The first Anglo-Boer War of 1881–82 led to an inconclusive British victory. A renewed uprising led to the Boer War of 1899–1902, which was fought with great ferocity between British regular troops and Afrikaner guerrilla forces. The eventual British victory led to the establishment of British rule in all of South Africa and to the formation of the Union of South Africa in 1910. The union became a self-governing state within the British Empire in 1934.

South African politics became dominated by friction between British and Afrikaner whites; no effective black participation in government was permitted. The United South African party, led by Jan C. Smuts, advocated cooperation between the two groups and led South Africa to join World War II on the Allied side, over the opposition of the pro-Afrikaner Nationalist party.

After the war the Nationalists prevailed and won control of the government in 1948. Racial politics became the country's paramount concern, and the Nationalists introduced the policy of "apartheid" (separateness), under which racial groups were rigidly defined as white, black, Asian (primarily Indian), and colored (mixed ancestry). Each group was to be kept physically separate and develop its own political institutions within defined areas of residence; mixed neighborhoods, intermarriage, and other relations were prohibited. Blacks, in particular, were restricted by "pass laws" that allowed them only temporary access to white areas for employment.

International condemnation of these policies began almost immediately, as India broke relations with South Africa in 1946 over discrimination against Asians, and South Africa became the focus of mounting protest, UN resolutions, and international sanctions beginning in the

1960s. On May 31, 1961, South Africa gave up its dominion status and became a republic; its application for membership in the British Commonwealth was withdrawn in the face of opposition from the Commonwealth community. The African National Congress (ANC), organized in 1912, was banned by South African authorities. The imprisonment of its leader, Nelson Mandela, provided a focus for black political protest and nationalist aspirations. An uprising in Soweto in 1976 was put down by South African police and armed forces with the loss of hundreds of lives, providing a further focus of black protest. Pieter Willem Botha was elected president in 1978, pledging to uphold apartheid while seeking solutions to racial problems. In 1983 a majority of white voters approved the adoption of a new constitution that provided for limited power sharing by coloreds and Asians; blacks continued to be excluded (see "South African Homelands," below).

In the early 1980s, South African troops intervened in civil wars in Angola and Mozambique and were deployed to counteract growing proindependence rebellions in Namibia. Within South Africa terrorism and uprisings led by the African National Union grew in intensity in 1983–84. A state of emergency was declared in 1985 accompanied by renewed political and economic pressure from abroad. In 1986, Bishop Desmond Tutu, a leading black nationalist, addressed the United Nations and called for renewed sanctions. The Botha government announced an end to the pass laws and promised limited black participation in government. Fighting between black groups in 1986–87 further increased domestic tension.

On May 19, 1987, South African troops conducted raids against ANC bases in Zambia, Zimbabwe, and Botswana. A new national state of emergency was declared in June, as strikes and riots marked the 10th anniversary of the Soweto uprising. The United States announced measures designed to end American investment in South Africa.

The Brazzaville accords of Dec. 13, 1988, designed to bring about political settlements in Angola and Namibia, have given the South African government some breathing space in settling the domestic political situation. In early 1989, in anticipation of elections to be held in September, various proposals were put forward for constitutional reform. Most called for expanded power sharing but still within the context of defined racial groups.

South Africa has the continent's most highly developed economy; it is a fully-developed, capitalist industrial-commercial society with manufacturing, mining, agricultural, service, and other sectors. International sanctions have hampered the economy to a limited extent, but their impact has been lessened by South Africa's status as the world's largest producer of gold, a key source of chromium and other strategic metals, and of gem-quality diamonds. There remains a wide economic gap between the white minority and the black majority.

In July 1989 Pres. Botha had an unprecedented meeting with Nelson Mandela, amid strong suggestions that the white government was seeking an accommodation with the anti-apartheid leadership. Botha's successor, F.W.

de Klerk, continued that policy.

A series of measures in 1989–90 resulted in the partial dismantling of apartheid, against the vehement opposition of the white right wing, but violence between supporters of the ANC and the Zulu Inkatha movement in Natal led to the declaration of a state of emergency in the province and overshadowed these positive signs.

Mandela was released from prison in the spring of 1990 and received a rapturous welcome from South Africa's blacks, and later made a triumphant tour of Western Europe and North America. His glory was short-lived however, as the struggle for supremacy again erupted in murder and violence between Mandela's ANC and Mangosuthu Buthelezi's Inkatha Freedom party throughout the latter part of 1990 and 1991.

At the same time, Pres. de Klerk and parliament continued to move the nation toward the ending of apartheid by repealing many of the segregation laws that affected hospitals, libraries, schools, and other public institutions for more than 60 years. The United States and other countries began lifting trade sanctions against South Africa in the summer of 1991.

**South African homelands** Homelands were established under the Promotion of Bantu Self-Government Act of 1959 to further the policy of apartheid by creating separate, but dependent, states for South Africa's blacks. Their form of government was set up in the Black Constitution Act of 1971. The South African government intended that the homelands be regarded as separate nations, but none has been internationally recognized. Swaziland has resisted attempts by South Africa to cede some homeland territories to that nation.

The scattered homeland territories comprise only a small portion of the total area of South Africa and tend to include marginal and underdeveloped lands. Residents of the homelands are not citizens of South Africa, and the policy allows the South African government to consider homeland citizens working in South Africa as temporary migrant workers rather than citizens, and therefore ineligible for employment and other benefits.

(See Part I, "The Year in Review.")

## Spain
### Spanish State

**Geography** **Location:** Iberian Peninsula in southwest Europe; Canary Is. off West Africa (28°07'N, 15°26'W). **Boundaries:** Bay of Biscay and France to N; Mediterranean Sea to E; Morocco 19 mi. (30 km) to S, across Strait of Gibraltar; Portugal to W. **Total land area:** 194,897 sq. mi. (504,782 sq km). **Coastline:** 3,085 mi. (4,964 km). **Comparative area:** between California and Texas. **Land use:** 31% arable land; 10% permanent crops; 21% meadows and pastures; 31% forest and woodland; 7% other; includes 6% irrigated. **Major cities:** (1987 est.) Madrid (capital) 3,100,507; Barcelona 1,703,744; Valencia 732,491; Sevilla (Seville) 655,435; Zaragoza (Saragossa) 575,317.

**People** **Population:** 39,268,715 (1990).

**Nationality:** noun—Spaniard(s); adjective—Spanish. **Ethnic groups:** composite of Mediterranean and Nordic types. **Languages:** Castilian Spanish; second langs. include 17% Catalán, 7% Galician, 2% Basque. **Religions:** 99% Roman Catholic, 1% other.

**Government Type:** parliamentary monarchy. **Independence:** N.A. **Constitution:** Dec. 6, 1978, effective Dec. 29, 1978. **National holiday:** June 24. **Heads of government:** Juan Carlos I, king (since Nov. 1975); Felipe Gonzalez Márquez, prime minister (since Dec. 1982). **Structure:** executive—with acts of king subject to countersignature—prime minister and his ministers responsible to lower house; bicameral legislature—Cortes Generales, consisting of more powerful Congress of Deputies (350 members) and Senate (208 members) with possible addition of one to six members from each new autonomous region; judiciary—independent.

**Economy Monetary unit:** peseta. **Budget:** (1987) *income:* $57.8 bil.; *expend.:* $66.7 bil. **GNP:** $398.7 bil., $10,100 per capita (1989 est.). **Chief crops:** grains, citrus fruits, vegetables, wine grapes; virtually self-sufficient in good crop years. **Livestock:** sheep, pigs, cattle, horses, mules. **Natural resources:** coal, lignite, iron ore, uranium, mercury. **Major industries:** textiles, apparel (including footwear), food and beverages, metals and metal manufacturing. **Labor force:** 14.2 mil. (1987 est.); 44.8% services, 30.9% industry, 15.6% agriculture, 9.1% construction, 8.7% other. **Exports:** $40.2 bil. (f.o.b., 1988); foodstuffs, live animals, wood, footwear, machinery, chemicals. **Imports:** $60.4 bil. (c.i.f., 1988); petroleum, footwear, machinery, chemicals, grain, soybeans, coffee. **Major trading partners:** *exports:* 66% EC, 9% other developed countries, 8% Switzerland; *imports:* 57% EC, 13% other developed countries, 9% U.S., 3% Middle East.

**Intl. Orgs.** EC, FAO, GATT, IAEA, IBRD, ICAO, IDA, IFAD, IFC, ILO, IMF, IMO, INTELSAT, INTERPOL, ITU, NATO, OAS (observer), OECD, UN, UNESCO, UPU, WHO, WIPO, WMO.

Prehistoric Spain was populated by Iberians, Basques, and Celts. Its Mediterranean ports were frequented by Phoenician traders, and part of the country was incorporated into the empire of Carthage. Spain fell under the Roman Empire around 200 B.C.; Roman rule ended when the Visigoths invaded and took control of the Iberian Peninsula in the fifth century. The Visigoths adopted Christianity but were in turn conquered by Moors from northwest Africa in A.D. 711. The Berber/Arab civilization of the Moors produced the most elegant and cultivated culture in medieval Europe, and was an important conduit for the reintroduction of Greek science into Europe in the 12th century.

The Christian reconquest of the Iberian Peninsula began almost immediately after the Moors had established themselves and proceeded slowly but steadily over a period of 750 years. The consolidation of the region's small, contentious Christian kingdoms came with the marital alliance of Ferdinand of Aragon and Isabella of Castile in 1469. Grenada, the last Moorish outpost in Spain, fell to the forces of Ferdinand and Isabella in 1492, just as Columbus, with their sponsorship, was discovering the lands that were to become Spain's New World empire. Under the Inquisition, begun in 1478, Jews were expelled from Spain in 1492, and Muslims were expelled in 1502.

Under the Habsburg dynasty (1516–1700), Spain reached the zenith of its power and prestige around the year 1600 (despite the 1588 defeat of the Spanish Armada by England), controlling an empire that embraced nearly all of South America (except Brazil), Central America, Mexico, western North America, the Philippines, and smaller territories in Africa and Asia. But Spain's loss of the Netherlands, endless struggles with the French in Europe and the Turks in the Mediterranean, and relentless inflation caused by imports of New World silver—all took their toll. During the 18th century, the Bourbons ruled a declining but still powerful Spain, until Napoleon installed his brother as king in 1808.

After Napoleon's defeat, the Bourbons returned in 1814, but in the 19th century, the loss of the South American colonies, three dynastic wars, and a brief republican interlude after 1868 were all signs of progressive weakness. The crowning blow to Spanish power and prestige was the loss of the Spanish-American War to the United States in 1898, leading to the independence of Cuba and the American takeover of Puerto Rico and the Philippines.

Spain remained neutral in World War I. In 1923 Primo de Rivera established a dictatorship; he was forced out of office by King Alfonso XIII in 1930, but in 1931 the king himself was forced to abdicate. A republic replaced the monarchy. Its volatile mixture of socialism, anticlericalism, and decentralization provoked a right-wing reaction and exacerbated regional separatist tendencies. The government moved to the Right, and in 1934 a miner's strike in Asturia was put down with great bloodshed. A left-wing government was elected in 1936 and deposed in a coup, which led to the terrible Civil War of 1936–39, in which Spain became a battleground for competing world ideologies. The Nationalists, aided by Hitler and Mussolini, defeated the Republicans, aided by Stalin and by leftist volunteers from many countries. Out of the wreckage emerged the dictatorship of the apolitical and intensely patriotic and Catholic Gen. Francisco Franco.

At the time of the Civil War, Spain was still largely an agricultural country, with smallholdings in the north and great estates in the south. Traditional crops included grains, grapes and wine, citrus fruits, olives, and olive oil. In the Basque country, the mining of iron, copper, and lead provided the basis for both exports and a domestic iron and steel industry, which had been the case since the 19th century. In the 20th century, shipbuilding and chemicals were added to the traditional textile industries of the Mediterranean coastal cities. The civil war largely destroyed this industrial base, which was not rebuilt until the 1950s.

Except for a contingent of troops sent to fight with the German invaders of the Soviet Union, Spain remained precariously neutral during World War II; Franco declined to repay Hitler for his support in the Civil War. But wartime Spain, despite its neutrality, could not muster the resources to undertake national reconstruction.

In postwar Europe, the Franco regime seemed like a remnant of the fascism of the 1930s; Stalin's active hostility led the United Nations to treat Spain as an international pariah. Despite foreign disapproval, however, at home Franco represented peace and stability; few Spaniards were willing to risk a return to civil strife by opposing him. Over time the military and Catholic aspects of the regime grew more pronounced, while fascist elements were downplayed. In 1947 the Law of Succession made Spain a monarchy without a king, awaiting the restoration of the throne in the post-Franco era.

In the 1950s the Cold War led to friendlier American relations with Spain and the establishment of American military bases there in 1953. UN membership followed in 1955. Despite some resultant growth in international trade, Spain's economy lagged, with industrialization barely beginning.

In 1958 Franco turned the direction of the economy over to a group of technocrats, mostly neoliberal members of the Opus Dei lay Catholic order. With U.S. economic and military aid, a growing tourist industry, increased foreign investment, and, especially, freer markets, the economy revived. Older industries like iron, steel, and textiles were rejuvenated, while newer ones, such as chemicals, plastics, automobile assembly, and power plants, were created. Agriculture was increasingly mechanized, and it shifted to export-oriented ranching and horticulture.

In 1967 Franco proclaimed the Organic Law, which, while confirming him as head of state, granted some independence to the Cortes (legislature) and permitted heads of families to vote for some of its delegates. This, along with a relaxation of censorship, softened the growing opposition to the regime among students, labor unions, and regional separatists. In 1969 Prince Juan Carlos was named heir apparent to the Spanish throne.

Franco died in 1975 and was duly succeeded by Juan Carlos. With the new prime minister, Adolfo Suarez, the king worked to liberalize the Franco inheritance: Political parties were legalized; the Cortes was transformed into a bicameral legislature, with both houses elected by universal suffrage; the first elections since 1936 were held; and a new constitution was promulgated—all by 1978.

In 1980 Catalonia and the Basque country were granted home rule, following overwhelming victories in home-rule plebiscites. In the Basque lands, however, violent terrorist agitation for complete independence continues.

In February 1981 a right-wing coup attempted to depose the government; armed conspirators entered the Cortes and held the legislators hostage. The coup collapsed in a day when the armed forces declared their loyalty to the king.

Since 1982 the Socialist Workers' party has controlled both houses of the Cortes. Although socialist, the party has abandoned both Marxism and the traditional labor radicalism of prewar Spain; it now resembles, under Prime Minister Filipe Gonzalez Márquez, the mainstream Social Democratic parties of the rest of Western Europe.

Under the new monarchy, Spain joined the Council of Europe in 1977, NATO in 1982, and the EC in 1986. Spain is now a full participant in the affairs of Western Europe.

## Sri Lanka
### Democratic Socialist Republic of Sri Lanka
**Geography Location:** Indian Ocean about 50 mi. (80 km) SE of India. Colombo 6°55'N, 79°52'E. **Boundaries:** Palk Strait to N, Bay of Bengal to E, Indian Ocean to S and SW, and Gulf of Mannar to NW. **Total land area:** 24,886 sq. mi. (64,454 sq km). **Coastline:** 833 mi. (1,340 km). **Comparative area:** about size of West Virginia. **Land use:** 16% arable land; 17% permanent crops; 7% meadows and pastures; 37% forest and woodland; 23% other; includes 8% irrigated. **Major cities:** (1988 est.) Colombo (capital) 609,000; Dehiwala-Mount Lavinia 190,000; Jaffna 127,000.

**People Population:** 17,196,436 (1990). **Nationality:** noun—Sri Lankan(s); adjective—Sri Lankan. **Ethnic groups:** 74% Sinhalese; 18% Tamil; 7% Moor; 1% Burgher, Malay, and Veddha. **Languages:** Sinhala (official); Sinhala and Tamil listed as national languages; Sinhala spoken by about 74% of population, Tamil spoken by about 18%; English commonly used in government and spoken by about 10% of population. **Religions:** 69% Buddhist, 15% Hindu, 8% Christian, 8% Muslim.

**Government Type:** republic. **Independence:** Feb. 4, 1948 (from UK). **Constitution:** Aug. 31, 1978. **National holiday:** Independence Day, May 22. **Heads of government:** Ranasinghe Premadasa, president (since Dec. 1988); Dingiri Banda Wijetunga, prime minister (since Mar. 1989). **Structure:** 1978 Constitution established strong presidential form of government.

**Economy Monetary unit:** Sri Lankan rupee. **Budget:** (1989) *income:* $1.5 bil.; *expend.:* $2.3 bil. **GDP:** $6.1 bil., $370 per capita (1987). **Chief crops:** rice, coconuts, tea, rubber; agriculture accounts for about 26% of GDP. **Livestock:** cattle, buffalo, goats, pigs, sheep. **Natural resources:** limestone, graphite, mineral sands, gems, phosphates. **Major industries:** processing of rubber, tea, coconuts, and other agricultural commodities; cement, petroleum refinery. **Labor force:** 6.6 mil. (1985 est.); 45.9% agriculture, 13.3% mining and manufacturing, 12.4% trade and transport, 28.4% services and other; extensive underemployment; 19% unemployment (1986 est.). **Exports:** $1.5 bil. (f.o.b., 1988); tea, textiles and garments, petroleum products, coconut, rubber. **Imports:** $2.3 bil. (c.i.f., 1988); petroleum, machinery and equipment, textiles and textile materials, wheat, transport equipment. **Major**

**trading partners:** (1987) *exports:* 26% U.S., Egypt, Iraq, UK, W. Germany; *imports:* Japan, Saudi Arabia, U.S., India, Singapore.

**Intl. Orgs.** Colombo Plan, Commonwealth, FAO, G-77, GATT, IAEA, IBRD, ICAO, IDA, IFAD, IFC, ILO, IMF, IMO, INTELSAT, INTERPOL, ITU, NAM, UN, UNESCO, UPU, WHO, WIPO, WMO.

The ancient Veddah inhabitants of Sri Lanka were conquered by Sinhalese migrants from northern India in the sixth century B.C. The island's spices and precious stones and its position on the trans-Indian Ocean trade routes made it well known in ancient times. Sri Lanka was known to the Greeks as Tabrobane and to the Arabs as Serendip. From the third century A.D., Sri Lanka became a major center of Buddhist culture. Despite numerous invasions from India, the island was usually ruled by native kingdoms, but the invasions added a Tamil community to the premodern population.

The Portuguese conquered the coastal areas after 1505 and also introduced Roman Catholicism. The Dutch displaced the Portugese in 1648; the British expelled the Dutch in 1795. Great Britain was the first foreign power to extend its rule over the entire island, with the defeat of the central kingdom of Kandy in 1833. In that year all of Sri Lanka was incorporated into the British Crown colony of Ceylon. Under British rule, tea and rubber plantations were established in the island's interior, and coconut plantations in coastal areas were consolidated under foreign control.

Ceylon became an independent member of the British Commonwealth on Feb. 4, 1948; the Republic of Sri Lanka was proclaimed on May 22, 1972.

Prime Minister W.R.D. Bandaranaike was assassinated on Sept. 25, 1959. His widow, Sirimavo Bandaranaike, leader of the Freedom party, was elected as his successor. In 1962 her government expropriated the property of foreign oil companies. The conservative United National party won a majority in parliament in March 1965 and agreed to pay compensation for the expropriated assets. In May 1970 Mrs. Bandaranaike was again elected prime minister. Leftists secured the nationalization of foreign plantations in the mid-1970s. Mrs. Bandaranaike's party was ousted again by the United National party in 1977. Constitutional reform in 1978 aimed at increasing stability by establishing a presidential form of government. Pres. J.R. Jayawardene was elected to office on Feb. 4, 1978.

Sri Lanka's economy continues to be dominated by plantation agriculture; tea, rubber, copra, spices, and forest products (timber, plywood, paper pulp) are major exports. Rice is the principal food crop. Gemstones, particularly sapphires, are an important mineral resource, along with graphite, phosphate, and limestone. Industrial development has centered on textiles and light manufacturing. Tourism was an important industry before the outbreak of separatist violence in 1986.

The political power acquired by the Tamil (mostly Hindu) middle class under the British was deeply resented by the Sinhalese (Bud-

dhist) majority, which after independence slowly eroded Tamil rights. In 1957 the government proposed a Tamil state in a federal union and gave Tamil the status of a national (but not official) language. The pact was not fully implemented, and in the 1970s extremists began agitating for an independent Tamil state. The Tamils' minority status was reaffirmed in the constitution of 1972, the year the oldest insurgent group, the Liberation Tigers or Tamil Tigers, was founded.

In July 1987 Pres. Jayawardene accepted an offer from India's Prime Minister Rajiv Gandhi to supervise a truce in the Jaffna region under which the government pledged to hold a referendum aimed at granting self-rule to Tamil majority areas in the north and northeast. The plan failed, however; Indian troops became bogged down in battling the rebels, while the planned referendum was disrupted by fighting between separatists who demanded total independence for Tamil areas and more moderate Tamil groups willing to accept self-rule.

At the Sri Lankan government's request, India withdrew its forces in March 1989, and the following month the Tamil Tigers agreed to a cease-fire as the government prepared its plan for Tamil-area autonomy.

Tamil-speaking Muslims have also been targeted by some Tamil extremists. In addition to the Tamil insurgency, the government has had to combat the People's Liberation Front (JVP), a nominally Marxist Sinhalese group that opposes any concessions to Tamils and that targets both Tamils and moderate Sinhalese government officials.

## Sudan
### Republic of the Sudan
**Geography Location:** northeastern Africa. **Boundaries:** Egypt to N, Red Sea and Ethiopia to E, Kenya, Uganda, and Zaire to S, Central African Republic, Chad and Libya to W. **Total land area:** 967,500 sq. mi. (2,505,813 sq km). **Coastline:** 530 mi. (853 km). **Comparative area:** about size of Alaska, Texas, and Nevada combined. **Land use:** 5% arable land; negl. % permanent crops; 24% meadows and pastures; 20% forest and woodland; 51% other; includes 1% irrigated. **Major cities:** (1983 census) Khartoum (capital) 476,218; Omdurman 526,287; Khartoum North 341,146; Port Sudan 206,727; Wadi Medani 141,065.

**People Population:** 24,971,000 (1990). **Nationality:** noun—Sudanese (sing., pl.); adjective—Sudanese. **Ethnic groups:** 52% black, 39% Arab, 6% Beja, 2% foreigners. **Languages:** Arabic (official), Nubian, Ta Bedawie, diverse dialects of Nilotic, Nilo-Hamitic, and Sudanic languages, English; program of Arabization in progress. **Religions:** 70% Sunni Muslim in north, 20% indigenous beliefs, 5% Christian (mostly in south).

**Government Type:** republic. **Independence:** Jan. 1, 1956 (from Egypt and UK). **Constitution:** Apr. 12, 1973, suspended following coup of Apr. 6, 1985; interim constitution Oct. 10, 1985. **National holiday:** Independence Day, Jan. 1. **Heads of government:** Gen. Omar

Ahmed al-Bashir, president (since June 1989). **Structure:** Supreme Council and Civilian Cabinet; regional military governors.

**Economy** **Monetary unit:** Sudanese pound. **Budget:** (1989 est.) *income:* $514 mil.; *expend.:* $1.3 bil. **GDP:** $8.5 bil., $340 per capita. **Chief crops:** cotton, sorghum, millet, wheat, sesame; not self-sufficient in food production; main cash crops—cotton, sesame, gum arabic, peanuts, sorghum. **Livestock:** cattle, sheep, goats, chickens, camels. **Natural resources:** modest reserves of crude oil, iron ore, copper, chromium ore, zinc. **Major industries:** cotton ginning, textiles, cement. **Labor force:** 6.5 mil. (1983); 80% agriculture, 10% industry and commerce; labor shortages for almost all categories of skilled employment; 52% of population of working age (1985). **Exports:** $550 mil. (f.o.b., 1989 est.); cotton (44%), sesame, gum arabic, peanuts. **Imports:** $1.2 bil. (c.i.f., 1989 est.); petroleum products, manufactured goods, machinery and equipment, medicines and chemicals. **Major trading partners:** *exports:* 46% Western Europe, 14% Saudi Arabia, 9% Eastern Europe, 9% Japan; *imports:* 32% Western Europe, 15% Africa and Asia, 13% U.S.

**Intl. Orgs.** Arab League, FAO, G-77, IAEA, IBRD, ICAO, IDA, IFAD, IFC, ILO, IMF, IMO, INTELSAT, INTERPOL, ITU, NAM, OAU, UN, UNESCO, UPU, WHO, WIPO, WMO.

The northern Sudan, the ancient land of Nubia, was loosely controlled by Egypt in antiquity and incorporated into the Arab world by the Islamic expansion of the seventh century. The southern Sudan was part of tribal black Africa, under no external control but subject to continual raids by slave traders from the north.

Ottoman Egypt conquered the northern Sudan in 1820–21; British influence in Egypt in the 19th century extended into the Sudan as well. In 1881 Muhammed Ahmed ibn Abdalla, a religious leader known as the Mahdi, united northern and north-central Sudan and led a resistance movement against Anglo-Egyptian control. Khartoum, defended by British Gen. Charles George Gordon, fell in 1885, but the Mahdi died soon thereafter, and his revolt came to an end. An Anglo-Egyptian force under Kitchener regained control in 1898; Anglo-Egyptian joint rule was established in the Sudan in 1899.

Great Britain and Egypt granted self-government and self-determination to the Sudan in 1953, and a Sudanese parliament was seated in 1954. Full independence came in 1956. Gen. Ibrahim Abboud took power in a bloodless coup in 1958 but was forced to resign after riots in 1964. In 1969 a new military coup installed a ruling Revolutionary Command Council and instituted a socialist regime. The council's leader, Gen. Muhammed Nimeiri, became prime minister. Disputes between Marxists and non-Marxists, and between arabized northerners and black southerners, led to continual difficulties. An attempted coup was foiled in 1971. In 1972 the Sudan's three black southern provinces were granted local autonomy. Another attempted coup in 1976 was put down by the Nimeiri government, and hundreds of prominent citizens were arrested and executed. The government accused Libya of sponsoring the coup.

In 1983 attempts by the Nimeiri government to institute Islamic law throughout the Sudan led to riots in the south and the imposition of a nationwide state of emergency in 1984. Popular unrest was exacerbated by drought and famine in 1985, leading to severe price increases for food and fuel. On Apr. 6, 1985, Nimeiri was overthrown in a coup led by Gen. Suwar El Dahab. After a brief period of rule by a transitional military council, a civilian cabinet was installed, and free parliamentary elections were held in 1986. In June 1989 the government was overthrown in a coup led by Lt. Gen. Omar Ahmed al-Bashir. The Bashir government renewed the fight against the southern rebels, and supported the imposition of Islamic law throughout the Sudan.

In October 1990, the U.S. government stopped aid to the Sudan, citing the Khartoum government's diversion of food and other supplies from the southern provinces to the Muslim north. The Sudan openly supported Iraq in the Persian Gulf War and in January 1991, concerned for the safety of its respresentatives, the UN suspended relief efforts to help the estimated 7.1 million Sudanese threatened by famine. In addition to drought and internal refugees from famine areas, Sudan is also burdened by refugees from war zones in Chad and Ethiopia.

## Suriname
### Republic of Suriname

**Geography** **Location:** northeastern coast of South America. **Boundaries:** North Atlantic Ocean to N, French Guiana to E, Brazil to S, Guyana to W. **Total land area:** 63,037 sq. mi. (163,265 sq km). **Coastline:** 240 mi. (386 km). **Comparative area:** between Georgia and Washington. **Land use:** negl. % arable land; negl. % permanent crops; negl. % meadows and pastures; 97% forest and woodland; 3% other; includes negl. % irrigated. **Major cities:** (1980 census) Paramaribo (capital) 67,718.

**People** **Population:** 396,813 (1990). **Nationality:** noun—Surinamer(s); adjective—Surinamese. **Ethnic groups:** 37% Hindustani (East Indian), 31% Creole (black and mixed), 15.3% Javanese, 10.3% Bush black. **Languages:** Dutch (official), English widely spoken, Sranan Tongo (sometimes called Taki-Taki, the native language of Creoles and much of younger population and lingua franca among others), Hindi Suriname Hindustani, Javanese. **Religions:** 27.4% Hindu, 25.2% Protestant (predominantly Moravian), 22.8% Roman Catholic, 19.6% Muslim.

**Government** **Type:** in transition from military to civilian rule as of Jan. 1988. **Independence:** Nov. 25, 1975 (from Netherlands). **National holiday:** Independence Day, Nov. 25. **Heads of government:** Johannes Samuel Petrus Kraag, president (since Jan. 1991); Jules Wijdenbosch, prime minister (since Jan. 1991). **Structure:** civilian government moving away from military control.

**Economy** **Monetary unit:** Suriname guilder. **Budget:** (1989 est.) *income:* $466 mil.; *expend.:* $716 mil. **GDP:** $1.3 bil., $3,215 per capita (1988 est.). **Chief crops:** rice, bananas, palm oil, timber. **Livestock:** cattle, pigs, goats, sheep, horses, mules, asses. **Natural resources:** timber, hydropower potential, fish, shrimp, bauxite. **Major industries:** bauxite mining, alumina and aluminum production, lumbering. **Labor force:** 104,000 (1984); 11% agriculture, animal husbandry, fishing; 25–30% unemployment (1987). **Exports:** $425 mil. (f.o.b., 1988 est.); alumina, bauxite, aluminum, agricultural products, wood and wood products. **Imports:** $365 mil. (c.i.f., 1988 est.); capital equipment, petroleum, iron and steel, cotton, flour. **Major trading partners:** (1986) *exports:* 28% Netherlands, 22% U.S., 18% Norway, 11% Japan, 10% Brazil; *imports:* 34% U.S., 20% Netherlands, 8% Trinidad and Tobago, 5% Brazil.

**Intl. Orgs.** FAO, GATT, G-77, IBRD, ICAO, IFAD, ILO, IMF, IMO, INTERPOL, ITU, NAM, OAS, UN, UNESCO, UPU, WHO, WIPO, WMO.

In the early 17th century, the Dutch and English settled Suriname, which became a Dutch colony in 1667. Except for brief episodes of British rule, Suriname remained under Dutch control until its independence in 1975, shifting toward authoritarian military rule in 1980. The military created its own political party (the February 25 movement) and banned opposition organizations. The 1988 National Assembly election of Pres. Ramsewak Shankar marked an end to direct military rule, but the restriction of civil liberties continued.

The Shankar government was overthrown in a bloodless coup led by Cdr. Ivan Graanoogst. In January 1991, Johannes Kraag and Jules Wijdenbosch assumed the presidency and prime ministry, respectively.

## Swaziland
### Kingdom of Swaziland

**Geography** **Location:** landlocked country in southern Africa. **Boundaries:** South Africa to N, SE, S, and W; Mozambique to E. **Total land area:** 6,704 sq. mi. (17,363 sq km). **Coastline:** none. **Comparative area:** between Connecticut and New Jersey. **Land use:** 8% arable land; negl. % permanent crops; 67% meadows and pastures; 6% forest and woodland; 19% other; includes 2% irrigated. **Major cities:** (1982) Mbabane (capital) 38,636; Manzini 13,893.

**People** **Population:** 778,525 (1990). **Nationality:** noun—Swazi(s); adjective—Swazi. **Ethnic groups:** 97% African, 3% European. **Languages:** English and siSwati (both official); government business conducted in English. **Religions:** 57% Christian, 43% indigenous beliefs.

**Government** **Type:** monarchy; independent member of Commonwealth. **Independence:** Sept. 6, 1968 (from UK). **Constitution:** suspended Apr. 12, 1973; new constitution promulgated Oct. 13, 1978 but not yet formally presented to people. **National holiday:** Somhlolo

(Independence) Day, Sept. 6. **Heads of government:** Mswati III, king (since Apr. 1986); Obed M. Dlamini, prime minister (since July 1989). **Structure:** executive—king or queen (with advice of Supreme Council of State), whose assent is required before parliamentary acts become law; king's authority exercised through prime minister and cabinet; legislative—bicameral parliament (Senate, House of Assembly) formally opened Jan. 1979; 80-member electoral college chose 40 members of lower house and 10 members of upper house; additional 10 members of each house chosen by king; judiciary—part of Ministry of Justice but otherwise independent of executive and legislative branches; cases can be appealed to high court and court of appeal.

**Economy Monetary unit:** Swazi lilangeni. **Budget:** (1991 est.) *income:* $255 mil.; *expend.:* $253 mil. **GNP:** $539 mil., $750 per capita (1989 est.). **Chief crops:** maize, cotton, rice, sugar, citrus fruits. **Livestock:** goats, cattle, sheep, pigs, asses. **Natural resources:** asbestos, coal, clay, tin, hydroelectric power. **Major industries:** mining (coal and asbestos), wood pulp, sugar. **Labor force:** 195,000 (1987); about 92,000 wage earners (many whose employment is off-and-on); with 36% agriculture and forestry, 20% community and social services, 14% manufacturing, 9% construction, 21% other; over 60,000 in subsistence agriculture; 24,000–29,000 employed in South Africa. **Exports:** $394 mil. (f.o.b., 1988); sugar, asbestos, wood and forest products, citrus, canned fruits. **Imports:** $386 mil. (c.i.f., 1988); motor vehicles, chemicals, petroleum products, foodstuffs. **Major trading partners:** South Africa, UK, U.S.

**Intl. Orgs.** FAO, G-77, GATT (de facto), IBRD, ICAO, IDA, IFAD, IFC, ILO, IMF, INTERPOL, ITU, NAM, UN, UNESCO, UPU, WHO.

The Kingdom of Swaziland, a landlocked African country, is surrounded on three sides by South Africa and on the fourth by Mozambique. The Swazi are of Bantu origin. They are believed to have migrated in the late 1700s, under their chief Ngwane II, into what is now southeastern Swaziland, finding several different peoples there. Ngwane II and his successors united these tribal clans by the beginning of the 19th century.

Although British and Boer traders began exploring the area in the 1830s, it was not until gold was discovered in the 1880s that settlers began coming in large numbers. They hoodwinked the illiterate Swazi leadership into signing away their rights to the land. The British and Boer governments agreed in 1894 that the Boers would control Swaziland, but power reverted to Great Britain after they defeated the Boers in the Boer War, which ended in 1902. Not until the 1967 did they give Swaziland authority over its internal affairs. Under the British-authored constitution, Swaziland gained its independence in September 1968 as a constitutional monarchy led by King Sobhuza II. He set aside the constitution in 1973 and disbanded the legislature. He ruled the country

with the aid of a council of conservative ministers and named a committee to write a new constitution that was supposed to be more in keeping with Swazi traditions. A new legislature was created in 1979. The king died in 1982 and was replaced by his 18-year-old son, who took the name King Mswati III, in 1986.

In 1986 South African forces conducted raids into Swaziland, allegedly in pursuit of African National Congress activists. Swaziland maintains cooperative but cool relations with South Africa and Mozambique.

---

# Sweden
## Kingdom of Sweden

**Geography Location:** Scandinavian peninsula, northwest Europe. **Boundaries:** Norway to NE and W, Finland to NE, Gulf of Bothnia to E, Baltic Sea to E and S, Skagerrak channel to SW. **Total land area:** 170,250 sq. mi. (440,945 sq km). **Coastline:** 2,000 mi. (3,218 km). **Comparative area:** slightly larger than California. **Land use:** 7% arable land; 0% permanent crops; 2% meadows and pastures; 64% forest and woodland; 27% other; includes negl. % irrigated. **Major cities:** (1987 est.) Stockholm (capital) 666,810; Göteburg (Gothenburg) 431,521; Malmö 230,838; Uppsala 159,962; Orebro 119,066.

**People Population:** 8,401,098 (1989). **Nationality:** noun—Swede(s); adjective—Swedish. **Ethnic groups:** homogeneous white population; small Lappish minority; about 12% foreign-born or first-generation immigrants (Finns, Yugoslavs, Danes, Norwegians, Greeks, Turks). **Languages:** Swedish, small Lapp- and Finnish-speaking minorities; immigrants speak native languages. **Religions:** 93.5% Evangelical Lutheran, 1.0% Roman Catholic, 5.5% other.

**Government Type:** constitutional monarchy. **Independence:** N.A. **Constitution:** Jan. 1, 1975. **National holiday:** Sweden Day, June 6; King's Birthday, Apr. 30. **Heads of government:** Carl XVI Gustaf, king (since Nov. 1973); prime ministry vacant as of Sept. 25, 1991. **Structure:** executive power vested in cabinet, responsible to parliament; legislative authority rests with unicameral parliament (Riksdag); Supreme Court, six superior courts, 108 lower courts.

**Economy Monetary unit:** Swedish krona. **Budget:** (1989) *income:* $58.0 bil.; *expend.:* $57.9 bil. **GDP:** $132.7 bil., $15,700 per capita. **Chief crops:** grain, sugar beets, potatoes; 100% self-sufficient in grains and potatoes, 85% self-sufficient in sugar beets; milk and dairy products account for 37% of farm income. **Livestock:** poultry, pigs, cattle, sheep, goats. **Natural resources:** zinc, iron ore, lead, copper, silver. **Major industries:** iron and steel, precision equipment (bearings, radio and telephone parts, armaments), wood pulp. **Labor force:** 4.39 mil. (1986); 32.8% private services, 30% government services, 22% mining and manufacturing; 1.9% unemployment (1987). **Exports:** $52.2 bil. (f.o.b., 1989 est.); machinery, motor

vehicles, paper products, pulp and wood, iron and steel products. **Imports:** $48.5 bil. (c.i.f., 1989 est.); machinery, petroleum and petroleum products, chemicals, motor vehicles, foodstuffs. **Major trading partners:** *exports:* 52% EC (12% W. Germany, 11% UK, 7% Denmark), 10% U.S., 9% Norway; *imports:* 56% EC (21% W. Germany, 9% UK, 7% Denmark), 8% U.S., 6% Norway.

**Intl. Orgs.** EC (Free Trade Agreement), EFTA, FAO, GATT, IAEA, IBRD, ICAO, IDA, IFAD, IFC, ILO, IMO, INTELSAT, INTERPOL, ITU, OECD, UN, UNESCO, UPU, WHO, WIPO, WMO.

The earliest Swedes, the Svear, conquered and merged with their southern neighbors, the Gotar, by the sixth century. Organized into petty kingdoms, Swedes joined with other Norsemen in the Viking raids of the seventh through 11th centuries; in the 10th century, they began to dominate a trading empire that stretched through Russia to the Black Sea. Christianity was introduced by St. Ansgar in 829 but became fully established only in the 12th century, during the reign of Eric IX, who also conquered Finland. For centuries Sweden warred with its neighbors, Norway and Denmark, for control in the north, and it competed with the German Hanseatic League for control of the Baltic trade.

The Swedish and Norwegian monarchies were merged in 1319 by Magnus VII, and in 1397 Queen Margaret effected the Kalmar Union, which united Sweden, Denmark, and Norway under a single monarchy. Sweden resisted Danish rule, and in 1520 King Christian II responded with the massacre of the Swedish nobility at Stockholm. Sweden then rose against the Danish throne and in 1523 enthroned Gustavus Wasa as Gustavus I, founder of the Swedish monarchy. The Wasa dynasty slowly introduced Lutheran Christianity and in 1604 banned Catholicism.

Sweden became a European champion of Protestantism in the 17th century, intervening against the Habsburgs in the Thirty Years' War. Emerging among the victors after 1648, Sweden successfully waged wars with Denmark and Poland, built a great northern empire, and made the Baltic Sea virtually a Swedish lake. But in the late 17th century and into the 18th, the Russians deprived Sweden of the Baltic's eastern shore and, in 1808, of Finland, while the Prussians drove Sweden from the southern Baltic coast.

The kings of Sweden during the 18th century pursued a pointless despotism that weakened the country politically and socially. Sweden joined the European powers against Napoleon in 1813 and was rewarded with Norway in 1814. In 1905 Norway gained its independence, and Sweden took on its modern boundaries.

Sweden's greatest natural resources are timber, iron ore, and hydroelectric power. The first two were exploited by traditional industries, which supplemented other long-term economic activities such as fishing, maritime trade, and agriculture. All three provided the basis for industrialization in the 19th and 20th centuries, leading to an economic prosperity that was enhanced and protected by political neutrality.

Sweden's neutality was largely respected by Hitler during World War II, though Sweden was forced to accede to transportation of German troops to Norway over Swedish rails. Through the war Sweden continued to be ruled, under King Gustavus V, by a national coalition government lasting until 1945. Sweden's gross national product (GNP) rose by 20 percent during the war years.

The Social Democratic party dominated the Swedish government after 1936, and after 1945 its governance was reestablished, lasting until 1976 under the leadership of Tage Erlander. Sweden, like its Scandinavian neighbors, constructed an economy based on free enterprise, public ownership of utilities, exports, social welfare, and high taxes.

A UN charter member, Sweden accepted Marshall Plan aid and joined the Council of Europe in 1948. Sweden's plan for a Nordic Defense Alliance failed when Norway and Denmark joined NATO (Sweden refused to join the North Atlantic pact), but the political and economic Nordic Council (Sweden, Norway, Denmark, Iceland, and, after 1956, Finland) was formed with strong Swedish backing in 1952–53. This consultative body backed the establishment of SAS as the joint national airline of the first three members; coordination of the welfare programs of member states; and abolition of passport controls and controls on the migration of labor within Scandinavia.

Sweden maintains its neutrality by means of one of the highest rates of defense spending in Western Europe—13 percent of GNP in 1970, declining to 8 percent by 1985. Swedish armed forces have mobilized on a number of occasions to defend Sweden's airspace from Soviet aircraft and its territorial waters from intrusions by Soviet submarines.

Erlander retired as prime minister in 1969 and was succeeded by Olaf Palme, who pursued a more rigid socialist program than his predecessor. He advocated legislation to make incomes more equal, provoking some labor unrest. When King Gustav VI Adolf died in 1973 the Palme government passed the 1974 Instrument of Government Act, divesting the king of his role as commander in chief of the armed forces and of his right to appoint prime ministers.

Economic growth came to a virtual halt in the 1970s; lacking petroleum and gas resources, Sweden's oil import costs rose 700 percent between 1972 and 1979. Consumer prices rose sharply, and labor unrest grew. The Social Democrats were turned out of office by a conservative coalition in 1976 but returned with a minority cabinet in 1982.

Palme was assassinated in 1986, a still-unsolved crime that shocked the nation. He was succeeded by Ingvar Carlsson, whose Social Democratic program has focused on a scheme whereby business profits are taxed to fund labor union purchases of sufficient stock to gain labor ownership of private enterprise.

# Switzerland
## Swiss Confederation

**Geography  Location:** landlocked country in central Europe. **Boundaries:** Germany to N, Austria to E, Italy to S, and France to W. **Total land area:** 15,943 sq. mi. (41,293 sq km). **Coastline:** none. **Comparative area:** between Maryland and West Virginia. **Land use:** 10% arable land; 1% permanent crops; 40% meadows and pastures; 26% forest and woodland; 23% other; includes 1% irrigated. **Major cities:** (1988 est.) Berne (Bern, capital) 135,147; Zürich 345,159; Basel (Bâle) 170,080; Genève (Geneva or Genf) 163,998; Lausanne 123,468.

**People  Population:** 6,742,461 (1990). **Nationality:** noun—Swiss (sing., pl.); adjective—Swiss. **Ethnic groups:** total population—65% German, 18% French, 10% Italian, 1% Romansh, 5% other; Swiss nationals—74% German, 20% French, 4% Italian, 1% Romansh, 1% other. **Languages:** total population—65% German, 18% French, 12% Italian, 1% Romansh, 4% other; Swiss nationals—74% German, 20% French, 4% Italian, 1% Romansh, 1% other. **Religions:** 49% Catholic, 48% Protestant.

**Government  Type:** federal republic. **Independence:** Aug. 1, 1291. **Constitution:** May 29, 1874. **National holiday:** National Day, Aug. 1. **Heads of government:** Arnold Kohler, president (since 1989; president rotates annually); Flavio Cotti, vice president (since 1989; term runs concurrently with that of president). **Structure:** federal council (Bundesrat) has executive authority; bicameral parliament (National Council, Council of States) has legislative authority; judiciary left chiefly to cantons.

**Economy  Monetary unit:** Swiss franc. **Budget:** (1988) *income:* $17.0 bil.; *expend.:* $16.8 bil. **GDP:** $119.5 bil., $17,800 per capita (1988). **Chief crops:** less than 50% self-sufficient; food shortages—fish, refined sugar, fats and oils (other than butter), grains, eggs, fruits, vegetables, meat; dairy farming predominates. **Livestock:** pigs, cattle, sheep, goats, horses. **Natural resources:** hydropower potential, timber, salt. **Major industries:** machinery, chemicals, watches. **Labor force:** 3.05 mil.; 822,746 foreign workers, mostly Italian (1987); 42% services, 39% industry and crafts, 11% government; 0.7% unemployment (1988 est.). **Exports:** $51.2 bil. (f.o.b., 1988); machinery and equipment, precision instruments, metal products, foodstuffs. **Imports:** $57.2 bil. (c.i.f., 1988); agricultural products, machinery and transport equipment, chemicals, textiles. **Major trading partners:** *exports:* 64% Europe (56% EC, 8% other), 9% U.S., 4% Japan; *imports:* 79% Europe (72% EC, 7% other), 5% U.S.

**Intl. Orgs.** EFTA, FAO, GATT, IAEA, ICAO, IFAD, ILO, IMO, INTELSAT, INTERPOL, ITU, OECD, UNESCO, UPU, WHO, WIPO, WMO; permanent observer status at UN.

Switzerland, the Roman province of Helvetia, began to assume its modern form in A.D. 1291, when three independent cantons formed a defensive league against the expansion of Habsburg power. The Swiss League grew to eight cantons in 1353, 13 in 1513, 22 in 1815. The league continues to evolve; it reached its present size of 20 cantons and six half-cantons with the creation of the Canton of Jura in 1979.

The Treaty of Westphalia, which ended the Thirty Years' War in 1648, gave international recognition to the independence of Switzerland from the Holy Roman Empire. Switzerland became a client state of France in the Napoleonic period; the European powers recognized and guaranteed Swiss independence and neutrality at the Congress of Vienna in 1815. Constitutional changes in 1848 and 1874 somewhat increased the power of the central government, but the individual cantons cling stubbornly to their independence within the confederation. This policy has helped ensure stability within a multilingual nation.

The Swiss government consists of an upper house, representing the cantons, and a lower house that is directly elected. No executive can veto, nor court disallow, a bill of the Swiss legislature. Executive power is vested in a seven-member committee chosen by the legislature, with a rotating presidency.

Swiss neutrality is defended by more than simply international guarantees. Switzerland is a highly militarized society; every male is required to serve in the citizen's militia until age 47, keeping an assault rifle and other equipment ready at home. The armed forces are equipped with sophisticated modern weapons, and military spending amounts to 30 percent of the Swiss federal budget.

Landlocked, with little fertile farmland and limited Alpine pastures, lacking both natural resources and a colonial empire, Switzerland was traditionally one of Europe's poorest countries. Until the 19th century, its principal export was soldiers, mercenaries who supplied military services to any European sovereign who could pay for them. (The pope's Swiss Guard is a remnant of this tradition.) With the spread in the late 18th century of the Romantic movement, Europeans learned to appreciate the glamour of Alpine scenery, and a tourist industry was born. It was much expanded in the 20th century with the development of Alpine skiing. Tourism remains a conspicuous, though relatively minor, part of the Swiss economy.

Swiss prosperity came in the 20th century with specialized manufacturing and free trade within the world economy. By 1940 half of the population was engaged in manufacturing, producing specialty products requiring high degrees of skill: processed foods, watches, electrical machinery, engines, fine textiles, and the like.

Neutral in both world wars, Switzerland required no postwar recovery in the 1940s. It capitalized on the restructuring of European politics and economics to expand into the service sector, which now employs half of the work force (while manufacturing has declined to about 40%). Tourism, banking, insurance, and clerical/bureaucratic services to the many international organizations with headquarters in Switzerland help give the nation one of Europe's highest standards of living.

In the postwar period, Switzerland has enjoyed both political and economic stability. Government is normally controlled by a three- or four-party coalition, representing about 70–80 percent of the total vote. A cautious approach to economic development led to annual growth rates of over 6 percent in the 1950s and early 1960s, declining to 2 percent in the 1970s; the world economic boom of the 1980s produced higher growth rates again in Switzerland. In general the economy has avoided inflation, and the stability of the Swiss franc has been maintained.

Switzerland is a member of the European Free Trade Association and has ties to the EC, although it is not a member. Recent referenda brought overwhelming rejection of UN membership (it currently has observer status), and support for restrictive immigration legislation. The most significant political change in the postwar period has been the gradual extension, canton by canton, of women's right to vote.

# Syria
## Syrian Arab Republic

**Geography  Location:** western Asia. **Boundaries:** Turkey to N, Iraq to E, Jordan to S, Lebanon and Israel to SW, Mediterranean Sea to W. **Total land area:** 71,043 sq. mi. (184,050 sq km). **Coastline:** 120 mi. (193 km). **Comparative area:** slightly larger than North Dakota. **Land use:** 28% arable land; 3% permanent crops; 46% meadows and pastures; 3% forest and woodland; 20% other; includes 3% irrigated. **Major cities:** (1985 est.) Damascus (capital) 1,269,000; Aleppo 985,413; Homs 347,000.

**People  Population:** 12,483,440 (1990). **Nationality:** noun—Syrian(s); adjective—Syrian. **Ethnic groups:** 90.3% Arab, 9.7% Kurds, Armenians, and other. **Languages:** Arabic (official), Kurdish, Armenian, Aramaic, Circassian; French and English widely understood. **Religions:** 74% Sunni Muslim; 16% Alawite, Druze, and other Muslim sects; 10% Christian.

**Government  Type:** republic; under left-wing military regime since Mar. 1963. **Independence:** Apr. 17, 1946 (from League of Nations Mandate under French administration). **Constitution:** Mar. 12, 1973. **National holiday:** Independence Day, Apr. 17. **Heads of government:** Lt. Gen. Hafez al-Assad, president (since Mar. 1971); Mahmoud Zoubi, prime minister (since Nov. 1987). **Structure:** executive powers vested in president and Council of Ministers; power rests in unicameral legislature (People's Council); seat of power is Baath party's Regional (Syrian) Command.

**Economy  Monetary unit:** Syrian pound. **Budget:** (1989) *income:* N.A.; *expend.:* $3.2 bil. **GDP:** $18.5 bil., $1,540 per capita (1985). **Chief crops:** cotton, wheat, barley, tobacco. **Livestock:** sheep, goats, cattle, asses, horses. **Natural resources:** crude oil, phosphates, chrome and manganese ores, asphalt, iron ore.

**Major industries:** textiles, food processing, beverages. **Labor force:** 2.4 mil. (1984); 36% miscellaneous services, 32% agriculture, 32% industry (including construction); majority unskilled; shortage of skilled labor; 5% unemployment (1986). **Exports:** $1.3 bil. (f.o.b., 1988 est.); petroleum, textiles, fruits, vegetables, phosphates. **Imports:** $1.9 bil. (f.o.b., 1988 est.); petroleum, machinery, base metals, foodstuffs, beverages. **Major trading partners:** *exports:* Italy, Romania, USSR, U.S., Iran, France; *imports:* Iran, W. Germany, USSR, France, E. Germany, Libya, U.S.

**Intl. Orgs.** Arab League, FAO, G-77, IAEA, IBRD, ICAO, IDA, IFAD, IFC, ILO, IMF, IMO, INTELSAT, INTERPOL, ITU, NAM, UN, UNESCO, UPU, WHO, WMO.

The home of some of the world's most ancient centers of civilization, Syria was successively part of the Hittite, Assyrian, and Persian empires. At various times it was conquered by the Babylonians and the Egyptians. From about 1250 B.C., the coastal cities came under Phoenician rule. Alexander the Great brought Syria into the Hellenic world with his conquests in 332 B.C. After the fall of the Alexandrian empire, Syria came under the domain of the Seleucid empire but was constantly threatened by the Hellenic kingdom of Egypt, based in Alexandria.

In the classical period, Syria embraced a much larger territory than that of the present Syrian nation; it included the entire Levant and parts of present-day Turkey, Iraq, Iran, and Jordan. Greater Syria was conquered by Rome in 63 B.C. Under Roman rule the oasis region of Palmyra grew into a powerful semiautonomous kingdom. With the division of the Roman Empire in the fourth century A.D., Syria became part of the Eastern Roman (Byzantine) Empire. Throughout the Roman and Byzantine periods, the country was an important center of Christianity.

Syria was one of the first areas conquered when Islam began expansion from Arabia; Islamic rule was established by 636. From 661 to 751, Damascus was the center of the Caliphate, the ruling body of the Islamic world. By the late 11th century, the Seljuk Turks had conquered Syria. The large Syrian Christian population welcomed the European Crusaders as liberators from the Turks, but both Christians and Turks were defeated by the Arab general Saladin in the late 12th century. Saladin's rule was followed by that of the Mamluk empire of Egypt. During the Mamluk period, Mongol armies twice invaded Syria, in the mid-13th century and at the turn of the 15th century.

An Ottoman army defeated the Mamluks in Syria in 1516, making Syria part of the Ottoman Empire. In the 18th century, France declared itself the protector of Syria's Christian community against Ottoman abuses. Napoleon invaded Syria in 1799 but withdrew after a brief occupation. In the 1830s Egyptian troops occupied Syria but were forced to withdraw under pressure from the European powers.

Syrian nationalist aspirations emerged as the Ottoman Empire began to crumble before World War I. During the war the British encouraged Syrians to rebel against Turkish rule. After World War I, France governed both Syria and Lebanon (the Levant States) under a League of Nations Mandate. Under French rule, the region was divided into small territorial states along communal lines; Lebanon became independent in 1926. After prolonged negotiations much of Syria was organized into a semiautonomous state in 1930–32.

In June 1940 the French administration in Syria declared its loyalty to the Vichy government. British and Free French forces invaded in June 1941, and an independent Syrian republic was established in September 1941. Separately administered territories were consolidated with the republic over the next two years, and full independence was declared on Jan. 1, 1944; foreign troops did not withdraw, however, until April 1946.

Syria became a founding member of the Arab League and participated in the first Arab-Israeli War in 1948. An armistice with Israel was signed in July 1949. Severe political instability marked the early years of Syrian independence; the government was overthrown by military coups three times in 1949 alone.

Most of Syria's Jews emigrated to Israel before or during 1948, and much of its once-substantial Christian population has emigrated also. Syrian politics remain dominated by communal concerns, however; the Arab majority is divided into Sunni, Shiite, Alawite, and Druze communities.

Syria and Egypt merged as the United Arab Republic in February 1958; Syria seceded from the federation on Sept. 30, 1961. In Mar. 1963 a military coup established the pan-Arab Socialist Baath party in power; all other political parties were abolished. The Baath party leadership is dominated by the minority Alawite community.

Pres. Hafez al-Assad took power on Feb. 22, 1971.

In the 1967 Arab-Israeli War (the Six Day War), Israel seized and held the Golan Heights region of Syria, from which Syria had long shelled Israeli communities and military installations. The Golan Heights have since been incorporated into Israeli territory.

Syrian troops aided Palestinian forces fighting government troops in Jordan in September 1970. After the expulsion of Palestinian forces from Jordan in July 1971, Syria broke off relations with Jordan; relations were restored in 1975.

On Oct. 6, 1973, Syrian and Egyptian forces attacked Israel, touching off the third Arab-Israeli War, the Yom Kippur War. A cease-fire took effect on Oct. 24; Syria failed to regain territory lost to Israel in 1967. Following the 1973 war, Syria became a major recipient of economic aid from the Arab oil states and of military equipment and supplies from the Soviet Union.

In 1976 Syrian troops entered Lebanon in an attempt to mediate in that nation's civil war and became enmeshed in that conflict. Major fighting between Syrian troops and Lebanese Christian militiamen broke out in April 1981. On June 6, 1982, Israeli troops invaded Lebanon and engaged Syrian troops in a five-day war in the Bekaa Valley. Following serious losses of aircraft and troops, Syria agreed to a cease-fire with Israel on June 11. Syrian troops continue to occupy parts of Lebanon.

An attempted coup, in February 1982, by the Moslem Brotherhood led to serious fighting within Syria, but the rebellion was put down; casualties on both sides were estimated at more than 5,000.

From the time of the 1973 Arab-Israeli War (the Yom Kippur War), Syria consistently adopted a radical stance in Middle Eastern politics, rejecting the 1979 Egyptian-Israeli accord and all other attempts at Arab-Israeli reconciliation. Supporting radical movements within the Palestine Liberation Organization, Syria aided Palestinian militants in driving Yasir Arafat's centrist faction of the PLO from its headquarters in Tripoli in 1983. The Syrian government has been implicated in various acts of international terrorism in support of Palestinian, Libyan, and Iranian causes.

Syria has played a major role in the Lebanese peace process, backing the governments in place since the Taif peace accord and accommodating a peace settlement between rival Shiite militias. Syria also took part in the anti-Iraq coalition in 1990–91, sending 20,000 troops to Saudi Arabia, as well as mobilizing forces on its common border with Iraq. Despite its enmity towards Israel, in 1991 it sought to avoid being singled out as an obstacle to regional peace talks. (See Part 1, "The Year in Review.")

## Taiwan
### Republic of China
### (also called Nationalist China, Formosa)
**Geography Location:** one large and several smaller islands about 100 mi. (160 km) off SE coast of mainland China. Taipei 25°03′N, 121°30′E. **Boundaries:** East China Sea to N, Pacific Ocean to E, Bashi Channel to S, and Formosa Strait to W; separated from mainland by Formosa Strait. **Total land area:** 13,900 sq. mi. (36,000 sq km). **Coastline:** 900 mi. (1,448 km). **Comparative area:** slightly larger than Maryland. **Land use:** 24% arable land; 1% permanent crops; 5% meadows and pastures; 55% forest and woodland; 15% other; includes 14% irrigated. **Major cities:** (1989 est.) Taipei (capital) 2,702,678; Kaohsiung 1,374,231; Taichung 746,780; Tainan 675,685; Panchiao 506,220.

**People Population:** 20,546,664 (1990). **Nationality:** noun—Chinese (sing., pl.); adjective—Chinese. **Ethnic groups:** 84% Taiwanese, 14% mainland Chinese, 2% aborigine. **Languages:** Mandarin Chinese (official); Taiwanese and Hakka dialects also used. **Religions:** 93% mixture of Buddhist, Confucian, and Taoist; 4.5% Christian, 2.5% other.

**Government Type:** one-party presidential regime; 1988 political organizations bill permits legal formation of new political parties. **Constitution:** Dec. 25, 1947. **National holiday:** Oct. 10. **Heads of government:** Li Teng-hui, president (since Jan. 1988); Yü Kuo-hua, premier (since June 1984). **Structure:** five independent branches (executive, legislative, judicial, plus traditional Chinese functions of examination and control), dominated by executive branch; president and vice president elected by National Assembly.

**Economy Monetary unit:** New Taiwan dollar. **Budget:** (1989) *income:* 25.9 bil.; *expend.:* $33.2 bil. **GNP:** $121.4 bil., $6,000 per capita. **Chief crops:** rice, sweet potatoes, sugarcane, bananas, pineapples. **Livestock:** chickens, ducks, pigs, geese, turkeys. **Natural resources:** small deposits of coal, natural gas, limestone, marble, and asbestos. **Major industries:** textiles, clothing, chemicals. **Labor force:** 7,880,000 (1986); 41% industry and commerce, 32% services, 20% agriculture; 2% unemployment (1988). **Exports:** $66.2 bil. (f.o.b., 1989); 19% electrical machinery, 14% general machinery and equipment, 10% textiles, 9% communications equipment, 7% basic metals and metal products. **Imports:** $52.2 bil. (c.i.f., 1989); 16% machinery and equipment, 11% chemicals and chemical products, 7% basic metals, 5% crude oil. **Major trading partners:** (1988) *exports:* 36% U.S., 14% Japan; *imports:* 31% Japan, 23% U.S., 9% Saudi Arabia.

**Intl. Orgs.** expelled from UN General Assembly and Security Council, Oct. 25, 1971, and withdrew from other subsidiary organs; expelled from IMF/World Bank group 1980; seeking to join GATT and/or MFA; attempting to regain membership in INTELSAT and INTERPOL; suspended from IAEA in 1972 but still allows IAEA controls over extensive atomic development.

Nominally part of the Chinese empire since the Song dynasty (960–1279), Taiwan was inhabited only by non-Chinese aboriginals before the 17th century. Around 1600 the Portuguese established a trading station on Taiwan; they named the island Ilha Formosa. In 1620 the Dutch built Fort Zeelandia near present-day Tainan, controlling the island until they were driven out by the Chinese pirate-patriot Koxinga (Zheng Chenggong). Remnants of the overthrown Ming dynasty (1368–1644) held out on the island until 1683, when it came under the sway of the Qing dynasty (1644–1911). Thereafter, substantial numbers of farmers from Fujian Province migrated to the fertile western lowlands of the island, driving the aboriginals into the central mountains. The Qing dynasty administered Taiwan as a semiautonomous subprovince of Fujian Province.

Following China's defeat by Japan in the Sino-Japanese War of 1894–95, Taiwan was ceded to Japan as a colony. The Japanese built roads and railroads to exploit Taiwan's resources of rice, timber, and minerals. In 1945, after Japan's defeat in World War II, Taiwan was returned to Chinese sovereignty.

As the Chinese civil war turned against the Nationalist party of Chiang Kai-shek (see "China"), Nationalist troops began to prepare Taiwan as a base for a retreat from the mainland. In 1947 Nationalist agents executed several thousand students and others suspected of favoring Taiwan's independence from China.

In 1949 approximately two million Nationalist soldiers, government officials, and civilian sympathizers retreated to Taiwan. The relocated Republic of China (ROC) continued to claim to be the legitimate government of all of China, now under Communist control. In addition to Taiwan proper, the Nationalists occupied the P'eng-hu islands in the Taiwan Straits and the small islands of Quemoy and Matsu just off the coast of Fujian. Recovery of the mainland became a cornerstone of ROC policy, but no serious attempt was made to do so. U.S. policy in the Taiwan Straits was to defend Taiwan against Communist attack but also to keep the two rival governments of China well separated from each other.

A successful program of land reform in the early 1950s led to the creation of surplus capital, which fueled the development of an industrial base on the island. Foreign investment from Japan and the United States, and American military and economic aid, also enhanced economic development. By the early 1970s, the island had developed an export-oriented economy, producing textiles, cement, plastics, assembled electronic appliances, and other manufactured goods.

Chiang Kai-shek, president of the Republic of China since 1928, died in 1975 and was succeeded by his son, Chiang Ching-kuo. Under both father and son, the Nationalist party (Kuomintang, or KMT) controlled both the ROC and the Taiwan Provincial governments; mainland refugees and their descendants (15% of the population) dominated senior government posts and the military officer corps. Native Taiwanese played the leading role in agriculture, industry, and, increasingly, in local and county governments.

In foreign affairs the Republic of China became more and more isolated from the world community. In 1971 China's seat in the United Nations was taken away from the ROC and awarded to the People's Republic of China; international diplomatic recognition of the ROC dwindled steadily thereafter. On Jan. 1, 1979, the United States withdrew its recognition of the ROC and inaugurated mutual diplomatic relations with the People's Republic. Under the Taiwan Relations Act of 1979, nominally nongovernmental relations were maintained between the United States and Taiwan through the American Institute in Taipei and Taiwan's Coordination Council for North American Affairs in Washington, D.C. Similar arrangements elsewhere ensured that Taiwan's trade and other interests would be secured throughout the noncommunist world. Taiwan's economy has continued to be one of the world's most vigorous; Taiwan enjoys a substantial favorable balance of trade with the United States and has foreign-exchange holdings in excess of $75 billion.

In 1986 Pres. Chiang Ching-kuo began a policy of liberalization; in the fall of 1987, he abolished martial law and allowed non-KMT political parties to function legally. Some barriers to travel to and communication with the mainland by ROC citizens were eased, but Taiwan's government continued to rebuff all calls from the mainland for direct contacts and discussions of reunification. Chiang Ching-kuo died in January 1988 and was succeeded by his vice president, Li Teng-hui. In March 1990, Li was overwhelmingly reelected by the National Assembly in the first election for the office. Under Pres. Li, Taiwan continues to be a de facto nation with a regime that claims to be the *de jure* government of China. This anomalous situation, with the voice of the Taiwanese opposition growing steadily stronger, has uncertain implications for the future of Taiwan and the Republic of China.

## Tanzania
### United Republic of Tanzania

**Geography** **Location:** Tanganyika, on eastern coast of Africa, and islands of Zanzibar and Pemba, about 25 mi. (40 km) off Tanganyika coast in Indian Ocean. **Boundaries:** Burundi, Rwanda to NW, Uganda, Kenya to N, Indian Ocean to E, Mozambique, Malawi to S, Zambia to SW, Zaire to W. **Total land area:** 342,102 sq. mi. (886,040 sq km). **Coastline:** 885 mi. (1,424 km). **Comparative area:** slightly larger than twice size of California. **Land use:** 5% arable land; 1% permanent crops; 40% meadows and pastures; 47% forest and woodland; 7% other; includes negl. % irrigated. **Major cities:** (1978 census) Dar es Salaam (capital) 757,346; Zanzibar 110,669; Mwanza 110,611; Tanga 103,409.

**People** **Population:** 25,970,843 (1990). **Nationality:** noun—Tanzanian(s); adjective—Tanzanian. **Ethnic groups:** mainland—99% native Africans of over 100 groups; 1% Asian, European, and Arab; Zanzibar—almost all Arab. **Languages:** Swahili and English (both official); English primary language of commerce, administration, and higher education; Swahili widely understood and generally used for communication between ethnic groups; first language of most people is one of local languages; primary education generally in Swahili. **Religions:** mainland—33% Christian, 33% Muslim, 33% indigenous beliefs; Zanzibar—almost all Muslim.

**Government** **Type:** republic. **Independence:** Tanganyika became independent Dec. 9, 1961 (from UN trusteeship under British administration); Zanzibar became independent Dec. 19, 1963 (from UK); Tanganyika united with Zanzibar Apr. 26, 1964. **Constitution:** Apr. 25, 1977 (Zanzibar has own Constitution but remains subject to provisions of union Constitution). **National holiday:** Union Day, Apr. 26; Independence Day, Dec. 9. **Heads of government:** Ali Hassan Mwinyi, president (since Nov. 1985); Joseph Sinde Warioba, prime minister (since Nov. 1985). **Structure:** executive—president has authority on mainland, with government policies subject to validation by party, which is technically superior to government; legislative—National Assembly with 233 members, 72 from Zanzibar, 65 appointed from mainland, and 96 directly elected from mainland; National Assembly dominated by Chama Cha Mapinduzi (Revolutionary party).

**Economy** **Monetary unit:** Tanzanian shilling. **Budget:** (1989) *income:* $568.0 mil.; *expend.:* $835.0 mil. **GDP:** $5.9 bil., $235 per capita. **Chief crops:** cotton, coffee, sisal, vegetables, fruits, grain on mainland; cloves and coconuts on Zanzibar. **Livestock:** N.A. **Natural resources:** hydropower potential, tin, phosphates, large unexploited deposits of iron ore and coal, gemstones. **Major industries:** agricultural processing (sugar, beer, cigarettes, sisal twine), diamond mine, oil refinery. **Labor force:** 208,680 wage earners (1983); 90% agriculture, 10% industry and commerce. **Exports:** $394 mil. (f.o.b., 1989); coffee, cotton, sisal, cashew nuts, meat, cloves. **Imports:** $1.3 bil. (f.o.b., 1989); manufactured goods, machinery and transport equipment, cotton piece goods, crude oil, foodstuffs. **Major trading partners:** *exports:* W. Germany, UK, U.S; *imports:* W. Germany, UK, U.S., Iran.

**Intl. Orgs.** Commonwealth, FAO, G-77, GATT, IAEA, IBRD, ICAO, IDA, IFAD, IFC, ILO, IMF, IMO, INTELSAT, INTERPOL, ITU, NAM, UN, UNESCO, UPU, WHO, WMO.

Tanganyika's indigenous population includes people of diverse ethnic background, including San, Bantu, and Nilotic peoples. It was the site of a number of relatively advanced and well-organized societies.

Zanzibar and the neighboring island of Pemba were a crossroads of trade in East Africa since ancient times. Trade via Zanzibar between the Tanganyika coast and the Middle East dates back to the late Roman Empire, with ivory, gold, and iron the main items of trade. The coast was dominated by various Arab and Persian powers, usually based in Zanzibar, from about the eighth century. Zanzibar and Tanganyika were visited by the Portuguese explorer Vasco da Gama in 1498, and Portugal claimed Zanzibar in 1503 and the entire Tanganyika coast in 1506. The Portuguese established coastal trading stations but did not colonize the interior.

The Portuguese were driven from Zanzibar in 1652 by the sultanate of Oman, which soon expelled them from the mainland as well. Under Omani rule, trade in gold, ivory, and gems was supplemented by a sizable slave trade, and the clove plantations of Zanzibar became commercially important. Under Sultan Seyyid Said, the capital of the sultanate of Oman was transferred to Zanzibar in 1824, and Zanzibar became independent of Oman upon his death in 1856.

Both Germany and Great Britain became active in the region in the 19th century, motivated by trade and, in the British case, by the antislavery movement. Tanganyika was organized as the colony of German East Africa in 1884, while Zanzibar became a British protectorate in 1890. Tanganyika became a secondary battlefield of World War I, with frequent clashes between German and British troops.

Britain assumed control of Tanganyika in 1920 under a League of Nations Mandate and maintained control under a UN trusteeship after 1946. The temperate southern highlands were extensively colonized by British immigrants, and railroads and mines were developed by the British administration.

Elections for a local legislature were held in Zanzibar in July 1957. The island's politics were dominated by a split between Arab and African residents. Zanzibar became independent on Dec. 19, 1963. In January 1964 an African revolt overthrew the sultan of Zanzibar and resulted in the deaths of thousands of Arab residents and the emigration of many more. Political control shifted to the African party and Abeid Karume became president.

Tanganyika became independent in 1961. Julius K. Nyerere was Tanganyika's dominant political figure. Tanzania was formed from the union of Tanganyika and Zanzibar on April 26, 1964, with Zanzibar retaining local autonomy.

The United Republic of Tanzania, under Nyerere's leadership, advocated an "African socialist" form of development and formed close ties with China. Some British settlers left the country, but despite tensions, relations with Great Britain remained important. The Tan-Zan Railroad between Dar es Salaam and Lusaka, Zambia, was built with Chinese aid between 1970 and 1975. The ruling parties of Tanganyika and Zanzibar were united in 1977 under Nyerere's leadership.

In 1979 Tanzanian troops invaded Uganda to drive Idi Amin from power there. Elections were held in 1981 and 1985, as political tensions eased and Tanzania adopted a more open and democratic political structure. Since 1985 Pres. Ali Hassan Mwinyi has pressed for free-market economic policies.

In May 1987 ministers from Kenya, Uganda, and Tanzania met to plan closer economic and political ties in East Africa. Despite some stagnation during the socialist period of 1967–85, Tanzania's economy remains fundamentally strong because of the country's extensive natural resources. Light industry, including clothing, textiles, and food processing, has been developed. The country has one of Africa's best educational systems, and literacy, in both English and Swahili, is high.

The Olduvai Gorge, part of East Africa's Great Rift Valley, has yielded extensive fossil remains of early hominids. Tanzania and Kenya supported a worldwide ban on trade in ivory.

## Thailand
### Kingdom of Thailand

**Geography** **Location:** extends southward, along isthmus of Kra, to Malay peninsula, in Southeast Asia. **Boundaries:** Myanmar to W and N, Laos to NE, Cambodia and Gulf of Thailand to E, Malaysia to S, Andaman Sea to SW. **Total land area:** 198,115 sq. mi. (513,115 sq km). **Coastline:** 2,001 mi. (3,219 km). **Comparative area:** between California and Texas. **Land use:** 34% arable land; 4% permanent crops; 1% meadows and pastures; 30% forest and woodland; 31% other; includes 7% irrigated. **Major cities:** Bangkok Metropolis (capital) 5,468,915 (1986 est.); Songkla 172,604; Chonburi 115,350; Nakhon Si Thammarat 102,123; Chiang Mai 101,594 (1980 census).

**People** **Population:** 55,115,683 (1990).

**Nationality:** noun—Thai (sing., pl.); adjective—Thai. **Ethnic groups:** 75% Thai, 14% Chinese, 11% other. **Languages:** Thai; English is secondary language of elite; ethnic and regional dialects. **Religions:** 95.5% Buddhist, 4% Muslim, 0.5% other.

**Government Type:** constitutional monarchy. **Constitution:** Dec. 22, 1978. **National holiday:** King's Birthday, Dec. 5. **Heads of government:** Bhumibol Adulyadej, king (since June 1946); Anand Panyarachun, prime minister (since Mar. 1991). **Structure:** king is head of state with nominal powers; bicameral legislature (National Assembly—Senate appointed by king, elected House of Representatives); judiciary relatively independent except in important political subversion cases.

**Economy Monetary unit:** baht. **Budget:** (1989) **income:** $12.1 bil. **expend.:** $9.7 bil. **GNP:** $64.5 bil., $1,160 per capita (1988 est.). **Chief crops:** rice, sugar, corn, rubber, manioc; illegal producer of opium poppy and cannabis for international drug trade. **Livestock:** buffalo, cattle, pigs, goats, sheep. **Natural resources:** tin, rubber, natural gas, tungsten, tantalum. **Major industries:** textiles and garments, agricultural processing, beverages; world's second-largest tungsten producer and third-largest tin producer; tourism—largest source of foreign exchange. **Labor force:** 26 mil. (1984); 73% agriculture, 11% industry and commerce, 10% services; 6.4% unemployment (1988). **Exports:** $19.9 bil. (f.o.b., 1989); 12% textiles, 12% fishery products, 8% rice, 8% tapioca, 6% jewelry. **Imports:** $25.1 bil. (c.i.f., 1989); 23% machinery and parts, 13% petroleum products, 11% chemicals. **Major trading partners:** (1987) **exports:** 18% U.S., 14% Japan, 9% Singapore, Netherlands, Malaysia, Hong Kong; **imports:** 26% Japan, 14% U.S., 7% Singapore, W. Germany, Malaysia, UK.

**Intl. Orgs.** ASEAN, Colombo Plan, FAO, G-77, GATT, IAEA, IBRD, ICAO, IDA, IFAD, IFC, ILO, IMF, IMO, INTELSAT, INTERPOL, ITU, UN, UNESCO, UPU, WHO, WMO.

Ethnic Thai migrating south from China after about A.D. 1000 created a number of petty states in the region, most notably the kingdom of Sukhothai. These came under the influence of Indian civilization from the adjacent states of Burma and the Khmer empire, and Buddhism became established as the dominant religion of the Thai. A unified kingdom of Siam was established c. 1350, with its capital at Ayutthaya. Portuguese and other European traders and missionaries were active in Siam after 1511.

In 1767 Ayutthaya was destroyed in a war with Burma. In 1782 the Chakkri dynasty was established at Bangkok and restored the power of the Thai monarchy. By skillfully playing off the European powers against one another, Kings Mongkut (reigned 1851–68) and Chulalongkorn (reigned 1868–1910) enabled Siam to be the only Southeast Asian nation to escape European colonization or political domination. In a series of treaties with Great Britain and France, however, King Chulalongkorn was forced to renounce Siam's claims to portions of Malaya, Laos, and Cambodia.

Absolute monarchy ended in 1932, when a military coup forced the granting of a constitution. Japanese troops occupied Siam in December 1941. Siam concluded a nominal alliance with Japan in 1942 and declared war on Great Britain and the United States, while at the same time the monarchy secretly supported a strong anti-Japanese resistance movement. A period of postwar political turmoil ended with the accession in 1950 of King Phumiphon, who instituted a reformist and pro-Western policy. Thai politics since World War II have been democratic but dominated by an oligarchy of military officers and civilians with strong military ties.

On Dec. 8, 1990, Prime Minister Chatichai Choonhavan resigned amid charges of corruption and incompetence. Though reappointed by the king the next day, Chatichai was overthrown on Feb. 23 by military forces, who invited former diplomat and businessman Anand Panyarachun to serve as prime minister. Under an interim constitution, new elections must be held by Apr. 30, 1992.

During the Vietnam War, Thailand was an important staging area for American forces. U.S. and other foreign investment has contributed to significant industrialization and economic growth. Large numbers of Lao, Vietnamese, and Cambodian refugees have created a significant foreign-policy problem for Thailand; still, despite these problems and the constant political infighting that destabilizes the Thai government, Thailand has emerged as one of Asia's fastest growing economies.

# Togo
## Republic of Togo

**Geography Location:** western coast of Africa. **Boundaries:** Burkina Faso to N, Benin to E, Gulf of Guinea to S, Ghana to W. **Total land area:** 21,925 sq. mi. (56,785 sq km). **Coastline:** 35 mi. (56 km). **Comparative area:** between Maryland and West Virginia. **Land use:** 25% arable land; 1% permanent crops; 4% meadows and pastures; 28% forest and woodland; 42% other; includes negl. % irrigated. **Major cities:** (1977 est.) Lomé (capital) 229,400; Sokodé 33,500; Palimé 25,500; Atakpamé 21,800; Bassari 17,500.

**People Population:** 3,674,355 (1990). **Nationality:** noun—Togolese (sing., pl.); adjective—Togolese. **Ethnic groups:** 37 groups; largest are Ewe, Mina, and Kabyè; under 1% European and Syrian-Lebanese. **Languages:** French (both official and language of commerce); Ewe and Mina in south, Dagomba and Kabyè in north. **Religions:** about 70% indigenous beliefs, 20% Christian, 10% Muslim.

**Government Type:** republic; one-party presidential regime. **Independence:** Apr. 27, 1960 (from UN trusteeship under French administration). **Constitution:** Dec. 30, 1979. **National holiday:** Independence Day, Apr. 27. **Heads of government:** Gen. Gnassingbé Eyadema, president (since 1967); Kokou J. Koffigoh, prime minister (since Sept. 1991). **Structure:** executive-president; unicameral legislature—National Assembly; judiciary, including State Security Court,

established 1970; Constitution provides for elective presidential system and 67-member National Assembly.

**Economy Monetary unit:** Communauté Financière Africaine (CFA) franc. **Budget:** (1988 est.) **income:** $354.0 mil.; **expend.:** $399.0 mil. **GDP:** $1.4 bil., $405 per capita (1985). **Chief crops:** cash crops—coffee, cocoa, cotton; food crops—yams, cassava, corn, beans, rice. **Livestock:** sheep, goats, pigs, cattle. **Natural resources:** phosphates, limestone, marble. **Major industries:** phosphate mining, agricultural processing, cement, handicrafts, textiles, beverages. **Labor force:** 78% agriculture, 22% industry; about 88,600 wage earners, evenly divided between public and private sectors (1985); 50% of population of working age. **Exports:** $344 mil. (f.o.b., 1988); phosphates, cocoa, coffee, palm kernels. **Imports:** $369 mil. (c.i.f., 1988); food, fuels, durable goods, other intermediate goods, capital goods. **Major trading partners:** (1985) **exports:** 70% EC, 9% Africa, 2% U.S.; **imports:** 69% EC, 10% Africa, 7% Japan, 4% U.S.

**Intl. Orgs.** FAO, G-77, GATT, IBRD, ICAO, IDA, IFAD, IFC, ILO, IMF, IMO, INTERPOL, ITU, NAM, UN, UNESCO, UPU, WHO, WIPO, WMO.

Ewe-speaking peoples began to migrate into what is now Togo, located on Africa's west coast, early in the 14th century. Portuguese explorers arrived in the late 15th century, turning the coast into a point of departure for slaves captured from nearby villages, and between the 1600s and 1800s, the region became known as the "Slave Coast." Germans started to explore and trade in the region in the mid-19th century and declared a protectorate over the area in 1884. After World War I, however, Britain and France divided the nation between them, Britain receiving the western third, France the eastern two-thirds. The League of Nations confirmed this arrangement, giving mandates to British Togoland (later a part of Ghana) and French Togoland.

In 1956 France made French Togo an autonomous republic but retained control of its foreign affairs, defense, and currency; Nicholas Grunitzky was prime minister. The United Nations rejected this plan and in elections in 1958 advocates of complete independence won control of the legislature. On Apr. 27, 1960, French Togo cut its ties with France and became the fully independent Republic of Togo. Sylvanus Olympio became the new nation's first prime minister. Grunitzky went into exile but returned when Olympio was assassinated in January 1963. He led the new government and oversaw the writing of a new constitution allowing more political freedoms.

In 1967 army officers led by Lt. Col. Gnassingbé Eyadema overthrew Grunitzky, suspended the constitution, and named Eyadema president; he has been elected president in 1972, 1979, and 1986.

A new constitution in 1979 provided for a national assembly to serve as a consultative body. A 1986 coup against Eyadema was unsuccessful.

## Tonga
### Kingdom of Tonga

**Geography  Location:** 172 islands in South Pacific Ocean, 36 permanently inhabited. Nuku'alofa 21°09'S, 175°14'W. **Boundaries:** surrounded by South Pacific Ocean; Fiji is about 400 mi. (650 km) to NW and Western Samoa lies N. **Total land area:** 289 sq. mi. (748 sq km). **Coastline:** 260 mi. (419 km). **Comparative area:** about four times size of Washington, D.C. **Land use:** 25% arable land; 55% permanent crops; 6% meadows and pastures; 12% forest and woodland; 2% other. **Major cities:** (1986 census) Nuku'alofa (capital) 28,899; Tongatapu 63,614; Vava'u 15,170; Ha'apai 8,979; 'Eua 4,393.

**People  Population:** 101,313 (1990). **Nationality:** noun—Tongan(s); adjective—Tongan. **Ethnic groups:** Polynesian; about 300 Europeans. **Languages:** Tongan, English. **Religions:** Christian: Free Wesleyan Church claims over 30,000 adherents.

**Government  Type:** constitutional monarchy within Commonwealth. **Independence:** June 4, 1970 (from UK). **Constitution:** Nov. 4, 1875; revised Jan. 1, 1967. **National holiday:** King's Birthday, July 4; Constitution Day, Nov. 4. **Heads of government:** Taufa'ahau Tupou IV, king (since Dec. 1965); Prince Fatafehi Tu'ipelehake, premier (since Dec. 1965). **Structure:** executive—king, cabinet, and privy council; unicameral legislature—28-seat Legislative Assembly consists of king, privy council (composed of eight ministers and governors of Vava'u and Ha'apai), nine representatives of nobles elected by their peers, nine elected representatives of the people elected by the people; king appoints one noble as speaker; judiciary—Supreme Court, magistrate's court, land court.

**Economy  Monetary unit:** Tonga dollar. **Budget:** (1988) *income:* $54.8 mil.; *expend.:* $56.2 mil. **GDP:** $86 mil., $850 per capita (1983). **Chief crops:** dominated by coconut, copra, and banana production; vanilla beans, cocoa, coffee, ginger, black pepper. **Livestock:** poultry, pigs, goats, horses, cattle. **Natural resources:** fish, fertile soil. **Major industries:** tourism, fishing. **Labor force:** 70% engaged in agriculture; 600 engaged in mining. **Exports:** $9.1 mil. (1988 est.); coconut oil, desiccated coconut, vanilla, copra, bananas. **Imports:** $60.1 mil. (1988 est.); textiles, food, consumer products, machinery, petroleum. **Major trading partners:** (1987) *exports:* 54% New Zealand, 30% Australia, 8% U.S., 5% Fiji; *imports:* 39% New Zealand, 25% Australia, 9% Japan, 6% U.S., 5% EC.

**Intl. Orgs.** Commonwealth, FAO, GATT (de facto), IFAD, ITU, UNESCO, UPU, WHO.

The Polynesian islands that now compose Tonga were settled some 3,000 years ago. A highly stratified society evolved; the kings of Tonga dominated much of Polynesia by the 13th century. The islands were visited in 1643 by Abel Tasman, and in 1773 by Capt. James Cook, who named them the Friendly Islands. English missionaries arrived in 1797, and the islands came under British political influence. A code of laws was promulgated in 1862, and a constitutional monarchy established in 1875. A series of treaties with Western powers recognized Tonga's independence, but the kingdom became a British protectorate in 1900.

The islands were outside the Japanese perimeter in the Pacific theater of World War II. On June 4, 1970, the British dissolved their protectorate and the Kingdom of Tonga became independent as a member of the British Commonwealth. The present king, Taufa'ahau Tupou IV, came to the throne in 1965.

The Tongan economy is based on subsistence farming and fishing, with some handicraft industries and light manufacturing. Exports include copra, bananas, and vanilla. The tourist industry is developing rapidly. Remittances from Tongans temporarily working abroad (especially in New Zealand) are an important source of income.

## Trinidad and Tobago
### Republic of Trinidad and Tobago

**Geography  Location:** two islands (Port of Spain, Trinidad Is., 10°38'N, 61°31'W; Tobago Is., 11°11'N, 60°45'W) in southeastern Caribbean Sea, off northeastern South America. **Boundaries:** Caribbean Sea to N and W, Atlantic Ocean to E and S. **Total land area:** 1,980 sq. mi. (5,128 sq km). **Coastline:** 225 mi. (362 km). **Comparative area:** about size of Delaware. **Land use:** 14% arable land; 17% permanent crops; 2% meadows and pastures; 44% forest and woodland; 23% other; includes 4% irrigated. **Major cities:** (1988) Port of Spain (capital) 59,200; San Fernando 33,600; Arima (borough) 29,000.

**People  Population:** 1,344,639 (1990). **Nationality:** noun—Trinidadian(s), Tobagonian(s); adjective—Trinidadian, Tobagonian. **Ethnic groups:** 43% black, 40% East Indian, 14% mixed, 1% white. **Languages:** English (official), Hindi, French, Spanish. **Religions:** 36.2% Roman Catholic, 23% Hindu, 13.1% Protestant, 6% Muslim, 21.7% unknown.

**Government  Type:** parliamentary democracy. **Independence:** Aug. 31, 1962 (from UK). **Constitution:** Aug. 31, 1976. **National holiday:** Independence Day, Aug. 31. **Heads of government:** Noor Mohammed Hassanali, president (since Mar. 1987); Arthur Robinson, prime minister (since Dec. 1976). **Structure:** executive is cabinet led by prime minister; bicameral legislature (36-member elected House of Representatives and 31-member appointed Senate); judiciary headed by chief justice and includes court of appeal, high court, and lower courts.

**Economy  Monetary unit:** Trinidad and Tobago dollar. **Budget:** (1988 est.) *income:* $1.4 bil.; *expend.:* $2.1 bil. **GDP:** $3.75 bil., $3,070 per capita (1986). **Chief crops:** sugar, cocoa, coffee, rice, citrus, bananas; largely dependent on food imports. **Livestock:** pigs, cattle, goats, sheep, buffalo. **Natural resources:** crude oil, natural gas, asphalt. **Major industries:** petroleum, chemicals, tourism. **Labor force:** 463,900 (1986); 47.9% services (1985 est.), 18.1% construction and utilities, 14.8% manufacturing, mining, and quarrying, 10.9% agriculture; 17% unemployment (1986). **Imports:** $1.4 bil. (c.i.f., 1987); 70% petroleum and petroleum products, 15% fertilizer and chemicals, steel products, sugar. **Exports:** $1.2 bil. (c.i.f., 1987); 41% raw materials, 30% capital goods, 29% consumer goods. **Major trading partners:** *exports:* 61% U.S., 15% EC, 9% CARICOM, 7% Latin America; *imports:* 42% U.S., 21% EC, 10% Japan, 6% Canada, 6% Latin America.

**Intl. Orgs.** Commonwealth, FAO, G-77, GATT, IBRD, ICAO, IDA, IFC, ILO, IMF, IMO, INTELSAT, INTERPOL, ITU, NAM, OAS, UN, UNESCO, UPU, WHO, WMO.

Trinidad was a possession of Spain from 1498 to 1797, when it was surrendered to the British. England took control of Tobago in 1802. Together the two islands achieved independence from the UK in 1962. Prime Minister Arthur Robinson's National Alliance for Reconstruction currently governs the country. Civil and political rights are well respected, and political party competition tends to divide along ethnic (black, East Indian) lines. Agrarian reform designed to create tenable landholdings is a central political issue.

In July 1990 militant Muslims seized the prime minister and dozens of others, paralyzing the government and allowing widespread looting. Peace was restored when the government promised reforms.

## Tunisia
### Republic of Tunisia

**Geography  Location:** northern coast of Africa. **Boundaries:** Mediterranean to N and E, Libya to SE, Algeria to W. **Total land area:** 63,170 sq. mi. (163,610 sq km); includes land and inland waters. **Coastline:** 714 mi. (1,148 km). **Comparative area:** between Georgia and Washington. **Land use:** 20% arable land; 10% permanent crops; 19% meadows and pastures; 4% forest and woodland; 47% other; includes 1% irrigated. **Major cities:** (1984 census) Tunis (capital) 596,654; Sfax (Safaqis) 231,911; Ariana 98,655; Bizeria (Bizerie) 94,509; Djerba 92,269.

**People  Population:** 8,095,492 (1990). **Nationality:** noun—Tunisian(s); adjective—Tunisian. **Ethnic groups:** 98% Arab, 1% European, less than 1% Jewish. **Languages:** Arabic (official), Arabic and French (commerce). **Religions:** 98% Muslim, 1% Christian, less than 1% Jewish.

**Government  Type:** republic. **Independence:** Mar. 20, 1956 (from France). **Constitution:** June 1, 1959. **National holiday:** Independence Day, June 1. **Heads of government:** Zine el-Abidine Ben Ali, president (since Nov. 1987); Dr. Hamed Karoui, prime minister (since Sept. 1989). **Structure:** executive dominant; unicameral legislative (National Assembly) largely advisory; judiciary patterned on French and Koranic systems.

**Economy** **Monetary unit:** Tunisian dinar. **Budget:** (1989 est.) **income:** $2.9 bil.; **expend.:** $3.2 bil. **GDP:** $8.7 bil., $1,105 per capita (1987 est.). **Chief crops:** cereals (barley and wheat), olives, grapes, citrus fruits, vegetables; not self-sufficient in food. **Livestock:** sheep, goats, cattle, asses, camels. **Natural resources:** crude oil, phosphates, iron ore, lead, zinc, salt. **Major industries:** petroleum, mining (particularly phosphates and iron ore), textiles. **Labor force:** 2.25 mil.; 32% agriculture; 18% unemployment (1987 est.); shortage of skilled labor. **Exports:** $3.1 bil. (f.o.b., 1989); 40% hydrocarbons, 18% agricultural, 18% phosphates and chemicals. **Imports:** $4.4 bil. (c.i.f., 1989); 57% industrial goods, 13% hydrocarbons, 12% food. **Major trading partners:** **exports:** 73% EC, 9% Middle East, U.S., Turkey, USSR. **imports:** 68% EC, 7% U.S., Canada, Japan, USSR, China.

**Intl. Orgs.** Arab League, FAO, G-77, GATT (de facto), IAEA, IBRD, ICAO, IDA, IFAD, IFC, ILO, IMF, IMO, INTELSAT, INTERPOL, ITU, NAM, OAU, UN, UNESCO, UPU, WHO, WIPO, WMO.

The Phoenicians, an ancient seafaring people from the eastern Mediterranean, founded settlements in Tunisia dating back to 1000 B.C. The most important of these was Carthage, which dominated trade in the central Mediterranean until it was conquered and destroyed by Rome in 146 B.C. Tunisia remained part of the Roman Empire until it was conquered by the Vandals in the mid-fifth century A.D. The Byzantine Empire reconquered Tunisia in the sixth century.

Tunisia became part of the Arab world with the expansion of Islam in the seventh century and soon emerged as a principal center of Islamic culture in North Africa. Tunisia was incorporated into the Ottoman Empire in 1574 and was ruled from Constantinople by Turkish governors, or beys.

With the waning of Ottoman power in the 19th century, Tunisia became a French protectorate in 1881. Nationalist movements began in the early 20th century. During World War II Tunisia was under Vichy French rule and was the scene of fighting between the Axis and Allies in 1942–43. Nationalist unrest resumed when France reestablished its rule in the postwar period. Widespread popular unrest in the early 1950s led to a French grant of self-rule in 1954. Full independence was proclaimed on March 20, 1956; large numbers of French settlers returned to France. The French-sponsored monarchy was abolished in 1957, and the Neo-Destour (New Constitution) party under the leadership of Habib Bourguiba took power. Bourguiba was elected president in 1959 without opposition and was later named president for life. Under Bourguiba's rule, political parties ranging from Communist to monarchist flourished, leading to both democratic politics and political confusion.

Relations with France were strained in 1964 when Tunisia nationalized foreign assets but have since improved. The basic thrust of Tunisian government has been socialist, with state ownership of principal industries and heavy subsidies of basic commodities. In foreign affairs Tunisia has been closely tied to France and has been a moderate voice within the Arab League. The southern Tunisian mining town of Gafsa was invaded by Libya in 1980, but the invasion was repulsed. Tunisia restored diplomatic relations with Libya in 1989.

Popular unrest and labor strife have characterized Tunisia's internal situation in the 1980s, as political maneuvering began in anticipation of the end of the Bourguiba era, which came in 1987 when the aged leader was overthrown by Ben Ali. In 1989 the World Bank approved a loan of $130 million to Tunisia, and new elections were planned as part of a political and economic restructuring.

Tunisia's economy, though plagued by labor difficulties, has developed rapidly, led by textiles, food processing and other light industry, tourism, phosphate mining, and other mineral processing. The large agricultural sector includes grain, olives, dates, and winter fruit and vegetables for export to Europe.

# Turkey
## Republic of Turkey

**Geography** **Location:** partly in southeastern Europe and partly in western Asia. **Boundaries:** Black Sea to N; USSR to NE; Iran to E; Iraq, Syria, Mediterranean Sea to S; Aegean Sea, Greece to W; and Bulgaria to NW. **Total land area:** 300,948 sq. mi. (779,452 sq km). **Coastline:** 4,471 mi. (7,200 km). **Comparative area:** about twice size of California. **Land use:** 30% arable land; 4% permanent crops; 12% meadows and pastures; 26% forest and woodland; 28% other; includes 3% irrigated. **Major cities:** (1985 census) Ankara (capital) 2,235,035; Istanbul 5,475,982; Izmir 1,489,772; Adana 777,554; Bursa 612,510.

**People** **Population:** 56,704,327 (1990). **Nationality:** noun—Turk(s); adjective—Turkish. **Ethnic groups:** 85% Turkish, 12% Kurd, 3% other. **Languages:** Turkish (official), Kurdish, Arabic. **Religions:** 98% Muslim (mostly Sunni), 2% other (mostly Christian and Jewish).

**Government** **Type:** republican parliamentary democracy. **Independence:** Oct. 29, 1923 (from Ottoman Empire). **Constitution:** Nov. 7, 1982. **National holiday:** Republic Day, Oct. 29. **Heads of government:** Turgut Özal, president (since Oct. 1989), Mesut Yilmaz, prime minister (since June 1991). **Structure:** executive—president empowered to call new elections, promulgate laws (elected for 7-year term); unicameral legislature (450-member Grand National Assembly); independent judiciary.

**Economy** **Monetary unit:** Turkish lira. **Budget:** (1988 est.) **income:** $12.1 bil.; **expend.:** $14.5 bil. **GDP:** $75.0 bil., $1,350 per capita. **Chief crops:** cotton, tobacco, cereals, sugar beets, fruits; self-sufficient in food in average years; legal producer of opium poppy for pharmaceutical trade. **Livestock:** sheep, cattle, goats, asses, horses. **Natural resources:** antimony, coal, chromium, mercury, copper. **Major industries:** textiles, food processing, mining (coal, chromite, copper, boron minerals). **Labor force:** 18.8 mil.; 56% agriculture, 30% services, 14% industry; about one million Turks work abroad; 15.3% unemployment (1987). **Exports:** $11.7 bil. (f.o.b., 1988); 70% industrial products, 25% crops and livestock products. **Imports:** $14.3 bil. (c.i.f., 1988); crude oil, machinery, transport equipment, metals, pharmaceuticals. **Major trading partners:** **exports:** 18% W. Germany, 9% Iraq, 8% Italy, 7% U.S., 5% UK, 5% Iran; **imports:** 14% W. Germany, 11% U.S., 10% Iraq, 7% Italy, 6% France.

**Intl. Orgs.** EC (associate member), FAO, GATT, IAEA, IBRD, ICAO, IDA, IFAD, IFC, ILO, IMF, IMO, INTELSAT, INTERPOL, ITU, NATO, UN, UNESCO, UPU, WHO, WIPO, WMO.

The Hittites, an Indo-European people, created an empire in Anatolia before 2000 B.C. and controlled most of what is modern-day Turkey for nearly 1,000 years. The rise of Troy and other Hellenic city-states on the coast of Asia Minor and the expansion of the Assyrian empire led to the collapse of Hittite power by around 900 B.C. Except for some Hellenic enclaves on the Aegean Coast (Ionia), all of Turkey was incorporated into the Persian empire of Cyrus and Darius in the sixth century B.C. Alexander the Great conquered Turkey, but it returned to Persian rule following the collapse of his empire, c. 300 B.C.

All of Turkey, comprising Thracia, Galatia, Cappadocia, Cilicia, and other provinces, was incorporated into the Roman Empire by the end of the first century A.D. Constantine the Great founded the city of Constantinople on the site of ancient Byzantium in 330 as the empire's eastern capital. Following the decline of the western Roman Empire in the seventh century, Constantinople became the capital of the independent Eastern Roman (Byzantine) Empire. The Byzantine Empire fought off repeated attacks by Arab Islamic forces in the seventh and eighth centuries but lost control of central Anatolia to the Seljuk Turkish rulers of Persia after 1038.

The 13th-century Mongol invasions left Turkey largely untouched but weakened both Byzantine and Seljuk power. At the end of the 13th century, the Ottomans, a small Turkish tribe, expanded from their stronghold in western Anatolia and within a century captured most of Turkey, Bulgaria, and Serbia. Constantinople fell to the Ottomans in 1453. By the middle of the 16th century, the Ottoman Empire extended from southeastern Europe into the Crimea and Iran and included most of the Middle East, Egypt, and Arabia.

At its height the Ottoman Empire was a great world power and a substantial participant in European international relations. But beginning in the 18th century, the empire lost much of its autonomy through unequal treaties with European powers, and throughout the 19th century, parts of the empire were detached and either granted independence or placed under European protection. The Ottoman Empire became the "Sick Man of Europe." A liberal constitution was adopted in 1876 but largely ignored until the Young Turk Rebellion of 1908 forced the sultan to accept its provisions.

Siding with the Central Powers in World

War I, the Ottoman Empire lost most of its non-Turkish possessions to the Allies. The Treaty of Sèvres (1920) reduced the Ottoman state to a small part of northern Anatolia. Before the treaty was ratified, however, Kemal Ataturk seized power and regained much territory in a series of campaigns with Soviet assistance. The Treaty of Lausanne (1923) established the present boundaries of Turkey, and Turkey was proclaimed a republic in October 1923. The Caliphate was renounced in 1924, ending the Ottoman claim of spiritual leadership in the Islamic world.

The Turkish Republic became officially a secular and multiethnic state. Large numbers of Armenians had been killed or driven from the country in widespread campaigns of persecution in the late 19th and early 20th centuries; after 1923 most Greek and Bulgarian residents were forcibly repatriated. The large minority of Kurds in southeastern Turkey were pressured to abandon their ethnic identity. Today more than 85 percent of the population is Turkish, ultimately of Central Asian origin. Islam is widely practiced, but the veil and other Islamic dress are prohibited, as are religious political parties. In 1928 the Latin alphabet was adopted in place of Arabic script for writing Turkish. In 1930 Constantinople was officially renamed Istanbul.

Turkey joined the League of Nations in 1932. A series of treaties in the 1930s made small adjustments to Turkey's borders and confirmed Turkey's status as a European nation. Under Ismet Inonu, who became president upon Ataturk's death in 1938, Turkey remained neutral throughout most of World War II but was on friendly terms with the Allied powers. Turkey declared war against Germany in January 1945 and became a founding member of the United Nations at the end of the war.

Following World War II, Turkish relations with the Soviet Union cooled; Turkey became a major recipient of American aid under the Truman Doctrine. Turkish troops joined UN forces in the Korean War. Continuing the Europe-oriented policy instituted by Ataturk, Turkey has joined both NATO and the OECD and is seeking membership in the European Community. Soviet warships are allowed passage through the Bosporus between the Black Sea and the Mediterranean.

In 1974, long-standing discord with Greece erupted over the status of Cyprus, an independent nation with strong ties to Greece. On July 20, 1974, Turkish troops invaded Cyprus, occupying the northeastern 40 percent of the island. The United States cut off military aid to Turkey in 1975. Turkey forced resettlement of Greek and Turkish Cypriot residents; the Turkish sector seceded from Cyprus and became a Turkish federated state on July 8, 1975. American aid was restored in 1978. Despite many attempts at reconciliation, relations between Turkey and Greece remain strained.

Politically, postwar Turkey has alternated between civil and military governments. In the wake of mounting violence, martial law was imposed in 1978, and a military takeover of the government occurred on Sept. 12, 1980. Civil government was restored in 1983, and martial

law lifted in 1984. Communism and other leftist political movements are strongly suppressed, as are Armenian and Kurdish nationalists.

Turkey has tried to remain aloof from the political turmoil of the Middle East, but it was a crucial member of the anti-Iraq coalition in the Persian Gulf War. It supported the UN trade embargo and allowed the allies to use Turkish bases. Turkey's Kurdish problem was aggravated after the war as the country tried to offer humanitarian assistance to Kurdish refugees from Iraq without encouraging Kurdish nationalists at home.

Turkey has a mixed economy. The traditional agricultural and pastoral sectors remain important, but it also has extensive coal reserves and is one of the world's major exporters of chromium. The industrial sector has developed rapidly, particularly in the Istanbul-Izmir region; iron, steel, machinery, automobiles, electric and electronic goods, and other products are made for both domestic use and exportation.

## Tuvalu

**Geography Location:** group of nine small atolls, about 350 mi. (560 km) from N to S, in South Pacific Ocean. Funafuti 8°30′S, 179°12′E. **Boundaries:** surrounded by South Pacific Ocean; Kiribati to N, Fiji to S, Solomon Islands to W. **Total land area:** 10 sq. mi. (26 sq km). **Coastline:** 15 mi. (24 km). **Comparative area:** about 1/10 size of Washington, D.C. **Land use:** 0% arable land; 0% permanent crops; 0% meadows and pastures; 0% forest and woodland; 100% other. **Major cities:** (by atoll; 1985 census) Funafuti (capital) 2,810; Vaitupu 1,231; Niutao 904; Nanumea 879; Nukufetau 694.

**People Population:** 9,136 (1990). **Nationality:** noun—Tuvaluan(s); adjective—Tuvaluan. **Ethnic groups:** 96% Polynesian. **Languages:** Tuvaluan, English. **Religions:** Christian, predominantly Protestant.

**Government Type:** independent state, special member of Commonwealth. **Independence:** Oct. 1, 1978 (from UK). **Constitution:** Oct. 1, 1978. **National holiday:** N.A. **Heads of government:** Tupua Leupena, governor-general (since Mar. 1986); Dr. Tomasi Puapua, prime minister (since Sept. 1981). **Structure:** executive—prime minister and cabinet; unicameral legislature—12-member House of Parliament; judicial—high court, 8 island courts with limited jurisdiction.

**Economy** (1983) **Monetary unit:** Australian dollar. **Budget:** *income:* $2.59 mil.; *expend.:* $3.6 mil. **GNP:** $4.6 mil., $530 per capita (1989 est.). **Chief crops:** coconuts, copra. **Livestock:** pigs. **Natural resources:** none. **Major industries:** fishing, tourism, copra. **Labor force:** N.A. **Exports:** (est.) $1.0 mil.; copra. **Imports:** $2.8 mil.; food, animals, mineral fuels, machinery, manufactured goods. **Major trading partners:** Fiji, Australia, New Zealand.

**Intl. Orgs.** Commonwealth (special member), GATT (de facto), UPU.

A British protectorate was established in 1892, and the islands were incorporated into the British colony of the Gilbert and Ellice Islands in 1915. The nine principal islands that make up the Ellice group escaped Japanese occupation in World War II and were used as Allied bases in the campaign to recapture the Pacific.

The Gilbert and Ellice Islands colony was granted self-rule in 1971. In 1975 the Ellice Islands, inhabited mainly by Polynesians, seceded from the other (mainly Micronesian) islands of the colony and became independent as Tuvalu on Oct. 1, 1978. (See also "Kiribati.") In a 1979 U.S.-Tuvalu friendship treaty, the United States relinquished claims, based on 19th-century guano mining, to the four southernmost islands, in return for access to World War II military airfields and veto power over other nations' use of the islands for military purposes.

The economy is based on subsistence farming and fishing. Exports include copra and woven palm-leaf products, and hydroponic agriculture and offshore fisheries are being developed. Tuvalu remains heavily dependent on foreign aid, principally from Australia, New Zealand, and the United Kingdom.

## Uganda
### Republic of Uganda

**Geography Location:** landlocked equatorial country in eastern Africa. **Boundaries:** Sudan to N, Kenya to E, Tanzania to S, Rwanda to SW, Zaire to W. **Total land area:** 76,084 sq. mi. (197,058 sq km). **Coastline:** none. **Comparative area:** about size of South Dakota. **Land use:** 23% arable land; 9% permanent crops; 25% meadows and pastures; 30% forest and woodland; 13% other; includes negl. % irrigated. **Major cities:** (1980 est.) Kampala (capital) 458,423; Jinja 45,060; Masaka 29,123; Mbale 28,039; Mbarara 23,155.

**People Population:** 17,960,262 (1990). **Nationality:** noun—Ugandan(s); adjective—Ugandan. **Ethnic groups:** 99% African, 1% European, Asian, Arab. **Languages:** English (official), Luganda, Swahili, other Bantu and Nilotic languages. **Religions:** 33% Roman Catholic, 33% Protestant, 16% Muslim, 18% indigenous beliefs.

**Government Type:** republic. **Independence:** Oct. 9, 1962 (from UK). **Constitution:** Sept. 8, 1967, suspended following coup of July 27, 1985. **National holiday:** Independence Day, Oct. 9. **Heads of government:** Yoweri Kaguta Museveni, president (since Jan. 1986); George Kosmas Adyebo, prime minister (since Jan. 1991). **Structure:** president heads National Resistance Council.

**Economy Monetary unit:** Ugandan shilling. **Budget:** (1989 est.) *income:* $365 mil.; *expend.:* $545 mil. **GDP:** $4.9 bil., $300 per capita (1988). **Chief crops:** coffee, cotton, tobacco, tea. **Livestock:** cattle, goats, sheep, pigs, asses. **Natural resources:** copper, cobalt, limestone, salt. **Major industries:** sugar, brewing, tobacco. **Labor force:** 4.5 mil. (1983 est.); 94% subsistence activities, 6% wage earners (est.); 50% of population of working age (1983); N.A. unemployment. **Exports:** $272 mil. (f.o.b., 1988); 97% coffee, cotton, tea. **Imports:** $626 mil. (c.i.f., 1988); petroleum products, machinery, cotton piece goods, metals, transport equipment, food. **Major trading partners: *exports:*** 25% U.S., 18% UK, 11% France, 10% Spain; ***imports:*** 25% Kenya, 14% UK, 13% Italy.

**Intl. Orgs.** Commonwealth, FAO, G-77, GATT, IAEA, IBRD, ICAO, IDA, IFAD, IFC, ILO, IMF, INTELSAT, INTERPOL, ITU, NAM, UN, UNESCO, UPU, WHO, WIPO, WMO.

Prior to 1800 Uganda was the site of several important kingdoms, notably Buganda, centered on Kampala on the northern shore of Lake Victoria. After 1830 Arabs from the sultanate of Oman, based in Zanzibar, asserted loose control over the region and dominated its trade. British explorers, seeking the source of the Nile, reached the Lake Victoria region in the mid-19th century. Mission stations were established in 1877; a Muslim rebellion destroyed the missions and occupied Kampala in 1888.

Buganda was brought under the control of the British East Africa Company in 1890, and Britain established a protectorate in 1894 that was expanded to include neighboring territories in 1896. In 1902 some of the protectorate's territory was transferred to Kenya. British immigrants extensively developed the agricultural potential of Uganda's fertile and temperate highlands, establishing large and prosperous farms. Lake Victoria was the scene of naval battles between Great Britain and Germany (established in neighboring Tanganyika) during World War I.

In 1955 the British administration created a local parliamentary government in which both whites and Africans held ministerial office. Talks on the terms for independence began in 1961 and after some difficulty arrived at a formula for a national structure in which Buganda and other traditional kingdoms would retain local autonomy. Several political parties competed for power; the Uganda People's Congress led by Milton Obote gradually became dominant. Uganda became independent within the British Commonwealth on Oct. 9, 1962.

Several constitutional changes in the early 1960s led to an end to the autonomy of the kingdoms and the effective concentration of all power in Obote's presidency. In 1967 a new constitution proclaimed Uganda an independent republic.

Obote was overthrown on Jan. 25, 1971, by Idi Amin Dada, commander of Uganda's armed forces. Amin declared himself president, dissolved the parliament, and assumed absolute powers. In 1972 he expelled nearly all of Uganda's Asians (primarily people of Indian and Pakistani descent), who controlled most of the country's small-scale commerce. The United States broke off diplomatic relations in 1973. In 1976 Amin declared himself president for life. His eight-year reign was marked by extreme violence and persecution of political and tribal opponents; as many as 300,000 Ugandans may have been killed between 1971 and 1979. The country's prosperous agricultural, mining, and commercial economy was devastated, and its infrastructure, including a good road and rail network and

Makerere University, one of Africa's preeminent educational institutions, fell into ruins.

On July 3, 1976, Israeli airborne troops landed at Entebbe and rescued 103 hostages who had been captured in a skyjacking carried out by Palestinian and German terrorists.

In 1978 Amin, with the aid of Libyan troops, invaded Tanzania. In the following year, Tanzanian troops countered by invading Uganda; they captured Kampala on Apr. 11, 1979, and drove Amin into exile. Diplomatic relations with the United States resumed. After a series of interim governments, elections in 1981 returned Obote to power. Obote's new regime was marked by fierce repression of opponents and by the outbreak of rebellion in the northern part of the country by the National Resistance Army (NRA) under Yoweri Museveni.

Obote fled into exile in 1985 and was succeeded by Lt. Gen. Basilio Olara-Okello, but the NRA rebellion continued. Kenyan president Daniel arap Moi mediated peace talks between Olara-Okello and the NRA in late 1985; in January 1986 Olara-Okello fled into exile, and Museveni organized a new government. Despite continued insurgencies by rival military factions and a rebellion led by the charismatic religious leader Alice Lakwena, the Museveni government has generally restored order and, with aid from the World Bank and the IMF, has begun to rebuild Uganda's shattered society. In 1987 Uganda joined in talks with Kenya and Tanzania designed to promote closer political and economic relations in East Africa.

Nearly three decades of misrule have left Uganda in desperate economic straits, and despite its resources it is one of the poorest countries in Africa. Inflation, corruption, and public disorder are continuing problems. In addition, the country is threatened by an extensive epidemic of AIDS.

# Union of Soviet Socialist Republics

**Geography  Location:** central Asia; largest country in world. **Boundaries:** Arctic Ocean to N; Pacific Ocean to E; China, Mongolia, Afghanistan, Iran, and Black Sea to S; Turkey, Bulgaria, Romania, Hungary, Czechoslovakia, Poland, and Baltic Sea to W; Finland and short frontier with Norway to NW. **Total land area:** 8,599,228 sq. mi. (22,272,000 sq km). **Coastline:** 26,582 mi. (42,777 km). **Comparative area:** slightly less than 2.5 times size of U.S. **Land use:** 10% arable land; negl. % permanent crops; 17% meadows and pastures; 41% forest and woodland; 32% other; includes 1% irrigated. **Major cities:** (1989 est.) Moskva (Moscow—capital) 8,967,000; St. Petersburg (Leningrad) 5,020,000; Kiyev (Kiev) 2,587,000; Tashkent 2,073,000; Baku 1,757,000.

**People  Population:** 290,938,469 (1990). **Nationality:** noun—Soviet(s); adjective—Soviet. **Ethnic groups:** 52% Russian, 16% Ukrainian, 32% other; 100 ethnic groups. **Languages:** Russian (official); more than 200 languages and dialects (at least 18 with more than one million speakers); 75% Slavic group, 12% Altaic,

8% other Indo-European, 3% Uralian, 2% Caucasian. **Religions:** 70% atheist, 18% Russian Orthodox, 9% Muslim, 3% Jewish, Protestant, Georgian Orthodox, or Roman Catholic.

**Government  Type:** communist state. **Independence:** N.A. **Constitution:** Oct. 7, 1977. **National holiday:** October Revolution Day, Nov. 7. **Heads of government:** Mikhail Sergeyevich Gorbachev, president (since Mar. 1985; title was general secretary prior to Mar. 15, 1990); Ivan Silayev, prime minister (since Sept. 1991). **Structure:** executive—State Council; legislative—Supreme Soviet, made up of the Council of the Republics and Council of the Union; judicial—Supreme Court of USSR.

**Economy  Monetary unit:** ruble. **Budget:** (1989 est.) *income:* $622 bil.; *expend.:* $781 bil. **GNP:** $2,659.9 bil., $9,211 per capita. **Chief crops:** grain (especially wheat), potatoes, sugar beets, cotton, sunflowers, flax; degree of self-sufficiency depends on fluctuations in crop yields, particularly grain; large grain importer over past decade. **Livestock:** sheep, cattle, pigs, goats, horses. **Natural resources:** self-sufficient in oil, natural gas, coal, and strategic minerals, except bauxite, alumina, tantalum, tin, tungsten, fluorspar, and molybdenum; timber, gold, manganese, lead, zinc, nickel, mercury, potash, phosphates. **Major industries:** diversified, highly developed capital goods industries; consumer goods industries comparatively less developed. **Labor force:** civilian 150 mil. (1988); 78% industry and other nonagricultural fields; 22% agriculture; shortage of skilled labor; **Exports:** $110.7 bil. (f.o.b., 1988); petroleum and petroleum products, natural gas, metals, wood, agricultural products, wide variety of manufactured goods (primarily capital goods and arms). **Imports:** $107.3 bil. (f.o.b.,1988); grain and other agricultural products, machinery and equipment, steel products (including large-diameter pipe), consumer manufactures. **Major trading partners: *exports:*** 49% Eastern Europe, 14% EC, 5% Cuba, U.S., Afghanistan; ***imports:*** 54% Eastern Europe, 11% EC, Cuba, China, U.S.

**Intl. Orgs.** IAEA, ICAO, ILO, IMO, ITU, UN, UPU, WHO, WIPO, WMO.

In the ninth century A.D., Viking traders organized a state, which they called Rus, in the river valleys between the Baltic and the Black seas, centered on the cities of Kiev and Novgorod. In time the Vikings were absorbed into the native Slavic population; in 998 a Ruthenian prince of Kiev accepted Christianity from Constantinople. In the 13th century, Mongols under Genghis Khan and his descendants conquered most of Russia, and the Mongol Golden Horde maintained its power through the 14th century, exercising loose control over Novgorod and Moscow.

From the mid-14th century, Moscow grew to become the center of a new state that gathered in other lands and territories as Mongol power waned. Ivan III (Ivan the Great, 1440–1505) consolidated the power of Moscow; his marriage to a Byzantine princess led him to regard his empire as a third Rome, heir to the religious tradition of Constantinople. His grandson, Ivan IV (Ivan the Terrible, 1530–84), adopted the title czar (from the Latin *caesar*) when he came to power. He broke the power of the aristocratic boyar class and greatly extended the power of Moscow through military conquest.

Over the next two centuries, Russia carried out a steady program of expansion eastward into Siberia and across the Bering Strait to Alaska, until the empire covered one-sixth of the land surface of the globe. Peter the Great (1672–1725) made Russia a Baltic and Black sea naval-power, brought Russia into the European state system, and instituted a sweeping, if superficial, Westernization of his realm. His new capital at St. Petersburg (now Leningrad) became one of the most splendid cities in Europe. At the end of the 18th century, Catherine the Great (1729–96) participated with Prussia and Austria in the partitions of Poland, and Russia thereby became a major power in central Europe.

Catherine's grandson Alexander I (1777–1825), member of the grand coalition that defeated Napoleon, was not only czar of Russia but also king of Poland and grand duke of Finland. His troops occupied Paris in 1815. The Russian aristocracy became ardent Francophiles in the 19th century, ignoring growing problems at home. After losing the Crimean War in 1856, Russia began to develop Siberia and the southern territories near the border of Persia. Alaska was sold to the United States in 1867. In a major reform of the agricultural system, serfdom was abolished under Alexander II in 1861, though the newly independent peasantry, organized into agricultural cooperatives, only slowly derived benefits from its freedom. The late 19th century also marked the beginning of modern industrialization in Russia and of extensive development in Siberia, aided by state investment in railroads and mining.

Under the last czar, Nicholas II (1868–1918), Russia was defeated by Japan in a war over Manchuria in 1905. The defeat sparked a naval mutiny and an abortive revolution, which led to the establishment of a constitutional monarchy and other limited political reforms. Further military losses in World War I set the stage for the monarchy's downfall in the Revolution of 1917.

The initial revolution of March 1917 brought a relatively moderate socialist (Menshevik) group to power. Its principal leader, Aleksandr Kerensky, organized a republican government and tried to maintain the Russian war effort but failed to gain control of the many contending revolutionary factions of the time. The Germans allowed the radical Bolshevik leader, V.I. Lenin, to return to Russia, where he and his followers organized workers' soviets hostile to the Menshevik republic. Bolshevik forces occupied Leningrad on Nov. 7, 1917 (October in the old Byzantine calendar, hence the name October Revolution), arrested the cabinet, and put in place a Council of People's Commissars, under Lenin's chairmanship. There followed four years of civil war between Bolshevik, Menshevik, and czarist forces, in the course of which Nicholas II and his family were executed in 1918.

Decreeing land to the peasants, worker management in industry, and repudiation of czarist

---

---

debts, the Bolsheviks won the survival of their regime by withdrawing from World War I. The 1918 Treaty of Brest-Litovsk, which gained peace with Germany, granted freedom to Finland, the Baltic republics, Poland, the Ukraine, and Bessarabia. At the conclusion of the civil war (complicated by a war with Poland) in 1921, the Soviet state was established, with the Ukraine reabsorbed into the Soviet Union. The Bolshevik victory also resulted in the creation in 1921 of the Mongolian People's Republic as a close Soviet ally.

The early 1920s are now remembered as a "golden age" of Soviet history. Lenin's "New Economic Policies" allowed some role for market forces and private ownership and led to a brief burst of economic growth. Art, literature, and science flourished in an atmosphere of revolutionary enthusiasm and little censorship.

Lenin died on Jan. 21, 1924, and after a power struggle, was succeeded by Josef Stalin. Stalin supported communist revolutions in China and elsewhere through the Communist International (Comintern) but generally withdrew from foreign engagements in order to concentrate on domestic affairs. Under Lenin, and even more under Stalin, the Communist party established a police state, condemning millions of people to internal exile in the 1920s and consolidating all power in the hands of the state. In 1929 agriculture was forcibly collectivized, leading to the starvation or execution of an estimated 10 million peasants, while forced industrialization was carried out under a series of five-year plans.

Stalin's chief rival, Leon Trotsky, was expelled from the USSR in 1929 (and assassinated by Stalinist agents in Mexico in 1940).

---

Stalin's obsession with eliminating all possible rivals for power led to a series of purges which, at their height in 1934–39, saw the summary execution of hundreds of thousands of presumed "enemies of the state" and the imprisonment in concentration camps of millions more.

Russia's reemergence as a world power was signaled by the signing in August 1939 of the Hitler-Stalin Pact, a nonaggression treaty through which Stalin aimed to recover territories lost to Russia in 1918. Poland was again partitioned, Bessarabia annexed (as the Moldavian Republic), Finland conquered and partitioned, and the Baltic republics absorbed.

When, in June 1941, Hitler turned against his ally and invaded Russia, unprepared and ill-equipped Russian armies retreated on a broad front. But Stalin emerged as a national leader in the "Great Patriotic War," restructuring the army and enlisting the support of the Orthodox church in rallying the population. In the early winter of 1942, the war changed course as Russia broke the German siege of Stalingrad, and Russian armies began their westward push that would carry them to the Elbe River by April 1945.

By the end of World War II, Stalin had reestablished the old czarist boundaries of Russia, and he had a ring of occupied states along his western boundary and a divided Germany beyond. Over the years 1945–48, he engineered a thorough communization of those occupied states, turning them into Russian satellites. Only Yugoslavia escaped total Russian domination.

Stalin died in March 1953. He was succeeded by a collegial form of party and government leadership, from which Nikita Khrushchev, the party chairman, gradually emerged as the paramount figure. In a secret speech to the party leadership in 1956, Krushchev denounced Stalin for crimes against the party. He announced a set of new policies designed to bring about rapid modernization and consolidated his power when he became premier in 1958. The Khrushchev years brought a small but steady rise in living standards and a "thaw" in police state methods, the KGB (state security police) being brought under party control.

In foreign policy there was a thaw as well. In 1953 the Soviets agreed to an armistice in Korea, and tolerated the formation of a more liberal government in Hungary. In 1955 Russia returned the Porkkala peninsula to Finland and agreed to the Austrian State Treaty, which created an independent and neutral Austria. But the limits of disengagement became clear in 1956 with the ruthless Soviet suppression of the Hungarian uprising. A summit conference between Khrushchev and Eisenhower in 1960 led to a propaganda victory for Russia when an American U-2 spy plane was shot down over Russian territory on May 1. And in 1962 Khrushchev tried to install Soviet missiles in Cuba, a reckless adventure from which he had to back down during the "Cuban Missile Crisis."

While on vacation in 1964, Khrushchev was removed from office and replaced as party secretary by Leonid Brezhnev and as premier by Aleksei Kosygin. His failure to deliver on extravagant promises for domestic economic growth and his recklessness in foreign affairs seem to have been responsible for his downfall. The new leaders embarked on an ambitious program of military (and especially naval) expansion. They also pressed ahead vigorously with a space program that had begun with the triumphant launching of Sputnik I in 1957.

Under Brezhnev and Kosygin the USSR became more aggressive in foreign policy. The severe suppression of Czechoslovakia's "Prague Spring" in 1968 occasioned development of the Brezhnev Doctrine, whereby Russia claimed the right to intervene militarily in any socialist state. Soviet involvement in the Third World grew, with Russia supporting Vietnam against China; Syria and the PLO against Israel; leftist regimes in Angola, Ethiopia, and elsewhere in Africa; and the Sandanistas in Nicaragua. Cuba emerged as the principal Soviet proxy in supplying troops for leftist causes in the Third World. In 1979 Soviet troops moved into Afghanistan, allegedly at the invitation of its Marxist government, and remained bogged down there for a decade. Under American pressure, Brezhnev permitted the emigration of about 130,000 Jews and 40,000 ethnic Germans in the 1970s.

Domestically, the regime grew more oppressive; censorship was tightened and dissidents sentenced to terms in penal mental institutions. Elitism and nepotism created a self-perpetuating and interlocking network of power at the top, while the nation as a whole stagnated.

Brezhnev's death in 1982 brought about a rapid series of leadership transfers. Yuri Andropov, for 15 years head of the KGB, succeeded Brezhnev as party secretary but died after only 15 months in office. The downing by Soviet fighters of a Korean Airlines 747 on Sept. 1, 1983, brought a chill to Soviet-U.S. relations. Andropov was succeeded by Konstantin Chernenko, who died 13 months later. In March 1985 Mikhail Gorbachev became party secretary, ushering in a new era in Soviet history.

Gorbachev first instituted a cautious shake-up of state and party bureaucrats, promoting younger men who were technocrats rather than party professionals. Under the slogan *glasnost* (openness, candor), censorship was relaxed; by 1988 criticism of not only Stalin but also Brezhnev was permitted, and policy was openly debated in the press. Jamming of broadcasts from the West was ended. By the end of 1990 freedom of the press and of religion had been approved, and private citizens were given the right to own small businesses.

Gorbachev's other motto, *perestroika* (restructuring), addresses his aim to boost morale and increase economic efficiency by devolving responsibility for economic decisions away from the party and government and toward industrial and agricultural managers. Borrowing from the Chinese experience in agricultural reform and the Hungarian model of decentralized industrial management, perestroika has so far raised expectations but not output; the system remains sluggish, inefficient, and burdened with the vested interests of state

## UNION REPUBLICS OF THE USSR

| Union republic[1] | Area (sq km) | Population | Capital |
|---|---|---|---|
| Armenia | 29,800 | 3,283,000 | Yerevan |
| Azerbaidzhan[2] | 86,600 | 7,029,000 | Baku |
| Byelorussia | 207,600 | 10,200,000 | Minsk |
| Estonia[3] | 45,100 | 1,573,000 | Tallinn |
| Georgia[4] | 69,700 | 5,449,000 | Tbilisi |
| Kazakhstan | 2,717,300 | 16,538,000 | Alma-Ata |
| Kirghizstan | 198,500 | 4,291,000 | Frunze |
| Latvia[3] | 64,600 | 2,681,000 | Riga |
| Lithuania[3] | 65,200 | 3,690,000 | Vilnius |
| Moldavia | 33,700 | 4,341,000 | Kishiniev |
| Russia[5] | 17,075,400 | 147,386,000 | Moscow |
| Tadzhikistan | 143,100 | 5,112,000 | Dushanbe |
| Turkmenistan | 488,100 | 3,534,000 | Ashkhabad |
| Ukraine | 603,700 | 51,704,000 | Kiev |
| Uzbekistan[2] | 447,400 | 19,906,000 | Tashkent |

**Note:** One square kilometer equals 0.386 square miles. 1. All are designated Soviet Socialist Republics (SSR), except Russian Soviet Federated Socialist Republic (RSFSR). 2. Includes one autonomous republic. 3. Granted independence Sept. 6, 1991. 4. Includes two autonomous republics. 5. Includes 16 autonomous republics. **Source:** State Committee on Statistics of the USSR (1990).

planners. The nuclear power plant disaster at Chernobyl in April 1986 and a gas pipeline fire that killed hundreds of passengers in passing railroad trains in June 1989 exemplify the industrial mismanagement against which Gorbachev's policies are aimed. During 1989–91 there were strikes by coal miners, and shortages of food and consumer goods worsened.

In foreign policy Gorbachev has pursued arms reduction agreements with the United States and has withdrawn Soviet forces from Afghanistan. His international stature exceeds that of any previous Soviet leader; but his principal problems remain at home.

Foremost among these is the nationalities question. The southern Muslim regions of the USSR have been the scene of turmoil since the anti-Russian riots in Kazakhstan in 1986; in 1988 riots broke out in the Christian republic of Armenia over the status of ethnic Armenians in the neighboring Muslim republic of Azerbaidzhan, while the disastrous Armenian earthquake of 1988, and the ineptness of disaster relief efforts, added fuel to Armenian grievances against the central government. Fighting in Armenia and Azerbaidzhan worsened in 1989–90, leading to a breakdown of government control in some areas. Ethnic warfare between Uzbeks and Turks in Uzbekistan led to numerous deaths, and sporadic violence in other Central Asian republics broke out in 1990.

In the northwest, the Baltic republics of Estonia, Latvia, and Lithuania raised their old national flags over their parliaments, enacted laws giving their native languages priority over Russian, and proclaimed the superiority of local republican law over the laws of the Soviet Union. Lithuania proclaimed its independence from the USSR in December 1989, provoking a confrontation with strong international ramifications; Lithuania finally agreed to postpone its independence in 1990 pending negotiations with the Soviet government. Meanwhile, Latvia also signaled its intention to declare inde-

pendence in the near future. Within the USSR itself, the Russian Republic elected maverick Boris Yeltsin as president and pressed for greater autonomy; Yeltsin resigned from the Communist party in July 1990.

The total collapse of communist governments in Eastern Europe in 1989–90 added to Gorbachev's problems and led to the dissolution of the Warsaw Pact and the Council for Mutual Economic Assistance (COMECON) in 1991.

Gorbachev responded to these problems by assuming the presidency of the USSR and increasing the powers of that office, and he held off challenges to his leadership in 1990–91. Yet defections from the party by both right- and left-wing groups threw the party's future role in the USSR itself into doubt. Public demonstrations against Gorbachev and the Communist party took place in Moscow and elsewhere as the economy worsened and food supplies dwindled

In the spring of 1991, Boris Yeltsin was elected president of the Russian Republic in the first direct elections for the post. His stature soared when he rallied opposition to an unsuccessful coup to topple Gorbachev in August. In the wake of the coup, the Baltic republics of Estonia, Latvia, and Lithuania were granted independence.

(See Part I, "The Year in Review.")

## United Arab Emirates

**Geography Location:** eastern Arabian peninsula. **Boundaries:** Persian Gulf to N, Gulf of Oman to NE, Oman to E, Saudi Arabia to S and W, short frontier with Qatar to NW. **Total land area:** 32,270 sq. mi. (83,600 sq km). **Coastline:** 899 mi. (1,448 km). **Comparative area:** between South Carolina and Maine. **Land use:** negl. % arable land; negl. % permanent crops; 2% meadows and pastures; negl. % forest and woodland; 98% other; includes negl. % irrigated. **Major cities:** (1980 census) Abu Dhabi (capital) 242,975; Dubai 265,702; Sharjah 125,149; Ras al-Khaimah 42,000.

**People Population:** 2,253,624 (1990). **Nationality:** noun—Emirian(s); adjective—Emirian. **Ethnic groups:** 19% Emirian, 23% other Arab, 50% South Asian (fluctuating), 8% other expatriates (includes Westerners and East Asians); less than 20% of population are UAE citizens (1982). **Languages:** Arabic (official), Hindi, Urdu; Farsi and English widely spoken in major cities. **Religions:** 96% Muslim (16% Shia), 4% Christian, Hindu, and other.

**Government Type:** federation with specified powers delegated to UAE central government and other powers reserved to member sheikhdoms. **Independence:** Dec. 2, 1971 (from UK). **Constitution::** Dec. 2, 1971 (provisional). **National holiday:** Dec. 2. **Head of government:** Sheikh Zayed bin Sultan al-Nahyan of Abu Dhabi, president (since Dec. 1971); Maktoum Bin Rashid Al-Makoum, vice president (since Nov. 1990) and prime minister (since July 1979). **Structure:** executive—Supreme Council of Rulers (seven members), from which president and vice president are elected; prime minister and Council of Ministers; unicameral legislature—Federal National Council; judicial—Union Supreme Court.

**Economy Monetary unit:** UAE dirham. **Budget:** (1989 est.) *income:* $3.5 bil.; *expend.:* $4.0 bil. **GNP:** $23.3 bil., $11,680 per capita. **Chief crops:** food imported; some dates, alfalfa, vegetables, fruit, tobacco. **Livestock:** goats, sheep, camels, cattle. **Natural resources:** crude oil, natural gas. **Major industries:** petroleum, fishing, petrochemicals. **Labor force:** 580,000 (1986 est.); 85% industry and commerce; 80% of labor force is foreign; negl. unemployment (1987). **Exports:** $10.6 bil. (f.o.b., 1988 est.); 75% crude oil, natural gas, reexports, dried fish, dates. **Imports:** $8.5 bil. (f.o.b., 1988 est.); food, consumer and capital goods. **Major trading partners:** *exports:* U.S., EC, Japan; *imports:* EC, Japan, U.S.

**Intl. Orgs.** Arab League, FAO, G-77, GATT (de facto), IAEA, IBRD, ICAO, IDA, IFAD, IFC, ILO, IMF, IMO, INTELSAT, INTERPOL, ITU, NAM, OPEC, UN, UNESCO, UPU, WHO, WIPO.

In the 1820s Great Britain established protectorates over seven small sheikhdoms along the gulf coast between Qatar and Oman—Abu Dhabi, Dubai, Sharjah, Ajmar, Fujairah, and Umm al-Qaiwain. The region, which had been known as the Pirate Coast, then was generally referred to as the Trucial Coast or Trucial Oman. Under terms of a supplementary treaty in 1892, the sheikhdoms agreed not to enter into relations with any other country.

After Great Britain announced that it would withdraw its forces from the gulf in 1971, the seven sheikhdoms formed a federation and became independent as the United Arab Emirates on Dec. 2, 1971.

The economy, formerly limited to herding of nomadic sheep and camels, oasis agriculture, coastal shipping, and pearl diving, is now almost entirely dominated by petroleum. Citizens of the UAE receive extensive social services and enjoy one of the world's highest per capita incomes.

Just prior to his invasion of Kuwait in August 1990, Saddam Hussein threatened both the UAE and Kuwait for overproduction of petroleum, and the UAE was an integral part of the allied coalition against Iraq.

# United Kingdom
### United Kingdom of Great Britain and Northern Ireland

**Geography Location:** northwestern Europe, occupying major portion of British Isles. **Boundaries:** Atlantic Ocean to NW and W, North Sea to E; separated from France by English Channel to S; Republic of Ireland to W. **Total land area:** 94,249 sq. mi. (244,103 sq km). **Coastline:** 7,723 mi. (12,429 km). **Comparative area:** slightly smaller than Oregon. **Land use:** 29% arable land; negl. % permanent crops; 48% meadows and pastures; 9% forest and woodland; 14% other; includes 1% irrigated. **Major cities:** (1988 est.) Greater London (capital) 6,735,400; Birmingham 993,700; Glasgow 703,200; Sheffield 528,300.

**People Population:** 57,365,665 (1990). **Nationality:** noun—Briton(s), British (collective pl.); adjective—British. **Ethnic groups:** 81.5% English, 9.6% Scottish, 2.4% Irish, 1.9% Welsh, 1.8% Ulster, 2.8% West Indian, Indian, Pakistani, and other. **Languages:** English, Welsh (about 26% of population of Wales), Scottish form of Gaelic (about 60,000 in Scotland). **Religions:** 27 mil. Anglican, 5.3 mil. Roman Catholic, 2.0 mil. Presbyterian, 760,000 Methodist, 450,000 Jewish (registered).

**Government Type:** constitutional monarchy. **Independence:** N.A. **Constitution:** unwritten; partly statutes, partly common law and practice. **National holiday:** birthday of queen, June 16. **Heads of government:** Elizabeth II, queen (since Feb. 1952); John Major, prime minister (since Nov. 1990). **Structure:** executive authority lies with collectively responsible cabinet led by prime minister; legislative authority rests with Parliament (House of Lords, House of Commons); House of Lords is supreme judicial authority and highest court of appeals.

**Economy Monetary unit:** British pound or pound sterling. **Budget:** (1989) *income:* $348.7 bil.; *expend.:* $327.8 bil. **GDP:** $818 bil., $14,300 per capita. **Chief crops:** wheat, barley, potatoes, sugar beets, dairy products; 62.1% self-sufficient (1983); dependent on imports for more than half of consumption of refined sugar, butter, oils and fats, bacon, ham. **Livestock:** chickens, sheep and lambs, cattle, pigs, ducks, geese. **Natural resources:** coal, crude oil, natural gas, tin, limestone. **Major industries:** machinery and transportation equipment, metals, food processing. **Labor force:** 28.2 mil. (1988); 52.1% services, 23.4% manufacturing and construction, 10.5% self-employed; 8.1% unemployment. **Exports:** $151 bil. (f.o.b., 1989); manufactured goods, machinery, fuels, chemicals, semifinished goods, transport equipment. **Imports:** $189.2 bil. (c.i.f., 1989); manufactured goods, machinery, semifinished goods, foodstuffs, consumer goods. **Major trading partners:** *exports:* 50% EC (12% W. Germany, 10% France, 7% Netherlands), 13% U.S., 2% communist countries; *imports:* 53% EC (17% W. Germany, 9% France, 8% Netherlands), 10% U.S., 2% communist countries.

**Intl. Orgs.** Colombo Plan, EC, FAO, GATT, IAEA, IBRD, ICAO, IDA, IFAD, IFC, ILO, IMF, IMO, INTELSAT, INTERPOL, ITU, NATO, OECD, UN, UPU, WHO, WIPO, WMO.

Early megalithic and Iron Age peoples of Britain, primarily Celtic, developed tribal petty states that were conquered by Roman invaders in A.D. 43. After Roman legions withdrew from Britain in 410, invasions of Jutes, Angles, and Saxons conquered much of England, while Celtic peoples flourished in Wales, Scotland, and especially Ireland. Viking invaders established settlements in the eighth century. A united Saxon kingdom fell to the Norman invasion of William the Conquerer in 1066.

An aristocratic rebellion against the royal absolutism of King John in 1215 led to the royal acceptance of the Magna Carta, guaranteeing legal rights and laying the foundations of parlia-

mentary government. From the 12th to the 15th century, the Plantagenet dynasty ruled England and claimed overlordship over Ireland; Wales was conquered in 1283. The Plantagenets also controlled sizable territories in France.

The Hundred Years' War (1337–1453) cost England its French possessions; the War of the Roses, (1455–85) ended the Plantagenet dynasty and brought Henry Tudor (Henry VII) to the throne. The Tudors gradually centralized royal control by bringing pressure against both the church and the nobility. Henry VIII broke with Rome in 1534 and established the Church of England. Under Elizabeth I, the last of the Tudors, England defeated Spain at sea and laid the foundations of later worldwide English sea power. The English Renaissance began under Elizabeth I (1533–1603) with the works of Shakespeare and continued into the 17th century with Milton and Newton.

The Stuart dynasty was founded by James I (1566–1625), uniting the crowns of England and Scotland. The English Civil War (1642–49) culminated in the execution of Charles I and the proclamation of the Commonwealth (later the Protectorate) under Oliver Cromwell. The monarchy was restored with Charles II in 1660. In the bloodless Glorious Revolution (1688), James II fled before a Protestant army under the Dutch William of Orange, who married and ruled jointly with James's daughter Mary II. The English Bill of Rights established the supremacy of Parliament and made the government a model of constitutional monarchy.

In the last gasp of the Stuart claimants to the throne, Irish supporters of James II were defeated at the Battle of the Boyne (1690), which temporarily crushed Irish resistance to annexation by England. The United Kingdom was created when Scotland was joined with England in a common Parliament by the Act of Union in 1707. A Scottish uprising led by the Young Pretender, Charles Edward Stuart, was crushed at Culloden Moor in 1745. Ireland was made part of the United Kingdom in 1801.

In the 1700s the United Kingdom became the greatest sea power in the world, controlling an empire that included much of North America and India. Agrarian "enclosures" of the 18th century ruined the British peasantry but created an entrepreneurial revolution in agriculture that ultimately led to greatly increased agricultural productivity. The capital created in the process contributed to the success of the Industrial Revolution, which over the next century made England the wealthiest land on Earth.

Despite the loss of the 13 colonies after the American Revolution (1775–83), England consolidated its holdings in the Indian subcontinent, Australia and New Zealand, Malaya, Hong Kong, much of eastern Africa from "Cape to Cairo," and elsewhere. Britain's prosperity and moral purpose were embodied in the person of Victoria, Queen of Great Britain and Ireland (1836–1901) and Empress of India (from 1836).

The repeal of the protectionist Corn Laws in 1846 led to an agricultural depression and hastened the migration of labor from the countryside to the industrial cities. The rise of labor activism led in 1906 to laws granting privileged status to trade unions, which organized the Labour party to promote their interests.

Britain's involvement in the Triple Entente with France and Russia ensured its participation in World War I (1914–18) against Germany, Italy, and Austria-Hungary. Victory came at the cost of an entire generation of British youth, but Britain emerged from the war with its empire at a high point, adding Tanganyika, Jordan, Palestine, and Iraq as part of the postwar division of spoils. Most of Ireland became independent in 1921, however, leaving only Northern Ireland as part of the United Kingdom.

Between the two world wars, Britain's navy and air force were the largest in the world, its army the third largest. Yet its industry was aging, the Great Depression hit especially hard in the British Isles, strikes and labor unrest weakened the social fabric, and colonial ties began to weaken in the 1930s. Economic retrenchment led to a failure to rearm in the face of the rising threat of Hitler's Germany and Mussolini's Italy.

The Munich Pact of 1938 gave Hitler a license for war; his invasion of Poland in 1939 forced Britain into the conflict. When Winston Churchill became prime minister in 1940, Britain was under daily air attack and in danger of an invasion by sea, and the country was dependent on American friendship and lend-lease war materials. But 1941 brought alliance with the United States and the Soviet Union, and a slowly turning tide of war leading to victory in 1945. Still, postwar Britain quickly dropped to the second rank of superpowers.

The coalition between the Conservative and Labour parties that had governed Great Britain during the war seemed no longer necessary in 1945 as the war wound down. Labour won a landslide victory in the 1945 elections; Churchill was recalled in the midst of the Potsdam Conference, and Clement Atlee became prime minister. A brief Labour flirtation with the USSR quickly ended in the postwar 1940s; England became a founding member of the United Nations and also, in 1949, of NATO. As the Cold War took shape, Britain developed its own nuclear arsenal.

The Labour party nationalized the Bank of England along with railroads, public utilities, and heavy industry. A comprehensive welfare state apparatus was created, including a national health service, unemployment and retirement benefits, and free education at all levels. But postwar Britain was in many respects too poor to afford such changes; in order to cut expenditures, the government hastened the process of withdrawal from colonies and military bases around the world. India was granted its independence in 1947, and Palestine, Burma, and Ceylon in 1948; others would follow later.

The elections of 1951 brought Churchill back to the prime ministership at the head of a Conservative majority that would last for 13 years. The Conservatives returned steel and trucking to the private sector but in general refrained from undoing the social policies of their Labour predecessors. Economic growth began in the 1950s and held steady at about 2.5 percent per year, a significantly lower rate than in contemporary continental Europe; obsolescence, excessive wage and benefit settlements with labor, and a low savings rate all took their toll. The coronation of Elizabeth II in 1953 added a much-needed element of national celebration.

Churchill retired in 1955 and was succeeded by Anthony Eden. Eden's government fell in 1956 over the failed and bungled Anglo-French invasion of Suez. Eden's fall in 1957 brought to power Harold Macmillan, who pursued close relations with the United States. Most important, he presided over the transformation of an empire to a commonwealth; in the early 1960s, Ghana, Nigeria, Malaya, Singapore, and numerous other colonies were granted independence and Commonwealth status. Immigrants from the Commonwealth promptly flocked to England, straining housing, social services, and the labor market and creating problems of assimilation that remain unsolved.

Britain under Macmillan was the moving force behind the European Free Trade Association in 1960. In 1961 Britain applied for membership in the EEC, but that application was humiliatingly vetoed by France's Charles de Gaulle in 1963. Macmillan's government fell with the Profumo Scandal of 1963, and Douglas Home became a caretaker prime minister pending new elections.

The 1964 elections brought the Labour party to power under Harold Wilson, whose moderate positions made him unpopular with his own party, especially when he sponsored legislation to ban wildcat strikes. Strikes, wage inflation, the steady growth of the public sector (including renationalization of the steel industry), and the rise of turmoil in Northern Ireland in 1968–69 combined to make public support for Labour evaporate.

The Conservative victory in the 1970 elections brought Edward Heath to the office of prime minister. Promising to cut expenditures and taxes, reward initiative, and curb union power, the Conservatives were able to accomplish none of those aims. Heath's government imposed ineffective wage controls in an attempt to slow inflation and passed the 1971 Industrial Relations Act to regulate unions. When unions defied that act, the government fell. Heath's major achievement was the United Kingdom's admission to the EC in 1973. Continued turmoil in Northern Ireland was met with the abolition of Ulster's Stormount Parliament in 1972 and the imposition of direct British rule—a policy that did nothing to stem the growing sectarian violence.

Wilson returned to the prime ministership in 1974 and retired in 1976, passing on the office to James Callaghan, who governed until 1979 at the head of a Labour-Liberal coalition. The continued power of trade unions was seen in the repeal of the Industrial Relations Act and the extension of union privileges. The left wing of the Labour party brought increasing pressure against defense spending, membership in NATO, and the policy of moderation in Rhodesia, and also loudly criticized American foreign policy.

The OPEC oil price rises of 1972–74 hurt Great Britain in the short run but also encouraged development of oil and gas fields in the North Sea, which made the nation a major petroleum exporter and helped revitalize its economy. Oil exploration in the North Sea also encouraged Scottish nationalism, with some damage to national unity, although in both Scotland and Wales, proposals in 1979 for separate parliaments were soundly defeated by plebiscites.

The 1979 elections brought the Conservatives to power again, behind Margaret Thatcher, Great Britain's (and Europe's) first female prime minister. She proved to be the only British prime minister in modern times to lead her party successfully in three elections. Thatcher took office with an agenda that involved undoing much of the course of postwar British history.

The first target was inflation, attacked through a freeze on expenditures and reduction of government borrowing. The policy was a success; inflation fell from 18 percent in 1980 to 3 percent in 1989. But the austerity program had a high cost in unemployment, which remained at 14 percent in the mid-1980s, higher in older industrial areas.

In 1982 national attention turned abruptly to overseas concerns, as Argentina invaded the Falkland ("Malvinas") Islands (only 300 miles east of Argentina), which it had long claimed as Argentine national territory, on April 2. On May 21 British forces launched a counteroffensive, and the invading Argentine forces surrendered on June 14. The nation's success in mounting an amphibious operation 6,500 miles away provoked an upsurge of British patriotism at home that swept Thatcher's party into a second term of office in 1983.

After the election the government turned to denationalization, or privatization, of industry. Over $30 billion in state property—from industrial giants, such as Britoil and British Gas, to individual apartments in municipal housing projects—was sold to private interests. This program was followed in 1986 by tax cuts, in which the top income-tax rate dropped from 98 percent to 60 percent. In foreign affairs, Britain agreed in 1985 to return Hong Kong to Chinese sovereignty in 1997.

The 1987 elections pitted the Conservatives against a weak Liberal-Social Democratic alliance that opposed NATO missile deployment in Great Britain, advocating unilateral disarmament and calling for renationalization of industry and a return to higher taxes for the wealthy. By 1989 the "Thatcher Revolution" had produced a decisive long-term economic recovery, but one that was unevenly distributed: the southern part of the country enjoyed an economic boom, while the older industrial cities of the north remained stagnant. In 1990 an economic slowdown and rising inflation led to a strong decline in support for Mrs. Thatcher and her government. The imposition of a per-capita tax, intended to replace property taxes, met with strong public opposition and led to her resignation in November 1990.

Thatcher was replaced by Chancellor of the Exchequer John Major, whose domestic policy problems include rebuilding university education, which was severely constrained by the spending cuts of the early 1980s, and imposing the central government's discipline on quasi-independent local government authorities. In foreign affairs the key question is Britain's role in the united Europe, which is scheduled to become a reality in 1992, and to which Britain will have a land link (for the first time in 9,000 years) via the 31-mile Channel Tunnel (Chunnel), as of 1993.

The British Empire, now a shadow of its former grandeur, remains a global responsibility for the British government. The governments of Britain and Ireland are actively cooperating to seek a peaceful solution to the perennial "Irish Question." The turmoil in China has raised questions about the security of the 1984 Sino-British Agreement on Hong Kong; Spain continues to call for a referendum aimed at returning Gibraltar to Spanish control. Other island possessions of long standing, such as the Isle of Man, the Channel Islands, and Bermuda, remain serene, enjoying their status as tourist economies and tax havens.

## United States of America

**Geography Location**: 48 conterminous states in North America, between Atlantic and Pacific Oceans; Alaska in northwest North America; Hawaiian islands in Pacific Ocean about 3,000 miles W of California. **Boundaries**: Canada to N; Atlantic Ocean to E; Gulf of Mexico, Mexico to S; Pacific Ocean to W. Alaska bounded on E by Canada, on S and W by Pacific Ocean, on W and N by Arctic Ocean. **Total land area**: 3,449,120 sq. mi. (9,372,610 sq km). **Coastline**: 11,954 mi. (19,924 km). **Comparative area**: between Brazil and Canada; fourth largest country. **Land use**: 20% arable land; negl. % permanent crops; 26% meadows and pastures; 29% forest and woodland; 25% other; includes 2% irrigated. **Major cities**: New York 7,322,564; Los Angeles 3,485,398; Chicago 2,783,726; Houston 1,630,533; Philadelphia 1,585,577; San Diego 1,110,549; Detroit 1,027,974; Dallas 1,006,877.

**People Population**: 248,709,873 (1990 census). **Nationality**: noun—American(s); adjective—American. **Ethnic groups**: 80.3% white, 12.1% black, 2.9% Asian or Pacific Islander, 0.8% American Indian, Eskimo, or Aleut, 3.9% other; 9% Hispanic origin (of any race) (1990 census). **Languages**: predominantly English; sizable Spanish-speaking minority. **Religions**: 61% Protestant (21% Baptist, 12% Methodist, 8% Lutheran, 4% Presbyterian, 3% Episcopalian, 13% other Protestant), 25% Roman Catholic, 2% Jewish, 5% other, 7% none.

**Government Type**: federal republic; strong democratic tradition. **Independence**: July 4, 1776 (from England). **Constitution**: Sept. 17, 1787, effective June 21, 1788. **National holiday**: Independence Day, July 4 (1776). **Head of government**: George Bush, president (since 1989); Dan Quayle, vice president (since 1989). **Structure**: executive—president, vice president, cabinet; legislative—bicameral congress (House of Representatives

and Senate); judicial—Supreme Court; branches, in principle, independent and maintain balance of power.

**Economy Monetary unit**: United States dollar ($); $1 = 100 cents. **Budget**: (1989 est.) **revenues**: $976.0 bil.; **expend.**: $1,137.0 bil. **GNP**: $5,233.3 bil., $21,082 per capita (1989). **Chief crops**: food grains, feed crops, oil-bearing crops; world's second-largest producer and number-one exporter of grain; an illegal producer of cannabis. **Livestock**: cattle, pigs, lamb. **Natural resources**: coal, copper, lead, molybdenum, phosphates, uranium, bauxite, gold, iron, mercury, nickel, potash, silver, tungsten, zinc, crude oil, natural gas, timber. **Major industries**: leading industrial power in the world, highly diversified; petroleum, steel, motor vehicles, aerospace, telecommunications, chemicals, electronics, food processing, consumer goods, fishing, lumber, mining. **Labor force**: 125,557,000 (includes armed forces and unemployed); civilian labor force 123,869,000 (1989); 5.5% unemployment (1988). **Exports**: $322.3 bil. (f.o.b., 1988); **commodities**—capital goods, automobiles, consumer goods, industrial raw materials, food and beverages. **Imports**: $440.9 bil. (f.o.b., 1988); **commodities**—crude and partly refined petroleum, machinery, automobiles, consumer goods, industrial raw materials, food and beverages. **Major trading partners**: exports: Canada 23%, Japan 12%; imports: Japan 20%, Canada 19%.

**Intl. Orgs.** Colombo Plan, FAO, GATT, IAEA, IBRD, ICAO, IDA, IFAD, IFC, ILO, IMF, IMO, INTELSAT, INTERPOL, ITU, NATO, OAS, OECD, UN, UPU, WHO, WIPO, WMO.

(For current events and history see Part I, "The Year in Review," and Part II, "Chronology of American History.")

## Uruguay
### Oriental Republic of Uruguay

**Geography Location**: southeastern coast of South America. **Boundaries**: Brazil to N, Atlantic Ocean to E and S, Argentina to W. **Total land area**: 68,037 sq. mi. (176,215 sq km). **Coastline**: 410 mi. (660 km). **Comparative area**: slightly smaller than Washington State. **Land use**: 8% arable land; negl. % permanent crops; 78% meadows and pastures; 4% forest and woodland; 10% other; includes 1% irrigated. **Major cities**: (1985 census) Montevideo (capital) 1,246,500; Salto 77,400; Paysandú 75,200; Las Piedras 61,300; Rivera 55,400.

**People Population**: 3,036,660 (1990). **Nationality**: noun—Uruguayan(s); adjective—Uruguayan. **Ethnic groups**: 88% white, 8% mestizo, 4% black. **Languages**: Spanish. **Religions**: 66% Roman Catholic, 2% Protestant, 2% Jewish, 30% nonprofessing or other (less than half adult population attends church regularly).

**Government Type**: republic. **Independence**: Aug. 25, 1828 (from Brazil). **Constitution**: Nov. 27, 1966; effective Feb. 1967; suspended June 27, 1972; new constitution rejected by referendum, Nov. 30, 1980. **Nation-**

**al holiday**: Independence Day, Aug. 25. **Heads of government**: Dr. Luis Alberto Lacalle, president (since Mar. 1990). **Structure**: executive, headed by president; bicameral legislature (Senate and House of Deputies); national judiciary headed by Court of Justice.

**Economy Monetary unit**: Uruguayan peso. **Budget**: (1988) **income**: $1.2 bil.; **expend.**: $1.4 bil. **GDP**: $8.8 bil., $2,950 per capita (1988 est.). **Chief crops**: wheat, rice, corn, sorghum; large areas devoted to extensive livestock grazing; self-sufficient in most basic foodstuffs. **Livestock**: sheep, cattle, horses, pigs. **Natural resources**: soil, hydropower potential, minor minerals. **Major industries**: meat processing, wool and hides, sugar. **Labor force**: 1.3 mil. (1988 est.); 25% government; 19% manufacturing; 12% commerce; 12% utilities, construction, transport, and communications; 11% agriculture; 9% unemployment (1988 est.). **Exports**: $1.5 bil. (f.o.b., 1989 est.); 17% hides and leather goods, 10% beef, 9% wool, 7% fish, 4% rice. **Imports**: $1.1 bil. (f.o.b., 1989 est.); fuels and lubricants (15%), metals, machinery, transportation equipment, industrial chemicals. **Major trading partners**: *exports*: 17% Brazil, 15% U.S., 10% W. Germany, 10% Argentina; *imports*: 24% Brazil, 14% Argentina, 8% U.S., 8% W. Germany.

**Intl. Orgs.** FAO, G-77, GATT, IAEA, IBRD, ICAO, IFAD, IFC, ILO, IMF, IMO, INTELSAT, INTERPOL, ITU, OAS, UN, UNESCO, UPU, WHO, WIPO, WMO.

Uruguay was known as the Banda Oriental del Uruguay (Eastern Shore of the Uruguay River) during the colonial period. Although the Spanish first explored the area in 1516, they did not immediately settle there. Instead, the Portuguese founded the Colonia de Sacramento, near Buenos Aires, in 1680. They did not permanently establish the settlement of Montevideo until 1726. Under the leadership of José Gervasio Artigas, Uruguayans fought against both the Portuguese and the junta of Buenos Aires between 1811 and 1814 in an effort to establish their independence; in 1815 they proclaimed the Autonomous Government of the Eastern Provinces.

In 1817 the Portuguese again took control of the region, but Uruguayan nationals ousted them in 1828. A new constitution for the country was promulgated in 1830; however, domestic rivalry among elites soon led to civil war. The two contending factions, Liberals (Colorados) and Conservatives (Blancos), wore red and white armbands, respectively. Civil war continued through the 1840s and 1850s, until the victory of the Colorados in 1865. In the War of the Triple Alliance (1865–70), Uruguay allied itself with Argentina and Brazil against Paraguay. The consequence of the war for Uruguay was the definitive establishment of its independence from the other regional powers.

The Colorado party dominated Uruguayan government from 1865 until 1958. Waves of European immigrants transformed Uruguayan society during the latter half of the 19th century, and by 1880 immigrants made up almost half of the population. The last civil war between the Blancos and the Colorados took place in 1904; the Colorados won a definitive victory under Pres. José Batlle y Ordóñez, one of Uruguay's major political figures.

Batlle inaugurated a labor and social-welfare reform program that created Latin America's first eight-hour working day as well as progressive legislation on women's rights. A proposal for the extension of the franchise to women was put forward in 1917. Impressed with the Swiss plural executive Federal Council during his stay in Switzerland, Batlle believed such a structure could help Uruguay avoid the Latin American hazard of *caudillismo* (authoritarian rule). Batlle proposed the idea of a plural executive, and a version of the idea became part of the constitution that went into effect in 1919. The new constitution provided for both a president and a collegial National Council, both of which would make up the executive structure of the government.

In 1933 Uruguay experienced a military coup sponsored by Pres. Gabriel Terra, who sought to dissolve both the legislature and the National Council and to reestablish the single executive presidential system. He managed this by sponsoring a constituent assembly that drew up a new constitution in 1934. In a 1951 plebiscite, Uruguayan voters approved a return to the plural executive system, and a new constitutional order reflecting this went into effect the following year. The debate over the form of the executive was not over, however; in 1966 the public voted for yet another constitution, which once again established the single president as the executive power.

Uruguay's economy began to falter during the 1950s. This, combined with the expansion of governmental bureaucracy tied to the country's social welfare programs, led to increasing popular discontent. In 1958 the Blancos won two successive victories at the polls (for the first time in nearly a century). A candidate from the conservative wing of the Colorado party, Jorge Pacheco Areco, regained the presidency for the traditional ruling party in 1967, but neither the Blancos nor the Colorados were able to effectively deal with Uruguay's deteriorating economy or with its growing political unrest.

Uruguay's politics became increasingly polarized during the 1960s and into the 1970s. The leftist National Liberation Movement (MLN or Tupamaros), formed in 1967 and began urban guerrilla activity that included robbery and kidnapping. The Tupamaros, many of whom were young and middle class, embarrassed government officials and the police and were largely successful in eroding the public image of the civilian government. Tupamaro activity generated violence from the military and police, and as the political situation deteriorated in the early seventies, the government granted the military ever-expanding authority to deal with the situation.

By 1973 the military was in control of the country, and they dissolved the Congress. The military allowed Pres. Juan María Bordaberry to remain in office until 1976, at which time they installed Aparicio Méndez in the presidency. It was Bordaberry, however, who proposed the dismantling of the political parties in 1976. Uruguayan military rule was brutally repressive, and the armed forces perpetrated many human rights abuses (kidnapping, torture, murder). By some estimates, the Uruguayan military regime had the world's largest number of political prisoners in proportion to the population.

The military government held a plebiscite in 1980 on a new constitution that would have amounted to continued de facto military control. The popular vote went against the military, and a slow process of political transition began, in which the military tried to bargain with civilian political elites. In 1984 the civilian Colorado candidate Julio María Sanguinetti was elected to the presidency. He took office the following year as the military withdrew from governance, restoring civilian rule.

Luis Alberto Lacalle, a conservative member of the Blanco party, won the November 1989 presidential election, but his party failed to win a legislative majority, forcing the new president into a political pact with some opposition Colorado party members.

## Vanuatu
### Republic of Vanuatu

**Geography Location:** chain of 12 principal and some 60 smaller islands in Pacific Ocean, about 500 mi. (800 km) W of Fiji and 1,100 mi. (2,800 km) E of Australia. Port Vila 17°45′S, 168°18′E. **Boundaries:** surrounded by South Pacific Ocean; nearest neighbor is Santa Cruz Islands to N. **Total land area:** 4,707 sq. mi. (12,190 sq km). **Coastline:** 1,571 mi. (2,528 km). **Comparative area:** slightly larger than Connecticut. **Land use:** 1% arable land; 5% permanent crops; 2% meadows and pastures; 1% forest and woodland; 91% other. **Major cities:** (1989) Port Vila (capital) 19,000.

**People Population:** 165,006 (1990). **Nationality: noun**—Vanuatuan(s); adjective—Vanuatuan. **Ethnic groups:** 94% indigenous Melanesian, 4% French; remainder Vietnamese, Chinese, and various Pacific Islanders. **Languages:** English and French (official); pidgin (known as Bislama or Bichelam). **Religions:** most at least nominally Christian.

**Government Type:** republic. **Independence:** July 30, 1980 (from France and UK). **Constitution:** July 30, 1980. **National holiday:** July 30. **Heads of government:** Fred Karlomoana Timakata, president (since Jan. 1989); Father Walter Hadye Lini, prime minister (since July 1980). **Structure:** unicameral legislature (46-member Parliament).

**Economy** (1988 est.) **Monetary unit:** vatu. **Budget: income:** $80.1 mil. **expend.:** $86.6 mil. **GDP:** $120 mil., $820 per capita. **Chief crops:** export crops of copra, cocoa, coffee, and fish; subsistence crops of copra, taro, yams, coconuts, fruits, vegetables. **Livestock:** poultry, cattle, pigs, goats, horses. **Natural resources:** manganese, hardwood forests, fish. **Major industries:** food and fish-freezing, forestry processing, meat cannning. **Labor force:** N.A. **Exports:** $16.0 mil. (f.o.b., 1988 est.); 37% copra, 11% cocoa, 9% meat, 8% fish, 4% timber. **Imports:** $58.0 mil. (c.i.f., 1988 est.); 25% machines and vehicles, 23% food and beverages, 18% basic manufactures, 11% raw materials and fuels, 6% chemicals. **Major trading partners: exports:** 34% Netherlands, 27% France, 17% Japan, 4% Belgium, 3% New Caledonia; **imports:** 36% Australia, 13% Japan, 10% New Zealand, 8% France, 5% Fiji.

**Intl. Orgs.** Commonwealth, FAO, G-77, IBRD, ICAO, IDA, IFC, IMF, ITU, NAM, UN, WHO, WMO.

Formerly known as the New Hebrides, Vanuatu is a rugged, volcanic island chain with heavily forested mountains; peaks rise to over 6,000 feet (on Espiritu Santo, the largest island). The people are Melanesians. In 1887 the islands were placed under the administration of an Anglo-French naval commission, becoming a joint Anglo-French colony (condominium) in 1906. The islands escaped Japanese occupation during World War II; they sided with the Free French and were used as bases for Allied campaigns in the Pacific. The New Hebrides were granted independence as Vanuatu on July 30, 1980, with membership in the British Commonwealth. The government is a parliamentary system, complemented by a National Council of Chiefs to decide matters of tradition and customary law.

The economy is based on subsistence agriculture, cattle raising, and fishing. Tourism is developing rapidly, and the sale of long-term tuna-fishing rights, principally to Japan, Australia, and the United States, is an important earner of foreign exchange.

## Venezuela
### Republic of Venezuela

**Geography Location:** northern coast of South America. **Boundaries:** Caribbean Sea to N, Guyana to E, Brazil to S, Colombia to W. **Total land area:** 352,144 sq. mi. (912,050 sq km). **Coastline:** 1,739 mi. (2,800 km). **Comparative area:** about 1.3 times size of Texas. **Land use:** 3% arable land; 1% permanent crops; 20% meadows and pastures; 39% forest and woodland; 37% other; includes negl. % irrigated. **Major cities:** (1989) Caracas (capital) 3,373,059; Maracaibo 1,365,308; Valencia 1,227,472; Maracay 923,673; Barquisimeto 764,216.

**People Population:** 19,698,104 (1990). **Nationality: noun**—Venezuelan(s); adjective—Venezuelan. **Ethnic groups:** 67% mestizo, 21% white, 10% black, 2% Indian. **Languages:** Spanish (official), Indian dialects (spoken by about 200,000 Amerindians in remote interior). **Religions:** 96% nominally Roman Catholic, 2% Protestant.

**Government Type:** republic. **Independence:** July 5, 1821 (from Spain). **Constitution:** Jan. 23, 1961. **National holiday:** Independence Day, July 5. **Head of government:** Dr. Carlos Andrés Pérez, president (since Feb. 2, 1988). **Structure:** executive (president); bicameral legislature (National Congress—Senate, Chamber of Deputies); judiciary.

**Economy** Monetary unit: bolívar. **Budget:** (1989) *income:* $8.4 bil.; *expend.:* $8.6 bil. **GDP:** $52.0 bil., $2,700 per capita. **Chief crops:** cereals, fruits, sugar, coffee, rice; illegal producer of cannabis for international drug trade. **Livestock:** cattle, pigs, goats, horses, asses, sheep. **Natural resources:** crude oil, natural gas, iron ore, gold, bauxite. **Major industries:** petroleum, iron ore mining, construction materials. **Labor force:** 5.8 mil. (1985); 56% services, 28% industry, 16% agriculture; 7% unemployment (1988). **Exports:** $10.4 bil. (f.o.b., 1988); 81% petroleum, bauxite, aluminum, iron ore, agricultural products. **Imports:** $10.9 bil. (f.o.b., 1988); foodstuffs, chemicals, manufactures, machinery, transport equipment. **Major trading partners:** (1987) *exports:* 50% U.S., 4.7% W. Germany, 3.1% Japan, 2.6% Netherlands; *imports:* 44% U.S., 8.5% W. Germany, 6% Japan, 5% Italy, 4.4% Brazil.

**Intl. Orgs.** FAO, G-77, IAEA, IBRD, ICAO, IFAD, IFC, ILO, IMF, IMO, INTELSAT, INTERPOL, ITU, OAS, OPEC, UN, UNESCO, UPU, WHO, WMO.

At the time of European contact in the early 16th century, coastal Venezuela was home to nearly 50,000 semisedentary Indians. Although the region was "discovered" by Christopher Columbus in 1498, European settlement of the area was slow in comparison with the neighboring region of New Granada. The Spaniards explored and exploited Venezuela in the 1520s, their activity originally characterized by gold and pearl expeditions.

Early attempts at agriculture by the Spaniards failed until they discovered that the area around Caracas (founded in 1567) could sustain the production of both wheat and cocoa. African slave labor was an important part of the economic structure of the area, and as markets for cocoa expanded, Caracas grew in importance. Venezuela became a captaincy general (an administrative region below the level of viceroyalty) with an *audiencia* (high court) established at Caracas in 1777–78.

As early as 1797, Venezuelan society was in rebellion against the Spanish empire. A major hindrance to the revolutionary leadership of Simón Bolívar was the need to accommodate both the conservative landowners of the white elite and the *pardos*, lower class citizens of mixed African and European ancestry.

The wars of independence were particularly destructive in Venezuela, but by 1821 the region had achieved its independence and had become part of the federation of Gran Colombia, which also included Colombia and Ecuador. By 1830 Gran Colombia was in a state of political collapse, and Venezuela became an independent republic.

The militarization of Venezuela that resulted from the protracted independence struggle had profound consequences for the country's politics. The military caudillo (leader) José Antonio Páez controlled the country for three decades. With the demise of Antonio Páez and his conservative allies in the 1860s, the forces of liberalism under the control of Guzmán Blanco took over. The Guzmán Blanco era ended during a brief civil war in 1889. The victor of the strug-

gle, Gen. Cipriano Castro, proceeded to establish his own rule. In 1909 Gen. Juan Vicente Gómez occupied the presidency, and he controlled the politics of Venezuela until his death, in 1935.

The shift from dictatorship to democracy began with the Generation of 28, a student movement that organized urban workers and peasants into a viable political opposition. The Generation of 28 later became the modern Democratic Action party. In 1945 a group of young military officers, the Patriotic Military Union, overthrew the conservative dictatorship and supported the Democratic Action group in writing a new democratic constitution. Democratic Action won the elections of 1947, but conservative military elements overthrew the new government the following year. The conservative coup brought Col. Marcos Pérez Jiménez to power until his ouster in 1958.

The election of Democratic Action candidate Romulo Betancourt as president marks the beginning of stable multiparty democratic politics in Venezuela. The stability of the system owes much to political possibilities provided by the country's petroleum revenues. Just as important has been an agreement between the major political parties and their respective elites that ensures that no one group will lose its political standing completely as a result of an electoral loss.

Despite the nationalization of foreign-owned oil and iron firms in 1976, Venezuela's dependence on petroleum revenues precipitated economic and political problems for the country in the 1980s. The downturn of the global oil market caused Venezuela's economic base to shrink, and the country's massive foreign debt has hindered the expansion of populist political strategies.

The Christian Democrats defeated Democratic Action in 1968 and again in 1978. Pres. Luis Herrera Campíns's administration took the country in a more conservative direction for a short time. The Christian Democrat government was a vociferous supporter of Argentina's claim to the Falkland Islands in Argentina's war against Great Britain. Democratic Action regained the presidency in 1983 under the leadership of Jaime Lusinchi. Venezuela, as an original member of the multinational Latin American diplomatic organization, the Contadora group, made an early contribution to the international effort to bring about a diplomatic solution to conflicts in Central America.

Venezuela's foreign debt has been a major issue. The Lusinchi administration successfully renegotiated a debt package in 1985, but the resulting constraints on social programs have posed serious problems for the peaceful governance of the country. Riots protesting government policy followed the inauguration of the new president in 1989.

---

# Vietnam
### Socialist Republic of Viet Nam
**Geography Location:** Southeast Asia. **Boundaries:** China to N, Gulf of Tonkin to NE, South China Sea to E, Laos and Cambodia to W.

**Total land area:** 127,246 sq. mi. (329,566 sq km). **Coastline:** 2,140 mi. (3,444 km) excluding islands. **Comparative area:** between New Mexico and Montana. **Land use:** 22% arable land; 2% permanent crops; 1% meadows and pastures; 40% forest and woodland; 35% other; includes 5% irrigated. **Major cities:** (1989) Hanoi (capital) 1,088,862; Ho Chi Minh City (formerly Saigon) 3,169,135; Haiphong 456,049; Da Nang 370,670; Long Xuyen 217,171.

**People Population:** 66,170,889 (1990). **Nationality:** noun—Vietnamese (sing., pl.); adjective—Vietnamese. **Ethnic groups:** 85-90% Vietnamese, 3% Chinese; ethnic minorities include Muong, Thai, Meo, Khmer, Man, Cham; other mountain groups. **Languages:** Vietnamese (official); French, Chinese, English, Khmer, ethnic langs. (Mon-Khmer and Malayo-Polynesian). **Religions:** Buddhist, Confucian, Taoist, Roman Catholic.

**Government Type:** communist state. **Independence:** Sept. 2, 1945 (from France). **Constitution:** Dec. 18, 1980. **National holiday:** Sept. 2. **Heads of government:** Vo Chi Cong, president, (since June 1987); Du Muoi, prime minister (since June 1988). **Structure:** highest authority of land is technically Council of State, whose chairman serves as country's president; Council of Ministers oversees implementation of party policies—chairman is equivalent of premier; unicameral legislature (National Assembly).

**Economy Monetary unit:** new dong. **Budget:** (1987 est.) *income:* $3.2 bil.; *expend.:* $4.3 bil. **GNP:** $14.2 bil., $215 per capita (1989 est.). **Chief crops:** rice, rubber, fruits, vegetables; some corn, manioc, sugarcane; major food imports—wheat, corn, dairy products. **Livestock:** pigs, buffalo, cattle, goats, horses. **Natural resources:** phosphates, coal, manganese, bauxite, apatite. **Major industries:** food processing, textiles, machine building. **Labor force:** 32.9 mil. civilians (1987); 10% unemployment (1988 est.). **Exports:** $1.1 bil. (f.o.b., 1988); agricultural and handicraft products, coal, minerals, ores. **Imports:** $2.5 bil. (c.i.f., 1988); petroleum, steel products, railroad equipment, chemicals, medicines. **Major trading partners:** USSR, Eastern Europe, Japan, Singapore.

**Intl. Orgs.** Colombo Plan, FAO, G-77, IAEA, IBRD, ICAO, IDA, IFAD, IFC, ILO, IMF, INTELSAT, ITU, NAM, UN, UNDP, UNESCO, UNICEF, UPU, WHO, WIPO, WMO.

The southward expansion of the Chinese empire in the first millennium B.C. drove the Vietnamese peoples southward into northern Vietnam (Tonkin). The area came under direct Chinese rule in 111 B.C. Chinese rule endured, with some interruptions, until A.D. 948; thereafter, Vietnam was independent under strong Chinese influence.

The Hindu-Buddhist kingdom of Annam, in central Vietnam, gradually increased in size and power at the expense of Tonkin, to the north, and the Khmer empire and Champa, to the west and south. In 1558 the Kingdom of Annam split, with independent courts established at Hanoi, controlling Tonkin and the Red

River valley, and Hue, in central Vietnam. A remnant of the old Champa state remained independent in the Mekong delta in the south. In 1802 the monarchy was reunited, with the court at Hue controlling all of Vietnam and exercising hegemony over Cambodia.

European penetration of the region began in the 16th century; by the early 19th century, France was the dominant foreign power in Indochina. Efforts to establish French military control began in 1858–59 with the establishment of a colony in Cochin China, in southern Vietnam. Campaigns in the Red River valley in 1873 and 1882 were complicated by Chinese intervention and the determined resistance of the Vietnamese court. In 1884 separate protectorates were established in Tonkin and Annam; in 1887 those, along with Cochin China and Cambodia, were combined into the Union of Indochina under French colonial rule. Rubber plantations were established, and rice and timber exports were under French control. A nationalist rebellion under Phan Boi Chau was suppressed in the early 20th century.

Nationalist resistance to French colonialism continued, resulting in the creation in 1939 of the Vietminh, or Independence League. In 1940 Japanese troops occupied French Indochina, with the collaboration of colonial administrators loyal to the Vichy regime. The Vietminh spearheaded anti-Japanese guerrilla resistance and in 1945 forced the abdication of King Bao Dai, head of a pro-Japanese puppet state. In 1945 France reoccupied Indochina; in 1946 the leader of the Vietminh, Ho Chi Minh, became president of a separatist government at Hanoi. France ceded local autonomy to Tonkin and Annam but sought to retain Cochin China as a colony. Fighting between the French and the Vietminh resumed. On July 1, 1949, the French reinstalled Bao Dai as king of Vietnam, and in February 1950 recognized the independence of Vietnam within the French Union. Ho Chi Minh's republican government also claimed control of all of Vietnam.

Fighting between the two rivals culminated in the French defeat at Dienbienphu on May 7, 1954. An armistice was concluded according to which the country was partitioned at a demilitarized zone at latitude 17° north, the northern part going to the communist-controlled Vietminh government, the southern to Bao Dai. Nearly one million refugees, including many ethnic Chinese, fled from the north to the south. An international conference in Geneva agreed that elections would be held throughout Vietnam in 1956. In June 1954 Ngo Dinh Diem became premier of South Vietnam; full sovereignty in the south was transferred by France to the Vietnamese government in December 1954. In October 1955 Diem held elections in the south that resulted in the dismissal of Bao Dai as king and the proclamation of an independent Republic of Vietnam.

The scheduled elections of 1956 were never held. French troops completed withdrawal from South Vietnam in that year. Fighting continued in the south, as the Vietminh-backed National Liberation Front (Vietcong) sought to overthrow the Diem government. On Dec. 31, 1959, the Democratic Republic of Vietnam in the north adopted a new constitution calling for the reunification of the country; northern aid to the Vietcong increased significantly, as did American aid to the south. After 1962 American military advisers steadily increased in number and combat exposure.

In 1963 widespread public demonstrations, under Buddhist leadership, led to a coup on Nov. 1–2 in which Diem was deposed and assassinated. A series of short-lived military regimes followed until September 1967, when Nguyen Van Thieu was elected president. U.S. air strikes against North Vietnam began in 1964. In the same year, the flow of troops and supplies from north to south increased markedly. American combat troops entered the war in 1965. Despite U.S.–South Vietnamese superiority in arms and troops, and total control of the air, Vietcong control over the countryside increased. Both Operation Phoenix, in which antigovernment rural leaders were assassinated, and the establishment of fortified strategic hamlets to control the rural population, failed to reverse the tide.

The combined Vietcong–North Vietnamese Tet Offensive in early 1968 resulted in serious losses for South Vietnamese and American forces. The war spread to Laos and to Cambodia, the latter bombed in 1969. American air strikes in North Vietnam were stepped up, and U.S. troop strength reached a maximum of 543,000 in 1969. In July 1969 a series of U.S. troop withdrawals began, and secret talks were initiated in search of a negotiated settlement of the war. Following heavy U.S. bombardment of the north in 1972, a cease-fire agreement was signed in Paris by South Vietnam, North Vietnam, the Vietcong, and the United States on Jan. 27, 1973. It was never implemented, but the American withdrawal continued. In early 1975 South Vietnamese forces collapsed in the face of a series of North Vietnamese–Vietcong offensives. Remaining U.S. personnel were evacuated, and Saigon fell on Apr. 30, 1975. Hundreds of thousands of refugees ("boat people") have fled the country since then.

Following the fall of Saigon, the country was occupied by northern troops and administrators. Businesses were nationalized, agriculture collectivized, and tens of thousands of people sent to labor camps for "reeducation." A unified National Assembly met in 1976, and the country was officially reunified on July 2, 1976, under the existing government of the north. Saigon was renamed Ho Chi Minh City. A Soviet naval base was established at the former U.S. base at Cam Ranh Bay.

In 1978 Vietnamese troops occupied Cambodia (called Kampuchea at the time) ousting the government of Pol Pot and installing Heng Samrin as premier. In February 1979 China launched an unsuccessful punitive attack over its border with Vietnam to display displeasure with the invasion of Cambodia and with the treatment of ethnic Chinese in Vietnam. In 1988 Vietnam pledged to withdraw its troops from Cambodia and completed the withdrawal in September 1989.

Vietnam's communist government rules through the party's powerful Central Committee; no strong personalities have emerged to replace the leaders of the wartime generation. The economy functions only at a basic level, with the infrastructure in disrepair and agriculture and small business hampered by excessive collectivization and central planning. The economy is heavily dependent on Soviet aid. Resumption of contacts with the U.S. has been precluded by American insistence that Vietnam account more fully for American prisoners of war and troops missing in action. But high-level talks on the normalization of relations and the Cambodian question opened in 1990.

Despite Soviet pressure, Vietnam's leadership has resisted political liberalization and perestroika-style economic reform.

## Western Samoa
### Independent State of Western Samoa

**Geography** **Location:** two large and seven small islands (five inhabited) in South Pacific Ocean, about 1,500 mi. (2,400 km) NE of New Zealand. Apia 13°49′S, 171°45′W. **Boundaries:** surrounded by Pacific Ocean; nearest neighbor is American Samoa to E. **Total land area:** 1,093 sq. mi. (2,831 sq km). **Coastline:** 250 mi. (403 km). **Comparative area:** slightly smaller than Rhode Island. **Land use:** 19% arable land; 24% permanent crops; negl. % meadows and pastures; 47% forest and woodland; 10% other. **Major cities:** (1981 census) Apia (capital) 33,170.

**People** **Population:** 186,031 (1990). **Nationality:** noun—Western Samoan(s); adjective—Western Samoan. **Ethnic groups:** Samoan; about 7% Euronesians (persons of European and Polynesian blood), 0.4% Europeans. **Languages:** Samoan (Polynesian), English. **Religions:** 99.7% Christian (about half of population associated with London Missionary Society; includes Congregational, Roman Catholic, Methodist, Latter-day Saints, Seventh-Day Adventist).

**Government** **Type:** constitutional monarchy under native chief. **Independence:** Jan. 1, 1962 (from UN trusteeship administered by New Zealand). **Constitution:** Jan. 1, 1962. **National holiday:** Independence Day, Jan. 1. **Heads of government:** Malietoa Tanumafili II, head of state (since 1962); Tofilau Eti, prime minister (since Feb. 1988). **Structure:** head of state and executive council; unicameral legislature (47-member Legislative Assembly); Supreme Court, court of appeal, land and titles court, village courts.

**Economy** **Monetary unit:** WS tala. **Budget:** (1988) **income:** $54 mil.; **expend.:** $54 mil. (including development expend. of $20 mil.). **GDP:** $112 mil., $615 per capita. **Chief crops:** coconuts, fruit (including bananas, taro, yams). **Livestock:** poultry, pigs, cattle, horses. **Natural resources:** hardwood forests, fish. **Major industries:** timber, tourism, food processing. **Labor force:** about 37,000 (1983); about 22,000 employed in agriculture. **Exports:** $9.9 mil. (1988); 42% coconut oil and cream, 19% taro, 14% cocoa. **Imports:** $51.8 mil. (c.i.f., 1988); 58% intermediate goods, 17% food, 12% capital goods. **Major trading partners: exports:**

(1987) 30% New Zealand, 24% EC, 21% Australia, 9% U.S., 7% American Samoa; *imports:* 31% New Zealand, 20% Australia, 15% Fiji, 15% Japan, 5% U.S., 4% E.C.

**Intl. Orgs.** Commonwealth, FAO, G-77, IBRD, IDA, IFAD, IFC, IMF, UN, UNESCO, WHO.

The Polynesian island group of Samoa (Navigator's Islands) was partitioned in 1899 between the United States, which had established a naval base at Pago Pago on Tutuila in 1878, and Germany, which organized the westerly islands into a colony in 1894. In 1914 New Zealand troops occupied the German-held islands. New Zealand administered Western Samoa under a League of Nations mandate beginning in 1920 and continued to control the islands as a UN Trust Territory after 1945. In 1959 home rule was established under an elected local government. Western Samoa became an independent nation on Jan. 1, 1962. The constitution blends Western parliamentary government and traditional Samoan forms of rule. The parliamentary electorate is limited to the malai, heads of extended families; the malai are wholly responsible for local affairs. The local culture is similarly a blend of Samoan tradition with Christianity.

The economy is based on subsistence agriculture, forestry, fishing, and tourism. Nearly 50 percent of the land area is forested; lumber and wood products (plywood, veneer) are important exports. Offshore fisheries are being developed, along with light industry, particularly food processing.

# Yemen
## Republic of Yemen
**Geography** **Location:** southern shore of Arabian peninsula and southwest corner of Arabian peninsula. **Boundaries:** Saudi Arabia to N, Oman to E, Gulf of Aden to S, Red Sea to W. **Total land area:** 207,286 sq. mi. (536,869 sq km). **Coastline:** 1,184 mi. (1,906 km). **Land use:** 15% arable land; negl. % permanent crops; 31% meadows and pastures; 7% forest and woodland; 53% other; includes 1% irrigated. **Major cities:** (1986 est.) San'a (capital) 427,150; Ta'lz 178,043 (1973 census); Aden 291,000; Hadhramaut 451,000; Abyan 311,000; Lahej 273,000.

**People** **Population:** 9,746,465 (1990). **Nationality:** noun—Yemini(s); adjective—Yemeni. **Ethnic groups:** mostly Arab, a few Indians, Somalis, Europeans. **Languages:** Arabic. **Religions:** Muslim (Sunni and Shia), some Christian, Hindu.

**Government** **Type:** republic. **Independence:** Nov. 1918 (from Ottoman Empire). **Constitution:** Dec. 28, 1970; suspended June 19, 1974; amended in 1990. **National holiday:** Proclamation of the Republic, Sept. 26. **Heads of government:** Lt. Gen. Ali Abdullah Saleh, president of Republic of Yemen (since May 1990); Haider Abubaker al-Attas, prime minister of Republic of Yemen (since May 1990). (Note: Lt. Gen. Ali Abdullah Saleh was president of Yemen Arab Republic—North Yemen

(since 1978); Haider Abubaker al-Attas was chairman of Presidium, Supreme People's Council of People's Democratic Republic of Yemen—South Yemen (since Feb. 1986). **Structure:** executive—president and cabinet; legislative—People's Constituent Assembly; judicial—Supreme Court and lesser courts.

**Economy** Because of the recent unification of South Yemen with North Yemen, the economic statistics of the two previously separate countries have not yet been unified.

**Intl. Orgs.** Arab League, FAO, GATT (de facto), G-77, IBRD, ICAO, IDA, IFAD, IFC, ILO, IMF, IMO, INTELSAT, INTERPOL, ITU, NAM, UN, UNESCO, UPU, WHO, WIPO, WMO.

Yemen—in ancient times Sheba or Saba—is strategically located in the southwestern corner of the Arabian peninsula, near the southern end of the Red Sea. In biblical times and for many centuries thereafter, Yemen dominated the caravan trade in spices, gold, and other luxury goods from India and Africa to the Middle East.

The Islamic unification of Arabia in 628 resulted in the incorporation of Yemen into Arabia as a whole, but many local uprisings broke out over the course of the following three centuries. In the 10th century, control passed to a line of Yemeni kings who were simultaneously imams of the Zaidi sect of Islam; the Zaidi imams ruled until 1962.

Aden was the most important port of the ancient kingdom of Sheba and retained that status under the Zaidi imams of Yemen. Portuguese activity around Aden began in the 15th century; from the mid-16th century, control of the port was disputed by the Portuguese, the Yemeni kings, the Ottoman Turks, and, later, the British.

In 1839, Aden was made a British Crown Colony; the Hadramaut region of southern Arabia, north and east of Aden, became the British Protectorate of Aden. The colony and protectorate were both administered as part of British India.

Yemen came under the control of the Ottoman Empire from the mid-16th to the mid-17th centuries, and again from 1849 to 1918. The Turks were expelled at the end of World War I, and Yemen became an independent kingdom in 1918. The kingdom's independence was threatened by a short-lived Saudi invasion in 1934 and by a 1954 dispute with Great Britain over the status of Aden, which had become the key to British military power in the western Indian Ocean and Persian Gulf after India's independence in 1947.

Imam Ahmed came to the throne of Yemen in 1948, following the assassination of his predecessor. Most of Yemen's large Jewish population was evacuated to Israel in 1949–50. A palace coup against the imam in 1955 failed, but after he died on Sept. 19, 1962, his successor was quickly driven from the throne and the country was proclaimed the Yemen Arab Republic (North Yemen) under the leadership of Brig. Gen. Abdullah al-Salal.

A struggle for independence began in Aden and the protectorate in 1963, with two rival groups competing for power. The National Lib-

eration Front (NLF) gained the upper hand over the Egyptian-backed Front for the Liberation of Occupied South Yemen, as both groups waged guerrilla war against the British. Most of the country's Jewish population fled to Israel. British forces withdrew in 1967, and South Yemen became independent on Nov. 30 of that year. The nation's territory included Socotra and adjacent islands off the Horn of Africa, which had been British possessions since 1876.

In 1969 a leftist faction of the NLF seized power, nationalized key industries, and instituted a socialist regime. In the mid-1970s, South Yemeni troops aided leftist guerrillas in Oman, and fought in Ethiopia against Eritrean rebels. Subsequently Pres. Salem Robaye Ali took a more moderate stance and improved relations with Oman and Saudi Arabia. He was overthrown in a coup in June 1978 and executed. The succeeding government was overthrown in another coup on Jan. 13, 1986; on Feb. 8, Hasin Said Numan became prime minister of the new government.

In North Yemen, civil war between royalist and republican factions lasted until April 1970, when a coalition republican government was formed with the aid of Saudi mediation. Col. Ibrahim al-Hamidi came to power in a military coup on June 13, 1974; he was assassinated on Oct. 11, 1977. Pres. Ali Abdullah Saleh assumed office on July 17, 1978, following the assassination of previously elected president al-Gashmi.

Border skirmishes between North Yemen and South Yemen broke out during 1972–73. After several years of uneasy peace, South Yemen launched a full-scale war against the north on Feb. 24, 1979. Arab League pressure quickly led to a mutual disengagement on March 19. A cease-fire agreement between the two Yemeni nations was signed on March 29, 1979.

Relations improved during the 1980s, and following an agreement reached in November 1989, North Yemen and South Yemen merged as the Republic of Yemen on May 22, 1990. Ali Abdullah Saleh, president of North Yemen, became the new country's president; Ali Salem Al-Baidh, secretary of the South Yemeni Socialist party, was elected vice president by the unified parliament. The two are assisted by a ruling council, with three members from the south and two from the north. Elections are scheduled for 1992. San'a was proclaimed the capital of the United Yemen, though Aden will remain its most important economic center.

Yemen's economy has remained largely agricultural until recent years. Cotton is the chief agricultural export. The chewing of qat, a mildly stimulant leaf, is widespread; cultivation of qat bushes has replaced traditional coffee plantations in many areas. Oil was discovered in North Yemen in 1984 and in South Yemen in 1987; commercial deliveries of crude oil from both areas commenced in 1987. Additional petroleum fields are to be developed in the south. Shipping services in the port of Aden form an important part of the country's commercial economy; remittances from the more than 400,000 Yemenis working in other Arab nations provide the bulk of Yemen's nonpetroleum foreign earnings.

# Yugoslavia
## Socialist Federal Republic of Yugoslavia

**Geography Location:** southeastern Europe. **Boundaries:** Austria, Hungary to N, Romania, Bulgaria to E, Greece, Albania to S, Adriatic Sea to W; short frontier with Italy to NW. **Total land area:** 98,766 sq. mi. (255,804 sq km). **Coastline:** 2,446 mi. (3,935 km). **Comparative area:** slightly larger than Wyoming. **Land use:** 28% arable land; 3% permanent crops; 25% meadows and pastures; 36% forest and woodland; 8% other; includes 1% irrigated. **Major cities:** (1981 census) Beo Grad (Belgrade, capital) 1,470,073; Osijek 867,646; Zagreb 768,700; Nis 643,470; Skoplje (Skopje) 506,547.

**People Population:** 23,841,608 (1990). **Nationality:** noun—Yugoslav(s); adjective—Yugoslav. **Ethnic groups:** (1981 census) 19.7% Croat, 8.9% Muslim, 7.8% Slovene, 7.7% Albanian, 6.3% Serb, 5.9% Macedonian, 5.4% Yugoslav, 2.5% Montenegrin, 1.9% Hungarian, 3.9% other. **Languages:** Serbo-Croatian, Slovene, Macedonian (all official), Albanian, Hungarian. **Religions:** 50% Eastern Orthodox, 30% Roman Catholic, 10% Muslim, 1% Protestant, 9% other.

**Government Type:** federal republic in form. **Independence:** N.A. **Constitution:** Feb. 21, 1974; amendments in 1989 established more market economy and other economic and political changes. Additional amendments under discussion will continue to restructure the government. **National holiday:** Day of the Republic, Nov. 29. **Heads of government:** Stjepan Mesic, president (since June 1991); Ante Markovic, prime minister (since Mar. 1989). **Structure:** Executive branch—president is chairman of the Presidency, a collective body of representatives of the eight republics and autonomous provinces; legislative—two chambers: Federal Chamber and Chamber of Nationalities; judicial—Constitutional Court is only federal court, hears limited cases; each region has its own Supreme Court and lesser courts. (Note: as of July 1990, two of the six republics have held multiparty elections. The remaining four republics plan to hold multiparty elections in late 1990 or early 1991.)

**Economy Monetary unit:** dinar. **Budget:** (1990) *income:* $6.4 bil., *expend.:* $6.4 bil. **GNP:** $129.5 bil., $5,464 per capita (1989 est.). **Chief crops:** corn, wheat, tobacco, sugar beets, sunflowers; diversified agriculture with many small private holdings and large agricultural combines; occasionally net exporter of corn, tobacco, foodstuffs, live animals. **Livestock:** poultry, sheep, cattle, pigs, horses. **Natural resources:** coal, copper, bauxite, timber, iron ore. **Major industries:** metallurgy, machinery and equipment, petroleum. **Labor force:** 9.6 mil. (1986); 27% mining and manufacturing, 22% agriculture; about 5% of labor force are guest workers in Western Europe; unemployment about 10% of domestic labor force, including private agriculture (1987). **Exports:** $13.1 bil. (f.o.b., 1988); 50% raw

## YUGOSLAVIA'S REPUBLICS

| Republic | Area (sq km) | Population | Capital |
|---|---|---|---|
| Serbia | 88,361 | 9,313,676 | Belgrade |
| Vojvodina[1] | 21,506 | 2,034,772 | Novi Sad |
| Kosovo[1] | 10,887 | 1,584,440 | Pristina |
| Croatia[2] | 56,538 | 4,601,469 | Zagreb |
| Bosnia-Hercegovina | 51,129 | 4,124,256 | Sarajevo |
| Macedonia[3] | 25,713 | 1,909,112 | Skopje |
| Slovenia[2] | 20,251 | 1,891,864 | Ljubljana |
| Montenegro | 13,812 | 584,310 | Titograd |
| **Yugoslavia** | **255,804** | **22,424,687** | **Belgrade** |

**Note:** One square kilometer equals 0.386 square miles. 1. Autonomous provinces within Serbian republic. 2. Declared independence June 25, 1991. 3. Voted for independence Sept. 9, 1991.

materials and manufactures, 31% consumer goods, 19% capital goods and equipment. **Imports:** $13.8 bil. (c.i.f., 1988); 79% raw materials and semimanufactures, 15% capital goods, 6% consumer goods. **Major trading partners:** 30% EC, 45% CMEA, 14% less developed countries, 5% U.S., 6% other.

**Intl. Orgs.** FAO, G-77, GATT, IAEA, IBRD, ICAO, IDA, IFAD, IFC, ILO, IMF, IMO, INTELSAT, INTERPOL, ITU, NAM, OECD (participant in some activities), UN, UNESCO, UPU, WHO, WIPO, WMO.

The lands that now compose Yugoslavia were incorporated into the Roman Empire as the province of Illyricum in the first century A.D. Christianity became dominant by A.D. 600. With the fall of Rome, most of the territory was conquered by the Bulgars before being incorporated into the Byzantine Empire. Bulgarians were largely displaced by Slavic immigrants in the ninth century. Dalmatia and Serbia were detached from the Byzantine Empire at the time of the First Crusade in the 11th century; Serbia was conquered by the Ottoman Empire at the Battle of Kosovo in 1389, gaining its independence from the Ottoman Empire at the Congress of Berlin in 1878.

The complexities of Balkan politics occupied European statesmen throughout the late 19th century, and the Balkan Wars of 1912 and 1913 led directly to the outbreak of World War I. After the collapse of the Austro-Hungarian empire during the war, the multiethnic and multinational state of Yugoslavia was patched together in 1918–19. To Serbia were annexed the old Austro-Hungarian lands of Slovenia and Croatia, as well as the ethnically Croatian and Serbian lands of Bosnia and Herzegovina in the northwest, and, in the south and southwest, Montenegro, Macedonia, and Kosovo.

The nationalities coexisted in a state of mutual hostility, provoking a royal dictatorship instituted by King Alexander in 1929 and enduring after his assassination in 1934. Hitler invaded Yugoslavia in 1941; German troops were welcomed in Croatia as liberators from the Serbs. Resistance began almost immediately, split into two mutually hostile groups: Draža Mihajlović's Serbian royalist Chetniks, and Tito's leftist Partisans, composed of pan-Yugoslav Communists and non-Serbian anti-German forces. By the end of the war, over 2 million Yugoslavs had died and 3½ million were

homeless. Marshall Tito (whose real name was Josip Broz), backed by both Churchill and Stalin, ruled over a ruined land, the newly created Federal People's Republic of Yugoslavia.

Until World War II, Yugoslavia was primarily agricultural and pastoral, with a feudal peasantry living on a subsistence level in a largely infertile land. Agriculture was more prosperous in the northern river valleys formerly under Austro-Hungarian control, and there was some industrialization in those areas as well. Virtually all these areas had to be rebuilt after the war.

Tito imposed agricultural collectivization on the Stalinist model and pushed for the development of industry under state ownership. Politically, harsh repression fell on members of the Chetnik resistance as well as on wartime collaborators. But the postwar period of tyranny was short-lived.

Tito had achieved power as an independent Communist leader and refused to permit Yugoslavia to become a Soviet satellite. In March 1948 he expelled Russian military advisers and was himself expelled from the Comintern.

Despite economic pressure and military threats, Tito turned westward. Stalinism yielded to decentralized communism. The 1953 Agrarian Reform laws permitted private agricultural smallholdings, and over 80 percent of the land returned to private ownership; in the rest, "self-management" rather than central control was encouraged. Self-management was instituted in the industrial sector as well, with emphasis varying between capital goods and consumer goods. Economic growth averaged over 7 percent per year for three decades, lifting Yugoslavia into the ranks of the semideveloped countries.

Despite a reconciliation with Nikita Khrushchev's Soviet Union in 1955–56, Tito continued to chart an independent course, taking a leading role in the Third World Non-Aligned Movement and providing a political and economic alternative model for Eastern Europe. But Yugoslavian nationalism in foreign affairs masked the development of separate nationalisms within the Yugoslavian federation. By the time Tito died in 1980, there was a real question as to whether the nation could survive without his leadership.

In the 1980s, the country was plagued by an economic slowdown. Inflation and chronic trade deficits led to soaring national debt, bringing austerity measures and a decline in the standard of living.

The post-Tito "collegial rule," whereby the presidency of the country and the chairmanship of the Party Presidium rotate annually among the six republics and two autonomous provinces worked well for most of the 1980s. But since the summer of 1988, ethnic protests and riots have broken out in Serbia's autonomous provinces of Kosovo and Vojvodina, in Slovenia, in Serbia, and in Montenegro. Escalating violence between Serbs and Croats, the two largest ethnic groups, and declarations of independence by Slovenia (the richest republic) and Croatia in June 1991 threaten the very survival of Yugoslavia as a nation. (See Part I, "The Year in Review.")

## Zaire
### Republic of Zaire

**Geography Location:** equatorial country in central Africa. **Boundaries:** Central African Republic, Sudan to N, Uganda, Rwanda, Burundi, Tanzania to E, Zambia to S, Angola to SW, Atlantic Ocean, Cabinda district of Angola, Congo to W. **Total land area:** 875,525 sq. mi. (2,267,600 sq km). **Coastline:** 23 mi. (37 km). **Comparative area:** about 1.5 times size of Alaska. **Land use:** 3% arable land; negl. % permanent crops; 4% meadows and pastures; 78% forest and woodland; 15% other; includes negl. % irrigated. **Major cities:** (1984 census) Kinshasa (capital) 2,653,558; Lubumbashi (Elizabethville) 543,268; Mbuji-Mayi (Bakwanga) 423,363; Kananga (Luluabourg) 290,898; Kisangani (Stanleyville) 282,650.

**People Population:** 36,589,468 (1990). **Nationality:** noun—Zairian(s); adjective—Zairian. **Ethnic groups:** 45% of the people belong to one of four largest groups—Mongo, Luba, Kongo (all Bantu), and Mangbetu-Azande; over 200 other ethnic groups. **Languages:** French (official), English, Lingala, Swahili, Kingwana, Kikongo, Tshiluba. **Religions:** 50% Roman Catholic, 20% Protestant, 10% Kimbanguist, 10% Muslim, 10% other syncretic sects and traditional beliefs.

**Government Type:** republic with strong presidential system. **Independence:** June 30, 1960 (from Belgium). **Constitution:** June 24, 1967, amended Aug. 1974, revised Feb. 15, 1978. **National holiday:** Independence Day, June 30. **Heads of government:** Marshal Mobutu Sese Seko, president (since 1965); Lunda Bululu, prime minister (since May 1990). **Structure:** executive—president elected originally for seven-year term; Marshal Mobutu reelected July 1984 and limits on reelection removed by new constitution; legislative—unicameral National Legislative Council with 310 members elected for five-year terms; official party is supreme political institution.

**Economy Monetary unit:** zaïre. **Budget:** (1988) *income:* $856 mil.; *expend.:* $2.3 bil. **GDP:** $6.5 bil., $195 per capita. **Chief crops:** cash crops—coffee, palm oil, rubber, quinine; food crops—manioc, bananas, root crops, corn; some provinces self-sufficient; illegal producer of cannabis for international drug trade. **Livestock:** goats, cattle, pigs, sheep. **Natural resources:** cobalt, copper, cadmium, crude oil, industrial and gem diamonds. **Major industries:** mining, mineral processing, consumer products (including textiles, footwear, cigarettes). **Labor force:** about 15 mil., but only 13% wage earners (1985); 75% agriculture, 13% industry, 12% services; 51% of population of working age (1981); N.A. unemployment. **Exports:** $2.2 bil. (f.o.b., 1988); 37% copper, 24% coffee, 12% diamonds, cobalt, crude oil. **Imports:** $1.9 bil. (f.o.b., 1988); consumer goods, foodstuffs, mining and other machinery, transport equipment, fuels. **Major trading partners:** U.S., Belgium, France, W. Germany, Italy, UK, Japan.

**Intl. Orgs.** FAO, G-77, GATT, IAEA, IBRÐ, ICAO, IDA, IFAD, IFC, ILO, IMF, IMO, INTELSAT, INTERPOL, ITU, NAM, UN, UNESCO, UPU, WHO, WIPO, WMO.

Pygmies were probably the earliest inhabitants of the Congo region, followed much later by Bantu and Nilotic peoples. By the eighth century A.D., a number of well-established kingdoms and empires occupied the lower reaches of the Congo (now Zaire) River and the coastal plain; these included Kongo (Bakongo), Kuba, Luba, and Lunda.

Portuguese explorers and merchants arrived along the coast in the 1480s and initially traded with these kingdoms on a basis of relative equality; an indigenous Catholic church became established. Soon, however, the Portuguese established a slave trade that brought turmoil and decline to the native states. Europeans did not penetrate the interior of Zaire until the 19th century, but the slave trade (partly in Arab hands, in inland regions) had repercussions everywhere.

Henry Stanley descended the Congo River from east to west in 1876, opening the area for further exploration. In 1878 Stanley was engaged by King Leopold II of Belgium to establish Belgian trading stations along the river. King Leopold established the Congo Free State in 1885, not as a Belgian colony but as a personal possession of which he was king as well as chief stockholder.

The management corporation that ran the Free State abolished slavery but instituted a harsh and exploitative regime that reduced native peoples to a condition of involuntary servitude. Forced labor and harsh suppression of rebellion resulted in the deaths of unnumbered thousands of people. Protests against these conditions, led by Great Britain and the United States, led to the transformation of the Free State into the colony of the Belgian Congo in 1908 with promises of reforms.

By the 1920s the Belgian Congo had become a major world producer of copper, diamonds, gold, rubber, palm oil, and other commodities. Railroads were developed to bring these goods to market, notably the line from Elizabethville (now Lubumbashi) in the Katanga region through Angola to the Atlantic coast. River navigation on the Congo was also developed. All mining, plantation agriculture, industry, and administration was in Belgian hands with no native participation in government except at the most local level.

The depression of the 1930s led to reduced commodity prices worldwide and hurt the Belgian Congo badly. But the colony recovered swiftly after World War II.

In the 1950s agitation for increased native participation in government led, in 1957, to elections for local councils. In 1959 rioting against Belgian rule broke out. Elections were held on May 31 in anticipation of independence. Joseph Kasavubu became president, and Patrice Lumumba, head of the Congolese National Movement, became prime minister. On June 30, 1960, Belgium granted independence to the Congo; many Europeans fled the country. On July 4 the army mutinied, and on July 11 the southern province of Katanga (now Shaba), under the leadership of Moise Tshombe, seceded from the Congo and declared its independence. Belgium sent troops to quell the disorder.

On Aug. 9 the United Nations called on Belgium to withdraw its troops. Kasavubu removed Lumumba as prime minister. Lumumba, with the backing of Ghana, fought for control. He fled to Stanleyville (now Kisangani) but was kidnapped in January 1961 and taken to Katanga, where he was murdered, apparently with American and Belgian complicity. Fighting continued in Katanga, where Tshombe's regime was supported by European mercenaries and opposed by UN peacekeeping forces. The Katangan rebellion ended in late 1963; rebels fled to Angola, and UN forces were withdrawn in June 1964. In a surprising political settlement, Tshombe became president of the Congo on June 30. On Sept. 7 leftist rebels attempted to establish a "people's republic" based in Stanleyville. Tshombe again resorted to the use of mercenaries to put down the rebellion. Many white settlers, as well as Congolese, were killed in fierce fighting and terrorist atrocities. The rebellion ended in July 1965. In November 1965 Tshombe was deposed in a military coup led by Joseph Mobutu, whose government took immediate steps to consolidate its control and reduce European influence and struggled to rebuild the country's shattered economic infrastructure.

In 1971 Mobutu changed the country's name to Zaire and renamed Leopoldville Kinshasa. In 1972 he ordered all Zairians with European names to change them to African names; he became Mobutu Sese Seko. Attempts in 1974 to force foreign investors to sell their holdings to Zairians brought economic disruption, and foreign investors were invited back into the country in 1977.

In 1977 another rebellion broke out in Katanga (now Shaba) Province; the government put down the rebellion with the aid of France, Egypt, and Morocco. The rebels fled to Angola, but the province's rich mining economy was again disrupted; many European technical workers fled, and production plummeted.

Despite Zaire's rich natural resources in minerals, forest products, hydroelectric potential, and agriculture, the country has been impoverished by the nearly unprecedented corruption of the Mobutu regime. The president personally is estimated to have amassed a fortune of $3 billion during his term in office. In January 1989 Belgium suspended development projects in Zaire after the country defaulted on a $7 billion loan. Rival political leaders attempted to organize opposition to the Mobutu government in late 1987 and 1988, but most were arrested or driven into exile. In April 1990 Mobutu ended a 20-year ban on opposition parties.

In June 1989 Mobutu won international acclaim for his role in bringing together the leaders of rival factions in Angola in an attempt to end that country's long-standing civil war.

## Zambia
### Republic of Zambia

**Geography** **Location:** landlocked country in southern central Africa. **Boundaries:** Zaire to N, Tanzania to NE, Malawi to E, Mozambique to SE, Zimbabwe to S, Namibia to SW, Angola to W. **Total land area:** 285,994 sq. mi. (740,720 sq km). **Coastline:** none. **Comparative area:** slightly larger than Texas. **Land use:** 7% arable land; negl. % permanent crops; 47% meadows and pastures; 27% forest and woodland; 19% other; includes negl. % irrigated. **Major cities:** (1988 est.) Lusaka (capital) 870,030; Kitwe 472,255; Ndola 442,666; Kabwe (Broken Hill) 199,368.

**People** **Population:** 7,875,448 (1989). **Nationality:** noun—Zambian(s); adjective—Zambian. **Ethnic groups:** 98.7% African, 1.1% European, 0.2% other. **Languages:** English (official), about 70 indigenous languages. **Religions:** 50–75% Christian, 1% Muslim and Hindu, indigenous beliefs.

**Government** **Type:** one-party state. **Independence:** Oct. 24, 1964 (from UK). **Constitution:** Aug. 25, 1973. **National holiday:** Independence Day, Oct. 24. **Heads of government:** Kenneth David Kaunda, president (since Oct. 1964); Kebby Musokotwane, prime minister (since June 1985). **Structure:** executive—modified presidential system; legislative—unicameral National Assembly; judiciary.

**Economy** **Monetary unit:** kwacha. **Budget:** (1988 est.) *income:* $570 mil.; *expend.:* $939 mil. **GDP:** $4.0 bil., $530 per capita. **Chief crops:** corn, tobacco, cotton; net importer of most major agricultural products. **Livestock:** cattle, goats, pigs, sheep. **Natural resources:** copper, cobalt, zinc, lead, coal. **Major industries:** copper mining and processing, transport, construction. **Labor force:** 2.5 mil.; 85% agriculture, 9% transport and services, 6% mining, manufacturing, and construction. **Exports:** $1.2 bil. (f.o.b., 1988); copper, zinc, cobalt, lead, tobacco. **Imports:** $687 mil. (c.i.f., 1988); machinery, transport equipment, foodstuffs, fuels, manufactures. **Major trading partners:** EC, Japan, South Africa, U.S.

**Intl. Orgs.** Commonwealth, FAO, G-77, GATT (de facto), IAEA, IBRD, ICAO, IDA, IFAD, IFC, ILO, IMF, INTELSAT, INTERPOL, ITU, NAM, UN, UNESCO, UPU, WHO, WIPO, WMO.

Bantu peoples—including Luba, Lunda, Ngoni, and others—moved into what is now Zambia between the 15th and the 19th centuries, displacing or absorbing aboriginal populations. Occasional Portuguese explorers from Angola and Mozambique entered the region, and Angolan slave-raiders were active in the late 18th and early 19th centuries, but serious European influence did not begin until the mid-19th century. At that time British missionaries and merchants arrived, most notably David Livingstone and Cecil Rhodes.

Local rulers granted mineral concessions to Rhodes in both Northern and Southern Rhodesia (now Zambia and Zimbabwe). Rhodesia was declared a British sphere of influence in 1888; a British protectorate was established in 1891 and enlarged in 1894–95. The borders of Northern Rhodesia were established in 1911. The country was administered by the British South Africa Co. until 1924, when direct colonial rule began. Large numbers of British settlers arrived and developed extensive farms and ranches and mined the region's substantial copper deposits. A railroad was built linking Northern Rhodesia with Elizabethville in the Belgian Congo (now Lubumbashi, Zaire).

In 1953 Northern and Southern Rhodesia (Zimbabwe) were joined with Nyasaland (now Malawi) to form the Federation of Rhodesia and Nyasaland. The country entered a period of unrest with native peoples demanding greater participation in government, while white settlers clung to their privileged positions.

As the result of an election in 1962, the federation was dissolved in 1963. A national assembly was created on the basis of a broader, multiracial electorate. Northern Rhodesia became independent as the Republic of Zambia on Oct. 24, 1964. Relations between Zambia and white-ruled Rhodesia (formerly Southern Rhodesia) became strained in 1965 in a dispute over ownership and administration of the railway that spanned both countries. A new constitution was promulgated in 1973, creating a stronger presidency and a unicameral legislature; the United National Independence party was made the sole legal political party. Opposition parties were allowed to form again starting in December 1990.

Pres. Kenneth Kaunda, in office since Zambia's independence, has led a generally moderate government that has won the support of both whites and blacks, despite some early white emigration from the country. Even when there was only one legal political party, elections were, and are, freely contested, and there is substantial freedom of the press.

Zambia's economy, however, has not fared well under independence. The nation's wildlife supports a small tourist industry, and ivory is exported (both legally and illegally). The agricultural sector, which produces corn, tobacco, peanuts, cotton, rubber, sugar, and livestock, was hurt by the departure of some white settlers and subsequent land redistribution. Although the country has diverse mineral resources, copper is overwhelmingly the nation's main earner of foreign exchange. A steep decline in the world price of copper since the mid-1970s has led to massive foreign debt and labor unrest at home. The IMF has demanded reforms as a condition for future aid, and in 1987 Pres. Kaunda announced a program of economic restructuring to deal with these problems. In 1990 the government survived an attempted coup precipitated by a doubling in the price of the staple food, maize meal.

In April 1987 South African troops raided Zambian bases of the African National Congress in an action that led to heavy casualties and was condemned by the United Nations. Zambia, under Pres. Kaunda, has played an active role in pan-African affairs and actively supports anticommunist and anti-South African movements in neighboring countries.

## Zimbabwe
### Republic of Zimbabwe

**Geography** **Location:** landlocked country in southern Africa. **Boundaries:** Zambia to NW, Mozambique to E, South Africa to S, Botswana to SW. **Total land area:** 149,293 sq. mi. (386,670 sq km). **Coastline:** none. **Comparative area:** slightly larger than Montana. **Land use:** 7% arable land; negl. % permanent crops; 12% meadows and pastures; 62% forest and woodland; 19% other; includes negl. % irrigated. **Major cities:** (1982 census) Harare (Salisbury, capital) 656,000; Bulawayo 413,800; Chitungwiza 172,600; Gweru (Gwelo) 78,900; Mutare (Umtali) 69,600.

**People** **Population:** 10,392,161 (1990). **Nationality:** noun—Zimbabwean(s); adjective—Zimbabwean. **Ethnic groups:** 98% African (71% Shona, 16% Ndebele, 11% other), 1% white, 1% mixed and Asian. **Languages:** English (official), ChiShona, Si Ndebele. **Religions:** 50% syncretic (part Christian, part indigenous beliefs), 25% Christian, 24% indigenous beliefs, 1% Muslim.

**Government** **Type:** presidential system with bicameral legislature. **Independence:** Apr. 18, 1980 (from UK). **Constitution:** Dec. 21, 1979. **National holiday:** Apr. 18. **Heads of government:** Robert Gabriel Mugabe, president (since Dec. 1987). **Structure:** executive—cabinet led by president; legislative—parliament consisting of 100-member House of Assembly and 40-member Senate; judiciary—high court is supreme judicial authority.

**Economy** **Monetary unit:** Zimbabwean dollar. **Budget:** (1990) *income:* $2.4 bil.; *expend.:* $3.0 bil. **GDP:** $4.6 bil., $470 per capita (1988 est.). **Chief crops:** tobacco, corn, tea, sugar, cotton. **Livestock:** cattle, goats, sheep, pigs, asses. **Natural resources:** coal, chromium ore, asbestos, gold, nickel. **Major industries:** mining, steel, clothing and footwear. **Labor force:** 3.1 mil. (1987); 74% agriculture, 16% transport and services, 10% mining, manufacturing, construction. **Exports:** $1.6 bil. (f.o.b., 1988); 34% agricultural (21% tobacco, 13% other), 19% manufactures, 11% gold, 11% ferrochrome. **Imports:** $1.1 bil. (c.i.f., 1988); 37% machinery and transport equipment, 22% manufactures, 16% chemicals, 15% fuels. **Major trading partners:** *exports:* 55% Europe (41% EC, 6% Netherlands, 8% other), 25% Africa (12% S. Africa, 10% other), 6% U.S; *imports:* 31% EC, 29% Africa (21% S. Africa, 8% other), 8% U.S., 4% Japan.

**Intl. Orgs.** Commonwealth, FAO, G-77, GATT, IBRD, ICAO, IDA, IFAD, IFC, ILO, IMF, INTERPOL, NAM, UN, UNESCO, UPU, WHO, WMO.

Massive stone structures at Great Zimbabwe give evidence of a sizable urban society that flourished from the ninth to the 13th centuries and dominated iron-age trade in southeastern Africa. Bantu peoples migrated into the region beginning in the 15th century; the Mashona dominated until the early 19th century, when they were displaced by the Matebele.

Portuguese slave raiders from Mozambique were active in Zimbabwe from the 16th to the mid-19th centuries. Mineral concessions were granted to Cecil Rhodes by local rulers in the late 19th century, and the region became a British protectorate in 1888. Salisbury (now Harare) was founded in 1890, and the territory comprising Zimbabwe and Zambia was named Rhodesia in 1895. Rhodesia was governed by the British South Africa Co. until 1923, when it was partitioned into Northern and Southern Rhodesia. Northern Rhodesia became a British colony, whereas Southern Rhodesia, rejecting union with South Africa, became a self-governing (and white-ruled) state within the British Empire.

Southern Rhodesia had been heavily settled by whites from Great Britain, South Africa, and elsewhere, who developed extensive farms and ranches, forest products industries, and the country's rich mines. The country prospered but with little native participation in government except at the most local level.

In 1953 Northern Rhodesia, Southern Rhodesia, and Nyasaland were joined in the Federation of Rhodesia and Nyasaland. Increasing agitation for black participation in government, especially in the north and in Nyasaland, led to the dissolution of the federation in 1963; Northern Rhodesia subsequently became independent as Zambia, Nyasaland as Malawi. In 1961 Southern Rhodesia had adopted a constitution that guaranteed the continuation of white rule. White resistance to black political demands led to the rise of the Rhodesian Front party, whose leader, Ian D. Smith, became prime minister of Rhodesia (formerly Southern Rhodesia). After British-led negotiations for a biracial political compromise broke down, the Smith government on Nov. 11, 1965, issued a unilateral declaration of independence, which was declared illegal and invalid by the British government.

The UN condemned the Smith government and imposed economic sanctions; the government was supported by South Africa and Mozambique (before that country's independence in 1975). In May 1968 the UN voted to impose a trade embargo on Rhodesia.

A constitution adopted in 1970 effectively barred black participation in national politics. A British-initiated political settlement of 1972 was dropped because of black opposition. By 1974 mounting pressure from other African countries led the Smith government to enter into more serious negotiations. Guerrilla warfare pitting black nationalist groups against white settlers and mercenaries raged sporadically throughout the country, and many white settlers emigrated. A conference in Geneva in 1976 broke down, but a 1977 British-American proposal for majority rule provided the basis for a settlement of the crisis. An "internal settlement" was announced in April 1978 by Smith and three major nationalist leaders: Bishop Abel Muzorewa, leader of the United African National Congress, the Rev. Ndabaningi Sithole, former leader of the Zimbabwe African National Union (ZANU), and Chief Jeremiah Chirau. The settlement was rejected by the Patriotic Front that united ZANU (now led by Robert Mugabe) and Joshua Nkomo's Zimbabwe African People's Union (ZAPU).

Elections were held in April 1979 and Bishop Muzorewa assumed office on June 1 as prime minister of "Zimbabwe-Rhodesia," but the Patriotic Front continued to oppose the government. On Dec. 10 the "Zimbabwe-Rhodesia" parliament dissolved itself, and the country reverted briefly to British colonial rule. On Dec. 21 all parties agreed to a ceasefire and to a period of transitional British rule leading to independence. International economic sanctions were lifted.

Elections held in February 1980 resulted in a clear majority for Mugabe's ZANU party. Zimbabwe became independent, with Mugabe as prime minister, on April 18. As Mugabe embarked on an ambitious program of national reconstruction, Nkomo became leader of the opposition. Guerrillas linked to ZAPU, with Nkomo's tacit (or perhaps active) leadership and with alleged support from South Africa, continued to engage in sporadic warfare against Mugabe's government, and banditry and sabotage disrupted the countryside.

The elections of 1985 increased ZANU's majority in parliament. In 1987 the constitution was amended to strengthen the presidency and to end the separate role of blacks and whites in government; new elections were held for black members of parliament to fill seats formerly reserved for whites. Guerrillas renewed attacks on white-owned farms.

In December 1987 Mugabe and Nkomo agreed to merge ZANU and ZAPU, creating a de facto one-party state under Mugabe's leadership. This fragile political settlement remains in force, though scattered political and ethnic armed unrest persists, and Nkomo's commitment to Mugabe's government remains in doubt. In 1989 a new opposition party was organized by Edgar Z. Tekere.

Zimbabwe's economy is one of the strongest in sub-Saharan Africa. Agriculture is the major employer, and mineral resources are the country's major source of foreign earnings. An excellent transportation network and ample electric power (both hydroelectric and coal-fired) support a strong industrial base; major industries include steel, heavy equipment, ore processing, motor vehicle assembly, textiles, and food processing. Drought in the 1980s led to some food shortages, but Zimbabwe has exported food to all its neighbors, including South Africa, and as far afield as Ethiopia.

# Territories of the World

## NON-SELF-GOVERNING STATES

The community of nations has long recognized the existence of territories that do not have the status of independent states and that are subordinate in some degree to another power. The United Nations refers to these as "non-self-governing territories." Except for mandates and trusteeships specified by the League of Nations and the UN, the relationships between more and less powerful states have tended to evolve outside any rigid legal framework, and none of the following terms has an absolutely fixed meaning.

**Colonies** are dependent possessions whose inhabitants are not constitutionally under the dominant state's system of government but whose inhabitants are nationals of that state.

**Commonwealths** are autonomous states equal in status, united in their allegiance to a central power but not subordinate either to it or to one another in internal or external affairs.

**Dependencies** are states, provinces, or other places subject to the control of another power of which they do not form an integral part. The best known is Hong Kong, which China ceded to the United Kingdom in perpetuity in 1842, but which reverts to Chinese rule in 1997. The governor is appointed by the British monarch and foreign relations and defense are the responsibility of the UK, but Hong Kong has substantial autonomy in commercial relations.

**Mandates** were territories surrendered by Turkey and Germany after World War I and, according to the League of Nations, "inhabited by peoples not yet able to stand by themselves" and therefore placed under the "tutelage" of different members of the League as "mandatories on behalf of the League." The last mandate to gain independence was South West Africa, now Namibia.

**Protectorates** (*associated states*) are states or territories partly under the control of another state but autonomous in domestic and certain external affairs. Protectorates are established by treaties.

**Territories** are regions (especially of Australia, Canada, and the United States) administered by a federal government and having some degree of self-government but not organized as a province or a state.

**Trust territories** are administered on behalf of the UN by a designated power. The Trust Territory of the Pacific Islands (Palau) is the only one of the 11 trusteeships established by the UN that has not achieved self-government or independence either as a new sovereign state or by joining a neighboring independent country. (See Part II, "United States Territories and Possessions.")

## FORMER NAMES OF MODERN COUNTRIES

Throughout history, the names of nations change. These changes reflect a variety of trends—assimilation by other countries or the ascendancy of one group over another, to name only two. The accompanying list shows selected political entities whose names have changed or which have become part of another nation during the 20th century, and the countries or territories under whose description information about them can be found. Independent states that were constituent republics of either the Soviet Union or Yugoslavia as of June 1991 (Latvia and Serbia, for example) are not listed here but are listed with the descriptions of those nations.

| Former name | Country write-up | Former name | Country write-up |
|---|---|---|---|
| Abyssinia | Ethiopia | Friendly Islands | Tonga |
| Aden Protectorate | Yemen | German East Africa | Tanzania |
| Afars and Issas | Djibouti | German Southwest Africa | Namibia |
| Anglo-Egyptian Sudan | Sudan | Gilbert Islands | Kiribati |
| Annam | Vietnam | Gold Coast Colony | Ghana |
| Armenia | Turkey, USSR | Italian East Africa | Ethiopia, Somalia |
| Basutoland | Lesotho | Italian Somaliland | Somalia |
| Bechuanaland | Botswana | Kampuchea | Cambodia |
| Belgian Congo | Zaire | Line Islands | Kiribati, United States |
| Belgian East Africa | Burundi, Rwanda | Malagasy Republic | Madagascar |
| British East Africa | Kenya, Tanzania, Uganda | Malaya, Federation of | Malaysia, Singapore |
| British Guiana | Guyana | Marianas Islands | Guam, Northern Mariana |
| British Honduras | Belize | | Islands |
| British Solomon Islands | Solomon Islands | Mesopotamia | Iraq |
| British Somaliland | Somalia | Middle Congo | Congo |
| British West Indies | Antigua and Barbuda, | Muscat and Oman | Oman |
| | Bahamas, Barbados, | Netherlands East Indies | Indonesia |
| | British Virgin Islands, | New Guinea | Papua-New Guinea |
| | Cayman Islands, Grenada, | New Hebrides | Vanuatu |
| | Jamaica, Montserrat, St. | Northern Rhodesia | Zambia |
| | Kitts and Nevis, St. Lucia, | Nyasaland | Malawi |
| | St. Vincent and the | Outer Mongolia | Mongolia |
| | Grenadines, Trinidad and | Palestine | Israel |
| | Tobago | Persia | Iran |
| Burma | Myanmar | Pleasant Island | Nauru |
| Cameroons | Cameroon, Nigeria | Portuguese Congo | Angola (Cabinda) |
| Caroline Islands | Marshall Islands, | Portuguese East Africa | Mozambique |
| | Micronesia, Palau (Trust | Portuguese Guinea | Guinea-Bissau |
| | Territory of the Pacific) | Portuguese West Africa | Angola |
| Ceylon | Sri Lanka | Rhodesia | Zimbabwe |
| Cochin China | Vietnam | Río de Oro | Western Sahara |
| Congo Free State | Zaire | Ruanda-Urundi | Burundi, Rwanda |
| Congo, Democratic Republic of | Zaire | St. Christopher and Nevis | St. Kitts and Nevis |
| Congo, People's Republic of | Congo | Siam | Thailand |
| Dahomey | Benin | South-West Africa | Namibia |
| Dutch Guiana | Suriname | Southern Rhodesia | Zimbabwe |
| East Pakistan | Bangladesh | Spanish Guinea | Equatorial Guinea |
| Ellice Islands | Tuvalu | Spanish Morocco | Morocco |
| Eritrea | Ethiopia | Spanish Sahara | Western Sahara |
| Formosa | Taiwan | Straits Settlements | Malaysia, Singapore |
| French Congo | (see French Equatorial | Tanganyika | Tanzania |
| | Africa) | Togoland | Ghana, Togo |
| French Equatorial Africa | Central African Republic, | Tonkin | Vietnam |
| | Chad, Congo, Gabon | Transjordan | Jordan |
| French Guinea | Guinea | Trucial States | United Arab Emirates |
| French Indo-China | Cambodia, Laos, Vietnam | Ubangi-Shari | Central African Republic |
| French Somaliland | Djibouti | United Arab Republic | Egypt, Syria |
| French Sudan | Mali | Upper Volta | Burkina Faso |
| French Togo | Togo | West Pakistan | Pakistan |
| French West Africa | Benin, Guinea, Ivory | Zanzibar | Tanzania |
| | Coast, Mali, Mauritania, | | |
| | Niger, Senegal | | |

## Australia

### Christmas Island
#### Territory of Christmas Island

**Geography** **Location:** eastern Indian Ocean; 10°25'S, 105°39'E. **Boundaries:** Java Head, Indonesia, 224 mi. (360 km) to N, North West Cape, Australia, 875 mi. (1,408 km) to SE. **Total land area:** 52 sq. mi. (135 sq km). **Coastline:** 34 mi. (54 km). **Comparative area:** about 7/10 size of Washington, D.C. **Land use:** 0% arable land; 0% permanent crops; 0% meadows

and pastures; 0% forest and woodland; 100% other. **Major cities:** The Settlement (capital).

**People** **Population:** 2,278 (1990). **Nationality:** noun—Christmas Islander(s); adjective—Christmas Island. **Ethnic groups:** 61% Chinese, 25% Malay, 11% European, 3% other; no indigenous population. **Languages:** English.

**Government** **Type:** territory of Australia. **Heads of government:** A.D. Taylor, administrator. **Structure:** Advisory Council advises appointed administrator.

**Economy** **Monetary unit:** Australian dollar.

**Natural resources:** phosphates. **Major industries:** phosphate extraction (near depletion). **Labor force:** all workers are employees of Phosphate Mining Co. of Christmas Island, Ltd. **Exports:** about 1.2 million metric tons of phosphate exported to Australia, New Zealand, and some Asian nations. **Major trading partners:** Australia, New Zealand.

### Cocos (Keeling) Islands
#### Territory of Cocos (Keeling) Islands

**Geography** **Location:** 27 islands in eastern Indian Ocean. West Island 12°05'S, 96°53'E. **Boundaries:** island of Sumatra (part of Indonesia) about 932 mi. (1,500 km) to NE; Perth, Australia 1,720 mi. (2,768 km) to SE. **Total land area:** 5.4 sq. mi. (14.0 sq km). **Coastline:** undetermined. **Comparative area:** about 24 times size of the Mall in Washington, D.C. **Land use:** 0% arable land; 0% permanent crops; 0% meadows and pastures; 0% forest and woodland; 100% other. **Major cities:** West Island (capital).

**People** **Population:** 670 (1990). **Nationality:** noun—Cocos Islander(s); adjective—Cocos Islander. **Ethnic groups:** mostly Europeans on West Island and Cocos Malays on Home Island. **Languages:** English.

**Government** **Type:** territory of Australia. **Heads of government:** D. Lawrie, administrator; Parson bin Yapat, chairman of Islands Council. **Structure:** administrator, appointed by governor-general of Australia; Cocos Malay community is represented by Cocos (Keeling) Islands Council; supreme court.

**Economy** **Monetary unit:** Australian dollar. **Chief crops:** vegetables, bananas, pawpaws, coconuts. **Natural resources:** fish. **Major industries:** copra products. **Exports:** (1984) 202 metric tons of copra. **Imports:** foodstuffs from Australia, fuel, consumer items. **Major trading partners:** Australia.

### Norfolk Island
#### Territory of Norfolk Island

**Geography** **Location:** island in western Pacific Ocean; 29°04'S, 167°57'E. **Boundaries:** Vanuatu to N, New Zealand to SE, Brisbane, Australia 870 mi. (1,400 km) to W. **Total land area:** 13.3 sq. mi. (34.5 sq km). **Coastline:** 20 mi. (32 km). **Comparative area:** about 1/5 size of Washington, D.C. **Land use:** 0% arable land; 0% permanent crops; 25% meadows and pastures; 0% forest and woodland; 75% other. **Major cities:** Kingston (capital).

**People** **Population:** 2,533 (1990). **Nationality:** noun—Norfolk Islander(s); adjective—Norfolk Islander. **Ethnic groups:** descendants of *Bounty* mutiny; more recently, Australian and New Zealand settlers. **Languages:** English (official), Norfolk (a mixture of 18th century English and ancient Tahitian). **Religions:** Church of England, Roman Catholic, Uniting Church in Australia, Seventh-Day Adventist.

**Government** **Type:** territory of Australia. **National holiday:** Pitcairners Arrival Day Anniversary, June 8. **Heads of government:** John

Terence Brown, chief minister (since N.A.). **Structure:** nine-member elected Legislative Assembly; chief executive is Australian administrator named by governor-general.

**Economy Monetary unit:** Australian dollar. **Budget:** (1988) *income:* $3.4 mil.; *expend.:* $3.4 mil. **Chief crops:** Kentia palm seed, cereals, vegetables, fruit. **Natural resources:** fish. **Major industries:** tourism. **Exports:** $1.8 mil. (f.o.b. 1985); postage stamps, seeds of Norfolk Island pine and Kentia Palm, small quantities of avocados. **Imports:** $16.3 mil. (c.i.f. 1985). **Major trading partners:** Australia, Pacific Islands, New Zealand, Asia, Europe.

---

### Uninhabited Territories

Ashmore Is. (12°15′S, 123°05′E); Cartier Is. (12°30′S, 123°30′E); Coral Sea Is. (18°00′S, 158°00′E); Heard Is. (53°00′S, 73°35′E); McDonald Is. (52°29′S, 72°50′E).

---

## Denmark
### Faeroe Islands

**Geography Location:** group of 18 islands (17 inhabited) in Atlantic Ocean SE of Iceland. Tórshavn 62°02′N, 6°47′W. **Boundaries:** Iceland to NW, Norwegian Sea to N, Norway to E, Shetland Islands to SE, UK to S. **Total land area:** 540 sq. mi. (1,399 sq km). **Coastline:** 475 mi. (764 km). **Comparative area:** slightly less than eight times size of Washington, D.C. **Land use:** 2% arable land; 0% permanent crops; 0% meadows and pastures; 0% forest and woodland; 98% other. **Major cities:** (1986 est.) Tórshavn (capital) 15,300.

**People Population:** 47,715 (1990). **Nationality:** noun—Faeroese (sing., pl.); adjective—Faeroese. **Ethnic groups:** homogeneous Scandinavian population. **Languages:** Faeroese (derived from Old Norse), Danish. **Religions:** Evangelical Lutheran.

**Government Type:** self-governing overseas administrative division of Denmark. **Heads of government:** Margrethe II, queen (since Jan. 1972); Jógvan Sundstein, prime minister (since Jan. 1989). **Structure:** legislative authority lies jointly with Crown, acting through appointed high commissioner, and 32-member provincial parliament (Lagting) in matters of strictly Faeroese concern; executive power vested in Crown, acting through high commissioner, but exercised by provincial cabinet responsible to provincial parliament.

**Economy Monetary unit:** Danish krone. **Budget:** (1986) *income:* $176 mil.; *expend.:* $176 mil. **GDP:** $773 mil., $16,800 per capita (1986). **Chief crops:** sheep and cattle grazing. **Natural resources:** fish. **Major industries:** fishing. **Labor force:** 17,585; fishing, manufacturing, transportation, commerce. **Exports:** $267 mil. (f.o.b., 1986); 86% fish and fish products, animal feedstuffs, transport equipment. **Imports:** $363 mil. (c.i.f., 1986); 38% machinery and transport equipment, 11% food and livestock, 10% fuels, 10% chemicals. **Major trading partners:** (1986) *exports:* 18% Denmark, 14% U.S., W.

Germany, France, UK; *imports:* 46% Denmark, W. Germany, Norway, Japan, UK.

---

## Greenland

**Geography Location:** North Atlantic Ocean, largely within Arctic Circle. Godthåb 64°11′N, 51°44′W. **Boundaries:** Iceland about 190 mi. (300 km) to E across Denmark Strait, Canada to SW and W across Baffin Bay and Davis Strait. **Total land area:** 840,000 sq. mi. (2,175,600 sq km); land area 131,931 sq. mi. (341,700 sq km) ice free. **Coastline:** 27,400 mi. (44,087 km). **Comparative area:** slightly more than three times size of Texas. **Land use:** 0% arable land; 0% permanent crops; 1% meadows and pastures; negl. % forest and woodland; 99% other. **Major cities:** (1989) Godthåb (Nuuk, capital), 12,426.

**People Population:** 56,078 (1990). **Nationality:** noun—Greenlander(s); adjective—Greenlandic. **Ethnic groups:** 86% Greenlander (Eskimos and Greenland-born whites), 14% Danish. **Languages:** Danish, Eskimo dialects. **Religions:** Evangelical Lutheran.

**Government Type:** self-governing overseas administrative division of Denmark. **National holiday:** Apr. 16. **Heads of government:** Margrethe II, queen (since Jan. 1972); Jonathan Motzfeldt, home-rule chairman (since May 1979). **Structure:** executive—home-rule chairman and four-person council; legislative—elected 27-seat Landsting and Danish parliament.

**Economy Monetary unit:** Danish krone. **Budget:** (1985) *income:* $380 mil.; *expend:* $380 mil. **GNP:** $374 mil., $7,000 per capita. **Chief crops:** arable land largely in hay; sheep grazing, garden produce. **Natural resources:** zinc, lead, iron ore, coal, molybdenum. **Major industries:** mining, fishing, sealing. **Labor force:** 22,800; largely engaged in fishing, hunting, sheep breeding. **Exports:** $386.2 mil. (f.o.b., 1988); fish and fish products, metallic ores and concentrates. **Imports:** $445.6 mil. (c.i.f., 1988); petroleum and petroleum products, machinery and transport equipment, food products. **Major trading partners:** (1986) *exports:* 76% Denmark, 5% Sweden, 1% W. Germany; *imports:* 66% Denmark, 5% Norway, 4% Sweden, 4% W. Germany, 4% Japan, 3% U.S.

---

## France
### French Guiana
#### Department of Guiana

**Geography Location:** NE coast of South America. **Boundaries:** North Atlantic Ocean to N, Brazil to E and S across Oyapock River, Suriname to W across Maroni River. **Total land area:** 34,750 sq. mi. (90,000 sq km). **Coastline:** 235 mi. (378 km). **Comparative area:** slightly smaller than Indiana. **Land use:** negl. % arable land; negl. % permanent crops; negl. % meadows and pastures; 82% forest and woodland; 18% other. **Major cities:** (1989 est.) Cayenne (capital) 43,500.

**People Population:** 97,781 (1990). **Nationality:** noun—French Guianese (sing., pl.); ad-

jective—French Guiana. **Ethnic groups:** 66% black or mulatto, (2%) Caucasian, 12% East Indian, Chinese or Amerindian, 10% other. **Languages:** French. **Religions:** predominantly Roman Catholic.

**Government Type:** overseas department of France. **Heads of government:** Jean-Pierre Lacroix, commissioner (since Aug. 1988). **Structure:** executive—prefect appointed by Paris; legislative—popularly elected 16-member General Council and Regional Council composed of members of the local General Council and the locally elected deputy and senator to the French parliament; judicial—under jurisdiction of French judicial system.

**Economy Monetary unit:** French franc. **Budget:** (1985) *income:* $735 mil.; *expend.:* $735 mil. **GDP:** $210 mil., $3,230 per capita (1982). **Chief crops:** limited vegetables for local consumption; rice, corn, manioc, cocoa, bananas, sugar. **Livestock:** cattle, pigs, goats. **Natural resources:** bauxite, timber, gold, cinnabar, kaolin, fish. **Major industries:** construction, shrimp processing, forestry products. **Labor force:** 23,265 (1980); 60.6% services, government, and commerce, 21.2% industry, 18.2% agriculture; 15% unemployment (1987). **Exports:** $37.0 mil. (f.o.b., 1986); shrimp, timber, rum, rosewood essence. **Imports:** $297.7 mil. (c.i.f., 1986); food (grains, processed meat), other consumer goods, producer goods, petroleum. **Major trading partners:** (1984) *exports:* 41% U.S., 18% Japan, 9% France; *imports:* 55% France, 13% Trinidad and Tobago, 3% U.S.

---

## French Polynesia
### Territory of French Polynesia

**Geography Location:** five island groups (Gambier, Marquesas, Society, Tuamotu, and Tubuaï) in South Pacific Ocean about two-thirds of way from Panama Canal to New Zealand. Papeete (Society Is.) 17°32′S, 149°34′W. **Boundaries:** Kiribati to NE, Cook Islands to E. **Total land area:** 1,622 sq. mi. (4,200 sq km). **Coastline:** 1,569 mi. (2,525 km). **Comparative area:** slightly less than ⅓ size of Connecticut. **Land use:** 1% arable land; 19% permanent crops; 5% meadows and pastures; 31% forest and woodland; 44% other. **Major cities:** (1983) Papeete (capital) 23,496.

**People Population:** 190,181 (1990). **Nationality:** noun—French Polynesian(s); adjective—French Polynesian. **Ethnic groups:** 78% Polynesian, 12% Chinese, 6% local French, 4% metropolitan French. **Religions:** 55% Protestant, 32% Roman Catholic, 13% other.

**Government Type:** overseas territory of France. **Heads of government:** Jean Montpezat, high commissioner; Alexandre Leontieff, president of territorial government (since Dec. 1987). **Structure:** 30-member Territorial Assembly, popularly elected; five-member Council of Government, elected by assembly; popular election of two deputies to National Assembly and one senator to Senate in Paris.

**Economy Monetary unit:** Colonial Francs Pacifique (CFP). **Budget:** (1984) *income:* $431 mil.; *expend.:* $418 mil. **GDP:** $2.24 bil., $6,400 per capita (1986). **Chief crops:** coconuts. **Livestock:** pigs, cattle, goats, sheep, horses. **Natural resources:** timber, fish, cobalt. **Major industries:** tourism, pearls, agricultural processing. **Labor force:** N.A. **Exports:** $75 mil. (f.o.b., 1987); 79% coconut products, 14% mother-of-pearl, vanilla. **Imports:** $767 mil. (c.i.f., 1986); fuels, foodstuffs, equipment. **Major trading partners: exports:** 44% France, 21% U.S.; **imports:** 50% France, 16% U.S., 6% New Zealand.

## Guadeloupe
### Department of Guadeloupe
**Geography Location:** eastern Caribbean Sea: Guadeloupe 16°00'N, 61°42'W; St. Barthélemy 17°55'N, 63°50'W; Marie Galante 15°57'N, 61°20'W. **Boundaries:** Antigua to N, Dominica to S. **Total land area:** 687 sq. mi. (1,780 sq km). **Coastline:** 190 mi. (306 km). **Comparative area:** 10 times size of Washington, D.C. **Land use:** 18% arable land; 5% permanent crops; 13% meadows and pastures; 40% forest and woodland; 24% other; includes 1% irrigated. **Major cities:** (1982 census) Basse-Terre (capital) 13,656; Les Abymes 56,165; Pointe à Pitre 25,310.

**People Population:** 342,175 (1990). **Nationality:** noun—Guadeloupian(s); adjective—Guadeloupe. **Ethnic groups:** 90% black or mulatto, 5% white, 5% East Indian, Lebanese, Chinese. **Languages:** French, Creole patois. **Religions:** 95% Roman Catholic, 5% Hindu and African.

**Government Type:** overseas department of France. **Heads of government:** Jean-Paul Proust, prefect (since Nov. 1989). **Structure:** executive—prefect appointed by Paris; legislative—popularly elected General Council of 36 members and Regional Council composed of members of local General Council and locally elected deputies and senators to French parliament; judicial—under jurisdiction of French judicial system.

**Economy Monetary unit:** French franc. **Budget:** (1985) $380.5 mil. **GDP:** $1.1 bil., $3,300 per capita (1987). **Chief crops:** sugarcane, bananas, pineapples, vegetables. **Livestock:** cattle, pigs, goats. **Natural resources:** cultivable land, beaches and climate that foster tourism. **Major industries:** construction, cement, rum. **Labor force:** 120,000; 53% services, government, and commerce, 25.8% industry, 21.2% agriculture; 25% unemployment. **Exports:** $109 mil. (1986); bananas, sugar, rum. **Imports:** $792 mil. (1986); vehicles, foodstuffs, clothing and other consumer goods, construction materials, petroleum products. **Major trading partners:** (1984) **exports:** 72% France, 16% Martinique; **imports:** 59% France.

## Martinique
### Department of Martinique
**Geography Location:** eastern Caribbean Sea (14°36'N, 61°05'W). **Boundaries:** Dominica to N, St. Lucia to S. **Total land area:** 425 sq. mi. (1,100 sq km). **Coastline:** 180 mi. (290 km). **Comparative area:** slightly more than six times size of Washington, D.C. **Land use:** 10% arable land; 8% permanent crops; 30% meadows and pastures; 26% forest and woodland; 26% other; includes 5% irrigated. **Major cities:** (1989 est.) Fort-de-France (capital) 110,000.

**People Population:** 340,381 (1990). **Nationality:** noun—Martiniquais (sing., pl.); adjective—Martiniquais. **Ethnic groups:** 90% African and African-Caucasian-Indian mixture, 5% Caucasian, 5% East Indian, Lebanese, Chinese. **Languages:** French, Creole patois. **Religions:** 95% Roman Catholic, 5% Hindu and African beliefs.

**Government Type:** overseas department of France. **Heads of government:** Jean Claude Roure, commissioner (since 1989). **Structure:** executive—prefect appointed by Paris; legislative—popularly elected General Council of 36 members and Regional Council, including all members of local General Council and locally elected deputies and senators to French parliament; judicial—under jurisdiction of French judicial system.

**Economy Monetary unit:** French franc. **Budget:** (1981) **income:** $223 mil.; **expend.:** $223 mil. **GDP:** $1.3 bil., $3,650 per capita (1984). **Chief crops:** bananas, pineapples, vegetables, flowers, sugarcane for rum. **Livestock:** sheep, cattle, pigs, goats. **Natural resources:** coastal scenery and beaches, cultivable land. **Major industries:** construction, rum, cement. **Labor force:** 100,000; 31.7% service industry, 29.4% construction and public works, 13.1% agriculture; 25–30% unemployment (1985). **Exports:** $209 mil. (1986): refined petroleum products, bananas, rum, pineapples. **Imports:** $879 mil. (1986); petroleum products, foodstuffs, construction materials, vehicles, clothing and other consumer goods. **Major trading partners:** (1984) **exports:** 65% France, 26% Guadeloupe; **imports:** 64% France.

## Mayotte
### Territorial Collectivity of Mayotte
**Geography Location:** Comoros archipelago in eastern Indian Ocean (12°47'S, 45°12'E). **Boundaries:** Indian Ocean to N, Madagascar 300 mi. (480 km) to SE, Mozambique Channel to S, Mozambique to W. **Total land area:** 145 sq. mi. (376 sq km). **Coastline:** 5,798 mi. (9,330 km). **Comparative area:** slightly more than twice size of Washington, D.C. **Land use:** N.A. **Major cities:** (1985 census) Dzaoudzi (capital) 5,865; Mamoudzou 12,026; Pamanzi-Labattoir 4,106.

**People Population:** 72,186 (1990). **Nationality:** noun—Mahorais (sing., pl.); adjective—Mahoran. **Languages:** Mahorian (a Swahili dialect), French. **Religions:** 99% Muslim, 1% Christian (mostly Roman Catholic).

**Government Type:** territorial collectivity of France. **Heads of government:** Akli Khider, representative of government (since 1983); Younoussa Bamana, president of General Council (since 1976). **Structure:** elected 17-member General Council; appointed representative.

**Economy Monetary unit:** French franc. **Budget:** (1985). **income:** N.A.; **expend.:** $37.3 mil. **Chief crops:** vanilla, ylang-ylang, coffee, copra. **Natural resources:** none. **Major industries:** newly created lobster and shrimp industry. **Exports:** $4 mil. (1984); ylang-ylang, vanilla. **Imports:** $21.8 mil. (1984); building materials, transport equipment, rice, clothing, flour. **Major trading partners: exports:** 79% France, 10% Comoros, 9% Réunion; **imports:** 57% France, 16% Kenya, 11% South Africa, 8% Pakistan.

## New Caledonia
### Territory of New Caledonia and Dependencies
**Geography Location:** one large and several smaller islands in western South Pacific. Nouméa 22°16'S, 166°26'E. **Boundaries:** Vanuatu to N, Australia about 930 mi. (1,500 km) to W. **Total land area:** 7,376 sq. mi. (19,103 sq km). **Coastline:** 1,401 mi. (2,254 km). **Comparative area:** slightly smaller than Massachusetts. **Land use:** negl. % arable land; negl. % permanent crops; 14% meadows and pastures; 51% forest and woodland; 35% other. **Major cities:** (1983 census) Nouméa (capital) 60,112.

**People Population:** 153,215 (1990). **Nationality:** noun—New Caledonian(s); adjective—New Caledonian. **Ethnic groups:** 42.5% Melanesian, 37.1% European, 8.4% Wallisian, 3.8% Polynesian, 3.6% Indonesian, 1.6% Vietnamese, 3.0% other. **Languages:** French, Melanesian-Polynesian dialect. **Religions:** 60% Roman Catholic, 30% Protestant, 10% other.

**Government Type:** overseas territory of France. **Heads of government:** Bernard Grasset, high commissioner and president of Council of Government (since July 1988); Kanak Provisional Government—Jean-Marie Tjibaou, president (since Dec. 1984). **Structure:** administered by high commissioner, responsible to French Ministry for Overseas France and Council of Government; 46-seat Territorial Assembly.

**Economy Monetary unit:** Colonial Francs Pacifique (CFP). **Budget:** (1981) **income:** $110.5 mil.; **expend.:** $110.5 mil. **GNP:** $860 mil., $5,810 per capita (1985). **Chief crops:** coffee, maize, wheat, vegetables. **Livestock:** cattle, goats, pigs, horses. **Natural resources:** nickel, chrome, iron, cobalt, manganese, silver. **Major industries:** nickel mining. **Labor force:** 50,469 (1980 est.); immigrant labor now coming from Wallis and Futuna, Vanuatu, and French Polynesia; N.A. unemployment. **Exports:** $75 mil. (f.o.b., 1986); 95% nickel metal, nickel ore. **Imports:** $180 mil. (c.i.f., 1986); foodstuffs, fuels and minerals, machines and electrical equipment. **Major trading partners: exports:** 56.3% France, Japan; **imports:** 50.3% France, Australia.

**Intl. Orgs.** WMO.

## Réunion
### Department of Réunion
**Geography Location:** southwestern Indian Ocean (20°15'S, 55°27'E). **Boundaries:** 500 mi. (800 km) E of Madagascar. **Total land area:** 970 sq. mi. (2,512 sq km). **Coastline:** 125 mi. (201 km). **Comparative area:** slightly smaller than Rhode Island. **Land use:** 20% arable land; 2% permanent crops; 4% meadows and pastures; 35% forest and woodland; 39% other;

includes 2% irrigated. **Major cities:** (1989 est.) Saint-Denis (capital) 120,000; Saint-Paul 58,000; Saint-Pierre 50,061.

**People Population:** 595,583 (1990). **Nationality:** noun–Réunionese (sing., pl.); adjective–Réunionese. **Ethnic groups:** mostly intermixed French, African, Malagasy, Chinese, Pakistani, Indian ancestry. **Languages:** French (official), Creole. **Religions:** 94% Roman Catholic.

**Government Type:** overseas department of France. **Heads of government:** Daniel Contantin, commissioner. **Structure:** administered by prefect appointed by French minister of interior, assisted by secretary general and elected 36-man General Council; in 1974 France created an elected 45-member Regional Assembly to coordinate economic and social development policies; in 1981 both General Council and Regional Assembly received greater authority for fiscal policy.

**Economy Monetary unit:** French franc. **Budget:** (1986) *income:* $358 mil.; *expend.:* $914 mil. **GDP:** $2.4 bil., $4,290 per capita (1985). **Chief crops:** cash crops–almost entirely sugarcane, small amounts of vanilla and perfume plants; food crops–tropical fruit and vegetables, manioc, bananas, corn, market garden produce; most food imported. **Livestock:** pigs, goats, cattle, sheep. **Natural resources:** negl. **Major industries:** sugar, rum, cigarettes, handicraft items. **Labor force:** (1981) 49% services, 30% agriculture, 21% industry; 32% unemployment (1986) (high seasonal unemployment); 63% of population of working age (1983). **Exports:** $136 mil. (f.o.b., 1986); 75% sugar, 4% rum and molasses, 4% perfume essences, 1% vanilla and tea. **Imports:** $1.1 mil. (c.i.f., 1986); manufactured goods, food, beverages, tobacco, machinery and transportation equipment, raw materials, petroleum products. **Major trading partners:** France, Mauritius, Bahrain, S. Africa, Italy.

### St. Pierre and Miquelon
Department of St. Pierre and Miquelon
**Geography Location:** North Atlantic off east coast of Canada. St. Pierre 46°46′N, 56°12′W. **Boundaries:** Newfoundland, Canada 16 mi. (25 km) to N, North Atlantic Ocean to E and S. **Total land area:** 93 sq. mi. (242 sq km). **Coastline:** 75 mi. (120 km). **Comparative area:** slightly less than 1.5 times size of Washington, D.C. **Land use:** 13% arable land; 0% permanent crops; 0% meadows and pastures; 4% forest and woodland; 83% other. **Major cities:** (1982 census) St. Pierre (capital) 5,415; Miquelon 626.

**People Population:** 6,330 (1990). **Nationality:** noun–Frenchmen; adjective–French. **Ethnic groups:** originally Basques and Bretons (French fishermen). **Languages:** French. **Religions:** 98% Roman Catholic.

**Government Type:** territorial collectivity of France. **National holiday:** National Day, July 14. **Heads of government:** Jean-Pierre Marquie, commissioner; Marc Plantegenest, president of the General Council. **Structure:** executive–government commissioner appointed by Paris; legislative–popularly elected 14-member General

Council elected for six-year terms; judiciary–under jurisdiction of French judicial system.

**Economy Monetary unit:** French franc. **Budget:** (1987) *income:* N.A.; *expend.:* $13.9 mil. **GDP:** N.A., $2,495 per capita (1984). **Chief crops:** vegetables. **Livestock:** cattle, sheep, pigs. **Natural resources:** N.A. **Major industries:** fishing, supply base for fishing fleets, tourism. **Labor force:** 2,510 (1982); N.A. unemployment. **Exports:** $23.3 mil. (f.o.b., 1986); fish and fish products, fox and mink pelts. **Imports:** $50.3 mil. (c.i.f., 1986); meat, clothing, fuel, electrical equipment, machinery, building materials. **Major trading partners:** (1983) *exports:* 58% U.S., 17% France, 11% Canada; *imports:* Canada, France, U.S., Netherlands, UK.

### Wallis and Futuna
Territory of the Wallis and Futuna Islands
**Geography Location:** two island groups (Wallis to NE, Hooru, incl. Futuna Is., to SW) in South Pacific. Mata-Utu (Wallis group) 13°22′S, 176°12′W. **Boundaries:** Western Samoa to E, Fiji to SW. **Total land area:** 106 sq. mi. (274 sq km). **Coastline:** 80 mi. (129 km). **Comparative area:** slightly larger than Washington, D.C. **Land use:** 5% arable land; 20% permanent crops; 0% meadows and pastures; 0% forest and woodland; 75% other. **Major cities:** Mata-Utu (capital) (1983 census) 815.

**People Population:** 14,910 (1990). **Nationality:** noun–Wallisian(s), Futunan(s), or Wallis and Futuna Islander(s); adjective–Wallisian, Futunan, or Wallis and Futuna Islander. **Ethnic groups:** almost entirely Polynesian. **Languages:** French (official). **Religions:** largely Roman Catholic.

**Government Type:** overseas territory of France. **Heads of government:** Roger Dumec, high administrator (since July 1988). **Structure:** Territorial Assembly of 20 members; popular election of one deputy to National Assembly in Paris and one senator.

**Economy Monetary unit:** Colonial Francs Pacifique (CFP). **Budget:** N.A. **Chief crops:** dominated by coconuts, subsistence crops of yams, taro, bananas. **Livestock:** pigs, goats. **Natural resources:** none. **Major industries:** copra, handicrafts. **Exports:** negl. **Imports:** $3.4 mil. (1977); largely foodstuffs and some equipment associated with development programs.

### Uninhabited Territories
Bassas da India (21°25′S, 39°42′E); Clipperton Is. (22°20′S, 40°22′E); Europa Is. (22°20′S, 40°22′E); French Southern and Antarctic Lands (Kerguelen Is. 49°20′S, 69°30′E); Glorioso Is. (11°30′S, 47°20′E); Tromelin Is. (15°52′S, 54°25′E).

## Morocco
### Western Sahara
**Geography Location:** northwestern coast of Africa. **Boundaries:** Morocco to N, Algeria, Mauritania to E, Atlantic Ocean to W. **Total land area:** 102,703 sq. mi. (266,000 sq km).

**Coastline:** 690 mi. (1,110 km). **Comparative area:** between Wyoming and Colorado. **Land use:** negl. % arable land; 0% permanent crops; 19% meadows and pastures; 0% forest and woodland; 81% other. **Major cities:** (1982) El Aaiun (capital) 93,785.

**People Population:** 191,707 (1990). **Nationality:** noun–Saharan(s), Moroccan(s); adjective–Saharan, Moroccan. **Ethnic groups:** Arab, Berber. **Languages:** Hassaniya Arabic, Moroccan Arabic. **Religions:** Muslim.

**Government Type:** legal status of territory and question of sovereignty still unresolved. **Independence:** N.A. **Constitution:** N.A. **National holiday:** N.A. **Heads of government:** None. **Structure:** N.A.

**Economy Monetary unit:** Moroccan dirham. **Budget:** N.A. **GDP:** N.A. **Chief crops:** practically none; some barley grown in non-drought years; fruit and vegetables in the few oases; food imports; water shortage. **Livestock:** N.A. **Natural resources:** phosphates, iron ore. **Major industries:** phosphate, fishing, handicrafts. **Labor force:** 12,000; 50% animal husbandry and subsistence farming. **Exports:** $8 mil. (f.o.b., 1982 est.); 62% phosphates. **Imports:** $30 mil. (c.i.f., 1982); fuel for fishing fleet, foodstuffs. **Major trading partners:** Morocco claims administrative control over Western Sahara and controls all trade with country; trade figures are included in overall Moroccan accounts.

## Netherlands
### Aruba
**Geography Location:** southern Caribbean Sea (12°32′N, 70°02′W), off NW Venezuela. **Boundaries:** Curaçao, Netherlands Antilles 42 mi. (68 km) to E, Venezuela 16 mi. (25 km) to S. **Total land area:** 74.5 sq. mi. (193.0 sq km). **Coastline:** about 45 mi. (about 72 km). **Comparative area:** slightly larger than Washington, D.C. **Land use:** 0% arable land; 0% permanent crops; 0% meadows and pastures; 0% forest and woodland; 100% other. **Major cities:** Oranjestad (capital).

**People Population:** 62,656 (1990). **Nationality:** noun–Aruban(s); adjective–Aruban. **Ethnic groups:** 80% mixed European/Caribbean Indian. **Languages:** Dutch (official), Papiamento (a Spanish-Portuguese-Dutch-English dialect); English widely spoken. **Religions:** 82% Roman Catholic, 8% Protestant; also small Hindu, Muslim, Confucian, Jewish minorities.

**Government Type:** self-governing until complete independence from Netherlands is granted in 1996. **Heads of government:** Felipe (Felepito) Tromp, governor (since 1986); Nelson O. Oduber, prime minister (since Feb. 1989).

**Economy Monetary unit:** Aruban florin. **Budget:** (1987) *income:* $145 mil.; *expend.:* $185 mil. **GDP:** $620 mil., $8,210 per capita (1987). **Chief crops:** negl. **Livestock:** N.A. **Natural resources:** negl.; white sandy beaches. **Major industries:** tourism, light manufacturing (tobacco, beverages, consumer goods). **Labor force:** (1986) mostly tourism; 14.5% unemployment (1987). **Exports:** $47.5 mil. (f.o.b., 1988); mostly petroleum products. **Imports:** $296 mil. (c.i.f., 1988); foodstuffs, consumer goods. **Major trading partners:** *exports:* 64% U.S., EC; *imports:* 8% U.S., EC.

## Netherlands Antilles

**Geography  Location:** two island groups in Caribbean Sea, about 500 mi. (800 km) apart. Curaçao Is. 12°12′N, 68°56′W; St. Maarten Is. 18°03′N, 63°05′W. **Boundaries:** southern group (Curaçao and Bonaire)—Venezuela to S; northern group (St. Eustatius, Saba, and St. Maarten)—Antigua to E, Virgin Islands to W. **Total land area:** 309 sq. mi. (800 sq km). **Coastline:** 226 mi. (364 km). **Comparative area:** slightly less than 5.5 times size of Washington, D.C. **Land use:** 8% arable land; 0% permanent crops; 0% meadows and pastures; 0% forest and woodland; 92% other. **Major cities:** Willemstad (capital).

**People  Population:** 183,503 (1990). **Nationality:** noun—Netherlands Antillean(s); adjective—Netherlands Antillean. **Ethnic groups:** 85% mixed African; remainder Carib Indian, European, Latin, Oriental. **Languages:** Dutch (official), Papiamento (a Spanish-Portuguese-Dutch-English dialect) predominates; English widely spoken; Spanish. **Religions:** predominantly Roman Catholic; Protestant, Jewish, Seventh-Day Adventist.

**Government  Type:** autonomous part of Netherlands. **Constitution:** Dec. 29, 1954. **Heads of government:** Jaime Saleh, governor-general (since 1989); Maria Liberia-Peters, prime minister (since May 1988). **Structure:** executive—governor (appointed by Crown); actual power exercised by eight-member Council of Ministers or cabinet presided over by minister-president; legislative—22-member Legislative Council; judicial—independent court system under control of chief justice of Supreme Court of Justice; each island territory has island council headed by lieutenant governor.

**Economy  Monetary unit:** Netherlands Antillean guilder or florin. **Budget:** (1987 est.) *income:* $180 mil.; *expend.:* $289 mil. **GDP:** $1.0 bil., $5,500 per capita (1985). **Chief crops:** corn, pulses. **Livestock:** goats, sheep, cattle, pigs. **Natural resources:** phosphates (Curaçao only), salt (Bonaire only). **Major industries:** tourism on Curaçao and St. Maarten; petroleum refining on Curaçao; petroleum transshipment facilities on Curaçao and Bonaire; light manufacturing on Curaçao. **Labor force:** 89,000 (1983); 65% government, 28% industry and commerce; 8% unemployment (1987). **Exports:** $1.3 bil. (f.o.b., 1988); 98% petroleum products, phosphates. **Imports:** 1.5 bil. (c.i.f., 1988); 64% crude petroleum, food, manufactures. **Major trading partners:** *exports:* 55% U.S., 7% UK, 5% Jamaica; *imports:* 52% Venezuela, 15% Nigeria, 12% U.S.

## New Zealand

### Cook Islands

**Geography  Location:** 15 islands (13 inhabited) in South Pacific. Avarua 21°12′S, 159°46′W. Boundaries: French Polynesia to E, American Samoa to W. **Total land area:** 91.5 sq. mi. (237.0 sq km). **Coastline:** 75 mi. (120 km). **Comparative area:** slightly less than 1.5 times size of Washington, D.C. **Land use:** 4% arable land; 22% permanent crops; 0% meadows and pastures; 0% forest and woodland; 74% other. **Major cities:** Avarua (capital).

**People  Population:** 18,187 (1990). **Nationality:** noun—Cook Islander(s); adjective—Cook Islander. **Ethnic groups:** 81.3% Polynesian (full blood), 7.7% Polynesian and European, 7.7% Polynesian and other, 2.4% European, 0.9% other. **Languages:** English. **Religions:** Christian; majority of populace members of Cook Islands Christian Church.

**Government  Type:** self-governing in free association with New Zealand; Cook Islands government fully responsible for internal affairs and has right at any time to move to full independence by unilateral action; New Zealand responsible for external affairs, in consultation with Cook Islands government. **Heads of government:** Geoffrey Henry, prime minister (since Feb. 1989). **Structure:** New Zealand governor-general appoints representative to Cook Islands, who represents Queen of England and New Zealand government; representative appoints prime minister; popularly elected 24-member parliament; 15-member House of Arikis (chiefs), appointed by representative, is advisory body only.

**Economy  Monetary unit:** New Zealand dollar. **Budget:** (1987 est.) *income:* $33.8 mil.; *expend.:* $34.4 mil. **GDP:** $40.0 mil., $2,200 per capita (1988 est.). **Chief crops:** cash crops—copra, citrus fruits, pineapples, tomatoes, bananas; food crops—yams, taro. **Livestock:** poultry, pigs, horses, goats. **Natural resources:** negl. **Major industries:** fruit processing, tourism. **Exports:** $4.0 mil. (f.o.b., 1988); copra, fresh and canned fruit. **Imports:** $38.7 mil. (c.i.f., 1988); foodstuffs, textiles, fuels. **Major trading partners:** *exports:* 80% New Zealand, Japan; *imports:* 49% New Zealand, Japan, Australia.

**Intl. Orgs.**  IFC, IMF.

### Niue

**Geography  Location:** coral island in western South Pacific (19°02′S, 169°55′W). **Boundaries:** Tonga 300 mi. (480 km) to W, southern Cook Islands 580 mi. (930 km) to E. **Total land area:** 100 sq. mi. (259 sq km). **Coastline:** 40 mi. (64 km). **Comparative area:** slightly less than 1.5 times size of Washington, D.C. **Land use:** 61% arable land; 4% permanent crops; 4% meadows and pastures; 19% forest and woodland; 12% other. **Major cities:** Alofi (capital).

**People  Population:** 2,019 (1990). **Nationality:** noun—Niuean(s); adjective—Niuean. **Ethnic groups:** Polynesian, with about 200 Europeans, Samoans, Tongans. **Languages:** Polynesian dialect closely related to Tongan and Samoan; English. **Religions:** 75% Ekalesia Nieue Niue (Niuean Church)—a Christian Protestant church closely related to London Missionary Society, 10% Mormon, 5% Roman Catholic, Jehovah's Witnesses, Seventh-Day Adventist.

**Government  Type:** self-governing territory in free association with New Zealand. **Heads of government:** Sir Robert R. Rex, premier (since early 1950s); John Springford, New Zealand representative (since 1974). **Structure:** executive cabinet of four members—premier (elected by assembly) and three ministers (chosen by premier from among assembly members); Legislative Assembly consists of 20 members (14 village representatives and six elected on a common roll); if requested by assembly, New Zealand will also legislate for island.

**Economy  Monetary unit:** New Zealand dollar. **Budget:** (1985 est.) *income:* $5.5 mil.; *expend.:* $6.3 mil. **GNP:** $3 mil., $1,080 per capita (1984). **Chief crops:** cash crops—copra, coconuts, passion fruit, honey, limes; food crops—taro, yams, cassava (tapioca). **Livestock:** chickens, pigs, cattle. **Natural resources:** negl. **Major industries:** tourism, handicrafts. **Labor force:** about 1,000 (1981 est.); most Niueans work on family plantations; paid work exists only in government service, small industry, and Niue Development Board. **Exports:** $175,274 (f.o.b., 1985); canned coconut cream, copra, honey, passion fruit products, pawpaw. **Imports:** $3.8 mil. (c.i.f., 1985); food, live animals, manufactured goods, machinery, fuels, lubricants, chemicals, drugs. **Major trading partners:** *exports:* New Zealand, Fiji, Cook Islands, Australia; *imports:* New Zealand, Fiji, Japan, Western Samoa, Australia, U.S.

### Tokelau

**Geography  Location:** three atolls (Atafu, Nukunonu, Fakaofo) in South Pacific. Atafu 8°33′S, 172°30′W. **Boundaries:** northern Cook Islands to E, Western Samoa 300 mi. (480 km) to S, Tuvalu to W. **Total land area:** 3.9 sq. mi. (10.1 sq km). **Coastline:** 62 mi. (101 km). **Comparative area:** about 17 times size of the Mall in Washington, D.C. **Land use:** 0% arable land; 0% permanent crops; 0% meadows and pastures; 0% forest and woodland; 100% other. **Major cities:** none; each atoll has own administrative center.

**People  Population:** 1,700 (1990). **Nationality:** noun—Tokelauan(s); adjective—Tokelauan. **Ethnic groups:** all Polynesian, with cultural ties to Western Samoa. **Languages:** Tokelauan (a Polynesian language), English. **Religions:** 70% Congregational Christian Church, 30% Roman Catholic—on Atafu, all Congregational Christian Church of Samoa; on Nukunonu, all Roman Catholic; on Fakaofo, both denominations.

**Government  Type:** territory of New Zealand. **National holiday:** Waitangi Day, Feb. 6. **Heads of government:** Neil Walter, administrator. **Structure:** minister of foreign affairs of New Zealand is empowered to appoint administrator to region; powers of administrator are delegated to official secretary at Office of Tokelau Affairs, Apia, Western Samoa.

**Economy  Monetary unit:** New Zealand dollar and Tokelau souvenir coin; Western Samoan tala also used. **Budget:** (1987) *income:* $430,830; *expend.:* $2.8 mil. **GDP:** $1.4 mil., $670 per capita (1983). **Chief crops:** cash crops—coconuts, copra; food crops—pulaka, breadfruit, pawpaw, bananas. **Livestock:** pigs. **Natural resources:** negl. **Major industries:** small-scale enterprises for copra production, woodwork, plaited craft goods, stamps, coins. **Labor force:** N.A. **Exports:** $98,000 (f.o.b., 1983); stamps, handicrafts. **Imports:** $323,400 (c.i.f., 1983); foodstuffs, machinery, fuel. **Major trading partners:** New Zealand.

## Norway

### Svalbard

**Geography** **Location:** nine large and numerous smaller islands in Arctic Ocean. **Boundaries:** Longyearbyen (Spitsbergen Is.) 78° 13′N, 15°38′W; Bear Is. 74°30′N, 19°00′E. Norway to S, Greenland to W. **Total land area:** 24,000 sq. mi. (62,000 sq km). **Coastline:** undetermined. **Comparative area:** slightly smaller than West Virginia. **Land use:** 0% arable land; 0% permanent crops; 0% meadows and pastures; 0% forest and woodland; 100% other; no trees; only bushes are crowberry and cloudberry. **Major cities:** Longyearbyen (capital).

**People** **Population:** 3,942 (1990). **Ethnic groups:** 64% Russian, 35% Norwegian, 1% other. **Languages:** Russian, Norwegian.

**Government** **Type:** territory of Norway. **Heads of government:** Leif Eldring, governor.

**Economy** **Monetary unit:** Norwegian krone. **Budget:** (1986) $73 mil. kroner. **Natural resources:** coal, copper, iron ore, phosphate, zinc, wildlife, fish. **Major industries:** coal mining; trapping of seal, polar bear, fox, walrus. **Exports:** 507,000 metric tons of coal from Norwegian mines, 500,000 tons of coal from Soviet mines (1987).

### Uninhabited Territories

Bouvet Is. (54°26′S, 3°24′E); Jan Mayen Is. (71°00′N, 8°30′W).

## Portugal

### Macau

**Geography** **Location:** peninsula of Macau, on mainland of southern China, and three nearby islands. **Boundaries:** China to N, Hong Kong to NE, South China Sea to S. **Total land area:** 6.5 sq. mi. (16.9 sq km). **Coastline:** 25 mi. (40 km). **Comparative area:** about 1/10 size of Washington, D.C. **Land use:** 0% arable land; 0% permanent crops; 0% meadows and pastures; 0% forest and woodland; 100% other. **Major cities:** Macau (capital).

**People** **Population:** 441,691 (1990). **Nationality:** noun—Macanese (sing., pl.); adjective—Macau. **Ethnic groups:** 95% Chinese, 3% Portuguese, 2% other. **Languages:** Portuguese (official); Cantonese is language of commerce. **Religions:** mainly Buddhist; 17,000 Catholics, of whom half are Chinese.

**Government** **Type:** Chinese territory under Portuguese administration. **Heads of government:** Carlos Melancia, governor (since July 1987). **Structure:** governor assisted by five secretaries-adjunct (all appointed by president of Portugal), 17-member Legislative Assembly (five appointed by governor, six elected by direct and universal suffrage, six elected indirectly by various groups and associations).

**Economy** **Monetary unit:** pataca. **Budget:** (1986) *income:* $305 mil.; *expend.:* $298 mil. **GDP:** $2.7 bil., $6,300 per capita (1989 est.). **Chief crops:** rice, vegetables; food shortages—rice, vegetables; not self-sufficient in food production. **Livestock:** pigs, buffalo, cattle. **Natural resources:** none. **Major industries:** clothing, textiles, toys, plastic products, furniture, tourism. **Labor force:** 180,000 (1986); N.A. unemployment. **Exports:** $1.7 bil. (1989); textiles, clothing. **Imports:** $1.6 bil. (1989); raw materials, foodstuffs. **Major trading partners:** (1987) *exports:* 33% U.S., 15% Hong Kong, 12% W. Germany, 10% France; *imports:* 39% Hong Kong, 21% China, Japan 10%.

## United Kingdom

### Anguilla

**Geography** **Location:** island in northeastern Caribbean (18°03′N, 63°04′W). **Boundaries:** St. Martin 5 mi. (8 km) to S, St. Kitts 70 mi. (113 km) to SE. **Total land area:** 36 sq. mi. (96 sq km). **Coastline:** 38 mi. (61 km). **Comparative area:** about 1/2 size of Washington, D.C. **Land use:** N.A.; mostly rock with sparse scrub oak, few trees, some commercial salt ponds. **Major cities:** The Valley (capital).

**People** **Population:** 6,883 (1990). **Nationality:** noun—Anguillan(s); adjective—Anguillan. **Ethnic groups:** mainly of black African descent. **Languages:** English. **Religions:** Anglican, Methodist, Roman Catholic.

**Government** **Type:** dependent territory of UK. **Constitution:** Apr. 1, 1982. **Heads of government:** Geoffrey O. Whittaker, governor and president of Executive Council (since 1987). **Structure:** 11-member House of Assembly, seven-member Executive Council.

**Economy** **Monetary unit:** East Caribbean dollar. **Budget:** (1988 est.) *income:* $9.0 mil.; *expend.:* $8.8 mil. **GDP:** $23 mil., $3,350 per capita (1983 est.). **Chief crops:** pigeon peas, corn, sweet potatoes. **Natural resources:** negl.; salt, fish, lobsters. **Major industries:** tourism, boat building, salt, fishing. **Labor force:** 2,780 (1984); 30% unemployment (1985). **Exports:** lobsters.

**Intl. Orgs.** Commonwealth.

### Bermuda

**Geography** **Location:** archipelago of about 150 islands, in southern North Atlantic Ocean (32°18′N, 64°47′W). **Boundaries:** Cape Hatteras 580 mi. (933 km) to W. **Total land area:** 21 sq. mi. (53 sq km). **Coastline:** 64 mi. (103 km). **Comparative area:** about 3/10 size of Washington, D.C. **Land use:** 0% arable land; 0% permanent crops; 0% meadows and pastures; 20% forest and woodland; 80% other. **Major cities:** (1987 est.) Hamilton (capital) 3,000.

**People** **Population:** 58,337 (1990). **Nationality:** noun—Bermudian(s); adjective—Bermudian. **Ethnic groups:** 61% black, 39% white and other. **Languages:** English. **Religions:** 37% Anglican, 14% Roman Catholic, 10% African Methodist Episcopal (Zion), 6% Methodist, 5% Seventh-Day Adventist, 28% other.

**Government** **Type:** British dependent territory. **Constitution:** June 8, 1968. **Heads of government:** Sir Desmond Langley, governor (since Oct. 1988); John William David Swan, premier (since 1982). **Structure:** cabinet (Executive Council) appointed by governor, led by government leader; bicameral legislature with appointed Senate and 40-member directly elected House of Assembly; supreme court.

**Economy** **Monetary unit:** Bermuda dollar. **Budget:** (1989 est.) *income:* $280 mil.; *expend.:* $279 mil. **GDP:** $1.3 bil., $23,000 per capita (1987). **Chief crops:** bananas, vegetables, Easter lilies, dairy products, citrus fruits. **Livestock:** poultry, pigs, cattle. **Natural resources:** limestone, pleasant climate fostering tourism. **Major industries:** tourism, finance, structural concrete products. **Labor force:** 32,000 (1984); 25% clerical, 22% services, 21% laborers, 13% professional and technical, 10% administrative and managerial. **Exports:** $23 mil. (f.o.b., 1985); semitropical produce, light manufactures. **Imports:** $402 mil. (c.i.f., 1985); fuel, foodstuffs, machinery. **Major trading partners:** *exports:* 25% U.S., 25% Italy, 14% UK, 6% Canada, 31% other; *imports:* 58% U.S., 9% Netherlands Antilles, 8% UK, 6% Canada, 5% Japan, 14% other.

**Intl. Orgs.** INTERPOL, WHO.

### British Virgin Islands

**Geography** **Location:** more than 40 mountainous islands (15 inhabited) in northeastern Caribbean. Road Town (Tortola Is.), 18°26′N, 64°32′W. **Boundaries:** Puerto Rico about 100 mi. (161 km) to W. **Total land area:** 59 sq. mi. (153 sq km). **Coastline:** 50 mi. (80 km). **Comparative area:** about 4/5 size of Washington, D.C. **Land use:** 20% arable land; 7% permanent crops; 33% meadows and pastures; 7% forest and woodland; 33% other. **Major cities:** Road Town (capital).

**People** **Population:** 12,258 (1990). **Nationality:** noun—Virgin Islander(s); adjective—Virgin Islander. **Ethnic groups:** over 90% black, remainder of white and Asian origin. **Languages:** English. **Religions:** majority Methodist; others include Anglican, Church of God, Seventh-Day Adventist, Baptist, Roman Catholic.

**Government** **Type:** dependent territory of UK. **Constitution:** June 1, 1977. **National holiday:** Territory Day, July 1. **Heads of government:** Mark Herdman, governor and chairman of Executive Council (since 1986); H. Lavitty Stout, chief minister (since 1986). **Structure:** cabinet (Executive Council) consists of governor as chairman, four ministers of legislature, and ex officio member, who is attorney general;

Legislative Council consists of Speaker (elected from outside council), nine elected members, and ex officio member, who is attorney general.

**Economy** **Monetary unit:** U.S. dollar. **Budget:** (1988 est.) *income:* $26.2 mil.; *expend.:* $25.4 mil. **GDP:** $106.7 mil., $8,900 per capita (1987). **Chief crops:** limited—fruit, vegetables. **Natural resources:** negl. **Major industries:** tourism, construction, rum. **Labor force:** 4,911 (1980). **Exports:** $2.3 mil. (f.o.b., 1985); rum, fresh fish, gravel, sand, fruits, vegetables. **Imports:** $72 mil. (c.i.f., 1985); building materials, automobiles, foodstuffs, machinery. **Major trading partners:** Virgin Islands (U.S.), Puerto Rico, U.S.

**Intl. Orgs.** Commonwealth.

### Cayman Islands

**Geography** **Location:** three main and numerous smaller islands in western Caribbean. George Town (Grand Cayman Is.) 19°20′N, 81°23′W. **Boundaries:** Cuba to N, Jamaica 180 mi. (290 km) to SE. **Total land area:** 100 sq. mi. (259 sq km). **Coastline:** 100 mi. (160 km). **Comparative area:** slightly less than 1.5 times size of Washington, D.C. **Land use:** 0% arable land; 0% permanent crops; 8% meadows and pastures; 23% forest and woodland; 69% other. **Major cities:** (1987 est.) Georgetown (capital) 9,500.

**People** **Population:** 26,356 (1990). **Nationality:** noun—Caymanian(s); adjective—Caymanian. **Ethnic groups:** 40% mixed, 20% white, 20% black, 20% expatriates of various ethnic groups. **Languages:** English. **Religions:** United Church (Presbyterian and Congregational), Anglican, Baptist, Roman Catholic, Church of God, other Protestant denominations.

**Government** **Type:** British dependent territory. **National holiday:** Constitution Day, July 8. **Heads of government:** Alan Scott, governor and president of Executive Council (since 1987). **Structure:** executive—governor and Executive Council; legislative—unicameral Legislative Assembly; judicial—Summary Court, Supreme Court, Cayman Islands Court of Appeals, Her Majesty's Privy Council.

**Economy** **Monetary unit:** Cayman dollar. **Budget:** (1986) *income:* $46.2 mil.; *expend.:* $47 mil. **GDP:** $238 mil., $10,000 per capita (1989). **Chief crops:** minor production of vegetables; turtle farming. **Natural resources:** fish, climate and beaches that foster tourism. **Major industries:** tourism, banking, insurance, finance. **Labor force:** 8,061 (1979); 18.7% service workers, 18.6% clerical, 12.5% construction. **Exports:** $2.2 mil. (f.o.b., 1986 est.); turtle products, manufactured consumer goods. **Imports:** $134 mil. (c.i.f., 1986 est.); foodstuffs, manufactured goods. **Major trading partners:** *exports:* mostly U.S.; *imports:* U.S., Trinidad and Tobago, UK, Netherlands Antilles, Japan.

**Intl. Orgs.** Commonwealth.

### Falkland Islands
#### Colony of the Falkland Islands
**Geography** **Location:** two large and about 2,000 smaller islands in southwestern Atlantic

Ocean. Stanley (East Falkland) 51°45′S, 57°56′W. **Boundaries:** Cape Horn, South America, about 480 mi. (770 km) to SW. **Total land area:** 4,700 sq. mi. (12,173 sq km). **Coastline:** 800 mi. (1,288 km). **Comparative area:** slightly smaller than Connecticut. **Land use:** 0% arable land; 0% permanent crops; 99% meadows and pastures; 0% forest and woodland; 1% other. **Major cities:** (1986) Stanley (capital) 1,239.

**People** **Population:** 1,958 (1990). **Nationality:** noun—Falkland Islander(s); adjective—Falkland Island. **Ethnic groups:** mostly British. **Languages:** English. **Religions:** predominantly Anglican.

**Government** **Type:** colony of UK. **Constitution:** Oct. 3, 1985. **Heads of government:** William H. Fullerton, governor (since 1988). **Structure:** governor advised by Executive Council; Legislative Council.

**Economy** **Monetary unit:** Falkland Island pound. **Budget:** (1987) *income:* $11 mil.; *expend.:* $11.8 mil. **GNP:** N.A., N.A. per capita. **Livestock:** sheep, cattle, horses. **Natural resources:** fish, wildlife. **Major industries:** wool processing. **Labor force:** 1,100 (est.); 95% agriculture, mostly sheepherding. **Exports:** at least $14.7 mil. (1987); wool, hides, skins, other. **Imports:** at least $13.9 mil. (1987); food, clothing, fuels, machinery. **Major trading partners:** (1987 est.) *exports:* UK, Netherlands, Japan; *imports:* UK, Netherlands Antilles (Curaçao), Japan.

### Gibraltar
#### Colony of Gibraltar
**Geography** **Location:** narrow peninsula running southward from southwest coast of Spain, to which it is connected by an isthmus. **Boundaries:** Spain to W and N, Mediterranean Sea to E, Morocco to S across Strait of Gibraltar. **Total land area:** 2.125 sq. mi. (5.5 sq km). **Coastline:** 7.5 mi. (12 km). **Comparative area:** about 11 times size of the Mall in Washington, D.C. **Land use:** 0% arable land; 0% permanent crops; 0% meadows and pastures; 0% forest and woodland; 100% other. **Major cities:** Gibraltar (capital).

**People** **Population:** 29,572 (1990). **Nationality:** noun—Gibraltarian(s); adjective—Gibraltar. **Ethnic groups:** Italian, English, Maltese, Portuguese, and Spanish descent. **Languages:** English and Spanish are primary languages; Italian, Portuguese, Russian also spoken; English used in schools and for official purposes. **Religions:** 75% Roman Catholic, 8% Church of England, 2% Jewish.

**Government** **Type:** colony of UK. **Constitution:** May 30, 1969. **Heads of government:** Air Chief Marshal Sir Peter Terry, governor (since 1985); Joe Bossano, chief minister (since Mar. 1988). **Structure:** parliamentary system comprising Gibraltar House of Assembly, Council of Ministers headed by chief minister, and Gibraltar Council; governor appointed by Crown.

**Economy** **Monetary unit:** Gibraltar pound. **Budget:** (1987) *income:* $105 mil.; *expend.:* $104 mil. **GNP:** $129 mil., $4,450 per capita (1985). **Chief crops:** N.A. **Livestock:** N.A. **Natu-**

ral resources: none. **Major industries:** tourism, banking and finance, construction; support to large UK naval and air bases. **Labor force:** about 14,800 (including non-Gibraltar laborers); UK military establishments and civil government employ nearly 50% of insured labor force. **Exports:** $62.2 mil. (1985); principally re-exports—75% petroleum, 12% beverages and tobacco, 8% manufactured goods. **Imports:** $147 mil. (1985); manufactured goods, fuels, foodstuffs. **Major trading partners:** UK, Morocco, Portugal, Netherlands, Spain, U.S., W. Germany.

### Hong Kong
**Geography** **Location:** southern coast of China; consists of island of Hong Kong (22°17′N, 114°10′E), Stonecutters Island, Kowloon peninsula, and New Territories, which are partly on mainland. **Boundaries:** China to N, China sea to E, S, and W. **Total land area:** 413 sq. mi. (1,069 sq km). **Coastline:** 456 mi. (733 km). **Comparative area:** slightly less than six times size of Washington, D.C. **Land use:** 7% arable land; 1% permanent crops; 1% meadows and pastures; 12% forest and woodland; 79% other; includes 3% irrigated. **Major cities:** Victoria (capital).

**People** **Population:** 5,759,990 (1990). **Nationality:** adjective—Hong Kong. **Ethnic groups:** 98% Chinese, 2% other. **Languages:** Chinese (Cantonese), English. **Religions:** 90% eclectic mixture of local religions, 10% Christian.

**Government** **Type:** colony of UK; scheduled to revert back to China on June 30, 1997. **Heads of government:** Sir David Cline Wilson, governor (since Apr. 1987). **Structure:** governor, assisted by advisory Executive Council, legislates with advice and consent of Legislative Council; Executive Council composed of governor, four ex officio senior officials, and 12 nominated members; Legislative Council composed of governor, three ex officio members, seven official members, 22 appointed unofficial members, and 24 unofficial members elected indirectly by functional constituencies and by an electoral college; Urban Council, consisting of 15 elected members and 18 appointed by governor, responsible for health, recreation, and resettlement in urban areas; Regional Council (established Apr. 1, 1986)—composed of 12 directly elected members, nine indirectly elected, 12 appointed, and three ex officio—has similar responsibilities in nonurban areas; independent judiciary.

**Economy** **Monetary unit:** Hong Kong dollar. **Budget:** (1988) $6.9 bil. **GDP:** $57 bil., $10,000 per capita (1989). **Chief crops:** rice, vegetables, dairy products; minor part of economy. **Livestock:** chickens, pigeons, quail, ducks. **Natural resources:** none. **Major industries:** textiles, clothing, tourism, electronics, plastics, toys, watches, clocks. **Labor force:** 2.64 mil. (1986); 35.8% manufacturing, 22.7% wholesale and retail trade, restaurants, and hotels, 17.1% services; 1.8% unemployment. (1987). **Exports:** $63.2 bil. (f.o.b., 1988), including $22.9 bil. re-exports; clothing, plastic articles, textiles, electrical goods. **Imports:** $63.9 bil. (c.i.f., 1988). **Major trading partners:** (1987) *exports:*

31% U.S., 14% China, 8% W. Germany, 6% UK, 5% Japan; *imports:* 31% China, 20% Japan, 9% Taiwan, 8% U.S.

**Intl. Orgs.** GATT, IMO, INTERPOL, Multifiber Arrangement, WMO.

## Montserrat

**Geography** **Location:** eastern Caribbean Sea (16°44'N, 62°14'W). **Boundaries:** Guadeloupe 35 mi. (55 km) to S, Antigua 27 mi. (47 km) to NE. **Total land area:** 102 sq. mi. (264 sq km). **Coastline:** 25 mi. (40 km). **Comparative area:** about 3/5 size of Washington, D.C. **Land use:** 20% arable land; 0% permanent crops; 10% meadows and pastures; 40% forest and woodland; 30% other. **Major cities:** (1980) Plymouth (capital) 3,500.

**People** **Population:** 12,467 (1990). **Nationality:** noun—Montserratian(s); adjective—Montserratian. **Ethnic groups:** mostly black, with a few Europeans. **Languages:** English. **Religions:** Anglican, Methodist, Roman Catholic, Pentecostal, Seventh-Day Adventist, other Christian denominations.

**Government** **Type:** colony of UK. **Heads of government:** Christopher J. Turner, governor (since 1987); John A. Osborne, chief minister (since 1978). **Structure:** Executive Council presided over by governor, consisting of two ex officio members (attorney general and financial officer) and four unofficial members (chief minister and three other ministers); Legislative Council presided over by speaker chosen by council, seven elected, two official, and two nominated members.

**Economy** **Monetary unit:** East Caribbean dollar. **Budget:** (1987) *income:* $10 mil.; *expend.:* $9.4 mil. **GDP:** $45.5 mil., $3,780 per capita (1988). **Chief crops:** cotton, limes, potatoes, tomatoes, hot peppers. **Livestock:** sheep, goats, cattle, pigs. **Natural resources:** negl. **Major industries:** tourism, light manufacturing—rum, textiles, electronic appliances. **Labor force:** 5,100 (1983 est.); 40.5% community, social, and personal services, 13.5% construction, 12.3% trade, restaurants, and hotels, 10.5% manufacturing. **Exports:** $3 mil. (f.o.b., 1987); plastic bags, electronic parts, textiles, hot peppers, live plants, cattle. **Imports:** $25.3 mil. (c.i.f., 1987); machinery and transport equipment, foodstuffs, manufactured goods, fuels, lubricants, related materials. **Major trading partners:** N.A.

## Pitcairn Islands
### Pitcairn, Henderson, Ducie, and Oeno Islands

**Geography** **Location:** group of islands (one inhabited) in South Pacific. Pitcairn 25°04'S 130°04'W. **Boundaries:** about halfway between Panama and New Zealand; French Polynesia to NW. **Total land area:** 1.75 sq. mi. (4.5 sq km). **Coastline:** 32 mi. (51 km). **Comparative area:** 3/10 size of Washington, D.C. **Major cities:** Adamstown (capital).

**People** **Population:** 56 (1990). **Nationality:** noun—Pitcairn Islander(s); adjective—Pitcairn Islander. **Ethnic groups:** descendants of *Bounty* mutineers. **Languages:** English (official), also a Tahitian/English dialect. **Religions:** 100% Seventh-Day Adventist.

**Government** **Type:** colony of UK. **Heads of government:** Robin A. Byatt, governor and UK high commissioner to New Zealand (since 1988). **Structure:** administered locally by Island Council consisting of four elected island officers, a secretary, and five nominated members.

**Economy** **Monetary unit:** New Zealand dollar. **Budget:** (1987 est.) *income:* $430,440; *expend.:* $429,983. **Chief crops:** citrus, sugarcane, watermelons, bananas, yams. **Natural resources:** miro trees (used for handicrafts), fish. **Major industries:** postage stamp sales. **Labor force:** no business community in usual sense; some public works; subsistence farming and fishing. **Exports:** fruits, vegetables, curios. **Imports:** fuel oil, machinery, building materials, flour, sugar, other foodstuffs.

## St. Helena

**Geography** **Location:** eastern South Atlantic (15°58'S, 5°43'W). Dependencies are Ascension Is. (7°56'S, 14°25'W) 700 mi. to NW, and Tristan da Cunha (37°05'S, 12°17'W) 1,500 mi to SSW. **Boundaries:** Angola about 1,200 mi. (1,930 km) to E. **Total land area:** 47 sq. mi. (122 sq km). **Coastline:** 37 mi. (60 km). **Comparative area:** slightly more than 1.5 times size of Washington, D.C. **Land use:** 7% arable land; 0% permanent crops; 7% meadows and pastures; 3% forest and woodland; 83% other. **Major cities:** (1976) Jamestown (capital) 1,516.

**People** **Population:** 6,657 (1990). **Nationality:** noun—St. Helenian(s); adjective—St. Helenian. **Languages:** English. **Religions:** Anglican majority; also Baptist, Seventh-Day Adventist, Roman Catholic.

**Government** **Type:** colony of UK. **Constitution:** Jan. 1, 1967. **Heads of government:** Robert F. Stimson, governor (since 1987). **Structure:** Executive Council, 12-member elected Legislative Council.

**Economy** **Monetary unit:** British pound. **Budget:** (1984) *income:* $3.2 mil.; *expend.:* $2.9 mil. **Chief crops:** maize, potatoes, vegetables;

timber production being developed; crawfishing on Tristan de Cunha. **Livestock:** poultry, goats, sheep, cattle. **Natural resources:** fish; Ascension is sea turtle and sooty tern breeding ground; no minerals. **Major industries:** crafts (furniture, lacework, fancy woodwork), fish. **Labor force:** large proportion employed overseas. **Exports:** fish (frozen skipjack), tuna, saltdried skipjack), handicrafts. **Imports:** food, drink, tobacco, fuel oils, animal feed, building materials. **Major trading partners:** UK, South Africa.

## Turks and Caicos Islands

**Geography** **Location:** more than 30 islands forming southeastern end of Bahamas Islands in Caribbean Sea. **Boundaries:** Haiti 90 mi (145 km) to S. **Total land area:** 166 sq. mi. (430 sq km). **Coastline:** about 186 mi. (about 300 km). **Comparative area:** slightly less than 2.5 times size of Washington, D.C. **Land use:** 2% arable land; 0% permanent crops; 0% meadows and pastures; 0% forest and woodland; 98% other. **Major cities:** Jamestown (capital).

**People** **Population:** 9,761 (1990). **Ethnic groups:** mostly African descent. **Languages:** English. **Religions:** Anglican, Roman Catholic, Baptist, Methodist, Church of God, Seventh-Day Adventist.

**Government** **Type:** colony of UK. **Constitution:** introduced on Aug. 30, 1976, suspended in 1986, and at present a constitutional commission is reviewing its contents. **National holiday:** Commonwealth Day, May 31. **Heads of government:** Michael J. Bradley, governor (since 1987). **Structure:** executive, bicameral legislature (Executive Council, 14-member Legislative Council), judicial (Supreme Court).

**Economy** **Monetary unit:** U.S. dollar. **Budget:** (1987) *income:* $12.4 mil.; *expend.:* $15.8 mil. **GDP:** $44.9 mil., $5,000 per capita (1986). **Chief crops:** corn, beans. **Natural resources:** spiny lobster, conch. **Major industries:** fishing, tourism, offshore financial services. **Labor force:** some subsistence agriculture; majority engaged in fishing and tourist industries. **Exports:** $2.9 mil. (f.o.b., 1984); crawfish, dried and fresh conch, conch shells. **Imports:** $26.3 mil. (c.i.f., 1984); foodstuffs, drink, tobacco, clothing. **Major trading partners:** U.S. (lobster, conch, tourism), UK; considering trade agreement with Canada.

## Uninhabited Territories

British Indian Ocean Territory (Diego Garcia 6°34'S, 72°24'E); South Georgia Is. (54°15'S, 36°45'W); South Orkney Is. (60°35'S, 45°30'W); South Sandwich Is. (56°00'S, 26°30'W); South Shetland Is. (62°00'S, 58°00'W).

# Astronomy

Astronomy is the oldest science, but it continues to be at the forefront of scientific thought. The ancients of the Northern Hemisphere knew the skies, probably better than most of us do. They recognized that most stars appear to rise in the east at night and travel in circular paths across the sky, and that a few are wanderers—planets—that move among the other stars. They named the groups of stars that we call constellations and recognized that constellations visible in winter were different from those visible in summer (although some were visible all year). They recognized that one star, Polaris, or the North Star, was always in the north, and other stars seemed to move around it. They learned how to find the extremities of the sunrise and built giant stone structures, such as Stonehenge, probably to locate certain of the positions of the Sun or other stars.

In 1609 Galileo introduced the first artificial device for exploring the universe—the astronomical telescope. Even in that first year, he saw wonders the ancients never knew. Since then, we have built larger and better telescopes, devices for detecting radio waves, microwaves, X rays, infrared waves, and gamma rays from space, and have even traveled to our own Moon. We have sent space probes to eight of the nine known planets. Astronomers have learned that the universe is vastly more complex than the ancients thought and that it contains many secrets of nature we hope to unlock.

## MAJOR DISCOVERIES AND EVENTS IN ASTRONOMY AND SPACE

*B.C.*

**2296** Chinese astronomers begin recording appearance of "hairy stars" (comets).

**585** Thales of Miletus (Greek: c. 625–c. 547) predicts solar eclipse in Asia Minor.

**c. 480** Astronomer Oenopides of Chios (Greek: 5th cent.) discovers that Earth is tilted with respect to Sun.

**c. 410** First horoscopes developed in Mesopotamia.

**352** Chinese report "guest star," or supernova, the earliest known sighting.

**c. 340** Astronomer Kidinnu (Kidenas; Babylon: fl. c. 379) discovers precession of equinoxes, the apparent change in position of stars caused by Earth's wobbling on its orbit.

**c. 300** Chinese astronomers compile accurate star maps.

**c. 240** Chinese astronomers observe Halley's comet.
Eratosthenes of Cyrene (Greek: c. 276–c. 194) correctly calculates Earth's size.

**165** Chinese astronomers are first to notice sunspots.

**c. 130** Astronomer Hipparchus of Nicea (Greek: fl. 147–127) correctly determines distance to Moon and rediscovers precession of equinoxes (see 340 B.C.).

*A.D.*

**c. 140** *Almagest* of Ptolemy (Greek: c. 90–168) develops astronomy of solar system in form based on Sun and planets rotating about Earth.

**1543** *De Revolutionibus* by Nicholas Copernicus (Polish: 1473–1543) presents convincing arguments that Earth and other planets orbit Sun.

**1577** Tycho Brahe (Danish: 1546–1601) proves that comets are visitors from space, not weather phenomena as previously believed.

**1592** David Fabricius (German: 1564–1617) discovers star, later named Mira, that gradually disappears; in studying it in 1638, Phocylides Holawarda recognizes that it appears and reappears on regular basis—the first-known variable star.

**1609** Johannes Kepler (German: 1571–1630) discovers that the planets move in elliptical orbits.

**1610** Galileo observes Jupiter's moons, phases of Venus, and (although he does not recognize what they are) rings of Saturn.

**1611** Several astronomers simultaneously discover sunspots for first time in West.

**1633** Roman Catholic Church forces Galileo to recant his support of Copernicus's theory that Earth revolves about Sun.

**1671** Giovanni Domenico Cassini (Italian-French: 1625–1712) correctly determines distances of the planets from Sun.

**1682** Edmond Halley (English: 1656–1742) describes comet now known by his name and in 1705 correctly predicts its return in 1758.

**1718** Halley discovers that stars move with respect to each other.

**1755** Immanuel Kant (German: 1724–1804) proposes that many nebulas are actually composed of millions of stars and that solar system formed when giant cloud of dust condensed.

**1773** William Herschel (German-English: 1738–1822) shows that solar system is moving toward constellation Hercules.

**1781** Herschel discovers planet Uranus.

**1785** Herschel demonstrates that Milky Way is disk- or lens-shaped group of many stars, one of which is the Sun.

**1801** Guiseppe Piazzi (Italian; 1746–1826) discovers first-known asteroid, Ceres.

**1838** Friedrich W. Bessel (German: 1784–1846) is first to determine distance to star other than the Sun.

**1846** Johann G. Galle (German: 1812–1910) discovers planet Neptune using predictions of Urbain J.J. Leverrier (French: 1811–77) and John Couch Adams (English: 1819–92).

**1924** Edwin Hubble (American: 1889–1953) shows that galaxies are "island universes"—giant aggregations of stars as large as Milky Way.

**1929** Hubble establishes that universe is expanding.

**1930** Clyde Tombaugh (American: 1906– ) discovers planet Pluto.

**1931** Karl Jansky (American: 1905–50) discovers that radio waves are coming from space, leading to founding of radio astronomy.

**1948** George Gamow (Russian-American: 1904–68), Ralph Alpher (American: 1921– ), and Robert Herman (American: 1914– ) develop Big Bang theory of origin of universe.

**1957** USSR launches *Sputnik I*, the first man-made satellite.

**1961** Soviet cosmonaut Yuri A. Gagarin (Russian: 1934–68) is first human to orbit Earth.

**1963** Maarten Schmidt (Dutch-American: 1929– ) is first astronomer to recognize a quasar.

**1965** Arno Penzias (German-American: 1933– ) and Robert Wilson (American: 1936– ) find radio waves proving to most astronomers that Big Bang actually occurred.

**1967** Joycelyn Bell (English: 1943– ) discovers first-known pulsar while working for Antony Hewish (English: 1924– ); Hewish later gets Nobel Prize for discovery.

**1969** Neil Armstrong (American: 1930– ) and Edwin E. ("Buzz") Aldrin (American: 1930– ) walk on Moon.

**1971** American spacecraft, *Mariner 9*, is first to orbit another planet, Mars.

**1975** Soviet space probe transmits pictures from surface of Venus.

**1976** U.S. *Viking* space probes begin transmitting pictures of surface of Mars—unsuccessful in detecting life on planet.

**1977** Rings of Uranus are discovered.

**1979** U.S. space probe *Voyager 1* discovers that, like Saturn, Jupiter has rings.

**1980** Alan Guth (American: 1947– ) develops theory of inflationary universe, an explanation of how Big Bang occurred.

**1981** U.S. introduces reusable spacecraft, the space shuttle.

**1987** The explosion of Supernova 1987A, the nearest supernova that has been visible from Earth since 1604, is observed.

## THE SOLAR SYSTEM

Earth is one of nine known planets. A *planet* is a large, fairly cool body traveling in a path, called its orbit, around a star. All of the bodies under the gravitational influence of our local star, the Sun, together with the Sun, form the solar system. All nine of the known planets are in the solar system, although there is some evidence for planets around other stars. Many stars are orbited by large, hot bodies—other stars—but these are not considered planets. Cool bodies smaller than planets that orbit the Sun are called *asteroids* if they have fairly regular orbits and are called comets if their orbits take them from the edge of the system to locations near the Sun (some actually hit the Sun and burn up). Very small objects in space are called *meteoroids*. A meteoroid that burns up in Earth's atmosphere is called a *meteor*. One that reaches Earth's surface without burning completely is a meteorite.

Often smaller, cool bodies orbit planets. These are called satellites or moons.

It is currently believed that the solar system formed when a cloud of gas condensed to form the Sun. Parts of the cloud formed small bodies similar to today's asteroids, comets, and meteoroids. Collectively, these small bodies are called *planetesimals* or *planetoids*. Early in the history of the solar system, about 4.6 billion years ago or even before, the planetoids frequently crashed into one another. While this sometimes resulted in one or more of the planetoids breaking up, a small planetoid would often stick to a larger one, making it larger still. The end results of this process, it is proposed, are the nine known planets and their moons, along with the existing asteroids, comets, and meteoroids.

Although six of the nine planets were known to the ancients, and astronomers found the remaining three by early in the 20th century, observations from Earth had not prepared us for what we learned when we began exploring the solar system with space probes in 1962. Radar observations, both from Earth and from space probes, provided still more information. Satellite observation has also told us much we did not know about our own planet, Earth. While this age of exploration is far from over, here is an interim report.

### The Terrestrial Planets

In terms of distance from the Sun, these are the first four planets of the solar system—Mercury, Venus, Earth, and Mars. Terrestrial planets all have a comparatively high density, a concentration of metallic elements, and hard, rocky surfaces. Earth is the largest of the terrestrial planets but is dwarfed by the enormous sizes of the outer "gas giant" planets (Jupiter, Saturn, Uranus, and Neptune). Mercury, Earth, and Mars have magnetic fields, but Venus does not. Earth and Venus have thick atmospheres, Mars has a thin atmosphere, and Mercury's atmosphere is almost nonexistent.

**Mercury** is the planet closest to the Sun and in keeping with its namesake—Mercury, the winged messenger—moves the fastest in its

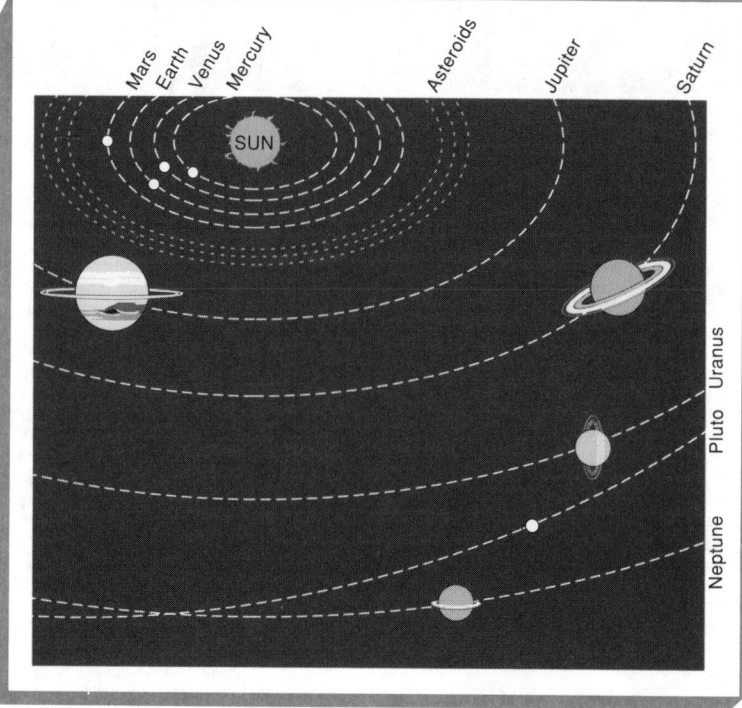

orbit. Mercury orbits the Sun at a mean velocity of 29.7 miles (47.9 km) per second and completes one revolution every 88 days. Its period of rotation is 59 days. Usually obscured from view from Earth by the Sun's glare, it is sometimes visible on Earth's horizon just after sunset, when it is called the Evening Star, or just before dawn, when it is the Morning Star. About 14 times every 100 years, Mercury can also be seen crossing directly in front of the Sun's disk.

Mercury was long thought to be the smallest planet, but better measurements of Pluto's size have shown that Pluto is even smaller.

The U.S. *Mariner 10* space probe provided the first detailed pictures of Mercury's surface during flybys in 1974 and 1975. *Mariner 10* mapped about 35% of the planet's heavily cratered, moonlike surface. No space probe has visited the planet since.

Mercury is a waterless, airless world that alternately bakes and freezes as it orbits the Sun. Its tenuous atmosphere is thought to be one-trillionth the density of Earth's atmosphere and largely composed of helium. On Mercury's sunlit side temperatures reach 950°F (510°C) and plummet to –346°F (–210°C) on the dark side. These extremes are largely due to Mercury's slow rate of rotation; one Mercury "day" (or *sol*, as astronomers call a single rotation of a planet or satellite) is two-thirds of one Mercury year. Because it takes 59 Earth days to complete one sol, there is time for the surface to heat up or cool off. In 1990 it was discovered that two spots on the surface are much hotter

than other places on the planet. This is caused by the combined action of the planet's rotation and revolution, which have a ratio of 3 to 2.

Mercury's surface is scarred with hundreds of thousands of meteor craters. Many such craters were probably formed during the planetoid showers believed to have occurred soon after the formation of the solar system. Many areas have had the craters smoothed over by ancient lava flows, however. This indicates extensive volcanic activity on Mercury during and after the time of the planetoid showers. The surface is also crisscrossed by huge cliffs, or scarps. These probably formed as Mercury's surface cooled and shrank. Some of the scarps are up to 1.2 miles (1.9 km) high and 932 miles (1,500 km) long.

Mercury is so dense for its size that astronomers think that its rocky outer crust is very thin and that the planet is mostly iron. It probably was once larger. During the early bombardment, it is conjectured that one of the larger planetoids (about a sixth of the size of the early planet) hit Mercury so hard that it blasted most of the rocky crust away.

**Venus,** as seen in the night sky from Earth, is second only to the Moon in brightness. Venus, named for the Roman goddess of love, is the planet that passes closest to Earth (26,000,000 mi., or 42,000,000 km). Since it is between Earth and the Sun, Venus, like Mercury, is seen either as the Morning Star or the Evening Star.

Because of its closer proximity to Earth and its position between Earth and the Sun, Venus became (in 1962) the first planet beyond Earth to be scanned by a space probe in its neighborhood (*Mariner 2*). The pull of the Sun's gravity makes Venus and Mercury "downhill" from the Earth; one must travel against the Sun's gravity to reach other planets. Since 1962 Venus has been visited by numerous U.S. and Soviet spacecraft. Soviet space probes *Venera 13* and *Venera 14* were the first to make a soft landing and send back pictures from the Venusian surface.

The Venusian atmosphere is thick with clouds that have shrouded the planet's surface from view, making the planet somewhat mysterious. This dense atmosphere has been studied extensively by a series of U.S. and Soviet space probes. The atmospheric pressure at the surface is 90 times that of Earth, its atmosphere composed of 96% carbon dioxide ($CO_2$) and nitrogen, with small amounts of other substances. The Venusian clouds range from about 28 to 37 miles (45 to 60 km) above the planet's surface and are differentiated into three layers. Droplets of sulfuric acid and water have been identified in the clouds.

The clouds and high level of $CO_2$ in the atmosphere have combined to trap heat in the lower atmosphere of Venus. This is an extreme form of the greenhouse effect and is responsible for high temperatures in the lower atmosphere, 900°F (482°C)—hot enough to melt lead. Radiation of heat from the lower atmosphere is so inefficient that there is little variation of temperature between night and day.

One feature of the Venusian upper atmosphere is markedly different from that of Earth. The atmosphere superrotates on Venus—that is, the atmosphere above the clouds moves 60 times faster than the planet rotates—whereas the Earth and its atmosphere rotate at the same speed. So, high winds are a dominant part of Venusian weather. Even at only 31 miles (50 km) above the surface, which is just under the cloud layer, the winds blow steadily at 109 miles (175 km) per hour.

Soviet space probes that soft-landed on Venus have provided photographs of the planet's surface; radar maps of 93% of the Venusian surface, completed by the U.S. *Pioneer* Venus spacecraft (from 1978), now give a detailed picture of the planet's surface. A new U.S. Venus orbiter, *Magellan*, is now completing its radar mapping at a higher resolution.

About 10% of the surface is highland terrain, 70% rolling uplands, and 20% lowland plains. There are two major highland areas: one about half the size of Africa and located in the equatorial region and the other, about the size of Australia, located to the north. The highest mountain on Venus—Maxwell Montes—is in the northern highlands and is higher than Earth's Mt. Everest. Two major areas of suspected volcanic activity have been found and make Venus only the fourth body in the solar system thought to be volcanically active (along with Earth; Io, a satellite of Jupiter; and Triton, a satellite of Neptune).

Venus is thought to have an internal structure like that of Earth. The outer crust may be thicker than that of Earth, which averages 12.5 miles (20 km). Below that is a thick mantle. The core is believed to be composed of molten nickel-iron.

**Earth** is the third planet from the Sun and the only one in the solar system known to harbor life. From out in space, our planet appears as a bright, blue-and-white sphere—blue because some 70% of the surface is covered by water, and white because clouds cover about half the planet's surface.

Earth's atmosphere is composed of about 78% nitrogen, 21% oxygen, and traces of other gases. The tenuous outer layer of the atmosphere—the thermosphere—begins about 310 miles (500 km) above Earth's surface. Between about 62 miles down to about 31 miles (100 to 50 km) is the mesosphere; below this is the stratosphere (down to about 8 mi., or 13 km); finally, there is the troposphere, the bottom layer. The atmosphere, along with Earth's magnetic field, shields us from nearly all harmful radiation coming from the Sun and from outer space.

The interior consists of three main layers. The outer crust, largely made up of granite and basalt rock, varies from 55 miles (89 km) deep under the continents to 3 miles (5 km) deep under the oceans. The second main layer, the mantle, extends down to about 1,900 miles (3,060 km) below the surface and is composed of silicate rock rich in iron. The top part of the mantle is semiliquid, down to about 150 miles (250 km). The rigid upper crust is broken into large plates that move slowly on this partially fluid layer, which is termed the asthenosphere. Beneath this lies the Earth's iron and nickel core. Scientists believe the temperature at the center of the core could be 7,200°F (4,000°C). The outer core is liquid due to the great heat, while an inner core is solid as a result of the great pressure at Earth's center.

**The Moon** is Earth's only natural satellite. Just over one-quarter the size of Earth in diameter, it is the brightest object in Earth's nighttime sky. The Moon regularly changes in appearance as seen from Earth. The main apparent changes are called phases; for example, the new moon, when the Moon is between Earth and the Sun, is the phase when the Moon cannot be seen; at full moon, when Earth is between the Moon and the Sun, the Moon is seen as completely round. When we see the moon as half a circle, the phase is called a quarter, with the first quarter appearing as the moon goes from a new moon toward a full moon, and the last quarter as the moon passes from a full moon toward a new moon. The full cycle, from new moon to new moon, takes about 28 days. It is believed that the lunar phases gave rise to both the week (7 days from one phase to the next) and the month.

Because the Moon is slightly egg-shaped, the same side of the satellite always faces Earth—this side being the elongated small end. As a result, the Moon rotates once during each revolution. The side we do not see is called the far side (not the dark side)—all parts of the moon undergo 14 Earth days of light, followed by 14 days of darkness.

Over a decade of exploration of the Moon by U.S. and Soviet space probes was capped by the landing of two U.S. astronauts on the Moon on July 20, 1969. A total of six two-man crews of American astronauts eventually landed on the

Moon between 1969 and 1972, and they brought back some 842 pounds (382 kg) of samples.

The world these astronauts found was airless, waterless, and devoid of life. Temperatures on the Moon range from up to 273°F (134°C) on the bright side to –274°F (–170°C) on the unlighted side.

The lunar surface is pockmarked with craters up to 56 miles (90 km) across and is broken by huge mountain ranges. The near side also has large regions (called maria, or seas) of solidified lava, indicating that the Moon was once volcanically active. Lunar soil, a mixture of fine powder and broken rock, blankets the Moon's surface.

**Mars** is the outermost of the four terrestrial planets and has a distinctive reddish coloring, coming from iron oxide in the Martian soil. The Romans named the planet after their god of war, and the two irregularly shaped satellites of Mars have been named after the horses—Deimos (terror) and Phobos (fear)—that pulled the war god's chariot. Mars is visible in Earth's nighttime sky and is lined up with Earth between it and the Sun once every 780 days, though its closest approach to Earth (35,000,000 mi., or 56,000,000 km) comes at 15- or 17-year intervals.

The so-called canals on Mars—later found to be optical illusions—were first observed by 19th-century astronomers and led to the widespread belief that there was life on Mars. (In 1900 the French Academy offered a prize to the first person to find life on any planet *except* Mars, presumably because everyone knew that there was life on that planet.) The planet thus became the target of numerous space probes, both U.S. and Soviet, from the early years of interplanetary exploration.

The first successful flyby of Mars was achieved by the U.S. spacecraft *Mariner 4* in 1965. The Soviets became the first to land a probe successfully on the surface of Mars in 1971, but the probe malfunctioned and stopped transmitting after only 20 seconds. It was not until 1976, when the U.S. *Viking 1* and *Viking 2* landers touched down on Mars, that extensive study of the planet from its surface became possible. In fact, the *Viking 1* lander continued to function long after its mission had been completed and sent back information on Martian weather until 1982, when communications with Earth at last failed.

The big question of whether there is (or was) life on Mars has yet to be answered with certainty. The *Viking* landers conducted three experiments on Martian soil to check for biological processes. Some of the tests yielded positive results, but these could also be explained by the soil chemistry. The lack of other evidence of organic molecules adds to the case against life on Mars.

Orbiting satellites have mapped the entire planet down to a resolution of 492–984 feet (150–300 m).

The planet's surface is heavily cratered, and there is extensive evidence of once-active volcanoes. There are also such spectacular features as Olympus Mons (an extinct volcano three times as high as Earth's Mt. Everest); mammoth canyons, one of which is four times

## Glossary of Planetary Terms

**Bar** A measure of pressure slightly less than Earth's air pressure at sea level under normal conditions, or about 29.53 (75 cm) inches of mercury, the measurement used in giving the weather report of barometric pressure; *bar* is derived from the Greek word for "weight." Earth's air pressure at sea level is 0.98 bar.

**Eccentricity** A number that measures the shape of a planet's orbit; all the planetary orbits are curves called ellipses, which are "squashed" circles; the smaller the eccentricity, the more an ellipse is like a circle, which has an eccentricity of 0.

**Ecliptic** The apparent path of the Sun through the stars as viewed from Earth, which is in a plane inclined 23.5° to Earth's equator. The planets are all roughly in the same plane, so like the Sun, they seem to move through the same groups of stars as the Sun does over the course of a year.

**Escape velocity** The speed needed for an object to be propelled from the surface of a planet and not fall back. Since the escape velocity for Earth is 6.96 miles per second (11.2 km), a rocket expected to reach the Moon or another planet must develop a speed of at least 7 miles (12 km) per second.

**Inclination of axis** The angle that the line about which a planet rotates makes with the plane defined by its path around the Sun.

**Inclination of orbit to the ecliptic** The angle that the plane defined by a planet's path around the Sun makes with the plane defined by the apparent path of the Sun among the stars as seen from Earth.

**Orbital velocity** The speed of a planet in its path around the Sun.

**Retrograde** In the opposite direction of other planets.

## BASIC FACTS ABOUT THE PLANETS

| Characteristic | Terrestrial Planets | | | |
| --- | --- | --- | --- | --- |
| | Mercury | Venus | Earth | Mars |
| Average distance from Sun | 35,900,000 mi. | 67,200,000 mi. | 92,960,000 mi. | 141,600,000 mi. |
| | 57,900,000 km | 108,200,000 km | 149,600,000 km | 227,900,000 km |
| Rotation period (hours) | 1,407.6 hrs. | −5,832.2 hrs. | 23.9 hrs. | 24.6 hrs. |
| | (59 d.) | (243 d., retrograde) | | |
| Period of revolution (in Earth days) | 88 d. | 224.7 d. | 365.26 d. | 687 d. |
| Average orbital velocity in miles per second | 29.8 | 21.75 | 18.46 | 14.98 |
| Inclination of axis | 2° | 3° | 23°27′ | 25°12′ |
| Inclination of orbit to the ecliptic | 7° | 3.39° | 0° | 1.9° |
| Eccentricity of orbit | 0.206 | 0.007 | 0.017 | 0.093 |
| Equatorial diameter | 3,030 mi. | 7,517 mi. | 7,926 mi. | 4,217 mi. |
| | 4,880 km | 12,104 km | 12,756 km | 6,787 km |
| Diameter relative to Earth | 38.2% | 94.9% | 100% | 53.2% |
| Mass | $3.303 \times 10^{23}$ kg | $4.87 \times 10^{24}$ kg | $5.97 \times 10^{24}$ kg | $6.42 \times 10^{23}$ kg |
| Mass relative to Earth | 5.58% | 81.5% | 100% | 10.74% |
| Average density | 3.13 oz./in.³ | 3.03 oz./in.³ | 3.19 oz./in.³ | 2.27 oz./in.³ |
| Gravity (at equator surface) | 12.4 ft./sec.² | 28.2 ft./sec.² | 32.1 ft./sec.² | 12.2 ft./sec.² |
| Gravity (relative to Earth) | 38% | 88% | 100% | 38% |
| Escape velocity at equator | 2.7 mi/sec. | 6.40 mi/sec. | 6.96 mi/sec. | 3.1 mi/sec. |
| | 4.3 km/sec. | 10.3 km/sec. | 11.2 km/sec. | 5 km/sec. |
| Average surface temperature | 332°F | 854°F | 59°F | −67°F |
| | 167°C | 457°C | 15°C | −55°C |
| Atmospheric pressure at surface | $10^{-15}$ bar | 90 bars | 0.98 bar | 0.007 bar |
| Atmosphere (main components) | Virtually none | Carbon dioxide | Nitrogen 77%; | Carbon dioxide |
| | (of that present, | 96%; nitrogen | oxygen 21%; | 95%; nitrogen |
| | 98% helium; | 3.5% | water 1%; | 2.7%; argon |
| | 2% hydrogen) | | argon 0.93% | 1.6% |
| Planetary satellites | None | None | 1 moon | 2 moons |

**Revolution** The trip a planet makes about the Sun.
**Rotation** The turning of a planet about a line through its center.

The numbers used in tables are sometimes given in scientific notation. A large number, such as 1,840,000,000, might be written as $1.84 \times 10^9$.

The exponent $9$ signifies the number of places after the first digit. A small number such as 0.00000000000001 is written as $10^{-15}$, where the exponent $-15$ tells the number of zeroes—counting the one before the decimal place—before the numeral *1*.

---

deeper than the Grand Canyon; and a gigantic basin (larger than Alaska) in the southern hemisphere that was probably created by a single, huge asteroid. The planet has ice caps at both poles (frozen carbon dioxide with some water), and the ice caps advance and recede with changes in the seasons.

But the most intriguing aspect of the Martian surface is an indication that water once flowed there in great quantities. Parts of the terrain apparently have sedimentary origins, and there are many long channels, complete with smaller tributary channels and islands, that extend for hundreds of kilometers. Scientists speculate that Mars once had a much thicker atmosphere, made up of gases vented during volcanic eruptions, which would have made it possible for water in its liquid state to exist on the surface. Martian atmospheric pressure is now so low, however, that surface water would immediately vaporize. It is conjectured that the water in the past flowed through the channels to lowland areas and then sank into the Martian regolith, or upper soil layer, since there is no geologic evidence that standing bodies of water ever existed. Astronomers believe that at least some of the primordial water may still be trapped as ice in the regolith.

Mars is too small to sustain continual volcanic activity. Its atmosphere apparently thinned out after volcanic activity ceased. Atmospheric pressure is now just two one-hundredths of that on Earth at sea level, and the predominant gas is carbon dioxide, which is relatively heavy. A small amount of water vapor in the atmosphere is enough to form some clouds, small patches of fog in some valleys, and occasionally even patches of frost. Surface temperatures vary from about 39°F (4°C) at the equator to about −189°F (−123°C) at the poles.

By far the most pronounced feature of Martian weather (apart from the bone-chilling cold) is the dust storms. Whipped by hurricane-force winds, these dust storms sometimes engulf the entire planet for weeks on end.

**The asteroids** The asteroid belt—first crossed by the U.S. space probe *Pioneer 10* on its way to Jupiter in 1973—lies between Mars and Jupiter. The name *asteroid* means "starlike" and was given to asteroids because they are so small they appear as points of light (as do stars) even in powerful telescopes. Otherwise, asteroids are not like stars at all. Astronomers once thought the asteroid belt had been formed by the breakup of a planet between Mars and

Jupiter, but they now think it is debris left over from the formation of the solar system. For some reason the asteroids did not accrete into a planet, perhaps because of Jupiter's strong gravitational pull.

Not all asteroids are found in the asteroid belt. Some cross Earth's orbit, for example.

## The Outer Planets

Beyond Mars and the asteroid belt lie the five known outer planets of our solar system. Four of these planets—Jupiter, Saturn, Uranus, and Neptune—are the so-called gas giants. Many times larger than the terrestrial planets, these planets are huge, dense balls of hydrogen and other gases. Beyond them (most of the time) lies the solar system's outermost and smallest known planet, Pluto, which may be nothing more than a tiny ball of frozen gases.

**Jupiter** is the largest planet in the solar system. It has 2.5 times more mass than all the other planets of the solar system together and is 11 times as large as Earth in diameter. Jupiter is so large that scientists believe it almost became a star: as the gases and dust contracted to form the planet, gravitational forces created tremendous pressure and temperature inside the core—perhaps as high as tens of thousands

## OUTER PLANETS

| Characteristic | Gas giants | | | | Pluto |
|---|---|---|---|---|---|
| | Jupiter | Saturn | Uranus | Neptune | |
| Average distance from Sun | 483,600,000 mi. | 886,700,000 mi. | 1,782,000,000 mi. | 2,794,000,000 mi. | 3,666,000,000 mi. |
| | 778,300,000 km | 1,427,000,000 km | 2,869,000,000 km | 4,496,000,000 km | 5,900,000,000 km |
| Rotation period (hours) | 9.8 hrs. | 10.2 hrs. | 17.2 hrs. | 16.1 hrs. | −153.3 hrs. |
| | | | | | (6.4 d., retrograde) |
| Period of revolution (in Earth days) | 4,332.6 | 10,759.2 | 30,685.4 | 60,189 | 90,465 |
| | (11.86 yrs.) | (29.46 yrs.) | (84.01 yrs.) | (164.8 yrs.) | (247.7 yrs.) |
| Average orbital velocity | 8.1 mi./sec. | 5.99 mi./sec. | 4.2 mi./sec. | 3.35 mi./sec. | 2.9 mi./sec. |
| | 13.06 km/sec. | 9.64 km/sec. | 6.8 km/sec. | 5.4 km/sec. | 4.7 km/sec. |
| Inclination of axis | 3°5′ | 26°44′ | 97°55′ | 28°48′ | 60° |
| Inclination of orbit to the ecliptic | 1.3° | 2.5° | 0.8° | 1.8° | 17.2° |
| Eccentricity of orbit | 0.048 | 0.056 | 0.047 | 0.009 | 0.25 |
| Equatorial diameter | 88,700 mi. | 74,800 mi. | 32,200 mi. | 30,800 mi. | 1,423 mi. |
| | 142,800 km | 120,400 km | 51,800 km | 49,500 km | 2,290 km |
| Diameter relative to Earth | 1,121% | 941% | 410% | 388% | 18% |
| Mass | $1.899 \times 10^{27}$ kg | $5.686 \times 10^{26}$ kg | $8.66 \times 10^{25}$ kg | $1.030 \times 10^{26}$ kg | c. $1.3 \times 10^{22}$ kg |
| Mass relative to Earth | 31,790% | 9,520% | 1,460% | 1,723% | c. 0.21% |
| Average density | 0.759 oz./in.$^3$ | 0.40 oz./in.$^3$ | 0.7 oz./in.$^3$ | 9.4 oz./in.$^3$ | c. 1 oz./in.$^3$ |
| Gravity (at equator surface) | 75.06 ft./sec.$^2$ | 29.69 ft./sec.$^2$ | 25.5 ft./sec.$^2$ | 36 ft./sec.$^2$ | 5.4 ft./sec.$^2$ |
| Gravity (relative to Earth) | 234% | 92% | 79% | 112% | 16% |
| Escape velocity at equator | 37.0 mi./sec. | 22.1 mi./sec. | 13.2 mi./sec. | 14.66 mi./sec. | 1.2 mi./sec. |
| | 59.5 km/sec. | 35.6 km/sec. | 21.2 km/sec. | 23.6 km/sec. | 1.9 km/sec. |
| Average temperature | (at surface) | (at surface) | (cloud tops) | (cloud tops) | (at surface) |
| in atmosphere | −162°F | −208°F | −344°F | −261°F | c. −355°F |
| | −108°C | −133°C | −209°C | −177°C | c. −215°C |
| Atmospheric pressure at surface | 3,000,000 bars | 8,000,000 bars | N.A. | N.A. | 0.1 millibar (?) |
| Atmosphere (main components) | (near cloud tops) | hydrogen 94%; | hydrogen, helium, | hydrogen, helium, | methane, possibly |
| | hydrogen 90%; | helium c. 6% | methane % N.A. | methane % N.A. | nitrogen % N.A. |
| | helium c. 10% | | | | |
| Other atmospheric gases | methane, water, | methane, ammonia | Unknown | Unknown | possibly carbon |
| | ammonia, ethane, | | | | monoxide and |
| | acetylene, phosphine, | | | | argon |
| | hydrogen cyanide, | | | | |
| | carbon monoxide | | | | |
| Planetary satellites | 16 | 18 | 15 | 8 | 1 |

of degrees. But there was not enough mass available to create the temperatures needed to start a fusion reaction such as that of the Sun (above 18,000,000°F or 10,000,000°C, at the sun's core); thus Jupiter has been slowly cooling down ever since. Even so, Jupiter still radiates about 2.5 times as much heat as it receives from the Sun.

The first object to reach Jupiter from Earth was *Pioneer 10*. It returned the first close-up pictures of the giant planet in 1973. Subsequently, the more sophisticated space probes *Voyager 1* and *Voyager 2* passed by Jupiter in 1979 and sent back images and more data on the planet. One of the most exciting discoveries by *Voyager 1* was that Jupiter has a faint but extensive ring system that extends almost 186,000 miles (300,000 km) out from the planet's surface. And in 1983 a study of *Voyager 2* readings indicated that Jupiter's magnetic field—stretched by solar wind into a long "tail" on the side away from the Sun—had actually reached Saturn when Jupiter and Saturn were aligned with the Sun (which occurs about once every 20 years).

Jupiter's thick atmosphere, which may extend downward by as much as 620 miles (1,000 km), is primarily made up of hydrogen,

some helium, and traces of methane, water, and ammonia. Because the planet spins so fast (one rotation in just under 10 hours), its clouds tend to form bands. They give the planet its red-, brownish-, and white-striped appearance. Bands of clouds at higher altitudes are carried eastward by jet streams, while those at lower levels are blown westward.

There are numerous eddies and swirls in Jupiter's atmosphere, but none can compare with the Great Red Spot, apparently a massive hurricane (rotating counterclockwise) located in the southern hemisphere near the equator. The Great Red Spot was first observed some 300 years ago, and this storm continues unabated today. Since 1938 three smaller white ovals have been observed to the south of the Great Red Spot.

Jupiter's cloud tops are extremely cold (about −202°F, or −130°C), but temperatures increase deeper inside the atmosphere. Pressure also increases, and at about 620 miles (1,000 km) below the outermost atmospheric layers, great oceans of liquid hydrogen form Jupiter's surface. These may be some 12,000 miles (20,000 km) deep. Beneath them the hydrogen is so densely compacted it is in a metallic state. Within this is the core, thought to be an iron

and silicate rock ball about the size of Earth.

Jupiter is now known to have 16 moons, the four largest being the Galilean moons, so called because they were first observed by Galileo. The Galilean moons are Ganymede, Callisto, Europa, and Io—after the Roman god Jupiter's cupbearer (Ganymede) and three of Jupiter's inamorata. Ganymede is the largest moon in the solar system—although previously this honor was accorded to Saturn's Titan—and is larger even than the planets Pluto and Mercury. It is a huge, cratered ball of ice and may have a core of solid silicate rock. Callisto, with an orbit outside that of Ganymede, is also covered with ice and is riddled with thousands of craters. Europa, which orbits inside Ganymede, is about the size of our Moon and has a smooth surface marked by networks of cracks. The most interesting of Jupiter's moons is Io, which of all four Galilean moon orbits is closest to Jupiter. *Voyager 1* photographed volcanoes erupting on Io. Orange-red patches on Io's mottled surface are apparently molten sulfur beds, but most other parts of Io's surface are apparently very cold (about −229°F, or −145°C). The volcanic activity is caused by gravitational force from Jupiter, Europa, and Ganymede.

**Saturn** is the sixth planet of the solar system and the second largest, after Jupiter. The outermost of the planets that can be identified easily in Earth's nighttime sky with the unaided eye, Saturn has a pale yellowish color and is not nearly so bright as Mars. Saturn's spectacular ring system, which makes it one of the most interesting of the planets, is visible only through a telescope. Its rings are more extensive than those of any other planet.

Like Jupiter, Saturn is composed of densely compacted hydrogen, helium, and other gases. Liquid or metallic hydrogen probably exists underneath the planet's thick atmosphere, and scientists believe there is a solid core of rock about two times the size of Earth at its center. Saturn's high rotational speed (once every 10 hours, 12 minutes) makes it the most oblate (flattened) of all the planets; it is almost 6,800 miles (11,000 km) wider at the equator than on a line through the poles.

Though exploration of Saturn began in 1979 with the first flyby (*Pioneer 11*), the *Voyager 1* and *Voyager 2* missions in 1980 and 1981, respectively, provided the first detailed look at the planet. Scientists have spent years sifting through the data gathered, and, though there were important new findings, many questions about Saturn remain unanswered.

The *Voyagers* found a huge storm thousands of miles across on Saturn, along with a wide band of extremely high winds—up to 994 miles (1,600 km) per hour—at the equator. Winds in this band all travel in the direction of the planet's rotation (unlike bands of wind on Jupiter). The *Voyagers* also discovered a vast hydrogen cloud circling the planet above the equator.

The *Voyagers'* most exciting discoveries concern the planetary rings. Previously, about six different rings had been identified within the ring system, but *Voyager 1* pictures show as many as 1,000 separate rings. Narrow rings can even be seen within the Cassini Division, once thought to be an empty gap between the two major parts of the ring system. Some rings are not circular, and at least two rings are intertwined, or "braided." A strange new phenomenon was also discovered in the rings. *Voyager 1* pictures clearly show dark, radial fingers—"spokes"—moving inside the rings in the direction of rotation. Scientists speculate that they are made of ice crystals.

*Voyager 2* pictures show that Saturn has far more than 1,000 rings—perhaps as many as a hundred thousand or more. One of the brightest rings is shown to be under 152 meters (500 ft.) thick. The pictures do not show signs of moonlets that some scientists had thought were the cause of gaps between individual rings.

Twelve of Saturn's moons were known before the arrival of the *Voyagers*, and instruments aboard the space probe helped locate three new ones. Most of Saturn's moons are relatively small and composed of rock and ice. All but one of the small moons are pockmarked by meteor craters, and in some cases the moons appear to have been cracked by collisions with especially large meteors. But *Voyager* pictures show that one moon, Enceladus, is smooth in large regions apparently unmarked by collisions with meteors. Scientists believe that

Enceladus is being pulled and stretched by the combined gravities of a nearby moon and Saturn itself. Tidal forces have apparently heated the core of Enceladus and made its surface soft enough to smooth over any craters formed by meteor impacts.

Titan, Saturn's largest moon (3,000 mi., or 4,800 km in diameter) is the only moon in the solar system known to have an atmosphere of any substance. Scientists suspect that at least some precursors of life may have formed there. For this reason *Voyager 1* was guided to within about 2,500 miles (4,000 km) of Titan during the Saturn flyby. Though Titan's surface was obscured by dense clouds, *Voyager's* sensors nevertheless returned a considerable amount of information about the moon and its atmosphere. Titan's atmosphere is composed mostly of nitrogen, like that of Earth, with only a small percentage of methane and carbon monoxide. Atmospheric pressure is at least 1.5 times that on Earth and temperatures range around –294°F (–181°C). Titan in fact appears to be a frozen version of Earth before life evolved.

The possibility of oceans of liquid methane (or of nitrogen or methane rain) on Titan was a matter of considerable controversy for some time after *Voyager 1* investigated the moon. But Titan is "dry," at least in the regions investigated. Pools of liquid methane might still exist in other low-lying regions, but it is unlikely that either methane or nitrogen condenses to liquid form on Titan.

*Voyager 2* also found seasonal differences between the planet's two hemispheres and photographed the storm some 4,000 miles (6,500 km) wide.

**Uranus** is the seventh planet in the solar system and the third of the gas giants. The planet is barely visible in Earth's nighttime sky (it looks like a faint star) and for that reason, it went undiscovered until 1781.

Nearly the same size as Neptune and only about 5% of Jupiter's mass, Uranus is a faintly greenish color, perhaps because its atmosphere contains methane. The planet's axis of rotation is tipped over on its side, and in 1977 a system of nine faint rings was discovered. There are five known moons of Uranus, which range between about 186 and 621 miles (300 and 1,000 km) in diameter.

The atmosphere of Uranus is composed of hydrogen, helium, and methane and is very clear and cold (–355°F, or –215°C). No clouds and little haze have been observed.

Scientists speculate that, as on Jupiter and Saturn, temperatures and pressures increase dramatically down through the outer layer of atmosphere. At some point the hydrogen and helium would be sufficiently compressed to form a liquid or slushy surface "crust." Underneath this crust they believe is a mantle of solidified methane, ammonia, and water; and inside this mantle, a rocky core of silicon and iron about 15 times as massive as Earth. The core is hot, probably about 12,000°F (7,000°C).

**Neptune,** the last of the gas giants, is the eighth planet in the solar system. It was discovered in 1846 after mathematical calcula-

tions based on irregularities in the orbit of Uranus provided astronomers with the correct location of the planet. Neptune, like Uranus, has been surrounded by considerable uncertainty because of its enormous distance from Earth. The 1989 visit by *Voyager 2* contributed greatly to improved understanding of the planet.

Neptune is a pale bluish color, and its atmosphere is composed of hydrogen and helium. Unlike Uranus, Neptune's atmosphere is often hazy—perhaps because of ice or other particles formed from an unknown substance—and it is very cold at the cloud tops (about –261°F, or –177°C).

Scientists believe that Neptune has a three-layered structure similar to that of Uranus: a crust of solidified or liquid hydrogen and helium that gradually thins outward into an atmosphere; a mantle of solidified gases and water; and a hot, rocky core (about 12,000°F or 7,000°C) some 15 times as massive as Earth. But one aspect of Neptune remains a mystery. Despite similarities with Uranus, Neptune has been found to radiate more heat than it receives from the Sun (at a rate of 0.03 microwatts per ton of mass). Uranus, on the other hand, does not emit excess heat.

Neptune has eight known moons, Triton and Nereid, discovered from Earth, and six others discovered by *Voyager 2*, and a ring system containing three rings and two ringlike features. Triton is the largest moon and has an atmosphere. Triton is unusual in that it travels in a direction opposite that of Neptune's rotation, suggesting that it has a different origin from the planet.

**Pluto,** the ninth and outermost (most of the time) known planet of the solar system, is a ball of frozen gases probably only about the size of Earth's Moon. Because of its relatively small size and chaotic orbit (which at times crosses inside Neptune's orbit), some scientists think that Pluto is not really a planet at all. Instead, they theorize that Pluto is only a former moon of Neptune that has been pulled out of orbit by some other celestial body.

Pluto was discovered in 1930 as a result of an extensive search by Clyde Tombaugh. Although his search was based on mathematical calculations derived from deviations in the orbit of Neptune, most astronomers now think that Tombaugh found Pluto as a result of a lucky accident.

Frozen methane and a thin atmosphere of methane and some other gases have been detected on Pluto. Pluto has one known moon, Charon, discovered in 1978. Charon is about one-half the size of Pluto. Pluto and Charon rotate and revolve synchronously like a double planet system.

## The Sun

Virtually all of the energy used by living things comes from the Sun. The Sun's light causes photosynthesis in green plants, and its heat causes winds. Fossil fuels, such as coal, oil, and natural gas, got their energy originally from photosynthesis, as did wood. Animals derive their energy from plants that photosynthesize, either directly or indirectly. The only natural nonsolar energy sources are nuclear reactions (which also produce geothermal energy), some bacteria that metabolize sulfur, and the tides, which are produced largely by the Moon, but in part by the Sun.

## CHARACTERISTICS OF THE SUN

| | |
|---|---|
| Position in solar system | Center |
| Mean distance from Earth | 92,960,000 mi. |
| | (149,600,000 km) |
| Distance from center of | 27,710 light-yrs. |
| Milky Way galaxy | |
| Estimated velocity of revolution | 175 mi./sec. |
| | (282 km/sec.) |
| Period of rotation | 27 d. on average |
| Inclination (relative to Earth's orbit) | 7° |
| Equatorial diameter | 865,000 mi. (1,392,000 km) |
| Diameter relative to Earth | 109 times |
| Mass | $1.8 \times 10^{27}$ tons |
| Gravity relative to Earth's | 27.8 times |
| Temperature at core | 27,000,000°F (15,000,000°C) |
| Temperature at surface | 10,260°F (5,700°C) |
| Main components | Hydrogen and helium |
| Expected life of hydrogen fuel supply | 5 billion years |

Because the Sun is a ball of gases, it does not rotate as a whole. The equator rotates in about 25 days, while gas near the poles rotates in about 30 days. The period of rotation at each latitude can be found by observing sunspots, which are magnetic storms. Sunspots appear and disappear in a mysterious 22-year cycle that many think influences weather on Earth, although convincing proof is lacking. Sometimes sunspots disappear for tens of years at a time, as during the period from 1645 to 1715. It may or may not be a coincidence that those years coincided with the "Little Ice Age" in Europe, when temperatures were far below average.

Like Earth the Sun is composed of various layers. The part we see is called the photosphere. In the Sun's interior, energy is generated when hydrogen in the core fuses to become helium. Above the photosphere is a region of pinkish gases, the chromosphere. Above that is a large halo, visible only in eclipses, called the corona. Particles from the Sun, the solar wind, stream through the solar system, creating auroras on Earth. Strong increases in solar wind during solar flares can interfere with radio communication.

The Sun will eventually—in five billion years—burn all its hydrogen fuel into helium. When that happens, the nature of the Sun will change from a yellow dwarf to a red giant. Such a star is typically larger in diameter than the orbit of Venus, and may be larger than Earth's orbit. In either case Earth would be burned to a cinder, and no life could survive on it.

## STARS AND THE UNIVERSE
### The Constellations

Constellations are small groups of stars that from our vantage point on Earth seem to form some particular shape. In actuality, however, the stars forming a constellation are usually at vastly different distances from the solar system. They only appear to form a particular figure from Earth.

Long ago, before recorded history, people began naming these groups. By Sumerian times (3000–2500 B.C.), stories were already being told about how particular constellations were formed. Most of our present knowledge of such stories comes from the Greeks, much of whose mythology was reflected in the names of stars, planets, and constellations.

One group of constellations has exerted a special influence on human thought, at least since 1500 B.C. As the Sun, Moon, and planets move through the sky, they pass through a group of 12 constellations, called the constellations of the zodiac. Chaldean astronomers believed that the presence of the Sun, a planet, or even the Moon in one of these constellations at a person's birth (or at other significant times) influenced happenings on Earth. We call this belief astrology. Because of the precession of the equinoxes (see the section, "The Calendar of the Year"), the traditional 12 constellations are no longer where they were 3,500 years ago. Modern astrologers have divided the year into 12 "houses," based on where the signs of the zodiac used to be. Thus, when an astronomer and an astrologer refer to the zodiac, they mean quite different things.

Today astronomers use constellations for their own purposes, such as for mapping the sky. Each part of the sky is named by a particular constellation. These constellations, especially in the southern hemisphere, may not be traditional ones, but rather, groups of stars astronomers have named so that for reference purposes all of the sky is labeled. The International Astronomical Union has decreed that each such constellation be bounded by straight north-south and east-west lines. As a result, many of the larger traditional constellations extend beyond the boundaries of modern astronomical constellations.

While astronomers often use the traditional names of stars, most of which come to us from Latin or Arabic sources, they also use another system for naming objects in the sky (galaxies, radio sources, quasars, etc.) that is based on constellations. Generally, the brightest star in a particular astronomical constellation is called alpha, the next brightest beta, and so on, through several letters of the Greek alphabet, although stars of comparable brightness are assigned Greek letters on the basis of position rather than brightness. Thus Sirius is also known as alpha Canis Majoris, usually abbreviated as α CMa, which means it is the brightest star in the constellation of Canis Major (Latin for "big dog"; Sirius has long been known as the "dog star"). Since Sirius is a binary star (see "The Universe" below), the brighter main star is officially α CMa A. Bright radio sources were once designated by the name of a constellation followed by a letter of the Roman alphabet, such as Cassiopeia A (Cassiopeia is a character from Greek mythology) or Cygnus A (the Swan). Unfortunately, this system has been largely abandoned, so the same radio source may have several different names, depending on the astronomer. X-ray sources are still designated by the name of the constellation, followed by a hyphenated X and number. The number 1 is the brightest X-ray source in a given constellation, so Scorpius X-1 is the brightest X-ray source in the constellation Scorpio.

### The Universe

Most of the universe was greatly misunderstood until the 20th century. The most common notion from the time of the ancient Greek philosophers until the end of the middle ages was that a number of crystal spheres revolved about Earth, and that each of the planets and Earth's Moon occupied one of these spheres. All the stars occupied the farthest sphere. There were only about 6,000 stars known, those visible to the naked eye (and about half of these were south of the equator, so few Europeans had ever seen them).

In 1609 Galileo of Italy turned the first astronomical telescope on the heavens. Galileo's early telescopes were good enough to show that the Milky Way was not merely a whitish band across the sky but consisted of a vast number of stars, far more than the few thousand visible with the naked eye. People began to speculate about astronomical entities beyond a simple sphere of stars. Not until 1924 were telescopes sufficiently powerful to show that many cloudy patches in the sky consisted of millions of stars far away from the Milky Way. This discovery led to the recognition of the enormous complexity and diversity of the universe.

**Big Bang** The accepted theory of how the universe began is known as the Big Bang theory, since it proposes that the universe began as something like an explosion, which has caused all parts of the universe to rush away from one another (the expansion of the universe). Such an expansion is observed. Other evidence for the Big Bang theory is the discovery of cosmic background radiation, a radiation that seems to come equally from all directions. Cosmic background radiation has the characteristics expected if the universe resulted from a small, dense region exploding.

**Binary stars** Almost half the stars in the visible universe are actually pairs of stars that orbit each other. Astronomers can sometimes see both stars, but more commonly they recognize that a star is part of a binary because of the influence of the dimmer star's gravitational pull on the other star.

**Black holes** When a body becomes so massive for its size that not even light can escape the powerful gravitational pull it exerts, it is called a black hole. Black holes were predicted as early as 1784 (by John Michell) and invoked later by various astronomers and physicists to explain many strange astronomical phenomena. It is still not completely clear that any black holes have been found, but they are widely suspected of being at the center of many galaxies, including our own Milky Way.

**Brown dwarfs** are bodies too small to be stars (since they emit no visible light and are not undergoing fusion) but too large to be planets (they give off a lot of energy in the infrared part of the electromagnetic spectrum as a result of gravitational contraction). No brown dwarfs have been positively identified, but some astronomers think there might be enough of them to account for the "missing mass" (see below).

**Dwarfs** All stars can be plotted on a graph where the horizontal axis is spectral class (temperature) and the vertical axis is absolute magnitude (true brightness); such a graph is called a Hertzsprung-Russell (H-R) diagram. On an H-R diagram, most stars fall along the main sequence, a slightly curvy line from the top left to the bottom right of the graph. Stars above the line are giants. White and brown dwarfs fall below the line. Dwarfs are small stars that lie on the main sequence—the brightest are red dwarfs, the dimmest blue dwarfs. The Sun, near the middle of the main sequence, is a yellow dwarf.

**Expanding universe** The farther away something is from us, the faster it is moving away from us. When Albert Einstein developed his general theory of relativity, he found it predicted that the universe would expand as if it were exploding. He tried to correct this prediction by inserting a factor in his equations to counteract the prediction, but in the 1920s, Edwin Hubble discovered that the universe actually was expanding. It is easier to measure the speed of recession than the distance, so astronomers commonly use the speed something is moving away as the measure of its distance from us. Of course, it is not just moving away from us. In the expanding universe, everything is moving away from everything else.

**Galaxies** are systems of very many stars separated from one another by largely empty space (sometimes called island universes). In the 18th century, William Herschel concluded that many cloudy patches of light seen among the stars were actually giant systems of billions of stars, but so far away from Earth as to look like clouds. Better telescopes proved him right in the early 20th century, and these far-off, great masses of stars became known as galaxies, after our own Milky Way, the galaxy that includes the Sun. Observation with large telescopes in the 20th century has revealed two main types of galaxy—spiral and elliptical—although some galaxies are neither (irregular).

**Milky Way** This is the galaxy to which the Sun and Earth belong. If you are in a place unafflicted with much light pollution, when you look at the night sky, you can see a faint band crossing it. The ancient Greeks named this the Milky Way (*galaxy* in Greek). Early in the 19th century, William Herschel determined that our Sun was a star in a vast lens-shaped star system, and that the Milky Way was the part of the star system we see from our vantage point inside it. Today, recognizing there are very many other such star systems, scientists often call it the Milky Way galaxy.

**Missing mass** is matter that is apparently in the universe but that has not been observed. Astronomers note that galaxies are rotating as if they were embedded in larger, invisible bodies. Furthermore, there are the-

oretical reasons to believe there is even more matter in the universe than can be accounted for by the invisible matter surrounding galaxies. Ideas as to what this "missing mass" might be include everything from brown dwarfs to undiscovered subatomic particles.

**Nebulae** are patches of gas and dust observable in telescopes. Before Herschel discovered that some cloudy patches seen through telescopes were vast collections of stars, all such patches were called nebulae (meaning *clouds*). Some "clouds" turned out to be gal-

## CONSTELLATIONS AND BRIGHT STARS

The 25 brightest stars are listed in the constellation where they can be seen. The number following the official name is their rank. Thus Sirius is listed under Canis Major as "Contains Sirius ($\alpha$ CMa A) – 1," which means it is the brightest star in the sky, while Canopus, the second brightest, is followed by "– 2." Constellations are named in Latin. When citing a constellation to locate a star, astronomers use the genitive (or possessive) form of the constellation's name, which differs slightly from the common (or nominative) form. Thus, in the constellation Canis Major, the star Sirius is alpha Canis Majoris, or "alpha of Canis Major."

| Name | Genitive | Abbreviation | Translation | Remarks |
|------|----------|--------------|-------------|---------|
| Andromeda | Andromedae | And | Andromeda | Character in Greek myth |
| Antlia | Antliae | Ant | Air Pump | Of modern origin |
| Apus | Apodis | Aps | Bird of Paradise | Of modern origin |
| Aquarius | Aquarii | Aqr | Water Bearer | In zodiac |
| Aquila | Aquilae | Aql | Eagle | Contains Altair ($\alpha$ Aql) – 12 |
| Ara | Arae | Ara | Altar | — |
| Aries | Arietis | Ari | Ram | In zodiac |
| Auriga | Aurigae | Aur | Charioteer | Contains Capella ($\alpha$ Aur) – 6 |
| Boötes | Boötis | Boo | Herdsman | Contains Arcturus ($\alpha$ Boo) – 3 |
| Caelum | Caeli | Cae | Chisel | Of modern origin |
| Camelopardalis | Camelopardalis | Cam | Giraffe | Of modern origin |
| Cancer | Cancri | Cnc | Crab | In zodiac |
| Canes Venatici | Canum Venaticorum | CVn | Hunting Dogs | Of modern origin |
| Canis Major | Canis Majoris | CMa | Big Dog | Contains Sirius ($\alpha$ CMa A) – 1 and Adhara ($\epsilon$ CMa A) – 22 |
| Canis Minor | Canis Minoris | CMi | Little Dog | Contains Procyon ($\alpha$ CMi A) – 8 |
| Capricornus | Capricorni | Cap | Goat | In zodiac |
| Carina | Carinae | Car | Ship's Keel[1] | Of modern origin; contains Canopus ($\alpha$ Car) – 2 |
| Cassiopeia | Cassiopeiae | Cas | Cassiopeia | Character in Greek myth |
| Centaurus | Centauri | Cen | Centaur | Character in Greek myth; contains Rigil Kentaurus ($\alpha$ Cen A) – 4 and Hadar/Agena ($\beta$ Cen A) – 11 |
| Cepheus | Cephei | Cep | Cepheus | Character in Greek myth |
| Cetus | Ceti | Cet | Whale | — |
| Chamaeleon | Chamaeleonis | Cha | Chameleon | Of modern origin |
| Circinus | Circini | Cir | Compass | Of modern origin |
| Columba | Columbae | Col | Dove | Of modern origin |
| Coma Berenices | Comae Berenices | Com | Berenice's Hair | Third-century B.C. Egyptian queen |
| Corona Australis | Coronae Australis | CrA | Southern Crown | Of modern origin |
| Corona Borealis | Coronae Borealis | CrB | Northern Crown | — |
| Corvus | Corvi | Crv | Crow | — |
| Crater | Crateris | Crt | Cup | — |
| Crux | Crucis | Cru | Southern Cross | Of modern origin; contains Beta Crucis ($\beta$ Cru) – 19 and Acrux ($\alpha$ Cru A) – 21; smallest constellation |
| Cygnus | Cygni | Cyg | Swan | Contains Deneb ($\alpha$ Cyg) – 18 |
| Delphinus | Delphini | Del | Dolphin | — |
| Dorado | Doradus | Dor | Goldfish | Of modern origin |
| Draco | Draconis | Dra | Dragon | — |
| Equuleus | Equulei | Equ | Little Horse | — |
| Eridanus | Eridani | Eri | River Eridanus | Contains Achernar ($\alpha$ Eri) – 10 |
| Fornax | Fornacis | For | Furnace | Of modern origin |
| Gemini | Geminorum | Gem | Twins | In zodiac; contains Pollux ($\beta$ Gem) – 17 |
| Grus | Gruis | Gru | Crane | Of modern origin |
| Hercules | Herculis | Her | Hercules | Character from Greek myth |
| Horologium | Horologii | Hor | Clock | Of modern origin |
| Hydra | Hydrae | Hya | Hydra | Monster from Greek myth; largest constellation |

axies, but many did not. The patches of gas emit light, often by the same mechanism that a fluorescent light does; energy ionizes the gas, which gives off visible light. Some patches of dust also glow, usually reflecting the light of nearby stars. Other patches of dust are opaque or nearly so, blocking out part of the sky. Some of the most striking nebulae consist of glowing gas surrounded by opaque dust or vice versa, which give the nebulae a definite shape, such as the North America Nebula (shaped like the continent of North America) or the Horsehead Nebula (which looks like a black horse's head against a glowing background). Herschel also studied a class of nebulae that looked to be giant spheres. He correctly concluded that these planetary nebulae were balls of gas produced when a star exploded.

**Novae** are stars that seem to appear in place of dim stars or out of nowhere. Early peoples were surprised from time to time by the appearance of a new (*nova*) star in the sky. Ancient Chinese astronomers called them guest stars. It is now clear that a truly new star does not appear; instead, a dim, existing star suddenly brightens. In early days, before the telescope, the dim stars could not be seen at all, so it looked as if a star came from nowhere. Today we know that there are two different types of "guest star," and we reserve the name nova for one type and call the other a supernova (see below). The type referred to today as novae are less bright than supernovae and may appear more than once. It is thought that they occur when material from one star in a binary pair falls on the other star, causing it suddenly to flare up.

**Neutron stars** are those composed of neutrons instead of atoms. When a star's core collapses, it may collapse so much that the electrons and protons in the core are squeezed together to become neutrons. Such a star may be only a dozen miles in diameter but may have a mass twice that of the Sun.

**Pulsars** are neutron stars that emit electromagnetic signals from their magnetic poles in a direction that reaches Earth. All neutron stars emit signals and rotate very rapidly (at least when they are first formed); they gradually slow down. These signals form a tight beam. If the beam intersects Earth, a radio telescope observes a fast pulsing on and off of the signal. The pulses are so regular that when they were first discovered, they were thought to be the work of extraterrestrial beings.

**Quasars** are distant sources of great energy. The name *quasar* is short for Quasi-Stellar Object, and the objects are so called because they seem to be about the size and general appearance of stars, but produce far too much energy for sure. No one knows for sure what they are, but there is some evidence that quasars are the central part of distant galaxies. The stars in the galaxies cannot be seen because of the great distance, so we see only the central part, which is the quasar.

**Red giants** are stars that have used their hydrogen fuel and expanded as a result. Young stars "burn" hydrogen in a nuclear fusion process that leads to helium. When a star has consumed the hydrogen in its core, new fusion reactions that start with helium begin, leading to carbon. The new reactions are hotter than the fusion of hydrogen to helium. This added energy causes the hydrogen and helium outside the core to expand. When the Sun becomes a red giant in the distant future, it will expand almost to the orbit of Earth, completely engulfing Mercury and Venus, and charring Earth to a cinder. The star is red because the outer layers are relatively cool, but its large size makes it visible. Hotter stars are yellow, and still-hotter stars are blue-white, just as heated iron

| Name | Genitive | Abbreviation | Translation | Remarks |
|---|---|---|---|---|
| Hydrus | Hydri | Hyi | Sea Serpent | Of modern origin |
| Indus | Indi | Ind | Indian | Of modern origin |
| Lacerta | Lacertae | Lac | Lizard | Of modern origin |
| Leo | Leonis | Leo | Lion | In zodiac; contains Regulus ($\alpha$ Leo A) – 20 |
| Leo Minor | Leonis Minoris | LMi | Little Lion | Of modern origin |
| Lepus | Leporis | Lep | Hare | — |
| Libra | Librae | Lib | Scales | In zodiac |
| Lupus | Lupi | Lup | Wolf | — |
| Lynx | Lyncis | Lyn | Lynx | Of modern origin |
| Lyra | Lyrae | Lyr | Harp | Contains Vega ($\alpha$ Lyr) – 5 |
| Mensa | Mensae | Men | Table (mountain) | Of modern origin |
| Microscopium | Microscopii | Mic | Microscope | Of modern origin |
| Monoceros | Monocerotis | Mon | Unicorn | Of modern origin |
| Musca | Muscae | Mus | Fly | Of modern origin |
| Norma | Normae | Nor | Carpenter's Square | Of modern origin |
| Octans | Octanis | Oct | Octant | Of modern origin |
| Ophiuchus | Ophiuchi | Oph | Ophiuchus (serpent bearer) | Character in Greek myth |
| Orion | Orionis | Ori | Orion | The hunter, character in Greek myth; contains Rigel ($\beta$ Ori A) – 7, Betelgeuse ($\alpha$ Ori) – 9, and Bellatrix ($\gamma$ Ori) – 24 |
| Pavo | Pavonis | Pav | Peacock | — |
| Pegasus | Pegasi | Peg | Pegasus | Winged horse in Greek myth |
| Perseus | Persei | Per | Perseus | Character in Greek myth |
| Phoenix | Phoenicis | Phe | Phoenix | Of modern origin |
| Pictor | Pictoris | Pic | Painter | Of modern origin |
| Pisces | Piscium | Psc | Fish | In zodiac |
| Piscis Austrinus | Piscis Austrini | PsA | Southern Fish | Contains Fomalhaut ($\alpha$ PsA) – 16 |
| Puppis | Puppis | Pup | Ship's Stern[1] | Of modern origin |
| Pyxis | Pyxidis | Pyx | Ship's Compass[1] | Of modern origin |
| Reticulum | Reticuli | Ret | Net | Of modern origin |
| Sagitta | Sagittae | Sge | Arrow | — |
| Sagittarius | Sagittarii | Sgr | Archer | In zodiac |
| Scorpius | Scorpii | Sco | Scorpion | In zodiac; contains Antares ($\alpha$ Sco A) – 15 and Shaula ($\lambda$ Sco) – 23 |
| Sculptor | Sculptoris | Scl | Sculptor | Of modern origin |
| Scutum | Scuti | Sct | Shield | Of modern origin |
| Serpens | Serpentis | Ser | Serpent | — |
| Sextans | Sextantis | Sex | Sextant | Of modern origin |
| Taurus | Tauri | Tau | Bull | In zodiac; contains Aldebran ($\alpha$ Tau A) – 13 and Elnath ($\beta$ Tau) – 25 |
| Telescopium | Telescopii | Tel | Telescope | Of modern origin |
| Triangulum | Trianguli | Tri | Triangle | — |
| Triangulum Australe | Trianguli Australis | TrA | Southern Triangle | Of modern origin |
| Tucana | Tucanae | Tuc | Toucan | Of modern origin |
| Ursa Major | Ursae Majoris | UMa | Big Bear | Big Dipper |
| Ursa Minor | Ursae Minoris | UMi | Little Bear | Little Dipper |
| Vela | Velorum | Vel | Ship's Sails[1] | Of modern origin |
| Virgo | Virginis | Vir | Virgin | In zodiac; contains Spica ($\alpha$ Vir) – 14 |
| Volans | Volantis | Vol | Flying Fish | Of modern origin |
| Vulpecula | Vulpeculae | Vul | Little Fox | Of modern origin |

1. Formerly part of the constellation Argo Navis, the Argonaut's Ship.

goes from red to blue-white with increased temperature. The hotter or larger a star is, the brighter it is.

**Stars** are bodies of gas large enough to undergo fusion reactions in their core. As a result of the energy produced by fusion, stars emit visible light, as well as electromagnetic radiation at other wavelengths. The Sun is a star.

**Superclusters and clusters of galaxies** are groups of galaxies associated in space. There may be just a few members of a cluster or as many as thousands. About two dozen galaxies near us form, with the Milky Way, our Local Group. The members of the Local Group also include the Andromeda galaxy and the Large and Small Magellanic Clouds. All are traveling through the universe together. The Local Group is a member of a supercluster of galaxies, called the Local Supercluster, that contains about 100 clusters. Clusters and superclusters are primarily recognized because the average distance within a cluster or a supercluster from one galaxy or cluster to another is much less than the distance to other galaxies or clusters.

**Supernovae** are large stars that explode. A supernova explosion is much more dramatic than the brightening of a nova. A supernova reported by Chinese astronomers from A.D. 1054 was visible in the daytime. The remnants of this explosion are known today as the Crab Nebula. At its heart the Crab Nebula has a pulsar, all that is left of the star that exploded.

**Variable stars** Any star that periodically changes brightness is called a variable (a nova changes brightness but not at regular intervals). The period varies with the cause of the change and the individual star. Some variables are part of a binary system in which one star periodically passes in front of the other. Other kinds of variables are called Mira variables and Cepheid variables, after the first stars known of each type. It is not clear what causes the brightness to vary.

**White dwarfs** are stars whose cores have collapsed until all the atoms are pressed very close together. A single teaspoonful of the matter in a white dwarf weighs about 5 tons. The core collapses because a red giant has used all its helium for fuel, but the star is too small to start burning carbon.

## Elements in the Universe

Astronomers and physicists believe that the Big Bang produced a universe that contained 80% hydrogen, 20% helium, and probably no other elements at all. When clouds of hydrogen and helium began to collapse into small spaces as a result of gravitational forces, the nuclei of hydrogen atoms were pressed so close together that they fused into heavier hydrogen (deuterium and tritium), which in turn fused to form helium. The process released energy, and the balls of hydrogen and helium became stars. The energy released balanced the force of gravity, and the stars stabilized in size. This is the source of the Sun's energy, and the process continues today for other small stars. In larger stars the helium

and hydrogen continue to fuse, producing nitrogen, carbon, neon, and some oxygen, as well as more helium. Still-larger stars go farther, and are able to produce heavier elements, including magnesium, silicon, and iron.

Iron is the end of the line for this process, because fusing iron nuclei takes more energy than the process produces. Gravitational energy, however, causes the star's core to contract with great speed when the fusion process begins to slacken. This contraction provides the necessary energy to fuse iron, but it provides so much energy that the star blows up, becoming a supernova. In the process of exploding, elements heavier than iron are created. Furthermore, the explosion sends all the elements from the supernova into space, creating clouds that contain all elements. The solar system apparently formed from such a cloud, since silicon, oxygen, and iron are abundant, and elements as heavy as uranium occur in smaller amounts.

Since the Big Bang, some hydrogen and helium have remained as interstellar gases, and some have formed smaller stars in which the fusion process does not go beyond fusion of helium. As a result more hydrogen and helium are still present than any other elements. Carbon, nitrogen, and oxygen are the main components of the medium-size star's fusion cycle, so they are the next most abundant elements. After iron is produced, the amount of heavier elements present through supernovae explosions goes down considerably, although nickel occurs in quantities near that of iron. With few exceptions fusion produces elements with even atomic numbers more easily than those with odd atomic numbers. (See "The Periodic Table.")

---

## EXPLORING THE UNIVERSE

**Optical telescopes** Telescopes were first developed in Holland about 400 years ago. The first telescopes used lenses to gather light and focus it. Later in the 17th century, scientists realized that curved mirrors could also gather and focus light. Since the light did not need to pass through the mirror (as light passes through a lens), mirrors proved to be more efficient than lenses for large telescopes.

| Year | Type | Importance |
|------|------|------------|
| 1608 | Lens | Hans Lipperhey in Holland applies for first patent on a telescope |
| 1609 | Lens | Galileo builds first astronomical telescopes, eventually reaching 30 power |
| 1611 | Lens | Johannes Kepler introduces convex lens, producing greater power |
| 1663 | Mirror | James Gregory is first to think that reflecting telescope can be made |
| 1668 | Mirror | Isaac Newton builds first telescope to use mirror to collect light, rather than lens |
| 1723 | Mirror | John Hadley invents reflecting telescope based on parabola, which concentrates light at a point |
| 1789 | Mirror | William Herschel builds telescope with 48-in. (122-cm) mirror, largest for many years |
| 1897 | Lens | Alvan Clark builds what is still world's largest telescope to use lens instead of mirror, 40 in. (102 cm) |
| 1917 | Mirror | Hooker Telescope at Mount Wilson in California is put into operation; it will be world's largest for about 30 years |
| 1930 | Combination | Bernard Schmidt makes first telescopes combining lenses and mirrors; they become workhorse of astronomy |
| 1948 | Mirror | Hale Telescope (200 in., or 5 m), located on Mt. Palomar in California, becomes largest and best on Earth |
| 1962 | Mirror | Largest telescope devoted to observing the Sun is erected at Kitt Peak in Arizona |
| 1976 | Mirror | Soviet Zelenchukskaya becomes largest telescope, but various problems limit effectiveness |
| 1979 | Mirrors | MMT on Mt. Hopkins in Arizona uses six mirrors to obtain equivalent light-gathering power of 177-in. (4.5 m) reflector |
| 1990 | Mirror | Hubble Space Telescope (94 in., or 2.4 m) becomes first optical telescope in space |
| 1991 | Mirror | Keck Telescope on Mauna Kea in Hawaii uses world's largest mirror, 396 in. in diameter, with 4 times light-gathering capacity of Hale |

**Radio telescopes** Before 1931 all telescopes were optical—i.e., they gathered and focused electromagnetic radiation in the range people can sense with their eyes. Stars, planets, and other objects in the universe also produce other wavelengths of radiation, however. A radio telescope gathers and focuses radiation at long wavelengths, the same kind of electromagnetic radiation used for transmission of radio signals.

| Year | Type | Importance |
|------|------|------------|
| 1931 | Ordinary antenna | Karl Jansky accidentally discovers, in trying to track down sources of static, that radio waves are coming from space |
| 1937 | Parabolic dish | Grote Reber builds first intentional radio telescope in dish, Wheaton, Ill. |
| 1957 | Steerable dish | Parabolic dish (250 ft., or 75 m) at Jodrell Bank in England is first major radio telescope |
| 1962 | Steerable dish | Dish (300 ft., or 90 m) at Green Bank, W.Va., first used to search for extraterrestrial life; it collapses mysteriously on Nov. 15, 1988 |
| 1963 | Fixed dish | Largest fixed-dish radio telescope, 1,000 ft. (305 m) across, is built in valley at Arecibo, Puerto Rico |

| Year | Type | Importance |
|------|------|------------|
| 1970 | Steerable dish | World's largest steerable dish, at Effelsberg, W. Germany is 328 ft. (100 m) in diameter |
| 1977 | Several antennae | First Very Long Baseline Interferometry begins operating at Cal Tech's Owens Valley Radio Observatory |
| 1980 | 27 antennae | Very Long Array (VLA) is built in 13 mi. (21 km) Y shape near Socorro, New Mexico |

**Other telescopes** Since both short wavelengths and long ones coming from space had been studied by optical and radio telescopes, it seemed likely that other wavelengths could also be detected. The problem was that Earth's atmosphere, relatively transparent to optical and radio waves, is almost opaque to other wavelengths of electromagnetic radiation. The solution to making telescopes that could detect other wavelengths was to put telescopes in satellites traveling above Earth's atmosphere. An entirely different problem faced designers of telescopes studying energetic particles called neutrinos. To eliminate "noise" from other particles, they located telescopes deep under the earth's surface.

| Year | Type | Importance |
|------|------|------------|
| 1961 | Gamma rays | First telescope in space observes gamma rays that do not penetrate Earth's atmosphere |
| 1968 | Neutrinos | First neutrino telescope built, at the Homestake Gold Mine in Lead, S.Dak.; first takes data on solar neutrinos in 1970 |
| 1970 | X rays | First telescope to detect X rays, known as Uhuru ("Freedom" in Swahili), is launched into space |
| 1972 | Ultraviolet radiation | Copernicus spacecraft has a telescope designed to collect ultraviolet radiation |
| 1978 | X rays | Einstein Observatory, which detects X rays from space, becomes one of most productive satellite-based telescopes |
| 1983 | Infrared radiation | Infrared Astronomy Satellite (IRAS) becomes most successful satellite-based telescope, detecting possible new planetary systems and formation of stars |
| 1990 | Gamma rays | Gamma Ray Observatory with more sensitive telescope and wider range than previous satellite telescopes |
| 1991 | Ultraviolet radiation | Extreme Ultraviolet Explorer (EUVE) to study short ultraviolet wavelengths; U.S. observatory planned for August launch |

## MAJOR ACCOMPLISHMENTS OF SATELLITES AND SPACE PROBES, 1957–91

While much attention is focused on human beings in space, most of the serious scientific progress has been made by satellites or probes—the general name for space vehicles that neither carry humans nor orbit Earth—that are directed internally or from Earth. Since 1957 there have been hundreds of such satellites and probes.

| Launch date | Name | Accomplishment |
|-------------|------|----------------|
| 10/4/57 | Sputnik 1 | First satellite to orbit Earth (USSR) |
| 11/3/57 | Sputnik 2 | Carries Laika, first dog in space; burns in atmosphere 4/14/58 |
| 1/31/58 | Explorer 1 | First satellite to detect Van Allen radiation belts; first U.S. satellite |
| 3/17/58 | Vanguard | Demonstrates that Earth is pear shaped with slight bulge in Southern Hemisphere (U.S.) |
| 1/2/59 | Mechta | First space probe to go into orbit around Sun, passing 5,000 mi. from Moon (at which it was aimed) (USSR) |
| 3/3/59 | Pioneer IV | First American probe aimed at Moon; like Mechta it misses and goes into orbit about Sun |
| 9/12/59 | Lunik II | First space probe to reach Moon, where it crash lands (USSR) |
| 10/4/59 | Lunik III | First space probe to return photographs of far side of Moon (USSR) |
| 4/1/60 | Tiros I | First weather satellite (U.S.) |
| 6/22/60 | Transit I-B | First navigational satellite (U.S.) |
| 8/12/60 | Echo I | First communications satellite—actually a large balloon off which radio signals could be bounced (U.S.) |
| 8/18/60 | Corona | First U.S. spy satellite |
| 8/19/60 | Sputnik 5 | Carries dogs Belka and Streika and successfully returns them to Earth; 18 orbits |
| 12/12/61 | Venera 1 | First space probe intended to reach another planet—Venus (USSR) |
| 3/7/62 | OSO I | Orbiting Solar Observatory—first major astronomical satellite (U.S.) |
| 4/23/62 | Ranger IV | First U.S. space probe to reach Moon |
| 4/26/62 | Cosmos 4 | First Soviet spy satellite |
| 7/10/62 | Telstar | First active communications satellite, allowing direct television between Europe and U.S. (U.S.) |
| 8/27/62 | Mariner II | First space probe to reach vicinity of another planet (Venus) and return scientific information (U.S.) |
| 10/31/62 | Anna I-B | First satellite intended for accurately measuring shape of Earth (U.S.) |
| 11/1/62 | Mars I | First space probe aimed at Mars; contact lost about 66 million mi. from Earth (USSR) |
| 6/26/63 | Syncom II | First communications satellite to go into synchronous orbit with Earth (U.S.) |
| 7/28/64 | Ranger VII | Returns close-up photographs of Moon before crashing into it (U.S.) |
| 8/28/64 | Nimbus I | First weather satellite to be stabilized so that its cameras always point toward Earth (U.S.) |
| 11/28/64 | Mariner IV | Flies by Mars and takes 21 pictures of its surface, successfully transmitting them back to Earth; its closest approach is 6,118 mi. (U.S.) |
| 4/6/65 | Early Bird | First commercial satellite (U.S.) |
| 4/23/65 | Molniya I | First Soviet communications satellite |
| 7/16/65 | Proton I | At 26,896 lbs., it is largest Earth satellite to this date (USSR) |
| 11/16/65 | Venera 3 | Crash-lands on Venus; first space probe to make physical contact with another planet; radio contact lost before it reaches immediate vicinity of planet (USSR) |
| 11/26/65 | A-1 | First satellite to be launched by nation other than the USSR or U.S. (France) |
| 12/16/65 | Pioneer 6 | Launched into solar orbit; still functions today |
| 1/31/66 | Luna 9 | Although main vehicle crash-lands, ejected capsule lands safely on Moon and transmits photographs to Earth (USSR) |
| 5/30/66 | Surveyor 1 | First soft landing of complete vehicle on Moon (U.S.) |
| 3/31/66 | Luna 10 | First space vehicle to go into orbit about Moon (USSR) |
| 8/10/66 | Lunar Orbiter 1 | First American space vehicle to go into orbit about Moon |
| 6/12/67 | Venera 4 | Ejects instrument package into atmosphere of Venus; package parachutes toward surface; contact lost before reaching surface (USSR) |
| 6/14/67 | Mariner 5 | Second American satellite to reach vicinity of Venus |
| 9/15/68 | Zond 5 | First Soviet satellite to return to Earth from vicinity of Moon |
| 2/11/70 | Ohsumi | First satellite to be launched by Japan |
| 4/24/70 | Mao 1 | First Chinese satellite; it broadcasts song "The East Is Red" once a minute, pausing at the end for other signals |
| 8/17/70 | Venera 7 | First Venus probe to return signals from planet's surface (USSR) |
| 9/12/70 | Luna 16 | First space probe to land on Moon without humans aboard, scoop up samples, and return them to Earth (USSR) |
| 11/10/70 | Luna 17 | Carries roving vehicle to Moon's surface; vehicle roams for 2 weeks at a time (during daylight), then "sleeps"; as it roams, it returns photos and other data to Earth (USSR) |
| 12/12/70 | Uhuru | First X-ray satellite telescope (U.S.) |
| 5/28/71 | Mars 3 | First space probe to soft-land on Mars, although it quickly ceases functioning (USSR) |
| 5/30/71 | Mariner 9 | First space probe to orbit another planet (Mars); returns 7,329 photographs of planet (U.S.) |
| 3/2/72 | Pioneer 10 | First space probe to study Jupiter and, on June 13, 1983, first to leave solar system (U.S.) |

| Launch date | Name | Accomplishment |
|---|---|---|
| 7/23/72 | Landsat I | First Earth resources satellite (U.S.) |
| 3/6/73 | Pioneer 11 | First space probe to reach vicinity of Saturn (U.S.) |
| 11/3/73 | Mariner 10 | First space probe to observe 2 planets, Venus and Mercury, and only probe ever to observe Mercury (U.S.) |
| | Venera 9 | Returns first photographs from surface of Venus (USSR) |
| 12/10/74 | Helios | First W. German space probe |
| 8/20/75 | Viking 1 | First American space probe to soft-land on Mars; continues to return data until May 1983 |
| 9/20/75 | Viking 2 | Successfully soft-lands on Mars (U.S.) |
| 8/20/77 | Voyager 2 | After studying Jupiter and Saturn, it becomes first space probe to reach vicinities of Uranus and Neptune (U.S.) |
| 9/5/77 | Voyager 1 | After studying Jupiter, it becomes first space probe to reach vicinity of Saturn (U.S.) |
| 1/26/78 | IUE | International Ultraviolet Explorer—the only astronomical satellite to be placed in geosynchronous orbit; it is still sending back data |
| 5/20/78 | Pioneer Venus 1 | First space probe to go into orbit about Venus (U.S.) |
| 6/26/78 | Seasat | Analyzes ocean currents and ice flow (U.S.) |
| 8/12/78 | ISEE-3 | Originally the third International Sun-Earth Explorer, space probe is renamed International Cometary Explorer (ICE) when it is redirected to study tail of comet Giacobini-Zinner in 1983 (U.S.) |
| 12/13/78 | HEAO-2 | High-Energy Astronomy Observatory, also known as the Einstein Observatory—it makes high-resolution X-ray images of the universe (U.S.) |
| 2/24/79 | P78-1 | Studies solar radiation until purposely shot down by U.S. Air Force 9/13/85; still working at time of its destruction, satellite is deemed by many scientists to be too valuable to be used as target (U.S.) |
| 2/14/80 | Solar Max | Studies solar radiation; after failure in Nov. 1980, it is repaired and relaunched from space shuttle in April 1984; finally pushed to its destruction by massive solar flare, Dec. 2, 1989 (U.S.) |

| Launch date | Name | Accomplishment |
|---|---|---|
| 1/25/83 | IRAS | Infrared Astronomical Satellite studies galactic and extragalactic infrared sources and discovers new stars forming as well as possible planet formation (U.S.) |
| 12/15/84 | Vega 1 | First Soviet mission to study Halley's comet; along the way it drops balloon probe into atmosphere of Venus |
| 12/21/84 | Vega 2 | Second Soviet mission to Halley's comet; it also releases a balloon probe at Venus |
| 1/7/85 | Sakigake | First Japanese mission to study Halley's comet (this one from far away) |
| 7/2/85 | Giotto | Joint European mission to Halley's comet; passes closest to the comet—375 mi. |
| 8/18/85 | Suisei | Japanese mission to Halley's comet |
| 2/21/86 | SPOT | French satellite designed to photograph surface details of Earth as small as 30 ft. across |
| 5/4/89 | Magellan | American probe now orbiting Venus and mapping it in detail with radar |
| 10/18/89 | Galileo | After passing near Venus and Earth (twice), it will orbit Jupiter, report on Jovian moons, and drop probe into Jupiter's atmosphere (U.S.) |
| 11/18/89 | Cosmic Background Explorer (COBE) | To study cosmic background radiation in hopes of learning cause of galaxy formation |
| 4/24/90 | Hubble Space Telescope | First optical telescope placed in orbit about Earth (U.S.) |
| 10/5/90 | Ulysses | U.S.–European Space Agency to study previously unobserved north and south poles of the Sun |
| 4/5/91 | Gamma Ray Observatory | A 17-ton telescope for observing the universe at very short wavelengths |
| 8/91 (sched.) | Extreme Ultraviolet Explorer (EUVA) | American satellite to study high range of ultraviolet radiation in universe |

## SPACEFLIGHTS CARRYING PEOPLE, 1961–91

The space programs of the Soviet Union and the United States both had dramatic flights by human pilots as an important component, although many scientists felt that most goals of the space program could be achieved without risking lives. The *Vostok, Voskhod,* and *Soyuz* missions are part of the Soviet program; *Mercury, Gemini, Apollo, Skylab,* and the shuttle are part of the U.S. program.

| Date | Craft | Duration | Crew | Remarks | Date | Craft | Duration | Crew | Remarks |
|---|---|---|---|---|---|---|---|---|---|
| | | | | **Proving that people can venture into space** | | | | | |
| 4/12/61 | Vostok 1 | 1 hr. 48 min. | Yuri A. Gagarin | First spaceflight by human | 8/12/62 | Vostok 4 | 70 hrs. 57 min. | Pavel R. Popovitch | Dual launch with Vostok 3; 48 orbits |
| 5/5/61 | Mercury 3 | 15 min. | Alan B. Shepard, Jr. | Suborbital | 10/3/62 | Mercury 8 | 9 hrs. 13 min. | Walter M. Schirra | 6 orbits |
| 7/21/61 | Mercury 4 | 16 min. | Virgil I. Grissom | Suborbital | 5/15/63 | Mercury 9 | 34 hrs. 20 min. | L. Gordon Cooper | 22 orbits |
| 8/6/61 | Vostok 2 | 25 hrs. 18 min. | Gherman S. Titov | First multiorbit flight; 17 orbits | 6/14/63 | Vostok 5 | 119 hrs. 6 min. | Valery F. Bikovsky | 81 orbits |
| 2/20/62 | Mercury 6 | 5 hrs. 55 min. | John H. Glenn, Jr. | First orbital flight by American; 3 orbits | 6/16/63 | Vostok 6 | 70 hrs. 50 min. | Valentina V. Tereshkova | First woman cosmonaut; 48 orbits; dual launch with Vostok 5 |
| 5/24/62 | Mercury 7 | 4 hrs. 56 min. | M. Scott Carpenter | 3 orbits | | | | | |
| 8/11/62 | Vostok 3 | 94 hrs. 24 min. | Andrian G. Nikolayev | 64 orbits; landing by parachute | 10/12/64 | Voskhod 1 | 24 hrs. 17 min. | Vladimir M. Komarov Konstantin P. Feoktistov Boris B. Yegorov | First multihuman crew; 3 cosmonauts make 16 orbits |
| | | | | **Planning for operations in space** | | | | | |
| 3/18/65 | Voskhod 2 | 26 hrs. | Aleksei A. Leonov Pavel I. Belyayev | First extravehicular activity (EVA) by Leonov (20 min.); 17 orbits | 8/21/65 | Gemini 5 | 190 hrs. 56 min. | L. Gordon Cooper Charles Conrad, Jr. | 120 orbits; demonstrates feasibility of lunar mission; simulated rendezvous |
| 3/23/65 | Gemini 3 | 4 hrs. 53 min. | Virgil I. Grissom John W. Young | First American multiperson crew; 3 orbits | 12/4/65 | Gemini 7 | 330 hrs. 35 min. | Frank Borman James A. Lovell, Jr. | 206 orbits; extensions of testing and performance; target for first rendezvous |
| 6/3/65 | Gemini 4 | 97 hrs. 56 min. | James A. McDivitt Edward H. White II | 62 orbits; first American EVA: first use of personal propulsion unit | 12/15/65 | Gemini 6A | 25 hrs. 51 min. | Walter M. Schirra Thomas P. Stafford | 15 orbits; rendezvous with Gemini 7 |

| Date | Craft | Duration | Crew | Remarks | Date | Craft | Duration | Crew | Remarks |
|------|-------|----------|------|---------|------|-------|----------|------|---------|
| 3/16/66 | Gemini 8 | 10 hrs. 42 min. | Neil A. Armstrong<br>David R. Scott | 6.5 orbits; first dual launch and docking; first Pacific landing | 7/18/66 | Gemini 10 | 70 hrs. 47 min. | John W. Young<br>Michael Collins | 43 orbits; first dual rendezvous, docked vehicle maneuvers; umbilical EVA |
| 6/3/66 | Gemini 9A | 72 hrs. 21 min. | Thomas P. Stafford<br>Eugene A. Cernan | 44 orbits; unable to dock with target vehicle; 2 hrs. 7 min. of EVA | 9/12/66 | Gemini 11 | 71 hrs. 17 min. | Charles Conrad, Jr.<br>Richard F. Gordon, Jr. | 44 orbits; rendezvous and docking |
| | | | | | 11/11/66 | Gemini 12 | 94 hrs. 34 min. | James A. Lovell, Jr.<br>Edwin A. Aldrin | 59 orbits; final Gemini mission; 5 hrs. of EVA |

## To the Moon and experiments in space

| Date | Craft | Duration | Crew | Remarks | Date | Craft | Duration | Crew | Remarks |
|------|-------|----------|------|---------|------|-------|----------|------|---------|
| 4/23/67 | Soyuz 1 | 26 hrs. 48 min. | Vladimir M. Komarov | 18 orbits; Komarov is killed when parachute fails, first fatality of space program | 10/11/69 | Soyuz 6 | 118 hrs. 42 min. | Georgi S. Shonin<br>Valery N. Kubasov | First triple launch (with Soyuz 7 and 8) |
| 10/11/68 | Apollo 7 | 260 hrs. 8 min. | Walter M. Schirra<br>Donn F. Eisele<br>R. Walter Cunningham | 8 service propulsion firings; 7 live TV sessions with crew; rendezvous with S-IVB stage performed | 10/12/69 | Soyuz 7 | 118 hrs. 41 min. | Anatoly V. Filipchenko<br>Vladislav N. Volkov<br>Viktor V. Gorbatko | With Soyuz 7 and 8, conducts experiments in navigation and photography |
| | | | | | 10/13/69 | Soyuz 8 | 118 hrs. 59 min. | Vladimir A. Shatalov<br>Aleksei S. Yeliseyev | 80 orbits |
| 10/26/68 | Soyuz 3 | 94 hrs. 51 min. | Georgi T. Beregovoi | 64 orbits; approaches unpiloted Soyuz 2 to distance of 650 ft. (198 m) | 11/14/69 | Apollo 12 | 244 hrs. 36 min. | Charles Conrad, Jr.<br>Richard F. Gordon, Jr.<br>Alan L. Bean | Second lunar landing; demonstrates point landing capability; samples more area; total EVA time: 15 hrs. 32 min. |
| 12/21/68 | Apollo 8 | 147 hrs. | Frank Borman<br>James A. Lovell, Jr.<br>William A. Anders | First Saturn-V propelled flight; first lunar orbital mission (10 orbits); returns good lunar photography | 4/11/70 | Apollo 13 | 142 hrs. 55 min. | James A. Lovell, Jr.<br>Fred W. Haise, Jr.<br>John L. Swigert, Jr. | Third lunar landing attempt aborted owing to loss of pressure in liquid oxygen in service module and fuel cell failure |
| 1/14/69 | Soyuz 4 | 71 hrs. 14 min. | Vladimir A. Shatalov | 48 orbits; docks with Soyuz 5 in first linkup of 2 space vehicles both carrying people | 6/2/70 | Soyuz 9 | 424 hrs. 59 min. 17 d. 16 hrs. | Andrian G. Nikolayev<br>Vitaly I. Sevastianov | Longest spaceflight to this time |
| 1/15/69 | Soyuz 5 | 72 hrs. 46 min. | Boris V. Volynov<br>Alexei S. Yeliseyev<br>Yevgeni V. Khrunov | 3 cosmonauts perform EVA, transferred to Soyuz 4 in rescue rehearsal | 1/31/71 | Apollo 14 | 9 d. 42 min. | Alan B. Shepard, Jr.<br>Stuart A. Roosa<br>Edgar D. Mitchell | Third lunar landing, returns 98 lbs. of lunar material |
| 3/3/69 | Apollo 9 | 241 hrs. 1 min. | James A. McDivitt<br>David R. Scott<br>Russell L. Schweickart | First flight of all lunar hardware in Earth orbit, incl. lunar module (LM) | 4/23/71 | Soyuz 10 | 47 hrs. 46 min. | Vladimir A. Shatalov<br>Aleksei S. Yeleseyev<br>Nikolai N. Rukavishnikov | Docks with Salyut 1, the first space station |
| 5/18/69 | Apollo 10 | 192 hrs. 3 min. | Eugene A. Cernan<br>John W. Young<br>Thomas P. Stafford | Lunar mission development flight to evaluate LM performance in lunar environment; descent to within 50,000 ft. of Moon | 6/6/71 | Soyuz 11 | 23 d. 18 hrs. 22 min. | Georgi T. Dobrovolsky<br>Viktor I. Patsayev<br>Vladislav N. Volkov | All 3 cosmonauts killed during reentry |
| | | | | | 7/26/71 | Apollo 15 | 12 d. 7 hrs. 12 min. | David R. Scott<br>Alfred M. Worden<br>James B. Irwin | Fourth lunar landing; first to carry Lunar Roving Vehicle (LVR); total EVA time: 18 hrs. 46 min.; returns 173 lbs. of material |
| 7/16/69 | Apollo 11 | 165 hrs. 18 min. | Neil A. Armstrong<br>Michael Collins<br>Edwin E. Aldrin, Jr. | First lunar landing; limited inspection, photography, evaluation, and sampling of lunar soil; touchdown: July 20 | 4/16/72 | Apollo 16 | 11 d. 14 hrs. 51 min. | John W. Young<br>Thomas K. Mattingly II<br>Charles M. Duke, Jr. | Fifth lunar landing; second to carry LRV; total EVA time: 20 hrs. 14 min.; returns 213 lbs. of material |
| | | | | | 12/7/72 | Apollo 17 | 12 d. 13 hrs. 52 min. | Eugene A. Cernan<br>Ronald E. Evans<br>Harrison H. Schmitt | Last manned lunar landing; third with LRV; total EVA time: 44 hrs. 8 min.; returns 243 lbs. of material |

## First stations in space

| Date | Craft | Duration | Crew | Remarks | Date | Craft | Duration | Crew | Remarks |
|------|-------|----------|------|---------|------|-------|----------|------|---------|
| 5/25/73 | Skylab 2 | 28 d. 49 min. | Charles Conrad, Jr.<br>Joseph P. Kerwin<br>Paul J. Weitz | First Skylab launch; establishes Skylab Orbital Assembly in earth orbit; conducts medical and other experiments | 7/29/73 | Skylab 3 | 59 d. 11 hrs. 9 min. | Alan L. Bean<br>Owen K. Garriott<br>Jack R. Lousma | Second Skylab; crew performs systems and operational tests, experiments, and thermal shield deployment |

| Date | Craft | Duration | Crew | Remarks | Date | Craft | Duration | Crew | Remarks |
|------|-------|----------|------|---------|------|-------|----------|------|---------|
| 9/27/73 | Soyuz 12 | 47 hrs. 16 min. | Vasily G. Lazarev<br>Oleg G. Makarov | First Soviet space flight to carry humans since the Soyuz 11 tragedy | 12/2/74 | Soyuz 16 | 5 d. 22 hrs. 24 min. | Anatoly V. Filipchenko<br>Nikolai N. Rukavishnikov | Taken to check modifications in Saylut system |
| 11/16/73 | Skylab 4 | 84 d. 1 hr. 7 min. | Gerald P. Carr<br>Edward G. Gibson<br>William R. Pogue | Third Skylab; crew services unmanned Saturn workshop; obtains medical data for extending space flights | 1/10/75 | Soyuz 17 | 29 d. 13 hrs. 20 min. | Alexei A. Gubarev<br>Georgi M. Grechko | Docks with Salyut 4; sets Soviet endurance record at this time |
| 12/18/73 | Soyuz 13 | 7 d. 20 hrs. 55 min. | Pyotr I. Klimuk<br>Valentin Lebedev | Performs astrophysical and biological experiments | 4/5/75 | Soyuz 18A | 22 min. | Vasily G. Lazarev<br>Oleg G. Makarov | Separation from booster fails, and craft fails to reach orbit, but crew successfully lands in western Siberia |
| 7/3/74 | Soyuz 14 | 15 d. 17 hrs. 30 min. | Pavel R. Popovich<br>Yuri P. Artyukhin | Crew occupies Salyut 3 space station; studies Earth resources | 5/24/75 | Soyuz 18B | 63 d. | Pyotr I. Klimuk<br>Vitaly I. Sevastyanov | Docks with Salyut 4 |
|  |  |  |  |  | 7/15/75 | ASTP | 9 d. 1 hr. 30 min. | Thomas P. Stafford<br>Vance D. Brand<br>Donald K. Slayton | Apollo-Soyuz Test Project, cooperative U.S.-Soviet mission |
| 8/26/74 | Soyuz 15 | 48 hrs. 12 min. | Gennady Sarafanov<br>Lev Demin | Makes unsuccessful attempt to dock with Salyut 3 | 7/15/75 | Soyuz 19 | 5 d. 23 hrs. 31 min. | Alexei A. Leonov<br>Valery N. Kubasov | Docks with ASTP, the U.S. Apollo capsule |

### The Soviet study of human biology in space

| Date | Craft | Duration | Crew | Remarks | Date | Craft | Duration | Crew | Remarks |
|------|-------|----------|------|---------|------|-------|----------|------|---------|
| 11/17/75 | Soyuz 20 | 90 d. | No crew | Biological mission; docks with Salyut 4 | 2/25/79 | Soyuz 32 | 175 d. | Vladimir Lyakhov<br>Valery Ryumin | Carries crew to Salyut 6; new endurance record set |
| 7/6/76 | Soyuz 21 | 49 d. | Boris V. Volynov<br>Vitaly Zholobov | Docks with Salyut 5 and performed Earth resource work | 4/10/79 | Soyuz 33 | 2 d. | Nikolai N. Rukavishnikov<br>Georgi Ivanov | Engine failure prior to docking forces early termination; first Bulgarian, Ivanov |
| 9/15/76 | Soyuz 22 | 8 d. | Valery F. Bykovsky<br>Vladimir Aksenov | Takes Earth-resources photographs |  |  |  |  |  |
| 10/14/76 | Soyuz 23 | 2 d. | Vyacheslav Zudov<br>Valery Rozhdestvensky | Unsuccessful attempt to dock with Salyut 5; first landing in water for Soviet program (in Lake Tengiz; unplanned, but crew survives) | 6/6/79 | Soyuz 34 | 74 d. | No crew | Launches with no crew; returns with crew from Salyut 6 |
|  |  |  |  |  | 4/9/80 | Soyuz 35 | 185 d. | Valery Ryumin<br>Leonid Popov | Carries 2 crew members to Salyut 6 |
|  |  |  |  |  | 5/26/80 | Soyuz 36 | 8 d. | Valery N. Kubasov<br>Bertalan Farkas | Carries 2 crew members to Salyut 6; crew returns in Soyuz 35; first Hungarian, Farkas |
| 2/7/77 | Soyuz 24 | 7 d. | Viktor G. Gorbatko<br>Yuri N. Glazkov | Docks with Salyut 5 for 18 d. of experiments |  |  |  |  |  |
| 10/9/77 | Soyuz 25 | 2 d. | Vladimir Kovalyonok<br>Valery Ryumin | Unsuccessful attempt to dock with Salyut 6 | 6/5/80 | Soyuz T-2 | 4 d. | Yuri Malyshev<br>Vladimir Aksenov | Test of modified Soyuz craft; docks with Salyut 6 |
| 12/10/77 | Soyuz 26 | 96 d. | Yuri V. Romanenko<br>Georgi M. Grechko | Docks with Salyut 6; crew sets endurance record | 7/23/80 | Soyuz 37 | 8 d. | Viktor F. Gorbatko<br>Pham Tuan | Exchanges cosmonauts in Salyut 6; returns Soyuz 35 crew after 185 days in orbit; first Vietnamese in space, Tuan |
| 1/10/78 | Soyuz 27 | 6 d. | Valdimir Dzhanibekov<br>Oleg G. Makarov | Carries second crew to dock with Salyut 6 space station |  |  |  |  |  |
| 3/2/78 | Soyuz 28 | 8 d. | Vladimir Remek<br>Alexi A. Gubarev | Carries third crew to board Salyut 6; Remek first non-Russian, non-American in space (Czech) | 9/18/80 | Soyuz 38 | 8 d. | Yuri V. Romanenko<br>Arnaldo Tamayo-Mendez | Ferries to Salyut 6; first Cuban in space, Tamayo-Mendez |
|  |  |  |  |  | 11/27/80 | Soyuz T-3 | 13 d. | Leonard Kizim<br>Oleg G. Makarov<br>Gennadi M. Strekalov | Ferries to Salyut 6; first 3-person crew since Soyuz 11 |
| 6/15/78 | Soyuz 29 | 140 d. | Vladimir Kovalyonok<br>Aleksander S. Ivanchenkov | Docks with Salyut 6; crew sets new space endurance record | 3/12/81 | Soyuz T-4 | 75 d. | Vladimer Kovalyonok<br>Viktor Savinykh | Mission to Salyut 6 |
|  |  |  |  |  | 3/22/81 | Soyuz 39 | 8 d. | Vladimir Dzhanibekov<br>Jugderdemuduyn Gurragcha | Docks with Salyut 6; first Mongolian, Gurragcha |
| 6/27/78 | Soyuz 30 | 8 d. | Pyotr I. Klimuk<br>Miroslaw Hermaszewski | Carries second international crew to Salyut 6; first Polish cosmonaut, Hermaszewski |  |  |  |  |  |
| 8/25/78 | Soyuz 31 | 8 d. | Valery F. Bykovsky<br>Sigmund Jahn | Carries third international crew to Salyut 6; first East German, Jahn |  |  |  |  |  |

## The space shuttle: U.S. reentry in space

| Date | Craft | Duration | Crew | Remarks | Date | Craft | Duration | Crew | Remarks |
|---|---|---|---|---|---|---|---|---|---|
| 4/12/81 | *Columbia* | 2 d. 6 hrs. | John W. Young<br>Robert L. Crippen | First flight of reusable space shuttle *Columbia*; first landing of U.S. spacecraft on land | 2/3/84 | *Challenger* | 8 d. | Vance Brand<br>Bruce McCandless<br>Robert Stewart<br>Ronald McNair<br>Robert Gibson | Jet-propelled backpacks carry 2 astronauts on first untethered space walks; 2 satellites (Western Union and Indonesia) lost; first landing at Kennedy Space Center |
| 5/14/81 | *Soyuz 40* | 8 d. | Leonid Popov<br>Dumitru Prunariu | First Romanian (Prunariu) in space | | | | | |
| 11/12/81 | *Columbia* | 2 d. 6 hrs. | Joe H. Engle<br>Richard H. Truly | First reuse of space shuttle; ended early due to loss of fuel cell | 2/8/84 | *Soyuz T-10B* | 237 d. | Leonard Kizim<br>Oleg Atkov<br>Vladimir Solovyov | Mission to *Salyut 7* to repair propulsion system; sets new duration-in-space record for crew |
| 3/22/82 | *Columbia* | 8 d. | Jack R. Lousma<br>C. Gordon Fullerton | Third shuttle flight; payload includes space science experiments | 4/2/84 | *Soyuz T-11* | 8 d. | Yuri Malyshev<br>Gennadi M. Strekalov<br>Rakesh Sharma | Docks with *Salyut 7*; first Indian cosmonaut, Sharma |
| 5/13/82 | *Soyuz T-5* | 211 d. | Anatoly Berezovoy<br>Valentin Lebedev | First flight to *Salyut 7*; space station equipped to measure body functions | 4/7/84 | *Challenger* | 8 d. | Robert L. Crippen<br>Richard Scobee<br>Terry Hart<br>George Nelson<br>James van Hoften | Deploys Long Duration Exposure Facility for experiments in space durability; snares Solar Max satellite and repairs attitude-control system |
| 6/24/82 | *Soyuz T-6* | 8 d. | Vladimir Dzhanibekov<br>Jean-Loup Chrétien<br>Aleksandr Ivanchenkov | Mission to *Salyut 7*; Soviet/French team; first French cosmonaut, Chrétien | | | | | |
| 6/27/82 | *Columbia* | 7 d. 1 hr. | Thomas Mattingly II<br>Henry Hartsfield, Jr. | Fourth shuttle mission; first landing on hard surface | 7/18/84 | *Soyuz T-12* | 12 d. | Svetlana Savitskaya<br>Vladimir Dzhanibekov<br>Igor Volk | Savitskaya becomes first woman to walk in space |
| 8/16/82 | *Soyuz T-7* | 8 d. | Leonid I. Popov<br>Svetlana Savitskaya<br>Alexander Serebrov | Mission to *Salyut 7*; second Soviet woman in space, Savitskaya | 8/30/84 | *Discovery* | 6 d. | Henry W. Hartsfield Jr.<br>Michael L. Coates<br>Steven A. Hawley<br>Judith Resnik<br>Richard M. Mullane<br>Charles D. Walker | Third shuttle in fleet; deploys 3 satellites and tests a solar sail |
| 11/11/82 | *Columbia* | 5 d. 2 hrs. | Vance D. Brand<br>Robert F. Overmyer<br>Joseph P. Allen<br>William B. Lenoir | First operational mission; first 4-man crew; first deployment of satellites from shuttle | | | | | |
| 4/4/83 | *Challenger* | 5 d. | Paul J. Weitz<br>Karol J. Bobko<br>Donald H. Peterson<br>F. Story Musgrave | Second shuttle joins fleet; deploys TDRS tracking satellite; first shuttle EVA | 10/5/84 | *Challenger* | 7 d. | Robert L. Crippen<br>Jon A. McBride<br>Kathryn D. Sullivan<br>Sally K. Ride<br>Marc Gameau<br>David C. Leestma<br>Paul D. Scully-Power | Carries first Canadian astronaut, Gameau; deploys Earth Radiation Budget Satellite and monitors land formations, ocean currents, and wind patterns; uses Sir-B radar system to see beneath surface of sand |
| 4/20/83 | *Soyuz T-8* | 48 hrs. | Vladimir G. Titov<br>Gennadi M. Strekalov<br>Aleksandr A. Serebrov | 3 cosmonauts fail in planned rendezvous with *Salyut 7* | | | | | |
| 6/18/83 | *Challenger* | 6 d. 2 hrs. | Robert L. Crippen<br>Frederick H. Hauck<br>John M. Fabian<br>Sally K. Ride<br>Norman E. Thagard | First 5-person crew; first U.S. woman in space; first use of Remote Manipulator Structure ("Arm") to deploy and retrieve satellite | 11/8/84 | *Discovery* | 7 d. | Frederick H. Hauck<br>David M. Walker<br>Anna L. Fisher<br>Joseph P. Allen<br>Dale A. Gardner | Salvages 2 inoperative satellites and returns them to Earth |
| 6/27/83 | *Soyuz T-9* | 150 d. | Vladimir Lyakhov<br>Aleksandr Aleksandrov | Crew spends 149 days in *Salyut 7* after *Soyuz 10* fails in relief mission | 1/24/85 | *Discovery* | 2 d. | Thomas K. Mattingly<br>Loren J. Shriver<br>James F. Buchli<br>Ellison S. Onizuka<br>Gary E. Payton | Secret military mission |
| 8/30/83 | *Challenger* | 6 d. | Richard Truly<br>Daniel Brandenstein<br>William Thornton<br>Guion Bluford, Jr.<br>Dale Gardner | First night launch; first black American (Bluford); launches weather/communications satellite for India | 4/12/85 | *Discovery* | 6 d. | Karol J. Bobko<br>Donald E. Williams<br>Jake Garn<br>Charles D. Walker<br>Jeffrey A. Hoffman<br>S. David Griggs<br>M. Rhea Seddon | First U.S. senator in space, Garn |
| 11/28/83 | *Columbia* | 10 d. | John Young<br>Brewster Shaw, Jr.<br>Robert Parker<br>Owen Garriott<br>Byron Lichtenberg<br>Ulf Merbold | Launches Spacelab; crew performs experiments in astronomy and medicine | | | | | |

| Date | Craft | Duration | Crew | Remarks | Date | Craft | Duration | Crew | Remarks |
|------|-------|----------|------|---------|------|-------|----------|------|---------|
| 4/29/85 | *Challenger* | 7 d. | Robert F. Overmyer<br>Frederick D. Gregory<br>Don L. Lind<br>Taylor G. Wang<br>Lodewijk van den Berg<br>Norman Thagard<br>William Thornton | Carries European<br>Spacelab module<br>and conducts 15<br>experiments in<br>space | 10/4/85 | *Atlantis* | 2 d. | Karol J. Bobco<br>Ronald J. Grabe<br>David C. Hilmers<br>William A. Pailes<br>Robert C. Stewart | Fourth shuttle brings<br>fleet up to target<br>size |
| 6/6/85 | *Soyuz T-13* | 112 d. | Vladimir Dzhanibekov<br>Viktor Savinykh | Successful mission to<br>repair damage to<br>*Salyut 7*, which had<br>suffered power<br>failure | 10/30/85 | *Challenger* | 7 d. | Henry W. Hartsfield, Jr.<br>Steven R. Nagel<br>Bonnie J. Dunbar<br>Guion S. Bluford, Jr.<br>Ernst Messerschmid<br>Reinhard Furrer<br>Wubbo J. Ockels | Carries Spacelab 1-D;<br>scientific experi-<br>ments conducted<br>by Germans |
| 6/17/85 | *Discovery* | 6 d. | John O. Creighton<br>Shannon W. Lucid<br>Steven R. Nagel<br>Daniel C. Brandenstein<br>John W. Fabian<br>Salman al-Saud<br>Patrick Baudry | First Arabian in<br>space, Prince Sul-<br>tan Salman al-Saud;<br>successfully<br>launches 4 satellites | 11/26/85 | *Atlantis* | 7 d. | Brewster H. Shaw, Jr.<br>Bryan D. O'Conner<br>Charles Walker<br>Rudolfo Neri Vela<br>Jerry L. Ross<br>Sherwood C. Spring<br>Mary L. Cleave | First Mexican in space,<br>Vela; works on as-<br>sembling structures |
| 7/29/85 | *Challenger* | 7 d. | Roy D. Bridges, Jr.<br>Anthony W. England<br>Karl G. Henize<br>F. Story Musgrave<br>C. Gordon Fullerton<br>Loren W. Acton<br>John-David F. Bartoe | Carries Spacelab 2, a<br>group of scientific<br>experiments | 1/12/86 | *Columbia* | 5 d. | Robert L. Gibson<br>Charles F. Bolden, Jr.<br>George D. Nelson<br>Franklin R. Chang-Diaz<br>Steven A. Hawley<br>Robert J. Cenker | First U.S. congressman<br>in space, Nelson |
| 8/27/85 | *Discovery* | 7 d. | John M. Lounge<br>James D. van Hoften<br>William F. Fisher<br>Joe H. Engle<br>Richard O. Covey | Repairs satellite<br>Syncom 3 | 1/28/86 | *Challenger* | 73 sec. | Francis R. Scobee<br>Michael J. Smith<br>Robert E. McNair<br>Ellison S. Onizuka<br>Judith A. Resnik<br>Gregory B. Jarvis<br>Christa McAuliffe | *Challenger* disaster:<br>O-rings in solid-fuel<br>boosters wear<br>through, and fuel<br>supply explodes,<br>killing all 6 regular<br>astronauts and<br>school teacher<br>McAuliffe |
| 9/17/85 | *Soyuz T-14* | 65 d. | Vladimir Vasyutin<br>Aleksandr N. Volkov<br>Georgi M. Grechko | Takes supplies to *Sal-<br>yut 7*; terminated<br>early to return Vas-<br>yutin to Earth<br>because he was ill | | | | | |

### After the *Challenger* disaster: the first actual space station

| Date | Craft | Duration | Crew | Remarks | Date | Craft | Duration | Crew | Remarks |
|------|-------|----------|------|---------|------|-------|----------|------|---------|
| 2/20/86 | *Mir* | | Variable | Soviet space station,<br>launched without<br>crew | 8/29/88 | *Soyuz TM-6* | 9 d. | Vladimir Lyakhov<br>Valery Polyakov<br>(Abdul) Ahad (Mohmand) | Ahad first Afghan in<br>space; on 9/6/88<br>Lyakhov and Ahad<br>are stranded 24 hrs.<br>as they attempt to<br>return in *Soyuz<br>TM-5*, but land<br>safely on 9/7/88 |
| 5/5/86 | *Soyuz T-15* | 125 d. | Vladimir Solovyev<br>Leonid Kizim | First cosmonauts to<br>board *Mir* space<br>station | | | | | |
| 2/7/87 | *Soyuz TM-2* | 326 d. | Yuri Romanenko<br>Aleksandr Laveykin | Romanenko and<br>Laveykin begin mar-<br>athon tours in<br>space, thought to<br>be leading toward a<br>Mars expedition | 9/29/88 | *Discovery* | 4 d. | John M. Lounge<br>David C. Hilmers<br>Frederick H. Hauck<br>George D. Nelson<br>Richard O. Covey | Redesigned shuttle<br>makes first flight<br>since the *Challenger*<br>disaster |
| 7/23/87 | *Soyuz TM-3* | 8 d. | Aleksandr Alexandrov<br>Aleksandr Viktorenko<br>Muhammad Faris | First Syrian in space,<br>Faris | 11/26/88 | *Soyuz TM-7* | 152 d. | Aleksandr Volkov<br>Sergei Krikalev<br>Jean-Loup Chrétien | *Mir* is temporarily<br>abandoned for first<br>time after cos-<br>monauts return<br>to Earth |
| 12/20/87 | *Soyuz TM-4* | 366 d. | Vladimir G. Titov<br>Musa Manarov<br>Anatoly Levchenko | Cosmonauts set new<br>record of a year in<br>space, mostly in *Mir*<br>space station—366<br>days | | | | | |
| 6/7/88 | *Soyuz TM-5* | 10 d. | Aleksandr Alexandrov<br>Viktor P. Savinykh<br>Anatoly Y. Solovyov | Alexandrov becomes<br>the first Bulgarian in<br>space; not same<br>Aleksanderov as<br>*Soyuz TM-3* flight | 12/2/88 | *Atlantis* | 4 d. | Robert L. Gibson<br>Jerry L. Ross<br>William M. Shepherd<br>Guy S. Gardner<br>Richard M. Mullane | Secret military mission<br>widely known to<br>have deployed radar<br>spy satellite |

| Date | Craft | Duration | Crew | Remarks |
|------|-------|----------|------|---------|
| 3/13/89 | Discovery | 4 d. | Michael L. Coats<br>John E. Blaha<br>James F. Buchli<br>James P. Bagian<br>Robert C. Springer | Deploys NASA's third relay satellite and tests thermal control system for proposed U.S. space station |
| 5/4/89 | Atlantis | 4 d. | David M. Walker<br>Ronald J. Grabe<br>Mary L. Cleave<br>Norman E. Thagard<br>Mark C. Lee | Launches space probe Magellan on its way to map Venus with radar |
| 5/9/89 | Soyuz TM–8 | 6 d. | Alexander S. Vitorenko<br>Alexander A. Serebrov | Reoccupy Mir |
| 8/9/89 | Columbia | 5 d. | Brewster H. Shaw, Jr.<br>Richard N. Richards<br>David C. Leestma<br>James C. Adamson<br>Mark N. Brown | Secret military mission to launch spy satellite |
| 10/18/89 | Atlantis | 5 d. | Donald E. Williams<br>Michael J. McCulley<br>Shannon W. Lucid<br>Franklin R. Chang-Diaz<br>Ellen S. Baker | Launches Galileo space probe that travels to Venus, returns twice to vicinity of Earth, and then will take up a long-term orbit around Jupiter |
| 11/22/89 | Discovery | 5 d. | Frederick D. Gregory<br>John E. Blaha<br>F. Story Musgrave<br>Kathryn C. Thornton<br>Manley Lanier Carter, Jr. | Secret military mission |
| 1/9/90 | Columbia | 10 d. 21 hrs. | Daniel C. Brandenstein<br>Bonnie J. Dunbar<br>Marsha S. Ivens<br>G. David Low<br>James D. Wetherbee | Launches communication satellite Syncom IV and retrieves the Long Duration Exposure Facility (see 4/7/84); longest shuttle flight to date |
| 2/11/90 | Soyuz TM–9 | 6 d. | Anatoly Solovyev<br>Aleksandr Balandin | To relieve Vitorenko and Serebrov; July 18, Solovyev and Balandin briefly locked out of Mir by faulty hatch |

| Date | Craft | Duration | Crew | Remarks |
|------|-------|----------|------|---------|
| 2/28/90 | Atlantis | 6 d. | John O. Creighton<br>John H. Caspar<br>David C. Hilmers<br>Richard M. Mullane<br>Pierre J. Thuot | Secret military mission launches spy satellite that fails and burns in atmosphere |
| 4/24/90 | Discovery | 5 d. | Loren J. Shriver<br>Charles F. Bolden, Jr.<br>Bruce McCandless 2nd<br>Steven H. Hawley<br>Kathryn D. Sullivan | Launches Hubble Space Telescope |
| 5/8/90 | Soyuz TM–10 | 6 d. | Gennadi Manakov<br>Gennadi Strekalov | To replace Solovyev and Balandin |
| 10/6/90 | Discovery | 4 d. | Richard N. Richards<br>Robert D. Cabana<br>Bruce E. Melnick<br>William M. Shepherd<br>Thomas D. Akers | Launches Ulysses space probe into solar orbit |
| 11/15/90 | Atlantis | 6 d. | Richard O. Covey<br>Frank L. Culbertson, Jr.<br>Charles D. Gemar<br>Carl J. Meade<br>Robert C. Springer | NASA announces this as last secret military mission |
| 12/2/90 | Columbia | 9 d. | Vincent D. Brand<br>Guy S. Gardner<br>Jeffrey A. Hoffman<br>John M. (Mike) Lounge<br>Robert A.R. Parker<br>Samuel T. Durrance<br>Ronald A. Parise | Carries set of 3 UV and 1 X-ray telescopes; launch delayed by hydrogen leak |
| 12/2/90 | Soyuz TM–11 | 9 d. | Viktor Afansev<br>Musa Manarov<br>Toyohiro Akiyama | Journalist Akiyama, sponsored by Japanese corporations, visits Mir; others replace Manakov and Strekalov |
| 4/5/91 | Atlantis | 6 d. | Steven R. Nagel<br>Kennety D. Cameron<br>Linda M. Godwin<br>Jerry L. Ross<br>Jerome Apt | Launches 17-ton Gamma Ray Observatory; unscheduled spacewalk required to properly open satellite's antenna; high winds delay landing one day |
| 4/23/91 | Discovery | 5 d. | Michael L. Coats<br>L. Blaine Hammond, Jr.<br>Gregory J. Harbaugh<br>Charles Lacy Veach<br>Guion S. Bluford, Jr.<br>Richard J. Hieb<br>Donald R. McMonagle | Tests detection devices developed for space use and recovers Star Wars satellite |

# Earth Sciences

Earth sciences include geology (the study of Earth's rocks and interior), oceanography (the study of ocean water, currents, and the ocean floor), paleontology (the study of fossils and ancient life-forms), parts of astronomy, and meteorology (the study of the atmosphere, including weather). Except for astronomy and weather, which are covered elsewhere, this section deals with all of these studies.

## MAJOR DISCOVERIES IN EARTH SCIENCES

*B.C.*

**c. 300** Dicaearchus (Greek: fl.c. 320) develops map of Earth on a sphere using lines of latitude.

*A.D.*

**132** Zhang Heng (Chinese: 78–139) develops first crude seismograph.

**1600** William Gilbert (English: 1544–1603) suggests that Earth is giant magnet, which is why magnetic compasses indicate north.

**1669** Nicolaus Steno (Niels Stensen; Danish: 1638–86) correctly explains origin of fossils.

**1777** Nicolas Desmarest (French: 1725–1815) proposes that the rock basalt is formed from lava.

**1785** James Hutton (Scottish: 1726–97) explains features of Earth on basis of tiny changes taking place over very long periods of time (uniformitarianism).

**1795** Baron Georges Cuvier (French: 1769–1832) shows that giant bones found in Meuse River are remains of extinct giant reptile.

**1797** Sir James Hall (Scottish: 1761–1832) shows that melted rocks form crystals upon cooling.

**1822** Gideon A. Mantell (English: 1790–1852) and his wife, Mary Ann, are first to discover and recognize dinosaur bones as those of a giant, extinct reptile.

**1830** Sir Charles Lyell (Scottish: 1797–1875) begins to publish *Principles of Geology*, the work that convinced geologists that Earth is at least several hundred million years old.

**1880** John Milne (English: 1850–1913) invents modern seismograph.

**1896** Svante A. Arrhenius (Swedish: 1859–1927) discovers that global temperatures rise with higher levels of carbon dioxide in atmosphere (greenhouse effect).

**1902** Léon-Philippe Teisserenc de Bort (French: 1855–1913) discovers the stratosphere.

**1906** Richard D. Oldham (English: 1858–1936) establishes existence of Earth's core.

**1907** Bertram B. Boltwood (American: 1870–1927) shows that age of rocks containing uranium can be determined by measuring ratio of uranium to lead.

**1909** Andrija Mohorovičić (Croatia: 1857–1936) discovers boundary between Earth's crust and mantle, now known as Mohorovičić discontinuity, or "Moho."

**1912** Alfred L. Wegener (German: 1880–1930) proposes theory of continental drift, idea that a single continent—Pangaea—split into present-day continents, which have drifted away from each other.

**1925** The German *Meteor* expedition discovers Mid-Atlantic Ridge, a giant mountain range in middle of the Atlantic Ocean.

**1929** Motonori Matuyama (Japanese: 1884–1958) shows that Earth's magnetic field reverses every few hundred million years.

**1943** Mexican farmer discovers volcano—eventually named Mt. Parícutin—in his field; first observation of a volcano's genesis.

**1946** Vincent J. Schaefer (American: 1906– ) discovers that dry ice can be used to cause clouds to release rain.

**1953** Maurice Ewing (American: 1906–74) discovers rift that runs down middle of Mid-Atlantic Ridge.

**1958** James A. Van Allen (American: 1914– ) discovers belts of radiation that surround Earth in space, now known as Van Allen belts.

**1960** Harry H. Hess (American: 1906–69) develops theory of seafloor spreading—oceans are getting wider as new seafloor is formed at midocean ridges.

**1979** American oceanographers discover hot vents in oceans, surrounded by exotic forms of life based on sulfur, not oxygen.

**1980** Walter Alvarez (American: 1940– ) and co-workers discover geologic layer of iridium in region identified with the demise of the dinosaurs; he attributes both iridium and extinction to impact of a large comet or meteorite on Earth.

**1987** NASA determines that continents are moving in ways predicted by theory of plate tectonics, a theory based on idea that Earth's crust is broken into huge plates that are moving with respect to each other.

**1990** Kathleen Crane (American) and a Soviet-American team discover hot vents in the floor of Lake Baikal in the USSR, suggesting that this is a "spreading center," a widening crack in the Asian landmass.

# COMPOSITION OF THE EARTH

In their study of the Earth, scientists distinguish a number of distinct layers from the inner core—the center of which is about 6,400 km (roughly 4,000 mi.) below the surface—to the farthest limit of the atmosphere, about 1,000 km (620 mi.) above the surface. This section describes these layers, from the innermost to the outermost.

**Core** The core consists of two parts—one liquid, the other solid—both thought to be a mixture of iron and nickel. The solid inner core begins about 5,000 km (3,100 mi.) from the surface, and the liquid outer core at about 1,100 km (1,800 mi.) from the surface.

**Mantle** The bulk of the Earth—roughly two-thirds of its mass—is composed of the mantle, which extends from the outer core to within about 90 km (55 mi.) of the Earth's surface below the higher mountains, and to within only 5 to 8 km (3 to 5 mi.) of the Earth's surface below some areas of the oceans. Silicon dioxide constitutes almost half of the mantle, and there is an abundance of magnesium oxide, some iron oxide, and smaller amounts of oxides of other metals. (Although silicon dioxide is known as quartz when found in the Earth's crust, under the heat and pressure of the mantle it may have very different properties from the form we know.) Part of the upper mantle is somewhat liquid and known as the asthenosphere.

**Crust** The crust is the outermost solid layer of the Earth. Under the continents, the crust varies from 30 to 60 km (19 to 37 mi.) in thickness, while under the oceans it is generally only 5 to 8 km (3 to 5 mi.) thick. Continental and oceanic crust differ from each other in thickness and composition. Continental crust consists of granite and other relatively light rocks, while oceanic crust is made up chiefly of basalt. The crust is separated from the mantle by the Mohorovičić discontinuity, or Moho. The crust that is accessible to accurate measurements contains the following principle elements:

| Element | Percent[1] |
|---|---|
| Oxygen | 45.6% |
| Silicon | 27.3 |
| Aluminum | 8.4 |
| Iron | 6.2 |
| Calcium | 4.7 |
| Magnesium | 2.8 |
| Sodium | 2.3 |
| Potassium | 1.8 |
| Hydrogen | 1.5 |
| Titanium | 0.6 |

1. Adds to more than 100% due to rounding.

**Hydrosphere** Water—virtually all of it sea water—covers about 71% of the Earth's surface and thereby constitutes a distinct layer of the Earth. Sea water varies in composition from place to place, but on average it is about 3.5% salts—that is, evaporating 100 lb. of sea water would yield 3.5 lb. of salt. Sodium chloride (ordinary table salt) constitutes 2.7% of sea water, or 77.8% of total solids in sea water. The typical composition of solids in sea water is as follows:

| Compound | Percent |
|---|---|
| Sodium chloride | 77.8% |
| Magnesium chloride | 10.9 |
| Magnesium sulfide | 4.7 |
| Calcium sulfate | 3.6 |
| Potassium sulfate | 2.5 |
| Calcium carbonate | 0.3 |
| Magnesium bromide | 0.2 |
| Other compounds | trace |

**Atmosphere** The atmosphere is the gaseous layer that envelopes the Earth. The lower atmosphere consists of the troposphere and the stratosphere. The *troposphere* has an average thickness of about 11 km (7 mi.), although it is only 8 km (5 mi.) at the poles and as much as 16 km (10 mi.) around the equator. Most clouds and weather phenomena occur in this region. The composition of dry air at sea level is: nitrogen, 78.08%; oxygen, 20.05%; argon, 0.93%; and carbon dioxide, 0.03%. There are also lesser amounts of neon, helium, krypton, and xenon. These proportions change with altitude, lighter gases being more common at higher altitudes, but they are approximately the same everywhere on Earth at the same altitude. There are also variable quantities of water vapor, dust particles, and other compounds whose proportions change from place to place at the same altitude—fewer dust particles being found over oceans, and less water vapor over deserts. Temperature decreases with altitude in the troposphere.

The *stratosphere* is found between 11 km and 50 km (7–50 mi.) out from the Earth's surface. Temperatures in this region rise slightly as altitude increases, to a maximum of about 0°C (32°F). Virtually coextensive with the stratosphere is the *ozonosphere*, or ozone layer, region in which most of the atmosphere's ozone is found. Because ozone absorbs most of the sun's ultraviolet radiation, it is vital to the continued existence of life on the planet.

Beyond the stratosphere is the upper atmosphere, or *ionosphere*, so called because it is the layer in which atmospheric gases have been ionized by solar radiation. The ionosphere reflects certain wavelengths back to the surface, making it possible to transmit radiowaves around the curve of the Earth. The ionosphere is further divided into the *mesosphere*, between 50 km and 80 km (30–50 mi.), in which the temperature decreases with altitude to –90°C (–130°F); and the *thermosphere*, from about 80 km to 450 km (50–280 mi.), in which the temperature increases to as much as 1475°C (2690°F). Beyond the thermosphere is the *exosphere*, extending to about 1,000 km (625 mi.). In this layer, temperature no longer has the customary meaning. (See also "Global Warming" and "The Ozone Layer.")

# THE CHANGING EARTH

Despite its apparent solidity, the interior of the Earth is constantly changing. Although most of its movements are slow and seldom affect people, there are some significant exceptions. Most notable of these are large earthquakes and volcanic eruptions, together with their associated tsunamis and landslides.

**Plate tectonics** The earth's outer crust is composed of lithospheric (or tectonic) plates that move from a few millimeters to several centimeters per year. Hundreds of millions of years ago, these plates formed a continuous landmass known as Pangaea and surrounded by ocean. Eventually the plates separated, until they reached the positions they occupy today.

As plates move away from each other, molten rock emerges from the mantle to form oceanic crust. Where they come together, one plate is forced under the other, forming either oceanic trenches or mountain ranges. These areas are also the site of greatest volcanic and earthquake activity.

The relative position of the major tectonic plates can be gathered from their names: Antarctic, African, Indo-Australian (including most of the Indian subcontinent), Pacific, South American, North American, and Eurasian (including Southeast Asia). The seven smaller plates are the Nazca, bounded by (in clockwise order) the Cocos, South American, Antarctic, and Pacific; the Cocos, bounded by the North American, Caribbean, South American, Nazca, and Pacific; the Caribbean, bounded by the North American, South American, and Cocos; the Hellenic, bounded by the Eurasian, Arabian, and African; the Arabian, bounded by the Hellenic, Iranian, Indo-Australian, and African; the Iranian, bounded by the Eurasian, Indo-Australian, and Arabian; and the Philippine, bounded by the Pacific to the east and the Eurasian to the west.

**Earthquakes and tsunamis** Most earthquakes are caused when rock on one side of a fault (or crack) in the Earth's crust moves with respect to the rock on the other side of the fault. The motion causes vibrations in the crust that travel through the rock as shock waves. When these reach the surface, they cause it to move in various ways, which is called seismic motion. (Small earthquakes that accompany volcanic eruptions are caused by the motion of liquid rock, or magma.)

More than 800,000 earthquakes are registered by seismographs each year, but the overwhelming majority go unnoticed by anyone. However, large earthquakes are of great concern to many people living in regions of significant seismic activity. Although earthquake prediction is an inexact science, thanks to advances in engineering technology and a better understanding of how earthquakes affect physical structures, it is now possible to minimize the destruction of human lives and property caused by earthquakes. A comparison of two recent earthquakes of virtually the same magnitude bears this out. Nearly 29,000 people died in the Armenian earthquake in 1988, which registered 6.9 on the Richter Scale,

## GEOLOGIC TIME SCALE

Geologists and other earth scientists divide the history of the planet into periods of varying length based on the fossils found in rock strata. Geologists often speak of the period before 570 million years ago as Precambrian Time. The eras after 570 million years ago are grouped into the Phanerozoic Eon.

| Era or Eon | Period | Epoch | Organisms | Time before present (millions of years) |
|---|---|---|---|---|
| ARCHEAN EON | | | Monerans: bacteria and blue-green algae | 4,600 |
| PROTEROZOIC EON | | | Protists, algae, and soft-bodied creatures similar to jellyfish and worms | 2,500 |
| PHANEROZOIC EON PALEOZOIC ERA | Cambrian | | Tiny fossils with skeletons followed by animals with shells, notably trilobites | 570 |
| | Ordovician | | Brachiopods (shellfish similar to clams), corals, starfish, and some organisms that have no modern counterparts, called sea scorpions, conodonts, and graptolites | 500 |
| | Silurian | | Snails, clams and mussels, ammonoids (similar to the nautilus), jawless fish, sea scorpions, first land plants and animals (club mosses, land scorpions); modern groups of algae and fungi | 425 |
| | Devonian | | Spiders, amphibians, jawed fish, lobe-finned fish, sharks, lungfish, and ferns | 395 |
| | Carboniferous | | Insects, land snails, amphibians, early reptiles, sea lilies, giant club mosses, and seed ferns | 350 |
| | Permian | | Mammal-like reptiles and fin-backed reptiles, cycads, ginkgoes, and conifers | 290 |
| MESOZOIC ERA | Triassic | | Marine reptiles (plesiosaurs and ichthyosaurs), crocodiles, frogs, turtles, early mammals, and early dinosaurs | 235 |
| | Jurassic | | Dinosaurs (such as stegosaurus), pterosaurs (such as pterodactyl), early birds, dinoflagellates, diatoms, early flowering plants | 190 |
| | Cretaceous | | Dinosaurs (such as tyrannosaurus, triceratops, and brontosaurus), salamanders, modern bony fishes, mosasaurs (marine lizards), flowering plants, placental and marsupial mammals | 130 |
| CENOZOIC ERA | Tertiary | Paleocene | Early primates, early horses, rodents, sycamores | 65 |
| | | Eocene | Whales, penguins, roses, bats, camels, early elephants, dogs, cats, weasels | 55 |
| | | Oligocene | Deer, pigs, saber-toothed cats, monkeys | 38 |
| | | Miocene | Seals, dolphins, grasses, daisies, asters, sunflowers, lettuce, giraffes, bears, hyenas, early apes | 26 |
| | | Pliocene | Apes, australopithecines (early hominids), *Homo habilis* (first human species), mammoths, giant sloths, and armadillos | 6 |
| | Quaternary | Pleistocene | *Homo erectus* (ancestor of modern humans), modern humans, and Neanderthal humans; large mammals, such as giant bison and beavers; many kinds of hoofed animals | 1.8 |
| | | Holocene | Modern humans and flora and fauna of today | 0.01 (11,000 yrs) |

while only 61 lives were lost in the Loma Prieta earthquake near San Francisco in 1989, which registered 7.1 and occurred in a much more densely populated area.

One common side effect of undersea earthquakes are *tsunamis*—or (incorrectly) tidal waves—against which there is little protection. Tsunamis are caused when an earthquake raises or lowers a section of seabed, thereby producing a wave that, while not generally noticeable at sea, can reach great heights as it approaches land. Similar to and as destructive as tsunamis, harbor waves are generated when a landslide falls into a bay, strait, or other confined body of water causing almost immediate flooding. High waves are also caused by volcanic explosions or collapses, such as the explosion and collapse of Krakatau in 1883.

**Volcanoes** are openings in the Earth's crust that emit molten or partially molten rock (lava), various hot gases, and ash. (A volcano is also the mountain formed by solidified lava ejected from the opening.) If the opening is like a crack, it is called a vent. If it is larger and fairly circular, it is called a crater. A caldera is a basin formed by the settling of the top of a volcanic mountain, and it may have several vents or craters on its floor.

Most volcanoes are found where two tectonic plates meet, such as along the famous "Ring of Fire" around the Pacific Ocean. A few, such as the volcanoes of the Hawaiian islands, appear to be over "hot spots" in the Earth's crust where liquid rock flows upward with sufficient force to burn through the crust. Although volcanoes are associated with destruction, they have many positive effects. Minerals from deep within the Earth make the land around many volcanoes extremely fertile; volcanoes can create new landforms in the sea; and the study of volcanoes contributes enormously to our understanding of the Earth's interior.

Although geologists consider a volcano active if it has shown signs of activity in historic times, it is not usually clear whether a volcano is extinct or only dormant and could be active again. (Thus Tambora, which has not erupted since 1815, is considered active.) Some volcanoes once thought to be extinct have become active, and there are now about 600 volcanoes that are considered active. The accompanying list contains about a third of all volcanoes known to have been active in recent years, volcanoes in the United States, and volcanoes that have had famous eruptions.

Although the destruction caused by volcanoes is usually localized, their effects can be felt around the world and take many forms. At their worst, volcanoes can blow themselves to pieces, as the island of Thera did about 1650 B.C. More often, volcanic ash blankets an area (as Mt. Vesuvius did at Pompeii), or clouds of hot gases and dust sweep down the side of the volcano poisoning the air. Although lava generally moves too slowly to be a menace to people, it can sometimes flow too quickly to be outrun. Even more unpredictable, heat from a volcano can melt glaciers or snowcaps, triggering massive mud slides or releasing lakes of boiling water (as happened in Colombia in 1985).

## MEASURING EARTHQUAKES

The size of an earthquake is generally reported in the United States using the Richter scale, a system developed by American geologist Charles Richter in 1935. The Richter scale measures the magnitude of an earthquake, that is, the size of ground waves generated by an earthquake as shown on a measuring device called a seismograph. Each whole number on the scale represents a tenfold increase (or decrease) in magnitude: a magnitude 6 earthquake produces a ground wave 10 times greater than a magnitude 5.

This does not mean, however, that a magnitude 6 earthquake has 10 times the energy as one of magnitude 5. Measuring the actual energy requires instruments placed at the site of the earthquake. Various methods have been developed for inferring energy from magnitude and these suggest that one magnitude corresponds to a thirty- to sixtyfold change in energy. So the energy of a magnitude 8 earthquake, a very serious event, can be as much as 1 million to 10 million times as much as that of a magnitude 4 earthquake, one that can be felt but causes almost no damage.

A very different scale, developed by Giuseppe Mercalli in 1902 and modified by Harry Wood and Frank Neumann for the U.S. in the 1930s, is widely used to describe the intensity of earthquakes. The modified Mercalli scale, as it is known, describes the effects of earthquake shocks; comparing the Mercalli and Richter scales helps one to understand the relative energy of earthquakes.

### RICHTER AND MERCALLI SCALES COMPARED

| Richter scale | | Mercalli earthquake intensity scale |
|---|---|---|
| 2.5 | Generally not felt, but recorded on seismometers. | **I.** Not felt except by a very few under specially favorable circumstances. |
| | | **II.** Felt only by a few persons at rest, especially on upper floors of buildings. |
| 3.5 | Felt by many people. | **III.** Felt quite noticeably indoors, especially on upper floors of buildings, but many people do not recognize as an earthquake. |
| | | **IV.** During the day, felt indoors by many; outdoors by few. Sensation like heavy truck striking building. |
| | | **V.** Felt by nearly everyone; many awakened. Disturbances of trees, poles, and other tall objects sometimes noticed. |
| 4.5 | Some local damage may occur. | **VI.** Felt by all; many frightened and run outdoors. Some heavy furniture moved; few instances of fallen plaster or damaged chimneys. Damage slight. |
| | | **VII.** Everybody runs outdoors. Damage negligible in buildings of good design and construction; slight to moderate in well-built ordinary structures; considerable in poorly built or badly designed structures. |
| 6.0 | A destructive earthquake. | **VIII.** Damage slight in specially designed structures; considerable in ordinary substantial buildings with partial collapse; great in poorly built structures. (Collapse of chimneys, factory stacks, columns, monuments, walls.) |
| | | **IX.** Damage considerable in specially designed structures. Buildings shifted off foundations. Ground cracked conspicuously. |
| 7.0 | A major earthquake. About 10 occur each year. | **X.** Some well-built wooden structures destroyed. Most masonry and frame structures destroyed with foundations. Ground badly cracked. |
| 8.0 and above | Great earthquakes. These occur once every five to 10 years. | **XI.** Few, if any (masonry) structures remain standing. Bridges destroyed. Broad fissures in ground. |
| | | **XII.** Damage total. Waves seen on ground surfaces. Objects thrown upward into air. |

## MAJOR EARTHQUAKES, 526–1991

| Date | Location and remarks | Estimated deaths | Richter magnitude |
|---|---|---|---|
| May 29, 526 | Antioch, Turkey | 250,000 | — |
| 856 | Corinth, Greece | 45,000 | — |
| 1036 | Shanxi, China | 23,000 | — |
| 1057 | Chihli (Hopeh), China | 25,000 | — |
| 1170 | Sicily | 15,000 | — |
| 1268 | Cilicia (Turkey) | 60,000 | — |
| Sept. 27, 1290 | Chihli (Hopeh), China | 100,000 | — |
| May 20, 1293 | Kamakura, Japan | 30,000 | — |
| Jan. 26, 1531 | Lisbon, Portugal | 30,000 | — |
| Jan. 24, 1556 | Shanxi, China | 830,000 | — |
| Nov. 1667 | Shemakha, Azerbaijan (USSR) | 80,000 | — |
| June 7, 1692 | Port Royal, Jamaica | 30,000 | — |
| Jan. 11, 1693 | Catania province, Sicily | 60,000 | — |
| 1693 | Naples, Italy | 93,000 | — |
| 1707 | Tsunami hits Japan | 30,000 | — |
| Dec. 30, 1730 | Hokkaido Island, Japan | 137,000 | — |
| 1731 | Beijing, China | 100,000 | — |
| Oct. 11, 1737 | Calcutta, India | 300,000 | — |
| June 7, 1755 | Northern Persia | 40,000 | — |
| Nov. 1, 1755 | Lisbon, Portugal (earthquake and tsunami) | 60,000 | 8.7 |
| Nov. 18, 1755 | Boston, Massachusetts | 0 | — |
| Feb. 4-5 and Mar. 28, 1783 | Calabria, Italy | 35,000 | — |
| Feb. 4, 1797 | Quito, Ecuador, and Cuzco, Peru | 41,000 | — |
| Dec. 16, 1811 | New Madrid, Missouri | 10 | — |
| Jan. 23, 1812 | New Madrid, Missouri | 0 | — |
| Feb. 7, 1812 | New Madrid, Missouri | 0 | — |
| Sept. 5, 1822 | Aleppo (Syria) | 22,000 | — |
| Dec. 28, 1828 | Echigo, Japan | 30,000 | — |
| June 1838 | San Francisco, California | — | — |
| Dec. 24, 1854 | Tokai, Japan | 3,000 | 8.4 |
| Oct. 1855 | Tokyo, Japan | 2,000+ | — |
| Jan. 9, 1857 | Fort Tejon, California | 2 | 8.3 |
| 1857 | East of Naples, Italy | 10,000+ | — |
| Aug. 13-15, 1868 | Peru and Ecuador | 40,000 | — |
| Mar. 26, 1872 | Owens Valley, California | 60 | — |
| May 16, 1875 | Venezuela and Colombia | 16,000 | — |
| Aug. 31, 1886 | Charleston, South Carolina | 83 | 7.0 |
| Oct. 28, 1891 | Central Japan | 7,300 | — |
| June 15, 1896 | Sanriku and Kamaish, Japan (tsunami) | 26,000 | — |
| Sept. 3, 1899 | Yakatanga, Alaska | 0 | 8.3 |
| Sept. 10, 1899 | Yakatanga, Alaska | 0 | 8.6 |
| Apr. 4, 1905 | Kangra, India | 20,000 | — |
| Apr. 18, 1906 | San Francisco, California | 667 | 8.3 |
| Aug. 16, 1906 | Valparaiso, Chile | 20,000 | 8.6 |
| 1907 | Tadzhikistan, USSR | 40,000 | — |
| Dec. 28, 1908 | Messina, Sicily | 75,000 | 7.5 |
| Jan. 13, 1915 | Avezzano, Italy | 30,000 | — |
| Oct. 2, 1915 | Pleasant Valley, Nevada | 0 | 7.8 |
| Jan. 13, 1916 | Avezzano, Italy | 29,980 | 7.5 |
| Oct. 11, 1918 | Mona Passage, Caribbean Sea | 116 | 7.5 |
| Dec. 16, 1920 | Kansu, China | 180,000+ | 8.6 |
| Sept. 1, 1923 | Tokyo and Yokohama, Japan | 143,000 | 8.3 |
| June 27, 1925 | Helena, Montana | 0 | 6.8 |
| Mar. 7, 1927 | Tango, Japan | 1,120 | 8.0 |
| May 22, 1927 | Nan-Shan, China | 200,000 | 8.3 |
| Aug. 16, 1931 | Mt. Livermore, Texas | 0 | 6.4 |
| Dec. 20, 1932 | Cedar Mountain, Nevada | 0 | 7.3 |
| Dec. 26, 1932 | Kansu, China | 70,000 | 7.6 |
| Mar. 2, 1933 | Sanriku, Japan (tsunami) | 2,990 | 8.9 |
| Mar. 10, 1933 | Long Beach, California | 120 | 6.3 |
| Jan. 15, 1934 | India, Bihar, and Nepal | 10,700 | 8.4 |
| Mar. 12, 1934 | Great Salt Lake, Utah | 0 | 6.6 |
| May 31, 1935 | Quetta, India (Pakistan) | 50,000 | 7.5 |
| Oct.–Nov. 1936 | Helena, Montana | 2 | — |
| Jan. 24, 1939 | Concepción, Chile | 30,000 | 8.3 |
| Dec. 27, 1939 | Erzincan, Turkey | 30,000 | 7.9 |
| May 18, 1940 | Imperial Valley, California | 9 | 7.1 |
| Apr. 1, 1946 | Earthquake at Unimak Island, Alaska, causes tsunami in Hawaii that strikes Hilo | 173 | 7.2 |
| Dec. 21, 1946 | Honshu Island, Japan | 2,000 | 8.4 |
| June 28, 1948 | Fukui, Japan | 3,500+ | 7.3 |
| Oct. 1948 | Ashkhabad, USSR | 20,000 | — |
| July 10, 1949 | Tadzhikistan, USSR | 120,000 | 7.5 |
| Aug. 5, 1949 | Pelileo, Ecuador | 6,000 | 6.8 |
| Aug. 15, 1950 | Assam State, India | 1,500 | 8.7 |
| July 21, 1952 | Bakersfield, California | 12 | 7.7 |
| Mar. 18, 1953 | Northwest Turkey | 1,200 | 7.2 |
| Sept. 9–12, 1954 | Orléansville, Algeria | 1,660 | — |
| Dec. 16, 1954 | Frenchman's Station, Nevada | 0 | 7.1 |
| June 10–17 1956 | Northern Afghanistan | 2,000 | 7.7 |
| July 2, 1957 | Northern Iran | 2,500 | 7.4 |
| Dec. 13, 1957 | Western Iran | 2,000 | 7.1 |
| July 9, 1958 | Lituya Bay, Alaska | 3 | 7.9 |
| Aug. 17, 1959 | Hebgen Lake, Montana | 28 | 7.1 |
| Feb. 29, 1960 | Agadir, Morocco | 12,000 | 5.8 |
| May 21–30, 1960 | Southern Chile; on May 22, a tsunami strikes various Pacific islands, including Hawaii, killing 61 in Hilo | 5,700 | 8.3 |
| Sept. 1, 1962 | Northwestern Iran | 12,403 | 7.1 |
| Feb. 21–22, 1963 | El Marj, Libya | 260 | 5.0 |
| July 26, 1963 | Skopje, Yugoslavia | 1,011 | 5.5 |
| Mar. 27, 1964 | Southern Alaska | 131 | 8.3 |
| Mar. 28, 1965 | Central Chile | 420 | — |
| Aug. 19, 1966 | Eastern Turkey | 2,520 | 6.9 |
| July 27, 1967 | Caracas, Venezuela | 250+ | 6.5 |
| Dec. 11, 1967 | Konya, India (extra pressure from water filling a reservoir caused earth to shift) | 117 | 6.5 |
| Aug. 31, 1968 | Khurasan, Iran | 12,000 | 7.8 |
| July 25, 1969 | Eastern China | 3,000 | — |
| Jan. 5, 1970 | Yunnan Province, China | 10,000 | 7.7 |
| Mar. 28, 1970 | Gediz, Turkey | 1,086 | 7.4 |
| May 31, 1970 | Yungay, Ranrahirca, Huarás, and other cities in Peru | 66,794 | 7.7 |
| Feb. 9, 1971 | San Fernando Valley, California | 64 | 6.6 |
| Apr. 10, 1972 | Ghir, Iran | 5,057 | 6.9 |
| Dec. 23, 1972 | Managua, Nicaragua | 10,000+ | 5.6 |
| Apr. 28, 1973 | Puebla, Mexico | 527 | 6.8 |
| Dec. 28, 1974 | North Pakistan | 5,200+ | 6.3 |
| Feb. 5, 1975 | Liaoning Province, China (predicted) | 300 | — |
| Sept. 6, 1975 | Lice, Turkey | 2,312 | 6.8 |
| Feb. 4, 1976 | Guatemala City, Guatemala | 22,778 | 7.5 |
| May 6, 1976 | Northeast Italy | 946 | 6.5 |
| June 26, 1976 | New Guinea and Irian Java | 8,000+ | 7.1 |
| July 28, 1976 | Tangshan, China | 750,000 | 8.0 |
| Aug. 17, 1976 | Philippine island of Mindanao (earthquake and tsunami) | 8,000 | 7.3 |
| Nov. 24, 1976 | Eastern Turkey | 4,000 | 7.9 |
| Mar. 4, 1977 | Bucharest, Romania | 1,541 | 7.5 |
| Aug. 19, 1977 | Indonesia | 200 | 8.0 |
| Nov. 23, 1977 | Northwestern Argentina | 100 | 8.2 |
| Dec. 20, 1977 | Central Iran | 500+ | — |
| Jan. 14, 1978 | Tokai region, Japan | 25 | 7.0 |
| June 12, 1978 | Sendai, Japan | 27+ | 7.5 |
| June 20, 1978 | Salonika, Greece | 51 | — |
| Aug. 18, 1978 | Tsunami strikes Acajutla, El Salvador | 100+ | — |
| Sept. 16, 1978 | Northeast Iran | 25,000 | 7.7 |

| Date | Location and remarks | Estimated deaths | Richter magnitude |
|------|----------------------|------------------|-------------------|
| Jan. 17, 1979 | Eastern Iran | 200 | 6.7–7.5 |
| Apr. 15, 1979 | Yugoslavia and Albania | 129 | 7.2 |
| Nov. 14, 1979 | Meshed, Iran | 500 | 6.7 |
| Dec. 12, 1979 | Colombia and Ecuador | 800 | 7.9 |
| Dec. 18, 1979 | Bali, Indonesia | 100 | 6.1 |
| Oct. 10, 1980 | Northwestern Algeria | 4,500 | 7.3 |
| Nov. 23, 1980 | Southern Italy | 4,800 | 7.2 |
| July 28, 1981 | Kerman province, Iran | 8,000 | — |
| Dec. 13, 1982 | Yemen | 2,800 | 6.0 |
| Mar. 31, 1983 | Popayán, Colombia | 200,000 | 5.7 |
| Oct. 28, 1983 | Challis, Idaho | 2 | 6.9 |
| Oct. 30, 1983 | Turkey | 2,000 | 7.2 |
| Mar. 3, 1985 | Algarrobo, Chile | 177 | 7.8 |
| Sept. 19, 21, 1985 | Mexico City | 4,200 | 8.1 |
| Oct. 10, 1986 | San Salvador, El Salvador | 1,000+ | 7.5 |
| Mar. 5–6, 1987 | Ecuador | 2,000 | 7.0 |
| Aug. 20, 1988 | Nepal and India | 700+ | 6.5 |
| Nov. 6, 1988 | Yunnan Province, China and Burma | 730 | 7.6 |
| Dec. 6, 1988 | Mamasani, Iran | 7 | 5.6 |
| Dec. 7, 1988 | Armenia, USSR | 28,854 | 6.9 |
| Jan. 22, 1989 | Tadzhikistan, USSR | 274 | 5.5 |
| Mar. 10, 1989 | Malawi | 9 | 6.2 |
| May 23, 1989 | Macquarie Ridge, 300 mi. SE of New Zealand | 0 | 8.2–8.3 |
| Aug. 1, 1989 | West Irian, Indonesia | 120 | 5.9 |
| Oct. 17, 1989 | Loma Prieta, California (Santa Cruz Mountains), destructive in San Francisco and Oakland | 67 | 7.1 |
| Oct. 18, 1989 | Shanxi-Hebei border, China | 29+ | 7.1 |
| Oct. 19, 1989 | Cherchell, Algeria | 30 | 6.0 |
| Dec. 15, 1989 | Off coast of Mindanao, Philippines | 2 | 7.3 |
| Dec. 27, 1989 | Newcastle, Australia | 11 | 5.4 |
| Mar. 4, 1990 | West-central Pakistan | 11 | 6.1 |
| Apr. 26, 1990 | Qinghai Province, China | 126 | 6.8 |
| June 20, 1990 | Caspian Sea, near Rasht, Iran | 60,000 | 7.7 |
| July 16, 1990 | Cabanatuan (Luzon I.), Philippines | 1,650+ | 7.7 |
| Oct. 25, 1990 | Afghanistan and Pakistan | 11 | 6.0 |
| Nov. 6, 1990 | Southern Iran | 22+ | 6.8 |
| Dec. 13, 1990 | Carlentini, Sicily | 15 | 5.1 |
| Feb. 1, 1991 | Hindu Kush, Afghanistan | 300 | 6.8 |
| Apr. 22, 1991 | Cobano, Costa Rica | N.A. | 7.4 |

## VOLCANOES AND LANDSLIDES, 1628 B.C.–A.D. 1991

| Date | Event | Deaths |
|------|-------|--------|
| 1628 or 1645 B.C. | Mediterranean volcanic island of Thera (Santorini) explodes. | N.A. |
| Aug. 24–26, A.D. 79 | Mt. Vesuvius, near Naples, Italy, erupts, destroying towns of Pompeii and Herculaneum. | 2,000+ |
| 260 | Mt. Ilopango in El Salvador erupts, apparently destroying the early Maya civilization. | N.A. |
| Sept. 4, 1618 | Landslides hit Chiavenna Valley, Italy. | 2,420 |
| Dec. 16, 1631 | Mt. Vesuvius erupts. | 4,000+ |
| Mar. 25, 1669 | Mt. Etna at Catania, Sicily, erupts. | 20,000 |
| Jan. 11, 1683 | Mt. Etna erupts, accompanied by earthquakes. | 60,000 |
| Aug. 11–12, 1772 | Mt. Papandayan on Java explodes. | 3,000+ |
| June 1783–Feb. 1784 | Laki fissure on Mt. Skaptar in Iceland erupts; poisonous gases kill crops and livestock, and thick haze interrupts fishing on oceans. | 9,800 |
| Sept. 2, 1806 | Rossberg Peak collapses, causing landslides in Goldau Valley, Switzerland. | 500 |
| Apr. 5, 1815 | Mt. Tambora on Sumbawa in East Indies begins series of eruptions that results in immediate death of about 10,000 people; another 80,000 die of famine and disease locally; eruptions also alter weather around world. | 162,000 |
| Oct. 8 and 12, 1822 | Mt. Galunggung on Java erupts, causing slides of mud and boiling water. | 4,000 |
| 1845 | Eruption of Nevada del Ruiz in northern Colombia causes mudslides from melting snow. | 1,000 |
| July 28, 1883 | Epomeo volcano on Italian Isle of Ischia erupts, causing destructive earthquakes. | 2,000+ |
| Aug. 26, 1883 | Krakatau volcano in East Indies erupts, producing giant waves that strike nearby islands. | 37,000 |
| July 15, 1888 | Bandai volcano in Japan erupts, causing steaming mud slides. | 500+ |
| May 7, 1902 | La Soufrière on St. Vincent in West Indies erupts. | 1,500–2,000 |
| May 8, 1902 | Pelée volcano on neighboring Martinique erupts, pouring cloud of flaming gas on city of St. Pierre. | 29,000 |
| Aug. 30, 1902 | Mt. Pelée erupts. | 2,000 |
| Apr. 18, 1906 | Mt. Vesuvius near Naples erupts. | 150+ |
| 1911 | Taal volcano, near Manila, Philippines, erupts. | 1,300 |
| May 1919 | Crater lake of Mt. Kelut in Indonesia, boiling by volcanic activity, breaks through side of the mountain. | 5,000 |
| Jan. 15, 1951 | Mt. Lamington on New Guinea produces cloud of hot gas and dust, similar to that at Mt. Pelée in 1902 and Mt. St. Helens in 1980. | 3,000–5,000 |
| Dec. 4, 1951 | Mt. Catarman (Hibokhibok) in Philippines releases cloud of hot gas. | 500 |
| Sept. 24, 1952 | Japanese research ship investigating undersea volcano is destroyed in eruptive event. | 29 |
| Dec. 25, 1953 | Dam, created by 1945 eruption of Ruapehu volcano on New Zealand, gives way; avalanche of mud and snow strikes passenger train. | 150 |
| Sept. 28, 1956 | Taal volcano, near Manila, Philippines, erupts. | 350 |
| Jan. 10, 1962 | Landslide on Mt. Huascarán, Peru. | 3,000 |
| Mar. 14, 1962 | Two landslides near Paucartambno Hydroelectric Station in Peru. | 204 |
| Mar. 17–21, 1963 | Mt. Agung volcano in Bali, Indonesia, has second eruption of year. | 1,584 |
| Aug. 10, 1963 | Landslide in Nepal sweeps villages into Trisuli River. | 200 |
| Oct. 9, 1963 | Flood occurs when Valont Dam near Langarone, Italy, overflows as result of landslide into its reservoir. | 2,200 |

| Date | Event | Deaths |
|------|-------|--------|
| Aug. 30, 1965 | Avalanche near Saas-Fee, Switzerland, from Allalin glacier strikes workers building dam. | 40–100 |
| July 22, 1970 | Landslide diverts course of Alaknanda River in India, causing sudden flood. | 600 |
| Mar. 18, 1971 | Landslide into Lake Yanahuani, creates 60-foot wave that sweeps over Chungar, Peru. | 200 |
| July 29, 1971 | Landslide into high lake in Hindu Kush mountains of Afghanistan, causes instant flood. | 1,000+ |
| June 28, 1974 | Landslides along Quebrada Blanca Canyon in Eastern Colombia. | 200 |
| Jan. 10, 1977 | Fast-moving stream of lava from volcano near Goma, Zaire, overtakes fleeing residents. | 70 |
| Feb. 21, 1979 | Volcano in Java, Indonesia, erupts. | 175+ |
| Apr. 30, 1979 | Landslide covers side of Merapi volcano in Sumatra, Indonesia. | 82+ |
| July 18, 1979 | Landslide on Mt. Werung causes wave to strike beach areas on Lomblen island, Indonesia. | 539 |
| May 18, 1980 | Mt. St. Helens volcano erupts in Washington. | 61 |

| Date | Event | Deaths |
|------|-------|--------|
| Mar. 28, Apr. 3–4, 1982 | El Chichón in Chiapas State, Mexico, erupts; major blast on Apr. 4, sends cloud of volcanic ash around world. | 2,000 |
| Aug. 16, 1984 | Carbon dioxide emitted by Lake Monoun, Cameroon, spreads in region around lake. | 37 |
| Nov. 13, 1985 | Eruption of Nevada del Ruiz in northern Colombia melts snow on its summit, causing massive mud slide that covers town of Armero. | 25,000 |
| Aug. 21, 1986 | Carbon dioxide from Lake Nyos, Cameroon, caused either by underwater volcano or overturning of water layers, spreads through surrounding region. | 1,700+ |
| July 13, 1990 | Earthquake triggers landslide in Pamir Mts., USSR. | 40+ |
| Oct. 13, 1990 | Geyserlike explosion in the Ahuachapán Geothermal Field, El Salvador, releases wave of carbon dioxide and water. | 26 |
| Jan. 5, 1991 | Landslide at Zunil Geothermal Field, western Guatemala | 33 |

## MAJOR ACTIVE VOLCANOES

| Volcano | Location | Height (ft. above sea level) | Last reported eruption |
|---------|----------|------------------------------|------------------------|
| **AFRICA AND THE INDIAN OCEAN** | | | |
| Cameroon Mt. | Cameroon | 13,354 | 1982 |
| Erta-Ale | Ethiopia | 1,650 | 1973 |
| Karthala | Comoros | 8,000 | 1977 |
| Nyamuragira | Zaire | 10,028 | 1989 |
| Nyiragongo | Zaire | 11,400 | 1977 |
| Ol Doinyo Lengai | Tanzania | N.A. | 1990 |
| Piton de la Fournaise | Réunion Island | 8,638 | 1990 |
| **ANTARCTICA** | | | |
| Big Ben | Heard Island | 9,007 | 1986 |
| Deception Island | South Shetland Is. | 1,890 | 1970 |
| Mount Erebus | Ross Island | 12,450 | 1989 |
| **ASIA** | | | |
| Agung | Bali, Indonesia | 10,308 | 1964 |
| Akita Komaga-take | Japan | 5,449 | 1970 |
| Alaid | Kuril Islands, USSR | 7,674 | 1972 |
| Amburomrribu | Indonesia | 7,051 | 1969 |
| Asama | Honshu, Japan | 8,300 | 1983 |
| Aso | Kyushu, Japan | 5,223 | 1989 |
| Awu | Indonesia | 4,350 | 1968 |
| Azuma | Honshu, Japan | 6,700 | 1978 |
| Batur | Bali, Indonesia | 5,636 | 1974 |
| Bezymianny | USSR | 9,514 | 1986 |
| Bulusan | Philippines | 5,115 | 1988 |
| Chokai | Honshu, Japan | 7,300 | 1974 |
| Dukono | Indonesia | 3,566 | 1971 |
| Gamalama | Ternate Is., Indonesia | 5,625 | 1990 |
| Galunggug | Java, Indonesia | 7,113 | 1982 |
| Gamkonora | Indonesia | 5,365 | 1981 |
| Gerde | Indonesia | 9,705 | 1949 |
| Karymsky | USSR | 4,869 | 1982 |
| Kelimutu | Indonesia | 5,460 | 1968 |
| Kelut | Java, Indonesia | 5,679 | 1990 |
| Kerinci | Sumatra, Indonesia | 12,467 | 1987 |
| Kirishima | Japan | 5,577 | 1982 |

| Volcano | Location | Height (ft. above sea level) | Last reported eruption |
|---------|----------|------------------------------|------------------------|
| Kliuchevskoi | USSR | 15,584 | 1990 |
| Korayskaya | USSR | 11,339 | 1957 |
| Krakatau (or Anak Krakatau) | Indonesia | 330 | 1972 |
| Lewotobi Laki-Laki | Indonesia | 5,217 | 1968 |
| Lokon-Empung | Indonesia | 5,187 | 1988 |
| Mayon | Philippines | 9,991 | 1978 |
| Me-akan | Japan | 4,931 | 1966 |
| Merapi | Sumatra, Indonesia | 9,485 | 1988 |
| Nasu | Japan | 6,210 | 1977 |
| Niigata-yakeyama | Japan | 8,064 | 1989 |
| On-Take | Kyushu, Japan | 10,049 | 1980 |
| Oshima | Japan | 2,550 | 1990 |
| Raung | Java, Indonesia | 10,932 | 1990 |
| Rindjani | Indonesia | 12,224 | 1981 |
| Sakura-jima | Japan | 2,640 | 1990 |
| Sangeang Api | Indonesia | 6,351 | 1988 |
| Sarychev | Kuril Islands, USSR | 5,115 | 1976 |
| Semeru | Java, Indonesia | 12,060 | 1989 |
| Shiveluch | USSR | 10,771 | 1964 |
| Siau | Indonesia | 5,853 | 1976 |
| Sinila | Indonesia | 7,000 | 1979 |
| Slamet | Java, Indonesia | 11,247 | 1967 |
| Soputan | Indonesia | 5,994 | 1989 |
| Suwanose-jima | Japan | 2,640 | 1987 |
| Taal | Luzon, Philippines | 4,752 | 1977 |
| Tambora | Sumbawa, Indonesia | 9,000 | 1815 |
| Tangkuban Prahu | Java, Indonesia | 6,637 | 1967 |
| Ternate | Indonesia | 5,627 | 1963 |
| Tiatia | Kuril Islands, USSR | 6,013 | 1973 |
| Tjarme | Indonesia | 10,098 | 1938 |
| Usu | Japan | 2,390 | 1978 |
| Yake Dake | Japan | 8,064 | 1963 |
| **CENTRAL AMERICA AND THE CARIBBEAN** | | | |
| Acatenango | Guatemala | 12,992 | 1972 |
| Arenal | Costa Rica | 5,092 | 1990 |
| Conchagua | El Salvador | 4,100 | 1947 |

| Volcano | Location | Height (ft. above sea level) | Last reported eruption |
|---------|----------|------------------------------|------------------------|
| El Viejo (San Cristóbal) | Nicaragua | 5,840 | 1987 |
| Fuego | Guatemala | 12,582 | 1987 |
| Irazú | Costa Rica | 11,260 | 1965 |
| Izalco | El Salvador | 7,749 | 1966 |
| Kick-'em-Jenny | Subocean, off Grenada | −160 | 1988 |
| Momotombo | Nicaragua | 4,199 | 1905 |
| Mount Pelée | Martinique | 4,500 | 1930 |
| Ometepe (Concepción) | Nicaragua | 5,106 | 1986 |
| Pacaya | Guatemala | 8,346 | 1990 |
| Póas | Costa Rica | 8,930 | 1990 |
| Rincon de la Vieja | Costa Rica | 6,234 | 1987 |
| San Miguel | El Salvador | 6,994 | 1986 |
| Santiaguito Dome (Santa Maria) | Guatemala | 12,362 | 1990 |
| San Salvador | El Salvador | 6,187 | 1923 |
| Soufrière | St. Vincent and the Grenadines | 4,048 | 1979 |
| Tacaná | Guatemala | 12,400 | 1988 |
| Telica | Nicaragua | 3,409 | 1982 |
| **EUROPE AND THE ATLANTIC OCEAN** | | | |
| Askja | Iceland | 4,594 | 1961 |
| Beerenberg | Jan Mayen Island, Norway | 7,470 | 1985 |
| Eldfell | Iceland | 327 | 1973 |
| Etna | Italy | 11,053 | 1990 |
| Fogo | Cape Verde Islands | 9,300 | 1951 |
| Hekla | Iceland | 4,892 | 1980 |
| Krafla | Iceland | 2,145 | 1984 |
| Leirhnukur | Iceland | 2,145 | 1975 |
| Stromboli | Italy | 3,038 | 1990 |
| Surtsey | Iceland | 568 | 1967 |
| Tristan da Cunha | St. Helena | 6,760 | 1961 |
| Vesuvius | Italy | 4,203 | 1944 |
| Vulcano | Lipari Is., Italy | N.A. | 1890 |
| **NORTH AMERICA** | | | |
| Akutan | Alaska | 4,265 | 1989 |
| Amukta | Alaska | 3,490 | 1963 |

| Volcano | Location | Height (ft. above sea level) | Last reported eruption |
|---|---|---|---|
| Aniakchak | Alaska | 4,450 | 1931 |
| Augustine | Alaska | 3,995 | 1986 |
| Bogoslof | Alaska | 150 | 1931 |
| Carlisle | Alaska | 5,315 | 1838 |
| Chiginagak | Alaska | 7,985 | 1929 |
| Cleveland | Alaska | 5,710 | 1987 |
| Colima | Mexico | 14,003 | 1987 |
| El Chichón | Mexico | 7,300 | 1983 |
| Gareloi | Alaska | 5,370 | 1982 |
| Great Sitkin | Alaska | 5,775 | 1974 |
| Iliamna | Alaska | 10,140 | 1978 |
| Isanotski | Alaska | 8,185 | 1845 |
| Kagamil | Alaska | 2,945 | 1929 |
| Kanaga | Alaska | 4,450 | 1933 |
| Katmai | Alaska | 7,540 | 1974 |
| Kiska | Alaska | 4,025 | 1969 |
| Korovin | Alaska | 4,885 | 1987 |
| Lassen Peak | California | 10,453 | 1921 |
| Little Sitkin | Alaska | 3,945 | 1828 |
| Mageik | Alaska | 7,295 | 1946 |
| Makushin | Alaska | 6,720 | 1987 |
| Martin | Alaska | 6,050 | 1960 |
| Mt. Baker | Washington | 10,778 | 1870 |
| Mt. Hood | Oregon | 11,245 | 1801 |
| Mt. Rainier | Washington | 14,410 | 1882 |
| Mt. Shasta | California | 14,161 | 1855 |
| Mt. St. Helens | Washington | 9,671 | 1986 |
| Novarupta | Alaska | N.A. | 1912 |

| Volcano | Location | Height (ft. above sea level) | Last reported eruption |
|---|---|---|---|
| Okmok | Alaska | 3,540 | 1988 |
| Parícutin | Mexico | 1,500 | 1952 |
| Pavlof | Alaska | 8,960 | 1988 |
| Peulik | Alaska | 5,030 | 1852 |
| Pogromni | Alaska | 7,545 | 1964 |
| Redoubt | Alaska | 10,265 | 1990 |
| Seguam | Alaska | 3,465 | 1977 |
| Shishaldin | Alaska | 9,430 | 1987 |
| Spurr | Alaska | 11,070 | 1953 |
| Tanaga | Alaska | 7,015 | 1914 |
| Tobert | Alaska | 11,413 | 1953 |
| Trident | Alaska | 6,830 | 1974 |
| Veniaminof | Alaska | 8,450 | 1987 |
| Vsevidof | Alaska | 6,965 | 1880 |
| Westdahl | Alaska | 5,055 | 1964 |
| Yunaska | Alaska | 1,980 | 1937 |
| **OCEANIA** | | | |
| Ambrym | Vanuatu | 4,376 | 1990 |
| Bagana | Bougainville Is., Papua New Guinea | N.A. | 1990 |
| Hualalai | Hawaii | 8,251 | 1801 |
| Karkar | Papua New Guinea | 4,920 | 1981 |
| Kilauea | Hawaii | 4,090 | 1990 |
| Langila | New Britain, Papua New Guinea | 3,586 | 1990 |
| Lopevi | Vanuatu | 4,755 | 1982 |
| Manam | Papua New Guinea | 6,000 | 1989 |

| Volcano | Location | Height (ft. above sea level) | Last reported eruption |
|---|---|---|---|
| Mauna Loa | Hawaii | 13,680 | 1987 |
| Ngauruhoe | North Island, New Zealand | 7,515 | 1975 |
| Pagan | Mariana Islands | 1,870 | 1988 |
| Ruapehu | New Zealand | 9,175 | 1982 |
| Tarawera | North Island, New Zealand | 3,645 | 1886 |
| Ulawun | New Britain, Papua New Guinea | 7,532 | 1990 |
| White Island | New Zealand | 1,075 | 1990 |
| **SOUTH AMERICA** | | | |
| Alcedo | Galapagos Islands, Ecuador | 3,599 | 1970 |
| Cotacachi | Ecuador | 16,204 | 1955 |
| Cotopaxi | Ecuador | 19,347 | 1975 |
| Guagua Pichincha | Ecuador | 15,696 | 1982 |
| Guallatiri | Chile | 19,882 | 1987 |
| Hudson | Chile | 8,580 | 1973 |
| Lascar | Chile | 18,372 | 1990 |
| Llaima | Chile | 10,239 | 1984 |
| Lonquimay | Chile | 9,400 | 1990 |
| Nevado del Ruiz | Colombia | 17,720 | 1989 |
| Puracé | Colombia | 15,604 | 1977 |
| Reventador | Ecuador | 11,434 | 1976 |
| Sangay | Ecuador | 17,159 | 1976 |
| Shoshuenco | Chile | 7,743 | 1960 |
| Tupungatito | Chile | 18,504 | 1986 |
| Villarica | Chile | 9,318 | 1984 |

# Chemistry

Chemistry is concerned with the way substances interact with one another. These interactions are chiefly the result of outer electrons of an atom interacting with the outer electrons of another atom. It has increasingly become clear that the shapes of the various combinations of atoms (called molecules) also affect chemical reactions, and physical chemistry is one of the most vital parts of chemistry today. Another vital branch is biochemistry, the study of the chemistry of molecules in living organisms. Organic chemistry generally deals with chemicals formed by living organisms and other chemicals containing carbon, but it treats them as chemicals outside the organism. Inorganic chemistry is concerned with chemicals that do not contain carbon.

## MAJOR DISCOVERIES IN CHEMISTRY

*B.C.*

**c. 450** Leucippus of Miletus (Greek: 5th cent.) introduces concept of atom, later expanded upon by his pupil Democritus of Abdera (c. 460–c. 370).

*A.D.*

**1662** Robert Boyle (Anglo-Irish: 1627–91) announces what becomes known as Boyle's law: For gas kept at constant temperature, pressure and volume vary inversely.

**1755** Joseph Black (Scottish: 1728–99) discovers carbon dioxide.

**1766** Henry Cavendish (English: 1731–1810) discovers hydrogen.

**1772** Joseph Priestley (English-American: 1733–1804) notes that burning hydrogen produces water.
Daniel Rutherford (Scottish: 1749–1819) and several other chemists discover nitrogen.
Karl Wilhelm Scheele (Swedish: 1742–86) discovers oxygen but does not announce discovery until after independent discovery by Joseph Priestly in 1774.

**1777** Antoine-Laurent Lavoisier (French: 1743–94) discovers that air is mostly mixture of nitrogen and oxygen.

**1784** Cavendish announces water is compound of hydrogen and oxygen.

**1789** Lavoisier explicitly states law of conservation of matter: In chemical change, matter is neither created nor destroyed.

**1791** Jeremias Benjamin Richter (German: 1762–1807) shows that acids and bases always neutralize each other in same proportion.

**1803** John Dalton (English: 1766–1844) establishes atomic theory of matter.

**1811** Amedeo Avogadro (Italian: 1776–1856) proposes that equal volumes of gas at same temperature and pressure contain same number of molecules (Avogadro's law).

**1824** Joseph-Louis Gay-Lussac (French: 1778–1850) discovers chemical isomers, chemicals with same formula but different structures.

**1828** Friedrich Wöhler (German: 1800–82) prepares organic compound from inorganic chemicals, showing that life is basically same as other matter.

**1859** Gustav Robert Kirchhoff (German: 1824–87) and Robert Wilhelm Bunsen (German: 1811–99) introduce use of spectroscope to identify elements from light they give off when heated or burned.

**1868** Pierre-Jules-César Janssen (French: 1824–1907) and Sir Joseph Norman Lockyer (English: 1836–1920) discover helium by observing sun's spectrum.

**1869** Dmitry Ivanovich Mendeleyev (Russian: 1834–1907) publishes his first version of periodic table of elements.

**1875** Paul-Emile Lecoq de Boisbaudran (French: 1838–1912) discovers gallium, the first discovery of an element predicted by Mendeleyev on basis of his periodic table.

**1906** Mikhail Tsvett (Russian: 1872–1919) develops paper chromotography, the beginning of modern methods of chemical analysis.

**1908** Fritz Haber (German: 1868–1934) develops cheap process for making ammonia from nitrogen in the air.

**1943** Albert Hofmann (Swiss: 1906– ) discovers that LSD is hallucinogenic.

**1962** Neil Bartlett (English: 1932– ) creates xenon, showing that the noble gases can form compounds.

**1982** W. German scientists produce one atom of element 109.

**1984** Dany Shechtman (American) and co-workers discover first quasicrystal, a "crystal" that violates the symmetry rules of all other crystals.

**1985** Richard E. Smalley (American: 1943– ) and Harry Kroto (English) discover buckminsterfullerene, a carbon molecule containing 60 carbon atoms arranged in a geodesic sphere (nicknamed "bucky balls").

## PROPERTIES, ABUNDANCE, AND DISCOVERY OF THE ELEMENTS

All ordinary matter is made from one or more substances called elements (because they cannot be changed by chemical means). Ninety elements are found in nature, and people have created others, for a current total of 109. In this table each of the elements is listed in alphabetical order along with several of its important properties. The chemical symbol and the atomic number can be used to locate other information about the elements in the periodic table reprinted below. The relative abundance of the elements is given as parts per million in the Earth's crust—83,600 parts per million for aluminum means that of a million atoms chosen at random from the crust, 83,600 atoms, on average, would be aluminum atoms. Some elements have so few parts per million that they are simply listed as rare, whereas others are "synthetic"—artificial elements not found in the crust at all. Many elements, known from ancient times, are labeled "prehistoric." Others are given with their first discovery—many elements having been independently rediscovered by others.

| Element | Symbol/ atomic number | Type[1] | Melting point[1] | Boiling point[1] | Parts per million in crust | Year discovered and by whom | Derivation of name |
|---|---|---|---|---|---|---|---|
| Actinium | Ac 89 | Radioactive metal | 1920°F 1050°C | 5790°F 3200°C | Rare | 1899 André-Louis Debierne | Greek *aktis*, a ray |
| Aluminum | Al 13 | Metal | 1220°F 660°C | 4473°F 2467°C | 83,600 | 1825 Hans Christian Oersted | Latin *alumen*, a substance having astringent taste |
| Americium | Am 95 | Radioactive metal | 1821°F 994°C | 4725°F 2607°C | Synthetic | 1944 Glenn T. Seaborg & co-workers | For America |
| Antimony | Sb 51 | Metal | 1167°F 631°C | 3180°F 1750°C | 0.2 | c. 900 Rhazes | Greek *antimonos*, opposed to solitude; symbol Sb from Latin *stibium* |
| Argon | Ar 18 | Gas | −308.6°F −189.2°C | −302.3°F −185.7°C | Rare | 1892 Sir William Ramsay | Greek *argus*, neutral inactive |
| Arsenic | As 33 | Nonmetal | 1503°F[2] 817°C[2] | 1135°F[2] 613°C[2] | 1.8 | 1649 J. Schroeder & N. Lémery | Latin *arsenicum*; folk etymology connects with yellow and maleness |
| Astatine | At 85 | Radioactive nonmetal | 576°F 302°C | 639°F 337°C | Synthetic | 1940 Emilio Segrè, D.R. Corson, K.R. MacKenzie | Greek *astatos*, unstable |
| Barium | Ba 56 | Metal | 1337°F 725°C | 2980°F 1640°C | 390 | 1808 Humphry Davy | Greek *baros*, heavy; because its compounds are dense |
| Berkelium | Bk 97 | Radioactive metal | N.A. | N.A. | Synthetic | 1949 Glenn T. Seaborg & co-workers | First made at Univ. of California at Berkeley |
| Beryllium | Be 4 | Metal | 2332°F 1278°C | 5380°F 2970°C | 2 | 1798 Louis-Nicolas Vauquelin | Latin *beryllus*, Greek *beryllos*, gem |
| Bismuth | Bi 83 | Metal | 520°F 271°C | 2840°F 1560°C | 0.008 | 1753 Claude J. Geoffrey | German *weisse masse*, white mass; changed to *bismat* |
| Boron | B 5 | Nonmetal | 3774°F 2079°C | 4620°F 2550°C | 9 | 1808 Joseph-Louis Gay-Lussac & Louis-Jacques Thénard | Arabic *borak* (borax); BORax + carbON |
| Bromine | Br 35 | Liquid nonmetal | 19°F −7.2°C | 137.8°F 58.8°C | 2.5 | 1825 Carl Löwig | Greek *bromos*, a stench; because of odor of its vapors |
| Cadmium | Cd 48 | Metal | 609.6°F 320.9°C | 1409°F 765°C | 0.16 | 1817 Friedrich Strohmeyer | Greek *cadmia*, earthy |
| Calcium | Ca 20 | Metal | 1542°F 839°C | 2703°F 1484°C | 46,600 | 1808 Humphry Davy | Latin *calx, calcis*, lime |
| Californium | Cf 98 | Radioactive metal | N.A. | N.A. | Synthetic | 1950 Glenn T. Seaborg & co-workers | First made at Univ. of California |
| Carbon | C 6 | Nonmetal | 6420°F 3550°C | 8721°F 4827°C | 180 | Prehistoric | Latin *carbo*, coal |
| Cerium | Ce 58 | Rare earth | 1468°F 798°C | 5875°F 3246°C | 66.4 | 1803 Martin Klaproth | For asteroid Ceres, discovered in 1801 |
| Cesium | Cs 55 | Metal | 83.1°F 28.4°C | 1236.7°F 669.3°C | 2.6 | 1860 Gustav Kirchhoff & Robert Bunsen | Latin *caesius*, bluish gray |
| Chlorine | Cl 17 | Gas | −150°F −101°C | −30.3°F −34.6°C | 126 | 1774 Karl Wilhelm Scheele | Greek *chloros*, grass-green; from color of gas |
| Chromium | Cr 24 | Metal | 3375°F 1857°C | 4842°F 2672°C | 122 | 1797 Louis-Nicolas Vauquelin | Greek *chroma*, color; because many of its compounds are colored |
| Cobalt | Co 27 | Metal | 2723°F 1495°C | 5200°F 2870°C | 29 | 1735 George Brandt | German *Kobalt*, a goblin |
| Copper | Cu 29 | Metal | 1981°F 1083°C | 4653°F 2567°C | 68 | Prehistoric | Latin *cuprum*; for island of Cyprus |
| Curium | Cm 96 | Radioactive metal | 2444°F 1340°C | N.A. | Synthetic | 1944 Glenn T. Seaborg & co-workers | After Pierre and Marie Curie |
| Dysprosium | Dy 66 | Rare earth | 2574°F 1412°C | 4653°F 2567°C | Rare | 1886 Paul-Emile Lecoq de Boisbaudran | Greek *dysprositos*, difficult of access |
| Einsteinium | Es 99 | Radioactive | N.A. | N.A. | Synthetic | 1952 Albert Ghiorso & co-workers | After Albert Einstein |
| Element 106 | N.A. 106 | Radioactive metal | N.A. | N.A. | Synthetic | 1974 N.A. | Claimed by Russia and U.S. |
| Element 107 | N.A. 107 | Radioactive metal | N.A. | N.A. | Synthetic | 1981 N.A. | Identified in W. Germany following earlier disputed claim by Soviet Union |

| Element | Symbol/atomic number | Type[1] | Melting point[1] | Boiling point[1] | Parts per million in crust | Year discovered and by whom | Derivation of name |
|---|---|---|---|---|---|---|---|
| Element 108 | N.A. 108 | Radioactive metal | N.A. | N.A. | Synthetic | 1984 N.A. | Created in W. Germany by bombarding lead with iron ions |
| Element 109 | N.A. 109 | Radioactive metal | N.A. | N.A. | Synthetic | 1982 N.A. | Created in W. Germany by bombarding bismuth with iron ions |
| Erbium | Er 68 | Rare earth | 2784°F 1529°C | 4334°F 2868°C | 3.46 | 1843 Carl Gustav Mosander | For Ytterby, village in Sweden |
| Europium | Eu 63 | Rare earth | 1512°F 822°C | 2907°F 1597°C | 2.1 | 1896 Eugène-Anatole Demarçay | For Europe |
| Fermium | Fm 100 | Radioactive metal | N.A. | N.A. | Synthetic | 1952 Albert Ghioroso & co-workers | After Enrico Fermi, Italian physicist |
| Fluorine | F 9 | Gas | −363.3°F −219.6°C | −306.7°F −188.1°C | 544 | 1886 Ferdinand-Frédéric-Henri Moissan | Latin *fluere*, to flow |
| Francium | Fr 87 | Radioactive metal | 80.6°F 27°C | 1256°F 677°C | Rare | 1939 Marguerite Perey | For France |
| Gadolinium | Gd 64 | Rare earth | 2395°F 1313°C | 5923°F 3273°C | 6.1 | 1880 Jean-Charles Marignac | After gadolinite, mineral named for Johan Gadolin, Finnish chemist |
| Gallium | Ga 31 | Metal | 86.6°F 29.8°C | 4357°F 2403°C | 19 | 1875 Paul-Emile Lecoq de Boisbaudran | Latin *Gallia*, France; also latin gallus, a cock—pun on Lecoq de Boisbaudran |
| Germanium | Ge 32 | Metal | 1719°F 937°C | 5126°F 2830°C | 1.5 | 1886 Clemens Winkler | For Germany |
| Gold | Au 79 | Metal | 1947°F 1064°C | 5086°F 2808°C | 0.002 | Prehistoric | Anglo-Saxon *gold*; Sanskrit *juel*, to shine; symbol from Latin *aurum*, shining down |
| Hafnium | Hf 72 | Metal | 4041°F 2227°C | 8316°F 4602°C | 2.8 | 1923 Dirk Coster & György Hevesy | From *Hafnia*, ancient name of Copenhagen |
| Hahnium (nielsbohrium) | Ha 105 | Radioactive metal | N.A. | N.A. | Synthetic | 1970 Albert Ghiorso & co-workers | Hahnium, the name used in U.S., after German physicist Otto Hahn; nielsbohrium, name used in USSR, after the Danish physicist Niels Bohr |
| Helium | He 2 | Gas | −458°F −272°C | −452°F −269°C | Rare | 1868 Pierre-Jules-César Janssen & Sir Joseph Norman Lockyer | Greek *helios*, the sun; first observed in sun's atmosphere |
| Holmium | Ho 67 | Rare earth | 2678°F 1470°C | 4928°F 2720°C | 1.26 | 1879 Per Teodor Cleve | From *Holmia*, Latinized form of *Stockholm* |
| Hydrogen | H 1 | Gas | −434.6°F −259.1°C | −423.2°F −252.9°C | 1520 | 1766 Henry Cavendish | Greek *hydor*, water, plus *gen*, forming |
| Indium | In 49 | Metal | 313.9°F 156.6°C | 3776°F 2080°C | 0.24 | 1863 Ferdinand Reich & Hieronymus Theodor Richter | Latin *indicum*, indigo |
| Iodine[3] | I 53 | Nonmetal | 236.3°F 113.5°C | 363.9°F 184.4°C | 0.46 | 1811 Bernard Courtois | Greek *iodes*, violet; from color of its vapor |
| Iridium | Ir 77 | Metal | 4370°F 2410°C | 7466°F 4130°C | 0.001 | 1803 Smithson Tennant | Greek *iris*, a rainbow, from changing color of its salts |
| Iron | Fe 26 | Metal | 2795°F 1535°C | 4982°F 2750°C | 62,200 | Prehistoric | Anglo-Saxon *iren*; symbol from Latin *ferrum* |
| Krypton | Kr 36 | Gas | −249.9°F −156.6°C | −242.1°F −152.3°C | Rare | 1898 Alexander Ramsay & Morris William Travers | Greek *kryptos*, hidden |
| Lanthanum | La 57 | Rare earth | 1684°F 918°C | 6267°F 3464°C | 34.6 | 1839 Carl Mosander | Greek *lanthanein*, to be concealed |
| Lawrencium | Lr 103 | Radioactive metal | N.A. | N.A. | Synthetic | 1961 Albert Ghiorso & co-workers | After Ernest Lawrence, American physicist |
| Lead | Pb 82 | Metal | 621.5°F 327.5°C | 3164°F 1740°C | 13 | Prehistoric | Anglo-Saxon *lead*; symbol from Latin *plumbum* |
| Lithium | Li 3 | Metal | 356.9°F 180.5°C | 2248°F 1342°C | 18 | 1817 J.A. Arfvedson | Greek *lithos*, stony |
| Lutetium | Lu 71 | Rare earth | 3025°F 1663°C | 6157°F 3402°C | Rare | 1907 Georges Urbain | Latin *Lutetia*, ancient name for Paris |
| Magnesium | Mg 12 | Metal | 1200°F 649°C | 1994°F 1090°C | 27,640 | 1808 Humphry Davy | Latin *Magnesia*, a district in Asia Minor |
| Manganese | Mn 25 | Metal | 2271°F 1244°C | 3564°F 1962°C | 1060 | 1774 Johann Gottlieb Gahn | Latin *magnes*, magnet; because of confusion with magnetic iron ores |
| Mendelevium | Md 101 | Radioactive metal | N.A. | N.A. | Synthetic | 1955 Albert Ghiorso & co-workers | After Dmitri Mendeléev, Russian chemist |
| Mercury | Hg 80 | Liquid metal | −38.0°F −38.9°C | 673.9°F 356.6°C | 0.08 | Prehistoric | For Roman god Mercurius; symbol from Latin *hydrargyrum* |
| Molybdenum | Mo 42 | Metal | 4743°F 2617°C | 8334°F 4612°C | 1.2 | 1778 Karl Wilhelm Scheele | Greek *molybdos*, lead |
| Neodymium | Nd 60 | Rare earth | 1870°F 1021°C | 5565°F 3074°C | 39.6 | 1885 Karl Auer (Baron von Welsbach) | Greek *neo*, new, plus *didymon*, twin (with the element praseodymium) |

| Element | Symbol/ atomic number | Type[1] | Melting point[1] | Boiling point[1] | Parts per million in crust | Year discovered and by whom | Derivation of name |
|---|---|---|---|---|---|---|---|
| Neon | Ne 10 | Gas | −416.7°F −248.7°C | −411°F −246°C | Rare | 1898 Alexander Ramsay & Morris William Travers | Greek *neo*, new |
| Neptunium | Np 93 | Radioactive metal | 1184°F 640°C | 7056°F 3902°C | Synthetic | 1940 Edwin McMillan & Philip Abelson | For planet Neptune |
| Nickel | Ni 28 | Metal | 2647°F 1453°C | 4950°F 2732°C | 99 | 1751 Axel Cronstedt | German *Nickel*, Satan (Old Nick) |
| Niobium | Nb 41 | Metal | 4474°F 2468°C | 8568°F 4742°C | 20 | 1801 Charles Hachett | Latin *Niobe*, daughter of Tantalus |
| Nitrogen | N 7 | Gas | −345.8°F −209.9°C | −320.4°F −195.8°C | 19 | 1772 Daniel Rutherford | Latin, forming *niter*, a compound of nitrogen |
| Nobelium | No 102 | Radioactive metal | N.A. | N.A. | Synthetic | 1957 P.R. Fields & co-workers | After Alfred Nobel; made at Nobel Institute |
| Osmium | Os 76 | Metal | 5513°F 3045°C | 9081°F 5027°C | 0.005 | 1803 Smithson Tennant | Greek *osme*, smell; for malodorousness |
| Oxygen | O 8 | Gas | −361°F −218.4°C | −297°F −183°C | 456,000 | 1774 Joseph Priestley | Greek *oxys*, sharp, plus *gen*, forming; from incorrect belief that oxygen forms acids |
| Palladium | Pd 46 | Metal | 2829°F 1554°C | 5684°F 3140°C | 0.015 | 1803 William Hyde Wollaston | For Greek goddess Pallas; from asteroid Pallas |
| Phosphorus | P 15 | Nonmetal | 111.4°F 44.1°C | 536°F 280°C | 1120 | 1669 Hennig Brand | Greek *phosphoros*, light-bringer; glows because of rapid oxidation |
| Platinum | Pt 78 | Metal | 3222°F 1772°C | 6921°F 3827°C | 0.01 | 1735 Antonio de Ulloa | Diminutive of Spanish *plata*, silver, *platina* |
| Plutonium | Pu 94 | Radioactive metal | 1186°F 641°C | 5850°F 3232°C | Synthetic | 1940 Glenn T. Seaborg & co-workers | For planet Pluto |
| Polonium | Po 84 | Radioactive metal | 489°F 254°C | 1764°F 962°C | Rare | 1898 Marie Curie & Pierre Curie | Named by Marie Curie for her native Poland |
| Potassium | K 19 | Metal | 145.9°F 63.3°C | 1399.8°F 759.9°C | 18,400 | 1807 Humphry Davy | For potash, a compound of potassium; symbol from Latin *kalium* |
| Praseodymium | Pr 59 | Rare earth | 6368°F 3520°C | 5814°F 3212°C | 9.1 | 1885 Karl Auer (Baron von Welsbach) | Greek *prasios*, green, plus *didymos*, twin (with the element Neodymium) |
| Promethium | Pm 61 | Radioactive rare earth | 1908°F 1042°C | 5430°F(est.) 3000°C(est.) | Rare | 1945 J.A. Marinsky, L.E. Glendenin, & C.D. Coryell | For Greek god Prometheus, who stole fire from heaven |
| Protactinium | Pa 91 | Radioactive metal | 2912°F 1600°C | N.A. N.A. | Rare | 1917 Otto Hahn & Lise Meitner | Latin *proto*, first, plus actinium, one of the elements |
| Radium | Ra 88 | Radioactive metal | 1292°F 700°C | 2084°F 1140°C | Rare | 1898 Marie Curie & Pierre Curie | Latin *radius*, ray |
| Radon | Rn 86 | Radioactive gas | −96°F −71°C | −79°F −61.8°C | Rare | 1900 Friedrich Ernst Dorn | *Radium* plus *on*, as in *neon* |
| Rhenium | Re 75 | Metal | 5756°F 3180°C | 10,161°F 5627°C | 0.0007 | 1925 Walter Noddack, Ida Tacke, & Otto Berg | Latin *Rhenus*, Rhine |
| Rhodium | Rh 45 | Metal | 3571°F 1966°C | 6741°F 3727°C | Rare | 1803 William Hyde Wollaston | Greek *rhodon*, rose; for red color of its salts |
| Rubidium | Rb 37 | Metal | 102°F 38.9°C | 1267°F 686°C | 78 | 1861 Gustav Kirchhoff & Robert Bunsen | Latin *rubidus*, red; from red lines in its spectrum |
| Ruthenium | Ru 44 | Metal | 4190°F 2310°C | 7052°F 3900°C | Rare | 1844 Carl Claus | For Ruthenia in Urals, where ore was first found |
| Rutherfordium | Rf 104 | Radioactive metal | N.A. | N.A. | Synthetic | 1969 Albert Ghiorso & co-workers | After Ernest Rutherford, British physicist |
| Samarium | Sm 62 | Rare earth | 1965°F 1074°C | 3261°F 1794°C | 7 | 1879 Paul-Emile Lecoq de Boisbaudran | For Scandinavian mineral samarskite |
| Scandium | Sc 21 | Metal | 2806°F 1541°C | 5128°F 2831°C | 25 | 1879 Lars Fredrik Nilson | For Scandinavia |
| Selenium | Se 34 | Nonmetal | 423°F 217°C | 1265°F 685°C | 0.05 | 1817 Jöns Jakob Berzelius | Greek *selene*, the moon |
| Silicon | Si 14 | Nonmetal | 2570°F 1410°C | 4271°F 2355°C | 273,000 | 1824 Jöns Jakob Berzelius | Latin *silex*, flint |
| Silver | Ag 47 | Metal | 1763.4°F 961.9°C | 4014°F 2212°C | 0.08 | Prehistoric | Anglo-Saxon *sealfor;* symbol is from Latin *argentum* |
| Sodium | Na 11 | Metal | 208.0°F 97.8°C | 1621.2°F 882.9°C | 22,700 | 1807 Humphry Davy | English soda, compound of sodium; symbol from Latin *natrium* |
| Strontium | Sr 38 | Metal | 1416°F 769°C | 2523°F 1384°C | 384 | 1808 Humphry Davy | For Strontian, a town in Scotland |
| Sulfur | S 16 | Nonmetal | 235.0°F 112.8°C | 832.5°F 444.7°C | 340 | Prehistoric | Sanskrit *solvere*, Latin *sulphur* |
| Tantalum | Ta 73 | Metal | 5425°F 2996°C | 9797°F 5425°C | 1.7 | 1802 Anders Ekeberg | For mythical king Tantalus, condemned to thirst; because of its insolubility |

| Element | Symbol/ atomic number | Type[1] | Melting point[1] | Boiling point[1] | Parts per million in crust | Year discovered and by whom | Derivation of name |
|---|---|---|---|---|---|---|---|
| Technetium | Tc 43 | Radioactive metal | 3942°F 2172°C | 8811°F 4877°C | Synthetic | 1937 Emilio Segrè | Greek *technetos*, artificial; first artificial element |
| Tellurium | Te 52 | Metal | 841.1°F 449.5°C | 1814°F 990°C | Rare | 1782 Franz Joseph Müller | Latin *tellus*, the earth |
| Terbium | Tb 65 | Rare earth | 2473°F 1356°C | 5846°F 3230°C | 1.18 | 1843 Carl Gustav Mosander | For Ytterby, village in Sweden |
| Thallium | Tl 81 | Metal | 578.3°F 303.5°C | 2655°F 1457°C | 0.7 | 1861 William Crookes | Greek *thallos*, a young, or green, twig (after color of its spectrum) |
| Thorium | Th 90 | Radioactive metal | 3182°F 1750°C | 8654°F 4790°C | 8.1 | 1829 Jöns Jakob Berzelius | For Norse god Thor |
| Thulium | Tm 69 | Rare earth | 2813°F 1545°C | 3542°F 1950°C | 0.5 | 1879 Per Teodor Cleve | Greek *Thule*, Greek name for land north of Britain |
| Tin | Sn 50 | Metal | 450°F 232°C | 4118°F 2270°C | 2.1 | Prehistoric | Anglo-Saxon *tin*; symbol from Latin *stannum* |
| Titanium | Ti 22 | Metal | 3020°F 1660°C | 5949°F 3287°C | 6,320 | 1791 William Gregor | For Titans of classical mythology |
| Tungsten | W 74 | Metal | 6170°F 3410°C | 10,220°F 5660°C | 1.2 | 1783 Fausto and Juan José d'Elhuyar | Swedish *tung sten*, heavy stone; symbol from German *Wolfram* |
| Uranium | U 92 | Radioactive metal | 2070°F 1132°C | 6904°F 3818°C | 2.3 | 1789 Martin Klaproth | For planet Uranus |
| Vanadium | V 23 | Metal | 3434°F 1890°C | 6116°F 3380°C | 136 | 1801 Andrès del Rio | For Scandinavian goddess Vanadis |
| Xenon | Xe 54 | Gas | −169.4°F −111.9°C | −161°F −107°C | Rare | 1898 Alexander Ramsay & Morris William Travers | Greek *xenon*, stranger |
| Ytterbium | Yb 70 | Rare earth | 1506°F 819°C | 2185°F 1196°C | 3.1 | 1907 George Urbain | For Ytterby, a village in Sweden |
| Yttrium | Y 39 | Rare earth | 2826°F 1552°C | 9640°F 3338°C | 31 | 1794 Johan Gadolin | For Ytterby, a village in Sweden |
| Zinc | Zn 30 | Metal | 787.3°F 419.6°C | 1665°F 907°C | 76 | Prehistoric | German *zink* |
| Zirconium | Zr 40 | Metal | 3366°F 1852°C | 7911°F 4377°C | 162 | 1789 Martin Klaproth | Arabic *zargun*, gold color |

1. At a pressure of one atmosphere and, for type, at room temperature. 2. At a pressure of 28 atmospheres. 3. This element sublimes (slowly evaporates from its solid form) at room temperature and one atmosphere.

## THE PERIODIC TABLE

In the 19th century, chemists began to determine how much one atom of an element weighed with respect to another—the atomic weight (now known as the atomic mass and measured in atomic mass units, or amu, a mass equal to one-twelfth the mass of the most common form of carbon atom). The first comprehensive list was prepared by Jöns Jakob Berzelius in 1828. When chemists made lists of elements in the order of atomic weights, they noticed that every seven or eight elements in the list had similar properties. In 1869 Dmitri Mendeleyev went further and boldly interchanged some elements in the list and left blanks for others to make sure the properties matched for every "period" of eight elements. This was the first periodic table. Mendeleyev had only 63 elements to work with, but he correctly predicted three more that would make his list more complete. Today there are 109 elements in the periodic table.

Early in the 20th century, atoms were discovered to consist of protons and electrons (in 1932 it was discovered that neutrons also are found in atoms). Normally, the number of protons and electrons is equal. This number is the atomic number, which is a different counting number for every element from hydrogen (atomic number 1) to the unnamed element numbered 109. When the concept of atomic number was discovered, it was possible to improve the periodic table by arranging the elements in order of atomic number instead of atomic weight. This did not require the rearrangements Mendeleyev had to make, and it clearly showed where the blanks were—all of which have been filled in since 1940. Any other newly discovered or created elements must go at the end of the table.

Each column of the periodic table includes elements with similar properties, although hydrogen in the first column is less typical in this respect. But the other elements in the first column are all soft metals that react strongly. Similarly, the last column of the table contains only the gases that react very minimally. In general, elements are metals on the left side of the table (except for hydrogen), becoming mostly nonmetals in the last six columns. These last columns include some elements that are metals, such as aluminum. (A broken, heavy line separates the metals from the nonmetals.)

The row of rare-earth elements beginning with lanthanum and the row of actinide elements beginning with actinium do not fit neatly into the rest of the table. Elements from atomic number 57 to 71 are all similar to lanthanum, while elements from atomic number 89 to 103 are similar to actinium. The rare earths are not generally rare, nor do they resemble soil. They are moderately common metals that, because of atomic structure, are very similar chemically. The actinide elements are radioactive metals.

The periodic table also includes the atomic mass as well as the atomic number. The atomic mass is essentially the sum of the protons and neutrons in an atom of an element, although different standards have been used at various times to measure this. As protons and neutrons join to form an atomic nucleus, a little of their energy becomes mass, the amount of which depends on how many protons and neutrons there are (this effect is exploited in nuclear fission, in which the reverse process—splitting the nucleus—releases the energy). Consequently, a particular atom is chosen upon which to base the amu. Today the atomic mass is adjusted to make the most common form of carbon have an atomic mass of exactly 12 (6 protons and 6 neutrons). Most elements occur with several different atomic masses (in addition to carbon-12, for example, there are both carbon-13 and carbon-14; carbon-14 has 6 protons and 8 neutrons and is radioactive). These different forms are called isotopes. Therefore, in the periodic table, the atomic mass given for most elements is the one that would be found by averaging the different isotopes in the amounts they naturally occur. Carbon is given an atomic mass of 12.01 because there is so much more carbon-12 than there is carbon-13 or carbon-14 in an ordinary sample of carbon. For some radioactive elements, natural abundance is meaningless, since there is no stable form. For these, the atomic mass of the most stable form is given, indicated by putting the atomic mass in parentheses.

# THE PERIODIC TABLE OF THE ELEMENTS

Legend:
- 6 — atomic number
- **C** — chemical symbol
- 12.01 — atomic mass
- Carbon — name of element

**Main table**

| IA | IIA | IIIB | IVB | VB | VIB | VIIB | VIII | | | IB | IIB | IIIA | IVA | VA | VIA | VIIA | O (noble gases) |
|---|---|---|---|---|---|---|---|---|---|---|---|---|---|---|---|---|---|
| 1 **H** 1.01 Hydrogen | | | | | | | | | | | | | | | | | 2 **He** 4.00 Helium |
| 3 **Li** 6.94 Lithium | 4 **Be** 9.01 Beryllium | | | | | | | | | | | 5 **B** 10.81 Boron | 6 **C** 12.01 Carbon | 7 **N** 14.01 Nitrogen | 8 **O** 16.00 Oxygen | 9 **F** 19.00 Fluorine | 10 **Ne** 20.18 Neon |
| 11 **Na** 22.99 Sodium | 12 **Mg** 24.31 Magnesium | | | | | | | | | | | 13 **Al** 26.98 Aluminum | 14 **Si** 28.09 Silicon | 15 **P** 30.97 Phosphorus | 16 **S** 32.07 Sulfur | 17 **Cl** 35.45 Chlorine | 18 **Ar** 39.95 Argon |
| 19 **K** 39.10 Potassium | 20 **Ca** 40.08 Calcium | 21 **Sc** 44.96 Scandium | 22 **Ti** 47.88 Titanium | 23 **V** 50.94 Vanadium | 24 **Cr** 52.00 Chromium | 25 **Mn** 54.94 Manganese | 26 **Fe** 55.85 Iron | 27 **Co** 58.93 Cobalt | 28 **Ni** 58.70 Nickel | 29 **Cu** 63.55 Copper | 30 **Zn** 65.39 Zinc | 31 **Ga** 69.72 Gallium | 32 **Ge** 72.61 Germanium | 33 **As** 74.92 Arsenic | 34 **Se** 78.96 Selenium | 35 **Br** 79.90 Bromine | 36 **Kr** 83.80 Krypton |
| 37 **Rb** 85.47 Rubidium | 38 **Sr** 87.62 Strontium | 39 **Y** 88.91 Yttrium | 40 **Zr** 91.22 Zirconium | 41 **Nb** 92.91 Niobium | 42 **Mo** 95.94 Molybdenum | 43 **Tc** (98) Technetium | 44 **Ru** 101.07 Ruthenium | 45 **Rh** 102.91 Rhodium | 46 **Pd** 106.4 Palladium | 47 **Ag** 107.87 Silver | 48 **Cd** 112.41 Cadmium | 49 **In** 114.82 Indium | 50 **Sn** 118.71 Tin | 51 **Sb** 121.75 Antimony | 52 **Te** 127.60 Tellurium | 53 **I** 126.90 Iodine | 54 **Xe** 131.29 Xenon |
| 55 **Cs** 132.91 Cesium | 56 **Ba** 137.33 Barium | Lanthanide series (see below) | 72 **Hf** 178.49 Hafnium | 73 **Ta** 180.95 Tantalum | 74 **W** 183.85 Tungsten | 75 **Re** 186.21 Rhenium | 76 **Os** 190.2 Osmium | 77 **Ir** 192.22 Iridium | 78 **Pt** 195.08 Platinum | 79 **Au** 196.97 Gold | 80 **Hg** 200.59 Mercury | 81 **Tl** 204.38 Thallium | 82 **Pb** 207.2 Lead | 83 **Bi** 208.98 Bismuth | 84 **Po** (209) Polonium | 85 **At** (210) Astatine | 86 **Rn** (222) Radon |
| 87 **Fr** (223) Francium | 88 **Ra** 226.03 Radium | Actinide series (see below) | 104 **Rf** (261) Rutherfordium | 105 **Ha** (262) Hahnium | 106 (263) | 107 (262) | 108 (265) | 109 (266) | | | | | | | | | |

alkali metals — IA
alkaline earth metals — IIA
transition metals
other metals
nonmetals
noble gases — O

**rare earth elements — Lanthanide series**

| 57 **La** 138.91 Lanthanum | 58 **Ce** 140.12 Cerium | 59 **Pr** 140.91 Praseodymium | 60 **Nd** 144.24 Neodymium | 61 **Pm** (145) Promethium | 62 **Sm** 150.4 Samarium | 63 **Eu** 151.96 Europium | 64 **Gd** 157.25 Gadolinium | 65 **Tb** 158.93 Terbium | 66 **Dy** 162.50 Dysprosium | 67 **Ho** 164.93 Holmium | 68 **Er** 167.26 Erbium | 69 **Tm** 168.93 Thulium | 70 **Yb** 173.04 Ytterbium | 71 **Lu** 174.97 Lutetium |
|---|---|---|---|---|---|---|---|---|---|---|---|---|---|---|

**Actinide series**

| 89 **Ac** 227.03 Actinium | 90 **Th** 232.04 Thorium | 91 **Pa** 231.04 Protactinium | 92 **U** 238.03 Uranium | 93 **Np** 237.05 Neptunium | 94 **Pu** (244) Plutonium | 95 **Am** (243) Americium | 96 **Cm** (247) Curium | 97 **Bk** (247) Berkelium | 98 **Cf** (251) Californium | 99 **Es** (252) Einsteinium | 100 **Fm** (257) Fermium | 101 **Md** (258) Mendelevium | 102 **No** (259) Nobelium | 103 **Lr** (260) Lawrencium |
|---|---|---|---|---|---|---|---|---|---|---|---|---|---|---|

Period 1, Period 2, Period 3, Period 4, Period 5, Period 6, Period 7

# Physics

Physics is the basis of the other sciences because it is concerned with the fundamental interactions of matter and energy. The first physicists studied how ordinary objects and very large objects (moon, planets, and stars) moved in response to forces. Their study was extremely successful. Near the end of the 19th century, physicists began to investigate radiation in detail, leading to the discovery of various forms of electromagnetic radiation (of which only ordinary light was known previously) and particles smaller than the atom (subatomic particles, such as the electron and proton). In the 20th century, the study of subatomic particles, called particle physics, has become a major branch of the science. Many particle physicists limit their work to the particles in the nucleus of atoms and to the behavior of nuclei. Another major branch, condensed-matter physics, is concerned with the physical behavior of materials—for example, their electrical and magnetic properties. Major successes in condensed-matter physics include development of the transistor and related devices (chips) and superconductivity, a state in which electric currents can be transmitted with no resistance. Today many physicists are also cosmologists, who study how the universe began and is constructed, or astrophysicists, who study processes in stars.

## MAJOR DISCOVERIES IN PHYSICS

**1586** Simon Stevinus (Belgian-Dutch: 1548–1620) shows that two different weights dropped at same time from same height will reach ground at same time.

**1604** Galileo (Italian: 1564–1642) announces his discovery that a body falling freely will increase its distance as square of time.
Johannes Kepler (German: 1571–1630) shows that light diminishes as square of distance from source.

**1663** Blaise Pascal (French: 1623–62) proposes what becomes known as Pascal's Law: pressure in fluid is transmitted equally in all directions. (Published year after his death.)

**1675** Ole Rømer (Danish: 1644–1710) becomes first to measure speed of light, although his value is somewhat too slow by today's standards.

**1676** Robert Hooke (English: 1635–1703) discovers what becomes known as Hooke's Law: The amount a spring stretches varies directly with its tension.

**1678** Christiaan Huygens (Dutch: 1629–95) develops wave theory of light.

**1687** Sir Isaac Newton's (English: 1642–1727) *Principia* is published, containing his laws of motion and theory of gravity.

**1746** At least two experimenters in Leyden, the Netherlands, invent method for storing static electricity, which becomes known as Leyden jar.

**1752** Benjamin Franklin (American: 1706–90) performs kite experiment, demonstrating that lightning is form of electricity.

**1787** Jacques A.C. Charles (French: 1746–1823) discovers what is later known as Charles's law: All gases expand same amount with given rise in temperature; e.g., same rise in temperature that will cause hydrogen to double in volume will also cause air to double in volume.

**1791** Luigi Galvani (Italian: 1737–98) announces his discovery that when two different metals touch in frog's muscle, they produce electric current.

**1798** Benjamin Thompson, Count von Rumford (American-German: 1753–1814) shows that heat is form of motion.
Henry Cavendish (English: 1731–1810) determines gravitational constant and mass of Earth.

**1801** Johann W. Ritter (German: 1776–1810) discovers ultraviolet light.

**1802** Thomas Young (English: 1773–1829) develops his wave theory of light—more detailed than ideas of Christiaan Huygens and based on convincing experiments.

**1819** Hans Christian Oersted (Danish: 1777–1851) discovers that magnetism and electricity are two different manifestations of same force (not published until 1820).

**1820** André-Marie Ampère (French: 1775–1836) formulates first laws of electromagnetism.

**1831** Michael Faraday (English: 1791–1867) in England and Joseph Henry (American: 1797–1878) in U.S. (in 1830) independently discover principle of electrical dynamo.

**1842** Julius Robert von Mayer (German: 1814–78) is first scientist to state law of conservation of energy: In chemical reactions energy is neither created nor destroyed.

**1848** William Thompson, Baron Kelvin (Scottish: 1824–1907), proposes concept of absolute zero, the lowest theoretically possible temperature (−460°F, or −273°C).

**1850** Rudolf J.E. Clausius (German: 1822–88) makes first clear statement of second law of thermodynamics: Energy in closed system tends to degrade into heat.

**1873** James Clerk Maxwell (Scottish: 1831–79) publishes complete theory of electromagnetism, which includes his prediction that radio waves must exist.

**1887** Albert A. Michelson (German-American: 1852–1931) and Edward Morley (American: 1838–1923) attempt to measure changes in velocity of light produced by motion of Earth through space; inability to find such changes is later interpreted as helping to establish Einstein's special theory of relativity.

**1888** Heinrich P. Hertz (German: 1857–94) produces and detects radio waves.

**1895** Wilhelm Konrad Röntgen (German: 1845–1923) discovers X rays.

**1896** Henri Becquerel (French: 1852–1908) discovers natural radioactivity.

**1897** Sir Joseph John Thomson (English: 1856–1940) discovers electron.

**1900** Max K.E.L. Planck (German: 1858–1947) explains behavior of light by proposing that there is smallest step a physical process can take, which he names quantum.

**1905** Albert Einstein (German-American: 1879–1955) shows that photoelectric effect—ejection of electrons from metal by action of light—can be explained if light has particle nature as well as wave nature.
Einstein shows that motion of small particles in liquid ("Brownian motion") can be explained by assuming that the liquid is made of molecules.
Einstein develops his special theory of relativity and the law $E = mc^2$ (energy equals mass times square of speed of light).

**1911** Heike Kamerlingh Onnes (Dutch: 1853–1926) discovers superconductivity in metals cooled near to absolute zero.
Ernest Rutherford (British: 1871–1937) discovers the proton.

**1915** Einstein completes his general theory of relativity, a theory of gravity more accurate than that of Sir Isaac Newton, and publishes it the following year.

**1919** An expedition led by Sir Arthur S. Eddington (English: 1882–1944) to observe bending of starlight by sun's gravity during eclipse confirms that Einstein's theory of gravity is more accurate than Newton's in predicting effect of gravity on light.

**1924** Louis-Victor de Broglie (French: 1892–1987) publishes his theory that particles, such as electron, also have wave nature.

**1925** Wolfgang Pauli (Austrian-American: 1900–58) discovers exclusion principal: Two electrons or protons described by same numbers (called quantum numbers) cannot exist in same atom.
Werner Karl Heisenberg (German: 1901–76) develops matrix version of quantum mechanics, a mathematical treatment that explains behavior of electrons and protons.

**1926** Erwin Schrödinger (Austrian: 1887–1961) develops wave version of quantum mechanics, a different mathematical treatment of behavior of electrons and protons producing same results as Heisenberg's matrix mechanics.

**1927** Heisenberg develops his uncertainty principle: It is impossible to measure accurately position and momentum of electron or proton at same time.

**1932** Sir James Chadwick (British: 1891–1974) discovers neutron, a neutral particle about same mass as proton.
Carl D. Anderson (American: 1905–91) discovers positron, a positively charged analog of electron.
Sir John G. Cockcroft (English: 1897–1967) and Ernest Walton (Irish: 1903– ) develop first particle accelerator, a device for speeding subatomic particles, which causes them to react more intensely with atoms or other particles (often still known as "atom smasher").

**1937** Anderson, with several other physicists, performs the work that culminates in the discovery of the muon.

**1938** Otto Hahn (German: 1879–1968) splits uranium atom, opening way for nuclear bombs and nuclear power.

**1945** Scientists funded by U.S. government and

led by J. Robert Oppenheimer (American: 1904–67) detonate first nuclear-fission explosion (atomic bomb).

**1947** Quantum electrodynamics (QED) is born, with many parents: notably, Richard P. Feynman (American: 1918–88), Julian S. Schwinger (American: 1918– ), Schin'ichiro Tomonaga (Japanese: 1906–79), Willis E. Lamb, Jr. (American: 1913– ) (all of whom received Nobel Prizes for this concept), and Hans A. Bethe (German-American: 1906– ).

Cecil Frank Powell (English: 1903–69) and coworkers discover pion, first-known meson, a subatomic particle involved in holding nucleus of atom together.

**1952** Group of scientists in U.S. led by Edward Teller (Hungarian-American: 1908– ) develops first artificial nuclear-fusion device (hydrogen bomb).

**1955** Owen Chamberlain (American: 1920– ) and Emilio Segrè (Italian-American: 1905–89) produce first-known antiprotons, negatively charged analogs of proton.

Clyde Cowan, Jr. (American: 1919– ) and Frederick Reines (American: 1918– ) are first to observe neutrino, a subatomic particle with no mass or charge produced in certain forms of radioactive decay (technically, they observe antineutrinos, which have opposite spin of neutrinos).

**1957** Experiments by group led by Chien-Shiung Wu (Chinese-American: 1912– ) and quickly confirmed by others show that Law of Conservation of Parity does not hold for weak interaction; broadly speaking, right and left are distinguished by behavior of electrons emitted in certain forms of radioactivity.

John Bardeen (American: 1908–91), Leon Cooper (American: 1930– ), and John Schrieffler (American: 1931– ) develop a theory explaining superconductivity.

**1960** Rudolf Ludwig Mössbauer (German: 1929– ) discovers way to make gama rays with very narrow wavelengths and to measure changes in wavelength; Mössbauer effect confirms Einstein's general relativity theory.

**1961** Murray Gell-Mann (American: 1929– ) and, independently, Yu'val Ne'eman (Israeli: 1925– ) and others develop method of classifying heavy subatomic particles that comes to be known as "eight-fold way."

**1964** Gell-Mann introduces concept of quarks as components of heavy subatomic particles, such as protons and mesons.

**1967** Steven Weinberg (American: 1933– ), Abdus Salam (Pakistani-British: 1926– ), and Sheldon Lee Glashow (American: 1932– ) independently develop theory that combines electromagnetic force with weak force.

**1980** Heinrich Rohrer (Swiss: 1933– ) and Gerd Binning (German) invent the scanning-tunneling microscope, a device with which it is possible to produce images of individual atoms or crystal surfaces.

**1986** Karl Alexander Müller (Swiss: 1927– ) and Johannes Georg Bednorz (German: 1950– ) discover first "warm-temperature" superconductor.

# THE BASIC LAWS OF PHYSICS

**Key Terms** *Mass* is a measure of the amount of matter; it is proportional to weight. Near the surface of Earth it is roughly equivalent to weight.

*Velocity* measures how an object changes position with time.

*Acceleration* is how an object changes velocity with time.

*Momentum* is the product of mass and velocity.

*Energy* is the ability to do work.

## Law of Gravity

*The gravitational force between any two objects is proportional to the product of their masses and inversely proportional to the square of the distance between them.* If $F$ is the force, $G$ is the number that represents the ratio (the gravitational constant), $m$ and $M$ are the two masses, and $r$ is the distance between the objects:

$$F = \frac{GmM}{r^2} .$$

In metric measure, the gravitational constant is 0.00000000006672 (6.67 × $10^{-11}$) N $m^2/kg^2$, so another way of writing the basic law of gravity is

$$F = \frac{0.0000000000667 mM}{r^2} .$$

This law implies that objects falling near the surface of Earth will fall with the same rate of acceleration (ignoring drag caused by air). This rate is 32.174 feet per second per second (ft./ sec²), or 9.8 m/sec², and is conventionally labeled $g$. Applying this rate to falling objects gives the velocity, $v$, and distance, $d$, after any amount of time, $t$, in seconds. If the object starts at rest and 32 ft./sec² is used as an approximation for $g$,

$$v = 32t$$
$$d = 16t^2.$$

For example, after 3 seconds, a dropped object that is still falling will have a velocity of 32 × 3 = 96 feet per second and will have fallen a distance of 16 × $3^2$ = 144 feet.

If the object has an initial velocity $v_0$ and an initial height above the ground of $a$, the equations describing the velocity and the distance, $d$, above the ground (a positive velocity is *up* and a negative velocity is *down*) become

$$v = v_0 - 32t$$

and

$$d = -16t^2 + v_0 t + a.$$

After 3 seconds, an object tossed in the air from a height of 6 feet with a velocity of 88 feet per second will reach a speed of 88 – 96 = –8 feet per second, meaning that it has begun to descend, and will have a height of (–16 × 9) + (88 × 3) + 6 = –144 + 264 + 6 = 126 feet above the ground.

The maximum height, $H$, reached by the object with an initial velocity $v_0$ and initial height $a$ is

$$H = a + \frac{v_0^2}{64} .$$

For the object tossed upward at 88 feet per second from a height of 6 feet, the maximum height reached would be 6 + 88²/64 = 6 + 121 = 127 feet. Therefore, after 3 seconds, the object has just reached its peak and has fallen back only 1 foot.

Albert Einstein's general theory of relativity introduced laws of gravity more accurate than those just given, which were discovered by Sir Isaac Newton. Newton's gravitational theory is extremely accurate for most practical situations, however. For example, Newton's theory is used to determine how to launch satellites into proper orbits.

## Newton's Laws of Motion

Newton's Laws of Motion also apply to objects in a vacuum and are not easily observed in the real world, where forces such as friction tend to overwhelm the natural motion of objects. To obtain realistic solutions to problems, however, physicists and engineers begin with Newton's laws and then add in the various forces that also affect motion.

1. *Any object at rest tends to stay at rest. A body in motion moves at the same velocity in a straight line unless acted upon by a force.* This is also known as the law of inertia. Note that this law implies that an object will travel in a curved path only so long as a force is acting on it. When the force is released, the object will travel in a straight line. A weight on a string swung in a circle will travel in a straight line when the string is released, for the string was supplying the force that caused circular motion.

2. *The acceleration of an object is directly proportional to the force acting on it and inversely proportional to the mass of the object.* This law, for an acceleration $a$, a force $F$, and a mass $m$, is more commonly expressed in terms of finding the force when you know the mass and the acceleration. In this form it is written as

$$F = ma.$$

The implication of this law is that a constant force will produce acceleration, which is an increase in velocity. Thus, a rocket, which is propelled by a constant force as long as its fuel is burning, constantly increases in velocity. If there were enough fuel, the rocket would eventually cease to increase in velocity, however, because Einstein's other relativity theory, the special theory of relativity, states that no object can exceed the speed of light in a vacuum (see "Conservation of Mass-Energy" below). Nevertheless, even a small force, constantly applied, can cause a large mass to reach velocities near the speed of light if enough time is allowed.

3. *For every action there is an equal and opposite reaction.*

## Conservation Laws

Many results in physics come from various conservation laws. A conservation law is a rule that a certain entity must not change in amount during a certain class of operations. All such conservation laws treat closed systems. Anything added from outside the system could affect the amount of the entity being conserved.

**Conservation of momentum** In a closed system, momentum stays the same. This law is equivalent to Newton's third law. Since momentum is the product of mass and velocity, if the mass of a system changes, then the velocity must change. For example, consider a person holding a heavy anchor in a stationary rowboat in the water. The momentum of the system is 0, since the masses have no velocity. Now the person in the rowboat tosses the anchor toward the shore. The momentum of the anchor is now a positive number if velocity toward the shore is measured as positive. To conserve momentum, the rowboat has to be accelerated in the opposite direction, away from the shore. The positive momentum of the anchor is balanced by the negative momentum of the rowboat and its cargo. In terms of two masses, $m$ and $M$, and matching velocities $v$ and $V$,

$$mv = MV.$$

**Conservation of angular momentum** An object moving in a circle has a special kind of momentum, called angular momentum. As noted above, motion in a circle requires some force. Angular momentum combines mass, velocity, and acceleration (produced by the force). For a body moving in a circle, the acceleration depends on both the speed of the body in its path and the square of the radius of the circle. The product of this speed, the mass, and the square of the radius is the angular momentum of the mass.

*In a closed system, angular momentum is conserved.* This effect is used by skaters to change their velocity of spinning. Angular momentum is partly determined by the masses of a skater's arms combined with the rate of rotation and the square of the radius to the center of mass of each arm (the point that can represent the total mass of the arm). When skaters bring their arms close to their body, this would tend to reduce the angular momentum, because the center of mass is closer to the body. But, since angular momentum is conserved, the rate of rotation has to increase to compensate for the decreased radius. Because the rate depends on the square of the rotation, the rate increases dramatically.

**Conservation of mass** *In a closed system, the total amount of mass appears to be conserved in all but nuclear reactions and other extreme conditions.*

**Conservation of energy** *In a closed system, energy appears to be conserved in all but nuclear reactions and other extreme conditions.* Energy comes in very many forms: mechanical, chemical, electrical, heat, and so forth. As one form is changed into another (excepting nuclear reactions and extreme conditions), this law guarantees that the total amount remains the same. Thus, when you change the chemical energy of a dry cell into electrical energy and use that to turn a motor, the total amount does not change (although some becomes heat energy—see "Laws of Thermodynamics" below).

**Conservation of mass-energy** Einstein discovered that his special theory of relativity implied that energy and mass are related. Consequently, mass and energy by themselves are not conserved, since one can be converted into the other. Mass and energy appear to be conserved in ordinary situations because the

effect of Einstein's discovery is very small most of the time. The more general law, then, is the law of conservation of mass-energy: *The total amount of mass and energy must be conserved.* Einstein found the following equation that links mass and energy.

$$E = mc^2$$

In this equation, $E$ is the amount of energy, $m$ is the mass, and $c$ is the speed of light in a vacuum.

One instance of energy changing to mass occurs in Einstein's equation for how the mass increases with velocity. If $m_0$ is the mass of the object when it is not moving, $v$ is the velocity of the object in relation to an observer who is considered to be at rest, and $c$ is the speed of light in a vacuum, then the mass, $m$, is given by the equation

$$m = \frac{m_0}{\sqrt{1 - \dfrac{v^2}{c^2}}}.$$

This accounts for the rule that no object can exceed the speed of light in a vacuum. As the object approaches this speed, so much of the energy is converted to mass that it cannot continue to accelerate.

In both nuclear fission (splitting of the atomic nucleus) and nuclear fusion (the joining of atomic nuclei, producing the energy of a hydrogen bomb), mass is converted into energy.

**Conservation for particles** Many properties associated with atoms and subatomic particles are also conserved. Among them are charge, spin, isospin, and a combination known as CPT for *charge conjugation, parity,* and *time.*

## First and Second Laws of Thermodynamics

**First law** This is the same as the law of conservation of energy. It is a law of thermodynamics, or the movement of heat, because heat must be treated as a form of energy to keep the total amount of energy constant. All bodies contain heat as energy no matter how cold they are, although there is not much heat at temperatures close to absolute zero.

**Second law** *Heat in a closed system can never travel from a low temperature region to one of higher temperature in a self-sustaining process.* Self-sustaining in this case means a process that does not need energy from outside the system to keep it going. In a refrigerator, heat from the cold inside of the refrigerator is transferred to a warmer room, but energy from outside is required to make the transfer happen, so the process is not self-sustaining.

The second law has many implications. One of them is that no perpetual motion machine can be constructed. Another is that all energy in a closed system eventually becomes heat that is diffused equally throughout the system, so that one can no longer obtain work from the system.

The equations that describe the behavior of heat also can be applied to order and therefore to information. The word *entropy* refers to diffused heat, disorder, or lack of information. Another form of the second law of thermodynamics is that in a closed system, entropy

always increases.

## Laws of Current Electricity

**Key terms** When electrons flow in a conductor, the result is electric *current*. The amount of current is based on an amount of electric charge called the *coulomb*, which is the charge of about 6.25 quintillion ($6.25 \times 10^{18}$) electrons. When 1 coulomb of charge moves past a point in 1 second, it creates a current of 1 ampere. Just as a stream can carry the same amount of water swiftly through a narrow channel or slowly through a broad channel, the energy of an electric current varies depending on the difference in charge between places along the conductor. This is called *potential difference* and is measured in *volts*. The voltage is affected by the nature of the conductors. Some substances conduct an electric current much more easily than others. This *resistance* to the current is measured in ohms. *Electric power* is the rate at which electricity is used.

**Ohm's law** *Electric current is directly proportional to the potential difference and inversely proportional to resistance.* If you measure current, $I$, in amperes, potential difference, $V$, in volts, and resistance, $R$, in ohms, then the current is equal to the potential difference divided by the resistance. $$I = \frac{V}{R}$$

**Law of electric power** *If electric power, P, is measured in watts, then the power is equal to the product of the current measured in amperes and the potential difference measured in volts.*
$$P = IV$$

## Laws of Waves, Light, and Electromagnetic Radiation

**Key terms** Light is a part of a general form of radiation known as *electromagnetic waves,* or, when thought of as particles, *photons.* Here, electromagnetic radiation is considered as a wave phenomenon for the most part. The *velocity* of a wave is how fast the wave travels as a whole. The *wavelength* is the distance between one crest of the wave and the next crest. The *frequency* is how many crests pass a particular location in a unit of time.

**Law of wave motion** All waves (including water waves and sound waves) obey the wave equation that relates the velocity of the wave to its frequency and wavelength. *For all waves, the velocity is equal to the product of the frequency and wavelength.* The letters traditionally used in this equation have already been used in the equations above to mean something else, so here, $W$ will be used for the velocity of the wave, $f$ for the frequency, and $l$ for the wavelength. $$W = fl$$

**Law of electromagnetic energy** The energy of an electromagnetic wave depends on a small number known as Planck's constant. Measured in joules per hertz (energy per frequency), Planck's constant is $6.626196 \times 10^{-34}$. *The energy is equal to the product of Planck's constant and the frequency.* Using $E$ for energy, $h$ for Planck's constant, and $f$ for frequency, $$E = hf.$$

When thought of in terms of the particles called photons, the energy of a photon obeys the same law. The law of wave motion and the law of electromagnetic energy can be combined with the speed of light in a vacuum (c) to give

$$E = \frac{hc}{l} \ .$$

The energy of a photon is the product of Planck's constant and the speed of light, divided by the wavelength of the photon.

**Inverse-square law** All radiation obeys an inverse-square law, which is similar to the law of gravity. *The intensity of the radiation decreases as the inverse of the square of the distance from a point source radiation.*

## Two Basic Laws of Quantum Physics

When one considers effects on very small masses and at very small distances, different forces begin to affect how objects behave than occur at the sizes and distances one can observe directly. Since these effects occur in discrete steps based upon Planck's constant times the frequency, called the quantum—which is the size by which energy changes in steps (instead of continuously)—the science of such effects is called quantum physics. Small masses act sometimes like particles and sometimes like waves and sometimes like nothing we know about at the scale we live. Two laws in particular that describe the behavior of small masses are basic and easily stated.

**Heisenberg's uncertainty principle** *It is impossible to specify completely the position and momentum of a particle, such as an electron.*

**Pauli's exclusion principle** *Two particles of a certain class that are essentially the same cannot be in the same exact state.* This class, the fermions, includes such particles as the electron, neutron, and proton. Bosons, particles of a different class, do not obey Pauli's exclusion principle. (See "Subatomic Particles.")

## SUBATOMIC PARTICLES

During the 19th century, most scientists came to believe that everything was made from atoms, even though they had no way then to observe atoms. It is now known they were right, and there are even "photographs" of individual atoms available, images made with the scanning tunneling microscope. At the turn of the 20th century, physicists discovered that atoms themselves were made from smaller pieces—subatomic particles. These smaller pieces seemed at first to be the ultimate limit of matter, but in the 1960s, physicists proposed that many subatomic particles were themselves made from smaller particles that could not be detected. Like the unobserved atoms of the 19th century, the undetectable smaller particles, called quarks, have come to be accepted. Perhaps in the next century, there will be "photographs" of quarks.

Quarks are considered to be "fundamental" in that scientists believe they are not made up of still smaller pieces. Beside the quarks, vari-

ous other groups of particles are thought to be fundamental. Among these are the leptons. Together, quarks and leptons form what we think of as matter. They are characterized by a spin of ½, as are the particles made from three quarks, the baryons. *Spin* is a number for each particle that has a behavior similar to angular momentum (see "Basic Laws of Physics"). All particles with a spin of ½ are called fermions. Other apparently fundamental subatomic particles are similar to the photon, the particle that makes up light. Particles such as the photon and other particles with a spin of either 0 or 1 are called bosons, and they act as "glue" that holds matter together. Bosons produce the four known forces: gravity, electromagnetism, the strong force, and the weak force. (Under certain conditions electromagnetism and the weak force become a single force, the electroweak force.)

Many subatomic particles carry a charge, which is a unit of electromagnetism. Nearly all charges are counted as either –1 or +1 or 0 (no charge), based on the charge of the electron, which is –1. Quarks, however, have charges in multiples of ⅓. No one knows why charges come only in these particular amounts and do not occur in other amounts. No known law, for example, predicts that the charge of the large proton will be exactly the same amount (but opposite: +1) as the charge of the small electron.

The masses of subatomic particles are measured in terms of the particle's energy, for energy, *E*, is related to mass, *m*, and the speed of light, *c*, by Albert Einstein's famous equation $E = mc^2$. Since *c* is a very large number, the energy of a particle is much larger than its mass. Even so, the energy is expressed in a very small unit, the MeV, which is a million electron volts. An electron volt is 0.000000000000000001602 (1.602 × $10^{-19}$) joule.

Recently, many physicists have proposed various other still-undetected particles, called WIMPs (for Weakly Interacting Massive Particles); these are far from being fully accepted at this time and are omitted from the following list. Every particle mentioned has an antiparticle whose charge is the opposite (negative particles have positive antiparticles) and whose spin is in the opposite direction. Unless there is something special about the antiparticle, it will not be mentioned.

### Fermions
#### Fundamental Particles of Matter
**The Electron (A Lepton)** Movement of electrons is the source of current electricity, while an excess or deficit of electrons causes static electricity. The properties of the electron form the basis of electronic devices, such as computer chips. Electrons are found in all atoms, where they occupy several shells around the outside of the atom. Interactions between electrons account for all chemical reactions. The electron is stable and very light. Its mass is 0.511 MeV. Its charge is –1. Like all subatomic particles, it has a related particle, the antiparticle, known as the positron. The positron is a mirror-image of the electron with a charge of +1. The positron was the first antiparticle to be discovered. It was proposed in 1931 by Paul Adrien Maurice

Dirac and discovered (accidentally) in 1932 by Carl David Anderson.

**Muons and Tauons (Leptons)** The muon is often described as a "fat electron," since it has all the properties of an electron except that its mass is 200 times as great—105.7 MeV. Similarly, the tauon is a "fat muon," with a mass of 1,750 MeV. No one predicted these particles, and no one knows what their role in the universe is.

**Neutrinos (Leptons)** form a group of leptons associated with electrons, muons, and tauons, with which they form three "families." A family consists of a charged particle, such as an electron, its antiparticle, such as a positron, and an associated neutrino and antineutrino. Aside from their separate associations, there would seem to be no differences among the three types of neutrino. All have no charge and probably no mass and a spin of ½. (Some evidence suggests that neutrinos have a very small mass.) They do not interact strongly with anything. Neutrinos are passing through your body all the time, and most go on to pass through the earth and out the other side.

**Quarks** were first proposed by Murray Gell-Mann in 1964 to account for the relationships between various kinds of baryons (see below). Each baryon is composed of three quarks, and each meson (see below) of two quarks. Common baryons and mesons are composed of quarks known as *up* (charge +⅔ and mass 1.0 MeV) and *down* (charge –⅓ and mass 3.0 MeV). Even though their individual masses are small, the binding energy between them in a baryon produces most of the mass in the universe. Other baryons or mesons have a quality known as "strangeness," which is conferred by the *strange quark* (charge –⅓ and mass 102.2 MeV), or a quality known as "charm," conferred by the *charm quark* (charge –⅔ and mass 1,530 MeV). Two other quarks, variously known as *top* and *bottom* or as *truth* and *beauty* complete the list of six "flavors." Each quark also comes in one of three "colors," although physicists disagree on what to call the colors (red, blue, and green are one of the popular choices.) In a meson or a baryon, the colors are always combined so as to produce absence of color; thus color cannot be detected directly. Furthermore, quarks are confined within the particles they make up, making direct detection impossible; but various experiments have established that all, except possibly top or truth, actually exist.

### Baryons
**The Proton** is found in the nucleus of the atom. For about 20 years, it was assumed that atoms consisted of a core of protons surrounded by electrons, although the true situation is somewhat more complex. The proton appears to be stable, although recently some theorists have proposed that protons may decay into pure energy after about 10,000,000,000,000,000,-000,000,000,000,000 ($10^{31}$) years. So far, although much watched, no one has seen a proton decay. Protons are heavy particles with a mass of 938.3 MeV, and they have a charge of +1. Every atom contains an equal number of +1 protons and –1 electrons, giving a total charge to the atom of 0. (An atom that has lost or gained an electron—and therefore a charge—is called an ion.)

**The Neutron** is almost exactly like a proton but with no charge and therefore much harder to detect. Neutrons in the nuclei of atoms are stable, but outside the nucleus, each neutron soon decays into a proton, an electron, and an electron antineutrino. All atoms except hydrogen must have neutrons in their nuclei to be stable. Neutrons have a mass of 939.6 MeV.

**Other Baryons** These include two hyperons, three sigmas, two xis, and an omega. Except for the omega, none was predicted. Instead they were found in cosmic-ray and particle-accelerator experiments in the late 1940s and in the 1950s. In 1961 Murray Gell-Mann predicted the omega on the basis of a theory preliminary to the quark theory. The omega was discovered in 1964. None of these particles is stable, decaying after much less than a second into other particles. They are not constituents of ordinary matter; i.e., they do not exist at ordinary energies on Earth.

## Bosons

### Mesons
### (Bosons made from Quarks)

**Pions** are the bosons that hold the nucleus of atoms together, producing the strong force. Pions come in positive, negative, and neutral forms. In 1935 Hideki Yukawa predicted the pion in his theory of the strong force. When a pion is exchanged between a proton and a neutron, it can change each into the other particle. In the process, it produces the strong force, which is needed to keep the positively charged protons from rushing apart because of the electromagnetic force (positive charges repel each other). When the muon was first discovered in 1937, scientists thought it was the particle Yukawa predicted, but by 1945 it was known that the muon's properties were wrong for that role. In 1947 Cecil Frank Powell and co-workers located the pion in cosmic rays. Each form of the pion has a slightly different mass (positive 139.6 MeV, negative 189.6 MeV, and neutral 135 MeV), and all decay in much less than a second. Pions, like all mesons, are composite particles made from two quarks. Other bosons are thought to be elementary particles, not made up of other particles.

**Other Mesons** Various short-lived mesons heavier than the pion incorporate such quarks as strange, top, and bottom. None of them are constituents of ordinary matter, but the neutral K mesons, or kaons, have been very important in experiments extending basic physical theories.

### Bosons not made from Quarks

**Gluons** Although the Yukawa theory of the pion seemed to explain the strong force, the quark theory soon led to the understanding that pions and the strong force are side effects of a more essential strong force, one carried by eight neutral particles called gluons. Exchanging gluons between quarks usually causes quarks to change from one color to another, keeping the quarks attracted to each other. Gluons have no mass and a spin of 1.

**The Photon** is the agent of electromagnetic radiation, including ordinary light, radio waves, microwaves, X rays, and gamma rays. In the 19th century, Thomas Young demonstrated the wave nature of electromagnetic radiation, but in 1905 Albert Einstein showed that it also had a particle nature. The particle, a vector boson (see "Vector Bosons" below) came to be called the photon. It has no mass and a spin of 1. Exchanging photons causes charged particles to be attracted (if the charges are unlike) or repelled (if the charges are alike). When an electron absorbs or emits a photon of sufficient energy, it can change into a positron. If a positron and an electron meet, they disappear, leaving an energetic photon. Electrons can emit and absorb photons in other ways as well. The photon has no mass and a spin of 1.

**Other Vector Bosons** The *positive and negative W particles* and the *neutral Z particle* were predicted by the electroweak theory and produced and detected by Carlo Rubbia and co-workers in 1983. They are quite massive (W particles 81,000 MeV and Z particle 93,800 MeV) and have a spin of 1. Two other particles of this class have been predicted but not detected: the *Higgs particle*, a massive particle that helps give mass to the W and Z particles, and the massless *graviton*, which should have the same relation to gravity as the photon does to electromagnetism. Both have a spin of 0.

---

# Life Sciences

While the scientific study of living creatures seems to have begun with Aristotle, there was much practical experimentation with living things much earlier, going back to the domestication of a species, the dog, around 10,000 B.C. In the years that followed the Scientific Revolution of the 17th century, the science of biology came to include most of the then-known life sciences: zoology (the study of animals), botany (the study of plants), and taxonomy (the classification of living things). In the 19th century, biology began to fragment into other studies: microbiology (the study of creatures visible only through the microscope), genetics (the study of how traits are inherited), biochemistry (the study of molecules created by living things), and so forth. At the same time, different ways of studying living organisms were developed, among them anthropology (the study of human beings), ecology (the study of interactions between different living things and their environment), and ethology (the study of animal behavior).

## MAJOR DISCOVERIES IN LIFE SCIENCES

B.C.

**c. 9000** Agricultural Revolution starts in Near East with domestication of sheep and goats in Persia (Iran) and Afghanistan and cultivation of wheat in Canaan (Israel).

**c. 8000** Agricultural Revolution starts independently in what are now Peru, Central America, and Indochina.

**c. 350** Aristotle (Greek: 384–322 B.C.) classi-

fies known animals in system that will continue to be used until 1735.

A.D.

**1548** Jan Baptista van Helmont (Flemish: 1580–1644) shows that plants do not obtain large amounts of material for their growth from soil.

**1665** Robert Hooke (English: 1635–1703) describes and names the cell.

**1668** Francesco Redi (Italian: 1626–97) shows that maggots in meat do not arise spontaneously but are hatched from flies' eggs.

**1669** Anton van Leeuwenhoek (Dutch: 1632–1723) discovers microorganisms—creatures too small to see with naked eye—and recognizes that sperm are part of reproduction.

**1683** Leeuwenhoek is first to observe bacteria.

**1735** Carolus Linnaeus (Carl Linné; Swedish: 1707–78) introduces system in use today for classifying plants and animals.

**1779** Jan Ingenhousz (Dutch: 1730–99) discovers that plants release oxygen when exposed to sunlight and that they consume carbon dioxide; this is first step in our understanding of photosynthesis.

**1827** John James Audubon (American: 1785–1851) starts publication of *Birds of America*, a collection of engravings of

435 detailed paintings Audubon had made of American birds.

**1839** Theodor A.H. Schwann (German: 1810–82), building on work of Matthias Jakob Schleiden (German: 1804–81) in 1838, develops cell theory of life.

**1856** First skeleton of what we now call Neanderthals is found in cave in Neander valley, near Düsseldorf (Germany). Louis Pasteur (French: 1822–95) discovers that fermentation is caused by microorganisms.

**1858** Charles R. Darwin (English: 1809–82) and Alfred R. Wallace (English: 1823–1913) announce their theory of evolution by natural selection to the Linnean Society.

**1859** Darwin's *On the Origin of Species* is published.

**1865** Gregor Johann Mendel's (Austrian: 1822–84) theory of dominant and recessive genes is published in obscure local journal.

**1868** Workers building road in France discover skeletons of first-known Cro-Magnons in cave.

**1894** Eugène Dubois (Dutch: 1858–1940) announces discovery of "Java ape-man," now known to be first-discovered specimen of *Homo erectus*.

**1898** Mosaic disease of tobacco plants is recognized as being caused by virus, the first identification of a virus (viruses cannot be seen at this time, being known only from their effects).

**1900** Three different biologists rediscover laws of genetics originally found by Mendel.

**1919** Karl von Frisch (Austrian–German: 1886–1982) discovers that bees have language that can be used to communicate where to find good source of flower nectar.

**1924** Raymond A. Dart (Australian–South African: 1893–1988) identifies first fossil of an australopithecine, a close relative of early humans.

**1937** The kouprey, a species of wild ox, is found in Indonesia; it is the last large land animal to become known to science.

**1938** First-known live coelacanth, a lobe-finned fish believed to have been extinct for 60 million years, is captured in waters off Comoro Islands.

**1952** Eugene Aserinsky (American: 1921– ) discovers that sleep with rapid eye movements (REMs) is a distinct stage of sleep, later found to be associated with dreams.

**1953** James D. Watson (American: 1928– ) and Francis Crick (English: 1916– ) determine structure of DNA, the basis of heredity.

**1961** Louis S.B. Leakey (English: 1903–72) and Mary D. Leakey (English: 1913– ) discover a previously unknown ancestor of humans, *Homo habilis*, in the Olduvai Gorge of northern Tanzania.
Marshall W. Nirenberg (American: 1927– ) learns to read one of "letters" of genetic code.

**1968** Werner Arber (Swiss: 1929– ) discovers restriction enzymes, a class of proteins that will make genetic engineering possible.

**1969** Jonathan Beckwith (American: 1935– ) and co-workers are first to isolate a single gene.

**1970** Har Gobind Khorana (Indian-American: 1922– ) and co-workers produce first artificial gene. Howard Temin (American: 1934– ) and David Baltimore (American: 1938– ) discover enzyme that causes RNA to be transcribed to DNA, a key step in development of genetic engineering.

**1973** Stanley Cohen (American: 1922– ) and Herbert Boyer (American: 1936– ) succeed in putting specific gene into bacterium, the first instance of true genetic engineering.

**1974** Donald C. Johanson (American: 1943– ) and co-workers discover Lucy in Afar region of Ethiopia, the nearly complete skeleton of *Australopithecus afarensis*, an early relative of humans (more than 3 million years old).

**1975** César Milstein (Argentine-English: 1927– ) announces discovery of how to produce monoclonal antibodies, highly specific chemicals that can be made to react with particular proteins or other chemicals in the body.

**1980** Martin Cline (American: 1934– ) and co-workers succeed in transferring functioning gene from one mouse to another.

**1981** Chinese scientists succeed in cloning a fish.

**1982** Kary B. Bullis invents the use of the polymerase chain reaction to make copies of DNA sequences, a vital tool in finding specific genes.

**1985** Alan Walker finds "the black skull," (officially KNM-WT 17000), the stained skull of an unknown Australopithecan species that has greatly puzzled anthropologists since.

**1990** Michael T. Clegg (American: 1941– ), Edward M. Golenburg, and co-workers isolate DNA and a gene for photosynthesis from a fossilized 17-million-year-old magnolia leaf.

## MAJOR GROUPS OF LIVING ORGANISMS

Biologists classify all living things (organisms) according to a system first introduced by Carolus Linnaeus in 1735. At that time Linnaeus and other scientists divided all life forms into two kingdoms—plants and animals. Since then, biologists have learned that there are fundamental differences among organisms that go beyond the differences between plants and animals and have added three kingdoms. The five kingdoms recognized today are: Monerans, Protists, Fungi, Plants, and Animals.

Following Linnaeus, all classification terms are usually given in Latin. In the following list, English terms are substituted when they are an exact translation—for example, *animals* instead of *animalia* and *birds* instead of *aves*. If there is no exact English translation, the Latin form is kept.

Each kingdom is divided into two or more phyla (singular: phylum). Organisms within one phylum are more closely related to one another than they are to members of other phyla.

The phyla are also divided into parts, which are then further divided, each time on the basis of closer and closer relationships. In descending order of size, the main divisions are as follows:

Kingdom
  Phylum
    Class
      Order
        Family
          Genus
            Species

Many biologists add to this list by classifying groups of species with *sub-* or *super-*, as in subphylum or superfamily.

By convention, Latin names except for genus and species are given in Roman type; genus and species are italicized.

**Kingdom: Monerans** One-celled organisms with simple cells that lack a membrane around the genetic material. Bacteria do not produce their own food; blue-green algae do.
*Phylum:* Bacteria
*Phylum:* Blue-green algae, also called blue-green bacteria or cyano bacteria

**Kingdom: Protists** One-celled or colonial; complex cells that have a membrane around their genetic material; protozoans and slime molds do not produce their own food; all other phyla in this kingdom can.

*Phylum:* Protozoans
  *Class:* Ciliophora (ciliated protozoans such as Paramecium)
  *Class:* Mastigophora (protozoans with flagella such as trypanosomes; the cause of sleeping sickness)
  *Class:* Sarcodina (protozoans that move by flowing, such as amoebas)
  *Class:* Sporozoa (parasitic protozoans with no means of motion during most of their lives, such as Plasmodium, the cause of malaria)
*Phylum:* Euglenas
*Phylum:* Golden algae and diatoms
*Phylum:* Fire or golden brown algae
*Phylum:* Green algae
*Phylum:* Brown algae
*Phylum:* Red algae
*Phylum:* Slime molds

**Kingdom: Fungi** One-celled or multicelled; cells have nuclei, which stream between cells, giving the appearance that cells have many nuclei; fungi do not produce their own food.
*Phylum:* Zygomycetes (e.g., black bread-mold)
*Phylum:* Ascomycetes (includes Penicillium, truffles, yeasts)
*Phylum:* Basidiomycetes (includes mushrooms)

**Kingdom: Plants** Multicellular organisms that carry out photosynthesis; cells have nuclei and cell walls.
*Phylum:* Mosses and liverworts
*Phylum:* Horsetails
*Phylum:* Ferns
*Phylum:* Conifers
*Phylum:* Cone-bearing desert plants
*Phylum:* Cycads
*Phylum:* Ginkgoes
*Phylum:* Flowering plants
  *Subphylum:* Dicots (plants with two seed leaves—e.g., most fruits and vegetables, common flowers, and trees)
  *Subphylum:* Monocots (plants with a single seed leaf—e.g., onions, lilies, and grasses)

**Kingdom: Animals** Multicellular organisms that get their food by ingestion; most are able to move from place to place; cells have nuclei but not cell walls.
*Phylum:* Porifera (sponges)
*Phylum:* Cnidaria (jellyfish, anemones, corals)
*Phylum:* Platyhelminthes (flatworms)
*Phylum:* Nematodes (roundworms)
*Phylum:* Rotifers (microscopic wormlike or spherical animals)
*Phylum:* Bryozoa (moss animals)
*Phylum:* Brachiopods (lampshells)
*Phylum:* Phoronidea (tube worms)
*Phylum:* Annelids (segmented worms, such as earthworms, leeches)
*Phylum:* Mollusks (soft-bodied animals with a mantle and foot)
  *Class:* Chitons
  *Class:* Bivalves (clams, oysters, mussels)
  *Class:* Scaphopoda (tooth or tusk shells)
  *Class:* Gastropods (slugs and snails)
  *Class:* Cephalopods (octopus, squid)
*Phylum:* Arthropods (segmented animals with an external skeleton)
  *Class:* Horseshoe crabs

*Class:* Crustaceans (lobsters, crabs, shrimp)
*Class:* Arachnids (spiders, mites, ticks)
*Class:* Insects
*Class:* Centipedes
*Class:* Millipedes
*Phylum:* Echinoderms (starfish, brittle stars)
*Phylum:* Hemichordata (acorn worms)
*Phylum:* Chordates
  *Subphylum:* Tunicates
  *Subphylum:* Lancelets
  *Subphylum:* Vertebrates (animals with back-bones)
  *Class:* Agnatha (lampreys, hagfish)
  *Class:* Sharks and rays
  *Class:* Bony fish
  *Class:* Amphibians
  *Class:* Reptiles
  *Class:* Birds
  *Class:* Mammals
    *Subclass:* Monotremes (egg-laying mammals)
    *Subclass:* Marsupials
    *Subclass:* Placentals
      *Order:* Insectivores (shrews)
      *Order:* Flying lemurs
      *Order:* Bats
      *Order:* Primates (lemurs, monkeys, apes, humans)
      *Order:* Edentates (anteaters)
      *Order:* Pangolins
      *Order:* Lagomorphs (rabbits, hares)
      *Order:* Rodents (squirrels, rats, mice, porcupines)
      *Order:* Cetaceans (whales, dolphins)
      *Order:* Carnivores (wolves, cats, bears, raccoons, weasels, badgers, skunks, otters, hyenas)
      *Order:* Seals
      *Order:* Aardvarks
      *Order:* Elephants
      *Order:* Hyraxes
      *Order:* Sirenians (dugongs, manatees)
      *Order:* Odd-toed ungulates (horses, tapirs, rhinoceroses)
      *Order:* Even-toed ungulates (pigs, hippopotamuses, camels, deer, giraffes, pronghorns, cattle, goats, sheep)

## EVOLUTION OF THE HUMAN FAMILY

The understanding of the various relatives of modern human beings and just how they are related is undergoing great changes. Often what seems to be true one year is overturned the next. Currently there is little consensus among paleoanthropologists, the people who study early humans and their relatives, about the details of who is related to whom.

The first column below gives scientific and common names (modern paleoanthropologists shun the use of *man* to mean "human") along with the time and place in which the animal is known to have flourished.

## CLASSIFYING HUMANS

**KINGDOM: Animals** Organisms that use other organisms for food and that sometimes move rapidly.
**PHYLUM: Chordates** Animals that are partially supported by a rod of cartilage or bone vertebrae and an internal skeleton.
**SUBPHYLUM: Vertebrates** Chordates that have vertebrae, such as fish, amphibians, reptiles, birds, and mammals.
**CLASS: Mammals** Vertebrates that have hair and suckle their young.
**ORDER: Primates** Mammals that use sight more than scent, have nails instead of claws on grasping hands and feet, are mostly active in daylight, and have relatively large brains.
**SUPERFAMILY: Hominoids** Primates that are tailless, generally large in size, can climb trees, and have relatively flat faces; specifically, the great apes, australopithecines, and human beings.
**FAMILY: Hominids** Hominoids that walk upright, have small canines, and large brains; specifically, the australopithecines and human beings.
**GENUS: *Homo*** Hominids with especially large brains that make tools and show other signs of culture; specifically, *Homo habilis*, *Homo erectus*, and *Homo sapiens*.
**SPECIES: *Homo sapiens*** Modern human beings.

## THE HUMAN FAMILY TREE

| | |
|---|---|
| ***Catopithecus browni*** c. 40 million years ago Egypt | Earliest known representative of higher primates, which include Old World monkeys, apes, and humans. |
| ***Aegyptopithecus*** c. 30 million years ago Egypt | Monkeylike creature; may be earliest-known ancestor of hominoids. |
| ***Proconsul;*** three known species c. 20 million years ago East Africa | Oddly named after popular chimpanzee, Consul, in London Zoo (hence, *Proconsul*— "before Consul"); generally recognized as an ancestor of all hominoids. |
| ***Sivepithecus*** c. 10 million years ago Asia and Turkey | Once believed to be directly on he line to humans, today *Sivepithecus* is thought to be ancestor of orangutan. |
| ***Pan troglodytes*** ***Pan paniscus*** Chimpanzee c. 7 million years ago to present Sub-Saharan African forests | Several studies of proteins and DNA suggest chimpanzee is our closest living relative; some evidence indicates we are more closely related to pygmy chimpanzee or bonobo, *P. paniscus*, than to common chimp. |
| ***Australopithecus afarensis*** c. 4 million years ago Ethiopia and East Africa | Many believe *A. afarensis* is ultimate ancestor of humans, but it is not all that clear who ultimate ancestor of *A. afarensis* is. Famous fossil known as "Lucy" is member of this species, as well as group known as "The First Family." |
| ***Australopithecus africanus*** | First nonhuman hominid to be discovered (1924) and widely |

"The Taung Child"
c. 2.5 million years ago
South Africa

***Homo habilis***
"Handy Man"
c. 2.2 million years ago
East Africa

***Australopithecus boisei***
"Zinj"
"Nutcracker man"
c. 2 million years ago
East Africa

***Homo erectus***
"Java Ape Man"
"Peking Man"
c. 2 million–90,000 years ago
Africa, Asia, and Europe

***Australopithecus robustus***
c. 1.5 million years ago
South Africa

***"Neanderthal Man"***
100,000–35,000 years ago
Mostly European, but some fossils from Africa and Near East

***Archaic Homo sapiens***
c. 90,000–? years ago
Africa and possibly Europe

***Homo sapiens***
"Cro-Magnon Man"
Since 35,000 years ago
Worldwide

doubted at first. Like all australopithecines, walked upright and had brain much smaller than members of *Homo* of same size. May be an ancestor of humans.
First-known member of our own genus, and—if classified correctly—probably direct ancestor; widely believed that stone tools found that date from the same time were made by *H. habilis*. Not clear whether *H. habilis* was hunter or scavenger or both. May actually be two related species.
A still controversial classification that some would label merely East African subspecies of *A. robustus*. When first specimen was found by L.S.B. Leakey (1959), he thought it was new genus, *Zinjanthropus*—hence, nickname.
Depending on how one classes Neanderthals, this is first non-human hominid discovered (1890, by Eugène Dubois). It was successful creature who could make fire and was probably good hunter. That it did not change its basic tool kit for 1.5 million years suggests limited intelligence. Generally thought to be immediate ancestor of *Homo sapiens*. Other hominids became extinct, and by at least million years ago, *H. erectus* was only hominid on Earth, with possible exception of very early archaic *H. sapiens*.
Despite name, not especially "robust" by modern human standards; however, compared with "gracile" *A. afarensis* and *A. africanus*, this is larger and stronger species.
While general sentiment among paleoanthropologists since World War II has classified this well-known group as subspecies of modern humans—*Homo sapiens neandertalis*—current thinking is that this "cave man" of ice age may be separate species. They share certain traits with modern human, e.g., large brain and customs such as burial of dead. Anatomical differences between Neanderthals and modern humans not pronounced but are clear.
Today many anthropologists recognize that our species evolved about 90,000 years ago from *Homo erectus* but that first humans were not fully evolved. This is us! We may have started with Archaic *H. sapiens* (see above), and we may—although most think it is not likely—have evolved from Neanderthals around 35,000 years ago. In any case, we replaced all other hominids about 35,000 years ago.

# THE HUMAN BODY

**Systems** The human body consists of nine main systems: the skeleton, the muscles, the nervous system, the hormonal system, the circulatory system, the digestive system, the respiratory system, the immune system, and the reproductive system.

**Organs** Each system is made up of a number of organs. An organ is a part of the body with a specific purpose. Some organs, such as the liver or the skin, have more than one function.

**Tissues** Organs are made from tissues. A tissue is a part of the organ made from similar cells and, in some cases, extracellular material (for example, bone tissue consists of bone cells and extracellular minerals).

**Cells** are the fundamental components of all organisms. Even they are composed of several different parts—the nucleus, the cytoplasm, the cell membrane, and various smaller parts—that have different functions.

## Skeleton

**Bones** There are 206 bones in the human body, or one or two more or less, depending on how they are counted. Their main function is to provide a structural support for everything else, but they also have other vital functions. Bones might be classified as part of the circulatory system, for example, since they produce all of the body's blood cells within their marrow. Bones are also part of the hormonal system in that they are an important reservoir for calcium, an element necessary for life. If the body's intake of calcium is too low, the bones make up the deficit. This weakens their role as structural support and can result in the condition osteoporosis, or fragile bone structure.

**Cartilage** is a flexible substance that precedes bone development in children and that is found in adults at joints, places where bones meet, as well as in the nose and ears.

**Ligaments** Bones are attached to each other by flexible tissues called ligaments. A few bones, such as those in the skull, grow together, forming rigid attachments.

## Muscles

There are over 600 muscles in the body that have been named. They occur in three different systems.

**Skeletal muscles** are used to move various parts of the body. They are what one normally thinks of when one thinks of muscles, and nearly all of them are attached to bones by tendons, long or flat sheets of tough tissue. Made from fibers that are striped (or striated) in appearance under a microscope, each fiber can contract or lengthen when the muscle receives a message from the brain. Because the individual controls the use of these muscles, they are also called voluntary muscles.

**Smooth muscles** are found in the walls of the stomach and intestines, in the walls of veins and arteries, and in various other internal organs. They are for the most part not controlled by the will, so they also are known as the involuntary muscles. People do have partial control over some of the "involuntary" muscle, however; for example, you can stop the smooth muscle of the diaphragm from causing you to breathe for a time.

**Cardiac muscle** The muscles of the heart resemble both skeletal muscle in being striped and smooth muscle in its involuntary nature.

## Nervous System and Senses

**Brain** The organ that controls the rest of the body and undertakes thought is composed of three main parts. Located in the head, it is protected by the bones of the skull. The cerebrum is the folded, outer part of each half of the brain; it governs thought, the senses, and movement. The cerebellum controls balance and muscle coordination. Deep in the brain is the brain stem, which governs involuntary muscles. A small, but important, part of the human brain is the hypothalamus, which controls the hormonal system (see below).

**Spinal cord** Extending from the brain to the base of the torso, protected by the vertebrae, the spinal cord is the main highway for messages to and from the brain. The spinal cord can initiate actions on its own, which are known as reflexes.

**Nerves** Twelve pairs of cranial nerves connect directly to the brain. Ten of these pairs are connected to parts of the head concerned with sight, sound, smell, and taste, such as the optic nerves to the eyes and the auditory nerves to the ears. One part of the eye, the retina, is actually an exposed part of the brain, the only part in direct contact with the outside world. The vagus nerves extend to various organs of the torso, where they control involuntary muscles. The twelfth pair of cranial nerves are connected to the shoulder, where they are mostly involved in the sense of position (e.g., knowing in what position your arms are).

Thirty-one pairs of spinal nerves connect to the spinal cord and are the nerves involved in touch and other sensations, in control of skeletal muscles, and in partial control over internal organs. For example, the median nerve connects from the spinal cord to the finger muscles. Some nerves connected to the cranial and spinal nerves form the autonomic nervous system, one set of nerves that handles stress and another set of nerves that directly controls most of the organs of the body.

**Sense organs** Specialized organs mediate several of the senses—sight, sound, smell, and taste. The eye contains a lens that focuses light upon the retina, where it sends signals to the rest of the brain. The ear consists of the outer (visible) ear that gathers sounds, a middle ear with an ingenious arrangement for transmitting sound, and an inner ear that uses tiny hairs in a liquid to detect sound waves and transmit them to the auditory nerve. Both the nose and tongue contain cells that detect chemicals, resulting in the senses of smell and taste.

## Hormonal System

Hormones are chemicals produced in the body that control various body processes. The important chemicals used to regulate activity of the nervous system (such as dopamine and serotonin) and various other chemical messengers are not considered hormones, however. See the chart "Human Hormones—Their Function and Gland(s) of Origin" for the main hormones and their purposes.

Many hormones are produced by organs called glands. Some hormones are produced by organs that have other purposes as well and are not considered glands. For example, the stomach, the heart, and the small intestine all produce important hormones. For the most part, glands come in two varieties—those that release hormones into the blood and those that release chemicals through tubes called ducts. The former are called endocrine glands, and the latter are known as exocrine glands. Some glands, such as the pancreas, have both endocrine and exocrine functions. The exocrine glands are all part of the digestive system, and, with the exception of the pancreas, are included under that heading.

**Major endocrine glands** are the following:
**Pineal** Responds to light and helps regulate reproduction. Located in the forehead.
**Pituitary** Under control of the brain, this "master gland" produces hormones that control many other glands and also produces growth hormone. Located in the head, below the center of the brain.
**Thyroid** Regulates metabolism, growth, and calcium uptake by bones. Located in the neck or just below it.
**Parathyroids** Regulate the release of stored calcium from bones. Located on the thyroid gland.
**Adrenals** Help regulate blood pressure, blood sugar, and the sex drive and also partially control metabolism. Located in the abdomen.
**Pancreas** Controls blood sugar. The pancreas, located in the abdomen, is also a part of the digestive system; acting as an exocrine gland, it releases chemicals that break down fats, carbohydrates, and proteins in the small intestine.
**Ovaries** Produce hormones that regulate pregnancy, produce female secondary sexual characteristics, and also help control calcium uptake into bones. Located in the pelvis in women.
**Testes** Produce secondary sexual characteristics in males and are involved in sperm production. Located in a sack suspended below the penis in men.

## Circulatory System

Blood is the main messenger that carries chemicals around the body, although its white cells are essentially part of the immune system and are treated under that heading. If blood flow is cut off from any organ, the organ cannot obtain oxygen, it has no nutrients, and it cannot get rid of wastes. After a short time, the cells of the organ die.

**Blood** is a complex substance that contains a number of different kinds of cells and extracellular substances. It can be described as the body's only liquid organ. Its red color comes from erythrocytes, commonly known as red blood cells. Unlike true cells, erythrocytes lack nuclei and internal structure. They are produced by true cells in the bone marrow (called stem cells). Erythrocytes carry oxygen needed by cells for metabolism and to remove carbon dioxide, produced when cells metabolize. Another component of blood is also made by the bone's stem cells—the platelets, which are even less like cells than erythrocytes. Their function is to keep blood from flowing out of the body when there is a break in the circulatory system—to cause clotting. About half of blood is an extracellular mix of water and chemicals that is called plasma or (when separated from proteins that, with the platelets, are involved in clotting) serum. Lymphocytes and phagocytes (white blood cells) are found in the blood, also (see "Immune System").

**Blood vessels** are a closed system of tubes that carry blood throughout the body. Vessels carrying blood away from the heart are called arteries. Arteries have strong, four-layered walls to maintain blood under pressure. Arteries connect to very tiny tubes with quite thin walls called capillaries. The walls are so thin that oxygen and nutrients pass through them to reach the cells, while carbon dioxide and wastes from the cells enter through the walls into the blood. The waste-carrying blood then passes into vessels that lead back to the heart, the veins. Most of the blood pressure has been lost by this point, so veins do not need the strong walls of arteries. Instead, veins need and have valves that ensure the blood does not travel in the wrong direction.

**Heart** Primarily a pump that pushes the blood through blood vessels, it consists of four chambers. Blood from the body enters the chamber known as the right atrium and is pumped through a valve to a larger chamber below the atrium called the right ventricle, which pumps the blood into an artery leading to the lungs. After picking up oxygen and leaving carbon dioxide behind, the blood returns to the heart, entering the left atrium. The blood is pumped through a valve to the left ventricle, which is the largest chamber (and therefore the most powerful pump). The left ventricle sends the blood into the arteries that lead to the body. The heart is also an endocrine gland, secreting a hormone that helps regulate blood pressure.

**Spleen** This organ is a cleaner and storehouse for blood. Chiefly, it removes damaged red blood cells or platelets. It also stores excess blood and red blood cells until they are needed. Some now believe it may have a role in the immune system. A person can live without a spleen.

**Kidneys** and the bladder and associated tubes are often considered the urinary system. Technically, however, kidneys are part of the circulatory system in that they remove chemical wastes from blood. They also act as an endocrine gland by secreting hormones that aid in regulating blood pressure. Additionally, they regulate the composition of blood, keeping it from becoming too acid or alkaline. The wastes removed by the kidneys are dissolved in water as urine, which is stored in the bladder before passing through the urethra to leave the body.

## Digestive System

The digestive system consists largely of a pathway for food from the mouth to the anus with several ducted or exocrine glands that empty into it (the pancreas, one of these, is treated as part of the hormonal system).

**Teeth** Thirty-two permanent teeth (if none have been lost) in an adult are used to chop food into small bits.

**Salivary glands** release saliva, the first of many enzymes (proteins that promote particular chemical reactions) that are used to break down large molecules, such as carbohydrates, proteins, and fats, into smaller molecules that the body can then reassemble to meet its needs. Saliva breaks down some starches into sugars, as you can tell by noticing how much sweeter a cracker becomes if you chew it and then keep it in your mouth for a short while.

**Tongue** While an important organ of speech in humans, the tongue is basically the part of the digestive system that moves food around and pushes it down the throat.

**Esophagus** This is a tube through which food moves on its way to the stomach. The pyloric valve at its base prevents food from traveling back up again.

**Stomach** This organ produces enzymes (and therefore acts as a gland) and hydrochloric acid. These are mixed with the food by churning motions of the stomach, which also tend to break food into smaller particles, even as the stomach enzymes and acid are chemically changing food. From this point forward, one can no longer call this soup of nutrients food.

**Liver** The main chemical factory of the body and, after the skin, the largest organ in the body is the liver. As part of the digestive system, it acts as a ducted, or exocrine, gland that produces bile, a substance that helps reduce the acidity of the nutrient mixture and also helps break down fats. The liver is also part of the circulatory system, since it cleans poisons out of the blood and regulates blood's composition in various other ways. In many cases the liver scavenges unwanted chemicals from the blood, takes them apart, and reassembles the parts into needed chemicals.

**Gall bladder** This organ simply stores bile from the liver until food is consumed, at which time it releases the bile into the small intestine.

**Small intestine** Like the stomach, the 21-foot-long small intestine produces enzymes that further break down the nutrients that pass through it. The upper portion of the small intestine is called the duodenum. As nutrients become broken into small enough molecules, they are able to pass through projections, or villi, in the wall of the small intestine into the blood.

**Large intestine** With most of the nutrients gone, the remains of the food pass into the 5-foot-long large intestine as a kind of soup. Water is transferred to the blood from the soup through the walls of the capillaries that line the large intestine.

**Rectum** A short tube collects the partially dehydrated waste in preparation for evacuation, which is through a valve called the anus.

## Respiratory System

The main purpose of the respiratory system is to get oxygen to the blood and to remove carbon dioxide. Along the way, the air is sampled for chemicals (smelled), partly cleaned, and frequently used to make sounds.

**Nose** In addition to being an organ of smell, the nose is the place best designed to admit air into the body, for it can warm and moisten it, and hairs in the nose can filter out dust. Often

there is a need for more air than can pass through the nose, however, and the mouth is used as a supplemental way to take in air. From either the nose or the mouth, air then passes through the throat (also called the pharynx). The sinuses are air-filled cavities in the skull that are connected to the nose.

**Trachea** After passing through your throat, air goes into a tube called the trachea. A flap called the epiglottis closes the top of the trachea when food or water is being swallowed and opens to permit air to enter the trachea. The trachea branches into two tubes called bronchi (singular, *bronchus*) that carry the air into the lungs.

**Larynx** Near the top of the trachea is the larynx, or voice box. The main feature of the larynx is a pair of membranes that stretch across the air passageway. As air is exhaled, these membranes can be tightened across the passage to produce sound.

**Lungs,** the principal organs of respiration, are two large spongy masses located in the chest that are protected by the ribs. Air enters a lung through a bronchus. The bronchus is divided into smaller bronchial tubes, which continue to divide until they become very fine tubes called bronchioles. Each bronchiole ends in a cluster of tiny round bodies called an air sac. As small as air sacs are, each of these contains even smaller cavities called alveoli. It is in the thin-walled alveoli that the exchange of oxygen to and carbon dioxide from the blood actually takes place. The lungs contain about 300 million aveoli, and although each alveolus is tiny, the total surface area they present is about 40 times the surface area of the skin.

**Diaphragm** The reason air moves in and out of the body is that the volume of the lungs is continually being changed. The principal agent of change is the diaphragm, a muscle stretched across the abdomen just below the lungs. When the diaphragm is pulled down, the volume of the chest cavity is increased, causing air to enter the lungs. Similarly, when the diaphragm is pulled up, it reduces the volume of the chest cavity and expels air. This process is aided by the muscles of the rib case, which also expand and contract the size of the chest cavity.

## Immune System

The immune system was not recognized as a separate system until recently. Although evidence of immune protection was known in ancient times, the first inkling of how the body develops immunity was in 1884, when macrophages (see "Phagocytes" below) were first observed. Since then, many different components of the system have been found. Much still remains to be learned about this system, however.

**Skin** Although a part of the immune system, skin is often viewed as simply a barrier between the body and the outside world. The largest organ in the body, the skin is far more complex. Its immune functions include not only the barrier against invaders but also production of oil and sweat, both of which kill or retard many bacteria and fungi. On the other hand, the skin harbors millions of helpful bacteria that resist invasion by other bacteria. The skin even has a role in the development of some lymphocytes (white blood cells—see below).

Skin also helps regulate body temperature, helps produce cholesterol (a necessary body chemical, even though it is inadvisable to have too much of it in our blood), and is the location of sensors for heat, cold, and pressure.

**Thymus** The thymus is a medium-size organ in the upper chest that looks as if it could be an endocrine gland (and was often identified as one in the past). It becomes smaller as a person ages. In some as-yet-unknown way, the thymus "trains" certain lymphocytes to be part of the immune system. If the thymus is removed from a very young animal, the animal does not develop the immune response that causes transplant rejection, for example.

**Lymphatic system** When blood passes through capillaries, it loses some of its plasma, which becomes part of a liquid between the cells. This liquid is known as lymph. Lymph needs to be returned to the circulatory system to keep the blood volume fairly constant, so a system of tubes called the lymphatic system drains the lymph back into the blood. Along the way it passes through masses of spongy tissue called lymph nodes that filter out any debris, including bacteria, from the lymph. Lymph nodes are made of lymphoid tissue, but they are not the only organs where lymphoid tissue is found; it is found everywhere that bacteria or other germs can easily invade the body, specifically in the linings of the parts of the body exposed to the outside, such as the respiratory system and parts of the digestive system. Most of the action of the immune system takes place in lymphoid tissue.

**Lymphocytes** Although lymphocytes are known as white blood cells, they are found in the lymph as well as in the blood. Draining all the lymph from an animal's body would remove all the lymphocytes, which would suppress immune reactions. Like red blood cells, lymphocytes are produced in bone marrow, a very well-protected place, suggesting their importance to the body. Scientists have found and continue to find many distinct types of lymphocytes, but there seem to be two main varieties.

The T lymphocytes are those that must mature in the thymus before they can be involved in the immune response. The *T* is for *thymus*. They are the principal cells involved in graft rejection, but they also play a role in fighting bacteria and other invaders. A deficiency of one type of T cell is a major symptom of the disease AIDS, although AIDS seems to affect the immune system in many other ways as well.

The B lymphocytes mature directly in the bone, but the *B* does not stand for *bone*. In birds, B lymphocytes mature in an organ that humans do not have, the bursa of Fabricius, and the *B* stands for *bursa*. B cells react to invaders by releasing chemicals called antibodies. An antibody is a chemical that is specific to a particular protein, sugar, nucleic acid, or fat, but the strongest reaction is with proteins. If, for example, a measles virus is in the blood or lymph, a B lymphocyte will release an antibody that attaches to a protein on the surface of the virus. In some unknown way, one kind of T cell then stimulates the production of many B cells

## HUMAN HORMONES—THEIR FUNCTION AND GLAND(S) OF ORIGIN

| Hormone | Associated gland(s) | Function |
|---|---|---|
| Adrenaline (epinephrine) | Adrenal medulla | Increases blood sugar, pulse, and blood pressure |
| Adrenocorticotropic hormone (ACTH) | Anterior pituitary | Stimulates adrenal cortex |
| Aldosterone | Adrenal cortex | Controls reabsorption of sodium and potassium by kidneys |
| Calcitonin (Thyrocalcitonin) | Thyroid gland | Lowers level of calcium in blood by inhibiting calcium release from bones |
| Cholecystokinin (CCK) | Glands in small intestine | Stimulates pancreatic secretions and contraction of gall bladder |
| Chorionic gonadotropin | Placenta | Stimulates ovaries to continue producing estrogens and progesterone during early stages of pregnancy; hormone detected in pregnancy test |
| Cortisol and related hormones | Adrenal cortex | Affect metabolism of proteins, carbo-hydrates, and lipids; reduce inflammation |
| Estrogens | Ovaries and placenta | Stimulate development of secondary sexual characteristics in females; help regulate ovaries and uterus during menstrual cycle and pregnancy |
| Follicle-stimulating hormone (FSH) | Anterior pituitary | Stimulates follicle development in females and sperm production in males |
| Gastrin | Glands in stomach | Stimulates secretion of gastric juice |
| Glucagon | Pancreas (Islet cells) | Increases blood sugar level by stimulating breakdown of glycogen |
| Growth hormone (somatotropin or somatotrophic hormone or STP) | Anterior pituitary | Stimulates bone and muscle growth |
| Insulin | Pancreas (Islet cells) | Lowers blood sugar level and increases storage of glycogen |
| Luteinizing hormone (LH) | Anterior pituitary | Stimulates ovulation and formation of corpus luteum in females and testosterone production in males |
| Norepinephrine | Adrenal medulla | Increases metabolic rate and constricts blood vessels |
| Oxytocin | Produced in hypothalamus, stored in posterior pituitary | Causes sex to be pleasurable; stimulates uterine contractions during childbirth and milk release |
| Parathormone (Parathyroid hormone or PTH) | Parathyroid glands | Increases level of calcium in blood by increasing calcium release from bones; decreases blood phosphate level |
| Progesterone | Ovaries and placenta | Helps regulate uterus during menstrual cycle and pregnancy |
| Prolactin (lactogenic hormone or LTH) | Anterior pituitary | Stimulates milk production (lactation) |
| Secretin | Glands in small intestine | Stimulates secretion of pancreatic digestive juices |
| Testosterone (androgens) | Testes | Stimulates development of male sex organs and secondary sexual characteristics; supports sperm production |
| Thyroid-stimulating hormone (TSH) | Anterior pituitary | Stimulates thyroid gland to produce and secrete thyroxin |
| Thyroxin (Thyroxine) | Thyroid gland | Controls rate of metabolism and growth |
| Vasopressin | Produced in hypothalamus, stored in posterior pituitary | Controls reabsorption of water by kidneys; increases blood pressure |

that release the same antibody. The next measles virus that comes along is met with great amounts of the antibody, causing immunity to measles.

**Phagocytes** There are many other cells produced as part of the immune system by the bone marrow that were formerly grouped under the general heading "white blood cell," including neutrophils, mast cells, and macrophages. When an antibody binds to a protein, it attracts a macrophage, which proceeds to "eat" it, thus removing it. The ability to ingest cells indicates that macrophages are phagocytes, or "eaters of cells." The macrophage also pushes the original protein that triggered the antibody to its surface, where it projects from the cell membrane and causes more B lymphocytes to make the antibody against it. Neutrophils are smaller phagocytes than macrophages, or "big eaters." Mast cells collect near a source of infection and release the chemical histamine, which causes phagocytes to gather and quell the infection.

## Reproductive System

The male and female reproductive systems differ in fundamental ways.

**Male reproductive system** Sperm are formed in the two testes, which hang below the groin, so situated because human body temperature is too high for proper sperm formation. Sperm are stored in the epididymis, just above the testes. During sex the sperm move through tubes and are mixed with secretions from the prostate and Cowper's gland, both ducted glands. The result is called semen. Semen exits the body through a tube in the penis called the urethra, which is otherwise used for excretion of urine.

**Female reproductive system** Corresponding to the testes in males, the ovaries produce eggs (also known as ova). Unlike sperm, eggs can be produced at human body temperature, allowing for the ovaries and related organs to be located inside the pelvis. Eggs pass through the Fallopian tubes to the uterus, or womb, which is sealed at the other end by the cervix. On the other side of the cervix is a muscular tube called the vagina, or birth canal.

**Pregnancy and birth** Female physiology changes considerably during pregnancy, although the organs remain the same, with one exception. Sperm that have been implanted in the vagina swim to the uterus, where they fertilize an egg. The egg gradually develops into an embryo attached to a new organ, which consists of the placenta and cord. The placenta has many functions, including the production of hormones, making it an endocrine gland. It is formed from tissue both from the embryo and from the uterus. When the baby is fully formed, the cervix opens and the baby passes through the vagina, still attached to its mother by the cord, which is cut at the navel. The placenta also passes through the vagina and is discarded.

## Human Hormones

Hormones are chemicals made in the body that regulate body functions or achieve specific tasks. Some are fairly familiar, such as insulin and estrogen. Others, though less familiar, are clear from their description or name, for example, growth hormone. Increasingly, hormones are available either as products of genetic engineering (human insulin and human growth hormone, for example) or as synthetics. The notorious steroids used for body building are synthetic testosterone. (See "Health and Medicine.") Such manufactured hormones offer both the promise of relief from hormone-deficiency diseases and the possibility of hormone abuse.

## Elements of the Human Body

The normal human body contains almost all of the chemical elements, mostly in small amounts. Not all are used by the body, and some elements found in tiny quantities in the body are poisonous, such as lead.

The elements that the body uses are necessary for health. For the body to grow, it needs large amounts of elements found in four major nutrients—proteins, carbohydrates, fats, and water—as well as smaller amounts of other elements, known as minerals. When very small amounts are needed, the minerals are called trace elements. Vitamins, the remaining nutrient, are needed compounds that the body cannot make itself in sufficient quantity.

## ELEMENTS IN A 150-POUND INDIVIDUAL

| Element | Weight (lbs.) | Use by the body | Element | Weight (lbs.) | Use by the body |
|---|---|---|---|---|---|
| Oxygen | 97.5 | Part of all major nutrients, which make up tissues of the body, but also vital to production of energy in form of elemental oxygen obtained from air. | Magnesium | 0.06 | Required by both plants (it is in chlorophyll) and animals. In humans, works with enzymes to speed chemical reactions, is involved in transmission of messages between nerves, and has a role in bone structure. |
| Carbon | 27.0 | Essential element for life—most compounds based on carbon are called organic, meaning "from life." An essential part of proteins, carbohydrates, and fats, the building blocks of human cells. | Iron | 0.006 | Essential for carrying oxygen to cells and carbon dioxide waste away, although present only in small amount; lack of iron causes anemia. |
| Hydrogen | 15.0 | Part of each of major nutrients, and thus a building block of every cell. Unlike oxygen, has no part in respiration. | Cobalt | 0.00024 | Part of vitamin $B_{12}$, found in meats and dairy products; its exact role in the body is not well understood. |
| Nitrogen | 4.5 | Essential part of proteins, DNA, and RNA, the compounds most active in controlling cells; most of the body's functions depend on nitrogen compounds at one stage or another. | Copper | 0.00023 | Helps form red blood cells, maintain nervous system, and regulate cholesterol levels. |
| Calcium | 3.0 | Mostly locked into hard compounds that form nonliving parts of bone. One of principal messengers between cells, telling them when to act and when to stay quiet. | Manganese | 0.00020 | Aids in bone formation, helps regulate nervous system, and is part of sex hormones. |
| Phosphorus | 1.8 | Important element in bone building, but, like calcium, has another role: it is essential in producing energy in cell. | Iodine | 0.00006 | Part of thyroid hormone that controls rate at which food is burned for energy. |
| Potassium | 0.3 | Regulates contraction of muscle cells (and some other cell functions) along with sodium. In general, potassium is involved with muscle contractions and general maintenance of pressure a cell exerts on its covering membrane. | Zinc | trace | Needed for some enzymes, for proper sex development, in healing wounds, for sense of taste, and for normal sperm count. |
| Sulfur | 0.3 | Essential to most forms of life. An important constituent of proteins. | Boron | trace | Low levels required by plants, and hence, element appears in human body, but its role, if any, is not known. |
| Chlorine | 0.3 | Used in form of chloride ions to transport messages from the body to cells; helps regulate electrical activity. | Aluminum | trace | Its role in the body is not clear, but too much aluminum may have role in Alzheimer's disease or other neurological disorders. |
| Sodium | 0.165 | Required by vertebrates to control fluid pressure in cells. | Vanadium | trace | Its role, if any, in the body is poorly understood. |
| | | | Molybdenum | trace | Contained in various enzymes. |
| | | | Silicon | trace | Among most abundant elements on Earth, so is not surprising to find silicon in the body, but its necessity to any essential function is unclear. |
| | | | Fluorine | trace | Strengthens teeth and bones. |
| | | | Chromium | trace | Used in metabolism of sugar and the regulation of fats. |
| | | | Selenium | trace | In small amounts, may reduce cell damage and promote growth. |

# Mathematics

Strictly speaking, mathematics is not considered a science but a separate branch of learning on its own. Because the use of mathematics has been so important to science, however, it is generally treated along with sciences.

Mathematics consists of a set of abstract symbols and of rules for manipulating them, along with the results of that manipulation. Because of this, some have classified mathematics as a kind of game, while others view it as a kind of language. Many mathematicians believe there is a much deeper reality than those classifications, but it is one that is very difficult to explain. Even when mathematics is treated as a game, the results seem to be strongly connected to the real world.

Most people learn numbers, arithmetic, and some geometry in elementary school. In high school more mathematics is taught, perhaps including the calculus. Almost all the mathematics taught in elementary school or high school is at least 300 years old. In the past 300 years, mathematicians have developed many new branches of the subject often requiring years of special training even to understand the basic parts. This section, however, focuses on aspects of mathematics useful in daily life or that may be encountered in school by non-mathematicians.

## MILESTONES IN THE HISTORY OF MATHEMATICS

*B.C.*

**c. 20,000** People in Near East begin using notches to record numbers.

**c. 3500** Egyptians develop numeration system that can record very large numbers, with different symbols for ones, tens, hundreds, etc.

**c. 2400** A numeration system based on place value (similar to Hindu-Arabic system) is introduced in Mesopotamia.

**c. 2000** Mesopotamian mathematicians learn how to solve quadratic equations.

**c. 1900** Mesopotamian mathematicians discover what we now call the Pythagorean theorem: The sum of the squares of the legs of a right triangle equals the square of the hypotenuse.

**c. 470** Mathematician Hippasus of Metapontum (Greek: fl.c. 500) discovers dodecahedron, a regular solid with 12 faces.

**c. 450** Pythagoreans show that some measures, such as $\sqrt{2}$, cannot be measured in units; today we call these irrational numbers.

**c. 300** Euclid's (Greek: fl.c. 300) *Elements* shows that virtually all parts of mathematics known at the time could be proved from short list of assumptions.

**c. 260** In Central America, Maya develop numeration system based on place value.

**c. 230** Apollonius of Perga (Greek: c. 262– 190) writes *Conics*, an analysis of such curves as parabola, ellipse, and hyperbola.

*A.D.*

**876** The first-known use of a symbol for zero occurs in India.

**c. 1100** Poet, mathematician, and astronomer Omar Khayyám (Persian: 1048–c. 1131) develops geometric methods for solving cubic equations.

**1321** Levi ben Gershom (Gersonides; French: 1288-1344) is first to use mathematical induction in a proof.

**c. 1515** Scipione del Ferro (Italian: 1465–1526) discovers algebraic method for solving one form of cubic equations.

**1536** Niccolò Tartaglia (Italian: 1499–1557) announces he is able to solve two types of cubic equations.

**1545** Girolamo Cardano's (Italian: 1501–76) *Ars Magna* contains Lodovico Ferrari's (Italian: 1522–65) complete solution of the quartic as well as complete solution of the cubic based on Tartaglia's work.

**1572** Rafael Bombelli (Italian: 1526–c. 1573) uses complex numbers to solve equations.

**1614** John Napier (Scottish: 1550–1617) describes logarithms.

**1637** René Descartes (French: 1596–1650) publishes first account of analytic geometry; also discovered by Pierre de Fermat (French: 1601–65).

**1639** Gérard Desargues (French: 1591–1661) introduces projective geometry.

**1654** Blaise Pascal (French: 1623–62) and Pierre de Fermat (French: 1601–65) develop basic laws of probability.

**1666** Sir Isaac Newton (English: 1642–1727) describes his invention of the calculus but does not have it published at this time.

**1684** Gottfried Wilhelm Leibniz (German: 1646–1716) publishes first account of his independent discovery of the calculus, the first description to reach print.

**1763** Gaspard Monge (French: 1746–1818) invents descriptive geometry, the mathematical techniques that are basis of mechanical drawing and most architects' plans.

**1799** Karl Friedrich Gauss (German: 1777– 1855) proves fundamental theorem of algebra, which is that every polynomial equation has solution.
Paolo Ruffini (Italian: 1765–1822) offers first proof that not all polynomial equations of fifth degree can be solved by algebraic methods.

**1801** Gauss publishes *Disquisitiones arithmeticae*, greatly extending number theory.

**1822** Jean-Victor Poncelet (French: 1788–1867) further develops projective geometry.

**1826** Nikolai Ivanovich Lobachevski (Russian: 1793–1856) gives first public address concerning non-Euclidean geometry.

**1837** Pierre Wantzel (French: 1814–48) proves an angle cannot be trisected with compass and straightedge alone.

**1854** Georg F.B. Riemann (German: 1826–66) shows that several non-Euclidean geometries are possible (including one Albert Einstein (German-American: 1879– 1955) later demonstrated was the most likely geometry of the universe).

**1873** Charles Hermite (French: 1822–1901) shows that the number *e* is not solution to any polynomial equation with rational numbers as coefficients; *e* is therefore transcendental number.

**1877** Georg F.L.P. Cantor (German: 1845– 1918) shows that number of points in a line segment is same as number in interior of a square.

**1881** Josiah Willard Gibbs (American: 1839– 1903) introduces vector analysis.

**1882** Ferdinand von Lindemann (German: 1852– 1939) proves that $\pi$ is transcendental, implying the circle cannot be squared with straightedge and compass.

**1892** Cantor proves there are at least two types of infinities—specifically, that infinity of real numbers (including all infinite decimals) is bigger than infinity of counting numbers (1, 2, 3, . . .).

**1900** David Hilbert (German: 1862–1943) proposes his famous list of 23 unsolved problems.

**1931** Kurt Gödel (Austrian-American: 1906–78) shows that any formal system strong enough to include laws of arithmetic is either incomplete or inconsistent: *incomplete* if not all true theorems can be proved or *inconsistent* if two contradictory theorems can be proved.

**1936** Independently, Alan M. Turing (English: 1912–54) and Alonzo Church (American: 1903– ) discover there is no single infallible method for proving whether a statement in mathematics is true or false.

**1949** Claude E. Shannon (American: 1916– ) publishes his work on information thery, a general approach to handling communications.

**1976** In first major computer-assisted proof, it is shown that any map can be colored with four colors in such a way that no two regions of the same color share common border.

**1980** Classification of all finite simple groups, started in 1830, is completed, perhaps longest proof in history of mathematics.

**1989** Miklos Laczkovich (Hungarian) proves that a circle can be cut into a finite number of pieces that can be reassembled into a square.

## COMMONLY USED MATHEMATICAL FORMULAS

Most formulas needed in solving everyday problems are collected below, with special emphasis on formulas relating to measurements, as these are used in everything from sewing to building a house. However, some important formulas from algebra, graphing, and trigonometry are at the end. Additional formulas can also be found in "Basic Laws of Physics."

**General** The **distance *d*,** given the rate *r* and the time *t*:

$$d = rt$$

**Length** The **perimeter (distance around) *p* of any polygon** (closed plane figure with straight sides that do not cross), given the lengths of the sides $a$, b, c, and so forth:

$$p = a + b + c + \ldots$$

**Perimeter $p$ of a rectangle**, given the length $l$ and the width $w$:

$$p = 2l + 2w$$

**Perimeter $p$ of a square**, given the length of a side $s$:

$$p = 4s$$

**Circumference (distance around) $C$ of a circle**, given the diameter $d$ (distance across) or the radius $r$ (distance from the center to the circle):

$$C = \pi d$$
or
$$C = 2\pi r$$

The number $\pi$ is an infinite decimal that begins 3.14159 . . ., which is often approximated as either 3.14 or as 22/7.

**Area** In each of the following, the area (amount of surface) is $A$. For three-dimensional figures, $A$ is the total surface area.

**Rectangle**, given the length $l$ and the width $w$:
$$A = lw$$

**Square**, given the length of a side $s$:
$$A = s^2$$

**Circle**, given the radius $r$:
$$A = \pi r^2$$

**Triangle**, given the base $b$ and the height $h$:
$$A = \tfrac{1}{2} bh$$

**Right triangle**, given the lengths $a$ and $b$ of the two sides (legs) that form the right angle:
$$A = \tfrac{1}{2} ab$$

**Parallelogram**, given the base $b$ and the height $h$:
$$A = bh$$

**Trapezoid**, given the two bases $B$ and $b$ and the height $h$:
$$A = \tfrac{1}{2} h(B + b)$$

**Kite**, given the lengths of the two diagonals $D$ and $d$:
$$A = \tfrac{1}{2} Dd$$

**Regular polygon** (polygon with all sides of equal length and all angles of equal measure), given the perimeter $p$ and the apothem $a$ (the distance from the center of the regular polygon to one of its sides):
$$A = \tfrac{1}{2} ap$$

**Equilateral triangle** (all sides the same length), given the length of a side $s$:
$$A = \frac{s^2 \sqrt{3}}{4}$$

**Heron's Formula** Any **triangle**, given half the length of the perimeter (the semiperimeter) $s$ and the lengths of the sides $a$, $b$, and $c$:
$$A = \sqrt{s(s-a)(s-b)(s-c)}$$

**Right circular cylinder** (a cylinder with a circular region as its base whose sides make a right angle with the base), given the radius $r$ of the base and the height $h$ of the cylinder:
$$A = 2\pi r(h + r)$$

**Right circular cone** (a cone with a circular region as its base and whose altitude makes a right angle with the base), given the radius $r$ of the base and the slant height $l$ of the cone (the shortest distance from the tip of the cone to the circle of the base):
$$A = \pi r(l + r)$$

**Sphere**, given the radius $r$:
$$A = 4\pi r^2$$

**Volume** In each of the following, the volume (space enclosed) is $V$.

**Cube**, given the length of an edge $e$:
$$V = e^3$$

**Right rectangular prism** (box), given the length $l$, the width $w$, and the height $h$
$$V = lwh$$

**Prism**, given the area of the base $B$ and the height $h$:
$$V = Bh$$

**Right circular cylinder**, given the radius $r$ of the base and the height $h$:
$$V = \pi r^2 h$$

**Right circular cone**, given the radius $r$ of the base and the height $h$:
$$V = \tfrac{1}{3} \pi r^2 h$$

**Pyramid**, given the area of the base $B$ and the height $h$:
$$V = \tfrac{1}{3} Bh$$

**Sphere**, given the radius $r$:
$$V = \tfrac{4}{3} \pi r^3$$

**Algebra** If $a$, $b$, and $x$ are any numbers or variables ("unknowns"):

$$(a + b)^2 = a^2 + 2ab + b^2$$
$$(a - b)^2 = a^2 - 2ab + b^2$$
$$x^2 - a^2 = (x + a)(x - a)$$
$$x^3 - a^3 = (x - a)(x^2 + ax + a^2)$$
$$x^3 + a^3 = (x + a)(x^2 - ax + a^2)$$

If $a$, $b$, $c$, and $d$ are any numbers or variables except that neither $b$ nor $d$ can be zero:

$$a/b + c/d = (ad + bc)/bd$$
$$a/b - c/d = (ad - bc)/bd$$
$$a/b \times c/d = ac/bd$$
$$a/b \div c/d = ad/bc \ (c \neq 0)$$

**Quadratic formula** for the solutions of a second degree polynomial equation in one variable of the form $ax^2 + bx + c = 0$:
$$x = \frac{-b \pm \sqrt{b^2 - 4ac}}{2a}$$

**Laws of exponents**, given that $a$, $b$, $x$, and $y$ are numbers or variables:

$$a^x a^y = a^{x+y}$$
$$(a^x)^y = a^{xy}$$
$$(ab)^x = a^x b^x$$
$$(a/b)^x = a^x/b^x$$
$$a^x/a^y = a^{x-y}$$
$$a^{-x} = 1/a^x$$
$$a^0 = 1$$
$$a^1 = a$$

**Laws of logarithms**, given that $a$, $b$, $x$, and $y$ are positive numbers, $c$ is any real number, and $a \neq 1$, $b \neq 1$.

$$\log_a (xy) = \log_a x + \log_a y$$
$$\log_a 1/x = -\log_a x$$
$$\log_a (x/y) = \log_a x - \log_a y$$
$$\log_a (x^c) = c \log_a x$$
$$\log_b x = (\log_a x)/(\log_a b)$$
$$\log_a 1 = 0$$
$$\log_a a = 1$$
$$a^{\log_a x} = x$$
$$\log_a (a^c) = c$$

**Graphs** In a rectangular (Cartesian) coordinate plane, where the horizontal axis is $x$ and the vertical axis is $y$:

**Slope of a line**, $m$, given two particular points $(x_1, y_1)$ and $(x_2, y_2)$ where $x_1 \neq x_2$:
$$m = (y_2 - y_1)/(x_2 - x_1)$$

**Point-slope equation** of a line, given the slope $m$ and a point on the nonvertical line $(x_1, y_1)$:
$$y - y_1 = m(x - x_1)$$

**Slope-intercept equation** of a line, given the slope $m$ and the $y$-intercept $b$ (the number on the $y$ axis where the line crosses the $y$ axis):
$$y = mx + b$$

**Distance $d$ between any two points, $(x_1, y_1)$ and $(x_2, y_2)$:**
$$d = \sqrt{(x_2 - x_1)^2 + (y_2 - y_1)^2}$$

**Trigonometry** In a **right triangle** whose two shorter sides (or legs) are $a$ and $b$, opposite angles $A$ and $B$ respectively, and whose longest side (or hypotenuse, always the side opposite the right angle, $C$) is $c$:

**Pythagorean Theorem:**
$$c^2 = a^2 + b^2$$

**Trigonometric Functions:**

sine: $\sin A = a/c$
cosine: $\cos A = b/c$
tangent: $\tan A = a/b$
cotangent: $\cot A = b/a$
secant: $\sec A = c/b$
cosecant: $\csc A = c/a$

In any triangle labeled such that side $a$ is opposite angle $A$, side $b$ is opposite angle $B$, and side $c$ is opposite angle $C$:

**Angle sum:**
$$A + B + C = 180°$$

**Law of Sines:**
$$(\sin A)/a = (\sin B)/b = (\sin C)/c$$

**Law of Cosines:**
$$c^2 = a^2 + b^2 - 2ab \cos C$$

If $x$ is any real number or a measure of an angle in degrees, the following statements are true for all:

**Defining Trigonometric Identities:**

$$\tan x = \sin x/\cos x$$
$$\cot x = \cos x/\sin x$$
$$\sec x = 1/\cos x$$
$$\csc x = 1/\sin x$$
$$\cot x = 1/\tan x$$

**Trigonometric Identities of Symmetry:**

$$\sin (-x) = -\sin x \quad \cos (-x) = \cos x$$
$$\tan (-x) = -\tan x \quad \cot (-x) = -\cot x$$
$$\sec (-x) = \sec x \quad \csc (-x) = -\csc x$$

**Pythagorean Identities:**

$$\sin^2 x + \cos^2 x = 1$$
$$\tan^2 x + 1 = \sec^2 x$$
$$\cot^2 x + 1 = \csc^2 x$$

**Sum and Difference Formulas:** If $x$ and $y$ are any two real numbers or measures of angles:

$$\sin (x + y) = \sin x \cos y + \cos x \sin y$$
$$\cos (x + y) = \cos x \cos y - \sin x \sin y$$
$$\tan (x + y) = (\tan x + \tan y)/(1 - \tan x \tan y)$$
$$\sin (x - y) = \sin x \cos y - \cos x \sin y$$
$$\cos (x - y) = \cos x \cos y + \sin x \sin y$$
$$\tan (x - y) = (\tan x - \tan y)/(1 + \tan x \tan y)$$

## LARGE NUMBERS

There are two primary naming systems for large numbers. The U.S. and French (among others) use one system, while Germany and Great Britain use the other. (Googol and googolplex, invented by the nephew of mathematician and author Edward Kasner, are rarely used outside the United States.) (See also "Standard Weights and Measures.")

| Number of zeroes after 1 | American name | British name |
|---|---|---|
| 6 | million | million |
| 9 | billion | milliard |
| 12 | trillion | billion |
| 15 | quadrillion | 1,000 billion |
| 18 | quintillion | trillion |
| 21 | sextillion | 1,000 trillion |
| 24 | septillion | quadrillion |
| 27 | octillion | 1,000 quadrillion |
| 30 | nonillion | quintillion |
| 33 | decillion | 1,000 quintillion |
| 100 | googol | googol |
| googol | googolplex | googolplex |

## FRACTIONS AND DECIMALS

To find the equivalent of a fraction in decimal form, divide the numerator (top number) by the denominator (bottom number). To change from a decimal to a percentage, multiply by 100. To change from a percentage to a decimal, divide by 100.

| Fraction | Decimal | Percentage |
|---|---|---|
| 1/16 | 0.0625 | 6.25 % |
| 1/8 (=2/16) | 0.125 | 12.5 |
| 3/16 | 0.1875 | 18.75 |
| 1/4 (=2/8; =4/16) | 0.25 | 25.0 |
| 1/3 | $0.\overline{3}\ldots$ | $33.\overline{3}\ldots$ |
| 5/16 | 0.3125 | 31.25 |
| 3/8 (=6/16) | 0.375 | 37.5 |
| 7/16 | 0.4375 | 43.75 |
| 1/2 (=2/4; =4/8; =8/16) | 0.5 | 50.0 |
| 9/16 | 0.5625 | 56.25 |
| 2/3 | $0.\overline{6}\ldots$ | $66.\overline{6}\ldots$ |
| 5/8 (=10/16) | 0.625 | 62.5 |
| 11/16 | 0.6875 | 68.75 |
| 3/4 (=6/8; =12/16) | 0.75 | 75.0 |
| 13/16 | 0.8125 | 81.25 |
| 7/8 (=14/16) | 0.875 | 87.5 |
| 15/16 | 0.9375 | 93.75 |
| 1 (=2/2; =4/4; =8/8; =16/16) | 1.0 | 100.0 |

# Technology

In our modern world, most technological advances are closely related to and driven by science, but the inventors of better ways to chip flint or forge iron were not scientists. Even Thomas Alva Edison, perhaps the greatest single contributor to modern technology, made only one scientific discovery (the Edison effect, an electric current produced when a hot wire is near a conductor in a vacuum). Instead, Edison was an inventor. The list of major discoveries in technology is essentially a list of inventions.

Since the Industrial Revolution in the late 18th century, the pace of invention has increased. This is shown dramatically by the rise in the number of U.S. patents issued. At the same time, there are fewer lone inventors—in fact, Edison himself was only a lone inventor in the beginning, and he pioneered the idea of a large group of people working together on new inventions. The creations of the lone inventor gradually have been overtaken by inventions patented by corporations. As technology has become a mainstay of business worldwide, the number of foreign patents issued to corporations has surpassed those obtained by U.S. corporations.

Although the lone inventor is to some degree gone, he or she is not forgotten by the U.S. Patent Office, which maintains the Inventors Hall of Fame.

*"Genius is one percent inspiration, ninety-nine percent perspiration."*

—Attributed to Thomas Alva Edison, c. 1903

## MAJOR DISCOVERIES IN THE HISTORY OF TECHNOLOGY

(See also "Chronology of Information Processing" in "The Computer.")

**B.C.**

**2,400,000** Ancestors of human beings begin to manufacture stone tools.

**1,000,000** Ancestors of human beings learn to control fire.

**23,000** Bow and arrow developed in Mediterranean regions of Europe and Africa.

**7000** People in Asia Minor begin to make pottery and cloth.

**5000** Egyptians start mining and smelting copper ore.

**3500** Potter's wheel and (shortly after) wheeled vehicles appear in Mesopotamia.

**2900** Great Pyramid of Giza and first form of Stonehenge (having only three stones) are built.

**2000** Interior bathrooms are built in palaces in Crete.

**1500** Earliest glass vessels from Egypt.

**522** Eupalinus of Megara (Greek: 6th cent.) constructs 3,600-ft. tunnel on Samos to supply water from one side of Mt. Castro to other.

**290** Pharos lighthouse at Alexandria is built.

**260** Archimedes (Greek: c. 287–212 B.C.) develops mathematical descriptions of the lever and other simple machines.

**200** Romans develop concrete.

**140** Chinese start making paper but do not use it for writing.

**100** In Illyria (now Yugoslavia and Albania), water-powered mills are introduced.

*A.D.*

**c. 1** Chinese invent centerline rudder for ships and magnetic compass; neither found in West for 1,000 years.

**190** Chinese develop porcelain.

**600** First windmills are built in what is now Iran.

**704** Between 704 and 751, Chinese start printing with woodblocks.

**1040** Chinese develop gunpowder.

**1041** Between 1041 and 1048, Chinese inventor Pi Sheng develops movable type.

**1190** First-known reference to a compass, in Europe.

**1267** Book written by Roger Bacon (English: c. 1220–92) in 1267 mentions eyeglasses to correct farsightedness.

**1288** First-known gun, a small cannon, is made in China.

**1310** Mechanical clocks driven by weights begin to appear in Europe.

**c. 1440** Johannes Gutenberg (German: c. 1398–1468) reinvents printing with movable type.

**1450** Nicholas of Cusa (German: 1401–64) develops eyeglasses for the nearsighted.

**1555** Georg Bauer (Georgius Agricola; German: 1494–1555) writes *De re metallica*, a handbook of mining techniques.

**c. 1590** Compound microscope (using two lenses) developed in Holland.

**1608** Telescope developed in Holland, probably by Hans Lippershey (German-Dutch: c. 1570–1619).

**1620** Cornelis Jacobszoon Drebbel (Dutch: 1572–1633) builds first navigable submarine.

**1643** Evangelista Torricelli (Italian: 1608–

47) makes first barometer, thereby producing first vacuum known to science.

**1654** Christiaan Huygens (Dutch: 1629–95) develops pendulum clock.

**1658** Robert Hooke (English: 1635–1703) invents balance spring for watches.

**1698** Thomas Savery (English: c. 1650–1715) patents the "Miner's Friend," first practical steam engine.

**1701** Jethro Tull (English: 1674–1741), possibly inspired by Chinese devices, invents device for planting seeds called a seed drill.

**1709** Daniel Gabriel Fahrenheit (German-Dutch: 1686–1736) invents alcohol thermometer; 1714, mercury thermometer.

**1733** John Kay (English: 1704–64) invents flying-shuttle loom, which, along with the steam engine and improvements in making iron, is a key to the start of Industrial Revolution.

**1751** Benjamin Huntsman (English: 1704–76) invents crucible process for casting steel.

**1762** John Harrison (English: 1693–1776) designs a marine chronometer (clock) accurate enough to enable navigators to calculate longitude at sea.

**1764** James Hargreaves (English: 1720–78) introduces spinning jenny, a machine that spins from 8 to 120 threads at once.

**1765** James Watt (Scottish: 1736–1819) builds model of his improved steam engine.

**1769** Sir Richard Arkwright (English: 1732–92) patents the water frame, a spinning machine that complements spinning jenny.

**1783** Joseph-Michel and Jacques-Etienne Montgolfier (French: 1740–1810; 1745–99) develop first hot-air balloon. Jacques A.C. Charles (French: 1746–1823) builds first hydrogen balloon.

**1785** Edmund Cartwright (English: 1743–1823) invents first form of the power loom.

**1792** William Murdock (Scottish: 1754–1839) is first to use coal gas for lighting.

**1793** Eli Whitney (American: 1765–1825) invents cotton gin, a machine for separating cotton fibers from seeds.

**1800** Alessandro G.A.A. Volta (Italian: 1745–1827) invents first form of chemical battery for producing electric current.

**1804** Nicolas-François Appert (French: c.1750–1841) develops canning as means of preserving food.

**1807** Robert Fulton (American: 1765–1815) introduces first commercially successful steamboat.

**1816** Sir David Brewster (Scottish: 1781–1868) invents kaleidoscope.

**1822** Joseph N. Niepce (French: 1765–1833) produces earliest form of the photograph.

**1823** Charles Macintosh (Scottish: 1766–1843) patents a waterproof fabric.

**1825** George Stephenson (English: 1781–1848) develops first steam-powered locomotive to carry both passengers and freight.

**1835** William Henry Fox Talbot (English: 1800–77) invents photographic negative using silver chloride, essentially how black-and-white pictures are made today.

**1837** Samuel Finley Breese Morse (American: 1791–1872) patents first commercially successful version of the telegraph.

**1839** Louis J.M. Daguerre (French: 1789–1851) announces his process for making photographs, which come to be called daguerreotypes.

Charles Goodyear (American: 1800–60) discovers how to make rubber resistant to heat and cold, a process called vulcanization.

**1842** Sir John Bennet Lawes (English: 1814–99) patents manufacture of superphosphate, the first manufactured fertilizer.

**1843** Isambard Kingdom Brunel's (English: 1806–59) *Great Britain* is first iron-hulled screw-propellor ship to cross the Atlantic.

**1846** Elias Howe (American: 1819–67) patents lock-stitch sewing machine.

Richard March Hoe (American: 1812–96) invents rotary printing press.

**1851** Isaac Merrit Singer (American: 1811–75) patents continuous-stitch sewing machine.

**1852** Elisha Graves Otis (American: 1811–61) installs first elevator incorporating safety device that prevents cage from falling if the cable breaks.

**1856** Henry Bessemer (English: 1813–98) develops way of making inexpensive steel (Bessemer process).

**1859** Edwin L. Drake (American: 1819–80) drills first oil well, in Titusville, Pa.

**1862** Richard Jordan Gatling (American: 1818–1903) invents first form of machine gun.

**1866** Robert Whitehead (English: 1823–1905) invents naval torpedo.

Georges Leclanché (French: 1839–82) develops first form of dry cell for producing electricity.

**1867** Christopher L. Sholes (American: 1819–90) and two others invent first practical typewriter.

**1869** Hippolyte Mège Mouriés (French: 1817–80) patents margarine.

**1874** Joseph Farwell Glidden (American: 1813–1906) invents the kind of barbed wire used today.

**1876** Alexander Graham Bell (Scottish-American: 1847–1922) invents telephone.

Karl von Linde (German: 1842–1934) invents first practical refrigerator.

**1877** Nikolaus A. Otto (German: 1832–91) invents type of internal combustion engine still used in most automobiles.

Thomas Alva Edison (American: 1847–1931) invents phonograph, which uses a wax cylinder.

**1878** Louis-Marie-Hilaire Bernigaud (French: 1839–1924) develops rayon.

Carl Gustaf Patrik de Laval (Swedish: 1845–1913) invents turbine-operated centrifugal cream separator.

**1879** Edison and Sir Joseph W. Swan (English: 1828–1914) independently discover how to make practical electric lights.

**1885** Karl Benz (German: 1844–1929) builds precursor of modern automobile.

Rover Safety Bicycle, built in England, is first bicycle with essentially modern features.

**1886** George Westinghouse (American: 1846–1914) invents airbrake for railroad cars.

**1888** Emile Berliner (German: 1851–1929) invents phonograph disk.

John B. Dunlop (Scottish: 1840–1921) patents air-filled tire.

George Eastman (American: 1854–1932) develops first camera using roll film.

**1889** Gustave Eiffel (French: 1832–1923) builds his famous tower in Paris; at 993 ft. it is tallest freestanding structure of the time.

**1893** Rudolf Diesel (German: 1858–1913) describes diesel engine.

**1895** First public showing of a motion picture, "Workers Leaving the Lumière Factory" by Auguste and Louis Lumière (French: 1862–1954; 1864–1948), in Paris.

Guglielmo Marconi (Italian: 1874–1937) transmits signals for a mile with his wireless telegraph (a precursor of radio) near Bologna, Italy.

**1897** Karl Ferdinand Braun (German: 1850–1918) invents cathode-ray tube oscilloscope.

**1898** Valdemar Poulsen (Danish: 1869–1942) invents magnetic wire recorder, the precursor to the modern tape recorder.

**1902** Willis H. Carrier (American: 1876–1950) invents air conditioning.

**1903** Orville and Wilbur Wright (American: 1871–1948; 1867–1912) fly the first successful airplane at Kitty Hawk, N.C.

**1904** John Fleming (English: 1849–1945) develops first vacuum tube, a device for changing alternating current to direct.

**1907** Lee De Forest (American: 1873–1961) patents Audion vacuum tube, a device for magnifying weak electronic signals.

**1908** Henry Ford (American: 1863–1947) introduces Model T, the first affordable automobile.

**1909** Leo Baekeland (Belgian-American: 1863–1944) patents Bakelite, the first truly successful plastic.

**1912** Reginald Aubrey Fessenden (Canadian-American: 1866–1932) develops heterodyne circuit, an important improvement in radio reception.

**1917** Clarence Birdseye (American: 1886–1956) develops freezing as a means of preserving food.

**1919** Sir Arthur W. Brown (British: 1886–1948) and Sir John W. Alcock (British: 1892–1919) make first transatlantic flight, Newfoundland to Ireland.

**1924** Vladimir Kosma Zworykin (Russian-American: 1889–1982) develops iconoscope, the beginning of modern television.

**1929** Robert H. Goddard (American: 1882–1945) launches first instrumented, liquid-fueled rocket.

**1930** Sir Frank Whittle (British: 1907– ) patents jet engine.

**1931** Ernst A.F. Ruska (German: 1906– ) builds first electron microscope.

**1934** Wallace Hume Carothers (American: 1896–1937) invents nylon, first marketed in 1938.

**1935** Sir Robert Alexander Watson-Watt (Scottish: 1892–1973) begins work on radio detection and ranging (radar).

**1937** Chester F. Carlson (American: 1906–68) invents xerography, the first method of photocopying.

**1939** Paul H. Müller (Swiss: 1899–1965) discovers that DDT is potent and long-lasting insecticide.
Igor I. Sikorsky (Russian-American: 1889–1972) designs and flies first helicopter developed for mass production.

**1940** Peter Carl Goldmark (Hungarian-American: 1906–77) demonstrates first successful color television system.

**1941** John Rex Whinfield (English: 1901–66) invents Dacron.

**1942** Enrico Fermi (Italian-American: 1901–54) builds first nuclear reactor.

**1947** Dennis Gabor (Hungarian-British: 1900–79) develops holography, a method of recording and displaying a three-dimensional object.

**1948** Goldmark develops the 33⅓ rpm long-playing phonograph record.
Georges de Mestral (Swiss: 1908–90) invents Velcro, patented in 1955.

**1957** Gordon Gould (American: 1920– ) develops basic idea for the laser, which he succeeds in patenting in 1986 after long struggle.

**1958** U.S. opens first experimental nuclear power plant.

**1962** First industrial robot is marketed.
First active communications satellite, Telstar, goes into orbit.

**1963** Audio cassettes introduced.

**1982** Compact disc players introduced.

**1990** Scientists at Bell Labs develop first all-optical computer.

## NATIONAL INVENTORS HALL OF FAME

In 1973 the U.S. Patent Office began the practice of naming certain American and foreign inventors with U.S. patents to the National Inventors Hall of Fame. Although many of those honored have many patents, the committee selects one for each inventor as the occasion for the award, which they identify by the title of the original patent application. The date at the end of each of the following entries denotes the year of induction.

**Ernst Alexanderson** (Swedish-American: 1881?–1975) HIGH FREQUENCY ALTERNATOR This is the basic device that makes it possible for radio (and television) to transmit voices and music, not just dots and dashes. (1983)

**Andrew Alford** (Russian-American: 1904– ) LOCALIZER ANTENNA SYSTEM With this and other inventions, Alford developed the radio system for navigation as well as instrument landing systems for airplanes. (1983)

**Luis Walter Alvarez** (American: 1911–88) RADIO DISTANCE AND DIRECTION INDICATOR (1978)

**Edwin Howard Armstrong** (American: 1890–1954) METHOD OF RECEIVING HIGH FREQUENCY OSCILLATIONS Armstrong's several inventions connected with radio broadcasting and reception made possible the "radio days" of the 1920s through the 1940s. In 1939 he invented FM broadcasting and reception, which helped lead to another revolution in radio. (1980)

**Leo Hendrik Baekeland** (Belgian-American: 1863–1944) SYNTHETIC RESINS Baekeland's plastic (synthetic resin) that he named Bakelite was not the first plastic to be manufactured (that was celluloid), but it was the first to make people realize the potential of plastics in general. (1978)

**John Bardeen** (American: 1908– ) TRANSISTOR Invented by Bardeen, William Shockley, and Walter Brattain, the transistor is the essential semiconductor device used on microprocessors and other chips. (1974)

**Arnold O. Beckman** (American: 1900– ) APPARATUS FOR TESTING ACIDITY Beckman developed a precise instrument to measure how acid a substance is as well as other precision instruments. (1987)

**Alexander Graham Bell** (Scottish-American: 1874–1922) TELEGRAPHY Despite the title of this patent, the invention here was the telephone. Another important Bell invention was the disk phonograph. (1974)

**Willard H. Bennett** (American: 1903–87) RADIO FREQUENCY MASS SPECTROMETER Measures chemical composition of elements; patented in 1955. (1991)

**Harold Stephen Black** (American: 1898– ) NEGATIVE FEEDBACK AMPLIFIER The basic principle of the negative feedback amplifier has become fundamental to many other devices since Black first used it to control distortion. (1981)

**Walter H. Brattain** (American: 1902–87) TRANSISTOR (See John Bardeen) (1974)

**Luther Burbank** (American: 1849–1926) PEACH Burbank's work in developing more than 800

## NUMBER OF PATENTS ISSUED FOR INVENTIONS BY DECADE, 1790–1990

| Period | Patents issued |
|---|---|
| 1790–1800 | 309 |
| 1801–10 | 1,093 |
| 1811–20 | 1,930 |
| 1821–30 | 3,086 |
| 1831–40 | 5,519 |
| 1841–50 | 5,933 |
| 1851–60 | 23,065 |
| 1861–70 | 79,459 |
| 1871–80 | 125,438 |
| 1881–90 | 207,514 |
| 1891–1900 | 220,608 |
| 1901–10 | 315,193 |
| 1911–20 | 383,117 |
| 1921–30 | 423,089 |
| 1931–40 | 439,863 |
| 1941–50 | 308,436 |
| 1951–60 | 430,120 |
| 1961–70 | 585,115 |
| 1971–80 | 687,800[1] |
| 1981–90 | 744,000[1] |

**Note:** Excludes patents granted for designs and botanical plants. 1. Numbers rounded in source. **Sources:** U.S. Bureau of the Census, *The Statistical History of the United States* (1976), and U.S. Patent Office.

new varieties of plants contributed to the development of the Plant Patent program in 1930. Burbank holds 16 plant patents, all issued posthumously. (1986)

**William Seward Burroughs** (American: 1857–98) CALCULATING MACHINE Although the calculating machine dates from the 17th century, Burroughs's was the first that could be mass produced and easily used. (1987)

**William Meriam Burton** (American: 1865–1954) MANUFACTURE OF GASOLINE Burton developed the first commercially successful cracking process, a method that yielded twice the amount of gasoline from crude oil than previous methods had. (1984)

**Marvin Camras** (American: 1916– ) METHOD AND MEANS OF MAGNETIC RECORDING Before the tapes currently used to record sound and pictures, sound was recorded on the wire recorder that Camras invented in the 1930s. He went on to develop over 500 inventions, most connected with improvements in recording methods. (1985)

**Chester F. Carlson** (American: 1906–68) ELECTROPHOTOGRAPHY Carlson invented the dry copying method called xerography. Although patented in 1940, the dry copier was not marketed until 1958, by which time Carlson had patented many improvements. (1981)

**Wallace Hume Carothers** (American: 1896–1937) DIAMINE-DICARBOXYLIC ACID SALTS AND PROCESS OF PREPARING SAME AND SYNTHETIC FIBER Carothers's invention—known as nylon—contributed an important fiber to the world; he also developed the first commercially successful synthetic rubber. (1984)

**Willis Haviland Carrier** (American: 1876–1950) APPARATUS FOR TREATING AIR Carrier invented the first successful air-conditioning system, and many of the techniques used in modern refrigerators. (1985)

**George Washington Carver** (American: 1864–1943) PRODUCTS USING PEANUTS AND SWEET POTATOES A successful scientist in Iowa who later taught at the prestigious black Tuskegee Institute, Carver developed over 300 uses for the peanut and 118 sweet potato by-products as an incentive for farmers to plant regenerative crops rather than the traditional soil-destroying cotton and tobacco. (1990)

**Frank B. Colton** (Polish-American: 1923– ) ORAL CONTRACEPTIVES Colton not only developed the first "pill" in 1960, but he also pioneered the development of anabolic steroids. (1988)

**William D. Coolidge** (American: 1873–1974) VACUUM TUBE The "Coolidge tube" is actually an X-ray generator. Among his many other inventions was the modern tungsten-filament electric light. (1975)

**Raymond V. Damadian** (American: 1936– ) APPARATUS AND METHOD FOR DETECTING CANCER IN TISSUE Damadian was the first to realize that the nuclear magnetic resonance technique could be used on living creatures (it was already a success as a laboratory tool used by chemists) and that it could detect cancer cells. (1989)

**John Deere** (American: 1804–86) PLOW Anyone who grew up near a farm knows the name John Deere. His vastly improved plow was the start of his commercial success, and the company he founded still makes farm tools. (1989)

**Lee De Forest** (American: 1873–1961) AUDION AMPLIFIER Although he eventually acquired more than 300 patents related to radio, De Forest's invention of the triode was the key to modern radio and later developments in the amplification of signals. (1977)

**Rudolf Diesel** (German: 1858–1913) INTERNAL COMBUSTION ENGINE The pressure-ignited heat engine is still called the diesel engine. (1976)

**Carl Djerassi** (Austrian-American: 1923– ) ORAL CONTRACEPTIVES A major influence on modern organic chemistry, Djerassi's research into the chemistry of steroids and his synthesis of antihistamines are two of his many contributions. (1978)

**Herbert Henry Dow** (Canadian-American: 1866–1930) BROMINE Besides new methods of extracting bromine and chlorine from naturally occurring salt deposits, Dow patented over 90 inventions and founded the Dow Chemical Company. (1983)

**Charles Stark Draper** (American: 1901–87) GYROSCOPIC EQUIPMENT Draper's gyroscopic stabilizer helped both antiaircraft guns and falling bombs hit their targets during World War II. Later he developed gyroscopic systems for air and marine navigation and for guided missiles. (1983)

**Graham J. Durant** (British-American: 1934– ) CIMETIDINE (TAGAMET®) With John C. Emmet and C. Robin Ganellin, Durant developed the major drug used to suppress acid in stomach and intestinal ulcers. Introduced in the U.S. in 1977, by 1980 Tagamet® was the best-selling drug in America. (1990)

**George Eastman** (American: 1854–1932) METHOD AND APPARATUS FOR COATING PLATES FOR USE IN PHOTOGRAPHY Eastman developed the dry plate negative and transparent roll film for still cameras, and a motion picture film for

use in the newly invented cinema. (1977)

**Harold E. Edgerton** (American: 1903– ) STROBOSCOPE Edgerton created this device to produce flashes that would stop action in a photograph at regular intervals. (His classic photograph of the crown produced by a drop of milk falling into a bowl of milk dates from the 1930s.) He also contributed inventions to underwater photography. (1986)

**Thomas Alva Edison** (American: 1847–1931) ELECTRIC LAMP In addition to the carbonfilament electric lamp, Edison patented a phonograph, the mimeograph, the fluoroscope, and motion picture cameras and projectors. (1973)

**Gertrude B. Elion** (American: 1918– ) DNA-BLOCKING DRUGS Crucial to cancer treatment and antiviral research. First woman elected to National Inventors Hall of Fame. (1991)

**John C. Emmet** (British: 1938– ) CIMETIDINE (TAGAMET®) (see Graham J. Durant) (1990)

**Philo Taylor Farnsworth** (American: 1906–71) TELEVISION SYSTEM Farnsworth patented many components of all-electronic television. He also worked on the electronic microscope, radar, the use of ultraviolet light for seeing in the dark, and nuclear fusion. (1984)

**Enrico Fermi** (Italian-American: 1901–54) NEUTRONIC REACTOR Fermi's nuclear reactor is the basis of nuclear power today. His many contributions to modern physics include basic theoretical work as well as experimental physics. (1976)

**Henry Ford** (American: 1863–1947) TRANSMISSION MECHANISM Best remembered for his innovative business practices, Ford also invented and patented numerous mechanisms used in automobiles. (1982)

**Jay W. Forrester** (American: 1918– ) MULTI-COORDINATED DIGITAL INFORMATION STORAGE DEVICE A pioneer in the development of electronic computers after World War II, Forrester's main invention was the magnetic storage of information. Most computers today, from giant mainframes to lightweight laptops, still use magnetic storage to store data even when the computer has been shut off. (1979)

**C. Robin Ganellin** (British: 1934– ) CIMETIDINE (TAGAMET®) (see Graham J. Durant) (1990)

**Charles P. Ginsburg** (American: 1920– ) VIDEOTAPE RECORDER The now ubiquitous VCR was originally developed by an engineering team led by Ginsburg. (1990)

**Robert Hutchings Goddard** (American: 1882–1945) CONTROL MECHANISM FOR ROCKET APPARATUS The father of American rocketry, Goddard devised successful rocket weapons and rocket-assisted take-off mechanisms for carrier-based airplanes for the military. He obtained 214 patents on various aspects of rocketry. (1979)

**Charles Goodyear** (American: 1800–60) IMPROVEMENT IN INDIA-RUBBER FABRICS In 1844 Goodyear discovered vulcanization, a process to make rubber resistant to heat and cold. (1976)

**Gordon Gould** (American: 1920– ) OPTICALLY PUMPED LASER AMPLIFIERS Gould envisioned the basic idea for the laser in 1957, but did not win his first patent until 1977. (1991)

**Wilson Greatbatch** (American: 1919– ) MEDICAL CARDIAC PACEMAKER Greatbatch's pace-

## PATENTS GRANTED, BY PATENTEE, 1901–90

| Year | Total number granted | Individuals | Corporations U.S. | Corporations Foreign | U.S. government[1] |
|---|---|---|---|---|---|
| 1901 | 25,546 | 20,896 | 4,370 | 280 | N.A. |
| 1921 | 37,798 | 27,098 | 9,860 | 840 | N.A. |
| 1930 | 45,226 | 23,726 | 19,700 | 1,800 | N.A. |
| 1940 | 42,238 | 17,627 | 22,165 | 2,406 | 40 |
| 1950 | 43,040 | 18,960 | 21,782 | 1,660 | 622 |
| 1960 | 47,170 | 13,069 | 28,187 | 4,670 | 1,244 |
| 1965 | 62,857 | 16,063 | 37,158 | 8,096 | 1,540 |
| 1970 | 64,427 | 13,511 | 36,896 | 12,294 | 1,726 |
| 1980[2] | 61,800 | 13,300 | 29,400 | 18,200 | 1,232 |
| 1985[2] | 71,700 | 12,900 | 31,300 | 26,400 | 1,125 |
| 1987[2] | 83,000 | 15,300 | 33,800 | 32,900 | 975 |
| 1988[2] | 77,900 | 14,300 | 31,400 | 31,450 | 728 |
| 1989 | 102,712 | 23,624 | 77,034 | 2,054 | 700[2] |
| 1990 | 90,366 | 17,293 | 36,113 | 35,983 | 977 |

1. Excludes patents issued to Alien Property Custodian until 1942. 2. Figures rounded in source. **Sources:** U.S. Bureau of the Census, *The Statistical History of the United States* (1976), and U.S. Patent Office.

maker has helped millions of people with heart disease. He also invented batteries to keep the pacemaker running without adverse physical effects from the battery chemicals. (1986)

**Leonard M. Greene** (American: 1918– ) AIRPLANE STALL WARNING DEVICE Patented in 1949. (1991)

**Charles Martin Hall** (American: 1863–1914) MANUFACTURE OF ALUMINUM In 1886, Hall developed a cheap method to make aluminum (then selling at $5 a pound). That same year, French metallurgist Paul-Louis-Toussaint Héroult discovered the same process. Patent litigation between the two was resolved amicably. (1976)

**W.E. "Butch" Hanford** (U.S.: 1908– ) POLYURETHANE This 1942 patent (won with Donald F. Holmes) remains basis for chemistry used in manufacture of all polyurethanes. (1991)

**René Alphonse Higonnet** (French: 1902–83) PHOTO COMPOSING MACHINE Along with Louis Marius Moyroud, Higonnet developed (in 1946) the first machine to set type by recording the images of letters on film. Film composition became the standard way of setting type, replacing type set from metal for the next 40 years, after which it was replaced by electronic composition. (1985)

**James Hillier** (Canadian-American: 1915– ) ELECTRON LENS CORRECTION DEVICE Although Hillier was not the first to make a microscope using electrons, his microscopes became the standard in the field. Electron microscopes can enlarge much smaller details than light microscopes because the wavelength of an electron is much smaller than the wavelength of a photon of visible light. (1980)

**Herman Hollerith** (American: 1869–1929) STORAGE AND PROCESSING OF NUMERICAL DATA Hollerith's punched cards and readers, developed for the 1890 U.S. Census, became the basis of modern data processing. (1990) (see also "Chronology of Information Processing")

**Donald Fletcher Holmes** (American: 1910–80) POLYURETHANE (see W.E. "Butch" Hanford). (1991)

**Eugene J. Houdry** (French: 1892–1962) CATALYTIC CRACKING OF PETROLEUM Houdry developed a process to make high-grade gasoline and airplane fuel from crude oil, as well as other catalytic processes and devices, including the basic catalytic converter used in automobile mufflers. (1990)

**Percy F. Julian** (American: 1899–1975) SYNTHESIS OF CORTISONE AND OTHER HORMONES Julian developed many important industrial products derived from soybeans before discovering that soybeans could be used as the basis for synthesizing cortisone, an important hormone with many medical applications. (1990)

**Charles Franklin Kettering** (American: 1875–1958) ENGINE STARTING DEVICES AND IGNITION SYSTEM Kettering's Delco company produced the self-starter for automobiles and a small generator for use in isolated farms. (1980)

**Jack S. Kilby** (American: 1923– ) MINIATURIZED ELECTRONIC CIRCUITS A number of people worked on putting many transistors and other solid-state electronic devices on a single chip, but the monolithic integrated circuit that Kilby developed for Texas Instruments in 1959 was the beginning of the modern integrated circuit. (1982)

**Willem J. Kolff** (Dutch-American: 1911– ) SOFT-SHELL MUSHROOM-SHAPED HEART Although the patent cited is for an early version of an artificial heart, Kolff's most important work was the development of the artificial-kidney dialysis machine. (1985)

**Edwin Herbert Land** (American: 1909–91) PHOTOGRAPHIC PRODUCT COMPRISING A RUPTURABLE CONTAINER CARRYING A PHOTOGRAPHIC PROCESSING LIQUID Land's first success was the development and application of substances that polarize light. In addition to this and his celebrated instant camera, he also made important contributions to the theory of color vision. (1977)

**Irving Langmuir** (American: 1881–1957) INCANDESCENT ELECTRIC LAMP In 1913 Langmuir realized that filling the original Edison-Swan lightbulb with a nonburning gas would result in a longer-lasting light. His later work on the chemistry of surfaces won him a Nobel Prize in 1932. (1989)

**Ernest Orlando Lawrence** (American: 1901–58) METHOD AND APPARATUS FOR THE ACCELERATION OF IONS Although Lawrence did not develop the very first particle accelerator (popularly known as an "atom smasher"), his 1930 cyclotron has been the basic pattern for the most successful and powerful machines of its kind ever since. (1982)

**Robert S. Ledley** (American: 1926– ) WHOLE-BODY CAT SCANNER Ledley's device for making three-dimensional images of living tissues quickly became an established medical technique for looking inside the human body. (1990)

**Theodore Harold Maiman** (American: 1927– ) RUBY LASER SYSTEMS Although there has been much dispute about the invention of the laser, Maiman's ruby laser was the first to be recognized worldwide and to be commercially successful. (1984)

**Guglielmo Marconi** (Italian: 1874–1937) TRANSMITTING ELECTRICAL SIGNALS Marconi's patent for using radio waves to carry coded messages is best known as wireless telegraphy. (1975)

**Cyrus McCormick** (American: 1809–84) REAPER McCormick's machine for harvesting grain (patented in 1834) and other inventions revolutionized American agriculture. (1976)

**Ottmar Mergenthaler** (German-American: 1854–99) MACHINE FOR PRODUCING PRINTING BARS Mergenthaler's invention, known as the Linotype, was the first major improvement in printing since Gutenberg's movable type in the 15th century. This machine, which is controlled by a keyboard, casts individual lines of type from melted lead. (1982)

**Samuel F.B. Morse** (American: 1791–1872) TELEGRAPH SIGNALS Morse developed the first commercially successful telegraph. Joseph Henry was the genius behind the electronics, but Morse and his dot-dash code made instantaneous long-distance communications possible. (1975)

**Andrew J. Moyer** (American: 1899–1959) METHOD FOR PRODUCTION OF PENICILLIN Moyer, a microbiologist at the U.S. Department of Agriculture's Northern Regional Research Laboratory in Peoria, Ill., developed a way of producing penicillin in bulk during World War II. The basic method is still used in manufacture of antibiotics and other substances produced by microorganisms. (1987)

**Louis Marius Moyroud** (French: 1914– ) PHOTO COMPOSING MACHINE (see René Alphonse Higonnet.) (1985)

**Robert N. Noyce** (American: 1927–90) SEMICONDUCTOR DEVICE-AND-LEAD STRUCTURE Noyce has been at the center of development for two important semiconductor producers, the Fairchild and Intel corporations. Intel today makes the most widely used microprocessor chips for personal computers, those at the heart of various IBM models and their clones. (1983)

**Kenneth H. Olsen** (American: 1926– ) IMPROVED MAGNETIC CORE MEMORY Olsen founded Digital Equipment Corp. to manufacture computers based on his new memory devices; he has also contributed extensively to the development of the minicomputer. (1990)

**Elisha Graves Otis** (American: 1811–61) IMPROVEMENT IN HOISTING APPARATUS Otis devised the safety elevator in 1853, when his employer asked him to build a hoist to lift heavy equipment. Eight years later Otis installed the first passenger elevators. (1988)

**Nikolaus August Otto** (German: 1832–91) GAS MOTOR ENGINE Otto's four-stroke engine of 1876 is the basis of the modern internal combustion engine. It ran on compressed natural gas instead of gasoline (a development pioneered by Gottlieb Daimler and Wilhelm Maybach in 1889). (1981)

**Louis W. Parker** (Hungarian-American: 1906– ) TELEVISION RECEIVER Parker invented both the basic type of television receiver in common use today, and the type of color television transmission and reception that is most commonly used. (1988)

**Louis Pasteur** (French: 1822–95) BREWING OF BEER AND ALE Pasteur's work on beer and ale is generally considered unsuccessful, but he invented several vaccines, and he developed pasteurization, the heating process that protects beverages and food from microbe contamination. (1978)

**Charles J. Plank** (American: 1915– ) CATALYTIC CRACKING OF HYDROCARBONS WITH A CRYSTALLINE ZEOLITE CATALYST COMPOSITE Along with Edward J. Rosinski, Plank discovered in the early 1960s that zeolites (various aluminum silicates, a fairly common kind of mineral) could be used to improve the production of gasoline and other petroleum products. (1979)

**Roy J. Plunkett** (American: 1910– ) TETRAFLUOROETHYLENE POLYMERS In 1938 Plunkett discovered the tetrafluoroethylene polymer known as Teflon. He later developed many of the hydrofluorocarbons (Freons) since found to be eroding the ozone layer. (1985)

**Edward J. Rosinski** (American: 1921– ) CATALYTIC CRACKING OF HYDROCARBONS WITH A CRYSTALLINE ZEOLITE CATALYST COMPOSITE (see Charles J. Plank) (1979)

**Lewis Hastings Sarett** (American: 1917– ) THE PROCESS OF TREATING PREGNENE COMPOUNDS In 1944 Sarett found a way to produce cortisone as an artificial steroid. By 1949 he and his collaborators had learned to make cortisone from simple inorganic chemicals. Cortisone and related steroids are used for medical treatment of conditions ranging from psoriasis to arthritis. (1980)

**William Bradford Shockley** (English-American: 1910–89) TRANSISTOR (see John Bardeen) (1974)

**Igor I. Sikorsky** (Russian-American: 1889–1972) HELICOPTER CONTROLS Sikorsky designed and built many successful airplanes, but in 1931, he made a critical breakthrough in helicopter design. His continued developments led to the helicopter of today. (1987)

**Elmer A. Sperry** (American: 1860–1930) SHIP'S GYROSCOPIC COMPASS Patented in 1917. (1991)

**Charles Proteus Steinmetz** (German-American: 1865–1923) SYSTEM OF ELECTRICAL DISTRIBUTION Steinmetz was an important theoretician and inventor whose most significant work was in developing the theory of alternating current that made power grids possible. Among his inventions was a machine that produced "lightning in the laboratory." (1977)

**George R. Stibitz** (American: 1904– ) COMPLEX COMPUTER Stibitz was one of several scientists who developed electromechanical computers in the late 1930s and during World War II. His innovations at Bell Telephone Laboratories and in the U.S. Office of Scientific Research and Development include floating decimal arithmetic and taped computer programs. (1983)

**Donalee L. Tabern** (American: 1900–74) THIOBARBITURIC ACID DERIVATIVES Along with Ernest H. Volwiler, Tabern in 1936 discovered Pentothal, anesthetic of choice for short surgical procedures. Tabern later introduced therapeutic use of radioactive chemicals. (1986)

**Nikola Tesla** (Croatian-American: 1857–1943) ELECTRO-MAGNETIC MOTOR Tesla's induction motor was simpler than previous electric motors and was powered by alternating current (AC), which can be distributed more easily over a long distance than direct current (DC). (1975)

**Max Tishler** (American: 1906– ) RIBOFLAVIN AND SULFAQUINOXALINE In the late 1930s,

Tishler developed an economical method for synthesizing riboflavin–vitamin $B_2$. Later he and his co-workers developed a way to produce sulfaquinoxaline (an antibiotic that prevents and cures a disease common in poultry) commercially. (1982)

**Charles Hard Townes** (American: 1915– ) MASERS The maser, which preceded the better-known laser, is essentially a laser that works at microwave wavelengths instead of at the shorter wavelength of visible light. Masers are used in many applications. Solely responsible for the maser, Townes also contributed to the development of the laser. (1976)

**Ernest H. Volwiler** (American: 1893– ) THIOBARBITURIC ACID DERIVATIVES (see Donalee L. Tabern) (1986)

**An Wang** (Chinese-American: 1920–90) MAGNETIC PULSE CONTROLLING DEVICE Although best known for his state-of-the-art word processor of the 1960s and 1970s, Wang contributed many fundamental ideas to the development of electronic computers, including the principle on which magnetic core memory is built. (1988)

**George Westinghouse** (American: 1846–1914) STEAM-POWERED BRAKE DEVICES In 1869 Westinghouse patented an air brake for locomotives, his most important contribution to railroad safety. His later work on signals and switches led him to form the Westinghouse Electric Co. in 1884. (1989)

**Eli Whitney** (American: 1765–1825) COTTON GIN By making it possible to remove seeds from cotton mechanically, the gin made large-scale cotton farming possible. Whitney also introduced interchangeable parts, the beginning of mass production. (1974)

**Robert R. Williams** (American: 1886–1965) ISOLATION OF VITAMIN $B_1$ (THIAMINE) He later synthesized thiamine for commercial production in 1935. (1991)

**Orville Wright** (American: 1871–1948) & **Wilbur Wright** (American: 1867–1912) FLYING MACHINE The Wright brothers not only invented the first airplane in 1903, they also popularized, manufactured, and sold the new machines. (1975)

**Vladimir Kosma Zworykin** (Russian-American: 1889–1982) CATHODE RAY TUBE The cathode ray tube that Zworykin invented in 1928 is the kinescope, the basic picture tube used in modern television. Ten years later he developed the iconoscope, the first practical television camera. He also contributed to the development of the electron microscope. (1977)

# Computers

A computer is a machine for storing and processing information. It converts any information that it receives into a binary code—a string of signals, in which each signal is either *1* or *0*. The basic working component of a computer is a series of electronic switches, each of which can be set either "off" or "on" and thus represent 1 or 0 in the binary system. The history of computers is, to some extent, a history of the electronic switching devices that have been used to represent 1 and 0. These fall into three main categories: vacuum tubes, transistors, and integrated circuits.

The relative size and power of these three types are so disparate that it is almost impossible to compare them; there is no single scale against which they can be measured. In 1946 the ENIAC (Electronic Numerical Integrator and Calculator)—which occupied 2,000 square feet, weighed 50 tons, and used 18,000 vacuum tubes—could perform about 10,000 multiplications per second and had an internal memory capacity of 200 decimal digits, or about 20 words. By 1990 a silicon chip measuring a quarter of an inch across could outperform ENIAC by a factor of about one million and had a memory capable of storing 50,000 words. As one computer analyst calculated in the 1980s, comparable efficiencies in car manufacturing would have yielded a Rolls Royce costing $2.70 and getting 2 million mpg.

## CHRONOLOGY OF INFORMATION PROCESSING

*B.C.*
**500** Bead-and-wire abacus in use in Egypt.
*A.D.*
**200** Computing trays in use in China and Japan.
**1340** Double-entry bookkeeping originates in Lombardy.
**c. 1621** Mathematician William Oughtred (English: 1574–1660) invents slide rule, which he first describes in 1632.

**1642** Blaise Pascal (French: 1623–62) invents "pascaline"—the first calculating machine, capable of addition and subtraction.

**1666** Gottfried Wilhelm Leibniz (German: 1646–1716) argues that all reasoning is reducible to an ordered combination of elements—the first principle of computer theory.

**1679** Leibniz perfects binary system of notation that eventually will be used by all computers; also develops improved version of pascaline, capable of multiplication and division.

**1801** Joseph-Marie Jacquard (French: 1752–1834) uses punched cards to control operation of his mechanical loom—precursor of cards used in modern data-storage systems.

**1822** Charles Babbage (English: 1792–1871) designs and builds prototype of "Difference Engine" for calculating logarithms.

**1833** Babbage designs "Analytical Engine," a computing machine featuring printed-card input, memory, and printed output, and capable of being programmed to perform different tasks. Forerunner of modern computer, it never goes beyond design stage.

**1847** George Boole (English: 1815–64) publishes *Mathematical Analysis of Logic*, which treats logic as a branch of mathematics (Boolean Algebra).

**1853** Pehr Georg Scheutz and his son Edvard G.R. Scheutz (Swedish: 1785–1873; 1821–81) complete version of Babbage's Difference Engine. One client is British government, which uses Scheutz engine to calculate life expectancy tables.

**1886** William S. Burroughs (American: 1855–98) develops first commercially successful mechanical adding machine.

**1887** U.S. Census Bureau holds competition for device to speed up computation of census information; Herman Hollerith (American: 1860–1929) designs winning tabulating machine. Later develops mechanical sorting machine (1896).

His Tabulating Machine Co. (founded 1911) becomes IBM in 1924.

**1890** Hollerith's electromechanical machine, using perforated cards, processes U.S. census results in six weeks—one-third the time taken in 1880.

**1894** Otto Steiger develops "Millionaire," the first commercially successful machine capable of direct multiplication, as opposed to multiplication by repeated addition. Nearly 5,000 sold between 1894 and 1935.

**1931** Vannevar Bush (American: 1890–1974) completes "differential analyser," first computing machine to use electronic components (vacuum tubes in which values could be stored as voltages).

**1936** Mathematician Alan M. Turing (English: 1912–54) publishes "On Computable Numbers," which describes hypothetical computer with infinite storage capacity, capable of performing any conceivable calculation.

**1937** John V. Atanasoff (American: 1903– ) starts work on first electronic computer.

**1938** Konrad Zuse (German: 1910– ) builds "Z1," the first computing machine to use binary, instead of decimal, method of operation. Other features include keyboard to input information and system of electric bulbs to signal results of calculations.

**1939** Atanasoff and Clifford Berry complete ABC device, first digital computer.

**1940** Zuse's Z2 machine introduces electromagnetic relays (as used in telephone switching gear) to store numbers. (Relays were capable of switching, i.e., calculating, 5 times per second.)

### First Generation: Vacuum Tubes

**1943** British government uses first fully electronic computer to crack German military codes. Designed by Turing, "Colossus" uses 2,000 vacuum tubes to perform calculations and digest information at rate of 5,000 characters per second.

**1944** Completion of "Harvard Mark I," designed by Howard H. Aiken (American: 1900–73) and built by IBM. Vast, over 50 ft. long, it was obsolete almost immediately because it used electromagnetic relays rather than vacuum tubes.

**1946** At press conference at University of Pennsylvania, the ENIAC (Electronic Numerical Integrator and Calculator) multiplies five-digit number by itself 5,000 times in half a second. Designed by J. Presper Eckert, Jr. (American: 1919– ) and John W. Mauchly (American: 1907–80) to calculate ballistic trajectories, ENIAC occupies 2,000 sq. ft., weighs 50 tons, uses 18,000 vacuum tubes, and can store about 20 words in its memory.

John von Neumann (Hungarian-American: 1903–57) publishes paper suggesting that instructions given to computer—"programs"—can themselves be stored by computer in numerical form.

First use of term *bit* to mean binary digit.

**1948** "Mark I," designed by Tom Kilburn (English: 1921– )and Sir Frederic C. Williams (English: 1911–77) at Manchester University, England, is first computer to utilize von Neumann's concept of stored programs. It can thus be "programmed" to perform infinite variety of functions.

John Bardeen (American: 1908– ), Walter H. Brattain (American: 1902–87), and William B. Shockley (English-American: 1910–89) invent the transistor; it will eventually replace vacuum tube and make computers faster and more reliable.

IBM, Bell Telephone, and Sperry-Rand each begin production of commercial computers.

First chess-playing computer built at M.I.T.

**1950** Eckert and Mauchly's EDVAC (*E*lectronic *D*iscrete *V*ariable *A*utomatic *C*omputer) is first to use magnetic disks for storage.

**1951** Lyons Tea Shop Co. in England uses specially designed computer ("LEO") to perform routine administrative functions.

Eckert and Mauchly's UNIVAC (*Universal Automatic Computer*) is installed at U.S. Bureau of Census. UNIVAC uses magnetic tape for input and becomes first commercially successful machine, selling over 50 models.

Wang Laboratories founded in Boston.

**1952** One hour after polls close, CBS television network uses UNIVAC to predict Eisenhower's landslide victory in U.S. presidential election. Prediction was based on less than 10% of the votes.

**1953** First high-speed printer linked to a computer.

IBM introduces its first stored-program computer, the vacuum-tube based "701."

**1956** First use of term *artificial intelligence*.

## Second Generation: Transistors

**1958** Control Data Corp. introduces first fully transistorized computer, the CDC 1604, designed by Seymour Cray (American: 1925– ).

Jack St.C. Kilby (American: 1923– ) of Texas Instruments and Robert Noyce (American: 1927–90) of Intel Corp. independently produce first integrated circuits.

**1959** First commercially marketed program. IBM markets its first transistorized computers, the 1620 and 1790.

**1960** First minicomputer, the PDP-1, developed by Digital Equipment Corp.

Introduction of removable magnetic disks for data storage.

## Third Generation: Integrated Circuits

**1965** IBM markets its first integrated-circuit based computer, the 360.

**1968** Stanley Kubrick's (American: 1928– ) *2001: A Space Odyssey* stars supercomputer called "Hal," which critics complain is the most "human" character in film.

**1969** Graduate student Alan Kay, later to become top designer with Apple Computer Co., writes doctoral thesis describing hypothetical "personal computer."

First international conference on artificial intelligence.

**1970** Lexitron introduces first word processor, a computer designed specifically to handle written text. It features a cathode ray tube (CRT) terminal, as used in television sets, to display information.

Floppy disk is introduced for data storage.

**1971** Intel Corp. announces first microprocessor, several integrated circuits contained on one silicon chip.

First electronic pocket calculator produced by Texas Instruments; it weighs about 2½ lbs. and costs about $150.

**1973** IBM introduces "Winchester" disk drive, a sealed storage module containing several rotating magnetic disks.

Introduction of "bit-mapped" monitor capable of high-resolution graphics display.

Xerox markets first hand-held "mouse," a time-saving device for giving commands to computer.

Intel introduces 8080 microprocessor, which will become the central processing unit (CPU) of several microcomputers.

**1975** First personal computer, the MITS Altair 8800, is marketed in kit form, with memory capacity of 256 bytes.

Cray Research (founded 1972) announces the Cray-1 supercomputer, capable of 100 million operations per second.

**1976** Apple Computer Co. founded by Stephen Wozniak and Steven Jobs (American: 1955– ) in the Wozniak family garage; first Apple "boards" (self-assembly personal computer kits) go on sale.

**1977** Apple markets Apple II—the first widely accepted personal computer. Commodore and Tandy also begin to sell personal computers.

Microsoft Corp. is founded to produce microcomputer operating systems—programs allowing a central processing unit to control and coordinate the different elements of computer's hardware. Microsoft systems used for Radio Shack TRS-80 and Altair PC.

**1978** Hayes Microcomputer Products introduces Micromodem 100, the first microcomputer-compatible modem.

**1979** Micropro International releases Word-Star, popular word-processing program for personal computers.

WordPerfect Corp., producers of rival WordPerfect program, begins operation.

**1980** Microsoft adapts UNIX (an operating system for mainframe and minicomputers) for use with microcomputers; paves way for personal computers to begin performing tasks associated with larger machines.

**1981** IBM introduces its first personal computer, the IBM PC. Using operating system called PC-DOS, developed by Microsoft, it almost immediately becomes the industry standard.

First fully portable computer, the Osborne 1, is introduced.

Xerox markets the Star, a mouse-driven computer that prefigures many features of Apple Macintosh.

Ashton-Tate introduces dBASE II, the first popular database program for microcomputers.

**1982** Microsoft introduces MS-DOS, a version of the PC-DOS operating system designed for IBM PC; allows other manufacturers to produce copies ("clones") of the IBM machine.

Compaq announces its first portable computer (IBM compatible).

**1983** Apple introduces Apple IIe and "Lisa," an important step toward development of the Macintosh.

IBM announces PC Junior, which is commercially unsuccessful.

Radio Shack markets Model 100 portable, weighing just 4 lbs.

First IBM-compatible "laptop" computer introduced by Gavilan Corp.

Lotus Development Corp. introduces 1-2-3, a best-selling program for managing business spreadsheets.

Introduction of optical (laser-readable) storage disks.

Cray 2 supercomputer capable of 1 million operations per second.

**1984** Apple introduces "Macintosh." With list price of $2,495, it includes Apple's first "Mac" software programs, MacWrite (for text) and MacPaint (for graphics). Fifty thousand are sold within three months.

IBM markets the PC AT (Advanced Technology) model; features include

Enhanced Graphics Adapter (EGA) for improved screen resolution.

**1985** Apple's LaserWriter printer and Aldus Corp.'s PageMaker program usher in age of desktop publishing—electronic, rather than mechanical, production of documents and books.

Introduction of erasable optical storage disks.

Voice-data entry becomes feasible.

Toshiba markets first laptop computer.

**1986** IBM announces OS/2, a new operating system that allows personal computers to run several programs simultaneously (called multitasking).

**1987** Apple introduces Macintosh SE and Macintosh II. IBM introduces Personal System/2 (PS/2), features of which include high-resolution VGA (Video Graphics Array) display.

**1988** Computer security becomes an urgent issue when a "worm" program penetrates thousands of systems on Internet information network.

Steven Jobs, now with Next, Inc., unveils "computer workstation," featuring an optical disk drive capable of storing 250 times as much data as floppy disks used by IBM and Apple.

Motorola announces new microprocessor, the 88000.

First IBM PS/2 "clones" announced by rival manufacturers.

Compaq markets SLT/286, the first laptop with VGA display.

IBM and Sears launch Prodigy, a videotex service enabling subscribers with a computer and modem to access a central information bank.

**1989** Intel announces the 80860 chip, containing 1 million transistors; designed to give a microcomputer the power and speed normally associated with supercomputers.

IBM announces production of commercial quantities of 4-megabyte chips.

First portable computers with color liquid crystal displays (LCDs) announced.

**1990** Clifford Stoll's *The Cuckoo's Egg*, an account of tracking down an East European "hacker" who gains access to U.S. military files, dramatizes vulnerability of computer systems, becomes best-seller.

# A GLOSSARY OF COMPUTER TERMS

**Artificial intelligence (AI)** The underlying assumption of artificial intelligence is that machines can be programmed to perform human functions. The primary AI functions are *expert systems*, programs that contain a body of knowledge (contributed by experts) that the machine can draw on to solve specific types of problems; *natural language interfaces* that make it possible for users to access a computer's database with commands entered in ordinary written or spoken language (for example, "Give me a list of countries bordering the Atlantic Ocean"); *speech recognition, speech synthesis,* and *optical recognition* systems that enable computers to understand spoken commands, make speech, and interpret visible images (such as bar codes on retail goods); and *robotics,* machines whose design and systems enable them to imitate complex "eye-hand" coordination of humans.

**ASCII (American Standard Code for Information Exchange)** Computers work with numbers, not letters. ASCII is the numerical code used by personal computers (*microcomputers*). While many programs also use special codes of their own, data from one computer to another are best transmitted in "pure ASCII."

**Baud rate** A transmission rate used in sending data from one computer to another, with a baud approximately equal to one *bit* per second. Most *modems* use either 1,200 or 2,400 baud. Rates must be the same between modems for data to be transmitted.

**Bit** In the binary system, a bit is either of the digits *0* or *1*. The bit (for *binary digit*) is the basic unit for storing data, with "off" representing 0 and "on" representing 1.

**Buffer** Any memory location where data can be stored temporarily while the computer is doing something else; specifically, a memory location in the computer, in a printer, or in a separate storage device (*peripheral*) that stores a file being printed so that the computer is not tied up waiting for the printing to finish.

**Bug** An error in a *software* program or in the *hardware.*

**Byte** A group of 8 *bits* that together represent one character, whether alphabetic, numeric, or otherwise. A byte is the smallest accessible unit in a computer's memory.

**Cathode ray tube (CRT)** The display device, or *monitor,* similar to a television screen, used with most desktop computers.

**Central processing unit (CPU)** The group of circuits that directs the entire computer system by (1) interpreting and executing *program* instruction and (2) coordinating the interaction of input, output, and storage devices.

**Chip** See "Silicon chip."

**Computer-aided design (CAD), engineering (CAE)** and **manufacturing (CAM)** Systems that automate many complex tasks such as drafting, computation, or repetitive actions. CAM is closely related to *robotics* (see "Artificial intelligence").

**Cursor** A marker on the computer display that shows which region of the screen is active.

**Database** Either a *program* for arranging facts in the computer and retrieving them (the computer equivalent of a filing system) or a *file* set up by such a system. Often databases are central files that can be accessed by a *modem* for a fee.

**Desktop publishing** The electronic, rather than mechanical, production of books and documents. A combination of *hardware* (laser printers capable of printing a range of type sizes and styles) and *software* (programs such as Aldus's PageMaker and Xerox's Ventura) enables the writer to design, typeset, and print his or her own work.

**Disk drive** A mechanism for retrieving information stored on a magnetic disk. The drive rotates the disk at high speed and "reads" the data with a magnetic head similar to those used in tape recorders.

**File** Any group of data treated as a single entity by the computer, such as a word processor document, a *program,* or a *database.*

**Floppy disk** A thin, flexible magnetic disk encased in a protective jacket. On the surface of the disk are a number of "tracks" on which data may be recorded in the form of magnetic spots.

**Graphical user interface (GUI)** A system that uses icons (symbols) seen on the screen to represent available functions. These icons are generally manipulated by a mouse and/or a keyboard. This approach contrasts with the more traditional method of using typed commands.

**Hard disk** A sealed cartridge containing magnetic storage disk(s) that holds much more memory—typically 20 to 90 *megabytes*—than *floppy disks.* Usually a hard disk is built into the computer, but it can be a *peripheral.*

**Hardware** The physical equipment, as opposed to the *programs* and procedures, used in data processing. The term covers not only computers themselves but also *peripherals* (see "Software").

**Integrated circuit** An entire electronic circuit contained on one piece of material. Originally, electronic components (transistors, capacitors, etc.) were placed on a metal chassis and then wired together. The first integrated circuit began with a single board (originally plastic), onto which strips of conducting material were sprayed. Electronic components could then be inserted directly onto the board (see "Silicon chip").

**Kilobyte (K)** A unit of measurement for storage capacity; equivalent to 1,024 *bytes,* but often rounded to 1,000 (see "Megabyte").

**Lapstation** A portable *workstation* with processing and storage capacity for many design and engineering functions; their use is restricted by reliance on AC power and limitations of display resolution.

**Laptop** A portable *microcomputer* small enough to operate in one's lap (for example, on a commuter train or an airplane). Generally a laptop weighs less than 15 pounds and uses a liquid-crystal display rather than a *cathode ray tube.*

**Liquid crystal display (LCD)** A type of flat-panel display monitor used in *portable computers.*

**Local area networks (LANs)** Systems that allow users to connect *PCs* to one another or to *minicomputers* or *mainframes.*

**Mainframe computer** Generally the largest, fastest, and most expensive kind of computer, usually costing millions of dollars and requiring special cooling. Mainframe computers can accommodate hundreds of simultaneous users and normally are run around the clock; typically they are owned by large companies (see "Microcomputer"; "Minicomputer"; "Supercomputer").

**Megabyte (M)** A unit of measurement for storage capacity equivalent to one million *bytes.*

**Menu-driven** A *program* that uses a number of "menus," or lists of possible activities from which the operator chooses in order to activate the appropriate commands. This is the alternative to a command-driven program, for which the operator must remember a number of commands in order to tell the computer what to do.

> *"One evening I was sitting in the rooms of the Analytical Society at Cambridge . . . with a table of logarithms lying before me. Another member coming into the room, and seeing I was half asleep, called out, 'Well, Babbage, what are you dreaming about?' to which I replied, 'I am thinking that all these tables might be calculated by machinery.'"*
>
> —Charles Babbage, whose "Analytical Engine" (1822) did just that

## COMPUTER LANGUAGES

| Name | Source of name | Introduced | Creators | Uses |
|------|---------------|-----------|----------|------|
| ADA | For Lady Ada Lovelace, who wrote a description of Charles Babbage's "analytical engine" | 1979 | Team headed by Jean Ichbiah of Honeywell | Based on Pascal; devised to manage complex computing activities needed by U.S. Army, Navy, and Air Force. |
| Algol | *Algo*rithmic *L*anguage | 1960 | International committee | Designed for solving math problems; both readable and practical, forerunner of many other languages, including Pascal. |
| APL | *A* *P*rogramming *L*anguage | 1961 | Kenneth Iverson of IBM | First used for expressing problems in applied mathematics because it can handle large numbers easily; now useful to airlines for complex routing and scheduling. |
| BASIC | *B*eginners *A*ll-purpose *S*ymbolic *I*nstruction *C*ode | 1965 | John Kemeny and Thomas Kurtz of Dartmouth College | Most popular and versatile of all computer languages; most often used as introduction to computing. |
| C | Successor to B language (Bell Computer programming Language/BCPL) | early 1970s | Dennis Ritchie at Bell Laboratories | Unusually flexible language; coming into wide use because programs are easily transferable between types of computers. |
| COBOL | *Co*mmon *B*usiness *O*riented *L*anguage | 1959 | Grace Murray Hopper and committee of computer manufacturers | Principal language for large-scale data processing in government, banking, and insurance. |
| Forth | *Fourth* generation language | 1970 | Charles Moore of National Radio Astronomy Observatory | Originally invented to control telescope at Kitts Peak Observatory, Ariz.; has been adapted for many mini- and microcomputer uses, including robotics and arcade games. |
| FORTRAN | *For*mula *Tran*slator | 1954 | John Backus and team at IBM | Standard computer language for scientists and mathematicians; first designed for large computers, now used by microcomputers for many business calculations. |
| LISP | *Lis*t *P*rocessing | 1956 | John McCarthy at M.I.T. | Used primarily for research in artificial intelligence; not mathematical, but composed of words. |
| Logo | From Greek *logos*, meaning "word" | late 1960s | Seymour Papert and others at M.I.T. | A learning language, simple enough for a child to program, but complex enough to use in higher education. |
| Pascal | For Blaise Pascal, French mathematician and inventor of first computing device | 1971 | Niklaus Wirth of the Swiss Federal Institute of Technology | Noted for its simplicity, was devised as a tool for teaching but later adapted to many other uses; is becoming most popular language for application software. |
| PILOT | *P*rogrammed *I*nquiry, *L*earning *o*r *T*eaching | 1969 | University of California at San Francisco | First language for computer-aided instruction; can be used by teachers with little computer experience to devise learning programs. |
| PL/1 | *P*rogramming *L*anguage *One* | 1964 | Team at IBM | Designed by IBM to run its mainframe computer, now becoming popular with users of minicomputers; rich in useful features, but more difficult to master than other languages. |

**Microcomputer** Generally the smallest and least expensive kind of computer, usually costing hundreds or thousands of dollars and small enough to fit on a desk top. The heart of the microcomputer is the *microprocessor* (see "Mainframe computer"; "Minicomputer").

**Microprocessor** A complete *Central processing unit* assembled on one, single *silicon chip*.

**Minicomputer** A small computer, usually used by medium-size or smaller businesses. Minicomputers often perform scientific or industrial tasks, cost tens or hundreds of thousands of dollars, and are housed in large cabinets (see "Mainframe computer"; "Microcomputer").

**MIPS (million instructions per second)** A measure of computer processing speed.

**Modem (modulator-demodulator)** A device capable of converting a digital (computer-compatible) signal to an analog signal, which can be transmitted via a telephone line, reconverted, and then "read" by another computer.

**Monitor** The display device on a computer, similar to a television screen.

**Mouse** A small box connected by cable to a computer and featuring one or more button-style switches. When moved around a desk, the mouse causes a symbol on the computer screen to make corresponding movements. By selecting items on the screen and pressing a button on the mouse, the user can perform certain functions much more quickly than by typing commands on the keyboard.

**Network** An interconnected group of computers that can exchange information or work together on different parts of the same problem.

**Notebook** A type of full-function *portable computer* that uses miniaturized components, weighs about 4–6 pounds, and can be carried in a briefcase.

**Operating system** A sequence of programming codes that instructs a computer about its various parts and peripherals and how to operate them. Operating systems deal only with the workings of the *hardware* and are separate from *software* programs.

**Peripheral** A device connected to the computer that provides communication or auxiliary functions. There are three types of peripherals: input devices, such as keyboards; output devices, such as *monitors* and printers; and storage devices, such as magnetic disks.

**Personal computer** A *microcomputer* used by an individual at home or in the office.

**Portable computer** A *personal computer* with all the functions of a desktop computer but which has a full-size keyboard in the same physical unit as the display and some type of mass storage device. (See also *lapstation, laptop,* and *notebook*.)

**Program** As a noun, a prepared set of instructions for the computer, often with provisions for the operator to choose among various options. As a verb, to create such a set of instructions.

**Random access memory (RAM)** A temporary storage space in which data may be held on a *chip* rather than being stored on disk or tape. The contents of RAM may be accessed or altered at any time during a session, but will be lost when the computer is turned off (see "ROM").

**Read-only memory (ROM)** A type of *chip* memory, the contents of which have been permanently recorded in a computer by the manufacturer and cannot be altered by the user (see "RAM").

**Silicon chip** A special kind of *integrated circuit* in which traditional electronic components have been replaced by chemicals. Tiny wafers (chips) of silicon are covered with layers of chemicals, each of which acts as an electrical component (a *transistor*, capacitor, etc.). The first chips, made in the early 1960s, contained two transistors. By 1989 chips existed that contained 10 million transistors. The industry standard is one million transistors per chip.

**Software** The *programs* and procedures, as opposed to the physical equipment, used in data processing (see "Hardware").

**Spreadsheet** A *program*, such as Lotus 1-2-3, that performs mathematical operations on numbers arranged in large arrays; used mainly for accounting and other record keeping.

**Supercomputer** The fastest of the *mainframe* class of computers, usually used for complex scientific calculations.

**Transistor** A small piece of semiconducting material (material that conducts electricity better than, say, wood but not as well as metal).

Flows of electrons within the transistor can be controlled, enabling it to act as an electronic "switching" device. In other words, it can record information in the form of an "on" or an "off" signal. Early transistors were about one-hundredth the size of *vacuum tubes*, required very little energy, and generated no heat.

**Vacuum tube** A glass tube, shaped like a light bulb, that contains a heating element that pumps electrons through a vacuum. In the earliest computers, the status of the electrical current—"on" or "off"—was used as a means of storing information. Two major drawbacks of the vacuum tube were that it generated excessive heat and used large amounts of energy.

**Window** A portion of the screen display used to view simultaneously a different part of the file in use or a part of a different file than the one in use.

**Workstation** High-performance *microcomputers* with advanced graphics capabilities designed for use by scientists and engineers.

## SYSTEMS OF MEASUREMENT

There are two measurement systems that are widely used. Most of the world uses a system known as the metric system, or the International System (abbreviated SI from *Système internationale*, its name in French). The United States continues to use a system called U.S. customary measure which derives from (and differs from) the British imperial system. From time to time, our government has taken steps to change from the customary system to the International System, but these efforts have failed. Metric measure is legal in the United States, but nearly everyone continues to use the customary system in everyday use. The International System is generally used in scientific pursuits and increasingly in international trade.

The following tables show first the U.S. customary system, then the International System, and finally some important conversion factors between the two.

### Length or Distance

U.S. CUSTOMARY

1 foot (ft.) = 12 inches (in.)
1 yard (yd.) = 3 feet = 36 inches
1 rod (rd.) = 5½ yards = 16½ feet
1 furlong (fur.) = 40 rods = 220 yards
= 660 feet
1 mile (mi.) = 8 furlongs
= 1,760 yards = 5,280 feet

An International nautical mile has been defined as 6,076.1155 feet.

INTERNATIONAL SYSTEM

The basic unit for length is the meter, which is slightly longer than the customary yard. Other units of length are decimal subdivisions or multiples of the meter.

1 decimeter (dm) = 10 centimeters
= 0.1 meter
1 centimeter (cm) = 0.01 meter
1 millimeter (mm) = 0.1 centimeter
= 0.001 meter
1 micrometer ($\mu$m) = 0.001 millimeter
= 0.0001 centimeter
= 0.000001 meter
1 angstrom (Å) = 0.0001 micron
= 0.0000001 millimeter
1 dekameter (dam) = 10 meters
1 hectometer (hm) = 10 dekameters
= 100 meters
1 kilometer (km) = 10 hectometers
= 100 dekameters
= 1,000 meters

# Standard Weights & Measures

CONVERSIONS

In 1959 the relationship between customary and international measures of length was officially defined as follows:

0.0254 meter (exactly) = 1 inch
0.0254 meter × 12 = 0.3048 meter
= 1 international foot.

This definition, which makes many conversions simple, defines a foot that is shorter (by about 6 parts in 10,000,000) than the survey foot, which had earlier been defined as exactly 1200/3937, or 0.3048006, meter.

Following the international foot standard, the major equivalents are as listed below:

1 in. = 2.54 cm = 0.0254 m
1 ft. = 30.48 cm = 0.3048 m
1 yd. = 91.44 cm = 0.9144 m
1 mi. = 1,609.344 m
= 1.609344 km

1 cm = 0.3937 in.
1 m = 1.093613 yd.
= 3.28084 ft.
= 0.00062137 mi.

### Area

CUSTOMARY

Areas are derived from lengths as follows:
1 square foot = 144 square inches
1 square yard = 9 sq. ft.
1 square rod = 30¼ square yards
= 272¼ sq. ft.
1 acre = 160 square rods
= 4,840 sq. yd.
= 43,560 sq. ft.
1 square mile = 640 acres =
1 section = 1 mile square
1 township = 6 miles square
= 36 square miles

INTERNATIONAL SYSTEM

1 sq. millimeter (mm²) = 1,000,000 sq. microns
1 sq. centimeter (cm²) = 100 mm²
1 sq. meter (m²) = 10,000 cm²
1 are (a) = 100 m²
1 hectare (ha) = 100 ares
= 10,000 m²
1 sq. kilometer (km²) = 100 hectares
= 1,000,000 m²

CONVERSIONS

1 sq. inch = 6.4516 cm²
1 sq. foot = 929.0304 cm²
= 0.09290304 m²
1 sq. yard = 8,361.2736 cm²
= 0.83612736 m²
1 acre = 4,046.8564 m²
= 0.40468564 ha
1 sq. mile = 2,589,988.11 m²
= 258.998811 ha
= 2.58998811 km²

1 cm² = 0.1550003 sq. in.
1 m² = 1,550.003 sq. in.
= 10.76391 sq. ft.
= 1.195990 sq. yd.
1 hectare = 107,639.1 sq. ft.
= 11,959.90 sq. yd.
= 2.4710538 acres
= 0.003861006 sq. mi.
1 km² = 247.10538 acres
= 0.3861006 sq. mi.

### Cubic Measure

CUSTOMARY

1 cubic foot (ft³) = 1,728 cubic inches (in³)
1 cubic yard (yd³) = 27 cubic feet

INTERNATIONAL SYSTEM

1 cubic centimeter = 1,000 cubic millimeters
(cm³)      (mm³)
1 cubic decimeter = 1,000 cm³
(dm³)
1 cubic meter (m³) = 1,000 dm³
= 1,000,000 cm³

Cubic centimeter is sometimes abbreviated *cc* and is used in fluid measure interchangeably with milliliter (ml).

CONVERSIONS

1 in³ = 16.387064 cm³
1 ft³ = 28,316.846592 cm³
= 0.028316847 m³
1 yd³ = 764,554.857984 cm³
= 0.764554858 m³

1 cm³ = 0.06102374 in³
1 m³ = 61,023.74 in³
= 35.31467 ft³
= 1.307951 yd³

### Fluid Volume

CUSTOMARY MEASURE

A gallon is equal to 231 cubic inches of liquid or capacity.

1 tablespoon (tbs.) = 3 teaspoons (tsp.)
= 0.5 fluid ounce (fl. oz.)
1 cup = 8 fl. oz.
1 pint (pt.) = 2 cups = 16 fl. oz.

1 quart (qt.) = 2 pt. = 4 cups
          = 32 fl. oz.
1 gallon (gal.) = 4 qt. = 8 pt. = 16 cups
1 bushel (bu.) = 8 gal. = 32 qt.

### INTERNATIONAL SYSTEM

Fluid-volume measurements are directly tied to cubic measure. One milliliter of fluid occupies a volume of 1 cubic centimeter. A liter of fluid (slightly more than the customary quart) occupies a volume of 1 cubic decimeter, or 1,000 cubic centimeters.

1 centiliter (cl) = 10 milliliters (ml)
1 deciliter (dl) = 10 cl
          = 100 ml
     1 liter (L) = 10 dl
          = 1,000 ml
1 dekaliter (dal) = 10 L
1 hectoliter (hl) = 10 dal
          = 100 L
1 kiloliter (kl) = 100 hl
          = 1,000 L

#### CONVERSIONS

1 fluid ounce = 29.573528 ml = 0.02957 L
     1 cup = 236.588 ml = 0.236588 L
     1 pint = 473.176 ml = 0.473176 L
     1 quart = 946.3529 ml
          = 0.9463529 L
     1 gallon = 3,785.41 ml = 3.78541 L

1 milliliter = 0.0338 fluid ounce
     1 liter = 33.814 fluid ounces
          = 4.2268 cups = 2.113 pints
          = 1.0567 quarts = 0.264 gallon

### Dry Volume

#### CONVERSIONS

1 pint, dry = 33.600 cu. in. = 0.551 L
1 quart, dry = 67.201 cu. in. = 1.101 L

### Mass and Weight

Mass and weight are often confused. Mass is a measure of the quantity of matter in an object and does not vary with changes in altitude or in gravitational force (as on the moon or another planet). Weight, on the other hand, is a measure of the force of gravity on an object and so does change with altitude or gravitational force.

#### CUSTOMARY

In customary measure it is more common to measure weight than mass. The most common customary system of weight is avoirdupois:

1 pound (lb.) = 16 ounces (oz.)
1 (short) hundred- = 100 lb.
     weight (cwt.)
     1 (short) ton = 20 hundredweights
          = 2,000 lb.
1 long hundred- = 112 lb.
     weight
     1 long ton = 20 long hundred-
          weights = 2,240 lb.

A different system called troy weight is used to weigh precious metals. In troy weight the ounce is slightly larger than in avoirdupois, but there are only 12 ounces to the troy pound.

---

## SIMPLIFIED CONVERSION TABLE (alphabetical order)

| To convert | to | multiply by: |
|---|---|---|
| centimeters | feet | 0.0328 |
| centimeters | inches | 0.3937 |
| cubic cm | cubic in. | 0.0610 |
| cubic ft. | cubic m | 0.0283 |
| degrees | radians | 0.0175 |
| feet | cm | 30.48 |
| feet | meters | 0.3048 |
| gallons | liters | 3.785 |
| gal. water | lb. water | 8.3453 |
| grams | ounces | 0.0353 |
| inches | cm | 2.54 |
| kilograms | pounds | 2.205 |
| kilometers | feet | 3,280.8 |
| kilometers | miles | 0.6214 |
| knots | mi./hr. | 1.151 |
| liters | gallons | 0.2642 |
| liters | pints | 2.113 |
| meters | feet | 3.281 |
| miles | km | 1.609 |
| ounces | grams | 28.3495 |
| pounds | kg | 0.4536 |

---

## PREFIXES USED IN THE METRIC SYSTEM

| Prefix | Abbreviation | Factor by which unit is multiplied | Scientific notation |
|---|---|---|---|
| Exa- | E | 1,000,000,000,000,000,000 | $10^{18}$ |
| Peta- | P | 1,000,000,000,000,000 | $10^{15}$ |
| Tera- | T | 1,000,000,000,000 | $10^{12}$ |
| Giga- | G | 1,000,000,000 | $10^{9}$ |
| Mega- | M | 1,000,000 | $10^{6}$ |
| Kilo- | k | 1,000 | $10^{3}$ |
| Hecto- | h | 100 | $10^{2}$ |
| Deka- | da | 10 | $10^{1}$ |
| Deci- | d | 0.1 | $10^{-1}$ |
| Centi- | c | 0.01 | $10^{-2}$ |
| Milli- | m | 0.001 | $10^{-3}$ |
| Micro- | μ | 0.000 001 | $10^{-6}$ |
| Nano- | n | 0.000 000 001 | $10^{-9}$ |
| Pico- | p | 0.000 000 000 001 | $10^{-12}$ |
| Femto- | f | 0.000 000 000 000 001 | $10^{-15}$ |
| Atto- | a | 0.000 000 000 000 000 001 | $10^{-18}$ |

### INTERNATIONAL SYSTEM

Instead of weight, the International System generally uses to measure mass. The International System's basic unit for measurement of mass is the gram, which was originally defined as the mass of 1 milliliter (= 1 cm³) of water at 4 degrees Celsius (about 39°F). Today the official standard of measure is the kilogram (1,000 g).

1 centigram (cg) = 10 milligrams (mg)
1 decigram (dg) = 10 cg = 100 mg
     1 gram (g) = 10 dg = 100 cg = 1,000 mg
1 kilogram (kg) = 10 hectograms (hg)
          = 100 dekagrams (dag)
          = 1,000 g
1 metric ton (t) = 1,000 kg

---

#### CONVERSIONS

Since mass and weight are identical at standard conditions (sea level on earth), grams and other International System units of mass are often used as measures of weight or converted into customary units of weight. Under standard conditions:

1 ounce = 28.3495 grams
1 pound = 453.59 grams
          = 0.45359 kilogram
1 short ton = 907.18 kilograms
          = 0.907 metric ton

1 milligram = 0.000035 ounce
     1 gram = 0.03527 ounce
1 kilogram = 35.27 ounces
          = 2.2046 pounds
1 metric ton = 2,204.6 pounds
          = 1.1023 short ton

### Time

#### CUSTOMARY AND INTERNATIONAL SYSTEM

The International System in 1967 adopted a second that is based on the microwaves emitted by the vibrations of hot cesium atoms. A second (abbreviated sec. in customary usage, s in SI usage) is the time it takes the atoms to vibrate exactly 9,192,631,770 times. In the customary measure of time, the day is divided into 24 hours, the hour into 60 minutes, and the minute into 60 seconds. Since the Earth's rotation is gradually slowing, scientists must periodically add a second to a day to keep the year in sequence with their clocks (most recently done on Dec. 31, 1989). The change is so small that for almost all practical purposes an International System second and a customary second are the same.

Decimal fractions of time are used to measure smaller time intervals:

millisecond (ms) = 0.001 second $(10^{-3})$
microsecond (μs) = 0.000001 second $(10^{-6})$
nanosecond (ns) = 0.000000001 second
          $(10^{-9})$
picosecond (ps) = 0.000000000001
          second $(10^{-12})$

### Temperature

#### U.S. CUSTOMARY

In the United States, temperature is usually measured in degrees Fahrenheit: water freezes at 32°F and boils at 212°F. The basis of the Fahrenheit scale was 0°F, the coldest temperature that its originator, G.D. Fahrenheit (1686–1736), could obtain under laboratory conditions.

#### INTERNATIONAL SYSTEM

The Swedish astronomer Anders Celsius (1701–44) devised the temperature scale that bears his name in 1742. On the Celsius scale water freezes at 0°C and boils at 100°C. Very low temperatures are measured on the Kelvin scale, named for William Thomson, Baron Kelvin (1824–1907). It is also called the absolute scale because absolute zero—0 K (-273.15° C)—is the temperature at which no body can give up heat. The interval of a degree Kelvin equals the interval of a degree Celsius. At very high temperatures, differences between the

## TEMPERATURE CONVERSIONS

Often you need to know only the approximate values to convert a weather report or temperature in a recipe from Celsius to Fahrenheit. The following table can be used to get an approximate conversion between the two scales for temperatures frequently encountered. Note that −40°F is the same temperature as −40°C.

| Celsius | Fahrenheit | Fahrenheit | Celsius |
|---|---|---|---|
| −45° = −49° | | −45° = −42.8° | |
| −40 = −40 | | −40 = −40.0 | |
| −35 = −31 | | −35 = −37.2 | |
| −30 = −22 | | −30 = −34.4 | |
| −25 = −13 | | −25 = −31.7 | |
| −20 = −4 | | −20 = −28.9 | |
| −15 = 5 | | −15 = −26.1 | |
| −10 = 14 | | −10 = −23.3 | |
| −5 = 23 | | −5 = −20.6 | |
| **0 = 32** | | 0 = −17.8 | |
| 5 = 41 | | 5 = −15.0 | |
| 10 = 50 | | 10 = −12.2 | |
| 15 = 59 | | 15 = −9.4 | |
| 20 = 68 | | 20 = −6.7 | |
| 25 = 77 | | 25 = −3.9 | |
| 30 = 86 | | 30 = −1.1 | |
| 35 = 95 | | **32 = 0.0** | |
| 40 = 104 | | 35 = 1.7 | |
| 45 = 113 | | 40 = 4.4 | |
| 50 = 122 | | 45 = 7.2 | |
| 55 = 131 | | 50 = 10.0 | |
| 60 = 140 | | 55 = 12.8 | |
| 65 = 149 | | 60 = 15.6 | |
| 70 = 158 | | 65 = 18.3 | |
| 75 = 167 | | 70 = 21.1 | |
| 80 = 176 | | 75 = 23.9 | |
| 85 = 185 | | 80 = 26.7 | |
| 90 = 194 | | 85 = 29.4 | |
| 95 = 203 | | 90 = 32.2 | |
| **100 = 212** | | 95 = 35.0 | |
| 125 = 257 | | 100 = 37.8 | |
| 150 = 302 | | 105 = 40.6 | |
| 175 = 347 | | 110 = 43.3 | |
| 200 = 392 | | **212 = 100.0** | |
| 225 = 437 | | 225 = 107.2 | |
| 250 = 482 | | 250 = 121.1 | |
| 275 = 527 | | 275 = 135.0 | |
| 300 = 572 | | 300 = 148.9 | |
| 325 = 617 | | 325 = 162.8 | |
| 350 = 662 | | 350 = 176.7 | |
| 375 = 707 | | 375 = 190.6 | |
| 400 = 752 | | 400 = 204.4 | |
| 425 = 797 | | 425 = 218.3 | |
| 450 = 842 | | 450 = 232.2 | |
| 475 = 887 | | 475 = 246.1 | |

Kelvin and Celsius scales are insignificant.

*Fahrenheit to Celsius*: Subtract 32 from the temperature and multiply the difference by 5; then divide the product by 9. The formula is: C = 5⁄9 (F − 32)

*Celsius to Fahrenheit*: Multiply the temperature by 1.8, then add 32. The formula is often given with the fraction 9⁄5 instead of the equivalent decimal, 1.8. The formula is: F = 9⁄5 C + 32

*Celsius to Kelvin*: Add 273.15 to the temperature. The formula is: K = C + 273.15

KELVIN, CELSIUS, AND FAHRENHEIT EQUIVALENTS

| Characteristic | K | C° | F° |
|---|---|---|---|
| Absolute zero | 0 | −273.15° | −459.7° |
| Freezing point, water | 273.15 | 0° | 32° |
| Normal human body temp. | 310.15 | 37° | 98.6° |
| Boiling point, water | 373.15 | 100° | 212° |

### Force, Work/Energy, Power

CUSTOMARY SYSTEM

The foot/pound/second system of reckoning includes the following units:

slug = the mass to which a force of 1 poundal will give an acceleration of 1 foot per second per second ( = approximately 32.17 lbs.)

poundal = fundamental unit of force

foot-pound = the work done when a force of 1 poundal produces a movement of 1 foot

foot-pound/second = the unit of power equal to 1 foot/pound per second.

Another common unit of power is horsepower, which is equal to 550 foot-pounds per second.

Thermal work or energy is often measured in British thermal units (Btu), which are defined as the energy required to increase the temperature of 1 pound of water by 1 degree Fahrenheit. The Btu is equal to about 0.778 foot-pound.

INTERNATIONAL SYSTEM

In physics, compound measurements of force, work or energy, and power are essential. There are two parallel systems using International System units: the centimeter/gram/second system (cgs) is used for small measurements, and the meter/kilogram/second system (mks) is used for larger measurements. The mks system is the official one for SI. They are described below.

Measurement of Force

| cgs unit | dyne (dy) | The force required to accelerate a mass of 1 g 1 cm/s² (cm/s² means "centimeter per second per second") |
|---|---|---|
| mks unit | newton (new) | The force required to accelerate a mass of 1 kg 1 m/s² |

Measurement of Work or Energy

| cgs unit | erg | The dyne-centimeter, i.e., the work done when a force of 1 dy produces a movement of 1 cm |
|---|---|---|
| mks unit | joule (j) | The newton-meter, i.e., the work done when a force of 1 new produces a movement of 1 m ( = 10,000,000 ergs) |

Measurement of Power

| cgs unit | erg/second | A rate of 1 erg per second |
|---|---|---|
| mks unit | watt (w) | The joule/second, i.e., a rate of 1 joule per second ( = 10,000,000 erg-seconds) |

Heat energy is also measured using the calorie (cal), which is defined as the energy required to increase the temperature of 1 cubic centimeter (1 ml) of water by 1 degree C. One calorie is equal to about 4.184 joules. The kilocalorie (Kcal or Cal) is equal to 1,000 calories and is the unit in which the energy values of food are measured. This more familiar unit, also commonly referred to as a Calorie, is equal to about 4,184 joules.

CONVERSIONS

Measurement of Force
1 poundal = 13,889 dynes
= 0.13889 newtons
1 dyne = 0.000072 poundals
1 newton = 7.2 poundals

Measurement of Work/Energy
1 foot-pound = 1,356 joules
British thermal unit = 1,055 joules
= 252 gram calories
1 joule = 0.0007374 foot-pounds
1 (gram) calorie = 0.003968 Btu
1 (kilo) Calorie = 3.968 Btu

Measurement of Power
1 foot-pound/second = 1.3564 watts
1 horsepower = 746 watts
= 0.746 kilowatts
1 watt = 0.73725 foot-pound/second
= 0.00134 horsepower
1 kilowatt = 737.25 ft.-lb./sec.
= 1.34 horsepower

### Electrical Measure

Originally, the basic unit of quantity in electricity was the coulomb. A coulomb is equal to the passage of $6.25 \times 10^{18}$ electrons past a given point in an electrical system.

The unit of electrical flow is the ampere, which is equal to a coulomb/second, i.e., the flow of 1 coulomb per second. The ampere is analogous in electrical measure to a unit of flow such as gallons-per-minute in physical measure. In SI, the ampere is taken as the basic unit.

The unit for measuring electrical potential energy is the volt, which is defined as 1 joule/coulomb, i.e., 1 joule of energy per coulomb of electricity. The volt is analogous to a measure of pressure in a water system.

The unit for measuring electrical power is the watt as defined in the previous section. Power in watts (P) is the product of the electrical flow in amperes (I) and the potential electrical energy in volts (E):

$$P = I \times E$$

Since the watt is such a small unit for practical applications, the kilowatt ( = 1,000 watts) is often used. A kilowatt-hour is the power of 1,000 watts over an hour's time.

The unit for measuring electrical resistance is the ohm, which is the resistance offered by a circuit to the flow of 1 ampere being driven by the force of 1 volt. It is derived from Ohm's law, which defines the relationship between flow or current (amperes), potential energy (volts), and resistance (ohms). It states that the current in amperes (I) is proportional to potential energy in volts (E) and inversely proportional to resistance in ohms (R). Thus, when voltage and resistance are known, amperage can be calculated by the simple formula

$$I = \frac{E}{R}$$

### Measure of Angles and Arcs

Angles are measured by systems based on arcs (portions) of circles. Arcs of a circle can be measured by length, but they are also often measured by angles. In the latter case, the measure of the arc is the same as the measure of an angle whose vertex is at the center of the circle and whose sides pass through the ends of the arc. Such an angle is said to be subtended by the arc.

The most commonly used angle measure is degree measure. One degree is the angle subtended by an arc that is 1/360 of a circle. This is an ancient system of measurement probably originally developed by Sumerian astronomers. These astronomers used a numeration system based on 60 (60 x 6 = 360), as well as a 360-day year. They divided the day into 12 equal periods of 30 smaller periods each (12 ×

30 = 360) and used roughly the same system for dividing the circle. Even when different years and numeration systems were adopted by later societies, astronomers continued to use a variation of the Sumerian system.

1 degree (1°) = 60 minutes (60′)
           = 3,600 seconds (3,600″)
1 minute = 60 seconds

When two lines are perpendicular to each other, they form four angles of the same size, which are called right angles. Two right angles make up a line, which in this context is considered a straight angle.

1 right angle = 90°
1 straight angle = 180°

While this system is workable for most purposes, it is artificial. Mathematicians discovered that using a natural system of angle measurement produces results that make better sense in mathematical and many scientific applications. This system is called radian measure. Radian measure is considered a supplement to SI. One radian is the measure of the angle subtended by an arc of a circle that is exactly as long as the radius of the circle.

1 radian = about 57° 17′ 45″

The circumference, $C$, of a circle is given by the formula $C = 2\pi r$, where $\pi$ is a number (approximately 3.14159) and $r$ is the radius. Therefore, a semicircle whose radius is 1 is $\pi$ units long, which implies that there are $\pi$ radians in a straight angle. Many of the angles commonly encountered are measured in multiples of $\pi$ radians:

| | |
|---|---|
| 0° = 0 radians | 90° = $\pi/2$ radians |
| 30° = $\pi/6$ radians | 180° = $\pi$ radians |
| 45° = $\pi/4$ radians | 270° = $3\pi/2$ radians |
| 60° = $\pi/3$ radians | 360° = $2\pi$ radians |

To convert from radians to degrees, use the formula $t \text{ radians} = (180/\pi) \, t°$. To convert from degrees to radians, use the formula $\theta° = (\pi/180)\theta \text{ radians}$.

The U.S. artillery uses the mil to measure angles. A mil is the angle subtended by an arc that is 1/6400 of a circle.

1 mil = 0.05625° = 3′ 22.5″
1 mil = almost 0.001 radian

### Astronomical Distances

One very large measure of distance useful in astronomy is the light-year. It is defined as the distance light travels through a vacuum in a year (approximately 365¼ days). Light travels though a vacuum at the rate of about 186,250 miles per second (exactly 299,792,458 m/s —exact because the meter is defined in terms of the speed of light in a vacuum). It is approximately equivalent to 5,880 billion miles (9,460 billion km).

Astronomers also use a measure even larger than the light-year, the parsec, equal to 3.258 light-years, or about 19,180 billion miles (30,820 billion km).

A smaller unit, for measurements within the solar system, is the astronomical unit, which is the average distance between the earth and the sun, or about 93 million miles (150 million km).

---

The environmental movement in the United States dates from Earth Day 1969, when the American public first began to take stock of the ecological devastation going on around them. Then there were no pollution controls on cars; people and municipalities dumped untreated sewage into the nation's rivers, some of which were so saturated with chemical waste that they actually caught fire; and industrial cities were routinely shrouded with thick acrid smoke.

Many of these problems have been effectively addressed and dramatically diminished. Today the Environmental Protection Agency (EPA) routinely monitors air quality at thousands of sites around the country. Toxic emissions from smokestacks at smelters, factories, and garbage incinerators have been sharply reduced. Mandatory pollution control standards on automobiles have led to an overwhelming drop in lead emissions—96% in the last 10 years alone. Recycling as a way of reducing solid waste has taken hold in cities and towns throughout the country.

## Costing the Earth

Spending on the environment is one of the fastest growing sectors of the economy. In current (1990) dollars, pollution control expenditures in the U.S. rose from $30 billion in 1972 to $115 billion in 1990, and they are expected to reach anywhere from $171 to $185 billion by 2000. As a percentage of GNP, this represents a three-fold increase in spending over the

# The Environment

30 years, from 0.9% of GNP in 1972 to between 2.6% and 2.8% in 2000. This level of expenditure is comparable with that of many Western European nations.

By far the biggest source of funds for environmental cleanup is the private sector, which in 1987 accounted for about 63% of total spending. State and local governments chipped in about 22.5%, followed by the EPA with 7%, the states with 3.5%, and non-EPA federal spending of 3.1%. The EPA predicts that the federal government share will more than double by the year 2000, while the private sector share will shrink to about 60% of the total. The growth in federal spending is due to increased expenditures for military and nuclear waste cleanup by the departments of defense and energy; EPA funding is expected to shrink.

Although their share of total environmental spending will go down, annual local government costs are expected to increase from $19 billion in 1987 to over $32 billion in 2000, a 69% increase. These increases are driven by higher costs for wastewater treatment and compliance with broader and more stringent standards for drinking-water treatment, sewage sludge disposal, and solid waste dis-

posal. The EPA predicts that average household costs for environmental cleanup in 2000 will be 60% to 120% higher than at present, and that the average household will pay an additional $100 annually for locally provided environmental services. Municipalities with populations under 2,500 and over 250,000 will be hardest hit: households in these cities will pay an average 0.7% and 0.5% of their incomes for environmental services, respectively.

### Assessing Environmental Risk

While expenditures for environmental protection are significant, many feel they are misapportioned. Based on the findings of a scientific advisory group, the EPA has ranked the major environmental issues as follows:

**High risk** Habitat destruction; global warming; ozone layer depletion; species extinction; biological diversity.

**Medium risk** Herbicides and pesticides; surface water pollution; airborne toxic substances.

**Low risk** Oil spills; radioactive materials; groundwater pollution.

**Human health risks** Indoor air pollution; outdoor air pollution; drinking water; exposure to chemicals.

Despite such findings, the EPA expects that over the next decade there will be a major reallocation of the percentage of pollution control expenditures to land pollution control (including groundwater protection) and away from air and water pollution control.

## MAJOR EVENTS IN THE HISTORY OF THE ENVIRONMENT

**1775** Sir Percival Potts observes that chimney sweeps develop cancer as a result of their contact with soot, the first recognition of environmental factors on cancer.

**1872** Robert Angus Smith (Scottish: 1817–84) describes acid rain.
Yellowstone, world's first national park, opens.

**1885** Canada establishes first national park at Banff, Alberta.

**1892** John Muir (Scottish-American: 1838–1914) founds the Sierra Club.

**1905** U.S. Forest Service established.

**1914** Passenger pigeon and Carolina parakeet declared extinct.

**1916** National Park Service established.

**1939** Paul Müller (Swiss: 1899–1965) discovers insecticidal properties of DDT.

**1948** Five days of smog kills 20 people in Donora, Pennsylvania.

**1952** Smog blamed for 4,000 deaths in London.

**1953** Smog blamed for 200 deaths in New York.

**1955** Link between exposure to asbestos and lung cancer established.

**1957** Nuclear wastes stored by the Soviet Union in a remote mountain region of the Urals explode; radioactive contamination affects thousands of square miles; several villages permanently evacuated.

**1961** Investigations in Scandinavia and the U.S. Adirondacks confirm that acid rain kills some species living in lakes.

**1962** *Silent Spring* by Rachel Carson (American: 1907–64) attacks pesticide use and stimulates major environmental movement.

**1964** Congress passes Wilderness Act, setting up the National Wilderness Preservation System.

**1965** Congress passes Highway Beautification Act, banning many highway billboards.

**1966** Congress passes Rare and Endangered Species Act.

**1967** S. Manabe and R.T. Wetherald predict that increased amounts of carbon dioxide in the atmosphere will lead to greenhouse effect.

**1968** Congress passes Wild and Scenic River Act.

**1970** First Earth Day celebrated on April 22.

**1972** Congress passes Clean Air Act.

**1974** F. Sherwood Rowland and Mario Molinas warn that chlorofluorocarbons (CFCs) are destroying ozone layer.

**1976** Congress passes Toxic Substances Control Act to control hazardous industrial chemicals.

**1977** U.S. signs Convention of International Trade in Endangered Species.

**1978** Community of Love Canal, near Niagara, N.Y., evacuated after hazardous waste dumps are uncovered. EPA declares site safe in 1990.

**1979** Nuclear reactor at Three Mile Island, near Harrisburg, Pa., suffers partial meltdown; radiation confined to reactor dome.

**1980** Congress passes Comprehensive Environmental Response, Compensation and Liability Act (the "Superfund") to clean up hazardous waste sites.

**1983** Scientists predict that a large-scale nuclear war could produce "nuclear winter," cold global temperatures that might destroy most living creatures.
Community of Times Beach, Mo., evacuated after soil is found to be contaminated with dioxin from waste oil used to keep down road dust.

**1984** More than 2,000 die and thousands are injured from toxic gas in an industrial accident at the U.S.-owned Union Carbide plant in Bhopal, India.

**1985** British scientists discover a "hole" in the ozone layer develops over Antarctica during the warmer months.

**1986** A worldwide ban on whaling (with limited exceptions) begins.
Chernobyl nuclear reactor number 4 explodes and burns causing 31 deaths within days, shortening the lives of thousands, and forcing the evacuation of hundreds of square miles in the Soviet Ukraine for an unknown length of time; radioactivity also contaminates food products across northern Europe.

**1987** Last-known wild California condor trapped and moved to a zoo to save species from extinction.

**1989** *Exxon Valdez* grounds, leaking 35,000 tons of oil into Prince William Sound in southern Alaska.
Thirteen industrial nations agree to halt production of CFCs by the year 2000.

**1990** Federal panel reports that low-level radiation from sources such as power lines, toasters, and electric blankets can cause leukemia in children.

## GLOBAL WARMING

Many scientists today believe that over the past century the Earth has begun to warm significantly—about 0.5°C—and that at its current rate, it is likely to warm as much as 1.5° to 2.5°C more over the next 50 to 60 years. According to measurements by scientists working independently in Great Britain and the United States, eight of the 10 warmest years recorded since 1880 were 1983 through 1990, and 1990 was the warmest year on record—15.45°C (59.81°F). The magnitude of such climatic change is staggering—the temperature has risen only 5°C since the end of the last ice age 18,000 years ago. The additional warming would raise sea level a meter or more, threatening water supplies, forests, and agriculture in many parts of the world.

Sunlight that reaches the surface of the earth is partly absorbed and partly reflected. The absorbed light heats the surface and is later emitted from the surface as infrared radiation. Gases that are not transparent to infrared radiation (carbon dioxide is one) collect this heat and keep it in the atmosphere. Our atmosphere is only 0.03% carbon dioxide, but combined with other gases this is enough to trap 30% of the reflected heat (the rest is radiated out to space) and maintain the Earth's average temperature at about 15°C (59°F).

Since the Industrial Revolution, an unprecedented amount of four primary greenhouse gases has been released into the atmosphere. In addition to carbon dioxide, these are chlorofluorocarbons (CFCs), methane, and nitrogen oxide. The worst offenders are CFCs, which in addition to contributing to the greenhouse effect also destroy stratospheric ozone which shields the Earth's surface (and inhabitants) from ultraviolet rays. Countries of the European Community, the United States, the USSR, and Japan have agreed to a 100% phaseout of CFCs by the year 2000.

The sources of methane and nitrogen oxide are neither as easy to identify nor as easy to control. Methane is emitted by decomposing organic waste, natural-gas leaks, and fermenting rice paddies. The primary sources of nitrogen oxide are automobile exhaust and industrial smoke stacks, especially coal-fired plants. The increased presence of carbon dioxide is due primarily to the burning of carbon fuels including oil, coal, and natural gas, as well as burning trees for deforestation.

Most of the consequences of global warming would result from one of three physical changes:

**Sea level rise** Climatologists generally expect the sea level to rise at least 30–40 cm (1 ft.), and possibly as much as 200 cm (6.6 ft.) in the next century. Generally speaking, a rise in sea level would be uniform—both geographically and seasonally—because sea level is a global phenomenon. The impact of such a rise, however, would vary greatly from place to place. A one-meter (3-ft.) rise would inundate 18,000 square kilometers (7,000 sq. mi.) of dry land—an area the size of Massachusetts—in the United States, mostly in the southeast. It would also destroy a comparable area of coastal wetlands, erode recreational beaches 100 to 200 meters, exacerbate coastal flooding, and increase the salinity of aquifers and estuaries. It is likely that the people of an industrialized continental nation such as the United States could sustain the population shifts caused by such climatic changes. However, an estimated one-third of the world's population—about 1.75 billion people, today—lives within 40 miles of the sea, mostly along low-lying flood plains and estuaries. How the low-lying Netherlands or Bangladesh or the island nations of the Pacific can or will respond to such forces is impossible to see.

**Higher temperatures** Temperature change from global warming is expected to have more seasonal and geographical variation, with warming greater in the winter and at high latitudes (closer to the poles than to the equator). The predicted effects on some major cities show how severe the effects might be: Rio de Janeiro will experience 52 days a year with temperatures over 95°F, as opposed to only 5 days now; Singapore will go from 95 days to 124 days; Rome from 6 to 55 days; and Tokyo from 5 to 41 days.

**Rainfall patterns** Climatologists expect rainfall patterns to follow the same pattern of change as temperatures. Although there is a general expectation of wetter winters and drier summers in midlatitude continental areas, the possibility of wetter summers cannot be ruled out for any particular location.

A change in rainfall patterns and increased temperatures could have a severe impact on agricultural crops and other forms of vegetation, as well as the animals that depend on them, by disrupting their natural growing seasons. Rising temperatures would also enable insects and fungal pests to migrate to previously unaffected farming regions. Plants that spread easily can adapt to new climates, but trees do not migrate, as scientists call it, very fast, and many types of forests and their ecosystems could be permanently lost.

## THE OZONE LAYER

There are two distinct problems associated with the chemical ozone ($O_3$): ground-level ozone, the main component of smog, which is discussed under "Air Pollution," and stratospheric ozone. The primary difference between the two problems is that at ground level there is too much ozone, while in the stratosphere there is not enough.

The problem of stratospheric ozone depletion is closely related to global warming in terms of its causes and its remedies. Stratospheric ozone (sometimes referred to as upper-atmosphere or atmospheric ozone) absorbs most of the Sun's ultraviolet radiation. A significant reduction of the ozone layer would lead to sharp increases in the incidence of skin cancer and cataracts in humans. It is also thought that there would be serious losses of small ocean algae, which produce oxygen and break down carbon dioxide, and of bacteria important to crop production.

Complex natural forces are continually at work creating and destroying ozone in the atmosphere. This involves first the breakdown of individual molecules of oxygen ($O_2$) into atomic oxygen (O), through the absorption of ultraviolet radiation. In turn, each atomic oxygen normally combines with an additional molecule of $O_2$ to form ozone ($O_3$). Destruction of ozone can be caused by the occasional recombination of ozone with atomic oxygen to form two molecules of $O_2$. As long as the Earth's sunlit atmosphere contains molecular oxygen, as it has for more than one billion years, ozone will be maintained in this dynamic balance.

This balance can be altered, however, by the introduction into the atmosphere of ozone-destroying chemicals that shift the equilibrium toward smaller average concentrations of ozone. In 1974, scientists saw the first suggestion that a group of chemicals known as chlorofluorocarbons (CFCs) could be a major avenue for adding chlorine to the atmosphere and disturbing the ozone balance.

CFCs were developed in the 1930s after a search for an ammonia substitute in refrigeration use. The results of this search produced a family of chemicals with properties ideal for many applications beyond refrigeration. Chemically inert, nontoxic, and easily liquified, CFC use became widespread in air conditioning, packaging and insulation, as a solvent for cleaning electronic circuit boards, and as an aerosol propellant.

It is this very absence of chemical reactivity that makes CFCs so dangerous to the ozone layer. Unlike less inert compounds, CFCs are not destroyed or removed in the lower atmosphere by rain, oxidation, or sunlight. Instead they drift into the upper atmosphere, where their chlorine components are released into the atmosphere under the effects of ultraviolet radiation. Almost all of these freed chlorine atoms find and react with the ozone, creating chlorine monoxide. In a subsequent reaction, the chlorine monoxide releases its oxygen atom to form molecular oxygen, and the chlorine atom is freed once again to repeat the process. The atmospheric lifetimes for the most commonly used CFC compounds have been estimated to be between 75 and 110 years, so through this continuing cycle of reactions, each chlorine atom can destroy about 100,000 molecules of ozone before the chain reaction ends.

To combat ozone depletion, there have been stringent reductions in CFC use. The United States, the USSR, Japan, and the nations of the European Community have agreed to reduce CFC production and use 100 percent by 2000. Even so, it will be many decades before the amount of chlorine in the ozone layer begins to decline.

## U.S. WETLANDS

Marshes, swamps, bogs, small ponds, sloughs, potholes, river overflows, oxbows, mud flats, wet meadows—in general, wetlands are lands where saturation with water is the dominant factor in determining the nature of soil development and the types of plant and animal communities living in the soil and on its surface. Technically, wetlands are lands transitional between terrestrial and aquatic systems, where the water table is usually at or near the surface, or the land is covered by shallow water.

Throughout the United States, a wide variety of wetland types exist, ranging from permafrost-underlain wetlands in Alaska, to tropical rain forests in Hawaii, to riparian wetlands in the arid Southwest. Found in every state in the nation, wetlands vary in size, shape, and type because of differing climate, vegetation, soils, and hydrologic conditions. They are characterized both by their location (coastal, upland, estuarine, and so on) and by their dominant vegetation. Emergent wetlands (marshes and wet meadows) are dominated by grasses, sedges, and other herbaceous (nonwoody) plants. Shrub wetlands (shrub swamps and bogs) are represented by woody plants less than 20 feet tall. And forested wetlands (wooded swamps and bottomland hardwood forests) are dominated by trees greater than 20 feet tall.

Wetlands produce numerous benefits for society, benefits that are either irreplaceable if lost or that can be replaced only at immense expense. Broadly, wetlands regulate water flows, storing water and buffering the effects of storms; they filter and help to purify water; and they provide essential habitats for flora and fauna.

Wetlands are among the most productive natural ecosystems in the world, and certain types of wetlands rival our best corn fields. Wetlands can be regarded as the farmlands of the aquatic environment since they produce great volumes of food. Although direct grazing of most wetland plants is generally limited, their major food value comes from dead leaves and stems that break down in the water to form small particles of organic material called detritus. This serves as the principal food for many small aquatic invertebrates and forage fishes that are food for larger predatory fishes and so on, up the food chain.

As the nursery of much of life, wetlands provide habitats for many species of fish and wildlife, including migratory birds, endangered species, commercially and recreationally important fish, shellfish, and fur-bearing animals, as well as many unique species and communities of wild plants. One-third of the nation's endangered or threatened species live in or are dependent on wetlands. Coastal wetlands are spawning grounds and nurseries for between 60% and 90% of U.S. commercial fisheries, and they are vital to the nation's $10-

## STATES WITH MOST WETLAND ACREAGE, 1780s-1980s

| | Wetlands in 1780s | | Wetlands in 1980s | | |
| State | Acres | Percent of area | Acres | Percent of area | Percent lost |
|---|---|---|---|---|---|
| Alaska | 170,200,000 | 45.3% | 170,000,000 | 45.3% | −0.1% |
| Florida | 20,325,013 | 54.2 | 11,038,300 | 29.5 | −46 |
| Louisiana | 16,194,500 | 52.1 | 8,784,200 | 28.3 | −46 |
| Minnesota | 15,070,000 | 28.0 | 8,700,000 | 16.2 | −42 |
| Texas | 15,999,700 | 9.4 | 7,612,412 | 4.4 | −52 |
| North Carolina | 11,089,500 | 33.0 | 5,689,500 | 16.9 | −49 |
| Michigan | 11,200,000 | 30.1 | 5,583,400 | 15.0 | −50 |
| Wisconsin | 9,800,000 | 27.3 | 5,331,392 | 14.8 | −46 |
| Georgia | 6,843,200 | 18.2 | 5,298,200 | 14.1 | −23 |
| Maine | 6,460,000 | 30.4 | 5,199,200 | 24.5 | −20 |

**Note:** Ranked by wetlands acreage in the 1980s. **Source:** U.S. Dept. of Interior, Fish and Wildlife Service, *Wetlands in the United States, 1780s to 1980s* (1990).

billion-per-year fishing harvest. Wetlands also support a major portion of the nation's multi-million-dollar annual fur and hide harvest. Sport fishing, hunting, bird-watching, and other wetland-related recreational activities also generate billions of dollars annually.

Wetlands provide a natural means of flood control, slowing and retaining water during periods of high runoff. This buffers the impact of storms and reduces shoreline erosion, thereby protecting against the loss of life and property. Moreover, through processes not yet thoroughly understood, wetlands can moderate local temperature and precipitation.

By filtering out pollutants and trapping sediment, wetlands help maintain water quality. Artificial wetlands are now being created as a means of treating sewage. When wetlands are seriously altered or destroyed, rivers, lakes, and streams are subjected to more agricultural and urban runoff, which can flow into sensitive estuaries, harming fisheries and also impairing drinking-water supplies. The ability of wetlands to assimilate wastes can be exceeded, however, and such degradation of wetland water quality is becoming a serious problem.

**Wetlands losses** From colonial times until just recently, wetlands have been regarded as nuisances, wastelands, habitats for pests, and threats to public health. They have been drained, cleared, filled, exploited for whatever resources could be extracted from them, and altered in every conceivable way. They have been everything but appreciated. One indicator of how vital wetlands are can be seen in the effect of the Midwest drought of 1988: the number of migratory ducks and other waterfowl fell to 64 million per year, from an average of 92 million per year in the 1970s.

According to a U.S. Fish and Wildlife Department report issued in 1990, the land area that now comprises the United States contained an estimated 392 million acres of wetlands 200 years ago—221 million acres in the lower 48 states. By the 1980s, only an estimated 104 million acres of wetlands remained in the lower 48 states: as a percentage of surface land area, wetlands declined from 12% to 5%. Ten states have lost at least 70% of their wetlands, and 22 states have lost more than 50%. Alaska, Florida, Louisiana, Minnesota, and Texas have the greatest wetland acreage.

Wetlands are naturally changing environments subject to both human-induced and natural forces. Almost all wetland losses have been due to draining and clearing wetlands for cropland. In the 1980s, there were an estimated 107.5 million acres of artificially drained agricultural land. Among the other human causes of wetland loss are pond and lake construction for water supply, flood protection, and recreation; filling wetlands for houses and other buildings, highways, and waste disposal; dredging and channelizing wetlands for navigation or to facilitate timber harvest; peat, coal, sand, and gravel mining; and pollution by direct or indirect discharge of pesticides, sediment, domestic sewage, and agricultural wastes.

Natural forces affecting wetlands include the subsidence of coastal areas from sea level rise; natural succession from one wetland type to another; erosion and accretion; animal actions, including beaver impoundments and muskrat and goose "eat-outs"; droughts; and hurricanes and other major storms.

## AIR POLLUTION

The Environmental Protection Agency (EPA) monitors the nation's air quality at approximately 3,000 sites around the country. Of special concern are six pollutants for which the EPA has set National Ambient Air Quality Standards (NAAQS). Primary standards are designed to protect public health, while secondary standards protect public welfare, including the effects of air pollution on vegetation, materials, and visibility. The six pollutants are: particulate matter ($PM_{10}$), sulfur dioxide ($SO_2$), carbon monoxide (CO), nitrogen dioxide ($NO_2$), lead (Pb), and ozone ($O_3$). (This is ground level, or tropospheric, ozone, not stratospheric ozone, which is a beneficial screen to the Sun's ultraviolet rays.) The EPA estimates that pollution controls have substantially decreased the emissions of these pollutants since 1970 as follows: particulate matter emissions are 30% what they would be without controls, sulphur dioxide 58%, nitrogen oxides 72%, carbon dioxide 43%, lead 3%, and volatile organic compounds (VOCs) 58%. (Because ozone is a secondary pollutant formed by the reaction of reactive volatile organic compounds and nitrogen oxides, emissions of VOCs are measured rather than ozone.)

**Particulate matter ($PM_{10}$)** The EPA measures particulate matter with an aerodynamic diameter smaller than 10 micrometers. This includes dust, dirt, soot, smoke, and liquid droplets directly emitted into the air from factories, power plants, cars, construction sites, fires, and natural erosion, as well as particles

## NUMBER OF UNHEALTHY DAYS IN SELECTED METROPOLITAN AREAS, 1980–89

| PMSA | 1980 | 1985 | 1986 | 1987 | 1988 | 1989 | Total 1985–89 |
|---|---|---|---|---|---|---|---|
| Atlanta | 7 | 9 | 17 | 19 | 15 | 3 | 63 |
| Boston | 8 | 2 | 0 | 5 | 11 | 1 | 19 |
| Chicago | 34 | 6 | 5 | 9 | 18 | 2 | 40 |
| Dallas | 19 | 12 | 5 | 6 | 3 | 3 | 29 |
| Denver | 35 | 32 | 42 | 33 | 15 | 10 | 132 |
| Houston | 10 | 19 | 24 | 20 | 25 | 12 | 100 |
| Kansas City | 13 | 4 | 8 | 5 | 3 | 2 | 22 |
| Los Angeles | 220 | 189 | 208 | 185 | 218 | 206 | 1,006 |
| New York | 119 | 21 | 16 | 16 | 35 | 9 | 97 |
| Philadelphia | 52 | 25 | 30 | 33 | 34 | 18 | 140 |
| Pittsburgh | 20 | 6 | 9 | 15 | 31 | 11 | 72 |
| San Francisco | 2 | 5 | 4 | 1 | 1 | 0 | 11 |
| Seattle | 33 | 26 | 18 | 13 | 8 | 4 | 69 |
| Washington, D.C. | 38 | 14 | 10 | 23 | 34 | 7 | 88 |

**Note:** Unhealthy days are those with PSI numbers greater than 100. **Source:** Environmental Protection Agency, *National Air Quality and Emissions Trends Report, 1989* (1991).

## EMISSIONS ESTIMATES FOR EPA-MONITORED POLLUTANTS BY SOURCE, 1980–89 (million metric tons)

| Year | Transpor-tation | Fuel combustion | Industrial processes | Solid waste | Miscel-laneous | Total |
|---|---|---|---|---|---|---|
| | Particulate matter ($PM_{10}$) | | | | | |
| 1980 | N.A. | N.A. | N.A. | N.A. | N.A. | N.A. |
| 1985 | 1.3 | 1.2 | 2.4 | 0.2 | 0.8 | 5.9 |
| 1989 | 1.5 | 1.3 | 2.3 | 0.2 | 0.7 | 5.9 |
| | Sulfur oxides ($SO_x$) | | | | | |
| 1980 | 0.9 | 18.7 | 3.8 | 0.0 | 0.0 | 23.4 |
| 1985 | 0.9 | 17.0 | 3.2 | 0.0 | 0.0 | 20.9 |
| 1989 | 1.0 | 16.8 | 3.3 | 0.0 | 0.0 | 21.1 |
| | Carbon monoxide (CO) | | | | | |
| 1980 | 56.1 | 7.4 | 6.3 | 2.2 | 7.6 | 79.6 |
| 1985 | 47.9 | 7.5 | 4.4 | 1.9 | 7.9 | 69.6 |
| 1989 | 40.0 | 7.8 | 4.6 | 1.7 | 6.7 | 60.9 |
| | Ozone ($O_3$) | | | | | |
| 1980 | 9.0 | 0.9 | 9.2 | 0.6 | 2.9 | 22.7 |
| 1985 | 7.6 | 0.9 | 8.5 | 0.6 | 2.6 | 20.2 |
| 1989 | 6.4 | 0.9 | 8.1 | 0.6 | 2.5 | 18.5 |

**Source:** Environmental Protection Agency, *National Air Quality and Emissions Trends Report, 1989* (1991).

formed in the atmosphere by condensation or transformation of emitted gases such as sulfur dioxide and volatile organic compounds.

Particulate matter is responsible for most adverse health effects in the lower regions of the respiratory tract. People with chronic obstructive pulmonary or cardiovascular disease, individuals with influenza, asthmatics, the elderly, and children are especially sensitive. $PM_{10}$ also causes material soiling and is responsible for substantial visibility impairment in many parts of the United States.

**Sulfur dioxide (SO₂)** Ambient sulfur dioxide comes mostly from stationary-source coal and oil combustion, refineries, pulp and paper mills, and nonferrous smelters. The health hazards associated with exposure to $SO_2$ include impaired breathing, respiratory illness, alterations in the lungs' defenses, and aggravation of existing respiratory and cardiovascular disease. Those most sensitive to $SO_2$ include asthmatics and people with chronic lung disease or cardiovascular disease, children, and the elderly. Sulfur dioxide also damages leaves on trees and crops and it is an agent of acid rain.

Electric utilities generate two-thirds of all $SO_2$ emissions, 95% of which come from coal-fired power plants. Sulfur dioxide emissions decreased 10% between 1980 and 1989 due to three factors: installation of desulfurization controls at new coal-fired electric-generating stations and a reduction in the average sulfur content of fuels; implementation of emission-reduction controls at sulfuric acid manufacturing plants and nonferrous smelters, and the shutdown of some large smelters; and decreased use of coal by other stationary-source fuel combustors.

**Carbon monoxide (CO)** Carbon monoxide is a colorless, odorless, and poisonous gas produced by incomplete burning of carbon in fuels. Carbon monoxide enters the bloodstream and disrupts delivery of oxygen to the body's organs and tissues. The health threat from carbon monoxide is serious for those who suffer from cardiovascular diseases. Healthy individuals are also affected, and exposure to elevated carbon monoxide levels is associated with impairment of visual perception and manual dexterity.

Although carbon monoxide emissions from highway vehicles decreased 33% between 1980 and 1989 (this despite a 39% increase in vehicle miles traveled), CO remains a concern in many urban areas.

**Nitrogen dioxide (NO₂)** Nitrogen dioxide is a yellowish brown, highly reactive gas that plays a major role, together with volatile organic compounds, in the formation of ozone. Nitrogen oxides form when fuel is burned at high temperatures. The two major emissions sources are cars and trucks, and stationary fuel-combustion sources such as electric-utility and industrial boilers.

Nitrogen oxides can irritate the lungs and lower resistance to respiratory infections such as influenza. Prolonged exposure to higher than normal concentrations can cause pulmonary angina. Nitrogen dioxide is also an agent of acid rain and plays a key role in nitrogen loading of forests and ecosystems. Over the past decade, Los Angeles is the only urban area in the United States that has recorded violations of the EPA's annual $NO_2$ standards.

**Ozone (O₃)** Ground-level ozone is a colorless gas and the main component of smog. Unlike most other air pollutants, ozone is not emitted by factories or automobiles, but is formed by the interaction of volatile organic compounds and nitrous oxide. These reactions are stimulated by sunlight and temperature so that peak ozone levels occur typically during the warmer times of year. The severity of a smog problem in a given locale is directly related to the temperature and ultraviolet radiation intensity in that area. While the problems associated with ozone depletion (see "The Ozone Layer") and ground-level ozone are usually viewed separately, it is worth noting that as upper-atmosphere ozone is depleted, more ultraviolet radiation reaches the Earth and stimulates the production of ozone/smog.

Both VOCs and nitrous oxide are emitted by transportation and industrial sources as diverse as autos, chemical manufacturing, dry cleaners, paint shops, and other solvent-using industries. High levels of ozone affect people with impaired respiratory systems, such as asthmatics, and exposure to relatively low concentrations of ozone for only a few hours has been found to significantly reduce lung function in normal, healthy people during exercise. This is generally accompanied by symptoms including chest pain, coughing, sneezing, and pulmonary congestion. Ozone is also responsible each year for several billion dollars worth of domestic crop yield losses, and it causes noticeable damage to leaves in many crops and species of trees. Forest and ecosystem damage may result from high ambient ozone levels.

**Lead (Pb)** People can be exposed to lead via air, diet, and ingestion of lead in soil and dust. Lead accumulates in the body in blood, bone, and soft tissue, and because it is not readily excreted, it also affects the kidneys, nervous system, and blood-forming organs. Excessive exposure to lead may cause seizures, mental retardation, and/or behavioral disorders. Even at low doses, lead exposure is associated with changes in fundamental enzymatic, energy transfer, and homeostatic mechanisms in the body. Infants and children are especially susceptible to low doses of lead and often suffer central nervous system damage. Recent studies have also shown that lead may be a factor in high blood pressure and subsequent heart disease.

Lead gasoline additives, nonferrous smelters, and battery plants are the most significant contributors to atmospheric lead emissions. The decline in the share of lead emissions from transportation sources (mostly cars and trucks) is due to the reduction of the lead content of gasoline since the 1970s (to 0.1 grams/gallon as of Jan. 1986) and to the introduction of unleaded gasoline in 1975 for use in automobiles equipped with catalytic control devices, which reduce emissions of carbon monoxide, VOCs, and nitrogen oxides. Unleaded gasoline accounts for about 90% of total gasoline sales.

**Metropolitan area trends** The EPA's pollution standards index (PSI) simplifies the presentation of air quality data by taking data on many pollutants across an urban area and producing a single number ranging from 0 to 500. The health effect descriptions are: 0–50 good; 51–100 moderate; 101–199 unhealthy; 200–299 very unhealthy; and 300–500 hazardous. The PSI is frequently reported as a regular feature on local TV and radio news programs and in newspapers.

## ACID RAIN

Acid rain refers to acidic precipitation of all kinds, including rain, snow, and fog, as well as acidic dust particles. The main component of acid rain is sulfuric acid, a product of reactions of sulfur dioxide released by industrial and power plants fueled by coal or oil. Another major agent of acid rain is nitrogen oxides, which form nitric acid and which are found in motor vehicle exhaust and in emissions from industrial plants that burn any fuel at high temperatures. Burning vegetation also produces nitric acid, as well as formic acid and acetic acid. Acid rain can travel great distances from its source: 10% to 80% increases in acidity have been detected as far away as 2,500 miles from a source.

Acid rain has been implicated in the destruction of lakes, the weathering of man-made structures, and the destruction of forests and crops. When acid rain winds up in lakes, it can increase the level of acidity to such an extent that the lake loses its ability to buffer the acidity with alkaline chemicals from the surrounding soil and rocks. How quickly this occurs is to some extent determined by the nature of the surrounding soil, which means that lakes in some regions are more vulnerable to the effects of acid rain than others.

As lakes become more acidic, small invertebrates die off. This begins a reaction up the food chain: as the smallest organisms disappear, the food supply for larger invertebrates such as fish and frogs is depleted. Because lakes are not closed ecosystems, the demise of fish and other native populations also affects other forms of wildlife that depend on them at some level for their survival. Lakes in the Appalachian and Adirondack mountains, southeastern Canada, and Scandinavia have been severely affected in this way by acid rain; one 1988 study estimated that 25% of the lakes in New York's Adirondack Mountains had become too acidic to support life.

Another clear effect of acid rain is the weathering of marble, limestone, sandstone, and bronze. Statues, sculptures, and tombstones lose their features or become illegible. This effect is not confined to industrial cities, where it is certainly most noticeable. Weathering of the 1,600 tombstones in Gettysburg National Military Park in Pennsylvania has worsened dramatically in recent years.

Although there is evidence that acid rain is a factor in the depletion of forests in some parts of the United States and Europe, whether it is the sole, or even primary, factor is unknown.

Acid rain is also known to be harmful to certain food crops such as broccoli, spinach, and beans. However, few major food crops are grown in regions of high acid precipitation, so the effect of acid rain on the food supply is not considered great.

In China, some of the worst acid rain damage occurs in the Xishuangbanna National Nature Reserve, which is home to several rare mammals, 35% of all of China's bird species, half of its butterfly species, and 4,000 types of flowering plants. In sub-Saharan Africa, acid rain falls on the tropical rain forest as a result of year-round burning of the savannah to clear the land for crops. The Amazonian rain forest also receives acid rain from land clearing on a seasonal basis.

## MAJOR INDOOR AIR POLLUTANTS IN THE HOME

Until recently, most air pollution was viewed as something that occurred outside the house and was in the house only when it drifted in through open windows. Today, with better sealed houses, it has become clear that the house itself, chemicals or activities within it, and even the ground the house is built upon may contribute to air pollution indoors. Some of the pollutants found indoors are more dangerous to individuals than any outdoor air pollution. One estimate is that one-fifth to one-third of office buildings in America have polluted indoor air.

| Pollutant | Sources | Effects | Levels in homes | Steps to reduce exposure |
|---|---|---|---|---|
| Asbestos | Old or damaged insulation, fireproofing, or acoustical tiles. | Many years later, chest and abdominal cancers and lung diseases. | Elevated levels can occur where asbestos-containing materials are damaged or disturbed. | Seek professional help from trained contractors; follow proper procedures for replacing wood stove gaskets that may contain asbestos. |
| Biological pollutants | Bacteria, mold and mildew, viruses, animal dander and cat saliva, mites, cockroaches, and pollen. | Eye, nose, and throat irritation; shortness of breath; dizziness, lethargy; fever; digestive problems; asthma; influenza and other infectious diseases. | Higher levels occur in homes with wet or moist walls, ceilings; poorly maintained humidifiers, dehumidifiers, or air conditioners; and household pets. | Use fans vented to outdoors in kitchens and bathrooms; vent clothes dryers outdoors; clean humidifiers daily; empty water trays in appliances frequently; clean and dry or remove water-damaged carpets; use basement living areas only if they are leakproof and have adequate ventilation, keeping humidity at 30–50%. |
| Carbon monoxide | Unvented kerosene and gas heaters; leaking chimneys and furnaces; wood stoves and fireplaces; gas stoves; automobile exhaust from attached garages; tobacco smoke. | At low levels, fatigue in healthy people and chest pain in people with heart disease. At higher levels, impaired vision and coordination; headaches; dizziness, confusion; nausea. Fatal at very high concentrations. | Homes without gas stoves vary from 0.5 to 5 ppm. Levels near properly adjusted gas stoves are often 5–15 ppm; near poorly adjusted gas stoves, can be 30 ppm. | Keep gas appliances properly adjusted; use vented gas space heaters and furnaces; use proper fuel in kerosene space heaters; install exhaust fan vented to outside over gas stoves; open flues when gas fireplaces are used; choose wood stoves that meet EPA emission standards; have annual inspection of home heating system; do not idle car inside garage. |
| Formaldehyde | Plywood, wall paneling, particleboard, fiberboard; foam insulation; fire and tobacco smoke; durable press drapes, textiles, and glues. | Eye, nose, and throat irritation; wheezing and coughing; fatigue; skin rash; severe allergic reactions; may cause cancer. | Average concentration in older homes without urea-formaldehyde foam insulation generally below 0.1 ppm, but may be greater that 0.3 ppm in newer homes using pressed-wood products. | Use interior-grade wood products; use air conditioners and dehumidifiers to maintain moderate temperatures and reduce humidity levels; increase ventilation after bringing new formaldehyde sources into home. |
| Lead | Automobile exhaust; sanding or burning of lead paint; soldering. | Impaired mental and physical development in fetus and children; decreased coordination and mental abilities; damage to kidneys, nervous system, and red blood cells; may raise blood pressure. | Lead dust levels are 10–100 times greater in homes where sanding or burning of lead paint has occurred. | Have paint tested before removing it in older homes; if it is lead based, cover it with wallpaper or other building material and replace moldings and woodwork; use no-lead solder; have drinking water tested for lead; if exposure is suspected, consult your health department. |
| Mercury | Some latex paints. | Vapors can cause kidney damage; long-term exposure can cause brain damage. | Vapors seldom found outside of homes. | Use paints that are certified free of mercury; do not use exterior latex paints inside the home. |
| Nitrogen dioxide | Kerosene heaters, unvented gas stoves and heaters; tobacco smoke. | Eye, nose, and throat irritation; may impair lung function and increase respiratory infections in young children. | Average levels in homes without heaters is about half that of outdoors; homes with gas stoves or unvented gas or kerosene heaters often exceed outdoor levels. | Same steps that prevent carbon monoxide should be taken to prevent build-up of nitrogen dioxide. |
| Organic gases | Paints, paint strippers, solvents, wood preservatives; aerosol sprays; cleansers and disinfectants; moth repellents; air fresheners; stored fuels; hobby supplies; dry-cleaned clothing. | Eye, nose, and throat irritation; headaches; loss of coordination; nausea; damage to liver, kidney, and nervous system; some organics cause cancer in animals and are suspected of causing cancer in humans. | May average 2–5 times higher indoors than outside; activities such as paint stripping can raise levels to 1,000 times outdoor levels. | Follow manufacturers instructions when using household products; use volatile products outdoors or in well-ventilated places; dispose of unused or little-used products safely; buy volatiles in quantities you will use soon. |

| Pollutant | Sources | Effects | Levels in homes | Steps to reduce exposure |
|---|---|---|---|---|
| Particles (soot) | Fireplaces, wood stoves, kerosene heaters, and tobacco smoke. | Eye, nose, and throat irritation; respiratory infections and bronchitis; lung cancer. | Unless the home contains smokers or other strong particle sources, levels are same as or lower than outdoors | Vent all furnaces outdoors; keep doors to rest of house open when using unvented heaters; choose wood stoves that meet EPA standards; have annual tune-up of heating system; change filters on central-heating and cooling systems and air cleaners according to manufacturer's directions. |
| Pesticides | Products used to kill household pests and products used on lawns or gardens that drift or are tracked inside the house. | Irritation to eye, nose, and throat; damage to nervous system and kidneys; cancer. | Preliminary research shows widespread presence of pesticide residues in homes. | Use strictly according to manufacturer's instructions; mix or dilute outdoors; take plants or pets outside when possible; increase ventilation when using indoors; use other methods of pest control when possible; do not store pesticides indoors; dispose of unwanted containers safely. |
| Radon | Earth and rock beneath home; well water; building materials. | No immediate symptoms; estimated to cause about 10% of lung cancer deaths; smokers at higher risk. | Estimated national average is 1.5 picocuries per liter, but levels in homes have been found as high as 200 picocuries per liter. EPA believes levels in homes should be less than 4 picocuries per liter. | Test your home for radon; get professional advice if radon reduction is indicated; seal cracks and other openings in basement floor; ventilate crawl space; install subslab ventilation or air-to-air heat exchangers; treat well water by aerating or filtering through granulated activated charcoal. |
| Tobacco smoke | Cigarette, pipe, and cigar smoking. | Eye, nose, and throat irritation; headaches; bronchitis; pneumonia; increased risk of respiratory and ear infections in children; causes lung cancer; contributes to heart disease. | Homes with one or more smokers may have level several times higher than outdoor levels. | Stop smoking and discourage others from smoking; if you do smoke, smoke outdoors. |

**Note:** ppm = parts per million. **Source:** U.S. Environmental Protection Agency, adapted from *The Inside Story: A Guide to Indoor Air Quality* (1988).

## OCEAN POLLUTION

In 1989, the grounding of the *Exxon Valdez* resulted in the release of 35,000 tons of toxic petroleum into an environmentally sensitive region in Alaska. Missteps that caused and then followed the spill outraged much of the American public against Exxon in particular and against environmental pollution in general. The story stayed alive into 1990 as the beaches near the oil spill were still polluted, and various legal battles continued in the spring.

While the *Exxon Valdez* captured the largest headlines, the worst problems of ocean pollution were elsewhere. In the United States, various forms of ocean pollution were outlawed or restricted in the 1970s and early 1980s, but lack of compliance has rendered the laws almost useless. One example is pollution by municipal sewage systems, restricted by a 1972 law that set 1977 as a date for compliance. Gradually, that date was extended to July 1, 1988, but on that date, 34 cities on the U.S. East Coast still were not treating their sewage except to screen out large, floating objects.

Another example concerns New York City, its suburbs, and parts of New Jersey, which dump sewage sludge in the oceans. Currently, they dump about 5.5 million gallons a day into a site on the edge of the continental shelf, having had to abandon a previous site closer to the New Jersey shore when it became completely

## OIL SPILLS OF 100,000 TONS OR MORE

| Date | Cause | Location | Tons spilled |
|---|---|---|---|
| Jan.–June/42 | German U-boat attacks on tankers after U.S. enters World War II | U.S., East Coast | 590,000 |
| 3/18/67 | Tanker *Torrey Canyon* grounds | English Channel, off Land's End, UK | 119,000 |
| 3/20/70 | Tanker *Othello* collides with another ship | Tralhavet Bay, Sweden | 60,000–100,000 |
| 12/19/72 | Tanker *Sea Star* collides with another ship | Gulf of Oman | 115,000 |
| 5/12/76 | *Urquiola* grounds | La Coruña, Spain | 100,000 |
| 3/16/78 | Tanker *Amoco Cadiz* grounds | Northwest France | 223,000 |
| 6/3/79 | Itox I oil well blows | Southern Gulf of Mexico | 600,000 |
| 7/1/79 | Tankers *Atlantic Empress* and *Aegean Captain* collide | Off Trinidad and Tobago | 300,000 |
| Feb./83 | Blowout in Norwuz oil field | Persian Gulf | 600,000 |
| 8/6/83 | Fire aboard *Castillio de Beliver* | Off Cape Town, South Africa | 250,000 |
| 1/25/91 | Iraq begins deliberately dumping oil into Persian Gulf | Sea Island, Kuwait | 1,450,000[1] |

**Note:** One ton equals approximately 269 gallons or 6.4 barrels. For comparison, the 1989 *Exxon Valdez* grounding in Prince William Sound, Alaska, spilled 35,000 tons of oil. 1. Based on UN mission estimates.

unable to support life. The dumping was outlawed in 1981, but New York State has been able to get a reprieve from the courts. New Jersey now has a law on the books calling for its dumping to end in 1991. The U.S. Congress has once again outlawed all ocean dumping, this time by 1992. It is not clear how New York City will solve its sludge problem if the 1992 ban is enforced, although the city and nearby Westchester County have agreed to comply with the deadline.

Yet another problem afflicting the oceans

has been an increase in algae, some of it toxic to fish or shellfish. The famous bay scallops of Long Island disappeared from the market completely in 1987–89 as a result of an algal bloom, and millions of fish in various parts of the ocean were killed in the summer of 1988 by other algal blooms. Although part of the problem is caused by untreated sewage, other factors are thought to be agricultural runoff carried to the ocean by rivers and streams and the nitric-acid component of acid rain.

Plastic, which generally does not break

down in the ocean, is another hazard. Although the U.S. Senate has ratified an international treaty to prohibit disposal of plastic wastes that can kill or maim marine creatures becoming entangled in them, the new treaty is difficult to enforce.

Toxic wastes have affected ocean wildlife. Striped bass along the East Coast, which breed in rivers, are polluted with PCBs, potentially cancer-causing chemicals, and the commercial fishery industry has had to be closed. Nearly a third of Louisiana's oyster beds and half of Texas's shellfish beds were closed in 1988 because of toxic pollution of one form or another.

The amount of oil spilled has declined somewhat since 1979, when the amount spilled worldwide on both land and sea was estimated at 1,116,000 tons. Since 1983, total oil spills have stayed in a range between 82,000 and 187,000 tons. Although ship accidents and oil-well blowouts command the public's main attention, most oil pollution in the ocean actually comes from municipal and industrial runoff, cleaning of ships' bilges or tanks, and other routine events.

## SOLID WASTE

Many areas of the United States currently face serious problems in safely and effectively managing the garbage they generate. As a nation, we are generating more trash than ever before, and as the generation of municipal solid waste (MSW) increases, the capacity to handle it is decreasing. Limits to traditional trash management practices such as landfills and incineration are forcing many communities to increase source reduction and recycling programs.

Municipal solid waste is distinct from industrial wastes produced by factories, tailings from mines, construction and demolition waste, sludge from sewage treatment, and junked machinery. MSW is characterized either by the source materials or the end products involved; these characterizations are used to highlight opportunities for source reduction and recycling, and provide information on waste-disposal tendencies.

### Disposing of Solid Waste

Total generation of municipal solid waste more than doubled between 1960 and 1988, from 88 million to nearly 180 million tons per year, while per capita generation increased almost 50%, from 2.7 pounds to 4.0 pounds per person per day. The EPA projects the per capita figure will grow to 4.4 pounds by 2000. The four primary methods of dealing with solid waste are putting it in landfills, incineration, recycling, and composting.

**Landfills** By far the greatest amount of MSW is sent to landfills, of which there are more than 9,000 in the United States. Landfill use fluctuates with changes in the use of alternative waste management methods such as incineration and recycling. In 1960 approximately 62% of all garbage was sent to landfills; in 1980 this figure grew to 81%, and in 1988 it decreased to 73%.

Landfills pose a number of problems. Most landfills are dry and preserve garbage by cutting it off from the rotting influences of air and moisture. William L. Rathje, a professor of anthropology at the University of Arizona and director of The Garbage Project, found that even biodegradable material in landfills does not decay. Newspapers 40 years old can still be read, and hot dogs thrown out years before look more or less unchanged. Some food debris and yard wastes do degrade, but very slowly—about 25% in the first 15 years, with almost no visible change thereafter for the 65-year period Rathje studied.

EPA regulations favor dry landfills for two reasons. As biodegradation in wet landfills occurs there is a buildup of hazardous methane gas, and contaminated water leaching out of landfills (leachate) can pollute the surrounding groundwater. But wet landfills have their supporters, who argue that by enhancing decay, a landfill's biological life can be compressed from 40-to-50 years to 5-to-10 years. Since landfills can contain up to 200 hazardous chemicals, they require continuous monitoring anyway; so shortening their active life can yield significant savings. Moreover, by decreasing the volume of trash in a landfill through biodegradation, it can be kept open longer. This is important because some estimates indicate that 80% of the nation's landfills will be closed within 20 years, and people are increasingly adamant about not having landfills in their communities, which makes it harder to site new landfills.

To create efficient wet landfills, scientists seek to manipulate the levels of three types of bacteria that ultimately convert wood, paper, and other plant wastes to carbon dioxide and methane. The buildup of methane gas, which is produced through the anaerobic decomposition of organic waste, is a hazard the EPA seeks to avoid. Between 1984 and 1989, explosions and fires from high concentrations of methane killed eight people. But despite methane's potential danger, it can be harnessed efficiently, and methane collection projects are in place at approximately 100 landfills for the primary purpose of resource recovery and energy production.

**Incineration/combustion** One popular method of disposing of municipal waste used to be simply to burn it. In the 1940s there were approximately 700 municipal incinerators in the United States. Despite the efficiency with which they reduced the volume of waste, they stank, and their stacks emitted sizable particles of ash, and they produced noxious gases. For these aesthetic rather than environmental reasons, their numbers declined dramatically in the 1950s. By the time of the Clean Air Act of 1970, there were only 67 incinerators still in operation—most with no energy recovery and no air pollution controls.

By 1991, there were 128 incinerators in operation in the United States, 19 under construction, and 70 in the planning stages. Combusted waste represented only 10% of all waste generated in 1980 and 14% in 1988. The EPA estimates that combustion will account for 23% of municipal waste in 1995 and 26% in 2000.

Today, MSW is burned either in "resource-recovery" incinerators or in mass-burn incinerators. The resource-recovery systems, a direct result of the energy crisis in the 1970s, are complex enterprises that depend on the sale of recyclable material and waste-generated power for profits. Although these incinerators were designed with pollution controls, they frequently violate emissions standards.

Mass-burning has been in use in Europe and Japan for a quarter century. In this technique, waste burned at about 2000°F is used to boil water for a steam generator, which produces electricity. In addition to producing a useful by-product, mass-burning reduces the waste to as little as 10% of its original volume, so it takes up less room in landfills. The drawback to mass-burning is that when burned, much of the garbage generates toxic wastes such as lead, cadmium, dioxins, and mercury that wind up in the ash, which then must be buried in landfills.

**Recycling/composting** Recycling of manufactured goods (such as paper, cans, and glass) and composting of organic goods (food and yard waste) are two ways of significantly reducing the amount of waste that winds up in landfills or incinerators. Although composting of municipal waste has been practiced in Europe for more than 30 years—Sweden composts over one-fourth of all its solid waste—it has only recently taken root in the United States. Composted MSW accounted for 0.3% of MSW generated in 1988, but this figure is expected to grow to 4.3% by 1995.

Between 1960 and 1988, the amount of recycled materials in municipal waste nearly doubled, from 7% to 13%. Paper and paperboard are recycled more than any other material. In 1988, 45% of all corrugated boxes, 33% of all newspapers, and 22% of all office paper were recovered. Over 18 million tons of post-consumer wastepaper (that is paper purchased, discarded, and recycled, as distinct from paper damaged and "recycled" in production) were recovered in 1988—25% of all paper waste generated. Based on current trends, the EPA projects that 20% to 28% of MSW will be recovered annually by 1995. Exceeding this projected range will require fundamental changes in government programs, technology, and corporate and consumer behavior.

Recycling is considered vital to reducing the nation's waste. In addition to diverting large volumes of waste from landfills and combustors, it also stops the unnecessary depletion of natural resources and raises awareness about solid waste disposal, because people must become conscious of what they do and do not discard. One impediment to increased recycling is the economic disincentives to processing and purchasing secondary materials, such as the cost of developing new or adapting existing technologies to accommodate recycled materials.

New materials being targeted for increased recycling are plastics and lead-acid batteries. The problem with plastics is that they are made from a wide variety of chemical mixes that, so far, must be recycled independently of one another. Coloring agents in plastics pose additional problems.

## MUNICIPAL SOLID WASTE GENERATED, RECOVERED, COMBUSTED, AND DISCARDED, 1960–88

| Category | 1960 | 1965 | 1970 | 1975 | 1980 | 1985 | 1988 |
|---|---|---|---|---|---|---|---|
| | | | Millions of tons | | | | |
| Generation | 87.8 | 103.4 | 121.9 | 128.1 | 149.6 | 161.6 | 179.6 |
| Materials recovery | 5.9 | 6.8 | 8.6 | 9.9 | 14.5 | 16.4 | 23.5 |
| Recovery for recycling | 5.9 | 6.8 | 8.6 | 9.9 | 14.5 | 16.4 | 23.1 |
| Recovery for composting | 0.0 | 0.0 | 0.0 | 0.0 | 0.0 | 0.0 | 0.5 |
| Combustion | 27.0 | 27.0 | 25.1 | 18.5 | 13.7 | 11.7 | 25.5 |
| Combustion with energy recovery | 0.0 | 0.2 | 0.4 | 0.7 | 2.7 | 7.6 | 24.5 |
| Combustion without energy recovery | 27.0 | 26.8 | 24.7 | 17.8 | 11.0 | 4.1 | 1.0 |
| Landfill or other | 54.9 | 69.6 | 88.2 | 99.7 | 121.4 | 133.5 | 130.5 |
| | | | Percent of total generation | | | | |
| Generation | 100.0% | 100.0% | 100.0% | 100.0% | 100.0% | 100.0% | 100.0% |
| Materials recovery | 6.7 | 6.6 | 7.1 | 7.7 | 9.7 | 10.1 | 13.1 |
| Recovery for recycling | 6.7 | 6.6 | 7.1 | 7.7 | 9.7 | 10.1 | 12.9 |
| Recovery for composting | 0.0 | 0.0 | 0.0 | 0.0 | 0.0 | 0.0 | 0.3 |
| Combustion | 30.8 | 26.1 | 20.6 | 14.4 | 9.2 | 7.2 | 14.2 |
| Combustion with energy recovery | 0.0 | 0.2 | 0.3 | 0.5 | 1.8 | 4.7 | 13.6 |
| Combustion without energy recovery | 30.8 | 25.9 | 20.3 | 13.9 | 7.4 | 2.5 | 1.5 |
| Landfill or other | 62.5 | 67.3 | 72.4 | 77.8 | 81.1 | 82.6 | 72.7 |

**Source:** Environmental Protection Agency, *Characterization of Municipal Solid Waste in the United States: 1990 Update* (1990).

## GENERATION AND RECOVERY OF SELECTED MATERIALS IN MUNICIPAL SOLID WASTE, 1960-88 (millions of tons)

| Item and material | 1960 | 1965 | 1970 | 1975 | 1980 | 1985 | 1988 |
|---|---|---|---|---|---|---|---|
| | | | Gross waste generated | | | | |
| Paper and paperboard | 29.8 | 37.9 | 43.9 | 42.6 | 53.9 | 61.7 | 71.8 |
| Ferrous metals | 9.9 | 10.1 | 12.6 | 12.3 | 11.6 | 10.7 | 11.6 |
| Aluminum | 0.4 | 0.5 | 0.9 | 1.1 | 1.8 | 2.3 | 2.5 |
| Glass | 6.5 | 8.6 | 12.7 | 13.9 | 14.9 | 13.2 | 12.5 |
| Plastics | 0.4 | 1.4 | 3.0 | 4.4 | 7.6 | 9.8 | 14.4 |
| | | | Materials recovered | | | | |
| Paper and paperboard | 5.4 | 5.7 | 7.4 | 8.2 | 11.8 | 13.0 | 18.4 |
| Ferrous metals | 0.1 | 0.1 | 0.2 | 0.4 | 0.3 | 0.3 | 0.7 |
| Aluminum | N.A. | N.A. | N.A. | 0.1 | 0.3 | 0.6 | 0.8 |
| Glass | 0.1 | 0.1 | 0.2 | 0.4 | 0.8 | 1.1 | 1.5 |
| Plastics | N.A. | N.A. | N.A. | N.A. | N.A. | 0.1 | 0.2 |
| | | | Percent of gross discards recovered | | | | |
| Paper and paperboard | 18.1% | 15.0% | 16.9% | 19.2% | 21.9% | 21.1% | 25.6% |
| Ferrous metals | 0.5 | 1.0 | 1.6 | 1.6 | 3.4 | 2.8 | 5.8 |
| Aluminum | N.A. | N.A. | N.A. | 9.1 | 16.7 | 26.1 | 31.7 |
| Glass | 1.5 | 1.2 | 2.3 | 2.9 | 5.4 | 8.3 | 12.0 |
| Plastics | N.A. | N.A. | N.A. | N.A. | N.A. | 1.0 | 1.1 |

**Note:** Covers post consumer residential and commercial solid wastes, which comprise the major portion of typical municipal collections. Excludes mining, agricultural and industrial processing, demolition and construction wastes, sewage sludge, and junked autos and obsolete equipment wastes. Based on material flows estimating procedure and net weight as generated. **Source:** Environmental Protection Agency, *Characterization of Municipal Solid Waste in the United States: 1990 Update* (1990).

**Source reduction** Many experts believe that the key to solving the municipal waste problem is source reduction—minimizing the volume of products and the toxics they contain, and extending their useful life. Removal of toxics enhances the safety of recycling, landfilling, and combustion, while volume reduction helps to extend the capacity of existing waste systems. Without source reduction, the amount of waste generated in 1995 is expected to reach 200 million tons, or 4.2 pounds per person per day. By 2010 generation is projected to reach 4.9 pounds per person per day—a 23% increase over 1988 levels and nearly twice as much as in 1960.

### Waste Characterizations

**Glass** enters the waste stream primarily as discarded containers for food, beverages, and cosmetics, as well as in some durable goods. The increased use of plastic and aluminum for containers has led to a decline in the amount of glass in MSW.

**Metals** are classified as either ferrous metals, aluminum, or other nonferrous metals. Ferrous metals—mostly from durable goods, containers, and packaging—are the largest category of metals in MSW. Recovery rates for ferrous metals are low: in 1988 only 15% of steel cans and 2% of ferrous metals in durable goods were recovered.

Aluminum, used primarily in the making of containers, has largely displaced ferrous metals in that area. About 1.8 million tons of aluminum containers were recycled in 1988. Aluminum is recovered at a rate of about 44%, nearly all of that total coming from recycled beer and soda drink cans.

Other nonferrous metals in the waste stream—chiefly copper, lead, and zinc—amounted to 1.1 million tons. While 73% of this was lead in lead-acid batteries, it is estimated that 90% of all battery lead is recovered.

**Plastics** are the most rapidly growing segment of MSW, increasing 34-fold from 400,000 tons in 1960 to 14 million tons in 1988. But while the uses and demand for plastic grew at a staggering rate, the technology for using recycled plastics is still in its infancy. In 1988, only 200,000 tons, or 1.5%, of plastics were recycled.

**Food waste** includes uneaten food and food scraps from residences, restaurants, and commercial and institutional establishments. The decline of food waste as a percentage of MSW from 15% in 1960 to 9% in 1988 is attributed to the increased use of garbage disposals which send food waste straight to sewer systems, and to the increase in prepared foods, since food preparation waste from foods prepared and packaged off-site is classified as industrial waste.

**Yard wastes,** including grass clippings and leaves from residential, commercial, and industrial sources, made up 31.6 million tons of MSW in 1988. While composting will probably become a significant factor in reducing the amount of yard waste in MSW, only 2% of the total yard waste generated in 1988 was so handled.

## HAZARDOUS WASTE

### Superfund

In 1980, Congress enacted the Comprehensive Environmental Response, Compensation, and Liability Act (CERCLA), better known as the Superfund, a $1.6 billion, five-year program to clean up thousands of hazardous waste sites. The fund was renewed in 1986 and again in 1991. The EPA, which administers the Superfund, can take two types of action when a hazardous substance is released into the environment. It can remove the threat, in an emergency action limited to one year and/or $2 million. Or it can provide a permanent remedial response; this is generally longer-term and more expensive than removal. The money for cleaning up hazardous waste comes from several sources. The preferred source is the individuals or companies responsible for the problem, who can clean up the site voluntarily or after action has been taken by the government. In cases where the original polluters are bankrupt or cannot be found, the Superfund can be used to pay for the costs entirely. Generally speaking, the EPA estimates the average cost of a long-term solution at $25–$30 million.

Before work begins on a long-term solution to a hazardous-waste site, the site must be listed on the EPA's National Priorities List (NPL). Whether a site makes the NPL depends on its score on a numerically based system that factors in risks to groundwater, surface water, and air. CERCLA also allows states and territo-

## STATES WITH MOST NATIONAL PRIORITY LIST SITES, 1991

| State | Nonfederal | Federal | Total |
|---|---|---|---|
| New Jersey | 103 | 6 | 109 |
| Pennsylvania | 91 | 4 | 95 |
| California | 68 | 20 | 88 |
| New York | 79 | 4 | 83 |
| Michigan | 77 | 0 | 77 |
| Florida | 47 | 4 | 51 |
| Washington | 31 | 14 | 45 |
| Minnesota | 40 | 2 | 42 |
| Wisconsin | 39 | 0 | 39 |
| Illinois | 32 | 4 | 36 |

**Source:** Environmental Protection Agency, *National Priorities List, Supplementary Lists and Supporting Materials*, February 1991 (1991).

ries to designate one top-priority site regardless of its score, and there are seven such sites that would not make the NPL on the basis of their numerical score alone.

The Superfund restricts the EPA's authority to respond to certain sites by expressly excluding some substances—most notably petroleum—from the definition of "release." However, in some cases other laws may enable the federal government to undertake or enforce cleanup actions of these excluded substances. Since the Superfund's enactment, it has evaluated 31,000 sites, of which 5% to 10% have been placed on the NPL. As of February 1991, there were 1,189 sites listed, including 116 federal facilities. Groundwater was contaminated at 73% of these sites, surface water at 30%, and air at 12%.

### Hazardous Chemicals

By law the EPA must determine which substances used in the United States that might be released into the environment are hazardous. Hundreds of substances are classified as hazardous, and releases of more than a specified amount must be reported to the U.S. Coast Guard's National Response Center—the 24-hour toll-free number is 1-800-424-8802—who pass on information to the EPA and other appropriate agencies. Substances are considered hazardous if they catch fire easily, are corrosive, react easily with other chemicals, or are toxic. Some substances are hazardous because they cause cancer, such as asbestos.

Toxic chemicals must also be reported annually, and extremely hazardous substances require emergency planning if you possess over a certain amount, called the Threshold Planning Quantity (TPQ). If you exceed the TPQ, you must have a plan for emergencies.

Since 1963 there have been 17 U.S. industrial accidents in which the amounts and toxicity of chemicals released exceeded that of the accident in Bhopal, India (1984), which killed about 3,000 people and seriously injured many more. Luck, planning, and other circumstances, however, resulted in fatalities in only a single accident, a release of vinyl chloride in Maine in 1964 that took five lives. It is disturbing, however, to note that 15 of the 17 accidents of this magnitude took place in the 1980s.

Smaller toxic releases have also caused

death and injury. From 1982 to 1988, 11,048 toxic spills caused a total of 309 deaths and 11,341 injuries.

The accompanying table describes some of the most commonly used substances in the United States, general information about them, and the amount that must be reported to the National Response Center if any are released into the environment.

### Nuclear Waste

Nuclear waste in the United States comes from either nuclear-weapons production facilities, or from nuclear power plants, some of which are operated by the federal government. The problem with nuclear waste is that it is radioactive and can remain that way for years—in some cases, thousands of years. For this reason, and because the technology to con-

## THE WORST SUPERFUND HAZARDOUS WASTE SITES, 1991

| State | Site | City/County | Rank | When listed |
|---|---|---|---|---|
| Alabama | Triana/Tennessee River | Limestone/Morgan | 31 | Oct. 1981 |
| Arkansas | Vertac, Inc. | Jacksonville | 18 | Oct. 1981 |
| California | Riverbank Army Ammunition Plant | Riverbank | Fed. | June 1988 |
| California | Stringfellow | Glen Avon Heights | 32 | Oct. 1981 |
| Colorado | Rocky Flats Plant (USDOE) | Golden | Fed. | Oct. 1984 |
| Colorado | Sand Creek Industrial | Commerce City | 36 | Dec. 1982 |
| Delaware | Army Creek Landfill | New Castle County | 9 | Oct. 1981 |
| Delaware | Tybouts Corner Landfill | New Castle County | 2 | Oct. 1981 |
| Florida | Reeves Southeast Galvanizing Corp. | Tampa | 46 | Oct. 1981 |
| Florida | Schuylkill Metals Corp. | Plant City | 43 | Dec. 1982 |
| Iowa | LaBounty Site | Charles City | 8 | Dec. 1982 |
| Maine | McKin Co. | Gray | 33 | Dec. 1982 |
| Massachusetts | Baird & McGuire | Holbrook | 14 | Dec. 1982 |
| Massachusetts | Industri-Plex | Woburn | 5 | Oct. 1981 |
| Massachusetts | Nyanza Chemical Waste Dump | Ashland | 11 | Oct. 1981 |
| Massachusetts | W.R. Grace & Co. Inc. (Acton Plant) | Acton | 38 | Dec. 1982 |
| Michigan | Berlin & Farro | Swartz Creek | 13 | July 1982 |
| Michigan | Liquid Disposal, Inc. | Utica | 23 | July 1982 |
| Minnesota | FMC Corp. (Fridley Plant) | Fridley | 17 | July 1982 |
| Minnesota | New Brighton/Arden Hills | New Brighton | 39 | July 1982 |
| Minnesota | Reilly Tar (St. Louis Park Plant) | St. Louis Park | 40 | Oct. 1981 |
| Missouri | Weldon Spring (USDOE/Army) | St. Charles County | Fed. | Oct. 1984 |
| Montana | Anaconda Co. Smelter | Anaconda | 48 | Dec. 1982 |
| Montana | East Helena Site | East Helena | 29 | Sept. 1983 |
| Montana | Silver Bow Creek/Butte Area | Sil Bow/Deer Lodge | 20 | Dec. 1982 |
| New Hampshire | Keefe Environmental Services | Epping | 19 | Oct. 1981 |
| New Hampshire | Somersworth Sanitary Landfill | Somersworth | 16 | Dec. 1982 |
| New Hampshire | Sylvester | Nashua | 24 | Oct. 1981 |
| New Jersey | Bridgeport Rental & Oil Services | Bridgeport | 35 | Oct. 1981 |
| New Jersey | Burnt Fly Bog | Marlboro Township | 42 | Oct. 1981 |
| New Jersey | CPS/Madison Industries | Old Bridge Township | 10 | Dec. 1982 |
| New Jersey | GEMS Landfill | Gloucester Township | 12 | July 1982 |
| New Jersey | Helen Kramer Landfill | Mantua Township | 4 | July 1982 |
| New Jersey | Lipari Landfill | Pitman | 1 | Oct. 1981 |
| New Jersey | Lone Pine Landfill | Freehold Township | 15 | Oct. 1981 |
| New Jersey | Price Landfill | Pleasantville | 6 | Oct. 1981 |
| New Jersey | Shieldalloy Corp. | Newfield Borough | 47 | Sept. 1983 |
| New Jersey | Vineland Chemical Co. Inc. | Vineland | 41 | Sept. 1983 |
| New Mexico | Cal West Metals (USSBA) | Lemitar | Fed. | June 1988 |
| New York | Old Bethpage Landfill | Oyster Bay | 45 | Oct. 1981 |
| New York | Pollution Abatement Services | Oswego | 7 | Oct. 1981 |
| Ohio | Arcanum Iron & Metal | Darke County | 28 | Dec. 1982 |
| Pennsylvania | Bruin Lagoon | Bruin Borough | 3 | Oct. 1981 |
| Pennsylvania | McAdoo Associates | McAdoo Borough | 26 | Oct. 1981 |
| Pennsylvania | Publicker Industries, Inc. | Philadelphia | 44 | May 1989 |
| Pennsylvania | Tysons Dump | Upper Merion Township | 25 | Sept. 1983 |
| South Dakota | Whitewood Creek | Whitewood | 21 | Oct. 1981 |
| Texas | Crystal Chemical Co. | Houston | 34 | July 1982 |
| Texas | French, Ltd. | Crosby | 22 | Oct. 1981 |
| Texas | Geneva Industries/Fuhrmann Energy | Houston | 37 | Sept. 1983 |
| Texas | Motco, Inc. | La Marque | 27 | Oct. 1981 |
| Texas | Sikes Disposal Pits | Crosby | 30 | Oct. 1981 |
| Washington | Hanford 200-Area (USDOE) | Benton County | Fed. | June 1988 |
| Washington | Hanford 300-Area (USDOE) | Benton County | Fed. | June 1988 |
| Washington | Western Processing Co., Inc. | Kent | 49 | July 1982 |
| Wisconsin | Omega Hills North Landfill | Germantown | 50 | Sept. 1983 |

**Source:** Environmental Protection Agency, *National Priorities List* (Feb. 1991).

tain or neutralize radioactive waste is not very sophisticated, it is very difficult to find states that will allow either the temporary or permanent storage of nuclear waste on their land.

The explosion at the Chernobyl nuclear reactor number 4 in 1986 was the worst publicly documented nuclear accident. According to Soviet government reports, 31 people died in the explosion, but outside experts think the toll was closer to 300 people. The real tragedy and suffering resulted from the release of radioactive materials into the atmosphere which resulted in the evacuation of 100,000 people from a 1,000 square mile area around Chernobyl. Seventy percent of the radiation fell in Byelorussia; as many as 3 million people live on land irradiated by the fallout, and a further 14,000 people were evacuated in 1990. In the city of Minsk incidence of leukemia rose from 41 per million in 1985 to 93 per million in 1990. It is estimated that cleanup will cost more than $45 billion, and that there will be 5,000 to 150,000 more deaths from cancer than if the accident had not happened.

**Nuclear weapons waste** The Nuclear Regulatory Commission is the agency charged with monitoring the disposal of waste generated by civilian-operated nuclear reactors. How-

ever, most of the nuclear waste in the United States is the byproduct of the federal government's nuclear weapons programs. Disposal and monitoring of this waste—which includes millions of cubic yards of contaminated soil and other debris at more than 100 sites in 32 states and the Marshall Islands— is the responsibility of the Department of Energy, the Department of Defense, the Nuclear Waste Technical Review Board, and the Office of the Nuclear Waste Negotiator. Total cost of the cleanup will be about $200 billion, and by fiscal year 1992 the Department of Energy will be the government's largest environmental agency.

The Nuclear Waste Technical Review Board evaluates the technical and scientific validity of the Department of Energy's nuclear waste disposal program undertaken after the enactment of the Nuclear Waste Policy Amendments Act of 1987.

The Office of the Nuclear Waste Negotiator is directed to attempt to find and to negotiate with any state or Indian tribe willing to host a nuclear waste repository or monitored retrievable storage facility at a technically qualified site on reasonable terms.

## ACTIVITIES AT TOXIC WASTE SITES, 1991

| Activity | Number of sites |
|---|---|
| Surface impoundments | 437 |
| Landfills, commercial/industrial | 418 |
| Containers/drums | 301 |
| Other manufacturing/industrial | 235 |
| Landfills, municipal | 231 |
| Spills | 196 |
| Chemical processing/manufacturing | 168 |
| Leaking containers | 117 |
| Waste piles | 116 |
| Tanks, above ground | 111 |
| Tanks, below ground | 81 |
| Ground-water plumes | 70 |
| Electroplating | 69 |
| Military testing and maintenance | 62 |
| Wood-preserving | 55 |

**Note:** Several activities may take place at one site. **Source:** U.S. Environmental Protection Agency, *National Priorities List, Supplementary Lists and Supporting Materials*, February 1991 (1991).

## COMMON HAZARDOUS CHEMICALS REQUIRING NATIONAL RESPONSE CENTER NOTIFICATION (partial list)

| Substance | Remarks | Amount to be reported if released | Substance | Remarks | Amount to be reported if released |
|---|---|---|---|---|---|
| Acetic acid | Vinegar is generally 2% acetic acid, but acetic acid is used in many manufacturing processes; Toxic as vapor at 10 parts per million in air. | 5,000 lbs. (2,270 kg) | Formaldehyde | Used in wood substitutes and plastics; toxic and may cause cancer; extremely hazardous; requires emergency planning if 500 lbs. possessed. | 100 lbs. (45.4 kg) |
| Acetone | Toxic chemical (1,000 parts per million in air) used in large amounts as solvent for resins and fats. | 5,000 lbs. (2,270 kg) | Hydrochloric acid | Used in petroleum, manufacturing, and metals industries; toxic; as the gas hydrogen chloride, it is extremely hazardous and requires emergency planning if 500 lbs. possessed. | 5,000 lbs. (2,270 kg) |
| Aluminum sulfate | Used sometimes in dyeing or in foam fire extinguishers. | 1,000 lbs. (454 kg) | Methanol | Commonly called wood alcohol; used as antifreeze, solvent, and starting material for other compounds; toxic. | 5,000 lbs. (2,270 kg) |
| Ammonia | Use as fertilizer does not need to be reported; however, it is toxic and extremely hazardous; emergency planning required if 500 lbs. possessed. | 100 lbs. (45.4 kg) | Nitric acid | Used in preparing fertilizers and explosives; toxic and extremely hazardous; requires emergency planning if 1,000 lbs. possessed. | 1,000 lbs. (454 kg) |
| Benzene | Used in drugs, dyes, explosives, plastics, detergents, and paint remover; can cause cancer; toxic. | 10 lbs. (4.54 kg) | Phenol | Used in making plastics; vapor is toxic to skin at 5 parts per million in air; extremely hazardous; requires emergency planning if 500 pounds possessed and further planning if 10,000 pounds possessed. | 1,000 lbs. (454 kg) |
| Chlorine | Widely used to disinfect water, the gas is toxic at concentration of one part per million in air; extremely hazardous; requires emergency planning if 100 lbs. is possessed. | 10 lbs. (4.54 kg) | | | |
| Cumene | Additive for high-octane fuels; toxic to skin at 50 parts per million in air. | 5,000 lbs. (2,270 kg) | Phosphoric acid | Used as flavoring agent, in pharmaceuticals, and in manufacturing fertilizers; toxic. | 5,000 lbs. (2,270 kg) |
| Cyclohexane | Petroleum derivative. | 1,000 lbs. (454 kg) | Sodium hydroxide | Commonly known as lye or as caustic soda; toxic. | 1,000 lbs. (454 kg) |
| Ethylbenzene | Toxic at 100 parts per million in air. | 1,000 lbs. (454 kg) | Styrene | Used in manufacture of styrene plastics and artificial rubber; toxic. | 1,000 lbs. (454 kg) |
| Ethylene dichloride | Additive to gasoline that combines with lead to make "Ethyl" gasoline; also used in making plastics. | 100 lbs. (45.4 kg) | Sulfuric acid | Most common chemical used in U.S.; toxic and extremely hazardous; emergency planning required if 1,000 lbs. possessed. | 1,000 lbs. (454 kg) |
| Ethylene oxide | Widely used in making plastics; toxic at 50 parts per million in air; extremely hazardous; requires emergency planning if 1,000 lbs. possessed. | 1–10 lbs. (0.454 kg– 4.54 kg) | Toluene | Used in making explosives, drugs, and dyes; toxic. | 1,000 lbs. (454 kg) |
| | | | Vinyl chloride | Used to make plastics and aerosols; causes cancer; toxic. | 1 lb. (0.454 kg) |
| | | | Xylene | Used to make other compounds; toxic. | 1,000 lbs. (454 kg) |

**Source:** Environmental Protection Agency, *Title 3: List of Lists* (Jan. 1990).

# Endangered Species

A species is a specific kind of organism, such as the common earthworm, the daffodil, the American opossum, or the human. All told there are about 1.4 million classified species of all kinds, including plants, microorganisms, mammals, and fish. This is thought to represent no more than about 10% of all species. (And if the results of some surveys of rain forest canopies in Panama are correct, there may be as many as 30 million insect species alone.) Since life developed more than 600 million years ago, innumerable species have appeared and become extinct. Today, biological diversity faces a rate of species destruction greater than any since the mass extinctions of the dinosaurs 65 million years ago.

Animal and plant species are threatened on a number of fronts. Their natural habitats face destruction through deforestation, wetlands loss, and urban sprawl, and are also affected by processes that derive from global warming such as shifting climate and vegetation zones. Another problem is the shift to "monocultures" in agriculture, producing only one strain of crop for food.

**Biological diversity** What makes monoculture risky is that all plants are equally vulnerable to one parasite. It was just such a circumstance that caused the Irish potato famine in 1848 in which millions died or were forced to emigrate; and in 1970, the United States lost 15% of its corn crop in a similar situation. In many parts of the world, the change to monocultures is a relatively recent phenomenon. In the 1950s, Sri Lankan farmers grew 2,000 varieties of rice; today they rely primarily on only five. In India, where a 15% drop in production could cause widespread starvation, 75% of its rice harvest comes from only 10 strains. The total medicinal value of the world's plants can only be guessed. Not only is their use widespread in "folk" medicine around the world, but even in the United States they are the basis of a quarter of all prescription medicine.

To reverse the trend toward species extinction, governments around the world have set aside a total of about 425 million hectares (about 16.4 million square miles) of protected lands in about 3,500 parks and preserves. In addition, many countries try to identify species threatened with extinction.

In the United States, species are classified as threatened or endangered by the U.S. Fish and Wildlife service in accordance with the 1973 Endangered Species Act, renewed and extended in 1988. The list of endangered species maintained by the Department of the Interior goes back to the original Endangered Species Act of 1966. The first list of endangered species, in March 1967, included 78 species. The current list contains more than 2,000 species. Species listed are protected in various ways, most specifically by a prohibition against killing them. Also, a critical habitat can be protected against change if the change would contribute to species extinction.

## SELECTED ENDANGERED SPECIES OF THE WORLD

### Mammals

**Cheetah** (*Acinonyx jubatus*) It is believed the cheetah almost became extinct at some time in the recent past, causing a "genetic bottleneck" when the population contained only a few closely related individuals. One cause of the fragility of the present cheetah population, which ranges from Africa to India, is this lack of genetic variability—although all the big cats are under pressure from changes in the environment and from hunters.

**Chimpanzee, African** (*Pan troglodytes*) Endangered status applies to chimpanzees in Africa only; the 600 or so chimpanzees in the United States are classified as threatened and may continue to be used in research.

**Dugong, or sea cow** (*Dugong dugon*) An inoffensive sea mammal living in shallow waters around the coasts of the Western Pacific, and Indian Ocean from East Africa to Japan, the dugong is easy to capture and desirable as food. Its hide makes excellent leather. It is so vulnerable, however, that any organized hunting soon leads to local extinction. Although the dugong is protected by law in large parts of its range, controlling hunting at sea is difficult.

**Gibbon** (*Hylobates*, all species) As recently as 1969, a major list of endangered species failed to include any gibbon species. Today all species of this most primitive of apes are endangered, primarily because of habitat destruction.

**Gorilla** (*Gorilla gorilla*) The gorilla is thought to have been endangered since 1933, only 31 years after its "discovery." The causes are habitat destruction, the use of gorillas as a food source, and the sale of baby gorillas to people outside Africa.

**Jaguar** (*Panthera onca*) It is surprising that an animal with a historic range extending from the U.S. Southwest to practically the southern tip of South America could become endangered. Habitat destruction and hunting for its pelt are the most likely causes.

**Leopard** (*Panthera pardus, P. uncia*, and *Neofelis nebulosa*) Three species of leopard are endangered, although the common leopard, *P. pardus*, in the southern part of its African range is not endangered, only threatened. The other two are commonly called the clouded leopard (*N. nebulosa*), found in southeast and south central Asia and Taiwan, and the snow leopard (*P. uncia*), found in the Himalaya mountains and central Asia.

**Monkey** Many species of monkey, especially those from Latin America, such as the howler monkey (*Alouatta palliata*) and the spider monkey (*Ateles geoffroyi*), are endangered. A few African species, such as some colobus monkeys (e.g., *Colobus kirki*) are also endangered. The colobus monkeys are hunted for their fur, while habitat destruction and collecting for pets have been problems for Latin American monkeys. Another group of endangered Latin American monkeys are the tamarins (*Leontopithecus* ssp.).

**Orangutan** (*Pongo pygmaeus*) This great ape has seen its range shrink from much of southern Asia to parts of the islands of Sumatra and Borneo. Habitat destruction and the capture of animals for pets or zoos have been factors, but also young orangutans are likely to catch human diseases. Orangutans also have a very low reproductive rate.

**Panda, giant** (*Ailuropoda melanoleuca*) One of the last large mammals to become known to Western science (brought to its attention in 1869), the giant panda has been one of the favorite creatures of all who have seen it. Its restricted habitat in China's western mountains and restricted diet of bamboo shoots contribute greatly to its endangered status. There are so few individual pandas that collecting them for zoos probably is a factor as well. Some attempts to breed pandas in zoos have been successful, but it is not easy to accomplish.

**Rhinoceros** Most species of rhinoceros are endangered, with the black rhinoceros (*Diceros bicornis*) and the northern white rhinoceros (*Ceratotherium simum cottoni*) the principal foci of concern. Several other rhinoceros species in Asia have been close to extinction for many years. Poachers kill rhinos for the horns, which are valued in traditional medicine and for knife or sword handles.

**Tiger** (*Panthera tigris*) Habitat destruction and excessive hunting have nearly done in the species in temperate and tropical Asia.

**Whale** The blue whale (*Balaenoptera musculus*), bowhead whale (*Balaena mysticetus*), finback whale (*Balaenoptera physalus*), gray whale (*Eschrichtius robustus*), humpback whale (*Megaptera novaeangliae*), right whale (*Balaena glacialis*), Sei whale (*Balaenoptera borealis*), and sperm whale (*Physeter catodon*) are all listed as endangered by the United States. Since 1986 the International Whaling Commission has prohibited essentially all whaling, although a few whales are allowed to be taken by traditional whalers such as the Inuit (or Eskimo) or for research purposes (often disputed). The blue whale, the largest animal of any kind that has ever lived, is most at risk. A 1989 survey estimated that only 1,200 to 1,500 blue whales survive from a population estimated to have been as high as 225,000 before commercial whale hunting started.

### Other Species

**Birds** There are about 9,000 species of birds currently identified around the world. According to the International Council on Bird Preservation, more than 1,000 of these species are threatened or endangered, three times the number at risk in 1978. Dramatic changes in their populations have occurred especially in the tropics, where the number of threatened parrot species has almost doubled since 1978. In Indonesia, for example, the number of threatened species rose from 14 to 126 in the period 1978–88.

Birds have been particularly vulnerable to human-caused extinctions. The first extinctions definitely known to be caused by humans were the extinctions of some 20 species of flightless moas in New Zealand by the Maori, who probably arrived around A.D. 800. The last moa of any species was killed about the time of Capt. James Cook's voyage around the islands in 1769-70. Together with the Europeans who colonized the islands, the Maoris caused the extinction of about a third of the 150 bird species.

Some bird extinctions are well known, such as the dodo (late 17th century), the passenger pigeon (1914), and the Carolina parakeet (1914). But these are only the tip of the iceberg, since about 100 species of birds are known to have become extinct since A.D. 1600 (about the time that good worldwide records of species first became available).

**Reptiles** Many species or subspecies of alligators, crocodiles, iguanas, and sea turtles are endangered. In the United States, protection of alligators has produced a resurgence in the species. Probably the greatest problem is the sea turtles, hunted from the egg to the adult for their food value or their shells. Beaches where they lay their eggs are raided. Another problem contributing to their endangered status is plastic debris in the ocean, which they often ingest with fatal consequences.

**Amphibians** In 1990 amphibian specialists comparing notes at international meetings realized that amphibians were diminishing in number around the world, frogs of many types and habitats among them. While as yet there is no tested explanation for this phenomenon, since amphibians breathe and drink partly through their skins, they may directly absorb toxins from the environment that creatures with less permeable skins are able to shield against.

## SPECIES LISTED AS ENDANGERED OR THREATENED, 1991

| Status, location | Mammals | Birds | Reptiles | Amphibians | Fishes | Snails | Clams | Crustaceans | Insects[1] | Plants |
|---|---|---|---|---|---|---|---|---|---|---|
| Endangered species, total | 303 | 225 | 74 | 14 | 64 | 5 | 39 | 8 | 11 | 187 |
| U.S. only | 35 | 57 | 8 | 6 | 51 | 4 | 37 | 8 | 10 | 180 |
| U.S. and foreign | 19 | 15 | 8 | 0 | 2 | 0 | 0 | 0 | 1 | 6 |
| Foreign only[2] | 249 | 153 | 58 | 8 | 11 | 1 | 2 | 0 | 0 | 1 |
| Threatened species, total | 30 | 12 | 32 | 5 | 33 | 6 | 0 | 2 | 9 | 62 |
| U.S. only | 5 | 7 | 14 | 4 | 27 | 6 | 2 | 2 | 9 | 51 |
| U.S. and foreign | 3 | 5 | 4 | 1 | 6 | 0 | 0 | 0 | 0 | 9 |
| Foreign only[2] | 22 | 0 | 14 | 0 | 0 | 0 | 0 | 0 | 0 | 2 |

1. Includes arachnids. 2. Species outside U.S. and outlying areas as determined by the U.S. Fish and Wildlife Service. **Source:** U.S. Fish and Wildlife Service, *Endangered Species Technical Bulletin* (Mar. 1991).

**Fish** Most ocean fish are thought to be so numerous that they are not endangered, but overfishing has drastically reduced stocks of commercial fish in many specific grounds. Many Pacific salmon runs have been cut in half as a result of fishing in the ocean, mainly by Japanese and Korean vessels, with plastic mesh nets 40 miles long. These nets not only catch salmon but also trap marine mammals, sea birds, and any other fish in the area. Much of this fishing is conducted illegally in waters where it is banned by international agreements. The productive Georges Bank region off the coast of Massachusetts has seen takes of cod, flounder, and haddock drop to a quarter of what they were in the 1960s as a result of overfishing, first by foreign factory ships and later, when the region was restricted to U.S. fishing, by a modernized fishing fleet from New England.

Pressures on freshwater fish can also be heavy, and most endangered species are ones with a limited habitat, which can be altered by dam building or introduction of foreign species.

**Plants** Worldwide the most concern for plant extinctions is in the tropical rain forest. Tropical rain forests have a greater number of species per unit of area than any other type of environment. This is true for all kinds of organisms in tropical rain forests, not just plants, but plant extinctions are of particular concern because of the possibility of extracting useful products, such as medicines, from them.

In the United States, a survey by the Center for Plant Conservation claims that about 8% of all plant species are endangered, for a total of 3,000 species. (This is much higher than the approximately 200 U.S. plant species listed as threatened or endangered by the U.S. Fish and Wildlife Service.) The CPC projects that up to 700 may become extinct by the year 2000.

## MAJOR ENVIRONMENTAL ORGANIZATIONS

**American Forestry Association** 1516 P St. NW, Washington, DC 20005. (202) 667-3300. Concerned with management of forests, soil, water, wildlife; Global ReLeaf tree-planting program; publishes *American Forests*. Estab. 1875. Mem. 40,000.

**Conservation International,** 1015 18th St. NW, Ste. 1000, Washington, DC 20036. (202) 429-5660. Works in partnership with local groups in developing countries to conserve rain forests and other high-biodiversity ecosystems. Estab. 1987. Mem. 45,000.

**Friends of the Earth** 218 D St. SE, Washington, DC 20003. (202) 544-2600. Formed by merger of Friends of the Earth, Environmental Policy Institute, and Oceanic Society; lobbies federal and state governments; publishes *Friends of the Earth*. Estab. 1969. Mem. 50,000.

**Greenpeace, USA,** 1436 U St. NW, Washington, DC 20009. (202) 462-1177. Conducts nonviolent direct action against environmental destruction. Estab. 1971. Mem. 2,300,000 U.S.; 4 mil. worldwide.

**International Union for the Conservation of Nature and Natural Resources (IUCN),** World Conservation Center, Avenue du Mont-Blanc, CH-1196 Gland, Switz. Alliance of conservation authorities, government departments, and independent organizations. Estab. 1948. Mem. 500.

**National Audubon Society,** 950 Third Ave., New York, NY 10022. (212) 832-3200. Local groups (500) interested in ecology and conservation of wildlife and their habitats. Estab. 1905. Mem. 400,000.

**National Wildflower Research Center** 2600 FM 973 North, Austin, TX 78725. (512) 929-3600. Researches wildflowers and other native plants; promotes their conservation and use in planned landscapes; publishes *Wildflower Journal*. Estab. 1982. Mem. 15,000.

**National Wildlife Federation,** 1400 16th St. NW, Washington, DC 20036. (202) 797-6800. Federation of state and territorial conservation organizations working for intelligent management of life-sustaining resources. Estab. 1936. Mem. 5,800,000.

**Natural Resources Defense Council (NRDC),** 40 W. 20th St., New York, NY 10011. (212) 727-2700. Works for legislative change by drafting laws and public education. Estab. 1970. Mem. 170,000.

**The Nature Conservancy,** 1815 N. Lynn St., Arlington, VA 22209. (703) 841-5300. Protects endangered species and habitats through land acquisition. Estab. 1951. Mem. 570,000.

**Sierra Club,** 730 Polk St., San Francisco, CA 94109. (415) 776-2211. Undertakes scientific studies concerning the protection of the world's ecosystems. Estab. 1892. Mem. 633,000.

**United Nations Environment Programme (UNEP),** New York Liaison Office, 2 United Nations Plaza, Room 812, New York, NY 10017. (212) 963-8139. UN coordinating body on the environment. Estab. 1972.

**Wilderness Society,** 900 17th St. NW, Washington, DC 20006. (202) 833-2300. Focus is on issues involving federal public lands, including national parks and wildlife preserves. Estab. 1935. Mem. 400,000.

**World Wildlife Fund/Conservation Foundation,** 1250 24th St. NW, Washington, DC 20037. (202) 293-4800. Promotes appropriate use of the world's natural resources and energy. Merged on July 1, 1990. Mem. 1 mil.

## ENDANGERED ANIMALS IN THE UNITED STATES

Although the world's attention is often on large endangered mammals from Africa or the oceans, the United States is home to many endangered species and subspecies. A subspecies, sometimes called a race, is a local population of a given animal that has some distinctive trait, such as size or color that sets it apart from the main species but is still classed as part of the species because the two populations can and sometimes do breed with each other.

Many endangered species and subspecies, especially birds, live on islands. Of the 100 or so known species of birds that have become extinct since 1600, 85 lived on islands. Because islands have small populations, limited habitats and allow the introduction of new species easily, they are especially vulnerable environments.

In 1989 the General Accounting Office reported that only 16% of endangered or threatened species in the United States were improving their status, while a third were deteriorating. Since the Endangered and Threatened Wildlife and Plants listing was started in 1967, seven listed species have become extinct: the Tecopa pupfish (*Cyprinodon nevadensis calidae*, 1982),

the longjaw cisco (*Coregonus alpenae*, 1983), the blue pike (*Stizostedion vitreum glaucum*, 1983), the Santa Barbara song sparrow (*Melospiza melodia graminea*, 1983), Sampson's pearly mussel (*Epioblasma* (= *Dysnomia*) sampsoni, 1984), the Amistad gambusia (*Gambusia amistadensis*, 1987), and the dusky seaside sparrow (*Ammodramus* (= *Ammospiza*) maritimus nigrescens, 1990). Three species listed as either threatened or endangered have recovered sufficiently to be removed from the list altogether: the Palau dove (*Gallicolumba canifrons*, 1985), the Palau fantail (or Old World flycatcher; *Rhipidura lepida*, 1985), and the Palau owl (*Pyroglaux* (= *Otus*) podargina*, 1985).

## ANIMALS IN THE U.S. OFFICIALLY LISTED AS ENDANGERED, 1991

| Common name | Scientific name | Remarks | Common name | Scientific name | Remarks |
|---|---|---|---|---|---|
| | | **Mammals endangered in the U.S.** | | | |
| Bat, gray | *Myotis grisescens* | Found in central and southeastern U.S. | Mouse, Key Largo cotton | *Peromyscus gossypinus allapaticola* | Subspecies of white-footed beach mouse found in Florida |
| Bat, Hawaiian hoary | *Lasiurus cinereus semotus* | Related to hairy-tailed bats found on the mainland of the Americas | Mouse, Perdido Key beach | *Peromyscus polionotus trissyllepsis* | Subspecies of white-footed beach mouse found in Florida and Alabama |
| Bat, Indiana | *Myotis sodalis* | Found both in East and Midwest | Mouse, salt marsh harvest | *Reithrodontomys raviventris* | Species of American harvest mouse found in California |
| Bat, Mexican long-nosed | *Leptonycteris nivalis* | Found in New Mexico, Texas, and Central America, as well as Mexico | Ocelot | *Felis pardalis* | Small spotted cat found in Arizona and Texas; endangered throughout Central and South America as well |
| Bat, Ozark big-eared | *Plecotus townsendii ingens* | Lives in caves in Missouri, Oklahoma, and Arkansas | | | |
| Bat, Sanborn's long-nosed | *Leptonycteris sanborni* (= *yerbabuenae*) | Found in New Mexico, Texas, and Central America, as well as Mexico | Panther, Florida | *Felis concolor coryi* | Formerly found throughout Southeast, now confined to Florida; estimated that only 30–50 survive |
| Bat, Virginia big-eared | *Plecotus townsendii virginianus* | A subspecies of big-eared bat found in Kentucky, North Carolina, West Virginia, and Virginia | Pronghorn, Sonoran | *Antilocapra americana sonoriensis* | Desert subspecies of the pronghorn found in Arizona and Mexico |
| Caribou, woodland | *Rangifer tarandus caribou* | Endangered in Washington, Idaho, and Canada | Rabbit, Lower Keys | *Sylvilagus palustris hefneri* | Found in Florida Keys |
| Deer, Columbian white-tailed | *Odocoileus virginianus leucurus* | Subspecies of white-tailed deer found in Washington and Oregon | Rat, Fresno kangaroo | *Dipodomys nitratoides exilis* | California subspecies of kangaroo rat, desert rodent not closely related to true rats |
| Deer, key | *Odocoileus virginianus clavium* | Subspecies of white-tailed deer found in Florida | Rat, giant kangaroo | *Dipodomys ingens* | California species of kangaroo rat |
| Ferret, black-footed | *Mustela nigripes* | Found in Western U.S. | Rat, Morro Bay kangaroo | *Dipodomys heermanni morroensis* | California subspecies of kangaroo rat |
| Fox, San Joaquin kit | *Vulpes macrotis mutica* | California subspecies of kit fox; smaller than red fox | Rat, Stephens' kangaroo | *Dipodomys stephensi* (incl. *D. cascus*) | Historic range: California |
| Jaguarundi | *Felis jagouaroundi cacomitli* | Found in Texas and Mexico; northern subspecies of small wildcat | Rat, Tipton kangaroo | *Dipodomys nitratoides nitratoides* | California subspecies of kangaroo rat |
| Jaguarundi | *Felis jagouaroundi tolteca* | Subspecies of small wildcat found in Mexico and Arizona | Seal, Hawaiian monk | *Monachus schauinslandi* | Related species in Caribbean and Mediterranean also endangered |
| Manatee, West Indian (= Florida) | *Trichechus manatus* | Large, plant-eating water mammal believed to have been the inspiration for the mermaid legend | Squirrel, Carolina northern flying | *Glaucomys sabrinus coloratus* | Subspecies of northern flying squirrel found in North Carolina and Tennessee |
| Mouse, Alabama beach | *Peromyscus polionotus ammobates* | Subspecies of white-footed beach mouse found in Alabama | Squirrel, Delmarva Peninsula fox | *Sciurus niger cinereus* | Subspecies of fox squirrel found on Delmarva Peninsula and in eastern Pennsylvania |
| Mouse, Anastasia Island beach | *Peromyscus polionotus phasma* | Subspecies of white-footed beach mouse found in Florida | Squirrel, Mt. Graham red | *Tamiasciurus hudsonicus grahamensis* | Status has prevented construction of telescopes on Mt. Graham, Arizona |
| Mouse, Choctawhatchee beach | *Peromyscus polionotus allophrys* | Subspecies of white-footed beach mouse found in Florida | Squirrel, Virginia northern flying | *Glaucomys sabrinus fuscus* | Subspecies of northern flying squirrel found in Virginia and West Virginia |
| | | | Vole, Amargosa | *Microtus californicus scirpensis* | California subspecies of vole |
| | | | Vole, Florida salt marsh | *Microtus pennsylvanicus dukecampbelli* | Florida subspecies of vole |

| Common name | Scientific name | Remarks | Common name | Scientific name | Remarks |
|---|---|---|---|---|---|
| Vole, Hualapai Mexican | *Microtus mexicanus hualpaiensis* | Arizona subspecies of Mexican vole | Wolf, red | *Canis rufus* | Found in southeastern U.S.; considered endangered except for an experimental population in North Carolina |
| Wolf, gray | *Canis lupus* | Most common wolf; endangered in continental U.S. except Minnesota, where it is threatened | Woodrat, Key Largo | *Neotoma floridana smalli* | Historic range: Florida |

### Birds endangered in the U.S.

| Common name | Scientific name | Remarks | Common name | Scientific name | Remarks |
|---|---|---|---|---|---|
| Akepa, Hawaii (honeycreeper) | *Loxops coccineus coccineus* | Subspecies of 1 of the 22 known species of Hawaiian honeycreepers; 8 species are extinct and 8 are threatened or endangered | Falcon, northern aplomado | *Falco femoralis septentrionalis* | Found in southwest U.S., Mexico, and Guatemala |
| Akepa, Maui (honeycreeper) | *Loxops coccineus ochraceus* | Subspecies of Akepa found on Maui | Falcon, peregrine | *Falco peregrinus* | Although population declined severely because DDT interferes with breeding, they have been making a comeback; continued concern about use of DDT in their winter range in Latin America |
| Akialoa, Kauai (honeycreeper) | *Hemignathus procerus* | Species of Hawaiian honeycreeper | | | |
| Akiapolaau (honeycreeper) | *Hemignathus munroi (=wilsoni)* | Species of Hawaiian honeycreeper | Finch, Laysan (honeycreeper) | *Telespyza (=Psittirostra) cantans* | Found on island of Laysan, in Hawaiian chain |
| Blackbird, yellow-shouldered | *Agelaius xanthomus* | Relative of common red-winged blackbird found in Puerto Rico | Finch, Nihoa (honeycreeper) | *Telespyza (=Psittirostra) ultima* | Found on island of Nihoa, in Hawaiian chain |
| Bobwhite, masked (quail) | *Colinus virginianus ridgwayi* | Subspecies of common bobwhite found in Sonora desert of Arizona and Mexico | Goose, Hawaiian (=nene) | *Nesochen (=Branta) sandvicensis* | Once almost extinct; captive breeding program successful in preserving species and reintroducing it to the wild |
| Broadbill, Guam | *Myiagra freycineti* | Historic range: Guam | | | |
| Condor, California | *Gymnogyps californianus* | Species continues only in captivity; there are plans to reintroduce it to the wild | Hawk, Hawaiian (=Io) | *Buteo solitarius* | Found in upland forests on island of Hawaii |
| Coot, Hawaiian (=alae keo keo) | *Fulica americana alai* | Hawaiian subspecies of common American coot | Honeycreeper, crested (='akohekohe) | *Palmeria dolei* | Found on Maui in Hawaii; now rarely sighted or heard |
| Crane, Mississippi sandhill | *Grus canadensis pulla* | Subspecies of sandhill crane found in Mississippi | Kingfisher, Guam Micronesian | *Halcyon cinnamomina cinnamomina* | Historic range: Guam, Western Pacific |
| Crane, whooping | *Grus americana* | Among most famous endangered species; making a comeback, in part due to program in which sandhill cranes hatch and rear whooping cranes | Kite, Everglade snail | *Rostrhamus sociabilis plumbeus* | Loss of habitat in Florida has confined this bird to one small nesting population; also found in Cuba, where it is not endangered |
| Creeper, Hawaii | *Oreomystis (=Loxops) mana* | Subspecies of either finch or honeycreeper found in Hawaii | Mallard, Mariana | *Anas oustaleti* | Historic range: Guam, Western Pacific |
| Creeper, Molokai (=kakawahie) | *Paroreomyza (=Oreomystis, =Loxops) flammea* | Subspecies of either finch or honeycreeper found in Hawaii | Millerbird, Nihoa (Old World warbler) | *Acrocephalus familiaris kingi* | Found on Hawaiian island of Nihoa; one of the rarest birds on Earth |
| Creeper, Oahu (=alauwahio) | *Paroreomyza (=Oreomystis, =Loxops) maculata* | Subspecies of either finch or honeycreeper found in Hawaii | Moorhen (=gallinule), Hawaiian common | *Gallinula chloropus sandvicensis* | Revered by Hawaiians as bird that brought fire to islands; extinct on Hawaii and Maui, endangered on other islands |
| Crow, Hawaiian (='alala) | *Corvus hawaiiensis (=tropicus)* | Species of crow found in Hawaii | Moorhen (=gallinule), Mariana common | *Gallinula chloropus guami* | Historic range: Western Pacific, Guam |
| Crow, Mariana | *Corvus kubaryi* | Historic range: Guam, Western Pacific | Nightjar (=whippoorwill), Puerto Rican | *Caprimulgus noctitherus* | Puerto-Rican relative of American whippoorwill; once thought extinct |
| Curlew, Eskimo | *Numenius borealis* | One of the rarest birds on Earth; until near turn of the century, large flocks seen and hunted in eastern U.S. during migration from Alaska and Canada to Argentina | Nukupu'u (honeycreeper) | *Hemignathus lucidus* | Originally found on Maui, Oahu, and Kauai; now only occasional sightings on Kauai |
| | | | 'O'o, Kauai (='O'o 'A'a) (honeyeater) | *Moho braccatus* | Of 5 species of honeyeaters in Hawaii, 4 have become extinct since 1859, leaving only the 'O'o, on Kauai |
| Duck, Hawaiian (=koloa) | *Anas wyvilliana* | Closely related to common mallard | 'O'u (honeycreeper) | *Psittirostra psittacea* | Once common on all Hawaiian islands, 'O'u now extinct on Oahu, Lanai, and Molokai |
| Duck, Laysan | *Anas laysanensis* | Historic range: Hawaii | | | |
| Eagle, Bald | *Haliaeetus leucocephalus* | Endangered in all states except Alaska, Washington, Oregon, Minnesota, Wisconsin, and Michigan, where they are threatened | Palila (honeycreeper) | *Loxioides (=Psittirostra) bailleiu* | Once common throughout islands, now found only on Hawaii |
| Falcon, American peregrine | *Falco peregrinus anatum* | Subspecies of peregrine falcon endangered throughout Americas | | | |

| Common name | Scientific name | Remarks |
|---|---|---|
| Parrot, Puerto Rican | *Amazona vittata* | Once common on Puerto Rico and nearby islands, sole remaining population is in Luquillo National Forest, P.R. |
| Parrotbill, Maui (honeycreeper) | *Pseudonestor xanthophrys* | Extremely rare Hawaiian honeycreeper occasionally sighted on Maui |
| Pelican, brown | *Pelecanus occidentalis* | Endangered along Pacific coast and in Central and South America; has made comeback in southeastern U.S. since ban of DDT |
| Petrel, Hawaiian dark-rumped | *Pterodroma phaeopygia sandwichensis* | Subspecies of gadfly petrel; endangered because of predation by rats introduced onto Hawaiian islands where it breeds |
| Pigeon, Puerto Rican plain | *Columba inornata wetmorei* | Subspecies of pigeon related to common pigeons |
| Plover, piping | *Charadrius melodus* | Endangered in Great Lakes region and part of Canada |
| Po'ouli (honeycreeper) | *Melamprosops phaeosoma* | One of 28 species of Hawaiian finches, of which 20 are either endangered or threatened |
| Prairie chicken, Attwater's greater | *Tympanuchus cupido attwateri* | One of 4 subspecies of prairie chickens once found in U.S.; limited to Texas |
| Rail, California clapper | *Rallus longirostris obsoletus* | Historic range: California |
| Rail, Guam | *Rallus owstoni* | Historic range: Western Pacific, Guam |
| Rail, light-footed clapper | *Rallus longirostris levipes* | Historic range: California and Baja California |
| Rail, Yuma clapper | *Rallus longirostris yumanensis* | One of a trio of clapper rail subspecies; endangered in Arizona and California |
| Shrike, San Clemente loggerhead | *Lanius ludovicianus mearnsi* | California subspecies of loggerhead shrike |
| Sparrow, Cape Sable seaside | *Ammodramus (= Ammospiza) maritimus mirabilis* | Subspecies of seaside sparrow, found in Florida |
| Sparrow, Florida grasshopper | *Ammodramus savannarum floridanus* | Like the Cape Sable seaside sparrow, this subspecies is actually a New World bunting |
| Stilt, Hawaiian (= Ae'o) | *Himantopus mexicanus (= himantopus) knudseni* | Subspecies of the black-winged stilt, a wading bird |

| Common name | Scientific name | Remarks |
|---|---|---|
| Stork, wood | *Mycteria americana* | Endangered in Southeastern U.S. |
| Swiftlet, Mariana gray (= Vanikoro) | *Aerodramus (= Collocalia) vanikorensis bartschi* | Historic range: Western Pacific, Marianas, Guam |
| Tern, California least | *Sterna antillarum (= albifrons) browni* | Historic range: Mexico, California |
| Tern, least | *Sterna antillarum* | Endangered throughout Mississippi River basin in U.S. |
| Tern, roseate | *Sterna dougallii dougallii* | Endangered along Atlantic Coast between North Carolina and Newfoundland |
| Thrush, large Kauai | *Myadestes (= Phaeornis) myadestinus* | Subspecies of this Hawaiian thrush became extinct on Oahu (1825), Lanai (1931), and Molokai (1936); there is a subspecies on Hawaii |
| Thrush, Molokai (= oloma'o) | *Myadestes (= Phaeornis) lanaiensis (= obscurus) rutha* | Species of the "Hawaiian thrush"; once believed to have become extinct in 1936 |
| Thrush, small Kauai (= puaiohi) | *Myadestes (= Phaeornis) palmeri* | Found only in forests on Kauai; probably rarest of surviving Hawaiian thrushes |
| Vireo, black-capped | *Vireo atricapillus* | Vireo found in Kansas, Oklahoma, Texas, and Mexico |
| Vireo, least Bell's | *Vireo bellii pusillus* | Subspecies of Bell's vireo found in California and Mexico |
| Warbler (wood), Bachman's | *Vermivora bachmanii* | Considered the rarest North American native songbird; Bachman's may have been near extinction when first noticed by science in 1833 |
| Warbler (wood), golden-cheeked | *Dendroica chrysoparia* | Affected range from Texas to Nicaragua |
| Warbler (wood), Kirtland's | *Dendroica kirtlandii* | Nesting only in Michigan and wintering in the Bahamas, about 1,000 of these birds survive with human help |
| White-eye bridled | *Zosterops conspicillatus conspicillatus* | Historic range: Western Pacific, Guam |
| Woodpecker, ivory-billed | *Campephilus principalis* | Large American woodpecker close to extinction due to destruction of old growth forests in southeast and Cuba |
| Woodpecker, red-cockaded | *Picoides (= Dendrocopos) borealis* | Woodpecker of Southeast U.S.; related to more common downy and hairy woodpeckers |

### Reptiles endangered in the U.S.

| Common name | Scientific name | Remarks |
|---|---|---|
| Anole, Culebra Island giant | *Anolis roosevelti* | Lizard endangered in Puerto Rico and Culebra Island |
| Boa, Puerto Rican | *Epicrates inornatus* | Boa found in Puerto Rico |
| Boa, Virgin Islands tree | *Epicrates monensis granti* | Subspecies of boa found in U.S. and British Virgin Islands |
| Crocodile, American | *Crocodylus acutus* | In U.S., found only in Florida; endangered throughout range in Americas |
| Gecko, Monito | *Sphaerodactylus micropithecus* | Puerto-Rican lizard |
| Iguana, Mona ground | *Cyclura stejnegeri* | Large lizard found on Mona Island (Puerto Rico) |
| Lizard, blunt-nosed leopard | *Gambelia (= Crotaphytus) silus* | California lizard |
| Lizard, St. Croix ground | *Ameiva polops* | Found in U.S. Virgin Islands |

| Common name | Scientific name | Remarks |
|---|---|---|
| Snake, San Francisco garter | *Thamnophis sirtalis tetrataenia* | California subspecies of garter snake |
| Turtle, Alabama red-bellied | *Pseudemys alabamensis* | Alabama freshwater turtle |
| Turtle, green sea | *Chelonia mydas (incl. agassizi)* | Florida breeding ground populations endangered |
| Turtle, Kemp's (= Atlantic) ridley sea | *Lepidochelys kempii* | One of its few remaining breeding grounds is on Padre Island, Texas |
| Turtle, leatherback sea | *Dermochelys coriacea* | Although it no longer breeds in the U.S., the leatherback is found sometimes in U.S. waters |
| Turtle, Plymouth red-bellied | *Pseudemys (= Chrysemys) rubriventris bangsi* | Subspecies of freshwater turtle found in Massachusetts |

| Common name | Scientific name | Remarks | Common name | Scientific name | Remarks |
|---|---|---|---|---|---|

### Amphibians endangered in the U.S.

| Common name | Scientific name | Remarks | Common name | Scientific name | Remarks |
|---|---|---|---|---|---|
| Salamander, desert slender | *Batrachoseps aridus* | Lungless salamander found in California | Salamander, Texas blind | *Typhlomolge rathbuni* | Lives in caves and has external gills, vestigial eyes, and white body |
| Salamander, Santa Cruz long-toed | *Ambystoma macrodactylum croceum* | Mole salamander subspecies found in California | Toad, Houston | *Bufo houstonensis* | True toad found in Texas |
| Salamander, Shenandoah | *Plethodon shenandoah* | Virginia salamander; classified as endangered in 1989 | Toad, Wyoming | *Bufo hemiophrys baxteri* | Subspecies of true toad found in Wyoming |

### Fish endangered in the U.S.

| Common name | Scientific name | Remarks | Common name | Scientific name | Remarks |
|---|---|---|---|---|---|
| Cavefish, Alabama | *Speoplatyrhinus poulsoni* | Found in caves in Alabama | Madtom, Scioto | *Noturus trautmani* | Historic range: Ohio |
| Chub, bonytail | *Gila elegans* | Historic range: Arizona, California, Colorado, Nevada, Utah, and Wyoming | Madtom, Smoky | *Noturus baileyi* | Historic range: Tennessee |
| | | | Pupfish, Ash Meadows Amargosa | *Cyprinodon nevadensis mionectes* | Historic range: Nevada |
| Chub, Borax Lake | *Gila boraxobius* | Historic range: Oregon | Pupfish, Comanche Springs | *Cyprinodon elegans* | Historic range: Large springs in Pecos County, Texas; these have gone dry and now the pupfish survives only in irrigation ditches |
| Chub, humpback | *Gila cypha* | Historic range: Arizona, Colorado, Utah, and Wyoming | | | |
| Chub, Mohave tui | *Gila bicolor mohavensis* | Historic range: California | | | |
| Chub, Owens tui | *Gila bicolor snyderi* | Historic range: California | | | |
| Chub, Pahranagat roundtail | *Gila robusta jordani* | Historic range: Nevada | Pupfish, desert | *Cyprinodon macularius* | Historic range: Arizona, California, Mexico |
| Chub, Virgin River | *Gila robusta seminuda* | Southwestern subspecies classified as endangered in 1989 | Pupfish, Devils Hole | *Cyprinodon diabolis* | Historic range: One spring hole in Nevada; perhaps most restricted range of any vertebrate |
| Chub, Yaqui | *Gila purpurea* | Historic range: Arizona, Mexico | | | |
| Cui-ui | *Chasmistes cujus* | Historic range: Nevada | | | |
| Dace, Ash Meadows speckled | *Rhinichthys osculus nevadensis* | Historic range: Nevada | | | |
| | | | Pupfish, Leon Springs | *Cyprinodon bovinus* | Historic range: Leon Springs, near Fort Stockton, Texas |
| Dace, Clover Valley speckled | *Rhinichthys osculus oligoporus* | Nevada subspecies classified as endangered in 1989 | Pupfish, Owens | *Cyprinodon radiosus* | Historic range: California |
| Dace, Independence Valley speckled | *Rhinichthys osculus lethoporous* | Nevada subspecies classified as endangered in 1989 | Pupfish, Warm Springs | *Cyprinodon nevadensis pectoralis* | Historic range: Nevada |
| Dace, Kendall Warm Springs | *Rhinichthys osculus thermalis* | Historic range: Wyoming | Shiner, Cahaba | *Notropis cahabae* | Found only in Alabama |
| | | | Shiner, Cape Fear | *Notropis mekistocholas* | Minnow found in North Carolina |
| Dace, Moapa | *Moapa coriacea* | Historic range: Warm springs in southern Nevada | Spinedace, White River | *Lepidomeda albivallis* | Historic range: Nevada |
| Darter, amber | *Percina antesella* | Historic range: Georgia, Tennessee | Springfish, Hiko White River | *Crenichthys baileyi grandis* | Historic range: Nevada |
| Darter, boulder (= Elk River) | *Etheostoma wapiti* | Historic range: Alabama, Tennessee | Springfish, White River | *Crenichthys baileyi baileyi* | Subspecies of springfish found in Nevada |
| Darter, fountain | *Etheostoma fonticola* | Historic range: Texas | Squawfish, Colorado | *Ptychocheilus lucius* | Historic range: Southwestern U.S., Mexico |
| Darter, Maryland | *Etheostoma sellare* | Historic range: Maryland | Stickleback, unarmored three-spine | *Gasterosteus aculeatus williamsoni* | Historic range: California |
| Darter, Okaloosa | *Etheostoma okaloosae* | Historic range: Florida | | | |
| Darter, watercress | *Etheostoma nuchale* | Historic range: Alabama | Sturgeon, pallid | *Scaphirhynchus albus* | Affected in a broad range from Montana to Mississippi |
| Gambusia, Big Bend | *Gambusia gaigei* | Historic range: Two springs near Big Bend National Park in Texas; in 1957 there were only 2 males and 1 female; has recovered somewhat since | Sturgeon, shortnose | *Acipenser brevirostrum* | Historic Range: Atlantic coast of U.S. and Canada |
| | | | Sucker, June | *Chasmistes liorus* | Historic range: Utah Lake, a spawning run on Provo River; nearly became extinct during droughts of 1930s |
| Gambusia, Clear Creek | *Gambusia heterochir* | Historic range: Headwaters of 1 creek in Texas; threatened by competition from interbreeding with introduced mosquito fish | Sucker, Lost River | *Deltistes luxatus* | Historic range: California, Oregon |
| | | | Sucker, Modoc | *Catostomus microps* | Historic range: California |
| | | | Sucker, shortnose | *Chasmistes brevirostris* | Historic range: California, Oregon |
| Gambusia, Pecos | *Gambusia nobilis* | Historic range: New Mexico, Texas; now confined to region around Toyahvale, Texas | Topminnow, Gila (incl. Yaqui) | *Poeciliopsis occidentalis* | Historic range: Lower Gila River basin of Arizona and New Mexico and northern Mexico; competition from introduced mosquito fish |
| Gambusia, San Marcos | *Gambusia georgei* | Historic range: Texas | | | |
| Killifish, Pahrump | *Empetrichthys latos* | Found in 1 spring in western Nevada | Trout, Gila | *Onchorhychus (= Salmo) gilae* | Historic range: Gila River basin of Arizona and New Mexico; suffers from competition with introduced trout and from habitat destruction |
| Logperch, Conasauga | *Percina jenkinsi* | Historic range: Georgia, Tennessee | | | |
| Logperch, Roanoke | *Percina rex* | Classified as endangered in 1989 | | | |
| | | | Woundfin | *Plagopterus argentissimus* | Historic range: Arizona, Nevada, and New Mexico |

## Clams, crustaceans, and snails endangered in the U.S.

| Common name | Scientific name | Remarks | Common name | Scientific name | Remarks |
|---|---|---|---|---|---|
| Amphipod, Hay's Spring | Stygobromus hayi | Historic range: District of Columbia | Pearly mussel, pale lilliput | Toxolasma (=Carunculina) cylindrellus | Historic range: Alabama, Tennessee |
| Crayfish (no common name) | Cambarus zophonastes | Historic range: Arkansas | Pearly mussel, pink mucket | Lampsilis orbiculata | Historic range: Midwestern U.S. |
| Crayfish, Nashville | Orconectes shoupi | Historic range: Tennessee | Pearly mussel, purple cat's paw | Epioblasma (=Dysnomia) obliquata (=sulcata) o. | Affected range: Alabama, Kentucky, Tennessee |
| Crayfish, Shasta (=Placid) | Pacifastacus fortis | Historic range: California | Pearly mussel, tubercled-blossom | Epioblasma (=Dysnomia) torulosa torulosa | Historic range: Midwestern U.S. |
| Fanshell | Cyprogenia stegaria (=irrorata) | Affected range along Ohio and Mississippi valleys from Pennsylvania to Alabama | Pearly mussel, turgid-blossom | Epioblasma (=Dysnomia) turgidula | Historic range: Alabama, Tennessee |
| Isopod, Socorro | Thermosphaeroma (=Exosphaeroma) thermophilus | Historic range: New Mexico | Pearly mussel, white cat's paw | Epioblasma (=Dysnomia) sulcata delicata | Historic range: Indiana, Michigan, Ohio |
| Mussel, Curtus' | Pleurobema curtum | Historic range: Alabama, Mississippi | Pearly mussel, white wartyback | Plethobasus cicatricosus | Historic range: Alabama, Indiana, Tennessee |
| Mussel, dwarf wedge | Alasmidonta heterodon | Historic range: Mid Atlantic and New England states | Pearly mussel, yellow-blossom | Epioblasma (=Dysnomia) florentina florentina | Historic range: Alabama, Tennessee |
| Mussel, Judge Tait's | Pleurobema taitianum | Historic range: Mid Atlantic and New England states | Pigtoe, fine-rayed | Fusconaia cuneolus | Clamlike mollusk found in Alabama, Tennessee, Virginia |
| Mussel, Marshall's | Pleurobema marshalli | Historic range: Mid Atlantic and New England states | Pigtoe, rough | Pleurobema plenum | Historic range: Indiana, Kentucky, Tennessee, Virginia |
| Mussel, penitent | Epioblasma (=Dysomia) penita | Historic range: Mid Atlantic and New England states | Pigtoe, shiny | Fusconaia edgariana | Historic range: Alabama, Tennessee, Virginia |
| Mussel, ring pink (=golf stick pearly) | Obovaria retusa | Mississippi mussel, classified as endangered in 1989 | Pocketbook, fat | Potamilus (=Proptera) capax | Clamlike mollusk found in Arkansas, Indiana, Missouri, Ohio |
| Pearlshell, Louisiana | Margaritifera hembeli | Historic range: Louisiana | Pocketbook, speckled | Lampsilils streckeri | Arkansas mussel classified as endangered in 1989 |
| Pearly mussel, Alabama lamp | Lampsilis virescens | Historic range: Alabama, Tennessee | Riffle-shell, tan | Epioblasma walkeri | Pearly mussel found in Kentucky, Tennessee, Virginia |
| Pearly mussel, Appalachian monkeyface | Quadrula sparsa | Historic range: Tennessee, Virginia | Shrimp, Alabama cave | Palaemonias alabamae | Historic range: Alabama |
| Pearly mussel, birdwing | Conradilla caelata | Historic range: Tennessee, Virginia | Shrimp, California freshwater | Syncaris pacifica | Classified endangered in 1988 |
| Pearly mussel, cracking | Hemistena (=Lastena) lata | Mississippi mussel, classified as endangered in 1989 | Shrimp, Kentucky cave | Palaemonias ganteri | Found in Mammoth Cave system |
| Pearly mussel, Cumberland bean | Villosa (=Micromya) trabalis | Historic range: Tennessee, Virginia | Snail, Iowa Pleistocene | Discus macclintocki | Historic range: Iowa |
| Pearly mussel, Cumberland monkeyface | Quadrula intermedia | Historic range: Alabama, Tennessee, Virginia | Snail, Oahu tree | Achatinella (all species) | Historic range: Hawaii |
| Pearly mussel, Curtis' | Epioblasma (=Dysnomia) florentina curtsi | Historic range: Missouri | Snail, tulotoma | Tulotoma magnifica | Historic range: Alabama |
| | | | Snail, Virginia fringed mountain | Polygyriscus virginianus | Historic range: Virginia |
| Pearly mussel, dromedary | Dromus dromas | Historic range: Tennessee, Virginia | Spinymussel, James (=Virginia) | Pleurobema (=Fusconaia =Elliptio =Canthyria) collina | Historic Range: Virginia, West Virginia |
| Pearly mussel, green-blossom | Epioblasma (=Dysnomia) torulosa gubermaculum | Historic range: Tennessee, Virginia | Spinymussel, Tar River | Elliptio (Canthyria) steinstansana | Historic range: North Carolina |
| Pearly mussel, Higgins' eye | Lampsilis higginsi | Historic range: Midwestern U.S. | Stirrup shell | Quadrula stapes | Pearly mussel found in Alabama and Mississippi |
| Pearly mussel, little wing | Pegias fabula | Found from Alabama to Virginia | | | |
| Pearly mussel (=pimple back) orange-footed | Plethobasus cooperianus | Historic range: Midwestern U.S. | | | |

## Insects and arachnids endangered in the U.S.

| Common name | Scientific name | Remarks | Common name | Scientific name | Remarks |
|---|---|---|---|---|---|
| Beetle, American burying (=giant carrion beetle) | Nicrophorus americanus | Midwestern beetle classified as endangered in 1989 | Butterfly, San Bruno elfin | Callophrys mossii bayensis | Historic range: California |
| Beetle, Kretschmarr Cave mold | Texamaurops reddelli | Historic range: Texas | Butterfly, Schaus swallowtail | Heraclides (=Papilio) aristodemus ponceanus | Historic range: Florida |
| Beetle, Tooth Cave ground | Rhadine persephone | Historic range: Texas | Butterfly, Smith's blue | Euphilotes (=Shijimiaeoides) enoptes smithi | Historic range: California |
| Butterfly, El Segundo blue | Euphilotes (=Shijimiaeoides) battoides allyni | Historic range: California | Harvestman, Bee Creek Cave | Texella reddelli | "Daddy longlegs" found in Texas |
| Butterfly, Lange's metalmark | Apodemia mormo langei | Historic range: California | Pseudoscorpion, Tooth Cave | Microcreagris texana | Historic range: Texas |
| Butterfly, lotis blue | Lycaeides argyrognomon lotis | Historic range: California | Spider, Tooth Cave | Leptoneta myopica | Historic range: Texas |
| Butterfly, mission blue | Icaricia icarioides missionensis | Historic range: California | | | |
| Butterfly, Palos Verdes blue | Glaucopsyche lygdamus palosverdesensis | Historic range: California | | | |

**Source:** U.S. Fish and Wildlife Service, *Endangered and Threatened Wildlife and Plants* (1991).

# ARTS AND ENTERTAINMENT

## THE ACADEMY AWARDS

The "Oscars" are officially known as the Academy of Motion Picture Arts and Sciences Awards; they were inaugurated in 1928 as part of Hollywood's drive to improve its less-than-respectable image. (The stated aim of the academy, founded in 1927, was to raise the "cultural, educational, and scientific standards" of the motion picture industry.) Membership in the academy (currently over 3,000) is by invitation only, with members divided into 13 branches. Each branch selects up to five nominees for awards in its own area of expertise, with the entire membership making "Best Film" nominations, and then voting on all the categories. Major awards are shown in the chart. The year 1934 marked a growing number of award categories. "Best Foreign Film" awards, which began in 1956, are listed in a separate table at the end of this section. "Best Directors" are named for films winning "Best Picture" except where indicated.

## THE ACADEMY AWARDS, 1928–90

| Year | Best Picture | Best Director | Best Actor | Best Actress | Best Cinematographer |
|---|---|---|---|---|---|
| 1928 | *Wings* | Frank Borzage *Seventh Heaven* Lewis Milestone *2 Arabian Knights* | Emil Jannings *The Way of All Flesh, The Last Command* | Janet Gaynor *Seventh Heaven, Sunrise, Street Angel* | Charles Rosher, Karl Struss *Sunrise* |
| 1929 | *Broadway Melody* | Frank Lloyd *The Divine Lady* | Warner Baxter *In Old Arizona* | Mary Pickford *Coquette* | Clyde DeVinna *White Shadows, In the South Seas* |
| 1930 | *All Quiet on the Western Front* | Lewis Milestone | George Arliss *Disraeli* | Norma Shearer *The Divorcee* | Joseph T. Rucker, Willard Van Der Veer *With Byrd at the South Pole* |
| 1931 | *Cimarron* | Norman Taurog *Skippy* | Lionel Barrymore *A Free Soul* | Marie Dressler *Min and Bill* | Floyd Crosby *Tabu* |
| 1932 | *Grand Hotel* | Frank Borzage *Bad Girl* | Wallace Beery *The Champ* Fredric March *Dr. Jekyll and Mr. Hyde* | Helen Hayes *The Sin of Madelon Claudet* | Lee Garmes *Shanghai Express* |
| 1933 | *Cavalcade* | Frank Lloyd | Charles Laughton *The Private Life of Henry VIII* | Katharine Hepburn *Morning Glory* | Charles Bryant Lang, Jr. *A Farewell to Arms* |

| Year | Best Picture | Best Director | Best Actor | Best Actress | Best Supporting Actor | Best Supporting Actress | Best Song (from film) | Original Score | Best Cinematographer |
|---|---|---|---|---|---|---|---|---|---|
| 1934 | *It Happened One Night* | Frank Capra | Clark Gable *It Happened One Night* | Claudette Colbert *It Happened One Night* | — | — | "The Continental" *The Gay Divorcee* | Louis Silvers[1] *One Night of Love* | Victor Milner *Cleopatra* |
| 1935 | *Mutiny on the Bounty* | John Ford *The Informer* | Victor McLaglen *The Informer* | Bette Davis *Dangerous* | — | — | "Lullaby of Broadway" *Lullaby of Broadway* | Max Steiner[1] *The Informer* | Hal Mohr *A Midsummer Night's Dream* |
| 1936 | *The Great Ziegfeld* | Frank Capra *Mr Deeds Goes to Town* | Paul Muni *The Story of Louis Pasteur* | Luise Rainer *The Great Ziegfeld* | Walter Brennan *Come and Get It* | Gale Sondergaard *Anthony Adverse* | "The Way You Look Tonight" *Swing Time* | Leo Forbstein[1] *Anthony Adverse* | Gaetano Gaudio *Anthony Adverse* |
| 1937 | *The Life of Emile Zola* | Leo McCarey *The Awful Truth* | Spencer Tracy *Captains Courageous* | Luise Rainer *The Good Earth* | Joseph Schildkraut *The Life of Emile Zola* | Alice Brady *In Old Chicago* | "Sweet Leilani" *Waikiki Wedding* | Charles Previn[1] *100 Men and a Girl* | Karl Freund *The Good Earth* |

1. From 1934 to 1937, the "Best Original Score" award was presented to the head of the music department of the relevant studio, and not necessarily to the composer of the score.

| Year | Best Picture | Best Director | Best Actor | Best Actress | Best Supporting Actor | Best Supporting Actress | Best Song (from film) | Original Score | Best Cinematographer |
|------|--------------|---------------|------------|--------------|----------------------|------------------------|----------------------|----------------|----------------------|
| 1938 | You Can't Take It with You | Frank Capra | Spencer Tracy *Boys Town* | Bette Davis *Jezebel* | Walter Brennan *Kentucky* | Fay Bainter *Jezebel* | "Thanks for the Memory" *Big Broadcast of 1938* | Alfred Newman *Alexander's Ragtime Band* Erich Wolfgang Korngold *The Adventures of Robin Hood* | Joseph Ruttenberg *The Great Waltz* |
| 1939 | Gone with the Wind | Victor Fleming | Robert Donat *Goodbye, Mr. Chips* | Vivien Leigh *Gone with the Wind* | Thomas Mitchell *Stagecoach* | Hattie McDaniel *Gone with the Wind* | "Over the Rainbow" *The Wizard of Oz* | Herbert Stothart *The Wizard of Oz* Richard Hageman, Frank Harling, John Leipold, Leo Shuken *Stagecoach* | Gregg Toland *Wuthering Heights* Ernest Haller, Ray Rennahan *Gone with the Wind* |
| 1940 | Rebecca | John Ford *The Grapes of Wrath* | James Stewart *The Philadelphia Story* | Ginger Rogers *Kitty Foyle* | Walter Brennan *The Westerner* | Jane Darwell *The Grapes of Wrath* | "When You Wish upon a Star" *Pinocchio* | Alfred Newman *Tin Pan Alley* Leigh Harline, Paul J. Smith, Ned Washington *Pinocchio* | George Barnes *Rebecca* George Perinal *Thief of Bagdad* |
| 1941 | How Green Was My Valley | John Ford | Gary Cooper *Sergeant York* | Joan Fontaine *Suspicion* | Donald Crisp *How Green Was My Valley* | Mary Astor *The Great Lie* | "The Last Time I Saw Paris" *Lady Be Good* | Bernard Herrmann *All That Money Can Buy* Frank Churchill, Oliver Wallace *Dumbo* | Arthur Miller *How Green Was My Valley* Ernest Palmer, Ray Rennahan *Blood and Sand* |
| 1942 | Mrs. Miniver | William Wyler | James Cagney *Yankee Doodle Dandy* | Greer Garson *Mrs. Miniver* | Van Heflin *Johnny Eager* | Teresa Wright *Mrs. Miniver* | "White Christmas" *Holiday Inn* | Max Steiner *Now, Voyager* Ray Heindorf, Heinz Roemheld *Yankee Doodle Dandy* | Joseph Ruttenberg *Mrs. Miniver* Leon Shamroy *The Black Swan* |
| 1943 | Casablanca | Michael Curtiz | Paul Lukas *Watch on the Rhine* | Jennifer Jones *The Song of Bernadette* | Charles Coburn *The More the Merrier* | Katina Paxinou *For Whom the Bell Tolls* | "You'll Never Know" *Hello, Frisco, Hello* | Alfred Newman *The Song of Bernadette* Ray Heindorf *This Is the Army* | Arthur Miller *The Song of Bernadette* Hal Mohr, W. Howard Greene *The Phantom of the Opera* |
| 1944 | Going My Way | Leo McCarey | Bing Crosby *Going My Way* | Ingrid Bergman *Gaslight* | Barry Fitzgerald *Going My Way* | Ethel Barrymore *None But the Lonely Heart* | "Swinging on a Star" *Going My Way* | Max Steiner *Since You Went Away* Carmen Dragon, Morris Stoloff *Cover Girl* | Joseph LaShelle *Laura* Leon Shamroy *Wilson* |
| 1945 | The Lost Weekend | Billy Wilder | Ray Milland *The Lost Weekend* | Joan Crawford *Mildred Pierce* | James Dunn *A Tree Grows in Brooklyn* | Anne Revere *National Velvet* | "It Might As Well Be Spring" *State Fair* | Miklos Rozsa *Spellbound* Georgie Stoll *Anchors Aweigh* | Harry Stradling *The Picture of Dorian Gray* Leon Shamroy *Leave Her to Heaven* |
| 1946 | The Best Years of Our Lives | William Wyler | Fredric March *The Best Years of Our Lives* | Olivia de Havilland *To Each His Own* | Harold Russell *The Best Years of Our Lives* | Anne Baxter *The Razor's Edge* | "On the Atchison, Topeka and Santa Fe" *The Harvey Girls* | Hugo Friedhofer *The Best Years of Our Lives* Morris Stoloff *The Jolson Story* | Arthur Miller *Anna and the King of Siam* Charles Rosher, Leonard Smith, Arthur Arling *The Yearling* |
| 1947 | Gentleman's Agreement | Elia Kazan | Ronald Colman *A Double Life* | Loretta Young *The Farmer's Daughter* | Edmund Gwenn *Miracle on 34th Street* | Celeste Holm *Gentleman's Agreement* | "Zip-A-Dee-Doo-Dah" *Song of the South* | Miklos Rozsa *A Double Life* Alfred Newman *Mother Wore Tights* | Guy Green *Great Expectations* Jack Cardiff *Black Narcissus* |

| Year | Best Picture | Best Director | Best Actor | Best Actress | Best Supporting Actor | Best Supporting Actress | Best Song (from film) | Original Score | Best Cinematographer |
|---|---|---|---|---|---|---|---|---|---|
| 1948 | *Hamlet* | John Huston *Treasure of the Sierra Madre* | Laurence Olivier *Hamlet* | Jane Wyman *Johnny Belinda* | Walter Huston *Treasure of the Sierra Madre* | Claire Trevor *Key Largo* | "Buttons and Bows" *The Paleface* | Brian Easdale *The Red Shoes* Johnny Green, Roger Edens *Easter Parade* | William Daniels *The Naked City* Joseph Valentine, William V. Skall, Winton Hoch *Joan of Arc* |
| 1949 | *All the King's Men* | Joseph L. Mankiewicz *A Letter to Three Wives* | Broderick Crawford *All the King's Men* | Olivia de Havilland *The Heiress* | Dean Jagger *Twelve O'Clock High* | Mercedes McCambridge *All the King's Men* | "Baby, It's Cold Outside" *Neptune's Daughter* | Aaron Copeland *The Heiress* Roger Edens, Lenny Hayton *On the Town* | Paul C. Vogel *Battleground* Winton Hoch *She Wore a Yellow Ribbon* |
| 1950 | *All About Eve* | Joseph L. Mankiewicz | Jose Ferrer *Cyrano de Bergerac* | Judy Holliday *Born Yesterday* | George Sanders *All About Eve* | Josephine Hull *Harvey* | "Mona Lisa" *Captain Carey, USA* | Franz Waxman *Sunset Boulevard* Adolph Deutsch, Roger Edens *Annie Get Your Gun* | Robert Krasker *The Third Man* Robert Surtees *King Solomon's Mines* |
| 1951 | *An American in Paris* | George Stevens *A Place in the Sun* | Humphrey Bogart *The African Queen* | Vivien Leigh *A Streetcar Named Desire* | Karl Malden *A Streetcar Named Desire* | Kim Hunter *A Streetcar Named Desire* | "In the Cool, Cool, Cool of the Evening" *Here Comes the Groom* | Franz Waxman *A Place in the Sun* Saul Chaplin, Johnny Green *An American in Paris* | William C. Mellor *A Place in the Sun* Alfred Gilks, John Alton (ballet) *An American in Paris* |
| 1952 | *The Greatest Show on Earth* | John Ford *The Quiet Man* | Gary Cooper *High Noon* | Shirley Booth *Come Back, Little Sheba* | Anthony Quinn *Viva Zapata!* | Gloria Grahame *The Bad and the Beautiful* | "High Noon (Do Not Forsake Me, Oh My Darlin')" *High Noon* | Dimitri Tiomkin *High Noon* Alfred Newman *With a Song in My Heart* | Robert Surtees *The Bad and the Beautiful* Winton Hoch, Archie Stout *The Quiet Man* |
| 1953 | *From Here to Eternity* | Fred Zinnemann | William Holden *Stalag 17* | Audrey Hepburn *Roman Holiday* | Frank Sinatra *From Here to Eternity* | Donna Reed *From Here to Eternity* | "Secret Love" *Calamity Jane* | Bronislau Kaper *Lili* Alfred Newman *Call Me Madam* | Burnett Guffey *From Here to Eternity* Loyal Griggs *Shane* |
| 1954 | *On the Waterfront* | Elia Kazan | Marlon Brando *On the Waterfront* | Grace Kelly *The Country Girl* | Edmond O'Brien *The Barefoot Contessa* | Eva Marie Saint *On the Waterfront* | "Three Coins in the Fountain" *Three Coins in the Fountain* | Dimitri Tiomkin *The High and the Mighty* Saul Chaplin, Adolph Deutsch *Seven Brides for Seven Brothers* | Boris Kaufman *On the Waterfront* Milton Krasner *Three Coins in the Fountain* |
| 1955 | *Marty* | Delbert Mann | Ernest Borgnine *Marty* | Anna Magnani *The Rose Tattoo* | Jack Lemmon *Mister Roberts* | Jo Van Fleet *East of Eden* | "Love Is a Many-Splendored Thing" *Love Is a Many-Splendored Thing* | Alfred Newman *Love Is a Many-Splendored Thing* Robert Russell Bennett, Jay Blackton, Adolph Deutsch *Oklahoma!* | James Wong Howe *The Rose Tattoo* Robert Burks *To Catch a Thief* |
| 1956 | *Around the World in 80 Days* | George Stevens *Giant* | Yul Brynner *The King and I* | Ingrid Bergman *Anastasia* | Anthony Quinn *Lust for Life* | Dorothy Malone *Written on the Wind* | "Whatever Will Be, Will Be (Que Sera, Sera)" *The Man Who Knew Too Much* | Victor Young *Around the World in 80 Days* Alfred Newman, Ken Darby *The King and I* | Joseph Ruttenberg *Somebody Up There Likes Me* Lionel Lindon *Around the World in 80 Days* |
| 1957 | *The Bridge on the River Kwai* | David Lean | Alec Guinness *The Bridge on the River Kwai* | Joanne Woodward *The Three Faces of Eve* | Red Buttons *Sayonara* | Miyoshi Umeki *Sayonara* | "All the Way" *The Joker Is Wild* | Malcolm Arnold *The Bridge on the River Kwai* | Jack Hildyard *The Bridge on the River Kwai* |
| 1958 | *Gigi* | Vincente Minnelli | David Niven *Separate Tables* | Susan Hayward *I Want to Live!* | Burl Ives *The Big Country* | Wendy Hiller *Separate Tables* | "Gigi" *Gigi* | Dimitri Tiomkin *The Old Man and the Sea* Andre Previn *Gigi* | Sam Leavitt *The Defiant Ones* Joseph Ruttenberg *Gigi* |

| Year | Best Picture | Best Director | Best Actor | Best Actress | Best Supporting Actor | Best Supporting Actress | Best Song (from film) | Original Score | Best Cinematographer |
|------|-------------|---------------|------------|--------------|----------------------|------------------------|----------------------|----------------|---------------------|
| 1959 | *Ben Hur* | William Wyler | Charlton Heston *Ben Hur* | Simone Signoret *Room at the Top* | Hugh Griffith *Ben Hur* | Shelley Winters *The Diary of Anne Frank* | "High Hopes" *A Hole in the Head* | Miklos Rosza *Ben Hur* Andre Previn, Ken Darby *All That Jazz* | William C. Mellor *The Diary of Anne Frank* Robert L. Surtees *Ben Hur* |
| 1960 | *The Apartment* | Billy Wilder | Burt Lancaster *Elmer Gantry* | Elizabeth Taylor *Butterfield 8* | Peter Ustinov *Spartacus* | Shirley Jones *Elmer Gantry* | "Never on Sunday" *Never on Sunday* | Ernest Gold *Exodus* Morris Stoloff, Harry Sukman *Song without End* | Freddie Francis *Sons and Lovers* Russell Metty *Spartacus* |
| 1961 | *West Side Story* | Jerome Robbins, Robert Wise | Maximilian Schell *Judgment at Nuremberg* | Sophia Loren *Two Women* | George Chakiris *West Side Story* | Rita Moreno *West Side Story* | "Moon River" *Breakfast at Tiffany's* | Henry Mancini *Breakfast at Tiffany's* Saul Chaplin, Johnny Green, Sid Ramin, Irwin Kostal *West Side Story* | Eugen Shuftan *The Hustler* Daniel L. Fapp *West Side Story* |
| 1962 | *Lawrence of Arabia* | David Lean | Gregory Peck *To Kill a Mockingbird* | Anne Bancroft *The Miracle Worker* | Ed Begley *Sweet Bird of Youth* | Patty Duke *The Miracle Worker* | "Days of Wine and Roses" *Days of Wine and Roses* | Maurice Jarre *Lawrence of Arabia* | Jean Bourgoin, Walter Wottitz *The Longest Day* Fred A. Young *Lawrence of Arabia* |
| 1963 | *Tom Jones* | Tony Richardson | Sidney Poitier *Lilies of the Field* | Patricia Neal *Hud* | Melvyn Douglas *Hud* | Margaret Rutherford *The V.I.P.s* | "Call Me Irresponsible" *Papa's Delicate Condition* | John Addison *Tom Jones* | James Wong Howe *Hud* Leon Shamroy *Cleopatra* |
| 1964 | *My Fair Lady* | George Cukor | Rex Harrison *My Fair Lady* | Julie Andrews *Mary Poppins* | Peter Ustinov *Topkapi* | Lila Kedrova *Zorba the Greek* | "Chim Chim Cher-ee" *Mary Poppins* | Richard M. Sherman, Robert B. Sherman *Mary Poppins* | Walter Lassally *Zorba the Greek* Harry Stradling *My Fair Lady* |
| 1965 | *The Sound of Music* | Robert Wise | Lee Marvin *Cat Ballou* | Julie Christie *Darling* | Martin Balsam *A Thousand Clowns* | Shelley Winters *A Patch of Blue* | "The Shadow of Your Smile" *The Sandpiper* | Maurice Jarre *Dr. Zhivago* | Ernest Laszlo *Ship of Fools* Freddie Young *Dr. Zhivago* |
| 1966 | *A Man for All Seasons* | Fred Zinnemann | Paul Scofield *A Man for All Seasons* | Elizabeth Taylor *Who's Afraid of Virginia Woolf?* | Walter Matthau *The Fortune Cookie* | Sandy Dennis *Who's Afraid of Virginia Woolf?* | "Born Free" *Born Free* | John Barry *Born Free* | Haskell Wexler *Who's Afraid of Virginia Woolf?* Ted Moore *A Man for All Seasons* |
| 1967 | *In the Heat of the Night* | Mike Nichols *The Graduate* | Rod Steiger *In the Heat of the Night* | Katharine Hepburn *Guess Who's Coming to Dinner* | George Kennedy *Cool Hand Luke* | Estelle Parsons *Bonnie and Clyde* | "Talk to the Animals" *Doctor Dolittle* | Elmer Bernstein *Thoroughly Modern Millie* | Burnett Guffey *Bonnie and Clyde* |
| 1968 | *Oliver!* | Carol Reed | Cliff Robertson *Charly* | Katharine Hepburn *The Lion in Winter* Barbra Streisand *Funny Girl* | Jack Albertson *The Subject Was Roses* | Ruth Gordon *Rosemary's Baby* | "The Windmills of Your Mind" *The Thomas Crown Affair* | John Barry *The Lion in Winter* | Pasqualino DeSantis *Romeo and Juliet* |
| 1969 | *Midnight Cowboy* | John Schlesinger | John Wayne *True Grit* | Maggie Smith *The Prime of Miss Jean Brodie* | Gig Young *They Shoot Horses Don't They?* | Goldie Hawn *Cactus Flower* | "Raindrops Keep Fallin' on My Head" *Butch Cassidy and the Sundance Kid* | Burt Bacharach *Butch Cassidy and the Sundance Kid* | Conrad Hall *Butch Cassidy and the Sundance Kid* |
| 1970 | *Patton* | Franklin Schaffner | George C. Scott *Patton* | Glenda Jackson *Women in Love* | John Mills *Ryan's Daughter* | Helen Hayes *Airport* | "For All We Know" *Lovers and Other Strangers* | Francis Lai *Love Story* The Beatles (music, lyrics) *Let It Be* | Freddie Young *Ryan's Daughter* |
| 1971 | *The French Connection* | William Friedkin | Gene Hackman *The French Connection* | Jane Fonda *Klute* | Ben Johnson *The Last Picture Show* | Cloris Leachman *The Last Picture Show* | "Theme from Shaft" *Shaft* | Michel Legrand *The Summer of '42* | Oswald Morris *Fiddler on the Roof* |
| 1972 | *The Godfather* | Bob Fosse *Cabaret* | Marlon Brando *The Godfather* | Liza Minnelli *Cabaret* | Joel Grey *Cabaret* | Eileen Heckart *Butterflies Are Free* | "The Morning After" *The Poseidon Adventure* | Charles Chaplin, Raymond Rasch, Larry Russell *Limelight* | Geoffrey Unsworth *Cabaret* |

| Year | Best Picture | Best Director | Best Actor | Best Actress | Best Supporting Actor | Best Supporting Actress | Best Song (from film) | Original Score | Best Cinematographer |
|------|-------------|---------------|------------|--------------|----------------------|------------------------|----------------------|----------------|---------------------|
| 1973 | *The Sting* | George Roy Hill | Jack Lemmon *Save the Tiger* | Glenda Jackson *A Touch of Class* | John Houseman *The Paper Chase* | Tatum O'Neal *Paper Moon* | "The Way We Were" *The Way We Were* | Marvin Hamlisch *The Way We Were* | Sven Nykvist *Cries and Whispers* |
| 1974 | *The Godfather Part II* | Francis Ford Coppola | Art Carney *Harry and Tonto* | Ellen Burstyn *Alice Doesn't Live Here Anymore* | Robert DeNiro *The Godfather Pt. II* | Ingrid Bergman *Murder on the Orient Express* | "We May Never Love Like This Again" *The Towering Inferno* | Nino Rota, Carmine Coppola *The Godfather Pt. II* | Fred Koenekamp, Joseph Biroc *The Towering Inferno* |
| 1975 | *One Flew over the Cuckoo's Nest* | Miloš Forman | Jack Nicholson *One Flew over the Cuckoo's Nest* | Louise Fletcher *One Flew over the Cuckoo's Nest* | George Burns *The Sunshine Boys* | Lee Grant *Shampoo* | "I'm Easy" *Nashville* | John Williams *Jaws* | John Alcott *Barry Lyndon* |
| 1976 | *Rocky* | John G. Avildsen | Peter Finch *Network* | Faye Dunaway *Network* | Jason Robards *All the President's Men* | Beatrice Straight *Network* | "Evergreen" (love theme) *A Star Is Born* | Jerry Goldsmith *The Omen* | Haskell Wexler *Bound for Glory* |
| 1977 | *Annie Hall* | Woody Allen | Richard Dreyfuss *The Goodbye Girl* | Diane Keaton *Annie Hall* | Jason Robards *Julia* | Vanessa Redgrave *Julia* | "You Light Up My Life" *You Light Up My Life* | John Williams *Star Wars* | Vilmos Zsigmond *Close Encounters of the Third Kind* |
| 1978 | *The Deer Hunter* | Michael Cimino | Jon Voight *Coming Home* | Jane Fonda *Coming Home* | Christopher Walken *The Deer Hunter* | Maggie Smith *California Suite* | "Last Dance" *Thank God It's Friday* | Giorgio Moroder *Midnight Express* | Nestor Almendros *Days of Heaven* |
| 1979 | *Kramer vs. Kramer* | Robert Benton | Dustin Hoffman *Kramer vs. Kramer* | Sally Field *Norma Rae* | Melvyn Douglas *Being There* | Meryl Streep *Kramer vs. Kramer* | "It Goes Like It Goes" *Norma Rae* | Georges Delerue *A Little Romance* | Vittorio Storaro *Apocalypse Now* |
| 1980 | *Ordinary People* | Robert Redford | Robert DeNiro *Raging Bull* | Sissy Spacek *Coal Miner's Daughter* | Timothy Hutton *Ordinary People* | Mary Steenburgen *Melvin and Howard* | "Fame" *Fame* | Michael Gore *Fame* | Geoffrey Unsworth, Ghislain Cloquet *Tess* |
| 1981 | *Chariots of Fire* | Warren Beatty *Reds* | Henry Fonda *On Golden Pond* | Katharine Hepburn *On Golden Pond* | John Gielgud *Arthur* | Maureen Stapleton *Reds* | "Arthur's Theme" (Best That You Can Do) *Arthur* | Vangelis *Chariots of Fire* | Vittorio Storaro *Reds* |
| 1982 | *Gandhi* | Richard Attenborough *Gandhi* | Ben Kingsley *Gandhi* | Meryl Streep *Sophie's Choice* | Lou Gossett, Jr. *An Officer and a Gentleman* | Jessica Lange *Tootsie* | "Up Where We Belong" *An Officer and a Gentleman* | John Williams *E.T.* | Billy Williams, Ronnie Taylor *Gandhi* |
| 1983 | *Terms of Endearment* | James L. Brooks | Robert Duvall *Tender Mercies* | Shirley MacLaine *Terms of Endearment* | Jack Nicholson *Terms of Endearment* | Linda Hunt *The Year of Living Dangerously* | "Flashdance . . . What a Feeling" *Flashdance* | Bill Conti *The Right Stuff* | Sven Nykvist *Fanny and Alexander* |
| 1984 | *Amadeus* | Miloš Forman | F. Murray Abraham *Amadeus* | Sally Field *Places in the Heart* | Haing S. Ngor *The Killing Fields* | Peggy Ashcroft *A Passage to India* | "I Just Called to Say I Love You" *The Woman in Red* | Maurice Jarre *A Passage to India* Prince *Purple Rain* | Chris Menges *The Killing Fields* |
| 1985 | *Out of Africa* | Sydney Pollack | William Hurt *Kiss of the Spider Woman* | Geraldine Page *The Trip to Bountiful* | Don Ameche *Cocoon* | Anjelica Huston *Prizzi's Honor* | "Say You, Say Me" *White Nights* | John Barry *Out of Africa* | David Watkin *Out of Africa* |
| 1986 | *Platoon* | Oliver Stone | Paul Newman *The Color of Money* | Marlee Matlin *Children of a Lesser God* | Michael Caine *Hannah and Her Sisters* | Dianne Wiest *Hannah and Her Sisters* | "Take My Breath Away" *Top Gun* | Herbie Hancock *'Round Midnight* | Chris Menges *The Mission* |
| 1987 | *The Last Emperor* | Bernardo Bertolucci | Michael Douglas *Wall Street* | Cher *Moonstruck* | Sean Connery *The Untouchables* | Olympia Dukakis *Moonstruck* | "(I've Had) the Time of My Life" *Dirty Dancing* | Ryuichi Sakamoto, David Byrne, Cong Su *The Last Emperor* | Vittorio Storaro *The Last Emperor* |
| 1988 | *Rain Man* | Barry Levinson | Dustin Hoffman *Rain Man* | Jodie Foster *The Accused* | Kevin Kline *A Fish Called Wanda* | Geena Davis *The Accidental Tourist* | "Let the River Run" *Working Girl* | Dave Grusin *The Milagro Beanfield War* | Peter Biziou *Mississippi Burning* |
| 1989 | *Driving Miss Daisy* | Oliver Stone *Born on the Fourth of July* | Daniel Day-Lewis *My Left Foot* | Jessica Tandy *Driving Miss Daisy* | Denzel Washington *Glory* | Brenda Fricker *My Left Foot* | "Under the Sea" *The Little Mermaid* | Alan Menken *The Little Mermaid* | Freddie Francis *Glory* |
| 1990 | *Dances With Wolves* | Kevin Costner | Jeremy Irons *Reversal of Fortune* | Kathy Bates *Misery* | Joe Pesci *GoodFellas* | Whoopi Goldberg *Ghost* | "Sooner or Later (I Always Get My Man)" *Dick Tracy* | John Barry *Dances With Wolves* | Dean Semler *Dances With Wolves* |

**Source:** BASELINE II, INC.

## ACADEMY AWARDS FOR BEST FOREIGN LANGUAGE FILM, 1956–90

| Year | Film | Country | Director |
|------|------|---------|----------|
| 1956 | La Strada | Italy | Federico Fellini |
| 1957 | The Nights of Cabiria | Italy | Federico Fellini |
| 1958 | Mon Oncle | France | Jacques Tati |
| 1959 | Black Orpheus | France/Italy/Brazil | Marcel Camus |
| 1960 | The Virgin Spring | Sweden | Ingmar Bergman |
| 1961 | Through a Glass Darkly | Sweden | Ingmar Bergman |
| 1962 | Sundays and Cybele | France | Serge Bourguignon |
| 1963 | 8½ | Italy | Federico Fellini |
| 1964 | Yesterday, Today and Tomorrow | Italy/France | Vittorio de Sica |
| 1965 | The Shop on Main Street | Czechoslovakia | Jan Kadar |
| 1966 | A Man and a Woman | France | Claude Lelouch |
| 1967 | Closely Watched Trains | Czechoslovakia | Jirí Menzel |
| 1968 | War and Peace | USSR | Sergei Bondarchuk |
| 1969 | Z | France/Algeria | Costa-Gavras |
| 1970 | Investigation of a Citizen above Suspicion | Italy | Elio Petri |
| 1971 | The Garden of the Finzi-Continis | Italy | Vittorio de Sica |
| 1972 | The Discreet Charm of the Bourgeoisie | France | Luis Buñuel |

| Year | Film | Country | Director |
|------|------|---------|----------|
| 1973 | Day for Night | France/Italy | Francois Truffaut |
| 1974 | Amarcord | Italy/France | Federico Fellini |
| 1975 | Dersu Uzala | USSR/Japan | Akira Kurosawa |
| 1976 | Black and White in Color | France/Switzerland/Ivory Coast | Jean-Jacques Annaud |
| 1977 | Madame Rosa | France | Moshe Mizrahi |
| 1978 | Get Out Your Handkerchiefs | France | Bertrand Blier |
| 1979 | The Tin Drum | Germany | Volker Scholondorff |
| 1980 | Moscow Does Not Believe in Tears | USSR | Vladimir Menshov |
| 1981 | Mephisto | Austria/Germany/Hungary | Istvan Szabo |
| 1982 | To Begin Again | Spain | Jose Luis Garci |
| 1983 | Fanny and Alexander | Sweden | Ingmar Bergman |
| 1984 | Dangerous Moves | France | Richard Dembo |
| 1985 | The Official Story | Argentina | Luis Puenzo |
| 1986 | The Assault | Netherlands | Fons Rademakers |
| 1987 | Babette's Feast | Denmark | Gabriel Axel |
| 1988 | Pelle the Conqueror | Denmark | Bille August |
| 1989 | Cinema Paradiso | Italy | Giuseppe Tornatore |
| 1990 | Journey of Hope | Switzerland | Xavier Koller |

**Source:** BASELINE II, INC.

## AMERICAN FILM INSTITUTE LIFE ACHIEVEMENT AWARDS, 1973–91

Awarded to individuals whose "talent has fundamentally advanced the art of American film or television . . . and whose work has withstood the test of time."

| | | | | |
|------|------|------|------|------|
| 1973 John Ford | 1977 Henry Fonda | 1981 Fred Astaire | 1985 Gene Kelly | 1989 Gregory Peck |
| 1974 James Cagney | 1978 Bette Davis | 1982 Frank Capra | 1986 Billy Wilder | 1990 David Lean |
| 1975 Orson Welles | 1979 Alfred Hitchcock | 1983 John Huston | 1987 Barbara Stanwyck | 1991 Kirk Douglas |
| 1976 William Wyler | 1980 James Stewart | 1984 Lillian Gish | 1988 Jack Lemmon | |

**Source:** American Film Institute.

## CANNES FESTIVAL BEST FILM AWARDS, 1946–91

The Festival International du Film was scheduled to make its debut in September 1939, but was cancelled that year due to the outbreak of World War II. The first festival was held in 1946. The official name for the best film award has been Grand Prix (1949–54 and 1964–74) and the Palme d'Or (1955–63 and 1975–present).

| Year | Film and director |
|------|-------------------|
| 1946 | La Bataille du Rail, René Clément[1] |
| 1949[2] | The Third Man, Carol Reed |
| 1951 | Miracle in Milan, Vittorio De Sica |
| | Miss Julie, Alf Sjöberg |
| 1952 | Two Cents Worth of Hope, Renato Castellani |
| | Othello, Orson Welles |
| 1953 | The Wages of Fear, Georges Clouzot |
| 1954 | Gate of Hell, Teinosuke Kinugasa |
| 1955 | Marty, Delbert Mann |
| 1956 | The Silent World, Jacques Cousteau, Louis Malle |
| 1957 | Friendly Persuasion, William Wyler |
| 1958 | The Cranes are Flying, Mikhail Kalatozov |
| 1959 | Black Orpheus, Marcel Camus |
| 1960 | La Dolce Vita, Federico Fellini |
| 1961 | Viridiana, Luis Buñuel |
| 1962 | The Given Word, Anselmo Duarte |
| 1963 | The Leopard, Luchino Visconti |
| 1964 | The Umbrellas of Cherbourg, Jacques Demy |
| 1965 | The Knack, and How to Get It, Richard Lester |
| 1966 | A Man and a Woman, Claude Lelouch |
| 1967 | Blow-Up, Michelangelo Antonioni[1] |
| 1968 | No award[3] |
| 1969 | If . . . , Lindsay Anderson |
| 1970 | M*A*S*H, Robert Altman |

| Year | Film and director |
|------|-------------------|
| 1971 | The Go-Between, Joseph Losey |
| 1972 | The Working Class Goes to Heaven, Elio Petri |
| | The Mattei Afair, Francesco Rosi |
| 1973 | Scarecrow, Jerry Schatzberg |
| | The Hireling, Alan Bridges |
| 1974 | The Conversation, Francis Ford Coppola |
| 1975 | Chronique des Années de Braise, M. Lakhdar Hamina |
| 1976 | Taxi Driver, Martin Scorsese |
| 1977 | Padre Padrone, Paolo and Vittorio Taviani |
| 1978 | The Tree of Wooden Clogs, Ermanno Olmi |
| 1979 | The Tin Drum, Volker Schlöndorff |
| 1980 | Kagemusha, Akira Kurosawa |
| 1981 | Man of Iron, Andrzej Wajda |
| 1982 | Missing, Costa-Gavras |
| | Yol, Yilmar Güney |
| 1983 | The Ballad of Narayama, Shohei Imamura |
| 1984 | Paris, Texas, Wim Wenders |
| 1985 | When Father Was Away on Business, Emir Kusturica |
| 1986 | The Mission, Roland Joffé |
| 1987 | Under Satan's Sun, Maurice Pialat |
| 1988 | Pelle the Conqueror, Bille August |
| 1989 | sex, lies, and videotape, Steven Soderbergh |
| 1990 | Wild at Heart, David Lynch |
| 1991 | Barton Fink, Joel Coen |

1. Winner of the International Jury Prize. 2. In 1947, there was no "best film" award, but prizes were given to outstanding works in several categories, including "Psychological and Love Films," "Adventure and Police Films," and so on. The festival was canceled in 1948 and 1950. 3. Festival canceled because of student riots in Paris. **Source:** BASELINE II, INC.

## THE EMMY AWARDS, 1948–91

The National Academy of Television Arts and Sciences Awards, formed in 1946, presented the first Emmy Awards in 1949. Only a selection is printed here; not only has the number of awards changed from year to year (peaking in 1978 with a total of 75 categories), but the categories themselves have fluctuated to reflect change in the industry.

### 1948

Outstanding TV Personality: Shirley Dinsdale (and her puppet Judy Splinters) (KTLA)
Most Popular TV Program: *Pantomime Quiz Time* (KTLA)
Best Film Made for Television: "The Necklace," *Your Show Time* (NBC)
Special Award: Louis McManus, original designer of the Emmy.

### 1949

Best Live Show: *The Ed Wynn Show* (CBS)
Best Kinescope[1] Show: *Texaco Star Theater* (NBC)
Outstanding Live Personality: Ed Wynn (CBS)
Outstanding Kinescope Personality: Milton Berle (NBC)
Best Film Made for TV: *The Life of Riley* (NBC)

### 1950

Best Actor: Alan Young (CBS)
Best Actress: Gertrude Berg (CBS)
Outstanding Personality: Groucho Marx (NBC)
Best Variety Show: *The Alan Young Show* (CBS)
Best Dramatic Show: *Pulitzer Prize Playhouse* (ABC)
Best Game Show: *Truth or Consequences* (CBS)

### 1951

Best Dramatic Show: *Studio One* (CBS)
Best Comedy Show: *The Red Skelton Show* (CBS)
Best Variety Show: *Your Show of Shows* (NBC)
Best Actor: Sid Caesar (NBC)
Best Actress: Imogene Coca (NBC)
Best Comedian or Comedienne: Red Skelton (NBC)

### 1952

Best Dramatic Program: *Robert Montgomery Presents* (NBC)
Best Variety Program: *Your Show of Shows* (NBC)
Best Mystery, Action, or Adventure Program: *Dragnet* (NBC)
Best Situation Comedy: *I Love Lucy* (CBS)
Best Actor: Thomas Mitchell
Best Actress: Helen Hayes

### 1953

Best Dramatic Program: *The U.S. Steel Hour* (ABC)
Best Situation Comedy: *I Love Lucy* (CBS)
Best Variety Program: *Omnibus* (CBS)
Best Male Star of Regular Series: Donald O'Connor, *Colgate Comedy Hour* (NBC)
Best Female Star of Regular Series: Eve Arden, *Our Miss Brooks* (CBS)
Best Mystery, Action, or Adventure Program: *Dragnet* (NBC)

### 1954

Best Actor Starring in a Regular Series: Danny Thomas, *Make Room for Daddy* (ABC)
Best Actress Starring in a Regular Series: Loretta Young, *The Loretta Young Show* (NBC)
Best Mystery or Intrigue Series: *Dragnet* (NBC)

1. Kinescope was an early method of recording TV shows, before the advent of videotape. A movie camera was placed in front of a monitor in the TV studio and would "film" the show directly off the screen. The finished program could then be broadcast at a later date.

Best Variety Series Including Musical Varieties: *Disneyland* (ABC)
Best Situation Comedy Series: *Make Room for Daddy* (ABC)
Best Dramatic Series: *The U.S. Steel Hour* (ABC)

### 1955

Best Action or Adventure Series: *Disneyland* (ABC)
Best Comedy Series: *The Phil Silvers Show* (CBS)
Best Variety Series: *The Ed Sullivan Show* (CBS)
Best Dramatic Series: *Producers' Showcase* (NBC)
Best Actor (Continuing Performance): Phil Silvers, *The Phil Silvers Show* (CBS)
Best Actress (Continuing Performance): Lucille Ball, *I Love Lucy* (CBS)

### 1956

Best Single Program of the Year: "Requiem for a Heavyweight," *Playhouse 90* (CBS)
Best Series (Half Hour or Less): *The Phil Silvers Show* (CBS)
Best Series (One Hour or More): *Caesar's Hour* (NBC)
Best Continuing Performance by an Actor in a Dramatic Series: Robert Young, *Father Knows Best* (NBC)
Best Continuing Performance by an Actress in a Dramatic Series: Loretta Young, *The Loretta Young Show* (NBC)

### 1957

Program of the Year: "The Comedian," *Playhouse 90* (CBS)
Best Dramatic Series with Continuing Characters: *Gunsmoke* (CBS)
Best Comedy Series: *The Phil Silvers Show* (CBS)
Best Musical, Variety, Audience Participation, or Quiz Series: *The Dinah Shore Chevy Show* (NBC)
Best Continuing Performance by an Actor in a Leading Role in a Dramatic or Comedy Series: Robert Young, *Father Knows Best* (NBC)
Best Continuing Performance by an Actress in a Leading Role in a Dramatic or Comedy Series: Jane Wyatt, *Father Knows Best* (NBC)

### 1958–59

Program of the Year: "An Evening with Fred Astaire" (NBC)
Best Dramatic Series (One Hour or Longer): *Playhouse 90* (CBS)
Best Dramatic Series (Less Than One Hour): *Alcoa-Goodyear Theatre* (NBC)
Best Comedy Series: *The Jack Benny Show* (CBS)
Best Musical or Variety Series: *The Dinah Shore Chevy Show* (NBC)
Best Western Series: *Maverick* (ABC)
Best Actor in a Leading Role (Continuing Character) in a Dramatic Series: Raymond Burr, *Perry Mason* (CBS)
Best Actress in a Leading Role (Continuing Character) in a Dramatic Series: Loretta Young, *The Loretta Young Show* (NBC)
Best Actor in a Leading Role (Continuing Character) in a Comedy Series: Jack Benny, *The Jack Benny Show* (CBS)
Best Actress in a Leading Role (Continuing Character) in a Comedy Series: Jane Wyatt, *Father Knows Best* (CBS and NBC)

### 1959–60

Outstanding Program Achievement in the Field of Humor: "The Art Carney Special" (NBC)
Outstanding Program Achievement in the Field of Drama: *Playhouse 90* (CBS)
Outstanding Program Achievement in the Field of Variety: "The Fabulous Fifties" (CBS)

Outstanding Performance by an Actor in a Series (Lead or Support): Robert Stack, *The Untouchables* (ABC)
Outstanding Performance by an Actress in a Series (Lead or Support): Jane Wyatt, *Father Knows Best* (CBS)
Outstanding Performance in a Variety or Musical Program or Series: Harry Belafonte, "Tonight with Belafonte," *The Revlon Revue* (CBS)

### 1960–61

Program of the Year: "Macbeth," *Hallmark Hall of Fame* (NBC)
Outstanding Program Achievement in the Field of Humor: *The Jack Benny Show* (CBS)
Outstanding Program Achievement in the Field of Drama: "Macbeth," *Hallmark Hall of Fame* (NBC)
Outstanding Program Achievement in the Field of Variety: "Astaire Time" (NBC)
Outstanding Performance by an Actor in a Series (Lead): Raymond Burr, *Perry Mason* (CBS)
Outstanding Performance by an Actress in a Series (Lead): Barbara Stanwyck, *The Barbara Stanwyck Show* (NBC)
Outstanding Performance in a Variety or Musical Program or Series: Fred Astaire, "Astaire Time" (NBC)

### 1961–62

Program of the Year: "Victoria Regina," *Hallmark Hall of Fame* (NBC)
Outstanding Program Achievement in the Field of Humor: *The Bob Newhart Show* (NBC)
Outstanding Program Achievement in the Field of Drama: *The Defenders* (CBS)
Outstanding Program Achievement in the Field of Variety: *The Garry Moore Show* (CBS)
Outstanding Continued Performance by an Actor in a Series (Lead): E.G. Marshall, *The Defenders* (CBS)
Outstanding Continued Performance by an Actress in a Series (Lead): Shirley Booth, *Hazel* (NBC)
Outstanding Performance in a Variety or Musical Program or Series: Carol Burnett, *The Garry Moore Show* (CBS)

### 1962–63

Program of the Year: "The Tunnel" (NBC)
Outstanding Program Achievement in the Field of Humor: *The Dick Van Dyke Show* (CBS)
Outstanding Program Achievement in the Field of Drama: *The Defenders* (CBS)
Outstanding Program Achievement in the Field of Music: "Julie and Carol at Carnegie Hall" (CBS)
Outstanding Program Achievement in the Field of Variety: *The Andy Williams Show* (NBC)
Outstanding Continued Performance by an Actor in a Series (Lead): E.G. Marshall, *The Defenders* (CBS)
Outstanding Continued Performance by an Actress in a Series (Lead): Shirley Booth, *Hazel* (NBC)
Outstanding Performance in a Variety or Musical Program or Series: Carol Burnett, "Julie and Carol at Carnegie Hall" (CBS) and "Carol and Company" (CBS)

### 1963–64

Program of the Year: "The Making of the President 1960" (ABC)
Outstanding Program Achievement in the Field of Comedy: *The Dick Van Dyke Show* (CBS)
Outstanding Program Achievement in the Field of Drama: *The Defenders* (CBS)
Outstanding Program Achievement in the Field of Variety: *The Danny Kaye Show* (CBS)
Outstanding Continued Performance by an Actor in a Series (Lead): Dick Van Dyke, *The Dick Van Dyke Show* (CBS)

Outstanding Continued Performance by an Actress in a Series (Lead): Mary Tyler Moore, *The Dick Van Dyke Show* (CBS)

Outstanding Performance in a Variety or Musical Program or Series: Danny Kaye, *The Danny Kaye Show* (CBS)

### 1964–65

Outstanding Achievements in Entertainment: *The Dick Van Dyke Show* (CBS); "The Magnificent Yankee," *Hallmark Hall of Fame* (NBC); "My Name Is Barbra" (CBS)

Outstanding Individual Achievements in Entertainment (Actors and Performers): Lynn Fontanne, "The Magnificent Yankee," *Hallmark Hall of Fame* (NBC); Barbra Streisand, "My Name Is Barbra" (CBS); Dick Van Dyke, *The Dick Van Dyke Show* (CBS)

### 1965–66

Outstanding Comedy Series: *The Dick Van Dyke Show* (CBS)

Outstanding Variety Series: *The Andy Williams Show* (NBC)

Outstanding Dramatic Series: *The Fugitive* (ABC)

Outstanding Continued Performance by an Actor in a Leading Role in a Dramatic Series: Bill Cosby, *I Spy* (NBC)

Outstanding Continued Performance by an Actress in a Leading Role in a Dramatic Series: Barbara Stanwyck, *The Big Valley* (ABC)

Outstanding Continued Performance by an Actor in a Leading Role in a Comedy Series: Dick Van Dyke, *The Dick Van Dyke Show* (CBS)

Outstanding Continued Performance by an Actress in a Leading Role in a Comedy Series: Mary Tyler Moore, *The Dick Van Dyke Show* (CBS)

### 1966–67

Outstanding Comedy Series: *The Monkees* (NBC)

Outstanding Variety Series: *The Andy Williams Show* (NBC)

Outstanding Dramatic Series: *Mission: Impossible* (CBS)

Outstanding Continued Performance by an Actor in a Leading Role in a Dramatic Series: Bill Cosby, *I Spy* (NBC)

Outstanding Continued Performance by an Actress in a Leading Role in a Dramatic Series: Barbara Bain, *Mission: Impossible* (CBS)

Outstanding Continued Performance by an Actor in a Leading Role in a Comedy Series: Don Adams, *Get Smart* (NBC)

Outstanding Continued Performance by an Actress in a Leading Role in a Comedy Series: Lucille Ball, *The Lucy Show* (CBS)

### 1967–68

Outstanding Comedy Series: *Get Smart* (NBC)

Outstanding Dramatic Series: *Mission: Impossible* (CBS)

Outstanding Continued Performance by an Actor in a Leading Role in a Dramatic Series: Bill Cosby, *I Spy* (NBC)

Outstanding Continued Performance by an Actress in a Leading Role in a Dramatic Series: Barbara Bain, Mission: Impossible (CBS)

Outstanding Continued Performance by an Actor in a Leading Role in a Comedy Series: Don Adams, *Get Smart* (NBC)

Outstanding Continued Performance by an Actress in a Leading Role in a Comedy Series: Lucille Ball, *The Lucy Show* (CBS)

### 1968–69

Outstanding Comedy Series: *Get Smart* (NBC)

Outstanding Dramatic Series: *NET Playhouse* (NET)

Outstanding Musical or Variety Series: *Rowan and Martin's Laugh-In* (NBC)

Outstanding Continued Performance by an Actor in a Leading Role in a Dramatic Series: Carl Betz, *Judd, for the Defense* (ABC)

Outstanding Continued Performance by an Actress in a Leading Role in a Dramatic Series: Barbara Bain, *Mission: Impossible* (CBS)

Outstanding Continued Performance by an Actor in a Leading Role in a Comedy Series: Don Adams, *Get Smart* (NBC)

Outstanding Continued Performance by an Actress in a Leading Role in a Comedy Series: Hope Lange, *The Ghost and Mrs. Muir* (NBC)

### 1969–70

Outstanding Comedy Series: *My World and Welcome to It* (NBC)

Outstanding Dramatic Series: *Marcus Welby, M.D.* (ABC)

Outstanding Variety or Musical Series: *The David Frost Show* (syndicated)

Outstanding Continued Performance by an Actor in a Leading Role in a Dramatic Series: Robert Young, *Marcus Welby, M.D.* (ABC)

Outstanding Continued Performance by an Actress in a Leading Role in a Dramatic Series: Susan Hampshire, *The Forsythe Saga* (NET)

Outstanding Continued Performance by an Actor in a Leading Role in a Comedy Series: William Windom, *My World and Welcome to It* (NBC)

Outstanding Continued Performance by an Actress in a Leading Role in a Comedy Series: Hope Lange, *The Ghost and Mrs. Muir* (ABC)

### 1970–71

Outstanding Series—Comedy: *All in the Family* (CBS)

Outstanding Series—Drama: *The Senator* (NBC)

Outstanding Variety Series—Musical: *The Flip Wilson Show* (NBC)

Outstanding Continued Performance by an Actor in a Leading Role in a Dramatic Series: Hal Holbrook, *The Senator* (NBC)

Outstanding Continued Performance by an Actress in a Leading Role in a Dramatic Series: Susan Hampshire, *The First Churchills (Masterpiece Theatre)* (PBS)

Outstanding Continued Performance by an Actor in a Leading Role in a Comedy Series: Jack Klugman, *The Odd Couple* (CBS)

Outstanding Continued Performance by an Actress in a Leading Role in a Comedy Series: Jean Stapleton, *All in the Family* (CBS)

### 1971–72

Outstanding Series—Comedy: *All in the Family* (CBS)

Outstanding Series—Drama: *Elizabeth R (Masterpiece Theatre)* (PBS)

Outstanding Variety Series—Musical: *The Carol Burnett Show* (CBS)

Outstanding Variety Series—Talk: *The Dick Cavett Show* (ABC)

Outstanding Continued Performance by an Actor in a Leading Role in a Dramatic Series: Peter Falk, *Columbo* (NBC)

Outstanding Continued Performance by an Actor in a Leading Role in a Comedy Series: Carroll O'Connor, *All in the Family* (CBS)

Outstanding Continued Performance by an Actress in

a Leading Role in a Comedy Series: Jean Stapleton, *All in the Family* (CBS)

### 1972–73

Outstanding Comedy Series: *All in the Family* (CBS)

Outstanding Drama Series: *The Waltons* (CBS)

Outstanding Variety Musical Series: *The Julie Andrews Hour* (ABC)

Outstanding Continued Performance by an Actor in a Leading Role (Drama Series—Continuing): Richard Thomas, *The Waltons* (CBS)

Outstanding Continued Performance by an Actress in a Leading Role (Drama Series—Continuing): Michael Learned, *The Waltons* (CBS)

Outstanding Continued Performance by an Actor in a Leading Role in a Comedy Series: Jack Klugman, *The Odd Couple* (ABC)

Outstanding Continued Performance by an Actress in a Leading Role in a Comedy Series: Mary Tyler Moore, *The Mary Tyler Moore Show* (CBS)

### 1973–74

Outstanding Comedy Series: *M*A*S*H* (CBS)

Outstanding Drama Series: *Upstairs, Downstairs (Masterpiece Theatre)* (PBS)

Outstanding Music-Variety Series: *The Carol Burnett Show* (CBS)

Best Lead Actor in a Comedy Series: Alan Alda, *M*A*S*H* (CBS)

Best Lead Actor in a Drama Series: Telly Savalas, *Kojak* (CBS)

Best Lead Actress in a Comedy Series: Mary Tyler Moore, *The Mary Tyler Moore Show* (CBS)

Best Lead Actress in a Drama Series: Michael Learned, *The Waltons* (CBS)

### 1974–75

Outstanding Comedy Series: *The Mary Tyler Moore Show* (CBS)

Outstanding Drama Series: *Upstairs, Downstairs (Masterpiece Theatre)* (PBS)

Outstanding Comedy-Variety or Music Series: *The Carol Burnett Show* (CBS)

Outstanding Lead Actor in a Comedy Series: Tony Randall, *The Odd Couple* (ABC)

Outstanding Lead Actor in a Drama Series: Robert Blake, *Baretta* (ABC)

Outstanding Lead Actress in a Comedy Series: Valerie Harper, *Rhoda* (CBS)

Outstanding Lead Actress in a Drama Series: Jean Marsh, *Upstairs, Downstairs (Masterpiece Theatre)* (PBS)

### 1975–76

Outstanding Comedy Series: *The Mary Tyler Moore Show* (CBS)

Outstanding Drama Series: *Police Story* (NBC)

Outstanding Comedy-Variety or Music Series: *NBC's Saturday Night Live* (NBC)

Outstanding Lead Actor in a Comedy Series: Jack Albertson, *Chico and the Man* (NBC)

Outstanding Lead Actor in a Drama Series: Peter Falk, *Columbo* (NBC)

Outstanding Lead Actress in a Comedy Series: Mary Tyler Moore, *The Mary Tyler Moore Show* (CBS)

Outstanding Lead Actress in a Drama Series: Michael Learned, *The Waltons* (CBS)

### 1976–77

Outstanding Comedy Series: *The Mary Tyler Moore Show* (CBS)

Outstanding Drama Series: *Upstairs, Downstairs (Masterpiece Theatre)* (PBS)

Outstanding Comedy-Variety or Music Series: *Van Dyke and Company* (NBC)

Outstanding Lead Actor in a Comedy Series: Carroll O'Connor, *All in the Family* (CBS)

Outstanding Lead Actor in a Drama Series: James Garner, *The Rockford Files* (NBC)

Outstanding Lead Actress in a Comedy Series: Beatrice Arthur, *Maude* (CBS)

Outstanding Lead Actress in a Drama Series: Lindsay Wagner, *The Bionic Woman* (ABC)

### 1977–78

Outstanding Comedy Series: *All in the Family* (CBS)

Outstanding Drama Series: *The Rockford Files* (NBC)

Outstanding Comedy-Variety or Music Series: *The Muppet Show* (syndicated)

Outstanding Lead Actor in a Comedy Series: Carroll O'Connor, *All in the Family* (CBS)

Outstanding Lead Actor in a Drama Series: Ed Asner, *Lou Grant* (CBS)

Outstanding Lead Actress in a Comedy Series: Jean Stapleton, *All in the Family* (CBS)

Outstanding Lead Actress in a Drama Series: Sada Thompson, *Family* (ABC)

### 1978–79

Outstanding Comedy Series: *Taxi* (ABC)

Outstanding Drama Series: *Lou Grant* (CBS)

Outstanding Comedy-Variety or Music Program (Special or Series): *Steve & Eydie Celebrate Irving Berlin* (NBC)

Outstanding Lead Actor in a Comedy Series (Continuing or Single Performance): Carroll O'Connor, *All in the Family* (CBS)

Outstanding Lead Actor in a Drama Series (Continuing or Single Performance): Ron Leibman, *Kaz* (CBS)

Outstanding Lead Actress in a Comedy Series (Continuing or Single Performance): Ruth Gordon, *Taxi* ("Sugar Mama") (ABC)

Outstanding Lead Actress in a Drama Series (Continuing or Single Performance): Mariette Hartley, *The Incredible Hulk* ("Married") (CBS)

### 1979–80

Outstanding Comedy Series: *Taxi* (ABC)

Outstanding Drama Series: *Lou Grant* (CBS)

Outstanding Variety or Music Program (Special or Series): *IBM Presents Baryshnikov on Broadway* (ABC)

Outstanding Lead Actor in a Comedy Series (Continuing or Single Performance): Richard Mulligan, *Soap* (ABC)

Outstanding Lead Actor in a Drama Series (Continuing or Single Performance): Ed Asner, *Lou Grant* (CBS)

Outstanding Lead Actress in a Comedy Series (Continuing or Single Performance): Cathryn Damon, *Soap* (ABC)

Outstanding Lead Actress in a Drama Series (Continuing or Single Performance): Barbara Bel Geddes, *Dallas* (CBS)

### 1980–81

Outstanding Comedy Series: *Taxi* (ABC)

Outstanding Drama Series: *Hill Street Blues* (NBC)

Outstanding Variety, Music, or Comedy Program: *Lily: Sold Out* (CBS)

Outstanding Lead Actor in a Drama Series: Daniel J. Travanti, *Hill Street Blues* (NBC)

Outstanding Lead Actor in a Comedy Series: Judd Hirsch, *Taxi* (ABC)

Outstanding Lead Actress in a Drama Series: Barbara Babcock, *Hill Street Blues* (NBC)

Outstanding Lead Actress in a Comedy Series: Isabel Sanford, *The Jeffersons* (CBS)

### 1981–82

Outstanding Comedy Series: *Barney Miller* (ABC)

Outstanding Drama Series: *Hill Street Blues* (NBC)

Outstanding Variety, Music, or Comedy Program: *Night of 100 Stars* (ABC)

Outstanding Lead Actor in a Drama Series: Daniel J. Travanti, *Hill Street Blues* (NBC)

Outstanding Lead Actor in a Comedy Series: Alan Alda, *M*A*S*H* (CBS)

Outstanding Lead Actress in a Drama Series: Michael Learned, *Nurse* (CBS)

Outstanding Lead Actress in a Comedy Series: Carol Kane, *Taxi* ("Simka Returns") (ABC)

### 1982–83

Outstanding Comedy Series: *Cheers* (NBC)

Outstanding Drama Series: *Hill Street Blues* (NBC)

Outstanding Variety, Music, or Comedy Program: *Motown 25: Yesterday, Today, Forever* (NBC)

Outstanding Lead Actor in a Drama Series: Ed Flanders, *St. Elsewhere* (NBC)

Outstanding Lead Actor in a Comedy Series: Judd Hirsch, *Taxi* (ABC)

Outstanding Lead Actress in a Drama Series: Tyne Daly, *Cagney & Lacey* (CBS)

Outstanding Lead Actress in a Comedy Series: Shelley Long, *Cheers* (NBC)

### 1983–84

Outstanding Comedy Series: *Cheers* (NBC)

Outstanding Drama Series: *Hill Street Blues* (NBC)

Outstanding Variety, Music, or Comedy Program: "The 6th Annual Kennedy Center Honors: A Celebration of the Performing Arts" (CBS)

Outstanding Lead Actor in a Drama Series: Tom Selleck, *Magnum, P.I.* (CBS)

Outstanding Lead Actor in a Comedy Series: John Ritter, *Three's Company* (ABC)

Outstanding Lead Actress in a Drama Series: Tyne Daly, *Cagney & Lacey* (CBS)

Outstanding Lead Actress in a Comedy Series: Jane Curtin, *Kate & Allie* (CBS)

### 1984–85

Outstanding Comedy Series: *The Cosby Show* (NBC)

Outstanding Drama Series: *Cagney & Lacey* (CBS)

Outstanding Variety, Music, or Comedy Program: "Motown Returns to the Apollo" (NBC)

Outstanding Lead Actor in a Drama Series: William Daniels, *St. Elsewhere* (NBC)

Outstanding Lead Actor in a Comedy Series: Robert Guillaume, *Benson* (ABC)

Outstanding Lead Actress in a Drama Series: Tyne Daly, *Cagney & Lacey* (CBS)

Outstanding Lead Actress in a Comedy Series: Jane Curtin, *Kate & Allie* (CBS)

### 1985–86

Outstanding Comedy Series: *The Golden Girls* (NBC)

Outstanding Drama Series: *Cagney & Lacey* (CBS)

Outstanding Variety, Music, or Comedy Program: "The Kennedy Center Honors: A Celebration of the Performing Arts" (CBS)

Outstanding Lead Actor in a Drama Series: William Daniels, *St. Elsewhere* (NBC)

Outstanding Lead Actor in a Comedy Series: Michael J. Fox, *Family Ties* (NBC)

Outstanding Lead Actress in a Drama Series: Sharon Gless, *Cagney & Lacey* (CBS)

Outstanding Lead Actress in a Comedy Series: Betty White, *The Golden Girls* (NBC)

### 1986–87

Outstanding Comedy Series: *The Golden Girls* (NBC)

Outstanding Drama Series: *L.A. Law* (NBC)

Outstanding Variety, Music, or Comedy Program: "The 1987 Tony Awards" (CBS)

Outstanding Lead Actor in a Drama Series: Bruce Willis, *Moonlighting* (ABC)

Outstanding Lead Actor in a Comedy Series: Michael J. Fox, *Family Ties* (NBC)

Outstanding Lead Actress in a Drama Series: Sharon Gless, *Cagney & Lacey* (CBS)

Outstanding Lead Actress in a Comedy Series: Rue McClanahan, *The Golden Girls* (NBC)

### 1987–88

Outstanding Comedy Series: *The Wonder Years* (ABC)

Outstanding Drama Series: *thirtysomething* (ABC)

Outstanding Variety, Music, or Comedy Program: "Irving Berlin's 100th Birthday Celebration" (CBS)

Outstanding Lead Actor in a Comedy Series: Michael J. Fox, *Family Ties* (NBC)

Outstanding Lead Actor in a Drama Series: Richard Kiley, *A Year in the Life* (NBC)

Outstanding Lead Actress in a Comedy Series: Beatrice Arthur, *The Golden Girls* (NBC)

Outstanding Lead Actress in a Drama Series: Tyne Daly, *Cagney & Lacey* (CBS)

### 1988–89

Outstanding Comedy Series: *Cheers* (NBC)

Outstanding Drama Series: *L.A. Law* (NBC)

Outstanding Variety, Music, or Comedy Program: *The Tracey Ullman Show* (Fox)

Outstanding Lead Actor in a Comedy Series: Richard Mulligan, *Empty Nest* (NBC)

Outstanding Lead Actor in a Drama Series: Carroll O'Connor, *In the Heat of the Night* (NBC)

Outstanding Lead Actress in a Comedy Series: Candice Bergen, *Murphy Brown* (CBS)

Outstanding Lead Actress in a Drama Series: Dana Delany, *China Beach* (ABC)

### 1989–90

Outstanding Comedy Series: *Murphy Brown* (CBS)

Outstanding Drama Series: *L.A. Law* (NBC)

Outstanding Variety, Music, or Comedy Series: *In Living Color* (Fox)

Outstanding Lead Actor in a Comedy Series: Ted Danson, *Cheers* (NBC)

Outstanding Lead Actor in a Drama Series: Peter Falk, *Columbo* (ABC)

Outstanding Lead Actress in a Comedy Series: Candice Bergen, *Murphy Brown* (CBS)

Outstanding Lead Actress in a Drama Series: Patricia Wettig, *thirtysomething* (ABC)

### 1990–91

Outstanding Comedy Series: *Cheers* (NBC)

Outstanding Drama Series: *L.A. Law* (NBC)

Outstanding Variety, Music, or Comedy Series: *The 63rd Annual Academy Awards* (ABC)

Outstanding Lead Actor in a Comedy Series: Burt Reynolds, *Evening Shade* (CBS)

Outstanding Lead Actor in a Drama Series: James Earl Jones, *Gabriel's Fire* (ABC)

Outstanding Lead Actress in a Comedy Series: Kirstie Alley, *Cheers* (NBC)

Outstanding Lead Actress in a Drama Series: Patricia Wettig, *thirtysomething* (ABC)

## THE GRAMMYS, 1958–90

The "Grammys" are officially known as the National Academy of Recording Arts and Sciences Awards. Winners (in almost 70 categories) are selected yearly by the 6,000 or so voting members of the academy. The five award categories listed below have remained fairly constant over the years, although the overall "Best Vocal Performance" award was phased out in 1968; from that year on, our listing is for "Best Pop Vocal Performance" except where indicated.

| Year | Record of the year | Album of the year | Song of the year[1] | Best vocal performance (male) | Best vocal performance (female) |
|------|--------------------|--------------------|--------------------|-------------------------------|----------------------------------|
| 1958 | Domenico Modugno *Nel Blu Dipinto di Blu (Volare)* | Henry Mancini *The Music from Peter Gunn* | Domenico Modugno "Nel Blu Dipinto di Blu" ("Volare") | Perry Como *Catch a Falling Star* | Ella Fitzgerald *Ella Fitzgerald Sings the Irving Berlin Songbook*[2] |
| 1959 | Bobby Darin *Mack the Knife* | Frank Sinatra *Come Dance with Me* | Jimmy Driftwood "The Battle of New Orleans" | Frank Sinatra *Come Dance with Me* | Ella Fitzgerald *But Not for Me* |
| 1960 | Percy Faith *Theme from a Summer Place* | Bob Newhart *Button-Down Mind* | Ernest Gold "Theme from Exodus" | Ray Charles *Georgia on My Mind* | Ella Fitzgerald *Mack the Knife* |
| 1961 | Henry Mancini *Moon River* | Judy Garland *Judy at Carnegie Hall* | Henry Mancini, Johnny Mercer "Moon River" | Jack Jones *Lollipops and Roses* | Judy Garland *Judy at Carnegie Hall*[2] |
| 1962 | Tony Bennett *I Left My Heart in San Francisco* | Vaughn Meader *The First Family* | Leslie Bricusse, Anthony Newley "What Kind of Fool Am I?" | Tony Bennett *I Left My Heart in San Francisco*[2] | Ella Fitzgerald *Ella Swings Brightly with Nelson Riddle*[2] |
| 1963 | Henry Mancini *The Days of Wine and Roses* | Barbra Streisand *The Barbra Streisand Album* | Henry Mancini, Johnny Mercer "The Days of Wine and Roses" | Jack Jones *Wives and Lovers* | Barbra Streisand *The Barbra Streisand Album*[2] |
| 1964 | Stan Getz, Astrud Gilberto *The Girl from Ipanema* | Stan Getz, Astrud Gilberto *Getz/Gilberto* | Jerry Herman "Hello, Dolly!" | Louis Armstrong *Hello, Dolly!* | Barbra Streisand *People* |
| 1965 | Herb Alpert & the Tijuana Brass *A Taste of Honey* | Frank Sinatra *September of My Years* | Paul Francis Webster, Johnny Mandel "The Shadow of Your Smile" | Frank Sinatra *It Was a Very Good Year* | Barbra Streisand *My Name Is Barbra*[2] |
| 1966 | Frank Sinatra *Strangers in the Night* | Frank Sinatra *A Man and His Music* | John Lennon, Paul McCartney "Michelle" | Frank Sinatra *Strangers in the Night* | Eydie Gorme *If He Walked into My Life* |
| 1967 | 5th Dimension *Up, Up and Away* | The Beatles *Sgt. Pepper's Lonely Hearts Club Band* | Jim Webb "Up, Up and Away" | Glen Campbell *By the Time I Get to Phoenix* | Bobbie Gentry *Ode to Billie Joe* |
| 1968 | Simon & Garfunkel *Mrs. Robinson* | Glen Campbell *By the Time I Get to Phoenix* | Bobby Russell "Little Green Apples" | Jose Feliciano[3] *Light My Fire* | Dionne Warwick[3] *Do You Know the Way to San Jose?* |
| 1969 | 5th Dimension *Aquarius/Let the Sunshine In* | Blood, Sweat & Tears *Blood, Sweat & Tears* | Joe South "Games People Play" | Harry Nilsson[4] *Everybody's Talkin'* | Peggy Lee[4] *Is That All There Is?* |
| 1970 | Simon & Garfunkel *Bridge over Troubled Water* | Simon & Garfunkel *Bridge over Troubled Water* | Paul Simon "Bridge over Troubled Water" | Ray Stevens[4] *Everything Is Beautiful* | Dionne Warwick[4] *I'll Never Fall in Love Again*[2] |
| 1971 | Carole King *It's Too Late* | Carole King *Tapestry* | Carole King "You've Got a Friend" | James Taylor[5] *You've Got a Friend* | Carole King[5] *Tapestry*[2] |
| 1972 | Roberta Flack *The First Time Ever I Saw Your Face* | George Harrison, Ravi Shankar, Bob Dylan et al *Concert for Bangladesh* | Ewan McColl "The First Time Ever I Saw Your Face" | Harry Nilsson *Without You* | Helen Reddy *I Am Woman* |
| 1973 | Roberta Flack *Killing Me Softly with His Song* | Stevie Wonder *Innervisions* | Norman Gimbel, Charles Fox "Killing Me Softly with His Song" | Stevie Wonder *You Are the Sunshine of My Life* | Roberta Flack *Killing Me Softly with His Song* |
| 1974 | Olivia Newton-John *I Honestly Love You* | Stevie Wonder *Fulfillingness' First Finale* | Marilyn & Alan Bergman, Marvin Hamlisch "The Way We Were" | Stevie Wonder *Fulfillingness' First Finale*[2] | Olivia Newton-John *I Honestly Love You* |

| Year | Record of the year | Album of the year | Song of the year[1] | Best vocal performance (male) | Best vocal performance (female) |
|------|--------------------|--------------------|---------------------|-------------------------------|----------------------------------|
| 1975 | Captain & Tennille *Love Will Keep Us Together* | Paul Simon *Still Crazy after All These Years* | Stephen Sondheim "Send in the Clowns" | Paul Simon *Still Crazy after All These Years*[2] | Janis Ian *At Seventeen* |
| 1976 | George Benson *This Masquerade* | Stevie Wonder *Songs in the Key of Life* | Bruce Johnston "I Write the Songs" | Stevie Wonder *Songs in the Key of Life*[2] | Linda Ronstadt *Hasten Down the Wind*[2] |
| 1977 | The Eagles *Hotel California* | Fleetwood Mac *Rumours* | Barbra Streisand, Paul Williams "Evergreen" | James Taylor *Handy Man* | Barbra Streisand *Evergreen* |
| 1978 | Billy Joel *Just the Way You Are* | Various Artists *Saturday Night Fever* | Billy Joel "Just the Way You Are" | Barry Manilow *Copacabana (At the Copa)* | Anne Murray *You Needed Me* |
| 1979 | The Doobie Brothers *What a Fool Believes* | Billy Joel *52nd Street* | Kenny Loggins, Michael McDonald "What a Fool Believes" | Billy Joel *52nd Street*[2] | Dionne Warwick *I'll Never Love This Way Again* |
| 1980 | Christopher Cross *Sailing* | Christopher Cross *Christopher Cross* | Christopher Cross "Sailing" | Kenny Loggins *This Is It* | Bette Midler *The Rose* |
| 1981 | Kim Carnes *Bette Davis Eyes* | John Lennon/Yoko Ono *Double Fantasy* | Donna Weiss, Jackie DeShannon "Bette Davis Eyes" | Al Jarreau *Breakin' Away*[2] | Lena Horne *Lena Horne: The Lady and Her Music Live on Broadway*[2] |
| 1982 | Toto *Rosanna* | Toto *Toto IV* | Johnny Christopher, Mark James, Wayne Carson "Always on My Mind" | Lionel Richie *Truly* | Melissa Manchester *You Should Hear How She Talks about You* |
| 1983 | Michael Jackson *Beat It* | Michael Jackson *Thriller* | Sting "Every Breath You Take" | Michael Jackson *Thriller*[2] | Irene Cara *Flashdance . . . What a Feeling* |
| 1984 | Tina Turner *What's Love Got to Do with It?* | Lionel Richie *Can't Slow Down* | Graham Lyle, Terry Britten "What's Love Got to Do with It?" | Phil Collins *Against All Odds (Take a Look at Me Now)* | Tina Turner *What's Love Got to Do with It?* |
| 1985 | USA for Africa *We Are the World* | Phil Collins *No Jacket Required* | Michael Jackson, Lionel Richie "We Are the World" | Phil Collins *No Jacket Required*[2] | Whitney Houston *Saving All My Love for You* |
| 1986 | Steve Winwood *Higher Love* | Paul Simon *Graceland* | Various Artists "That's What Friends Are For" | Steve Winwood *Higher Love* | Barbra Streisand *The Broadway Album*[2] |
| 1987 | Paul Simon *Graceland* | U2 *The Joshua Tree* | Linda Ronstadt, James Ingram "Somewhere Out There" | Sting *Bring On the Night*[2] | Whitney Houston *I Wanna Dance with Somebody (Who Loves Me)* |
| 1988 | Bobby McFerrin *Don't Worry, Be Happy* | George Michael *Faith* | Bobby McFerrin "Don't Worry, Be Happy" | Bobby McFerrin *Don't Worry, Be Happy* | Tracy Chapman *Fast Car* |
| 1989 | Bette Midler *Wind Beneath My Wings* | Bonnie Raitt *Nick of Time* | Bette Midler "Wind Beneath My Wings" | Michael Bolton *How Am I Supposed to Live Without You* | Bonnie Raitt *Nick of Time* |
| 1990 | Phil Collins *Another Day in Paradise* | Quincy Jones *Back on the Block* | Julie Gold "From a Distance" | Roy Orbison *Oh Pretty Woman* | Mariah Carey *Vision of Love* |

**Notes:** 1. Awarded to the composer, rather than the performer, of the song. 2. Awarded for an album, rather than an individual song. 3. Award given for "Best Contemporary – Pop Vocal Performance." 4. Award given for "Best Contemporary Vocal Performance." 5. From 1971 on, all awards in these columns are for "Best Pop Vocal Performance." **Source:** National Academy of Recording Arts and Sciences.

## MTV VIDEO MUSIC AWARDS, 1984–91

Each year MTV Networks recognizes outstanding achievement in the field of video music with the MTV Video Music Awards. Since their inception in 1984, the number of awards has grown to 21. In addition to those listed below, there are special categories for rap, heavy metal and dance videos, as well as for technical achievement in choreography, direction and cinematography.

| Year | Best video | Best male video | Best female video | Best group video | Best new artist in a video |
|------|------------|-----------------|-------------------|------------------|----------------------------|
| 1984 | Cars, "You Might Think" | David Bowie, "China Girl" | Cyndi Lauper, "Girls Just Want to Have Fun" | ZZ Top, "Legs" | Eurythmics, "Sweet Dreams (Are Made of This)" |
| 1985 | Don Henley, "The Boys of Summer" | Bruce Springsteen, "I'm on Fire" | Tina Turner, "What's Love Got to Do With It?" | USA for Africa, "We Are the World" | til' tuesday, "Voices Carry" |

| Year | Best video | Best male video | Best female video | Best group video | Best new artist in a video |
|------|-----------|-----------------|-------------------|------------------|----------------------------|
| 1986 | Dire Straits, "Money for Nothing" | Robert Palmer, "Addicted to Love" | Whitney Houston, "How Will I Know?" | Dire Straits, "Money for Nothing" | a-Ha, "Take On Me" |
| 1987 | Peter Gabriel, "Sledgehammer" | Peter Gabriel, "Sledgehammer" | Madonna, "Papa Don't Preach" | Talking Heads, "Wild Wild Life" | Crowded House, "Don't Dream It's Over" |
| 1988 | INXS, "Need You Tonight/Mediate" | Prince, "U Got the Look" | Suzanne Vega, "Luka" | INXS, "Need You Tonight/Mediate" | Guns N' Roses, "Welcome to the Jungle" |
| 1989 | Neil Young, "This Note's for You" | Elvis Costello, "Veronica" | Paula Abdul, "Straight Up" | Living Colour, "Cult of Personality" | Living Colour, "Cult of Personality" |
| 1990 | Sinead O'Connor, "Nothing Compares 2 U" | Don Henley, "The End of the Innocence" | Sinead O'Connor, "Nothing Compares 2 U" | B-52s, "Love Shack" | Michael Penn, "No Myth" |
| 1991 | R.E.M., "Losing My Religion" | Chris Isaak, "Wicked Game" | Janet Jackson, "Love Will Never Do Without You" | R.E.M., "Losing My Religion" | Jesus Jones, "Right Here, Right Now" |

**Source:** MTV Networks.

## THE ROCK AND ROLL HALL OF FAME, 1986–91

The Rock and Roll Hall of Fame has three categories. Artists are eligible for induction 25 years after the release of their first recording. Early influences are prerock musical pioneers, usually blues or jazz artists. The nonperformance category includes producers, disc jockeys, agents, and others whose work behind the scenes has had a lasting impact on rock and roll. The hall of fame itself will be located in Cleveland.

**1986**
*Artists:*
  Chuck Berry
  James Brown
  Ray Charles
  Sam Cooke
  Fats Domino
  The Everly Brothers
  Buddy Holly
  Jerry Lee Lewis
  Elvis Presley
  Little Richard
*Early Influences:*
  John Hammond
  Robert Johnson
  Jimmie Rodgers
  Jimmy Yancey

*Nonperformers:*
  Alan Freed
  Sam Philips
**1987**
*Artists:*
  The Coasters
  Eddie Cochran
  Bo Diddley
  Aretha Franklin
  Marvin Gaye
  Bill Haley
  B.B. King
  Clyde McPhatter
  Ricky Nelson
  Roy Orbison
  Carl Perkins
  Smokey Robinson
  Joe Turner

Muddy Waters
  Jackie Wilson
*Early Influences:*
  Louis Jordan
  T-Bone Walker
  Jerry Wexler
  Hank Williams
*Nonperformers:*
  Leonard Chess
  Ahmet Ertegun
  Jerome Lieber and
    Michael Stoller
**1988**
*Artists:*
  The Beach Boys
  The Beatles
  The Drifters
  Bob Dylan

The Supremes
*Early Influences:*
  Woody Guthrie
  Leadbelly
  Les Paul
*Nonperformer:*
  Berry Gordy, Jr.
**1989**
*Artists:*
  Dion DiMucci
  Otis Redding
  The Rolling Stones
  The Temptations
  Stevie Wonder
*Early Influences:*
  The Ink Spots
  Bessie Smith
  The Soul Stirrers

*Nonperformer:*
  Phil Spector
**1990**
*Artists:*
  Hank Ballard
  Bobby Darin
  The Four Seasons
  The Four Tops
  The Kinks
  The Platters
  Simon & Garfunkel
  The Who
*Early Influences:*
  Louis Armstrong
  Charlie Christian
  Ma Rainey
*Nonperformers:*
  Gerry Goffin and

Carole King
  Lamont Dozier,
  Brian Holland, and
  Eddie Holland
**1991**
*Artists:*
  LaVern Baker
  The Byrds
  John Lee Hooker
  The Impressions
  Wilson Pickett
  Jimmy Reed
  Ike and Tina Turner
*Early Influences:*
  Howlin' Wolf
*Nonperformers:*
  Dave Bartholomew
  Ralph Bass

## THE TONY AWARDS, 1947–91

The Tony Awards are presented each year by the American Theatre Wing for distinguished achievement in the Broadway theater. Named for Antoinette Perry, an actress, producer, director, and chairman of the American Theatre Wing who died in 1946, the Tonys were first presented in 1947. Awards are given to performers, authors, producers, directors, composers, and choreographers, and scenic, costume, and lighting designers. Listed here is a selection of major awards for each year: best play (author), best performance by an actor in a play, best performance by an actress in a play, best musical (composer and lyricist), best performance by an actor in a musical, best performance by an actress in a musical.

**PLAY**

| Year | Best play | Best actor | Best actress |
|------|-----------|-----------|-------------|
| 1947 | no play | José Ferrer, *Cyrano de Bergerac*; Frederic March, *Year 1790* | Ingrid Bergman, *Joan of Lorraine*; Helen Hayes, *Happy Birthday*. |
| 1948 | *Mister Roberts*, Thomas Heggen and Joshua Logan | Henry Fonda, *Mister Roberts*; Paul Kelly, *Command Decision*; Basil Rathbone, *The Heiress* | Judith Anderson, *Medea*; Katharine Cornell, *Antony and Cleopatra*; Jessica Tandy, *A Streetcar Named Desire* |
| 1949 | *Death of a Salesman*, Arthur Miller | Rex Harrison, *Anne of a Thousand Days* | Martita Hunt, *The Mad Woman of Chaillot* |
| 1950 | *The Cocktail Party*, T.S. Eliot | Sidney Blackmer, *Come Back, Little Sheba* | Shirley Booth, *Come Back, Little Sheba* |
| 1951 | *The Rose Tattoo*, Tennessee Williams | Claude Rains, *Darkness at Noon* | Uta Hagen, *The Country Girl* |
| 1952 | *The Fourposter*, Jan de Hartog | José Ferrer, *The Shrike* | Julie Harris, *I Am a Camera* |
| 1953 | *The Crucible*, Arthur Miller | Tom Ewell, *The Seven Year Itch* | Shirley Booth, *Time of the Cuckoo* |
| 1954 | *The Teahouse of the August Moon*, John Patrick | David Wayne, *The Teahouse of the August Moon* | Audrey Hepburn, *Ondine* |
| 1955 | *The Desperate Hours*, Joseph Hayes | Alfred Lunt, *Quadrille* | Nancy Kelly, *The Bad Seed* |
| 1956 | *The Diary of Anne Frank*, Frances Goodrich and Albert Hackett | Paul Muni, *Inherit the Wind* | Julie Harris, *The Lark* |

| Year | Best play | Best actor | Best actress |
|------|-----------|------------|--------------|
| 1957 | *Long Day's Journey Into Night*, Eugene O'Neill | Frederic March, *Long Day's Journey Into Night* | Margaret Leighton, *Separate Tables* |
| 1958 | *Sunrise at Campobello*, Dore Schary | Ralph Bellamy, *Sunrise at Campobello* | Helen Hayes, *Time Remembered* |
| 1959 | *J.B.*, Archibald MacLeish | Jason Robards, *The Disenchanted* | Gertrude Berg, *A Majority of One* |
| 1960 | *The Miracle Worker*, William Gibson | Melvyn Douglas, *The Best Man* | Anne Bancroft, *The Miracle Worker* |
| 1961 | *Becket*, Jean Anouilh | Zero Mostel, *Rhinoceros* | Joan Plowright, *A Taste of Honey* |
| 1962 | *A Man for All Seasons*, Robert Bolt | Paul Scofield, *A Man for All Seasons* | Margaret Leighton, *Night of The Iguana* |
| 1963 | *Who's Afraid of Virginia Woolf?* Edward Albee | Arthur Hill, *Who's Afraid of Virginia Woolf?* | Uta Hagen, *Who's Afraid of Virginia Woolf?* |
| 1964 | *Luther*, John Osborne | Alec Guiness, *Dylan* | Sandy Dennis, *Any Wednesday* |
| 1965 | *The Subject was Roses*, Frank Gilroy | Walter Matthau, *The Odd Couple* | Irene Worth, *Tiny Alice* |
| 1966 | *Marat/Sade*, Peter Weiss | Hal Holbrook, *Mark Twain Tonight!* | Rosemary Harris, *The Lion in Winter* |
| 1967 | *The Homecoming*, Harold Pinter | Paul Rogers, *The Homecoming* | Beryl Reid, *The Killing of Sister George* |
| 1968 | *Rosencrantz and Guildenstern Are Dead*, Tom Stoppard | Martin Balsam, *You Know I Can't Hear You When the Water's Running* | Zoe Caldwell, *The Prime of Miss Jean Brodie* |
| 1969 | *The Great White Hope*, Howard Sackler | James Earl Jones, *The Great White Hope* | Julie Harris, *Forty Carats* |
| 1970 | *Borstal Boy*, Frank McMahon | Fritz Weaver, *Child's Play* | Tammy Grimes, *Private Lives* (R) |
| 1971 | *Sleuth*, Anthony Shaffer | Brian Bedford, *The School for Wives* | Maureen Stapleton, *Gingerbread Lady* |
| 1972 | *Sticks and Bones*, David Rabe | Cliff Gorman, *Lenny* | Sada Thompson, *Twigs* |
| 1973 | *That Championship Season*, Jason Miller | Alan Bates, *Butley* | Julie Harris, *The Last of Mrs. Lincoln* |
| 1974 | *The River Niger*, Joseph A. Walker | Michael Moriarty, *Find Your Way Home* | Colleen Dewhurst, *A Moon for the Misbegotten* (R) |
| 1975 | *Equus*, Peter Shaffer | John Kani, *Sizwe Banzi Is Dead;* Winston Ntshona, *The Island* | Ellen Burstyn, *Same Time, Next Year* |
| 1976 | *Travesties*, Tom Stoppard | John Wood, *Travesties* | Irene Worth, *Sweet Bird of Youth* (R) |
| 1977 | *The Shadow Box*, Michael Cristofer | Al Pacino, *The Basic Training of Pavlo Hummel* | Julie Harris, *The Belle of Amherst* |
| 1978 | *Da*, Hugh Leonard | Barnard Hughes, *Da* | Jessica Tandy, *The Gin Game* |
| 1979 | *The Elephant Man*, Bernard Pomerance | Tom Conti, *Whose Life Is It Anyway?* | Constance Cummings, *Wings* |
| 1980 | *Children of a Lesser God*, Mark Medoff | John Rubenstein, *Children of a Lesser God* | Phyllis Frelich, *Children of a Lesser God* |
| 1981 | *Amadeus*, Peter Shaffer | Ian McKellen, *Amadeus* | Jane Lapotaire, *Piaf* |
| 1982 | *Nicholas Nickleby*, David Edgar | Roger Rees, *Nicholas Nickleby* | Zoe Caldwell, *Medea* |
| 1983 | *Torch Song Trilogy*, Harvey Fierstein | Harvey Fierstein, *Torch Song Trilogy* | Jessica Tandy, *Foxfire* |
| 1984 | *The Real Thing*, Tom Stoppard | Jeremy Irons, *The Real Thing* | Glenn Close, *The Real Thing* |
| 1985 | *As Is*, William Hoffman | Derek Jacobi, *Much Ado About Nothing* | Stockard Channing, *Joe Egg* (R) |
| 1986 | *I'm Not Rappaport*, Herb Gardner | Judd Hirsch, *I'm Not Rappaport* | Lily Tomlin, *The Search for Intelligent Life in the Universe* |
| 1987 | *Fences*, August Wilson | James Earl Jones, *Fences* | Linda Lavin, *Broadway Bound* |
| 1988 | *M. Butterfly*, David Henry Hwang | Ron Silver, *Speed-The-Plow* | Joan Allen, *Burn This* |
| 1989 | *The Heidi Chronicles*, Wendy Wasserstein | Philip Bosco, *Lend Me a Tenor* | Pauline Collins, *Shirley Valentine* |
| 1990 | *The Grapes of Wrath*, adapted from John Steinbeck's novel by Frank Galati | Robert Morse, *Tru* | Maggie Smith, *Lettice and Lovage* |
| 1991 | *Lost In Yonkers*, Neil Simon | Nigel Hawthorne, *Shadowlands* | *Mercedes Rule, Lost in Yonkers* |

## MUSICAL

| Year | Best musical | Best actor | Best actress |
|------|--------------|------------|--------------|
| 1947 | no award | no award | no award |
| 1948 | *Angel in the Wings*, Paul Hartman (M & L) | Paul Hartman, *Angel in the Wings* | Grace Hartman, *Angel in the Wings* |
| 1949 | *Kiss Me Kate*, Cole Porter (M & L) | Ray Bolger, *Where's Charley?* | Nanette Fabray, *Love Life* |
| 1950 | *South Pacific*, Richard Rodgers (M), Oscar Hammerstein, (L) | Ezio Pinza, *South Pacific* | Mary Martin, *South Pacific* |
| 1951 | *Guys and Dolls*, Frank Loesser (M & L) | Robert Alda, *Guys and Dolls* | Ethel Merman, *Call Me Madam* |
| 1952 | *The King and I*, Richard Rodgers (M), Oscar Hammerstein (L) | Phil Silvers, *Top Banana* | Gertrude Lawrence, *The King and I* |
| 1953 | *Wonderful Town*, Leonard Bernstein (M), Betty Comden and Adolph Green (L) | Thomas Mitchell, *Hazel Flagg* | Rosalind Russell, *Wonderful Town* |
| 1954 | *Kismet*, Alexander Borodin (M), adapted by Robert Wright and George Forrest (L) | Alfred Drake, *Kismet* | Dolores Gray, *Carnival in Flanders* |
| 1955 | *The Pajama Game*, Richard Adler and Jerry Ross (M & L) | Walter Slezak, *Fanny* | Mary Martin, *Peter Pan* |
| 1956 | *Damn Yankees*, Richard Adler and Jerry Ross (M & L) | Ray Walston, *Damn Yankees* | Gwen Verdon, *Damn Yankees* |
| 1957 | *My Fair Lady*, Frederick Loewe (M), Alan Jay Lerner (L) | Rex Harrison, *My Fair Lady* | Judy Holliday, *Bells Are Ringing* |
| 1958 | *The Music Man*, Meredith Willson (M & L) | Robert Preston, *The Music Man* | Thelma Ritter, *New Girl in Town* |

| Year | Best musical | Best actor | Best actress |
|------|-------------|-----------|-------------|
| 1959 | *Redhead*, Albert Hague (M), Dorothy Fields (L) | Richard Kiley, *Redhead* | Gwen Verdon, *Redhead* |
| 1960 | (tie) *Fiorello*, Jerry Bock (M), Sheldon Harnick (L); *The Sound of Music*, Richard Rodgers (M), Oscar Hammerstein (L) | Jackie Gleason, *Take Me Along* | Mary Martin, *The Sound of Music* |
| 1961 | *Bye, Bye, Birdie*, Charles Strouse (M), Lee Adams (L) | Richard Burton, *Camelot* | Elizabeth Seal, *Irma la Douce* |
| 1962 | *How to Succeed in Business without Really Trying*, Frank Loesser (M & L) | Robert Morse, *How to Succeed in Business without Really Trying* | (tie) Anna Maria Alberghetti, *Carnival*; Diahann Carroll, *No Strings* |
| 1963 | *A Funny Thing Happened on the Way to the Forum*, Stephen Sondheim (M & L) | Zero Mostel, *A Funny Thing Happened on the Way to the Forum* | Vivien Leigh, *Tovarich* |
| 1964 | *Hello, Dolly!* Jerry Herman (M & L) | Bert Lahr, *Foxy* | Carol Channing, *Hello, Dolly!* |
| 1965 | *Fiddler on the Roof*, Jerry Bock (M), Sheldon Harnick (L) | Zero Mostel, *Fiddler on the Roof* | Liza Minnelli, *Flora, the Red Menace* |
| 1966 | *Man of La Mancha*, Mitch Leigh (M), Joe Darion (L) | Richard Kiley, *Man of La Mancha* | Angela Lansbury, *Mame* |
| 1967 | *Cabaret*, John Kander (M), Fred Ebb (L) | Robert Preston, *I Do! I Do!* | Barbara Harris, *The Apple Tree* |
| 1968 | *Hallelujah, Baby!* Jule Styne (M), Betty Comden and Adolph Green (L) | Robert Goulet, *The Happy Time* | Patricia Routledge, *Darling of the Day* |
| 1969 | *1776*, Sherman Edwards (M & L) | Jerry Orbach, *Promises, Promises* | Angela Lansbury, *Dear World* |
| 1970 | *Applause*, Charles Strouse (M), Lee Adams (L) | Cleavon Little, *Purlie* | Lauren Bacall, *Applause* |
| 1971 | *Company*, Stephen Sondheim (M & L) | Hal Linden, *The Rothchilds* | Helen Gallagher, *No, No, Nannette* (R) |
| 1972 | *Two Gentlemen of Verona* [best score: *Follies*, Stephen Sondheim (M & L)] | Phil Silvers, *A Funny Thing Happened on the Way to the Forum* (R) | Alexis Smith, *Follies* |
| 1973 | *A Little Night Music*, Stephen Sondheim (M & L) | Ben Vereen, *Pippin* | Glynis Johns, *A Little Night Music* |
| 1974 | *Raisin* [best score: *Gigi*, Frederick Loewe (M), Alan Jay Lerner (L)] | Christopher Plummer, *Cyrano* | Virginia Capers, *Raisin* |
| 1975 | *The Wiz*, Charlie Smalls (M & L) | John Cullum, *Shenandoah* | Angela Lansbury, *Gypsy* (R) |
| 1976 | *A Chorus Line*, Marvin Hamlisch (M), Edward Kleban (L) | George Rose, *My Fair Lady* (R) | Donna McKenchie, *A Chorus Line* |
| 1977 | *Annie*, Charles Strouse (M), Martin Charnin (L) | Barry Bostwick, *The Robber Bridegroom* | Dorothy Loudon, *Annie* |
| 1978 | *Ain't Misbehavin'* [best score: *On the Twentieth Century*, Cy Coleman (M), Betty Comden and Adolph Green (L)] | John Cullum, *On the Twentieth Century* | Liza Minelli, *The Act* |
| 1979 | *Sweeney Todd*, Stephen Sondheim (M & L) | Len Cariou, *Sweeney Todd* | Angela Lansbury, *Sweeney Todd* |
| 1980 | *Evita*, Andrew Lloyd Webber (M), Tim Rice (L) | Jim Dale, *Barnum* | Patti LuPone, *Evita* |
| 1981 | *42nd Street*, [best score: *Woman of the Year*, John Kander (M), Fred Ebb (L)] | Kevin Kline, *The Pirates of Penzance* | Lauren Bacall, *Woman of the Year* |
| 1982 | *Nine*, Maury Yeston (M & L) | Ben Harney, *Dreamgirls* | Jennifer Holliday, *Dreamgirls* |
| 1983 | *Cats*, Andrew Lloyd Webber (M), T.S. Eliot (L) | Tommy Tune, *My One and Only* | Natalia Makarova, *On Your Toes* (R) |
| 1984 | *La Cage Aux Folles*, Jerry Herman (M & L) | George Hearn, *La Cage Aux Folles* | Chita Rivera, *The Rink* |
| 1985 | *Big River*, Roger Miller (M & L) | no award | no award |
| 1986 | *The Mystery of Edwin Drood*, Rupert Holmes (M & L) | George Rose, *The Mystery of Edwin Drood* | Bernadette Peters, *Song and Dance* |
| 1987 | *Les Misérables*, Claude-Michel Schönberg (M), Herbert Kretzmer and Alain Boublil (L) | Robert Lindsay, *Me and My Girl* (R) | Maryann Plunkett, *Me and My Girl* (R) |
| 1988 | *The Phantom of the Opera* [best score: *Into the Woods*, Stephen Sondheim (M & L)] | Michael Crawford, *The Phantom of the Opera* | Joanna Gleason, *Into the Woods* |
| 1989 | *Jerome Robbins' Broadway* | Jason Alexander, *Jerome Robbins' Broadway* | Ruth Brown, *Black and Blue* |
| 1990 | *City of Angels*, Cy Coleman and David Zippel (M); Larry Gelbart (L) | James Naughton, *City of Angels* | Tyne Daly, *Gypsy* |
| 1991 | *The Will Rogers Follies* | Jonathan Price, *Miss Saigon* | Lea Salonga, *Miss Saigon* |

M = music; L = lyrics; R = revival. **Note:** Since 1971 "Musical" and "Score" have been separate categories. See listing for 1972, 1974, 1978, 1981, and 1988. **Source:** Isabelle Stevenson, *The Tony Award* (1987)—supplement, American Theatre Wing (1988), reprinted with permission.

## THE NATIONAL BOOK AWARDS, 1950–90

The National Book Awards are given annually for outstanding literary works by American citizens. In the past the number of prizes has varied and has included such categories as poetry, fiction, biography, science, philosophy, religion, and history. Currently only two awards are made each year, one for fiction and one for nonfiction.

| Year | Author/Title | Year | Author/Title | Year | Author/Title |
|------|-------------|------|-------------|------|-------------|

### National book awards for fiction, 1950–90

| Year | Author/Title | Year | Author/Title | Year | Author/Title |
|------|-------------|------|-------------|------|-------------|
| 1950 | Nelson Algren, *The Man with the Golden Arm* | 1958 | John Cheever, *The Wapshot Chronicle* | 1966 | Katherine Anne Porter, *The Collected Stories* |
| 1951 | William Faulkner, *The Collected Stories* | 1959 | Bernard Malamud, *The Magic Barrel* | 1967 | Bernard Malamud, *The Fixer* |
| 1952 | James Jones, *From Here to Eternity* | 1960 | Philip Roth, *Goodbye, Columbus* | 1968 | Thornton Wilder, *The Eighth Day* |
| 1953 | Ralph Ellison, *Invisible Man* | 1961 | Conrad Richter, *The Waters of Kronos* | 1969 | Jerzy Kosinski, *Steps* |
| 1954 | Saul Bellow, *The Adventures of Augie March* | 1962 | Walker Percy, *The Moviegoer* | 1970 | Joyce Carol Oates, *Them* |
| 1955 | William Faulkner, *A Fable* | 1963 | J.F. Powers, *Morte d'Urban* | 1971 | Saul Bellow, *Mr. Sammler's Planet* |
| 1956 | John O'Hara, *Ten North Frederick* | 1964 | John Updike, *The Centaur* | 1972 | Flannery O'Connor, *The Complete Stories* |
| 1957 | Wright Morris, *Field of Vision* | 1965 | Saul Bellow, *Herzog* | 1973 | John Barth, *Chimera* |

1974 Thomas Pynchon, *Gravity's Rainbow*
     Isaac Bashevis Singer, *A Crown of Feathers & Other Stories*
1975 Robert Stone, *Dog Soldiers*
     Thomas Williams, *The Hair of Harold Roux*
1976 William Gaddis, *JR*
1977 Wallace Stegner, *The Spectator Bird*

1978 Mary Lee Settle, *Blood Ties*
1979 Tim O'Brien, *Going After Cacciato*
1980 William Styron, *Sophie's Choice*
1981 Wright Morris, *Plains Song*
1982 John Updike, *Rabbit Is Rich*
1983 Alice Walker, *The Color Purple*
1984 Ellen Gilchrist, *Victory Over Japan*

1985 Don DeLillo, *White Noise*
1986 E.L. Doctorow, *World's Fair*
1987 Larry Heinemann, *Paco's Story*
1988 Pete Dexter, *Paris Trout*
1989 John Casey, *Spartina*
1990 Charles Johnson, *The Middle Passage*

### National book awards for nonfiction, 1950–90

1950 Ralph L. Rusk, *Ralph Waldo Emerson*
1951 Newton Arvin, *Herman Melville*
1952 Rachel Carson, *The Sea Around Us*
1953 Bernard De Voto, *Course of Empire*
1954 Bruce Catton, *A Stillness at Appomattox*
1955 Joseph Wood Krutch, *The Measure of Man*
1956 Herbert Kubly, *An American in Italy*
1957 George F. Kennan, *Russia Leaves the War*
1958 Catherine Drinker Bowen, *The Lion and the Throne*
1959 J. Christopher Herold, *Mistress to an Age*
1960 Richard Ellman, *James Joyce*
1961 William L. Shirer, *The Rise and Fall of the Third Reich*
1962 Lewis Mumford, *The City in History*
1963 Leon Edel, *Henry James*, vols. 2 and 3
1964 Aileen Ward, *John Keats: The Making of a Poet*
1965 Louis Fisher, *The Life of Lenin*
1966 Arthur M. Schlesinger Jr., *A Thousand Days: JFK in the White House*

1967 Justin Kaplan, *Mr. Clemens and Mark Twain*
1968 Jonathan Kozol, *Death at an Early Age*
1969 Norman Mailer, *The Armies of the Night*
1970 Lillian Hellman, *An Unfinished Woman, a Memoir*
1971 James MacGregor Burns, *Roosevelt: The Soldier of Freedom*
1972 Joseph P. Lash, *Eleanor and Franklin*
1973 Frances Fitzgerald, *Fire in the Lake: The Vietnamese and the Americans in Vietnam*
1974 Pauline Kael, *Deeper into the Movies*
1975 Richard B. Sewall, *The Life of Emily Dickinson*
     Lewis Thomas, *The Lives of a Cell*
1976 Paul Fussell, *The Great War and Modern Memory*
1977 Bruno Bettelheim, *The Uses of Enchantment: The Meaning and Importance of Fairy Tales*
1978 Walter Jackson Bate, *Samuel Johnson*
1979 Arthur M. Schlesinger Jr., *Robert Kennedy and His Times*
1980 Tom Wolfe, *The Right Stuff*

1981 Maxine Hong Kingston, *China Men*
1982 Tracy Kidder, *The Soul of a New Machine*
1983 Fox Butterfield, *China: Alive in the Bitter Sea*
1984 Robert V. Remini, *Andrew Jackson and the Course of American Democracy, 1833–1845*, vol. 5
1985 J. Anthony Lukas, *Common Ground: A Turbulent Decade in the Lives of Three American Families*
1986 Barry Lopez, *Arctic Dreams*
1987 Richard Rhodes, *The Making of the Atom Bomb*
1988 Neil Sheehan, *A Bright and Shining Lie: John Paul Vann and America in Vietnam*
1989 Thomas L. Friedman, *From Beirut to Jerusalem*
1990 Ron Chernow, *The House of Morgan: An American Banking Dynasty and the Rise of Modern Finance*

### National book awards for poetry, 1950–84

1950 William Carlos Williams, *Paterson: Book III* and *Selected Poems*
1951 Wallace Stevens, *The Auroras of Autumn*
1952 Marianne Moore, *Collected Poems*
1953 Archibald MacLeish, *Collected Poems 1917–1952*
1954 Conrad Aiken, *Collected Poems*
1955 Wallace Stevens, *The Collected Poems*
1956 W.H. Auden, *The Shield of Achilles*
1957 Richard Wilbur, *Things of this World*
1958 Robert Penn Warren, *Promises: Poems, 1954–56*
1959 Theodore Roethke, *Words for the Wind*
1960 Robert Lowell, *Life Studies*

1961 Randall Jarrell, *The Woman at the Washington Zoo*
1962 Alan Dugan, *Poems*
1963 William Stafford, *Traveling Through the Dark*
1964 John Crowe Ransom, *Selected Poems*
1965 Theodore Roethke, *The Far Field*
1966 James Dickey, *Buckdancer's Choice*
1967 James Merrill, *Nights and Days*
1968 Robert Bly, *The Light Around the Body*
1969 John Berryman, *His Toy, His Dream, His Rest*
1970 Elizabeth Bishop, *The Complete Poems*
1971 Mona Van Duyn, *To See, To Take*
1972 Howard Moss, *Selected Poems*
1973 A.R. Ammons, *Collected Poems: 1951–1971*

1974 Allen Ginsberg, *The Fall of America: Poems of These States, 1965–71*
     Adrienne Rich, *Diving into the Wreck: Poems, 1971–72*
1975 Marilyn Hacker, *Presentation Piece*
1976 John Ashbery, *Self-Portrait in a Convex Mirror*
1977 Richard Eberhart, *Collected Poems, 1930–1976*
1978 Howard Nemerov, *The Collected Poems*
1979 James Merrill, *Mirabell: Books of Number*
1980 Philip Levine, *Ashes*
1981 Lisel Mueller, *The Need to Hold Still*
1982 William Bronk, *Life Supports*
1983 Galway Kinnell, *Selected Poems*
1984 Charles Wright, *Country Music*

**Source:** National Book Awards, Inc.

## THE NATIONAL BOOK CRITICS CIRCLE AWARD, 1975–90

Selected by a 24-member board of critics (who serve three-year terms) from around the country, this award has been increasingly important in the last few years. Books are often recommended to the board by the more than 500 general members of the Circle.

| Year | Author/Title | Year | Author/Title | Year | Author/Title |
|------|-------------|------|-------------|------|-------------|
| | | | **Fiction, 1975–90** | | |
| 1975 | E.L. Doctorow, *Ragtime* | 1981 | John Updike, *Rabbit is Rich* | 1987 | Phillip Roth, *The Counterlife* |
| 1976 | John Gardner, *October Light* | 1982 | Stanley Elkin, *George Mills* | 1988 | Bharati Mukherjee, *The Middleman and Other Stories* |
| 1977 | Toni Morrison, *Song of Solomon* | 1983 | William Kennedy, *Ironweed* | | |
| 1978 | John Cheever, *The Stories of John Cheever* | 1984 | Louise Erdrich, *Love Medicine* | 1989 | E.L. Doctorow, *Billy Bathgate* |
| 1979 | Thomas Flanagan, *The Year of the French* | 1985 | Anne Tyler, *The Accidental Tourist* | 1990 | John Updike, *Rabbit at Rest* |
| 1980 | Shirley Hazzard, *The Transit of Venus* | 1986 | Reynolds Price, *Kate Vaiden* | | |

| | | | **General nonfiction, 1975–90** | | |
|------|-------------|------|-------------|------|-------------|
| 1975 | R.W.B. Lewis, *Edith Wharton* | 1977 | Walter Jackson Bate, *Samuel Johnson* | 1980 | Ronald Steel, *Walter Lippmann and the American Century* |
| 1976 | Maxine Hong Kingston, *The Woman Warrior: Memoirs of a Girlhood Among Ghosts* | 1978 | Maureen Howard, *Facts of Life* | | |
| | | 1979 | Telford Taylor, *Munich: The Price of Peace* | 1981 | Stephen Jay Gould, *The Mismeasure of Man* |

1982 Robert A. Caro, *The Path of Power: The Years of Lyndon Johnson*
1983 Seymour M. Hersh, *The Price of Power: Kissinger and the Nixon White House*
1984 Freeman Dyson, *Weapons and Hope*
1985 J. Anthony Lukas, *Common Ground: A Turbulent Decade in the Lives of Three American Families*
1986 John W. Dower, *War Without Mercy: Race and Power in the Pacific War*
1987 Richard Rhodes, *The Making of the Atomic Bomb*
1988 Taylor Branch, *Parting the Waters: America in the King Years, 1954–63*
1989 Michael Dorris, *The Broken Cord*
1990 Shelby Steele, *The Content of Our Character: A New Vision of Race in America*

### Biography/Autobiography, 1983–90

1983 Joyce Johnson, *Minor Characters*
1984 Joseph Frank, *Dostoevsky: The Years of Ordeal: 1850–1859*
1985 Leon Edel, *Henry James: A Life*
1986 Theodore Rosengarten, *Tombee: Portrait of a Cotton Planter*
1987 Donald R. Howard, *Chaucer: His Life, His Works, His World*
1988 Richard Ellman, *Oscar Wilde*
1989 Geoffrey C. Ward, *A First-Class Temperament: The Emergence of Franklin Roosevelt*
1990 Robert A. Caro, *Means of Ascent: The Years of Lyndon Johnson, Vol. 2*

### Poetry, 1975–90

1975 John Ashbery, *Self-Portrait in a Convex Mirror*
1976 Elizabeth Bishop, *Geography III*
1977 Robert Lowell, *Day by Day*
1978 L.E. Sissman, *Hello Darkness: The Collected Poems of L.E. Sissman*
1979 Philip Levine, *Ashes and Seven Years from Somewhere*
1980 Frederick Seidel, *Sunrise*
1981 A.R. Ammons, *A Coast of Trees*
1982 Katha Pollitt, *Antarctic Traveler*
1983 James Merrill, *The Changing Light at Sandover*
1984 Sharon Olds, *The Dead and the Living*
1985 Louise Gluck, *The Triumph of Achilles*
1986 Edward Hirsch, *Wild Gratitude*
1987 C.K. Williams, *Flesh and Blood*
1988 Donald Hall, *The One Day*
1989 Rodney Jones, *Transparent Gestures*
1990 Amy Gerstler, *Bitter Angel*

### Criticism, 1975–90

1975 Paul Fussell, *The Great War and Modern Memory*
1976 Bruno Bettelheim, *The Uses of Enchantment: The Meaning and Importance of Fairy Tales*
1977 Susan Sontag, *On Photography*
1978 Meyer Schapiro, *Modern Art: 19th and 20th Centuries, Selected Papers*
1979 Elaine Pagels, *The Gnostic Gospels*
1980 Helen Vendler, *Part of Nature, Part of Us: Modern American Poets*
1981 Virgil Thompson, *A Virgil Thompson Reader*
1982 Gore Vidal, *The Second American Revolution and Other Essays, 1976–82*
1983 John Updike, *Hugging the Shore*
1984 Robert Hass, *Twentieth Century Pleasures: Prose on Poetry*
1985 William H. Gass, *Habitations of the Word: Essays*
1986 Joseph Brodsky, *Less Than One: Selected Essays*
1987 Edwin Denby, *Dance Writings*
1988 Clifford Geertz, *Works and Lives: The Anthropologist as Author*
1989 John Clive, *Not by Fact Alone: Essays on the Writing and Reading of History*
1990 Arthur C. Danto, *Encounters and Reflections: Art in the Historical Present*

**Source:** The National Book Critics Circle.

## BOLLINGEN PRIZE FOR POETRY, 1949–91

First awarded annually, and biennially since 1963, the Bollingen Prize for Poetry is given by Yale University to an American citizen for a distinguished book of poetry, or in recognition of a poet's entire achievement. The award now carries a stipend of $10,000.

| Year | Recipient | Year | Recipient | Year | Recipient | Year | Recipient |
|---|---|---|---|---|---|---|---|
| 1949 | Wallace Stevens | 1956 | Allen Tate | 1967 | Robert Penn Warren | 1981 | May Swenson |
| 1950 | John Crowe Ransom | 1957 | e.e. cummings | 1969 | John Berryman | | Howard Nemerov |
| 1951 | Marianne Moore | 1958 | Theodore Roethke | | Karl Shapiro | 1983 | Anthony E. Hecht |
| 1952 | Archibald MacLeish | 1959 | Delmore Schwartz | 1971 | Richard Wilbur | | John Hollander |
| | William Carlos Williams | 1960 | Ivor Winters | | Mona Van Duyn | 1985 | John Ashbery |
| 1953 | W.H. Auden | 1961 | Richard Eberhart | 1973 | James Merrill | | Fred Chappel |
| 1954 | Leonie Adams | | John Hall Wheelock | 1975 | A.R. Ammons | 1987 | Stanley Kunitz |
| | Louise Bogan | 1962 | Robert Frost | 1977 | David Ignatow | 1989 | Edgar Bowers |
| 1955 | Conrad Aiken | 1965 | Horace Gregory | 1979 | W. S. Merwin | 1991 | Laura Riding Jackson |
| | | | | | | | Donald Justice |

**Source:** Yale University.

## CHILDREN'S BOOK AWARDS

### THE NEWBERY MEDAL, 1922–91

The Newbery Medal, presented by the American Library Association, is awarded annually to the author of the most distinguished contribution to American literature for children published in the United States during the previous year. The award is named in honor of John Newbery (1713–1767), the first English publisher of books for children.

| Year | Author/Title | Year | Author/Title | Year | Author/Title |
|---|---|---|---|---|---|
| 1922 | Willem Van Loon, *The Story of Mankind* | 1929 | Eric P. Kelly, *The Trumpeter of Krakow* | 1935 | Monica Shannon, *Dobry* |
| 1923 | Hugh Lofting, *The Voyages of Doctor Dolittle* | 1930 | Rachel Field, *Hitty, Her First Hundred Years* | 1936 | Carol Brink, *Caddie Woodlawn* |
| 1924 | Charles Hawes, *The Dark Frigate* | 1931 | Elizabeth Coatsworth, *The Cat Who Went to Heaven* | 1937 | Ruth Sawyer, *Roller Skates* |
| 1925 | Charles Finger, *Tales from Silver Lands* | | | 1938 | Kate Seredy, *The White Stag* |
| 1926 | Arthur Bowie Chrisman, *Shen of the Sea* | 1932 | Laura Adams Armer, *Waterless Mountain* | 1939 | Elizabeth Enright, *Thimble Summer* |
| 1927 | Will James, *Smoky, The Cowhorse* | 1933 | Elizabeth Foreman Lewis, *Young Fu of the Upper Yangtze* | 1940 | James Daugherty, *Daniel Boone* |
| 1928 | Dhan Gopal Mukerji, *Gayneck, The Story of a Pigeon* | 1934 | Cornelia Meigs, *Invincible Louisa* | 1941 | Armstrong Sperry, *Call It Courage* |
| | | | | 1942 | Walter D. Edmonds, *The Matchlock Gun* |

| | | | |
|---|---|---|---|
| 1943 | Elizabeth Janet Gray, *Adam of the Road* | 1961 | Scott O'Dell, *Island of the Blue Dolphins* |
| 1944 | Esther Forbes, *Johnny Tremain* | 1962 | Elizabeth George Speare, *The Bronze Bow* |
| 1945 | Robert Lawson, *Rabbit Hill* | 1963 | Madeleine L'Engle, *A Wrinkle in Time* |
| 1946 | Lois Lenski, *Strawberry Girl* | 1964 | Emily Cheney Neville, *It's Like This, Cat* |

1943 Elizabeth Janet Gray, *Adam of the Road*
1944 Esther Forbes, *Johnny Tremain*
1945 Robert Lawson, *Rabbit Hill*
1946 Lois Lenski, *Strawberry Girl*
1947 Carolyn Sherwin Bailey, *Miss Hickory*
1948 William Pène du Bois, *The Twenty-One Balloons*
1949 Marguerite Henry, *King of the Wind*
1950 Marguerite de Angeli, *The Door in the Wall*
1951 Elizabeth Yates, *Amos Fortune, Free Man*
1952 Eleanor Estes, *Ginger Pye*
1953 Ann Nolan Clark, *Secret of the Andes*
1954 Joseph Krumgold, *...And Now Miguel*
1955 Meindert DeJong, *The Wheel on the School*
1956 Jean Lee Latham, *Carry On, Mr. Bowditch*
1957 Virginia Sorensen, *Miracles on Maple Hill*
1958 Harold Keith, *Rifles for Watie*
1959 Elizabeth George Speare, *The Witch of Blackbird Pond*
1960 Joseph Krumgold, *Onion John*

1961 Scott O'Dell, *Island of the Blue Dolphins*
1962 Elizabeth George Speare, *The Bronze Bow*
1963 Madeleine L'Engle, *A Wrinkle in Time*
1964 Emily Cheney Neville, *It's Like This, Cat*
1965 Maia Wojciechowska, *Shadow of a Bull*
1966 Elizabeth Borten de Trevino, *I, Juan de Pareja*
1967 Irene Hunt, *Up a Road Slowly*
1968 E.L. Konigsburg, *From the Mixed-up Files of Mrs. Basil E. Frankweiler*
1969 Lloyd Alexander, *The High King*
1970 William H. Armstrong, *Sounder*
1971 Betsy Byars, *Summer of the Swans*
1972 Robert C. O'Brien, *Mrs. Frisby and the Rats of NIMH*
1973 Jean George, *Julie of the Wolves*
1974 Paula Fox, *The Slave Dancer*
1975 Virginia Hamilton, *M.C. Higgins the Great*
1976 Susan Cooper, *The Grey King*
1977 Mildred D. Taylor, *Roll of Thunder, Hear My Cry*

1978 Katherine Paterson, *Bridge to Terabithia*
1979 Ellen Raskin, *The Westing Game*
1980 Joan Blos, *A Gathering of Days: A New England Girl's Journal, 1830–32*
1981 Katherine Paterson, *Jacob Have I Loved*
1982 Nancy Willard, *A Visit to William Blake's Inn: Poems for Innocent and Experienced Travelers*
1983 Cynthia Voigt, *Dicey's Song*
1984 Beverly Cleary, *Dear Mr. Henshaw*
1985 Rolin McKinley, *The Hero and the Crown*
1986 Patricia MacLachlan, *Sarah, Plain and Tall*
1987 Sid Fleischman, *The Whipping Boy*
1988 Russell Freedman, *Lincoln: A Photobiogrqaphy*
1989 Paul Fleischman, *Joyful Noise: Poems for Two Voices*
1990 Lois Lowry, *Number the Stars*
1991 Jerry Spinelli, *Maniac Magee*

**Source:** American Library Association.

## THE CALDECOTT MEDAL, 1938–91

The Caldecott Medal, presented by the American Library Association, is awarded annually to the illustrator of the most distinguished picture book for children published in the United States during the preceding year. The award is named in honor of the English illustrator Randolph Caldecott (1846–1886). In cases where only one name is given, the book was written and illustrated by the same person.

| Year | Illustrator/Author/Title | Year | Illustrator/Author/Title | Year | Illustrator/Author/Title |
|---|---|---|---|---|---|

1938 Dorothy Lathrop; Helen Dean Fish, *Animals of the Bible*
1939 Thomas Handforth, *Mei Li*
1940 Ingri and Edgar Parin d'Aulaire, *Abraham Lincoln*
1941 Robert Lawson, *They Were Strong and Good*
1942 Robert McCloskey, *Make Way for Ducklings*
1943 Virginia Lee Burton, *The Little House*
1944 Louis Slobodkin; James Thurber, *Many Moons*
1945 Elizabeth Orton Jones; Rachel Jones, *Prayer for a Child*
1946 Maude and Miska Petersham, *The Rooster Crows* (traditional Mother Goose)
1947 Leonard Weisgard; Golden MacDonald, *The Little Island*
1948 Roger Duvoisin; Alvin Tresselt, *White Snow, Bright Snow*
1949 Bert and Elmer Hader, *The Big Snow*
1950 Leo Politi, *Song of the Swallows*
1951 Katherine Milhous, *The Egg Tree*
1952 Nicolas Mordvinoff; Will Mordvinoff, *Finders Keepers*
1953 Lynd Ward, *The Biggest Bear*
1954 Ludwig Bemelmans, *Madeline's Rescue*
1955 Marcia Brown; Charles Perault, *Cinderella, or the Little Glass Slipper*

1956 Feodor Rojankovsky; John Langstaff, *Frog Went A-Courtin'*
1957 Marc Simont; Janice May Udry, *A Tree is Nice*
1958 Robert McCloskey, *Time of Wonder*
1959 Barbara Cooney, *Chanticleer and the Fox* (adapted from Geoffrey Chaucer)
1960 Marie Hall Ets and Aurora Labastida, *Nine Days to Christmas*
1961 Nicolas Sidjakov; Ruth Robbins, *Baboushka and the Three Kings*
1962 Marcia Brown, *Once a Mouse...*
1963 Ezra Jack Keats, *The Snowy Day*
1964 Maurice Sendak, *Where the Wild Things Are*
1965 Beni Montresor; Beatrice Schenk de Regniers, *May I Bring a Friend?*
1966 Nonny Hogrogian; Sorche Nic Leodhas, *Always Room for One More*
1967 Evaline Ness, *Sam, Bangs & Moonshine*
1968 Ed Emberley; Barbara Emberley, *Drummer Hoff*
1969 Uri Shulevitz; Arthur Ransome, *The Fool of the World and the Flying Ship*
1970 William Steig, *Sylvester and the Magic Pebble*
1971 Gail E. Haley, *A Story—A Story*
1972 Nonny Hogrogian, *One Fine Day*
1973 Blair Lent; retold by Arlene Mosel, *The Funny Little Woman*

1974 Margot Zemach; Harve Zemach, *Duffy and the Devil*
1975 Gerald McDermott, *Arrow to the Sun*
1976 Leo and Diane Dillon; retold by Verna Aardema, *Why Mosquitoes Buzz in People's Ears*
1977 Leo and Diane Dillon; Margaret Musgrove, *Ashanti to Zulu: African Traditions*
1978 Peter Spier, *Noah's Ark*
1979 Paul Goble, *The Girl Who Loved Wild Horses*
1980 Barbara Cooney; Donald Hall, *Ox-Cart Man*
1981 Arnold Lobel, *Fables*
1982 Chris Van Allsburg, *Jumanji*
1983 Marcia Brown, *Shadow*
1984 Martin and Alice Provensen, *The Glorious Flight*
1985 Trina Schart Hyman, *Saint George and the Dragon*
1986 Chris Van Allsburg, *The Polar Express*
1987 Richard Egielski; Arthur Yorinks, *Hey, Al*
1988 John Schoenherr, *Owl Moon*
1989 Stephen Gammell; Karen Ackerman, *Song and Dance Man*
1990 Ed Young, *Lon Po Po: A Red-Riding Hood Story from China*
1991 David Macaulay, *Black and White*

**Source:** American Library Association.

# AMERICAN INSTITUTE OF ARCHITECTS GOLD MEDALISTS, 1907–91

First awarded in 1907, the American Institute of Architects Gold Medal recognizes outstanding lifetime achievement by an architect.

| Year | Medalists | Year | Medalists | Year | Medalists |
|---|---|---|---|---|---|

1907 Sir Aston Webb, London
1909 Charles Follen McKim, New York
1911 George B. Post, New York
1914 Jean Louis Pascal, Paris
1922 Victor Laloux, Paris
1923 Henry Bacon, New York
1925 Sir Edwin Landseer Lutyens, London
1925 Bertram Grosvenor Goodhue, New York

1927 Howard Van Doren Shaw, Chicago
1929 Milton Bennett Medary, Philadelphia
1933 Ragnar Ostberg, Stockholm
1938 Paul Philippe Cret, Philadelphia
1944 Louis Henri Sullivan, Chicago
1947 Eliel Saarinen, Bloomfield Hills, Mich.
1948 Charles Donagh Maginnis, Boston
1949 Frank Lloyd Wright, Spring Green, Wis.

1950 Sir Patrick Abercrombie, London
1951 Bernard Ralph Maybeck, San Francisco
1952 Auguste Perret, Paris
1953 Williams Adams Delano, New York
1955 Willem Marinus Dudok, Hilversum, Holland
1956 Clarence S. Stein, New York
1957 Ralph Walker, New York
1957 Louis Skidmore, New York

| Year | Medalists |
|------|-----------|
| 1958 | John Wellborn Root, Chicago |
| 1959 | Walter Gropius, Cambridge, Mass. |
| 1960 | Ludwig Mies van der Rohe, Chicago |
| 1961 | Le Corbusier (Charles Edouard Jeanneret-Gris), Paris |
| 1962[1] | Eero Saarinen, Bloomfield Hills, Mich. |
| 1963 | Alvar Aalto, Helsinki |
| 1964 | Pier Luigi Nervi, Rome |
| 1966 | Kenzo Tange, Tokyo |

| Year | Medalists |
|------|-----------|
| 1967 | Wallace K. Harrison, New York |
| 1968 | Marcel Breuer, New York |
| 1969 | William Wilson Wurster, San Francisco |
| 1970 | Richard Buckminster Fuller, Carbondale, Ill. |
| 1971 | Louis I. Kahn, Phildadelphia |
| 1972 | Pietro Belluschi, Boston |
| 1977[1] | Richard Joseph Neutra, Los Angeles |
| 1978 | Philip Johnson, New York |
| 1979 | Ieoh Ming Pei, New York |

| Year | Medalists |
|------|-----------|
| 1981 | Josep Lluis Sert, Cambridge, Mass. |
| 1982 | Romaldo Giurgola, New York |
| 1983 | Nathaniel A. Owings, San Francisco |
| 1985[1] | William Caudill, Houston |
| 1986 | Arthur Erickson, Canada |
| 1989 | Joseph Esherick, San Francisco |
| 1990 | Fay Jones, Fayetteville, Ark. |
| 1991 | Charles Willard Moore, Austin, Tex. |

1. Awarded posthumously. **Source:** American Institute of Architects.

**PULITZER PRIZES**

The Pulitzer Prizes are named for their benefactor, Joseph Pulitzer (1847–1911), a Hungarian-born journalist. Pulitzer founded the *St. Louis Post-Dispatch* (1878) and later purchased the *New York World* (1883), under whose banner he revolutionized journalism for mass readership. He bequeathed $2 million to found the Columbia School of Journalism, whose trustees make annual awards ($3,000 in 1990) for outstanding achievement in journalism (13 prizes), literature and drama (6 prizes), and musical composition (1 prize).

## PULITZER PRIZES IN JOURNALISM, 1917–91

### MERITORIOUS PUBLIC SERVICE, 1918–91

| Year | Winner | Distinction |
|------|--------|-------------|
| 1918 | New York Times | Reports, documents, and speeches relating to World War I. |
| 1919 | Milwaukee Journal | Campaign for Americanism. |
| 1920 | No award | |
| 1921 | Boston Post | Articles exposing operations and leading to arrest of Charles Ponzi. |
| 1922 | New York World | Articles exposing operations of Ku Klux Klan. |
| 1923 | Memphis Commercial Appeal | News and cartoons about Ku Klux Klan. |
| 1924 | New York World | Exposure of Florida peonage evil. |
| 1925 | No award | |
| 1926 | Columbus (Ga.) Enquirer Sun | Articles decrying Ku Klux Klan, dishonest public officials, lynching, and a law barring teaching of evolution. |
| 1927 | Canton (Ohio) Daily News | Articles about collusion between city government and organized crime, resulting in assassination of editor, Don R. Mellett. |
| 1928 | Indianapolis Times | Exposure of political corruption in Indiana. |
| 1929 | New York Evening World | Campaign to correct evil and corruption in administration of justice. |
| 1930 | No award | |
| 1931 | Atlanta Constitution | Municipal graft exposure leading to convictions. |
| 1932 | Indianapolis News | Campaign to eliminate waste in city management and reduce tax levy. |
| 1933 | New York World-Telegram | Series of articles on veterans' relief, real estate bond evil, campaign urging New York City voters to "write in" name of Joseph V. McKee, and articles exposing lottery schemes of various fraternal organizations. |
| 1934 | Medford (Ore.) Mail Tribune | Campaign against unscrupulous politicians in Jackson County, Ore. |
| 1935 | Sacramento (Calif.) Bee | Campaign against political machine influence in appointment of two federal judges in Nevada. |
| 1936 | Cedar Rapids (Iowa) Gazette | Crusade against corruption and misgovernment in state of Iowa. |
| 1937 | St. Louis Post-Dispatch | Exposure of registration fraud in St. Louis resulting in invalidation of more than 40,000 fraudulent ballots and appointment of new election board. |

| Year | Winner | Distinction |
|------|--------|-------------|
| 1938 | Bismarck (N.D.) Tribune | News reports and editorials entitled "Self Help in the Dust Bowl." |
| 1939 | Miami Daily News | Campaign for recall of Miami City Commission. |
| 1940 | Waterbury (Conn.) Republican & American | Campaign exposing municipal graft. |
| 1941 | St. Louis Post-Dispatch | Campaign against city smoke nuisance. |
| 1942 | Los Angeles Times | Campaign resulting in clarification and confirmation of freedom of press rights for all American newspapers. |
| 1943 | Omaha (Neb.) World-Herald | Campaign for collection of scrap metal for war effort. Plan was adopted on national scale by daily newspapers. |
| 1944 | New York Times | Survey of teaching of American History. |
| 1945 | Detroit Free Press | Investigation of legislative graft and corruption at Lansing, Mich. |
| 1946 | Scranton (Pa.) Times | Fifteen-year investigation of judicial practices in U.S. District Court for middle district of Pennsylvania, resulting in removal of district judge and indictment of many others. |
| 1947 | Baltimore Sun | Series of articles by Howard M. Norton dealing with administration of unemployment compensation in Maryland, resulting in 93 criminal convictions and/or guilty pleas. |
| 1948 | St. Louis Post-Dispatch | Coverage of Centralia, Ill., mine disaster and follow-up articles resulting in reforms in mine safety laws and regulations. |
| 1949 | Nebraska State Journal | Campaign establishing "Nebraska All-Star Primary" that called attention to issues early in presidential campaign. |
| 1950 | Chicago Daily News and St. Louis Post-Dispatch | Work of George Thiem and Roy J. Harris, respectively, in exposing presence of 37 Illinois newspapermen on an Illinois state payroll. |
| 1951 | Miami Herald and Brooklyn Eagle | Crime reporting during year. |
| 1952 | St. Louis Post-Dispatch | Investigation and disclosures of corruption in Internal Revenue Bureau and other government departments. |
| 1953 | Whiteville (N.C.) News Reporter and Tabor City (N.C.) Tribune | Campaign against Ku Klux Klan by two weekly North Carolina newspapers. |

| Year | Winner | Distinction |
|---|---|---|
| 1954 | Newsday (Garden City, L.I., N.Y.) | Exposé of New York State's race track scandals and labor racketeering, leading to extortion indictment, guilty plea, and imprisonment of racketeer William C. DeKoonig, Sr. |
| 1955 | Columbus (Ga.) Ledger and Sunday Ledger-Enquirer | News coverage and editorial attack on corruption in neighboring Phenix City, leading to destruction of racket-ridden city government. |
| 1956 | Watsonville (Calif.) Register-Pajaronion | Exposure of corruption in public office leading to resignation of a district attorney and conviction of one of his associates. |
| 1957 | Chicago Daily News | Exposure of $2.5 million in office of Illinois state auditor, resulting in his indictment and reorganization of state procedures. |
| 1958 | Arkansas Gazette | Civic leadership, journalistic responsibility, and moral courage during school integration crisis of 1957. |
| 1959 | Utica (N.Y.) Observer-Dispatch and Utica Daily Press | Campaign against corruption, gambling, and vice and achievement of sweeping civic reforms. |
| 1960 | Los Angeles Times | Attack on narcotics traffic; reporting of Gene Sherman, which led to opening of negotiations between U.S. and Mexico to halt flow of illegal drugs into California and other border states. |
| 1961 | Amarillo (Tex.) Globe-Times | Exposure of lax law enforcement resulting in punitive action sweeping officials from their posts and creating election of reform slate. |
| 1962 | Panama City (Fla.) News-Herald | Three-year campaign against entrenched power and corruption, resulting in reforms in Panama City and Bay County. |
| 1963 | Chicago Daily News | Articles calling public attention to providing birth control services in public health programs. |
| 1964 | St. Petersburg (Fla.) Times | Investigation of illegal activity within Florida Turnpike Authority, resulting in major reorganization of state's road construction program. |
| 1965 | Hutchinson (Kans.) News | Campaign for more equitable reapportionment of Kansas legislature. |
| 1966 | Boston Globe | Campaign to prevent confirmation of Francis X. Morrissey as federal district judge in Massachusetts. |
| 1967 | Louisville Courier Journal and Milwaukee Journal | Campaign to control Kentucky strip-mining industry; campaign to stiffen water pollution laws in Wisconsin. |
| 1968 | Riverside (Calif.) Press-Enterprise | Exposure of corruption in courts in connection with handling of property and estates of an Indian tribe in California. |
| 1969 | Los Angeles Times | Exposure of wrongdoing within Los Angeles city government commissions, resulting in criminal convictions, resignations, and sweeping reforms. |
| 1970 | Newsday (Garden City, L.I., N.Y.) | Three-year investigation and exposure of secret land deals in eastern Long Island, leading to criminal convictions, resignations, and discharges among public and political officials. |
| 1971 | Winston-Salem (N.C.) Journal and Sentinel | Coverage of environmental problems, as exemplified by campaign to block a strip-mining operation that would have caused irreparable damage to northwest North Carolina hill country. |

| Year | Winner | Distinction |
|---|---|---|
| 1972 | New York Times | Publication of Pentagon Papers. |
| 1973 | Washington Post | Investigation of Watergate case. |
| 1974 | Newsday (Garden City, L.I., N.Y.) | Definitive report on illicit narcotics traffic in U.S. and abroad, entitled "The Heroin Trail." |
| 1975 | Boston Globe | Coverage of Boston school desegregation crisis. |
| 1976 | Anchorage Daily News | Disclosures of impact and influence of Teamsters Union on Alaska's economy and politics. |
| 1977 | Lufkin (Tex.) News | Obituary of local man who died in Marine training camp, which grew into investigation of that death and fundamental reform in Marine Corps' recruiting and training practices. |
| 1978 | Philadelphia Inquirer | Series of articles showing abuses of power by Philadelphia police. |
| 1979 | Point Reyes (Calif.) Light | Investigation of Synanon. |
| 1980 | Gannett News Service | Series on financial contributions to Pauline Fathers. |
| 1981 | Charlotte (N.C.) Observer | Series called "Brown Lung: A Case of Deadly Neglect." |
| 1982 | Detroit News | Series by Sydney P. Freedberg and David Ashenfelter exposing U.S. Navy's cover-up of circumstances surrounding deaths of seamen aboard ship and leading to significant reforms in naval procedures. |
| 1983 | Jackson (Miss.) Clarion-Ledger | Campaign supporting Gov. Winter in his legislative battle for reform of Mississippi's public education system. |
| 1984 | Los Angeles Times | In-depth examination of southern California's growing Latino community. |
| 1985 | Fort Worth (Tex.) Star-Telegram | Reporting by Mark J. Thompson revealing that nearly 250 U.S. servicemen died because of a design problem in helicopters built by Bell Helicopter—causing the army to ground almost 600 Huey helicopters pending their modification. |
| 1986 | Denver Post | In-depth study of "missing children," revealing that most are involved in custody disputes or are runaways, and helping to mitigate national fears stirred by exaggerated statistics. |
| 1987 | Pittsburgh Press | Reporting by Andrew Schneider and Matthew Brelis, revealing inadequacy of FAA's medical screening of airline pilots, and leading to reform. |
| 1988 | Charlotte (N.C.) Observer | Revealing misuse of funds by the PTL television ministry, despite massive campaign by PTL to discredit the newspaper. |
| 1989 | Anchorage Daily News | For series revealing high incidence of alcoholism and suicide among Native Alaskans. |
| 1990 | Philadelphia Inquirer | For series by Gilbert M. Gaul disclosing shortcomings in federal regulation of the nation's blood banks. |
| | Washington (N.C.) Daily News | For series by Betty Gray and Mike Voss revealing contamination of the municipal water supply in the town of 9,000 and the 8-year cover-up by elected officials. |
| 1991 | Des Moines Register | For series by Jane Schorer about a rape and its aftermath that reopened debate over whether rape victims should be identified by name. |

## REPORTING, 1917–91

The Pulitzer Prize for Reporting is the oldest given in journalism. Various journalism prizes have been established over the years, reflecting the changing nature and public perception of reporting. Originally, the reporting prize recognized excellence irrespective of the journalist's beat; it could be local, national, or international. Also, the prize could be awarded for reporting under the pressure of a deadline or investigative reporting carried out over a longer period. In 1929 a correspondence category was created to distinguish reporters stationed in Washington or abroad from local journalists. From 1942 to 1947 two prizes were added for national and international telegraphic reporting. In 1948, these categories and the correspondence category were consolidated into two—national reporting and international reporting. These categories are still recognized today.

In 1953, the original reporting category was broken down into reporting, on deadline; and reporting, not on deadline. The names of these two categories have changed over the years. From 1964 to 1983, they were known as local general or spot news reporting, and local investigative or specialized reporting, respectively. In 1984, they became general local reporting and special local reporting. The following year, general local reporting was changed to general news reporting, and special local reporting was split into three categories: investigative reporting, explanatory journalism, and specialized reporting.

| Year | Winner, Newspaper | Year | Winner, Newspaper | Year | Winner, Newspaper |
|---|---|---|---|---|---|
| 1917 | Herbert Bayard Swope, New York World | 1932 | W.C. Richards, D.D. Martin, J.S. Pooler, F.D. Webb and J.N.W. Sloan, Detroit Free Press | 1941 | Westbrook Pegler, New York World-Telegram |
| 1918 | Harold A. Littledale, New York Evening Post | | | 1942 | Stanton Delaplane, San Francisco Chronicle |
| 1919 | No award | 1933 | Francis A. Jameson, Associated Press | 1943 | George Weller, Chicago Daily News |
| 1920 | John J. Leary, Jr., New York World | 1934 | Royce Brier, San Francisco Chronicle | 1944 | Paul Schoenstein and Associates, New York Journal American |
| 1921 | Louis Seibold, New York World | 1935 | William H. Taylor, New York Herald Tribune | | |
| 1922 | Kirke L. Simpson, Associated Press | 1936 | Lauren D. Lyman, New York Times | 1945 | Jack S. McDowell, San Francisco Call-Bulletin |
| 1923 | Alva Johnston, New York Times | 1937 | John J. O'Neill, New York Herald Tribune | | |
| 1924 | Magner White, San Diego Sun | | William L. Laurence, New York Times | 1946 | William Leonard Laurence, New York Times |
| 1925 | James W. Mulroy and Alvin H. Goldstein, Chicago Daily News | | Howard W. Blakeslee, Associated Press | 1947 | Frederick Woltman, New York World-Telegram |
| | | | Gobind Behari Lal, Universal Service | | |
| 1926 | William Burke Miller, Louisville Courier-Journal | | David Dietz, Scripps-Howard Newspaper Alliance | 1948 | George E. Goodwin, Atlanta Journal |
| | | | | 1949 | Malcolm Johnson, New York Sun |
| 1927 | John T. Rogers, St. Louis Post-Dispatch | 1938 | Raymond Sprigle, Pittsburgh Post-Gazette | 1950 | Meyer Berger, New York Times |
| 1928 | No award | 1939 | Thomas Lunsford Stokes, Scripps-Howard Newspaper Alliance (articles published in New York World-Telegram) | 1951 | Edward S. Montgomery, San Francisco Examiner |
| 1929 | Paul Y. Anderson, St. Louis Post-Dispatch | | | | |
| 1930 | Russell D. Owen, New York Times | | | 1952 | George de Carvalho, San Francisco Chronicle |
| 1931 | A.B. MacDonald, Kansas City Star | 1940 | S. Burton Heath, New York World-Telegram | | |

### REPORTING, EDITION TIME, 1953–63

| Year | Winner, Newspaper | Year | Winner, Newspaper | Year | Winner, Newspaper |
|---|---|---|---|---|---|
| 1953 | Editorial Staff, Providence Journal and Evening Bulletin | 1958 | Staff, Fargo (N.D.) Forum | 1962 | Robert D. Mullins, Deseret News, Salt Lake City |
| 1954 | Staff, Vicksburg (Miss.) Sunday Post-Herald | 1959 | Mary Lou Werner, Evening Star, Washington, D.C. | 1963 | Sylvan Fox, Anthony Shannon, and William Longgood, New York World-Telegram and Sun |
| 1955 | Caro Brown, Alice (Tex.) Daily Echo | 1960 | Jack Nelson, Atlanta Constitution | | |
| 1956 | Lee Hills, Detroit Free Press | 1961 | Sanche de Gramont, New York Herald-Tribune | | |
| 1957 | Staff, Salt Lake (Utah) Tribune | | | | |

### LOCAL GENERAL/SPOT NEWS REPORTING, 1964–83, 1991

| Year | Winner, Newspaper | Year | Winner, Newspaper | Year | Winner, Newspaper |
|---|---|---|---|---|---|
| 1964 | Norman C. Miller, Jr., Wall Street Journal | 1970 | Thomas Fitzpatrick, Chicago Sun-Times | 1977 | Margo Huston, Milwaukee Journal |
| 1965 | Melvin H. Ruder, Hungry Horse News, Columbia Falls, Mont. | 1971 | Staff, Akron (Ohio) Beacon Journal | 1978 | Richard Whitt, Louisville Courier-Journal |
| | | 1972 | Richard Cooper and John Machacek, Rochester (N.Y.) Times-Union | 1979 | Staff, San Diego Evening Tribune |
| 1966 | Staff, Los Angeles Times | | | 1980 | Staff, Philadelphia Inquirer |
| 1967 | Robert V. Cox, Chambersburg (Pa.) Public Opinion | 1973 | Staff, Chicago Tribune | 1981 | Staff, Longview (Wash.) Daily News |
| | | 1974 | Arthur M. Petacque and Hugh F. Hough, Chicago Sun-Times | 1982 | Staffs, Kansas City Star and Kansas City Times |
| 1968 | Staff, Detroit Free Press | | | | |
| 1969 | John Fetterman, Louisville Times and Courier-Journal | 1975 | Staff, Xenia (Ohio) Daily Gazette | 1983 | Editorial staff, Fort Wayne (Ind.) News-Sentinel |
| | | 1976 | Gene Miller, Miami Herald | 1991 | Staff, Miami Herald |

### SPECIAL LOCAL REPORTING, 1984

| Year | Winner, Newspaper |
|---|---|
| 1984 | Kenneth Cooper, Jonathan Kaufman, Joan Fitzgerald, Norman Lockman, Gary McMillan, Kirk Scharfenberg, David Wessel, Boston Globe |

### REPORTING, NO EDITION TIME, 1953–63

| Year | Winner, Newspaper | Year | Winner, Newspaper | Year | Winner, Newspaper |
|---|---|---|---|---|---|
| 1953 | Edward J. Mowery, New York World-Telegram & Sun | 1957 | Wallace Turner and William Lambert, Portland Oregonian | 1960 | Miriam Ottenberg, Evening Star, Washington, D.C. |
| 1954 | Alvin Scott McCoy, Kansas City Star | 1958 | George Beveridge, Evening Star, Washington, D.C. | 1961 | Edgar May, Buffalo (N.Y.) Evening News |
| 1955 | Roland Kenneth Towery, Cuero (Tex.) Record | | | 1962 | George Bliss, Chicago Tribune |
| 1956 | Arthur Daley, New York Times | 1959 | John Harold Brialin, Scranton (Pa.) Tribune and Scrantonian | 1963 | Oscar Griffin, Jr., Pecos (Tex.) Independent and Enterprise |

## LOCAL INVESTIGATIVE/SPECIALIZED REPORTING, 1964–83

| Year | Winner, Newspaper | Year | Winner, Newspaper | Year | Winner, Newspaper |
|------|-------------------|------|-------------------|------|-------------------|
| 1964 | James V. Magee, Albert V. Gaudiosi, and Frederick A. Meyer, Philadelphia Bulletin | 1972 | Timothy Leland, Gerard M. O'Neill, Stephen A. Kurkjian, and Ann DeSantis, Boston Globe | 1979 | Gilbert M. Gaul and Elliot G. Jaspin, Pottsville (Pa.) Republican |
| 1965 | Gene Goltz, Houston Post | 1973 | Staffs, Sun Newspapers of Omaha | 1980 | Stephen A. Kurkjian, Nils Bruzelius, Alexander B. Hawes, Jr., Joan Vennochi, and Robert M. Porterfield, Boston Globe Spotlight |
| 1966 | John Anthony Frasca, Tampa Tribune | 1974 | William Sherman, New York Daily News | | |
| 1967 | Gene Miller, Miami Herald | 1975 | Staff, Indianapolis Star | | |
| 1968 | J. Anthony Lukas, New York Times | 1976 | Staff, Chicago Tribune | 1981 | Clark Hallas and Robert B. Lowe, Arizona Daily Star |
| 1969 | Albert L. Delugach and Denny Walsh, St. Louis Globe-Democrat | 1977 | Acel Moore and Wendell Rawls, Jr., Philadelphia Inquirer | 1982 | Paul Henderson, Seattle Times |
| 1970 | Harold Eugene Martin, Montgomery Adviser and Alabama Journal | 1978 | Anthony R. Dolan, Stamford (Conn.) Advocate | 1983 | Loretta Tofani, Washington Post |
| 1971 | William Jones, Chicago Tribune | | | | |

## GENERAL LOCAL REPORTING, 1984

1984  Team of reporters, Newsday (Garden City, L.I., N.Y.)

## GENERAL NEWS REPORTING, 1985–90

| Year | Winner, Newspaper | Year | Winner, Newspaper | Year | Winner, Newspaper |
|------|-------------------|------|-------------------|------|-------------------|
| 1985 | Thomas Turcol, Virginian-Pilot and Ledger-Star (Norfolk, Va.) | 1987 | Staff, Akron (Ohio) Beacon Journal | 1989 | Staff, Louisville (Ky.) Courier-Journal |
| 1986 | Edna Buchanan, Miami Herald | 1988 | Staff, Alabama Journal / Staff, Lawrence (Mass.) Eagle-Tribune | 1990 | Staff, San Jose (Calif.) Mercury News |

## INVESTIGATIVE REPORTING, 1985–91

| Year | Winner, Newspaper | Year | Winner, Newspaper | Year | Winner, Newspaper |
|------|-------------------|------|-------------------|------|-------------------|
| 1985 | William K. Marimow, Philadelphia Inquirer / Lucy Morgan and Jack Reed, St. Petersburg Times | 1987 | Daniel R. Biddle, H.G. Bissinger, Fredric N. Tulsky, and John Woestendiek, Philadelphia Inquirer | 1989 | Bill Dedman, Atlanta Journal and Constitution |
| 1986 | Jeffrey A. Marx and Michael M. York, Lexington (Ky.) Herald Leader | 1988 | Dean Baquet, William Gaines and Ann Marie Lipinski, Chicago Tribune | 1990 | Lon Kilzer and Chris Ison, Minneapolis-St. Paul Star Tribune |
| | | | | 1991 | Joseph T. Hallinan and Susan M. Headden, Indianapolis Star |

## EXPLANATORY JOURNALISM, 1985–91

| Year | Winner, Newspaper | Year | Winner, Newspaper | Year | Winner, Newspaper |
|------|-------------------|------|-------------------|------|-------------------|
| 1985 | Jon Franklin, Baltimore Evening Sun | 1988 | Daniel Hertzberg and James B. Stewart, Wall Street Journal | 1990 | David A. Vise and Steve Coll, Washington Post |
| 1986 | Staff, New York Times | 1989 | David Hanners, William Snyder, and Karen Blessen, Dallas Morning News | 1991 | Susan C. Faludi, Wall Street Journal |
| 1987 | Jeff Lyon and Peter Gorner, Chicago Tribune | | | | |

## SPECIALIZED/BEAT REPORTING, 1985–91

| Year | Winner, Newspaper | Year | Winner, Newspaper | Year | Winner, Newspaper |
|------|-------------------|------|-------------------|------|-------------------|
| 1985 | Randall Savage and Jackie Crosby, Macon (Ga.) Telegraph News | 1987 | Alex S. Jones, New York Times | 1990 | Tamar Sieber, Albuquerque Journal |
| 1986 | Andrew Schneider and Mary Pat Flaherty, Pittsburgh Press | 1988 | Walt Bogdanich, Wall Street Journal | 1991 | Natalie Angier, New York Times |
| | | 1989 | Edward Humes, Orange County (Calif.) Register | | |

## CORRESPONDENCE, 1929–47

| Year | Winner, Newspaper | Year | Winner, Newspaper | Year | Winner, Newspaper |
|------|-------------------|------|-------------------|------|-------------------|
| 1929 | Paul Scott Mowrer, Chicago Daily News | 1935 | Arthur Krock, New York Times | 1942 | Carlos P. Romulo, Philippines Herald |
| 1930 | Leland Stowe, New York Herald Tribune | 1936 | Wilfred C. Barber (posthumous), Chicago Tribune | 1943 | Hanson W. Baldwin, New York Times |
| 1931 | H.R. Knickerbocker, Philadelphia Public Ledger and New York Evening Post | 1937 | Anne O'Hare McCormick, New York Times | 1944 | Ernest Taylor Pyle, Scripps-Howard Newspaper Alliance |
| 1932 | Walter Duranty, New York Times / Charles G. Ross, St. Louis Post-Dispatch | 1938 | Arthur Krock, New York Times | 1945 | Harold V. (Hal) Boyle, Associated Press |
| 1933 | Edgar Ansel Mowrer, Chicago Daily News | 1939 | Louis P. Lochner, Associated Press | 1946 | Arnaldo Cortesi, New York Times |
| 1934 | Frederick T. Birchall, New York Times | 1940 | Otto D. Tolischus, New York Times | 1947 | Brooks Atkinson, New York Times |
| | | 1941 | Group award[1] | | |

1. Instead of an individual prize, the trustees commissioned the creation of a bronze plaque to symbolize the services and achievements of all American news reporters in the war zones of Europe, Asia, and Africa.

## TELEGRAPHIC REPORTING (NATIONAL), 1942–47

| Year | Winner, Newspaper | Year | Winner, Newspaper | Year | Winner, Newspaper |
|------|-------------------|------|-------------------|------|-------------------|
| 1942 | Louis Stark, New York Times | 1944 | Dewey L. Fleming, Baltimore Sun | 1946 | Edward A. Harris, St. Louis Post-Dispatch |
| 1943 | No award | 1945 | James B. Reston, New York Times | 1947 | Edward T. Folliard, Washington Post |

## TELEGRAPHIC REPORTING (INTERNATIONAL), 1942–47

| Year | Winner, Newspaper | Year | Winner, Newspaper | Year | Winner, Newspaper |
|------|-------------------|------|-------------------|------|-------------------|
| 1942 | Lawrence Edmund Allen, Associated Press | 1944 | Daniel DeLuce, Associated Press | 1946 | Homer William Bigart, New York Herald Tribune |
| 1943 | Ira Wolfert, North American Newspaper Alliance, Inc. | 1945 | Mark S. Watson, Baltimore Sun | 1947 | Eddy Gilmore, Associated Press |

## NATIONAL REPORTING, 1948–91

| Year | Winner, Newspaper |
|------|-------------------|
| 1948 | Bert Andrews, New York Herald Tribune |
| | Nat S. Finney, Minneapolis Tribune |
| 1949 | C.P. Trussell, New York Times |
| 1950 | Edwin O. Guthman, Seattle Times |
| 1951 | No award[1] |
| 1952 | Anthony Leviero, New York Times |
| 1953 | Don Whitehead, Associated Press |
| 1954 | Richard Wilson, Des Moines Register and Tribune |
| 1955 | Anthony Lewis, Washington Daily News |
| 1956 | Charles L. Bartlett, Chattanooga Times |
| 1957 | James B. Reston, New York Times |
| 1958 | Relman Morin, Associated Press |
| | Clark Mollenhoff, Des Moines Register and Tribune |
| 1959 | Howard Van Smith, Miami News |
| 1960 | Vance Trimble, Scripps-Howard Newspaper Alliance |
| 1961 | Edward R. Cony, Wall Street Journal |
| 1962 | Nathan G. Caldwell and Gene S. Graham, Nashville Tennessean |
| 1963 | Anthony Lewis, New York Times |
| 1964 | Merriman Smith, United Press International |
| 1965 | Louis M. Kohlmeier, Wall Street Journal |
| 1966 | Haynes Johnson, Washington Evening Star |
| 1967 | Stanley Penn and Monroe Karmin, Wall Street Journal |
| 1968 | Howard James, Christian Science Monitor |
| | Nathan K. (Nick) Kotz, Des Moines Register and Minneapolis Tribune |
| 1969 | Robert Cahn, Christian Science Monitor |
| 1970 | William J. Eaton, Chicago Daily News |
| 1971 | Lucinda Franks and Thomas Powers, United Press International |
| 1972 | Jack Anderson, Syndicated columnist |
| 1973 | Robert Boyd and Clark Hoyt, Knight Newspapers |
| 1974 | James R. Polk, Washington Star-News |
| | Jack White, Providence Journal and Evening Bulletin |
| 1975 | Donald L. Barlett and James B. Steele, Philadelphia Inquirer |
| 1976 | James Risser, Des Moines Register |
| 1977 | Walter Mears, Associated Press |
| 1978 | Gaylord D. Shaw, Los Angeles Times |
| 1979 | James Risser, Des Moines Register |
| 1980 | Bette Swenson Orsini and Charles Stafford, St. Petersburg Times |
| 1981 | John M. Crewdson, New York Times |
| 1982 | Rick Atkinson, Kansas City Times |
| 1983 | Staff, Boston Globe |
| 1984 | John Noble Wilford, New York Times |
| 1985 | Thomas J. Knudson, Des Moines Register |
| 1986 | Arthur Howe, Philadelphia Inquirer |
| | Craig Flournoy and George Rodrigue, Dallas Morning News |
| 1987 | Staff, Miami Herald |
| | Staff, New York Times |
| 1988 | Tim Weiner, Philadelphia Inquirer |
| 1989 | Donald L. Barlett and James B. Steele, Philadelphia Inquirer |
| 1990 | Ross Anderson, Bill Dietrich, Mary Ann Gwinn, and Eric Nalder, Seattle Times |
| 1991 | Marjie Lundstrom and Rochelle Sharpe, Gannett News Service |

1. The board decided that Arthur Krock of the *New York Times* deserved the prize for National Reporting, but he could not accept the award because he was a board member.

## INTERNATIONAL REPORTING, 1948–91

| Year | Winner, Newspaper |
|------|-------------------|
| 1948 | Paul W. Ward, Baltimore Sun |
| 1949 | Price Day, Baltimore Sun |
| 1950 | Edmund Stevens, Christian Science Monitor |
| 1951 | Keyes Beech, Chicago Daily News |
| | Homer William Bigart, New York Herald Tribune |
| | Marguerite Higgins, New York Herald Tribune |
| | Relman Morin, Associated Press |
| | Fred Sparks, Chicago Daily News |
| | Don Whitehead, Associated Press |
| 1952 | John M. Hightower, Associated Press |
| 1953 | Austin Wehrwein, Milwaukee Journal |
| 1954 | Jim G. Lucas, Scripps-Howard Newspaper Alliance |
| 1955 | Harrison E. Salisbury, New York Times |
| 1956 | William Randolph Hearst, Jr., Kingsbury Smith, and Frank Conniff, International News Service |
| 1957 | Russell Jones, United Press |
| 1958 | Staff, New York Times |
| 1959 | Joseph Martin and Philip Santora, New York Daily News |
| 1960 | A.M. Rosenthal, New York Times |
| 1961 | Lynn Heinzerling, Associated Press |
| 1962 | Walter Lippmann, New York Herald Tribune Syndicate |
| 1963 | Hal Hendrix, Miami News |
| 1964 | Malcolm W. Browne, Associated Press |
| | David Halberstam, New York Times |
| 1965 | J.A. Livingston, Philadelphia Bulletin |
| 1966 | Peter Arnett, Associated Press |
| 1967 | R. John Hughes, Christian Science Monitor |
| 1968 | Alfred Friendly, Washington Post |
| 1969 | William Tuohy, Los Angeles Times |
| 1970 | Seymour M. Hersh, Dispatch News Service |
| 1971 | Jimmie Lee Hoagland, Washington Post |
| 1972 | Peter R. Kann, Wall Street Journal |
| 1973 | Max Frankel, New York Times |
| 1974 | Hedrick Smith, New York Times |
| 1975 | William Mullen (reporter), Ovie Carter (photographer), Chicago Tribune |
| 1976 | Sydney H. Schanberg, New York Times |
| 1977 | No award |
| 1978 | Henry Kamm, New York Times |
| 1979 | Richard Ben Cramer, Philadelphia Inquirer |
| 1980 | Joel Brinkely (reporter), Jay Mather (photographer), Louisville Courier-Journal |
| 1981 | Shirley Christian, Miami Herald |
| 1982 | John Darnton, New York Times |
| 1983 | Thomas L. Friedman, New York Times |
| | Loren Jenkins, Washington Post |
| 1984 | Karen Elliott House, Wall Street Journal |
| 1985 | Josh Friedman and Dennis Bell (reporters) and Ozier Muhammad (photographer), Newsday (Garden City, L.I., N.Y.) |
| 1986 | Lewis M. Simons, Pete Carey, and Katherine Ellison, San Jose (Calif.) Mercury News |
| 1987 | Michael Parks, Los Angeles Times |
| 1988 | Thomas L. Friedman, New York Times |
| 1989 | Glenn Frankel, Washington Post |
| | Bill Keller, New York Times |
| 1990 | Nicholas D. Kristof and Sheryl WuDunn, New York Times |
| 1991 | Caryle Murphy, Washington Post |
| | Serge Schmemann, New York Times |

## EDITORIAL WRITING, 1917–91

| Year | Winner, Newspaper |
|------|-------------------|
| 1917 | Luisitania editorial article, New York Tribune |
| 1918 | War editorials and articles, Lousiville Courier Journal |
| 1919 | No award |
| 1920 | Harvey E. Newbranch, Evening World Herald |
| 1921 | No award |
| 1922 | Frank M. O'Brien, New York Herald |
| 1923 | William Allen White, Emporia (Kans.) Gazette |
| 1924[1] | Coolidge editorial, Boston Herald |
| 1925 | "Plight of the South" editorial, Charleston (S.C.) News and Courier |
| 1926 | Edward M. Kingsbury, New York Times |
| 1927 | F. Lauriston Bullard, Boston Herald |
| 1928 | Grover Cleveland Hall, Montgomery (Ala.) Advertiser |
| 1929 | Louis Isaac Jaffe, Norfolk Virginian-Pilot |
| 1930 | No award |
| 1931 | Charles S. Ryckman, Fremont (Nebr.) Tribune |
| 1932 | No award |
| 1933 | Series of editorials, Kansas City Star |
| 1934 | E.P. Chase, Atlantic (Iowa) News-Telegraph |
| 1935 | No award |
| 1936 | Felix Morley, Washington Post |
| | George B. Parker, Scripps-Howard Newspapers |
| 1937 | John W. Owens, Baltimore Sun |
| 1938 | William Wesley Waymack, Des Moines Register and Tribune |
| 1939 | Ronald G. Callvert, Portland Oregonian |
| 1940 | Bart Howard, St. Louis Post-Dispatch |
| 1941 | Reuben Maury, New York Daily News |
| 1942 | Geoffrey Parsons, New York Herald Tribune |
| 1943 | Forrest W. Seymour, Des Moines Register and Tribune |
| 1944 | Henry J. Haskell, Kansas City Star |
| 1945 | George W. Potter, Providence Journal-Bulletin |
| 1946 | Hodding Carter, Delta Democrat-Times (Greenville, Miss.) |
| 1947 | William H. Grimes, Wall Street Journal |
| 1948 | Virginius Dabney, Richmond Times-Dispatch |
| 1949 | John H. Crider, Boston Herald |
| | Herbert Elliston, Washington Post |
| 1950 | Carl M. Saunders, Jackson (Mich.) Citizen Patriot |
| 1951 | William Harry Fitzpatrick, New Orleans States |
| 1952 | Louis LaCoss, St. Louis Globe Democrat |
| 1953 | Vermont Connecticut Royster, Wall Street Journal |

1. A special prize was awarded to the widow of the late Frank I. Cobb of the *New York World* in recognition of his lifetime of editorial writing and service.

| Year | Winner, Newspaper | Year | Winner, Newspaper | Year | Winner, Newspaper |
|---|---|---|---|---|---|
| 1954 | Don Murray, Boston Herald | 1966 | Robert Lasch, St. Louis Post-Dispatch | 1978 | Meg Greenfield, Washington Post |
| 1955 | Royce Howes, Detroit Free Press | 1967 | Eugene Patterson, Atlanta Constitution | 1979 | Edwin M. Yoder, Jr., Washington Star |
| 1956 | Lauren K. Soth, Des Moines Register and Tribune | 1968 | John S. Knight, Knight Newspapers | 1980 | Robert L. Bartley, Wall Street Journal |
| | | 1969 | Paul Greenberg, Pine Bluff (Ark.) Commercial | 1981 | No award |
| 1957 | Buford Boone, Tuscaloosa (Ala.) News | 1970 | Philip L. Geyelin, Washington Post | 1982 | Jack Rosenthal, New York Times |
| 1958 | Harry S. Ashmore, Arkansas Gazette | 1971 | Horance G. Davis, Jr., Gainesville (Fla.) Sun | 1983 | Editorial board, Miami Herald |
| 1959 | Ralph McGill, Atlanta Constitution | 1972 | John Strohmeyer, Bethlehem (Pa.) Globe-Times | 1984 | Albert Scardino, Georgia Gazette |
| 1960 | Lenoir Chambers, Norfolk Virginian-Pilot | | | 1985 | Richard Aregood, Philadelphia Daily News |
| 1961 | William J. Dorvillier, San Juan (Puerto Rico) Star | 1973 | Roger B. Linscott, Berkshire Eagle (Pittsfield, Mass.) | 1986 | Jack Fuller, Chicago Tribune |
| | | | | 1987 | Jonathan Freedman, San Diego Tribune |
| 1962 | Thomas M. Storke, Santa Barbara (Calif.) News-Press | 1974 | F. Gilman Spencer, Trentonian (Trenton, N.J.) | 1988 | Jane Healy, Orlando Sentinel |
| | | 1975 | John Daniell Maurice, Charleston (W.Va.) Daily Mail | 1989 | Lois Wille, Chicago Tribune |
| 1963 | Ira B. Harkey, Jr., Pascagoula (Miss.) Chronicle | | | 1990 | Thomas J. Hylton, Pottstown (Pa.) Mercury |
| | | 1976 | Philip P. Kerby, Los Angeles Times | 1991 | Ron Casey, Harold Jackson, and Joey Kennedy, Birmingham (Ala.) News |
| 1964 | Hazel Brannon Smith, Lexington (Miss.) Advertiser | 1977 | Warren L. Lerude, Foster Church, and Norman F. Cardoza, Reno (Nev.) Evening Gazette and Nevada State Journal | | |
| 1965 | John R. Harrison, Gainesville (Fla.) Daily Sun | | | | |

## EDITORIAL CARTOONING, 1922–91

| Year | Winner, Newspaper | Year | Winner, Newspaper | Year | Winner, Newspaper |
|---|---|---|---|---|---|
| 1922 | Rollin Kirby, New York World | 1947 | Vaughn Shoemaker, Chicago Daily News | 1971 | Paul Conrad, Los Angeles Times |
| 1923 | No award | 1948 | Reuben L. Goldberg, New York Sun | 1972 | Jeffrey K. MacNelly, Richmond News-Leader |
| 1924 | Jay Norwood Darling, Des Moines Register and Tribune | 1949 | Lute Pease, Newark Evening News | 1973 | No award |
| | | 1950 | James T. Berryman, Evening Star (D.C.) | 1974 | Paul Szep, Boston Globe |
| 1925 | Rollin Kirby, New York World | 1951 | Reg Manning, Arizona Republic | 1975 | Garry Trudeau, Universal Press Syndicate |
| 1926 | Daniel R. Fitzpatrick, St. Louis Post-Dispatch | 1952 | Fred L. Packer, New York Mirror | 1976 | Tony Auth, Philadelphia Inquirer |
| 1927 | Nelson Harding, Brooklyn Daily Eagle | 1953 | Edward D. Kuekes, Cleveland Plain Dealer | 1977 | Paul Szep, Boston Globe |
| 1928 | Nelson Harding, Brooklyn Daily Eagle | 1954 | Herbert L. Block ("Herblock"), Washington Post & Times Herald | 1978 | Jeffrey K. MacNelly, Richmond News-Leader |
| 1929 | Rollin Kirby, New York World | | | 1979 | Herbert L. Block ("Herblock"), Washington Post |
| 1930 | Charles R. Macauley, Brooklyn Daily Eagle | 1955 | Daniel R. Fitzpatrick, St. Louis Post-Dispatch | | |
| 1931 | Edmund Duffy, Baltimore Sun | 1956 | Robert York, Louisville (Ky.) Times | 1980 | Don Wright, Miami News |
| 1932 | John T. McCutcheon, Chicago Tribune | 1957 | Tom Little, Nashville Tennessean | 1981 | Mike Peters, Dayton (Ohio) Daily News |
| 1933 | H.M. Talburt, Washington Daily News | 1958 | Bruce M. Shanks, Buffalo (N.Y.) Evening News | 1982 | Ben Sargent, Austin (Tex.) American-Statesman |
| 1934 | Edmund Duffy, Baltimore Sun | | | | |
| 1935 | Ross A. Lewis, Milwaukee Journal | 1959 | William H. ("Bill") Mauldin, St. Louis Post-Dispatch | 1983 | Richard Locher, Chicago Tribune |
| 1936 | No award | | | 1984 | Paul Conrad, Los Angeles Times |
| 1937 | C.D. Batchelor, New York Daily News | 1960 | No award | 1985 | Jeffrey K. MacNelly, Chicago Tribune |
| 1938 | Vaughn Shoemaker, Chicago Daily News | 1961 | Carey Orr, Chicago Tribune | 1986 | Jules Feiffer, Village Voice (New York City) |
| 1939 | Charles G. Werner, Daily Oklahoman | 1962 | Edmund S. Valtman, Hartford (Conn.) Times | 1987 | Berke Breathed, Washington Post Writers Group |
| 1940 | Edmund Duffy, Baltimore Sun | 1963 | Frank Miller, Des Moines Register | | |
| 1941 | Jacob Burck, Chicago Times | 1964 | Paul Conrad, Denver Post | 1988 | Doug Marlette, Atlanta Constitution and Charlotte Observer |
| 1942 | Herbert L. Block ("Herblock"), NEA Service | 1965 | No award | | |
| 1943 | Jay Norwood Darling, Des Moines Register and Tribune | 1966 | Don Wright, Miami News | 1989 | Jack Higgins, Chicago Sun-Times |
| | | 1967 | Patrick Oliphant, Denver Post | 1990 | Tom Toles, Buffalo News |
| 1944 | Clifford K. Berryman, Evening Star (D.C.) | 1968 | Eugene Gray Payne, Charlotte (N.C.) Observer | 1991 | Jim Borgman, Cincinnati Enquirer |
| 1945 | Sgt. Bill Mauldin, United Feature Syndicate, Inc. | 1969 | John Fischetti, Chicago Daily News | | |
| 1946 | Bruce Alexander Russell, Los Angeles Times | 1970 | Thomas F. Darcy, Newsday (Garden City, L.I., N.Y.) | | |

## PHOTOGRAPHY, 1942–67[1]

| Year | Winner, Newspaper | Year | Winner, Newspaper | Year | Winner, Newspaper |
|---|---|---|---|---|---|
| 1942 | Milton Brooks, Detroit News | 1951 | Max Desfor, Associated Press | 1960 | Andrew Lopez, United Press International |
| 1943 | Frank Noel, Associated Press | 1952 | John Robinson and Don Ultang, Des Moines Register and Tribune | 1961 | Yasushi Nagao, Mainichi (Tokyo); photo distributed by United Press International |
| 1944 | Frank Filan, Associated Press Earle L. Bunker, World-Herald (Omaha, Nebr.) | | | | |
| | | 1953 | William M. Gallagher, Flint (Mich.) Journal | 1962 | Paul Vathis, Associated Press |
| 1945 | Joe Rosenthal, Associated Press | 1954 | Mrs. Walter M. Schau, Amateur; photo published by the Akron (Ohio) Beacon Journal | 1963 | Hector Rondon, La Republica (Caracas, Venezuela); photo distributed by the Associated Press |
| 1946 | No award | | | | |
| 1947 | Arnold Hardy, Amateur; photo distributed by the Associated Press | 1955 | John L. Gaunt, Jr., Los Angeles Times | 1964 | Robert H. Jackson, Dallas Times-Herald |
| | | 1956 | Photography staff, New York Daily News | 1965 | Horst Faas, Associated Press |
| 1948 | Frank Cushing, Boston Traveler | 1957 | Harry A. Trask, Boston Traveler | 1966 | Kyoichi Sawada, United Press International |
| 1949 | Nathaniel Fein, New York Herald-Tribune | 1958 | William C. Beall, Washington Daily News | 1967 | Jack R. Thornell, Associated Press |
| 1950 | Bill Crouch, Oakland (Calif.) Tribune | 1959 | William Seaman, Minneapolis Star | | |

1. In 1968 the Photography category was divided into two groups: Spot News Photography and Feature Photography.

## SPOT NEWS PHOTOGRAPHY, 1968–91

| Year | Winner, Newspaper | Year | Winner, Newspaper | Year | Winner, Newspaper |
|---|---|---|---|---|---|
| 1968 | Rocco Morabito, Jacksonville Journal | 1972 | Horst Faas and Michel Laurent, Associated Press | 1976 | Stanley Forman, Boston Herald American |
| 1969 | Edward T. Adams, Associated Press | | | 1977 | Neal Ulevich, Associated Press |
| 1970 | Steve Starr, Associated Press | 1973 | Huynh Cong Ut, Associated Press | | Stanley Forman, Boston Herald American |
| 1971 | John Paul Filo, Valley Daily News and Daily Dispatch (New Kensington, Pa.) | 1974 | Anthony K. Roberts, Freelance photographer, Beverly Hills, Calif. | 1978 | John H. Blair, United Press International |
| | | 1975 | Gerald H. Gay, Seattle Times | 1979 | Thomas J. Kelly III, Pottstown (Pa.) Mercury |

| Year | Winner, Newspaper | Year | Winner, Newspaper | Year | Winner, Newspaper |
|------|-------------------|------|-------------------|------|-------------------|
| 1980 | Unnamed photographer, United Press International | 1984 | Stan Grossfeld, Boston Globe | 1988 | Scott Shaw, Odessa (Tex.) American |
| 1981 | Larry C. Price, Fort Worth (Tex.) Star-Telegram | 1985 | Photography staff, Register (Santa Ana, Calif.) | 1989 | Ron Olshwanger, St. Louis Post-Dispatch |
| 1982 | Ron Edmonds, Associated Press | 1986 | Carol Guzy and Michel duCille, Miami Herald | 1990 | Photography staff, Oakland Tribune |
| 1983 | Bill Foley, Associated Press | 1987 | Kim Komenich, San Francisco Examiner | 1991 | Greg Marinovich, Associated Press |

## FEATURE PHOTOGRAPHY, 1968–91

| Year | Winner, Newspaper | Year | Winner, Newspaper | Year | Winner, Newspaper |
|------|-------------------|------|-------------------|------|-------------------|
| 1968 | Toshio Sakai, United Press International | 1976 | Photography staff, Louisville Courier-Journal and Times | 1984 | Anthony Suau, Denver Post |
| 1969 | Moneta Sleet, Jr., Ebony magazine | | | 1985 | Stan Grossfeld, Boston Globe |
| 1970 | Dallas Kinney, Palm Beach Post (West Palm Beach, Fla.) | 1977 | Robin Hood, Chattanooga News-Free Press | | Larry C. Price, Philadelphia Inquirer |
| | | 1978 | J. Ross Baughman, Associated Press | 1986 | Tom Gralish, Philadelphia Inquirer |
| 1971 | Jack Dykinga, Chicago Sun-Times | 1979 | Photography staff, Boston Herald American | 1987 | David Peterson, Des Moines Register |
| 1972 | Dave Kennerly, United Press International | 1980 | Erwin H. Hagler, Dallas Times Herald | 1988 | Michel duCille, Miami Herald |
| 1973 | Brian Lanker, Topeka Capital-Journal | 1981 | Taro M. Yamasaki, Detroit Free Press | 1989 | Manny Crisostomo, Detroit Free Press |
| 1974 | Slava Veder, Associated Press | 1982 | John H. White, Chicago Sun-Times | 1990 | David C. Turnley, Detroit Free Press |
| 1975 | Matthew Lewis, Washington Post | 1983 | James B. Dickman, Dallas Times Herald | 1991 | William Snyder, Dallas Morning News |

## COMMENTARY, 1970–91

| Year | Winner, Newspaper | Year | Winner, Newspaper | Year | Winner, Newspaper |
|------|-------------------|------|-------------------|------|-------------------|
| 1970 | Marquis W. Childs, St. Louis Post-Dispatch | 1977 | George F. Will, Washington Post Writers Group | 1984 | Vermont Royster, Wall Street Journal |
| 1971 | William A. Caldwell, Record (Hackensack, N.J.) | | | 1985 | Murray Kempton, Newsday (Garden City, L.I., N.Y.) |
| | | 1978 | William Safire, New York Times | | |
| 1972 | Mike Royko, Chicago Daily News | 1979 | Russell Baker, New York Times | 1986 | Jimmy Breslin, New York Daily News |
| 1973 | David S. Broder, Washington Post | 1980 | Ellen H. Goodman, Boston Globe | 1987 | Charles Krauthammer, Washington Post |
| 1974 | Edwin A. Roberts, Jr., National Observer | 1981 | Dave Anderson, New York Times | 1988 | Dave Barry, Miami Herald |
| 1975 | Mary McGrory, Washington Star | 1982 | Art Buchwald, Los Angeles Times Syndicate | 1989 | Clarence Page, Chicago Tribune |
| 1976 | Walter ("Red") Smith, New York Times | 1983 | Claude Sitton, Raleigh (N.C.) News & Observer | 1990 | Jim Murray, Los Angeles Times |
| | | | | 1991 | Jim Hoagland, Washington Post |

## CRITICISM, 1970–91

| Year | Winner, Newspaper | Year | Winner, Newspaper | Year | Winner, Newspaper |
|------|-------------------|------|-------------------|------|-------------------|
| 1970 | Ada Louise Huxtable, New York Times | 1978 | Walter Kerr, New York Times | 1986 | Donal Henahan, New York Times |
| 1971 | Harold C. Schonberg, New York Times | 1979 | Paul Gapp, Chicago Tribune | 1987 | Richard Eder, Los Angeles Times |
| 1972 | Frank Peters, Jr., St. Louis Post-Dispatch | 1980 | William A. Henry III, Boston Globe | 1988 | Tom Shales, Washington Post |
| 1973 | Ronald Powers, Chicago Sun-Times | 1981 | Jonathan Yardley, Washington Star | 1989 | Michael Skube, Raleigh (N.C.) News and Observer |
| 1974 | Emily Genauer, Newsday syndicate | 1982 | Martin Bernheimer, Los Angeles Times | | |
| 1975 | Roger Ebert, Chicago Sun-Times | 1983 | Manuela Hoelterhoff, Wall Street Journal | 1990 | Allan Temko, San Francisco Chronicle |
| 1976 | Alan M. Kriegsman, Washington Post | 1984 | Paul Goldberger, New York Times | 1991 | David Shaw, Los Angeles Times |
| 1977 | William McPherson, Washington Post | 1985 | Howard Rosenberg, Los Angeles Times | | |

## FEATURE WRITING, 1979–91

| Year | Winner, Newspaper | Year | Winner, Newspaper | Year | Winner, Newspaper |
|------|-------------------|------|-------------------|------|-------------------|
| 1979 | Jon D. Franklin, Baltimore Evening Sun | 1984 | Peter Mark Rinearson, Seattle Times | 1988 | Jacqui Banaszynski, St. Paul Pioneer Press and Dispatch |
| 1980 | Madeleine Blais, Miami Herald | 1985 | Alice Steinbach, Baltimore Sun | | |
| 1981 | Teresa Carpenter, Village Voice (New York City) | 1986 | John Camp, St. Paul Pioneer Press and Dispatch | 1989 | David Zucchino, Philadelphia Inquirer |
| | | | | 1990 | Dave Curtin, Colorado Springs Gazette Telegram |
| 1982 | Saul Pett, Associated Press | 1987 | Steve Twomey, Philadelphia Inquirer | | |
| 1983 | Nan Robertson, New York Times | | | 1991 | Sheryl James, St. Petersburg Times |

## SPECIAL AWARDS AND CITATIONS, 1930–87

| 1930 | William O. Dapping, Auburn (N.Y.) Citizen, Prison reporting | 1947 | Columbia University and Graduate School of Journalism, Governing Pulitzer prizes | 1958 | Walter Lippmann, New York Herald Tribune, Lifetime achievement |
|------|--|------|--|------|--|
| 1938 | Edmonton (Alberta) Journal, Freedom-of-the-press editorials | | St. Louis Post-Dispatch, Adherence to ideals of journalism | 1964 | Gannett Newspapers, "The Road to Integration" program |
| 1941 | New York Times, Foreign news reporting | 1948 | Dr. Frank Diehl Fackenthal, Interest and service | 1976 | Professor John Hohenberg, Administration of Pulitzer prizes |
| 1944 | Byron Price, director of the Office of Censorship, Creation and administration of newspaper and radio codes | 1951 | Cyrus L. Sulzberger, New York Times, Interview with Archbishop Stepinac | 1978 | Richard Lee Strout, Christian Science Monitor, Lifetime achievement |
| | Mrs. William Allen White, Services to Advisory Board, Graduate School of Journalism, Columbia University | 1952 | Max Kase, N.Y. Journal-American, Corruption in basketball | 1987 | Joseph Pulitzer, Jr., Lifetime services to Pulitzer Board |
| | | | Kansas City Star, Coverage of regional flood | | |
| 1945 | American press cartographers, Maps of war fronts | 1953 | New York Times, Sunday "Review of the Week" section | | |

# PULITZER PRIZES IN LETTERS, 1917–91

## THE PULITZER PRIZE FOR THE NOVEL/FICTION, 1918–91

| Year | Author/Title | Year | Author/Title | Year | Author/Title |
|---|---|---|---|---|---|
| 1918 | Ernest Poole, *His Family* | 1942 | Ellen Glasgow, *In This Our Life* | 1968 | William Styron, *The Confessions of Nat Turner* |
| 1919 | Booth Tarkington, *The Magnificent Ambersons* | 1943 | Upton Sinclair, *Dragon's Teeth* | 1969 | N. Scott Momaday, *House Made of Dawn* |
| 1920 | No award | 1944 | Martin Flavin, *Journey in the Dark* | 1970 | Jean Stafford, *Collected Stories* |
| 1921 | Edith Wharton, *The Age of Innocence* | 1945 | John Hersey, *A Bell for Adano* | 1971 | No award |
| 1922 | Booth Tarkington, *Alice Adams* | 1946 | No award | 1972 | Wallace Stegner, *Angle of Repose* |
| 1923 | Willa Cather, *One of Ours* | 1947 | Robert Penn Warren, *All the King's Men* | 1973 | Eudora Welty, *The Optimist's Daughter* |
| 1924 | Margaret Wilson, *The Able McLaughlins* | 1948[1] | James A. Michener, *Tales of the South Pacific* | 1974 | No award |
| 1925 | Edna Ferber, *So Big* | 1949 | James Gould Cozzens, *Guard of Honor* | 1975 | Michael Shaara, *The Killer Angels* |
| 1926 | Sinclair Lewis, *Arrowsmith* | 1950 | A.B. Guthrie, Jr., *The Way West* | 1976 | Saul Bellow, *Humboldt's Gift* |
| 1927 | Louis Bromfield, *Early Autumn* | 1951 | Conrad Richter, *The Town* | 1977 | No award |
| 1928 | Thornton Wilder, *The Bridge of San Luis Rey* | 1952 | Herman Wouk, *The Caine Mutiny* | 1978 | James Alan McPherson, *Elbow Room* |
| 1929 | Julia Peterkin, *Scarlet Sister Mary* | 1953 | Ernest Hemingway, *The Old Man and the Sea* | 1979 | John Cheever, *The Stories of John Cheever* |
| 1930 | Oliver LaFarge, *Laughing Boy* | 1954 | No award | 1980 | Norman Mailer, *The Executioner's Song* |
| 1931 | Margaret Ayer Barnes, *Years of Grace* | 1955 | William Faulkner, *A Fable* | 1981 | John Kennedy Toole, *A Confederacy of Dunces* |
| 1932 | Pearl S. Buck, *The Good Earth* | 1956 | MacKinlay Kantor, *Andersonville* | 1982 | John Updike, *Rabbit Is Rich* |
| 1933 | T.S. Stribling, *The Store* | 1957 | No award | 1983 | Alice Walker, *The Color Purple* |
| 1934 | Caroline Miller, *Lamb in His Bosom* | 1958 | James Agee, *A Death in the Family* | 1984 | William Kennedy, *Ironweed* |
| 1935 | Josephine Winslow Johnson, *Now in November* | 1959 | Robert Lewis Taylor, *The Travels of Jaimie McPheeters* | 1985 | Alison Lurie, *Foreign Affairs* |
| 1936 | Harold L. Davis, *Honey in the Horn* | 1960 | Allen Drury, *Advise and Consent* | 1986 | Larry McMurtry, *Lonesome Dove* |
| 1937 | Margaret Mitchell, *Gone with the Wind* | 1961 | Harper Lee, *To Kill a Mockingbird* | 1987 | Peter Taylor, *A Summons to Memphis* |
| 1938 | John Phillips Marquand, *The Late George Apley* | 1962 | Edwin O'Connor, *The Edge of Sadness* | 1988 | Toni Morrison, *Beloved* |
| 1939 | Marjorie Kinnan Rawlings, *The Yearling* | 1963 | William Faulkner, *The Reivers* | 1989 | Anne Tyler, *Breathing Lessons* |
| 1940 | John Steinbeck, *The Grapes of Wrath* | 1964 | No award | 1990 | Oscar Hijuelos, *The Mambo Kings Play Songs of Love* |
| 1941 | No award | 1965 | Shirley Ann Grau, *The Keepers of the House* | 1991 | John Updike, *Rabbit at Rest* |
| | | 1966 | Katherine Anne Porter, *Collected Stories* | | |
| | | 1967 | Bernard Malamud, *The Fixer* | | |

1. In 1948 the name of the category was changed to Fiction.

## THE PULITZER PRIZE FOR DRAMA, 1918–91

| Year | Author/Title | Year | Author/Title | Year | Author/Title |
|---|---|---|---|---|---|
| 1918 | Jesse Lynch Williams, *Why Marry* | 1946 | Russel Crouse and Howard Lindsay, *State of the Union* | 1968 | No award |
| 1919 | No award | 1947 | No award | 1969 | Howard Sackler, *The Great White Hope* |
| 1920 | Eugene O'Neill, *Beyond the Horizon* | 1948 | Tennessee Williams, *A Streetcar Named Desire* | 1970 | Charles Gordone, *No Place to Be Somebody* |
| 1921 | Zona Gale, *Miss Lulu Bett* | | | 1971 | Paul Zindel, *The Effect of Gamma Rays on Man-in-the-Moon Marigolds* |
| 1922 | Eugene O'Neill, *Anna Christie* | 1949 | Arthur Miller, *Death of a Salesman* | |  |
| 1923 | Owen Davis, *Icebound* | 1950 | Richard Rodgers, Oscar Hammerstein II, and Joshua Logan, *South Pacific* | 1972 | No award |
| 1924 | Hatcher Hughes, *Hell–Bent Fer Heaven* | | | 1973 | Jason Miller, *That Championship Season* |
| 1925 | Sidney Howard, *They Knew What They Wanted* | 1951 | No award | 1974 | No award |
| 1926 | George Kelly, *Craig's Wife* | 1952 | Joseph Kramm, *The Shrike* | 1975 | Edward Albee, *Seascape* |
| 1927 | Paul Green, *In Abraham's Bosom* | 1953 | William Inge, *Picnic* | 1976 | Michael Bennett; Nicholas Dante and James Kirkwood (book); Marvin Hamlisch (music); and Edward Kleban (lyrics), *A Chorus Line* |
| 1928 | Eugene O'Neill, *Strange Interlude* | 1954 | John Patrick, *The Teahouse of the August Moon* | | |
| 1929 | Elmer L. Rice, *Street Scene* | | | | |
| 1930 | Marc Connelly, *The Green Pastures* | 1955 | Tennessee Williams, *Cat on a Hot Tin Roof* | 1977 | Michael Cristofer, *The Shadow Box* |
| 1931 | Susan Glaspell, *Alison's House* | 1956 | Albert Hackett and Frances Goodrich, *The Diary of Anne Frank* | 1978 | Donald L. Coburn, *The Gin Game* |
| 1932 | George S. Kaufman, Morrie Ryskind, and Ira Gershwin, *Of Thee I Sing* | | | 1979 | Sam Shepard, *Buried Child* |
| | | 1957 | Eugene O'Neill, *Long Day's Journey Into Night* | 1980 | Lanford Wilson, *Talley's Folly* |
| 1933 | Maxwell Anderson, *Both Your Houses* | 1958 | Ketti Frings, *Look Homeward, Angel* | 1981 | Beth Henley, *Crimes of the Heart* |
| 1934 | Sidney Kingsley, *Men in White* | 1959 | Archibald MacLeish, *J.B.* | 1982 | Charles Fuller, *A Soldier's Play* |
| 1935 | Zoe Akins, *The Old Maid* | 1960 | Jerome Weidman and George Abbott (book); Jerry Bock (music); and Sheldon Harnick (lyrics), *Fiorello!* | 1983 | Marsha Norman, *'night Mother* |
| 1936 | Robert E. Sherwood, *Idiot's Delight* | | | 1984 | David Mamet, *Glengarry Glen Ross* |
| 1937 | Moss Hart and George S. Kaufman, *You Can't Take It with You* | | | 1985 | Stephen Sondheim (music and lyrics); James Lapine (book), *Sunday in the Park with George* |
| 1938 | Thornton Wilder, *Our Town* | 1961 | Tad Mosel, *All the Way Home* | | |
| 1939 | Robert E. Sherwood, *Abe Lincoln in Illinois* | 1962 | Frank Loesser and Abe Burrows, *How to Succeed in Business Without Really Trying* | 1986 | No award |
| 1940 | William Saroyan, *The Time of Your Life* | | | 1987 | August Wilson, *Fences* |
| 1941 | Robert E. Sherwood, *There Shall Be No Night* | 1963 | No award | 1988 | Alfred Uhry, *Driving Miss Daisy* |
| 1942 | No award | 1964 | No award | 1989 | Wendy Wasserstein, *The Heidi Chronicles* |
| 1943 | Thornton Wilder, *The Skin of Our Teeth* | 1965 | Frank D. Gilroy, *The Subject Was Roses* | 1990 | August Wilson, *The Piano Lesson* |
| 1944 | No award | 1966 | No award | 1991 | Neil Simon, *Lost in Yonkers* |
| 1945 | Mary Chase, *Harvey* | 1967 | Edward Albee, *A Delicate Balance* | | |

## THE PULITZER PRIZE FOR HISTORY, 1917–91

| Year | Author/Title |
|------|--------------|
| 1917 | His Excellency J.J. Jusserand, French ambassador to the U.S., *With Americans of Past and Present Days* |
| 1918 | James Ford Rhodes, *A History of the Civil War, 1861–1865* |
| 1919 | No award |
| 1920 | Justin H. Smith, *The War with Mexico* |
| 1921 | William Sowden Sims, with Burton J. Hendrick, *The Victory at Sea* |
| 1922 | James Truslow Adams, *The Founding of New England* |
| 1923 | Charles Warren, *The Supreme Court in United States History* |
| 1924 | Charles Howard McIlwain, *The American Revolution—A Constitutional Interpretation* |
| 1925 | Frederic L. Paxson, *A History of the American Frontier* |
| 1926 | Edward Channing, *The History of the United States* |
| 1927 | Samuel Flagg Bemis, *Pinckney's Treaty* |
| 1928 | Vernon Louis Parrington, *Main Currents in American Thought* |
| 1929 | Fred Albert Shannon, *The Organization and Administration of the Union Army, 1861–1865* |
| 1930 | Claude H. Van Tyne, *The War of Independence* |
| 1931 | Bernadotte E. Schmitt, *The Coming of the War: 1914* |
| 1932 | John J. Pershing, *My Experiences in the World War* |
| 1933 | Frederick J. Turner, *The Significance of Sections in American History* |
| 1934 | Herbert Agar, *The People's Choice* |
| 1935 | Charles McLean Andrews, *The Colonial Period of American History* |
| 1936 | Andrew C. McLaughlin, *The Constitutional History of the United States* |
| 1937 | Van Wyck Brooks, *The Flowering of New England* |
| 1938 | Paul Herman Buck, *The Road to Reunion 1856–1900* |
| 1939 | Frank Luther Mott, *A History of American Magazines* |
| 1940 | Carl Sandburg, *Abraham Lincoln: The War Years* |

| Year | Author/Title |
|------|--------------|
| 1941 | Marcus Lee Hansen, *The Atlantic Migration, 1607–1860* |
| 1942 | Margaret Leech, *Reveille in Washington* |
| 1943 | Esther Forbes, *Paul Revere and the World He Lived In* |
| 1944 | Merle Curti, *The Growth of American Thought* |
| 1945 | Stephen Bonsal, *Unfinished Business* |
| 1946 | Arthur Meier Schlesinger, Jr., *The Age of Jackson* |
| 1947 | James Phinney Baxter III, *Scientists Against Time* |
| 1948 | Bernard DeVoto, *Across the Wide Missouri* |
| 1949 | Roy Franklin Nichols, *The Disruption of American Democracy* |
| 1950 | Oliver W. Larkin, *Art and Life in America* |
| 1951 | R. Carlyle Buley, *The Old Northwest, Pioneer Period 1815–1840* |
| 1952 | Oscar Handlin, *The Uprooted* |
| 1953 | George Dangerfield, *The Era of Good Feelings* |
| 1954 | Bruce Catton, *A Stillness at Appomattox* |
| 1955 | Paul Horgan, *Great River: The Rio Grande in North American History* |
| 1956 | Richard Hofstadter, *The Age of Reform* |
| 1957 | George F. Kennan, *Russia Leaves the War: Soviet American Relations, 1917–1920* |
| 1958 | Bray Hammond, *Banks and Politics in America* |
| 1959 | Leonard D. White, with Jean Schneider, *The Republican Era: 1869–1901* |
| 1960 | Margaret Leech, *In the Days of McKinley* |
| 1961 | Herbert Feis, *Between War and Peace: The Potsdam Conference* |
| 1962 | Lawrence H. Gipson, *The Triumphant Empire, Thunder Clouds in the West* |
| 1963 | Constance McLaughlin Green, *Washington, Village and Capital, 1800–1878* |
| 1964 | Sumner Chilton Powell, *Puritan Village: The Formation of a New England Town* |
| 1965 | Irwin Unger, *The Greenback Era* |
| 1966 | Perry Miller, *Life of the Mind in America* |
| 1967 | William H. Goetzmann, *Exploration and Empire: The Explorer and the Scientist in the Winning of the American West* |
| 1968 | Bernard Bailyn, *The Ideological Origins of the American Revolution* |

| Year | Author/Title |
|------|--------------|
| 1969 | Leonard W. Levy, *Origins of the Fifth Amendment* |
| 1970 | Dean Acheson, *Present at the Creation: My Years in the State Department* |
| 1971 | James MacGregor Burns, *Roosevelt, The Soldier of Freedom* |
| 1972 | Carl N. Degler, *Neither Black Nor White* |
| 1973 | Michael Kammen, *People of Paradox: An Inquiry Concerning the Origins of American Civilization* |
| 1974 | Daniel J. Boorstin, *The Americans: The Democratic Experience* |
| 1975 | Dumas Malone, *Jefferson and His Time, Vols. I-V* |
| 1976 | Paul Horgan, *Larry of Santa Fe* |
| 1977 | David M. Potter (manuscript finished by Don E. Fehrenbacher), *The Impending Crisis* |
| 1978 | Alfred D. Chandler, Jr., *The Visible Hand: The Managerial Revolution in American Business* |
| 1979 | Don E. Fehrenbacher, *The Dred Scott Case* |
| 1980 | Leon F. Litwack, *Been in the Storm So Long* |
| 1981 | Lawrence A. Cremin, *American Education: The National Experience, 1783–1876* |
| 1982 | C. Vann Woodward (ed.), *Mary Chesnut's Civil War* |
| 1983 | Rhys L. Isaac, *The Transformation of Virginia, 1740–1790* |
| 1984 | No award |
| 1985 | Thomas K. McCraw, *Prophets of Regulation* |
| 1986 | Walter A. McDougall, *...the Heavens and the Earth: A Political History of the Space Age* |
| 1987 | Bernard Bailyn, *Voyagers to the West: A Passage in the Peopling of America on the Eve of the Revolution* |
| 1988 | Robert V. Bruce, *The Launching of Modern American Science 1846–1876* |
| 1989 | Taylor Branch, *Parting the Waters: America in the King Years, 1954–63* |
| | James M. McPherson, *Battle Cry of Freedom: The Civil War Era* |
| 1990 | Stanley Karnow, *In Our Image: America's Empire in the Philippines* |
| 1991 | Laurel Thatcher Ulrich, *A Midwife's Tale: The Life of Martha Ballard, Based on Her Diary 1785–1812* |

## THE PULITZER PRIZE FOR BIOGRAPHY OR AUTOBIOGRAPHY, 1917–91

| Year | Author/Title |
|------|--------------|
| 1917 | Laura E. Richards and Maude Howe Elliott, with Florence Howe Hall, *Julia Ward Howe* |
| 1918 | William Cabell Bruce, *Benjamin Franklin, Self-Revealed* |
| 1919 | Henry Adams, *The Education of Henry Adams* |
| 1920 | Albert J. Beveridge, *The Life of John Marshall* |
| 1921 | Edward Bok, *The Americanization of Edward Bok* |
| 1922 | Hamlin Garland, *A Daughter of the Middle Border* |
| 1923 | Burton J. Hendrick, *The Life and Letters of Walter H. Page* |
| 1924 | Michael Idvorsky Pupin, *From Immigrant to Inventor* |
| 1925 | M.A. DeWolfe Howe, *Barrett Wendell and His Letter* |
| 1926 | Harvey Cushing, *The Life of Sir William Osler* |
| 1927 | Emory Holloway, *Whitman* |
| 1928 | Charles Edward Russell, *The American Orchestra and Theodore Thomas* |

| Year | Author/Title |
|------|--------------|
| 1929 | Burton J. Hendrick, *The Training of an American: The Earlier Life and Letters of Walter H. Page* |
| 1930 | Marquis James, *The Raven* |
| 1931 | Henry James, *Charles W. Eliot* |
| 1932 | Henry F. Pringle, *Theodore Roosevelt* |
| 1933 | Allan Nevins, *Grover Cleveland* |
| 1934 | Tyler Dennett, *John Hay* |
| 1935 | Douglas S. Freeman, *R.E. Lee* |
| 1936 | Ralph Barton Perry, *The Thought and Character of William James* |
| 1937 | Allan Nevins, *Hamilton Fish* |
| 1938 | Odell Shepard, *Pedlar's Progress* |
| | Marquis James, *Andrew Jackson* |
| 1939 | Carl Van Doren, *Benjamin Franklin* |
| 1940 | Ray Stannard Baker, *Woodrow Wilson, Life and Letters, vols. 7 & 8* |
| 1941 | Ola Elizabeth Winslow, *Jonathan Edwards* |
| 1942 | Forrest Wilson, *Crusader in Crinoline* |
| 1943 | Samuel Eliot Morison, *Admiral of the Ocean Sea* |

| Year | Author/Title |
|------|--------------|
| 1944 | Carleton Mabee, *The American Leonardo: The Life of Samuel F.B. Morse* |
| 1945 | Russell Blaine Nye, *George Bancroft: Brahmin Rebel* |
| 1946 | Linnie Marsh Wolfe, *Son of the Wilderness* |
| 1947 | William Allen White, *The Autobiography of William Allen White* |
| 1948 | Margaret Clapp, *Forgotten First Citizen: John Bigelow* |
| 1949 | Robert E. Sherwood, *Roosevelt and Hopkins* |
| 1950 | Samuel Flagg Bemis, *John Quincy Adams and the Foundations of American Foreign Policy* |
| 1951 | Margaret Louise Coit, *John C. Calhoun: American Portrait* |
| 1952 | Merlo J. Pusey, *Charles Evan Hughes* |
| 1953 | David J. Mays, *Edmund Pendleton 1721–1803* |
| 1954 | Charles A. Lindbergh, *The Spirit of St. Louis* |
| 1955 | William S. White, *The Taft Story* |

| Year | Author/Title |
|------|-------------|
| 1956 | Talbot Faulkner Hamlin, *Benjamin Henry Latrobe* |
| 1957 | John F. Kennedy, *Profiles in Courage* |
| 1958 | Douglas Southall Freeman, John Alexander Carroll, Mary Wells Ashworth, *George Washington,* vols. 1–4; and vol. 7, written after Dr. Freeman's death in 1953 |
| 1959 | Arthur Walworth, *Woodrow Wilson, American Prophet* |
| 1960 | Samuel Eliot Morison, *John Paul Jones* |
| 1961 | David Donald, *Charles Sumner and the Coming of the Civil War* |
| 1962 | No award |
| 1963 | Leon Edel, *Henry James* |
| 1964 | Walter Jackson Bate, *John Keats* |
| 1965 | Ernest Samuels, *Henry Adams* |
| 1966 | Arthur M. Schlesinger, Jr., *A Thousand Days: JFK in the White House* |
| 1967 | Justin Kaplan, *Mr. Clemens and Mark Twain* |

| Year | Author/Title |
|------|-------------|
| 1968 | George F. Kennan, *Memoirs* |
| 1969 | Benjamin Lawrence Reid, *The Man From New York: John Quinn and His Friends* |
| 1970 | T. Harry Williams, *Huey Long* |
| 1971 | Lawrance Thompson, *Robert Frost: The Years of Triumph, 1915–1938* |
| 1972 | Joseph P. Lash, *Eleanor and Franklin* |
| 1973 | W.A. Swanberg, *Luce and His Empire* |
| 1974 | Louis Sheaffer, *O'Neill, Son and Artist* |
| 1975 | Robert A. Caro, *The Power Broker: Robert Moses and the Fall of New York* |
| 1976 | R.W.B. Lewis, *Edith Wharton: A Biography* |
| 1977 | John E. Mack, *A Prince of Our Disorder: The Life of T.E. Lawrence* |
| 1978 | Walter Jackson Bate, *Samuel Johnson* |
| 1979 | Leonard Baker, *Days of Sorrow and Pain: Leo Baeck and the Berlin Jews* |
| 1980 | Edmund Morris, *The Rise of Theodore Roosevelt* |

| Year | Author/Title |
|------|-------------|
| 1981 | Robert K. Massie, *Peter the Great: His Life and World* |
| 1982 | William S. McFeely, *Grant: A Biography* |
| 1983 | Russell Baker, *Growing Up* |
| 1984 | Louis R. Harlan, *Booker T. Washington: The Wizard of Tuskegee, 1901–1915* |
| 1985 | Kenneth Silverman, *The Life and Times of Cotton Mather* |
| 1986 | Elizabeth Frank, *Louise Bogan: A Portrait* |
| 1987 | David J. Garrow, *Bearing the Cross: Martin Luther King, Jr. and the Southern Christian Leadership Conference* |
| 1988 | David Herbert Donald, *Look Homeward: A Life of Thomas Wolfe* |
| 1989 | Richard Ellman, *Oscar Wilde* |
| 1990 | Sebastian de Grazia, *Machiavelli in Hell* |
| 1991 | Steven Naifeh, Gregory White Smith, *Jackson Pollock : An American Saga* |

## THE PULITZER PRIZE FOR POETRY, 1922–91

Pulitzer Prizes in poetry were first awarded in 1922. The Poetry Society awarded prizes in 1918 to Sara Teasdale for *Love Songs,* and in 1919 to Margaret Widdemer for *Old Road to Paradise* and to Carl Sandburg for *Corn Huskers.*

| Year | Author/Title |
|------|-------------|
| 1922 | Edward Arlington Robinson, *Collected Poems* |
| 1923 | Edna St. Vincent Millay, *The Ballad of the Harp–Weaver; A Few Figs from Thistles; Eight Sonnets in American Poetry, 1922, A Miscellany* |
| 1924 | Robert Frost, *New Hampshire: A Poem with Notes and Grace Notes* |
| 1925 | Edward Arlington Robinson, *The Man Who Died Twice* |
| 1926 | Amy Lowell, *What's O'Clock* |
| 1927 | Leonora Speyer, *Fiddler's Farewell* |
| 1928 | Edward Arlington Robinson, *Tristram* |
| 1929 | Stephen Vincent Benét, *John Brown's Body* |
| 1930 | Conrad Aiken, *Selected Poems* |
| 1931 | Robert Frost, *Collected Poems* |
| 1932 | George Dillon, *The Flowering Stone* |
| 1933 | Archibald MacLeish, *Conquistador* |
| 1934 | Robert Hillyer, *Collected Verse* |
| 1935 | Audrey Wurdemann, *Bright Ambush* |
| 1936 | Robert P. Tristram Coffin, *Strange Holiness* |
| 1937 | Robert Frost, *A Further Range* |
| 1938 | Marya Zaturenska, *Cold Morning Sky* |
| 1939 | John Gould Fletcher, *Selected Poems* |
| 1940 | Mark Van Doren, *Collected Poems* |
| 1941 | Leonard Bacon, *Sunderland Capture* |
| 1942 | William Rose Benét, *The Dust Which Is God* |
| 1943 | Robert Frost, *A Witness Tree* |

| Year | Author/Title |
|------|-------------|
| 1944 | Stephen Vincent Benét, *Western Star* |
| 1945 | Karl Shapiro, *V–Letter and Other Poems* |
| 1946 | No award |
| 1947 | Robert Lowell, *Lord Weary's Castle* |
| 1948 | W.H. Auden, *The Age of Anxiety* |
| 1949 | Peter Viereck, *Terror and Decorum* |
| 1950 | Gwendolyn Brooks, *Annie Allen* |
| 1951 | Carl Sandburg, *Complete Poems* |
| 1952 | Marianne Moore, *Collected Poems* |
| 1953 | Archibald MacLeish, *Collected Poems 1917–1952* |
| 1954 | Theodore Roethke, *The Waking* |
| 1955 | Wallace Stevens, *Collected Poems* |
| 1956 | Elizabeth Bishop, *Poems—North & South* |
| 1957 | Richard Wilbur, *Things of This World* |
| 1958 | Robert Penn Warren, *Promises: Poems 1954–1956* |
| 1959 | Stanley Kunitz, *Selected Poems 1928–1958* |
| 1960 | W.D. Snodgrass, *Heart's Needle* |
| 1961 | Phyllis McGinley, *Times Three: Selected Verse from Three Decades* |
| 1962 | Alan Dugan, *Poems* |
| 1963 | William Carlos Williams, *Pictures from Breughel* |
| 1964 | Louis Simpson, *At the End of the Open Road* |
| 1965 | John Berryman, *77 Dream Songs* |
| 1966 | Richard Eberhart, *Selected Poems* |

| Year | Author/Title |
|------|-------------|
| 1967 | Anne Sexton, *Live or Die* |
| 1968 | Anthony Hecht, *The Hard Hours* |
| 1969 | George Oppen, *Of Being Numerous* |
| 1970 | Richard Howard, *Untitled Subjects* |
| 1971 | William S. Merwin, *The Carrier of Ladders* |
| 1972 | James Wright, *Collected Poems* |
| 1973 | Maxine Kumin, *Up Country* |
| 1974 | Robert Lowell, *The Dolphin* |
| 1975 | Gary Snyder, *Turtle Island* |
| 1976 | John Ashbery, *Self-Portrait in a Convex Mirror* |
| 1977 | James Merrill, *Divine Comedies* |
| 1978 | Howard Nemerov, *Collected Poems* |
| 1979 | Robert Penn Warren, *Now and Then* |
| 1980 | Donald Justice, *Selected Poems* |
| 1981 | James Schuyler, *The Morning of the Poem* |
| 1982 | Sylvia Plath, *The Collected Poems*[3] |
| 1983 | Galway Kinnell, *Selected Poems* |
| 1984 | Mary Oliver, *American Primitive* |
| 1985 | Carolyn Kizer, *Yin* |
| 1986 | Henry Taylor, *The Flying Change* |
| 1987 | Rita Dove, *Thomas and Beulah* |
| 1988 | William Meredith, *Partial Accounts: New and Selected Poems* |
| 1989 | Richard Wilbur, *New and Collected Poems* |
| 1990 | Charles Simic, *The World Doesn't End* |
| 1991 | Mona Van Duyn, *Near Changes* |

## THE PULITZER PRIZE FOR GENERAL NONFICTION, 1962–91

| Year | Author/Title |
|------|-------------|
| 1962 | Theodore H. White, *The Making of the President 1960* |
| 1963 | Barbara W. Tuchman, *The Guns of August* |
| 1964 | Richard Hofstadter, *Anti-Intellectualism in American Life* |
| 1965 | Howard Mumford Jones, *O Strange New World* |
| 1966 | Edwin Way Teal, *Wandering Through Winter* |
| 1967 | David Brion Davis, *The Problem of Slavery in Western Culture* |
| 1968 | Will and Ariel Durant, *Rousseau and Revolution,* vol. 10 of the *Story of Civilization* |
| 1969 | René Jules Dubos, *So Human An Animal* Norman Mailer, *The Armies of the Night* |
| 1970 | Erik H. Erikson, *Gandhi's Truth* |
| 1971 | John Toland, *The Rising Sun* |
| 1972 | Barbara W. Tuchman, *Stilwell and the American Experience in China, 1911–1945* |

| Year | Author/Title |
|------|-------------|
| 1973 | Robert Coles, *Children of Crisis,* vols. 2 & 3 Frances Fitzgerald, *Fire in the Lake: The Vietnamese and the Americans in Vietnam* |
| 1974 | Ernest Becker, *The Denial of Death* |
| 1975 | Annie Dillard, *Pilgrim at Tinker Creek* |
| 1976 | Robert N. Butler, *Why Survive? Being Old in America* |
| 1977 | William N. Warner, *Beautiful Swimmers* |
| 1978 | Carl Sagan, *The Dragons of Eden* |
| 1979 | Edward O. Wilson, *On Human Nature* |
| 1980 | Douglas R. Hofstadter, *Gödel, Escher, Bach: An Eternal Golden Braid* |
| 1981 | Carl E. Schorske, *Fin-de-Siècle Vienna: Politics and Culture* |
| 1982 | Tracy Kidder, *The Soul of a New Machine* |
| 1983 | Susan Sheehan, *Is There No Place on Earth for Me?* |

| Year | Author/Title |
|------|-------------|
| 1984 | Paul Starr, *The Social Transformation of American Medicine* |
| 1985 | Studs Terkel, *The Good War: An Oral History of World War Two* |
| 1986 | Joseph Lelyveld, *Move Your Shadow: South Africa, Black and White* J. Anthony Lukas, *Common Ground: A Turbulent Decade in the Lives of Three American Families* |
| 1987 | David K. Shipler, *Arab and Jew: Wounded Spirits in a Promised Land* |
| 1988 | Richard Rhodes, *The Making of the Atomic Bomb* |
| 1989 | Neil Sheehan, *A Bright Shining Lie: John Paul Vann and America in Vietnam* |
| 1990 | Dale Maharidge, Michael Williamson, *And Their Children After Them* |
| 1991 | Bert Holldobler, Edward O. Wilson, *The Ants* |

## PULITZER SPECIAL CITATIONS IN LETTERS, 1944–84

| Year | Author/Title | Year | Author/Title | Year | Author/Title |
|------|-------------|------|-------------|------|-------------|
| 1944 | Richard Rodgers and Oscar Hammerstein II, *Oklahoma!* | 1961 | N.A., *The American Heritage Picture History of the Civil War* | 1977 | Alex Haley, *Roots* |
| 1957 | Kenneth Roberts, for his historical novels | 1973 | James Thomas Flexner, *George Washington*, vols. 1–4 | 1978 | E.B. White, lifetime achievement |
| 1960 | Garret Mattingly, *The Armada* | | | 1984 | Theodore Seuss Geisel, lifetime achievement (Dr. Seuss) |

**Note:** N.A. = not applicable. **Source:** Columbia University.

## THE PULITZER PRIZE FOR MUSIC, 1943–91

| Year | Composer | Title | Year | Composer | Title | Year | Composer | Title |
|------|----------|-------|------|----------|-------|------|----------|-------|
| 1943 | William Schuman | Secular Cantata No. 2, *A Free Song* | 1961 | Walter Piston | Symphony No. 7 | 1980 | David Del Tredici | *In Memory of a Summer Day* |
| 1944 | Howard Hanson | Symphony No. 4, Opus 34 | 1962 | Robert Ward | *The Crucible* (opera) | 1981 | No award | |
| 1945 | Aaron Copland | *Appalachian Spring* | 1963 | Samuel Barber | Piano Concerto No. 1 | 1982 | Roger Sessions | Concerto for Orchestra |
| 1946 | Leo Sowerby | *The Canticle of the Sun* | 1964 | No award | | 1983 | Ellen Taaffe Zwilich | Symphony No. 1 |
| 1947 | Charles Ives | Symphony No. 3 | 1965 | No award | | 1984 | Bernard Rands | "Canti del Sole" for Tenor and Orchestra |
| 1948 | Walter Piston | Symphony No. 3 | 1966 | Leslie Bassett | Variations for Orchestra | | | |
| 1949 | Virgil Thomson | Music for the film *Louisiana Story* | 1967 | Leon Kirchner | Quartet No. 3 | 1985 | Stephen Albert | Symphony *RiverRun* |
| | | | 1968 | George Crumb | *Echoes of Time and the River* (orchestral suite) | 1986 | George Perle | Wind Quintet IV |
| 1950 | Gian Carlo Menotti | Music for *The Consul* | | | | 1987 | John Harbison | *The Flight into Egypt* |
| 1951 | Douglas S. Moore | Music for the opera *Giants in the Earth* | 1969 | Karel Husa | String Quartet No. 3 | 1988 | William Bolcom | 12 New Etudes for Piano |
| | | | 1970 | Charles Wuorinen | *Time's Encomium* | 1989 | Roger Reynolds | *Whispers Out of Time* |
| 1952 | Gail Kubik | *Symphony Concertante* | 1971 | Mario Davidovsky | Synchronisms No. 6 for Piano and Electronic Sound | 1990 | Mel Powell | *Duplicates: A Concerto for Two Pianos and Orchestra* |
| 1953 | No award | | | | | | | |
| 1954 | Quincy Porter | Concerto for Two Pianos and Orchestra | 1972 | Jacob Druckman | *Windows* | 1991 | Shulamit Ran | *Symphony* |
| | | | 1973 | Elliott Carter | String Quartet No. 3 | | | |
| 1955 | Gian Carlo Menotti | *The Saint of Bleecker Street* (opera) | 1974 | Donald Martino | *Notturno* (chamber music piece) | **SPECIAL CITATIONS IN MUSIC** | | |
| | | | | | | 1974 | Roger Sessions | Lifetime achievement |
| 1956 | Ernest Toch | Symphony No. 3 | 1975 | Dominick Argento | *From the Diary of Virginia Woolf* | 1976 | Scott Joplin[1] | Contributions to American music |
| 1957 | Norman Dello Joio | *Meditations on Ecclesiastes* | 1976 | Ned Rorem | *Air Music: Ten Etudes for Orchestra* | | | |
| 1958 | Samuel Barber | *Vanessa* (opera) | 1977 | Richard Wernick | *Visions of Terror and Wonder* | 1982 | Milton Babbitt | Lifetime achievement |
| 1959 | John LaMontaine | Concerto for Piano and Orchestra | 1978 | Michael Colgrass | *Déjà Vu* for Percussion Quartet and Orchestra | 1985 | William Schuman | Lifetime achievement |
| 1960 | Elliott Carter | Second String Quartet | 1979 | Joseph Schwantner | *Aftertones of Infinity* | | | |

1. Awarded posthumously. **Source:** Columbia University.

# THE NOBEL PRIZES

First awarded in 1901, the Nobel Prizes were established through a bequest of $9.2 million from Alfred Bernhard Nobel (1833–1896), a Swedish chemical engineer and the inventor of dynamite and other explosives, and by a gift from the Bank of Sweden. Nobel's will directed that the interest from the fund be divided annually among people who have made significant discoveries or inventions in the fields of chemistry, physics, and physiology or medicine, as well as to that author who has "produced in the field of literature the most outstanding work of an idealistic tendency," and to that individual or group that has "done the most or the best work for fraternity between nations, for the abolition or reduction of standing armies and for the holding and promotion of peace congresses." In 1968, the 300th anniversary of the Bank of Sweden, an additional prize for outstanding work in the economic sciences was established; it was first granted the following year.

Today, all of the prizes are funded with the help of the Bank of Sweden. Final decisions are made for physics, chemistry, and economics by the Royal Swedish Academy of Sciences, Stockholm; for physiology or medicine by the Nobel Assembly at the Karolinska Institute, Stockholm; for literature by the Swedish Academy, Stockholm; and for peace by the Norwegian Nobel Committee, Olso.

The prizes are formally awarded annually on December 10, the anniversary of Nobel's death, but announced earlier in the fall. For a list of 1991 winners, see "Late Breaking News." The peace prize is presented in Olso and other awards are given in Stockholm, by the king of Sweden. The amount of each prize varies according to the interest from the fund. Each 1989 award was approximately $653,000, up from $489,000 in 1988 and $362,500 in 1987. Each prize includes a gold medal, a diploma, and a gift of money which is awarded at a formal ceremony. There were no prizes awarded from 1940 to 1942.

## NOBEL PEACE PRIZE RECIPIENTS

**1901 Jean-Henri Dunant** (Switzerland) Founder of International Committee of the Red Cross; **Frédéric Passy** (France) Founder of first French peace society.

**1902 Elie Ducommun** (Switzerland) Director of Permanent International Peace Bureau; **Charles A. Gobat** (Switzerland) Secretary-general of Inter-Parliamentary Union.

**1903 Sir William R. Cremer** (Great Britain) Founder of International Arbitration League.

**1904 Institute of International Law** Founded in 1873.

**1905 Baroness Bertha S.F. von Suttner** (Austria) Author of antiwar novel *Lay Down Your Arms.*

**1906 Theodore Roosevelt** (U.S.) President; mediated Russo-Japanese War.

**1907 Ernesto T. Moneta** (Italy) Founder of Lombard League of Peace; **Louis Renault** (France) Leading jurist at Hague Peace Conferences.

**1908 Klas P. Arnoldson** (Sweden) Founder of Swedish Peace and Arbitration League;

**Fredrik Bajer** (Denmark) Writer and peace activist.

**1909 Auguste M.F. Beernaert** (Belgium) Prime minister and peace activist; **Paul H.B.B. D'Estournelles de Constant (Baron de Constant de Rebecque)** (France) Founder of French parliamentary group for voluntary arbitration.

**1910 Permanent International Peace Bureau** Founded 1891.

**1911 Tobias M.C. Asser** (Netherlands) A founder of Institute of International Law; **Alfred H. Fried** (Austria) Journalist and founder of many peace publications.

**1912 Elihu Root** (U.S.) Secretary of state and originator of several arbitration treaties.

**1913 Henri Lafontaine** (Belgium) President of Permanent International Peace Bureau in Bern.

**1914–16** No award.

**1917 International Committee of the Red Cross** Founded 1863.

**1918** No award.

**1919 Thomas Woodrow Wilson** (U.S.) President; instrumental in establishing League of Nations.

**1920 Léon Victor A. Bourgeois** (France) Drafted framework for League of Nations.

**1921 Karl H. Branting** (Sweden) Prime minister and pacifist; **Christian L. Lange** (Norway) A founder of Inter-Parliamentary Union.

**1922 Fridtjof Nansen** (Norway) Scientist, explorer, originator of "Nansen passports" for refugees.

**1923–24** No award.

**1925 Sir Austen Chamberlain** (Great Britain) Foreign secretary; worked for Locarno Pact; **Charles G. Dawes** (U.S.) Vice president; drafted Dawes Plan settling German reparations issue.

**1926 Aristide Briand** (France) and **Gustav Stresemann** (Germany) Creators of Locarno Pact.

**1927 Ferdinand Buisson** (France) Human rights advocate; **Ludwig Quidde** (Germany) Lifelong peace activist.

**1928** No award.

**1929 Frank B. Kellogg** (U.S.) Secretary of state; a creator of Kellogg-Briand Pact.

**1930 L.O. Nathan Söderblom** (Sweden) Archbishop; leader in the ecumenical movement.

**1931 Jane Addams** (U.S.) President of Women's International League for Peace and Freedom; **Nicholas M. Butler** (U.S.) Promoter of Kellogg-Briand Pact.

**1932** No award.

**1933 Sir Norman Angell (Ralph Lane)** (Great Britain) Author of antiwar book *The Great Illusion*.

**1934 Arthur Henderson** (Great Britain) President of League of Nations World Disarmament Conference 1932.

**1935 Carl von Ossietzky** (Germany) Journalist and pacifist.

**1936 Carlos Saavedra Lamas** (Argentina) Secretary of state; president of League of Nations and mediator in a conflict between Paraguay and Bolivia.

**1937 Lord Edgar Algernon R.G. Cecil** (Great Britain) An architect of League of Nations.

**1938 Nansen International Office for Refugees** Founded 1921.

**1939–43** No award.

**1944 International Committee of the Red Cross** Founded 1863.

**1945 Cordell Hull** (U.S.) Secretary of state; instrumental in creating UN.

**1946 Emily G. Balch** (U.S.) Leader of international women's movement for peace; **John R. Mott** (U.S.) Leader of Christian ecumenical movement.

**1947 The Friends Service Council** and **The American Friends Service Committee (The Quakers).**

**1948** No award.

**1949 Lord John Boyd Orr** (Great Britain) Nutritionist; worked to eliminate world hunger.

**1950 Ralph Bunche** (U.S.) Mediator in Middle East war.

**1951 Léon Jouhaux** (France) Advocate of improved working-class conditions.

**1952 Albert Schweitzer** (France) Missionary surgeon and founder of Lambarene Hospital in Africa.

**1953 George C. Marshall** (U.S.) General; originator of Marshall Plan, which provided recovery loans and technical aid to European nations after World War II.

**1954 Office of the United Nations High Commissioner for Refugees.**

**1955–56** No award.

**1957 Lester B. Pearson** (Canada) Secretary of state; worked to resolve Suez Canal Crisis of 1956.

**1958 Georges Pire** (Belgium) Dominican priest and leader of relief organization for refugees, l'Europe du Coeur au Service du Monde.

**1959 Philip J. Noel-Baker** (Great Britain) Lifelong worker for international peace through disarmament.

**1960 Albert J. Luthuli** (South Africa) President of the African National Congress; led peaceful resistance to apartheid.

**1961 Dag Hammarskjöld** (Sweden) Secretary-general of UN; worked for peace in the Congo.

**1962 Linus C. Pauling** (U.S.) Chemist; warned against dangers of radioactive fallout in nuclear weapons testing and war.

**1963 International Committee of the Red Cross** and **League of Red Cross Societies.**

**1964 Martin Luther King, Jr.** (U.S.) Leader of American civil rights movement.

**1965 United Nations Children's Fund (UNICEF).**

**1966–67** No award.

**1968 René Cassin** (France) President of European Court for Human Rights.

**1969 International Labour Organization** UN agency involved in improving worldwide working and social conditions.

**1970 Norman Borlaug** (U.S.) Agricultural scientist and developer of high-yield grains credited with helping to alleviate world hunger.

**1971 Willy Brandt** (Federal Republic of Germany) Chancellor; champion of East-West détente.

**1972** No award.

**1973 Henry A. Kissinger** (U.S.) Secretary of state and **Le Duc Tho** (Democratic Republic of Viet Nam) Foreign minister; negotiated Vietnam cease-fire agreement. Mr. Tho declined the prize.

**1974 Seán MacBride** (Ireland) President of International Peace Bureau and UN commissioner for Namibia; **Eisaku Sato** (Japan) Prime minister of Japan and campaigner against nuclear weapons.

**1975 Andrei Sakharov** (USSR) Nuclear physicist and human rights campaigner.

**1976 Betty Williams** and **Mairead Corrigan** (Northern Ireland) Founders of Northern Ireland Peace Movement.

**1977 Amnesty International** A human rights organization.

**1978 Anwar el-Sadat** (Egypt) President and **Menachem Begin** (Israel) Prime minister; negotiated Israeli-Egyptian peace accord.

**1979 Mother Teresa** (India) Worker for the poor in Calcutta.

**1980 Adolfo Pérez Esquivel** (Argentina) Architect, sculptor, and human rights leader.

**1981 Office of the United Nations High Commissioner for Refugees.**

**1982 Alva Myrdal** (Sweden) and **Alfonso García Robles** (Mexico) Campaigners for disarmament.

**1983 Lech Walesa** (Poland) Leader of the Solidarity trade union federation.

**1984 Desmond M. Tutu** (South Africa) Bishop of Johannesburg; a leader of the anti-apartheid movement.

**1985 International Physicians for the Prevention of Nuclear War** Organization jointly headed by a Soviet and an American doctor.

**1986 Elie Wiesel** (U.S.) Writer on the Holocaust and Nazi death camp survivor.

**1987 Oscar Arias Sánchez** (Costa Rica) President of Costa Rica; creator of a peace plan for Central America.

**1988 United Nations Peacekeeping Forces** (see "The United Nations").

**1989 Dalai Lama** (Tibet) Exiled religious and political leader of Tibet for his nonviolent campaign to end China's domination of his country.

**1990 Mikhail Gorbachev** (USSR) President of the Soviet Union; "for his leading role in the peace process which today characterizes important parts of the international community."

# NOBEL PRIZES IN PHYSIOLOGY OR MEDICINE

**1901 Emil A. von Behring** (Germany) Marburg Univ. "for his work on serum therapy, especially its application against diphtheria, by which he has opened a new road in the domain of medical science and thereby placed in the hands of the physician a victorious weapon against illness and deaths."

**1902 Sir Ronald Ross** (Great Britain) University College "for his work on malaria, by which he has shown how it enters the organism and thereby has laid the foundation for successful research on this disease and methods of combating it."

**1903 Niels R. Finsen** (Denmark) Finsen Medical Light Institute "in recognition of his contribution to the treatment of diseases, especially lupus vulgaris, with concentrated light radiation, whereby he has opened a new avenue for medical science."

**1904 Ivan P. Pavlov** (Russia) Military Medical Academy "in recognition of his work on the physiology of digestion, through which knowledge on vital aspects of the subject has been transformed and enlarged."

**1905 Robert Koch** (Germany) Institute for Infectious Diseases "for his investigations and discoveries in relation to tuberculosis."

**1906 Camillo Golgi** (Italy) Pavia Univ., and **Santiago Ramon Y Cajal** (Spain) Madrid Univ. "in recognition of their work on the structure of the nervous system."

**1907 Charles L.A. Laveran** (France) Institut Pasteur "in recognition of his work on the role played by protozoa in causing diseases."

**1908 Il'ja I. Mecnikov** (Russia) Institut Pasteur (Paris), and **Paul Ehrlich** (Germany) Goettingen Univ. and Royal Institute for Experimental Therapy "in recognition of their work on immunity."

**1909 Emil T. Kocher** (Switzerland) Berne Univ. "for his work on the physiology, pathology, and surgery of the thyroid gland."

**1910 Albrecht Kossel** (Germany) Heidelberg Univ. "in recognition of the contributions to our knowledge of cell chemistry made through his work on proteins, including the nucleic substances."

**1911 Allvar Gullstrand** (Sweden) Uppsala Univ. "for his work on the dioptrics of the eye."

**1912 Alexis Carrel** (France) Rockefeller Institute for Medical Research (New York) "in recognition of his work on vascular suture and the transplantation of blood-vessels and organs."

**1913 Charles R. Richet** (France) Sorbonne Univ. "in recognition of his work on anaphylaxis."

**1914 Robert Bárány** (Austria) Vienna Univ. "for his work on the physiology and pathology of the vestibular apparatus."

**1915–18** No award.

**1919 Jules Bordet** (Belgium) Brussels Univ. "for his discoveries relating to immunity."

**1920 Schack A.S. Krough** (Denmark) Copenhagen Univ. "for his discovery of the capillary motor regulating mechanism."

**1921** No award.

**1922 Sir Archibald V. Hill** (Great Britain) London Univ. "for his discovery relating to the production of heat in the muscle";

**Otto F. Meyerhof** (Germany) Kiel Univ. "for his discovery of the fixed relationship between the consumption of oxygen and the metabolism of lactic acid in the muscle."

**1923 Sir Frederick B. Banting** (Canada) Toronto Univ., and **John J.R. Macleod** (Canada) Toronto Univ. "for the discovery of insulin."

**1924 Willem Einthoven** (Netherlands) Leyden Univ. "for his discovery of the mechanism of the electrocardiogram."

**1925** No award.

**1926 Johannes A.G. Fibiger** (Denmark) Copenhagen Univ. "for his discovery of the Spiroptera carcinoma."

**1927 Julius Wagner-Jauregg** (Austria) Vienna Univ. "for his discovery of the therapeutic value of malaria inoculation in the treatment of dementia paralytica."

**1928 Charles J.H. Nicolle** (France) Institut Pasteur "for his work on typhus."

**1929 Christiaan Eijkman** (Netherlands) Utrecht Univ. "for his discovery of the antineuritic vitamin"; **Sir Frederick G. Hopkins** (Great Britain) Cambridge Univ. "for his discovery of the growth-stimulating vitamins."

**1930 Karl Landsteiner** (Austria) Rockefeller Inst. for Medical Research (New York) "for his discovery of human blood groups."

**1931 Otto H. Warburg** (Germany) Kaiser-Wilhelm-Institut (now Max-Planck-Institut) "for his discovery of the nature and mode of action of the respiratory enzyme."

**1932 Sir Charles S. Sherrington** (Great Britain) Oxford Univ., and **Lord Edgar D. Adrian** (Great Britain) Cambridge Univ. "for their discoveries regarding the functions of neurons."

**1933 Thomas H. Morgan** (U.S.) California Institute of Technology "for his discoveries concerning the role played by the chromosome in heredity."

**1934 George H. Whipple** (U.S.) Rochester Univ., **George R. Minot** (U.S.) Harvard Univ., and **William P. Murphy** (U.S.) Harvard Univ. "for their discoveries concerning liver therapy in cases of anaemia."

**1935 Hans Spemann** (Germany) Univ. of Freiburg im Breisgau "for his discovery of the organizer effect in embryonic development."

**1936 Sir Henry H. Dale** (Great Britain) National Institute for Medical Research, and **Otto Loewi** (Austria) Graz Univ. "for their discoveries relating to chemical transmission of nerve impulses."

**1937 Albert Szent-Györgyi von Nagyrapolt** (Hungary) Szeged Univ. "for his discoveries in connection with the biological combustion processes, with special reference to vitamin C and the catalysis of fumaric acid."

**1938 Corneille J.F. Heymans** (Belgium) Ghent Univ. "for the discovery of the role played by the sinus and aortic mechanisms in the regulation of respiration."

**1939 Gerhard Domagk** (Germany) Munster

Univ. "for the discovery of the antibacterial effects of prontosil."

**1940–42** No award.

**1943 Henrik C.P. Dam** (Denmark) Polytechnic Institute "for his discovery of vitamin K"; **Edward A. Doisy** (U.S.) St. Louis Univ. "for his discovery of the chemical nature of vitamin K."

**1944 Joseph Erlanger** (U.S.) Washington Univ., and **Herbert S. Gasser** (U.S.) Rockefeller Institute for Medical Research "for their discoveries relating to the highly differentiated functions of single nerve fibres."

**1945 Sir Alexander Fleming** (Great Britain) London Univ., **Sir Ernst B. Chain** (Great Britain) Oxford Univ., and **Lord Howard W. Florey** (Great Britain) Oxford Univ. "for the discovery of penicillin and its curative effect in various infectious diseases."

**1946 Hermann J. Muller** (U.S.) Indiana Univ. "for the discovery of the production of mutations by means of X-ray irradiation."

**1947 Carl F. Cori** (U.S.) Washington Univ., and his wife **Gerty T. Cori** (U.S.) Washington Univ. "for their discovery of the course of the catalytic conversion of glycogen"; **Bernardo A. Houssay** (Argentina) Institute for Biology and Experimental Medicine "for his discovery of the part played by the hormone of the anterior pituitary lobe in the metabolism of sugar."

**1948 Paul H. Müller** (Switzerland) Laboratory of the J.R. Geigy Dye-Factory Co. "for his discovery of the high efficiency of DDT as a contact poison against several arthropods."

**1949 Walter R. Hess** (Switzerland) Zurich Univ. "for his discovery of the functional organization of the interbrain as a coordinator of the activities of the internal organs; **Antonio Caetano de Abreu F.E. Moniz** (Portugal) Univ. of Lisbon "for his discovery of the therapeutic value of leucotomy in certain psychoses."

**1950 Edward C. Kendall** (U.S.) Mayo Clinic, **Tadeus Reichstein** (Switzerland) Basel Univ., and **Philip S. Hench** (U.S.) Mayo Clinic "for their discoveries relating to the hormones of the adrenal cortex, their structure, and biological effects."

**1951 Max Theiler** (Union of South Africa) Laboratories Division of Medicine and Public Health, Rockefeller Foundation (New York) "for his discoveries concerning yellow fever and how to combat it."

**1952 Selman A. Waksman** (U.S.) Rutgers Univ. "for his discovery of streptomycin, the first antibiotic effective against tuberculosis."

**1953 Sir Hans A. Krebs** (Great Britain) Sheffield Univ. "for his discovery of the citric acid cycle"; **Fritz A. Lipmann** (U.S.) Harvard Medical School and Massachusetts General Hospital "for his discovery of co-enzyme A and its importance for intermediary metabolism."

**1954 John F. Enders** (U.S.) Harvard Medical School and Research Division of Infectious Diseases, Children's Medical Center; **Thomas H. Weller** (U.S.) Research Division of Infectious Diseases, Children's Medical Center; and **Frederick C. Robbins** (U.S.) Western Reserve Univ. "for their discovery of the ability of poliomyelitis viruses to grow in cultures of various types of tissue."

1955 **Axel H.T. Theorell** (Sweden) Nobel Medical Institute "for his discoveries concerning the nature and mode of action of oxidation enzymes."

1956 **Andre F. Cournand** (U.S.) Cardio-Pulmonary Laboratory, Columbia Univ. Division, Bellevue Hospital; **Werner Forssmann** (Germany) Mainz Univ. and Bad Kreuznach; and **Dickinson W. Richards** (U.S.) Columbia Univ. "for their discoveries concerning heart catheterization and pathological changes in the circulatory system."

1957 **Daniel Bovet** (Italy) Chief Institute of Public Health "for his discoveries relating to synthetic compounds that inhibit the action of certain body substances, and especially their action on the vascular system and the skeletal muscles."

1958 **George W. Beadle** (U.S.) California Institute of Technology, and **Edward L. Tatum** (U.S.) Rockefeller Institute for Medical Research "for their discovery that genes act by regulating definite chemical events"; **Joshua Lederberg** (U.S.) Wisconsin Univ. "for his discoveries concerning genetic recombination and the organization of the genetic material of bacteria."

1959 **Severo Ochoa** (U.S.) New York Univ., College of Medicine, and **Arthur Kornberg** (U.S.) Stanford Univ. "for their discovery of the mechanisms in the biological synthesis of ribonucleic acid and deoxyribonucleic acid."

1960 **Sir Frank M. Burnet** (Australia) Walter and Eliza Hall Institute for Medical Research, and **Sir Peter B. Medawar** (Great Britain) University College "for discovery of acquired immunological tolerance."

1961 **Georg von Békésy** (U.S.) Harvard Univ. "for his discoveries of the physical mechanism of stimulation within the cochlea."

1962 **Francis H.C. Crick** (Great Britain) Institute of Molecular Biology, **James D. Watson** (U.S.) Harvard Univ., and **Maurice H.F. Wilkins** (Great Britain) University of London "for their discoveries concerning the molecular structure of nuclear acids and its significance for information transfer in living material."

1963 **Sir John C. Eccles** (Australia) Australian National Univ., **Sir Alan L. Hodgkin** (Great Britain) Cambridge Univ., and **Sir Andrew F. Huxley** (Great Britain) University of London "for their discoveries concerning the ionic mechanisms involved in excitation and inhibition in the peripheral and central portions of the nerve cell membrane."

1964 **Konrad Bloch** (U.S.) Harvard Univ., and

**Feodor Lynen** (Germany) Max-Planck-Institut fur Zellchemie "for their discoveries concerning the mechanism and regulation of the cholesterol and fatty acid metabolism."

1965 **François Jacob** (France) Institut Pasteur, **André Lwoff** (France) Institut Pasteur, and **Jacques Monod** (France) Institut Pasteur "for their discoveries concerning genetic control of enzyme and virus synthesis."

1966 **Peyton Rous** (U.S.) Rockefeller Univ. "for his discovery of tumor-inducing viruses"; **Charles B. Huggins** (U.S.) Ben May Laboratory for Cancer Research, Univ. of Chicago "for his discoveries concerning hormonal treatment of prostatic cancer."

1967 **Ragnar Granit** (Sweden) Karolinska Institutet, **Haldan K. Hartline** (U.S.) The Rockefeller Univ., and **George Wald** (U.S.) Harvard Univ. "for their discoveries concerning the primary physiological and chemical visual processes in the eye."

1968 **Robert W. Holley** (U.S.) Cornell Univ., **Har G. Khorana** (U.S.) Univ. of Wisconsin, and **Marshall W. Nirenberg** (U.S.) National Institutes of Health "for their interpretation of the genetic code and its functions in protein synthesis."

1969 **Max Delbrück** (U.S.) California Institute of Technology, **Alfred D. Hershey** (U.S.) Carnegie Institution of Washington, and **Salvador Luria** (U.S.) M.I.T. "for their discoveries concerning the replication mechanism and the genetic structure of viruses."

1970 **Sir Bernard Katz** (Great Britain) University College, **Ulf von Euler** (Sweden) Karolinska Institutet, and **Julius Axelrod** (U.S.) National Institutes of Health "for their discoveries concerning the humoral transmitters in the nerve terminals and the mechanism for their storage, release, and inactivation."

1971 **Earl W. Sutherland, Jr.** (U.S.) Vanderbilt Univ. "for his discoveries concerning the mechanisms of the action of hormones."

1972 **Gerald M. Edelman** (U.S.) Rockefeller Univ., and **Rodney R. Porter** (Great Britain) Oxford Univ. "for their discoveries concerning the chemical structure of antibodies."

1973 **Karl von Frisch** (W. Germany) Zoologisches Institut der Universitat Munchen; **Konrad Lorenz** (Austria) Osterreichische Akademie der Wissenschaften, Institut fur vergleichende Verhaltensforschung; and **Nikolaas Tinbergen** (Great Britain) Dept. of Zoology, University Museum "for their discoveries concerning organization and elicitation of individual and social behavior patterns."

1974 **Albert Claude** (Belgium) Université Catholique de Louvain, **Christian de Duve** (Belgium) Rockefeller Univ. (New York), and **George E. Palade** (U.S.) Yale Univ. School of Medicine "for their discoveries concerning the structural and functional organization of the cell."

1975 **David Baltimore** (U.S.) M.I.T., **Renato Dulbecco** (U.S.) Imperial Cancer Research Fund Laboratory (London), and **Howard M. Temin** (U.S.) Univ. of Wisconsin "for their discoveries concerning the interaction between tumour viruses and the genetic material of the cell."

1976 **Baruch S. Blumberg** (U.S.) The Institute for Cancer Research, and **D. Carleton Gajdusek** (U.S.) National Institutes of Health "for their discoveries concerning new mechanisms for the origin and dissemination of infectious diseases."

1977 **Roger Guillemin** (U.S.) The Salk Institute, and **Andrew V. Schally** (U.S.) Veterans Administration Hospital, New Orleans "for their discoveries concerning the peptide hormone production of the brain"; **Rosalyn Yalow** (U.S.) Veterans Administration Hospital, Bronx "for the development of radioimmunoassays of peptide hormones."

1978 **Werner Arber** (Switzerland) Biozentrum der Universitat, **Daniel Nathans** (U.S.) Johns Hopkins Univ. School of Medicine, and **Hamilton O. Smith** (U.S.) Johns Hopkins Univ. School of Medicine "for the discovery of restriction enzymes and their application to problems of molecular genetics."

1979 **Allan M. Cormack** (U.S.) Tufts Univ., and **Sir Godfrey N. Hounsfield** (Great Britain) "for the development of computer-assisted tomography."

1980 **Baruj Benacerraf** (U.S.) Harvard Medical School; **Jean Dausset** (France) Université de Paris, Laboratoire Immuno-Hemetologie; and **George D. Snell** (U.S.) Jackson Laboratory "for their discoveries concerning genetically determined structures on the cell surface that regulate immunological reactions."

1981 **Roger W. Sperry** (U.S.) California Institute of Technology "for his discoveries concerning the functional specialization of the cerebral hemispheres"; **David H. Hubel** (U.S.) Harvard Medical School, and **Torsten N. Wiesel** (Sweden) Harvard Medical School "for their discoveries concerning information processing in the visual system."

1982 **Sune K. Bergström** (Sweden) Karolinska Institutet, **Bengt I. Samuelsson** (Sweden) Karolinska Institute, and **Sir John R. Vane** (Great Britain) The Wellcome Research Laboratories "for their discoveries concerning prostaglandins and related biologically active substances."

1983 **Barbara McClintock** (U.S.) Cold Spring Harbor Laboratory "for her discovery of mobile genetic elements."

1984 **Niels K. Jerne** (Denmark) Basel Institute for Immunology (Basel, Switzerland), **Georges J.F. Köhler** (W. Germany) Basel Institute for Immunology, and **César Milstein** (Great Britain and Argentina) Medical Research Council Laboratory of Molecular Biology (Cambridge) "for theories concerning the specificity in development and control of the immune system and the discovery of the principle for production of monoclonal antibodies."

**1985 Michael S. Brown** (U.S.) Univ. of Texas Health Science Center at Dallas, and **Joseph L. Goldstein** (U.S.) Univ. of Texas Health Science Center at Dallas "for their discoveries concerning the regulation of cholesterol metabolism."

**1986 Stanley Cohen** (U.S.) Vanderbilt Univ. School of Medicine, and **Rita Levi-Montalcini** (Italy and U.S.) Institute of Cell Biology of the C.N.R. (Rome) "for their discoveries of growth factors."

**1987 Susumu Tonegawa** (U.S.) M.I.T. "for discovery of the genetic principle for generation of antibody diversity."

**1988 Sir James W. Black** (United Kingdom) King's College Hospital Medical School, **Gertrude B. Elion** (U.S.) Wellcome Research Laboratories, and **George H. Hitchings** (U.S.) Wellcome Research Laboratories "for their discoveries of Important Principles for Drug Treatment."

**1989 J. Michael Bishop** and **Harold E. Varmus** (U.S.) Univ. of California School of Medicine, San Francisco "for their discovery of 'The Cellular Origin of Retroviral Oncogenes.'"

**1990 Joseph E. Murray** (U.S.) Brigham and Women's Hospital, Boston, who performed the first kidney transplant (1954), and **E. Donnall Thomas** (U.S.), Fred Hutchinson Cancer Research Center, Seattle, who performed the first successful bone marrow transplant between two people who were not twins (1970).

## NOBEL PRIZES IN ECONOMIC SCIENCES

**1969 Ragnar Frisch** (Norway) Oslo Univ., and **Jan Tinbergen** (Netherlands) The Netherlands School of Economics "for having developed and applied dynamic models for the analysis of economic processes."

**1970 Paul A. Samuelson** (U.S.) M.I.T. "for the scientific work through which he has developed static and dynamic economic theory and actively contributed to raising the level of analysis in economic science."

**1971 Simon Kuznets** (U.S.) Harvard Univ. "for his empirically founded interpretation of economic growth which has led to new and deepened insight into the economic and social structure and process of development."

**1972 Sir John R. Hicks** (Great Britain) All Souls College, and **Kenneth J. Arrow** (U.S.) Harvard Univ. "for their pioneering contributions to general economic equilibrium theory and welfare theory."

**1973 Wassily Leontief** (U.S.) Harvard Univ. "for the development of the input-output method and for its application to important economic problems."

**1974 Gunnar Myrdal** (Sweden), **Friedrich A. von Hayek** (Great Britain) "for their pioneering work in the theory of money and economic fluctuations and for their penetrating analysis of the interdependence of economic, social and institutional phenomena."

**1975 Leonid Kantorovich** (USSR) Academy of Sciences, and **Tjalling C. Koopmans** (U.S.) Yale Univ. "for their contributions to the theory of optimum allocation of resources."

**1976 Milton Friedman** (U.S.) Univ. of Chicago "for his achievements in the fields of consumption analysis, monetary history and theory, and for his demonstration of the complexity of stabilization policy."

**1977 Bertil Ohlin** (Sweden) Stockholm School of Economics, and **James E. Meade** (Great Britain) Cambridge Univ. "for their pathbreaking contribution to the theory of international trade and international capital movements."

**1978 Herbert A. Simon** (U.S.) Carnegie-Mellon Univ. "for his pioneering research into the decision-making process within economic organizations."

**1979 Theodore W. Schultz** (U.S.) Univ. of Chicago, and **Sir Arthur Lewis** (Great Britain) Princeton Univ. "for their pioneering research into economic development research with particular consideration of the problems of developing countries."

**1980 Lawrence R. Klein** (U.S.) Univ. of Pennsylvania "for the creation of economic models and their application to the analysis of economic fluctuations and economic policies."

**1981 James Tobin** (U.S.) Yale Univ. "for his analysis of financial markets and their relations to expenditure decisions, employment, production, and prices."

**1982 George J. Stigler** (U.S.) Univ. of Chicago "for his seminal studies of industrial structures, functioning of markets, and causes and effects of public regulation."

**1983 Gerard Debreu** (U.S.) University of California, Berkeley "for having incorporated new analytical methods into economic theory and for his rigorous reformulation of the theory of general equilibrium."

**1984 Sir Richard Stone** (Great Britain) Cambridge Univ. "for having made fundamental contributions to the development of systems of national accounts and hence greatly improved [sic] the basis for empirical economic analysis."

**1985 Franco Modigliani** (U.S.) M.I.T. "for his pioneering analyses of saving and of financial markets."

**1986 James M. Buchanan, Jr.** (U.S.) Center for Study of Public Choice "for his development of the contractual and constitutional bases for the theory of economic and political decision-making."

**1987 Robert M. Solow** (U.S.) M.I.T. "for his contributions to the theory of economic growth."

**1988 Maurice Allais** (France) Centre d'analyse économique "for his pioneering contributions to the theory of markets and efficient utilization of resources."

**1989 Trygve Haavelmo** (Norway) Univ. of Oslo "for his clarification of the probability theory foundations of econometrics and his analyses of simultaneous economic structures."

**1990 Harry Markowitz** (U.S.) Baruch College of City Univ. of New York, for his Portfolio Theory; **William F. Sharpe** (U.S.) Stanford Univ., for his Capital Asset Pricing Model; and **Merton Miller** (U.S.) Univ. of Chicago, for his work on the Miller-Modigliani Theory. Taken together, their work revolutionized the financial and business industries.

## NOBEL PRIZES IN CHEMISTRY

**1901 Jacobus H. Van't Hoff** (Netherlands) Berlin Univ. (Germany) "in recognition of the extraordinary services he has rendered by the discovery of the laws of chemical dynamics and osmotic pressure in solutions."

**1902 Hermann E. Fischer** (Germany) Berlin Univ. "in recognition of the extraordinary services he has rendered by his work on sugar and purine syntheses."

**1903 Svante A. Arrhenius** (Sweden) Stockholm Univ. "in recognition of the extraordinary services he has rendered to the advancement of chemistry by his electrolytic theory of dissociation."

**1904 Sir William Ramsay** (Great Britain) London Univ. "in recognition of his services in the discovery of the inert gaseous elements in air, and his determination of their place in the periodic system."

**1905 Johann F.W.A. von Baeyer** (Germany) Munich Univ. "in recognition of his services in the advancement of organic chemistry and the chemical industry, through his work on organic dyes and hydroaromatic compounds."

**1906 Henri Moissan** (France) Sorbonne Univ. "in recognition of the great services rendered by him in his investigation and isolation of the element fluorine, and for the adoption in the service of science of the electric furnace called after him."

**1907 Eduard Buchner** (Germany) Agricultural College "for his biochemical researches and his discovery of cell-free fermentation."

**1908 Lord Ernest Rutherford** (Great Britain) Victoria Univ. "for his investigations into the disintegration of the elements, and the chemistry of radioactive substances."

**1909 Wilhelm Ostwald** (Germany) Leipzig Univ. "in recognition of his work on catalysis, and for his investigations into the fundamental principles governing chemical equilibria and rates of reaction."

**1910 Otto Wallach** (Germany) Goettingen Univ. "in recognition of his services to organic chemistry and the chemical industry by his pioneer work in the field of alicyclic compounds."

**1911 Marie Curie** (France) Sorbonne Univ. "in recognition of her services to the advancement of chemistry by the discovery of the elements radium and polonium, by the isolation of radium and the study of the nature and compounds of this remarkable element."

**1912 Victor Grignard** (France) Nancy Univ. "for the discovery of the so-called Grignard reagent, which in recent years has greatly advanced the progress of organic chemistry"; **Paul Sabatier** (France) Toulouse Univ. "for his method of hydrogenating organic compounds in the presence of finely disintegrated metals whereby the progress of organic chemistry has been greatly advanced in recent years."

**1913 Alfred Werner** (Switzerland) Zurich Univ. "in recognition of his work on the linkage of atoms in molecules by which he has thrown new light on earlier investigations and opened up new fields of research especially in inorganic chemistry."

**1914 Theodore W. Richards** (U.S.) Harvard Univ. "in recognition of his accurate determinations of the atomic weight of a large number of chemical elements."

**1915 Richard M. Willstätter** (Germany) Munich Univ. "for his researches on plant pigments, especially chlorophyll."

**1916–17** No award.

**1918 Fritz Haber** (Germany) Kaiser-Wilhelm-Institut (now Fritz-Haber-Institut) "for the synthesis of ammonia from its elements."

**1919** No award.

**1920 Walther H. Nernst** (Germany) Berlin Univ. "in recognition of his work in thermochemistry."

**1921 Frederick Soddy** (Great Britain) Oxford Univ. "for his contributions to our knowledge of the chemistry of radioactive substances, and his investigations into the origin and nature of isotopes."

**1922 Francis W. Aston** (Great Britain) Cambridge Univ. "for his discovery, by means of his mass spectrograph, of isotopes in a large number of nonradioactive elements, and for his enunciation of the whole-number rule."

**1923 Fritz Pregl** (Austria) Graz Univ. "for his invention of the method of microanalysis of organic substances."

**1924** No award.

**1925 Richard A. Zsigmondy** (Germany) Goettingen Univ. "for his demonstration of the heterogeneous nature of colloid solutions and for the methods he used, which have since become fundamental in modern colloid chemistry."

**1926 The (Theodor) Svedberg** (Sweden) Uppsala Univ. "for his work on disperse systems."

**1927 Heinrich O. Wieland** (Germany) Munich Univ. "for his investigations of the constitution of the bile acids and related substances."

**1928 Adolf O.R. Windaus** (Germany) Goettingen Univ. "for the services rendered through his research into the constitution of the sterols and their connection with the vitamins."

**1929 Sir Arthur Harden** (Great Britain) London Univ., **Hans K.A. von Euler-Chelpin** (Sweden) Stockholm Univ. "for their in-

vestigations on the fermentation of sugar and fermentative enzymes."

**1930 Hans Fischer** (Germany) Institute of Technology "for his researches into the constitution of haemin and chlorophyll, and especially for his synthesis of haemin."

**1931 Carl Bosch** (Germany) Heidelberg Univ. and I.G. Farbenindustrie A.G., and **Friedrich Bergius** (Germany) Heidelberg Univ. and I.G. Farbenindustrie A.G. "in recognition of their contributions to the invention and development of chemical high pressure methods."

**1932 Irving Langmuir** (U.S.) General Electric Co. "for his discoveries and investigations in surface chemistry."

**1933** No award.

**1934 Harold C. Urey** (U.S.) Columbia Univ. "for his discovery of heavy hydrogen."

**1935 Frédéric Joliot** (France) Institut du Radium, and his wife **Irène Joliot-Curie** (France) Institut du Radium "in recognition of their synthesis of new radioactive elements."

**1936 Petrus (Peter) J.W. Debye** (Netherlands) Berlin Univ. and Kaiser-Wilhelm-Institut (now Max-Planck-Institut) für Physik (Berlin-Dahlem) "for his contributions to our knowledge of molecular structure through his investigations on dipole moments and on the diffraction of X-rays and electrons in gases."

**1937 Sir Walter N. Haworth** (Great Britain) Birmingham Univ. "for his investigations on carbohydrates and vitamin C"; **Paul Karrer** (Switzerland) Zurich Univ. "for his investigations on carotenoids, flavins, and vitamins A and B-2."

**1938 Richard Kuhn** (Germany) Heidelberg Univ. and Kaiser-Wilhelm-Institut (now Max-Planck-Institut) für Medizinische Forschung "for his work on carotenoids and vitamins." (Compelled by the authorities of his country to decline the award, but later received the diploma and the medal.)

**1939 Adolf F.J. Butenandt** (Germany) Berlin Univ. and Kaiser-Wilhelm-Institut (now Max-Planck-Institut) für Biochemie "for his work on sex hormones." (Compelled by the authorities of his country to decline the award, but later received the diploma and the medal); **Leopold Ruzicka** (Switzerland) Federal Institute of Technology "for his work on polymethylenes and higher terpenes."

**1940–42** No award.

**1943 George de Hevesy** (Hungary) Stockholm Univ. (Sweden) "for his work on the use of isotopes as tracers in the study of chemical processes."

**1944 Otto Hahn** (Germany) Kaiser-Wilhelm-Institut (now Max-Planck-Institut) für Chemie "for his discovery of the fission of heavy nuclei."

**1945 Artturi I. Virtanen** (Finland) Helsinki Univ. "for his research and inventions in agricultural and nutrition chemistry, especially for his fodder preservation method."

**1946 James B. Sumner** (U.S.) Cornell Univ. "for his discovery that enzymes can be crystallized"; **John H. Northrop** (U.S.) Rockefeller Institute for Medical Research, and **Wendell M. Stanley** (U.S.) Rockefeller Institute for Medical Research "for their preparation of enzymes and virus proteins in a pure form."

**1947 Sir Robert Robinson** (Great Britain) Oxford Univ. "for his investigations on plant products of biological importance, especially the alkaloids."

**1948 Arne W.K. Tiselius** (Sweden) Uppsala Univ. "for his research on electrophoresis and adsorption analysis, especially for his discoveries concerning the complex nature of the serum proteins."

**1949 William F. Giauque** (U.S.) Univ. of California, Berkeley "for his contributions in the field of chemical thermodynamics, particularly concerning the behavior of substances at extremely low temperatures."

**1950 Otto P.H. Diels** (Germany) Kiel Univ., and **Kurt Alder** (Germany) Cologne Univ. "for their discovery and development of the diene synthesis."

**1951 Edwin M. McMillan** (U.S.) Univ. of California, Berkeley, and **Glenn T. Seaborg** (U.S.) Univ. of California, Berkeley "for their discoveries in the chemistry of the transuranium elements."

**1952 Archer J.P. Martin** (Great Britain) National Institute for Medical Research, and **Richard L.M. Synge** (Great Britain) Rowett Research Institute (Scotland) "for their invention of partition chromatography."

**1953 Hermann Staudinger** (Germany) State Research Institute for Macromolecular Chemistry "for his discoveries in the field of macromolecular chemistry."

**1954 Linus C. Pauling** (U.S.) California Institute of Technology "for his research into the nature of the chemical bond and its application to the elucidation of the structure of complex substances."

**1955 Vincent du Vigneaud** (U.S.) Cornell Univ. "for his work on biochemically important sulphur compounds, especially for the first synthesis of a polypeptide hormone."

**1956 Sir Cyril N. Hinshelwood** (Great Britain) Oxford Univ., and **Nikolaj N. Semenov** (USSR) Institute for Chemical Physics of the Academy of Sciences of the USSR "for their researches into the mechanism of chemical reactions."

**1957 Lord Alexander R. Todd** (Great Britain) Cambridge Univ. "for his work on nucleotides and nucleotide co-enzymes."

**1958 Frederick Sanger** (Great Britain) Cambridge Univ. "for his work on the structure of proteins, especially that of insulin."

**1959 Jaroslav Heyrovsky** (Czechoslovakia) Polarographic Institute of the Czechoslovak Academy of Science "for his discovery and development of the polarographic methods of analysis."

**1960 Willard F. Libby** (U.S.) Univ. of California,

Los Angeles "for his method to use carbon-14 for age determination in archaeology, geology, geophysics, and other branches of science."

**1961 Melvin Calvin** (U.S.) Univ. of California, Berkeley "for his research on the carbon dioxide assimilation in plants."

**1962 Max F. Perutz** (Great Britain) Laboratory of Molecular Biology, and **Sir John C. Kendrew** (Great Britain) Laboratory of Molecular Biology "for their studies of the structures of globular proteins."

**1963 Karl Ziegler** (Germany) Max-Planck-Institut for Carbon Research, and **Giulio Natta** (Italy) Institute of Technology "for their discoveries in the field of the chemistry and technology of high polymers."

**1964 Dorothy C. Hodgkin** (Great Britain) Royal Society, Oxford Univ. "for her determinations by X-ray techniques of the structures of important biochemical substances."

**1965 Robert B. Woodward** (U.S.) Harvard Univ. "for his outstanding achievements in the art of organic synthesis."

**1966 Robert S. Mulliken** (U.S.) Univ. of Chicago "for his fundamental work concerning chemical bonds and the electronic structure of molecules by the molecular orbital method."

**1967 Manfred Eigen** (W. Germany) Max-Planck-Institut für Physikalische Chemie, **Ronald G.W. Norrish** (Great Britain) Institute of Physical Chemistry, and **Sir George Porter** (Great Britain) The Royal Institution "for their studies of extremely fast chemical reactions, effected by disturbing the equilibrium by means of very short pulses of energy."

**1968 Lars Onsager** (U.S.) Yale Univ. "for the discovery of the reciprocal relations bearing his name, which are fundamental for the thermodynamics of irreversible processes."

**1969 Sir Derek H.R. Barton** (Great Britain) Imperial College of Science and Technology, and **Odd Hassel** (Norway) Kjemisk Institut "for their contributions to the development of the concept of conformation and its application in chemistry."

**1970 Luis F. Leloir** (Argentina) Institute for Biochemical Research "for his discovery of sugar nucleotides and their role in the biosynthesis of carbohydrates."

**1971 Gerhard Herzberg** (Canada) National Research Council of Canada "for his contributions to the knowledge of electronic structure and geometry of molecules, particularly free radicals."

**1972 Christian B. Anfinsen** (U.S.) National Institutes of Health "for his work on ribonuclease, especially concerning the connection between the amino acid sequence and the biologically active conformation"; **Stanford Moore** (U.S.) Rockefeller Univ., and **William H. Stein** (U.S.) Rockefeller Univ. "for their contribution to the understanding of the connection between chemical structure and catalytic activity of the active center of the ribonuclease molecule."

**1973 Ernst O. Fischer** (W. Germany) Technical Univ. of Munich, and **Sir Geoffrey Wilkinson** (Great Britain) Imperial College "for their pioneering work, performed independently, on the chemistry of the organometallic, so-called sandwich compounds."

**1974 Paul J. Flory** (U.S.) Stanford Univ. "for his fundamental achievements, both theoretical and experimental, in the physical chemistry of the macromolecules."

**1975 Sir John W. Cornforth** (Australia and Great Britain) Univ. of Sussex "for his work on the stereochemistry of enzyme-catalyzed reactions"; **Vladimir Prelog** (Switzerland) Eidgenossische Technische Hochschule "for his research into the stereochemistry of organic molecules and reactions."

**1976 William N. Lipscomb** (U.S.) Harvard Univ. "for his studies on the structure of boranes illuminating problems of chemical bonding."

**1977 Ilya Prigogine** (Belgium) Université Libre de Bruxelles, (Univ. of Texas, U.S.) "for his contributions to nonequilibrium thermodynamics, particularly the theory of dissipative structures."

**1978 Peter D. Mitchell** (Great Britain) Glynn Research Laboratories "for his contribution to the understanding of biological energy transfer through the formulation of the chemiosmotic theory."

**1979 Herbert C. Brown** (U.S.) Purdue Univ., and **Georg Wittig** (Germany) Univ. of Heidelberg "for their development of the use of boron- and phosphorus-containing compounds, respectively, into important reagents in organic synthesis."

**1980 Paul Berg** (U.S.) Stanford Univ. "for his fundamental studies of the biochemistry of nucleic acids, with particular regard to recombinant-DNA"; **Walter Gilbert** (U.S.) Biological Laboratories, and **Frederick Sanger** (Great Britain) MRC Laboratory of Molecular Biology "for their contributions concerning the determination of base sequences in nucleic acids."

**1981 Kenichi Fukui** (Japan) Kyoto Univ., and **Roald Hoffmann** (U.S.) Cornell Univ. "for their theories, developed independently, concerning the course of chemical reactions."

**1982 Aaron Klug** (Great Britain) MRC Laboratory of Molecular Biology "for his development of crystallographic electron microscopy and his structural elucidation of biologically important nucleic acid-protein complexes."

**1983 Henry Taube** (U.S.) Stanford Univ. "for his work on the mechanisms of electron transfer reactions, especially in metal complexes."

**1984 Robert B. Merrifield** (U.S.) Rockefeller Univ. "for his development of methodology for chemical synthesis on a solid matrix."

**1985 Herbert A. Hauptman** (U.S.) The Medical Foundation of Buffalo, and **Jerome Karle** (U.S.) U.S. Naval Research Laboratory

"for their outstanding achievements in the development of direct methods for the determination of crystal structures."

**1986 Dudley R. Herschbach** (U.S.) Harvard Univ., **Yuan T. Lee** (U.S.) Univ. of California, Berkeley, and **John C. Polanyi** (Canada) Univ. of Toronto "for their contributions concerning the dynamics of chemical elementary processes."

**1987 Donald J. Cram** (U.S.) Univ. of California, Los Angeles, **Jean-Marie Lehn** (France) Université Louis Pasteur, and **Charles J. Pedersen** (U.S.) Du Pont Laboratory "for their development and use of molecules with structure-specific interactions of high selectivity."

**1988 Johann Deisenhofer** (U.S.) Howard Hughes Medical Institute, **Robert Huber** (W. Germany) Max-Planck-Institut für Biochemie, and **Hartmut Michel** (W. Germany) Max-Planck-Institut für Biophysik "for the determination of the three-dimensional structure of a photosynthetic reaction centre."

**1989 Sidney Altman** (U.S.) Yale Univ., and **Thomas Cech** (U.S.) Univ. of Colorado "for their discovery of the catalytic properties of RNA." (They worked independently.)

**1990 Elias James Coret** (U.S.) Harvard Univ., for developing new ways to synthesize complex molecules ordinarily found in nature, work that has contributed to "the high standard of living and health, and the longevity enjoyed at least in the Western world."

# NOBEL PRIZES IN PHYSICS

**1901 Wilhelm C. Rüntgen** (Germany) Munich Univ. "in recognition of the extraordinary services he has rendered by the discovery of the remarkable rays subsequently named after him."

**1902 Hendrik A. Lorentz** (Netherlands) Leyden Univ., and **Pieter Zeeman** (Netherlands) Amsterdam Univ. "in recognition of the extraordinary service they rendered by their researches into the influence of magnetism upon radiation phenomena."

**1903 Antoine H. Becquerel** (France) Ecole Polytechnique "in recognition of the extraordinary services he has rendered by his discovery of spontaneous radioactivity"; **Pierre Curie** (French) Municipal School of Industrial Physics and Chemistry, and his wife **Marie Curie** (France [born in Poland]) "in recognition of the extraordinary services they have rendered by their joint researches on the radiation phenomena discovered by Professor Henri Becquerel."

**1904 Lord Rayleigh (John W. Strutt)** (Great Britain) Royal Institution of Great Britain "for his investigations of the densities of the most important gases and for his discovery of argon in connection with these studies."

**1905 Philipp E.A. Lenard** (Germany) Kiel

Univ. "for his work on cathode rays."

**1906 Sir Joseph J. Thomson** (Great Britain) Cambridge Univ. "in recognition of the great merits of his theoretical and experimental investigations on the conduction of electricity by gases."

**1907 Albert A. Michelson** (U.S.) Univ. of Chicago "for his optical precision instruments and the spectroscopic and metrological investigations carried out with their aid."

**1908 Gabriel Lippmann** (France) Sorbonne Univ. "for his method of reproducing colours photographically based on the phenomenon of interference."

**1909 Guglielmo Marconi** (Italy) Marconi Wireless Telegraph Co., Ltd., and **Carl F. Braun** (Germany) Strasbourg Univ. "in recognition of their contributions to the development of wireless telegraphy."

**1910 Johannes D. van der Waals** (Netherlands) Amsterdam Univ. "for his work on the equation of state for gases and liquids."

**1911 Wilhelm Wien** (Germany) Würzburg Univ. "for his discoveries regarding the laws governing the radiation of heat."

**1912 Nils G. Dalén** (Sweden) Swedish Gas-Accumulator Co. "for his invention of automatic regulators for use in conjunction with gas accumulators for illuminating lighthouses and buoys."

**1913 Heike Kamerlingh-Onnes** (Netherlands) Leyden Univ. "for his investigations on the properties of matter at low temperatures which led, inter alia, to the production of liquid helium."

**1914 Max von Laue** (Germany) Frankfurt-am-Main Univ. "for his discovery of the diffraction of X-rays by crystals."

**1915 Sir William Henry Bragg** (Great Britain) London Univ., and his son **Sir William Lawrence Bragg** (Great Britain) Victoria Univ. "for their services in the analysis of crystal structure by means of X-rays."

**1916** No award.

**1917 Charles G. Barkla** (Great Britain) Edinburgh Univ. "for his discovery of the characteristic Röntgen radiation of the elements."

**1918 Max K.E.L. Planck** (Germany) Berlin Univ. "in recognition of the services he rendered to the advancement of Physics by his discovery of energy quanta."

**1919 Johannes Stark** (Germany) Greifswald Univ. "for his discovery of the Doppler effect in canal rays and the splitting of spectral lines in electric fields."

**1920 Charles E. Guillaume** (Switzerland) International Bureau of Weights and Measures "in recognition of the service he has rendered to precision measurements in physics by his discovery of anomalies in nickel steel alloys."

**1921 Albert Einstein** (Germany) Kaiser-Wilhelm-Institut für Physik (now Max-Planck-Institut) "for his services to theoretical physics, and especially for his discovery of the law of the photoelectric effect."

**1922 Niels Bohr** (Denmark) Copenhagen Univ.

"for his services in the investigation of the structure of atoms and of the radiation emanating from them."

**1923 Robert A. Millikan** (U.S.) California Institute of Technology "for his work on the elementary charge of electricity and on the photoelectric effect."

**1924 Karl M.G. Siegbahn** (Sweden) Uppsala Univ. "for his discoveries and research in the field of X-ray spectroscopy."

**1925 James Franck** (Germany) Goettingen Univ., and **Gustav Hertz** (Germany) Halle Univ. "for their discovery of the laws governing the impact of an electron upon an atom."

**1926 Jean B. Perrin** (France) Sorbonne Univ. "for his work on the discontinuous structure of matter, and especially for his discovery of sedimentation equilibrium."

**1927 Arthur H. Compton** (U.S.) Univ. of Chicago "for his discovery of the effect named after him"; **Charles T.R. Wilson** (Great Britain) Cambridge Univ. "for his method of making the paths of electrically charged particles visible by condensation of vapour."

**1928 Sir Owen W. Richardson** (Great Britain) London Univ. "for his work on the thermionic phenomenon and especially for the discovery of the law named after him."

**1929 Prince Louis-Victor de Broglie** (France) Sorbonne Univ. "for his discovery of the wave nature of electrons."

**1930 Sir Chandrasekhara V. Raman** (India) Calcutta Univ. "for his work on the scattering of light and for the discovery of the effect named after him."

**1931** No award.

**1932 Werner Heisenberg** (Germany) Leipzig Univ. "for the creation of quantum mechanics, the application of which, has, inter alia, led to the discovery of the allotropic forms of hydrogen."

**1933 Erwin Schrödinger** (Austria) Berlin Univ., and **Paul A.M. Dirac** (Great Britain) Cambridge Univ. "for the discovery of new productive forms of atomic theory."

**1934** No award.

**1935 Sir James Chadwick** (Great Britain) Liverpool Univ. "for his discovery of the neutron."

**1936 Victor F. Hess** (Austria) Innsbruck Univ. "for his discovery of cosmic radiation"; **Carl D. Anderson** (U.S.) California Institute of Technology "for his discovery of the positron."

**1937 Clinton J. Davisson** (U.S.) Bell Telephone Laboratories, and **Sir George P. Thomson** (Great Britain) London Univ. "for their experimental discovery of the diffraction of electrons by crystals."

**1938 Enrico Fermi** (Italy) Rome Univ. "for his demonstrations of the existence of new radioactive elements produced by neutron irradiation, and for his related discovery of nuclear reactions brought about by slow neutrons."

**1939 Ernest O. Lawrence** (U.S.) Univ. of California, Berkeley "for the invention and

development of the cyclotron and for results obtained with it, especially with regard to artificial radioactive elements."

**1940–42** No award.

**1943 Otto Stern** (U.S.) Carnegie Institute of Technology (now Carnegie Mellon Univ.) "for his contribution to the development of the molecular ray method and his discovery of the magnetic moment of the proton."

**1944 Isidor I. Rabi** (U.S.) Columbia Univ. "for his resonance method for recording the magnetic properties of atomic nuclei."

**1945 Wolfgang Pauli** (Austria) Princeton Univ. "for the discovery of the Exclusion Principle, also called the Pauli Principle."

**1946 Percy W. Bridgman** (U.S.) Harvard Univ. "for the invention of an apparatus to produce extremely high pressures, and for the discoveries he made therewith in the field of high-pressure physics."

**1947 Sir Edward V. Appleton** (Great Britain) Dept. of Scientific and Industrial Research "for his investigations of the physics of the upper atmosphere, especially for the discovery of the so-called Appleton layer."

**1948 Lord Patrick M.S. Blackett** (Great Britain) Victoria Univ. "for his development of the Wilson cloud chamber method, and his discoveries therewith in the fields of nuclear physics and cosmic radiation."

**1949 Hideki Yukawa** (Japan) Kyoto Imperial Univ. and Columbia Univ. "for his prediction of the existence of mesons on the basis of theoretical work on nuclear forces."

**1950 Cecil F. Powell** (Great Britain) Bristol Univ. "for his development of the photographic method of studying nuclear processes and his discoveries regarding mesons made with this method."

**1951 Sir John D. Cockcroft** (Great Britain) Atomic Energy Research Establishment, and **Ernest T.S. Walton** (Ireland) Dublin Univ. "for their pioneer work on the transmutation of atomic nuclei by artifically accelerated atomic particles."

**1952 Felix Block** (U.S.) Stanford Univ., and **Edward M. Purcell** (U.S.) Harvard Univ. "for their development of new methods for nuclear magnetic precision measurements and discoveries in connection therewith."

**1953 Frits (Frederik) Zernike** (Netherlands) Groningen Univ. "for his demonstration of the phase contrast method, especially for his invention of the phase contrast microscope."

**1954 Max Born** (Great Britain) Edinburgh Univ. "for his fundamental research in quantum mechanics, especially for his statistical interpretation of the wave-function"; **Walther Bothe** (Germany) Heidelberg Univ., Max-Planck-Institut "for the coincidence method and his discoveries made therewith."

**1955 Willis E. Lamb** (U.S.) Stanford Univ. "for his discoveries concerning the fine structure of the hydrogen spectrum"; **Polykarp Kusch** (U.S.) Columbia Univ. "for his precision determination of the magnetic moment of the electron."

**1956 William Shockley** (U.S.) Semiconductor Laboratory of Beckman Instruments, Inc., **John Bardeen** (U.S.) Univ. of Illinois, and **Walter H. Brattain** (U.S.) Bell Telephone Laboratories "for their researches on semiconductors and their discovery of the transistor effect."

**1957 Chen N. Yang** (China) Institute for Advanced Study (Princeton, N.J.), and **Tsung-Dao Lee** (China) Columbia Univ. "for their penetrating investigation of the so-called parity laws which has led to important discoveries regarding the elementary particles."

**1958 Pavel A. Cherenkov** (USSR) Physics Institute of USSR Academy of Sciences, **Il'ja M. Frank** (USSR) Univ. of Moscow and Physics Institute of USSR Academy of Sciences, and **Igor J. Tamm** (USSR) Univ. of Moscow and Physics Institute of USSR Academy of Sciences "for the discovery and the interpretation of the Cherenkov effect."

**1959 Emilio G. Segrè** (U.S.) Univ. of California, Berkeley, and **Owen Chamberlain** (U.S.) Univ. of California, Berkeley "for their discovery of the antiproton."

**1960 Donald A. Glaser** (U.S.) Univ. of California, Berkeley "for the invention of the bubble chamber."

**1961 Robert Hofstadter** (U.S.) Stanford Univ. "for his pioneering studies of electron scattering in atomic nuclei and for his thereby achieved discoveries concerning the structure of the nucleons"; **Rudolf L. Mössbauer** (Germany) Technische Hochschule (Munich), and California Institute of Technology "for his researches concerning the resonance absorption of gamma radiation and his discovery in this connection of the effect which bears his name."

**1962 Lev D. Landau** (USSR) Academy of Sciences "for his pioneering theories for condensed matter, especially liquid helium."

**1963 Eugene P. Wigner** (U.S.) Princeton Univ. "for his contributions to the theory of the atomic nucleus and the elementary particles, particularly through the discovery and application of fundamental symmetry principles"; **Maria Goeppert-Mayer** (U.S.) Univ. of California, La Jolla, and **J. Hans D. Jensen** (Germany) Univ. of Heidelberg "for their discoveries concerning nuclear shell structure."

**1964 Charles H. Townes** (U.S.) M.I.T., and **Nikolai G. Basov** (USSR) Lebedev Institute for Physics, and **Aleksandre M. Prochorov** (USSR) Lebedev Institute for Physics "for fundamental work in the field of quantum electronics, which has led to the construction of oscillators and amplifiers based on the maser-laser-principle."

**1965 Sin-Itiro Tomonaga** (Japan) Tokyo Univ. of Education, **Julian Schwinger** (U.S.) Harvard Univ., and **Richard Feynman**

(U.S.) California Institute of Technology "for their fundamental work in quantum electrodynamics, with deep-ploughing consequences for the physics of elementary particles."

**1966 Alfred Kastler** (France) Ecole Normale Supérieure, Université de Paris "for the discovery and development of optical methods for studying hertzian resonances in atoms."

**1967 Hans A. Bethe** (U.S.) Cornell Univ. "for his contributions to the theory of nuclear reactions, especially his discoveries concerning the energy production in stars."

**1968 Luis W. Alvarez** (U.S.) Univ. of California, Berkeley "for his decisive contributions to elementary particle physics, in particular the discovery of a large number of resonance states, made possible through his development of the technique of using hydrogen bubble chamber and data analysis."

**1969 Murray Gell-Mann** (U.S.) California Institute of Technology "for his contributions and discoveries concerning the classification of elementary particles and their interactions."

**1970 Hannes Alfvén** (Sweden) Royal Institute of Technology "for fundamental work and discoveries in magneto-hydrodynamics with fruitful applications in different parts of plasma physics"; **Louis Neel** (France) Univ. of Grenoble "for fundamental work and discoveries concerning antiferromagnetism and ferrimagnetism which have led to important applications in solid-state physics."

**1971 Dennis Gabor** (Great Britain) Imperial College of Science and Technology "for his invention and development of the holographic method."

**1972 John Bardeen** (U.S.) Univ. of Illinois, **Leon N. Cooper** (U.S.) Brown Univ., and **Robert J. Schrieffer** (U.S.) Univ. of Pennsylvania "for their jointly developed theory of superconductivity, usually called the BCS-theory."

**1973 Leo Esaki** (Japan) IBM Thomas J. Watson Research Center (Yorktown Heights, N.Y.), and **Ivar Giaever** (U.S.) General Electric Co. "for their experimental discoveries regarding tunneling phenomena in semiconductors and superconductors, respectively"; **Brian D. Josephson** (Great Britain) Cambridge Univ. "for his theoretical predictions of the properties of a supercurrent through a tunnel barrier, in particular those phenomena which are generally known as the Josephson effects."

**1974 Sir Martin Ryle** (Great Britain) Cambridge Univ., and **Antony Hewish** (Great Britain) Cambridge Univ. "for their pioneering research in radio astrophysics: Ryle for his observations and inventions, in particular of the aperture synthesis technique, and Hewish for his decisive role in the discovery of pulsars."

**1975 Aage Bohr** (Denmark) Niels Bohr Institute, **Ben Mottelson** (Denmark) Nordita, and **James Rainwater** (U.S.) Columbia Univ. "for the discovery of the connec-

tion between collective motion and particle motion in atomic nuclei and the development of the theory of the structure of the atomic nucleus based on this connection."

**1976 Burton Richter** (U.S.) Stanford Linear Accelerator Center, and **Samuel C.C. Ting** (U.S.) M.I.T. "for their pioneering work in the discovery of a heavy elementary particle of a new kind."

**1977 Philip W. Anderson** (U.S.) Bell Laboratories, **Sir Nevill F. Mott** (Great Britain) Cambridge Univ., and **John H. van Vleck** (U.S.) Harvard Univ. "for their fundamental theoretical investigations of the electronic structure of magnetic and disordered systems."

**1978 Peter L. Kapitsa** (USSR) Academy of Sciences "for his basic inventions and discoveries in the area of low-temperature physics; **Arno A. Penzias** (U.S.) Bell Laboratories, and **Robert W. Wilson** (U.S.) Bell Laboratories "for their discovery of cosmic microwave background radiation."

**1979 Sheldon L. Glashow** (U.S.) Lyman Laboratory, Harvard Univ., **Abdus Salam** (Pakistan) International Centre for Theoretical Physics (Trieste) and Imperial College of Science and Technology (London), and **Steven Weinberg** (U.S.) Harvard Univ. "for their contributions to the theory of the unified weak and electromagnetic interaction between elementary particles, including, inter alia, the prediction of the weak neutral current."

**1980 James W. Cronin** (U.S.) Univ. of Chicago, and **Val L. Fitch** (U.S.) Princeton Univ. "for the discovery of violations of fundamental symmetry principles in the decay of neutral K-mesons."

**1981 Nicolaas Bloembergen** (U.S.) Harvard Univ., and **Arthur L. Schawlow** (U.S.) Stanford Univ. "for their contributions to the development of laser spectroscopy"; **Kai M. Siegbahn** (Sweden) Uppsala Univ. "for his contribution to the development of high-resolution electron spectroscopy."

**1982 Kenneth G. Wilson** (U.S.) Cornell Univ. "for his theory for critical phenomena in connection with phase transitions."

**1983 Subrahmanyan Chandrasekhar** (U.S.) Univ. of Chicago "for his theoretical studies of the physical processes of importance to the structure and evolution of the stars"; **William A. Fowler** (U.S.) California Institute of Technology "for his theoretical and experimental studies of the nuclear reactions of importance in the formation of the chemical elements in the universe."

**1984 Carlo Rubbia** (Italy) CERN, Geneva, and **Simon van der Meer** (Netherlands) CERN, Geneva "for their decisive contributions to the large project, which led to the discovery of the field particles W and Z, communicators of weak interaction."

**1985 Klaus von Klitzing** (W. Germany) Max-Planck-Institut for Solid State Research "for the discovery of the quantized Hall effect."

**1986** **Ernst Ruska** (W. Germany) Fritz-Haber-Institut der Max-Planck-Gesellschaft "for his fundamental work in electron optics, and for the design of the first electron microscope"; **Gerd Binnig** (W. Germany) IBM Zurich Research Laboratory, and **Heinrich Rohrer** (Switzerland) IBM Zurich Research Laboratory "for their design of the scanning tunneling microscope."

**1987** **Georg J. Bednorz** (Switzerland) IBM Zurich Research Laboratory, and **Dr. K. Alex Müller** (Switzerland) IBM Zurich Research Laboratory "for the discovery of new superconducting materials."

**1988** **Leon M. Lederman** (U.S.) Fermi National Accelerator Laboratory, **Melvin Schwartz** (U.S.) Digital Pathways, Inc., and **Jack Steinberger** (Switzerland) CERN "for the neutrino beam method and the demonstration of the doublet structure of the leptons through the discovery of the muon neutrino."

**1989** **Norman F. Ramsey** (U.S.) Harvard Univ. "for the invention of the separated oscillatory fields method and its use in . . . atomic clocks." **Hans G. Dehmelt** (U.S.) Univ. of Washington, and **Wolfgang Paul**, Univ. of Bonn (W. Germany) "for the development of the ion trap technique," which allows detailed study of subatomic particles.

**1990** **Richard E. Taylor** (Canada) Stanford Univ., **Jerome I. Friedman** (U.S.) M.I.T., and **Henry W. Kendall** (U.S.) M.I.T., whose experiments between 1967 and 1973 confirmed the existence of quarks, the fundamental building blocks of matter.

# NOBEL PRIZES
# FOR LITERATURE

**1901** **Sully Prudhomme (pen name of René F.A. Prudhomme)** (France) "in special recognition of his poetic composition, which gives evidence of lofty idealism, artistic perfection, and a rare combination of the qualities of both heart and intellect."

**1902** **Christian M.T. Mommsen** (Germany) "the greatest living master of the art of historical writing, with special reference to his monumental work, *A History of Rome*."

**1903** **Bjørnstjerne M. Bjørnson** (Norway) "as a tribute to his noble, magnificent, and versatile poetry, which has always been distinguished by both the freshness of its inspiration and the rare purity of its spirit."

**1904** **Frederic Mistral** (France) "in recognition of the fresh orginality and true inspiration of his poetic production, which faithfully reflects the natural scenery and native spirit of his people, and, in addition, his significant work as a Provencal philologist"; **José Echegaray y Eizaguirre** (Spain) "in recognition of the numerous and brilliant compositions which, in an individual and original manner, have revived the great traditions of the Spanish drama."

**1905** **Henryk Sienkiewicz** (Poland) "because of his outstanding merits as an epic writer."

**1906** **Giosuè Carducci** (Italy) "not only in consideration of his deep learning and critical research, but above all as a tribute to the creative energy, freshness of style, and lyrical force which characterize his poetic masterpieces."

**1907** **Rudyard Kipling** (Great Britain) "in consideration of the power of observation, originality of imagination, virility of ideas, and remarkable talent for narration which characterize the creations of this world-famous author."

**1908** **Rudolf C. Eucken** (Germany) "in recognition of his earnest search for truth, his penetrating power of thought, his wide range of vision, and the warmth and strength in presentation with which in his numerous works he has vindicated and developed an idealistic philosophy of life."

**1909** **Selma O.L. Lagerlöf** (Sweden) "in appreciation of the lofty idealism, vivid imagination, and spiritual perception that characterize her writings."

**1910** **Paul J.L. Heyse** (Germany) "as a tribute to the consummate artistry, permeated with idealism, which he has demonstrated during his long productive career as lyric poet, dramatist, novelist, and writer of world-renowned short stories."

**1911** **Count Maurice (Mooris) P.M.B. Maeterlinck** (Belgium) "in appreciation of his many-sided literary activities, and especially of his dramatic works, which are distinguished by a wealth of imagination and by a poetic fancy."

**1912** **Gerhart J.R. Hauptmann** (Germany) "primarily in recognition of his fruitful, varied, and outstanding production in the realm of dramatic art."

**1913** **Rabindranath Tagore** (India) "because of his profoundly sensitive, fresh, and beautiful verse, by which, with consummate skill, he has made his poetic thought, expressed in his own English words, a part of the literature of the West."

**1914** No award.

**1915** **Romain Rolland** (France) "as a tribute to the lofty idealism of his literary production and to the sympathy and love of truth with which he has described different types of human beings."

**1916** **Carl G.V. von Heidenstam** (Sweden) "in recognition of his significance as the leading representative of a new era in our literature."

**1917** **Karl A. Gjellerup** (Denmark) "for his varied and rich poetry, which is inspired by lofty ideals"; **Henrik Pontoppidan** (Denmark) "for his authentic descriptions of presentday life in Denmark."

**1918** No award.

**1919** **Carl F.G. Spitteler** (Switzerland) "in special appreciation of his epic, *Olympian Spring*."

**1920** **Knut P. Hamsun** (Norway) "for his monumental work, *Growth of the Soil*."

**1921** **Anatole France (pen name of Jacques A. Thibault)** (France) "in recognition of his brilliant literary achievements, characterized as they are by a nobility of style, a profound human sympathy, grace, and a true Gallic temperament."

**1922** **Jacinto Benavente** (Spain) "for the happy manner in which he has continued the illustrious traditions of the Spanish drama."

**1923** **William B. Yeats** (Ireland) "for his always inspired poetry, which in a highly artistic form gives expression to the spirit of a whole nation."

**1924** **Wladyslaw S. Reymont (pen name of Reyment)** (Poland) "for his great national epic, *The Peasants*."

**1925** **George B. Shaw** (Great Britain) "for his work which is marked by both idealism and humanity, its stimulating satire often being infused with a singular poetic beauty."

**1926** **Grazia Deledda (pen name of Grazia Madesani)** (Italy) "for her idealistically inspired writings which with plastic clarity picture the life on her native island and with depth and sympathy deal with human problems in general."

**1927** **Henri Bergson** (France) "in recognition of his rich and vitalizing ideas and the brilliant skill with which they have been presented."

**1928** **Sigrid Undset** (Norway) "principally for her powerful descriptions of Northern life during the Middle Ages."

**1929** **Thomas Mann** (Germany) "principally for his great novel *Buddenbrooks*, which has won steadily increased recognition as one of the classic works of contemporary literature."

**1930** **Sinclair Lewis** (U.S.) "for his vigorous and graphic art of description and his ability to create, with wit and humour, new types of characters."

**1931** **Erik A. Karlfeldt** (Sweden) "the poetry of Erik Axel Karlfeldt."

**1932** **John Galsworthy** (Great Britain) "for his distinguished art of narration which takes its highest form in *The Forsythe Saga*."

**1933** **Ivan A. Bunin** (stateless domicile in France) "for the strict artistry with which he has carried on the classical Russian traditions in prose writing."

**1934** **Luigi Pirandello** (Italy) "for his bold and ingenious revival of dramatic and scenic art."

**1935** No award.

**1936** **Eugene G. O'Neill** (U.S.) "for the power, honesty, and deep-felt emotions of his dramatic works, which embody an original concept of tragedy."

**1937** **Roger Martin du Gard** (France) "for the artistic power and truth with which he has depicted human conflict as well as some fundamental aspects of contemporary life in his novel-cycle *Les Thibault*."

**1938** **Pearl Buck (pen name of Pearl Walsh)** (U.S.) "for her rich and truly epic descriptions of peasant life in China and for her biographical masterpieces."

**1939 Frans E. Sillanpää** (Finland) "for his deep understanding of his country's peasantry and the exquisite art with which he has portrayed their way of life and their relationship with Nature."

**1940–43** No award.

**1944 Johannes V. Jensen** (Denmark) "for the rare strength and fertility of his poetic imagination with which is combined an intellectual curiosity of wide scope and bold, freshly creative style."

**1945 Gabriela Mistral (pen name of Lucila Godoy y Alcayaga)** (Chile) "for her lyric poetry which, inspired by powerful emotions, has made her name a symbol of the idealistic aspirations of the entire Latin American world."

**1946 Hermann Hesse** (Switzerland) "for his inspired writings which, while growing in boldness and penetration, exemplify the classical humanitarian ideals and high qualities of style."

**1947 André P.G. Gide** (France) "for his comprehensive and artistically significant writings, in which human problems and conditions have been presented with a fearless love of truth and keen psychological insight."

**1948 Thomas S. Eliot** (Great Britain) "for his outstanding, pioneer contribution to presentday poetry."

**1949 William Faulkner** (U.S.) "for his powerful and artistically unique contribution to the modern American novel."

**1950 Earl (Bertrand) Russell** (Great Britain) "in recognition of his varied and significant writings in which he champions humanitarian ideals and freedom of thought."

**1951 Pär F. Lägerkvist** (Sweden) "for the artistic vigour and true independence of mind with which he endeavours in his poetry to find answers to the eternal questions confronting mankind."

**1952 François Mauriac** (France) "for the deep spiritual insight and the artistic intensity with which he has in his novels penetrated the drama of human life."

**1953 Sir Winston L.P. Churchill** (Great Britain) "for his mastery of historical and biographical description as well as for brilliant oratory in defending exalted human values."

**1954 Ernest M. Hemingway** (U.S.) "for his mastery of the art of narrative, most recently demonstrated in *The Old Man and the Sea*, and for the influence that he has exerted on contemporary style."

**1955 Halldór K. Laxness** (Iceland) "for his vivid epic power which has renewed the great narrative art of Iceland."

**1956 Juan R. Jiménez** (Spain [domicile in Puerto Rico]) "for his lyrical poetry, which in Spanish language constitutes an example of high spirit and artistical purity."

**1957 Albert Camus** (France) "for his important literary production, which with clearsighted earnestness illuminates the problems of the human conscience in our times."

**1958 Boris L. Pasternak** (USSR) "for his important achievement both in contemporary lyrical poetry and in the field of the great Russian epic tradition." (Declined the prize.)

**1959 Salvatore Quasimodo** (Italy) "for his lyrical poetry, which with classical fire expresses the tragic experience of life in our own times."

**1960 Saint-John Perse (pen name of Alexis Léger)** (France) "for the soaring flight and the evocative imagery of his poetry which in a visionary fashion reflects the conditions of our time."

**1961 Ivo Andrić** (Yugoslavia) "for the epic force with which he has traced themes and depicted human destinies drawn from the history of his country."

**1962 John Steinbeck** (U.S.) "for his realistic and imaginative writings, combining as they do sympathetic humour and keen social perception."

**1963 Giorgos Seferis (pen name of Giorgos Seferiades)** (Greece) "for his eminent lyrical writing, inspired by a deep feeling for the Hellenic world of culture."

**1964 Jean-Paul Sartre** (France) "for his work which, rich in ideas and filled with the spirit of freedom and the quest for truth, has exerted a far-reaching influence on our age." (Declined the prize.)

**1965 Michail A. Solochov** (USSR) "for the artistic power and integrity with which, in his epic of the Don, he has given expression to a historic phase in the life of the Russian people."

**1966 Shmuel Y. Agnon** (Israel) "for his profoundly characteristic narrative art with motifs from the life of the Jewish people; **Nelly Sachs** (Germany [domiciled in Sweden]) "for her outstanding lyrical and dramatic writing, which interprets Israel's destiny with touching strength."

**1967 Miguel A. Asturias** (Guatemala) "for his vivid literary achievement, deep-rooted in the national traits and traditions of Indian peoples of Latin America."

**1968 Yasunari Kawabata** (Japan) "for his narrative mastery, which with great sensibility expresses the essence of the Japanese mind."

**1969 Samuel Beckett** (Ireland) "for his writing, which—in new forms for the novel and drama—in the destitution of modern man acquires its elevation."

**1970 Alexandr Solzhjenitsyn** (USSR) "for the ethical force with which he has pursued the indispensable traditions of Russian literature."

**1971 Pablo Neruda** (Chile) "for a poetry that with the action of an elemental force brings alive a continent's destiny and dreams."

**1972 Heinrich Böll** (W. Germany) "for his writing which through its combination of a broad perspective on his time and a sensitive skill in characterization has contributed to a renewal of German literature."

**1973 Patrick White** (Australia) "for an epic and psychological narrative art which has

introduced a new continent into literature."

**1974 Eyvind Johnson** (Sweden) "for a narrative art, far-seeing in lands and ages, in the service of freedom"; **Harry Martinson** (Sweden) "for writings that catch the dewdrop and reflect the cosmos."

**1975 Eugenio Montale** (Italy) "for his distinctive poetry which, with great artistic sensitivity, has interpreted human values under the sign of an outlook on life with no illusions."

**1976 Saul Bellow** (U.S.) "for the human understanding and subtle analysis of contemporary culture that are combined in his work."

**1977 Vicente Aleixandre** (Spain) "for a creative poetic writing which illuminates man's condition in the cosmos and in present-day society, at the same time representing the great renewal of the traditions of Spanish poetry between the wars."

**1978 Isaac B. Singer** (U.S.) "for his impassioned narrative art which, with roots in a Polish-Jewish cultural tradition, brings universal human conditions to life."

**1979 Odysseus Elytis (pen name of Odysseus Alepoudhelis)** (Greece) "for his poetry, which against the background of Greek tradition, depicts with sensuous strength and intellectual clear-sightedness modern man's struggle for freedom and creativeness."

**1980 Czeslaw Milosz** (U.S. and Poland) "who with uncompromising clear-sightedness voices man's exposed condition in a world of severe conflicts."

**1981 Elias Canetti** (Great Britain) "for writings marked by a broad outlook, a wealth of ideas, and artistic power."

**1982 Gabriel García Marquez** (Colombia) "for his novels and short stories, in which the fantastic and the realistic are combined in a richly composed world of imagination, reflecting a continent's life and conflicts."

**1983 William Golding** (Great Britain) "for his novels which, with the perspicuity of realistic narrative art and the diversity and universality of myth, illuminate the human condition in the world of today."

**1984 Jaroslav Seifert** (Czechoslovakia) "for his poetry which, endowed with freshness, sensuality, and rich inventiveness, provides a liberating image of the indomitable spirit and versatility of man."

**1985 Claude Simon** (France) "who in his novel combines the poet's and the painter's creativeness with a deepened awareness of time in the depiction of the human condition."

**1986 Wole Soyinka** (Nigeria) "who in a wide cultural perspective and with poetic overtones fashions the drama of existence."

**1987 Joseph Brodsky** (U.S.) "for his all-embracing authorship imbued with clarity of thought and poetic intensity."

**1988 Naguib Mahfouz** (Egypt) "who, through works rich in nuance—now clear-sight-

edly realistic, now evocatively ambiguous—has formed an Arabian narrative art that applies to all mankind."
**1989 Camilo José Cela** (Spain) a novelist

whose "rich and inventive prose, which . . . forms a challenging vision of man's vulnerability." His most famous work is *The Family of Pascual Duarte* (1942).

**1990 Octavio Paz** (Mexico) poet and social essayist. Volumes include *The Labyrinth of Solitude* (1950), *Sunstone* (1957), and *Sor Juana: Or, the Traps of Faith* (1990).

# SCIENCE AWARDS

The National Medal of Science is the highest science award given by the United States government. Since 1962, it has been presented by the president for achievement in physical, biological, mathematical, engineering, behavioral, or social science.

The medal itself is intended to symbolize science. It shows a human being, surrounded by earth, sea, and sky, contemplating and seeking to understand nature. The scientist holds a

crystal in one hand, intended to symbolize the universal order and also the basic unit of living things. With the other hand the scientist is sketching a formula in the sand.

The nominees are selected by a presidential committee of twelve members acting with the president's science advisor and the president of the National Academy of Sciences. The medals are not awarded every year.

## NATIONAL MEDAL OF SCIENCE AWARDS, 1962–90

| Year | Winner, Field, Affiliation |
|---|---|
| 1962 | Theodore von Karman, Aeronautics, Cal Tech |
| 1963 | Luis Walter Alvarez, Physics, Univ. of California, Berkeley |
| | Vannevar Bush, Electronics, Carnegie Institute |
| | John Robinson Pierce, Communications, Bell Labs |
| | Cornelius B. van Niel, Microbiology, Stanford Univ. |
| | Norbert Wiener, Mathematics, M.I.T. |
| 1964 | Roger Adams, Chemistry, Univ. of Illinois |
| | Othmar H. Ammann, Engineering, Ammann & Whitney |
| | Theodosius Dobzhansky, Medicine, Rockefeller Univ. |
| | Charles Stark Draper, Astronautics, M.I.T. |
| | Solomon Lefschetz, Mathematics, Princeton Univ. |
| | Neal Elgar Miller, Psychology, Yale Univ. |
| | Harold Marston Morse, Mathematics, Institute for Advanced Studies |
| | Marshall W. Nirenberg, Genetics, National Institutes of Health |
| | Julian Schwinger, Physics, Harvard Univ. |
| | Harold C. Urey, Chemistry, Univ. of California, Berkeley |
| | Robert B. Woodward, Chemistry, Harvard Univ. |
| 1965 | John Bardeen, Electronics, Univ. of Illinois |
| | Peter J.W. Debye, Chemistry, Cornell Univ. |
| | Hugh L. Dryden, Administration, NASA |
| | Clarence L. Johnson, Aeronautics, Lockheed |
| | Leon M. Lederman, Physics, Columbia Univ. |
| | Warren K. Lewis, Chemical eng., M.I.T. |
| | Francis Peyton Rous, Medicine, Rockefeller Univ. |
| | William W. Rubey, Geophysics, UCLA |
| | George. G. Simpson, Paleontology, Harvard Univ. |
| | Donald Van Slyke, Chemistry, Brookhaven National Lab |
| | Oscar Zariski, Mathematics, Harvard Univ. |
| 1966 | Jacob Bjerknes, Meteorology, UCLA |
| | S. Chandrasekhar, Astrophysics, Univ. of Chicago |
| | Henry Eyring, Administration, Univ. of Utah |
| | E.F. Knipling, Entomology, U.S. Dept. of Agriculture |
| | Fritz A. Lipmann, Biochemistry, Rockefeller Univ. |
| | John W. Minor, Administration, Princeton Univ. |
| | William C. Rose, Chemistry, Univ. of Illinois |
| | Claude E. Shannon, Science history, M.I.T. |
| | J.H. Van Vleck, Physics, Harvard Univ. |
| | Sewall Wright, Genetics, Univ. of Wisconsin |
| | Vladimir Zworykin, Physics, RCA |
| 1967 | J.W. Beams, Physics, Univ. of Virginia |
| | A. Francis Birch, Geology, Harvard Univ. |
| | Gregory Breit, Physics, Yale Univ. |
| | Paul J. Cohen, Mathematics, Stanford Univ. |
| | Kenneth S. Cole, Biophysics, National Institutes of Health |
| | Louis P. Hammett, Chemistry, Columbia Univ. |
| | Harry F. Harlow, Psychology, Univ. of Wisconsin |
| | Michael Heidelberger, Immunology, New York Univ. |

| Year | Winner, Field, Affiliation |
|---|---|
| | G.S. Kistiakowsky, Chemistry, Harvard Univ. |
| | Edwin H. Land, Photography, Polaroid Corporation |
| | Igor I. Sikorsky, Aeronautics, United Aircraft |
| | Alfred H. Sturtevant, Biology, Cal Tech |
| 1968 | Horace A. Barker, Biochemistry, Univ. of California, Berkeley |
| | Paul D. Bartlett, Chemistry, Harvard Univ. |
| | Bernard B. Brodie, Pharmacology, National Institutes of Health |
| | Detlev W. Bronk, Medicine, Rockefeller Univ. |
| | J. Presper Eckert, Computer science, Sperry-Rand Corporation |
| | Herbert Friedman, Astrophysics, Naval Research Lab |
| | Jay L. Lush, Genetics, Iowa State Univ. |
| | N.M. Newmark, Civil eng., Univ. of Illinois |
| | Jerzy Neyman, Mathematics, Univ. of California, Berkeley |
| | Lars Onsager, Chemistry, Yale Univ. |
| | B.F. Skinner, Psychology, Harvard Univ. |
| | Eugene P. Wigner, Physics, Princeton Univ. |
| 1969 | Herbert C. Brown, Chemistry, Purdue Univ. |
| | William Feller, Mathematics, Princeton Univ. |
| | Robert J. Huebner, Medicine, National Institutes of Health |
| | Jack S.C. Kilby, Computer science, Texas Instruments |
| | Ernst Mayr, Zoology, Harvard Univ. |
| | W.K.H. Panofsky, Physics, Stanford Univ. |
| 1970 | Richard D. Brauer, Mathematics, Harvard Univ. |
| | Robert H. Dicke, Physics, Princeton Univ. |
| | Barbara McClintock, Genetics, Carnegie Institute |
| | George E. Mueller, Administration, General Dynamics |
| | Albert B. Sabin, Medicine, Weizmann Institute |
| | Allan R. Sandage, Astronomy, Cal Tech |
| | John C. Slater, Physics, Univ. of Florida |
| | John A. Wheeler, Physics, Princeton Univ. |
| | Saul Winstein, Chemistry, UCLA |
| 1973 | Daniel I. Arnon, Biochemistry, Stanford Univ. |
| | Carl Djerassi, Chemistry, Stanford Univ. |
| | Harold E. Edgerton, Mathematics, M.I.T. |
| | William M. Ewing, Electrical eng., Univ. of Texas |
| | Arie J. Haagen-Smit, Biochemistry, Cal Tech |
| | Vladimir Haensel, Geology, Universal Oil |
| | Frederick Seitz, Administration, Rockefeller Univ. |
| | Earl W. Sutherland, Physics, Univ. of Miami |
| | John W. Tukey, Statistics, Princeton Univ. |
| | Richard T. Whitcomb, Aeronautics, Langley Center |
| | Robert P. Wilson, Administration, Fermilab |
| 1974 | Nicolaas Bloembergen, Physics, Harvard Univ. |
| | Britton Chance, Physics, Univ. of Pennsylvania |
| | Erwin Chargaff, Chemistry, Columbia Univ. |
| | Paul J. Flory, Chemistry, Stanford Univ. |
| | William A. Fowler, Physics, Cal Tech |
| | Kurt Gödel, Mathematics, Institute for Advanced Study |

| Year | Winner, Field, Affiliation |
|---|---|
| | Rudolf Kompfner, Physics, Stanford Univ. |
| | James V. Neel, Genetics, Univ. of Michigan |
| | Linus Pauling, Chemistry, Stanford Univ. |
| | Ralph B. Peck, Engineering, Univ. of Illinois |
| | K.S. Pitzer, Chemistry, Univ. of California, Berkeley |
| | James A. Shannon, Medicine, Rockefeller Univ. |
| | Abel Wolman, Engineering, Johns Hopkins Univ. |
| 1975 | John Backus, Computer science, San Jose Laboratory |
| | Manson Benedict, Mathematics, M.I.T. |
| | Hans A. Bethe, Physics, Cornell Univ. |
| | Shiing-shen Chern, Mathematics, Univ. of California, Berkeley |
| | George B. Dantzig, Computer science, Stanford Univ. |
| | Hallowell Davis, Medicine, Washington Univ. |
| | Paul Gyorgy, Pediatrics, Univ. of Pennsylvania |
| | Sterling B. Hendricks, Chemistry, U.S. Dept. of Agriculture |
| | Joseph O. Hirschfelder, Chemistry, Univ. of Wisconsin |
| | William H. Pickering, Physics, Jet Propulsion Laboratory |
| | Lewis H. Sarett, Administration, Merck, Sharp, and Dohme |
| | Frederick E. Terman, Administration, Stanford Univ. |
| | Orville A. Vogel, Agronomy, Washington State Univ. |
| | Wernher von Braun, Administration, NASA |
| | E. Bright Wilson, Chemistry, Harvard Univ. |
| | Chien-Shiung Wu, Physics, Columbia Univ. |
| 1976 | Morris Cohen, Metallurgy, M.I.T. |
| | Kurt O. Friedrichs, Mathematics, New York Univ. |
| | Peter C. Goldmark, Communications, Goldmark Corporation |
| | Samuel A. Goudsmit, Physics, Univ. of Nevada |
| | Roger C. Guillemin, Neurology, Salk Institute |
| | Herbert S. Gutowsky, Chemistry, Univ. of Illinois |
| | Erwin W. Mueller, Physics, Pennsylvania State Univ. |
| | Keith R. Porter, Biology, Univ. of Colorado |
| | Efraim Racker, Biochemistry, Cornell Univ. |
| | Frederick D. Rossini, Chemistry, Rice Univ. |
| | Verner E. Suomi, Meteorology, Univ. of Wisconsin |
| | Henry Taube, Chemistry, Stanford Univ. |
| | George E. Uhlenbeck, Physics, Rockefeller Univ. |
| | Hassler Whitney, Physics, Princeton Univ. |
| | Edward O. Wilson, Zoology, Harvard Univ. |
| 1979 | Robert H. Burris, Biochemistry, Univ. of Wisconsin |
| | Elizabeth C. Crosby, Anatomy, Univ. of Michigan |
| | Joseph L. Doob, Mathematics, Univ. of Illinois |
| | Richard P. Feynman, Physics, Cal Tech |
| | Donald E. Knuth, Computer science, Stanford Univ. |
| | Arthur Kornberg, Biochemistry, Stanford Univ. |
| | Emmett N. Leith, Electrical eng., Univ. of Michigan |
| | Herman F. Mark, Administration, Brooklyn Polytech |
| | Raymond D. Mindlin, Civil eng., Columbia Univ. |
| | Robert N. Noyce, Computer science, Intel Corp. |

| Year | Winner, Field, Affiliation | Year | Winner, Field, Affiliation | Year | Winner, Field, Affiliation |
|---|---|---|---|---|---|

Severo Ochoa, Biochemistry, New York Univ.
Earl R. Parker, Metallurgy, Univ. of California, Berkeley
Edward M. Purcell, Physics, Harvard Univ.
Simon Ramo, Administration, Thompson, Ramo, Wooldridge, Inc.
John H. Sinfelt, Science adviser, Exxon
Lyman Spitzer, Jr., Astronomy, Princeton Univ.
Earl R. Stadtman, Biochemistry, National Institutes of Health
G. Ledyard Stebbins, Genetics, Univ. of California, Davis
Paul A. Weiss, Biology, Rockefeller Univ.
Victor F. Weisskopf, Physics, M.I.T.
1981 Philip Handler, Biochemistry, National Academy of Sciences
1982 Philip W. Anderson, Physics, Bell Labs
Seymour Benzer, Biology, Cal Tech
Glenn W. Burton, Biology, U.S. Dept. of Agriculture
Mildred Cohn, Chemistry, Univ. of Pennsylvania
F. Albert Cotton, Chemistry, Texas A&M
Edward H. Heinemann, Engineering, General Dynamics
Donald Katz, Chemistry, Univ. of Michigan
Yoichiro Nambu, Physics, Univ. of Chicago
Marshall H. Stone, Mathematics, Univ. of Massachusetts
Gilbert Stork, Chemistry, Columbia Univ.
Edward Teller, Physics, Stanford Univ.
Charles H. Townes, Physics, Univ. of California, Berkeley
1985 Howard L. Bachrach, Biochemistry, U.S. Dept. of Agriculture
Paul Berg, Biology, Stanford Univ.
Margaret Burbidge, Astronomy, Univ. of California, San Diego
Maurice Goldhaber, Physics, Brookhaven National Lab
Herman H. Goldstine, Computer science, American Philosophical Society
William R. Hewlett, Electronics, Hewlett-Packard Company
Roald Hoffmann, Chemistry, Cornell Univ.
Helmut Landsberg, Climatology, Resources for the Future
George M. Low, Space science, Rensselaer Polytechnic Inst.
Walter Munk, Geophysics, Univ. of California, San Diego
George C. Pimentel, Chemistry, Univ. of California, Berkeley
Frederick Reines, Physics, Univ. of California, Irvine
Wendell L. Roelofs, Biology, Cornell Univ.
Bruno Rossi, Astronomy, M.I.T.
Berta Scharrer, Medicine, Albert Einstein College of Medicine
Robert Schrieffer, Physics, Univ. of California, Santa Barbara
Isadore Singer, Mathematics, Univ. of California, Berkeley
John G. Trump, Medicine, M.I.T.
Richard N. Zare, Chemistry, Stanford Univ.
1986 Solomon J. Buchsbaum, Physics, Bell Labs
Stanley Cohen, Biochemistry, Vanderbilt Univ.
Horace R. Crane, Biophysics, Univ. of Michigan
Herman Feshbach, Physics, M.I.T.
Harry B. Gray, Chemistry, Cal Tech

Donald A. Henderson, Medicine, Johns Hopkins Univ.
Robert Hofstadter, Physics, Stanford Univ.
Peter D. Lax, Mathematics, New York Univ.
Yuan Tseh Lee, Chemistry, Univ. of California, Berkeley
Hans W. Liepmann, Physics, Cal Tech
Tung Yen Lin, Engineering, T.Y. Lin, International
Carl S. Marvel, Chemistry, Univ. of Arizona
Vernon B. Mountcastle, Medicine, Johns Hopkins Univ.
Bernard M. Oliver, Electronics, NASA
George E. Palade, Biology, Yale Univ.
Herbert A. Simon, Psychology, Carnegie Mellon Univ.
Joan A. Steitz, Biochemistry, Yale Univ.
Frank H. Westheimer, Chemistry, Harvard Univ.
Chen Ning Yang, Physics, State Univ. of N.Y., Stony Brook
Antoni Zygmund, Mathematics, Univ. of Chicago
1987 Philip H. Abelson, Physics, American Association of Allied Sciences
Anne Anastasi, Psychology, Fordham Univ.
Robert Bird, Physics, Univ. of Wisconsin
Raoul Bott, Mathematics, Harvard Univ.
Michael E. DeBakey, Medicine, Baylor College of Medicine
Theodor Diener, Biology, U.S. Dept. of Agriculture
Harry Eagle, Biology, Albert Einstein College of Medicine
Walter M. Elsasser, Physics, Johns Hopkins Univ.
Michael Freedman, Mathematics, Univ. of California, San Diego
William S. Johnson, Biochemistry, Stanford Univ.
Har Gobind Khorana, Biology, M.I.T.
Paul C. Lauterbur, Medicine, Univ. of Illinois
Rita Levi-Montalcini, Medicine, Lab. of Cell Biology, Rome
George E. Pake, Administration, Xerox Corporation
H. Bolton Seed, Engineering, Univ. of California, Berkeley
George J. Stigler, Economics, Univ. of Chicago
Walter H. Stockmayer, Chemistry, Dartmouth College
Max Tishler, Chemistry, Wesleyan Univ.
James A. Van Allen, Astronomy, Univ. of Iowa
Ernest Weber, Engineering, Polytechnic Inst. of N.Y.
1988 William O. Baker, Chemistry, Bell Labs
Konrad E. Bloch, Medicine, Harvard Univ.
D. Allan Bromley, Physics, Yale Univ.
Michael S. Brown, Medicine, Univ. of Texas Medical Center
Paul C.W. Chu, Physics, Univ. of Houston
Stanley N. Cohen, Genetics, Stanford Univ.
Elias J. Corey, Chemistry, Harvard Univ.
Daniel C. Drucker, Engineering, Univ. of Florida
Milton Friedman, Economics, Hoover Institution, Stanford
Joseph L. Goldstein, Medicine, Univ. of Texas Medical Center
Ralph E. Gomery, Mathematics, IBM Corporation
Willis M. Hawkins, Aeronautics, Lockheed Corporation
Maurice R. Hillerman, Medicine, Merck Institute

George W. Housner, Earth science, Cal Tech
Eric R. Kandel, Biochemistry, Columbia Univ.
Joseph B. Keller, Physics, Stanford Univ.
Walter Kohn, Physics, Univ. of California, Santa Barbara
Norman F. Ramsey, Physics, Harvard Univ.
Jack Steinberger, Physics, CERN (European Center for Nuclear Research), Geneva
Rosalyn S. Yalow, Medicine, Mt. Sinai School of Medicine
1989 Arnold O. Beckman, Chemistry, Cal Tech
Richard B. Bernstein, Chemistry, Univ. of California, Los Angeles
Melvin Calvin, Biochemistry, Univ. of California, Berkeley
Harry G. Drinkamer, Physics, Univ. of Illinois
Katherine Esau, Biology, Univ. of California, Santa Barbara
Herbert E. Grier, Electronics, CER Corporation
Viktor Hamburger, Biology, Washington Univ., St. Louis
Samuel Karlin, Mathematics, Stanford Univ.
Philip Leder, Biochemistry, Harvard Medical School
Joshua Lederberg, Biochemistry, Rockefeller Univ.
Saunders Mac Lane, Mathematics, Univ. of Chicago
Rudolph A. Marcus, Chemistry, Cal Tech
Harden M. McConnell, Biochemistry, Stanford Univ.
Eugene N. Parker, Astrophysics, Univ. of Chicago
Robert P. Sharp, Astronomy, Cal Tech
Donald C. Spencer, Oceanography, Woods Hole
Harland G. Wood, Biochemistry, Case Western Reserve
1990 Baruj Benacerraf, Medicine, Dana-Farber Cancer Inst.
Elkan R. Blount, Medicine, Harvard School of Public Health
Herbert W. Boyer, Biology, Univ. of California
George F. Carrier, Mathematics, Harvard Univ.
Allan M. Cormack, Physics, Tufts Univ.
Mildred S. Dresselhaus, Physics, M.I.T.
Karl Folkers, Biochemistry, Inst. for Biomedical Research, Univ. of Texas
Nick Holonyak, Jr., Physics, Univ. of Illinois
Leonid Hurwicz, Economics, Univ. of Minnesota
Stephen C. Kleene, Mathematics, Univ. of Wisconsin
Daniel E. Koshland, Jr., Biochemistry, Univ. of California, Berkeley
Edward B. Lewis, Anthropology, Cal Tech
John McCarthy, Computer science, Stanford Univ.
Edwin M. McMillan, Physics, Univ. of California, Berkeley
David G. Nathan, Medicine, The Children's Hospital, Boston
Robert V. Pound, Physics, Harvard Univ.
R.D. Revelle, Oceanography, Scripps Institution of Oceanography, Univ. of California, La Jolla
John D. Roberts, Chemistry, Cal Tech
Patrick Suppes, Mathematics, Stanford Univ.
E. Donnall Thomas, Medicine, Fred Hutchinson Cancer Research Center, Seattle

## FERMI AWARDS, 1954–90

The Enrico Fermi Award is given by the U.S. Department of Energy for exceptional scientific and technical achievement in the development, use, or control of atomic energy. The award is named for Enrico Fermi, the first recipient and the scientist who constructed the first nuclear reactor (called an atomic pile at the time). Since the award is for a lifetime achievement, a specific work is not cited. The Fermi Award includes a prize of $100,000.

| Year | Winners | Year | Winners | Year | Winners | Year | Winners |
|---|---|---|---|---|---|---|---|
| 1954 | Enrico Fermi | | Fritz Strassman | 1980 | Alvin M. Weinberg and Rudolf E. Peierls | | Marshall N. Rosenbluth |
| 1956 | John von Neumann | 1968 | John A. Wheeler | | | 1986 | Ernest D. Courant and M. Stanley Livingstone |
| 1957 | Ernest O. Lawrence | 1969 | Walter H. Zinn | 1981 | W. Bennett Lewis | | |
| 1958 | Eugene P. Wigner | 1970 | Norris E. Bradbury | 1982 | Herbert Anderson and Seth Neddermeyer | 1987 | Luis W. Alvarez and Gerald F. Tape |
| 1959 | Glenn T. Seaborg | 1971 | Shields Warren and Stafford L. Warren | | | | |
| 1961 | Hans A. Bethe | | | 1983 | Alexander Hollaender and John H. Lawrence | 1988 | Richard B. Setlow and Victor F. Weisskopf |
| 1962 | Edward Teller | 1972 | Manson Benedict | | | | |
| 1963 | J. Robert Oppenheimer | 1976 | William L. Russell | 1984 | Robert R. Wilson and Georges Vendryès | 1990 | George A. Cowan and Robley D. Evans |
| 1964 | Adm. Hyman G. Rickover | 1978 | Harold M. Agnew and Wolfgang K.H. Panofsky | | | | |
| 1966 | Otto Hahn, Lise Meitner, and | | | 1985 | Norman C. Rasmussen and | | |

# COLLEGE SPORTS

## THE NCAA

The NCAA acts as the governing body of intercollegiate athletics, setting the playing rules for each sport and eligibility standards for participating athletes. Its other major functions are to conduct championships and maintain historical records. The organization grew out of a series of meetings convened by President Theodore Roosevelt, who was concerned about the number of serious injuries and deaths in college football games. In 1905 alone, 18 players died.

# Football

## NCAA NATIONAL FOOTBALL CHAMPIONS

The NCAA Football Guide recognizes as unofficial national champion the team selected each year by press association polls. Where the Associated Press poll (of writers) does not agree with the United Press International poll (of coaches), the guide lists both teams selected.

| Year | Team | Year | Team |
|------|------|------|------|
| 1936 | Minnesota | 1964 | Alabama |
| 1937 | Pittsburgh | 1965 | Alabama and Michigan State |
| 1938 | Texas Christian | 1966 | Notre Dame |
| 1939 | Texas A&M | 1967 | Southern California |
| 1940 | Minnesota | 1968 | Ohio State |
| 1941 | Minnesota | 1969 | Texas |
| 1942 | Ohio State | 1970 | Nebraska and Texas |
| 1943 | Notre Dame | 1971 | Nebraska |
| 1944 | Army | 1972 | Southern California |
| 1945 | Army | 1973 | Notre Dame |
| 1946 | Notre Dame | 1974 | Oklahoma and Southern California |
| 1947 | Notre Dame | 1975 | Oklahoma |
| 1948 | Michigan | 1976 | Pittsburgh |
| 1949 | Notre Dame | 1977 | Notre Dame |
| 1950 | Oklahoma | 1978 | Alabama and Southern California |
| 1951 | Tennessee | 1979 | Alabama |
| 1952 | Michigan State | 1980 | Georgia |
| 1953 | Maryland | 1981 | Clemson |
| 1954 | Ohio State and UCLA | 1982 | Penn State |
| 1955 | Oklahoma | 1983 | Miami (Fla.) |
| 1956 | Oklahoma | 1984 | Brigham Young |
| 1957 | Auburn and Ohio State | 1985 | Oklahoma |
| 1958 | Louisiana State | 1986 | Penn State |
| 1959 | Syracuse | 1987 | Miami (Fla.) |
| 1960 | Minnesota | 1988 | Notre Dame |
| 1961 | Alabama | 1989 | Miami (Fla.) |
| 1962 | Southern California | 1990 | Colorado and Georgia Tech |
| 1963 | Texas | | |

Source: NCAA.

## NCAA FOOTBALL CAREER LEADERS

### CAREER POINTS (Nonkickers)

| Player, team | Years | TD | XPt. | FG | Pts. |
|--------------|-------|----|------|----|----|
| Anthony Thomson, Indiana | 1986–89 | 65 | 4 | 0 | 394 |
| Tony Dorsett, Pittsburgh | 1973–76 | 59 | 2 | 0 | 356 |
| Glenn Davis, Army | 1943–46 | 59 | 0 | 0 | 354 |
| Art Luppino, Arizona | 1953–56 | 48 | 49 | 0 | 337 |
| Steve Owens, Oklahoma | 1967–69 | 56 | 0 | 0 | 336 |
| Wilford White, Arizona State | 1947–50 | 48 | 27 | 4 | 327 |
| Barry Sanders, Oklahoma State | 1986–88 | 54 | 0 | 0 | 324 |
| Allen Pinkett, Notre Dame | 1982–85 | 53 | 2 | 0 | 320 |
| Ed Marinaro, Cornell | 1969–71 | 52 | 6 | 0 | 318 |
| Pete Johnson, Ohio State | 1973–76 | 53 | 0 | 0 | 318 |

### CAREER POINTS (Kickers)

| Player, team | Years | PAT | Att. | FG | Att. | Pts. |
|--------------|-------|-----|------|----|------|------|
| Derek Schmidt, Florida State | 1984–87 | 174 | 178 | 73 | 102 | 393 |
| Luis Zendejas, Arizona State | 1981–84 | 134 | 135 | 78 | 105 | 368 |
| Jeff Jaeger, Washington | 1983–86 | 118 | 123 | 80 | 99 | 358 |
| Roman Anderson, Houston | 1988–90 | 174 | 176 | 60 | 86 | 354 |
| John Lee, UCLA | 1982–85 | 116 | 117 | 79 | 92 | 353 |
| Max Zendejas, Arizona | 1982–85 | 122 | 124 | 77 | 104 | 353 |
| Kevin Butler, Georgia | 1981–84 | 122 | 125 | 77 | 98 | 353 |
| Philip Doyle, Alabama | 1987–90 | 105 | 108 | 78 | 105 | 345 |
| Barry Belli, Fresno State | 1984–87 | 116 | 123 | 70 | 99 | 326 |
| R.D. Lashar, Oklahoma | 1987–90 | 194 | 200 | 42 | 60 | 320 |

### RUSHING, Career yards

| Player, team | Years | Carries | Yards | Avg. | Long |
|--------------|-------|---------|-------|------|------|
| Tony Dorsett, Pittsburgh | 1973–76 | 1,074 | 6,082 | 5.66 | 73 |
| Charles White, Southern California | 1976–79 | 1,023 | 5,598 | 5.47 | 79 |
| Herschel Walker, Georgia | 1980–82 | 994 | 5,259 | 5.29 | 76 |
| Archie Griffin, Ohio State | 1972–75 | 845 | 5,177 | 6.13 | 75 |
| Darren Lewis, Texas A&M | 1987–90 | 909 | 5,012 | 5.51 | 84 |
| Anthony Thomson, Indiana | 1986–89 | 1,089 | 4,965 | 4.56 | 52 |
| George Rogers, South Carolina | 1977–80 | 902 | 4,958 | 5.50 | 80 |
| Paul Palmer, Temple | 1983–86 | 948 | 4,895 | 5.16 | 78 |
| Steve Bartalo, Colorado State | 1983–86 | 1,215 | 4,813 | 3.96 | 39 |
| Mike Rozier, Nebraska | 1981–83 | 668 | 4,780 | 7.16 | 93 |

### RECEIVING, Career catches

| Player, team | Years | Catches | Yards | Avg. | TD |
|--------------|-------|---------|-------|------|----|
| Terance Mathis, New Mexico | 1985–87, 1989 | 263 | 4,254 | 16.2 | 36 |
| Mark Templeton, Long Beach State | 1983–86 | 262 | 1,969 | 7.5 | 11 |
| Howard Twilley, Tulsa | 1963–65 | 261 | 3,343 | 12.8 | 32 |
| David Williams, Illinois | 1983–85 | 245 | 3,195 | 13.0 | 22 |
| Marc Zeno, Tulane | 1984–87 | 236 | 3,725 | 15.8 | 25 |
| Kenny Hazzard, Houston | 1989–90 | 220 | 2,635 | 12.0 | 31 |
| Darrin Nelson, Stanford | 1977–78, 1980–81 | 214 | 2,368 | 11.1 | 16 |
| Ron Sellers, Florida State | 1966–68 | 212 | 3,598 | 17.0 | 23 |
| Jason Phillips, Houston | 1987–88 | 207 | 2,319 | 11.2 | 18 |
| Hart Lee Dykes, Oklahoma State | 1985–88 | 203 | 3,171 | 15.5 | 29 |

### PASSING, Career yards

| Player, team | Years | Att. | Comp. | Int. | Pct. | Yards | TD |
|--------------|-------|------|-------|------|------|-------|----|
| Todd Santos, San Diego State | 1984–87 | 1,484 | 910 | 57 | .613 | 11,425 | 70 |
| Ty Detmer, Brigham Young | 1988–90 | 1,127 | 709 | 53 | .629 | 11,000 | 86 |
| Kevin Sweeney, Fresno State | 1982–86 | 1,336 | 731 | 48 | .547 | 10,623 | 66 |
| Doug Flutie, Boston College | 1981–84 | 1,270 | 677 | 54 | .533 | 10,579 | 67 |
| Brian McClure, Bowling Green | 1982–85 | 1,427 | 900 | 58 | .631 | 10,280 | 63 |
| Ben Bennett, Duke | 1980–83 | 1,375 | 820 | 57 | .596 | 9,614 | 53 |
| Jim McMahon, Brigham Young | 1977–78, 1980–81 | 1,060 | 653 | 34 | .616 | 9,536 | 84 |
| Todd Ellis, South Carolina | 1986–89 | 1,266 | 704 | 66 | .556 | 9,516 | 49 |
| Erik Wilhelm, Oregon | 1985–88 | 1,480 | 870 | 61 | .588 | 9,393 | 52 |
| John Elway, Stanford | 1979–82 | 1,246 | 774 | 39 | .621 | 9,349 | 77 |

## NCAA FOOTBALL—MAJOR BOWL GAMES, 1975–91

### ROSE BOWL (Pasadena, Calif.)

1902 Michigan 49, Stanford 0
1916 Washington State 14, Brown 0
1917 Oregon 14, Pennsylvania 0
1918 Mare Island 19, Camp Lewis 7
1919 Great Lakes 17, Mare Island 0
1920 Harvard 7, Oregon 6
1921 California 28, Ohio State 0
1922 Washington and Jefferson 0, Cal. 0
1923 Southern Cal. 14, Penn State 3
1924 Navy 14, Washington 14
1925 Notre Dame 27, Stanford 10
1926 Alabama 20, Washington 19
1927 Alabama 7, Stanford 7
1928 Stanford 7, Pittsburgh 6
1929 Georgia Tech 8, California 7
1930 Southern Cal. 47, Pittsburgh 14
1931 Alabama 24, Washington State 0
1932 Southern California 21, Tulane 12
1933 Southern Cal. 35, Pittsburgh 0
1934 Columbia 7, Stanford 0
1935 Alabama 29, Stanford 13
1936 Stanford 7, Southern Methodist 0
1937 Pittsburgh 21, Washington 0
1938 California 13, Alabama 0
1939 Southern California 7, Duke 0
1940 Southern Cal. 14, Tennessee 0
1941 Stanford 21, Nebraska 13
1942 Ore. St. 20, Duke 16 (at Durham)
1943 Georgia 9, UCLA 0
1944 Southern Cal. 29, Washington 0
1945 Southern Cal. 25, Tennessee 0
1946 Alabama 34, Southern Cal. 14
1947 Illinois 45, UCLA 14
1948 Michigan 49, Southern California 0
1949 Northwestern 20, California 14
1950 Ohio State 17, California 14
1951 Michigan 14, California 6
1952 Illinois 40, Stanford 7
1953 Southern California 7, Wisconsin 0
1954 Michigan State 28, UCLA 20
1955 Ohio State 20, Southern Cal. 7
1956 Michigan State 17, UCLA 14
1957 Iowa 35, Oregon State 19
1959 Iowa 38, California 12
1960 Washington 44, Wisconsin 8
1961 Washington 17, Minnesota 7
1962 Minnesota 21, UCLA 3
1963 Southern Cal. 42, Wisconsin 37
1964 Illinois 17, Washington 7
1965 Michigan 34, Oregon State 7
1966 UCLA 14, Michigan State 12
1967 Purdue 14, Southern California 13
1968 Southern California 14, Indiana 3
1969 Ohio State 27, Southern Cal. 16
1970 Southern California 10, Michigan 3
1971 Stanford 27, Ohio State 17
1972 Stanford 13, Michigan 12
1973 Southern Cal. 42, Ohio State 17
1974 Ohio State 42, Southern Cal. 21
1975 Southern Cal. 18, Ohio State 17
1976 UCLA 23, Ohio State 10
1977 Southern California 14, Michigan 6
1978 Washington 27, Michigan 20
1979 Southern Cal. 17, Michigan 10
1980 Southern Cal. 17, Ohio State 16
1981 Michigan 23, Washington 6
1982 Washington 28, Iowa 0
1983 UCLA 24, Michigan 14
1984 UCLA 45, Illinois 9
1985 Southern Cal. 20, Ohio State 17
1986 UCLA 45, Iowa 28
1987 Arizona State 22, Michigan 15
1988 Michigan St. 20, Southern Cal. 17
1989 Michigan 22, Southern Cal. 14
1990 Southern Cal. 17, Michigan 10
1991 Washington 46, Iowa 34

### COTTON BOWL (Dallas, Tex.)

1937 Texas Christian 16, Marquette 6
1938 Rice 28, Colorado 14
1939 St. Mary's 20, Texas Tech 13
1940 Clemson 6, Boston College 3
1941 Texas A&M 13, Fordham 12
1942 Alabama 29, Texas A&M 21
1943 Texas 14, Georgia Tech 7
1944 Texas 7, Randolph Field 7
1945 Okla. State 34, Texas Christian 0
1946 Texas 40, Missouri 27
1947 Arkansas 0, Louisiana State 0
1948 So. Methodist 13, Penn State 13
1949 Southern Methodist 21, Oregon 13
1950 Rice 27, North Carolina 13
1951 Tennessee 20, Texas 14
1952 Kentucky 20, Texas Christian 7
1953 Texas 16, Tennessee 0
1954 Rice 28, Alabama 0
1955 Georgia Tech 14, Arkansas 6
1956 Mississippi 14, Texas Christian 13
1957 Texas Christian 28, Syracuse 27
1958 Navy 20, Rice 7
1959 Texas Christian 0, Air Force 0
1960 Syracuse 23, Texas 14
1961 Duke 7, Arkansas 6
1962 Texas 12, Mississippi 7
1963 Louisiana State 13, Texas 0
1964 Texas 28, Navy 6
1965 Arkansas 10, Nebraska 7
1966 Louisiana State 14, Arkansas 7
1967 Georgia 24, Southern Methodist 9
1968 Texas A&M 20, Alabama 16
1969 Texas 36, Tennessee 13
1970 Texas 21, Notre Dame 24
1971 Notre Dame 24, Texas 11
1972 Penn State 30, Texas 6
1973 Texas 17, Alabama 13
1974 Nebraska 19, Texas 3
1975 Penn State 41, Baylor 20
1976 Arkansas 31, Georgia 10
1977 Houston 30, Maryland 21
1978 Notre Dame 38, Texas 10
1979 Notre Dame 35, Houston 34
1980 Houston 17, Nebraska 14
1981 Alabama 30, Baylor 2
1982 Texas 14, Alabama 12
1983 Southern Methodist 7, Pittsburgh 3
1984 Georgia 10, Texas 9
1985 Boston College 45, Houston 28
1986 Texas A&M 36, Auburn 16
1987 Ohio State 28, Texas A&M 12
1988 Texas A&M 35, Notre Dame 10
1989 UCLA 17, Arkansas 3

### ORANGE BOWL (Miami, Fla.)

1935 Bucknell 26, Miami (Fla.) 0
1936 Catholic U. 20, Mississippi 19
1937 Duquesne 13, Miss. State 12
1938 Auburn 6, Michigan State 0
1939 Tennessee 17, Oklahoma 0
1940 Georgia Tech 21, Misouri 7
1941 Miss. State 14, Georgetown 7
1942 Georgia 40, Texas Christian 26
1943 Alabama 37, Boston College 21
1944 Louisiana St. 19, Texas A&M 14
1945 Tulsa 26, Georgia Tech 12
1946 Miami (Fla.)13, Holy Cross 6
1947 Rice 8, Tennessee 0
1948 Georgia Tech 20, Kansas 14
1949 Texas 41, Georgia 28
1950 Santa Clara 21, Kentucky 13
1951 Clemson 15, Miami (Fla.) 14
1952 Georgia Tech 20, Baylor 14
1953 Alabama 61, Syracuse 6
1954 Oklahoma 7, Maryland 0
1955 Duke 34, Nebraska 7
1956 Oklahoma 20, Maryland 6
1957 Colorado 27, Clemson 21
1958 Oklahoma 48, Duke 21
1959 Oklahoma 21, Syracuse 6
1960 Georgia 14, Missouri 0
1961 Missouri 21, Navy 14
1962 Louisiana State 25, Colorado 7
1963 Alabama 17, Oklahoma 0
1964 Nebraska 13, Auburn 7
1965 Texas 21, Alabama 17
1966 Alabama 39, Nebraska 28
1967 Florida 27, Georgia Tech 12
1968 Oklahoma 26, Tennessee 24
1969 Penn State 15, Kansas 14
1970 Penn State 10, Missouri 3
1971 Nebraska 17, Louisiana State 12
1972 Nebraska 38, Alabama 6
1973 Nebraska 40, Notre Dame 6
1974 Penn State 16, Louisiana State 9
1975 Notre Dame 13, Alabama 11
1976 Oklahoma 14, Michigan 6
1977 Ohio State 27, Colorado 10
1978 Arkansas 31, Oklahoma 6
1979 Oklahoma 31, Nebraska 24
1980 Oklahoma 24, Florida State 7
1981 Oklahoma 18, Florida State 17
1982 Clemson 22, Nebraska 15
1983 Nebraska 21, Louisiana State 20
1984 Miami (Fla.) 31, Nebraska 30
1985 Washington 28, Oklahoma 17
1986 Oklahoma 25, Penn State 10
1987 Oklahoma 42, Arkansas 8
1988 Miami (Fla.) 20, Oklahoma 14
1989 Miami (Fla.) 23, Nebraska 3
1990 Notre Dame 21, Colorado 6
1991 Colorado 10, Notre Dame 9

### SUGAR BOWL (New Orleans, La.)

1935 Tulane 20, Temple 14
1936 Texas Christian 3, Louisiana St. 2
1937 Santa Clara 21, Louisiana State 14
1938 Santa Clara 6, Louisiana State 0
1939 Tex. Christian 15, Carnegie Tech 7
1940 Texas A&M 14, Tulane 13
1941 Boston College 19, Tennessee 13
1942 Fordham 2, Missouri 0
1943 Tennessee 14, Tulsa 7
1944 Georgia Tech 20, Tulsa 18
1945 Duke 29, Alabama 26
1946 Oklahoma State 33, St. Mary's 13
1947 Georgia 20, North Carolina 10
1948 Texas 27, Alabama 7
1949 Oklahoma 14, North Carolina 6
1950 Oklahoma 35, Louisiana State 0
1951 Kentucky 13, Oklahoma 7
1952 Maryland 28, Tennessee 13
1953 Georgia Tech 24, Mississippi 7
1954 Georgia Tech 42, West Virginia 19
1955 Navy 21, Mississippi 0
1956 Georgia Tech 7, Pittsburgh 0
1957 Baylor 13, Tennessee 7
1958 Mississippi 39, Texas 7
1959 Louisiana State 7, Clemson 0
1960 Mississippi 21, Louisiana State 0
1961 Mississippi 14, Rice 6
1962 Alabama 10, Arkansas 3
1963 Mississippi 17, Arkansas 13
1964 Alabama 12, Mississippi 7
1965 Louisiana State 13, Syracuse 10
1966 Missouri 20, Florida 18
1967 Alabama 34, Nebraska 7
1968 Louisiana State 20, Wyoming 13
1969 Arkansas 16, Georgia 2
1970 Mississippi 27, Arkansas 22
1971 Tennessee 34, Air Force 13
1972 Oklahoma 40, Auburn 22
1973 Oklahoma 14, Penn State 0
1974 Notre Dame 24, Alabama 23
1975 Nebraska 13, Florida 10
1976 Alabama 13, Penn State 6
1977 Pittsburgh 27, Georgia 3
1978 Alabama 35, Ohio State 6
1979 Alabama 14, Penn State 7
1980 Alabama 24, Arkansas 9
1981 Georgia 17, Notre Dame 10
1982 Pittsburgh 24, Georgia 20
1983 Penn State 27, Georgia 23
1984 Auburn 9, Michigan 7
1985 Nebraska 28, Louisiana State 10
1986 Tennessee 35, Miami (Fla.) 7
1987 Nebraska 30, Louisiana State 15
1988 Syracuse 16, Auburn 16
1989 Florida State 13, Auburn 7
1990 Miami (Fla.) 33, Alabama 25
1991 Tennessee 23, Virginia 22

## OUTLAND TROPHY

Honoring the outstanding interior lineman, as selected by the Football Writers Association of America, this trophy commemorates John Outland, a two-time consensus All-American guard for Penn State (1897–98).

| Year | Player | College | Position |
|------|--------|---------|----------|
| 1946 | George Connor | Notre Dame | T |
| 1947 | Joe Steffy | Army | G |
| 1948 | Bill Fischer | Notre Dame | G |
| 1949 | Ed Bagdon | Michigan State | G |
| 1950 | Bob Gain | Kentucky | T |
| 1951 | Jim Weatherall | Oklahoma | T |
| 1952 | Dick Modzelewski | Maryland | T |
| 1953 | J.D. Roberts | Oklahoma | G |
| 1954 | Bill Brooks | Arkansas | G |
| 1955 | Calvin Jones | Iowa | G |
| 1956 | Jim Parker | Ohio State | G |
| 1957 | Alex Karras | Iowa | T |
| 1958 | Zeke Smith | Auburn | G |
| 1959 | Mike McGee | Duke | T |
| 1960 | Tom Brown | Minnesota | G |
| 1961 | Merlin Olsen | Utah State | T |
| 1962 | Bobby Bell | Minnesota | T |
| 1963 | Scott Appleton | Texas | T |
| 1964 | Steve DeLong | Tennessee | T |
| 1965 | Tommy Nobis | Texas | G |
| 1966 | Loyd Phillips | Arkansas | T |
| 1967 | Ron Yary | Southern California | T |
| 1968 | Bill Stanfill | Georgia | T |
| 1969 | Mike Reid | Penn State | DT |
| 1970 | Jim Stillwagon | Ohio State | MG |
| 1971 | Larry Jacobson | Nebraska | DT |
| 1972 | Rich Glover | Nebraska | MG |
| 1973 | John Hicks | Ohio State | OT |
| 1974 | Randy White | Maryland | DE |
| 1975 | Lee Roy Selmon | Oklahoma | DT |
| 1976 | Ross Browner | Notre Dame | DE |
| 1977 | Brad Shearer | Texas | DT |
| 1978 | Greg Roberts | Oklahoma | G |
| 1979 | Jim Ritcher | North Carolina State | C |
| 1980 | Mark May | Pittsburgh | OT |
| 1981 | Dave Rimington | Nebraska | C |
| 1982 | Dave Rimington | Nebraska | C |
| 1983 | Dean Steinkuhler | Nebraska | G |
| 1984 | Bruce Smith | Virginia Tech | DT |
| 1985 | Mike Ruth | Boston College | NG |
| 1986 | Jason Buck | Brigham Young | DT |
| 1987 | Chad Hennings | Air Force | DT |
| 1988 | Tracy Rocker | Auburn | DT |
| 1989 | Mohammed Elewonibi | Brigham Young | G |
| 1990 | Russell Maryland | Miami (Fla.) | DT |

## HEISMAN MEMORIAL TROPHY

Honoring the outstanding college football player in the United States.

| Year | Player | College | Position |
|------|--------|---------|----------|
| 1935 | Jay Berwanger | Chicago | HB |
| 1936 | Larry Kelley | Yale | E |
| 1937 | Clint Frank | Yale | HB |
| 1938 | Davey O'Brien | Texas Christian | QB |
| 1939 | Nile Kinnick | Iowa | HB |
| 1940 | Tom Harmon | Michigan | HB |
| 1941 | Bruce Smith | Minnesota | HB |
| 1942 | Frank Sinkwich | Georgia | HB |
| 1943 | Angelo Bertelli | Notre Dame | QB |
| 1944 | Les Horvath | Ohio State | QB |
| 1945 | Doc Blanchard | Army | FB |
| 1946 | Glenn Davis | Army | HB |
| 1947 | John Lujack | Notre Dame | QB |
| 1948 | Doak Walker | Southern Methodist | HB |
| 1949 | Leon Hart | Notre Dame | E |
| 1950 | Vic Janowicz | Ohio State | HB |
| 1951 | Dick Kazmaier | Princeton | HB |
| 1952 | Billy Vessels | Oklahoma | HB |
| 1953 | John Lattner | Notre Dame | HB |
| 1954 | Alan Ameche | Wisconsin | FB |
| 1955 | Howard Cassady | Ohio State | HB |
| 1956 | Paul Hornung | Notre Dame | QB |
| 1957 | John Crow | Texas A&M | HB |
| 1958 | Pete Dawkins | Army | HB |
| 1959 | Billy Cannon | Louisiana State | HB |
| 1960 | Joe Bellino | Navy | HB |
| 1961 | Ernie Davis | Syracuse | HB |
| 1962 | Terry Baker | Oregon State | QB |
| 1963 | Roger Staubach | Navy | QB |
| 1964 | John Huarte | Notre Dame | QB |
| 1965 | Mike Garrett | Southern California | HB |
| 1966 | Steve Spurrier | Florida | QB |
| 1967 | Gary Beban | UCLA | QB |
| 1968 | O.J. Simpson | Southern California | HB |
| 1969 | Steve Owens | Oklahoma | HB |
| 1970 | Jim Plunkett | Stanford | QB |
| 1971 | Pat Sullivan | Auburn | QB |
| 1972 | Johnny Rodgers | Nebraska | FL |
| 1973 | John Cappelletti | Penn State | HB |
| 1974 | Archie Griffin | Ohio State | HB |
| 1975 | Archie Griffin | Ohio State | HB |
| 1976 | Tony Dorsett | Pittsburgh | HB |
| 1977 | Earl Campbell | Texas | HB |
| 1978 | Billy Sims | Oklahoma | HB |
| 1979 | Charles White | Southern California | HB |
| 1980 | George Rogers | South Carolina | HB |
| 1981 | Marcus Allen | Southern California | HB |
| 1982 | Herschel Walker | Georgia | HB |
| 1983 | Mike Rozier | Nebraska | HB |
| 1984 | Doug Flutie | Boston College | QB |
| 1985 | Bo Jackson | Auburn | HB |
| 1986 | Vinny Testaverde | Miami (Fla.) | QB |
| 1987 | Tim Brown | Notre Dame | WR |
| 1988 | Barry Sanders | Oklahoma State | RB |
| 1989 | Andre Ware | Houston | QB |
| 1990 | Ty Detmer | Brigham Young | QB |

# Basketball

## NCAA BASKETBALL CAREER LEADERS

### SCORING LEADERS

| Player, team | Points |
|--------------|--------|
| Pete Maravich, Louisiana State | 3,667 |
| Freeman Williams, Portland St. | 3,249 |
| Lionel Simmons, LaSalle | 3,217 |
| Harry Kelly, Texas Southern | 3,066 |
| Hersey Hawkins, Bradley | 3,008 |
| Oscar Robertson, Cincinnati | 2,973 |
| Danny Manning, Kansas | 2,951 |
| Alfredrick Hughes, Loyola (Ill.) | 2,914 |
| Elvin Hayes, Houston | 2,884 |
| Larry Bird, Indiana State | 2,850 |

### ASSIST LEADERS

| Player, team | Assists |
|--------------|---------|
| Chris Corchiani, N. Carolina St. | 1,038 |
| Keith Jennings, E. Tennessee St. | 983 |
| Sherman Douglas, Syracuse | 960 |
| Greg Anthony, UNLV | 950 |
| Gary Payton, Oregon State | 938 |
| Andre Lafleur, Northeastern | 894 |
| Jim Les, Bradley | 884 |
| Frank Smith, Old Dominion | 883 |
| Taurence Chisholm, Delaware | 877 |
| Grayson Marshall, Clemson | 857 |

### REBOUNDING LEADERS

| Player, team | Rebounds | Player, team | Rebounds |
|--------------|----------|--------------|----------|
| Tom Gola, LaSalle | 2,201 | Paul Silas, Creighton | 1,751 |
| Joe Holup, George Washington | 2,030 | Art Quimby, Connecticut | 1,716 |
| Charlie Slack, Marshall | 1,916 | Jerry Harper, Alabama | 1,688 |
| Ed Conlin, Fordham | 1,884 | Jeff Cohen, William and Mary | 1,679 |
| Dickie Hemric, Wake Forest | 1,802 | Steve Hamilton, Morehead State | 1,675 |

## NCAA DIVISION I MEN'S BASKETBALL FINAL FOUR RESULTS

The first NCAA men's basketball tournament was held in 1939, when eight teams, selected by committee, from eight geographical regions gathered in Evanston, Ill. In the past 52 years, the tournament has grown tremendously, and 64 teams now compete for the title of national champion. The tournament field, consisting of 30 conference champions and 34 "at-large" bids, is divided into four regions, each one sending a team to the Final Four through a single-game elimination process.

| Year | Champion | Score | Runner-up | Third place | Fourth place | Champion coach | Outstanding player award | |
|------|----------|-------|-----------|-------------|--------------|----------------|-------------------------|---|
| 1939 | Oregon | 46–33 | Ohio State | Oklahoma[1] | Villanova[1] | Howard Hobson | None selected | |
| 1940 | Indiana | 60–42 | Kansas | Duquesne[1] | Southern California[1] | Branch McCracken | Marvin Huffman | Indiana |
| 1941 | Wisconsin | 39–34 | Washington State | Pittsburgh[1] | Arkansas[1] | Harold Foster | John Kotz | Wisconsin |
| 1942 | Stanford | 53–38 | Dartmouth | Colorado[1] | Kentucky[1] | Everett Dean | Howard Dallmar | Stanford |
| 1943 | Wyoming | 46–34 | Georgetown | Texas[1] | DePaul[1] | Everett Shelton | Ken Sailors | Wyoming |
| 1944 | Utah | 42–40[2] | Dartmouth | Iowa State[1] | Ohio State[1] | Vadal Peterson | Arnold Ferrin | Utah |
| 1945 | Oklahoma State | 49–45 | New York Univ. | Arkansas[1] | Ohio State[1] | Henry Iba | Bob Kurland | Oklahoma State |
| 1946 | Oklahoma State | 43–40 | North Carolina | Ohio State | California | Henry Iba | Bob Kurland | Oklahoma State |
| 1947 | Holy Cross | 58–47 | Oklahoma | Texas | CCNY | Alvin Julian | George Kaftan | Holy Cross |
| 1948 | Kentucky | 58–42 | Baylor | Holy Cross | Kansas State | Adolph Rupp | Alex Groza | Kentucky |
| 1949 | Kentucky | 46–36 | Oklahoma State | Illinois | Oregon State | Adolph Rupp | Alex Groza | Kentucky |
| 1950 | CCNY | 71–68 | Bradley | North Carolina State | Baylor | Nat Holman | Irwin Dambrot | CCNY |
| 1951 | Kentucky | 68–58 | Kansas State | Illinois | Oklahoma State | Adolph Rupp | None selected | |
| 1952 | Kansas | 80–63 | St. John's | Illinois | Santa Clara | Forrest Allen | Clyde Lovellette | Kansas |
| 1953 | Indiana | 69–68 | Kansas | Washington | Louisiana State | Branch McCracken | B.H. Born | Kansas |
| 1954 | La Salle | 92–76 | Bradley | Penn State | Southern California | Kenneth Loeffler | Tom Gola | La Salle |
| 1955 | San Francisco | 77–63 | La Salle | Colorado | Iowa | Phil Woolpert | Bill Russell | San Francisco |
| 1956 | San Francisco | 83–71 | Iowa | Temple | Southern Methodist | Phil Woolpert | Hal Lear | Temple |
| 1957 | North Carolina | 54–53[3] | Kansas | San Francisco | Michigan State | Frank McGuire | Wilt Chamberlain | Kansas |
| 1958 | Kentucky | 84–72 | Seattle | Temple | Kansas State | Adolph Rupp | Elgin Baylor | Seattle |
| 1959 | California | 71–70 | West Virginia | Cincinnati | Louisville | Pete Newell | Jerry West | West Virginia |
| 1960 | Ohio State | 75–55 | California | Cincinnati | New York Univ. | Fred Taylor | Jerry Lucas | Ohio State |
| 1961 | Cincinnati | 70–65[2] | Ohio State | St. Joseph's (Pa.)[4] | Utah | Edwin Jucker | Jerry Lucas | Ohio State |
| 1962 | Cincinnati | 71–59 | Ohio State | Wake Forest | UCLA | Edwin Jucker | Paul Hogue | Cincinnati |
| 1963 | Loyola (Ill.) | 60–58[2] | Cincinnati | Duke | Utah | George Ireland | Art Heyman | Duke |
| 1964 | UCLA | 98–83 | Duke | Michigan | Kansas State | John Wooden | Walt Hazzard | UCLA |
| 1965 | UCLA | 91–80 | Michigan | Princeton | Wichita State | John Wooden | Bill Bradley | Princeton |
| 1966 | UTEP | 72–65 | Kentucky | Duke | Utah | Don Haskins | Jerry Chambers | Utah |
| 1967 | UCLA | 79–64 | Dayton | Houston | North Carolina | John Wooden | Lew Alcindor | UCLA |
| 1968 | UCLA | 78–55 | North Carolina | Ohio State | Houston | John Wooden | Lew Alcindor | UCLA |
| 1969 | UCLA | 92–72 | Purdue | Drake | North Carolina | John Wooden | Lew Alcindor | UCLA |
| 1970 | UCLA | 80–69 | Jacksonville | New Mexico State | St. Bonaventure | John Wooden | Sidney Wicks | UCLA |
| 1971 | UCLA | 68–62 | Villanova[4] | Western Kentucky[4] | Kansas | John Wooden | Howard Porter | Villanova |
| 1972 | UCLA | 81–76 | Florida State | North Carolina | Louisville | John Wooden | Bill Walton | UCLA |
| 1973 | UCLA | 87–66 | Memphis State | Indiana | Providence | John Wooden | Bill Walton | UCLA |
| 1974 | North Carolina State | 76–64 | Marquette | UCLA | Kansas | Norm Sloan | David Thompson | North Carolina State |
| 1975 | UCLA | 92–85 | Kentucky | Louisville | Syracuse | John Wooden | Richard Washington | UCLA |
| 1976 | Indiana | 86–68 | Michigan | UCLA | Rutgers | Bob Knight | Kent Benson | Indiana |
| 1977 | Marquette | 67–59 | North Carolina | UNLV | N. Carolina, Charlotte | Al McGuire | Butch Lee | Marquette |
| 1978 | Kentucky | 94–88 | Duke | Arkansas | Notre Dame | Joe Hall | Jack Givens | Kentucky |
| 1979 | Michigan State | 75–64 | Indiana State | DePaul | Penn | Jud Heathcote | Earvin Johnson | Mighigan State |
| 1980 | Louisville | 59–54 | UCLA[4] | Purdue | Iowa | Denny Crum | Darrell Griffith | Louisville |
| 1981 | Indiana | 63–50 | North Carolina | Virginia | Louisiana State | Bob Knight | Isiah Thomas | Indiana |
| 1982 | North Carolina | 63–62 | Georgetown | Houston[1] | Louisville[1] | Dean Smith | James Worthy | North Carolina |
| 1983 | North Carolina State | 54–52 | Houston | Georgia[1] | Louisville[1] | Jim Valvano | Akeem Olajuwon | Houston |
| 1984 | Georgetown | 84–75 | Houston | Kentucky[1] | Virginia[1] | John Thompson | Patrick Ewing | Georgetown |
| 1985 | Villanova | 66–64 | Georgetown | St. John's[1] | Memphis State[1, 4] | Rollie Massemino | Ed Pinckney | Villanova |
| 1986 | Louisville | 72–69 | Duke | Kansas[1] | Louisiana State[1] | Denny Crum | Pervis Ellison | Louisville |
| 1987 | Indiana | 74–73 | Syracuse | UNLV[1] | Providence[1] | Bob Knight | Keith Smart | Indiana |
| 1988 | Kansas | 83–79 | Oklahoma | Arizona[1] | Duke[1] | Larry Brown | Danny Manning | Kansas |
| 1989 | Michigan | 80–79[2] | Seton Hall | Illinois[1] | Duke[1] | Steve Fisher | Glen Rice | Michigan |
| 1990 | UNLV | 103–73 | Duke | Georgia Tech[1] | Arkansas[1] | Jerry Tarkanian | Anderson Hunt | UNLV |
| 1991 | Duke | 72–65 | Kansas | UNLV[1] | North Carolina[1] | Mike Krzyzewski | Christian Laettner | Duke |

1. Tied for third place. 2. Overtime. 3. Triple overtime. 4. Later declared ineligible.

## NATIONAL INVITATION TOURNAMENT CHAMPIONS

| | | | | | |
|---|---|---|---|---|---|
| 1938 Temple | 1945 DePaul | 1952 La Salle | 1959 St. John's | 1966 Brigham Young | 1975 Princeton | 1984 Michigan |
| 1939 Long Island Univ. | 1946 Kentucky | 1953 Seton Hall | 1960 Bradley | 1967 Southern Illinois | 1976 Kentucky | 1985 UCLA |
| 1940 Colorado | 1947 Utah | 1954 Holy Cross | 1961 Providence | 1968 Dayton | 1977 St. Bonaventure | 1986 Ohio State |
| 1941 Long Island Univ. | 1948 St. Louis | 1955 Duquesne | 1962 Dayton | 1969 Temple | 1978 Texas | 1987 S. Mississippi |
| 1942 West Virginia | 1949 San Francisco | 1956 Louisville | 1963 Providence | 1970 Marquette | 1979 Indiana | 1988 Connecticut |
| 1943 St. John's | 1950 CCNY | 1957 Bradley | 1964 Bradley | 1971 North Carolina | 1980 Virginia | 1989 St. John's |
| 1944 St. John's | 1951 Brigham Young | 1958 Xavier (Ohio) | 1965 St. John's | 1972 Maryland | 1981 Tulsa | 1990 Vanderbilt |
| | | | | 1973 Virginia Tech | 1982 Bradley | 1991 Stanford |
| | | | | 1974 Purdue | 1983 Fresno State | |

# OTHER MEN'S NCAA CHAMPIONS

## BASEBALL

**Year Champion**

1947 California
1948 Southern California
1949 Texas
1950 Texas
1951 Oklahoma
1952 Holy Cross
1953 Michigan
1954 Missouri
1955 Wake Forest
1956 Minnesota
1957 California
1958 Southern California
1959 Oklahoma State
1960 Minnesota
1961 Southern California
1962 Michigan
1963 Southern California
1964 Minnesota
1965 Arizona State
1966 Ohio State
1967 Arizona State
1968 Southern California
1969 Arizona State
1970 Southern California
1971 Southern California
1972 Southern California
1973 Southern California
1974 Southern California
1975 Texas
1976 Arizona
1977 Arizona State
1978 Southern California
1979 California State,
    Fullerton
1980 Arizona
1981 Arizona State
1982 Miami (Fla.)
1983 Texas
1984 California State,
    Fullerton
1985 Miami (Fla.)
1986 Arizona
1987 Stanford
1988 Stanford
1989 Wichita State
1990 Georgia
1991 Louisiana State

## ICE HOCKEY

**Year Champion**

1948 Michigan
1949 Boston College
1950 Colorado College
1951 Michigan
1952 Michigan
1953 Michigan
1954 Rensselaer
1955 Michigan
1956 Michigan
1957 Colorado College
1958 Denver
1959 North Dakota
1960 Denver
1961 Denver
1962 Michigan Tech

1963 North Dakota
1964 Michigan
1965 Michigan Tech
1966 Michigan State
1967 Cornell
1968 Denver
1969 Denver
1970 Cornell
1971 Boston University
1972 Boston University
1973 Wisconsin
1974 Minnesota
1975 Michigan Tech
1976 Minnesota
1977 Wisconsin
1978 Boston University
1979 Minnesota
1980 North Dakota
1981 Wisconsin
1982 North Dakota
1983 Wisconsin
1984 Bowling Green
1985 Rensselaer
1986 Michigan State
1987 North Dakota
1988 Lake Superior State
1989 Harvard
1990 Wisconsin
1991 Northern Michigan

## LACROSSE

**Year Champion**

1971 Cornell
1972 Virginia
1973 Maryland
1974 Johns Hopkins
1975 Maryland
1976 Cornell
1977 Cornell
1978 Johns Hopkins
1979 Johns Hopkins
1980 Johns Hopkins
1981 North Carolina
1982 North Carolina
1983 Syracuse
1984 Johns Hopkins
1985 Johns Hopkins
1986 North Carolina
1987 Johns Hopkins
1988 Syracuse
1989 Syracuse
1990 Syracuse
1991 North Carolina

## SOCCER

**Year Champion**

1959 St. Louis
1960 St. Louis
1961 West Chester
1962 St. Louis
1963 St. Louis
1964 Navy
1965 St. Louis
1966 San Francisco
1967 Michigan State
    St. Louis

1968 Maryland
    Michigan State
1969 St. Louis
1970 St. Louis
1971 vacated
1972 St. Louis
1973 St. Louis
1974 Howard
1975 San Francisco
1976 San Francisco
1977 Hartwick
1978 vacated
1979 Southern
    Illinois Univ. at
    Edwardsville
1980 San Francisco
1981 Connecticut
1982 Indiana
1983 Indiana
1984 Clemson
1985 UCLA
1986 Duke
1987 Clemson
1988 Indiana
1989 Santa Clara
    Virginia
1990 UCLA

## TENNIS

**Year Champion**

1946 Southern California
1947 William and Mary
1948 William and Mary
1949 San Francisco
1950 UCLA
1951 Southern California
1952 UCLA
1953 UCLA
1954 UCLA
1955 Southern California
1956 UCLA
1957 Michigan
1958 Southern California
1959 Notre Dame
    Tulane
1960 UCLA
1961 UCLA
1962 Southern California
1963 Southern California
1964 Southern California
1965 UCLA
1966 Southern California
1967 Southern California
1968 Southern California
1969 Southern California
1970 UCLA
1971 UCLA
1972 Trinity (Tex.)
1973 Stanford
1974 Stanford
1975 UCLA
1976 Southern California
    UCLA
1977 Stanford
1978 Stanford
1979 UCLA
1980 Stanford
1981 Stanford
1982 UCLA
1983 Stanford
1984 UCLA

1985 Georgia
1986 Stanford
1987 Georgia
1988 Stanford
1989 Stanford
1990 Stanford
1991 Southern California

## VOLLEYBALL

**Year Champion**

1970 UCLA
1971 UCLA
1972 UCLA
1973 San Diego State
1974 UCLA
1975 UCLA
1976 UCLA
1977 Southern California
1978 Pepperdine
1979 UCLA
1980 Southern California
1981 UCLA
1982 UCLA
1983 UCLA
1984 UCLA
1985 Pepperdine
1986 Pepperdine
1987 UCLA
1988 Southern California
1989 UCLA
1990 Southern California
1991 California State,
    Long Beach

## WATER POLO

**Year Champion**

1969 UCLA
1970 Univ. of California,
    Irvine
1971 UCLA
1972 UCLA
1973 California
1974 California
1975 California
1976 Stanford
1977 California
1978 Stanford
1979 Univ. of California,
    Santa Barbara
1980 Stanford
1981 Stanford
1982 Univ. of California,
    Irvine
1983 California
1984 California
1985 Stanford
1986 Stanford
1987 California
1988 California
1989 California
1990 California

## SWIMMING
## AND DIVING

**Year Champion**

1937 Michigan
1938 Michigan
1939 Michigan
1940 Michigan
1941 Michigan

1942 Yale
1943 Ohio State
1944 Yale
1945 Ohio State
1946 Ohio State
1947 Ohio State
1948 Michigan
1949 Ohio State
1950 Ohio State
1951 Yale
1952 Ohio State
1953 Yale
1954 Ohio State
1955 Ohio State
    Michigan
1956 Ohio State
1957 Michigan
1958 Michigan
1959 Michigan
1960 Southern California
1961 Michigan
1962 Ohio State
1963 Southern California
1964 Southern California
1965 Southern California
1966 Southern California
1967 Stanford
1968 Indiana
1969 Indiana
1970 Indiana
1971 Indiana
1972 Indiana
1973 Indiana
1974 Southern California
1975 Southern California
1976 Southern California
1977 Southern California
1978 Tennessee
1979 California
1980 California
1981 Texas
1982 UCLA
1983 Florida
1984 Florida
1985 Stanford
1986 Stanford
1987 Stanford
1988 Texas
1989 Texas
1990 Texas
1991 Texas

## WRESTLING

**Year Champion**

1928 Oklahoma State[1]
1929 Oklahoma State
1930 Oklahoma State[1]
1931 Oklahoma State[1]
1932 Indiana
1933 Oklahoma State[1]
    Iowa State[1]
1934 Oklahoma State
1935 Oklahoma State
1936 Oklahoma
1937 Oklahoma State
1938 Oklahoma State
1939 Oklahoma State
1940 Oklahoma State
1941 Oklahoma State
1942 Oklahoma State
1946 Oklahoma State

1947 Cornell College
1948 Oklahoma State
1949 Oklahoma State
1950 Northern Iowa
1951 Oklahoma
1952 Oklahoma
1953 Penn State
1954 Oklahoma State
1955 Oklahoma State
1956 Oklahoma State
1957 Oklahoma
1958 Oklahoma State
1959 Oklahoma State
1960 Oklahoma
1961 Oklahoma State
1962 Oklahoma State
1963 Oklahoma
1964 Oklahoma State
1965 Iowa State
1966 Oklahoma State
1967 Michigan State
1968 Oklahoma State
1969 Iowa State
1970 Iowa State
1971 Oklahoma State
1972 Iowa State
1973 Iowa State
1974 Oklahoma
1975 Iowa
1976 Iowa
1977 Iowa State
1978 Iowa
1979 Iowa
1980 Iowa
1981 Iowa
1982 Iowa
1983 Iowa
1984 Iowa
1985 Iowa
1986 Iowa
1987 Iowa State
1988 Arizona State
1989 Oklahoma State
1990 Oklahoma State
1991 Iowa
1. Unofficial champions.

## CROSS-COUNTRY

**Year Champion**

1938 Indiana
1939 Michigan State
1940 Indiana
1941 Rhode Island
1942 Indiana
1944 Drake
1945 Drake
1946 Drake
1947 Penn State
1948 Michigan State
1949 Michigan State
1950 Penn State
1951 Syracuse
1952 Michigan State
1953 Kansas
1954 Oklahoma State
1955 Michigan State
1956 Michigan State
1957 Notre Dame
1958 Michigan State
1959 Michigan State
1960 Houston
1961 Oregon State

| | |
|---|---|
| 1962 | San Jose State |
| 1963 | San Jose State |
| 1964 | Western Michigan |
| 1965 | Western Michigan |
| 1966 | Villanova |
| 1967 | Villanova |
| 1968 | Villanova |
| 1969 | UTEP |
| 1970 | Villanova |
| 1971 | Oregon |
| 1972 | Tennessee |
| 1973 | Oregon |
| 1974 | Oregon |
| 1975 | UTEP |
| 1976 | UTEP |
| 1977 | Oregon |
| 1978 | UTEP |
| 1979 | UTEP |
| 1980 | UTEP |
| 1981 | UTEP |
| 1982 | Wisconsin |
| 1983 | vacated |
| 1984 | Arkansas |
| 1985 | Wisconsin |
| 1986 | Arkansas |
| 1987 | Arkansas |
| 1988 | Wisconsin |
| 1989 | Iowa State |
| 1990 | Arkansas |

## OUTDOOR TRACK
**Year Champion**

| | |
|---|---|
| 1921 | Illinois |
| 1922 | California |
| 1923 | Michigan |
| 1925 | Stanford |
| 1926 | Southern California |
| 1927 | Illinois |
| 1928 | Stanford |
| 1929 | Ohio State |
| 1930 | Southern California |
| 1931 | Southern California |
| 1932 | Indiana |
| 1933 | Louisiana State |
| 1934 | Stanford |
| 1935 | Southern California |
| 1936 | Southern California |
| 1937 | Southern California |
| 1938 | Southern California |
| 1939 | Southern California |
| 1940 | Southern California |
| 1941 | Southern California |
| 1942 | Southern California |
| 1943 | Southern California |
| 1944 | Illinois |
| 1945 | Navy |
| 1946 | Illinois |
| 1947 | Illinois |
| 1948 | Minnesota |
| 1949 | Southern California |
| 1950 | Southern California |
| 1951 | Southern California |
| 1952 | Southern California |
| 1953 | Southern California |
| 1954 | Southern California |
| 1955 | Southern California |
| 1956 | UCLA |
| 1957 | Villanova |
| 1958 | Southern California |
| 1959 | Kansas |

| | |
|---|---|
| 1960 | Kansas |
| 1961 | Southern California |
| 1962 | Oregon |
| 1963 | Southern California |
| 1964 | Oregon |
| 1965 | Oregon |
| | Southern California |
| 1966 | UCLA |
| 1967 | Southern California |
| 1968 | Southern California |
| 1969 | San Jose State |
| 1970 | Brigham Young |
| | Kansas |
| 1971 | UCLA |
| 1972 | UCLA |
| 1973 | UCLA |
| 1974 | Tennessee |
| 1975 | UTEP |
| 1976 | Southern California |
| 1977 | Arizona State |
| 1978 | UCLA |
| | UTEP |
| 1979 | UTEP |
| 1980 | UTEP |
| 1981 | UTEP |
| 1982 | UTEP |
| 1983 | Southern Methodist |
| 1984 | Oregon |
| 1985 | Arkansas |
| 1986 | Southern Methodist |
| 1987 | UCLA |
| 1988 | UCLA |
| 1989 | Louisiana State |
| 1990 | Louisiana State |
| 1991 | Tennessee |

## INDOOR TRACK
**Year Champion**

| | |
|---|---|
| 1965 | Missouri |
| 1966 | Kansas |
| 1967 | Southern California |
| 1968 | Villanova |
| 1969 | Kansas |
| 1970 | Kansas |
| 1971 | Villanova |
| 1972 | Southern California |
| 1973 | Manhattan |
| 1974 | UTEP |
| 1975 | UTEP |
| 1976 | UTEP |
| 1977 | Washington State |
| 1978 | UTEP |
| 1979 | Villanova |
| 1980 | UTEP |
| 1981 | UTEP |
| 1982 | UTEP |
| 1983 | Southern Methodist |
| 1984 | Arkansas |
| 1985 | Arkansas |
| 1986 | Arkansas |
| 1987 | Arkansas |
| 1988 | Arkansas |
| 1989 | Arkansas |
| 1990 | Arkansas |
| 1991 | Arkansas |

## GYMNASTICS
**Year Champion**

| | |
|---|---|
| 1938 | Chicago |
| 1939 | Illinois |

| | |
|---|---|
| 1940 | Illinois |
| 1941 | Illinois |
| 1942 | Illinois |
| 1948 | Penn State |
| 1949 | Temple |
| 1950 | Illinois |
| 1951 | Florida State |
| 1952 | Florida State |
| 1953 | Penn State |
| 1954 | Penn State |
| 1955 | Illinois |
| 1956 | Illinois |
| 1957 | Penn State |
| 1958 | Michigan State |
| | Illinois |
| 1959 | Penn State |
| 1960 | Penn State |
| 1961 | Penn State |
| 1962 | Southern California |
| 1963 | Michigan |
| 1964 | Southern Illinois |
| 1965 | Penn State |
| 1966 | Southern Illinois |
| 1967 | Southern Illinois |
| 1968 | California |
| 1969 | Iowa |
| | Michigan[1] |
| 1970 | Michigan |
| | Michigan[1] |
| 1971 | Iowa State |
| 1972 | Southern Illinois |
| 1973 | Iowa State |
| 1974 | Iowa State |
| 1975 | California |
| 1976 | Penn State |
| 1977 | Indiana State |
| | Oklahoma |
| 1978 | Oklahoma |
| 1979 | Nebraska |
| 1980 | Nebraska |
| 1981 | Nebraska |
| 1982 | Nebraska |
| 1983 | Nebraska |
| 1984 | UCLA |
| 1985 | Ohio State |
| 1986 | Arizona State |
| 1987 | UCLA |
| 1988 | Nebraska |
| 1989 | Illinois |
| 1990 | Nebraska |
| 1991 | Oklahoma |

1. Trampoline.

## GOLF
**Year Champion**

| | |
|---|---|
| 1897 | Yale |
| 1898 | Harvard (spring) |
| | Yale (fall) |
| 1899 | Harvard |
| 1901 | Harvard |
| 1902 | Yale (spring) |
| | Harvard (fall) |
| 1903 | Harvard |
| 1904 | Harvard |
| 1905 | Yale |
| 1906 | Yale |
| 1907 | Yale |
| 1908 | Yale |
| 1909 | Yale |
| 1910 | Yale |
| 1911 | Yale |

| | |
|---|---|
| 1912 | Yale |
| 1913 | Yale |
| 1914 | Princeton |
| 1915 | Yale |
| 1916 | Princeton |
| 1919 | Princeton |
| 1920 | Princeton |
| 1921 | Dartmouth |
| 1922 | Princeton |
| 1923 | Princeton |
| 1924 | Yale |
| 1925 | Yale |
| 1926 | Yale |
| 1927 | Princeton |
| 1928 | Princeton |
| 1929 | Princeton |
| 1930 | Princeton |
| 1931 | Yale |
| 1932 | Yale |
| 1933 | Yale |
| 1934 | Michigan |
| 1935 | Michigan |
| 1936 | Yale |
| 1937 | Princeton |
| 1938 | Stanford |
| 1939 | Stanford |
| 1940 | Princeton |
| | Louisiana State |
| 1941 | Stanford |
| 1942 | Louisiana State |
| | Stanford |
| 1943 | Yale |
| 1944 | Notre Dame |
| 1945 | Ohio State |
| 1946 | Stanford |
| 1947 | Louisiana State |
| 1948 | San Jose State |
| 1949 | North Texas |
| 1950 | North Texas |
| 1951 | North Texas |
| 1952 | North Texas |
| 1953 | Stanford |
| 1954 | Southern Methodist |
| 1955 | Louisiana State |
| 1956 | Houston |
| 1957 | Houston |
| 1958 | Houston |
| 1959 | Houston |
| 1960 | Houston |
| 1961 | Purdue |
| 1962 | Houston |
| 1963 | Oklahoma State |
| 1964 | Houston |
| 1965 | Houston |
| 1966 | Houston |
| 1967 | Houston |
| 1968 | Florida |
| 1969 | Houston |
| 1970 | Houston |
| 1971 | Texas |
| 1972 | Texas |
| 1973 | Florida |
| 1974 | Wake Forest |
| 1975 | Wake Forest |
| 1976 | Oklahoma |
| 1977 | Houston |
| 1978 | Oklahoma State |
| 1979 | Ohio State |
| 1980 | Oklahoma State |
| 1981 | Brigham Young |
| 1982 | Houston |

| | |
|---|---|
| 1983 | Oklahoma State |
| 1984 | Houston |
| 1985 | Houston |
| 1986 | Wake Forest |
| 1987 | Oklahoma State |
| 1988 | UCLA |
| 1989 | Oklahoma |
| 1990 | Arizona |
| 1991 | Oklahoma State |

## FENCING
**Year Champion**

| | |
|---|---|
| 1941 | Northwestern |
| 1942 | Ohio State |
| 1947 | New York University |
| 1949 | Army |
| | Rutgers |
| 1950 | Navy |
| 1951 | Columbia |
| 1952 | Columbia |
| 1953 | Pennsylvania |
| 1954 | Columbia |
| | New York University |
| 1955 | Columbia |
| 1956 | Illinois |
| 1957 | New York University |
| 1958 | Illinois |
| 1959 | Navy |
| 1960 | New York University |
| 1961 | New York University |
| 1962 | Navy |
| 1963 | Columbia |
| 1964 | Princeton |
| 1965 | Columbia |
| 1966 | New York University |
| 1967 | New York University |
| 1968 | Columbia |
| 1969 | Pennsylvania |
| 1970 | New York University |
| | Columbia |
| 1971 | New York University |
| 1972 | Detroit |
| 1973 | New York University |
| 1974 | New York University |
| 1975 | Wayne State |
| 1976 | New York University |
| 1977 | Notre Dame |
| 1978 | Notre Dame |
| 1979 | Wayne State |
| 1980 | Wayne State |
| 1981 | Pennsylvania |
| 1982 | Wayne State |
| 1983 | Wayne State |
| 1984 | Wayne State |
| 1985 | Wayne State |
| 1986 | Notre Dame |
| 1987 | Columbia |
| 1988 | Columbia |
| 1989 | Columbia |
| 1990 | Penn State |

## MEN'S AND WOMEN'S RIFLE
**Year Champion**

| | |
|---|---|
| 1980 | Tennessee Tech |
| 1981 | Tennessee Tech |
| 1982 | Tennessee Tech |
| 1983 | West Virginia |

| | |
|---|---|
| 1984 | West Virginia |
| 1985 | Murray State |
| 1986 | West Virginia |
| 1987 | Murray State |
| 1988 | West Virginia |
| 1989 | West Virginia |
| 1990 | West Virginia |
| 1991 | West Virginia |

## MEN'S AND WOMEN'S SKIING
**Year Champion**

| | |
|---|---|
| 1954 | Denver |
| 1955 | Denver |
| 1956 | Denver |
| 1957 | Denver |
| 1958 | Dartmouth |
| 1959 | Colorado |
| 1960 | Colorado |
| 1961 | Denver |
| 1962 | Denver |
| 1963 | Denver |
| 1964 | Denver |
| 1965 | Denver |
| 1966 | Denver |
| 1967 | Denver |
| 1968 | Wyoming |
| 1969 | Denver |
| 1970 | Denver |
| 1971 | Denver |
| 1972 | Colorado |
| 1973 | Colorado |
| 1974 | Colorado |
| 1975 | Colorado |
| 1976 | Colorado |
| | Dartmouth |
| 1977 | Colorado |
| 1978 | Colorado |
| 1979 | Colorado |
| 1980 | Vermont |
| 1981 | Utah |
| 1982 | Colorado |
| 1983 | Utah |
| 1984 | Utah |
| 1985 | Wyoming |
| 1986 | Utah |
| 1987 | Utah |
| 1988 | Utah |
| 1989 | Vermont |
| 1990 | Vermont |
| 1991 | Colorado |

## MEN'S AND WOMEN'S FENCING
**Year Champion**

| | |
|---|---|
| 1990 | Penn State |
| 1991 | Penn State |

## NCAA WOMEN'S MAJOR SPORTS

### NCAA DIVISION I WOMEN'S BASKETBALL CHAMPIONSHIPS

| Year | Champion | Coach | Outstanding player | Score | Runner-up |
|------|----------|-------|--------------------|-------|-----------|
| 1982 | Louisiana Tech | Sonja Hogg | Janice Lawrence | 76–62 | Cheyney |
| 1983 | Southern California | Linda Sharp | Cheryl Miller | 69–67 | Louisiana Tech |
| 1984 | Southern California | Linda Sharp | Cheryl Miller | 72–61 | Tennessee |
| 1985 | Old Dominion | Marianne Stanley | Tracy Claxton | 70–65 | Georgia |
| 1986 | Texas | Jody Conradt | Clarissa Davis | 97–81 | Southern California |
| 1987 | Tennessee | Pat Summitt | Tonya Edwards | 67–44 | Louisiana Tech |
| 1988 | Louisiana Tech | Leon Barmore | Erica Westbrooks | 56–54 | Auburn |
| 1989 | Tennessee | Pat Summitt | Bridgette Gordon | 76–60 | Auburn |
| 1990 | Stanford | Tara VanderVeer | Jennifer Azzi | 88–81 | Auburn |
| 1991 | Tennessee | Pat Summitt | Dawn Staley | 70–67 | Virginia |

### CROSS-COUNTRY

| Year | Champion |
|------|----------|
| 1981 | Virginia |
| 1982 | Virginia |
| 1983 | Oregon |
| 1984 | Wisconsin |
| 1985 | Wisconsin |
| 1986 | Texas |
| 1987 | Oregon |
| 1988 | Kentucky |
| 1989 | Villanova |
| 1990 | Villanova |

### FENCING

| Year | Champion |
|------|----------|
| 1982 | Wayne State |
| 1983 | Penn State |
| 1984 | Yale |
| 1985 | Yale |
| 1986 | Pennsylvania |
| 1987 | Notre Dame |
| 1988 | Wayne State |
| 1989 | Wayne State |
| 1990 | Wayne State |

### FIELD HOCKEY

| Year | Champion |
|------|----------|
| 1981 | Connecticut |
| 1982 | Old Dominion |
| 1983 | Old Dominion |
| 1984 | Old Dominion |
| 1985 | Connecticut |
| 1986 | Iowa |
| 1987 | Maryland |
| 1988 | Old Dominion |
| 1989 | North Carolina |
| 1990 | Old Dominion |

### GOLF

| Year | Champion |
|------|----------|
| 1982 | Tulsa |
| 1983 | Texas Christian |
| 1984 | Miami (Fla.) |
| 1985 | Florida |
| 1986 | Florida |
| 1987 | San Jose State |
| 1988 | Tulsa |
| 1989 | San Jose State |
| 1990 | Arizona State |
| 1991 | UCLA |

### GYMNASTICS

| Year | Champion |
|------|----------|
| 1982 | Utah |
| 1983 | Utah |
| 1984 | Utah |
| 1985 | Utah |
| 1986 | Utah |
| 1987 | Georgia |
| 1988 | Alabama |
| 1989 | Georgia |
| 1990 | Utah |
| 1991 | Alabama |

### TENNIS

| Year | Champion |
|------|----------|
| 1982 | Stanford |
| 1983 | Southern California |
| 1984 | Stanford |
| 1985 | Southern California |
| 1986 | Stanford |
| 1987 | Stanford |
| 1988 | Stanford |
| 1989 | Stanford |
| 1990 | Stanford |
| 1991 | Stanford |

### SWIMMING AND DIVING

| Year | Champion |
|------|----------|
| 1982 | Florida |
| 1983 | Stanford |
| 1984 | Texas |
| 1985 | Texas |
| 1986 | Texas |
| 1987 | Texas |
| 1988 | Texas |
| 1989 | Stanford |
| 1990 | Texas |
| 1991 | Texas |

### SOCCER

| Year | Champion |
|------|----------|
| 1982 | North Carolina |
| 1983 | North Carolina |
| 1984 | North Carolina |
| 1985 | George Mason |
| 1986 | North Carolina |
| 1987 | North Carolina |
| 1988 | North Carolina |
| 1989 | North Carolina |
| 1990 | North Carolina |

### SOFTBALL

| Year | Champion |
|------|----------|
| 1982 | UCLA |
| 1983 | Texas A&M |
| 1984 | UCLA |
| 1985 | UCLA |
| 1986 | California State, Fullerton |
| 1987 | Texas A&M |
| 1988 | UCLA |
| 1989 | UCLA |
| 1990 | UCLA |
| 1991 | Arizona |

### LACROSSE

| Year | Champion |
|------|----------|
| 1982 | Massachusetts |
| 1983 | Delaware |
| 1984 | Temple |
| 1985 | New Hampshire |
| 1986 | Maryland |
| 1987 | Penn State |
| 1988 | Temple |
| 1989 | Penn State |
| 1990 | Harvard |
| 1991 | Virginia |

### VOLLEYBALL

| Year | Champion |
|------|----------|
| 1981 | Southern California |
| 1982 | Hawaii |
| 1983 | Hawaii |
| 1984 | UCLA |
| 1985 | Pacific |
| 1986 | Pacific |
| 1987 | Hawaii |
| 1988 | Texas |
| 1989 | California State, Long Beach |
| 1990 | UCLA |

### INDOOR TRACK

| Year | Champion |
|------|----------|
| 1983 | Nebraska |
| 1984 | Nebraska |
| 1985 | Florida State |
| 1986 | Texas |
| 1987 | Louisiana State |
| 1988 | Texas |
| 1989 | Louisiana State |
| 1990 | Texas |
| 1991 | Louisiana State |

### OUTDOOR TRACK

| Year | Champion |
|------|----------|
| 1982 | UCLA |
| 1983 | UCLA |
| 1984 | Florida State |
| 1985 | Oregon |
| 1986 | Texas |
| 1987 | Louisiana State |
| 1988 | Louisiana State |
| 1989 | Louisiana State |
| 1990 | Louisiana State |
| 1991 | Louisiana State |

### WOMEN'S TEAM TITLES

| College | Number |
|---------|--------|
| Texas | 13 |
| Utah[1] | 11 |
| Stanford | 11 |
| UCLA | 11 |
| North Carolina | 9 |
| Louisiana State | 8 |
| Old Dominion | 6 |
| West Virginia[1] | 6 |
| Southern California | 5 |

**Note:** Total team titles since 1981.
1. Includes co-ed championships in Skiing and Rifle.

---

## AMATEUR ATHLETIC UNION OF THE U.S. (AAU)
**AAU House**
**3400 West 86th Street**
**P.O. Box 68207**
**Indianapolis, IN 46268**
**(317) 872-2900**
President: Richard Harkins
Founded: 1888

### SULLIVAN AWARD

James E. Sullivan was a longtime official of the Amateur Athletic Union. The AAU awards the trophy annually "to the amateur athlete who, by performance, example, and good influence, did the most to advance the cause of good sportsmanship."

| Year | Winner (sport) |
|------|----------------|
| 1930 | Bobby Jones (golf) |
| 1931 | Barney Berlinger (track and field) |
| 1932 | Jim Bausch (track and field) |
| 1933 | Glenn Cunningham (track and field) |
| 1934 | Bill Bonthron (track and field) |
| 1935 | Lawson Little (golf) |

| 1936 | Glenn Morris (track and field) |
|------|--------------------------------|
| 1937 | Don Budge (tennis) |
| 1938 | Don Lash (track and field) |
| 1939 | Joe Burk (rowing) |
| 1940 | Greg Rice (track and field) |
| 1941 | Leslie MacMitchell (track and field) |
| 1942 | Cornelius Warmerdam (track and field) |
| 1943 | Gilbert Dodds (track and field) |
| 1944 | Ann Curtis (swimming) |
| 1945 | Doc Blanchard (football) |
| 1946 | Arnold Tucker (football) |
| 1947 | John Kelly, Jr. (rowing) |
| 1948 | Robert Mathias (track and field) |
| 1949 | Dick Button (figure skating) |
| 1950 | Fred Wilt (track and field) |
| 1951 | Rev. Robert Richards (track and field) |
| 1952 | Horace Ashenfelter (track and field) |
| 1953 | Dr. Sammy Lee (diving) |
| 1954 | Mal Whitfield (track and field) |
| 1955 | Harrison Dillard (track and field) |
| 1956 | Patricia McCormick (diving) |
| 1957 | Bobby Joe Morrow (track and field) |
| 1958 | Glenn Davis (track and field) |
| 1959 | Parry O'Brien (track and field) |
| 1960 | Rafer Johnson (track and field) |
| 1961 | Wilma Rudolph (track and field) |
| 1962 | James Beatty (track and field) |
| 1963 | John Pennel (track and field) |

| 1964 | Don Schollander (swimming) |
|------|----------------------------|
| 1965 | Bill Bradley (basketball) |
| 1966 | Jim Ryun (track and field) |
| 1967 | Randy Matson (track and field) |
| 1968 | Debbie Meyer (swimming) |
| 1969 | Bill Toomey (track and field) |
| 1970 | John Kinsella (swimming) |
| 1971 | Mark Spitz (swimming) |
| 1972 | Frank Shorter (track and field) |
| 1973 | Bill Walton (basketball) |
| 1974 | Rick Wohlhuter (track and field) |
| 1975 | Tim Shaw (swimming) |
| 1976 | Bruce Jenner (track and field) |
| 1977 | John Naber (swimming) |
| 1978 | Tracy Caulkins (swimming) |
| 1979 | Kurt Thomas (gymnastics) |
| 1980 | Eric Heiden (speed skating) |
| 1981 | Carl Lewis (track and field) |
| 1982 | Mary Decker (track and field) |
| 1983 | Edwin Moses (track and field) |
| 1984 | Greg Louganis (diving) |
| 1985 | Joan Benoit Samuelson (marathon) |
| 1986 | Jackie Joyner-Kersee (track and field) |
| 1987 | Jim Abbott (baseball) |
| 1988 | Florence Griffith Joyner (track and field) |
| 1989 | Janet Evans (swimming) |
| 1990 | John Smith (wrestling) |

**Source:** Amateur Athletic Union.

# PROFESSIONAL SPORTS

## Basketball

### National Basketball Association

Olympic Tower
645 Fifth Avenue
New York, NY 10022
(212) 826–7000

Commissioner: David Stern
Founded: 1946
Number of teams: 27

The first pro game was played in 1896 in Trenton, New Jersey, and by 1898 the fledgling National Basketball League and several others were organized. The Buffalo Germans were the first powerhouse, winning 792 games against only 86 losses from 1895 to 1925. In 1914 the New York Celtics (later renamed the Original Celtics) were organized, playing a "modern" style of basketball using zone defenses, the fast break, and a pivot man.

Other "ethnic" teams dominated in the 1930s, including the Philadelphia SPHAs (South Philadelphia Hebrew Association) under Eddy Gottlieb, and the black barnstorming New York Renaissance—the Rens. Several weak leagues continued to compete until the end of World War II. The Basketball Association of America was formed in 1946 by hockey arena managers seeking additional tenants. By 1949 it had merged with its last rival, to form the modern NBA.

Dr. James Naismith invented basketball in 1891 only after his indoor versions of lacrosse, rugby, and soccer proved too violent for the intended use in a YMCA fitness program. Yet even his "noncontact" amateur sport proved too rough for many YMCAs, which dropped basketball. Teams were forced to rent halls; they charged an admission fee to pay the rent, and split any leftover cash among the players. Thus was born professional basketball.

> *"You gotta love the NBA: where else could you see the greatest athletes in the world under one roof . . . and Michael Jordan above it?"*
>
> —Frank Layden,
> former NBA coach

## NBA LEADERS, 1990–91

### SCORING

| | G | Pts. | Avg. |
|---|---|---|---|
| Michael Jordan, Chicago | 82 | 2,580 | 31.5 |
| Karl Malone, Utah | 82 | 2,382 | 29.0 |
| Bernard King, Washington | 64 | 1,817 | 28.4 |
| Charles Barkley, Philadelphia | 67 | 1,849 | 27.6 |
| Patrick Ewing, New York | 81 | 2,154 | 26.6 |
| Michael Adams, Denver | 66 | 1,752 | 26.5 |
| Dominique Wilkins, Atlanta | 81 | 2,101 | 25.9 |
| Chris Mullin, Golden State | 82 | 2,107 | 25.7 |
| David Robinson, San Antonio | 82 | 2,101 | 25.6 |
| Mitch Richmond, Golden State | 77 | 1,840 | 23.9 |
| Tim Hardaway, Golden State | 82 | 1,881 | 22.9 |
| Reggie Miller, Indiana | 82 | 1,855 | 22.6 |
| Kevin Johnson, Phoenix | 77 | 1,710 | 22.2 |
| Hersey Hawkins, Philadelphia | 80 | 1,767 | 22.1 |
| Tony Campbell, Minnesota | 77 | 1,678 | 21.8 |
| Brad Daugherty, Cleveland | 76 | 1,645 | 21.6 |
| Clyde Drexler, Portland | 82 | 1,767 | 21.5 |
| James Worthy, L.A. Lakers | 78 | 1,670 | 21.4 |
| Ricky Pierce, Seattle | 78 | 1,598 | 20.5 |
| Joe Dumars, Detroit | 80 | 1,629 | 20.4 |

### REBOUNDS

| | G | Tot. | Avg. |
|---|---|---|---|
| David Robinson, San Antonio | 82 | 1,063 | 13.0 |
| Dennis Rodman, Detroit | 82 | 1,026 | 12.5 |
| Charles Oakley, New York | 76 | 920 | 12.1 |
| Karl Malone, Utah | 82 | 967 | 11.8 |
| Patrick Ewing, New York | 81 | 905 | 11.2 |
| Brad Daugherty, Cleveland | 76 | 830 | 10.9 |
| Robert Parish, Boston | 81 | 856 | 10.6 |
| Benoit Benjamin, Seattle | 70 | 723 | 10.3 |
| Otis Thorpe, Houston | 82 | 846 | 10.3 |
| Derrick Coleman, New Jersey | 74 | 759 | 10.3 |

Source: NBA.

### FIELD GOAL PERCENTAGE

| | FGM | FGA | Pct. |
|---|---|---|---|
| Buck Williams, Portland | 358 | 595 | .602 |
| Robert Parish, Boston | 485 | 811 | .598 |
| Kevin Gamble, Boston | 548 | 933 | .587 |
| Charles Barkley, Philadelphia | 665 | 1,167 | .570 |
| Vlade Divac, L.A. Lakers | 360 | 637 | .565 |
| Olden Polynice, L.A. Clippers | 316 | 564 | .560 |
| Otis Thorpe, Houston | 549 | 988 | .556 |
| Kevin McHale, Boston | 504 | 912 | .553 |
| David Robinson, San Antonio | 754 | 1,366 | .552 |
| John Paxson, Chicago | 317 | 578 | .548 |

### FREE THROW PERCENTAGE

| | FTM | FTA | Pct. |
|---|---|---|---|
| Reggie Miller, Indiana | 551 | 600 | .918 |
| Jeff Malone, Utah | 231 | 252 | .917 |
| Ricky Pierce, Seattle | 430 | 471 | .913 |
| Kelly Tripucka, Charlotte | 152 | 167 | .910 |
| Magic Johnson, L.A. Lakers | 519 | 573 | .906 |
| Scott Skiles, Orlando | 340 | 377 | .902 |
| Kiki Vandeweghe, New York | 259 | 288 | .899 |
| Jeff Hornacek, Phoenix | 201 | 224 | .897 |
| Eddie Johnson, Seattle | 229 | 257 | .891 |
| Larry Bird, Boston | 163 | 183 | .891 |

### 3-PT. FIELD GOALS

| | FGM | FGA | Pct. |
|---|---|---|---|
| Jim Les, Sacramento | 71 | 154 | .461 |
| Trent Tucker, New York | 64 | 153 | .418 |
| Jeff Hornacek, Phoenix | 61 | 146 | .418 |
| Terry Porter, Portland | 130 | 313 | .415 |
| Scott Skiles, Orlando | 93 | 228 | .408 |
| Danny Ainge, Portland | 102 | 251 | .406 |
| Hersey Hawkins, Philadelphia | 108 | 270 | .400 |
| Larry Bird, Boston | 77 | 198 | .389 |
| Glen Rice, Miami | 71 | 184 | .386 |
| Tim Hardaway, Golden State | 97 | 252 | .385 |

### ASSISTS

| | G | No. | Avg. |
|---|---|---|---|
| John Stockton, Utah | 82 | 1,164 | 14.2 |
| Magic Johnson, L.A. Lakers | 79 | 989 | 12.5 |
| Michael Adams, Denver | 66 | 693 | 10.5 |
| Kevin Johnson, Phoenix | 77 | 781 | 10.1 |
| Tim Hardaway, Golden State | 82 | 793 | 9.7 |
| Isiah Thomas, Detroit | 48 | 446 | 9.3 |
| Pooh Richardson, Minnesota | 82 | 734 | 9.0 |
| Gary Grant, L.A. Clippers | 68 | 587 | 8.6 |
| Sherman Douglas, Miami | 73 | 624 | 8.5 |
| Scott Skiles, Orlando | 79 | 660 | 8.4 |

### STEALS

| | G | No. | Avg. |
|---|---|---|---|
| Alvin Robertson, Milwaukee | 81 | 246 | 3.04 |
| John Stockton, Utah | 82 | 234 | 2.85 |
| Michael Jordan, Chicago | 82 | 223 | 2.72 |
| Tim Hardaway, Golden State | 82 | 214 | 2.61 |
| Scottie Pippen, Chicago | 82 | 193 | 2.35 |
| Mookie Blaylock, New Jersey | 72 | 169 | 2.35 |
| Michael Adams, Denver | 66 | 147 | 2.23 |
| Hersey Hawkins, Philadelphia | 80 | 178 | 2.23 |
| Kevin Johnson, Phoenix | 77 | 163 | 2.12 |
| Chris Mullin, Golden State | 82 | 173 | 2.11 |

### BLOCKED SHOTS

| | G | No. | Avg. |
|---|---|---|---|
| Hakeem Olajuwon, Houston | 56 | 221 | 3.95 |
| David Robinson, San Antonio | 82 | 320 | 3.90 |
| Patrick Ewing, New York | 81 | 258 | 3.19 |
| Manute Bol, Philadelphia | 82 | 247 | 3.01 |
| Chris Dudley, New Jersey | 61 | 153 | 2.51 |
| Larry Nance, Cleveland | 80 | 200 | 2.50 |
| Mark Eaton, Utah | 80 | 188 | 2.35 |
| Kevin McHale, Boston | 68 | 146 | 2.15 |
| Benoit Benjamin, Seattle | 70 | 145 | 2.07 |
| Pervis Ellison, Washington | 76 | 157 | 2.07 |

## NBA FINAL STANDINGS, 1990-91

| EASTERN CONFERENCE | W | L | Pct. | Home | Away | 1989-90 |
|---|---|---|---|---|---|---|
| 1. Chicago Bulls | 61 | 21 | .744 | 35–6 | 26–15 | 55–27 |
| 2. Boston Celtics | 56 | 26 | .683 | 35–6 | 21–20 | 52–30 |
| 3. Detroit Pistons | 50 | 32 | .610 | 32–9 | 18–23 | 59–23 |
| 4. Milwaukee Bucks | 48 | 34 | .585 | 33–8 | 15–26 | 44–38 |
| 5. Philadelphia 76ers | 44 | 38 | .537 | 29–12 | 15–26 | 53–29 |
| 6. Atlanta Hawks | 43 | 39 | .524 | 29–12 | 14–27 | 41–41 |
| 7. Indiana Pacers | 41 | 41 | .500 | 29–12 | 12–29 | 42–40 |
| 8. New York Knicks | 39 | 43 | .476 | 21–20 | 18–23 | 45–37 |
| 9. Cleveland Cavaliers | 33 | 49 | .402 | 23–18 | 10–31 | 42–40 |
| 10. Washington Bullets | 30 | 52 | .366 | 21–20 | 9–32 | 31–51 |
| 11. Charlotte Hornets | 26 | 56 | .317 | 17–24 | 9–32 | 19–63 |
| 12. New Jersey Nets | 26 | 56 | .317 | 20–21 | 6–35 | 17–65 |
| 13. Miami Heat | 24 | 58 | .293 | 18–23 | 6–35 | 18–64 |

| WESTERN CONFERENCE | W | L | Pct. | Home | Away | 1989-90 |
|---|---|---|---|---|---|---|
| 1. Portland Trail Blazers | 63 | 39 | .768 | 36–5 | 27–14 | 59–23 |
| 2. Los Angeles Lakers | 58 | 24 | .707 | 33–8 | 25–16 | 63–19 |
| 3. San Antonio Spurs | 55 | 27 | .671 | 33–8 | 22–19 | 56–26 |
| 4. Phoenix Suns | 55 | 27 | .671 | 32–9 | 23–18 | 54–28 |
| 5. Utah Jazz | 54 | 28 | .659 | 36–5 | 18–23 | 55–27 |
| 6. Houston Rockets | 52 | 30 | .634 | 31–10 | 21–20 | 41–41 |
| 7. Golden State Warriors | 44 | 38 | .537 | 30–11 | 14–27 | 37–45 |
| 8. Seattle SuperSonics | 41 | 41 | .500 | 28–13 | 13–28 | 41–41 |
| 9. Orlando Magic | 31 | 51 | .378 | 24–17 | 7–34 | 18–64 |
| 10. Los Angeles Clippers | 31 | 51 | .378 | 23–18 | 8–33 | 30–52 |
| 11. Minnesota Timberwolves | 29 | 53 | .354 | 21–20 | 8–33 | 22–60 |
| 12. Dallas Mavericks | 28 | 54 | .341 | 20–21 | 8–33 | 47–35 |
| 13. Sacramento Kings | 25 | 57 | .305 | 24–17 | 1–40 | 23–59 |
| 14. Denver Nuggets | 20 | 62 | .244 | 17–24 | 3–38 | 43–39 |

**Note:** The top eight teams from each conference qualified for the playoffs. **Source:** The NBA.

## NBA CHAMPIONSHIP COMPOSITE BOX, 1991

**CHICAGO BULLS**

| Player | G. | Min. | FG M–A | Pct. | FT M–A | Pct. | Reb. O–T | A | Pts. | Avg. |
|---|---|---|---|---|---|---|---|---|---|---|
| Jordan | 5 | 220 | 63–113 | .558 | 28–33 | .848 | 8–33 | 57 | 156 | 31.2 |
| Pippen | 5 | 218 | 39–86 | .453 | 25–29 | .862 | 15–47 | 33 | 104 | 20.8 |
| Grant | 5 | 198 | 32–51 | .627 | 9–12 | .750 | 14–39 | 8 | 73 | 14.6 |
| Paxson | 5 | 159 | 32–49 | .653 | 2–2 | 1.000 | 2–10 | 17 | 67 | 13.4 |
| Cartwright | 5 | 160 | 20–46 | .435 | 4–6 | .667 | 5–25 | 12 | 44 | 8.8 |
| Hodges | 5 | 53 | 9–23 | .391 | 0–0 | — | 0–3 | 1 | 19 | 3.8 |
| Levingston | 5 | 90 | 8–13 | .615 | 0–0 | — | 5–14 | 3 | 16 | 3.2 |
| Armstrong | 5 | 37 | 5–11 | .455 | 0–0 | — | 1–3 | 4 | 10 | 2.0 |
| Williams | 4 | 45 | 2–4 | .500 | 4–6 | .667 | 2–9 | 3 | 8 | 2.0 |
| Perdue | 5 | 37 | 3–5 | .600 | 2–2 | 1.000 | 3–12 | 1 | 8 | 1.6 |
| King | 2 | 6 | 0–3 | .000 | 2–2 | 1.000 | 0–1 | 0 | 2 | 1.0 |
| Hopson | 1 | 2 | 0–0 | — | 0–0 | — | 0–0 | 0 | 0 | 0.0 |
| Totals | 5 | 1,225 | 213–404 | .527 | 76–92 | .826 | 55–196 | 139 | 507 | 101.4 |

**LOS ANGELES LAKERS**

| Player | G. | Min. | FG M–A | Pct. | FT M–A | Pct. | Reb. O–T | A | Pts. | Avg. |
|---|---|---|---|---|---|---|---|---|---|---|
| Worthy | 4 | 164 | 35–73 | .479 | 6–9 | .667 | 4–12 | 8 | 77 | 19.3 |
| Johnson | 5 | 228 | 25–58 | .431 | 39–41 | .951 | 8–40 | 62 | 93 | 18.6 |
| Divac | 5 | 208 | 39–69 | .565 | 13–13 | 1.000 | 17–44 | 10 | 91 | 18.2 |
| Perkins | 5 | 206 | 28–69 | .406 | 22–29 | .759 | 14–38 | 5 | 83 | 16.6 |
| Campbell | 3 | 33 | 10–16 | .625 | 3–4 | .750 | 1–4 | 0 | 23 | 7.7 |
| Smith | 2 | 32 | 5–7 | .714 | 2–3 | .667 | 1–1 | 2 | 12 | 6.0 |
| Green | 5 | 113 | 10–32 | .313 | 7–12 | .583 | 13–28 | 1 | 29 | 5.8 |
| Teagle | 5 | 71 | 7–21 | .333 | 11–14 | .786 | 1–2 | 1 | 25 | 5.0 |
| Scott | 4 | 140 | 5–18 | .278 | 7–10 | .700 | 0–7 | 7 | 18 | 4.5 |
| Drew | 4 | 20 | 3–8 | .375 | 1–2 | .500 | 0–2 | 0 | 7 | 1.8 |
| Thompson | 1 | 10 | 0–3 | .000 | 0–0 | — | 0–0 | 0 | 0 | 0.0 |
| Totals | 5 | 1,225 | 167–374 | .447 | 111–137 | .810 | 59–178 | 96 | 456 | 91.6 |

**Source:** NBA

## NBA PLAYOFF RESULTS, 1991

### FIRST ROUND

**EASTERN CONFERENCE**

**Chicago vs. New York**
(Chicago wins series, 3–0)
Chicago 126 New York 85
Chicago 89 New York 79
Chicago 103 New York 94

**Boston vs. Indiana**
(Boston wins series, 3–2)
Boston 127 Indiana 120
Indiana 130 Boston 118
Boston 112 Indiana 105
Indiana 116 Boston 113
Boston 124 Indiana 121

**Philadelphia vs. Milwaukee**
(Philadelphia wins series, 3–0)
Philadelphia 99 Milwaukee 90
Philadelphia 116 Milwaukee 112 (ot)
Philadelphia 121 Milwaukee 100

**Detroit vs. Atlanta**
(Detroit wins series, 3–2)
Atlanta 103 Detroit 98
Detroit 101 Atlanta 88
Detroit 103 Atlanta 91
Atlanta 123 Detroit 111
Detroit 113 Atlanta 81

**WESTERN CONFERENCE**

**San Antonio vs. Golden State**
(Golden State wins series, 3–1)
San Antonio 130 Golden State 121
Golden State 111 San Antonio 98
Golden State 109 San Antonio 106
Golden State 110 San Antonio 97

**Utah vs. Phoenix**
(Utah wins series, 3–1)
Utah 129 Phoenix 90
Phoenix 102 Utah 92
Utah 107 Phoenix 98
Utah 101 Phoenix 93

**Portland vs. Seattle**
(Portland wins series, 3–2)
Portland 110 Seattle 102
Portland 115 Seattle 106
Seattle 102 Portland 99
Seattle 101 Portland 89
Portland 119 Seattle 107

**L.A. Lakers vs. Houston**
(Los Angeles wins series, 3–0)
Los Angeles 94 Houston 92
Los Angeles 109 Houston 98
Los Angeles 94 Houston 90

### CONFERENCE SEMIFINALS

**Chicago vs. Philadelphia**
(Chicago wins series, 4–1)
Chicago 105 Philadelphia 92
Chicago 112 Philadelphia 100
Philadelphia 99 Chicago 97
Chicago 101 Philadelphia 85
Chicago 100 Philadelphia 95

**Detroit vs. Boston**
(Detroit wins series, 4–2)
Detroit 86 Boston 75
Boston 109 Detroit 103
Boston 115 Detroit 83
Detroit 104 Boston 97
Detroit 116 Boston 111
Detroit 117 Boston 113 (ot)

**L.A. Lakers vs. Golden State**
(Los Angeles wins series, 4–1)
Los Angeles 126 Golden State 116
Golden State 125 Los Angeles 124
Los Angeles 115 Golden State 114
Los Angeles 123 Golden State 107
Los Angeles 124 Golden State 119 (ot)

**Portland vs. Utah**
(Portland wins series, 4–1)
Portland 117 Utah 97
Portland 118 Utah 116
Utah 107 Portland 101
Portland 104 Utah 101
Portland 103 Utah 96

### CONFERENCE FINALS

**Chicago vs. Detroit**
(Chicago wins series, 4–0)
Chicago 94 Detroit 83
Chicago 105 Detroit 97
Chicago 113 Detroit 107
Chicago 115 Detroit 94

**L.A. Lakers vs. Portland**
(Los Angeles wins series, 4–2)
Los Angeles 111 Portland 106
Portland 109 Los Angeles 98
Los Angeles 106 Portland 92
Portland 95 Los Angeles 84
Los Angeles 91 Portland 90

### NBA CHAMPIONSHIP SERIES

**Chicago vs. L.A. Lakers**
(Chicago wins series, 4–1)
Los Angeles 93 Chicago 91
Chicago 107 Los Angeles 86
Chicago 104 Los Angeles 96 (ot)
Chicago 97 Los Angeles 82
Chicago 108 Los Angeles 101

## NBA ALL-TIME CAREER LEADERS

| Games | | Rebounds | | Field Goals Made | | Assists | | Points | |
|---|---|---|---|---|---|---|---|---|---|
| Kareem Abdul-Jabbar | 1,560 | Wilt Chamberlain | 23,924 | Kareem Abdul-Jabbar | 15,837 | Magic Johnson | 9,921 | Kareem Abdul-Jabbar | 38,387 |
| Elvin Hayes | 1,303 | Bill Russell | 21,620 | Wilt Chamberlain | 12,681 | Oscar Robertson | 9,887 | Wilt Chamberlain | 31,419 |
| John Havlicek | 1,270 | Kareem Abdul-Jabbar | 17,440 | Elvin Hayes | 10,976 | Isiah Thomas | 7,431 | Elvin Hayes | 27,313 |
| Paul Silas | 1,254 | Elvin Hayes | 16,279 | Alex English | 10,659 | Len Wilkens | 7,211 | Oscar Robertson | 26,710 |
| Alex English | 1,193 | Moses Malone | 15,150 | John Havlicek | 10,513 | Maurice Cheeks | 7,100 | John Havlicek | 26,395 |
| Robert Parish | 1,181 | Nate Thurmond | 14,464 | Oscar Robertson | 9,508 | Bob Cousy | 6,955 | Moses Malone | 25,737 |
| Moses Malone | 1,164 | Walt Bellamy | 14,241 | Jerry West | 9,016 | Guy Rodgers | 6,917 | Alex English | 25,613 |
| Hal Greer | 1,122 | Wes Unseld | 13,769 | Moses Malone | 8,867 | Nate Archibald | 6,476 | Jerry West | 25,192 |
| Jack Sikma | 1,107 | Jerry Lucas | 12,942 | Elgin Baylor | 8,693 | John Lucas | 6,454 | Adrian Dantley | 23,177 |
| Dennis Johnson | 1,100 | Bob Pettit | 12,849 | Hal Greer | 8,504 | Reggie Theus | 6,453 | Elgin Baylor | 23,149 |

**Note**: At the end of 1990-91 season. **Source**: NBA

## NBA WORLD CHAMPIONSHIP SERIES

| Year | Winner | Loser | Games |
|---|---|---|---|
| 1947 | Philadelphia Warriors | Chicago Stags | 4–1 |
| 1948 | Baltimore Bullets | Philadelphia Warriors | 4–2 |
| 1949 | Minneapolis Lakers | Washington Capitols | 4–2 |
| 1950 | Minneapolis Lakers | Syracuse Nationals | 4–2 |
| 1951 | Rochester Royals | N.Y. Knicks | 4–3 |
| 1952 | Minneapolis Lakers | N.Y. Knicks | 4–3 |
| 1953 | Minneapolis Lakers | N.Y. Knicks | 4–1 |
| 1954 | Minneapolis Lakers | Syracuse Nationals | 4–3 |
| 1955 | Syracuse Nationals | Ft. Wayne Pistons | 4–3 |
| 1956 | Philadelphia Warriors | Ft. Wayne Pistons | 4–1 |
| 1957 | Boston Celtics | St. Louis Hawks | 4–3 |
| 1958 | St. Louis Hawks | Boston Celtics | 4–2 |
| 1959 | Boston Celtics | Minneapolis Lakers | 4–0 |
| 1960 | Boston Celtics | St. Louis Hawks | 4–3 |
| 1961 | Boston Celtics | St. Louis Hawks | 4–1 |
| 1962 | Boston Celtics | L.A. Lakers | 4–3 |
| 1963 | Boston Celtics | L.A. Lakers | 4–2 |
| 1964 | Boston Celtics | San Francisco Warriors | 4–1 |
| 1965 | Boston Celtics | L.A. Lakers | 4–1 |
| 1966 | Boston Celtics | L.A. Lakers | 4–3 |
| 1967 | Philadelphia 76ers | San Francisco Warriors | 4–2 |
| 1968 | Boston Celtics | L.A. Lakers | 4–2 |
| 1969 | Boston Celtics | L.A. Lakers | 4–3 |
| 1970 | N.Y. Knicks | L.A. Lakers | 4–3 |
| 1971 | Milwaukee Bucks | Baltimore Bullets | 4–0 |
| 1972 | L.A. Lakers | N.Y. Knicks | 4–1 |
| 1973 | N.Y. Knicks | L.A. Lakers | 4–1 |
| 1974 | Boston Celtics | Milwaukee Bucks | 4–3 |
| 1975 | Golden State Warriors | Washington Bullets | 4–0 |
| 1976 | Boston Celtics | Phoenix Suns | 4–2 |
| 1977 | Portland Trail Blazers | Philadelphia 76ers | 4–2 |
| 1978 | Washington Bullets | Seattle SuperSonics | 4–3 |
| 1979 | Seattle SuperSonics | Washington Bullets | 4–1 |
| 1980 | L.A. Lakers | Philadelphia 76ers | 4–2 |
| 1981 | Boston Celtics | Houston Rockets | 4–2 |
| 1982 | L.A. Lakers | Philadelphia 76ers | 4–2 |
| 1983 | Philadelphia 76ers | L.A. Lakers | 4–0 |
| 1984 | Boston Celtics | L.A. Lakers | 4–3 |
| 1985 | L.A. Lakers | Boston Celtics | 4–2 |
| 1986 | Boston Celtics | Houston Rockets | 4–2 |
| 1987 | L.A. Lakers | Boston Celtics | 4–2 |
| 1988 | L.A. Lakers | Detroit Pistons | 4–3 |
| 1989 | Detroit Pistons | L.A. Lakers | 4–0 |
| 1990 | Detroit Pistons | Portland Trail Blazers | 4–1 |
| 1991 | Chicago Bulls | L.A. Lakers | 4–1 |

## NBA FIRST ROUND DRAFT PICKS, 1991

| Rank/Team | | Player | Position | School |
|---|---|---|---|---|
| 1. | Charlotte | Larry Johnson | F | UNLV |
| 2. | New Jersey | Kenny Anderson | G | Georgia Tech |
| 3. | Sacramento | Billy Owens | F | Syracuse |
| 4. | Denver | Dikembe Mutombo | C | Georgetown |
| 5. | Miami | Steve Smith | G | Michigan State |
| 6. | Dallas | Doug Smith | F | Missouri |
| 7. | Minnesota | Luc Longley | C | New Mexico |
| 8. | Denver | Mark Macon | G | Temple |
| 9. | Atlanta | Stacey Augmon | F | UNLV |
| 10. | Orlando | Brian Williams | F | Arizona |
| 11. | Cleveland | Terrell Brandon | G | Oregon |
| 12. | New York | Greg Anthony | G | UNLV |
| 13. | Indiana | Dale Davis | C | Clemson |
| 14. | Seattle | Rick King | C | Nebraska |
| 15. | Atlanta | Anthony Avent | F | Seton Hall |
| 16. | Golden State | Chris Gatling | F | Old Dominion |
| 17. | Golden State | Victor Alexander | C | Iowa State |
| 18. | Milwaukee | Kevin Brooks | F | Southwestern Louisiana |
| 19. | Washington | LaBradford Smith | G | Louisville |
| 20. | Houston | John Turner | F | Phillips |
| 21. | Utah | Erick Murdock | G | Providence |
| 22. | L.A. Clippers | LeRon Ellis | C | Syracuse |
| 23. | Orlando | Stanley Roberts | C | Real Madrid |
| 24. | Boston | Rick Fox | F | North Carolina |
| 25. | Golden State | Shaun Vandiver | F | Colorado |
| 26. | Chicago | Mark Randall | F | Kansas |
| 27. | Sacramento | Pete Chilcutt | F | North Carolina |

Source: NBA.

## NBA MOST VALUABLE PLAYERS

| Year | Name | Team | Pts. | Avg. | Reb. |
|---|---|---|---|---|---|
| 1955–56 | Bob Pettit | St. Louis Hawks | 1,849 | 25.7 | 1,164 |
| 1956–57 | Bob Cousy | Boston Celtics | 1,319 | 20.6 | 309 |
| 1957–58 | Bill Russell | Boston Celtics | 1,142 | 16.6 | 1,564 |
| 1958–59 | Bob Pettit | St. Louis Hawks | 2,105 | 29.2 | 1,182 |
| 1959–60 | Wilt Chamberlain | Philadelphia Warriors | 2,207 | 37.6 | 1,941 |
| 1960–61 | Bill Russell | Boston Celtics | 1,322 | 16.9 | 1,868 |
| 1961–62 | Bill Russell | Boston Celtics | 1,436 | 18.9 | 1,790 |
| 1962–63 | Bill Russell | Boston Celtics | 1,309 | 16.8 | 1,843 |
| 1963–64 | Oscar Robertson | Cincinnati Royals | 2,480 | 31.4 | 783 |
| 1964–65 | Bill Russell | Boston Celtics | 1,102 | 14.1 | 1,878 |
| 1965–66 | Wilt Chamberlain | Philadelphia 76ers | 2,649 | 33.5 | 1,943 |
| 1966–67 | Wilt Chamberlain | Philadelphia 76ers | 1,956 | 24.1 | 1,957 |
| 1967–68 | Wilt Chamberlain | Philadelphia 76ers | 1,992 | 24.3 | 1,952 |
| 1968–69 | Wes Unseld | Baltimore Bullets | 1,131 | 13.8 | 1,491 |
| 1969–70 | Willis Reed | N.Y. Knicks | 1,755 | 21.7 | 1,126 |
| 1970–71 | Kareem Abdul-Jabbar | Milwaukee Bucks | 2,596 | 31.7 | 1,311 |
| 1971–72 | Kareem Abdul-Jabbar | Milwaukee Bucks | 2,822 | 34.8 | 1,346 |

| Year | Name | Team | Pts. | Avg. | Reb. |
|---|---|---|---|---|---|
| 1972–73 | Dave Cowens | Boston Celtics | 1,684 | 20.5 | 1,329 |
| 1973–74 | Kareem Abdul-Jabbar | Milwaukee Bucks | 2,191 | 27.0 | 1,178 |
| 1974–75 | Bob McAdoo | Buffalo Braves | 2,831 | 34.5 | 1,155 |
| 1975–76 | Kareem Abdul-Jabbar | L.A. Lakers | 2,275 | 27.7 | 1,383 |
| 1976–77 | Kareem Abdul-Jabbar | L.A. Lakers | 2,152 | 26.2 | 1,090 |
| 1977–78 | Bill Walton | Portland Trail Blazers | 1,097 | 18.9 | 766 |
| 1978–79 | Moses Malone | Houston Rockets | 2,031 | 24.8 | 1,444 |
| 1979–80 | Kareem Abdul-Jabbar | L.A. Lakers | 2,034 | 24.8 | 886 |
| 1980–81 | Julius Erving | Philadelphia 76ers | 2,014 | 24.6 | 657 |
| 1981–82 | Moses Malone | Houston Rockets | 2,520 | 31.1 | 1,188 |
| 1982–83 | Moses Malone | Philadelphia 76ers | 1,908 | 24.5 | 1,194 |
| 1983–84 | Larry Bird | Boston Celtics | 1,908 | 24.2 | 796 |
| 1984–85 | Larry Bird | Boston Celtics | 2,295 | 28.7 | 842 |
| 1985–86 | Larry Bird | Boston Celtics | 2,115 | 25.8 | 805 |
| 1986–87 | Magic Johnson | L.A. Lakers | 1,909 | 23.9 | 504 |
| 1987–88 | Michael Jordan | Chicago Bulls | 2,868 | 35.0 | 449 |
| 1988–89 | Magic Johnson | L.A. Lakers | 1,730 | 22.5 | 607 |
| 1989–90 | Magic Johnson | L.A. Lakers | 1,765 | 22.3 | 525 |
| 1990–91 | Michael Jordan | Chicago Bulls | 2,580 | 31.5 | 492 |

## NBA ROOKIES OF THE YEAR

| Year | Name | Team |
|---|---|---|
| 1952–53 | Don Meineke | Fort Wayne Pistons |
| 1953–54 | Ray Felix | Baltimore Bullets |
| 1954–55 | Bob Pettit | Milwaukee Hawks |
| 1955–56 | Maurice Stokes | Rochester Royals |
| 1956–57 | Tom Heinsohn | Boston Celtics |
| 1957–58 | Woody Sauldsberry | Philadelphia Warriors |
| 1958–59 | Elgin Baylor | Minneapolis Lakers |
| 1959–60 | Wilt Chamberlain | Philadelphia Warriors |
| 1960–61 | Oscar Robertson | Cincinnati Royals |
| 1961–62 | Walt Bellamy | Chicago Bulls |
| 1962–63 | Terry Dischinger | Chicago Bulls |
| 1963–64 | Jerry Lucas | Cincinnati Royals |
| 1964–65 | Willis Reed | N.Y. Knicks |
| 1965–66 | Rick Barry | San Francisco Warriors |
| 1966–67 | Dave Bing | Detroit Pistons |
| 1967–68 | Earl Monroe | Baltimore Bullets |
| 1968–69 | Wes Unseld | Baltimore Bullets |
| 1969–70 | Kareem Abdul-Jabbar | Milwaukee Bucks |
| 1970–71 | Dave Cowens | Boston Celtics |
|  | Geoff Petrie (tie) | Portland Trail Blazers |
| 1971–72 | Sidney Wicks | Portland Trail Blazers |
| 1972–73 | Bob McAdoo | Buffalo Braves |
| 1973–74 | Ernie DiGregorio | Buffalo Braves |
| 1974–75 | Keith Wilkes | Golden State Warriors |
| 1975–76 | Alvin Adams | Phoenix Suns |
| 1976–77 | Adrian Dantley | Buffalo Braves |
| 1977–78 | Walter Davis | Phoenix Suns |
| 1978–79 | Phil Ford | Kansas City Kings |
| 1979–80 | Larry Bird | Boston Celtics |
| 1980–81 | Darrell Griffith | Utah Jazz |
| 1981–82 | Buck Williams | New Jersey Nets |
| 1982–83 | Terry Cummings | San Diego Clippers |
| 1983–84 | Ralph Sampson | Houston Rockets |
| 1984–85 | Michael Jordan | Chicago Bulls |
| 1985–86 | Patrick Ewing | N.Y. Knicks |
| 1986–87 | Chuck Person | Indiana Pacers |
| 1987–88 | Mark Jackson | N.Y. Knicks |
| 1988–89 | Mitch Richmond | Golden State Warriors |
| 1989–90 | David Robinson | San Antonio Spurs |
| 1990–91 | Derrick Coleman | New Jersey Nets |

## NBA NAISMITH MEMORIAL HALL OF FAME

Although the Basketball Hall of Fame elected its first members in 1959, its cornerstone was not laid until 1961. The original Hall of Fame in Springfield, Mass., was opened to the public on Feb. 17, 1968, where it remained for 17 years. On June 30, 1985, the Hall of Fame was reopened in a new, $11.5-million building. Dr. James Naismith, the game's originator, was among the members elected in 1959.

| Player (year elected) | Games | Points | FG% | FT% | Rebs. | Assts. |
|---|---|---|---|---|---|---|
| **Archibald, Nate (Tiny)** (1991) | 876 | 16,481 | .467 | .810 | 2,046 | 6,476 |
| Averaged 18.8 ppg over 13 seasons; six-time All-Star | | | | | | |
| **Arizin, Paul J.** (1977) | 713 | 16,266 | .421 | .810 | 6,129 | 1,665 |
| NBA scoring leader in 1952 (25.4 ppg) and 1957 (25.6 ppg) | | | | | | |
| **Barry, Rick** (1986–87) | 794 | 18,395 | .449 | .900 | 5,168 | 4,017 |
| (ABA) | 226 | 6,884 | .477 | .880 | 1,695 | 935 |
| NBA all-time free-throw percentage leader | | | | | | |
| **Baylor, Elgin** (1976) | 846 | 23,149 | .431 | .780 | 11,463 | 3,650 |
| Named to NBA All-Star First Team 10 times | | | | | | |
| **Bing, Dave** (1990) | 901 | 18,327 | .441 | .775 | 3,420 | 5,397 |
| NBA rookie of the year, 1967, MVP 1976 | | | | | | |
| **Bradley, Bill** (1982) | 742 | 9,217 | .448 | .840 | 2,533 | 2,363 |
| Averaged 30.2 ppg in 83 games at Princeton University | | | | | | |
| **Chamberlain, Wilt** (1978) | 1,045 | 31,419 | .540 | .511 | 23,924 | 4,643 |
| Holds NBA single-game records for points (100) and rebounds (55); all-time rebound leader | | | | | | |
| **Cousy, Bob** (1970) | 924 | 16,960 | .375 | .803 | 4,786 | 6,955 |
| Led NBA in assists eight consecutive seasons (1953–60) | | | | | | |
| **Cowens, Dave** (1991) | 766 | 13,516 | .460 | .783 | 10,444 | 2,950 |
| Seven-time All-Star; three-time All-Defensive team | | | | | | |
| **Cunningham, Billy** (1985–86) | 654 | 13,626 | .446 | .720 | 6,638 | 2,625 |
| (ABA) | 116 | 2,684 | .483 | .791 | 1,343 | 680 |
| Coached Philadelphia 76ers to 454–196 record in eight years | | | | | | |
| **Davies, Bob** (1969) | 462 | 6,594 | .378 | .759 | 980[1] | 2,050 |
| NBL MVP, 1947 (NBL)[2] | 107 | 1,177 | | .747 | | |
| **DeBusschere, Dave** (1982) | 875 | 14,053 | .432 | .699 | 2,497 | 2,801 |
| NBA All-Defensive team six consecutive seasons (1969–74) | | | | | | |
| **Frazier, Walt (Clyde)** (1986–87) | 825 | 15,581 | .490 | .786 | 4,830 | 5,040 |
| NBA All-Defensive team seven consecutive seasons (1969–75) | | | | | | |
| **Fulks, Joe** (1977) | 489 | 8,003 | .302 | .766 | 1,382[1] | 587 |
| NBA scoring leader in 1947 (23.2 ppg) | | | | | | |
| **Gallatin, Harry** (1991) | 682 | 8,843 | .398 | .773 | 6,684 | 1,208 |
| Seven-time All-Star | | | | | | |
| **Gola, Tom** (1975) | 698 | 7,871 | .431 | .760 | 5,605 | 2,953 |
| One of only two major-college players with more than 2,000 points and 2,000 rebounds in career | | | | | | |
| **Greer, Harold (Hal)** (1981) | 1,122 | 21,586 | .452 | .801 | 5,665 | 4,540 |
| Scored 19 points in one quarter of 1968 All-Star game | | | | | | |
| **Hagan, Cliff** (1977) | 746 | 13,447 | .450 | .798 | 5,019 | 2,236 |
| (ABA) | 94 | 1,423 | .496 | .807 | 436 | 398 |
| Helped St. Louis to 1958 championship with 27.7 ppg in playoffs | | | | | | |
| **Havlicek, John J. (Hondo)** (1983) | 1,270 | 26,395 | .439 | .815 | 8,007 | 6,114 |
| Fifth among NBA career scoring leaders | | | | | | |
| **Hayes, Elvin** (1990) | 1,303 | 27,313 | .452 | .670 | 16,279 | 2,398 |
| Third all-time NBA scorer, fourth all-time rebounder | | | | | | |
| **Heinsohn, Tom** (1985–86) | 654 | 12,194 | .405 | .790 | 5,749 | 1,318 |
| Played for eight NBA championship teams and coached two others | | | | | | |
| **Houbregs, Robert J.** (1986–87) | 281 | 2,611 | .404 | .771 | 1,552 | 500 |
| NCAA Player of the Year, 1953 | | | | | | |
| **Johnston, Neil** (1990) | 516 | 10,023 | .444 | .768 | 5,856 | 1,269 |
| Named to four straight all-NBA First Teams (1953–56) | | | | | | |
| **Jones, K.C.** (1988–89) | 676 | 5,011 | .387 | .647 | 2,399 | 2,908 |
| High scorer in 1955 NCAA finals (24 points), while holding Tom Gola scoreless for 21 min. | | | | | | |
| **Jones, Sam** (1983) | 871 | 15,411 | .456 | .803 | 4,305 | 2,209 |
| Member of 10 NBA championship teams | | | | | | |
| **Lovellette, Clyde** (1987–88) | 704 | 11,947 | .443 | .756 | 6,663 | 1,165 |
| Three-time All-American at University of Kansas (1950–52) | | | | | | |
| **Lucas, Jerry Ray (Luke)** (1979) | 829 | 14,053 | .499 | .783 | 12,942 | 2,730 |
| NBA Rookie of the Year and field-goal percentage leader (.527) in 1964 | | | | | | |
| **Macauley, Edward (Easy Ed)** (1960) | 641 | 11,234 | .436 | .761 | 2,079 | 1,667 |
| NBA All-Star Game MVP, 1951 | | | | | | |

| Player (year elected) | Games | Points | FG% | FT% | Rebs. | Assts. |
|---|---|---|---|---|---|---|
| Maravich, Pete (Pistol) (1986–87) | 658 | 15,948 | .441 | .820 | 2,747 | 3,563 |

NCAA career record holder for points scored (3,667) and average (44.2 ppg)

| | | | | | | |
|---|---|---|---|---|---|---|
| Martin, Slater (1981) | 745 | 7,337 | .364 | .762 | 2,302[1] | 3,160 |

Played in seven straight All-Star Games, 1953–59

| | | | | | | |
|---|---|---|---|---|---|---|
| Mikan, George L. (1959) | 439 | 10,156 | .404 | .782 | 4,167[1] | 1,245 |
| (NBL)[2] | 81 | 1,608 | | .756 | | |

Three-time NBA scoring leader (1949, 1950, 1952)

| | | | | | | |
|---|---|---|---|---|---|---|
| Monroe, Earl (The Pearl) (1990) | 926 | 17,454 | .464 | .807 | 2,796 | 3,594 |

NBA Rookie of the Year, 1968

| | | | | | | |
|---|---|---|---|---|---|---|
| Pettit, Robert L. (1970) | 792 | 20,880 | .436 | .761 | 12,849 | 2,369 |

Led NBA in scoring (25.7 ppg) and rebounds (1,164) in 1956

| | | | | | | |
|---|---|---|---|---|---|---|
| Phillip, Andy (1961) | 701 | 6,384 | .368 | .695 | 2,395[1] | 3,759 |

Led NBA in assists, 1951 and 1952

| | | | | | | |
|---|---|---|---|---|---|---|
| Pollard, Jim (1977) | 438 | 5,762 | .360 | .750 | 2,487[1] | 1,417 |
| (NBL)[2] | 59 | 760 | | .676 | | |

Started in four NBA All-Star Games

| | | | | | | |
|---|---|---|---|---|---|---|
| Ramsey, Frank (1981) | 623 | 8,378 | .402 | .804 | 3,410 | 1,136 |

Member of seven NBA championship teams

| | | | | | | |
|---|---|---|---|---|---|---|
| Reed, Willis (1981) | 650 | 12,183 | .476 | .747 | 8,414 | 1,186 |

In 1970 was named NBA MVP, All-Star Game MVP, and Playoff MVP

| | | | | | | |
|---|---|---|---|---|---|---|
| Robertson, Oscar (1979) | 1,040 | 26,710 | .485 | .838 | 7,804 | 9,887 |

NBA all-time leader in rebounds by a guard, assists, and free throws made (7,694)

| | | | | | | |
|---|---|---|---|---|---|---|
| Russell, Bill (1974) | 963 | 14,522 | .440 | .561 | 21,620 | 4,100 |

Five-time NBA MVP; 32 rebounds in one half vs. Philadelphia, 1957

| | | | | | | |
|---|---|---|---|---|---|---|
| Schayes, Adolph (Dolph) (1972) | 996 | 18,438 | .380 | .849 | 11,256[1] | 3,072 |
| (NBL)[2] | 63 | 811 | | .724 | | |

NBA Coach of the Year (1966)

| | | | | | | |
|---|---|---|---|---|---|---|
| Sharman, Bill (1974) | 711 | 12,665 | .426 | .883 | 2,779 | 2,101 |

Led NBA in free-throw percentage for seven seasons

| | | | | | | |
|---|---|---|---|---|---|---|
| Thurmond, Nate (1984) | 964 | 14,437 | .421 | .667 | 14,464 | 2,575 |

Holds NCAA tournament record for most rebounds in one game (31)

| | | | | | | |
|---|---|---|---|---|---|---|
| Twyman, Jack (1982) | 823 | 15,840 | .450 | .778 | 5,421 | 1,969 |

Led NBA in field-goal percentage, 1958 (.452)

| | | | | | | |
|---|---|---|---|---|---|---|
| Unseld, Wes (1987–88) | 984 | 10,624 | .509 | .633 | 13,769 | 3,822 |

Named NBA MVP and Rookie of the Year in same year (1969)

| | | | | | | |
|---|---|---|---|---|---|---|
| Wazner, Robert (1986–87) | 502 | 5,891 | .388 | .800 | 1,652[1] | 1,575 |

Free-throw percentage leader, 1952 (.904)

| | | | | | | |
|---|---|---|---|---|---|---|
| West, Jerry Alan (1979) | 932 | 25,192 | .474 | .814 | 5,376 | 6,238 |

All-time playoff scoring average leader (29.1 ppg)

| | | | | | | |
|---|---|---|---|---|---|---|
| Wilkens, Lenny (1988–89) | 1,077 | 17,772 | .432 | .774 | 5,030 | 7,211 |

Ranks third in the NBA in career assists

**Note:** All statistics for NBA career unless otherwise noted. NBL = National Basketball League; ABA = American Basketball Association. 1. Does not include seasons played prior to 1950–51, when the NBA first began keeping statistics for rebounds. 2. The National Basketball League did not keep statistics for field-goal percentage, rebounds, or assists.

## COACHES

Anderson, W. Harold 1984
Auerbach, Arnold J. "Red" 1968
Barry, Justin "Sam" 1978
Blood, Ernest A. 1960
Cann, Howard G. 1967
Carlson, Dr. H. Clifford 1959
Carnevale, Ben 1969
Case, Everett 1981
Dean, Everett S. 1966
Diddle, Edgar A. 1971
Drake, Bruce 1972
Gaines, Clarence 1981
Gardner, James H. "Jack" 1983
Gill, Amory T. 1967
Harshman, Marv 1984
Hickey, Edgar S. "Eddie" 1978
Hobson, Howard A. 1965
Holzman, William "Red" 1986
Iba, Henry P. 1968
Julian, Alvin F. 1967

Keaney, Frank W. 1960
Keogan, George E. 1961
Knight, Bob 1991
Lambert, Ward L. 1960
Litwack, Harry 1975
Leoffler, Kenneth D. 1964
Lonborg, Arthur C. 1972
McCutchan, Arad A. 1980
McGuire, Frank J. 1976
Meanwell, Dr. Walter E. 1959
Meyer, Raymond J. 1978
Miller, Ralph 1987
Rupp, Adolph F. 1968
Sachs, Leonard D. 1961
Shelton, Everett F. 1979
Smith, Dean 1982
Taylor, Fred R. 1985–86
Wade, L. Margaret 1984
Watts, Stanley H. 1985–86
Wooden, John R. 1972

# Football

**National Football League**
**410 Park Avenue**
**New York, NY 10022**
**(212) 758-1500**

Commissioner: Paul Tagliabue
Founded: 1920—Number of Teams: 28

## 1990 NFL REGULAR SEASON FINAL STANDINGS

### AMERICAN FOOTBALL CONFERENCE

| EASTERN DIVISION | W | L | T | Pct. | Pts. | Op. |
|---|---|---|---|---|---|---|
| Buffalo Bills[1] | 13 | 3 | 0 | .813 | 428 | 263 |
| Miami Dolphins[2] | 12 | 4 | 0 | .750 | 336 | 242 |
| Indianapolis Colts | 7 | 9 | 0 | .438 | 281 | 353 |
| New York Jets | 6 | 10 | 0 | .375 | 295 | 345 |
| New England Patriots | 1 | 15 | 0 | .063 | 181 | 446 |
| **CENTRAL DIVISION** | | | | | | |
| Cincinnati Bengals[1] | 9 | 7 | 0 | .563 | 360 | 352 |
| Houston Oilers[2] | 9 | 7 | 0 | .563 | 405 | 307 |
| Pittsburgh Steelers | 9 | 7 | 0 | .563 | 292 | 240 |
| Cleveland Browns | 3 | 13 | 0 | .188 | 228 | 462 |
| **WESTERN DIVISION** | | | | | | |
| Los Angeles Raiders[1] | 12 | 4 | 0 | .750 | 337 | 268 |
| Kansas City Chiefs[2] | 11 | 5 | 0 | .688 | 369 | 257 |
| Seattle Seahawks | 9 | 7 | 0 | .563 | 306 | 286 |
| San Diego Chargers | 6 | 10 | 0 | .375 | 315 | 281 |
| Denver Broncos | 5 | 11 | 0 | .313 | 331 | 374 |

### NATIONAL FOOTBALL CONFERENCE

| EASTERN DIVISION | W | L | T | Pct. | Pts. | Op. |
|---|---|---|---|---|---|---|
| New York Giants[1] | 13 | 3 | 0 | .813 | 335 | 211 |
| Philadelphia Eagles[2] | 10 | 6 | 0 | .625 | 396 | 299 |
| Washington Redskins[2] | 10 | 6 | 0 | .625 | 381 | 301 |
| Dallas Cowboys | 7 | 9 | 0 | .438 | 244 | 308 |
| Phoenix Cardinals | 5 | 11 | 0 | .313 | 268 | 396 |
| **CENTRAL DIVISION** | | | | | | |
| Chicago Bears[1] | 11 | 5 | 0 | .688 | 348 | 280 |
| Tampa Bay Buccaneers | 6 | 10 | 0 | .375 | 264 | 367 |
| Detroit Lions | 6 | 10 | 0 | .375 | 373 | 413 |
| Green Bay Packers | 6 | 10 | 0 | .375 | 271 | 347 |
| Minnesota Vikings | 6 | 10 | 0 | .375 | 351 | 326 |
| **WESTERN DIVISION** | | | | | | |
| San Francisco 49ers[1] | 14 | 2 | 0 | .875 | 353 | 239 |
| New Orleans Saints[2] | 8 | 8 | 0 | .500 | 274 | 275 |
| Los Angeles Rams | 5 | 11 | 0 | .313 | 345 | 412 |
| Atlanta Falcons | 5 | 11 | 0 | .313 | 348 | 365 |

1. Division champion. 2. Wild Card for playoffs.

## 1990 POSTSEASON AT A GLANCE

**AFC First Round**
MIAMI 17, Kansas City 16
CINCINNATI 41, Houston 14

**NFC First Round**
Washington 20, PHILADELPHIA 6
CHICAGO 16, New Orleans 6

**AFC Divisional Playoff**
BUFFALO 44, Miami 34
L.A. RAIDERS 20, Cincinnati 10

**NFC Divisional Playoff**
SAN FRANCISCO 28, Washington 10
N.Y. GIANTS 31, Chicago 3

**AFC Championship Game**
BUFFALO 51, L.A. Raiders 3

**NFC Championship Game**
N.Y. Giants 15, SAN FRANCISCO 13

**Super Bowl XXV at Tampa Stadium, Tampa, Florida**
N.Y. GIANTS 20, Buffalo 19

**AFC-NFC Pro Bowl at Honolulu, Hawaii**
AFC 23, NFC 21

**Note**: Home team in capital letters.

## NFL LEADERS, 1990

### RUSHING

| AFC | No. | Yds. | Avg. | Long | TD |
|-----|-----|------|------|------|-----|
| Thurman Thomas, Buffalo | 271 | 1,297 | 4.8 | 80 | 11 |
| Marion Butts, San Diego | 265 | 1,225 | 4.6 | 52 | 8 |
| Bobby Humphrey, Denver | 288 | 1,202 | 4.2 | 37 | 7 |
| Barry Word, Kansas City | 204 | 1,015 | 5.0 | 53 | 4 |
| James Brooks, Cincinnati | 195 | 1,004 | 5.1 | 56 | 5 |
| Derrick Fenner, Seattle | 215 | 859 | 4.0 | 36 | 14 |
| Sammie Smith, Miami | 226 | 831 | 3.7 | 33 | 8 |
| John Stephens, New England | 212 | 808 | 3.8 | 26 | 2 |
| Christian Okoye, Kansas City | 245 | 805 | 3.3 | 32 | 7 |
| **NFC** | | | | | |
| Barry Sanders, Detroit | 255 | 1,304 | 5.1 | 45 | 13 |
| Earnest Byner, Washington | 297 | 1,219 | 4.1 | 22 | 6 |
| Neal Anderson, Chicago | 260 | 1,078 | 4.1 | 52 | 10 |
| Randall Cunningham, Philadelphia | 118 | 942 | 8.0 | 52 | 5 |
| Emmitt Smith, Dallas | 241 | 937 | 3.9 | 48 | 11 |
| Johnny Johnson, Phoenix | 234 | 926 | 4.0 | 41 | 5 |
| Cleveland Gary, L.A. Rams | 204 | 808 | 4.0 | 48 | 14 |
| Ottis Anderson, N.Y. Giants | 225 | 784 | 3.5 | 28 | 11 |
| Herschel Walker, Minnesota | 184 | 770 | 4.2 | 58 | 5 |

### PASSING

| AFC | Att. | Comp. | Yds. | TD | Int. | Rating |
|-----|------|-------|------|-----|------|--------|
| Jim Kelly, Buffalo | 346 | 219 | 2,829 | 24 | 9 | 101.2 |
| Warren Moon, Houston | 584 | 362 | 4,689 | 33 | 13 | 96.8 |
| Steve DeBerg, Kansas City | 444 | 258 | 3,444 | 23 | 4 | 96.3 |
| Jay Schroeder, L.A. Raiders | 334 | 182 | 2,849 | 19 | 9 | 90.8 |
| Dan Marino, Miami | 531 | 306 | 3,563 | 21 | 11 | 82.6 |
| Bubby Brister, Pittsburgh | 387 | 223 | 2,725 | 20 | 14 | 81.6 |
| John Elway, Denver | 502 | 294 | 3,526 | 15 | 14 | 78.5 |
| Ken O'Brien, N.Y. Jets | 411 | 226 | 2,855 | 13 | 10 | 77.3 |
| Boomer Esiason, Cincinnati | 402 | 224 | 3,031 | 24 | 22 | 77.0 |
| **NFC** | | | | | | |
| Phil Simms, N.Y. Giants | 311 | 184 | 2,284 | 15 | 4 | 92.7 |
| Randall Cunningham, Phil. | 465 | 271 | 3,466 | 30 | 13 | 91.6 |
| Joe Montana, San Francisco | 520 | 321 | 3,944 | 26 | 16 | 89.0 |
| Jim Harbaugh, Chicago | 312 | 180 | 2,178 | 10 | 6 | 81.9 |
| Rodney Peete, Detroit | 271 | 142 | 1,974 | 13 | 8 | 79.8 |
| Jim Everett, L.A. Rams | 554 | 307 | 3,989 | 23 | 17 | 79.3 |
| Chris Miller, Atlanta | 388 | 222 | 2,735 | 17 | 14 | 78.7 |
| Mark Rypien, Washington | 304 | 166 | 2,070 | 16 | 11 | 78.4 |
| Vinny Testaverde, Tampa Bay | 365 | 203 | 2,818 | 17 | 18 | 75.6 |

**Note:** Rating based on percentage of completions, percentage of touchdowns, percentage of interceptions, and average gain per attempt.

### RECEIVING

| AFC | No. | Yds. | Avg. gain | TD |
|-----|-----|------|-----------|-----|
| Haywood Jeffries, Houston | 74 | 1,048 | 14.2 | 8 |
| Drew Hill, Houston | 74 | 1,019 | 13.8 | 5 |
| John L. Williams, Seattle | 73 | 699 | 9.6 | 0 |
| Ernest Givins, Houston | 72 | 979 | 13.6 | 9 |
| Andre Reed, Buffalo | 71 | 945 | 13.3 | 8 |
| Albert Bentley, Indianapolis | 71 | 664 | 9.4 | 2 |
| Curtis Duncan, Houston | 66 | 785 | 11.9 | 1 |
| Stephone Paige, Kansas City | 65 | 1,021 | 15.7 | 5 |
| Anthony Miller, San Diego | 63 | 933 | 14.8 | 7 |
| **NFC** | | | | |
| Jerry Rice, San Francisco | 100 | 1,502 | 15.0 | 13 |
| Andre Rison, Atlanta | 82 | 1,208 | 14.7 | 10 |
| Keith Byars, Philadelphia | 81 | 819 | 10.1 | 3 |
| Henry Ellard, L.A. Rams | 76 | 1,294 | 17.0 | 4 |
| Gary Clark, Washington | 75 | 1,112 | 14.8 | 8 |
| Anthony Carter, Minnesota | 70 | 1,008 | 14.4 | 8 |
| Art Monk, Washington | 68 | 770 | 11.3 | 5 |
| Sterling Sharpe, Green Bay | 67 | 1,105 | 16.5 | 6 |
| Kelvin Martin, Dallas | 64 | 732 | 11.4 | 0 |

## NFL 1991 FIRST-ROUND DRAFT CHOICES

| Team | Choice | Pos. | College |
|------|--------|------|---------|
| Dallas | Russell Maryland | DT | Miami (Fla.) |
| Cleveland | Eric Turner | S | UCLA |
| Atlanta | Bruce Pickens | CB | Nebraska |
| Denver | Mike Croel | LB | Nebraska |
| Los Angeles Rams | Todd Lyght | CB | Notre Dame |
| Phoenix | Eric Swann | DL | none |
| Tampa Bay | Charles McRae | T | Tennessee |
| Philadelphia | Antone Davis | T | Tennessee |
| San Diego | Stanley Richard | DB | Texas |
| Detroit | Herman Moore | WR | Virginia |
| New England | Pat Harlow | T | Southern California |
| Dallas | Alvin Harper | WR | Tennessee |
| Atlanta | Mike Pritchard | WR | Colorado |
| New England | Leonard Russell | RB | Arizona St. |
| Pittsburgh | Hoey Richardson | LB | Florida |
| Seattle | Dan McGwire | QB | San Diego St. |
| Washington | Bobby Wilson | DT | Michigan St. |
| Cincinnati | Alfred Williams | LB | Colorado |
| Green Bay | Vincent Clark | DB | Ohio St. |
| Dallas | Kelvin Pritchett[1] | DT | Mississippi |
| Kansas City | Harvey Williams | RB | Louisiana St. |
| Chicago | Stan Thomas | T | Texas |
| Miami | Randal Hill | WR | Miami (Fla.) |
| Los Angeles Raiders | Todd Marinovich | QB | Southern California |
| San Francisco | Ted Washington | DL | Louisville |
| Buffalo | Henry Jones | S | Illinois |
| New York Giants | Jarrod Bunch | RB | Michigan |

1. Traded to Detroit. **Source:** NFL.

## NFL NUMBER-ONE DRAFT PICKS, 1936–91

| Year | Player | Team | Pos. | College |
|------|--------|------|------|---------|
| 1936 | Jay Berwanger | Philadelphia Eagles | RB | Chicago |
| 1937 | Sam Francis | Philadelphia Eagles | RB | Nebraska |
| 1938 | Corbett Davis | Cleveland Rams | RB | Indiana |
| 1939 | Charles Aldrich | Chicago Cardinals | OL | Texas Christian |
| 1940 | George Cafego | Chicago Cardinals | QB | Tennessee |
| 1941 | Tom Harmon | Chicago Bears | RB | Michigan |
| 1942 | Bill Dudley | Pittsburgh Steelers | RB | Virginia |
| 1943 | Frank Sinkwich | Detroit Lions | RB | Georgia |
| 1944 | Angelo Bertelli | Boston Yanks | QB | Notre Dame |
| 1945 | Charley Trippi | Chicago Cardinals | RB | Georgia |
| 1946 | Frank Dancewicz | Boston Yanks | QB | Notre Dame |
| 1947 | Bob Fenimore | Chicago Bears | RB | Oklahoma A&M |
| 1948 | Harry Gilmer | Washington Redskins | QB | Alabama |
| 1949 | Chuck Bednarik | Philadelphia Eagles | OL | Pennsylvania |
| 1950 | Leon Hart | Detroit Lions | RB | Notre Dame |
| 1951 | Kyle Rote | New York Giants | E/K | Southern Methodist |
| 1952 | Bill Wade | Los Angeles Rams | QB | Vanderbilt |
| 1953 | Harry Babcock | San Francisco 49ers | E | Georgia |
| 1954 | Bobby Garrett | Cleveland Browns | QB | Stanford |
| 1955 | George Shaw | Baltimore Colts | QB | Oregon |
| 1956 | Gary Glick | Pittsburgh Steelers | QB | Colorado State |
| 1957 | Paul Hornung | Green Bay Packers | RB | Notre Dame |
| 1958 | King Hill | St. Louis Cardinals | QB | Rice |
| 1959 | Randy Duncan | Green Bay Packers | QB | Iowa |
| 1960 | Billy Cannon | Los Angeles Rams | RB | Louisiana State |
| 1961 | Tommy Mason | Minnesota Vikings | RB | Tulane |
| 1962 | Ernie Davis | Washington Redskins | RB | Syracuse |
| 1963 | Terry Baker | Los Angeles Rams | QB | Oregon State |
| 1964 | Dave Parks | San Francisco 49ers | E | Texas Tech |
| 1965 | Tucker Frederickson | New York Giants | RB | Auburn |
| 1966 | Tommy Nobis | Atlanta Falcons | LB | Texas |
| 1967 | Bubba Smith | Baltimore Colts | DL | Michigan State |
| 1968 | Ron Yary | Minnesota Vikings | OL | USC |
| 1969 | O.J. Simpson | Buffalo Bills | RB | USC |
| 1970 | Terry Bradshaw | Pittsburgh Steelers | QB | Louisiana Tech |

| Year | Player | Team | Pos. | College |
|------|--------|------|------|---------|
| 1971 | Jim Plunkett | Boston Patriots | QB | Stanford |
| 1972 | Walt Patulski | Buffalo Bills | DL | Notre Dame |
| 1973 | John Matuszak | Houston Oilers | DL | Tampa |
| 1974 | Ed Jones | Dallas Cowboys | DL | Tennessee State |
| 1975 | Steve Bartkowski | Atlanta Falcons | QB | California |
| 1976 | Lee Roy Selmon | Tampa Bay Buccaneers | DL | Oklahoma |
| 1977 | Ricky Bell | Tampa Bay Buccaneers | RB | USC |
| 1978 | Earl Campbell | Houston Oilers | RB | Texas |
| 1979 | Tom Cousineau | Buffalo Bills | LB | Ohio State |
| 1980 | Billy Sims | Detroit Lions | RB | Oklahoma |
| 1981 | George Rogers | New Orleans Saints | RB | South Carolina |
| 1982 | Kenneth Sims | New England Patriots | DL | Texas |
| 1983 | John Elway | Baltimore Colts | QB | Stanford |
| 1984 | Irving Fryar | New England Patriots | WR | Nebraska |
| 1985 | Bruce Smith | Buffalo Bills | DL | Virginia Tech |
| 1986 | Bo Jackson | Tampa Bay Buccaneers | RB | Auburn |
| 1987 | Vinny Testaverde | Tampa Bay Buccaneers | QB | Miami (Fla.) |
| 1988 | Aundray Bruce | Atlanta Falcons | LB | Auburn |
| 1989 | Troy Aikman | Dallas Cowboys | QB | UCLA |
| 1990 | Jeff George | Indianapolis Colts | QB | Illinois |
| 1991 | Russell Maryland | Dallas Cowboys | DT | Miami (Fla.) |

## ALL-TIME PRO FOOTBALL RECORDS

### RUSHING

| | Player | League | Yrs. | Yds. | Att. | Avg. |
|---|--------|--------|------|------|------|------|
| 1. | Walter Payton | NFL | 13 | 16,726 | 3,838 | 4.4 |
| 2. | Tony Dorsett | NFL | 12 | 12,739 | 2,936 | 4.3 |
| 3. | Jim Brown | NFL | 9 | 12,312 | 2,359 | 5.2 |
| 4. | Franco Harris | NFL | 13 | 12,120 | 2,949 | 4.1 |
| 5. | Eric Dickerson[1] | NFL | 8 | 11,903 | 2,816 | 4.6 |
| 6. | John Riggins | NFL | 14 | 11,352 | 2,916 | 3.9 |
| 7. | O.J. Simpson | AFL–NFL | 11 | 11,236 | 2,404 | 4.7 |
| 8. | Ottis Anderson[1] | NFL | 12 | 10,101 | 2,499 | 4.0 |
| 9. | Joe Perry | AAFC–NFL | 16 | 9,723 | 1,929 | 5.0 |
| 10. | Earl Campbell | NFL | 8 | 9,407 | 2,187 | 4.3 |

### RECEIVING

| | Player | League | Yrs. | No. | Yds. | Avg. |
|---|--------|--------|------|-----|------|------|
| 1. | Steve Largent | NFL | 14 | 819 | 13,089 | 16.0 |
| 2. | Charlie Joiner | AFL–NFL | 18 | 750 | 12,146 | 16.2 |
| 3. | Art Monk[1] | NFL | 11 | 730 | 9,835 | 13.6 |
| 4. | Ozzie Newsome | NFL | 13 | 662 | 7,960 | 12.1 |
| 5. | Charley Taylor | NFL | 13 | 649 | 9,110 | 14.0 |
| 6. | James Lofton[1] | NFL | 13 | 642 | ·11,963 | 18.6 |
| 7. | Don Maynard | NFL–AFL | 15 | 633 | 11,834 | 18.7 |
| 8. | Raymond Berry | NFL | 13 | 631 | 9,275 | 14.7 |
| 9. | Harold Carmichael | NFL | 14 | 590 | 8,985 | 15.2 |
| 10. | Fred Biletnikoff | AFL–NFL | 14 | 589 | 8,974 | 15.2 |

### SCORING

| | Player | League | Yrs. | Total | TD | PAT | FG |
|---|--------|--------|------|-------|-----|-----|-----|
| 1. | George Blanda | NFL–AFL | 26 | 2,002 | 9 | 943 | 335 |
| 2. | Jan Stenerud | AFL–NFL | 19 | 1,699 | — | 580 | 373 |
| 3. | Lou Groza | AAFC–NFL | 21 | 1,608 | 1 | 810 | 264 |
| 4. | Jim Turner | AFL–NFL | 16 | 1,439 | 1 | 521 | 304 |
| 5. | Mark Moseley | NFL | 16 | 1,382 | — | 482 | 300 |
| 6. | Jim Bakken | NFL | 17 | 1,380 | — | 534 | 282 |
| 7. | Fred Cox | NFL | 15 | 1,365 | — | 519 | 282 |
| 8. | Pat Leahy[1] | NFL | 17 | 1,362 | — | 528 | 278 |
| 9. | Chris Bahr | NFL | 14 | 1,213 | — | 490 | 241 |
| 10. | Nick Lowery[1] | NFL | 12 | 1,152 | — | 375 | 259 |

**Note**: Through end of 1990 season. 1. Active player. **Source**: NFL.

## NFL ALL-TIME PASSING LEADERS

| | | | PASSING | | | | | | |
|---|--------|--------|------|------|------|------|-----|-----|--------|
| Rank | Player | League | Yrs. | Att. | Comp. | Yds. | TD | Int. | Rating |
| 1. | Joe Montana | NFL | 12 | 4,570 | 2,914 | 34,986 | 242 | 123 | 93.4 |
| 2. | Dan Marino | NFL | 8 | 4,181 | 2,480 | 31,416 | 241 | 136 | 88.5 |
| 3. | Jim Kelly | NFL | 5 | 2,041 | 1,251 | 15,730 | 105 | 72 | 85.8 |
| 4. | Boomer Esiason | NFL | 7 | 2,007 | 1,520 | 21,381 | 150 | 96 | 85.3 |
| 5. | Roger Staubach | NFL | 11 | 2,958 | 1,685 | 22,700 | 153 | 109 | 83.4 |
| 6. | Neil Lomax | NFL | 8 | 3,153 | 1,817 | 22,771 | 136 | 90 | 82.7 |
| 7. | Sonny Jurgensen | NFL | 18 | 4,262 | 2,433 | 32,224 | 255 | 189 | 82.6 |
| 8. | Len Dawson | AFL–NFL | 19 | 3,741 | 2,136 | 28,711 | 239 | 183 | 82.6 |
| 9. | Dave Krieg | NFL | 11 | 3,291 | 1,908 | 24,062 | 184 | 136 | 82.3 |
| 10. | Jim Everett | NFL | 5 | 2,036 | 1,154 | 15,345 | 101 | 73 | 82.2 |

**Note**: Rating points based on a combination of performances in the following four categories: percentage of completions, percentage of touchdown passes, percentage of interceptions, and average gain per pass attempt.

### TOTAL PASSES ATTEMPTED

| | | |
|---|--------|-------|
| 1. | Fran Tarkenton | 6,467 |
| 2. | Dan Fouts | 5,604 |
| 3. | Johnny Unitas | 5,186 |
| 4. | Jim Hart | 5,076 |
| 5. | John Hadl | 4,687 |
| 6. | Joe Montana | 4,570 |
| 6. | Joe Ferguson | 4,519 |
| 8. | Roman Gabriel | 4,498 |
| 9. | John Brodie | 4,491 |
| 10. | Ken Anderson | 4,475 |
| 11. | Y.A. Tittle | 4,395 |
| 12. | Norm Snead | 4,353 |
| 13. | Sonny Jurgensen | 4,262 |
| 14. | Dan Marino | 4,181 |
| 15. | Ron Jaworski | 4,117 |
| 16. | George Blanda | 4,007 |
| 17. | Terry Bradshaw | 3,901 |
| 18. | Ken Stabler | 3,793 |
| 19. | Craig Morton | 3,786 |
| 20. | Joe Namath | 3,762 |

### TOTAL TOUCHDOWN PASSES

| | | |
|---|--------|-----|
| 1. | Fran Tarkenton | 342 |
| 2. | Johnny Unitas | 290 |
| 3. | Sonny Jurgensen | 255 |
| 4. | Dan Fouts | 254 |
| 5. | John Hadl | 244 |
| 6.(T) | Joe Montana | 242 |
| 6.(T) | Y.A. Tittle | 242 |
| 8. | Dan Marino | 241 |
| 9. | Len Dawson | 239 |
| 10. | George Blanda | 236 |
| 11. | John Brodie | 214 |
| 12. | Terry Bradshaw | 212 |
| 13. | Jim Hart | 209 |
| 14. | Roman Gabriel | 201 |
| 15. | Ken Anderson | 197 |
| 16.(T) | Bobby Layne | 196 |
| 16.(T) | Norm Snead | 196 |
| 16.(T) | Joe Ferguson | 196 |
| 19. | Ken Stabler | 194 |
| 20. | Bob Griese | 192 |

### TOTAL PASSES COMPLETED

| | | |
|---|--------|-------|
| 1. | Fran Tarkenton | 3,686 |
| 2. | Dan Fouts | 3,297 |
| 3. | Joe Montana | 2,914 |
| 4. | Johnny Unitas | 2,830 |
| 5. | Ken Anderson | 2,654 |
| 6. | Jim Hart | 2,593 |
| 7. | Dan Marino | 2,480 |
| 8. | John Brodie | 2,469 |
| 9. | Sonny Jurgensen | 2,433 |
| 10. | Y.A. Tittle | 2,427 |
| 11. | Joe Ferguson | 2,369 |
| 12. | Roman Gabriel | 2,366 |
| 13. | John Hadl | 2,363 |
| 14. | Norm Snead | 2,276 |
| 15. | Ken Stabler | 2,270 |
| 16. | Ron Jaworski | 2,187 |
| 17. | Len Dawson | 2,136 |
| 18. | Craig Morton | 2,053 |
| 19. | Joe Theismann | 2,044 |
| 20. | Terry Bradshaw | 2,025 |

**Note**: Through the end of 1990 season. **Source**: NFL.

### TOTAL YARDS PASSING

| | | |
|---|--------|--------|
| 1. | Fran Tarkenton | 47,003 |
| 2. | Dan Fouts | 43,040 |
| 3. | Johnny Unitas | 40,239 |
| 4. | Joe Montana | 34,986 |
| 5. | Jim Hart | 34,665 |
| 6. | John Hadl | 33,513 |
| 7. | Y.A. Tittle | 33,070 |
| 8. | Ken Anderson | 32,838 |
| 9. | Sonny Jurgensen | 32,224 |
| 10. | John Brodie | 31,548 |
| 11. | Dan Marino | 31,416 |
| 12. | Norm Snead | 30,797 |
| 13. | Joe Ferguson | 29,817 |
| 14. | Roman Gabriel | 29,444 |
| 15. | Len Dawson | 28,711 |
| 16. | Ron Jaworski | 28,190 |
| 17. | Terry Bradshaw | 27,989 |
| 18. | Ken Stabler | 27,938 |
| 19. | Craig Morton | 27,908 |
| 20. | Joe Namath | 27,663 |

## NFL ROOKIE OF THE YEAR, 1970–90

| Year | | Player | Pos. | Team | Year | | Player | Pos. | Team |
|------|------|--------|------|------|------|------|--------|------|------|
| 1970 | NFC: | Bruce Taylor | CB | San Francisco 49ers | 1978 | NFC: | Al Baker | DE | Detroit Lions |
| | AFC: | Dennis Shaw | QB | Buffalo Bills | | AFC: | Earl Campbell | RB | Houston Oilers |
| 1971 | NFC: | John Brockington | RB | Green Bay Packers | 1979 | NFC: | Ottis Anderson | RB | St. Louis Cardinals |
| | AFC: | Jim Plunkett | QB | New England Patriots | | AFC: | Jerry Butler | WR | Buffalo Bills |
| 1972 | NFC: | Chester Marcol | PK | Green Bay Packers | 1980 | | Billy Sims | RB | Detroit Lions |
| | AFC: | Franco Harris | RB | Pittsburgh Steelers | 1981 | | George Rogers | RB | New England Patriots |
| 1973 | NFC: | Chuck Foreman | RB | Minnesota Vikings | 1982 | | Marcus Allen | RB | Los Angeles Raiders |
| | AFC: | Boobie Clark | RB | Cincinnati Bengals | 1983 | | Dan Marino | QB | Miami Dolphins |
| 1974 | NFC: | Wilbur Jackson | RB | San Francisco 49ers | 1984 | | Louis Lipps | WR | Pittsburgh Steelers |
| | AFC: | Don Woods | RB | San Diego Chargers | 1985 | | Eddie Brown | WR | Cincinnati Bengals |
| 1975 | NFC: | Steve Bartkowski | QB | Atlanta Falcons | 1986 | | Rueben Mayes | RB | New Orleans Saints |
| | AFC: | Robert Brazile | LB | Houston Oilers | 1987 | | Robert Awalt | TE | St. Louis Cardinals |
| 1976 | NFC: | Sammy White | WR | Minnesota Vikings | 1988 | | Keith Jackson | TE | Philadephia Eagles |
| | AFC: | Mike Haynes | CB | New England Patriots | 1989 | | Barry Sanders | RB | Detroit Lions |
| 1977 | NFC: | Tony Dorsett | RB | Dallas Cowboys | 1990 | | Richmond Webb | OL | Miami Dolphins |
| | AFC: | A.J. Duhe | DT | Miami Dolphins | | | | | |

**Note:** In 1980 *The Sporting News* began selecting one rookie as Rookie of the Year for the entire NFL. **Source:** NFL

## NFL PLAYER OF THE YEAR

| Year | | Player | Pos. | Team | Year | | Player | Pos. | Team |
|------|------|--------|------|------|------|------|--------|------|------|
| 1957 | | Jim Brown | RB | Cleveland Browns | 1975 | NFC: | Fran Tarkenton | QB | Minnesota Vikings |
| 1958 | | Jim Brown | RB | Cleveland Browns | | AFC: | O.J. Simpson | RB | Buffalo Bills |
| 1959 | | Johnny Unitas | QB | Baltimore Colts | 1976 | NFC: | Walter Payton | RB | Chicago Bears |
| 1960 | | Norm Van Brocklin | QB | Philadelphia Eagles | | AFC: | Ken Stabler | QB | Oakland Raiders |
| 1961 | | Paul Hornung | HB | Green Bay Packers | 1977 | NFC: | Walter Payton | RB | Chicago Bears |
| 1962 | | Y.A. Tittle | QB | New York Giants | | AFC: | Craig Morton | QB | Denver Broncos |
| 1963 | | Y.A. Tittle | QB | New York Giants | 1978 | NFC: | Archie Manning | QB | New Orleans Saints |
| 1964 | | Johnny Unitas | QB | Baltimore Colts | | AFC: | Earl Campbell | RB | Houston Oilers |
| 1965 | | Jim Brown | RB | Cleveland Browns | 1979 | NFC: | Ottis Anderson | RB | St. Louis Cardinals |
| 1966 | | Bart Starr | QB | Green Bay Packers | | AFC: | Dan Fouts | QB | San Diego Chargers |
| 1967 | | Johnny Unitas | QB | Baltimore Colts | 1980 | | Brian Sipe | QB | Cleveland Browns |
| 1968 | | Earl Morrall | QB | Baltimore Colts | 1981 | | Ken Anderson | QB | Cincinnati Bengals |
| 1969 | | Roman Gabriel | QB | Los Angeles Rams | 1982 | | Mark Moseley | PK | Washington Redskins |
| 1970 | NFC: | John Brodie | QB | San Francisco 49ers | 1983 | | Eric Dickerson | RB | Los Angeles Rams |
| | AFC: | George Blanda | QB-PK | Oakland Raiders | 1984 | | Dan Marino | QB | Miami Dolphins |
| 1971 | NFC: | Roger Staubach | QB | Dallas Cowboys | 1985 | | Marcus Allen | RB | Los Angeles Raiders |
| | AFC: | Bob Griese | QB | Miami Dolphins | 1986 | | Lawrence Taylor | LB | New York Giants |
| 1972 | NFC: | Larry Brown | RB | Washington Redskins | 1987 | | Jerry Rice | WR | San Francisco 49ers |
| | AFC: | Earl Morrall | QB | Miami Dolphins | 1988 | | Boomer Esiason | QB | Cincinnati Bengals |
| 1973 | NFC: | John Hadl | QB | Los Angeles Rams | 1989 | | Joe Montana | QB | San Francisco 49ers |
| | AFC: | O.J. Simpson | RB | Buffalo Bills | 1990 | | Jerry Rice | WR | San Francisco 49ers |
| 1974 | NFC: | Chuck Foreman | RB | Minnesota Vikings | | | | | |
| | AFC: | Ken Stabler | QB | Oakland Raiders | | | | | |

**Note:** In 1970–79 a player was selected as Player of the Year for both the NFC and AFC. In 1980 *The Sporting News* reinstated the selection of one player as Player of the Year for the entire NFL. **Source:** *The Sporting News.*

## NFL CHAMPIONS, 1921–66

| Year | Team | Year | Team | Year | Team |
|------|------|------|------|------|------|
| 1921 | Chicago Staleys (10–1–1)[1] | 1936 | Green Bay Packers (10–1–1) | 1951 | Los Angeles Rams (8–4–0) |
| 1922 | Canton Bulldogs (10–0–2) | 1937 | Washington Redskins (8–3–0) | 1952 | Detroit Lions (9–3–0) |
| 1923 | Canton Bulldogs (11–0–1) | 1938 | New York Giants (8–2–1) | 1953 | Detroit Lions (10–2–0) |
| 1924 | Cleveland Bulldogs (7–1–1)[2] | 1939 | Green Bay Packers (9–2–0) | 1954 | Cleveland Browns (9–3–0) |
| 1925 | Chicago Cardinals (11–2–1) | 1940 | Chicago Bears (8–3–0) | 1955 | Cleveland Browns (9–2–1) |
| 1926 | Frankford Yellowjackets (14–1–1) | 1941 | Chicago Bears (10–1–1) | 1956 | New York Giants (8–3–1) |
| 1927 | New York Giants (11–1–1) | 1942 | Washington Redskins (10–1–1) | 1957 | Detroit Lions (8–4–0) |
| 1928 | Providence Steamrollers (8–1–2) | 1943 | Chicago Bears (8–1–1) | 1958 | Baltimore Colts (9–3–0) |
| 1929 | Green Bay Packers (12–0–1) | 1944 | Green Bay Packers (8–2–0) | 1959 | Baltimore Colts (9–3–0) |
| 1930 | Green Bay Packers (10–3–1) | 1945 | Cleveland Rams (9–1–0) | 1960 | Philadelphia Eagles (10–2–0) |
| 1931 | Green Bay Packers (12–2–0) | 1946 | Chicago Bears (8–2–1) | 1961 | Green Bay Packers (11–3–0) |
| 1932 | Chicago Bears (7–1–6) | 1947 | Chicago Cardinals (9–3–0) | 1962 | Green Bay Packers (13–1–0) |
| 1933 | Chicago Bears (10–2–1) | 1948 | Philadelphia Eagles (9–2–1) | 1963 | Chicago Bears (11–1–2) |
| 1934 | New York Giants (8–5–0) | 1949 | Philadelphia Eagles (11–1–0) | 1964 | Cleveland Browns (10–3–1) |
| 1935 | Detroit Lions (7–3–2) | 1950 | Cleveland Browns (10–2–0) | 1965 | Green Bay Packers (10–3–1) |
| | | | | 1966 | Green Bay Packers (12–2–0) |

1. Later called the Chicago Bears. 2. Franchise moved from Canton.

# SUPER BOWL RESULTS

### Super Bowl I
Jan. 15, 1967, Memorial Coliseum
Los Angeles, California
### Green Bay Packers 35
### Kansas City Chiefs 10

Green Bay's Max McGee was a surprise star, as he filled in for ailing Boyd Dowler. McGee had caught only three passes all year, but in Super Bowl I he caught seven from quarterback Bart Starr for 138 yards and two touchdowns. Starr himself was the game's MVP, as he completed 16 of 23 passes for 250 yards and two touchdowns. Green Bay broke open the game with three second-half touchdowns, the first of which was set up by all-pro safety Willie Wood's 40-yard return of an interception to the Chiefs' five-yard line.

### Super Bowl II
Jan. 14, 1968, Orange Bowl
Miami, Florida
### Green Bay Packers 33
### Oakland Raiders 14

Bart Starr again dominated proceedings with 13 completions in 24 passing attempts, totaling 202 yards and a touchdown, winning his second straight MVP award. The Pack attack was in control all the way after building a 16–7 halftime lead. Don Chandler kicked four field goals and all-pro cornerback Herb Adderley capped the Green Bay scoring with a 60-yard run on an interception.

### Super Bowl III
Jan. 12, 1969, Orange Bowl
Miami, Florida
### New York Jets 16
### Baltimore Colts 7

Joe Namath became a prophet with honor—on the Thursday before the game, he "guaranteed" victory for New York. He did just that, earning MVP honors by completing 17 of 28 passes for 206 yards and directing a steady attack that racked up 337 total yards. Three times in the first half, the Jet defense intercepted Colts quarterback Earl Morrall, who was playing for an injured Johnny Unitas. With the Jets ahead 16–0 in the fourth quarter, Unitas came off the bench and orchestrated Baltimore's sole touchdown.

### Super Bowl IV
Jan. 11, 1970, Tulane Stadium
New Orleans, Louisiana
### Kansas City Chiefs 23
### Minnesota Vikings 7

Superb quarterbacking continued to be the key to Super Bowl victory as MVP Len Dawson called a nearly flawless game for Kansas City, completing 12 of 17 passes and hitting Otis Taylor on a 46-yard pass for the final Chiefs touchdown. The Kansas City defense limited Minnesota's strong rushing game to 67 yards and had three interceptions and two fumble recoveries. The Chiefs rolled up a 16–0 halftime lead and stood off the Vikings after that.

### Super Bowl V
Jan. 17, 1971, Orange Bowl
Miami, Florida
### Baltimore Colts 16
### Dallas Cowboys 13

First-year kicker Jim O'Brien booted a 32-yard field goal to give the Colts a victory over the Cowboys in the final seconds of the Super Bowl. Dallas led 13–6 at halftime, but two Colt interceptions set up a Baltimore touchdown and O'Brien's crucial kick. Earl Morrall relieved an injured Johnny Unitas in the first half. Unitas's lone scoring pass was dramatic—the ball caromed off receiver Eddie Hinton's fingertips, off Dallas defensive back Mel Renfro, and finally settled into the grasp of tight end John Mackey, who went 45 yards to score on a 75-yard play. Dallas linebacker Chuck Howley was the MVP.

### Super Bowl VI
Jan. 16, 1972, Tulane Stadium
New Orleans, Louisiana
### Dallas Cowboys 24
### Miami Dolphins 3

The Cowboys rushed for a record 252 yards, and their defense limited the Dolphins to a record low 185 while not permitting a touchdown. Dallas converted Chuck Howley's recovery of Larry Csonka's first fumble of the season into a 3–0 advantage. At halftime Dallas led 10–3. An eight-play, 71-yard march made it a 17–3 game. Cowboys' quarterback Roger Staubach was voted MVP for his 12 completions in 19 attempts, 119 yards passing, and two touchdowns.

### Super Bowl VII
Jan. 14, 1973, Memorial Coliseum
Los Angeles, California
### Miami Dolphins 14
### Washington Redskins 7

The Dolphins dominated the first half. On its third possession, Miami opened its first scoring drive from the Dolphins' 37-yard line. An 18-yard pass from Bob Griese to Paul Warfield was quickly followed by a Griese 28-yard touchdown pass to Howard Twilley. Miami scored its second touchdown in the first half with 18 seconds to go, after Nick Buoniconti's interception of Billy Kilmer's pass at the Miami 41 started the scoring drive. Safety Jake Scott was the MVP. Washington's sole touchdown came with 7:07 left in the game and resulted from a misplayed field goal attempt and a fumble.

### Super Bowl VIII
Jan. 13, 1974, Rice Stadium
Houston, Texas
### Miami Dolphins 24
### Minnesota Vikings 7

On their first two possessions, Miami scored, on 62- and 56-yard marches. The initial 10-play drive was climaxed by a Larry Csonka touchdown bolt through right guard after 5:27 had elapsed. Four plays later, Miami's second assault sent Jim Kiick bursting one yard through the middle for the second touchdown. By halftime Miami led 17–0. Minnesota came back from its 20 to a second-and-two situation on the Miami seven-yard line with 1:18 left in the half, but Miami limited Minnesota's Oscar

Reed to one yard. On the fourth-and-one from the six, Reed went over right tackle, but Dolphin middle linebacker Nick Buoniconti jarred the ball loose and Jake Scott recovered for Miami to end the Minnesota threat. Csonka rushed 33 times for a Super Bowl record 145 yards, winning the MVP.

### Super Bowl IX
Jan. 12, 1975, Tulane Stadium
New Orleans, Louisiana
### Pittsburgh Steelers 16
### Minnesota Vikings 6

Steeler Dwight White downed Fran Tarkenton's fumbled pass attempt in the end zone for a safety to put the Steelers on the board in the second quarter. They took advantage of another break in the second half, when Minnesota's Bill Brown fumbled on the kickoff and Marv Kellum recovered for Pittsburgh on the Vikings' 30. Franco Harris carried three straight times for 27 yards and a touchdown, putting the Steelers in front 9–0. Minnesota was able to block Bobby Walden's punt attempt, and Terry Brown recovered the ball for a touchdown. But the Steelers roared back with a 66-yard march, climaxed by Terry Bradshaw's four-yard scoring pass to Larry Brown. Pittsburgh's defense controlled the game by permitting Minnesota only 119 yards total offense and a record low 17 yards rushing. Franco Harris's record 158 yards rushing on 34 carries won him MVP honors, and paced the Steelers' 333-yard rushing attack.

### Super Bowl X
Jan. 18, 1976, Orange Bowl
Miami, Florida
### Pittsburgh Steelers 21
### Dallas Cowboys 17

Steeler quarterback Terry Bradshaw hurled a 64-yard touchdown pass to Lynn Swann to win the game, while his aggressive defense stopped the Cowboys' last rally with an end-zone interception in the game's final play. It was a battle of quarterbacks, with Cowboy Roger Staubach and Bradshaw both hurling two touchdowns. Lynn Swann earned his MVP award with a record 161 yards gained on his four receptions. The Steelers blasted out in front with a 14-point fourth quarter.

### Super Bowl XI
Jan. 9, 1977, Rose Bowl
Pasadena, California
### Oakland Raiders 32
### Minnesota Vikings 14

A record 81 million TV viewers watched the Raiders gain a record-breaking 429 yards, including running back Clarence Davis's 137 yards rushing. Wide receiver Fred Biletnikoff made four key receptions, which earned him the game's MVP trophy. Oakland scored on three successive possessions in the second quarter to build a 16–0 halftime lead. Minnesota's Fran Tarkenton passed for a touchdown in the third to cut the deficit, but two fourth-quarter interceptions clinched the title for the Raiders. One set up Pete Banaszak's second touchdown run, the other resulted in cornerback Willie Brown's Super Bowl record 75-yard interception return.

## Super Bowl XII
Jan. 15, 1978, Louisiana Superdome
New Orleans, Louisiana
### Dallas Cowboys 27
### Denver Broncos 10

The TV audience climbed to 102 million, a new record, as Dallas converted two interceptions into 10 points and Efren Herrera added a 35-yard field goal for a 12–0 Dallas halftime lead. Butch Johnston made a spectacular diving catch in the end zone of a Roger Staubach pass to make it 20-3. Dallas clinched the victory when running back Robert Newhouse threw a 29-yard touchdown pass to Golden Richards with 7:04 remaining in the game. It was the first pass thrown by Newhouse since 1975. Co-MVPs Harvey Martin and Randy White led the Cowboys' defense, which recovered four fumbles and intercepted four passes.

## Super Bowl XIII
Jan. 21, 1979, Orange Bowl
Miami, Florida
### Pittsburgh Steelers 35
### Dallas Cowboys 31

Terry Bradshaw hurled a record four touchdown passes to lead the Steelers to victory, making them the first team to win three Super Bowls. His accurate arm enabled the Steelers to outlast the Cowboys in a mean-fought contest. Bradshaw completed 17 of 30 passes for 318 yards, a personal high. Cowboy quarterback Roger Staubach threw two touchdown passes himself. In the fourth quarter, the Steelers broke open the contest with two touchdowns in 19 seconds. Franco Harris rambled 22 yards up the middle to put Pittsburgh in front 28-17. The Steelers got the ball right back when Randy White fumbled the kickoff and Dennis Winston recovered for the Steelers. On first down Bradshaw hit Lynn Swann with an 18-yard scoring pass to boost the Steelers to 35-17. The Cowboys came back with a Staubach touchdown pass to Billy Joe DuPree and by recovering an onside kick. But Rocky Bleier recovered another onside kick with 17 seconds remaining to seal the victory for Pittsburgh—and the MVP award for Bradshaw.

## Super Bowl XIV
Jan. 20, 1980, Rose Bowl
Pasadena, California
### Pittsburgh Steelers 31
### Los Angeles Rams 19

It was all Terry Bradshaw again as he completed 14 of 21 passes for 309 yards and set two passing records as the Steelers became the first team to win four Super Bowls. Despite three interceptions by the Rams, Bradshaw brought the Steelers back from behind twice in the second half. On Pittsburgh's first possession of the final period, Bradshaw lofted a 73-yard scoring pass to John Stallworth to put the Steelers in front to stay, 24–19. Franco Harris scored on a one-yard run later to seal the verdict. A 45-yard pass from Bradshaw to Stallworth was the key play in the drive to Harris's score. Bradshaw was the MVP for the second straight Super Bowl and set career Super Bowl records for most touchdown passes (nine) and most passing yards (932). Vince Ferragamo passed for 212 yards, completing 15 of 25.

## Super Bowl XV
Jan. 25, 1981, Louisiana Superdome
New Orleans, Louisiana
### Oakland Raiders 27
### Philadelphia Eagles 10

Jim Plunkett threw three touchdown passes, including an 80-yarder to Kenny King—the longest play in Super Bowl history—to give Oakland a decisive 14-0 advantage nine seconds before halftime. Oakland linebacker Rod Martin intercepted three passes for a Super Bowl record, as the Raiders completely stifled Eagle quarterback Ron Jaworski's offense. Jaworski managed an eight-yard touchdown pass in the fourth quarter, but the issue had been decided by Plunkett, who completed 13 of the 21 pass attempts for 261 yards and was named MVP. The Raiders dedicated their win to the newly freed 52 American hostages, who had been held in Tehran by Iranian militants. Many of the former hostages watched the game on a wide-screen television at West Point while resting from their ordeal.

## Super Bowl XVI
Jan. 24, 1982, Pontiac Silverdome
Pontiac, Michigan
### San Francisco 49ers 26
### Cincinnati Bengals 21

This was a game of a failed comeback, as the 49ers led 20–0 at halftime and barely hung on to their lead. Ray Wersching kicked a record-tying four field goals for San Francisco. Quarterback Joe Montana capped a San Francisco 11-play, 68-yard drive with a one-yard run. Another key was a record 92-yard drive, which ended in a touchdown pass by Montana. The Bengals rebounded in the second half as quarterback Ken Anderson ran in a touchdown and passed for another. He set Super Bowl records for completions, 25, and completion percentage, 73.5% on 25 of 34. With 16 seconds remaining, the Bengals managed to score on an Anderson-to-Dan Ross three-yard pass, but it was too little too late. Ross set a Super Bowl record with 11 receptions for 104 yards. Montana, the MVP, completed 14 of 22 passes for 157 yards. Cincinnati compiled 345 yards to San Francisco's 275, which marked the first time in Super Bowl history that the team that gained more yards from scrimmage lost the game.

## Super Bowl XVII
Jan. 30, 1983, Rose Bowl
Pasadena, California
### Washington Redskins 27
### Miami Dolphins 17

Washington fullback John Riggins ran the ball for a record 166 yards on 38 carries to lead Washington to victory, their first NFL title since 1942. Their 400 total yards offense, a Super Bowl record 276 yards rushing and 124 yards passing, was paced by Riggins, the MVP, and quarterback Joe Theismann, who passed 23 times for 15 completions and two touchdowns. He also notched two interceptions. Miami tied the score with help from a 76-yard touchdown pass from quarterback David Woodley to wide receiver Jimmy Cefalo. But the game's main force was Riggins, who took the ball on fourth-and-one and ran 43 yards off left tackle for a touchdown to put Washington in front.

## Super Bowl XVIII
Jan. 22, 1984, Tampa Stadium
Tampa, Florida
### Los Angeles Raiders 38
### Washington Redskins 9

This hopelessly lopsided victory set records. Raider reserve linebacker Jack Squirek intercepted a Joe Theismann pass at the Redskins' five-yard line and ran the ball in for a touchdown with seven seconds left in the first half. Raiders' Marcus Allen rushed for a record 191 yards on 20 carries, including two touchdowns, one of which was on a record 74-yard run. Allen was voted game MVP. The 38 points was the highest total scored by a Super Bowl team.

## Super Bowl XIX
Jan. 20, 1985, Stanford Stadium
Stanford, California
### San Francisco 49ers 38
### Miami Dolphins 16

The Dolphins led 10–7 at the end of the first period, but 49er running back Roger Craig set a Super Bowl record by scoring three touchdowns. Joe Montana dominated the game with an MVP performance—24 of 35 passes for a record 331 yards and three touchdowns. He also rushed five times for 59 yards and a touchdown. Craig had 56 yards on 15 carries and caught seven passes for 77 yards. Wendell Tyler rushed 13 times for 65 yards, as San Francisco's running game racked up mileage. As a team San Francisco gained 537 yards, setting a new record, while holding the ball for 37:11 as opposed to Miami's 22:49.

## Super Bowl XX
Jan. 26, 1986, Louisiana Superdome
New Orleans, Louisiana
### Chicago Bears 46
### New England Patriots 10

The Patriots took the quickest lead in Super Bowl history when Tony Franklin kicked a 36-yard field goal with 1:19 elapsed in the first period. But the Bears rebounded by mauling the Pats. Chicago tied the record for sacks (seven) and limited the Pats to a record-low seven yards rushing. Total yardage on the day told the story: Chicago 236, New England minus 19. The 46 points scored by the Bears was also a record. The Bears ran up a fat 23–3 lead by halftime. In the second half, the Bears marched 96 yards in nine plays, and capped it as quarterback Jim McMahon rushed one yard for a touchdown. He became the first quarterback in Super Bowl history to rush for two touchdowns. Bears defensive end Richard Dent won the MVP after contributing one-and-a-half sacks and leading the ferocious Chicago defense. McMahon completed 12 of 20 passes for 256 yards before leaving the game with an injury. NFL all-time rushing leader Walter Payton carried 22 times for 61 yards.

## Super Bowl XXI
Jan. 25, 1987, Rose Bowl
Pasadena, California
### New York Giants 39
### Denver Broncos 20

The Broncos got off to a 10-9 lead at halftime, the narrowest such margin in Super Bowl history, backed by the passing of John Elway.

He capped a 58-yard scoring drive on six plays with a four-yard touchdown run. But in the second half, the Giants' defense took over, sacking Elway in his end zone for a safety. The Broncos had a first-and-goal but failed to score on three plays and a field goal attempt. After that the Giants took over, scoring 30 points in the second half, a record, one a nine-play, 63-yard touchdown drive that included a fourth-and-one situation on the Giants' 46-yard line and ended with Mark Bavaro's 13-yard touchdown catch. MVP Giants' quarterback Phil Simms set Super Bowl records for most consecutive completions (10) and highest completion percentage (88% on 22 completions in 25 attempts). He passed for 268 yards and three touchdowns. The Giants' top rusher was Joe Morris with 20 carries for 67 yards.

### Super Bowl XXII
Jan. 31, 1988, Jack Murphy Stadium
San Diego, California
### Washington Redskins 42
### Denver Broncos 10

A record 35-point second quarter was the key to Washington's convincing Super Bowl triumph. The Broncos jumped in front early as John Elway hurled a 56-yard touchdown pass to wide receiver Ricky Nattiel on the Broncos' first play from scrimmage. But the Redskins erupted for 35 points on five straight possessions. Redskins' quarterback Doug Williams led the assault, hurling a record-tying four touchdown passes, including 80- and 50-yarders to wide receiver Gary Clark and an 8-yarder to tight end Clint Didier. Washington scored five touchdowns in 18 plays in 5:47 of possession. MVP Williams completed 18 of 29 passes for 340 yards, a new Super Bowl record. Rookie running back Timmy Smith ran 22 times for a record 204 yards. Washington's six touchdowns and 602 total yards gained also set Super Bowl records, as the Redskins coasted after the decisive second quarter.

### Super Bowl XXIII
Jan. 22, 1989, Joe Robbie Stadium
Miami, Florida
### San Francisco 49ers 20
### Cincinnati Bengals 16

San Francisco captured its third Super Bowl of the 1980s by defeating the Bengals in a rematch of Super Bowl XVI. The 49ers thus became the first NFC team to capture three Super Bowl trophies. Even though San Francisco held an advantage in total yards (454 vs. 229), they found themselves trailing late in the game. With the score tied at 13 points each, Cincinnati took a 16–13 lead on Jim Breech's 40-yard field goal with 3:20 remaining. Breech's kick capped a 46-yard ball-control effort, which had consumed 5:27. The 49ers started their winning drive at their own eight yard line. Over the next 11 plays, they drove 92 yards to the winning score, a 10-yard touchdown pass from Joe Montana to wide receiver John Taylor with only 34 seconds remaining. San Francisco's swift wide receiver Jerry Rice won the MVP after catching 11 passes for a Super Bowl record 215 yards. Montana completed 23 of 36 passes for a record 357 yards and two touchdowns.

### Super Bowl XXIV
Jan. 28, 1990, Louisiana Superdome
New Orleans, Louisiana
### San Francisco 49ers 55
### Denver Broncos 10

San Francisco demolished the Broncos and became the first team to repeat as champions since the 1979–80 Steelers. The 49ers' diverse offense was magnificently orchestrated by quarterback Joe Montana, who completed 22 of 29 passes for 297 yards and five touchdowns, en route to winning the MVP. Montana raised his record to 122 total Super Bowl pass attempts without an interception. Fiercely protected by his offensive line, he was able to study the defense and complete passes to nine different teammates. His primary receiver was the fleet Jerry Rice, who hauled in seven passes for 148 yards and three touchdowns. Running backs Tom Rathman and Roger Craig ran for three touchdowns, while combining for nine receptions which gained an additional 77 yards. Denver had not given up more than 28 points all season, yet was down by 27 at halftime. The San Francisco defense completely dominated John Elway and the high-powered Bronco offense, limiting them to 167 total yards while sacking Elway six times, intercepting him twice, and harrying him into numerous mistakes.

### Super Bowl XXV
Jan. 27, 1991, Tampa Stadium
Tampa, Florida
### New York Giants 20
### Buffalo Bills 19

The Giants edged the Bills in a tightly contested, nearly error-free game; victory was secured only when the Bills' Scott Norwood missed what would have been the winning field goal with eight seconds to play. The key ingredient to the Giants' victory was a ball-control offense, led by reserve quarterback Jeff Hostetler and veteran running back Ottis Anderson, which set a Super Bowl record for possession time of 40 minutes, 33 seconds. Anderson, who carried the ball 21 times for 102 yards, was named Most Valuable Player. After falling behind 12–3, the Giants, led by 21 players with Super Bowl experience, refused to panic. Their defense slowed Buffalo's vaunted "hurry-up" offense to a crawl, surrounding Jim Kelly's receivers with extra defensive backs and linebackers playing a physical, "bump and run" style. Kelly finished the day with 18 completions in 30 attempts for 205 yards, but could rarely convert on crucial third down opportunities. Hostetler, substituting for the injured Phil Simms, directed the Giants on touchdown drives of 75 and 87 yards, while completing 20 of 32 passes for 214 yards and allowing no turnovers.

---

# PRO FOOTBALL HALL OF FAME MEMBERS

Alphabetical listing of the members of the Professional Football Hall of Fame. Listing includes enshrinee's name, year of enshrinement, position(s), and pro team(s).

**Herb Adderley** (1980) CB, Packers, Cowboys.
**Lance Alworth** (1978) WR, Chargers, Cowboys.
**Doug Atkins** (1982) DE, Browns, Bears, Saints.
**Morris (Red) Badgro** (1981) E, Yankees, Giants, Dodgers.
**Cliff Battles** (1968) HB, QB, Braves, Redskins. Coach, Dodgers.
**Sammy Baugh** (1963 Charter) QB, Redskins. Coach, Titans, Oilers, Lions.
**Chuck Bednarik** (1967) C, LB, Eagles.
**Bert Bell** (1963 Charter) Commissioner, NFL. Founder, Eagles, 1933. Coach Eagles, Steelers. Club president, Eagles, Steelers.
**Bobby Bell** (1983) LB, DE, Chiefs.
**Raymond Berry** (1973) E, Colts. Coach, Patriots.
**Charles W. Bidwill, Sr.** (1967) Owner and president, Chicago Cardinals.
**Fred Biletnikoff** (1988) WR, Raiders.

**George Blanda** (1981) QB, PK, Bears, Colts, Oilers, Raiders.
**Mel Blount** (1989) CB, Steelers.
**Terry Bradshaw** (1989) QB, Steelers.
**Jim Brown** (1971) RB, Browns.
**Paul E. Brown** (1967) Coach and GM, Browns, Bengals.
**Roosevelt Brown** (1975) OT, Giants.
**Willie Brown** (1984) CB, Broncos, Raiders.
**Buck Buchanan** (1990) DT, Chiefs.
**Dick Butkus** (1979) LB, Bears.
**Earl Campbell** (1991) RB, Oilers, Saints.
**Tony Canadeo** (1974) HB, Packers.
**Joe Carr** (1963) NFL President.
**Guy Chamberlin** (1965) E, Bulldogs, Staleys, Yellowjackets, Cardinals. Coach, Bulldogs, Yellowjackets, Cardinals.
**Jack Christiansen** (1970) DB, Spartans, Lions. Coach, 49ers.
**Earl (Dutch) Clark** (1970) DB, Spartans, Lions, Rams.
**George Connor** (1975) OT, DT, LB, Bears.
**Jimmy Conzelman** (1964) QB, Staleys, Independents, Badgers, Panthers. Owner, Steamrollers, Cardinals, Panthers.
**Larry Csonka** (1987) RB, Dolphins, Giants.
**Willie Davis** (1981) DE, Browns, Packers.
**Len Dawson** (1987) QB, Steelers, Browns, Texans, Chiefs.
**Mike Ditka** (1988) TE, Bears, Eagles, Cowboys. Coach, Bears.
**Art Donovan** (1968) DT, Colts, Yankees, Texans.
**John (Paddy) Driscoll** (1965) QB, Pros, Staleys, Cardinals, Bears. Coach, Cardinals, Bears.
**Bill Dudley** (1966) RB, Steelers, Lions, Redskins.
**Albert Glen (Turk) Edwards** (1969) OT, Braves, Redskins. Coach, Redskins.

**Weeb Ewbank** (1978) Coach, Colts, Jets.
**Tom Fears** (1970) E, Rams. Coach, Saints.
**Ray Flaherty** (1976) E, Wildcats, Yankees, Giants. Coach, Redskins, Yankees.
**Leonard (Len) Ford** (1976) DE, OE, Dons. Browns, Packers.
**Daniel J. Fortmann, M.D.** (1965) G, Bears.
**Frank Gatski** (1985) C, Browns, Lions.
**Bill George** (1974) LB, Bears, Rams.
**Frank Gifford** (1977) RB, Giants.
**Sid Gillman** (1983) Head coach, Rams, Chargers, Oilers.
**Otto Graham** (1965) QB, Browns. Head coach, Redskins.
**Harold (Red) Grange** (1963 Charter) RB, Bears, Yankees.
**(Mean) Joe Greene** (1987) DT, Steelers.
**Forrest Gregg** (1977) OL, Packers, Cowboys. Head coach, Browns, Bengals, Packers.
**Bob Griese** (1990) QB, Dolphins.
**Lou Groza** (1974) OT, PK, Browns.
**Joe Guyon** (1966) RB, Bulldogs, Indians, Independents, Cowboys, Giants.
**George Halas** (1963) Founder, head coach, player, Staleys. President, head coach, player, Bears.
**Jack Ham** (1988) LB, Steelers.
**John Hannah** (1991) G, Patriots.
**Ed Healey** (1964) OT, Independents, Bears.
**Mel Hein** (1963) C, Giants. Head coach, Dons.
**Wilbur (Pete) Henry** (1963) OT, Bulldogs, Giants, Maroons.
**Arnie Herber** (1966) QB, Packers, Giants.
**Bill Hewitt** (1971) E, Bears, Eagles, Phil-Pitt.
**Clarke Hinkle** (1964) RB, Packers.
**Elroy (Crazy Legs) Hirsch** (1968) RB, E, Rockets, Rams.

Paul Hornung (1986) RB, Packers.
Ken Houston (1986) DB, Oilers, Redskins.
Robert (Cal) Hubbard (1963) OT, Giants, Packers, Pirates.
Sam Huff (1982) LB, Giants, Redskins.
Lamar Hunt (1972) Founder, AFL. Owner, Texans, Chiefs.
Don Hutson (1963) E, Packers.
John Henry Johnson (1987) RB, 49ers, Lions, Steelers, Oilers.
David (Deacon) Jones (1980) DE, Rams, Chargers, Redskins.
Stan Jones (1991) G, DT, Bears, Redskins. Asst. coach Browns, Bills, Patriots.
Sonny Jurgensen (1983) QB, Eagles, Redskins.
Walt Kiesling (1966) G, Eskimos, Maroons, Chicago Cardinals, Bears, Packers, Pirates. Head coach, Pirates, Steelers.
Frank (Bruiser) Kinard (1971) OT, Dodgers, Yankees.
Early (Curly) Lambeau (1963) HB, Packers. Founder, Packers. Head coach, Packers, Cardinals, Washington Redskins.
Jack Lambert (1990) LB, Steelers.
Tom Landry (1990) Head coach, Cowboys.
Dick (Night Train) Lane (1974) DB, Rams, Cardinals, Lions.
Jim Langer (1987) C, Dolphins, Vikings.
Willie Lanier (1986) LB, Chiefs.
Yale Lary (1979) DB, Lions.
Dante Lavelli (1975) E, Browns.
Bobby Layne (1967) QB, Bears, Bulldogs, Lions, Steelers.
Alphonse (Tuffy) Leemans (1978) RB, Giants.
Bob Lilly (1980) DT, Cowboys.
Vince Lombardi (1971) Head coach, Packers, Redskins.
Sid Luckman (1965) QB, Bears.
William Roy (Link) Lyman (1964) OT, Bulldogs, Yellowjackets, Bears.
Tim Mara (1963) Founder, president, Giants.
Gino Marchetti (1972) DE, Texans, Colts.
George Preston Marshall (1963) Founder, president, Braves (Redskins).
Ollie Matson (1972) RB, Cardinals, Rams, Lions, Eagles.
Don Maynard (1987) WR, Giants, Titans, Jets, Cardinals.
George McAfee (1966) RB, Bears.
Mike McCormack (1984) OT, Yankees, Browns. Head coach, Eagles, Colts, Seahawks.
Hugh McElhenny (1970) RB, 49ers, Vikings, Giants, Lions.
John (Blood) McNally (1963) RB, Badgers, Eskimos, Maroons, Packers, Pirates. Head coach and player, Pirates.
August (Mike) Michalske (1964) G, Yankees, Packers.
Wayne Millner (1968) E, Redskins. Head coach, Eagles.
Bobby Mitchell (1983) WR, RB, Browns, Redskins.
Ron Mix (1979) OT, Chargers, Raiders.
Leonard (Lenny) Moore (1975) WR, RB, Colts.
Marion Motley (1968) RB, Browns, Steelers.
George Musso (1982) OT, G, Bears.
Bronko Nagurski (1963) RB, Bears.
Joe Namath (1985) QB, Jets, Rams.
Earle (Greasy) Neale (1969) E, Bulldogs. Head coach, Eagles.
Ernie Nevers (1963) RB, Eskimos, Cardinals. Head coach, Eskimos, Cardinals.
Ray Nitschke (1978) LB, Packers.
Leo Nomellini (1969) DT, 49ers.
Merlin Olsen (1982) DT, Rams.
Jim Otto (1980) C, Raiders.
Steven Owen (1966) OT, Cowboys, Giants. Head coach, Giants.
Alan Page (1988) DT, Vikings, Bears.
Clarence (Ace) Parker (1972) QB, Dodgers, Yankees.
Jim Parker (1973) G, OT, Colts.
Fletcher (Joe) Perry (1969) RB, 49ers, Colts.
Pete Pihos (1970) E, Eagles.
Hugh (Shorty) Ray (1966) Supervisor of officals.
Dan Reeves (1967) Owner, Rams.
Jim Ringo (1981) C, Packers, Eagles. Head coach, Bills.
Andy Robustelli (1971) DE, Rams, Giants.
Art Rooney (1964) Founder, president, Pirates, Steelers.
Pete Rozelle (1985) Commissioner, NFL.
Gale Sayers (1977) RB, Bears.
Joe Schmidt (1973) LB, Lions. Head coach, Lions.
Tex Schramm (1991) GM, Cowboys.
Art Shell (1989) OT, Raiders. Head coach, Raiders.
O.J. Simpson (1985) RB, Bills, 49ers.
Bart Starr (1977) QB, Packers. Head coach, Packers.
Roger Staubach (1985) QB, Cowboys.
Ernie Stautner (1969) DT, Steelers.
Jan Stenerud (1991) PK, Chiefs, Packers, Vikings.
Bob St. Clair (1990) OT, 49ers.
Ken Strong (1967) RB, Stapletons, Giants, Yankees.
Joe Stydahar (1967) OT, Bears. Head coach, Rams, Cardinals.

Fran Tarkenton (1986) QB, Vikings, Giants.
Charley Taylor (1984) WR, RB, Redskins.
Jim Taylor (1976) RB, Packers, Saints.
Jim Thorpe (1963) RB, Bulldogs, Indians, Maroons, Independents, Giants, Cardinals. Head coach, Bulldogs.
Y.A. Tittle (1971) QB, Colts, 49ers, Giants.
George Trafton (1964) C, Staleys, Bears.
Charley Trippi (1968) RB QB, Cardinals.
Emlen Tunnell (1967) DB, Giants, Packers.
Clyde (Bulldog) Turner (1966) C, LB, Bears. Head coach, Titans.
Johnny Unitas (1979) QB, Colts, Chargers.
Gene Upshaw (1987) G, Raiders.
Norm Van Brocklin (1971) QB, Rams, Eagles. Head coach, Vikings, Falcons.
Steve Van Buren (1965) RB, Eagles.
Doak Walker (1986) RB, Lions.
Paul Warfield (1983) WR, Browns, Dolphins.
Bob Waterfield (1965) QB, Rams. Head coach, Rams.
Arnie Weinmeister (1984) DT, Yankees, Giants.
Bill Willis (1977) G, MG, Browns.
Larry Wilson (1978) DB, Cardinals.
Alex Wojciechowicz (1968) C, LB, Lions, Eagles.
Willie Wood (1989) DB, Packers.

# Ice Hockey

**National Hockey League
650 Fifth Avenue
New York, NY 10019
(212) 398-1100**

**Montreal Address
1155 Metcalfe, Ste. 960
Montreal, Quebec H3B 2W2
(514) 871-9220**

President: John A. Ziegler, Jr.
Chairman of the Board: William W. Wirtz
Number of Teams: 22    Founded: 1917

## NHL STANDINGS, 1990-91

### CAMPBELL CONFERENCE

| NORRIS DIVISION | W | L | T | Pts. |
|---|---|---|---|---|
| Chicago Blackhawks | 49 | 23 | 8 | 106 |
| St. Louis Blues | 47 | 22 | 11 | 105 |
| Detroit Red Wings | 34 | 38 | 8 | 76 |
| Minnesota North Stars | 27 | 39 | 14 | 68 |
| Toronto Maple Leafs | 23 | 46 | 11 | 57 |

| SMYTHE DIVISION | W | L | T | Pts. |
|---|---|---|---|---|
| Los Angeles Kings | 46 | 24 | 10 | 102 |
| Calgary Flames | 46 | 26 | 8 | 100 |
| Edmonton Oilers | 37 | 37 | 6 | 80 |
| Vancouver Canucks | 28 | 43 | 9 | 65 |
| Winnipeg Jets | 26 | 43 | 11 | 63 |

### WALES CONFERENCE

| ADAMS DIVISION | W | L | T | Pts. |
|---|---|---|---|---|
| Boston Bruins | 44 | 24 | 12 | 100 |
| Montreal Canadiens | 39 | 30 | 11 | 89 |
| Buffalo Sabres | 31 | 30 | 19 | 81 |
| Hartford Whalers | 31 | 38 | 11 | 73 |
| Quebec Nordiques | 16 | 50 | 14 | 46 |

| PATRICK DIVISION | W | L | T | Pts. |
|---|---|---|---|---|
| Pittsburgh Penguins | 41 | 33 | 6 | 88 |
| N.Y. Rangers | 36 | 31 | 13 | 85 |
| Washington Capitals | 37 | 36 | 7 | 81 |
| New Jersey Devils | 32 | 33 | 15 | 79 |
| Philadelphia Flyers | 33 | 37 | 10 | 76 |
| N.Y. Islanders | 25 | 45 | 10 | 60 |

## STANLEY CUP PLAYOFFS 1991
### (All rounds are seven-game series)
### ROUND 1
#### PRINCE OF WALES CONFERENCE

| | | | |
|---|---|---|---|
| Boston Bruins 4 | Hartford Whalers 2 |
| Montreal Canadiens 4 | Buffalo Sabres 2 |
| Pittsburgh Penguins 4 | New Jersey Devils 3 |
| Washington Capitals 4 | New York Rangers 2 |

#### CLARENCE CAMPBELL CONFERENCE

| | |
|---|---|
| Minnesota North Stars 4 | Chicago Blackhawks 2 |
| St. Louis Blues 4 | Detroit Red Wings 3 |
| Los Angeles Kings 4 | Vancouver Canucks 2 |
| Edmonton Oilers 4 | Calgary Flames 3 |

### ROUND 2
#### PRINCE OF WALES CONFERENCE

| | |
|---|---|
| Boston Bruins 4 | Montreal Canadiens 3 |
| Pittsburgh Penguins 4 | Washington Capitals 1 |

#### CLARENCE CAMPBELL CONFERENCE

| | |
|---|---|
| Minnesota North Stars 4 | St. Louis Blues 2 |
| Edmonton Oilers 4 | Los Angeles Kings 2 |

### CONFERENCE CHAMPIONSHIPS
#### PRINCE OF WALES CONFERENCE

| | |
|---|---|
| Pittsburgh Penguins 4 | Boston Bruins 2 |

#### CLARENCE CAMPBELL CONFERENCE

| | |
|---|---|
| Minnesota North Stars 4 | Edmonton Oilers 1 |

### STANLEY CUP CHAMPIONSHIP

| | |
|---|---|
| Pittsburgh Penguins 4 | Minnesota North Stars 2 |

## THE STANLEY CUP

The Stanley Cup, awarded annually to the team winning the National Hockey League's best-of-seven final playoff round, is symbolic of the World Professional Hockey Championship. The oldest trophy competed for by professional athletes in North America, it was donated by Frederick Arthur, Lord Stanley of Preston and son of the Earl of Derby, in 1893. Lord Stanley purchased the trophy for 10 guineas ($50 at that time) for presentation to the amateur hockey champions of Canada. Since 1910, when the National Hockey Association took possession of the Stanley Cup, the trophy has been the symbol of professional hockey supremacy. Since 1926 only NHL teams have competed for the Stanley Cup. It has been under the exclusive control of the NHL since 1946.

## STANLEY CUP CHAMPIONS, 1917-91

| Season | Champion | Finalist | GP in final |
|---|---|---|---|
| 1917-18 | Toronto Arenas | Vancouver Millionaires | 5 |
| 1918-19 | No decision[1] | No decision | 5 |
| 1919-20 | Ottawa Senators | Seattle Metropolitans | 5 |
| 1920-21 | Ottawa Senators | Vancouver Millionaires | 5 |
| 1921-22 | Toronto St. Pats | Vancouver Millionaires | 5 |
| 1922-23 | Ottawa Senators | Edmonton Eskimos | 2 |
| 1923-24 | Montreal Canadiens | Calgary Tigers | 2 |
| 1924-25 | Victoria Cougars | Montreal Canadiens | 4 |
| 1925-26 | Montreal Maroons | Victoria Cougars | 4 |
| 1926-27 | Ottawa Senators | Boston Bruins | 2 |
| 1927-28 | New York Rangers | Montreal Maroons | 5 |
| 1928-29 | Boston Bruins | New York Rangers | 2 |
| 1929-30 | Montreal Canadiens | Boston Bruins | 2 |
| 1930-31 | Montreal Canadiens | Chicago Blackhawks | 5 |
| 1931-32 | Toronto Maple Leafs | New York Rangers | 3 |
| 1932-33 | New York Rangers | Toronto Maple Leafs | 4 |

| Season | Champion | Finalist | GP in final |
|---|---|---|---|
| 1933–34 | Chicago Blackhawks | Detroit Red Wings | 4 |
| 1934–35 | Montreal Maroons | Toronto Maple Leafs | 3 |
| 1935–36 | Detroit Red Wings | Toronto Maple Leafs | 4 |
| 1936–37 | Detroit Red Wings | New York Rangers | 5 |
| 1937–38 | Chicago Blackhawks | Toronto Maple Leafs | 4 |
| 1938–39 | Boston Bruins | Toronto Maple Leafs | 5 |
| 1939–40 | New York Rangers | Toronto Maple Leafs | 6 |
| 1940–41 | Boston Bruins | Detroit Red Wings | 4 |
| 1941–42 | Toronto Maple Leafs | Detroit Red Wings | 7 |
| 1942–43 | Detroit Red Wings | Boston Bruins | 4 |
| 1943–44 | Montreal Canadiens | Chicago Blackhawks | 4 |
| 1944–45 | Toronto Maple Leafs | Detroit Red Wings | 7 |
| 1945–46 | Montreal Canadiens | Boston Bruins | 5 |
| 1946–47 | Toronto Maple Leafs | Montreal Canadiens | 6 |
| 1947–48 | Toronto Maple Leafs | Detroit Red Wings | 4 |
| 1948–49 | Toronto Maple Leafs | Detroit Red Wings | 4 |
| 1949–50 | Detroit Red Wings | New York Rangers | 7 |
| 1950–51 | Toronto Maple Leafs | Montreal Canadiens | 5 |
| 1951–52 | Detroit Red Wings | Montreal Canadiens | 4 |
| 1952–53 | Montreal Canadiens | Boston Bruins | 5 |
| 1953–54 | Detroit Red Wings | Montreal Canadiens | 7 |
| 1954–55 | Detroit Red Wings | Montreal Canadiens | 7 |
| 1955–56 | Montreal Canadiens | Detroit Red Wings | 5 |
| 1956–57 | Montreal Canadiens | Boston Bruins | 5 |
| 1957–58 | Montreal Canadiens | Boston Bruins | 6 |
| 1958–59 | Montreal Canadiens | Toronto Maple Leafs | 5 |
| 1959–60 | Montreal Canadiens | Toronto Maple Leafs | 4 |
| 1960–61 | Chicago Blackhawks | Detroit Red Wings | 6 |
| 1961–62 | Toronto Maple Leafs | Chicago Blackhawks | 6 |
| 1962–63 | Toronto Maple Leafs | Detroit Red Wings | 5 |
| 1963–64 | Toronto Maple Leafs | Detroit Red Wings | 7 |
| 1964–65 | Montreal Canadiens | Chicago Blackhawks | 7 |
| 1965–66 | Montreal Canadiens | Detroit Red Wings | 6 |
| 1966–67 | Toronto Maple Leafs | Montreal Canadiens | 6 |
| 1967–68 | Montreal Canadiens | St. Louis Blues | 4 |
| 1968–69 | Montreal Canadiens | St. Louis Blues | 4 |
| 1969–70 | Boston Bruins | St. Louis Blues | 4 |
| 1970–71 | Montreal Canadiens | Chicago Blackhawks | 7 |
| 1971–72 | Boston Bruins | New York Rangers | 6 |
| 1972–73 | Montreal Canadiens | Chicago Blackhawks | 6 |
| 1973–74 | Philadelphia Flyers | Boston Bruins | 6 |
| 1974–75 | Philadelphia Flyers | Buffalo Sabres | 6 |
| 1975–76 | Montreal Canadiens | Philadelphia Flyers | 4 |
| 1976–77 | Montreal Canadiens | Boston Bruins | 4 |
| 1977–78 | Montreal Canadiens | Boston Bruins | 6 |
| 1978–79 | Montreal Canadiens | New York Rangers | 5 |
| 1979–80 | New York Islanders | Philadelphia Flyers | 6 |
| 1980–81 | New York Islanders | Minnesota North Stars | 5 |
| 1981–82 | New York Islanders | Vancouver Canucks | 4 |
| 1982–83 | New York Islanders | Edmonton Oilers | 4 |
| 1983–84 | Edmonton Oilers | New York Islanders | 5 |
| 1984–85 | Edmonton Oilers | Philadelphia Flyers | 5 |
| 1985–86 | Montreal Canadiens | Calgary Flames | 5 |
| 1986–87 | Edmonton Oilers | Philadelphia Flyers | 7 |
| 1987–88 | Edmonton Oilers | Boston Bruins | 4 |
| 1988–89 | Calgary Flames | Montreal Canadiens | 6 |
| 1989–90 | Edmonton Oilers | Boston Bruins | 5 |
| 1990–91 | Pittsburgh Penguins | Minnesota North Stars | 5 |

1. In the spring of 1919 the Montreal Canadiens traveled to Seattle to meet Seattle, champs of the Pacific Coast Hockey League. After five games had been played—teams were tied at 2 wins and 1 tie—the series was called off by the local Department of Health because of the influenza epidemic.

## TOP 10 SCORERS 1990–91

| Player | Team | GP | G | A | Pts. |
|---|---|---|---|---|---|
| Wayne Gretzky | Los Angeles | 78 | 41 | 122 | 163 |
| Brett Hull | St. Louis | 78 | 86 | 45 | 131 |
| Adam Oates | St. Louis | 61 | 25 | 90 | 115 |

| Player | Team | GP | G | A | Pts. |
|---|---|---|---|---|---|
| Mark Recchi | Pittsburgh | 78 | 40 | 73 | 113 |
| John Cullen | Pittsburgh-Hartford | 78 | 39 | 71 | 110 |
| Joe Sakic | Quebec | 80 | 48 | 61 | 109 |
| Steve Yzerman | Detroit | 80 | 51 | 57 | 108 |
| Theo Fleury | Calgary | 79 | 51 | 53 | 104 |
| Al Macinnis | Calgary | 78 | 28 | 75 | 103 |
| Steve Larmer | Chicago | 80 | 44 | 57 | 101 |

## TOP 10 ALL-TIME NHL SCORING LEADERS

| Player | GOALS | | | Goals/ |
|---|---|---|---|---|
| | Seasons | Games | Goals | game |
| Gordie Howe | 26 | 1,767 | 801 | .453 |
| Marcel Dionne | 18 | 1,348 | 731 | .542 |
| Wayne Gretzky | 12 | 925 | 718 | .776 |
| Phil Esposito | 18 | 1,282 | 717 | .572 |
| Bobby Hull | 16 | 1,063 | 610 | .574 |
| Mike Bossy | 10 | 752 | 573 | .762 |
| Guy Lafleur | 17 | 1,126 | 560 | .497 |
| John Bucyk | 23 | 1,540 | 556 | .361 |
| Maurice Richard | 18 | 978 | 544 | .556 |
| Stan Mikita | 22 | 1,394 | 541 | .388 |

| Player | ASSISTS | | | Assts./ |
|---|---|---|---|---|
| | Seasons | Games | Assists | game |
| Wayne Gretzky | 12 | 925 | 1,424 | 1.539 |
| Gordie Howe | 26 | 1,767 | 1,049 | .593 |
| Marcel Dionne | 18 | 1,348 | 1,040 | .771 |
| Stan Mikita | 22 | 1,394 | 926 | .664 |
| Phil Esposito | 18 | 1,282 | 873 | .681 |
| Bryan Trottier | 16 | 1,175 | 872 | .742 |
| Bobby Clarke | 15 | 1,144 | 852 | .745 |
| Alex Delvecchio | 23 | 1,549 | 825 | .533 |
| Gilbert Perreault | 17 | 1,191 | 814 | .683 |
| John Bucyk | 23 | 1,540 | 813 | .528 |

| Player | POINTS | | | | |
|---|---|---|---|---|---|
| | Seasons | Games | Goals | Assists | Points |
| Wayne Gretzky | 12 | 925 | 718 | 1,424 | 2,142 |
| Gordie Howe | 26 | 1,767 | 801 | 1,049 | 1,850 |
| Marcel Dionne | 18 | 1,348 | 731 | 1,040 | 1,771 |
| Phil Esposito | 18 | 1,282 | 717 | 873 | 1,590 |
| Stan Mikita | 22 | 1,394 | 541 | 926 | 1,467 |
| Bryan Trottier | 16 | 1,175 | 509 | 872 | 1,381 |
| John Bucyk | 23 | 1,540 | 556 | 813 | 1,369 |
| Gilbert Perreault | 17 | 1,191 | 512 | 814 | 1,326 |
| Guy Lafleur | 16 | 1,067 | 548 | 777 | 1,325 |
| Alex Delvecchio | 23 | 1,549 | 456 | 825 | 1,281 |

**Note:** As of end of 1990–91 season. **Source:** The National Hockey League.

## CONN SMYTHE TROPHY WINNERS, 1965–91

The Conn Smythe Trophy is an annual award "to the most valuable player for his team in the playoffs." The winner is selected by the Professional Hockey Writers' Association at the conclusion of the final game in the Stanley Cup Finals and receives $3,000.

| Season | Player | Team |
|---|---|---|
| 1965 | Jean Béliveau | Montreal |
| 1966 | Roger Crozier | Detroit |
| 1967 | Dave Keon | Toronto |
| 1968 | Glenn Hall | St. Louis |
| 1969 | Serge Savard | Montreal |
| 1970 | Bobby Orr | Boston |
| 1971 | Ken Dryden | Montreal |
| 1972 | Bobby Orr | Boston |

| Season | Player | Team |
|---|---|---|
| 1973 | Yvan Cournoyer | Montreal |
| 1974 | Bernie Parent | Philadelphia |
| 1975 | Bernie Parent | Philadelphia |
| 1976 | Reggie Leach | Philadelphia |
| 1977 | Guy Lafleur | Montreal |
| 1978 | Larry Robinson | Montreal |
| 1979 | Bob Gainey | Montreal |
| 1980 | Bryan Trottier | N.Y. Islanders |
| 1981 | Butch Goring | N.Y. Islanders |
| 1982 | Mike Bossy | N.Y. Islanders |
| 1983 | Bill Smith | N.Y. Islanders |
| 1984 | Mark Messier | Edmonton |
| 1985 | Wayne Gretzky | Edmonton |
| 1986 | Patrick Roy | Montreal |
| 1987 | Ron Hextall | Philadelphia |
| 1988 | Wayne Gretzky | Edmonton |
| 1989 | Al MacInnis | Calgary |
| 1990 | Bill Ranford | Edmonton |
| 1991 | Mario Lemieux | Pittsburgh |

## HART TROPHY WINNERS, 1924–91

The Hart Trophy is an annual award "to the player adjudged the most valuable to his team." The winner is selected in a poll of the Professional Hockey Writers' Association in the 21 NHL cities at the end of the regular schedule. The winner receives $3,000, and the runner-up $1,500.

| Season | Player | Team |
|---|---|---|
| 1924 | Frank Nighbor | Ottawa Senators |
| 1925 | Billy Burch | N.Y. Americans |
| 1926 | Nels Stewart | Montreal Maroons |
| 1927 | Herb Gardiner | Montreal |
| 1928 | Howie Morenz | Montreal |
| 1929 | Roy Worters | N.Y. Americans |
| 1930 | Nels Stewart | Montreal Maroons |
| 1931 | Howie Morenz | Montreal |
| 1932 | Howie Morenz | Montreal |
| 1933 | Eddie Shore | Boston |
| 1934 | Aurel Joliat | Montreal |
| 1935 | Eddie Shore | Boston |
| 1936 | Eddie Shore | Boston |
| 1937 | Babe Siebert | Montreal |
| 1938 | Eddie Shore | Boston |
| 1939 | Toe Blake | Montreal |
| 1940 | Ebbie Goodfellow | Detroit |
| 1941 | Bill Cowley | Boston |
| 1942 | Tom Anderson | N.Y. Americans |
| 1943 | Bill Cowley | Boston |
| 1944 | Babe Pratt | Toronto |
| 1945 | Elmer Lach | Montreal |
| 1946 | Max Bentley | Toronto |
| 1947 | Maurice Richard | Montreal |
| 1948 | Buddy O'Connor | N.Y. Rangers |
| 1949 | Sid Abel | Detroit |
| 1950 | Charlie Rayner | N.Y. Rangers |
| 1951 | Milt Schmidt | Boston |
| 1952 | Gordie Howe | Detroit |
| 1953 | Gordie Howe | Detroit |
| 1954 | Al Rollins | Toronto |
| 1955 | Ted Kennedy | Toronto |
| 1956 | Jean Béliveau | Montreal |
| 1957 | Gordie Howe | Detroit |
| 1958 | Gordie Howe | Detroit |
| 1959 | Andy Bathgate | N.Y. Rangers |
| 1960 | Gordie Howe | Detroit |
| 1961 | Bernie Geoffrion | Montreal |
| 1962 | Jacques Plante | Montreal |
| 1963 | Gordie Howe | Detroit |

| 1964 | Jean Béliveau | Montreal |
|---|---|---|
| 1965 | Bobby Hull | Chicago |
| 1966 | Bobby Hull | Chicago |
| 1967 | Stan Mikita | Chicago |
| 1968 | Stan Mikita | Chicago |
| 1969 | Phil Esposito | Boston |
| 1970 | Bobby Orr | Boston |
| 1971 | Bobby Orr | Boston |
| 1972 | Bobby Orr | Boston |
| 1973 | Bobby Clarke | Philadelphia |
| 1974 | Phil Esposito | Boston |
| 1975 | Bobby Clarke | Philadelphia |
| 1976 | Bobby Clarke | Philadelphia |
| 1977 | Guy Lafleur | Montreal |
| 1978 | Guy Lafleur | Montreal |
| 1979 | Bryan Trottier | N.Y. Islanders |
| 1980 | Wayne Gretzky | Edmonton |
| 1981 | Wayne Gretzky | Edmonton |
| 1982 | Wayne Gretzky | Edmonton |
| 1983 | Wayne Gretzky | Edmonton |
| 1984 | Wayne Gretzky | Edmonton |
| 1985 | Wayne Gretzky | Edmonton |
| 1986 | Wayne Gretzky | Edmonton |
| 1987 | Wayne Gretzky | Edmonton |
| 1988 | Mario Lemieux | Pittsburgh |
| 1989 | Wayne Gretzky | Los Angeles |
| 1990 | Mark Messier | Edmonton |
| 1991 | Brett Hull | St. Louis |

## ART ROSS TROPHY WINNERS, 1918–91

The Art Ross Trophy is an annual award "to the player who leads the league in scoring points at the end of the regular season." The overall winner receives $3,000, and the runner-up $1,500.

| Season | Player | Team |
|---|---|---|
| 1918 | Joe Malone | Montreal |
| 1919 | Newsy Lalonde | Montreal |
| 1920 | Joe Malone | Quebec |
| 1921 | Newsy Lalonde | Montreal |
| 1922 | Punch Broadbent | Ottawa |
| 1923 | Babe Dye | Toronto |
| 1924 | Cye Denneny | Ottawa |
| 1925 | Babe Dye | Toronto |
| 1926 | Nels Stewart | Montreal Maroons |
| 1927 | Bill Cook | N.Y. Rangers |
| 1928 | Howie Morenz | Montreal |
| 1929 | Ace Bailey | Toronto |
| 1930 | Cooney Weiland | Boston |
| 1931 | Howie Morenz | Montreal |
| 1932 | Harvey Jackson | Toronto |
| 1933 | Bill Cook | N.Y. Rangers |
| 1934 | Charlie Conacher | Toronto |
| 1935 | Charlie Conacher | Toronto |
| 1936 | Dave Shriner | N.Y. Americans |
| 1937 | Dave Shriner | N.Y. Americans |
| 1938 | Gordie Drillon | Toronto |
| 1939 | Toe Blake | Montreal |
| 1940 | Milt Schmidt | Boston |
| 1941 | Bill Cowley | Boston |
| 1942 | Bryan Hextall | N.Y. Rangers |
| 1943 | Doug Bentley | Chicago |
| 1944 | Herbie Cain | Boston |
| 1945 | Elmer Lach | Montreal |
| 1946 | Max Bentley | Chicago |
| 1947 | Max Bentley | Chicago |
| 1948 | Elmer Lach | Montreal |
| 1949 | Roy Conacher | Chicago |
| 1950 | Ted Lindsay | Detroit |

| 1951 | Gordie Howe | Detroit |
|---|---|---|
| 1952 | Gordie Howe | Detroit |
| 1953 | Gordie Howe | Detroit |
| 1954 | Gordie Howe | Detroit |
| 1955 | Bernie Geoffrion | Montreal |
| 1956 | Jean Béliveau | Montreal |
| 1957 | Gordie Howe | Detroit |
| 1958 | Dickie Moore | Montreal |
| 1959 | Dickie Moore | Montreal |
| 1960 | Bobby Hull | Chicago |
| 1961 | Bernie Geoffrion | Montreal |
| 1962 | Bobby Hull | Chicago |
| 1963 | Gordie Howe | Detroit |
| 1964 | Stan Mikita | Chicago |
| 1965 | Stan Mikita | Chicago |
| 1966 | Bobby Hull | Chicago |
| 1967 | Stan Mikita | Chicago |
| 1968 | Stan Mikita | Chicago |
| 1969 | Phil Esposito | Boston |
| 1970 | Bobby Orr | Boston |
| 1971 | Phil Esposito | Boston |
| 1972 | Phil Esposito | Boston |
| 1973 | Phil Esposito | Boston |
| 1974 | Phil Esposito | Boston |
| 1975 | Bobby Orr | Boston |
| 1976 | Guy Lafleur | Montreal |
| 1977 | Guy Lafleur | Montreal |
| 1978 | Guy Lafleur | Montreal |
| 1979 | Bryan Trottier | N.Y. Islanders |
| 1980 | Marcel Dionne | Los Angeles |
| 1981 | Wayne Gretzky | Edmonton |
| 1982 | Wayne Gretzky | Edmonton |
| 1983 | Wayne Gretzky | Edmonton |
| 1984 | Wayne Gretzky | Edmonton |
| 1985 | Wayne Gretzky | Edmonton |
| 1986 | Wayne Gretzky | Edmonton |
| 1987 | Wayne Gretzky | Edmonton |
| 1988 | Mario Lemieux | Pittsburgh |
| 1989 | Mario Lemieux | Pittsburgh |
| 1990 | Wayne Gretzky | Los Angeles |
| 1991 | Wayne Gretzky | Los Angeles |

## JAMES NORRIS MEMORIAL TROPHY WINNERS, 1954–91

The James Norris Memorial Trophy is an annual award "to the defense player who demonstrates throughout the season the greatest all-round ability in the position." The winner is selected in a poll of the Professional Hockey Writers' Association at the end of the regular schedule. The winner receives $3,000, and the runner-up $1,500.

| Season | Player | Team |
|---|---|---|
| 1954 | Red Kelly | Detroit |
| 1955 | Doug Harvey | Montreal |
| 1956 | Doug Harvey | Montreal |
| 1957 | Doug Harvey | Montreal |
| 1958 | Doug Harvey | Montreal |
| 1959 | Tom Johnson | Montreal |
| 1960 | Doug Harvey | Montreal |
| 1961 | Doug Harvey | Montreal |
| 1962 | Doug Harvey | N.Y. Rangers |
| 1963 | Pierre Pilote | Chicago |
| 1964 | Pierre Pilote | Chicago |
| 1965 | Pierre Pilote | Chicago |
| 1966 | Jacques Laperrière | Montreal |
| 1967 | Harry Howell | N.Y. Rangers |
| 1968 | Bobby Orr | Boston |
| 1969 | Bobby Orr | Boston |
| 1970 | Bobby Orr | Boston |

| 1971 | Bobby Orr | Boston |
|---|---|---|
| 1972 | Bobby Orr | Boston |
| 1973 | Bobby Orr | Boston |
| 1974 | Bobby Orr | Boston |
| 1975 | Bobby Orr | Boston |
| 1976 | Denis Potvin | N.Y. Islanders |
| 1977 | Larry Robinson | Montreal |
| 1978 | Denis Potvin | N.Y. Islanders |
| 1979 | Denis Potvin | N.Y. Islanders |
| 1980 | Larry Robinson | Montreal |
| 1981 | Randy Carlyle | Pittsburgh |
| 1982 | Doug Wilson | Chicago |
| 1983 | Rod Langway | Washington |
| 1984 | Rod Langway | Washington |
| 1985 | Paul Coffey | Edmonton |
| 1986 | Paul Coffey | Edmonton |
| 1987 | Ray Bourque | Boston |
| 1988 | Ray Bourque | Boston |
| 1989 | Chris Chelios | Montreal |
| 1990 | Ray Bourque | Boston |
| 1991 | Ray Bourque | Boston |

## VEZINA TROPHY WINNERS, 1927–90

The Vezina Trophy is an annual award "to the goalkeeper adjudged to be the best at his position" as voted by the general managers of the 21 clubs. The overall winner receives $3,000, runner-up $1,500.

| Season | Player | Team |
|---|---|---|
| 1927 | George Hainsworth | Montreal |
| 1928 | George Hainsworth | Montreal |
| 1929 | George Hainsworth | Montreal |
| 1930 | Tiny Thompson | Boston |
| 1931 | Roy Worters | N.Y. Americans |
| 1932 | Charlie Gardiner | Chicago |
| 1933 | Tiny Thompson | Boston |
| 1934 | Charlie Gardiner | Chicago |
| 1935 | Lorne Chabot | Chicago |
| 1936 | Tiny Thompson | Boston |
| 1937 | Normie Smith | Detroit |
| 1938 | Tiny Thompson | Boston |
| 1939 | Frank Brimsek | Boston |
| 1940 | Dave Kerr | N.Y. Rangers |
| 1941 | Turk Broda | Toronto |
| 1942 | Frank Brimsek | Boston |
| 1943 | Johnny Mowers | Detroit |
| 1944 | Bill Durnan | Montreal |
| 1945 | Bill Durnan | Montreal |
| 1946 | Bill Durnan | Montreal |
| 1947 | Bill Durnan | Montreal |
| 1948 | Turk Broda | Toronto |
| 1949 | Bill Durnan | Montreal |
| 1950 | Bill Durnan | Montreal |
| 1951 | Al Rollins | Toronto |
| 1952 | Terry Sawchuk | Detroit |
| 1953 | Terry Sawchuk | Detroit |
| 1954 | Harry Lumley | Toronto |
| 1955 | Terry Sawchuk | Detroit |
| 1956 | Jacques Plante | Montreal |
| 1957 | Jacques Plante | Montreal |
| 1958 | Jacques Plante | Montreal |
| 1959 | Jacques Plante | Montreal |
| 1960 | Jacques Plante | Montreal |
| 1961 | Johnny Bower | Toronto |
| 1962 | Jacques Plante | Montreal |
| 1963 | Glenn Hall | Chicago |
| 1964 | Charlie Hodge | Montreal |
| 1965 | Terry Sawchuk | Toronto |
|  | Johnny Bower |  |
| 1966 | Lorne Worsley | Montreal |
|  | Charlie Hodge |  |

| | | |
|---|---|---|
| 1967 | Glenn Hall | Chicago |
| | Denis Dejordy | |
| 1968 | Lorne Worsley | Montreal |
| | Rogie Vachon | |
| 1969 | Jacques Plante | St. Louis |
| | Glenn Hall | |
| 1970 | Tony Esposito | Chicago |
| 1971 | Ed Giacomin | N.Y. Rangers |
| | Gilles Villemure | |
| 1972 | Tony Esposito | Chicago |
| | Gary Smith | |
| 1973 | Ken Dryden | Montreal |
| 1974 | Bernie Parent | Philadelphia |
| | Tony Esposito | Chicago |
| 1975 | Bernie Parent | Philadelphia |
| 1976 | Ken Dryden | Montreal |
| 1977 | Ken Dryden | Montreal |
| | Michel Larocque | |
| 1978 | Ken Dryden | Montreal |
| | Michel Larocque | |
| 1979 | Ken Dryden | Montreal |
| | Michel Larocque | |
| 1980 | Bob Sauvé | Buffalo |
| | Don Edwards | |
| 1981 | Richard Sevigny | Montreal |
| | Denis Herron | |
| | Michel Larocque | |
| 1982 | Bill Smith | N.Y. Islanders |
| 1983 | Pete Peeters | Boston |
| 1984 | Tom Barrasso | Buffalo |
| 1985 | Pele Lindbergh | Philadelphia |
| 1986 | John Vanbiesbrouck | N.Y. Rangers |
| 1987 | Ron Hextall | Philadelphia |
| 1988 | Grant Fuhr | Edmonton |
| 1989 | Patrick Roy | Montreal |
| 1990 . | Patrick Roy | Montreal |
| 1991 | Ed Belfour | Chicago |

## LADY BYNG TROPHY WINNERS, 1925–91

The Lady Byng Trophy is an annual award "to the player adjudged to have exhibited the best type of sportsmanship and gentlemanly conduct combined with a high standard of playing ability." The winner is selected in a poll of the Professional Hockey Writers' Association at the end of the regular schedule. The winner receives $3,000, and the runner-up $1,500.

| Season | Player | Team |
|---|---|---|
| 1925 | Frank Nighbor | Ottawa |
| 1926 | Frank Nighbor | Ottawa |
| 1927 | Billy Burch | N.Y. Americans |
| 1928 | Frank Boucher | N.Y. Rangers |
| 1929 | Frank Boucher | N.Y. Rangers |
| 1930 | Frank Boucher | N.Y. Rangers |
| 1931 | Frank Boucher | N.Y. Rangers |
| 1932 | Joe Primeau | Toronto |
| 1933 | Frank Boucher | N.Y. Rangers |
| 1934 | Frank Boucher | N.Y. Rangers |
| 1935 | Frank Boucher | N.Y. Rangers |
| 1936 | Doc Romnes | Chicago |
| 1937 | Marty Barry | Detroit |
| 1938 | Gordie Drillon | Toronto |
| 1939 | Clint Smith | N.Y. Rangers |
| 1940 | Bobby Bauer | Boston |
| 1941 | Bobby Bauer | Boston |
| 1942 | Syl Apps | Toronto |
| 1943 | Max Bentley | Chicago |
| 1944 | Clint Smith | Chicago |
| 1945 | Bill Mosienko | Chicago |

| | | |
|---|---|---|
| 1946 | Toe Blake | Montreal |
| 1947 | Bobby Bauer | Boston |
| 1948 | Buddy O'Connor | N.Y. Rangers |
| 1949 | Bill Quackenbush | Detroit |
| 1950 | Edgar Laprade | N.Y. Rangers |
| 1951 | Red Kelly | Detroit |
| 1952 | Sid Smith | Toronto |
| 1953 | Red Kelly | Detroit |
| 1954 | Red Kelly | Detroit |
| 1955 | Sid Smith | Toronto |
| 1956 | Earl Reibel | Detroit |
| 1957 | Andy Hebenton | N.Y. Rangers |
| 1958 | Camille Henry | N.Y. Rangers |
| 1959 | Alex Delvecchio | Detroit |
| 1960 | Don McKenney | Boston |
| 1961 | Red Kelly | Toronto |
| 1962 | Dave Keon | Toronto |
| 1963 | Dave Keon | Toronto |
| 1964 | Ken Wharram | Chicago |
| 1965 | Bobby Hull | Chicago |
| 1966 | Alex Delvecchio | Detroit |
| 1967 | Stan Mikita | Chicago |
| 1968 | Stan Mikita | Chicago |
| 1969 | Alex Delvecchio | Detroit |
| 1970 | Phil Goyette | St. Louis |
| 1971 | John Bucyk | Boston |
| 1972 | Jean Ratelle | N.Y. Rangers |
| 1973 | Gilbert Perreault | Buffalo |
| 1974 | John Bucyk | Boston |
| 1975 | Marcel Dionne | Detroit |
| 1976 | Jean Ratelle | N.Y. Rangers-Boston |
| 1977 | Marcel Dionne | Los Angeles |
| 1978 | Butch Goring | Los Angeles |
| 1979 | Bob MacMillan | Atlanta |
| 1980 | Wayne Gretzky | Edmonton |
| 1981 | Rick Kehoe | Pittsburgh |
| 1982 | Rick Middleton | Boston |
| 1983 | Mike Bossy | N.Y. Islanders |
| 1984 | Mike Bossy | N.Y. Islanders |
| 1985 | Jari Kurri | Edmonton |
| 1986 | Mike Bossy | N.Y. Islanders |
| 1987 | Joe Mullen | Calgary |
| 1988 | Mats Naslund | Montreal |
| 1989 | Joe Mullen | Calgary |
| 1990 | Brett Hull | St. Louis |
| 1991 | Wayne Gretzky | Los Angeles |

## FRANK J. SELKE TROPHY WINNERS, 1978–91

The Frank J. Selke Trophy is an annual award "to the forward who best excels in the defensive aspects of the game." The winner is selected in a poll of the Professional Hockey Writers' Association at the end of the regular schedule. The winner receives $3,000, and the runner-up $1,500.

| | | |
|---|---|---|
| 1978 | Bob Gainey | Montreal |
| 1979 | Bob Gainey | Montreal |
| 1980 | Bob Gainey | Montreal |
| 1981 | Bob Gainey | Montreal |
| 1982 | Steve Kasper | Boston |
| 1983 | Bobby Clarke | Philadelphia |
| 1984 | Doug Jarvis | Washington |
| 1985 | Craig Ramsay | Buffalo |
| 1986 | Troy Murray | Chicago |
| 1987 | Dave Poulin | Philadelphia |
| 1988 | Guy Carbonneau | Montreal |
| 1989 | Guy Carbonneau | Montreal |
| 1990 | Rick Meagher | St. Louis |
| 1991 | Dirk Graham | Chicago |

## CALDER MEMORIAL TROPHY WINNERS, 1933–90

The Calder Memorial Trophy is an annual award "to the player selected as the most proficient in his first year of competition in the National Hockey League." The winner is selected in a poll of the Professional Hockey Writers' Association at the end of the regular schedule. The winner receives $3,000, and the runner-up $1,500.

| Season | Player | Team |
|---|---|---|
| 1933 | Carl Voss | Detroit |
| 1934 | Russ Blinko | Montreal Maroons |
| 1935 | Dave Schriner | N.Y. Americans |
| 1936 | Mike Karakas | Chicago |
| 1937 | Syl Apps | Toronto |
| 1938 | Cully Dahlstrom | Chicago |
| 1939 | Frank Brimsek | Boston |
| 1940 | Kilby MacDonald | N.Y. Rangers |
| 1941 | Johnny Quilty | Montreal |
| 1942 | Grant Warwick | N.Y. Rangers |
| 1943 | Gaye Stewart | Toronto |
| 1944 | Gus Bodnar | Toronto |
| 1945 | Frank McCool | Toronto |
| 1946 | Edgar Laprade | N.Y. Rangers |
| 1947 | Howie Meeker | Toronto |
| 1948 | Jim McFadden | Detroit |
| 1949 | Pentti Lund | N.Y. Rangers |
| 1950 | Jack Gelineau | Boston |
| 1951 | Terry Sawchuk | Detroit |
| 1952 | Bernie Geoffrion | Montreal |
| 1953 | Lorne Worsley | N.Y. Rangers |
| 1954 | Camille Henry | N.Y. Rangers |
| 1955 | Ed Litzenberger | Chicago |
| 1956 | Glenn Hall | Detroit |
| 1957 | Larry Regan | Boston |
| 1958 | Frank Mahovlich | Toronto |
| 1959 | Ralph Backstrom | Montreal |
| 1960 | Bill Hay | Chicago |
| 1961 | Dave Keon | Toronto |
| 1962 | Bobby Rousseau | Montreal |
| 1963 | Kent Douglas | Toronto |
| 1964 | Jacques Laperrière | Montreal |
| 1965 | Roger Crozier | Detroit |
| 1966 | Brit Selby | Toronto |
| 1967 | Bobby Orr | Boston |
| 1968 | Derek Sanderson | Boston |
| 1969 | Danny Grant | Minnesota |
| 1970 | Tony Esposito | Chicago |
| 1971 | Gilbert Perreault | Buffalo |
| 1972 | Ken Dryden | Montreal |
| 1973 | Steve Vickers | N.Y. Rangers |
| 1974 | Denis Potvin | N.Y. Islanders |
| 1975 | Eric Vail | Atlanta |
| 1976 | Bryan Trottier | N.Y. Islanders |
| 1977 | Willie Plett | Atlanta |
| 1978 | Mike Bossy | N.Y. Islanders |
| 1979 | Bobby Smith | Minnesota |
| 1980 | Raymond Bourque | Boston |
| 1981 | Peter Stastny | Quebec |
| 1982 | Dale Hawerchuk | Winnipeg |
| 1983 | Steve Larmer | Chicago |
| 1984 | Tom Barrasso | Buffalo |
| 1985 | Mario Lemieux | Pittsburgh |
| 1986 | Gary Suter | Calgary |
| 1987 | Luc Robitaille | Los Angeles |
| 1988 | Joe Nieuwendyk | Calgary |
| 1989 | Brian Leetch | N.Y. Rangers |
| 1990 | Sergei Makarov | Calgary |
| 1991 | Ed Belfour | Chicago |

# Baseball

**Major League Baseball**
**Office of the Commissioner**
**350 Park Avenue**
**New York, NY 10022**
**(212) 339-7800**
**FAX: (212) 355-0007**

Commissioner: Francis T. Vincent, Jr.
Deputy Commissioner and Chief Operating Officer:
Steve Greenberg
Number of teams—26

**The National League of**
**Professional Baseball Clubs**
**350 Park Avenue**
**New York, NY 10022**
**(212) 339-7700**
**FAX: (212) 935-5069**

President and Treasurer: Bill White
President Emeritus: Charles S. "Chub" Feeney
Founded: 1876

**The American League of**
**Professional Baseball Clubs**
**350 Park Ave., 18th Floor**
**New York, NY 10022**
**(212) 339-7600**
**FAX: (212) 593-7138**

President: Dr. Bobby Brown
Vice Presidents: John E. Fetzer and Gene Autry
Founded: 1901

## MAJOR LEAGUE BASEBALL ALL-TIME CAREER LEADERS

### BATTING AVERAGE
1. Ty Cobb .367
2. Rogers Hornsby .358
3. Joe Jackson .356
4. Pete Browning .354
5. Dan Brouthers .349
6. Ed Delahanty .346
7. Willie Keeler .345
8. Tris Speaker .345
9. Ted Williams .344
10. Billy Hamilton .344

### TOTAL BASES
1. Hank Aaron 6,856
2. Stan Musial 6,134
3. Willie Mays 6,066
4. Ty Cobb 5,863
5. Babe Ruth 5,793
6. Pete Rose 5,752
7. Carl Yastrzemski 5,539
8. Frank Robinson 5,373
9. Tris Speaker 5,105
10. Lou Gehrig 5,059

### SLUGGING AVERAGE
1. Babe Ruth .690
2. Ted Williams .634
3. Lou Gehrig .632
4. Jimmie Foxx .609
5. Hank Greenberg .605
6. Joe DiMaggio .579
7. Rogers Hornsby .577
8. Johnny Mize .562
9. Stan Musial .559
10. Willie Mays .557

### RUNS BATTED IN
1. Hank Aaron 2,297
2. Babe Ruth 2,204
3. Lou Gehrig 1,991
4. Ty Cobb 1,959
5. Stan Musial 1,951
6. Jimmie Foxx 1,922
7. Willie Mays 1,903
8. Mel Ott 1,860
9. Carl Yastrzemski 1,844
10. Ted Williams 1,839

### RUNS
1. Ty Cobb 2,245
2. Babe Ruth 2,174
  Hank Aaron 2,174
4. Pete Rose 2,165
5. Willie Mays 2,062
6. Stan Musial 1,949
7. Lou Gehrig 1,888
8. Tris Speaker 1,881
9. Mel Ott 1,849
10. Frank Robinson 1,829

### HITS
1. Pete Rose 4,256
2. Ty Cobb 4,191
3. Hank Aaron 3,771
4. Stan Musial 3,630
5. Tris Speaker 3,515
6. Honus Wagner 3,430
7. Carl Yastrzemski 3,419
8. Eddie Collins 3,309
9. Willie Mays 3,283
10. Nap Lajoie 3,252

### EXTRA BASE HITS
1. Hank Aaron 1,477
2. Stan Musial 1,377
3. Babe Ruth 1,356
4. Willie Mays 1,323
5. Lou Gehrig 1,190
6. Frank Robinson 1,186
7. Carl Yastrzemski 1,157
8. Ty Cobb 1,139
9. Tris Speaker 1,133
10. Jimmie Foxx 1,117
  Ted Williams 1,117

### GAMES PLAYED
1. Pete Rose 3,562
2. Carl Yastrzemski 3,308
3. Hank Aaron 3,298
4. Ty Cobb 3,093
5. Stan Musial 3,026
6. Willie Mays 2,992
7. Rusty Staub 2,951
8. Brooks Robinson 2,896
9. Al Kaline 2,834
10. Eddie Collins 2,826

### STOLEN BASES
1. Rickey Henderson 994
2. Lou Brock 938
3. Ty Cobb 892
4. Eddie Collins 742
5. Max Carey 738
6. Honus Wagner 703
7. Joe Morgan 689
8. Bert Campaneris 649
9. Willie Wilson 632
10. Maury Wills 586

### CONSECUTIVE GAMES
1. Lou Gehrig 2,130
2. Cal Ripken, Jr. 1,573
3. Everett Scott 1,307
4. Steve Garvey 1,207
5. Billy Williams 1,117
6. Joe Sewell 1,103
7. Stan Musial 895
8. Eddie Yost 829
9. Gus Sur 822
10. Nellie Fox 798

## LIFETIME PITCHING LEADERS

### WINS
1. Cy Young 511
2. Walter Johnson 416
3. Christy Mathewson 373
  Grover Alexander 373
5. Warren Spahn 363
6. Pud Galvin 361
7. Kid Nichols 360
8. Tim Keefe 344
9. Steve Carlton 329
10. Eddie Plank 327

### INNINGS PITCHED
1. Cy Young 7,356
2. Pud Galvin 5,941
3. Walter Johnson 5,924
4. Phil Niekro 5,404
5. Gaylord Perry 5,362
6. Don Sutton 5,281
7. Warren Spahn 5,244
8. Steve Carlton 5,216
9. Grover Alexander 5,189
10. Kid Nichols 5,089

### EARNED RUN AVG.
1. Ed Walsh 1.82
2. Addie Joss 1.88
3. Mordecai "Three Finger" Brown 2.06
4. Christy Mathewson 2.13
5. Rube Waddell 2.16
6. Walter Johnson 2.17
7. Orval Overall 2.24
8. Ed Reulbach 2.28
9. Jim Scott 2.32
10. Eddie Plank 2.34

### STRIKEOUTS
1. Nolan Ryan 5,511
2. Steve Carlton 4,136
3. Tom Seaver 3,640
4. Bert Blyleven 3,631
5. Don Sutton 3,574
6. Gaylord Perry 3,534
7. Walter Johnson 3,508
8. Phil Niekro 3,342
9. Ferguson Jenkins 3,192
10. Bob Gibson 3,117

### SHUTOUTS
1. Walter Johnson 113
2. Grover Alexander 90
3. Christy Mathewson 83
4. Cy Young 77
5. Eddie Plank 70
6. Warren Spahn 63
  Mordecai "Three Finger" Brown 63
7. Tom Seaver 61
8. Don Sutton 58
  Ed Walsh 58
10. Pud Galvin 57

**Note:** As of the end of the 1991 season. For home run leaders, see "Major League Players, 400 or More Home Runs." **Source:** Major League Baseball.

## BATTING CHAMPIONS

### NATIONAL LEAGUE

| Year | Name | Team | Avg. |
|---|---|---|---|
| 1876 | Roscoe Barnes | Chicago Cubs | .403 |
| 1877 | James White | Boston Braves | .385 |
| 1878 | Abner Dalrymple | Milwaukee Brewers | .356 |
| 1879 | Cap Anson | Chicago Cubs | .407 |
| 1880 | George Gore | Chicago Cubs | .365 |
| 1881 | Cap Anson | Chicago Cubs | .399 |
| 1882 | Dan Brouthers | Buffalo Bisons | .367 |
| 1883 | Dan Brouthers | Buffalo Bisons | .371 |
| 1884 | Jim O'Rourke | Buffalo Bisons | .350 |
| 1885 | Roger Connor | N.Y. Giants | .371 |
| 1886 | Mike Kelly | Chicago Cubs | .388 |
| 1887 | Cap Anson | Chicago Cubs | .421 |
| 1888 | Cap Anson | Chicago Cubs | .343 |
| 1889 | Dan Brouthers | Boston Braves | .373 |
| 1890 | Jack Glasscock | N.Y. Giants | .336 |
| 1891 | Billy Hamilton | Philadelphia Phillies | .338 |
| 1892 | "Cupid" Childs | Cleveland Spiders | .335 |
| | Dan Brouthers | Brooklyn Dodgers | .335 |
| 1893 | Hugh Duffy | Boston Braves | .378 |
| 1894 | Hugh Duffy | Boston Braves | .438 |
| 1895 | Jesse Burkett | Cleveland Spiders | .423 |
| 1896 | Jesse Burkett | Cleveland Spiders | .410 |
| 1897 | Willie Keeler | Baltimore Orioles | .432 |
| 1898 | Willie Keeler | Baltimore Orioles | .379 |
| 1899 | Ed Delahanty | Philadelphia Phillies | .408 |
| 1900 | Honus Wagner | Pittsburgh Pirates | .380 |
| 1901 | Jesse Burkett | St. Louis Cardinals | .382 |
| 1902 | C.H. Beaumont | Pittsburgh Pirates | .357 |
| 1903 | Honus Wagner | Pittsburgh Pirates | .355 |
| 1904 | Honus Wagner | Pittsburgh Pirates | .349 |
| 1905 | J. Bentley Seymour | Cincinnati Reds | .377 |
| 1906 | Honus Wagner | Pittsburgh Pirates | .339 |
| 1907 | Honus Wagner | Pittsburgh Pirates | .350 |
| 1908 | Honus Wagner | Pittsburgh Pirates | .354 |
| 1909 | Honus Wagner | Pittsburgh Pirates | .339 |
| 1910 | Sherwood Magee | Philadelphia Phillies | .331 |
| 1911 | Honus Wagner | Pittsburgh Pirates | .334 |
| 1912 | Heinie Zimmerman | Chicago Cubs | .372 |
| 1913 | Jake Daubert | Brooklyn Dodgers | .350 |
| 1914 | Jake Daubert | Brooklyn Dodgers | .329 |
| 1915 | Larry Doyle | N.Y. Giants | .320 |
| 1916 | Hal Chase | Cincinnati Reds | .339 |
| 1917 | Edd Roush | Cincinnati Reds | .341 |
| 1918 | Zack Wheat | Brooklyn Dodgers | .335 |
| 1919 | Edd Roush | Cincinnati Reds | .321 |
| 1920 | Rogers Hornsby | St. Louis Cardinals | .370 |
| 1921 | Rogers Hornsby | St. Louis Cardinals | .397 |
| 1922 | Rogers Hornsby | St. Louis Cardinals | .401 |
| 1923 | Rogers Hornsby | St. Louis Cardinals | .384 |
| 1924 | Rogers Hornsby | St. Louis Cardinals | .424 |
| 1925 | Rogers Hornsby | St. Louis Cardinals | .403 |
| 1926 | Bubbles Hargrave | Cincinnati Reds | .353 |
| 1927 | Paul Waner | Pittsburgh Pirates | .380 |
| 1928 | Rogers Hornsby | Boston Braves | .387 |
| 1929 | Lefty O'Doul | Philadelphia Phillies | .398 |
| 1930 | Bill Terry | N.Y. Giants | .401 |
| 1931 | Chick Hafey[1] | St. Louis Cardinals | .349 |
| 1932 | Lefty O'Doul | Brooklyn Dodgers | .368 |
| 1933 | Chuck Klein | Philadelphia Phillies | .368 |
| 1934 | Paul Waner | Pittsburgh Pirates | .362 |
| 1935 | Arky Vaughan | Pittsburgh Pirates | .385 |
| 1936 | Paul Waner | Pittsburgh Pirates | .373 |
| 1937 | Joe Medwick | St. Louis Cardinals | .374 |
| 1938 | Ernie Lombardi | Cincinnati Reds | .342 |
| 1939 | Johnny Mize | St. Louis Cardinals | .349 |
| 1940 | Debs Garms | Pittsburgh Pirates | .355 |
| 1941 | Pete Reiser | Brooklyn Dodgers | .343 |
| 1942 | Ernie Lombardi | Boston Braves | .330 |
| 1943 | Stan Musial | St. Louis Cardinals | .357 |
| 1944 | Dixie Walker | Brooklyn Dodgers | .357 |
| 1945 | Phil Cavarretta | Chicago Cubs | .355 |
| 1946 | Stan Musial | St. Louis Cardinals | .365 |
| 1947 | Harry Walker | St. Louis-Philadelphia | .363 |
| 1948 | Stan Musial | St. Louis Cardinals | .376 |
| 1949 | Jackie Robinson | Brooklyn Dodgers | .342 |
| 1950 | Stan Musial | St. Louis Cardinals | .346 |
| 1951 | Stan Musial | St. Louis Cardinals | .355 |
| 1952 | Stan Musial | St. Louis Cardinals | .336 |
| 1953 | Carl Furillo | Brooklyn Dodgers | .344 |
| 1954 | Willie Mays | N.Y. Giants | .345 |
| 1955 | Richie Ashburn | Philadelphia Phillies | .338 |
| 1956 | Hank Aaron | Milwaukee Braves | .328 |
| 1957 | Stan Musial | St. Louis Cardinals | .351 |
| 1958 | Richie Ashburn | Philadelphia Phillies | .350 |
| 1959 | Hank Aaron | Milwaukee Braves | .355 |
| 1960 | Dick Groat | Pittsburgh Pirates | .325 |
| 1961 | Roberto Clemente | Pittsburgh Pirates | .351 |
| 1962 | Tommy Davis | L.A. Dodgers | .346 |
| 1963 | Tommy Davis | L.A. Dodgers | .326 |
| 1964 | Roberto Clemente | Pittsburgh Pirates | .339 |
| 1965 | Roberto Clemente | Pittsburgh Pirates | .329 |
| 1966 | Matty Alou | Pittsburgh Pirates | .342 |
| 1967 | Roberto Clemente | Pittsburgh Pirates | .357 |
| 1968 | Pete Rose | Cincinnati Reds | .335 |
| 1969 | Pete Rose | Cincinnati Reds | .348 |
| 1970 | Rico Carty | Atlanta Braves | .366 |
| 1971 | Joe Torre | St. Louis Cardinals | .363 |
| 1972 | Billy Williams | Chicago Cubs | .333 |
| 1973 | Pete Rose | Cincinnati Reds | .338 |
| 1974 | Ralph Garr | Atlanta Braves | .353 |
| 1975 | Bill Madlock | Chicago Cubs | .354 |
| 1976 | Bill Madlock | Chicago Cubs | .339 |
| 1977 | Dave Parker | Pittsburgh Pirates | .338 |
| 1978 | Dave Parker | Pittsburgh Pirates | .334 |
| 1979 | Keith Hernandez | St. Louis Cardinals | .344 |
| 1980 | Bill Buckner | Chicago Cubs | .324 |
| 1981 | Bill Madlock | Pittsburgh Pirates | .341 |
| 1982 | Al Oliver | Montreal Expos | .331 |
| 1983 | Bill Madlock | Pittsburgh Pirates | .323 |
| 1984 | Tony Gwynn | San Diego Padres | .351 |
| 1985 | Willie McGee | St. Louis Cardinals | .353 |
| 1986 | Tim Raines | Montreal Expos | .334 |
| 1987 | Tony Gwynn | San Diego Padres | .370 |
| 1988 | Tony Gwynn | San Diego Padres | .313 |
| 1989 | Tony Gwynn | San Diego Padres | .336 |
| 1990 | Willie McGee | St. Louis Cardinals | .335 |
| 1991 | Terry Pendleton | Atlanta Braves | .319 |

### AMERICAN LEAGUE

| Year | Player | Team | Avg. |
|---|---|---|---|
| 1901 | Nap Lajoie | Philadelphia A's | .422 |
| 1902 | Ed Delahanty | Washington Senators | .376 |
| 1903 | Nap Lajoie | Cleveland Indians | .355 |
| 1904 | Nap Lajoie | Cleveland Indians | .381 |
| 1905 | Elmer Flick | Cleveland Indians | .306 |
| 1906 | George Stone | St. Louis Browns | .358 |
| 1907 | Ty Cobb | Detroit Tigers | .350 |
| 1908 | Ty Cobb | Detroit Tigers | .324 |
| 1909 | Ty Cobb | Detroit Tigers | .377 |
| 1910 | Ty Cobb | Detroit Tigers | .385 |
| 1911 | Ty Cobb | Detroit Tigers | .420 |
| 1912 | Ty Cobb | Detroit Tigers | .410 |
| 1913 | Ty Cobb | Detroit Tigers | .390 |
| 1914 | Ty Cobb | Detroit Tigers | .368 |
| 1915 | Ty Cobb | Detroit Tigers | .370 |
| 1916 | Tris Speaker | Cleveland Indians | .386 |
| 1917 | Ty Cobb | Detroit Tigers | .383 |
| 1918 | Ty Cobb | Detroit Tigers | .382 |
| 1919 | Ty Cobb | Detroit Tigers | .407 |
| 1920 | George Sisler | St. Louis Browns | .407 |
| 1921 | Harry Heilmann | Detroit Tigers | .394 |
| 1922 | George Sisler | St. Louis Browns | .420 |
| 1923 | Harry Heilmann | Detroit Tigers | .403 |
| 1924 | Babe Ruth | N.Y. Yankees | .378 |
| 1925 | Harry Heilmann | Detroit Tigers | .393 |
| 1926 | Heinie Manush | Detroit Tigers | .377 |
| 1927 | Harry Heilmann | Detroit Tigers | .398 |
| 1928 | Goose Goslin | Washington Senators | .379 |
| 1929 | Lew Fonseca | Cleveland Indians | .369 |
| 1930 | Al Simmons | Philadelphia A's | .381 |
| 1931 | Al Simmons | Philadelphia A's | .390 |
| 1932 | Dale Alexander | Detroit-Boston | .367 |
| 1933 | Jimmie Foxx | Philadelphia A's | .356 |
| 1934 | Lou Gehrig | N.Y. Yankees | .363 |
| 1935 | Buddy Myer | Washington Senators | .349 |
| 1936 | Luke Appling | Chicago White Sox | .388 |
| 1937 | Charlie Gehringer | Detroit Tigers | .371 |
| 1938 | Jimmie Foxx | Boston Red Sox | .349 |
| 1939 | Joe DiMaggio | N.Y. Yankees | .381 |
| 1940 | Joe DiMaggio | N.Y. Yankees | .352 |
| 1941 | Ted Williams | Boston Red Sox | .406 |
| 1942 | Ted Williams | Boston Red Sox | .356 |
| 1943 | Luke Appling | Chicago White Sox | .328 |
| 1944 | Lou Boudreau | Cleveland Indians | .327 |
| 1945 | Snuffy Stirnweiss | N.Y. Yankees | .309 |
| 1946 | Mickey Vernon | Washington Senators | .352 |
| 1947 | Ted Williams | Boston Red Sox | .343 |
| 1948 | Ted Williams | Boston Red Sox | .369 |
| 1949 | George Kell | Detroit Tigers | .343 |
| 1950 | Billy Goodman | Boston Red Sox | .354 |
| 1951 | Ferris Fain | Philadelphia A's | .344 |
| 1952 | Ferris Fain | Philadelphia A's | .327 |
| 1953 | Mickey Vernon | Washington Senators | .337 |
| 1954 | Bobby Avila | Cleveland Indians | .341 |
| 1955 | Al Kaline | Detroit Tigers | .340 |
| 1956 | Mickey Mantle | N.Y. Yankees | .353 |
| 1957 | Ted Williams | Boston Red Sox | .388 |
| 1958 | Ted Williams | Boston Red Sox | .328 |
| 1959 | Harvey Kuenn | Detroit Tigers | .353 |
| 1960 | Pete Runnels | Boston Red Sox | .320 |
| 1961 | Norm Cash | Detroit Tigers | .361 |
| 1962 | Pete Runnels | Boston Red Sox | .326 |
| 1963 | Carl Yastrzemski | Boston Red Sox | .321 |
| 1964 | Tony Oliva | Minnesota Twins | .323 |
| 1965 | Tony Oliva | Minnesota Twins | .321 |
| 1966 | Frank Robinson | Baltimore Orioles | .316 |
| 1967 | Carl Yastrzemski | Boston Red Sox | .326 |
| 1968 | Carl Yastrzemski | Boston Red Sox | .301 |
| 1969 | Rod Carew | Minnesota Twins | .332 |
| 1970 | Alex Johnson | California Angels | .329 |
| 1971 | Tony Oliva | Minnesota Twins | .337 |
| 1972 | Rod Carew | Minnesota Twins | .318 |
| 1973 | Rod Carew | Minnesota Twins | .350 |
| 1974 | Rod Carew | Minnesota Twins | .364 |
| 1975 | Rod Carew | Minnesota Twins | .359 |
| 1976 | George Brett | K.C. Royals | .333 |
| 1977 | Rod Carew | Minnesota Twins | .388 |
| 1978 | Rod Carew | Minnesota Twins | .333 |
| 1979 | Fred Lynn | Boston Red Sox | .333 |
| 1980 | George Brett | K.C. Royals | .390 |
| 1981 | Carney Lansford | Boston Red Sox | .336 |
| 1982 | Willie Wilson | K.C. Royals | .332 |
| 1983 | Wade Boggs | Boston Red Sox | .361 |
| 1984 | Don Mattingly | N.Y. Yankees | .343 |
| 1985 | Wade Boggs | Boston Red Sox | .368 |
| 1986 | Wade Boggs | Boston Red Sox | .357 |
| 1987 | Wade Boggs | Boston Red Sox | .363 |
| 1988 | Wade Boggs | Boston Red Sox | .366 |
| 1989 | Kirby Puckett | Minnesota Twins | .339 |
| 1990 | George Brett | K.C. Royals | .329 |
| 1991 | Julio Franco | Texas Rangers | .341 |

1. Hafey led with .3489, Bill Terry, N.Y., second with .3486, Jim Bottomley, St. Louis, third with .3482

## CY YOUNG AWARD WINNERS

| Year | Name | Team | Won | Lost | ERA |
|------|------|------|-----|------|-----|
| 1956 | Don Newcombe | Brooklyn Dodgers | 27 | 7 | 3.06 |
| 1957 | Warren Spahn | Milwaukee Braves | 21 | 11 | 2.69 |
| 1958 | Bob Turley | N.Y. Yankees | 21 | 7 | 2.97 |
| 1959 | Early Wynn | Chicago White Sox | 22 | 10 | 3.17 |
| 1960 | Vernon Law | Pittsburgh Pirates | 20 | 9 | 3.08 |
| 1961 | Whitey Ford | N.Y. Yankees | 25 | 4 | 3.21 |
| 1962 | Don Drysdale | L.A. Dodgers | 25 | 9 | 2.83 |
| 1963 | Sandy Koufax | L.A. Dodgers | 25 | 5 | 1.88 |
| 1964 | Dean Chance | L.A. Angels | 20 | 9 | 1.65 |
| 1965 | Sandy Koufax | L.A. Dodgers | 26 | 8 | 2.04 |
| 1966 | Sandy Koufax | L.A. Dodgers | 27 | 9 | 1.73 |

### NATIONAL LEAGUE

| Year | Name | Team | Won | Lost | ERA |
|------|------|------|-----|------|-----|
| 1967 | Mike McCormick | S.F. Giants | 22 | 10 | 2.85 |
| 1968 | Bob Gibson | St. Louis Cardinals | 22 | 9 | 1.12 |
| 1969 | Tom Seaver | N.Y. Mets | 25 | 7 | 2.21 |
| 1970 | Bob Gibson | St. Louis Cardinals | 23 | 7 | 3.12 |
| 1971 | Ferguson Jenkins | Chicago Cubs | 24 | 13 | 2.77 |
| 1972 | Steve Carlton | Philadelphia Phillies | 27 | 10 | 1.97 |
| 1973 | Tom Seaver | N.Y. Mets | 19 | 10 | 2.08 |
| 1974 | Mike Marshall[1] | L.A. Dodgers | 15 | 12 | 2.42 |
| 1975 | Tom Seaver | N.Y. Mets | 22 | 9 | 2.38 |
| 1976 | Randy Jones | San Diego Padres | 22 | 14 | 2.74 |
| 1977 | Steve Carlton | Philadelphia Phillies | 23 | 10 | 2.64 |
| 1978 | Gaylord Perry | San Diego Padres | 21 | 6 | 2.72 |
| 1979 | Bruce Sutter[2] | Chicago Cubs | 6 | 6 | 2.23 |
| 1980 | Steve Carlton | Philadelphia Phillies | 24 | 9 | 2.34 |
| 1981 | Fernando Valenzuela | L.A. Dodgers | 13 | 7 | 2.48 |
| 1982 | Steve Carlton | Philadelphia Phillies | 23 | 11 | 3.10 |
| 1983 | John Denny | Philadelphia Phillies | 19 | 6 | 2.37 |
| 1984 | Rick Sutcliffe | Chicago Cubs | 20 | 6 | 3.64 |
| 1985 | Dwight Gooden | N.Y. Mets | 24 | 4 | 1.53 |
| 1986 | Mike Scott | Houston Astros | 18 | 10 | 2.22 |
| 1987 | Steve Bedrosian[3] | Philadelphia Phillies | 5 | 3 | 2.83 |
| 1988 | Orel Hershiser | L.A. Dodgers | 23 | 8 | 2.26 |
| 1989 | Mark Davis[4] | San Diego Padres | 4 | 3 | 1.85 |
| 1990 | Doug Drabek | Pittsburgh Pirates | 22 | 6 | 2.76 |

### AMERICAN LEAGUE

| Year | Name | Team | Won | Lost | ERA |
|------|------|------|-----|------|-----|
| 1967 | Jim Lonborg | Boston Red Sox | 22 | 9 | 3.16 |
| 1968 | Denny McLain | Detroit Tigers | 31 | 6 | 1.96 |
| 1969 | Mike Cuellar | Baltimore Orioles | 23 | 11 | 2.38 |
| | Denny McLain (tie) | Detroit Tigers | 24 | 9 | 2.80 |
| 1970 | Jim Perry | Minnesota Twins | 24 | 12 | 3.03 |
| 1971 | Vida Blue | Oakland A's | 24 | 8 | 1.82 |
| 1972 | Gaylord Perry | Cleveland Indians | 24 | 16 | 1.92 |
| 1973 | Jim Palmer | Baltimore Orioles | 22 | 9 | 2.40 |
| 1974 | Catfish Hunter | Oakland A's | 25 | 12 | 2.49 |
| 1975 | Jim Palmer | Baltimore Orioles | 23 | 11 | 2.09 |
| 1976 | Jim Palmer | Baltimore Orioles | 22 | 13 | 2.51 |
| 1977 | Sparky Lyle[5] | N.Y. Yankees | 13 | 5 | 2.17 |
| 1978 | Ron Guidry | N.Y. Yankees | 25 | 3 | 1.74 |
| 1979 | Mike Flanagan | Baltimore Orioles | 23 | 9 | 3.08 |
| 1980 | Steve Stone | Baltimore Orioles | 25 | 7 | 3.23 |
| 1981 | Rollie Fingers[6] | Milwaukee Brewers | 6 | 3 | 1.04 |
| 1982 | Peter Vuckovich | Milwaukee Brewers | 18 | 6 | 3.34 |
| 1983 | LaMarr Hoyt | Chicago White Sox | 24 | 10 | 3.66 |
| 1984 | Willie Hernandez[7] | Detroit Tigers | 9 | 3 | 1.92 |
| 1985 | Bret Saberhagen | K.C. Royals | 20 | 6 | 2.87 |
| 1986 | Roger Clemens | Boston Red Sox | 24 | 4 | 2.48 |
| 1987 | Roger Clemens | Boston Red Sox | 20 | 9 | 2.97 |
| 1988 | Frank Viola | Minnesota Twins | 24 | 7 | 2.64 |
| 1989 | Bret Saberhagen | K.C. Royals | 23 | 6 | 2.16 |
| 1990 | Bob Welch | Oakland Athletics | 27 | 6 | 3.06 |

1. In 1974, 21 saves. 2. In 1979, 37 saves. 3. In 1987, 40 saves. 4. In 1989, 44 saves. 5. In 1977, 26 saves. 6. In 1981, 28 saves. 7. In 1984, 32 saves.

## A MOST VALUABLE TEAM

Only nine players have won the Most Valuable Player Award in consecutive seasons; oddly enough there is only one from each fielding position.

| Position | Player | Team | Years |
|----------|--------|------|-------|
| First Base | Jimmie Foxx | Philadelphia A's | 1932–33 |
| Second Base | Joe Morgan | Cincinnati Reds | 1975–76 |
| Third Base | Mike Schmidt | Philadelphia Phillies | 1980–81 |
| Shortstop | Ernie Banks | Chicago Cubs | 1958–59 |
| Outfield | Mickey Mantle | N.Y. Yankees | 1956–57 |
| Outfield | Roger Maris | N.Y. Yankees | 1960–61 |
| Outfield | Dale Murphy | Atlanta Braves | 1982–83 |
| Catcher | Yogi Berra | N.Y. Yankees | 1954–55 |
| Pitcher | Hal Newhouser | Detroit Tigers | 1944–45 |

## TRIPLE CROWN WINNERS

Only 11 players have led their league in home runs, runs batted in, and batting average in one season.

| Player | Team | Year | HRs | RBIs | Avg. |
|--------|------|------|-----|------|------|
| Ty Cobb | Detroit Tigers | 1909 | 9 | 115 | .377 |
| Heinie Zimmerman | Chicago Cubs | 1912 | 14 | 98 | .372 |
| Rogers Hornsby | St. Louis Cardinals | 1922 | 42 | 152 | .401 |
| Rogers Hornsby | St. Louis Cardinals | 1925 | 39 | 143 | .403 |
| Chuck Klein | Philadelphia Phillies | 1933 | 28 | 120 | .368 |
| Jimmie Foxx | Philadelphia A's | 1933 | 48 | 163 | .356 |
| Lou Gehrig | N.Y. Yankees | 1934 | 49 | 165 | .363 |
| Joe Medwick | St. Louis Cardinals | 1937 | 31 | 154 | .374 |
| Ted Williams | Boston Red Sox | 1942 | 36 | 137 | .356 |
| Ted Williams | Boston Red Sox | 1947 | 32 | 114 | .343 |
| Mickey Mantle | N.Y. Yankees | 1956 | 52 | 130 | .353 |
| Frank Robinson | Baltimore Orioles | 1966 | 49 | 122 | .316 |
| Carl Yastrzemski | Boston Red Sox | 1967 | 44 | 121 | .326 |

## MAJOR LEAGUE PITCHERS, 300 OR MORE VICTORIES

| Name | Years | Won | Lost | Name | Years | Won | Lost |
|------|-------|-----|------|------|-------|-----|------|
| Denton T. "Cy" Young | 22 | 511 | 313 | John Clarkson | 12 | 326 | 177 |
| Walter Johnson | 21 | 416 | 279 | Don Sutton | 23 | 324 | 256 |
| Grover Alexander | 20 | 373 | 208 | Phil Niekro | 24 | 318 | 274 |
| Christy Mathewson | 17 | 373 | 168 | Nolan Ryan | 24 | 314 | 278 |
| Warren Spahn | 21 | 363 | 245 | Gaylord Perry | 22 | 314 | 265 |
| James F. "Pud" Galvin | 15 | 361 | 310 | Tom Seaver | 20 | 311 | 205 |
| Charles "Kid" Nichols | 15 | 360 | 203 | Mickey Welch | 13 | 311 | 207 |
| Tim Keefe | 14 | 344 | 225 | Charles "Old Hoss" Radbourne | 11 | 308 | 191 |
| Steve Carlton | 24 | 329 | 244 | Robert "Lefty" Grove | 17 | 300 | 141 |
| Eddie Plank | 17 | 327 | 193 | Early Wynn | 23 | 300 | 244 |

## MAJOR LEAGUE PLAYERS, 400 OR MORE HOME RUNS

| Player | HRs | Player | HRs |
|--------|-----|--------|-----|
| Hank Aaron | 755 | Eddie Mathews | 512 |
| Babe Ruth | 714 | Mel Ott | 511 |
| Willie Mays | 660 | Lou Gehrig | 493 |
| Frank Robinson | 586 | Stan Musial | 475 |
| Harmon Killebrew | 573 | Willie Stargell | 475 |
| Reggie Jackson | 563 | Carl Yastrzemski | 452 |
| Mike Schmidt | 548 | Dave Kingman | 442 |
| Mickey Mantle | 536 | Billy Williams | 426 |
| Jimmie Foxx | 534 | Darrell Evans | 414 |
| Willie McCovey | 521 | Duke Snider | 407 |
| Ted Williams | 521 | Dave Winfield[1] | 406 |
| Ernie Banks | 512 | | |

1. Active during the 1991 season.

## MOST VALUABLE PLAYER AWARD WINNERS

Between 1911 and 1914 the Chalmers Award was given to the player judged to be the most valuable in each league. It was not until 1922 that the American League began to select a league MVP. The National League began to do so as well two years later. By the end of the decade, though, both leagues failed to select an MVP. In 1931 the Baseball Writers Association of America began to select the league MVPs, and has continued to do so through today.

### NATIONAL LEAGUE

| Year | Name | Team | HRs | RBIs | Avg. |
|---|---|---|---|---|---|
| 1911 | Frank Schulte | Chicago Cubs | 21 | 121 | .300 |
| 1912 | Larry Doyle | N.Y. Giants | 10 | 90 | .330 |
| 1913 | Jake Daubert | Brooklyn Dodgers | 2 | 52 | .350 |
| 1914 | Johnny Evers | Chicago Cubs | 1 | 40 | .279 |
| | | | | | |
| 1924 | Dazzy Vance (P) | Brooklyn Dodgers | 28W | 6L | 2.16 ERA |
| 1925 | Rogers Hornsby | St. Louis Cardinals | 29 | 143 | .403 |
| 1926 | Bob O'Farrell | St. Louis Cardinals | 7 | 68 | .293 |
| 1927 | Paul Waner | Pittsburgh Pirates | 9 | 131 | .380 |
| 1928 | Jim Bottomley | St. Louis Cardinals | 31 | 136 | .325 |
| 1929 | Rogers Hornsby | St. Louis Cardinals | 39 | 149 | .380 |
| | | | | | |
| 1931 | Frankie Frisch | St. Louis Cardinals | 4 | 82 | .311 |
| 1932 | Chuck Klein | Philadelphia Phillies | 38 | 137 | .348 |
| 1933 | Carl Hubbell (P) | N.Y. Giants | 23W | 12L | 1.66 ERA |
| 1934 | Dizzy Dean (P) | St. Louis Cardinals | 30W | 7L | 2.66 ERA |
| 1935 | Gabby Hartnett | Chicago Cubs | 13 | 91 | .344 |
| 1936 | Carl Hubbell (P) | N.Y. Giants | 26W | 6L | 2.31 ERA |
| 1937 | Joe Medwick | St. Louis Cardinals | 31 | 154 | .374 |
| 1938 | Ernie Lombardi | Cincinnati Reds | 19 | 95 | .342 |
| 1939 | Bucky Walters (P) | Cinncinati Reds | 27W | 11L | 2.29 ERA |
| 1940 | Frank McCormick | Cinncinati Reds | 19 | 127 | .309 |
| 1941 | Dolph Camilli | Brooklyn Dodgers | 34 | 120 | .285 |
| 1942 | Mort Cooper (P) | St. Louis Cardinals | 22W | 7L | 1.78 ERA |
| 1943 | Stan Musial | St. Louis Cardinals | 13 | 81 | .357 |
| 1944 | Marty Marion | St. Louis Cardinals | 6 | 63 | .267 |
| 1945 | Phil Cavarretta | Chicago Cubs | 6 | 97 | .355 |
| 1946 | Stan Musial | St. Louis Cardinals | 16 | 103 | .365 |
| 1947 | Bob Elliott | Boston Braves | 22 | 113 | .317 |
| 1948 | Stan Musial | St. Louis Cardinals | 39 | 131 | .376 |
| 1949 | Jackie Robinson | Brooklyn Dodgers | 16 | 124 | .342 |
| 1950 | Jim Konstanty (P)[1] | Philadelphia Phillies | 16W | 7L | 2.66 ERA |
| 1951 | Roy Campanella | Brooklyn Dodgers | 33 | 108 | .325 |
| 1952 | Hank Sauer | Chicago Cubs | 37 | 121 | .270 |
| 1953 | Roy Campanella | Brooklyn Dodgers | 41 | 142 | .312 |
| 1954 | Willie Mays | N.Y. Giants | 41 | 110 | .345 |
| 1955 | Roy Campanella | Brooklyn Dodgers | 32 | 107 | .318 |
| 1956 | Don Newcombe (P) | Brooklyn Dodgers | 27W | 7L | 3.06 ERA |
| 1957 | Hank Aaron | Milwaukee Braves | 44 | 132 | .322 |
| 1958 | Ernie Banks | Chicago Cubs | 47 | 129 | .313 |
| 1959 | Ernie Banks | Chicago Cubs | 45 | 143 | .304 |
| 1960 | Dick Groat | Pittsburgh Pirates | 2 | 50 | .325 |
| 1961 | Frank Robinson | Cincinnati Reds | 37 | 124 | .323 |
| 1962 | Maury Wills | L.A. Dodgers | 6 | 48 | .299 |
| 1963 | Sandy Koufax (P) | L.A. Dodgers | 25W | 5L | 1.88 ERA |
| 1964 | Ken Boyer | St. Louis Cardinals | 24 | 119 | .295 |
| 1965 | Willie Mays | San Francisco Giants | 52 | 112 | .317 |
| 1966 | Roberto Clemente | Pittsburgh Pirates | 29 | 119 | .317 |
| 1967 | Orlando Cepeda | San Francisco Giants | 25 | 111 | .325 |
| 1968 | Bob Gibson (P) | St. Louis Cardinals | 22W | 9L | 1.12 ERA |
| 1969 | Willie McCovey | San Francisco Giants | 45 | 126 | .320 |
| 1970 | Johnny Bench | Cincinnati Reds | 45 | 148 | .293 |
| 1971 | Joe Torre | St. Louis Cardinals | 45 | 137 | .363 |
| 1972 | Johnny Bench | Cincinnati Reds | 40 | 125 | .270 |
| 1973 | Pete Rose | Cincinnati Reds | 5 | 64 | .338 |
| 1974 | Steve Garvey | L.A. Dodgers | 21 | 111 | .312 |
| 1975 | Joe Morgan | Cincinnati Reds | 17 | 94 | .327 |
| 1976 | Joe Morgan | Cincinnati Reds | 27 | 111 | .320 |
| 1977 | George Foster | Cincinnati Reds | 52 | 149 | .320 |
| 1978 | Dave Parker | Pittsburgh Pirates | 30 | 117 | .334 |

| Year | Name | Team | HRs | RBIs | Avg. |
|---|---|---|---|---|---|
| 1979 | Keith Hernandez | St. Louis Cardinals | 11 | 105 | .344 |
| | Willie Stargell | Pittsburgh Pirates | 32 | 82 | .281 |
| 1980 | Mike Schmidt | Philadelphia Phillies | 48 | 121 | .286 |
| 1981 | Mike Schmidt | Philadelphia Phillies | 31 | 91 | .316 |
| 1982 | Dale Murphy | Atlanta Braves | 36 | 109 | .281 |
| 1983 | Dale Murphy | Atlanta Braves | 36 | 121 | .302 |
| 1984 | Ryne Sandberg | Chicago Cubs | 19 | 84 | .314 |
| 1985 | Willie McGee | St. Louis Cardinals | 10 | 82 | .353 |
| 1986 | Mike Schmidt | Philadelphia Phillies | 37 | 119 | .290 |
| 1987 | Andre Dawson | Chicago Cubs | 49 | 137 | .287 |
| 1988 | Kirk Gibson | L.A. Dodgers | 25 | 76 | .290 |
| 1989 | Kevin Mitchell | San Francisco Giants | 47 | 125 | .291 |
| 1990 | Barry Bonds | Pittsburgh Pirates | 33 | 114 | .301 |

1. Twenty-two saves in 1950. **Source:** Baseball Writers' Assn.

### AMERICAN LEAGUE

| Year | Name | Team | HRs | RBIs | Avg. |
|---|---|---|---|---|---|
| 1911 | Ty Cobb | Detroit Tigers | 8 | 144 | .420 |
| 1912 | Tris Speaker | Boston Red Sox | 10 | 98 | .383 |
| 1913 | Walter Johnson (P) | Washington Senators | 36W | 7L | 1.09 ERA |
| 1914 | Eddie Collins | Philadelphia A's | 2 | 85 | .344 |
| 1922 | George Sisler | St. Louis Browns | 8 | 105 | .420 |
| 1923 | Babe Ruth | N.Y. Yankees | 41 | 131 | .393 |
| 1924 | Walter Johnson (P) | Washington Senators | 23W | 7L | 2.72 ERA |
| 1925 | Roger Peckinpaugh | Washington Senators | 4 | 64 | .294 |
| 1926 | George Burns | Cleveland Indians | 4 | 114 | .358 |
| 1927 | Lou Gehrig | N.Y. Yankees | 47 | 175 | .373 |
| 1928 | Mickey Cochrane | Philadelphia A's | 10 | 57 | .293 |
| 1931 | Lefty Grove (P) | Philadelphia A's | 31W | 4L | 2.06 ERA |
| 1932 | Jimmie Foxx | Philadelphia A's | 58 | 169 | .364 |
| 1933 | Jimmie Foxx | Philadelphia A's | 48 | 163 | .356 |
| 1934 | Mickey Cochrane | Detroit Tigers | 2 | 76 | .320 |
| 1935 | Hank Greenberg | Detroit Tigers | 36 | 170 | .328 |
| 1936 | Lou Gehrig | N.Y. Yankees | 49 | 152 | .354 |
| 1937 | Charley Gehringer | Detroit Tigers | 14 | 96 | .371 |
| 1938 | Jimmie Foxx | Boston Red Sox | 50 | 175 | .349 |
| 1939 | Joe DiMaggio | N.Y. Yankees | 30 | 126 | .381 |
| 1940 | Hank Greenberg | Detroit Tigers | 41 | 150 | .340 |
| 1941 | Joe DiMaggio | N.Y. Yankees | 30 | 125 | .357 |
| 1942 | Joe Gordon | N.Y. Yankees | 18 | 103 | .322 |
| 1943 | Spud Chandler (P) | N.Y. Yankees | 20W | 4L | 1.64 ERA |
| 1944 | Hal Newhouser (P) | Detroit Tigers | 29W | 9L | 2.22 ERA |
| 1945 | Hal Newhouser (P) | Detroit Tigers | 25W | 9L | 1.81 ERA |
| 1946 | Ted Williams | Boston Red Sox | 38 | 123 | .342 |
| 1947 | Joe DiMaggio | N.Y. Yankees | 20 | 97 | .315 |
| 1948 | Lou Boudreau | Cleveland Indians | 18 | 106 | .355 |
| 1949 | Ted Williams | Boston Red Sox | 43 | 159 | .343 |
| 1950 | Phil Rizzuto | N.Y. Yankees | 7 | 66 | .324 |
| 1951 | Yogi Berra | N.Y. Yankees | 27 | 88 | .294 |
| 1952 | Bobby Shantz (P) | Philadelphia A's | 24W | 7L | 2.48 ERA |
| 1953 | Al Rosen | Cleveland Indians | 43 | 145 | .336 |
| 1954 | Yogi Berra | N.Y. Yankees | 22 | 125 | .307 |
| 1955 | Yogi Berra | N.Y. Yankees | 27 | 108 | .272 |
| 1956 | Mickey Mantle | N.Y. Yankees | 52 | 130 | .353 |
| 1957 | Mickey Mantle | N.Y Yankees | 34 | 94 | .365 |
| 1958 | Jackie Jensen | Boston Red Sox | 35 | 122 | .286 |
| 1959 | Nelson Fox | Chicago White Sox | 2 | 70 | .306 |
| 1960 | Roger Maris | N.Y. Yankees | 39 | 112 | .283 |
| 1961 | Roger Maris | N.Y. Yankees | 61 | 142 | .269 |
| 1962 | Mickey Mantle | N.Y. Yankees | 30 | 89 | .321 |
| 1963 | Elston Howard | N.Y. Yankees | 28 | 85 | .287 |
| 1964 | Brooks Robinson | Baltimore Orioles | 28 | 118 | .317 |
| 1965 | Zoilo Versalles | Minnesota Twins | 19 | 77 | .273 |
| 1966 | Frank Robinson | Baltimore Orioles | 49 | 122 | .316 |
| 1967 | Carl Yastrzemski | Boston Red Sox | 44 | 121 | .326 |
| 1968 | Denny McLain (P) | Detroit Tigers | 31W | 6L | 1.96 ERA |
| 1969 | Harmon Killebrew | Minnesota Twins | 49 | 140 | .276 |
| 1970 | Boog Powell | Baltimore Orioles | 35 | 114 | .297 |

| Year | Name | Team | HRs | RBIs | Avg. |
|------|------|------|-----|------|------|
| 1971 | Vida Blue (P) | Oakland A's | 24W | 8L | 1.82 ERA |
| 1972 | Dick Allen | Chicago White Sox | 37 | 113 | .308 |
| 1973 | Reggie Jackson | Oakland A's | 32 | 117 | .293 |
| 1974 | Jeff Burroughs | Texas Rangers | 25 | 118 | .301 |
| 1975 | Fred Lynn | Boston Red Sox | 21 | 105 | .331 |
| 1976 | Thurman Munson | N.Y. Yankees | 17 | 105 | .302 |
| 1977 | Rod Carew | Minnesota Twins | 14 | 100 | .388 |
| 1978 | Jim Rice | Boston Red Sox | 46 | 139 | .315 |
| 1979 | Don Baylor | California Angels | 36 | 139 | .296 |
| 1980 | George Brett | Kansas City Royals | 24 | 118 | .390 |
| 1981 | Rollie Fingers (P)[1] | Milwaukee Brewers | 6W | 3L | 1.04 ERA |
| 1982 | Robin Yount | Milwaukee Brewers | 29 | 114 | .331 |
| 1983 | Cal Ripken, Jr. | Baltimore Orioles | 27 | 102 | .318 |

| Year | Name | Team | HRs | RBIs | Avg. |
|------|------|------|-----|------|------|
| 1984 | Willie Hernandez (P)[2] | Detroit Tigers | 9W | 3L | 2.48 ERA |
| 1985 | Don Mattingly | N.Y. Yankees | 35 | 145 | .324 |
| 1986 | Roger Clemens (P) | Boston Red Sox | 24W | 4L | 2.48 ERA |
| 1987 | George Bell | Toronto Blue Jays | 47 | 134 | .308 |
| 1988 | Jose Canseco | Oakland A's | 42 | 124 | .307 |
| 1989 | Robin Yount | Milwaukee Brewers | 21 | 103 | .318 |
| 1990 | Rickey Henderson | Oakland A's | 28 | 61 | .325 |

1. Had 28 saves in 1981. 2. Had 32 saves in 1984. **Source:** Baseball Writers' Assn.

## ROOKIE OF THE YEAR

### NATIONAL LEAGUE

| Year | Name | Team |
|------|------|------|
| 1947[1] | Jackie Robinson | Brooklyn Dodgers |
| 1948[1] | Alvin Dark | Boston Braves |
| 1949 | Don Newcombe (P) | Brooklyn Dodgers |
| 1950 | Sam Jethroe | Boston Braves |
| 1951 | Willie Mays | N.Y. Giants |
| 1952 | Joe Black (P) | Brooklyn Dodgers |
| 1953 | Junior Gilliam | Brooklyn Dodgers |
| 1954 | Wally Moon | St. Louis Cardinals |
| 1955 | Bill Virdon | St. Louis Cardinals |
| 1956 | Frank Robinson | Cincinnati Reds |
| 1957 | Jack Sanford (P) | Philadelphia Phillies |
| 1958 | Orlando Cepeda | S.F. Giants |
| 1959 | Willie McCovey | S.F. Giants |
| 1960 | Frank Howard | L.A. Dodgers |
| 1961 | Billy Williams | Chicago Cubs |
| 1962 | Ken Hubbs | Chicago Cubs |
| 1963 | Pete Rose | Cincinnati Reds |
| 1964 | Richie Allen | Philadelphia Phillies |
| 1965 | Jim Lefebvre | L.A. Dodgers |
| 1966 | Tommy Helms | Cincinnati Reds |
| 1967 | Tom Seaver (P) | N.Y. Mets |
| 1968 | Johnny Bench | Cincinnati Reds |
| 1969 | Ted Sizemore | L.A. Dodgers |
| 1970 | Carl Morton (P) | Montreal Expos |
| 1971 | Earl Williams | Atlanta Braves |
| 1972 | Jon Matlack (P) | N.Y. Mets |
| 1973 | Gary Matthews | S.F. Giants |
| 1974 | Bake McBride | St. Louis Cardinals |
| 1975 | John Montefusco (P) | S.F. Giants |
| 1976 | Pat Zachry (P) | Cincinnati Reds |
|  | Butch Metzger (P) | San Diego Padres |
| 1977 | Andre Dawson | Montreal Expos |
| 1978 | Bob Horner | Atlanta Braves |
| 1979 | Rick Sutcliffe (P) | L.A. Dodgers |
| 1980 | Steve Howe (P) | L.A. Dodgers |
| 1981 | Fernando Valenzuela (P) | L.A. Dodgers |
| 1982 | Steve Sax | L.A. Dodgers |
| 1983 | Darryl Strawberry | N.Y. Mets |
| 1984 | Dwight Gooden (P) | N.Y. Mets |
| 1985 | Vince Coleman | St. Louis Cardinals |
| 1986 | Todd Worrell (P) | St. Louis Cardinals |
| 1987 | Benito Santiago | San Diego Padres |
| 1988 | Chris Sabo | Cincinnati Reds |
| 1989 | Jerome Walton | Chicago Cubs |
| 1990 | Dave Justice | Atlanta Braves |

### AMERICAN LEAGUE

| Year | Player | Team |
|------|--------|------|
| 1949 | Roy Sievers | St. Louis Browns |
| 1950 | Walt Dropo | Boston Red Sox |
| 1951 | Gil McDougald | N.Y. Yankees |
| 1952 | Harry Byrd (P) | Philadelphia A's |
| 1953 | Harvey Kuenn | Detroit Tigers |
| 1954 | Bob Grim (P) | N.Y. Yankees |
| 1955 | Herb Score (P) | Cleveland Indians |
| 1956 | Luis Aparicio | Chicago White Sox |
| 1957 | Tony Kubek | N.Y. Yankees |
| 1958 | Albie Pearson | Washington Senators |
| 1959 | Bob Allison | Washington Senators |
| 1960 | Ron Hansen | Baltimore Orioles |
| 1961 | Don Schwall (P) | Boston Red Sox |
| 1962 | Tom Tresh | N.Y. Yankees |
| 1963 | Gary Peters (P) | Chicago White Sox |
| 1964 | Tony Oliva | Minnesota Twins |
| 1965 | Curt Blefary | Baltimore Orioles |
| 1966 | Tommie Agee | Chicago White Sox |
| 1967 | Rod Carew | Minnesota Twins |
| 1968 | Stan Bahnsen (P) | N.Y. Yankees |
| 1969 | Lou Piniella | K.C. Royals |
| 1970 | Thurman Munson | N.Y. Yankees |
| 1971 | Chris Chambliss | Cleveland Indians |
| 1972 | Carlton Fisk | Boston Red Sox |
| 1973 | Al Bumbry | Baltimore Orioles |
| 1974 | Mike Hargrove | Texas Rangers |
| 1975 | Fred Lynn | Boston Red Sox |
| 1976 | Mark Fidrych (P) | Detroit Tigers |
| 1977 | Eddie Murray | Baltimore Orioles |
| 1978 | Lou Whitaker | Detroit Tigers |
| 1979 | John Castino | Minnesota Twins |
|  | Alfredo Griffin | Toronto Blue Jays |
| 1980 | Joe Charboneau | Cleveland Indians |
| 1981 | Dave Righetti (P) | N.Y. Yankees |
| 1982 | Cal Ripken, Jr. | Baltimore Orioles |
| 1983 | Ron Kittle | Chicago White Sox |
| 1984 | Alvin Davis | Seattle Mariners |
| 1985 | Ozzie Guillen | Chicago White Sox |
| 1986 | Jose Canseco | Oakland A's |
| 1987 | Mark McGwire | Oakland A's |
| 1988 | Walt Weiss | Oakland A's |
| 1989 | Greg Olson (P) | Baltimore Orioles |
| 1990 | Sandy Alomar, Jr. | Cleveland Indians |

1. One player selected as Major League Rookie of the Year. Policy of naming a player from each league was inaugurated in 1949. **Source:** Baseball Writers' Assn.

## MOST WINS BY MANAGERS

| Manager | Wins | Losses | Pct. |
|---------|------|--------|------|
| 1. Connie Mack | 3,776 | 4,025 | .484 |
| 2. John McGraw | 2,840 | 1,984 | .589 |
| 3. Bucky Harris | 2,159 | 2,219 | .493 |
| 4. Joe McCarthy | 2,126 | 1,335 | .614 |
| 5. Walter Alston | 2,040 | 1,613 | .558 |
| 6. Leo Durocher | 2,010 | 1,710 | .540 |
| 7. Casey Stengel | 1,926 | 1,867 | .508 |
| 8. Sparky Anderson[1] | 1,921 | 1,524 | .558 |
| 9. Gene Mauch | 1,901 | 2,037 | .483 |
| 10. Bill McKechnie | 1,898 | 1,724 | .524 |

1. Active in 1991 season.

## The World Series

A championship series between the winners of two leagues was held in 1882 between the National League and the American Association and was played at the end of each season until the AA folded in 1890. Following this, the top two NL clubs played each other for the "Temple Cup," but the idea never really caught on with the public. When the American League began operations again in 1901, there was great animosity between the two circuits due to bidding wars for the services of star players. Peace was established before the 1903 season, and when it became clear that Pittsburgh would win the NL and Boston the AL, the owners of each club reached a private agreement to hold a "World Series" in October. Many were surprised when the newer American League won the title.

There was no agreement to play such a series every year, however, and in 1904 the New York Giants refused to meet the Boston club, probably because of John McGraw's dislike of American League President Ban Johnson. But the baseball public wanted a championship series, and by 1905 Giants' owner John Brush proposed rules governing a mandatory series to be played every year. With minute changes, those rules stand to this day.

**1903. Boston (A) over Pittsburgh (N), 5–3.** The upstart American League emerged victorious in the first World Series, a best-of-nine affair. The "Pilgrims" (Red Sox) staged one of the greatest comebacks in history by sweeping the final four games. Bill Dineen and Cy Young each won two for Boston, and held Pirate immortal Honus Wagner to one harmless single in those four contests.

**1904. No series.** New York Giants owner John T. Brush and manager John McGraw refused to play the World Champion Boston club, dismissing them as representative of an "inferior league."

**1905. New York (N) over Philadelphia (A), 4–1.** Every game was won by a shutout, with Christy Mathewson throwing three for the Giants. In 27 innings, he allowed 14 hits, striking out 18 and walking one. The Athletics committed five errors in Game three, the pivotal contest.

**1906. Chicago (A) over Chicago (N), 4–2.** The first "subway series" was a stunning upset. The "Hitless Wonders" White Sox had batted .230 with seven home runs during the season, while the Cubs were winning 116 games, still the all-time record. Utility man George Rohe hit two game-winning triples for the Sox and Ed Walsh pitched two of their wins.

**1907. Chicago (N) over Detroit (A), 4–0.** Avenging the past year, the Cubs shut down Ty Cobb, Sam Crawford et al, behind a superb four-man pitching performance, and the hitting of Harry Steinfeldt (.471) and Johnny Evers (.350).

**1908. Chicago (N) over Detroit (A), 4–1.** Only a little closer this year. Johnny Evers repeated his .350 average of 1907, joining player-manager Frank Chance (.421) and outfielder Wildfire Schulte (.389) in the Cub attack. Ty Cobb led Detroit (.368), to no avail.

**1909. Pittsburgh (N) over Detroit (A), 4–3.** The Tigers lost their third straight series, as Honus Wagner won the "Battle of the Titans" with Ty Cobb. The Pirate shortstop hit .333 with six RBIs and six stolen bases, and Babe Adams pitched in with three complete-game victories.

**1910. Philadelphia (A) over Chicago (N), 4–1.** Connie Mack's infielders combined to bat .364 as the A's rolled to an easy title. Jack Coombs pitched three wins and tossed in a .385 batting average. The great Cubs pitching staff was growing old.

**1911. Philadelphia (A) over New York (N), 4–2.** Regarded by some as the greatest team ever, the A's wrestled down a strong New York club featuring Christy Mathewson and Rube Marquard. Frank "Home Run" Baker got his nickname from game-winning blasts in Games Two and Three.

**1912. Boston (A) over New York (N), 4–3.** This thrill-a-minute series featured an 11-inning tie in Game Two, and an extra-inning final game. Two Giant errors, by Freds Merkle and Snodgrass, enabled Boston to score two runs in the bottom of the 10th inning of the final contest.

**1913. Philadelphia (A) over New York (N), 4–1.** Home Run Baker again hammered Giant pitching, batting .450 with seven RBIs. Eddie Collins also starred for the A's, hitting .421 with three stolen bases.

**1914. Boston (N) over Philadelphia (A), 4–0.** The red-hot "Miracle Braves" swept the heavily favored Athletics, who scored only six runs in the four games. Catcher Hank Gowdy (.545) and second baseman Johnny Evers (.438) led the Boston offense.

**1915. Boston (A) over Philadelphia (N), 4–1.** The famous Red Sox outfield of Speaker, Lewis, and Hooper combined to bat .364 while Rube Foster pitched two complete-game wins. Foster also batted .500, driving in the winning run in Game Two.

**1916. Boston (A) over Brooklyn (N), 4–1.** After three one-run games, Boston took charge with 6–2 and 4–1 victories. A young lefthander named Babe Ruth twirled a 14-inning six hitter in Game Two.

**1917. Chicago (A) over New York (N), 4–2.** The pitching of Red Faber (3–1, 2.33) and the hitting of Eddie Collins, Buck Weaver, and Joe Jackson were too much for the Giants in a sloppy (23 errors) series.

**1918. Boston (A) over Chicago (N), 4–2.** Every game a pitchers duel, the losing Cubs posted a 1.04 ERA over the six games. The Boston staff allowed but nine runs in the series, led by Babe Ruth, who extended his consecutive scoreless inning streak to 29⅔.

**1919. Cincinnati (N) over Chicago (A), 5–3.** Results declared invalid after eight Chicago "Black Sox" were found to have acted to lose games intentionally. All eight, plus 14 other major leaguers, were barred from baseball for life in the ensuing scandal.

**1920. Cleveland (A) over Brooklyn (N), 5–2.** Game Five was surely the most freakish in series history. It featured a) the first World Series grand slam home run (Indians right-fielder Elmer Smith), b) the first World Series home run by a pitcher (Indians Jim Bagby), and c) the first and only unassisted triple play in series action (Indians second baseman Billy Wambsganss).

**1921. New York (N) over New York (A), 5–3.** Six Giants batted over .300, and their pitchers held Babe Ruth to a .500 slugging average. Giant hurler Jesse Barnes won two games and batted .444.

**1922. New York (N) over New York (A), 4–0.** The result was said to be final proof that "brains beat brawn." Giant pitching shut down Ruth & Co., allowing only 11 runs in the five contests (one tie).

**1923. New York (A) over New York (N), 4–2.** The Yankees took the last three to break the spell of their cross-river rivals, behind Babe Ruth's three homers and eight RBIs. Casey Stengel hit two home runs for the losers.

**1924. Washington (A) over New York (N), 4–3.** A 12-inning seventh game won by Walter Johnson in relief capped an exciting affair. Twenty-seven-year-old player-manager Bucky Harris starred for the Senators (.333, 7 RBIs), as did outfielder Goose Goslin (.344, 7 RBIs).

**1925. Pittsburgh (N) over Washington (A), 4–3.** Pirate centerfielder Max Carey had 11 hits and three stolen bases, as Pittsburgh became the first team since 1903 to come back from a three games to one deficit.

**1926. St. Louis (N) over New York (A), 4–3.** Babe Ruth hit three homers in Game Four, but in the seventh inning of the seventh contest Grover Cleveland Alexander struck out Tony Lazzeri with the bases loaded, saving the game and the series for the Cardinals.

## WORLD SERIES MVP WINNERS

| Year | Name | Team |
|------|------|------|
| 1955 | Johnny Podres | Brooklyn Dodgers |
| 1956 | Don Larsen | N.Y. Yankees |
| 1957 | Lew Burdette | Milwaukee Braves |
| 1958 | Bob Turley | N.Y. Yankees |
| 1959 | Larry Sherry | L.A. Dodgers |
| 1960 | Bobby Richardson | N.Y. Yankees |
| 1961 | Whitey Ford | N.Y. Yankees |
| 1962 | Ralph Terry | N.Y. Yankees |
| 1963 | Sandy Koufax | L.A. Dodgers |
| 1964 | Bob Gibson | St. Louis Cardinals |
| 1965 | Sandy Koufax | L.A. Dodgers |
| 1966 | Frank Robinson | Baltimore Orioles |
| 1967 | Bob Gibson | St. Louis Cardinals |
| 1968 | Mickey Lolich | Detroit Tigers |
| 1969 | Donn Clendenon | N.Y. Mets |
| 1970 | Brooks Robinson | Baltimore Orioles |
| 1971 | Roberto Clemente | Pittsburgh Pirates |
| 1972 | Gene Tenace | Oakland A's |
| 1973 | Reggie Jackson | Oakland A's |
| 1974 | Rollie Fingers | Oakland A's |
| 1975 | Pete Rose | Cincinnati Reds |
| 1976 | Johnny Bench | Cincinnati Reds |
| 1977 | Reggie Jackson | N.Y. Yankees |
| 1978 | Bucky Dent | N.Y. Yankees |
| 1979 | Willie Stargell | Pittsburgh Pirates |
| 1980 | Mike Schmidt | Philadelphia Phillies |
| 1981 | Ron Cey | L.A. Dodgers |
|      | Pedro Guerrero | L.A. Dodgers |
|      | Steve Yeager | L.A. Dodgers |
| 1982 | Darrell Porter | St. Louis Cardinals |
| 1983 | Rick Dempsey | Baltimore Orioles |
| 1984 | Alan Trammell | Detroit Tigers |
| 1985 | Bret Saberhagen | Kansas City Royals |
| 1986 | Ray Knight | N.Y. Mets |
| 1987 | Frank Viola | Minnesota Twins |
| 1988 | Orel Hershiser | L.A. Dodgers |
| 1989 | Dave Stewart | Oakland A's |
| 1990 | José Rijo | Cincinnati Reds |

**1927. New York (A) over Pittsburgh (N), 4–0.** Generally regarded as the greatest team of all time, the "Murderers' Row" Yankees disposed of the Pirates behind two more Babe Ruth homers, plus the pitching of Wilcy Moore, Herb Pennock, and George Pipgras.

**1928. New York (A) over St. Louis (N), 4–0.** Another Yankee sweep. Ruth and Lou Gehrig combined to bat .593, with seven home runs and 13 RBIs. Waite Hoyt pitched two complete-game victories.

**1929. Philadelphia (A) over Chicago (N), 4–1.** Trailing 8–0 in Game Four, the A's roared back to score 10 runs in the seventh inning, a series record. In the next contest, the Mackmen took the series with a three-run ninth inning.

**1930. Philadelphia (A) over St. Louis (N), 4–2.** Lefty Grove and George Earnshaw pitched well, while Al Simmons, Jimmie Foxx, and Mickey Cochrane combined for 11 extra-base hits. Cardinal regulars batted only .185 in the six games.

**1931. St. Louis (N) over Philadelphia (A), 4–3.** Cardinal centerfielder Pepper Martin set a record that stood for 33 years with his 12 hits. Martin also stole five bases and hit a home run. Bill Hallahan and Burleigh Grimes handled the pitching, combining for a 4–0, 1.25 ERA.

**1932. New York (A) over Chicago (N), 4–0.**
The Yankees completed a streak of 12 straight World Series victories in sweeping the Cubs. This time Ruth and Gehrig combined to bat .438, with five homers and 14 RBIs.

**1933. New York (N) over Washington (A), 4–1.**
Same teams as 1924, different result. Bill Terry's Giants defeated Joe Cronin's Senators in a battle of player-managers. Carl Hubbell won two for New York and did not allow an earned run.

**1934. St. Louis (N) over Detroit (A), 4–3.**
Dizzy and Paul Dean hurled the Cardinals to the title, winning all four Redbird victories. A bad defensive series, with 27 errors and 13 unearned runs.

**1935. Detroit (A) over Chicago (N), 4–2.** The Cubs won 21 straight games in September, but came up short when faced with Mickey Cochrane's Tigers. Charlie Gehringer and Tommy Bridges starred for Detroit, while Lou Warneke (2–0, 0.54) was superb for the losers.

**1936. New York (A) over New York (N), 4–2.**
The Yankees hammered Giant pitching in Games Two and Six, ending with 43 runs for the series. Tony Lazzeri and Bill Dickey each drove in runs in five games in the second contest, when Joe McCarthy's "Windowbreakers" scored 18 times to set a record.

**1937. New York (A) over New York (N), 4–1.**
Lefty Gomez pitched two of the Yankee wins and drove in the winning run with a single in the final game. The Yanks scored seven runs in the sixth inning of Game One, then coasted to an easy championship.

**1938. New York (A) over Chicago (N), 4–0.** In a replay of 1932, the Bronx Bombers blew out an overmatched Cub squad. Cub fans are still waiting for their team's first series victory over the Yankees.

**1939. New York (A) over Cincinnati (N), 4–0.**
New York won its fourth straight World Championship the same way they won the first three—easily. Charlie Keller batted .438 with three homers, and scored as many runs as the entire Reds team, eight.

**1940. Cincinnati (N) over Detroit (A), 4–3.**
The Reds repeated as NL champs, then prevailed over the Tigers when Paul Derringer beat Bobo Newsome 2–1 in the seventh game. Derringer and Bucky Walters each won two games.

**1941. New York (A) over Brooklyn (N), 4–1.**
With two outs in the ninth inning of Game Four, Dodger catcher Mickey Owen dropped a third strike on Tommy Henrich, allowing him to reach first base. The Yankees then scored four times to win the ballgame, and finished Brooklyn off the next day.

**1942. St. Louis (N) over New York (A), 4–1.**
The Cardinals, winners of 106 games during the regular season, lost Game One with the tying run at bat. They then swept four in a row, behind the pitching of Johnny Beazley (2–0, 2.50) and Ernie White's shutout in Game Three.

**1943. New York (A) over St. Louis (N), 4–1.** In a turnaround from 1942, the Yanks held St. Louis to nine runs in the five games. Joe Gordon and Bill Dickey homered, while third baseman Billy Johnson drove in three runs for New York.

**1944. St. Louis (N) over St. Louis (A), 4–2.**
The Browns struggled valiantly in their only World Series appearance, but fell short against a strong Cardinal club left relatively intact by World War II. Ten Brown errors gave the Redbirds seven unearned runs.

**1945. Detroit (A) over Chicago (N), 4–3.** Tiger Ace Hal Newhouser was hit hard in Game One, but he bounced back to win Games Five and Seven. Doc Cramer (.379) and Hank Greenberg (2 HRs, 7 RBIs) led the Detroit offense.

**1946. St. Louis (N) over Boston (A), 4–3.** Enos Slaughter scored from first on a base-hit by Harry Walker in the eighth inning of the seventh game, giving St. Louis its third title in five years. Harry Brecheen won three games for the Cardinals, allowing but one run.

**1947. New York (A) over Brooklyn (N), 4–3.**
Yankee pitcher Bill Bevens had a no-hitter for 8 2/3 innings in Game Four, but lost the game on a double by Cookie Lavagetto. Tommy Henrich (.323) had the game winning RBIs in Games One, Two, and Seven.

**1948. Cleveland (A) over Boston (N), 4–2.**
The series featured fine pitching on both sides, including the first game, when Boston's Johnny Sain beat Bob Feller 1–0. Cleveland's Gene Beardon did not allow a run in 10²⁄₃ innings.

**1949. New York (A) over Brooklyn (N), 4–1.**
Game One was 0–0 until Tommy Henrich led off the bottom of the ninth with a home run off Don Newcombe. Bobby Brown (currently president of the American League) batted .500 with five RBIs.

**1950. New York (A) over Philadelphia (N), 4–0.** New York struggled to win the first three contests by scores of 1–0, 2–1, and 3–2, in a series that was closer than it looks. The "Whiz Kid" Phillies held the Yanks to a .222 batting average but managed to hit only .203 themselves.

**1951. New York (A) over New York (N), 4–2.** A tired Giant pitching staff held the Yankees in check for three games, but the AL champs broke out to score 23 runs in the final three. Eddie Lopat (2–0, 0.50) starred for the winners.

**1952. New York (A) over Brooklyn (N), 4–3.**
Allie Reynolds and Vic Raschi each won two games, combining for a 1.69 ERA. Johnny Mize hit three homers, and Mickey Mantle and Yogi Berra each hit two. Duke Snider batted .345 with four roundtrippers in a losing cause.

**1953. New York (A) over Brooklyn (N), 4–2.**
The Yankees won their fifth straight World Championship as second baseman Billy Martin tied a record with 12 hits. Martin slugged .958 and drove in eight runs.

**1954. New York (N) over Cleveland (A), 4–0.**
The Indians won 111 games during the season, still an AL record. The Giants, sparked by a spectacular Willie Mays catch in the first game, went on to defeat Cleveland easily. Pinch-hitter-outfielder Dusty Rhodes drove in seven runs on two homers and two singles in six at bats.

**1955. Brooklyn (N) over New York (A), 4–3.**
The Dodgers finally won a World Series in their eighth try, behind the pitching of series MVP Johnny Podres (2–0, 1.00). Duke Snider hit four homers in a series for the second time, and

Dodger leftfielder Sandy Amoros made a game-saving catch in the seventh game.

**1956. New York (A) over Brooklyn (N), 4–3.**
Yankee righthander and series MVP Don Larsen pitched a perfect game in the fifth contest, while Mickey Mantle and Yogi Berra each hit three homers for the winners.

**1957. Milwaukee (N) over New York (A), 4–3.**
Lew Burdette won three times for the Braves, allowing but two runs in 27 innings, and won the MVP. Milwaukee's hitting was led by Hank Aaron (.393, 3 HRs, 7 RBIs).

**1958. New York (A) over Milwaukee (N), 4–3.**
Yankees Hank Bauer and Moose Skowron combined for six homers and 15 RBIs as the Bronx Bombers came back from a 3–1 deficit to sweep the last three games. Yankee pitcher "Bullet" Bob Turley earned MVP honors.

**1959. Los Angeles (N) over Chicago (A), 4–2.** Los Angeles enjoyed its first World Championship as the transplanted Dodgers prevailed, aided by the relief pitching of MVP Larry Sherry (2 wins, 2 saves). Ted Kluszewski of the "Go-Go" White Sox hit .391, with three homers and 10 RBIs.

**1960. Pittsburgh (N) over New York (A), 4–3.**
Pirate second baseman Bill Mazeroski's home run in the bottom of the ninth in the seventh game capped one of the most exciting contests in history. In the 10–9 ballgame, 10 of the runs were scored in the last two innings. Yankee second baseman Bobby Richardson, a hitting star throughout the series, was named MVP.

**1961. New York (A) over Cincinnati (N), 4–1.**
Whitey Ford tossed two shutouts in winning the MVP, and the Yankee offense pounded out 16 extra-base hits in the five games. Bobby Richardson (.391) and John Blanchard (.400, 2 HRs) starred for New York.

**1962. New York (A) over San Francisco (N), 4–3.** Ralph Terry's four-hit shutout won the seesaw affair for the Yanks, and earned him the MVP. Whitey Ford completed his series record 33 consecutive scoreless innings in the first game, and for the Giants, Chuck Hiller hit the first National League series grand slam home run in Game Four.

**1963. Los Angeles (N) over New York (A), 4–0.**
Dodger pitchers held New York to four runs, led by Sandy Koufax's two wins and 23 strikeouts, including a record-breaking 15 in the first game. Koufax was the runaway choice for MVP.

**1964. St. Louis (N) over New York (A), 4–3.**
Ten Yankee home runs were not enough to beat the Cardinals. Bob Gibson was the series MVP, and Tim McCarver (.478) also starred. Highlights included Ken Boyer's game-winning grandslam in Game Four, and Bobby Richardson's record 13 hits.

**1965. Los Angeles (N) over Minnesota (A), 4–3.** As in 1963, MVP Sandy Koufax again excelled for the Dodgers, allowing only two runs in 24 innings, striking out 29. Jim "Mudcat" Grant won two games and hit a three-run homer for the Twins.

**1966. Baltimore (A) over Los Angeles (N), 4–0.** The Orioles made the most of their first World Series appearance, as their young pitchers did not allow a run after the third inning of the first game. Slugger Frank Robinson capped a great year with the series MVP award.

## MAJOR LEAGUE BASEBALL LEAGUE CHAMPIONSHIP SERIES RESULTS (Divisional play began in 1969)

| | AMERICAN LEAGUE | | | | NATIONAL LEAGUE | | |
|---|---|---|---|---|---|---|---|
| Year | Winner | Loser | MVP | Year | Winner | Loser | MVP |
| 1969 | Baltimore Orioles·3 | Minnesota Twins·0 | | 1969 | N.Y. Mets·3 | Atlanta Braves·0 | |
| 1970 | Baltimore Orioles·3 | Minnesota Twins·0 | | 1970 | Cincinnati Reds·3 | Pittsburgh Pirates·0 | |
| 1971 | Baltimore Orioles·3 | Oakland A's·0 | | 1971 | Pittsburgh Pirates·3 | S.F. Giants·1 | |
| 1972 | Oakland A's·3 | Detroit Tigers·2 | | 1972 | Cincinnati Reds·3 | Pittsburgh Pirates·2 | |
| 1973 | Oakland A's·3 | Baltimore Orioles·2 | | 1973 | N.Y. Mets·3 | Cincinnati Reds·2 | |
| 1974 | Oakland A's·3 | Baltimore Orioles·1 | | 1974 | L.A. Dodgers·3 | Pittsburgh Pirates·1 | |
| 1975 | Boston Red Sox·3 | Oakland A's·0 | | 1975 | Cincinnati Reds·3 | Pittsburgh Pirates·0 | |
| 1976 | N.Y. Yankees·3 | Kansas City Royals·2 | | 1976 | Cincinnati Reds·3 | Philadelphia Phillies·0 | |
| 1977 | N.Y. Yankees·3 | Kansas City Royals·2 | | 1977 | L.A. Dodgers·3 | Philadelphia Phillies·1 | Dusty Baker, L.A. |
| 1978 | N.Y. Yankees·3 | Kansas City Royals·1 | | 1978 | L.A. Dodgers·3 | Philadelphia Phillies·1 | Steve Garvey, L.A. |
| 1979 | Baltimore Orioles·3 | California Angels·1 | | 1979 | Pittsburgh Pirates·3 | Cincinnati Reds·0 | Willie Stargell, Pittsburgh |
| 1980 | Kansas City Royals·3 | N.Y. Yankees·0 | Frank White, Kansas City | 1980 | Philadelphia Phillies·3 | Houston Astros·2 | Manny Trillo, Philadelphia |
| 1981 | N.Y. Yankees·3 | Oakland A's·0 | Graig Nettles, N.Y. | 1981 | L.A. Dodgers·3 | Montreal Expos·2 | Burt Hooton, L.A. |
| 1982 | Milwaukee Brewers·3 | California Angels·2 | Fred Lynn, California | 1982 | St. Louis Cardinals·3 | Atlanta Braves·0 | Darrell Porter, St. Louis |
| 1983 | Baltimore Orioles·3 | Chicago White Sox·1 | Mike Boddicker, Baltimore | 1983 | Philadelphia Phillies·3 | L.A. Dodgers·1 | Gary Matthews, Philadelphia |
| 1984 | Detroit Tigers·3 | Kansas City Royals·0 | Kirk Gibson, Detroit | 1984 | San Diego Padres·3 | Chicago Cubs·2 | Steve Garvey, San Diego |
| 1985[1] | Kansas City Royals·4 | Toronto Blue Jays·3 | George Brett, Kansas City | 1985[1] | St. Louis Cardinals·4 | L.A. Dodgers·2 | Ozzie Smith, St. Louis |
| 1986 | Boston Red Sox·4 | California Angels·3 | Marty Barrett, Boston | 1986 | N.Y. Mets·4 | Houston Astros·2 | Mike Scott, Houston |
| 1987 | Minnesota Twins·4 | Detroit Tigers·1 | Gary Gaetti, Minnesota | 1987 | St. Louis Cardinals·4 | S. F. Giants·3 | Jeff Leonard, S.F. |
| 1988 | Oakland A's·4 | Boston Red Sox·0 | Dennis Eckersley, Oakland | 1988 | L.A. Dodgers·4 | N.Y. Mets·3 | Orel Hershiser, L.A. |
| 1989 | Oakland A's·4 | Toronto Blue Jays·1 | Rickey Henderson, Oakland | 1989 | S.F. Giants·4 | Chicago Cubs·1 | Will Clark, S.F. |
| 1990 | Oakland A's·4 | Boston Red Sox·0 | Dave Stewart, Oakland | 1990 | Cincinnati Reds·4 | Pittsburgh Pirates·2 | Rob Dibble, Randy Myers, Cincinnati |

1. In 1985 the League Championship Series was switched to a best-of-seven format.

**1967. St. Louis (N) over Boston (A), 4–3.** Bob Gibson pitched three complete game victories, added a home run in Game Seven, and was named MVP. Lou Brock batted .414 and stole seven bases, tying Eddie Collins's record and pacing the Cards.

**1968. Detroit (A) over St. Louis (N), 4–3.** The Cardinals were rolling behind Bob Gibson's record 17 strikeouts in Game One and his record seventh straight series win in Game Four. Again Lou Brock joined him in the record books with 13 hits and seven stolen bases. But their feats couldn't stop the Tigers, led by the MVP pitching of Mickey Lolich (3–0, 1.67).

**1969. New York (N) over Baltimore (A), 4–1.** The Mets stunned the baseball world by winning four in a row after dropping the opener. Their young pitchers held the Orioles to only nine runs, aided by the great outfield catches of Ron Swoboda and Tommie Agee. Series MVP Donn Clendenon (.357, 3 HRs) and Al Weis (.455, 1 HR) led the Met attack.

**1970. Baltimore (A) over Cincinnati (N), 4–1.** Brooks Robinson almost singlehandedly beat the Reds with spectacular defense at third base and a .429 average with two homers and two doubles. His dominance of the series earned the MVP. Also chipping in for the O's were Paul Blair (.474), Frank Robinson, and Boog Powell (two homers each).

**1971. Pittsburgh (N) over Baltimore (A), 4–3.** Roberto Clemente played in 14 World Series games and hit safely in every one. Here he batted .414, slugged .759, and won MVP honors. Steve Blass, Nelson Briles, and Bruce Kison won all the Pirate victories with a combined ERA of 0.54.

**1972. Oakland (A) over Cincinnati (N), 4–3.** A's backup catcher Gene Tenace hit home runs in his first two series at bats, then went on to hit two more, becoming the surprise star and

MVP selection. Rollie Fingers relieved in six of the contests, winning one and saving two.

**1973. Oakland (A) over New York (N), 4–3.** The Mets had the worst record of any pennant winner ever (82–79), but they lasted till the seventh game in a sloppily played (19 errors) affair. Darold Knowles pitched in all seven games for the A's, saving two. Reggie Jackson slugged his way to the first of his two series MVP awards.

**1974. Oakland (A) over Los Angeles (N), 4–1.** The A's won their third straight World Championship behind the three saves and one win of MVP Rollie Fingers. Joe Rudi (.333) and Bert Campaneris (.353) starred with the bats.

**1975. Cincinnati (N) over Boston (A), 4–3.** Five of the seven games were decided by one run, including the famous twelve-inning sixth contest won on a Carlton Fisk home run. Cincinnati used 23 relief pitchers to set a record. Pete Rose, the heart and soul of the Big Red Machine, hustled his way to MVP honors.

**1976. Cincinnati (N) over New York (A), 4–0.** The Big Red Machine drove over the Yankees, slugging .522 as a team. Seven of nine Reds hitters batted over .300, led by MVP Johnny Bench's .533 (1.133 slugging average).

**1977. New York (A) over Los Angeles (N), 4–2.** Reggie Jackson hit five homers, including three in the final game, to equal records set by Babe Ruth and win the MVP for the second time. Mike Torrez won two for the Yankees.

**1978. New York (A) over Los Angeles (N), 4–2.** Shortstop Bucky Dent and backup infielder Brian Doyle batted .417 and .438 respectively, pacing New York in its second straight six-game triumph. Dent was named MVP. In the last four contests, the Yankees outscored L.A. 28–8.

**1979. Pittsburgh (N) over Baltimore (A), 4–3.** The Pirates overcame a three games to one defi-

cit as Earl Weaver's Orioles waited for the three-run homer that never came. Led by Willie Stargell (.400, 3 HRs) and Phil Garner (.500), Pittsburgh batted .323 as a team. "Pops" Stargell's on-field performance and team leadership of the Pirates' "family" were honored with the MVP.

**1980. Philadelphia (N) over Kansas City (A), 4–2.** The two teams batted .292 in a series decided largely by the relief pitching of Tug McGraw (1–1, 2 saves) vs. Dan Quisenberry (1–2, 1 save). Mike Schmidt took MVP honors with a .381 average and seven RBIs.

**1981. Los Angeles (N) over New York (A), 4–2.** Many observers called this sloppy series a fitting end to this strike-stricken 1981 season. Even the MVP award proved impossible to settle, as Pedro Guerrero, Steve Yeager, and Ron Cey shared the honor.

**1982. St. Louis (N) over Milwaukee (A), 4–3.** Joaquin Andujar won two games for the Cardinals, and Willie McGee had perhaps the greatest single series game by a rookie, with two homers and two great catches in Game Four. American League MVP Robin Yount batted .414 for the losers.

**1983. Baltimore (A) over Philadelphia (N), 4–1.** The Phillies couldn't hit Orioles' pitching, scoring but nine runs in the five games. Catcher Rick Dempsey hit four doubles and a home run, held the Phils to one stolen base, and was named MVP.

**1984. Detroit (A) over San Diego (N), 4–1.** The Tigers belted seven homers and backed them up with the pitching of Jack Morris (2–0, 2.00). Sparky Anderson become the first manager to win World Championships in both leagues. The Tigers' sure-handed shortstop, Alan Trammell, fielded flawlessly and hit with power to earn MVP honors.

**1985.** Kansas City (A) over St. Louis (N), 4–3. The Cards were one inning away from the title, but a disputed call at first base opened the door for the Royals in Game Six. They won that contest, then blew St. Louis away 11–0 in the finale. Bret Saberhagen won three for Kansas City, and the MVP.

**1986.** New York (N) over Boston (A), 4–3. As in 1985, misplays in the final inning of Game Six caused the series to turn around, as the Red Sox lost their fourth straight seven game series. Mets third baseman Ray Knight capped a comeback year with clutch hitting and the series MVP.

**1987.** Minnesota (A) over St. Louis (N), 4–3. The Twins won their first championship by taking all four games in their exotic home park, the Metrodome. Cardinal pitching held them to five runs in the three games in St. Louis, but in Minnesota the Twins could not be contained, scoring 33 times. Frank Viola (2–1, ERA 3.72) was the MVP.

**1988.** Los Angeles (N) over Oakland (A), 4–1. Series MVP Orel Hershiser (2–0, 17 Ks) dazzled the powerful A's. Injured Dodger Kirk Gibson's dramatic two-out home run in the bottom of the ninth in Game One set the tone for the unexpected Los Angeles triumph.

**1989.** Oakland (A) over San Francisco (N), 4–0. The A's thoroughly dominated a weak Giants' pitching staff, pounding out 32 runs, 44 hits (including nine home runs) in only four games. Series MVP Dave Stewart and reliever Dennis Eckersley led an Oakland staff to shut down the Giants. This series will be long remembered for the major earthquake that struck the Bay area just before Game Three and delayed the contest for 12 days.

**1990.** Cincinnati (N) over Oakland (A), 4–0. Cincinnati dominated the heavily favored A's in a stunning series sweep. The Reds hit .317 as a team, while their pitchers, led by MVP José Rijo, held Oakland's vaunted offense to a mere .207 series average. Billy Hatcher broke Babe Ruth's World Series record by hitting .750, and he set two other records, with seven consecutive hits and four doubles.

## WORLD SERIES RECORDS

### BATTING

| Runs scored | | Home runs | |
|---|---|---|---|
| Mickey Mantle | 42 | Mickey Mantle | 18 |
| Yogi Berra | 41 | Babe Ruth | 15 |
| Babe Ruth | 37 | Yogi Berra | 12 |
| **Hits** | | Most home runs in one series: | 5 |
| Yogi Berra | 71 | (Reggie Jackson, 1977). | |
| Mickey Mantle | 59 | **Runs batted in** | |
| Frankie Frisch | 58 | | |
| Most hits in one series: | 13 | Mickey Mantle | 40 |
| (Bobby Richardson, 1960; | | Yogi Berra | 39 |
| Lou Brock, 1968; | | Lou Gehrig | 35 |
| Marty Barrett, 1986). | | Most runs batted in one series: | 12 |
| | | (Bobby Richardson, 1960). | |

**Source:** Major League Baseball.

## 1991 SEASON

### FINAL STANDINGS, 1991

| Division/ Team | W | L | Pct. | GB |
|---|---|---|---|---|
| **National League East** | | | | |
| Pittsburgh | 98 | 64 | .605 | — |
| St. Louis | 84 | 78 | .519 | 14 |
| Philadelphia | 78 | 84 | .481 | 20 |
| Chicago | 77 | 83 | .481 | 20 |
| New York | 77 | 84 | .478 | 20½ |
| Montreal | 71 | 90 | .441 | 20½ |
| **National League West** | | | | |
| Atlanta | 94 | 68 | .580 | — |
| Los Angeles | 93 | 69 | .574 | 1 |
| San Diego | 84 | 78 | .519 | 10 |
| San Francisco | 75 | 87 | .463 | 19 |
| Cincinnati | 74 | 88 | .457 | 20 |
| Houston | 65 | 97 | .401 | 29 |
| **American League East** | | | | |
| Toronto | 91 | 71 | .562 | — |
| Boston | 84 | 78 | .519 | 7 |
| Detroit | 84 | 78 | .519 | 7 |
| Milwaukee | 83 | 79 | .512 | 8 |
| New York | 71 | 91 | .438 | 20 |
| Baltimore | 67 | 95 | .414 | 24 |
| Cleveland | 57 | 105 | .352 | 34 |
| **American League West** | | | | |
| Minnesota | 95 | 67 | .586 | — |
| Chicago | 87 | 75 | .537 | 8 |
| Texas | 85 | 77 | .525 | 10 |
| Oakland | 84 | 78 | .519 | 11 |
| Seattle | 83 | 79 | .512 | 12 |
| Kansas City | 82 | 80 | .506 | 13 |
| California | 81 | 81 | .500 | 14 |

### 1991 LEAGUE CHAMPIONSHIP SERIES
#### American League

| Game 1 | Minnesota 5 | Toronto 4 |
|---|---|---|
| Game 2 | Toronto 5 | Minnesota 2 |
| Game 3 | Minnesota 3 | Toronto 2 |
| Game 4 | Minnesota 9 | Toronto 3 |
| Game 5 | Minnesota 8 | Toronto 5 |

The Twins, who finished last one year earlier, won three consecutive times in Toronto's SkyDome, continuing the Blue Jays' postseason frustration. Led by MVP Kirby Puckett, Minnesota outhit Toronto .276 to .249. Twins pitchers, behind veteran Jack Morris (2–0) had a combined 3.33 ERA.

#### National League

| Game 1 | Pittsburgh 5 | Atlanta 1 |
|---|---|---|
| Game 2 | Atlanta 1 | Pittsburgh 0 |
| Game 3 | Atlanta 10 | Pittsburgh 3 |
| Game 4 | Pittsburgh 3 | Atlanta 2 |
| Game 5 | Pittsburgh 1 | Atlanta 0 |
| Game 6 | Atlanta 1 | Pittsburgh 0 |
| Game 7 | Atlanta 4 | Pittsburgh 0 |

Atlanta's young pitching staff overpowered the Pirates' big hitters, holding Barry Bonds, Andy Van Slyke, and Bobby Bonilla to a collective .200 with only three RBIs. MVP Steve Avery won two shutouts, late-season acquisition Alejandro Peña provided dominating relief, and starters Tom Glavine and John Smoltz pitched like veterans. The Braves thus joined Minnesota in a World Series featuring two "last to first" teams.

## THE 1991 WORLD SERIES

| Game | Winner | Loser |
|---|---|---|
| **Game 1** | **Minnesota 5** | **Atlanta 2** |

Atlanta manager Bobby Cox's controversial decision to start lefthander Charlie Leibrandt in the deafening Metrodome backfired. Leibrandt surrendered seven hits in four-plus innings, including shortstop Greg Gagne's three-run homer to left. Veteran starter Jack Morris easily held the Braves at bay.

| **Game 2** | **Minnesota 3** | **Atlanta 2** |
|---|---|---|

Minnesota's rookie third baseman, Scott Leius, hit a first-pitch leadoff home run in the bottom of the eighth inning, breaking a 2–2 tie. Twins starter Kevin Tapani scattered seven hits before giving way to ace reliever Rick Aguilera, who struck out the last three batters in the ninth. Atlanta's Tom Glavine pitched a complete-game four-hitter in a losing cause.

| **Game 3** | **Atlanta 5** | **Minnesota 4** |
|---|---|---|

Playing before a raucous home crowd, the Braves pulled out a thrilling 12-inning win when diminutive second baseman Mark Lemke drove in David Justice with a single to left. Justice stumbled rounding third, and just beat Dan Gladden's throw to catcher Brian Harper. The two teams used a series-record 42 players and 12 pinch hitters.

| **Game 4** | **Atlanta 3** | **Minnesota 2** |
|---|---|---|

The Braves pulled out a squeaker in the bottom of the ninth when Lemke again came through in the clutch with a triple to left center. Pinch hitter Jerry Willard hit a short sacrifice fly to right, and Lemke was safe by inches when catcher Brian Harper tagged him with his elbow, not with the ball. Atlanta's John Smoltz pitched seven strong innings, striking out seven and walking none before yielding a home run to Mike Pagliarulo.

| **Game 5** | **Atlanta 14** | **Minnesota 5** |
|---|---|---|

Atlanta's offense was in high gear all game, driving a succession of Twins pitchers, including starter Tapani, from the mound. Although players up and down the Braves lineup contributed, the scoring was again led by the unlikely duo of Lemke and Lonnie Smith. Lemke had two triples and three RBIs, while Smith hit his third home run of the series.

| **Game 6** | **Minnesota 4** | **Atlanta 3** |
|---|---|---|

The Twins returned home and pulled out a victory with a sensational 11th-inning home run by Kirby Puckett. The homer capped a sterling performance by the Twins centerfielder, whose triple in the first led to two runs, and whose catch of a Gant fly ball in the third was the defensive play of the series. The Atlanta offense seemed snakebitten, failing to score runners with less than two out in the ninth, 10th, and 11th innings.

| **Game 7** | **Minnesota 1** | **Atlanta 0** |
|---|---|---|

Twins pinch hitter Gene Larkin's 10th-inning single drove in Gladden with the winning run and ended one of the most dramatic seventh games in World Series history. The star of the game and the MVP of the series was Morris, who went the distance for Minnesota, giving up seven hits and working out of several jams. The game capped one of the most spectacular series in recent history, with four games decided in the last at-bat, five decided by one run, and three going into extra innings.

## 1991 INDIVIDUAL LEADERS

### AMERICAN LEAGUE

| BATTING AVERAGE | | HOME RUNS | | RUNS BATTED IN | | PITCHING—WINS | | PITCHING—ERA | |
|---|---|---|---|---|---|---|---|---|---|
| Franco, Texas | .341 | Canseco, Oakland | 44 | Fielder, Detroit | 133 | Erickson, Minnesota | 20 | Clemens, Boston | 2.62 |
| Boggs, Boston | .332 | Fielder, Detroit | 44 | Canseco, Oakland | 122 | Gullickson, Detroit | 20 | Candiotti, Cleveland/ | |
| Randolph, Milwaukee | .327 | C. Ripken, Baltimore | 34 | Sierra, Texas | 116 | Langston, California | 19 | Toronto | 2.65 |
| Griffey, Jr., Seattle | .327 | Carter, Toronto | 33 | C. Ripken, Baltimore | 114 | Finley, California | 18 | Wegman, Milwaukee | 2.84 |
| Molitor, Milwaukee | .325 | Thomas, Chicago | 31 | Thomas, Chicago | 109 | Clemens, Boston | 18 | J. Abbott, California | 2.89 |
| C. Ripken, Baltimore | .323 | Tartabull, Kansas City | 31 | Carter, Toronto | 108 | J. Abbott, California | 18 | Ryan, Texas | 2.91 |
| Palmeiro, Texas | .322 | Tettleton, Detroit | 31 | Gonzalez, Texas | 102 | Morris, Minnesota | 18 | Moore, Oakland | 2.96 |
| Puckett, Minnesota | .319 | Davis, Minnesota | 29 | Griffey, Jr., Seattle | 100 | Moore, Oakland | 17 | Tapani, Minnesota | 2.99 |
| Thomas, Chicago | .318 | 3 tied | 28 | Tartabull, Kansas City | 100 | McDowell, Chicago | 17 | Langston, California | 3.00 |
| Tartabull, Kansas City | .316 | | | Ventura, Chicago | 100 | | | Key, Toronto | 3.05 |
| | | | | | | | | Saberhagen, Kansas City | 3.07 |

### NATIONAL LEAGUE

| BATTING AVERAGE | | HOME RUNS | | RUNS BATTED IN | | PITCHING—WINS | | PITCHING—ERA | |
|---|---|---|---|---|---|---|---|---|---|
| Pendleton, Atlanta | .319 | Johnson, New York | 38 | Johnson, New York | 117 | Smiley, Pittsburgh | 20 | De. Martinez, Montreal | 2.39 |
| Morris, Cincinnati | .318 | Williams, San Francisco | 34 | Bonds, Pittsburgh | 116 | Glavine, Atlanta | 20 | Rijo, Cincinnati | 2.51 |
| Gwynn, San Diego | .317 | Gant, Atlanta | 32 | Clark, San Francisco | 116 | Avery, Atlanta | 18 | Glavine, Atlanta | 2.55 |
| McGee, San Francisco | .312 | Dawson, Chicago | 31 | McGriff, San Diego | 106 | Martinez, Los Angeles | 17 | Belcher, Los Angeles | 2.62 |
| Jose, St. Louis | .305 | McGriff, San Diego | 31 | Gant, Atlanta | 105 | Smith, Pittsburgh | 16 | Harnisch, Houston | 2.70 |
| Larkin, Cincinnati | .302 | Clark, San Francisco | 29 | Dawson, Chicago | 104 | Mulholland, Philadelphia | 16 | DeLeon, St. Louis | 2.71 |
| Bonilla, Pittsburgh | .302 | O'Neill, Cincinnati | 28 | Bonilla, Pittsburgh | 100 | 6 tied | 15 | Morgan, Los Angeles | 2.78 |
| Clark, San Francisco | .301 | Strawberry, Los Angeles | 28 | Sandberg, Chicago | 100 | | | Tomlin, Pittsburgh | 2.98 |
| Sabo, Cincinnati | .301 | Mitchell, San Francisco | 27 | Strawberry, Los Angeles | 99 | | | Benes, San Diego | 3.03 |
| Calderon, Montreal | .300 | 2 tied | 26 | Williams, San Francisco | 98 | | | Drabek, Pittsburgh | 3.07 |

## ALL STAR GAME RESULTS, 1933–91

| Year | Winner | Score | Year | Winner | Score |
|---|---|---|---|---|---|
| 1933 | American | 4–2 | 1963 | National | 5–3 |
| 1934 | American | 9–7 | 1964 | National | 7–4 |
| 1935 | American | 4–1 | 1965 | National | 6–5 |
| 1936 | National | 4–3 | 1966 | National | 2–1 |
| 1937 | American | 8–3 | 1967 | National | 2–1 |
| 1938 | National | 4–1 | 1968 | National | 1–0 |
| 1939 | American | 3–1 | 1969 | National | 9–3 |
| 1940 | National | 4–0 | 1970 | National | 5–4 |
| 1941 | American | 7–5 | 1971 | American | 6–4 |
| 1942 | American | 3–1 | 1972 | National | 4–3 |
| 1943 | American | 5–3 | 1973 | National | 7–1 |
| 1944 | National | 7–1 | 1974 | National | 7–2 |
| 1945 | No game due to wartime | | 1975 | National | 6–3 |
| 1946 | American | 12–0 | 1976 | National | 7–1 |
| 1947 | American | 2–1 | 1977 | National | 7–5 |
| 1948 | American | 5–2 | 1978 | National | 7–3 |
| 1949 | American | 11–7 | 1979 | National | 7–6 |
| 1950 | National | 4–3 | 1980 | National | 4–2 |
| 1951 | National | 8–3 | 1981 | National | 5–4 |
| 1952 | National | 3–2 | 1982 | National | 4–1 |
| 1953 | National | 5–1 | 1983 | American | 13–3 |
| 1954 | American | 11–9 | 1984 | National | 3–1 |
| 1955 | National | 6–5 | 1985 | National | 6–1 |
| 1956 | National | 7–3 | 1986 | American | 3–2 |
| 1957 | American | 6–5 | 1987 | National | 2–0 |
| 1958 | American | 4–3 | 1988 | American | 2–1 |
| 1959(1)[1] | National | 5–4 | 1989 | American | 5–3 |
| 1959(2) | American | 5–3 | 1990 | American | 2–0 |
| 1960(1) | National | 5–3 | 1991 | American | 4–2 |
| 1960(2) | National | 6–0 | | | |
| 1961(1) | National | 5–4 | | | |
| 1961(2) | Tie[2] | 1–1 | | | |
| 1962(1) | National | 3–1 | | | |
| 1962(2) | American | 9–4 | | | |

1. Two All Star games were played 1959–62. 2. Game was called after nine innings because of rain.

## THE BASEBALL HALL OF FAME

National Baseball Hall of Fame and Museum
Main Street, Cooperstown, NY 13326
(607) 547–9988

Hours: From May 1 to Oct. 31—9:00 a.m. to 9:00 p.m.
From Nov. 1 to Apr. 30—9:00 a.m. to 5:00 p.m.
(Every day of the year except Thanksgiving, Christmas,
and New Year's.)

The Hall of Fame was established in 1936 and opened in Cooperstown, N.Y., in 1939. From the start there were two ways to be elected: by receiving 75 percent of the votes cast by the Baseball Writers Association of America or 75 percent of the votes cast by a Committee on Old Timers. In the first year, the writers picked the top five players of the post-1900 era: Ty Cobb, Walter Johnson, Christy Mathewson, Babe Ruth, and Honus Wagner. To be elected, a player must have played at least 10 years in the major leagues and been retired for at least five years. The Committee on Old Timers, originally created to consider 19th century players, was replaced by a Special Veterans Committee whose scope includes all players retired for a minimum of 25 years who may have been overlooked when they were first eligible. In 1971 a Special Committee on the Negro Leagues was set up to consider ballplayers who played in the old Negro Leagues.

## BASEBALL HALL OF FAME

| Player/Position/Year Inducted | Games | At bats | HRs | BA | Hits | RBIs |
|---|---|---|---|---|---|---|
| **Aaron, Henry (Hank)** OF 1982 | 3,298 | 12,364 | 755 | .305 | 3,771 | 2,297 |
| All-time leader in home runs and RBIs | | | | | | |
| **Anson, Adrian (Cap)** 1B 1939 | 2,276 | 9,108 | 96 | .334 | 3,041 | 1,715 |
| Managed 20 years, 1879–98, winning five pennants | | | | | | |
| **Aparicio, Luis** SS 1984 | 2,599 | 10,230 | 83 | .262 | 2,677 | 791 |
| 2,581 games at shortstop, most all-time | | | | | | |
| **Appling, Luke** SS 1964 | 2,422 | 8,857 | 45 | .310 | 2,749 | 1,116 |
| Batted .388 in 1936 | | | | | | |
| **Averill, Earl** OF 1975 | 1,669 | 6,358 | 238 | .318 | 2,020 | 1,165 |
| 232 hits in 1936 | | | | | | |

| Player/Position/Year Inducted | Games | At bats | HRs | BA | Hits | RBIs |
|---|---|---|---|---|---|---|
| **Baker, Frank (Home Run)** 3B 1955 | 1,575 | 5,985 | 96 | .307 | 1,838 | 1,013 |
| Batted .363 in six World Series | | | | | | |
| **Bancroft, Dave** SS 1971 | 1,913 | 7,182 | 32 | .279 | 2,004 | 591 |
| Modern leader in total chances per game among shortstops | | | | | | |
| **Banks, Ernie** SS, 1B 1977 | 2,528 | 9,421 | 512 | .274 | 2,583 | 1,636 |
| Consecutive MVP awards, 1958–59 | | | | | | |
| **Beckley, Jake** 1B 1971 | 2,386 | 9,527 | 88 | .308 | 2,931 | 1,575 |
| 244 career triples, mostly in 19th century | | | | | | |
| **Bench, Johnny** C 1989 | 2,158 | 7,658 | 389 | .267 | 2,048 | 1,376 |
| All-time HR leader for catchers; MVP 1970, 1972 | | | | | | |
| **Berra, Lawrence (Yogi)** C, OF 1972 | 2,120 | 7,555 | 358 | .285 | 2,150 | 1,430 |
| Three MVP awards, 1951, 1954, 1955 | | | | | | |
| **Bottomley, Jim** 1B 1974 | 1,991 | 7,471 | 219 | .310 | 2,313 | 1,422 |
| Twelve RBIs in one game, 1924 | | | | | | |
| **Boudreau, Lou** SS 1970 | 1,646 | 6,030 | 68 | .295 | 1,779 | 789 |
| MVP in 1948; managed 16 years | | | | | | |
| **Bresnahan, Roger** C, OF 1945 | 1,430 | 4,478 | 26 | .279 | 1,251 | 530 |
| 212 stolen bases, most ever by a catcher | | | | | | |
| **Brock, Lou** OF 1985 | 2,616 | 10,332 | 149 | .293 | 3,023 | 900 |
| 938 stolen bases; batted .391 in three World Series | | | | | | |
| **Brouthers, Dan** 1B 1945 | 1,673 | 6,716 | 106 | .343 | 2,304 | 1,056 |
| Seven slugging and five batting titles during 19th century | | | | | | |
| **Burkett, Jesse** OF 1946 | 2,072 | 8,430 | 75 | .341 | 2,873 | 952 |
| Led NL in batting three times and in hits four times | | | | | | |
| **Campanella, Roy** C 1969 | 1,215 | 4,205 | 242 | .276 | 1,161 | 856 |
| Three MVP awards, 1951, 1953, 1955 | | | | | | |
| **Carew, Rod** IF 1991 | 2,469 | 9,315 | 92 | .328 | 3,053 | 1,015 |
| Seven batting titles; 18 All-Star Game appearances | | | | | | |
| **Carey, Max** OF 1961 | 2,476 | 9,363 | 69 | .285 | 2,665 | 800 |
| 738 stolen bases | | | | | | |
| **Chance, Frank** 1B 1946 | 1,286 | 4,295 | 20 | .297 | 1,274 | 596 |
| Managed Chicago (NL) to four pennants in five years, 1906–10 | | | | | | |
| **Clarke, Fred** OF 1945 | 2,245 | 8,588 | 67 | .315 | 2,708 | 1,015 |
| 223 career triples, sixth-best ever | | | | | | |
| **Clemente, Roberto** OF 1973 | 2,433 | 9,454 | 240 | .317 | 3,000 | 1,305 |
| Career average of over 18 outfield assists per season | | | | | | |
| **Cobb, Ty** OF 1936 | 3,034 | 11,429 | 118 | .367 | 4,191 | 1,961 |
| Batted .320 or better for 23 straight years | | | | | | |
| **Cochrane, Mickey** C 1947 | 1,482 | 5,169 | 119 | .320 | 1,652 | 832 |
| Two MVP awards, 1928 and 1934 | | | | | | |
| **Collins, Eddie** 2B 1939 | 2,826 | 9,949 | 47 | .333 | 3,311 | 1,299 |
| All-time leader in games, putouts, and assists at second base | | | | | | |
| **Collins, Jimmy** 3B 1945 | 1,728 | 6,796 | 64 | .294 | 1,997 | 982 |
| Led NL in home runs, 1898 | | | | | | |
| **Combs, Earle** OF 1970 | 1,454 | 5,748 | 58 | .325 | 1,866 | 629 |
| Averaged 127 runs scored per season | | | | | | |
| **Comiskey, Charles** 1B 1939 | 1,390 | 5,796 | 29 | .264 | 1,531 | 467 |
| Manager and owner of Chicago White Sox | | | | | | |
| **Connor, Roger** 1B 1976 | 1,998 | 7,798 | 136 | .318 | 2,480 | 1,078 |
| 233 career triples in 19th century, fifth-best all-time | | | | | | |
| **Crawford, Sam** OF 1957 | 2,517 | 9,580 | 97 | .309 | 2,964 | 1,525 |
| 312 triples, best ever | | | | | | |
| **Cronin, Joe** SS 1956 | 2,124 | 7,579 | 170 | .301 | 2,285 | 1,424 |
| MVP in 1930; managed 1933–47 | | | | | | |
| **Cuyler, Hazen (Kiki)** OF 1968 | 1,879 | 7,161 | 127 | .321 | 2,299 | 1,065 |
| Led NL in runs scored twice, stolen bases four times | | | | | | |
| **Delahanty, Ed** IF, OF 1945 | 1,834 | 7,502 | 100 | .345 | 2,591 | 1,464 |
| Batted .408 in 1899 | | | | | | |
| **Dickey, Bill** C 1954 | 1,789 | 6,300 | 202 | .313 | 1,969 | 1,209 |
| Catcher on eight AL pennant winning teams | | | | | | |
| **DiMaggio, Joe** OF 1955 | 1,736 | 6,821 | 361 | .325 | 2,214 | 1,537 |
| 56-game hitting streak in 1941 | | | | | | |
| **Doerr, Bobby** 2B 1986 | 1,865 | 7,093 | 223 | .288 | 2,042 | 1,247 |
| Led AL in slugging 1944 | | | | | | |
| **Duffy, Hugh** OF 1945 | 1,736 | 7,062 | 103 | .328 | 2,314 | 1,299 |
| Batted .438 in 1894, highest ever | | | | | | |
| **Evers, Johnny** 2B 1946 | 1,783 | 6,134 | 12 | .270 | 1,658 | 538 |
| NL MVP in 1914 | | | | | | |
| **Ewing, Buck** C, IF, OF 1939 | 1,315 | 5,363 | 70 | .303 | 1,625 | 733 |
| Regarded as greatest player of 19th century | | | | | | |

| Player/Position/Year Inducted | Games | At bats | HRs | BA | Hits | RBIs |
|---|---|---|---|---|---|---|
| **Ferrell, Rick** C 1984 | 1,884 | 6,028 | 28 | .281 | 1,692 | 734 |
| Led AL catchers at times in putouts, assists, fielding average, and double plays | | | | | | |
| **Flick, Elmer** OF 1963 | 1,484 | 5,603 | 47 | .315 | 1,767 | 756 |
| Led AL in triples 1905, 1906, 1907 | | | | | | |
| **Foxx, Jimmie** 1B, 3B 1951 | 2,317 | 8,134 | 534 | .325 | 2,646 | 1,921 |
| Slugged over .700 three seasons | | | | | | |
| **Frisch, Frank** 2B, 3B 1947 | 2,311 | 9,112 | 105 | .316 | 2,880 | 1,244 |
| Highest career batting average ever for a switch hitter | | | | | | |
| **Gehrig, Lou** 1B 1939 | 2,164 | 8,001 | 493 | .340 | 2,721 | 1,990 |
| 2,130 consecutive games played | | | | | | |
| **Gehringer, Charlie** 2B 1949 | 2,323 | 8,860 | 184 | .320 | 2,839 | 1,427 |
| 60 doubles in 1936 | | | | | | |
| **Goslin, Leon (Goose)** OF 1968 | 2,287 | 8,655 | 248 | .316 | 2,735 | 1,609 |
| 100+ RBIs 11 years | | | | | | |
| **Greenberg, Hank** 1B 1956 | 1,394 | 5,193 | 331 | .313 | 1,628 | 1,276 |
| 58 home runs in 1938; 183 RBIs in 1937 | | | | | | |
| **Hafey, Charles (Chick)** OF 1971 | 1,283 | 4,625 | 164 | .317 | 1,466 | 833 |
| NL batting title (.349) in 1931 | | | | | | |
| **Hamilton, Billy** OF 1961 | 1,593 | 6,284 | 40 | .344 | 2,163 | 736 |
| Scored 196 runs in 1894, with a .509 on-base average and 99 stolen bases | | | | | | |
| **Hartnett, Charles** C 1955 | 1,990 | 6,432 | 236 | .297 | 1,912 | 1,179 |
| Played on four NL pennant winners, managed one | | | | | | |
| **Heilmann, Harry** OF, 1B 1952 | 2,146 | 7,787 | 183 | .342 | 2,660 | 1,551 |
| Batted .403 in 1923 | | | | | | |
| **Herman, Billy** 2B 1975 | 1,922 | 7,707 | 47 | .304 | 2,345 | 839 |
| 57 doubles in 1935 | | | | | | |
| **Hooper, Harry** OF 1971 | 2,308 | 8,785 | 75 | .281 | 2,466 | 817 |
| 375 career stolen bases | | | | | | |
| **Hornsby, Rogers** 2B, IF 1942 | 2,259 | 8,173 | 301 | .358 | 2,930 | 1,584 |
| Batted .402 in years 1921–25; nine slugging titles | | | | | | |
| **Huggins, Miller** 2B 1964 | 1,585 | 5,557 | 9 | .265 | 1,474 | 318 |
| Managed N.Y. Yankees 1913–29; 1,002 career walks | | | | | | |
| **Jackson, Travis** SS 1982 | 1,656 | 6,086 | 135 | .291 | 1,768 | 929 |
| Batted over .300 six times in 1920s and 1930s | | | | | | |
| **Jennings, Hugh** SS 1945 | 1,285 | 4,905 | 18 | .312 | 1,531 | 840 |
| Managed Detroit 1907–20; batted .398 in 1896 | | | | | | |
| **Kaline, Al** OF 1980 | 2,834 | 10,116 | 399 | .297 | 3,007 | 1,583 |
| 3,007 career hits; 11 Gold Gloves | | | | | | |
| **Keeler, Willie** OF 1939 | 2,124 | 8,591 | 34 | .345 | 2,962 | 810 |
| Batted .432 in 1897; 495 career stolen bases | | | | | | |
| **Kell, George** 3B 1983 | 1,795 | 6,702 | 78 | .306 | 2,054 | 870 |
| AL batting champ (.343) in 1949 | | | | | | |
| **Kelley, Joe** OF 1971 | 1,845 | 7,018 | 65 | .319 | 2,242 | 1,193 |
| Averaged 151 runs scored, 1894–96 | | | | | | |
| **Kelly, George** 1B 1973 | 1,622 | 5,993 | 148 | .297 | 1,778 | 1,020 |
| Led NL in RBIs, 1920 and 1925 | | | | | | |
| **Kelly, Mike (King)** OF, C 1945 | 1,463 | 5,923 | 69 | .307 | 1,820 | 794 |
| Two batting titles, 1884 and 1886; 315 career stolen bases | | | | | | |
| **Killebrew, Harmon** 1B, 3B, OF 1984 | 2,435 | 8,147 | 573 | .256 | 2,086 | 1,584 |
| 40+ home runs eight years | | | | | | |
| **Kiner, Ralph** OF 1975 | 1,472 | 5,205 | 369 | .279 | 1,451 | 1,015 |
| Second-highest home run per at bat ratio of all-time | | | | | | |
| **Klein, Chuck** OF 1980 | 1,753 | 6,486 | 300 | .320 | 2,076 | 1,201 |
| 44 outfield assists in 1930 | | | | | | |
| **Lajoie, Napoleon (Larry)** 2B 1937 | 2,479 | 9,589 | 82 | .338 | 3,244 | 1,599 |
| Batted .422 in 1901 | | | | | | |
| **Lazzeri, Tony** IF 1991 | 1,740 | 6,297 | 178 | .292 | 1,840 | 1,191 |
| Batted .300 or better five times; clutch hitter in World Series | | | | | | |
| **Lindstrom, Fred** 3B, OF 1976 | 1,438 | 5,611 | 103 | .311 | 1,747 | 779 |
| 231 hits in 1928 | | | | | | |
| **Lombardi, Ernie** C 1986 | 1,853 | 5,855 | 190 | .306 | 1,792 | 990 |
| Two NL batting titles, 1938 and 1942 | | | | | | |
| **Lopez, Al** C 1977 | 1,950 | 5,916 | 52 | .261 | 1,547 | 652 |
| Managed 17 years; 1,918 games caught is second-highest all-time | | | | | | |
| **Mantle, Mickey** OF 1974 | 2,401 | 8,102 | 536 | .298 | 2,415 | 1,509 |
| 52 home runs in 1956, 54 in 1961 | | | | | | |
| **Manush, Heinie** OF 1964 | 2,009 | 7,653 | 110 | .330 | 2,524 | 1,173 |
| Hit .378 in 1926 | | | | | | |
| **Maranville, Walter (Rabbit)** SS, 2B 1954 | 2,670 | 10,078 | 28 | .258 | 2,605 | 884 |
| 23-year career; hit .308 in two World Series | | | | | | |

| Player/Position/Year Inducted | Games | At bats | HRs | BA | Hits | RBIs |
|---|---|---|---|---|---|---|
| **Mathews, Eddie** 3B 1978 | 2,388 | 8,537 | 512 | .271 | 2,315 | 1,453 |
| 1,444 career walks | | | | | | |
| **Mays, Willie** OF 1979 | 2,992 | 10,881 | 660 | .302 | 3,283 | 1,903 |
| Slugged over .600 six seasons | | | | | | |
| **McCarthy, Tommy** OF 1946 | 1,275 | 5,128 | 44 | .292 | 1,496 | 666 |
| Averaged 122 runs scored, 1888–94 | | | | | | |
| **McCovey, Willie** 1B, OF 1986 | 2,588 | 8,197 | 521 | .270 | 2,211 | 1,555 |
| 45 intentional walks in 1969, an NL record | | | | | | |
| **McGraw, John** 3B, SS 1937 | 1,009 | 3,922 | 13 | .334 | 1,308 | 462 |
| .549 on-base average in 1899; 2,840 career wins as manager | | | | | | |
| **Medwick, Joe** OF 1968 | 1,984 | 7,635 | 205 | .324 | 2,471 | 1,383 |
| Won NL Triple Crown in 1937 | | | | | | |
| **Mize, Johnny** 1B 1981 | 1,884 | 6,443 | 359 | .312 | 2,011 | 1,337 |
| Four-time NL home run champ | | | | | | |
| **Morgan, Joe** 2B 1990 | 2,649 | 9,277 | 268 | .271 | 2,517 | 1,133 |
| Won back-to-back MVP awards, 1975, 1976 | | | | | | |
| **Musial, Stan** OF, 1B 1969 | 3,026 | 10,972 | 475 | .331 | 3,630 | 1,951 |
| 725 doubles and 177 triples | | | | | | |
| **O'Rourke, Jim** OF 1945 | 1,774 | 7,435 | 51 | .310 | 2,304 | 830 |
| Batted .300+ 11 times in the 19th century | | | | | | |
| **Ott, Mel** OF 1951 | 2,732 | 9,456 | 511 | .304 | 2,876 | 1,860 |
| Averaged 121 RBIs 1929–38 | | | | | | |
| **Reese, Harold (Pee Wee)** SS 1984 | 2,166 | 8,058 | 126 | .269 | 2,170 | 885 |
| Finished in top 10 in MVP balloting nine times | | | | | | |
| **Rice, Sam** OF 1963 | 2,404 | 9,269 | 34 | .322 | 2,987 | 1,078 |
| Only 18 strikeouts per 154 games | | | | | | |
| **Robinson, Brooks** 3B 1983 | 2,896 | 10,654 | 268 | .267 | 2,848 | 1,357 |
| 16 consecutive Gold Gloves, 1960–75 | | | | | | |
| **Robinson, Frank** OF 1982 | 2,808 | 10,006 | 586 | .294 | 2,943 | 1,812 |
| MVP in both leagues; AL Triple Crown in 1966 | | | | | | |
| **Robinson, Jackie** 2B 1972 | 1,382 | 4,877 | 137 | .311 | 1,518 | 734 |
| First black player in MLB; Rookie of the Year 1947; MVP and batting champ 1949 | | | | | | |
| **Robinson, Wilbert** C 1945 | 1,347 | 5,077 | 18 | .273 | 1,399 | 740 |
| Managed Brooklyn 1914–31, winning two pennants | | | | | | |
| **Roush, Edd** OF 1962 | 1,967 | 7,363 | 68 | .323 | 2,376 | 981 |
| Two NL batting titles, 1917 and 1919 | | | | | | |
| **Ruth, George (Babe)** OF, P 1936 | 2,503 | 8,399 | 714 | .342 | 2,873 | 2,211 |
| Slugged .847 1920–21 | | | | | | |
| **Schalk, Ray** C 1955 | 1,760 | 5,306 | 12 | .253 | 1,345 | 594 |
| 176 stolen bases | | | | | | |
| **Schoendienst, Albert (Red)** 1989 | 2,216 | 8,479 | 84 | .289 | 2,449 | 773 |
| Managed Cards to two pennants and 1967 World Series crown | | | | | | |
| **Sewell, Joe** SS, 3B 1977 | 1,902 | 7,132 | 49 | .312 | 2,226 | 1,051 |
| Only 22 strikeouts in his last 2,500 at bats, 1929–33 | | | | | | |
| **Simmons, Al** OF 1953 | 2,215 | 8,761 | 307 | .334 | 2,927 | 1,827 |
| Drove in over 100 runs in each of his first 11 years, 1924–34 | | | | | | |
| **Sisler, George** 1B 1939 | 2,055 | 8,267 | 100 | .340 | 2,812 | 1,175 |
| Batted .400 1920–22 | | | | | | |
| **Slaughter, Enos** OF 1985 | 2,380 | 7,946 | 169 | .300 | 2,383 | 1,304 |
| 52 doubles in 1939 | | | | | | |
| **Snider, Edwin (Duke)** OF 1980 | 2,143 | 7,161 | 407 | .295 | 2,116 | 1,333 |
| Averaged 41 home runs, 1953–57 | | | | | | |
| **Speaker, Tris** OF 1937 | 2,789 | 10,208 | 117 | .344 | 3,515 | 1,559 |
| 793 doubles, best all-time | | | | | | |
| **Stargell, Willie** OF, 1B 1988 | 2,360 | 7,927 | 475 | .282 | 2,232 | 1,540 |
| MVP in 1979 | | | | | | |
| **Terry, Bill** 1B 1954 | 1,721 | 6,428 | 154 | .341 | 2,193 | 1,078 |
| Last NL .400 hitter, .401 in 1930 | | | | | | |
| **Thompson, Sam** OF 1974 | 1,410 | 6,005 | 128 | .331 | 1,986 | 1,299 |
| 166 RBIs in 1887, 165 in 1895 | | | | | | |
| **Tinker, Joe** SS 1946 | 1,805 | 6,441 | 31 | .263 | 1,695 | 782 |
| Played in four World Series with Chicago Cubs | | | | | | |
| **Traynor, Pie** 3B 1948 | 1,941 | 7,559 | 58 | .320 | 2,416 | 1,273 |
| 100+ RBIs seven years | | | | | | |
| **Vaughan, Joseph (Arky)** SS 1985 | 1,817 | 6,622 | 96 | .318 | 2,103 | 926 |
| .385 in 1935 | | | | | | |
| **Wagner, Honus** SS 1936 | 2,786 | 10,427 | 101 | .327 | 3,418 | 1,732 |
| Eight batting titles, four in a row 1906–1909 | | | | | | |

| Player/Position/Year Inducted | Games | At bats | HRs | BA | Hits | RBIs |
|---|---|---|---|---|---|---|
| **Wallace, Bobby** SS 1953 | 2,386 | 8,652 | 35 | .267 | 2,314 | 1,121 |
| 6.1 chances per game at shortstop, fifth-best all-time | | | | | | |
| **Waner, Lloyd** OF 1967 | 1,992 | 7,772 | 28 | .316 | 2,459 | 598 |
| 234 hits in 1929 | | | | | | |
| **Waner, Paul** OF 1952 | 2,549 | 9,459 | 112 | .333 | 3,152 | 1,309 |
| 62 doubles in 1932 | | | | | | |
| **Wheat, Zack** OF 1959 | 2,410 | 9,106 | 132 | .317 | 2,884 | 1,261 |
| Batted .375 at age 36 in 1924 | | | | | | |
| **Williams, Billy** OF 1987 | 2,488 | 9,350 | 426 | .290 | 2,711 | 1,475 |
| 30+ home runs in five seasons | | | | | | |
| **Williams, Ted** OF 1966 | 2,292 | 7,706 | 521 | .344 | 2,654 | 1,839 |
| Last .400 hitter in majors, .406 in 1941 | | | | | | |
| **Wilson, Lewis (Hack)** OF 1979 | 1,348 | 4,760 | 244 | .307 | 1,461 | 1,062 |
| 56 home runs and 190 RBIs in 1930, both NL records | | | | | | |
| **Wright, George** SS 1937 | 329 | 1,494 | 2 | .256 | N/A | N/A |
| Pioneer of professional baseball | | | | | | |
| **Yastrzemski, Carl (Yaz)** OF, 1B 1989 | 3,308 | 11,988 | 452 | .285 | 3,419 | 1,844 |
| Won Triple Crown in 1967; three batting titles; most games played in AL history | | | | | | |
| **Youngs, Ross** OF 1972 | 1,211 | 4,627 | 42 | .322 | 1,491 | 592 |
| Killed at age 30; .398 on-base average in four World Series, 1921–24 | | | | | | |

## HALL OF FAME—PITCHERS

| Player/Year Inducted | Wins | Losses | ERA | Games | IP | SOs |
|---|---|---|---|---|---|---|
| **Alexander, Grover Cleveland** 1938 | 373 | 208 | 2.56 | 696 | 5,189 | 2,199 |
| Won 30 games three years; led NL in ERA five times | | | | | | |
| **Bender, Charles (Chief)** 1953 | 210 | 127 | 2.46 | 459 | 3,017 | 1,711 |
| Led AL in winning percentage three seasons | | | | | | |
| **Brown, Mordecai (Three Finger)** 1949 | 239 | 129 | 2.06 | 481 | 3,172 | 1,375 |
| 1.04 ERA in 1906 | | | | | | |
| **Chesbro, Jack** 1946 | 198 | 132 | 2.68 | 392 | 2,897 | 1,265 |
| 41 wins in 1904 | | | | | | |
| **Clarkson, John** 1963 | 326 | 177 | 2.81 | 531 | 4,536 | 2,015 |
| 53 wins in 1885, with 623 innings pitched | | | | | | |
| **Coveleski, Stan** 1969 | 215 | 142 | 2.88 | 450 | 3,093 | 981 |
| Led AL in ERA in 1925, 2.84 | | | | | | |
| **Cummings, William (Candy)** 1939 | 21 | 22 | 2.78 | 43 | 372 | 37 |
| Inventor of the curveball | | | | | | |
| **Dean, Jay (Dizzy)** 1953 | 150 | 83 | 3.03 | 317 | 1,966 | 1,155 |
| 30 wins in 1934 | | | | | | |
| **Drysdale, Don** 1984 | 209 | 166 | 2.95 | 518 | 3,432 | 2,486 |
| 56⅔ consecutive scoreless innings, 1968 | | | | | | |
| **Faber, Urban (Red)** 1964 | 254 | 212 | 3.15 | 669 | 4,088 | 1,471 |
| Led AL in ERA in 1921 and 1922 | | | | | | |
| **Feller, Bob** 1962 | 266 | 162 | 3.25 | 570 | 3,827 | 2,581 |
| Led AL in wins six times, in shutouts seven | | | | | | |
| **Ford, Edward (Whitey)** 1974 | 236 | 106 | 2.75 | 498 | 3,170 | 1,956 |
| 25–4 in 1961, 24–7 in 1963 | | | | | | |
| **Galvin, James (Pud)** 1965 | 361 | 310 | 2.87 | 697 | 5,941 | 1,799 |
| 46 wins in 1883 and 1884 | | | | | | |
| **Gibson, Bob** 1981 | 251 | 174 | 2.91 | 528 | 3,885 | 3,117 |
| 1.12 ERA in 1968; seven straight wins in World Series play | | | | | | |
| **Gomez, Vernon (Lefty)** 1972 | 189 | 102 | 3.34 | 368 | 2,503 | 1,468 |
| Led AL in shutouts three years | | | | | | |
| **Grimes, Burleigh** 1964 | 270 | 212 | 3.53 | 617 | 4,180 | 1,512 |
| Last legal spitball pitcher; won 20+ five times | | | | | | |
| **Grove, Robert (Lefty)** 1947 | 300 | 141 | 3.06 | 616 | 3,941 | 2,266 |
| Led AL in ERA nine times, in strikeouts seven | | | | | | |
| **Haines, Jesse** 1970 | 210 | 158 | 3.64 | 555 | 3,209 | 981 |
| Twice led NL in shutouts, 1921 and 1927 | | | | | | |
| **Hoyt, Waite** 1969 | 237 | 182 | 3.59 | 674 | 3,763 | 1,206 |
| 1.83 ERA in 84 World Series innings | | | | | | |
| **Hubbell, Carl** 1947 | 253 | 154 | 2.97 | 535 | 3,589 | 1,678 |
| 26–6 in 1936; 1.66 ERA in 1933 | | | | | | |
| **Hunter, Jim (Catfish)** 1987 | 224 | 166 | 3.26 | 500 | 3,448 | 2,012 |
| 21 or more wins, 1971–75 | | | | | | |
| **Jenkins, Ferguson** 1991 | 284 | 226 | 3.34 | 664 | 4,499 | 3,192 |
| Cy Young Award winner (1971); three-time All-Star | | | | | | |
| **Johnson, Walter** 1936 | 416 | 279 | 2.17 | 802 | 5,924 | 3,508 |
| 36–7, 1.09 ERA in 1913 | | | | | | |

| Player/Year Inducted | Wins | Losses | ERA | Games | IP | SOs |
|---|---|---|---|---|---|---|
| **Joss, Addie** 1978 | 160 | 97 | 1.88 | 286 | 2,336 | 926 |
| Averaged 21–11, 1.66 ERA in years 1904–08 | | | | | | |
| **Keefe, Tim** 1964 | 344 | 225 | 2.62 | 601 | 5,072 | 2,533 |
| Averaged 37 wins 1883–85 | | | | | | |
| **Koufax, Sandy** 1972 | 165 | 87 | 2.76 | 397 | 2,324 | 2,396 |
| 95–27, 1.85 ERA for seasons 1963–66 | | | | | | |
| **Lemon, Bob** 1976 | 207 | 128 | 3.23 | 460 | 2,850 | 1,277 |
| Won 20 or more seven times | | | | | | |
| **Lyons, Ted** 1955 | 260 | 230 | 3.67 | 594 | 4,161 | 1,073 |
| Pitched 27 shutouts | | | | | | |
| **Marichal, Juan** 1983 | 243 | 142 | 2.89 | 471 | 3,509 | 2,303 |
| Only 1.8 walks per nine innings over career | | | | | | |
| **Marquard, Richard (Rube)** 1971 | 201 | 177 | 3.08 | 536 | 3,307 | 1,593 |
| 73–23 in years 1911–13 | | | | | | |
| **Mathewson, Christy** 1936 | 373 | 188 | 2.13 | 636 | 4,782 | 2,502 |
| 80 career shutouts | | | | | | |
| **McGinnity, Joe** 1946 | 247 | 144 | 2.64 | 466 | 3,459 | 1,068 |
| 35–8 in 1904, with an ERA of 1.61 | | | | | | |
| **Nichols, Charles (Kid)** 1949 | 360 | 203 | 2.94 | 621 | 5,084 | 1,885 |
| Won 30 or more games seven straight seasons, 1891–97 | | | | | | |
| **Palmer, Jim** 1990 | 268 | 152 | 2.86 | 558 | 3,948 | 2,212 |
| Won Cy Young Award 1973, 1975, 1976 | | | | | | |
| **Pennock, Herb** 1948 | 240 | 162 | 3.61 | 617 | 3,558 | 1,227 |
| 162–90 as a New York Yankee, 1923–33 | | | | | | |
| **Perry, Gaylord** 1991 | 314 | 265 | 3.10 | 777 | 5,352 | 3,534 |
| Won Cy Young Award in both leagues | | | | | | |
| **Plank, Eddie** 1946 | 327 | 193 | 2.34 | 622 | 4,505 | 2,246 |
| 1.32 ERA in seven World Series games | | | | | | |
| **Radbourn, Charles (Old Hoss)** 1939 | 308 | 191 | 2.67 | 528 | 4,535 | 1,830 |
| 60–12 in 1884, with 679 innings pitched | | | | | | |
| **Rixey, Eppa** 1963 | 266 | 251 | 3.15 | 692 | 4,495 | 1,350 |
| Won 25 games in 1922 | | | | | | |
| **Roberts, Robin** 1976 | 286 | 245 | 3.41 | 676 | 4,689 | 2,357 |
| 28–7 in 1952; five-time NL leader in complete games | | | | | | |
| **Ruffing, Charles (Red)** 1967 | 273 | 225 | 3.80 | 624 | 4,344 | 1,987 |
| .645 winning percentage as a New York Yankee | | | | | | |
| **Rusie, Amos** 1977 | 243 | 160 | 3.07 | 462 | 3,770 | 1,957 |
| Won 30+ games three years | | | | | | |
| **Spahn, Warren** 1973 | 363 | 245 | 3.09 | 750 | 5,244 | 2,583 |
| Won 20 or more games 13 times, including 23 at age 42 | | | | | | |
| **Spalding, Al** 1939 | 48 | 13 | 1.78 | 65 | 540 | 41 |
| First 200-game winner (207–56 from 1871 to 1875 in National Association) | | | | | | |
| **Vance, Clarence (Dazzy)** 1955 | 197 | 140 | 3.24 | 442 | 2,697 | 2,045 |
| 60–15 over two years, 1924–25 | | | | | | |
| **Waddell, George (Rube)** 1946 | 191 | 145 | 2.16 | 407 | 2,961 | 2,316 |
| 349 strikeouts in 1904 | | | | | | |
| **Walsh, Ed** 1946 | 195 | 126 | 1.82 | 430 | 2,964 | 1,736 |
| 40–15 in 1908 with 11 shutouts; all-time ERA leader | | | | | | |

| Player/Year Inducted | Wins | Losses | ERA | Games | IP | SOs |
|---|---|---|---|---|---|---|
| **Ward, Montgomery** 1964 | 161 | 101 | 2.10 | 291 | 2,462 | 920 |
| 87 wins 1879–80 | | | | | | |
| **Welch, Mickey** 1973 | 311 | 207 | 2.71 | 564 | 4,802 | 1,850 |
| 44–11 in 1885 | | | | | | |
| **Wilhelm, Hoyt** 1985 | 143 | 122 | 2.52 | 1,070 | 2,254 | 1,610 |
| All-time leader in games pitched; 227 career saves | | | | | | |
| **Wynn, Early** 1972 | 300 | 244 | 3.54 | 691 | 4,564 | 2,334 |
| Led AL in shutouts at age 40 in 1960 | | | | | | |
| **Young, Denton (Cy)** 1937 | 511 | 313 | 2.63 | 906 | 7,359 | 2,799 |
| All-time leader in wins, losses, complete games, and innings pitched | | | | | | |

## ELECTED FOR MANAGING

Alston, Walter 1983
Comiskey, Charles 1939
Griffith, Clark 1946
Harris, Bucky 1975
Huggins, Miller 1964
Lopez, Al 1977
Mack, Connie 1937

McCarthy, Joe 1957
McGraw, John 1937
McKechnie, Bill 1962
Robinson, Wilbert 1945
Stengel, Casey 1966
Wright, George 1937
Wright, Harry 1953

## ELECTED FOR MERITORIOUS SERVICE

Barlick, Al
Barrow, Edward
Bulkeley, Morgan
Cartwright, Alexander
Chadwick, Henry
Chandler, Happy
Conlan, John (Jocko)
Connolly, Thomas
Evans, William
Foster, Andrew (Rube)
Frick, Ford

Giles, Warren
Harridge, William
Hubbard, Cal
Johnson, B. Bancroft
Klem, William
Landis, Kenesaw Mountain
MacPhail, Larry
Rickey, W. Branch
Veeck, Bill
Weiss, George
Yawkey, Tom

In 1971 Satchel Paige became the first player admitted to Cooperstown based on achievement in the old Negro Leagues. Since then, the following men have been granted the same honor.

Gibson, Josh 1972
Leonard, William "Buck" 1972
Irvin, Monte 1973
Bell, James "Cool Papa" 1974
Johnson, Judy 1975

Charleston, Oscar 1976
DiHigo, Martin 1977
Lloyd, John Henry 1977
Dandridge, Ray 1987

# Other Professional Sports

## GOLF—MEN

### THE SENIOR PGA TOUR

The Senior Tour began with two tournaments in 1980, which offered a total of $250,000 in prize money. In 1991, 42 tournaments were held, paying more than $17 million. All entrants must be qualified members of the PGA, at least 50 years of age. Currently, there are 122 participating players.

### PGA LEADING CAREER MONEY WINNERS

| | | |
|---|---|---|
| 1. | Tom Kite | $6,542,364 |
| 2. | Tom Watson | 5,632,628 |
| 3. | Curtis Strange | 5,614,988 |
| 4. | Jack Nicklaus | 5,268,936 |
| 5. | Lanny Wadkins | 5,172,454 |
| 6. | Payne Stewart | 4,687,959 |
| 7. | Ben Crenshaw | 4,624,941 |
| 8. | Hale Irwin | 4,398,156 |
| 9. | Greg Norman | 4,321,018 |
| 10. | Paul Azinger | 4,117,807 |

**Note**: As of May 19, 1991.

## LEADING MONEY WINNERS, 1934–90
### MEN

| Year | Name | Winnings | Year | Name | Winnings |
|------|------|----------|------|------|----------|
| 1934 | Paul Runyan | $ 6,767 | 1963 | Arnold Palmer | $ 128,230 |
| 1935 | Johnny Revolta | 9,543 | 1964 | Jack Nicklaus | 113,284 |
| 1936 | Horton Smith | 7,682 | 1965 | Jack Nicklaus | 140,752 |
| 1937 | Harry Cooper | 14,138 | 1966 | Billy Casper | 121,944 |
| 1938 | San Snead | 19,534 | 1967 | Jack Nicklaus | 188,998 |
| 1939 | Henry Picard | 10,303 | 1968 | Billy Casper | 205,168 |
| 1940 | Ben Hogan | 10,655 | 1969 | Frank Beard | 164,707 |
| 1941 | Ben Hogan | 18,358 | 1970 | Lee Trevino | 157,037 |
| 1942 | Ben Hogan | 13,143 | 1971 | Jack Nicklaus | 244,490 |
| 1943 | No statistics compiled | | 1972 | Jack Nicklaus | 320,542 |
| 1944 | Byron Nelson | 37,967[1] | 1973 | Jack Nicklaus | 308,362 |
| 1945 | Byron Nelson | 63,335[1] | 1974 | Johnny Miller | 353,021 |
| 1946 | Ben Hogan | 42,556 | 1975 | Jack Nicklaus | 298,149 |
| 1947 | Jimmy Demaret | 27,936 | 1976 | Jack Nicklaus | 266,438 |
| 1948 | Ben Hogan | 32,112 | 1977 | Tom Watson | 310,653 |
| 1949 | San Snead | 31,593 | 1978 | Tom Watson | 362,428 |
| 1950 | San Snead | 35,758 | 1979 | Tom Watson | 462,636 |
| 1951 | Lloyd Mangrum | 26,088 | 1980 | Tom Watson | 530,808 |
| 1952 | Julius Boros | 37,032 | 1981 | Tom Kite | 375,698 |
| 1953 | Lew Worsham | 34,002 | 1982 | Craig Stadler | 446,462 |
| 1954 | Bob Toski | 65,819 | 1983 | Hal Sutton | 426,668 |
| 1955 | Julius Boros | 63,121 | 1984 | Tom Watson | 476,260 |
| 1956 | Ted Kroll | 72,835 | 1985 | Curtis Strange | 542,321 |
| 1957 | Dick Mayer | 65,835 | 1986 | Greg Norman | 653,296 |
| 1958 | Arnold Palmer | 42,607 | 1987 | Curtis Strange | 925,941 |
| 1959 | Art Wall | 53,167 | 1988 | Curtis Strange | 1,147,644 |
| 1960 | Arnold Palmer | 75,262 | 1989 | Tom Kite | 1,395,278 |
| 1961 | Gary Player | 64,540 | 1990 | Greg Norman | 1,165,477 |
| 1962 | Arnold Palmer | 81,448 | | | |

1. Paid in war bonds. **Source:** Professional Golfer's Assn.

## U.S. OPEN

| Year | Winner | Year | Winner |
|------|--------|------|--------|
| 1895 | Horace Rawlins | 1932 | Gene Sarazen |
| 1896 | James Foulis | 1933 | Johynny Goodman |
| 1897 | Joe Lloyd | 1934 | Olin Dutra |
| 1898 | Fred Herd | 1935 | San Parks, Jr. |
| 1899 | Willie Smith | 1936 | Tony Manero |
| 1900 | Harry Vardon | 1937–38 | Ralph Guldahl |
| 1901 | Willie Anderson | 1939 | Byron Nelson |
| 1902 | Laurie Auchterlonie | 1940 | Lawson Little |
| 1903–05 | Willie Anderson | 1941 | Craig Wood |
| 1906 | Alex Smith | 1942–45 | No championship |
| 1907 | Alex Ross | 1946 | Lloyd Mangrum |
| 1908 | Fred McLeod | 1947 | Lew Worsham |
| 1909 | George Sargent | 1948 | Ben Hogan |
| 1910 | Alex Smith | 1949 | Cary Middlecoff |
| 1911–12 | John McDermott | 1950–51 | Ben Hogan |
| 1913 | Francis Ouimet | 1952 | Julius Boros |
| 1914 | Walter Hagen | 1953 | Ben Hogan |
| 1915 | Jerome Travers | 1954 | Ed Furgol |
| 1916 | Charles Evans, Jr. | 1955 | Jack Fleck |
| 1917–18 | No championship | 1956 | Cary Middlecoff |
| 1919 | Walter Hagen | 1957 | Dick Mayer |
| 1920 | Edward Ray | 1958 | Tommy Bolt |
| 1921 | James M. Barnes | 1959 | Billy Casper |
| 1922 | Gene Sarazen | 1960 | Arnold Palmer |
| 1923 | Robert T. Jones, Jr. | 1961 | Gene Littler |
| 1924 | Cyril Walker | 1962 | Jack Nicklaus |
| 1925 | W. MacFarlane | 1963 | Julius Boros |
| 1926 | Robert T. Jones, Jr. | 1964 | Ken Venturi |
| 1927 | Tommy Armour | 1965 | Gary Player |
| 1928 | Johnny Farrell | 1966 | Billy Casper |
| 1929–30 | Robert T. Jones, Jr. | 1967 | Jack Nicklaus |
| 1931 | Billy Burke | 1968 | Lee Trevino |

| Year | Winner | Year | Winner |
|------|--------|------|--------|
| 1969 | Orville Moody | 1980 | Jack Nicklaus |
| 1970 | Tony Jacklin | 1981 | David Graham |
| 1971 | Lee Trevino | 1982 | Tom Watson |
| 1972 | Jack Nicklaus | 1983 | Larry Nelson |
| 1973 | Johnny Miller | 1984 | Fuzzy Zoeller |
| 1974 | Hale Irwin | 1985 | Andy North |
| 1975 | Lou Graham | 1986 | Ray Floyd |
| 1976 | Jerry Pate | 1987 | Scott Simpson |
| 1977 | Hubert Green | 1988–89 | Curtis Strange |
| 1978 | Andy North | 1990 | Hale Irwin |
| 1979 | Hale Irwin | 1991 | Payne Stewart |

## BRITISH OPEN

| Year | Winner | Year | Winner |
|------|--------|------|--------|
| 1860 | Willie Park | 1926–27 | Robert T. Jones, Jr. |
| 1861–62 | Tom Morris, Sr. | 1928–29 | Walter Hagen |
| 1863 | Willie Park | 1930 | Robert T. Jones, Jr. |
| 1864 | Tom Morris, Sr. | 1931 | Tommy D. Armour |
| 1865 | Andrew Strath | 1932 | Gene Sarazen |
| 1866 | Willie Park | 1933 | Denny Shute |
| 1867 | Tom Morris, Sr. | 1934 | Henry Cotton |
| 1868–70 | Tom Morris, Sr. | 1935 | Alfred Perry |
| 1871 | No championship | 1936 | Alfred Padgham |
| 1872 | Tom Morris, Jr. | 1937 | Henry Cotton |
| 1873 | Tom Kidd | 1938 | R.A. Whitcombe |
| 1874 | Mungo Park | 1939 | Richard Burton |
| 1875 | Willie Park | 1940–45 | No championship |
| 1876 | Bob Martin | 1946 | Sam Snead |
| 1877–79 | Jamie Anderson | 1947 | Fred Daly |
| 1880–82 | Robert Ferguson | 1948 | Henry Cotton |
| 1883 | Willie Fernie | 1949–50 | Bobby Locke |
| 1884 | Jack Simpson | 1951 | Max Faulkner |
| 1885 | Bob Martin | 1952 | Bobby Locke |
| 1886 | David Brown | 1953 | Ben Hogan |
| 1887 | Willie Park, Jr. | 1954–56 | Peter Thomson |
| 1888 | Jack Burns | 1957 | Bobby Locke |
| 1889 | Willie Park, Jr. | 1958 | Peter Thomson |
| 1890 | John Ball | 1959 | Gary Player |
| 1891 | Hugh Kirkaldy | 1960 | Ken Nagle |
| (Championship extended from | | 1961–62 | Arnold Palmer |
| 36 to 72 holes) | | 1963 | Bob Charles |
| 1892 | Harold H. Hilton | 1964 | Tony Lema |
| 1893 | William Auchterlonie | 1965 | Peter Thomson |
| 1894–95 | John H. Taylor | 1966 | Jack Nicklaus |
| 1896 | Harry Vardon | 1967 | Roberto DeVicenzo |
| 1897 | Harold H. Hilton | 1968 | Gary Player |
| 1898–99 | Harry Vardon | 1969 | Tony Jacklin |
| 1900 | John H. Taylor | 1970 | Jack Nicklaus |
| 1901 | James Braid | 1971–72 | Lee Trevino |
| 1902 | Alexander Hord | 1973 | Tom Weiskopf |
| 1903 | Harry Vardon | 1974 | Gary Player |
| 1904 | Jack White | 1975 | Tom Watson |
| 1905–06 | James Braid | 1976 | Johnny Miller |
| 1907 | Arnaud Massy | 1977 | Tom Watson |
| 1908 | James Braid | 1978 | Jack Nicklaus |
| 1909 | John H. Taylor | 1979 | Seve Ballesteros |
| 1910 | James Braid | 1980 | Tom Watson |
| 1911 | Harry Vardon | 1981 | Bill Rogers |
| 1912 | Edward ("Ted") Ray | 1982–83 | Tom Watson |
| 1913 | John H. Taylor | 1984 | Seve Ballesteros |
| 1914 | Harry Vardon | 1985 | Sandy Lyle |
| 1915–19 | No championship | 1986 | Greg Norman |
| 1920 | George Duncan | 1987 | Nick Faldo |
| 1921 | Jock Hutchison | 1988 | Seve Ballesteros |
| 1922 | Walter Hagen | 1989 | Mark Calcavecchia |
| 1923 | Arthur G. Havers | 1990 | Nick Faldo |
| 1924 | Walter Hagen | 1991 | Ian Baker-Finch |
| 1925 | James M. Barnes | | |

## MASTERS

| Year | Winner | Year | Winner |
|------|--------|------|--------|
| 1934 | Horton Smith | 1963 | Jack Nicklaus |
| 1935 | Gene Sarazen | 1964 | Arnold Palmer |
| 1936 | Horton Smith | 1965–66 | Jack Nicklaus |
| 1937 | Byron Nelson | 1967 | Gay Brewer, Jr. |
| 1938 | Henry Picard | 1968 | Bob Goalby |
| 1939 | Ralph Guldahl | 1969 | George Archer |
| 1940 | Jimmy Demaret | 1970 | Billy Casper |
| 1941 | Craig Wood | 1971 | Charles Coody |
| 1942 | Byron Nelson | 1972 | Jack Nicklaus |
| 1943–45 | No tournament | 1973 | Tommy Aaron |
| 1946 | Herman Keiser | 1974 | Gary Player |
| 1947 | Jimmy Demaret | 1975 | Jack Nicklaus |
| 1948 | Claude Harman | 1976 | Ray Floyd |
| 1949 | Sam Snead | 1977 | Tom Watson |
| 1950 | Jimmy Demaret | 1978 | Gary Player |
| 1951 | Ben Hogan | 1979 | Fuzzy Zoeller |
| 1952 | Sam Snead | 1980 | Seve Ballesteros |
| 1953 | Ben Hogan | 1981 | Tom Watson |
| 1954 | Sam Snead | 1982 | Craig Stadler |
| 1955 | Cary Middlecoff | 1983 | Seve Ballesteros |
| 1956 | Jack Burke, Jr. | 1984 | Ben Crenshaw |
| 1957 | Doug Ford | 1985 | Bernhard Langer |
| 1958 | Arnold Palmer | 1986 | Jack Nicklaus |
| 1959 | Art Wall, Jr. | 1987 | Larry Mize |
| 1960 | Arnold Palmer | 1988 | Sandy Lyle |
| 1961 | Gary Player | 1989–90 | Nick Faldo |
| 1962 | Arnold Palmer | 1991 | Ian Woosnam |

**Note:** All Masters tournaments are held on the same course at the Augusta National Golf Club, Augusta, Ga.

## PGA

| Year | Winner | Year | Winner |
|------|--------|------|--------|
| 1916 | James M. Barnes | 1958 | Dow Finsterwald |
| 1917–18 | No championship | 1959 | Bob Rosburg |
| 1919 | James M. Barnes | 1960 | Jay Hebert |
| 1920 | Jock Hutchison | 1961 | Jerry Barber |
| 1921 | Walter Hagen | 1962 | Gary Player |
| 1922–23 | Gene Sarazen | 1963 | Jack Nicklaus |
| 1924–27 | Walter Hagen | 1964 | Bobby Nichols |
| 1928–29 | Leo Diegel | 1965 | Dave Marr |
| 1930 | Tommy Armour | 1966 | Al Geiberger |
| 1931 | Tom Creavy | 1967 | Don January |
| 1932 | Olin Dutra | 1968 | Julius Boros |
| 1933 | Gene Sarazen | 1969 | Ray Floyd |
| 1934 | Paul Runyan | 1970 | Dave Stockton |
| 1935 | Johnny Revolta | 1971 | Jack Nicklaus |
| 1936–37 | Denny Shute | 1972 | Gary Player |
| 1938 | Paul Runyan | 1973 | Jack Nicklaus |
| 1939 | Henry Picard | 1974 | Lee Trevino |
| 1940 | Byron Nelson | 1975 | Jack Nicklaus |
| 1941 | Vic Ghezzi | 1976 | Dave Stockton |
| 1942 | Sam Snead | 1977 | Lanny Wadkins |
| 1943 | No championship | 1978 | John Mahaffey |
| 1944 | Bob Hamilton | 1979 | David Graham |
| 1945 | Byron Nelson | 1980 | Jack Nicklaus |
| 1946 | Ben Hogan | 1981 | Larry Nelson |
| 1947 | Jim Ferrier | 1982 | Raymond Floyd |
| 1948 | Ben Hogan | 1983 | Hal Sutton |
| 1949 | Sam Snead | 1984 | Lee Trevino |
| 1950 | Chandler Harper | 1985 | Hubert Green |
| 1951 | Sam Snead | 1986 | Bob Tway |
| 1952 | Jim Turnesa | 1987 | Larry Nelson |
| 1953 | Walter Burkemo | 1988 | Jeff Sluman |
| 1954 | Chick Harbert | 1989 | Payne Stewart |
| 1955 | Doug Ford | 1990 | Wayne Grady |
| 1956 | Jack Burke | 1991 | John Daly |
| 1957 | Lionel Hebert | | |

## GOLF—WOMEN

### LPGA LEADING CAREER MONEY WINNERS

| | | |
|---|---|---|
| 1. | Pat Bradley | $3,639,683 |
| 2. | Betsy King | 3,182,322 |
| 3. | Nancy Lopez | 3,160,017 |
| 4. | Beth Daniel | 3,101,430 |
| 5. | Patty Sheehan | 3,097,350 |
| 6. | Amy Alcott | 2,658,339 |
| 7. | JoAnne Carner | 2,431,899 |
| 8. | Ayako Okamoto | 2,201,955 |
| 9. | Jan Stephenson | 1,868,762 |
| 10. | Cathy Whitworth | 1,721,942 |
| 11. | Hollis Stacy | 1,562,138 |
| 12. | Jane Geddes | 1,445,439 |
| 13. | Rosie Jones | 1,399,541 |
| 14. | Donna Caponi | 1,387,919 |
| 15. | Sally Little | 1,305,893 |

**Note:** As of June 10, 1991.

### LEADING MONEY WINNERS, 1956–90

#### WOMEN

| Year | Name | Winnings | Year | Name | Winnings |
|------|------|----------|------|------|----------|
| 1956 | Marlene Bauer Hagge | $ 20,235 | 1974 | JoAnne Carner | $ 87,094 |
| 1957 | Patty Berg | 16,272 | 1975 | Sandra Palmer | 76,374 |
| 1958 | Beverly Hanson | 12,629 | 1976 | Judy T. Rankin | 150,734 |
| 1959 | Betsy Rawls | 26,774 | 1977 | Judy T. Rankin | 122,890 |
| 1960 | Louis Euggs | 16,892 | 1978 | Nancy Lopez | 189,813 |
| 1961 | Mickey Wright | 22,238 | 1979 | Nancy Lopez | 197,488 |
| 1962 | Mickey Wright | 21,654 | 1980 | Beth Daniel | 231,000 |
| 1963 | Mickey Wright | 31,269 | 1981 | Beth Daniel | 206,977 |
| 1964 | Mickey Wright | 29,800 | 1982 | JoAnne Carner | 310,399 |
| 1965 | Kathy Whitworth | 28,658 | 1983 | JoAnne Carner | 291,404 |
| 1966 | Kathy Whitworth | 33,517 | 1984 | Betsy King | 266,771 |
| 1967 | Kathy Whitworth | 32,937 | 1985 | Nancy Lopez | 416,472 |
| 1968 | Kathy Whitworth | 48,379 | 1986 | Pat Bradley | 492,021 |
| 1969 | Carol Mann | 49,152 | 1987 | Ayako Okamoto | 466,034 |
| 1970 | Kathy Whitworth | 30,235 | 1988 | Sherri Turner | 350,851 |
| 1971 | Kathy Whitworth | 41,181 | 1989 | Betsy King | 654,132 |
| 1972 | Kathy Whitworth | 65,063 | 1990 | Beth Daniel | 863,578 |
| 1973 | Kathy Whitworth | 82,864 | | | |

**Source:** Professional Golfer's Assn.

### U.S. WOMEN'S OPEN

| Year | Winner | Year | Winner |
|------|--------|------|--------|
| 1946 | Patty Berg | 1968 | Susie Berning |
| 1947 | Betty Jameson | 1969–70 | Donna Caponi |
| 1948 | Babe Zaharias | 1971 | JoAnne Carner |
| 1949 | Louise Suggs | 1972–73 | Susie Berning |
| 1950 | Babe Zaharias | 1974 | Sandra Haynie |
| 1951 | Betsy Rawls | 1975 | Sandra Palmer |
| 1952 | Louise Suggs | 1976 | JoAnne Carner |
| 1953 | Betsy Rawls | 1977–78 | Hollis Stacy |
| 1954 | Babe Zaharias | 1979 | Jerilyn Britz |
| 1955 | Fay Crocker | 1980 | Amy Alcott |
| 1956 | Kathy Cornelius | 1981 | Pat Bradley |
| 1957 | Betsy Rawls | 1982 | Janet Anderson |
| 1958–59 | Mickey Wright | 1983 | Jan Stephenson |
| 1960 | Betsy Rawls | 1984 | Hollis Stacy |
| 1961 | Mickey Wright | 1985 | Kathy Baker |
| 1962 | Murle Breer | 1986 | Jane Geddes |
| 1963 | Mary Mills | 1987 | Laura Davies |
| 1964 | Mickey Wright | 1988 | Liselotte Neumann |
| 1965 | Carol Mann | 1989–90 | Betsy King |
| 1966 | Sandra Spuzich | 1991 | Meg Mallon |
| 1967 | Catherine LaCoste | | |

## LPGA CHAMPIONSHIP

| Year | Winner | Year | Winner |
|------|--------|------|--------|
| 1955 | Beverly Hanson | 1974 | Sandra Haynie |
| 1956 | Marlene Hagge | 1975 | Kathy Whitworth |
| 1957 | Louise Suggs | 1976 | Betty Burfeindt |
| 1958 | Mickey Wright | 1977 | Chako Higuchi |
| 1959 | Betsy Rawls | 1978 | Nancy Lopez |
| 1960–61 | Mickey Wright | 1979 | Donna Caponi |
| 1962 | Judy Kimball | 1980 | Sally Little |
| 1963 | Mickey Wright | 1981 | Donna Caponi |
| 1964 | Mary Mills | 1982 | Jan Stephenson |
| 1965 | Sandra Haynie | 1983–84 | Patty Sheehan |
| 1966 | Gloria Ehret | 1985 | Nancy Lopez |
| 1967 | Kathy Whitworth | 1986 | Pat Bradley |
| 1968 | Sandra Post | 1987 | Jane Geddes |
| 1969 | Betsy Rawls | 1988 | Sherri Turner |
| 1970 | Shirley Englehorn | 1989 | Nancy Lopez |
| 1971 | Kathy Whitworth | 1990 | Beth Daniel |
| 1972 | Kathy Ahern | 1991 | Meg Mallon |
| 1973 | Mary Mills | | |

## TENNIS—MEN

### THE GRAND SLAM OF TENNIS

Only six players have won the French Open, the Australian Open, the U.S. Open, and Wimbledon in the same year. Don Budge became the first "grand slammer" in 1938. Maureen Connolly became the first woman winner in 1953 when she won straight-set victories in all four final-round matches. Australian Rod Laver won the Grand Slam in 1962 and 1969, making him the only repeat winner. Margaret Court swept through the tournaments in 1970. Steffi Graf became the youngest to accomplish the feat in 1988. Martina Navratilova won the four tournaments consecutively but not in the same calendar year; she won the French Open in 1984, following 1983 victories in the other three.

Eleven players have won each of the four tournaments but never in the same year. Several others have dominated tennis without winning all the events. Sweden's Bjorn Borg won five consecutive Wimbledon titles but failed to win the U.S. Open in nine attempts.

### MEN'S TENNIS COUNCIL

Modern "open" tennis tournaments, in which both professionals and amateurs compete, began in 1968, although World Championship Tennis staged an abbreviated professional tour the previous year. In 1985 the WCT merged with the Grand Prix Circuit. What is now the Men's Tennis Council was formed in 1974 to administer professional tennis. More than $42 million in prize money was awarded in 77 tournaments in 1990.

### U.S. CHAMPIONSHIPS

| Year | Winner | Year | Winner |
|------|--------|------|--------|
| 1881–87 | Richard D. Sears | 1906 | William J. Clothier |
| 1888–89 | H.W. Slocum, Jr. | 1907–11 | William A. Larned |
| 1890–92 | Oliver S. Campbell | 1912–13 | Maurice E. McLoughlin |
| 1893–94 | Robert D. Wrenn | 1914 | Richard N. Williams |
| 1895 | Frederick H. Hovey | 1915 | William M. Johnston |
| 1896–97 | Robert D. Wrenn | 1916 | Richard N. Williams |
| 1898–1900 | Malcolm D. Whitman | 1917–18 | R.L. Murray |
| 1901–02 | William A. Larned | 1919 | William M. Johnston |
| 1903 | H. Laurie Doherty | 1920–25 | Bill Tilden |
| 1904 | Holcombe Ward | 1926–27 | Rene Lacoste |
| 1905 | Beals C. Wright | 1928 | Henri Cochet |

| Year | Winner | Year | Winner |
|------|--------|------|--------|
| 1929 | Bill Tilden | 1962 | Rod Laver |
| 1930 | John H. Doeg | 1963 | Rafael Osuna |
| 1931–32 | H. Ellsworth Vines | 1964 | Roy Emerson |
| 1933–34 | Fred J. Perry | 1965 | Manuel Santana |
| 1935 | Wilmer L. Allison | 1966 | Fred Stolle |
| 1936 | Fred J. Perry | 1967 | John Newcombe |
| 1937–38 | Don Budge | 1968[1] | Arthur Ashe |
| 1939 | Bobby Riggs | 1969 | Rod Laver |
| 1940 | Donald McNeill | 1970 | Ken Rosewall |
| 1941 | Bobby Riggs | 1971 | Stan Smith |
| 1942 | Frederick R. Schroeder, Jr. | 1972 | Ilie Nastase |
| 1943 | Joseph R. Hunt | 1973 | John Newcombe |
| 1944–45 | Frank Parker | 1974 | Jimmy Connors |
| 1946–47 | Jack Kramer | 1975 | Manuel Orantes |
| 1948–49 | Pancho Gonzales | 1976 | Jimmy Connors |
| 1950 | Arthur Larsen | 1977 | Guillermo Vilas |
| 1951–52 | Frank Sedgman | 1978 | Jimmy Connors |
| 1953 | Tony Trabert | 1979–81 | John McEnroe |
| 1954 | E. Victor Seixas, Jr. | 1982–83 | Jimmy Connors |
| 1955 | Tony Trabert | 1984 | John McEnroe |
| 1956 | Ken Rosewall | 1985–87 | Ivan Lendl |
| 1957 | Malcolm J. Anderson | 1988 | Mats Wilander |
| 1958 | Ashley J. Cooper | 1989 | Boris Becker |
| 1959–60 | Neale Fraser | 1990 | Pete Sampras |
| 1961 | Roy Emerson | 1991 | Stefan Edberg |

1. Became Open Championships (amateurs and professionals).

## WIMBLEDON

| Year | Winner | Year | Winner |
|------|--------|------|--------|
| 1877 | Spencer W. Gore | 1940–45 | Not held |
| 1878 | P. Frank Hadow | 1946 | Yvon Petra |
| 1879–80 | John T. Hartley | 1947 | Jack Kramer |
| 1881–86 | William Renshaw | 1948 | Bob Falkenburg |
| 1887 | Herbert F. Lawford | 1949 | Ted Schroeder |
| 1888 | Ernest Renshaw | 1950 | Budge Patty |
| 1889 | William Renshaw | 1951 | Dick Savitt |
| 1890 | William J. Hamilton | 1952 | Frank Sedgman |
| 1891–92 | Wilfred Baddeley | 1953 | Vic Seixas |
| 1893–94 | Joshua Pim | 1954 | Jaroslav Drobny |
| 1895 | Wilfred Baddeley | 1955 | Tony Trabert |
| 1896 | Harold S. Mahoney | 1956–57 | Lew Hoad |
| 1897–1900 | Reggie F. Doherty | 1958 | Ashley Cooper |
| 1901 | Arthur W. Gore | 1959 | Alex Olmedo |
| 1902–06 | H. Laurie Doherty | 1960 | Neale Fraser |
| 1907 | Norman E. Brooks | 1961–62 | Rod Laver |
| 1908–09 | Arthur W. Gore | 1963 | Chuck McKinley |
| 1910–13 | Anthony F. Wilding | 1964–65 | Roy Emerson |
| 1914 | Norman E. Brookes | 1966 | Manuel Santana |
| 1915–18 | Not held | 1967 | John Newcombe |
| 1919 | Gerald L. Patterson | 1968–69[1] | Rod Laver |
| 1920–21 | Bill Tilden | 1970–71 | John Newcombe |
| 1922 | Gerald L. Patterson | 1972 | Stan Smith |
| 1923 | William M. Johnston | 1973 | Jan Kodes |
| 1924 | Jean Borotra | 1974 | Jimmy Connors |
| 1925 | Rene Lacoste | 1975 | Arthur Ashe |
| 1926 | Jean Borotra | 1976–80 | Bjorn Borg |
| 1927 | Henri Cochet | 1981 | John McEnroe |
| 1928 | Rene Lacoste | 1982 | Jimmy Connors |
| 1929 | Henri Cochet | 1983–84 | John McEnroe |
| 1930 | Bill Tilden | 1985–86 | Boris Becker |
| 1931 | Sidney B. Wood, Jr. | 1987 | Pat Cash |
| 1932 | Ellsworth Vines | 1988 | Stefan Edberg |
| 1933 | Jack Crawford | 1989 | Boris Becker |
| 1934–36 | Fred J. Perry | 1990 | Stefan Edberg |
| 1937–38 | Don Budge | 1991 | Michael Stich |
| 1939 | Bobby Riggs | | |

1. Became Open Championships (amateurs and professionals).

## FRENCH CHAMPIONSHIPS

| Year | Winner | Year | Winner |
|------|--------|------|--------|
| 1925 | Rene Lacoste | 1958 | Mervyn Rose |
| 1926 | Henri Cochet | 1959–60 | Nicola Pietrangeli |
| 1927 | Rene Lacoste | 1961 | Manuel Santana |
| 1928 | Henri Cochet | 1962 | Rod Laver |
| 1929 | Rene Lacoste | 1963 | Roy Emerson |
| 1930 | Henri Cochet | 1964 | Manuel Santana |
| 1931 | Jean Borotra | 1965 | Fred Stolle |
| 1932 | Henri Cochet | 1966 | Tony Roche |
| 1933 | John H. Crawford | 1967 | Roy Emerson |
| 1934 | Gottfried von Cramm | 1968[1] | Ken Rosewall |
| 1935 | Fred J. Perry | 1969 | Rod Laver |
| 1936 | Gottfried von Cramm | 1970–71 | Jan Kodes |
| 1937 | Henner Henkel | 1972 | Andres Gimeno |
| 1938 | Don Budge | 1973 | Ilie Nastase |
| 1939 | Donald McNeill | 1974–75 | Bjorn Borg |
| 1940 | Not held | 1976 | Adriano Panatta |
| 1941–42 | Bernard Destremau | 1977 | Guillermo Vilas |
| 1943–45 | Yvon Petra | 1978–81 | Bjorn Borg |
| 1946 | Marcel Bernard | 1982 | Mats Wilander |
| 1947 | Joseph Asboth | 1983 | Yannick Noah |
| 1948–49 | Frank Parker | 1984 | Ivan Lendl |
| 1950 | Budge Patty | 1985 | Mats Wilander |
| 1951–52 | Jaroslav Drobny | 1986–87 | Ivan Lendl |
| 1953 | Ken Rosewall | 1988 | Mats Wilander |
| 1954–55 | Tony Trabert | 1989 | Michael Chang |
| 1956 | Lew Hoad | 1990 | Andrés Gómez |
| 1957 | Sven Davidson | 1991 | Jim Courier |

1. Became Open Championships (amateurs and professionals).

## AUSTRALIAN CHAMPIONSHIPS

| Year | Winner | Year | Winner |
|------|--------|------|--------|
| 1905 | Rodney Heath | 1949–50 | Frank Sedgman |
| 1906 | Tony Wilding | 1951 | Richard Savitt |
| 1907 | Horace M. Rice | 1952 | Ken McGregor |
| 1908 | Fred Alexander | 1953 | Ken Rosewall |
| 1909 | Tony Wilding | 1954 | Mervyn Rose |
| 1910 | Rodney Heath | 1955 | Ken Rosewall |
| 1911 | Norman Brooks | 1956 | Lew Hoad |
| 1912 | J. Cecil Parke | 1957–58 | Ashley Cooper |
| 1913 | E.F. Parker | 1959 | Alex Olmedo |
| 1914 | Pat O'Hara Wood | 1960 | Rod Laver |
| 1915 | Francis G. Lowe | 1961 | Roy Emerson |
| 1916–18 | Not held | 1962 | Rod Laver |
| 1919 | A.R.F. Kingscote | 1963–67 | Roy Emerson |
| 1920 | Pat O'Hara Wood | 1968 | Bill Bowrey |
| 1921 | Rhys H. Gemmell | 1969[1] | Rod Laver |
| 1922–23 | Pat O'Hara Wood | 1970 | Arthur Ashe |
| 1924–25 | James Anderson | 1971–72 | Ken Rosewall |
| 1926 | John Hawkes | 1973 | John Newcombe |
| 1927 | Gerald Patterson | 1974 | Jimmy Connors |
| 1928 | Jean Borotra | 1975 | John Newcombe |
| 1929 | John C. Gregory | 1976 | Mark Edmondson |
| 1930 | Gar Moon | 1977 | Roscoe Tanner |
| 1931–33 | Jack Crawford | 1977 | Vitas Gerulaitis |
| 1934 | Fred J. Perry | 1978–79 | Guillermo Vilas |
| 1935 | Jack Crawford | 1980 | Brian Teacher |
| 1936 | Adrian Quist | 1981–82 | Johan Kriek |
| 1937 | Vivian B. McGrath | 1983–84 | Mats Wilander |
| 1938 | Don Budge | 1985 | Stefan Edberg |
| 1939 | John Bromwich | 1986 | Not held; moved to Jan. 1987 |
| 1940 | Adrian Quist | | |
| 1941–45 | Not held | 1987 | Stefan Edberg |
| 1946 | John Bromwich | 1988 | Mats Wilander |
| 1947 | Dinny Pails | 1989–90 | Ivan Lendl |
| 1948 | Adrian Quist | 1991 | Boris Becker |

1. Became Open Championships (amateurs and professionals).

## TENNIS—WOMEN

### BEST ANNUAL W-L RECORDS 1980–90

| Player | W-L | Pct. | Year |
|--------|-----|------|------|
| Martina Navratilova | 86–1 | .989 | 1983 |
| Steffi Graf | 86–2 | .977 | 1989 |
| Martina Navratilova | 78–2 | .975 | 1984 |
| Steffi Graf | 75–2 | .974 | 1987 |
| Martina Navratilova | 90–3 | .968 | 1982 |
| Martina Navratilova | 89–3 | .967 | 1986 |
| Steffi Graf | 72–3 | .960 | 1988 |
| Martina Navratilova | 84–5 | .944 | 1985 |
| Steffi Graf | 72–5 | .935 | 1990 |
| Chris Evert | 75–6 | .926 | 1982 |

## U.S. CHAMPIONSHIPS

| Year | Winner | Year | Winner |
|------|--------|------|--------|
| 1887 | Ellen Hensell | 1938–40 | Alice Marble |
| 1888–89 | Bertha L. Townsend | 1941 | Sarah Palfrey Cooke |
| 1890 | Ellen C. Roosevelt | 1942–44 | Pauline Betz |
| 1891–92 | Mabe Caty | 1945 | Sarah Palfrey Cooke |
| 1893 | Aline Terry | 1946 | Pauline Betz |
| 1894 | Helen Hellwig | 1947 | Louise Brough |
| 1895 | Juliette Atkinson | 1948–50 | Margaret Osborne duPont |
| 1896 | Elizabeth Moore | 1951–53 | Maureen Connolly |
| 1897–98 | Juliette Atkinson | 1954–55 | Doris Hart |
| 1899 | Marion Jones | 1956 | Shirley Fry |
| 1900 | Myrtle McAleer | 1957–58 | Althea Gibson |
| 1901 | Elizabeth Moore | 1959 | Maria Bueno |
| 1902 | Marion Jones | 1960–61 | Darlene Hard |
| 1903 | Elizabeth Moore | 1962 | Margaret Smith |
| 1904 | May Sutton | 1963–64 | Maria Bueno |
| 1905 | Elizabeth Moore | 1965 | Margaret Smith |
| 1906 | Helen Homans | 1966 | Maria Bueno |
| 1907 | Evelyn Sears | 1967 | Billie Jean King |
| 1908 | Maud Barger-Wallach | 1968[1] | Virginia Wade |
| 1909–11 | Hazel Hotchkiss | 1969–70 | Margaret Smith Court |
| 1912–14 | Mary Browne | 1971–72 | Billie Jean King |
| 1915–16 | Molla Bjurstedt | 1973 | Margaret Smith Court |
| 1917 | Not held | 1974 | Billie Jean King |
| 1918 | Molla Bjurstedt | 1975–78 | Chris Evert |
| 1919 | Hazel Hotchkiss Wightman | 1979 | Tracy Austin |
| 1920–22 | Molla Bjurstedt Mallory | 1980 | Chris Evert Lloyd |
| 1923–25 | Helen Wills | 1981 | Tracy Austin |
| 1926 | Molla Bjurstedt Mallory | 1982 | Chris Evert Lloyd |
| 1927–29 | Helen Wills | 1983–84 | Martina Navratilova |
| 1930 | Betty Nuthall | 1985 | Hanna Mandlikova |
| 1931 | Helen Wills Moody | 1986–87 | Martina Navratilova |
| 1932–35 | Helen Jacobs | 1988–89 | Steffi Graf |
| 1936 | Alice Marble | 1990 | Gabriela Sabatini |
| 1937 | Anita Lizana | 1991 | Monica Seles |

1. Became Open Championships (amateurs and professionals).

## WIMBLEDON

| Year | Winner | Year | Winner |
|------|--------|------|--------|
| 1884–85 | Maud Watson | 1897 | Blanche Hillyard |
| 1886[1] | Blanche Bingley | 1898 | Charlotte Cooper |
| 1887–88 | Charlotte Dod | 1899–1900 | Blanche Hillyard |
| 1889 | Blanche Bingley Hillyard | 1901 | Charlotte Cooper Sterry |
| 1890 | Lena Rice | 1902 | Muriel Robb |
| 1891–93 | Charlotte Dod | 1903–04 | Dorothea Douglass |
| 1894 | Blanche Hillyard | 1905 | May Sutton |
| 1895–96 | Charlotte Cooper | 1906 | Dorothea Douglass |

| Year | Winner | Year | Winner |
|------|--------|------|--------|
| 1907 | May Sutton | 1951 | Doris Hart |
| 1908 | Charlotte Sterry | 1952–54 | Maureen Connolly |
| 1909 | Dora Boothby | 1955 | Louise Brough |
| 1910–11 | Dorothea Lambert Chambers | 1956 | Shirley Fry |
| | | 1957–58 | Althea Gibson |
| 1912 | Ethel Larcombe | 1959–60 | Maria Bueno |
| 1913–14 | Dorothea Lambert Chambers | 1961 | Angela Mortimer |
| | | 1962 | Karen Hantze Susman |
| 1915–18 | Not held | 1963 | Margaret Smith |
| 1919–23[2] | Suzanne Lenglen | 1964 | Maria Bueno |
| 1924 | Kathleen McKane | 1965 | Margaret Smith |
| 1925 | Suzanne Lenglen | 1966–68[3] | Billie Jean King |
| 1926 | Kathleen McKane Godfree | 1969 | Ann Jones |
| | | 1970 | Margaret Smith Court |
| 1927–29 | Helen Wills | 1971 | Evonne Goolagong |
| 1930 | Helen Wills Moody | 1972–73 | Billie Jean King |
| 1931 | Cilly Aussem | 1974 | Chris Evert |
| 1932–33 | Helen Wills Moody | 1975 | Billie Jean King |
| 1934 | Dorothy Round | 1976 | Chris Evert |
| 1935 | Helen Wills Moody | 1977 | Virginia Wade |
| 1936 | Helen Jacobs | 1978–79 | Martina Navratilova |
| 1937 | Dorothy Round | 1980 | Evonne Goolagong Cawley |
| 1938 | Helen Wills Moody | | |
| 1939 | Alice Marble | 1981 | Chris Evert Lloyd |
| 1940–45 | Not held | 1982–87 | Martina Navratilova |
| 1946 | Pauline Betz | 1988–89 | Steffi Graf |
| 1947 | Margaret Osborne | 1990 | Martina Navratilova |
| 1948–50 | Louise Brough | 1991 | Steffi Graf |

1. Through 1921, championship decided on challenge round system. If no finalist, holder did not defend.
2. Challenge round abolished.  3. Became Open Championships (amateurs and professionals).

## FRENCH CHAMPIONSHIPS

| Year | Winner | Year | Winner |
|------|--------|------|--------|
| 1897–99 | Adine Massor | 1955 | Angela Mortimer |
| 1900 | Y. Prevost | 1956 | Althea Gibson |
| 1901 | P. Girod | 1957 | Shirley Bloomer |
| 1902–03 | Adine Massor | 1958 | Zsuzsi Kormoczy |
| 1904–05 | Katie Gilou | 1959 | Christine Truman |
| 1906 | Katie Gilou Fenwick | 1960 | Darlene Hard |
| 1907 | Casse De Kerme | 1961 | Ann Haydon |
| 1908 | Katie Gilou Fenwick | 1962 | Margaret Smith |
| 1909–12 | Jeanne Matthey | 1963 | Lesley Turner |
| 1913–14 | Marguerite Broquedis | 1964 | Margaret Smith |
| 1915–19 | Not held | 1965 | Lesley Turner |
| 1920–23 | Suzanne Lenglen | 1966 | Ann Jones |
| 1924 | Diddie Vlasto | 1967 | Francoise Durr |
| 1925[1]–26 | Suzanne Lenglen | 1968[2] | Nancy Richey |
| 1927 | Kea Bouman | 1969–70 | Margaret Smith Court |
| 1928–29 | Helen Wills | 1971 | Evonne Goolagong |
| 1930 | Helen Wills Moody | 1972 | Billie Jean King |
| 1931 | Cilly Aussem | 1973 | Margaret Smith Court |
| 1932 | Helen Wills Moody | 1974–75 | Chris Evert |
| 1933–34 | Margaret Scriven | 1976 | Sue Barker |
| 1935–37 | Hilde Sperling | 1977 | Mima Jausovec |
| 1938–39 | Simone Mathieu | 1978 | Virginia Ruzici |
| 1940–45 | Not held | 1979–80 | Chris Evert Lloyd |
| 1946 | Margaret Osborne | 1981 | Hana Mandlikova |
| 1947 | Patricia Todd | 1982 | Martina Navratilova |
| 1948 | Nelly Landry | 1983 | Chris Evert Lloyd |
| 1949 | Margaret Osborne duPont | 1984 | Martina Navratilova |
| 1950 | Doris Hart | 1985–86 | Chris Evert Lloyd |
| 1951 | Shirley Fry | 1987–88 | Steffi Graf |
| 1952 | Doris Hart | 1989 | Arantxa Sanchez Vicario |
| 1953–54 | Maureen Connolly | 1990–91 | Monica Seles |

1. Before 1925 the French Championships were limited to residents of France.  2. Became Open Championships (amateurs and professionals).

## AUSTRALIAN CHAMPIONSHIPS

| Year | Winner | Year | Winner |
|------|--------|------|--------|
| 1922–23 | Margaret Molesworth | 1959 | Mary Carter Reitano |
| 1924 | Sylvia Lance | 1960–66 | Margaret Smith |
| 1925–26 | Daphne Akhurst | 1967 | Nancy Richey |
| 1927 | Edna Boyd | 1968 | Billie Jean King |
| 1928–30 | Daphne Akhurst | 1969[1]–71 | Margaret Smith Court |
| 1931–32 | Coral Buttsworth | 1972 | Virginia Wade |
| 1933–34 | Joan Hartigan | 1973 | Margaret Smith Court |
| 1935 | Dorothy Round | 1974–75 | Evonne Goolagong |
| 1936 | Joan Hartigan | 1976 | Evonne Goolagong Cawley |
| 1937 | Nancye Wynne Bolton | 1977 | Kerry Melville Reid |
| 1938 | Dorothy Bundy | 1977 | Evonne Goolagong Cawley |
| 1939 | Emily Westacott | 1978 | Chris O'Neil |
| 1940 | Nancye Wynne Bolton | 1979 | Barbara Jordan |
| 1941–45 | Not held | 1980 | Hana Mandlikova |
| 1946–48 | Nancye Wynne Bolton | 1981 | Martina Navratilova |
| 1949 | Doris Hart | 1982 | Chris Evert Lloyd |
| 1950 | Louise Brough | 1983 | Martina Navratilova |
| 1951 | Nancye Wynne Bolton | 1984 | Chris Evert Lloyd |
| 1952 | Thelma Long | 1985 | Martina Navratilova |
| 1953 | Maureen Connolly | 1986 | Not held; |
| 1954 | Thelma Long | | moved to Jan. 1987 |
| 1955 | Beryl Penrose | 1987 | Hana Mandlikova |
| 1956 | Mary Carter | 1988–90 | Steffi Graf |
| 1957 | Shirley Fry | 1991 | Monica Seles |
| 1958 | Angela Mortimer | | |

1. Became Open Championships (amateurs and professionals).

## PROFESSIONAL BOWLERS ASSOCIATION

The PBA was founded by 33 charter members who competed in three 1959 tournaments for prizes worth a total of $49,500. The traditional Winter Tour, which has been augmented and expanded into three separate seasonal tours, now pays more than $6 million in prize money.

**Source:** Professional Bowlers Assn.

## PBA LEADING MONEY WINNERS, 1959–90

| Year | Name | Winnings | Year | Name | Winnings |
|------|------|----------|------|------|----------|
| 1959 | Dick Weber | $ 7,672 | 1975 | Earl Anthony | $107,585 |
| 1960 | Don Carter | 22,525 | 1976 | Earl Anthony | 110,833 |
| 1961 | Dick Weber | 26,280 | 1977 | Mark Roth | 105,583 |
| 1962 | Don Carter | 49,972 | 1978 | Mark Roth | 134,500 |
| 1963 | Dick Weber | 46,333 | 1979 | Mark Roth | 124,517 |
| 1964 | Bob Strampe | 33,592 | 1980 | Wayne Webb | 116,700 |
| 1965 | Dick Weber | 47,675 | 1981 | Earl Anthony | 164,735 |
| 1966 | Wayne Zahn | 54,720 | 1982 | Earl Anthony | 134,760 |
| 1967 | Dave Davis | 54,165 | 1983 | Earl Anthony | 135,605 |
| 1968 | Jim Stefanich | 67,375 | 1984 | Mark Roth | 158,712 |
| 1969 | Billy Hardwick | 64,160 | 1985 | Mike Aulby | 201,200 |
| 1970 | Mike McGrath | 52,049 | 1986 | Walter Ray Williams, Jr. | 145,550 |
| 1971 | Johnny Petraglia | 85,065 | 1987 | Pete Weber | 179,516 |
| 1972 | Don Johnson | 56,648 | 1988 | Brian Voss | 225,485 |
| 1973 | Don McCune | 69,000 | 1989 | Mike Aulby | 298,237 |
| 1974 | Earl Anthony | 99,585 | 1990 | Auleto Monacelli | 204,775 |

## LADIES PRO BOWLING TOUR (LPBT) LEADING CAREER MONEY WINNERS, 1981–90

| | Bowler | Winnings | | Bowler | Winnings |
|--|--------|----------|--|--------|----------|
| 1. | Lisa Wagner | $396,549 | 6. | Lorrie Nichols | $284,787 |
| 2. | Aleta Sill | 380,721 | 7. | Cindy Coburn-Carroll | 241,474 |
| 3. | Robin Romeo | 327,590 | 8. | Jeanne Maiden | 221,959 |
| 4. | Tish Johnson | 295,192 | 9. | Cheryl Daniels | 204,372 |
| 5. | Nikki Gianulias | 288,619 | 10. | Leanne Barrette | 190,530 |

**Source:** LPBT.

# BOXING CHAMPIONS

Although many governing bodies now issue and certify their own championships, the two most widely accepted are the World Boxing Association (WBA) and World Boxing Council (WBC). In addition, the International Boxing Federation (IBF) has recently risen to a position of near parity with the WBA and WBC.

## HEAVYWEIGHTS (over 195 lbs.)

| Year | Name |
|------|------|
| 1882–92 | John L. Sullivan |
| 1892–97 | James J. Corbett |
| 1897–99 | Robert Fitzsimmons |
| 1899–1905 | James J. Jeffries |
| 1905–06 | Marvin Hart |
| 1906–08 | Tommy Burns |
| 1908–15 | Jack Johnson |
| 1915–19 | Jess Willard |
| 1919–26 | Jack Dempsey |
| 1926–28 | Gene Tunney[1] |
| 1928–30 | vacant |
| 1930–32 | Max Schmeling |
| 1932–33 | Jack Sharkey |
| 1933–34 | Primo Carnera |
| 1934–35 | Max Baer |
| 1935–37 | James J. Braddock |
| 1937–49 | Joe Louis[1] |
| 1949–51 | Ezzard Charles |
| 1951–52 | Joe Walcott |
| 1952–56 | Rocky Marciano[1] |
| 1956–59 | Floyd Patterson |
| 1959–60 | Ingemar Johansson |
| 1960–62 | Floyd Patterson |
| 1962–64 | Sonny Liston |
| 1964–67 | Cassius Clay[1] (Muhammad Ali) |
| 1970–73 | Joe Frazier |
| 1973–74 | George Foreman |
| 1974–78 | Muhammad Ali |
| 1978–79 | Leon Spinks, Muhammad Ali[1] |
| 1978 | Ken Norton (WBC), Larry Holmes (WBC) |
| 1979 | John Tate (WBA) |
| 1980 | Mike Weaver (WBA) |
| 1982 | Michael Dokes (WBA) |
| 1983 | Gerrie Coetzee (WBA) |
| 1984 | Tim Witherspoon (WBC), Pinklon Thomas (WBC), Greg Page (WBA) |
| 1985 | Tony Tubbs (WBA) |
| 1986 | Tim Witherspoon (WBA), Trevor Berbick (WBC), Mike Tyson (WBC), James "Bonecrusher" Smith (WBA) |
| 1987–89 | Mike Tyson |
| 1990 | Buster Douglas, Evander Holyfield |

## LIGHT HEAVYWEIGHTS (175–194 lbs.)

| Year | Name |
|------|------|
| 1903 | Jack Root, George Gardner |
| 1903–05 | Bob Fitzsimmons |
| 1905–12 | Philadelphia Jack O'Brien[1] |
| 1912–16 | Jack Dillon |
| 1916–20 | Battling Levinsky |
| 1920–22 | Georges Carpentier |
| 1922–23 | Battling Siki |
| 1923–25 | Mike McTigue |
| 1925–26 | Paul Berlenbach |
| 1926–27 | Jack Delaney[1] |
| 1927–29 | Tommy Loughran[1] |
| 1930–34 | Maxie Rosenbloom |
| 1934–35 | Bob Olin |
| 1935–39 | John Henry Lewis[1] |
| 1939 | Melio Bettina |
| 1939–41 | Billy Conn[1] |
| 1941 | Anton Christoforidis |
| 1941–48 | Gus Lesnevich, Freddie Mills |
| 1948–50 | Freddie Mills |
| 1950–52 | Joey Maxim |
| 1952–60 | Archie Moore |
| 1961–62 | vacant |
| 1962–63 | Harold Johnson |
| 1963–65 | Willie Pastrano |
| 1965–66 | Jose Torres |
| 1966–68 | Dick Tiger |
| 1968–74 | Bob Foster,[1] John Conteh (WBA) |
| 1975–77 | John Conteh (WBC), Miguel Cuello (WBC), Victor Galindez (WBA) |
| 1978 | Mike Rossman (WBA), Mate Parlov (WBC), Marvin Johnson (WBC) |
| 1979 | Victor Galindez (WBA), Matthew Saad Muhammad (WBC) |
| 1980 | Eddie Mustafa Muhammad (WBA) |
| 1981 | Michael Spinks (WBA), Dwight Braxton (WBC) |
| 1983 | Michael Spinks undisputed |
| 1986 | Marvin Johnson (WBA), Dennis Andries (WBC) |
| 1987 | Thomas Hearns (WBC), Leslie Stewart (WBA), Virgil Hill (WBA), Don Lalonde (WBC) |
| 1988 | Ray Leonard (WBC)[2], Dennis Andries |
| 1989 | Virgil Hill (WBA), Jeff Harding (WBC) |
| 1990 | Dennis Andries (WBC), Prince Charles Williams (IBF) |
| 1991 | Thomas Hearns (WBA) |

## CURRENT BOXING CHAMPIONS

| Class | WBA | WBC | IBF |
|-------|-----|-----|-----|
| Heavyweight | Evander Holyfield United States | Evander Holyfield United States | Evander Holyfield United States |
| Cruiserweight | Bobby Czyz United States | Massimiliano Duran Italy | Jeff Lampkin United States |
| Light Heavyweight | Thomas Hearns United States | Dennis Andries United States | Charles Williams United States |
| Super Middleweight | Victor Cordoba Panama | Mauro Galvano Italy | Lindell Holmes United States |
| Middleweight | Mike McCallum Jamaica | Julian Jackson Virgin Islands | James Toney United States |
| Jr. Middleweight | Gilbert Dele France | Terry Norris United States | Gianfranco Rosi Italy |
| Welterweight | Meldrick Taylor United States | Simon Brown United States | Simon Brown United States |
| Jr. Welterweight | Loreto Garza United States | Julio Cesar Chavez Mexico | Vacant |
| Lightweight | Pernell Whitaker United States | Pernell Whitaker United States | Pernell Whitaker United States |
| Jr. Lightweight | Brian Mitchell South Africa | Azumah Nelson Ghana | Troy Dorsey United States |
| Featherweight | Park Yung-Kyun South Korea | Marcos Villasana Mexico | Troy Dorsey United States |
| Jr. Featherweight | Luis Mendoza Colombia | Kiyoshi Hatanaka Japan | Welcome N'Cita South Africa |
| Bantamweight | Luisito Espinosa Phillipines | Greg Richardson United States | Orlando Canizales United States |
| Flyweight | Kim Yong-Gang South Korea | Muangchai Kittikasem Taiwan | Dave McCauley Ireland |

**Note**: As of Aug. 1, 1991. **Source**: Ring magazine.

## MIDDLEWEIGHTS (160–174 lbs.)

| Year | Name |
|------|------|
| 1884–91 | Jack "Nonpareil" Dempsey |
| 1891–97 | Bob Fitzsimmons[2] |
| 1897–1907 | Tommy Ryan[2] |
| 1907–08 | Stanley Ketchel, Billy Papke |
| 1908–10 | Stanley Ketchel |
| 1911–13 | vacant |
| 1913 | Frank Klaus, George Chip |
| 1914–17 | Al McCoy |
| 1917–20 | Mike O'Dowd |
| 1920–23 | Johnny Wilson |
| 1923–26 | Harry Greb |
| 1926–31 | Tiger Flowers, Mickey Walker |
| 1931–32 | Gorilla Jones (NBA) |
| 1932–37 | Marcel Thil |
| 1938 | Al Hostak (NBA), Solly Krieger (NBA) |
| 1939–40 | Al Hostak (NBA) |
| 1941–47 | Tony Zale |
| 1947–48 | Rocky Graziano |
| 1948 | Tony Zale, Marcel Cerdan |
| 1949–51 | Jake LaMotta |
| 1951 | Ray Robinson, Randy Turpin, Ray Robinson[2] |
| 1953–55 | Carl "Bobo" Olson |
| 1955–57 | Ray Robinson |
| 1957 | Gene Fullmer (NBA), Ray Robinson, Carmen Basilio |
| 1958 | Ray Robinson |
| 1959 | Gene Fullmer (NBA), Ray Robinson (N.Y.) |
| 1960 | Gene Fullmer (NBA), Paul Pender (N.Y. & Mass.) |
| 1961 | Gene Fullmer (NBA), Terry Downes (N.Y., Mass., and Europe) |
| 1962 | Gene Fullmer (NBA), Dick Tiger (NBA), Paul Pender (N.Y. and Mass.) |
| 1963 | Dick Tiger |
| 1963–65 | Joey Giardello |
| 1965–66 | Dick Tiger |

| Year | Name |
|---|---|
| 1966–67 | Emile Griffith |
| 1967 | Nino Benvenuti |
| 1967–68 | Emile Griffith |
| 1968–70 | Nino Benvenuti |
| 1970–77 | Carlos Monzon |
| 1977–78 | Rodrigo Valdez |
| 1978–79 | Hugo Corro |
| 1979–80 | Alan Minter, Marvin Hagler |
| 1987 | Ray Leonard[2] (WBC), Thomas Hearns (WBC), Sumbo Kalambay (WBA) |
| 1988 | Iran Barkley (WBC) |
| 1989 | Sumbo Kalambay (WBA), Mike McCallum (WBA), Roberto Duran (WBC) |
| 1990 | Julian Jackson (WBC), James Toney (IBF) |

## WELTERWEIGHTS (147–153 lbs.)

| Year | Name |
|---|---|
| 1892–94 | Billy Smith |
| 1894–96 | Tommy Ryan |
| 1896 | Kid McCoy[2] |
| 1900 | Rube Ferns, Matty Matthews |
| 1901 | Rube Ferns |
| 1901–04 | Joe Walcott |
| 1904–06 | Dixie Kid, Joe Walcott, Honey Mellody |
| 1907–11 | Mike Sullivan |
| 1911–15 | vacant |
| 1915–19 | Ted Lewis |
| 1919–22 | Jack Britton |
| 1922–26 | Mickey Walker |
| 1926 | Pete Latzo |
| 1927–29 | Joe Dundee |
| 1929 | Jackie Fields |
| 1930 | Jack Thompson, Tommy Freeman |
| 1931 | Tommy Freeman, Jack Thompson, Lou Brouillard |
| 1932 | Jackie Fields |
| 1933 | Young Corbett, Jimmy McLarnin |
| 1934 | Barney Ross, Jimmy McLarnin |
| 1935–38 | Barney Ross |
| 1938–40 | Henry Armstrong |
| 1940–41 | Fritzie Zivic |
| 1941–46 | Fred Cochrane |
| 1946 | Marty Servo,[2] Ray Robinson |
| 1946–50 | Ray Robinson[2] |
| 1951 | Johnny Bratton (NBA) |
| 1951–54 | Kid Gavilan |
| 1954–55 | Johnny Saxton |
| 1955 | Tony De Marco, Carmen Basilio |
| 1956 | Carmen Basilio, Johnny Saxton, Carmen Basilio |
| 1957 | Carmen Basilio[2] |
| 1958–60 | Virgil Akins, Don Jordan |
| 1960 | Benny Paret |
| 1961 | Emile Griffith, Benny Paret |
| 1962 | Emile Griffith |
| 1963 | Luis Rodriguez, Emile Griffith |
| 1964–66 | Emile Griffith[2] |
| 1966–69 | Curtis Cokes |
| 1969–70 | Jose Napoles, Billy Backus |
| 1971–75 | Jose Napoles |
| 1975–76 | John Stracey (WBC), Angel Espada (WBA) |
| 1976–79 | Carlos Palomino (WBC), Jose Cuevas (WBA) |
| 1979 | Wilfredo Benitez (WBC), Sugar Ray Leonard (WBC) |
| 1980 | Roberto Duran (WBC), Thomas Hearns (WBA), Sugar Ray Leonard (WBC) |
| 1981–82 | Sugar Ray Leonard[2] |
| 1983 | Donald Curry (WBA), Milton McCrory (WBC) |
| 1985 | Donald Curry |

| Year | Name |
|---|---|
| 1986 | Lloyd Honeyghan (WBC) |
| 1987 | Mark Breland (WBA), Marlon Starling (WBA), Jorge Vaca (WBC) |
| 1988 | Thomas Molinares (WBA), Lloyd Honeyghan (WBC) |
| 1989 | Thomas Molinares (WBA),[1] Mark Breland (WBA), Marlon Starling (WBC) |
| 1990 | Aaron Davis (WBA), Maurice Blocker (WBC), Meldrick Taylor (WBA) |
| 1991 | Simon Brown (WBC, IBF) |

## LIGHTWEIGHTS (131–135 lbs.)

| Year | Name |
|---|---|
| 1896–99 | Kid Lavigne |
| 1899–1902 | Frank Erne |
| 1902–08 | Joe Gans |
| 1908–10 | Battling Nelson |
| 1910–12 | Ad Wolgast |
| 1912–14 | Willie Ritchie |
| 1914–17 | Freddie Welsh |
| 1917–25 | Benny Leonard[2] |
| 1925 | Jimmy Goodrich, Rocky Kansas |
| 1926–30 | Sammy Mandell |
| 1930 | Al Singer, Tony Canzoneri |
| 1930–33 | Tony Canzoneri |
| 1933–35 | Barney Ross[2] |
| 1935–36 | Tony Canzoneri |
| 1936–38 | Lou Ambers |
| 1938 | Henry Armstrong |
| 1939 | Lou Ambers |
| 1940 | Lew Jenkins |
| 1941–43 | Sammy Angott |
| 1944 | Sammy Angott (NBA), J. Zurita (NBA) |
| 1945–51 | Ike Williams |
| 1951–52 | James Carter |
| 1952 | Lauro Salas, James Carter |
| 1953–54 | James Carter |
| 1954 | Paddy De Marco, James Carter |
| 1955 | James Carter, Bud Smith |
| 1956 | Bud Smith, Joe Brown |
| 1956–62 | Joe Brown |
| 1962–65 | Carlos Ortiz |
| 1965 | Ismael Laguna |
| 1965–68 | Carlos Ortiz |
| 1968–69 | Teo Cruz |
| 1969–70 | Mando Ramos |
| 1970 | Ismael Laguna, Ken Buchanan (WBA) |
| 1971 | Mando Ramos (WBC), Pedro Carrasco (WBC) |
| 1972–79 | Roberto Duran[1] (WBA) |
| 1972 | Pedro Carrasco, Mando Ramos, Chango Carmona, Rodolfo Gonzalez (all WBC) |
| 1974–76 | Guts Ishimatsu (WBC) |
| 1976–77 | Esteban De Jesus (WBC) |
| 1979 | Jim Watt (WBC), Ernesto Espana (WBA) |
| 1980 | Hilmer Kenty (WBA) |
| 1981 | Alexis Arguello (WBC), Sean O'Grady (WBA), Arturo Frias (WBA) |
| 1982–84 | Ray Mancini (WBC) |
| 1983 | Edwin Rosario (WBC) |
| 1984 | Livingstone Bramble (WBA), Jose Luis Ramirez (WBC) |
| 1985 | Hector (Macho) Camacho (WBC) |
| 1986 | Edwin Rosario (WBA), Jose Luis Ramirez (WBC) |
| 1987 | Julio Cesar Chavez (WBA) |
| 1988 | Julio Cesar Chavez[1] (WBA) |
| 1989 | Edwin Rosario (WBA) |
| 1990 | Juan Nazario (WBA), Pernell Whitaker |

## FEATHERWEIGHTS (126–129 lbs.)

| Year | Name |
|---|---|
| 1900–01 | Terry McGovern, Young Corbett[2] |
| 1901–12 | Abe Attell |
| 1912–23 | Johnny Kilbane |
| 1923 | Eugene Criqui, Johnny Dundee |
| 1923–25 | Johnny Dundee[2] |
| 1925–27 | Kid Kaplan[2] |
| 1927–28 | Benny Bass, Ton Canzoneri |
| 1928–29 | Andre Routis |
| 1929–32 | Battling Battalino[2] |
| 1932–34 | Tommy Paul |
| 1933–36 | Freddie Miller |
| 1936–37 | Petey Sarron |
| 1937–38 | Henry Armstrong[2] |
| 1938–40 | Joey Archibald |
| 1940–41 | Harry Jeffra |
| 1942–48 | Willie Pep |
| 1948–49 | Sandy Saddler |
| 1949–50 | Willie Pep |
| 1950–57 | Sandy Saddler[2] |
| 1957–59 | Hogan (Kid) Bassey |
| 1959–63 | Davey Moore |
| 1963–64 | Sugar Ramos |
| 1964–67 | Vicente Saldivar[2] |
| 1968–71 | Paul Rojas (WBA), Sho Saijo (WBA) |
| 1971 | Antonio Gomez (WBA), Kuniaki Shibada (WBC) |
| 1972 | Ernesto Marcel[2] (WBA), Clemente Sanchez[2] (WBC), Jose Legra (WBA) |
| 1973 | Eder Jofre (WBC) |
| 1974 | Ruben Olivares (WBA), Alexis Arguello (WBA), Bobby Chacon (WBC) |
| 1975 | Ruben Olivares (WBA), David Kotey (WBC) |
| 1976 | Danny Lopez (WBC) |
| 1977 | Rafael Ortega (WBA) |
| 1978 | Cecillio Lastra (WBA), Eusebio Pedrosa (WBA) |
| 1980 | Salvador Sanchez (WBC) |
| 1982 | Juan LaPorte (WBC) |
| 1984 | Wilfredo Gomez (WBC), Azumah Nelson (WBC) |
| 1985 | Barry McGuigan (WBA) |
| 1986 | Steve Cruz (WBA) |
| 1987 | Antonio Esparragoza (WBA) |
| 1988 | Jeff Fenech (WBC) |
| 1990 | Park Young-Kyun (WBA) |
| 1991 | Troy Dorsey (IBF) |

**Note:** WBC = World Boxing Council; WBA = World Boxing Assn.; NBA = National Boxing Assn. 1. Stripped of title. 2. Abandoned title.
**Sources:** *KO* magazine; *Ring* magazine.

## AUTOMOBILE RACING
### Grand Prix Racing

The tradition of road racing in Formula One cars developed in Europe, with the French inaugurating the Grand Prix in 1906; the winner averaged about 12 miles per hour. For many years the races were held on public roadways, but safety considerations have encouraged the building of specialized race courses.

"Formula One" refers to certain weight and engine size restrictions placed on the cars. Although the exact specifications have been changed many times, this standardization is intended to emphasize competitiveness and driving skill. The cars today are powered by rear-mounted, V-8 gasoline engines producing 450–475 horsepower, and can attain speeds of approximately 200 miles per hour.

## FORMULA ONE CHAMPIONS, 1950–90

| Year | Driver | Country | Car |
|------|--------|---------|-----|
| 1950 | Giuseppe Farina | Italy | Alfa Roméo |
| 1951 | Juan Manuel Fangio | Argentina | Alfa Roméo |
| 1952 | Alberto Ascari | Italy | Ferrari |
| 1953 | Alberto Ascari | Italy | Ferrari |
| 1954 | Juan Manuel Fangio | Argentina | Mercedes/Maserati |
| 1955 | Juan Manuel Fangio | Argentina | Mercedes |
| 1956 | Juan Manuel Fangio | Argentina | Lancia/Ferrari |
| 1957 | Juan Manuel Fangio | Argentina | Maserati |
| 1958 | Mike Hawthorne | Great Britain | Ferrari |
| 1959 | Jack Brabham | Australia | Cooper Climax |
| 1960 | Jack Brabham | Australia | Cooper Climax |
| 1961 | Phil Hill | United States | Ferrari |
| 1962 | Graham Hill | Great Britain | BRM |
| 1963 | Jim Clark | Great Britain | Lotus Climax |
| 1964 | John Surtees | Great Britain | Ferrari |
| 1965 | Jim Clark | Great Britain | Lotus Climax |
| 1966 | Jack Brabham | Australia | Brabham Repco |
| 1967 | Denis Hulme | New Zealand | Brabham Repco |
| 1968 | Graham Hill | Great Britain | Lotus Ford |
| 1969 | Jackie Stewart | Great Britain | Matra Ford |
| 1970 | Jochen Rindt | Austria | Lotus Ford |
| 1971 | Jackie Stewart | Great Britain | Tyrrell Ford |
| 1972 | Emerson Fittipaldi | Brazil | Lotus Ford |
| 1973 | Jackie Stewart | Great Britain | Tyrrell Ford |
| 1974 | Emerson Fittipaldi | Brazil | McLaren Ford |
| 1975 | Niki Lauda | Austria | Ferrari |
| 1976 | James Hunt | Great Britain | McLaren Ford |
| 1977 | Niki Lauda | Austria | Ferrari |
| 1978 | Mario Andretti | United States | Lotus Ford |
| 1979 | Jody Scheckter | South Africa | Ferrari |
| 1980 | Alan Jones | Australia | Williams Ford |
| 1981 | Nelson Piquet | Brazil | Brabham Ford |
| 1982 | Keke Rosberg | Finland | Williams Ford |
| 1983 | Nelson Piquet | Brazil | Brabham BMW Turbo |
| 1984 | Niki Lauda | Austria | McLaren TAG Porsche Turbo |
| 1985 | Alain Prost | France | McLaren TAG Porsche Turbo |
| 1986 | Alain Prost | France | McLaren TAG Porsche Turbo |
| 1987 | Nelson Piquet | Brazil | Williams Honda Turbo |
| 1988 | Ayrton Senna | Brazil | McLaren Honda Turbo |
| 1989 | Alain Prost | France | McLaren Honda Turbo |
| 1990 | Ayrton Senna | Brazil | McLaren Honda Turbo |

## Indianapolis 500

A number of U.S. states and cities banned automobile racing on public roads during the early 1900s, leading to the development of closed-circuit courses. The Indianapolis Motor Speedway, a 2.5-mile macadam oval, was built in 1909 (it was paved with brick in 1911). The first Indy 500 was run two years later. The American Automobile Association, troubled by a series of fatal crashes, stopped sactioning races, and in 1956, the United States Auto Club (USAC) took over the Indy 500.

## INDY 500 TOTAL PRIZE MONEY, SELECTED YEARS

| Year | Total | Year | Total |
|------|-------|------|-------|
| 1911 | $ 27,550 | 1983 | $2,411,450 |
| 1920 | 93,550 | 1984 | 2,795,899 |
| 1930 | 96,250 | 1985 | 3,271,025 |
| 1940 | 85,525 | 1986 | 4,001,450 |
| 1950 | 201,035 | 1987 | 4,490,375 |
| 1960 | 369,150 | 1988 | 5,025,400 |
| 1970 | 1,000,002 | 1989 | 5,723,725 |
| 1980 | 1,503,225 | 1990 | 6,325,803 |
| 1981 | 1,605,375 | 1991 | 7,009,150 |
| 1982 | 2,067,475 | | |

## INDY 500, 1911–91

| Year | Winner | Time | MPH |
|------|--------|------|-----|
| **UNDER AAA SANCTION** | | | |
| 1911 | Ray Harroun | 6:42:08 | 74.602 |
| 1912 | Joe Dawson | 6:21:06 | 78.719 |
| 1913 | Juses Goux | 6:35:05 | 75.933 |
| 1914 | Rene Thomas | 6:03:45 | 82.474 |
| 1915 | Ralph DePalma | 5:33:55 | 89.840 |
| 1916 | Dario Resta | 3:34:17[1] | 84.001 |
| 1919 | Howard Wilcox | 5:40:42 | 88.050 |
| 1920 | Gaston Chevrolet | 5:38:32 | 88.618 |
| 1921 | Tommy Milton | 5:34:34 | 89.621 |
| 1922 | Jimmy Murphy | 5:17:30 | 94.484 |
| 1923 | Tommy Milton | 5:29:50 | 90.954 |
| 1924 | L.L. Corum and Joe Boyer | 5:05:23 | 98.234 |
| 1925 | Peter DePaolo | 4:56:39 | 101.127 |
| 1926 | Frank Lockhart | 4:10:14[2] | 95.904 |
| 1927 | George Souders | 5:07:33 | 97.545 |
| 1928 | Louis Meyer | 5:01:33 | 99.482 |
| 1929 | Ray Keech | 5:07:25 | 97.585 |
| 1930 | Billy Arnold | 4:58:39 | 100.448 |
| 1931 | Louis Schneider | 5:10:27 | 96.629 |
| 1932 | Fred Frame | 4:48:03 | 104.144 |
| 1933 | Louis Meyer | 4:48:00 | 104.162 |
| 1934 | William Cummings | 4:46:05 | 104.863 |
| 1935 | Kelly Petillo | 4:42:22 | 106.240 |
| 1936 | Louis Meyer | 4:35:03 | 109.069 |
| 1937 | Wilbur Shaw | 4:24:07 | 113.580 |
| 1938 | Floyd Roberts | 4:15:58 | 117.200 |
| 1939 | Wilbur Shaw | 4:20:47 | 115.035 |
| 1940 | Wilbur Shaw | 4:22:31 | 114.277 |
| 1941 | Floyd Davis and Mauri Rose | 4:20:36 | 115.117 |
| 1946 | George Robson | 4:21:16 | 114.820 |
| 1947 | Mauri Rose | 4:17:52 | 116.338 |
| 1948 | Mauri Rose | 4:10:23 | 119.814 |
| 1949 | Bill Holland | 4:07:15 | 121.327 |
| 1950 | Johnnie Parsons | 2:46:55[3] | 124.002 |
| 1951 | Lee Wallard | 3:57:38 | 126.244 |
| 1952 | Troy Ruttman | 3:52:41 | 128.922 |
| 1953 | Bill Vukovich | 3:53:01 | 128.740 |
| 1954 | Bill Vukovich | 3:49:17 | 130.840 |
| 1955 | Bob Sweikert | 3:53:59 | 128.209 |
| **UNDER USAC SANCTION** | | | |
| 1956 | Pat Flaherty | 3:53:28 | 128.490 |
| 1957 | Sam Hanks | 3:41:14 | 135.601 |
| 1958 | Jim Bryan | 3:44:13 | 133.791 |
| 1959 | Rodger Ward | 3:40:49 | 135.857 |
| 1960 | Jim Rathmann | 3:36:11 | 138.767 |
| 1961 | A.J. Foyt, Jr. | 3:35:37 | 139.131 |
| 1962 | Rodger Ward | 3:33:50 | 140.293 |
| 1963 | Parnelli Jones | 3:29:35 | 143.137 |
| 1964 | A.J. Foyt, Jr. | 3:23:35 | 147.350 |
| 1965 | Jim Clark | 3:19:05 | 150.686 |
| 1966 | Graham Hill | 3:27:52 | 144.317 |
| 1967 | A.J. Foyt, Jr. | 3:18:24 | 151.207 |
| 1968 | Bobby Unser | 3:16:13 | 152.882 |
| 1969 | Mario Andretti | 3:11:14 | 156.867 |
| 1970 | Al Unser | 3:12:37 | 155.749 |
| 1971 | Al Unser | 3:10:11 | 157.735 |
| 1972 | Mark Donohue | 3:04:05 | 162.962 |
| 1973 | Gordon Johncock | 2:05:26[4] | 159.036 |
| 1974 | Johnny Rutherford | 3:09:10 | 158.589 |
| 1975 | Bobby Unser | 2:54:55[5] | 149.213 |
| 1976 | Johnny Rutherford | 1:42:52[6] | 148.725 |
| 1977 | A.J. Foyt, Jr. | 3:05:57 | 161.331 |
| 1978 | Al Unser | 3:05:54 | 161.363 |
| 1979 | Rick Mears | 3:08:47 | 158.899 |
| 1980 | Johnny Rutherford | 3:29:59 | 142.862 |
| 1981 | Bobby Unser | 3:35:41 | 139.084 |
| 1982 | Gordon Johncock | 3:05:09 | 162.029 |
| 1983 | Tom Sneva | 3:05:03 | 162.117 |
| 1984 | Rick Mears | 3:30:21 | 163.612 |
| 1985 | Danny Sullivan | 3:16:06 | 152.982 |
| 1986 | Bobby Rahal | 2:55:43 | 170.722 |
| 1987 | Al Unser | 3:04:59 | 162.175 |
| 1988 | Rick Mears | 3:27:10 | 144.809 |
| 1989 | Emerson Fittipaldi | 2:59:01 | 167.581 |
| 1990 | Arie Luyendyk | 2:41:18 | 185.984[7] |
| 1991 | Rick Mears | 2:50:01 | 176.457 |

1. 300 miles (scheduled). 2. 400 miles (rain). 3. 345 miles (rain). 4. 332.5 miles (rain). 5. 435 miles (rain). 6. 255 miles (rain). 7. Track record.
**Source:** Indianapolis Motor Speedway Hall of Fame and Museum.

## Stock Car Racing

### DAYTONA 500 WINNERS, 1959–91

| Year | Driver | Avg. speed (mph) |
|------|--------|------------------|
| 1959 | Lee Petty | 135.521 |
| 1960 | Junior Johnson | 124.740 |
| 1961 | Marvin Panch | 149.601 |
| 1962 | Fireball Roberts | 152.529 |
| 1963 | Tiny Lund | 151.566 |
| 1964 | Richard Petty | 154.334 |
| 1965 | Fred Lorenzen | 141.539 |
| 1966 | Richard Petty | 160.627 |
| 1967 | Mario Andretti | 146.926 |
| 1968 | Cale Yarborough | 143.251 |
| 1969 | LeeRoy Yarbrough | 157.950 |
| 1970 | Pete Hamilton | 149.601 |
| 1971 | Richard Petty | 144.462 |
| 1972 | A.J. Foyt, Jr. | 161.550 |
| 1973 | Richard Petty | 157.205 |
| 1974 | Richard Petty | 140.894 |
| 1975 | Benny Parsons | 153.649 |
| 1976 | David Pearson | 152.181 |
| 1977 | Cale Yarborough | 153.218 |
| 1978 | Bobby Allison | 159.730 |
| 1979 | Richard Petty | 143.977 |
| 1980 | Buddy Baker | 177.602 |
| 1981 | Richard Petty | 169.651 |
| 1982 | Bobby Allison | 153.991 |
| 1983 | Cale Yarborough | 155.979 |
| 1984 | Cale Yarborough | 150.994 |
| 1985 | Bill Elliott | 172.265 |
| 1986 | Geoff Bodine | 148.124 |
| 1987 | Bill Elliott | 176.263 |
| 1988 | Bobby Allison | 137.531 |
| 1989 | Darrell Waltrip | 148.466 |
| 1990 | Derrike Cope | 165.761 |
| 1991 | Ernie Irvan | 148.148 |

**Source:** NASCAR.

## NASCAR

The National Association for Stock Car Auto Racing (NASCAR) first sponsored a Grand National championship in 1949. The 27 Winston Cup races, covering at least 400 miles, are now contested on 17 designated speedways around the country.

### 1990 WINSTON CUP MONEY LEADERS

| Position | Driver | Money won |
|---|---|---|
| 1 | Dale Earnhardt | $3,083,056 |
| 2 | Mark Martin | 1,302,958 |
| 3 | Geoff Bodine | 1,131,222 |
| 4 | Bill Elliott | 1,090,730 |
| 5 | Morgan Shepherd | 666,915 |

### WINSTON CUP WINNERS, 1959–90

| Year | Driver | Points |
|---|---|---|
| 1959 | Lee Petty | 11,792 |
| 1960 | Rex White | 21,164 |
| 1961 | Ned Jarrett | 27,272 |
| 1962 | Joe Weatherly | 30,836 |
| 1963 | Joe Weatherly | 33,398 |
| 1964 | Richard Petty | 40,252 |
| 1965 | Ned Jarrett | 38,824 |
| 1966 | David Pearson | 35,638 |
| 1967 | Richard Petty | 42,472 |
| 1968 | David Pearson | 3,499 |
| 1969 | David Pearson | 4,170 |
| 1970 | Bobby Isaac | 3,911 |
| 1971 | Richard Petty | 4,435 |
| 1972 | Richard Petty | 8,701 |
| 1973 | Benny Parsons | 7,173 |
| 1974 | Richard Petty | 5,037 |
| 1975 | Richard Petty | 4,783 |
| 1976 | Cale Yarborough | 4,644 |
| 1977 | Cale Yarborough | 5,000 |
| 1978 | Cale Yarborough | 4,841 |
| 1979 | Richard Petty | 4,830 |
| 1980 | Dale Earnhardt | 4,661 |
| 1981 | Darrell Waltrip | 4,880 |
| 1982 | Darrell Waltrip | 4,489 |
| 1983 | Bobby Allison | 4,667 |
| 1984 | Terry Labonte | 4,508 |
| 1985 | Darrell Waltrip | 4,292 |
| 1986 | Dale Earnhardt | 4,468 |
| 1987 | Dale Earnhardt | 4,696 |
| 1988 | Bill Elliott | 4,488 |
| 1989 | Rusty Wallace | 4,176 |
| 1990 | Dale Earnhardt | 4,430 |

## THOROUGHBRED RACING

### HORSE OF THE YEAR (ECLIPSE AWARD)

| Year | Horse | Year | Horse |
|---|---|---|---|
| 1936 | Granville | 1941 | Whirlaway |
| 1937 | War Admiral | 1942 | Whirlaway |
| 1938 | Seabiscuit | 1943 | Count Fleet |
| 1939 | Challedon | 1944 | Twilight Tear |
| 1940 | Challedon | 1945 | Busher |

| | | | |
|---|---|---|---|
| 1946 | Assault | 1969 | Arts and Letters |
| 1947 | Armed | 1970 | Personality |
| 1948 | Citation | 1971 | Ack Ack |
| 1949 | Capot | 1972 | Secretariat |
| 1950 | Hill Prince | 1973 | Secretariat |
| 1951 | Counterpoint | 1974 | Forego |
| 1952 | Native Dancer | 1975 | Forego |
| 1953 | Tom Fool | 1976 | Forego |
| 1954 | Native Dancer | 1977 | Seattle Slew |
| 1955 | Nashua | 1978 | Affirmed |
| 1956 | Swaps | 1979 | Affirmed |
| 1957 | Bold Ruler | 1980 | Spectacular Bid |
| 1958 | Round Table | 1981 | John Henry |
| 1959 | Sword Dancer | 1982 | Conquistador Cielo |
| 1960 | Kelso | 1983 | All Along |
| 1961 | Kelso | 1984 | John Henry |
| 1962 | Kelso | 1985 | Spend a Buck |
| 1963 | Kelso | 1986 | Lady's Secret |
| 1964 | Kelso | 1987 | Ferdinand |
| 1965 | Moccasin | 1988 | Alysheba |
| 1966 | Buckpasser | 1989 | Sunday Silence |
| 1967 | Damascus | 1990 | Criminal Type |
| 1968 | Dr. Fager | | |

**Source:** The Jockey Club.

## THE BREEDERS' CUP

Billed as thoroughbred racing's most glamorous and exciting day of the year, these races (one for each standard category of sex, distance, and surface) attract the finest horses in the world, with unprecedented purses of $1 million to $3 million per race. The site changes from year to year.

### JUVENILE

Purse: $1 mil.; distance: 1 1/16 miles (previous years 1 mile, except 1986).

| Year | Winner | Jockey | Time |
|---|---|---|---|
| 1984 | Chief's Crown | Don MacBeth | 1:36.1 |
| 1985 | Tasso | Laffit Pincay, Jr. | 1:36.1 |
| 1986 | Capote | Laffit Pincay, Jr. | 1:43.4 |
| 1987 | Success Express | José Santos | 1:35.1 |
| 1988 | Is It True | Laffit Pincay, Jr. | 1:36.3 |
| 1989 | Rhythm | Craig Perret | 1:43.3 |
| 1990 | Fly So Free | José Santos | 1:43.2 |

### JUVENILE FILLIES

Purse: $1 mil.; distance: 1 1/16 miles (1 mile in 1984, '85, '87).

| | | | |
|---|---|---|---|
| 1984 | Outstandingly | Walter Guerra | 1:37.4 |
| 1985 | Twilight Ridge | Jorge Velasquez | 1:35.4 |
| 1986 | Brave Raj | Pat Valenzuela | 1:43.1 |
| 1987 | Epitome | Pat Day | 1:36.2 |
| 1988 | Open Mind | Angel Cordero, Jr. | 1:46.3 |
| 1989 | Go For Wand | Randy Romero | 1:44.1 |
| 1990 | Meadow Star | José Santos | 1:44.0 |

### BREEDERS' CUP SPRINT

Purse: $1 mil.; distance: 6 furlongs.

| | | | |
|---|---|---|---|
| 1984 | Eillo | Craig Perret | 1:10.1 |
| 1985 | Precisionist | Chris McCarron | 1:08.2 |
| 1986 | Smile | Jacinto Vasquez | 1:08.2 |
| 1987 | Very Subtle | Pat Valenzuela | 1:08.4 |
| 1988 | Gulch | Angel Cordero, Jr. | 1:10.2 |
| 1989 | Dancing Spree | Angel Cordero, Jr. | 1:09.0 |
| 1990 | Safely Kept | Craig Perret | 1:09.3 |

### BREEDERS' CUP MILE

Purse: $1 mil.; distance: 1 mile, turf.

| | | | |
|---|---|---|---|
| 1984 | Royal Heroine | Fernando Toro | 1:32.3 |
| 1985 | Cozzene | Walter Guerra | 1:35.0 |
| 1986 | Last Tycoon | Yves Saint-Martin | 1:35.1 |
| 1987 | Miesque | Freddie Head | 1:32.4 |
| 1988 | Miesque | Freddie Head | 1:38.3 |
| 1989 | Steinlen | José Santos | 1:37.1 |
| 1990 | Royal Academy | Lester Piggott | 1:35.1 |

### THE DISTAFF

Purse: $1 mil.; distance: 1 1/4 miles. (1 1/8 mi. after 1987.)

| | | | |
|---|---|---|---|
| 1984 | Princess Rooney | Ed Delahoussaye | 2:02.2 |
| 1985 | Life's Magic | Angel Cordero, Jr. | 2:01.0 |
| 1986 | Lady's Secret | Pat Day | 2:01.1 |
| 1987 | Sacahuista | Randy Romero | 2:02.4 |
| 1988 | Personal Ensign | Randy Romero | 1:52.0 |
| 1989 | Bayakoa | Laffit Pincay, Jr. | 1:47.2 |
| 1990 | Bayakoa | Laffit Pincay, Jr. | 1:49.1 |

### BREEDERS' CUP TURF

Purse: $2 mil.; distance: 1 1/2 miles, turf.

| | | | |
|---|---|---|---|
| 1984 | Lashkari | Yves Saint-Martin | 2:25.1 |
| 1985 | Pebbles | Pat Eddery | 2:27.0 |
| 1986 | Manila | José Santos | 2:25.2 |
| 1987 | Theatrical | Pat Day | 2:24.2 |
| 1988 | Great Communicator | Roy Sibille | 2:35.1 |
| 1989 | Prized | Ed Delahoussaye | 2:28.0 |
| 1990 | In The Wings | Gary Stevens | 2.29.3 |

### CLASSIC

Purse: $3 mil.; distance: 1 1/4 miles.

| | | | |
|---|---|---|---|
| 1984 | Wild Again | Pat Day | 2:03.2 |
| 1985 | Proud Truth | Jorge Velasquez | 2:00.4 |
| 1986 | Skywalker | Laffit Pincay, Jr. | 2:00.2 |
| 1987 | Ferdinand | Bill Shoemaker | 2:01.2 |
| 1988 | Alysheba | Chris McCarron | 2:04.4 |
| 1989 | Sunday Silence | Chris McCarron | 2:00.1 |
| 1990 | Unbridled | Pat Day | 2.02.1 |

**Source:** Breeders' Cup Limited.

### THE TRIPLE CROWN WINNERS

In more than 100 years, only 11 horses have won all three jewels of the triple crown, the Kentucky Derby, the Preakness, and the Belmont Stakes:

| Horse | Year |
|---|---|
| Sir Barton | 1919 |
| Gallant Fox | 1930 |
| Omaha | 1935 |
| War Admiral | 1937 |
| Whirlaway | 1941 |
| Count Fleet | 1943 |
| Assault | 1946 |
| Citation | 1948 |
| Secretariat | 1973 |
| Seattle Slew | 1977 |
| Affirmed | 1978 |

## KENTUCKY DERBY, 1900–91

Site: Churchill Downs, Louisville, Kentucky
Distance: 1¼ miles

| Year | Horse | Jockey | Time |
|---|---|---|---|
| 1900 | Lt. Gibson | J. Boland | 2:06¼ |
| 1901 | His Eminence | J. Winkfield | 2:07¾ |
| 1902 | Alan-a-Dale | J. Winkfield | 2:08¾ |
| 1903 | Judge Himes | H. Booker | 2:09.0 |
| 1904 | Elwood | F. Prior | 2:08½ |
| 1905 | Agile | J. Martin | 2:10¾ |
| 1906 | Sir Huon | R. Troxler | 2:08.4 |
| 1907 | Pink Star | A. Minder | 2:12.3 |
| 1908 | Stone Street | A. Pickens | 2:15.1 |
| 1909 | Wintergreen | V. Powers | 2:08.1 |
| 1910 | Donau | F. Herbert | 2:06.2 |
| 1911 | Meridan | G. Archibald | 2:05.0 |
| 1912 | Worth | C. H. Shilling | 2:09.2 |
| 1913 | Donerall | R. Goose | 2:04.4 |
| 1914 | Old Rosebud | J. McCabe | 2:03.2 |
| 1915 | Regret | J. Notter | 2:05.2 |
| 1916 | George Smith | J. Loftus | 2:04.3 |
| 1917 | Omar Khayyam | C. Borel | 2:04.0 |
| 1918 | Exterminator | W. Knapp | 2:10.4 |
| 1919 | Sir Barton | J. Loftus | 2:09.4 |
| 1920 | Paul Jones | T. Rice | 2:09.0 |
| 1921 | Behave Yourself | C. Thompson | 2:04.1 |
| 1922 | Morvich | A. Johnson | 2:04.3 |
| 1923 | Zev | E. Sande | 2:05.2 |
| 1924 | Black Gold | J.D. Mooney | 2:05.1 |
| 1925 | Flying Ebony | E. Sande | 2:07.3 |
| 1926 | Bubbling Over | A. Johnson | 2:03.4 |
| 1927 | Whiskery | L. McAtee | 2:06.0 |
| 1928 | Reigh Count | C. Lang | 2:10.2 |
| 1929 | Clyde Van Dusen | L. McAtee | 2:10.4 |
| 1930 | Gallant Fox | E. Sande | 2:07.3 |
| 1931 | Twenty Grand | C. Kurtsinger | 2:01.4 |
| 1932 | Burgoo King | E. James | 2:05.1 |
| 1933 | Brokers Tip | D. Meade | 2:06.4 |
| 1934 | Cavalcade | M. Garner | 2:04.0 |
| 1935 | Omaha | W. Saunders | 2:05.0 |
| 1936 | Bold Venture | I. Hanford | 2:03.3 |
| 1937 | War Admiral | C. Kurtsinger | 2:03.1 |
| 1938 | Lawrin | E. Arcaro | 2:04.4 |
| 1939 | Johnstown | J. Stout | 2:03.2 |
| 1940 | Gallahadion | C. Bierman | 2:05.0 |
| 1941 | Whirlaway | E. Arcaro | 2:01.2 |
| 1942 | Shut Out | W.D. Wright | 2:04.2 |
| 1943 | Count Fleet | J. Longden | 2:04.0 |
| 1944 | Pensive | C. McCreary | 2:04.1 |
| 1945 | Hoop Jr. | E. Arcaro | 2:07.0 |
| 1946 | Assault | W. Mehrtens | 2:06.3 |
| 1947 | Jet Pilot | E. Guerin | 2:06.3 |
| 1948 | Citation | E. Arcaro | 2:05.2 |
| 1949 | Ponder | S. Brooks | 2:04.1 |
| 1950 | Middleground | W. Boland | 2:01.3 |
| 1951 | Count Turf | C. McCreary | 2:02.3 |
| 1952 | Hill Gail | E. Arcaro | 2:01.3 |
| 1953 | Dark Star | H. Moreno | 2:02.0 |
| 1954 | Determine | R. York | 2:03.0 |
| 1955 | Swaps | W. Shoemaker | 2:01.4 |
| 1956 | Needles | D. Erb | 2:03.2 |
| 1957 | Iron Liege | W. Hartack | 2:02.1 |
| 1958 | Tim Tam | I. Valenzuela | 2:05.0 |
| 1959 | Tommy Lee | W. Shoemaker | 2:02.1 |
| 1960 | Venetian Way | W. Hartack | 2:02.2 |
| 1961 | Carry Back | J. Sellers | 2:04.0 |
| 1962 | Decidedly | W. Hartack | 2:00.2 |
| 1963 | Chateaugay | B. Baeza | 2:01.4 |
| 1964 | Northern Dancer | W. Hartack | 2:00.0 |
| 1965 | Lucky Debonair | W. Shoemaker | 2:01.1 |
| 1966 | Kauai King | D. Brumfield | 2:02.0 |
| 1967 | Proud Clarion | R. Ussery | 2:00.3 |
| 1968 | Forward Pass[1] | I. Ussery | 2:02.1 |
| 1969 | Majestic Prince | W. Hartack | 2:01.4 |
| 1970 | Dust Commander | M. Manganello | 2:03.2 |
| 1971 | Canonero II | G. Avila | 2:03.1 |
| 1972 | Riva Ridge | R. Turcotte | 2:01.4 |
| 1973 | Secretariat | R. Turcotte | 1:59.2[2] |
| 1974 | Cannonade | A. Cordero, Jr. | 2:04.0 |
| 1975 | Foolish Pleasure | J. Vasquez | 2:02.0 |
| 1976 | Bold Forbes | A. Cordero, Jr. | 2:01.3 |
| 1977 | Seattle Slew | J. Cruquet | 2:02.1 |
| 1978 | Affirmed | S. Cauthen | 2:01.1 |
| 1979 | Spectacular Bid | R. Franklin | 2:02.2 |
| 1980 | Genuine Risk | J. Vasquez | 2:02.0 |
| 1981 | Pleasant Colony | J. Velasquez | 2:02.0 |
| 1982 | Gato Del Sol | E. Delahoussaye | 2:02.2 |
| 1983 | Sunny's Halo | E. Delahoussaye | 2:02.1 |
| 1984 | Swale | L. Pincay | 2:02.2 |
| 1985 | Spend A Buck | A. Cordero, Jr. | 2:00.1 |
| 1986 | Ferdinand | W. Shoemaker | 2:02.4 |
| 1987 | Alysheba | C. McCarron | 2:03.2 |
| 1988 | Winning Colors | G. Stevens | 2:02.2 |
| 1989 | Sunday Silence | P. Valenzuela | 2:05.0 |
| 1990 | Unbridled | C. Perret | 2:02.0 |
| 1991 | Strike the Gold | C. Antley | 2:03.0 |

**Note:** Race first run in 1875. Prior to 1896 the distance was 1½ miles. 1. In 1968 Dancer's Image finished first but was later disqualified from the purse money, and Forward Pass was declared winner. 2. Record. **Source:** *Daily Racing Form.*

## PREAKNESS STAKES, 1900–91

Site: Pimlico Racetrack, Baltimore, Maryland
Distance: 1³⁄₁₆ miles

| Year | Horse | Jockey | Time |
|---|---|---|---|
| 1900 | Hindus | H. Spencer | 1:48.2 |
| 1901 | The Parader | F. Landry | 1:47.1 |
| 1902 | Old England | L. Jackson | 1:45.4 |
| 1903 | Flocarline | W. Gannon | 1:44.4 |
| 1904 | Bryn Mawr | E. Hildebrand | 1:44.1 |
| 1905 | Cairngorm | W. Davis | 1:45.4 |
| 1906 | Whimsical | W. Miller | 1:45.0 |
| 1907 | Don Enrique | G. Mountain | 1:45.2 |
| 1908 | Royal Tourist | E. Dugan | 1:46.2 |
| 1909 | Effendi | W. Doyle | 1:39.4 |
| 1910 | Layminister | R. Estep | 1:40.3 |
| 1911 | Watervale | E. Dugan | 1:51.0 |
| 1912 | Colonel Holloway | C. Turner | 1:56.3 |
| 1913 | Buskin | J. Butwell | 1:53.2 |
| 1914 | Holiday | A. Schuttinger | 1:53.4 |
| 1915 | Rhine Maiden | D. Hoffman | 1:58.0 |
| 1916 | Damrosch | L. McAtee | 1:54.4 |
| 1917 | Kalitan | E. Haynes | 1:54.2 |
| 1918 | Jack Hare, Jr. | C. Peak | 1:53.2 |
| | War Cloud | J. Loftus | 1:53.3 |
| 1919 | Sir Barton | J. Loftus | 1:53.0 |
| 1920 | Man O' War | C. Kummer | 1:51.3 |
| 1921 | Broomspun | F. Coltiletti | 1:54.1 |
| 1922 | Pillory | L. Morris | 1:51.3 |
| 1923 | Vigil | B. Marinelli | 1:53.3 |
| 1924 | Nellie Morse | C. Merimee | 1:57.1 |
| 1925 | Coventry | C. Kummer | 1:59.0 |
| 1926 | Display | J. Maiben | 1:59.4 |
| 1927 | Bostonian | A. Abel | 2:01.3 |
| 1928 | Victorian | R. Workman | 2:00.1 |
| 1929 | Dr. Freeland | L. Schaefer | 2:01.3 |
| 1930 | Gallant Fox | E. Sande | 2:00.3 |
| 1931 | Mate | G. Ellis | 1:59.0 |
| 1932 | Burgoo King | E. James | 1:59.4 |
| 1933 | Head Play | C. Kurtsinger | 2:02.0 |

**Note:** Race first run in 1873. Distance varied from 1 mile 70 yds to 1⅛ miles until 1925. **Source:** *Daily Racing Form.*

| 1934 | High Quest | R. Jones | 1:58.1 |
|---|---|---|---|
| 1935 | Omaha | W. Saunders | 1:58.2 |
| 1936 | Bold Venture | G. Woolf | 1:59.0 |
| 1937 | War Admiral | C. Kurtsinger | 1:58.2 |
| 1938 | Dauber | M. Peters | 1:59.4 |
| 1939 | Challedon | G. Seabo | 1:59.4 |
| 1940 | Bimelech | F. A. Smith | 1:58.3 |
| 1941 | Whirlaway | E. Arcaro | 1:58.4 |
| 1942 | Alsab | B. James | 1:57.0 |
| 1943 | Count Fleet | J. Longden | 1:57.2 |
| 1944 | Pensive | C. McCreary | 1:59.1 |
| 1945 | Polynesian | W.D. Wright | 1:58.4 |
| 1946 | Assault | W. Mehrtens | 2:01.2 |
| 1947 | Faultless | D. Dodson | 1:59.0 |
| 1948 | Citation | E. Arcaro | 2:02.2 |
| 1949 | Capot | T. Atkinson | 1:56.0 |
| 1950 | Hill Prince | E. Arcaro | 1:59.1 |
| 1951 | Bold | E. Arcaro | 1:56.2 |
| 1952 | Blue Man | C. McCreary | 1:57.2 |
| 1953 | Native Dancer | E. Guerin | 1:57.4 |
| 1954 | Hasty Road | J. Adams | 1:57.2 |
| 1955 | Nashua | E. Arcaro | 1:54.3 |
| 1956 | Fabius | W. Hartack | 1:58.2 |
| 1957 | Bold Ruler | E. Arcaro | 1:56.1 |
| 1958 | Tim Tam | I. Valenzuela | 1:57.1 |
| 1959 | Royal Orbit | W. Harmatz | 1:57.0 |
| 1960 | Bally Ache | R. Ussery | 1:57.3 |
| 1961 | Carry Back | J. Sellers | 1:57.3 |
| 1962 | Greek Money | J. L. Rotz | 1:56.1 |
| 1963 | Candy Spots | W. Shoemaker | 1:56.1 |
| 1964 | Northern Dancer | W. Hartack | 1:56.4 |
| 1965 | Tom Rolfe | R. Turcotte | 1:56.1 |
| 1966 | Kauai King | D. Brumfield | 1:55.2 |
| 1967 | Damascus | W. Shoemaker | 1:55.1 |
| 1968 | Forward Pass | I. Valenzuela | 1:56.4 |
| 1969 | Majestic Prince | W. Hartack | 1:55.3 |
| 1970 | Personality | E. Belmonte | 1:56.1 |
| 1971 | Canonero II | G. Avila | 1:54.0 |
| 1972 | Bee Bee Bee | E. Nelson | 1:55.3 |
| 1973 | Secretariat | R. Turcotte | 1:54.2 |
| 1974 | Little Current | M. Rivera | 1:54.3 |
| 1975 | Master Derby | D. McHargue | 1:56.2 |
| 1976 | Elocutionist | J. Lively | 1:55.0 |
| 1977 | Seattle Slew | J. Cruguet | 1:54.2 |
| 1978 | Affirmed | S. Cauthen | 1:54.2 |
| 1979 | Spectacular Bid | R. Franklin | 1:54.1 |
| 1980 | Codex | A. Cordero, Jr. | 1:54.1 |
| 1981 | Pleasant Colony | J. Velasquez | 1:54.3 |
| 1982 | Aloma's Ruler | J. Kaenel | 1:55.2 |
| 1983 | Deputed Testamony | D. Miller | 1:55.2 |
| 1984 | Gate Dancer | A. Cordero, Jr. | 1:53.3 |
| 1985 | Tank's Prospect | P. Day | 1:53.2 |
| 1986 | Snow Chief | A. Solis | 1:54.4 |
| 1987 | Alysheba | C. McCarron | 1:55.4 |
| 1988 | Risen Star | E. Delahoussaye | 1:56.1 |
| 1989 | Sunday Silence | P. Valenzuela | 1:53.4 |
| 1990 | Summer Squall | P. Day | 1:53.3 |
| 1991 | Hansel | J. Bailey | 1:54.0 |

## BELMONT STAKES, 1900–91

Site: Belmont Park, New York    Distance: 1½ miles

| Year | Horse | Jockey | Time |
|---|---|---|---|
| 1900 | Ildrim | N. Turner | 2:21½ |
| 1901 | Commando | H. Spencer | 2:21.0 |
| 1902 | Masterman | J. Bullman | 2:22½ |
| 1903 | Africander | J. Bullman | 2:23.1 |
| 1904 | Delhi | G. Odom | 2:06.3 |
| 1905 | Tanya | E. Hildebrand | 2:08.0 |

| Year | Horse | Jockey | Time | Year | Horse | Jockey | Time | Year | Horse | Jockey | Time |
|---|---|---|---|---|---|---|---|---|---|---|---|
| 1906 | Burgomaster | L. Lyne | 2:20.0 | 1937 | War Admiral | C. Kurtsinger | 2:28.3 | 1966 | Amberoid | W. Boland | 2:29.3 |
| 1907 | Peter Pan | G. Mountain | No Time | 1938 | Pasteurized | J. Stout | 2:29.2 | 1967 | Damascus | W. Shoemaker | 2:28.4 |
| 1908 | Colin | J. Notter | No Time | 1939 | Johnstown | J. Stout | 2:29.2 | 1968 | Stage Door Johnny | H. Gustines | 2:27.1 |
| 1909 | Joe Madden | E. Dugan | 2:21.3 | 1940 | Bimelech | F.A. Smith | 2:29.3 | 1969 | Arts and Letters | B. Baeza | 2:28.4 |
| 1910 | Sweep | J. Butwell | 2:22.0 | 1941 | Whirlaway | E. Arcaro | 2:31.0 | 1970 | High Echelon | J.L. Rotz | 2:34.0 |
| 1913 | Prince Eugene | R. Troxler | 2:18.0 | 1942 | Shut Out | E. Arcaro | 2:29.1 | 1971 | Pass Catcher | W. Blum | 2:30.2 |
| 1914 | Luke McLuke | M. Buxton | 2:20.0 | 1943 | Count Fleet | J. Longden | 2:28.1 | 1972 | Riva Ridge | R. Turcotte | 2:28.0 |
| 1915 | The Finn | G. Byrne | 2:18.2 | 1944 | Bounding Home | G.L. Smith | 2:32.1 | 1973 | Secretariat | R. Turcotte | 2:24.0 |
| 1916 | Friar Rock | E. Haynes | 2:22.0 | 1945 | Pavot | E. Arcaro | 2:30.1 | 1974 | Little Current | M. Rivera | 2:29.1 |
| 1917 | Hourless | J. Butwell | 2:17.4 | 1946 | Assault | W. Mehrtens | 2:30.4 | 1975 | Avatar | W. Shoemaker | 2:28.1 |
| 1918 | Johren | F. Robinson | 2:20.2 | 1947 | Phalanx | R. Donoso | 2:29.2 | 1976 | Bold Forbes | A. Cordero, Jr. | 2:29.0 |
| 1919 | Sir Barton | J. Loftus | 2:17.2 | 1948 | Citation | E. Arcaro | 2:28.1 | 1977 | Seattle Slew | J. Cruguet | 2:29.3 |
| 1920 | Man O' War | C. Kummer | 2:14.1 | 1949 | Capot | T. Atkinson | 2:30.1 | 1978 | Affirmed | S. Cauthen | 2:26.4 |
| 1921 | Grey Lag | E. Sande | 2:16.4 | 1950 | Middleground | W. Boland | 2:28.3 | 1979 | Coastal | R. Hernandez | 2:28.3 |
| 1922 | Pillory | C. H. Miller | 2:18.4 | 1951 | Counterpoint | D. Gorman | 2:29.0 | 1980 | Temperance Hill | E. Maple | 2:29.4 |
| 1923 | Zev | E. Sande | 2:19.0 | 1952 | One Count | E. Arcaro | 2:30.1 | 1981 | Summing | G. Martens | 2:29.0 |
| 1924 | Mad Play | E. Sande | 2:18.4 | 1953 | Native Dancer | E. Guerin | 2:28.3 | 1982 | Conquistador Cielo | L. Pincay | 2:28.1 |
| 1925 | American Flag | A. Johnson | 2:16.4 | 1954 | High Gun | E. Guerin | 2:30.4 | 1983 | Caveat | L. Pincay | 2:27.4 |
| 1926 | Crusader | A. Johnson | 2:32.1 | 1955 | Nashua | E. Arcaro | 2:29.0 | 1984 | Swale | L. Pincay | 2:27.1 |
| 1927 | Chance Shot | E. Sande | 2:32.2 | 1956 | Needles | D. Erb | 2:29.4 | 1985 | Creme Fraiche | E. Maple | 2:27.0 |
| 1928 | Vito | C. Kummer | 2:33.1 | 1957 | Gallant Man | W. Shoemaker | 2:26.3 | 1986 | Danzig Connection | C. McCarron | 2:29.4 |
| 1929 | Blue Larkspur | M. Garner | 2:32.4 | 1958 | Cavan | P. Anderson | 2:30.1 | 1987 | Bet Twice | C. Perret | 2:28.1 |
| 1930 | Gallant Fox | E. Sande | 2:31.1 | 1959 | Sword Dancer | W. Shoemaker | 2:28.2 | 1988 | Risen Star | E. Delahoussaye | 2:26.2 |
| 1931 | Twenty Grand | C. Kurtsinger | 2:29.3 | 1960 | Celtic Ash | W. Hartack | 2:29.3 | 1989 | Easy Goer | P. Day | 2:26.0 |
| 1932 | Faireno | T. Malley | 2:32.4 | 1961 | Sherluck | B. Baeza | 2:29.1 | 1990 | Go And Go | M. Kinane | 2:27.1 |
| 1933 | Hurryoff | M. Garner | 2:32.3 | 1962 | Jaipur | W. Shoemaker | 2:28.4 | 1991 | Hansel | J. Bailey | 2:28.0 |
| 1934 | Peace Chance | W.D. Wright | 2:29.5 | 1963 | Chateaugay | B. Baeza | 2:30.1 | | | | |
| 1935 | Omaha | W. Saunders | 2:30.3 | 1964 | Quadrangle | M. Ycaza | 2:28.2 | | | | |
| 1936 | Granville | J. Stout | 2:30.0 | 1965 | Hail to All | J. Sellers | 2:28.2 | | | | |

**Note:** Race first run in 1867. Distance varied until 1926. **Source:** *Daily Racing Form.*

# HARNESS RACING

## HAMBLETONIAN WINNERS

| Year | Horse | Driver | Best time | Heats | Purses | Year | Horse | Driver | Best time | Heats | Purses |
|---|---|---|---|---|---|---|---|---|---|---|---|
| 1926 | Guy McKinney | N. Ray | 2:04¾ | 2 | $ 73,451 | 1960 | Blaze Hanover | J. O'Brien | 1:59.3 | 4 | $ 144,590 |
| 1927 | Iosola's Worthy | M. Childs | 2:03¾ | 2 | 54,694 | 1961 | Harlan Dean | J. Arthur | 1:58.2 | 2 | 131,573 |
| 1928 | Spenser | W. H. Leese | 2:03½ | 2 | 66,226 | 1962 | A.C.'s Viking | S. Russell | 1:59.3 | 2 | 116,613 |
| 1929 | Walter Dear | W. Cox | 2:02¾ | 2 | 60,310 | 1963 | Speedy Scot | R. Baldwin | 1:57.3 | 3 | 115,549 |
| 1930 | Hanover's Bertha | T. Berry | 2:03.0 | 3 | 56,860 | 1964 | Ayres | J. Simpson, Jr. | 1:56.4 | 2 | 115,281 |
| 1931 | Calumet Butler | R. McMahon | 2:03¼ | 3 | 50,921 | 1965 | Egyptian Candor | A. Cameron | 2:03.4 | 4 | 122,246 |
| 1932 | The Marchioness | W. Caton | 2:01¼ | 4 | 48,339 | 1966 | Kerry Way | F. Ervin | 1:58.4 | 2 | 122,540 |
| 1933 | Mary Reynolds | B. White | 2:03¾ | 3 | 40,461 | 1967 | Speedy Streak | A. Cameron | 2:00.0 | 2 | 122,650 |
| 1934 | Lord Jim | H. M. Parshall | 2:02¾ | 4 | 25,844 | 1968 | Nevele Pride | S. Dancer | 1:59.2 | 2 | 116,190 |
| 1935 | Greyhound | S. Palin | 2:02¼ | 2 | 33,321 | 1969 | Lindy's Pride | H. Beissinger | 1:57.3 | 2 | 124,910 |
| 1936 | Rosalind | B. White | 2:01¾ | 2 | 35,644 | 1970 | Timothy T. | J. Simpson, Jr. | 1:58.2 | 3 | 143,620 |
| 1937 | Shirley Hanover | H. Thomas | 2:01½ | 2 | 37,913 | 1971 | Speedy Crown | H. Beissinger | 1:57.2 | 2 | 129,770 |
| 1938 | McLin Hanover | H. Thomas | 2:02¼ | 2 | 37,962 | 1972 | Super Bowl | S. Dancer | 1:56.2 | 2 | 119,090 |
| 1939 | Peter Astra | H. M. Parshall | 2:04¼ | 2 | 40,502 | 1973 | Flirth | R. Baldwin | 1:57.1 | 2 | 144,710 |
| 1940 | Spencer Scott | F. Egan | 2:02.0 | 2 | 43,658 | 1974 | Christopher T. | W. Haughton | 1:58.3 | 3 | 160,150 |
| 1941 | Bill Gallon | L. Smith | 2:05.0 | 3 | 38,730 | 1975 | Bonefish | S. Dancer | 1:59.0 | 4 | 232,192 |
| 1941 | The Ambassador | B. White | 2:04.0 | 2 | 38,854 | 1976 | Steve Lobell | W. Haughton | 1:56.2 | 4 | 263,524 |
| 1943 | Volo Song | B. White | 2:02½ | 3 | 42,298 | 1977 | Green Speed | W. Haughton | 1:55.3 | 2 | 284,131 |
| 1944 | Yankee Maid | H. Thomas | 2:04.0 | 2 | 34,427 | 1978 | Speedy Somolli | H. Beissinger | 1:55.0 | 3 | 241,280 |
| 1945 | Titan Hanover | H. Pownall | 2:04.0 | 2 | 51,047 | 1979 | Legend Hanover | G. Sholty | 1:56.1 | 2 | 300,000 |
| 1946 | Chestertown | T. Berry | 2:02½ | 2 | 51,846 | 1980 | Burgomeister | W. Haughton | 1:56.3 | 3 | 293,570 |
| 1947 | Hoot Mon | S. Palin | 2:00.0 | 3 | 46,268 | 1981 | Shiaway St. Pat | R. Remmen | 2:01.1 | 3 | 838,000 |
| 1948 | Demon Hanover | H. Hoyt | 2:02.0 | 2 | 59,941 | 1982 | Speed Bowl | T. Haughton | 1:56.4 | 2 | 875,000 |
| 1949 | Miss Tilly | F. Egan | 2:01.2 | 2 | 69,791 | 1983 | Duenna | S. Dancer | 1:57.2 | 2 | 1,080,000 |
| 1950 | Lusty Song | D. Miller | 2:02.0 | 2 | 75,209 | 1984 | Historic Freight | B. Webster | 1:56.2 | 3 | 1,219,000 |
| 1951 | Mainliner | G. Crippen | 2:02.3 | 2 | 95,264 | 1985 | Prakas | W. O'Donnell | 1:54.3 | 2 | 1,272,000 |
| 1952 | Sharp Note | B. Shively | 2:02.3 | 3 | 87,638 | 1986 | Nuclear Kosmos | J. Campbell | 1:55.2 | 2 | 1,172,082 |
| 1953 | Helicopter | H. Harvey | 2:01.3 | 3 | 117,118 | 1987 | Mack Lobell | J. Campbell | 1:53.3 | 2 | 1,046,300 |
| 1954 | Newport Dream | A. Cameron | 2:02.4 | 2 | 106,831 | 1988 | Armbro Goal | J. Campbell | 1:54.3 | 2 | 1,156,800 |
| 1955 | Scott Frost | J. O'Brien | 2:00.3 | 3 | 86,863 | 1989[1] | Park Ave Joe | R. Naples | 1:55.3 | 3 | 565,500 |
| 1956 | The Intruder | W. Bower | 2:01.2 | 3 | 100,604 | | Probe | W. Fahy | 1:54.3 | 3 | 282,750 |
| 1957 | Hickory Smoke | J. Simpson, Sr. | 2:00.1 | 5 | 111,126 | 1990 | Harmonious | J. Campbell | 1:54.1 | 2 | 1,346,000 |
| 1958 | Emily's Pride | F. Nipe | 1:59.4 | 3 | 106,719 | 1991 | Giant Victory | J. Moiseyev | 1:54.4 | 3 | 1,238,000 |
| 1959 | Diller Hanover | F. Ervin | 2:01.1 | 2 | 125,283 | | | | | | |

1. Co-winners. **Source:** U.S. Trotting Association.

# International Sports

## THE WORLD CUP, 1990

West Germany, led by Rudi Vohler, Lothar Matthaeus, and Guido Buchwald, defeated defending champ Argentina 1–0 to capture its third World Cup. The championship game, as many others during the tournament, was decided by penalties, and a penalty kick scored by Andreas Brehme in the closing stages. Argentina entered the game less four starters who had been disqualified for previous infractions, and lost two more to penalties, in the second half. The Argentine star Diego Maradona, hero of the 1986 Cup, did not score a single goal this year. In many ways the game was typical of the entire tournament, which featured rough play, a record number of penalties, and very little scoring; Argentina managed only one shot on goal the entire championship game.

Host country Italy's beloved Azzurri, heavy favorites to win their fourth Cup, had to settle for beating England 2–1 for third place. Italy's only consolation was the play of Salvatore (Toto) Schillaci, who led the tournament in scoring with six goals, five of them game-winners. Other notable teams among the 106 competing for the championship were Cameroon,

which won a string of upsets to become the first African nation ever to compete in the elimination round, and surprisingly successful squads from Ireland, Yugoslavia, and Romania.

The U.S. qualified for the tournament for the first time in 40 years, only to be crushed by Czechoslovakia 5–1 in its opening game; the inexperienced young Americans subsequently played much better and saved considerable face in later losing to Italy by only 1–0. The U.S. will host the next World Cup in 1994. The U.S. team, coached by Yugoslavian Bora Milutinovic, who has extensive World Cup experience, continues to prepare by playing strong international schedule.

## Round-by-Round Results

### Eliminated in First Phase

Results are given as Wins, Ties, Losses: Austria (1–0–2), Egypt (0–2–1), South Korea (0–0–3), Soviet Union (1–0–2), Sweden (0–0–3), United Arab Emirates (0–0–3), United States (0–0–3)

### Second Phase

Cameroon 2    Colombia 1
Czechoslovakia 4    Costa Rica 1
Argentina 1    Brazil 0

West Germany 2    Netherlands 1
Ireland 1    Romania 0*
Italy 2    Uruguay 0
Yugoslavia 2    Spain 1*
England 1    Belgium 0*

### Quarterfinals

Argentina 1    Yugoslavia 0*
Italy 1    Ireland 0*
West Germany 1    Czechoslovakia 0
England 3    Cameroon 2*

### Semifinals

Argentina 2    Italy 1*
West Germany 2    England 1*

### Match for Third Place

Italy 2    England 1

### Finals

West Germany 1    Argentina 0

(*) Game tied in regulation, and won in penalty kick "shootout."

## FIGURE SKATING

While the Dutch are credited with inventing ice skating, it was British soldiers stationed in Philadelphia who brought it to colonial America. The nation's first skating club was established there in 1849.

---

## THE WORLD CUP

From its origins in various "football" games dating back to ancient Greece and China, soccer (as it is called in the United States) has become the world's most popular sport, with over 20 million participants in over 140 nations. The World Cup championship, modern soccer's most spectacular event, is staged by the Federation Internationale de Football Association (FIFA). Formally known as the Jules Rimet Trophy, the World Cup is awarded every four years to the victor in a 24-nation, 52-game final tournament. Players must represent their home country, regardless of where they regularly play. Millions attend the Cup's many contests and in recent years the televised final has been viewed by over a billion people worldwide. In 1986 12.8 billion viewers saw at least some live coverage. The host country for the 1994 tournament is the United States.

| Year | Host | Winner | Leading scorer, goals | PN[1] |
|---|---|---|---|---|
| 1930 | Uruguay | Uruguay | Stabile, Argentina (8) | 13 |
| 1934 | Italy | Italy | Conen, Germany (4) | 29 |
| | | | Nejedly, Czechoslovakia (4) | |
| | | | Schiavo, Italy (4) | |
| 1938 | France | Italy | Leonidas, Brazil (8) | 26 |
| 1942 | No tournament—World War II | | | |
| 1946 | No tournament—World War II | | | |
| 1950 | Brazil | Uruguay | Ademir, Brazil (7) | 28 |
| 1954 | Switzerland | West Germany | Kocsis, Hungary (11) | 36 |
| 1958 | Sweden | Brazil | Fontaine, France (11) | 53 |
| 1962 | Chile | Brazil | Jerkovic, Yugoslavia (5) | 57 |
| 1966 | England | England | Eusebio, Portugal (9) | 71 |
| 1970 | Mexico | Brazil | Muller, West Germany (10) | 73 |
| 1974 | West Germany | West Germany | Lato, Poland (7) | 95 |
| 1978 | Argentina | Argentina | Kempes, Argentina (6) | 105 |
| 1982 | Spain | Italy | Rossi, Italy (6) | 109 |
| 1986 | Mexico | Argentina | Lineker, England (6) | 112 |
| 1990 | Italy | West Germany | Schillaci, Italy (6) | 106 |

1. PN: Participating Nations. **Source:** FIFA.

## FIGURE SKATING CHAMPIONS

### U.S. CHAMPIONS

| Year | Men | Women |
|---|---|---|
| 1952 | Richard Button | Tenley Albright |
| 1953 | Hayes Jenkins | Tenley Albright |
| 1954 | Hayes Jenkins | Tenley Albright |
| 1955 | Hayes Jenkins | Tenley Albright |
| 1956 | Hayes Jenkins | Tenley Albright |
| 1957 | Dave Jenkins | Carol Heiss |
| 1958 | Dave Jenkins | Carol Heiss |
| 1959 | Dave Jenkins | Carol Heiss |
| 1960 | Dave Jenkins | Carol Heiss |
| 1961 | Bradley Lord | Laurence Owen |
| 1962 | Monty Hoyt | Barbara Roles Pursley |
| 1963 | Tommy Litz | Lorraine Hanlon |
| 1964 | Scott Allen | Peggy Fleming |
| 1965 | Gary Visconti | Peggy Fleming |
| 1966 | Scott Allen | Peggy Fleming |
| 1967 | Gary Visconti | Peggy Fleming |
| 1968 | Tim Wood | Peggy Fleming |
| 1969 | Tim Wood | Janet Lynn |
| 1970 | Tim Wood | Janet Lynn |
| 1971 | John Misha Petkevich | Janet Lynn |
| 1972 | Ken Shelley | Janet Lynn |
| 1973 | Gordon McKellen, Jr. | Janet Lynn |
| 1974 | Gordon McKellen, Jr. | Dorothy Hamill |
| 1975 | Gordon McKellen, Jr. | Dorothy Hamill |
| 1976 | Terry Kubicka | Dorothy Hamill |
| 1977 | Charles Tickner | Linda Fratianne |
| 1978 | Charles Tickner | Linda Fratianne |
| 1979 | Charles Tickner | Linda Fratianne |
| 1980 | Charles Tickner | Linda Fratianne |
| 1981 | Scott Hamilton | Elaine Zayak |

| 1982 | Scott Hamilton | Rosalynn Sumners |
| 1983 | Scott Hamilton | Rosalynn Sumners |
| 1984 | Scott Hamilton | Rosalynn Sumners |
| 1985 | Brian Boitano | Tiffany Chin |
| 1986 | Brian Boitano | Debi Thomas |
| 1987 | Brian Boitano | Jill Trenary |
| 1988 | Brian Boitano | Debi Thomas |
| 1989 | Christopher Bowman | Jill Trenary |
| 1990 | Todd Eldridge | Jill Trenary |
| 1991 | Todd Eldridge | Tonya Harding |

## WORLD CHAMPIONS

| Year | Men | Women |
|------|-----|-------|
| 1952 | Richard Button, U.S. | Jacqueline du Bief, France |
| 1953 | Hayes Jenkins, U.S. | Tenley Albright, U.S. |
| 1954 | Hayes Jenkins, U.S. | Gundi Busch, W. Germany |
| 1955 | Hayes Jenkins, U.S. | Tenley Albright, U.S. |
| 1956 | Hayes Jenkins, U.S. | Carol Heiss, U.S. |
| 1957 | Dave Jenkins, U.S. | Carol Heiss, U.S. |
| 1958 | Dave Jenkins, U.S. | Carol Heiss, U.S. |
| 1959 | Dave Jenkins, U.S. | Carol Heiss, U.S. |
| 1960 | Alain Giletti, France | Carol Heiss, U.S. |
| 1961 | No champion | No champion |
| 1962 | Don Jackson, Canada | Sjoukje Dijkstra, Netherlands |
| 1963 | Don McPherson, Canada | Sjoukje Dijkstra, Netherlands |
| 1964 | Manfred Schnelldorfer, W. Germany | Sjoukje Dijkstra, Netherlands |
| 1965 | Alain Calmat, France | Petra Burka, Canada |
| 1966 | Emmerich Danzer, Austria | Peggy Fleming, U.S. |
| 1967 | Emmerich Danzer, Austria | Peggy Fleming, U.S. |
| 1968 | Emmerich Danzer, Austria | Peggy Fleming, U.S. |
| 1969 | Tim Wood, U.S. | Gabriele Seyfert, E. Germany |
| 1970 | Tim Wood, U.S. | Gabriele Seyfert, E. Germany |
| 1971 | Ondrej Nepela, Czechoslovakia | Beatrix Schuba, Austria |
| 1972 | Ondrej Nepela, Czechoslovakia | Beatrix Schuba, Austria |
| 1973 | Ondrej Nepela, Czechoslovakia | Karen Magnussen, Canada |
| 1974 | Jan Hoffmann, E. Germany | Christine Errath, E. Germany |
| 1975 | Sergei Volkov, USSR | Dianne de Leeuw, Netherlands-U.S. |
| 1976 | John Curry, Great Britain | Dorothy Hamill, U.S. |
| 1977 | Vladimir Kovalev, USSR | Linda Fratianne, U.S. |
| 1978 | Charles Tickner, U.S. | Anett Potzsch, E. Germany |
| 1979 | Vladimir Kovalev, USSR | Linda Fratianne, U.S. |
| 1980 | Jan Hoffmann, E. Germany | Anett Potzsch, E. Germany |
| 1981 | Scott Hamilton, U.S. | Denise Biellmann, Switzerland |
| 1982 | Scott Hamilton, U.S. | Elaine Zayak, U.S. |
| 1983 | Scott Hamilton, U.S. | Rosalynn Sumners, U.S. |
| 1984 | Scott Hamilton, U.S. | Katarina Witt, E. Germany |
| 1985 | Aleksandr Fadeev, USSR | Katarina Witt, E. Germany |
| 1986 | Brian Boitano, U.S. | Debi Thomas, U.S. |
| 1987 | Brian Orser, Canada | Katarina Witt, E. Germany |
| 1988 | Brian Boitano, U.S. | Katarina Witt, E. Germany |
| 1989 | Kurt Browning, Canada | Midori Ito, Japan |
| 1990 | Kurt Browning, Canada | Jill Trenary, U.S. |
| 1991 | Kurt Browning, Canada | Kristi Yamaguchi, U.S. |

# CYCLING

## THE TOUR DE FRANCE

Established in 1903, the world's most important bicycle road race covers between 2,500 and 3,000 miles, including at least one mountain with an elevation of over 7,500 feet.

| Year | Champion | Year | Champion |
|------|----------|------|----------|
| 1903 | Maurice Garin | 1953 | Louison Bobet |
| 1904 | Henri Cornet | 1954 | Louison Bobet |
| 1905 | Louis Trousselier | 1955 | Louison Bobet |
| 1906 | Rene Pottier | 1956 | Roger Walkowiak |
| 1907 | Lucien Petit-Breton | 1957 | Jacques Anquetil |
| 1908 | Lucien Petit-Breton | 1958 | Charly Gaul |
| 1909 | Francois Faber | 1959 | Federico Bahamontes |
| 1910 | Octave Lapize | 1960 | Gastone Nencini |
| 1911 | Gustave Garrigou | 1961 | Jacques Anquetil |
| 1912 | Odile Defraye | 1962 | Jacques Anquetil |
| 1913 | Philippe Thijs | 1963 | Jacques Anquetil |
| 1914 | Philippe Thijs | 1964 | Jacques Anquetil |
| 1919 | Firmin Lambot | 1965 | Felice Gimondi |
| 1920 | Philippe Thijs | 1966 | Lucien Aimar |
| 1921 | Leon Scieur | 1967 | Roger Pingeon |
| 1922 | Firmin Lambot | 1968 | Jan Janssen |
| 1923 | Henri Pelissier | 1969 | Eddy Merckx |
| 1924 | Ottavio Bottecchia | 1970 | Eddy Merckx |
| 1925 | Ottavio Bottecchia | 1971 | Eddy Merckx |
| 1926 | Lucien Buysse | 1972 | Eddy Merckx |
| 1927 | Nicolas Frantz | 1973 | Luis Ocana |
| 1928 | Nicolas Frantz | 1974 | Eddy Merckx |
| 1929 | Maurice Dewaele | 1975 | Bernard Thevenet |
| 1930 | Andre Leducq | 1976 | Lucien Van Impe |
| 1931 | Antonin Magne | 1977 | Bernard Thevenet |
| 1932 | Andre Leducq | 1978 | Bernard Hinault |
| 1933 | Georges Speicher | 1979 | Bernard Hinault |
| 1934 | Antonin Magne | 1980 | Joop Zoetemelk |
| 1935 | Romain Maes | 1981 | Bernard Hinault |
| 1936 | Sylvere Maes | 1982 | Bernard Hinault |
| 1937 | Roger Lapebie | 1983 | Laurent Fignon |
| 1938 | Gino Bartali | 1984 | Laurent Fignon |
| 1939 | Sylvere Maes | 1985 | Bernard Hinault |
| 1947 | Jean Robic | 1986 | Greg Le Mond |
| 1948 | Gino Bartali | 1987 | Stephen Roche |
| 1949 | Fausto Coppi | 1988 | Pedro Delgado |
| 1950 | Ferdi Kubler | 1989 | Greg Le Mond |
| 1951 | Hugo Koblet | 1990 | Greg Le Mond |
| 1952 | Fausto Coppi | 1991 | Miguel Indurain |

# YACHTING
## THE AMERICA'S CUP

In 1851 the Royal Yacht Squadron (United Kingdom) presented a "hundred guinea cup" to the winning yacht in a race around the Isle of Wight in the English Channel. The cup was won by the U.S. schooner *America* and thereafter became known as the America's Cup, which was held by the New York Yacht Club. A fitting name it was, for in 24 challenges held over the next 132 years, it remained in the hands of U.S. yachtsmen.

In 1983, the Australian challenger *Australia II* beat the defender *Liberty*. In 1987, an American syndicate out of the San Diego Yacht Club successfully challenged the Australians and brought the cup back to the States. While in recent years it has been customary to hold races once every three or four years, a New Zealand syndicate launched a radically designed monohull, *New Zealand,* to challenge the Americans the following year. Unable to develop as sophisticated a monohull on such short notice, the Americans decided to defend the America's Cup with a catamaran. Though they handily defeated *New Zealand,* the New Zealand syndicate protested the result and finally won a judgment in U.S. court that the catamaran violated the original Cup Deed of Gift, and the San Diego Yacht Club surrendered the Cup to New Zealand. In early 1990 the ruling was reversed. San Diego will defend the cup in May 1992, when 20 syndicates from 15 countries, including the Soviet Union, Switzerland, and Japan, will challenge in a new class of 70 ft. monohulls.

## AMERICA'S CUP RESULTS, 1870–1988

| Year | Challenger, rig, country | Defender, rig, country |
|------|--------------------------|------------------------|
| 1870 | *Cambria*, schooner, UK | *Magic*, schooner, U.S. |
| 1871 | *Livonia*, schooner, UK | *Columbia* and *Sappho*, schooners, U.S. |
| 1876 | *Countess of Dufferin*, schooner, Canada | *Madeleine*, schooner, U.S. |
| 1881 | *Atalanta*, sloop, Canada | *Mischief*, cutter, U.S. |
| 1885 | *Genesta*, cutter, UK | *Puritan*, cutter, U.S. |
| 1886 | *Galatea*, cutter, UK | *Mayflower*, cutter, U.S. |
| 1887 | *Thistle*, cutter, UK | *Volunteer*, cutter, U.S. |
| 1893 | *Valkyrie II*, cutter, UK | *Vigilant*, cutter, U.S. |
| 1895 | *Valkyrie III*, cutter, UK | *Defender*, cutter, U.S. |
| 1899 | *Shamrock*, cutter, UK | *Columbia*, cutter, U.S. |
| 1901 | *Shamrock II*, cutter, UK | *Columbia*, cutter, U.S. |
| 1903 | *Shamrock III*, cutter, UK | *Reliance*, cutter, U.S. |
| 1920 | *Shamrock IV*, cutter, UK | *Resolute*, cutter, U.S. |
| 1930 | *Shamrock V*, J-class sloop, UK | *Enterprise*, J-class sloop, U.S. |
| 1934 | *Endeavor*, J-class sloop, UK | *Rainbow*, J-class sloop, U.S. |
| 1937 | *Endeavor II*, J-class sloop, UK | *Ranger*, J-class sloop, U.S. |
| 1958 | *Sceptre*, 12–m, UK | *Columbia*, 12–m, U.S. |
| 1962 | *Gretel*, 12–m, Australia | *Weatherly*, 12–m, U.S. |
| 1964 | *Sovereign*, 12–m, UK | *Constellation*, 12–m, U.S. |
| 1967 | *Dame Pattie*, 12–m, Australia | *Intrepid*, 12–m, U.S. |
| 1970 | *Gretel II*, 12–m, Australia | *Intrepid*, 12–m, U.S. |
| 1974 | *Southern Cross*, 12–m, Australia | *Courageous*, 12–m, U.S. |
| 1977 | *Australia*, 12–m, Australia | *Courageous*, 12–m, U.S. |
| 1980 | *Australia*, 12–m, Australia | *Freedom*, 12–m, U.S. |
| 1983 | *Australia II*, 12–m, Australia | *Liberty*, 12–m, U.S. |
| 1987 | *Stars & Stripes*, 12–m, U.S. | *Kookaburra III*, 12–m, Australia |
| 1988 | *New Zealand*, sloop, New Zealand | *Stars & Stripes*, catamaran, U.S. |

**Note:** 12–m = international 12-meter class.

## CHESS

### CHESS—WORLD CHAMPIONS

| Year | Name | Country |
|------|------|---------|
| 1886–94 | Wilhelm Steinitz | Austria |
| 1894–1921 | Emanuel Lasker | Germany |
| 1921–27 | José R. Capablanca | Cuba |
| 1927–35 | Alexander A. Alekhine | France |
| 1935–37 | Max Euwe | Netherlands |
| 1937–48 | Alexander A. Alekhine | France |
| 1948–57 | Mikhail Botvinnik | USSR |
| 1957–58 | Vassily Smyslov | USSR |
| 1958–60 | Mikhail Botvinnik | USSR |
| 1960–61 | Mikhail Tal | USSR |
| 1961–63 | Mikhail Botvinnik | USSR |
| 1963–69 | Tigran Petrosian | USSR |
| 1969–72 | Boris Spassky | USSR |
| 1972–75 | Bobby Fischer | U.S. |
| 1975–85 | Anatoly Karpov | USSR |
| 1985– | Gary Kasparov | USSR |

**Source:** U.S. Chess Federation.

### U.S. CHESS CHAMPIONS

| Year | Name |
|------|------|
| **EARLY MATCHES** | |
| 1845–57 | Charles Henry Stanley |
| 1857–71 | Paul Morphy |
| 1871–90 | Capt. George Mackenzie |
| 1890–91 | Jackson Showalter |
| 1891–94 | Soloman Lipschutz |
| 1894 | Jackson Showalter |
| 1894–95 | Albert B. Hodges |
| 1895–97 | Jackson Showalter |
| 1897–1906 | Harry Pillsbury |
| 1906–09 | Jackson Showalter |
| 1909–36 | Frank J. Marshall |
| **MODERN TOURNAMENTS** | |
| 1936–44 | Sammy Reshevsky |
| 1944–46 | Arnold Denker |
| 1946–48 | Sammy Reshevsky |
| 1948–51 | Herman Steiner |
| 1951–54 | Larry Evans |
| 1954–57 | Arthur Bosguier |
| 1957–61 | Bobby Fischer |
| 1961–62 | Larry Evans |
| 1962–68 | Bobby Fischer |
| 1968–69 | Larry Evans |
| 1969–72 | Sammy Reshevsky |
| 1972–73 | Robert Byrne |
| 1973–74 | John Grefe, Lubosh Kavalek (tie) |
| 1974–78 | Walter Browne |
| 1978–80 | Lubosh Kavalek |
| 1980–81 | Walter Brown, Larry Evans, Larry Christiansen (tie) |
| 1981–83 | Walter Browne, Yasser Seirawan (tie) |
| 1983–84 | Walter Browne, Larry Christiansen, Roman Dzhindzhikashvili (tie) |
| 1984–86 | Lev Alburt |
| 1986–87 | Yasser Seirawan |
| 1987–88 | Joel Benjamin, Nick Defirmian (tie) |
| 1988–90 | Michael Wilder |
| 1990– | Lev Alburt |

## MARATHON RUNNING

Most marathons are approximately 26 miles, 385 yards long, the distance purportedly run by the Athenian messenger who announced his city-state's victory over the Persian Empire on the Plains of Marathon in 490 B.C. The oldest and best-known U.S. marathon covers a route from Hopkinton, Massachusetts, to downtown Boston. For many years, the Boston Athletic Association organized the race on an amateur basis, and winners received only a laurel wreath and the traditional pot of beef stew. In 1986, John Hancock Financial Services began sponsoring the race, and by 1990 it was paying $1.3 million in fees, prizes, and performance bonuses; 13 other corporate sponsors provide goods and services. Winners receive $50,000 and a free car.

### BOSTON MARATHON CHAMPIONS

#### MEN

| Year | Name, city/state/country | Time |
|------|--------------------------|------|
| 1897 | John J. McDermott, New York | 2:55:10 |
| 1898 | Ronald J. McDonald, Cambridge, Mass. | 2:42:00 |
| 1899 | Lawrence J. Brignolia, Cambridge, Mass. | 2:54:38 |
| 1900 | James J. Caffrey, Hamilton, Ont. | 2:39:44 |
| 1901 | James J. Caffrey, Hamilton, Ont. | 2:29:23 |
| 1902 | Samuel A. Mellor, Yonkers, N.Y. | 2:43:12 |
| 1903 | John C. Lorden, Cambridge, Mass. | 2:41:29 |
| 1904 | Michael Spring, New York | 2:38:04 |
| 1905 | Fred Lorz, Yonkers, N.Y. | 2:38:25 |
| 1906 | Timothy Ford, Cambridge, Mass. | 2:45:45 |
| 1907 | Thomas Longboat, Hamilton, Ont. | 2:24:24 |
| 1908 | Thomas P. Morrissey, Yonkers, N.Y. | 2:25:43 |
| 1909 | Henri Renaud, Nashua, N.H. | 2:53:36 |
| 1910 | Fred L. Cameron, Amherst, Nova Scotia | 2:28:52 |
| 1911 | Clarence H. DeMar, Melrose, Mass. | 2:21:39 |
| 1912 | Michael J. Ryan, New York | 2:21:18 |
| 1913 | Fritz Carlson, Minneapolis | 2:25:14 |
| 1914 | James Duffy, Hamilton, Ont. | 2:25:01 |
| 1915 | Edouard Fabre, Montreal | 2:31:41 |
| 1916 | Arthur V. Roth, Roxbury, Mass. | 2:27:16 |
| 1917 | William K. Kennedy, Port Chester, N.Y. | 2:28:37 |
| 1918 | (WWI) Service team race won by Camp Devens | |
| 1919 | Carl W. A. Linder, Quincy, Mass. | 2:29:13 |
| 1920 | Peter Trivoulidas, Greece | 2:29:31 |
| 1921 | Frank Zuna, Newark, N.J. | 2:18:57 |
| 1922 | Clarence H. DeMar, Dorchester Club, Mass. | 2:18:10 |
| 1923 | Clarence H. DeMar, Melrose, Mass. | 2:23:37 |
| 1924 | Clarence H. DeMar, Melrose, Mass. | 2:29:40 |
| 1925 | Charles L. Mellor, Chicago | 2:33:00 |
| 1926 | John C. Miles, Sidney Mines, Nova Scotia | 2:25:40 |
| 1927 | Clarence H. DeMar, Melrose, Mass. | 2:40:22 |
| 1928 | Clarence H. DeMar, Melrose, Mass. | 2:37:07 |
| 1929 | John C. Miles, Hamilton, Ont. | 2:33:08 |
| 1930 | Clarence H. DeMar, Melrose, Mass. | 2:34:48 |
| 1931 | James P. Henigan, Medford, Mass. | 2:46:45 |
| 1932 | Paul deBruyn, Germany | 2:33:36 |
| 1933 | Leslie Pawson, Pawtucket, R.I. | 2:33:01 |
| 1934 | Dave Komonen, Sudbury, Ont. | 2:32:53 |
| 1935 | John A. Kelley, Arlington, Mass. | 2:32:07 |
| 1936 | Ellison M. (Tarzan) Brown, Alton, R.I. | 2:33:40 |
| 1937 | Walter Young, Verdun, Quebec | 2:33:20 |
| 1938 | Leslie Pawson, Pawtucket, R.I. | 2:35:34 |
| 1939 | Ellison M. (Tarzan) Brown, Alton, R.I. | 2:28:51 |
| 1940 | Gerard Cote, Ste.-Hyacinthe, Quebec | 2:33:20 |
| 1941 | Leslie Pawson, Pawtucket, R.I. | 2:30:38 |
| 1942 | Bernard Joe Smith, Medford | 2:26:51 |
| 1943 | Gerard Cote, Ste.-Hyacinthe, Quebec | 2:28:25 |
| 1944 | Gerard Cote, Ste.-Hyacinthe, Quebec | 2:31:50 |
| 1945 | John A. Kelley, West Acton, Mass. | 2:30:40 |
| 1946 | Stylianos Kyriakides, Greece | 2:29:27 |
| 1947 | Yun Bok Suh, Korea | 2:25:39 |
| 1948 | Gerard Cote, Ste.-Hyacinthe, Quebec | 2:31:02 |
| 1949 | Karle Gosta Leandersson, Sweden | 2:31:50 |
| 1950 | Kee Yong Ham, Korea | 2:32:39 |
| 1951 | Shigeki Tanaka, Japan | 2:27:45 |
| 1952 | Doroteo Flores, Guatemala | 2:31:53 |
| 1953 | Keizo Yamada, Japan | 2:18:51 |
| 1954 | Veikko L. Karvonen, Finland | 2:20:39 |
| 1955 | Hideo Hamamura, Japan | 2:18:22 |
| 1956 | Antti Viskari, Finland | 2:14:14 |
| 1957 | John J. Delley, Boston | 2:20:05 |
| 1958 | Franjo Mihalic, Yugoslavia | 2:25:54 |
| 1959 | Eino Oksanen, Finland | 2:22:42 |
| 1960 | Paavo Kotila, Finland | 2:20:54 |
| 1961 | Eino Oksanen, Finland | 2:23:39 |
| 1962 | Eino Oksanen, Finland | 2:23:48 |
| 1963 | Aurele Vandriessche, Belgium | 2:18:58 |
| 1964 | Aurele Vandriessche, Belgium | 2:19:59 |
| 1965 | Morio Shigematsu, Japan | 2:16:33 |
| 1966 | Kenji Kimihara, Japan | 2:17:11 |
| 1967 | David McKenzie, New Zealand | 2:15:45 |
| 1968 | Ambrose Burfoot, Wesleyan University | 2:22:17 |
| 1969 | Yoshiaki Unetani, Japan | 2:13:49 |
| 1970 | Ron Hill, England | 2:10:30 |
| 1971 | Alavaro Mejia, West Valley TC, Calif. | 2:18l45 |
| 1972 | Olavi Suomalainen, Finland | 2:15:39 |
| 1973 | Jon Anderson, Oregon | 2:16:03 |
| 1974 | Neil Cusack, East Tennessee State | 2:13:39 |
| 1975 | Bill Rodgers, Melrose, Mass. | 2:09:55 |
| 1976 | Jack Fultz, Georgetown University | 2:20:19 |
| 1977 | Jerome Drayton, Toronto, Ont. | 2:14:46 |
| 1978 | Bill Rodgers, Melrose, Mass. | 2:10:13 |
| 1979 | Bill Rodgers, Melrose, Mass. | 2:09:27 |
| 1980 | Bill Rodgers, Melrose, Mass. | 2:12:11 |
| 1981 | Toshihiko Seko, Japan | 2:09:26 |
| 1982 | Alberto Salazar, Wayland, Mass. | 2:08:52 |
| 1983 | Gregory A. Meyer, Wellesley, Mass. | 2:09:00 |
| 1984 | Geoff Smith, Rhode Island | 2:10:34 |
| 1985 | Geoff Smith, Massachusetts | 2:14:05 |
| 1986 | Robert de Castella, Australia | 2:07:51 |
| 1987 | Toshihiko Seko, Japan | 2:11:50 |
| 1988 | Ibrahim Hussein, Kenya | 2:08:43 |
| 1989 | Abebe Mekonnen, Ethiopia | 2:09:06 |
| 1990 | Gelindo Bordin, Italy | 2:08:20 |
| 1991 | Ibrahim Hussein, Kenya | 2:11:06 |

#### WOMEN

| Year | Name, city/state/country | Time |
|------|--------------------------|------|
| 1972 | Nina Kuscsik, New York | 3:10:26 |
| 1973 | Jacqueline Hansen, California | 3:05:59 |
| 1974 | Miki Gorman, California | 2:47:11 |
| 1975 | Liane Winter, West Germany | 2:42:24 |
| 1976 | Kim Merritt, Wisconsin | 2:47:10 |
| 1977 | Miki Gorman, California | 2:46:22 |
| 1978 | Gayle Barron, Georgia | 2:44:52 |
| 1979 | Joan Benoit, Maine | 2:35:15 |
| 1980 | Jacqueline Gareau, Canada | 2:34:28 |
| 1981 | Allison Roe, New Zealand | 2:26:46 |
| 1982 | Charlotte Teske, West Germany | 2:29:33 |
| 1983 | Joan Benoit, Massachusetts | 2:22:43 |
| 1984 | Lorraine Moller, New Zealand | 2:29:28 |
| 1985 | Lisa Larsen-Weidenbach, Massachusetts | 2:34:06 |
| 1986 | Ingrid Kristiansen, Norway | 2:24:55 |
| 1987 | Rosa Mota, Portugal | 2:25:21 |
| 1988 | Rosa Mota, Portugal | 2:24:30 |
| 1989 | Ingrid Kristiansen, Norway | 2:24:33 |
| 1990 | Rosa Mota, Portugal | 2:25:24 |
| 1991 | Wanda Panfil, Poland | 2:24:18 |

**Source:** Boston Athletic Assn.

## NEW YORK MARATHON

### CHAMPIONS

| Year | Men | Time |
|---|---|---|
| 1970 | Gary Muhrcke | 2:31:39 |
| 1971 | Norman Higgins | 2:22:55 |
| 1972 | Sheldon Karlin | 2:27:53 |
| 1973 | Tom Fleming | 2:21:55 |
| 1974 | Norbert Sander | 2:26:31 |
| 1975 | Tom Fleming | 2:19:27 |
| 1976 | Bill Rodgers | 2:10:10 |
| 1977 | Bill Rodgers | 2:11:28 |
| 1978 | Bill Rodgers | 2:12:12 |
| 1979 | Bill Rodgers | 2:11:42 |
| 1980 | Alberto Salazar | 2:09:41 |
| 1981 | Alberto Salazar | 2:08:13 |
| 1982 | Alberto Salazar | 2:09:29 |
| 1983 | Rod Dixon | 2:08:59 |
| 1984 | Orlando Pizzolato | 2:14:53 |
| 1985 | Orlando Pizzolato | 2:11:34 |
| 1986 | Gianni Poli | 2:11:06 |
| 1987 | Ibrahim Hussein | 2:11:01 |
| 1988 | Steve Jones | 2:08:20 |
| 1989 | Jumo Ikangaa | 2:08:01 |
| 1990 | Douglas Wakiihuri | 2:12:39 |

| Year | Women | Time |
|---|---|---|
| 1971 | Beth Bonner | 2:55:22 |
| 1972 | Nina Kuscsik | 3:08:42 |
| 1973 | Nina Kuscsik | 2:57:08 |
| 1974 | Katherine Switzer | 3:07:29 |
| 1975 | Kim Merritt | 2:46:15 |
| 1976 | Miki Gorman | 2:39:11 |
| 1977 | Miki Gorman | 2:43:10 |
| 1978 | Grete Waitz | 2:32:30 |
| 1979 | Grete Waitz | 2:27:33 |
| 1980 | Grete Waitz | 2:25:41 |
| 1981 | Allison Roe | 2:25:29 |
| 1982 | Grete Waitz | 2:27:14 |
| 1983 | Grete Waitz | 2:27:00 |
| 1984 | Grete Waitz | 2:29:30 |
| 1985 | Grete Waitz | 2:28:34 |
| 1986 | Grete Waitz | 2:28:06 |
| 1987 | Priscilla Welch | 2:30:17 |
| 1988 | Grete Waitz | 2:28:07 |
| 1989 | Ingrid Kristiansen | 2:25:30 |
| 1990 | Wanda Panfil | 2:30:45 |

**Source:** New York Roadrunners Club.

# TRACK AND FIELD

## TRACK AND FIELD WORLD RECORDS (as of Sept. 5, 1991)

These are the recognized records of the IAAF (International Amateur Athletic Federation). Marks pending approval by the IAAF are denoted by 'P.' All walk records must have been made on a track, and all relay records must be made by teams composed of individuals from the same country.

### MEN

| Event | Time | Record holder (country) | Date |
|---|---|---|---|
| 100 m | 9.86p | Carl Lewis (U.S.) | 8/25/91 |
| 200 m | 19.72 | Pietro Mennea (Italy) | 9/17/79 |
| 400 m | 43.29 | Butch Reynolds (U.S.) | 8/17/88 |
| 800 m | 1:41.73 | Sebastian Coe (U.K.) | 6/10/81 |
| 1,500 m | 3:29.46 | Said Aouita (Morocco) | 8/23/85 |
| Mile | 3:46.32 | Steve Cram (U.K.) | 7/27/85 |
| Steeplechase | 8:05.35 | Peter Koech (Kenya) | 7/3/89 |
| 5,000 m | 12:58.39 | Said Aouita (Morocco) | 7/22/87 |
| 10,000 m | 27:08.23 | Arturo Barrios (Mexico) | 8/18/89 |
| Marathon | 2:06:50 | Belayneh Densimo (Ethiopia) | 4/17/88 |
| 110-m hurdles | 12.92 | Roger Kingdom (U.S.) | 8/16/89 |
| 400-m hurdles | 47.02 | Edwin Moses (U.S.) | 8/31/83 |
| 20-km walk | 1:18:40.00 | Ernesto Canto (Mexico) | 5/5/84 |
| 50-km walk | 3:41:38.40 | Raul Gonzales (Mexico) | 5/25/79 |
| 4 x 100 m | 37.50 | United States | 9/1/91 |
| | | (Andre Cason, Leroy Burrell, Dennis Mitchell, Carl Lewis) | |
| 4 x 400 m | (tie) 2:56.16 | United States | 10/20/68 |
| | | (Vince Matthews 45.0, Ron Freeman 43.2, Larry James 43.8, Lee Evans 44.1) | |
| | 2:56.16 | United States | 10/10/88 |
| | | (Danny Everett 43.79, Steve Lewis 43.69, Kevin Robinzine 44.74, Butch Reynolds 43.94) | |

| Event | Meters | Ft./in. | Record holder (country) | Date |
|---|---|---|---|---|
| High jump | 2.44 | 8-0 | Javier Sotomayor (Cuba) | 7/29/89 |
| Pole vault | 6.10p | 20-0 | Sergey Bubka (USSR) | 8/5/91 |
| Long jump | 8.95p | 29-4 1/2 | Mike Powell (U.S.) | 8/30/91 |
| Triple jump | 17.97 | 58-11 1/2 | Willie Banks (U.S.) | 6/16/85 |
| Shot put | 23.12 | 75-10 1/4 | Randy Barnes (U.S.) | 5/20/90 |
| Discus | 74.08 | 243-0 | Jurgen Schult (E. Ger.) | 6/6/86 |
| Hammer | 86.74 | 284-7 | Yuriy Syedikh (USSR) | 8/30/86 |
| Javelin | 96.96p | 318-1 | Seppo Raty (Finland) | 6/3/91 |
| Decathlon | 8,847 points | | Daley Thompson (U.K.) | 8/9/84 |
| | (10.44, 26-3 1/2, 51-7, 6-8, 46.97, 14.33, 152-9, 16-4-3/4, 214-0, 4:35.00) | | | |

### WOMEN

| Event | Time | Record holder (country) | Date |
|---|---|---|---|
| 100 m | 10.49 | Florence Griffith Joyner (U.S.) | 7/16/88 |
| 200 m | 21.34 | Florence Griffith Joyner (U.S.) | 9/29/88 |
| 400 m | 47.60 | Marita Koch (E. Ger.) | 10/6/85 |
| 800 m | 1:53.28 | Jarmila Kratochvilova (Czech.) | 7/26/83 |
| 1,500 m | 3:52.47 | Tatyana Kazankina (USSR) | 8/13/80 |
| Mile | 4:15.61 | Paula Ivan (Romania) | 7/10/89 |
| 3,000 m | 8:22.62 | Tatyana Kazankina (USSR) | 8/26/84 |
| 5,000 m | 14:37.33 | Ingrid Kristiansen (Norway) | 8/5/86 |
| 10,000 m | 30:13.74 | Ingrid Kristiansen (Norway) | 7/5/86 |
| Marathon | 2:21:06 | Ingrid Kristiansen (Norway) | 4/21/85 |
| 100-m hurdles | 12.21 | Yordanka Donkova (Bulgaria) | 8/20/88 |
| 400-m hurdles | 52.94 | Marina Stepanova (USSR) | 9/17/86 |
| 4 x 100 m | 41.37 | East Germany | 10/6/85 |
| | | (Silke Moller, Sabine Rieger, Ingrid Auerswald, Marlies Gohr) | |
| 4 x 400 m | 3:15.18 | Soviet Union | 10/1/88 |
| | | (Tatyana Ledovskaya 50.12, Olga Nazarova 47.82, Maria Pinigina 49.43, Olga Bryzgina 47.78) | |
| 10-km walk | 41:46.21 | Nadezhda Ryashkina (USSR) | 7/24/90 |

| Event | Meters | Ft./in. | Record holder (country) | Date |
|---|---|---|---|---|
| High jump | 2.09 | 6-10 1/4 | Stefka Kostadinova (Bulgaria) | 8/30/87 |
| Long jump | 7.52 | 24-8 1/4 | Galina Chistyakova (USSR) | 6/11/88 |
| Shot put | 22.63 | 74-3 | Natalya Lisovskaya (USSR) | 6/7/87 |
| Discus | 76.80 | 252-0 | Gabriele Reinsch (E. Ger.) | 7/9/88 |
| Javelin | 80.00 | 262-5 | Petra Felke (E. Ger.) | 9/9/88 |
| Heptathalon | 7,291 points | | Jackie Joyner-Kersee (U.S.) | 9/24/88 |
| | (12.69, 6-1 1/4, 51-10, 22.56, 23-10 1/4, 149-10, 2:08.51) | | | |
| Triple jump | 14.95p | 49-3/4 | Inessa Kravets (USSR) | 7/10/91 |

**Source:** International Amateur Athletic Federation.

## WORLD INDOOR RECORDS

### MEN

| Event | Time | Record holder (country) | Date |
|---|---|---|---|
| 50 yds. | 5.22 | Stanley Floyd (U.S.)[1] | 2/1/82 |
| | 5.00 | Kirk Clayton (U.S.)[2] | 10/1/70 |
| | | Herb Washington (U.S.)[2] | 2/4/72 |
| 440 yds. | 46.40 | Sunder Nix (U.S.) | 3/3/84 |
| 500 yds. | 54.40 | Lee Evans (U.S.) | 1/8/71 |
| | | Lee Evans (U.S.) | 1/30/71 |
| 500 m | 1:00.17 | Ken Lowery (U.S.) | 1/16/87 |
| 600 yds. | 1:07.60 | Martin McGrady (U.S.) | 2/27/70 |
| 600 m | 1:15.77 | Donato Sabia (Italy) | 2/4/84 |
| 800 m | 1:44.84 | Paul Ereng (Kenya) | 3/4/89 |
| 880 yds. | 1:46.80 | Johnny Gray (U.S.) | 1/17/86 |
| 1,000 yds. | 2:04.39 | Johnny Gray (U.S.) | 2/23/86 |
| 1,000 m | 2:16.40 | Rob Druppers (Holland) | 2/20/88 |
| 1,500 m | 3:34.16p | Nourredine Motceli (Algeria) | 2/28/91 |
| Mile | 3:49.78 | Eamonn Coghlan (Ireland) | 2/27/83 |
| 2,000 m | 4:54.07 | Eamonn Coghlan (Ireland) | 2/21/87 |
| 3,000 m | 7:39.20 | Emiel Puttemans (Belgium) | 2/18/73 |
| 2 mi. | 8:13.20 | Emiel Puttemans (Belgium) | 2/18/73 |
| 3 mi. | 12:54.60 | Emiel Puttemans (Belgium) | 1/10/76 |
| 5,000 m | 13:20.40 | Suleiman Nyambi (Tanzania) | 2/6/81 |
| 50-yd. hurdles | 5.88 | Greg Foster (U.S.) | 1/17/86 |
| 50-m hurdles | 6.25 | Mark McKoy (Canada) | 3/5/86 |
| 60-yd. hurdles | 6.82 | Renaldo Nehemiah (U.S.) | 1/30/82 |
| 60-m hurdles | 7.36 | Greg Foster (U.S.) | 1/16/87 |
| 110-m hurdles | 13.58 | Arto Bryggare (Finland) | 12/30/82 |
| 1,500-m walk | 5:13.53 | Tim Lewis (U.S.) | 2/13/88 |
| Mile walk | 5:33.53 | Tim Lewis (U.S.) | 2/5/88 |
| 3,000-m walk | 10:54.61 | Carlo Mattioli (Italy) | 2/6/80 |
| 2-mi. walk | 11:54.50 | Valdas Kazlaukas (USSR) | 2/24/90 |
| 3-mi. walk | 18:23.88p | Frants Kostyukevich (USSR) | 2/10/91 |
| 5,000-m walk | 18:23.55p | Frants Kostyukevich (USSR) | 3/10/91 |
| 10-km walk | 38:31.40 | Werner Heyer (E. Ger.) | 1/12/80 |
| 15-km walk | 1:00:09 | Ronald Weigel (E. Ger.) | 1/27/80 |
| 20-km walk | 1:20:40 | Ronald Weigel (E. Ger.) | 1/27/80 |
| 4 x 200 m | 1:22.11 | Great Britain | 3/3/91 |
| 4 x 220 yds. | 1:26.90 | Idaho State (U.S.) | 2/29/71 |
| 4 x 400 m | 3:05.05 | Germany | 3/3/91 |
| 4 x 440 yds. | 3:09.40 | Pacific Coast Club (U.S.) | 2/27/71 |
| 4 x 800 m | 7:17.80 | USSR | 3/14/71 |
| 4 x 880 yds. | 7:20.80 | Univ. of Chicago Track Club (U.S.) | 2/9/74 |
| 4 x mile | 16:19.00 | Villanova (U.S.) | 1/16/76 |
| Sprint medley | 3:18.70 | Eastern Michigan (U.S.) | 1/28/84 |
| Distance medley | 9:36.90 | Michigan (U.S.) | 2/18/83 |
| 4 x 60-yd. hurdles | 27.60 | Air Force Academy (U.S.) | 2/22/75 |

| Event | Ft./in. | Record holder (country) | Date |
|---|---|---|---|
| High jump | 7-11 1/4 | Javier Sotomayor (Cuba) | 3/4/89 |
| Pole vault | 20-1 | Sergey Bubka (USSR) | 3/23/91 |
| Long jump | 28-10-1/4 | Carl Lewis (U.S.) | 1/27/84 |
| Triple jump | 58-3-1/4 | Mike Conley (U.S.) | 2/27/87 |
| Shot put | 74-4 1/4 | Randy Barnes (U.S.) | 1/20/89 |
| Weight throw | 79-3-3/4 | Lance Deal (U.S.) | 2/22/91 |

### WOMEN

| Event | Time | Record holder (country) | Date |
|---|---|---|---|
| 50 yds. | 5.74 | Evelyn Ashford (U.S.)[1] | 2/18/83 |
| | 5.50 | Iris Davis (U.S.)[2] | 2/2/73 |
| | | Alice Annum (Ghana)[2] | 1/5/75 |
| 50 m | 6.00 | Barbara Ferrell (U.S.)[2] | 2/17/68 |
| | | Barbara Ferrell (U.S.)[2] | 2/21/69 |
| | | Renate Stecher (E. Ger.)[2] | 2/14/71 |
| | | Renate Stecher (E. Ger.)[2] | 2/20/71 |
| | | Renate Stecher (E. Ger.)[2] | 2/28/71 |
| 60 yds. | 6.54 | Evelyn Ashford (U.S.) | 2/26/82 |
| | | Jeanette Bolden (U.S.) | 2/21/86 |
| 60 m | 7.00 | Nellie Cooman (Holland)[1] | 2/23/86 |
| | 6.90 | Alice Annum (Ghana)[2] | 6/17/75 |
| | | Marlies Gohr (E. Ger.)[2] | 2/10/79 |
| 100 yds. | 10.15 | Heike Drechsler (E. Ger.) | 2/8/87 |
| 100 m | 11.15 | Marita Koch (E. Ger.) | 1/12/80 |
| 200 m | 22.24 | Merlene Ottey (Jamaica) | 3/10/91 |
| 220 yds. | 22.89 | Marita Koch (E. Ger.) | 2/28/86 |
| 300 yds. | 32.63 | Merlene Ottey (Jamaica) | 3/13/82 |
| 300 m | 35.83 | Merlene Ottey (Jamaica)[1] | 3/14/81 |
| | 35.50 | Jarmila Kratochvilova (Czech.)[2] | 3/7/82 |
| 400 m | 49.59 | Jarmila Kratochvilova (Czech.) | 3/7/82 |
| 440 yds. | 52.20 | Diane Dixon (U.S.) | 2/22/85 |
| 500 yds. | 1:02.09 | Diane Dixon (U.S.) | 2/21/86 |
| 500 m | 1:07.67 | Olga Nazarova (USSR) | 1/10/88 |
| 600 yds. | 1:17.38 | Delisa Walton-Floyd (U.S.) | 3/13/82 |
| 600 m | 1:25.46 | Lyubov Kiryukhina (USSR) | 2/15/87 |
| 800 m | 1:56.40 | Christine Wachtel (E. Ger.) | 2/13/88 |
| 880 yds. | 1:59.70 | Mary Decker (U.S.) | 2/22/80 |
| 1,000 yds. | 2:23.50 | Joetta Clark (U.S.) | 3/9/86 |
| 1,000 m | 2:34.80 | Brigitte Kraus (E. Ger.) | 2/19/78 |
| 1,500 m | 4:00.27 | Doina Melinte (Romania) | 2/9/90 |
| Mile | 4:17.13 | Doina Melinte (Romania) | 2/9/90 |
| 2,000 m | 5:34.52 | Mary Decker (U.S.) | 1/18/85 |
| 3,000 m | 8:33.82 | Elly van Hulst (Holland) | 3/4/89 |
| 2 mi. | 9:28.15 | Lynn Jennings (U.S.) | 2/28/86 |
| 3 mi. | 14:53.80 | Christine McMiken (New Zeal.) | 2/22/85 |
| 5,000 m | 15:13.72 | Uta Pippig (Germany) | 2/10/91 |
| 50-yd. hurdles | 6.20 | Johanna Klier (E. Ger.) | 2/10/78 |
| 50-m hurdles | 6.58 | Cornelia Oschkenat (E. Ger.) | 2/20/88 |
| 60-yd. hurdles | 7.36 | Stephanie Hightower (U.S.) | 2/25/83 |
| 60-m hurdles | 7.69 | Lyudmila Narozhilenko (USSR) | 2/4/90 |
| 100-m hurdles | 13.12 | Anneliese Ehrhardt (E. Ger.)[1] | 1/14/76 |
| | 12.60 | Svetlana Gusova (USSR)[2] | 3/2/85 |
| 1,500-m walk | 5:54.35 | Debbie Lawrence (U.S.) | 2/8/91 |
| Mile walk | 6:28.46 | Giuliana Salce (Italy) | 2/16/85 |
| 3,000-m walk | 11:50.90 | Beate Anders (Germany) | 3/9/91 |
| 5,000-m walk | 21:44.52 | Giuliana Salce (Italy) | 2/20/85 |
| 4 x 200 m | 1:32.55 | SC Eintracht Hamm (W. Ger.) | 2/20/88 |
| 4 x 220 yds. | 1:36.50 | Tennessee State (U.S.) | 2/10/79 |
| 880 medley | 1:41.90 | The Colorado Gold (U.S.) | 3/19/72 |
| 4 x 400 m | 3:27.22 | German National Team | 3/10/91 |
| 4 x 440 yds. | 3:39.58 | Morgan State (U.S.) | 3/12/83 |
| 4 x 800 m | 8:25.50 | Villanova (U.S.) | 2/7/87 |
| 4 x 880 yds. | 8:41.60 | USSR | 3/17/72 |
| Sprint medley | 3:58.50 | Michigan State (U.S.) | 2/6/81 |
| Distance medley | 10:54.34 | Villanova (U.S.) | 1/30/88 |

| Event | Ft./in. | Record holder (country) | Date |
|---|---|---|---|
| High jump | 6-9 | Stefka Kostadinova (Bulgaria) | 2/20/88 |
| Long jump | 24-2 1/4 | Heike Drechsler (E. Ger.) | 2/13/88 |
| Triple jump | 47-4 1/2 | Inessa Kravets (USSR) | 3/9/91 |
| Shot put | 73-10 | Helena Fibingerova (Czech.) | 2/19/77 |

1. Timed by electronic device. 2. Timed by hand. **Source:** The Athletics Congress/USA.

# THE OLYMPIC GAMES

## WINTER OLYMPICS CHAMPIONS

### ICE HOCKEY

1920  Canada, U.S., Czechoslovakia
1924  Canada, U.S., Great Britain
1928  Canada, U.S., Switzerland
1932  Canada, U.S., Germany
1936  Great Britain, Canada, U.S.
1948  Canada, Czechoslovakia, Switzerland
1952  Canada, U.S., Sweden
1956  USSR, U.S., Canada
1960  U.S., Canada, USSR
1964  USSR, Sweden, Czechoslovakia
1968  USSR, Czechoslovakia, Canada
1972  USSR, U.S., Czechoslovakia
1976  USSR, Czechoslovakia
1980  U.S., USSR, Sweden
1984  USSR, Czechoslovakia, Sweden
1988  USSR, Finland, Sweden

### ALPINE SKIING—MEN   Time

**DOWNHILL**
1948  Henri Oreiller, France    2:55.00
1952  Zeno Colo, Italy    2:30.80
1956  Anton Sailer, Austria    2:52.20
1960  Jean Vuarnet, France    2:06.00
1964  Egon Zimmerman, Austria    2:18.16
1968  Jean-Claude Killy, France    1:59.85
1972  Bernhard Russi, Switzerland    1:51.43
1976  Franz Klammer, Austria    1:45.73
1980  Leonhard Stock, Austria    1:45.50
1984  William Johnson, U.S.    1:45.59
1988  Pirmin Zurbriggen, Switzerland    1:59.63

**GIANT SLALOM**
1952  Stein Eriksen, Norway    2:25.00
1956  Anton Sailer, Austria    3:00.10
1960  Roger Staub, Switzerland    1:48.30
1964  François Bonlieu, France    1:46.71
1968  Jean-Claude Killy, France    3:29.28
1972  Gustavo Thöni, Italy    3:09.62
1976  Heini Hemmi, Switzerland    3:26.97
1980  Ingemar Stenmark, Sweden    2:40.74
1984  Max Julen, Switzerland    2:41.18
1988  Alberto Tomba, Italy    2:06.37

**SUPER GIANT SLALOM**
1988  Frank Piccard, France    1:39.66

**SLALOM**
1948  Edi Reinalter, Switzerland    2:10.30
1952  Othmar Schneider, Austria    2:00.00
1956  Anton Sailer, Austria    3:14.70
1960  Ernst Hinterseer, Austria    2:08.90
1964  Josef Stiegler, Austria    2:11.13

1968  Jean-Claude Killy, France    1:39.73
1972  Francisco Fernandez Ochoa,
     Spain    1:39.73
1976  Piero Gros, Italy    2:03.29
1980  Ingemar Stenmark, Sweden    1:44.26
1984  Philip Mahre, U.S.    1:39.41
1988  Alberto Tomba, Italy    1:39.47

### ALPINE SKIING—WOMEN   Time

**DOWNHILL**
1948  Hedi Schlunegger, Switzerland    2:28.30
1952  Trude Jochum-Beiser, Austria    1:47.10
1956  Madeleine Berthod, Switzerland    1:40.70
1960  Heidi Biebl, Germany    1:37.60
1964  Christl Haas, Austria    1:55.39
1968  Olga Pall, Austria    1:40.87
1972  Marie-Theres Nadig, Switzerland    1:36.68
1976  Rosi Mittermaier, West Germany    1:46.16
1980  Annemarie Moser-Pröll, Austria    1:37.52
1984  Michela Figini, Switzerland    1:13.361
1988  Marina Kiehl, West Germany    1:25.86
1. Race shortened by weather conditions.

**GIANT SLALOM**
1952  Andrea Mead Lawrence, U.S.    2:06.80
1956  Ossi Reichert, Germany    1:56.50
1960  Yvonne Rüegg, Switzerland    1:39.90
1964  Marielle Goitschel, France    1:52.24
1968  Nancy Greene, Canada    1:51.97
1972  Marie-Theres Nadig, Switzerland    1:29.90
1976  Kathy Kreiner, Canada    1:29.13
1980  Hanni Wenzel, Liechtenstein    2:41.66
1984  Debbie Armstrong, U.S.    2:20.98
1988  Vreni Schneider, Switzerland    2:06.49

**SUPER GIANT SLALOM**
1988  Sigrid Wolf, Austria    1:19.03

**SLALOM**
1948  Gretchen Fraser, U.S.    1:57.20
1952  Andrea Mead Lawrence, U.S.    2:10.60
1956  Renèe Colliard, Switzerland    1:52.30
1960  Anne Heggtveigt, Canada    1:49.60
1964  Christine Goitschel, France    1:29.86
1968  Marielle Goitschel, France    1:25.86
1972  Barbara Cochran, U.S.    1:31.24
1976  Rosi Mittermaier, West Germany    1:30.54
1980  Hanni Wenzel, Liechtenstein    1:25.09
1984  Paoletta Magoni, Italy    1:36.47
1988  Vreni Schneider, Switzerland    1:36.69

### NORDIC SKIING AND JUMPING—MEN   Time

**15-KILOMETER (9.3-MI.) CROSS-COUNTRY**
1968  Harald Grönningen, Norway    47:54.20
1972  Sven-Ake Lundbäck, Sweden    45:28.24
1976  Nikolai Bazhukov, USSR    43:58.47
1980  Thomas Wassberg, Sweden    41:57.63
1984  Gunde Svan    41:25.60
1988  Mikhail Deviatiarov, USSR    41:18.90

**30-KILOMETER (18.6-MI.) CROSS-COUNTRY**
1956  Veikko Hakulinen, Finland    1:44:06.00
1960  Sixten Jernberg, Sweden    1:51:03.90
1964  Eero Mäntyranta, Finland    1:30:50.70
1968  Franco Nones, Italy    1:35:39.20
1972  Vyacheslav Vedenin, USSR    1:36:31.15
1976  Sergei Saveliev, USSR    1:30:29.38
1980  Nikolai Zimyatov, USSR    1:27:02.80
1984  Nikolai Zimyatov, USSR    1:28:56.30
1988  Aleksei Prokourorov, USSR    1:24:26.30

**50-KILOMETER (31.2-MI.) CROSS-COUNTRY**
1924  Thorleif Haug, Norway    3:44:32.00
1928  Per Erik Hedlund, Sweden    4:52:03.00
1932  Veli Saarinen, Finland    4:28:00.00
1936  Elis Viklund, Sweden    3:30:11.00
1948  Nils Karlsson, Sweden    3:47:48.00
1952  Veikko Hakulinen, Finland    3:33:33.00
1956  Sixten Jernberg, Sweden    2:50:27.00
1960  Kalevi Hamalainen, Finland    2:59:06.30
1964  Sixten Jernberg, Sweden    2:43:52.60
1968  Ole Ellefsaeter, Norway    2:28:45.80
1972  Pål Tyldum, Norway    2:43:14.75
1976  Ivar Formo, Norway    2:37:30.05
1980  Nikolai Zimyatov, USSR    2:27:24.60
1984  Thomas Wassberg, Sweden    2:15:55.80
1988  Gunde Svan, Sweden    2:04:30.90

**40-KILOMETER (24.8-MI.) CROSS-COUNTRY RELAY (4 × 10)**
1936  Finland, Norway, Sweden    2:41:33.00
1948  Sweden, Finland, Norway    2:32:08.00
1952  Finland, Norway, Sweden    2:20:16.00
1956  USSR, Finland Sweden    2:15:30.00
1960  Finland, Norway, USSR    2:18:45.60
1964  Sweden, Finland, USSR    2:18:34.60
1968  Norway, Sweden, Finland    2:08:33.50
1972  USSR, Norway, Switzerland    2:04:47.94
1976  Finland, Norway, Switzerland    2:07:59.72
1980  USSR, Norway, Finland    1:57:03.46
1984  Sweden, USSR, Finland    1:55:06.30
1988  Sweden, USSR, Czechoslovakia    1:43:58.60

**SKI JUMP**   Points

**70-METER (229.7 FT.) JUMP**
1964  Veikko Kankkonen, Finland    229.90
1968  Jiri Raska, Czechoslovakia    216.50
1972  Yukio Kasaya, Japan    244.20
1976  Hans-Georg Aschenbach,
     East Germany    252.00
1980  Anton Innauer, Austria    266.30
1984  Jens Weissflog, East Germany    215.20
1988  Matti Nykänen, Finland    229.10

**90-METER (295.3 FT.) JUMP**
1924  Jacob Tullin Thambs, Norway    18.960
1928  Alf Andersen, Norway    19.208
1932  Birger Ruud, Norway    228.10
1936  Birger Ruud, Norway    232.00
1948  Petter Hugsted, Norway    228.10
1952  Arnfinn Bergmann, Norway    226.00
1956  Antti Hyvarinen, Finland    227.00
1960  Helmut Recknagel, East Germany    227.20
1964  Toralf Engan, Norway    230.70
1968  Vladimir Beloussov, USSR    231.30
1972  Wojiech Fortuna, Poland    219.90
1976  Karl Schnabl, Austria    234.80
1980  Jouko Tormanen, Finland    271.00
1984  Matti Nykänen, Finland    231.20
1988  Matti Nykänen, Finland    224.00

**90-METER (295-FT.) JUMP, TEAM**
1988  Finland, Yugoslavia, Norway    634.40

**NORDIC COMBINED (15-KM [9.3-MI.] CROSS-COUNTRY AND 70-METER [229.7-FT.] SKI JUMP)[1]**
1924  Thorleif Haug, Norway    18.906
1928  Johan Gröttumsbraaten, Norway    17.833
1932  Johan Gröttumsbraaten, Norway    446.00
1946  Oddbjörn Hagen, Norway    430.30
1952  Simon Slåttvik, Norway    451.62
1956  Sverre Stenersen, Norway    455.00
1960  George Thoma, West Germany    457.95
1964  Tormod Knutsen, Norway    469.28

1968  Franz Keller, West Germany    449.04
1972  Ulrich Wehling, East Germany    413.34
1976  Ulrich Wehling, East Germany    423.39
1980  Ulrich Wehling, East Germany    432.20
1984  Tom Sandberg, Norway    422.59
1988  Hippolyt Kempf, Switzerland    235.80

1. Until 1956, 18 kilometers.

### NORDIC SKIING —WOMEN   Time

**10-KILOMETER (6.2-MI.) CROSS-COUNTRY**
1952  Lydia Wideman, Finland    41:40.00
1956  Lyubov Kosyreva, USSR    38:11.00
1960  Maria Gusakova, USSR    39:46.60
1964  Claudia Boyarskikh, USSR    40:24.30
1968  Toini Gustafsson, Sweden    36:46.50
1972  Galina Kolakova, USSR    34:17.82
1976  Raisa Smetanina, USSR    30:31.54
1980  Barbara Petzoid, East Germany    30:31.54
1984  Marja-Liisa Hämäläinen, Finland    31:44.20
1988  Vida Ventsene, USSR    30:08.20

**20-KILOMETER (12.4 MI.) CROSS-COUNTRY**
1984  Marja-Liisa Hämäläinen, Finland    1:01:45.00
1988  Tamara Tikhonova, USSR    55:53.60

**15-KILOMETER (9.3 MI.) RELAY (3 x 5)**
1956  Finland    1:09:01.00
1960  Sweden    1:04:21.00
1964  USSR    0:59:20.00
1968  Norway    0:57:30.00
1972  USSR    48:46.15

**20-KILOMETER (12.4 MI.) RELAY (4 x 5)**
1976  USSR    1:07:49.75
1980  East Germany    1:02:11.10
1984  Norway    1:06:49.70
1988  USSR    0:59:51.10

### BOBSLEDDING

| | Time | | Time |
|---|---|---|---|
| **TWO-MAN** | | | |
| 1932  U.S. | 8:14.74 | 1968  Italy | 4:41.54 |
| 1936  U.S. | 5:29.29 | 1972  West Germany | 4:57.07 |
| 1948  Switzerland | 5:29.20 | 1976  East Germany | 3:44.42 |
| 1952  Germany | 5:24.54 | 1980  Switzerland | 4:09.36 |
| 1956  Italy | 5:30.14 | 1984  East Germany | 3:25.56 |
| 1964  Great Britain | 4:21.90 | 1988  USSR | 3:54.19 |
| **FOUR-MAN** | | | |
| 1924  Switzerland | 5:45.54 | 1964  Canada | 4:14.46 |
| 1928  U.S. (5-Man) | 3:20.50 | 1968  Italy (2 races) | 2:17.39 |
| 1932  U.S. | 7:53.68 | 1972  Switzerland | 4:43.07 |
| 1936  Switzerland | 5:19.85 | 1976  East Germany | 3:40.43 |
| 1948  U.S. | 5:20.10 | 1980  East Germany | 3:59.42 |
| 1952  Germany | 5:07.84 | 1984  East Germany | 3:20.22 |
| 1956  Switzerland | 5:10.44 | 1988  Switzerland | 3:47.51 |

### LUGE   Time

**SINGLES (men)**
1964  Thomas Köhler, East Germany    3:26.77
1968  Manfred Schmid, Austria    2:52.48
1972  Wolfgang Scheidel, East Germany    3:27.58
1976  Dettlef Günther, East Germany    3:27.68
1980  Bernhard Glass, East Germany    2:54.79
1984  Paul Hildgartner, Italy    3:04.25
1988  Jens Mueller, East Germany    3:05.54

| | | | Competitors | | Nations | | | | Competitors | | Nations |
|---|---|---|---|---|---|---|---|---|---|---|---|
| Olympics/year | | Place | Men | Women | Represented | Olympics/year | | Place | Men | Women | Represented |
| I | 1924 | Chamonix, France | 281 | 13 | 16 | VIII | 1960 | Squaw Valley, U.S. | 521 | 144 | 30 |
| II | 1928 | St. Moritz, Switzerland | 468 | 27 | 25 | IX | 1964 | Innsbruck, Austria | 986 | 200 | 36 |
| III | 1932 | Lake Placid, U.S. | 274 | 32 | 17 | X | 1968 | Grenoble, France | 1,081 | 212 | 37 |
| IV | 1936 | Garmisch-Parten-kirchen, Germany | 675 | 80 | 28 | XI | 1972 | Sapporo, Japan | 1,015 | 217 | 35 |
| | | | | | | XII | 1976 | Innsbruck, Austria | 900 | 228 | 37 |
| V | 1948 | St. Moritz, Switzerland | 636 | 77 | 28 | XIII | 1980 | Lake Placid, U.S. | 833 | 234 | 37 |
| VI | 1952 | Oslo, Norway | 623 | 109 | 30 | XIV | 1984 | Sarajevo, Yugoslavia | 1,002 | 276 | 49 |
| VII | 1956 | Cortina D'Ampezzo, Italy | 686 | 132 | 32 | XV | 1988 | Calgary, Canada | 1,445 (total) | | 57 |

**Sources:** David Wallechinsky, *The Complete Book of the Olympics* (1988), reprinted by permission; U.S. Olympic Committee.

## THE SUMMER GAMES

| Olympics/Year | Place | Competitors Men | Women | Nations represented | | Olympics/Year | Place | Competitors Men | Women | Nations represented |
|---|---|---|---|---|---|---|---|---|---|---|
| I | 1896 | Athens, Greece | 311 | — | 13 | | XI | 1936 | Berlin, Germany | 3,738 | 328 | 49 |
| II | 1900 | Paris, France | 1,319 | 11 | 22 | | XII | 1948 | London, UK | 3,714 | 385 | 59 |
| III | 1904 | St. Louis, U.S. | 681 | 6 | 12 | | XIII | 1952 | Helsinki, Finland | 4,407 | 518 | 69 |
| — | 1906 | Athens, Greece | 877 | 7 | 20 | | XIV | 1960 | Rome, Italy | 4,738 | 610 | 83 |
| IV | 1908 | London, UK | 1,999 | 36 | 23 | | XV | 1964 | Tokyo, Japan | 4,457 | 683 | 93 |
| V | 1912 | Stockholm, Sweden | 2,490 | 57 | 28 | | XVI | 1968 | Mexico City, Mexico | 4,750 | 781 | 112 |
| VI | 1916 | Berlin, Germany | — | — | — | | XVII | 1972 | Munich, W. Germany | 5,848 | 1,299 | 122 |
| VII | 1920 | Antwerp, Belgium | 2,543 | 64 | 29 | | XVIII | 1976 | Montreal, Canada | 4,834 | 1,251 | 92 |
| VIII | 1924 | Paris, France | 2,956 | 136 | 44 | | XIX | 1980 | Moscow, USSR | 4,265 | 1,088 | 81 |
| IX | 1928 | Amsterdam, Holland | 2,724 | 290 | 46 | | XX | 1984 | Los Angeles, U.S. | 5,458 | 1,620 | 141 |
| X | 1932 | Los Angeles, U.S. | 1,281 | 127 | 37 | | XXI | 1988 | Seoul, South Korea | 9,593 (total)[1] | | 160 |

1. Gender breakdown not available. **Source:** David Wallechinsky, *The Complete Book of the Olympics* (1988), reprinted by permission.

## TWO-SEATER (men)

| | | |
|---|---|---|
| 1964 | Austria | 1:41.62 |
| 1968 | East Germany | 1:35.85 |
| 1972 | Italy, East Germany (tie) | 1:28.35 |
| 1976 | East Germany | 1:25.60 |
| 1980 | East Germany | 1:19.33 |
| 1984 | West Germany | 1:23.62 |
| 1988 | East Germany | 1:31.94 |

## SINGLES (women)

| | | |
|---|---|---|
| 1964 | Ortrun Enderlein, East Germany | 3:24.67 |
| 1968 | Erica Lechner, Italy | 2:28.66 |
| 1972 | Anna M. Müller, East Germany | 2:59.18 |
| 1976 | Margit Schumann, East Germany | 2:50.62 |
| 1980 | Vera Zozulya, USSR | 2:36.53 |
| 1984 | Steffi Martin, East Germany | 2:46.57 |
| 1988 | Steffi Walter, East Germany | 3:03.97 |

## FIGURE SKATING

### MEN

| | | |
|---|---|
| 1908 | Ulrich Salchow, Sweden |
| 1920 | Gillis Grafstrom, Sweden |
| 1924 | Gillis Grafstrom, Sweden |
| 1928 | Gillis Grafstrom, Sweden |
| 1932 | Karl Schafer, Austria |
| 1936 | Karl Schafer, Austria |
| 1948 | Richard Button, U.S. |
| 1952 | Richard Button, U.S. |
| 1956 | Hayes Alan Jenkins, U.S. |
| 1960 | David W. Jenkins, U.S. |
| 1964 | Manfred Schnelldorfer, West Germany |
| 1968 | Wolfgang Schwartz, Austria |
| 1972 | Ondrej Nepela, Czechoslovakia |
| 1976 | John Curry, Great Britain |
| 1980 | Robin Cousins, Great Britain |
| 1984 | Scott Hamilton, U.S. |
| 1988 | Brian Boitano, U.S. |

### WOMEN

| | | |
|---|---|
| 1908 | Madge Syers, Great Britain |
| 1920 | Magda Julin-Mauroy, Sweden |
| 1924 | Heima von Szabo-Planck, Austria |
| 1928 | Sonja Henie, Norway |
| 1932 | Sonja Henie, Norway |
| 1936 | Sonja Henie, Norway |
| 1948 | Barbara Ann Scott, Canada |
| 1952 | Jeanette Altwegg, Great Britain |
| 1956 | Tenley Albright, U.S. |
| 1960 | Carol Heiss, U.S. |
| 1964 | Sjoukje Dijkstra, Netherlands |
| 1968 | Peggy Fleming, U.S. |
| 1972 | Beatrix Schuba, Austria |
| 1976 | Dorothy Hamill, U.S. |
| 1980 | Annett Pötzsch, East Germany |
| 1984 | Katarina Witt, East Germany |
| 1988 | Katarina Witt, East Germany |

### PAIRS

| | | |
|---|---|
| 1908 | Germany—Anna Hubler, Heinrich Burger |
| 1920 | Finland—Ludovika & Walter Jakobsson |
| 1924 | Austria—Helene Engelman, Alfred Berger |
| 1928 | France—Andrée Joly, Pierre Brunet |
| 1932 | France—Andrée Joly, Pierre Brunet |
| 1936 | Germany—Maxie Herber, Ernst Baier |
| 1948 | Belgium—Micheline Lannoy, Pierre Baugniet |
| 1952 | Germany—Ria & Paul Falk |
| 1956 | Austria—Elisabeth Schwartz, Kurt Oppelt |
| 1960 | Canada—Barbara Wagner, Robert Paul |

| | | |
|---|---|
| 1964 | USSR—Ludmila Beloussova, Oleg Protopopov |
| 1968 | USSR—Ludmila Beloussova, Oleg Protopopov |
| 1972 | USSR—Irina Rodnina, Alexei Ulanov |
| 1976 | USSR—Irina Rodnina, Aleksandr Zaitsev |
| 1980 | USSR—Irina Rodnina, Aleksandr Zaitsev |
| 1984 | USSR—Elena Valova, Oleg Vassiliev |
| 1988 | USSR—Ekaterina Gordeeva, Sergei Grinko |

### ICE DANCING

| | | |
|---|---|
| 1976 | USSR—Lyudmila Pakhomova, Aleksandr Gorshkov |
| 1980 | USSR—Natalia Linichuk, Gennadi Karponosov |
| 1984 | Great Britain—Jayne Torvill, Christopher Dean |
| 1988 | USSR—Natalia Bestemianova, Andrei Bukin |

## SPEED SKATING—MEN   Time

### 500 METERS (1,641 FT.)

| | | |
|---|---|---|
| 1924 | Charles Jewtraw, U.S. | 0:44.00 |
| 1928 | Clas Thunberg, Finland, and Bernst Evensen, Norway (tie) | 0:43.40 |
| 1932 | John A. Shea, U.S. | 0:43.40 |
| 1936 | Ivar Ballangrud, Norway | 0:43.40 |
| 1948 | Finn Helgesen, Norway | 0:43.10 |
| 1952 | Ken Henry, U.S. | 0:43.20 |
| 1956 | Yevgeny Grishin, USSR | 0:40.20 |
| 1960 | Yevgeny Grishin, USSR | 0:40.20 |
| 1964 | Terry McDermott, U.S. | 0:40.10 |
| 1968 | Erhard Keller, West Germany | 0:40.30 |
| 1972 | Erhard Keller, West Germany | 0:39.40 |
| 1976 | Yergeny Kulikov, USSR | 0:39.17 |
| 1980 | Eric Heiden, U.S. | 0:38.03 |
| 1984 | Sergei Fokichev, USSR | 0:38.19 |
| 1988 | Jens-Uwe Mey, East Germany | 0:36.45 |

### 1,000 METERS (3,281 FT.)

| | | |
|---|---|---|
| 1976 | Peter Mueller, U.S. | 1:19.32 |
| 1980 | Eric Heiden, U.S. | 1:15.18 |
| 1984 | Gaétan Boucher, Canada | 1:15.80 |
| 1988 | Nikolai Guiliaev, USSR | 1:13.03 |

### 1,500 METERS (4,922 FT.)

| | | |
|---|---|---|
| 1924 | Clas Thunberg, Finland | 2:20.80 |
| 1928 | Clas Thunberg, Finland | 2:21.10 |
| 1932 | John A. Shea, U.S. | 2:57.50 |
| 1936 | Charles Mathisen, Norway | 2:19.20 |
| 1948 | Sverre Farstad, Norway | 2:17.60 |
| 1952 | Hjalmar Andersen, Norway | 2:20.40 |
| 1956 | Yevgeni Grishin and Yuri Mikhailov, USSR (tie) | 2:08.60 |
| 1960 | Roald Aas, Norway, and Yevgeni Grishin, USSR (tie) | 2:10.40 |
| 1964 | Ants Anston, USSR | 2:10.30 |
| 1968 | Cornelis Verkerk, Netherlands | 2:03.40 |
| 1972 | Ard Schenk, Netherlands | 2:02.90 |
| 1976 | Jan Egil Storholt, Norway | 1:59.38 |
| 1980 | Eric Heiden, U.S. | 1:55.40 |
| 1984 | Gaétan Boucher, Canada | 1:58.36 |
| 1988 | Andre Hoffmann, East Germany | 1:52.06 |

### 5,000 METERS (16,405 FT.)

| | | |
|---|---|---|
| 1924 | Clas Thunberg, Finland | 8:39.00 |
| 1928 | Ivar Ballangrud, Norway | 8:50.50 |
| 1932 | Irving Jaffee, U.S. | 9:40.80 |
| 1936 | Ivar Ballangrud, Norway | 8:19.60 |
| 1948 | Reidar Liaklev, Norway | 8:29.40 |
| 1952 | Hjalmar Andersen, Norway | 8:10.60 |

| | | |
|---|---|---|
| 1956 | Boris Shilkov, USSR | 7:48.70 |
| 1960 | Viktor Kosichkin, USSR | 7:51.30 |
| 1964 | Knut Johannesen, Norway | 7:38.40 |
| 1968 | F. Anton Maier, Norway | 7:22.40 |
| 1972 | Ard Schenk, Netherlands | 7:23.61 |
| 1976 | Sten Stensen, Norway | 7:24.48 |
| 1980 | Eric Heiden, U.S. | 7:02.29 |
| 1984 | Sven Tomas Gustafson, Sweden | 7:12.28 |
| 1988 | Tomas Gustafson, Sweden | 6:44:63 |

### 10,000 METERS (32,810 FT.)

| | | |
|---|---|---|
| 1924 | Julien Skutnabb, Finland | 18:04.80 |
| 1928 | (ice thawed, so event canceled) | |
| 1932 | Irving Jaffee, U.S. | 19:13.60 |
| 1936 | Ivar Ballangrud, Norway | 17:24.30 |
| 1948 | Ake Seyffarth, Sweden | 17:26.30 |
| 1952 | Hjalmar Andersen, Norway | 16:45.80 |
| 1956 | Sigvard Ericsson, Sweden | 16:35.90 |
| 1960 | Knut Johannessen, Norway | 15:46.60 |
| 1964 | Jonny Nilsson, Sweden | 15:50.10 |
| 1968 | Johnny Hoeglin, Sweden | 15:23.60 |
| 1972 | Ard Schenk, Netherlands | 15:01.30 |
| 1976 | Piet Kleine, Netherlands | 14:50.59 |
| 1980 | Eric Heiden, U.S. | 14:28.13 |
| 1984 | Igor Malikov, USSR | 14:39.90 |
| 1988 | Tomas Gustafson, Sweden | 13:48.20 |

## SPEED SKATING—WOMEN   Time

### 500 Meters (1,641 ft.)

| | | |
|---|---|---|
| 1960 | Helga Haase, Germany | 0:45.90 |
| 1964 | Lydia Skoblikova, USSR | 0:45.00 |
| 1968 | Ludmila Titova, USSR | 0:46.10 |
| 1972 | Anne Henning, U.S. | 0:43.30 |
| 1976 | Sheila Young, U.S. | 0:42.76 |
| 1980 | Karin Enke, East Germany | 0:41.78 |
| 1984 | Christa Rothenburger, East Germany | 0:41.02 |
| 1988 | Bonnie Blair, U.S. | 0:39.10 |

### 1,000 METERS (3,281 FT.)

| | | |
|---|---|---|
| 1960 | Klara Guseva, USSR | 1:34.10 |
| 1964 | Lydia Skoblikova, USSR | 1:33.20 |
| 1968 | Carolina Geiissen, Netherlands | 1:32.60 |
| 1972 | Monika Pflug, West Germany | 1:31.40 |
| 1976 | Tatiana Averina, USSR | 1:28.43 |
| 1980 | Natalia Petruseva, USSR | 1:24.10 |
| 1984 | Karin Enke, East Germany | 1:21.61 |
| 1988 | Christa Rothenburger, East Germany | 1:17.65 |

### 1,500 METERS (4,922 FT.)

| | | |
|---|---|---|
| 1960 | Lydia Skoblikova, USSR | 2:25.20 |
| 1964 | Lydia Skoblikova, USSR | 2:22.60 |
| 1968 | Kaija Mustonen, Finland | 2:22.40 |
| 1972 | Dianne Holum, U.S. | 2:20.80 |
| 1976 | Galina Stepanskaya, USSR | 2:16.58 |
| 1980 | Annie Borchink, Netherlands | 2:10.95 |
| 1984 | Karin Enke, East Germany | 2:03.42 |
| 1988 | Yvonne Van Gennip, Netherlands | 2:00.68 |

### 3,000 METERS (9,843 FT.)

| | | |
|---|---|---|
| 1960 | Lydia Skoblikova, USSR | 5:14.30 |
| 1964 | Lydia Skoblikova, USSR | 5:14.90 |
| 1968 | Johanna Schut, Netherlands | 4:56.20 |
| 1972 | Stien Kaiser-Baas, Netherlands | 4:52.10 |
| 1976 | Tatiana Averina, USSR | 4:45.19 |
| 1980 | Bjoerg Eva Jensen, Norway | 4:32.13 |
| 1984 | Andrea Schöne, East Germany | 4:24.79 |
| 1988 | Yvonne Van Gennip, Netherlands | 4:11.94 |

## Summer Olympics Champions

### SWIMMING AND DIVING—MEN

| Year | Champion, country | Time |
|---|---|---|
| **50-METER FREESTYLE** | | |
| 1988 | Matt Biondi, U.S. | 22.14 |
| **100-METER FREESTYLE** | | |
| 1896 | Alfred Hajos, Hungary | 1:22.20 |
| 1904 | Zoltan de Halmay, Hungary (100 yds.) | 1:02.80 |
| 1908 | Charles Daniels, U.S. | 1:05.60 |
| 1912 | Duke Kahanamoku, U.S. | 1:03.40 |
| 1920 | Duke Kahanamoku, U.S. | 1:01.40 |
| 1924 | John Weissmuller, U.S. | 0:59.00 |
| 1928 | John Weissmuller, U.S. | 0:58.60 |
| 1932 | Yasuji Miyazaki, Japan | 0:58.20 |
| 1936 | Ferenc Csik, Hungary | 0:57.60 |
| 1948 | Walter Ris, U.S. | 0:57.30 |
| 1952 | Clarke Scholes, U.S. | 0:57.40 |
| 1956 | Jon Hendricks, Australia | 0:55.40 |
| 1960 | John Devitt, Australia | 0:55.20 |
| 1964 | Donald A. Schollander, U.S. | 0:53.40 |
| 1968 | Michael Wenden, Australia | 0:52.20 |
| 1972 | Mark Spitz, U.S. | 0:51.20 |
| 1976 | Jim Montgomery, U.S. | 0:49.99 |
| 1980 | Jorg Woithe, East Germany | 0:50.40 |
| 1984 | Ambrose ("Rowdy") Gaines, U.S. | 0:49.80 |
| 1988 | Matt Biondi, U.S. | 0:48.63 |
| **200-METER FREESTYLE** | | |
| 1968 | Michael Wenden, Australia | 1:55.20 |
| 1972 | Mark Spitz, U.S. | 1:52.80 |
| 1976 | Bruce Furniss, U.S. | 1:50.29 |
| 1980 | Sergei Kopliakov, USSR | 1:49.81 |
| 1984 | Michael Gross, West Germany | 1:47.44 |
| 1988 | Duncan Armstrong, Australia | 1:47.25 |
| **400-METER FREESTYLE** | | |
| 1896 | Paul Neumann, Austria (500 m) | 8:12.60 |
| 1904 | Charles Daniels, U.S. (440 yds.) | 6:16.20 |
| 1908 | Henry Taylor, Great Britain | 5:36.80 |
| 1912 | George Hodgson, Canada | 5:24.40 |
| 1920 | Norman Ross, U.S. | 5:26.80 |
| 1924 | John Weissmuller, U.S. | 5:04.20 |
| 1928 | Albert Zorilla, Argentina | 5:01.60 |
| 1932 | Clarence "Buster" Crabbe, U.S. | 4:48.40 |
| 1936 | Jack Medica, U.S. | 4:44.50 |
| 1948 | William Smith, U.S. | 4:41.00 |
| 1952 | Jean Boiteux, France | 4:30.70 |
| 1956 | Murray Rose, Australia | 4:27.30 |
| 1960 | Murray Rose, Australia | 4:18.30 |
| 1964 | Donald A. Schollander, U.S. | 4:12.20 |
| 1968 | Michael Burton, U.S. | 4:09.00 |
| 1972 | Bradford Cooper, Australia | 4:00.30 |
| 1976 | Brian Goodell, U.S. | 3:51.93 |
| 1980 | Vladimir Salnikov, USSR | 3:51.31 |
| 1984 | George DiCarlo, U.S. | 3:51.23 |
| 1988 | Ewe Dassler, East Germany | 3:46.95 |
| **1,500-METER FREESTYLE** | | |
| 1896 | Alfred Hajos, Hungary (1,200 m) | 18:22.20 |
| 1900 | John Jarvis, Great Britain (1,000 m) | 13:40.20 |

1904 Emil Rausch, Germany (1,609 m) 27:18.20
1908 Henry Taylor, Great Britain 22:48.40
1912 George Hodgson, Canada 22:00.00
1920 Norman Ross, U.S. 22:23.20
1924 Andrew Charlton, Australia 20:06.60
1928 Arne Borg, Sweden 19:51.80
1932 Kusuo Kitamura, Japan 19:12.40
1936 Noboru Terada, Japan 19:13.70
1948 James P. McLane, U.S. 19:18.50
1952 Ford Konno, U.S. 18:30.00
1956 Murray Rose, Australia 17:58.90
1960 John Konrads, Australia 17:19.60
1964 Robert Windle, Australia 17:01.70
1968 Michael Burton, U.S. 16:38.90
1972 Michael Burton, U.S. 15:52.60
1976 Brian Goodell, U.S. 15:02.40
1980 Vladimir Salnikov, USSR 14:58.27
1984 Michael O'Brien, U.S. 15:05.20
1988 Vladimir Salnikov, USSR 15:00.40

**100-METER BACKSTROKE**
1904 Walter Brack, Germany (100 yds.) 1:16.80
1908 Arno Bieberstein, Germany 1:24.60
1912 Harry Hebner, U.S. 1:21.20
1920 Warren Kealoha, U.S. 1:15.20
1924 Warren Kealoha, U.S. 1:13.20
1928 George Kojac, U.S. 1:08.20
1932 Masaji Kiyokawa, Japan 1:08.60
1936 Adolph Kiefer, U.S. 1:05.90
1948 Allen Stack, U.S. 1:06.40
1952 Yoshinobu Oyakawa, U.S. 1:05.40
1956 David Thiele, Australia 1:02.20
1960 David Thiele, Australia 1:01.90
1964 Not on program
1968 Roland Matthes, East Germany 0:58.70
1972 Roland Matthes, East Germany 0:56.60
1976 John Naber, U.S. 0:55.49
1980 Bengt Baron, Sweden 0:56.33
1984 Richard Carey, U.S. 0:55.79
1988 Daichi Suzuki, Japan 0:55.05

**200-METER BACKSTROKE**
1900 Ernest Hoppenberg, Germany 2:47.00
1964 Jed R. Graef, U.S. 2:10.30
1968 Roland Matthes, East Germany 2:09.60
1972 Roland Matthes, East Germany 2:02.80
1976 John Naber, U.S. 1:59.19
1980 Sandor Wladar, Hungary 2:01.93
1984 Richard Carey, U.S. 2:00.23
1988 Igor Polianski, USSR 1:59.37

**100-METER BREASTSTROKE**
1968 Donald McKenzie, U.S. 1:07.70
1972 Nobutaka Taguchi, Japan 1:04.90
1976 John Hencken, U.S. 1:03.11
1980 Duncan Goodhen, Great Britain 1:03.44
1984 Steve Lundquist, U.S. 1:01.99
1988 Adrian Moorhouse, Great Britain 1:02.04

**200-METER BREASTSTROKE**
1908 Frederick Holman, Great Britain 3:09.20
1912 Walter Bathe, Germany 3:01.80
1920 Haken Malmroth, Sweden 3:04.40
1924 Robert Skelton, U.S. 2:56.60
1928 Yoshiyuki Tsuruta, Japan 2:48.80
1932 Yoshiyuki Tsuruta, Japan 2:45.40
1936 Tetsuo Hamuro, Japan 2:41.50
1948 Joseph Verdeur, U.S. 2:39.30
1952 John Davies, Australia 2:34.40
1956 Masura Furukawa, Japan 2:34.70
1960 William Mulliken, U.S. 2:37.40
1964 Ian O'Brien, Australia 2:27.80
1968 Felipe Muñoz, Mexico 2:28.70
1972 John Hencken, U.S. 2:21.50
1976 David Wilkie, Great Britain 2:15.11
1980 Robertas Zhulpa, USSR 2:15.85
1984 Victor Davis, Canada 2:13.34
1988 Jozsef Szabo, Hungary 2:13.52

**100-METER BUTTERFLY**
1968 Douglas Russell, U.S. 0:55.90
1972 Mark Spitz, U.S. 0:54.30
1976 Matt Vogel, U.S. 0:54.35
1980 Par Arvidsson, Sweden 0:54.92
1984 Michael Gross, West Germany 0:53.08
1988 Anthony Nesty, Suriname 0:53.00

**200-METER BUTTERFLY**
1956 William Yorzyk, U.S. 2:19.30
1960 Michael Troy, U.S. 2:12.80
1964 Kevin Berry, Australia 2:06.60
1968 Carl Robie, U.S. 2:08.70
1972 Mark Spitz, U.S. 2:00.70
1976 Michael Bruner, U.S. 1:59.23
1980 Sergei Fesenko, USSR 1:59.76
1984 Jon Sieben, Australia 1:57.04
1988 Michael Gross, West Germany 1:56.94

**200-METER INDIVIDUAL MEDLEY**
1968 Charles Hickcox, U.S. 2:12.00
1972 Gunnar Larsson, Sweden 2:07.20
1984 Alex Baumann, Canada 2:01.42
1988 Tamas Darnyi, Hungary 2:00.17

**400-METER INDIVIDUAL MEDLEY**
1964 Richard W. Roth, U.S. 4:45.40
1968 Charles Hickcox, U.S. 4:48.40
1972 Gunnar Larsson, Sweden 4:32.00
1976 Rod Strachan, U.S. 4:23.68
1980 Aleksandr Sidorenko, USSR 4:22.89
1984 Alex Baumann, Canada 4:17.41
1988 Tamas Darnyi, Hungary 4:14.75

**400-METER FREESTYLE RELAY**

| | | | | | |
|---|---|---|---|---|---|
| 1964 | U.S. | 3:33.20 | 1984 | U.S. | 3:19.03 |
| 1968 | U.S. | 3:31.70 | 1988 | U.S. | 3:16.53 |
| 1972 | U.S. | 3:26.40 | | | |

**400-METER MEDLEY RELAY**

| | | | | | |
|---|---|---|---|---|---|
| 1960 | U.S. | 4:05.40 | 1976 | U.S. | 3:42.22 |
| 1964 | U.S. | 3:58.40 | 1980 | Australia | 3:45.70 |
| 1968 | U.S. | 3:54.90 | 1984 | U.S. | 3:39.30 |
| 1972 | U.S. | 3:48.20 | 1988 | U.S. | 3:36.93 |

**800-METER FREESTYLE RELAY**

| | | | | | |
|---|---|---|---|---|---|
| 1908 | Great Britain | 10:55.60 | 1956 | Australia | 8:23.60 |
| | | | 1960 | U.S. | 8:10.20 |
| 1912 | Australia | 10:11.20 | 1964 | U.S. | 7:52.10 |
| 1920 | U.S. | 10:04.40 | 1968 | U.S. | 7:52.30 |
| 1924 | U.S. | 9:53.40 | 1972 | U.S. | 7:38.80 |
| 1928 | U.S. | 9:36.20 | 1976 | U.S. | 7:23.22 |
| 1932 | Japan | 8:58.20 | 1980 | USSR | 7:23.50 |
| 1936 | Japan | 8:51.50 | 1984 | U.S. | 7:15.69 |
| 1948 | U.S. | 8:31.10 | 1988 | U.S. | 7:12.51 |
| 1952 | U.S. | 8:31.10 | | | |

**SPRINGBOARD DIVING** **Points**
1908 Albert Zurner, Germany 85.50
1912 Paul Guenther, Germany 79.23
1920 Louis Kuehn, U.S. 675.00
1924 Albert C. White, U.S. 696.40
1928 Pete Desjardins, U.S. 185.04
1932 Michael Galitzen, U.S. 161.38
1936 Richard Degener, U.S. 163.57
1948 Bruce Harlan, U.S. 163.64
1952 David Browning, U.S. 205.29
1956 Robert L. Clotworthy, U.S. 159.56
1960 Gary Tobian, U.S. 170.00
1964 Kenneth R. Sitzberger, U.S. 159.90
1968 Bernard Wrightson, U.S. 170.15
1972 Vladimir Vasin, USSR 594.09
1976 Phil Boggs, U.S. 619.52
1980 Aleksandr Portnov, USSR 905.02
1984 Gregory Louganis, U.S. 754.41
1988 Gregory Louganis, U.S. 730.80

**PLATFORM DIVING**
1904 Dr. G. E. Sheldon, U.S. 12.75
1908 Hjalmar Johansson, Sweden 83.75
1912 Erik Adlerz, Sweden 73.94
1920 Clarence Pinkston, U.S. 100.67
1924 Albert C. White, U.S. 97.46
1928 Pete Desjardins, U.S. 98.74
1932 Harold Smith, U.S. 124.80
1936 Marshall Wayne, U.S. 113.58
1948 Dr. Samuel Lee, U.S. 130.05
1952 Dr. Samuel Lee, U.S. 156.28
1956 Joaquin Capilla, Mexico 152.44
1960 Robert Webster, U.S. 165.56
1964 Robert Webster, U.S. 148.58
1968 Klaus DiBiasi, Italy 164.18
1972 Klaus DiBiasi, Italy 504.12
1976 Klaus DiBiasi, Italy 600.51
1980 Falk Hoffmann, East Germany 835.65
1984 Gregory Louganis, U.S. 710.91
1988 Gregory Louganis, U.S. 638.61

## SWIMMING AND DIVING—WOMEN

**50-METER FREESTYLE**
1988 Kristin Otto, East Germany 25.49

**100-METER FREESTYLE**
1912 Fanny Durack, Australia 1:22.20
1920 Ethelda Bleibtrey, U.S. 1:13.60
1924 Ethel Lackie, U.S. 1:12.40
1928 Albina Osipowich, U.S. 1:11.00
1932 Helene Madison, U.S. 1:06.80
1936 Hendrika Mastenbroek, Netherlands 1:05.90
1948 Greta Andersen, Denmark 1:06.30
1952 Katalin Szoke, Hungary 1:06.80
1956 Dawn Fraser, Australia 1:02.00
1960 Dawn Fraser, Australia 1:01.20
1964 Dawn Fraser, Australia 0:59.50
1968 Margo Jan Henne, U.S. 1:00.00
1972 Sandra Neilson, U.S. 0:58.60
1976 Kornelia Ender, East Germany 0:55.65
1980 Barbara Krause, East Germany 0:54.79
1984 Nancy Hogshead, U.S. 0:55.92
1988 Kristin Otto, East Germany 0:54.93

**200-METER FREESTYLE**
1968 Deborah Meyer, U.S. 2:10.50
1972 Shane Gould, Australia 2:03.60
1976 Kornelia Ender, East Germany 1:59.26
1980 Barbara Krause, East Germany 1:58.33
1984 Mary Wayte, U.S. 1:59.23
1988 Heike Friederich, East Germany 1:57.65

**400-METER FREESTYLE**
1920 Ethelda Bleibtrey, U.S. (300 m) 4:34.00
1924 Martha Norelius, U.S. 6:02.20
1928 Martha Norelius, U.S. 5:42.40
1932 Helene Madison, U.S. 5:28.50
1936 Hendrika Mastenbroek, Netherlands 5:26.40
1948 Ann Curtis, U.S. 5:17.80
1952 Valeria Gyenge, Hungary 5:12.10
1956 Lorraine Crapp, Australia 4:54.60
1960 S. Chris Von Saltza, U.S. 4:50.60
1964 Virginia Duenkel, U.S. 4:43.30
1968 Deborah Meyer, U.S. 4:31.80
1972 Shane Gould, Australia 4:19.00
1976 Petra Thuemer, East Germany 4:09.89
1980 Ines Diers, East Germany 4:08.76
1984 Tiffany Cohen, U.S. 4:07.10
1988 Janet Evans, U.S. 4:03.85

**800-METER FREESTYLE**
1968 Deborah Meyer, U.S. 9:24.00
1972 Keena Rothhammer, U.S. 8:53.70
1976 Petra Thuemer, East Germany 8:37.14
1980 Michelle Ford, Australia 8:28.90
1984 Tiffany Cohen, U.S. 8:24.95
1988 Janet Evans, U.S. 8:20.20

**100-METER BACKSTROKE**
1924 Sybil Bauer, U.S. 1:23.20
1928 Marie Braun, Netherlands 1:22.00
1932 Eleanor Holm, U.S. 1:19.40
1936 Dina Senff, Netherlands 1:18.90
1948 Karen Harup, Denmark 1:14.40
1952 Joan Harrison, South Africa 1:14.30
1956 Judy Grinham, Great Britain 1:12.90
1960 Lynn Burke, U.S. 1:09.30
1964 Cathy Ferguson, U.S. 1:07.70
1968 Kaye Hall, U.S. 1:06.20
1972 Melissa Belote, U.S. 1:05.80
1976 Ulrike Richter, East Germany 1:01.83
1980 Rica Reinisch, East Germany 1:00.86
1984 Theresa Andrews, U.S. 1:02.55
1988 Kristin Otto, East Germany 1:00.89

**200-METER BACKSTROKE**
1968 Lillian "Pokey" Watson, U.S. 2:24.80
1972 Melissa Belote, U.S. 2:19.20
1976 Ulrike Richter, East Germany 2:13.43
1980 Rica Reinisch, East Germany 2:11.77
1984 Jolanda de Rover, Netherlands 2:12.38
1988 Krisztina Egerszegi, Hungary 2:09.29

**100-METER BUTTERFLY**
1956 Shelley Mann, U.S. 1:11.00
1960 Carolyn Schuler, U.S. 1:09.50
1964 Sharon Stouder, U.S. 1:04.70
1968 Lynn McClements, Australia 1:05.50
1972 Mayumi Aoki, Japan 1:03.30
1976 Kornelia Ender, East Germany 1:00.13
1980 Caren Metschuck, East Germany 1:00.42
1984 Mary T. Meagher, U.S. 0:59.26
1988 Kristin Otto, East Germany 0:59.00

**200-METER BUTTERFLY**
1968 Ada Kok, Netherlands 2:24.70
1972 Karen Moe, U.S. 2:15.60
1976 Andrea Pollack, East Germany 2:11.41
1980 Ines Geissler, East Germany 2:10.44
1984 Mary T. Meagher, U.S. 2:06.90
1988 Kathleen Nord, East Germany 2:09.51

**100-METER BREASTSTROKE**
1968 Djurdjica Bjedov, Yugoslavia 1:15.80
1972 Cathy Carr, U.S. 1:13.60
1976 Hannelore Anke, East Germany 1:11.16
1980 Ute Geweniger, East Germany 1:10.22
1984 Petra Van Staveren, Netherlands 1:09.69
1988 Tania Dangalakova, Bulgaria 1:07.95

**200-METER BREASTSTROKE**
1924 Lucy Morton, Great Britain 3:33.20
1928 Hilde Schrader, Germany 3:12.60
1932 Clare Dennis, Australia 3:06.30
1936 Hideko Maehata, Japan 3:03.60
1948 Nelly Van Vliet, Netherlands 2:57.20
1952 Eva Szekely, Hungary 2:51.70
1956 Ursula Happe, Germany 2:53.10
1960 Anita Lonsbrough, Great Britain 2:49.50
1964 Galina Prozumenshikova, USSR 2:46.40
1968 Sharon Wichman, U.S. 2:44.40
1972 Beverly Whitfield, Australia 2:41.70
1976 Marina Koshevaya, USSR 2:33.35
1980 Lina Kaciusyte, USSR 2:29.54
1984 Anne Ottenbrite, Canada 2:30.38
1988 Silke Hoerner, East Germany 2:26.71

**400-METER FREESTYLE RELAY**

| | | | | | |
|---|---|---|---|---|---|
| 1912 | Great Britain | 5:52.80 | 1960 | U.S. | 4:08.90 |
| 1920 | U.S. | 5:11.60 | 1964 | U.S. | 4:03.80 |
| 1924 | U.S. | 4:58.80 | 1968 | U.S. | 4:02.50 |
| 1928 | U.S. | 4:47.60 | 1972 | U.S. | 3:55.20 |
| 1932 | U.S. | 4:38.00 | 1976 | U.S. | 3:44.82 |
| 1936 | Netherlands | 4:36.00 | 1980 | East Germany | 3:42.71 |
| 1948 | U.S. | 4:29.20 | 1984 | U.S. | 3:43.43 |
| 1952 | Hungary | 4:24.40 | 1988 | East Germany | 3:40.63 |
| 1956 | Australia | 4:17.10 | | | |

**400-METER MEDLEY RELAY**

| | | | | | |
|---|---|---|---|---|---|
| 1960 | U.S. | 4:41.10 | 1980 | East Germany | 4:06.67 |
| 1964 | U.S. | 4:33.90 | | | |
| 1968 | U.S. | 4:28.30 | 1984 | U.S. | 4:08.34 |
| 1972 | U.S. | 4:20.70 | 1988 | East Germany | 4:03.74 |
| 1976 | East Germany | 4:07.95 | | | |

**200-METER INDIVIDUAL MEDLEY**
1968 Claudia Kolb, U.S. 2:24.70
1972 Shane Gould, Australia 2:23.10
1984 Tracy Caulkins, U.S. 2:12.64
1988 Daniela Hunger, East Germany 2:12.59

**400-METER INDIVIDUAL MEDLEY**
1964 Donna de Varona, U.S. 5:18.70
1968 Claudia Kolb, U.S. 5:08.50
1972 Gail Neall, Australia 5:03.00
1976 Ulrike Tauber, East Germany 4:42.77
1980 Petra Schneider, East Germany 4:36.29
1984 Tracy Caulkins, U.S. 4:39.24
1988 Janet Evans, U.S. 4:37.76

**SPRINGBOARD DIVING** **Points**
1920 Aileen Riggin, U.S. 539.90
1924 Elizabeth Becker, U.S. 474.50
1928 Helen Meany, U.S. 78.62
1932 Georgia Coleman, U.S. 87.52
1936 Marjorie Gestring, U.S. 89.27
1948 Victoria Draves, U.S. 108.74
1952 Patricia McCormick, U.S. 147.30
1956 Patricia McCormick, U.S. 142.36
1960 Ingrid Kramer, Germany 155.81
1964 Ingrid Engle-Kramer, East Germany 145.00
1968 Sue Gossick, U.S. 150.77
1972 Micki King, U.S. 450.03
1976 Jennifer Chandler, U.S. 506.19
1980 Irina Kalinina, USSR 725.91
1984 Sylvie Bernier, Canada 530.70
1988 Gao Min, China 580.23

**PLATFORM DIVING**
1912 Greta Johansson, Sweden 39.90
1920 Stefani Fryland-Clausen, Denmark 34.60
1924 Caroline Smith, U.S. 33.20
1928 Elizabeth Pinkston, U.S. 31.60
1932 Dorothy Poynton, U.S. 40.26
1936 Dorothy Poynton Hill, U.S. 33.93
1948 Victoria Draves, U.S. 68.87
1952 Patricia McCormick, U.S. 79.37
1956 Patricia McCormick, U.S. 84.85
1960 Ingrid Kramer, Germany 91.28
1964 Lesley Bush, U.S. 99.80
1968 Milena Duchkova, Czechoslovakia 109.59
1972 Ulrika Knape, Sweden 390.00
1976 Yelena Vaitsekhovskaya, USSR 406.49
1980 Martina Jäschke, East Germany 596.25
1984 Zhou Jihong, China 435.51
1988 Xu Yahmei, China 445.20

## TRACK AND FIELD—MEN

### 100-METER DASH

| | | Time |
|---|---|---|
| 1896 | Thomas E. Burke, U.S. | 12.00 |
| 1900 | Francis W. Jarvis, U.S. | 10.80 |
| 1904 | Archie Hahn, U.S. | 11.00 |
| 1908 | Reginald E. Walker, South Africa | 10.80 |
| 1912 | Ralph C. Craig, U.S. | 10.80 |
| 1920 | Charles W. Paddock, U.S. | 10.80 |
| 1924 | Harold M. Abrahams, Great Britain | 10.60 |
| 1928 | Percy Williams, Canada | 10.80 |
| 1932 | Eddie Tolan, U.S. | 10.30 |
| 1936 | Jesse Owens, U.S. | 10.30 |
| 1948 | Harrison Dillard, U.S. | 10.30 |
| 1952 | Lindy J. Remigino, U.S. | 10.40 |
| 1956 | Bobby J. Morrow, U.S. | 10.50 |
| 1960 | Armin Hary, Germany | 10.20 |
| 1964 | Robert L. Hayes, U.S. | 10.00 |
| 1968 | James Hines, U.S. | 9.90 |
| 1972 | Valery Borzov, USSR | 10.10 |
| 1976 | Hasely Crawford, Trinidad and Tobago | 10.06 |
| 1980 | Allan Wells, Great Britain | 10.25 |
| 1984 | Carl Lewis, U.S. | 9.99 |
| 1988 | Carl Lewis, U.S. | 9.92 |

### 200 METERS

| | | |
|---|---|---|
| 1900 | John W.B. Tewksbury, U.S. | 22.20 |
| 1904 | Archie Hahn, U.S. | 21.60 |
| 1908 | Robert Kerr, Canada | 22.60 |
| 1912 | Ralph C. Craig, U.S. | 21.70 |
| 1920 | Allan Woodring, U.S. | 22.00 |
| 1924 | Jackson V. Scholz, U.S. | 21.60 |
| 1928 | Percy Williams, Canada | 21.80 |
| 1932 | Eddie Tolan, U.S. | 21.20 |
| 1936 | Jesse Owens, U.S. | 20.70 |
| 1948 | Melvin Patton, U.S. | 21.10 |
| 1952 | Andrew W. Stanfield, U.S. | 20.70 |
| 1956 | Bobby J. Morrow, U.S. | 20.60 |
| 1960 | Livio Berruti, Italy | 20.50 |
| 1964 | Henry Carr, U.S. | 20.30 |
| 1968 | Tommie Smith, U.S. | 19.80 |
| 1972 | Valery Borzov, USSR | 20.00 |
| 1976 | Donald Quarrie, Jamaica | 20.23 |
| 1980 | Pietro Mennea, Italy | 20.19 |
| 1984 | Carl Lewis, U.S. | 19.80 |
| 1988 | Joe DeLoach, U.S. | 19.75 |

### 400 METERS

| | | |
|---|---|---|
| 1896 | Thomas E. Burke, U.S. | 54.20 |
| 1900 | Maxwell W. Long, U.S. | 49.40 |
| 1904 | Harry I. Hillman, U.S. | 49.20 |
| 1908 | Wyndham Halswelle, Great Britain | 50.00 |
| 1912 | Charles D. Reidpath, U.S. | 48.20 |
| 1920 | Bevil G.D. Rudd, South Africa | 49.60 |
| 1924 | Eric H. Liddel, Great Britain | 47.60 |
| 1928 | Ray Barbuti, U.S. | 47.80 |
| 1932 | William A. Carr, U.S. | 46.20 |
| 1936 | Archie Williams, U.S. | 46.50 |
| 1948 | Arthur Wint, Jamaica | 46.20 |
| 1952 | George Rhoden, Jamaica | 45.90 |
| 1956 | Charles L. Jenkins, U.S. | 46.70 |
| 1960 | Otis Davis, U.S. | 44.90 |
| 1964 | Michael D. Larrabee, U.S. | 45.10 |
| 1968 | Lee Evans, U.S. | 43.80 |
| 1972 | Vince Matthews, U.S. | 44.70 |
| 1976 | Alberto Juantorena, Cuba | 44.26 |
| 1980 | Viktor Markin, USSR | 44.60 |
| 1984 | Alonzo Babers, U.S. | 44.27 |
| 1988 | Steven Lewis, U.S. | 43.87 |

### 800 METERS

| | | |
|---|---|---|
| 1896 | Edwin H. Flack, Australia | 2:11.00 |
| 1900 | Alfred E. Tysoe, Great Britain | 2:01.40 |
| 1904 | James D. Lightbody, U.S. | 1:56.00 |
| 1908 | Melvin W. Sheppard, U.S. | 1:52.80 |
| 1912 | James E. Meredith, U.S. | 1:51.90 |
| 1920 | Albert G. Hill, Great Britain | 1:53.40 |
| 1924 | Douglas G.A. Lowe, Great Britain | 1:52.40 |
| 1928 | Douglas G.A. Lowe, Great Britain | 1:51.80 |
| 1932 | Thomas Hampson, Great Britain | 1:49.80 |
| 1936 | John Woodruff, U.S. | 1:52.90 |
| 1948 | Malvin Whitfield, U.S. | 1:49.20 |
| 1952 | Malvin Whitfield, U.S. | 1:49.20 |
| 1956 | Thomas W. Courtney, U.S. | 1:47.70 |
| 1960 | Peter Snell, New Zealand | 1:46.30 |
| 1964 | Peter Snell, New Zealand | 1:45.10 |
| 1968 | Ralph Doubell, Australia | 1:44.30 |
| 1972 | Dave Wottle, U.S. | 1:45.90 |
| 1976 | Alberto Juantorena, Cuba | 1:43.50 |
| 1980 | Steven Ovett, Great Britain | 1:45.40 |
| 1984 | Joaquim Cruz, Brazil | 1:43.00 |
| 1988 | Paul Ereng, Kenya | 1:43.45 |

### 1,500-METER RUN

| | | |
|---|---|---|
| 1896 | Edwin H. Flack, Australia | 4:33.20 |
| 1900 | Charles Bennett, Great Britain | 4:06.20 |
| 1904 | James D. Lightbody, U.S. | 4:05.40 |
| 1908 | Melvin W. Sheppard, U.S. | 4:03.40 |
| 1912 | Arnold N.S. Jackson, Great Britain | 3:56.80 |
| 1920 | Albert G. Hill, Great Britain | 4:01.80 |
| 1924 | Paavo Nurmi, Finland | 3:53.60 |
| 1928 | Harry E. Larva, Finland | 3:53.20 |
| 1932 | Luigi Beccali, Italy | 3:51.20 |
| 1936 | Jack E. Lovelock, New Zealand | 3:47.80 |
| 1948 | Henry Eriksson, Sweden | 3:49.80 |
| 1952 | Joseph Barthel, Luxembourg | 3:45.20 |
| 1956 | Ronald Delany, Ireland | 3:41.20 |
| 1960 | Herbert Elliott, Australia | 3:35.60 |
| 1964 | Peter Snell, New Zealand | 3:38.10 |
| 1968 | Kipchoge Keino, Kenya | 3:34.90 |
| 1972 | Pekka Vasala, Finland | 3:36.30 |
| 1976 | John Walker, New Zealand | 3:39.17 |
| 1980 | Sebastian Coe, Great Britain | 3:38.40 |
| 1984 | Sebastian Coe, Great Britain | 3:32.53 |
| 1988 | Peter Rono, Kenya | 3:35.96 |

### 5,000 METERS

| | | |
|---|---|---|
| 1912 | Hannes Kolehmainen, Finland | 14:36.60 |
| 1920 | Joseph Guillemot, France | 14:55.60 |
| 1924 | Paavo Nurmi, Finland | 14:31.20 |
| 1928 | Willie Ritola, Finland | 14:38.00 |
| 1932 | Lauri Lehtinen, Finland | 14:30.00 |
| 1936 | Gunnar Hocket, Finland | 14:22.20 |
| 1948 | Gaston Reiff, Belgium | 14:17.60 |
| 1952 | Emil Zatopek, Czechoslovakia | 14:06.60 |
| 1956 | Vladimir Kuts, USSR | 13:39.60 |
| 1960 | Murray Halberg, New Zealand | 13:43.40 |
| 1964 | Robert K. Schul, U.S. | 13:48.80 |
| 1968 | Mohamed Gammoudi, Tunisia | 14:05.10 |
| 1972 | Lasse Viren, Finland | 13:26.40 |
| 1976 | Lasse Viren, Finland | 13:24.76 |
| 1980 | Miruts Yifter, Ethiopia | 13:21.00 |
| 1984 | Said Aouita, Morocco | 13:05.59 |
| 1988 | John Ngugi, Kenya | 13:11.70 |

### 10,000 METERS

| | | |
|---|---|---|
| 1912 | Hannes Kolehmainen, Finland | 31:20.80 |
| 1920 | Paavo Nurmi, Finland | 31:45.80 |
| 1924 | Willie Ritola, Finland | 30:23.20 |
| 1928 | Paavo Nurmi, Finland | 30:18.80 |
| 1932 | Janusz Kusocinski, Poland | 30:11.40 |
| 1936 | Ilmari Salminen, Finland | 30:15.40 |
| 1948 | Emil Zatopek, Czechoslovakia | 29:59.60 |
| 1952 | Emil Zatopek, Czechoslovakia | 29:17.00 |
| 1956 | Vladimir Kuts, USSR | 28:45.60 |
| 1960 | Petr Bolotnikov, USSR | 28:32.20 |
| 1964 | William Mills, U.S. | 28:24.40 |
| 1968 | Naftali Temu, Kenya | 29:27.40 |
| 1972 | Lasse Viren, Finland | 27:38.40 |
| 1976 | Lasse Viren, Finland | 27:40.38 |
| 1980 | Miruts Yifter, Ethiopia | 27:42.70 |
| 1984 | Alberto Cova, Italy | 27:47.54 |
| 1988 | Brahim Boutaib, Morocco | 27:21.46 |

### MARATHON

| | | |
|---|---|---|
| 1896 | Spyros Loues, Greece | 2:58:50.00 |
| 1900 | Michel Theato, France | 2:59:45.00 |
| 1904 | Thomas J. Hicks, U.S. | 3:28:53.00 |
| 1908 | John J. Hayes, U.S. | 2:55:18.40 |
| 1912 | Kenneth McArthur, South Africa | 2:36:54.80 |
| 1920 | Hannes Kolehmainen, Finland | 2:32:35.80 |
| 1924 | Albin Stenroos, Finland | 2:41:22.60 |
| 1928 | A.B. El Quafi, France | 2:32:57.00 |
| 1932 | Juan Zabala, Argentina | 2:31:36.00 |
| 1936 | Kitei Son, Japan | 2:29:19.20 |
| 1948 | Delfo Cabrera, Argentina | 2:34:51.60 |
| 1952 | Emil Zatopek, Czechoslovakia | 2:23:03.20 |
| 1956 | Alain Mimoun, France | 2:25:00.00 |
| 1960 | Abebe Bikila, Ethiopia | 2:15:16.20 |
| 1964 | Abebe Bikila, Ethiopia | 2:12:11.20 |
| 1968 | Mamo Wolde, Ethiopia | 2:20:26.40 |
| 1972 | Frank Shorter, U.S. | 2:12:19.70 |
| 1976 | Waldemar Cierpinski, East Germany | 2:09:55.00 |
| 1980 | Waldemar Cierpinski, East Germany | 2:11.03.00 |
| 1984 | Carlos Lopes, Portugal | 2:09.21.00 |
| 1988 | Gelindo Bordin, Italy | 2:10.32.00 |

### 110-METER HURDLES

| | | |
|---|---|---|
| 1896 | Thomas P. Curtis, U.S. | 17.60 |
| 1900 | Alvin E. Kraenzlein, U.S. | 15.40 |
| 1904 | Frederick W. Schule, U.S. | 16.00 |
| 1908 | Forrest Smithson, U.S. | 15.00 |
| 1912 | Frederick W. Kelley, U.S. | 15.10 |
| 1920 | Earl J. Thomson, Canada | 14.80 |
| 1924 | Daniel C. Kinsey, U.S. | 15.00 |
| 1928 | Sydney Atkinson, South Africa | 14.80 |
| 1932 | George Saling, U.S. | 14.60 |
| 1936 | Forrest Towns, U.S. | 14.20 |
| 1948 | William Porter, U.S. | 13.90 |
| 1952 | Harrison Dillard, U.S. | 13.70 |
| 1956 | Lee Q. Calhoun, U.S. | 13.50 |
| 1960 | Lee Q. Calhoun, U.S. | 13.80 |
| 1964 | Hayes W. Jones, U.S. | 13.60 |
| 1968 | Willie Davenport, U.S. | 13.30 |
| 1972 | Rod Milburn, U.S. | 13.20 |
| 1976 | Guy Drut, France | 13.30 |
| 1980 | Thomas Munkelt, East Germany | 13.39 |
| 1984 | Roger Kingdom, U.S. | 13.20 |
| 1988 | Roger Kingdom, U.S. | 12.98 |

### 400-METER HURDLES

| | | |
|---|---|---|
| 1900 | John W.B. Tewksbury, U.S. | 57.60 |
| 1904 | Harry L. Hillman, U.S. | 53.00 |
| 1908 | Charles J. Bacon, U.S. | 55.00 |
| 1920 | Frank F. Loomis, U.S. | 54.00 |
| 1924 | F. Morgan Taylor, U.S. | 52.60 |
| 1928 | Lord David Burghley, Great Britain | 53.40 |
| 1932 | Robert Tisdall, Ireland | 51.80 |
| 1936 | Glenn Hardin, U.S. | 52.40 |
| 1948 | Roy Cochran, U.S. | 51.10 |
| 1952 | Charles Moore, U.S. | 50.80 |
| 1956 | Glenn A. Davis, U.S. | 50.10 |
| 1960 | Glenn A. Davis, U.S. | 49.30 |
| 1964 | Warren "Rex" Cawley, U.S. | 49.60 |
| 1968 | David Hemery, Great Britain | 48.10 |
| 1972 | John Akii-Bau, Uganda | 47.80 |
| 1976 | Edwin Moses, U.S. | 47.64 |
| 1980 | Volker Beck, East Germany | 48.70 |
| 1984 | Edwin Moses, U.S. | 47.75 |
| 1988 | Andre Phillips, U.S. | 47.19 |

### 3,000-METER STEEPLECHASE

| | | |
|---|---|---|
| 1920 | Percy Hodge, Great Britain | 10:00.40 |
| 1924 | Willie Ritola, Finland | 9:33.60 |
| 1928 | Toivo A. Loukola, Finland | 9:21.80 |
| 1932 | Volmari Iso-Hollo, Finland (3,460 m—extra lap by official error) | 10:33.40 |
| 1936 | Volmari Iso-Hollo, Finland | 9:03.80 |
| 1948 | Thore Sjostrand, Sweden | 9:04.60 |
| 1952 | Horace Ashenfelter, U.S. | 8:45.40 |
| 1956 | Chris Brasher, Great Britain | 8:41.20 |
| 1960 | Zdzislaw Krzyszkowiak, Poland | 8:34.20 |
| 1964 | Gaston Roelants, Belgium | 8:30.80 |
| 1968 | Amos Biwott, Kenya | 8:51.00 |
| 1972 | Kipchoge Keino, Kenya | 8:23.60 |
| 1976 | Anders Gärderud, Sweden | 8:08.20 |
| 1980 | Bronislaw Malinowski, Poland | 8:09.70 |
| 1984 | Julius Korir, Kenya | 8:11.80 |
| 1988 | Julius Karuiki, Kenya | 8:05.51 |

### 20-KILOMETER WALK

| | | |
|---|---|---|
| 1956 | Leonid Spirine, USSR | 1:31:27.4 |
| 1960 | Vladimir Golubnichy, USSR | 1:34:07.2 |
| 1964 | Kenneth Matthews, Great Britain | 1:29:34.0 |
| 1968 | Vladimir Golubnichy, USSR | 1:33:58.4 |
| 1972 | Peter Frenkel, East Germany | 1:26:42.4 |
| 1976 | Daniel Bautista, Mexico | 1:24:40.6 |
| 1980 | Maurizio Damilano, Italy | 1:23:35.5 |
| 1984 | Ernesto Canto, Mexico | 1:23:13.0 |
| 1988 | Josef Pribilinec, Czechoslovakia | 1:19:57.0 |

### 50-KILOMETER WALK

| | | |
|---|---|---|
| 1932 | Thomas W. Green, Great Britain | 4:50:10.0 |
| 1936 | Harold Whitlock, Great Britain | 4:30:41.4 |
| 1948 | John A. Ljunggren, Sweden | 4:41:52.0 |
| 1952 | Giuseppe Dordoni, Italy | 4:28:07.8 |
| 1956 | Norman Read, New Zealand | 4:30:42.8 |
| 1960 | Donald Thompson, Great Britain | 4:25:30.0 |
| 1964 | Abdon Pamich, Italy | 4:11:12.4 |
| 1968 | Christoph Kohne, East Germany | 4:20:13.6 |
| 1972 | Bernd Kannenberg, West Germany | 3:56:11.6 |
| 1980 | Hartwig Gauter, East Germany | 3:49:24.0 |
| 1984 | Raul Gonzalez, Mexico | 3:47:26.0 |
| 1988 | Vayachselav Ivanenko, USSR | 3:38:29.0 |

### 400-METER RELAY

| | | | | | |
|---|---|---|---|---|---|
| 1912 | Great Britain | 42.40 | 1952 | U.S. | 40.10 |
| 1920 | U.S. | 42.20 | 1956 | U.S. | 39.50 |
| 1924 | U.S. | 41.00 | 1960 | West Germany | 39.50 |
| 1928 | U.S. | 41.00 | | | |
| 1932 | U.S. | 40.00 | 1964 | U.S. | 39.00 |
| 1936 | U.S. | 40.00 | 1968 | U.S. | 38.20 |
| 1948 | U.S. | 40.30 | 1972 | U.S. | 38.19 |
| 1976 | U.S. | 38.33 | 1984 | U.S. | 37.83 |
| 1980 | USSR | 38.26 | 1988 | USSR | 38.19 |

### 1,600-METER RELAY

| | | | | | |
|---|---|---|---|---|---|
| 1908 | U.S. | 3:29.40 | 1956 | U.S. | 3:04.80 |
| 1912 | U.S. | 3:16.60 | 1960 | U.S. | 3:02.20 |
| 1920 | Great Britain | 3:22.20 | 1964 | U.S. | 3:00.70 |
| 1924 | U.S. | 3:16.00 | 1968 | U.S. | 2:56.10 |
| 1928 | U.S. | 3:14.20 | 1972 | Kenya | 2:59.80 |
| 1932 | U.S. | 3:08.20 | 1976 | U.S. | 2:58.65 |
| 1936 | Great Britain | 3:09.00 | 1980 | USSR | 3:01.10 |
| 1948 | U.S. | 3:10.40 | 1984 | U.S. | 2:57.91 |
| 1952 | Jamaica | 3:03.90 | 1988 | U.S. | 2:56.16 |

### POLE VAULT

| | | Height |
|---|---|---|
| 1896 | William W. Hoyt, U.S. | 10'9 3/4" |
| 1900 | Irving K. Baxter, U.S. | 10'9 9/10" |
| 1904 | Charles E. Dvorak, U.S. | 11'6" |
| 1908 | Albert C. Gilbert, U.S. / Edward T. Cook, Jr., U.S. | 12'2" |
| 1912 | Harry S. Babcock, U.S. | 12'11 1/2" |
| 1920 | Frank K. Foss, U.S. | 12'5 9/16" |
| 1924 | Lee S. Barnes, U.S. | 12'11 1/2" |
| 1928 | Sabin W. Carr, U.S. | 13'9 3/8" |
| 1932 | William Miller, U.S. | 14'1 7/8" |
| 1936 | Earle Meadows, U.S. | 14'3 1/4" |
| 1948 | O. Guinn Smith, U.S. | 14'1 1/4" |
| 1952 | Robert Richards, U.S. | 14'11 1/4" |
| 1956 | Robert Richards, U.S. | 14'11 1/2" |
| 1960 | Donald Bragg, U.S. | 15'5 1/8" |
| 1964 | Fred M. Hansen, U.S. | 16'8 3/4" |
| 1968 | Robert Seagren, U.S. | 17'8 1/2" |
| 1972 | Wolfgang Nordwig, East Germany | 18'1/2" |
| 1976 | Tadeusz Slusarki, Poland | 18'1/2" |
| 1980 | Wladyslaw Kozakiewicz, Poland | 18'11 1/2" |
| 1984 | Pierre Quinon, France | 18'10 1/4" |
| 1988 | Sergei Bubka, USSR | 19'9 1/4" |

### HIGH JUMP

| | | |
|---|---|---|
| 1896 | Ellery Clark, U.S. | 5'11 1/4" |
| 1900 | Irving K. Baxter, U.S. | 6'2 4/5" |
| 1904 | Samuel Jones, U.S. | 5'11" |
| 1908 | Harry Porter, U.S. | 6'3" |
| 1912 | Almer Richards, U.S. | 6'4" |
| 1920 | Richmond Landon, U.S. | 6'4 1/4" |
| 1924 | Harold Osborn, U.S. | 6'5 15/16" |
| 1928 | Robert W. King, U.S. | 6'4 3/8" |
| 1932 | Duncan McNaughton, Canada | 6'5 5/8" |
| 1936 | Cornelius Johnson, U.S. | 6'7 15/16" |
| 1948 | John Winter, Australia | 6'6" |
| 1952 | Walter Davis, U.S. | 6'8 1/4" |
| 1956 | Charles E. Dumas, U.S. | 6'11 1/4" |
| 1960 | Robert Shavlakadze, USSR | 7'1" |
| 1964 | Valery Brumel, USSR | 7'1 3/4" |
| 1968 | Richard Fosbury, U.S. | 7'4 1/4" |
| 1972 | Juri Tarmak, USSR | 7'3 3/4" |
| 1976 | Jacek Wszola, Poland | 7'4 1/2" |
| 1980 | Gerd Wessig, East Germany | 7'8 3/4" |
| 1984 | Dietmar Mogenburg, West Germany | 7'8 1/2" |
| 1988 | Guennadi Avdeenko, USSR | 7'9 1/2" |

### LONG JUMP

| | | Distance |
|---|---|---|
| 1896 | Ellery Clark, U.S. | 20'10" |
| 1900 | Alvin Kraenzlein, U.S. | 23'6 7/8" |
| 1904 | Meyer Prinstein, U.S. | 24'1" |
| 1908 | Francis Irons, U.S. | 24'6 1/2" |
| 1912 | Albert Gutterson, U.S. | 24'11 1/4" |
| 1920 | William Pettersson, Sweden | 23'5 1/2" |
| 1924 | DeHart Hubbard, U.S. | 24'5 1/8" |
| 1928 | Edward Hamm, U.S. | 25'4 3/4" |
| 1932 | Edward Gordon, U.S. | 25'3/4" |
| 1936 | Jesse Owens, U.S. | 26'5 3/8" |
| 1948 | Willie Steel, U.S. | 25'8" |
| 1952 | Jerome Biffle, U.S. | 24'10" |
| 1956 | Gregory C. Bell, U.S. | 25'8 1/4" |
| 1960 | Ralph H. Boston, U.S. | 26'7 3/4" |
| 1964 | Lynn Davies, Great Britain | 26'5 3/4" |
| 1968 | Robert Beamon, U.S. | 29'2 1/2" |
| 1972 | Randy Williams, U.S. | 27'1/2" |
| 1976 | Arnie Robinson, U.S. | 27'4 3/4" |
| 1980 | Lutz Dombrowski, East Germany | 28'1/4" |
| 1984 | Carl Lewis, U.S. | 28'1/4" |
| 1988 | Carl Lewis, U.S. | 28'7 1/4" |

### TRIPLE JUMP

| | | |
|---|---|---|
| 1896 | James B. Connolly, U.S. | 45'0" |
| 1900 | Myer Prinstein, U.S. | 47'4 1/4" |
| 1904 | Myer Prinstein, U.S. | 47'0" |
| 1908 | Timothy Ahearne, Great Britain | 48'11 1/4" |
| 1912 | Gustaf Lindblom, Sweden | 48'5 1/8" |

| | | |
|---|---|---|
| 1920 | Vilho Tuulos, Finland | 47'6 7/8" |
| 1924 | Archibald Winter, Australia | 50'11 1/8" |
| 1928 | Mikio Oda, Japan | 49'10 13/16" |
| 1932 | Chuhei Nambu, Japan | 51'7" |
| 1936 | Naoto Tajima, Japan | 52'5 7/8" |
| 1948 | Arne Ahman, Sweden | 50'6 1/4" |
| 1952 | Adhemar Ferreira da Silva, Brazil | 53'2 1/2" |
| 1956 | Adhemar Ferreira da Silva, Brazil | 53'7 1/2" |
| 1960 | Jozef Schmidt, Poland | 55'1 3/4" |
| 1964 | Jozef Schmidt, Poland | 55'3 1/4" |
| 1968 | Viktor Saneyev, USSR | 57'3/4" |
| 1972 | Viktor Saneyev, USSR | 56'11" |
| 1976 | Viktor Saneyev, USSR | 56'8 3/4" |
| 1980 | Jaak Uudmae, USSR | 56'11 1/4" |
| 1984 | Al Joyner, U.S. | 56'7 1/2" |
| 1988 | Hristo Markov, Bulgaria | 57'9 1/4" |

**16-POUND SHOT PUT**

| | | |
|---|---|---|
| 1896 | Robert Garrett, U.S. | 36'9 3/4" |
| 1900 | Richard Sheldon, U.S. | 46'3 1/8" |
| 1904 | Ralph Rose, U.S. | 48'7" |
| 1908 | Ralph Rose, U.S. | 46'7 1/2" |
| 1912 | Patrick McDonald, U.S. | 50'4" |
| 1920 | Ville Porhola, Finland | 48'7 1/8" |
| 1924 | Clarence Houser, U.S. | 49'2 1/2" |
| 1928 | John Kuck, U.S. | 52'13/16" |
| 1932 | Leo Sexton, U.S. | 52'6 3/16" |
| 1936 | Hans Woellke, Germany | 53'1 3/4" |
| 1948 | Wilbur Thompson, U.S. | 56'2" |
| 1952 | William Parry O'Brien, Jr., U.S. | 57'1 1/2" |
| 1956 | William Parry O'Brien, Jr., U.S. | 60'11" |
| 1960 | William Nieder, U.S. | 64'6 3/4" |
| 1964 | Dallas C. Long, U.S. | 66'8 1/2" |
| 1968 | James Randel Matson, U.S. | 67'4 3/4" |
| 1972 | Wladyslaw Komar, Poland | 69'6" |
| 1976 | Udo Beyer, East Germany | 69'6 7/10" |
| 1980 | Vladimir Kiselyov, USSR | 70'1/2" |
| 1984 | Allesandro Andrei, Italy | 69'9" |
| 1988 | Ulf Timmermann, East Germany | 73'8 3/4" |

**DISCUS THROW**

| | | |
|---|---|---|
| 1896 | Robert Garrett, U.S. | 95'7 1/2" |
| 1900 | Rudolf Bauer, Hungary | 118'2 9/10" |
| 1904 | Martin Sheridan, U.S. | 128'10 1/2" |
| 1908 | Martin Sheridan, U.S. | 134'2" |
| 1912 | Armas Taipale, Finland | 145'9/16" |
| 1920 | Elmer Niklander, Finland | 146'7" |
| 1924 | Clarence Houser, U.S. | 151'5 1/4" |
| 1928 | Clarence Houser, U.S. | 155'2 4/5" |
| 1932 | John Anderson, U.S. | 162'4 7/8" |
| 1936 | Kenneth Carpenter, U.S. | 165'7 1/2" |
| 1948 | Adolfo Consolini, Italy | 173'2" |
| 1952 | Sim Iness, U.S. | 180'6 1/2" |
| 1956 | Alfred A. Oerter, U.S. | 184'10 1/2" |
| 1960 | Alfred A. Oerter, U.S. | 194'2" |
| 1964 | Alfred A. Oerter, U.S. | 200'1 1/2" |
| 1968 | Alfred A. Oerter, U.S. | 212'6 1/2" |
| 1972 | Ludwick Danek, Czechoslovakia | 211'3 1/2" |
| 1976 | Mac Wilkins, U.S | 221'5 2/5" |
| 1980 | Viktor Raschupkin, USSR | 218'8" |
| 1984 | Rolf Danneberg, West Germany | 218'6" |
| 1988 | Jurgen Schult, East Germany | 225'9 1/4" |

**16-POUND HAMMER THROW**

| | | |
|---|---|---|
| 1900 | John Flanagan, U.S. | 167'4" |
| 1904 | John Flanagan, U.S. | 168'1" |
| 1908 | John Flanagan, U.S. | 170'4 1/4" |
| 1912 | Matthew McGrath, U.S. | 179'7 1/8" |
| 1920 | Patrick Ryan, U.S. | 173'5 5/8" |
| 1924 | Frederick Tootell, U.S. | 174'10 1/4" |
| 1928 | Patrick O'Callaghan, Ireland | 168'7 1/2" |
| 1932 | Patrick O'Callaghan, Ireland | 176'11 1/8" |
| 1936 | Karl Hein, Germany | 185'4 1/4" |
| 1948 | Imre Nemeth, Hungary | 183'11 1/2" |
| 1952 | Jozsef Csermak, Hungary | 197'11 3/4" |
| 1956 | Harold V. Connolly, U.S. | 207'3 1/2" |
| 1960 | Vasiliy Rudenkov, USSR | 220'1 5/8" |
| 1964 | Romuald Klim, USSR | 229'9 1/2" |
| 1968 | Gyula Zsivotzky, Hungary | 240'8" |
| 1972 | Anatol Bondarchuk, USSR | 247'8" |
| 1976 | Yuri Sedykh, USSR | 254'4" |
| 1980 | Yuri Sedykh, USSR | 268'4" |
| 1984 | Juha Tiainen, Finland | 256'2" |
| 1988 | Sergei Litinov, USSR | 278'2 1/2" |

**JAVELIN THROW**

| | | |
|---|---|---|
| 1908 | Erik Lemming, Sweden | 179'10 1/2" |
| 1912 | Erik Lemming, Sweden | 198'11 1/4" |
| 1920 | Jonni Myyra, Finland | 215'9 3/4" |
| 1924 | Jonni Myyra, Finland | 206'6 3/4" |
| 1928 | Erik Lundquist, Sweden | 218'6 1/8" |
| 1932 | Matti Jarvinen, Finland | 238'7" |
| 1936 | Gerhard Stock, Germany | 235'8 5/16" |
| 1948 | Tapio Rautavaara, Finland | 228'10 1/2" |
| 1952 | Cyrus Young, U.S. | 242'3/4" |
| 1956 | Egil Danielson, Norway | 281'2 1/4" |
| 1960 | Viktor Tsibulenko, USSR | 277'8 3/8" |
| 1964 | Pauli Nevala, Finland | 271'2 1/4" |
| 1968 | Janis Lusis, USSR | 295'7 1/4" |
| 1972 | Klaus Wolfermann, West Germany | 296'10" |
| 1976 | Miklos Nemeth, Hungary | 310'4 1/2" |
| 1980 | Dainis Kula, USSR | 299'2" |
| 1984 | Arto Harkonen, Finland | 284'8" |
| 1988 | Tapio Korjus, Finland | 276'6" |

**DECATHLON**

| | | Points |
|---|---|---|
| (Old point system, 1912–32) | | |
| 1912 | Hugo Wieslander, Sweden | 7,724.49 |
| 1920 | Helge Lovland, Norway | 6,804.35 |
| 1924 | Harold Osborn, U.S. | 7,710.77 |
| 1928 | Paavo Yrjola, Finland | 8,053.29 |
| 1932 | James Bausch, U.S. | 8,462.23 |
| (Revised point system, 1936–60) | | |
| 1936 | Glenn Morris, U.S. | 7,900.00 |
| 1948 | Robert Mathias, U.S. | 7,139.00 |
| 1952 | Robert Mathias, U.S. | 7,887.00 |
| 1956 | Milton G. Campbell, U.S. | 7,937.00 |
| 1960 | Rafer Johnson, U.S. | 8,392.00 |
| (New scoring system) | | |
| 1964 | Willi Holdorf, West Germany | 7,887.00 |
| 1968 | William Toomey, U.S. | 8,193.00 |
| 1972 | Nikolai Avilov, USSR | 8,454.00 |
| 1976 | Bruce Jenner, U.S. | 8,618.00 |
| 1980 | Francis Thompson, Great Britain | 8,495.00 |
| 1984 | Francis Thompson, Great Britain | 8,798.00 |
| 1988 | Christian Schenk, East Germany | 8,488.00 |

## TRACK AND FIELD—WOMEN

Time

**100-METER DASH**

| | | |
|---|---|---|
| 1928 | Elizabeth Robinson, U.S. | 12.20 |
| 1932 | Stanislawa Walasiewicz, Poland | 11.90 |
| 1936 | Helen Stephens, U.S. | 11.50 |
| 1948 | Francina Blankers-Koen, Netherlands | 11.90 |
| 1952 | Marjorie Jackson, Australia | 11.50 |
| 1956 | Betty Cuthbert, Australia | 11.50 |
| 1960 | Wilma Rudolph, U.S | 11.00 |
| 1964 | Wyomia Tyus, U.S. | 11.40 |
| 1968 | Wyomia Tyus, U.S. | 11.00 |
| 1972 | Renate Stecher, East Germany | 11.10 |
| 1976 | Annegret Richter, West Germany | 11.01 |
| 1980 | Lyudmila Kondratyeva, USSR | 11.06 |
| 1984 | Evelyn Ashford, U.S. | 10.97 |
| 1988 | Florence Griffith-Joyner, U.S. | 10.54 |

**200 METERS**

| | | |
|---|---|---|
| 1948 | Francina Blankers-Koen, Netherlands | 24.40 |
| 1952 | Marjorie Jackson, Australia | 23.70 |
| 1956 | Betty Cuthbert, Australia | 23.40 |
| 1960 | Wilma Rudolph, U.S. | 24.00 |
| 1964 | Edith McGuire, U.S. | 23.00 |
| 1968 | Irena Kirszenstein Szewinska, Poland | 22.50 |
| 1972 | Renate Stecher, East Germany | 22.40 |
| 1976 | Bärbel Eckert, East Germany | 22.37 |
| 1980 | Bärbel Wöckel (Eckert), East Germany | 22.03 |
| 1984 | Valerie Brisco-Hooks, U.S. | 21.81 |
| 1988 | Florence Griffith-Joyner, U.S. | 21.34 |

**400 METERS**

| | | |
|---|---|---|
| 1964 | Betty Cuthbert, Australia | 52.00 |
| 1968 | Colette Besson, France | 52.00 |
| 1972 | Monika Zehrt, East Germany | 51.10 |
| 1976 | Irena Szewinska, Poland | 49.29 |
| 1980 | Marita Koch, East Germany | 48.88 |
| 1984 | Valerie Brisco-Hooks, U.S. | 48.83 |
| 1988 | Olga Bryzgina, USSR | 48.65 |

**800 METERS**

| | | |
|---|---|---|
| 1928 | Linda Radke-Batschauer, Germany | 2:16.80 |
| 1960 | Lyudmila Shevcova-Lysenko, USSR | 2:04.30 |
| 1964 | Ann Packer, Great Britain | 2:01.10 |
| 1968 | Madeline Manning, U.S. | 2:00.90 |
| 1972 | Hildegard Falck, West Germany | 1:58.60 |
| 1976 | Tatyana Kazankina, USSR | 1:54.94 |
| 1980 | Nadezhda Olizarenko, USSR | 1:53.42 |
| 1984 | Doina Melinte, Romania | 1:57.60 |
| 1988 | Sigrun Wodars, East Germany | 1:56.10 |

**1,500 METERS**

| | | |
|---|---|---|
| 1972 | Lyudmila Bragina, USSR | 4:01.40 |
| 1976 | Tatyana Kazankina, USSR | 4:05.48 |
| 1980 | Tatyana Kazankina, USSR | 3:56.60 |
| 1984 | Gabrielle Dorio, Italy | 4:03.25 |
| 1988 | Paula Ivan, Romania | 3:53.96 |

**3,000 METERS**

| | | |
|---|---|---|
| 1984 | Maricica Puica, Romania | 8:35.96 |
| 1988 | Tatyana Samolenko, USSR | 8:26.53 |

**10,000 METERS**

| | | |
|---|---|---|
| 1988 | Olga Boldarenko, USSR | 31:44.69 |

**MARATHON**

| | | |
|---|---|---|
| 1984 | Joan Benoit, U.S. | 2:24.52 |
| 1988 | Rosa Mota, Portugal | 2:25.40 |

**400-METER RELAY**

| | | | | | |
|---|---|---|---|---|---|
| 1928 | Canada | 48.40 | 1968 | U.S. | 42.80 |
| 1932 | U.S. | 47.00 | 1972 | West Germany | 42.80 |
| 1936 | U.S. | 46.90 | 1976 | East Germany | 42.55 |
| 1948 | Netherlands | 47.50 | 1980 | East Germany | 41.60 |
| 1952 | U.S. | 45.90 | 1984 | U.S. | 41.65 |
| 1956 | Australia | 44.50 | 1988 | U.S. | 41.98 |
| 1960 | U.S. | 44.50 | | | |
| 1964 | Poland | 43.60 | | | |

**1,600-METER RELAY**

| | | | | | |
|---|---|---|---|---|---|
| 1972 | East Germany | 3:23.00 | 1980 | USSR | 3:20.02 |
| 1976 | East Germany | 3:19.23 | 1984 | U.S. | 3:18.29 |
| | | | 1988 | USSR | 3:15.18 |

**100-METER HURDLES**

| | | |
|---|---|---|
| 1972 | Annelie Erhardt, East Germany | 12.60 |
| 1976 | Johanna Schaller, East Germany | 12.77 |
| 1980 | Vera Komisova, USSR | 12.56 |
| 1984 | Benita Brown-Fitzgerald | 12.84 |
| 1988 | Jordanka Donkova, Bulgaria | 12.38 |

**HIGH JUMP**

| | | Height |
|---|---|---|
| 1928 | Ethel Catherwood, Canada | 5'3" |
| 1932 | Jean Shiley, U.S. | 5'5 1/4" |
| 1936 | Ibolya Csak, Hungary | 5'3" |
| 1948 | Alice Coachman, U.S. | 5'6 1/8" |
| 1952 | Esther Brand, South Africa | 5'5 3/4" |
| 1956 | Mildred McDaniel, U.S. | 5'9 1/4" |
| 1960 | Iolanda Balas, Romania | 6'1/4" |
| 1964 | Iolanda Balas, Romania | 6'2 3/4" |
| 1968 | Miloslava Rezkova, Czechoslovakia | 5'11 3/4" |
| 1972 | Ulrika Meyfarth, West Germany | 6'3 1/2" |
| 1976 | Rosemarie Ackermann, East Germany | 6'4" |
| 1980 | Sara Simeoni, Italy | 6'5 1/2" |
| 1984 | Ulrike Meyfarth, West Germany | 6'7 1/2" |
| 1988 | Louise Ritter, U.S. | 6'8" |

**LONG JUMP**

| | | Distance |
|---|---|---|
| 1948 | Olga Gyarmati, Hungary | 18'8 1/4" |
| 1952 | Yvette Williams, New Zealand | 20'5 3/4" |
| 1956 | Elizbieta Krzeskinska, Poland | 20'9 3/4" |
| 1960 | Vyera Krepkina, USSR | 20'10 3/4" |
| 1964 | Mary Rand, Great Britain | 22'2" |
| 1968 | Viorica Viscopoleanu, Romania | 22'4 1/2" |
| 1972 | Heidemarie Rosendahl, West Germany | 22'3" |
| 1976 | Angela Voigt, East Germany | 22'2 1/2" |
| 1980 | Tatiana Kolpakova, USSR | 23'2" |
| 1984 | Anisoara Cusmir-Stanciu, Romania | 22'10" |
| 1988 | Jackie Joyner-Kersee, U.S. | 24'3 1/2" |

**DISCUS THROW**

| | | |
|---|---|---|
| 1928 | Helena Konopacka, Poland | 129'11 7/8" |
| 1932 | Lillian Copeland, U.S. | 133'2" |
| 1936 | Gisela Mauermayer, Germany | 156'3 3/16" |
| 1948 | Micheline Ostermeyer, France | 137'6 1/2" |
| 1952 | Nina Romaschkova, USSR | 168'8 1/2" |
| 1956 | Olga Fikotova, Czechoslovakia | 176'1 1/2" |
| 1960 | Nina Ponomareva, USSR | 180'8 1/4" |
| 1964 | Tamara Press, USSR | 187'10 3/4" |
| 1968 | Lia Manoliu, Romania | 191'2 1/2" |
| 1972 | Faina Melnik, USSR | 218'7" |
| 1976 | Evelin Schlaak, East Germany | 226'4 1/2" |
| 1980 | Evelin Jahl (Schaak), East Germany | 229'6" |
| 1984 | Ria Stalman, Netherlands | 214'5" |
| 1988 | Martina Hellmann, East Germany | 237'2 1/4" |

**8-LB. 13-OZ. SHOT PUT**

| | | |
|---|---|---|
| 1948 | Micheline Ostermeyer, France | 45'1 1/2" |
| 1952 | Galina Zybina, USSR | 50'1 1/2" |
| 1956 | Tamara Tishkyevich, USSR | 54'5" |
| 1960 | Tamara Press, USSR | 56'9 3/4" |
| 1964 | Tamara Press, USSR | 59'6" |
| 1968 | Margitta Gummel, East Germany | 64'4" |
| 1972 | Nadezhda Chizhova, USSR | 69'0" |
| 1976 | Ivanka Khristova, Bulgaria | 69'5" |
| 1980 | Ilona Slupianek, East Germany | 73'6 1/4" |
| 1984 | Claudia Losch, West Germany | 67'2 1/4" |
| 1988 | Natalya Lisovskaya, USSR | 72'11 1/2" |

**JAVELIN THROW**

| | | |
|---|---|---|
| 1932 | Mildred Didrikson, U.S. | 143'4" |
| 1936 | Tilly Fleischer, Germany | 148'2 3/4" |
| 1948 | Herma Bauma, Austria | 149'6" |
| 1952 | Dana Zatopekova, Czechoslovakia | 165'7" |
| 1956 | Inessa Janzeme, USSR | 176'8" |
| 1960 | Elvira Ozolina, USSR | 183'8" |
| 1964 | Mihaela Penes, Romania | 198'7 1/2" |
| 1968 | Angela Nemeth, Hungary | 198'1/2" |
| 1972 | Ruth Fuchs, East Germany | 209'7" |
| 1976 | Ruth Fuchs, East Germany | 216'4" |
| 1980 | Maria Colon Ruenes, Cuba | 224'5" |
| 1984 | Theresa Sanderson, Great Britain | 228'2" |
| 1988 | Petra Felke, East Germany | 245'0" |

**PENTATHLON**

| | | Points |
|---|---|---|
| 1964 | Irina Press, USSR | 5,246 |
| 1968 | Ingrid Becker, West Germany | 5,098 |
| 1972 | Mary Peters, Great Britain | 4,801 |
| 1976 | Siegrun Siegl, East Germany | 4,745 |
| 1980 | Nadezhda Tkachenko, USSR | 5,083 |

**HEPTATHLON**

| | | |
|---|---|---|
| 1984 | Glynis Nunn, Australia | 6,390 |
| 1988 | Jackie Joyner-Kersee, U.S. | 7,215 |

## TEAM SPORTS (since 1948)

**BASKETBALL—MEN**

| | | | |
|---|---|---|---|
| 1948 | U.S. | 1972 | USSR |
| 1952 | U.S. | 1976 | U.S. |
| 1956 | U.S. | 1980 | Yugoslavia |
| 1960 | U.S. | 1984 | U.S. |
| 1964 | U.S. | 1988 | USSR |
| 1968 | U.S. | | |

**BASKETBALL—WOMEN**

| | |
|---|---|
| 1976 | USSR |
| 1980 | USSR |
| 1984 | U.S. |
| 1988 | U.S., Yugoslavia, USSR |

**SOCCER (FOOTBALL)**

| | | | |
|---|---|---|---|
| 1948 | Sweden | 1976 | East Germany |
| 1952 | Hungary | 1980 | Czechoslovakia |
| 1956 | USSR | 1984 | France |
| 1960 | Yugoslavia | 1988 | USSR |
| 1964 | Hungary | | |
| 1968 | Hungary | | |
| 1972 | Poland | | |

**VOLLEYBALL—MEN**

| | | | |
|---|---|---|---|
| 1964 | USSR | 1980 | USSR |
| 1968 | USSR | 1984 | U.S. |
| 1972 | Japan | 1988 | U.S. |
| 1976 | Poland | | |

**VOLLEYBALL—WOMEN**

| | | | |
|---|---|---|---|
| 1964 | Japan | 1980 | USSR |
| 1968 | USSR | 1984 | China |
| 1972 | USSR | 1988 | USSR |
| 1976 | Japan | | |

**WATER POLO**

| | | | |
|---|---|---|---|
| 1948 | Italy | 1972 | USSR |
| 1952 | Hungary | 1976 | Hungary |
| 1956 | Hungary | 1980 | USSR |
| 1960 | Italy | 1984 | Yugoslavia |
| 1964 | Hungary | 1988 | Yugoslavia |
| 1968 | Yugoslavia | | |

**645**

**661**